The New
INTERNATIONAL DICTIONARY OF THE BIBLE
Pictorial Edition

The New INTERNATIONAL DICTIONARY OF THE BIBLE

Pictorial Edition

J. D. Douglas
REVISING EDITOR

Merrill C. Tenney
GENERAL EDITOR

Consulting Editors for the Revision
F. F. Bruce
Walter A. Elwell
Thomas E. McComiskey
J. A. Motyer
Peter Toon

Regency Reference Library
Zondervan Publishing House
Grand Rapids, MI, U.S.A.

MARSHALL·PICKERING
3 Beggarwood Lane
Basingstoke, Hants, U.K.

THE NEW INTERNATIONAL DICTIONARY OF THE BIBLE

REGENCY REFERENCE LIBRARY is an imprint of
Zondervan Publishing House, 1415 Lake Drive S.E., Grand Rapids, Michigan 49506

First published 1987 in the UK by Marshall Pickering,
3 Beggarwood Lane, Basingstoke, Hants, RG23 7LP

Library of Congress Cataloging in Publication Data

The new international dictionary of the Bible.

Originally published as: The Zondervan pictorial Bible dictionary. 1963.
1. Bible—Dictionaries. I. Tenney, Merrill Chapin, 1904– II. Douglas, J. D. (James Dixon). III. Zondervan Pictorial Bible Dictionary.
BS440.N44 1987 220.3 87-2220
ISBN 0-310-33190-0 (Zondervan Publishing House)
ISBN 0-551-01570-5 (Marshall Pickering)

Edited by Jean Syswerda, Lyman Rand Tucker, Jr., and Gerard H. Terpstra

Scripture Index compiled by Claire M. Hughes

Printed in the United States of America

87 88 89 90 91 92 93 94 95 96 / DC / 10 9 8 7 6 5 4 3 2 1

Contents

Revising Editor's Preface

For more than two decades *The Zondervan Pictorial Bible Dictionary* has been a best-seller. During that period, however, more background information has become available. Archaeological excavations have been carried out on biblical sites. New books have been written to enhance our understanding of the Bible. A further dimension was added with the publication of the New International Version of the Bible.

These developments are reflected in this revision. The revision has been so thorough, in fact, that the dictionary merits a new name: *The New International Dictionary of the Bible*. There is, for example, a completely new entry on archaeology, and, where necessary, notes have been added to the individual entries dealing with particular sites.

More emphasis has been placed on bibliography. To all the articles on biblical books are appended some suggestions for further reading. So, too, with most of the longer articles. Some entries call for bibliography more than others, hence the apparent anomaly that sees none attached to a sizable entry, but, for exceptional reasons, finds one in a shorter entry.

This revision is based on the NIV, but there are frequent comparisons with the KJV. Other versions—notably JB, NASB, NEB, and RSV—have been cited where it was considered helpful. While the spelling of places and personal names follows NIV usage, preference is occasionally given to the KJV rendering in order to avoid confusion or perhaps because of editorial affinity with some old and much-loved landmark.

Every reviser is in debt to the original editors and writers and lives with a nagging feeling of presumptuousness in setting out to amend or supersede the work of bygone saints. Why did they say this or that? Did they know something we don't know? This haunting and not-unlikely possibility is a healthy inhibiting factor for brandishers of blue pencils.

This is especially relevant when confronting a presentation that is put a little more forcefully than one would expect in a dictionary of the Bible. In the following pages a reasonable amount of idiosyncrasy has been perpetuated in certain entries; with a certain affectionate indulgence we recognize that that was the way in which some of our elders drew attention to the importance of their topics.

A few brief explanations are called for. In articles where only minor revision has been carried out or bibliography updated, the name of the original author has been retained. Where there has been substantial alteration or addition, the name of the reviser also has been supplied. Where more than two writers have been involved, the article is left unsigned, a procedure that is followed with most of the shorter entries.

Cross-references are an editorial nightmare; too many of them make for confusion and untidiness. We reduced them to a minimum, knowing that readers would, without prompting from us, be enterprising enough to look up other subjects. Most of them involve related entries that are mentioned at the end of an entry.

Dictionaries are particularly vulnerable because a writer has to say in a few words what others expand into whole books. Contributors to dictionaries of the Bible are further at risk because some of their subjects lend themselves to controversy. In treating them, mention may be made either of opinions not within the Evangelical tradition or of widely divergent interpretations within that tradition. We hope that this policy will have no adverse effect on anyone's blood pressure. It was, indeed, an eminent physician, Sir Wilfred Grenfell, who reminded us that two men can think differently without either being wicked.

The consulting editors are not to be held accountable for the finished revision. None of them has seen all of it. All of them responded to the initial invitation to comment on what needed to be done. Moreover, all were contributors as well as consultants, and the work has greatly benefited. But someone had to see the work last, so for the final choice of material the revising editor alone is responsible.

In addition to article writers, a number of people worked very hard and lightened the editorial task. Doug Buckwalter and David Lazell shared their expertise in the peculiarly demanding job of adapting some of the omnibus articles to NIV usage. Myra Wilson cheerfully did a mass of accurate typing and checking; Ruj Vanavisut meticulously performed a daunting load of secretarial and kindred chores; Louan and Walter Elwell selflessly provided a second home and library facilities for a traveling editor. For the publisher, Stan Gundry was a model of restraint in letting the editor get on with the project unhindered but was ready to respond promptly to editorial requests.

J. D. DOUGLAS

Preface to First Edition

Robert A. Millikan, American physicist and Nobel prizewinner, once said that a knowledge of the Bible is an indispensable qualification of a well-educated man. No other single book in the history of literature has been so widely distributed or read, or has exercised so powerful an influence upon civilization. It is the fountainhead of Western culture, and is the sole source of spiritual life and revelation for all Christians. For the development of Christian experience and for the propagation of faith, a study of the Scriptures is absolutely necessary. The history, laws, prophecies, sermons and letters which they contain provide God's estimate of man and His disclosure of Himself through the historic process of revelation culminating in the person of His Son, Jesus Christ.

Understanding the Bible is often difficult for the average reader because of the unfamiliar names of persons, places, and objects to which it alludes. The historical and cultural backgrounds are alien to those of the modern day and presuppose knowledge that is not easily attainable. The function of a Bible dictionary is to render accessible a body of information that will enable one to comprehend the meaning of the text he is reading, and to obtain ready and complete data concerning any related subject.

Within recent years, the need for a new, up-to-date reference work has become increasingly urgent. Fresh discoveries in archaeology, better understanding of the history and geography of the Middle East, and the fruit of multiplied research have provided new insights and interpretations. The advance of the graphic arts has improved greatly the effectiveness of photography, so that the artifacts and inscriptions of the past can be reproduced vividly for public exhibition. Realizing the opportunity for a fresh venture in this field, the Zondervan Publishing House, inspired by the interest and foresight of Mr. Peter deVisser, Director of Publications, has undertaken the task of creating a totally new dictionary, enlisting the cooperation of sixty-five competent scholars in every field from archaeology to zoology. The content includes more than five thousand entries, among which may be found a number of important monographs on biblical and theological topics. In addition, the dictionary contains an extensive series of articles on Christian doctrines.

This *Pictorial Bible Dictionary* is a completely new, fully illustrated one-volume work. It is designed to provide quick access to explanatory data, both by the verbal exposition of biographical, chronological, geographical, and historical aspects of the Bible, and by the illustrations related to them. The pictures have been selected for their relevance to the subject matter, for their historical value, and also with an eye to human interest.

The scope of a one-volume dictionary is necessarily limited. The articles are not intended to be exhaustive, nor are they planned primarily for professional scholars. They are gauged for the use of pastors, Sunday-school teachers, Bible-class leaders, and students who desire concise and accurate information on questions raised by ordinary reading. For intensive research, a more detailed and critical work is recommended.

Although the articles are written from a conservative viewpoint, each writer has been free to express his own opinions and is responsible for the material that appears over his signature. There may be minor disagreements between statements by different persons; in such instances there is room for debate, and the contributors have liberty to differ. Uncertainty still exists in some fields, since sufficient data are not available for final conclusions.

While the writers are indebted to many sources, no previously published work has been incorporated in these pages. The pictures have been taken chiefly from recent photographs, and are not old reprints. No expense has been spared to prepare the best possible aid for the Bible student.

In the matter of illustrations, special thanks are due Mr. and Mrs. G. Eric Matson of the Matson Photo Service, Los Angeles, formerly of the American Colony in Jerusalem, for placing at our disposal their vast and unsurpassed collection of photographs gathered in a lifetime career of professional photography in the Bible lands. We wish herewith also to thank all organizations and individuals who have extended their help in supplying photos and illustrations, including: the Oriental Institute of the University of Chicago; the British Museum of London; the University Museum of Pennsylvania; the Radio Times Hulton Picture Library of London; Dr. Edward F. Campbell, Jr., Editor of *The Biblical Archaeologist;* the American Schools of Oriental Research; the University of Michigan Library; Dr. John F. Walvoord and Dr. Merrill F. Unger of Dallas Theological Seminary; Dr. and Mrs. Henry H. Halley of Chicago; Dr. Siegfried H. Horn of Andrews University, and others.

A complete bibliography of all sources of information would obviously be impossible. Selected references have been appended to major articles in order to afford opportunity for further research.

Names of persons and places, for the most part, have been taken from the King James Version, which is still more widely read than any other, but variants occurring in the American Standard Version and in the Revised Standard Version have been noted. Pronunciation follows the practice of the unabridged second edition of Webster's *New International Dictionary of the English Language*. All Hebrew and Greek names, as well as other names and terms, are followed by their English pronunciations in parentheses. Transliterated Hebrew and Greek words appear in italics, with their meaning when it can be identified. A list of symbols and abbreviations appears on pages xiii and xiv.

Special acknowledgments are due to Dr. Steven Barabas, Associate Editor, who collaborated in preparing articles for publication, and who contributed many himself; to Dr. E. M. Blaiklock, Professor Wick Broomall, Dr. Howard Z. Cleveland, the Rev. Charles Cook, Dr. Carl De Vries, the Rev. Arthur B. Fowler, the Rev. J. P. Freeman, Dr. Guy B. Funderburk, the Rev. Clyde E. Harrington, Dr. D. Edmond Hiebert, the Rev. John G. Johansson, the Rev. Brewster Porcella, Professor Arthur M. Ross, Dr. Emmet Russell, and Dr. Walter Wessel, who, in addition to the initialed articles published under their names, contributed many of the unsigned articles; to Miss Verda Bloomhuff and the Rev. Briggs P. Dingman, who assisted in correction of copy and proof; and to Mrs. Carol Currie and Mrs. Alice Holmes for invaluable secretarial service. The General Editor wishes to express his gratitude to all those scholars named in the list of contributors who have lent their time and counsel to the production of this book.

MERRILL C. TENNEY

Contributors and Editors

ABBREVIATIONS

AAM	Allan A. MacRae
ABF	Arthur B. Fowler
ABM	A. Berkeley Mickelsen
ACS	Arnold C. Schultz
AMR	Arthur M. Ross
BLD	Burton L. Goddard
BP	Brewster Porcella
BPD	Briggs P. Dingman
CBB	Clarence B. Bass
CEC	Charles E. Cook
CED	Carl E. DeVries
CEH	Clyde E. Harrington
CFP	Charles F. Pfeiffer
DCB	Donald Chapin Boardman
DEH	D. Edmond Hiebert
EFH	Everett F. Harrison
EJY	Edward J. Young
EMB	Edward M. Blaiklock
ER	Emmet Russell
ERT	Edwin R. Thiele
FFB	F. F. Bruce
GBF	Guy B. Funderburk
GEL	George Eldon Ladd
GFO	G. Frederick Owen
GLA	Gleason L. Archer, Jr.
GWB	Geoffrey W. Bromiley
HHH	H. Harold Hartzler
HPH	H. Paul Holdridge
HWP	Hazel W. Perkin
HZC	Howard Z. Cleveland
JAM	J. A. Motyer
JBG	John B. Graybill
JBP	J. Barton Payne
JCW	John C. Whitcomb, Jr.
JDD	J. D. Douglas
JDF	John D. Freeman
JFG	John F. Gates
JGJ	John G. Johansson
JHG	J. Harold Greenlee
JLL	John L. Leedy
JOB	James Oliver Buswell, Jr.
JR	John Rea
JRM	John Robert McRay
KSK	Kenneth S. Kantzer
LGO	Lee G. Olson
LMP	Lorman M. Petersen
MCT	Merrill C. Tenney
MFU	Merrill F. Unger
MGK	Meredith G. Kline
OTA	Oswald T. Allis
PEA	Paul E. Adolph
PT	Peter Toon
RE	Ralph Earle
RKH	Roland Kenneth Harrison
RLH	R. Laird Harris
SB	Steven Barabas
SJS	Samuel J. Schultz
TEM	Thomas Edward McComiskey
VCG	Vernon C. Grounds
WAE	Walter A. Elwell
WB	Wick Broomall
WH	William Hendriksen
WMS	Wilbur M. Smith
WSLS	William Sanford LaSor
WWW	Walter W. Wessel

ALPHABETICAL LISTING

PAUL E. ADOLPH
M.D. (School of Medicine, University of Pennsylvania). Former Medical Director, Chicago Missionary Medical Office.

OSWALD T. ALLIS
B.D. (Princeton Theological Seminary), Ph.D. (University of Berlin). Former Professor Emeritus of Old Testament, Westminster Theological Seminary.

GLEASON L. ARCHER, JR.
B.A., (Harvard University), LL.B. (Suffolk University Law School), B.D. (Princeton Theological Seminary), A.M., Ph.D. (Harvard University). Professor of Old Testament and Semitic Languages, Trinity Evangelical Divinity School.

STEVEN BARABAS
A.B. (Princeton University), B.D., Th.D. (Princeton Theological Seminary). Former Professor of Theology, Wheaton College.

CLARENCE B. BASS
B.A., M.A. (Wheaton College), Th.D. (University of Edinburgh). Professor of Systematic Theology, Bethel Theological Seminary.

EDWARD M. BLAIKLOCK
M.A., Litt. D. (University of Auckland). Former Professor Emeritus of Classics, University of Auckland, New Zealand.

DONALD CHAPIN BOARDMAN
B.S. (Wheaton College), M.S. (Iowa), Ph.D. (Wisconsin). Professor Emeritus of Geology, Department Chairman, Wheaton College.

GEOFFREY W. BROMILEY
M.A. (University of Cambridge), Ph.D., D.Litt., D.D. (University of Edinburgh). Senior Professor of Church History and Historical Theology, Fuller Theological Seminary.

WICK BROOMALL
A.B. (Maryville College), Th.B., Th.M. (Princeton Theological Seminary), M.A. (Princeton University). Former Pastor, Westminster Presbyterian Church, Augusta, Georgia.

F. F. BRUCE
M.A. (Universities of Aberdeen, Cambridge, Manchester), D.D. (University of Aberdeen). Rylands Professor Emeritus of Biblical Criticism and Exegesis, University of Manchester, England.

JAMES OLIVER BUSWELL, JR.
B.D. (McCormick Theological Seminary), M.A. (University of Chicago), Ph.D. (New York University). Former Dean of the Graduate Faculty, Covenant College and Seminary.

HOWARD Z. CLEVELAND
Th.D. (Dallas Theological Seminary). Former Chairman, Departments of Theology and Greek, Oak Hills Bible Institute.

CHARLES E. COOK
Th.M. (Westminster Theological Seminary). Former Pastor, First Baptist Church, Concord, New Hampshire. Former Instructor, Barrington College.

CARL E. DEVRIES
S.B., A.M., B.D. (Wheaton College), Ph.D. (University of Chicago). Former Research Associate (Associate Professor), Oriental Institute, University of Chicago.

BRIGGS P. DINGMAN
A.B. (Southwestern Bible College), Moody Bible Institute, Dickinson College, Xenia Theological Seminary. Former Instructor, Modern Languages and History, Elim Bible Institute.

J. D. DOUGLAS
M.A., B.D. (University of St. Andrews), S.T.M. (Hartford Theological Seminary), Ph.D. (Hartford Seminary Foundation). Editor and writer.

RALPH EARLE
A.B. (Eastern Nazarene College), M.A. (Boston University), B.D., Th.D. (Gordon Divinity School), D.D. (Eastern Nazarene College). Distinguished Professor Emeritus of New Testament, Nazarene Theological Seminary.

WALTER A. ELWELL
B.A., M.A. (Wheaton College), Ph.D. (University of Edinburgh). Professor of Bible and Theology, Wheaton College Graduate School.

ARTHUR B. FOWLER
B.A. (Princeton University), B.D. (Princeton Theological Seminary). Dean Emeritus, Buffalo Bible Institute.

JOHN D. FREEMAN
Th.M. (Southern Baptist Theological Seminary), Ph.D. (University of Arkansas). Editor.

GUY B. FUNDERBURK
A.B. (Furman University), Th.M., Ph.D. (Southern Baptist Theological Seminary). Former Chairman, Department of Religion and Philosophy, Salem College, West Virginia.

JOHN F. GATES
S.T.D. (Temple University School of Theology). Former Professor of Bible and Philosophy, St. Paul Bible College.

BURTON L. GODDARD
A.B. (University of Minnesota), Th.B. (Westminster Theological Seminary), S.M. (Simmons College), S.T.M., Th.D. (Harvard University). Dean Emeritus and Professor of Biblical Languages and Exegesis, Gordon-Conwell Divinity School.

JOHN B. GRAYBILL
B.D. (Faith Theological Seminary), Ph.D. (Brandeis University). Barrington Presbyterian Church, Barrington, Rhode Island.

J. HAROLD GREENLEE
A.B. (Asbury College), B.D. (Asbury Theological Seminary), M.A. (University of Kentucky), Ph.D. (Harvard University). Missionary of OMS International, International Translation Consultant for Wycliffe Bible Translators, and Professor, United Biblical Seminary of Colombia.

VERNON C. GROUNDS
A.B. (Rutgers University), B.D. (Faith Theological Seminary), Ph.D. (Drew University), D.D. (Wheaton College). President Emeritus and Cauwels Professor Emeritus of Pastoral Care and Christian Ethics, Conservative Baptist Theological Seminary.

CLYDE E. HARRINGTON
B.D. (Faith Theological Seminary), Ph.D. (Dropsie College). Former Instructor, Lancaster School of the Bible. Former Editor, American Sunday School Union.

R. LAIRD HARRIS
B.S. (University of Delaware), Th.B., Th.M. (Westminster Theological Seminary), M.A. (University of Pennsylvania), Ph.D. (Dropsie Col-

lege). Professor Emeritus of Old Testament, Covenant Theological Seminary.

EVERETT F. HARRISON
B.A. (University of Washington), M.A. (Princeton University), Th.B. (Princeton Theological Seminary), Th.D. (Dallas Theological Seminary), Ph.D. (University of Pennsylvania). Professor Emeritus of New Testament, Fuller Theological Seminary.

ROLAND KENNETH HARRISON
B.D., M.Th., Ph.D. (University of London), D.D. (University of Western Ontario). Professor of Old Testament, Wycliffe College, University of Toronto.

H. HAROLD HARTZLER
Ph.D. (Rutgers University). Professor Emeritus of Mathematics, Mankato State College.

WILLIAM HENDRIKSEN
Th.B. (Princeton Theological Seminary). Former Pastor, Christian Reformed Church, Boca Raton, Florida.

D. EDMOND HIEBERT
A.B. (John Fletcher College), Th.M., Th.D. (Southern Baptist Theological Seminary). Professor Emeritus of New Testament, Mennonite Brethren Biblical Seminary.

H. PAUL HOLDRIDGE
B.A. (Central Pilgrim College). Pastor and editor, Bartlesville, Oklahoma.

JOHN G. JOHANSSON
A.B. (Methodist Theological School, Uppsala, Sweden). Former Production Manager, *Christianity Today*.

KENNETH S. KANTZER
A.B. (Ashland College), A.M. (Ohio State University), B.D., S.T.M. (Faith Theological Seminary), Ph.D. (Harvard University). Dean Emeritus, Distinguished Professor of Biblical and Systematic Theology, Trinity Evangelical Divinity School.

MEREDITH G. KLINE
A.B. (Gordon College), Th.B., Th.M. (Westminster Theological Seminary), Ph.D. (Dropsie College). Professor of Old Testament, Westminster Theological Seminary in California.

GEORGE ELDON LADD
B.D. (Gordon Divinity School), Ph.D. (Harvard University). Former Professor Emeritus of New Testament Theology and Exegesis, Fuller Theological Seminary.

WILLIAM SANFORD LASOR
A.B. (University of Pennsylvania), Th.B., Th.M., (Princeton Theological Seminary), A.M. (Princeton University), Ph.D. (Dropsie College), Th.D. (University of Southern California). Professor Emeritus of Old Testament, Fuller Theological Seminary.

JOHN L. LEEDY
Ph.D. (University of Minnesota). Professor Emeritus of Botany, Wheaton College.

THOMAS EDWARD MCCOMISKEY
B.A. (The King's College), M.Div. (Faith Theological Seminary), Th.M. (Westminster Theological Seminary), M.A.. Ph.D. (Brandeis University). Professor of Old Testament and Semitic Languages, Trinity Evangelical Divinity School.

ALLAN A. MACRAE
A.B. (Occidental College), A.M., Th.B. (Princeton Theological Seminary), A.M. (Princeton University), Ph.D. (University of Pennsylvania). Chancellor and Professor Emeritus of Old Testament, Biblical Theological Seminary.

JOHN ROBERT MCRAY
B.A. (David Lipscomb College), M.A. (Harding Graduate School of Religion), Ph.D. (University of Chicago). Professor of New Testament and Coordinator of Biblical Studies Concentration, Wheaton College Graduate School.

A. BERKELEY MICKELSEN
B.A. (Wheaton College), B.D., M.A. (Wheaton College Graduate School), Ph.D. (University of Chicago). Professor Emeritus of New Testament Interpretation, Bethel Theological Seminary.

J. A. MOTYER
A.B., M.A., B.D. (Trinity College, University of Dublin). Minister of Christ Church, Westbourne, Dorset, England; Former Principal, Trinity College, Bristol.

LEE G. OLSON
S.M.M., S.M.D. (Union Theological Seminary). Former Professor Emeritus, Division of Sacred Music, Nyack College.

G. FREDERICK OWEN
A.B., M.A., B.D. (Vanderbilt University), M.A., D.Ed. (George Washington University). Former Professor of Archaeology, Pasadena College; Carver Foundation Lecturer; Member, Society of Oriental Research.

J. BARTON PAYNE
B.A. (University of California), Th.B. (San Francisco Theological Seminary), M.A., B.D., Th.D. (Princeton Theological Seminary). Former Professor of Old Testament, Covenant Theological Seminary.

HAZEL W. PERKIN
B.A. (Sir George Williams University), M.A. (McGill University). Principal, St. Clement's School, Toronto.

LORMAN M. PETERSEN
B.D., M.S.T., Th.D. (Concordia Theological Seminary). Former Professor of New Testament Interpretation, Academic Dean, Concordia Theological Seminary, Fort Wayne, Indiana.

CHARLES F. PFEIFFER
B.A. (Temple University), B.D. (Reformed Episcopal Theological Seminary), Th.M. (Chicago Lutheran Theological Seminary), Ph.D. (Dropsie College). Former Professor of Ancient Literature, Central Michigan University.

BREWSTER PORCELLA
A.B., A.M. (Wheaton College), B.D. (Faith Theological Seminary), M.S., Ph.D. (University of Illinois). Librarian, Trinity Evangelical Divinity School.

JOHN REA
B.S. (Princeton University), M.A. (Wheaton College), B.D., Th.M., Th.D. (Grace Theological Seminary). Professor of Biblical Studies (Old Testament), CBN University.

ARTHUR M. ROSS
B.S., B.D., A.M. (Wheaton College). Dean of College-Credit Instruction, Correspondence School, Moody Bible Institute.

EMMET RUSSELL
A.B. (Harvard College), LL.B. (Harvard Law School), B.D., S.T.D. (Gordon College of Theology and Missions). Former pastor of Short Beach United Church, Short Beach, Connecticut.

ARNOLD C. SCHULTZ
B.A., M.A. (University of Chicago), B.D., Th.D. (Northern Baptist Theological Seminary). Former Lecturer in Near Eastern Studies, Roosevelt University.

SAMUEL J. SCHULTZ
B.A. (John Fletcher College), B.D. (Faith Theological Seminary), S.T.M., Th.D. (Harvard Divinity School). Chairman Emeritus, Division of Biblical Studies, and Samuel Robinson Professor Emeritus of Biblical Studies, Wheaton College Graduate School.

WILBUR M. SMITH
D.D. (Dallas Theological Seminary), D.Litt. (Trinity Evangelical Divinity School). Former Professor Emeritus of English Bible, Trinity Evangelical Divinity School.

MERRILL C. TENNEY
Th.B. (Gordon College of Theology and Missions), A.M. (Boston University), Ph.D. (Harvard University). Former Dean and J. P. Williston Professor of Bible and Theology, Wheaton College Graduate School.

EDWIN R. THIELE
M.A., Ph.D. (University of Chicago), D.D. (Andrews University). Professor Emeritus of Religion and Philosophy and Professor Emeritus of Antiquity, Andrews University.

PETER TOON
M.A. (University of Liverpool), M.Th. (University of London), D.Phil. (Oxford University). Director of Post-Ordination Training, Diocese of St. Edmundsbury and Ipswich.

MERRILL F. UNGER
A.B., Ph.D. (Johns Hopkins University), Th.M., Th.D. (Dallas Theological Seminary). Former Department Chairman and Professor Emeritus of Old Testament and Semitics, Dallas Theological Seminary.

WALTER W. WESSEL
Th.B. (Biola College), M.A. (University of California at Los Angeles), Ph.D. (University of Edinburgh). Professor of New Testament and Greek, Bethel Theological Seminary, West Campus.

JOHN C. WHITCOMB, JR.
A.B. (Princeton University), B.D., Th.M., Th.D. (Grace Theological Seminary). Professor of Theology and Old Testament, Director of Post-Graduate Studies, Grace Theological Seminary.

EDWARD J. YOUNG
A.B. (Leland Stanford Junior University), Th.B., Th.M. (Westminster Theological Seminary), Ph.D. (Dropsie College). Former Professor of Old Testament, Westminster Theological Seminary.

Abbreviations

GENERAL ABBREVIATIONS

Aram.	Aramaic
c.	about, approximately
cent.	century
cf.	compare
ch.	chapter (*pl.* chs.)
cm.	centimeters
contra	in contrast to
ed.	editor (*pl.* eds.); edition; edited by
e.g.	for example
et al.	and others
EV	English version of Bible
f.	and following (*pl.* ff.)
ft.	feet
Gr.	Greek
Heb.	Hebrew
ibid.	in the same place
id.	the same
i.e.	that is
in.	inches
in loc.	in the place cited
km.	kilometers
l.	liters
Lat.	Latin
lit.	literal; literally
LXX	Septuagint
m.	meters
mg.	margin
mi.	miles
MS	manuscript (*pl.* MSS)
MT	Masoretic Text
n.	note (*pl.* nn.)
n.d.	no date
no.	number
NT	New Testament
OT	Old Testament
p.	page (*pl.* pp.)
pl.	plural
repr.	reprint; reprinted
s.v.	under the word
TR	Textus Receptus
trans.	translated by; translation
v.	verse (*pl.* vv.)
vol.	volume (*pl.* vols.)

BOOKS OF THE BIBLE

The following abbreviations are used for books of the Bible (Old Testament, New Testament, and Apocrypha) when mentioned in parenthetical references. When the name of the Bible book is in the text of an article, it is ordinarily not abbreviated.

Old Testament

Gen
Exod
Lev
Num
Deut
Josh
Judg
Ruth
1 Sam
2 Sam
1 Kings
2 Kings
1 Chron
2 Chron
Ezra
Neh
Esth
Job
Ps
Prov
Eccl
S of Sol
Isa
Jer
Lam
Ezek
Dan
Hos
Joel
Amos
Obad
Jonah
Mic
Nah
Hab
Zeph
Hag
Zech
Mal

New Testament

Matt
Mark
Luke
John
Acts
Rom
1 Cor
2 Cor
Gal
Eph
Phil
Col
1 Thess
2 Thess
1 Tim
2 Tim
Titus
Philem
Heb
James
1 Peter
2 Peter
1 John
2 John
3 John
Jude
Rev

Apocrypha

1 Esd	1 Esdras
2 Esd	2 Esdras
Tobit	Tobit
Jud	Judith
Add Esth	Additions to Esther
Wisd Sol	Wisdom of Solomon
Ecclus	Ecclesiasticus (Wisdom of Jesus the Son of Sirach)
Baruch	Baruch
Ep Jer	Epistle of Jeremy
S Th Ch	Song of the Three Children (or Young Men)
Sus	Susanna
Bel	Bel and the Dragon
Pr Man	Prayer of Manasseh
1 Macc	1 Maccabees
2 Macc	2 Maccabees

BIBLE VERSIONS, PERIODICALS, REFERENCE BOOKS, AND OTHER SOURCES

Anab	Zenophon, *Anabasis*
AB	*Anchor Bible*
A-S	Abbott-Smith, *Manual Greek Lexicon of the New Testament*
Alf	Alford's Greek Testament
Antiq	Josephus, *Antiquities of the Jews*
Arndt	Arndt-Gingrich, *A Greek-English Lexicon of the New Testament and Other Early Christian Literature*
ARAB	*Ancient Records of Assyria and Babylonia* (D. D. Luckenbill, 1926)
ARC	*Archaeology*
ASV	The American Standard Version
AThR	*The Anglican Theological Review*
AV	The Authorized Version (The King James Version)
BA	*The Biblical Archaeologist*
BASOR	*Bulletin of American Schools of Oriental Research*
Beng	Bengel's *Gnomon*
BETS	*Bulletin of the Evangelical Theological Society*
Blunt	Blunt's *Dictionary of Doctrinal and Historical Theology*
BS	*Bibliotheca Sacra*
BTh	*Biblical Theology*
CBC	*Cambridge Bible Commentary*
CBQ	*Catholic Biblical Quarterly*
CGT	*Cambridge Greek Testament*
ChT	*Christianity Today*
Corp Herm	*Corpus Hermeticum*
Crem	Cremer's *Biblico-Theological Lexicon of New Testament Greek*
DeissBS	Deissmann, *Bible Studies*
DeissLAE	Deissmann, *Light from the Ancient East*
DSS	Dead Sea Scrolls
EB	*The Expositor's Bible*
EBC	*The Expositor's Bible Commentary*
EGT	*The Expositor's Greek Testament*
EQ	*The Evangelical Quarterly*
ERV	The English Revised Version (Revised Version)
ETh	*Evangelische Theologie*
EXP	*The Expositor*
ExpT	*The Expository Times*
GNB	The Good News Bible
GNC	*Good News Commentary*
GR	*Gordon Review*
HDAC	Hastings' *Dictionary of the Apostolic Church*
HDB	Hastings' *Dictionary of the Bible*
HDCG	Hastings' *Dictionary of Christ and the Gospels*
HERE	Hastings' *Encyclopedia of Religion and Ethics*
HJ	*Hibbert Journal*
HNTC	*Harper's New Testament Commentaries*
HR	Hatch and Redpath, *A Concordance to the Septuagint & Other Greek Versions of the Old Testament*
HTR	*The Harvard Theological Review*
HZNT	*Handbuch zum Neuen Testament* (Lietzmann)
IB	*The Interpreter's Bible*
ICC	*International Critical Commentary*
IDB	*The Interpreter's Dictionary of the Bible*
INT	*Interpretation*
ISBE	*The International Standard Bible Encyclopaedia*
JB	The Jerusalem Bible
JBL	*Journal of Biblical Literature*
JBR	*Journal of Bible and Religion*
JewEnc	*Jewish Encyclopaedia*
JNES	*Journal of Near Eastern Studies*
JQR	*Jewish Quarterly Review*
JTS	*Journal of Theological Studies*
KD	Keil and Delitzsch, *Commentaries on the Old Testament*
KJV	The King James Version (The Authorized Version)
LBC	*Liberty Bible Commentary*
Life	Josephus, *The Life of Flavius Josephus*
LSJ	Liddell, Scott, Jones, *Greek-English Lexicon*
MLB	The Modern Language Bible
MM	Moulton and Milligan, *The Vocabulary of the Greek Testament*
MNT	Moffatt's *New Testament Commentary*

Mof	James Moffatt, *The Bible: A New Translation*
MSt	McClintock and Strong, *Cyclopaedia of Biblical, Theological and Ecclesiastical Literature*
NASB	The New American Standard Bible
NBCrev	*The New Bible Commentary: Revised*
NBD	*The New Bible Dictionary*
NCB	*New Century Bible Commentary*
NEB	The New English Bible
Nestle	Nestle (ed.), *Novum Testamentum Graece*
NIC	*New International Commentary*
NICNT	*New International Commentary New Testament*
NIGTC	*New International Greek Testament Commentary*
NIV	The New International Version
NovTest	*Novum Testamentum*
NTS	*New Testament Studies*
PTR	*Princeton Theological Review*
RB	*Révue Biblique*
RGG	*Die Religion in Geschichte und Gegenwart*
RSV	The Revised Standard Version
RTWB	Richardson's *Theological Word Book of the Bible*
RV	The Revised Version, 1881 (English Revised Version)
SBK	*Kommentar zum Neuen Testament aus Talmud und Midrasch* (Strack and Billerbeck)
SHERK	*The New Schaff-Herzog Encyclopedia of Religious Knowledge*
ST	*Studia Theologica*
TBC	*Torch Bible Commentaries*
TCERK	*The Twentieth Century Encyclopedia of Religious Knowledge*
TDNT	*Theological Dictionary of the New Testament*
ThLZ	*Theologische Literaturzeitung*
ThR	*Theologische Rundschau*
ThT	*Theology Today*
TNTC	*Tyndale New Testament Commentaries*
TOTC	*Tyndale Old Testament Commentaries*
Trench	Trench's *Synonyms of the New Testament*
TWNT	*Theologisches Wörterbuch zum Neuen Testament*
VT	*Vetus Testamentum*
War	Josephus, *The Jewish War*
WBC	*Word Biblical Commentary*
WC	*Westminster Commentaries*
Wett	Wettstein's *Novum Testamentum Graecum*
Wey	R. F. Weymouth, *The New Testament in Modern Speech*
WH	B. F. Westcott and F. J. A. Hort, *The New Testament in Greek*
WTJ	*The Westminster Theological Journal*
ZAW	*Zeitschrift für die alttestamentliche Wissenschaft*
ZNW	*Zeitschrift für die neutestamentliche Wissenschaft*

English Pronunciation

VOWELS		CONSONANTS	
ā	as in tāme, hāte, chā'ŏs, dāte	b	bed, dub
ă	as in hat, ask, glass, add, lap	d	did, had
â	as in câre, bâre, râre	g	get, dog
ȧ	as in ȧh, ȧrm, fȧ'thêr, sō'fȧ	h	he, ahead
		j	joy jump
ē	as in ēve, hēre, ēvĕnt', mēēt	k	kill, bake
ĕ	as in ĕnd, sīlĕnt, pĕt, ēvĕnt	l	let, ball
êr	as in mākêr, ōvêr, ŭndêr, fȧthêr, êrr	m	met, trim
		n	not, ton
ī	as in īce, bīte, mīle, fīne	p	put, tap
ĭ	as in ĭll, hĭt, hĭm, chârĭty	r	red, dear
î	as in bîrth, mîrth	s	sell, pass
		t	top, hat
		v	vat, have
ō	as in ōld, ōbey, gō, tōne, bōwl	w	will, always
ŏ	as in ŏn, ŏdd, cŏnnĕct, lŏt, tŏp	y	yet, yard
ô	as in ôrb, sôft, hôrn, fôrk, nôr	z	zebra, haze
o͞o	as in fo͞od, lo͞ot, tro͞op		—
o͝o	as in fo͝ot, bo͝ok, ho͝ok	ch	chin, arch
		n	ring, drink
		sh	she, dash
ū	as in tūne, rūde, ūnīte', ūse, cūte	th	thin, truth
ŭ	as in ŭs, ŭp, bŭt	*th*	then, father
û	as in ûrn, tûrn, fûr	zh	azure, leisure

For other variations, also double vowels and consonants, the dictionary uses simplified and phonetic spelling to indicate pronunciation:

â	for e as in where, there	oi	for oy, oi, as in boy, boil, oil, foil
â	for ei, ai, ea as in their, fair, bear	ow	for ou as in about, shout
ā	for ai as in hail, pail	ū	for eu as in neuter
aw	for au, ou as in ought, caught	egs	for x in example
ē	for ee, ea, as in heed, meat, meal, dear	j	for soft g as in giant
ē	for i as in machine	k	for hard ch as in character
ē	for y as in belly, fully, charity	s	for soft c as in celestial
ī	for ei as in heil	sh	for s as in pressure
ī	for y as in type, why	shun	for tion as in attention
ĭ	for y as in typical, hypnosis	z	for soft s as in his

Transliterations

Hebrew

א = ʼ	ד = *dh*	י = *y*	ס = *s*	ר = *r*
בּ = *b*	ה = *h*	כּ = *k*	ע = ʻ	שׂ = *s*
ב = *v*	ו = *w*	ךְ כ = *kh*	פּ = *p*	שׁ = *sh*
גּ = *g*	ז = *z*	ל = *l*	ף פ = *ph*	תּ = *t*
ג = *gh*	ח = *ch*	ם מ = *m*	ץ צ = *ts*	ת = *th*
דּ = *d*	ט = *ṭ*	ן נ = *n*	ק = *q*	

(ה)ָ = *â (h)*	ָ = *ā*	ַ = *a*	ֲ = ^{a}
יֵ = *ê*	ֵ = *ē*	ֶ = *e*	ֱ = ^{e}
יִ = *î*	ֹ = *ō*	ִ = *i*	ְ = ^{e} *(if vocal)*
וֹ = *ô*		ָ = *o*	ֳ = ^{o}
וּ = *û*		ֻ = *u*	

Greek

α = *a*	η = *ē*	ν = *n*	τ = *t*
β = *b*	θ = *th*	ξ = *x*	υ = *y*
γ = *g*	ι = *i*	ο = *o*	φ = *ph*
δ = *d*	κ = *k*	π = *p*	χ = *ch*
ε = *e*	λ = *l*	ρ = *r*	ψ = *ps*
ζ = *z*	μ = *m*	σ,ς = *s*	ω = *ō*

αυ = *au*	γγ = *ng*	ᾳ = *ā*	῾ = *h*
ευ = *eu*	γκ = *nk*	ῃ = *ē*	ῥ = *rh*
ηυ = *ēu*	γξ = *nx*	ῳ = *ō*	
ου = *ou*	γχ = *nch*		
υι = *ui*			

The New INTERNATIONAL DICTIONARY OF THE BIBLE

Pictorial Edition

A

AARON (âr'ŭn, Heb. *'ahărôn,* meaning uncertain). The oldest son of Amram and Jochebed, of the tribe of Levi, and brother of Moses and Miriam (Exod 6:2; Num 26:59). He was born during the captivity in Egypt, before Pharaoh's edict that all male infants should be destroyed, and was three years older than Moses (Exod 7:7). His name first appears in God's commission to Moses. When Moses protested that he did not have sufficient ability in public speaking to undertake the mission to Pharaoh, God declared that Aaron should be spokesman for his brother (4:10–16). So Aaron met Moses at "the mountain of God" (4:27) after forty years' separation, and took him back to the family home in Goshen. Aaron introduced him to the elders of the people and persuaded them to accept him as their leader. Together Moses and Aaron went to Pharaoh's court, where they carried on the negotiations that finally brought an end to the oppression of the Israelites and precipitated the Exodus from Egypt.

During Moses' forty years in the wilderness Aaron had married Elisheba, daughter of Amminadab and sister of Nahshon, a prince of the tribe of Judah (Exod 6:23; 1 Chron 2:10). They had four sons: Nadab, Abihu, Eleazar, and Ithamar (Exod 6:23).

After Israel left Egypt, Aaron assisted his brother during the wandering in the wilderness. On the way to Sinai, in the battle with Amalek, Aaron and Hur held up Moses' hands (Exod 17:9–13), in which was the staff of God. Israel consequently won the battle. With the establishment of the tabernacle, Aaron became high priest in charge of the national worship and the head of the hereditary priesthood.

In character he was weak and occasionally jealous. He and Miriam criticized Moses for having married a Cushite woman (Num 12:1–2). This may have been an intentionally insulting reference to Zipporah. (See Hab 3:7 for a linking of Midian and Cush; Zipporah is always elsewhere described as a Midianite.) Behind this personal slight lies a more serious threat to Moses' position. Aaron was high priest and thus the supreme religious leader of Israel; Miriam was a prophetess (Exod 15:20). The great issue is not whom Moses had married but whether Moses could any longer be considered the sole, authoritative mouthpiece of God. As Aaron and Miriam said, "Hasn't he also spoken through us?" (Num 12:2). It is in the light of this basic challenge to Moses' God-given status that we must understand and appreciate the prompt and dramatic response of the Lord (12:4ff.).

We may further note that Aaron's own authority as priest did not go unchallenged. It becomes clear that when Korah and his company (Num 16) challenged Moses' leadership, Aaron's priesthood was also called into question. By the miraculous sign of the flowering and fruitbearing staff, the Lord identified Aaron as his chosen priest (17:1–9) and accorded him a perpetual priesthood by ordering his staff to be deposited in the sanctuary (17:10).

When Moses went up Mount Sinai to receive the tables of the law from God, Aaron acceded to the people's demand for a visible god that they could worship. Taking their personal jewelry, he melted it in a furnace and made a golden calf similar to the familiar bull-god of Egypt. The people hailed this image as the god who had brought them out of Egypt. Aaron did not remonstrate with them but built an altar and proclaimed a feast to the Lord on the next day, which the people celebrated with revelry and debauchery (Exod 32:1–6). When Moses returned from the mountain and rebuked Aaron for aiding this abuse, Aaron gave this naïve answer: "They gave me the gold, and I threw it into the fire, and out came this calf!" (32:24). It may be that Aaron meant to restrain the people by a compromise, but he was wholly unsuccessful.

Much is made of the consecration of Aaron and his sons as priests. The "dignity and honor" (Exod 28:2) of their office was expressed in garments of great beauty and significance: the breastpiece, ephod, robe, tunic, turban, and sash. The ceremony of appointment is described in Exodus 29 and enacted in Leviticus 8. It involved offering a sin offering and a burnt offering on behalf of the priests-to-be (Exod 29:10–14, 15–18), for though they were priests, they were first of all sinners needing the grace of God in atonement (Heb 5:2–3).

The consecration included three special ceremonies: (1) their ears, hands, and feet were touched with the blood of a ram, signifying the hallowing of the mind and of the acts and directions of life (what they would hear, what they would do, where they would go), respectively (Exod 29:19–20); (2) they were anointed with oil mingled with the sacrificial blood, symbolizing the grace of God in atonement (blood) and endowment (oil) (29:21); (3) their hands were filled with some of the fat of the slain beasts along with various sorts of bread, and the whole was lifted up in offering to the Lord (29:22–23). Just as we say that a busy person "has his hands full," so they consecrated the whole business of living—life's special duties, seen in the fat of the

Mount Hor (Jebel Haroun), just west of Petra, one of the traditional sites associated with the death and burial of Aaron. Courtesy Garo Nalbandian.

sacrifices; life's ordinary cares and needs, seen in the bread—to the Lord. After eight days (Lev 9:1) Aaron and his sons entered their public ministry, offering the sin offering, burnt offering, and fellowship offering on behalf of the people. This first act of ministry received divine ratification in the appearing of the glory of the Lord and the fire of God that fell on the offering (9:23–24).

At the end of the wilderness wandering, Aaron was warned of his impending death. He and Moses went up Mount Hor, where Aaron was stripped of his priestly robes, which passed in succession to his son Eleazar. Aaron died at the age of 123 and was buried on the mountain (Num 20:22–29; 33:38; Deut 10:6; 32:50). The people mourned for him thirty days.

The Psalms speak of the priestly line as the "house of Aaron" (Ps 115:10, 12; 118:3; 135:19), and Aaron is mentioned in the Book of Hebrews as a type of Christ, who was "called by God, just as Aaron was" (Heb 5:4–5), though the eternal priesthood of Christ is stated explicitly to be derived from Melchizedek and not from Aaron (7:11). SB and JAM

AARONITES (âr'ŭn-īts). Descendants of Aaron who fought with David against Saul (1 Chron 12:27; NIV "family of Aaron"). They were distinguished from the Levites (27:17).

AB. The fifth month of the Hebrew year, coinciding approximately with early August (Num 33:38). See CALENDAR.

ABADDON (à-băd'ŭn, Heb. *'ăvaddôn, ruin, perdition, destruction*). The term is found once in the NT (Rev 9:11), where its Greek equivalent is Apollyon, the angel who reigns over the infernal regions. Its general meaning of "ruin, destruction" is variously translated in such passages as Job 26:6; 28:22; 31:12; Psalm 88:11; Proverbs 15:11; 27:20.

ABAGTHA (à-băg'thà, Heb. *'ăvaghethā'*). One of the seven eunuchs who served King Xerxes (Ahasuerus) as chamberlains (Esth 1:10). The king had the eunuchs bring Queen Vashti before him. Oriental kings customarily had eunuchs to supervise their harems.

ABANA (à-băn'à, Heb. *'ăvānâ,* KJV, RSV, NIV; Abanah, ASV). The name of a river that flows through Damascus. Mentioned in the Bible only in 2 Kings 5:12, where Naaman asks, "Are not Abana and Pharpar, the rivers of Damascus, better than any of the waters of Israel?" The Greeks called it the Chrysorrhoas ("golden stream"); it is the same as the modern Barada River. Beginning twenty-three miles (thirty-eight km.) NW of Damascus in the Anti-Lebanon Mountains, it flows through Damascus, making the city, though bordering on a desert, one of the loveliest and most fertile on earth. It divides into nine or ten branches and spreads out like an open fan into the plain east of Damascus.

Engraving of the Abana River at Damascus, based on a late nineteenth-century photograph by Bonfils.

ABARIM (ăb'à-rĭm, Heb. *'avārîm, those beyond,* or *on the other side*). Either the region east of the Jordan or the name of a mountain range NW of Moab. The Israelites encamped here just before crossing the Jordan (Num 33:47), and from one of its peaks Moses saw the Promised Land (Num 27:12).

ABBA (ăb'à, Heb. *'abbā'*). Aramaic word for *father,* transliterated into Greek and thence into English. The corresponding Hebrew word is Ab. Abba is found three times in the NT (Mark 14:36; Rom 8:15; Gal 4:6).

ABDA (ăb'dà, Heb. *'avdā',* probably *servant of God*). 1. The father of Adoniram (1 Kings 4:6).

2. A Levite, the son of Shammua (Neh 11:17), called "Obadiah the son of Shemaiah" (1 Chron 9:16).

ABDEEL (ăb'dē-ĕl, Heb. *'avde'ēl, servant of God*). The father of Shelemiah, ordered by King Jehoiakim to arrest Jeremiah the prophet and his scribe, Baruch (Jer 36:26).

ABDI (ăb'dī, Heb. *'avdî, probably servant of Jehovah*). 1. A Levite, father of Kishi, the grandfather of David's singer Ethan (1 Chron 6:44). It is uncertain whether the Abdi of 2 Chronicles 29:12 is the same man.

2. One of the sons of Elam who in Ezra's time had married foreign wives (Ezra 10:26).

ABDIEL (ăb'dī-ĕl, Heb. *'avdî 'ēl, servant of God*). A Gadite who lived in Gilead (1 Chron 5:15).

ABDON (ăb'dŏn, Heb. *'avdôn*, meaning uncertain, may be *servant, service*, or *servile*). 1. One of the judges of Israel—the eleventh one mentioned. Nothing is said about his rule except that he judged Israel for eight years (Judg 12:13–15). Josephus says that his reign was a peaceful one, and therefore "he had no occasion to perform glorious actions" (*Antiq.*, 5.7.15).

2. One of the sons of Shashak, a Benjamite, living in Jerusalem (1 Chron 8:23, 28).

3. The son of Jeiel of Gibeon (1 Chron 8:30; 9:35–36).

4. An official of King Josiah, sent by him to Huldah the prophetess (2 Chron 34:20; called Acbor in 2 Kings 22:12).

ABDON. One of four Levitical cities in the tribe of Asher (Josh 21:30; 1 Chron 6:74). It may be the same as "Hebron" in Joshua 19:28. Now called Abdeh, near the Mediterranean and about fifteen miles (twenty-five km.) south of Tyre.

ABEDNEGO (ȧ-bĕd'nē-gō, Heb. *'ăvēdhneghô, servant of Nego*). One of the three Hebrews (the other two were Shadrach and Meshach) whom Daniel requested be appointed over the affairs of the province of Babylon. The three were later saved from the fiery furnace (Dan 1:7; 3:12–30).

ABEL (ā'bĕl, Heb. *hevel*). A Hebrew word of this spelling means "breath," "vapor," that which is "insubstantial"; but more likely the name should be linked with an Accadian word meaning "son." He was Adam and Eve's second son, who was murdered by his brother Cain (Gen 4). "Abel kept flocks, and Cain worked the soil" (4:2). The problem that caused disaffection between the brothers arose when Cain brought a vegetable offering to the Lord, and Abel brought a lamb from the flock. "The Lord looked with favor on Abel and his offering, but on Cain and his offering he did not look with favor" (4:4–5). What this precisely means the Bible does not make clear. The Lord had previously made his will known that man must approach him with blood-sacrifice (possibly the revelation was made at 3:21); or possibly with this incident between Cain and Abel the Lord revealed that he required animal sacrifice. Two things tend to suggest an earlier revelation of this requirement: first, the Genesis account has "Abel and his offering," "Cain and his offering," in each case putting the person first and suggesting that the one came in a correct spirit whereas the other did not. Second, the Book of Hebrews suggests the same view: "By faith Abel offered God a better sacrifice than Cain did" (Heb 11:4). How could he have acted in faith if there had not been a prior word from the Lord for him to believe and obey? Cain, by contrast, came in a defiant spirit, as is revealed in his hurt refusal of the Lord's reminder that the right way was open to him and in his resentful murder of his brother. Thus Abel became the first exemplar of the way of righteousness through faith (Matt 23:35; 1 John 3:12). JAM

ABEL (ā'bĕl, Heb. *'āvēl, a meadow*). 1. The name of a city involved in the rebellion of Sheba (2 Sam 20:14, 18); the same as Abel Beth Maacah (20:15).

2. In 1 Samuel 6:18, KJV has "the great stone of Abel," but NIV has "the large rock."

ABEL BETH MAACAH (ā'bel bĕth mā'ȧ-kȧ, Heb. *'āvēl bêth ma'ăkhâh*). *Abel of Beth-Maacah*, in KJV written "Maachah"; Abel, i.e., "meadow,"

The large, ancient mound of Abel Beth Maacah, looking north-northeast. In the days of David, it was a fortified place and "a city that is a mother in Israel" (2 Sam 20:19). Courtesy Duby Tal.

or perhaps "brook," near Beth Maacah. A town in the extreme north of Palestine, probably about twelve miles (twenty km.) north of Lake Huleh, in the tribe of Naphtali (2 Sam 20:15; 1 Kings 15:20). Sheba, son of Bicri, fled to it when his revolt against David failed. The town was saved from assault by Joab when, with its proverbial shrewdness, it followed the advice of "a wise woman" that the people sacrifice Sheba (2 Sam 20:14–22). About eighty years later it was seized by Benhadad (1 Kings 15:20) and in 734 B.C. by Tiglath-Pileser, who carried off its inhabitants to Assyria (2 Kings 15:29).

ABEL KERAMIM (ā'bĕl kĕr-ȧ-mĭm, Heb. *'avēl-kerāmîm, meadow of vineyards* or *brook of vineyards*). A place in Ammon, east of the Jordan, to which Jephthah pursued the Ammonites (Judg 11:33).

ABEL MAIM (ā'bel ma'ĭm, Heb. *'āvēl-mayim, meadow of waters* or *brook of waters*). A variant of Abel Beth Maacah (2 Chron 16:4).

ABEL MEHOLAH (ā'bĕl mē-hō'lȧ, *meadow of dancing* or *brook of dancing*). A town not certainly identified, but probably in the Jordan valley, where Elisha was born and lived (1 Kings 19:16). The Midianites routed by Gideon fled to its environs (Judg 7:22).

ABEL MIZRAIM (ā'bĕl mĭz'rā-ĭm, Heb. *'āvēl-mitsrayim, meadow* or *mourning of Egypt*). A place east of the Jordan at which the funeral cortege of Jacob stopped to mourn for seven days before entering Canaan to bury the patriarch (Gen 50:11). It had been called the "threshing floor of Atad," but the Canaanites now called it the "mourning of Egypt" or the "funeral from Egypt," because the princes and chief men of Egypt, with their chariots and horsemen, took part in the funeral rites.

ABEL SHITTIM (ā'bĕl shĭt'ĭm, Heb. *'āvēl ha-shittîm, acacia meadow*). A locality in the plains of Moab where Israel rested for the last time before crossing the Jordan (Num 33:49).

ABEZ (See EBEZ)

ABIA (See ABIJAH)

ABI-ALBON (See ABIEL)

ABIASAPH (ȧ-bī'ă-săf, Heb. *'ăvî'āsāph, the father gathers,* or *adds*). A descendant of Levi through Korah (Exod 6:24).

ABIATHAR (ȧ-bī'ă-thȧr, Heb. *'evîāthār, father of abundance*). Son of Ahimelech, who with eighty-four other priests was killed at Nob on Saul's instructions, after Doeg had told the king that Ahimelech had helped David by inquiring of the Lord for him and by giving him Goliath's sword (1 Sam 22). Abiathar somehow escaped the slaughter and joined David, bringing the oracular ephod with him (22:20ff.). The term "high priest" is not actually used throughout these narratives, but it is clear that Abiathar and Zadok were in effect joint high priests when David brought the ark to Jerusalem (1 Chron 15:11f.). This situation continued through David's reign, as the references to the two men during Absalom's rebellion indicate (e.g., 2 Sam 15:24, 27, 29). Abiathar did not, however, give the same loyalty to Solomon, but associated himself with the cause of Adonijah, the eldest surviving son of David (1 Kings 1:7, 19, 25). It would appear that, even after the failure of Adonijah's attempt to succeed David, Abiathar was in some way still linked with him, for when Adonijah was executed on suspicion of plotting a coup, Abiathar was banished from Jerusalem (2:22–27). This terminated the joint priesthood of Zadok and Abiathar, as referred to in 1 Kings 4:4, and also fulfilled the prediction, made 150 years earlier, of the end of the priestly rule of the house of Eli (1 Sam 2:31–35). JAM

ABIB (ā'bĭb, Heb. *'āvîv, an ear of corn*). The preexilic name for the first month of the year (Exod 13:4; 23:15; 34:18). After the Exile the name was changed to Nisan. It fell about the time of March and early April. See also CALENDAR.

ABIDA (ȧ-bī'dȧ, Heb. *'ăvîdhā', the father knows*). This appears as Abidah in KJV of Genesis 25:4. A son of Midian and grandson of Abraham and Keturah (Gen 25:4; 1 Chron 1:33).

ABIDAN (ȧ-bī'dăn, Heb. *'ăvîdhān, the father is judge*). A prince of the tribe of Benjamin chosen to represent his tribe at the census in the wilderness of Sinai (Num 1:11; 2:22). He was present at the dedication of the tabernacle, making an offering as one of the heads of Israel (7:60, 65).

ABIEL (ā'bĭ-ĕl, Heb. *'ăvî'ēl, the father is God,* or *God is father*). 1. The grandfather of Saul and Abner (1 Sam 9:1; 14:51).

2. One of David's mighty men (1 Chron 11:32), also called Abi-Albon (2 Sam 23:31).

ABIEZER (ā'bī-ē'zêr, Heb. *'ăvî'ezer, father of help,* or *father is help*). 1. A descendant of Joseph and head of one of the families of Manasseh. Gideon belonged to this family (Judg 6:11–12; 8:2, 32). In Numbers 26:30, NASB and NIV have "Iezerrm," and KJV and NEB have "Jeezer."

2. One of David's mighty men (2 Sam 23:27; 1 Chron 11:28; 27:12).

ABIGAIL (ăb'ĭ-gāl, Heb. *'ăvîghayil, father is rejoicing*). 1. The wife of Nabal, and, after his death, of David (1 Sam 25:3, 14–44; 27:3; 2 Sam 3:3), to whom she bore his second son, Kileab (or 1 Chron 3:1, Daniel).

2. Hebrew *'ăvîghal.* A sister or stepsister of David. In 1 Chronicles 2:13–17 she apparently belongs to Jesse's family and is, along with Zeruiah, a sister of David. But in 2 Samuel 17:25 she is mentioned as a daughter of Nahash. The probability is that Nahash was the first husband of Jesse's wife—this would account for the slightly unusual way in which she and Zeruiah are recorded in Chronicles, not as Jesse's daughters but as his sons' sisters. She was married to an Ishmaelite, Jether (1 Chron 2:17; on 2 Sam 17:27 see NIV footnote), and became the mother of Amasa, Absalom's commander-in-chief (2 Sam 17:2), who was also for a time David's commander-in-chief (19:13). JAM

ABIHAIL (ăb'i-hāl, Heb. *'ăvîhayil, the father is strength*). 1. A Levite, the father of Zuriel, who in the wilderness was the head of the house of Merari (Num 3:25).

2. The wife of Abishur of the tribe of Judah (1 Chron 2:29).

3. A Gadite who lived in Gilead of Bashan (1 Chron 5:14).

4. The wife of Rehoboam, king of Judah. She

was a daughter of Eliab, David's oldest brother (2 Chron 11:18).

5. The father of Queen Esther (Esth 2:15; 9:29).

ABIHU (ȧ-bī'hū, Heb. *'ăvîhû, the father is he*). Second son of Aaron (Exod 6:23). With Aaron, Nadab his brother, and the seventy elders he went with Moses up Mount Sinai for a limited distance (24:1). It was his privilege to see the God of Israel (24:9–11), but subsequently he died under divine judgment because he offered "unauthorized fire before the LORD" (Num 10:1).

ABIHUD (ȧ-bī'hŭd, Heb. *'ăvîhûdh, the father is majesty*). The son of Bela, the eldest son of Benjamin (1 Chron 8:3).

ABIJAH (ȧ-bī'jȧ, Heb. *'ăvîyâh* or *'ăvîyāhû, Jehovah is father*). 1. The wife of Judah's grandson Hezron (1 Chron 2:24).

2. The seventh son of Beker, the son of Benjamin (1 Chron 7:8).

3. The second son of the prophet Samuel. Appointed a judge by his father, he became corrupt (1 Sam 8:2; 1 Chron 6:28).

4. A descendant of Aaron. The ancestral head of the eighth of the twenty-four groups into which David had divided the priests (1 Chron 24:10). The father of John the Baptist belonged to this group (Luke 1:5).

5. A son of Jeroboam I of Israel (1 Kings 14:1–18). He died from illness when still a child, in fulfillment of a prediction by the prophet Ahijah, to whom the queen had gone in disguise to inquire regarding the outcome of the child's illness. The death was a judgment for the apostasy of Jeroboam.

6. King of Judah, the son and successor of Rehoboam. He made war on Jeroboam in an effort to recover the ten tribes of Israel. In a speech before an important battle in which his army was greatly outnumbered, he appealed to Jeroboam not to oppose the God of Israel, for God had given the kingdom to David and his sons forever. Abijah gained a decisive victory. Prosperity tempted him to multiply wives and to follow the evil ways of his father. He reigned three years (2 Chron 12:16–14:1).

7. Hezekiah's mother (2 Chron 29:1), "Abi" in 2 Kings 18:2 (KJV, NASB, NEB, RSV).

8. A chief of the priests who returned from Babylon with Zerubbabel (Neh 12:4, 17).

9. A priest of Nehemiah's time (Neh 10:7).

ABILENE (ăb'ĭ-lēn, Gr. *Abilēnē,* probably from Heb., *meadow*). A tetrarchy near Anti-Lebanon. Luke 3:1 mentions it as the tetrarchy of Lysanias when John the Baptist began his ministry. Its capital, Abela, was about eighteen miles (thirty km.) NW of Damascus. In A.D. 37 the tetrarchy, with other territories, was given to Agrippa. When he died in 44, it was administered by procurators until 53, when the emperor of Rome conferred it on Agrippa II; on Agrippa II's death, toward the end of the century, it was made a part of the province of Syria.

ABIMAEL (ȧ-bĭm'ā-ĕl, Heb. *'ăvîmā'ēl, God is father*). The ninth of the thirteen sons or descendants of Joktan, who was descended from Shem (Gen 10:28; 1 Chron 1:22).

ABIMELECH (ȧ-bĭm'ĕ-lĕk, Heb. *'ăvîmelekh,* probably either *the father is king* or *the father of a king*). 1. A Philistine king of Gerar, near Gaza. It was at his court that Abraham, out of fear, said that Sarah was his sister. Struck by her beauty, Abimelech took her to marry her but when he was warned by God in a dream, he immediately returned her to Abraham (Gen 20:1–18). Later, when their servants contended over a well, the two men made a covenant (21:22–34).

2. A second king of Gerar, probably the son of the first-mentioned Abimelech. At his court Isaac tried to pass off his wife Rebekah as his sister (Gen 26:1–11). Abimelech rebuked Isaac when the falsehood was detected. Later their servants quarreled, and they made a covenant between them, as Abraham and the first Abimelech had done.

3. The son of Gideon by a concubine (Judg 8:31; 9:1–57). After the death of his father, aspiring to be king, he murdered seventy sons of his father. Only one son, Jotham, escaped. Abimelech was then made king of Shechem. After he had reigned only three years, rebellion broke out against him; in the course of the rebellion he attacked and destroyed his own city of Shechem. Later he was killed while besieging the nearby Thebez.

4. A Philistine king mentioned in the title of Psalm 34. He is very likely the same as Achish, king of Gath (1 Sam 21:10–22:1), with whom David sought refuge when he fled from Saul. It is possible that Abimelech was a royal title of Philistine kings, not a personal name.

5. A priest in the days of David, a son of Abiathar; also called Ahimelech (1 Chron 18:16; 24:6).

ABINADAB (ȧ-bĭn'ȧ-dăb, Heb. *'ăvînādhāv, the father is generous*). 1. A man living in Kiriath Jearim to whose home the ark was brought from the land of the Philistines. About a century later, David removed the ark to Jerusalem (1 Sam 7:1–2; 2 Sam 6:3; 1 Chron 13:7).

2. The second of the eight sons of Jesse. He was in Saul's army when Goliath gave his challenge (1 Sam 16:8; 17:13; 1 Chron 2:13).

3. A son of Saul. He was killed with his father by the Philistines at Mount Gilboa (1 Sam 17:13; 31:2; 1 Chron 8:33; 9:39; 10:2).

4. The father of a son-in-law of Solomon (1 Kings 4:11).

ABINOAM (ȧ-bĭn'ō-ăm, Heb. *'ăvînōam, the father is pleasantness*). The father of Barak (Judg 4:6; 5:12).

ABIRAM (ȧ-bī'răm, Heb. *'ăvîrām, the father is*

exalted). 1. A Reubenite who with his brothers Dathan and Korah conspired against Moses and was destroyed by God (Num 16).

2. The eldest son of Hiel the Bethelite, who rebuilt Jericho (1 Kings 16:34).

ABISHAG (ăb'ĭ-shăg, Heb. *'ăvîshagh, the father wanders,* or *errs*). A Shunamite woman who nursed David in his old age (1 Kings 1:3, 15). She reappears in the story (2:17ff.) when Adonijah, Solomon's elder half-brother, asked permission to marry her. For this Solomon had Adonijah executed. It may help us to understand Solomon's action when we consider that Absalom's behavior (2 Sam 16:20–22) shows that the household women of a former king were used as pawns in registering a claim to the throne. This may have been Adonijah's motive.

ABISHAI (ȧ-bĭsh'ā-ī, Heb. *'ăvîshay,* meaning is doubtful). Son of David's sister Zeruiah, and brother of Joab and Asahel. He was impetuous and courageous, cruel and hard to his foes, but always intensely loyal to David. He counseled David to kill the sleeping Saul (1 Sam 26:6–9). He aided Joab in the murder of Abner, an act of revenge for the slaying of their brother Asahel (2 Sam 3:30). He was loyal to David when Absalom and Sheba revolted, and he wanted to kill Shimei for cursing David (16:5–14). He defeated a large army of Edomites (1 Chron 18:12–13). Late in David's life he rescued the king in the fight with Ishbi-Benob, the Philistine giant (2 Sam 21:17).

ABISHALOM (See ABSALOM)

ABISHUA (ȧ-bĭsh'ū-ȧ, Heb. *'ăvîshûa'*, perhaps *the father is salvation* or *noble*). 1. The son of Phinehas the priest (1 Chron 6:4–5, 50; Ezra 7:5).

2. A Benjamite of the family of Bela (1 Chron 8:4).

ABISHUR (ȧ-bī'shêr, Heb. *'ăvîshûr, the father is a wall*). A man of Judah, the son of Shammai (1 Chron 2:28–29).

ABITAL (ȧ-bī'tăl, Heb. *'ăvîtāl, the father is dew*). One of the wives of David (2 Sam 3:4; 1 Chron 3:3).

ABITUB (ȧ-bī'tŭb, Heb. *'ăvîtûv, the father is goodness*). A Benjamite, son of Shaharaim and Hushim (1 Chron 8:8–11).

ABIUD (ȧ-bī'ŭd, Gr. *Abioud,* probably the Greek form of Abihud). The son of Zerubbabel. Mentioned only in the genealogy of Jesus (Matt 1:13).

ABNER (ăb'nêr, Heb. *'ăvnēr, the father is a lamp*). The son of Ner, who was the brother of Kish, the father of King Saul. Abner and Saul were therefore cousins. During Saul's reign, Abner was the commander-in-chief of Saul's army (1 Sam 14:50). It was Abner who brought David to Saul following the slaying of Goliath (17:55–58). He accompanied Saul in his pursuit of David (26:5ff.) and was rebuked by David for his failure to keep better watch over his master (26:13–16).

At Saul's death, Abner espoused the cause of Saul's house and had Ish-Bosheth, Saul's son, made king over Israel (2 Sam 2:8). Abner and his men met David's servants in combat by the pool of Gibeon and were overwhelmingly defeated. During the retreat from this battle, Abner was pursued by Asahel, Joab's brother, and in self-defense killed him (2:12–32).

Soon after this, Abner and Ish-Bosheth had a quarrel over Saul's concubine. Ish-Bosheth probably saw Abner's behavior with Rizpah as tantamount to a claim to the throne. This resulted in Abner's entering into negotiations with David to go to his side, and he promised to bring all Israel with him. David graciously received him; Abner had not been gone long when Joab heard of the affair, and, believing or pretending to believe that Abner had come as a spy, Joab invited him to a friendly conversation and murdered him "to avenge the blood of his brother Asahel" (2 Sam 3:6–27). This seems to have been a genuine grief to David, who composed a lament for the occasion (3:33–34).

ABOMINATION, ABOMINATION OF DESOLATION. The word *abomination* occurs rarely in the NIV (e.g., Prov 26:25; Isa 66:3; Dan 9:27; 11:31; 12:11; cf. "abominable," Isa 66:17; Jer 32:34). The idea is, however, much more widespread, most often expressed in the NIV by the verb *detest* and the adjective *detestable.* Two main Hebrew words are involved: (1) *shiqqutz,* used of idols (e.g., 2 Kings 23:24; Jer 7:30), of the gods represented by idols (e.g., 2 Kings 23:13), of forbidden practices (e.g., 23:24), and generally of anything contrary to the worship and religion of the Lord (e.g., 2 Chron 15:8; Isa 66:3; Jer 4:1). The related noun *sheqetz* is used of idols in animal form (Ezek 8:10), forbidden foods (Lev 11:10, 13, 42), and generally of anything bringing ceremonial defilement (7:21). (2) *tô'evah.* This word is often synonymous with *shiqqutz,* but is also used in wider areas of life. It is used of things related to idols (Deut 7:25; 27:15) and of the false gods themselves (32:16); but it is used also, for example, of forbidden sexual practices (e.g., Lev 18:22, 26–27), of prophecy leading to the worship of other gods (Deut 13:13–14), of offering blemished animals in sacrifice (17:1), and of heathen divination (18:9, 12). Basic to the use of these words, then, is the active abhorrence the Lord feels toward that which challenges his position as the sole God of his people, or contradicts his will, whether in the way he is to be worshiped or the way his people are to live.

The interpretation of the references of Daniel to some notable and frightful abomination (Dan 9:27; 11:31; 12:11) has caused much difficulty and difference among interpreters. Many continue to hold that Daniel 11:31 was fulfilled in 186 B.C., when the Syrian Antiochus Epiphanes set up an altar in the Jerusalem temple and sacrificed a pig on it. But Matthew 24:15 and Mark 13:14 make it clear that the Lord Jesus understood the "abomination" as still to come. Some understand the Lord to refer to some horrifying act of sacrilege during the period of the Jewish revolt and the sack of Jerusalem by the Romans in A.D. 70. It cannot, however, be the entry of the Romans into the Most Holy Place, for the setting up of the abomination is offered by the Lord as a sign to his true followers that they must leave the city without delay to avoid being caught up in its overthrow. Once the city fell to the Romans, the time of flight would be past. It is more likely, therefore, that the reference is to Jewish zealot rebels who actually set up their military headquarters in the Holy Place. Other interpreters, however, understand the Lord to be speaking not of the fall of Jerusalem but of the end-time itself, immediately prior to his own coming; and they link the setting up of the abomination with the appearance and activity of the man of sin (2 Thess 2:3–4, 8–9).

Bibliography: C. R. Erdman, *The Gospel of Mark,* 1945; R. T. France, *Jesus and the Old Testament,* 1971; W. L. Lane, *The Gospel of Mark,* 1974. JAM

ABRAHAM (ā'brȧ-hăm, Heb. *'avrāhām, father of a multitude;* earlier name Abram, Heb. *'avram, exalted father*). Son of Terah, founder of the Hebrew nation and father of the people of God, he traced his ancestry back to Noah through Shem (Gen 11:10ff.) and came into the Bible story out of an idolatrous background (Josh 24:2). After the death of his brother Haran (Gen 11:28), Abram moved in obedience to a divine vision (Acts 7:2–4) from Ur of the Chaldees in Mesopotamia to the city of Haran in the extreme north of Palestine. He was accompanied by his father Terah, his wife and half-sister Sarai, and his nephew Lot (Gen 11:31–32).

Abraham's renown in the Bible as a man of faith and the father of the people of faith is a direct consequence of the way the Bible tells his story. Like all history writing, the Bible is selective in the facts it records, choosing those that are most significant to bring out the meaning of the events. The Genesis account of Abraham's life records the development of his faith—from the imperfect faith of Genesis 12–13, through the growing faith of Genesis 14–17, and on to the mature faith of Genesis 18–25:10.

At age seventy-five (Gen 12:4) Abram was commanded to leave all and go out into the unknown, sustained only by the promises of God (12:1–3). In faith he obeyed, but with an imperfect obedience. Contrary to the command to leave his "father's household," he took his nephew Lot with him, laying the foundation for considerable future trouble (chs 13, 19). When Abram arrived in Canaan (12:6), God confirmed the promise that this was the land Abram's descendants would possess (12:7), but the imperfection of Abram's faith again appeared. Although as-

Ancient Oak of Mamre, about two miles north of Hebron, thought to be the site where Abram pitched his tent (Gen 13:18). The picture was taken around the turn of the century. From the private collection of the Ottoman Sultan Abdul-Hamid (1876–1909). Courtesy University Library, Istanbul.

sured by God that he was in the right place, Abram deserted Canaan for Egypt in a time of famine and, still uncertain whether the Lord could preserve him in trouble, tried to pass off Sarai as his sister, hoping to purchase his own safety at her expense (12:10–20). Yet Abram's imperfection of faith did not shake the promises of God, who first acted to protect the chosen family in Egypt (12:17–20) and then, when Abram tried to solve family problems (13:7) by dividing up the Promised Land, reaffirmed (13:14–17) that none but Abram and his descendants could inherit the promises.

The fascinating glimpse into the international tensions of the ancient world given in Genesis 14 allows us to see Abram's growing faith. Clearly he is now more aware of himself as the man separated to God from the world. He first opposed the kings (14:13–16) and then refused the world's wealth (14:21–24). These are plainly the acts of a man confident in the protection and provision of God. The Lord was not slow to respond in both regards (15:1). But the richness of the divine response provoked Abram to question the point of it all, for he had no son to inherit what the Lord would give him. This leads to that high moment of faith when Abram, fully aware that every human aspect of the situation was against him (Rom 4:18–21), rested wholly and absolutely on God's word of promise; this is the faith that justifies (Gen 15:4–6). But though Abram had leaped onto a pinnacle of faith, he was still only learning to walk in the way of faith.

The Lord confirmed his promises of children and land in a great covenant sign (Gen 15:7–21), but Abram and Sarai, tired of waiting (ch 16), turned from the way of faith to a human expedient that was permitted—even expected—by the laws of the day: a childless couple might "have children" through the medium of a secondary wife. Poor, mistreated Hagar fell into this role. Yet the Lord was not diverted from his chosen course: in gentle grace he picked up the pieces of Hagar's broken life (16:7–16) and reaffirmed his covenant with Abram (17:1ff.). In three ways the Lord made his promises more sure. First, by making Abram and Sarai into new people (17:3–5, 15–16). This is the significance of the gift of new names: they are themselves made new, with new capacities. Second, the Lord restated and amplified his spoken promises so as to leave no doubt of his seriousness in making them (17:6–8). Third, he sealed his promises with the sign of circumcision (17:9–14) so that forever after Abraham and his family would be able to look at their own bodies and say, "The Lord has indeed kept his promises to me!"

Out of this experience of becoming the new man, Abraham, and having the promises confirmed and sealed, Abraham's faith grew to maturity. Genesis 17:17–22:19 is the tale of two sons. Abraham deeply loved his sons Ishmael and Isaac (17:18; 21:11–12), yet he was called to give them both up—in faith that the Lord would keep his promises concerning them (21:11–13; 22:1–18). The Lord did not spring these great decisions on Abraham, but prepared him for them by his experience over Lot and Sodom (chs 18–19). In this connection Abraham would learn two lessons: First, that it is not a vain thing to leave matters in the hand of God—he prayed, and the Lord answered prayer (18:22–33); second, that the Lord really meant the "family" aspect of his promises—even Lot was preserved because the Lord "remembered Abraham" (19:29). To be linked with the covenant man was to come under the sovereign hand of the covenant God. And if Lot, how much more Ishmael, and how very much more the son of promise himself, Isaac! Thus Abraham came to the maturity of faith that enabled him to say (22:5), "We will go . . . we will worship . . . we will come back"—knowing that the worship in question involved raising the knife over Isaac.

Quietly the underlining of the maturity of Abraham's faith proceeds: Sarah was laid to rest within the Promised Land by her husband, who was planning to be buried there himself, awaiting the fulfillment of the promise of possession. Sternly Abraham's servant was forbidden to move Isaac away from the place of promise (Gen 24:6–7), for even if Isaac had to marry a Canaanite girl (24:8), he was not to leave the land designated by God.

Three main streams of NT thought focus on Abraham as the exemplar of faith. Paul stresses faith as simple trust in the promises of God (Rom 4:18–22); Hebrews takes note especially of the patience of faith (11:8–16; cf. 6:11–13); and James brings out the essential obedience that proves faith to be geniune (2:21–23).

Bibliography: A. M. Stibbs, *God's Friend,* 1964; R. E. Clements, *Abraham and David,* 1967; D. J. Wiseman, "Abraham Re-assessed," in *Essays on the Patriarchal Narratives,* ed. A. R. Millard and D. J. Wiseman, 1980; R. S. Wallace, *Abraham,* 1981.
JAM

ABRAHAM'S SIDE (Luke 16:22–23; "Abraham's bosom" in JB, KJV, NASB, and RSV). It indicates *blessedness after death.* The figure derives either from the Roman custom of reclining on the left side at meals, Lazarus being in the place of honor at Abraham's right, leaning on his breast, or from its appropriateness as expressing closest fellowship (John 1:18; 13:23). Since Abraham was the founder of the Hebrew nation, such closeness was the highest honor and bliss.

ABRAM (See ABRAHAM)

ABRECH (ăb'rĕk). Found only in Genesis 41:43 in ASV margin, it is a word of unknown meaning. Other versions have "Abrek" (JB, RSVMG), "Bow down" (note in NIV), "Bow the knee!" (KJV, MLB, NASB, RSV), and "Make way!" (NEB, NIV). "Attention," "kneel," and "pay homage" have also been suggested. It was the word shouted to warn of the approach of Joseph, presumably so proper respect could be shown to him.

ABRONAH (à-brō'nà, Heb. *'avrōnâ,* possible meaning, *crossing, ford*). A camping place of the Israelites in the wilderness, one march before Ezion-Geber on the Gulf of Aqabah (Num 33:34–35). The exact location is uncertain.

ABSALOM (ăb'sà-lŏm, Heb. *'avshālôm, father [is] peace,* written Abishalom in 1 Kings 15:2, 10). Third son of David, by Maacah, daughter of Talmai, king of Geshur, a small district NE of Lake Galilee (2 Sam 3:3; 1 Chron 3:2). Amnon, David's eldest son and Absalom's half-brother, raped Absalom's sister Tamar (2 Sam 13:1–19). David, though greatly angered, never punished Amnon (13:21). Absalom nursed his hatred for two years, then treacherously plotted Amnon's assassination (13:22–29). Absalom fled to his grandfather and remained with him three years (13:37–38), while David "longed to go to Absalom, for he was consoled concerning Amnon's death" (13:39). At the end of that time Joab by strategem induced David to recall Absalom, but David would not see him for two years more (14:1–24). Then Absalom by a trick of his own moved Joab to intercede with the king and was restored to favor (14:28, 33).

"In all Israel there was not a man so highly praised for his handsome appearance as Absalom," and for the abundance of his hair (2 Sam 14:25–27). He had three sons and a daughter, whom he named Tamar after his sister. Absalom now began to act like a candidate for the kingship (15:1–6), parading a great retinue and subtly

The so-called Tomb of Absalom, located in the Kidron Valley in Jerusalem. Built by wealthy citizens of Jerusalem in the Herodian period. In its lower part, hewn out of rock, was the burial chamber, on top of which was constructed the cone-shaped memorial. In due course, this tomb came to be associated with such notables as the kings of the House of David. Although popularly identified with Absalom, son of King David, this attribution is only legend. Courtesy Zev Radovan.

indicating how he would improve the administration of justice in the interests of the people.

At the end of four years (2 Sam 15:7; see NIV text and footnote for uncertainties surrounding the Hebrew text at this point), Absalom pretended a proper motive for visiting Hebron, the capital of Judah when David began his reign and Absalom's birthplace (3:2–3). There Absalom proclaimed himself king and attracted the disaffected to his standard (15:7–14). David realized at once that this was a serious threat to his throne. He plainly could have chosen to remain in the safety of the all-but-impregnable fortress city of Jerusalem, but this would have been both strategically a mistake and practically a needless involvement of an innocent population in the harsh realities of a prolonged siege. David did not explain his decision to depart hastily from the city, but what we know of him from the Bible suggests these two motives: first, out in the open country he was in his natural element both as a man and as a soldier; second, he could rally troops to his cause and, as a commander actually in the field—not confined in the city—he could direct operations. But it was a sad and hurried flight, marked by partings from friends and the defection of valued counselors such as Ahithophel. David sent back to the capital the intensely loyal priests, Zadok and Abiathar, that with their sons as messengers they might keep David informed of events. Hushai the Arkite also was asked to return and feign loyalty to Absalom, and so help David by "frustrating Ahithophel's advice" (15:20–37).

Ahithophel advised Absalom to attack David at once, before he could gather a large following (2 Sam 17:1–4). Hushai advised delay until all the military power of the realm could be gathered under the command of Absalom himself, to make sure they had a force large enough to defeat the warlike David and his loyal soldiers (17:5–14). Absalom actually followed a compromise plan. The armies met in the wood of Ephraim, where Absalom's forces were disastrously defeated (18:1–8). Absalom was caught by his head in the branches of an oak, and the mule he was riding went on and left him dangling helpless there. Joab and his men killed him, though David, in the hearing of the whole army, had forbidden anyone to harm him. Absalom was buried in a pit and covered with a heap of stones in the wood where he fell (18:9–17).

David's great and prolonged grief over the death of his son nearly cost him the loyalty of his subjects (2 Sam 18:33–19:8). Absalom's rebellion was the most serious threat to David's throne, but its significance for the future lay in the weakness already existing in the kingdom in David's day. Plainly David's administration was faulty. The ease with which Absalom detached the northern tribes from allegiance to David not only exposed the fact that as a Judahite David was guilty of neglecting the Israelite section of his kingdom, but also, more seriously, showed how fragile were the bonds between Judah and Israel. Solomon's more rigorous administrative methods staved off the inevitable division that needed only the ineptitude of his son and successor Rehoboam to make it a reality (1 Kings 12:1–19). In these ways, as much as in its more explicit predictions, the OT prepared the way for Christ. It records the golden days of David, yet the flaws in David's character and kingdom give rise to the people's yearning for great David's greater Son.

ER and JAM

ABSTINENCE (ăb'stĭ-nĕns, Gr. *apechomai*). The verb *abstain* occurs six times and means "hold oneself away from." The noun *abstinence* occurs once in the KJV (Gr. *asitia,* Acts 27:2) and means abstinence from food. The decree of the Jerusalem council (15:20, 29) commanded abstinence from "food sacrificed to idols, from blood, from the meat of strangled animals and from sexual immorality," practices abhorrent to Jewish Christians. Paul (1 Thess 4:3) connects abstaining from fornication with sanctification. In 1 Thessalonians 5:22 he exhorts abstinence from all appearance of evil. In 1 Timothy 4:3 he refers to false teachers who commanded believers "to abstain from certain foods, which God created to be received with thanksgiving by those who believe and who know the truth." In 1 Peter 2:11, Peter exhorts, "Dear friends, I urge you, as aliens and strangers in the world, to abstain from sinful desires, which war against your soul."

Abstinence from eating blood antedates the Mosaic Law (see Gen 9:4) but was rigorously reinforced when the Lord spoke through Moses. The sacred function of blood within the sacrificial system (Lev 17:11) made it something set apart from any common use. Israel abstained voluntarily from eating the sinew on the thigh for the reason given in Genesis 32:32. Leviticus 11 defined what animals the children of Israel might not eat, "to distinguish between the unclean and the clean" (11:47), and to keep Israel separate from other nations. The priests were forbidden to drink wine while they were ministering (Lev 10:8–9). The Nazirites were to abstain from the fruit of the vine absolutely. The Recabites took such a vow in deference to their ancestor Jonadab (Jer 35). God's people are to abstain from participation in idol feasts (Exod 34:15; Ps 106:28; Rom 14:21; 1 Cor 8:4–13).

The injunctions regarding drunkenness and sobriety (1 Cor 5:11; 6:9–10; Eph 5:18; 1 Tim 3:3, 8; Titus 2:2–4) point to the wisdom of total abstinence from alcoholic beverages if one would be at his best for the Lord. They are reinforced by the fact that the believer's body is the temple of the Holy Spirit (1 Cor 6:19; 2 Cor 6:16), and by such words as those found in Colossians 3:17. Paul's advice to Timothy (1 Tim 5:23) sanctions no more than medicinal use of wine mixed with water.

Abstinence is not a virtue in itself, but it can be a means to make virtue possible.

See also FASTING.

ABYSS (à-bĭs', Gr. *abyssos*). In the NT it refers to the world of the dead (Rom 10:7) or the nether world, the prison of disobedient spirits (Luke 8:31; Rev 9:1–2, 11; 11:7; 17:8; 20:1–3). KJV renders the Greek word as "the deep" in Luke 8:31 and Romans 10:7 and "the bottomless pit" in Revelation. The ASV and NIV uniformly have "the abyss." RSV has "the abyss" in Luke 8:31 and Romans 10:7, "the pit" in Revelation 20:3, and "the bottomless pit" elsewhere in Revelation.

In classical Greek *abyssos* was an adjective meaning "bottomless," applied to the primeval deep of ancient cosmogonies, an ocean surrounding and under the earth. In the LXX it translates Hebrew *tehôm*, meaning the primal waters of Genesis 1:2; once the world of the dead (Ps 71:20). In later Judaism it means also the interior depths of the earth and the prison of evil spirits.

The use of abyss in Romans 10:7 is parallel with the use of "the lower, earthly regions" in Ephesians 4:9 (see Ps 106:28); both contrast the highest heaven and the lowest depth. In Luke 8:31 the demons had a great dread of the primal abyss; even so, they may have caused themselves to go there when the pigs were drowned in the sea. In Revelation the horror of infinite deeps is intensified. ER

ACACIA (See PLANTS)

ACBOR (ăk'bôr, Heb. *'akhbôr, mouse*). 1. The father of a king of Edom (Gen 36:38–39; 1 Chron 1:49).

2. A messenger sent by King Josiah to inquire of the Lord concerning the book found by Hilkiah (2 Kings 22:12, 14; called Abdon in 2 Chron 34:20); father of Elnathan (Jer 26:22; 36:12).

ACCAD (See AKKAD)

ACCO, ACCHO (ăk'ō, Heb. *'akkô*, Judg 1:31; KJV Accho; in ASV, RSV, and NIV, Acco). The name occurs in some manuscripts and versions of Joshua 19:30. In the NT, Ptolemais; modern Arabic, 'Akka; English, Acre. A seaport, eight miles (thirteen km.) north of Mount Carmel, thirty miles (fifty km.) south of Tyre. The river Belus flows into the Mediterranean Sea close to the town. Acco was in the portion assigned to the tribe of Asher, but the Hebrews did not drive out the original inhabitants (Judg 1:31). It received the name Ptolemais from the Ptolemies of Egypt, from whom it was wrested by the Romans. Paul stayed there a day with Christian brethren on his way from Tyre to Caesarea (Acts 21:7). The Crusaders occupied the town and named it St. Jean d'Acre. In modern times it was part of the Turkish Empire, except for a time when it was occupied by Egypt, being restored to the Turks with British help. Today it is in the nation of Israel, opposite the larger city of Haifa.

ACCUSER (See SATAN)

ACELDAMA (See AKELDAMA)

ACHAIA (à-kā'yà, Gr. *Achaia*). In NT times a Roman province that included the Peloponnesus and northern Greece south of Illyricum, Epirus, and Thessaly, which were districts of Macedonia. Corinth was the capital. Used together, "Macedonia and Achaia" generally mean all Greece (Acts 19:21; Rom 15:26; 1 Thess 1:7–8). In Acts 20:2 "Greece" refers to Achaia. In Acts 18:12, Gallio is accurately called "proconsul" (RSV, NIV) of Achaia; for Claudius had just made Achaia a senatorial province, the governors of which were called proconsuls, while the governors of imperial provinces were called procurators. In Romans 16:5, KJV has "Achaia," but most other versions have "Asia." Achaia is mentioned in five other NT passages (Acts 18:27; 1 Cor 16:15; 2 Cor 1:1; 9:2; 11:10).

ACHAICUS (à-kā'ĭ-kŭs, Gr. *Achaikos*). A Corinthian Christian, named for his country of origin, who accompanied Stephanas and Fortunatus to bring supplies to Paul at Ephesus (1 Cor 16:17–19).

ACHAN (ā'kan, Heb. *'ākhān*). An Israelite whose tragic experience is recorded in Joshua 7. Achan took a garment, silver, and gold—part of the spoil of Jericho. Joshua had devoted the metals to God (Josh 6:17–19). All else was to be

A splendid view of Acre (Acco) and its port. The chief center of Christian power in Palestine in the 1200s, it is now a part of Israel. Courtesy Israel Government Press Office.

destroyed. Because of one man's disobedience, Israel was defeated at Ai. God revealed the reason to Joshua. By a process of elimination Achan was found out. He confessed, and he and his family and possessions were brought down to the valley of Achor. In spite of some difficulty in understanding the Hebrew text in verses 25–26, there is little ground for holding that Joshua's command (6:17) was not carried out in the execution of both Achan and his entourage. In the Scriptures the Lord often allows us to see the full significance of our sinful ways. Achan's experience illustrates the biblical revelation that we never sin alone: there is always a family involvement (cf. Exod 20:5–6) and also a wider pollution touching the whole people of God and bringing them under judgment. Joshua expressed this thought in his epitaph: "Why have you brought this disaster on us?" (7:25), allowing the name Achan to slip over into the similar-sounding verb *'āchar,* "to trouble, bring disaster." This in turn became the name of the place itself, Achor, "disaster." In 2 Chronicles 2:7, Achan's name reads "Achar," the man of disaster.

ACHAR (See ACHAN)

ACHAZ (See AHAZ)

ACHBOR (See ACBOR)

ACHIM (See AKIM)

ACHISH (ā'kĭsh, Heb. *'ākhîsh*). King of Gath, to whom David fled for protection (1 Sam 21:10–15). David became fearful and pretended insanity. Achish repulsed him, and David fled. David again sought refuge with Achish, this time behaving so as to win his confidence (27:1–12). David consented to join Achish against Israel, but when the Philistine lords objected, Achish sent David away (29:1–11). He may be the same Achish to whom Shimei's servant fled (1 Kings 2:39–40). Achish is called Abimelech in the title to Psalm 34. Genesis 20:2, 22; 26:1, 26 suggest that Abimelech was a dynastic name of Philistine kings.

ACHMETHA (See ECBATANA)

ACHOR (ā'kôr, Heb. *'ākhôr, disaster;* see ACHAN). The location of this valley is uncertain. Joshua 15:7 situates a place named Achor somewhere south of Debir, but this can hardly be the same Achor in which Achan played so tragic a role. A site near Jericho is required, and this certainly suits the symbolic reference in Hosea

2:15 where the transformation of Achor into "a door of hope" typifies the changed expectations of the people of God in the messianic day (cf. Isa 65:10).

ACHSAH, ACHSA (See ACSAH)

ACHSHAPH (See ACSHAPH)

ACHZIB (See ACZIB)

ACRE (ā'kêr, Heb. *tsemedh*). In both occurrences of this word (1 Sam 14:14; Isa 5:10) the area involved is the average amount a "yoke" (*tsemedh*) of oxen could plow in a day. What actual area is involved is not known, and the translation "acre" is merely conventional.

ACROPOLIS (ȧ-krŏp'ō-lĭs, Gr. *akropolis,* from *akros, highest,* and *polis, city*). The upper or higher city, citadel, or castle of a Greek municipality; especially the citadel of Athens, where the treasury was. Athens's crowning glory is the Parthenon, the finest exemplar of Greek architecture. During Paul's stay in Athens (Acts 17:15–18:1), "he was greatly distressed to see that the city was full of idols" (17:16). The images of gods and of heroes worshiped as gods filled Athens and were inescapably conspicuous on the Acropolis. As Paul stood on Mars Hill, before the court of the Areopagus, he could see the temples on the Acropolis directly to the east, and the Agora (marketplace) below it.

Many NT towns—e.g., Corinth, Philippi, Samaria—had an Acropolis, which served as the town's civic and religious centers, while the Agora constituted the central shopping plaza.

ACROSTIC (ȧ-krôs'tĭc, Gr. *akrostichis,* from *okros, topmost,* and *stichos, a line of poetry*). In the common form of acrostic found in OT poetry, each line or stanza begins with a letter of the Hebrew alphabet in order. This literary form may have been intended as an aid to memory, but more likely it was a poetic way of saying that a total coverage of the subject was being offered—as we would say, "from A to Z." Acrostics occur in Psalms 111 and 112, where each letter begins a line; in Psalms 25, 34, and 145, where each letter begins a half-verse; in Psalm 37, Proverbs 31:10-31, and Lamentations 1, 2, and 4, where each letter begins a whole verse; and in Lamentations 3, where each letter begins three verses. Psalm 119 is the most elaborate demonstration of the acrostic method where, in each section of eight verses, the same opening letter is used, and the twenty-two sections of the psalm move through the Hebrew alphabet, letter after letter. It is the genius of Hebrew poetry to allow the demands of the sense to take precedence over the demands of form, and this accounts for "broken acrostics" (there is a letter missing in each of Pss 25 and 34) or acrostics in which letters are taken out of order (as in Lam 2:16–17). JAM

ACSAH (āk'să, Heb. *'akhsâ, anklet*). The story of Acsah is charmingly told in Joshua 15:16–19; Judges 1:12–15. She was the daughter of Caleb the son of Hephunneh, who was given in marriage to Othniel, son of Kenaz, Caleb's younger brother, in keeping a promise Caleb had made to give his daughter to him who "captures Kiriath Sepher" (Josh 15:16). The bride persuaded her husband to ask her father for a field. It was given him, but Acsah was not satisfied. Out riding one day, she met Caleb and asked him for springs to water the field. Caleb gave her both the upper and lower springs.

ACSHAPH (ȧk'shăf, Heb. *'akhshāph*). A city (Josh 11:1) that Joshua captured with its king (12:7, 20). It is on the border of the lot assigned to Asher (19:24–25). Acshaph is now tentatively identified with Tell Keisan, a few miles SE of Acco (Acre; Ptolemais), NE of Mount Carmel.

ACTS OF THE APOSTLES. The book that gives the history of early Christianity from the ascension of Christ to the end of two years of Paul's imprisonment in Rome.

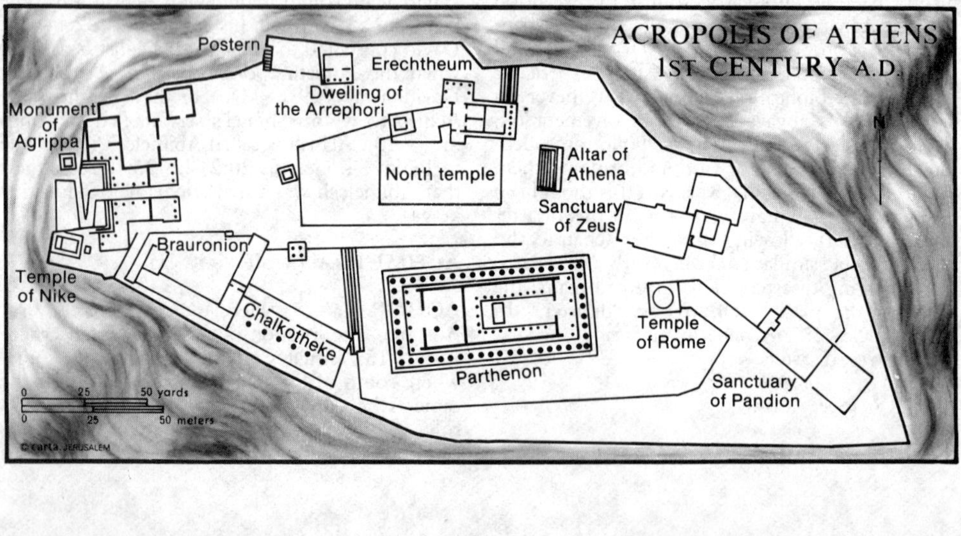

I. Title of the Book. An early MS has the title "Acts" (Gr. *praxeis, doings, transactions, achievements*). Other early titles are "Acts of Apostles," "The Acts of the Apostles," "Acts of the Holy Apostles." Acts narrates actions and speeches chiefly of Peter and Paul. There is some information about Judas (1:16–20), the man chosen to succeed him (1:21–26), John (3:1–4:31; 8:14–17), and James (12:12). The Twelve, except the betrayer, are listed in 1:13. Acts is not a history of all the apostles; rather, it is a selection from the deeds and words of some who illustrate the progress of first-century Christianity in those phases that interested the author as he was moved by the Holy Spirit. The title "Acts of the Holy Spirit" has often been suggested, and the contents of the book bear out the appropriateness of such a title.

II. Author. Not until A.D. 160–200 do we have positive statements as to the authorship of Acts. From that time onward, all who mention the subject agree that the two books dedicated to Theophilus (Luke and Acts) were written by "Luke, the beloved physician." Only in modern times have there been attempts to ascribe both books to Titus or some other author.

By writing "we" instead of "they" in recounting events when he was present, the author indicates that he was a companion of Paul. Luke joined Paul, Silas, and Timothy at Troas during the second missionary journey and accompanied them to Philippi but did not go on with them when they left there (Acts 16:10–17). Luke is next mentioned as being at Philippi toward the end of the third missionary journey, when Paul was about to sail for Palestine with the contributions of the Gentile churches for the poor at Jerusalem (20:4ff.; Rom 15:25ff.). We do not know whether Luke spent all the interval at Philippi. From this point Luke accompanied Paul to Jerusalem (Acts 20:5–21:18). Nor do we know how Luke spent the two years during which Paul was imprisoned at Caesarea, but Luke enters the narrative again in 27:1 ("when it was decided that we should sail for Italy"); he continued with Paul, giving us a vivid account of the voyage to Rome. Acts breaks off abruptly at the end of Paul's two years of ministry when he was enjoying the relative freedom of "his own rented house," where he "welcomed all who came to see him. Boldly and without hindrance he preached the kingdom of God and taught about the Lord Jesus Christ" (28:30–31). If a later writer had incorporated these "we" sections, he would have named their author to enhance their authority. But the style of the "we" passages cannot be distinguished from the style of the rest of Acts nor from that of Luke's Gospel. The author of Luke and Acts is the author of the "we" sections of Acts and a companion of Paul.

The question remains: Which of the companions of Paul is the author of Acts? He cannot be one of those named in the "we" sections as distinct from the author. He is not likely to have been one of those named in Paul's letters written at times other than those included in the "we" sections. Of those named in Paul's letters written when the "we" author might have been with Paul, early Christian writers chose "our dear friend Luke, the doctor" (Col 4:14). Luke is not otherwise prominent in the NT. Why should he have been chosen, unless he was the author? The medical language in Acts is not sufficient to prove that the author was a physician, but it is sufficient to confirm other evidence to that effect. Luke was with Paul shortly before his expected death (2 Tim 4:11).

Luke cannot be certainly identified with Lucius of Acts 13:1 or with Lucius of Romans 16:21. There is wide and ancient support for connecting Luke with Antioch in Syria. It is not probable that he was from Philippi. The tradition that he was a painter cannot be traced earlier than the tenth century. From 2 Corinthians 8:18 it is possible to infer that Titus was Luke's brother and that Luke was "the brother who is praised by all the churches for his service to the gospel." Titus and Luke are named together in 2 Timothy 4:10–11. The conjecture that Luke was the "man of Macedonia" of Paul's vision (Acts 16:9) is attractive and inherently possible but not certain.

III. Place. The place where Acts was written is not named, though the sudden ending of the book, while Paul is residing at Rome awaiting trial, makes Rome an appropriate choice. The question of place is tied in with that of Luke's purpose in writing and with the occasion for the publication of the book.

IV. Date. Allusions to the book in the Apostolic Fathers are too indefinite to compel the setting of a date much before the end of the first century A.D. If Acts is dependent on Josephus for information, it cannot be earlier than 93. But such dependence is not proved and is highly unlikely. Acts must have been finished after the latest date mentioned in the book, in 28:30. The abrupt close indicates that it was written at that time, c. 61 or 62. Luke's Gospel has an appropriate ending; Acts does not. We are not told how the trial of Paul came out. There is no hint of Paul's release or of his death. The attitude toward Roman officials is friendly, and that would not have been the case after the persecution under Nero in 64. The Jewish War of 66–70 and the destruction of Jerusalem are not referred to. Chapters 1–15 accurately picture conditions in Jerusalem before its destruction. It would be attractive to think that Luke's two books were written to inform and influence well-disposed Roman officials in their handling of Paul's case.

V. The Speeches in Acts. Do the speeches report what was actually said? We do not expect stenographic reporting, but Luke is a careful writer, as a comparison of his Gospel with Mark and Matthew shows. The style of the speeches in Acts is not Luke's, but that which is appropriate to each speaker: Peter, Stephen, Paul, even the minor characters such as Gamaliel (5:25ff.), the Ephesian town clerk (19:35ff.), and Tertullus (24:2ff.). Similarities between the speeches of Peter and Paul are explained by the fact that Paul explicitly preached the same gospel as Peter did.

Speeches by the same person are varied in type, each suited to the occasion.

VI. Summary of the Contents. Introduction. (1) Summary of ground covered by the "former treatise," especially the resurrection ministry of Jesus, 1:1–11. (2) The period of waiting; a ten-day prayer meeting in the Upper Room, 1:12–14. (3) The choice of a successor to the betrayer as one of the Twelve, 1:15–26.

1. Pentecost, the birthday of the church. (a) The occasion and the event, 2:1–13. (b) Peter's sermon, 2:14–36. (c) The result: the beginning of the church, 2:37–47.

2. Pictures of the first church in Jerusalem. (a) A lame man healed, 3:1–11. (b) Peter's sermon to the crowd on this occasion, 3:12–26. (c) Attempted suppression of the new church met by prayer-power, 4:1–30. (d) A contrast in givers, 4:31–5:11: Barnabas, the generous giver, 4:31–37; Ananias and Sapphira, the grudging givers, 5:1–11. (e) Growth of the healing ministry of the church, 5:12–16. (f) Another attempt at suppression of the church met by obedience to God, 5:17–42. (g) An administrative problem solved leads to further advance, 6:1–8. (h) The attempt of the Council (Sanhedrin) to suppress the new leader, Stephen, 6:9–15. (i) Stephen's defense, 7:1–53. (j) Stephen's martyrdom, 7:54–60.

3. The gospel spread to all Judea and Samaria, 8:1–25. (a) The stimulus to expansion: Saul as persecutor, 8:1–4. (b) Problems in Samaria, 8:5–25.

4. Three "continental" conversions. (a) From Africa: the eunuch from Ethiopia, 8:26–40. (b) From Asia: Saul of Tarsus, 9:1–31. (Interlude: Peter in western Palestine, 9:32–43.) (c) From Europe: Cornelius of Italy, 10:1–48.

5. The Judean church accepts the mission to the Gentiles, 11:1–30. (a) Peter convinces the Jewish Christians, 11:1–18. (b) The extent of the early mission to the Gentiles, 11:19–21. (c) Barnabas and Saul minister in Antioch of Syria, 11:22–26. "The disciples were called Christians first at Antioch," 11:26. (d) Response of the church in Antioch to need in Judea, 11:27–30. (e) A further attempt to suppress the Christian movement frustrated by the miraculous escape of Peter from prison, 12:1–19. (Note: The death of Herod, 12:20–23.)

6. Paul's first missionary journey. (a) The church at Antioch commissions Barnabas and Saul as missionaries to the Gentiles, 12:24–13:3. (b) The mission to Cyprus, 13:4–12. (c) The mission at Antioch in Pisidia, 13:13–50. (d) The mission to Iconium, 13:51–14:5. (e) The mission to Lystra, 14:6–20. (f) The mission to Derbe, 14:20–21. (g) Return through the cities visited and formally established churches, 14:21–25. (h) Furlough in Antioch, 14:26–28.

7. The Church Council at Jerusalem: Terms of admission of Gentile believers settled, 15:1–29.

8. Paul's second missionary journey. (a) Completion of furlough in Antioch and reporting the Council's proceedings, 15:30–35. (b) Paul and Barnabas part, Barnabas to Cyprus, Paul to Cilicia, 15:36–41. (c) The journey to Troas, 16:1–8. (d) Invitation to Europe accepted, 16:9–11. (e) The mission to Philippi, 16:12–40. (f) The mission to Thessalonica, 17:1–9. (g) The mission to Berea, 17:10–14. (h) The mission to Athens, 17:15–34. (i) The mission to Corinth, 18:1–18. (j) Beginning of the mission to Ephesus and the journey to Jerusalem and Antioch, 18:18–23.

9. Paul's third missionary journey. (a) Confirming the disciples in Galatia and Phrygia, 18:23. (b) Apollos at Ephesus, 18:24–28. (c) The mission to Ephesus, 19:1–20:1. (d) Journeyings through Greece and Macedonia to Troas, 20:1–6. (e) The mission to Troas, 20:6–12. (f) The journey to Jerusalem, 20:13–21:16.

10. Paul's arrest and voyage to Rome. (a) Paul in Jerusalem, 21:17–23:30. (b) Paul in Caesarea, 23:31–26:32. (c) The voyage to Rome, 27:1–28:15. (d) Paul in Rome, 28:16–31.

Bibliography: F. F. Bruce, *The Acts of the Apostles,* 1952 (on the Greek text), and *The Book of the Acts* (NICNT), 1954; E. Haenchen, *The Acts of the Apostles,* 1971; W. W. Gasque, *A History of the Acts of the Apostles,* 1975; M. Hengel, *Acts and the History of Earliest Christianity,* 1979; I. H. Marshall, *The Acts of the Apostles* (TNTC), 1980.

ER

ACZIB (ăk'zĭb, Heb. *'akhzîv, a lie*). 1. A city of Judah (Josh 15:44) perhaps Tell el-Beida, SW of Adullam. Called Kezib (Gen 38:5) and Cozeba (1 Chron 4:22). See Micah 1:14.

2. A town in Asher (Judg 1:31; Josh 19:29) on the coast north of Acco. The Hebrews did not drive out the earlier inhabitants. In NT times Ecdippa, modern ez-Zib.

Clay figurine of a horse, from Phoenician cemetery at Aczib, c. sixth to fifth century B.C. Courtesy Israel Department of Antiquities and Museums.

ADADAH (ă-dā'da, Heb. *'adh' ādhâh*). A city in Judah (Josh 15:22). Its identity is not certain.

ADAH (ā'dȧ, Heb. *'ādhâh, ornament*). 1. One of Lamech's two wives (Gen 4:19–20, 23), mother of Jabal and Jubal. Lamech spoke a poem in praise of himself to his wives.

2. One of Esau's wives (Gen 36:2, 4, 10, 12, 16), daughter of Elon the Hittite. In Genesis 26:34 Esau married Basemath, daughter of Elon the Hittite, Basemath being either another name for Adah, or her sister. Adah's son is Eliphaz (36:10), and his sons are called hers (36:12, 16), not Esau's.

ADAIAH (ȧ-dā'yȧ, Heb. *'ădhāyâh, Jehovah has adorned,* or *pleasing to Jehovah*). 1. A man of Boscath, father of Josiah's mother (2 Kings 22:1).

2. A Levite descended from Gershom (1 Chron 8:1, 21).

3. A son of Shimshi the Benjamite (1 Chron 6:41–43).

4. A Levite of the family of Aaron, head of a family living in Jerusalem (1 Chron 9:10–12).

5. The father of Captain Maaseiah who helped Jehoiada put Joash on the throne of Judah (2 Chron 23:1).

6. A son of Bani who married a foreign wife during the Exile (Ezra 10:29).

7. Another of a different Bani family who did the same (Ezra 10:34).

8. A descendant of Judah by Perez (Neh 11:5).

9. A Levite of the family of Aaron. Most likely the same as no. 4 (Neh 11:12).

ADALIA (ȧd-ā-lī'ȧ, Heb. *'ădhalyā'*). The fifth of Haman's sons, all of whom were hanged with their father (Esth 9:8).

ADAM (Heb. *'ādhām,* Gr. *Adam, of the ground* or *taken out of the red earth*). In Hebrew this is both a personal name and a general noun, "mankind." The latter meaning is found over five hundred times in the OT. Both usages are found in Genesis 1–3, where Adam as a personal name occurs at 2:20 (for further references see 3:17, 21; 4:25; 5:2–5; 1 Chron 1:1). As the first and representative man, Adam was made in God's image, provided with a garden and a wife and given work to do (Gen 1–2). His rejection of God's authority led to the breaking of communion with God (see FALL), his expulsion from the Garden, and a life of toil (Gen 3). From the physical descendants of Adam and Eve the human race emerged.

Adam is mentioned nine times in the NT (Luke 3:38; Rom 5:14 [twice]; 1 Cor 15:22, 45 [twice]; 1 Tim 2:13–14; Jude 14). In all these he is assumed to be the first human being to live on the earth. Paul developed a theology of the identity and role of Jesus through a comparison with the identity and role of Adam (Rom 5:12ff.; 1 Cor 15:20–22, 45–49). In these comparisons Paul made use of the double meaning of the Hebrew word for Adam. He also developed a theology of the submission of the woman to the man from the details of the Genesis account of Adam and Eve (1 Tim 2:11ff.). Jesus referred to the union of Adam and Eve in marriage as a union of one flesh (Matt 19:4–6 and Mark 10:6–9, where Gen 1:27 and 2:24 are cited).

Bibliography: J. de Fraine, *Adam and the Family of Man,* 1965; and E. K. V. Pearce, *Who Was Adam?* 1969. PT

ADAM (Heb. *'ādhām, red*). A city near Zarethan (Josh 3:16), seventeen miles (twenty-eight km.) north of Jericho. At this spot the waters of the Jordan River were stopped to create a dry pathway for Israel to enter Canaan. Now identified with Tell ed-Damiyeh.

Aerial view of the winding course of the Jordan River, with Adam Bridge, the bridge at center, marking the apparent site of the Israelite crossing (Josh 3:16) near the ancient town of Adam. Courtesy Carta, Jerusalem.

ADAMAH (ăd'ȧ-mȧ, Heb. *'ădhāmâh, red ground*). A fortified city of Naphtali (Josh 19:36). It is thought to be Qarn Hattin.

ADAMANT. The Hebrew word *shāmîr,* in NIV translated "flint" (Jer 17:1) and "hardest stone" (Ezek 3:9), is spelled identically with the word translated "brier" in Isaiah 5:6, but is not now thought to be the same word. See also MINERALS: *Precious Stones.*

ADAMI NEKEB (ăd'ȧ-mī nē'kĕb). A place on the border of Naphtali (Josh 19:33). Modern Khirbet ed-Damiyeh.

ADAR (ā'dȧr, Heb. *'ădār*) The twelfth month of the calendar used by the Israelites after the Exile. It is roughly equivalent to mid-February to mid-March. See also CALENDAR..

ADBEEL (ăd'bē-ĕl, Heb. *'adhbe'ēl, languishing for God*). The third son of Ishmael and grandson of Abraham (Gen 25:13; 1 Chron 1:29).

ADDAN (See ADDON)

ADDAR (ā'dȧr, Heb. *'ăddār*). A place on the southern border of Judah (Josh 15:3).

ADDAR (ăd'ȧr, Heb. *'addār, threshing floor*). Son of Bela, grandson of Benjamin (1 Chron 8:3). Called Ard in Genesis 46:21 and Numbers 26:40; counted as a son of Benjamin and head of a family in the tribe.

ADDER (See ANIMALS: *Snake*)

ADDI (ăd'ī, Gr. *Addi, Addei, my witness,* or *adorned*). An ancestor of Joseph, the husband of Mary, our Lord's mother (Luke 3:28).

ADDON (ăd'ŏn, Heb. *'addān, 'addon*). A place in Babylonia from which exiles named in Ezra 2:60–63 and Nehemiah 7:62–65 returned home.

ADER (See EDER)

ADIEL (ā'dĭ-ĕl, Heb. *'ădhiēl, ornament of God*).

1. A descendant of Simeon (1 Chron 4:36).
2. A priest, son of Jahzerah (1 Chron 9:12).
3. Father of Azmaveth, who was supervisor of David's treasuries (1 Chron 27:25). Perhaps the same as no. 2.

ADIN (ā'dĭn, Heb. *'ādhîn, voluptuous*). 1. One whose family returned from exile with Zerubbabel (Ezra 2:15; Neh 7:20).

2. One whose posterity came back with Ezra (Ezra 8:6).

3. The name of a family sealing the covenant (Neh 10:16). These are all thought to be the same family. The list in Ezra 2 appears to include both exiles who returned with Zerubbabel and some who returned later. The family included "chiefs of the people" (Neh 10:14).

ADINA (ăd'ĭ-nȧ, Heb. *'ădhînā,* perhaps *voluptuous*). A Reubenite and one of David's military officers (1 Chron 11:42).

ADINO (ăd'ĭ-nō, ȧ-dī'nō, Heb. *'ădhînô*). The word occurs in a footnote to 2 Samuel 23:8 (NIV); see 1 Chronicles 11:11. With such textual uncertainty surrounding him it is not possible to be certain what Adino did; we know only that he was among David's mighty men. The NIV footnote is probably as near as we can get to the meaning.

ADITHAIM (ăd-ĭ-thā'ĭm, Heb. *'ădhîtayim*). An unidentified site in the southern lowlands of Judah (Josh 15:33–36).

ADJURATION (See CURSE)

ADLAI (ăd'lā-ī, Heb. *'adhlay, justice of Jehovah,* or *weary*). Father of Shaphat, who was overseer of David's cattle in the lowlands (1 Chron 27:29).

ADMAH (ăd'mȧ, Heb. *'adhmâh, red earth*). A city near Gomorrah and Zeboiim (Gen 10:19) with a king (14:2, 8), destroyed with Sodom and Gomorrah (cf. Deut 29:23 with Gen 19:24–28; see Hos 11:8).

ADMATHA (ăd'mȧ-thȧ, Heb. *'adhmāthā', unrestrained*). A prince of Persia and Media (Esth 1:14).

ADNA (ăd'nȧ, Heb. *'adhnā, pleasure*). 1. A son of Pahath-Moab who had married a foreign wife during the Exile (Ezra 10:30).

2. A priest, head of his father's house in the days of Joiakim (Neh 12:12–15).

ADNAH (ăd'nȧ, Heb. *'adhnāh, pleasure*). 1. A Manassite who joined David at Ziklag (1 Chron 12:20).

2. A man of Judah who held high military rank under Jehoshaphat (2 Chron 17:14).

ADONI-BEZEK (ȧ-dō'nī-bē'zĕk, Heb. *'ădhōnî-vezeq, lord of lightning,* or *of the city of Bezek*). A king of Bezek, captured by the men of Judah and Simeon and taken to Jerusalem, where he was mutilated. The cutting off of his thumbs and great toes not only rendered him harmless, but reminded him that man reaps what he sows (Judg 1:5–7; Gal 6:7).

ADONIJAH (ăd'ō-nī'jȧ, Heb. *'ădhōnîyāhû, my Lord is Jehovah*). 1. The fourth son of David, by Haggith, born at Hebron (2 Sam 3:2–4; 1 Chron 3:2). Ammon and Absalom, David's first and third sons, had died; the second, Kileab, had not been mentioned since his birth and might have died also. Adonijah, as the eldest living son, aspired to the throne. The story of his attempt and failure to seize the crown is told in 1 Kings 1:5–2:25.

He was a spoiled, handsome lad (1:6), and now he "got chariots and horses ready, with fifty men to run ahead of him" (1:5). He won over Joab and Abiathar the priest, but failed to gain Zadok the priest and Nathan the prophet. Moreover, "David's special guard did not join Adonijah" (1:7–8). He held a great feast at En-Rogel, to which he invited "all his brothers, the king's sons, and all the men of Judah who were royal officials, but he did not invite Nathan the prophet or Benaiah or the special guard or his brother Solomon" (1:9–10). Nathan spoke to Bathsheba, Solomon's mother, and together they warned David of what Adonijah was doing. David, roused to action, had Solomon proclaimed king at Gihon (1:11–40). Adonijah and his guests heard the shout and the sound of the trumpet (1:41). Immediately Jonathan, the son of Abiathar, brought a full account of what had happened (1:42–48). The guests fled, and Adonijah sought refuge at the altar (1:49–50). Solomon pardoned him, and he returned home (1:51–53). But after the death of David, Adonijah emboldened himself to ask Bathsheba to persuade King Solomon to give him Abishag, David's nurse in his last illness, for a wife (2:13–18). This revived Solomon's suspicions, for in ancient times claiming a former monarch's concubines was tantamount to claiming his throne. Solomon had Adonijah killed (2:19–25).

2. A Levite, sent by Jehoshaphat to teach the law (2 Chron 17:8).

3. A chieftain who with Nehemiah sealed the covenant (Neh 10:14–16). ER

ADONIKAM (ăd-ō-nī'kăm, Heb. *'ădhōnîqām, my Lord has arisen*). The ancestor of a family, 666 of whom returned from exile with Zerubbabel (Ezra 2:13). Among the chiefs of the people who returned with Ezra are three sons and sixty males of this family (8:13). In the list of exiles whose genealogy proved them Israelites are 667 of this family (Neh 7:18). The Adonijah of Nehemiah 10:16, because of his position among those who sealed the covenant, is thought to be the same as Adonikam.

ADONIRAM (ăd-ō-nī'răm, Heb. *'ădhōnîrām, my Lord is exalted*). He first appears by the name Adoram as an officer of David "in charge of forced labor" (2 Sam 20:24). He held the same office under Solomon (1 Kings 4:6). Rehoboam sent him on a mission of some kind to the now rebel tribes of Israel (1 Kings 12:18) who stoned him to death. Another variant of his name, Hadoram, appears in the NIV footnote to 2 Chronicles 10:18.

ADONI-ZEDEK (ȧ-dō'nī-zē'dĕk, Heb. *'ădhōnîtsedheq, lord of righteousness,* or, *my lord is righteous*). Amorite king of Jerusalem (Josh 10:1–27). Having heard how Joshua destroyed Ai and Jericho and how Gibeon made peace with Israel, Adoni-Zedek invited four other Amorite kings to join him in attacking Gibeon. Joshua came to the aid of Gibeon. God defeated the kings, both in battle and with great hailstones. This was the day when Joshua called on the sun and moon to stand still until the people had avenged themselves on their enemies. The kings hid in a cave, which Joshua sealed with great stones. When he had completed the victory, Joshua ordered the kings brought out. He killed them and hanged them on trees until sunset, when they were cut down and buried in the cave where they had hidden. An earlier king of Jerusalem (Salem) bore a name of similar form and identical meaning: Melchizedek, "king of righteousness" (Gen 14:18–20). This may well indicate the continuation of the same dynasty with the same dynastic name; at all events it indicates that even if the dynasty changed, there was some reason why the pre-Davidic kings of Jerusalem thought it important to preserve the same name or title. See also MELCHIZEDEK.

ADOPTION (ȧ-dŏp'shŭn, Gr. *huiothesia* in the NT). The practice of adoption is exemplified in the OT: Pharaoh's daughter adopted Moses (Exod 2:10) as her son; Hadad the Edomite married the sister of the Egyptian queen, and

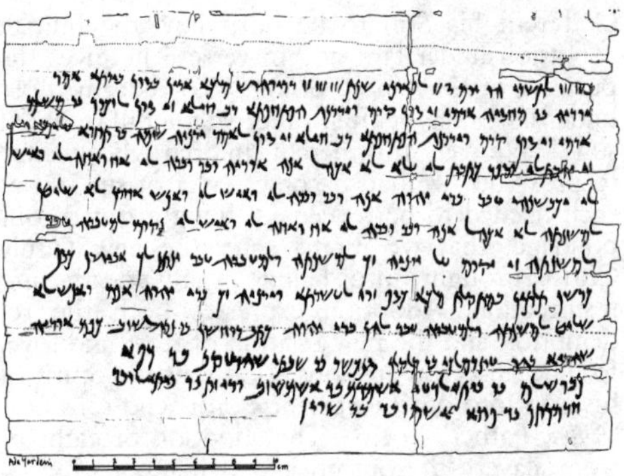

Facsimile of papyrus document (from Elephantine, 416 B.C.) in which Zakkur ben Meshullam deeds the slave Yedoniah to Uriah ben Mahseiah for adoption. Courtesy Prof. B. Porten and A. Yardeni.

their son Genubath was brought up "with Pharaoh's own children," whether formally adopted or not (1 Kings 11:20); Esther was adopted by Mordecai (Esth 2:7, 15). These cases were outside Palestine, in Egypt or Persia. Whether adoption was practiced in the Hebrews' own land is not clear. Abram thinks of Eliezer of Damascus as his heir, but God tells him this will not be (Gen 15:2–4). Sarai gave her maid Hagar to Abram that she might obtain children by her (16:1–3). Rachel (30:1–5) and Leah (30:9–12) gave Jacob their maids for a like purpose, a kind of adoption by the mother but not by the father. Jacob adopted his grandsons Manasseh and Ephraim to be as Reuben and Simeon (48:5). The case of Jair (1 Chron 2:21–22) is one of inheritance rather than adoption. Whether Mary the mother of Jesus, or Joseph her husband, or both, were adopted, is a matter of inference incapable of direct proof (Matt 1:16; Luke 3:23). Levirate marriage (Deut 25:5–6) involved a sort of posthumous adoption of a brother's later-born son.

But none of the OT instances have a direct bearing on the NT usage of the term. Paul is the only writer to use it, and with him it is a metaphor derived from Hellenistic usage and Roman law. The legal situation of a son in early Roman times was little better than that of a slave, though in practice its rigor would vary with the disposition of the father. A son was the property of his father, who was entitled to the son's earnings. The father could transfer ownership of him by adoption or by a true sale and could, under certain circumstances, even put him to death. An adopted son was considered like a son born in the family. He could no longer inherit from his natural father. He was no longer liable for old debts (a loophole eventually closed). So far as his former family was concerned, he was dead. Modifications of the rigor of sonship were at intervals introduced into Roman law, and a more liberal Hellenistic view was doubtless in the mind of Paul.

In Galatians 4:1–3 Paul states accurately the Roman law of sonship. In verse 4 he says that

God sent his Son to be born into the human condition under law, and in verse 5 he gives the purpose of God in so doing: "To redeem those under law, that we might receive the full rights of sons." We were not merely children who needed to grow up; we had become slaves of sin and as such needed to be redeemed, bought out of our bondage, that we might enter the new family Christ brought into being by his death and resurrection. Adoption expresses both the redemption and the new relation of trust and love, for "because you are sons, God sent the Spirit of his Son into our hearts, the Spirit who calls out, '*Abba*, Father' " (4:6). The adoption brought us from slavery to sonship and heirship (4:7).

The same thought appears in Romans 8:15. Verses 1–14 demonstrate that the adoption is more than a matter of position or status; when God adopted us, he put his Spirit within us, and we became subject to his control. This involves chastisement (Heb 12:5–11) as well as inheritance (Rom 8:16–18).

In Romans 8:23 "our adoption" is spoken of as future, in the sense that its full effects are to be consummated at the time of "the redemption of our bodies." This "redemption" is not the "buying out" of Galatians 4:5, but a word (Gr. *apolytrōsis*) emphasizing the release, the loosing from all restraints that the limitation of a mortal body imposes. We are part of a suffering creation (Rom 8:22). The spiritual body, the resurrection body, pictured in the vivid terms of 1 Corinthians 15:35–57, is the object of Paul's longing (2 Cor 5:1–8; Phil 3:21). The present effects of God's adoption of us as sons are marvelous, yet they are only a small indication (2 Cor 1:22; 5:5; Eph 1:13–14) of what the adoption will mean when we come into our inheritance in heaven.

In Romans 9:4 Paul begins with enumeration of the privileges of Israelites with "the adoption." Although God said, "Israel is my firstborn son" (Exod 4:22); and "When Israel was a child, I loved him, and out of Egypt I called my son" (Hos 11:1); and Moses expressed the relationship in this way, "You are the children of the LORD your God" (Deut 14:1); yet Israel's sonship was not the natural relationship by creation, but a peculiar one by a covenant of promise, a spiritual relationship by faith, under the sovereign grace of God, as Paul goes on to explain in Romans 9–11. Thus a clear distinction is drawn between the "offspring" of God by creation (Acts 17:28) and the children of God by adoption into the obedience of faith.

With utmost compression of language Paul expresses, in Ephesians 1:4–5, God's action that resulted in his adoption of us and enumerates its effects in verses 6–12. This action began with God's election: "For he chose us in him before the creation of the world," using predestination as the mode ("he predestined us"); Christ is the agent (by Jesus Christ); and he himself is the adopting parent (to himself). God's sovereign act is stressed by the concluding phrase of verse 5: "in accordance with his pleasure and will." That adoption is not a mere matter of position is made plain in the statement of the purpose of election: "he chose us . . . to be holy and blameless in his sight" (1:4).

Adoption is a serious matter under any system of law. As a figure of speech expressing spiritual truth it emphasizes the sovereign and gracious character of the act of God in our salvation, our solemn obligation as adopted sons of our adopting Parent, the newness of the family relationship established, a climate of intimate trust and love, and the immensity of an inheritance that eternity alone can reveal to us.

Bibliography: D.J. Theron, "Adoption in the Paul Corpus," EQ 28 (1956): 1ff.; F. Lyall, "Roman Law in the Writings of Paul—Adoption," JBL 88 (1969): 458–66; G. Braumann NIDNTT (1975), 1:280–91. ER

ADORAIM (ăd'ō-rām, Heb. *'ădhōrayim*). A fortress built by Rehoboam in Judah (2 Chron 11:9). Probably now Dura, a large village on rising ground west of Hebron.

ADORAM (See ADONIRAM)

ADORATION (See WORSHIP)

ADRAMMELECH (ăd-răm'ĕ-lĕk, Heb. *'adhrammelekh, Addar is king*). 1. The name that the author of 2 Kings 17:31 gives to Addar, the god the Sepharvites brought to Samaria when the king of Assyria settled them there, and in the worship of whom children were burned in fire. It was a time of syncretism, when Israelites and Assyrian colonists both paid service to God and to heathen deities alike (2 Kings 17:24–41).

2. A son of Sennacherib, who, with his brother Sharezer, murdered their father in the temple of Nisroch (2 Kings 19:37; Isa 37–38).

ADRAMYTTIUM (ăd'ră-mĭt'ĭ-ŭm). An old port city of Mysia, in the Roman province of Asia, near Edremit. Paul sailed in a ship of Adramyttium along the coast from Caesarea in Palestine to Myra in Lycia, where an Alexandrian ship bound for Italy took him on board (Acts 27:2–6).

ADRIA (ā'drĭ-ă). Originally that part of the gulf between Italy and the Dalmatian coast near the mouth of the Po River, named for the town of Adria. Later it was extended to include what is now the Adriatic Sea; and in NT times it included also that part of the Mediterranean between Crete and the Peloponnesus on the east and Sicily and Malta on the west. This extended meaning appears in Acts 27:27, where Paul's ship is "driven across the Adriatic Sea." "The sailors sensed that they were approaching land," and that land proved to be Malta (Acts 28:1 RSV, NIV; Melita in KJV).

ADRIEL (ā'drĭ-ĕl, Heb. *'adhrî'ēl, God is my help*). Son of Barzillai the Meholathite, to whom Merab, Saul's daughter, was given in marriage, though she had been promised to David (1 Sam 18:19;

2 Sam 21:8). According to 2 Samuel 21:8 he had five sons, all of whom perished in David's dreadful and sinful acquiescence in the demand of the Gibeonites for scapegoats. As in the NIV of 2 Samuel 21:8 the correct form is "Merab," not "Michal" (as explained in the footnote).

ADULLAM (à-dŭl'ăm, Heb. *'ădhullām, retreat, refuge*). A city in the Shephelah or low country, between the hill country of Judah and the sea, thirteen miles (twenty-two km.) SW of Bethlehem; very ancient (Gen 38:1, 12, 20; Josh 15:35); the seat of one of the thirty-one petty kings conquered by Joshua (Josh 12:15). It was fortified by Rehoboam (2 Chron 11:7). Because of its beauty it was called "the glory of Israel" (Mic 1:15). It was reoccupied on the return from the Babylonian exile (Neh 11:30).

David hid with his family and about four hundred men in one of the many limestone caves near the city (1 Sam 22:1–2) at a time when Saul sought his life. While David was here, three of his "mighty men" risked their lives to fulfill his expressed desire for water from the well of Bethlehem, but David refused to drink it, rightly recognizing that the extreme devotion that put life itself at risk was due to the Lord alone. For this reason he "poured it out before the LORD" (2 Sam 23:13–17; 1 Chron 11:15–19).

ADULTERY. In the OT sexual intercourse, usually of a man, married or unmarried, with the wife of another. One of the Ten Commandments forbids it (Exod 20:14; Deut 5:18). The punishment for both man and woman was death, probably by stoning (Deut 22:22–24; John 8:3–7). "Adultery" and related words translate derivatives of the Hebrew root *n'ph* (*nā 'aph*), conveying the one plain meaning.

From the earliest times (Gen 39:9), even outside the people of God (26:10), adultery was regarded as a serious sin. Along with other sexual offenses (e.g., Gen 34:7; Deut 22:21; Judg 19:23; 2 Sam 13:12) it is a wicked outrage (Jer 29:23), the word being *nĕvālāh,* behavior lacking moral principle or any recognition of proper obligation. Marriage is a covenant relationship (e.g., Mal 2:14), and for this reason it not only imposes obligations on the partners, but also on the community within which they have entered into their solemn, mutual vows.

The OT finds adultery a ready figure for apostasy from the Lord and attachment to false gods, as can be seen in Isaiah 57:3; Jeremiah 3:8–9; 13:27; Ezekiel 23:27, 43; Hosea 2:4; and similar passages.

While fornication is frequently and severely condemned in the OT, special solemnity attaches to the reproof of adultery, both in the relations of individual men and women and, figuratively, in the relations of the covenant people Israel, conceived of as a wife with God, their spiritual husband. Isaiah, Jeremiah, and Ezekiel use the figure (see references above). Hosea develops from personal experience with an adulterous wife an allegory of God's love for his unfaithful people. Adultery in the marriage relation is reprehensible; how much more infidelity in the behavior of human beings toward a God who loves them with a love that can well be expressed as that of a husband for his wife! Thus the figurative use enhances the literal sense, emphasizing the divine institution and nature of marriage.

In the NT "adultery" translates Greek *moicheuō* and related words, which the LXX had already used for Hebrew *nā'aph*. The meaning throughout the Bible widens and deepens, first with the prophets, then with Jesus and his apostles.

Jesus quotes the commandment (Matt 5:27–30; 19:18; Mark 10:19; Luke 18:20), broadening its application to include the lustful look that betrays an adulterous heart. He teaches that such evils as adultery come from the heart (Matt 15:19; Mark 7:21). Dealing with divorce, Jesus declares remarriage of a divorced man or woman to be adultery (Matt 5:31–32; 19:3–9; Mark 10:2–12; Luke 16:18), with one exception (Matt 5:32; 19:9), the interpretation of which by various interpreters differs. The Pharisee in a parable rejoices that he is not an adulterer (Luke 18:11). Jesus uses the term figuratively of a people unfaithful to God (Matt 12:39; 16:4; Mark 8:38). In John 8:2–11, the account of a woman taken in adultery reveals Jesus' insistence on the equal guilt of the man. Without belittling the seriousness of adultery, Jesus exercises the sovereign pardoning power of the grace of God, coupled with a solemn injunction against future offenses. Jesus' attitude toward adultery springs from his conception of marriage as God intended it and as it must be in the new Christian society.

Paul names adultery as one of the tests of obedience to the law (Rom 2:22), quotes the commandment (13:9), uses adultery as an analogy of our relation to God (7:3), says that adulterers "will not inherit the kingdom of God" (1 Cor 6:9), and lists adultery among works of the flesh (Gal 5:19). The sanctity of marriage is the point stressed in Hebrews 13:4. James 2:1 uses adultery and murder as examples of the equal obligation of all the commandments of God. In James 4:4 adultery is a figure of speech for unfaithfulness to God. Revelation 2:20–23 condemns spiritual adultery.

The NT treatment of adultery, following the implications of the OT concept, supports marriage as a lifelong monogamous union. Adultery is a special and aggravated case of fornication. In the teaching of Jesus and the apostles in the NT, all sexual impurity is sin against God, against self, and against others. Spiritual adultery (unfaithfulness to God) violates the union between Christ and his own.

Bibliography: J. Murray, *Divorce,* 1953; D. Atkinson, *To Have and to Hold,* 1979; G. Bromiley, *God and Marriage,* 1980. ER

ADUMMIM (à-dŭm'ĭm, Heb. *'ădhummîm,* perhaps *red spots*). A pass, the ascent of Addummim, on the road between Jerusalem and Jericho (Josh 15:7; 18:17). It was on the northern border of Judah and the southern border of Benjamin and is convincingly held to be the scene of Jesus' parable of the Good Samaritan (Luke 10:30–35).

ADVENT (See ESCHATOLOGY)

ADVOCATE (ăd'vōkāt, Gr. *paraklētos, counselor, comforter, supporter, backer, helper, Paraclete*). The Holy Spirit is the Advocate of the Father with us, therefore our Comforter (KJV, John 14:16, 26; 15:26; 16:7; RSV, NIV translate, "Counselor"). As applied to the Holy Spirit, the Greek word is so rich in meaning that adequate translation by any one English word is impossible. The KJV "Comforter" is as satisfactory as any, if it is taken in the fullest sense of one who not only consoles but also strengthens, helps, and counsels, with such authority as a legal advocate has for his client. Jesus speaks of the Holy Spirit as "another Comforter" (NIV "Counselor," John 14:16), using the same Greek word, thereby implying that he himself is a "Comforter." In 1 John 2:1 the meaning is narrowed to that of Christ being our Advocate with the Father, "one who speaks to the Father in our defense."

AENEAS (ē-nē'ăs). A paralytic, healed at Lydda by Peter (Acts 9:32–35).

AENON (ē'nŏn; in Aramaic means *springs*). A place near Salim, where John the Baptist was baptizing during the time Jesus was baptizing in Judea (John 3:22–23). The site of Aenon is unknown. Two possibilities are suggested for Salim—one east of Mount Gerizim, the other six miles (ten km.) south of Scythopolis. There are springs near both places. It would have been unnecessary to mention "much water" (3:23) if Aenon had been close to the Jordan River. John seems to have moved from "Bethany on the other side of the Jordan," where we find him in John 1:28.

AEON (ē'ŏn, Gr. *aiōn*). The word *aeon* does not occur in the English Bible but is variously translated. Its original meaning is "relative time duration, limited or unlimited," i.e., a period of time, or eternity. A common translation in the NT is "world" (RSV often "age"). Frequently it occurs in phrases meaning "for ever" (e.g., Matt 6:13 KJV). KJV has "ages" twice (Eph 2:7; Col 1:26). When aeon is the word translated "world," its duration in time is involved, though aeon is sometimes synonymous with Greek *kosmos,* world-order (e.g., Mark 4:19; 1 Cor 1:20; 2:6; 3:19). Good examples of the meaning of aeon as a period of time are Hebrews 9:26, where "the end of the ages" is the period ushered in by the first coming of Christ; and Matthew 24:3; 28:20, where "the end of the age" is its culmination at his second coming. We live in the in-between period (1 Cor 10:11). "This present age [time]" and "the age [world] to come" are distinguished (e.g., Matt 12:32; Mark 10:30). "This [the present] world [age]" (e.g., Rom 12:2; 2 Tim 4:10; Titus 2:12) implies the existence of another world. In Ephesians 1:21 "the present age" precedes "the one to come." Hebrews 6:5 speaks of "the powers of the coming age," which believers already experience. The Gnostic concept of aeons as beings emanating from and standing between God and the world is foreign to the NT.

ER

AFRICA. Either the whole continent or Roman Proconsular Africa (that is, modern Tunisia, to which were added Numidia and Mauretania). In the OT there are many references to Egypt and a few to Ethiopia (e.g., Isa 45:14; Jer 13:23). In the NT, Egypt, its Greek city of Alexandria (Acts 18:24), Ethiopia (8:27), and the port of Cyrene (in modern Libya) (Mark 15:21) are mentioned primarily because of the Jewish settlements there. Jesus himself went into Egypt (Matt 2:13–14), and Jews from Africa were present on the Day of Pentecost (Acts 2:10).

AGABUS (ăg'à-bŭs). One of the prophets from Jerusalem who came to Antioch and prophesied that there would be "a severe famine . . . over the entire Roman world." "This happened during the reign of Claudius." The prophecy led Christians at Antioch "to provide help for . . . Judea . . . by Barnabas and Saul" (Acts 11:27–30). Years later, a "prophet named Agabus" came down from Jerusalem to Caesarea and by a dramatic action warned Paul that he would be put in bonds if he persisted in going to Jerusalem (21:10–11). Although we cannot prove that the two prophets are the same man, there is no reason to doubt it.

AGAG (ā'găg, Heb. *'ăghāgh,* perhaps meaning *violent*). An important king of Amalek (Num 24:7). Balaam prophesied that a king of Jacob (Israel) would surpass him. In Numbers 24:3–9 Balaam began to predict the coming prosperity of Israel. Israel's oldest enemy following the Exodus was Amalek (Exod 17:8–15), and Balaam foresaw Israel's future glory in terms of the defeat of Amalek under a king whom he identified as Agag. This prediction was fulfilled when Saul and Agag met in battle (1 Sam 15:1–33). Saul defeated Agag, but he only partly obeyed the command to wreak the Lord's vengeance on the Amalekites. See also SAUL.

AGAGITE (See HAMAN)

AGAPE (ăg'à-pā, Gr. *agapē*). The more frequent of two NT words for love, connoting the preciousness or worthiness of the one loved. It is used in Jude 12 (KJV "feasts of charity," ASV, RSV, NIV "love feasts") of common meals that cultivated brotherly love among Christians. They may be referred to in Acts 20:11; 1 Corinthians 11:21–22, 33–34; 2 Peter 2:13. In Acts 2:46, "broke bread" refers to the Lord's Supper (cf. v. 42), but "ate together" requires a full meal. Paul rebukes Christians for the abuses that had crept into the love feasts and had marred the Lord's Supper (1 Cor 11:20–34). The Lord's Supper properly followed, but was distinct from, the love feast.

Main altar of the Basilica of the Agony in Gethsemane, at the foot of the Mount of Olives in Jerusalem. The mosaic depicts the scene of Jesus' agony (Luke 22:43–44). In front of the altar is the traditional Rock of Agony. Courtesy Duby Tal.

AGAR (ā'găr). The Greek name of Sarai's handmaid (Gal 4:24–25). See HAGAR.

AGATE (See MINERALS)

AGE (See AEON)

AGE, OLD AGE. Called the reward of filial obedience according to the commandment (Exod 20:12). The Mosaic legislation spelled out the respect to be shown the aged (Lev 19:32). Younger men waited till they had spoken (Job 32:4). God promised Abraham "a good old age" (Gen 15:15). When Pharaoh received him, Jacob lamented that he had not lived as long as his ancestors (47:7–9). There are many Hebrew words relating to old age in the OT, showing the honor in which the aged were usually held; yet the gray hairs that were so much respected also had their sorrows (44:29–31). Official positions went to older men (elders, e.g., Exod 3:16; Matt 21:23). Elders were ordained for the early Christian churches (e.g., Acts 14:23). Aged men and women are given sound advice in Titus 2:2–5. There is a fine picture of old age in Ecclesiastes 12:1–7. Jesus Christ is portrayed with the white hair of old age in Revelation 1:14.

AGEE (ā'gĕ, Heb. *'agē', fugitive*). The father of Shammah, one of David's mighty men (1 Sam 23:11). He is called a Hararite.

AGONY (Gr. *agōnia, agony, anguish*). The word is derived from the Greek *agōn,* "contest, struggle," and depicts severe conflict and pain. Luke 22:44 tells us that Christ's agony was such that "his sweat was like drops of blood falling to the ground." (See also Matt 26:36–46; Mark 14:32–42; Heb 5:7–8.) While Luke alone records the bloody sweat and the appearance of an angel from heaven strengthening Jesus, Matthew and Mark speak of the change in his countenance and manner and record his words as he spoke of his overwhelming sorrow "even unto death." The passage in Hebrews is the only clear reference in the NT apart from the Gospels to this agonizing crisis. Jesus' struggle was in part with the powers of darkness, which were then returning with double force, having retreated after Satan's defeat at the temptation (Luke 4:13) "until an opportune time" (Gr. "until the season," i.e., in Gethsemane, Luke 22:53). Chiefly, however, Jesus' agony was caused by the prospect of the darkness on Calvary, when he was to experience a horror never known before, the hiding of the Father's face, the climax of his vicarious suffering for our sins. The one who knew no sin was to be made sin for mankind. The hour was before him when he would cry out in wretchedness of soul, "My God, my God, why have you forsaken me?" The prospect of this dreadful cup caused the struggle in the Garden. In this supreme spiritual conflict, the Captain of our salvation emerged triumphant, as is evident in the language of his final victory of faith over the sinless infirmity of his flesh: "Shall I not drink the cup the Father has given me?" (John 18:11). BP

AGORA (ă'gō-rȧ, Gr. *agora, marketplace*). In ancient cities the town meeting place, where the public met for the exchange of merchandise, information, and ideas. As centers where people congregated, the agorae of Galilee and Judea were the scenes for many of the healing miracles of Christ (Mark 6:56). Here the village idlers, as well as those seeking work, would gather (Matt 20:3). Here the vain and the proud could parade

Remains of the Agora in Athens, the central market place and meeting ground for various public activities. It was here that Paul had his daily disputations with the citizens (Acts 17:17). The temple of Hephaestus is viewed in background. Courtesy Gerald Nowotny.

in order to gain public recognition (Matt 23:7; Mark 12:38; Luke 11:43; 20:46). Here also the children would gather for play (Matt 11:16–17; Luke 7:32). In Gentile cities, the agorae served also as forums and tribunals. The agora of Philippi was the scene of the trial of Paul and Silas following the deliverance of a "slave girl who had a spirit by which she predicted the future" (Acts 16:16ff.). In Athens Paul's daily disputations in the agora led directly to his famed message before the Areopagus (17:17ff.), the court that met on Mars Hill, north of the Acropolis.

AGRAPHA (ăg'rȧ-fȧ, Gr. *agrapha, unwritten things*). These are units of tradition concerning Christ, mostly sayings ascribed to him, transmitted to us outside of the canonical Gospels. The entire collection of agrapha, gathered from all sources, is not large; and when what is obviously apocryphal or spurious is eliminated, the small remainder is of very little value.

Several sources of agrapha may be noted. The best authenticated are those found in the NT outside of the Gospels: four in Acts (1:4–5; 1:7–8; 11:16; 20:35); two in Paul's letters (1 Cor 11:24–25; 1 Thess 4:15ff.); and one in James (1:12). A second source of agrapha is found in ancient manuscripts of the NT. Most often, sayings preserved in such manuscripts are of the nature of textual variations: parallel forms or expansions or combinations of sayings found in the canonical Gospels. A few, however, cannot be fitted into this category; the following, for example, is found after Luke 6:5 in Codex Bezae: "On the same day, seeing someone working on the Sabbath, he [Jesus] said to him, 'Man, if indeed you know what you are doing, you are blessed; but if you do not know, you are cursed and a transgressor of the Law.' " A third source of agrapha is patristic literature. Papias, bishop of Hierapolis (c. A.D. 80–155), was the first of the church fathers to make a collection of the sayings of Jesus not recorded in the Gospels, but very little of his work survives. Agrapha are found in the works of Justin Martyr, Clement of Alexandria, Origen, and a few others. Origen, for example, wrote, "I have read somewhere that the Saviour said . . . 'He that is near me is near the fire; he that is far from me is far from the kingdom.' " Still another source of agrapha is the papyri that have been discovered in Egypt during the past century, especially those found by Grenfell and Hunt at Oxyrhynchus. In some of these papyri one agraphon follows another without context, introduced by the simple formula, "Jesus says," as in the following: "Jesus says: Wheresoever there are two, they are not with God, and where there is one alone, I say, I am with him. Lift up the stone, and there shalt thou find me; cleave the wood, and I am there." Agrapha are found also in the apocryphal gospels, like the *Gospel According to the Hebrews* and the *Gospel According to the Egyptians*, but few, if any, of these can be regarded as genuine. The recently discovered (1945 or 1946) Gnostic Coptic *Gospel of Thomas*, found near Nag Hammadi in Upper Eygpt, which is dated around 150, consists of more than one hundred short sayings of Jesus, the majority of which begin with the words, "Jesus said," or they give a reply by Jesus when asked by his disciples to instruct them on a doubtful point. Many sayings ascribed to Jesus are found in Islamic sources, but these traditions are for the most part of no value.

Although the number of agrapha collected by scholars seems imposing, only a very few have anything like a strong claim to acceptance on the grounds of early and reliable source and internal character. Some scholars reject the agrapha completely; others think that they are the remains of a considerable body of extracanonical sayings that circulated in early Christian circles, and that a few of them, at least, may be genuine. See also THOMAS, GOSPEL OF.

Bibliography: M. R. James, *The Apocryphal New Testament,* 1924, pp. 33–37; J. Donovan, *The Logia in Ancient and Recent Literature,* 1924; J. Jeremias, *Unknown Sayings of Jesus,* 1957. SB

AGRICULTURE. Not a Bible word; "husbandry" and "husbandman" are used for the activity and the one who practices it. In the form of horticulture, it is as old as Adam (Gen 2:5, 8–15). Caring for the Garden of Eden became

The Gezer calendar on a tablet of limestone (4¼ in. x 3⅛ in.) that records the annual cycle of agricultural activities. Evidently a schoolboy's exercises from about the time of Solomon. The script is ancient Hebrew. Courtesy Israel Department of Antiquities and Museums.

A peasant with a primitive plow, "plowing in hope" (1 Cor 9:10), near Hebron. Courtesy Zev Radovan.

labor after the curse (3:17–19). Nomad and farmer began to be differentiated with Abel and Cain (4:2–4). As animal husbandry took its place along with tillage as part of the agricultural economy, the farmer gained in social status. Yet as late as shortly before the Babylonian exile, nomads still felt a sense of superiority over the settled agricultural people (cf. the Recabites, Jer 35:1–11).

"Noah, a man of the soil, proceeded to plant a vineyard" (Gen 9:20). Abraham and his descendants were nomad herdsmen in Canaan, though Isaac and Jacob at times also tilled the soil (26:12; 37:7). Recurrent famines and the sojourn in Egypt taught the Israelites to depend more on agriculture, so that the report of the spies regarding the lush growth in Canaan interested them (Num 13:23; Deut 8:8). Agriculture became the basis of the Mosaic commonwealth, since the land of Palestine was suited to an agricultural rather than a pastoral economy. The soil is fertile wherever water can be applied abundantly. The Hauran district (Perea) is productive. The soil of Gaza is dark and rich, though porous, and retains rain; olive trees abound there. The Israelites cleared away most of the wood that they found in Canaan (Josh 17:18). Wood became scarce; dung and hay heated their ovens (Ezek 4:12–15; Matt 6:30). Their water supply came from rain, from brooks that ran from the hills, and from the Jordan. Irrigation was made possible by ducts from cisterns hewn out of rock. As population increased, the more difficult cultivation of the hills was resorted to and yielded abundance. Terraces were cut, one above another, and faced with low stone walls. Rain falls chiefly in autumn and winter, November and December, rarely after March, almost never as late as May. The "early" rain falls from about the September equinox to sowing time in November or December, the "latter" rain comes in January and February (Joel 2:23; James 5:7). Drought two or three months before harvest meant famine (Amos 4:7–8). Wheat, barley, and rye (millet rarely) were the staple cereals. "Corn" in the KJV, according to British usage, refers to any grain, not specifically to maize (NIV renders "grain"). The barley harvest was earlier than the wheat harvest: "The flax and the barley were destroyed, since the barley had headed and the flax was in bloom. The wheat and spelt, however, were not destroyed, because they ripen later" (Exod 9:31–32). Accordingly, at the Passover the barley was ready for the sickle, and the wave sheaf was offered. At the Pentecost feast fifty days later, the wheat was ripe for cutting, and the firstfruit loaves were offered. The vine, olive, and fig abounded, and traces remain everywhere of wine and olive presses. Cummin, peas, beans, lentils, lettuce, endive, leek, garlic, onion, cucumber, and cabbage were also cultivated.

The Passover in the month of Nisan occurred in the green stage of produce; the feast of weeks in Sivan, to the ripening stage; and the Feast of Tabernacles in Tisri, to the harvest. The six months from Tisri to Nisan were occupied with cultivation; the six months from Nisan to Tisri, with gathering fruits. Rain from the equinox in Tisri to Nisan was pretty continuous but was heavier at the beginning (the early rain) and the end (the latter rain). Rain in harvest was almost unknown (Prov 26:1).

Viticulture (the cultivation of grapes) is pictured in Isaiah 5:1–7 and Matthew 21:33–41. Some farming procedures are described in Isaiah 28:24–28. The plow was light and drawn by yokes of oxen (1 Kings 19:19). Oxen were urged

A wooden model of a man guiding a two-handled plow drawn by two oxen. The yoke consists of a bar placed on the necks of the oxen just behind the long horns. From Egypt, c. 2350–2000 B.C. Reproduced by courtesy of the Trustees of the British Museum.

on with a spearlike goad, which could double as a deadly weapon (Judg 3:31). Fallow ground was broken and cleared early in the year (Jer 4:3; Hos 10:1). Seed was scattered broadcast, as in the parable of the sower (Matt 13:1–8), and plowed in afterward, the stubble of the preceding crop becoming mulch by decay. In irrigated fields, the seed was trodden in by cattle (Isa 32:20). The contrast between the exclusive dependence on irrigation in Egypt and the larger dependence on rain in Palestine is drawn in Deuteronomy 11:10–12. To sow among thorns was deemed bad husbandry (Job 5:5; Prov 24:30–32). Hoeing and weeding were seldom needed in their fine tilth. Seventy days sufficed between barley sowing and the offering of the wave sheaf of ripe grain at Passover. Harvesting and harvest customs in the time of the Judges are described in Ruth 2 and 3. Sowing varied seed in a field was forbidden (Deut

Wooden sledge with stones fastened to the underside, for threshing, similar to the type used in ancient times. It is commonly used by Arab peasants. Courtesy Israel Government Press Office.

22:9). Oxen, unmuzzled (25:4) and five abreast, trod out the grain on a threshing floor of hard beaten earth, to separate the grain from chaff and straw. Flails were used for small quantities and lighter grains (Isa 28:27). A threshing sledge (41:15) was also used, probably like the Egyptian sledge still in use (a stage with three rollers ridged with iron, which cut the straw for fodder, while crushing out the grain). The shovel and fan winnowed the grain afterward with the help of the evening breeze (Ruth 3:2; Isa 30:24); lastly it was shaken in a sieve (Amos 9:9; Luke 22:31). The fruit of newly planted trees was not to be eaten for the first three years. In the fourth it was offered as firstfruits. In the fifth year it might be eaten freely (Lev 19:23–25).

We have glimpses of the relations of farm laborers, steward (manager or overseer), and owner in the Book of Ruth, in Matthew 20:1–16, and in Luke 17:7–9.

Agriculture was beset with pests: locust, cankerworm, caterpillar, and palmerworm (Joel 2:25 KJV); God calls them "my great army," as destructive as an invasion by human enemies. Haggai speaks (2:17) of blight, mildew, and hail. Modern development of agriculture in Palestine under the British mandate and since the establishment of the State of Israel, and parallel but lesser development in the country of Jordan, are restoring the coastal plain, the plains of Esdraelon and Dothan, the Shephelah, the Negev, and the Hauran to their ancient prosperity. See also FARMING; OCCUPATIONS AND PROFESSIONS ER

AGRIPPA I (ȧ-grĭp'ȧ). Known in history as King Herod Agrippa I and in the NT, where he is mentioned in Acts 12, as Herod. He was the son of Aristobulus and Bernice and grandson of Herod the Great. Through friendship with the

Bronze coin depicting the portrait of King Agrippa I with the Greek inscription, "Of the great King Agrippa the friend of the Emperor." Reverse depicts the city-goddess of Caesarea and the inscription, "Caesarea which is near by the Augustan harbor, year 7 (A.D. 43)." Courtesy Carta, Jerusalem.

emperors Caligula and Claudius he gained the rulership first of Iturea and Trachonitis, then of Galilee and Perea, and ultimately of Judea and Samaria. He ruled over this reunited domain of Herod the Great from A.D. 40 until his death in 44 at the age of fifty-four. While owing his position to the favor of Rome, he recognized the importance of exercising great tact in his contacts with the Jews. Thus it was that his natural humanity gave way to expediency in the severe conflict between Judaism and the growing Christian movement. He killed James, an act that "pleased the Jews," and imprisoned Peter with the intention of bringing him before the people for execution after the Passover (Acts 12:2–4). Agrippa's sudden death shortly thereafter, noted in Acts 12:20–23, is fully recorded by Josephus (*Antiq.* 19.8). On the second day of a festival held in Caesarea in honor of Claudius, Agrippa put on a silver garment of "wonderful" texture and entered the amphitheater early in the morning. When the sun's rays shone on his garment, the brilliant glare caused his flatterers to cry out that he was a god. Josephus adds that "the king did neither rebuke them nor reject their impious flattery." Almost immediately a severe pain arose in his abdomen; five days later he died in great agony. See also HEROD.

AGRIPPA II (à-grĭp'à). Known in history as King Herod Agrippa II and in the NT (where he is mentioned only in Acts 25 and 26) as Agrippa. He was the son of Agrippa I. Only seventeen at the death of his father, he was thought too young to succeed to the throne. Six years later (A.D. 50), he was placed over the kingdom of Chalcis, which included the right to appoint the high priest of the temple in Jerusalem. In 53 he was transferred to the tetrarchies formerly held by Philip (Iturea and Trachonitis) and Lysanias (Abilene) and given the title of king. After the death of Claudius in 54 Nero added to Agrippa's realm several cities of Galilee and Perea. When Festus became procurator of Judea, Agrippa, accompanied by his sister (and consort) Bernice, went to Caesarea to pay his respects. It was at this time that Paul appeared before him, as recorded in Acts 25:23–26:32. In the final revolt of the Jews against Rome, Agrippa sided with the Romans in the destruction of his nation in the same cynical spirit with which he met the impassioned appeal of the apostle. Following the fall of Jerusalem in 70, he retired with Bernice to Rome, where he died in 100.

AGUE (See DISEASES)

AGUR (ā'gûr, Heb. *'āghûr, gatherer*). The otherwise unknown author of Proverbs 30. His words are described as "an oracle," thus claiming divine inspiration. Many, however, follow the suggestion of a place name—"of Massa" (cf. NIV footnote). See also Genesis 25:14, 16.

AHAB (ā'hăb, Heb. *'ah'āv, father's brother*). 1. Son of Omri and seventh king of the northern kingdom of Israel. He reigned twenty-two years, 873–851 B.C. Politically, Ahab was one of the strongest kings of Israel. In his days Israel was at peace with Judah and maintained her dominion over Moab, which paid a considerable tribute (2 Kings 3:4). He went into battle on three different occasions in later years against Ben-Hadad, king of Syria. While he had great success in the first two campaigns, he was defeated and mortally wounded in the third. Not mentioned in the Bible is Ahab's participation in the Battle of Karkar in 854. The "Monolith Inscription" of the Assyrian king Shalmanezer III contains a description of this battle that the Assyrians fought against a Syrian coalition of twelve kings. Of these, "Hadad-ezer," king of Damascus, is named first. Irhuleni of Hamath follows and in third place is "Ahab, the Israelite." The inscription states that Ahab commanded two thousand chariots and ten thousand men. The number of his chariots was far greater than the number credited to any other king.

Israelite remains of city wall at Ahab's capital, Samaria. The wall was c. 5 feet (1.6 m.) thick and built of fine ashlar masonry laid in headers and stretchers carefully fitted together. Courtesy Israel Department of Antiquities and Museums.

Successful as he might have been politically, however, Ahab owes his prominence in the OT to the religious apostasy that occurred in Israel during his reign. Of him it is said, he "did more evil in the eyes of the LORD than any of those before him" (1 Kings 16:30). His marriage to Jezebel, daughter of the king of the Zidonians, was politically advantageous but religiously disastrous. Jezebel introduced the idolatrous worship of Baal into Israel as well as the licentious orgies of the goddess Ashtoreth. She also instituted a severe persecution against the followers of the Lord and killed all the prophets of the Lord with the sword, except the one hundred who were hidden by Obadiah (18:4; cf. 19:14). At this critical period in the history of Israel, God raised up Elijah, whose faithful ministry culminated in the conflict with the prophets of Baal on Mount Carmel (ch 18).

Ahab's religious corruption was equaled by his love of material wealth and display. He was well known, for example, for his elaborately ornamented ivory palace (1 Kings 22:39). Not content with what he had, however, he coveted the vineyard of Naboth, which adjoined his palace at Jezreel. Naboth refused to sell the land and Ahab was utterly dejected. Seeing his state, Jezebel asked him to remember who was king in Israel, and proceeded unscrupulously to charge Naboth with blasphemy, doing so in the name of the king, who weakly maintained silence. False witnesses testified against Naboth, he was stoned to death, and Ahab took possession of the vineyard. This crime sealed the doom not only of Ahab, but also of his family. The judgment of the Lord was that all of his posterity would be cut off (21:21), even as had been the case with the two previous dynasties, those of Jeroboam and Baasha. The ringing condemnatory sentence of Elijah (21:19) was fulfilled to the letter on Ahab's son Joram (2 Kings 9:24–26) and in part on Ahab himself (1 Kings 22:38). Execution of the sentence was, however, delayed by Ahab's repentance (21:27–29). Ahab also sinned by failing to discern the Lord's will and sparing the defeated Ben-Hadad of Syria (20:20–43). The prediction of his own death (20:42) was fulfilled when he was killed in battle at Ramoth Gilead (22:34).

Ahab's character is succinctly summarized by the historian: "There was never a man like Ahab, who sold himself to do evil in the eyes of the LORD, urged on by Jezebel his wife" (1 Kings 21:25).

2. A false prophet who deceived the Jews in Babylon. Joining with Zedekiah, another false prophet, Ahab predicted an early return to Jerusalem. For this sin and for their immoral conduct, Jeremiah prophesied that they would be burned to death by the king of Babylon and that their names would become a byword (Jer 29:21–23). BP

AHARAH (à-hâr'àh, Heb. *'ahrah*). The third son of Benjamin, probably the founder of a family (1 Chron 8:1).

AHARHEL (à-hàr'hel, Heb. *'ăharhēl*). A son of Harum, founder of a family enrolled in the tribe of Judah (1 Chron 4:8).

AHASAI (See AHZAI)

AHASBAI (à-hăs'bī, Heb. *'ăhasbay*). The father of Eliphelet, one of David's heroes (2 Sam 23:34).

AHASUERUS (See XERXES)

AHAVA (à-hā'và, Heb. *'ahăwā'*). A river in Babylonia named after a place by which it flowed (Ezra 8:15, 21), where Ezra assembled the Jewish exiles to seek God's guidance and protection for the long and dangerous journey to Jerusalem.

AHAZ (ā'hăz, Heb. *'āhāz, he has grasped*). Reigning over the southern kingdom of Judah, 735–715 B.C., Ahaz was a king of great significance. Historically during his reign and as a result of his policies, the people of God became vassals of Assyria and never again did the throne of David exist in its own sovereign right. Ahaz began that prolonged period of foreign domination that continued beyond the time of the coming of Christ. The dominant political power changed—Assyria, Babylon, Persia, Greece, Rome—but the vassalage did not. In addition, Ahaz is significant theologically, for his policies involved a denial of the way of faith. The essential cause of the demeaning of the throne of David and its enslavement was unbelief. The message of the reign of Ahaz remains as Isaiah summarized it: "If you do not stand firm in your faith, you will not stand at all" (Isa 7:9).

Ahaz is often represented as a weak, ineffective king. This is not the case. He gave his country firm and resolute leadership—but in the wrong direction. In 745 B.C. Tiglath-Pileser gained the throne of Assyria, the contemporary "super-power"; at once the Assyrians threw off the lethargy of the previous years and began to pursue imperialist policies. The states of Western Palestine, particularly Syria (Aram) and Israel (the northern kingdom of the people of God), felt their security threatened and determined on a defensive, military alliance. Desiring a united Palestinian front, these northern powers determined to coerce Judah into their anti-Assyrian bloc. From the time of Jotham, Ahaz's father, Judah had been under this pressure (2 Kings 15:37), but it was not until Ahaz's day that events reached a climax. A large-scale invasion brought the northern powers the successes reported in 2 Chronicles 28:5–8, though for reasons no longer clear they failed to capitalize on success by taking Jerusalem (Isa 7:1). A further incursion was planned. This time Edomite and Philistine (2 Chron 28:17–18) armies also took the field, with the clearly defined objective of bringing the monarchy of David to an end and replacing the Davidic king, perhaps with an Aramean puppet (Isa 7:6). This threat to the dynasty of David made the events of the reign of Ahaz crucially significant. In the face of the threat we may well ask, "What made the people of God secure? How did they keep hold of their God-given possessions and privileges?"

Isaiah answered these questions with one word: "Faith." Those who trust the Lord's promises will find that he keeps his promises. Isaiah revealed the Lord's mind in Isaiah 7:7–8. The dreaded threat from the north would come to nothing (7:7); trusting in the apparent security of her military alliance with Syria would bring Ephraim (Israel) to a total end (7:8). Only the way of faith would keep Judah secure (7:9). When Isaiah made this appeal to Ahaz, that resolute monarch was already committed to the beginning of a militarist solution. Isaiah 7:3 reveals him reviewing Jerusalem's most vulnerable point: its overground water supply that could easily be cut off by a besieging enemy. King Ahaz could not be moved to the position of simple faith. To the offer of a sign from the Lord of even cosmic proportions (7:10–11) he gave the sort of answer that is often the resort of the outwardly religious man (7:12), and the die was cast. Ahaz refused the way of faith and embraced instead the way of works—the military-political solution. He showed all his astute hard-headedness in the course he followed. In fear of Assyria, Syria and Israel were threatening him. What better way to deal with them than to appeal over their heads to Assyria, secure an alliance with the super-power, and leave it to Assyrian armed might to disperse the Syro-Ephraimite armies? This is exactly what Ahaz did (2 Kings 16:7ff.; 2 Chron 28:16ff.). But he learned the risk of taking a tiger by the tail: once Assyria had disposed of the north Palestine kingdoms it was the turn of Judah, and Ahaz became the first vassal king in David's line.

The Bible makes it clear that Ahaz had prepared the way for his own spiritual downfall by religious apostasy long before the decisive moment came (2 Kings 16:14; 2 Chron 28:1–4). It comes as no surprise that his decisions to abandon the way of faith opened the door to further and greater religious decline (2 Kings 16:10–18; 2 Chron 28:22–23).

2. A great-grandson of Jonathan, son of King Saul; one of four sons of Micah and the father of Jehoaddah (1 Chron 8:35–36). JAM

AHAZIAH (ā'hȧ-zī'ȧ, Heb. *'ăhazyâh, Jehovah hath grasped*). 1. Son of Ahab and Jezebel, eighth king of Israel. He reigned only briefly, 851–850 B.C. Ahaziah was a worshiper of Jeroboam's calves and of his mother's idols, Baal and Ashtoreth. The most notable event of his reign was the revolt of the Moabites, who had been giving a yearly tribute of a hundred thousand lambs and a hundred thousand rams (2 Kings 1:1; 3:4–5). Ahaziah was prevented from trying to put down the revolt by a fall through a lattice in his palace at Samaria. Injured severely, he sent messengers to inquire of Baalzebub, god of Ekron, whether he would recover. Elijah the prophet was sent by God to intercept the messengers and proclaimed to them that Ahaziah would die. The king in anger tried to capture the prophet, but two groups of fifty men were consumed by fire from heaven in making the attempt. A third contingent was sent to seize the prophet but instead implored Elijah to deliver them from the fate of their predecessors (2 Kings 1:13, 14). Elijah then went down to Samaria and gave the message directly to the king, who died shortly afterward. He was succeeded by his brother Jehoram (1:17; cf. 8:16).

2. Son of Jehoram of Judah and Athaliah; thus grandson of Jehoshaphat and Ahab, and nephew of Ahaziah of Israel. He was the sixth king of Judah in the divided monarchy and reigned only one year (2 Chron 22:2), 843 B.C. In 2 Chronicles 21:17 and 25:23, his name appears also as Jehoahaz (a simple transposition of the component parts of the compound name), and in 2 Chronicles 22:6 (KJV) he is called Azariah. According to 2 Kings 8:26, Ahaziah was twenty-two years old when he began to reign, and his father, Jehoram, only lived to age forty (21:20). However, 2 Chronicles 22:2 states that he was forty-two years old when he ascended the throne. Some have thought that this last reference is a scribal error, but it may indicate a co-regency. Ahaziah walked in all the idolatries of the house of Ahab, "for his mother encouraged him in doing wrong" (22:3). He sinned also in allying himself with Joram (KJV "Jehoram") of Israel against Hazael of Syria, going into battle at Ramoth Gilead (22:5). Joram was wounded and Ahaziah went to see him at Jezreel. Here judgment came on him through the hand of Jehu, who fell on Joram and all the house of Ahab. When Ahaziah saw the slaughter, he fled, but "they wounded him in his chariot . . . he escaped to Megiddo and died there" (2 Kings 9:27). The account given in Chronicles presents different though not irreconcilable details of his death (2 Chron 22:6–9). Ahaziah was buried with his fathers in Jerusalem (2 Kings 9:28). Jehu allowed this honorable burial because Ahaziah was the grandson of Jehoshaphat, who sought the Lord with all his heart (2 Chron 22:9). Following the death of Ahaziah, his mother Athaliah seized the throne. She killed all the royal sons of the house of Judah except Joash, Ahaziah's son, who was hidden by Jehosheba, sister of Ahaziah and wife of Jehoiada the high priest (22:10–12).

AHBAN (ȧ'băn, Heb. *'ahbān*). A man of Judah, of the house of Jerahmeel (1 Chron 2:29).

AHER (ā-hêr, Heb. *'ahēr*). A Benjamite (1 Chron 7:12).

AHI (ā'hī, Heb. *'ăhî*). 1. Chief of the Gadites in Gilead (1 Chron 5:15).

2. A man of Asher, son of Shamer (1 Chron 7:34).

AHIAH (See AHIJAH)

AHIAM (ā-hī'ăm, Heb. *'ăhî 'ām, mother's brother*). One of David's thirty heroes (2 Sam 23:33).

AHIAN (ȧ-hī'ăn, Heb. *'ahyān*). A Manassite of the family of Shemida (1 Chron 7:19).

AHIEZER (ā-hī-ē' zêr, Heb. *'ahî 'ezer, brother of help*). 1. The head of the tribe of Dan in the wilderness (Num 1:12; 2:25; 7:66).

2. A Gibeonite who joined David at Ziklag (1 Chron 12:3).

AHIHUD (ȧ-hī'hŭd, Heb. *'ăhîhûdh, brother is majesty*). 1. Prince of the tribe of Asher; selected by Moses to help divide the land of Canaan (Num 34:27).

2. A son of Ehud (1 Chron 8:7).

AHIJAH (ȧ-hī'jȧ, Heb. *'ăhîyâ, brother of Jehovah*). 1. One of the sons of Jerahmeel, a great-grandson of Judah and brother of Caleb (1 Chron 2:25).

2. A descendant of Benjamin, mentioned in connection with an intra-family conflict (1 Chron 8:7).

3. Son of Ahitub. He was priestly successor to the great priest of Shiloh, Eli, and after the destruction of Shiloh, served as priest under King Saul. In particular he was asked to inquire of the Lord for Saul in the course of the Philistine war recorded in 1 Samuel 13–14. See especially 14:3, 18–19.

4. The Pelonite, one of the valiant men of David's armies (1 Chron 11:36).

5. A Levite who was in charge of the treasures

of the house of God in David's reign (1 Chron 26:20).

6. Son of Shisha and brother of Elihoreph. He was a scribe of Solomon (1 Kings 4:3).

7. A prophet of Shiloh (1 Kings 11:29–39; 12:15; 14:2; 15:29). He predicted to Jeroboam that he would reign over ten of the twelve tribes, and that his dynasty would be an enduring one if he did what was right in the eyes of the Lord. However, Jeroboam ignored the condition attached to the prediction, and it fell to Ahijah to foretell not only the death of Jeroboam's son but also the end of Jeroboam's line.

8. The father of Baasha, king of Israel, of the tribe of Issachar (1 Kings 15:27).

9. One of the men who set their seal to the covenant drawn up before the Lord in the days of Nehemiah (Neh 10:26).

AHIKAM (à-hī'kăm, Heb. *'ăhîqām, my brother has risen up*). Son of Shaphan the scribe, sent by Josiah to ask the meaning of the Book of the Law that was found (2 Kings 22:12). Later he successfully pleaded before the princes and elders that Jeremiah should not be put to death for his warnings of impending doom (Jer 26:24). After the deportation to Babylon, Ahikam's son Gedaliah became governor over the people who remained in the cities of Judah (2 Kings 25:22; Jer 40:5).

AHILUD (à-hī'lŭd, Heb. *'ăhîlûdh, a child's brother*). Father of Jehoshaphat the recorder (2 Sam 8:16; 20:24; 1 Kings 4:3; 1 Chron 18:15).

AHIMAAZ (à-hĭm'ā-ăz, Heb. *'ăhîma'ats, brother of anger*). 1. The father of Ahinoam, wife of King Saul (1 Sam 14:50).

2. Son of Zadok the high priest (1 Chron 6:8). During Absalom's rebellion he and Jonathan, son of Abiathar, served as messengers between David and Hushai, David's counselor and spy. They brought to David Hushai's news that Ahithophel had urged Absalom to make an immediate attack and Hushai's warning that David should cross the Jordan at once (2 Sam 15:24–27; 17:15–22). David's estimate of Ahimaaz appears in his remark at his approach after the battle: "He's a good man . . . He comes with good news" (18:27). Ahimaaz announced the victory but evaded the question concerning Absalom's fate, wishing to spare the feelings of the king. While he was still in David's presence the Cushite arrived and unfeelingly broke the news concerning Absalom's death. Comparing 1 Kings 4:2 with 1 Chronicles 6:8–10, some infer that Ahimaaz died before he attained the priesthood and before the death of his father Zadok, who was succeeded by Ahimaaz's son, Azariah.

3. One of Solomon's twelve commissary officers (1 Kings 4:15). He married Basemath, the daughter of Solomon. Some suggest that he should be identified with the son of Zadok.

AHIMAN (à-hī'măn, Heb. *'ăhîman, my brother is a gift*). 1. One of the three giant sons of Anak seen in Mount Hebron by the spies (Num 13:22). The Anakim race was cut off from the land of Israel and Judah by Joshua (11:21–22). The three sons—Sheshai, Ahiman, and Talmai—were driven by Caleb from Hebron (Josh 15:14) and killed (Judg 1:10).

2. A Levite gatekeeper (1 Chron 9:17).

AHIMELECH (à-hĭm'-ĕ-lĕk, Heb. *'ăhîmelekh, brother of a king*). 1. A priest serving in the priestly center of Nob in the time of Saul. He assisted David, not knowing that he was a fugitive from the king, by giving him Goliath's sword and allowing him to eat the consecrated bread. Doeg the Edomite denounced him to Saul and, at Saul's command, massacred all the priests at Nob except Abiathar, who fled to David (1 Sam 21–22).

2. Son of Abiathar and grandson of Ahimelech (2 Sam 8:17; 1 Chron 18:16; 24:6).

3. A Hittite who, with Abishai, was asked to accompany David to Saul's camp (1 Sam 26:6).

AHIMOTH (à-hī'mŏth, Heb. *'ăhîmôth, brother of death*). Son of Elkanah (1 Chron 6:25), descendant of Kohath, and a Levite.

AHINADAB (à-hĭn'à-dăb, Heb. *'ăhînādhāv*). A commissary officer of Solomon (1 Kings 4:14).

AHINOAM (à-hĭn'ō-ăm, Heb. *'ăhînō'am, my brother is delight*). 1. Wife of King Saul (1 Sam 14:50).

2. One of David's wives, a Jezreelitess (1 Sam 25:43), who lived with him at Gath (27:3). She and Abigail were captured by the Amalekites at Ziklag (30:5) but were rescued by David (30:18). They were with David in Hebron (2 Sam 2:2), where Ahinoam bore Amnon, his first son (3:2).

AHIO (à-hī'ō, Heb. *'ahyô, brotherly*). 1. Son of Abinadab. He and his brother Uzzah accompanied the ark of God from Gibeah on David's first attempt to remove it to Jerusalem (2 Sam 6:2–22; 1 Chron 13:1–14). Ahio walked before, guiding the oxen that drew the cart, while Uzzah walked alongside.

2. A Benjamite (1 Chron 8:14).

3. A Gibeonite, son of Jehiel (1 Chron 8:31; 9:37).

AHIRA (à-hī'rà, Heb. *'ăhîra', brother of evil*). Prince captain of the tribe of Naphtali (Num 1:15; 2:29; 7:78, 83; 10:27).

AHIRAM (à-hī'răm, Heb. *'ăhîrām, brother of height, exalted brother*). Son of Benjamin (Num 26:38). Although his name does not appear in the list of Benjamin's sons given in Genesis 46:21, it is thought that Ehi is perhaps a shortened form of Ahiram. In the list of five sons given in 1 Chronicles 8:1–2 the name of Aharah, expressly mentioned as "the third" son, is thought to be a variant of Ahiram or a different name for the same person (cf. Num 26:38–39, where Ahiram is the third name in a list of five).

AHIRAMITE (à-hī'rà-mīt, Heb. *'ăḥîrāmî, of the family of Ahiram*). A Benjamite clan mentioned in Numbers 26:38.

AHISAMACH (à-hĭs'à-măk, Heb. *'ăḥîsāmākh, my brother supports*). A Danite, the father of Oholiab (Exod 31:6; 35:34; 38:23).

AHISHAHAR (à-hĭsh'à-här, Heb. *'ăḥîshaḥar, brother of dawn*). A descendant of Benjamin through Jediael and Bilhan (1 Chron 7:10).

AHISHAR (à-hī'shär, Heb. *'ăḥîshār, my brother has sung*). An official over Solomon's household (1 Kings 4:6).

AHITHOPHEL (à-hĭth'ō-fĕl, Heb. *'ăḥîthōphel, brother of folly*). David's counselor who joined the conspiracy of Absalom. His oracular wisdom was proverbial (2 Sam 16:23), and it seems clear that he was a mainspring of the rebellion (15:12). Some suggest, in looking for motivation for his treachery, that he was the grandfather of Bathsheba, for she was the daughter of Eliam (11:3), and an Eliam, the son of Ahithophel the Gilonite, is listed as one of David's valiant men (23:34). Thus it is suggested that Ahithophel had a certain bitterness toward David, the murderer of his grandson by marriage and the corrupter of his grandaughter. Others note, however, that the time element seems insufficiently long for Ahithophel to have a married granddaughter at the time of David's great sin, and that it seems easier to believe that there was more than one man in Israel named Eliam. Furthermore, it seems unlikely that a man such as Ahithophel would conspire against the interests of his grandaughter and her son. His main motivation appears to have been ambition for personal power. His proposal to Absalom that he pursue David immediately with twelve thousand men, smiting the king while he was still weary and underprotected, indicates his wisdom and boldness. David's prayer turned his counsel into foolishness (15:31), for Absalom deferred to Hushai's advice that they take time to muster all Israel against such a mighty man of war as David. Ahithophel, seeing his counsel rejected, realized that the cause of Absalom was lost; he went to his home and hanged himself (17:1–23). BP

AHITUB (à-hī'tŭb, Heb. *'ăḥîṭûb, brother of goodness*). 1. The brother of Ichabod and son of Phinehas the son of Eli; father of Ahiah (1 Sam 14:3) and Ahimelech (22:9, 11, 20). Although he is a son and father of priests, nothing is said of his own priestly office.

2. Son of Amariah and father of Zadok the high priest (2 Sam 8:17; 1 Chron 6:7–8). He appears as grandfather of Zadok in 1 Chronicles 9:11 and Nehemiah 11:11. A descendant of Aaron through Eleazar, he is to be distinguished from Ahitub no. 1, who descended through Ithamar (1 Chron 24).

3. Son of another Amariah and father of another Zadok (1 Chron 6:11–12). Cf. the list in Ezra 7:1–5. It is possible that because of compression of names or a copyist's error this man may be the same as no. 2.

AHLAB (à'lăb, Heb. *'aḥlāv, fat or fruitful*). A town of Asher whose inhabitants the Israelites were not able to drive out (Judg 1:31). Some identify Ahlab with Gush Chaleb or Giscala, in the hills NW of the Sea of Galilee, home of John of Giscala.

AHLAI (à'lī, Heb. *'aḥlay, O would that!*). 1. The father of Zabad, one of David's soldiers (1 Chron 11:41).

2. A daughter of Sheshan who married her father's Egyptian slave Jarha. They had a son named Attai (1 Chron 1:31–35).

AHOAH (à-hō'à, Heb. *'ăḥôaḥ, brotherly*). A son of Bela (1 Chron 8:4) and the one from whom is derived the term "Ahohite" (2 Sam 23:9, 28; 1 Chron 11:12).

AHOHITE (à-hō'hīt, Heb. *'ăḥôḥî*). A patronymic given to the descendants of Ahoah: Dodo (2 Sam 23:9), Zalmon (23:28), and Ilai (1 Chron 11:29).

AHOLAH (See OHOLAH)

AHOLIAB (See OHOLIAB)

AHOLIBAH (See OHOLIBAH)

AHOLIBAMAH (See OHOLIBAMAH)

AHUMAI (à-hū'mī, Heb. *'ăḥûmay*). A descendant of Judah (1 Chron 4:2).

AHUZZAM (à-hŭz'ăm, Heb. *'ăḥuzzām, possessor*). A man of the tribe of Judah, one of four sons born to Ashur by his wife Naarah (1 Chron 4:6).

AHUZZATH (à-hŭz'ăth, Heb. *'ăḥuzzath, possession*). A "friend" of Abimelech. These men and Phicol, chief of the Philistine army, made a peace treaty with Isaac at Beersheba after they saw that the Lord had blessed him (Gen 26:23–33). The ending *-ath* is in other Philistine names, e.g., Gath, Goliath.

AHZAI (à-zī', Heb. *'aḥzay, my protector*). A priest who lived in Jerusalem (Neh 11:13).

AI (ā'ī, Heb. *'ay, ruin*). A city of central Palestine, east of Bethel. Abraham pitched his tent between Ai and Bethel when he arrived in Canaan (Gen 12:8). Ai figures most prominently in the account of the conquest of the land; it was the second Canaanite city taken by the forces under Joshua (Josh 7–8). Having conquered Jericho, the Israelites felt that a portion of the armies would be sufficient to conquer the much smaller Ai. The Israelite contingent was routed, however. It was then disclosed that Achan had sinned in taking articles from the consecrated spoil of Jericho. After Achan had confessed his sin and he and his family had been stoned to death, the Israelites made a second attack, which resulted in the total destruction of the city and the annihila-

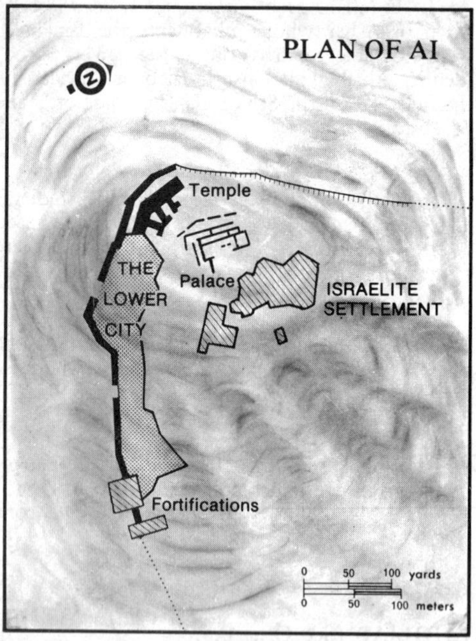

The city captured, after initial defeat, by Joshua and his men (Josh 7:2–8:29). Courtesy Carta, Jerusalem.

tion of all its twelve thousand inhabitants. The city, the site of which belonged to the tribe of Benjamin following the partition of the land, had not been rebuilt when the Book of Joshua was written (Josh 8:28). It was, however, rebuilt in later days, for men of Ai returned from Babylon with Zerubbabel (Ezra 2:28; Neh 7:32).

The work of Joseph Callaway (1964–72) at Et-Tell, generally identified with biblical Ai, has shown that no city stood here from the Early Bronze Age destruction in about 2300 B.C. till a pre-Israelite settlement was built in the Early Iron Age (c. 1200 B.C.). Thus no town existed here in the time of the conquest under Joshua during the Late Bronze Age (c. 1550 to 1200 B.C.). Either the biblical record may be somewhat misleading in its account of Ai's demise or the site is not actually that of Ai. There is no certain evidence confirming this identity.

AIAH (ā'yȧ, Heb. *'ayyâh, falcon*). 1. A Horite (Gen 36:24; 1 Chron 1:40).

2. The father of Rizpah, Saul's concubine (2 Sam 3:7; 21:8).

AIATH (ā'yăth, Heb. *'ayyāth*). Feminine form of the city Ai (Isa 10:28).

AIJA (ā-ī'jȧ, Heb. *'ayyā'*). Another form of the city Ai (Neh 11:31).

AIJALON (ā'jȧ-lŏn, Heb. *'ayyālôn, place of gazelles*). 1. A city of Dan (Josh 19:42), assigned to the Levite sons of Kohath (1 Chron 6:69). It is mentioned most notably in the memorable words of Joshua, "O sun, stand still over Gibeon, O moon, over the Valley of Aijalon" (Josh 10:12). It is identified with the modern Yalo, fourteen miles (twenty-two km.) from Jerusalem, north of the Jaffa road.

2. The burial place of the judge Elon, in Zebulun (Judg 12:12).

AIJELETH SHAHAR (ā'jĕ-lĕth shā'hȧr, Heb. *'ayyeleth hash-shahar, the hind of the morning*). The term is found in the title to Psalm 22. NIV commits itself to one traditional explanation: "To the tune 'The Doe of the Morning,' " and this, of course, remains a possible interpretation. It is somewhat more common at present to take *'ayyeleth* as related to the word *'ayaluth* (v. 19), "strength," or "help." If this is correct, the words actually entitle the psalm "Help at Daybreak" suitably, as verses 22–31 show.

AIN (ȧ'ēn, Heb. *'ayin, eye, fountain*). From the basic meaning of "eye," the word "fountain" is derived by the vivid imagery of the East, for the spring flashes in the landscape like a gleaming eye. This differs from *beer,* which is a dug well. This word is usually found in such names as En Gedi and Endor.

1. A landmark on the eastern border of the Promised Land; west of Riblah (Num 34:11). It is usually thought to be the modern Ain el ' Azy, the main source of the Orontes River.

2. A southern city of Judah (Josh 15:32), later of Simeon (19:7), and still later assigned to the priests (21:16).

AIR. In the OT and the Gospels this word is usually found in expressions speaking of the birds or fowl of the air (Job 41:16 is the only exception) and representing words normally translated "heaven." Elsewhere in the NT it stands for *aēr,* the atmosphere. An ineffective Christian is pictured as a boxer "beating the air" (1 Cor 9:26). "Speaking into the air" describes unintelligible

The Valley of Aijalon with the hills of Shephelah in background. Courtesy Seffie Ben-Joseph.

utterance (14:9). Satan is called "the prince of the power of the air" (Eph 2:2)—i.e., the ruler of the demonic beings that fill the air. The rapture of the church will culminate in her meeting the Lord and Savior, Jesus Christ, "in the air" (1 Thess 4:17).

AJAH (See AIAH)

AJALON (See AIJALON)

AKAN (ā'kăn, Heb. *'ăqān, twisted*). A descendant or branch of the Horites of Mount Seir (Gen 36:27).

AKELDAMA (ȧ-kĕl'dȧ-mȧ, ASV, NIV, RSV; Aceldama, ȧ-sĕl'dȧ-mȧ, KJV; Hakeldama, hȧ-kĕl'dȧ-mȧ, JB, NASB; Gr. *Akeldama*). The field purchased with the money Judas received for betraying Christ (Acts 1:18–19). Matthew 27:3–10, with a fuller account of the purchase, says the priests bought it "as a burial place for foreigners." Acts 1:18–19 is a parenthesis, an explanation by Luke, not part of Peter's speech. These verses say that "with the reward he got for his wickedness, Judas bought a field." The priests apparently bought it in Judas' name, the money having been his. The field was called "the place of blood" in Aramaic. Some think the Aramaic word means "field of sleep," or "cemetery," but the meaning "field of blood" is preferable, and it is appropriate because of the manner of Judas' death, the gruesome details being given in Acts 1:18.

Akeldama, or the Field of Blood, on the southern slope of the Hinnom Valley in Jerusalem. Courtesy Zev Radovan.

AKHENATON (ȧ'kĕn-ȧ't'n, *he who is beneficial to Aton*). The name chosen by Amenhotep IV (1377–1360 B.C.), ruler in the Eighteenth Dynasty of Egypt, when he changed the religion of his country, demanding that all his subjects worship only the sun god under the name Aton. Politically his reign was disastrous. Internal disorders prevailed, and Egypt's Asian possessions began to slip away. His external troubles are illustrated by clay tablets found at Tell el-Amarna, the site of Akhetaton, the capital he established. Hundreds of letters from vassal governors in Syria and Palestine tell of invasions and intrigue and make appeals for help. Many of these tablets refer to invaders called the Habiru. Some feel that this name designates the Hebrews; others say that it speaks of a non-Semitic people. Akhenaton is credited by many as being the first monotheist and, indeed, the inspiration for the monotheism of Moses. However, Akhenaton clearly worshiped the sun itself and not the Creator of the sun.

Drawing of a colossal statue of Akhenaton (Amenhotep IV), a pharaoh in the fourteenth century B.C. He wears the ceremonial beard on which is drawn the *ankh* sign. He holds a flail in his right hand and a crook in his left, and he wears a tightly pleated skirt. Courtesy Carta, Jerusalem.

AKIM (ā'kĭm, Gr. *Achim,* from Heb., meaning *Jehovah will establish*). A descendant of Zerubbabel (Matt 1:14). One of the ancestors of Christ, after the Babylonian captivity.

AKKAD (ăk'ăd, Heb. *'akkadh,* Gen 10:10). One of the cities or districts of Nimrod's kingdom,

Bronze head of an Akkadian ruler thought to represent Niram-Sin of Agade. From Nineveh (c. 2500 B.C.). Courtesy Bildarchiv Foto, Marburg.

with Babel, Erech, and Calneh. Babel and Erech are located on or near the lower Euphrates, Erech being not far from what was then the head of the Persian Gulf. Calneh, formerly identified with Nippur between Babel and Erech, is now generally thought to be, not the name of a city, but a word meaning "all of them," referring to Babel, the capital, and to Akkad and Erech, the chief cities of the northern and southern districts of Babylonia respectively. The location of Akkad is uncertain, though it is thought to be identified with Agade, the chief city of a district of the same name in northern Babylonia, which Sargon I, the Semitic conqueror of the Sumerian Akkadians, made his capital in c. 2350 B.C. The kingdom called Nimrod's had evidently fallen into disorder, and Sargon united the warring city-states under his firm rule. With the help of invaders, first from the NE and then from the NW, Akkadian civilization flourished sporadically and precariously until Semitic Amorites from the west founded a dynasty at Babylon about 1894. The most illustrious ruler of this dynasty was Hammurabi (1792–1750). Sumerian or Akkadian civilization now finally came to an end. As Nimrod cannot be certainly identified with any person otherwise known, so Akkad remains a shadowy city or region (Gen. 10:10).

AKKUB (ăk'ŭb, Heb. *'aqqûv, pursuer*). 1. Son of Elioenai (1 Chron 3:24).

2. A Levite who founded a family of temple porters (1 Chron 9:17).

3. The head of a family of temple servants (KJV Nethinim) (Ezra 2:45).

4. A Levite who helped expound the Law (Neh 8:7).

Sandstone stele, 6½ feet (2 m.), c. 2250 B.C., of Naram-Sin of Agade, from Susa (Shushan), depicting the king standing before a stylized mountain as the victor over the Lullu(bians). Courtesy Réunion des Musées Nationaux.

AKRABBIM (ăk-răb'ĭm, Heb. *'aqrabbîm, scorpions*). A word always found with *ma'ăleh* (mā'a-la), meaning "the going up to," "ascent of," or "pass." So "Scorpion Pass" (NIV), rising between the SW corner of the Dead Sea and Zin, was the southern boundary between Judah and Edom (Num 34:4; Josh 15:3) and the boundary of the Amorites (Judg 1:36). It was the scene of Judas Maccabeus' victory over the Edomites. It is now identified as the pass Es-Sufah.

ALABASTER (See MINERALS)

ALAMETH (See ALEMETH)

ALAMMELECH (See ALLAMMELECH)

ALAMOTH (ăl'à-mŏth, Heb. *'ălāmôth, maidens, virgins*). A musical term of uncertain meaning (1 Chron 15:20; Ps 46:1). It may indicate a women's choir, musical instruments set in a high pitch, or instruments plays by virgins.

ALCIMUS (ăl'sĭ-mŭs, Heb. *'elyāqûm, God will rise*; Gr. *Alkimos, valiant*). A wicked high priest who was opposed by the Maccabees (1 Macc 7:9).

ALEMETH (ăl'ĕ-mĕth, Heb. *'ālāmeth, concealment*). 1. A son of Beker and grandson of Benjamin (1 Chron 7:8).

2. Son of Jehoaddah (1 Chron 8:36), Jarah (9:42, JB, KJV, MLB, NASB, NEB, RSV; Jadah NIV).

ALEMETH, ALMON (ăl'ĕ-mĕth, ăl'mŏn, *hidden*). A priests' city (Josh 21:18; 1 Chron 6:60). It is the modern Almit.

ALEPH (ă'lĕf, *ox*). The first letter of the Hebrew alphabet. Although a consonant, it is the forerunner of the Greek *alpha* and the English *a*.

ALEXANDER (ăl'ĕg-zăn'dêr, Gr. *Alexandros, man-defending*). A common Greek name belonging to five Jews to whom reference is made in the NT:

1. Alexander, brother of Rufus and son of Simon of Cyrene, the man who carried the cross of Jesus (Mark 15:21).

2. A kinsman of the Jewish high priest Annas (Acts 4:6).

3. A Jew of Ephesus who was pushed forward to speak to a noisy crowd that had been listening to Paul (Acts 19:33).

4. A false teacher whom Paul handed over to Satan for punishment (1 Tim 1:20).

5. A metalworker who did Paul harm (2 Tim 4:14). It is possible that nos. 3 and 5 are identical, or nos. 4 and 5; our knowledge is too sketchy to be sure.

ALEXANDER THE GREAT (ăl'ĕg-zăn'dêr, Gr. *Alexandros, man-defending*). Son of Philip, king of Macedon, and Olympias, an Epirote princess; born 356 B.C. Although not named in the Bible, he is described prophetically in Daniel, the "goat" from the west with a notable horn between his eyes. He came against the ram with two horns, who was standing before the river, defeated the ram, and became very great until the great horn was broken and four notable ones came up from it (Dan 8:5–8). The prophecy identifies the ram as the kings of Media and Persia, the goat as the king of Greece, the great horn being the first king. When he fell, four kings arose in his place (8:18–22). The historical fulfillment is striking: Alexander led the Greek armies across the Hellespont into Asia Minor in 334 B.C. and defeated the Persian forces at the river Granicus. Moving with amazing rapidity ("without touching the ground," 8:5), he again met and defeated the Persians at Issus. Turning south, he moved down the Syrian coast, advancing to Egypt, which fell to him without a blow. Turning again to the east, he met the armies of Darius for the last time, defeating them in the battle of Arbela, east of the Tigris River. Rapidly he occupied Babylon, then Susa and Persepolis, the capitals of Persia. The next years were spent in consolidating the new empire. Alexander took Persians into his army, encouraged his soldiers to marry Asians, and began to Hellenize Asia through the establishment of Greek cities in the Eastern Empire. He marched his armies eastward as far as India, where they won a great battle at the Hydaspes River. The army, however, refused to advance farther, and Alexander was forced to return to Persepolis. While still making plans for further conquests, he contracted a fever. Weakened by the strenuous campaign and his increasing dissipation, he was unable to throw off the fever and died in Babylon in 323 at the age of thirty-three. His empire was then divided among four of his generals. While Alexander was outstanding as a conqueror, his notable contributions to civilization came via his Hellenizing efforts. The fact that Greek became the language of literature and commerce throughout the "inhabited world," for example, was of inestimable importance to the spread of the gospel. BP

Drawing of Alexander the Great, from a mosaic found at Pompeii (c. 300 B.C.). Courtesy Carta, Jerusalem.

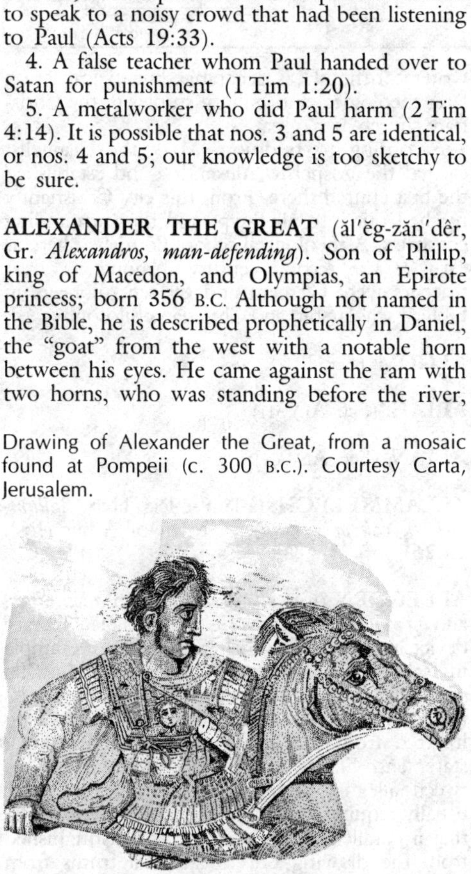

ALEXANDRA (ăl-ĕg-zăn'drȧ, Gr. *Alexandra*). Wife of Aristobulus, king of the Jews (105–104 B.C.). Upon his death, she made her brother-in-law, Jannaeus Alexander, king and married him. After he died, Alexandra ruled from 78–69. John Hyrcanus II and Aristobulus II were her sons.

ALEXANDRIA (ăl'ĕg-zăn'drĭ-ȧ, Gr. *Alexandreia*). Founded by Alexander the Great, 332 B.C.; successively the Ptolemaic, Roman, and Christian capital of Lower Egypt. Its harbors, formed by the island Pharos and the headland Lochias, were suitable for both commerce and war. It was the chief grain port for Rome. Its merchant ships, the largest and finest of the day, usually sailed directly to Puteoli, but at times because of the severity of the weather sailed under the coast of Asia Minor, as did the vessel that carried Paul (Acts 27:6). Alexandria was also an important cultural center, boasting an excellent university. Patterned after the great school at Athens, it soon outstripped its model. It was especially noted for the study of mathematics, astronomy, medicine, and poetry. Literature and art also flourished. The library of

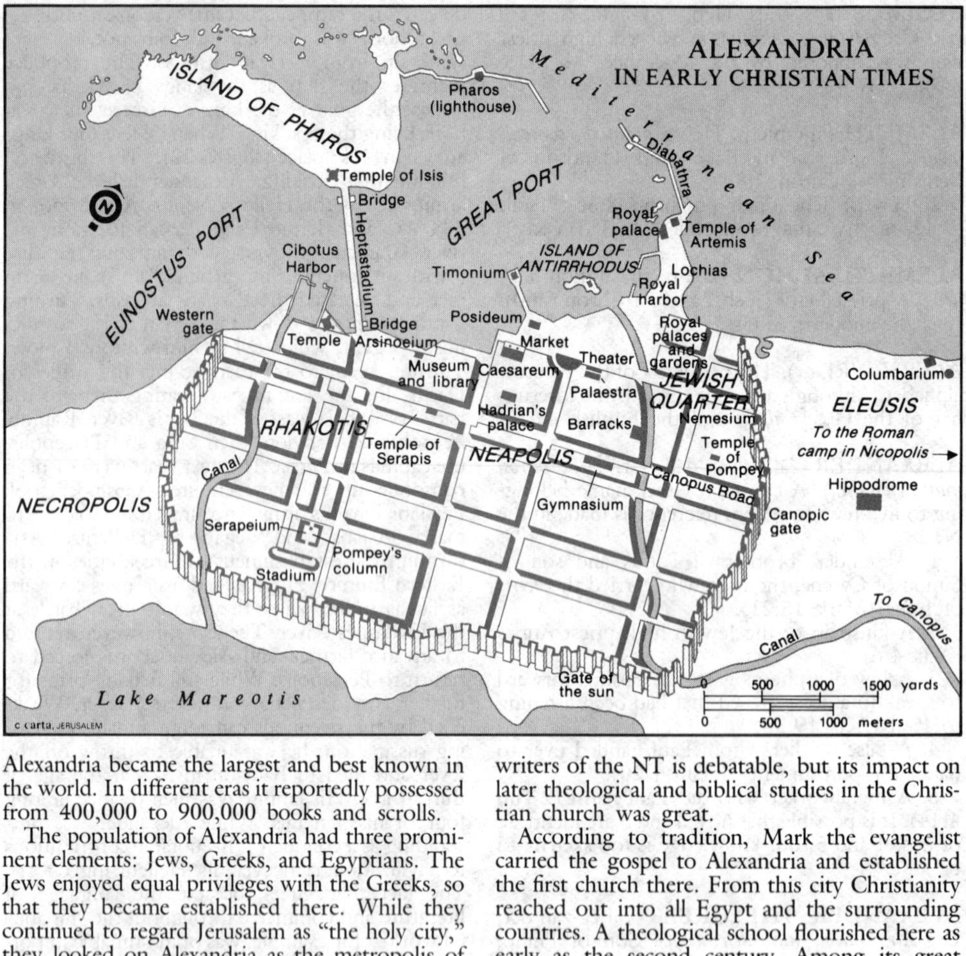

Alexandria became the largest and best known in the world. In different eras it reportedly possessed from 400,000 to 900,000 books and scrolls.

The population of Alexandria had three prominent elements: Jews, Greeks, and Egyptians. The Jews enjoyed equal privileges with the Greeks, so that they became established there. While they continued to regard Jerusalem as "the holy city," they looked on Alexandria as the metropolis of the Jews throughout the world. Here the translation of the OT into Greek, known as the Septuagint, was made in the third century before Christ. It became the popular Bible of the Jews of the Dispersion, generally used by the writers of the NT. At Alexandria the OT revelation was brought into contact with Greek philosophy. The consequent synthesis became of great importance in subsequent religious thought. The influence of Alexandrian philosophy on the thought of the writers of the NT is debatable, but its impact on later theological and biblical studies in the Christian church was great.

According to tradition, Mark the evangelist carried the gospel to Alexandria and established the first church there. From this city Christianity reached out into all Egypt and the surrounding countries. A theological school flourished here as early as the second century. Among its great teachers were Clement and Origen, pioneers in biblical scholarship and Christian philosophy. BP

The modern port at Alexandria. Courtesy B. Brandl.

ALGUM (See PLANTS)

ALIAH (See ALVAH)

ALIAN (See ALVAN)

ALLAMMELECH (ȧ-lăm′-ĕ-lĕk, Heb. *'allammelekh, oak of a king*). A town of Asher (Josh 19:26).

ALLEGORY (Gr. *allēgoreuein,* from *allos, other,* and *agoreuein, to speak in the assembly*). The literary device is used extensively in Scripture, for example in Isaiah 5:1–7 and in the Song of Songs. To speak allegorically is to set forth one thing in the image of another, the principal subject being inferred from the figure rather than by direct statement. Clarity of inference differentiates between allegory and parable, because the latter usually requires an interpretation for the teaching that it parallels. Allegorizing (to be distinguished from the drawing out of spiritual truths from factual presentations) has had broad application in Bible teaching. Alexandrian Jews spiritualized Scripture. The church fathers followed, reaching an extreme in the school of Origen in which spiritualization attained great heights in mystical and moral meanings. In the allegory in Galatians 4:24 Isaac, the child of promise, typifies the Christian who is justified in Christ and is free to love and serve his Father; while Ishmael, the child of contrivance, typifies the legalist who is under the law and is bound to serve it and to seek justification in obedience to it. CEC

ALLELUIA (See HALLELUJAH)

ALLIANCES (See COVENANT)

ALLON (ăl'ŏn, Heb. *'allôn, oak*). 1. A prince of Simeon (1 Chron 4:37).

2. Otherwise "Elon" (Heb. *'ēlôn*), a town, or "*the large tree* in Zaanannim" (NIV), a southern boundary point in Naphtali (Josh 19:33; cf. Judg 4:11).

3. *Allon Bachuth,* "the oak of weeping," a tree marking the burial place of Deborah, the nurse of Rebekah (Gen 35:8).

ALMIGHTY (Heb. *shadday,* meaning uncertain). Gr. *pantokratōr, all powerful.* Used with *el, Kurios, Theos,* for identification (Gen 17:1), invocation (28:3), description (Ezek 10:5), praise (Rev 4:8). See also EL SHADDAI.

ALMODAD (ăl-mō'dăd, Heb. *'almôdhādh, the beloved*). First-mentioned of Joktan's thirteen sons (Gen 10:26; 1 Chron 1:20). This Arabian name is preserved in El-Mudad, famous in Arabian history as reputed father of Ishmael's Arab wife and as chief of Jurham, a Joktanite tribe.

ALMON (See ALEMETH, ALMON)

ALMON DIBLATHAIM (ăl'mŏn dĭb-là-thā'ĭm, Heb. *'almōn divlāthayim, Almon of two cakes of figs*). One of the last stops of the Israelites on their journey from Egypt to the Jordan. Lying between Dibon-Gad and the mountains of Abarim (Num 33:46–47), it is probably the same as Beth Diblathaim of Moab (Jer 48:22), which King Mesha boasts in the famous Moabite stone as "built" by him.

ALMOND TREE (See PLANTS)

ALMS (ähms). Kind deeds arising out of compassion, mercy, and pity for the unfortunate. The word itself is not found in the NIV, though the practice is of Mosaic legislation and NT injunction. Greek *eleēmosynē,* also in LXX for Hebrew *tsedhāqâh,* "righteousness," and *hesedh,* "kindness." Matthew 6:1 has *dikaiosynē,* "alms" (KJV), "acts of righteousness" (NIV). The verb *poiein,* "to do, perform," is often used with the noun to convey the meaning of helping the poor and needy (cf. Matt 6:2–3; Acts 9:36; 10:2; 24:17). In the OT the law prescribed gleanings from the harvest, the vineyards, and the grain in the corners of the field for the poor (Lev 19:9–10). Deuteronomy 24:10–22 stipulated further gleanings from the orchards and olive groves. It also protected the rights of the poor and unfortunate concerning wages, working conditions, and pledges, preventing the poor from being deprived of necessary garments or other needs. Almsgiving is set forth in Deuteronomy 15:11: "There will always be poor people in the land. Therefore I command you to be openhanded toward your brothers and toward the poor and needy in your land."

In later Judaism the righteousness of almsgiving became somewhat legalistic and professional. The lame man at the Gate Beautiful exemplified professional begging in that daily he "asked . . . for money" (Acts 3:2–3 NIV; "ask alms" KJV, RSV; "beg alms" MLB, NASB). Perversion in receiving alms is seen in a beggar's cry, couching the idea "bless yourself by giving to me." Perversion in giving alms is seen in benefactors who "announce it with trumpets," probably to be taken figuratively, and who want "to be seen" by people, involving the word from which we derive "theater" (Matt 6:1–2). Almsgiving was of two kinds: "alms of the dish" (food and money received daily for distribution) and "alms of the chest" (coins received on the Sabbath for widows, orphans, strangers, and the poor). The practice of the NT church was foreshadowed in Jesus' admonitions: "give to the poor" (Luke 11:41; cf. 1 Cor 16:2) and "sell your possessions and give to the poor" (Luke 12:33; cf. 2 Cor 8:3). Alms in the NT church were seen in the churches of Macedonia, who in "their extreme poverty . . . beyond their ability . . . [shared] in this service to the saints" (2 Cor 8:1–4). True purpose and spirit were shown: "At the present time your plenty will supply what they need, so that in turn their plenty will supply what you need" (8:14). The full measure of ministry, blessings, and ability to give by God's grace is delineated in 2 Corinthians 8 and 9, to be done liberally, prayerfully, and cheerfully. See also James 2:15–16 and 1 John 3:17. A primary function of deacons was to distribute alms (Acts 6).

Bibliography: C. H. Dodd, *The Bible and the Greeks,* 1936, pp. 59–62; M. Weber, *Ancient Judaism,* ET 1952, pp. 255–67; R. Bultmann, TDNT, 1964, 2:485–87. CEC

ALMUG (See PLANTS)

ALOE (See PLANTS)

ALOTH (ā'lŏth, Heb. *'ālôth*). A town or district mentioned with Asher and of which Baanah was Solomon's commissary (1 Kings 4:16). ASV has Bealoth.

ALPHA (ăl'fà). First letter of the Greek alphabet (A). The word "alphabet," indicating a list of elementary sounds in any language, comes from the first two Greek letters, alpha and beta. In contrast is omega, the last letter of the Greek alphabet. Combined with alpha it signifies completeness, as "from A to Z" in modern usage. So God is the Alpha and the Omega, the First and the Last, the Beginning and the End (Rev 1:8), as is also Christ (21:6; 22:13). Compare Isaiah 41:4; 44:6.

ALPHABET (See WRITING)

ALPHAEUS (ăl-fē'ŭs, Gr. *Alphaios*). 1. Father of Levi (Mark 2:14).

2. Father of James the apostle (Matt 10:3; Mark 3:18; Luke 6:15; Acts 1:13) and named with him to distinguish him from James the brother of John.

3. Possibly Clopas (KJV Cleophas), husband of the Mary at the cross (John 19:25; cf. Mark 15:40), as *Cleophas* (Gr. *Klopas*) and *Alphaeus* are of Semitic derivation. He is unlikely to be Cleopas of the Emmaus road (Luke 24:18); *Cleopas* was a common Greek name.

ALTAR (Heb. *mizbēah, place of slaughter,* Gr. *bomos,* in Acts only, and *thysiastērion*). In OT times altars were many and varied, their importance seen in the fact that the Hebrew and Greek words appear some 360 times.

The first Hebrew altar we read about (Gen 8:20) was erected by Noah after leaving the ark. Subsequent altars were built by Abraham (12:7–8; 13:4, 18; 22:9), Isaac (26:25), Jacob (35:1–7), Moses (Exod 17:15), and Joshua (Josh 8:30–31). Some of these must have been very simple in structure, as the context of Genesis 22:9 seems to indicate. Most of the altars were built for sacrificial purposes, but some seem to have been largely memorial in character (Exod 17:15–16; Josh 22:26–27). Sometimes God stated just how the altar was to be built and of what materials (e.g., Exod 20:24–26).

With the erection of the tabernacle, altars were constructed by the Hebrews for two chief purposes: the offering of sacrifices and the burning of incense. Moses was commanded to make the altar of burnt offering for the tabernacle exactly as God had commanded him (Exod 25:9). It was to be made of acacia (shittim) wood, which was to be overlaid with brass or, as is more probable, bronze. The shape was a square of five cubits, three cubits high. At each corner of the altar there was to be a projection or "horn." This feature is found outside Israel, as in the tenth-century B.C. altar discovered at Megiddo. The purpose of the horns is not known, and the popular belief that clinging to the horns gave security from justice is disproved by 1 Kings 1:50–53; 2:28–34. A bronze grating was placed in the center of the altar that projected through the opening on two sides. Four rings were fastened to it in which two poles of the same material as the altar were to be placed to carry the altar. Steps leading up to the altar were forbidden (Exod 20:26). For seven days atonement was to be made for the altar—apparently to sanctify it for the uses to which it was to be devoted (29:37); it was to be cleansed on the Day of Atonement after the presentation

Remains of the Canaanite temple at Megiddo, with a large oval altar and a small square one (c. 2500–1850 B.C.). Large temple compounds served those who worshiped many gods. Courtesy Israel Department of Antiquities and Museums.

Model of the altar in the main hall of the Canaanite fosse temple at Lachish, thirteenth century B.C. (about the time of Deborah and Barak, Judg 5). This temple was erected in the fosse that has been dug around the mound as a part of the city's outer defense. On and around the altar were placed offering vessels. Courtesy Israel Museum, Jerusalem. Photo Nahum Slapak.

of sin offerings for the high priest and the nation (Lev 16:19–20).

Certain bronze utensils were made in connection with the altar. There were pans to hold the ashes, shovels for removing the ashes, basins to receive the blood and to convey it to the varied places for sprinkling, three-pronged flesh hooks with which to remove the flesh, and censers for carrying coals from the altar (Exod 27:3). Once the fire on this altar was kindled, it was required that it burn continually (Lev 6:13).

The altar of burnt offering was also in Solomon's temple, the second temple, and in the temple built by Herod. Its form was altered to fit into the varying sizes of these structures. Solomon made his altar of bronze twenty cubits square and twenty cubits high (2 Chron 4:1). After its construction it had a very interesting history. Because idols had polluted it, King Asa rededicated it (15:8). Later on Uriah removed it from its regular place, in order it seems to make room for another altar that he had patterned after the one King Ahaz had seen in Damascus (2 Kings 16:11–14). The terrible pollution of spiritual things in the reign of Ahaz led Hezekiah to cleanse the altar (2 Chron 29:12–18). Finally it was repaired and restored to its place by Manasseh (33:16).

In Zerubbabel's temple the altar was built first (Ezra 3:2), on the exact spot where it previously stood (Jos. *Antiq.,* 11.4.1). After it had been desecrated by Antiochus Epiphanes, it was rebuilt by Judas Maccabeus, apparently with unhewn stone (1 Macc 4:47).

Moses was also commanded by God to make "an altar . . . for burning incense" (Exod 30:1), sometimes called "the gold altar" (Exod 39:38; Num 4:11). It was to be a cubit square and two cubits high (Exod 30:2) with horns at each corner. It was made of acacia (shittim) wood overlaid with pure gold. Around the top of this structure a crown of gold was placed, beneath which were fixed two golden rings, one on each side. Staves of the same construction as the altar were placed through these rings to carry it (30:1–5).

This altar was to be located before the veil that separated the Holy Place from the Most Holy Place, midway between the walls (Exod 30:6; 40:5). Because of its special location, it was referred to as "the altar before the LORD" (Lev 16:12). Elsewhere in the Bible it is referred to as "the altar that belonged to the inner sanctuary" (1 Kings 6:22; cf. Heb 9:3–4) and "the golden altar before the throne" (Rev 8:3). Incense was burned on this altar twice each day (Exod 30:7–8), and the blood of the atonement was sprinkled on it (30:10). The burning of incense on this altar symbolized the offering up of the believers' prayers (Rev 8:3). It was while Zechariah was officiating at this altar that the angel appeared to him (Luke 1:10).

Three-footed stone altar with round top. Each of the altar's legs is shaped in the form of a lion's foot and is set upon a tripod base. An inscription of Sargon II (721–705 B.C.) is incised around the edge of the top. Perhaps from Khorsabad. Courtesy Istanbul Museum. Photo: B. Brandl.

There are no altars recognized in the NT church. While Hebrews 13:10 is sometimes used to prove the contrary, a careful study of this passage in its context is fatal to such an idea. The concept in this passage is that Jesus Christ is the true altar of each believer. Paul mentions in Acts 17:23 the inscription on an altar, "TO AN UNKNOWN GOD," which he saw in Athens. Such inscriptions were common in pagan cultures and are referred to by a number of early writers (see Augustine, *The City of God,* 3:12).

There is good reason to believe that the need for altars was revealed to man very early as basic in approaching God. The altar played a leading role in all OT worship of the true God, as well as a prominent part in most pagan religions. A careful study of the use of this article of furniture in Israel's worship furnishes us with many spiritual lessons today. It was the place of sacrifice where God was propitiated and where man was pardoned and sanctified. It looked to the great sacrifice that the Son of God was about to make on the cross. The altar of sacrifice, the first thing visible as one approached the tabernacle, spoke loudly to man that without the shedding of blood there would be no access to God and no forgiveness of sin (Heb 9:9, 22). Most scholars say that the brass or bronze speaks of divine judgment.

Bibliography: G. B. Gray, *Sacrifice in the Old Testament,* 1925; W. F. Albright, *Archeology and the Religion of Israel,* 2d ed., 1946; R. de Vaux, *Ancient Israel, Its Life and Institutions,* 1961, pp. 406–14; F. F. Bruce, IDB (Supp. Vol.), 1976, pp. 19ff. HZC

ALTASCHITH (ăl-tăs'chĭth, Heb. *'al tashēth, destroy not*). A title notation in Psalms 57, 58, 59, 75, rightly translated in NIV as "Do not destroy." It may perhaps indicate the melody to be used (cf. Isa 65:8, where it is possibly a snatch from a vintage song). But David's word about Saul, "Don't destroy him" (1 Sam 26:9), and the words of Moses' prayer (Deut 9:26) both imply a spirit of trust in the Lord suited to the content of these psalms. The purpose of the title may, therefore, be to indicate the type of praise that follows. See also AIJELETH SHAHAR.

ALUSH (ā'lŭsh, Heb. *'ālŭsh*). A desert campsite of the Israelites between Dophkah and Rephidim (Num 33:13–14).

ALVAH (ăl'vȧ, Heb. *'alwâh*). A chief of Edom (Gen 36:40).

ALVAN, ALIAN (ăl'văn, Heb. *'alwān,* tall). A son of Shobal the Horite (Gen 36:23; 1 Chron 1:40).

AMAD (ā'măd, Heb. *'am' ādh*). A town of the tribe of Asher (Josh 19:26).

AMAL (ā'măl, Heb. *'āmāl*). An Asherite (1 Chron 7:35).

AMALEK (ăm'ȧ-lĕk, Heb. *'ămālēq*). Son of Eliphaz (eldest son of Esau) by his concubine Timna (Gen 36:12; 1 Chron 1:36). A "chief" of Edom (Gen 36:16).

AMALEKITES (ă-măl'ĕk-īts, ăm'ȧ-lĕk-īts Heb. *'ămālēqî*). An ancient and nomadic marauding people dwelling mainly in the Negev from the times of Abraham to Hezekiah, c. 2000–700 B.C.

The first mention of them is among those conquered by Kedorlaomer in the days of Abraham (Gen 14:7). Moses felt their fury in the unprovoked attack on the Israelites at Rephidim, for which God decreed continual war and ultimate obliteration (Exod 17:8ff.). Joshua and the spies encountered them in Canaan, and they and the Canaanites repulsed the Israelites at Hormah (Num 14:45). During the period of the judges they sided with the Ammonites and Moabites against the Israelites in the days of Ehud (Judg 3:13) and with the Midianites and other eastern peoples against Gideon (6:3, 33). Abdon was buried "in the hill country of the Amalekites" (12:15). Saul was commissioned to destroy them utterly but failed to do so and spared Agag (1 Sam 15:8ff.). An Amalekite later killed Saul (2 Sam 1:8ff.). David invaded the land of the Amalekites and other ancient inhabitants from Shur to Egypt (1 Sam 27:8) and struck them severely in recovering his wives and property stolen during the raid on Ziklag (30:18). They are numbered among nations subdued by him (2 Sam 8:12; 1 Chron 18:11). The Simeonites during the time of Hezekiah finally exterminated them (1 Chron 4:43).

Distribution of the Amalekites was primarily in the Negev SW of the Dead Sea but also in the Sinai Peninsula from Rephidim (Exod 17:8) to the border of Egypt (1 Sam 27:8); northward at Jezreel (Judg 6:33), Pirathon (12:15), and at or near Jericho (3:13); and eastward to Mount Seir (1 Chron 4:42). See also Numbers 13:29.

The origin of the Amalekites is not known for sure. If Amalek, the grandson of Esau (Gen 36:12), is the nation's father, the note in Genesis 14:7 must be seen as proleptic. Accordingly, "first among the nations" in Numbers 24:20 can be first in time, first in preeminence, or first to molest liberated Israel (at Rephidim). Arab traditions, late and conflicting, have the Amalekites stem from Ham.

In character the Amalekites were warlike, usually confederate with the Canaanites (Num 14:45) or Moabites (Judg 3:13), but sometimes alone, as at Rephidim (Exod 17:8) and Ziklag (1 Sam 10:1). They "cut off all who were lagging behind; they had no fear of God" (Deut 25:18), and they destroyed crops (Judg 6:4).

At Rephidim the Lord said, "I will completely blot out the memory of Amalek from under heaven" (Exod 17:14), and through Balaam, "Amalek . . . will come to ruin at last" (Num 24:20). Saul failed to destroy the Amalekites, but David reduced them to inactivity, and the Simeonites at Mount Seir "killed the remaining Amalekites who had escaped" (1 Chron 4:43). Archaeology has produced no evidence of them thus far.

AMAM (ā'măm, Heb. *'ămām*). An unidentified southern town belonging to Judah (Josh 15:26).

AMANA, AMANAH (ȧ-mā'nȧ, Heb. *'ămānâh, constant* [?]). A mountain near Lebanon (Song of Songs 4:8), from which flow the Amana springs. (See ABANA)

AMARANTHINE (ăm-ȧ-răn'thĭn, *fades not away*). An inheritance (1 Peter 1:4), glory (5:4). From *amaranth,* a flower that when picked does not wither; the unfading flower of the poets.

AMARIAH (ăm'ȧ-rī'ăh). 1. A Levite and ancestor of Ezra (1 Chron 6:7, 11, 52; Ezra 7:3).

2. A Levite serving in the house of the Lord under David (1 Chron 23:19; 24:23).

3. Chief priest under Jehoshaphat (2 Chron 19:11).

4. A Levite under Hezekiah (2 Chron 31:15).

5. A man who was guilty of marrying a foreign woman (Ezra 10:42).

6. A covenant signer (Neh 10:3).

7. A Levite under Zerubbabel (Neh 12:2).

8. Son of Hezekiah and great-grandfather of Zephaniah (Zeph 1:1). See also Nehemiah 11:4; 12:13.

AMARNA, TELL EL (tĕll ĕl ȧ-mȧr'nȧ, *the hill amarna*). A name used to describe a mound of ruins in Egypt, halfway between Memphis and Luxor. It is the modern name for the ancient capital of Amenhotep IV (c. 1387–1366 B.C.). In A.D. 1887, a peasant woman, seeking the dust from ancient buildings with which to fertilize her garden, dug in the ruins of Tell El Amarna. She found some clay tablets, which she pulverized and took to her home. Finally an American missionary stationed at Luxor, Chauncey Murch, heard of this and notified some cuneiform scholars. After

Plan of Tell el-Amarna, showing the main excavations. Courtesy Carta, Jerusalem.

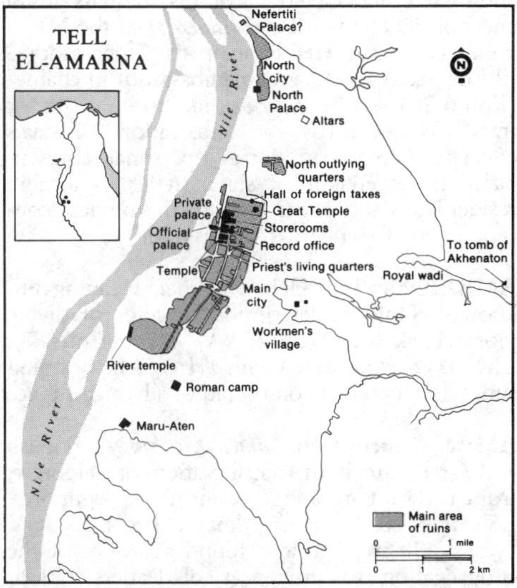

Part of the ruins at Tell el-Amarna, showing the building in which the famous Amarna Letters were found. Courtesy B. Brandl.

the site producing these tablets had been identified, it was excavated by Sir Flinders Petrie.

The excavation yielded 320 clay tablets of varying sizes with cuneiform writing on both sides. There are now 82 in the British Museum, 160 in Berlin, 60 at Gizeh Museum, and the rest in private hands. They contain the private correspondence between the ruling Egyptian pharaohs at the time and the political leaders in Palestine. It is believed they reflect the prevailing conditions that existed during the time Joshua carried on his campaigns in Palestine. Aside from confirming certain biblical facts, they reveal the plan of Egyptian houses, throwing light on the early activities of Joseph in Egypt. These tablets have also provided valuable aid to scholars in establishing the Egyptian vowel system.

AMASA (ă-mā'sȧ, Heb. *'ămāsā'*). 1. Captain of the rebel forces under Absalom. According to 2 Samuel 17:25, his father was Ithra the Israelite, whereas he is called Jether the Ishmaelite in 1 Chronicles 2:17. In either case Abigail, sister of Zeruiah and David, was his mother, making him nephew to David and cousin to Absalom. Following the defeat of the rebels under Amasa and the death of Absalom by Joab in the wood of Ephraim (2 Sam 18:6ff.), David made Amasa captain of the army in place of Joab (19:13). When Sheba and the men of Israel rebelled, David set three days for Amasa to assemble the men of Judah (20:4). Amasa delayed beyond the set time, so David sent Abishai, brother of Joab, and a body of armed men after Sheba. Amasa joined forces with Abishai at "the great rock in Gibeon," where Joab, in feigned greeting, "took Amasa by the beard with his right hand to kiss him" and ran him through with his sword (20:8–10).

2. A prince of Ephraim, son of Hadlai, among those who sided with the prophet Oded in opposition to the intentions of Pekah of Israel to hold as slaves the Jews taken in an attack on Ahaz of Judah (1 Chron 28:12–13).

AMASAI (ȧ-măs'ā-ī). 1. Chief of the captains and spokesman for some men of Benjamin and Judah who joined David at his stronghold at Ziklag. The Spirit came on Amasai, whereupon

Amasai assured David of their loyalty to him (1 Chron 12:18).

2. A trumpeter among the priests in the procession bringing the ark to Jerusalem during the reign of David (1 Chron 15:24).

3. Father of Mahath, one of several Levites who sanctified themselves for the repairing of the temple during the time of Hezekiah (2 Chron 29:12). Possibly identified with "Mahath, the son of Amasai, the son of Elkanah" in 1 Chronicles 6:35–36, which would make him a Levite in the line of Kohath and progenitor of Samuel. See also 1 Chronicles 6:25.

AMASHSAI (ȧ-măsh′sā-ī). A priest of the house of God at Jerusalem under Nehemiah (Neh 11:13).

AMASIAH (ăm′ȧ-sī′ȧ, Heb. *'ămasyăh, Yahweh bears*). Son of Zicri who offered himself to the Lord as a captain under Jehoshaphat (2 Chron 17:16).

AMAZIAH (ăm-ȧ-zī′ȧ, Heb. *'ămatsyâh, whom Jehovah strenghtens*). 1. The ninth king of Judah (including Athaliah), of the lineage of David through Rehoboam (1 Chron 3:12), succeeding his father Joash who had been murdered by conspirators (2 Kings 12:21). Seemingly he was co-regent with his father, who was sick (2 Chron 24:23–25), for we read concerning Joash that the departing Syrians "left Joash severely wounded," and the conspirators subsequently "killed him in his bed." Jehoash of Israel came to the throne in the thirty-seventh year of Joash of Judah (2 Kings 13:10). Amaziah began to rule in the second year of Jehoash of Israel, which would be the thirty-ninth year of Joash of Judah (14:1). Since Joash ruled for forty years (2 Chron 24:1), there must have been a co-regency for at least a year.

The account of Amaziah is found chiefly in 2 Kings 14, with a parallel and supplementary account in 2 Chronicles 25. Amaziah came to the throne when twenty-five years old and ruled for twenty-nine years, doing right as did his father "but not wholeheartedly," for the high places were not taken away and the people continued to offer sacrifices and burn incense. His first act was to execute his father's murderers, though he spared their children, as Moses had ruled in Deuteronomy 24:16. He then assembled an army of 300,000 men of Judah, appointed captains over thousands and hundreds (2 Chron 25:5–6), and hired an additional 100,000 men of Israel for one hundred talents of silver. Warned by a man of God against using the Israelite mercenaries, Amaziah protested the loss of his one hundred talents but was assured, "The LORD can give you much more than that." He dismissed the Israelites, who returned home in anger, raiding certain cities of Judah along the way and taking much spoil (25:13).

In the meantime Amaziah went against Edom and took Sela (2 Kings 14:7), possibly the rock-city now identified as Petra. He killed ten thousand Edomites in battle and put to death another ten thousand captives by hurling them from "the top of a cliff" (2 Chron 25:11–12). He brought back the gods of the Edomites and bowed down to them, burning sacrifices, for which his destruction was foretold (25:14–16). Amaziah then challenged Jehoash of Israel to war. In reply Jehoash likened Amaziah to a "thistle" making demands of a "cedar" and advised him to be content with his victory over Edom. Amaziah persisted, so they joined in battle at Beth Shemesh. The men of Judah were routed; Amaziah was captured and returned to Jerusalem. Six hundred feet (188 m.) of Jerusalem's wall facing Israel was broken down, after which Jehoash returned to Samaria, taking along hostages and treasures from the house of God and the house of the king. Fifteen years later a conspiracy made Amaziah flee to Lachish, but he was followed and killed. His body was brought back to Jerusalem for burial.

2. A priest of Bethel during the reign of Jeroboam II. He complained to Jeroboam about the prophet Amos and advised him to go back to Judah. Amos prophesied his death in a foreign land and the tragic end of his wife and family (Amos 7:10–17).

3. A Simeonite, whose son Joshah was among those who killed the remnant of Amalekites who had fled to Mount Seir (1 Chron 4:34, 43).

4. A Levite in the ancestry of the Ethan who served in the tabernacle about the time of David (1 Chron 6:45, 48). CEC

AMBASSADOR. The OT has three Hebrew words that express the idea of "ambassador." (1) *Tzîr* (e.g., Isa 18:2) probably denotes "going," i.e., away from home in a foreign land; (2) *mal'ākh* (e.g., Isa 37:9, 14; cf. 37:36 where it is the Lord's "angel" as his ambassador), meaning "messenger," therefore one sent on higher authority; (3) *lûts* (2 Chron 32:31), literally "interpreter" (e.g., Gen 42:23), i.e., one carrying an authorized understanding of his master's mind and policy. The word *ambassador(s)* in the NT—e.g.,"We are therefore Christ's ambassadors" (2 Cor 5:20) and "I am an ambassador in chains" (Eph 6:20)—is from *presbeuein,* "to be, work, or travel as an envoy or ambassador." Today's concept of an ambassador as a personal representative of sovereigns of state, living in foreign residence, is somewhat alien to the biblical concept of a messenger as ambassador.

AMBER (ăm′bêr, Heb. *hash-mal,* meaning unknown). Only in description of color of divine glory (Ezek 1:4, 27; 8:2; NIV "glowing metal"). LXX has *ēlektron,* allied with *ēlektōr,* "the beaming sun," designating a compound of silver and gold.

AMEN (ā-mĕn, Heb. *'āmēn,* Gr. *amēn*). English and Greek are both transliterations of Hebrew, from the root meaning "confirm" or "support." LXX translates it *genoito,* "may it become," KJV "verily." In the NT it is found as assent of the congregation to utterances of leaders (1 Cor

14:16); it is also equated with certainty of the promises of God (2 Cor 1:20). The general sense is "so let it be," "truly," "indeed." In the OT it appears with doxologies (1 Chron 16:36; Neh 8:6; Ps 41:13) as an assent by the congregation to laws (Num 5:22; Deut 27:15–26), with oaths (Neh 5:13), with appointments (1 Kings 1:36), and as a call to divine witness (Jer 28:6). In the NT it is used to introduce a solemn saying of Jesus, always in the sense of "I tell you the truth" (KJV, "Verily I say," John 3:5; cf. Ps 41:13). It is also used following a doxology (Rom 11:36), following a benediction (15:33), as a concluding particle at the end of a writing (all but Acts, James, and 3 John end with "Amen"—fifteen are with benedictions, three are with doxologies, and six are unrelated), as an assent to forebodings (Rev 1:7; 22:20), in reverence to God (Rom 1:25; 9:5; Rev 1:18), and as a title of God (Rev 3:14; cf. Isa 65:15).

AMERICAN STANDARD VERSION (See BIBLE, ENGLISH VERSIONS)

AMETHYST (See MINERALS)

AMI (ā'mī, Heb. *'āmî*). A servant of Solomon (Ezra 2:57), called Amon in Neḥemiah 7:59.

AMIL-MARDUK (See EVIL-MERODAK)

AMINADAB (See AMMINIDAB)

AMITTAI (ȧ-mĭt'ī, Heb. *'ămittay, faithful*). Father of Jonah (2 Kings 14:25; Jonah 1:1).

AMMAH (ām'ȧ, Heb. *'ammâh, mother,* or *beginning*). A hill facing Giah by way of the wilderness of Gibeon, where Joab and Abishai stopped at sundown in their pursuit of Abner after Asahel's death (2 Sam 2:24).

AMMAN (See RABBAH)

AMMI (ăm'ī, Heb. *'ammî, my people*). A symbolic name given to Israel (Hos 2:1 KJV, NASB), it is predictive of God's reconciliation to them, in contrast to sinful Israel, which is represented by Hosea's son Lo-Ammi, "not my people" (Hos 1:9). See Romans 9:25–26.

AMMIEL (ăm'ĭ-ĕl, Heb. *'ammî'ēl, my kinsman is God*). 1. The son of Gemalli and spy of the tribe of Dan sent out by Moses (Num 13:12).

2. The father of Machir of Lo Debar (2 Sam 9:4–5; 17:27).

3. The father of Bathsheba, one of David's wives (1 Chron 3:5).

4. The sixth son of Obed-Edom who, with his family, was associated with the temple gatekeepers (1 Chron 26:5).

AMMIHUD (ă-mī'hŭd, Heb. *'ammîhûdh, my kinsman is glorious*). 1. The father of Elishama, chief of Ephraim (Num 1:10; 2:18; 7:48, 53).

2. A man of Simeon and father of Shemuel (Num 34:20).

3. A Naphtalite whose son Pedahel assisted in the division of the land (Num 34:28).

4. Father of Talmai and king of Geshur. Absalom fled to Talmai after he murdered his brother Amnon (2 Sam 13:37).

5. Son of Omri, father of Uthai (1 Chron 9:4).

AMMINADAB (ă-mĭn'ȧ-dăb, Heb. *'ammînādhāv, my people are willing,* or *my kinsman is generous*). 1. A Levite, Aaron's father-in-law (Exod 6:23).

2. A prince of Judah (Num 1:7; 2:3; 7:12, 17; 10:14; Ruth 4:19–20; 1 Chron 2:10).

3. A son of Kohath, son of Levi (1 Chron 6:22). Perhaps the same as no. 1.

4. A Kohathite who assisted in the return of the ark from the house of Obed-Edom (1 Chron 15:10–11).

AMMISHADDAI (ăm-ĭ-shăd'ī, *an ally is the Almighty*). Father of Abiezer, captain of the tribe of Dan in Moses' time (Num 1:12; 2:25; 7:66, 71; 10:25).

AMMIZABAD (ȧ-mĭz'ȧ-băd, Heb. *'ammîzāvādh, my kinsman has endowed*). Son of Benaiah, third of David's captains (1 Chron 27:6).

AMMON (ăm'ŏn, Heb. *'ammôn, a people*). Ammon or Ben-Ammi is the name of one of the sons of Lot born to him by his youngest daughter in the neighborhood of Zoar (Gen 19:38). He was the father of the Ammonites, who occupied the area east of the Dead Sea in the land of Gilead.

AMMONITES (ăm'ŏn-īts, Heb. *'ammônîm*). The name given to the descendants of Ben-Ammi or Ammon (Gen 19:38). They were related to the Moabites by ancestry and often appear in Scripture in united effort with them. Because by ancestry they were related to Israel, "children of my people" (see the NIV footnote to Gen 19:38), the Israelites were told by the Lord not to enter into battle with them as they journeyed toward the land of Canaan (Deut 2:19). Lot fled from the destruction of the cities of Sodom and Gomorrah and dwelt in the mountains to the east of the Dead Sea. The land God gave the Ammonites stretched to the north as far as the Jabbok River and to the south to the hills of Edom. Many years later the Ammonites made war with Israel in order to extend their borders farther west. Although this land never really belonged to the Ammonites, they claimed it and gave this as a reason for their aggression (Judg 11:13).

Unable to expand westward and not desiring the desert tract of land on the east, the Ammonites were confined to a small area. Although they were a nomadic people, they did have a few cities, their capital Rabbath-Ammon being the most famous.

The people were fierce in nature and rebellious and, apart from the period when Nahash was a friendly ally of David's (2 Sam 10:1ff.), hostile to Israel. They threatened to gouge out the right eyes of all in Jabesh Gilead (1 Sam 11:2). They

Stone statue of an Ammonite god or king, found in Rabbath Ammon (Amman, capital of Jordan); from Iron Age (c. 1200–300 B.C.). Courtesy Studium Biblicum Franciscanum, Jerusalem.

were given to brutal murder (Jer 40:14; 41:5–7; Amos 1:14). Though related to Israel, they refused to help them when asked, and they joined with Moab in securing Balaam to curse them (Deut 23:3–4). Later in Israel's history they united with Sanballat to oppose the work of Nehemiah in restoring the walls of Jerusalem (Neh 2:10–19). In religion the Ammonites were a degraded, idolatrous people. Their chief idol was Molech, to whom they were guilty of offering human sacrifices (1 Kings 11:7).

Because of their sins and especially because they constantly opposed Israel, Ezekiel predicted their complete destruction (Ezek 25:1–7). Their last stand seems to have been against Judas Maccabeus (1 Macc 5:6). HZC

AMNON (ăm′nŏn). 1. Son of David by Ahinoam. By contrivance he raped his half-sister Tamar as she tended him during a pretended sickness; for this he was later murdered by Tamar's brother Absalom (2 Sam 13:1–29).

2. A son of the Judahite Shimon (1 Chron 4:20).

AMOK (ā′mŏk, Heb. *'āmôq*). Chief of priests who returned with Zerubbabel from the Exile (Neh 12:7, 20).

AMON (ā′mŏn, Heb. *'āmôn*). 1. The successor and son of King Manasseh and the father of the illustrious King Josiah. Since this name was identical with that of the Egyptian deity, it is thought that perhaps Manasseh named him while he was still in idolatry. He was an evil king and after two years of reign (642–640 B.C.) was slain by officials of his household (2 Kings 21:19–26; 2 Chron 33:21–25).

2. The governor of Samaria to whom Micaiah the prophet was committed by Ahab, king of Israel, because he had predicted the king's death (1 Kings 22:15–28).

3. One of Solomon's servants (Neh 7:57–59), though sometimes he is called Ami (Ezra 2:57).

4. The name of an Egyptian deity that appears in the OT linked with his city, No (Jer 46:25; Nah 3:8, see NIV footnote). Better known by its Greek name, Thebes, No was 318 miles (530 km.) south of Cairo and is now known by the names Karnak and Luxor and is famed for its huge necropolis. Little is known of Amon for sure. During the period of the Theban Dynasties (from 1991 B.C.) Amon became the state god of the Egyptian empire. His city and priesthood came to such glory that Nahum was able to recall its downfall as evidence to great Nineveh that its time of desolation would surely come also.

The Egyptian god Amon, wearing the headdress of a cylindrical cap surmounted by two feathers. The ceremonial beard worn by the god has been broken off. Courtesy B. Brandl.

AMORITE (ăm'ō-rīt, Heb. *'ĕmōrî, mountain dwellers*). Although this word in the Hebrew is always in the singular, it is used collectively of that tribe of people who, according to Genesis 10:16, descended from Canaan. They probably were east Semites and although not Akkadians were very closely akin to them.

They were a prominent people in pre-Israelite days, for it is believed that at one time their kingdom occupied the larger part of Mesopotamia and Syria, with their capital at Haran. The Mari tablets throw a flood of light on them, and it is now thought that Amraphel of Shinar (Gen 14:1) was one of their kings. When people from the north drove them from this region, they settled Babylonia and brought the entire area under their control, giving to Babylonia one of the richest periods in her history. After several hundred years they were defeated by the Hittites, and they settled throughout a large portion of Canaan. They may even have ruled in Egypt for a time.

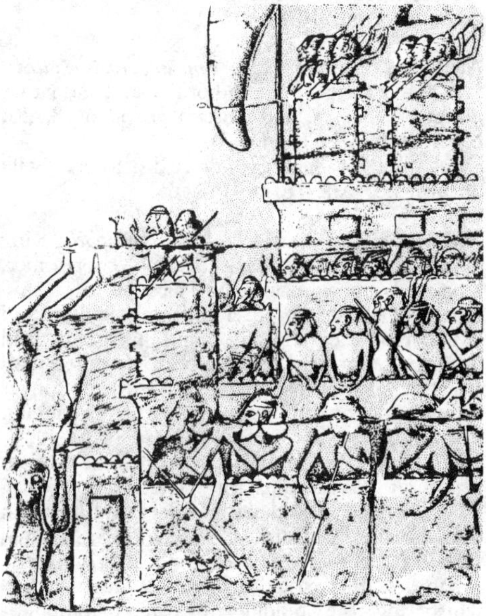

Siege of fortified town in the land of Amurru. The drawing is from relief of Ramses III at Medinet Habu, (c. 1195–1164 B.C.). The towers and walls of the fortress are manned by Syrian lancers as the chief of town stands on one of the gate towers at left holding out a brazier as a sign of surrender. Above, two towers, before which is the town's triangular standard hanging from a pole. Courtesy Carta, Jerusalem.

We do know that during their supremacy in Canaan they marched on the kingdom of Moab and under the leadership of King Sihon subdued a large portion of this land, in which they settled (Num 21:13, 26–31). Joshua speaks of their land as east of the Jordan (Josh 24:8), but Moses describes it as being on the western shore of the Dead Sea (Gen 14:7), on the plain of Mamre (14:13), and around Mount Hermon (Deut 3:8). They were apparently a very wicked people, for God told Abraham that his descendants would mete out divine vengeance on them when their iniquity was full (Gen 15:16). Under Moses' leadership this judgment was dealt to Og, king of Bashan, and to Sihon, king of Heshbon—the kings of the Amorites east of the Jordan. Their territory was subdued and given to Reuben, who held it for five hundred years until it fell to Moab. This land was very rich, attractive to both farmers and herdsmen. Joshua met these people in battle in the united campaign of the five Amorite kings of Jerusalem, Hebron, Marmuth, Lachish, and Eglon (Josh 10:1–43). These battles (11:1–14), fought by Joshua under divine leadership, ended forever Amorite hostilities against Israel (1 Sam 7:14; 1 Kings 9:20–21). HZC

AMOS (ā'mŏs, Heb. *'āmôs*, Gr. *amos, burden-bearer*). One of the colorful personalities in an era that saw the rise of several towering prophetic figures. His ministry occurred in the reign of Jeroboam II (c. 786–746 B.C.), son of King Jehoash of the Jehu dynasty of Israel. Due to the removal of Benhadad III of Syria as a military threat, the northern kingdom had been able to consolidate its hold on Damascus and extend its borders northward to the pass of Hamath. To the south and east, its territorial acquisitions equaled those of the early kingdom period under David and Solomon. While Assyria was becoming an increasingly serious political threat, its military might under Tiglath-Pileser III was still a distant prospect when Jeroboam II began to rule Israel.

Jeroboam's forty-year reign was one of great prosperity for the northern kingdom, approaching in character the "golden age" of David and Solomon. With the threat of war removed, a cultural, social, and economic revival took place. The expansion of trade and commerce resulted in a steady drift from country to city, and the small towns in the northern kingdom gradually became overcrowded. But prosperity was accompanied by an almost unprecedented degree of social corruption (Amos 2:6–8; 5:11–12), caused principally by the demoralizing influence of Canaanite Baal worship, which had been fostered at the local shrines from the time when the northern kingdom had assumed a separate existence.

Archaeological discoveries in Palestine have furnished a dramatic picture of the extent to which this depraved, immoral religion exerted its corrupting influences over the Israelites. Characteristic of the ritual observances were drunkenness, violence, gross sensuality, and idolatrous worship. The effect was seen in the corruption of justice, in wanton and luxurious living, and in the decay of social unity in Hebrew society. The rich manifested no sense of responsibility toward the poor, and instead of relieving their economic distress seemed bent on devising new means of depriving them of their property.

To this perilous situation Amos brought a message of stern denunciation. Although he was not an inhabitant of the northern kingdom, he was painfully aware of its moral, social, and religious shortcomings. Amos lived in the small mountain village of Tekoa, which lay to the south of Jerusalem on the borders of the extensive upland pastures of Judah. By trade he was a herdsman of sheep and goats (Amos 7:14) and was also engaged in dressing the sycamore-fig tree, whose fruit needs to be incised about four days before the harvest to hasten the ripening process. His background was of a strictly agricultural nature, and his work afforded him ample time for meditating on God's laws and their meaning for wayward Israel.

On receiving his call, Amos protested vigorously against the luxurious and careless lifestyle characteristic of Samaria, castigated the elaborate offerings made at the shrines of Beersheba and Gilgal, and stated flatly that ritual could never form an acceptable substitute for righteousness. He asserted the moral jurisdiction of God over all nations (Amos 1:3, 6, 9, 11, 13; 2:1, 4, 6) and warned the Israelites that unless they repented of their idolatry and, following a renewed spiritual relationship with God, commenced to redress social inequalities, they would fall victim to the invader from the east. So great was the impact of this vigorous personality that Amos was accused of sedition by Amaziah, the idolatrous high priest of Bethel (7:10ff.). In reply, Amos pointed out that he had no connection with any prophetic order, nor was he linked in any way politically with the house of David. Instead he was called by God to prophesy the captivity of an unrepentant Israel.

The style of his book, though simple, is picturesque, marked by striking illustrations taken from his rural surroundings. His work as a herdsman was clearly not incompatible either with a knowledge of history (Amos 9:7) or with an ability to assess the significance of contemporary political and religious trends. The integrity of his book has suffered little at the hands of modern critical scholars.

Analysis

1–2. The indictment of foreign nations, including Judah and Israel.

3:1–5:17. The condemnation of wicked Samaria.

5:18–6:14. False security exposed; judgment foretold.

7:1–9:10. Five visions illustrate divine forbearance and justice; Amos's reception at Bethel (7:10–17).

9:11–15. Epilogue promising restoration and prosperity.

Bibliography: J. K. Howard, *Amos Among the Prophets,* 1968; J. L. Mays, *Amos: A Commentary,* 1969; J. A. Motyer, *The Day of the Lion,* 1974.

RKH

AMOZ (ā'mŏz, Heb. *'āmôts*). The father of the prophet Isaiah (2 Kings 19:2, 20; Isa 1:1).

AMPHIPOLIS (ăm-fip'ō-lĭs, Gr. *Amphipolis, a city pressed on all sides*). A city of Macedonia, situated on a bend of the River Strymon. It was founded by the Athenians in the fifth century B.C. and under the Romans it became the capital of one of the four districts into which Macedonia was divided. It was a military post on the Via Egnatia, thirty-three miles (fifty-five km.) SW of Philippi. Paul passed through it on the way from Philippi to Thessalonica (Acts 17:1).

AMPLIATUS (ăm'plĭ-ā'tŭs, Gr. *Ampliatus,* KJV Amplias). A Christian to whom Paul sent a greeting (Rom 16:8).

AMRAM (ăm'răm, Heb. *'amrām, people exalted*). 1. A descendant of Levi and of Kohath, and father of Aaron, Moses, and Miriam (Exod 6:18, 20; Num 26:59; 1 Chron 6:3).

2. A son of Bani. He married a foreign wife during the Exile (Ezra 10:34).

AMRAPHEL (ăm'rà-fĕl, Heb. *'amrāphel*). King of Shinar, one of four kings, led by Kedorlaomer, king of Elam, who invaded Palestine to crush a rebellion (Gen 14). After pillaging Sodom and Gomorrah, they took Lot and his goods and departed. Amraphel has not been identified with any king known in secular history. It is no longer thought that he can be equated with Hammurabi.

AMULETS. Isaiah (3:20) speaks of the women of his day as wearing charms. The Hebrew word, *lāhash,* is used in Ecclesiastes 10:11 and Jeremiah 8:17 specifically of snake-charming (cf. the related verb in Ps 58:4–5). At root it means "a whisper." Isaiah sees the existence of those "instructed in whispering" (i.e., holding whispered communication with the dead, with spirits, or making whispered communication purporting to come from "the other side") as evidence that society is about to collapse. The same word (Isa 3:20) also means objects, personal ornaments, into which some magic charm has been whispered, supposed therefore to afford protection or some other

Gold amulets (in the shape of an eight-pointed star) and a plaque (representing the goddess Astarte) worn as pendants. Tell el-Ajjul, Late Bronze Age (c. 1550–1400 B.C.). Courtesy Israel Department of Antiquities and Museums.

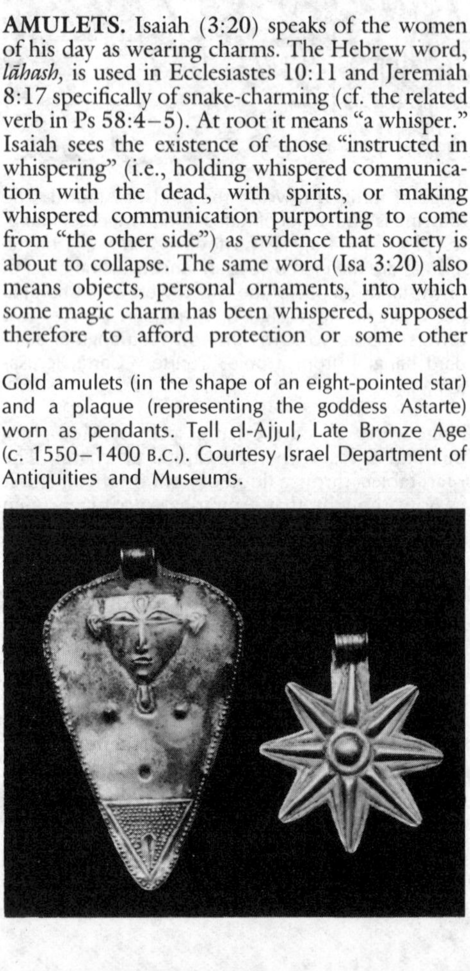

"lucky" benefit to the wearer. Archaeology has revealed such practices all over the ancient world. The same Hebrew word is used in Isaiah 26:16 without any overtones of superstition or magic to mean "whisper a prayer."

AMZI (ăm'zī, Heb. *'amtsî*). 1. A descendant of Merari and of Levi, and progenitor of Ethan, whom David set over the service of song (1 Chron 6:44–46).

2. Ancestor of Adaiah, a priest in the second temple (Neh 11:12).

ANAB (ā'năb, Heb. *'ănāv, grapes*). A city of the Anakim, taken by Joshua (Josh 11:21). It was part of the inheritance of Judah (15:50). It lies SE of Debir, SW of Hebron, and retains its ancient name.

ANAH (ā'nȧ, Heb. *'ănâh*). See Genesis 36:2, 14, 18, 20, 24–25, 29; 1 Chronicles 1:40–41. While all the other references make Anah a male descended from Seir the Horite and in the immediate family of Zibeon, Genesis 36:14 has often been understood to make Anah the daughter of Zibeon. Some (see RSV) solved this problem by following Greek and Syriac texts that read "son." NIV wisely offers "Oholibamah daughter of Anah and granddaughter of Zibeon," for as the word "son" is used in Hebrew of immediate and remote male descendants, so is the word "daughter" here. The family tree, therefore, runs from Seir through the males, Zibeon and Anah, to the female Oholibamah, whom Esau married.

ANAHARATH (ȧ-nā'hȧ-răth, Heb. *'anāhărāth*). A town in the territory of Issachar, in the valley of Jezreel near Shunem, Nain, and Endor. It is the modern en-Naura (Josh 19:19).

ANAIAH (ȧ-nī'ȧh, Heb. *'ănāyâh, Jehovah has answered*). 1. A prince or priest who assisted in the reading of the law to the people (Neh 8:4).

2. One of those who, with Nehemiah, sealed the covenant (Neh 10:22). Nos. 1 and 2 may be the same person.

ANAK (ā'năk, Heb. *'ănāq, long-necked*). A descendant of Arba (Josh 15:13) and ancestor of the Anakites (Num 13:22, 28, 33).

ANAKITES, ANAKIM (ăn'ȧ-kīts, ăn'ȧ-kĭm, Heb. *'ănāqîm*). Also called "sons [children] of Anak." The spies compared them to the giants of Genesis 6:4 (RSV, NIV, Nephilim); also they were reckoned among the Rephaites (Deut 2:11, RSV, NIV). Three chiefs of the Anakites were in Hebron (Num 13:22) from the time of the spies until Caleb took it (Josh 15:13–14). Remnants of them remained in Gaza, Gath, and Ashod (11:21–22).

ANAMITES (ăn'ȧ-mīts, Heb. *'ănāmîm*). A people descended from Mizraim (Gen 10:13; 1 Chron 1:11), of whom nothing further is known.

ANAMMELECH (ȧ-năm'ĕ-lĕk, Heb. *'ănammelekh*). One of the gods of Sepharvaim, worshiped by colonists from that city who were settled in Samaria by order of the king of Assyria. The identity and location of Sepharvaim and the character of Anammelech are disputed (2 Kings 17:31).

ANAN (ā'năn, Heb. *'ānān, cloud*). A returned exile who sealed the covenant with Nehemiah (Neh 10:26).

ANANI (ȧ-nā'nī, Heb. *'ănānî*). A son of Elioenai, of the family of David (1 Chron 3:24).

ANANIAH (ăn'ȧ-nī'ȧh, Heb. *'ănanyâh, Jehovah is a protector*). 1. The father of Maaseiah and grandfather of Azariah (Neh 3:23).

2. A town of Benjamin (Neh 11:32).

ANANIAS (ăn'ȧ-nī'ăs, Gr. form of Heb. *hănanyâh, Jehovah has been gracious*). 1. Husband of Sapphira (Acts 5:1–11). He and his wife pretended to give to the church all they received from a sale of property but kept back part. When Peter denounced his deceit, Ananias fell down dead. The generosity of others (4:32–37) accentuates the meanness of Ananias. Yet lying to the Holy Spirit, rather than greed, was the sin for which he was punished. That his was the first gross act of disobedience within the church justifies the severity of the punishment. Peter prophesied rather than decreed his death, which was a penalty God inflicted.

2. A disciple at Damascus who, obeying a vision, was the means of healing the sight of Saul of Tarsus and of introducing him to the Christians of Damascus (Acts 9:10–19). In Acts 22:12–16 Paul recalls Ananias's part in his conversion and speaks of him as "a devout observer of the law and highly respected by all the Jews living" in Damascus.

3. A high priest before whom Paul was tried in Jerusalem (Acts 23:1–5). Paul, whether because of poor eyesight or momentary forgetfulness or Ananias's unpriestly behavior, reviled him, was rebuked, and promptly apologized. Ananias came down to Caesarea in person to accuse Paul before the Roman governor Felix (24:1). ER

ANATH (ā'năth, Heb. *'ănāth*). Father of Shamgar, third judge after Joshua (Judg 3:31; 5:6).

ANATHEMA (ȧ-năth'ĕ-mȧ, Gr. *anathema*, the rendering in the LXX and in the NT of the Hebrew *herem, anything devoted*). A thing devoted to God becomes his and is therefore irrevocably withdrawn from common use. A person so devoted is doomed to death—a death implying moral worthlessness (Lev 27:28–29; Rom 3:9; 1 Cor 12:3; 16:22; Gal 1:9). See also DEVOTED THING.

ANATHEMA MARANATHA (ȧ-năth'ĕ-mȧ mâr'ȧ-năth'ȧ). These words (1 Cor 16:22) have been taken as being a double imprecation (KJV) or as having no necessary connection. Maranatha (NASB) may be a distinct sentence made up of two Aramaic words, either *Maran atha* (JB)—"Our Lord is come [or comes]"—or *Marana tha* (NEB)—"Our Lord, come" (MLB, RSV). It may have been an expression among early Christians to indicate their fervent hope in Christ's early return. See MARANATHA.

ANATHOTH (ăn'à-thŏth, Heb. *'ănāthôth,* probably the plural of *anath, goddess*). 1. A city of Benjamin assigned to the priests (Josh 21:18), the native place of Abiathar the priest (1 Kings 2:26) and Jeremiah the prophet (Jer 1:1). Two of David's distinguished soldiers, Abiezer (2 Sam 23:27) and Jehu (1 Chron 12:3), also lived there.

2. A Benjamite, the son of Beker (1 Chron 7:8).

3. A leader of the men of Anathoth who sealed the covenant (Neh 10:19).

ANCHOR (Gr. *ankyra*). In ancient times every ship carried several anchors. In successive periods they were made of stone, iron, lead, and perhaps other metals. Each had two flukes and was held by a cable or a chain. The word is used in Acts 27:13, 17, 29, 30, 40 and Hebrews 6:19; in Acts in connection with Paul's journey to Rome, and in Hebrews in a figurative sense.

ANCIENT OF DAYS. In Daniel 7:9, 13, 22 the reference is to God, as he appeared in a vision to the prophet. See DANIEL; SON OF MAN.

ANDREW (ăn'drū, Gr. *Andreas, manly*). The brother of Simon Peter and son of Jonas of Bethsaida on the Sea of Galilee (John 1:44). He was a fisherman, like his brother, with whom he lived at Capernaum (Mark 1:29). He was a disciple of John the Baptist, who directed him to Jesus as the Lamb of God. Convinced that Jesus was the Messiah, he quickly brought his brother Peter to Jesus (John 1:25–42). Subsequently Jesus called the two brothers to abandon their fishing and take up permanent fellowship with him (Matt 4:18–19); later Jesus appointed Andrew an apostle (Matt 10:2; Mark 3:18; Luke 6:14; Acts 1:13). In the lists of the apostles his name always appears next to that of Philip, who was also from Bethsaida. He is associated with the feeding of the five thousand, where he expressed doubt that the multitude could be fed with the lad's five loaves and two fishes (John 6:6–9), and also with the request of the Greeks to see Jesus (12:22). Andrew was one of the four who asked Jesus about the destruction of the temple and the time of the Second Coming. After Acts 1:13 he is never mentioned again. According to tradition he preached in Scythia and suffered martyrdom in Achaia, crucified on an X-shaped cross, now called a St. Andrew's cross.

ANDRONICUS (ăn'drō-nī'kŭs, Gr. *Andronikos*). A Jewish believer, once a fellow-prisoner of Paul, to whom the apostle sent a greeting (Rom 16:7).

ANEM (ā'nĕm, Heb. *'ānēm*). A city of Issachar, set aside for the Levites (1 Chron 6:73). Omitted in the parallel list in Joshua 21:29.

ANER (ā'nêr, Heb. *'ānēr*). 1. A brother of Mamre the Amorite, Abraham's ally in battle (Gen 14:13, 24).

2. A Levitical city in Manasseh (1 Chron 6:70).

ANGEL (Gr. *angelos, messenger*). A supernatural, heavenly being, a little higher in dignity than man. Angels are created beings (Ps 148:2–5; Col 1:16). Scripture does not tell us the time of their creation, but it was certainly before the creation of man (Job 38:7). They are described as "spirits" (Heb 1:14). Although without a bodily organism, they have often revealed themselves in bodily form to man. Jesus said that they do not marry and do not die (Luke 20:34–36). They therefore constitute a company, not a race developed from one original pair. Scripture describes them as personal beings, not mere personifications of abstract good and evil. Although possessed of superhuman intelligence, they are not omniscient (Matt 24:36; 1 Peter 1:12); and although stronger than men, they are not omnipotent (Ps 103:20; 2 Thess 1:7; 2 Peter 2:11). They are not glorified human beings but are distinct from man (1 Cor 6:3; Heb 1:14). There is a vast multitude of them. John said, "I . . . heard the voice of many angels, numbering thousands upon thousands, and ten thousand times ten thousand" (Rev 5:11). They are of various ranks and endowments (Col 1:16), but only one—Michael—is expressly called an archangel in Scripture (Jude 9). The great hosts of angels, both good and bad, are highly organized (Rom 8:38; Eph 1:21; 3:10; Col 1:16; 2:15).

Angels were created holy (Gen 1:31; Jude 6), but after a period of probation some fell from their state of innocence (2 Peter 2:4; Jude 6). Scripture is silent regarding the time and cause of their fall, but it is clear that it occurred before the fall of man (for Satan deceived Eve in the Garden of Eden) and that it was due to a deliberate, self-determined rebellion against God. As a result these angels lost their original holiness, became corrupt, and were confirmed in evil. Some were "sent . . . to hell," where they are held in chains until the Day of Judgment (2 Peter 2:4); others were left free, and they oppose the work of God.

The work of the angels is varied. Good angels stand in the presence of God and worship him (Matt 18:10; Heb 1:6; Rev 5:11). They assist, protect, and deliver God's people (Gen 19:11; Ps 91:11; Dan 3:28; 6:22; Acts 5:19). The author of Hebrews says (1:14), "Are not all angels ministering spirits sent to serve those who will inherit salvation?" They sometimes guide God's children, as when one told Philip to go into the desert near Gaza (Acts 8:26); and they bring encouragement, as when one spoke to Paul in Corinth (27:23–24). Sometimes they interpret God's will to people (Dan 7:16; 10:5, 11; Zech 1:9, 13–14, 19). They execute God's will toward individuals and nations (Gen 19:12, 13; 2 Sam

24:16; Ezek 9:2, 5, 7; Acts 12:23). The affairs of nations are guided by them (Dan 10:12–13, 20). God uses them to punish his enemies (2 Kings 19:35; Acts 12:23).

Angels had a large place in the life and ministry of Christ. At his birth they made their appearance to Mary, Joseph, and the shepherds. After the wilderness temptation of Christ they ministered to him (Matt 4:11); an angel strengthened him in the Garden (Luke 22:43); an angel rolled away the stone from the tomb (Matt 28:2–7); and angels were with him at the Ascension (Acts 1:10–11).

As for the evil angels, it is clear that their principal purpose is to oppose God and to try to defeat his will and frustrate his plans. Evil angels endeavor to separate believers from God (Rom 8:38). They oppose good angels in their work (Dan 10:12–13). They hinder man's temporal and eternal welfare by a limited control over natural phenomena (Job 1:12–13, 19; 2:7), by inflicting disease (Luke 13:11, 16; Acts 10:38; 2 Cor 12:7), by tempting man to sin (Matt 4:3; John 13:27; 1 Peter 5:8), and by spreading false doctrine (1 Kings 22:21–23; 2 Thess 2:2; 1 Tim 4:1). They cannot, however, exercise over people any moral power independent of the human will, and whatever power they have is limited by the permissive will of God. The word *Satan* means "adversary," and Scripture shows him to be the adversary of both God and man. All of his many other names show his extremely wicked character.

Scripture shows that good angels will continue in the service of God in the future age, whereas evil angels will have their part in the eternal fire (Matt 25:41).

Bibliography: E. Langton, *The Angel Teaching of the New Testament,* 1937; W. G. Heidt, *Angelology in the Old Testament,* 1949; W. O. E. Oesterley, *Angelology and Demonology in Early Judaism,* 1950; W. Carr, *Angels and Principalities,* 1981. SB

ANGEL OF THE LORD. In the OT we often find the phrase "the angel of the Lord." In almost every case, this messenger is regarded as deity and yet is distinguished from God (Gen 16:7–14; 22:11–18; 31:11, 13; Exod 3:2–5; Num 22:22–35; Judg 6:11–23; 13:2–25; 1 Kings 19:5–7; 1 Chron 21:15–17). These references show that the Angel is the Lord himself adopting a visible form (and therefore a human appearance) for the sake of speaking with people (e.g., Judg 13:6, 10, 21). While himself holy as God is holy (e.g., Exod 3:2–5), the Angel expresses the Holy One's condescension to walk among sinners (32:34; 33:3). He is also the executant of divine wrath (e.g., 2 Sam 24:16; 2 Kings 19:35). In all these ways, as we can see from the NT perspective, the Angel is part of the OT preparation for the Lord Jesus Christ.

ANGER. The English rendering of at least ten biblical words, of which the most common is Heb. *'aph,* which could also mean "snorting." The OT condemns anger because it encourages folly and evil (Ps 37:8; Prov 14:29) and because vengeance belongs to God (Deut 32:35). Elsewhere it calls for restraint from those confronted by anger (Prov 16:14; Eccl 10:4). In the NT anger is among those emotions that provoke God's wrath (Eph 5:6) and is regarded as alien to godliness (1 Tim 2:8; James 1:19–20). There is righteous anger, however, as when Jesus condemned the misuse of the temple (John 2:12–17), the corruption of children (Mark 9:42), and lack of compassion (3:5). See also WRATH. JDD

ANIAM (à-nī'ăm, Heb. *'ănî'ām, lament of the people*). A son of Shemidah, a Manassite (1 Chron 7:19).

ANIM (ā'nim, Heb. *'ānîm*). A city in the southern hill country of Judah (Josh 15:50), probably the ruins of el-Ghuwein, south of Eshtemoa.

ANIMALS. This article deals with all kinds of animal life appearing in the Bible, with the exception of birds, which are the subject of a separate entry. The word "animal" itself is used in Genesis 7 in connection with all wild creatures taken into the ark by Noah.

Adder. See Snake.

Ant. The two references in Proverbs (6:6; 30:25) cite the excellent example given to a

Ancient clay vessel with spout in the shape of a monkey. Ancient people showed much interest in apes, and Solomon imported them, probably to provide amusement in his court (cf. 1 Kings 10:22). Courtesy Israel Department of Antiquities and Museums.

sluggard and no doubt other people. Study of the ant's behavior will provide wisdom, declares the author, drawing special attention to the ant's wise use of its "little strength" to "store up [its] food" and prepare for the future.

The type of ant mentioned here is the harvester ant, found in regions of relative food shortage and therefore dependent on a diet of seeds. There are thousands of species world-wide belonging to this insect family, *Formicidae.* Most species maintain underground colonies that, like those of bees, work on a division-of-labor principle. Some attend to the cultivation of fungi, others milk the aphids for their secreted honeydew, others guard the colony. Most ants are wingless sterile workers, but the short-lived male has wings.

Antelope. See Gazelle.

Ape. The modern use of the word has more specific reference to a species excluding the monkey. The biblical record did not anticipate our contemporary classification when it recorded that King Solomon's fleet journeyed to Tarshish every three years and returned with "gold, silver and ivory, and apes and baboons" (1 Kings 10:22; 2 Chron 9:21). Although the precise location of Tarshish is uncertain, it is likely that the rhesus monkey of India is meant by the word "ape."

Asp. See Snake.

Ass. See Donkey.

Baboon. The NIV translation (1 Kings 10:22; 2 Chron 9:21) rendered by KJV, NASB, and RSV as "peacock." (Peacocks were for generations an adornment of royal courts.) A large, short-tailed monkey, the baboon is found mainly in Africa, but the Arabian baboon was once considered sacred to the Egyptians. With its doglike appearance, the baboon lives in the wild in large social groups.

Badger. The badger, species *Meles meles,* is found throughout Europe and northern Asia, while the American badger, *Taxidea taxus,* is a smaller species. This mainly underground dweller is not found in Bible lands. In Exodus 25:5 and Numbers 4:6, the uncertain word for the coverings used in the tabernacle is rendered in various ways: "fine leather" (JB), "badgers' skins" (KJV), "goatskins" (MLB), "leather" (MOF), "porpoise skins" (NASB), "porpoise-hides" (NEB), "hides of sea cows" (NIV), and "goats' skins" (RSV). It is true that there was widespread ownership of goats; but the dimensions of the covering were 75 x 45 feet, so that "the hides of sea cows" also represents a realistic translation of the original.

The coney is confirmed as unclean (Lev 11:5) and is a rock-dweller (hence, perhaps, "rock badger"; see NIV footnote in Lev 11:5; Ps 104:18). It is similar in appearance to a rabbit, but for the absence of a tail and comparatively short legs and ears. The four-toed foot of the coney has earned it the description, "little cousin of the elephant." Vegetarian, with molars similar to those of the rhinoceros, the coney has a jaw action reminiscent of an animal "chewing the cud," though its digestive system does not allow for rumination. Although it is timid, the coney is

Among the four things on earth that "are small, yet extremely wise" are the coneys (Hyrax or rock badger—Prov 30:26). About the size of the hare, their fur is thick, fine, and soft gray in color. The webbed feet function like suction cups enabling coneys to climb steep slippery rock surfaces. Especially prevalent in the rocky region surrounding the Dead Sea. Courtesy Seffie Ben-Yoseph.

a very active creature. It is found throughout the Middle East and much of Africa.

Bald Locust. See Grasshopper, Locust, Cricket.

Bat. The Bible classifies bats as unclean (Lev 11:19; Deut 14:18), while Isaiah's vision of the last days refers to people throwing their various idols made of precious metals to "rodents and bats" (Isa 2:20). Although since biblical times rumor and legend have given the bat an unfavorable reputation, this only true flying mammal is wonderfully equipped with a natural radar system for locating its prey—usually insects. An estimated two thousand different types of bats are found throughout the world, most of them nocturnal in habit. Some tropical species are fruit-eating, but those found in Bible lands are usually insect-eating. Gregarious creatures—living in great numbers in remote caves, for example—bats are classified with birds in Scripture, as in the Leviticus and Deuteronomy references above.

Bear. With a mainly vegetable diet, the bear could have been far more frequently encountered in an afforested Palestine than is sometimes supposed. The bear killed by David (1 Sam 17:34–37) was the Syrian brown bear, *Ursus syriacus,* the species referred to elsewhere in the OT. Reference is made to the ferocity of a female bear robbed of her cubs (2 Sam 17:8), and a readiness to attack humans is indicated in 2 Kings 2:23–25, when two bears mauled some forty-two youths who had been jeering at Elisha's bald head. A bald man was not a common sight, and the attitude of the youths seems to have been more threatening than mere banter. The RSV refers to the attacking animals as "she bears," surmising perhaps that they had been provoked to defend their cubs, apparently or really threatened by the youths. The sole reference to cubs is made in 2 Samuel 17:8. In terms of a symbol for other powers, the bear featured prominently in visions given to Isaiah, Daniel, and John.

Beast. This generic description is derived from some thirteen Hebrew and five Greek words, providing the following criteria:

1. A mammal, not including man and clearly different from birds and fishes and sometimes from reptiles also. Genesis 1:30 refers to "all the beasts of the earth," as distinct from "birds of the air and all the creatures that move on the ground."

2. A wild, undomesticated animal, as in Leviticus 26:22 and Isaiah 13:21; 34:14 ("desert creatures"). Mark 1:13 refers to the Lord's time in the desert with "wild animals."

3. Any of the "inferior" animals, in relation to the Mosaic Law's definition of ceremonially clean or unclean animals or beasts. Ecclesiastes 3:19 mentions the general mortality of the animal creation and of man himself. Acts 28:5 alludes to one of the inferior creatures, as Paul shakes from his hand and into the fire a viper that attacked him, with no ill effects to himself.

4. An apocalyptic symbol of brute force, opposed to God's rule and thereby to man's best interests. In Daniel 7:3 four great beasts symbolize four successive world empires—Babylon, Medo-Persia, Greece, and Rome. In Revelation 13:1–10 a beast coming out of the sea is identified as a world ruler with great, if temporary, authority. Many take the beast that comes out of the earth (Rev 13:11–18) to be Antichrist.

5. Celestial beings that worship God, reflect his qualities, and perform his will (Rev 4:6–9; 5:6, 8, 11, 14; 6:1, 3, 5–7; 7:11; 14:3; 15:7; 19:4). Various translations speak of them as "animals" (JB), "beasts" (KJV), "living beings" (MLB), and "living creatures" (NIV, RSV).

Bee, Hornet. The description "hornet" applies to several species of large social asps belonging to the family *Vespidae*. Usually colored yellow and black, the hornet is a medium-sized insect deriving its diet from flies. Its paper nest may be above or below ground level and, though basically beneficial to man, the hornet possesses a severe sting and an evident determination to deliver it when stimulated to do so.

Bees—the agents of pollination—have four wings. They may be social or solitary in behavior.

A nest of hornets suspended from a tree branch. When hornets fear their nest is in danger they will swarm out in large numbers and recklessly attack the intruder. Courtesy Seffie Ben-Yoseph.

Colonies function on what may be described as a division-of-labor system, with as many as fifty thousand members. Expansion is not unlimited, however, and swarms represent waves of emigration from the old hive (which remains in use) to a new home to be created elsewhere. Honey is made from the nectar collected by bees in their pollination activity, developed in the honey sac of the workers, and stored in the wax cells of the honeycomb.

Although there is little evidence that the ancient Hebrews cultivated bees for the manufacture of honey, the link was obvious enough. Bees would be plentiful in any land flowing with milk and honey, as indeed they always have been in Palestine. The abundance of flora in the land insured a large bee community.

Biblical references indicate God's use of the hornet in driving away the enemies of Israel (Exod 23:28; Deut 7:20; Josh 24:12). On occasion, enemies of Israel were compared to a swarm of bees, e.g., the Amorites (Deut 1:44) and other nations (Ps 118:12). Isaiah's prophecy included their response from the land of Assyria, when "the LORD will whistle" for them (Isa 7:18). In Judges 14:8, Samson finds a swarm of bees and honey in a lion's carcass, a discovery that shaped one of the most famous riddles in history (Judg 14:14).

Beetle. See Grasshopper, Locust, Cricket.

Behemoth. The graphic description in Job 40:15–24 has a footnote in the NIV and KJV suggesting the hippopotamus or the elephant. The footnote in the RSV suggests "hippopotamus."

Sometimes described as "the river horse of Africa," the hippopotamus is certainly a herbivorous heavyweight, sometimes reaching four tons (three and one-half metric tons). Despite its ungainly, even lethargic appearance, it is versatile in terms of its environment. It can swim or float, sink to the bottom of the river bed, and run along on the bottom. The species *Hippopotamus amphibius* is found in Central Africa; the pygmy hippopotamus, *Choeropsis liberiensis,* is found in Liberia. Like the elephant, the hippopotamus is a source of ivory through the large tusks in its lower jaw. There was extensive trading in ivory in biblical times, with at least a dozen biblical references to its use. King Solomon overlaid his ivory throne with gold (1 Kings 10:18); King Ahab made great use of ivory in his palace.

The elephant had many practical uses in ancient times, even in battle, as 1 and 2 Maccabees confirm. The elephant, with its instinctive grandeur, may better fit some of Job's words, as when "his tail sways like a cedar" (Job 40:17). This could possibly, and certainly more appropriately, refer to the elephant's trunk. One scholar has suggested that Job might have seen one of the last dinosaurs, but the identity of "behemoth" may never be decided.

Boar. See Pig.

Bull. See Cattle.

Butterfly. See Moth, Butterfly.

Calf. See Cattle.

Camel, Dromedary. The importance of the camel to life in Bible lands is confirmed by the many references (over sixty) to it in Scripture. As the original root word is almost identical in Hebrew and Arabic, one may conclude that the camel was well known to the patriarchs, long before the horse came into widespread use. Despite its reportedly grumbling disposition, the camel is well named the "ship of the desert," with its marvelous adaptation to terrain and climate. It can travel long distances without the need to take in water and can withstand high temperatures while being surefooted in undulating terrain. Of further value to the desert-dweller is the camel's long life, perhaps forty or fifty years.

Two basic forms are found: the single-humped dromedary and the slower-moving Bactrian camel with its two humps. The dromedary has longer legs and can move considerably faster than the other. With a load that may be up to 400 pounds (182 kg.), the Bactrian camel may cover little more than 30 miles (50 km.) in a single day; a dromedary, lightly burdened, can cover up to 150 miles (250 km.). The two forms are thus complementary: the dromedary for personal travel or the fast conveying of important messages, the Bactrian camel for commerce and trade.

Probably the most familiar biblical reference to the camel is that of Matthew 19:24, in which our Lord compares the difficulty of rich men securing entry into the kingdom of God with that of a camel making its way through the eye of a needle, i.e., the small gate permitting travelers to enter a city after the main gates have been closed. In order to get through the small gateway, the camel had to kneel, be relieved of its load, and then be urged through the gateway on its knees. As camels are as likely to complain when being unloaded as when being loaded, the illustration would have reminded hearers of the late traveler's exasperation on occasion.

Young camel quenching its thirst in the Negev. The Bible variety of camel is a single humped dromedary. Its many chambered stomach is lined with cells that can hold 15–30 quarts of liquid, allowing it to go from 5–25 days (depending on the heat) without drinking. Courtesy Israel Government Press Office.

Camels feature prominently in OT narrative and are included among Abraham's acquisitions while in Egypt (Gen 12:16). Genesis 24 focuses on aspects of contemporary travel, as Abraham's servant goes out to find a wife for Isaac. The journey to NW Mesopotamia is accomplished with ten camels—the encounter with Rebekah commencing as the camels are watered.

Inventory of Jacob's wealth includes camels (Gen 30:43), as does that of Job (Job 1:3; 42:12).

The camel was ceremonially unclean (Lev 11:4), though its milk was utilized (Gen 32:15). Even in our technologically advanced age, the camel remains an important aspect of economy in Bible lands. Its flesh and milk are valued by some inhabitants, together with the use of its hair.

Earlier translations, especially KJV, referred to dromedaries in 1 Kings 4:28 and Esther 8:10, but these are now translated as (swift) horses. Elsewhere the NIV refers to camel in a generic sense, i.e., dromedary as well as Bactrian.

Cankerworm. See Grasshopper, Locust, Cricket.

Caterpillar. See Moth, Butterfly.

Cattle. Cattle are mentioned in the first chapter of the Bible ("livestock" in NIV), symbolic of their importance to the well-being of the human race. Eleven Hebrew and two Greek words are translated to indicate cattle, the species descended from wild members of the family *Bovidae,* true ruminants with four-chambered stomachs for leisurely and thorough mastication.

Canaan was portrayed as a place of great prosperity, a place flowing with milk and honey—an abundance of cattle and good grazing ground. The patriarchs were accounted wealthy largely on the basis of their ownership of cattle, as in the case of Abraham (Gen 13:2). Included in Jacob's gift for his brother Esau were "forty cows and ten bulls" (32:15) taken from his own substantial herds. Joseph's destiny was shaped by Pharaoh's dream of seven cows, sleek and fat, succeeded by seven cows, ugly and gaunt (41:1–7), symbolic of years of plenteous harvests followed by bad ones. Joseph's life as prime minister and his relationship to his formerly estranged brothers includes reference to their cattle (45:10; 46:34). Loss of cattle represented a catastrophe, yet the Egyptians did not heed Moses' warning (Exod 9:1–7) of the destruction of their cattle as part of God's judgment. Later, Moses' defeat of the Midianites brought considerable "plunder" includng 72,000 cattle (Num 31:33).

A young cowherder with his cattle near the Sea of Galilee. Cattle were an important form of wealth in Bible times. The "cattle on a thousand hills" (Ps 50:10) belong to the Lord. Courtesy Israel Government Press Office.

Calves (young bulls or cows) were valued for food as well as sacrifice. A choice, tender calf was chosen by Abraham in entertaining his three mysterious visitors (Gen 18:7). Visions given to Isaiah, Ezekiel, and John included the calf, and Jesus concluded the story of the prodigal's homecoming with a great feast—at which a calf was prepared as appropriate to the celebration.

Calves used for sacrifice were usually one-year-old males, specified by Moses in Leviticus 9:3, 8. Corruption of the sacrificial aspect resulted in occasional lapses into calf worship, similar to that followed by the Egyptians. Moses' anger at witnessing such behavior was so great that he broke the tablets of the law that were in his hands (Exod 32:19).

A young bull was brought as a sin offering (Lev 4:15ff.), whereas Gideon's sacrifice (Judg 6:25–28) involved the use of a fully grown bull from his father's herd. At times of national and religious revival in the OT, substantial numbers of bulls, as well as rams and lambs, were offered in sacrifice. King Solomon's temple included a molten sea of brass supported by twelve bulls cast in bronze (1 Kings 7:25). Bulls were important in the lives of the people and for the nation, playing a part in the sin offerings for the congregation and in consecration of the Levites and the work of the priests. Yet David also made the bull a figure of threat in distress when, hunted by Saul, he wrote, "Many bulls surround me; strong bulls of Bashan encircle me" (Ps 22:12).

A heifer is a young cow. It was often used in sacrifice, or at the direct request of the Lord. Abraham killed a heifer on direct instruction (Gen 15:9), and Samuel was instructed by the Lord to take a heifer for sacrifice. Religious ceremonial law involving the use of a heifer is restricted to Deuteronomy 21:1–9. Ashes of the red heifer were used to remove ceremonial uncleanness, as in purification of the leper or of one who had touched a dead person (Num 19:9).

From the bright perspective of the Christian era, Paul encouraged converts from the Jewish tradition by referring to the fact that Christ's finished work superseded the old forms of sacrifice (Heb 9:13).

While found in the KJV, the word "kine" is no longer widely used, and in NIV it is translated "cow."

During the creation, God made the livestock according to their kinds (Gen 1:25). In Exodus 9 the word is used in referring to the disaster that would befall Egypt if Pharaoh refused to permit the Israelites to leave in peace: the plague would fall "on your livestock in the field—on your horses and donkeys and camels and on your cattle and sheep and goats." In Numbers 32 the word "livestock" is synonymous with "very large herds and flocks" (32:1).

Oxen, in addition to their use for food and in religious ceremonies, were important working members of the agricultural community. Six covered carts and twelve oxen were presented to the Lord's work at the dedication of the tabernacle (Num 7:3), to "be used in the work at the Tent of Meeting" (7:5). Property rights pertaining to oxen, as well as those relevant to other animals, were defined by the Lord (Exod 22:1) in recognition of their importance to the well-being of man. Jesus referred to the care owed to animals (including oxen) in his reponse to those who attacked him for healing on the Sabbath (Luke 13:15). There were, even for the strict Sabbatarians, "animal rights" that were to be observed, whatever the day of the week.

Elisha was plowing with twelve yoke of oxen when Elijah encountered him (1 Kings 19:19), just as Amos was following the plow when he heard the call of God. Although the ox is not especially regarded today as a religious symbol, it should be noted that Ezekiel's vision of the four celestial living creatures referred to one having the face of an ox (Ezek 1:10).

The unicorn, distinct from the mythological figure of that name, was probably the extinct auroch. When seen in profile, it gave the appearance of having one horn rather than two. A very powerful animal, standing some six feet (two m.) high, the auroch was once a familiar sight in Bible lands. NIV, ASV, and RSV all render "wild ox" to correct the mistranslation in KJV (Num 23:22; Deut 33:17).

The yearling is referred to in Isaiah's vision of the Millennium (Isa 11:6; "fatling" in KJV, NASB). "Fattened calf" is found in NIV in 2 Samuel 6:13 and 1 Kings 1:9–25.

Chameleon. See Lizard.

Chamois. See Sheep.

Cobra. See Snake.

Cockatrice. See Snake.

Colt. See Horse.

Coney. See Badger.

Coral. Red Coral, *Corallium nobile*, is native to the central and western Mediterranean and was greatly prized in ancient times. Its substance consists of the calcareous skeleton of a branching colony of polyps that remains long after the jellylike body of the polyp has perished and disappeared. Used in the making of jewelry, coral is mentioned in Job 28:18 in a celebrated passage on the value of wisdom. Ezekiel's lament concerning Tyre (Ezek 27:16) includes reference to trade in coral, which might be expected of a coastal city.

The Hebrew word translated as "coral" in the passages above has the alternative translation of "too high" in Proverbs 24:7, where wisdom is said to be "too high" to a fool.

Cow. See Cattle.

Creeping Thing, Crawling Thing. The description is used in several versions including NIV in referring to various land animals.

Cricket. See Grasshopper, Locust, Cricket.

Crocodile. See Lizard.

Deer. The family of ruminant mammals, *Cervidae,* which includes deer, elks, reindeer, moose, found world-wide except in Australia. The deer is included in the list of animals that may be eaten (Deut 14:5) and also in Solomon's list of daily provisions (1 Kings 4:23). As with other Bible animals, the special qualities of the deer are praised as models for human brings. David's song of praise compares his feet to those of the deer (2 Sam 22:34). Psalm 42 begins with a comparison of David's soul's thirst for God with that of a deer panting for streams of water. The writer of Lamentations likens the plight of princes to that of deer without pasture (Lam 1:6). Isaiah's description of the job of the redeemed anticipates the leaping of the lame like a deer (Isa 35:6).

The doe, the female of the species (traditionally of the fallow deer), "bears beautiful fawns" (Gen 49:21). Proverbs 5:19 compares the wife of one's youth with "a loving doe, a graceful deer." The Lord inquires of Job, "Do you watch when the doe bears her fawn?" (Job 39:1).

The word "fallow deer" is rendered "deer" by NIV. The meaning of fallow deer more particularly applies today to a smaller deer found in the forests and mountains of Europe and northern Asia. KJV uses "fallow deer" and "roebuck" in 1 Kings 4:23.

The "hart" of KJV and RSV (NIV "deer") was either the red deer of Europe and Asia (*Cervus elephus*) or the Syrian deer (*Cervus barbatus*). The former is similar to the American elk, but smaller. Harts are stags, or male deer, the word "stag" appearing only in the Song of Songs (2:9, 17; 8:14), and then in a lyrical sense. A single hart may weigh as much as 300 pounds (136 kg.). Every year the six-branched antlers are shed, to be replaced by new ones in due course.

Relief showing a hunt for wild asses. One ass is held with ropes by two attendants as two others flee. From the palace of Ashurbanipal (668–633 B.C.) at Nineveh. Reproduced by courtesy of the Trustees of the British Museum.

The female hind is also translated in NIV as "deer" (Ps 18:13). Habakkuk's well-known statement that the Lord made his "feet like hinds' feet" in KJV (Hab 3:19) becomes "like the feet of a deer" in NIV. Female red deer, i.e., hinds, are not listed as items of food in the original Hebrew text. See also Gazelle.

Desert Creature. A term used in Isaiah's prophecies against Babylon (Isa 13:21), Tyre (23:13), and Edom (34:14). Jeremiah's prophecy against Babylon also refers to desert creatures (Jer 50:39). No particular species is intended, and the description seemingly applies to a variety of wild creatures, great or small (though primarily the latter) that would be found in places remote from human habitation.

Devourer. See Grasshopper, Locust, Cricket.

Doe. See Deer.

Dog. Domesticated members of the *Canidae* family to which the wolf and jackal also belong. The Bible's forty references to dogs are not complimentary to these unclean animals. Proverbs 26:11 reflects a contemporary opinion that dogs return to their own vomit, while their readiness to bark at people or animals is mentioned in Exodus 11:7. Here, however, God declares that among the Israelites not a dog will bark at any man or animal. In NT times dogs—often strays—were regarded as nuisances. One licked the sores of the beggar named Lazarus (Luke 16:21). Job's reference to his sheep dogs (Job 30:1) suggests that good training could make even these despised animals useful, since he was hardly a man to take chances with his stock. Especially evocative is the Canaanite woman's plea for help, met when she reminded the Lord that "even the dogs" were permitted to eat the crumbs from the master's table (Matt 15:26–27).

KJV uses the word "greyhound" once (Prov 30:31), listed among things that move well. NASB, NEB, and RSV opt for "strutting cock"—an ancient breed of dog known in Egypt and thought of being capable of speeds up to forty miles (sixty-seven km.) an hour. It is also translated "war-horse" (ASV), "fighting cock" (MLB), and "a strutting rooster" (NIV).

Donkey. This small mammal, genus *equus,* with some similarity in appearance to a horse (though usually smaller), has served mankind for thousands of years. It is probably descended from the Abyssinian or Somali wild ass (donkey). Among its special characteristics are endurance and surefootedness, though occasional stupidity is not unknown. Found wild in semidesert regions, the species includes the African and Asian varieties.

NIV and NASB usually translate as "donkey" the six Hebrew and three Greek words rendered as "ass" in KJV and RSV. NIV translates the Hebrew for "he-ass" and "she-ass" as "male donkey" and "female donkey."

Abraham's journey of testing, with his son

Isaac, was made with a donkey (Gen 22:3, 5). Balaam's donkey was given the temporary power of speech in order to rebuke the foolish prophet (Num 22:21–33). In a rhetorical question Job (Job 6:5) asks if a wild donkey would bray if preoccupied with good pasture.

Donkeys were a fundamental part of the economy, and a man's wealth was measured by the number he owned. Sometimes donkeys were acquired in battle as plunder, as when the Israelites captured some 61,000 from the Midianites (Num 31:34). But Israelites were commanded neither to covet a donkey nor to attempt to plow with a donkey and an ox together (Deut 5:21; 22:10).

Donkeys undertook heavy work on the farm but were used for personal transportation too. White donkeys were highly prized by their owners, who would in any case be careful of their choice of an animal for a long journey. Jesus' triumphal entry into Jerusalem, celebrated on Palm Sunday in the church calendar, fulfilled the prophecy of Zechariah 9:9 as he came "riding on a donkey, on a colt, the foal of a donkey" (Matt 21:2–7). The donkey did not then have the lowly status it has today but was an appropriate choice for a procession of importance.

The mule is the offspring of a male donkey and a horse mare, and is itself sterile. The Israelites were forbidden to breed mules under a general prohibition on mating different animals (Lev 19:19), but mules were secured in the course of trading and were used for carrying goods and merchandise, as well as for personal transportation. King David reputedly introduced the use of the mule for riding. That mules might be urged to move quickly if required is indicated in 2 Samuel 13:29, where the king's sons mounted their mules and fled. Absalom was deserted by his mule when his head became caught in the branches of a thick oak (2 Sam 18:9), the mule plodding on while his master remained suspended in midair.

In warmer climates the donkey grows into a large, stately, and speedy animal. Shown here is a wild donkey and her colt in the Judean wilderness. Courtesy Israel Government Press Office.

Mules ridden by kings, officials, and army officers were chosen with care, but at the best of times the mule might prove unpredictable. In comparatively recent times itinerant preachers used mules as transportion to local engagements.

Dragon. KJV has some thirty-five references to "dragon." NASB, NIV, and RSV translate a number of them as "jackal." Where the Hebrew word is *tannîm,* a jackal or some kind of lizard might be intended.

Dragon (*mushhushshu*) in brick, one of several that ornamented the Ishtar Gate at Babylon. This hybrid creature (c. 600 B.C.) has a serpent's head, scaly-coated body, hind claws of an eagle, and front legs of a feline. From *Excavations at Babylon,* R. Koldewey, 1914. By permission of Macmillan, London and Basinstoke.

NIV does not use "dragon" for any OT translation. The word "monster" occurs in Psalm 74:13 and Ezekiel 32:2, both having a maritime significance. Sea voyagers for many centuries have reported "monsters of the sea," and no doubt such stories were well known in biblical times. "Jackal" is used in Job 30:29; Psalm 44:19; and Isaiah 13:22, all of them referring to situations of isolation and desolation, likely places in which jackals would be found. NIV, in common with other versions, refers to Satan as a dragon in Revelation 12:13; 20:2, but this language of imagery is characteristic of the final book of the Bible, referring to the ferocity of Satan's personality rather than to any physical attribute.

Dromedary. See Camel.

Ewe. See Sheep.

Elephant. See Behemoth.

Fallow Deer. See Deer.

Fatling. See Cattle.

Fawn. See Deer.

Fish. In Genesis 1, Adam is instructed to rule over the fish of the sea, as well as the rest of creation. Many references to fish and the means of catching them are found in the Scriptures, while the outline of a fish became symbolic in the early church. Specific species are not mentioned, though the striped mullet *(Mugil cephalus)* was well known in Bible times, found in the Mediterranean area, and the barbel—represented by

Vessel shaped in the form of a fish, made from alabaster, sixteenth century B.C. (Bronze) period. Courtesy Israel Museum, Jerusalem.

various species—was almost certainly known too, being found from British waters eastward to the East Indies.

There is no doubt about the importance of fish in everyday diet. One of the judgments that befell Egypt was the destruction of the nation's fish stock, and during their sojourn in the desert the Israelites grieved for the good fish they had eaten in Egypt (Num 11:5).

The great fish that swallowed Jonah (Jonah 1:17) is not identified by species, though in popular parlance it is thought of as a "whale." Our Lord's miraculous feeding of the five thousand involved use of five loaves and two fishes (Matt 14:17). Significantly, the final chapter of John's Gospel records Christ's resurrection appearance to the disciples as coinciding with a miraculous draught of fish, caught after the previously daunted fishermen let down their nets at his command (John 21).

Flea. Common throughout Bible lands, as elsewhere in the world, the flea is mentioned in 1 Samuel 24:14; 26:20. The flea is any of the *Aphaniptera* order of small, wingless insects possessing a flattened body and legs highly developed for leaping. An estimated five hundred species of fleas present a threat as well as an irritant to mankind, as their bite can transmit disease, more particularly bubonic plague. Endemic typhus is also transmitted by fleas.

David's rhetorical question in 1 Samuel 24:14 refers to the folly of pursuing a flea, while 1 Samuel 26:20 compares the task of looking for a flea with that of hunting a partridge in the mountains. With its natural agility and tiny size, the flea is difficult to catch. Some reportedly can jump thirteen inches (thirty-three cm.) horizontally and almost eight inches (twenty-one cm.) vertically.

Fly. This widely occurring species includes not only the house fly, but the tsetse fly and the malaria-carrying mosquito. Flies may carry disease by germs on their body or by bloodsucking. True flies have a single pair of functional membranous wings, plus a pair of halteres, i.e., small clublike appendages that by rapid movement in flight are the fly's gyro, or balance mechanism.

Ruination of Egypt by flies (Exod 8:24) was one of God's judgments described (8:20–32) as the plague of flies, following the plague of gnats described in earlier verses. The flies were possibly mosquitoes, for the original Hebrew word means "to suck."

In addition to threats to health, flies could also ruin crops. Failure of the olive crop (Deut 28:40) was due to the olive fly, a pest that deposits its eggs beneath the skin of the ripening olive. The maggot emerging from the egg destroys the fruit. Such loss is anticipated by Micah 6:15 in speaking to an unrepentant Israel, while Habakkuk also refers to the failure of the olive crop (Hab 3:17), apparently through similar assault.

The threat to Egypt prophesied by Jeremiah (Jer 46:20) is described as "destruction" in KJV, but NIV renders the word as "gadfly"—a biting, pestering nuisance. Socrates was described as "the gadlfy of Athens," suggesting that the ancients were well aware of the gadfly's persistent attacks.

The gnat, a sharp-biting member of the mosquito family, was used in one of the judgments on Egypt, though the gnats (Exod 8:16–18) may have been some kind of sandfly with an especially painful sting. An alternative rendering of the Hebrew is "lice" (so KJV; see also Ps 105:31). Jesus rebuked the teachers of the law for straining at a gnat but swallowing a camel (Matt 23:24). Man's insignificant status is emphasized in Job 25:6 as that of a maggot. In ancient times the fate of corpses, as of unguarded or unfresh food, was obvious enough. Isaiah's prophecy against the king of Babylon (Isa 14:11) refers to the presence of maggots in his grave. The narrative of the manna and quail in the wilderness (Exod 16:20, 24) demonstrates that food could not be stored, except by the grace of God, as when it remained fresh over the Sabbath.

In every mention of the worm in Scripture, the reference is to the maggot rather than to the earthworm, which is apparently nowhere mentioned in the Bible. Maggots are hatched from eggs laid by flies such as the flesh fly (of the family *Sarcophagidae*) or the blow fly (of the family *Calliphoridae*). The blow fly is well known to even our hygienic times, being the large and noisy fly with blue or green iridescent body. Such flies lay their eggs in the bodies of dead animals, in effect accelerating the decaying process, as the maggots feed on the corpse during their larval period. In that sense they serve a beneficial purpose in the natural process.

Herod's death (Acts 12:23) is described as caused by his being eaten by worms. This demise was probably accomplished by the screw worm, as the adult female fly lays eggs not only on decaying animal matter, but in wounds and sores and even in the nostrils and ears of people and cattle. In severe attacks, in the ancient world especially, infection of the nasal passages by larvae could produce collapse of the septum and palate. Herod's affliction is not, however, regarded as accidental, but as a judgment arising from his pride and his aspiration to divine status.

The presence of worms on the human body,

alive (Job 7:5) or dead (Job 17:14, 21:26; Isa 14:11; 66:24), was a further reminder of the transient nature of life. The condition of hell, warned Mark, was one in which the worm does not die (Mark 9:48).

Foal. See Horse.

Fox. The nine references in Scripture are to the common fox of Palestine, *Vulpes vulgaris,* a wild carnivore of the dog family, living usually on a diet of small animals and fruit, though its European relations may sometimes be found looking into trash cans during daylight hours as well as at night. This natural predator usually lives in burrows, the American red fox being a related species.

Damage to vineyards by "the little foxes" (Song of Songs 2:15) may have been a reference to jackals rather than to foxes. Similarly the three hundred foxes caught by Samson in order to pair them for raids on Philistine corn fields, with lit torches tied to their tails (Judg 15:4–5), may have been jackals, which would have been more readily caught. Tobiah the Ammonite poured scorn on the rebuilding of the wall of Jerusalem by suggesting that even the tread of a fox would break the stones (Neh 4:3).

"Foxes have holes. . . ." (Matt. 8:20). A fox peering out from his den in the Judean desert. Courtesy Seffie Ben-Yoseph.

The craftiness of the fox was emphasized by our Lord's description of Herod (Luke 13:32).

Frog. Exodus 8 speaks of the plague of frogs, summoned by Aaron from their natural habitat of streams, canals, and ponds. References in Psalms 78:45 and 105:30 recall the plague, and as the frog had some cultic significance to the Egyptians the significance of the plague would not have been overlooked.

A tailless amphibian of the order *Anura,* the frog was represented by two species in Egypt, toads by three. Revelation 16:13 tells of evil spirits with the appearance of frogs, possibly with the plague narrative in mind.

Gadfly. See Fly.

Gazelle. KJV usually translates "roe" or "roebuck" rather than "gazelle" (see Deer). The Dorcas gazelle was, however, known in Bible lands—a swift-running antelope having its natural habitat in barren wilderness areas. Over sixty types exist or have existed in southern Asia and northern Africa. Traditionally the gazelle has been hunted by desert people with the aid of falcons and, on occasion, greyhounds. The fast-moving gazelle is stunned by a blow from the falcon, permitting the rider on horseback to catch up and trap it.

A one-horned ibex (the other horn was apparently lost in an attack with another animal) roaming the hills of the Judean wilderness. At En Gedi (see 1 Sam 24:1–2) there is today a wildlife sanctuary especially to preserve the Nubian ibex. Courtesy Seffie Ben-Yoseph.

The delicacy of the meat is indicated in Deuteronomy 12:15, 22, coupled with that of the deer. Solomon's list of provisions included gazelles (1 Kings 4:23). One of Zeruiah's sons is reported as having been "as fleet-footed as a wild gazelle" (2 Sam 2:18).

The antelope is included among the permitted edible animals in Deuteronomy 14:5. A hoofed ruminant of the *Bovidae* family, it is most often found in Africa. Hunting of antelope, using net, is indicated in Isaiah 51:20. KJV sometimes translates antelope as "wild bull."

Ibex is a description that may be generally applied to any of several species of mountain goats, with their horns curving backward. Included in the list of permitted edible animals (Deut 14:5), the variety known to the people was that of the Nubian ibex, occurring in Palestine as well as in Egypt and Arabia. KJV translates the word as "gazelle" or "roe."

In Deuteronomy 14:5 KJV uses the word "pygarg" (which means "white rumped"). The species is uncertain, but the word is thought to refer to a type of antelope known as the addax, a native of desert areas of northern Africa and the Sudan. RSV renders this word as "ibex," NIV "roe deer."

More than a dozen times KJV uses the word "roebuck," "roe" (e.g., Deut 12:15; 1 Chron 18:3; Isa 13:14). This translation is not used in RSV, which, like ASV, most often has "gazelle"—a translation favored also by NIV in a majority of cases. NIV has "roe deer" in Deuteronomy 14:5, however, and "roebuck" (in addition to "gazelles") in 1 Kings 4:23.

Gecko. See Lizard.

Gnat. See Fly.

Grasshopper, Locust, Cricket. Grasshoppers and locusts are included in the insect family *Locustidae,* itself part of the order *Orthoptera,* which includes crickets, katydids, cockroaches, mantids, and walking sticks as well. Grasshoppers are the most frequently mentioned insects in the Bible, and man is sometimes compared to them in terms of his insignificance before great enemies (Num 13:3) or in the sight of God (Isa 40:22). In Ecclesiastes 12:5 the grasshopper's painful progress as he "drags himself along" is contained in a passage pointing to man's own mortality.

Locusts had significance beyond the natural order, often having been sent as a judgment from God (Exod 10:4). Such visitations could be devastating, and even in our technological age, locust swarms can quickly denude an area of its vegetation. Most species of locust are nonmigratory, but some migrate in great swarms, traveling over great distances if necessary and proving themselves omnivorous consumers of all kinds of vegetation. Where natural food is lacking, they can become cannibalistic and carnivorous.

The awesome sight and power of locusts depicted in Revelation 9:3, 7 is beyond anything yet known to man's experience. The author of the book knew well the tradition of locusts as a form of judgment from God. Joel's description of utter devastation through a visitation by locusts (Joel 1:4) precedes a passage (2:1–11) in which locusts are described in terms of a great army.

Locusts, however, were not without benefit to the human race and represented a useful diet for the poor—that is, in normal times. Edible locusts are listed in Leviticus 11:21–22, while the Talmud provides a description of edible locusts in order that readers could identify them. John the Baptist ate locusts and wild honey (Mark 1:6), a diet that was not considered unusual by his contemporaries. One of the edible locusts is rendered "bald locust" by KJV and RSV, and "katydid" by NIV (Lev 11:22). This is an insect of the long-horned grasshopper family found in the tropics and in the eastern USA.

In Leviticus 11:22, KJV has "beetle," and NIV "cricket," referring to an insect of the *Gryllidae* family related to the grasshopper and locust, but with long antennae and an apparent liking for human company.

The cankerworm, the larval state of the locust (Joel 1:4; 2:25; Nah 3:15–16), is rendered in NIV as "young locust."

KJV and NASB use "devourer" as a description of the locust in Malachi 3:11; NIV, "pest." "Hopper" is the RSV description in Joel 2:25 where NIV has "locust." The KJV "palmerworm" (Joel 1:4; 2:25; Amos 4:9) is "cutting locust" in RSV, "locust" in NIV.

Great Lizard. See Lizard.

Greyhound. See Dog.

Hare. See Rabbit.

Hart. See Deer.

Heifer. See Cattle.

Hind. See Deer.

Hippopotamus. See Behemoth.

Hopper. See Grasshopper, Locust, Cricket.

Hornet. See Bee, Hornet.

Horse. Most references concern the use of the horse in warfare, though some religious significance is attached to the appearance of the horse, as in the visions of Revelation 9:17–19; 6:1–8. Domesticated on the plains of Asia more than four thousand years ago, the horse—a herbivorous hoofed mammal, *Equus caballus*—was used in the military campaigns of Alexander the Great and was probably introduced into the American continent by conquerors from Europe. Scripture refers to the beneficial use of the horse among its more than 150 references. Joseph exchanged food for horses and for other animals during the great famine in Egypt (Gen 47:17). A very large company of chariots and horses accompanied the body of Jacob to his last resting place (50:9).

"Well-coiffured" and "crowned" horses, the tribute paid by a Mede to King Sargon of the Persians. This fragment of wall relief was found in Sargon II's palace (722–705 B.C.) at Khorsabad. Courtesy The Metropolitan Museum of Art; gift of John D. Rockefeller, Jr., 1933.

Although horses, with other livestock, perished under the judgment of God (Exod 9:3), Pharaoh secured further war horses and chariots in order to pursue the departing Israelites (14:23), though the Lord swept them into the sea (14:27–28). David's victories included the acquisition of large numbers of chariots, charioteers, and horses (2 Sam 8:4; 10:18).

Solomon's accumulation of chariots and horses (1 Kings 10:26) involved importation of horses from Egypt and Kue at considerable expense that, in view of his drift away from his former moral convictions, would have affronted the prophets (Isa 31).

Isaiah refers to the agricultural use of the horse,

i.e., for plowing (Isa 28:24–29). The use of horsemen to convey messages (2 Kings 9:18) and for royal processions (Esth 6:8–11) was familiar to the ancients. Ending of the idolatrous use of horses and chariots dedicated to the sun is reported in 2 Kings 23:11 as Josiah renewed the covenant with God. The sun religion, like the horses, was probably imported from Egypt.

The colt—the foal of a donkey—is included in Jacob's blessing (Gen 49:11) and in the narrative of our Lord's triumphal entry into Jerusalem (Matt 21:2–7; John 12:15).

As the stallion is a horse used for breeding purposes, its use in the OT is aligned to the sinful behavior of the people. Jeremiah likens his careless contemporaries to well-fed, lusty stallions considering their neighbors' wives (Jer 5:8; cf. 50:11). Stallions were large and strong and were used as symbols of enemy power, as in the Lord's declaration that the whole land trembled at the neighing of the enemy's stallions (8:16).

The steed was a horse especially chosen for battle, probably for its speed and daring. Deborah's song recites the galloping of the mighty steeds (Judg 5:22). We learn that the Israelites used steeds for battle against Egypt (Jer 46:4) and against the Philistines (47:3).

Horse Leech. See Leech.

Hyena. This carnivorous animal allied to the dog was common in Palestine. Isaiah's prophecy against Babylon speaks of hyenas howling in the strongholds of the fallen city (Isa 13:22)—a fate reserved for the citadels of Edom (34:14). Jeremiah speaks in similar vein against Babylon (Jer 50:39). The hyena, like the jackal, was associated with desolation and with dwelling among ruins.

Ibex. See Gazelle.

Katydid. See Grasshopper, Locust, Cricket.

Kine. See Cattle.

Leech. The word is derived from a Hebrew term meaning "sucking" (Prov 30:15). KJV renders "horseleach," though its attentions are not restricted to animals. The leech is of the class of annelids (*Hirudinea*) living in water or swampy territory. A sucker at either end of its segmented body fixes onto the body of an animal or human, sucking blood. A natural anticoagulant (hirudin) keeps the blood liquid. At one time the use of leeches was thought to have beneficial properties, and a type of leech, *Hirudo medicinalis,* was well known to physicians of past generations.

Leopard. The reference to "mountain haunts of the leopards" (Song of Songs 4:8) reminds us that these awesome animals were well known in Palestine, as well as in the mountainous regions of Lebanon, at the time of Solomon's reign. A mammal of the cat family (*panthera pardus*) with a black-spotted yellowish coat, the leopard is today found only in Africa and Asia. Its ferocity and intelligence were apparent to dwellers in Bible lands, though, as with the rest of the wayward creation, transformation was promised in the messianic age (Isa 11:6). Jeremiah regarded the leopard as an instrument of God's judgment on the wicked (Jer 5:6), and in a later passage raised the rhetorical question whether a leopard could change his spots (13:23). Several references to the leopard appear in KJV, RSV, and NIV, including the figurative usage in Daniel 7:6 and Revelation 13:2.

Leviathan. That the Leviathan was strong and probably very large is confirmed by the question put in Job 41:1. The NIV footnote suggests a hippopotamus or elephant, neither of which would be pulled in with a fishhook. Job's cursing (3:8) refers to those who are ready to rouse Leviathan.

Crushing the heads of Leviathan (Ps 74:14) immediately follows reference to the destruction of monsters of the sea. This may echo the song of praise to God following the safe journey of the Israelites through the Red Sea. Crocodiles or other threatening creatures would have been rendered harmless to the Israelites, as the pursuing Egyptians were. Not all allusions to Leviathan concern threatening species, however; Psalm 104:26 refers to its frolicking in the sea. Probably this is the sperm whale, which has been seen in the Mediterranean and which surfaces suddenly before submerging, giving the impression of play activity.

Lice. See Fly.

Lion. A large carnivore of the cat family (*Panthera leo*) today found in Africa south of the Sahara and in NW India. In biblical times the lion was far more widespread and was found even in Greece as well as in Asia Minor, Iran and Iraq, Syria and Turkey. A social animal, the lion is a member of a group known as a pride and will live in isolation only when old or wounded—conditions in which it is most dangerous to man. In usual circumstances the lion will not attack man, though "man-eaters" have been known, becoming part of local legends and hunters' tales.

Daniel's testing in the lions' den (Dan 6) demonstrates an oriental ruler's use of lions as a means of execution, but it is more importantly an example of protection by the Almighty. A wayward prophet was killed by a lion (1 Kings 13:24–28), but this event is told in terms of God's judgment rather than any initiative by a roving lion. A young lion attacked Samson but was speedily dealt with (Judg 14:5–6), and David also killed a lion (1 Sam 17:34–37), both

The lion, "mighty among beasts, who retreats before nothing" (Prov 30:30), symbolizes the unvanquished hero. Shown here is a lion orthostat found at Hazor (1500–1200 B.C.). Courtesy Dvir, Tel-Aviv.

"The lion has roared—who will not fear?" (Amos 3:8). Pottery figurine from the Judean hills of a roaring lion, bearing a strong resemblance to the lion depicted on the Hebrew seal of "Shema servant of Jeroboam," from Megiddo. Late Israelite (Iron) period. Courtesy Reuben and Edith Hecht Museum, University of Haifa. Photo Zev Radovan.

triumphs being ascribed to God's protection.

The power, speed, and ferocity of the lion were compared to those of Israel's foes; and throughout Scripture the lion is used as a symbol of might. Jacob compared his son Judah to a lion (Gen 49:9), and the Lord Jesus Christ is often called the Lion of the Tribe of Judah (or the Lion of Judah). Daniel described Babylon as a winged lion—a religious symbol used in the ancient pagan world—while Peter warned his contemporaries that the devil prowls around like a roaring lion (1 Peter 5:8).

Lioness. Ezekiel's lament on the princes of Israel refers to the lioness as their mother (Ezek 19:2), whose cubs might be scattered (Job 4:11). Joel's prophecy (Joel 1:6) speaks of the fangs of the lioness as a characteristic of an invading nation.

Livestock. See Cattle.

Lizard. A reptile of the suborder *Lacertila,* with four legs usually, but some species—like the slow-worm—have none. With scaly skin and long body and tail, the lizard may be small or comparatively large. The species includes the iguana, monitor, and gecko. Leviticus 11:29–30 classifies as unclean any kind of great lizard, the gecko, monitor lizard, wall lizard, skink, and chameleon. The most common lizard in Palestine was the *Agama stellio,* part of a family of dragon lizards. These reptiles are active during the daylight hours, possess crests and dewlaps, and somewhat resemble the iguanids.

The chameleon (Lev 11:30) is any member of the *Chamaeleontidae* family of reptiles, resembling lizards, but having the interesting characteristic of controlling its color to match its environment. This reptile catches insects by its tongue. Its eyes are able to operate independently of each other.

The crocodile (Lev 11:30 NASB, RSV) is rendered by the NIV as "monitor lizard." The gecko (11:30) is a harmless lizard, a member of the *Gekkonidae* family, found in tropical or subtropical regions. Some geckos are able to move readily on a vertical wall or other smooth surface, using a natural adhesive pad on their feet. Their diet consists of insects. An interesting feature is the gecko's ability to grow a new tail when its old one is broken off by a predator or overinquisitive human being.

The great lizard (Lev 11:29), another unclean animal, is possibly the Arabian thorny-tailed, color-changing lizard (*Uromastix spinipes*) common in Egypt and also found in Syria and Arabia. The monitor lizard (11:30) is a member of the *Varanidae* family of large carnivorous lizards and is found in Africa, Asia, and Australia, its largest species being the Komodo Dragon. It is recognized additionally by its elongated snout, long neck, and forked tongue. The Nile monitor, *Varanus niloticus,* is the largest four-footed reptile in Africa, with the exception of the crocodile, and may attain a length of six feet (almost two m.).

A reptile called the sand lizard (Lev 11:30 RSV), *Lacerta agilis,* is found in sandy regions in central and western Europe. The same verse in the NIV lists the skink, some six hundred species of which represent the largest family of lizards. Snakelike and found most often in desert regions, their features include a scaly tongue and elongated body, with limbs either of small size or absent altogether. The skink mentioned in Leviticus 11:30 was the common skink *(Scincus scincus)* of Africa.

In Leviticus 11:29, KJV has "tortoise" where RSV and NIV have "great lizard." In the next verse the wall lizard is included in the list of unclean reptiles, but its precise species is uncertain. Small lizards or reptiles living close to human habitation would be commonly found on walls.

Locust. See Grasshopper, Locust, Cricket.

The chameleon of Palestine. It lives in the more wooded areas and can make itself inconspicuous by changing the color of its skin to yellow, green, and black. It is listed among the unclean animals (Lev 11:30). Courtesy Seffie Ben-Yoseph.

Maggot. See Fly.
Mole. See Rodent.
Monitor Lizard. See Lizard.
Monster. The word formerly meant little more than "large" or "extensive." Job's debate speaks of the monster of the deep (Job 7:14), as does Psalm 74:13. Notwithstanding the traditional Israelite awe of the sea, the references suggest great wonders of creation rather than any frightening or aggressive beast. Genesis 1:21 alludes to the "great creatures of the sea" (NIV), which KJV translates as "great whales." The KJV of Lamentations 4:3 has "sea monsters," NEB has "whales," and ASV, NIV, and RSV translate this word as "jackals."

Moth, Butterfly. Both belong to the order *Lepidoptera,* the moth being distinguished from the butterfly by its nocturnal activity, its thread-like antenna, and wings that wrap around its body (most butterflies fold their wings vertically). Butterflies have two pairs of wings, and most have eye-catching color displays, using their proboscis to suck nectar. America has more than nine thousand species of moths and butterflies. Throughout the world some species have either disappeared or seem to be on the verge of extinction. To counter this problem, at least in part, new work in butterfly farming is occurring.

The moth of Scripture is usually the clothes moth of the large family, *Tineidae.* The frailty of man is like that of the moth (Job 4:19), a sentiment echoed in Job 13:28, where man's own wasting away is likened to that of a garment eaten by moths (or moth larvae). Psalm 39:11 and Isaiah 50:9; 51:8 offer similar reflections. Man's habitation is akin to that of a moth's cocoon (Job 27:18).

Insignificant and fragile though it is (Hos 5:12), the clothes moth is no less able to destroy those transient possessions that people set their hearts on (Matt 6:19). It lays its eggs at night on wool, fur, feathers, or other materials; when the larvae hatch about ten days later, they immediately start eating the host material.

Silkworms, larvae of the Chinese silkworm moth (*Bombyx mori*), produce the natural fiber of silk garments known to the ancients and worn by the most wealthy. Silk is included among the cargoes of merchants that in the apocalyptic vision of Revelation 18:12 no one buys any more. Raw silk is derived from the cocoon of larvae that pupate in thick oval, white or yellow silken cocoons. As larvae are easily reared on a commercial basis—if one has the appropriate skills and resources—silk has been a source of wealth to many traders over the centuries. Even in our age of modern fibers, silk remains a symbol of luxury and status.

A Lepidopterous larva was probably the "worm" that chewed the vine under which Jonah sat (Jonah 4:7), since such larvae have voracious appetites. Most references to "worm" in Scripture refer to the larvae of flies, generally known as "maggots" (see Fly).

The caterpillar, larva of a butterfly or moth, is a word not found in NIV. It is variously translated as "young locust" (Isa 33:4), "grasshopper" (Ps 78:46; 105:34), and "locusts" (Amos 4:9).

Mouse. See Rat.
Mule. See Donkey.
Ox. See Cattle.
Palmerworm. See Grasshopper, Locust, Cricket.
Peacock. See Baboon.
Pig. The pig is stated to be an unclean animal (Lev 11:7; Deut 14:8), yet it seems to have been present in considerable numbers in Palestine. Destruction of a large herd occurred when evil spirits entered them following Jesus' healing of a demon—possessed man (Mark 5:1–17; Luke 8:27–39). The parable of the prodigal son demonstrated the desperate plight of the young man, becoming a pig-feeder (Luke 15:15), employment degrading to any self-respecting Israelite.

Jesus advised against throwing pearls before pigs (Matt 7:6), as they are likely to be trampled underfoot by the undiscerning creatures. Solomon compared a beautiful woman devoid of discretion with a gold ring in a pig's snout (Prov 11:22). Peter speaks of a washed sow returning to wallow in the mud (2 Peter 2:22).

The domestic pig, member of the *Suidae* family of hoofed animals, was probably developed from the wild boar of the Orient, with widespread domestication for food and other uses.

The sole reference to "boar" is in Psalm 80:13, where the ravaging actions of wild boars are indicated. With its enlarged canine tusk, the wild boar could cause damage to property or crops and inflict wounds on the unsuspecting.

Where NASB and NIV translate Hebrew and Greek as "pig," KJV and RSV use "swine," the name given to members of the *Suidae* family, especially the domestic variety. In Isaiah's rebuke (Isa 65:4) of the people for eating the flesh of pigs, the latter phrase is "swine's flesh" in KJV and RSV.

Pygarg. See Gazelle.
Rabbit. The rabbit was classified as unclean (Lev 11:6; Deut 14:7) because it did not have a split hoof. KJV and RSV have the word "hare," because some think rabbits did not exist in Palestine at the time of the Pentateuch's composition. However, at least two species of hare were thought to be present, both members of the order *Lagomorpha,* though the hare was originally classified as a rodent. Rabbits live in burrows and are born hairless and blind. Hares do not use burrows and are born with a coat of hair and with effective vision. The hare also has longer ears and hind legs. Like the rabbit, it is found extensively in Europe.

Ram. See Sheep.
Rat. Rats, like mice—to which they are related—followed man's exploitation and habitation of previously inhabited areas. Rats are mentioned in the list of unclean animals in Leviticus 11:29 (KJV, RSV, "mouse"), and in the narrative of the plague on the Philistines (1 Sam 6 KJV, RSV, "mice"). Isaiah prophesied against those who had followed heathen practices of eating pig's flesh

and rats (Isa 66:17); RSV, KJV translate the latter word in Isaiah 66 as "mice," and "mouse," respectively, one of the many long-tailed rodents of the *Muridae* family.

Red Heifer. See Cattle.

Reptile. See Snake.

Rock Badger. See Badger.

Rodent. In Isaiah 2:20 NIV has "rodents," where KJV, RSV, and NASB have "moles." Isaiah is prophesying that in the Day of the Lord men will throw their idols of silver and gold away to the lowly rodents. KJV and NASB have "mole" also in Leviticus 11:30 (NIV "chameleon"). Isaiah's reference was probably to the mole rat found in SE Europe, rather than to the mole as known in Britain and the USA.

Roe. See Gazelle.

Roe Deer. See Gazelle.

Sand Lizard. See Lizard.

Sand Reptile. See Lizard.

Scorpion. Found in the vast, thirsty land of the wilderness journey, the scorpion (Deut 8:15) is notorious for its venomous sting delivered from its long, segmented tail. Rehoboam unwisely threatened to scourge the people with scorpions (1 Kings 12:11, 14). Followers of Jesus were given authority to tread on scorpions (Luke 10:19), an authority related to the work of the kingdom of God. In Luke 11:12 Jesus mentions the scorpion in a rhetorical question.

"Which of you fathers, if your son asks for . . . an egg, would give him a scorpion?" asks Jesus (Luke 11:11–12). Known for their ability to sting, scorpions have always been surrounded by an aura of horror and mystery. Courtesy Carta, Jerusalem.

The name scorpion applies to any of the order *Scorpionidae* of arachnids of tropical or hot regions. Large pincers at the front of the body, as well as the curving, sting-laden tail, give the scorpion a distinctive and formidable appearance.

Sea Cow. See Badger.

Serpent. See Snake.

Sheep. This animal is the most often mentioned in Scripture, perhaps because of its importance in the economy of the age. The most familiar picture of Jesus Christ is probably that of the Good Shepherd, the most easily recalled parable that of the lost sheep.

A ruminant mammal of the *Ovidae* family, sheep come in many breeds today, some with special advantages for their wool, others for meat. For centuries sheep have been largely domesticated. In Bible lands sheep were kept for their milk more than for their meat. Religious ceremonies included the sacrifice of sheep, and rams' horns were used to summon the congregation.

"With curds and milk from herd and flock and with fattened lambs and goats. . ." (Deut 32:14). Courtesy Seffie Ben-Yoseph.

Job's wealth consisted of flocks and herds, including seven thousand sheep (Job 1:3), which were all destroyed by a divinely permitted catastrophe (1:16). The life of shepherds and their flocks is reported in several places (Gen 29; Exod 22:1, 4; Num 31:36). Sheep were watered at midday, and the well became an important meeting place. Need for water and at least reasonable pasture shaped the shepherd's way of life. His care for his sheep is reflected in Psalm 23. The Bible often refers to bad or good shepherds in terms of their care not merely of sheep but also of their fellow human beings in the eyes of God. Women also served as shepherds, as in the case of seven daughters of the priest of Midian (Exod 2:16).

Several Hebrew words are translated "ewe," i.e., a female sheep. Seven ewe lambs were presented by Abraham to Abimelech (Gen 21:28, 29) to seal the treaty made at Beersheba. Jacob's gift to Esau included two hundred ewes and twenty rams (32:14). Use of a female lamb without defect was permitted as a sin offering (Lev 4:32). Nathan's parable (2 Sam 12:3) referred to a man whose "one ewe lamb" was taken from him by a rich and greedy man.

The list of unclean foods in Deuteronomy 14:5 includes "mountain sheep," KJV "chamois," a ruminant mammal halfway between a goat and an antelope, found usually in mountainous regions of Europe and SW Asia.

The ram, the horned male sheep, was used in breeding. Although most biblical references are to the ram's role in priestly ceremony or sacrifice (Gen 15:9; Exod 29; Num 7), the skipping action of the ram is poetically portrayed by the psalmist (Ps 114).

Skink. See Lizard.

Slug, Snail. The slug is herbivorous and often

creates considerable damage to plant life. Like the snail the slug is a gastropod mollusc, moving on a muscular foot with a natural form of lubrication that appears as a trail of slime. The snail has a spiral protective shell and exists in varying species in salt water, fresh water, and on land. The most common species is that of the garden snail (*Helix aspera*), to be distinguished from the edible variety (*Helix pomatia*). The action of the slug (KJV, RSV, NASB "snail") is described in Psalm 58:8. The list of prohibited food in Leviticus 11:30 includes the snail (KJV).

Snake. Member of the suborder *Ophidia* of limbless, elongated reptiles, with scaly skin, a forked tongue, and a mouth that opens sufficiently wide to swallow prey, e.g., rodents, or eggs. Poisonous snakes carry venom in their salivary glands, delivered through the fangs and acting either on the central nervous system to paralyze or on cells to cause hemorrhages. The snake has special significance in the OT. One of the signs of authority given to Moses was that of his staff turning into a snake when thrown to the ground (Exod 3:3–4). Venomous snakes invaded the Israelite camp when the people complained about God and Moses. They were healed when they looked at an emblem of a snake cast in bronze by Moses (Num 21). The symbol of the snake on the staff is today an emblem of healing used by the medical profession.

Serpents decorating a pottery stand (c. 60 cm. high), a cult object found in a Canaanite temple at Beth Shan (eleventh century B.C.). Courtesy Israel Department of Antiquities and Museums.

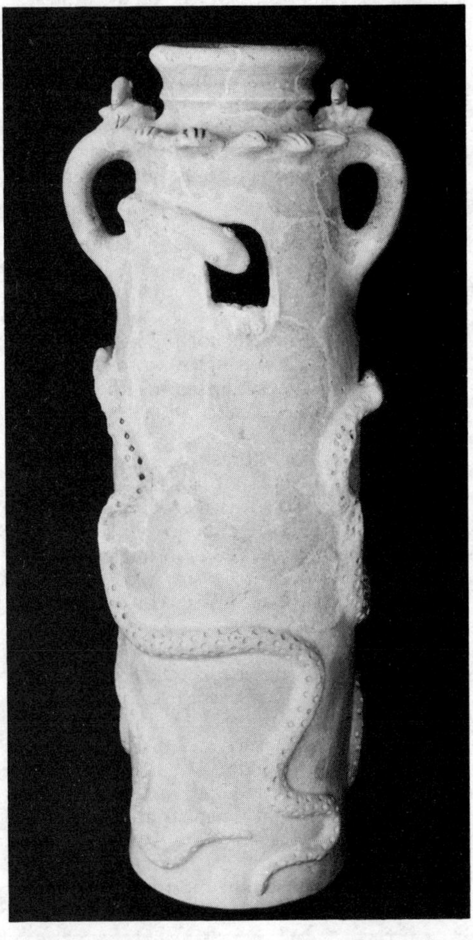

Translations of various poisonous snakes differ. Jeremiah 8:17 speaks of "vipers that cannot be charmed" as one of God's judgments—an allusion perhaps to the so-called charming of snakes that are actually not "charmed" but controlled more subtly by their masters. Job 20:16 refers to the destruction of the wicked by the fangs of the adder, just as Isaiah 59:5 anticipates the infliction of vipers on the wicked. In modern language the viper and adder are the same species, but the scriptural reference is probably to the northern viper, *Vipera berus,* found also in Africa.

Psalm 91:13 assures the godly that they will tread on the cobra and the serpent without any harm, through divine protection. The cobra was doubtless the Egyptian cobra, used throughout Egypt as a religious symbol and attaining a length of at least 8½ feet (2½ m.). It is found along the coast of north and east Africa, with a subspecies occurring in the Arabian peninsula.

In the millennial age the cobra and the viper will be the harmless companions of children (Isa 11:8)—further confirmation of the reconciliation of man with the natural order following the creation's renewal. Isaiah, then, does not anticipate a banishing of such reptiles but their transformation. His prophecy against the Philistines (14:29) involves a viper. The use of the word "asp" in some translations denotes a poisonous reptile, i.e., the Egyptian cobra.

Where "cockatrice" is used in some translations (RSV, NASB, and NIV refer more specifically to adder, viper, or cobra), the word was associated with a poisonous reptile generally, rather than with specific species (Isa 11:8; 14:29; 59:5; Jer 8:17).

Solomon's wisdom led him to teach about reptiles, as well as mammals, birds, and fish (1 Kings 4:33). Peter's remarkable vision included reptiles to be eaten, confirming that nothing God had made could now be called unclean (Acts 10:12; 11:6), symbolizing the now-clean Gentiles in the new covenant.

Man could tame a serpent, observed James (3:7 KJV), but could not control his own tongue.

No single species is identified in the word "serpent," but the meaning is that of a crafty and very dangerous creature, albeit a persuasive one. It was a symbol of evil (Gen 3), but God was able to pierce it (Job 26:13). Paul referred to the cunning of the serpent (2 Cor 11:3). KJV prefers the word "serpent" to "snake."

Spider. Member of the order *Araneida* of arachnids, many species of which are armed with poison glands for killing prey. The black widow spider and the Australian funnel-web spider are especially dangerous to man, unlike most species. The spider's abdomen has two or more pairs of

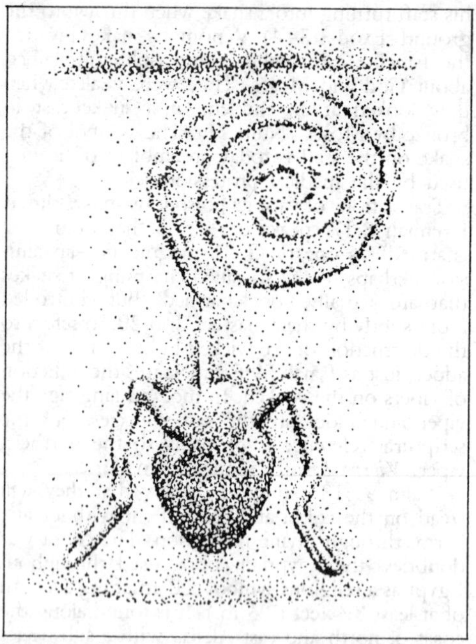

Drawing of a spider pictured on a cylinder seal from Ur, c. 3000 B.C. As always, it is the web constructed from a fluid in the spider's body that fascinates people. Courtesy Carta, Jerusalem.

spinnerets that produce the silk thread for webs and cocoons. One who forgets God has hope as fragile as a spider's web (Job 8:14) and finds his own fabrications useless (Isa 59:5). Proverbs 30:28 refers to the presence of spiders in kings' palaces, though NIV here has the word "lizard" rather than "spider."

Sponge. Known scientifically as *Porifera,* the sponge is a class of the sessile aquatic animal family. A sponge filled with wine vinegar was offered to Jesus on the cross (Matt 27:48; Mark 15:36). John notes that a stalk of the hyssop plant was used to lift the sponge to the Lord's lips (John 19:29). Such use of a sponge to provide liquid refreshment was common in biblical times. The sponge would absorb the wine or water in a vessel, then was usually squeezed into the upturned mouth of the user.

Stag. See Deer.

Stallion. See Horse.

Steed. See Horse.

Steer. See Cattle.

Swarming Thing. Creatures that swarmed over the earth were among every living thing that perished during the Flood (Gen 7:21). Prohibition on swarming things as food is stated in Leviticus 11:10, the description applying, for example, to swarms of flies or plagues of locusts.

Swine. See Pig.

Tortoise. See Lizard.

Unicorn. See Cattle.

Viper. See Snake.

Weasel. Classed as unclean (Lev 11:29), the weasel is a small, carnivorous mammal, genus *Mustela,* resembling a small ermine. Its diet consists of small rodents and its distribution is apparently world-wide.

Well Lizard. See Lizard.

Whale. KJV translates as "whale" those words rendered by NIV as "great creatures" (Gen 1:21), "monster of the deep" (Job 7:12), and "monster in the seas" (Ezek 32:2). In KJV, RSV, and NIV the "great fish" describes the animal that swallowed Jonah (Jonah 1:17); KJV and RSV mention "whale" in Matthew 12:40, where NIV keeps to "huge fish."

The whale, a large marine fishlike mammal (order *Cetacea*), is one of nature's most amazing wonders. One group includes the toothed whales, another the whalebone or buleen whales in which teeth are not present, using instead thin, parallel whalebone plates to extract plankton from sea water. Toothed whales include porpoises, dolphins, and sperm whales. Whalebone whales include the blue whale, largest of all mammals.

Wolf. A carnivorous, intelligent mammal, genus *Canis,* the wolf usually hunts in packs and will readily attack more powerful animals. The North American timber or grey wolf is a subspecies of the European *Canis lupus*. The behavior of this animal has fascinated many writers. Mentioned thirteen times in Scripture, the wolf would have been a familiar threat to shepherds, especially in Palestine with its forest terrain. False prophets were described as "ferocious wolves" in sheep's clothing (Matt 7:15), while Genesis 49:27 declares the tribe of Benjamin to be like the ravenous wolf. Isaiah's anticipation of the Millennium includes the wolf living with the lamb (Isa 11:6; 65:25).

Worm. See Fly.

Yearling. See Cattle.

ANISE (See PLANTS)

ANKLET. An ornament for the ankles, consisting of metal or glass spangles, worn by women. Sometimes anklets were linked together by ankle chains (Isa 3:20). See also DRESS.

ANNA (ăn'ȧ, Gr. form of *Hannah, grace*). Daughter of Phanuel of the tribe of Asher. Widowed after seven years of marriage, she became a prophetess. At the age of eighty-four, when the infant Jesus was brought into the temple to be dedicated, she recognized and proclaimed him as the Messiah (Luke 2:36–38).

ANNAS (ăn'ȧs, Gr. for Hanan, contraction for Hananiah, *merciful, gracious;* called "Ananos" by Josephus). In his thirty-seventh year (c. A.D. 6), he was appointed high priest by Quirinius, governor of Syria. He was deposed c. A.D. 15 by Valerius Gratus, governor of Judea. His five sons became high priests, and he was father-in-law of Caiaphas (John 18:13). He and Caiaphas are described as the high priests when John the Baptist began his public ministry (Luke 3:2), perhaps because as family head Annas was the most influential priest and still bore the title. Therefore when Jesus was arrested, he was led first to Annas (John 18:13), and only later was sent bound to Caiaphas (18:24). Similarly, Annas is called the high priest in Acts 4:6 when Peter and John were arrested, although Caiaphas was probably the actual high priest.

ANNUNCIATION (from Lat. *annuntiatio, an announcement*). The word itself is not found in Scripture but is the name given to the announcement made by the angel Gabriel to Mary that she would conceive and give birth to a son to be called Jesus (Luke 1:26–38). Mary, a virgin, was betrothed but not yet married to Joseph. They lived in Nazareth, a town of Galilee. In his message Gabriel assured the frightened Mary that she was highly favored and that the Lord was with her. The young lady was overcome with surprise and fear, not only by the presence of the angel, but also by his message. Gabriel, however, assured her that she had no need to fear. God had chosen her to be the mother of a unique boy: "He will be great and will be called the Son of the Most High" (1:32). Her son would be God's Son, and, like David, he would reign over the people of God; yet, unlike David's kingdom, his would be an everlasting kingdom. When Mary asked how this could occur since she was not yet married, Gabriel explained that she would conceive through the direct agency of the Holy Spirit. Like her relative Elizabeth (who had conceived in her old age and was carrying John the Baptist), she would know the power of God in her life. Overwhelmed by this amazing message, Mary submitted to the will of the Lord, and the angel left her.

The word is used also of the festival held on March 25 (nine months before Chrismas Day) to celebrate the visit of Gabriel to the Virgin Mary. PT

ANOINT. To apply oil to a person or thing, a practice common in the East. Anointing was of three kinds: ordinary, sacred, and medical. Ordinary anointing with scented oils was a common operation (Ruth 3:3; Ps 104:15; Prov 27:9). It was discontinued during a time of mourning (2 Sam 14:2; Dan 10:3; Matt 6:17). Guests were anointed as a mark of respect (Ps 23:5; Luke 7:46). The dead were prepared for burial by anointing (Mark 14:8; 16:1). The leather of shields was rubbed with oil to keep it from cracking (Isa 21:5), but this could be called also a sacred anointing—i.e., consecration to the war in the name of whatever god was invoked to bless the battle.

The purpose of sacred anointing was to dedicate the thing or person to God. Jacob anointed the stone he had used for a pillow at Bethel (Gen 28:18). The tabernacle and its furniture were anointed (Exod 30:22–29). Prophets (1 Kings 19:16; 1 Chron 16:22), priests (Exod 28:41; 29:7; Lev 8:12, 30), and kings (Saul—1 Sam 9:16; 10:1; David—1 Sam 16:1, 12–13; 2 Sam 2:7; Solomon—1 Kings 1:34; Jehu—1 Kings 19:16) were anointed, the oil symbolizing the Holy Spirit. They were thus set apart and empowered for a particular work in the service of God. "The Lord's anointed" was the common term for a theocratic king (1 Sam 12:3; Lam 4:20).

Wall painting from tomb of Sebekhotep, Thebes (c. 1421–1413 B.C.) depicting a Syrian envoy carrying an anointing horn, to which has been added a neck and head surmounted by a hand in the form of a spoon. The ointment is apparently passed from the head into the spoon when the flask is turned upside down. Reproduced by courtesy of the Trustees of the British Museum.

Messiah, from the Hebrew word *mashach,* and Christ, from the Greek *chrein,* mean "the anointed one." The word is twice used of the coming Redeemer in the OT (Ps 2:2; Dan 9:25–26). Jesus was anointed with the Holy Spirit at his baptism (John 1:32–33), marking him as the Messiah of the OT (Luke 4:18, 21; Acts 9:22; 17:2–3; 18:5, 28). His disciples, through union with him, are anointed with the Holy Spirit too (2 Cor 1:21; 1 John 2:20).

Medical anointing, not necessarily with oil, was customary for the sick and wounded (Isa 1:6; Luke 10:34). Mark 6:13 and James 5:14 speak of the use of anointing oil by disciples of Jesus. SB

ANT (See ANIMALS)

ANTELOPE (See ANIMALS)

ANTHOTHIJAH (ăn′thō-thī′jà) Heb., *'anthōthîyâh*). A son of Shashak, a Benjamite (1 Chron 8:24–25).

ANTICHRIST (Gr. *antichristos, against* or *instead of Christ*). The word *antichrist* may mean either an enemy of Christ or one who usurps Christ's name and rights. The word is found in only four verses of Scripture (1 John 2:18, 22; 4:3; 2 John 7), but the idea conveyed by the word appears throughout Scripture. It is evident from the way John and Paul refer to the Antichrist that they took for granted a tradition well known at the time (2 Thess 2:6, "you know"; 1 John 4:3, "you have heard").

The OT gives evidence of a belief in a hostile person or power who in the end time will bring an attack against God's people—an attack that will be crushed by the Lord or his Messiah. Psalm 2 gives a picture of the rebellion of the world kingdoms "against the LORD and against his Anointed One." The same sort of contest is described in Ezekiel 38–39 and in Zechariah 12–14. In the Book of Daniel there are vivid descriptions of the Antichrist that find their echo in the writings of the apostles (cf. 2 Thess 2:4 with Dan 11:36–37; and cf. Rev 13:1–8 with Dan 7:8, 20–21; 8:24; 11:28, 30).

In his eschatological discourse Christ warns against the "false Christs" and the "false prophets" who would lead astray, if possible, even the elect (Matt 24:24; Mark 13:22). In Matthew 24:15 he refers to "the abomination that causes desolation" spoken of by Daniel.

In 2 Thessalonians 2:1–12 Paul gives us a very full description of the working of Antichrist, under the name of "the man of lawlessness," in which he draws on the language and imagery of the OT. The Thessalonian Christians seem to have been under the erroneous impression that the "day of the Lord" was at hand, and Paul told them that before that day could come two things would have to take place: an apostasy and the revelation of the man of lawlessness, the son of perdition. The "secret power of lawlessness" (2:7) is already at work, he said, but is held in check by some restraining person or power. With the removal of this restraining force, the man of lawlessness is revealed. He will oppose and exalt himself above God and will actually sit in the temple of God and claim to be God. With satanic power he will perform signs and deceitful wonders, bringing great deception to people who reject God's truth. In spite of his extraordinary power, however, "the Lord Jesus will overthrow [him] with the breath of his mouth" (2:8).

In 1 John 2:18 John shows that the coming of the Antichrist was an event generally expected by the church. It is apparent, however, that he is more concerned about directing the attention of Christians to anti-Christian forces already at work ("even now many antichrists have come"). He says that teachers of erroneous views of the person of Christ (evidently Gnostic and Ebionite) are antichrists (1 John 2:22; 4:3; 2 John 7).

In the Book of Revelation, the beast of Revelation 17:8 recalls the horned beast of Daniel 7–8. He claims and is accorded divine homage and makes war on God's people. For a period of three and one-half years he rules over the earth and is finally destroyed by the Lord in a great battle. With his defeat the contest of good and evil comes to its final decision.

Bibliography: W. Bousset, *The Antichrist Legend,* 1896; G. Vos, *The Pauline Eschatology,* 1961, pp. 94–135; G. C. Berkouwer, *The Return of Christ,* 1972, pp. 260–90. SB

ANTI-LEBANON (See LEBANON)

ANTINOMIANISM (ăn'tī-nō'mĭ-ăn-ĭsm Gr. *anti, against; nomos, law*). The view that the oral law does not apply to Christians, who are under the law of grace. Because salvation does not come through works but through grace, it is held, moral effort can be discounted. Paul found that this kind of heresy had crept into the church (1 Cor 5–6). Others had chosen to misrepresent his own teaching on grace (Rom 3:8), and he pointed out the absurdity of the charge (6:1, 15). From the first century to our own day, some individuals or groups have sought to combine the spiritual life with moral license, but Scripture leaves no doubt that the new life in Christ means death to the old evil desires (Gal 5:24). JDD

ANTIOCH (ăn'tĭ-ŏk, Gr. *Antiocheia*). 1. Antioch in Syria, the capital of Syria, built in 301 B.C. by Seleucus Nicator, founder of the Seleucid Empire, which had been the Asiatic part of the vast empire of Alexander the Great. It was the greatest of sixteen Antiochs he founded in honor of his father Antiochus. It was a great commercial center. Caravan roads converged on it from the east, and its situation on the Orontes River, fifteen navigable miles (twenty-five km.) from the Mediterranean, made it readily available to ships as well. The city was set in a broad and fertile valley, shielded by majestic snow-covered mountains, and was called "Antioch the Beautiful and the Golden." In 65 the Romans took the city and made it the capital of the Roman province of Syria. Seleucid kings and early Roman emperors extended and adorned the city until it became the third largest in the Roman Empire (after Rome and Alexandria), with a population in the first century A.D. of about 500,000. A cosmopolitan city from its foundation, its inhabitants included many Jews, who were given privileges similar to those of the Greeks. Its citizens were a vigorous and aggressive race, famous for their commercial aptitude, their licentiousness, and their biting wit.

Antioch has an important place in the early history of Christianity. One of the original deacons of the apostolic church was Nicolas, a proselyte of Antioch (Acts 6:5). The first Gentile church, the mother of all the others, was founded there. Many fugitive Christians, scattered at the death of Stephen, went to Antioch and inaugurated a new era by preaching not only to the Hellenist Jews but to "Greeks also" (11:20). The Jerusalem church sent Barnabas to assist in the work; after laboring there for a while Barnabas summoned Paul from Tarsus to assist him. After they had worked there for a year, they were sent with relief to the famine-stricken saints in Jerusa-

Antioch on the Orontes River in Syria, looking west from Mount Silpius. Courtesy Ecole Biblique et Archéologique Française, Jerusalem.

lem. The disciples were called Christians first in Antioch (11:19–26), a designation probably coming from the populace, who were well known for their invention of nicknames. The church at Antioch sent Paul and his companions out on his three missionary journeys (13:1ff.; 15:36ff.; 18:23), and he reported to it on his return from the first two (14:26ff.; 18:22). It submitted the question of the circumcision of Gentile converts to a council at Jerusalem (Acts 15), winning for the church at large a great victory over Judean narrowness.

Antioch gave rise to a school of thought distinguished by literal interpretation of the Scriptures. Between A.D. 252 and 380, ten church councils were held there. The city was taken and destroyed in 538 by the Persians, rebuilt by the Roman emperor Justinian shortly afterward, and in 635 was taken by the Muslims, by whom it has since, except for a brief period, been retained. The place, now called Antakiyeh, is unimportant today, with a population of about 42,000.

In 1916 an announcement was made that Arabs in or near Antioch had found what has come to be known as "The Chalice of Antioch." It is a plain silver cup surrounded by an outer shell decorated with vines and the figures of Christ and the apostles and is set on a solid silver base. The cup was vigorously claimed to be the Holy Grail, used by Jesus at the Last Supper, the figures on the shell interpreted as first-century portraits. But the authenticity of the chalice has been called into question. Serious scholars have virtually proved that at most the cup is a piece of early Christian silver from the fourth or fifth century and had nothing to do with the Last Supper in Jerusalem.

2. Antioch near Pisidia, a town in southern Asia Minor, founded by Seleucus Nicator, and named in honor of his father Antiochus. It was situated in Phrygia, not far from Pisidia, and was therefore called Antioch toward Pisidia and Pisidian Antioch to distinguish it from the other cities of the same name. In 25 B.C. it became a part of the Roman province of Galatia. Soon after, it was made the capital of southern Galatia, and a Roman colony. The Romans made it a strong garrison center to hold down the surrounding wild tribes. Paul and Barnabas preached in the synagogue there on their first missionary journey; but the Jews, jealous of the many Gentile converts that were made, drove the missionaries from the city to Iconium and followed them even to Lystra (Acts 13:14–14:19). On Paul's return journey he revisited Antioch to establish the disciples and probably returned on his second (16:6) and third journeys as well (18:23). SB

ANTIOCHUS (ăn-tī'ŏ-kŭs, Gr. *withstander*). 1. Antiochus III, the Great (223–187 B.C.), king of Syria and sixth ruler of the Seleucid dynasty. By his victory over the Egyptians in 198 Syria gained control of Palestine. He was decisively defeated by the Romans in 190 and thereby lost control over Asia Minor. He was murdered by a mob while plundering a temple.

2. Antiochus IV (Epiphanes), son of Antiochus III and eighth ruler of the Seleucid Dynasty, 175–163 B.C. (1 Macc 1:10; 6:16). In his attempt to Hellenize the Jews he had a pig sacrified on the altar in Jerusalem, forbade circumcision, and destroyed all the OT books he could find. These outrages involved him in the Maccabean war in

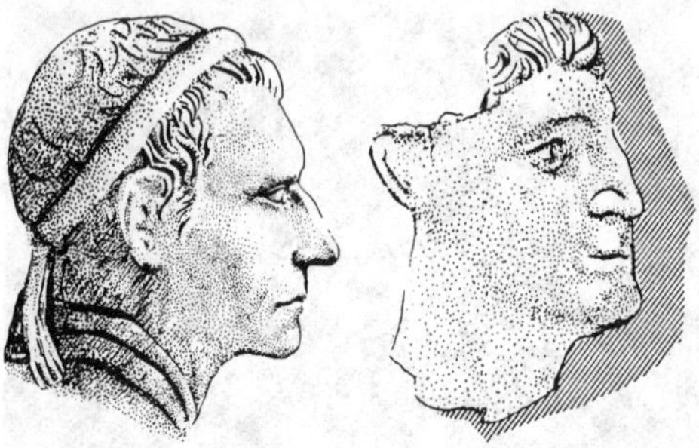

Drawing of Antiochus III (left) from a coin, and his son and successor, Antiochus IV, drawn from a bronze mask found at Susa. Courtesy Carta, Jerusalem.

which the Syrian armies were repeatedly defeated by the brilliant Judas Maccabeus.

3. Antiochus V (Eupator), son of no. 2. He reigned as a minor for two years and then was assassinated.

ANTIPAS (ăn'-tĭ-pȧs, Gr. *Antipas*). A contraction of Antipater. 1. An early Christian martyr of Pergamum, described as "my faithful witness" (Rev 2:13).

2. Herod Antipas, son of Herod the Great and brother of Philip the Tetrarch and of Archelaus, both of whom, like him, were rulers of parts of Palestine. See HEROD.

ANTIPATER (See HEROD)

ANTIPATRIS (ăn-tĭp'ȧ-trĭs, Gr. *antipatris, belonging to Antipater*). A city built (or rebuilt) by Herod the Great and named after his father Antipater. It lay on the road between Jerusalem and Caesarea. There is only one reference to it in Scripture, when Paul was taken following his arrest in Jerusalem from that city to Caesarea (Acts 23:31). It marked the NW limit of Judea.

"So the soldiers took Paul with them . . . and brought him as far as Antipatris" (Acts 23:31), a city on the way to Caesarea. This aerial view of Antipatris shows the remains of a crusader fortress. Courtesy Israel Government Press Office.

ANTONIA, TOWER OF. A castle connected with the temple at Jerusalem, rebuilt by Herod the Great and named by him in honor of Mark Antony, his patron. A Roman legion was stationed in the castle to guard against excesses on the part of the people. When Paul was seized in the temple by the Jews, he was carried to this castle, from the stairs of which he addressed the people (Acts 21:30ff.; see "the barrack" in 21:34).

Reconstruction of the Tower of Antonia at the northwest corner of the temple area. Many scholars believe this is the place where Christ was tried before Pilate. Paul was imprisoned here (Acts 21:31–22:24). Courtesy Zev Radovan.

ANUB (ā'nŭb, Heb. *'ānûv*). A son of Coz, descendant of Judah (1 Chron 4:8).

ANVIL. The Heb. *pa'am* originally meant "strike," "hit." The word occurs in several senses in the OT, but only once with the meaning "anvil" (Isa 41:7), in a passage concerning the encouragement given by one workman to another.

APE (See ANIMALS)

APELLES (ȧ-pĕl'ēz, Gr. *Apellēs*). An approved Christian at Rome to whom Paul sent a greeting (Rom 16:10).

APHEK (ā'fĕk, Heb. *'ăpēk, strength, fortress*). 1. A city NE of Beirut, identified with Afqa (Josh 13:4).

2. A city in the territory of Asher, never wrested from its Canaanite inhabitants (Josh 19:30; Judg 1:31).

3. A town in the Plain of Sharon (Josh 12:18), probably within twenty-five miles (forty-two km.) of Shiloh (1 Sam 4:1, 12). The Philistines may have encamped here before the first battle with Israel at Ebenezer.

4. A town west of the Jordan in the Plain of Jezreel. The Philistines used it as a base in two important campaigns against Israel (1 Sam 1:4; 29:1). It may also have been the town where a wall fell and killed 27,000 of Ben-Hadad's soldiers (1 Kings 20:26–30), and where, according to prophecy, the Syrians were to be destroyed (2 Kings 13:14–19).

APHEKAH (à-fē′kȧ, Heb. *'ăphēqâh*). A city in the hill country of Judah (Josh 15:53). Its location is unknown.

APHIAH (ȧ-fī′ȧ, Heb. *'ăphîah*). One of Saul's ancestors (1 Sam 9:1).

APHIK (See APHEK)

APHRAH (See BETH OPHRAH)

APHSES (See HAPPIZZEZ)

APOCALYPSE (See APOCALYPTIC LITERATURE)

APOCALYPTIC LITERATURE. A type of Jewish and Christian religious writing that developed between the testaments and had it roots in OT prophecy. The word *apocalyptic,* derived from the Greek word *apokalypsis,* means "revelation" or "unveiling," and is applied to these writings because they contain alleged revelation of the secret purposes of God, the end of the world, and the establishment of God's kingdom on earth. The same Greek word is translated "revelation" in Revelation 1:1.

After the days of the postexilic prophets, God no longer spoke to Israel through the living voice of inspired prophecy. The prophetic forecasts of the coming of God's kingdom and the salvation of Israel had not been fulfilled. Instead of God's kingdom, a succession of evil kingdoms ruled over Israel: Medo-Persia, Greece, and finally Rome. Evil reigned supreme. The hope of God's kingdom grew dim. God no longer offered words of comfort and salvation to his people.

The apocalypses were written to meet this religious need. Following the pattern of canonical Daniel, various unknown authors wrote alleged revelations of God's purposes that explained present evils, comforted Israel in her sufferings and afflictions, and gave fresh assurances that God's kingdom would shortly appear. Many modern critics place Daniel in these times, but there are valid reasons for an earlier date.

The outstanding apocalypses are *1 Enoch* or *Ethiopic Enoch,* a composite book written during the first two centuries B.C. that is notable for its description of the heavenly Son of Man; *Jubilees,* an alleged revelation to Moses of the history of the world from creation to the end, written in the second century B.C.; the *Assumption of Moses,* late first century B.C.; *Fourth Ezra* or *Second Esdras* and the *Apocalypse of Baruch,* both written after the fall of Jerusalem in A.D. 70 and reflecting the tragic fall of God's people; *Second Enoch* or *Slavonic Enoch,* date uncertain. Other writings have been discovered among the Dead Sea Scrolls that have not yet been made available for study.

A number of other writings are usually included in the discussion of apocalyptic literature, although they are not, properly speaking, apocalypses. *The Testaments of the Twelve Patriarchs,* written in the second century B.C., imitating OT predictive prophecy rather than apocalyptic, contain important eschatological materials. The seventeenth and eighteenth *Psalms of Solomon,* first century B.C., portray the hope of the coming of the Lord's Anointed to establish God's kingdom. The *Sibylline Oracles,* which follow the pattern of Greek oracular literature, also contain eschatological passages.

Certain characteristics mark these apocalypses. (1) *Revelation.* They describe alleged revelations of God's purposes given through the media of dreams, visions, or journeys to heaven by which the seer learns the secrets of God's world and the future. (2) *Imitation.* These writings seldom embody any genuine subjective visionary experiences. Their "revelations" have become a literary form imitating the visions of the true prophets in a thinly veiled literary fiction. (3) *Pseudonymity.* These books, although actually written close to NT times, are usually attributed to some OT saint who lived long ago. Pseudonymity was used as a means of validating the message of these authors to their own generation. Since God was no longer speaking through the spirit of prophecy, no man could speak in his own name or directly in the name of the Lord. Instead, the apocalyptists placed their "revelations" in the mouths of OT saints. (4) *Symbolism.* These works employ an elaborate symbolism, similar to that appearing in Daniel, as a means of conveying their predictions of the future. (5) *Pseudo-predictive.* The authors take their stand in the distant past and rewrite history under the guise of prophecy down to their own day when the end of the world and the kingdom of God were expected shortly to come.

There are distinct similarities but even more important differences between canonical and noncanonical apocalypses. The visions of Daniel provide the archetype that the later apocalypses imitate, and the Revelation of John records visions given to the apostle in similar symbolic forms. Both Daniel and the Revelation contain revelations conveyed through symbolism; but they differ from noncanonical apocalypses in that they are genuine experiences rather than imitative literary works, are not pseudonymous, and do not rewrite history under the guise of prophecy.

The importance of these apocalyptic writings is that they reveal first-century Jewish ideas about God, evil, and history, and they disclose Jewish hopes for the future and the coming of God's kingdom. They show us what such terms as the "kingdom of God," "Messiah," and the "Son of Man" meant to first-century Jews to whom our Lord addressed his gospel of the kingdom.

Bibliography: F.C. Burkitt, *Jewish and Christian Apocalypses,* 1914; H. H. Rowley, *The Relevance of Apocalyptic;* D. S. Russell, *The Method and Message of Jewish Apocalyptic,* 1964; L. Morris, *Apocalyptic,* 1973; G. W. E. Nickelsburg, *Jewish Literature Between the Bible and the Mishna,* 1981.

GEL

APOCRYPHA. Interspersed among the canonical books of the OT in the old Latin Vulgate Bible are certain additional books and chapters. It is to these that Protestant usage generally assigns the term "Apocrypha." In English versions the Apocrypha are usually presented as fifteen separate books. (See below for individual treatment of these.)

At the Council of Trent (A.D. 1546) the Roman Catholic church received as canonical all the additional materials in the Vulgate except for 1 and 2 Esdras and the Prayer of Manasseh. That decision was made in contradiction of the best tradition of even the Roman church itself. It was a reaction to the Reformers, who recognized as divinely inspired and as their infallible rule of faith and practice only those books that were in the canon of the Jews (cf. esp., Josephus, *Contra Apionem* 1:8), the canon sanctioned by the Lord Jesus Christ.

1 Esdras: It is called 3 Esdras in post-Trentian editions of the Vulgate, where the canonical Ezra and Nehemiah are called 1 and 2 Esdras ("Esdras" being the Greek form of Ezra). Except for the story of the wisdom contest (3:1–5:6), the contents are a version of the history narrated in 2 Chronicles 35–36:23, Ezra, and Nehemiah 7:73–8:12, embracing the period from Josiah's Passover to Ezra's reformation. Nothing is known of the author (or translator) of the LXX form except that he produced it some time before Josephus, who in his *Antiquities* strangely prefers it to the canonical record.

2 Esdras: The Vulgate designation is 4 Esdras. Some call it Apocalyptic Esdras because the central kernel (chapters 3–14) presents seven revelations allegedly given to Ezra in exile, several in visionary form and of largely eschatological import. To this original composed by an unknown Jew, probably near the end of the first century A.D., and later translated into Greek, Christian authors subsequently added in Greek the chapters 1, 2, 15, and 16. The Jewish original offers its apocalyptic prospects as an answer to the theodicy problem (God's goodness in relation to the evil in the world), acutely posed for Judaism by the fall of Jerusalem in A.D. 70. The Christian addition assigns the casting off of Israel in favor of the Gentiles to Israel's apostasy.

Tobit: This romantic tale with religious didactic purpose was composed at least as early as the second century B.C. It is named after its hero, who is pictured as an eighth-century B.C. Naphtalite carried into exile to Nineveh. His story becomes entwined with that of his kinswoman Sarah, exiled in Ecbatana. The tragedies of both are remedied through the adventures of Tobit's son Tobias, whom Sarah marries, and all under the angel Raphael's supervision. Prayer, fasting, and almsgiving are stressed but unfortunately in a context of autosoterism, i.e., works righteousness.

Judith: Judith, like Tobit, is Jewish historical fiction with a religious moral. It includes elements from two centuries (seventh to fifth B.C.) of Israelite fortunes, not always in their proper historical order or setting. Using Jael-like (Judg 4:14–22) tactics, Judith, a beautiful Jewess, saves besieged "Bethulia" by slaying Holofernes, the enemy commander. Possibly the grotesque anachronisms are intentional; Luther interpreted it as an allegory of Israel's triumphing, under God, over her enemies. The book evidences appreciation of Israel's peculiar theocratic privileges but magnifies a ceremonial piety that would exceed the requirements of Moses. Some think it was composed to inspire zeal during the Maccabean revolt in the second century B.C.

Additions to Esther: The canonical Hebrew text of Esther has 163 verses; the Greek version has 270. The additional material is divided into seven sections and is distributed at the appropriate points throughout the narrative in this way: (1) before 1:1; (2) after 3:13; (3) and (4) after 7:17; (5) after 8:12; (6) after 10:3. Inasmuch as genuine Esther contains explicit references neither to God nor traditional Jewish religious practices other than fasting, it is significant that prayers of Mordecai and Esther and also frequent mention of God are included in the additions. The Greek additions contradict details of canonical Esther and contain other obviously fictional elements. They appeared as an appendix to Esther in the Vulgate and this fusion of disconnected fragments constitutes a "book" in the Apocrypha.

Wisdom of Solomon: The LXX uses this title; the Vulgate, *Liber Sapientiae*. The author, who identifies himself with the figure of Solomon, apparently was an Alexandrian Jew writing in Greek in the first century B.C. or A.D. (some, however, judge the book to be of composite authorship). The influence of Greek philosophy is evidenced by the dependence on *logos* speculations in the treatment of personified Wisdom and by the acceptance of various pagan teachings: the creation of the world out of preexistent matter; the preexistence of souls; the impedimentary character of the body; perhaps too, the doctrine of emanation. In tracing Wisdom's government of history from Adam to Moses, numerous fanciful and false embellishments of the biblical record are intruded.

Ecclesiasticus: This second representative of the wisdom style of literature in the Apocrypha is also called, after its author, The Wisdom of Jesus ben Sira. Written in Hebrew, 180 B.C. or earlier, it was translated into Greek for the Alexandrian Jews by the author's grandson c. 130. Ben Sira, apparently a professional scribe and teacher, patterned his work after the style of Proverbs. In it he expounds the nature of wisdom, applying its counsel to all areas of social and religious life. Though often reflecting sentiments of the canonical books, Ben Sira also echoes the ethical motivations of pagan wisdom literature. Moreover, he contradicts the biblical teaching that salvation is through Christ alone by writing that almsgiving makes atonement for sin.

Baruch: This pseudepigraphic book was evidently written by several authors at different times. The first part, 1:1–3:8, dated by some as early as the third century B.C., was probably written in Hebrew, as was possibly also the remainder, which is of later origin. Composed in a prophetic prose, 1:1–3:8 purports to have been produced by Jeremiah's secretary in Babylonian exile and sent to Jerusalem. It is a confession of national sin (in imitation of Daniel's), petitioning for God's mercy. Actually Baruch went to Egypt with Jeremiah, and there is no evidence that he was ever in Babylonia. From 3:9 the book is poetry. In 3:9–4:4 Israel is recalled to wisdom. In 4:5–5:9 Jerusalem laments her exiled children, but assurances of restoration are offered.

Epistle of Jeremy: In some Greek and Syriac manuscripts this "epistle" is found after Lamentations; in others and in the Vulgate it is attached to Baruch and therefore appears as a sixth chapter of Baruch in most English editions. A superscription describes it as an epistle sent by Jeremiah to certain captives about to be led into Babylon (cf. Jer. 29:1ff.). The true author is unknown and the original language uncertain. A baffling reference to "seven generations" of exile (contrast Jer 29:10) has figured in speculation as to its date, which was no later than the second century B.C. It ridicules the foolishness of idol worship as represented by the worship of the god Bel and so served as a warning to the Jews and as an accusation against Gentiles.

The Prayer of Azariah and the Song of the Three Children: This is one of the three sections (see also Susanna and Bel and the Dragon) added to the canonical Daniel in the "Septuagint" translation (whether in the first edition, i.e., probably by the early second century B.C., or in a later edition is not known) and afterward in Theodotion's Greek version. From the latter Jerome translated the additions into Latin, commenting that they did not exist in manuscripts of the Hebrew-Aramaic original of Daniel.

Between 3:23 and 3:24 of canonical Daniel both Greek and Latin versions insert: (1) a prayer of national confession with supplication for deliverance, which Daniel's friend Azariah (cf. Dan 1:7) offers while he and his two companions are in the fiery furnace; (2) a psalm of praise (dependent on Pss 148 and 136), uttered by the three; and (3) a narrative framework containing details not warranted by the genuine Daniel. This section is itself perhaps of composite authorship and was probably written in Hebrew.

Susanna: In the Vulgate, Susanna follows canonical Daniel as chapter 13; in Greek manuscripts it is prefixed to chapter 1. Two crucial word plays at the climax of the tale suggest it was composed in Greek but there is no consensus. Its origin and date are unknown; Alexandria about 100 B.C. is one theory. The story relates how two Israelite elders in Babylon, their lustful advances having been resisted by Susanna, falsely accuse her of adultery. But young Daniel effects Susanna's deliverance and the elders' doom by ensnaring them in contradictory testimony.

Bel and the Dragon: These fables ridiculing heathenism appear as chapter 13 of Daniel in Greek and as chapter 14 in the Vulgate. They date from the first or second century B.C.; their original language is uncertain. Daniel plays detective to expose to Cyrus the fraud of the priests who clandestinely consumed the food-offerings of Bel (Baal—i.e., Marduk). After destroying Bel, Daniel concocts a recipe that explodes a sacred dragon. Consigned to a den of lions, Daniel is miraculously fed and delivered.

The Prayer of Manasseh: According to 2 Chronicles 33:11ff., when the wicked King Manasseh had been carried into exile, he repented and God restored him to Jerusalem. Verses 18–19 refer to sources that contained Manasseh's prayer of repentance. The origin of the apocryphal book that purports to be that prayer is unknown; possibly it was produced in Palestine a century or two before Christ. It contains confession of sin and petition for forgiveness. The view is expressed that certain sinless men need no repentance. In Greek manuscripts the prayer appears in the Odes attached to the Psalter. In the old Vulgate it came to be placed after 2 Chronicles.

1 Maccabees: Beginning with the accession of Antiochus Epiphanes (176 B.C.), the history of the Jewish struggle for religious-political liberation is traced to the death of Simon (136 B.C.). This apocryphal book is our most valuable historical source for that period. It narrates the exploits of the priest Mattathias and of his sons—Judas, Jonathan, and Simon—who successively led the Hasidim to remarkable victories. Judas was given the surname "Maccabee," afterward applied to his brothers and four books (1–4 Maccabees). The author wrote in Hebrew and was a contemporary of John Hyrcanus, son and successor of Simon. According to one theory, the last three chapters were added and the whole reedited after the destruction of the temple.

2 Maccabees: Independent of 1 Maccabees, this history partly overlaps it, extending from the last year of Seleucus IV (176 B.C.) to the defeat of Nicanor by Judas (161). The author states that he has epitomized the (now lost) five-volume history of Jason of Cyrene (1 Macc 2:23). Both Jason and the Epitomist wrote in Greek. Suggested dates for 2 Maccabees vary from c. 120 B.C. to the early first century A.D. Two introductory letters (1:1–2:18) were perhaps lacking in the first edition. While there are various errors in 1 Maccabees, legendary exaggeration is characteristic of the moralizing in 2 Maccabees. It also includes doctrinal errors such as the propriety of prayers for the dead.

Bibliography: R. H. Charles, *The Apocrypha and Pseudepigrapha of the Old Testament in English,* 2 vols., 1913; W. O. E. Oesterley, *The Books of the Apocrypha,* 1915; C. C. Torrey, *The Apocryphal Literature: A Brief Introduction,* 1945; R. H. Pfeiffer, *History of New Testament Times, With an Introduction to the Apocrypha,* 1949; W. O. E. Oesterley, *An Introduction to the Books of the Apocrypha,* 1953; B. M. Metzger, *An Introduction to the Apocrypha,* 1957. MGK

APOLLONIA (ăp'ŏ-lō'nĭ-à, Gr. *Apollōnia, pertaining to Apollo*). A town of Macedonia on the celebrated Egnatian Way, twenty-eight miles (forty-seven km.) west of Amphipolis and thirty-eight miles (sixty-three km.) east of Thessalonica (Acts 17:1).

APOLLOS (à-pŏl'ŏs, Gr. *Apollōs*). The short

form of Apollonius, an Alexandrian Jew, described in Acts 18:24–25 as a man mighty in the Scriptures, eloquent, fervent in the Spirit, instructed in the way of the Lord, but knowing only the baptism of John. He came to Ephesus after Paul had visited that city on his second missionary journey. There he met Aquila and Priscilla, who had been left there to minister pending the apostle's return. They heard Apollos speak boldly in the synagogue and, observing that he was deficient in his knowledge of the gospel, they "explained to him the way of God more adequately" (18:26). It is not easy to determine from the brief account in Acts the precise character of his religious knowledge. Before long he went to Achaia with letters of recommendation from the Ephesian brothers. When he arrived in Corinth, "he was a great help to those who by grace had believed. For he vigorously refuted the Jews in public debate, proving from the Scriptures that Jesus was the Christ" (18:27–28).

Apollos's gifts and methods of presenting the gospel were undoubtedly different from those of Paul, and he put the impress of his own mode of thinking on many who heard him. Before long a party arose in the Corinthian church with the watchword, "I follow Apollos" (1 Cor 3:4). There does not, however, appear to have been any feeling of rivalry between Paul and Apollos. Paul urged Apollos to revisit Corinth (16:12), and he also asked Titus to help Apollos, apparently then or when he was on his way to Crete (Titus 3:13).

Luther suggested the theory, since accepted by some scholars, that Apollos wrote the Letter to the Hebrews. SB

APOLLYON (See ABADDON)

APOSTASY (à-pŏs'tà-sē, Gr. *apostasia, a falling away, a withdrawal, a defection*). The word is seldom found in English translations of the Bible, but it is a description of Israel's rebellion against God (Josh 22:22; 2 Chron 29:19; Jer 2:19). In Greek, where it has the implication of deserting a post, it refers generally to the abandonment of Christianity for unbelief (1 Tim 4:1; 2 Tim 2:18), perhaps on the part of those who had never truly believed (1 John 1:19; cf. John 15:6). The writer of the Letter to the Hebrews declares apostasy to be irrevocable (Heb 6:4–6; 10:26), and Paul applies it eschatologically to the coming of a time of great rebellion against God (2 Thess 2:3).

APOSTLE (à-pŏs'l, Gr. *apostolos, messenger, envoy, ambassador*). This title is used to describe various men in the NT. First of all, it once described Jesus himself—"Jesus, the apostle and high priest . . ." (Heb 3:1), pointing to Jesus' role on earth as the ambassador of the Father. Second, the twelve disciples whom Jesus chose to be with him and whom he commissioned and sent out to preach are also called "apostles" (Matt 10:2; Mark 3:14; 6:30; Luke 6:13; 9:10; 11:49; 17:5; 22:14; 24:10). These men (without Judas but with Matthias, Acts 1:26) were primary witnesses of the resurrection of Jesus, and their task was to proclaim the gospel of God, establish churches, and teach sound doctrine (Acts 4:33; 5:12; 5:29; 8:1, 14–18). They did this as they lived in spiritual union with the exalted Jesus through the Holy Spirit promised by Jesus in John 14–16.

Since Paul met the resurrected and glorified Jesus and was given a commission by him to be the messenger to the Gentiles and the planter of churches in Gentile cities, he called himself an apostle (Rom 1:1; Gal 1:1), he defended his right to be known as an apostle (2 Cor 11–12; Gal 1), and he was described as an apostle by Luke (Acts 14:14). He believed that suffering was an inescapable part of his apostolic role (1 Cor 4:9–13; 2 Cor 4:7–12; 11:23–29), and he held that the church of God was built on Christ as the chief cornerstone and on the apostles as primary foundational stones (Eph 2:20).

Further, and this information prevents neat and tidy definitions of an apostle, there are others who are called "apostles" in the NT. James, brother of the Lord Jesus (Gal 1:19; 2:9); Barnabas, a fellow worker with Paul (Acts 14:4, 14); Andronicus and Junias (Rom 16:7); and Silas (1 Thess 2:6) were probably known as "apostles" within the early church. But they were not of the Twelve (Rev 21:14) and not on the same footing as Paul, who was uniquely *the* apostle to the Gentiles.

The teaching contained within the pages of the NT is apostolic teaching, and its authority rests on the relation of the apostles to Christ.

Bibliography: A. T. Hanson, *The Pioneer Ministry,* 1961; E. M. B. Green, *Called to Serve,* 1964; Leon Morris, *Minister of God,* 1964; C. K. Barrett, *The Sign of an Apostle,* 1970. PT

APOSTOLIC AGE. The period in the history of the Christian church when the apostles were alive, beginning with the Day of Pentecost and ending with the death of the apostle John near the end of

Section of the Appian Way with remains of Roman structures alongside. Built in 312 B.C., this is the oldest of the famous Roman Roads that first ran 132 miles (c. 210 km.) from Rome to Capua and later extended to Brundisium. In places the ancient road is still in use. Paul must have traversed a part of the Appian Way in his journey from Puteoli to Rome (Acts 28:13–16). Courtesy Gerald Nowotny.

the first century. Our only source for the period is the NT, especially Acts and the Epistles.

APOTHECARY (See Occupations and Professions)

APPAIM (ăp'ā-ĭm, Heb. *'appayim*). Son of Nadab, of the family of Hezron (1 Chron 2:30–31).

APPAREL (See Dress)

APPEAL. No provision was made in the OT for the reconsideration from a lower to a higher court of a case already tried. Exodus 18:26 shows, however, that Moses provided for lower and higher courts: "The difficult cases they brought to Moses, but the simple ones they decided themselves." In Deuteronomy 17:8–13 provision was made for a lower court, under certain conditions, to seek instructions as to procedure from a higher court; but the decision itself belonged to the lower court.

In NT times the Roman government allowed each synagogue to exercise discipline over Jews, but only the Romans had the power of life and death. A Roman citizen could, however, claim exemption from trial by the Jews and appeal to be tried by a Roman court. Paul did this when he said, "I appeal to Caesar!" (Acts 25:11). In such cases the litigant either pronounced the word *appellō*, as Paul did, or submitted the appeal in writing. In either case the presiding magistrate was under obligation to transmit the file, together with a personal report, to the competent higher magistrate.

APPHIA (ăf'ĭ-à, ăp'fĭ-à, Gr. *Apphia*). Called "our beloved" in KJV, "our sister" in ASV, RSV, NIV, following a different text. A Christian of Colosse, believed to be the wife of Philemon and mother of Archippus (Philem 2).

APPIAN WAY (ăp'ĭ-ăn). Oldest of the Roman roads, begun in 312 B.C., which originally ran from Rome to Capua and was later extended to Brundisium. Parts of the road are still in use. Paul must have traveled by it from Puteoli to Rome (Acts 28:13–16).

APPIUS, FORUM OF (ăp'ĭ-ŭs). A town on the Appian Way, a day's journey for sturdy travelers, about forty miles (sixty-seven km.) from Rome toward Naples, where Paul was met by Christian brothers from Rome (Acts 28:15, "Market of Appius" in ASV).

APPLE (See Plants)

APPLE OF THE EYE (Heb. *'ishôn, little man,* Deut 32:10; Ps 17:8; Prov 7:2; *babhâh, gate,* Zech 2:8). The eyeball or the pupil in its center, protected by the eyelids automatically closing when anything approaches too near. A symbol of that which is precious and protected.

APRON (See Dress)

The Gulf of Aqabah, looking east from the hills of Elath. Courtesy Duby Tal.

AQABAH, GULF OF (à'kà-bà). The eastern arm of the Red Sea between the Sinai Peninsula on the west and Midian on the east. Solomon's seaport of Ezion Geber is located at its head, where the Wadi Arabah empties into it (1 Kings 9:26).

AQUEDUCT. A channel, covered or open, cut in the rock; a waterway built of stone and sometimes faced with smooth cement; a waterway carried on stone arches across depressions; used to convey water from reservoirs, pools, cisterns, or springs to the places where it is to be used. Aqueducts may have existed even in pre-Israelite times, and continued to be developed until the excellent work of the Nabatean period (100 B.C. to A.D. 100). The Roman period shows many fine examples. Hezekiah excavated the Siloam tunnel (conduit) to bring water into Jerusalem by a way that could not be stopped up in time of siege (2 Kings 20:20; 2 Chron 32:30), and this served the purpose of an aqueduct.

Ruins of the Roman aqueduct at Caesarea, built during Herod's time. It extended some 5½ miles (9 km.), bringing water to the city from Mount Carmel. Courtesy Israel Government Press Office.

AQUILA (ăk'wĭ-là, Gr. *Akylos,* Latin for "eagle"). A Jew whom Paul found at Corinth on his arrival from Athens (Acts 18:2, 18, 26; Rom 16:3–4; 1 Cor 16:19; 2 Tim 4:19). A characteristic feature of Aquila and his wife Priscilla is that their names are always mentioned together. All that they accomplished was the result of their unity of spiritual nature and purpose in Christ. Having been expelled from Rome, they opened a

A typical desert scene in the Arabah, the great rift valley running from the Sea of Galilee, including the Jordan Valley and the Dead Sea, and extending to the Gulf of Aqabah. Courtesy Seffie Ben-Yoseph.

tentmaking business in Corinth. Because Paul followed the same trade, he was attracted to them. Being in full sympathy with Paul, they hospitably received him into their home, where he remained for a year and a half. Their willingness to "risk their lives" for him earned the gratitude of all the churches. Apollos and many others were helped by their spiritual insight. Aquila and Priscilla had a "church that [met] at their house." Priscilla is usually named first, whether because she became a Christian first or was more active or for some other reason is a matter of conjecture.

AR (Heb. *'ār*). A city or district of Moab, referred to in a song quoted in Numbers 21:15, named in Deuteronomy 2:9, 18, 29 and in a prophecy of Isaiah (Isa 15:1).

ARA (ā'rȧ, Heb. *'ărā'*). Son of Jether, of the tribe of Asher (1 Chron 7:38).

ARAB (ăr'ăb, Heb. *'ărāv*). A city in the hill country of Judah, probably er-Rabiyeh, south of Hebron (Josh 15:52).

ARABAH (ăr'ȧ-bȧ, Heb. *'ărāvâh, desert plain, steppe*). El-Ghor (the Jordan Valley) north of the Dead Sea; Wadi el-Arabah, south of it. The remarkable rift running from Mount Hermon to the Gulf of Aqabah. Its northern portion drains into the Dead Sea, and from above the Sea of Gennesaret (Kinnereth) it is below sea level. South of the Dead Sea it is higher and drains into the Gulf of Aqabah at Ezion Geber. The southern portion is referred to in Deuteronomy 1:1, 2:8. It is associated with the Dead Sea and the Sea of Galilee in Deuteronomy 3:17, 4:49; Joshua 3:16, 12:3; 2 Kings 14:25. It was used in the most extended sense, as appears from Deuteronomy 11:30; Joshua 8:14, 12:1, 18:18; 2 Samuel 2:29, 4:7; 2 Kings 25:4; Jeremiah 39:4, 52:7. The Arabah represents one of the major natural divisions of Palestine in Joshua 11:16, 12:8. It is a narrow valley of varying breadth; the productivity of various sections depends on the availability of water. Populated intermittently from early ages, it lay in the path of caravan traffic between the Arabian and Sinai deserts and Canaan to the north. The Israelites made stops here in their wilderness wanderings. Solomon got iron and copper from the mines of the Arabah, which was part of the extended kingdom of David and Solomon when they ruled over Edom. The name Arabah itself signifies that which is arid or even waste, as references such as Isaiah 33:9 indicate.

ARABIA (ȧ-rā'bĭ-ȧ, Heb. *'ărāv, steppe*). The large peninsula consisting of Arabia Petraea, including Petra and the peninsula of Sinai; Arabia Deserta, the Syrian desert, between the Jordan Valley and the Euphrates; Arabia Felix, the south; bounded east, south, and west by the Persian Gulf, Indian Ocean, and Red Sea, north by the Fertile Crescent. Arabia is an arid steppe, a rocky tableland with enough rainfall in the interior and south to support considerable population, yet with resources so meager they encourage emigration. With water barriers on three sides, expansion was toward the more fertile lands northward, in successive waves of Canaanites, Israelites, Amorites, Babylonians, Assyrians, Arameans (called Syrians in the Bible, except NIV), Idumeans, and Nabateans, all Semitic peoples. They collided with Indo-Europeans pressing down from Asia Minor and Iran. The proximity of Arabia, with a border ill-defined and difficult to

Aerial view of the Arabah (the "waste land") between the Dead Sea and the Gulf of Aqabah. The Dead Sea is sometimes referred to as the "Sea of the Arabah" (Deut 4:49). Courtesy S. Zur Picture Library.

Drawing of Arabian warriors mounted on camels. The relief is from palace of Ashurbanipal at Nineveh, 668–633 B.C. Courtesy Carta, Jerusalem.

defend, and with a "have-not" population ready to plunder, was a major factor influencing the history of Israel.

The first mention of Arabia in the Bible by name is in the reign of Solomon, when its king brought gold and spices, either as tribute or in trade (1 Kings 10:15; 2 Chron 9:14). Arabians brought tribute to Jehoshaphat (2 Chron 17:11). They joined the Philistines against Jehoram, defeating him disastrously (21:16–22:1). At desolate Babylon not even the Arabian nomad would pitch his tent (Isa 13:20). Isaiah 21:13–17 laid a burden on Arabia. Moral depravity is indicated in Jeremiah 3:2. The kings of Arabia were involved in judgment on the nations after the Babylonian captivity (Jer 25:24). Arabia sold cattle to Tyre (Ezek 27:21). Arabians gave Nehemiah trouble when he was rebuilding the walls of Jerusalem (Neh 2:19; 4:7; 6:1). Arabians were among those present at Pentecost (Acts 2:11). Paul went into Arabia (Gal 1:17). The belief that he went to Mount Sinai is based on the experiences of Moses and Elijah there and on his mention of "Mount Sinai in Arabia" (4:25). ER

ARAD (ā'răd, Heb. *'ărādh*). 1. A descendant of Benjamin (1 Chron 8:15).

2. A city, now Tell Arad, about seventeen miles (twenty-eight km.) south of Hebron. Its king opposed Israel and his city was destroyed and renamed Hormah (Num 21:1–3; 33:40; cf. Josh

General view of the excavations at Tell Arad in the Negev. The area was conquered by the Israelites at the time of their wilderness journey (Num 21:1–3). On top of the mound are remains of an Iron Age citadel, some remains showing Israelite occupation between the eleventh and sixth centuries B.C. Courtesy Israel Government Press Office.

12:14). According to Judges 1:16, Kenites settled in the area.

ARAH (ā′rȧ, Heb. *ʾārah, wayfarer*). 1. A son of Ulla, an Asherite (1 Chron 7:39).

2. The father of a family that returned from exile (Ezra 2:5; Neh 7:10). Perhaps the same as no. 1 above.

3. A man into whose family Tobiah the Ammonite married (Neh 6:18). This also may be the same Arah as no. 1 above.

ARAM (ā′răm, Heb. *ʾărām*). 1. A son of Shem (Gen 10:22–23; 1 Chron 1:17).

2. Son of Kemuel, Abraham's nephew (Gen 22:21).

3. Son of Shamer, of the tribe of Asher (1 Chron 7:34).

4. In KJV, for the Greek form of Ram (Matt 1:3–4 ASV, RSV, NIV), called Arni in ASV, RSV of Luke 3:33.

5. A district of the hill country belonging to Gilead (1 Chron 2:23).

6. Usually appearing as "Syria" in English Bibles, Aram broadly describes the area north of Israel and extending eastward to Mesopotamia. The latter was itself Aram Naharaim, i.e., Aram of the two rivers (Gen 24:10). In the title to Psalm 60 we hear of the two divisions, Aram Naharaim and Aram Zobah, conquered by David. The Aramean kingdom of Damascus, though once conquered by David, was able later to reassert itself and was continually hostile to the northern kingdom of Israel until it fell before the westward thrust of Assyria in 732 B.C. ER

ARAMAIC (âr′ȧ-mā′ĭk, Heb. *ʾărāmîth*). A West Semitic language, closely related to Hebrew, which developed various dialects. Genesis 31:47 calls attention to Laban's use of Aramaic in contrast to Jacob's use of Hebrew. That Aramaic

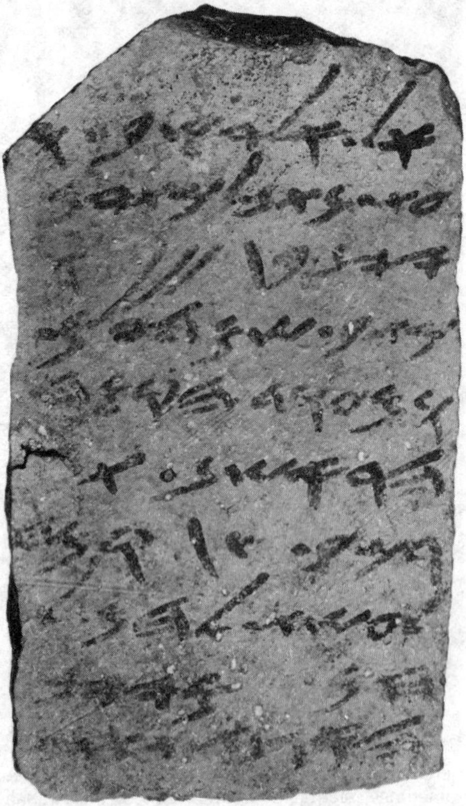

Arad ostracon, a letter in Aramaic addressed to Eliashib, believed to have been the commander of the fortress. According to Numbers 21:1–3, the "king" (or chieftain) of Arad joined battle with Israel and was defeated. Courtesy Israel Department of Antiquities and Museums. Exhibited and photographed by Israel Museum, Jerusalem.

had become the language of Assyrian diplomacy is clear from 2 Kings 18:26; Isaiah 36:11 (see NIV). Aramaic and Hebrew were so different that the people of Jerusalem did not understand the former. Jeremiah 10:11 is in Aramaic, an answer by the Jews to their Aramaic-speaking conquerors who would seduce them to worship idols. Daniel 2:4–7:28 is in Aramaic, also Ezra 4:8–6:18 and 7:12–26. It is not surprising that men in government circles in their period of history should write Aramaic, but why these particular parts of their books should be in Aramaic is not clear. Some Aramaic place names and personal names occur in the OT, as Tabrimmon (1 Kings 15:18) and Hazael (2 Kings 8:8ff.). There are several Aramaic words and phrases in the NT, such as *Talitha koum* (Mark 5:41), *Ephphatha* (7:34), *Eloi, Eloi, lama sabachthani* (Matt 27:46; Mark 15:34), *Maranatha* (1 Cor 16:22 footnote), *Abba* (Mark 14:36; Rom 8:15; Gal 4:6), and many other words and names. It has been generally assumed as proven that Aramaic was the colloquial language of Palestine from the time of the return of the exiles from Babylon. But some believe that Hebrew was spoken in Galilee in NT times. It is probably safe to assert that our Lord habitually spoke Aramaic and occasionally Greek and could read and speak Hebrew.

ARAN (ā'răn, Heb. *'ărān*). One of the two sons of Dishan, and grandson of Seir the Horite (Gen 26:28; 1 Chron 1:42).

ARARAT (âr'à-răt, Heb. *'ărārāt*). A country in eastern Armenia, a mountainous tableland from which flow the Tigris, Euphrates, Aras (Araxes), and Choruk rivers. Near its center lies Lake Van, which, like the Dead Sea, has no outlet. Its general elevation is about 6,000 feet (1,875 m.),

The snowcapped Mount Ararat, now part of Turkey. Courtesy B. Brandl.

above which rise mountains to as high as 17,000 feet (5,313 m.), the height of the extinct volcano that in modern times is called Mount Ararat and on which the ark is supposed to have rested, though Genesis 8:4 is indefinite: "On the mountains of Ararat" (plural). There the sons of Sennacherib fled after murdering their father (2 Kings 19:37; Isa 37:38). Jeremiah 51:27 associates the kingdoms of Ararat, Minni, and Ashkenaz with the kings of the Medes as prophesied conquerors of Babylonia. The region is now part of Turkey. The Babylonian name was Urartu, having the same consonants as the Hebrew *'ărārāt*. Its meaning cannot be determined with certainty.

ARAUNAH (à-rô'nà, Heb. *'ărawnâh*). The Jebusite who owned the threshing floor on Mount Moriah that David purchased in order to erect an altar. Because of David's sin in numbering the people, the land was stricken with a plague. When the plague was stayed, David presented a costly offering to the Lord (2 Sam 24:15–25). Araunah is called Ornan in 1 Chronicles 21:18–28 (KJV). The difference between 2 Samuel 24:24 and 1 Chronicles 21:25 may be explained if we consider that in 2 Samuel we are told of an immediate transaction covering what David purchased then and there, while 1 Chronicles records a subsequent purchase of the whole site. In 2 Samuel 24:16 the Hebrew text has "the Araunah" and in verse 23 "Araunah the king." Was Araunah, then, the last Jebusite king of Jerusalem, permitted to live on in his city after David captured it? This is no more than an interesting conjecture.

ARBA (àr'ba', Heb., *'arba'*). The father of Anak. He founded the city that bore his name, Kiriath Arba of Hebron (Josh 14:15; 15:13).

ARBATHITE (àr'bà-thīt, Heb. *'arvāthî*). One of David's thirty heroes, a native of the Arabah or of Beth Arabah, called Abi-Albon in 2 Samuel 23:31, Abiel in 1 Chronicles 11:32.

ARBITE (àr'bīt, Heb. *'ārbî*). One of David's mighty men in 2 Samuel 23:35 is called Paarai the Arbite. In his place in 1 Chronicles 11:37 is Naarai the son of Ezbai.

ARCHAEOLOGY.

I. The Meaning of Archaeology. By definition archaeology is the study of antiquity. In modern times it has graduated from a treasure hunt into a highly scientific discipline, a branch of history that works with the unwritten material remains of antiquity. W. F. Albright once wrote that next to nuclear science, archaeology has become the fastest-growing discipline in the country. Excavation is only one aspect of the total effort of an archaeological enterprise. Geographical regional surveys, geological analyses, evaluation of artifacts, translation of inscriptions, reconstruction of architecture, examination of human remains, identification of art forms, construction of ceramic pottery typology for chronological purposes, and many other highly complex scientific endeavors constitute a major part of the expedition's work. The end result of it all is to enrich our understanding of unknown aspects of ancient civilizations.

II. Biblical Archaeology. G. E. Wright has insisted that biblical archaeology is an armchair variety of general archaeology, but William Dever has correctly emphasized that archaeology is biblical only where and when the scientific methodology of general archaeology uncovers something relative to the Bible. There is no special science or technique available to the biblical scholar. One who digs a biblical site is a biblical archaeologist in the same way that one who digs a classical site is a classical archaeologist. The methods are the same. There are no special methods or aims for biblical archaeology. Special emphasis should be given to the fact that all reputable archaeology strives for the same total reconstruction of the past and presupposes the same standards of objectivity. As Roland de Vaux pointed out, archaeology cannot prove the Bible. Spiritual truth is of such a nature that it cannot be proven or disproven by the material discoveries of archaeology. The truths of the Bible do not need proving; they are self-evident. But as the Israeli scholar Gaalyah Cornfeld commented in a recent book, "The net effect of archaeology has been to support the general trustworthiness and substantial historicity of the biblical traditon where data are available." The study of the Bible and the pursuit of archaeology belong together. When Middle-Eastern archaeology began about a century ago, the majority of the excavators were biblical scholars. They recognized the fact that the greatest contribution archaeology could make to biblical studies would be to illuminate our understandings of the cultural settings in which the various books of the Bible were written and which they reflect. That information will, at times, significantly affect our interpretation of relevant sections of the text.

III. The History of Palestinian Archaeology. Although some exploration had been done in the Middle Ages, no real interest was kindled in Middle-Eastern antiquities until after 1600 when cuneiform documents from Persepolis reached Europe. Napoleon took a team of scholars with him in 1798 to study the antiquities of Egypt once he had conquered it. One of his officers discovered the Rosetta Stone, whose identical inscription in three languages unlocked the mystery of Egyptian hieroglyphs and opened the history of Egypt. Palestine was explored in the mid-1800s by Edward Robinson, Charles Warren, C. R. Conder, H. H. Kitchener, and others. A British officer named Henry Rawlinson found a trilingual inscription at Behistun, Persia, that unlocked the mysteries of cuneiform, and this "Rosetta Stone of Persia" further heightened interest in the lands of the Bible.

Although exploration of Palestine had been remarkably well done by the end of the century, excavation was quite rare and virtually worthless. Systematic excavation got underway only after 1870 when Heinrich Schliemann discovered in Troy on the west coast of Turkey that the mounds dotting the horizon all over Bible lands were actually the remains of ancient cities successively destroyed and rebuilt, one on top of another. Lack of understanding about these mounds had reflected itself in Bible translations prior to that time—for example, Joshua 11:13 in the KJV: "But as for the cities that stood still in their strength, Israel burned none of them save Hazor only." The Hebrew word *tell,* whose meaning was unknown at that time, was translated "strength." Schliemann's work showed that the word rather meant "mound" and later revisions of the KJV translate the phrase correctly: "the cities that stood on their mounds."

Nevertheless, his work was still of little influence in Palestinian excavation. He realized that these mounds consisted of strata, layers of civilization superimposed one on the other like layers of cake, but he did not know how to date them other than the obvious fact that the oldest ones were at the bottom. It remained for Sir Flinders Petrie to provide the means of dating these strata that has remained our most important method until the present time. In Egypt he became familiar with ceramic pottery that could be dated by tomb inscriptions. In his work in Israel in 1890 he discovered that the same forms of pottery could be found in various strata of his excavation at Tell el Hesi. He observed that the pottery styles changed from layer to layer and that he could date the strata by the changing forms, in much the same way that automobiles can be dated by their changing forms. His work was supplemented by that of W. F. Albright at Tell Beit Mirsim in 1926–32, and an extensive ceramic typology was published that has become a standard basis of comparison for Palestinian archaeologists. This has proven to be the single most important method of dating ancient sites, because the pottery is virtually indestructible and was so easily made that people never bothered to take it when they moved.

IV. The Future of Palestinian Archaeology. Albright trained a generation of archaeologists, both American and Israeli, and work today continues at a feverish pace both by his students and those whom they have trained. These in turn are training a new generation. The "new archaeology," which has become prominent in the past decade, is seeking to go beyond the concern these men had with structures and chronology and is attempting to reconstruct the total picture of the society that lived in a given period of history. Such an approach to excavation requires a vast array of expertise, and expeditions are regularly staffed now with such specialists as paleoethnobotanists, geologists, architects, ceramicists, numismatists, stratigraphers, historians, linguists, photographers, geographers, and the like. The days of treasure hunting are over; excavations have become scientific expeditions.

Archaeology is a rapidly developing science. Its potential for significant contribution to the interpretation of the Bible is well established and the future is bright for the discipline. There is much that remains to be done. Paul Lapp estimated in 1963 that of a total of 5,000 sites in Palestine there had been scientific excavations at about 150, including only 26 major excavations. Of the more than 5,000 mounds located in Iraq, ancient Babylonia, and Assyria, fewer than 30 major excavations are documented in Beek's *Atlas of Mesopotamia,* less than 1 percent of the total sites. Little more than 10 percent of the 500,000 cuneiform tablets found in Mesopotamia had been published when another 17,000 were found in 1974 and 1975 at Tel Mardikh (Ebla) in Syria. Yigael Yadin estimated that at the rate of his normal excavation progress at Hazor in Galilee it would take 8,000 years to thoroughly excavate the site. Hazor covers about 200 acres in its upper and lower sections. How long would it take to thoroughly excavate the 8,000 acres of Caesarea Maritima? Work has been going on there since 1972 and fewer than 5 acres have been excavated!

V. Recent Contributions of Archaeology to the Study of the Bible.

A. **Old Testament.** Until recently it was commonly felt that Abraham lived in the Middle Bronze Period (c. 2000–1500 B.C.), but an electrifying new discovery in Syria in 1974 at Tell Mardikh (Ebla) has caused Noel Freedman to place him in the Early Bronze period at a time when Ebla was at its height of power and influence. A royal library was found here consisting of 20,000 clay tablets, 80 percent of which were written in Sumerian and the rest in an unknown Semitic language akin to Hebrew that is now called Eblaite. Located halfway between modern Aleppo and Hama, at the top of the Fertile Crescent, the city was in the heart of Abraham's ancestral home territory of Haran and flourished in c. 2200 B.C. Names like David, Micah, Jerusalem, Sodom, Gomorrah, Haran, and Ur appear in the texts. Here we have a cultural area as large and influential as either Egypt or Lower Mesopotamia at the time civilization began.

The impact of archaeology has been felt recently on the interpretation of the date of the Exodus of Moses and the Israelites out of Egypt. A thirteenth-century B.C. date has been indicated by destruction levels that date to that century in excavations of Hazor, Jericho, Ai, Lachish, and other sites mentioned in the Book of Joshua. John Bimson argued in a publication in 1978 that neither the archaeological nor the biblical evidence militates against an early date. His selectivity in handling archaeological data, however, has limited the influence of his book among archaeologists. A growing trend sees the Exodus not as an event but as a series of events beginning with some sort of violent intrusion followed by a more socio-economic upheaval of people within the land. Both Yigael Yadin and Yohanan Aharoni held such a view. However, a restatement of the early date of the Exodus and conquest has been made by a leading Egyptologist: Hans Goedicke, chairman of the department of Near Eastern Studies at Johns Hopkins University, puts the Exodus in the spring of 1477 at the time Thera/Santorini was blown apart by a volcano that, he argues, caused tidal waves that drowned the Egyptians in the Red Sea. Conservatives will not be happy, however, with Goedicke's rejection of the Bible as descriptive historiography. The early date has also been argued recently (1982) by Eugene Merrill, who deprecates the archaeological evidence that does not reveal the destruction in the fifteenth century B.C. of the cities Joshua is said to have conquered. Merrill argues that the thirteenth-century evidence of destruction is irrelevant because the Bible does not really say Joshua destroyed these cities, only that he conquered them and reused them. He considers Hazor an exception to this policy (Josh 11:13). Therefore he does not expect to find destruction levels associated with Joshua's conquest. But it should be pointed out that Jericho was burned (6:24)! The more daring views of Norman Gottwald and Robert Boling, that the conquest was not a military invasion at all, are so at variance with the straightforward reading of the biblical text that they will not likely secure a large following. To call it merely an economically based sociological upheaval is inadequate. A final resolution of the issue, however, is still not possible.

The period of the monarchy has been significantly touched by the excavations at Hazor, Megiddo, Jerusalem, and Gezer. These cities, which were renovated by Solomon (1 Kings 9:15), have been found to have unique water systems, and all but Jerusalem have unique city gates. Jerusalem has not been thoroughly excavated, however, because it continues to be a living city. The water systems consist of hidden underground springs outside the city walls. Water is brought through a secret tunnel into the city to a pool that is reached by a stairway. The gates have four protruding sections facing each other from two separate structures, producing three compartments within, and are unique in ancient Palestine. Excavations on Mount Ophel by Yigal Shiloh in the early 1980s have produced a part of the city wall just south of the temple mount that may belong to Solomon, extending below and not into sixth-century-B.C. buildings as Kathleen Kenyon had previously thought when she first excavated the wall and dated it to the time of Nehemiah.

The water tunnel at Megiddo, built during Solomon's time. Part of a water system consisting of a pit 81 feet (25 m.) deep, with stairs leading to the horizontal tunnel 224 feet (70 m.) long (viewed here) and to a spring at the foot of the mound. This great engineering feat served to convey water from the spring through the tunnel to the shaft inside the city wall, thus making it safe for the inhabitants to draw water from inside the city in times of siege. Courtesy Israel Government Press Office.

Asher Kaufmann has found convincing evidence of foundational cuttings for the temples of Solomon and Zerubbabel/Herod on the NW corner of the temple platform. The cuttings coincide with the 16.7 inch (42.8 cm.) cubit used in the construction of the first temple and the 17

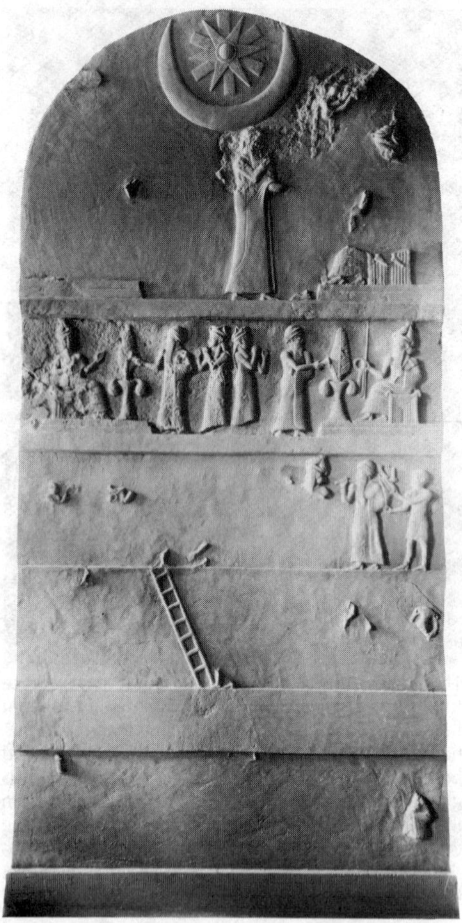

Obverse of the restored stele of Ur-Nammu from Ur, c. 2060–1955 B.C. The top register shows king standing before a deity seated on a throne. Two scenes in second register each show the king offering libations to a deity. What remains of the third and fourth registers shows the king carrying a basket and surveying and building instruments; part of a ladder and bricks (at lower right of fourth register) built into a wall suggest that the subject was the building of a ziggurat. Courtesy The University Museum, University of Pennsylvania.

inch (43.7 cm.) cubit used in the second temple. These line up the Most Holy Place with the modern Golden Gate, solving a previously inexplicable problem of the misalignment of the Gate in relation to the current Dome of the Rock, which has been assumed to sit over the temple site. In 1983 James Fleming published his discovery of another gate beneath this one belonging either to the second or tenth centuries B.C., possibly built by Solomon.

A stunning discovery was made in 1980 during the excavation of a sixth-century-B.C. burial cave in Jerusalem. It was a silver amulet, 3.82 inches (9.8 cm.) long, containing the ancient Hebrew name of God (Yahweh or Jehovah) inscribed on it. Although the name is found more than 6,800 times in the OT, this is the first time that the name has been found in excavations in Jerusalem.

In 1977 the tomb of Philip II of Macedon was found in Vergina, Greece, containing the bones, armor, and gold diadem of this man. His son Alexander the Great made Greek the universal language of the empire, the language in which the books of the NT were originally written. The lid of his golden casket was decorated with the golden sunburst, symbol of the Macedonian kings.

Equally important but not so recent are a number of finds that significantly contribute to our understanding of the OT. A number of discoveries have greatly weakened the Wellhausian theory of the evolutionary development of the Israelite religion. This theory advocated that Moses could not have written the Pentateuch because neither language nor the concept of law had yet developed to the advanced stage represented in the Law of Moses. In refutation of this, James Pritchard has published in ANET four laws found in Mesopotamia that are older than those of Moses and are almost identical in the casuistic (if . . . then) portions. The Ur-Nammu Law Code was produced by the founder of the third dynasty of Ur and builder of the best preserved ziggurat in Mesopotamia. He ruled from 2112 to 2095 B.C. Twenty-nine laws are extant. The Eshunna Code found in a suburb of Baghdad (also called the Code of Bilalama) was published by Bilalama, who reigned about 1950 B.C. Sixty laws are extant. The Lipit Ishtar Code was produced by this fifth ruler of the dynasty of Isin who ruled from 1864 to 1854. Thirty-eight laws are extant. The Hammurabi Code dates from his reign, 1728 to 1686, and there are 282 laws inscribed on a stela preserved in the Louvre in Paris. All of these are casuistic in nature; i.e., like the Book of the Covenant in Exodus 21–24, they are written in the form "if . . . then." No apodictic laws ("You shall not . . .") have yet been found in the Middle East corresponding to Exodus 20.

An account of the Flood, called the Gilgamesh Epic, was found in 1853 in the midst of a long and beautiful Babylonian poem, excavated as a part of Ashurbanipal's library in Nineveh. It contains remarkable parallels to the biblical account, such as a warning of the coming flood, the building of an ark, the flood coming, the ark resting on a mountain, and birds being sent out to find land. The hero of the story corresponding to the biblical Noah is Utnapishtim who, like Noah, offers a sacrifice after the Flood. Pritchard dates the original composition of the work to c. 2000 B.C. The story is found in many ancient languages including Assyrian, Hittite, Hurrian, and Sumerian.

The period of the patriarchs has been illuminated by the discovery in 1925 of approximately one thousand clay tablets at Nuzi in Mesopotamia, written in Akkadian cuneiform and dating to the fifteenth century B.C. Even though they were written about three centuries after the patriarchal period, they are generally acknowledged as reflecting much older material, throwing light on customs that existed in the very region inhabited by the family of Abraham. There are parallels to numerous customs mentioned in Genesis, such as the importance of the patriarchal blessing that Isaac gave Jacob, the giving of a handmaid to one's husband as Sarah gave Hagar to Abraham, the transfer of a birthright as Isaac did from Esau to Jacob, the proof of ownership of property by the possession of one's family idols explaining why Rachel stole her father's teraphim. These indicate that the appropriate setting for the stories told in Genesis is the second millennium B.C. and not the first, as some radical critics claimed.

For the period of the Exodus and conquest much of the older evidence has been reevaluated by later digs and better dating techniques, though, as discussed above, there is still no substantial agreement about either the nature or date of these events. Garstang's dates for Jericho and Hazor have been shown to be wrong by Kenyon and Yadin respectively, while work in the past fifty years at other sites mentioned in Joshua—such as Gibeon, Ai, Azekah, and Lachish—have yielded dates for destruction levels later than most readings of the biblical data will easily warrant. Kenyon dated the fall of Jericho earlier than the usual late date (thirteenth century B.C.) but much later than the early date (fifteenth century). Both archaeological methodology and the handling of biblical numerology are still imperfect, and the results yielded are less than certain.

Our understanding of the religion of the Canaanites at the time of the conquest has been greatly increased by the discovery of ancient Ugarit in 1928 and its excavation until the 1950s. A library was found there by Claude Schaeffer dating to the period of the city's greatest literary and cultural achievements (1600–1200 B.C.), and written in what we now call Ugaritic. It testifies to the depraved nature of Canaanite religion at this time, including the boiling of a goat kid in its mother's milk, a practice warned against in Exodus 23:19 and 34:26 and which probably lies at the heart of the kosher laws. In addition to considerable information about the Canaanite idol Baal, against whom strong invectives are made in the Bible, there appears also the astonishing fact that the chief deity of the Canaanites was named El, the same name used by the Jews for their God. Help is being found in this library for correcting our misimpressions of some words in our Hebrew Bibles. For example, we should probably render *bamoth* as "backs" rather than "high places" in Deuteronomy 33:29, and "fields that yield offerings" as "upsurging of the deep" in 2 Samuel 1:21.

Considerably more information was gained about the various cities of Palestine about the time of the Exodus and conquest by the discovery of the Amarna Letters dating to the reign of Amenhotep IV (Akhenaton) and his father in the late fourteenth century B.C. These clay tablets, written in the Babylonian language, were found

The Hammurabi Code (dated c. 1765–1686 B.C.), the name given to the inscription of nearly 282 laws in Old Babylonian cuneiform on a diorite stele. The top of the stele, itself a pillar of black diorite 8 feet high, shows Hammurabi receiving the command to inscribe the laws from the god Shamash. Courtesy Réunion des Musées Nationaux.

One of the "Amarna Letters," the cuneiform tablets accidentally found by a peasant woman in 1887. The tablets, which reflect the socio-political situation of Canaan just prior to the Hebrew conquest, comprise the diplomatic correspondence between Egyptian Pharaohs Amenhotep III and IV (Akhenaton) and the kings of the city-states in western Asia. Fourteenth century B.C. Courtesy The Metropolitan Museum of Art, Rogers Fund, 1924.

in Tell-el-Amarna, Egypt, in 1887. They refer to a marauding class of people called Habiru, who may possibly be the Hebrews, though this is not certain.

In the fifth year of the Pharaoh Merneptah (c. 1223–1211 B.C.) he commemorated his military achievements over the eastern Mediterranean by setting up a black granite stela with an extensive inscription containing among other references these words: "Canaan is plundered with every evil; Ashkelon is taken; Gezer is captured . . . Israel lies desolate." This is the earliest reference to Israel in antiquity.

Important references to people mentioned in the Bible have been found in the centuries following the monarchy (this was discussed in the beginning of this section). The divided kingdom after Solomon (ninth to sixth centuries B.C.) was affected by Syrians, Moabites, Assyrians, and Babylonians, all of whom left witness of their relation to biblical events in official monuments. The ninth-century Moabite stone, published by Mesha, king of Moab, was found at Diban in Jordan in 1868. It contains references to Omri, king of Israel (2 Kings 3). The Milgart Stele from the same century, found apparently in 1939 north of Aleppo, Syria, contains the name of Ben-Hadad the king of Syria referred to in 1 Kings 15:18. The Zakir Stele, also ninth century, found in 1907 south of Aleppo, commemorates a victory of Zakir, king of Hamath, over this same Ben-Hadad. The Assyrian sources have been found to be basically reliable as have those of the Neo-Babylonian period. Historical texts from these two empires have been found in Nineveh, Nimrud (Calah of Gen 10:10–11), Ashur, and Babylon. The Kurkh Stele, erected in the mid-ninth century, contains the name of Ahab the Israelite (1 Kings 16:29). The Black Obelisk of Shalmaneser III not only contains the name of "Jehu, Son of Omri," a king of Israel (2 Kings 10:28–29) in the late ninth century, but also has a depiction of him bowing before Shalmaneser. Jehu is bearded and wears a sleeveless mantle over a long fringed and girded tunic. This is the only contemporary depiction of any Israelite king.

In the eighth century B.C. the Annals of Tiglath-Pileser III mention that Menahem paid tribute, the amount being clearly stated in 2 Kings 15:19–20. Azriau of Yaudi is also referred to, probably Azariah of Judah (2 Chron 26:6–15).

The Zakir Stele, commemorating the victory of Zakir, king of Hamath over Ben-Hadad, king of Syria. Ninth century B.C. Courtesy Encyclopaedia Judaica Photo Archive, Jerusalem.

The Nimrud Tablet of the same century claims that Tiglath-Pileser set Hoshea over Israel after Pekah was deposed (2 Kings 15:29–31). A slab inscription from the SE palace at Nimrud states that Jehoahaz (long form of Ahaz) of Judah paid tribute to Tiglath-Pileser (16:8). There is frequent mention in this century of Israel, called "the House of Omri," in the various inscriptions of Sargon II (722–205). Sennacherib, his successor (705–681), left a fascinating reference to a Jewish king in the Taylor Prism, which says that "Hezekiah the Jew [literally Judean]" resisted the Assyrian monarch and "he himself I shut up like a caged bird within Jerusalem" (18:13–14). Interestingly the Prism makes no mention of the actual conquest of Jerusalem. The reason is that he never conquered it. He lost 185,000 troops by the hand of God during the siege, and he went back to Nineveh (19:35–36). The Bull Inscription, however, boasts that Sennacherib "laid waste the district of Judah [Iaudi] and made the overbearing and proud Hezekiah, its king, bow submissively at my feet." A slab inscription found at Nineveh claims, "I overthrew the wide district of Judah. I imposed my [yoke-] ropes upon Hezekiah, its king." The Annals of Assyria, which detail the exploits of Esarhaddon (681–669), the successor of Sennacherib, mention the subservience of "Manasseh, king of Judah" (2 Kings 21). Esarhaddon is mentioned in 2 Kings 19:37; Isaiah 37:38; Ezra 4:2.

One of the most important documents of the period is the Babylonian Chronicle containing a running and probably contemporary record of the exploits of the Babylonians in Syria, Palestine, and other countries. It states that "the Babylonian king [Nebuchadnezzar] . . . on the second day of the month of Adar [March 16, 597 B.C.] took the city and captured the king [Jehoichin]" (2 Kings 24:12–13). This gives a firm date for OT and Babylonian chronology. Cyrus the Persian, who conquered the Babylonians in October of 539, left a clay cylinder inscribed in cuneiform that tells of his decree allowing conquered peoples to rebuild their cities and religious shrines. This is consistent with the biblical record of the return of the Jews from Persia to Palestine in the books of Ezra and Nehemiah.

B. **The New Testament.** Herod the Great was king of the Jews when Jesus was born. He was the greatest builder in Jewish history, having built in twenty sites in Palestine and thirteen outside the land. Extensive remains of his program have been found in recent excavations that supplement what we already know about him. At Casearea Maritima portions of his wall around the city have been found since 1972, including the northern gate. His harbor and about a hundred vaulted warehouses stretching along the harbor have been found in underwater excavation. The high-level aqueduct and the small theater in which he dedicated his newly built city have long been identified. An inscription bearing the name of Pontius Pilate was found in the theater. His desert palace at Herodium, south of Bethlehem, has recently been shown to have seven levels in the

The "Black Obelisk of Shalmaneser," a four-sided object of black limestone, 6½ feet (2.02 m.) high, from the reign of Shalmaneser III (858–824 B.C.), king of Assyria. The pillar is composed of five rows of bas-relief panels, intended to be read around the four sides of the pillar. Of special interest is one panel in which a bearded Semite bows before the king while his servants present gifts. The text refers to the suppliant as Jehu, son of Omri. Reproduced by courtesy of the Trustees of the British Museum.

Frontal view of Masada, with the three-tiered remains of a palace in the foreground. Two years after the fall of Jerusalem (A.D. 70), Zealots occupying this last stronghold to survive the war with the Romans had to defend themselves against the vast Roman army. The leader and 960 followers, rather than surrender, chose to take their own lives. Courtesy Israel Government Press Office.

large donut-shaped mound. The lower palace has an esplanade and large square pool found by Ehud Netzer. The esplanade leads to a building complex that Netzer thinks may contain the tomb of Herod. A unique circular pavilion with concentric walls stood in the middle of a pool, its unique design appearing in Palestine only in Herod's building projects; e.g., in the middle level pavilion at Masada's northern palace and in the frigidarium (unheated bathing pool) of the Roman bath in his palace at Jericho. A portion of a similar structure has been found in the area just north of the Damascus Gate in Jerusalem which Netzer thinks may be the family tomb of Herod. This structural oddity may have influenced the design of the similar edifice in Hadrian's villa outside Rome. Yadin's excavation of Masada, on the west side of the Dead Sea, revealed a massive complex of buildings constructed by Herod, consisting of casemate walls, a northern palace in three tiers, a large bathhouse, a swimming pool, many huge cisterns, warehouses, and a dining hall later converted into a synagogue. In the 1970s Herod's winter palace at Jericho was found by Ehud Netzer and Eric Meyers and was extensively excavated, revealing a large reception hall with an adjoining apse leading to a large Roman bath. Included in the complex was the older Hasmonean winter palace containing many pools, including the large one in which Herod had Aristobulus drowned. It also contained several of the oldest mikvehs (Jewish pools for ritual bathing) yet found in Palestine (second century B.C.). Evidence of his work in Jerusalem is seen in the tower still standing in the Jaffa Gate, which Titus left to show the greatness of the city he had conquered. A considerable portion of the Herodian courses of stone undergirding his expansion of the temple mount have been exposed, including some monoliths that weigh 400 tons (364 metric tons). The arches holding up the southern end of the temple mount are Herodian, not Solomonic.

Excavations at Capernaum in the past decade have revealed that the synagogue there is not earlier than the fourth century A.D. but that it was built over a first-century synagogue whose basalt stone floors and walls have been found directly beneath the floor of the fourth-century prayer hall. This no doubt was the synagogue that Jesus attended while in Capernaum with Simon Peter. The house of Peter may have been located immediately south of the synagogue, built of the same basalt stone found in the earlier synagogue. A large room in the center of the house has evidently been venerated since the mid-first century when the pottery found in the room ceased to be domestic. The walls were plastered about this time, the only excavated house in Capernaum so done. On the wall 130 grafitti in several languages mention Jesus as Lord and Christ, among other things. The room was designated by an arch and then covered in the fourth century by a square Byzantine church building, over which a fifth-century octagonal church was built with a mosaic floor that remained there until the recent excavations.

In Jerusalem the pool of Bethesda (John 5:2) has been excavated just inside the eastern Lion Gate, and further to the south the pool of Siloam (9:7) is easily identified by Hezekiah's tunnel connecting it with the Gihon spring. Thirty steps leading up to the temple mount through the southern gates of Hulda, two hundred feet (sixty-three m.) in width, have been found along with adjacent houses from the time of Christ. Underground walkways and aqueducts have been excavated in this area dating to the same period. A portion of an aqueduct built by Pontius Pilate has recently been found in Bethlehem; this aqueduct brought water to Jerusalem from south of Hebron. The stone pavement on which Jesus stood before Pilate (John 19:13) is almost certainly to be identified with the courtyard of the Fortress of Antonia, beneath the Sisters of Zion Convent. Excavations of Kathleen Kenyon have shown that the modern Church of the Holy Sepulchre, the probable site of the crucifixion and burial of Jesus, was outside the first-century city wall. Ancient burials for everyone but kings and high officials were outside the walls.

In 1947 the Dead Sea Scrolls were found on the NW shore of the Dead Sea in a number of caves, deposited there by a sect of Jews generally identified as Essenes. Their walled community nearby was excavated from 1953 to 1956, revealing several large cisterns used for baptisms and for storage of water brought in by aqueduct from the cliffs to the west. John the Baptist may have been closely acquainted with this sect in his earlier life. They not only baptized, but, like John, used Isaiah 40:3 to justify their being in the wilderness. He preached in this area and baptized Jesus not far away. Ten of eleven caves found produced tens of thousands of fragments of ancient books including some of every book of the OT. A full copy of Isaiah was found dating to the second century B.C., the oldest copy of a book of the Hebrew Bible. The Essenes' documents were produced between 200 B.C. and A.D. 50. The community, consisting of perhaps two hundred members, was destroyed by the Romans about A.D. 68.

In recent decades many papyri containing books of the NT dating into the second and third centuries A.D. have been found; e.g., the Bodmer II papyrus of the complete Gospel of John, the Chester Beatty papyri of Paul's Letters, and the John Rylands fragment of John 18 (which dates to the early second century, making it the oldest surviving piece of any book of the NT). A third-century Greek inscription of Romans 13:3 was found in 1972 in excavations at Caesarea Maritima. It is part of a mosaic floor belonging to a building that was constructed in the third and destroyed in the seventh century. Some of the missing pages in Codex Sinaiticus, a fourth-century manuscript of the Bible, have just been found in St. Catherine's Convent at Sinai.

In 1945 a complete library was discovered at Nag Hammadi, Egypt, that contains many apocryphal NT books along with other books related to the religion of second-century Gnostic sects. Originally produced in Greek, they were translated into Coptic in the fourth century. These documents are extremely valuable for studying the milieu of early Christianity and have been recently published by James Robinson. Gnostic-type groups constituted a challenge to mainline Christianity in these early centuries, replacing the biblical emphasis on faith with that of a special kind of knowledge (gnosis). They seem to have prompted the finalizing of the limits of the NT canon.

An important discovery bearing on the chronology of the NT has been reported by Jerry Vardaman, who has found coins with an accession date of A.D. 56 for Festus, before whom Paul appeared (Acts 25:1). This is a pivotal date for establishing the chronology of the activities of Paul. Equally important is the older discovery of the Gallio inscription in Delphi, Greece, which places this proconsul in Greece in the spring of 51, and thus Paul's arrival there about eighteen months earlier (Acts 18:11). Although Vardaman has not yet published his material, it is accepted by Jack Finegan in his *Archaeology of the New Testament: Mediterranean World of the Early Christian Apostles* (1981).

No less exciting is Vardaman's discovery of "micrographic" letters on coins and inscriptions of the first century that date the proconsulship of Quirinius in Syria and Cilicia from 11 B.C. Although not yet published, this new evidence will erase doubt as to the accuracy of Luke's statement (Luke 2:2) that Quirinius ruled Syria at the time Christ was born and the census was taken.

An inscription dating probably to the middle of the first century A.D. was found in the pavement NE of the large theater in Corinth, reading ERASTUS. PRO. AED/S.P.STRAVIT. It means that Erastus, in return for his aedileship (an aedile was a Roman official in charge of public works), laid the pavement at his own expense. Unabbreviated it would read "Erastus pro aedilitate sua pecunia stragit." This must refer to the same Erastus whom Paul mentions as "treasurer of the city" of Corinth, for whom Romans 16:23 was undoubtedly written! Also found in excavations at Corinth is the Bema (referred to in a Latin inscription in Corinth as *rostra*), the tribunal or platform where Paul stood before Gallio (Acts 18:12–17).

Excavations in Ephesus have revealed the 22,000-seat theater mentioned in Acts 19:29 where an irate crowd assembled to express opposition to Paul's attack on Diana (Greek, Artemis), the patron goddess of the city. Her temple was one of the seven wonders of the ancient world. Two magnificent statues of Diana were found, illuminating references to her in Acts 19:24–25.

Luke's accuracy as a witness to the historical circumstances of early Christian missionary activity is indicated by the discovery of an inscription, now in the British Museum, that stood in an arch at the west end of the Egnatia Odos in Thessalonica. It begins "In the days of the politarchs . . . ," using a word for Roman officials that critics said Luke had mistakenly used in Acts 17:6, since it has not been found anywhere else in Greek literature. A number of inscriptions have now been found that contain the word.

Bibliography: J. Pritchard, *Ancient Near Eastern Texts* (3 vols.), 1950; W. F. Albright, *The Archaeology of Palestine: From the Stone Age to Christianity,* 1956; G. E. Wright, *Biblical Archaeology,* 1957; D. W. Thomas (ed.), *Documents from Old Testament Times,* 1958; J. A. Thompson, *The Bible and Archaeology,* 1962; J. Finegan, *The Archaeology of the New Testament* (2 vols.), 1969; A. Negev, *Archaeological Encyclopedia of the Holy Land,* 1972; M. Avi-Yonah (ed.), *Encyclopedia of Archaeology Excavations in the Holy Land* (4 vols.), 1975–78; J. J. Hester, *Introduction to Archaeology,* 1976; J. Wilkinson, *Jerusalem as Jesus Knew It,* 1978; K. Schoville, *Biblical Archaeology in Focus,* 1978; W. Ashmore and R. J. Sharer, *Fundamentals of Archaeology,* 1979; N. Avigad, *Discovering Jerusalem,* 1980; E. Meyers and J. Strange, *Archaeology, the Rabbis and Early Christianity,* 1981; B. Fagan, *Archaeology: A Brief Introduction,* 1983.

JRM

ARCHANGEL (See ANGEL)

ARCHELAUS (är′kĕ-lā′ŭs). Son of Herod the Great, who succeeded his father as ruler of Idumea, Samaria, and Judea in 4 B.C. He was deposed by the Roman government in A.D. 6 (Matt 2:22).

ARCHERS. Bowmen, hunters, or warriors with bow and arrows. Ishmael is the first man so named in the Bible (Gen 21:20). Joseph is represented as victor in a battle of archery (49:23–24). RSV has "sound of musicians" and NIV has "voice of the singers" in Judges 5:11 where KJV has "noise of archers." Archery plays a

Two Elamite warriors carrying bows and a quiver, a limestone relief from Nineveh, c. 668-633 B.C. "See, I will break the bow of Elam, the mainstay of their might" (Jer 49:35). The Elamites were a warlike people who periodically threatened the Babylonians and Assyrians. Courtesy S.P.Q.R. Musei Capitolini, Rome.

part in a crisis in the relations of David and Jonathan (1 Sam 20:17–42). Philistine archers mortally wounded Saul (1 Sam 31:3; 1 Chron 10:3). The sons of Ulam, Benjamites, "were brave warriors who could handle the bow" (1 Chron 8:40). Josiah was killed by archers (2 Chron 35:23). Job compares his troubles to being surrounded by archers (Job 16:13). Archers are mentioned in Isaiah 21:17; 22:3; Jeremiah 50:29. Light-armed, mobile, effective at a distance, archers were valuable in any army, and their skill was no less useful in hunting.

ARCHEVITES (är'kē-vīts). Colonists in Samaria who complained to Artaxerxes when the Jews began rebuilding Jerusalem (Ezra 4:9). They are identified in NIV as the men of Erech.

ARCHIPPUS (är-kĭp'ŭs, *master of the horse*). A Christian at Colosse, conspicuous as a champion of the gospel, a close friend (perhaps the son) of Philemon, an office-bearer in the church (Col 4:17; Philem 2). Because of the spiritual laxity at Colosse (like Laodicea, Rev 3:14–19), it is not surprising to find that Paul exhorts his fellow soldier to maintain his zeal and fidelity.

ARCHITE (See ARKITE)

ARCHITECTURE. This may be defined as the art or science of building. As a form of art, architecture is the effort to make a building aesthetically pleasing as well as useful. It must be classified as an abstract art, for it is the least representational of all the arts. For example, an artist who wished to portray the Madonna and Child could hardly use architecture as his medium; modern architects do indeed attempt to use symbolism in order to make it representational, but even this is greatly limited. Architecture could further be described as the most social of the arts, since a building is usually designed for more than one person, whether it is a church, a railroad station, or a home. The sole exception probably would be the monument or tomb that is intended simply to contain the remains of a single individual.

The materials of architecture in antiquity were wood, clay, brick (formed of clay, whether sun-baked or kiln-fired), and stone—in general, local availability determined the material used. It is well-known that wooden beams were exported from Lebanon (the famed "cedars of Lebanon") to practically all parts of the ancient Middle East; likewise the beautiful and distinctive rose granite was exported from the quarries at Aswan in Upper Egypt to many lands to be used for columns and statues, but these are notable exceptions.

One of the earliest materials for building is known as "wattle and daub," formed by driving stakes into the ground and interlacing reeds or flexible twigs to form the framework, and then covering both sides with clay. When the clay had dried in the sun it was quite permanent and required only a periodic coat of plaster to preserve it. Wattle-and-daub walls have been found dating back to the earliest period of building, namely the late Neolithic period. Buildings of this material can be included under the subject of architecture only in the broadest sense of the word, however, for they give little indication of any aesthetic quality.

Clay bricks seem to have been invented by the Obeid people in Persia before they descended to the Mesopotamian plain early in the fourth millennium B.C. The temple of Abu Shahrein (known in ancient times as Eridu) in southern Mesopotamia and that at Tepe Gawra in northern Mesopotamia (both from the early part of the fourth millennium) can clearly be described as architectural buildings, incorporating several features that became characteristic of Mesopotamian architecture. We mention here only the use of the buttress, designed not so much to strengthen the construction as to break up the monotonous expanse of a clay-brick wall.

In Egypt early builders experimented not only with clay and brick but also with wood, and then they made a remarkable transition to stone masonry. The genius traditionally connected with this new building technique was Imhotep, the designer and builder of the Step Pyramid at Saqqara in the time of Zoser (or Djoser) of the Third Dynasty (c. 2780 B.C.). From an examination of the remains at Saqqara there seems to be little doubt that the builders were seeking to imitate wood through the medium of stone. We find simulated hinges, boards carved in stone doors that obviously could not function, and other features that would be useful in wood but only ornamental in stone.

The Step Pyramid at Saqqara in Egypt, designed and built by Imhotep in the time of Djoser, 3rd Dynasty. Courtesy Seffie Ben-Yoseph.

In the same building compound at Saqqara are found such remarkable features as the Proto-Doric column (which seems to have been formed in stone after the pattern of papyrus bundles), the cornice, corner posts, and other architectural elements. The columns, it should be added, are not freestanding but are an integral part of the stone building; yet they cannot properly be identified as pilasters, since they have all of the other features of the column. Fluting is not only concave in the customary Doric manner but also convex, and the capitals appear to be papyrus and palm leaves, which compare to the acanthus leaves of the Corinthian columns of Greek architecture

A close-up view of the Step Pyramid at Saqqara, built in the time of Djoser (c. 2630 B.C.). Courtesy Zev Radovan.

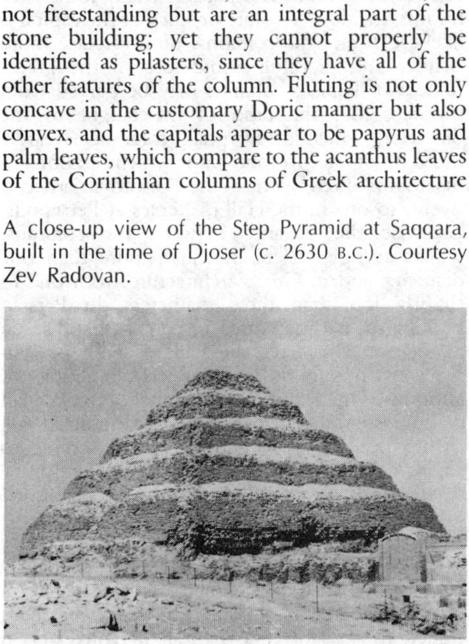

Reconstruction of Mesopotamian ziggurat, a pyramid-shaped building of clay brick with exterior staircases, sloping ramps, and shrine on top. The "Tower of Babel" (Gen 11:1–5) may well have been a ziggurat. Courtesy Carta, Jerusalem.

of a much later period. If the columns were freestanding, the fluting would number from fourteen to twenty around the circumference of the column, which compares to twenty flutes in the classical Doric order.

One of the early problems to be faced in building was the construction of the roof, and the solutions led to two main forms of architecture: trabeated and arcuated. The trabeated form is designed and constructed using horizontal beams supported by vertical posts, commonly called "post and lintel." The arcuated form makes use of various modifications of the arch. In the trabeated form the length of span between vertical supports is limited by the strength of the material used for the lintel. If, for example, the lintels were constructed of stone, as in ancient Egypt, it was only by using stone of great thickness that a span of any reasonable length could be obtained; as a result the space between columns in Egyptian temples is not much greater than the diameter of the columns. Wooden beams, on the other hand, permitted more useful space between the uprights. With the modern invention of structural steel and reinforced concrete, the span reaches probably its greatest limit.

An attempt to solve this problem resulted in the development of the arch. The first step was probably the corbelled vault, which is formed by stepping out successive courses of brick or stone beyond the supporting wall or column to meet similar corbelling from the adjacent vertical support. Corbelled vaults can be found at Ur in Mesopotamia as early as the Early Dynastic Period (c. 3000–2340 B.C.) and in Egypt as early as the tombs of the Third Dynasty (c. 2780–2680) at Reqaqnah and Beit Khallaf. To judge from predynastic drawings from Egypt, the true arch may have developed from the practice of bending reeds, which had been erected vertically to form side walls, so they would join overhead to form a roof. The arch, which is but a refinement of corbelling to effect a curved line rather than a steplike appearance, is found also in some of the buildings of Ur. However, the arch does not seem to have been used successfully in large buildings until the Roman period and is generally attributed to the Etruscans. A modification of the corbelled vault, in which the stones form the sides of a triangle coming to an apex overhead, is found in Mycenaean tombs at Mycenae and Ugarit, dating from the fifteenth or fourteenth century B.C.

Unusual styles of architecture include the pyramid-shaped building. The ziggurat in Mesopotamia is generally believed to be the representative of a mountain; it was built of clay brick with exterior staircases or a sloping ramp and probably a shrine at the top. One of the best preserved has recently been excavated at Choga Zambil, twenty miles (thirty-three kms.) SE of Susa in Iran. The pyramids in Egypt were built as tombs and were constructed of stone, having an inner room or rooms. The Egyptians developed great precision in squaring and orienting their pyramids.

The Levant (the lands on the eastern shore of the Mediterranean) exhibited very poor architecture in the early second millennium B.C., and what little there is of quality can be traced to external origins. Original architecture does, however, seem to have developed in northern Syria, the most characteristic being the *bit hilani*, a temple or palace compound that incorporates a portico and a throne room with their long axis parallel to the façade, behind which are small rooms, probably bedrooms and a storeroom. This pattern was developed in the second millennium but became characteristic of the early first millennium B.C. One feature of north Syrian architecture that should be mentioned is the use of a zoomorphic (animal form) base to support a column and often a human figure for the column itself.

Among the Israelites architecture does not seem to have been developed as an art or a skill; rather, Phoenician craftsmen were brought in to build Solomon's palace and temple. Phoenician elements appear to be present also in the buildings of subsequent Israelite periods; it is difficult to classify these, however, for the Phoenicians made use of many techniques and styles, some of which can be traced to Cyprus and Egypt. Their use of metal work in architecture (e.g., the columns in front of Solomon's temple) was possibly derived from Asia Minor.

The Hittites made use of stone foundations, often using large stones, at first rough but later dressed; characteristically the first course was set with the long dimension vertical. The upper portions of their buildings were frequently built of sun-dried brick strengthened by wooden beams, a type of architecture that can be found in the same areas of Asia Minor to the present time.

Late Assyrian architecture is perhaps best understood through the excavations of the palace of Sargon II at Khorsabad (720–704 B.C.). Regularity and a notable use of symmetry in the buildings are chracteristic. Much of the work was still of clay brick, with the use of glazed bricks (a technique that had been imported by the Mitanni from Crete) to protect the exterior or exposed surfaces, as well as to lend a decorative element.

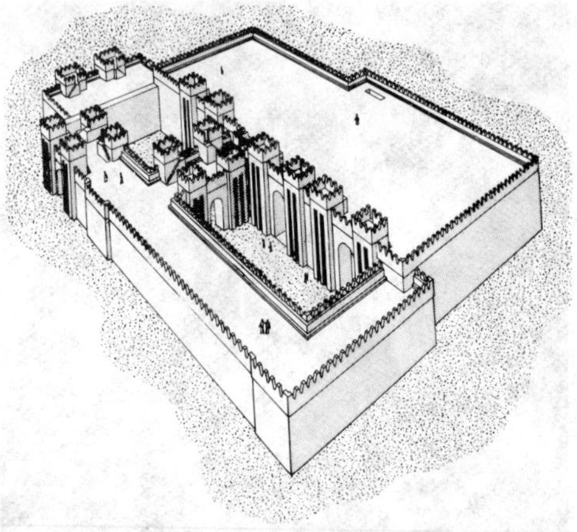

Reconstruction of the temple of King Sin-sharishkum, a last testimony to Assyrian architecture at the close of the seventh century. The king of Assyria said: "As one reaches into a nest, so my hand reached for the wealth of nations . . ." (Isa 10:14). Courtesy Carta, Jerusalem.

Persian architecture seems to have developed the use of the cyclopean foundation, which may have come from the Urartians in the region of Lake Van. This use of huge stones, sometimes with drafting around the edges, is comparable to the well-known Herodian use of large stones; particularly true of Taht-i-Sulayman north of Pasargadae in Iran, the foundation stones there could easily be mistaken for those at Ramat el-Khalil near Hebron, a town built by Herod several centuries later. The Persians apparently brought in the Ionic column from the Greek world and developed and used it widely. The base of Persian columns is characteristically Ionic with fluting; the double volute or spiral at the capital is likewise Ionic; the columns, however, are more slender and graceful. Some idea of the gracefulness of Persian columns may be gained from the fact that the ratio of the height to the diameter, which in Egyptian columns is rarely more than six to one and which attained a maximum of ten to one in the Corinthian order, is twelve to one in the Hall of Xerxes at Persepolis. Likewise the distance between the columns, which in Egypt is rarely much more than one diameter and in Greek architecture from one to slightly less than three diameters, in Persian buildings is between three and one-half and seven diameters. This gave the halls a sense of spaciousness not found in other large buildings of antiquity. One feature of the capital of the Persian column is unique, namely the use of a stylized bull with a head at either end, the heads serving to support the longitudinal beams, while the hollow of the back supported the transverse beams.

The supreme achievement in architecture is admittedly the Periclean architecture of Greece (460–400 B.C.). This is the Doric order characterized by simplicity and symmetry. There are certain optical refinements, among which may be mentioned the use of entasis (a slight convexity in

Remains of the Parthenon (447–432 B.C.), the chief temple of Athena on the Acropolis at Athens, as viewed from the northwest. Designed by the architects Ictinus and Callicrates, it represents the peak of the Doric order in Greek architecture. Courtesy Gerald Nowotny.

Ionic capital, partly restored, from the temple of Artemis at Ephesus, fourth century. It is now in the British Museum. Reproduced by courtesy of the Trustees of the British Museum.

columns to avoid the impression of hollowness that straight lines would give), similarly a slight convexity of long horizontal lines (to avoid the appearance of sagging), deviation from perpendicular at the corners of the building and from exact intervals of spacing between the columns (to avoid the appearance that the end columns are leaning outward and the central columns are too close together). We can clearly see the developments of the Doric order if we consult first of all the Temple of Apollo at Corinth (about the sixth century), then the great temple of Poseidon at Paestum in Italy (early fifth century). The Ionic order achieved its classical form during this same period, having originated along the Asiatic coast of the Aegean Sea. The Corinthian order developed toward the end of the fifth and the beginning of the fourth century and reached its zenith in the Greco-Roman period a few centuries later.

Roman architecture owed much to the Greeks but adopted some elements from the Etruscans; among the latter is principally the arch. In general we may say that Roman is not as subtle as Greek architecture, but at the same time it is more utilitarian. The Greeks had developed the skill of masonry to a high degree of perfection and fit marble blocks together with remarkable accuracy without mortar or cement. The Romans, on the other hand, developed the use of pozzolana, a volcanic earth that was mixed with lime to make a hydraulic cement. Using this as mortar, they were able to bond courses of stone without exact precision in masonry, increase the span in arches, and build two-story structures. Roman architecture, even more than Greek, included memorial arches and columns, amphitheaters, theaters, forums (or marketplaces), and many other forms familiar to us from the numerous remains of the Roman world to be found all over the Middle East.

Bibliography: A. W. Lawrence, *Greek Architecture,* 1937; H. Frankfort, *The Art and Architecture of the Ancient Orient,* 1955; W. S. Smith, *The Art and Architecture of Ancient Egypt,* 1958; Seaton Lloyd, *The Art of the Ancient Near East,* 1961; V. Scully, *The Earth, The Temple, and the Gods: Greek Sacred Architecture,* 1979 WSLS.

ARD, ARDITE (ȧrd, ȧr′dīt). Ard is listed as a son of Benjamin in Genesis 46:21, but as a son of Bela, son of Benjamin, in Numbers 26:40; the latter reference mentions also "the Ardite clan." Ard is called Addar (with the Hebrew consonants transposed) in 1 Chronicles 8:3.

ARDON (ȧr′dŏn). A son of Caleb (1 Chron 2:18).

ARELI (ȧ-rē′lī). A son of Gad and founder of the tribal family, the Arelites (Gen 46:16; Num 26:17).

AREOPAGITE (See DIONYSIUS)

AREOPAGUS (âr′ē-ŏp′ȧ-gŭs, Gr. *Areios pagos*). The rocky hill of the god Ares, or Mars. A spur

A view of the Acropolis in Athens looking west from the Areopagus, the low hill in the foreground noted as the meeting place of the earliest aristocratic council of the city. The name was extended to refer to the council itself. It was here that Paul was summoned to defend himself (Acts 17:22–34). Courtesy Gerald Nowotny.

jutting out from the western side of the Acropolis at Athens, separated from it by a short saddle. To the north directly below was the Agora or marketplace.

Areopagus is also the name of the council that met on Mars Hill, a court dating back to legendary times, in NT days still charged with questions of morals and the rights of teachers who lectured in public. Its importance was enhanced under the Romans. Paul was brought to the Areopagus (Acts 17:19) to be examined regarding his teaching. KJV says that "Paul stood in the midst of Mars hill," where ASV and RSV have "in the midst [middle] of the Areopagus," referring to the court, not the hill (17:22). NIV, even more specific, says that Paul stood up "in the meeting of the Areopagus." Before these "solid citizens," the bulwark of civic and religious conservatism, Paul met the mocking taunts of adherents of two of that day's most popular philosophies, Epicureanism and Stoicism. His address is today more widely read than any of the writings of the philosophers and is almost the only means by which we remember the Council of Areopagus. Paul's mission in Athens produced numerically scant results, and the founding of no church is recorded; but Dionysius the Areopagite, one of the members of this honorable court, was among those who "became followers of Paul and believed" (17:34). ER

ARETAS (ār'ē-tăs, *pleasing* or *virtuous*). A Nabatean king, father-in-law of Herod the tetrarch, whose deputy sought to apprehend Paul at Damascus (2 Cor 11:32; cf. Acts 9:24).

ARGOB (ȧr'gŏb, Heb. *'argōv, heap,* or *region of clods*). 1. A well-defined region of Bashan, identified with the kingdom of Og in Deuteronomy 3:4, 13–14 and 1 Kings 4:13. This land of sixty strong, fortified cities was taken by the Israelites under Moses (Deut 3:4) and was given to the half-tribe of Manasseh (3:13), because Jair of this tribe conquered the region. He gave it his own name, Bashan-Navoth-Jair (3:14). In Solomon's reign, one of his princes, the son of Geber, held Argob, which still had "sixty large walled cities with bronze gate bars" (1 Kings 4:13).

2. The reference in 2 Kings 15:25 is either to a place or to a person. If a place, it may signify the location of one of the king's houses. If a person, he may have been either a follower of Pekahiah, killed with him, or a follower of Pekah who took part in the murder of Pekahiah. The Hebrew text is uncertain. RSV omits mention of Argob here.

ARIDAI (ȧ-rĭd'ā-ī, ȧ-rĭd'ī). One of Haman's ten sons, killed by the Jews (Esth 9:9).

ARIDATHA (ȧ-rĭd'ȧ-thȧ, ăr-ĭ-dā'thȧ). A son of Haman, killed by the Jews (Esth 9:8).

ARIEH (ȧ-rī'ĕ, ār'ĭ-ĕ). Named with Argob in 2 Kings 15:25, KJV, ASV, NIV, either as places or as persons, but omitted in RSV. The Hebrew text is uncertain.

ARIEL (âr'ĭ-ĕl, Heb. *'ărî 'ēl, lion of God*). 1. One of an embassy sent by Ezra to "bring attendants to us for the house of our God" to the returning exiles from Babylonia (Ezra 8:16–17).

2. In 2 Samuel 23:20 and 1 Chronicles 11:22, where KJV has "two lionlike men of Moab"; ASV conjectures "two sons of Ariel of Moab"; RSV has "two ariels of Moab" (marginally explaining that the meaning of *ariel* is unknown); and NIV renders "two of Moab's best men." The text is uncertain.

3. A poetic name, "lion of God," according to some versions; "hearth of God," according to others, given to Jerusalem (Isa 29:1–2, 7).

ARIMATHEA (âr'ĭ-mȧ-thē'ȧ). The city of the Joseph who buried the body of Jesus in his own new tomb near Jerusalem (Matt 27:57; Mark 15:43; Luke 23:51; John 19:38). The location of Arimathea is in doubt but is conjectured to be Ramathaim-Zophim, the Ramah of Samuel's residence, in the hill country of Ephraim, about twenty miles (thirty-three km.) NW of Jerusalem and six miles (ten km.) SE of Antipatris.

ARIOCH (ăr'ĭ-ŏk). 1. The king of Ellasar in Syria and confederate with Kedorlaomer (Gen 14:1, 4, 9).

2. Captain of the king's guard at Babylon under Nebuchadnezzar (Dan 2:14–25).

ARISAI (ȧ-rĭs'ā-ī, ăr'ĭ-sī). A son of Haman who was killed by the Jews (Esth 9:9).

ARISTARCHUS (ăr'ĭs-tȧr'kŭs, *the best ruler*). A Macedonian of Thessalonica, one of Paul's travel companions. This convert from Judaism is spoken of as Paul's "fellow prisoner," implying imprisonment for the gospel's sake (Acts 19:29; 20:4; 27:2; Col 4:10; Philem 24).

ARISTOBULUS (ă-rĭstŏ-bū'lŭs, *the best counselor*). A Christian in Rome, whose household Paul greeted. There is a tradition that he was one of the seventy disciples and that he preached in Britain (Rom 16:10).

ARK (Heb. *tēvâh, a chest* or *a vessel to float;* in the Bible the Hebrew word always has the second meaning). It is used of the vessel that God directed Noah to build (Gen 6:14–16). God told Noah what to bring into it (6:18–21), and Noah obeyed (6:22–7:10). The ark floated during the Flood (7:11–8:3), then came to rest "on the mountains of Ararat" (8:4). After Noah abandoned the ark (8:18–19), what happened to it is unknown, despite many traditions and expeditions. We do not even know on which peak of the mountains in the land of Ararat the ark grounded.

The ark of Noah is referred to in Matthew 24:38 and Luke 17:27 in a warning of coming judgment; in Hebrews 11:7 its copnstruction is an example of faith; and in 1 Peter 3:20 "the days of Noah while the ark was being built" are held up as an example of the long-suffering of God, followed by disaster for the disobedient and salvation for the few who entered the ark. The same Hebrew word is used of the basket of bulrushes in which Moses was cast out to float on the Nile (Exod 2:2–5).

ARKITE (àr'kīt). 1. A member of the clan of Ataroth in Ephraim (Josh 16:2). Hushai, David's friend (1 Chron 27:33), acted as his secret agent in the rebellion of Absalom, to defeat the counsel of Ahithophel (2 Sam 15:32–17:23). KJV, Archite.

2. People of Arka, a Phoenician town a few miles NE of Tripoli, and near but not on the sea. The Arkites are named among the descendants of Canaan (Gen. 10:17; 1 Chron 1:15).

ARK OF THE COVENANT, ARK OF THE TESTIMONY (Heb. *'ărôn ha-berîth, chest of the covenant*). The word used for ark is the same as that used of the coffin (mummy case) of Joseph (Gen 50:26); elsewhere of the chest containing the tables of the law, resting in the tabernacle or in the temple. God directed Moses (Exod 25:10–22; Deut 10:2–5) to make the ark of acacia (shittim) wood, of precise dimensions, and to overlay it with pure gold within and without, with a crown of gold about it. Rings of gold at the corners and staves covered with gold to put through the rings were made to carry the ark. Moses placed inside the ark the stone tablets on which the commandments were written. An atonement cover of gold, with two winged cherubim of gold, covered the top of the ark. There God promised to meet and talk with Moses. Moses made the ark after the golden calf was destroyed (Deut 10:1, "at that time") and set it up in the tabernacle (Exod 40:20).

The ark went before Israel in the wilderness journeys "to find them a place to rest" (Num 10:33). The ark was instrumental in the crossing of Jordan on dry land under Joshua (Josh 3) and in the capture of Jericho (4:7–11). Joshua prayed before the ark after the defeat at Ai (7:6) and after the subsequent victory at Mount Ebal with the ark present (8:33). In the days of Eli the ark was in the tabernacle at Shiloh (1 Sam 3:3). Eli's sons took it into battle against the Philistines, and they captured it, and because of this, it was said, "The glory has departed from Israel" (4:3–22). The Philistines held the ark until a plague convinced them that it was too dangerous to keep, and they ceremoniously sent it back to Beth Shemesh (5:1–6:16). The men of this place also suffered a plague for looking into the ark, and it was removed to Kiriath Jearim (6:19–21). Here it was treated with due respect, kept in the house of Abinadab under the care of his son Eleazar (7:1–2).

Relief of a structure on wheels representing the ark of the covenant, found in third century ruins at Capernaum. The original ark of the covenant was a portable wooden chest decorated with cherubim and containing the tablets of stone with the Ten Commandments. Courtesy Israel Government Press Office.

David brought the ark to Jerusalem, after some misadventures (2 Sam 6; 1 Chron 13 and 15). When Uriah said to David, "The ark and Israel and Judah are staying in tents" (2 Sam 11:11), he may have meant that the ark had been taken by the army into the field or merely that the ark was in a tent (the tabernacle) just as the armies of Israel and Judah were in tents. At the time of Absalom's rebellion, Zadok and the Levites carried the ark out of Jerusalem, but David had them take it back (15:24–29). The priests brought the ark into Solomon's temple (1 Kings 8:3–9). There was nothing in it at this time "except the two stone tablets that Moses had placed in it at Horeb" (8:9).

Before the ark was made, Moses directed that a pot of manna be kept before the Lord (Exod 16:32–34) and Hebrews 9:4 says that the "ark contained the gold jar of manna, Aaron's staff that had budded, and the stone tablets of the covenant," though it need not be understood to imply that these were the contents of the ark throughout its history. Jeremiah, writing after the destruction of Jerusalem by Nebuchadnezzar, prophesied that in time to come the ark would no longer be of significance for worship (Jer 3:16). Psalm 132:8 speaks of the ark poetically as representing the strength of the Lord. Hebrews 9 uses the tabernacle and all its furnishings, including the ark, in explaining by analogy salvation by the high priesthood of Christ. After the destruction of the first temple, there is no evidence as to what happened to the ark, but only highly speculative tradition and conjecture. Synagogues, from our earliest knowledge of them to the present, have had arks in the side wall toward Jerusalem; the scrolls of the Law are stored in them behind a curtain.

The ark was set in the very heart of the tabernacle, the Most Holy Place (Exod 26:34), symbolizing its central significance in Israel. When the high priest, once each year (Lev 16:15; Heb 9:7), penetrated to the innermost shrine, he came into the very presence of the God of Israel (Exod 30:6; Lev 16:1–2). But that presence was not visibly expressed in any image form (Deut 4:12), but by the presence of the Law of the Lord (the stone tablets) and the atonement cover that was over the Law. In other words, the ark by its contents declared the divine holiness by which all stand condemned and by its form (specifically the atonement cover) declared the divine redeeming mercy through the shed blood. See also ATONEMENT. ER

ARM. Used as a figure for personal, active power. Thus the Lord lays "bare his holy arm" (Isa 52:10), rather as we might say of someone about to undertake some task, "he rolled up his sleeves." The Lord's arm (53:1) is figurative of his personal intervention. In particular the figure of the "arm" looks back to what the Lord did at the Exodus (Exod 6:6; Deut 4:34; 5:15; Isa 51:9–11).

ARMAGEDDON (ȧr-mȧ-gĕd'ŏn, Gr. *Armagedōn,* from Heb., *har-mĕgiddôn*; ASV, Mount Megiddo). A word found only in Revelation 16:16 for the final battleground between the forces of good and the forces of evil. The Valley of Jezreel and the Plain of Esdraelon at the foot of Mount Megiddo were the scene of many decisive incidents in the history of Israel: the victory over Sisera sung by Deborah and Barak (Judg 5:19–20); Gideon's defeat of Midian (6:33); Saul's death at the hands of the Philistines (1 Sam 31; cf. 2 Sam 4:4); Josiah's death in battle with Pharaoh Neco (2 Kings 23:29–30); Ahaziah's death when he fled there (9:27). The town of Megiddo guarded the pass that formed the easiest caravan route between the Plain of Sharon and the Valley of Jezreel, and the low mountains around were silent witnesses of perhaps more bloody encounters than any other spot on earth, continuing down to recent times. Hence the appropriateness of this place for the vast conflict pictured in Revelation 16.

ARMENIA (ȧr-mē'nĭ-ȧ). Occurs only in KJV of 2 Kings 19:37 and Isaiah 37:38, where it is said that the two sons of Sennacherib, king of Assyria, "escaped into the land of Armenia" after murdering their father. ASV, RSV, NIV, and KJV elsewhere (e.g., Gen 8:4; Jer 51:27) have Ararat, following the Hebrew and LXX. The same mountainous country, north of Assyria, is meant by both names.

ARMLET, BRACELET. An ornament for men and women, usually worn on the upper arm. The precise meanings of the several different Hebrew words thus translated are uncertain; archaeological finds illustrate possible armlets. In seven verses, both KJV and NIV have "bracelets" (Gen 24:22, 30, 47; Num 31:50; Isa 3:19; Ezek 16:11; 23:42); once (Num 31:50) KJV has 'chains," NIV has "armlets." "Armlets" appears more in other versions—twice in ASV (Exod 35:22; Num 31:50), four times in RSV (Exod 35:22; Num 31:50; 2 Sam 1:10; Isa 3:20).

ARMONI (ȧr-mō'nī, *belonging to the palace*). A son of Saul by his concubine Rizpah. He was killed by the Gibeonites to satisfy justice (2 Sam 21:8–11).

ARMOR (See ARMS AND ARMOR)

ARMOR-BEARER. One who bears weapons. Abimelech (Judg 9:54), Saul (1 Sam 31:4), Jonathan (14:12), and Joab (2 Sam 23:37) each had one. Cf. Goliath (1 Sam 17:7, 41).

ARMORY. Three Hebrew words: *'ôtsār* (Jer 50:25), figurative for the "Lord's means of judgment" rendered also "treasury," "store house"; *nesheq* (Neh 3:19), "storehouse for valuables and arms"; *talpîyôth* (Song of Songs 4:4), used figuratively for "beauty."

ARMS AND ARMOR. These are mentioned often in the Bible, both literally and as illustrative of spiritual conflicts. Here only hand weapons and body armor are considered, not chariots or machines used in siege.

A. **Offensive weapons.** (1) *Sword* is the first offensive weapon mentioned in the Bible: "A flaming sword flashing back and forth to guard the way to the tree of life" (Gen 3:24). Hebrew *hereb,* a weapon for killing, is the common sword (Gen 27:40; Exod 17:13); a sword for punishment is ascribed to God (Exod 5:3; 22:24). Figurative and literal are united in "a sword for

Egyptian bronze sword, bent deliberately and buried with its owner, from Late Canaanite (Bronze) period, c. 1550–1200 B.C. Courtesy Reuben and Edith Hecht Museum, University of Haifa. Photo Zev Radovan.

A gold helmet that was worn over a quilted cap with laces that passed through the small holes around the rim to hold the helmet in place. Found in the tomb of Meskalamdug, from Ur, 25th century B.C. Goliath (late 11th century B.C.) had a bronze helmet on his head and wore a coat of scale armor weighing about 125 pounds (1 Sam 17:5). Courtesy the University Museum, University of Pennsylvania.

the Lord and for Gideon" (Judg 7:20). Gideon's men were executing the judgment of God. In NT Greek the more common word is *machaira,* short sword, dagger, or saber (Matt 26:27–53; Rom 8:35; 13:4); figuratively "the sword of the Spirit" (Eph 6:17). *Rhomphaia,* once a large, broad sword, occurs with symbolic meaning once in Luke 2:35 and six times in the Book of Revelation (e.g. 1:16). (2) *Rod,* a stick loaded at one end. It could be for reassurance (Ps 23:4), to count sheep (Lev 27:32), or as a weapon (Ps 2:9). (3) *Sling,* a band of leather, wide in the middle to receive a stone. With the ends held together, it was swung around the head, then one end was released so that the stone could fly to its mark (1 Sam 17:40, 49; Judg 20:16; 2 Kings 3:25). (4) *Bow,* sometimes of bronze (2 Sam 22:35; Job 20:24; Ps 18:34), and *arrows.* First mentioned (Gen 27:3) as used in hunting, except that the same word is used for the rainbow in Genesis 9:13–16. The practice of archery is described in 1 Samuel 20:20–22, 35–40. The bow is mentioned only once in the NT (Rev 6:2). (5) *Spear, lance, javelin, or dart,* sharp-pointed instruments to be thrust or thrown (Josh 8:18; Judg 5:8; 1 Sam 17:7; 18:11; Ps 68:30, different Heb. words). Spearmen are mentioned in Acts 23:23, and a Roman lance pierced the body of Jesus on the cross (John 19:34). Flame-tipped darts were used also (Eph 6:16).

B. **Defensive armor.** (1) *Shields* were either small and round, Hebrew *maghēn* (Gen 15:1; Judg 5:8) or large, Hebrew *tsinnâh* (1 Sam 17:7, 41), and were sometimes used for display (2 Chron 9:16), called *thyreos,* "like a door" in Greek (Eph 6:16). (2) *Helmet* (1 Sam 17:5; Isa 59:17), sometimes of bronze (1 Sam 17:38), surrounding the head (Eph 6:17; 1 Thess 5:8). (3) *Coat of mail,* only in 1 Samuel 17:5, 38, called "breastplate" in Isaiah 59:17. In the NT, Greek *thorax* (Eph 6:14; 1 Thess 5:8, figuratively; Rev 9:9, 17, symbolic). (4) *Greaves,* for the legs, only in 1 Samuel 17:6. (5) *Girdle,* or belt from which the sword hung (2 Sam 20:8). Ephesians 6:14 implies it as part of the equipment of a heavily armed soldier; the description of this equipment in Ephesians 6:11–18 is evidently drawn from Paul's intimate contact, as a prisoner, with Roman guards. "The whole armor," Greek *panoplia,* is a technical term for such armament. Note also the detailed description of the armor of Goliath (1 Sam 17:4–7). ER

ARMY. A collection of men armed and organized for warfare. Of the several words used for army, *gedhûdh* is used thirty-two times and generally means a band of light troops going out on forays (1 Sam 30:8; 2 Sam 22:30), though in the time of Amaziah (ninth century B.C.) it was used (2 Chron 25) of his great army of 300,000 chosen men of Judah and Benjamin with, at first, 100,000 mercenaries from the northern kingdom. These were drafted and put under colonels and captains. The armies of Israel, when directed and led by God, were uniformly successful (Josh 1:3, 5:14), but when men like Saul (1 Sam 15) and Amaziah (2 Chron 25:14) refused to listen to God, defeat and death followed. *Hayil,* used 231 times and translated "army" 54 times, implies might, valor, wealth, or, in military contexts, warlike resources in general. For some reason, God did not want Israel to use or to depend on

A scale of armor from copper hoard found at Kefar Monash in the Sharon plain, c. 3000–1000 B.C. Courtesy Israel Department of Antiquities and Museums.

Group of model Egyptian soldiers (made of painted wood) armed with spears and shields, from tomb at Asyut (12th Dynasty). Now in Egyptian Museum, Cairo. Courtesy Giraudon.

cavalry (Deut 17:16; 20:1; Isa 31:1). *Mahăneh*, used over 200 times, generally means "encampment" but is sometimes used of an army in the field (e.g., Judg 4:15).

The word *ma'ărākhâh* comes from a verb meaning "to set in order" and is used of the army actually drawn up for or involved in battle—"the ranks of Israel" (1 Sam 17:8, 10). The word *tsāvā'* properly means "host," e.g., "Lord God of Sabaoth" (Isa 22:15; NIV "the LORD Almighty") or "LORD God of hosts." It is used nearly five hundred times and is rendered "army" twenty-nine times. The word emphasizes the vast number of the soldiers. When used of God's army, the "soldiers" may be people (Exod 7:4), angels (Ps 103:21), or, by implication, locusts (Joel 2). The corresponding Greek word *stratia* is used of angels (Luke 2:13) and of stars and planets (Acts 7:42).

In the days of the judges, God raised up from time to time men of special ability to save Israel when she had suffered for her apostasies and had been brought to repentance. These judges saved Israel from her foreign oppressors and they varied greatly in character, from the godly Deborah (Judg 4–5) to the rather erratic champion Samson (Judg 14–16). Israel's armies down to Solomon's time were composed mostly of footmen, armed with swords, spears, bows and arrows, and slings, and protected by small shields, with a judge, general, or king at the head.

Numbers 1 contains a military census of Israel at Sinai just after the Exodus, and Numbers 26 records a second census taken forty years later in the plains of Joab. According to the plain sense of the English versions, the number of military men was immense: over 603,000 at the Exodus and nearly as many at the Jordan. These figures imply a total population of something like three million men, women, and children, accompanied by herds and flocks. It is hard to picture them drinking at a common spring, even a large one. The Hebrew word *'eleph* means either a thousand or a family, and by reading "families" in the censuses, some would make the numbers more comprehensible; e.g., Numbers 1:21 could read "forty-six families, five hundred men" instead of "46,500." This would not only make the story more easy to comprehend, but it would explain the very remarkable numerical phenomenon in censuses. In all the twenty-four numbers recorded, in the hundreds' digits we have not a single "zero," "one," "eight," or "nine," and only one "two" in the whole list. The trouble with this theory, however, lies in the totals: if *'eleph* here means family, the total in Numbers 1:46 would become 598 families, 5,500 men instead of 603,500 men, for we could not "carry over" the hundreds' digit.

Israel, on the condition of obedience (Deut 28:1–7), could have become the paramount power of the earth; but when she had gone into hopeless apostasy, God began to raise up great universal world powers (Dan 2) to overturn (Ezek 21:27) Israel, preparing for the coming of our Lord. The Babylonians with their hordes were overthrown by the Persians, originally a hardy race whose armies were mostly cavalry; but when the Persian king Xerxes (Esth 1) attempted to invade Europe, he was defeated. The Book of Esther tells of his great "feast" of six months, which was really a military council preparing for his invasion of Greece in 480 B.C. The eastern army was defeated by the Greeks with their phalanxes of heavily armed infantry, arranged closely in ranks and files. The Greek armies, in turn, were conquered by the Romans. The Romans had a genius for government and for military organization, and the various NT references mention their "commanders" (Acts 21:31), whom we would call colonels, and their "centurions" (10:1), implying their organization into legions and armies. Jesus (Matt 26:53) hints at a possible angelic army divided into legions like the Roman army. The smallest group mentioned in reference to the Roman army is the quaternion (Acts 12:4), comprising only four soldiers. ABF

ARNAN (ȧr'năn). Head of a noble family about 500 B.C. (1 Chron 3:21).

ARNON (ȧr'nŏn). The swift "roaring stream" and the valley of the same name that descend to the east side of the Dead Sea a little north of its center. The river begins in the hills of northern Arabia, flows NW a while, and then turns westward to descend precipitously into the Dead Sea, emptying at about the lowest point on the

Gorge of the Arnon River where it enters the Dead Sea. Courtesy Ecole Biblique et Archéologique Française, Jerusalem.

The rolling hills of Moab east of the Dead Sea. The river Arnon, today a wadi, cuts through the mountains, in ancient days forming the natural northern border of Moab (Num 21:13). Courtesy Studium Biblieum Franciscanum, Jerusalem.

earth's surface. It is now a "wadi," implying that it is dry most of the year. It is first mentioned (Num 21:13) as the boundary between the Moabites and the Amorites in the time of Moses; Israel encamped on its north side so as not to invade Moab. In Judges 11:18–26 Jephthah tells the Ammonites how Israel had held the land north of the Arnon for three hundred years previous to this time (c. 1560–1260 B.C.). For all those years, and for a long time after, the Arnon was the southern boundary of the tribe of Reuben. In the days of Jehu (ninth century), Hazael, king of Syria, overpowered Israel east of the Jordan as far as Arnon (2 Kings 10:32–33). The Arnon now flows through the kingdom of Jordan.

ARODI, AROD (ȧrō'dī, ā'rŏd). A son of Gad (Gen 46:16). Head of the Arodites in the time of Moses (Num 26:17).

AROER (ȧ-rō'êr, Heb. *'aro'ēr, poor, naked, helpless*). The same word is translated "bush" in Jeremiah 17:6; 48:6. 1. A town on a branch of the brook Jabbok, fortified early by the tribe of Gad (Num 32:34), having been taken from Sihon, king of the Amorites (cf. Josh 13:25). A camping place of Joab (2 Sam 24:5) when taking a census in the days of David. Isaiah speaks of it as being deserted in his time (Isa 17:2).

2. A town about thirty-five miles (fifty-eight km.) south of no. 1, on the north bank of the Arnon, located in the tribe of Reuben just across from Moab. Moses took this town also from Sihon (Deut 2:36) and gave it to Reuben (Josh 13:9). Hazael, king of Syria, took it from Israel in the days of Jehu (2 Kings 10:33). Jeremiah scoffs at its inhabitants (Jer 48:19).

3. A town in the southern part of Judah (1 Sam 30:28).

ARPAD (ȧr'păd). A town and its surrounding region in the northern part of Syria near Hamath (modern Hamah), with which it is associated in all six biblical references. Rabshakeh, representing Sennacherib before Jerusalem in 701 B.C., boasts that the gods of Arpad could not stand before his master, therefore neither could the Lord deliver Jerusalem (2 Kings 18:34–35). In Jeremiah's time (c. 580) Arpad had lost its power (Jer 49:23).

ARPHAXAD, ARPACHSHAD (ȧr-făk'săd, Heb. *Arpachshad*). Third son of Shem, c. 2479 B.C., the first birth recorded after the Flood. He lived 438 years and was the ancestor of the Hebrews and of many Arab tribes. In fact, all Semites descend from him except Arameans, Assyrians, Elamites, and Lydians, (Gen 10:22– 11:13). The name is so far unknown outside the Bible.

ARROW (See ARMS AND ARMOR)

ARSENAL (See ARMS AND ARMOR)

ART. The application of human skills to produce a pleasing effect. The word is also used in a broader sense with reference to the good and the useful, but the narrower meaning, referring to the beautiful, is more common. The six major arts are music, dance, architecture, sculpture, painting, and literature.

It is difficult to date the beginning of art. If some human being found pleasure in the shape of a stone axe or flint sickle, this might be described as the beginning of art. By any definition, the line drawings in the cave of La Madelaine from the Old Stone Age seem to be art. Architecture might be traced to the first building of a house, although some effort at an aesthetic quality should be added to the utilitarian value in order for the building to qualify as "art." Artistic attempts can be found in the early temples in Mesopotamia from the fourth millennium B.C. and in Egypt only slightly later. Sculpture is found in Mesopotamia and Egypt as early as the beginning of the third millennium. Literature must be placed before the time of writing, for the folk stories and legends had already taken on forms that gave pleasure to the hearers in the preliterary period—again toward the end of the fourth millennium. To judge from wall paintings in Egypt, music and dance must go back to about the same time. Hence it seems reasonable to date the beginning of art in historical cultures to some time in the fourth millennium. The origin of the arts may be intended in Genesis 4:21–22, where Jubal and Tubal-Cain are mentioned.

The arts can be classified as spatial (architecture, sculpture, painting) and temporal (music, literature), with the dance extending over both categories. Spatial art can be seen as a whole before the parts become meaningful; temporal art on the other hand must be seen or heard in the parts before the whole is comprehended. The temporal forms therefore require a greater use of the memory on the part of the observer, and a certain amount of repetition and interpretation on the part of the artist. Music and in many cases literature might be called aural arts, whereas the others are visual arts.

In each of the arts, categories of matter, form, and content can be distinguished. Matter involves all the material available to the artist to select, arrange, and use for the purpose intended; form involves all the ways in which the artist can organize the material; content involves what is actually expressed when the work of art is finished. The artist's innate ability is discernible in the selection of matter and form; it would be ludicrous if an artist were to attempt to present a sunset at sea by sculpturing in marble, or a thunderstorm by a piccolo solo.

It becomes increasingly apparent, as we think on the subject of art, that something of the image of God as Creator is to be found in humans as artists. Artists create. In fact, some authors claim that there is no art in nature and no art without the creativity of the artist.

Each art has certain limitations imposed on it. Music and dance can convey certain emotional messages, but in spite of the saying that "music is the universal language," it is seriously limited in the intellectual message it can convey. Sculpture and painting can convey messages from the visible world but are more limited in conveying ideas or emotions. Literature is by far the most communicative of all the arts and can be used to convey conceptual, emotional, and other ideas. In keeping with this fact is the presentation of God's revelation through the medium of literature.

In Israel, probably because of the commandment against representational art (Exod 20:4), there were no great contributions to the arts of painting or sculpturing. The major architectural work in Israel—the temple—is a notable exception, yet even that was constructed with some help from Phoenician craftsmen. References to dance in the OT are extremely limited and afford no information on the form or content. The development of music in Israel, on the other hand, is noteworthy; and to judge from the titles we may assume that many of the psalms, if not all, were sung to music and accompanied by musical instruments. Literature, however, was the most thoroughly developed art in Israel and reached a level not surpassed in all antiquity.

ARTAXERXES (ȧr-tȧ-zûrk'sēz). A proper name or possibly a title, like *Pharaoh* or *Caesar* for several kings of Persia. The name is variously derived by scholars but perhaps "strong king" (Gesenius) is as good as any. Herodotus said it meant "great warrior." It is the name or title of three Persian kings in the OT.

1. The pseudo-Smerdis of Ezra 4:7–23, a Magian usurper who claimed to be Smerdis, a son of Syrus who had died. This false Smerdis took the title Artaxerxes and reigned about seven months in 522–521 B.C. He was opposed to the liberal policies of Cyrus and Cambyses (called Xerxes, NIV; Ahasuerus, KJV, RSV in Ezra 4:6) and was glad to prohibit the Jews from building the temple.

2. A Persian king (Ezra 7:1–8; Neh 2:1; 5:14; 13:6) who was nicknamed "Longimanus" ("Long-handed") because of a deformity of his right hand. He granted the requests of Ezra (Ezra 7:6) in 457 B.C. and of Nehemiah (Neh 2:1–8) in 444 to go to Jerusalem and gave them power, supplies, and authority.

3. Possibly another king who must have reigned before 516 B.C. (Ezra 6:14). WSLS

ARTEMAS (ȧr'tĕ-măs). A companion of Paul at Nicopolis whom Paul expected to send to Crete. He is mentioned only in Titus 3:12. In tradition, he is a bishop of Lystra.

ARTEMIS (Gr. *Artemis,* Lat. *Diana*). Diana was the Roman goddess of the moon. A daughter of Jupiter, she was a twin sister of Apollo, who was associated with the sun, as she was with the moon. She was represented as a virgin huntress and was widely worshiped. When the Greek worship penetrated Italy about 400 B.C., the Italians identified Diana with their Artemis, her Greek counterpart. Her worship was pure compared with the sensual worship of eastern gods and goddesses.

"Artemis of the Ephesians" is mentioned only in Acts 19:24–35 ("Diana" in JB, KJV, NEB), and her myths were of a very different sort. Her silver "shrines" (19:24) were little "temples" containing an image of Artemis as imagined by the Asiatics, a combination of the Greek virgin goddess with the many-breasted and lewd Semitic moon goddess Ashtoreth. For the Ephesians, Artemis was the great Asiatic nursing mother of gods, men, animals, and plants, and was the patroness of the sexual instinct. Her images, instead of being artistically beautiful like those of the Greeks, were ugly, more like the lascivious images of India and Tyre and Sidon. Her special worship was centered in the great temple at Ephesus, probably because of the discovery of a very interesting aerolite that supposedly fell from

A statue of Artemis, dating from the second century A.D. in Ephesus. This is the Artemis "whom all Asia and the world worship" (Acts 19:27). Courtesy Duby Tal.

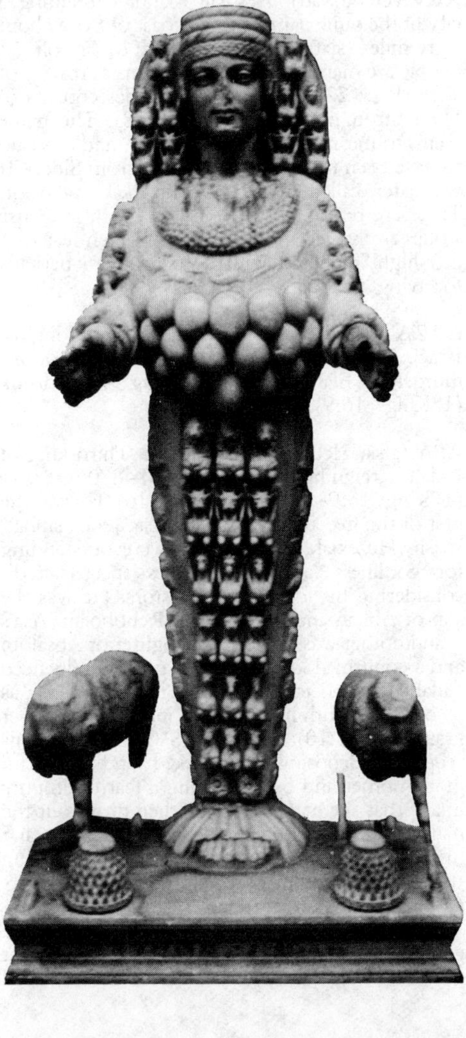

heaven (19:35). The feasts of Diana, "who is worshiped throughout the province of Asia and the world" (19:27), were commercialized, and among the silversmiths there was a large industry in making shrines and idols for the worship of this goddess. The preaching of Paul interfered with this commerce and aroused violent opposition. It seems that Paul and his companions had preached the gospel from the positive side instead of directly attacking the idolatry, for the city clerk testified that they "neither robbed temples nor blasphemed our goddess" (19:37). ABF

ARTIFICER (See OCCUPATIONS AND PROFESSIONS)

ARUBBOTH (ȧ-rŭb'ŏth). A region of the Shephelah in Judah assigned to Ben-Hesed to provide food for Solomon's court (1 Kings 4:10).

ARUMAH (ȧ-rū'mȧ). A place near Shechem in Ephraim where Abimelech lived (Judg 9:41). Variously placed NE or south of modern Nablus.

ARVAD (ar'văd). A small island, containing a city of the same name, off the coast of Syria about forty miles (sixty-seven km.) north of Tripoli. Its people are mentioned with Sidonians as rowers of Tyre (Ezek 27:8, 11). They were descendants of Ham through Canaan (Gen 10:18). The name seems to mean "a place of fugitives," and it is said to have been first built by fugitives from Sidon. It was later called "Ruad," from the same root. There are remains of the sea walls with immense stones twelve feet (3.8 m.) long and ten feet (3.1 m.) high, indented with deep grooves, perhaps for tying up boats.

ARZA (ăr'zȧ). A steward of Elah, a king of Israel. It was in his house at Tirzah that Zimri murdered Elah while the king was drunk (1 Kings 16:9).

ASA (ā'sȧ, Heb. *'āsā'*, *healer*). 1. Third king of Judah, reigning from 911/10–870/69 B.C. (1 Kings 15:9–24; 2 Chron 14–16). He was the first of the five kings of Judah (Asa, Jehoshaphat, Joash, Hezekiah, Josiah) who were outstanding for godliness, and he deserves special credit considering his idolatrous ancestors. He was the son of Abijah and grandson of Rehoboam. Asa's grandmother was Maacah, a daughter of Absalom and a confirmed idolatress who greatly influenced Judah toward idolatry. She is spoken of as "mother" of both her son (1 Kings 15:2) and her grandson (15:10) in KJV, RSV. Asa began his reign by deposing his wicked and powerful grandmother and by destroying a fearful, impure image that she had set up. He then drove out the male shrine prostitutes and destroyed idols that his fathers had worshiped (15:12), commanding Judah to seek the Lord God of their fathers (2 Chron 14:4).

In the early peaceful days of his reign, he gathered into the temple the dedicated things that he and his father had dedicated to the Lord (1 Kings 15:15). Then about 897 B.C. Zerah the Ethiopian came against him with an immense force. The Lord helped Judah defeat them at Mareshah in the west-central part of Judah, because Asa trusted the Lord (2 Chron 14:9–15). In 2 Chronicles 15:1–13 we see how the Lord approved and encouraged Asa in his faith and in his work of reformation. Later, c. 895/94, Baasha of the northern kingdom made war against Judah. Judah this time did not put her whole trust in the Lord, but Asa bribed Ben-Hadad of Syria to break his league with Baasha so as to draw off the forces of Israel. This Ben-Hadad did, but the Lord, through his prophet Hanani, rebuked Asa for trusting in politics rather than in God (1 Kings 15:16–22; 2 Chron 16:1–10). In the thirty-ninth year of his reign Asa was taken with a severe disease of the feet, and because he trusted his physicians rather than the Lord, he died two years later (2 Chron 16:11–14).

2. A Levite among those who had returned from captivity (1 Chron 9:16).

ASAHEL (ăs'ȧ-hĕl, *whom God made*). 1. The youngest son of Zeruiah, David's sister; brother of Joab and Abishai. These three were among the mighty men of David; Asahel was over 24,000 men (1 Chron 27:7). A fast runner, he pursued Abner, Saul's former general (2 Sam 2:18–23), who killed him.

2. A teaching Levite in the reign of Jehoshaphat (2 Chron 17:8).

3. A Levite in Hezekiah's reign, who oversaw the offerings (2 Chron 31:13).

4. Father of a certain Jonathan (Ezra 10:15).

ASAIAH, ASAHIAH (ȧ-sā'yȧ, ăs'ȧ-hī'ȧ, *whom Jehovah made*). 1. One of Josiah's officers whom he sent to inquire of the Lord concerning the words of the law that Shaphan had read to the king (2 Kings 22:12–14).

2. A Simeonite, c. 800 B.C. (1 Chron 4:36).

3. A Levite of the family of Merari in the time of David (1 Chron 6:30).

4. A Shilonite, one of the first after the Captivity to dwell in Jerusalem (1 Chron 9:5).

5. One of the chief Levites of the family of Merari in David's day (1 Chron 15:6, 11). This may be the same as no. 3 above. He seems to have been the leader of about 220 Levites who assisted in bringing the ark from the house of Obed-Edom in Jerusalem.

ASAPH (ā'săf). 1. A Levite of the Gershonite family, appointed over the service of praise in the time of David and Solomon (1 Chron 16:5; 2 Chron 5:12). He led the singing and sounded cymbals before the ark and apparently set up a school of music (Neh 7:44). Twelve psalms are credited to Asaph (Pss 50, 73–83). This accreditation does not necessarily imply authorship (see PSALMS) and may mean no more than that these psalms constituted an Asaphic collection, begun by the great man and then prolonged over the years by the Asaph singers. The psalms themselves cover a long span of time, for psalms like 74 are best understood in an exilic context. The psalms of Asaph have certain points in common: God as Judge (50:3–4; 75:8; 76:8–9), a call to true spirituality reminiscent of the prophets (50:7, 14–15, 22–23; 81:8–10), the use of history to teach spiritual lessons (78), the Lord as Shepherd (74:1; 77:20; 79:13; 80:1). These psalms have a deep and contemplative nature.

2. Father of Hezekiah's recorder (2 Kings 18:18).

3. An official under Artaxerxes Longimanus, king of Persia (Neh 2:8).

4. In 1 Chronicles 26:1 read Ebiasaph (cf. 9:19).

ASAREL (ăs′à-rĕl). A descendant of Judah and a son of Jehallel (1 Chron 4:16).

ASARELAH (ăs′à-rē′là). A Levite singer of the sons of Asaph in David's time (1 Chron 25:2). Called Jesarelah in 1 Chron 25:14.

ASCENSION OF CHRIST. The movement of the eternal Son, in his assumed and glorified humanity, from earth to heaven in order to sit at the right hand of the Father as co-regent. The witness of the NT to the Ascension is of three kinds. First, there is the descriptive material in Mark 16:19; Luke 24:51; Acts 1:9–11. Second, there is the prophetic or anticipatory reference found in John 6:62; 20:17. Third, there is the reference that assumes that Christ is ascended and exalted and therefore proclaims his present exalted position or future coming in glory (Eph 4:8–11; Heb 4:14; 6:19–20; Rev 12:1–6). Much of the latter teaching is molded in the light of Psalm 110:1, 4. Ascension presupposes bodily resurrection, for it was in his body that Jesus went up (*anabainō*). "Exaltation" covers both resurrection and ascension, while "session" means his sitting at the Father's right hand. The position of the exalted Jesus has often been portrayed in biblical imagery as that of King (= Lord) of the universe and church, Priest of the people of God, and Prophet to the people of God and the world. The Holy Spirit is sent by the Father in the name of the Lord Jesus so that he comes bearing the virtues and characteristics of Christ and so is the Paraclete (John 16:5–14). As Jesus ascended into heaven, so he will return from heaven to judge the world (Acts 1:11).

Bibliography: B. K. Donne, *Christ Ascended,* 1983; Peter Toon, *The Ascension of Our Lord,* 1984. PT

ASCENTS (Heb. *ma'ălâh, a going up* or *ascent,* Gr. *tapeinos, low*). The word "ascent" (KJV 'degrees') occurs in the titles of fifteen psalms (120–134), which are called songs of ascents (KJV, 'songs of degrees'). The common opinion regarding the meaning is that they were sung by the pilgrims as they went up to Jerusalem (cf. 1 Sam 1:3; Ps 42:4; 122:4; Isa 30:29). The word is also used in 2 Kings 20:9–10 (translated "steps" in NIV, "degrees" in KJV), where Hezekiah

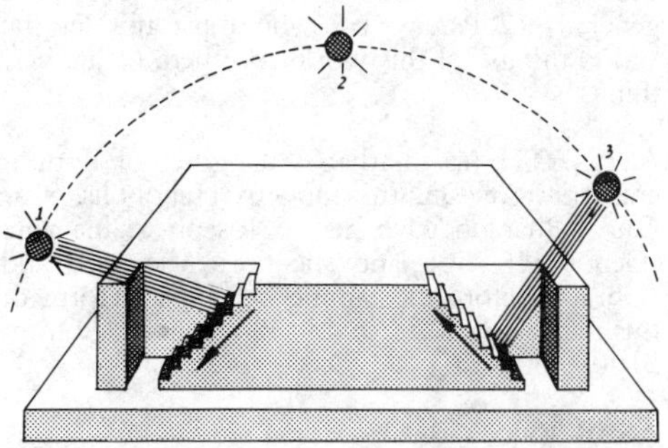

Representation of the shadow on the stairway of Ahaz in the (1) morning, (2) afternoon, and (3) evening, as related in 2 Kings 20:9–10. Courtesy Carta, Jerusalem.

is told that his sundial would go back ten degrees as a sign that the Lord would heal him. It is also used in a secondary sense of rank or order (1 Chron 15:18; 17:17; Ps 62:9; Luke 1:52; James 1:9).

ASCENTS, SONGS OF. The title given to Psalms 120–34. There is uncertainty about the origin of the title. Some Jewish authorities attributed it to the use made of fifteen steps leading from the court of men to the court of women in the temple. The Levitical musicians performed with these steps as the stage. Some scholars attribute the title to the way in which the thought advances from step to step, as seen in 121:4–5, 124:1–4, but not all these songs do this. Because Ezra (7:9) used the word *hamma'lah,* meaning "a going up from Babylon," some have thought the title originated when exiles were returning to Jerusalem during the reign of Artaxerxes in Babylon. The most logical explanation is that the title was given the series of hymns because they were used by pilgrims *going up* to the three annual pilgrimage feasts of Jerusalem (see FEASTS).

These lovely pilgrim songs should be studied in groups of three: In each triad the first finds the pilgrim far away (e.g., Ps 120, he feels himself an alien in Kedar; Ps 129, still among enemies); the second in each triad concentrates on the Lord's power to preserve, whatever the vicissitudes of the way; and the third is a psalm of arrival and security in Zion. In this way the whole "pilgrim hymnbook" is vibrant with the theme of going up and going home to Zion.

ASCETICISM (ă-sĕ′tĭ-sĭz′m). Although this word is not used in the Bible, the concept is found frequently. In the sense of self-discipline, asceticism normally occurs in the OT in connection with particular circumstances such as repentance (1 Sam 7:6) or religious regulations (Lev 10:9; Num 6:1–8). In the NT, however, it affects the whole lifestyle, calling for renunciation of everything that hinders discipleship (Matt 19:21–22; Mark 10:29–30). Self-control is listed as a fruit of the Spirit (Gal 5:23). It is demanded of the contestant (1 Cor 9:25), of church elders (Titus 1:8), and of Christians generally (2 Peter 1:6), who must not let the "good things" of this world rob them of the best things.

ASENATH (ăs'ĕn-ăth). A daughter of Potiphera, priest of On, the modern Heliopolis, near Cairo. Pharaoh gave her to Joseph as his wife (Gen 41:45–50), and she bore Manasseh and Ephraim before the famine began. The form of this name is well attested in Egyptian usage from 2100–1600 B.C.

ASER (See ASHER)

ASHAN (ā'shăn). A town in the tribe of Judah, later given to Simeon because Judah's territory was too large, then given to the priests (Josh 15:42; 19:7; 1 Chron 4:32; 6:59). This was one of about a dozen towns mentioned in the lists of both Judah and Simeon, as the boundary was indistinct and the territories overlapped.

ASHBEA (ăsh'bē-à). Head of a family in Judah that worked in fine linen (1 Chron 4:21). He was a descendant of Shelah. In NIV and RSV it is the name of the place where this family lived, Beth Ashbea.

ASHBEL (ăsh'bĕl). The second son of Benjamin, son of Jacob (1 Chron 8:1). The Ashbelites (Num 26:38) descended from him.

ASHDOD (ăsh'dŏd, *stronghold, fortress*). One of the five chief cities of the Philistines: Ashdod, Gaza, Ashkelon, Gath, and Ekron (Josh 13:3). They were assigned to Judah, but Judah failed to drive out the inhabitants "because they had iron chariots" (Judg 1:19). Ashdod was a center of Dagon worship, but when the Philistines thought to honor the ark of the Lord by placing it in the house of Dagon (1 Sam 5:1–7), God cast down and destroyed their idol. The Philistines found by careful testing that their plagues (1 Sam 5–6) were from God, so they sent back the ark with a guilt offering. Uzziah, king of Judah early in the eighth century B.C., conquered the city (2 Chron 26:6). Amos predicted Ashdod's destruction (Amos 1:8). About 711 Sargon II of Assyria took it (Isa 20:1). In Jeremiah's prophecy (Jer 25:15–29) Ashdod was to drink with the nations "this cup filled with the wine" of God's wrath. Zephaniah prophesied the destruction of the Philistines (Zeph 2:4), and Zechariah said that "foreigners will occupy Ashdod" (Zech 9:6). In Nehemiah's time (c. 444) the men of Ashdod combined with others to hinder the Jews (Neh 4:7–9). Failing in this, they tried intermarrying with them (13:23–24) to produce a mongrel race, but Nehemiah foiled them. In the LXX and in the NT Ashdod is "Azotus." Philip the evangelist found himself there after the Holy Spirit had taken him away from the Ethiopian eunuch (Acts 8:40).

Philistine clay figurine representing a fertility goddess in the form of a throne (from Ashdod, 12th century B.C.). It is something Samson might have seen when he sought an occasion to confront the Philistines (Judg 14:4). Courtesy Zev Radovan.

Fragments of Sargon's victory stele set up in Ashdod following the abortive rebellion of 712 B.C. Courtesy Israel Department of Antiquities and Museums.

ASHDOTH PISGAH (See PISGAH)

ASHER, ASER (ăsh'êr, ˇa'sêr, *happy*). 1. The second son of Zilpah, the handmaid whom Laban gave to Leah his daughter and whom she gave to Jacob; named "Happy" by Leah in her happiness at his birth. He was born at Padan-Aram (in the plain of Mesopotamia) during Jacob's service with

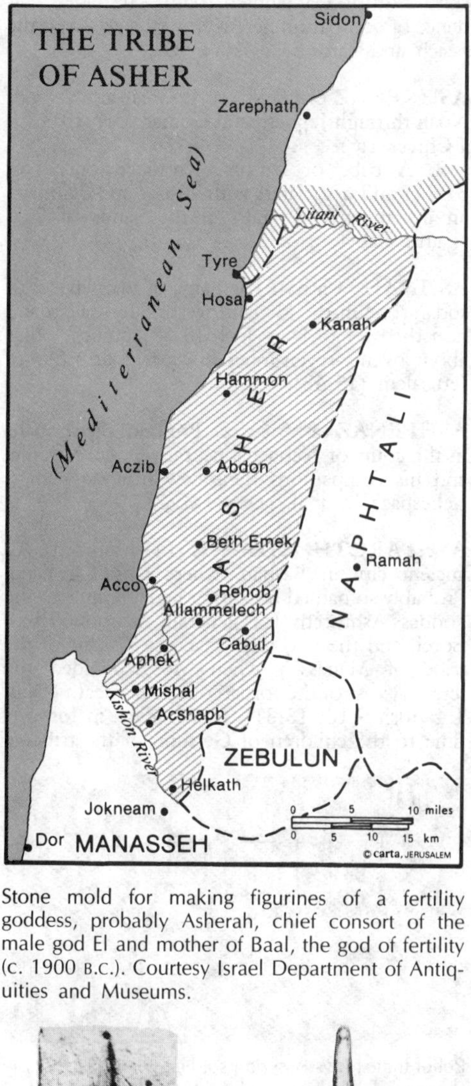

Stone mold for making figurines of a fertility goddess, probably Asherah, chief consort of the male god El and mother of Baal, the god of fertility (c. 1900 B.C.). Courtesy Israel Department of Antiquities and Museums.

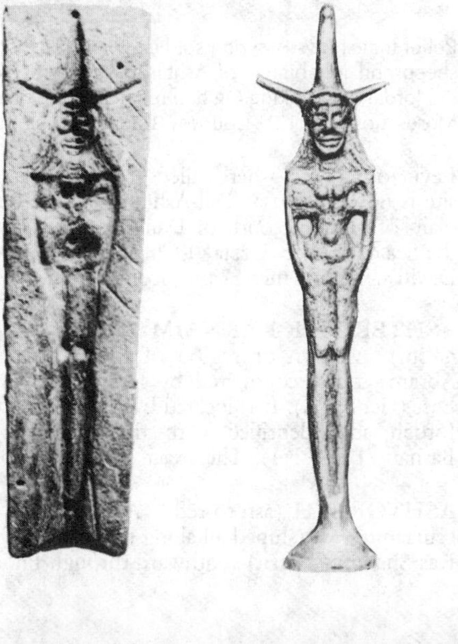

Figure of a Canaanite goddess (probably Asherah), made from bronze. Dressed in full-length clothes and with veil. Late Bronze Age (c. 1500–1200 B.C.). Courtesy Reuben and Edith Hecht Museum, University of Haifa.

Laban (Gen 30:13). We know little of his personal history except the names of his five children (46:17).

2. The tribe that descended from Asher (Josh 19:24–31). It was given the territory along the Mediterranean in the NW corner of Palestine, but failed to drive out the inhabitants of Sidon, Acco, and other Canaanite towns, and settled down to dwell among them. By David's time Asher seems to have become insignificant, for this tribe is omitted in the list of David's chief rulers (1 Chron 27:16–22).

ASHERAH (à-shē'rà). 1. A goddess of the Phoenicians and Syrians, taken over by the Israelites when they fell into idolatry.

2. Images representing this goddess whose worship was lewd and associated with Baal (Exod 34:13; 1 Kings 16:29–33). They are called "Asherah poles" in the NIV.

ASHES. The expression "dust and ashes" (e.g., Gen 18:27) is a play on words (*aphar* and *epher*) and signifies the origin of the human body from the ordinary chemical elements. It contrasts the lowliness of man with the dignity of God. Ashes were sprinkled over a person, or a person sat among ashes, as a sign of mourning (2 Sam 13:19; Job 2:8). The word is often united with "sackcloth" to express mourning (Jer 6:26).

The lovely expression "beauty for ashes" (Isa 61:3) is also a play on words. Another word for ashes, *deshen,* is used for the remains of the burnt offering (e.g., Lev 6:10–11).

ASHHUR (ăsh'ėr). Great grandson of Judah through Perez and Hezron (1 Chron 2:24; 4:5).

ASHIMA (ȧ-shī'mȧ). A god of the Hamathites, whose worship was brought to Samaria at its repopulation by the king of Assyria about 715 B.C. (2 Kings 17:30). There is no certain reference to Ashima outside the OT.

ASHKELON (ăsh'kĕ-lŏn). One of the five chief cities of the Philistines, located on the seacoast about twelve miles (twenty km.) NE of Gaza. It was taken by the tribe of Judah shortly after the death of Joshua (Judg 1:18), but was retaken by the Philistines and remained in their hands through much of the OT period. In the eighth century B.C. Amos denounced the city for its complicity with Phoenicia and Edom in their warfare on Israel (Amos 1:6–8). Zephaniah, writing in the dark days before the captivity of Judah (Zeph 2:4, 7) and looking far into the future, saw the restoration of Judah and the Jews occupying the desolate ruins of Ashkelon. Zechariah, writing about 518 B.C., prophesied that Ashkelon would see the destruction of Tyre and then that Ashkelon itself would be destroyed (Zech 9:5). Apparently it was rebuilt, for Herod the Great was born there and Roman ruins have been found. During the Crusades, it came to life again, and Richard Coeur de Lion held court there. Later the town reverted to the Saracens.

Archaeological remains are sparse: a ruined and overgrown Byzantine church, a quadrangle with some preserved columns and foundation walls of an odeum (tiered council chamber) attributed to Herod the Great by the excavators, some statues belonging to the façade of the odeum, and a third-century A.D. painted tomb. The oldest evidence of occupation here is from the area near the beach and dates to c. 2000 B.C.

City coin of Ashkelon; silver tetradrachm from second half of first century B.C. Obverse: head of Talmai XV. Reverse: eagle standing on thunderbolt, with small dove on the left (symbol of Ashkelon). Greek inscription reads: "Ashkelon the holy, city of asylum." Courtesy Israel Department of Antiquities and Museums.

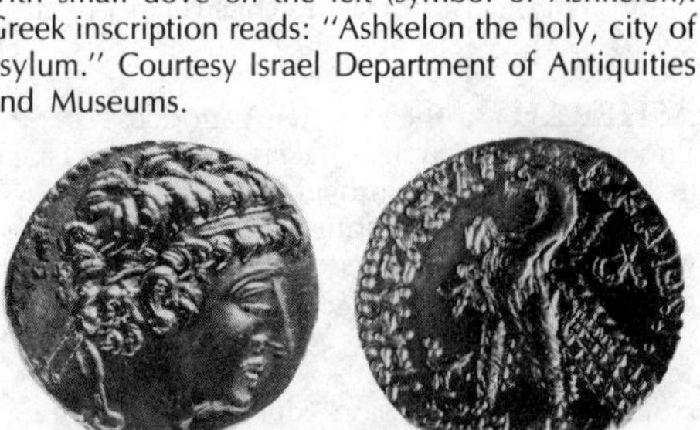

ASHKENAZ (ăsh'kĕ-năz). 1. Great-grandson of Noah through Japheth and Gomer (Gen 10:3; cf. 1 Chron 1:6).

2. A tribe or nation mentioned once (Jer 51:27) and associated with Ararat and Minni as an instrument of wrath in the hands of God against Babylon.

ASHNAH (ăsh'nȧ). The name of two villages of Judah, one in the lowland west of Jerusalem and near the tribe of Dan (Josh 15:33), and the other about twenty-seven miles (forty-five km.) SW of Jerusalem (15:43).

ASHPENAZ (ăsh'pĕ-năz). Prince of the eunuchs in the court of Nebuchadnezzar. He gave Daniel and his companions their new heathen names: Belteshazzar, et al. (Dan 1:3, 7).

ASHTAROTH, ASTAROTH (ăsh'tȧ-rŏth). An ancient city in Bashan, where king Og lived. Probably so named because it had a temple to the goddess Ashtoreth. It is generally mentioned with Edrei, and the two were given to Machir of the tribe of Manasseh when Moses divided the territory east of the Jordan before his death (Deut 1:4; Josh 9:10; 13:31). It was given in Joshua's time to the children of Gershon of the tribe of Levi (Josh 21:27—here called "Be Eshterah"). Its site is now known as Tell-Ashtarah, in the fertile plain of Hauran south of Damascus and east of the Sea of Galilee. Uzzia (1 Chron 11:44), one of David's mighty men, came from this town.

Relief that shows Assyrian soldiers leading away the sheep and inhabitants of Ashtaroth, a town east of the Jordan where king Og had reigned in the days of Moses (Josh 13:12). Courtesy Carta, Jerusalem.

ASHTEROTH KARNAIM (ăsh'tĕ-rŏth kăr-nā'ĭm). A town or region of the Rephaim in Abram's time, conquered by four kings of the East (Gen 14:5). It is located by some east of the Jordan and identified with the Ashtaroth of Bashan (Deut 1:4). The exact site is unknown.

ASHTORETH (ăsh'tō-rĕth). A goddess of the Canaanites, worshiped all along the seacoast from Ras Shamra (Ugarit) southward through Phoeni-

Pottery figurine of fertility-goddess Ashtoreth, who was indistinguishable from Ashera. It dates from just before or after the Israelite conquest of Canaan. Courtesy Zev Radovan.

cia and Philistia. The plural Ashtaroth (NIV "the Ashtoreths") is found commonly and refers to the idols representing her. Her male consort was apparently Baal, and the two were worshiped with lewd rites. In Judges 2:11–23 we are told that Israel forsook their God and served "Baal and the Ashtoreths." The prophet Samuel brought about a great revival, but before Israel could be saved from the Philistines, they had to give up Ashtoreth and turn to the Lord (1 Sam 7:3–4). Israel kept fairly close to the Lord through the times of Samuel, Saul, and David, and the early days of Solomon, until that "wise" man lost his wisdom by marrying various heathen women for political reasons. They succeeded in turning his heart from the Lord to worship of the Ashtoreth and other idols (1 Kings 11:4–8). These idols remained more than three and a half centuries till Josiah defiled and demolished them (2 Kings 23:13–14). Biblical scholar Gesenius related the name Ashtoreth to the Persian word "sitarah" or "star" and connected it with Venus, goddess of love.

ASHUR (See ASHHUR)

ASHURBANIPAL (ă-shĕr-bă'nĕ-păl, *Ashur creates a son*). King of Assyria. He was grandson of the famous Sennacherib and son of Esarhaddon. Ashurbanipal, or, as he was known to the Greeks, Sardanapalus, reigned from 668 to 626 B.C. and therefore was contemporary with Manasseh, Jotham, and Josiah of Judah. Modern scholars have reason to be grateful to Ashurbanipal because he was a lover of learning and collected a great library of cuneiform tablets (over

The "great and honorable Ashurbanipal" (Ezra 4:10), soldier, hunter, scholar, shown carrying a basket for the rebuilding of a temple in Babylon. He is best known for amassing a library of literary texts including an epic of creation. The relief is from the north palace of Ashurbanipal (668–633 B.C.) at Nineveh. Reproduced by courtesy of the Trustees of the British Museum.

22,000 in number) that have given to us most of what we know of Babylonian and Assyrian literature. In Ezra 4:10, his name is also rendered "Asnapper" (KJV, MLB, NEB) and Osnapper (NASB, RSV); see NIV footnote to this passage.

ASHURI (ăsh'ŭr-ē; KJV, RSV, Ashurites). Mentioned as a part of the realm of Ish-Bosheth, son of Saul (2 Sam 2:9 and NIV footnote). Possibly the same as the Asherites or people of Asher (Judg 1:32). The "Asshurites" of Genesis 25:3, mentioned among the Arabian descendants of Abraham through Keturah, may be the same. In Ezekiel 27:6 the Hebrew text reads "daughter of Ashurites" (cf. KJV), but most prefer to translate as NIV; see also NIV footnote.

ASHVATH (ăsh'văth). An early descendant of Asher (1 Chron 7:33).

ASIA. Proconsular Asia in NT times was the Roman province that contained the SW part of Asia Minor, and in particular "the seven churches in the province of Asia" addressed in the first three chapters of Revelation. In the NT the word "Asia" occurs nineteen times and always refers to this division, not to the whole continent, nor even to Anatolia. Its capital was Ephesus, where both Paul and John labored. Most of its cities have disappeared, but Smyrna (Rev 2:8–11) remains a great city even now (called Izmir, in modern Turkey). Philadelphia remained till the Middle Ages.

ASIEL (ā'sĭ-ĕl, *God is maker*). A Simeonite, mentioned only in 1 Chronicles 4:35 as a prince in his family.

ASNAH (ăs'nȧ). Head of a family of temple servants who returned from the Captivity with Zerubbabel, 536 B.C. (Ezra 2:50). See NETHINIM.

ASNAPPER (See ASHURBANIPAL)

ASP (See ANIMALS)

ASPATHA (ăs-pā'thȧ). Third son of Haman (Esth 9:7).

ASRIEL (ăs'rĭ-ĕl). 1. Grandson of Manasseh and son of Gilead, and head of the family of Asrielites (Num 26:31; Josh 17:2).

2. A son of Manasseh by his Aramean concubine (1 Chron 7:14).

ASS (See ANIMALS)

The national god Asshur, represented with spread wings and drawn bow and placed within a disc of flames and among rain clouds. This god's name appears as an element in many personal names (cf. Ashurbanipal: "Asshur has created an heir"). Courtesy Staatliche Museen zu Berlin.

ASSHUR (ăsh'ûr, Heb. *'ashshûr*). The god of the Assyrians; their reputed human founder; the ancient capital of the country; often the nation Assyria. Asshur is the builder of Nineveh and nearby cities (Gen 10:11 JB, KJV). He comes from the kingdom of Nimrod, a descendant of Ham, but may not be of his race, for in Genesis 10:22 and 1 Chronicles 1:17 Asshur is a descendant of Shem. ASV, NIV, and RSV render Genesis 10:11 to read that Nimrod went into Assyria and founded Nineveh. In Balaam's prophecy (Num 24:22, 24) Asshur appears to be Assyria. Assur (KJV) in Ezra 4:2 is translated "Assyria" in ASV, NIV, and RSV. In Psalm 83:8, in a list of enemies of Israel, ASV, NIV, and RSV have "Assyria," while JB, KJV, and NEB have "Assur." In Ezekiel 27:23, Asshur is in a list of nations with whom Israel traded; but in 32:22, in a list of nations to be destroyed, ASV and KJV retain "Asshur," while NIV and RSV have "Assyria." KJV, NIV, and RSV all have "Assyria" in Hosea 14:3. For most occurrences of the Hebrew word, KJV has "Assyria," which is the probable meaning in every case.

ASSIR (ăs'êr, *captive*). 1. Moses' first cousin once removed (Exod 6:24).

2. Great-grandson of no. 1 (1 Chron 6:23).

3. In 1 Chronicles 3:17, the name of a son of Jeconiah (KJV) or a modifier of "Jehoiachin" ("the captive" NIV).

Ruins of the temple of Athena at Assos, looking toward the south. Courtesy Ecole Biblique et Archéologique Française, Jerusalem.

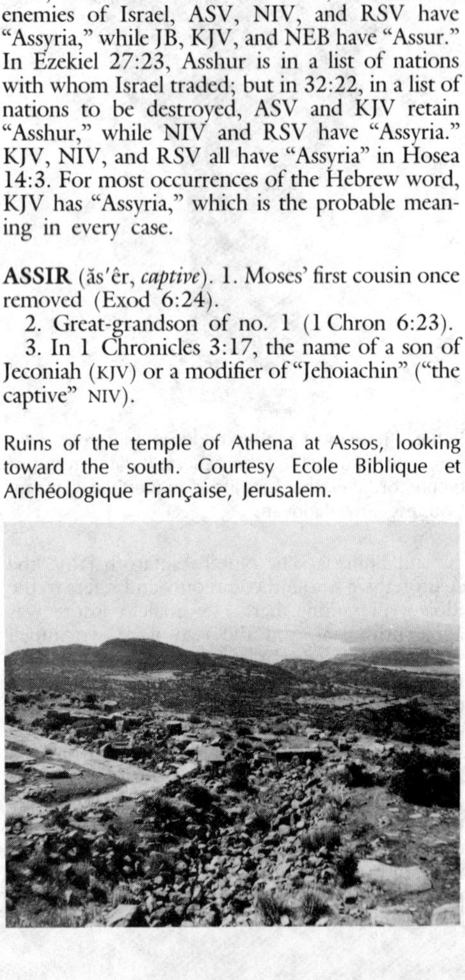

ASSOS (ăs'ŏs). Modern Behramkoy, seaport of Mysia in Asia Minor on the north coast of the gulf of Adramyttium, seven miles (twelve km.) from the island of Lesbos to the south near Methymna, twenty miles (thirty-three km.) south of Troas (Acts 20:13–14). The ship with Luke and others sailed from Troas around Cape Lectum, while Paul walked the shorter way (twenty miles) overland to Assos, where he reached the ship in time for her arrival that evening at Mitylene, a port on the SE coast of Lesbos.

ASSURANCE. The internal and external evidence by which Christians may have confidence to believe that God is their Father and Christ their Savior and Lord. Thus they know that what the gospel declares about Jesus is true and that in Jesus they have a new relationship with God.

Faith (*pistis*) as belief in, trust of, and commitment to God through Jesus Christ carries with it a certain assurance. This is because true faith includes the acceptance of God's own testimony concerning himself and his relation to a sinner (Acts 17:31; 1 Cor 2:10–13; 1 Thess 2:13). Thus the believer approaches the Father in prayer and worship with *plērophoria* (humble conviction and "full assurance"—Col 2:2; Heb 6:11; 10:22 KJV). In fact the Christian is "fully persuaded" that God is what he says he is and does what he claims to do (Rom 4:21; 8:38; 2 Tim 1:12 KJV).

There is also the internal witness of the Holy Spirit bringing the knowledge that the believer is truly a child of God (Rom 8:15–16) as well as the external testimony of a changed life (1 John 2:3–5, 29; 3:9–14, 18–19; 4:7). Because of the presence of the indwelling Spirit, assurance in the new covenant is of a much deeper order than in the old covenant. However, assurance was a reality for believers within the Mosiac covenant (Isa 32:17).

Bibliography : J. C. P. Cockerton, *To Be Sure: Christian Assurance—Presumption or Privilege?* (1967). PT

ASSYRIA (ȧ-sĭr'ĭ-ȧ, Heb. *'ashshûr*). Originally a land between the upper Tigris and Zab rivers, with its capital first at Assur, later at Nineveh. Assyria was taken over in the third millennium B.C. by Semites from Arabia. First mentioned in the Bible in Genesis 2:14, Assyria and the Assyrians are frequently named, sometimes as Asshur or Assur. By 1900 Assyrian traders had a colony in Hittite territory, at Kanish in Asia Minor. In the thirteenth century Assyrian military expeditions crossed the Euphrates, and by 1100 they reached the Mediterranean. But Assyria was not strong enough to maintain their advance. By 1000 the Aramean kingdom of Zobah reached the Euphrates, but David conquered Zobah and stopped its invasion of Assyria, an irony of history enabling Assyria to become strong. The tenth century was one of powerful and systematic advance. Assyria rounded out its borders north and east, conquered Babylonia, and advanced westward through Aramean territory to the Mediterranean. Under Shalmaneser III the Assyrians turned toward Palestine. In 853 they were defeated at Karkar but claimed a victory over Ben-Hadad of Damascus and a coalition incuding Ahab, king of Israel. They failed to follow up their effort.

After the religious revival under Elijah and Elisha, the coalition of Israel with Syria broke up. When Jehu gained the throne (2 Kings 9–10),

Limestone relief (2.18 meters high) of Shamshi-Adad V, king of Assyria, 823–811 B.C., from Nimrud. He wears a long garment fringed at the bottom and two shoulder straps that cross his chest diagonally. Suspended from his neck is a cross. He also wears the royal headdress and sandals and holds a mace in his left hand. Reproduced by courtesy of the Trustees of the British Museum.

Shalmaneser III seized the opportunity to claim tribute from Jehu and to weaken Damascus. Internal difficulties kept Assyria from further Palestinian inroads for nearly a century, until shortly after the middle of the eighth century B.C., when Tiglath-Pileser III invaded the west, divided the territory into subject provinces, and exchanged populations on a large scale to make rebellion more difficult. In 733–732 he conquered Galilee, the Plain of Sharon, and Gilead and made both Israel and Judah pay tribute (15:29; 16:9). Isaiah prophesied that this attempt to subjugate Judah would eventually fail. Shalmaneser V besieged Samaria for three years. He died during the siege, and his successor Sargon II (now called Sargon III) took the city in 721 and carried its more prosperous citizens into exile, replacing them with colonists from other provinces of his empire (17:6–41).

For nearly a century thereafter, Assyria was troubled from all sides—from Babylon, Elam, the Medes, Phrygia, and Egypt. Yet Sennacherib nearly captured Jerusalem in 701–700 B.C. (2 Kings 18:13–19:37; Isa 36–37), the danger ending only when "the angel of the LORD went out and put to death a hundred and eighty-five thousand men in the Assyrian camp" followed by the assassination of Sennacherib. Manasseh, king of Judah, paid tribute to Assyria, except during a short rebellion for which he was carried to Babylon but released after he sought the Lord (2 Chron 33:11–13). The last quarter of the seventh century saw the fall and decline of the Assyrian empire and its subjugation by the Chaldean conquerors of Babylonia with the Medes. Nineveh was taken in 612. For a short time Babylonia replaced Assyria as the great power. The prophets Elijah, Elisha, and Isaiah are largely concerned with Assyria; several other prophets—Jeremiah, Ezekiel, Hosea, Micah, Nahum, Zephaniah, and Zechariah—refer to it. Jonah was actually sent to prophesy to Nineveh, and the revival he unwillingly promoted saved the city from destruction for a long period of time.

Assyrian kings during the centuries in which Assyria had its closest contact with Israel and Judah, with approximate dates for their reigns (all B.C.) from the list found at Khorsabad in Mesopotamia, are as follows:

Shalmaneser III	859–824
Shamshi–Adad V	823–811
Adad-Nirari III	810–783
Shalmaneser IV	782–772
Ashur-dan III	771–754
Ashur-Nirari V	753–746
Tiglath-Pileser III	745–727
Shalmaneser V	726–722
Sargon III (II)	722–705
Sennacherib	705–681
Esarhaddon	681–669
Ashurbanipal	669–627
Ashur-eti-ilani	627–623
Sin-shum-lishir	623–623
Sin-shar-ishkun	623–612
Ashur-uballit	611–608

Assyrian art, architecture, and technology were successively influenced by Sumerians, Akkadians, and Babylonians and early attained high levels, exciting the admiration and imitation of Ahaz, king of Judah (2 Kings 16:10–13). Literature was largely utilitarian—legal, historical, commercial, scientific, pseudo-scientific, and religious—but it exists in abundance, notably the library of Ashurbanipal, consisting of thousands of clay tablets. The Assyrians early added to their worship of the primitive national god Asshur the Babylonian deities with their cultic apparatus. Wherever they influenced Israel and Judah, the effort was demoralizing, as the historical books of the Bible and the prophets bear abundant witness.
ER

ASTROLOGY, ASTROLOGER. In warning his people against Canaanite superstition (Deut 18:10–13), Moses made no reference to astrology or any sort of fortunetelling by means of the stars, for, though this later came into western Palestine, it was essentially a Babylonian or Mesopotamian study. Although the translation "astrologer" appears several times in the English Bible (e.g., Dan 2:2; 5:7 NIV), the only unequivocal reference to the practice and its practitioners is found in Isaiah 47:13 ("those stargazers who make predictions month by month") and in Jeremiah 10:2 (where people are urged not to be "terrified by signs in the sky"). It was a characteristic of Babylonian wisdom, as well as Egyptian, to ponder the movement of the stars, taking note of variations and conjunctions, so as to predict events on earth. The Hebrew word *'ashshāph* (e.g., in Dan 1:20; 2:2, 10, 17; 4:7; 5:7, 11, 17) has often been translated "astrologer," though not by the NIV. It refers to the general practice of "magic" or the casting of spells and pronouncing of "charms." The NIV does, however, use "astrologer" to represent "Chaldean" in some of these same verses as well as others (e.g., Dan 2:2, 4–5, 10; 5:7, 11), a needless restriction of meaning for a word that covers, for example, philosophy as well as astrology and, in general, refers to educated or knowledgeable people. JAM

ASTRONOMY. While the word *astronomy* is not found in the Bible, there are many passages that refer to some aspect of the subject. God is recognized as the maker of the stars (Gen 1:16) as well as the One who knows their number and names (Ps 147:4). In Psalm 19 there is a beautiful poem telling how the heavenly bodies (referring to the stars) show forth the glory of their Creator. A reference is made also to the sun as another of the heavenly bodies.

There are hundreds of biblical references to stars, sun, moon, and planets. Evidently the early Bible writers were much better acquainted with the subject of astronomy than are many modern people. When God wished to tell Abraham how numerous his descendants would be, he took him out and showed him the stars. Then God said, "Look up at the heavens and count the stars—if indeed you can count them" (Gen 15:5). Later

God compared the number of Abraham's descendants not only with the stars, but also with the sand on the seashore (22:17). For many years it was not clear that this was a fair comparison. Before the invention of the astronomical telescope it was not at all certain that the number of stars was as great as the number of grains of sand on the seashore. Modern discoveries, however, have proved the Bible correct. The total number of stars is approximately equal to the number of grains of sand on the seashore, a number so large it is impossible for the human mind to comprehend.

The Bible refers in a most striking manner to the height of the stars—that is, to their distance from the earth: "Is not God in the heights of heaven? And see how lofty are the highest stars!" (Job 22:12). Another reference to the great height of the stars is found in Isaiah 14:13. Here Satan says, "I will ascend to heaven; I will raise my throne above the stars of God." The inference here is that it must be a very great distance to the stars. The true distances to the stars were not known until 1838 when Bessel first computed the distance to a star. Before that time astronomers had little idea how far stars were from the earth. Now the distances to many stars have been measured, and it turns out that the distances to the most distant stars known are more than one hundred thousand times the diameter of our solar system.

It appears that the biblical writers were aware that the stars differ greatly from each other. Paul, writing to the church at Corinth, says, "The sun has one kind of splendor, the moon another and the stars another; and star differs from star in splendor" (1 Cor 15:41). This has been verified by the astronomers. Not only do stars have different colors, but they also differ widely in size, in density, in temperature, and in total amount of light emitted. The sun, around which the earth revolves, is an average star. While it is over one million times as large as the earth, there are some stars that are one million times as large as the sun. On the other hand, there are other stars smaller than the planet Mercury.

Painting of astronomical chart on ceiling of tomb of Senenmut in the time of Hatshepsut and Thutmose III. The three columns represent (from the left) Jupiter, Sirius, and Orion. The "egg" in the center is probably Pleiades, and the V-shaped constellation between Orion and Pleiades is Ursa Major over Ursa Minor.

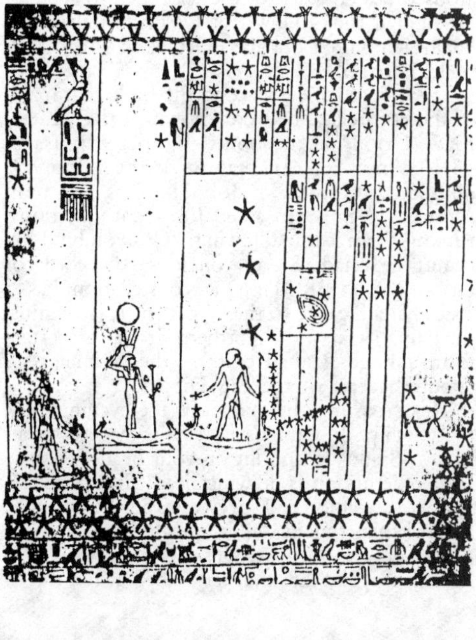

One of the many sins of the children of Israel was that of worshiping idols. They wanted to worship also the sun, the moon, and the stars. In Deuteronomy 4:19 they were warned not to indulge in such worship. In spite of such warnings, sun worship prevailed many times. Asa and Josiah, kings of Judah, found it necessary to take away the sun images that had been kept at the entrance to the temple.

While there is little evidence in the Bible that the Hebrew people had indulged very much in the study of astronomy, it is very clear that they recognized a sublime order in the movements of the heavenly bodies. They observed carefully the daily rising of the sun, its majestic movement across the sky, and its final setting in the west. This is vividly portrayed in the story of the battle with the Amorites as recorded in Joshua 10, when the sun stood still in the middle of the sky. Many theories have been proposed in an attempt to give a scientific explanation to this "long day of Joshua." None is completely satisfactory, and they will not be discussed here. It is sufficient to add that this is one of many miracles recorded in the Bible to show us that God is the ruler and sustainer of the universe.

More remarkable than the long day of Joshua when the sun apparently stood still, is the story of the return of the shadow on the sundial of Ahaz. In this case the Lord gave King Hezekiah a sign saying, "I will make the shadow cast by the sun go back the ten steps it has gone down on the stairway of Ahaz" (Isa 38:8). This is, indeed, a remarkable miracle. If taken literally, this means not only that the earth stopped rotating on its axis, but that it reversed its direction of rotation for a short time. Again the scientists have no answer to explain such an event.

There are a number of allusions in the Bible to eclipses of the sun and of the moon. In Isaiah 13:10 it is stated, "The rising sun will be darkened," while in Joel 2:31 we have the statement, "The sun will be turned to darkness and the moon to blood." These two descriptions accord quite well with observations of eclipses of the sun and of the moon. As the shadow of the moon sweeps across the face of the sun it appears that the sun is turned to darkness. When the earth comes directly between the sun and the moon, there is an eclipse of the moon. When the eclipse is complete, it is still possible to see the surface of the moon, due to the fact that the atmosphere of the earth bends the light rays from their straight

Seleucid astrological text of the time of Antiochus I, found at Uruk. It is divided into twelve compartments, corresponding to the twelve months and the twelve zodiacal signs, beginning with Virgo, represented by the figure at upper right holding an ear of barley. In the center is the planet Mercury and, at left, a raven representing the constellation Hydra. Each month is associated with different stones, plants, and trees. Courtesy Réunion des Musées Nationaux.

line path. Thus sunlight is bent somewhat as it passes the earth, is then reflected by the moon and returned to the earth. Just as the sun appears to be red when it is setting, due to the passage of the light through more atmosphere, so the eclipsed moon appears strange in color. The Bible uses the apt expression "turned . . . to blood" to describe this astronomical phenomenon.

Calculated eclipses of the sun that occurred in Palestine during OT times are as follows: July 31, 1063 B.C.; August 15, 831; June 15, 763; May 18, 603; May 28, 585. Very likely the prophets Amos and Joel witnessed the eclipse of August 15, 831. Such an eclipse is vividly described by Amos: "I will make the sun go down at noon and darken the earth in broad daylight" (Amos 8:9).

The subject of astrology has been connected with astronomy since early times. The reference in Judges 5:20 no doubt refers to the influence of the stars in the lives of people. The writer states, "From the heavens the stars fought, from their courses they fought against Sisera." However, the Hebrew people seemed to have had little to do with the subject. In the Book of Daniel there are repeated statements made concerning the astrologers. It is to be noted that Daniel and his three friends, though closely associated with astrologers, are always mentioned as keeping themselves separated and undefiled. Again and again when the magicians and the astrologers were unable to perform a task, it was Daniel who was able to do important things for the king. Thus it is apparent that the Bible condemns the pseudo-science of astrology.

Probably the most fascinating part of biblical astronomy concerns the star of Bethlehem. This story is told in the second chapter of Matthew. When the wise men from the east came to Jerusalem they asked, "Where is the one who has been born king of the Jews? We saw his star in the east and have come to worship him" (Matt 2:2). Even the king was greatly disturbed over the news, for he inquired of them diligently at what time the star appeared. This star seemed to be their ever-present guide, for it is stated that "the star they had seen in the east went ahead of them until it stopped over the place where the child was" (2:9).

The question is: What kind of a star can continually guide travelers to a definite point on the earth? Many answers have been proposed. One is that this was an unusual conjunction of bright planets. A conjunction is the coming together on the same meridian at the same time of two or more celestial objects, so that they appear almost as one. It is known that in the year 6 B.C. there was a conjunction of Mars, Jupiter, and Saturn. However, the conjunction would not have been visible to the wise men for it was too near the sun, and 6 B.C. is two years too early for the birth of Christ.

Another theory is that this star was a nova. A nova is a star that suddenly becomes very bright. Ordinarily such a star is too dim to be seen by the unaided eye. Very quickly such a star becomes as bright or brighter than the brightest star in the sky. Many novae have been discovered and studied. The problem in this case is to explain how such a bright star could serve as a guide to the wise men.

Still another theory proposed to explain the star of Bethlehem is that this was the planet Venus at its greatest brilliance. It is true that this planet does appear at times as a very bright object in the winter sky. However, these wise men knew the movements of the planets, and therefore, the bright appearance of Venus would hardly have served as a guide to lead them to the Christ child.

Evidently here is another of the many biblical miracles that modern science is unable to explain. This miraculous appearance, which is called a star, aroused the curiosity of the wise men to such an extent that they followed it for many miles until finally it pointed out the exact place where they wished to go.

There is much evidence in the Bible that many of the constellations were known to the writers. *Kesil* (Orion) is mentioned in Job 9:9; Isaiah 13:10; Amos 5:8. *Ash* or *Ayish* occurs in Job 9:9; 38:32. Also found in Job 38:32 is the term *Mazzarot*. The Lord asked Job many questions. Among them is the following: "Can you bind the beautiful Pleiades? Can you loose the cords of Orion?" (Job 38:31). One constellation has a special significance to the Christian. It is Cygnus, the flying swan or the Northern Cross. Its six stars form a huge Roman cross in the summer sky, about the size of the Big Dipper.

This cross may be said to be the evening's call to worship. It reminds us of the passage from Luke, "Stand up and lift up your heads, because your redemption is drawing near" (Luke 21:28). This constellation sinks westward in the sky until at Christmas time it stands upright just above the horizon in the northwest. There is rich symbolism here in the fact that the star Deneb at the top of the cross, where the head of Christ was, is a supergiant, while the one at the bottom, Albireo, where his feet were, is a telescopic double; it is really very beautiful with one star yellow and the other blue.

In the last chapter of the last book of the Bible, the Lord Jesus is called "the bright Morning Star" (Rev 22:16). Evidently the writer, the apostle John, had frequently waited for the morning light and had watched for the bright morning star, which is usually a planet. Its beauty had greatly inspired him, so he used this striking figure for the Lord Jesus Christ. Many Christians watch for his coming as people of old have watched for the morning and have seen the bright stars of the morning!

Bibliography: G. V. Schiaporelli, *Astronomy in the Old Testament,* 1905; E. W. Maunder, *The Astronomy of the Bible,* 1935; G. Abetti, *The History of Astronomy,* 1952. HHH

ASWAN (ăs'wăn, Heb *sevēnēh*). An Egyptian city, identified as present-day Aswan, at the First Cataract of the Nile, on the east bank of the river, opposite the island of Elephantine, which is well-known to biblical students from the Aramaic papyri found there. During much of Egypt's history this area marked the effective southern boundary of Egypt. The name Aswan ("Syene" in JB, KJV, MLB, MOF, NASB, NEB, RSV) appears only twice in the OT (NIV—Ezek 29:10; 30:16), both times in prophecies against Egypt, geographically defining the extent of Egyptian territory, from Migdol in the north to Aswan in the south.

ASYNCRITUS (á-sĭng'krĭ-tŭs, *incomparable*). A Christian in Rome to whom Paul sent a salutation (Rom 16:14).

ATAD (ā'tăd, Heb. *'ātādh, thorn*). Name of a place, "the threshing floor of Atad," east of Jordan, where the Israelites mourned for Joseph. The Canaanites called the place Abel Mizraim (Gen 50:11).

ATARAH (ăt'á-rá). A wife of Jerahmeel and mother of Onam (1 Chron 2:26).

ATAROTH (ăt'á-rŏth, *crowns*). 1. Modern Khirbet-at-tarus, east of Jordan in the territory of Reuben, but fortified by Gad (Num 32:3, 34).

2. On the border between Ephraim and Benjamin, to the west (Josh 16:2), probably the same as Ataroth Addar (16:5; 18:13).

3. On the eastern border of Ephraim (Josh 16:7).

4. Near Bethlehem (1 Chron 2:54; Atroth Beth Joab in NIV). The locations of the last three are uncertain.

ATER (ā'tĕr). 1. The ancestor of an exiled family (Ezra 2:16; Neh 7:21).

2. Ancestor of a family of gatekeepers who returned from exile with Zerubbabel (Ezra 2:42; Neh 7:45).

3. The chief of the people who, with Nehemiah, sealed the covenant (Neh 10:17).

ATHACH (ā'thăk). A city of Judah, probably near Ziklag. David sent to it from Ziklag some of the spoil taken from the Amalekites (1 Sam 30:30).

ATHAIAH (á-thī'á, *Jehovah is helper*). The son of Uzziah a Judahite in Nehemiah's time (Neh 11:4).

ATHALIAH (ăth'á-lī'á). 1. The only woman who ever reigned over Judah (see 2 Kings 8:18, 25–28; 11:1–20; 2 Chron 22:1–23:21; 24:7).

The constellation of Orion, the moon, and Pleiades, as depicted on a clay tablet dating to about the third century B.C. Courtesy Staatliche Museen zu Berlin.

She was the daughter of Ahab (king of Israel) and Jezebel (a devotee of Baal). Omri (king of Israel) was her grandfather, and Jehoram (king of Judah) was her husband. After the death of their son Ahaziah, Athaliah reigned six years. She put to death all Ahaziah's sons except Joash, who was hidden by Jehosheba, sister of Ahaziah and wife of Jehoiada the priest. Then, in the seventh year, Jehoiada conspired to put Joash on the throne. Coming into the temple to see what the excitement meant, Athaliah found that the coronation had already taken place. She was allowed to leave the temple, that it might not be defiled with her blood, but was killed as she went out the door.

2. A son of Jeroham, a Benjamite (1 Chron 8:26).

3. The father of Jeshiah, a returned exile (Ezra 8:7).

ATHARIM (ăth'ăr-ĭm). The reading of RSV, ASV ("the way of Atharim"), and NIV ("the road to Atharim") in Numbers 21:1 which, following the LXX, regards Atharim as a place. Here the king of Arad attacked the Israelites and took some of them captive. The site is unknown. KJV reads "the way of the spies," following other ancient versions.

ATHENS (ăth'ĕnz, Gr. *Athēnai*). In ancient times the famous capital of Attica, one of the Greek states, now the capital of Greece. The city was named after its patron goddess Athene. It centered around a rocky hill called Acropolis and was four and one-half miles (seven and one-half km.) from the sea. Two walls, 250 feet (78 m.) apart, connected the city with its harbor (Peiraeus). According to tradition, the city was founded by Cecrops, who came from Egypt about 1556 B.C.; Athens sent fifty ships to the Trojan War. The city was ruled by kings until about 1068, when archons (magistrates) began to rule. Two of the most famous archons were Draco, who in c. 620 issued laws "written in blood," and Solon, who in 594 gave the state a constitution. The Athenians defeated the Persians at Marathon in 490 and again in 480 at Salamis. They then built a small empire, with a powerful fleet for its support. The period of Athens' greatest glory was during the rule of Pericles (459–431), who erected many beautiful public buildings in the city and under whose administration literature and art flourished. The Peloponnesian War (431–404) ended with the submission of Athens to Sparta. Later wars sapped the strength of Athens. Philip of Macedon crushed the city in 338. In 146 the Romans made it a part of the province of Achaea. The Roman general Sulla sacked the city in 86. It subsequently came into the hands of the Goths, the Byzantines, and other peoples. The Turks ruled it from A.D. 1458 until the emancipation of Greece in 1833.

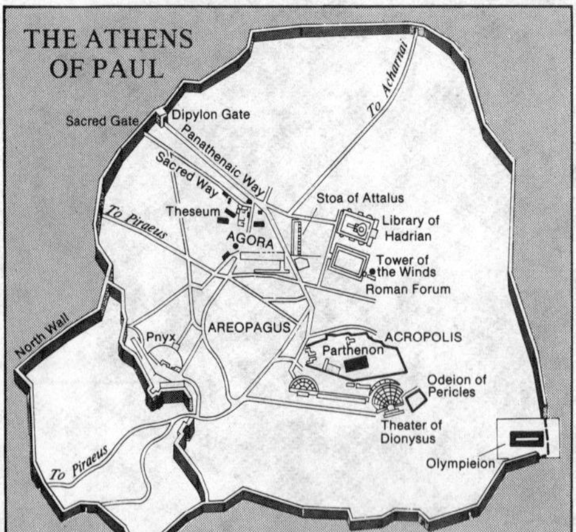

In ancient times Athens had a population of at least a quarter of a million. It was the seat of Greek art, science, and philosophy, and was the most important university city in the ancient world, even under Roman sway. Although politically conquered, it conquered its conquerors with its learning and culture.

Paul visited the city on his second missionary journey and spoke to an interested but somewhat disdainful audience (Acts 17). He reminded them of their altar inscribed with the words "TO AN UNKNOWN GOD," which he had seen in the city, and declared that he could tell them about this God. He made some converts in the city, but there is no record of his establishing a church there or of his returning on any later occasion. From Athens he went to Corinth, where he remained for a year and a half, establishing a strong church.

ATHLAI (ăth'lā-ī). A man of Israel who in the days of Ezra (c. 456 B.C.) divorced his foreign wife (Ezra 10:28).

ATONEMENT (ă-tōn'mĕnt). The root meaning in English, "reparation," leads to the secondary meaning of reconciliation, or "at-one-ment," the bringing together into harmony of those who have been separated, enemies. This double meaning brings a basic biblical concept into focus. But at the same time it leaves unanswered the really crucial questions: What has caused the separation? What has brought about peace? How has it been accomplished?

In the OT, atonement is mainly expressed by the verb *kāphar,* whose root meaning is "to cover over." In secular use, for example, Noah "covered over" the woodwork of the ark with pitch (Gen 6:14). The noun related to this verb, *kōpher,* while it has its secular use (6:14; NIV "pitch"), is mainly used of the ransom price that "covers" an offense—not by sweeping it out of sight but by making an equivalent payment so that the offense has been actually and exactly paid for (e.g., Exod 30:12, "ransom"; Num 35:31; Ps 49:7; Isa 43:3). Arising from this use of the noun, one whole section of the verb (in Heb. the Piel and Pual forms, *kippēr* and *kuppar*) came to be set aside to express only the idea of removing offense by equivalent payment and so bringing the offender and the offended together. The only secular uses of this word (in Gen 32:20; Lev 5:16; 16:30, 33; 17:11) show also that the means of atonement—the actual price paid as equivalent to the sin committed—was the sacrificial blood, the life laid down in death. See also BLOOD.

The ritual of the Day of Atonement should be studied, and in particular the part played by the two goats (Lev 16:15–17, 20–22). The Lord wanted his people to know the significance of what had happened in secret when the high priest sprinkled the blood on the "atonement cover" (Heb. *kappōreth*). Therefore he commanded the ceremony of the live goat so that they might actually see their sins being laid on another and see their sins being borne away never to return again. See also ATONEMENT, DAY OF; LAYING ON OF HANDS.

In Christian theology, atonement is the central doctrine of faith and can properly include all that Jesus accomplished for us on the cross. It was a vicarious (substitutionary) atonement. On the Day of Atonement, the goat that was substituted was in some sense not as valuable as a person, though the goat had never sinned; but God in his matchless grace provided a Substitute who was *infinitely* better than the sinner, absolutely sinless and holy, and dearer to the Father than all creation. "The wages of sin is death" (Rom 6:23) and "God made him who had no sin to be sin for us, so that in him we might become the righteousness of God" (2 Cor 5:21).

There are two opposite facts that the ingenuity of the theologians could not have reconciled without God's solution: First, that God is holy and he hates sin, and that by his holy law sin is a capital crime; and second, that "God is love" (1 John 4:8). So the problem was, "How can God be just and at the same time justify the sinner?" (cf. Rom 3:26). John 3:16 tells us that God so loved that he gave—but our blessed Lord was not just a means to an end, he was not a martyr to a cause. In the eternal counsels of the Trinity, he offered himself to bear our sins (Rev 13:8). He voluntarily emptied himself of the divine trappings of omnipotence, omniscience, and glory (Phil 2:5–8), that he might be truly human, becoming the babe of Bethlehem. For some thirty-three years he perfectly fulfilled the law on our behalf (Matt 5:18) and then paid the penalty for our sins in his death for us on the cross. Our Lord's work of atonement looks in three directions: toward sin and Satan (1 Peter 1:18–19), toward us (Rom 5:6–11), and toward the Holy Father (1 John 2:2).

Bibliography: L. Berkhof, *Vicarious Atonement Through Christ,* 1936; B. B. Warfield, *The Person and Work of Christ,* 1950; J. Denney, *The Death of Christ,* 1951; Leon Morris, *The Apostolic Preaching of the Cross,* 1955; J. B. Payne, *The Theology of the Older Testament,* 1962; I. H. Marshall, *The Work of Christ,* 1968; R. S. Wallace, *The Atoning Death of Christ,* 1981.

ATONEMENT, DAY OF. Theologically and spiritually, the Day of Atonement is the center of Leviticus, "the book of holiness." The sixteenth chapter gives the law for the Day of Atonement. The divinely inspired commentary on this chapter is found in Hebrews 9:1–10:25. Israel had two beginnings for its years, six months apart. In the first month on the fourteenth day, they ate the Passover as a memorial of the events leading to the Exodus from Egypt; half a year later, in the seventh month on the tenth day (Lev 16:29), they afflicted their souls and the priest made atonement for them. The Jews now celebrate their New Year's Day (Rosh Hashanah) on the first day of the seventh month (Sept.), and the Day of Atonement (Yom Kippur), properly *yom hakkippurim,* on the tenth.

The purpose of the Day of Atonement seems to have been at least fourfold: first, to show God's hatred of sin, that the "wages of sin is death" (Rom 6:23) and that "without the shedding of blood there is no forgiveness" (Heb 9:22); second, to show the contagious nature of sin, for even the Most Holy Place had to be cleansed (Lev 16:16) "because of the uncleanness and rebellion of the Israelites, whatever their sins have been"; third, to point forward by three types to the death of "the Lamb of God," our blessed Savior; and fourth, by its repetition year after year to signify that the way into the very presence of God had not been made manifest before the death of Christ (Heb 9:7–9). When our Lord offered himself on Calvary, the veil of the temple was torn (Mark 15:38), and God signified that from that moment on we were under a new covenant—a covenant of grace, not of law. "For the law was given through Moses; grace and truth came through Jesus Christ" (John 1:17). The OT ceremonies were but symbols and types and shadows: the NT records the realities. In OT times God was teaching his people by "kindergarten" methods—godliness brought health, long life, and prosperity; sin brought quick, visible, corporeal punishment. Today, under grace, we look back to Calvary, when the great Day of Atonement took place once for all.

ATROTH BETH JOAB (See ATAROTH)

ATROTH SHOPHAN (ăt′rŏth shō′făn). A town the tribe of Gad built and fortified east of Jordan (Num 32:35). The KJV reading ("Atroth, Shophan") may imply two towns.

ATTAI (ăt′ȧ-ī). 1. A half-Egyptian member of the tribe of Judah (1 Chron 2:35–36).

2. A mighty man of Gad who joined David (1 Chron 12:11).

3. Younger brother of Abijah, king of Judah (2 Chron 11:20).

ATTALIA (ăt′ȧ-lī′ȧ). A seaport of Pamphylia near Perga, mentioned in Acts 14:25. On Paul's first missionary journey he landed at Perga, several miles inland, but on his return he and Barnabas sailed for Antioch in Syria from Attalia, the main seaport on the Gulf of "Adalia," as it is spelled today. The city was founded by and

Drawing of a statue of the Roman emperor Augustus Caesar (63 B.C. to A.D. 14), the emperor who issued a decree "that all the world should be enrolled" (Luke 2:1). Courtesy Carta, Jerusalem.

named for Attalus Philadelphus, king of Pergammum from 159 to 138 B.C.

ATTIRE (see DRESS)

AUGUSTUS CAESAR (ô-gŭs'tŭs sē'zêr). Gaius Octavius, whose male ancestors for four generations had the same name, was born in Rome in 63 B.C., and early became influential through his great-uncle Julius Caesar. He was studying quietly in Illyria when he heard of Caesar's murder in 44. Hastening to Italy, he learned that Caesar had adopted him and made him his heir. Thus in his early manhood by skillful manipulation of his friends, he conquered his rival Antony at Actium. The beginning of the Roman Empire may be reckoned from that date—September 2, 31. By his adoption he had become "Caesar," and now the Roman senate added the title "Augustus." Although he preserved the forms of a republic, he gradually got all the power into his hands. He reigned till A.D. 14. Some of the secular histories omit the most important event in his reign—a Baby was born in Bethlehem! Augustus Caesar is mentioned just once in the NT (Luke 2:1).

AUTHORITY (Gr. *exousia*). The legal and/or moral right to exercise power, or power that is rightly possessed. In the Bible God is presented as the ultimate, personal authority and the source of all authority. All exercise of authority in the created order, by angels or men, is therefore subordinate and derivative. The important statements of Daniel (4:34–35; cf. 2:21; 7:13–14) and Paul (Rom 13:1) point to the sovereign, final, and incontestable authority of God, Creator, Judge, and Redeemer over and in his creation. Thus, the Lord exercises power as the One with authority.

In the life of the people of Israel, the Lord exercised his authority through the authority he gave to king, priest, and prophet. It was the duty of the king to reign in righteousness and justice, of the priest rightly to order the worship and service of God, and of the prophet to declare the word of the sovereign Lord, whether the people would or would not hear. When the word of the Lord came to be written down as Scripture it was seen as authoritative because of its source (see Ps 119).

Since Jesus is uniquely sent by God, he has authority; and since he is anointed by the Holy Spirit in order to perform the ministry of Messiah, he has power. Authority (*exousia*) and power (*dynamis*) are related but different (see Luke 4:36), "with authority and power he . . ."). Jesus is a man under authority and with authority (Matt 8:9; 7:29; Mark 1:27); he empowers his disciples to cast out demons (Matt 10:1; Mark 3:15); he does what only God can do—he forgives sins (Matt 9:6); he has control over nature (Mark 4:41); he exercises power over death (John 10:18); and as the resurrected Lord he has all authority in earth and heaven (Matt 28:18).

As those who believed that Jesus had been exalted to the right hand of the Father, the apostles developed the theme of the authority of Jesus, presenting him as coregent of the Father and possessing authority over the whole cosmos (Eph 1:20–23; Phil 2:1–11; Col 2:9–10). He is the "Lord of lords and King of kings" (Rev 17:14).

The NT also recognizes other forms of authority as delegated by God and Christ. There is the authority of the state (Rom 13:1ff.), of the apostles as unique pillars of the church and recipients of divine revelation (Luke 6:13; Eph 2:20), and of the husband as head of the family (1 Cor 11:3). In each case the exercise of power is to be within the will of God, and the one exercising authority must be mindful that God is Judge. The possession of authority and power by Satan (Luke 22:53; Col 1:13) has been abused and will be punished.

Bibliography: H. von Campenhausen, *Ecclesiastical Authority and Spiritual Power in the Church of the First Three Centuries,* 1969; B. Mickelson, "The Bible's Own Approach to Authority," in *Biblical Authority* (ed. Jack Rogers), 1977. PT

AUTHORIZED VERSION (See BIBLE, ENGLISH VERSIONS)

AVA (See AVVA)

AVEN (ā'vĕn, Heb. *'āwen, vanity*). Evidently a valley in Syria, dedicated to heathen worship (Amos 1:5), and thought by some to be Baalbek.

AVENGER. The Hebrew word *goēl* has a two-sided application of its basic meaning. At heart it is a very gracious word: It refers to the "next of kin" who possesses the right to take on himself whatever need may have overwhelmed his kinsman or kinswoman. We see this at its human best in the Book of Ruth (3:12–13; 4:2–10) and at its highest when the Lord himself is called our *goēl* (Isa 43:14). But there is a darker side. Suppose someone has committed the ultimate crime against us and we lie dead through murder. What then? The *goēl* comes to take our part and to exact the vengeance that the law demands (Num 35:11–34). This is how the word that means "redeemer" also means "avenger." OT law was rightly dominated by the concept of equality: an exact equivalence between crime and punishment. It expressed this in characteristically vigorous terms—for example, "an eye for an eye" (Exod 21:23–24; Lev 24:20; Deut 19:21). We should note that these passages all refer to punishments imposed by courts of law and are not rules for private conduct. In the case of murder, where life must be taken for life, the next of kin took up the dreadful duty, carefully circumscribed in his actions by the clear OT distinction between capital murder and accidental manslaughter and by the limitation of vengeance to the murderer only (Deut 24:16). JAM

AVIM, AVITES (See AVVITES, AVVIM)

AVITH (ā'vĭth). Name of a town or city that was the capital of Hadad, fourth king of Edom, before there were any kings in Israel (Gen 36:35).

AVVA (ăv'vȧ). A region in Assyria from which Sargon brought people to populate devastated Samaria (2 Kings 17:24), thought by some to be the Ivvah of 2 Kings 18:34. The people who were brought in worshiped the gods Nibhaz and Tartak (17:31).

AVVITES, AVVIM (ă'vīts, ā'vĭm). 1. An ancient people who dwelled in the region of Gaza before the time of Moses (Deut 2:23). When Joshua was an old man, these people still had not been rooted out (Josh 13:3).

2. Avvim was a city in the tribe of Benjamin (Josh 18:23), perhaps populated by the remains of this ancient tribe.

AWL. A sharp, piercing tool (Exod 21:6; Deut 15:17).

AYIN (ā'yēn, Heb. *'ayin, an eye, a spring or fountain*). 1. The sixteenth letter of the Hebrew alphabet, probably so named because originally in outline the letter resembled an eye. See also WRITING.

2. A place name. See AIN.

AYYAH (āy'yăh). In 1 Chronicles 7:28 (NIV, RSV), one of the towns possessed by the tribe of Ephraim. KJV and NEB have Gaza, though not the Philistine Gaza.

AZAL (See AZEL)

AZALIAH (ăz'ȧ-lī'ȧ, Heb. *'ătsalyâhû, probably Jehovah has set aside,* or *Jehovah has shown himself distinguished*). A son of Meshullam and father of Shaphan the scribe (2 Kings 22:3).

AZANIAH (ăz'ȧ-nī'ȧ, Heb. *'ăzanyâh, Jehovah has set aside,* or *Jehovah has given ear*). A son of Jeshua, a Levite who signed the covenant (Neh 10:9).

AZAREL, AZAREEL (ăz'âr-ĕl, ȧ-zā'rē-ĕl, Heb. *'ăzar'ēl, God is helper*). 1. A Levite who entered the army of David at Ziklag (1 Chron 12:6).

2. A musician in the temple in David's time (1 Chron 25:18).

3. A captain in the service of David (1 Chron 27:22).

4. A man Ezra persuaded to divorce his foreign wife (Ezra 10:41).

5. A priest who lived in Jerusalem after the Exile (Neh 11:13).

6. A musician who played in the procession when Jerusalem's new wall was dedicated (Neh 12:36).

AZARIAH (ăz'ȧ-rī'ȧ, Heb. *'ăzăryahu, Jehovah has helped*). 1. King of Judah. See UZZIAH.

2. A man of Judah of the house of Ethan the Wise (1 Chron 2:8).

3. The son of Jehu, descended from an Egyptian through the daughter of Sheshan (1 Chron 2:38).

4. A son of Ahimaaz (1 Chron 6:9).

5. A Levite of the family of Kohath (1 Chron 6:36).

6. A son of Zadok, the high priest under Solomon (1 Kings 4:2).

7. A high priest and son of Johanan (1 Chron 6:10).

8. Son of Nathan, an officer at Solomon's court (1 Kings 4:5).

9. A prophet, son of Obed, in the reign of King Asa (2 Chron 15:1–8).

10. Son of Jehoshaphat, listed with five others, of which one is called Azariahu (2 Chron 21:2).

11. A son of Jehoram (2 Chron 22:1).

12. Son of Jeroham. He helped to overthrow Athaliah (2 Chron 23:1).

13. Son of Johanan. He helped to get the captives of Judah released (2 Chron 28:12).

14. A Levite who assisted in purifying the temple in Hezekiah's reign (2 Chron 29:12).

15. A high priest who rebuked Uzziah's attempt to assume priestly functions (2 Chron 26:16–20).

16. A son of Hilkiah; a high priest not long before the Exile (1 Chron 6:13–14).

17. A man of Judah who bitterly opposed Jeremiah (Jer 43:2).

18. One of the captives taken to Babylon, whose name was changed to Abednego (Dan 1:7).

19. The son of Maaseiah. He helped repair the walls of Jerusalem (Neh 3:23).

20. A Levite who assisted Ezra in explaining the Law (Neh 8:7).
21. A priest who sealed the covenant (Neh 10:2).
22. A prince of Judah who marched in the procession at the dedication of the wall of Jerusalem (Neh 12:32–33).

AZARIAHU (See AZARIAH)

AZAZ (ā'zăz, Heb. *'āzāz, strong*). A Reubenite, the son of Shema (1 Chron 5:8).

AZAZEL (See SCAPEGOAT)

AZAZIAH (ăz'à-zī'à, Heb. *'ăzazyāhû, Jehovah is strong*). 1. A harpist during the reign of David (1 Chron 15:21).
2. The father of the prince of Ephraim in the reign of David (1 Chron 27:20).
3. A Levite overseer of the temple in the reign of Hezekiah (2 Chron 31:13).

AZBUK (ăz'bŭk). Father of a certain Nehemiah who lived at the same time as the famous governor of that name (Neh 3:16).

AZEKAH (à-zē'kà). A town in NW Judah, mentioned as a place to which Joshua pursued the kings at the battle of Gibeon (Josh 10:10–11). Other places where it is mentioned are Joshua 15:35; 1 Samuel 17:1; 2 Chronicles 11:9; Nehemiah 11:30; Jeremiah 34:7.

AZEL (ā'zĕl). 1. A descendant of Saul's son Jonathan (1 Chron 8:37–38; 9:43–44).
2. A place near Jerusalem (Zech 14:5).

AZGAD (ăz'găd, Heb. *'azgādh, Gad is strong,* or *fate is hard*). The ancestral head of a postexilic family (Ezra 2:12; 8:12; Neh 7:17; 10:15).

AZIEL (ā'zĭ-ĕl, Heb. *'ăzī'ēl, God is my strength*). A Levite musician (1 Chron 15:20; Jaaziel in 15:18, Jehiel in 16:5).

The large mound of Tell ez-Zakariyeh, identified with Azekah, on the northeastern edge of the Valley of Elah. Courtesy Ecole Biblique et Archéologique Française, Jerusalem.

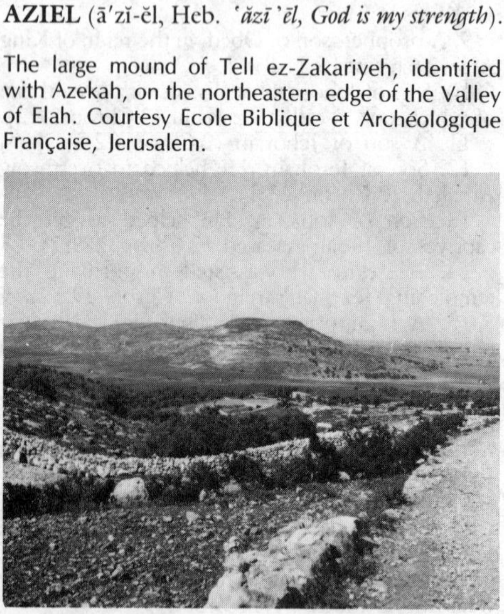

AZIZA (à-zī'zà, Heb. *'ăzîzā', strong*). A man in the time of Ezra who divorced his foreign wife (Ezra 10:27).

AZMAVETH (ăz-mā'vĕth, Heb. *'azmāweth, death is strong*). 1. One of David's heroes (2 Sam 23:31).
2. A Benjamite, one of whose sons followed David (1 Chron 12:3).
3. A man in charge of David's treasures (1 Chron 27:25).
4. A descendant of Saul's son Jonathan (1 Chron 8:36).
5. A place north of Amathoth to which some exiles returned (Ezra 2:24; Neh 12:29); also called Beth Azmaveth (Neh 7:28).

AZMON (ăz'mŏn, Heb. 'atsmôn, strong). A town on the south border of Judah (Num 34:4–5; Josh 15:4). The site is unknown.

AZNOTH TABOR (ăz'nŏth-tā'bôr, Heb. *'aznôth tāvōr, the ears,* i.e., slopes of Tabor). A place near Mount Tabor on the border of Naphtali (Josh 19:34).

AZOR (ā'zôr). A postexilic ancestor of Christ (Matt 1:13–14).

AZOTUS (See ASHDOD)

AZRIEL (ăz' rĭ-ĕl, Heb. *'azrî'ēl, God is help*). 1. A chieftain of the tribe of Manasseh east of the Jordan (1 Chron 5:24).
2. A Naphtalite of David's time (1 Chron 27:19).
3. The father of Seraiah of Jeremiah's time (Jer 36:26).

AZRIKAM (ăz'rĭ-kăm, Heb. *'azrîqām, my help has arisen*). 1. A son of Neariah (1 Chron 3:23).
2. A descendant of Saul (1 Chron 8:38; 9:44).
3. A Levite, descended from Merari (1 Chron 9:14).
4. An officer of Ahaz (2 Chron 28:7).

AZUBAH (à-zū'bà, *forsaken*). 1. A wife of Caleb (1 Chron 2:18–19).
2. The mother of Jehoshaphat (1 Kings 22:42).

AZUR (See AZZUR)

AZZAH (See GAZA)

AZZAN (ăz'ăn, *strong*). The father of Paltiel, who was prince of Issachar in the days of Moses (Num 34:26).

AZZUR (ăz'êr, Heb. *'azzur, helped*). 1. Father of Hananiah the false prophet (Jer 28:1).
2. Father of Jaazaniah (Ezek 11:1).
3. One of the signers of the covenant in the days of Nehemiah (Neh 10:17).

B

BAAL (bā'ăl, Heb. *ba'al, lord, possessor, husband*). 1. The word "baal" appears in the OT with a variety of meanings. Originally it was not a proper noun, but later it came to be so used. Sometimes it is used in the primary sense of "master" or "owner" (as in Exod 21:28, 34; Judg 19:22; Isa 16:8). Since the Hebrew husband was regarded as the literal owner of his wife, baal was the common term for husband (as in Exod 21:3; 2 Sam 11:26; Hos 2:16). Most often, however, the word refers to the Semitic deity or deities called Baal. Baal became the proper name for the most significant god in the Canaanite pantheon, or company of gods. He was the presiding deity in many localities. The plural word, Baalim, may be used of the different manifestations or attributes of the one Baal or may indicate that in popular thought local Baals came to have independent existence. The Baalim were the gods of the land, owning and controlling it; and the increase of crops, fruits, and cattle was under their control. The farmer was completely dependent on the Baalim. Some Baals were greater than others. Some were in control of cities, as Melkart of Tyre. The name Baal occurs as early as the Hyksos period (c. 1700 B.C.). The Amarna letters and the Ras Shamra texts (c. 1400) make Baal a prominent Semitic deity, and in the latter texts the name is not only applied to local gods but is also used as the name of a distinct god Baal.

Frontal and side view of bronze figurine of Canaanite god (Baal or Reshef). The god raises his hand in a smiting gesture. The headdress and the kilt show strong Egyptian influence. Late Canaanite period (c. 1550–1200 B.C.). Courtesy Reuben and Edith Hecht Museum, University of Haifa.

Baal was worshiped on high places in Moab in the time of Balaam and Balak (Num 22:41). In the period of the judges there were altars to Baal in Palestine (Judg 2:13; 6:28–32); and in the time of Ahab and Jezebel, the daughter of the heathen king of the Sidonians, the worship of the Lord was almost supplanted by that of Baal. The struggle between Baalism and the worship of the true God came to a head on Mount Carmel when the prophet Elijah met the priests of Baal and had 450 of them killed (1 Kings 16:32; 18:17–40). The cult quickly revived, however, and prospered until crushed by Jehu (2 Kings 10:18–28). Jezebel's daughter Athaliah, the wife of Jehoram, gave the worship of Baal a new impulse (2 Chron 17:3; 21:6; 22:2). When she was overthrown, the temple of Baal at Jerusalem was destroyed and the chief priest killed before the altar (2 Kings 11:18). Before long, however, there was another revival of the worship of Baal (2 Chron 28:2; 2 Kings 21:3). Josiah again destroyed the temple of Baal at Jerusalem and caused the public worship of the god to cease for a time (2 Kings 23:4–5). Prophets of Israel, especially Jeremiah, often denounced Baal worship (Jer 19:4–5).

Incense and sacrifice were offered to Baal (Jer 7:9)—even human sacrifice (19:5), but the worship of Baal was chiefly marked by fertility rites. The main function of Baal was thought to be to make land, animals, and people fertile. To prompt the god to perform these functions, worshipers themselves performed human sexual acts of fertility, and the Baal shrines were staffed with male and female attendants for this purpose. They were called *gedeshim* and *gedeshoth,* "holy men" and "holy women," not because they were morally holy but because they were wholly "separated" to the service of their god. The same function of prompting Baal to do what is sought from him is seen in 1 Kings 18:26, 28. The priests desired fire from heaven and tried to represent this by making blood pour down their bodies, hoping that Baal might see and perform a similar action himself.

In early years the title Baal seems to have been used for the Lord (Yahweh). When the Lord's people came into Canaan, they naturally and innocently began to think of him as the "possessor" and "lord" of the land—as indeed he was. Even David described the Lord as "Baal" (2 Sam 5:20). But later it was seen that this opened the door to thinking of the God of Israel as though he were only a Canaanite Baal, and the practice was dropped. We see this change in the alteration of names like Jerubaal to Jerubesheth (Judg 6:32; 2 Sam 11:21).

2. A descendant of Reuben, the firstborn son of Jacob (1 Chron 5:5).

3. A Benjamite (1 Chron 8:30).

4. A town somewhere on the border of Simeon (1 Chron 4:33).

5. In conjunction with another name it is often the name of a man and not of Baal, e.g., Baal-Manan, a king of Edom (Gen 36:38; 1 Chron 1:49). SB

BAALAH (See KIRIATH JEARIM)

BAALATH (bā'ălăth, Heb *ba'allāth*). A town in Dan (Josh 19:44) and a store city of Solomon (1 Kings 9:18; 1 Chron 8:6). In Joshua 15:9 it is identified with Kiriath Jearim.

BAALATH BEER (See RAMATH OF THE SOUTH)

BAALBEK (bāl'bĕk, *city of Baal*). A city of Coele-Syria, about forty miles (sixty-seven km.) NW of Damascus, celebrated for its magnificence in the first centuries of the Christian era and famous since then for its ruins. Because it was early identified with the worship of the sun god Baal, the Greeks named it Heliopolis, "City of the Sun." It cannot be identified with any Bible locality. It became a place of importance only after it was made a Roman colony. Chief of the ruins is the great Temple of the Sun, 290 feet (90.6 m.) x 160 feet (50 m.), built of incredibly huge stones from nearby quarries. The city was completely destroyed by earthquake in A.D. 1759. The Prussian government undertook its excavation in 1902.

Coffered ceiling of the peristyle, temple of Bacchus at Baalbek, ancient city in the valley of Beqa'a, which separates the Lebanon and Anti-Lebanon mountains. The ceiling is superbly decorated with intricate carvings and reaching a height of c. 42 feet (14 m.). Courtesy Studium Biblicum Franciscanum, Jerusalem.

BAAL-BERITH (bā'ăl-bĭr-īth, *lord of covenant*). A god Israel worshiped after Gideon's death (Judg 8:33). Abimelech was given seventy pieces of silver from the temple of this god, and he used this money "to hire reckless adventurers, who became his followers" (9:4).

BAALE OF JUDAH (See KIRIATH JEARIM)

BAAL GAD (bā'ăl găd, *Gad is Baal*). A place in the Valley of Lebanon at the foot of Mount Hermon that marked the northern limit of Israel's conquest of Canaan (Josh 11:17; 12:7; 13:5). Its site is unknown.

BAAL HAMON (bā'ăl hā'mŏn, *Baal of Hamon*). A place where Solomon had a vineyard (Song of Songs 8:11). Its location is unknown.

BAAL-HANAN (bā'ăl-hā'năn, *Baal is gracious*).

1. The son of Acbor and king of Edom (Gen 36:38; 1 Chron 1:49).

2. An official under David (1 Chron 27:28).

BAAL HAZOR (bā'ăl hā'zôr, *Baal of Hazor*). A place beside Ephraim where Absalom had a sheep range and where he brought about the death of Amnon in revenge for the rape of his sister (2 Sam 13:23).

BAAL HERMON (bā'ăl hûr'mŏn, *Baal of Hermon*). A town or place near Mount Hermon marking the NW limit of the half-tribe of Manasseh east of the Jordan (Judg 3:3; 1 Chron 5:23).

BAALIS (bā'ȧ-lĭs, Heb. *ba'alîs*). A king of the

The temple of the sun at Baalbek, or Heliopolis, "city of the sun." Built during the second and early third centuries A.D. Courtesy Studium Biblicum Franciscanum, Jerusalem.

A general view of the ruins at Baalbek, looking northwest. The great pillars of the temple of the sun are pictured at far left. Courtesy Studium Biblicum Franciscanum, Jerusalem.

Ammonites who reigned soon after Nebuchadnezzar's capture of Jerusalem. He instigated the murder of Gedaliah (Jer 40:14).

BAAL MEON (bā'ăl mē'ŏn, Heb. *ba'al me'ôn, Baal of Meon*). An old city on the frontiers of Moab, assigned to Reuben (Num 32:38). It is called Beth Meon in Jeremiah 48:23, and Beon in Numbers 32:3.

BAAL PEOR (bā'ăl pē'ôr, Heb. *ba'al pe'ôr, Baal of Peor*). A Moabite deity, probably Chemosh, worshiped on the top of Mount Peor. The Israelites, when encamped at Shittim, were induced by Moabite women to the worship of this deity and were severely punished by God as a result (Num 25:1–9; Ps 106:28; Hos 9:10).

BAAL PERAZIM (bā'ăl pē-rā'zĭm, Heb. *ba'al perātsîm, Baal of the breaking through*). A place near the Valley of Rephaim where David had a great God-given victory over the Philistines (2 Sam 5:18–20; 1 Chron 14:9–11).

BAAL SHALISHAH (bā'ăl shăl'ĭ-shȧ, Heb. *ba'al shālīshâh, Baal of Shalishah*). A place in Ephraim from which bread and corn were brought to Elisha when he was at Gilgal (2 Kings 4:42–44).

BAAL TAMAR (bā'ăl tā'mȧr, Heb. *ba'al tāmār, Baal of the palm tree*). A place in Benjamin, near Gibeah and Bethel (Judg 20:33).

BAAL-ZEBUB (bā'ăl-zē'bŭb, Heb. *ba'al zevûv, Baal,* or *lord of flies*). The name under which Baal was worshiped by the Philistines of Ekron (2 Kings 1:2, 3, 6, 16). Elijah rebuked Ahaziah for consulting this god to find out whether he would recover from his illness. This is almost certainly the same name as Baalzebub, or Beelzebul in the Greek text. Beelzebub is the prince of the demons (Matt 1:25; 12:24; Mark 3:22; Luke 11:15, 18–19), and is identified with Satan (Matt 12:26; Mark 3:23; Luke 11:18). Beelzebul signifies "lord of the dwelling," a meaning that is pertinent to the argument in Matthew 10:25; 12:29; Mark 3:27.

BAAL ZEPHON (bā'ăl zē'fŏn, Heb. *ba'al tsephôn, lord of the north*). A place near which the Israelites encamped just before they crossed the Red Sea (Exod 14:2, 9; Num 33:7). The site is unknown.

BAANA (bā'ȧ-nȧ, Heb. *ba'ănā', son of oppression*). 1. Two officers in the service of Solomon (1 Kings 4:12, 16).

2. The father of Zadok, one of those who helped in rebuilding the wall of Jerusalem in Nehemiah's time (Neh 3:4).

BAANAH (bā'ȧ-nȧ, Heb. *ba'ănā', son of oppression*). 1. A captain in the army of Ish-Bosheth. He and his brother murdered Ish-Bosheth and thus assisted in turning the kingdom to David. David, however, had them put to death as criminals (2 Sam 4).

2. The father of Heled, one of David's warriors (2 Sam 23:29; 1 Chron 11:30).

3. A Jew who returned from Babylon with Zerubbabel and was one of those who sealed the covenant (Ezra 2:2; Neh 7:7; 10:27).

BAARA (bā'à-rà, Heb. *ba'ărā', the burning one*). A wife of Shaharaim, a Benjamite (1 Chron 8:8).

BAASEIAH (bā'à-sē'yà, Heb. *ba'ăsēyâh, the Lord is bold*). An ancestor of Asaph, the musician (1 Chron 6:40).

BAASHA (bā'à-shà, Heb. *ba'shā', boldness*). The son of Ahijah, of the tribe of Issachar. He became the third king of Israel by assassinating Nadab, when that king, the son of Jeroboam, was directing the siege of Gibbethon in the land of the Philistines. Baasha exterminated the house of Jeroboam and made Tirzah his capital. He ascended the throne in the third year of Asa, king of Judah (1 Kings 15–16), and carried on a long war with him. About the sixteenth year of Asa, Baasha began to fortify Ramah, five miles (eight km.) north of Jerusalem, in order to blockade the northern frontier of Judah. He was prevented from completing this work by Ben-Hadad, king of Damascus, whom Asa had hired (1 Kings 15:16–21; 2 Chron 16:1–6). Asa then tore down Baasha's defenses, and for his own protection built up the bulwarks of Geba (between Ramah and Jerusalem). Baasha continued the calf worship begun by Jeroboam, and Jehu the prophet threatened him and his house with a worse fate than Jeroboam's. After a reign of twenty-four years he died a natural death and was succeeded by his son Elah, who, along with every member of the house of Baasha, was killed by Zimri (1 Kings 15–16). SB

BABEL, TOWER OF (bā'bĕl, *gate of God*). An expression not used as such in the OT, but found popularly for the structure built in the plain of Shinar, as the story is told in Genesis 11:1–9. The men of Shinar intended to build a tower that reached "to the heavens," but the Lord frustrated them by confusing their tongues. The author of Genesis assumes that before this the whole human species was a single tribe moving from place to place and speaking one language. The event took place not very long after the Flood.

The remains of large towers called "ziggurats" can be found at the sites of many ancient cities in Mesopotamia. These sacred temple-towers were built in steplike stages of brick and asphalt, usually with a shrine at the top. The Tower of Babel was, however, not a temple-tower but simply a tower, apparently the first one ever attempted. The ziggurats may have been imitations of this tower.

It is not known for certain whether the ruins of the Tower of Babel are still extant. There are rival claimants for the honor. SB

BABOON (See ANIMALS)

BABYLON (Băb'ĭ-lŏn). The Greek form of the Hebrew word *bāvel,* which was closely allied to and probably derived from the Akkadian *babilu* or "gate of God." The name referred not only to the city itself but also to the country of which it was the capital. Though not the oldest city in Babylonia, it soon became the most important from the standpoint of both size and influence.

Babylon was situated in central Mesopotamia on the river Euphrates, some fifty miles (eighty-three km.) south of modern Baghdad, capital of Iraq. A huge plantation of palm trees added to the beauty of the ancient city, and a permanent water supply assured fertility for the surrounding areas. It was within easy reach of the Persian Gulf and, being situated on an important caravan-trade route, was in contact with all the most important cultural centers of the ancient Near East.

The date of its foundation is still disputed. The connection between Akkad, Calneh, Erech, and Babylon (Gen 10:10) indicates a period at least as early as 3000 B.C. Babylon may have been founded originally by the Sumerians, and an early tablet recorded that Sargon of Akkad (c. 2400) destroyed Babylon and took some of its sacred earth to his own capital city, Akkad. Whatever the date of its foundation, the earliest archaeological levels of the mound that once was stately Babylon come from the first dynasty period, i.e., the nineteenth to sixteenth centuries B.C.

The history of Babylon is complicated by the fact that it was governed by rulers from several lands who were successively engaged in struggles

Clay tablet, from c. 600 B.C., illustrating the Babylonian concept of the world, with Babylon at its center. The inscription mentions the conquests of Sargon of Agade, who lived several centuries earlier. Reproduced by courtesy of the Trustees of the British Museum.

for its capture and retention. It was the scene of many a decisive battle, its magnificent buildings plundered in various periods and its walls and temples leveled from time to time. Yet this apparently indestructible city rose from its ruins on each occasion more splendid than before, until during the reign of Nebuchadnezzar II (c. 605–562 B.C.) it was probably the largest and most elaborate city in the ancient world. All that now remains of its former glory is a series of mounds some five miles (eight km.) in extent, lying mostly on the left bank of the Euphrates.

The political history of Babylon was bound up with that of Babylonia and Assyria, though from the beginning of the eighteenth century B.C. (about the period of Terah's migration from Ur, Gen 11:31) until the time of the Assyrian regime (ninth to sixth centuries), Babylon was the dominant influence in Mesopotamia. Under Hammurabi (c. 1704–1662), the last great king of the first dynasty, the Babylonian Empire stretched from the Persian Gulf to the middle Euphrates and upper Tigris regions. Archaeological discoveries have brought to light many of the achievements of this remarkable scholar-statesman, the most interesting of which is his celebrated legal code. His attempts to unify and organize social life led him to collect and expand existing minor law codes. The resulting legislation was of a most comprehensive nature, and Hammurabi ordered it to be incised on a basalt column and placed in the temple of Shamash, god of justice, for all to see. This column is in every sense a monument of ancient jurisprudence. It was carried away as a trophy by invading Elamites in a surprise raid during the twelfth century and was unearthed only in A.D. 1901 at Susa (biblical Shushan) by J. de Morgan.

The first dynasty of Babylon fell about 1596 B.C. when the Hittite king Mursilis I advanced from Anatolia (modern Turkey) with an army and sacked the city. For about three hundred years Babylon was at the mercy of the Kassites who lived to the north, the Elamites, and other warlike nomadic people. An early Assyrian monarch Tukulti-Ninurta I (c. 1250) occupied Babylon and took the sacred statue of Marduk, patron deity of the city, to Ashur. From the end of the tenth century Babylon became a vassal of Assyria, controlled by the kings of Nineveh. Occasionally the vassal ruler revolted and attempted to form a new dynasty in Babylon, but by the time of Tiglath-Pileser III of Assyria (c. 745–727) Babylon was completely under Assyrian control. This redoubtable monarch, known as Pul in 2 Kings 15:19 and 1 Chronicles 5:26, attacked the northern kingdom of Israel, carried away captives from Gilead, Galilee, and Naphtali (2 Kings 15:29), demanded booty, and reduced Israel to a series of provinces.

One of the more vigorous vassal rulers of Babylon who revolted against Assyria was Mardukapal-iddin (c. 722–711 B.C.), the Merodach-Baladan of 2 Kings 20:12–13 and Isaiah 39:1. He endeavored to organize a coalition against his overlord Sargon II (c. 722–705) and sought the kingdom of Judah as an ally. Isaiah dissuaded Hezekiah from such a course on the ground that it would be futile. A small stone tablet has been unearthed in Babylonia depicting Merodach-Baladan as a stout man with the long curled hair and beard typical of Babylonian men. He held a scepter in his left hand, and on his head he wore a conical helmet quite unlike the usual Assyrian crown. Merodach-Baladan's schemes were ended by Sargon, who subdued him with difficulty and occupied the throne of Babylon.

Sargon was succeeded by his son Sennacherib (c. 705–681 B.C.), who employed vassal princes to keep Babylon in subjugation. When this device failed, he attacked the city and sacked it in 689, removing the statues of its gods to Assyria. It was left to his son Esarhaddon (c. 681–669) to repair the damage and restore the city, perhaps at the instigation of his mother, who was apparently of Aramean descent. When Esarhaddon died, his kingdom was divided between his two sons. One of them, Ashurbanipal (c. 669–626), the last great Assyrian ruler, reigned in Nineveh while his brother Shamash-Shumukin occupied the throne of Babylon. They quarreled bitterly, and in 651 Ashurbanipal attacked and burned Babylon. His brother was killed, and a vassal was appointed to succeed him. Toward the end of Ashurbanipal's life this man became increasingly rebellious, and from 631–612 the influence of Babylon increased to the point where Nabopolassar founded an independent dynasty in 626, known as the neo-Babylonian, or Chaldean, regime.

Under Nabopolassar (c. 626–605) and his son Nebuchadnezzar II (c. 605–562), ancient Babylon attained the height of its splendor. While both men were notable military strategists they were also individuals of cultural interests, and they set about rebuilding the old Babylonian Empire so as to make it the most splendid and notable of all time. Military expeditions brought numbers of captive peoples to Babylonia, and these were employed as artisans and craftsmen on the vast reconstruction projects. As a result of the energy and imagination of Nabopolassar and his son, the influence of Babylon far outstripped that of Nineveh, and in 616 the Babylonians began a military campaign against the middle Euphrates region that ended in the destruction of the Assyrian Empire.

Nabopolassar first marched to the Balikh River and sacked a number of towns but returned to Babylon the same year. In 615 B.C. he set out to attack Ashur, and after a year's siege the city capitulated. A revolt in the central Euphrates region delayed a further attack on Assyria, but in 612 a combined force of Babylonians and Medes marched against Nineveh, captured it, and burned it to the ground. The remnant of the Assyrian forces fled to Haran in NW Mesopotamia, and despite their attempts to ally with Egypt they were decisively defeated in 610, ending the power of the Assyrian regime.

A battle at Carchemish in 605 B.C. against the Egyptians gave the Babylonian forces a decided military advantage, and Nabopolassar determined

The ruins of Babylon, with a view of the Ishtar Gate in foreground. Courtesy Staatliche Museen zu Berlin.

to occupy southern Palestine, probably intending to use it as an advance base for a subsequent attack on Egypt. Nebuchadnezzar directed the operation on the death of Nabopolassar in 605, and in 597 the first attack on Judah took place. This was followed by others in 586 and 581, when several thousand inhabitants of Judah were sent to Babylon as captives. This group joined other previously enslaved peoples, supplementing the already large labor force employed on the gigantic tasks of reconstruction and expansion current in the empire.

Once Nebuchadnezzar felt reasonably secure, he devoted an increasing amount of attention to the expansion of cultural interests in imperial territory, and more particularly in Babylon. His objective was to make this capital the most notable city in the world, and to this end he constructed new canals and navigable waterways, erected magnificent buildings, and laid out extensive parks. A number of travelers who visited Babylon at this time have left their impressions of the city. The description furnished by Herodotus in particular clearly indicates his amazement at the city's great size and splendor.

According to this notable historian of antiquity the city occupied an area of about two hundred square miles (513 square km.) and was built on both sides of the Euphrates. It was protected by a double defensive brick wall reinforced with towers. Outside the city wall, about twenty yards (nineteen m.) distant, was an additional defensive wall of burnt bricks set in bitumen. The outer portion of the twin walls extended over seventeen miles (twenty-eight km.) and was constructed under Nebuchadnezzar, while his predecessors were responsible for other parts of the fortification. Excavations at the mound have shown that the earliest attempt at constructing a defensive system goes back to the nineteenth century B.C.

According to cuneiform sources, access to the city was gained by eight gates, four of which have been excavated. Probably the most impressive of these is the Ishtar gate, located at the northern end of the mound. To reach it one passed down part of the great stone-paved processional street that was about one thousand yards (937.5 m.) in length. It was decorated on either side with figures of lions *passant* in enameled brick. Assyrian art was at its height at this period, and the draftmanship and execution of these animals indicates an advanced degree of artistic skill. The Ishtar gate was also decorated with animals, consisting of about a dozen rows of bulls and mythological dragons placed alternately. The decor was executed predominantly in blue and brown enamel and was done in the time of Nebuchadnezzar.

When the city was at the height of its influence, there were more than fifty temples in Babylon. When some of these were excavated, they were found to be in a reasonably good state of preservation. The temple of Ninmah, goddess of the underworld, was built by Ashurbanipal near the Ishtar gate. The ground plan indicated that when the city was approached from the north, a vestibule led into a larger courtyard, the south

Babylon's Ishtar Gate, set within a 40 feet high double tower, guarded the northern entrance to the city. The construction here shows the relief figures of bulls and dragons in alternate rows. Brick was the standard building material in a land almost totally lacking in stone. Courtesy Staatliche Museen zu Berlin.

end of which was decorated with pillars. Beyond these was an antechapel, while to the south of this area was the shrine of the deity; this shrine contained among other structures an elevated platform designed to support a statue of the goddess. In addition there were living quarters for the priests and stairways that gave access to other parts of the building. A great number of terra-cotta figurines were uncovered at the site but proved to be of little importance.

The southern citadel that was adjacent to the processional street comprised a huge complex of buildings whose main sections were the work of Nabopolassar and Nebuchadnezzar. Several blocks of buildings and courtyards finally led to the royal palace, many of whose rooms were ornately decorated with blue enameled bricks incorporating motifs similar to those used in Greece at a later time. The living quarters provided for the royal family, the court officers, and the retinue of servants, and displayed the grandeur and pomp characteristic of an eastern court.

In this complex was situated one of the seven wonders of the world, the celebrated "hanging gardens" of Babylon. They actually consisted of terraces supported on huge masonry arches, on which carefully tended gardens had been laid out at different levels. Most probably they were designed and executed under Nebuchadnezzar, who had married a Median princess and intended the raised gardens to be a comforting reminder of her mountainous homeland. They included many species of Babylonian and Persian plants in addition to the palm trees that were a characteristic feature of Babylonia at that time. Water was raised to these elevated terraces by a number of mechanical hoists. The interesting feature of these raised gardens was that they were visible above the tops of the buildings, providing a welcome contrast of greenery against an otherwise unrelieved expanse of white roofs or blue sky.

In an enclosed area southwest of the Ishtar gate was the huge ziggurat of Babylon, which was closely linked with the temple of Marduk lying immediately to the south. A ziggurat was a staged or terraced tower crowned with a small shrine dedicated to a particular deity. The structure was generally erected on a mound or artificial brick platform, presumably to serve as a protection against floodwaters. Sometimes the term *ziggurat* is used to include the platform as well as the tower itself. This great staged tower of Babylon may have been the original Tower of Babel (Gen 11:1–9), modified by subsequent reconstruction and additions, although efforts to prove so have been unsuccessful. From archaeological and other sources it appears that it was a seven-story building of sun-dried mud brick faced with kiln-dried brick. An eighth story probably consisted of a small shrine dedicated to Marduk, and in the time of Nebuchadnezzar it was faced with blue enameled bricks. Access to the various levels was gained by means of stairways or ramps. The ground plan of the ziggurat was approximately three hundred feet (ninety-four m.) square, and the structure as it stood in the sixth century B.C. exceeded three hundred feet (ninety-four m.) in height.

The associated temple of Marduk consisted of an annex leading to the principal building. In the latter were a number of chapels devoted to deities other than Marduk, but his shrine was by far the most ornate, richly decorated with gold, alabaster, cedar-wood paneling, lapis lazuli, obsidian, and other semiprecious stones. Much of this work was done in the sixth century B.C.

Nebuchadnezzar died in 562 B.C., and during the next five years three kings, one of whom was the Evil-Merodach of 2 Kings 25:27, occupied the throne until Nabonidus came to power in 556. Nabonidus was a mystic who had antiquarian interests, and after a short rule he made his son Bel-sharusur (Belshazzar) regent while he retired to Teima in Arabia. After nine years he returned to Babylon only to witness the overthrow of the city by Cyrus in 539. This conqueror did not pillage Babylon, but acted respectfully toward the shrines and deities of the land. Enslaved populations were liberated, including the captive Hebrews, and Cyrus, "king of Babylon," set about building up his vast Persian Empire.

Darius I (c. 521–485 B.C.) continued the political tendencies begun by Cyrus, but in later

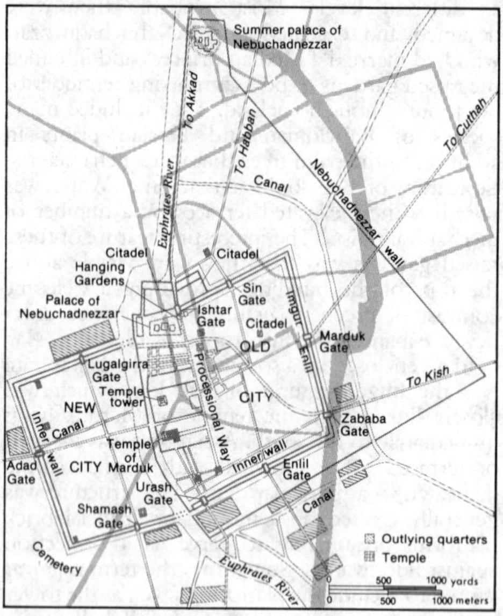

Babylon at the time of Nebuchadnezzar II (605–562 B.C.). Courtesy Carta, Jerusalem.

years the center of influence of the Achaemenid regime moved from Babylon to Persepolis and Ecbatana. When the Persian Empire fell to Alexander the Great in 330, Babylon was destroyed. Alexander intended to reconstruct the great ziggurat, and ordered the rubble removed from the site, but at his death in 323 the task was left unfinished.

Although remaining an inhabited site, Babylon declined still further in importance under the Parthians (c. 125 B.C.) and was last mentioned on a Babylonian clay tablet dated about 10 B.C. At the present time the Baghdad-to-Bassorah railway line passes within a few yards of the mound that was once the most splendid city of the world.
RKH

BACA (bā'kȧ, Heb. *bākhā, a balsam tree*). KJV, RSV, and NIV in Psalm 84:6 all have "the Valley of Baca" (ASV "the Valley of Weeping" but with a marginal variant "the valley of the balsam trees"). The tree was called a weeper probably because it exuded tears of gum. There is no trace of a real tree with this name. The phrase refers figuratively to an experience of sorrow turned into joy.

BACHRITES (See BEKER)

BADGER (See ANIMALS)

BAG. Various kinds of bags are mentioned in the Bible. 1. Hebrew *kelî;* Greek *pēra.* This was a kind of haversack made of skin, for the carrying of one or more days' provisions. This is the "scrip for your journey" mentioned in Matthew 10:10 KJV, where NEB reads "pack for the road."

2. Hebrew *kîs,* a bag for merchants' weights such as in Deuteronomy 25:13: "Do not have two differing weights in your bag—one heavy, one light."

3. Greek *ballantion,* a more finished leather pouch that served as a "purse": "Do not take a purse or bag" (Luke 10:4).

4. Hebrew *hărîț,* a large bag, one large enough to hold a talent of silver (2 Kings 5:23).

5. Hebrew *tserôr,* a bag that could be tied with a string and was a favorite receptacle for valuables. It is translated "pouch" in Genesis 42:35. In the NT this bag is expressed by Greek *zonē* (Matt 3:4; 10:9; Acts 21:11; Rev 1:13; 15:6).

BAHURIM (bȧ-hū'rĭm, Heb. *bahurîm*). A place in Benjamin on the road from Jerusalem to Jericho, not far from the Mount of Olives. It is frequently mentioned in the history of David. It was the home of Shimei, who cursed David on his flight from Absalom (2 Sam 16:5; 19:16; 1 Kings 2:8). Jonathan and Ahimaaz hid in a well there when acting as David's spies (2 Sam 17:18).

BAKBAKKAR (băk-băk'êr, Heb. *baqbaqqar, investigator*). A Levite (1 Chron 9:15).

BAKBUK (băk-bŭk, Heb. *baqbûq, bottle* [onomatopoeic]). The founder of a family of temple servants (KJV, Nethinim) who returned from the Captivity with Zerubbabel (Ezra 2:51; Neh 7:53).

BAKBUKIAH (băk'bū-kī'a, Heb. *buqbuqyâh, flask,* or perhaps, *the Lord pours out*). A name occurring three times in Nehemiah (11:17; 12:9, 25), all the references to one person, a Levite in high office in Jerusalem right after the Exile.

BAKER (See OCCUPATIONS AND PROFESSIONS)

BALAAM (bā'lăm, Heb. *bil'ām,* perhaps *devouring* or *devourer*). The son of Beor from the city of Pethor on the Euphrates, a diviner with a remarkable history (Num 22:22–24:25; 31:8, 16; Deut 23:4; Josh 13:22; 24:9; Neh 13:2; Mic 6:5; 2 Peter 2:15; Jude 11; Rev 2:14).

After their victory over Sihon and Og, the Israelites pitched their tents in the plains of Moab. Balak, the king of the Moabites, sent an embassy of elders of Moab and Midian to Balaam, offering to reward him if he would curse the Israelites. After looking to God about the matter, he replied that God had forbidden him to comply with the request. Balak then sent some messengers of a higher rank with more alluring promises. This time God permitted Balaam to go, cautioning him, however, to deliver only the message God gave him. On his way to Balak, Balaam had this command strongly impressed on his mind by the strange behavior of his donkey and his encounter with the angel of the Lord.

Balak took Balaam to the high places of Baal, from which a part of the camp of the Israelites could be seen. To Balak's disappointment, Balaam pronounced a blessing on the Israelites instead of a curse. Surprised and incensed at the words of the diviner, Balak thought that a fuller view of the camp of Israel might change his disposition. He took him to the top of Mount Pisgah, but the only result was further blessing instead of cursing. Balaam compared the children of Israel to a lion who will not lie down until he has eaten his prey. In desperation Balak now suggested that the issue be tried from a third locality. They went to the top of Peor, and there the Spirit of God came on Balaam and caused him to declare not only that God would bless Israel, but that he who blessed her would be blessed and he who cursed her would be cursed. In his bitter disappointment, Balak angrily reproached Balaam and ordered him to go home without the promised reward. Before he left, Balaam reminded the king that at the very beginning he had said that no amount of money could make him give anything other than the commandment of the Lord. He then uttered a last prophecy—the most remarkable so far—in which he foretold the coming of a star from Jacob and a scepter out of Israel that would defeat Israel's enemies, including Moab.

Nothing else is said of Balaam until Numbers 31. There the seer, who had failed to turn away the Lord from his people, tried before long to turn the people from the Lord. He knew that if he succeeded in this, the consequences to Israel would be just as Balak had desired, God's curse on Israel. By his advice the Israelites were seduced into idolatry and all the vile abominations connected with it. In the judgment that followed, no fewer than 24,000 Israelites perished, until it was evident that the nation abhorred idolatry as a great crime against God. By God's command Israel brought vengeance on her seducers the Midianites, and in the universal slaughter, Balaam also perished.

In the NT Balaam is several times held up as an example of the pernicious influence of hypocritical teachers who attempt to lead God's people astray. No Bible character is more severely excoriated.

The experience of Balaam brings into focus some basic elements in the biblical understanding of God's rule in the world. First, we see how the Lord overrules man's sinful will and desire to bring his own purposes to pass. Balaam already knew God's will (Num 22:12–13). The fact that he responded to the second deputation (22:15) with a reference to abundant reward (22:18) and a renewed approach to the Lord indicates not a sincere desire to do God's will but a determination if at all possible to do his own. It is in this light that we should understand what is expressed as a divine directive (22:20): Balaam hears from the Lord only what he wants to hear. But when he went to Balak, all he could do was what the Lord determined he should do. It is the Lord who reigns. Second, we ought to note that against all odds the Lord's promises prevail: Balak may wish to reverse them and Balaam, if only he could, might try to overturn them, but the promises stand. It is to highlight this truth that Balaam is brought before us in a manner that challenges the promise to Abraham (Num 22:6; cf. Gen 12:3). But in any event it is not the word that Balaam speaks but the people's attitude to the descendants of Abraham that is decisive: Balak is unable to hurt them; Balaam and the Midianites perish (Num 31:1ff.). Third, we learn that the Lord guards his people from overwhelming threats of which they are not even aware. Balaam certainly possessed a mysterious power (22:6) and, without their knowledge, it was to be directed against Israel from the hills overlooking their camp. But the Lord turned the curse into a blessing and they knew nothing about it until long after (31:8). This is the truth expressed in 1 Corinthians 10:13. Fourth, there is a marvelous correspondence between the story of Balaam and the Letter of Jude: to contradict the faith once delivered to us as saints (Jude 3) involves not only denying doctrine but also turning from holiness (Jude 4; cf. 11, 22; Num 25:1ff.). SB

BALAH (bā'lȧ, Heb. *bālâh*). A town in SW Palestine (Josh 19:3), called Bilhah in 1 Chronicles 4:29. The site is unknown. It may be the same as Baalah in Judah (Josh 15:29).

BALAK (bā'lăk, Heb. *bālāq, devastator*). A king of Moab in Moses' day who hired Balaam, a diviner from the Euphrates, to pronounce a curse on the Israelites (Num 22–24; Judg 11:25; Mic 6:5; Rev 2:14). Frightened by the story of Israel's victory over Sihon and Og, he evidently thought that the favor of the Lord could be turned from Israel to his own nation. Instead of cursings, he heard blessings; but he achieved his end in an indirect way when he followed Balaam's advice to seduce the people of Israel to idolatry, a sin that resulted in heavy judgment on the chosen people. See also BALAAM.

BALANCE. The English word is from the Latin *bilanx* and means "having two scales." It is used to

Man holding in his left hand a folded balance and in his right another balance ready for use, on sandstone relief from Mesopotamia, ninth-eighth century B.C. Courtesy Réunion des Musées Nationaux.

translate three Hebrew words: *mo'znayim, kaneh,* and *peles.* The balances of the Hebrews consisted of a horizontal bar, either suspended from a cord that was held in the hand, or pivoted on a perpendicular rod. Scales were suspended from the ends of the bar, one for the object to be weighed, the other for the weight. At first the weights were of stone. Weighing with such balances could be accurately done, but the system was liable to fraud, so that in the OT there is much denunciation of "dishonest scales" (Mic 6:11).

BALD LOCUST (See ANIMALS)

BALDNESS. Natural baldness is seldom mentioned in the Bible. It was believed to result from hard work (Ezek 29:18) or disease (Isa 3:17, 24). Baldness produced by shaving the head, however, is frequently referred to. It was done as a mark of mourning for the dead (Lev 21:5; Isa 15:2; 22:12; Mic 1:16). Shaving the head as a sacrifice to the deity was the custom of the heathens in the land, and the Israelites were strictly forbidden to practice it (Lev 21:5; Deut 14:1). The custom among neighboring nations of shaving all but a small patch in the center of the head was also forbidden (Lev 19:27; 21:5). When a Nazirite completed his vow, the shaven hair was offered as a sacrifice to the Lord (Num 6:18; cf. Acts 18:18; 21:24).

BALM (Heb. *tsŏrî*). An odoriferous resin perhaps obtained in Gilead (Gen 37:25; Jer 8:22; 46:11) and exported from Palestine. It was used as an ointment for healing wounds (Jer 51:8). It came from a small tree not now found in Gilead, and perhaps it never grew there. Seealso PLANTS.

BALSAM (See PLANTS)

BAMAH (bà'mà, Heb. *bāmâh, high place*). Ezekiel (20:29) plays on the two syllables *ba* (go) and *mah* (what), with evident contempt for the high place to which the word refers.

BAMOTH BAAL (bā'mŏth bā'ăl, Heb. *bāmôth ba'al, high places of Baal*). A place north of the Arnon, in the tribe of Reuben, to which Balak took Balaam (Num 22:41; Josh 13:17; also "Bamoth" in Num 21:19–20).

BANDS. In English the word has two common meanings: that which holds together or binds, and a company of men. Both meanings are found in Scripture. In the NT reference is made to the "Italian band" (Acts 10:1 KJV; NIV "Italian Regiment"), a cohort of Roman soldiers stationed at Caesarea, and the "Augustan Band" (Acts 27:1; NIV "Imperial Regiment"), a cohort to which the Roman centurion Julius, who had charge of Paul on his voyage to Rome, belonged.

BANI (bā'nī, Heb. *bānî, posterity*). 1. A Gadite, one of David's heroes (2 Sam 23:36).

2. A Levite whose son served in the tabernacle in David's time (1 Chron 6:46).

3. A descendant of Judah whose son lived in Jerusalem after the Captivity (1 Chron 9:4).

4. A Levite and builder (Neh 3:17).

5. A Levite (Neh 9:4).

6. A Levite who lived before the return from the Exile (Neh 11:22).

7. A Levite who sealed the covenant (Neh 10:13).

8. A leader who also signed the covenant (Neh 10:14).

9. Founder of a family, some of whom returned from Babylonia with Zerubbabel (Ezra 2:10). Some took foreign wives (Ezra 10:29).

10. Founder of a house (Ezra 10:34), a descendant of whom was also named Bani (Ezra 10:38).

BANK. In its modern form banking is of recent origin (seventeenth century A.D.), but banking of a primitive kind was known in ancient times among both Jews and Gentiles. Money was received on deposit, loaned out, exchanged for smaller denominations or for foreign money. Israelites were not permitted to charge each other interest (Exod 22:25) but could lend with interest to Gentiles (Deut 23:20).

BANNER (Heb. *nēs, deghel, banner, ensign, standard*). Banners were used in ancient times for military, national, and ecclesiastical purposes very much as they are today. In connection with Israel's wilderness journey we read, "The Israelites are to camp around the Tent of Meeting some distance from it, each man under his standard with the banners of his family" (Num 2:2). The word occurs frequently in the figurative sense of a rallying point for God's people (Isa 5:26; 11:10; Jer 4:21).

BANQUET. The Hebrews, like other peoples of the ancient East, were very fond of social feasting. At the three great religious feasts, which all males were expected to attend, the family had its feast. Sacrifices were accompanied by a feast (Exod 34:15; Judg 16:23–25). There were feasts on birthdays (Gen 40:20; Job 1:4; Matt 14:6), marriages (Gen 29:22; Matt 22:2), funerals (2 Sam 3:35; Jer 16:7), laying of foundations (Prov 9:1–5), vintage (Judg 9:27), sheep-shearing (1 Sam 25:2, 36), and on other occasions. A banquet always included wine drinking; it was not simply a feast in our sense. At a large banquet a second invitation was often sent on the day of the feast, or a servant brought the guests to the feast (Matt 22:2ff.; Luke 14:17). The host provided robes for the guests, and they were worn in his honor and were a token of his regard. Guests were welcomed by the host with a kiss (Luke 7:45), and their feet were washed because of the dusty roads (Gen 18:4; Judg 19:21; Luke 7:44). The head was anointed (Ps 23:5; Luke 7:46), and sometimes the beard, the feet, and the clothes were also anointed. The head was decorated with garlands (Isa 28:1). The guests were seated according to their respective rank (1 Sam 9:22;

Banquet scene with a bearded figure seated before a table, holding a cup, and attended by servants and a magician, limestone relief from Carchemish, second half of eight century B.C. Reproduced by courtesy of the Trustees of the British Museum.

Luke 14:8), the hands were washed (2 Kings 3:11), and prayers for blessing on the food were said (1 Sam 9:13; Matt 15:35; Luke 22:17). The Pharisees made hand washing and the blessing of food burdensome rituals. The feast was put under the superintendence of a "governor of the feast," usually one of the guests, whose task it was to taste the food and the drinks and to settle about the toasts and amusements. The most honored guests received either larger portions or more choice ones than the rest (Gen 43:34; 1 Sam 9:23–24). Portions were sometimes sent to friends not attending the feast (2 Sam 11:8; Neh 8:10). Often the meal was enlivened with music, singing, and dancing (2 Sam 19:35; Luke 15:25), or with riddles (Judg 14:12). A great banquet sometimes lasted seven days, but excess in eating and drinking was condemned by the sacred writers (Eccl 10:16–17; Isa 5:11–12). SB

BAPTISM (băp'tĭzm). A term derived from the Greek *baptisma* (antecedent, *baptizō*); the etymological significance of the word often has been obscured by a lack of exegetical clarity and by forced interpretation. Its true meaning can be found only in its usage and its theological significance. Its antecedent meaning involves the Judaic usage in the OT times and the practice of John the Baptist. Its incipient meaning lies in Christ's baptism and his interpretation of it. Its formal meaning is to be found in its apostolic interpretation, particularly by Paul.

The idea of ceremonial washing, or cleansing, appears repeatedly in the Mosaic laws of purification (e.g., Exod 29:4, 17; 30:17–21; 40:12, 30; Lev 1:9, 13; 6:27; 9:14; 11:25; 14:8, 9, 47; 15:5–27; 16:4-28; 17:15–16; 22:6; Num 8:7; 19:7–21; 31:23–24; Deut 21:6; 23:11). In the Septuagint version of the OT, translated into the Hellenistic idiom of the NT, the word *baptizō* is used twice: 2 Kings 5:14 (where the meaning is cleansing) and Isaiah 21:4 (where its meaning is obscured). It is clear, however, that later Judaism incorporated this connotation of cleansing and purification into its idea of the new covenant relation and used baptism as a rite of initiation, as reflected in the practices of the Qumran sect and the Dead Sea Scroll communities.

While later Judaism certainly attached a deeply pietistic significance to the cleansing act, John the Baptist, who followed in this tradition, infused into the ritual act of initiation and purification an ethical quality that baptism had not had before. His was a moral community of penitent souls seeking personal righteousness, and he associated with the act of baptism the imperative necessity for a thorough change in the condition of the soul, manifested in a remission of sins through repentance. His fervent exhortation to repent and flee from the wrath to come (Matt 3:7–8) was not a mere invitation to a religious ceremony, but was, rather, an indication of the change brought on by the act of baptism itself. The meaning of the act was deepened. Baptism was transformed from a rite to which one submitted oneself to a positive moral act initiated by the individual as a decisive commitment to personal piety.

John's baptism was, nevertheless, only transitory—his baptism of repentance was but preparatory to a baptism of identification. The meaning and efficacy of baptism can be understood only in the light of the redemptive death and resurrection of Christ. Christ referred to his death in the words "I have a baptism to undergo" (Luke 12:59) and "Can you drink the cup I drink or be baptized with the baptism I am baptized with?" (Matt 20:22; Mark 10:38). Here the word *baptisma,* which indicates the state or condition, is used instead of *baptismos,* which applies to Jewish rites and refers only to the act itself. *Baptisma,* used only in the NT and in Christian writings, never refers to the act alone but always incorporates into its meaning the entire scope of the redemptive significance of the incarnate person of Christ.

John's baptism of Jesus, therefore, connects the act of water baptism with the meaning of the salvation events through his own person and work. To the act of water baptism Jesus added the promise of the baptism with the Spirit, the means by which his redemptive work is applied to human beings (Matt 3:11; Mark 1:8; Luke 3:16; Acts 1:4ff.; 11:16). Using the initiatory and purificatory meaning found in water baptism, Christ made spiritual baptism (by the Holy Spirit) synonymous with the actual application of the virtues of his death and resurrection to sinners.

The apostolic writers, particularly Paul, related Spirit baptism to the whole of the redemptive act. The act of water baptism symbolizes cleansing, but Spirit baptism gives the believer entry into the righteousness of Christ through an identification with Christ himself. Through Spirit baptism the redeemed sinner is incorporated into the spiritual body of Christ, not merely as an act of initiation but as a state or condition of personal righteousness. It is, therefore, the only access to identification with the redeeming Christ.

Baptism may, therefore, be regarded from two perspectives. *Subjectively,* the baptism by the Holy Spirit brings the believer into positive relationship to God; *symbolically,* water baptism is the objective manifestation of the believer's acquiescence in that relationship.

Its subjective significance is represented in the NT by many analogies. It is regarded as the means of *participation in the death and resurrection* of Jesus. In Romans 6:3–5, Paul relates the actual spiritual condition of his readers to such a participation in Jesus' death and resurrection through Spirit baptism. "Do you not know that all of us who have been baptized into Christ Jesus were baptized into his death? We were buried therefore with him *by baptism* into death, so that as Christ was raised from the dead by the glory of the Father, we too might walk in newness of life." This identification is not merely to the death of Christ, in which the believer has also died to sin, but to the resurrection of Christ, in which the believer has found "newness of life." Spirit baptism is, therefore, an *entry into the new life in Christ*—a passage from the old creation into the new creation. This involves not merely forgiveness of sins but also an impartation of the life and righteousness of Christ to the believer (2 Peter 1:4). The believer is "in Christ," and Christ is in the believer. Moreover, the identification effected through Spirit baptism *cleanses the believer through the blood of Christ* (Titus 3:5–6). Thus, Spirit baptism is the incorporation of the believer into Christ's righteousness and an infusion of that righteousness into the believer.

Its symbolic significance is depicted in its objective form. While much debate has focused on the varying interpretations of the forms of

Baptism scene at the River Jordan. Courtesy Zev Radovan.

baptism, each form (immersion, sprinkling, or pouring) is clearly associated with the concept of cleansing and identification, which are the two integral parts of Spirit baptism. Immersion, however, depicts more clearly the symbolic aspect of baptism since its three steps—*im*mersion (going into the water), *sub*mersion (going under the water), and *e*mersion (coming out of the water)—more closely parallel the concept of entering into the death of Christ, experiencing the forgiveness of sins, and rising to walk in the newness of Christ's resurrected life (Rom 6:4).

The genius of Christian baptism, however, is to be found not merely in its symbolic significance but in its actual effect in the life of the believer. Spirit baptism is always vitally related to faith. Only through responsive faith to the regenerative work of Christ does the soul participate in Spirit baptism and, simultaneously, in vital union with God. Subsequently, the symbolic form of baptism (water baptism) should also be related to, and on the basis of, personal faith, as a public commitment to the person of Christ.

While much recent emphasis among Evangelicals has been on the "symbol only" concept of baptism, and while the NT pointedly abstains from ascribing a sacramental value to the act itself, a renewed emphasis on Spirit baptism will restore to its proper place a much neglected aspect of this doctrine. No statement of the doctrine can be a truly biblical one if it fails to emphasize that beyond the symbolic and commemorative act performed by a person there is also the Holy Spirit's inward operation. Spirit baptism brings the regenerated person into a redemptive relationship through his participation in and identification with the death, burial, and resurrection of Christ and the subsequent infusion of the merits of that death and resurrection into the life of the believer, by which he may live as one dead to sin but alive to God (Rom 6:11).

Bibliography: K. Barth. *The Teaching of the Church Regarding Baptism,* 1948; W. F. Flemington, *The New Testament Doctrine of Baptism,* 1948; O. Cullmann, *Baptism in the New Testament,* 1950; P. C. Marcel, *The Biblical Doctrine of Infant Baptism,* 1953; R. E. O. White, *The Biblical Doctrine of Initiation,* 1960; G. R. Beasley-Murray, *Baptism in the New Testament,* 1962, and *Baptism Today and Tomorrow,* 1966; E. Schlink, *The Doctrine of Baptism,* 1972; G. W. Bromiley, *Children of Promise,* 1979. CBB

BAR. An Aramaic word for the Hebrew *bēn,* "son." In the NT it is used as a prefix to the names of persons, e.g., Bar-Jonah, "son of Jonah" (Matt 16:17); Barabbas; Bar-Jesus; Barnabas; Barsabbas; Bartholomew; Bartimaeus.

BARABBAS (bȧr-ăb′ăs, Gr. *Barabbas,* for Aramaic *Bar-abba, son of the father,* or *teacher*). A criminal chosen by the Jerusalem mob, at the instigation of the chief priests, in preference to Christ, to be released by Pilate on the feast of the Passover. Matthew calls him a notorious prisoner, and the other evangelists say he was arrested with others for robbery, sedition, and murder (Matt 27:16; Mark 15:15; Luke 23:18; John 18:40). The custom here mentioned of releasing a prisoner on the Passover is otherwise unknown. The reading "Jesus Barabbas" for his full name in Matthew 27:16–17 was found by Origen in many MSS and is still found in some early versions and a few cursives. It is probably due to a scribe's error in transcription.

BARACHEL (See BARAKEL)

BARACHIAS (See BEREKIAH, BERAKIAH)

BARAK (bâr′ăk, Heb. *bārāq, lightning*). The son of Abinoam of Kedesh, a refuge city in Mount Naphtali. He was summoned by Deborah the judge and prophetess to lead the Israelites to war against the Canaanites who were under the leadership of Sisera, the commander in chief of Jaban, king of Canaan. For twenty years Israel had been oppressed by the Canaanites. The farm lands were plundered; traffic almost ceased; and the fighting men of Israel were disarmed, so that not a shield nor a spear was to be seen among them. Barak raised an army of one hundred thousand men, mostly from a few faithful tribes. They encamped on Mount Tabor, where wooded slopes would protect them against the chariots of the Canaanites. The army of Israel routed Jabin's eight hundred iron chariots and heavily armed host in the plain of Jezreel (Esdraelon). A heavy rainfall caused the alluvial plain to become a morass in which the Canaanite army found it impossible to move. Sisera abandoned his chariot and ran away on foot. Barak pursued him and found him killed by Jael in her tent. A peace of forty years followed (Judg 4–5). In Hebrews 11:32 Barak's name appears among those who achieved great things through faith. The period of the judges is probably to be dated from 1200 B.C., with Deborah and Barak c. 1125.

BARAKEL (băr′ȧ-kĕl, Heb. *bārakh'ēl, God blesses*). A Buzite, whose son Elihu was the last of Job's friends to reason with him (Job 32:2, 6).

BARBARIAN (bȧr-bâr′ĭ-ăn). Originally anyone who did not speak Greek. Paul uses it in this strict sense in Romans 1:14 (KJV; "non-Greeks" in NIV), where "Greeks" and "barbarians" mean the whole human race. Romans and Jews did not mind being called barbarians in this sense. In 1 Corinthians 14:11 (KJV) Paul uses the word to describe one who spoke in an unintelligible foreign tongue; and in Acts 28:2, 4 (KJV) the inhabitants of Malta are called barbarians (they spoke a Punic dialect). In Colossians 3:11 the word refers to those who did not belong to the cultivated Greek race.

BARBER (See OCCUPATIONS AND PROFESSIONS)

BARIAH (bȧ-rī′ȧ, *fugitive*). Son of Shemaiah, and a descendant of David through Solomon (1 Chron 3:22).

BAR-JESUS (Gr. *Bariesous, son of Jesus*). A Jewish magician and false prophet in the court of Sergius Paulus when the latter was proconsul of Cyprus. He was struck blind for interfering with Paul's work (Acts 13:6–12).

BARKOS (bȧr′kŏs, Heb. *barqôs*). One of the temple servants (KJV Nethinim) who founded a family, some members of which returned with Zerubbabel to Jerusalem (Ezra 2:53; Neh 7:55).

BARLEY (See PLANTS)

BARNABAS (bȧr′nȧ-băs, Gr. *Barnabas,* explained in Acts 4:36 to mean *son of exhortation* or *consolation*). The surname of Joseph, a Levite from Cyprus, who was an early convert to Christianity. He sold a field and gave the proceeds to the support of the poorer members of the church in Jerusalem (4:36ff.). In Acts 11:24 he is described as "a good man and full of the Holy Spirit and faith," traits that early brought him into leadership. When the church in Jerusalem hesitated to receive Paul into their fellowship, Barnabas removed their fears by speaking in the apostle's behalf (9:27).

After the start of the work at Antioch, the church in Jerusalem sent Barnabas there to give the work direction; after laboring there for some time, he went to Tarsus and brought back Paul as his associate (Acts 11:22–26). At the end of a year the two men were sent to carry alms from the infant church to the believers at Jerusalem, who were suffering from famine (11:27–30). Returning with John Mark from Jerusalem, they were ordained as missionaries and proceeded on a mission to the Gentiles (13:2–3). Barnabas as well as Paul is called an "apostle" (14:14). Together the two men labored at Cyprus, Antioch in Pisidia, Iconium, Lystra, and Derbe. Up to Acts 13:43 the leadership is ascribed to Barnabas; after that, Paul takes the lead. At Lystra, after a cripple was healed, the inhabitants worshiped Barnabas as Jupiter, and Paul, the chief speaker, as Mercury (13:3–14:28). After their return to Antioch, the church sent them to the council at Jerusalem (15:2). They were commissioned to carry the decrees of the council to the churches in Syria and Asia Minor (15:22–35).

The beginning of a difference between the two men is suggested by Paul in Galatians 2:13, where he says that Barnabas went along with Peter in the latter's inconsistent course. This was followed by a more serious break when, after Paul had suggested a second missionary journey, he refused to take along Barnabas's cousin Mark on the ground that he had left them on their first journey. The two men separated, Barnabas going with Mark to Cyprus, and Paul to Asia Minor (Acts 15:36–41). The mutual affection of the two evangelists did not cease, however. Paul's allusions to Barnabas in his letters shows that he continued to hold his former associate in high esteem (1 Cor 9:6; Gal 2:1, 9, 13; Col 4:10). Some early church leaders attributed the authorship of the Letter to the Hebrews to Barnabas.

BARSABBAS (bȧr-sȧb'ăs, Gr. from Aram., *son of Sabbas,* or perhaps, *son of,* i.e., *born on, the Sabbath*). 1. The surname of the Joseph who with Matthias was nominated by the apostles as the successor of Judas (Acts 1:23).

2. The surname of Judas, a prophet of the Jerusalem church, sent with Silas to Antioch with the decree of the Jerusalem council. Judas afterward returned to Jerusalem (Acts 15:22). Nothing further is recorded of him.

BARTHOLOMEW (bȧr-thŏl'ō-mū, Gr. from Aram., *son of Tolmai* or *Talmai,* Gr. *Bartholomaios*). One of the twelve apostles. He is mentioned in all four of the lists of the apostles in the NT (Matt. 10:3; Mark 3:18; Luke 6:14; Acts 1:13). There is no further reference to him in the NT, and the traditions concerning him are not trustworthy. Some scholars think that Bartholomew is the surname of Nathanael, who was led to Christ by Philip (John 1:45–46). The reason for this is that in the list of the apostles in the Gospels the name of Bartholomew immediately follows that of Philip, and the synoptic Gospels never mention Nathanael, while John never mentions Bartholomew. This view has, however, not been conclusively established.

BARTIMAEUS (bȧr'tĭ-mē'ŭs, Gr. *Bartimaios, son of Timaeus*). A blind man healed by Jesus as he went out from Jericho on his way to Jerusalem shortly before Passion Week (Mark 10:46–52). A similar account is given by Luke (18:35–43), except that the miracle occurred as Jesus drew near to Jericho, and the blind man's name is not given. Matthew (20:29–34) tells of Jesus healing two blind men on the way out of Jericho. On the surface the stories seem irreconcilable, but there is no doubt that if we knew some slight circumstance not mentioned, the difficulty would be cleared up. Various explanations, which may be found in the standard commentaries, have been suggested.

BARUCH (bâr'ŭk, Heb. *bārûkh', blessed*). 1. Son of Neriah and brother of Seraiah (Jer 36:32), of a princely family. He was the trusted friend (32:12) and secretary (36:4ff.) of the prophet Jeremiah. A man of unusual qualities, he might have risen to a high position if he had not thrown in his lot with Jeremiah (45:5). Jeremiah dictated his prophecies to Baruch, who read them to the people (ch 36). King Jehoiakim, on hearing the opening sentences of the prophecy, became greatly angered and burned the scroll. He ordered the arrest of Baruch and Jeremiah, but they escaped. Baruch rewrote the prophet's oracles with additions (36:27–32). In the reign of Zedekiah, during the final siege of Jerusalem, Jeremiah bought his ancestral estate in Anathoth. Since he was at that time a prisoner, he placed the deed in Baruch's hands and testified that Israel would again possess the land (ch 32). Josephus (*Antiq.* 10.9.1) says that Baruch continued to live with Jeremiah at Mizpah after the fall of Jerusalem. After the murder of Gedaliah, the leaders accused him of unduly influencing Jeremiah when the latter urged the people to remain in Judah (43:3), a fact that shows how great Baruch's influence was thought to be over his master. He was taken to Egypt with Jeremiah (43:6). After that, all reliable records about him cease. Jerome preserves a tradition that he died in Egypt soon after his arrival. Other traditions say that he was taken by Nebuchadnezzar to Babylon after this king conquered Egypt and that he died there twelve years later. The high regard in which Baruch was held is shown by the large number of spurious writings that were attributed to him, among them *The Apocalypse of Baruch,* the *Book of Baruch; The Rest of the Words of Baruch;* the *Gnostic Book of Baruch,* and others.

2. A man who helped Nehemiah in rebuilding the walls of Jerusalem (Neh 3:20).

3. A priest who signed the covenant with Nehemiah (Neh 10:6).

4. The son of Colhozeh, a descendant of Perez (Neh 11:5). SB

BARUCH, BOOK OF (See Apocrypha)

BARZILLAI (bȧr-zĭl'ā-ī, Heb. *bārzillay, made of iron*). 1. A wealthy Gileadite of Rogelim, east of the Jordan, who brought provisions to David and his army when the king fled from Absalom (2 Sam 17:27–29). When David was returning to Jerusalem, after Absalom's defeat, David invited Barzillai to come to live in the capital. Barzillai,

The southern area of Bashan bordered by the Yarmuk River was suitable for agriculture (cf. "The bulls of Bashan" [Ps 22:12]). Courtesy Zev Radovan.

who was then eighty, refused because of his age but arranged that his son Kimham should go instead (19:31–40). Before his death David charged Solomon to "show kindness to the sons of Barzillai" (1 Kings 2:7).

2. One of the returning exiles living in Ezra's time. He "married a daughter of Barzillai the Gileadite" and adopted his wife's family name (Ezra 2:61–62).

3. A Meholathite, whose son Adriel married Saul's daughter, either Michal (2 Sam 21:8) or Merab (1 Sam 18:19).

BASEMATH (băs'ē-măth, Heb. *bāsmath, fragrant,* "Bashemath" in KJV). 1. One of Esau's wives, daughter of the Hittite Elon (Gen 26:34). She is called Adah in the genealogy of Edom (36:2–3).

2. Ishmael's daughter and sister of Nebaioth, the last of Esau's three wives, according to the genealogy in Genesis 36:3–4, 13, 17. In Genesis 28:9 she is called Mahalath.

3. Solomon's daughter, married to Ahimaaz, Solomon's tax collector for Naphtali (1 Kings 4:15).

BASHAN (bā'shăn, Heb. *bāshān, smooth, fertile land*). The broad, fertile region east of the Sea of Galilee, extending roughly from Gilead in the south to Mount Hermon in the north. Josephus identifies Bashan with Gaulonitis and Batanea (cf. Jos. *Antiq*. 4.5.3 with 1 Kings 4:13; and *Antiq*. 9.8.1 with 2 Kings 10:33). In the days of Abraham it was occupied by a people called the Rephaites (Gen 14:5). Og, the last king of the race, was defeated and killed by the Israelites at Edrei in the time of Moses (Num 21:33–35; Deut 3:1–7). The entire district was assigned to the half-tribe of Manasseh (Deut 3:13). Edrei, Ashtaroth, Golan, and Salecah were its chief cities (1:4; 3:1, 10; 4:43). Solomon taxed the land (1 Kings 4:13). It was lost to Israel in the Syrian wars (1 Kings 22:3ff.; 2 Kings 8:28; 10:32, 35). Tiglath-Pileser incorporated it into the Assyrian Empire (2 Kings 15:29). The Nabateans held it in the second century B.C. It was included in the kingdom of Herod the Great and then belonged to Philip, Herod's son. It was celebrated for its cattle (Ps 22:12), its breed of sheep (Deut 32:14), and for its oak trees (Isa 2:13; Ezek 27:6). SB

BASHAN-HAVOTH-JAIR (see HAVVOTH JAIR)

BASHEMATH (See BASEMATH)

BASIN. A wide hollow vessel for holding water for washing and other purposes (John 13:5). The word is used for various kinds of bowls and dishes:

1. A small vessel used for wine and other liquids (Exod 24:6).

2. A shallow vessel used to receive the blood of sacrifices in the temple (Exod 12:22) and for domestic purposes.

3. A large bowl used in the temple for various purposes, especially at the great altar (Zech 9:15).

Detail of a limestone plaque from Tello (c. 2550 B.C.)—bas-relief of basket, perhaps containing the first brick for the foundation of a temple, borne by King Ur-nanshe of Lagash. Courtesy Réunion des Musées Nationaux.

BASKET. Four kinds of baskets are mentioned in the OT, but we cannot tell from their names their differences in size, shape, and use. They were made of various materials—leaves, reeds, rushes, twigs, or ropes; and they had various shapes and sizes. Some were small enough to be carried in the hands; others had to be carried on the shoulder or head or on a pole between two men. They were used for a variety of purposes: for carrying fruit (Deut 26:2); bread, cake, and meat (Gen 40:17; Exod 29:2–3); clay to make bricks, and earth for embankments (Ps 81:6). In the NT two kinds of baskets are referred to. The *kophinos* (Matt 14:20; Mark 6:43; John 6:13) was a relatively small basket that could be carried on the back to hold provisions. Twelve of these baskets were used to gather the food that remained after the feeding of the five thousand. The *spuris* was considerably larger, as we may be sure from its use in letting Paul down from the wall at Damascus (Acts 9:25). Seven of these were used to gather the food that was left after the feeding of the four thousand (Matt 16:9–10). SB

BASMATH (See BASEMATH)

BASTARD (Heb. *mamzēr,* Gr. *nothos, bastard,* specifically, *child of incest*). In Deuteronomy 23:2 the word probably means a "child of incest," not simply an illegitimate child (NIV "one born of a forbidden marriage"). There it says that a bastard and his descendants to the tenth generation are excluded from the assembly of the Lord. Jephthah, the "son of a strange woman" (KJV), a "prostitute" (NIV), was called to be a judge of Israel (Judg 11:1–2). In Zechariah 9:6 KJV reads, "And a bastard shall dwell in Ashdod," but NIV renders it, "Foreigners will occupy Ashdod." In Hebrews 12:8 the word is used in its proper sense of born out of wedlock. Bastards had no claim to paternal care or the usual privileges and discipline of legitimate children.

BAT (See ANIMALS)

BATH (See WEIGHTS AND MEASURES)

BATH, BATHING. Bathing in the ordinary, nonreligious sense, whether for physical cleanliness or refreshment, is not often mentioned in the Scriptures. The average Hebrew had neither the water nor the inclination for bathing. In most cases "bathe" means partial washing. Public baths of the Greek type were unknown among the Hebrews until Greek culture invaded Palestine under Antiochus Epiphanes (c. 168 B.C.). The dusty roads of Palestine made frequent washing of the feet necessary, and this was always done when staying at a house (Gen 18:4; 19:2; John 13:10). In the Bible bathing stands chiefly for ritual acts—purification from ceremonial defilement because of contact with the dead, defiled persons or things, or things under the ban. Priests washed

Interior of a bathhouse at Masada, from Herod's time. Courtesy S. Zur Picture Library.

their hands and feet before entering the sanctuary or making an offering on the altar (Exod 30:19–21). The high priest bathed on the Day of Atonement before each act of expiation (Lev 16:4, 24). In the time of Christ, the Jews washed their hands before eating (Mark 7:3–4). According to Josephus, the Essenes practiced daily bathing for ceremonial reasons. SB

BATH RABBIM (băth răb'ĭm, Heb. *bath-rabbîm, daughter of multitudes*). The name of a gate of Heshbon (Song of Songs 7:4). Near it were two pools that the Shulammite's eyes were compared to.

BATHSHEBA (băth-shē'bȧ, Heb. *bath-sheva', daughter of Sheba*). The daughter of Eliam (2 Sam 11:3) or Ammiel (1 Chron 3:5); both names have the same meaning. She was the wife of Uriah the Hittite, a soldier in David's army. During Uriah's absence in the wars David forced her to commit adultery with him (2 Sam 11). Uriah was then treacherously killed by David's order (11:6ff.). She became David's wife and lived with him in the palace. They had four sons, including Solomon (2 Sam 5:14; 1 Chron 3:5), after the first child had died (2 Sam 12:14ff.). With the help of the prophet Nathan she defeated the plot of Adonijah to usurp the kingdom and succeeded in having David choose Solomon as his successor. Adonijah was ultimately put to death. She was a woman of resourcefulness and energy, and retained her influence over David until his death. Her sons Nathan and Solomon were both ancestors of Jesus Christ (Matt 1:6; Luke 3:31).

BATHSHUA (băth'shūȧ, Heb. *bath-shûa', daughter of opulence,* or *daughter of Shua*). 1. In Genesis 38:2 (NIV has "daughter of a Canaanite man named Shua") and 1 Chronicles 2:3, where the name indicates daughter of Shua, wife of Judah.

2. In 1 Chronicles 3:5 as the mother of Solomon in most Hebrew manuscripts, but this is probably a misreading of Bathsheba due to a scribal error. The LXX has Bathsheba, and this is followed by NIV.

BATTERING RAM (See WAR)

BATTLE. In ancient times a trumpet signal by the commander opened each battle (Judg 7:18), and, when it was over, called the soldiers away from the fight (2 Sam 2:28; 18:16). Priests accompanied the army into war to ascertain God's will (Judg 6:36ff.; 1 Sam 14:8ff.). To make the Lord's help in battle more certain, the ark was taken along. When the army drew near the battle, a priest or the commander encouraged the soldiers by reminding them of God's presence and help. The fainthearted were exempted (Deut 20:8). Military science was relatively simple. A force was usually divided into two attacking divisions, the one in the rear serving as a reserve or as a means of escape for the leader in case of defeat. Spearmen probably formed the first line,

Drawing of a battle between cavalry and infantry, on sarcophagus found at Sidon. Courtesy Carta, Jerusalem.

bowmen or archers the second, and slingers the third. Horses and chariots were not used by Israel until quite late. Most of the fighting was done by footmen. Sometimes the battle was preceded by duels between individuals, and these on occasion determined the outcome of the battle (1 Sam 17:3ff.; 2 Sam 2:14ff.). Night attacks and ambushes were often resorted to (Judg 7:16; Josh 8:2). See also ARMS AND ARMOR; WAR. SB

BATTLEMENT (See PARAPET)

BAY TREE (See PLANTS)

BAZLUTH, BAZLITH (băz'lŭth, baž'lĭth, Heb. *batslûth, batslîth, stripping*). The ancestor of a family of temple servants (KJV Nethinim), members of which returned from captivity (Ezra 2:52; Neh 7:54).

BDELLIUM (dĕl'ĭ-ŭm, Heb. *bedhōlah*). A substance mentioned in Genesis 2:12 and Numbers 11:7, variously taken to be a gum or resin, a precious stone, or a pearl. It was the same color as manna and was found like gold and the onyx stone or the beryl in the land of Havilah. The Greeks gave the name bdellium to a gum obtained from a tree growing in Arabia, Babylonia, India, and Media. NIV renders "resin" or "aromatic resin."

BEALIAH (bē'ȧ-lī'a, Heb. *be'alyâh, Jehovah is Lord*). A Benjamite soldier who joined David at Ziklag (1 Chron 12:5).

BEALOTH (bē'ȧ-lŏth, Heb. *be'ālôth*). 1. A town in the south of Judah (Josh 15:24).

2. A locality in north Israel (1 Kings 4:16, Aloth in KJV and NIV). The text is uncertain.

BEAM. Used in the OT to refer to beams used in constructing the upper floors and roofs of buildings (1 Kings 7:3) and to the beam of a weaver's loom (Judg 16:14). Jesus uses the term in a figurative sense in Matthew 7:3 and Luke 6:41 (NIV "plank" in both cases) in contrast to a mote, in order to show how inconsistent it is to criticize minor faults in others when ours are so much greater.

BEAN (See PLANTS)

BEAR (See ANIMALS)

BEARD. With Asiatics a badge of manly dignity, in contrast to the Egyptians, who usually shaved the head and the face. As a sign of mourning, it was the custom to pluck it out or cut it off. The Israelites were forbidden to shave off the corners of their beards, probably because that act was regarded as a sign of paganism (Lev 19:27). To force a man to cut off his beard was to inflict on him a shameful disgrace (2 Sam 10:4–5).

BEAST (See ANIMALS)

BEATITUDES (bē-ăt'ĭ-tūds, Lat. *beatitudo, blessedness*). The word "beatitude" is not found in the English Bible. It means either (1) the joys of heaven or (2) a declaration of blessedness, especially as made by Christ. Beatitudes occur frequently in the OT (e.g., Ps 32:1–2; 41:1; 65:4). The Gospels contain isolated beatitudes by Christ (Matt 11:6; 13:16; 16:17; 24:46 with the Lukan parallels; John 13:17; 20:29). But the word is most commonly used of the declarations of blessedness made by Christ in the discourses recorded by Matthew (5:3–11) and Luke (6:20–22) that are called the "Sermon on the Mount" and the "Sermon on the Plain." Scholars are not agreed whether we have here two different records of the same discourse or records of two different but similar discourses.

The Beatitudes do not describe separate types of Christian character. Rather, they set forth qualities and experiences that are combined in the ideal character. In Matthew there are nine beatitudes and no woes; Luke has four beatitudes and four corresponding woes. In Matthew all the sayings except the last are in the third person; in Luke they are in the second. In Matthew all the blessings except the last are attached to spiritual qualities; in Luke they relate to outward conditions of poverty and suffering. The general declarations in Matthew require certain spiritual conditions, whereas the special declarations in Luke, since they were addressed to Jesus' disciples, do not. Luke omits the third, fifth, sixth, and seventh beatitudes of Matthew. Some scholars profess to find a gradation in the order in which the beatitudes are recorded. Much has been written on the grouping of the Beatitudes, but no grouping is generally accepted.

Bibliography: W. D. Davies, *The Sermon on the Mount,* 1966; C. H. Dodd, *More New Testament Studies,* 1968, pp. 1–10; R. A. Guelich, *The Sermon on the Mount,* 1982. SB

BEBAI (bē'bā-ī, Heb. *bēvay*). 1. The ancestral head of a family that returned from the Captivity (Ezra 2:11; 8:11; Neh 7:16; 10:15).

2. One of this family (Ezra 8:11).

BECHER (See BEKER)

BECORATH, BECHORATH (bē-kō'răth, Heb. *bekhôrath, the first birth*). An ancestor of Saul of the tribe of Benjamin (1 Sam 9:1).

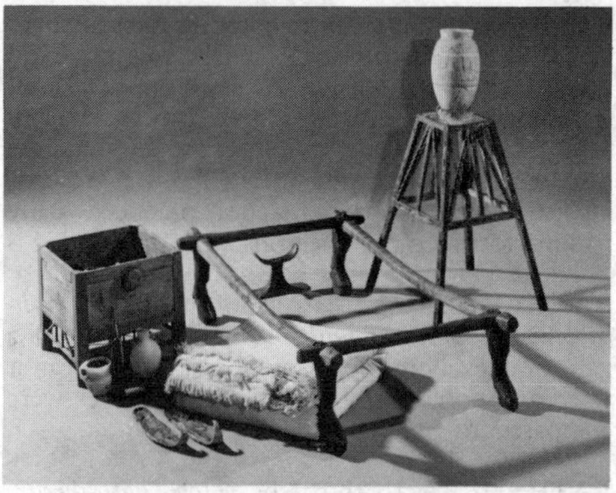

Wooden frame of a bed from Thebes (c. 1250 B.C.), perhaps that of a child. The feet are in the form of a bull's hooves. Also shown are a headrest, painted jar stand, coarsely woven piece of linen, fringed at one end, sandals, vessels, and a chest. Reproduced by courtesy of the Trustees of the British Museum.

BED. In the East, in ancient times as now, the very poor slept on the ground, their outer garments serving as both mattress and blanket. The law, therefore, did not allow such a garment to be kept in pledge after sunset, or the man would be without covering (Deut 24:13). In more advanced conditions a rug or a mat was used as a bed. At first it was laid on the floor, usually near a wall; later it was put on an elevation, either a raised part of the floor or a bedstead, which gave rise to the expression "go up into my bed" (Ps 132:3 KJV). Beds on raised platforms along the walls of a room were covered with cushions and used as sofas during the day. The mats from such beds were rolled up and put away in a closet or another room for the day. The bedroom where Joash was hidden was not a chamber for sleeping but a storeroom in which bedding was kept (2 Kings 11:2). Still later, in some cases, a mattress took the place of the mat, and a pillow was also used, along with a blanket of some kind. Bedsteads must have been used occasionally, for the giant Og had one made of iron, a marvel in those days (Deut 3:11). The very wealthy had more elaborate and ornamented bedsteads. Amos speaks of "beds inlaid with ivory" (Amos 6:4), and in Esther 1:6 we read of "couches of gold and silver." Such bedsteads were sometimes further furnished with posts and a canopy (Song of Songs 3:10), and they had silken cushions on them (Amos 3:12 RV) and rich coverings (Prov 7:16). SB

BEDAD (bē'dăd, Heb. *bedhadh, alone*). The father of Hadad, king of Edom (Gen 36:35; 1 Chron 1:46).

BEDAN (bē'dan, Heb. *bedhān,* perhaps *son of judgment*). 1. A Hebrew judge who with Jerubbaal, Jephthan, and Samuel is mentioned as a deliverer of the nation (1 Sam 12:11). The Book of Judges does not mention him. It is thought that "Bedan" is a misreading for "Abdon" (Judg

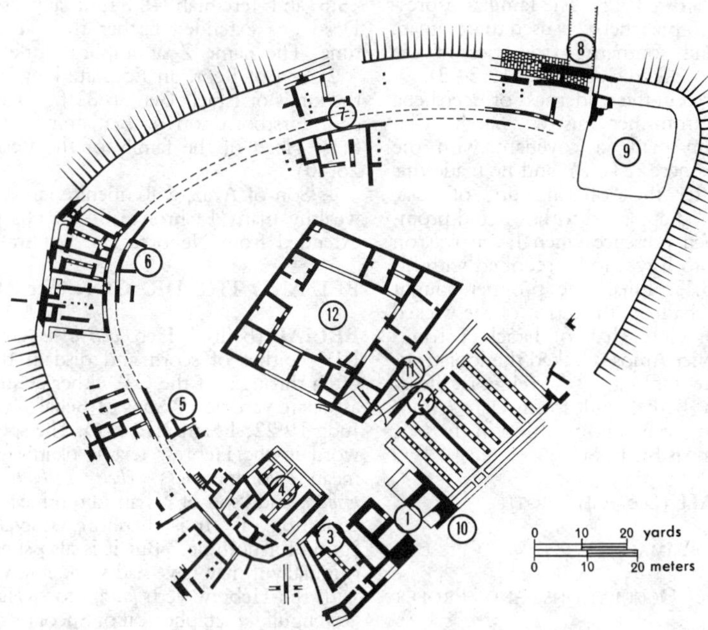

Plan of the excavated areas of Beersheba (Tell es-Seba): (1) city gate; (2) royal storehouses; (3,4) administration buildings; (5) cult area; (6,7) living quarters; (8) deep trench; (9) water system; (10) well; (11) Hellenistic fortress, (12) Roman fortress. Courtesy Carta, Jerusalem.

12:13) or for "Barak," which is found in the LXX and the Syriac.

2. A son of Ulam of the house of Manasseh (1 Chron 7:17).

BEDEIAH (bē-dē′yȧ, Heb. *bēdheyāh, servant of Jehovah*). A son of Bani who had taken a foreign wife (Ezra 10:35).

BEE (See ANIMALS)

BEELIADA (bē′ĕ-lī′ȧ-dȧ, Heb. *be'elyādhā', the Lord knows*). A son of King David (1 Chron 14:7); called Eliada in 2 Samuel 5:16 and 1 Chronicles 3:8.

BEELZEBUB (See BAALZEBUB)

BEELZEBUL (See BAALZEBUB)

BEER (bē′ēr, Heb. *be'ēr, a well*). 1. A place where the Israelites stopped during their wilderness journey (Num 21:16), possibly the same as Beer Elim (Isa 15:8).

2. A place to which Jotham fled from his brother Abimelech (Judg 9:21). The site is unknown.

BEERA (bē-êr′rȧ, Heb. *be'ērā', a well*). A descendant of Asher (1 Chron 7:37).

BEERAH (bē-ê′rȧ, Heb. *be'ērāh, a well*). A Reubenite prince whom Tiglath-Pileser carried away captive (1 Chron 5:6).

BEER ELIM (bē′êr ē′līm, Heb. *be'ēr 'ēlîm, well of Elim*). A village of Moab (Isa 15:8). See BEER.

BEERI (bē-ê′rī, Heb. *be'ērî, belonging to the well*). 1. A Hittite. He was the father of Judith, one of Esau's wives (Gen 26:34).

2. The father of the prophet Hosea (Hos 1:1).

BEER LAHAI ROI (bē′êr lȧ-hī′ roi, Heb. *be'ēr lahay rō'î, the well of the living one who sees me*). A well, probably near Kadesh, where the Lord appeared to Hagar (Gen 16:7, 14) and where Isaac lived for some time (24:62; 25:11).

BEEROTH (bē-ê′rŏth, Heb. *be'ērôth, wells*). A Canaanite town whose inhabitants succeeded in deceiving Israel by making a covenant with them (Josh 9:3ff.). When the deceit was discovered, they were made slaves by the Israelites (9:22–23). They were apparently Hivites (9:7), their village located in the territory assigned to Benjamin (Josh 18:25; 2 Sam 4:2). The murderers of Ish-Bosheth (2 Sam 4:2) and Naharai, Joab's armor-bearer (23:37) came from Beeroth; and Beerothites returned from Babylon after the Exile (Ezra 2:25).

BEERSHEBA (bē′êr shē′bȧ, Heb. *be'ēr shēva', well of seven* or *the seventh well*). The most southerly town in the kingdom of Judah; hence, its practical boundary line, with only the Wady el Arish (the river of Egypt, Gen 15:18) some sixty miles (one hundred km.) to the south. In the days of the conquest of Canaan, it was allotted to the tribe of Simeon (Josh 19:2). The familiar expression "from Dan to Beersheba" is used to designate the northern and southern extremities of the nation of Israel (2 Sam 3:10; 17:11; 24:2).

Hagar wandered in the wilderness of Beersheba when she fled from her mistress Sarah (Gen 21:14). Abraham made a covenant with the Philistine princes here (21:32), and he made this his residence after the "offering up" of Isaac (22:19). Here God appeared to Jacob and promised his continued presence when Jacob was on his way down into Egypt to be reunited with his son Joseph (46:1). Elijah the prophet sought refuge in Beersheba from the terror of the wicked Jezebel, wife of King Ahab of Israel (1 Kings 19:3). The prophet Amos rebuked the idolatrous tendencies he saw infiltrating the religious life of Beersheba from Bethel and from Dan (Amos 8:14). The town receives no mention in the NT. The modern name is Bir Es Seba. JFG

BE ESHTARAH (See ASHTAROTH)

BEETLE (See ANIMALS)

BEGGAR (See OCCUPATIONS AND PROFESSIONS)

BEHEMOTH (See ANIMALS)

BEKA (See WEIGHTS AND MEASURES)

BEKER (bē'kêr, Heb. *bekher, firstborn,* or *young camel*). 1. The second son of Benjamin (Gen 46:21; 1 Chron 7:6). His descendants are not listed in the registry of families (Num 26:38; 1 Chron 8:1–6), probably because they were too few in the beginning to form a tribal family. Beker's nine sons ultimately had 20,200 male descendants (1 Chron 7:8–9). They lived in Anathoth and other places in the territory of Benjamin.

2. A son of Ephraim, and founder of a family (Num 26:35, Bachrites in KJV). But in 1 Chronicles 7:20 we read "Bered," which may be the correct form.

BEL. The Baal of the Babylonians. The Babylonian Hymn to Bel translated from the cuneiform script reveals him as the supreme ruler, the life-giver, the god of justice, he who holds society together, controller of the elements, particularly fire (Isa 46:1; Jer 50:2; 51:44). See also BAAL.

BELA, BELAH (bē'là, Heb. *bela', destruction, belay*). 1. A neighboring city of Sodom and Gomorrah, in the vicinity of the Dead Sea. It was spared, through the intercession of Lot (Gen 19:15–30), from the fiery holocaust that overtook the cities of the plain. It was later known as Zoar (14:2). According to Deuteronomy 34:3, Moses is said to have viewed the southern sector of the Promised Land from Jericho, the city of palm trees, to Zoar. For all practical purposes this places its location at the southern end of the Dead Sea. On the basis of the LXX reading of Isaiah 15:5 and Jeremiah 48:34, it appears as if the Dead Sea extended farther than at the present time. The name Zoar implies "little one."

2. Son of Beor, an Edomite king, previous to the kings of Israel (Gen 36:32ff.; 1 Chron 1:43).

3. Firstborn son of Benjamin (1 Chron 7:6; 8:1). Head of the family of the Belaites (Num 26:40).

4. Son of Azaz, a Reubenite, an exceptionally wealthy man (1 Chron 5:8–9). His possessions extended from Nebo to the Euphrates.

BEL AND THE DRAGON (See APOCRYPHA)

BELIAL (bē'lĭ-ăl, Heb. *belîya'al,* Gr. *Beliar*). A KJV epithet of scorn and disdain that appears often throughout the OT, either as such or in its associate variation, "Sons of Belial" (Deut 13:13; Judg 19:22; 1 Sam 2:12 KJV). The spelling of the word in the Hebrew text is plainly intended to mean "worthlessness" (*beli, without* and *ya-al, profit*), and "son of" is an idiom meaning "in the condition of." It is therefore equivalent to our "good-for-nothing." But it is also suggested that originally it may have had some link with Baal or with the Hebrew verb *bala,* "to swallow down," "to engulf," metaphorical of Sheol or destruction. A "son of destruction" would be one set on a disasterous course and meriting the outcome of it. Nabal (1 Sam 25:25 KJV) receives such a description from the lips of Abigail, his wife (cf. "Raca," Matt 5:22). The apostle Paul employs the term once (2 Cor 6:15; the only place where the term appears in the NIV) where Belial (Beliar) stands as opposed to Christ, thus approaching the diabolical status of Antichrist. In this later usage it is often used by Jewish apocalyptic writers for both Satan and Antichrist.

BELL (Heb. *metsillôth, pa'amôn*). The latter of these terms rendered bell is found in Exodus 28:33ff.; 39:25–26. Bells were attached to the hem of the priestly robes worn by Aaron and his descendants as they performed service in the tabernacle. The tinkling of the bells gave assurance to the worshipers outside the tabernacle that the high priest had not incurred divine retribution but remained alive as their intercessor. The other Hebrew term is used just once, in Zechariah 14:20, where the bells bear the inscription "HOLY TO THE LORD." These "bells" are more like our cymbals than our bells. The bell was not used in biblical times for the purpose of religious convocation as today. The use of the bell to summon the worshipers is a distinctively Christian practice dating back to the end of the fourth century A.D. Its usage seems to have been introduced by Bishop Paulinus who lived during that time. Miniature bells were often fastened to the necks of goats and sheep, enabling the shepherd to more easily keep track of them. JFG

BELLOWS. An ancient device for fanning the flames of the fires of the smelting furnace. The Egyptian type of bellows was operated by the feet, as one alternately trod on two inflated skins.

This created a forced draft by means of reed tubes tipped with iron; the air thus jettisoned into the glowing fire caused the flames to burn more brilliantly and hotly. As each skin was exhausted of its supply of air, the workman would raise it by a cord attached for that purpose and inflate the skin again. This process was then repeated as many times as was necessary. See Jeremiah 6:29.

BELSHAZZAR (bĕl-shăz′àr, Heb. *bēlsha′tstsar, may Bel protect the king*). This was for many years regarded as a fictitious literary creation of a postcaptivity author assuming the pen name of Daniel (c. 165 B.C.). Now, however, it is well authenticated through archaeological studies that Belshazzar was a historic personage. In Daniel 5 he is referred to as the son of Nebuchadnezzar (vv. 2, 11, 13, 18, 22). This conforms with general Semitic usage where one's descendant is often referred to as his "son." Nebuchadnezzar died in 562 B.C., after a forty-two-year reign, and was followed in quick succession by Amel-Marduk (562–560), the Evil-Merodach of Jeremiah 52:31 and 2 Kings 25:27. He was replaced by Nergal Shar-usar (Nergal-Sharezer) who reigned from 560 to 556. He was succeeded by Labashi-Marduk, his weak son, who reigned but a few months and was then overthrown by revolution.

One of the conspirators, Nabonidus (Nabonaid), then ascended the throne. Though a revolutionary, he was still a man of culture and religious zeal for the gods of Babylon. He is sometimes styled "the world's first archaeologist." Nabonidus is thus the last true king of Babylon and the father of Belshazzar. Nabonidus made Belshazzar coregent when he retired to Arabia, presumably to consolidate the weakening empire. The Nabonidus chronicle was written after the capture of Babylon in 539 B.C. Cyrus of Persia declares how he was able to take the city without a struggle. He describes his leniency toward the population, regarding himself as an "Enlightened Despot" and executioner of the will of the gods. His estimation of the character of Belshazzar is exceedingly low, not at all out of harmony with that represented by the biblical account.

Regarding the latter account, Belshazzar's miserable doom came about at the end of, and largely as a consequence of, a drunken orgy held October 29, 539 B.C. (Dan 5). Suddenly the fingers of a man's hand appeared, writing in fiery letters a message that Belshazzar could not decipher but which he still recognized as ominous. After the failure of his advisers to decipher the "cryptogram," he followed the suggestion of the queen mother and summoned the venerable Hebrew prophet Daniel. After verbally castigating Belshazzar, Daniel interpreted the message ("You have been weighed on the scales and found wanting"). The judgment was swift and inevitable. Babylon fell to the Medo-Persians, Belshazzar was killed, and Darius in the name of Cyrus took the throne.

Bibliography: J. G. Baldwin, *Daniel* (TOTC), 21–23, 119ff. JBG

BELTESHAZZAR (bĕl′tĕ-shăz-àr, Heb. *beltsha tstsar, may Bel protect his life*). The name given to the Hebrew prophet Daniel by Nebuchadnezzar's steward (Dan 1:7; 2:26; 4:8; 5:12). Not to be confused with Belshazzar (5:1ff.).

BEN (Heb. *ben*). 1. In Semite usage a term used to designate a male descendant, without being limited to the father-son association of the west. Thus, Uzziah (Azariah) can be represented as Joram's son, despite the intervening generations (Matt 1:8). The term Ben is also used in connection with a clan, in plural only, as in the children of (sons of) Israel, children of (sons of) Ammon, etc. It is used also in prefixes of proper names such as Benjamin, Ben-Hadad, etc. It is found also connoting a class, as "sons of the prophets" (2 Kings 2:15, NIV "company of the prophets").

2. A Levite appointed by David to serve in a musical capacity before the ark of the Lord (1 Chron 15:18). The text is doubtful, because Ben is not mentioned in verse 20 and receives no reference at all in the LXX. NIV omits it.

BEN-ABINADAB (bĕnė-bĭn′e-dăb; KJV, "son of Abinadab"). An officer under Solomon responsible for providing the food necessary for one month of the year for the king and his household (1 Kings 4:11).

BENAIAH (bē-nā′yȧ, Heb. *benāyâh, Jehovah has built*). 1. According to 1 Chronicles 27:5, the son of Jehoiada the priest, and so of the tribe of Levi; probably from the village of Kabzeel in the south of Judah (2 Sam 23:30). He was appointed over David's personal bodyguard, the Kerethites and the Pelethites (1 Kings 1:38). He was a man of exceptional prowess and bravery. He earned this reputation by killing two "lionlike" men of Moab and killing a lion trapped in a pit in a snowstorm (2 Sam 23:20). Although outstanding for these achievements, Benaiah never gained the status of David's "original three" but is always listed as being next in order of rank (23:23). One of the special duties imposed on Benaiah by the rapidly failing monarch was the oversight of the coronation of his son Solomon (1 Kings 1:38–39). Benaiah played no part in the rebellion of Adonijah, but remained faithful to the cause of Solomon. He thus succeeded Joab as captain of the host (2:35; 4:4).

2. One of David's "valiant Thirty," the Pirathonite, tribe of Ephraim (2 Sam 23:30).

3. A prince from the tribe of Simeon who drove the Amalekites from the pastureland of Gedor (1 Chron 4:39–40).

4. A Levite who played with the psaltery "according to *alamoth*" at the return of the ark to Jerusalem (1 Chron 15:20).

5. A priest appointed to blow the trumpet on the same occasion (1 Chron 15:24).

6. Ancestor of Jahaziel the prophet who prophesied for Moab and Ammon in the days of Jehoshaphat, the good king (2 Chron 20:14).

7. One of the overseers for the offerings in the temple in the days of Hezekiah (2 Chron 31:13).

8. Father of Pelatiah who died as a judgment for false teaching in the days of Ezekiel (Ezek 11:13).

9. The name of four men, each of whom had taken a foreign wife in the time of Ezra (Ezra 10:25, 30, 35, 43).

BEN-AMMI (bĕn-ăm'ī, Heb. *ben' ammî, son of my people*). Son of the younger daughter of Lot (Gen 19:38) whom she conceived through her own father following the destruction of Sodom. The progenitor of the Ammonites. Moab shares a like origin through the older sister (19:37).

BEN-DEKER (bĕn-dĕ'ker; "Ben-dekar" in NEB; "Son of Dekar" in JB and KJV). One of twelve officers, each responsible to supply food one month each year for Solomon's household (1 Kings 4:13).

BENE BERAK (bĕn'ĕ bē'răk, Heb. *benê beraq*). A town allotted to the tribe of Dan (Josh 19:45). Its modern counterpart is represented by Ibn Ibrak, a few miles SE of Jaffa.

BENE JAAKAN (bĕn'ĕ jā'à-kăn, Heb. *benê ya' a-qān*). A desert encampment of the Israelites on their journey, placed immediately before Moserah, the site of Aaron's death in Deuteronomy 10:6. The Bene Jaakans are sometimes identified with the Horites.

BEN-GEBER (bĕn-gē'bėr; "son of Geber" in JB, KJV, AND MLB). One of twelve officers, each responsible to supply food one month each year for king Solomon's household (1 Kings 4:13).

BEN-HADAD (bĕn-hā'dăd, Heb. *ben hădhadh*). The name is titular, as opposed to a proper name. As the rulers in Egypt bore the title Pharaoh, so the rulers of Syria bore the designation Ben-Hadad, "son of [the god] Hadad." The Syrians believed their rulers were lineal descendants of the Syrian god Hadad, the deity of storm and thunder, to be identified with Rimmon (2 Kings 5:18). There are three individuals in the OT called Ben-Hadad.

Ben-Hadad I was a contemporary with Asa, king of Judah (1 Kings 15:18). It is plausible (913–873 B.C.) that he is to be identified with Rezon, the founder of the kingdom of Damascus (11:23–25). At the request of Asa of Judah, Ben-Hadad severed his alliance with Baasha of Israel and aligned himself with the southern kingdom (15:16ff.). Though his assistance was of temporary value, the price that Asa was obliged to pay for such aid was tremendous, as Ben-Hadad not only gained control of the treasures of Asa's kingdom but was able through his alliance to extend his territory into the Hebrew kingdoms themselves. Asa was sternly reprimanded by the prophet Hanani for this unfortunate alliance (2 Chron 16:7ff.).

Ben-Hadad II was in all probability the son of Ben-Hadad I. He is the Hadadezer of the monuments. He was contemporary with Ahab of Israel

Basalt stele dedicated to the god Milqart. The inscription on the lower part of stele mentions the name of Ben-Hadad, king of Aram. Dated c. ninth century B.C. Courtesy The University Museum, University of Pennsylvania.

(873–853 B.C.), against whom he waged war, laying siege to the newly constructed capital, Samaria. Because of the ungracious terms of surrender demanded by Ben-Hadad, Ahab refused to capitulate. With divine aid, Ahab was able to rout the Syrian army utterly at the battle of

Aphek (1 Kings 20:26ff.). Ahab spared the life of Ben-Hadad, thus never fully realizing the victory that otherwise would have been his.

Ben-Hadad III (796–770 B.C.) was son of the usurper Hazael, hence not in direct line. His name was adopted from the illustrious name before him. He was a contemporary of Amaziah, king of Judah, and Jehoahaz of Israel. He reduced the fighting personnel of Israel till it was "like the dust at threshing time" (2 Kings 13:7). It was at this time that God raised up a deliverer for Israel, most likely Ramman-Mirari III, as shown from an inscription. Joash was able to defeat Ben-Hadad on three difference occasions and to recover the cities of Israel (13:25). Under Jeroboam II the northern kingdom restored its prestige, but Amos had already prophesied of the time when Israel and Samaria would go into captivity beyond Damascus (Amos 1:4ff.; 5:27). JFG

BEN-HAIL (bĕn-hā'ĭl, Heb. *ben-hayil, son of strength*). One of the princes sent out by Jehoshaphat on a "teaching mission" to the cities of Judah (2 Chron 17:7).

BEN-HANAN (bĕn-hā'năn, Heb. *ben-hānān, son of grace*). A son of Shimon of the tribe of Judah (1 Chron 4:20).

BEN-HESED (bĕn-hĕs'ĕd; "son of Hesed" in JB, KJV, AND MLB). A commissary of Solomon who was to provide one month's food each year for the king's household (1 Kings 4:10).

BEN-HINNOM (See HINNOM, VALLEY OF)

BEN-HUR (bĕn-hûr'; "son of Hur" in JB, KJV, AND MLB). One of twelve officers Solomon commissioned to provide food for the king's household, each for one month a year (1 Kings 4:8).

BENINU (bĕ-nī'nū, Heb. *benînû,* our son). A Levite in postexilic days, one of the cosigners of the covenant with Nehemiah (Neh 10:13).

BENJAMIN (bĕn'jă-mĭn, Heb. *binyāmîn, son of my right hand,* Gen 35:17ff.). The youngest son of the patriarch Jacob whom his wife Rachel bore in her dying agony; named Ben-oni ("son of my sorrow") by Rachel, his mother, but renamed Benjamin ("son of my right hand") by his father Jacob. Of all the children of Jacob, he alone was born in Palestine, between Ephrathah and Bethel. Together with his elder brother Joseph, he appears as a special object of parental love and devotion, no doubt, in part at least, because of the sad circumstances surrounding his birth. He seems to have played no part in the sale of Joseph into Egypt. The intercession on the part of Judah in behalf of Benjamin (Gen 44:18–34) is one of the most moving speeches in all of literature. No doubt the brothers had been softened in their attitude as they had observed the continued suffering of their father over the fate of Joseph, whom he believed irrevocably lost.

2. A great-grandson of Benjamin, son of Jacob (1 Chron 7:10).

3. One of those who had married a foreign wife (Ezra 10:32).

BENJAMIN, TRIBE OF. Named for Jacob's youngest son. On the basis of the first census taken after the Exodus, the tribe numbered 35,400; at the second census, it numbered 45,600 (Num 1:37; 26:41).

In the division of territory by Joshua among the twelve tribes, Benjamin was assigned the portion between Judah on the south and Ephraim on the north (Josh 11:18ff.). Benjamin thus occupied a strategic position commercially and militarily. Benjamin loyally participated in Deborah's rebellion against Sisera (Judg 5:14). The civil war with Benjamin constitutes a sad and strange story (Judg 19–20).

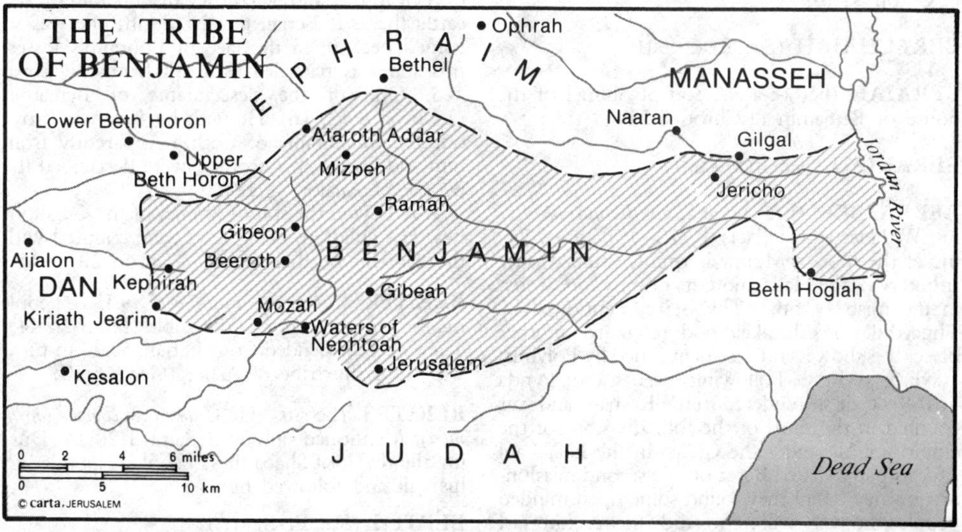

Saul, son of Kish, came from this tribe (1 Sam 9:1ff.). After the death of Saul there was tension and actual fighting between the forces of David and the men of Benjamin. Ish-Bosheth, Saul's weak son, was set up as David's rival (2 Sam 2:8). Shimei of Bahurim, who cursed David, was a Benjamite (2 Sam 16:5, 11). At the time of the schism after the death of Solomon, however, the Benjamites threw in their lot with the tribe of Judah and followed the Davidic house as represented by Rehoboam, against Jeroboam, the son of Nebat to the north. Benjamin was included in the restoration. Saul of Tarsus (Paul) was a member of the tribe of Benjamin (Phil 3:5). JBG

BENO (bē'nō, Heb. *benô, his son*). A Levite. The son of Jaaziah (1 Chron 24:26–27).

BEN-ONI (bĕn-ō'nī, Heb. *ben-'ônî, son of my sorrow*). The name given to Benjamin by his dying mother, Rachel (Gen 35:18). See BENJAMIN.

BEN-ZOHETH (bĕn-zō'hĕth, Heb. *ben-zôhēth,* probably *to be strong*). Son (or perhaps grandson) of Ishi of the tribe of Judah (1 Chron 4:20).

BEON (bē'ŏn, Num 32:3, known also as Baal Meon). A town built by the tribe of Reuben, who chose to remain on the east side of the Jordan. Under its new name it was allotted to the Reubenites after the conquest of Canaan (Josh 13:17). See BAAL MEON.

BEOR (See BALAAM)

BERA (bē'rȧ, Heb. *bera', gift*). King of Sodom, defeated by Kedorlaomer in the days of Abraham at the battle of Siddim (Gen 14:2, 8).

BERACAH, BERACHAH (bêr'ȧ-kȧ, *a blessing*). One of the thirty volunteers who came to the aid of David at Ziklag when he fled from Saul. These men were known for their ability as archers (1 Chron 12:3).

BERACHAIAH (See BEREKIAH)

BERAIAH (bêr'ă-ī-ȧ). A son of Shimei of the house of Benjamin (1 Chron 8:21).

BERAKIAH (See BEREKIAH)

BEREA, BEROEA (bêr-ē'ȧ, Gr. *Beroia*). A city in SW Macedeonia (Acts 17:10–15; 20:4). Lying at the foot of Mount Bermius, situated on a tributary of the Haliacmon, its origins appear lost in the mists of time. The Berea mentioned by Thucydides in all likelihood refers to another place. It is, however, twice mentioned by Polybius (xxvii:8, xxviii:8). Following the battle of Pynda in 168 B.C., it surrendered to the Romans and was counted in the third of the four divisions of the empire of Alexander the Great. In the NT, Paul and his party visited Berea on the second missionary journey. Here they found some open-minded people who were willing to study the teachings of Paul in the light of the Scripture. This happy situation was disrupted, however, when Jews from Thessalonica arrived, turning the Bereans against the message and forcing Paul to flee to Athens. Silas and Timothy remained there briefly instructing the true believers.

BERED (bē'rĕd, Heb. *beredh, to be cold*). Between Kadesh and Bered was the well-known well of Beer Lahai Roi (Gen 16:14). The various Targums render Bered as Shur, thus placing it in the vicinity of Kadesh-Barnea. That Bered is to be located in the region of the Negev cannot be doubted. It was called Elusa by Ptolemy. It formed a connecting link between Palestine, Kadesh, and Sinai.

BEREKIAH, BERAKIAH (bêr-ĕ-kī'ȧ, Heb. *Berekhyâh, Jehovah blesses*). 1. One of David's descendants (1 Chron 3:20).

2. Father of Asaph the singer (1 Chron 6:39).

3. A Levite dwelling in Jerusalem (1 Chron 9:16).

4. A custodian of the ark (1 Chron 15:23).

5. An Ephraimite who protested the sale of Hebrews to their fellows (2 Chron 28:12).

6. The father of Meshullam. He was a builder during the days of Nehemiah (Neh 3:4, 30; 6:18).

7. The father of Zechariah, a prophet of the restoration (Zech 1:1, 7).

BERI (bê'rī, Heb. *bērî, wisdom*). A descendant of Asher (1 Chron 7:36).

BERIAH (bē-rīȧ, Heb. *berî'âh,* meaning uncertain, perhaps *gift* or *evil*). 1. This name is given to a son of Asher the father of Heber and Malkiel (Gen 46:17; 1 Chron 7:30). The Beriites were descended from him (Num 26:44).

2. Ephraim called one of his sons Beriah "because there had been misfortune in his family" (1 Chron 7:23). Men of Gath had killed a number of men in the land when they made a raid on the cattle there. If Beriah means "a gift," he was so named because in the face of Ephraim's losses, this son was regarded as a gift from the Lord.

3. One of the descendants of Benjamin (1 Chron 8:13, 16). He with his brother "drove out the inhabitants of Gath." Apparently from him and Shema, his brother, were descended the people of Aijalon (8:13).

4. A Levite, the son of Shimei of the Gershonites. His children, being few, were counted with those of his brother, Jeush (1 Chron 23:7–11).

BERIITES (bē-rī'īts, Heb. *berî'îm*). A people mentioned only once in the Bible (Num 26:44). They were descended from Beriah, who, in turn, was from the tribe of Asher (Gen 46:17).

BERITES (bē'rīts, Heb. *bērîm, choice young men*). Mentioned only in 2 Samuel 20:14. During the revolt of Sheba these people responded to his call and followed him.

BERITH (See EL-BERITH)

BERNICE (bêr-nī'sē, Gr. *Bernikē, victorious*). Three times in the Book of Acts reference is made to Bernice (Acts 25:13, 23; 26:30), Herod Agrippa's eldest daughter (Acts 12:1), a wicked woman who lived an incestuous life. According to Josephus, she was first married to Marcus. After his death she became the wife of Herod of Chalcis, her own uncle (Jos. *Antiq.* 19.5.1; 20.7.1–3). After Herod's death she had evil relations with Agrippa, her own brother, and with him listened to Paul's noble defense at Caesarea. Later she was married to King Ptolemy of Sicily. This marriage was of short duration, as she returned to Agrippa. She was later the mistress of Vespasian and Titus, who finally cast her aside.

BERODACH-BALADAN (See MERODACH-* BALADAN)

BEROTHAH, BEROTHAI (bē-rō'thȧ, bē-rō'thī, Heb. *bērôthāh, well or wells*). A town situated between Hamath and Damascus (Ezek 47:16). Probably the same as a city of Hadadezer that David took (2 Sam 8:8). It has now been identified as Bereitan, north of Damascus.

BERYL (See MINERALS)

BESAI (bē'sī, Heb. *bēsay, down-trodden*). The founder of a family that returned to Jerusalem from Babylon under the leadership of Zerubbabel (Ezra 2:49; Neh 7:52).

BESODEIAH (bĕs'ō-dē'yȧ, Heb. *besôdheyâh, in the counsel of Jehovah*). The father of Meshullam, a builder under Nehemiah (Neh 3:6).

BESOR (bē'sôr, Heb. *besôr*). A brook five miles (eight km.) south of Gaza where David left two hundred of his men who were too faint to assist in pursuing the Amalekites (1 Sam 30:9–10, 21). Some identify this as Wady en Sheriah, while others think it is Wady Ghazzah.

BETAH (bē'tȧ, *confidence*). A city of Syria that David captured and from which he took much brass, later used by Solomon in making furnishings for the temple (2 Sam 8:8; NIV Tebah, cf. footnote). It is called "Tibhath" in 1 Chronicles 18:8 KJV (Tebah, NIV).

BETEN (bē'tĕn, Heb. *beten, hollow*). A city on Asher's border (Josh 19:25). Its location is uncertain.

BETH (bĕth, *house*). The name by which the second letter of the Hebrew alphabet is known. The Hebrew uses it also for the number two. It is the most common OT word for house. It designates a more permanent dwelling than tent. It is used often in connection with other words to form proper names, the most common of which are Bethel and Bethlehem.

BETHABARA (bĕth'ab'ȧ-rȧ, *house of the ford*). A place on the east bank of the Jordan where John baptized (John 1:28 KJV). The later and more reliable Greek manuscripts have rendered this word "Bethany." Care must be taken, however, not to confuse this with the city of the same name near Jerusalem, the home of Mary, Martha, and Lazarus. Its exact location is uncertain. Some identify it with Beth Barah (Judg 7:24).

BETH ANATH (bĕth' ā'năth, *the temple of Anath*). A city near Naphtali (Josh 19:38; Judg 1:33) identified with the modern el-Baneh.

BETH ANOTH (bĕth' ā'nŏth, *house of Anoth*). A town in the hill country of Judea (Josh 15:59). The name derives from Anoth, goddess of the Canaanites.

BETHANY (bĕth'ȧ-nē, Gr. *Bethania, house of unripe dates or figs*). 1. Town mentioned in John

Early photograph of the village of Bethany, home of Mary, Martha, and Lazarus, situated just east of Jerusalem. Courtesy Ecole Biblique et Archéologique Française, Jerusalem.

1:28, "Bethabara" being its name as given in the KJV. Nothing certain is known about it except what is found in this passage: it is beyond the Jordan, and it is where John the Baptist was accomplishing his work.

2. Another city of this name—the home of Mary, Martha, and Lazarus—situated about two miles (three km.) SE of Jerusalem (John 11:18) on the eastern slope of Mount Olivet. Some refer to this as the Judean home of Jesus. It was here that he raised Lazarus (John 11) and attended the feast at Simon's house (Matt 26; Mark 14; Luke 7). The ascension took place in the region of this city (Luke 24:50–51). It is known today as El-Azariyeh. The modern city contains the supposed tomb of Lazarus and house of Simon the leper.

BETH ARABAH (bĕth' ăr'à-bà, *house of the desert*, NIV; "Beth-arabah" in RSV; "Arabah" in JB, KJV, MOF, NASB, NEB). A town probably at the northern end of the Dead Sea, one of Judah's six northern border cities (Josh 18:18).

BETH ARBEL (bĕth' àr'bĕl, *house of Arbel*). Probably a town in the tribe of Naphtali, mentioned in Hosea 10:14 as the scene of a horrible destruction brought about by Shalmaneser. It is used to illustrate the disaster to come on Ephraim. It is unlikely that this name is used here of the well-known city by this name on the Euphrates. It is the modern Irbid, a few miles NW of Tiberias.

BETH ASHBEA (See ASHBEA)

BETH AVEN (bĕth' ā'vĕn, Heb. *bēth'āwen, house of vanity*). A town on the northern mountains of Benjamin (Josh 18:12), beside Ai, east of Bethel (7:2) and west of Michmash (1 Sam 13:5; 14:23). The name is used by Hosea (4:15; 5:8; 10:5) to reveal the fallen condition of Bethel due to the idolatry introduced by King Jeroboam. The house of God (Bethel) had become the house of vanity and idolatry (Beth Aven).

BETH AZMAVETH (bĕth' ăz-mā'vĕth, *house of the strong one of death*). A village belonging to Benjamin mentioned in Nehemiah 7:28. Forty-two former inhabitants of this city accompanied Zerubbabel from Babylon on his return to Jerusalem.

BETH BAAL MEON (bĕth' bā'ăl mē'ŏn, Heb. *bêth ba'al me'ôn, house of Baal Meon*). A place in the territory assigned to Reuben, east of the Jordan (Josh 13:17). This is the same as Baal Meon (Num 32:38) and Beon (32:3). Jeremiah speaks of it as belonging to Moab (Jer 48:23), confirmed by the appearance of this name on the Moabite Stone. Identified today with the ruins of Ma'in in northern Moab.

BETH BARAH (bĕth' bâr'à, Heb. *bethbarah, house of the ford*). One of the important fords of the Jordan, identified by some with Beth Arabah. The Midianites were expected to use it as they escaped from Gideon, thus Gideon's instruction to his messengers to "seize the waters of the Jordan ahead of them as far as Beth Barah" (Judg 7:24). Here Jephthah killed the Ephraimites (12:4), and here, some say, Jacob crossed the Jordan (Gen 32:33).

BETH BIRI (bĕth' bĭr'ī, *house of my creator*). A town of Simeon (1 Chron 4:31) in the southern part of Judah. Joshua refers to this place as Beth Lebaoth, "abode of lions," and as Lebaoth (Josh 19:6; 15:32). It has not yet been identified.

BETH CAR (bĕth' kăr', *house of sheep*). A place west of Mizpah to which Israel pursued the Philistines, "slaughtering them along the way to a point below Beth Car" (1 Sam 7:11). It has never been identified. In this area Samuel set up the stone called Ebenezer (7:12).

BETH DAGON (bĕth' dā'gŏn, *house of Dagon*). A town in the Shephelah of Judah (Josh 15:41), five miles (eight km.) from Lydda, and identified as Khirbet Dajun. The name suggests worship of the Philistine god Dagon, revealing how far such worship went beyond Philistine territory. This name was used also of a town on the border of Asher (19:27).

BETH DIBLATHAIM (bĕth' dĭb'là-thā'ĭm, *house of a double cake of figs*). A Moabitish town (Jer 48:22), known also as Almon Diblathaim (Num 33:46) and Diblath (Ezek 6:14) and mentioned on the Moabite Stone.

BETH EDEN (See EDEN)

BETH EKED (bĕth' ĕ'kĕd). Mentioned only in 2 Kings 10:12, 14. KJV translates it "shearing house."

BETHEL (bĕth'ĕl, Heb. *bêth'ēl, house of God*). 1. A town originally known as Luz, twelve miles (twenty km.) north of Jerusalem (Gen 28:19), west of Ai. Abraham stopped near this spot on his way to the Negev and offered a sacrifice (12:8;

Site of ancient Bethel, included in the tribal territory of Benjamin. Shown here are remains of a partly preserved basalt-stone fortress from Crusader times. Courtesy Zev Radovan.

13:3). Jacob called Luz "Bethel" (28:10–22), since God met him here and confirmed the Abrahamic covenant to him. Jacob revisited this town when he returned from Paddan Aram in response to the command of God (35:1). He built an altar and worshiped, calling the place El Bethel (35:7). Here Jacob buried Deborah, the nurse of Rebekah who had died (35:8). It was a logical stopping place, for it lay on a well-known route running from the Plain of Esdraelon to Beersheba.

Bethel seems to have been a Canaanite city originally, and after the conquest by Joshua was given to the tribe of Benjamin (Josh 18:21–22). Joseph's descendants, under the guidance of the Lord, went up against Bethel and took it (Judg 1:22–26). It remained on the southern border of Ephraim. During the period of the judges, because of the wickedness of the tribe of Ephraim, the Israelites marched against them. They stopped at Bethel to ascertain God's will (20:18). The ark was kept there at this time (20:26–28). Samuel went to this city from time to time to conduct business and to worship (1 Sam 7:16; 10:3).

Bone handle of a sistrum shaped as a Hathor column, found in the ruins of a sanctuary at Bethel (1550–1400 B.C.). Courtesy Israel Department of Antiquities and Museums.

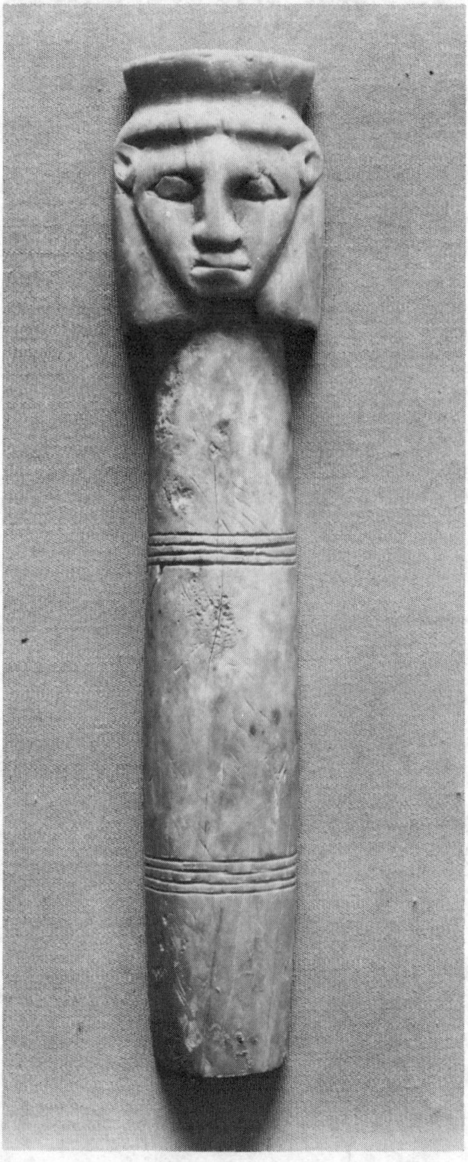

At a later period when the kingdom was divided, Jeroboam, in order to nullify the influence of Jerusalem as the center of religious activity for the people, chose Bethel as one of the two centers in which he set up golden calves (1 Kings 12:26–30). Here he sacrificed to the calves and placed priests to minister in the high places (12:32). Because of these and other sins, Amos cried out against this city (Amos 3:14; 4:4–6). Hosea too pronounced judgment on Bethel, even calling it "Beth Aven," "the house of wickedness" (Hos 4:15). An Israelite priest returned here to teach the people resettled here by Assyria about the Lord (2 Kings 17:27–28). They combined worship of their heathen gods with worship of the Lord (17:33). It was not until Josiah became king that this idolatry was removed from Bethel and the true worship of the Lord established (23:15–23). When the Jews returned from the Babylonian captivity, Ezra and Nehemiah both record that some returned to Bethel (Ezra 2:28; Neh 7:32) and, as one might suppose, they are listed as Benjamites (Neh 11:31).

Bethel is mentioned in the apocryphal books as being fortified by Bacchides (1 Macc 9:50).

Modern Beitin, Bethel was excavated by Albright and Kelso intermittently from 1934 to 1961. City walls from the Middle Bronze Age (2200 to 1550 B.C.), the time of the patriarchs, were found. In the Late Bronze Age (1550–1200) there were well-built houses here with much imported pottery. In the thirteenth century a destruction layer of ashes and burned bricks testifies to its demise that some attribute to Joshua.

2. Another city mentioned in southern Judah (1 Sam 30:27) is also called Bethel. Joshua refers to it as Bethul (Josh 19:4). It is noted again as "Bethuel" (1 Chron 4:30). This site has not yet been identified. HZC

BETH EMEK (bĕth′ ā′mĕk, *house of the valley*). A city mentioned in Joshua 19:27 as in the Valley of Iphtah El on the edge of Asher's territory. It is not yet identified.

BETHER (bē′thêr, Heb. *bether, separation*). A mountain range mentioned in the Song of Songs 2:17 (KJV, NASB "mountains of Bether"; RSV "rugged mountains"; NIV "rugged hills"). A proper name may not have been intended. The phrase "spice-laden mountains" (8:14) may refer to the same place.

BETHESDA (bĕ-thĕs′dȧ, Gr. *Bēthesda, house of grace*). A spring-fed pool at Jerusalem, surrounded by five porches and mentioned only in John 5:2. Sick people waited to step down into these waters that were thought to have healing properties. Here Jesus healed a man who had been sick for thirty-eight years (John 5:1–16). John 5:4, though appearing in most Greek MSS and in some versions (e.g., JB, KJV, MLB, MOF), is omitted by most other modern versions because some early MSS and versions omit it.

In A.D. 1888, while the church of St. Anne in NE Jerusalem was being repaired, a reservoir was discovered. On the wall is a faded fresco that depicts an angel troubling the water. It is thought, therefore, that this best fits the description in the NT. The reservoir is cut from the rock and is rain-filled. It is about fifty-five feet (seventeen m.) long and twelve feet (almost four m.) wide. It is approached by a flight of steps both steep and winding.

BETH EZEL (bĕth′ ē′zĕl, *a house adjoining*). A town in southern Judea in the Philistine plain (Mic 1:11). For a time this was thought to be the same as Azel (Zech 14:5), but now has been identified with Deir el-Asal.

BETH GADER (bĕth′ gā′dêr, *house of the wall*). A place in the tribe of Judah (1 Chron 2:51), probably to be identified with Geder (Josh 12:13).

BETH GAMUL (bĕth′ gā′mŭl, *house of recompense*). A Moabitish city (Jer 48:23). It is now

"Now there is in Jerusalem . . . a pool, which in Aramaic is called Bethesda and which is surrounded by five covered colonnades. Here a great number of disabled people used to lie . . ." (John 5:2–3). In the background is the Church of St. Anne. Courtesy Zev Radovan.

Reconstruction of the pool of Bethesda. According to archaeological evidence, the northern pool (left) was dug first, in the reign of Solomon, and the southern pool was added in the beginning of the second century B.C. (during the Hellenistic period). The drawing is based mainly on Christian sources, and the description given in John 5:1–16. Courtesy Carta, Jerusalem.

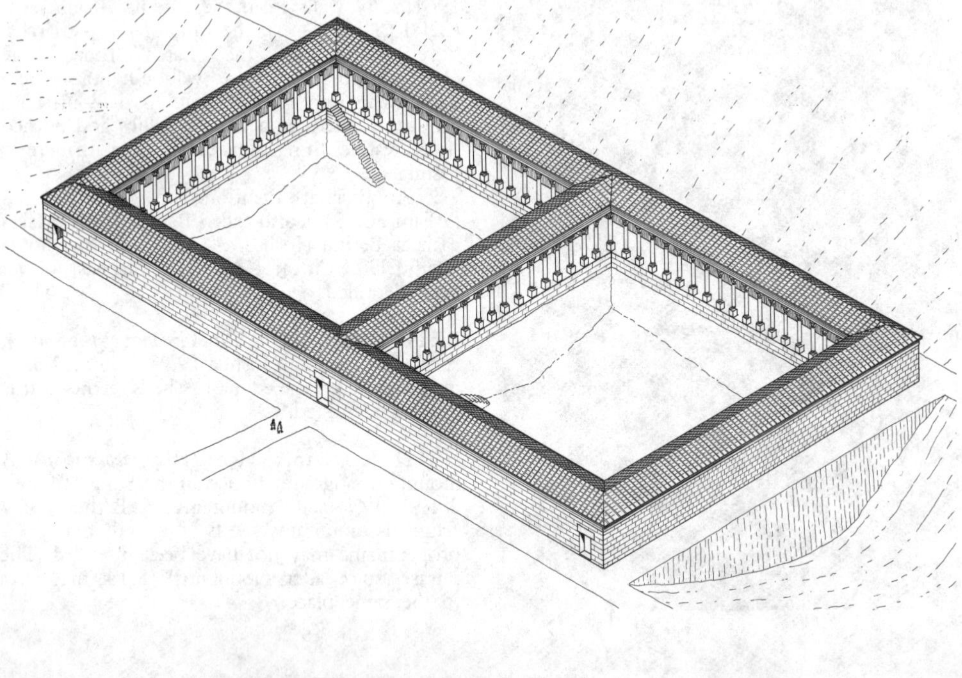

identified with Khirbet Jemeil. It has been cited as a good example of an unwalled town.

BETH GILGAL (bĕth' gĭl'găl, Heb. *bêth hagilgal, house of Gilgal*). A place from which singers came to the dedication of the Jerusalem wall. It is probably to be identified with Gilgal (Neh 12:27–29).

BETH HAGGAN (bĕth' hăg'ĕn, *house of the garden*). Mentioned in 2 Kings 9:27 (NIV; KJV and NASB have "garden house") as the place to which Ahaziah fled when chased by Jehu. It is possibly En-gannim (modern Jenin).

BETH HAKKEREM (bĕth' hă-kē'rĕm, *house of the vineyard*). A Judean town (Neh 3:14), ruled by Malkijah. Jeremiah notes it as a vantage site for signaling in time of danger (Jer 6:1). It is now identified with a place on top of Jebel Ali called ʿAin Karim. The cairns on top of this hill are thought to have been used for beacons.

BETH HARAM, BETH HARAN (bĕth' hā'răm, bĕth' hā'răn, *house of the mountaineer*). A fortified city built by the Gadites east of the Jordan (Num 32:36; Josh 13:27).

Beth Horon, the upper and lower towns, lying on the border between Benjamin and Ephraim. Upper Beth Horon (top picture) is situated east of the lower town. They were strategically located on the road between Gibeon and Aijalon and guarded the important "ascent of Beth Horon." For the battle of Beth Horon on the day the sun stood still, see Joshua 10:10–11. Courtesy Zev Radovan.

BETH HOGLAH (bĕth' hŏg'là, *house of a partridge*). A place belonging to Benjamin, lying between Jericho and the Jordan (Josh 15:6; 18:19, 21). It is now identified with Ain Hajlah.

BETH HORON (bĕth' hŏ'rŏn, Heb. *bêth-hôrōn, place of a hollow*). Two towns, the upper and the lower (Josh 16:3, 5; 1 Chron 7:24; 2 Chron 8:5), separated by a few miles. Beit Ur el foka ("the upper") is 800 feet (250 m.) higher than Beit Ur el tahta ("the lower"). Built by Sherah, a granddaughter of Ephraim (1 Chron 7:24), Beth Horon lay on the boundary line between Benjamin and Ephraim (Josh 16:3, 5), on the road from Gibeon to Azekah (10:10–11). It was assigned to Ephraim and given to the Kohathites (21:22).

For centuries a strategic route into the heart of Judea went up from Joppa (modern Jaffa) on the coast through the Valley of Aijalon (modern Yalo), ascending through the two Beth Horons to Gibeon (four miles [seven km.] distant) on its way to Jerusalem. It was in this valley that Joshua commanded the sun and moon to stand still while he fought the Amorite kings in his defense of the Gibeonites. He chased these five kings over the pass to Beth Horon (Josh 10:10–13). Along this route the Philistines fled after they had been defeated at Micmash (1 Sam 14:31), and it was there that Judas Maccabeus overthrew the army of Seron, a prince of Syria (1 Macc 3:13–24). The importance of the Beth Horon pass as a key route into Palestine explains the fortification of its towns by Solomon (2 Chron 8:5). It is no longer important, but great foundation stones can be seen there yet today.

BETH JESHIMOTH (bĕth' jĕsh'ĭ-mŏth, Heb. *bêth ha-yeshīmō, place of deserts*). A town east of the mouth of the Jordan, next to the last camp of the Israelites (Num 33:49). It was assigned to Reuben (Josh 13:20).

BETH LEBAOTH (See BETH BIRI)

BETHLEHEM (bĕth'lē-hĕm, Heb. *bêth-lehem, house of bread*). 1. A town five miles (eight km.) SW of Jerusalem, 2550 feet (797 m.) above sea level, in the hill country of Judea on the main highway to Hebron and Egypt. In Jacob's time it was called Ephrath ("fruitful") and was the burial place of Rachel (Gen 35:16, 19; 48:7). After the conquest of Canaan it was called Bethlehem in Judah (Ruth 1:1) to distinguish it from Bethlehem No. 2 (see below). It was the home of Ibzan, the tenth judge (Judg 12:8–10); of Elimelech, father-in-law of Ruth (Ruth 1:1–2), as well as of her husband Boaz (2:1, 4). Here their great-grandson David kept his father's sheep and was anointed king by Samuel (1 Sam 16:13, 15). Hence it was known as "the city of David" (Luke 2:4, 11). It was once occupied by a Philistine garrison (2 Sam 23:14–16), later fortified by Rehoboam (2 Chron 11:6).

In Jeremiah's time (Jer 41:17) the caravan inn of Kimham (see 2 Sam 19:37–40) near Bethlehem was the usual starting place for Egypt. The inn mentioned in Luke 2 was a similar one and may have been the same. Here the Messiah was born (Matt 2:1; Luke 2:1–7), for whom this town that was "small among the clans of Judah" (Mic 5:2) achieved its great fame. Its male children under two years of age were murdered in Herod's attempt to kill the King of the Jews (Matt 2:16).

Justin Martyr, second century A.D., said that our Lord's birth took place in a cave close to the village. Over this traditional manger site the emperor Constantine (A.D. 330) and Helena his mother built the Church of the Nativity. Rebuilt more sumptuously by Justinian in the sixth century, it still has part of the original structure and is a popular attraction for tourists today. The grotto of the nativity is beneath a crypt, thirty-nine feet (twelve m.) long, eleven feet (three and one-half m.) wide, and nine feet (three m.) high, hewn out of the rock and lined with marble. A rich altar is over the supposed site of the Savior's birth. In a part of this cave Jerome, the Latin scholar, spent thirty years translating the Bible into Latin.

Modern Bethlehem is a village of fewer than ten thousand inhabitants. The slopes abound in figs, vines, almonds, and olives. The shepherds' fields are still seen to the NE.

2. A town of Zebulun (Josh 19:15), now the village of Beit Lahm, seven miles (twelve km.) NW of Nazareth.

BETH MAACHAH (See ABEL BETH MAACAH)

BETH MARCABOTH (bĕth' mȧr'kȧ-bŏth, Heb. *bêth ha-markāvōth, the house of chariots*). A town of Simeon in the extreme south of Judah (Josh 19:5; 1 Chron 4:31). Possibly one of the cities that Solomon built for his chariots (1 Kings 9:19).

BETH MEON (bĕth' mē'ōn). A city of Moab (Jer 48:23), same as Beth Baal Meon (Josh 13:17).

BETH MILLO (See MILLO)

BETH NIMRAH (bĕth' nĭm'rȧ, Heb. *bêth nimrâh, house of leopard*). A fortified city of Gad east of the Jordan (Num 32:3, 36). The LXX

General view of modern Bethlehem, with the Church of the Nativity at top center. Ancient Bethlehem is definitely identified with the modern town located 5½ miles (9 km.) south of Jerusalem. It was a small town that acquired importance when Herod build his fortresses at Herodium and Masada, since it overlooked the roads leading to the fortresses. Courtesy Israel Government Press Office.

A view of Bethlehem from southeast to northwest. Courtesy Ecole Biblique et Archéologique Française, Jerusalem.

reading, "Beth-anabra," in Joshua 13:27 has led some to identify this with Bethabara in the NT, whose abundant waters were the scene of John's baptizing (John 1:28).

BETH OPHRAH (bĕth' ôf'rȧ). Named in parallelism with Gath in Micah 1:10. KJV has "the house of Aphrah"; ASV and RSV, "Beth-le-aphrah."

BETH PAZZEZ (bĕth' păz'ĕz). A town of Issachar (Josh 19:21).

BETH PELET, BETH PALET (bĕth' pē'lĕt, bĕth' pā'lĕt, Heb. *bêth pelet, house of escape*). A town in the south of Judah (Josh 15:27; Neh 11:26).

BETH PEOR (bĕth' pē'ôr, Heb. *bêth pe'ôr, house of Peor*). One of Israel's last campsites (Deut 3:29; 4:46). Here Moses was buried (34:6). A possession of Reuben (Josh 13:20).

BETHPHAGE (bĕth'fȧ-jē, Heb. *bêth paghah, house of unripe figs*). A village on the Mount of Olives, on the road going east from Jerusalem to Jericho. The traditional site is NW of Bethany, and it is mentioned twice in the NT (Mark 11:1–11; Luke 19:28–40). Here the colt was obtained for the Palm Sunday entry into Jerusalem (Matt 21:1–11). Jesus cursed the fruitless fig tree in the vicinity of Bethphage (Matt 21:18–20; Mark 11:12–14, 20–21).

BETH RAPHA (bĕth' rā'fȧ, Heb. *bêth rāphā*). Son of Eshton in the genealogy of Judah (1 Chron 4:12).

BETH REHOB (bĕth' rē'hŏb, Heb. *bêth rehôv, house of Rechob*). An Aramean town and district near the valley containing the town Laish or Dan (Judg 18:28). Probably to be identified with Rehob (Num 13:21), the northern limit of the spies' search. The Ammonites, having needlessly provoked David, hired the men of Beth Rehob in a futile defense against David's attack (2 Sam 10). It is thought to be the modern Hunin, site of the Crusaders' castle-fortress commanding the Huleh plain.

BETHSAIDA (bĕth'sā'ĭ-dȧ, Gr. *Bēthsaida, house of fishing*). 1. A village close to the west side of the Sea of Galilee in the land of Gennesaret, where Jesus sent his disciples by boat after he had fed the five thousand (Mark 6:45–53). John says that they headed for Capernaum (6:17), but when they were blown off their course they landed in Gennesaret and then went to Capernaum. Possibly, therefore, this Bethsaida was close to Capernaum and may have been its fishing district next to the lake. This would explain how Peter and Andrew are said to be of Bethsaida (John 1:44; 12:21), whereas Mark mentions their house close to the synagogue in Capernaum (Mark 1:29). Along with Chorazin and Capernaum, Jesus

Early twentieth-century view of Bethphage, looking northeast from across the Kidron Valley. The site is marked by a Greek-Orthodox church (1). Courtesy Ecole Biblique et Archéologique Française, Jerusalem.

The Valley of Bethsaida, at the northeastern edge of the Sea of Galilee, possible site of the feeding of the 5000 (Luke 9:10). Courtesy Duby Tal.

rebuked Bethsaida for unbelief (Matt 11:20–23; Luke 10:13–15).

2. Another Bethsaida, NE of the Sea of Galilee and the scene of the feeding of the five thousand (Luke 9:10). Jesus restored sight to a blind man in Bethsaida (Mark 8:22), which is on the east side of the lake, since Jesus had just come from Dalmanutha (Magdala, Matt 15:39) on the west side (Mark 8:10–13). This Bethsaida was a village in Gaulanitis (now Jaulan). Philip the tetrarch enlarged it to be the capital and called it Julias, after Julia, the daughter of Emperor Augustus. Its site is uncertain, but some identify it with et Tel, east of the Jordan and one mile (one and one-half km.) from the Sea of Galilee, from which it rises to a height of one hundred feet (thirty-one m.)

BETH SHAN, BETH SHEAN (bĕth' shăn, bĕth' shē'ăn, Heb. *bêth shan, bêth sheān, house of quiet*). A town of Manasseh in the territory of Issachar. The people of Israel were not able to drive the Canaanites out of this town (Josh 17:11–12; Judg 1:27). It lay fourteen miles (twenty-three km.) south of the Sea of Galilee, overlooking the Plain of Esdraelon in the Valley of Jezreel. After Saul died on Mount Gilboa, the Philistines fastened his body to the wall of Beth Shan and put his armor in the temple of the Ashtoreths as trophies of their victory (1 Sam 31:8–12). Later the men of Jabesh Gilead stole the bones of Saul and his sons from the street of Beth Shan, but David recovered them and gave them a proper burial (2 Sam 21:12–14).

Today the site of the city is a mound, called Tell el-Husn ("Mound of the Fortress"), located near the Arab village of Beisan (note the similarity to Beth Shan). Excavations by the University of Pennsylvania, A.D. 1921–33, have yielded rich finds, dating the history of the city from 3500 B.C. to the Christian era. A stratification of eighteen levels of debris and ruined houses can be seen as evidence of repeated destructions and eras of rebuilding. Because of its commanding location, it was fortified with double walls and was a strong Egyptian outpost from the fifteenth to the twelfth centuries. Temples and monument inscriptions by

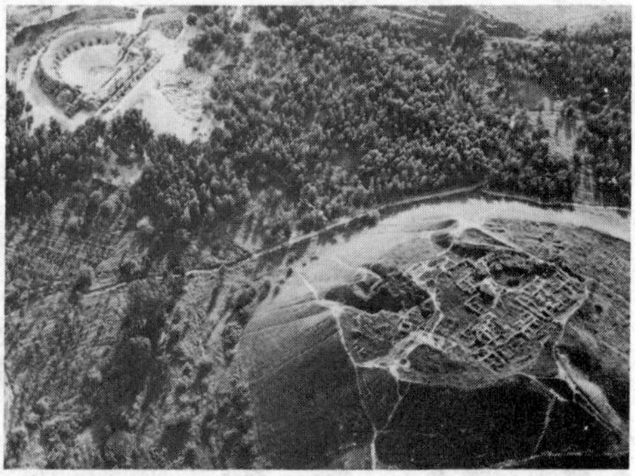

Aerial view of Tell el-Husn and the Greco-Roman theater at Beth Shan. Courtesy Israel Government Press Office.

Statue of Ramses III found at Beth Shan. Courtesy Israel Department of Antiquities and Museums.

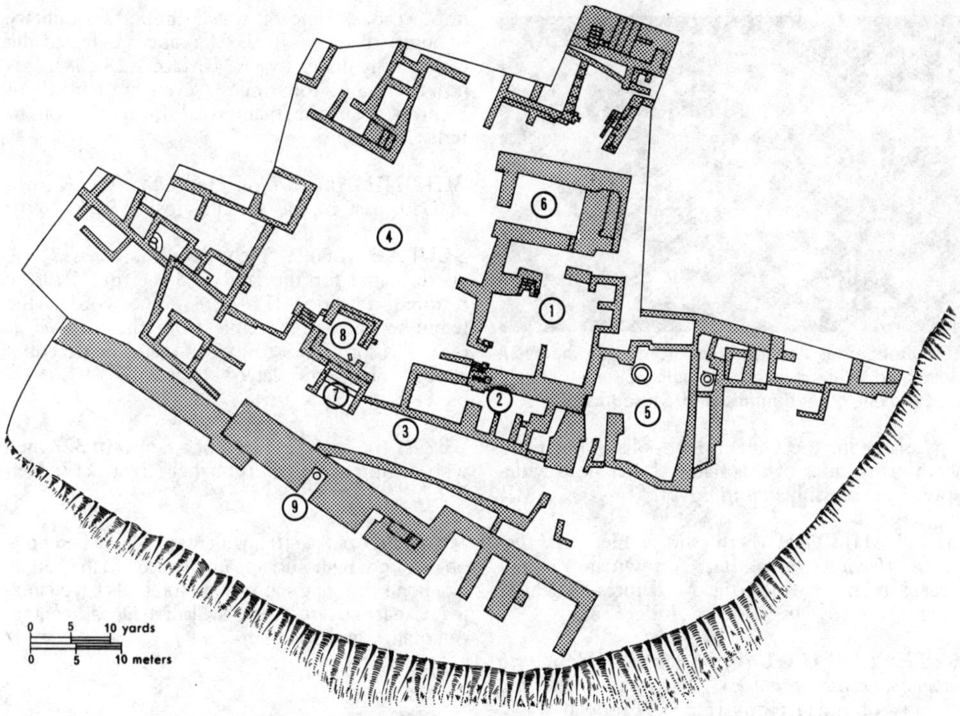

Plan of the temple dedicated to Mekal, the god of Beth Shan: (1) altar court; (2) inner altar; (3) entrance corridor; (4) inner court; (5) room with oven and well; (6) room north of the sanctuary; (7) altar(?); (8) guard room; (9) reservoir. Beth Shan was located as above in the eastern part of the valley of Jezreel. Courtesy Carta, Jerusalem.

three pharaohs were discovered and date back to this time. The excavators have shown that Beth Shan was destroyed between 1050 and 1000, the approximate time of King David, who may have destroyed it. Four Canaanite temples were unearthed at the site, one of which has been identified with the "temple of the Ashtoreths" (1 Sam 31:10), and another with the temple of Dagon where the Philistines fastened Saul's head (1 Chron 10:10). In Solomon's reign Beth Shan was included in one of his commissary districts (1 Kings 4:12).

A Roman theater, erected about A.D. 200, still stands, and the remains of a synagogue from the fourth century have been found. AMR

BETH SHEMESH (bĕth′ shē′mĕsh, Heb. *bêth-shemesh, house of the sun*). 1. A town of NW Judah near the Philistine border (Josh 15:10; 1 Sam 6:12). It was a priests' city given by Judah to the Levites (Josh 21:16; 1 Chron 6:50). The Philistines had been plagued for their seizure of the ark of God. Anxious to be rid of it, they put the ark on a cart pulled by two milking cows and tied their calves at home (1 Sam 6). They expected the cows to return instinctively to their young, but if they left their young behind, this would be a sure sign of guidance by Israel's God and of his influence on the Philistine's misery. The animals left Ekron and headed for Beth Shemesh seven miles (twelve km.) away, not turning aside until they came to the field of Joshua the Beth Shemite, where the ark was received and a sacrifice made to the Lord. Here, too, many died for their irreverence toward the ark; but perhaps only 70 were killed instead of 50,070 (1 Sam 6:19). The latter figure may be due to an error in later texts.

Beth Shemesh was in a commissary district of Solomon (1 Kings 4:9). It was here that Joash, king of Israel, encountered Amaziah, king of Judah, and took him prisoner (2 Kings 14:11–13; 2 Chron 25:21–23). Ir Shemesh ("city of the sun," Josh 19:41) may be the same city. Today the name is preserved as Ain Shems, SE of Gezer. Beth Shemesh was excavated in A.D. 1911–12 and 1928–33. Six levels of occupation were found. The third level dates to the time of Saul and David (Iron 1, 1200–1000 B.C.). Implements of the late Canaanite and early Israelite period have been discovered here, such as pottery, weapons, and jewelry. Quantities of Philistine pottery indicate their domination of the Israelite population and also suggest a later Philistine occupancy (2 Chron 28:18). Copper smelters and houses with underground cisterns were also found.

2. A city of Issachar (Josh 19:22).

3. A city of Naphtali (Josh 19:38; Judg 1:33), from which the Canaanites were not driven.

4. An idol city in Egypt (Jer 43:13), the

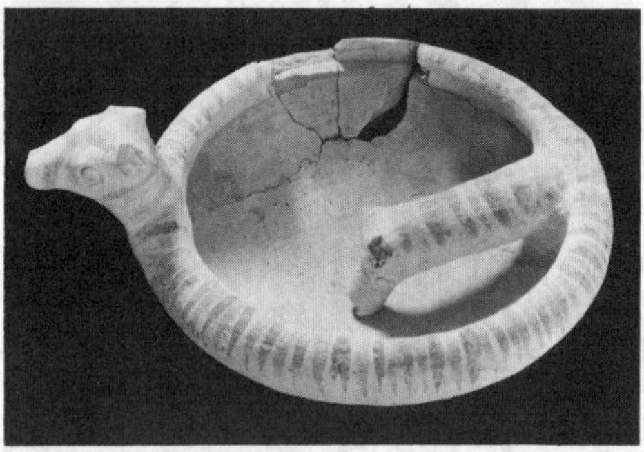

Late Bronze Age libation bowl (from Beth Shemesh) decorated with stylized animals. Courtesy Israel Department of Antiquities and Museums.

Egyptian On, the Greek Heliopolis. That there were many cities of this name shows how widespread sun worship was in Egypt. AMR

BETH SHITTAH (bĕth′ shĭt′á, Heb. *bêth ha-shittâh, house of the acacia*). A town in Zererah near Jordan to which the Midianites fled after their overthrow by Gideon (Judg 7:22).

BETH TAPPUAH (bĕth′ tăp′u-á, Heb. *bêth tappûah, house of apples*). A town in the hill country of Judah (Josh 15:53). Tappuah was a son of Hebron (1 Chron 2:43). Now identified with Taffuh, five miles (eight km.) west of Hebron, surrounded by fruitful terraces.

BETH TOGARMAH (See TOGARMAH)

BETHUEL, BETHUL (bē-thū′ĕl, bĕth′ŭl, Heb. *bethû'ēl, bethûl, abode of God*). 1. Son of Nahor and Milcah, nephew of Abraham, and father of Rebekah and Laban (Gen 22:22–23; 24:15, 24, 47; 28:2, 5). His insignificance in the arrangements for his daughter's marriage was conspicuous. When Abraham's servant asked Rebekah if there was room at her *father's* house, she ran and told those in her *mother's* house (24:28). Her *brother* invited him in, not Bethuel, the natural one to do so. Bethuel and Laban (the son mentioned first) acknowledged his mission to be from the Lord. Presents were given to Rebekah and to her mother and brother, not her father; and when the bride left home, it was not as a daughter but as a "sister" (24:55–60). These many references make Bethuel seem incapable, whether from age or imbecility, to manage his own affairs.

2. A town in the south of Simeon (Josh 19:4; 1 Chron 4:30). It is the same as Kesil (Josh 15:30).

BETH ZUR (bĕth zûr, Heb. *bêth tsûr, house of rock*). One of Judea's strongest natural fortresses in the mountains of Judah, near Halhul and Gedor (Josh 15:58). It was fortified by Rehoboam (2 Chron 11:7). Nehemiah, son of Azbuk and ruler of half of Beth Zur, helped to repair the wall of Jerusalem (Neh 3:16). Known as Bethsura in Maccabean times, it was an important military stronghold, where Judas Maccabeus defeated the Greek army under Lysias (1 Macc 4:28–34). It is now Beit Sur, four miles (seven km.) north of Hebron, near the main road from Hebron to Jerusalem.

BETONIM (bĕt′ō-nĭm, Heb. *betōnîm*). A town of Gad, east of the Jordan (Josh 13:26).

BEULAH (byū′lá, Heb. *be'ûlâh, married*). A poetic name for the land of Israel in its future restored condition (Isa 62:4). The word is the feminine passive participle from the verb *ba'al* ("to be a lord," or "to marry"), and hence could almost be translated "lorded" (cf. Isa 54:4–6; 1 Peter 3:6).

BEZAI (bē′zā-ī). 1. Head of a family of 323 men who returned with Zerubbabel (Ezra 2:17; Neh 7:23).

Middle Bronze Age (?) fragment of a decorated bone object, from Beth Zur, apparently used as the handle of a bone cosmetic spoon that represents Egyptianizing Canaanite art. Courtesy Israel Department of Antiquities and Museums.

2. Probably a member of the same family a century later (Neh 10:18).

BEZALEL (bē'zā-lĕl, *in the shadow of God*). 1. Son of Uri, son of Hur of the tribe of Judah, whom the Lord called by name (Exod 31:2; 35:30) and by his Spirit empowered to work in metals, wood, and stone for the tabernacle. He had as a helper Oholiab of the tribe of Dan, whom God similarly empowered for the work in textiles.

2. A descendant of Pahath-Moab, an official of Moab, who in the days of Ezra and Nehemiah was compelled to give up his foreign wife (Ezra 10:30).

BEZEK (bē'zĕk, *scattering, sowing*). 1. A town in the territory of Judah taken for Israel under Joshua from the Canaanites and Perizzites of whom more than ten thousand had congregated there. Its king had either the name or more probably the title Adoni-Bezek (i.e., lord of Bezek). The ruin Bezkah, about twenty miles (thirty-three km.) NW of Jerusalem, may mark the spot (Judg 1:4–5).

2. The place where Saul numbered his forces before going to relieve Jabesh Gilead (1 Sam 11:8), about fourteen miles (twenty-three km.) NE of Samaria.

BEZER (bē'zĕr, Heb. *betser, strong*). 1. A city in the wilderness plateau east of the Dead Sea and in the tribe of Reuben, set apart as a city of refuge (Deut 4:43) and as a home for Merarites of the tribe of Levi (Josh 21:36). On the Moabite Stone, Mesha, king of Moab, claims that he fortified it.

2. One of the mighty men of the tribe of Asher, known only as a son of Zophah (1 Chron 7:37).

BIBLE. The collection of books recognized and used by the Christian church as the inspired record of God's revelation of himself and of his will to mankind.

I. Names. The word "Bible" is from Greek *biblia,* plural of *biblion,* diminutive of *biblos* (book), from *byblos* (papyrus). In ancient times papyrus was used in making the paper from which books were manufactured. The words *biblion* and *biblia* are used in the OT (LXX) and the Apocrypha for the Scriptures (Dan 9:2; 1 Macc 1:56; 3:48; 12:9). By about the fifth century A.D. the Greek church fathers applied the term *biblia* to the whole Christian Scriptures. Later the word passed into the western church, and although it is really a plural neuter noun, it came to be used in the Latin as a feminine singular. Thus "The Books" became by common consent "The Book."

In the NT the OT is usually referred to as "the Scriptures" (Matt 21:42; 22:29; Luke 24:32; John 5:39; Acts 18:24). Other terms used are "Scripture" (Acts 8:32; Gal 3:22), the "holy Scriptures" (Rom 1:2; 2 Tim 3:15), and "sacred writings" (2 Tim 3:15 RSV).

The plural term *biblia* stresses the fact that the Bible is a collection of books. That the word came to be used in the singular emphasizes that behind these many books there lies a wonderful unity. That no qualifying adjective stands before it points to the uniqueness of this book.

The names "Old Testament" and "New Testament" have been used since the close of the second century A.D. to distinguish the Jewish and Christian Scriptures. The Old Testament is composed of books produced by writers under God's covenant with Israel; the New Testament contains writings of the apostles (members of God's new covenant people). The term *Novum Testamentum* occurs first in Tertullian (A.D. 190–220). "Testament" is used in the NT (KJV) to render the Greek word *diathēkē* (Latin *testamentum*), which in classical usage meant "a will" but in the LXX and in the NT was used to translate the Hebrew word *berîth* ("a covenant").

II. Languages. Most of the OT was written in Hebrew, the language spoken by the Israelites in Canaan before the Babylonian captivity. After the return from exile, Hebrew gave way to Aramaic, a related dialect generally spoken throughout SW Asia. A few parts of the OT are in Aramaic (Ezra 4:8–7:18; 7:12–26; Jer 10:11; Dan 2:4–7:28). The ancient Hebrew text consisted only of consonants, since the Hebrew alphabet had no written vowels. Vowel signs were invented by the Jewish Masoretic scholars in the sixth century A.D. and later.

Except for a few words and sentences, the NT was composed in Greek, the language of ordinary conversation in the Hellenistic world. The difference of NT Greek from classical Greek and the Greek of the LXX used to be a cause of bewilderment to scholars, but the discovery, since the 1890s, of many thousands of papyri documents in the sands of Egypt has shown that the Greek of the NT is identical with the Greek generally spoken in the Mediterranean world in the first century. The papyri have thrown a great deal of light on the meaning of many NT words.

III. Compass and Divisions. The Protestant Bible in general use today contains sixty-six books, thirty-nine in the OT and twenty-seven in the NT. The thirty-nine OT books are the same as those recognized by the Palestinian Jews in NT times. The Greek-speaking Jews of this period, on the other hand, recognized as Scripture a larger number of books, and the Greek OT (LXX), which passed from them to the early Christian church contained, in addition to the thirty-nine books of the Hebrew canon, a number of others, of which seven—Tobit, Judith, Wisdom, Ecclesiasticus, Baruch, 1 and 2 Maccabees, plus the two so-called additions to Esther and Daniel—are regarded as canonical by the Roman Catholic church, which therefore has an OT canon of forty-six books. Jews today consider canonical only the thirty-nine books accepted by Protestants.

The books in the Hebrew Bible are arranged in three groups: the Law, the Prophets, and the Writings. The Law comprises the Pentateuch. The Prophets consist of eight books: the Former Prophets (Joshua, Judges, Samuel, and Kings) and the Latter Prophets (Isaiah, Jeremiah, Ezekiel, and the Minor Prophets). The Writings are the remaining books: Psalms, Proverbs, Job, Song of Songs, Ruth, Lamentations, Ecclesiastes, Esther, Daniel, Ezra-Nehemiah, and Chronicles. The total is traditionally reckoned as twenty-four, but these correspond to the Protestant thirty-nine, since in the latter reckoning the Minor Prophets are counted as twelve books, and Samuel, Kings, Chronicles, and Ezra-Nehemiah as two each. In ancient times there were also other enumerations, notably one by Josephus, who held twenty-two books as canonical (after the number of letters in the Hebrew alphabet), but his twenty-two are the same as the twenty-four in the traditional reckoning.

In the LXX both the number of books and the arrangement of them differ from the Hebrew Bible. It is evident that the NT writers were familiar with the LXX, which contained the Apocrypha, but no quotation from any book of the Apocrypha is found in their pages. The books of the Apocrypha are all late in date and are in Greek, though at least one (Sirach) had a Hebrew origin. The more scholarly of the church fathers (Melito, Origen, Athanasius, Jerome) did not

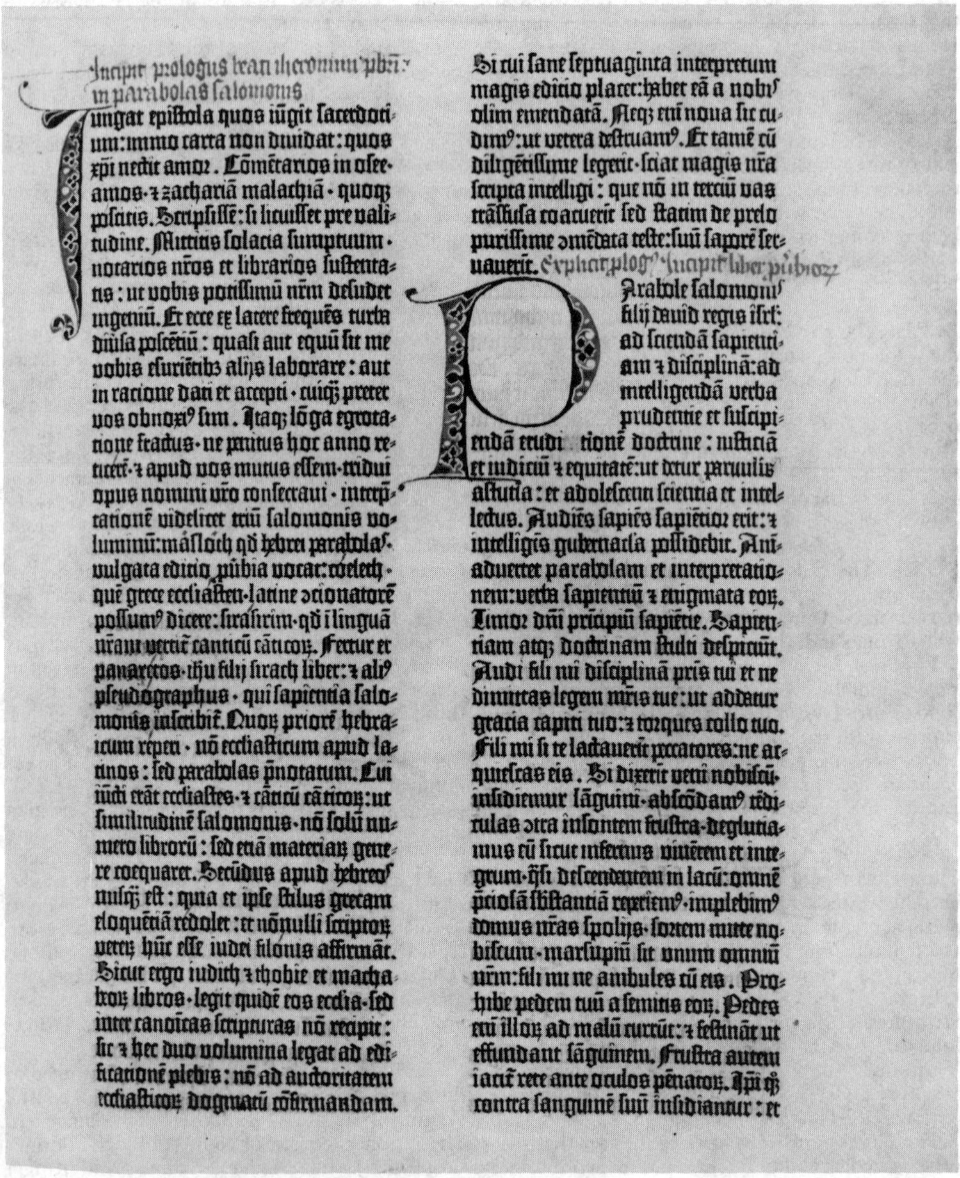
Incipit prologus beati iheronimi pbri in parabolas salomonis
Iungat epistola quos iūgit sacerdoci-
um: immo carta non dividat: quos
xpi nectit amor. Cōmētarios in osee-
amos- z zachariā malachiā- quoq;
poscitis. Scripsissē: si licuisset pre vali-
tudine. Mittitis solacia sumptuum.
notarios nr̄os et librarios sustenta-
tis: ut vobis potissimū nr̄m desudet
ingeniū. Et ecce ex latere frequēs turba
diūsa poscētiū: quasi aut equū sit me
vobis esurientib; aliis laborare: aut
in racione dati et accepti- cuiq; preter
vos obnoxi⁹ sim. Itaq; lōga egrota-
tione fractus- ne penitus hoc anno re-
ticerē- z apud vos mutus essem- tridui
opus nomini vr̄o consecraui- interp̄-
tationē videlicet triū salomonis vo-
luminū: masloth qd̄ hebrei parabolas.
vulgata edicio pūbia vocat: coeleth.
quē grece ecclesiasten- latine ɔcionatorē
possum⁹ dicere: sirasirim- qd̄ ī linguā
nr̄am vertit̄ canticū cāticoꝝ. Fertur et
panaretos- ihu filii sirach liber: z ali⁹
pseudographus- qui sapiencia salomonis inscribit̄. Quoꝝ priorē hebra-
icum reperi- nō ecclesiasticum apud la-
tinos: sed parabolas p̄notatum. Cui
iūcti erāt ecclesiastes- z cāticū cāticoꝝ: ut
similitudinē salomonis- nō solū nu-
mero librorū: sed etiā materiaꝝ gene-
re coequaret. Secūdus apud hebreos
nusq; est: quia et ipse stilus grecam
eloquētiā redolet: et nōnulli scriptoꝝ
veteꝝ hūc esse iudei filonis affirmāt.
Sicut ergo iudith z thobie et macha-
beoꝝ libros- legit quidē eos eccl'ia- sed
inter canōicas scripturas nō recipit:
sic z hec duo volumina legat ad edi-
ficationē plebis: nō ad auctoritatem
ecclesiasticoꝝ dogmatū cōfirmandam.
Si cui sane septuaginta interpretum
magis edicio placet: habet eā a nobis
olim emendatā. Neq; enī noua sic cu-
dim⁹: ut vetera destruam⁹. Et tamē cū
diligētissime legerit- sciat magis nr̄a
scripta intelligi: que nō in terciū vas
trāsfusa coacuerit sed statim de prelo
purissime ɔmēdata teste: suū saporē ser-
uauerit. Explicit prolog⁹ Incipit liber prouerbioꝝ
Parabole salomonis
filii david regis isrl̄:
ad sciendā sapienti-
am z disciplinā: ad
intelligendā verba
prudentie et suscipi-
endā erudi- tionē doctrine: iusticiā
et iudiciū z equitatē: ut detur paruulis
astutia: et adolescenti sciencia et intel-
lectus. Audiēs sapiēs sapiēcior erit: z
intelligēs gubernacla possidebit. Ani-
aduertet parabolam et interpretatio-
nem: verba sapientū z enigmata eoꝝ.
Timor dn̄i principiū sapiētie. Sapien-
tiam atq; doctrinam stulti despiciūt.
Audi fili mi disciplinā pris tui et ne
dimittas legem mr̄is tue: ut addatur
gracia capiti tuo: z torques collo tuo.
Fili mi si te lactauerit peccatores: ne ac-
quiescas eis. Si dixerit veni nobiscū.
insidiemur sāguini- abscōdam⁹ tedi-
culas ɔtra insontem frustra- degluciā-
mus eū sicut infernus viuētem et inte-
grum- q̄si descendentem in lacū: omnē
p̄ciosā sbstanciā reperiem⁹- implebim⁹
domus nr̄as spoliis- sortem mitte no-
biscum- marsupiū sit vnum omniū
nr̄m: fili mi ne ambules cū eis. Pro-
hibe pedem tuū a semitis eoꝝ. Pedes
enī illoꝝ ad malū currūt: z festināt ut
effundant sāguinem. Frustra autem
iacit̄ rete ante oculos pēnatoꝝ. Ipi q̄
contra sanguinē suū insidiantur: et

Reproduction of a page from the Gutenberg Bible, the first major book to be printed from movable type, c. 1455. This is the opening page of the Book of Proverbs. Courtesy The British Library.

regard the Apocrypha as canonical, although they permitted their use for edification.

The Protestant OT does not follow the grouping of either the Hebrew canon or the LXX. It has, first, the five books of the Pentateuch; then the eleven historical books, beginning with Joshua and ending with Esther; after that what are often called the poetical books: Job, Psalms, Proverbs, Ecclesiastes, and the Song of Songs; and finally the prophets, first the major and then the minor.

All branches of the Christian church are agreed on the NT canon. The grouping of the books is a natural one: first the four Gospels; then the one historical book of the NT, the Acts of the Apostles; after that the letters to the churches, first the letters of Paul and then the general letters; and finally the Revelation.

IV. Text. Although the Bible was written over a period of approximately 1,400 years, from the time of Moses to the end of the first century A.D., its text has come to us in a remarkable state of preservation. It is of course not identical with the text that left the hands of the original writers. Scribal errors have crept in. Until the invention of printing in the middle of the fifteenth century, all copies of the Scriptures were made by hand. There is evidence that the ancient Jewish scribes copied the books of the OT with extreme care. The recently discovered Dead Sea Scrolls, some going as far back as the second and third centuries B.C., contain either whole books or fragments of all but one (Esther) of the OT books; and they bear witness to a text remarkably like the Hebrew text left by the Masoretes (from A.D. 500 on). The Greek translation of the OT, the Septuagint, was begun about 250 B.C. and completed about one hundred years later. Although it differs in places from the Hebrew text current today, it is also a valuable witness to the accuracy of the OT text.

In the NT the evidence for the reliability of the text is almost embarrassingly large and includes about 4,500 Greek manuscripts, dating from A.D. 125 to the invention of printing; various versions, the Old Latin and Syriac going back to about A.D. 150; and quotations of Scripture in the writings of the church fathers, beginning with the end of the first century. The superabundance of textual evidence for the NT may be appreciated when it is realized that very few manuscripts of ancient Greek and Latin classical authors have survived, and those that have survived are all late in date. Among the oldest manuscripts of the Greek NT that have come down to us are the John Rylands fragment of the Gospel of John (c. 125); Papyrus Bodmer II, a manuscript of the Gospel of John dating c. 200; the Chester Beatty Papyri, consisting of three codices containing the Gospels and Acts, most of Paul's Letters, and the Revelation, dating from c. 200; and codices Vaticanus and Sinaiticus, both written about c. 350.

V. Chapters and Verses. The books of the Bible originally had no chapters or verses. For convenience of reference, Jews of pre-Talmudic times divided the OT into sections like our chapters and verses. The chapter divisions we use today were made by Stephen Langton, archbishop of Canterbury, who died in 1228. The division of the NT into its present verses is found for the first time in an edition of the Greek NT published in 1551 by a printer in Paris, Robert Stephens, who in 1555 also brought out an edition of the Vulgate that was the first edition of the entire Bible to appear with our present chapters and verses. The first English Bible to be so divided was the Genevan edition of 1560.

VI. Translations. The Old and New Testaments appeared very early in translations. The OT was translated into Greek (the LXX) between 250 and 150 B.C., and other translations in Greek appeared soon after the beginning of the Christian era. Parts, at least, of the OT were rendered into Syriac as early as the first century A.D., and a Coptic translation appeared probably in the third century. The NT was translated into Latin and Syriac c. 150 and into Coptic c. 200. In subsequent centuries versions appeared in the Armenian, Gothic, Ethiopic, Georgian, Arabic, Persian, and Slavonic languages. The Bible, in whole or in part, is now available in more than 1,100 different languages and dialects. Many languages have been reduced to writing in order that the Bible might be translated into them in written form, and this work still goes on in many lands.

VII. Message. Although the Bible consists of many different books written over a long period of time by a great variety of writers, most of whom did not know one another, it has an organic unity that can be explained only by assuming, as the book itself claims, that its writers were inspired by the Holy Spirit to give God's message to man. The theme of this message is the same in both Testaments, the redemption of man. The OT tells about the origin of man's sin and the preparation God made for the solution of this problem through his own Son the Messiah. The NT describes the fulfillment of God's redemptive plan; the four Gospels telling about the Messiah's coming; the Acts of the Apostles describing the origin and growth of the church, God's redeemed people; the Epistles giving the meaning and implication of the Incarnation; and the Revelation showing how some day all of history will be consummated in Christ. The two Testaments form two volumes of one work. The first is incomplete without the second; and the second cannot be understood without the first. Together they are God's revelation to people of the provision he has made for their salvation.

See also: TEXTS AND VERSIONS; OLD TESTAMENT; NEW TESTAMENT.

Bibliography: B. F. Westcott, *The Bible in the Church,* 1864; F. F. Bruce, *The Books and the Parchments,* 1953; C. F. H. Henry, *Revelation and the Bible,* 1959; P. R. Ackroyd et al., *The Cambridge History of the Bible,* 3 vols., 1970; A. C. Partridge, *English Bible Translation,* 1973; D. A. Carson, *King James Version Debate,* 1979; E. H. Glassman, *The Translation Debate,* 1981; J. P. Lewis, *The English Bible: From KJV to NIV,* 1981; M. A. Noll and N. O. Hatch (eds.), *The Bible in America,* 1982. SB

BIBLE, ENGLISH VERSIONS. In the earliest days of English Christianity the only known Bible was the Latin Vulgate, made by Jerome between A.D. 383 and 405. This could be read by the clergy and by monks, the only ones who were familiar with the language. In 670 Caedmon, a monk at Whitby, produced in Old English a metrical version of some of the more interesting narratives of the OT. The first straightforward translation of any part of the Bible into the language of the people was the Psalter, made in about 700 by Aldhelm, the first bishop of Sherborne in Dorset. Some parts of the NT were translated into English by Bede, the learned monk of Jarrow, author of the famous *Ecclesiastical History of the English Nation*. According to a letter of his disciple Cuthbert, Bede was still engaged in translating the Gospel of John into English on his deathbed. It is not certain whether he completed it, but, unfortunately, his translation has not survived. King Alfred (871–901) produced during his reign English versions of parts of the Old and New Testaments, including a part of the Psalter. Some Latin gospels that survive from this period have written between the lines what are known as "glosses," a word-for-word translation of the text into English, without regard to the idiom and usage of the vernacular. From the same period as these glosses come what are known as the Wessex Gospels, the first independent Old English version of the gospels. Toward the end of the tenth century Aelfric, archbishop of Canterbury, translated parts of the first seven books of the OT, as well as parts of other OT books.

For nearly three centuries after the Norman Conquest in 1066 the uncertain conditions of the language prevented any real literary progress, but some manuscripts of translations of parts of the Bible into Anglo-Norman French survive. About the beginning of the thirteenth century an Augustinian monk named Orm or Ormin produced a poetical version of the Gospels and the Acts of the Apostles called the *Ormulum*. From the first half of the fourteenth century there survive two prose translations of the Psalter, done in two different dialects; and from the end of the fourteenth century, a version of the principal NT letters, apparently made, however, not for the use of the common people but for monks and nuns. There was no thought as yet of providing ordinary layfolk with the Bible in their own tongue. It was Wycliffe who first entertained this revolutionary idea. And it was Wycliffe who first made the whole Bible available in English.

John Wycliffe. Born in Yorkshire about the year 1320, Wycliffe stands out as one of the most illustrious figures of the fourteenth century. This was a period of transition, neither the Middle Ages nor the Reformation—a kind of middle ground between the two. The old order was struggling with the new. Throughout the whole of this century the prestige of the Roman Catholic church was very low. The "Babylonian Captivity" of the popes at Avignon (1309–1378) was followed by the "Great Schism," when for forty years there were two rival popes, one at Rome and the other at Avignon. In the struggle between the papacy and the English parliament over the papal tribute, Wycliffe sided with the parliament. The outstanding Oxford theologian of his day and an ardent ecclesiastical reformer, he is called the "Morning-star of the Reformation." He was convinced that the surest way of defeating Rome was to put the Bible into the hands of the common people, and he therefore decided to make such a translation available. Under his auspices, the NT came out in 1380 and the OT two years later. It is uncertain exactly how much of the translation was done by Wycliffe himself. A number of scholars worked with him on the project, one of them, Nicholas Hereford, doing the greater part of the OT. The translation was made from the Latin, not from the original languages. Since printing was not known, copies were made by hand and were naturally very expensive. About 170 are in existence at present. It was never printed until 1850, when the Oxford Press published it. The original manuscript in the handwriting of at least five different men is preserved in the Bodleian Library at Oxford. To help him in his efforts for reform, Wycliffe organized a kind of religious order of poor preachers, called Lollards, whom he sent throughout England to preach his doctrines and to read the Scriptures to all who wished to hear. Foxe reports that the people were so eager to read it that they would give a whole load of hay for the use of the NT for one day. There was opposition to Wycliffe on the part of the church, but contrary to his own expectations, he was permitted to retire to his rectory of Lutterworth, where he quietly died in 1384. Twelve years later, however, his bones were disinterred and burned, and the ashes scattered over the river that flows through Lutterworth. His translation has indelibly stamped itself on our present-day Bible. Some of the familiar expressions that are first found in his version are "strait gate," "make whole," "compass land and sea," "son of perdition," "enter thou into the joy of thy Lord."

Four years after Wycliffe's death his secretary, John Purvey, issued a careful revision of his translation, introduced with an interesting prologue and accompanied by notes. The church, however, did not approve of the new Bible. In 1408 a decree, known as the "Constitutions of Oxford," was issued forbidding anyone to translate or read any part of the Bible in the vernacular without the approval of his bishop or of a provincial council. Six years later a law was enacted that all persons who should read the Scriptures in their own language should "forfeit land, catel, life, and goods from their heyres for ever." Nicholas Hereford and John Purvey were imprisoned. The public demand for the Bible continued, however, in spite of the severe penalties attached to its circulation.

The fifteenth century was one of the great epochs of human history. In that century there lived such men as Columbus, Galileo, Frances Bacon, Kepler, and Marco Polo. Another great man of the time was the inventor of printing,

Portrait presumed to be of William Tyndale, translator of the New Testament from the original Greek. Artist unknown. Courtesy National Portrait Gallery, London.

Gutenberg, who in 1454 brought out in Germany the first dated printed work, a Latin Psalter, and two years later the famous Gutenberg Bible in the Latin Vulgate. After the capture of Constantinople in 1453, Christian scholars were compelled to leave the capital of the Eastern Empire, where for a thousand years Greek learning had flourished. They brought with them to Western Europe many Greek manuscripts. This led to a revival of interest in biblical studies and made it possible for Erasmus to issue in 1516 the first printed edition of the Greek New Testament. At the beginning of the sixteenth century Greek was for the first time introduced as a subject of study in the universities of Oxford and Cambridge. By 1500 most of the countries of Europe had the Scriptures in the vernacular. England, however, had only scattered copies of the Wycliffe manuscript version, the language of which had by then become obsolete. The Constitutions of Oxford were still in force. England was ready for a new translation of the Bible, from the original languages.

William Tyndale. William Tyndale, the next great figure in the history of the English Bible, was born about the year 1494 and spent ten years studying at Oxford and Cambridge. Soon after leaving Cambridge, while working as a chaplain and tutor, he said in a controversy with a clergyman, "If God spare my life, ere many years I will cause a boy that driveth a plough to know more of the Scripture than thou dost." This became the fixed resolve of his life. In his projected translation he tried to get the support of the bishop of London, but without success. A wealthy London cloth merchant finally came to his support, but after six months, in 1524, Tyndale left for the Continent because, he said, he "understood at the last not only that there was no room in my lord of London's palace to translate the NT, but also that there was no place to do it in all England, as experience doth now openly declare." He was never able to return to England. He seems to have visited Luther at Wittenberg, and then went to Cologne, where he found a printer for his NT. A priest discovered his plan, and Tyndale was obliged to flee. In Worms he found another printer, and there, in 1525, three thousand copies of the first printed English NT were published. By 1530 six editions, numbering about fifteen thousand copies, were published. They were all smuggled into England—hidden in bales of cotton, sacks of flour, and bundles of flax.

As soon as Tyndale's NT reached England, there was a great demand for it: by the laity that they might read it, and by the ecclesiastical authorities, that they might destroy it! A decree was issued for its destruction. Bishops bought up whole editions to consign to the flames. As a result, only a few imperfect copies survive. Tyndale's English NT began a new epoch in the history of the English Bible. It was not a translation from the Latin, as Wycliffe's had been, but was translated from the original Greek, the text published by Erasmus. With each successive edition, Tyndale made corrections and improvements. So well did Tyndale do his work that the KJV reproduces about 90 percent of Tyndale in the NT. After the completion of the NT, Tyndale started to bring out a translation of the OT from the Hebrew text, but he lived only to complete the Pentateuch, Jonah, and probably the historical books from Joshua to 2 Chronicles. After ten years on the Continent, mostly in hiding, he was betrayed in Antwerp by an English Roman Catholic and was condemned to death for being a heretic. He was strangled and his body burned at the stake. His last words were a prayer, "Lord, open the King of England's eyes." But Tyndale had won his battle. Although his NT was burned in large quantities by the church, it contributed greatly toward creating an appetite for the Bible in English. The government, moreover, began to see the wisdom and necessity of providing the Bible in English for common use. The break with the papacy in 1534 helped greatly in this.

Miles Coverdale. While Tyndale was imprisoned in Belgium, an English Bible suddenly appeared in England in 1535. It had come from the Continent. The title page stated that it had been translated out of the German and Latin into English. This Bible was the rendering of Miles Coverdale, although in the NT and in those parts of the OT done by Tyndale, it was no more than a slight revision of the latter's work. It was the first complete printed Bible in the English language. It was not translated from the Hebrew and Greek, for in the dedication (to Henry VIII) Coverdale says that he used the work of five different translators. His version of the Psalms still appears in the Book of Common Prayer, used daily in the ritual of the Church of England. Two new

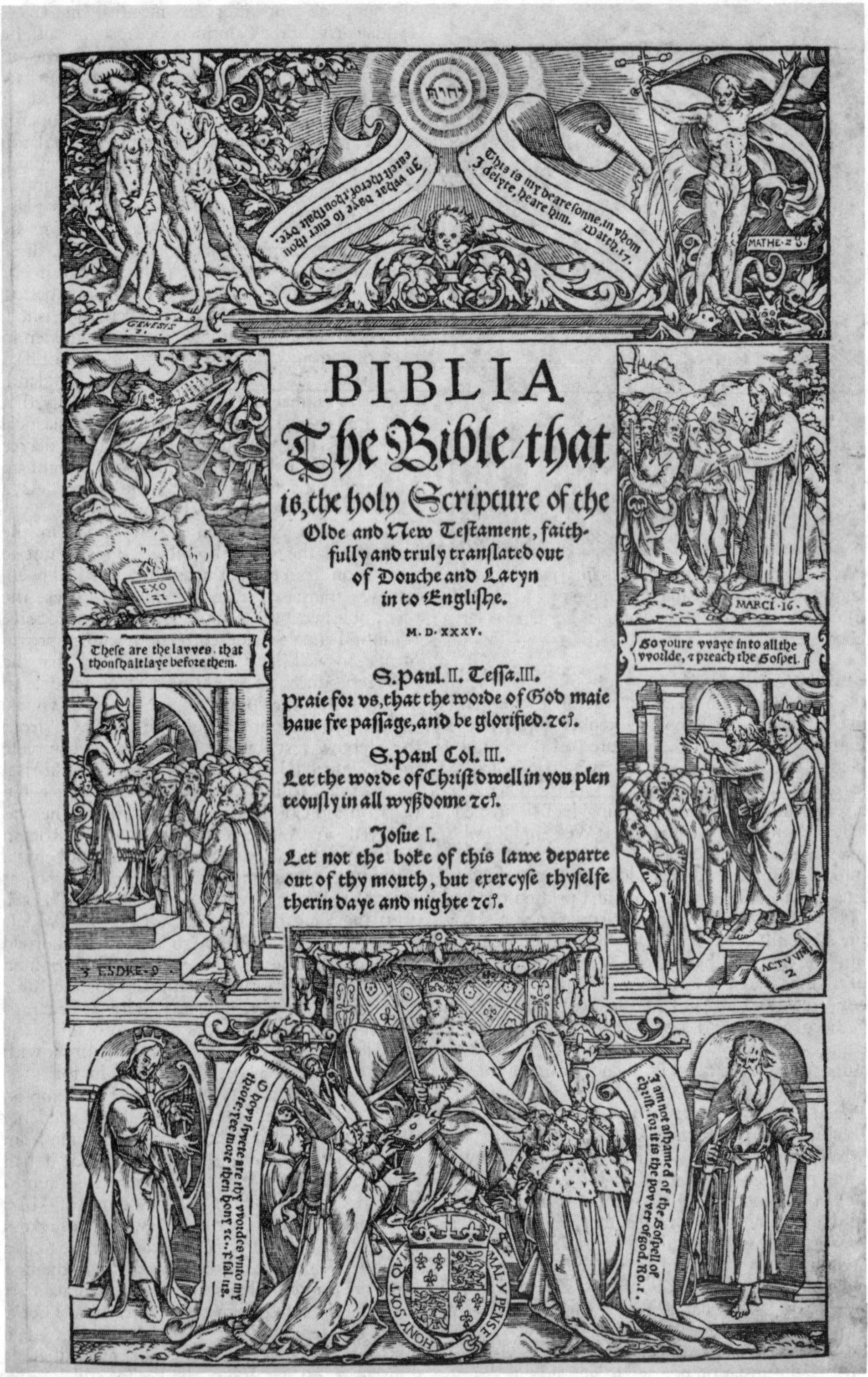

Title page of Coverdale's Bible, dated 1535, the first full Bible to be printed in English. Courtesy The British Library.

editions of Coverdale's Bible appeared in 1537, the title page containing the significant words "Set forth with the King's most gracious license." So within a year of Tyndale's death, the entire Bible was translated, printed, and distributed, apparently with royal approval.

Thomas Matthew. In 1537 another Bible appeared in England, this one by Thomas Matthew (a pen name for John Rogers, a former associate of Tyndale's), who was burned at the stake by Queen Mary in 1555. The whole of the NT and about half of the OT are Tyndale's, while the remainder is Coverdale's. It bore on its title page the words, "Set forth with the king's most gracious license." This Bible has the distinction of being the first edition of the whole English Bible actually to be printed in England. So now two versions of the English Bible circulated in England with the king's permission, Coverdale's and Matthew's, both of them heavily dependent on Tyndale.

The Great Bible. The next Bible to appear was a revision of the Matthew Bible, done by Coverdale. The printing of this was begun in Paris, but the Inquisition stepped in and the work was completed in England. It appeared in 1539 and was called the Great Bible because of its large size and sumptuousness. In his revision Coverdale made considerable use of the Hebrew and Greek texts then available. Subsequent editions were called Cranmer's Bible because of a preface he wrote for it in which he commended the widespread reading of the Scriptures and declared that they were the sufficient rule of faith and life. At the foot of the title page were the words "This is the Bible appointed to the use of the churches." This makes explicit an order that was issued in 1538, while this Bible was being printed, that a copy of it was to be placed in every church in the land. The people cordially welcomed the Great Bible, but its size and cost limited it largely to use in churches.

The later years of Henry VIII were marked by a serious reaction against the Reform movement. In 1543 Parliament passed an act to ban the use of Tyndale's NT, made it a crime for an unlicensed person to read or expound the Bible publicly to others, and restricted even the private reading of the Bible to the upper classes. Three years later Parliament prohibited the use of everything but the Great Bible. In London large quantities of Tyndale's NT and Coverdale's Bible were burned at St. Paul's Cross.

In the brief reign of Edward VI, who succeeded his father Henry VIII in 1547, no new translation work was done. However, great encouragement was given to the reading of the Bible and to the printing of existing versions, and injunctions were reissued that a copy of the Great Bible be placed in every parish church.

The Genevan Bible. With the accession of Mary in 1553, hundreds of Protestants lost their lives, among them some men closely associated with Bible translation, like John Rogers and Thomas Cranmer. Coverdale escaped martyrdom by fleeing to the Continent. Some of the English

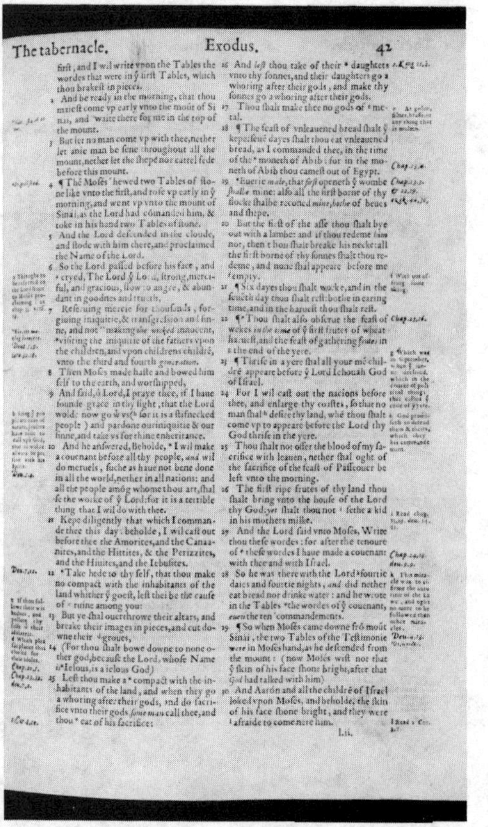
The tabernacle. Exodus. 42

firſt, and I wil write vpon the Tables the
wordes that were in ẏ firſt Tables, which
thou brakeſt in pieces.
2 And be ready in the morning, that thou
maieſt come vp early vnto the mount of Si
nai, and waite there for me in the top of
the mount.
3 But let no man come vp with thee, nether
let anie man be ſene throughout all the
mount, nether let the ſhepe nor cattel fede
before this mount.
4 ¶ Thē Moſes hewed two Tables of ſtone like vnto the firſt, and roſe vp early in ẏ
morning, and went vp vnto the mount of
Sinai, as the Lord had cōmanded him, &
toke in his hand two Tables of ſtone.
5 And the Lord deſcended in the cloude,
and ſtode with him there, and proclaimed
the Name of the Lord.
6 So the Lord paſſed before his face, and
cryed, The Lord ẏ Lord, ſtrong, merciful, and gracious, ſlow to angre, & abundant in goodnes and trueth,
7 Reſeruing mercie for thouſands, for-
giuing iniquitie, & tranſgreſſion and ſinne, and not making the wicked innocent,
viſiting the iniquitie of the fathers vpon
the children, and vpon childrens childrē,
vnto the third and fourth generation.
8 Then Moſes made haſte and bowed him
ſelf to the earth, and worſhipped,
9 And ſaid, ô Lord, I praye thee, if I haue
founde grace in thy ſight, that the Lord
wolde now go wt vs (for it is a ſtifnecked
people) and pardone our iniquitie & our
ſinne, and take vs for thine enheritance.
10 And he anſwered, Beholde, I wil make
a couenant before all thy people, and wil
do meruels, ſuche as haue not bene done
in all the world, nether in all nations: and
all the people amōg whome thou art, ſhal
ſe the worke of ẏ Lord: for it is a terrible
thing that I wil do with thee.
11 Kepe diligently that which I comman-
de thee this day: beholde, I wil caſt out
before thee the Amorites, and the Canaanites, and the Hittites, & the Perizzites,
and the Hiuites, and the Iebuſites.
12 Take hede to thy ſelf, that thou make
no compact with the inhabitants of the
land whither ẏ goeſt, leſt thei be the cauſe
of ruine among you:
13 But ye ſhal ouerthrowe their altars, and
breake their images in pieces, and cut downe their groues,
14 (For thou ſhalt bowe downe to none o-
ther god, becauſe the Lord, whoſe Name
is Ielous, is a ielous God)
15 Leſt thou make a compact with the inhabitants of the land, and when they go
a whoring after their gods, and do ſacrifice vnto their gods ſome man call thee, and
thou eat of his ſacrifice:
16 And leſt thou take of their daughters
vnto thy ſonnes, and their daughters go a
whoring after their gods, and make thy
ſonnes go a whoring after their gods.
17 Thou ſhalt make thee no gods of metal.
18 ¶ The feaſt of vnleauened bread ſhalt ẏ
kepe: ſeuē dayes ſhalt thou eat vnleauened
bread, as I commanded thee, in the time
of the moneth of Abib: for in the moneth of Abib thou cameſt out of Egypt.
19 Euerie male, that firſt openeth ẏ wombe
ſhalbe mine: alſo all the firſt borne of thy
flocke ſhalbe reconed mine, bothe of beues
and ſhepe.
20 But the firſt of the aſſe thou ſhalt bye
out with a lambe: and if thou redeme him
not, then thou ſhalt breake his necke: all
the firſt borne of thy ſonnes ſhalt thou redeme, and none ſhal appeare before me
empty.
21 ¶ Six dayes thou ſhalt worke, and in the
ſeuēth day thou ſhalt reſt: bothe in earing
time, and in the harueſt thou ſhalt reſt.
22 ¶ Thou ſhalt alſo obſerue the feaſt of
wekes in the time of ẏ firſt frutes of wheat
harueſt, and the feaſt of gathering frutes in
the end of the yere.
23 ¶ Thriſe in a yere ſhal all your mē childrē appeare before ẏ Lord Iehouah God
of Iſrael.
24 For I wil caſt out the nacions before
thee, and enlarge thy coſtes, ſo that no
man ſhal deſire thy land, whē thou ſhalt
come vp to appeare before the Lord thy
God thriſe in the yere.
25 Thou ſhalt not offer the blood of my ſacrifice with leauen, nether ſhal oght of
the ſacrifice of the feaſt of Paſſeouer be
left vnto the morning.
26 The firſt ripe frutes of thy land thou
ſhalt bring vnto the houſe of the Lord
thy God: yet ſhalt thou not ſethe a kid
in his mothers milke.
27 And the Lord ſaid vnto Moſes, Write
thou theſe wordes: for after the tenoure
of theſe wordes I haue made a couenant
with thee and with Iſrael.
28 So he was there with the Lord fourtie
daies and fourtie nights, and did nether
eat bread nor drinke water: and he wrote
in the Tables the wordes of ẏ couenant,
euen the ten commandements.
29 ¶ So when Moſes came downe frō mout
Sinai, the two Tables of the Teſtimonie
were in Moſes hand, as he deſcended from
the mount: (now Moſes wiſt not that
ẏ ſkin of his face ſhone bright, after that
God had talked with him)
30 And Aarōn and all the childrē of Iſrael
loked vpon Moſes, and beholde, the ſkin
of his face ſhone bright, and they were
afraide to come nere him.

L.ii.

A page from the Geneva Bible published in 1560; portion of Exodus 34. Courtesy The British Library.

Reformers escaped to Geneva, where the leading figure was John Calvin. One of their number, William Wittingham, who had married Calvin's sister, produced in 1557 a revision of the English NT. This was the first English NT printed in roman type and with the text divided into verses. He and his associates then undertook the revision of the whole Bible. This appeared in 1560 and is known as the Genevan Bible, or as the Breeches Bible from its rendering of Genesis 3:7, "They sewed fig tree leaves together, and made themselves breeches." It enjoyed a long popularity, going through 160 editions, 60 of them during the reign of Queen Elizabeth alone, and continued to be printed even after the publication of the KJV in 1611.

The Bishops' Bible. Queen Elizabeth, who succeeded Mary Tudor as queen, restored the arrangements of Edward VI. The Great Bible was again placed in every church, and people were encouraged to read the Scriptures. The excellence of the Genevan Bible made obvious the deficiencies of the Great Bible, but some of the Genevan Bible's renderings and the marginal notes made it unacceptable to many of the clergy. Archbishop Parker, aided by eight bishops and some other scholars, therefore made a revision of the Great Bible, which was completed and pub-

Title page of the King James Version (the Authorized Version) of the Bible, printed at London in 1611. Courtesy The British Library.

lished in 1568 and came to be known as the Bishops' Bible. It gained considerable circulation, but the Genevan Bible was far more popular and was used more widely.

Rheims and Douai Version. This came from the Church of Rome and is the work of Gregory Martin, who with a number of other English Romanists left England at the beginning of Elizabeth's reign and settled in NE France, where in 1568 they founded a college. The NT was published in 1582, and was done while the college was at Rheims, and hence is known as the Rheims NT; but the OT was not published until 1609–10, after the college had moved to Douai, and hence it is called the Douai OT. The preface warned readers against the then-existing "profane" translations and blames Protestants for casting what was holy to dogs. Like Wycliffe's version, this one was made not from the original languages but from Latin, and is therefore only a secondary translation. The main objection to the version is its too close adherence to the words of the original Latin and the too great Latinizing of the English. It included the Apocrypha and contained a large number of notes, most of them to interpret the sacred text in conformity with Roman Catholic teaching and to reply to the arguments of the Reformers. The Rheims-Douay Bible in use today is not the same as the one made by Gregory Martin, but is a thorough revision made of it between 1749 and 1763 by Bishop Richard Challoner. It was first authorized for use by American Roman Catholics in 1810.

King James (or Authorized) Version. When Elizabeth died in 1603, the crown passed to James I, who had been king of Scotland for thirty-six years as James VI. Several months after he ascended the throne of England he called a conference of bishops and Puritan clergy to harmonize the differences that existed in the church. At this conference Dr. John Reynolds, President of Corpus Christi College, Oxford, a leader of the Puritan party in the Church of England, suggested that a new translation of the Bible be made to replace the Bishops' Bible, which many people found unacceptable. The proposal pleased the king, who violently disliked the Genevan Bible; a resolution was passed to produce a new translation of the Bible from the original Hebrew and Greek, without any marginal notes, for the use of all the churches in England.

Without delay King James nominated fifty-four of the best Hebrew and Greek scholars of the day. Only forty-seven actually took part in the work, which did not begin until 1607. They were divided into six groups: three for the OT, two for the NT, and one for the Apocrypha. Two of the groups met at Oxford, two at Cambridge, and two at Westminster. Elaborate rules were laid down for their guidance. When a group had completed its task, its work was submitted to twelve men, two from each panel. Final differences of opinion were settled at a general meeting of each company. In cases of special difficulty, learned men outside the board of revisers were consulted. Marginal notes were used only to explain Hebrew and Greek words and to draw attention to parallel passages. Italics were used for words not found in the original but necessary to complete the sense.

Portrait of King James I, under whose authority the King James Version was prepared (published in 1611). After John de Critz the Elder. Courtesy National Portrait Gallery, London.

The revisers, who received no financial remuneration for their work, completed their task in two years; nine more months were devoted to a revision of their work by a special committee consisting of two members from each group. In 1611 the new version was published. Although the title page described it as "newly translated out of the original tongues" and as "appointed to be read in churches," neither statement is entirely in accord with the facts. The work was actually a revision of the Bishops' Bible on the basis of the Hebrew and Greek; and it was never officially sanctioned by king, Parliament, or the church. It did not win immediate universal acceptance, taking almost fifty years to displace the Genevan Bible in popular favor. In the course of time slight alterations were made, especially in spelling, to conform to changing usage, but these were all done piecemeal by private enterprise. Its excellence is shown by the fact that after 375 years it is still used in preference to any other version in the English-speaking Protestant world, for both public and private use.

English Revised Version. This version was seen as necessary for a number of reasons: (1) in the course of time some words in the KJV had become obsolete, (2) a number of Greek manuscripts were discovered that were older than those available to the KJV translators, and (3) scholars' knowledge of the Hebrew language had improved. It had its origin in 1870 when, at the Convocation of Canterbury of the Church of England, a committee was appointed to invite outstanding Hebrew and Greek scholars, irrespective of religious denomination, to join in revising the KJV. Eventually a committee of fifty-four was formed, divided into two groups of twenty-seven each—one for the OT, the other for the NT. American scholars were also invited to cooperate, and they formed two groups corresponding to the British groups. It was agreed that American suggestions not accepted by the British revisers be recorded in an appendix to the published volume and that the American revisers give their moral support to the new Bible and not issue an edition of their own until at least fourteen years later. The revisers were guided by a number of rules, the most important being that they were to make as few alterations as possible in the text of the KJV, while basing their translation on a different Greek text.

Altogether the Greek text underlying the revised NT differed in 5,788 readings from that used by the KJV translators—only about one-fourth of these making any material difference in the substance of the text, though none so seriously as to affect major Christian doctrines. In the English text of the NT there are about 36,000 changes. The new Bible differed from its predecessors in printing poetical passages in the OT as poetry and in grouping verses into paragraphs according to sense units.

The NT was published in 1881, the OT in 1885. The work occupied the NT translators for about 40 days each year for ten years, while the OT group was occupied for 792 days over a period of fourteen years. The revisers gave their time and labor without charge. When they completed their work, they disbanded. Although the new version was widely accepted (three million copies being sold within the first year), it did not meet with immediate approval, nor did it in succeeding years ever surpass the KJV for supremacy among Bible translations; the English of the Revised Version was not sufficiently readable to replace the time-honored KJV. Though not part of the original project, the Apocrypha was published in 1895.

American Standard Version. The American scholars who cooperated with the English revisers on the ERV were not entirely satisfied with it. The suggested changes printed in the appendix represented only a part of the changes they wanted made; and the English revisers retained a large number of words and phrases whose meanings and spellings were regarded as antiquated. These revisers also retained words that were English but not American in meaning. For these and other reasons the American scholars did not disband when the ERV was published, but their revision of the ERV was not published until 1901. It is regarded as being on the whole superior to the ERV, at least for American uses; but it has its defects, as, for example, the substitution of "Jehovah" for "Lord," especially in the Psalter.

Other Twentieth-Century Versions. The discovery at the end of the nineteenth century of many thousands of Greek papyri in the sands of Egypt, all written in the everyday Greek language of the people, had a revolutionary influence on the study of the Greek of the NT. NT Greek had hitherto presented a vexing problem, since it was neither classical Greek nor the Greek of the Septuagint. Now it was shown to be the Greek of the Papyri, and therefore the colloquial language of Greek-speaking people in the first century. Many felt, therefore, that the NT should be translated into today's everyday speech, not in stilted and antiquated English. These developments created a keen interest in bringing out fresh translations of the NT in the spoken English of today; and in the next forty-five years a number of new modern-speech versions came out, most of them by individuals but a few by groups of scholars.

The first of these to appear was *The Twentieth Century New Testament: A Translation into Modern English Made from the Original Greek* (Westcott and Hort's Text). This was published in 1902 (reprinted 1961) and was the work of about twenty translators whose names were not given. In 1903 R. F. Weymouth brought out *The New Testament in Modern Speech;* it was thoroughly revised in 1924 by J. A. Robertson. James Moffatt, the well-known Scottish NT scholar, brought out *The Bible: A New Translation* in 1913–14. The American counterpart of Moffatt was *The Complete Bible: An American Translation* (1927, revised 1935). The NT part first appeared in 1923 and was the work of E. J. Goodspeed; four scholars, headed by J. M. Powis Smith, did the OT. *The New Testament. A Translation in the Language of the People,* by C. B. Williams, came out in 1937. *The New Testament in Modern English* (1958) by J. B. Phillips, is one of the most readable of the modern-speech translations. *The Amplified New Testament* (1958), which gives variant shades of meaning in the original, was followed in 1961 by *The Amplified Old Testament.* It was the work of Frances E. Siewert and unnamed assistants. *The Holy Bible: The Berkeley Version in Modern English* (1959) was the work of Gerrit Verkuyl in the NT and of twenty American scholars in the OT. Kenneth Wuest's *The New Testament—An Expanded Translation* appeared complete in 1961. Also in 1961 *The Simplified New Testament* appeared, a new translation by Olaf M. Norlie.

During this period a number of new Roman Catholic versions were brought out also. *The New Testament of our Lord and Saviour Jesus Christ* (1941) was a revision of the Rheims-Challoner NT sponsored by the Episcopal Committee of the Confraternity of Christian Doctrine; therefore it was called the Confraternity Version. It was followed by the translation of the OT in four successive volumes (1948–69), which represented, not a revision of Douai-Challoner, but a new version from Hebrew. It seemed unreasonable to have a secondary version of the NT alongside a primary version of the OT; but when it was decided to make a new translation of the NT from Greek it was also decided to undertake a thorough revision of the whole Confraternity Version. This revision appeared in 1970 under the new title *The New American Bible*. *The Westminster Version of the Sacred Scriptures* appeared under the editorship of Cuthbert Lattey—the NT in 1935, followed by parts of the OT. It was discontinued after Lattey's death in 1954. R. A. Knox's translation from the Latin Vulgate (NT, 1941; OT, 1949; revision, 1955) is a literary masterpiece and retains the charm of a period piece. The *Jerusalem Bible* (1966), a scholarly and widely appreciated translation, follows the pattern of the French *Bible de Jerusalem* (1956), produced by the Dominican faculty of the Biblical and Archaeological School in Jerusalem.

Revised Standard Version. This is a revision of the ASV (1901), the NT appearing in 1946 and the OT in 1952. It was sponsored by the International Council of Religious Education and is the work of thirty-two American scholars who worked in two sections, one dealing with the OT, the other with the NT. It was designed for use in public and private worship. In this version the language is modernized; direct speech is regularly indicated by the use of quotation marks; and the policy is followed (as in the KJV) of using a variety of synonyms to translate the Greek words where it is thought to be advisable. Special Catholic editions of the RSV appeared in 1965 (NT) and 1966 (complete Bible). But a new edition of the RSV in 1973 was accepted as a "common Bible" for Catholic, Protestant, and Orthodox Christians alike.

New English Bible. This is a completely new translation, not a revision of previously existing versions. The first suggestion for this version came in 1946 from the General Assembly of the Church of Scotland, but it is the joint effort of all the major religious denominations (with the main Bible Societies) in the British Isles, apart from the Roman Catholic church. C. H. Dodd was the general director of the whole translation. The first requirement put on the translators was to produce a genuinely new translation, in which an attempt should be made consistently to use the idiom of contemporary English to convey the meaning of the original languages. The translators were assisted by a panel of advisors on literary and stylistic questions. The NT came out in 1961; the complete Bible (including the Apocrypha), in 1970. As with most earlier translations, this also was greeted with a mixture of praise and criticism. But criticisms of substance are under consideration by a revising committee, which plans to produce a new edition before long.

Other Recent Versions. The *New American Standard Bible* (completed 1971) was a revision and modernization of the American Standard Version of 1901. A more recent revision is the *New King James Version* (NT, 1979; complete Bible, 1982), a modernization of the KJV; although the OT is based on the most recent edition of the text of the Hebrew Bible, the NT stays with the type of Greek text used by the original KJV translators in 1611.

The year 1971 saw the completion of *The Living Bible,* a paraphrase into simple English, the work of one man, Kenneth N. Taylor. It attained widespread popularity, especially among young people, but has lost ground since 1976 to the *Good News Bible,* completed in that year. The NT part of this latter work had been published ten years earlier under the title *Today's English Version* or *Good News for Modern Man*. The translators had specially in mind the needs of those for whom English is an acquired language as well as those who speak it as their mother tongue. The idiom is contemporary; the aim has been to produce "dynamic equivalence"—the producing of the same effect on readers today as the Hebrew and Greek texts produced on the original readers or hearers.

The best English translation produced since 1970 is the *New International Version*. This was the work of a team of over one hundred evangelical scholars drawn from most of the English-speaking countries. A pilot scheme was launched in 1969—a version of the Gospel of John called *A Contemporary Translation*. The complete NT followed in 1973 and the entire Bible in 1978. Unlike RSV, and like NEB, it is a direct translation from the original languages, not a revision of any existing version. The sponsors claim that it is written in "the language of the common man," but its idiom is rather more elevated than that of the GNB. It is a thoroughly reliable and praiseworthy achievement.

For Bibliography, see under BIBLE. SB

BICRI (bĭk′rī, *firstborn*). Mentioned in 2 Samuel 20:1 as the father of Sheba, who led an insurrection against David.

BIDKAR (bĭd′kär). A military officer of Israel who joined Jehu in his revolt and was made his captain (2 Kings 9:25). He cast the body of Joram, king of Israel, into the plot of Naboth's vineyard, after Jehu had killed him.

BIGTHA (bĭg′thȧ). One of the seven chamberlains of Xerxes (Ahasuerus) (Esth 1:10).

BIGTHANA, BIGTHAN (bĭg′thā′nȧ, bĭg′-thăn). One of the chamberlains of King Xerxes (Ahasuerus) who with Teresh had plotted to kill the king. Mordecai heard of the plot and through Esther warned the king, who had the two men hanged (Esth 2:21–23; 6:2).

BIGVAI (bĭg′vā-ī, *fortunate*). 1. One of the eleven or twelve chief men who returned from captivity by permission of Cyrus in 536 B.C. (Ezra 2:2; Neh 7).

2. The ancestor of a family of over two thousand who returned with Zerubbabel from captivity (Ezra 2:14; Neh 7:19). Some think that the slight difference of numbers in the two verses quoted is due to the possibility that Ezra's was a list made in Babylon before starting, and Nehemiah's at Jerusalem after arriving. Some may have

dropped out and a few added during the migration.

3. Probably the same as no. 2. The ancestor of a family, seventy-two of whom returned with Ezra in 457 B.C. (Ezra 8:14).

BILDAD (bĭl′dăd). One of Job's three "comforters" (cf. Job 2:11–13 with 42:7–10). He was evidently a descendant of Shuah (Gen 25:2), a son of Abraham by Keturah, who became patriarch of an Arab tribe. Bildad made three speeches (Job 8, 18, 25), and his distinctive character as a "traditionalist" can best be seen in 8:8–10.

BILEAM (bĭl′ē-ăm). A town in the western half of the tribe of Manasseh given in Joshua's time to the Levites of the Kohathite family who were not priests (1 Chron 6:70). Perhaps the same as the Ibleam of Joshua 17:11; Judges 1:27; 2 Kings 9:27.

BILGAH (bĭl′gȧ, *cheerfulness*). 1. Head of the fifteenth course of priests in David's time (1 Chron 24:14).

2. A priest who returned with Zerubbabel in 536 B.C. (Neh 12:5).

BILGAI (bĭl′gā-ī). A priest in Nehemiah's time, 444 B.C. (Neh 10:8).

BILHAH (bĭl′hȧ, *foolish*). 1. Maidservant of Rachel, Jacob's beloved wife; she was later given to Jacob by Rachel that she might bear children who would be credited to Rachel (Gen 29:29; 30:1–8). She became ancestress of the two tribes, Dan and Naphtali. In the polygamous system of early Israel, she would be ranked higher than a mere concubine, but not as high as her free-born mistress.

2. A town in the tribe of Simeon; "Balah" in Joshua 19:3.

BILHAN (bĭl′hăn, *foolish*). 1. A son of Ezer, son of Seir the Horite (Gen 36:27; 1 Chron 1:42). Etymologically, the name is the same as Bilhah, but with the Horite ending.

2. An early Benjamite; son of Jediael, son of Benjamin (1 Chron 7:10). He had seven sons who were mighty men and heads of large families.

BILSHAN (bĭl′shăn). One of the eleven or twelve leaders of the Jews who returned from captivity in 536 B.C. (Ezra 2:2; Neh 7:7).

BIMHAL (bĭm′hăl). One of the three sons of Japhlet of the tribe of Asher (1 Chron 7:33).

BINDING AND LOOSING. The carrying of a key or keys was a symbol of the delegated power of opening and closing. In Matthew 16:19 our Lord gave the "power of the keys" to Peter, and Peter's use of the keys is narrated in what may be called the "three stages of Pentecost." On the Day of Pentecost (Acts 2:14–40) Peter preached the first Christian sermon and opened "the kingdom of heaven" to what became a Hebrew-Christian church; then, with John, he went to Samaria (8:14–17) and opened the same "kingdom" to the Samaritans; still later in the house of Cornelius (10:44–48) he opened it to the Gentiles. Thus, the church became universal. The medieval teaching about Peter standing at the gate of heaven to receive or reject souls of men has no basis in biblical teaching.

BINEA (bĭn′ē-ȧ). A Benjamite in the lineage of Saul (1 Chron 8:37; 9:43).

BINNUI (bĭn′ū-ī, *built*). 1. A Levite, whose son was partly in charge of the silver and gold at Ezra's return (Ezra 8:33).

2. One of the sons of Pahath-Moab who had married foreign wives (Ezra 10:30).

3. A son of Bani who had been similarly guilty (Ezra 10:38).

4. One of the rebuilders of Jerusalem in 444 B.C., who also became a covenanter under Nehemiah (Neh 3:24; 10:9).

5. Alternate spelling of Bani (cf. Ezra 2:10) whose family returned with Zerubbabel.

6. A Levite who returned with Zerubbabel (Neh 12:8).

BIRDS. Palestine is the home of some 375 kinds of birds, of which perhaps 25 are peculiar to that region. The Bible mentions about 50, using Hebrew or Greek names that can sometimes be identified with particular species of the present. Birds are mentioned in more than two-thirds of the biblical books. In English versions of the Bible there are often differences in the translations of the names of birds. Sometimes the identification of some creature as a bird has been questioned (see, e.g., *Peacock* and *Night Creature* below). Occasionally birds are dealt with in groups, but the listing will refer the reader to the main entry in that category.

Where there are differences of translation, comparisons are often made with terms as they occur in different versions—usually KJV, RSV, NASB, and NIV, with special attention given to the last-mentioned as the version on which this volume as a whole is primarily based. Some of the more speculative translations that occur in only one version have been omitted. While the main aim is to put birds in their biblical context, some brief general details of birds are also given.

Bird of Prey. Predators were described by the Hebrew word *'ayit,* the word possibly echoing the screaming cry made by hawks, falcons, or kites. However, as vultures grunt or hiss and do not cry, the word may equally be derived from the root meaning "flesh tearing," which would include vultures.

The Latin word *rapto* (to seize and carry off) is the root for the general description of birds of prey as raptors, a group that includes some of the largest and strongest birds, all with hook-tipped beaks and sharp, curving claws (talons).

Abraham drove away birds of prey from his sacrifice (Gen 15:11); this is the Bible's first reference to these troublesome creatures. Job

A buzzard in flight. Courtesy Seffie Ben-Yoseph.

reflected that no bird of prey knew the hidden path of a mine of precious metals (Job 28:7). Isaiah's prophecy against Cush (Isa 18:6) shows knowledge of the habits of birds of prey—which must also obey the call of God (46:11).

Bittern. A wading bird of the heron family, equipped with a long pointed bill used for spearing fish, frogs, and other prey. Its speckled plumage aids camouflage in the bittern's marshland environment, where it easily blends with reeds and other plant life.

With its somewhat mournful call, the bittern was considered a melancholy creature, and therefore likely to live in places far from human habitation, in the wasteland that followed the downfall of Edom (Isa 34:11 KJV) or the decay of Babylon (14:23 KJV). Nineveh would suffer a similar fate, its terrain becoming a home for the bittern (Zeph 2:14 KJV).

No reference to the bittern is found in the Pentateuch. An alternative translation is given as "porcupine" in ASV and RSV (Isa 34:11) and as "hedgehog" in NASB and RSV (Isa 14:23; RSV only: Zeph 2:14).

NIV translates this word "owl" (Isa 14:23) or specifies a variety of owl (Isa 34:11; Zeph 2:14); such translations are more likely, given the desolation that might be expected to follow the prophesied catastrophes.

Buzzard. A general description of any of a large number of heavily built hawks, mainly genus *Buteo.* With its short, broad wings and ability to soar, the buzzard is quite easily recognized. The European variety, *Buteo buteo,* is found from Scandinavia to the Mediterranean. The American use of "buzzard" is more widely applied to many types of hawk and vulture. Their main prey consists of small animals and insects, though the buzzard may occasionally attack small birds. It is included in the list of unclean birds (Lev 11:13; Deut 14:12 NASB, RSV).

Carrion Bird. The enemies of Israel would be given as food to all kinds of carrion birds, declared Ezekiel (39:4), the reference being to a variety of flesh-eating birds.

Carrion Vulture. As most vultures consume carrion, i.e., the flesh of dead animals or humans, the prohibition in Leviticus 11:18 NASB and in Deuteronomy 14:17 NASB, RSV, no doubt refers to any of this class of birds.

Chicken. Descended from the wild red jungle fowl of SE Asia, the domestic chicken or fowl is seen in many varieties throughout the world. It is mainly bred for food, the eggs of the female being a useful source of protein. Our Lord observed the hen's care of its chicks as a striking example of the concern he felt for Jerusalem (Matt 23:37; Luke 13:34). Immature males, cockerels, are usually bred for food purposes, mature males for breeding.

Cock. In biblical times its early morning crowing was associated with the start of a new day (Matt 13:35). The sound had a lamentable meaning for Peter, who denied his Lord before the cock crowed, according to Jesus' prophecy (Matt 26:74; Mark 14:30; Luke 22:34, 61; John 13:38; 18:27). NIV always renders the word "rooster."

Cormorant. A diving seabird of the Phalacrocoracidae family, equipped with a long neck and body that can reach a length of three feet (one m.). Although fast and powerful in flight—which is low over water—the cormorant has a rather laborious takeoff. With its diet of fish caught in short dives, the bird's hooked bill is ideal. Under water the cormorant swims with its feet only, while striking at its prey. Breeding harmoniously in colonies, the cormorant has been tamed in the Orient and trained to catch fish for its human owners. Because of its flesh-eating habits, the cormorant is included in the list of prohibited birds (Lev 11:17; Deut 14:17). In Isaiah 34:11 the word is translated as "pelican" in ASV, and "hawk" in RSV. Zephaniah 2:14 gives the word as "pelican" in ASV, and "vulture" in RSV. In both references NIV has "desert owl," but a marginal note concedes that precise identification is uncertain.

Crane. Any member of the Gruidae family of long-necked, long-legged wading birds, found throughout the world except for South America. The crane somewhat resembles the heron, but is larger and has a heavier bill, a partly naked head, and more compact plumage. When flying, it stretches its long neck forward, its stilt-like legs trailing behind.

The crane's croak, or honk, may be heard over distances of several miles and is unmistakable. Hezekiah's lament over his sickness was compared by Isaiah to the chatter of a crane, as if the king spoke loudly of his affliction, then fell away into muttering (Isa 38:14 KJV). NIV uses a different comparison, and there is a difference of opinion as to the bird precisely meant by Isaiah's text. The Hebrew word *'agar,* which means "traveler" or

The partridge (1) is mentioned only twice in Scripture. The sea gull (2), the kite (3) , and the heron (4) are all listed in Leviticus 11:13–18 as unclean or "detestable" (v. 13). In Israel, animals were expected to obey covenant law, and these did not. Their eating patterns involved eating flesh with blood in it. Courtesy Carta, Jerusalem.

"gatherer," could equally apply to a swallow as to a crane, especially if the spoken sound of the word is taken into account.

Jeremiah notes that birds, including the crane, know the time of their coming, i.e., their migratory journey (Jer 8:7 KJV), in contrast to man's often careless view of events. NIV uses "thrush" rather than "crane" in the passages mentioned above, i.e., a member of the family of songbirds, Turdidae.

Cuckoo. A member of the Cuculidae family of mainly insect-eating birds. Some species of cuckoo (KJV "cuckow") lay their eggs in other birds' nests, disposing of the existing eggs and/or young. They choose a particular bird species for a permanent fostering arrangement (i.e., they do not move from species to species). American cuckoos are not, however, parasitic in this way. The name of the bird comes from the male's distinctive cry. A long slender bird reaching a length of some twelve inches (thirty-one cm.), the cuckoo has a flying action similar to that of a hawk, but on ground level it hops in a rather clumsy fashion. It is classed as an unclean bird in Leviticus 11:16 and Deuteronomy 14:15, both KJV. ASV has "sea mew," RSV "seagull," NIV "gull." The gull is a flesh eater, hence condemned for human food.

Cuckow. See *Cuckoo.*

Desert Owl. See *Owl.*

Dove, Pigeon. The dove is a medium-sized bird of the family Columbidae, to which the pigeon also belongs, the latter being a somewhat larger bird. Domestic pigeons are descended from the rock dove, *Columba livia,* and a strong resemblance may be noted to the wild variety. A white domestic pigeon is usually called "the dove of peace," reproduction drawings showing a twig in its beak, commemorating the dispatch of the dove from the ark by Noah (Gen 8:8–12). Although not outstanding in its appearance, having a short neck and legs, nor in its cooing cry, the dove inspired the psalmist to write that he would indeed possess the wings of the dove (Ps 55:6). In God's good time, the believer will share such glory as may be compared to the wings of the dove being sheathed with silver, its feathers with shining gold (68:13).

Some biblical references to the dove probably refer to the turtle dove (see Turtle Dove) as in Song of Songs 2:12, where the cooing of doves was associated with the season of singing.

Hezekiah in contrast mourned about his illness, like a mourning dove (Isa 38:14), like the people in repentance (59:11). Ezekiel prophesied that those people who escaped the sword in the city would moan like doves of the valley (Ezek 7:16). Yet help was promised to those who flew like doves to their nests (Isa 60:8); that is, those who returned to their true home, which is God. The security of the dove in the clefts of the rocks was noted in Song of Songs 2:14. It was not, however, reckoned to be a very intelligent bird, and Ephraim was compared to one, in an unfavorable reflection on his good sense. Yet the NT spoke of the Holy Spirit descending like a dove onto the head of Jesus Christ at his baptism (Matt 3:18). This divinely given "dove" was indeed of power and grace, in contrast to the doves sold as merchandise in the temple, for ceremonial purification. The OT record clearly shows that doves were allowed for sacrifice because of their abundance: the temple authorities had made it hard for people to make their sacrifice by "cornering the market" in sacrificial doves. Jesus Christ charged his followers to be as shrewd as snakes and as innocent as doves (10:16), reflecting a prevailing public opinion of the bird.

Eagle. For many centuries the eagle has been adopted as a symbol of power and majesty, appropriately, it might be said, in view of its powers and regal appearance. Carnivorous, equipped with long talons and remarkably keen eyesight, the eagle is a member of the Accipitridae family and is monogamous—mating for life—and using the same nest every year. Nests are built in inaccessible places, far from human and animal marauders. For the most part, the eagle's diet consists of live prey, not carrion, and stories of the swift appearance of an eagle, carrying away a small animal (a baby lamb, for example) are commonly heard among shepherds. Although the eagle is superbly equipped for flying because of its exceptionally broad wings, it is somewhat ponderous in terms of effective pursuit of prey. Thus it uses a sudden descent and the element of surprise, these characteristics being duly noted by the bird-watchers of Bible times.

An eagle somewhat resembles a vulture, but it has a fully feathered head and, as already noted, prefers live prey. Among the many types found today is the crowned eagle, which may be some three feet (one m.) long and represents Africa's largest eagle; the snake-hunting harrier eagles of Europe, Asia, and Africa; as well as the lightly built hawk eagles found in the Mediterranean area and South Asia. Eagles were included among the unclean foods listed in Leviticus 11.

Although in normal circumstances the town-dweller in Bible times might see an eagle only rarely, such an appearance was not to be forgotten. Indeed, the people of Israel were reminded that they had been borne from Egyptian captivity, as it were, on the wings of eagles (Exod 19:4; Deut 32:11). In similar praise, the psalmist declares that his youth was renewed like that of the eagle (Ps 103:5). Isaiah promises similar power to those who hope in the Lord (Isa 40:31) Two eagle's wings were provided to transport the woman mentioned in Revelation 12 to the place prepared for her in the desert..

The power of the eagle was noted earlier; for example, the sudden descent of the eagle on its prey was appropriately compared to an attack of a nation that would be "like an eagle swooping down" on a careless Israel (Deut 28:49). Jeremiah prophesied in a similar vein, referring to an enemy equipped with horses swifter than eagles (Jer 4:13). Yet the Lord would prevail even against those enemies who built their nest as high as that of the eagle (49:16, echoed in Obad 4, in reference to Edom).

The face of the eagle was part of Ezekiel's great vision of living creatures (Ezek 1:10). Later, Ezekiel used two eagles and a vine in his allegory (ch 17); appropriately, both eagles were "great" and had "powerful wings." Daniel's dream of four beasts included a lion with the wings of an eagle (Dan 7:4)—a reference to the mighty kingdom of Nebuchadnezzar. Yet, among the warlike similes—necessary to warn a careless Israel—there is graciousness indeed, as that shown to Saul and Jonathan who were in life, swifter than eagles (2 Sam 1:23).

Job felt the passage of his days on earth as swift-passing as an eagle swooping on its prey (Job 9:26). In a no-less-reflective mood, the author of Proverbs believed that riches would fly away like an eagle (Prov 23:5).

Falcon. Found world-wide, this member of the Falconidae family is equipped with long, pointed wings, a powerful hooked beak, and a long tail. It is classed as unclean in Leviticus 11:14 and Deuteronomy 14:13; RSV translates the Hebrew word as "kite."

Species of falcon include the peregrine, kestrel, merlin, and South American caracara. Some nine classes of falcon were known in Bible times, though the Bible record may refer to kite or scavenger (Heb. *dayyāh*) or to falcon (Heb. *'ayyah*), according to the translator's preference. Isaiah's prophecy against Edom declared that falcons would gather there following the promised retribution (Isa 34:15).

Fowl. In modern speech "fowl" most often refers to "domestic fowl" and to poultry rather than to birds in general. Job 35:11 praises God for making men wiser than the birds of the air, or fowl, as the word might be translated. Jesus encouraged his disciples that they were indeed worth much more than many birds (Luke 12:24)—in the context of God's awareness of even a single bird's death, rather than to any thought about the cost of poultry in the marketplace.

However, fowl in the sense of poultry, or "choice fowl," is mentioned in the OT. It was included in Solomon's inventory of daily provisions (1 Kings 4:23), while the 150 Jews and officials who shared Nehemiah's table enjoyed meat of poultry as well as of oxen and choice sheep (Neh 5:18).

That people in Bible times set snares for wild fowl is clearly indicated in Psalms 91:3 and 124:7, where man's deliverance from his enemy is compared to the escape of a bird from a fowler's snare. An alternative translation of "fowler" (Heb. *yākôsh*) is "partridge catcher." The Hebrew word is also the root for the name "Jacob."

The partridge (1 Sam 26:20; Jer 17:11) was a medium-sized game bird, with plump body and a short tail. Known to the inhabitants of Bible lands as a delicacy, it was successfully introduced to the USA by European settlers.

Gier Eagle. An alternative translation in KJV (Lev 11:18; Deut 14:17) to "carrion vulture," which elsewhere is translated "osprey" (so NIV).

Glede. A vulture or hawk included in the list of unclean birds (Deut 14:13 KJV).

Great Owl. See *Owl.*

Gull. See *Cuckoo.*

Hawk. A general name applied to several small to medium-sized diurnal birds of prey, having short, rounded wings, hooked beaks, and claws. Kites, buzzards, harriers, falcons, and caracaras are included in the generic description, together with other members of the genus, *Accipiter.* All hawks were unclean and were not to be eaten (Lev 11:16; Deut 14:15). The impressive flying abilities of the hawk were compared to those of the eagle as the Lord answered Job out of the storm (Job 39:26–27). Found world-wide,

A hawk in flight. "Does the hawk take flight by your wisdom . . . ?" (Job 39:26). Courtesy Seffie Ben-Yoseph.

hawks usually nest in trees, though some, such as the marsh hawk, prefer a ground-level nest site in a suitable grassy environment. Others nest in cliffs.

Hen. See *Chicken.*

Heron. Listed among the unclean birds in Leviticus 11:19 and Deuteronomy 14:18, the heron is a long-necked, long-legged wading bird of the Ardeidae family, breeding in colonies with others in suitably high trees. Found throughout the world, herons are most concentrated in tropical regions, usually in marshy terrain. During biblical times large numbers of them populated the swamps surrounding Lake Huleh, and they were common also on the Jordan and the Kishon and on the coastal regions of Palestine. The heron's diet consists of fish, frogs, and other reptiles, caught while wading unobtrusively in shallow water. With its sharp-pointed, long and straight bill, the heron is ideally equipped to catch its prey.

Hoopoe. A solitary and somewhat timid bird, possessing a slender, down-curved bill and a long black-tipped erect crest, the hoopoe is found from southern Europe and Africa to SE Asia. It secures its diet of insects by thrusting its bill into the ground and foraging. This, together with its habit of fouling its own nest, may show why it was considered unclean (Lev 11:19; Deut 14:18 NASB, RSV, NIV).

A hoopoe, included in the lists of unclean birds (Lev 11:19). Courtesy Seffie Ben-Yoseph.

Horned Owl. See *Owl.*

Ibis. Included in the list of unclean birds (Lev 11:17 RSV), the ibis is a wading bird related to the stork and found mainly in tropical regions. It was regarded as sacred in ancient Egypt. The Greek historian Herodotus reported that the ibis was considered so sacred that anybody who killed one even accidentally was put to death.

Kite. A member of the hawk family, equipped with a short beak and long, pointed wings, the kite is found world-wide in warm regions. Its diet consists mostly of carrion and small birds, though some kites live on insects. Lightly built, the kite flies by a slow flapping of its wings and by effective gliding action. Its scavenging characteristics may account for its inclusion in the list of prohibited birds (Lev 11:14; Deut 14:13). American kites include the swallow-tailed kite, a black-and-white bird some two feet (one-half m.) in length, and the white-tailed kite, one of the few American birds of prey increasing in population.

Lapwing. A large, greenish-black and white plover found in Europe and Asia, the lapwing (sometimes known as the peewit) shows erratic flight during its breeding season. The Hebrew word in some versions (NIV, RSV, ASV) is rendered "hoopoe," but as "lapwing" in the KJV list of prohibited birds (Lev 11:19; Deut 14:18).

Lilith. See *Night Creature.*

Little Owl. See *Owl.*

Night Creature, Night Monster. A word appearing in an account of the desolation of Edom (Isa 34:14 ASV), and translated by many different terms. KJV has "screech owl," RV mg. "Lilith," RSV "night hag," NIV "night creature." Some have suggested a mythological interpretation of the term (Heb. *lîlîth*), but this finds scanty factual support. The reference could be to any of those nocturnal birds thought to bring omens, or to which superstitition might be attached.

Nighthawk. The name appears in the list of prohibited birds (Lev 11:16 KJV, RSV; Deut 14:15 KJV). Driver suggests "short-eared owl," NIV has "screech owl." The nighthawk, like the whippoorwill, is a small-beaked, insect-eating bird with impressive flying abilities.

Osprey, Ospray. The word is found among the list of unclean birds in Leviticus 11:18 and Deuteronomy 14:17 (RSV has "vulture" and "carrion vulture"). A large bird of the hawk family, the osprey is found in Europe, Asia, and North America. It has dark plumage with white underparts. Feeding on fish, the osprey is well-endowed with roughened pads on its feet in order to grasp its slippery prey.

Ossifrage. See *Osprey.*

Ostrich. The largest of all birds, up to eight feet (2.5 m.) tall, this nonflying, fast-running bird of Africa and Arabia is mainly vegetarian, able to

Wall relief (on the rock temple of Beit el-Wali in Nubia, Egypt) of an Ethiopian carrying an ostrich as a peace offering to Pharaoh Rameses II (thirteenth century B.C.). Courtesy B. Brandl.

do without water for considerable periods. Its long legs have two toes on each foot, and its long, featherless neck accounts for about half the total body weight. It is well adapted for its life in hot, dusty areas. In the wild, the ostrich lives in flocks and enjoys the company of other grazing animals. Job's essay on the ostrich (Job 39:13–18) confirms a keen observation of the bird. The author of Lamentations similarly thought ostriches were heartless (Lam 4:3). ASV translates Job's melancholy as being that of the ostrich's companion, rather than that of the owl, as translated elsewhere (Job 39:29). Jeremiah also referred to the dwelling of the ostrich among other desert creatures (Jer 50:39 NASB, RSV), just as Micah links the ostrich with desolation (Mic 1:18 ASV, RSV).

Owl. Any member of the order Strigformes, nocturnal birds of prey found throughout the world, in three families: typical owls (Strigidae), barn and grey owls (Tytonidae), and bay owls (Phodilidae). Equipped with a short, hooked beak set in a broad head, the owl has disc-shaped, forward-looking eyes, fringed with stiff feathers. Hearing and vision are acutely developed, fitting the owl for its nocturnal hunting pursuits. Prey consists of small birds and rodents. Hebrew names for the owl reflected the bird's own cry and nature. Thus Job confessed that he had become a companion of owls (Job 30:29), and the psalmist felt that he had become like an owl among the ruins (Ps 102:6). Isaiah declared that the great owl, desert owl, and screech owl would nest in the ruins of Edom (Isa 34:11), though the NIV footnote points out that precise identification is uncertain. Isaiah also referred to the owls nesting among the ruins of Edom in 34:15, in common with Jeremiah's own judgment on Babylon (Jer 50:39).

The "great owl" is listed among the unclean birds in Leviticus 11:18 (RSV "ibis") and in Deuteronomy 14:16. The "horned owl" also is listed among the unclean birds (Lev 11:16; Deut 14:15). Listed there also is the "little owl" (Lev 11:17; Deut 14:16), the most common owl in Palestine. The latter is noteworthy in its seeking of isolation, though its hoarse cry announces its presence to travelers.

Partridge. A member of the order of birds to which chickens belong. Because of their swift and sneaky running, they are excellent game birds. When Saul was hunting him, David compared himself to a partridge (1 Sam 26:20). It was supposed that partridges robbed eggs from other birds and hatched them, a symbol of getting riches unfairly (Jer 17:11).

Peacock. A male game bird, *Paro cristatus,* from India and SE Asia, best known for its handsome, long tail feathers, brought into a fan-shaped display during courtship. With their brightly colored bodies, peacocks were shown off in any self-respecting court in the ancient world and were a common feature of English country houses until fairly recent times. Large numbers of peacocks were imported for Solomon's palace (1 Kings 10:22; 2 Chron 9:21 KJV, RSV, NASB). NIV, however, translates the Hebrew as "baboon" (See ANIMALS). The Lord inquired of Job if he gave "goodly wings unto the peacocks" (Job

An owl perched between the rocks. Owls can be found in ruins, rock-hewn graves, and caves on both sides of the Jordan. "Their calls will echo through the windows" (Zeph 2:14). Courtesy Seffie Ben-Yoseph.

39:13 KJV), though NIV refers here to "ostrich" (cf. ASV).

Pelican. A gregarious web-footed water bird, equipped with a very large bill, beneath which is suspended a pouch for storing fish. The white pelican of Africa and Asia is the best known species, though pelicans may be found in many parts of the world. With a wingspan of up to ten feet (three m.) and a length up to six feet (almost two m.), the pelican is one of the world's largest birds. Its pursuit and capture of fish is helped by the webs between all four toes. Its flesh diet is one reason for its inclusion in the list of unclean birds (Lev 11:18; Deut 14:17 KJV, RSV, NASB; NIV has "desert owl").

The psalmist compared himself to a pelican in the wilderness (Ps 102:6 KJV, NASB, RSV), yet the pelican was to be incorporated into church tradition and even church architectural embellishment, because of a legend surrounding the bird. From early Christian times the pelican was regarded as pious. When feeding its young, the nesting adult excretes a liquid that adds a reddish tinge to its throat and breast, emphasized as the bird preens its feathers. It was suggested that the pelican was somehow sustaining its young with its own blood, and the "lesson drawn from nature" was soon offered to the saints.

Pigeon. See *Dove, Pigeon.*

Quail. A small migratory game bird, in some 130 species. The quail lives at ground level, in pasture, scrub-land, arable crops, etc. Ready to fly short distances at a comparatively rapid speed, the quail has some similarity to the partridge but is somewhat smaller, reaching a length of about seven inches (eighteen cm.). Like the partridge, the quail is a dust-bather and shares a similar diet of fruit, leaves, and insects.

In Bible times the quail was seen in large flocks, traveling most often over short distances. Its abundance as food for the Israelites in the wilderness came as large numbers of the Coturnix quail fell exhausted to the ground following the birds' long flight from Africa, where they had spent the winter (Exod 16:13; Ps 105:40). The abundance is graphically described in Numbers 11:31. The flesh of the quail is delicious, as are its eggs.

North American quail include the California or valley quail, as well as the desert quail—both being important game birds possessing forward curling head plume and somewhat stronger bills than are found in species of Europe, Asia, and Africa.

Raven. This large bird—the male of which can reach a length of two feet (one-half m.)—is a member of the crow family. It is found especially in the northern hemisphere in cliffs and mountainous terrain. In urban areas it is seen as a scavenger and will eat all kinds of animal flesh including carrion. Its head and shoulders are larger than those of a crow, and its soaring action is similar to that of a buzzard.

Leviticus 11:15 prohibits the eating of any kind of raven. Noah sent a raven from the ark to ascertain if a landfall might be made (Gen 8:7), apparently forgetting that, as the raven was a bird of prey, it was unlikely to return, given the abundance of carrion exposed by the receding waters. Nor did the raven have the homing instinct of the dove that subsequently carried out Noah's errand.

The record of Noah's dispatch of the raven and its apparent disloyalty, together with the bird's deep hoarse croak, accounts for some old beliefs. Proverbs 30:17 declares that any who mocked their fathers might expect to have their eye pecked out by the ravens of the valley. Yet ravens were used by God to feed Elijah (1 Kings 17:4), though some scholars have suggested here an alternative rendering to have Elijah fed by "human ravens," i.e., itinerant peddlers. Another suggestion is that Elijah was fed by citizens of the nearby town of Orbo. However, as ravens are ever generous in feeding their young, leaving some nests crowded with meat that could be eaten by a human being (after cooking or other preparation), the story has some validity. Ravens were themselves fed by the Lord (Job 38:41). Ravens would nest in the ruins of Edom, together with other birds of desolation (Isa 34:11).

Jesus referred to the ravens in his encouragement of the disciples and their immense significance to his heavenly Father (Luke 12:24).

Ravenous Bird. See *Bird of Prey.*

Rooster. See *Cock.*

Screech Owl. See *Owl; Night Monster.*

Sea Gull, Sea Mew. See *Cuckoo.*

Sparrow. A small, short-beaked, seed-eating bird—noisy, active, and prolific. The house sparrow, member of genus *Passer,* possesses brown/gray streaked plumage and was originally native to northern Europe and Asia. It has been introduced into Australasia and North America, where it is sometimes called the "English sparrow." In fact, it is classed by ornithologists as a finch, not as a sparrow. True sparrows, with other finches, buntings, and grosbeaks, are members of the family Fringillidae, a large group with many subdivisions.

In Bible times protection to the sparrow was provided within the temple precincts (Ps 84:3). Sparrows were so cheap to buy that the purchaser of four would get a fifth free. Yet even this seemingly unimportant bird was of great concern to the Lord, without whose knowledge no sparrow fell to the ground, but who accounted people far more highly (Matt 10:29, 31; Luke 12:6, 7). KJV refers to the psalmist's identification as being that of a sparrow alone on a housetop, a somewhat unusual sight (Ps 102:7). NIV renders "bird" rather than "sparrow," for the Hebrew word possibly means "rock thrust," a bird known to prefer isolated places.

Stork. A large migratory bird of the Ciconiidae family, nesting in trees. Equipped with long legs, neck, and bill, the stork usually lives on a diet of small animals caught at ground level. Some species, including the maribou stork of Africa and the adjutant stork of India, feed on carrion.

Nesting characteristics of the stork "in the pine trees" were noted by the psalmist (Ps 104:17),

Storks in their nest. Says the Psalmist: "The stork has its home in the pine trees" (Ps 104:17). Courtesy Seffie Ben-Yoseph.

and Jeremiah confirmed that the stork knew its appointed seasons (Jer 8:7). Here, as elsewhere in the passage, Jeremiah contrasted the alertness of the bird to natural law with the carelessness of men. Zechariah's vision included women equipped with the powerful wings of a stork (Zech 5:9). The stork was included in the list of prohibited birds (Lev 11:19; Deut 14:18).

Swallow. An insect-eating bird of the Hirundinidae family, small and with a long forked tail and long wings. Among the most agile of birds, it captures its insect prey while in flight. Its skill in executing maneuvers was noted by the author of Proverbs (26:2) while the piercing chatterlike call of the swallow was compared to the chattering of Hezekiah during his illness (Isa 38:14 NASB, KJV, RSV). Five species are still found in Bible lands. Two of these are known also in the United States—the bank swallow and the barn swallow, the latter recognized by its deeply forked tail feathers.

Swan. A large aquatic bird in the same family as the duck and goose, of genus *Cygnus*. Equipped with webbed feet and a long slender neck, the swan is usually white and mute. In the list of unclean birds it is called "water hen" in RSV, "horned owl" in ASV, and "white owl" in NIV (Lev 11:18; Deut 14:16).

Swift. Any member of the Apodidae family of migratory birds, resembling swallows and having long wings reminiscent of the shape of a scythe. That the swift knew the time of its seasons (i.e., for migration) was confirmed by Jeremiah (8:7, NASB, NIV). The record of Hezekiah's illness also refers to the swift (Isa 38:14 NIV) in preference to the use of "swallow" found in KJV, NASB, RSV.

Thrush. See *Crane*.

Turtledove. Found in southern Europe and in Africa, the turtledove—a wild pigeon of migratory habit (*Streptopelia turtur*)—is similar to the "mourning dove," which sings early in spring. Song of Songs 2:12 probably refers to such a bird. These were the birds that, abundant in number, were readily acquired for ceremonial sacrifice (Gen 15:9). Purification after childbirth involved sacrifice of this bird or a young pigeon (Lev 12:6–8). It was used in ceremonial cleansing (Num 6:10). Translations vary in Jeremiah 8:7: 'dove" (NEB, NIV), "turtle" (KJV), and "turtledove" (JB, MLB, NASB, RSV).

Vulture. A large carrion-eating bird equipped with a hooked beak and strong claws. Some twenty species in the order Falconiformes have featherless heads and necks, as well as large crops. The Andean condor is probably the best known of vultures found in the American continent, though vultures exist in central Europe, Asia, and parts of Africa. Also found in America is the black vulture, sometimes called "black buzzard" or "carrion crow," and the king vulture.

One of the largest and heaviest birds in the world, the cinereous (gray colored) vulture (*Aegypius monachus*) has a wingspread of some nine feet (three m.), is three or more feet (one m.) long, and weighs over twenty-seven pounds (twelve kg.). It is found in southern Europe, northern and eastern Africa, and the Middle East to Afghanistan and India. Another impressive member of the species is the Nubian or lappet-faced vulture found in Africa.

Little seems to discourage these large birds in their search for food, and the people of Bible times were accustomed to seeing vultures—and not merely on the battlefield or where carrion was plentiful. Sometimes they would descend to make a raid in some town. Some five species were known in those times. The bearded vulture was easily identified by its full-feathered head and black moustache feathers. The Egyptian vulture was a smaller bird with white feathers on its head, black flight feathers, and a weak, slender beak. Sometimes called Pharaoh's chicken, the Egyptian vulture grew to a length of about two feet (one-half m.). Three further types found in the area were all black and virtually bald.

Deuteronomy 14:12 prohibits eating the vulture. Jesus reminded his hearers that vultures eagerly gather around a carcass (Matt 24:28; Luke 17:37 NIV, NASB). Translations vary in Isaiah 34:15—"vultures" (KJV, MLB), "hawks" (NASB), "falcons" (NIV), and "kites" (RSV).

BIRSHA (bîr′shȧ). The king of Gomorrah who was defeated by Kedorlaomer (Gen 14:2).

BIRTH. The bringing forth of a separate life into the world. Although this is accompanied by rending pain, there is no evidence that such pain would have occurred had not sin entered the human race. (See Gen 3:16 where pain in childbearing is a part of the curse on Eve for her sin.) This pain is so uniquely severe that in nine-tenths of the forty-odd uses of the word "travail" in the KJV it is used as a figure for intense suffering (e.g., Jer 13:21; Rom 8:22; Gal 4:19). Apparently the ancient Hebrew women went

Terracotta figurine of a pregnant woman, carved in Syrian-Phoenician style, from Aczib, c. seventh century B.C. Courtesy Israel Department of Antiquities and Museums. Exhibited and photographed by Israel Museum, Jerusalem.

through travail more easily than the Egyptians did (Exod 1:19).

The day of one's birth is, in a sense, the most important day of one's life, for without it the individual would not have had life in the world; and so the celebration of birthdays goes back into very ancient times (Gen 40:20; Matt 14:6). The Hebrew ceremonies connected with childbirth are given in Leviticus 12. The permission to the poor to offer "a pair of turtledoves or two young pigeons" in place of a lamb (Luke 2:24) gives touching testimony to the comparative poverty of Mary, the mother of Jesus. Our Lord, in John 3:3–6, makes a clear distinction between the first and second births of a regenerate person; and when this distinction is applied, it seems almost to make two different species of the human race: the once-born and the regenerate. The former are depraved, and unless they repent they are destined for judgment (Heb 9:27; 10:31); the latter are being made partakers in the divine nature (2 Peter 1:4) and are destined for glory. ABF

BIRTHRIGHT. From time immemorial a man's firstborn son has been given privileges above those of his younger sons. This is illustrated today by the order of succession to the throne (in Britain, for instance). Among the Israelites God had a special claim on the firstborn, at least from the time of the Exodus, when he destroyed the firstborn of Egypt and claimed those of Israel by right of redemption (Exod 13:2, 12–16). The birthright included a double portion of the inheritance (Deut 21:15–17) and the privilege of priesthood (Exod 13:1–2; 24:5); but in Israel God later set apart the tribe of Levi instead of the firstborn for that service. (Note Num 3:38–51, where the Levites are about the same in number as the firstborn of Israel.) Esau lost his birthright by selling it to Jacob for some stew, and no regret could undo the loss he had brought on himself. (See Gen 25:27–34; Heb 12:16; and compare the destinies of Israel and of Edom; see also Obad 17–18.) In Israel, Reuben lost his birthright through sin, and his brothers Simeon and Levi lost theirs through violence; and so the blessing came to Judah (Gen 49:3–10).

BIRZAITH (bĭr-zā'ĭth). Either a son of Malkiel of the tribe of Asher (1 Chron 7:31) or a village whose people were descendants of Malkiel.

BISHLAM (bĭsh'lăm). An officer of Artaxerxes (Cambyses) who opposed the rebuilding of the temple (Ezra 4:7).

BISHOP (Gr. *episkopos, overseer*). Originally the principal officer of the local church, the other being the deacon or deacons (1 Tim 3:1–7). The title "elder" or "presbyter" generally applied to the same man; "elder" referring to his age and dignity, and "bishop" to his work of superintendence. As the churches multiplied, the bishop of a larger church would often be given special honor, and so gradually there grew up a hierarchy, all the way from presiding elders to bishops (over groups of churches), then archbishops.

BITHIAH (bĭ-thī'à, *daughter of Jehovah*). The name suggests that she was a convert to Judaism. She is called a daughter of Pharaoh. Mentioned only in 1 Chronicles 4:18 as wife of Mered of the tribe of Judah.

BITHRON (bĭth'rŏn, *rough country*). A region in the tribe of Gad between the Jordan and Mahanaim. Mentioned only in 2 Samuel 2:29.

BITHYNIA (bĭ-thĭn'ĭ-à, Gr. *Bithynia*). A region along the northern edge of Asia Minor fronting on the Black Sea, the Bosphorus, and the Sea of Marmara. Paul and his companions desired to enter Bithynia with the gospel (Acts 16:6–10), but the Holy Spirit was leading toward Europe, and so they could not enter. However, there were Christians there in the first century (1 Peter 1:1). The Roman governor Pliny the Younger complained to Trajan concerning the Christians and at the beginning of the second century asked how to deal with them.

Bithynia was settled very early, and its known history goes back past the sixth century B.C. when Croesus made it a part of his kingdom. A king of Bithynia in the third century B.C. invited the Gauls into Asia, so originating "Galatia." From the thirteenth century on, it has been Turkish, or at least ruled by the Turks.

BITTER HERBS (See PLANTS)

BITTERN (See BIRDS)

BITUMEN (bī-tū'mĕn). A mineral pitch widely scattered over the earth, and one of the best waterproofing substances known. It was used with tar to cover the ark of bulrushes (Exod 2:3) and to waterproof Noah's ark (Gen 6:14). It was also used for mortar in the tower of Babel (11:3), and to represent a curse on Edom (Isa 34:9). There were great deposits near the Dead Sea and at different places in Mesopotamia. The principal modern source is a great lake of pitch on the island of Trinidad.

BIZIOTHIAH (bĭz'ĭ-ō-thī'ăh, *contempt of Jehovah*). A town in southern Judah in Joshua's time (Josh 15:28).

BIZTHA, BIZTHAH (bĭz'thȧ). One of the seven chamberlains in the court of Xerxes (Ahasuerus) who were commanded to bring out Queen Vashti for exhibition (Esth 1:10).

BLACKSMITH (See OCCUPATIONS AND PROFESSIONS)

BLASPHEMY (blăs'fē-mē, Gr. *blasphēmia*). To reproach or to bring a railing accusation against any one is bad enough (Jude 9), but to speak lightly or carelessly of God is a mortal sin. The third commandment, "You shall not misuse the name of the LORD your God" (Exod 20:7), was observed so meticulously by the Jews that they would not speak the sacred name (Jehovah) at all, and so no one knows today for certain how it was pronounced. In the Hebrew Bible the consonants of the "sacred tetragrammaton" (YHWH) occur over six thousand times, always with the vowels for the Hebrew word for "LORD." Before his conversion, Paul blasphemed (1 Tim 1:13) and tried to force Christians to blaspheme (Acts 26:11). The Jews, with a peculiar sense of humor, sometimes used the word "to bless" to mean "to curse" or "to blaspheme" (1 Kings 21:10, 13; Job 1:5, 11; 2:5, 9). God prescribed that in Israel the punishment for blasphemy would be death by stoning (Lev 24:10–16). Naboth was falsely charged with blasphemy and was stoned to death (1 Kings 21:10–13), as was Stephen (Acts 6:11). Stoning was also in the minds of those who charged Jesus with blasphemy (Matt 9:3; 26:65; Luke 5:31; John 10:33); what Jesus said about himself would have been blasphemy were it not true. See also UNPARDONABLE SIN.

BLASTUS (blăs'tŭs, Gr. *Blastos*). A chamberlain of King Agrippa (Acts 12:20) who apparently was easily bribed. The men of Tyre and Sidon used him in approaching the king.

BLESS, BLESSING (Heb. *bārakh*). 1. God blesses nature (Gen 1:22), mankind (1:28), the Sabbath (2:3), nations (Ps 33:12), classes of men (1:1–3), and individuals (Gen 24:1).

2. Godly men should "bless" God; i.e., they should adore him, worship him, and praise him (Ps 103:1–2). The same word is used for what a worshiper offers to God (blessing) and seeks from him (blessing). When we "bless" God, we bring his glories before our mind and respond in worship and adoration; when we ask him to "bless" us, we invite him to call our needs to mind and respond in meeting them.

3. Godly people by words and actions can bestow blessings on their fellows (Matt 5:44; 1 Peter 3:9).

4. In Bible times, godly men under inspiration bestowed prophetic blessings on their progeny; e.g., Noah blessed Japheth and Shem (Gen 9:26–27), Isaac blessed Jacob and Esau (27:27–29, 39–40), Jacob blessed the tribes of Israel (ch 49), and Moses also blessed them (Deut 33).

5. We can bless things when we set them apart for sacred use, e.g., the "communion cup" (1 Cor 10:16).

BLESSING, THE CUP OF (KJV, RSV, ASV, "cup of thanksgiving" in NIV). In the "communion" service, the church blesses the cup when it is set apart for the Lord's Supper (1 Cor 10:16).

BLINDNESS (See DISEASES)

BLOOD. The word occurs over four hundred times in the Bible and is especially frequent in Leviticus. The circulation of the blood was not known until long after Scripture was written, and for the most part Bible references are directed toward the practical observation that loss of blood leads to loss of vitality and that a draining away of the blood leads to death. Genesis 9:5 says (literally), "Your blood, belonging to your lives, I will seek . . . from the hand of man . . . I will seek the life of man." "Seek" means, in this verse, "seek requital." In this verse "seeking your blood" is parallel with "seeking the life," and both mean exacting the death penalty. When blood is shed, life is terminated, and the Lord seeks requital for the shedding of blood by demanding the life of the murderer (cf. Gen 37:26; Ps 30:9; 58:10). The statement "Your blood be on your own head" (e.g., 2 Sam 1:16) witnesses to the same understanding of things: a person guilty of murder must pay with his life. Our concern here is not the question of the death penalty, but the way in which the Bible uses "blood" as a metaphor for "death." When blood is spoken of as the life of the flesh (Gen 9:4; cf. Lev 17:11), the meaning is the practical one that flesh and blood in their proper union constitute a living creature, beast or man, but that when they are separated death takes place. The bearing of this on the use of blood in the sacrifices is most important. For further discussion see SACRIFICE.

Bibliography: V. Taylor, *Jesus and His Sacrifice,* 1937; A. M. Stibbs, *The Meaning of the Word "Blood" in Scripture,* 1947; Leon Morris, *The Apostolic Preaching of the Cross,* 1955. JAM

BLOOD, AVENGER OF. Genesis 9:6 states the biblical law of equity that the taking of life by murder requires the taking of the life of the murderer as a judicial penalty. The OT recognizes in this connection both the function of the courts (e.g., Exod 24:12; Deut 19:15–21) and the rights of the family of the murdered person. The next of kin was permitted to exact the death penalty. The word that is questionably translated "avenger" (e.g., Num 35:12) is properly "next of kin" or "redeemer" (*go'el*). Not only in capital cases but in all the vicissitudes of life, the *go'el* was at hand to take on himself whatever need oppressed his close relative. For this reason "redeemer" became one of the most beautiful and theologically significant descriptions of the Lord in relation to his people (e.g., Isa 43:14). See also REDEMPTION. To prevent the work of the "avenger" from becoming a family vendetta, OT law appointed cities of refuge to which one guilty of manslaughter (not of murder) could flee for safety and where the avenger was not permitted to enter; also the OT insisted that children could not be punished for a parent's crime or vice versa (Deut 24:16). JAM

BLOOD, ISSUE OF (See DISEASES)

BLOODY SWEAT (See DISEASES)

BOANGERGES (bō'á-nûr'jēz, *sons of thunder*). A title given by the Lord to the two brothers James and John, the sons of Zebedee (Mark 3:17), probably because of their temperamental violence (cf. Luke 9:54–56).

BOAR (See ANIMALS)

BOAZ (bō'ăz, Heb. *bō'az*). A well-to-do Bethlehemite in the days of the judges who became an ancestor of Jesus by marrying Ruth, the Moabitess, widow of one of the sons of Elimelech (Ruth 2–4). This was in accordance with the levirate law of Deuteronomy 25:5–10; Boaz could marry Ruth only after the nearer kinsman (Ruth 3:12; 4:1–8) had refused the privilege—or the duty. The other refused because if he had married Ruth and had had a son, a portion of his property would have gone to the credit of Elimelech's posterity, instead of his own by a former marriage. It is impossible to date Boaz exactly, because the genealogy of Ruth 4:18–22 (given in Matt 1:4–6) is almost certainly a partial list, giving ten names to cover eight hundred years. The list in Matthew 1 is demonstrably schematic, as it omits names of four kings, and this one in Ruth is almost as surely partial also. They are both accurate but, like most genealogies, partial. Salmon (or Salmah), given here as the father of Boaz, lived at the time of the Conquest, for he married Rahab; but the general setting of the story is that of a later period of settled life.

BOAZ AND JACHIN (See TEMPLE)

BOCHERU (See BOKERU)

BOCHIM (See BOKIM)

BODY (Gr. *sōma*). The word has a wide range of meaning in the NT. It can refer to a corpse (Matt 27:52), one's physical body (Mark 5:29), and the human self expressed in and through a body (Heb 10:10; 1 Peter 2:24). As a Jewish thinker, Paul saw the body not merely as an outer shell to house the soul/spirit, but as the expression of the whole person (Rom 12:1). So he warned against the misuse of the body (1 Cor 6:13ff.), especially since it is the temple of the Holy Spirit in the case of the believer (6:15, 19). However, the body is affected by sin and so may be called the "body of sin" (Rom 6:6) and "body of death" (7:24). Even so, Paul's use of "body" must be distinguished from his use of "flesh." The latter always points to the principle of sin endemic in human nature.

As there is a physical body for this life, so there is a spiritual body for the life of the age to come after the resurrection (1 Cor 15:38ff.). The present body, which is affected by sin, will be replaced by a body whose nature is spirit and which is pure and glorious—like Christ's resurrection body.

In the Lord's Supper the bread symbolizes the body of Jesus offered as a sacrifice for sin (Mark 14:22; 1 Cor 11:24). Further, the local church, which meets for the Lord's Supper as believing disciples, is called by Paul a "body" (Rom 12:4–5; 1 Cor 12:12ff.) as is the universal church, "the body of Christ" (Eph 4:12).

The OT does not have one word that has the range of meaning possessed by *sōma.*

Bibliography: R. H. Gundry, *Sōma in Biblical Theology,* 1976. PT

BODY OF CHRIST. Within the NT this may be understood in three ways:

1. As the natural, human body of Jesus that the eternal Son made his own in the womb of Mary, and in which he offered himself as a sacrifice for the sin of the world (Heb 10:10). This body was transformed from a physical into a spiritual body in resurrection and then taken to heaven in ascension. Yet it remains a human body, and thus he who sits at the right hand of the Father as coregent is still the God-Man.

2. As the people of God or the church (local and universal) united to Christ in grace by faith and through baptism. Believers are "one body in Christ" (Rom 12:5) in each locality and, as a

universal community, are the "body of Christ" (Eph 4:12) ruled and sustained by Christ, the Head (5:23).

3. As the bread used at the Last Supper by Jesus and then as the bread used in Holy Communion by believers. "This is my body," said Jesus (Matt 26:26). As his body (bread) was broken on the cross and as by eating the Passover meal the Israelites had been associated with delivery from Egypt and bondage, so the believers participate in the saving work of Christ on the cross by taking this bread (and wine). PT

BOHAN (bō'hăn). A descendant of Reuben after whom a stone was named (Josh 15:6; 18:17). The stone was on the boundary between the tribes of Judah and Benjamin and was NW of the northern end of the Dead Sea and NE of Jerusalem.

BOIL (See DISEASES)

BOKERU (bō'kê-rū). A distant descendant of Saul, at the time of the return from captivity (1 Chron 8:38). One of the six sons of Azel.

BOKIM (bō'kĭm, *weepers*). A name given to the place where the angel of the Lord appeared and rebuked the children of Israel because of their failure to drive out the heathen and to destroy their places of worship (Judg 2:1–5).

BONE. In the living body, bones form the strong framework, and the connotation is one of strength. "Bone of my bones and flesh of my flesh" (Gen 2:23) was spoken in a literal sense of Eve; but almost the same words (29:14), spoken by Laban to Jacob, are figurative and show only kinship. Strong chastening is thought of as a bone-breaking experience (Ps 51:8), and the terrible writhing on the cross of Calvary literally threw bones out of joint (22:14). Dry bones form a picture of hopeless death (Ezek 37:1–12). The Passover lamb, without a broken bone (Exod 12:46), was a type of the Lamb of God (John 19:36).

BOOK. Generally a literary production having more or less unity of purpose. Books may be classified by their forms or subjects, but more particularly by the nature and quality of the written material within. In ancient Assyria and Babylonia much of the writing that was thought to be of value was done in wedge-shaped characters on soft clay that was then baked, and the "libraries" were, in form, almost like piles of brick.

In ancient Egypt, the people early learned to press and glue thin sheets of the papyrus plant into sheets of "paper"; the writing was in narrow columns on sheets of regular size that were then glued together and wound around two sticks, thus forming a "volumen" or roll. Still later, men learned to bind the sheets together into a "codex," very similar to our modern books. "Book" in the Bible always refers to a roll or scroll, a word that

Books from the Nag Hamadi library. (Nag Hamadi, the location where the papyri were found in 1946, is in Upper Egypt.) The library includes a collection (ascribed to the apostle Thomas) of 114 sayings of Christ. Courtesy Institute for Antiquity and Christianity, Claremont, California.

occurs fourteen times in Jeremiah 36. In Pergamum, in the second century B.C., due to the scarcity of paper, men learned to dress the skin of calves and of kids as a writing material. This new substance was named "parchment" in honor of its place of origin and almost displaced papyrus in many regions.

In ancient books made of papyrus or parchment, the writing was generally done on one side of each sheet, but occasionally, owing to afterthoughts, material was written also on the back side (see Rev 5:1). When a book was sealed, the contents were made secret, and when unsealed

Ancient scroll held by a Samaritan priest. Courtesy S. Zur Picture Library.

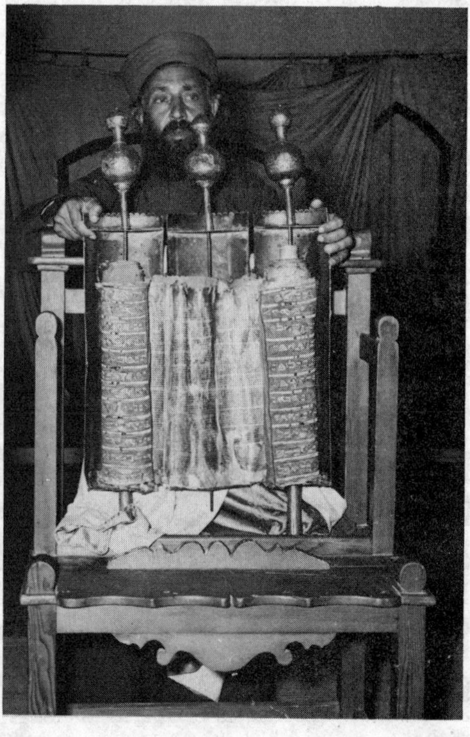

they were open (cf. Dan 12:4, 9; Rev 5:1–4 on the one hand and Rev 5:5; 22:10 on the other). Only the Son of God was found worthy to open the seals of the book of the future that had been locked in the hands of "him that sat on the throne."

Judaism, Christianity, and Islam are all religions of a book, and their main books have greatly changed the history of the human race.

The Bible is *the* book, God's Word, and it differs from all other books in that it alone is inspired (God-breathed). The Bible originally had sixty-three books, as the division of Samuel, Kings, and Chronicles into "First" and "Second" was not originally intended. The larger books were generally written on separate rolls (see Luke 4:17) but sometimes the "megilloth" (Ruth, Esther, Lamentations, Song of Songs, and Ecclesiastes) were bound together, as were also "The Twelve" (i.e., the Minor Prophets). Many books that have been lost are mentioned in the Bible: e.g., "the book of Jashar" (Josh 10:13), "the book of the annals of Solomon" (1 Kings 11:41). The word "book" is also used figuratively, as in "the Lamb's book of life" (Rev 21:27). ABF

Shelter or booth constructed of tree branches with leaves on the roof of a mud-brick house. Courtesy Seffie Ben-Yoseph.

BOOTH. A simple, temporary shelter generally constructed of tree branches with the leaves left on. It was used by the guardian of a vineyard or vegetable garden when the fruit was fit to be stolen. Sometimes this word describes a larger enclosure (Gen 33:17) such as Jacob built for his cattle (cf. Isa 1:8 ASV).

BOOTY. Goods taken from a defeated enemy. In the law as given through Moses, very different arrangements were made for varying circumstances. In the case of some cities whose people were extremely wicked, everything was to be "devoted" to the Lord; i.e., it was to be destroyed absolutely so as not to be used by anyone, except for some metallic vessels that could be sterilized by fire (Josh 6:18–21). Persons could sometimes be enslaved (Deut 20:14), but in other cases they had to be utterly destroyed (20:16–18). The purpose here was to prevent the pagans from teaching their abominations to God's people

Sennacherib seated on a high throne receiving prisoners and spoils from Lachish. Inscription before him reads: "Sennacherib, king of the world, king of Assyria, sat upon a . . . throne and passed in review the booty (taken) at Lachish." Gypsum relief from Kuyunjik, 704–681 B.C. Reproduced by courtesy of the Trustees of the British Museum.

Israel (cf. 1 Sam 15, where Saul's hypocritical half-obedience brought ruin on himself and his house).

The very practical question as to the division of the booty was solved partly by custom, as when Abram freely devoted a tenth of the spoil to the Lord by giving it to Melchizedek (Gen 14:20), and partly by legislation, as when David ordered that booty be shared equally by those who because of weariness could not continue in battle (1 Sam 30:21–25).

BOR ASHAN (See ASHAN)

BORROW, BORROWING. Several times in the OT the Hebrew word *shā'al* is translated by the verb "borrow." This occurs three times in the context of the people of Israel "borrowing" extensively from the Egyptians (Exod 3:22; 11:2; 12:35). The fact is that the Egyptians, thoroughly cowed by the rigors of the ten plagues, were willing to give generously in order to get rid of their troublesome "guests"; and God, in his providence, allowed Israel to despoil the Egyptians (Exod 12:36) in order to provide gold and silver for the tabernacle that was to be constructed. "Surely your wrath against men brings you praise" (Ps 76:10).

The Law of Moses gives careful direction concerning the responsibility of those who borrow or who hold property in trust or who are criminally careless in regard to the property of another (Exod 22:1–15). Among the blessings promised Israel on condition of obedience is that they would be lenders, not borrowers (Deut 15:6; 28:12). Also, Jesus instructed his followers to not turn away those who wanted to borrow from them (Matt 5:42). Generally the borrower is the servant of the lender (Prov 22:7), but God's judgment can erase differences (Isa 24:2).

Water carrier in Jerusalem bearing a container made from goat skin. Picture taken around the turn of the century. Courtesy University Library, Istanbul.

BOSCATH (See BOZKATH)

BOSOM. Although in English the word means the part of the body between the arms, in Scripture it is generally used in an affectionate sense, e.g., "the only Son, who is in the bosom of the Father" (John 1:18 RSV), carrying the lambs in his bosom (Isa 40:11 KJV), or Lazarus resting in Abraham's bosom (Luke 16:22–23 KJV). It can be almost synonymous with "heart" as the center of one's life (cf. Ps 35:13; Eccl 7:9 KJV). Quite commonly, of course, it refers to conjugal love, as in Micah 7:5 (KJV; NIV "embrace"). In Proverbs 17:23, KJV and RSV, we read of the bosom as a place of hiding money (NIV, "accepts a bribe in secret").

BOTCH (See DISEASES)

BOTTLE. 1. A container made of goat-skin, sewed up with the hair outside and used for carrying water (Gen 21:14–19), for storing wine (Josh 9:4, 13), and for fermenting milk into "leben" or "yogurt" (Judg 4:19). The fact that fermenting wine expands and stretches its container is used by Jesus in his discourse about putting new wine into old bottles (Luke 5:37–38). A new skin bottle would be elastic enough to stretch with the pressure of the fermenting wine, whereas an old, stiff wineskin would burst. Our Lord's teaching here is that Christianity cannot be contained in Judaism, nor can grace be confined in the bonds of the law. This meaning of "bottles" is used figuratively by Elihu in Job 32:19 as indicating his feeling that he must find relief by speaking.

2. A container made of baked clay, and therefore very fragile (Jer 19:1–11). As Jeremiah broke the bottle, so God would deal in fury with Israel.

3. Beautifully designed glass bottles, often found in Egyptian tombs, were used originally for burying some of the tears of the mourners with the deceased. See Psalm 56:8, KJV: "Put thou my tears into thy bottle"; NIV, "list my tears on your scroll," but with the footnote "put my tears in your wineskin."

4. The word translated "bottles" in Hosea 7:5 by KJV is handled differently by NIV, which makes the context "inflamed with wine."

5. Figuratively, the clouds as the source of rain (Job 38:37; NIV "water jars of the heavens").

6. Psalm 119:83: "Though I am like a wineskin [bottle] in the smoke" does not refer, as some think, to a custom, but rather to careless housekeeping. In the smoke of a kitchen without windows or chimney, a leather vessel that hung there would soon become brittle and dry. ABF

BOTTOMLESS PIT (See ABYSS)

BOUNDARY STONES. Our God is a God of order and not of confusion. He not only set careful bounds to the land of his people (Josh 13–21), but also provided a curse for those who removed their neighbors' landmarks (Deut 27:17;

cf. 19:14). Figuratively, the expression implies a decent regard for ancient institutions (Prov 22:28; 23:10).

BOW (See ARMS AND ARMOR; RAINBOW)

BOWELS. In the KJV the word occurs thirty-six times and in three principal senses:

1. Literally (2 Chron 21:15–19; Acts 1:18).
2. As the generative parts of the body, whether male or female (Gen 15:4; Ps 71:6).
3. The seat of the emotions, as we use the word "heart." See Lamentations 1:20 (ASV, NIV "heart"); Philippians 1:8 (ASV "tender mercies"; NIV "affection").

BOWL. A number of Hebrew and Greek words are rendered "bowl."

1. *Sēphel,* a large, flat earthenware dish for holding a liquid, such as milk (Judg 5:25).
2. *Mizrāq,* sometimes also translated "basin." Large costly bowls, like the silver bowls presented by the princes of the congregation (Num 7:13–14).
3. *Gāvia',* translated "pot" by the KJV in Jeremiah 35:5; a large silver bowl like the kind used at banquets to replenish drinking cups.
4. *Gullâh,* the receptacle for oil in the candlestick of Zechariah's vision (Zech 4:3), and the bowl-shaped capitals of the temple pillars Jachin and Boaz (1 Kings 7:41–42; 2 Chron 4:12–13).
5. *Kubba'ath kôs,* RV "bowl of the cup"; KJV "dregs of the cup" (Isa 51:21–22).
6. *Phialē,* RSV, NEB, NIV "bowl," KJV "vial" (Rev 5:8; 15:7; 16:1).

Boundary stone of Meli-Shipak, on which many symbols and objects are depicted. Text on back deals with a grant made to the son of the king, Marduk-apal-iddin, and ends with a list of gods invoked for cursing any who disrespect the terms of the grant. Apparently a boundary stone for an estate. Courtesy Carta, Jerusalem.

Boundary stone of Nebuchadnezzar I (65 cm. high), picturing symbols of gods and goddesses. The inscription (not shown) describes the military services that Ritti-Marduk rendered to Nebuchadnezzar and the terms of the charter granted to Ritti-Marduk by the king. Reproduced by courtesy of the Trustees of the British Museum.

BOX TREE (See Plants)

BOZEZ (bō'zĕz). A rocky crag near Gibeah (1 Sam 14:4). Because one of General Allenby's officers read this account, the British followed the route of Jonathan and attacked the Turks here in A.D. 1918, conquering them even as Jonathan and his armor-bearer defeated the Philistines.

BOZKATH, BOSCATH (bŏz'kăth). A city of Judah (Josh 15:39), the home of the maternal grandfather of King Josiah (2 Kings 22:1).

BOZRAH (bŏz'rȧ, Heb. *bōtsrâh, sheepfold*). 1. An important city of Edom, the residence of Jobab, one of Edom's early kings (Gen 36:33). In Jeremiah 49:13, 22, where the approaching doom of Edom is given, Bozrah is especially mentioned, and in Amos 1:12 we read of its palaces. The place is identified as the modern village of "el-Busaireh," i.e., "the little Bozrah," a few miles SE of the Dead Sea near the road toward Petra. In Micah 2:12 the word is probably Bozrah, though it can be read as a common noun, i.e., "a sheepfold," "sheep in a pen," NIV.

2. In Jeremiah 48:24 the word refers to a town in Moab. It lies about 75 miles (125 km.) south of Damascus and was enlarged and beautified (c. A.D. 106) by Emperor Trajan who made it the capital of the province of Arabia.

BRACELET. Properly a circlet for the wrist, but the word translates in the KJV five different Hebrew nouns. In 2 Samuel 1:10 the word probably means "armlet" as a mark of royalty (NIV, "band on his arm"); in Exodus 35:22 it could be "brooches" as in ASV, NIV, or "clasps"; in Genesis 38:18, 25 it represents the cord about the neck from which the signet ring was suspended; in Genesis 24:22, 30, 47, it is properly "bracelet" (so NIV), from the root meaning "something bound on"; in Ezekiel 16:11; 23:42; and in Isaiah 3:19, in the interesting inventory of twenty-one items of feminine adornment, it could be rendered "twisted chains." Bracelets and other showy adornments (anklets, nose-rings, armlets, etc.) were much admired in ancient days. See also Dress.

BRAMBLE (See Plants)

BRANCH. A word representing eighteen different Hebrew and four Greek words in the Bible, most notably as a title applied to the Messiah as the offspring of David (Jer 23:5; 33:15; Zech 3:8; 6:12).

BRASS (See Minerals)

BRAY. 1. The ass brays when hungry (Job 6:5), and some crude, uncouth people are described contemptuously as braying (30:7).

2. To pound as in a mortar (Prov 27:22 KJV; NIV "grind"). This word, related to the verb "to break," is rare both in English and in Hebrew, but is easily understood by the context.

BRAZEN SEA (See Bronze Sea)

BRAZEN SNAKE (See Bronze Snake)

BREAD. The "staff of life," generally baked from dough made of wheat flour that has been leavened (raised by means of fermenting yeast) and made into loaves of various shapes and sizes. At the time of the Passover (Exod 12) the Israelites ate unleavened bread because of their haste, and ever afterward they memorialized this in their annual feast of unleavened bread (12:15–20). The poorer people usually used barley instead of wheat to make the bread for this feast, and in times of distress and of famine most of the people used barley. In Judges 7:13, the Midianite's dream of a barley loaf, which was interpreted as "the sword of Gideon," perhaps hinted at the poverty of Israel under Midianite oppression; and in John

Wooden model of Egyptian bakery and brewery, from tomb of Meket-Re at Thebes, 11th Dynasty (c. 2000 B.C.). The room nearest entrance door (upper part of photo) is the brewery; the adjoining room is the bakery. The staff is shown treading and kneading dough, pounding grain with a pestle, mixing dough, and tending ovens. Courtesy The Metropolitan Museum of Art, Museum Excavations, 1919–20; Rogers Fund supplemented by contribution of Edward S. Harkness (20.3.12).

6:9 the boy's store of five barley loaves suggests that he came from a family or a region that could not afford the more delicious and nutritious wheat bread. Ezekiel 4:9–17 gives a vivid picture of baking in famine times.

In the more primitive parts of Syria today there are several sorts of wheat bread. In some villages a barrel-shaped hole in the ground is used as an oven; the women adroitly knead the bread into large thin sheets that they lay on cushions and slap against the hot wall of the oven. Though dried dung mixed with straw is used as fuel to preheat the oven, the taste is not impaired. In other villages of Syria, a convex sheet of iron is placed over an open fire and the bread is similarly baked; but in the larger towns and cities there are bakeries to which the people bring their loaves for baking. The long stone oven is heated for hours, then the raised loaves, about eight to ten inches (twenty-one to twenty-six cm.) in diameter and one-fourth inch (about one cm.) thick, are placed

Brickmaking scene from tomb painting at Thebes, fifteenth century B.C., showing workmen with hoes kneading clay as laborers carry material to brickmakers. Courtesy Carta, Jerusalem.

inside by means of a long wooden paddle. The heat quickly bakes the surface, and gas forming inside splits the loaves, which are then turned and soon removed (Hos 7:8).

The word "bread," depicting the most universal solid food, is often used figuratively for food in general. Genesis 3:19, "by the sweat of your brow you will eat your food" (KJV "bread"); Matthew 6:11, "Give us today our daily bread," and similar passages refer to all sustenance. The word "bread" is used by the Lord in a mystical but very true and precious sense in his discourse on "the bread of life" in John 6:43–59. As important as bread (i.e., solid food) is to our bodies, so necessary is the Lord to spiritual life. And so, in the "breaking of bread" at our "communion" services, some partake in a very real way of Christ, while others, not recognizing the body of the Lord, eat and drink judgment on themselves (1 Cor 11:29). In the tabernacle and in the temple, the "bread of the Presence" indicated the presence of the Lord, the "bread of life" among his people. ABF

BREAD OF THE PRESENCE (See TABERNACLE)

BREASTPLATE (See ARMS AND ARMOR)

BRETHREN OF THE LORD (See BROTHERS OF THE LORD)

BRICK. Building material made of clay dried in the sun. The word for "brick" in Hebrew is derived from the verb "to be white" and is almost identical with "Lebanon," so named for its snow-clad mountaintops. The very name would lead us to expect the oriental bricks to be whitish in color, rather than red like our more common bricks. The earliest mention of brick in the Bible (Gen 11:3) shows that the molding of clay into bricks and its thorough burning were known when the Tower of Babel was built, not more than a century after the Flood; and the finding of potsherds *under* the Flood deposits at Ur and Kish shows that the allied art of making clay into pottery was known before the Flood.

Owing to the prevalence of stone in Egypt and its comparative rarity in lower Mesopotamia, the use of brick for building was much more common in Chaldea than in Egypt, though the record of the bondage of Israel in Egypt (Exod 1:11–14; 5:7–19) shows that at least some cities in Egypt were built of brick rather than of stone. In fact, the ruins of Pithom have been found with three grades of brick *in situ:* bricks with binding material of straw at the bottom; above them, bricks made with stubble; and at the top, bricks of pure clay with no binding material at all. The ancient bricks were generally square instead of oblong and were much larger than ours, about 13 x 13 x 3½ inches (33 x 33 x 9 cm.). Before being baked they were often stamped with the name of the monarch—e.g., Sargon or Nebuchadnezzar. Much of the ancient brickwork was of bricks merely baked in the sun, especially in Egypt, but at Babylon the bricks were thoroughly burned. In Jeremiah 43:9 (KJV) we read of a "brickkiln" in Egypt in the sixth century B.C. The ASV renders the word "brickwork" (NIV "brick pavement"), but 2 Samuel 12:31 (KJV) clearly speaks of a brickkiln already in David's time; and Nahum, taunting the Ninevites four centuries later (Nah 3:14 KJV), tells them to "make strong the brickkiln." In Isaiah 9:9–10 the "pride and arrogance of heart" of the Israelites is rebuked because they intended to replace the overthrown bricks with stone, even as many a modern city has been rebuilt after a catastrophe. The sin was not in their desire for improvement, but in their impious and profane pride.

BRIDE, BRIDEGROOM (See WEDDING)

BRIDLE. The part of a harness that surrounds the head of the beast and connects the bit with the reins. It represents two words in the OT: one used in Proverbs 26:3 KJV (NIV "halter"), the other in Psalm 32:9. In Psalm 39:1 the word is correctly rendered "muzzle." In the NT the word occurs once (Rev 14:20), and the KJV so translates the corresponding verb twice (James 1:26; 3:2). The ancient Assyrians sometimes bridled their captives. In Isaiah 37:29 (KJV) God is represented as about to bridle the Assyrians in a similar way, but, of course, figuratively.

BRIER (See PLANTS)

BRIMSTONE. More properly translated "sulfur" in the NIV, the Hebrew word is related to "*gopher*," a resinous wood that was used in the construction of the ark. Its root meaning is "resinous" or "highly combustible." It is generally connected with judgment, as when the Lord rained brimstone and fire on Sodom and Gomorrah (Gen 19:24; cf. Ps 11:6 KJV) or as when the dust of Edom was to be turned into brimstone (Isa 34:9 KJV). In the NT "fire and brimstone" are principal elements in the punishment of the wicked in Gehenna, or the "lake of fire" (Rev 20:10; 21:8 KJV). In Revelation 9:17 KJV, "fire, jacinth, brimstone" refer to colors, as indicated in NIV: "fiery red, dark blue, and yellow as sulfur."

BRONZE (See MINERALS)

BRONZE SEA. In 2 Kings 25:13; 1 Chronicles 18:8; Jeremiah 52:17 (the KJV reads "sea of brass"), a rather exaggerated figure for the immense laver that Solomon placed in front of the temple for washing the sacrifices and the bodies of the priests.

BRONZE SNAKE. Numbers 21:4–9 records how the people of Israel complained against Moses and against God, who in judgment sent venomous snakes against them. When the people confessed their sin, Moses made a "bronze snake" (KJV "serpent of brass"), set it on a pole, and in effect said, "Look and live." Those who looked recovered. This bronze snake later was worshiped, but Hezekiah scornfully called it "Nehushtan" (which 2 Kings 18:4 NIV footnote describes as sounding like the Hebrew for "bronze" and "snake" and "unclean thing") and destroyed it. This bronze snake was a type of our Lord bearing our sins on the cross (John 3:14–16).

BROOK. A small stream. One of "the sweet words of Scripture," because the Bible was written in lands near the desert, and by men who therefore appreciated water. Many brooks are named in the Bible—e.g., Besor (1 Sam 30:9), Cherith (1 Kings 17:3–7), and Kidron (2 Sam 15:23). The word rendered "brooks" in the KJV in Isaiah 19:6–8 seems to refer to the Nile or its irrigating streams; in Psalm 42:1 it may refer to "channels" (NIV "streams"). The word *nahal*, translated "brook" over forty times in the KJV, often means "a wadi"—i.e., a torrent in winter and spring that dries up in summer.

Clay model of a horse with bridle, reins, and saddle. Persian period. Provenance unknown. Courtesy Reuben and Edith Hecht Museum, University of Haifa.

BROOM (See PLANTS)

BROTHER. 1. A male person related to another person or other persons by having the same parents (Gen 27:6) or the same father (28:2) or the same mother (Judg 8:19).

2. A man of the same country (Exod 2:11; Acts 3:22).

3. A member of the same tribe (2 Sam 19:12).

4. An ally (Amos 1:9).

5. One of a kindred people (Num 20:14).

6. A coreligionist (Acts 9:17; 1 Cor 6:6); often, Christian disciples (Matt 23:8; Rom 1:13). Someone spiritually akin (Matt 12:50).

7. A fellow office-bearer (Ezra 3:2).

8. Someone of equal rank or office (1 Kings 9:13).

9. Any member of the human race (Matt 7:3–5; Heb 2:17).

BROTHERS OF THE LORD. The term is used in the NT in identifying four men: James, Joseph, Simon, and Jude (Matt 13:55; Mark 6:3). It is also used collectively of a group of men whose names are not given (John 7:3; Acts 1:14; 1 Cor 9:5). The precise relationship of these men to Jesus has been much debated, with three different answers offered:

1. They were younger children of Mary and Joseph. This is suggested by the reference to Mary's "first" child (Luke 2:7) but is rejected by those who insist that Mary remained a virgin.

2. They were Joseph's children from a previous marriage. This view is possible, but it has no support in the NT.

3. They were cousins of Jesus, sons of his aunt Mary, wife of Cleopas (John 19:25), described as "the mother of James the Younger and of Joses" (Mark 15:40). But if this James is the apostle listed in Mark 3:18, Mary's husband was Alphaeus, not Cleopas, and this could be explained only if Alphaeus and Cleopas were alternative names for the same man, or if Mary had been married twice.

Evidence is too scanty for a firm conclusion. Moreover, the Lord's reference to his brothers in Matthew 28:10 implies a wider relationship than that of family only. JDD

BUBASTIS (bū-băs′tĭs, Gr. form of the Heb. *Pi-Beseth*). A city in the delta of Lower Egypt (Ezek 30:17) near Aven (On, or Heliopolis), on the western bank of the Pelusiac branch of the Nile. The names of Ramses II and of Shishak, conqueror of Rehoboam, are inscribed on the ruins. The red granite temple of the goddess Basht, admired by Herodotus, has been excavated. Also found was a unique cemetery of cats sacred to Basht; the cats had been buried, not mummified. Bubastis was occupied in the Fourth Dynasty of the Old Empire, the Middle Empire, Hyksos times, the New Empire to its end, and Roman times.

BUCKET OR PAIL. A vessel for drawing or holding water. In Isaiah 40:15 all the nations, compared with God, are but as the last drop in a bucket that has just been emptied. In Numbers 24:7 the reference is to a numerous posterity.

BUCKLER (See ARMS AND ARMOR)

BUKKI (bŭk'ī). 1. A prince of the tribe of Dan chosen to help Joshua divide the land (Num 34:22).

2. Son of Abishua, and high priest of Israel (1 Chron 6:5, 51; Ezra 7:4).

BUKKIAH (bŭ-kī'ȧ). One of the sons of Heman (1 Chron 25:4, 13) who were appointed over the service of song in the time of David. Bukkiah had in his group at least eleven of his "sons and relatives."

BUL (būl). The eighth month of the Jewish ecclesiastical year (1 Kings 6:38), fitting into November and/or December of our calendar. See CALENDAR.

BULL (See ANIMALS)

BULLOCK (See ANIMALS)

BULRUSH (See PLANTS)

BUNAH (bū'nȧ). A great-great-grandson of Judah (1 Chron 2:25) in the early days of the judges.

BUNNI (bŭn'ī). Three Levites mentioned in Nehemiah had this name: 1. A helper of Ezra (Neh 9:4).

2. An early dweller in Jerusalem in the fifth century B.C. (Neh 11:15).

3. One of the chief covenanters with Nehemiah (Neh 10:15).

BURDEN. That which is laid on an animal or person in order to be carried. The word translates eight different words in the OT and three in the NT. When it is literally used, it is easily understood and needs no special comment. Figuratively, it is used in the sense of "responsibility" (Num 11:11; Matt 11:30) or of a "sorrow" (Ps 55:22 KJV; "cares," NIV). The KJV translates "burden" where the NIV has "oracle" (Isa 15:1; 19:1; 22:1). These are generally "dooms," though in Zechariah 12:1 and in Malachi 1:1 the word is used simply for a "message" (NIV "oracle").

BURIAL. The act of placing a dead body in a tomb, in the earth or in the sea, generally with appropriate ceremonies; as opposed to exposure to the beasts, or abandonment or burning. Various peoples, notably the Egyptians, who believed that their dead would live and practice ordinary human occupations in "the land of the dead," often went to great lengths to preserve the bodies of their departed loved ones. They sometimes placed with the mummy tools or instruments or weapons, and occasionally killed and buried a wife or a servant to accompany the one whom they had buried.

Burial tomb from Jericho, Middle Bronze Age. Skeleton lying on burial bed is surrounded by pottery and other artifact remains. Courtesy Israel Department of Antiquities and Museums.

Partly because of God's declaration to fallen man, "For dust you are and to dust you will return" (Gen 3:19), the people of Israel almost always buried their dead; and because the land of Canaan had so many caves, these places were very frequently used as places of burial. Probably the prevailing motive for our respect for the dead, and even for the place of burial, is the sense of decency and our feeling of love for the person, often without regarding the fact that the real person has gone and that only his former "residence" remains.

The story of the treatment of the bodies of Saul and of his sons sheds light on the subject. The Philistines beheaded the bodies, exhibiting the heads throughout their land and fastening Saul's body to the wall of Beth Shan (1 Sam 31:8–13). The men of Israel rescued the bodies, burned them, reverently buried the bones under a tree, and mourned seven days.

It is remarkable that although God had given to Abraham the deed of the land of Canaan (Gen 15:18–21), the only land that the patriarchs possessed before Joshua's time was the burial places for the original family: a cave at Hebron and a field at Shechem (cf. Gen 23—the burial of Sarah; 49:29–32—Jacob's final request; and Josh 24:32–33—the burial of the mummy of Joseph and the body of Eleazar). In Canaan, in ancient times and in the more primitive parts of the land even today, there was (and is) no embalming in most cases but immediate burial to avoid unpleasant odors (Acts 5:5–10) and ceremonial uncleanness (Num 19:11–22). In the time of Christ, the bodies were wrapped in clean linen (Matt 27:57–60), and spices and ointments were prepared (Luke 23:56).

The strange story of the dead Moabite reviving when he touched the bones of Elisha (2 Kings 13:20–21) shows not only the speedy decomposition of a body but also the informality of burials in the time of war or necessity. The still stranger story of the disobedient prophet (1 Kings 13) shows how a heathen altar could be defiled by burning bones on it (13:1–3) and shows also the desire of a prophet to be buried near another whom he honored (13:30–31). In several cases of sinful rulers, ordinary burial was denied to their bodies: the dogs ate Jezebel (2 Kings 9:10); Jehoram of Judah, who died with incurable diseases, was not buried with the kings (2 Chron 21:18–20); Uzziah was buried in a field, not in the tombs of the kings (26:23); and Jehoiakim was given the burial of a donkey (Jer 22:18–19).

BURNING. God's judgments have often been accompanied with fire, as e.g., with Sodom and Gomorrah (Gen 19:24–28), Nadab and Abihu (Lev 10:1–6), and the 250 rebels in the wilderness (Num 16:2, 35). The final dissolution of "this present evil world" is to be with fierce fire (2 Peter 3:7–10, 12).

The traditional "burning bush," found at St. Catherine's Monastery in the Sinai Peninsula (cf. Exod 3:2). Courtesy Israel Government Press Office.

BURNING BUSH. A thorny bush that Moses saw burning and from which he heard the Lord speak (Exod 3:2–3; Deut 33:16; Mark 12:26). Many attempts have been made to identify the bush, but without success. The incident is important because it is the first direct statement in the Bible linking holiness with the very life of God and making fire the symbol of that holiness. The flame that needs no fuel to maintain it ("the bush . . . did not burn up") represents the eternal, self-sufficient life of God. Where this God is, holiness is, and sinners can draw near only by meeting the conditions God imposes ("take off your sandals"). This is the seed from which the whole Mosaic system grows. The unapproachable fire is seen in all its majesty on Mount Sinai (Exod 19:18), and this in turn is reflected in the undying fire on the altar (Lev 6:9). The same God who made the simple provision for Moses to draw nigh (Exod 3:5; cf. Josh 5:13) provided the sacrifices.

BURNT OFFERING (See SACRIFICE AND OFFERINGS)

BUSH (See PLANTS)

BUSHEL (See WEIGHTS AND MEASURES)

BUTLER (See OCCUPATIONS AND PROFESSIONS)

BUTTER. After the milk has been churned and the "butter" (in our sense of the word) produced, the butter is boiled and the curds separated from the almost pure oil; this is poured into a goatskin and kept until slightly rancid (to Western taste) and then is used with food, but more generally for frying eggs or vegetables. "Butter" is mentioned figuratively (Ps 55:21; in KJV, Job 20:17; 29:6, where NIV renders "cream"), as well as literally (Gen 18:8 KJV). Where KJV has "butter," NIV generally renders "curds" (e.g., Gen 18:8; Deut 32:14; 2 Sam 17:29).

A pottery churn from Abu Matar, a Bronze Age tell near Beersheba. Such a device was suspended with ropes and agitated to produce butter and other milk products. Courtesy Israel Department of Antiquities and Museums.

BUZ. 1. A nephew of Abraham and the second son of Nahor (Gen 22:21). His family apparently settled in Arabia. See Jeremiah 25:23, where Buz is mentioned with various districts of Arabia. The word means "contempt" and probably illustrates an Eastern superstition of giving a baby an unpleasant name so as "to avert the evil eye." One belonging to this region was a "Buzite" (see Job 32:2, 6).

2. Head of a family in the tribe of Gad (1 Chron 5:14), otherwise unknown.

BUZI (bū'zī). Ezekiel's father (Ezek 1:3).

BUZZARD (See BIRDS)

BYBLOS (See GEBAL)

BYWAYS. Literally "crooked paths." The word occurs only in Judges 5:6 (KJV, RSV; NIV "winding paths"). At certain times, on account of the oppression of the enemies of Israel (Philistines and Canaanites), people dared not walk on the highways, but kept out of sight by using little-known crooked paths.

C

CAB (kăb, *a hollow vessel,* ASV "kab"). A measure of capacity, a little less than two quarts, mentioned only in 2 Kings 6:25.

CABBON (kăb'ėn). A town in Judah, taken by Israel from the Amorites (Josh 15:40). It may be the same as Macbena (1 Chron 2:49).

CABUL (kā'bŭl). 1. A city of Galilee, mentioned in Joshua 19:27 as a border city of the tribe of Asher in the NE of Palestine. It lies between the hills about nine miles (fifteen km.) SE of Acre and is still inhabited.

2. A name given by Hiram of Tyre to a district in northern Galilee, including twenty cities, which Solomon ceded to him (1 Kings 9:13) and which probably included the original Cabul. It seems from 2 Chronicles 8:2 that Hiram (Huram) returned these cities and that Solomon rebuilt them.

The village of Cabul, a border city included in the territory of Asher. Courtesy Zev Radovan.

CAESAR (sē'zêr). 1. The name of a Roman family prominent from the third century B.C., of whom Caius Julius Caesar (c. 102–44) was by far the most prominent.

2. The title taken by each of the Roman emperors; e.g., Augustus Caesar, who reigned when Jesus was born (Luke 2:1); his successor Tiberius Caesar, who reigned A.D. 14–37 (3:1); Claudius Caesar, 41–54 (Acts 11:28; 18:2); and Nero, under whom Peter and Paul were martyred, 54–68 (Phil 4:22). Domitian was "Caesar" from 81 to 96, and it was under him that John was exiled to Patmos. "Caesar" is mentioned by our Lord (Luke 20:22–25) both literally as referring to Tiberius and figuratively as meaning any earthly ruler. The name Caesar came to be used as a symbol of the state in general and is often used in this sense in the NT (Matt 22:17, 21; Mark 12:14, 16–17; Luke 20:22, 25).

CAESAREA (sĕs'à-rē'à). A city built between 25 and 13 B.C. by Herod "the Great" at a vast cost and named in honor of his patron Augustus Caesar. It lay on the coast of the Mediterranean about twenty-five miles (forty-two km.) NW of the town of Samaria, which Herod had rebuilt and renamed "Sebaste," also in honor of Augustus. Herod intended it as the port of his capital, and a splendid harbor was constructed. Great stone blocks were used to top the reefs that helped to form the harbor. Being the military headquarters for the Roman forces and the residence of the procurators, it was the home of Cornelius in whose house Peter first preached to the Gentiles (Acts 10). It was the place of residence of Philip the evangelist with his four unmarried prophesying daughters (8:40; 21:8–9), who entertained Paul and Luke and their party on their return from the third missionary journey. Later it was the enforced residence of Paul while he was a prisoner for two years, and where he preached before King Agrippa (23:31–26:32). The Jewish war that Josephus described with such power and pathos, and that culminated in the destruction of Jerusalem, had its origin in a riot in Caesarea. Here Vespasian was proclaimed emperor of Rome in the year A.D. 69, while he was engaged in the Jewish war. Caesarea became the birthplace of Eusebius (c. 260) and

Drawing of a bust of Julius Caesar, Roman emperor c. 102–44 B.C. Courtesy Carta, Jerusalem.

"At Caesarea there was a man named Cornelius" (Acts 10:1). What Cornelius and his troops saw around them was a city, built by Herod the Great, almost dwarfed by the harbor, a magnificent feat of engineering. Courtesy Israel Government Press Office.

The Roman theater at Caesarea, built by Herod the Great, 25–13 B.C., and now partly restored. A surprising find here has been the name of Pontius Pilate in a fragmentary inscription. Courtesy Zev Radovan.

the seat of his bishopric. It is still called Kaysariyeh.

CAESAREA PHILIPPI (sĕs′á-rē′á fĭ-lĭp′ī, *Caesarea of Philip*). A town at the extreme northern boundary of Palestine, about thirty miles (fifty km.) inland from Tyre and fifty miles (eighty-three km.) SW of Damascus. It lies in the beautiful hill country on the southern slopes of Mount Hermon and was probably near the scene of Jesus' transfiguration (cf. Matt 16:13–17:8; Mark 8:27–9:8). The town was very ancient, being perhaps the Baal Gad of Joshua 12:7; 13:5, and for centuries it was a center of worship of the heathen god "Pan," whence it was known as "Paneas" and whence the modern name Banias (because there is no "p" in the Arabic alphabet). Augustus Caesar presented it, with the surrounding country, to Herod the Great, who built a temple there in honor of the emperor. Herod's son, Philip the Tetrarch, enlarged the town and named it Caesarea Philippi to distinguish it from the other Caesarea. It lies at the easternmost of

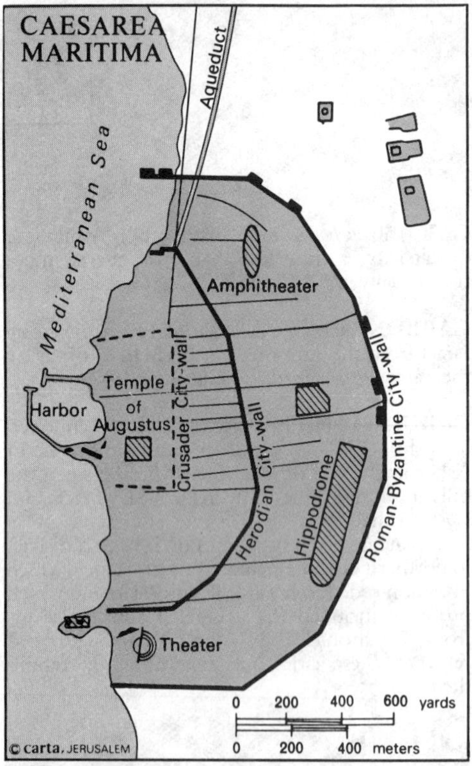

the four sources of the Jordan, and nearby these streams unite to form the main river. It was at a secluded spot near here that the Lord began to prepare his disciples for his approaching sufferings and death and resurrection, and that Peter made his famous confession (Matt 16:13–17).

CAGE. A device so-called when used by the fowler to keep his live birds, but "basket" when used for fruit (Jer 5:27; Amos 8:1–2). Cf. Revelation 18:2 KJV.

CAIAPHAS (kā′yȧ-făs). In the hundred years from 168 B.C., when Antiochus Epiphanes dese-

Site of Caesarea Philippi, known as Banias (Arab corruption of Paneas). Niches were used to place statues dedicated to the Greek god Pan. Courtesy Zev Radovan.

crated the temple, to 66, when the Romans took over, the high priesthood was almost a political office, the priests still coming from the descendants of Aaron but being generally appointed for worldly considerations.

From 66 B.C. the Romans rulers appointed not only the civil officers (e.g., Herod) but the high priests also, with the result that the office declined spiritually. Annas, father-in-law of Caiaphas (John 18:13), had been high priest by appointment of the Roman governor from A.D. 7 to 14 (see Luke 3:2), and though three of his sons succeeded for a short period, Caiaphas held the office from 18 to 36, with Annas still a sort of "high priest emeritus." After Jesus had raised Lazarus from the dead (John 11), many of the Jews believed in him (11:45–46), but some through jealousy reported the matter to the Pharisees. With the chief priests they gathered a council, fearing, or pretending to fear, that if Jesus were let alone many would accept him and the Romans would destroy what was left of Jewish autonomy. Caiaphas (11:41–53) declared that it would be better for Jesus to die than for the whole nation to be destroyed. When our Lord was betrayed into the hands of his enemies, the Roman soldiers and the Jewish officers took him first to the house of Annas, where by night he was given the pretense of a trial (18:12–23). Then Annas sent him bound to Caiaphas before whom the "trial" continued (18:24–27). Afterward he was delivered to Pilate because the Jews could not legally execute him.

CAIN (kān). 1. The first son of Adam and Eve, and a farmer by occupation. As an offering to God, he brought some of the fruits of the ground, while his brother brought an animal sacrifice (Gen 4). Angry when his offering was not received (Heb 11:4 shows that he lacked a right disposition toward God), he murdered his brother. He added to his guilt before God by denying the act and giving no evidence of repentance. He fled to the land of Nod and there built a city, becoming the ancestor of a line that included Jabal, forefather of tent-dwelling cattle-keepers; Jubal, forefather of musicians; Tubal-Cain, forefather of smiths; and Lamech, a man of violence. His wife must have been one of his own sisters—not an impropriety in those days.

2. The progenitor of the Kenites (Num 24:22).

3. A village in Judah (Josh 15:57, NIV "Kain").

ABF

CAINAN (kā-ī'năn). 1. In NIV, RSV, ASV "Kenan," the fourth from Adam in the messianic line (Gen 5:12-14; 1 Chron 1:2; Luke 3:37).

2. A son of Arphaxad (Luke 3:36), omitted in Genesis 10:24; 11:12, but found in the LXX, from which Luke quotes.

CALAH (kă'lă). A very ancient city of Assyria on the upper reaches of the Tigris River, built originally by Nimrod, who is listed in Genesis 10:6–12 as a grandson of Ham, son of Noah. According to KJV, the builder was "Asshur," from whom Assyria gets it name; but cf. NIV. The city was apparently rebuilt by Shalmanezer I (reigned c. 1456–1436 B.C.), then later abandoned for many centuries till Ashurnasirpal, who is pictured as "Ruthlessness Incarnate" (reigned c. 926–902), restored it. Aside from the mention in the Bible, the city is famous for its immense statuary in the form of winged lions and winged bulls, some of which can be seen in the British Museum today. Several great palaces have been excavated there, and the place is now known as "Nimrud."

Colossal human-headed winged lion that guarded the doorway to the palace of Ashurnasirpal II, 883–859 B.C., at Nimrud (Calah). Reproduced by courtesy of the Trustees of the British Museum.

CALAMUS (See PLANTS)

CALCOL, CHALCOL (kăl'kŏl). A son or descendant of Mahol. He was noted for his wisdom, yet Solomon was wiser than he (1 Kings 4:30–31). Calcol was also a son or descendant of Zerah (1 Chron 2:6).

CALDRON. A large pot or vessel in which meat is to be boiled; the word is sometimes translated "pot" in modern versions (Jer 52:18, 19; Ezek 11:3, 7, 11). Some scholars regard it as a mistranslation in Job 41:20.

CALEB (kā'lĕb, *dog*). 1. The son of Jephunneh, the Kenezite; the prince of Judah whom Moses sent with eleven others to spy out the Promised Land (Num 13:6). Most of the spies brought back a pessimistic report. Their names are almost forgotten; but two heroes of faith, Caleb and Joshua, who encouraged the people to go up and take the land, are still remembered. Because Israel in cowardice adopted the majority report, God imposed on them forty years of "wandering" in the wilderness until that generation died out. Caleb was forty years old when the spies were sent (Josh 14:7). At the age of eighty-five, when the land of Canaan was being distributed, he asked for, and received, Hebron and the hill country. There lived the fearful Anakim who had terrorized ten of the spies. Later he became father-in-law of Othniel, the first of the "judges," by giving him Acsah his daughter (Judg 1:12–15, 20).

2. A son of Hezron, son of Judah (1 Chron 2:18–19, 42), probably the same as the Caleb of 1 Chronicles 2:9 (KJV, Chelubai).

CALEB EPHRATHAH (kā'lĕb ĕf'rà-tà). Named in 1 Chronicles 2:24 as the place where Hezron died. The Hebrew and LXX texts differ here, and many scholars prefer the LXX reading, "after the death of Hezron, Caleb came unto Ephrath, the wife of Hezron, his father." When a son took his father's wife, it signified that he was claiming his father's possessions.

CALENDAR. Calendars are devised as a trustworthy means for recording history and determining dates in advance for social, civic, and religious anniversaries, and for economic planning. Comparatively little is known of the calendar of the early Israelites from the patriarchs to the Exile, but a critical study of the biblical records and archaeological discoveries is rewarding.

During the Bible period, time was reckoned solely on astronomical observations. The early Chaldean and Egyptian astrologers became quite learned in the movements of astronomical bodies. Their discoveries, as well as those of other Near Eastern neighbors, made their impact on the Jewish calendar. From earliest times the sun and moon were determinants of periods: days, months, and years.

I. Days in the biblical record of time begin with the account of creation. Various reckonings and measurements were derived from these early records. While the Babylonian day began at sunrise, the Bible reckoned the twenty-four-hour span from sunset to sunset (Deut 23:11), probably taking its clue from the repeated phrase of Genesis 1:5, 8, et al. Nehemiah 4:21 suggests that the end of one day and the beginning of the next was actually marked by the appearance of the stars.

Days of the week were not named but were designated by ordinal numbers. The term "sabbath" was not the name of the seventh day but a sacred designation.

Days were also subdivided in a manner set forth in the creation account. And God said, "Let there be lights in the expanse of the sky to separate the day from the night . . . the greater light to govern the day" (Gen 1:14–16; see also Num 9:16; Ruth 3:13). In the OT the day, as distinguished from the night, was not divided into exact periods but by broad terms such as evening, morning, midday, and (literally) "between the evenings" (e.g., Exod 12:6). The division of the day into hours is ancient in Babylonia, and Isaiah 39:8 (cf. 2 Kings 20:9–10) shows that timing devices were known among the Hebrews as well. Babylonians divided the day by sun-watches into twelve equal parts, which were subdivided by the sexagenary system into minutes and seconds. The Egyptians divided the day plus the night into twenty-four hours, for which they had at least two calibrated measuring devices. One was a shadow clock, comprised of a horizontal piece of wood with markings to which was attached at one end a short T-like piece, set toward the east in the morning and toward the west in the afternoon. A specimen, dating about 1400 B.C. is now in the Berlin Museum. Another Egyptian timepiece was the water-clock, clepsydra, the oldest-known specimen of which dates from the reign of Amenhotep III. It is of alabaster, shaped like a flower-pot, with calibrated marks inside and a small aperture near the bottom through which the water gradually flowed out. In the NT John 11:9 records the rhetorical question of Jesus, "Are there not twelve hours of daylight?"—as distinguished from night. This kind of daily reckoning is also seen in the crucifixion account that mentions the third, sixth, and ninth hours (Mark 15:25, 33, 34), referring to 9 a.m., noon, and 3 p.m.

Early Hebrews divided the night into three watches: "the morning watch" (Exod 14:24); "the middle watch" (Judg 7:19); and "at the beginning of the watches" (Lam 2:19 RSV). The Romans divided the night into four watches, from which Jesus drew an analogy in his eschatological warning of unpredictable time: ". . . in the evening, or at midnight, or when the rooster crows, or at dawn" (Mark 13:35).

II. Weeks constituted special and significant units of time for the "chosen people." The seven-day week is of Semitic origin, but reckoned from various reference points. The Babylonians and Assyrians bound their weeks to the lunar cycle, corresponding with the four phases of the moon, and began anew with each new moon. The biblical week had its origin in the seven-day creation account and ran consecutively in a free-week system irrespective of lunar or solar cycles. This was out of the high esteem held for the Sabbath. The Egyptian week had ten days.

Astronomical bodies were divinely ordained in creation to be time markers. Days and years were measured by the sun; months by the moon; and cycles by sun, moon, and stars. The week alone was not controlled by celestial bodies, but originated by divine command for man's economic, physical, and spiritual welfare.

Though God placed special emphasis on the seventh day at the time of creation (Gen 2:2–3), the records are silent as to its observance during the long interlude between then and Moses' day. If the people of the pre-Flood era or of the patriarchal period observed a "sabbath," there are no biblical records of it. However, since sabbath observance was kept alive in tradition until recorded in Genesis, it is a reasonable conjecture that it was preserved in practice also. Anyway, it was either revived or given special emphasis by Moses. The first recorded instance of the observance of "a day of rest, a holy Sabbath to the LORD" (Exod 16:23) was when the Israelites were gathering manna in the wilderness. Subsequently, the Sabbath became the most holy, as well as the most frequent, of all the sacred days observed by the Jews.

When Moses transmitted to Israel the fourth commandment in the Decalogue, "Remember the Sabbath day by keeping it holy" (Exod 20:8), it was designated as a perpetual memorial sign of the covenant between God and his chosen people. "Then the LORD said to Moses, 'Say to the Israelites, "You must observe my Sabbaths. This will be a sign between me and you for the generations to come, so you may know that I am the LORD, who makes you holy" ' " (31:12–13). It became a distinctive day with successive injunctions to observe it, describing the manner of doing so and the penalties for its desecration (23:12; 35:2–3). Emphasis on keeping "his holy sabbath" is seen in the Habakkuk (1:5) commentary of the Dead Sea Scrolls and the bitter accusations hurled at Jesus on this point (Mark

SYNCHRONIZED JEWISH CALENDAR

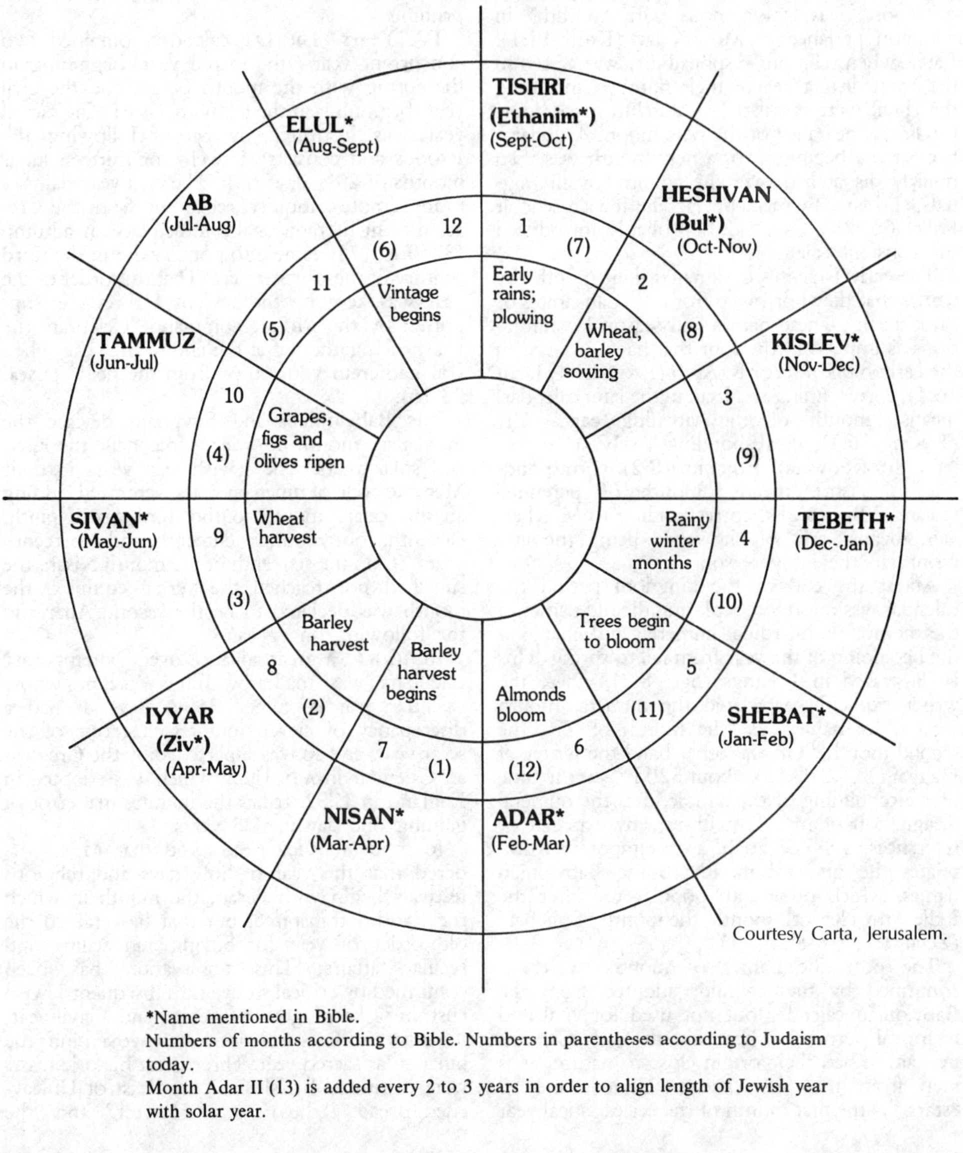

Courtesy Carta, Jerusalem.

*Name mentioned in Bible.
Numbers of months according to Bible. Numbers in parentheses according to Judaism today.
Month Adar II (13) is added every 2 to 3 years in order to align length of Jewish year with solar year.

2:24). However superficial the observance by some of Jesus' contemporaries might have been, he confirmed the divine authenticity of the Sabbath by going "into the synagogue, as was his custom" on the Sabbath day to teach, preach, and heal (Luke 4:16). Early Christian Jews made a habit of assembling on the first day of the week to commemorate Jesus' resurrection on that day (Luke 24:1); the first day instead of the seventh, became the day of worship and rest in Christendom.

III. Month, in effect, is a synonym for moon. Apparently all ancient peoples worshiped the moon. They also measured time by it, because of its regular cycles. The Arabic word for moon means "the measurer," and the Egyptian moon god Thoth was the god of measure. Even apostate Jews at times worshiped the moon along with other heavenly bodies (2 Kings 23:5; Jer 8:2).

"Moon" was synonymous with "month" in common parlance in Moses' day (Exod 19:1). Later, when religious responsibility was vested in the Sanhedrin, three of their number, including the chief, were entrusted as watchmen to report the first appearance of the new moon. A declaration of the beginning of a new month was then quickly dispatched over the country by fire signals, and later by messengers. The Jewish scholar Hillel (c. 60 B.C.–A.D. 20) probably introduced the constant calendar.

The early Israelites designated their months by names that they borrowed from the Canaanites or Phoenicians. These names had seasonal connotations as implied in the four that have survived in the early biblical records. Abib (Exod 13:4; Deut 16:1), corresonding to Nisan in the later calendar, means "month of the ripening ears." Ziv (1 Kings 6:1), corresponding to Iyyar, means "month of flowers." Ethanim (8:2), corresponding to Tishri, means "month of perennial streams." Bul (6:38), corresponding to Marchesvan, means "rain or showers," being the first month in the rainy season.

About the end of the kingdom period the calendar was reformed, replacing the old names of the months with ordinal numerals and changing the beginning of the year from fall to spring. This is illustrated in 1 Kings (6:1; 8:2), where the writer explicitly correlated the numeral month with older names, as "the month of Ziv, the second month." On the other hand the writer of Haggai (1:1; 2:1, 10), about 520 B.C., at the time of the rebuilding of the temple, uses the numeral designation of months without any explanatory references. Yet Zechariah, a contemporary work, relates the numeral month to the Babylonian names, which came into popular use after the Exile: "the eleventh month, the month of Shebat" (Zech 1:7; see also 7:1).

The postexilic names of months were, as confirmed by the Talmud, adopted from the Babylonian calendar but not used for civil and historical purposes. These, like the early Canaanite names, had their origin close to nature, as is seen from their derivations. Nisan—"move," "start," is the first month of the ecclesiastical year as well as of the vernal equinox. Iyyar—"to be bright," "flower." Sivan—"appoint," "mark." Tammuz—name of an ancient Akkadian god identified with vegetation. Ab—"hostile" heat, "bulrushes" growing. Elul—"to shout for joy" at vintage. Tishri—"begin" civil year, "dedicate" to the sun-god by Babylonians, and to which the Jews might have associated the Creation and the Day of Judgment. Marchesvan—"drop," "rainy season." Kislev—derivation uncertain. Tebeth—"to sink," "dip." Shebat—also uncertain. Adar—"to be dark."

The Gezer Calendar, dated in the tenth century B.C., gives an interesting glimpse into the agricultural life in Palestine at that early date. This archaeological find by Macalister is a limestone plaque bearing a Hebrew inscription enumerating farm operations for eight months, mentioning sowing, flax harvest, barley harvest, and vine pruning.

IV. Years. The OT calendar contained two concurrent years: the sacred year, beginning in the spring with the month Nisan, and the civil year, beginning in the fall with Tishri. The sacred year was instituted by Moses following the Exodus and consists of twelve or thirteen lunar months of 29½ days each. The civil year claims a more remote antiquity, reckoning from the Creation, which traditionally took place in autumn (3760 B.C.). It came into popular use in the third century of the Christian era. That this order of the year was kept by the ancient Hebrews is supported by the Mosaic command "Celebrate the Feast of Ingathering at the end of the year, when you gather in your crops from the field" (Exod 23:16).

The Babylonians and Egyptians devised the intercalary month in order to reconcile the lunar and solar years. The Jewish leap years in their Metonic cycle of nineteen years were fixed, adding an intercalary month to the third, sixth, ninth, eleventh, fourteenth, seventeenth, and nineteenth years. If, on the sixteenth of the month Nisan, the sun had not reached the vernal equinox, the month was declared to be the second Adar and the following one Nisan.

In 46 B.C., a great advance over contemporary calendars was made by Julius Caesar, whose calendar year contained 365¼ days. It had a discrepancy of eleven minutes in excess of the solar year, and so was superseded by the Gregorian Calendar in A.D. 1582, which was adopted in England in 1752. It has the infinitesimal error of gaining one day in 325 years.

Josephus (*Antiq.* 1.3.3) said that Moses ordered that the year of holy days and religious festivals begin with Nisan, the month in which the Exodus transpired, but that he retained the old order of year for buying and selling and secular affairs. This observation has been confirmed by critical study and subsequent Jewish custom of keeping both a sacred and a civil year.

Feasts and fasts were intricately woven into the lunar-solar sacred year. Three great historic feasts were instituted by Moses: "the Feast of Unleavened Bread," "the Feast of Harvest," and "the

Feast of Ingathering" (Exod 23:14–16), corresponding roughly to Passover, Pentecost, and Thanksgiving. There were also numerous minor feasts.

Beginning in the month Nisan or Abib (Neh 2:1; Exod 23:15), the sacred holidays of feasts and fasts came in the following order: On the fourteenth of Nisan, the first month, the Passover (Exod 12:18–19; 13:3–10) was observed in preparation for the following week's festival and in eating the paschal supper (see Matt 26:17–29). The fifteenth to twenty-first was the Feast of Unleavened Bread (Lev 23:6), which included, on the fifteenth, a Sabbath, a day of holy convocation; on the sixteenth, Omer, or presenting the first sheaves of harvest; and on the twenty-first, another holy convocation. This is also the month of latter or spring rains when the Jordan was in flood (Josh 3:15).

The Christian Easter, fulfilling the Passover, is reckoned on solar-lunar cycles, coming on the first full moon on or after the vernal equinox (March 21).

The name of the second month, Iyyar, known formerly as Ziv (1 Kings 6:1, 27), does not occur in the Bible, as is also true with Tammuz, Ab, and Marchesvan. The Jews fasted on the tenth in commemoration of the death of Elijah; the fourteenth was the Second or Little Passover for those who could not keep the regular one (Num 9:10–11); and on the sixteenth was a fast for the death of Samuel.

Pentecost or Feast of Weeks, or of Harvest, or of Firstfruits, when loaves as firstfruits of the gathered harvest were presented (Exod 23:16; 34:22; Lev 23:17, 20; Num 28:26; Deut 16:9–10), was celebrated on the sixth or seventh of Sivan (Esth 8:9; cf. Acts 2:1). This was the first of the two great agricultural feasts, coming at the end of seven weeks after the beginning of barley harvest, or fifty days after the Passover.

Next in annual order was the New Year (*Rosh Hashanah*), one of the most important and probably the oldest feast, observed on the first day of the civil year, in the month Tishri, the former Ethanim or seventh month (1 Kings 8:2). It was called the Feast of Trumpets, a precursor of one emblem of modern New Year's celebrations. It was a day of holy convocation, of reading the law (Neh 8:1–8), of blowing trumpets, of burnt offerings, of cereal offerings, and of profound solemnity, introducing "Ten Days of Repentance" (Num 29:1–16; Ezra 3:4–6). This protracted feast culminated in the Day of Atonement (*Yom Kippur*), the tenth of Tishri, one of the most holy days for the Jews. This is strictly a fast day and the only one commanded by law (Lev 16:26–34; 23:27–32), called "the fast" in Acts 27:9. The Jewish calendar makes "provision that neither *Rosh Hashanah* nor *Yom Kippur* may fall on the day before or the day after the sabbath, or the seventh day of Tabernacles on a sabbath." From the fifteenth to the twenty-first of Tishri the Jews held the Feast of Ingatherings (or Tabernacles or Booths—recalling the wilderness wandering), when the firstfruits of wine and oil were offered (Exod 23:16; Lev 23:34–42; Deut 16:13). It was a day of soul-searching and expiation of sins and of deep gratitude to God. It was the third of the three great feasts commanded by Moses, and the second of the two great agricultural feasts, corresponding to our modern Thanksgiving.

Winter holy days were few, though one of significance is mentioned in John 10:22–23: "Then came the Feast of Dedication at Jerusalem. It was winter, and Jesus was in the temple area . . . ." Dedication of the temple was instituted by Judas Maccabeus in 164 B.C. This feast was held on the twenty-fifth of Kislev (Zech 7:1), which was followed by the tenth month, Tebeth (Esth 2:16), and the eleventh month, Shebat (Zech 1:7).

Besides the one divinely ordained fast, the Day of Atonement, there were minor fasts, some temporary (Ezra 9:5; Neh 1:4) and some annual. One fast in memory of the destruction of Jerusalem by Nebuchadnezzar (2 Kings 25:1–7), instituted after the Exile, was observed on the ninth of Ab. Another, the fast of Esther, was observed on the thirteenth of Adar and was followed the next two days by the Feast of Purim.

V. Cycles. From God's hallowing of the seventh day there arose a special sacredness in relation to the number seven. Religious convocations and festivals were highly regarded on the seventh day, seventh week, seventh month, seventh year, and seven times seven years.

Hence, the epitome of the sabbatical feasts, of which the perennial ones have been mentioned, may thus appear. The sabbath of seven days; Pentecost, at the end of seven weeks after Passover; and the Feast of Trumpets, introducing the sacred seventh month, were all "appointed assemblies" (*mo'adhim*) of the Lord.

The sabbatical year was one of solemn rest for landlords, slaves, beasts of burden, and land, and of freedom for Hebrew slaves. Only what grew of itself on the farm and vineyard was to be gathered and consumed (Exod 23:10–11; Lev 25:3–7). The sabbatical and jubilee years were synchronized with the civil or agricultural year, beginning in autumn.

The Jubilee, every fiftieth year, following "seven weeks of years," was a hallowed year whose observance included family reunions, canceled mortgages, and the return of lands to their original owners (Lev 25:8–17).

VI. Eras in the Bible calendar constitute the whole span of time from the creation of the world to the consummation of the ages. Great events are terminal markers. These mountain peaks of time, in chronological sequence, are Creation, Flood, Abraham, Exodus, Exile, and Birth of Jesus. Consequently, the eras may be designated Ante-Diluvian, Post-Diluvian, Patriarchal, Israelite, Judean, and Christian. (Cf. Matt 1:2–17; Luke 3:23–37).

Astronomically, the phenomenal star that guided the Magi divided human history. It is the pivotal point from which all history is dated, terminating the old order and initiating the new. It stands as the signal reference point of all time, the preeminent red-letter date in the Bible calendar. In the Jewish Calendar it separates the history "Before the Common Era" (B.C.E.) from that of the "Common Era" (C.E.). In the Christian calendar it separates all "Before Christ" (B.C.) from that in *"Anno Domini"* (A.D.), "The year of our Lord." GBF

CALF (See ANIMALS)

CALF WORSHIP. A part of the religious worship of almost all ancient Semitic peoples. At least as early as the Exodus, living bulls were worshiped in Egypt. The Babylonians looked on the bull as the symbol of their greatest gods. The bull was a sacred animal in Phoenicia and Syria. Among the Semitic Canaanites the bull was the symbol of Baal. It appears that the bull was in some way connected with the reproductive processes of plants and animals and with the sun. It symbolized strength, vigor, and endurance.

Aaron made a golden image of a male calf in order that the people might worship the Lord under this form (Exod 32:4). It is very unlikely that the golden calf was a representation of an Egyptian deity. The feast held in connection with this worship was a "festival to the LORD" (32:5).

After the division of the kingdom, Jeroboam set up two golden calves in his kingdom, one at Bethel and one at Dan (1 Kings 12:28–29), because he feared that his people might desert him if they continued to worship in Jerusalem. He was not trying to make heathenism the state religion, for the bull images were erroneously supposed to represent God. In time, these images, at first recognized as symbols, came to be regarded as common idols (1 Kings 12:30; Hos 13:2).

Statuette of a bull, symbol of fertility and strength, found in northwest Samaria, and made from bronze, dated Israelite (Iron I) period, twelfth century B.C. Courtesy Israel Museum, Jerusalem.

CALL (Gr. *kaleō, to call*). One of the most common verbs in the Bible, representing over twenty words in the Hebrew and Greek text, but principally with four different meanings:

1. To speak out in the way of prayer—"Call to me and I will answer you" (Jer 33:3).
2. To summon or appoint—"I am about to summon all the peoples of the northern kingdoms" (Jer 1:15).
3. To name a person or thing—"God called the light 'day' " (Gen 1:5).
4. To invite people to accept salvation through Christ. This last is a call by God through the Holy Spirit; it is heavenly (Heb 3:1) and holy (2 Tim 1:9). This call comes to people in all situations and occupations (1 Cor 1:26; 7:20).

CALNEH (kăl'nĕ). One of the four cities—including also Babel, Erech (whence "Iraq"), and

Restored 15 by 20 cm. fragment of a clay tablet showing the plan of Nippur, a town identified by some scholars with Calneh. The locations of the temple, walls, gates, and canals are shown, with legends in cuneiform script. Courtesy University Museum, University of Pennsylvania.

Akkad—that were founded by Nimrod in the third generation after the Flood (Gen 10:10). It was in the land of Shinar in the southern part of Mesopotamia. It is not identified, but Kulunu and Nippur have been suggested.

CALNO (kăl'nō). A city named in Isaiah 10:9 in a list of the Assyrian victories. Almost certainly the same as Calneh.

CALVARY (kăl'vȧ-rē, Lat. *calvaria, skull*). A place not far from the walls of Jerusalem where Christ was crucified and near which he was buried (Luke 23:33). The Latin *calvaria* is a rendering of

Gordon's Calvary, located near the Garden Tomb. It is so named because in 1885 General Charles Gordon declared this to be the site of Jesus' crucifixion and burial. The rock formation resembles a skull, hence its popular identification as Golgotha, the "place of the skull." Courtesy Duby Tal.

The two domes of the Church of the Holy Sepulchre in Jerusalem, traditional site of Calvary. Courtesy Israel Government Press Office.

the Greek *kranion,* "skull," which renders the Hebrew *Gulgoleth* and the Aramaic *Gulgulta*. The common explanation is that the name was due to the cranial shape of the hill.

The exact site of Calvary is a matter of dispute. Two sites contend for acceptance, the Church of the Holy Sepulchre, which is within the walls of the modern city; and the Green Hill, or Gordon's Calvary, in which is Jeremiah's Grotto, a few hundred feet NE of the Damascus Gate. The first is supported by ancient tradition; but the second, suggested for the first time in 1849, has much to be said in its favor. See also GOLGOTHA.

CAMEL (See ANIMALS)

CAMEL'S HAIR. Mentioned only in Matthew 3:4 and Mark 1:6, where we are told that John the Baptist wore a garment of camel's hair. It is probable, however, that this was not a garment made of the relatively expensive woven camel's hair, but of dressed camel's skin. Such garments are still used in the Near East. Some think that Elijah's mantle was made of camel's hair (2 Kings 1:8; cf. Zech 13:4).

CAMON (See KAMON)

CAMP, ENCAMPMENT (Heb. *mahaneh*). A group of tents intended for traveling or for temporary residence as in case of war—contrasted with villages, towns, or cities that are composed of houses and other more or less permanent buildings. The word *mahaneh* occurs over two hundred times and is properly translated "camp," but it is often translated "host" and occasionally "army," indicating the military purpose of the encampment. In Genesis 32:1–2, when the angels of God met Jacob, Jacob exclaimed, "This is the camp of God!" and he named the place "Mahanaim," or "Two Camps," referring to God's host and his own.

In the wilderness the Israelites were given precise instructions as to the order and arrangements of their camp, both at rest and in traveling (Num 2). The tabernacle in the center indicated the centrality of God in their life and worship. It was surrounded rather closely by the three families of the priests and Levites, and then further back were the twelve tribes. In Deuteronomy 23:9–14 the sanitary and ceremonial observances, which were used to keep the camp clean and wholesome, are given. Three tribes were grouped on each side of the tabernacle under the banners of the leading tribes: Judah eastward, with Issachar and Zebulun; Reuben southward, with Simeon and Gad; Ephraim westward, with Manasseh and Benjamin; and Dan northward, with Asher and Naphtali. When they marched, the Levites, carrying the tabernacle, occupied the center of the line. The high command was located there. ABF

CAMPHIRE (See PLANTS: *Henna*)

CANA (kā'nȧ). Cana of Galilee is mentioned four times in the Gospel of John (2:1, 11; 4:46; 21:2) and nowhere else in Scripture. It was in the highlands of Galilee, as one had to go *down* from there to Capernaum; but opinions differ as to its exact location. It may have been at "Kefr Kenna," about five miles (eight km.) NE of Nazareth, or at "Khirbet Kana" a little farther north. Here Jesus performed his first miracle, graciously relieving the embarrassment caused by the shortage of wine at a marriage feast. It was here too (John 4:46) that he announced to the nobleman from Capernaum the healing of his apparently dying son. Nathanael came from Cana (John 21:2).

CANAAN, CANAANITES (kā'naň, kā'năn-īts). 1. Canaan was the son of Ham in the genealogical lists in Genesis 9–10. His descendants occupied Canaan and took their name from that country (Gen 9:18, 22; 10:6).

2. Canaan was one of the old names for Palestine, the land of the Canaanites dispossessed by the Israelites. The etymology of the name is unknown, as is also the earliest history of the name; but Egyptian inscriptions of c. 1800 B.C. use it for the coastland between Egypt and Asia Minor. In the Amarna letters of c. 1400 B.C. the name is applied to the Phoenician coast. According to Judges 1:9–10, Canaanites lived throughout the land. In Genesis 12:6; 24:3, 37; Joshua 3:10 the Canaanites included the whole pre-Israelite population, even east of the Jordan. The language of Canaan (Isa 19:18) refers to the group of West Semitic languages of which

Modern village of Cana of Galilee, site where Jesus performed His first miracle (John 2). Courtesy Zev Radovan.

Hebrew, Phoenician, and Moabite were dialects. The Canaanites were of Semitic stock and were part of a large migration of Semites (Phoenicians, Amorites, Canaanites) from NE Arabia in the third millennium B.C. They came under Egyptian control c. 1500. The Israelites were never able to exterminate the Canaanites completely, and many were undoubtedly absorbed by their Israelite conquerors. Their continued presence with their heathen practices created serious religious problems for the Israelites. SB

CANAANITE, SIMON THE. The KJV rendering of one of the apostles (Matt 10:4); the fuller designation distinguishes him from Simon Peter. Other versions have "the Cananaean" (ASV, NASB, RSV) or "the Zealot" (NIV). Differences also exist in Luke 6:15; KJV has "Zelotes," while ASV, NEB, NIV, and RSV have "the Zealot." See also SIMON.

CANDACE (kăn'dȧ-sē, Gr. *Kandakē*). The queen of Ethiopia mentioned only in Acts 8:27. The name seems to have been a general designation of Ethiopian queens (as "Pharaoh" was for Egyptian kings, and "Caesar" for Roman emperors). Her chief treasurer, a eunuch, went to Jerusalem to worship and was led by Philip the evangelist to faith in Christ.

Ivory palette (c. 10 inches [26 cm.], c. 1350–1150 B.C.) from Megiddo, showing a Canaanite ruler sitting on his throne, drinking from a bowl. The throne is supported by winged lions with human heads. Before him is pictured a celebration of victory with feasting and music and the procession of prisoners. Courtesy Collection of Israel Department of Antiquities, photographed Israel Museum.

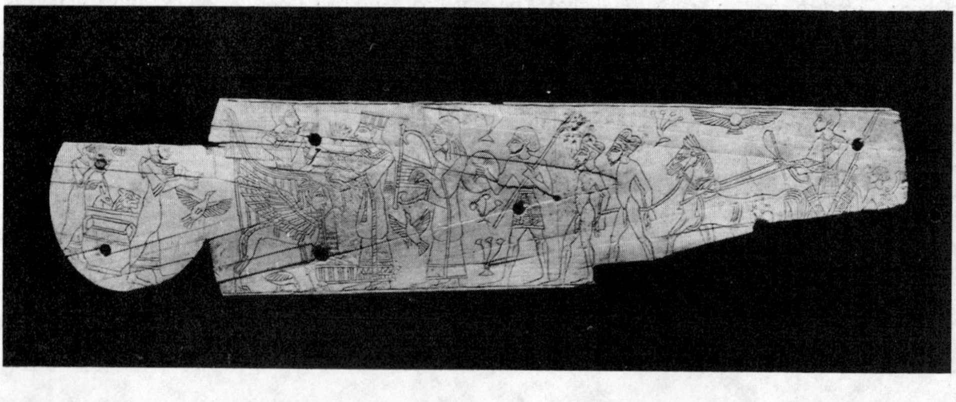

CANDLE (See LAMP)

CANDLESTICK (See LAMPSTAND)

CANE (See PLANTS)

CANKER (See DISEASES)

CANKERWORM (See ANIMALS)

CANNEH (kăn'nē). Mentioned only in Ezekiel 27:23 among the towns and regions with which Tyre traded. Some identify it with Calneh.

CANONICITY (kăn'ŏn-ĭc'itē). The word "canon" originally meant "measuring rule," hence "standard." In theology its chief application is to those books received as authoritative and making up our Bible. The Protestant canon includes thirty-nine books in the OT, twenty-seven in the NT. The Roman Catholic and Orthodox Canons add seven books and some additional pieces in the OT (See APOCRYPHA). The Jews accept as authoritative the same thirty-nine books of the OT as do Protestants.

It is commonly said that the Protestant test of canonicity is inspiration. That is, Protestants accept into their canon those books they believe to be immediately inspired by God and therefore true, infallible, and inerrant, the very Word of God. Creeds of the Reformation age often listed the books accepted as inspired, but the Protestant churches have accepted these books not because of the decision of a church or council, but because the books themselves were recognized as true and inspired, having God for their author. The history of the acceptance of these books and the study of the principles on which this acceptance occurred is an important phase of Bible introduction.

I. The Old Testament Canon. The Jewish Talmud of about A.D. 400 names the books of the Jewish canon in approximately the order found in our Hebrew Bibles today. By combining the twelve Minor Prophets, counting the books of Samuel, Kings, and Chronicles each as one book, etc., they arrive at the number of twenty-four books, divided into five of Law, eight of Prophets, and eleven books of Writings (Psalms, Proverbs, Job, Song of Songs, Ruth, Lamentations, Ecclesiastes, Esther, Daniel, Ezra-Nehemiah, Chronicles). The position of Chronicles at the end of the Canon is reflected in Luke 11:51, where Zechariah (cf. 2 Chron 24:20–22) is reckoned as the last martyr of pre-Christian times, as Abel was the first. In earlier days they combined Ruth with Judges, and Lamentations with Jeremiah and thus made twenty-two books equivalent to the twenty-two letters in the Hebrew alphabet. Origen, the Christian scholar of about A.D. 250, lists twenty-two OT books, but in the order of the Septuagint, not that of the Hebrew Bible (which is the order attested in the Talmud). Earlier, about 170, Melito of Sardis tells us that he went to Palestine to ascertain accurately the number of OT books. He lists the five books of the law first, then the others follow in an order based on the Septuagint and rather similar to that of our English Bible.

Before Melito, we have the vital witness of the Jewish historian Josephus. About A.D. 90 he wrote his work against Apion. In it he says that the Jews receive twenty-two books: five of the Law of Moses, thirteen of prophecy, and four of hymns to God and precepts for life. These books, he says, the pious Jew would rather die than alter or deny. He says these books were written by Moses and the succeeding prophets from that time to the days of Artaxerxes (around 400 B.C.) and that other later books, not written by prophets, were not so highly regarded. Josephus follows the order of books in the Septuagint and not that traditionally exhibited in the Hebrew Bible.

About A.D. 90 the Jews held the Council of Jamnia. We have only the later Talmudic reports concerning it, but apparently the canonicity of certain books was discussed—e.g., Ecclesiastes and Proverbs. This was not, of course, the time of original canonization of any book, as Josephus's witness assures us. Doubters arise in any age. But that Proverbs was already considered canonical in the second century B.C. we can now prove by reference to the Zadokite Documents (xi.20).

Earlier evidence on the OT canon gives us no listing but considerable valuable information. Philo, the Egyptian Jew of the first century A.D., evidently accepted the twenty-two Hebrew books, for he quotes from many of them and from them only, as authoritative. The NT evidence is in accord with this. Most of the OT books are quoted, and the seven apocryphal books are not. The NT gives no positive evidence on the order of the books, but it reveals in general a twofold division of the OT such as is found in Melito, rather than the threefold division. A dozen times the OT is referred to as the "Law and the Prophets" or "Moses and the Prophets." As is evident from NT usage, this twofold category included all twenty-two books. Only once does it adopt the threefold classification, "Moses, the Prophets and the Psalms" (Luke 24:44; but cf. 24:27).

Pre-Christian evidence has been greatly augmented by the discovery in A.D. 1947 of the Dead Sea Scrolls of the Qumran community. Previously, only the apocryphal books and other Jewish writings were available. These sources occasionally quoted books of the OT, but not with great frequency. Of special importance was the prologue to Ecclesiasticus, dated in 132 B.C. Three times it refers to the "law, and the prophets, and the other books of our fathers." One time it refers to these as already translated into Greek—the Septuagint. Because of the antiquity of this witness, the threefold canon was formerly held to be original. The twofold canon as referred to in the NT was not then explained. The Dead Sea Scrolls, however, give four places where the OT is referred to in two categories, the Law and the Prophets, as is usual in the NT. That this twofold canon included all our present books seems obvious from the fact that the Qumran community quoted from most of the OT books, including those later classified in the third division of "writings," and has left manuscripts of all the biblical books except Esther. Thus the twofold canon is as early as, or possibly earlier than, the threefold. In line with this evidence is the fact that the LXX translation, at least in later copies, accords with the twofold but not the threefold division.

From the above outline of evidence it is easily seen that the canonicity of the books of Tobit, Judith, Wisdom, Ecclesiasticus, Baruch, 1 and 2 Maccabees, and certain additions to Esther and Daniel, has no ancient authority and was not recognized by Christ, the apostles, or the Jewish people. The distinction between those books and the canonical OT writings was generally preserved by the Greek fathers; it was generally overlooked by the Latin fathers. Among the latter the outstanding exception was Jerome; his acquaintance with the Hebrew Bible enabled him to distinguish those books that belonged to the "Hebrew verity" from those of lesser authority. It was he who first called the latter the "apocryphal" books, meaning by that books that might be read in church "for example of life and instruction of manners," but not for the establishment of doctrine. Jerome's distinction was reaffirmed at the Reformation in the Anglican Articles of Religion (A.D. 1562) and has been generally recognized by Lutherans. Those churches, however, that followed the Reformed tradition of Geneva tended to give no canonical status to the Apocrypha. The Council of Trent, perhaps by reaction to the Reformers, affirmed the full canonicity of most of the Apocrypha in more uncompromising terms than had previously been used. This uncompromising position has been modified in recent practice: Catholic scholars tend to speak of the Apocrypha as the "deuterocanonical" books, which marks in effect a return to Jerome's position.

It also appears that the critical development theory that the Law was canonized in 400 B.C., the Prophets in 200 and the Writings in A.D. 90 is opposed to the facts. Some of the books that the Council at Jamnia in 90 had questions about were already accepted in the Qumran texts (e.g., Proverbs, in the Zadokite Documents, xi.20) or were in 90 actually counted among the Prophets by Josephus. The view is that Daniel was not classed among the Prophets because it was not written until 165 B.C., after the canon of the Prophets had closed. The designation "the prophet Daniel" that appears in the NT (Matt 24:15) is now known to have been anticipated in the Qumran literature.

The fact is that those who spoke the word of God to Israel were called prophets. There is no record of any group who were inspired without being prophets. Most of the OT books were clearly written by prophets. The authors of some others, like Joshua and Proverbs, Song of Songs, most of the Psalms, were also prophets—at least they received revelations from God (Num 12:6). For several books, information on authorship is lacking. Jewish tradition classifies the books of Joshua, Judges, Samuel, and Kings as "the Former Prophets" and represents them as having been written by prophets. One has as much right to hold that Ruth, Job, Esther, or Chronicles, were written by prophets as to say that Judges was. Certainly these books are included under the designation "Prophets" in the Qumran scrolls and in the NT. If books of prophetic origin were to be received by Israel, this is a practical test that would check on the authority of written teaching as well as oral (cf. Deut 13:1–5; 18:15–22). On this basis it can be explained how it was that the writings of prophets were accorded prompt acceptance by the faithful (cf. Josh 1:7, 8; Jer 36:8–16; 26:18; Dan 9:2). Hebrews 1:1 sums up the whole matter, "God spoke . . . through the prophets."

II. The New Testament Canon. Information on the early use of the NT books has been augmented in recent years both by the discovery of old portions of the NT and of early books that quote it.

Since the end of the fourth century A.D. there has been no question among most of the Christian churches as to which books belong in the NT. Nearly all branches of Christendom have accepted the current twenty-seven books as authoritative and canonical. They are so accepted because they are held to be true and immediately inspired by God.

Copies of the NT date from an early age. Already in the last century two remarkable old manuscripts had come to light—Sinaiticus and Vaticanus—from about 325. Since then, the discovery of the Chester Beatty papyri has given portions from the previous century that cover parts of the Gospels and Acts, most of Paul's letters, and about half of Revelation. In 1935 an even more remarkable fragment was published. Though small—parts of five verses of John 18—it is precious because it is the earliest. This Rylands papyrus is dated to the first half of the second century, or around 125.

Recently the sands of Egypt have yielded new treasures. The Bodmer papyrus of John, dating from about 200, is almost complete. Another Bodmer papyrus coming from the early third century contains the last part of Luke and the first part of John, while yet another comparable date includes 1 and 2 Peter and Jude along with a portion of the Psalms. Thus some actual NT manuscripts are now not too far removed from the days of the apostles themselves.

There was early a general agreement as to the books that the church at large accepted as canonical, but early evidence is not complete in detail for every book. Several books were accepted in some quarters but not in others. Contrary to statements sometimes made, no other books beside these twenty-seven were ever given significant or general acceptance. One must not, however, confuse the acceptance of the books with the establishment of the canon. In a sense, the canon was established at once as soon as there were inspired books, for the NT books claim authority and recognize the authority of one another. But while canonicity presupposes this recognition of authority, it implies also the collection of authoritative books, in such a way that it may be known by ordinary believers which books are authoritative and which are not by ascertaining which books are in the collection and which are not. Some churches had some of the books early but it took time for all of the books to be distributed and for the evidence of their genuineness to be given to all and accepted by all. Fortunately for us, the early Christians were not gullible; they had learned to try the spirits. This testing of the spirits became especially necessary in the second half of the second century because of the rise of the Montanists, with their claim to the renewed gift of prophecy; it was necessary to submit prophetic utterances to the judgment of holy Scripture, and this made it of practical importance to know what was holy Scripture and what was not. Furthermore, the Gnostic heresy rather soon began to multiply spurious writings and this made people cautious. It took time to convince everybody of every book. The history of the collection of the books traces this process.

A. **The Period of 170–200.** In brief survey we may take three early periods for analysis. Irenaeus of Lyons (c. 180) has not left us a specific list of NT books, but it is evident from his extant writings that, in addition to the self-evident canonicity of the four Gospels, he regarded as canonical Acts, Paul's letters (including the Pastorals), 1 Peter, 1 John, and Revelation. More or less contemporary with Irenaeus is the Muratorian Canon, a list of books acknowledged to be of apostolic authority. It includes the four Gospels and Acts, thirteen of Paul's letters (with a warning against some forgeries), two letters of John (probably in addition to 1 John, which is separately quoted), Jude, and Revelation. It mentions an apocalypse of Peter, "although some among us will not have this latter read in the churches." (This second-century apocalypse was popular because of its lurid description of the torments of the damned.) The Shepherd of Hermas is rejected from the canon because it is not apostolic and is too late to be included among the prophetic books. The omission of 1 Peter is surprising, especially if (as seems probable) the Muratorian list reflects the usage of the Roman church toward the end of the second century. The omission of Hebrews, on the other hand, is to be expected, because, while it was known in the Roman church from the first century on, it was not accepted there as canonical because it was known not to be the work of Paul.

B. **The Period of 140–170.** At the beginning of this period the most important figure is Marcion, who published an edition of Holy Scripture (an expurgated Greek New Testament) at Rome about 144. He rejected the OT as forming no part of Christian Scripture; his canon was a closed canon, comprising an edited text of the Gospel of Luke and ten letters of Paul (excluding the Pastorals). The use of Marcion's canon challenged orthodox churchmen to state more precisely what they believed constituted the canon of Christian Scripture. From this period we now have new evidence in the "Gospel of Truth" discovered recently in Egypt. This book, written by the Gnostic Valentinus, was referred to by Irenaeus in 170, and dates from about 150. It weaves into its pantheistic composition all our NT books except 1 and 2 Timothy, Titus, James, 2 Peter, 2 and 3 John, and Jude. Hebrews and Revelation are definitely included. One scholar has concluded that c. 140–150 a collection of writings known at Rome and accepted as authoritative was "virtually identical with our NT." Justin Martyr, who spent his later years in Rome and whose literary activity spans three decades (135–165), mentions "the memoirs of the apostles"—which, he says, "are called gospels"—and says that they were read in church along with the compositions of the prophets. His disciple Tatian showed his appreciation of the distinctive authority of the four Gospels by arranging their contents into a continuous narrative in the *Diatessaron*.

C. **The Period of 95–118.** Omitting many details, we may turn to the three great witnesses of the earliest age. Clement of Rome, Ignatius, and Polycarp all wrote between 95 and about 118. They show by quotation or clear allusion that they knew and used all our NT books except Luke, Colossians, Philemon, 2 Peter, 2 and 3 John, Jude, and Revelation. Moreover, these authors held the apostles in such high repute that their writings would obviously be treasured and accepted. Clement rather clearly ascribes inspiration to Paul.

D. **Later Problems.** Although our books were accepted at an early date, the history of their use is discontinuous. The Gospels were never challenged after the collection and publication of the fourfold Gospel, until a later group of heretics questioned all of John's writings, claiming that they were spurious. Note that here, as usual, denial of apostolicity involved denial of authority. The Book of Hebrews was continuously and from early days received and accepted as Pauline in Egypt. In Rome it was used by Clement, Justin, and Valentinus, although they did not accept it as the work of Paul. The witness of Irenaeus (c. 170) and Tertullian (c. 200) is hardly clear. Finally the views of Egypt and Palestine prevailed and Hebrews was fully accepted. The Roman church was persuaded to include it in the canon in the fourth century under pressure from Athanasius; they agreed to do so not because he convinced them of its Pauline authorship but because they did not wish to be out of step with the rest of Christendom. Second Peter had least external authority. It was certainly in circulation among the churches by the end of the second century. Its relation to Jude remains problematic. If 2 Peter 3:3 is quoted in Jude 18, 2 Peter belongs to the first century; the majority verdict seems to be, however, that 2 Peter is dependent on Jude rather than vice versa.

E. **The New Testament Witness.** We must not forget the vital witness of the NT itself. Paul claims the authority of an apostle (1 Cor 9:1;

2 Cor 12:11–12) and declares his letters are to be accepted (1 Cor 14:37; 2 Thess 3:14). John in Revelation does the same (Rev 1:3; 22:18–19). Peter insists that Paul's writings are Scripture (2 Peter 3:15; cf. 3:2). Jude quotes Peter as apostolic (Jude 18). It seems probable that 1 Timothy 5:18 quotes Luke 10:7 as Scripture. The fact is, as the early church knew, Christ had promised his apostles a special work of the Spirit, inspiring them as teachers of his revelation (John 14:25; 16:13). It is true that a few, a very few, of the books were actually written by those not themselves apostles. But it is clear that the apostles used helpers in their writing (Rom 16:22; 1 Peter 5:12). The early church fathers called such men as Mark, Luke, and the author of Hebrews helpers or disciples of the apostles, and accepted their work as that of the apostles with whom they labored. At least the books were all written and apparently were all accepted within the period of the apostles.

Other indications combine to teach us that these twenty-seven books are rightly in our canon. The Holy Spirit has witnessed through the generations to the saving truth contained in them. These books have brought untold blessing where they have been received and obeyed. The church with one voice finds them to be the very word of God.

Bibliography: B. F. Westcott, *The Canon of the New Testament,* 1870; Frants Buhl, *Canon and Text of the Old Testament,* 1892; H. E. Ryle, *The Canon of the Old Testament,* 2d ed., 1904; T. Zahn, *Introduction to the New Testament,* 3 vols., 1909; A. Harnack, *The Origin of the New Testament,* 1925; A. Souter, *The Text and Canon of the New Testament,* 2d ed., 1954; R. Laird Harris, *Inspiration and Canonicity of the Bible,* 1957; Hans von Campenhausen, *The Formation of the Christian Bible,* 1972. RLH

Floor plan of the synagogue at Capernaum, c. third century A.D.: (1) staircase; (2) platform; (3) main entrance; (4) side entrance; (5) nave; (6) aisle; (7) benches; (8) colonnade; (9) courtyard; (10) portico of the courtyard; (11) annexed back room. Courtesy Carta, Jerusalem.

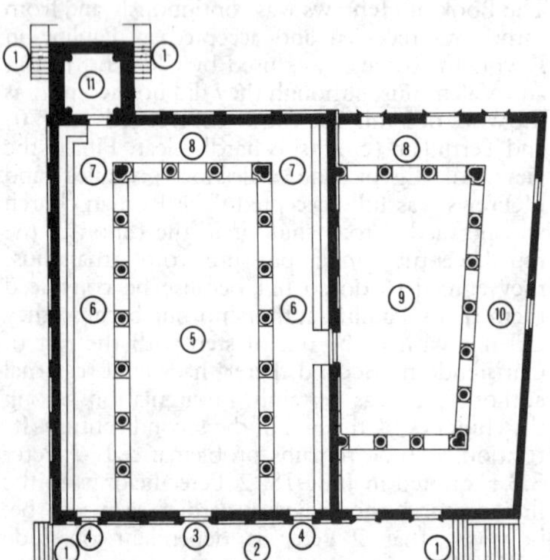

Aerial photo of remains of early type of synagogue at Capernaum on shore of Sea of Galilee. The façade in the foreground faces south and is oriented toward Jerusalem. Courtesy Israel Government Press Office.

CANTICLES (See SONG OF SONGS)

CAPERNAUM (kȧ-pûr'nā-ŭm, Gr. *Kapernaoum,* from Heb. *Kaphar-Nahum, village of Nahum*). A town on the NW shore of the Sea of Galilee where Jesus made his headquarters during his ministry in Galilee (Matt 4:13; Mark 2:1). In Scripture it is mentioned only in the Gospels, and perhaps did not arise until after the Captivity. That it was a town of considerable size in the days of Christ is shown by a number of facts: a tax collector had his office there (Mark 2:14); a high officer of the king (Herod Antipas) had his residence there and built a synagogue for the people there (Matt 8:5–13; Luke 7:1–10). Jesus performed many striking miracles there, among them the healing of the centurion's palsied servant (Matt 8:5–13), the paralytic who was lowered through a roof by four friends (Mark 2:1–13), and a nobleman's son (John 4:46–54). It was there that Jesus called Matthew to the apostleship as he was sitting at the tax-collector's booth (Matt 9:9–13). The discourse on the Bread of Life, which followed the feeding of the five thousand, and many other addresses were delivered there (Mark 9:33–50). In spite of Jesus' remarkable works and teachings, the people did not repent, and Jesus predicted the complete ruin of the place (Matt 11:23–24; Luke 10:15). His prophecy was so completely fulfilled that the town has disappeared and its very site is a matter of debate. There are two main claimants, about two and one-half miles (four km.) apart, for the honor of being the site: Tell Hum, which is about two and one-half miles (four km.) SW of the mouth of the Jordan, and Khan Minyeh, which is SW of Tell Hum. The present trend of opinion is in favor of Tell Hum. SB

CAPH (kȧf). The eleventh letter of the Hebrew alphabet, corresponding to our *k*. As a numeral it is eleven.

CAPHTOR (kăf'tôr, Heb. *kaphtôr*). The place from which the Philistines originally came (Amos 9:7). Jeremiah (47:4) calls it an island. There are a number of theories regarding the matter, but the one most widely accepted is that the Philistines came from the isle of Crete in the Mediterranean. There is evidence of ancient connection between Crete and Philistia (Ezek 25:16; Zeph 2:5, where the LXX renders Kerethites "Cretans"); and the Philistines are called Kerethites, which may mean Cretans. It is possible that Caphtor includes with Crete also the other islands in the vicinity, among them Caria and Lycia.

CAPPADOCIA (kăp'ȧ-dō'shĭ-ȧ). A large inland region of Asia Minor that apparently was given this name by the Persians, though its people were called "Syrians" by the Greeks. In the latter time of the Persian Empire the region was divided into two territories of which the more northerly was later named Pontus and the southerly Cappadocia, the name it retained in NT times. It was bounded on the north by Pontus, on the east by Syria and Armenia, on the south by Cilicia, and on the west by Lycaonia. The Romans built roads through the "Cilician gates" in the Taurus range so that Cappadocia could readily be entered from the south. The Cappadocians were Aryans. Jews from Cappadocia (Acts 2:9) were among the hearers of the first Christian sermon along with men from other Anatolian provinces; and Peter directed his first letter (1 Peter 1:1) in part to "God's elect . . . scattered throughout" various provinces in the north. It is almost certain that many of these Cappadocian Jews were converted on the Day of Pentecost, and so had the honor of being among the very earliest Christians. ABF

The land of Cappadocia, showing the dwelling caves at Göreme in the middle of Asia Minor. Courtesy B. Brandl.

Cappadocians bringing trousers and cloaks as tribute to the king (from the time of Xerxes, 485–465 B.C.). They are distinguished by the Phrygian fibula pinned to their cloaks. The hair and beard are elaborately curled. Cappadocia was one of twenty-three nations represented on the stairway of the apadana at Persepolis. Courtesy B. Brandl.

CAPTAIN. A word that in KJV translates sixteen different terms in the original text. By far the most frequent is *sar,* which can also mean "chief," "prince," "ruler." NIV has "captain" in Genesis 37:36; 2 Kings 1:9–11; Isaiah 3:3; et al. Apart from 1 Samuel 22:14, where translators differ, other Hebrew terms are *ba'al,* "lord," "owner" (Jer 37:13); *rab chōbēl,* "master of the pilots" (Jonah 1:6); *shālîsh,* "one of [or over] three" (1 Kings 9:22); and *chāqaq,* "to decree" (Judg 5:14). The Greek word *stratēgos,* "leader of any army," is rendered "captain" four times in NIV (Acts 4:1; 5:24, 26; Rev 18:17).

CAPTIVITY. When used of Israel, this term does not refer to the long series of oppressions and captivities of the Israelites by hostile peoples, beginning with the bondage in Egypt and ending with the domination of Rome, but to the captivity of the northern kingdom of Israel or Ephraim in 722 B.C. and the captivity of Judah in 586 B.C. The practice of making large-scale deportations of people as a punishment for rebellion was introduced by Assyria, but other nations adopted it.

I. The Captivity of the Northern Kingdom. Assyria first made contact with the northern kingdom when Shalmaneser II (860–825 B.C.) routed, in the battle of Karkar (854), the combined forces of Damascus, Hamath, Israel, and other states who had united to stop his westward progress. In another campaign Shalmaneser received tribute from Jehu, king of Israel. Not many years later, Rimmon-nirari III (810–781) compelled Syria to let go her hold of Israel. Tiglath-Pileser III (745–727), one of the greatest monarchs of antiquity, after capturing Samaria, put on the throne his vassal Hoshea, who had assassinated Pekah, king of Israel. With the death of Tiglath-Pileser III, Hoshea decided to strike a blow for independence. Help was promised by the king of Egypt, but it did not come. Hoshea was made a prisoner, and the capital was doomed to destruction, as the prophets had foretold (Isa 28:1; Hos 10:7–8; Mic 1:5–6). It was, however, only after a three-year siege that the city was captured. Before it fell, Shalmaneser had abdicated or died, and Sargon, who succeeded him, completed the conquest of the city and deported the inhabitants to Assyria (2 Kings 17:6–7; 18:11–12). Some time later Sargon's grandson Esarhaddon and his great-grandson Ashurbanipal imported to the region of Samaria some conquered peoples from the East (17:24). Not all of the inhabitants of the northern kingdom were taken into captivity. The very poor, who could cause no trouble in the future, were left (25:12). Intermarriage with the imported peoples resulted in the hybrid stock later known as the Samaritans. When the ten northern tribes were taken into captivity, some undoubtedly were absorbed into the pagan culture surrounding them, but for the most part they retained their identity, some returning to Judah at the end of the Exile, others remaining to become part of the Dispersion.

II. The Captivity of the Southern Kingdom. The Captivity of Judah was predicted 150 years before it occurred (Isa 6:11–12; 11:12). Isaiah (11:11; 39:6) and Micah (4:10) foretold that the place of the Captivity was to be Babylonia; and Jeremiah announced that it would be for seventy years (Jer 25:1, 11–12). The southern kingdom rested on a firmer foundation of faith than the northern and therefore survived longer, but it too had in it the seeds of moral and spiritual decay that caused its eventual disintegration.

Sargon was followed by a number of brilliant rulers, but by 625 B.C. the hold of Assyria over its tributary peoples had greatly slackened. Revolts broke out everywhere, and bands of Scythians swept through the empire as far as Egypt. Nineveh fell to the Babylonians in 606, never to rise again. A great new Babylonian empire was built up by Nebuchadnezzar (604–562). Judah became a vassal of Nebuchadnezzar, but Jehoiakim the king, though warned by Jeremiah, rebelled. Nebuchadnezzar therefore came into Jerusalem in 605 and carried off to Babylon the vessels of the house of God and members of the nobility of Judah, among them Daniel the prophet (2 Chron 36:2–7; Jer 45:1; Dan 1:1–3). Jehoiakim was taken in chains to Babylon (2 Chron 36:6). In 597, Nebuchadnezzar carried off Jehoiachin, his mother, his wives, three thousand princes, seven thousand men of might, and one thousand artisans (2 Kings 24:14–16). Among them was the prophet Ezekiel. This was the first large-scale deportation of the southern kingdom into Babylonia. Eleven years later (586) Nebuchadnezzar burned the temple, destroyed the city of Jerusalem, and deported into Babylonia all but the poorest of the land (2 Kings 25:2–21). A third group was taken into Babylonia five years after the destruction of the city (Jer 52:30).

The exiles were not heavily oppressed by their conquerors. They engaged in business, built houses (Ezra 2:65; Jer 29:5–7), and even held high positions in the state (Neh 1:11; Dan 2:48). They were not able to continue their system of sacrifices, but they had with them their priests and teachers (Ezra 1:5; Jer 29:1); and Ezekiel gave them constant encouragement (Ezek 1:1). In 539 B.C., Babylon fell to Cyrus king of Persia, who issued a decree permitting the Israelites to return

Limestone relief of a line of Syrian captives being led into the presence of Horemheb, on his tomb from Memphis, c. 1350–1300 B.C. Courtesy Rijksmuseum van Oudheden, Leiden, Netherlands.

Detail of a man leading a caravan of camels, as depicted on a mosaic from a Byzantine church in the Negev. Courtesy Zev Radovan.

to Jerusalem to rebuild the temple (Ezra 1:1–4). The next year, about 43,000 returned with Zerubbabel (Ezra 2:64). The rest preferred to remain in Mesopotamia (Zech 6:10). In 458, 1,800 returned with Ezra. SB

CARAVAN. A group of travelers united together for a common purpose or for mutual protection and generally equipped for a long journey, especially in desert country or through foreign and presumably hostile territory. Jacob's "company" (Gen 32–33) is a good example of a caravan organized to carry a clan to a new home; and the host of the Amalekites whom David destroyed (1 Sam 30:1–20) is another caravan, organized for raiding purposes. In the trackless desert where oases were few and far between and where savage beasts and more savage men were found, it was essential to go in caravans for protection. The word does not occur in the KJV, but "company" and "troop" could often have been "caravan."

CARAWAY (See PLANTS)

CARCAS (kȧr′kăs). A eunuch in the service of Xerxes (Ahasuerus) (Esth 1:10).

CARCASS, CARCASE. The dead body of a person or beast. The word is a translation of six different words in Scripture with root ideas of something fallen, faded, exhausted; or it may simply denote "body," such as the lion's carcass in Judges 14:8–9. The law of Moses, probably partly for sanitary reasons, required that carcasses of "unclean" beasts be considered abominable. See Leviticus 11:8–40.

CARCHEMISH, CHARCHEMISH (kȧr′kē-mĭsh). An ancient city of the Hittites located on the west bank of the Euphrates 63 miles (105 km.) NE of Aleppo. It was important commercially and militarily. For many years it paid tribute to the kings of Assyria. When Sargon captured it in 717 B.C., the Hittite Empire fell with it (Isa 10:9). It was the scene of a great victory by Nebuchadnezzar over Pharaoh Neco in 605 (Jer 46:2; 2 Chron 35:20). Its site is called Jerabis or Jerablus.

CAREAH (See KAREAH)

CARITES (See KERETHITES)

CARMEL (kȧr′mĕl, *garden*). 1. The mountainous promontory jutting into the Mediterranean Sea just south of the modern city Haifa and straight west of the Sea of Galilee. On the map of Palestine it forms the principal deviation from a comparatively straight coastline and forms the southern wall of the magnificent bay (or gulf) of Acre, the best natural harbor south of Beirut. When the word occurs with the definite article, it

Hills of the Carmel range. Courtesy Duby Tal.

generally refers to Mount Carmel and is often used to illustrate a beautiful and fruitful place (Isa 35:2; but see 33:9, which pictures God's judgment). South of Carmel lies the fruitful plain of Sharon and NE of it flows the river Kishon through the Plain of Esdraelon. At Carmel, Elijah stood against 450 heathen prophets and defeated them (1 Kings 18). Elisha also visited Carmel (2 Kings 2:25; 4:25).

Plan of the site of Carchemish, an important city of the Hittite empire. Courtesy Carta, Jerusalem.

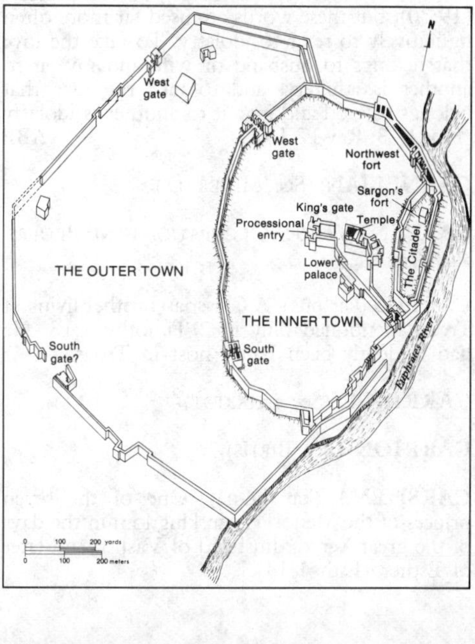

2. A very ancient town of Judah about seven miles (twelve km.) almost directly south of Hebron. First mentioned in Joshua 15:55, it is best known as the residence of the very churlish Nabal, who refused kindness to David (1 Sam 25:2–40) and whose life was saved by the tact of his beautiful wife Abigail. Abigail later became a wife of David.

CARMELITE (kàr'mĕl-īt). A native of Judean Carmel. This term was use in reference to David's wife Abigail, who had first married Nabal (1 Sam 27:3, KJV), and to Hezro, one of David's mighty men (1 Chron 11:37).

CARMI (kàr'mē). 1. One of the sons of Reuben, eldest son of Jacob, and head of the family of the "Carmites" (Gen 46:9; Num 26:6).

2. An early descendant of Judah (probably great-grandson) and father of Achan (Josh 7:1), mentioned in 1 Chronicles 4:1 KJV as "son" (NIV, "descendent") of Judah.

CARNAL. Fleshly, with reference to the body as the seat of the desires and appetites; usually used in Scripture in the negative sense, as opposed to the spiritual. In 1 Corinthians 2:14–3:4, Paul divides mankind into two classes—the natural and the spiritual; this corresponds to the classification of people as once-born and twice-born. Then he classifies Christians as "carnal" and "spiritual" (KJV; NIV has "worldly" and "spiritual") and lists the marks of carnality as "jealousy and quarreling" and undue emphasis on personalities: "I follow Paul—I follow Apollos." "Carnal" does not necessarily imply active and conscious sin but is opposed to "spiritual" (Rom 7:14; 2 Cor 10:4; Heb 7:16; 9:10). It describes the dominance of the lower side of human nature apart from God's work in one's life.

The KJV OT uses the expression "lie carnally" to describe adultery (Lev 18:20) and fornication (19:20), but these words are used far more often figuratively to refer to idolatry. To take the love that belongs to husband or wife and give it to another is adultery, and to take the love that belongs to God and give it to another is idolatry (Hos 1–3; Rev 17:18). ABF

CARNELIAN (See MINERALS)

CARPENTER (See OCCUPATIONS AND PROFESSIONS)

CARPUS (kàr'pŭs). A Christian brother living at Troas, mentioned only in 2 Timothy 4:13. He had evidently been Paul's host in Troas.

CARRIAGE (See CHARIOT)

CARRION (See BIRDS)

CARSHENA (kàr'shē-nȧ). One of the seven princes of the Medo-Persian kingdom in the days of the great Xerxes, husband of Vashti, and later of Esther (Esth 1:14).

CARTS. Carts and wagons are very ancient. In Genesis 45:19–21 Pharaoh provided carts for the wives and children of Jacob for their journey into Egypt. In the days of Eli, the Philistines took the ark of God, and, finding it a most unwelcome guest, put it on a cart and let it go back to Israel (1 Sam 6); but when David later desired to bring the same ark to his city, he used a cart, and there was a disastrous event connected with that arrangement (see 2 Sam 6:1–11).

CASIPHIA (kȧ-sĭf'ĭ-ȧ). A place near the river Ahava, a tributary of the Euphrates, twice mentioned in Ezra 8:17 as a place where exiled Levites lived.

CASLUHITES (kăs'lū-hīts). One of the seven tribes listed in Genesis 10:13–14 and its parallel passage in 1 Chronicles 1:11–12 as descended from "Mizraim," which is the name for Egypt. The Philistines are said to have come from this tribe.

CASSIA (See PLANTS)

CASTLE. A large fortified building or set of buildings, as that of a prince or nobleman. David took the Jebusite castle in Jerusalem and made it into his residence (1 Chron 11:5, 7). Castles were built in the cities of Judah by Jehoshaphat (2 Chron 17:12) and in its forests by Jotham (27:4). Where the KJV uses "castles," the RV sometimes uses "encampments," and the NIV "fortresses." Nehemiah erected a "castle" in Jerusalem that later became the Tower of Antonia, where Paul was confined.

CASTOR AND POLLUX (kăs'têr, pŏl'ŭks, Gr. *Dioskyroi, sons of Zeus*). In Greek mythology they were sons of Zeus by Leda, one of his numerous mistresses. Castor was a horseman and Pollux an adept boxer. They were later put in the sky in the constellation known as "Gemini," "the Twins," and were considered as tutelary deities favorable to sailors, a fact that explains why the ship mentioned in Acts 28:11, in which Paul sailed, was named in their honor. St. Elmo's fire used to be credited to Castor and Pollux.

CATERPILLAR (See ANIMALS)

CATHOLIC EPISTLES. A term applied to the Epistles of James, Peter, John, and Jude. It goes back to the early church fathers, but how it arose is unknown. The most commonly accepted explanation is that these epistles were addressed, not to individual churches or persons, but to a number of churches. They were addressed to the church at large, i.e., the universal church. The seeming exceptions, 2 and 3 John, were probably included as properly belonging with 1 John and of value to the general reader.

CATTLE (See ANIMALS)

CAUDA (kow'dȧ). A small island lying about

twenty-five (forty-two km.) miles to the south of Crete (Acts 27:16; KJV "Clauda") and now called Gavdo. Here Paul and his companions were almost wrecked on their journey toward Rome.

CAVE. A hollowed-out place in the earth, whether formed by nature or by man. In a mountainous land such as Palestine, where there is much limestone, caves are likely to be quite numerous. Caves were often used for regular human habitation, for hiding from the law or from enemies in warfare, for securing precious treasure (such as the Dead Sea Scrolls), for storehouses and cisterns, for stables and cattle, and for burial (Gen 19:30; 1 Kings 19:9).

CEDAR (See PLANTS)

CEDRON (See KIDRON)

CEILING. The word appears only in 1 Kings 6:15 (KJV "ceiling"), which says that Solomon built the walls of the ceiling with cedar. The reference here is not to the upper surface of a room, but to the inner walls. The word "ceiled" appears several times, but it usually means to panel the walls of a building.

CELIBACY. The state of being unmarried, particularly when this state is deliberately chosen. The Bible lays down no definitive rules about it. John the Baptist, for example, was unmarried, but Peter was married. Jesus himself did not marry, but he contributed notably to the wedding celebrations at Cana (John 2:1–11). He realized that some "have renounced marriage because of the kingdom of heaven" (Matt 19:12), and once he warned against wrong priorities if to become married would be a positive hindrance to discipleship (Luke 14:20). Paul recognized the dangers of earthly ties and stressed basic principles: God has an assignment for every life, and whatever our situation, married or single, the main thing is to be able to exercise our God-given gifts to the full (1 Cor 7:7–9, 17, 32–38).

CELLAR. A place for storage of wine (1 Chron 27:27, KJV, RSV) or oil (27:28 KJV). The root idea is not that of a room under a house, but that of a place of storage; thus NIV renders "vat" in 27:27, and in 27:28 prefers "supplies of olive oil."

CENCHREA (sĕn'krē-ȧ). The eastern harbor of Corinth, and the little town on the harbor. Paul in Romans 16:1 commends to the Roman church a deaconess called Phoebe of the church at Cenchrea, a church that Paul may have founded on his second missionary journey. Paul stopped here to have his head shaved in fulfillment of a vow (Acts 18:18).

CENSER. A vessel, probably shaped like a saucepan, for holding incense while it is being burned (Num 16:6–7, 39). The same Hebrew word is sometimes rendered "firepan" (Exod 27:3) or "snuffdish." NIV in certain contexts uses "wick trimmer" (Exod 25:28; 37:23; Num 4:9).

The renowned caves at Qumran, place where the Dead Sea Scrolls were discovered early in 1947 by a Bedouin goatherd. Courtesy S. Zur Picture Library.

CENSUS. A numbering and registration of a people. The OT tells of three different occasions when a formal census was taken. The first was at Mount Sinai, soon after the Israelites left Egypt (Num 1). The second was at Shittim near the end of the forty years' wilderness wandering. The third was made by David (2 Sam 24:1–9; 1 Chron 21:1–5). The exiles who returned from Babylonia with Zerubbabel were also numbered (Ezra 2). Shortly before the birth of Christ, Emperor Augustus ordered an enrollment in his empire (Luke 2:1).

CENTURION (cĕn-tū'rĭ-ŏn, Lat. *centum, one hundred*). A commander of a hundred soldiers in the Roman army. The word is mentioned first in connection with the centurion of Capernaum whose beloved servant was deathly sick (Matt 8:5–13; Luke 7:2–10). This officer had built a synagogue for the Jews, who therefore appreciated him and begged Jesus to heal the servant. The centurion showed real reverence for Jesus in saying, "I do not deserve to have you come under my roof," and Jesus responded, "I have not found anyone in Israel with such great faith." Cornelius (Acts 10), another centurion, was "devout and God-fearing." Peter was sent to him and "used the keys" to open up salvation to the Gentiles, as he had at Jerusalem for the Jews (Acts 2) and at Samaria for its people (Acts 8:14–17). Another centurion, Julius, of the Imperial Regiment (Acts 27:1–43), had the duty of taking Paul to Rome. He saved Paul's life when the soldiers wished to kill all the prisoners, and Paul by his presence and counsel saved the centurion and all the ship's company. Other centurions are mentioned elsewhere (Matt 27:54; Acts 22:25; 23:17). ABF

CEPHAS (sē′fās, Gr. *Kēphas,* from Aram. *Kepha, rock, or stone*). A name given by Jesus to the apostle Peter (John 1:42). See PETER.

CHAFF. The refuse of the grain that has been threshed and winnowed. This is partly dust and dirt, but the real chaff is the hard and inedible coat of the grain. By threshing, most of this is separated; then on a windy day the grain is tossed into the air and the chaff and the shorter pieces of straw are blown away. In Isaiah 5:24 and 33:11, the word properly means "dry hay" fit for burning. The more common Hebrew word is generally used as a figure for worthless or godless men (e.g., Ps 1:4—"Not so the wicked! They are like chaff that the wind blows away"). It is used also for godless nations (Isa 17:13). The evanescence of the wicked is likened in Hosea 13:3 to the morning mist, the early dew, "chaff swirling from a threshing floor," and "smoke escaping through a window" (KJV "chimney"). In Daniel 2:35 the Aramaic word rendered "chaff" signifies the small chaff that can get into the eye and irritate it. The word in Jeremiah 23:28 means the broken straw. In the preaching of John the Baptist (Matt 3:12; Luke 3:17) our Lord is to save the righteous ("gathering his wheat into his barn") and destroy the wicked ("burning up the chaff with unquenchable fire").

CHAIN. The English word represents many Hebrew words meaning "chain, necklace, band, bracelet, clasp, hook, ring, and rope." Chains were used for the following purposes:

1. As marks of distinction, in the cases of Joseph (Gen 41:42) and Daniel (Dan 5:7, 16, 29).

2. For ornaments. Chains were used to adorn the tabernacle (Exod 28:14, 22; 39:15, 17–18). Chains were among the atonement offerings (Num 31:50; NIV "Carmel"). Some people attached ornaments to their animals, such as the Midianites, who adorned their camels' necks (Judg 8:21, 26). Wreaths of chainwork ornamented the tops of the pillars (1 Kings 7:17; 2 Chron 3:16) and other places in Solomon's temple (1 Kings 6:21; 2 Chron 3:5). As jewelry, chains are referred to in Psalm 73:6 (NIV "hooks"); Proverbs 1:9; Song of Songs 4:9 (NIV "necklace"); Isaiah 3:20; 40:19 (idols); Ezekiel 16:11 (NIV "necklace").

3. For fetters (Ps 149:8 [NIV "fetters"]; Isa 45:14; Jer 39:7 [NIV "shackles"]; 40:1; Lam 3:7; Ezek 7:23; 19:4, 9 [NIV "hooks"]; Nah 3:10). In the NT most of the references represent the Greek *halysis, chain.* In Mark 5:3–4; Luke 8:29 chains are used to bind a demoniac; in Acts 12:6–7, Peter in prison was bound with two chains, but was quickly released. In Acts 28:20 Paul was bound by a chain on his right hand to a soldier's left. Paul refers to this in 2 Timothy 1:16; this circumstance offers one explanation of why Paul dictated his letters to a secretary. An angel binds Satan with a chain (Rev 20:1). In Jude 6 "chain" translates *desmos,* anything for tying or fastening. See also DRESS. ER

CHALCEDONY (See MINERALS)

CHALCOL (See CALCOL)

CHALDEA (kăl-dē′ă). The country of which Babylon was the capital, and which conquered Judah and carried its inhabitants into captivity. The name of the country and that of its people (Chaldeans) occurs fairly frequently (e.g., Gen 11:28; Job 1:17; Ezek 23:14–16; Acts 7:4), but sometimes NIV translates it "Babylonia" (Jer 50:10; 51:24, 35; Ezek 11:24; 16:29; but see footnote for each).

CHAMBERING. Repeated or habitual acts of illicit intercourse (Rom 13:13), rendered by NIV as "sexual immorality."

CHAMBERLAIN (See OCCUPATIONS AND PROFESSIONS)

CHAMELEON (See ANIMALS)

CHAMOIS (See ANIMALS)

CHANCELLOR. A Persian official in Palestine (Ezra 4:8–9, 17 KJV). RSV translates this word as "commander," NIV "commanding officer."

CHANGERS OF MONEY. Men who exchanged one currency for another at a premium. Coins issued by many governments circulated in Palestine; also Jews had to convert their currency into shekels for the temple tax. It was not the trade but the place where they plied it that led Christ to drive them out of the temple court (Matt 21:12; Mark 11:15; John 2:14–15); all three passages use the Greek *kollybistēs,* "a changer of small coin." John 2:14 has *kermatistēs,* with identical meaning. The word *trapezitēs,* found only in Matthew 25:27, is rendered "exchangers" (KJV) or "banker" (NIV, RSV), a lender of money at interest. Both used tables (*trapezas*) and often combined the two functions.

CHARASHIM (See GE HARASHIM)

CHARCHEMISH (See CARCHEMISH)

CHARCOAL (See COAL)

CHARGER. A dish or platter given as an offering for the tabernacle (Num 7:13–85); called "dishes" in Exodus 25:29; 37:16. NIV consistently renders as "plates." Another word (Ezra 1:9) refers to baskets or dishes (so NIV) belonging to the temple service. The NT word means a wooden dish or platter (Matt 14:8, 11; Mark 6:25, 28).

CHARIOT (Heb. *rekhev* and derivatives, from a root meaning *mount and ride*). A two-wheeled vehicle drawn by two horses. In Egypt, Joseph rode in Pharaoh's second chariot (Gen 41:43). Chariots were in Jacob's funeral procession (Gen 50:9). Pharaoh pursued the children of Israel into

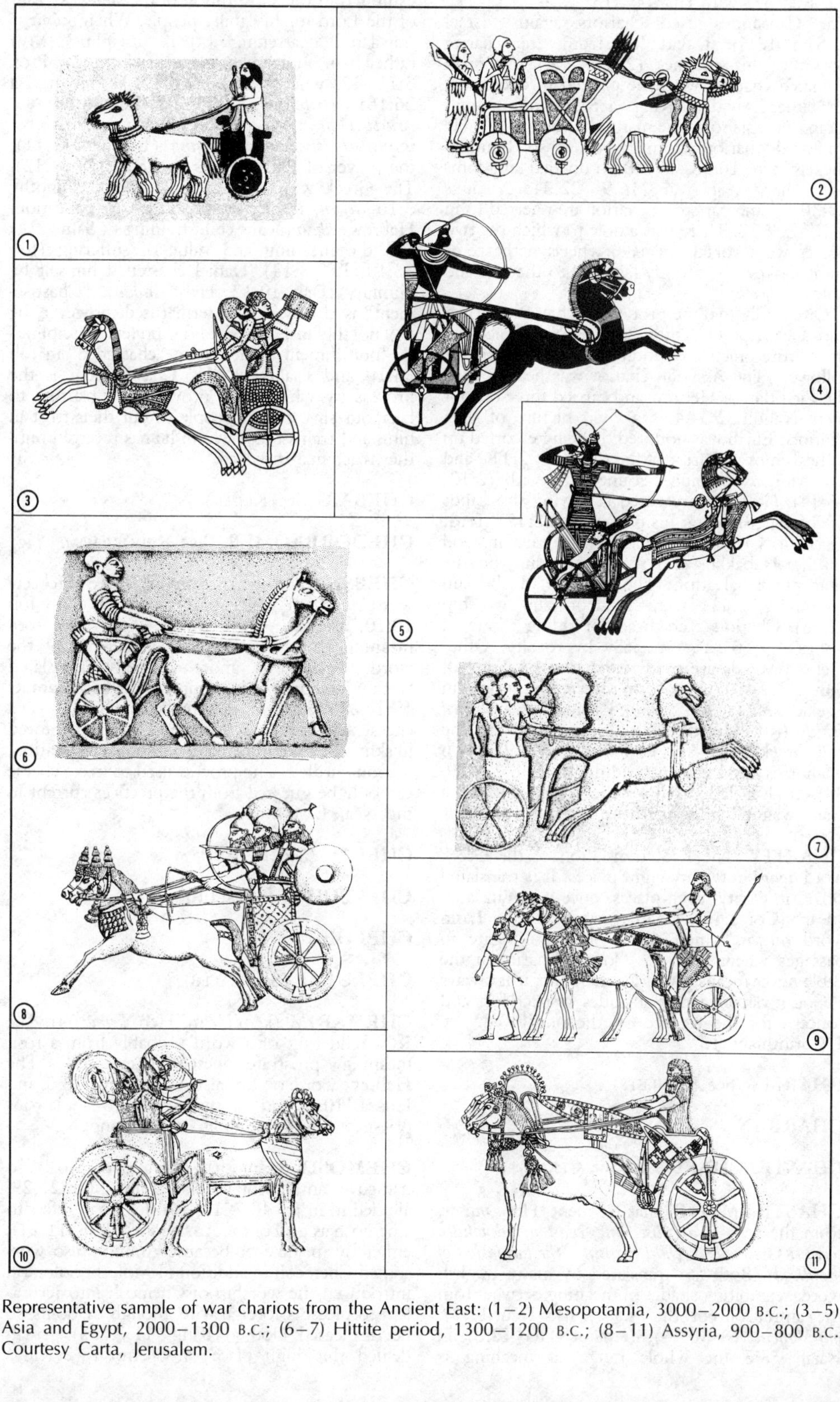

Representative sample of war chariots from the Ancient East: (1–2) Mesopotamia, 3000–2000 B.C.; (3–5) Asia and Egypt, 2000–1300 B.C.; (6–7) Hittite period, 1300–1200 B.C.; (8–11) Assyria, 900–800 B.C. Courtesy Carta, Jerusalem.

the Red Sea with chariots (Exod 14:7–15:19). The Canaanites used chariots against Israel (1 Sam 13:5). David hamstrung the chariot horses of his enemies (2 Sam 8:4). Adonijah prepared chariots when he plotted to overthrow his father David (1 Kings 1:5). Solomon built establishments to house many chariots (9:19). He imported chariots from Egypt at six hundred shekels each (10:28–29). Both divided kingdoms used chariots in war (16:9; 22:34; 2 Kings 23:30). Some parts of a chariot are referred to in 1 Kings 7:33. There was a pole to which the two horses were yoked, an axle, wheels with six or eight spokes, and a body fastened to the axle and pole.

Often only two men rode in a chariot, a driver and a warrior (1 Kings 22:34); but sometimes the Hittite practice of adding a shield-bearer was followed. The Assyrian chariot was heavier than the Egyptian or Hebrew and carried three or four men. Nahum 2:3–4 is a vivid picture of such chariots. Elijah was honored by being escorted up to heaven by a chariot of fire (2 Kings 2:11), and his manner of going became a proverb (2:12; 13:14). God is represented as having thousands of chariots, showing his power (Ps 68:17). Trust in chariots is vain compared with trust in God (20:7). Habakkuk 3:8 sees God riding on the chariots of salvation. The chariots of the sun (2 Kings 23:11) were used in sun worship (23:5). Chariots were used for riding (Song of Songs 1:9; 6:12), especially by royalty. Other Hebrew words are used for chariot: in Song of Songs 3:9–10, a *litter* or *carriage* is meant; in Ezekiel 23:24, a *war chariot;* Psalm 46:9, a *wheeled vehicle* (NIV "shields," but see footnote). In the NT, Greek *harma* is a *war chariot* (Rev 9:9) drawn by horses used also for riding (Acts 8:28–29, 38). In Revelation 18:13 the word is *rhedē,* a Gallic wagon with four wheels. ER

CHARITY. The KJV translation of the Greek word *agapē* in twenty-eight places. It is translated "love" in eighty-seven places; once it is translated "dear" (Col 1:13). Charity represents the Latin word *caritas,* which stands in the Vulgate in passages where KJV has "love." Charity in the Bible never means giving to the poor; it is always a God-given love that includes respect for, and concern for the welfare of, the one loved. See 1 Corinthians 13.

CHARMS (See AMULETS)

CHARRAN (See HARAN)

CHASTE, CHASTITY (See CLEAN)

CHASTISEMENT (chăs'tĭz-mĕnt, Heb. *mûsār,* from the verb *yāsar, discipline, chasten, admonish, correct;* Gr. *paideia, child-training, the formation of manhood*). Both are translated by many English words, exhibiting shades of meaning derived from the central concept: the widest sense (Deut 11:2); *punishment* (Jer 30:14); *discipline* (Heb 12:8); in Isaiah 53:5 the whole range of meaning is exhibited in the substitution of the sinless servant of the Lord for his guilty people. When *mûsār* is translated "chastening" (KJV), "discipline" (NIV) rather than punishment is meant (Job 5:17; Prov 3:11–12, whence Heb 12:5–11 is drawn; Isa 26:16); *retribution, punishment* (Lev 26:28); *instruction in wisdom* is prominent in Proverbs; *unjust chastisement, scourging* (1 Kings 12:11); the prayer of Psalm 6:1 is answered (Ps 94:12). The Greek word in Acts 7:22–23; 2 Timothy 3:16 (*learn, teach, instruct*) refers to education. Hebrew *yākah* means child-training (2 Sam 7:14) and the meaning and value of suffering (Job 33:19; Ps 73:14). Daniel chastened himself by humility (Dan 10:12, Heb. *'ānâh*). "Chastisement" is chiefly a KJV term (used, however, by RSV notably in Isa 53:5). NIV prefers "discipline" or "punishment," but retains "chastened" in Job 33:19 and Psalm 118:18. Chastisement is the process by which God provides a substitute to bear our sins, brings people to put their trust in him, and trains those whom he has received until they reach maturity. ER

CHEBAR (See KEBAR)

CHEDORLAOMER (See KEDORLAOMER)

CHEESE. The translation of three Hebrew words, each of which occurs only once. In Job 10:10, *gevînâh,* "curd, cheese," is from a root meaning "coagulate." In 2 Samuel 17:29 the word *shaphah* is more properly translated "cream," because it is skimmed off. In 1 Samuel 17:18 *hărītsî hehālāv* denotes "cuts of milk"—i.e., cheese. Milk of cows, goats, and sheep was stored in skins. In a warm climate, without refrigeration, it soon curdled. The process used to make cheese can only be guessed from the practices current in the Near East today.

CHELAL (See KELAL)

CHELLUH (See KELUHI)

CHELUB (See KELUB)

CHELUBAI (See CALEB)

CHEMARIM (kĕm'ȧ-rĭm, Heb. *kemārîm*). The KJV rendering of a word probably from a root meaning "prostrate oneself" (Zeph 1:4). The Hebrew word occurs also in 2 Kings 23:5 and Hosea 10:5 and always refers to idolatrous priests, thus the reading in RSV and NIV.

CHEMOSH (kē'mŏsh). The god of Moab, so named in an ancient Israelite song (Num 21:29, alluded to in Jer 48:7, 13, 46). Jephthah refers to Chemosh as god of the Ammonites (Judg 11:24), either by mistake or because Ammon also worshiped Chemosh in addition to Molech. Solomon introduced the worship of Chemosh into Jerusalem to please a foreign wife, though by doing so he displeased God (1 Kings 11:7, 33). Josiah defiled this high place of Chemosh (2 Kings

23:13), putting an end to its use as a place of worship. Mesha, king of Moab, suffered a great disaster in his rebellion against Israel, in consequence of which he offered his son, the heir to the throne of Moab, as a burnt offering (3:4–27). The inscription on the Moabite Stone shows that this sacrifice was made to Chemosh and describes the help that Mesha believed Chemosh had given his people in war and the chastisement that Chemosh meted out to them when they were unfaithful. The terms used are so similar in style to the terms used by the Israelites of the true God that they serve only to accentuate the contrast between the two.

CHENAANAH (See KENAANAH)

CHENANI (See KENANI)

CHENANIAH (See KENANIAH)

CHEPHAR-HAAMMONI (See KEPHAR AMMONI)

CHEPHIRAH (See KEPHIRAH)

CHERAN (See KERAN)

CHERETHITES, CHERETHIM (See KERETHITES)

CHERITH (See KERITH)

CHERUB, CHERUBIM (chĕr'ub, chĕr'ŭ-bĭm). In other than biblical usage the English plural is cherubs. The cherubim and a flaming sword were placed at the east of Eden to guard the way to the Tree of Life after Adam and Eve were expelled from the Garden of Eden (Gen 3:24). The curtains of the tabernacle were embroidered with cherubim (Exod 26:1). God directed Moses to place two cherubim of beaten gold on the mercy seat above the ark, where God would commune with Moses in the tabernacle (25:18–22; 37:7–9). God's glory rested between the cherubim (Num 7:89; 1 Sam 4:4; 2 Sam 6:2; 2 Kings 19:15; Ps 80:1; 99:1; Isa 37:16), in both the tabernacle and the temple. The cherubim in the temple were huge figures newly made for the purpose (1 Kings 6:23–28; 2 Chron 3:10–13; 5:7–8). Carved cherubim also ornamented the walls of the temple (1 Kings 6:29). Hebrews 9:5 mentions the cherubim in the tabernacle. David sings of God riding on a cherub (2 Sam 22:11; Ps 18:10). Psalm 18 pictures a storm with God riding on and speaking from the clouds.

That the cherubim were more than clouds or statues is plain from the description Ezekiel gives (Ezek 9:3; 10:1–22), which shows that they are the "living creatures" of the first chapter. The four faces of each of the cherubim (1:10) stand for the four "excellencies" of the created order: the lion, the greatest of the wild beasts; the eagle, the greatest of the birds; the ox, the greatest of the domestic beasts; and man, the crown of creation. Ezekiel sees, over the heads of the cherubim, the throne of the God who is thus absolutely sovereign over his whole creation, in all its variety of life and being and in all its complexity of movement. The same explanation of the cherub-form suits their function both in Eden (Creation in its ideal purity consents to the Creator's edict of exclusion from the Garden) and on the mercy seat (all the created excellencies marvel and adore the Triune God for the shed blood of atonement). At

"There above the cover between the two cherubim that are over the ark of the Testimony, I will meet with you and give you all my commands . . ." (Exod 25:22). These ivory carvings borrowed from Phoenician art are now understood to be winged sphinxes with human faces. (See also 1 Kings 6:23–29.) Reproduced by courtesy of the Trustees of the British Museum.

the same time, Ezekiel's vision explains the OT allusion to the Lord as seated (or enthroned) on/between the cherubim (e.g., Ps 99:1); it is a metaphor of his total sovereignty. Likewise when the Lord rides on the cherubim (e.g., Ps 18:10; Ezek 10 passim), the thought is that all creation is subject to his sovereign rule and "intervention," and all its powers are at his disposal.

In Revelation 4:6–9; 5:6–14; 6:1–11; 14:3; 15:7; 19:4 are four "beasts" (Gr. *zōa, living creatures;* so ASV, RSV, NIV; these are to be distinguished from the Gr. *thēria, wild beasts,* mentioned, e.g., in Rev 13:1). They are described in terms that identify them with Ezekiel's living creatures or cherubim (Ezek 1, 10). The first living creature was like a lion, the second like a calf, the third had a face as a man, the fourth was like a flying eagle (Rev 4:7). They are the bearers of the judgments that follow the breaking of the first four seals.

To sum up: The cherubim are the living chariot or carriers of God when appearing to men. They are heavenly creatures, servants of God in theophany and judgment, appearing in winged human-animal form with the faces of lion, ox, man, and eagle. Their representations in the tabernacle and temple as statues and in embroidery and carving are not a breach of the second commandment (Exod 20:4). They are significant in prophecy (Ezekiel) and in the Apocalypse (Revelation). Their service is rendered immediately to God. They never come closer to man than when one took fire in his hand and gave it into the hands of "the man in linen" (Ezek 10:7). Yet because the mercy seat, on which the blood of atonement was sprinkled, lay "between the cherubim," nothing can more nearly touch our salvation. In the OT sanctuary, where everything was done and taught by visible, tangible types and symbols, physical representations of the living heavenly cherubim were essential. In Ezekiel's new temple, and in the heavenly sanctuary of Hebrews and Revelation, they are no longer needed, for the redeemed themselves stand in the presence of the living cherubim. The carvings in Ezekiel 41:18 are memorials only. ER

CHERUB (See KERUB)

CHESALON (See KESALON)

CHESED (See KESED)

CHESIL (See KESIL)

CHEST. 1. Receptacles for money to repair the temple (2 Kings 12:9–10; 2 Chron 24:8, 10–11). Hebrew *'ărôn* is translated "coffin" once (Gen 50:26); elsewhere the "ark" in tabernacle and temple.

2. "Chests of rich apparel, bound with cords and made of cedar," of the merchandise of Tyre (Ezek 27:24 KJV) is renderd in NIV as "multicolored rugs with cords twisted and tightly knotted." Hebrew *genāzîm* is rendered "treasuries" in Esther 3:9 and 4:7, KJV, RSV; NIV has "treasury."

CHESTNUT TREE (See PLANTS)

CHESULLOTH (See KESULLOTH)

CHEZIB (See KEZIB)

CHICKEN (See BIRDS)

CHIDON (See KIDON)

CHILD, CHILDREN. Among the people of the OT and NT, as in most other cultures, children, especially male, were greatly desired (Gen 15:2; 30:1; 1 Sam 1:11, 20; Ps 127:3; 128:3; Luke 1:7, 28). Among the Hebrews all the firstborn belonged to God and had to be redeemed (Num 3:40–51). Children were sometimes dedicated to God for special service (Judg 13:2–7; 1 Sam 1:11; Luke 1:13–17, 76–79). Male descendants of Abraham were circumcised on the eighth day (Gen 17:12; 21:4; Luke 1:59; 2:21), when the name was given. Weaning often was delayed and then celebrated (Gen 21:8) with a feast. Education was primarily in the home and was the duty of parents (Exod 12:26–27; Deut 6:7; Josh 4:21–24; Prov 22:6; Eph 6:4; Col 3:21; 2 Tim 3:15). Discipline was to be firm, with corporal punishment (Prov 22:15; 23:13; 29:15). Much was expected of children (Prov 20:11). Obedience and respect to parents was commanded (Exod 21:17; Eph 6:1–3; Col 3:20; 1 Tim 3:4, 12; Titus 1:6). Favoritism was sometimes shown (Gen 25:28; 37:3). Affection for children is strikingly portrayed in many instances, as in David's love for a child who died (2 Sam 12:15–23); and in the raising of children to life by Elijah (1 Kings 17:17–24), by Elisha (2 Kings 4:18–37), and by Jesus (Matt 9:23–26; Mark 5:35–43; Luke 8:49–56). Jesus' love and concern for children is seen in Matthew 18:1–14; 19:13–15; Mark 9:35–37; 10:13–16; Luke 9:46–48; 18:15–17. Jesus recognized children's play (Matt 11:16). There are many reports of attractive childhood—e.g., Moses (Exod 2:1–10), Samuel (1 Sam 1:20–3:19), Jesus (Luke 2:7–40), Timothy (2 Tim 1:5; 3:14–15).

"Children" is an affectionate address, as in 1 John, of an old man to adults, who are nevertheless expected to act their age (1 Cor 13:11; 14:20). The attention given to the childhood of the Messiah in prophecy (Isa 7:14; 9:6) prepares us for the infancy narratives in Matthew 2 and Luke 2. The Savior came as a helpless babe and apparently had a normal childhood. A return to childlike receptiveness and trust is required of those who would enter the kingdom of heaven (Matt 18:1–14; 19:13–15; Mark 9:35–37; 10:13–16; Luke 9:46–48; 18:15–17). ER

CHILDBEARING. The word occurs in 1 Timothy 2:15 in a passage relating to the proper sphere and conduct of women. "Women will be saved through childbearing" (NIV; KJV, RSV are similar) cannot refer to salvation from sin, which is by grace through faith, but to safekeeping through the pain that became incidental to childbirth through the Fall (Gen 3:16). See NIV footnote: "restored." Hebrew mothers had the assistance of midwives (Exod 1:15–21). Newborn babies had the navel cut, were washed with water, salted, and wrapped in swaddling clothes (Ezek 16:4; Luke 2:7, 12). Purification rites were prescribed after childbirth (Lev 12; Luke 2:22–24).

CHILDREN OF GOD (See SON OF GOD and SONS OF GOD, CHILDREN OF GOD)

CHILEAB (See KILEAB)

CHILION (See KILION)

CHILMAD (See KILMAD)

CHIMHAM (See GERUTH KIMHAM)

CHINNERETH (See KINNERETH)

CHIOS (See KIOS)

CHISLEV (See KISLEV)

CHISLON (See KISLON)

CHISLOTH-TABOR (See KISLOTH TABOR)

CHITTIM (See KITTIM)

CHIUN (kī'ŭn). Possibly Saturn as god, but the meaning of the Hebrew word is uncertain. Thus in Amos 5:26 where KJV has "the tabernacle of your Molech and Chiun your images, the star of your god," NIV has "the shrine of your king, the pedestal of your idols, the star of your god" (but see footnote). RSV translates: "Sakkuth your king, and Kaiwan your star-god, your images."

CHLOE (klō'ē). A woman whose people informed Paul of contentions in the Corinthian church (1 Cor 1:11). Where she lived and how her people gained their information is not told. She was well known to the Corinthian Christians by her personal name.

CHORASHAN (See ASHAN)

CHRIST, JESUS (krīst, jē'zŭs, Gr. *Iēsous,* for Heb. *Jeshua, Jehoshua, Joshua, Jehovah is salvation;* Heb. *māshîah,* Gr. *Christos, anointed*).

I. Comprehensive Life and Work. Although the life of Christ, as ordinarily understood, embraces the years our Lord spent on this earth, as described in the four Gospels, his full career spans the ages and invites reflection on its several aspects. Fundamental to the various "I Am" sayings of Jesus is his assertion of absolute existence (John 8:58). Therefore it is reasonable to think of him as belonging to eternity. Scripture, in fact, affirms his preexistence and does so in terms of fellowship with the Father (1:1), glory (17:5), and designation in advance as the Savior of the world (1 Peter 1:20). His more immediate relation to the realm of people and things belongs to his activity in creation. All things came into being through him (John 1:3; 1 Cor 8:6; Heb 1:2) and in him continue to have their cohesive principle (Col 1:17). Evidence is not lacking for his presence also in the OT. The manifestations of God in this period are apparently connected with the preincarnate Christ. When Isaiah glimpsed the glory of God, he was seeing Christ (John 12:41). Moses and the prophets spoke of him (Luke 24:27, 44; John 5:46), with special reference to his sufferings and the glories that would follow (1 Peter 1:11). Some of the more important passages of a predictive nature are Genesis 3:15; Deuteronomy 18:15, 18; Psalms 2, 16, 22, 110; Isaiah 7:14; 9:6, 7, 11; 42:1–4; 52:13–53:12; 61:1, 2; Jeremiah 23:5–6; Micah 5:2. In addition there are covenantal statements that do not speak of the Messiah directly and personally, but that involve him in crucial ways (Gen 12:3; 2 Sam 7:12–16). As though in anticipation of the Incarnation, the Son of God showed himself at times to the faithful in visible form as the Angel of the Lord or the Angel of the covenant (Gen 18:1–19:1; Judg 13). Before his advent Christ had thoroughly identified himself with his people, so that when he came, he came to his own (John 1:11).

By the Incarnation, the Christ of God took on himself human nature in order to reveal God to people in a way they could grasp (1:14, 18), to become their Savior by ransoming them from their sins (Mark 10:45), and to deal sympatheti-

Aerial view (facing north) of Bethlehem, birthplace of Christ. Courtesy Israel Government Press Office.

cally with their needs (Heb 2:17–18). Today, in glory, he is still the God-man. The Incarnation persists.

The present ministry of Christ is being carried on in heaven, where he represents the saints before the throne of God (Heb 7:25; 1 John 2:1). By the successful completion of his work on earth he is exalted to be the head of the church (Eph 1:22; 4:15) and by the Spirit directs the life and service of his saints on earth (Matt 28:20).

One purpose of the Incarnation was not achieved during the earthly ministry of our Lord but is reserved for his second coming. His kingly rule will then be introduced following his work as judge (Matt 25:31–34). This future coming is one of the major truths set forth in the epistles (Phil 3:20–21; 2 Thess 1:7–10) and is the leading theme of the Revelation. After the millennial kingdom, Christ will enter with his people the blessedness of the eternal state, which will be unmarred by the inroads of sin or death.

II. Earthly Ministry. The long-heralded Christ came in the fullness of time (Gal 4:4). God providentially supplied the proper background for his appearing and mission. The world had become to a great extent homogeneous through the spread of the Greek language and culture and through the organizing genius of Rome. The means were thus provided for the spread of the gospel once it had been forged out in the career of the Son of God. His advent occurred at a point in human history when the law of Moses had done its work of demonstrating the sinfulness of man and the impossibility of achieving righteousness by human effort. Men here and there were looking with longing for spiritual deliverance.

Entirely in keeping with this divine control of the circumstances surrounding the Incarnation is the careful selection of the Virgin Mary as the mother of Jesus. The birth of the Savior was natural, but his conception was supernatural by the power of the Holy Spirit (Matt 1:18; Luke 1:35). Augustus, too, was drawn into the circle of the instruments chosen by God when he ordered a universal enrollment for taxation, not realizing that by doing so he would make possible the birth of Jesus in the place appointed by prophetic announcement (Mic 5:2; Luke 2:1–7). The shepherds, by their readiness to seek out the babe in the manger and by their joy at seeing him, became prototypes of the humble souls in Jewry who in coming days would recognize in Jesus their Savior. An intimation of Gentile desire to participate in the Christ may be seen in the coming of the Magi from the East. In darker perspective appears the figure of Herod, emblematic of the hatred and opposition that would meet Jesus of Nazareth and work for his death. In the scribes, who are conversant with the Scriptures but apathetic about seeking the One who fulfilled them, we see the shape of things to come—the leaders of a nation refusing to receive him when he came to his own.

In more theological terms the Christ-event is an incarnation. God was manifest in flesh. The One who was in the form of God took the form of a servant and was made in the likeness of men (Phil 2:6–7). Therefore, when the Scriptures assert from time to time that God sent his Son into the world, this affirmation is not to be treated as though Christ is merely a messenger of God, like the ancient prophets. Rather, he is the eternal Son of God now clothing himself with human nature to accomplish the salvation of people. Though the expression "God-man" is not found in the sacred records, it faithfully expresses the truth regarding the person of Jesus Christ. God did not appropriate a man who already existed and make of him an instrument for the working out of the divine purposes. He took what is common to us all, our human nature, yet free from any taint of sin, and combined it with deity to become an actual person with his own individuality. This is the mystery of the Incarnation. The gulf between the Creator and the creature is bridged, first by the person of Christ and then by his mediatorial work.

The boyhood of Jesus should be approached from the standpoint of the truth revealed about the Incarnation. Deity did not eclipse humanity so as to render the process of learning unnecessary. Christ grew in body and advanced in knowledge and in the wisdom that enabled him to make proper use of what he knew. He did not command his parents but rather obeyed them, fulfilling the law in this matter as in all others. The scriptural accounts have none of the fanciful extravagances of the Apocryphal Gospels, which present the boy Jesus as a worker of wonders during his early years. They emphasize his progress in the understanding of the OT and affirm his consciousness of a special relation to his Father in heaven (Luke 2:49).

Aerial view of modern Nazareth, place where Jesus grew to manhood. Archaeological evidence shows that Nazareth was already occupied in Early Bronze Age. To judge by some 25 graves accidentally uncovered during construction work, the town in New Testament times was higher up its western slope than the present Nazareth and apparently a small village of little importance (cf. John 1:46). Courtesy Israel Government Press Office.

At his baptism Jesus received divine confirmation of the mission now opening out before him and also the anointing of the Holy Spirit for the fulfillment of it. The days of preparation were definitely at an end, so that retirement was put aside and contact begun with his people Israel. By the Baptism he was fulfilling all righteousness (Matt 3:15) in the sense that he was identifying himself with those he came to redeem.

Closely related to the Baptism is the Temptation, for it also includes this representative character. The first Adam failed when put to the test; the last Adam succeeded, though weakened by hunger and harried by the desolation of the wilderness. In essence, the Temptation was the effort of Satan to break Christ's dependence on the Father, so that he would desert the standpoint of man and rely on special consideration as the Son of God. But Christ refused to be moved from his determined place of chosen identification with the human race. "Man does not live on bread alone. . ." was his first line of defense. He maintained it in the two following episodes, quoting the obligation of Israel in relation to God as his own reason for refusing to be moved from a place of trustful dependence on the Almighty (Matt 4:7, 10).

Only when equipped by the Baptism and seasoned by the ordeal of temptation was Jesus ready for his life and work. No word of teaching and no work of power is attributed to him prior to these events, but immediately afterward he began moving in the power of the Spirit to undertake the work the Father had given him to do (Luke 4:14).

The public ministry of Jesus was brief. Its length has to be estimated from the materials recorded in the Gospels. John gives more information on this point than the other Evangelists. Judging from the number of Passovers mentioned there (John 2:23; 5:1; 6:4; 13:1), the period was at least somewhat in excess of two years and possibly more than three.

John supplements the Synoptic Gospels also in the description of the place of ministry. Whereas the Synoptists put chief stress on Galilee, plus notice of a visit to the regions of Tyre and Sidon (Matt 15:21–28), Caesarea-Philippi (16:13ff.), the Gentile cities of the Decapolis (Mark 7:31; cf. also Mark 5:1–20), Samaria (Luke 9:51–56; 17:11), and the region east of the Jordan River known as Perea (Mark 10:1), John reports several visits to Jerusalem. In fact, most of his record is taken up with accounts of Jesus' ministry in Judea. The Synoptists hint at such a ministry (e.g., Matt 23:37; Luke 10:38–42) but give little information.

During his Galilean mission, Jesus made the city of Capernaum his headquarters. From this center he went out, usually in the company of his disciples, to challenge the people in city and town and village with his message. Several such tours are indicated in the sacred text (Mark 1:38, 6:6; Luke 8:1). A part of his ministry consisted in healings and exorcisms, for many had diseases of various sorts and many were afflicted with demon

The Mount of Temptation with a Greek Orthodox monastery built into its slopes. It is the traditional site where Jesus fasted and prayed for forty days and resisted the temptations of Satan (Matt 4:1–11). Courtesy Israel Government Press Office.

possession. These miracles were not only tokens of divine compassion but also signs that in the person of Jesus of Nazareth the Promised One had come (cf. Matt 11:2–6; Luke 4:16–19). They were revelations of the mercy and power of God at work in God's Anointed. Jesus found fault with the cities of Galilee for rejecting him despite the occurrence of so many mighty works in their midst (Matt 11:20–24).

The message proclaimed by Jesus during these journeys was epitomized in the phrase, "the kingdom of God." Fundamentally, this means the rule of God in human life and history. The phrase may have a more concrete significance at times, for Jesus spoke now and again about entering into the kingdom. In certain passages he spoke of the kingdom as future (Matt 25:31ff.), but in others of the kingdom as present (Luke 11:20). This last reference is of special importance, for it connects the kingdom with the activity of Jesus in casting out demons. To the degree that Jesus invades the kingdom of Satan in this fashion, the kingdom of God has already come. But in the more spiritual and positive aspects of kingdom teaching, where the individual life is concerned, the emphasis does not fall on invasion of personality or compulsive surrender to the power of God. The laws of discipleship are demanding indeed, but for their application they await the consent of the individual. No disciple is to be forced but is rather to be persuaded by the power of love and grace.

If we inquire more definitely into the relation of Jesus himself to the kingdom, we are obliged to conclude that he not only introduced the kingdom (in a sense, John the Baptist did that also) but also was its perfect embodiment. The appropriate response to the preaching of the kingdom is committal to the will of God (Matt 6:10), and it is crystal clear that doing the will of God was the mainspring of Jesus' ministry (Matt 12:50; Mark 14:36; John 4:34). It is evident, of course, that Jesus will also inaugurate the final phase of the kingdom when he comes again in power and glory. Entrance into the present aspect of the kingdom comes through faith in the Son of God and the successful completion of his mission. This could be done during his earthly ministry by anticipation of this redeeming work and thereafter by acceptance of the gospel message.

Much of our Lord's teaching was conveyed through parables. These were usually comparisons taken from various phases of nature or human life. "The kingdom of God is like . . . ." This method of teaching preserved the interest of the hearers until the spiritual application could be made. If the truth so taught was somewhat veiled by this method, this served to seal the spiritual blindness of the unrepentant and at the same time created a wholesome curiosity on the part of those who were disposed to believe, so that they could be led on to firm faith by more direct teaching.

The ministry of the Savior was predominantly to the multitudes during its earlier phase, as he sought out the people where they were, whether in the synagogue or on the city street or by the lakeside. "He went around doing good" is the way Peter described it (Acts 10:38). But much of Jesus' last year of ministry was given over to instruction of the twelve disciples whom he had chosen (for the two phases, see Matt 4:17 and 16:21). This shift of emphasis was not due primarily to the lack of response on the part of the multitudes, although his following faded at times (John 6:15, 66), but principally to his desire to instruct his disciples concerning himself and his mission. These men, nearly all Galileans and many of them fishermen, had been able to learn much through hearing Jesus address the crowds and through watching him heal the sick and relieve the distressed, and especially through being sent out by him to minister in his name (Luke 9:1–6). However, they needed more direct teaching to prepare them for the part they would play in the life of the church after the Ascension.

What they saw and heard during those early days confirmed their understanding of the person of Jesus as the Messiah and the Son of God (Matt 16:16), but they were quite unprepared to receive his teaching on the suffering and death that his earthly life would involve (16:21–23). Although this prospect was absolutely necessary for Jesus (16:21), for Peter it was something that the Lord could dismiss from consideration (16:22). If the most prominent one of the apostolic circle felt this way, no doubt the others were of the same mind. Their thoughts were so taken up with the prospect of a kingdom of external power and glory that they were perplexed and disturbed to find that their Master anticipated quite a different experience. His prediction of a resurrection from the dead fell on deaf ears, for the blow of the announcement about his forthcoming death had been too heavy. Even the lessons of the Transfiguration scene, where death was the theme under discussion and the glory beyond was presented to their sight, did not completely effect the orientation of the disciples to the teaching of Jesus. He had to repeat it more than once (Mark 10:33–45). Their sorrow in the garden of Gethsemane shows that they had reluctantly adjusted to it but could not look beyond it to resurrection nor could they realize how much that death itself could mean to their spiritual welfare. After the Resurrection they were much more open to the Lord's instruction, so when he appeared to them, he revealed from the OT the divine purpose prewritten there concerning himself (Luke 24:26–27, 44).

Christ's investment of time and patience with these men was well rewarded, for when the Spirit took up the work of instruction begun by him and gave them his own power for witness, they became effective instruments for declaring the Word of God and for the leadership of the Christian church. The record of the Book of Acts vindicates the wisdom of Christ and his understanding of the future.

In contrast to the Twelve in their attitude to Jesus are the scribes and Pharisees. The former were experts in the law and the traditions that had grown up around it, and the latter were men dedicated to a meticulous devotion to this heritage of Judaism. These groups usually worked together, and they collided with Jesus on many occasions over many issues. They were shocked that he would declare men's sins forgiven and claim a special relation to God as Son that others did not have. They resented his rejection of the traditions that they kept so carefully, and stood aghast at his willingness to break the Sabbath (in their way of thinking) by doing deeds of mercy on that day. It was tragic that men who held to the Scriptures as God's Word should fail to see in Jesus Christ the One of whom that Word spoke. They refused to put their trust in him despite all his miracles and the matchless perfection of his personal life. Because tradition meant more to them than truth, they stumbled in their apprehension of the Christ of God. In the end they plotted with their opponents the Sadducees in order to do away with Jesus.

Even as Christ was engaged in teaching his disciples from the days of the Transfiguration on, he was ever moving toward Jerusalem to fulfill his course at the cross (Luke 9:51). In those latter days some stirring events were unfolded—the triumphal entry into Jerusalem, the cleansing of the temple, the institution of the Lord's Supper, the soul conflict in the Garden of Gethsemane, the arrest and trial, the crucifixion, the resurrection, the appearances, the ascension into heaven. In all of them Jesus remained the central figure. In all of them he received testimony to himself or gave it. Nothing was unimportant. All contributed to the working out of the plan of God. The Cross was man's decision respecting Christ, but it had already been his own decision and that of the Father. It underscored the sins of some men even as it removed the sins of others. In the Cross man's day erupted in violence and blasphemy. In the Resurrection God's day began to dawn. It was his answer to the world and to the powers of darkness. In it Christ was justified and his claims illuminated.

III. Names, Titles, and Offices. Considerable help in understanding the person and work of Christ may be gleaned from a consideration of the terms used to designate him, especially as these are used by himself and his close associates. *Jesus* is used mostly in the narratives of the Gospels, and only rarely does it appear in direct address. It means "Savior" (Matt 1:21), being related philologically to the Hebrew name *Joshua*. Hebrews 4:8 in the KJV is rendered literally ("Jesus," instead of "Joshua"). For the most part the name *Jesus* is joined with other terms when used in the NT Epistles, but occasionally it stands alone, especially in Hebrews—doubtless for the purpose of emphasizing his humanity as a continuing element of his being. Thus, it is legitimate for us today to use the simple name in unadorned fashion, but to do so exclusively could indicate a lack of appreciation of the rounded presentation that Scripture gives of him.

Christ, meaning "anointed one," is the Greek equivalent of the Hebrew word *Messiah.* Its function as a title is emphasized by the fact that often it occurs with the definite article, which gives it the force of "the promised Christ," the one who fulfills the concept of Messiah as set forth in the OT Scriptures. Our Lord uses it of himself in Luke 24:46: "He told them, 'This is what is written: The Christ will suffer and rise from the dead on the third day.' " By extension of meaning, the same form is used by Paul as a synonym for the church (1 Cor 12:12), thus emphasizing the intimate bond between Christ and his people. Of special interest is the development that led to the use of "Christ" as a personal name. It must have taken place early in the life of the church, for we find it reflected, for example, in the opening verse of Mark's Gospel—"The beginning of the gospel of Jesus Christ, the Son of God." Possibly our Lord himself is responsible for this usage (John 17:3). In the NT letters there are numerous occurrences of Christ alone as a name (e.g., 1 Cor 15:3).

A circumstance that may strike the reader of the Gospels as odd is the prohibition against making Jesus known as the Christ during the days of his ministry. He imposed this restriction on the disciples (Matt 16:20) and somewhat similarly choked off any possible testimony from demons (Luke 4:41). If this title should be used freely of him among the Jews, it would excite the populace to expect in him a political Messiah who would gain for them their national freedom and many accompanying benefits. Since this was not the purpose of Jesus, he did what he could to suppress the use of the term *Messiah* with regard to himself, though he welcomed it in the circle of the apostles (Matt 16:16).

Only once does the name *Immanuel* occur, and then in connection with the conception of Jesus (Matt 1:23). It is a Hebrew word meaning "God with us," and is especially appropriate when describing the incarnation aspect of Jesus' birth. For some reason the name did not gain currency in the church, perhaps because it was crowded out by Jesus and Christ.

Among the ancients it was common to distinguish a person not only by name but also by place of residence. Consequently Jesus was often called the *Nazarene* because of his years spent in the village of Nazareth (Luke 24:19). When used of Jesus' followers by the Jews the term took on an element of reproach that it did not possess in any recognizable way during his life on earth.

When Jesus referred to himself, he most often used the title *Son of Man.* It was more than a means of identification, however, for it linked him to a conception of majesty that had gathered around the term since its use in Daniel 7:13. Although it is possible that occasionally the title stresses Jesus' humanity, in the main it serves to point to his transcendence as a heavenly figure. Certainly the widespread notion that Son of Man expresses the humanity of Jesus, as Son of God expresses his deity, is quite misleading (cf. Luke 22:69–70). By using this title publicly rather than Messiah, Jesus was able to avoid suggesting that his mission was political in nature, and instead could put into the title by his own use of it the content that he wanted to give it. The church recognized the Lord's right to exclusive use of the term and did not use it, out of deference to him (the one exception is Stephen in Acts 7:56).

One of the most familiar designations for Jesus is *Son of God.* Only in John's Gospel does he use it of himself (John 5:25; 10:36; 11:4). But elsewhere he uses its equivalent, the Son (Matt 11:27), which is especially appropriate when used opposite the Father, and which in such a passage clearly sets off the uniqueness of this particular Son. In the Synoptic Gospels considerable care is needed in order to impute to the term Son of God the exact nuance of meaning proper to its every occurrence. Geerhardus Vos discerned four meanings: the nativistic, which stresses the divine origination of the person of Jesus as a human figure; the ethico-religious, which points to the filial relation that Christ had with the Father within the context of his human life, similar to that which any child of God has; the messianic, which has to do with his appointment as the one anointed and sent by God, in fulfillment of OT prophecy; the trinitarian or ontological, in which the unique relation of Christ to the Father as the only Son is expressed. This latter, of course, represents the highest level of sonship (see G. Vos, *The Self-Disclosure of Jesus,* pp. 141ff.).

Rather frequently in the course of his ministry Jesus was addressed as *Son of David* (Matt 21:9; Luke 18:38), which is a distinctly messianic title pointing to him as the One who fulfilled the Davidic covenant, the One who was expected to establish the kingdom and bring Israel to freedom, peace, and glory (cf. Matt 1:1; Luke 1:32–33).

A few passages proclaim outright that Jesus is *God* (John 1:1 in a preincarnate setting; John

1:18, according to the strongest manuscript evidence; John 20:28; Rom 9:5, according to the most natural construction of the verse; Titus 2:13; Heb 1:8). That the passages are relatively few in number is probably due to the fact that Jesus Christ, as known to men, was in a position of subordination to the heavenly Father, his deity veiled by his humanity, so that it was much more natural to assign to him the predicates of deity than to refer to him directly as God. The monotheistic background of the early Hebrew Christians doubtlessly exercised a restraining influence also. Some moderns about whose orthodoxy there is no question have nevertheless confessed to a feeling of restraint in referring to Jesus as God, though they do not doubt his essential deity.

No term is more expressive of the faith of early believers in Jesus than *Lord* (Acts 2:36; 10:36; Rom 10:9; 1 Cor 8:6; 12:3; Phil 2:11). It denotes the sovereignty of Christ and his headship over the individual believer, the church as a body, and all things. For those who were strangers it was merely a title of respect and is translated "sir" (John 4:11); but for those who were deeply attached to the Savior it had the highest import, calling alike for homage and obedience (John 20:28; Acts 22:10). Used sparingly during the period of the earthly ministry prior to the Resurrection, it takes on an increased use and heightened significance as a result of that momentous event.

Some titles pertain to the mission of Christ more than to his person. One of these is *Word* (John 1:1, 14; 1 John 1:1). As such Christ is essentially the revealer of God, the One who opens to the understanding of people the nature and purposes of the Almighty and discloses the higher wisdom that stands in contrast to the wisdom of those who are merely human beings. In keeping with such a title is the designation *Teacher,* by which our Lord was customarily addressed in the days of his flesh. This attests to the impact of his instruction and the authority that lay behind it. Despite the fact that Jesus lacked rabbinic training, he could not be denied the recognition of the wisdom that shone through his spoken word.

The classic designation of Christ as *Servant* is given by Paul in Philippians 2:7, but it was widely recognized in the early church that our Lord fulfilled the servant-of-God role (see Matt 12:17–21). That it dominated the thinking of Christ himself may be safely affirmed in the light of such a passage as Mark 10:45.

Central to the mission of Christ was his work as *Savior.* We have already seen that the name Jesus has this meaning, the name suggesting the reason for his coming into the world. Luke 2:11 and John 4:42 are among the passages that herald Christ under the aspect of his saviorhood. The idea in the word is not merely deliverance from sin and all the other woes that afflict the human race, but the provision of a state of wholeness and blessedness in which a person realizes the purpose of God for him or her. In reports of the healings of Jesus, the verb form denotes the estate of soundness that results from the healing touch of the Savior.

Jesus' saving mission is declared also in the expression, *Lamb of God* (John 1:29, 36; cf. Rev 5:6). Peter likewise uses the word "lamb" in reference to Jesus, with special reference to his qualification of sinlessness (1 Peter 1:19).

The designation of Jesus as *High Priest* is confined to the Letter to the Hebrews, where it occurs some ten times, his work being described as taking place in the heavenly sanctuary, in the presence of God, where the fruits of his death for sinners on the earth are conserved in his work of intercession (Heb 9:11–12).

More general is the characterization of the Lord as the *Mediator* between God and men (1 Tim 2:5). This term takes account of the barrier that sin erected between the Creator and the creature, that Christ alone was qualified to remove. For the concept in the OT, see Job 9:33.

Paul uses the title *Last Adam* (1 Cor 15:45) in contrast to the first Adam, suggesting the undoing of the consequences of sin brought on by Adam's transgression (cf. Rom 5:12–21) and the new creation life that is to be the possession of all believers in resurrection glory even as it is already their portion in Christ in a spiritual sense.

This list of names and titles of Christ is not exhaustive. The resources of languages are taxed in the sacred record to set forth the full excellence and worth of the Son of God. When his work is considered in its broad sweep, the most satisfying analysis divides it into the offices that he fulfills—those of *prophet, priest,* and *king*. The prophetic ministry relates especially to the testimony given in the days of his flesh as he heralded the kingdom of God, warned of coming judgment, and encouraged the people of God. He is still the faithful and true witness as he speaks to the church through the Spirit. As priest our Lord made the one sacrifice of himself that brought to an end animal sacrifices and put away sin forever (Heb 9:26). Faithful and merciful, he ministers before God on behalf of this people who are compassed by sin and infirmity (2:17; 4:15–16). The term *king* relates especially to the future activity of our Lord as he comes again to supplant the kingdom of the world with his own gracious and sovereign rule (Rev 11:15). He will be no ordinary ruler, but King of kings, without a peer.

IV. Character. "What manner of man is this?" This was the amazed observation of the disciples of Jesus as they watched him in action and felt the strength and mystery of his personality as they associated with him. Certain ingredients of character deserve special mention, but it cannot be said that he was noted for some things above others, for this would involve disproportion and would reflect on the perfection of his being. He had integrity. After all, this is the kernel of character. The gospel appeal to put our faith in Christ would be impossible if he were not trustworthy. No taint of duplicity marred his dealings with others, for there was no mixture of motives within his heart. He could not deceive, for he was Truth incarnate. The claims of Jesus in areas where we have no means of testing them can be cordially received, because in areas where his affirmations can be judged they stand the test.

Christ had courage. When Aristotle advanced his famous doctrine of the mean, he illustrated it by courage, which lies midway between cowardice and recklessness. Judged by this standard the character of Jesus appears in a most favorable light, for in him one can detect no wild instability even in the most intense activity, nor any supineness in his passivity. Christ had physical courage. Without it he could never have cleared the temple single-handedly. He had the courage of conviction. Peter was probably his boldest disciple, yet he denied his Lord under pressure, whereas Jesus confessed his own person and mission before the Sanhedrin even though it meant his death. The stamina of men is often attributable, at least in part, to the help and sympathy of their fellows, but Jesus stood alone as he faced his final ordeal.

Our Lord showed great compassion as he dealt with people. This is the word used in the Gospels. In the NT epistles it is called love. The sight of multitudes forlorn and forsaken by those who should have been their spiritual shepherds stirred Christ to the depths of his being. Out of his compassion he ministered to their physical needs for food and health and went on to tell them the secrets of the life of true godliness. Compassion was more than an emotion with Jesus. It was a call to action, to selfless ministry on behalf of the needy. He gave himself to one with the same intensity that he showed in dealing with the many. Virtue went out of him and he did not regret the loss, for it is the nature of love to give. To love the loveless and love them to the end and to the uttermost—this is the love that Paul says "surpasses knowledge" (Eph 3:19). It is a love that proved itself through death—he "loved me and gave himself for me" (Gal 2:20)—and yet remains deathless.

Jesus clothed himself with humility. He could talk about this as his own possession without affectation (Matt 11:29). Christ wrought a revolution in ethics by dignifying humility in a world that despised it as weakness. Though the universe was his creation, though he was equal with the Father, and though every knee would one day bow before him, yet he was not lifted up with pride because of these things. The mind of Christ is that which takes every reason for exaltation and transforms it into a reason for selfless service. In essence his humility was his refusal to please himself. He came not to be ministered to but to minister.

Our Lord's character is crowned with perfection or sinlessness. This perfection was not simply the absence of sin, but the infusion of a heavenly holiness into all that he said and did. It may be objected that when Jesus gave way to anger and spoke out in bitter denunciation of the Pharisees (Matt 23), he revealed at least a trace of imperfection. But a character without the power of righteous indignation would be faulty. If Jesus had failed to expose these men, he would not have done his full duty as the exponent of truth. He is the image of the Father, and God is angry with the wicked every day.

V. Influence. A life so brief, so confined in its geographical orbit, so little noticed by the world in his own time, has yet become the most potent force for good in all of human history. This is seen in the Scriptures of the NT. In every single book that makes up this collection, Jesus Christ is the inevitable point of reference. Even so brief and personal a writing as Philemon owes its inspiration to the Son of God who came to make men free. The Gospels picture him in the flesh; the NT letters present him in the Spirit. The Acts of the Apostles depicts the victories of his grace in the extension of his church; the Revelation sets forth the triumph of his glory through his personal presence once more in history.

His influence on the saints is so radical and comprehensive that nothing can describe it better than the assertion that Christ is their life. They were not truly living until they came to know him by faith. Until he comes into the heart, self rules supreme. When he comes, he creates a new point of reference and a new set of values. To be Christ-centered is simply normal Christian experience.

What Christ can do in transforming a life may be seen to good advantage in the case of Saul of Tarsus. Apart from Christ the world might never have heard of him. Because in Christ he died to self and lived in the energy of the risen Christ to glorify God, his is a household name wherever Christians are found.

It is inevitable that sinners should feel the touch of Christ and never be the same afterward. Regarding the self-righteous leaders of his own time Jesus could say, "If I had not come and spoken to them, they would not be guilty of sin. Now, however, they have no excuse for their sin" (John 15:22). Christ is the conscience of the world. Because he is the light of the world, when people stand in that light but then turn from it, they walk in deeper darkness and are without hope.

In a more general sense, Christ has mightily affected society in its organized state. He has taught the world the dignity of human life, the worth of the soul, the preciousness of personality. Because of this the status of women has steadily been improved under Christian influence, slavery has been abolished, and children, instead of being exposed as infants and neglected in formative years, are recognized as a primary responsibility for the lavishing of love and care. Even when human life becomes weak or deformed or diseased, it is not regarded as forfeiting a right to a place in society, but as being entitled to assistance. The fact that governments and scientific groups are now engaged in social service on a large scale ought not to disguise the fact that the impulse for these works of mercy has been the Christian church acting in the name and spirit of Christ. The arts owe their sublimest achievements to the desire to honor the Son of God. Beethoven called Handel the greatest composer of all time, a man who could not complete his oratorio *The Messiah* without being moved repeatedly to tears as he thought about the Incarnation. Every cathedral spire that pierces the sky throughout Christendom bears its silent testimony to the loving outreach toward God that is induced through the knowledge of Christ the Lord. Moralists and philosophers, even when they lack faith in him for the saving of the soul, nevertheless are often found acknowledging wistfully that they wish they had a personal inheritance in him as they commend him to others as the one great hope for mankind.

Bibliography: B. B. Warfield, *The Lord of Glory,* 1907; T. W. Manson, *The Servant-Messiah,* 1953; G. C. Berkouwer, *The Person of Christ,* 1954; R. H. Fuller, *The Mission and Achievement of Jesus,* 1954; A. M. Hunter, *The Work and Words of Jesus,* 1954; James Denney, *The Death of Christ* (3d ed.), 1956; Vincent Taylor, *The Life and Ministry of Jesus,* 1954, and *The Atonement in New Testament Teaching,* 1958; E. Stauffer, *Jesus and His Story,* 1960; R. M. Grant, *The Earliest Lives of Jesus,* 1961; F. W. Beare, *The Earliest Records of Jesus,* 1962; O. Cullmann, *The Christology of the New Testament* (2d ed.), 1963; H. Zahrnt, *The Historical Jesus,* 1963; R. H. Fuller, *The Foundations of New Testament Christology,* 1965; L. Morris, *The Cross in the New Testament,* 1965; C. K. Barrett, *Jesus and the Gospel Tradition,* 1967; F. Hahn, *The Titles of Jesus in Christology,* 1969; I. H. Marshall, *The Work of Christ,* 1969; R. N. Longenecker, *The Christology of Early Jewish Christianity,* 1970; J. Jeremias, *New Testament Theology,* vol. 1, 1971; H. Conzelmann, *Jesus,* 1973; O. Cullmann, *Jesus and the Revolutionaries,* 1973; I. H. Marshall, *The Origins of New Testament Christology,* 1973; W. Karper, *Jesus the Christ,* 1976; H. E. W. Turner, *Jesus the Christ,* 1976; C. F. D. Moule, *The Origin of Christology,* 1977; F. Young, *Can These Bones Live?* 1982.

EFH

CHRISTIAN (Gr. *Christianos*). The biblical meaning is "adherent of Christ." The disciples were formally called Christians first in Antioch (Acts 11:26). Agrippa recognized that to believe what Paul preached would make him a Christian (Acts 26:28). Peter accepted the name as in itself a basis for persecution (1 Peter 4:16). Thus gradually a name imposed by Gentiles was adopted by the disciples of Jesus. Some Jews had referred to them as "the Nazarene sect" (Acts 24:5); and Paul, when he was a persecutor, referred to them as those "who belonged to the Way" (Acts 9:2). The Latin termination *-ianos,* widely used throughout the empire, often designated the slaves of the one with whose name it was compounded. This implication occurs in the NT (e.g., Rom 6:22; 1 Peter 2:16). The apostles wrote of themselves as servants (slaves) of Christ (Rom 1:1; James 1:1; 2 Peter 1:1; Jude 1; Rev 1:1). The NT calls the followers of Christ *brothers* (Acts 14:2); *disciples* (6:1–2); *saints* (Acts 9:13; Rom 1:7; 1 Cor 1:2); *believers* (1 Tim 4:12); *the church of God* (Acts 20:28); *all who call on your name* (Acts 9:14; Rom 10:12–13). To the first Christians, their own name mattered not at all; their concern was with the one Name of Jesus Christ (Acts 3:16; 4:10,12; 5:28). Inevitably, the name that they invoked was given to them: Christians, Christ's men. Its NT meaning is alone adequate for us. ER

CHRONICLES, 1 AND 2. These books are called in Hebrew *diverê ha-yāmîm,* "the words [affairs] of the days," meaning "the annals" (cf. 1 Chron 27:24). Similar annals, now lost, are mentioned in 1 and 2 Kings (e.g., 1 Kings 14:19, 29); they cannot, however, consist of our present books, which were not written until a century later. The church father Jerome (A.D. 400) first entitled them "Chronicles." Originally they formed a single composition but were divided into 1 and 2 Chronicles in the LXX, about 150 B.C. In the Hebrew they stand as the last book of the OT canon. Christ (Luke 11:51) thus spoke of all the martyrs from Abel in the first book (Gen 4) to Zechariah in the last (2 Chron 24).

Chronicles contains no statements about its own authorship or date. The last event it records is the decree of Cyrus in 538 B.C. that permitted the exiles to return from their Babylonian captivity (2 Chron 36:22); and its genealogies extend to approximately 500 B.C., as far, that is, as Pelatiah and Jeshaiah (1 Chron 3:21), two grandsons of Zerubbabel, the prince who led in the return from exile. The language, however, and the contents of Chronicles closely parallel that of the Book of Ezra, which continues the history of the Jews from the decree of Cyrus down to 457 B.C. Both documents are marked by lists and genealogies, by an interest in priestly ritual, and by devotion to the law of Moses. The closing verses, moreover, of Chronicles (2 Chron 36:22–23) are repeated as the opening verses of Ezra (1:1–3). Ancient Hebrew tradition and the modern scholarship of W. F. Albright therefore unite in suggesting that Ezra may have been the author of both volumes. His complete work would then have been finished some time around 450 B.C.

Ezra's position as a "scribe" (Ezra 7:6) may also explain the care that Chronicles shows in acknowledging its written source materials. These include such records as those of Samuel (1 Chron 29:29) and Isaiah (2 Chron 32:32) and a number of other prophets (9:29; 12:15; 20:34; 33:19) and above all else, "the book of the kings of Judah and Israel" (e.g., 16:11; 25:26). This latter work cannot be equated with our present-day 1–2 Kings, for verses such as 1 Chronicles 9:1 and 2 Chronicles 27:7 refer to "the book of the kings" for further details on matters about which 1–2 Kings is silent. The author's source must have been a larger court record, now lost, from which the authors of both Kings and Chronicles subsequently drew much of *their* information.

The occasion for the writing of Chronicles appears to be Ezra's crusade to bring postexilic Judah back into conformity with the Law of Moses (Ezra 7:10). From 458 B.C., Ezra sought to restore the temple worship (7:19–23, 27;

8:33–34), to eliminate the mixed marriages of Jews with their pagan neighbors (9–10), and to strengthen Jerusalem by rebuilding its walls (4:8–16). Chronicles, accordingly, consists of these four parts: genealogies, to enable the Jews to establish their lines of family descent (1 Chron 1–9); the kingdom of David, as a pattern for the ideal theocratic state (10–29); the glory of Solomon, with an emphasis on the temple and its worship (2 Chron 1–9); and the history of the southern kingdom, stressing in particular the religious reforms and military victories of Judah's more pious rulers (10–36).

As compared with the parallel histories in Samuel and Kings, the priestly annals of Chronicles put a greater emphasis on the structure of the temple (1 Chron 22) and on Israel's ark, the Levites, and the singers (1 Chron 13, 15–16). They omit, however, certain individualistic, moral acts of the kings (2 Sam 9; 1 Kings 3:16–28), as well as detailed biographies of the prophets (1 Kings 17–22:28; 2 Kings 1–8:15), features that account for the incorporation of Chronicles into the third (nonprophetic) section of the Hebrew canon, as distinguished from the location of the more homiletic books of Samuel and Kings in the second (prophetic) division. Finally, the chronicler foregoes discussion of David's disputed inauguration and later shame (2 Sam 1–4, 11–21), of Solomon's failures (1 Kings 11), and of the whole inglorious history of Saul (1 Sam 8–30, except his death, v. 31), and of the northern kingdom of Israel. The disillusioned, impoverished Jews of 450 B.C. knew enough of sin and defeat; they needed an encouraging reminder of their former, God-given victories (e.g., 2 Chron 13–14, 20, 25).

Because of these emphases, many modern critics have rejected Chronicles as being Levitical propaganda, a fiction of "what ought to have happened," with extensive (and conflicting) revisions as late as 250 B.C. The book's high numeric totals (such as the one million invading Ethiopians, 2 Chron 14:9) have been questioned despite the elucidations presented by several conservative scholars (see, e.g., E. J. Young, *An Introduction to the Old Testament,* 1949, pp. 388–90). Although Chronicles does stress the bright side of Hebrew history, it does not deny the defects (cf. 1 Chron 29:22 on the successful *second* anointing of Solomon, and 2 Chron 17:3 on the more exemplary *first* ways of David). The prophetic judgments of Kings and the priestly hopes of Chronicles are both true, and both are necessary. The morality of the former is invaluable, but the redemption of the latter constitutes the more distinctive feature of Christian faith.

While primarily historical in nature, the books of 1 and 2 Chronicles reflect a distinct theology. This theology is set forth in the selection and arrangement of historical events as well as in the chronicler's comments on these events.

One of the important theological themes of the books of Chronicles is the necessity of obedience for divine blessing. The chronicler observes that Saul's death was due to unfaithfulness (1 Chron 10:13–14), as was the exile of the southern kingdom (1 Chron 9:1; see also 2 Chron 6:24). On the other hand, obedience will bring blessing to the nation (1 Chron 28:8; 2 Chron 7:14–18). Even the lengthy genealogy that forms the preface to 1 Chronicles contains affirmations of this fact (4:10; 5:1, 25). The narration of selected events from the life of David focuses on the steps of obedience that led to his successful administration of the kingdom. Instances of David's disobedience are minimized. Thus the obedience of David was presented as an ideal for the postexilic community.

Another theological aspect of Chronicles is its emphasis on the Davidic theology. David's role in the establishment of Israelite worship receives prominence (1 Chron 22:2–5; 23:1–32; 25:1–26:32). But most important to the Davidic theology is the restatement of the terms of the Abrahamic covenant to David (1 Chron 17:1–27; cf. 2 Chron 6:1–11). The Davidic covenant established the divine authority of the Davidic dynasty and guaranteed its perpetuity (1 Chron 21:7).

The theology of worship in Chronicles acknowledges only one site where Israel may worship. The legitimacy of the postexilic temple and its personnel is established by virtue of its continuity with the temple built by Solomon under the sponsorship of David (1 Chron 17:24; 2 Chron 6:7–9).

Bibliography: J. M. Myers, *I Chronicles* (AB), 1965, and *II Chronicles* (AB), 1965; P. R. Ackroyd, *I & II Chronicles, Ezra, Nehemiah,* 1973; H. G. M. Williamson, *1 and 2 Chronicles* (NCB), 1982. JBP

CHRONOLOGY, NEW TESTAMENT. The science of determining the dates of the NT books and the historical events mentioned in them. The subject is beset with serious difficulty because sufficient data are often lacking and the computations must be based on ancient documents that did not record historical events under precise calendar dates as modern historical records do. Neither sacred nor secular historians of that time were accustomed to record history under exact dates; they felt that all demands were satisfied when some specific event was related to a well-known period, as the reign of a noted ruler or the time of some famous contemporary. Luke's method of dating the beginning of the ministry of John the Baptist (Luke 3:1–2) is typical of the historian's method of that day. Further, the use of different local chronologies and different ways of computing years often leave the results tentative. NT chronology naturally falls into two parts: the life of Christ and the apostolic age.

I. Life of Christ. The erection of a chronology of the life of Christ turns around three points: his birth, baptism, and crucifixion. Luke's statement of the age of Jesus at his baptism (Luke 3:23) links the first two, while the problem of the length of the ministry links the second and third.

The Christian era, now used almost exclusively in the Western world for civil chronology, was introduced at Rome by Abbot Dionysius Exiguus in the sixth century. It is now generally agreed that the beginning of the era should have been fixed at least four years later.

According to the Gospels, Jesus was born some time before the death of Herod the Great. Josephus, the Jewish historian who was born A.D. 37, affirms (*Antiq*. 17.6.4) that Herod died shortly after an eclipse of the moon, which is astronomically fixed at March 12–13, 4 B.C. His death occurred shortly before Passover, which that year fell on April 4. His death in 4 B.C. is also confirmed from the known commencement of the rule of his three sons in that year. The age of Jesus at Herod's death is not certain. The "two years" for the age of the children killed at Bethlehem (Matt 2:16) offers no sure indication, since Herod would allow a liberal margin for safety; also, part of a year might be counted as a year. It does show that Jesus was born at least some months before Herod's death. Christ's presentation in the temple after he was forty days old (Lev 12:1–8; Luke 2:22–24) makes it certain that the wise men came at least six weeks after his birth. The time spent in Egypt is uncertain, but it may have been several months. Thus, the birth of Jesus should be placed in the latter part of the year 5 B.C.

Luke's statement (2:1–2) that Jesus was born in connection with the "first census" when "Quirinius was governor of Syria" was once fiercely assailed as erroneous, since Quirinius was known to be governor in connection with the census of A.D. 6. But it is now known that he was also connected with the Syrian government at some previous time (see QUIRINIUS). Papyrus evidence shows that Augustus inaugurated a periodic census every fourteen years, from 8 B.C. onward. Herod's war with the king of Arabia and his troubles with Augustus, as well as the problem of the method of taking the census among the Jews, may have delayed the actual census in Palestine for several years, bringing it down to the year 5 B.C.

Luke gives the age of Jesus at his baptism as "about thirty years" (Luke 3:23). Although the statement of age is not specific, it naturally implies that his age was just about thirty, a few months under or over. Born in the latter part of 5 B.C., his baptism then occurred near the close of A.D. 26 or the beginning of 27. The forty-day period of the temptation, plus the events recorded in John 1:19–2:12 seem to require that the baptism occurred at least three months before the first Passover of his public ministry (John 2:13–22). Since Herod began the reconstruction of the temple in 20 B.C., the "forty and six years" mentioned by the Jews during this Passover, using the inclusive Jewish count, again brings us to A.D. 27 for this first Passover.

Apparently John began his ministry some six months before the baptism of Jesus, Scripture dating that beginning as "in the fifteenth year of the reign of Tiberius Caesar" (Luke 3:1). Augustus died in August of A.D. 14, but fifteen years added to that would be two years too late for our previous dates. Since Tiberius had been reigning jointly with Augustus in the provinces for two years before his death, it seems only natural that Luke would follow the provincial point of view and count the fifteen years from the time of Tiberius' actual assumption of authority in the provinces. Thus counted, the date is in harmony with our other dates. The ministry of John, begun about six months before the baptism of Jesus, commenced about the middle of A.D. 26.

The time of the Crucifixion will be determined by the length of the ministry of Jesus. Mark's Gospel seems to require at least two years: the plucking of the ears of grain (April–June) marks a first spring, the feeding of the five thousand when the grass was fresh green (March–April) was a second, and the Passover of the Crucifixion becomes the third. John's Gospel explicitly mentions three Passovers (John 2:23; 6:4; 11:55). If the feast of John 5:1 is also a Passover, as seems probable, a view having the traditional backing of Irenaeus, then the length of the ministry of Jesus was a full three years and a little over. This places the Crucifixion at the Passover of A.D. 30.

II. Apostolic Age. Due to the uncertainties connected with the limited data for an apostolic chronology, authorities have arrived at varied dates. The Book of Acts with its many notes of time, mostly indefinite, offers but few points for the establishment of even relatively fixed dates. Even Paul's apparently precise chronological notes in Galatians 1:18 and 2:1 leave us in doubt as to whether "after three years" and "fourteen years later" are to be regarded as consecutive or as both counting from his conversion.

The death of Herod Agrippa I (Acts 12:23) and the proconsulship of Gallio (18:12) are important for the chronology of the period. The death of Herod Agrippa I, one of the fixed dates of the NT, is known to have taken place in A.D. 44. It establishes the year of Peter's arrest and miraculous escape from prison. The proconsulship of Gallio is also strongly relied on for an apostolic chronology. A fragmentary inscription found at Delphi associates his proconsulship with the twenty-sixth acclamation of Claudius as Imperator. This would place his proconsulship between May 51 and 52, or May 52 and 53. The latter date is more probable since Gallio would assume office in May and not in midsummer as some advocates of the earlier date assumed. Since apparently Paul had already been at Corinth a year and a half when Gallio arrived, his ministry at Corinth began in the latter part of 50. Efforts to determine the time of the accession of Festus as governor, under whom Paul was sent to Rome, have not resulted in agreement. From the inconclusive data, advocates have argued for a date as early as 55 and as late as 60 or 61. The balance of the arguments seem to point to 60 or perhaps 59. If the latter, the suggested dates should be adjusted accordingly.

III. Chronological Table. The dates for many NT events must remain tentative, but as indicated by Luke (3:1–2), they have a definite correlation with secular history (as shown in the accompanying diagram). The following chronological table is regarded as approximately correct.

Birth of Jesus	5 B.C.
Baptism of Jesus	late A.D. 26 or early 27
First Passover of ministry	27
Crucifixion of Jesus	30
Conversion of Saul	34 or 35
Death of Herod Agrippa I	44
Letter of James	before 50
First missionary journey	48–49
Jerusalem conference	49 or 50
Second missionary journey	begun spring 50
Paul at Corinth	50–52
1 and 2 Thessalonians from Corinth	51
Galatians from Corinth (?)	early 52
Arrival of Gallio as proconsul	May 52
Third missionary journey	begun 54
Paul at Ephesus	54–57
1 Corinthians from Ephesus	spring 57
2 Corinthians from Macedonia	fall 57
Romans from Corinth	winter 57–58
Paul's arrest at Jerusalem	Pentecost 58
Imprisonment at Caesarea	58–60
On island of Malta	winter 60–61
Arrival at Rome	spring 61
Roman imprisonment	61–63
Colossians, Philemon, Ephesians	summer 62
Philippians	spring 63
Paul's release and further work	63–65
1 Timothy and Titus	63
Hebrews	64
Synoptic Gospels and Acts	before 67
1 and 2 Peter from Rome	64–65
Peter's death at Rome	65
Paul's second Roman imprisonment	66
2 Timothy	66
Death at Rome	late 66 or early 67
Jude	67–68
Writings of John	before 100
Death of John	98–100

Bibliography: George Ogg, *The Chronology of the Public Ministry of Jesus,* 1940, and *The Chronology of the Life of Paul,* 1968; J. Finegan , *Handbook of Biblical Chronology,* 1964; A. J. J. Gunther, *Paul, Messenger and Exile: A Study in the Chronology of His Life and Letters,* 1972. DEH

Chronological Chart of the New Testament

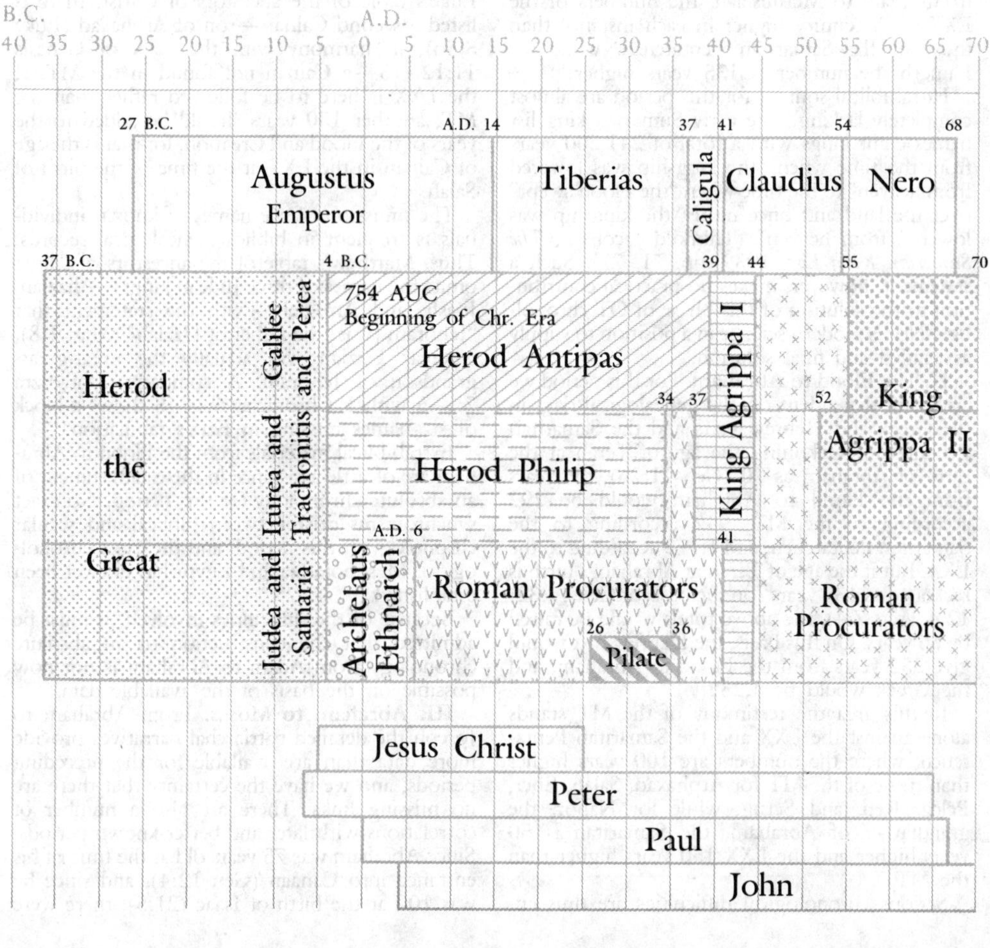

CHRONOLOGY, OLD TESTAMENT. This topic presents many complex and difficult problems. The data are not always adequate or clear; they are, at times, almost completely lacking. Because of insufficient data, many of the problems are at present insoluble. Even where the data are abundant, the exact meaning is often not immediately apparent, leaving room for considerable difference of opinion and giving rise to many variant chronological reconstructions. The chronological problem is thus one of the availability of evidence, of the correct evaluation and interpretation of that evidence, and of its proper application. Only the most careful study of all the data, both biblical and extrabiblical, can hope to provide a satisfactory solution.

I. From the Creation to the Flood. In this period the only biblical data are the ages of the patriarchs in Genesis 7:11 and the genealogical tables of Genesis 5. Calculations of the years from Adam to the Flood vary: 1,656 (Masoretic Text), 1,307 (Samaritan Pentateuch), and 2,242 (LXX). The numbers of the MT (Masoretic Text) are in agreement with the Samaritan except in the cases of Jared, Methuselah, and Lamech, where the numbers of the MT are higher by 100, 120, and 129 years respectively. For the eight patriarchs from Adam to Methuselah, the numbers of the LXX are a century higher in each instance than those of the Samaritan Pentateuch, while for Lamech the number is 135 years higher.

Extrabiblical sources for this period are almost completely lacking. The early Sumerian king list names eight kings with a total of 241,200 years from the time when "the kingship was lowered from heaven" to the time when "the Flood swept" over the land and once more "the kingship was lowered from heaven" (Thorkild Jacobsen, *The Sumerian King List,* 1939, pp. 71, 77). Such a statement, however, makes no practical contribution to the solution of this phase of OT chronology. Nor is modern science in a position to supply a detailed and final solution.

II. The Flood to Abraham. For this period we are again dependent on the genealogical data in the Greek and Hebrew texts and the Samaritan Pentateuch. Reckoning the age of Terah at the birth of Abraham as 70 (Gen 11:26), the years from the Flood to Abraham would be 292 according to the MT, 942 according to the Samaritan Pentateuch, and 1,172 according to the LXX. But if the age of Terah at Abraham's birth is reckoned as 130 years (on the basis of Gen 11:32; 12:4; Acts 7:4), the above totals would be raised by 60 years. On this basis, the Hebrew text would give 352 years from the Flood to Abraham, and the Greek would be 1,232.

In this area the testimony of the MT stands alone against the LXX and the Samaritan Pentateuch, where the numbers are 100 years higher than those of the MT for Arphaxad, Salah, Eber, Peleg, Reu, and Serug, while for Nahor, the grandfather of Abraham, the Samaritan is 50 years higher and the LXX 150 years higher than the MT.

Serious chronological difficulties are thus encountered in the period immediately beyond Abraham. Abraham was 86 years old at the birth of Ishmael (Gen 16:16) and 100 at the birth of Isaac (Gen 21:5). But how old was Terah at the birth of Abraham—70, 130, or some number not revealed? And how old was Nahor at the birth of Terah—29, 79, or 179? If Terah was 130 years old at the birth of Abraham, as seems to be indicated by the biblical evidence, it must be admitted that the numbers of the LXX for this period (135, 130, 130, 134, 130, 132, 130, 179, 130), are much more consistent with each other than the numbers of the Hebrew (35, 30, 34, 30, 32, 30, 29, 130). But notice that in the case of nine patriarchs in the LXX, five of them were 130 years old when their sons were born, while in the Hebrew three out of eight were 30, one was 130, while the others were all in their thirties with the exception of Nahor, who was 29—one year from 30. And if Terah was 130 years old when Abraham was born, why was it regarded as so very unusual for Abraham to have a son at the age of 100 (Gen 17:17; 18:11; 21:2, 5)?

An endeavor to assess the relative values of the three sources involved accomplishes little, for the indications are that none is complete. Certainly the LXX had great weight in NT times, for in Luke's table of the ancestors of Christ, there is listed a second Cainan—son of Arphaxad (Luke 3:36), in harmony with the LXX of Genesis 11:12–13—a Cainan not found in the MT. If the LXX is here to be followed rather than the MT, another 130 years should be added to the years of the Flood and Creation, for that is the age of Cainan in the LXX at the time of the birth of Salah.

The omission of the names of known individuals is frequent in biblical genealogical records. Thus, Matthew's table of the ancestors of Christ omits the names of three Judean kings—Ahaziah, Joash, and Amaziah—with the statement that "Jehoram [was] the father of Uzziah" (Matt 1:8), whereas Uzziah was actually the great-great-grandson of Jehoram. A comparison of Ezra 7:1–5 with 1 Chronicles 6:4–15 shows a block of six names missing in Ezra's tabulation.

Extrabiblical materials from the Flood to Abraham are of little assistance in the establishment of an absolute chronology for this period. No exact synchronisms exist between biblical and secular chronology of this period, and the exact chronology of Mesopotamia and Egypt has not yet been established.

Because of the difficulties involved, it must be admitted that the construction of an absolute chronology from Adam to Abraham is not now possible on the basis of the available data.

III. Abraham to Moses. From Abraham to Joseph the detailed patriarchal narratives provide more data than are available for the preceding periods, and we have the certainty that there are no missing links. There are also a number of correlations with later and better-known periods. Since Abraham was 75 years old at the time of his entrance into Canaan (Gen 12:4), and since he was 100 at the birth of Isaac (21:5), there were

25 years from the entry into Canaan to Isaac. Isaac was 60 at the birth of Jacob (25:26), and Jacob was 130 at his entrance into Egypt (47:9, 28), making 215 years from the beginning of the sojourn in Canaan to the beginning of the sojourn in Egypt. The total length of the sojourn was 430 years (Exod 12:40). Did this involve only the sojourn in Egypt or did it include also the sojourn in Canaan? If Israel was in Egypt 430 years, there were 645 years from the entrance into Canaan to Moses' departure from Egypt. However, if the 430 years includes the time spent by the patriarchs in Canaan, the length of the Egyptian sojourn would have been only 215 years.

According to 1 Kings 6:1, the temple was founded in the 480th year after the Exodus, which was the fourth year of Solomon's reign. On the basis of a 40-year reign for Solomon (1 Kings 11:42) and in accord with the established chronology of the kings, that was 966 B.C. This would provide 1445 as the date of the Exodus and 1525 as the year of Moses' birth (Exod 7:7). If the 430-year sojourn involved only the period in Egypt, Abraham entered Canaan in 2090. If it included the years in Canaan, the date was 1875. The answer depends on the meaning of the prophecy of Genesis 15:13–16 and the reconstruction of the details from Abraham to Moses. From Abraham to Joseph the details are known, but from Joseph to Moses there is only genealogical evidence.

Due to omissions, repetitions, and other variations in the genealogical lists, the endeavor to establish times by the evidence of such lists must be regarded as highly precarious. Compare, for instance, the line of descent of Samuel and his sons from Levi and Kohath as recorded in 1 Chronicles 6:22–28 and in verses 33–38, and see 1 Samuel 8:2 for the names of these sons. Compare also the various lists of the sons of Benjamin and their descendants as found in Genesis 46:21; Numbers 26:38–40; 1 Chronicles 7:6–12; 8:1–40. The variations in existence here and in many other lists indicate the dangers involved in dogmatic reconstructions based only on genealogical evidence.

The ancestry of Moses from Jacob through Levi, Kohath, and Amram is repeatedly given (Num 3:17–19; 26:57–59; 1 Chron 6:1–3; 23:6, 12–13), including the ages of these patriarchs at the time of death (Exod 6:16, 18, 20); but their ages at the time of their sons' births are not recorded. Jochebed, the wife of Amram and mother of Moses, is said to have been the sister of Kohath, who was the son of Levi and the grandfather of Moses (6:16, 18, 20), and to have been born to Levi in Egypt (Num 26:59). This might appear to be conclusive evidence of a comparatively brief period in Egypt and to make a sojourn there of 430 years impossible. But there are difficulties. While four to five generations from Jacob to Moses may be indicated in the above line of descent, eleven generations may be counted from Jacob to Joshua (1 Chron 7:20–27). And that some considerable period was involved is clear from the fact that Joseph before his death saw the children of the third generation of both his sons (Gen 50:23), and that at the time of the Exodus, Amram and his brothers were already regarded as founders of clans (Num 3:27).

Levi was the elder brother of Joseph and must have been born not more than ten years before Joseph (Gen 29:30–34; 30:22–43; 31:41). Since Joseph was 30 when he stood before Pharaoh (41:46), and since seven years of plenty and two years of famine had passed at the time Jacob entered Egypt (41:47, 53; 45:6), Joseph would have been 39 when Jacob was 130 (47:9, 28) and would thus have been born when Jacob was 91. That, however, would have made Jacob an old man of about 80 at the time of his marriage and the birth of his first-born. That is possible but hardly probable. In view of the frequency of the numbers of 30 or 130 in age lists of biblical patriarchs, and in view of the significance of the number 30 in connection with the Sed Festival in Egypt honoring a ruler on the thirtieth anniversary of his appointment as heir to the crown, the question might well be raised as to whether 130 as the age of Jacob is used in an absolute sense. If not, the chronological reckonings based on it are only approximate and not absolute.

We should also notice that if the sojourn in Egypt was 215 years and if there were only four generations from Jacob to Moses, then Levi must have been about 100 at the birth of Jochebed, and Jochebed 84 at the birth of Moses. Since the birth of Isaac to Sarah when she was 90 and to Abraham when he was 100 was regarded as in the nature of a miracle (Gen 17:17; 18:11–14; Rom 4:19), these ages are hardly probable.

On the basis of the OT data it is impossible to give a categorical answer as to exactly what was involved in the 430-year sojourn, nor is it possible to give an absolute date for Abraham's entry into Canaan. Paul regarded the 430 years as beginning at the time when the promises were made to Abraham (Gen 12:1–4) and terminating with the giving of the law at Sinai (Gal 3:16–17). On this basis the date of the entry into Canaan and the beginning of the sojourn was 1875 B.C.

An Exodus date of 1445 calls for 1405 as the beginning of the conquest (Num 33:38; Deut 1:3; Josh 5:6). According to these dates the Exodus took place during the reigns of the famous rulers of Egypt's Eighteenth Dynasty (c. 1570–1325). This fits in well with the Habiru inroads of the Amarna period and with the evidence of Israel's presence in Palestine during the Nineteenth Dynasty (c. 1325–1200). In view of recent evidence of a sedentary occupation of Trans-Jordan from the end of the Middle Bronze Age (c. 1550) to the end of the Late Bronze Age (c. 1250; see G. Lankester Harding, "Recent Discoveries in Jordan," *Palestine Exploration Quarterly,* January–June, 1958, pp. 10–12), the view is no longer tenable that nonoccupation of that area from the eighteenth to the thirteenth centuries B.C. makes a fifteenth-century date for the Exodus impossible.

IV. The Conquest to the Kingdom. The

establishment of absolute dates from Moses through Joshua and the judges to the setting up of the monarchy is again not possible with the available data. With the date 1405 B.C. for the beginning of the conquest, we secure 1399 as the year when Caleb received his inheritance, since he was 40 when he was sent as a spy from Kadesh-barnea (Josh 14:7) in the second year after the departure from Egypt (Num 10:11–12; Deut 2:14), and he was 85 when he received his inheritance 45 years later (Josh 14:10). The date of Joshua's death cannot be given, for we do not know how old he was when he was sent as a spy, although he was 110 when he died (24:29).

Many attempts have been made to set dates for the judges, but, with the data now available, absolute certainty regarding the chronology for this period is impossible. Here are the data:

	Reference	Years
Oppression under Cushan-Rishathaim	Judg 3:8	8
Deliverance under Othniel; peace	Judg 3:11	40
Oppression under Eglon of Moab	Judg 3:14	18
Deliverance by Ehud; peace	Judg 3:30	80
Oppression under Jabin of Hazor	Judg 4:3	20
Deliverance under Deborah; peace	Judg 5:31	40
Oppression under Midian	Judg 6:1	7
Deliverance under Gideon; peace	Judg 8:28	40
Reign of Abimelech	Judg 9:22	3
Judgeship of Tola	Judg 10:2	23
Judgeship of Jair	Judg 10:3	22
Oppression of Gilead by Ammon	Judg 10:8	18
Judgeship of Jephthah	Judg 12:7	6
Judgeship of Ibzan	Judg 12:9	7
Judgeship of Elon	Judg 12:11	10
Judgeship of Abdon	Judg 12:14	8
Oppression under the Philistines	Judg 13:1	40
Judgeship of Samson	Judg 15:20; 16:31	20
Judgeship of Eli	1 Sam 4:18	40
Judgeship of Samuel	1 Sam 7:2	20

The sum of the above numbers is 470 years. However, it seems clear that we can subtract the 20 years of Samson's judgship, because that period is included in the 40 years of oppression under the Philistines—he "led Israel for twenty years in the days of the Philistines" (Judg 15:20). This results in the grand total of 450 years for the period of the judges, the same number given by the apostle Paul when he spoke of this period in his speech in the synagogue at Antioch in Pisidia (Acts 13:20). On the other hand, some speculate that the judges were local rulers, exercising control over limited areas while others held office in other parts of the land—e.g., Jephthah, who ruled over Gilead (Judg 10:18; 11:5–11; 12:4). They argue that the judgeships and oppressions at times overlapped (as with Samson); two oppressions might have been simultaneous in different parts of the land, as with the Ammonites in the NE and the Philistines in the SW (10:6–7). Furthermore, they say, the numerous 40s or multiples and submultiples of 40 (40, 80, 20, 40, 40, 10, 40, 20, 40) and Jephthah's 300 years after the conquest (11:26) are to be understood as merely approximate.

V. The United Monarchy. Because of a number of uncertainties the absolute date for the establishment of the United Monarchy cannot be given. The OT does not give the length of the reign of Saul, but Paul in a sermon at Antioch referred to it as forty years (Acts 13:21). If Saul reigned a full forty years, David was not born until ten years after Saul began his reign, for he was thirty when he took the throne (2 Sam 5:4). The battle with the Philistines at Micmash, with Jonathan in command of a large part of the army, presumably took place early in Saul's reign, perhaps even in his second year (1 Sam 13:1–2). In such a case Jonathan would have been well advanced in years when David was a mere youth, which is out of harmony with the picture in the biblical record. Other difficulties are also involved, all making it clear that Saul either did not reign a full forty years or that he must have been very young when he took the throne.

The reign of David, on the other hand, may be regarded as a full forty years, for he reigned seven years in Hebron and thirty-three in Jerusalem (2 Sam 5:4–5; 1 Kings 2:11; 1 Chron 3:4), and one event is dated in the fortieth year (1 Chron 26:31).

Solomon began his reign before the death of David (1 Kings 1:32–48), but how long is not recorded. Presumably it was only a short time, but the indefiniteness of this period must be taken into consideration in any endeavor to establish an absolute chronology. And the forty years of his reign (11:42) might have been intended as a round number. Going back to the Exodus the recorded periods are as follows: 40, 8, 40, 18, 80, 20, 40, 7, 40, 3, 23, 22, 18, 6, 7, 10, 8, 40, 20, 40, 40, 40, 40. Unless we can be certain that all these numbers are absolute, we cannot be certain of an absolute chronology for the periods involved.

VI. The Divided Monarchy. For the period of the Divided Monarchy an entirely different situation is found. Here there are an abundance of data that may be checked against each other and the numbers are no longer round. Four biblical yardsticks are here provided—the lengths of reign of the rulers of Judah and those of Israel, and the synchronisms of Judah with Israel and of Israel with Judah. Furthermore, a number of synchronisms with the fixed years of contemporary Assyria make possible a check with an exact chronological yardstick and make possible the establishment of absolute years B.C. for the period of the kings.

Various methods were used in the ancient East for reckoning the official years of kings. During the Divided Monarchy, Judah used the method that the year when a ruler took the throne was his "accession year." Israel, on the other hand, followed those nations where a king termed his initial year his "first year." According to this latter method, the year when a king began to reign was always counted twice—as the last year of his predecessor and his own first official year. Thus, reigns reckoned according to this method were always one year longer in official length than those reckoned according to the former method, and for every reign there was always a gain of one year over absolute time. The following tables will make these two methods of reckoning clear and will show how for every reign the totals of Israel for this period increase by one year over those of Judah:

	Old king	New king			
Accession-year reckoning (Judah)	last year	Accession year	1st year	2nd year	3rd year
Non-accession-year reckoning (Israel)	last year	1st year	2nd year	3rd year	4th year

JUDAH, official years:	22	23	46	47	58	61	78	79
Rehoboam 17 Abijam 3 Asa	2nd	3rd	26th	27th	38th	41 Jehoshaphat	17th	18th
Jeroboam	22 Nadab 2	Baasha 24	Elah 2		Omri 12 Zimri	Ahab 4th	22 Ahaziah 2	Jehoram
ISRAEL, official years:	22	24	48	50	62	66	84	86
Excess years for Israel	0	1	2	3	4	5	6	7

The following table shows how the totals of both nations from the division to the death of Ahaziah in Israel in the eighteenth year of Jehoshaphat in Judah (omitting the seven-day reign of Zimri) are identical and perfectly correct when properly understood:

ISRAEL

King	Official years	Actual years
Jeroboam	22	21
Nadab	2	1
Baasha	24	23
Elah	2	1
Omri	12	11
Ahab	22	21
Ahaziah	2	1
Total	86	79

JUDAH

King	Years
Rehoboam	17
Abijam	3
Asa	41
Jehoshaphat	18
	79

The following are the conditions that make possible the construction of a chronological pattern of the kings based on the biblical data that possess internal harmony and are in accord with the years of contemporary Assyria and Babylon: Tishri regnal years for Judah and Nisan years for Israel; accession-year reckoning for Judah except for Jehoram, Ahaziah, Athaliah, and Joash, who followed the nonaccession-year system then employed in Israel; nonaccession-year reckoning in Israel for the early period, and from Jehoash to the end, accession-year reckoning; synchronisms of each nation in accord with its own current system of reckoning; a number of coregencies or of overlapping reigns when rival rulers exercised control; a double chronological pattern for both Israel and Judah involving the closing years of Israel's history.

The years of the kings based on the above principles are as follows:

ISRAEL Ruler	Overlapping Reign	Reign
Jeroboam I		931/30–910/9
Nadab		910/9 –909/8
Baasha		909/8 –886/85
Elah		886/85–885/84
Zimri		885/84
Tibni		885/84–880
Omri		885/84–880
Ahab		874/73–853
Ahaziah		853 –852
Joram		852 –841
Jehu		841 –814/13
Jehoahaz		814/13–798
Jehoash		798 –782/81
Jeroboam II	793/92–782/81	782/81–753
Zachariah		753 –752
Shallum		752
Menahem		752 –742/41
Pekahiah		742/41–740/39
Pekah		752 –740/39
Hoshea		732/31–723/22

JUDAH Ruler	Overlapping Reign	Reign
Rehoboam		931/30–913
Abijam		913 –911/10
Asa		911/10–870/69
Jehoshaphat	873/72–870/69	870/69–848
Jehoram	853 –848	848 –841
Ahaziah		841
Athaliah		841 –835
Joash		835 –796
Amaziah		796 –767
Azariah (Uzziah)	972/91–767	767 –740/39
Jotham	750 –740/39	740/39–732/31
Ahaz	735 –732/31	732/31–716/15
Hezekiah		716/15–687/86
Manasseh	697/96–687/86	687/86–643/42
Amon		643/42–641/40
Josiah		641/40–609
Jehoahaz		609
Jehoiakim		609 –598
Jehoiachin		598 –597
Zedekiah		597 –586

VII. The Exile and Return. The Book of Kings closes with the notice of the release of Jehoiachin from captivity on the twenty-seventh day of the twelfth month, in the thirty-seventh year of his captivity and the accession year of Evil-Merodach (2 Kings 25:27). That was April 2, 561 B.C.

Babylon fell to the Persians October 12, 539 B.C., and Cyrus in the first year of his reign issued a decree permitting the Jews to return and rebuild the temple (2 Chron 36:22; Ezra 1:1). On the basis of Nisan regnal years, this would have been 538 B.C. However, Nehemiah 1:1 and 2:1 give evidence that the author of Nehemiah reckoned the years of the Persian kings not from Nisan as was the Persian custom, but from Tishri, in accord with the Jewish custom. The Aramaic papyri from Elephantine in Egypt give evidence that the same custom was followed by the Jewish colony there in the fifth century B.C. Inasmuch as Chronicles-Ezra-Nehemiah were originally one and came from the same author, the indications are that the first year of Cyrus referred to in Ezra 1:1 was reckoned on a Tishri basis, and that it was, therefore, in 537 that Cyrus issued his decree.

Haggai began his ministry on the first day of the sixth month in the second year of Darius (Hag 1:1), August 29, 520 B.C.; and Zechariah commenced his work in the eighth month of the same year (Zech 1:1), in October or November 520. The temple was completed on the third of Adar, the sixth year of Darius (Ezra 6:15), March 12, 515.

The return of Ezra from Babylon was begun the first day of the first month, in the seventh year of Artaxerxes (Ezra 7:7, 9). Artaxerxes came to the throne in December, 465 B.C., and this would bring the first of Nisan of his seventh year on April 8, 458, according to Persian reckoning, but on March 27, 457, according to Judean years. The evidence that this was the custom then employed has already been given above.

Word was brought to Nehemiah of the sad state of affairs at Jerusalem in the month Kislev of the twentieth year of Artaxerxes (Neh 1:1), and in Nisan of that same twentieth year Nehemiah stood before the king and received permission to return to Jerusalem to rebuild the city (2:1–8). That was April, 444 B.C. With Nehemiah's return to Babylon in the thirty-second year of Artaxerxes (13:6), 433/32 B.C., the chronology of the OT proper comes to a close.

Bibliography: W. F. Albright, "The Chronology of the Divided Monarchy of Israel," BASOR, No. 100 (December 1945), pp. 16–22; P. Van der Meer, *The Ancient Chronology of Western Asia and Egypt,* 1955; R. A. Parker and W. H. Dubberstein, *Babylonian Chronology 626 B.C.–A.D. 75,* 1956; E. R. Thiele, *The Mysterious Numbers of the Hebrew Kings,* 1965; W. R. Wifall, Jr., "The Chronology of the Divided Monarchy of Israel," ZAW 80 (1968), pp. 319–37; R. K. Harrison, *Introduction to the Old Testament,* 1969, pp. 145–98.

ERT

CHRYSOLITE (See MINERALS)

CHRYSOPRASE (See MINERALS)

CHUN (See CUN)

CHURCH. The English word derives from the Greek *kuriakos* (belonging to the Lord), but it stands for another Greek word *ekklēsia* (whence "ecclesiastical"), denoting an assembly. This is used in its general sense in Acts 19:32, but had already been applied in the LXX as an equivalent for the "congregation" of the OT. Stephen's speech makes this equation (Acts 7:38), and in this sense it is adopted to describe the new gathering or congregation of the disciples of Jesus Christ.

In the Gospels the term is found only in Matthew 16:18 and 18:17. This paucity is perhaps explained by the fact that both these verses seem to envisage a situation that would follow Christ's earthly ministry. Yet the verses show that Christ has this reconstitution in view, that the church thus reconstituted will rest on the apostolic confession, and that it will take up the ministry of reconciliation.

When we turn to Acts, the situation changes. The saving work has been fulfilled, and the NT church can thus have its birthday at Pentecost. The term is now used regularly to describe local groups of believers. Thus, we read of the church at Jerusalem (Acts 5:11), Antioch (13:1), and Caesarea (18:22). At the same time the word is used for all believers (as is possibly the case in 9:31). From the outset the church has both a local and a general significance, denoting both the individual assembly and the world-wide community.

This twofold usage is also seen in Paul. He addresses his letters to specific churches, e.g., Corinth (1 Cor 1:2) or Thessalonica (1 Thess 1:1). Indeed, he seems sometimes to localize further by referring to specific groups within the local community as churches, as though sending greetings to congregations within the one city (e.g., Rom 16:5). Yet Paul also develops more fully the concept of a church that consists of all believers in all local churches, as in 1 Corinthians 10:32 and 1 Timothy 3:15, and with an even grander sweep in Colossians 1:18 and especially Ephesians. The other NT books give us mostly examples of the local usage (e.g., 3 John 9; Rev 1:4; 2:1).

There is no tension between the local and the universal sense. Each church or congregation is the church in its own setting, each a manifestation or concretion of the whole church. This means that there is room for great flexibility in organization and structure according to particular and varying needs. At the world-wide level, it is unlikely that there can ever be more than the loosest practical interconnection. Varying degrees of integration are possible at national, provincial, or municipal levels. But the basic unity is always the local church, not in isolation but as a concretion of the universal fellowship with a strong sense of belonging to it.

This leads us to the further consideration that the church is not primarily a human structure like a political, social, or economic organism. It is basically the church of Jesus Christ ("my church," Matt 16:18) or of the living God (1 Tim 3:15). The various biblical descriptions all emphasize this. It is a building of which Jesus Christ is the chief cornerstone or foundation, "a holy temple in the Lord . . . a dwelling in which God lives by his Spirit" (Eph 2:20–22). It is the fellowship of saints or people of God (1 Peter 2:9). It is the bride of Jesus Christ, saved and sanctified by him for union with himself (Eph 5:25–26). Indeed, it is the body of Jesus Christ, he being the head or whole body, and Christians the members (Rom 12:5; 1 Cor 12:12–13; Eph 4:4, 12, 16–17). As the body, it is the fullness of Christ, who himself fills all in all (Eph 1:23).

While there is an element of imagery in some of the terms used to refer to the church (Christ's temple, bride, or body), its true reality is found in the company of those who believe in Christ and are thus dead, buried, and raised in him, their Savior and substitute. Yet, this reality is not the visible one of earthly organization. The various local churches in this sinful age do not conform to their new and true reality any more than the believer conforms to what he now is in Christ. In its real life the church is known only in faith. It is, thus, hidden or, in the old phrase, "invisible." The visible life that it must also have, and that should be conformed to its true reality, may fall far short of it. Indeed, in visible organization even the membership cannot be fully identical with that of the true church (cf. Simon Magus). Yet the church invisible is not just ideal or mystical, but the real fact of the church is its being in Christ, as the new man of faith is the real fact of the believer. In every manifestation, there should thus be the aim, not of conformity to the world, but of transformation by renewal into the likeness of him in whom it has its true life (cf. Rom 12:2).

In this connection appears the relevance of the traditional marks or "notes" of the church. It is one (Eph 4:4), for Jesus Christ has only one temple, bride, and body, and all divisions are overcome in death and resurrection with him and by endowment of his Spirit. In all its legitimate multiformity, the visible church should thus seek a unity corresponding to this reality. It is holy, for it is set apart and sanctified by himself (Gal 1:4; Eph 5:26). Even in its pilgrimage in the world, it is thus to attest its consecration by the manner of its life and the nature of its service (cf. 1 Peter 1:15). It is catholic, constituted from among all people of all races, places, and ages (Eph 2:14; Col 1:6; 3:11; Rev 5:9). For all its diversity of membership and form, it is thus to maintain its universality of outreach, yet also its identity and relevance in every age and place. The church is apostolic, for it rests on the foundation of the apostles and prophets (Eph 2:20), the apostles being raised up as the first authoritative witnesses (Acts 1:8) whose testimony is basic and by whose teaching it is called, instructed, and directed. In all its activity it is thus "devoted . . . to the apostles' teaching and to the fellowship" (Acts 2:42), not finding apostolicity in mere externals but in conformity to apostolic teaching and practice as divinely perpetuated in Holy Scripture.

This brings us to the means of the church's life and its continuing function. It draws its life from Jesus Christ by the Holy Spirit; but it does so through the Word, from which it gets life (James 1:18) and by which it is nourished and sanctified

(Eph 5:26; 1 Peter 2:2). Receiving life by the Word, it also receives its function, namely, to pass on the Word that others may also be quickened and cleansed. It is to preach the gospel (Mark 16:15), to take up the ministry of reconciliation (2 Cor 5:19), to dispense the mysteries of God (1 Cor 4:1).

The ministry of the church arises in this connection. The apostles were first commissioned, and they ordained others, yet no rigid form of ministry arose in the NT. Rather, we are given patterns (notably of speech, action, and rule), historically focused in the elders, deacons, and overseers (or bishops). If it is essential that there should be the threefold pattern, there seems no biblical prescription for its discharge in a fixed order, nor for noninterchangeability of function, nor for the sharp isolation of an official ministry from the so-called laity or "mere" people of God. The Bible's concern is that there should be real ministry, i.e., service, not in self-assertion and pride but in humility, obedience, and self-offering that conforms to the example of him who was among us as one who serves (see Matt 23:11–12; Phil 2:5–6; 1 Peter 5:1–2).

Finally, the church's work is not merely for the salvation of people; it is primarily to the praise of God's glory (Eph 1:6; 2:7). Hence neither the church nor its function ceases with the completion of its earthly task. There is ground, therefore, for the old distinction between the church triumphant and the church militant. All the church is triumphant in its true reality. But the warring and wayfaring church is still engaged in conflict between the old reality and the new. Its destiny, however, is to be brought into full conformity to the Lord (1 John 3:2). Toward this it moves hesitantly yet expectantly, confident in its future glory when it will be wholly the church triumphant as graphically depicted in Revelation 7:9ff., enjoying its full reality as the bride and body of the Lord.

The Cilician Gates at Tarsus, a formidable pass through the Taurus range of mountains. Paul and his companions traveled through this pass on their missionary journeys. Courtesy Dan Bahat.

Bibliography: F. J. A. Hort, *The Christian Ecclesia,* 1897; R. N. Flew, *Jesus and His Church,* 1941; G. Johnston, *The Doctrine of the Church in the New Testament,* 1943; E. L. Mascall, *Christ, the Christian and the Church,* 1946; A. Schlatter, *The Church in the New Testament Period,* 1955; O. Cullmann, *The Early Church,* 1956; E. Schweizer, *Church Order in the New Testament,* 1961; A. Cole, *The Body of Christ,* 1964; G. C. Berkouwer, *The Church,* 1976. GWB

CHUSHAN-RISHATHAIM (See CUSHAN-RISHATHAIM)

CHUZA (See CUZA)

CILICIA (sĭ-lĭsh'ĭ-â, Gr. *Kilikia*). A country in SE Asia Minor, bounded on the north and west by the Taurus range, and on the south by the Mediterranean. It had two parts, the western one called the Rugged; the eastern one, the Plain Cilicia, the chief city of which was Tarsus, the birthplace of Paul (Acts 21:39; 22:3; 23:34). The early inhabitants must have been Hittites. Later, Syrians and Phoenicians settled there. It came under Persian sway. After Alexander, Seleucid rulers governed it from Antioch. It became a Roman province in 100 B.C. One of its governors was Cicero, the orator (51–50). Cilicia is accessible by land only by way of its two famous mountain passes, the Cilician Gates and the Syrian Gates. Jews from Cilicia disputed with Stephen (Acts 6:9). The gospel reached it early (15:23), probably through Paul (9:30; Gal 1:21). On Paul's second missionary journey he confirmed the churches that had been established there (Acts 15:41), and on his way to Rome as a prisoner he sailed over the sea of Cilicia (27:5).

CINNAMON (See PLANTS)

CIRCUMCISION (sĭr'kŭm-sĭ'shŭn, Lat. *a cutting around*). The cutting off of the foreskin, a custom that has prevailed, and still prevails, among many peoples in different parts of the world—in Asia, Africa, America, and Australia. In ancient times it was practiced among the western Semites—Hebrews, Arabians, Moabites, Ammonites, Edomites, and Egyptians, but not among the Babylonians, Assyrians, Canaanites, and Philistines. Various theories are held regarding the origin and original significance of circumcision, but there can be no doubt that it was at first a religious act.

Among the Hebrews the rite was instituted by

God as the sign of the covenant between him and Abraham, shortly after the latter's sojourn in Egypt. God ordained that it be performed on Abraham, on his posterity and slaves, and on foreigners joining themselves to the Hebrew nation (Gen 17:12). Every male child was to be circumcised on the eighth day. Originally the father performed the rite, but in exceptional cases a woman could do it (Exod 4:25). In later times a Hebrew surgeon was called in. The child was named at the ceremony. Today the rite is performed either in the parent's home or in the synagogue. In former times flint or glass knives were preferred, but now steel is usually used.

According to the terms of the covenant symbolized by circumcision, the Lord undertook to be the God of Abraham and his descendants, and they were to belong to him, worshiping and obeying only him. The rite effected admission to the fellowship of the covenant people and secured for the individual, as a member of the nation, his share in the promises God made to the nation as a whole. Circumcision reminded the Israelites of God's promises to them and of the duties they had assumed. The prophets often reminded them that the outward rite, to have any significance, must be accompanied by a "circumcision of the heart" (Lev 26:41; Deut 30:6; Ezek 44:7). Jeremiah said that his countrymen were no better than the pagans, for they were "uncircumcised in heart" (Jer 9:25–26). Paul used the word *concision* for this outward circumcision not accompanied by a spiritual change. In the early history of the Christian church, Judaizing Christians argued for the necessity of circumcising Gentiles who came into the church over against Paul, who insisted that the signs of the old covenant could not be forced on the children of the new covenant. Paul's view was affirmed by the Council of Jerusalem (Acts 15). SB

CISTERN (Heb. *bō'r* or *bôr*). An artificial tank or reservoir dug in the earth or rock for the collection and storage of rain water, or, sometimes, of spring water brought from a distance by a conduit. A cistern is distinguished from a pool by always being covered. Cisterns were very numerous in Palestine. The long, dry, rainless summers, lasting from May to September, and the small annual precipitation, together with a lack of natural springs, made the people largely dependent on rain water. Cisterns were fed from surface and roof drainage by gutters and pipes. The hilly character of the land allowed little rain to penetrate the soil. Most of it flowed down the steep hillsides through the many ravines and watercourses, and it was easily brought by conduits to pools and cisterns. Cisterns in Palestine varied in size and character. Some were cut wholly in the rock, often in the form of a bottle-shaped tank, with a long stairway leading to the surface of the ground. They were often of great depth, some more than one hundred feet (thirty-one m.) deep. Very large ones were supported by rock pillars. The temple area in Jerusalem had at least thirty-seven great cisterns, one of them holding between two and three million gallons (8 and 11 million liters). Public rock-cut cisterns were made within the city walls so that the inhabitants could hold out in time of siege.

Where the substratum of the soil was earth and not rock, cisterns of masonry were built. Some of these were large and had vaulted roofs supported by pillars. Besides the large public cisterns, there were many smaller private ones. Ancient sites are honeycombed with them. All cisterns had one or more openings for drawing water to the surface. They needed periodic cleaning because of the impurities washed in from the outside. Empty cisterns were sometimes used as prisons. Joseph was cast into one (Gen 37:22), and Jeremiah was let down into one with a muddy bottom (Jer 38:6). Zechariah 9:11 alludes to the custom of confining prisoners in an empty cistern. SB

CITADEL. Fortifications within Hebrew towns. The term should probably be applied only to the final defense unit of a city. This might include the palace (1 Kings 16:18) or sometimes the temple (Neh 2:8). See also CASTLE.

CITIES OF REFUGE. Six cities, three on each side of the Jordan, set apart by Moses and Joshua as places of asylum for those who had committed manslaughter. Those east of the Jordan were Bezer in Reuben, Ramoth Gilead in Gad, and Golan in Manasseh (Deut 4:41–43); those west of the Jordan were Hebron in Judah, Shechem in Ephraim, and Kedesh in Naphtali (Josh 20:7–8). To shelter the person guilty of manslaughter from the "avenger of blood," provision was made that the principal roads leading to these cities should always be kept open. No part of Palestine was more than thirty miles (fifty km.) away from a city of refuge—a distance that could easily be covered in one day. Cities of refuge were provided to protect a person until his case could be properly adjudged. The right of asylum was only for those who had taken life unintentionally. Willful murderers were put to death at once.

The regulations concerning these cities of refuge are found in Numbers 35; Deuteronomy 19:1–13; and Joshua 20. If one guilty of unintentional killing reached a city of refuge before the avenger of blood could kill him, he was given asylum until a fair trial could be held. The trial took place where the accused had lived. If proved innocent of willful murder, he was brought back to the city of refuge. There he had to stay until the death of the high priest. After that he was free to return to his own home. But if during that period he passed beyond the limits of the city of refuge, the avenger of blood could kill him without blame. See also AVENGER. SB

CITIES OF THE PLAIN (Heb. *kikkar hayardēn, circle of the Jordan*). Cities near the Dead Sea, including Sodom, Gomorrah, Admah, Zeboiim, and Zoar. They were first referred to in Genesis 13:10–12, where Lot, after Abraham had given him the choice of where he wanted to live, decided to dwell in the cities of the plain and pitched his tent near Sodom. Genesis 14 says that they were royal cities, each with its own king, and that Abraham delivered Lot when the cities were attacked and Lot taken captive. The story of the destruction of the cities because of their wickedness is given in Genesis 19. It is thought that God may have accomplished this by causing an eruption of gases and petroleum to ignite. Only Lot and his two daughters were spared. The exact site of the cities is unknown; but though there are weighty arguments for believing that they were at the north end of the Dead Sea, scholars favor the south end, especially since asphalt in large quantities has been found only at the south. It is believed that the sea covers the site. Sodom and Gomorrah are often used as a warning example of sin and divine punishment (Deut 29:23; Isa 1:9; 3:9; Jer 50:40; Ezek 16:46; Matt 10:15; Rom 9:29). SB

CITIZENSHIP (Gr. *politeuma, commonwealth*). In the NT the word for citizen often means nothing more than the inhabitant of a country (Luke 15:15; 19:14). Among the ancient Jews emphasis was placed on Israel as a religious organization, not on relationship to city and state. The good citizen was the good Israelite, one who followed not just civil law but religious law. Non-Israelites had the same protection of the law as native Israelites, but they were required not to perform acts hurting the religious feelings of the people. The advantage of a Jew over a Gentile was thus strictly spiritual. He was a member of the theocracy.

Among the Romans, citizenship brought the right to be considered equal to natives of the city of Rome. Emperors sometimes granted it to whole provinces and cities, and also to single individuals for services rendered to the state or to the imperial family, or even for a certain sum of money. Roman citizens were exempted from shameful punishments, such as scourging and crucifixion, and they had the right of appeal to the emperor with certain limitations.

Paul says he had become a Roman citizen by birth. Either his father or some other ancestor had acquired the right and had transmitted it to his son. He was proud of his Roman citizenship and when occasion demanded, availed himself of his rights. When writing to the Philippians, who were members of a Roman colony and therefore Roman citizens, Paul emphasized that Christians are citizens of a heavenly commonwealth and ought to live accordingly (Phil 1:27; 3:20). SB

City model of Megiddo, in the tenth century B.C., showing the gate area, stable complex, storehouses, and palace. Courtesy Israel Government Press Office.

CITRON (See PLANTS)

CITY. In ancient times cities owed their origin, not to organized manufacture, but to agriculture. When men left the pastoral life and settled down to the cultivation of the soil, they often found their cattle and crops endangered by wandering tribes of the desert; and it was to protect themselves from such enemies that they created first the village and then the city. Cities were built in areas where agriculture could be carried on, usually on the side of a mountain or the top of a hill, and where a sufficient supply of water was assured. The names of cities often indicate the feature that was determinative in the selection of the site. For example, the prefixes *Beer,* meaning "well," and *En,* meaning "spring," in such names as Beersheba and En Gedi, show that it was a local well or spring that determined the building of the city. Names like Ramah, Mizpah, and Gibeah (all from roots indicating height), which were very common in Palestine, indicate that a site on an elevation was preferred for a city. A ruling family sometimes gave its name to a city (*Beth,* meaning "house of").

Ancient farmers did not have their own farms. At the end of a day's work they retired for the night to the village or city. Smaller villages sought the protection of nearby cities. That is the meaning of the expression, added to the name of a city, "and its surrounding settlements" (Num 21:25; 32:42). In return for the protection offered against nomadic attacks, the cities received payment in service and produce. Sometimes a city was protected by a feudal lord around or near whose fortress the city was built. Often it depended entirely on the strength of its walls and the bravery of its men.

The chief feature distinguishing a city from a village was that it had a wall (Lev 25:29–30). Walls twenty and thirty feet (six to nine m.) thick were not unusual. Sometimes a city was also surrounded by a moat (Dan 9:25; KJV "wall;" NIV "trench"), and even by a second smaller wall acting as a rampart (2 Sam 20:15). The wall had one or more gates that were closed during the night (Josh 2:5, 7), and in later times on the sabbath (Neh 13:19). The gates were strengthened with iron or bronze bars and bolts (Deut 3:5; Judg 16:3) and had rooms overhead (2 Sam 18:24). From the top of the wall or from a tower by the gate, a watchman was on the lookout for approaching danger (Jer 6:17). The gates were approached by narrow roads easy to defend. From a distance, usually all that could be seen of a city was its walls, except possibly its inner fortress or citadel.

Area G of the City of David, excavated by Kathleen Kenyon, showing remains of Israelite structures and a strong retaining wall built by the Jebusites. Courtesy Zev Radovan.

Within the walls, the important features of a city were the stronghold or fortress, the high place, the broad place by the gate, and the streets. The stronghold was an inner fort protected by a garrison to which the inhabitants could run when the outer walls were taken by an enemy. The people of Shechem tried unsuccessfully to hold out against Abimelech in such a stronghold (Judg 9:49), and the king was afterward killed by a woman who dropped a stone from the tower within the city of Thebez (Judg 9:50, 53). When David captured the fortress of Zion, the whole city came into his possession (2 Sam 5:7). Sometimes towers abutted the inside of the city wall.

The high place was an important part of every Canaanite city and retained its place in Palestine to the time of Solomon's reign (1 Sam 9:12ff.). There sacrifices were offered and feasts held. Originally they were on an elevation, but the term became the general one for any local sanctuary even when it was on level ground.

The broad place was an open area—not a square, but only a widening of the street, just inside the city gate, serving as a place for social intercourse in general. It was the center of communal life. Here the people of the city administered justice, held deliberative assemblies, exchanged news, and transacted business. Strangers in the city passed the night there if they had no friends in the city. It had a defensive value in time of war, as it permitted the concentration of forces in front of the city gate.

The streets in ancient cities were not laid out on any fixed plan. They were narrow, winding, unpaved alleys. The streets of Jerusalem were not paved until the time of Herod Agrippa II. Cities built on steep hillsides had streets on the roofs of houses. Streets were rarely cleaned and were unlighted. Certain streets were allocated to particular trades and guilds—for bakers, cheesemakers, goldsmiths, etc.

Little is known about how city government was administered. In Deuteronomy 16:18 and 19:12 mention is made of elders and judges. Samaria had a governor (1 Kings 22:26). Jerusalem must have had several high officials (2 Kings 23:8). SB

CITY OF DAVID. 1. The Jebusite fortress of Zion that David captured and named the city of David (2 Sam 5:7, 9; 1 Kings 8:1; 1 Chron 11:5, 7; 2 Chron 5:2). It stood on a ridge near the later site of the temple. David made it his royal residence.

2. Bethlehem, the home of David (Luke 2:4).

CLAUDA (See CAUDA)

CLAUDIA (klô′dĭ-ȧ). A member of the Christian church at Rome who, along with other members of that church joined with Paul in sending greetings to Timothy (2 Tim 4:21).

CLAUDIUS (klô′dĭ-ŭs). The fourth Roman emperor (A.D. 41–54). He was a nephew of

Sketch of the Roman emperor Claudius, drawn from a statue now in the Vatican in Rome. Claudius is mentioned twice in the New Testament (Acts 11:28; 18:2). Courtesy Carta, Jerusalem.

Tiberius, the second Roman emperor. A weak, vacillating man, he was under the influence of unprincipled favorites and his wife Messalina. His second wife, Agrippina, poisoned him in 54. Herod Agrippa I, grandson of Herod the Great, had assisted him much in his advancement to the throne, and in consequence was given the whole of Palestine. Claudius also gave the Jews throughout the empire the right of religious worship, but later he banished all Jews from Rome (Acts 18:2; cf. Suet. *Claud.* 25). The famine foretold by Agabus took place in the reign of Claudius (11:28). Ancient writers say that from various causes his reign was a period of distress over the whole Mediterranean world.

CLAUDIUS LYSIAS (klô′dĭ-ŭs lĭs′ĭ-ăs). A chief captain who rescued Paul from fanatical Jewish rioters at Jerusalem (Acts 21:31; 24:22). He was a Greek, as his second name shows. He was a chiliarch (i.e., leader of a thousand men), in charge of the Roman garrison of Jerusalem, stationed in the Castle of Antonia, adjoining the temple. When Paul informed him that he was a Roman citizen and therefore could not legally be scourged, Claudias told Paul that he had purchased his Roman citizenship with a "big price" (22:28). To protect Paul, he soon afterward sent him to Caesarea to see Felix, the Roman governor.

CLAY. A word that translates a number of different Hebrew words and one Greek word and is often used in the Bible in a literal or a metaphorical sense—in the latter sense meaning "dust" or "flesh" (as made from earth). Clay was widely used in OT times for the making of brick, mortar, and pottery, and, in some countries, for the making of tablets on which inscriptions were impressed (see CLAY TABLETS). Mud bricks were not always made of true clay, but of mud mixed with straw. True clay was variable in composition, giving variety to quality and color, and thus was suited for different uses. As a building material, clay has been used from very ancient times. Babylon was made wholly of brick, either baked or dried in the sun. Nineveh, the capital of Assyria, was made mostly of brick. The villages of Egypt were constructed of sun-dried clay.

CLAY TABLETS. In ancient times writing was done on papyrus, parchment, potsherds, and clay tablets. The latter were made of clean-washed, smooth clay. While still wet, the clay had wedge-shaped letters (now called "cuneiform" from Latin *cuneus,* "wedge") imprinted on it with a stylus, and then was kiln fired or sun dried. Tablets were made of various shapes—cone-shaped, drum-shaped, and flat. They were often placed in a clay envelope. Vast quantities of these have been excavated in the Near East, of which about a half million are yet to be read. It is estimated that 99 percent of the Babylonian tablets have yet to be dug. The oldest ones go back to 3000 B.C. They are practically imperishable; fire only hardens them more. Personal and business letters, legal documents, books, and communications between rulers are represented.

Fragment of a clay tablet from Nineveh, with the Assyrian epic of Creation called *enuma elish* ("when the gods"), which tells of how Marduk slew the monster Tiamat and created the world out of her body. Reproduced by courtesy of the Trustees of the British Museum.

One of the most famous is the Code of Hammurabi, a Babylonian king who lived long before the time of Moses. The tablets reveal intimate details of everyday life in the Near East and shed light on many obscure customs mentioned in the OT. Some tell the story of the Creation, the Fall, and the Flood. They do much to verify the truth of the biblical record. SB

CLEAN (Heb. *tahor,* Gr. *hagnos, katharos*). The division found in the OT between clean and unclean is fundamental to Hebrew/Israelite religion. The Lord is to be served and worshiped only by a clean, pure, and chaste people. They were to be pysically clean (Exod 19:10ff.; 30:18–21), ritually and ceremonially clean (having offered the right sacrifices and been through the correct ceremonies [e.g., Lev 14:1ff.; 15:1ff.]), and morally clean in heart. David prayed, "Cleanse me with hyssop, and I will be clean; wash me, and I will be whiter than snow" (Ps 51:7). While the NT supplies examples of the need for ritual cleansing (e.g., Mark 1:44; Acts 21:26), its emphasis is on the clean heart and pure life. Jesus condemned the obsession with external purity with no related emphasis on internal purity/wholeness (Mark 7:1–23). Further, by his atoning work Jesus cleanses believers from all sin (Eph 5:25–26; 1 John 1:7). As High Priest, Jesus cleanses the heart as well as the body (Heb 10:2, 21–22). So believers are to be pure in heart (Matt 5:8; 1 Tim 1:5) and chaste in life (1 Tim 4:2; 5:2). It is their duty to purify themselves (1 Peter 2:22; 1 John 3:3). See also UNCLEAN. PT

CLEANTHES (klē-ăn'thēz). Son of Phanius of Assos and head of the Stoic school from 263 to 232 B.C. He infused religious fervor into Zeno's Stoicism. He taught that the universe was a living being and God its soul. He taught disinterestedness in ethics, maintaining that doing good to gain advantage was like feeding cattle for meat. He taught, too, that evil thoughts were worse than evil deeds. His *Hymn to Zeus,* a surviving poem, contains the words quoted by Paul in Athens (Acts 17:28).

CLEMENT (klĕm'ĕnt). A Christian who labored with Paul at Philippi (Phil 4:3). It is uncertain whether he was in Philippi when Paul wrote. Origen identifies him with the church father who afterward became bishop of Rome and wrote a letter to the Corinthian church, but if he is right, Clement must have lived to an extreme old age.

CLEOPAS (klē'ō-păs). One of the two disciples to whom the Lord appeared on the afternoon of the resurrection day. They walked with him on the road from Jerusalem to Emmaus, about seven miles (twelve km.) away (Luke 24:18). Nothing more is known about him. He is not to be confused with the Clopas (Cleophas, KJV) mentioned in John 19:25, although some church fathers assumed that the two were identical.

CLEOPHAS (See CLOPAS)

CLERK (See OCCUPATIONS AND PROFESSIONS)

CLOAK (See DRESS)

CLOPAS (klō'păs). Mentioned in John 19:25 (KJV, Cleophas) as the husband of Mary, one of the women who stood beside the cross and who is described as a sister of the mother of Jesus. He is not the same as the Cleopas who walked with Jesus to Emmaus (Luke 24:18).

CLOSET (Gr. *tameion*). Found in Matthew 6:6 and Luke 12:3, this word has been regarded as most probably referring to a special storage closet in which bedding was stored during the day. If required, it could also be used as a sleeping-room or for private conference. Our Lord advised that it be used for private prayer. RSV and NIV both render simply "room," in the first occurrence, "inner [or private] rooms" in the other.

CLOTH, CLOTHES, CLOTHING (See DRESS)

CLOUD. Few biblical references suggest that clouds have anything to do with actual weather conditions, because in Palestine the weather is not very varied. There were two recognized seasons: a rainy one from October to April, and one of sunshine from May to September. The Hebrews were not much given to making comments on the weather. In Scripture there are, however, many references to clouds in a metaphoric and figurative sense. They symbolize transitoriness. God says Judah's goodness is like a morning cloud (Hos 6:4 KJV; "mist" in NIV), and Job compares his prosperity to the passing clouds (Job 30:15). Sometimes they are used as a type of refreshment, for they bring shade from the oppressive sun and give promise of rain. Clouds without water, therefore, symbolize a person who promises much but does not perform (Prov 16:15; 25:14; Jude 12). The darkness of clouds is the symbol of mystery, especially that of creation (Job 3:5; 38:9; Ps 97:2). Their distance from the earth is made to typify the unattainable (Job 20:6; Ps 147:8; Isa 14:14). One of the most frequent and suggestive uses of the figure is in connection with the presence of God. Clouds both veil and reveal the divine presence. God rides on the clouds (Isa 19:1; Nah 1:3); he is present in the cloud (Exod 19:9; 24:16; 34:5). The pillar of cloud symbolized God's presence and guidance to the children of Israel in their wilderness journeys (Exod 40:36; Ps 78:14). A cloud appeared at our Lord's transfiguration (Matt 17:5) and at his ascension (Acts 1:9), and it has a place in his prediction of his coming again (Matt 24:30; 26:64). SB

CLOUD, PILLAR OF. A symbol of the presence and guidance of God in the forty-year wilderness journey of the Israelites from Egypt to Canaan (Exod 13:21–22). At night it became fire. When God wanted Israel to rest in any place, the cloud rested on the tabernacle above the mercy seat (29:42–43) or at the door of the tabernacle (33:9–10; Num 12:5), or it covered the tabernacle (Exod 40:34–38).

CLOUT (See DRESS)

CNIDUS (nī′dŭs). A city of Caria at the SW corner of Asia Minor, past which Paul sailed on his journey to Rome (Acts 27:7). It was situated at the end of a long, narrow peninsula projecting between the islands Cos and Rhodes, and had two excellent harbors. It had the rank of a free city. Jews lived there as early as the second century B.C. Only ruins are left of a once-flourishing city, especially noted for its temple of Venus and a statue of the goodness by Praxiteles.

COAL. Often found in the English Bible, the word never refers to true mineral coal, which has not been found in Palestine proper, where the geological formation as a whole is recent. Coal of a poor quality has been found at Sidon, and for a time some was mined in Lebanon. The half dozen Hebrew and Greek words rendered "coal" refer either to charcoal or to live embers of any kind. Charcoal was used by the Hebrews to provide warmth in winter (Isa 47:14; John 18:18), for cooking (Isa 44:19; John 21:9), and for blacksmith work (Isa 44:12; 54:16). It was made by covering a carefully stacked pile of wood with leaves and earth, and then setting fire to it. After several days of burning and smoldering, the wood was converted into charcoal and the pile was opened.

In Psalm 120:4 there is mention of "coals of the broom tree." In 1 Kings 19:6 and Isaiah 6:6 the Hebrew word denotes a hot stone. Frequently the word is used metaphorically, as in Proverbs 26:21 (NIV "charcoal"). In Proverbs 25:22 and Romans 12:20, where we are told to give to an enemy good in return for evil, thus heaping coals of fire on his head, the coals of fire are not meant to suggest the pain of punishment to the guilty but the softening of his heart as he thinks with burning shame of his unworthy hatred. Love will melt and purify. In Lamentations 4:8 the literal meaning of the Hebrew word translated "coal" by KJV, "soot" by NIV and RSV, is "blackness." SB

COAT (See DRESS)

COAT OF MAIL (See ARMS AND ARMOR)

COBRA (See ANIMALS)

COCK (See BIRDS)

COCKATRICE (See ANIMALS)

COCK CROWING. When referring to time, this is the third of the four watches into which the Romans divided the night: evening, midnight, cock crowing, morning. Cock crowing was between midnight and 3 a.m. (Matt 26:34; Mark 13:35). NIV reads "rooster."

COCKLE (See PLANTS)

Thirteenth century B.C. anthropoid coffin, stylistically similar to the mummy-cases found in Egypt, from Deir el-Balah in the Gaza region. Courtesy Zev Radovan.

COFFIN. This word is used only in Genesis 50:26; Luke 7:14. The literal meaning of the Hebrew word is "chest" or "box," but in this instance may mean "mummy case." Coffins were unknown among the Israelites, who were carried to the grave on a bier, a simple flat board with two or three staves. In Luke 7:14 where NIV has "coffin," KJV has "bier." In Egypt, where Joseph died, the dead were embalmed and put in a mummy case.

COIN (See MONEY)

COL-HOZEH (kŏl-hō′zĕ, *all-seeing one*). A Judahite of Nehemiah's day whose son Shallum rebuilt the fountain gate of Jerusalem (Neh 3:15; 11:5).

COLLAR (See DRESS)

COLONY (Gr. *kolōnia*, a transliteration of the Latin *colonus, farmer*). In the only occurrence of the word in the NT, Acts 16:12, Philippi is mentioned as a colony. A colony was a settlement of Roman citizens, authorized by the government, in conquered territory. The settlers were usually retired Roman soldiers, who settled in places where they could keep enemies of the empire in check. They were the aristocracy of the provincial towns where they lived. Such colonies had the rights of Italian cities: municipal self-government and exemption from poll and land taxes.

COLOSSE (kŏ-lŏs'ē, Gr. *Kolossai*). An ancient city of Phrygia, situated on the south bank of the Lycus River. It was about eleven miles (eighteen km.) from Laodicea and thirteen (twenty-one km.) from Hierapolis. Colosse stood on the most important trade route from Ephesus to the Euphrates and was a place of great importance from early times. Xerxes visited it in 481 B.C., and Cyrus the Younger in 401. The city was particularly renowned for a peculiar wool, probably purple in color (*colossinus*). The church at Colosse was established on Paul's third missionary journey, during his three years in Ephesus, not by Paul himself (Col 2:1), but by Epaphras (1:7, 12–13). Archippus also exercised a fruitful ministry there (4:17; Philem 2). Philemon was an active member of this church, and so also was Onesimus (Col 4:9). During Paul's first Roman imprisonment Epaphras brought him a report of the religious views and practices in Colosse that called forth his letter, in which he rebuked the church for its errors. Colosse lost its importance by the change of the road system. Laodicea became the greater city. During the seventh and eighth centuries A.D. its openness exposed it to the terrible raids of the Saracens, and the people moved to Chonae (now called Chonas), a fortress on the slope of Mount Cadmus, about three miles (five km.) farther south. In the twelfth century the Turks destroyed the city. Archaeologists have unearthed ruins of an ancient church. SB

COLOSSIANS, THE LETTER TO. A letter written by the apostle Paul when he was a prisoner (Col 4:3, 10, 18), about the year A.D. 62, probably during his first imprisonment in Rome (Acts 28:30–31), though Caesarea (23:35; 24:27) and Ephesus have also been suggested. The external and internal evidence for its genuineness is all that can be desired. The church at Colosse was very likely founded during Paul's three-year stay in Ephesus on his third missionary journey. It appears from Colossians 2:1 that Paul himself had never preached in Colosse. Epaphras, a native of Colosse (Col 4:12), was probably converted under Paul's ministry at Ephesus and was then sent by the apostle to preach in his native city (1:7). He also appears to have evangelized the nearby cities of Laodicea and Hierapolis (4:13). When Paul wrote this letter, the minister of the church at Colosse was Archippus (4:17), who may have been Philemon's son (Philem 2). Epaphras had recently come to Paul with a disturbing report of the condition of the church, and this led Paul to the writing of the letter. The bearer of the letter was Tychicus (Col 4:7, 8), to whom Paul also entrusted his letter to the Ephesians (Eph 6:21), which was probably written at the same time. With him went Onesimus (Col 4:9), a runaway slave converted by Paul, bearing Paul's letter to Philemon, a resident of Colosse, who was also one of Paul's converts, perhaps becoming a believer at Ephesus.

In the few years since Paul had been in the province of Asia an insidious error had crept into the church at Colosse. Who the false teachers were we do not know; but it is clear that the trouble was different from that faced by Paul at Galatia, where Judaizers had tried to undermine his work. The teaching attacked by Paul is described in Colossians 2:8, 16–23. It was, at least in part, Judaistic, as is seen in his reference to circumcision (2:11; 3:11), ordinances (2:14), meats and drinks, feast days, new moons, and Sabbaths (2:16). There was also in it a strong ascetic element. Special self-denying rules were given (2:16, 20–21) that had as their purpose the mortification of the body (2:23). Some sort of worship of angels was practiced—a worship that continued for several centuries, as we know from the fact that in the fourth century A.D. the Council of Laodicea condemned it in one of its canons, and in the fifth century Theodoret said that the archangel Michael was worshiped in the area. This heresy claimed to be a philosophy and made much of wisdom and knowledge (2:8). Plainly, the Colossians were beguiled by this religious syncretism and even took pride in it (2:8). The exact origin of the false teaching is unknown. Some find it in Essenism; others in incipient Gnosticism or in contemporary Judaism with a syncretistic addition of local Phrygian ideas.

Paul met these errors, not by controversy or personal authority, but by presenting the counter truth that Jesus Christ is the image of the invisible God (Col 1:15), in whom are hid all the treasures of wisdom and knowledge, and in whom the fullness of the divine perfections find their perfect embodiment (1:19). He is the creator of all, and all power is from him. On the cross he revealed the impotence of all the powers that had tried to thwart his purposes (2:15). Freedom from the corruption of human nature is found in the newness of life that the death and resurrection of Christ provide. The letter to the Colossians may be divided into four parts: (1) The salutation and thanksgiving (1:1–8); (2) the doctrinal section (1:9–2:5); (3) practical exhortations (2:6–4:6); (4) concluding salutations (4:7–18). Toward the end of the letter (4:16), Paul asks that the Colossian church exchange letters with the church at Laodicea, to which he has also written. It is likely that this letter to the Laodiceans is what we know as the letter to the Ephesians, sent as a circular letter to various churches in the Roman province of Asia.

Bibliography: J. B. Lightfoot, *Saint Paul's Epistles to the Colossians and to Philemon,* 1875; C. F. D. Moule, *The Epistles of Paul the Apostle to the Colossians and to Philemon* (CGTC), 1957; E. Lohse, *Colossians and Philemon,* 1971; R. P. Martin, *Colossians: The Church's Lord and the Christian's Liberty,* 1972, and *Colossians and Philemon* (NCB), 1974; P. T. O'Brien, *Colossians, Philemon* (WBC), 1982; E. Schweizer, *The Letter to the Colossians,* 1982; F. F. Bruce, *The Epistles to the Colossians, to Philemon and to the Ephesians* (NIC), 1984. SB

COLT (See ANIMALS)

COMFORTER, THE (See ADVOCATE; HOLY SPIRIT)

COMMANDMENT. The word is used in the English Bible to translate a number of Hebrew and Greek words meaning law, ordinance, statute, word, judgment, precept, saying, charge. The idea of authority conveyed by these words comes from the fact that God as sovereign Lord has a right to be obeyed. The instruction of Jesus is full of ethical teachings that have the force of divine commandments. What he says is as authoritative as what was said by God in OT times. That is true even when he does not use the word "commandment" or its equivalents, as he often does. But what is said of God and Jesus Christ is also true of the apostles. Paul, for example, does not hesitate to say, "What I am writing to you is the Lord's command" (1 Cor 14:37). The Bible makes it very clear that God is not satisfied with mere external compliance with his commandments but expects willing and joyful obedience, coming from the heart.

The Nash Papyrus, a second century (c. 150) B.C. papyrus fragment written in square Hebrew script. It contains the Ten Commandments and was the oldest biblical text known until the discovery of the Dead Sea Scrolls. Courtesy Encyclopaedia Judaica Photo Archive, Jerusalem.

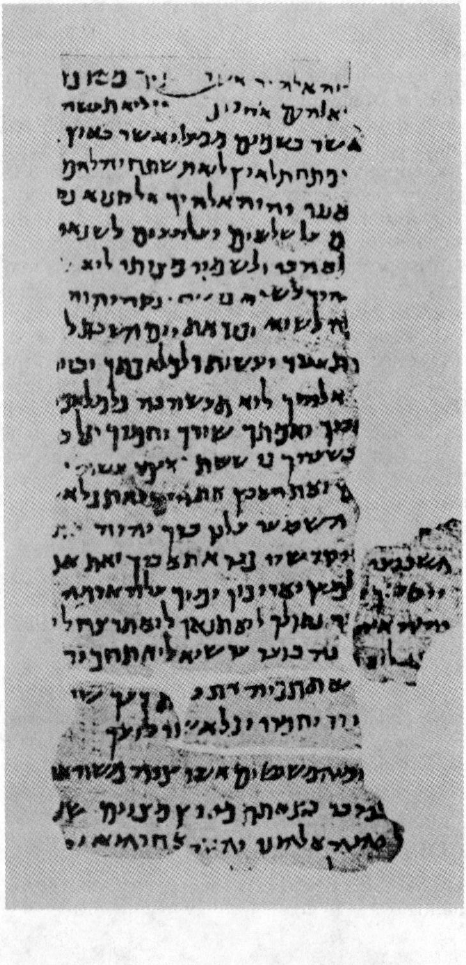

COMMANDMENTS, TEN. The OT is distinctly a religion of law, with creed, cult, and conduct prescribed minutely by God. The OT praises in the Torah (God's law or instruction as set forth in the first five books of the OT; cf. Ps 119:97) the revelational instruction that has come to the elect nation as a gift of grace and that has come to it invested with divine authority and sanction. The Torah is revered because it embodies the will and wisdom of the Creator. Expressing God's own nature, it demands of the creature only what the Creator's holiness requires for fellowship with himself. The climax of Torah is the Decalogue, the Code of the Ten Words, received by Moses on Mount Sinai. The Decalogue is specifically the gift of grace of God the Redeemer (Exod 20:2), given to his people, not to bring them into bondage but because they have been brought out of bondage. That it is unique among the several codes found in the OT can scarcely be disputed. Originally spoken by God in a context calculated to produce unforgettable awe (19:9–25), it was afterward inscribed by his finger on two tables of stone (31:18); in fact, it was inscribed by him a second time after Moses in anger shattered the first two tables (Deut 10:1–4). It was placed in the ark of the covenant (Exod 25:21) and thus enshrined at the very center of Israel's worship. All of its precepts, with the exception of sabbath-keeping, are repeated in the NT. Hence the Code of the Ten Words is indeed *sui generis,* a statement that gives the distillation of religion and morality: these principles, so simply phrased, are remarkably comprehensive and universally valid. Mount Sinai, therefore, was the scene of an epochal event in human history; from a religious standpoint, only Mount Calvary surpasses it.

Before examining this Code in any detail we must answer several questions concerning it. First, how do we explain the two somewhat dissimilar versions of it that the Pentateuch contains, one in Exodus 20:1–17, the other in Deuteronomy 5:6–21? In the Exodus version the fourth commandment grounds sabbath-keeping in God's sabbath-rest after his six days of creation; in the Deuteronomy version, however, sabbath-keeping is grounded in the Egyptian deliverance. Moreover, the two versions do not agree with respect to the tenth commandment, which forbids covetousness; different verbs are used and the order of clauses varies. But surely these are trivia that fade into nothingness when we remember that the Deuteronomic version is part of an address Moses delivered. In an oral recital one scarcely expects notarial precision. Also, Moses, because of the Spirit's guidance, was free to introduce new elements and slight changes.

Second, how are the Ten Words to be numbered? W. S. Bruce helpfully clears away the complexities of this question by pointing out that the commandments were not numbered by Moses, and thus down the ages different schemes of arrangement have been found. In the one most commonly known among English-speaking communities "the preface is not made a commandment or part of one: but the first commandment simply forbids the worship of false deities, and the second prohibits the use of idols; while all the prohibitions of covetousness are included under the last command" (*The Ethics of the Old Testament,* 1909, pp. 101–2).

Third, how are the Ten Words to be divided between the two tables? The Roman Catholic church puts three commandments on the first table, seven on the second. The Reformed church adheres to a four and six classification. Josephus, however, gives the traditional five and five arrangement, the first table dealing, as he says, with piety, the second with probity. Taking Josephus as his guide, C. E. Luthardt in his *History of Christian Ethics* gives what seems to be the most satisfactory division:

FIRST TABLE

1. No other gods.
2. No image of God.
3. No dishonoring of God's name.
4. No desecration of God's day.
5. No dishonoring of God's representatives (parents).

SECOND TABLE

1. No taking away of a neighbor's life.
2. No taking away of his wife—his home—his dearest good.
3. No taking away of his goods.
4. No taking away of his good name.
5. No coveting of his good or his goods.

Fourth, is there any significance to the fact that the Ten Words are inscribed on two tables rather than one? Traditionally the reference to "two tables" has been understood to refer to the fact that the Decalogue falls, as we have seen, into the two sections of our duty to God and our duty to man. It has been assumed that each of these sections was given a tablet to itself. This is intrinsically unlikely because it would put asunder what God has joined, making it appear as if the commandments Godward and the commandments manward are essentially separable. We ought therefore to follow the line opened up by more recent knowledge of ancient covenant forms in which the stipulations of the covenant—the laws imposed by the covenant-lord—were written in duplicate. The covenant-lord retained one copy and deposited the other in the sanctuary of the god of the people on whom he was imposing his covenant. In the case of the Decalogue, Yahweh is both Covenant-Lord and also God of Israel. He, therefore, takes both copies into his care: the whole care, continuance, and maintenance of the covenant relationship rests with him.

Fifth, is this Code merely negative or does it have a positive aspect also? Admittedly, the only commandment couched in positive terms is the fifth law, which enjoins respect for one's parents. But the seeming negativism of the Ten Words is only superficial. Whenever an evil is forbidden, the opposite good is implicitly demanded. Here we have far more than a forbidding: we have a requiring as well. When Jesus interprets and epitomizes this Code, he reduces it to the positive virtue of love. Paul does exactly the same thing in Romans 13:8–10. This Law cannot be fulfilled only by concern and care; it calls for loving obedience to God and loving service to man.

Sixth, is this Code really to be viewed as "a yoke of slavery" (Gal 5:1) or as a wise provision that God graciously made for his people? Undeniably in the course of the centuries rabbinic traditionalism perverted Torah into a grievous legalism; undeniably, too, the Law as a whole had a pedagogic function, revealing as it did—and still does—man's need of Jesus Christ (Rom 7:7; Gal 3:24). Yet the primary purpose of the Ten Words was to enable the Israelites, as the Lord's redeemed and peculiar treasure, to enter into a life of joyful fellowship with their Redeemer. This Code issued from God's sovereign and saving relationship with his elect nation. It was imposed at his initiative and as the result of his covenantal activity. Passages like Exodus 20:2 and Deuteronomy 4:32–40 show that Israel's Savior was Israel's Legislator. This Law, then, was designed to bring the Lord's saving deed to its fulfillment by creating a holy community, a community reflecting his own nature, a community in which he could dwell and by which he could be magnified (Lev 11:44; 20:8). Hence, used lawfully (1 Tim 1:8), this Code, which guided life rather than gave it, was a source of blessing (Ps 19:8–9; 119:54).

With these six questions answered, let us now analyze briefly each of the Ten Words. The first commandment (Exod 20:3) enjoins a confession of God's singularity, his absolute and exclusive deity. It predicates faith in him as the one and only God. Though not expressly teaching monotheism, it inferentially denounces polytheism as treason and unbelief. It demonstrates that God is not a class term but a proper name.

The second commandment (Exod 20:4–6) enjoins the adoration of God's spirituality. Forbidding his worship by any false means, it rebukes the gross idolatry that surrounded Israel. It shows that because of his very Being (John 4:24) no visible or material representation of true Deity is possible. Thus it prevents wrong concepts of God from taking root in man's mind (Rom 1:21–23).

The third commandment (Exod 20:7) enjoins the reverence of the Lord's name. Since in the OT name and person are equivalent, with the name practically a reification of the person, this law prohibits blasphemy and profanity. It also interdicts immorality, any conduct that causes God's honor to suffer defilement by the sinner who bears his name (Rom 2:24–25). With respect to the sacredness and significance of God's name, Malachi 3:16–17 is instructive.

The fourth commandment (Exod 20:8–11) enjoins the observance of the Lord's day. For both humanitarian (Amos 8:5–6) and religious (Isa 58:13–14) reasons, one day of rest in every seven is a blessed necessity. A Sabbath—whether on Saturday as commemorating a finished creation or on Sunday as commemorating a finished redemption—serves man's physical and spiritual welfare simultaneously (Mark 2:27).

The fifth commandment (Exod 20:12) enjoins the honor of God's surrogates, parents to whom he grants a kind of co-creatorship in the begetting of children and to whom he grants a kind of co-rulership in the governing of children. Let any nation abandon respect for the mystery, dignity, and authority of parenthood, and before long the moral fiber and social fabric of that nation are bound to disintegrate. That is why the OT statutes on this score are so severe (Exod 21:15; Deut 27:16; Prov 20:20).

The sixth commandment (Exod 20:13) is a prohibition of murder. A man's life is, patently, his one utterly indispensable possession; but, more than that, man is God's image-bearer, and murder wantonly destroys God's image. Hence capital punishment is the penalty affixed to breaking this law (Gen 9:5–6).

The seventh commandment (Exod 20:24) is a prohibition of adultery, a stringent prohibition that safeguards the sanctity of marriage and throws a bulwark around the home. In our day we are beginning to see what happens when the home is undermined by marital infidelity.

The eighth commandment (Exod 20:15) is a prohibition of theft in any and all forms. Property is essentially an extension of a man's personality, and thus this law indicates that the rights and achievements of one's neighbor must not be ignored.

The ninth commandment (Exod 20:16) is a prohibition of falsehood in its many varieties, whether perjury, slander, or defamation. Truth is the cement of community, the *sine qua non* of enduring interpersonal relationships on every level. Thus the OT, like the NT, stresses the need for a sanctified tongue (Ps 5:9; 15:1–4; Prov 18:21; Jer 9:1–5).

The tenth commandment (Exod 20:17) is a prohibition of covetousness, and as such reveals that the Ten Words are not simply a civil code, but form a moral and spiritual code that strikes beneath the surface of the overt act (which is the exclusive province of civil law), tracing evil conduct to evil desire, probing the hidden motives of people (which is the province of morality and religion, God's province). This tenth commandment, therefore, highlights the pivotal importance of wrong appetites and intentions; it agrees with Paul that covetousness is idolatry (Col 3:5), since inordinate craving means that man's ego has become man's god.

Except as the NT deepens and extends its principles, the Decalogue represents the high-water level of morality.

Bibliography: R. H. Charles, *The Decalogue,* 1923; G. Vos, *Biblical Theology,* 1954, pp. 145–59; Joy Davidman, *Smoke on the Mountain,* 1963; M. G. Kline, *The Structure of Biblical Authority,* 1975. VCG

CONANIAH (kŏn'á-nī'á, Heb. *kônanyāhû, Jehovah has founded*). 1. A Levite in charge of tithes and offerings in the reign of Hezekiah (2 Chron 31:12–13; KJV "Cononiah").

2. A Levite in Josiah's reign (2 Chron 35:9).

CONCUBINE. In the Bible, not a paramour, but a woman lawfully united in marriage to a man in a relation inferior to that of the regular wife. No moral stigma was attached to being a concubine. It was a natural part of a polygamous social system. Concubinage is assumed and provided for in the law of Moses, which tried to prevent its excesses and abuses (Exod 21:7–11; Deut 21:10–14). Concubines were commonly taken from among Hebrew or foreign slave girls, or Gentile captives taken in war, although free Hebrew women might also become concubines. They enjoyed no other right but lawful cohabitation. They had no authority in the family or in household affairs. Their husbands could send them away with a small present, and their children could, by means of small presents, be excluded from the heritage (Gen 25:6). The children were regarded as legitimate, although the children of the first wife were preferred in the distribution of the inheritance. In patriarchal times, at least, the immediate cause of concubinage was the barrenness of the lawful wife, who herself suggested that her husband have children by her maidservant (Gen 16; 30). Prominent OT figures who had concubines were Nahor (22:24), Abraham (25:6), Jacob (35:22), Eliphaz (36:12), Gideon (Judg 8:31), Saul (2 Sam 3:7), David (5:13; 15:16; 16:21), Solomon (1 Kings 11:3), Caleb (1 Chron 2:46), Manasseh (7:14), Rehoboam (2 Chron 11:21), Abijah (13:21), and Belshazzar (Dan 5:2). SB

CONDUIT (See AQUEDUCT)

CONEY (See ANIMALS)

CONFECTIONER (See OCCUPATIONS AND PROFESSIONS)

CONFESSION (Heb. *yādhâh,* Gr. *homologeō,* and their derivatives). Both the Hebrew and Greek words are capable of the same twofold meaning as the English. To confess is openly to acknowledge the truth in anything, as in the existence and authority of God or the sins of which one has been guilty. Occasionally it also means to concede or allow (John 1:20; Acts 24:14; Heb 11:13), or to praise God by thankfully acknowledging him (Rom 14:11; Heb 13:15). In the Bible, confession of sin before God is recognized as a condition of forgiveness. Christ taught the necessity of confessing offenses committed against other people (Matt 5:24; Luke 17:4). The Bible gives no instruction about the mode of confession or the person to receive it, but no authority is found in it for the auricular confession practiced in the Roman church.

CONGREGATION (Heb. *'ēdhâh* and *qāhāl,* Gr. *ekklēsia* and *synagōgē*). A word used in Scripture mainly to refer to the Hebrew people;

in its collective capacity regarded as God's people or as an assembly of the people summoned for a definite purpose (1 Kings 8:65) or met on a festive occasion (Deut 23:1). Sometimes it refers to an assembly of the whole people; sometimes, to any part of the people who might be present on a given occasion. Occasionally it conveys the idea of "horde." Every circumcised Hebrew was a member of the congregation and took part in its proceedings probably from the time he bore arms. He had, however, no political rights as an individual, but only as a member of a house, a family, or a tribe, which was usually represented by its head, known as an elder or a prince. The elders, summoned by the supreme governor or the high priest, represented the whole congregation, served as a national parliament, and had legislative and judicial powers. They sat as a court to deal with capital offenses (Num 15:32–33), declared war, made peace, and concluded treaties (Josh 9:15). The people were strictly bound by their acts, whether they approved of them or not (9:18). Occasionally the whole body of people was assembled for some solemn religious occasion (Exod 12:47; Num 25:6; Joel 2:15) or to receive some new commandments (Exod 19:7–8; Lev 8:4). After the conquest of Canaan the congregation was assembled only to consider very important matters. SB

CONIAH (kō-nī'a, Heb. *konyāhû, Jehovah is creating*). A form of the name Jehoiachin, found in Jeremiah 22:24, 28; 37:1. See also JEHOIACHIN.

CONSCIENCE. The OT has no separate word for "conscience," but it neither lacks the idea nor the means to express it. It is clear from Genesis 3:8 that the first result of the Fall was a guilty conscience, compelling Adam and Eve to hide from God. Likewise, we read that David's "heart smote him" (1 Sam 24:5 KJV, MLB, RSV); NIV interprets this as "David was conscience-stricken." In everyday Greek the word *syneidēsis* referred to the pain or guilt felt by persons who believed they had done wrong. Paul, who used the word more than other NT writers, refined and developed this meaning. (1) He described the universal existence of conscience (Rom 2:14–16) as the internal moral witness found in all human beings. (2) He believed that Christians should have clear and good consciences (2 Cor 1:12; 1 Tim 1:5, 19; 3:9), because their lives are lived for the glory of God and in the light of Christian teaching. (3) He knew of and gave advice about the weak or partially formed conscience of certain Christians ("conscience" occurs nine times in 1 Cor 8:1–13 and 10:23–11:1); in certain cases mature Christians are to restrict their liberty of action in order not to offend the undeveloped conscience of their weaker brothers and sisters. (4) He was aware of the existence of evil consciences, corrupted by false teaching (1 Tim 4:5; Titus 1:15). A person who rejects the gospel and resolutely opposes God has an evil conscience. (5) As a result of accepting the gospel, people receive a purified, or perfected, conscience (Heb 9:14; 10:22), through forgiveness and the gift of the Holy Spirit. Finally it may be said that while Paul's use of the word "conscience" is that of the internal witness of the mind/heart judging past actions in the light of Christian teaching, he also appears to suggest that the conscience will guide present and future actions (e.g., Rom 13:3; 1 Cor 10:25).

Bibliography: O. Hallesby, *Conscience,* 1960; Peter Toon, *Your Conscience as Your Guide,* 1984. SB

CONSECRATION. An act by which a person or thing is dedicated to the service and worship of God. In the KJV it translates several Hebrew and Greek words of different meanings. (1) Hebrew *hāram,* "devote" (Mic 4:13, NIV "devote"). (2) Hebrew *nāzar, nēzer,* "separate" (Num 6:7, 8, 12, NIV "separation"). (3) Hebrew *qādhēsh,* "to be set apart" (i.e., from that which is common or unclean: Exod 28:3; 30:30; 2 Chron 26:18; 29:33). (4) Heb. *millē' yadh,* literally, "to fill the hand," a peculiar idiom normally used for the installation of a priest into his office or of the installation offerings put into his hands (Exod 29:9, 29; Lev 8:33, NIV "ordain"). (5) Greek *teleioō,* "to make perfect" (Heb. 10:20, NIV "opened").

CONSOLATION (Gr. *paraklēsis, encouragement, comfort*). In the thought behind this word the "consolation of Israel" looked for by Simeon (Luke 2:25) is linked with the famous "comfort" mentioned by Isaiah in a passage about the fulfillment of the promises (Isa 40:1ff.). Yet "comfort" is more positive than "console," as can be seen in the description of the Holy Spirit as "the Comforter" (John 14:16–17 KJV), and of Barnabas as "Son of Encouragement" (Acts 4:36, RSV, NIV).

CONTEST (Gr. *athlēsis, fight*). The verb form is used in the NT in the sense of "to strive" or "to labor fervently." It is associated, for example, with the good fight of faith (1 Tim 6:12), consistent intercessory prayer (Col 4:12), and the struggle to overcome (1 Cor 9:25). As do athletes, so Timothy was exhorted to "strive for masteries" (2 Tim 2:5). Metaphors from the Greek athletic games would appeal particularly to the Corinthians, for games were regularly held in their city. The urgent advice to lay aside "every weight" (Heb 12:1–2 KJV, RSV) is probably taken from the athlete's shedding of weight during his preparation for a contest. NIV uses the noun once (10:32) in the context of "those earlier days . . . when you stood your ground in a great contest in the face of suffering."

CONVERSATION. A word often used in KJV to translate various terms signifying conduct or manner of life, especially with respect to morals. The Greek words rendered "conversation" in Philippians 1:27 and 3:20 refer to "civil life" or "citizenship" (so NIV). Paul means that we should live like citizens of heaven.

CONVERSION (Heb. *shûv*, Gr. *epistrophē*). The words commonly used in the English Bible as equivalent to the Hebrew and Greek words are "turn," "return," "turn back," "turn again." Thus conversion is synonymous with "turning." The turning may be in a literal or in a figurative, ethical, or religious sense, either from God or, more frequently, to God. It is significant that when the turning refers to a definite spiritual change, it almost invariably denotes an act of man: "Turn! Turn from your evil ways!" (Ezek 33:11; cf. Matt 18:3). Since the word implies both a turning *from* and a turning *to* something, it is not surprising that in the NT it is sometimes associated with repentance (Acts 3:19; 26:20) and faith (11:21). That is, conversion on its negative side is turning from sin and on its positive side is faith in Christ ("they must turn to God in repentance and have faith in our Lord Jesus," 20:21). Although conversion is an act of man, Scripture makes clear that it has a divine ground. The turning of sinful people is done by the power of God (3:26). In the process of salvation, conversion is the first step in the transition from sin to God. It is brought about by the Holy Spirit operating on the human mind and will, so that the course of one's life is changed. It is not the same as justification and regeneration, which are purely divine acts. It may come as a sudden crisis or as a more or less prolonged process.

Bibliography: E. S. Jones, *Conversion,* 1959; J. K. Grider, *Repentance Unto Life,* 1965; W. E. Conn, Conversion, 1978; E. Griffin, *Turning,* 1980.

CONVICTION (Gr. *elenchō, to convince or prove guilty*). Conviction is the first stage of repentance, experienced when in some way the evil nature of sin has been brought home to the penitent, and it has been proved to him that he is guilty of it. Although the word "conviction" is never used in KJV, both Testaments give many illustrations of the experience. In the OT one of the most notable is found in Psalm 51, where David, realizing he has sinned against God, is overwhelmed with sorrow for his transgression and cries out to God for forgiveness and cleansing. In the NT the central passage bearing on this theme is John 16:7–11, where Jesus says that when the Holy Spirit comes "he will reprove the world of sin, and of righteousness, and of judgment" (KJV). Here the word "reprove" (NIV "convict") means "convince" (so RSV) or "prove guilty." The thought is that the Holy Spirit addresses the heart of the guilty and shows how inadequate ordinary standards of righteousness are. The purpose of conviction is to lead to godly repentance. SB

CONVOCATION (Heb. *mikrā'*). The word is used in the expression "holy convocation," but it is sometimes used alone (Num 10:2, RSV "congregation," NIV "community"; Isa 1:13). A convocation was a religious festival during which no work could be done. The holy convocations were the Sabbath days (Lev 23:1–3); Pentecost (23:15–21); the first and seventh days of the feast of unleavened bread (Exod 12:16; Lev 23:6–7); the first and tenth days of the seventh month, the latter being the Day of Atonement (Lev 23:24–28); and the first and eighth days of the Feast of Tabernacles (23:34–36). The phrase "solemn assembly" is applied only to the concluding festivals at the end of Passover and the Feast of Tabernacles.

COOS (See COS)

COPPER (See MINERALS)

COPPERSMITH (See OCCUPATIONS AND PROFESSIONS)

COR (See WEIGHTS AND MEASURES)

CORAL (See ANIMALS; MINERALS)

CORBAN (Heb. *qorbān, an offering*). The word occurs in the Hebrew text of the OT and refers to an offering or sacrifice, whether bloody or unbloody, made to God (Lev 1:2–3; 2:1; 3:1; Num 7:12–17). It is found in our English versions in the NT in Mark 7:11, where it refers to money dedicated to God. The Talmud says that the Jews were much given to making rash vows to God, without any intention of carrying them out. By Christ's time there arose the reprehensible practice of children avoiding the responsibility of looking after their parents' material needs by telling them that their money was dedicated to God and that it would be wrong to divert it from this sacred purpose. This could be done by simply pronouncing the votive word "Corban." Ideally, the money thereafter belonged to God, but actually the one who made the vow might keep it in his possession. By referring to this custom Christ demonstrated the sophistry of tradition that enabled the Jews to disregard plain commandments of God, like the one requiring children to honor their parents.

CORD (Heb. *hevel, yether, mêthār,* Gr. *schoinion*). Throughout the East in ancient times, ropes and cords were made of goat's or camel's hair spun into threads and then plaited or twisted into the larger and stronger form. Sometimes they were made of strips of skin from goats and cows twisted together. Ropes for temporary fastenings were sometimes made from vines twisted together and also from the bark of the branches of the mulberry tree. Frequently the word is used in a figurative sense in the Bible. Thus Job speaks of being "held fast by cords of affliction" (Job 36:8), and Solomon says of the wicked man that "the cords of his sin hold him fast" (Prov 5:22). Other illustrations of this figurative use are Psalms 129:4; 140:5; Ecclesiastes 4:12; Isaiah 5:18, 54:2. The word is found also in the NIV translation of Hebrew *pāthîl* where the reference is to the "lace of blue" used to bind the high priest's breastplate to the ephod (Exod 28:28, 37; 39:21, 31). In these four occurrences KJV and

RSV have the word "lace." Jesus made a whip out of cords to clear the temple of moneychangers (John 2:15). Lifeboats were lashed to saling ships by means of cords, or ropes (Acts 27:32).

CORIANDER (See Plants)

CORINTH (Gr. *Korinthos, ornament*). A city of Greece on the narrow isthmus between the Peloponnesus and the mainland. Under the Romans, Athens was still the educational center of Greece, but Corinth was the capital of the Roman province they called Achaia and was the most important city in the country. Land traffic between the north and south of Achaia had to pass the city, and much of the commerce between Rome and the East was brought to its harbors.

Corinth occupied a strategic geographical position. It was situated at the southern extremity of the isthmus, at the northern foot of the lofty (2,000 ft. [625 m.]) and impregnable Acrocorinthus, which commanded a wonderful view over the Saronic Gulf on the east and the Corinthian Gulf on the west, as well as over central Greece and the Peloponnesus. From the Acrocorinthus it is possible on a clear day to see the Acropolis of Athens forty miles (sixty-seven km.) away. Corinth had three harbors: Lechaem to the west, Cenchreae and Schoenus to the east. Lechaeum was connected with Corinth by a double row of walls. Because of its highly favored commercial position, in ancient times the city was known as "two-sea'd Corinth."

Ancient sailors dreaded making the voyage round the southern capes of the Peloponnesus, and this, as well as the time saved caused many of the smaller ships and their cargoes to be hauled across the narrow isthmus on a track. Sometimes the cargo of large ships was removed at the harbor, carried across the isthmus, and then loaded onto another ship on the other side. Several attempts were made in ancient times to cut a ship canal across the isthmus, notably one by Nero about A.D. 66, but none was successful. One was opened in 1893 and is now in use.

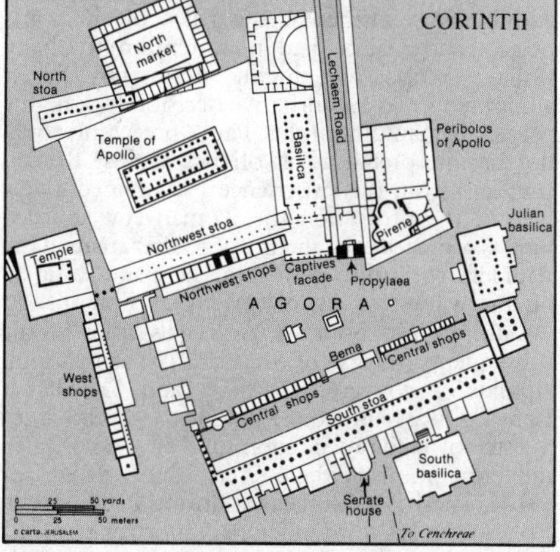

Corinth had an ancient and very interesting history. Phoenician settlers were early attracted to it. They introduced many profitable manufactures and established the impure worship of the Phoenician deities. Later, Greeks from Attica became supreme. They probably changed the name of the city to Corinth, and glorified the games held there in honor of Poseidon, the god of the sea. About 1074 B.C. the Dorians conquered the city. After the invention of triremes (ships with three tiers of oars on each side) about 585, a series of important colonies was founded, and Corinth became a strong maritime force. The city was lukewarm in the Persian Wars and opposed Athens in the Peloponnesian War. Except for a brief period the Macedonians held the city from 335 to 197. The Romans declared Greece and Corinth free in 196; but in 146, because of a rebellion against Rome, the city was totally destroyed by the Roman consul Mummius, and its famous art treasures were taken as spoil to Rome. Julius Caesar rebuilt it as a Roman colony and made it the capital of Achaia in 46, and after that it rapidly came into prominence again. The Goths raided it in the third and fourth centuries A.D.; the Normans sacked it in 1147; the Venetians and Turks held it in the Middle Ages; from 1715 until 1822 it remained with the Turks. A severe earthquake in 1858 caused the abandonment of the city and the building of a new town a few miles from the ancient site. Modern Corinth has a population of about 21,000. Until recent times when archaeologists began excavating the ancient city, nothing marked its site except seven columns of an old Doric temple.

In Roman times Corinth was a city of wealth, luxury, and immorality. It had no rivals as a city of vice. "To live like a Corinthian" meant to live a life of profligacy and debauchery. It was customary in a stage play for a Corinthian to come on the scene drunk. The inhabitants were naturally devoted to the worship of Poseidon, since they drew so much of their wealth from the sea, but their greatest devotion was given to Aphrodite, the goddess of love. Her temple on the Acrocorinthus had more than a thousand *hierodouloi*—priestesses of vice not found in other shrines of Greece, and she attracted worshipers from all over the ancient world. Besides drawing vast revenues from the sea, Corinth had many important industries, its pottery and brass especially being famous all over the world. The Isthmian games, held every two years, made Corinth a great center of Hellenic life.

At the height of its power, Corinth probably had a free population of 200,000 plus a half million slaves. Its residents consisted of the descendants of the Roman colonists who were established there in 46 B.C., many Romans who came for business, a large Greek population, and many strangers of different nationalities attracted to the city for various reasons. In the last group was a considerable body of Jews and also some Gentiles brought under the influence of Judaism because of its monotheism and lofty morality.

Paul visited Corinth for the first time on his second missionary journey (Acts 18). He had just

Ruins of the Forum at Corinth, with pillars of the temple of Apollo in the background. The surviving Doric columns of the temple are all that remains from a rectangle of six columns of the front and back and fifteen along the sides. Courtesy Gerald Nowotny.

come from Athens, where he had not been well received, and he began his work in Corinth with a sense of weakness, fear, and trembling (1 Cor 2:3). A special revelation from the Lord in a night vision altered his plans to return to Thessalonica (Acts 18:9–10; 1 Thess 2:17–18), and he was told to speak freely and boldly in the city. At his first arrival, he became acquainted with Aquila and Priscilla, fellow Christians and, like himself, tentmakers. During his stay of a year and a half he resided in their home. He labored with his own hands, so that his motives as a preacher would be above suspicion. Soon after his arrival, Silas and Timothy rejoined him, Timothy bringing news from the church at Thessalonica (1 Thess 3:6).

Every Sabbath Paul preached in the synagogue, but before long he met with strong opposition from the Jews, so that he turned from them and for the rest of his stay in Corinth gave his attention to the Gentiles (Acts 18:6). He was then offered the use of the house of Titus Justus, a God-fearing Gentile who lived next door to the synagogue. Many turned to Christ and were baptized as a result of Paul's preaching, among them Crispus, the ruler of the synagogue, and all his house. None of the baptisms in Corinth were performed by Paul himself, except those of Crispus, Gaius (Paul's host on his later visit, Rom 16:23), and the household of Stephanas, who were Paul's first converts (1 Cor 16:15).

During Paul's stay in Corinth, Gallio, the elder brother of the Roman philosopher Seneca, came to govern Achaia as proconsul. This was about the year A.D. 51, as an inscription found at Delphi in 1908 shows. The Jews brought an accusation before Gallio against Paul, charging that he was preaching a religion contrary to Roman law. Gallio, however, refused to admit the case to trial and dismissed them. It is evident that he looked on Christianity as being only an obscure variety of Judaism and that to him the quarrel between the Jews and Paul had its origin in nothing more than differing interpretations of the Jewish law. Following Gallio's decision, the Greek bystanders vented their hostility against the Jews by seizing and beating Sosthenes, the ruler of the synagogue, and Gallio paid no attention to them. Gallio's action was highly important, for it amounted to an authoritative decision by a highly placed Roman official that Paul's preaching could not be interpreted as an offense against Roman law; and from this experience Paul gained a new idea of the protection the Roman law afforded him as a preacher of the gospel. After many days, Paul left Corinth to go to Jerusalem and Antioch, on his way stopping off briefly at Ephesus.

Luke in the Book of Acts tells little of the subsequent history of the church at Corinth. Apollos, a convert of Aquila and Priscilla at Ephesus, was sent from Ephesus to Corinth with a letter of recommendation, and he exercised an influential ministry there (Acts 18:27–28; 1 Cor 1:12). There is evidence that during Paul's stay in Ephesus on his third missionary journey he paid a brief visit to Corinth (2 Cor 12:14; 13:1), though some hold that he did this later from Macedonia. While at Ephesus he wrote a letter to Corinth that has not been preserved (1 Cor 5:9). A reply to this, asking advice on important problems facing the church, and an oral report brought to him that all was not well in the church, led to his writing 1 Corinthians. This was probably brought by Titus, who was sent to Corinth by Paul about this time (2 Cor 7:13). Timothy was also sent there on some mission (1 Cor 4:17). After the silversmiths' riot at Ephesus, Paul went to Troas, hoping to meet Titus there with news from Corinth, but he was disappointed and went on to Macedonia, where he did meet him. From Titus's largely favorable report, Paul wrote 2 Corinthians, and probably sent Titus to deliver it. After some time in Macedonia, Paul went to Greece for three months (Acts 20:2–3), chiefly, no doubt, to Corinth. On Paul's third missionary journey he had busied himself getting offerings of money for the poor Christians in Jerusalem from the various churches he had founded. The Corinthian church responded generously (2 Cor 9:2–5). During this visit to Corinth, Paul wrote his letter to the Romans (Rom 16:23). Whether he ever returned to the city is unknown.

About A.D. 97, Clement of Rome wrote a letter, which survives, to the church at Corinth. It shows that in his time the Christians there were still vexed by divisions. SB

CORINTHIANS, 1 AND 2. The first letter to the Corinthians was written by Paul in Ephesus on his third missionary journey (Acts 19:1; 1 Cor 16:8, 19), probably in A.D. 56 or 57. He had previously written a letter to the Corinthians that has not come down to us; in it he had warned against associating with immoral persons (1 Cor 5:9). In reply Paul received a letter (alluded to several times in 1 Cor 5:10; 7:1; 8:1) in which they declared it was impossible to follow his advice without going out of the world altogether, and submitted to him a number of problems on which they asked his opinion. This letter from Corinth was probably brought by three of their number—Stephanas, Fortunatus, and Achaicus (16:17)—who came to visit Paul at Ephesus and undoubtedly told him about the condition of the church. Meanwhile, Paul had heard of factions in the church from the servants of Chloe (1:11), probably from Corinth, and this news caused him much pain and anxiety. It was these various circumstances that led to the writing of 1 Corinthians.

The following subjects are discussed in the letter, after the introductory salutation (1 Cor 1:1–9):

1. In the first four chapters the apostle takes up the reported factionalism in the church and points out the danger and scandal of party spirit. He reminds them that Christ alone is their Master, their Christian teachers being only servants of Christ and fellow workers with God.

2. In chapter 5 the apostle deals with a case of incestuous marriage and prescribes that the offender be put out of the church so that his soul may be saved.

3. In chapter 6 Paul addresses their practice of bringing disputes between themselves before heathen judges for litigation. He shows that this is morally wrong and out of harmony with the spirit of love by which they as Christians should be animated. Paul also pleads with Christians to keep their bodies pure for God's glory.

4. Various phases of the subject of marriage are considered in chapter 7. While commending a celibate life, Paul holds marriage to be wise and honorable. He forbids Christians from getting a divorce, even if they are married to unbelievers.

5. The eating of meat offered to idols was a problem of conscience to many Christians, and chapters 8–10 are devoted to it. Paul points out that while there is nothing inherently wrong in a Christian's eating such food, the law of love requires that it be avoided if it will offend another who regards the eating of it as sin. He illustrates this principle of self-control in his own life: lest his motives in preaching the gospel be misunderstood, he refuses to exercise his undoubted right of looking for material aid from the church. He warns against a spirit of self-confidence and urges them to be careful not to seem to countenance idolatry.

6. Paul next takes up certain abuses in public worship: the matter of appropriate head apparel for women in their assemblies (11:2–16) and the proper observance of the Lord's Supper (11:17–34), since there had been serious abuses in its administration.

7. There then follows a long discussion of the use and abuse of spiritual gifts, especially speaking in tongues (12–14). The apostle, while commending the careful exercise of all the gifts, bids them cultivate above all God's greatest gift, love (ch. 13).

8. In chapter 15 Paul turns to a consideration of one of the most important of their troubles—the doubt that some had concerning the resurrection of the dead. He meets the objections raised against the doctrine by showing that it is necessitated by the resurrection of Christ and that their salvation is inseparably connected with it.

9. The letter concludes with directions about the collections being made for the saints in Jerusalem, the mother church; with comments about Paul's plans; and with personal messages to various friends.

Second Corinthians was written by Paul on his third missionary journey somewhere in Macedonia, where he had just met Titus, who had brought him a report concerning the church at Corinth.

The letter reveals that Judaizing teachers—perhaps recent arrivals from Jerusalem—had sought to discredit the apostle and had succeeded in turning the church as a whole against him. Paul was denounced as no minister of Christ at all. This revolt caused Paul to make a brief visit to Corinth in order to restore his authority (2 Cor 12:14; 13:1–2), but the visit did not have its expected effect.

The report Titus brought Paul was, on the whole, most encouraging. The majority had repented of their treatment of Paul and had cast out of the church the man who had led the attack on him. Paul's authority was acknowledged once more. Titus seems to have helped greatly in bringing about this happy change. It was the report of Titus that chiefly occasioned the writing of this letter.

Paul's mention of a severe letter that had caused him great sorrow of heart to write (2 Cor 2:3–4, 9; 7:8–12) has naturally caused scholars to wonder what he had in mind. Some think he refers to 1 Corinthians; others hold that this letter, like the one referred to in 1 Corinthians 5:9, is wholly lost; while still others believe that it is preserved in 2 Corinthians 10–13, which, they say, was written by Paul at Ephesus some time after the writing of 1 Corinthians.

This second letter is the least methodical and the most personal of Paul's writings. It is very autobiographical and falls naturally into three main divisions:

1. In chapters 1–7 Paul, after giving thanks to God for his goodness to him in trial (1:1–11), shares some thoughts on the crisis through which the church has just passed.

2. In chapters 8 and 9 he admonishes the Corinthians to complete the collection for the poor in Jerusalem.

3. Chapters 10–13 are a defense of Paul's ministry against the attacks of his enemies and a vindication of his apostleship.

Bibliography: P. E. Hughes, *The Second Epistle to the Corinthians* (NIC), 1962; J. C. Hurd, *The Origin of 1 Corinthians,* 1965; C. K. Barrett, *The First Epistle to the Corinthians* (HNTC), 1968, and *The Second Epistle to the Corinthians* (HNTC), 1973; F. F. Bruce, *1 and 2 Corinthians* (NCB), 1971; H. Conzelmann, *1 Corinthians,* 1975; W. F. Orr and J. A. Walther, *1 Corinthians* (AB), 1976. SB

CORMORANT (See Birds)

CORN (See Plants)

CORNELIUS (kôr-nēl'yŭs, Gr. *Kornēlios, of a horn*). A name of ancient and honorable standing among the Romans. Before the NT age, it was borne by such distinguished families as the Scipios and Sulla. Acts 10:1 speaks of a Cornelius who was a centurion of the Italian Regiment. While stationed at Caesarea, in obedience to instructions received in a vision, he sent for Simon Peter, who was staying at Joppa, to learn from him how he and his household should be saved (11:14).

Cornelius is described as "devout and God-fearing" (Acts 10:2). His religious status prior to Peter's visit is ambiguous, but it is likely that Cornelius was a pious Roman, who, disillusioned by polytheism and disappointed by philosophy, had gravitated spiritually toward Judaism and was now a "proselyte of the Gate." Any doubts that Peter was acting improperly by sharing the message with this first Gentile convert are dispelled by the twofold consideration of Peter's preparatory vision (10:9–16) and the subsequent outpouring of the Holy Spirit on Cornelius's household (10:44–47). On these grounds, Peter defended his conduct before his critics at Jerusalem (11:1–18). JFG

CORNERSTONE (Heb. *pinnâh,* Gr. *akrogōniaios*). A term that has both a literal and figurative use in Scripture but is usually used figuratively (e.g., Job 38:6; Ps 118:22; Isa 28:16; Zech 10:4). Among the Canaanites, before the conquest of the land by Joshua, the laying of the foundation stone was accompanied by the dreadful rite of human sacrifice. Numerous skeletons have been unearthed, especially those of tiny babies in earthen jars.

Following rabbinical practice, which understood the term "cornerstone" in a messianic context, the synoptic Gospels validate the claim of Jesus of Nazareth to messiahship by citing Psalm 118:22 (Matt 21:42; Mark 12:10; Luke 20:17). Peter and Paul's use of the word must be understood in a similar fashion (see Rom 9:33, quoting Isa 28:16 and 8:14, following LXX; Eph 2:20; 1 Peter 2:6).

CORNET (See Music and Musical Instruments)

COS. An island off the coast of Asia Minor, one of the Sporades; mountainous in terrain, especially in the southern sector. The birthplace of Hippocrates, the father of medicine, and of Ptolemy Philadelphus. The name of its capital is also Cos. A large Jewish settlement was located there. It is mentioned in connection with Paul's third missionary journey (Acts 21:1).

COSAM (kō'săm). An ancestor of Christ (Luke 3:28).

COSMETICS. Any of the various preparations used for beautifying the hair and skin. Such

The Asclepieum was the main sanctuary on the island of Cos, birthplace of Hippocrates. Its impressive remains are spread over three terraces. Shown here are columns of one of the temples dedicated to the healing god Asclepius. Cos is mentioned in connection with Paul's third missionary journey (Acts 21:1). Courtesy Gerald Nowotny.

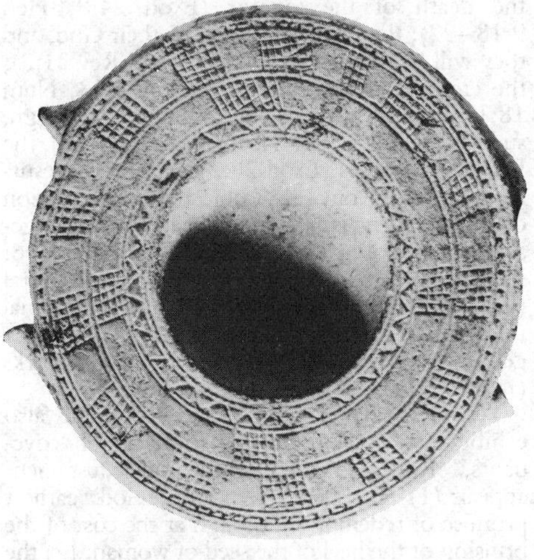

Small cosmetic palette made of hard limestone, with depression in the center, used for grinding and mixing ingredients. Late Israelite (Iron) period, c. 1000–586 B.C. Courtesy Reuben and Edith Hecht Museum, University of Haifa. Photo Zev Radovan.

practices were regarded with disfavor by the writers of Holy Writ. Jezebel, Ahab's wicked queen, painted her eyes immediately prior to her death (2 Kings 9:30). Ezekiel also refers to the practice of painting the eyes in an uncomplimentary vein in the parable of Oholah and Oholibah (Ezek 23:36, 40). "Why shade your eyes with paint?" demands Jeremiah 4:30. "You adorn yourself in vain."

COUCH. A piece of furniture for reclining. The couch became so ornate that Amos rebuked the rich for the costly display of their couches (Amos 6:4). Sometimes, however, the couch was no more than a rolled-up mat that could be easily transported (Matt 9:6). See also BED.

COULTER (See PLOWSHARE)

COUNCIL (Heb. *rigmâh,* Gr. *symboulion, synedrion*). A Jewish governing body, more or less informally held. David speaks of "the princes of Judah and their council" (Ps 68:27 KJV), rendered by NIV "the great throng of Judah's princes." He does not mean the Sanhedrin, which did not come into existence until after the Captivity. The heavenly host who surround the throne of the Lord are sometimes presented as the heavenly council of the Lord (Job 15:8; Ps 89:7). In the NT the "council" usually means the Sanhedrin consisting of seventy-one members (Matt 26:59; Mark 14:55; Acts 5:21, KJV; NIV renders "Sanhedrin"). The word also is used to refer to other local Jewish courts (Matt 10:17; Mark 13:9) and to Roman advisory boards (Acts 25:12).

The meeting of delegates of the church in Antioch with the apostles and elders in Jerusalem (Acts 15; Gal 2:1–10) is usually called the "Council of Jerusalem," though the text does not contain the word "council." Its primary concern was the admission of Gentile converts into what was up to that time a "Jewish" Christian church.

COUNSELOR (See ADVOCATE; HOLY SPIRIT; OCCUPATIONS AND PROFESSIONS)

COURT. On Jethro's advice Moses instituted a system of jurisprudence for the Israelites. He appointed judges over tens, fifties, hundreds, and thousands; Moses himself had the final decision in "difficult cases" (Exod 18:25–26). The office of judge was an elective one (Deut 1:13). Eventually judges were usually chosen from among the Levites, though this was not necessary. They were held in very high regard. In time the profession of law developed among the Hebrews, its members being called "lawyers," "scribes," or "doctors of the law" (Luke 2:46 KJV). These men studied and interpreted the law, decided questions of the law, and taught Hebrew boys the law. Technical knowledge of the law was not a prerequisite to become a judge. Under the Romans the supreme legislative and judicial body was the Sanhedrin. Its judgment was final except in cases involving capital punishment, when the consent of the procurator had to be secured. The Sanhedrin met in Jerusalem.

COVENANT. This translates the Hebrew noun *berîth.* The verbal root means either "to fetter" or "to eat with," which would signify mutual obligation, or "to allot" (1 Sam 17:8), which would signify a gracious disposition. Compare this with the Hittite "suzerainty covenant," in which a vassal swore fealty to his king out of gratitude for favors received.

In the OT, *berîth* identifies three different types of legal relationships. (1) A two-sided covenant between human parties who both voluntarily accept the terms of the agreement (for friendship, 1 Sam 18:3–4; marriage, Mal 2:14; or political alliance, Josh 9:15; Obad 7). God, however,

Relief from north palace of Ashurbanipal (668–633 B.C.) at Nineveh showing him reclining on a high couch as he drinks from a bowl and holds a blossom in his left hand. The queen sits on a high throne at the foot of the couch, also drinking from a bowl. Reproduced by courtesy of the Trustees of the British Museum.

never "enters in" to such a covenant of equality with men. The closest approximation is the "covenant of redemption" between God and Christ (mentioned in certain of the Psalms: 2:7–8; 40:6–8), under which the Son agrees to undertake man's salvation. But the actual term *berîth* is not used. (2) A one-sided disposition imposed by a superior party (Ezek 17:13–14). God the Lord thus "commands" a *berîth* that man, the servant, is to "obey" (Josh 23:16). In the original "covenant of works" (Hos 6:7 ASV), he placed Adam on probation, bestowing life, should he prove faithful (Gen 2:17). Humanity failed; but Christ, the last Adam (1 Cor 15:45), did fulfill all righteousness (Matt 3:15; Gal 4:4), thereby earning restoration for all who are his. (3) God's self-imposed obligation, for the reconciliation of sinners to himself (Deut 7:6–8; Ps 89:3–4). As he stated to Abraham, "I will establish my covenant . . . between me and you and your descendants after you for the generations to come (Gen 17:7).

The LXX avoided the usual Greek term for covenant, *synthēkē* (meaning a thing mutually "put together"), as unsuitable for the activity of the sovereign God. Instead, it used *diathēkē* (a thing, literally, "put through"), the primary meaning of which is "a disposition of property by a will." The LXX even used *diathēkē*, "will" (KJV "testament") for the human-agreement type of *berîth*.NT revelation, however, makes clear the wonderful appropriateness of *diathēkē*, "testament," for describing the instrument of God's redemptive love (see Heb 9:16–18). Indeed, "will," or "testament," signifies a specific form of covenant, the bequest; and it well describes God's OT *berîth*, because apart from the death of Christ the OT saints "should not be made perfect" (Heb 11:40 KJV).

The covenant then constitutes the heart of all God's special revelation; when put into writing, the "Book of the Covenant" becomes the objective source for man's religious hope (Exod 24:7). Scripture consists of the "Old Testament" and the "New Testament." For while there can be but one testament, corresponding to the one death of Christ ("my blood of *the* testament," according to the better MSS of Matt 26:28), revelation yet organizes itself under the older testament, with its anticipatory symbols of Christ's coming (Jer 31–32; 2 Cor 3:14), and the newer testament, commemorative of his accomplished redemption (Jer 31:31; 2 Cor 3:6).

The following aspects compose the testamentary arrangements: the testator, God the Son, "the mediator" (Heb 9:15); the heirs, "those who are called" (9:15); the objective method of effectuation, a gracious bequest (9:16); the subjective conditions by which the heir qualifies for the gift, namely, commitment (9:28: it is "to those who are waiting for him"); and the inheritance of reconciliation, eternal salvation (9:15, 28). Certain specific features then characterize this covenant. Its objective effectuation is always marked by a monergism ("one worker")—God exercising pure grace (cf. Gen 15:18; Exod 19:4), unassisted by man's works (Eph 2:8–9). Other features are the death of the testator (Exod 24:8; Heb 9:18–22); the promise, "I will be their God, and they will be my people" (Gen 17:7 to Rev 21:3); the eternity of the inheritance (Lev 2:13; Num 18:19; Ps 105:8–10); and a confirmatory sign, such as the rainbow to Noah (Gen 9:12–13), the Exodus to Moses (Exod 20:2), or Christ's resurrection to us (Rom 1:4). Subjective appropriation of the covenant is likewise marked by unchangeable features of human response: faith (Gen 15:6; Deut 6:5; Heb 11:6); and obedience, both moral (Gen 17:1; Matt 7:24; Eph 2:10) and ceremonial (Gen 17:10–14; Acts 22:16; 1 Cor 11:24)—for genuine faith must be demonstrated by works (James 2:14–26).

Yet God's revelations of his covenant also exhibit historical progression (note plural "covenants," Rom 9:4). Under the older testament appear: (1) The Edenic (Gen 3:15), God's earliest promise of redemption, though at the cost of the bruising of the heel of the seed of woman; (2) the Noachian (9:9), for the preservation of the seed; (3) the Abrahamic (15:18), granting blessing through Abram's family; (4) the Sinaitic (Exod 19:5–6), designating Israel as God's chosen people; (5) the Levitical (Num 25:12–13), making reconciliation through priestly atonement; (6) the Davidic (2 Sam 23:5), with messianic salvation promised through David's dynasty. Each of these covenants anticipated the same redemptive death; yet differences appear, particularly in their ceremonial response. A "dispensation" may thus be defined as a covenantal period during which faith in Christ is manifested by a distinct form of ceremonial obedience. Even our own, newer testament thus exhibits two stages: (7) The present new covenant in Christ, which is internal, "in their heart," reconciling (as always, "I will be their God"); direct, "they will all know me;" and with finished atonement, "for I will forgive their wickedness" (Jer 31:33–34; Heb 8:6–13). But its ceremony, the Lord's Supper, possesses a dispensational limit, exhibiting "the Lord's death *until he comes*" (1 Cor 11:26). For Ezekiel speaks of (8): the future covenant of peace, when our internal salvation will reach out to embrace external nature (Ezek 34:25), when direct spiritual communion will become "face to face" (20:35; 37:27), and when divine forgiveness will achieve the goal of peace among all nations (34:28).

Bibliography: E. J. Young, *The Study of Old Testament Theology Today,* 1958; J. B. Payne, *The Theology of the Older Covenant,* 1962; G. Vos, *Biblical Theology,* 1963, pp. 52–115; M. G. Kline, *The Treaty of the Great King,* 1963, and *The Structure of Biblical Authority,* 1975. JBP

COVERING THE HEAD. This is mentioned only in 1 Corinthians 11:15, where Paul says that a woman's hair is given her for a covering. In the preceding verses he says that women should have their heads covered in public worship. At that time in Greece only immoral women were seen with their heads uncovered. Paul means that Christian women cannot afford to disregard social convention; it would hurt their testimony. In giving them long hair, a natural veil, "nature" teaches the lesson that women should not be unveiled in public assemblies.

COVETOUSNESS (kŭv'ĕt-ŭs-nĕs). The word has various shades of meaning, among the most important are the following:

1. The desire to have something (1 Cor 12:31; 14:39).
2. The inordinate desire to have something (Luke 12:15ff.; Eph 5:5; Col 3:5).
3. Excessive desire of what belongs to another (Exod 20:17; Rom 7:7). A great deal of OT law was intended to counteract the spirit of covetousness. Outstanding examples of those who coveted in this sense are Achan (Josh 7), Saul (1 Sam 15:9, 19), Ananias and Sapphira (Acts 5:1–11).

COW (See ANIMALS)

COZ (See KOZ)

COZBI (kŏz'bī). A Midianite woman killed by Phinehas, Aaron's grandson, because through her the plague had come on Israel in the wilderness (Num 25:16–18).

CRAFT, CRAFTSMAN (See OCCUPATIONS AND PROFESSIONS)

CRAFTINESS. The determination to use any means, however bad, to attain one's purpose; guile; cunning (Luke 20:23 KJV; NIV has "duplicity"; also Eph 4:14).

CRANE (See BIRDS)

CRAWLING THING (See ANIMALS)

CREATION. The doctrine is clearly presented in certain key passages (Gen 1–2; Isa 40–51; Heb 11:3; the latter part of Job). The Bible teaches that the universe, including all matter, had a beginning and came into existence through the will of the eternal God. In Genesis 1:1 the words "the heavens and the earth" summarize all the various materials of the universe. This verse has been interpreted in various ways, but all agree in its essential significance. This is true even of the

Woodcuts illustrating the Creation, from Miles Coverdale's Bible of 1535. Courtesy The British Library.

new interpretation that takes it as a mere introduction to what follows (rendering it "When God began to create heaven and earth"). For even on this interpretation verse 2 would describe the situation that came into existence at the time God began to create, rather than contradict Hebrews 11:3 by implying that there was preexisting matter.

Some hold that there is a long gap between verses 1 and 2, in which God's perfect creation came into chaos through a great catastrophe. Hebrew syntax permits such a view but does not require it.

The length of the creative days of Genesis 1 is not stated in the Bible. The Hebrew word "day" may mean a period of light between two periods of darkness, a period of light together with the preceding period of darkness, or a long period of time. All three usages occur often in the Bible. No one of them is exactly twenty-four hours, though the second one is near it. There is no indisputable indication as to which of the three is meant. The Bible gives no specific statement as to how long ago matter was created, how long ago the first day of Creation began, or when the sixth day ended.

On the seventh day (Gen 2:2–3) God ceased from his labors. God refers to this as an example for Israel to have six days of labor followed by one day of rest (Exod 20:11). No end to the rest of the seventh day is mentioned. As far as the Bible tells us, God's rest from creating still continues.

There is much discussion about the question of "evolution" in relation to the Creation, but the word "evolution" is used in many different ways. If taken in its historic sense (the theory that everything now existing has come into its present condition as a result of natural development, all of it having proceeded by natural causes from one rudimentary beginning), such a theory is sharply contradicted by the divine facts revealed in Genesis 1–2. These chapters indicate a number of specific divine commands bringing new factors into existence. God's activity is indicated throughout the entire Creation narrative. It is explicitly stated several times that plants and animals are to reproduce "after their kind." Moses nowhere states how large a "kind" is, and there is no ground for equating it with any particular modern definition of "species." Yet it is clear that Genesis teaches that there are a number (perhaps a large number) of "kinds" of plants and of animals, which cannot reproduce in such a way as to evolve from one into the other. Nothing in the Bible denies the possibility of change and development within the limits of a particular "kind."

Moreover, the creation of Adam is sharply distinguished from other aspects of creation, and the creation of Eve is described as a distinct act of God. Genesis 2:7 (in the Hebrew) clearly teaches that Adam did not exist as an animate being before he was a man, created after the image of God.

It is sometimes said that the Bible begins with two contradictory accounts of Creation. To say this is like saying that an atlas begins with two maps. A map of the world and a map of the United States would overlap. The first would include a great deal of territory not included in the second. The second would include a great deal of detail not mentioned in the first.

This is exactly the relation between the two accounts. Genesis 1 describes the creation of the universe as a whole. Genesis 2:4–25 covers one special segment of that creation. The linking word (2:4) is translated in NIV as "account," but this is inadequate: it must mean "subsequent/emergent account," for the word (*tōledōth*) both in its individual meaning and in its OT use tells how something emerges from what has preceded. In this way, Genesis 2:4 "steps back" into Genesis 1 to begin the study of "what happened next," how out of God's creative work there came the beginnings of human life and history on earth. This explains the often-alleged differences and supposed contradictions between the chapters, for Genesis 2:4ff. alludes only to the creative work as a whole insofar as it is necessary to do so in recording the beginnings of human history. It is reasonable, therefore, that Genesis 2:4ff. gives a more detailed account of the creation of man but says nothing about that of matter, light, heavenly bodies, or plants.

Again, it is sometimes said that Genesis 1 begins with a watery chaos and Genesis 2:4ff. with a dry earth. But there is no contradiction, because the two have different starting points in the creative acts of God. Genesis 2:4ff. does not describe the creation of vegetation, as some assert; it simply mentions the planting of a garden. It is hardly reasonable to insist that God created man and then put him aside while the Garden was planted and given time to mature. The verbs in 2:8–9 must be understood (as is perfectly proper to do) as pluperfects, and the same is true of 2:19 where the previous creation of animals is alluded to. Genesis 2:4ff. does not contradict Genesis 1 in any way; instead, it opens up our understanding of the wonder of the creation of human beings and introduces us to the beginnings of human history on earth. Creation

Bibliography: N. H. Ridderbos, *Is There Conflict Between Genesis 1 and Natural Science?* 1957; L. Gilkey, *Maker of Heaven and Earth,* 1959; F. D. Kidner, *Genesis* (TOTC), 1967; J. A. Motyer, "Old Testament Theology," in NBC Revised, 1970, pp. 26–27; C. Westermann, *Creation,* 1974; D. J. Wiseman, *Clues to Creation in Genesis,* 1977.

AAM and JAM

CREATURE (Gr. *ktisis*). In the NT the word denotes that which has been created (Rom 1:25; 8:39; Heb 4:13). Sometimes it is used with the adjective *kainē* in the sense of the new creation (2 Cor 5:17) or in contrasting the old person with the new person (Gal 6:15).

CREEPING THING (See ANIMALS)

CRESCENS (Gr. *Krēskēs, increasing*). One of Paul's companions at Rome; he had departed for Galatia (2 Tim 4:10).

The land of Crete, showing the slopes of Mount Ida, the legendary birthplace of Zeus. Courtesy Gerald Nowotny.

CRETE, CRETANS (Gr. *Krētē, Krētes,* Acts 2:11; Titus 1:12). An island in the Mediterranean Sea with Cythera on the NW and Rhodes on the NE, forming a natural bridge between Europe and Asia Minor. Crete is about 156 (260 km.) miles long and from 7 to 30 miles (11½–50 km.) wide. Despite its enviable geographical position, Crete has never attained a prominent place in history, partly because of internal dissensions and, in more modern times, because of its acceptance of Turkish rule and the Islamic faith until A.D. 1913, when it was formally incorporated into Greece in which the Orthodox church predominates.

In mythology, Mount Ida is the legendary birthplace of Zeus, the head of the Greek Pantheon. King Minos, a half-historical and half-mythological character, alleged son of Zeus, was an early ruler of Crete. Both Thucydides and Aristotle accepted the existence of King Minos and claimed that he established maritime supremacy for Crete by putting down piracy. Aristotle compares the institutions of Crete to those of Sparta. Crete is said to have been colonized by the Dorians from Peloponnesus. The most important of the ancient cities of Crete are Knossos, excavated by Arthur Evans; Gortyna near the gulf of Messara; and Cydonia. Around 140 B.C. the Jews established a large enough colony on this island to be able to appeal successfully to the protection of Rome.

Remains of the Minoan palace of Knossos, one of the principal cities of ancient Crete. Now partly restored, the palace dates from the Bronze Age, c. 1700–1570 B.C. Courtesy Gerald Nowotny.

In the OT the Kerethites (1 Sam 30:14; Ezek 25:16), held to be a group of Philistines, are identified as Cretans. In the NT a number of Cretans are represented as being present on the Day of Pentecost. Paul visited Crete and left his assistant Titus in charge. In the opinion of the apostle Paul, even the Christians in Crete were not of high moral character: "Cretans are always liars . . . ." (Titus 1:12). The first words of this quotation are to be found in the hymn to Zeus by Callimachus. The particular lie of which the Cretans were always guilty was that they said the tomb of Zeus, a nonexistent personage, was located on their island. Laziness and gluttony also characterized them. Titus is charged sharply to rebuke them (1:13). A storm on his journey to Rome forced Paul's ship into the port of Cnidus (Acts 27:17). The narrative does not specifically indicate that Paul actually landed on the island.

CRIB (See MANGER)

CRICKET (See ANIMALS)

CRIMSON (Heb. *karmîl, tôlā'*). This refers to the brilliant red dye obtained from a bug. The word is applied to garments (2 Chron 2:7, 14; Jer 4:30 KJV). The best-known citation is doubtless the prophet's assurance in Isaiah 1:18.

CRISPUS (Gr. *Krispos, curled,* Acts 18:7–8; 1 Cor 1:14). Formerly the ruler of the Jewish synagogue at Corinth; converted under the preaching of Paul and subsequently baptized by him.

CROCODILE (See ANIMALS)

CROCUS (See PLANTS)

CROP (Lev 1:16). The enlargement of the gullet of a bird where food is partly macerated, removed by the priest for sacrificial purposes.

CROSS (Gr. *stauros*). There are three biblical uses of the term: first, the wooden instrument of torture; second, the cross as a symbolic representation of redemption; third, death on the cross, i.e., crucifixion. Our English word is derived from the Latin *Crux*. The cross existed in four different forms: (1) the *crux immissa,* the type usually presented in art in which the upright beam extends above the cross beam, traditionally held to be the cross on which the Redeemer suffered and died. (2) The *crux commissa,* or "Saint Anthony's Cross" in the form of the letter "T." (3) The Greek cross in which the cross beams are of equal length; (4) The *crux decussata,* or "Saint Andrew's Cross," in the shape of the letter "X." Antedating these forms, the Assyrians impaled the body with a crude pointed stick.

Because of the sacrificial death of the Savior on

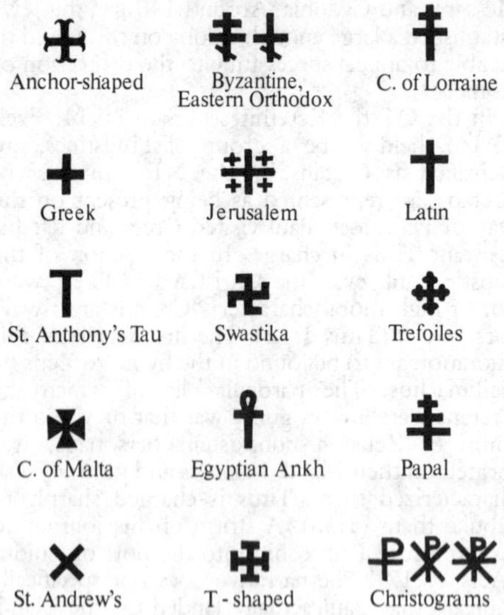

Chart showing the various forms of the cross. Courtesy Carta, Jerusalem.

the cross, the cross rapidly became interwoven into the theological construction of religious thinking, especially Paul's. In 1 Corinthians 1:17 the "preaching" (*kērygma*) of the Cross is set forth as the "divine folly" in sharp contrast to earthly wisdom. In Ephesians 2:16 it is presented as the medium of reconciliation. In Colossians 1:20 peace has been effected through the cross. In Colossians 2:14 the penalties of the law have been removed from the believer by the cross. How Paul as a pious Hebrew, to whom one hanged was accursed, and as a Roman to whom one crucified was an object of scorn (Gal 3:13), came to glory in the cross would be one of the absurdities of history were it not for the fact that the apostle held the Crucified as the Christ of God (2:20).

Crucifixion was one of the most cruel and barbarous forms of death known to man. It was practiced, especially in times of war, by the Phoenicians, Carthaginians, Egyptians, and later by the Romans. So dreaded was it that even in the pre-Christian era, the cares and troubles of life were often compared to a cross.

The details of the crucifixion of Christ are passed over, the Evangelists content with the simple statement, "They crucified him" (Matt 27:35; Mark 15:24). Following his trial before the Jewish and Roman authorities, Christ was led forth for crucifixion. Before the actual ordeal itself, he was scourged. The prisoner was bent over and tied to a post, while the Roman soldier applied blow after blow on his bared back with a lash intertwined with pieces of bone or steel. This in itself was frequently sufficient to cause death.

The agony of the crucified victim was brought about by a number of factors. First, the painful but nonfatal character of the wounds inflicted. Although there were two distinctive methods of affixing a living victim to a cross, tying or nailing, it is well established that Christ underwent the horror of the latter, or possibly both. The second factor causing great suffering was the abnormal position of the body. The slightest movement brought on additional torture. The third factor was the traumatic fever induced by hanging for such a long period of time.

What was the physical reason for Christ's death? Recent medical studies have sought an answer to the question. When a person is suspended by his two hands, the blood sinks rapidly into the lower extremities of the body. Within six to twelve minutes the blood pressure has dropped to half, while the rate of the pulse has doubled. The heart is deprived of blood, and fainting follows. This leads to an orthorastic collapse through insufficient circulation. Death during crucifixion is due to heart failure. Victims of crucifixion did not generally succumb for two or three days. Death was hastened by the "crucifragium" or the breaking of the legs. "But when they came to Jesus and found that he was already dead, they did not break his legs" (John 19:33). Sometimes a fire was built beneath the cross that its fumes might suffocate the sufferer.

Among the Jews, a stupefying potion was prepared by the merciful women of Jerusalem, a drink that Christ refused (Mark 15:23). To such a death, the one who was coequal with God descended (Phil 2:5).

Bibliography: H. W. Robinson, *The Cross in the Old Testament*, 1955; Leon Morris, *The Apostolic Preaching of the Cross*, 1960; C. Brown, NIDNTT, 1:389–404; M. Hengel, *Crucifixion*, 1977. JFG

CROW (See BIRDS)

CROWN. A band around the head to designate honor. There are three main types of crowns: the

Fragment of a gypsum slab from the central palace at Nimrud that shows Tiglath-pileser III, king of Assyria (744–727 B.C.), wearing the royal crown with pointed top. At the back hang two ribbons, which emerge from inside the headdress. Reproduced by courtesy of the Trustees of the British Museum.

The "double crown," as worn by the Egyptian god Atum. Part of a long, narrow, bronze box that probably served as a container for a mummified serpent, c. 525–30 B.C. Courtesy Carta, Jerusalem.

royal crown, the priestly crown, and the victor's crown. Among the terms used for "crown" in the OT are Hebrew *qodhqōth,* a part of the human anatomy, the "crown" of the head (Deut 28:35; 2 Sam 14:25); Hebrew *zēr,* that which encircles the head: a garland of flowers (Exod 25:11); Hebrew *nezer,* that which is a symbol of dedication to the priesthood; Hebrew *ʿăṭārâh,* the customary term (1 Chron 20:2; Prov 4:9). In the NT, Greek *stephanos* and *diadēma* are used. The first refers to a garland or chaplet such as worn by a victorious athlete—a figurative term used by Paul and John, symbolizing Christian triumph (2 Tim 4:8; Rev 2:10). The diadem was a symbol of the power to rule.

Of special interest is the crown of thorns worn by Jesus (Gr. *akanthinos stephanos,* Matt 27:29; Mark 15:17; John 19:2). It is impossible to determine the particular variety of thorn used here; many words in the Bible are used for the thorny plants, and the Greek word is a generic, not a specific term.

CRUCIBLE. A refining pot for silver and gold and other metals, made to resist great heat (Prov 17:3; 27:21).

CRUCIFIXION (See CROSS)

CRUSE. A small porous, earthen vessel for holding liquids (1 Sam 26:11–12, 16, NIV "water jug"; 1 Kings 19:6, NIV "jar"). *Alabastron* occurs in Matthew 26:7, Mark 14:3, and Luke 7:37—an alabaster "bottle" (NEB), "box" (KJV), "flask" (MLB, RSV), or "jar" (JB, NIV).

CRYSTAL. Both Hebrew and Greek terms can be translated "ice." More likely it means rock crystal or crystallized quartz. The reason for the meaning "ice" is that the ancients believed that crystal was formed by the process of intense cold (Job 28:17; Rev 4:6; 21:11; 22:1). See also MINERALS.

CUBIT (See WEIGHTS AND MEASURES)

CUCKOO (See BIRDS)

CUCKOW (See BIRDS)

CUCUMBER (See PLANTS)

CUMMIN (See PLANTS)

CUN (Heb. *kûn*). An Aramean city taken by David (1 Chron 18:8). In 2 Samuel 8:8 Berothai is given as the name of the city. The identification is uncertain.

CUP (Heb. *kôs,* Gr. *potērion*). A term used in a literal and figurative sense. Cups were of various forms and designs and were made of a variety of materials: gold, silver, earthenware, copper, bronze, etc. The cups of the Hebrews, whether metal or porcelain, often carried designs borrowed from Phoenicia and Egypt. All of Solomon's drinking vessels were of gold (1 Kings 10:21). The cups mentioned in the NT were doubtless of Roman style.

The word *cup* may also signify a laver (Exod 24:6) or goblet (1 Chron 28:17; Song of Songs 7:2). The cup is used as a symbol of prosperity or

Limestone relief of Ur-nanshe, king of Lagash, seated on a throne with a goblet in his hand and being served by a cupbearer who stands behind him. From Tello, first half of third millennium B.C. Courtesy Réunion des Musées Nationaux.

of the Lord's blessing and, in reverse, of his malediction on the wicked (Ps 11:6; 16:5; 23:5). The cup also represents drunkenness and other illicit pleasures (Prov 23:31; Rev 17:4; 18:6). "Cup of salvation" (Ps 116:13), "cup of thanksgiving" (1 Cor 10:16), and "cup of the Lord" (10:21) are also used. In the latter two passages, Paul is referring to the communion cup, over which the blessing is said prior to the feast that commemorates the Lord's death and burial. The cup from ancient times signified fellowship. Thus when the believer takes the cup of the Lord, he enters into fellowship with him. The "cup of demons" (10:21) mentioned in opposition to the cup of the Lord can best be understood in this context. The apostle is saying in a figurative way that we cannot have fellowship with Christ and with the forces of darkness at the same time. At heathen feasts the cup was sacred to the name of the god in whose name the feast was being held. Thus, in the communion service, the cup is sacred to the name of the Redeemer who instituted its practice (Matt 26:27; Mark 14:23–24; Luke 22:20). The "cup of his wrath" (Isa 51:17, 22), the "cup that sends all the surrounding peoples reeling" (Zech 12:2), and the "cup of ruin and desolation" (Ezek 23:33) are among other biblical occurrences of the term.

CUPBEARER (See OCCUPATIONS AND PROFESSIONS)

CURDS (See BUTTER)

CURSE (Heb. *'ālāh, me'ērâh, qelālâh,* Gr. *katapa*). The reverse of "to bless." On the human level, to wish harm or catastrophe. On the divine, to impose judgment. In the oriental mind the curse carried with it its own power of execution. A curse was imposed on the serpent (Gen 3:14). Noah cursed Canaan (9:25). The curse of Balaam, the pseudoprophet, turned to a blessing (Num 24:10). A curse was placed on Mount Ebal for disobedience to the law of Moses (Deut 27:1–9). The cursing of one's parents is sternly prohibited by Mosaic regulations. Christ commanded those who would be his disciples to bless and not to curse (Luke 6:28). When Peter, at Christ's trial, denied that he knew him, he invited a curse on himself (Matt 26:74); this passage is often misunderstood by Western readers. Paul represents the curse of the law as borne by Christ on the cross for the believer (Gal 3:13). The modern Western practice of cursing, i.e., using profane language, is never referred to in the Scriptures. See also BLASPHEMY.

CURTAINS (Heb. *yerî'âh*). 1. The curtains of fine linen and goats' hair that covered the tabernacle (Exod 26:1ff.; 38:9ff.). Gradually the "curtains" gave their name to the entire structure.

2. Employed figuratively by Isaiah (40:22), referring to the heavens. He uses the word *dōq,* literally, "gauze."

CUSH (Heb. *kûsh*). 1. The oldest son of Ham, one of the three sons of Noah (Gen 10:6–8; 1 Chron 1:8–10). Among the descendants were Seba, Havilah, Sabta, Raamah, and Sabtecha. They were mostly located in Arabia. Nimrod is likewise said to be the son of Cush, but the word "son" probably means "descendant."

2. "Cush, a Benjamite," in the title for Psalm 7, viewed as referring to King Saul, the Benjamite. Since Cush and Kish are similar in sound, they are held to be one. Saul's father's name was Kish.

3. Cush, the country. The name of the territory through which the Gihon flowed (Gen 2:13), translated "Ethiopia" by KJV, but NIV margin says "possibly southeast Mesopotamia." The wife of Moses is referred to as a Cushite, making her a target of criticism by Miriam and Aaron (Num 12:1). If this is Zipporah, the wife of Moses mentioned earlier, her origin was that of the land of Midian. The earlier passages seem to indicate Cush as African, the latter as Asian. The precise identification of either the woman or the country is an unsolved problem. See also ETHIOPIA.

CUSHAN-RISHATHAIM (kū'shăn-rĭsh'ā-thā'ĭm). A Mesopotamian king who held the Israelites in bondage for eight years. Othniel, Caleb's younger brother, put an end to his rule (Judg 3:5–11).

CUSHI (kū'shī). A member of the Cushite people. 1. The man sent by Joab to inform David that Absalom's rebellion was quelled and that the time was ripe for him to return to his throne (2 Sam 18:21–32).

2. A contemporary of Jeremiah, the great-grandfather of Jehudi (Jer 36:14).

3. The father of the prophet Zephaniah (Zeph 1:1).

CUSTOM. When not referring to a tax, usually means "manner," "way," or "statute" (Gen 31:35; Judg 11:39; Jer 32:11). Heathen religious practice is referred to in Leviticus 18:30 and Jeremiah 10:3. In the NT it means "manner," "usage" (Luke 1:9; Acts 6:14), and "religious practices."

CUSTOM, RECEIPT OF (NIV "tax collector's booth"). The post from which Matthew (Levi) was called to follow Christ (Matt 9:9). In postexilic days the tribute was usually in terms of a road toll. The Romans imposed tribute or tax on Jews as on all their subjects for the maintenance of their provincial government. Tax collectors or publicans were despised because of their notorious dishonesty and willingness to work for a foreign power.

CUTHAH, CUTHA, CUTH (kū'tha, kŭth). One of the cities from which Sargon, king of Assyria, brought immigrants to repopulate the area of Samaria that he had sacked in 720 B.C. (2 Kings 17:24–30). Because of their numerical predominance, the inhabitants of Samaria were henceforth referred to as Cutheans. They began a syncretistic form of religion, worshiping both the true God and the gods of the nations they came

Bronze jug of Cypriot ware, c. 1000–600 B.C. Courtesy Reuben and Edith Hecht Museum, University of Haifa. Photo Zev Radovan.

from. This is one of the explanations for the deep antipathy existing between the Jews and the Samaritans even to NT times (John 4:9).

From the contract tablets found by Rassam at Tel-Ibrahim it now appears that the ancient name of Cuthah was Gudua or Kuta. This city of high culture and commerce lay NE of Babylon and was one of its most important centers. Rassam describes its almost perfect ruins as being about 3,000 feet (937.5 m.) in circumference and 280 feet (87.5 m.) high. In it was a sanctuary dedicated to Ibrahim (Abraham). Both the city and its great temple, the latter dedicated to Nergal, appear to date back to Sumerian times.

CUZA (kū'zȧ, Gr. *Chouzas*). The steward of Herod Antipas. In Luke 8:3 we read that his wife Joanna, Susanna, and many others supported Christ and his disciples out of their own resources. Cuza was undoubtedly a man of rank and means.

CYMBAL (See MUSIC AND MUSICAL INSTRUMENTS)

CYPRESS (See PLANTS)

CYPRUS (sī'prŭs, Gr. *Kypros, copper*). An island in the eastern part of the Mediterranean directly off the coast of Syria and Cilicia, 148 miles (246.7 km.) long and about 40 miles (66.7 km.) across. Historically its roots are deep in the past. The OT refers to it as the "Isles of Chittim" (*Kittim,* Ezek 27:6; rendered by NIV as the "coasts of Cyprus").

The island is rich in copper deposits, hence its name. In the pre-Christian era, a large colony of Jews settled there and later formed the nucleus of the Christian church ministered to by Paul and company. During the Roman rule, the Jews were expelled from Cyprus in the days of Hadrian.

Barnabas, who accompanied Paul on his first missionary journey, was a native of the island (Acts 4:36); with John Mark he returned to evangelize Cyprus after they had left Paul's company (15:36–39). The apostolic party passed through the island from Salamis to Paphos. At Paphos, Sergius Paulus, the imperial deputy of the island, came to believe in Christ (13:12).

Cyprus has known various conquerors, in addition to the Assyrians, who had been attracted by its rich resources. The Egyptians, Hittites, Phoenicians, Greeks, Romans, Turks, and British have all taken advantage of its attractive character.

The aboriginal inhabitants of Cyprus seem to have been of Minoan stock. After the breakup of the Minoan civilization, the dark ages settled down on the island. The curtain rose again when Hellenistic settlers from the Greek mainland reached it. Sargon in 709 B.C. made himself ruler of Cyprus, and it paid tribute to Assyria until the days of Esarhaddon. The demise of the Assyrian Empire appears to have brought the island relative freedom, until it was annexed to Egypt in 540. With the rise of Cambyses (526), Cyprus passed under Persian rule until the time of Alexander the Great, to whom it surrendered voluntarily and helped with the siege of Tyre. During the late intertestamental period it fell into the hands of the Romans (cf. 1 Macc 10:13). A number of the ill-famed guard of Antiochus Epiphanes were Cypriots. In 58 Cyprus was accorded provincial status by the Romans. In 22 it was made the direct charge of the Senate. Roman coins of this particular period are numerous.

JFG

CYRENE (sīrē'nĭ, Gr. *Kyrēnē, wall*). A Libyan city in North Africa, west of Egypt, separated from it by a part of the Libyan Desert. It was situated some 2,000 feet (625 m.) above and ten miles (seventeen km.) away from the Mediterranean. The coastline afforded a natural shelter from the heat of the Sahara. It was protected by steps of descending ranges about 80 miles (133 km.) to the south. The fertility and climate of the city were delightful and productive.

Cyrene, originally a Greek colony, was founded by Battus in 603 B.C. This veritable "oasis in the desert" attracted travelers and commerce from early times. Among its distinguished citizens was Carneacles, the founder of the new academy at Athens. Aristippus, the Epicurean philosopher and friend of Socrates, also came from this city.

The famous Cylinder of Cyrus (the Lord's "anointed," Isa 45:1), which tells how he captured Babylon and liberated the prisoners from Babylonia. It was made of baked clay, from Babylon, c. 536 B.C. Reproduced by courtesy of the Trustees of the British Museum.

The Tomb of Cyrus, at Pasargadae in Iran. The tomb is constructed of white limestone and rests upon six steps of irregular height. The small entrance leads to a windowless chamber. Courtesy B. Brandl.

Ptolemy Euregets I incorporated Cyrene as a part of Egypt in 231. It later passed into the hands of the Romans, being willed to them by the last Ptolemy.

Cyrene is not mentioned in the OT but becomes important in the NT. A native of Cyrene, Simon by name, was impressed by the Roman soldiers into carrying the cross of Jesus (Luke 23:26); thus did Simon immortalize his city. There were also representatives of the city present in Jerusalem on the day of Pentecost (Acts 2:10). Its Jewish population warranted a synagogue (6:9). Lucius of Cyrene is mentioned in Acts 11:19–20. Archaeology has shown that it was the Greek plan to make Cyrene the "Athens of Africa." The most interesting remains are a great system of tombs cut out of solid rock into the cliff. Architecture and paintings adorn these tombs.

CYRENIUS (See QUIRINIUS)

CYRUS (sī'rŭs, Heb. *kôresh*). The son of Cambyses, king of Anshan. With the rise of Cyrus began the renowned Persian Empire that was to continue until the coming of Alexander the Great. Seven years after the death of Nebuchadnezzar, Nabonidus ascended the throne of Babylon, in 555 B.C. He was destined to be the last ruling sovereign of the neo-Babylonian Empire, for in the highlands of Iran another kingdom was forging out its own program of conquest. When the Medes and their king, Astyages, were defeated by Cyrus, the realm of Persia began to assume threatening proportions. Cyrus himself announced his genealogy: "I am Cyrus, king of the hosts, the great king, king of Babylon, king of Sumer and Akkad . . . son of Cambyses, the king, king of Anshan; the grandson of Cyrus . . . the great-grandson of Teispes . . . king of Anshan. . . ." In this same inscription Cyrus proceeds to relate how the city of Babylon opened its gates to him without resistance, confirming the biblical account recorded in Daniel 5 when Darius, acting as vice-regent for Cyrus, took the city of Babylon in the name of Cyrus the Great. The neo-Babylonian Empire was in no condition to resist the advance of Cyrus, and fell easily into the hands of the Persians. The OT sets the framework of reference against the backdrop of Belshazzar's impious feast (Dan 5:1–30).

Cyrus entered Babylon on October 29, 539 B.C., and presented himself in the role of the liberator of the people. He allowed the images of the gods to be transported back to their original cities and instituted a kindly policy of repatriation for captive peoples. His policies of moderation naturally extended to the Hebrews, whom he encouraged to return to Judea to rebuild their temple (2 Chron 36:22–23; Ezra 1:1–6). Isaiah refers to Cyrus as "his [i.e., the Lord's] anointed" (Isa 45:1).

Bibliography: R. K. Harrison, *Old Testament Times,* 1970, pp. 274ff.; C. F. Pfeiffer, *Old Testament History,* 1973, pp. 458ff.

JFG

D

DABBESHETH (dăb'ȧ-shĕth). Hill town of uncertain location, but adjoining the heritage of Zebulun (Josh 19:10).

DABERATH (dăb'ă-răth). An ancient town near the western side of Mount Tabor; part of the heritage of Issachar given to the Levites (Josh 19:12; 1 Chron 6:72). A strategic location, the probable site of the defeat of Sisera by Barak (Judg 4:14–22).

DAGON (dā'gŏn, Heb. *dāghôn,* probably *fish*). Chief god of the Philistines. Originally worshiped by the Canaanites before the Philistine invasion of Canaan, as indicated by place-names such as Beth Dagon in Judah (Josh 15:41) and in Asher (19:27). Either a fish god or the god of agriculture, from *Dab,* "fish," or *Dagan,* "grain." On a wall of a palace in Babylon he is shown as half fish. That he was god of agriculture is supported by the tribute that priests and diviners bade the rulers to send when the ark was returned to Israel. Five golden mice and five golden emerods ("tumors," NIV) were votive offerings expressing gratitude for Dagon's freeing their fields of mice and their bodies of tumors (1 Sam 5). Saul's head was placed in a temple of Dagon (1 Chron 10:10). Samson destroyed the temple of Dagon in Gaza (Judg 16:30). JDF

DALAIAH (See DELAIAH)

DALMANUTHA (dăl-mȧ-nū'thȧ). A village on the west coast of the Sea of Galilee, adjoining Magdala (Matt 15:39). Landing place of Jesus after feeding the multitude (Mark 8:10). It is mentioned only in the NT. Considerable ruins near modern Mejdel (Magdala) are considered to be the location.

DALMATIA (dăl-mā'shȧ, Gr. *Dalmatia, deceitful*). A mountainous province on the east shore of the Adriatic Sea. Christianity, implanted under Titus (2 Tim 4:10), continues until today. It was ruled by Rome as early as A.D. 160. Paul may have visited in the province (Rom 15:19); in his time it was regarded as part of Illyricum.

DALPHON (dăl'fŏn). A son of Haman who was executed and hanged after Esther became queen (Esth 9:6–13).

DAMARIS (dăm'ȧ-rĭs, Gr. *Damaris*). A convert of Paul at Mars Hill (Acts 17:34).

DAMASCUS (dȧ-măs'kŭs, Gr. *Damaskos*). For more than four thousand years the capital of one government after another, a prize for which nation after nation went to war, a city whose boast for centuries has been, "The world began at Damascus, and the world will end there." It is a modern focal point between the Christian and the Muslim worlds, center of tourist interest and of international unrest. Damascus is the capital of

Above, a general view of Damascus and, below, one of the city's narrow streets. Courtesy Ecole Biblique et Archéologique Française, Jerusalem.

The ancient wall of Damascus that is thought to be the site at which Paul escaped from the city. "I was let down in a basket through a window in the wall . . ." (2 Cor 11:33). Courtesy Studium Biblicum Franciscanum, Jerusalem.

Syria, a small region of unique geological formation, lying between Mount Hermon and the Syrian Desert. It is watered by the Barada and the Wady Awaj, Abana, and Pharpar of the OT (2 Kings 5:12). A 2,000-foot (625 m.) elevation gives it a delightful climate. Its gardens and olive groves still flourish after millennia of cultivation. Caravan routes from the east, west, and south once crossed in the city, carrying treasures of silks, perfumes, carpets, and foods. It was a rich city whose merchandise was far-famed (Ezek 27:16).

Damascus and Syria played an important part in biblical history. By the time of Abraham, Damascus was well enough known to be a landmark (Gen 14:15). En route from Ur, Abraham found in Syria a steward, Eliezer, who was his heir presumptive until Isaac came (15:2–3). From the days when Abraham liberated Lot (14:13–16), there were repeated periods of peace and war among his descendants, many of them involving Damascus. Abraham secured a wife for Isaac from Syria, hence Israel is of Syrian ancestry (Gen 24; Deut 26:5). Jacob labored long in Syria for Rachel (Gen 29).

According to Josephus, Hadad was the first king. David subjugated and ruled the city for a time (2 Sam 8:5–6; 1 Chron 18:3–6). Rezon, a deserter, killed King Hadadezer, whom David had defeated, and made himself king. He hated Israel and harassed Solomon all his life (1 Kings 11:23–25). Solomon had made extensive purchases from Syria (10:29). Asa, king of Judah, bribed Ben-Hadad, grandson of Rezon of Syria, to aid him against Israel, paying him with temple treasures (15:16–21). Elijah, acting on instructions from God, anointed Hazael to be king of Syria and Jehu to rule Israel, to the end that Judah might be punished (19:15–17). Elah succeeded Baasha in Israel (16:6) and, while drunk, was murdered by Zimri who usurped the throne and destroyed the house of Baasha (16:10–14). Zimri killed himself (16:18); his son Omri succeeded him, and was followed by Ahab (16:29). Ben-Hadad attacked Ahab with a great force, but during a drunken orgy was overwhelmed. Ahab foolishly allowed him to return to his throne (20:1–34). Later, becoming ill, Ben-Hadad sent Hazael to consult Elisha who made a prophecy that led Hazael to assassinate Ben-Hadad and usurp the throne for which Elijah had anointed him (19:15; 2 Kings 8:7–15). Hazael overcame Ahaziah and Joram (2 Kings 8:28), ravaged Reuben and Manasseh and Israel (10:32–33; 13:3).

A strong kingdom was developed under Ahab, with merchants in Damascus (1 Kings 20:34). Syrians defeated Joash after he failed in a test before Elisha (2 Kings 13:14–22). Ben-Hadad II succeeded Hazael, and Israel recovered her lost possessions (13:24–25). Under Jeroboam, Damascus was retaken by Israel (14:28). Ahaz, in order to save his kingdom from Syria, made an alliance with Tiglath-Pileser (Pul) who destroyed Damascus and ended Syria's power for many decades (16:7–9). The city remained of little importance until 333 B.C. when an army of Alexander the Great captured it. Then followed two centuries of rise and fall. In 63 Syria became a province of the Roman Empire.

During NT days, Damascus was an important center, ruled by Arabia under Aretas (2 Cor 11:32). A strong Christian community had developed by Paul's day. While en route there to arrest the believers, Saul was converted (Acts 9:1–18). He escaped his Jewish enemies of the city by being let down from a wall in a basket (Acts 9:25; 2 Cor 11:33). After a checkered history under Rome, Damascus was captured by Muslims in A.D. 635 and made the seat of the Muslim world. It remained the center of the Muslim faith until 1918 when it was put under French mandate after World War I. In 1946 it became a free state. JDF

DAMNATION (Heb. *rasha', to hold guilty,* Deut 25:1; Isa 50:9; 54:17; Gr. *krinō, to put under condemnation,* John 3:17–18; Rom 14:22; *katakrinō, to hold to be unpardonable,* Matt 12:41; 20:18; Rom 8:1, 3, 34; Heb 11:7; *krima* and *krisis, judgment, eternal punishment,* Matt 23:33; Mark 12:40; John 5:29; Rom 3:8; 5:16; 13:2; 1 Cor 11:29, 34; *apōleia, destruction, damnation,* 2 Peter 2:3). The penalty for unbelief (2 Thess 2:12), for adulterous relations (1 Tim 5:11–12), for hypocrisy (Matt 23:14); for treason (Rom 13:2). When referring to the future, the words mean primarily eternal separation from God with accompanying awful punishment (see Ps 88:10–12; Isa 38:18); being cast into hell (Matt 5:29; 10:28; 23:33; 24:51; Mark 9:43). The severity of the punishment is determined by the degree of sin (Luke 12:36–48), and it is eternal (Isa 66:24; Mark 3:29; 2 Thess 1:9; Jude 6–7). JDF

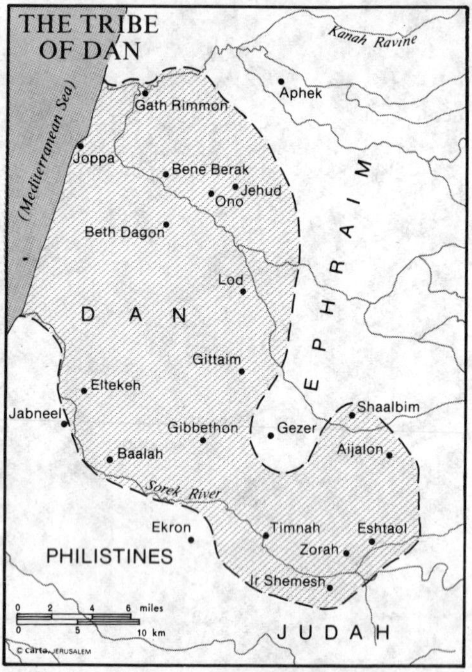

Remains of a large mud-brick gateway at Dan, complete with intact arch dated 1800–1500 B.C., which had apparently been used for only a few years when it was covered over completely in order to raise the level of the city walls. Courtesy Zev Radovan.

DAN. Northernmost city of Palestine. Originally Leshem (Josh 19:47; Judg 18:29). Captured by Danites and renamed Dan (Judg 18). It was a commercial center at one time (Ezek 27:19). Jeroboam I set up the golden calf here (1 Kings 12). The city marked the northern limit of Israel in the common phrase "from Dan to Beersheba" (e.g., Judg 20:1; 1 Sam 3:20).

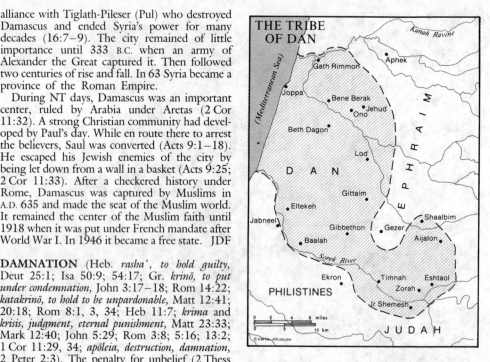

DAN. The tribe to which Dan, the fifth son of Jacob, gave origin, and the territory allotted it in Canaan. One son is mentioned among those who migrated to Egypt (Gen 46:8, 23). By the time of the Exodus his offspring had increased to 62,700 men (Num 1:39). The tribe acted as rear guard during the Exodus (10:25). They were given a fertile area lying between Judah and the Mediterranean Sea, occupied by the Philistines whose lands extended from Egypt to the coast west of Shechem (Josh 13:3). Failure to conquer Philistia made the Danites move northward, where by strategy they conquered Leshem (Laish of Judg 18:29) and renamed it Dan (Josh 19:47; Judg 18:1–29).

The heritage of Dan, though small, was productive and, with the acquisition of extra lands, provided for growth. Oholiab and Samson were Danites (Exod 31:6; Judg 13:2, 24). Jeroboam set up a golden calf in Dan and put high places throughout Israel (1 Kings 12:25–33). Menahem stopped Pul (Tiglath-Pileser) by bribery (2 Kings 15:14–20), but eventually Pul returned, overran Israel, and took many Danites into captivity (1 Chron 5:26). Little is known of the tribe from that time. JDF

DAN JAAN (dăn jā'ăn). A town covered by David's census (2 Sam 24:6). Hebrew *dān ya'an,* "Dan played a pipe," indicates it was a suburb of Dan. It was on the road to Ijon or Sidon (1 Kings 15:20; 2 Chron 16:4).

DANCING. This has formed a part of religious rites and has been associated with war and hunting, with marriage, birth, and other occasions since the records of man began to be written. It grew out of three basic human reactions: the desire to imitate movements of beasts, birds, even the sun and moon; the desire to express emotions by gestures; and gregarious impulses.

Throughout past ages, dancing has been linked with worship. In sacramental dance worshipers sought to express through bodily movements praise or penitence, worship or prayer. Out of the primitive dances the esthetic dance of civilized ancient nations slowly developed. In these the primary concern of the dancers was to reveal grace, speed, and rhythm, often to appeal to the carnal nature of both participants and spectators. Vashti refused to expose herself to this end (Esth 1:12). Priests of all pagan religions cultivated dancing but at times found it the source of dissipation and harm. For ages it has been accompanied by clapping of the hands. Percussion and other noise-making instruments seem to be native to dance (Judg 11:34; Ps 68:25).

The Hebrew people developed their own type of dancing, associated in the main with worship. Basically, it was more like modern religious shouting by individuals, or processions of exuberant groups. Three things characterized it. First, the sexes never intermingled in it, except where pagan influences had crept in (cf. Exod 32:19). Second, dancing was usually done by women, with one leading, as in the case of Miriam (15:20–21). In this incident, as well as on other occasions, a form of antiphonal singing was used. Third, dancing usually took place out of doors. For women dancers, see Exodus 15:20; Judges 21:19ff.; 1 Samuel 18:6; Psalm 68:25. Men danced solo, as in the case of David before the ark (2 Sam 6:14–16), and in groups, as when Israel celebrated the victory over the Amalekites (1 Sam 30:16). The time for dancing was recognized by the writer of Ecclesiates (3:4). Job complained against the rich because of their ability to dance (Job 21:11). Jeremiah bemoaned the tragedy that made singing and dancing out of place (Lam 5:15). The redemption of Israel was to be celebrated by dancing, both virgins and men and boys having part (Jer 31:13). The Romans introduced the Greek dance to Palestine. Primitive Christian churches allowed dance, but it soon caused degeneracy and was banned, as is indicated by many of the early Christian writers. JDF

DANIEL (dăn'yĕl, Heb. *dāniyē'l* or *dāni'ēl, God is my judge*). 1. David's second son (1 Chron 3:1; *Kileab,* 2 Sam 3:3).

2. A postexilic priest (Ezra 8:2; Neh 10:6).

3. The exilic seer of the Book of Daniel. The prophet was born into an unidentified family of Judean nobility at the time of Josiah's reformation (621 B.C.); he was among the select, youthful hostages of the first Jewish deportation, taken to Babylon by Nebuchadnezzar in 605, the third year of King Jehoiakim (Dan 1:1, 3). The reliability of this date and indeed, of the whole account has been questioned by some critics. However, the method of dating used in the Book of Daniel simply follows the customary Babylonian practice of numbering the years of a king's reign *after* his accession year (contrast Jer 46:2, which speaks of this date as Jehoiakim's fourth

Tomb painting (from Thebes, c. 1421–1377 B.C.) of two nude girls dancing to the music made by four seated women wearing unguent cones on their heads. To the right of the dancers are wine jars arranged in two tiers. Reproduced by courtesy of the Trustees of the British Museum.

year). The publication, moreover, of D. J. Wiseman's Nebuchadnezzar tablets demonstrates that after the Babylonian defeat of Egypt at Carchemish in 605 Nebuchadnezzar did "conquer the whole area of Hatti" (Syria and Palestine) and "took away the heavy tribute of Hatti to Babylon" just as claimed in Daniel 1:2 (cf. 2 Chron 36:6–7).

For three years Daniel was trained in all the wisdom of the Babylonians (Dan 1:4–5) and was assigned the Babylonian name Belteshazzar, "Protect his life!"—thereby invoking a pagan deity (4:8). Daniel and his companions, however, remained true to their ancestral faith, courteously refusing "the royal food and wine" (1:8, tainted with idolatry and contrary to the Levitical purity laws). God rewarded them with unsurpassed learning (1:20, qualifying them as official "wise men"; cf. 2:13). On Daniel, moreover, he bestowed the gift of visions and of interpreting dreams (1:17; cf. Daniel's wisdom in the apocryphal stories of *Susanna* and *Bel and the Dragon*).

Near the close of this second year (602 B.C.), Nebuchadnezzar required his fellow Babylonians, who as the ruling strata in society had assumed the position of priestly diviners (Dan 2:2; cf. Herodotus, I.191), to identify and interpret an undisclosed dream that had troubled him the preceding evening (2:5, 8). The hoax of spiritism and astrology was duly exposed; but when judgment was pronounced on the enchanters, Daniel and his companions were included under the death sentence. But the "God in heaven who reveals mysteries" (2:28; cf. 2:11) answered Daniel's prayer for illumination (2:18–19). Daniel revealed both the dream, depicting a fourfold image, and its import of four world empires (Babylon, Persia, Greece, and Rome) that would introduce God's messianic kingdom (2:44; see also DANIEL, BOOK OF). Nebuchadnezzar elevated Daniel to be chief over the wise men (2:48 does not, however, state that he became a pagan priest, as inferred by those who would discredit Daniel's historicity). He further offered him the governorship of the province of Babylon, though Daniel committed this latter appointment to his three friends (2:49).

In the latter years of Nebuchadnezzar's reign (604–562 B.C.), Daniel's courage was demonstrated (Dan 4:19; cf. 4:7) when he interpreted the king's dream of the fallen tree (4:13–27). He tactfully informed his despotic master that for seven "times" pride would reduce him to beastlike madness, and reiterated that "the Most High is sovereign over the kingdoms of men" (4:24–25; cf. its historical fulfillment twelve months later, 4:28–33).

In 552 B.C. after the retirement of King Nabonidus to Arabian Teima and the accession of his son Belshazzar, Daniel was granted his vision of the four great beasts (Dan 7) that parallels Nebuchadnezzar's earlier dream of the composite image. Then in 550, at the time of Cyrus's amalgamation of the Median and Persian states and of the growing eclipse of Babylon, Daniel received the prophecy of the ram and the goat

The traditional tomb of Daniel, marked by the mosque with its conical tower, at Susa. Courtesy B. Brandl.

concerning Persia and Greece (8:20–21) down to Antiochus IV (8:25). On October 12, 539, Cyrus's general, Gobryas, after having routed the Babylonian armies, occupied the city of Babylon. During the profane revelries of Belshazzar's court that immediately preceded the end, Daniel was summoned to interpret God's handwriting on the wall, and the prophet fearlessly condemned the desperate prince (5:22–23). He predicted Medo-Persian victory (5:28), and that very night the citadel fell and Belshazzar was slain.

When Darius the Mede (presumably Gobryas or another official of similar name) was made king of Babylon by Cyrus (Dan 5:31; 9:1), he at once sought out Daniel as one of his three "administrators" (6:2) because of his excellency, and was considering him for the post of chief administrator (6:3). Daniel's jealous colleagues, failing to uncover a valid charge of corruption (6:4), proceeded to contrive his downfall through a royal edict prohibiting for thirty days all prayers or petitions, except to Darius himself. Daniel was promptly apprehended in prayer to God; and Darius had no recourse but to cast him into a den of lions, as had been prescribed. God, however, intervened on behalf of his faithful servant (cf. 6:16) and shut the lion's mouths, though they subsequently devoured his accusers when they were condemned to a similar fate. It was in this same first year of Darius, as the seventy years of Babylonian exile drew to a close, that the angel Gabriel answered Daniel's prayers and confessions with a revelation of the seventy "sevens" (9:24–27). "So Daniel prospered during the reign of Darius" (6:28; cf. 1:21).

The last-known event in the life of Daniel took place in the third year of Cyrus (536 B.C.), when he was granted an overpowering vision of the archangel Michael contending with the demonic powers of pagan society (Dan 10:10–11:1); of the course of world history, through the persecutions of Antiochus IV (11:2–39); and of the eschatological Antichrist, the resurrections, and God's final judgment (11:40–12:4). The vision concluded with the assurance that though Daniel would go to his grave prior to these events he would yet receive his appointed reward in the consummation (12:13). Thus in his mid-eighties, after completing his inspired autobiography and apocalyptic oracles, he finished his honored course.

The history of Daniel the prophet is confirmed both by the words of Christ (Matt 24:15) and by references to his righteousness and wisdom by his prophetic contemporary Ezekiel (14:14, 20; 28:3, in 591 and 586 B.C., respectively, though some scholars relate the latter passages to the Daniel of the Ugaritic epic material). The name is spelled differently in Ezekiel from the way it is spelled in Daniel. The Book of Daniel presents a timeless demonstration of separation from impurity, of courage against compromise, of efficaciousness in prayer, and of dedication to him whose "kingdom endures from generation to generation" (Dan 4:34). JBP

DANIEL, BOOK OF. Although it stands as the last of the major prophets in the English Bible, this book appears in the Hebrew OT (which consists of "the law, prophets, and writings") as one of the "writings." For though Christ spoke of Daniel's *function* as prophetic (Matt 24:15), his *position* was that of a governmental official and inspired writer rather than ministering prophet (see Acts 2:29–30).

The first half of the book (chs. 1–6) consists of six narratives on the life of Daniel and his friends: their education (605–602 B.C.), Daniel's revelation of Nebuchadnezzar's dream-image, the trial by fiery furnance, Daniel's prediction of Nebuchadnezzar's madness, his interpretation of the handwriting on the wall (539, the fall of Babylon), and his ordeal in the lion's den (see also DANIEL; SHADRACH). The second half consists of four apocalyptic visions predicting the course of world history.

Daniel 7 envisions the rise of four beasts: a lion, bear, leopard, and monster with iron teeth explained as representing successive kings (kingdoms, 7:23). The description parallels that of Nebuchadnezzar's image, with its head, breast, trunk, and iron legs. The first empire must therefore be contemporary Babylon (2:38). The fourth kingdom is regarded by most conservative scholars as Rome. Between them lie Persia and Greece. The vision further describes the disintegration of Rome into a tenfold balance of power (2:42; 7:24; Rev 17:12, 16), the eventual rise of Antichrist for an indefinite period of "times" (Dan 7:8, 25), and his destruction when "one like a son of man" comes with the clouds of heaven (7:13). This figure is understood by most scholars as the Messiah because Christ applied this imagery to himself (Matt 24:30). However, some understand it to symbolize the saints of the Most High (7:18, 22) epitomized in Jesus Christ, the "last Adam" (Mark 14:62; 1 Cor 15:45). Some scholars understand the kingdom of God, represented by the rock (Dan 2:34–35; cf. vv. 44–45) to be the church. Others see it as the eschatological kingdom (the Millennium).

Daniel 2:4b–7:28 is composed in the international language of Aramaic. But with chapter 8, Daniel resumes his use of Hebrew, probably because of the more Jewish orientation of the three remaining visions. The ram and the goat depict the coming victory of Greece (331 B.C.) over the amalgamated empire of Media and Persia (8:20–21) and the subsequent persecution of Judah by Antiochus IV (168–165; 8:9–14, 23–26).

The prophecy of the seventy "sevens" in 9:20–27 was given in response to Daniel's prayer concerning the end of Jerusalem's desolations (9:16). The prophecy indicated that the desolations would cease at the end of seventy "sevens." Many scholars understand the designation "seven" to refer to a period of seven years. Sixty-nine "sevens" extend from the decree to rebuild Jerusalem (458—cf. Ezra 7:18, 25) to Messiah. Those who do not hold to the future significance of the seventieth "seven" propose that the "cutting off" (9:26) of the Messiah is Christ's crucifixion in the midst of the seventieth "seven." Other scholars terminate the sixty-ninth "seven" with Christ's death and place the seventieth "seven" in the last days. It is in the seventieth "seven" that Antichrist will destroy Jerusalem according to this view. If the pointing of the Masoretic tradition is observed, the first seven "sevens" are separated from the sixty-two, and the seventieth "seven" witnesses either the devastations under Antiochus Epiphanes or the eschatological Antichrist.

Chapters 10–12, after elaborating on the succession of Persian and Greek rulers through Antiochus, then move on to "the time of the end," foretelling Antichrist's tribulation (Dan 11:40–12:1), the resurrections of the saved and the lost (12:2; cf. Rev 20:4–6, 12), and the final judgment (Dan 12:2).

The authorship of the Book of Daniel is nowhere expressly defined but is indicated by the autobiographical, first-person compositon from 7:2 onward. Unity of style and content (as admitted by Driver, Rowley, and Pfeiffer), plus God's commitment of "the book" to Daniel (Dan 12:4) imply the latter's authorship, shortly after his last vision, 536 B.C. (10:1).

Modern criticism, however, overwhelmingly denies the authenticity of Daniel as a product of the sixth century B.C. Indeed, as early as A.D. 275 the neo-Platonic philosopher Porphyry categorically repudiated the possibility of Daniel's miraculous predictions. Antisupernaturalism must bring the "prophecy" down to a time after the events described (especially after Antiochus's sacrilege of 168 B.C.); or, if the latest possible date has been reached, it must then reinterpret the predictions to apply to other, already-accomplished events. Consequently, since Daniel was extensively quoted (and misunderstood) as early as 140 B.C. (Sibylline Oracles 3:381–400), rationalists have no alternative but to apply the supposed coming of the Messiah and the fulfillment of the seventy weeks to Maccabean times, rather than Christ's, even though this requires "surmising a chronological miscalculation on the part of the writer" (ICC, p. 393).

The arguments for a late (Maccabean) date for

the Book of Daniel may be classed as historical, literary, and theological. A number of specific censures have been advanced against Daniel's historical authenticity. These may, however, be dismissed, either as arguments from silence or as answered by recent archaeology (see DANIEL). More generally, it is asserted that Daniel conceived of a fictitious Median empire, existing as a separate kingdom between Babylon and Persia (thus allowing Daniel's fourth empire to be identified with Greece rather than Rome, as required by liberalism's presuppositions). But the very passage adduced (Dan 5:31–6:1) speaks of unified Medo-Persia (6:8, 12; cf. 7:5; cf. 8:3, 29) and this third, as the fourfold Greek (7:6; 8:8, 22). Again the fact that the apocryphal Book of Ecclesiasticus, written about 180 B.C., omits Daniel from its survey of Scripture, proves little other than the Sadducaic prejudice of its writer; for he likewise disregards the Book of Ezra, whose high theology parallels that of Daniel. Fragments of Daniel, moreover, have been discovered among the Dea Sea Scrolls of Qumran, datable to the very second century B.C., in which the book's fraudulent composition is commonly claimed.

Daniel has been questioned on literary grounds as well because it contains several terms of Persian or Greek origin. However, the Greek words are limited to the names of musical instruments, such as "harp" (Dan 3:5). These words may have been imported to Babylon at an earlier time. Among the apocryphal literature from Qumran, there has been recoverd a "Prayer of Nabonidu" that closely parallels Daniel's record of Nebuchadnezzar's madness (Dan 4). Far, however, from proving Daniel to be a corruption of this third-century work, the Qumranic legend, though garbled, serves to suggest the essential historicity of Daniel's account. As to the so-called "late" Aramaic and Hebrew languages of Daniel, E. J. Young has concluded that "nothing in them . . . necessarily precludes authorship by Daniel in the sixth century B.C."

Lastly, the theology of Daniel, with its apocalyptic eschatology, biblicism, and developed angelology, are said to prohibit exilic origin. Yet Isaiah had composed an apocalypse, describing the Resurrection in terms similar to Daniel's, as early as 711 B.C. (Isa 26:19—here, too, negative critics deny its authenticity); when Daniel in 538 B.C. devoted himself to the inspired "Scriptures" (Dan 9:2), the OT canon was complete, except for three minor prophets, the last two books of Psalms, and Chronicles-Esther (see also CANONICITY); and Daniel's angels, both in name and in function, stand naturally in the Hebraic religious development. His book was destined to inspire Jewish exiles with confidence in the Most High (4:34–37), and those of God's people today who will approach this book in faith believing will discover in it victorious supernaturalism that overcomes the world.

Bibliography: H. C. Leupold, *Exposition of Daniel,* 1949; E. J. Young, *The Prophecy of Daniel,* 1949; J. F. Walvoord, *Daniel: The Key to Prophetic Revelation,* 1971; J. G. Baldwin, *Daniel: An Introduction and Commentary* (TOTC), 1978.

JBP

DANNAH (dăn'ȧ). A mountain town given by Caleb as part of the heritage of Judah (Josh 15:49). Its location is uncertain, but it is not far from Hebron. Some authorities make it modern Idnah.

DARDA, DARA (dăr'dȧ, dă'rȧ). A member of a noted family of wise men. He was either a son of Mahol (1 Kings 4:31) or son of Zerah (1 Chron 2:6).

DARIC (dăr'ĭk). A Persian gold coin used in Palestine after the return from captivity (1 Chron 29:7; Ezra 8:27). It was worth about five dollars. See also MONEY.

DARIUS (dă-rī'ŭs, Heb. *dāryāwesh,* Gr. *Darios*). A common name for Medo-Persian rulers. Numerous cuneiform tablets contain references to them, especially to Darius Hystaspes. *Darius the Mede* is a more than mysterious figure who, so far, only appears in the Bible. He may have been Gubaru, an officer in Cyrus's army who became governor of the Persian province of northern Babylon, but the evidence is rather more suited by thinking that this is an alternative title for Cyrus the Persian himself. The only two references to him are in Daniel 5:31 and 9:1.

Darius Hytaspes was the greatest of the Persian rulers. Cambyses, the son of Cyrus, continued the conquests that his noted father had started. He did not, however, recognize the claims of the Jews (Jos. *Antiq.* 11.1.2). In one of his campaigns he was defeated by the Egyptians, and on his way home he committed suicide. Taking advantage of the king's defeat, a pretender named Smerdis was made king by zealots of the Magian religious sect, and he ruled one year until killed by Darius and other princes, Darius having had himself made king. He was of the same family line as Cyrus but

Darius I as depicted on relief on the cliff at Behistun in Iran. Courtesy Carta, Jerusalem.

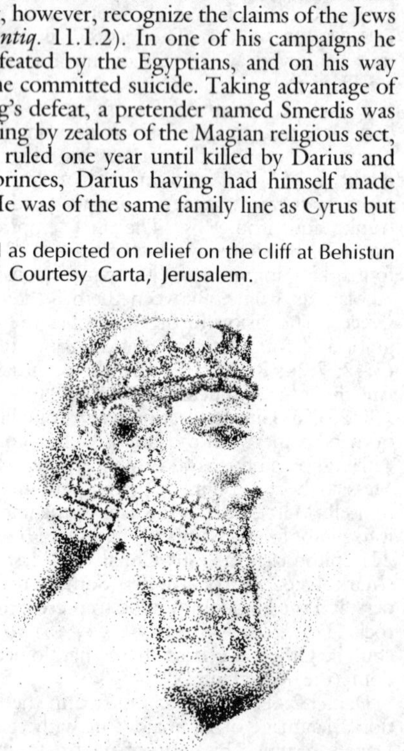

Remains of the palace of Darius I at Persepolis. Courtesy B. Brandl.

not a direct descendant. Cyrus, according to tradition, had selected Darius to succeed him. Between the reign of Cyrus and that of Darius, the Jews had been mistreated, and work on rebuilding Jerusalem had stopped (Ezra 4:1–6). An appeal was made to Darius who searched and discovered the original decree of Cyrus favoring the Jews. Under his lenient reign, they restored the walls of the city and rebuilt the temple (6:1–15). Darius was beset by rebellious subjects and spent much time in putting them down. He reorganized the government and extended its boundaries. He conducted many magnificent building enterprises and encouraged men of letters, especially the historians who extolled his prowess. The Greeks never yielded to him, however, and after some futile campaigns, his forces were overwhelmed in the battle at Marathon, 490 B.C. Darius planned another campaign against the Greeks, but rebellion in Egypt interfered, and death in 486 ended his career. He was succeeded by Xerxes, a grandson of Cyrus the Great.

Darius the Persian (Neh 12:22). There is uncertainty among scholars as to whether this was Darius Nothus or Darius Codomannus, but evidence favors the claim that he was the latter, whose kingdom was destroyed by Alexander the Great in 330 B.C. Following a disastrous defeat near Arbela, the Persian Empire crumbled, Darius the Persian being its last king.

Bibliography: D. J. Wiseman, *Notes on Some Problems in the Book of Daniel*, 1965, pp. 9–16; J. G. Baldwin, *Daniel* (TOTC), 1978, pp. 23–28.

JDF

DARKNESS (Heb. *hōshekh, the dark*, Gr. *skotos, darkness*). Used in the OT and NT both in a literal and in a figurative sense. Mankind has long associated it with evil, danger, crime; it has also been the metaphor that describes both mystery and the place of eternal punishment. Several uses of the term are found in the Scriptures:

1. To denote the absence of light (Gen 1:2–3; Job 34:22; Isa 45:7).
2. To depict the mysterious (Exod 20:21; 2 Sam 22:10; 1 Kings 8:12; Ps 97:2; Isa 8:22; Matt 10:27).
3. As ignorance, especially about God (Job 37:19; Prov 2:13; Eccl 2:14; John 12:35; 1 Thess 5:1–8).
4. To describe the seat of evil (Prov 4:19; Matt 6:23; Luke 11:34; 22:53; John 8:12; Rom 13:12; 1 Cor 4:5; Eph 5:11).
5. Presenting supernatural events (Gen 15:12; Exod 10:21; Matt 27:45; Rev 8:12; 16:10).
6. A sign of the Lord's return (Isa 60:2; Joel 2:2; Amos 5:8; Matt 24:29).
7. An agency of eternal punishment (Matt 22:13; 2 Peter 2:4, 17; Jude 6–7; see also Job 2:1–5; 20:20).
8. It describes spiritual blindness (Isa 9:2; John 1:5; Eph 5:8; 1 John 1:5; 2:8), sorrow and distress (Isa 8:22; 13:10; Ps 23:4). It never holds sway where the Redeemer has come to shed his light (Col 1:13).

DARKON. A descendant of Solomon's servant Jaala, who returned with Zerubbabel from exile (Ezra 2:56).

DART (See ARMS AND ARMOR)

DATHAN. A great-grandson of Reuben (Num 16:1). He, with his brothers Abiram and Korah,

A shepherd and his flock in the fields of Bethlehem, reminiscent of David's youth. Courtesy Zev Radovan.

rebelled against Moses (16:1–15), for which sin they were swallowed by the earth (16:31–35; see also ch. 26).

DAUGHTER. A word of various uses in the Bible. It referred to both persons and things, often without regard to kinship or sex. There was the familiar usage of child to parent (Gen 6:1; 20:12; 24:23; Judg 11:34; Matt 15:28). Not prized as highly as sons, they were sometimes sold into slavery (Exod 21:7). The word is used to indicate a remoter relationship, as when Rebekah is called "my master's brother's daughter" (Gen 24:48 KJV), though she was the speaker's granddaughter (so NIV; cf. Gen 24:15, 24). It often referred to any female descendant, regardless of the nearness of relations (Luke 1:5). Jacob's sons called their sister a daughter (Gen 34:13–17; cf. Ps 45:13; 144:12). The word could represent women in general (Gen 28:6; Num 25:1). It was often used in the figurative sense, referring to offspring (Isa 22.4; Jer 9:1; Lam 4:10) or to those who worshiped the true God (Ps 45:10; Song of Songs 1:5; 3:11; Isa 62:11; Zech 9:9; Matt 21:5; John 12:15). Physical means of making music, the mouth, ears, etc., were called daughters of music (Eccl 12:4 KJV).

DAVID (dā'vĭd, Heb. *Dāwîdh, beloved* or, as in ancient Mari, *chieftain*). Israel's greatest king, described in 1 Samuel 16–1 Kings 2:11 (1 Chron 11–29), plus many of the psalms, he ranks with Moses as one of the most commanding figures in the OT.

David was born in 1040 B.C. (2 Sam 5:4), the youngest son of Jesse of Bethlehem (1 Sam 16:10–11), and developed in strength, courage, and attractiveness while caring for his father's sheep (16:12; 17:34–36). When God rejected Saul, the prophet Samuel sought out David and secretly anointed him as Israel's next king; and God's Spirit came upon David from that time on (16:13). Saul, meanwhile, summoned David to periodic appearances at court to soothe his own troubled mind by skillful harp-playing (16:18; 17:15). While still in his teens, David gained national renown and the friendship of Saul's son Jonathan (18:1–3; cf. 20:12–16; 23:16–17) through his faith-inspired victory over the taunting Philistine champion Goliath (17:45–47). Saul's growing jealousy and four insidious attempts on David's life served only to increase the latter's popularity (cf. 18:13–16, 27). At length, urged on by David's rivals (cf. Ps 59:12), Saul openly sought his destruction; and though frustrated by Samuel and the priests at Nob, he did succeed in driving David into exile (1 Sam 19:11; 21:10).

David fled to Philistine Gath, but his motives became suspect. Only by a stratagem and by the grace of God (1 Sam 21:12; Ps 56:3; 34:6–8) did he reach the wilderness cave of Adullam in Judah (Ps 142:6). Here David was joined by a variety of malcontents (1 Sam 22:2) and by the priest Abiathar, who had escaped Saul's retaliatory attack upon Nob (cf. Ps 52:1). On three separate occasions Saul attempted to seize David: when fellow-Judeans from Ziph betrayed his presence, after his deliverance of Keilah (1 Sam 23; Ps 54:3); at the cave of En Gedi by the Dead Sea where Saul was caught in his own trap (1 Sam 24; Ps 7:4; 57:6); and on David's return to

Ziphite territory, when he again spared his pursuer's life (1 Sam 26). Near the end of 1012 B.C., however (27:7), David in despair sought asylum in Gath, feigning vassalage (27:8–28:25).

When David heard of the destruction of Saul at Mount Gilboa in 1010 B.C. and the Philistine domination of Israel from Beth Shan, David composed his moving lament of "The Bow" (2 Sam 1:19–27), the authenticity of which is unquestionable. Shortly thereafter, David's forces advanced inland to Hebron, where he was declared king over Judah. His appeal, however, to the northern and eastern tribes elicited no response (2:7); and for five years most of Israel lay under Philistine control.

In 1005 B.C. Saul's general, Abner, enthroned Ish-Bosheth, a son of the former monarch; but in the conflict that followed David's arms gained ascendancy. Abner himself eventually transferred his support to David, only to be treacherously murdered by David's vengeful commander Joab (2 Sam 3). Only after the death of Ish-Bosheth (ch. 4) did all Israel acclaim David king in 1003 (2 Sam 5:1–5; 1 Chron 11:10; 12:38).

Realizing that their "vassal" had gotten out of hand, the Philistines undertook an all-out attack on reunited Israel. David, however, after an initial retreat to Adullam (2 Sam 5:17; 23:13–17), expelled the enemy in two divinely directed campaigns (5:18–25). He next established a new capital by capturing the Jebusite stronghold of Jerusalem. This strategic site on the Benjamite border served not only as an incomparable fortress, vulnerable only to the "scaling hooks" of Joab (5:8 KJV; see NIV footnote), but also as a neutral location between the rival tribes of north and south. David then constructed "Millo," a fortification that "filled up" Jerusalem's breached northern wall. Because of Maccabean demolitions on the hill Ophel (David's City of Zion), no ruins survive that may be assigned him with confidence, though Davidic fortifications have been uncovered at Debir and Beth Shemesh. Joab, for his bravery, was appointed as commander (1 Chron 11:6). Twelve corps of militia were organized under him, each with twenty-four thousand men, on periods of one-month duty annually (ch. 27). David's military organization also included the professional Kerethites and Pelethites (Cretans and Philistines) and certain elite groups: "the six hundred" mighty men (2 Sam 15:18; cf. 1 Sam 27:2), "the thirty" heroes, and "the three" most distinguished (2 Sam 23; 1 Chron 11).

The spring at En Gedi, a place where David found refuge from Saul (1 Sam 23:29; 24:1–22). Courtesy S. Zur Picture Library.

The Citadel, which guards the western approach to Jerusalem and is made up of several towers, one of which dates from the second temple period. Courtesy Israel Government Press Office.

David also elevated Jerusalem into his religious capital by installing Moses' ark of the covenant in a tent on Zion (2 Sam 6; Ps 24; cf. Num 4:15 on the death of Uzzah, 2 Sam 6:6–7). He honored it, both with a dedicatory psalm (1 Chron 16, from Pss 96, 105, 106) and with a permanent ministry of Levitical singers under Asaph (1 Chron 16:5, 37, 42; 25:1–31). Once criticized as postexilic fiction, these regular *shārîm* have been authenticated by even earlier Canaanitish parallels from Ugarit. Eventually David organized thirty-eight thousand Levites under hereditary leaders, appointing them as doorkeepers, treasurers, or even district judges (chs. 23–26). The Aaronic priests he divided into twenty-four rotating courses, which were continued into NT times (1 Chron 24:10; Luke 1:5).

From 1002 to about 995 B.C. David expanded his kingdom on all sides: west against Philistia, taking Gath, one of its five ruling cities (2 Sam 8:1); east against Moab, (8:2); north against Syria, in two campaigns (10:13, 18; cf. 8:3) to the Euphrates River; and south against stubborn Edom (1 Kings 11:15; Ps 60:10). An alliance with Hiram of Tyre enabled David to construct a palace in Jerusalem (2 Sam 5:11). David's political organization shows analogies with Egypt's, his "cabinet" (8:15–18) including such officers as the recorder (public relations official), the scribe (secretary of state), and other later additions (20:23–26). Over all, however, whether tribal princes (1 Chron 27:16–24) or royal officials (27:25–31), David reigned supreme.

Rest from war followed (2 Sam 7:1; 22:1–51; Ps 18), and David proposed a permanent temple for the Lord in Jerusalem. But while the prophet Nathan denied David the privilege of building God's house (because of excessive bloodshed, 1 Chron 22:8; 28:3), he revealed that God would build David's "house," raising up his son to construct the temple (2 Sam 7:13a) and establishing his dynasty (7:13b), to culminate in the incarnation of God's eternal Son (7:14). This "Davidic covenant" (Ps 89:3; 132:12) mediates Christian salvation for all (Isa 55:3; Rev 22:16), climaxing God's promises begun in Genesis 3:15 and accomplished in the new testament of Jesus Christ. God's Spirit then inspired David to compose messianic psalms, depicting the deity of the Lord's anointed Son (Ps 2), his eternal priesthood (Ps 110), his atoning death (Ps 22), and his resurrection, ascension, and coming kingdom (Pss 2, 16, 68). Some of David's greatest achievements lie in this literary sphere. Of the 150 canonical psalms, 73 possess titles asserting Davidic authorship. These references, moreover, appear in the oldest MSS and warrant full acceptance. David also composed some of the titleless psalms (cf. Pss 2; 95; Acts 4:25; Heb 4:7); he stimulated Asaph and his associates to the inscripturation of others; and the king personally compiled the first book of the Psalter (Pss 1–41; cf. his closing doxology in 41:13). One of the world's best-loved compositions is David's heart-affirmation, "The Lord is my shepherd. . . ." (Ps 23).

Yet soon after this, David lapsed into a series of failures (Mephibosheth's appearance [2 Sam 9] could not have preceded 995 B.C. [4:4; 9:12], nor could Solomon's birth [12:24] have been long subsequent). He killed seven innocent descendants of Saul (but not Mephibosheth, 21:7) to enforce a promise rashly made to pagan Gibeonites (contrast Num 35:33). He committed adultery with Bathsheba and murdered her husband to conceal his crime (2 Sam 10–11). When exposed by Nathan, he humbly confessed his sin (the great penitential Pss 32 and 51); but the testimony of God's people had suffered compromise, and Nathan condemned the king to corresponding punishments (2 Sam 12:10–14). David also became guilty of ineffective control over his sons. Thus in about 990 Amnon, following his father's shameful example (13:1–14), raped his sister Tamar; and two years later Absalom avenged Tamar by murdering Amnon (13:23–29). Until about 983 (13:38; 14:28) David shunned Absalom's presence; and four years later (15:7 ASV mg.) Absalom revolted, driving his father from Jerusalem (cf. Pss 3, 63) and specifically fulfilling Nathan's curses (2 Sam 16:20–22). Through fatal delay, Absalom was defeated and killed by Joab, though only the latter's stern rebuke could shake David from irresponsible grief over the death of his son (18:33–19:8). Even after David's restoration to Jerusalem, intertribal jealousies led Sheba of Benjamin to prolong the disorder (ch. 20).

David's last years (975–970 B.C.) were occupied with Philistine wars (2 Sam 21:15–22) and with a military census, motivated by David's pride in his armed forces (24:3, 9; Ps 30:6). Plague resulted. But when the destroying angel halted at Araunah's threshing floor on Mount Moriah, just north of Jerusalem (2 Chron 3:1), this area became marked as David's place of sacrifice and the very house of God (1 Chron 22:1; Ps 30 title). David subsequently undertook massive preparations for the temple (1 Chron 22); he received in writing from God's Spirit the plans for its construction (28:12, 19); and he solemnly charged Solomon and the princes with their execution (chs. 22, 28, 29). As David became increasingly incapacitated by age, his oldest surviving son, Adonijah, attempted to usurp the throne from Solomon, the divinely designated heir. Nathan, however, aroused David to proclaim Solomon's coronation (1 Kings 1). Thus in 970, after a final charge to his son (2:2–9), David died. His last words were a prophecy of the future Davidic Messiah and of his own salvation, springing from this covenant (2 Sam 23:5). JBP

DAVID, CITY OF (See CITY OF DAVID; JERUSALEM)

DAY (Heb. *yôm*, Gr. *hēmera*). A word often misinterpreted because of its various uses in the Bible. It often denotes time from sunrise to sunset (Gen 1:5; Ps 74:16). At an early date it was divided into three parts—morning, noon, and evening (Ps 55:17; Dan 6:10). Probably due to Medo-Persian influence after the Exile, it was divided into twelve hours (John 11:9). Early morning was the first hour; the sixth hour was noon. Time could not be determined by clocks, so the length of an hour depended on the time of the year. The word also refers to time in general (Judg 18:30; Job 18:20; Obad 12). It is also used figuratively, referring to the day of judgment (Isa 2:12; Joel 1:15; Amos 5:18; Rom 13:12), the length of life (Gen 5:4), the time of opportunity (John 9:4), and any time (Prov 12:16, KJV, ASV, see footnote). JDF

DAY OF ATONEMENT (See ATONEMENT, DAY OF)

DAY OF CHRIST. A term used in the NT to indicate Jesus' intervention in human history. Sometimes it is called "that day" (Matt 7:22) and "the Day" (1 Cor 3:13). It refers to the return of Jesus for his own and for the judgment of unbelievers (1 Cor 1:8; 5:5; 2 Cor 1:14; Phil 1:6, 10; 2:16; 2 Thess 2:2–3). It will signal the completion of the redemptive work (2 Thess 2:1, 13), the day of triumph (Phil 2:9–11). Paul's letters, especially, are full of the longing for this day—when Christ will manifest himself in glory and establish his kingdom.

DAY OF THE LORD. An eschatological term referring to the consummation of God's kingdom and triumph over his foes and deliverance of his people. It begins at the Second Coming and will include the final judgment. It will remove class distinction (Isa 2:12–21), abolish sins (2 Peter 3:11–13), and will be accompanied by social calamities and physical cataclysms (Matt 24; Luke 21:7–33). It will include the millennial judgment (Rev 4:1–19:6) and culminate in the new heaven and the new earth (Isa 65:17; 66:22; Rev 21:1).

DAYSMAN (Heb *yākhah, to act as umpire*). A mediator or arbitrator—one who has set a day for hearing a dispute. As used in Job 9:33 (KJV; NIV "someone to arbitrate"), the word means an umpire or referee who hears two parties in a dispute and decides the merits of the case. In eastern lands it was the custom for the judge to put his hands on the heads of the two parties in disagreement to show his authority and his desire to render an unbiased verdict. Job's statement means that no human being is worthy of acting as judge of God.

DAYSPRING (Heb. *shāchar, to break forth*). A poetic name used in KJV for the dawn (Job 38:12; NIV "dawn"), and also in describing the advent of the Messiah (Luke 1:78; NIV "rising sun").

DAYSTAR (Gr. *phōsphoros, light-giving*). The planet Venus, seen as a morning star, heralding the dawn. The prophet compared the splendor of the king of Babylon to Lucifer, "son of the morning" (Isa 14:12 KJV; JB, NASB, RSV "son of [the] dawn"; NIV "morning star"). Jesus calls himself "the bright Morning Star" (Rev 22:16). He is called the "morning star" in 2 Peter 1:19.

DEACON, DEACONESS (Gr. *diakonos, servant*). Paul used the Greek word of himself (1 Cor 3:5; Eph 3:7). Jesus was declared to be a *diakonos* of the Jews (Rom 15:8). Household servants were *diakonoi* (Matt 22:13). Paul told Timothy how to be good *diakonos* (1 Tim 4:6). NIV usually renders "servant"; KJV, "minister."

The diaconate, as a church office, is inferred from Acts 6:1–8, but at least two of the seven men were evangelists. Ignatius, a contemporary of the apostle John, declared that the deacons were not mere servers of meat and drink. But the seven in Acts 6 did serve (*diakonein*) tables, so that the apostles could give themselves to the ministry (*diakonia*) of the Word. Their successors came to be recognized as church officers. Qualifications given in 1 Timothy 3 show that they were not considered ordinary lay members of the church. Paul's mention of deacons in connection with bishops (Phil 1:1) supports the view. Clement of Rome based the office on the two classes of synagogue workers mentioned in Isaiah 60:17 (LXX)—pastors and helpers.

The same Greek word is used of Phoebe in Romans 16:1—translated as "servant" (KJV, NASB, NIV) or "deaconess" (JB, RSV). Certain women ministered (*diakonein*) to Jesus (Luke 8:2–3). It does not appear from the Scripture or early church literature that deaconesses were ever church officers. JDF

DEAD SEA. Called in Scripture the Salt Sea (Gen 14:3), Sea of the Arabah (Deut 3:17), or the eastern sea (Joel 2:20; Zech 14:8). It has the earth's lowest surface, 1,290 feet (403 m.) below sea level. Occupying a geologic fault that extends from Syria through the Red Sea into Africa, it measures forty-seven by ten miles (seventy-eight by sixteen km.) (approximately 300 sq. mi. [789 sq. km.]). Cliffs rise 1,500–2,500 feet (469–781 m.) on either shore. North of Lisan, "the tongue" (Josh 15:2 ASV footnote), the water's depth attains 1,300 feet (406 m.), though southward it averages less than ten feet (three m.). The Sea is slowly expanding, as the muddy Jordan extends its northern delta. Salt concentration reaches 25 percent, four times that of ocean water. Magnesium bromide prevents organic life; the climate is arid, and the heat extreme.

Though man's historical access to the Dead Sea has been slight, five streams south of Lisan recommended the Plain of Siddim to Lot as a "well-watered . . . garden" (Gen 13:10). Yet writing some six hundred years later, Moses explained that the Valley of Siddim was the same as the Salt Sea (14:3), a fact suggested by the known growth of the Sea (once crossable at Lisan), by his mention of "tar pits" (14:10) now active on the Sea's floor (cf. Josephus's name, "Lake Asphaltites," *Antiq.* 1.9.1), and by contemporaneous ruins discoverd on Lisan. God's destruction of Sodom may thus reflect the area's combustibleness (Gen 19:24, 28); and Jebel Usdum, "mountain of Sodom," still identifies an extensive rock-salt formation opposite Zoar (cf. Gen 19:26; Luke 17:32).

The Dead Sea constituted Israel's eastern border (Num 34:12; Ezek 47:18). At En Gedi, which terminates the principal descent from

View of the Dead Sea, looking south from the ruins of the Essene community at Qumran. Courtesy S. Zur Picture Library.

Caves at Qumran, site where early in 1947 a Bedouin goatherd stumbled upon several jars containing leather scrolls now known as the Dead Sea Scrolls. Courtesy Israel Government Press Office.

Judah, a spring provided refuge for David (1 Sam 24:1). The Valley of Salt, south of the Sea, witnessed the victories of David and of Amaziah over Edom (2 Kings 14:7; 1 Chron 18:12) and countermarches in the days of Jehoshaphat (2 Kings 3:8–9; 2 Chron 20:1–2; the "Moabite Stone"). On the east shore above the Arnon, the springs of Callirhoe served Herod the Great during his final illness; and at Machaerus his son Herod Antipas imprisoned John the Baptist (Mark 1:14; 6:17). On the west shore, above En Gedi, lies Khirbet Qumran, site of the NT community with its famous scrolls; and opposite Lisan rises Masada, Palestine's finest natural fortress, the refuge of Herod against Parthians in 42 B.C., and the last stand of Jerusalem's zealots in A.D. 70 (Jos. *War* 7.10.1). In modern times the Dead Sea has produced potash; but Ezekiel predicts a healing of its waters, granting abundant life in God's kingdom age (Ezek 47:8–10). JBP

DEAD SEA SCROLLS. These were discovered, probably in A.D. 1947, by a Bedouin and brought to the attention of the scholarly world late that year and early in 1948. The discoveries were made in caves located in the marly cliffs a mile or so (1.6 km.) west of the NW corner of the Dead Sea, at a place known by the modern Arabic name of Qumran, which is near a copious spring of fresh water known as Ain Feshkha. This location is at the eastern edge of the Wilderness of Judah. Accordingly, alternate names for the discoveries include "Qumran," "Ain Feshkha," or "Wilderness of Judah."

The scrolls were seen by several scholars in the latter part of 1947, some of whom have admitted that they passed them up as forgeries. One of the scholars who recognized the antiquity of the scrolls was the late Professor Eleazar L. Sukenik of Hebrew University, who was subsequently successful in purchasing some of them. Other scrolls were taken to the American School of Oriental Research in Jerusalem, where the acting director, Dr. John C. Trever, was convinced of their value and arranged to photograph the portions that were brought to him. One of his photographs was sent to Professor William F. Albright, who promptly declared that this was "*the most important discovery ever made* in OT manuscripts."

The scrolls that were purchased by the Hebrew University included the *Hebrew University Isaiah Scroll* (1QIs[b]), which is a partial scroll of the book; the *Order of Warfare,* also known as the *War of the Sons of Light against the Sons of Darkness* (1QM); and the *Thanksgiving Hymns,* or *Hodayot* (1QH). The scrolls purchased by the Syrian archbishop and published by the American Schools of Oriental Research included the *St. Mark's Isaiah Scroll* (1QIs[a]), which is a complete scroll of the book, the *Habakkuk Commentary* (1QpHab) which contains the text of chapters 1 and 2 of Habakkuk with a running commentary; and the *Manual of Discipline* (1QS), which contains the rules for the members of the Qumran community. These all have subsequently come into the possession of the State of Israel and are housed in a shrine in the Hebrew University,

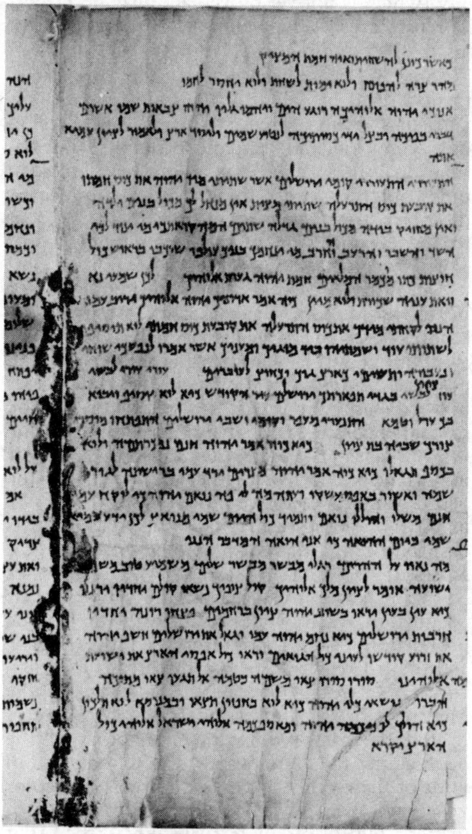

Fragment of the Isaiah Scroll found in Cave 1 at Qumran. The column shown here (c. 125–100 B.C.) contains Isaiah 51:13–52:12. Courtesy The Shrine of the Book, D. Samuel and Jeane H. Gottesman Center for Biblical Manuscripts, Israel Museum, Jerusalem.

Jerusalem, Israel. They have been published in numerous editions and translated into many languages, and are readily available for anyone who wishes to study them either in translation or in facsimile.

Following the discovery of these important scrolls, which are now all but unanimously accepted as having come from the last century B.C. and the first century A.D., the region from which they came was systematically explored. Numerous caves were found, and so far eleven caves have yielded materials from the same period as the original scrolls. Most of these materials have come from the fourth cave explored (known as Cave Four or 4Q); others of significance come from caves Two, Five, and Six. According to recent reports the most significant discoveries are those from Cave Eleven (11Q).

At least 382 manuscripts are represented by the fragments of Cave Four alone, about 100 of which are biblical manuscripts. These include fragments of every book of the Hebrew Bible except Esther. Some of the books are represented in many copies; e.g., 14 different manuscripts of Deuteronomy, 12 manuscripts of Isaiah, and 10 manuscripts of Psalms are represented in Cave Four; other fragments of these same books have been found in other caves. Almost complete scrolls of Psalms and Leviticus have been found in Cave Eleven, but these have not yet been published. One of the significant finds, which may turn out to have important bearing on the theories of date and authorship, concerns the Book of Daniel, fragments of which have been found with the change from Hebrew to Aramaic in Daniel 2:4 and from Aramaic to Hebrew in 7:28–8:1, exactly as in our modern texts of Daniel.

In addition to biblical books, fragments of deuterocanonical writings have been found, specifically Tobit and Ecclesiasticus, as well as fragments of several noncanonical writings. Some of these latter were already known, such as Jubilees, Enoch, and the Testament of Levi; others were not previously known, such as the peculiarly Qumranian documents: the Thanksgiving Psalms, the Book of Warfare, and the commentaries on portions of Scripture. These last give us insights into the nature and beliefs of the community at Qumran.

Near the cliffs on an alluvial plateau overlooking the shore of the Dead Sea is the site of an ancient building complex often referred to as the "Monastery." This was thoroughly excavated over several seasons and has yielded important data about the nature, size, and date of the Qumran community. From coins found there, together with other remains, the community has been dated within the limits of 140 B.C. and A.D. 67. The members were almost all male, although the literature contains provisions for the admission of women and children. The number of people living there at any one time was in the neighborhood of two to four hundred. A mile or so (1.6 km.) south at Ain Feshkha the remains of other buildings were found, the nature of which is not exactly clear. The fresh water of the spring probably was used for the growing of crops and

Part of the Habakkuk commentary (1 Qp Hab) from Cave 1 at Qumran, c. 30–1 B.C. Courtesy The Shrine of the Book, D. Samuel and Jeane H. Gottesman Center for Biblical Manuscripts, Israel Museum, Jerusalem.

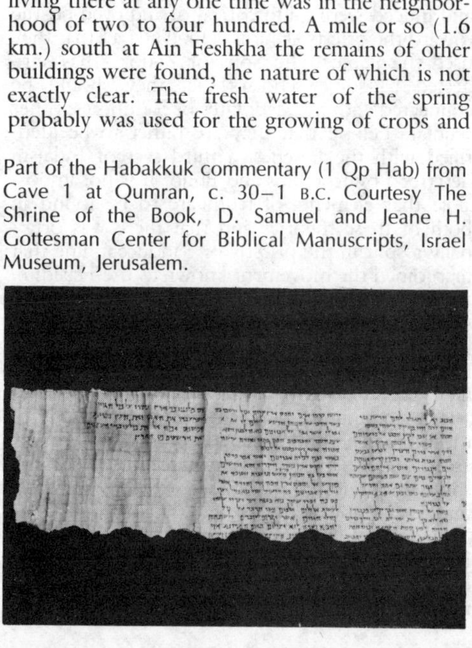

Section of the Thanksgiving Scroll found in one of the caves at Qumran. The complete scroll contains about forty hymns stylistically similar to the Psalms. Courtesy Shrine of the Book, D. Samuel and J. H. Gottesman, Center for Biblical Manuscripts, Israel Museum, Jerusalem.

other needs of the community.

From the sect's literature we know that the people of Qumran were Jews who had split off from the Jerusalem (or main) stream of Judaism, and indeed were quite critical of and even hostile toward the priests at Jerusalem. The fact that they used the name "The Sons of Zadok," has suggested to some scholars that they should be connected with the Zadokites or Sadducees; other scholars believe that they are rather to be identified with the Essenes, a third sect of Judaism described by Josephus and Philo. It is not impossible that elements of truth are to be found in both of these theories and that there was originally a split in the priestly or Sadducean line that first joined the movement known as the Hasidim, the forerunners of the Pharisees, ultimately to split again and form a narrow separatist group, part of which located at Qumran. We must await further discoveries before we attempt to give a final answer to this entire problem.

The community devoted itself to the study of the Bible. The life of the community was largely ascetic, and their practices included ritual bathing, sometimes referred to as baptism. This has been understood by some to be the origin of the baptism of John the Baptist. A study of John's baptism alongside that of the Qumranians shows, however, that the two practices were quite distinct: hence, if John did come from this community (which is not yet proven and may never be), he must have developed important distinctions in his own doctrine and practice of baptism.

Some scholars believe that Zoroastrian elements are to be found in the Qumran writings, particularly with reference to dualism and angelology. The problem is extremely complex. Zoroastrian dualism developed greatly in post-Christian times, and therefore it is precarious to assume that the Zoroastrian beliefs as we know them represent the beliefs a century or two before the time of Christ.

The discoveries of Qumran are important for biblical studies in general. The matter of the canon is not necessarily affected, since the group at Qumran was a schismatic group in the first place; and, moreover, the absence of Esther does not necessarily imply that they rejected this book from the canon. In the matter of the text of the OT, however, the Dead Sea Scrolls are of great importance. The text of the Greek OT (or the Septuagint), as well as the quotations of the OT in the NT, indicate that there were other texts besides the one that has come down to us (the Masoretic Text). The study of the Dead Sea Scrolls makes it clear that at the time of their production, which would be about the time of the production of the Scriptures used by the NT authors, there were at least three texts in existence: one we might call the ancestor of the Masoretic Text; the second was a text closely related to that used by the translators of the Septuagint; the third was a text differing from both of these other texts. The differences are not great and at no point do they involve doctrinal matters; but for careful textual study of the OT it is important that we free ourselves from the notion that the Masoretic Text is the only authentic text. As a matter of fact, the quotations of the OT found in the NT rather imply that it was not the Masoretic Text that was most commonly in use by NT authors. These statements should be qualified by pointing out that the quality of the text varies from book to book in the OT, and that there is much more uniformity in the text of the Pentateuch than in some of the other portions of the Hebrew Bible. The Dead Sea Scrolls have particularly made great contributions to the study of the text of Samuel.

In relation to the NT, the Dead Sea Scrolls are likewise of importance. There are no NT texts in the discoveries at Qumran, obviously, since the earliest book of the NT had been written only very shortly before the destruction of the Qumran community. Moreover, there was no reason why any of the NT writings should have reached Qumran. On the other hand, there are certain references and presuppositions found in the NT, particularly in the preaching of John the Baptist and Jesus Christ and in the writings of Paul and John, that are placed against a background now recognizably similar to that furnished by the documents from Qumran. Thus, for example, the Gnostic background found in certain Pauline writings and formerly thought to be second-century Greek Gnosticism—thus requiring a late

Section of the War Scroll from Qumran, also known as the War of the Sons of Light against the Sons of Darkness. Late first century B.C. Courtesy The Shrine of the Book, D. Samuel and Jeane H. Gottesman Center for Biblical Manuscripts, Israel Museum, Jerusalem.

date for the composition of Colossians—is now recognized as a Jewish Gnosticism of the first century or earlier. Similarly the fourth Gospel is shown to be Palestinian and not Hellenistic.

A great deal has been written concerning the relationship of Jesus Christ to the Qumran community. There is no evidence in the Qumran documents that Jesus was a member of the sect, and nothing in the NT requires such a position. Rather, the outlook of Jesus with reference to the world and particularly toward his own people is diametrically opposite that of Qumran, and it can be safely asserted that he was not a member of that group at any time. He may have had some disciples who had come out of that background, particularly those who were formerly disciples of John the Baptist—though this is far from proven. The attempt to show that the Qumran Teacher of Righteousness was the pattern for the gospel protrayal of Jesus cannot be established on the basis of the Dead Sea Scrolls. The Teacher of Righteousness was a fine young man with high ideals who died untimely; there is, however, no clear statement that he was put to death, certainly no indication that he was crucified or rose from the dead or that the Qumranians expected him to return. The difference between Jesus and the Teacher of Righteousness stands out clearly at several points: the Teacher of Righteousness was never referred to as the Son of God or God Incarnate; his death was not sacrificial in its nature; the sacramental meal (if such it was indeed) was not viewed as a memorial of his death or a pledge of his return in any way connected with the forgiveness of sin. Obviously in the case of Jesus Christ, all of these things are clearly asserted, not once but repeatedly in the NT, and indeed form a necessary basis without which there is no Christian faith.

WSLS

DEAFNESS (See DISEASES)

DEATH (Heb. *māweth*, Gr. *thanatos; nekros*). Both the OT and NT present death as an event belonging to our sinful existence, but also in relation to the living God, Creator, and Redeemer. Death means the end of a human life on earth—man is made from dust and to dust he returns (Gen 3:19). To ponder this may cause a sense of separation from God (e.g., Ps 6:5; 30:9; 88:5); but as death is faced it is recognized that total confidence should be placed in the Lord (Job 19:25–26; Ps 73:23–24; 139:8). The hope of bodily resurrection after death leading into life everlasting, which gradually emerges in the OT (Isa 26:19; Dan 12:2), is given prominence in the NT (e.g., 1 Cor 15).

In the NT, especially in Paul's letters, there is teaching on the cause of death; but this is death understood theologically, not biologically—not merely the end of physical existence on earth, but this together with the absence of a spiritual communion with God. (This understanding of death is also found in the OT—see, e.g., Deut 30:15; Jer 21:8; Ezek 18:21–22, 31–32.) Paul declares that "the wages of sin is death" (Rom 6:23) and "sin entered the world through one man, and death through sin" (5:12); thus he exclaims, "Who will rescue me from this body of death?" (7:24). In similar vein another writer declares that it is the devil who, in this age on this fallen earth, has power over death—until Christ takes it from him (Heb 2:15). Thus it is not surprising that the death of Jesus for the sins of the world is greatly emphasized as is also his victory over death in bodily resurrection. As Representative and Substitute Man, Jesus tastes death for every human being so that those who believe in him and are united to him have passed from death (separation from God) into life (that triumphs over physical death). Thus the Christian can say, "Whether we live or die, we belong to the Lord" (Rom 14:8).

The Book of Revelation contains the expression "the second death" (Rev 20:6, 14; 21:8), and it is defined in symbolic terms as "the fiery lake of burning sulfur" (21:8) and is the opposite of "the crown of life" (2:10–11). It will be experienced by those whose names are not written in the Lamb's Book of Life (20:15) and means everlasting separation from God and his redeemed people.

Bibliography: J. A. Motyer, *After Death,* 1965; M. J. Harris, *Raised Immortal,* 1983. PT

DEBIR (dē'bêr). A city of Judah, once a center of culture for the Canaanite people. Probably it took its name from the pagan temple in which the oracle occupied the holy place (see 1 Kings 6:5, where the word is translated "oracle" in KJV). In Joshua 15:15 it is called Kiriath Sepher, or "town of books." It could have been "town of scribes" (*sōphēr*). In Joshua 15:49 it is called Kiriath Sannah. It was SW of Jerusalem, some ten miles (seventeen km.) west of Hebron and was occupied by the Anakim (Josh 11:21; 15:14). It was captured by Joshua (10:38–39), evidently retaken by the Canaanites, and captured a second time under Caleb, who gave his daughter as reward to its captor, Othniel being the winner (15:13–17). It later became a priestly possession (Josh 21:15; 1 Chron 6:58).

2. A king of Eglon, who made an alliance with the king of Jerusalem against Joshua and was defeated at Gibeon (Josh 10:1–11).

3. A town on the border of Gad near Mahanaim (Josh 13:25–26).

4. A town on the border between Judah and Benjamin (Josh 1:7), on the road between Jerusalem and Jericho.

DEBORAH (dĕb'ō-rȧ, Heb. *devôrâh, bee*). 1. Rebekah's beloved wet nurse (Gen 24:59; 35:8), who accompanied her charge to Palestine—she became attached to Jacob's household and died at great age (cf. 25:20; 35:8) near Bethel. The tree under which she was buried was called "oak of weeping."

2. The fourth and greatest (with Gideon) of Israel's judges, a prophetess, a wife of Lappidoth (Judg 4–5). She resided near the border of Benjamin and Ephraim, probably belonging to the latter tribe, and administered justice "under the Palm of Deborah" (4:5). Like most Hebrew "judges," however, Deborah served primarily as a divinely appointed deliverer and executive leader of Israel.

After the death of Ehud, God's people had lapsed into apostasy, resulting in their subjection to the Canaanite king, Jabin II, of Hazor. Jabin's commander, Sisera, "had nine hundred iron chariots and had cruelly oppressed the Israelites for twenty years" (Judg 4:2–3). This period coincides with the unrest that followed the Hittite collapse and the death of Egypt's Rameses II, the treaties between which had preserved order in Palestine for eighty years (3:30). Rameses's successor, however, was the elderly Merneptah. Despite his claim to have pacified both Canaanites and Israelites, disorder became rampant: "The

The mound of Khirbet Rabud, identified with biblical Debir, in the Judean hills 7½ miles (12 km.) southwest of Hebron. Courtesy B. Brandl.

roads were abandoned . . . and not a shield or spear was seen . . . in Israel" (5:6–8).

Then arose Deborah, "a mother in Israel" (Judg 5:7). Summoning Barak of Naphtali, she prophesied that an offensive from Mount Tabor at the NE limit of Esdraelon would lure Sisera and Jabin's army to annihilation on the plains below (4:6–7). Barak agreed, provided Deborah's inspiring presence should accompany the troops, though Deborah predicted Sisera's death by a woman (4:8–9). Barak and Deborah then scouted Esdraelon around Kedesh; they mustered ten thousand men of Naphtali and Zebulun; and, together with princes of Issachar (5:15), they occupied Tabor (4:12). Deborah also summoned Dan and Asher in the north (cut off by Hazor) and Reuben and Gad in Transjordan, who failed to respond (5:16–17). But Benjamin, Ephraim, and Machir (Manasseh) answered the call (5:14), probably massing at Jenin at the SE edge of Esdraelon. Deborah thus accomplished Israel's first united action since the conquest, 175 years before.

Sisera, meanwhile, advanced from Harosheth Haggoyim in western Esdraelon, forded the Kishon southward to marshal the Canaanite kings from Jokneam, Megiddo, and Taanach (Judg 5:19), and pressed inland along its southern bank. But God fought against Sisera (5:20). A providential storm (cf. 5:4), which turned the plain into a morass, rendered Sisera's chariotry unmaneuverable, and they were cut to pieces by Israel's charging foot soldiers. The routed Canaanites, cornered at the Kishon ford, were then swept away by a flash flood (5:21). Sisera fled alone and was killed by the woman Jael at Kedesh (4:11, 17–22); Jabin was destroyed (4:24); and the land rested forty years (5:31), corresponding to the reign of Rameses III, the last great Pharaoh of Egypt's Twentieth Dynasty. After the battle Deborah and Barak sang Deborah's song of victory (5:2–31; cf. v. 7), the contemporaneous authenticity of which is universally recognized from its archaic language, vivid descriptions, and ringing faith (5:31).

Yet Deborah's record has occasioned manifold criticism against Scripture. 1. Textually, her song's admitted antiquity has been used to discredit the reliability of Scripture's earlier prose narratives. But while poetry does tend to preserve archaic forms, the modernized Hebrew of the Pentateuch need not affect true Mosaic authorship.

2. Confusion, furthermore, is alleged between Joshua 11 and Judges 4–5, as two garbled accounts of one actual battle against Jabin. Yet Joshua's opponent, in 1400 B.C., may have been a predecessor of Jabin; or "Jabin" may have been a hereditary title in Hazor.

3. Contradictions are discovered between the prose and the poem; fewer tribes fighting in chapter 4, and Sisera killed in his sleep. But the poetry intentionally singles out the tribes; and Sisera's sleeping in 5:26 is apparently understood; and his sinking and falling in 5:27 simply describes his subsequent death agonies.

4. Regarding the prose, some surmise that an account of King Jabin in Kedesh Naphtali and an account of King Sisera in Esdraelon were combined into one. Yet the Kedesh of 4:9–11 fits Esdraelon, not Naphtali; and Scripture never designates Sisera "king," only "captain" of Jabin.

5. The biblical date of Deborah is lowered a full century by Albright to 1125 B.C., but only because of his theory that no Philistines (cf. 5:6; 3:31) could reach Palestine before the 1100s; yet see Genesis 21:34; 26:1.

6. Morally, the charge that the scriptural account of Jael is "reprehensible . . . [and] cannot be justified" is made by one modern commentary. But while we question this Gentile's treacherous methods, Deborah's insight into her fearless and unsolicited devotion to God's people renders her "most blessed of women" (Judg 5:24). JBP

DEBT (Heb. *neshî*, Gr. *opheilēma, a sum owed, an obligation*). Under Mosaic Law Jews were not allowed to exact interest (usury) from other Jews (Exod 22:25). Special laws protected the poor against usurers (22:25–27; Deut 24:12–13). After the Exile cruel practices arose in collecting debts (2 Kings 4:1–7; Isa 50:1). A debtor had to make good his obligation, so land that was pledged (mortgaged) could be seized, but had to be restored during the Jubilee year (Lev 25:28). A house so pledged could be sold, or held in perpetuity if not redeemed during a year, unless it was an unwalled town (25:29–30). In NT times the Mosaic code was disregarded. We read of bankers, money-changers, interest, usury (Matt 25:16–27; John 2:13–17). Debtors were often thrown into prison (Matt 18:21–26). Jesus taught compassion toward those in debt (18:23–35). The prayer of Jesus, "forgive us our debts" (6:12), implies guilt from unpaid moral obligations to God. JDF

DECALOGUE (See COMMANDMENTS, TEN)

DECAPOLIS (dē-kăp'ô-lĭs, Gr. *deka, ten* and *polis, city*). A region east of Jordan that had been

Remains of an ancient church at Pella, one of the original ten cities of the Decapolis, located east of the Jordan. In A.D. 66 the Christians, in view of the predictions of Jerusalem's destruction (Mark 13:14), moved from there to Pella. Courtesy Studium Biblicum Franciscanum, Jerusalem.

The Roman ruins of Gerasa (modern Jerash in Jordan), one of the principal cities of the Decapolis, looking northward. In the foreground is shown the south theater and, to its right, the oval forum and colonnaded street. Courtesy Studium Biblicum Franciscanum, Jerusalem.

given to the tribe of Manasseh (Num 32:33–42). A league of ten cities, consisting of Greeks who had come in the wake of Alexander's conquests, was established after the Romans occupied the area (65 B.C.). According to Ptolemy, the number was later increased to eighteen. They had their own coinage, courts, and army. Ruins of temples, theaters, and other buildings tell of the high degree of culture that developed in these cities. Jesus drove the demons into swine near Gadara, one of these cities (Mark 5:1–20), and became popular in the Decapolis (Matt 4:24–25; Mark 7:31–37).

DECISION, VALLEY OF. The place where God will some day gather all nations for judgment (Joel 3:2, 12, 14). It is called the Valley of Jehoshaphat (*Jehovah judges*), and has been identified by some with the Valley of Kidron, but this is only conjecture. Perhaps no particular valley is intended, and the name may be only a symbol of the event.

DECREE. An official ruling or law. It translates various OT words such as *'ĕsār,* "interdict" (Dan 6:7); *gezērāh,* "decision" (4:17); *dāth,* "law" (2:9). In general it refers to any pronouncement of an official nature. In Esther 1:20; Daniel 3:10; Jonah 3:7, the word refers to laws governing special occasions. In Acts 16:4 the Greek *dogma* means rules for Christian living. God's decree is his settled plan and purpose (Ps 2:7–10; Dan 4:24; see also Exod 32:32; Rev 13:8).

DEDAN (dē′dăn). An Arabian people descended directly from Noah (Gen 10:6–7). They established themselves in the region around the NW end of the Persian Gulf. They were also related to Abraham by his concubine Keturah (25:3). Mention of these people occurs frequently in the Chaldean and Assyrian tablets. Israelites of later generations considered them kinsmen. Dedanites were warned by Jeremiah to flee to the back country (Jer 49:7–8). They were an important commercial people. Isaiah called the Dedanites traveling tradesmen (Isa 21:13). Ezekiel wrote of their connection with Tyre (Ezek 27:3, 15, 20), and foretold that the destruction of the Dedanites was to accompany that of the Edomites (25:13).

DEDICATION (Heb. *kādhēsh, to sanctify, hănukkâh, to consecrate*). An expression denoting dedication to holy ends. Often used of the consecration of persons, but usually of the setting apart of things for God's use. Consecration of the tabernacle (Num 7) was an elaborate ceremony, as was that of the temple (1 Kings 8). Among various dedicated things were: the city wall (Neh 12:27), private dwellings (Deut 20:5), the temple treasure (1 Chron 28:12), children (Exod 13:2), people (Exod 19:4; 1 Sam 16:5), and booty of war (2 Sam 8:10–11). The dedication of Nebuchadnezzar's image (Dan 3:2–3), and of Herod's temple (Jos. *Antiq.* 15.11.6) were elaborate occasions.

DEDICATION, FEAST OF. An annual festival of the Jews held throughout the country for eight days, celebrating the restoration of the temple following its desecration at the hands of the Syrians under Antiochus Epiphanes (1 Macc 4:52–59; 2 Macc 10:5), of which Josephus gives a graphic picture (*Antiq.* 12.5.4). The feast came on the twenty-fifth of Kislev (December). Josephus called it the "Feast of Lights." Like the Feast of Tabernacles, it was a time of pageantry and joy. It was at this feast that Jesus delivered the temple discourse recorded in John 10:22ff. JDF

DEEP. A translation of Hebrew and Greek words of varying meaning. Hebrew: *metsûlâh,* "the ocean" (Neh 9:11; Job 41:31; Ps 107:24; Isa 44:27); *metsôlâh,* "torment" (Ps 88:6); *tehôm,* "chaos" (Gen 1:2; 7:11); or "subterranean water" (Gen 49:25; Deut 33:13); *'ămîq,* "mysterious" (Dan 2:22); *'āmōq,* "depth" or "power" (Lev 13:4, 31; Job 11:8). Greek: *bathos,* of "water" or "condition" (Luke 5:4; John 4:11; Acts 20:9; 2 Cor 8:2); *bythos,* "sea" (2 Cor 11:25) or "abyss" (Luke 8:31; Rev 9:1; 11:7).

DEER (See ANIMALS)

DEFILE. There are a number of Hebrew and Greek words that in general mean "to profane, pollute, render unclean." In the OT defilement was physical (Song of Songs 5:3), sexual (Lev 18:20), ethical (Isa 59:3; Ezek 37:23), ceremonial (Lev 11:24, 17:15), and religious (Num 35:33; Jer 3:1). In the NT it is ethical or religious (Mark 7:19; Acts 10:15; Rom 14:20). In the NT the idea of ceremonial or ritual defilement does not exist. In OT times God's purpose in issuing laws regarding ceremonial defilement was clearly an educative one—to impress the Israelites with his holiness and the necessity of their living separate and holy lives.

DEGREE (See ASCENTS)

DEGREES, SONGS OF (See ASCENTS, SONGS OF)

DELAIAH (dē-lā'yȧ, *raised* or *freed by Jehovah*). 1. A descendant of David (1 Chron 3:1, 24).

2. A priest of David's time and leader of the twenty-third course of temple service (1 Chron 24:18).

3. A prince who urged King Jehoiakim not to burn the sacred roll containing the prophecy of Jeremiah (Jer 36:12, 25).

4. Head of a tribe that returned under Zerubbabel from captivity (Ezra 2:60; Neh 7:62).

5. The father of Shemaiah who advised Nehemiah to flee (Neh 6:10).

DELILAH (dē-lī'lȧ, *dainty one*). A Philistine woman from the Valley of Sorek, which extends from near Jerusalem to the Mediterranean. By her seductive wiles she learned the secret of Samson's strength and brought him to his ruin (Judg 16:4–20).

DELUGE (See FLOOD, THE)

DEMAS (dē'măs, Gr. *Dēmas, popular*). A faithful helper of Paul during his imprisonment in Rome (Col 4:14). Paul called him a "fellow worker" (Philem 24). He was probably a citizen of Thessalonica, where he went when he deserted Paul (2 Tim 4:10).

DEMETRIUS (dĕ-mē'trĭ-ŭs, Gr. *Dēmētrios, belonging to Demeter*). 1. The disciple whom John praised in his letter to Gaius (3 John 12).

2. The jeweler of Ephesus who raised a mob against Paul because his preaching had resulted in damage to his lucrative business of making silver images of the goddess Diana (Acts 19:23–27). The name of one Demetrius, a warden of the Ephesian temple, has been found by modern explorers; he probably was the silversmith.

DEMONS (Gr. *daimonia*). Evil spirits (Matt 8:16; Luke 10:17, 20; cf. Matt 17:18 and Mark 9:25). The immaterial and incorporeal nature of both Satan and his demon hosts is graphically set forth by the apostle Paul when he describes the believer's intense conflict as being "not against flesh and blood" but against "rulers," "authorities," "powers of this dark world," and "spiritual forces of evil in the heavenly realms" (Eph 6:12). Again the nonmaterial and incorporeal character of demons is hinted in the expression "The prince of the powers of the air, the spirits that are now at work in the hearts of the sons of disobedience" (2:2 WEYMOUTH).

The apostle John likewise stresses the incorporeality of demons in his reference to *pneumata daimoniōn* in Revelation 16:14. The construction is a genitive of apposition that defines the general term "spirits," which may be either good or bad, in this case bad or "demon-spirits."

As purely spiritual beings or personalities, demons operate above the laws of the natural realm and are invisible and incorporeal. The Bible presents them as such, and thus they are free from the magical rites and exorcistic rigmarole that contaminate ethnic and rabbinic demonology. The Word of God, however, does recognize the miracle whereby natural law may be temporarily transcended and residents of the spirit world glimpsed (2 Kings 2:11; 6:17). On this principle John in apocalyptic vision *saw* the awful last-day eruption of locust-demons from the abyss (Rev 9:1–12), as well as the three hideous frog-like spirits that emanate from the satanic trinity (the dragon, the beast, and the false prophet) in the Tribulation to muster the world's armies to their predestined doom at Armageddon (16:13–16).

As spirit personalities, demons have an intellectual nature through which they possess superhuman knowledge. Plato's etymology of *daimōn* from an adjective meaning "knowledge" or "intel-

Bronze figure of the Assyrian demon Pazuzu, seventh century B.C. Courtesy Réunion des Musées Nationaux.

ligent" points to these as the basic characteristics of demonic nature. Scripture features the shrewdness of demons. They know Jesus (Mark 1:24), bow to him (5:6), describe him as "the Son of the Most High God" (5:7), entreat him (Luke 8:31), obey him (Matt 8:16), corrupt sound doctrine (1 Tim 4:1–5), conceal the truth of Christ's incarnate deity and sole saviorhood (1 John 4:1–3), and comprehend prophecy and their inevitable doom (Matt 8:29).

Because of their superhuman knowledge, demons are consulted by spiritistic mediums, who allow themselves to get under the control of evil spirits for oracular purposes (1 Sam 28:1–25; Acts 16:16), as is seen in both ancient and modern spiritism, erroneously called "spiritualism."

In their moral nature all demons (as fallen angels) are evil and depraved, in distinction to the good spirits (the unfallen angels), who are sinless. The moral depravity of demons is everywhere evidenced in Scripture by the harmful effects they produce in their victims, deranging them mentally, morally, physically, and spiritually, and by the frequent epithet of "unclean," which often describes them (Matt 10:1; Mark 1:27; Luke 4:36; Acts 8:7; Rev 16:13 KJV; NIV renders "evil"). Fleshly uncleanness and base sensual gratification are the result of demon control of the human personality (Luke 8:27). Demons figure in the moral collapse of a people who yield to gross carnality and sexual sin, so rampant in the world today (2 Tim 3:1–9; Rev 9:21–22).

In addition to their superhuman intelligence and moral depravity, demons possess terrible physical strength, imparting it to the human body (Luke 8:29) and binding their victims as with chains and with physical defects and deformities (Luke 13:11–17) such as blindness (Matt 12:22), insanity (8:26–36), dumbness (Matt 9:32–33), and suicidal mania (Mark 9:22).

Demons under the leadership of Satan seek to oppose God's purposes and to hinder man's welfare. So intimately bound up are they with their prince leader that their work and his are identified rather than differentiated. Thus the earthly life of our Lord is said to have consisted in going about "doing good and healing all who were under the power of the devil" (Acts 10:38). Certainly much of this so-called oppression by the devil was the work of the demons, as a cursory examination of the gospel records will show.

Demons are of two classes—those who are free with the earth and the air as their abode (Eph 2:2; 6:11–12; Col 1:13) and those who are imprisoned in the abyss (Luke 8:31; Rev 9:1–11; 20:1–3). The abyss is only the temporary prison house of evil spirits, which must surrender its doleful inhabitants to Gehenna or the "lake of fire" (Matt 25:41), the eternal abode of Satan, demons, and unsaved human beings.

Bibliography: E. Langton, *The Essentials of Demonology,* 1949; G. B. Caird, *Principalities and Powers,* 1956; M. F. Unger, *Demons in the World Today,* 1971; J. Richards, *But Deliver Us From Evil,* 1974. MFU

DENARIUS (See MONEY)

DEPUTY (Heb. *nitstāv,* Gr. *anthypatos*). One appointed to rule under a higher authority, as a regent in place of a king (1 Kings 22:47) or a Roman consul or proconsul (Acts 13:7, 18:12, 19:38). Roman proconsuls were appointed by the Roman senate to govern senatorial provinces, usually for one year. They exercised judicial as well as military power in their province. During their term of office their power was absolute, but when it expired they were accountable for what they had done.

DERBE (dûr'bē, Gr. *Derbē*). A city in the SE corner of Lycaonia in Asia Minor. Paul visited it on the first journey after being stoned at Lystra (Acts 14:20), also on his second tour (16:1), and probably on the third. Gaius, who accompanied Paul to Jerusalem, was from this city (20:4). It was about three miles (five km.) NW of Zasta and forty-five miles (seventy-five km.) south of Iconium.

DESCENT INTO HELL. The familiar Apostles' Creed affirmation that Jesus descended into hell is based chiefly on two references by Peter, one of which (1 Peter 3:19) is more direct than the other (4:6), supported by implications to be taken from two other NT verses (Acts 2:27; Rom 10:7). The term is in harmony also with the language of Paul where he speaks of Christ's descending "to the lower earthly regions" (Eph 4:9), and with John's mention of "the First and the Last" who holds "the keys of death and Hades" (Rev 1:17–18). The lowest regions were recognized as the habitation of the disembodied spirits of the dead, but 1 Peter 4:6 may refer rather to fallen angels (cf. Jude 6).

DESERT. A rendering of a number of Hebrew and Greek words. 1. Hebrew *midbār* and Greek *erēmos,* "a wilderness," yet capable of pasturing flocks (Gen 16:7; 21:20; 1 Sam 17:28; Matt 3:1; Mark 1:13).

A view of the Judean Desert southeast of Jerusalem, on the way to the Dead Sea. Courtesy Zev Radovan.

2. Hebrew *'ărāvâh,* "an arid region." When used with the definite article, it denotes the plain of the Jordan and Dead Sea (2 Sam 2:29; Ezek 47:8).

3. Hebrew *yeshîmôn,* "a waste." With the definite article, it is rendered as a proper name, Jeshimon (Num 21:20).

4. Hebrew *hārbâh,* "waste, desolate place" (Isa 48:21; Ezek 13:4). It must not be thought that the deserts known to the Israelites were merely wastes of sand, like the Sahara. They were mostly latently fertile lands, needing only rain to make them fruitful.

DESERT CREATURE (See ANIMALS)

DESIRE (See PLANTS)

DESIRE OF ALL NATIONS. A phrase occurring only in Haggai 2:7 (KJV). RSV renders "treasures of all nations," NIV "desired of all nations." When the temple was erected in Ezra's time, the prophet was directed to encourage the older men who had seen the more magnificent temple of Solomon and were disappointed with what they now saw, by assuring them that God was with them, and in a little while he would shake the heavens, the earth, the sea, the dry land, and the nations, and "the desire of all nations" would come to fill the house with his glory. Many expositors refer the prophecy to Christ's first advent, and others to the second advent; still others deny a messianic application altogether, translating "the desire of all nations" by "the desirable things of all nations," i.e., their precious gifts (cf. Isa 60:5, 11; 61:6).

DEUEL (dū'ĕl). A Gadite, father of Eliasaph, prince of Gad in the wilderness just after the Exodus from Egypt (Num 1:14; 7:47; 10:20). In Numbers 2:14 most manuscripts of the Masoretic Text read "Reuel."

DEUTERONOMY (dū-têr-ŏn'ō-mē, Gr. *Deuteronomion, second law*). In sight of the Canaan he would not be allowed to enter, Moses gathered the hosts of Israel about him for his farewell addresses. These, set within the historical framework of several brief narrative passages, constitute the Book of Deuteronomy. Since the occasion of the renewal of the covenant made earlier at Sinai, the appropriate documentary pattern for covenant ratification supplied the pattern for Moses' speeches and thus for the book.

The English title is unfortunate, being based on the LXX's mistranslation of the phrase "a copy of this law" (Deut 17:18) as *to deuteronomion touto,* "this second law." The Jewish name *debārîm,* "words," derives from the opening expression, "These are the words Moses spoke" (1:1). This title is well-suited because it focuses attention on a clue to the peculiar literary character of the book; the treaties imposed by ancient imperial lords on their vassals began with such an expression. Deuteronomy is the text of "words" of a suzerainty covenant made by the Lord of heaven through the mediatorship of Moses with the servant people Israel beyond the Jordan.

The claims of Deuteronomy concerning its own authorship are plain. It consists almost entirely of the farewell speeches of Moses addressed to the new generation that had grown to manhood in the wilderness. The speeches are dated in the last month of the forty years of wandering (Deut 1:3), and it is stated that Moses wrote as well as spoke them (31:9, 24; cf. 31:22). Jesus affirmed the Mosaic authorship of the Law, i.e., the Pentateuch (cf. Mark 10:5; 12:26; John 5:46–47; 7:19). Modern orthodox Christian scholars, therefore, join older Jewish and Christian tradition in maintaining the Mosaic authorship of Deuteronomy as well as of the first four books of the Pentateuch. Almost all such scholars recognize that the account of Moses' death (Deut 34) is exceptional and must have been recorded by some other writer; some would attribute to a compiler (perhaps the unknown author of Deut 34) much of the narrative framework of Deuteronomy. Whether or not the biblical testimony allows the latter latitude, even that variety of the conservative position stands in clear opposition to modern negative theories of the origin of Deuteronomy.

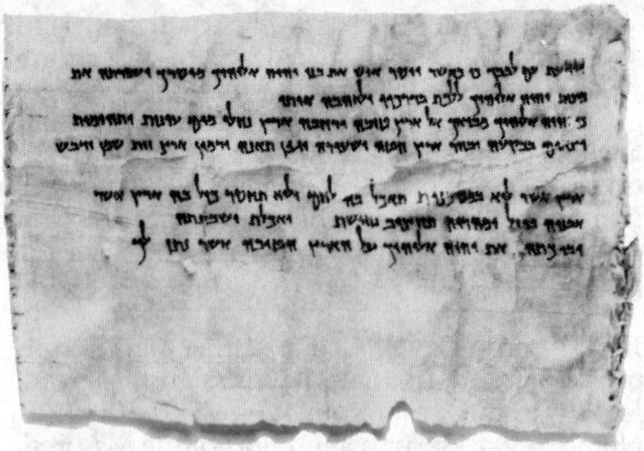

Deuteronomy 8:5–10, part of a leather scroll (c. first century B.C.) found at Qumran. Courtesy Israel Department of Antiquities and Museums.

According to the Development Hypothesis, popular among nineteenth-century negative critics, Deuteronomy was a product of the seventh century B.C. and provided the program for the reform of Josiah (cf. 2 Kings 22:3–23:25), allegedly introducing the concept of a centralized place of worship into Israelite religion at that late date. But unless a wholesale critical rewriting of the historical sources is undertaken, it is obvious that the concept of the central altar was normative during the entire life of Israel in Canaan. Moreover, it is equally apparent that, taken at face value, the covenant stipulations in Deuteronomy are directed to a unified young nation about to enter a program of conquest, not to a diminishing remnant of the divided kingdom. Indeed, many of those stipulations would be completely incongruous in a document produced in the seventh century. That dating, though still dominant, is being increasingly challenged even from the side of negative criticism. While some have suggested a postexilic origin, more have favored a date before Josiah's reign. There is a growing tendency to trace the sources of the deuteronomic legislation back to the early monarchy—if not earlier. The view that these traditions were preserved at a northern cult center, being shaped according to ritual patterns, is widespread. Some would detach Deuteronomy from the Pentateuch and treat Deuteronomy–2 Kings as a unit representing the historical-theological perspective of a distinctive school of thought, the "deuteronomic."

The unity, antiquity, and authenticity of Deuteronomy are evidenced by the conformity of its total structure to the pattern of Near Eastern suzerainty treaties dating from the second millennium B.C. The classic covenantal pattern consisted of the following sections: preamble, historical prologue, stipulations, curses and blessings, invocation of oath deities, directions for deposit of duplicate treaty documents in sanctuaries and periodic proclamation of the treaty to the vassal people.

This substantially is the outline of Deuteronomy:

1. Preamble: Covenant Mediator (1:1–5).
2. Historical Prologue: Covenant History (1:6–4:49).
3. Stipulations: Covenant Life (5–26).
4. Curses and Blessings: Covenant Ratification (27–30).
5. Succession Arrangements: Covenant Continuity (31–34).

In Deuteronomy 1:1–5 the speaker is identified as Moses, as the Lord's representative. Deuteronomy 1:6–4:49 is a rehearsal of God's past covenantal dealings with Israel from Horeb to Moab and serves to awaken reverence and gratitude as motives for renewed consecration. With 5:26 it is made clear that when covenants were renewed the former obligations were repeated and brought up to date. Thus chapters 5–11 review the Decalogue with its primary obligation of fidelity to Yahweh, while chapters 12–26 in considerable measure renew the stipulations of the Book of the Covenant (Exod 21–33) and other Sinaitic legislation, adapting where necessary to the new conditions awaiting Israel in Canaan. In chapters 27–30 directions are first given for the future and final act in this covenant renewal to be conducted by Joshua in Canaan (ch. 27). Moses then pronounces the blessings and curses as reasons for Israel's immediate ratification of the covenant, but also as a prophecy of Israel's future down to its ultimate exile and restoration (chs. 28–30). In chapters 31–34 preparations are made for the continuity of leadership through the succession of Joshua and for the continuing confrontation of Israel with the way of the covenant by periodic reading of the covenant document, which was to be deposited in the sanctuary, and by a prophetic song of covenant witness (chs. 31–32). The book ends with the final blessings and the death of Moses (chs. 33–34).

The similarity between the style of Deuteronomy and that of international suzerainty treaties is well worth noting. Also important is the overall oratorical nature of the book. The style is similar throughout, a fluent prose (chapters 32–33 are poetry) marked by majestic periods, warm eloquence, and the earnest exhortation of the preacher, calling the people to choose whom they would follow.

Deuteronomy is the Bible's full-scale exposition of the covenant concept and demonstrates that, far from being a contract between two parties, God's covenant with his people is a proclamation of his sovereignty and an instrument for binding his elect to himself in a commitment of absolute allegiance.

Israel is confronted with the demands of God's governmental omnipotence, redemptive grace, and consuming jealousy. They are to show their consecration to the Lord by obeying his mandate to establish his kingdom in his land. That involves conquering the land, by which divine judgment would be visited on those who worship alien gods in God's land, and also establishing a community of brotherly love in common service to the Lord within the Promised Land. This covenant calling was not an unconditional license to national privilege and prosperity. By the covenant oath Israel came under both the curses and the blessings that were to be meted out according to God's righteous judgment. The covenant relation called for responsible decision: "This day I call heaven and earth as witnesses against you that I have set before you life and death, blessings and curses. Now choose life, so that you and your children may live and that you may love the LORD your God. . . . For the LORD is your life" (30:19–20).

Bibliography: M. G. Kline, *Treaty of the Great King,* 1963; Anthony Phillips, *Deuteronomy* (CBC), 1973; J. A. Thompson, *Deuteronomy* (TOTC), 1974; P. C. Craigie, *The Book of Deuteronomy* (NIC), 1976; A. D. H. Mayes, *Deuteronomy* (NCB), 1979. MGK

DEVIL (Gr. *diabolos, slanderer*). One of the principal titles of Satan, the archenemy of God and of man. In the NT the word refers to Satan thirty-five times. The KJV uses the same word about sixty times to render the Greek *daimonion,* which the ASV and NIV translate as "demon." Three times the word *diabolos* is used for ill-natured persons, or "slanderers" (1 Tim 3:11; 2 Tim 3:3; Titus 2:3); in the KJV the last two of these passages have "false accusers." The plural word "devils" occurs four times in the OT (KJV)—twice representing *sa'îrim,* which means "he-goats" (Lev 17:7; 2 Chron 11:15), and twice translating *shēdîm,* or "demons" (Deut 32:17; Ps 106:37). (Cf. NIV for these four renderings.) The LXX renders "Satan" in the OT as *diabolos* (i.e., "devil"), but the Vulgate and the English versions rightly have "Satan" as the proper name. According to Numbers 22:22, the angel of the Lord stood in the way as an adversary (Heb. *Satan*) to the mad prophet Balaam, but generally the word is used in the bad sense.

How did Satan originate? "God is love," and God is holy. Because love is his predominating characteristic, God desired to surround his throne with creatures whom he might love and by whom he might be loved. Because of his holiness, these creatures must also be holy; and by logical necessity love and holiness cannot be forced. Compulsory love or holiness could not satisfy the all-wise Creator. Therefore these loving and holy creatures must be able to choose whether "to glorify God and to enjoy Him forever" or to reject him and suffer the consequences. The story of the beginning of sin is nowhere related explicitly in the Word; but certain passages seem to hint so strongly, that the following theory has long been held to explain them.

Apparently God first peopled the universe, or at least our part of it, with a hierarchy of holy angels, of whom one of the highest orders was (or contained) the cherubim. One of them, perhaps the highest of all, was "the anointed cherub that covereth," who was created beautiful and perfect in his ways. This cherub knew that he was beautiful, but pride entered his heart and the first sin in the whole history of eternity occurred. Pride led to self-will (Isa 14:13–14) and self-will to rebellion. This great cherub became the adversary ("Satan") of God and apparently led other angels into rebellion (cf. 2 Peter 2:4; Jude 6). God then created man in his own image (innocent but with the possibility of becoming holy on conditon of obedience). Because Satan already hated God, he hated man whom God loved, and tried to destroy him. It is evident that God could have destroyed Satan at the moment that he became "Satan," but God has tolerated him these many centuries and has used him for testing man until the days of testing will be over. Then Satan and all the other enemies of God will be cast into the "lake of burning sulfur" (Rev 20:10, 15). In the age-long (though not eternal) conflict between good and evil, it sometimes seems as though God has given Satan every advantage. Even so, God's victory is certain.

Among the devil's characterizations are "the god of this age" (2 Cor 4:4), "the ruler of the kingdom of the air" (Eph 2:2), and "the devil and his angels" (Matt 25:41). All these point to his immense power. In Ephesians 6:12 it is stated that our wrestling is "not against flesh and blood, but against the rulers, against the authorities, against the powers of this dark world and against the spiritual forces of evil in the heavenly realms." Our enemy is a murderer and a liar (John 8:44). On the other hand, he is a coward (James 4:7), and he can be defeated (Matt 4:1–11) by "the sword of the Spirit, which is the word of God" (Eph 6:17). His principal method of attack is that of temptation (Matt 4:3), and his leading temptations can be grouped under "the cravings of sinful man, the lust of his eyes and the boasting of what he has and does" (1 John 2:16). These he used effectively on Eve (Gen 3:6) and on her descendants, but ineffectively on our Lord (Matt 4:1–11). He is called "Abaddon" and "Apollyon" (i.e., "Destroyer") in Revelation 9:11, "Beelzebub, the prince of demons" in Matthew 12:24, and "that ancient serpent . . . the accuser of our brothers" in Revelation 12:9. Satan clearly showed his brazen shamelessness when, as recorded in Job 1–2, he came before God with "the angels" (literally, "the sons of God") and misrepresented the character and the purposes of Job. His end and our victory are sure. ABF

DEVOTED THING. That which is set apart to the Lord, and thus belongs no longer to the former owner and may not be used for sacrifice. A sacrifice or offering is a voluntary gift from the owner and can be recalled at any time before the ceremony, but not a devoted thing. Achan's sin at Jericho (Josh 6:17–19) was considered far more serious than mere stealing, for he had taken something devoted. Nations, cities, or men who were "devoted" were to be utterly destroyed: e.g., the Amalekites (1 Sam 15).

DEW. The moisture condensed from the air that forms in drops during a still, cloudless night on the earth or any warm surface. In Syria and most of Palestine these conditions are fulfilled through the cloudless summer and early autumn, and the dew is a great blessing to the fruits of the land. The word (Hebrew and Aramaic *tal*) occurs thirty-five times, almost always with pleasant connotation. Dew is often used in Scripture as a symbol of blessing (Gen 27:28; Mic 5:7) and of refreshment (Deut 32:2; Job 29:19; Ps 133:3; Isa 18:4).

DIADEM (Gr. *diadēma*). Properly an emblem of royalty, but in the OT the Hebrew word is generally rendered "mitre" and refers to the turban of the chief priest (Zech 3:5), a royal diadem (Isa 62:3), or a turban (Job 29:14). In the NT the word *diadem* does not occur in the KJV or NIV, but the Greek *diadēma* is used three times in Revelation (12:3; 13:1; 19:12) as an emblem of absolute power and is to be distinguished from the crown (Gr. *stephanos*) that is used elsewhere in the NT. The *stephanos* was given to victorious athletes, to generals and to the early emperors of Rome, until Diocletian (c. A.D. 284–305) transformed the empire into an Oriental absolutism and adopted the diadem as a symbol of his autocracy. Our Lord too will wear the diadem (Rev 19:12). See also CROWN.

DIAL. Properly, a graduated arc intended to mark the time of day by the shadow of a style or shaft falling on it. In modern times the style is generally (and properly) parallel to the axis of the earth. The word occurs twice in KJV (2 Kings 20:11; Isa 38:8), referring to the "sun-dial of Ahaz," which he may have introduced from Babylonia, where it was used as early as the eighth century B.C. The Hebrew *ma'ălâh* here translated "dial" is generally "degrees" or "steps" (so NIV), from the root meaning "to go up." It appears that the men of Hezekiah's day judged time by the shadow of a pillar as it ascended or descended the steps leading to the palace. The miracle recorded in connection with the dial can be compared with the "long day" in Joshua's time (Josh 10:12–14) and is equally inexplicable on natural grounds.

DIANA (See ARTEMIS)

DIASPORA (See DISPERSION)

DIBLAH (dĭb'lă). Occurs in Ezekiel 6:14; KJV has "Diblath." A few Hebrew manuscripts have "Diblah." It was a town about fifty miles (eighty-three km.) south of Hamath. In Ezekiel this place was the northern limit of God's judgments that were to fall on Palestine for its odious idolatry.

DIBLAIM (dĭb-lā'ĭm). Father-in-law of Hosea the prophet (Hos 1:3).

DIBLATH (See DIBLAH)

DIBON, DIBON GAD (dī'bŏn). 1. A place in the high plain of Moab about ten miles (seventeen km.) east of the Dead Sea. It was one of the stations of Israel in its journey toward the Promised Land (Num 33:45–46). It belonged to Sihon, king of the Amorites (21:21–31), who was conquered by Israel under Moses. The city was rebuilt by the tribe of Gad (32:34). Moses apparently gave it to Reuben (Josh 13–17). It was later taken by Moab under King Mesha, who rebelled against Israel after the death of Ahab 906 B.C. (2 Kings 1:1; 3:4–5). According to 2 Kings 3, Israel badly defeated Mesha at the ensuing battle, but Mesha set up a stele at Dibon (the famous "Moabite Stone") boasting of his defeat of Ahab.

2. A town in Judah, occupied by some of the Jews who returned with Zerubbabel (Neh 11:25).

DIBRI (dĭb'rē). A Danite, whose grandson fought with an Israelite in the camp, cursed, and then was stoned for his blasphemy (Lev 24:11–16).

DIDRACHMA (See MONEY)

DIDYMUS (dĭd'ĭ-mŭs, *a twin*). Surname of Thomas (John 11:16; 20:24; 21:2).

DIKLAH (dĭk'lă). Son of Joktan, and his descendants who probably lived in Arabia (Gen 10:27; 1 Chron 1:21).

DILEAN (dĭl'ē-ăn). A town in the lowlands of Judah (Josh 15:38).

DILL (See PLANTS)

DIMNAH (dĭm'nȧ). A town in Zebulun, given to the Merarite Levites (Josh 21:35). Rimmon (1 Chron 6:77) may be the same place.

DIMON (dī'mŏn). A town in Moab, generally called "Dibon" but in Isaiah 15:9 twice written "Dimon," about four (seven km.) miles north of Aroer.

DIMONAH (dī-mŏn'nȧ). A town in southern Judah (Josh 15:22), probably the same as the "Dibon" of Nehemiah 11:25.

DINAH (dī'nȧ). A daughter of Jacob and Leah (Gen 30:21), the only one mentioned in Scripture. While sightseeing (ch. 34) at the city near which Israel encamped, Shechem the prince violated her, for which crime Levi and Simeon, her brothers, destroyed the city.

DINAITE (dī'nȧ-īt). A member of the tribe of Dinaite whom Ashurbanipal had brought from Assyria to colonize Samaria (cf. 2 Kings 17:24 with Ezra 4:7–10 KJV).

DINHABAH (dĭn'hȧ-bȧ). The city of a king named Bela, the first known king of Edom (Gen 36:32).

DIONYSIUS (dī-ŏnĭsh'i-ŭs). A member of the Areopagus, the Athenian supreme court; mentioned as one of Paul's converts at Athens (Act 17:34).

DIOSCURI (See CASTOR AND POLLUX)

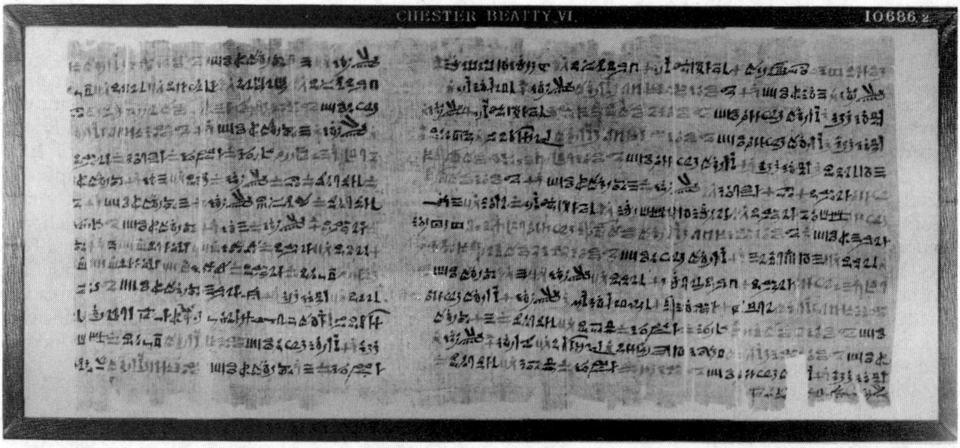

A medical treatise dealing with disorders of the anus and rectum. Forty-one disorders are mentioned, and for each disorder a remedy is prescribed. Among the ingredients prescribed for a seasonal disorder, mentioned at the top of the right-hand column, are dried carob beans, fresh dates, astor oil, honey, and water. Doses of this medicine were to be taken at four-hour intervals. Chester Beatty Medical Papyrus VI, 19th Dynasty (c. 1200 B.C.). Reproduced by courtesy of the Trustees of the British Museum.

DIOTREPHES (dī-ŏt′rĕ-fēz, Gr. *Diotrephēs, nurtured by Zeus*). A leading member, perhaps the bishop, of the church to which Gaius belonged, to whom John wrote his third letter. Few facts are known about him. His domineering attitude made him an obstacle to the progress of the church. The facts, though sad, have been a great blessing and comfort to many a minister who has had to serve a "one-man church." Pride and love of preeminence (Diotrephes loved "to be first" [3 John 9]) are of the devil and are exactly opposite to that unselfish humility that the Holy Spirit demands (Phil 2:3–8).

DISCERNING OF SPIRITS (KJV). The ability that the Holy Spirit gives to some Christians to discern between those who spoke by the Spirit of God and those who were moved by false spirits. The phrase occurs in 1 Corinthians 12:10 as one of the gifts of the Spirit. The NIV renders "distinguishing between spirits."

DISCIPLE (Gr. *mathētēs, a learner*). A pupil of some teacher. The word implies the acceptance in mind and life of the views and practices of the teacher. In the NT it means, in the widest sense, those who accept the teachings of anyone—like the disciples of John the Baptist (Matt 9:14), the Pharisees (22:16), Moses (John 9:28). Usually, however, it refers to the adherents of Jesus. Sometimes it refers to the twelve apostles (e.g., Matt 10:1; 11:1), but more often simply to Christians (Acts 6:1–2, 7; 9:36). Followers of Jesus were not called "Christians" until the founding of the church at Antioch (11:26).

DISCIPLINE (See CHASTISEMENT)

DISEASES. The diseases mentioned in Scripture appear largely to have been well-known entities—probably identical with those that now exist, especially in semitropical climates like that of Palestine. Instead of naming the disease involved, however, the Bible often simply mentions symptoms (e.g., fever, itch, sore).

I. Diseases With Primary Manifestations in Skin. The hygienic measures outlined in Leviticus agree with modern concepts of communicable disease control, especially regarding the availability of running water and the isolation of the patient. Two kinds of skin disease are recognized in Leviticus: (1) those classified as *tsāra'ath* (so-called leprosy in KJV), which were believed to require isolation, and (2) those not requiring isolation. Leviticus 13 gives clear diagnostic distinctions and procedural guides based on the developmental characteristics of the various diseases. Spinka believes that human *tsāra'ath* diseases include leprosy, syphilis, smallpox, boils, scabies, fungus infections (e.g., favus, tinea, actinomycosis), all of which are known to be potentially contagious, and also pemphigus, dermatitis herpetiformis, and skin cancer, which are doubtfully contagious. In addition there are classified as *tsāra'ath* certain mold and fungus growths in houses and on cloth, conditions assuming importance from the standpoint of human allergy, often with manifestations in the form of asthma.

A. **Diseases requiring isolation**

1. **Leprosy,** also known as Hansen's disease, as defined today, is the name for disease processes caused by the microorganism *Mycobacterium leprae*. There are two types: (a) the lepromatous type begins with brownish-red spots on the face, ears, forearms, thighs, and/or buttocks that later become thickened nodules and, losing their skin covering, become ulcers ("sores") with subsequent loss of tissue and then contraction and deformity. It was apparently the lepromatous type that was chiefly in view in the biblical cases of true leprosy. (b) The tuberculoid type is characterized by numbness of an affected area of skin and

deformity such as fingers like claws resulting from paralysis and consequent muscle wasting (atrophy). The advanced forms of leprosy are not described in Leviticus 13, presumably because this chapter is concerned with early diagnosis. Advanced leprosy would be seen only in isolation outside the camp.

2. **Syphilis** is regarded by Spinka as probably the disease called the "botch of Egypt" in Deuteronomy 28:27 (KJV; NIV "boils of Egypt"). It is a disease that from time to time throughout the ages has burst forth in virulent form with high mortality, e.g., Israel in Numbers 25:9. It is chiefly spread by sexual intercourse and is often associated with gonorrhea (cf. *tsāra'ath* associated with "bodily discharge" in Lev 22:4). Starting with a hard ulcer on the private parts, after some weeks raised spots (papular eruption) appear on the torso and extremities (almost never on the face), with no itching. Years later, syphilis of the vital organs such as heart, liver, or brain may become evident, often with fatal outcome. This late type of syphilis seems to be in view in Proverbs 7:22–23 where, referring to a harlot, it says, "He followed her like an ox going to the slaughter . . . till an arrow pierces his liver, like a bird darting into a snare, little knowing it will cost him his life." Syphilis may be present also from birth and give rise to abnormalities such as those listed in Leviticus 21:18ff.

3. **Smallpox,** uncontrolled, is a serious scourge of mankind, though over the last quarter of a century there has been a remarkable decrease of incidence. It consists of red spots that turn rapidly into blisterlike pustules over the entire body, including the face. A. R. Short suggested that Job's so-called boils (Heb. *sheḥîn*) were actually smallpox, since true boils do not occur in such profusion. This Hebrew word—occurring thirteen times in the OT and usually translated "boil(s)"—may indicate several types of diseased skin, today referred to as (a) papule (a raised red spot), (b) vesicle (a small blister containing yellow fluid; called "blain" in KJV and ASV), (c) pustule (a small blister containing pus), (d) boil (a deep, broad inflammation about a hair root resulting in death of the tissues in its center, with pus formation about this core, the pus discharging through an external opening), (e) carbuncle (a large boil with multiple openings), and (f) malignant pustule (anthrax).

4. **Hezekiah's "boil,"** which was almost fatal, may well have been a true boil or carbuncle. Another suggestion is that it was anthrax. The local application of a poultice of figs has been recognized therapy for gumboils in comparatively recent times. Its use by Hezekiah at the command of God's prophet (2 Kings 20:7) has often been cited as divine approval of the utilization of medicinal means of therapy.

5. **Festering boils** (Heb. *shehîn*, "boil breaking forth with blains," Exod 9:9 ASV) has provoked much speculation and two alternative explanations. (a) Both man and beast were infected with virtually the same disease called smallpox in man and cowpox in cattle, the germ of cowpox being originally utilized for vaccination against smallpox. (b) The "terrible plague" (Exod 9:3, ASV "very grievious murrain," the fifth plague) was anthrax of animals, later transmitted to man as malignant pustule (anthrax). Untreated, anthrax is a fatal infectious disease, chiefly of cattle and sheep, characterized by the formation of hard lumps and ulcers and symptoms of collapse. In man without modern therapy it is often fatal.

6. **Scabies** is called "the itch, from which you cannot be cured" (Deut 28:27). It is caused by a tiny insect allied to spiders that burrows under the skin. The itching is intense. Infection is spread to others through close bodily contact. The ancients knew no cure for it, but it readily responds to modern medicines.

B. **Diseases not requiring isolation.**

These are skin diseases (Heb. *gārāv* and *yallepheth*), called "scab," "scall," and "scurvy" in KJV. They probably include what today are known as eczema, psoriasis, and impetigo. Of these only impetigo is very contagious; it is of very superficial character without system manifestations.

Picture of a woman from Punt suffering from glandular-induced obesity drawn from painted relief from the temple of Queen Hatshepsut (c. 1490–1468 B.C.) at Deir el-Bahri. Courtesy Carta, Jerusalem.

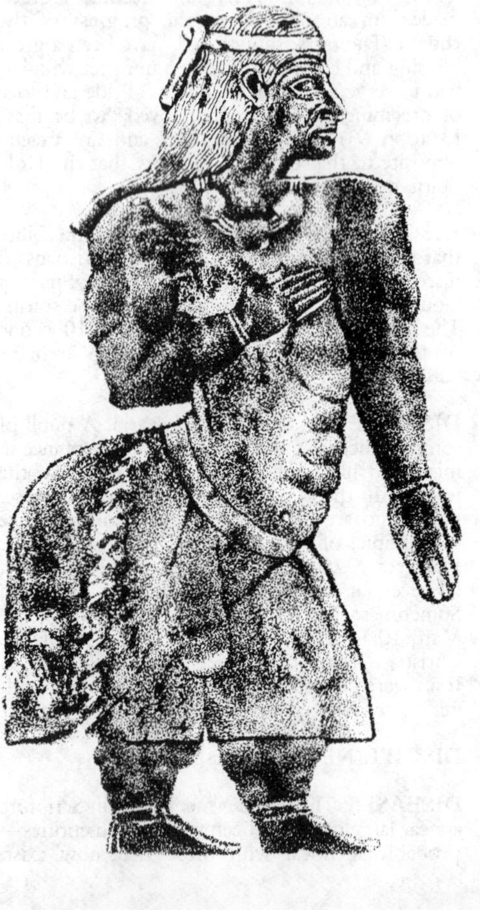

The scurvy of modern medicine, which is cured by eating high vitamin C citrus fruits, obviously is a different disease from the scurvy of KJV. Modern scurvy is not a skin disease and could not occur among the fruit and vegetable-eating Israelites.

Inflamation—which is present in wounds, bruises, and sores—is aggravated by accompanying infection when the skin is broken. "Wounds" are usually due to external violence; when the skin is unbroken they are called "bruises." A "sore," more properly called an ulcer, is a wound in which the skin and the underlying tissues are laid open, almost invariably becoming infected. For example, the Hebrew noun *yabbāl*, which occurs only once in the OT (Lev 22:22), was defined by Gesenius as a "running sore" (see NIV). It has been variously translated as "discharge" (RSV*KC), "INFECTED SORES" (MLB), AND "WEN" (ASV, KJV).

II. Diseases With Primarily Internal Manifestations.

A. **Plague** evidently played a major role in OT history. It begins with fever and chills that are followd by prostration, delirium, headache, vomiting, and diarrhea. Caused by the germ *Pasteurella pestis,* two forms of plague occur: (1) bubonic and (2) pneumonic, both forms being sudden in onset and very serious.

1. **Bubonic plague** apparently broke out among the Philistines when they placed the captured ark of God in an idol temple (1 Sam 5). This disease is transmitted by rats through infected fleas that they carry on their bodies, the fleas transferring to man for livelihood after the rat host dies of the disease. The disease causes the lymph nodes of the groin and armpits to enlarge to the size of walnuts. These enlarged nodes are known as buboes (Heb. *'ŏphālîm*, meaning "mounds")—"emerods" (KJV), "hemorrhoids" (MLB, NASB), "tumors" (NIV, RSV). This outbreak of bubonic plague was attributed to "rats that are destroying the country" (6:5). The LXX more vividly says: "In the midst of the land thereof mice were brought forth, and there was a great and deadly destruction in the city . . . and the land swarmed with mice." The Hebrew word *'akhbār* doubtless refers to rats as well as mice; no other word for rat occurs in the Bible, though rats evidently existed in the land, since archaeologists have found rat skeletons. Worthy of note is the ancient's recognition that plague broke out in dwellings (cf. Ps 91:10), followed lines of communication, and was transmitted by rats.

2. **Pneumonic plague** is transmitted by droplet spray from the mouth. The first case in an epidemic apparently arises from a case of bubonic plague that has been complicated by plague pneumonia. Untreated pneumonic plague is always fatal. The victim goes to bed apparently well and is found dead by morning. It appears very likely that it was either bubonic or pneumonic plague or both that destroyed Sennacherib's army (2 Kings 19:35) when 185,000 men were all "dead bodies" by early morning.

B. **Consumption** (Heb. *shahepheth,* "wasting disease") doubtless included tuberculosis, malaria, typhoid fever, typhus fever, dysentery, chronic diarrhea, and cholera. These diseases are contagious and are sometimes referred to as "pestilences," being especially prevalent under circumstances of impaired nutrition and crowding such as are encountered in the siege of a city, e.g., Deuteronomy 28:21–22; Jeremiah 21:6–7, 9.

1. **Tuberculosis** occurs in acute or chronic form, more commonly the latter. Under the living conditions of OT days, it probably not only attacked the lungs (common form in America today), but also the bones and joints (common in underdeveloped lands today). "Crookback," e.g., extreme hunchback of Leviticus 21:20, may result from tuberculosis of the spinal vertebrae or less commonly from severe back injury. Tuberculosis anywhere in the body may produce fever, defective nutrition with underweight, or discharge of infectious pus (referred to as an "issue" in Leviticus). The disease may produce chronic invalidism or death if the disease process is not arrested.

2. **Typhoid fever** and **typhus fever** both give rise to similar symptoms of steady fever and delirium lasting for a matter of weeks, often fatal. Typhoid fever is transmitted through contamination in water and contamination that flies carry to food and drink. Typhus fever is transmitted to humans by lice that have fed on infected human beings.

3. **Malaria** is believed to be the great fever with which Peter's mother-in-law was stricken. The "fever" (KJV "burning ague") of Leviticus 26:16 and the "extreme burning" (KJV) of Deuteronomy 28:22 were probably malaria. Transmitted by certain species of mosquito, malaria is responsible for much chronic illness. A chill followed by fever often subsides in a few hours only to recur more severely some hours later, continuing intermittently thereafter. Death may follow if the disease is not treated.

4. **Diarrhea, dysentery, and cholera,** caused by microorganisms taken into the body in contaminated food or drink, were doubtless prevalent in OT times. They are characterized by frequent watery bowel movements, often by vomiting and fever, and if protracted, by weakness and prostration. Publius's father's illness (Acts 28:8) is probably rightly translated by NIV as "fever and dysentery," a diarrhea associated with painful spasms of the bowel, ulceration, and infection, either amoebic or bacillary, giving rise to blood and pus in the excreta. As to cholera, it is fatal in half of the cases when modern treatment is not utilized.

III. Diseases Caused by Worms and Snakes.

1. **Intestinal roundworm infection** *(ascariasis)* is a common disease today in lands where sanitation is poor, and is believed to have been responsible for Herod Agrippa I's death (Acts 12:21–23). The pinkish yellow roundworm, *Ascaris lumbricoides,* is about ten to sixteen inches (twenty-six to forty-one cm.) long and one-fifth of an inch (one-half cm.) in diameter. Aggregated worms sometimes form a tight ball with their interlocking bodies so as to obstruct the intestine, producing severe pain and copious vomiting of

worms. If the obstruction is not promptly relieved by surgery, death may ensue. The roundworm does not chew and devour, but feeds on the nutrient fluids in the bowel and may work its way through diseased portions of the bowel as though it had eaten a hole through it. Josephus's account of Herod's death is highly suggestive of the intestinal obstruction produced by these worms.

2. **The Guinea worm,** *Dracunculus medinensis,* formerly called the serpent or dragon worm, has probably been known longer than any other human parasite. It is still found in interior Arabia and the adjacent Red Sea coast. Some regard it as the fiery serpent of Number 21. The infection enters the human body through drinking water containing *Cyclops* (a water insect one-fiftieth of an inch [.05 cm.] long) infected with tiny Guinea worm larvae. In about one year the female worm attains a length of three feet (one m.), being one-fifteenth inch (.17 cm.) in diameter, usually maturing under the skin of the leg or arm. A blister is raised in the skin through which a huge brood of tiny larvae are extruded. This area itches and burns intensely. Death may result from internal complications or severe secondary infection, particularly if the worm is broken. The ancient and modern treatment consists in hastening the extrusion of larvae with cold water followed by gradual extraction of the worm. This is done by winding the worm around a stick of wood without breaking it, taking a turn or two of the stick each day. Complete removal takes about three weeks. The implication is that Moses with his brass model of the Guinea worm twisted around a wooden stick taught the Israelites how to extract the worm.

3. **The snake-bite** that Paul received was doubtless inflicted by a venomous snake of the pit-viper type. Experts today stress that the bite of a venomous snake is not poisonous unless it is accompanied by envenomation, the latter failing to take place if the contents of the poison sac located at the base of the snake's hollow fangs have just previously been completely squeezed out, or if the sac is ineffectively squeezed when the snake strikes. Note that envenomation apparently did not take place in Acts 28:3, 6. The snake, enraged by the fire, probably repeatedly struck at surrounding objects and exhausted all its venom before fastening itself to Paul's hand. This is a frequent occurrence and makes for difficulty in assessing the degree of envenomation and evaluating the efficacy of one snake-bite treatment as compared with another. When envenomation with pit-viper venom takes place, the tissues may quickly swell to three or four times their normal size in the region of the bite.

IV. Diseases of the Eyes.

1. **Epidemic blindness,** described in 2 Kings 6:18, when a whole army was struck with blindness, is not the rarity that some may imagine. The writer, while a missionary in China, was in close contact with an army contingent that was decimated with blindness in a few days. Gonorrhea of the sexual organs had been occurring sporadically. Suddenly this same gonorrhea germ in the midst of unsanitary conditions changed its propensities to produce acute blinding inflammation of the eyes in violent epidemic form, spreading from eye to eye like wildfire, which is one of the recognized potentialities of this germ. Many of the soldiers were permanently blinded. The army troops that had been the most feared for their cruel depredations were suddenly rendered powerless, and the condition of the men was pitiful as one saw them trying to grope their way about, the totally blind being led about by the partially blind.

Limestone relief of a blind harpist, c. 1350 B.C., from the tomb of Paatenemheb near Saqqara. Courtesy Rijksmuseum van Oudheden, Leiden, Netherlands.

2. **Infirmity** (Gal 4:13, NIV "illness") of the apostle Paul, which he described as a "a thorn in my flesh," is considered by many authorities to have been *trachoma,* an infectious eye disease. Early in the disease there is often acute inflammation of the eyelids, which makes the lids feel like sandpaper. This frequently spreads on to the bulb of the eye, especially the cornea, the transparent part of the bulb, which becomes red and inflamed. At this state, infection with other germs is often added. Pus seeps out over the lid margins, forming a tough, crusting scab as it dries and unites with the greasy secretion of the glands of the lid margin.

It is possible that Paul's blindness encountered on the Damascus road was of this type. For three days the secretion was evidently so severe that it formed incrustations at the lid margins such as to glue and mat together the lashes of the lids, so that the eyelids could not be parted. At the end of this time we are told he saw again after scabs (Gr. *lepides,* which Hobart says is the medical term for particles or scaly substance thrown off from the body) fell (the Greek word was also used by Hippocrates, "the falling off of the scab, caused by burning in a medical operation, from the eyelid") from his eyes. Later Paul seemingly was afflicted with chronic trachoma as might well be expected. (a) He failed to recognize the high priest (Acts 23:2–5). (b) The Galatians offered their good eyes for his (Gal 4:13–15). (c) He wrote with "large letters" (6:11). (d) He used a secretary.

Severe chronic trachoma commonly produces scarring of the eyelids with incurving of the cartilage of the eyelid called entropion that makes the lashes poke into and rub back and forth on the cornea, resulting in a frosted appearance, impaired vision, and blindness if unrelieved. This condition comprises a literal thorn in the flesh of the eye. It is often encountered by medical missionaries in underdeveloped lands today. Modern surgery performed on these eyelids produces outcurving of the lids, the offending eyelashes either removed or transplanted. Without surgery the only recourse is to pluck out the lashes one by one, but this affords only transient relief since the lash soon reappears as a sharp, stiff stubble that even more effectively sticks into the cornea like a thorn.

V. Nervous and Mental Diseases.

While terminology and explanations of the causes of emotional and mental diseases have varied greatly through the centuries, there is clear insight in the Scriptures concerning the relationship between the emotional state and physical disease (psychosomatic medicine). This is exemplified in Proverbs 17:22: "A cheerful heart is good medicine, but a crushed spirit dries up the bones." The cheerful heart can resolve excessive emotional tension in a manner superior to that of any tranquilizer. In contrast, some forms of arthritis occur on an emotional basis, the outcome of a "crushed spirit," whereby the bones are seemingly dried of joint lubrication.

Both Elijah and Jonah were men who lapsed into states of extreme nervous exhaustion, often referred to as *neurasthenia,* a common condition amid the tension of modern days. God's method of dealing with this condition as outlined in 1 Kings 19 and in Jonah is a model for modern psychiatric therapy. In the case of Epaphroditus (Phil 2:25–30) there is clear recognition then as today of the role played by *pressure* of work and *anxiety* as he endeavored to accomplish a colossal task unaided by those who should have been his helpers. No doubt there was physical illness superimposed on the emotional tension in his case, often true in modern times as well. In addition, there are mental diseases that are recognized as disease entities just as distinctive as appendicitis or pneumonia. The general term used in KJV for those so afflicted is "lunatic," though formerly this term referred to epilepsy as well as insanity because of a supposed relationship to the phases of the moon. As today, legal responsibility for actions was regarded as tempered by proof of mental incompetence. Hence we find David escaping from Achish by pretending "insanity" (1 Sam 21:13–15). Perhaps he was even imitating some of Saul's actions. The modern psychiatrist would diagnose Saul's state as *manic-depressive insanity,* with its periods of black melancholy, flashes of homicidal violence, and deeply rooted delusion that people were plotting against him, characteristically ending in Saul's suicide. Nebuchadnezzar is considered by Short to have been a victim of paranoia, a delusional form of insanity well known to medical science.

VI. Miscellaneous Medical Disorders and Therapy.

1. The woman's **issue of blood** (NIV "bleeding") of twelve years' duration (Luke 8:43–44) was doubtless excessive menstrual flow, a fairly common condition. In its severe form, it is commonly due to fibroid tumors in the womb encroaching on the lining of the womb. A flow of blood with large clots occurs, depleting the body of blood and causing severe anemia. The modern remedy usually used in this condition is removal of the tumor from the womb or removal of the womb (hysterectomy). This surgery obviously was not available in NT times so that it is quite understandable that all this woman's living was spent on unsuccessful medical care.

2. In connection with Jesus' agony in Gethsemane, we read that "his sweat was like drops of blood falling to the ground" (Luke 22:44). Some have thought that this refers to actual blood-tinged sweat. Short tends to take this point of view despite his confession that this phenomenon must be very rare and is not well authenticated. Rather it seems that the emphasis here is to be put on the word "like," referring to the size and weight of the drops of sweat. It should be recalled that this occurred at night. Jesus' enemies carried lanterns and torches, but evidently he had neither. The color of the sweat was therefore unobservable. In the quiet of the garden the heavy drip of large drops of sweat was probably heard and not seen by the disciples particularly as Jesus came to arouse them from sleep. The word "drops" (Gr. *thromboi*) when used in connection with blood usually means "clots." It may be that the simile here includes that idea; i.e., the drops of sweat sounded like blood clots falling on the ground.

3. Timothy was admonished to shun profane babblings because "their teaching will spread like **gangrene"** (2 Tim 2:17). Gangrene means local death of the tissues. Common forms of gangrene are: (a) gas gangrene, a rapidly fatal type caused by a spreading gas-forming germ in muscles after recent injury; (b) diabetic gangrene, a "dry" gangrene that spreads less rapidly caused by circulatory impairment associated with uncontrolled diabetes; (c) septic gangrene that spreads from the edges of infected ulcers.

4. **Dropsy** (Luke 14:2), in modern medical language called edema, is a condition in which the tissues retain too much fluid. It may be caused by heart disease, kidney disease, or local infection, and may terminate fatally.

5. **Dwarfism** is referred to in Leviticus 21:20. One may have been dwarfed through tuberculosis or injury of the spine, but deficiency of thyroid function such as is found in cretinism is also a likely cause. In the latter condition there is also

usually mental deficiency and this gives added reason for not permitting such an individual to participate in priestly service. Cretinism today responds well to thyroid extract therapy if administered early in life.

6. As to orthopedic conditions, reference is made to the **maimed** (those whose bodies are deprived of a part) and the **halt** (those who limp in walking because of lameness from a disabled lower extremity). The latter may be due to a fracture that has healed in an unfavorable position or it may be due to atrophy (wasting) of the muscles. **Atrophy** of a hand is referred to as a "shriveled" hand in Luke 6:6 (KJV "withered"). Atrophy usually results from palsy or paralysis (synonymous terms), a condition characterized by loss of control of movement of muscles through disease or destruction of nerves or nervous tissue.

7. **Muteness,** i.e., inability to speak, may arise from deafness since one will naturally find it difficult to reproduce unheard sounds. It also may arise from hemorrhage (apoplexy) or thrombosis (clotting) in relation to the blood vessels of one or more of the speech centers of the brain. Often a marked degree of recovery takes place in these instances of so-called stroke as the clotted blood is gradually absorbed from the affected area. Such may have happened to Zacharias (Luke 1:20–22, 64), whereas Nabal (1 Sam 25:36–38) evidently experienced a fatal stroke.

8. Frequent instances of **unspecified sickness** occur throughout the biblical record. Some of the these cases of sickness did not experience divine healing. For example, Paul informs us, "I left Trophimus sick in Miletus" (2 Tim 4:20). Also Paul tells us that three times he prayed for the removal of his thorn in the flesh; he was answered not by removal of his infirmity but by being given more grace (2 Cor 12:8–10). Therefore, the Bible does not teach that all Christians are entitled to divine healing by virtue of being Christians.

James urges that the church elders be called to pray for the sick. He also directs that they "anoint him with oil in the name of the Lord" (James 5:14). The latter has perhaps wrongfully been assumed to refer to a church ritual. Bauer's Greek Lexicon states that the Greek verb *aleiphō,* used for "anointing," commonly referred to rubbing oil on the skin as a household remedy. It would seem to be James's meaning that the sick one is not only to be prayed for but the commonly accepted remedies are also to be applied as an indication of compassionate concern. Jesus' disciples made similar use of the application of oil to the sick (Mark 6:13).

Bibliography: A. R. Short, *The Bible and Modern Medicine,* 1953; W. K. Hobart, *Medical Language of Luke,* 1954; P. B. Beeson and W. McDermott, *Textbook of Medicine,* 1971; S. G. Browne, *Leprosy in the Bible,* 1974; F. MacNutt, *The Power to Heal,* 1977. PEA

It depicts a Syrian, afflicted with paralysis in his right leg, presenting offerings to his god. An Egyptian stele dated c. 1200 B.C. Courtesy The Ny Carlsberg Glyptotek.

DISH. A receptacle for food, generally made of baked clay or else of metal. The "chargers" (NIV "silver plates") of Numbers 7 were large flat dishes of beaten silver, but most of the dishes in Scripture were pottery. Orientals ate from a central platter or dish, generally using a thin piece of bread for a spoon and handling the food quite daintily (Matt 26:23). A special courtesy consisted in picking out a good piece of meat from the central dish and handing it to a guest. See also POTTERY.

DISHAN. The seventh son of Seir, the Horite (Gen 36:21).

DISHON. 1. A chief among the Horites, the name sometimes rendered Dishan (Gen 36:21).

2. A great-grandson of Seir the Horite (Gen 36:25). The two may, however, be the same.

DISPENSATION (Gr. *oikonomia*, law or arrangement of a house). A word that appears in the Bible four times, all of them in the NT (1 Cor 9:17; Eph 1:10; 3:2; Col 1:25). The first, third, and fourth occurrence mean "stewardship," "office," or "commission"—words involving the idea of administration (see NIV for each). In Ephesians 1:10 (KJV), a linguistically difficult passage, the reference is to God's plan of salvation that he is bringing to reality through Christ in the fullness of times (so rendered in NIV). The idea of administration is involved here, too, but it is considered from the divine side. The stewardship, or arrangement, for the redemption of human beings is God's. The NT, therefore, uses the word in a twofold sense: (1) with respect to one in authority, it means an arrangement or plan, and (2) with respect to one under authority, it means a stewardship or administration.

The modern theological use of the term as a "period of time during which man is tested in respect to obedience to some specific revelation of the will of God" (Scofield) is not found in Scripture. Nevertheless, the Scriptures do make a distinction between the way God manifested his grace in what may be called the "Old Covenant" and the way his grace has been manifested since the death of Christ in the "New Covenant," and there are accompanying differences in the requirements that God has for believers. Paul has this in mind when he speaks of God's dispensations in Ephesians and Colossians. In God's redemptive plan the era of law prepared the way, by types and shadows, for the new era of salvation through Christ, which in the NT is regarded as the climax of history (Heb 1:2). SB

DISPERSION (Gr. *diaspora, that which is sown*). The name applied to the Jews living outside of Palestine and maintaining their religious faith among the Gentiles. God had warned the Jews through Moses that dispersion among other nations would be their lot if they departed from the Mosaic Law (Deut 4:27; 28:64–68). These prophecies were largely fulfilled in the two captivities, by Assyria and Babylonia, but there were other captivities by the rulers of Egypt and Syria, and by Pompey, which helped scatter the Israelites. Especially from the time of Alexander the Great, many thousands of Jews emigrated for the purposes of trade and commerce into the neighboring countries, particularly the chief cities. By the time of Christ the dispersion must have been several times the population of Palestine. As early as 525 B.C. there had been a temple of the Lord in Elephantine, in the early years of the Maccabean struggle. The synagogues in every part of the known world helped greatly in the spread of Christianity, for Paul invariably went to them in every city he visited. The word *diaspora* occurs three times in the NT (John 7:35; James 1:1; 1 Peter 1:1). SB

DISTAFF. A stick used to hold the wool or flax fibers used in the process of spinning (Prov 31:19).

DIVES (dī'vēz, Lat. *rich*). A name applied in the Vulgate to the rich man in the parable of the rich man and Lazarus (Luke 16:19–31). It is a translation of the Greek word *plousios.*

DIVINATION (dĭv'ĭ-nā'shŭn). The attempt to obtain secret knowledge, especially of the future, either by inspiration (Acts 16:16) or by the reading and interpreting of certain signs called omens. Those who practice divination assume that the gods or spirits are in possession of secret knowledge desired by men and they can be induced to impart it. Divination was highly developed by all ancient peoples—the Babylonians, Egyptians, Greeks, Romans, etc.—and even the Hebrews practiced it, though it was severely condemned by Moses and the prophets. Deuteronomy 18:10–11 is the classical passage on this subject. There were various modes of divination: by reading omens; dreams, both involuntary and those induced by what is called "incubation," i.e., by sleeping in some sacred place where the god revealed his secrets to the sleeper; the use of the lot; hydromancy or foretelling from the appearance of water; astrology or the determination of the supposed influence of the heavenly bodies on the destiny of a person or nation; rhabdomancy or the use of the divining rod (Hos 4:12; Ezek 8:17); hepatoscopy or divination by an examination of the liver of animals; necromancy or consulting the dead; and the sacrifice of children by burning. SB

DIVORCE (Gr. *apostasion*). A divorce is a means whereby a legal marriage is dissolved publicly and the participants are freed from further obligations of the matrimonial relationship. It is an ancient device that has varied procedurally over the centuries, but in the main it has been instituted on the initiative of the husband.

Among the ancient Sumerians it was easy for a man to divorce his wife, especially if she had failed to produce children. Among the Babylonians, the Code of Hammurabi (eighteenth century B.C.) provided for divorce under certain circumstances but included the return of the dowry to the wife, a situation that would give many men pause for contemplation. Where there was no dowry, the husband was required to make a payment of silver according to a schedule that was organized in terms of the social status of the wife's family. But if the wife had been negligent in her household duties, she could be sent away without payment or simply replaced and demoted to the position of a servant or a slave (Code of Hammurabi, 141, 143). Simpler and more severe was the Middle Assyrian law code, which stated that, with no fault specified, the wife could be divorced and sent away empty-handed (Middle Assyrian Laws, 37). Generally speaking, it was an unusual and, therefore, more complex situation if a wife instituted divorce proceedings. Divorce was discouraged in the fourth century B.C. in Egypt, and later by the Hebrews, through the imposition of a substantial fine on the husband, known as "divorce money."

Although the Old Testament seems to permit divorce for rather general reasons (Deut. 24:1), it was usually either for adultery or childlessness. The bill of divorce could be a simple repudiation, such as, "She is not my wife, and I am not her husband" (Hos 2:2). Although either party could begin the divorce proceedings, it was considered a Gentile custom for the wife to do so (Mark 10:11–12). Because of the strength of the family unit, divorce was in actual fact not very common among the Hebrews. Nevertheless, in the postexilic period, in order for the purity of the Hebrew faith to be maintained, wholesale divorce was required by Ezra of those Jews who had married

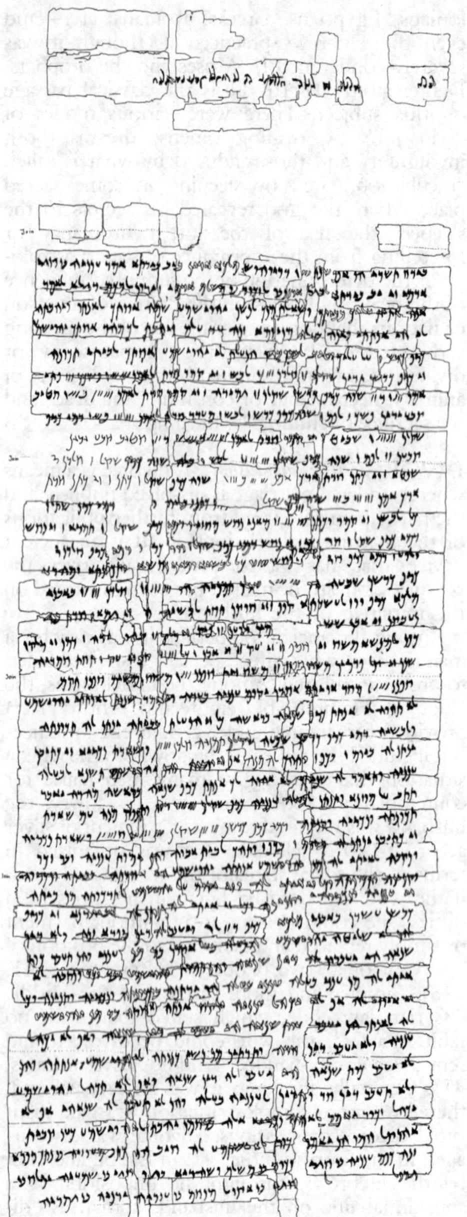

Facsimile of Aramaic marriage document (from Elephantine, c. 420 B.C.) that stipulates the terms in the event of divorce. If the husband seeks the divorce, he must restore to the wife her entire dowery; if the wife seeks the divorce, she receives all her orignial possessions but must pay her husband "divorce money" for the costs of the action. Courtesy Prof. B. Porten and A. Yardeni.

foreign wives in Babylonia (Ezra 9:2; 10:3, 16–17).

A Greek marriage could be dissolved at any time either by mutual consent or by the husband without cause, while the wife could institute divorce proceedings against her husband where she could prove persistent adultery on his part. In the early Roman period there was little divorce, but, typically, Roman law is quite specific about the marriage contract and its dissolution. The contract could be nullified by mutual consent, or for a variety of reasons that might be considered valid by the husband. If the wife proved to be barren, suffered from a chronic illness, or showed evidence of insanity, she could be divorced on those grounds. If she had attempted to kill her husband, or if she had committed adultery, she could also be divorced. In about 17 B.C. a law was passed that made it an offense for a husband to keep a wife known to be an adulteress. By the fourth and fifth centuries A.D. there was some curtailment of the grounds for divorce, but it was still relatively easy for either party to initiate proceedings.

The New Testament forbids divorce, and Jesus asserts that God had, under the Mosaic Law, allowed divorce as a concession to the hardness of the human heart (Matt. 19:8). Even the remarriage of widows was frowned upon by some in the apostolic period, though 1 Timothy 5:14 seems more lenient on this matter. Although in the early church the husband could not technically divorce an adulterous wife, he could separate from her or "put her away." Under such circumstances, neither party could marry without committing adultery. While a wife might emotionally reject a flagrantly unfaithful husband, she was nevertheless expected to show him an example of Christian love and stay with him if he wanted to continue the marriage. There were rare exceptions where a remarriage was permitted, but usually it was only for the pagan partner in a mixed Christian-pagan marriage. In any event the Christian partner was not permitted to remarry (1 Cor 7:10–15).

Bibliography: D. W. Amram, *The Jewish Law of Divorce* (1896); R. H. Charles, *The Teaching of the New Testament on Divorce* (1921); C. W. Johns, *Babylonian and Assyrian Laws, Contracts and Letters* (1904); S. E. Johnson, *Jesus' Teaching on Divorce* (1945); O. J. Baab, *IDB,* 1 (1962): 859; I. H. Marshall in *NIDNTT*, ed. C. Brown, 1:505–7. HWP

DIZAHAB (dī′zȧ-hăb). A place located in the region of Sinai, or possibly farther north where Moses gave his farewell address to the Israelites (Deut 1:1).

DOCTOR (Gr. *didaskalos, teacher*). The word *didaskolos* appears many times in the NT, but is rendered "doctor" by KJV only in Luke 2:46. It is usually rendered "master" or "teacher," whether referring to Jesus or other teachers. It is not to be confused with *iatros* ("physician") in passages such as Matthew 9:12; Mark 5:26; Luke 4:23.

DODAI (dō'dī). David's captain over twenty-four thousand men whose service culminated in the second month of each year (1 Chron 27:4).

DODANIM (See RODANIM)

DODAVAHU (dō'dȧ-vȧ'hū). Father of Eliezer, who prophesied against Jehoshaphat (2 Chron 20:37).

DODO (dō'dō). 1. A man of Issachar, grandfather of the judge Tola (Judg 10:1).

2. A son of Ahohi, and father of Eleazar the second of David's mighty men (2 Sam 23:9).

3. A man of Bethlehem whose son Elhanan was one of David's mighty men (2 Sam 23:24).

DOE (See ANIMALS)

DOEG (dō'ĕg). An Edomite whom Saul had made chief of his herdsmen. When David, fleeing from Saul, came to Nob, Doeg was being "detained before the LORD" for some reason. He reported to Saul about the help Ahimelech the priest gave David (1 Sam 21:1–9). In revenge Saul gathered all the house of Ahimelech and Doeg killed them, eighty-five priests, all the women and children of the village, and even the cattle (1 Sam 22:11–23).

DOG (See ANIMALS)

DONKEY (See ANIMALS)

DOOR (Heb. *pethah, opening, doorway; deleth, door;* Gr. *thyra*). Doors in ancient times moved on pivots turning in sockets above and below, and were frequently double doors. The word is often used in the NT in a figurative sense, many times referring to Christ (John 10:1, 2, 7; NIV "gate"; Rev 3:20); but also to opportunity (Matt 25:10; Acts 14:27; 1 Cor 16:9), and freedom and power (Col 4:3).

DOORKEEPER. Public buildings, temples, and walled cities had special officers to keep the doors; see Psalm 84:10: "I would rather be a doorkeeper," and John 18:17: "The girl at the door." Many English versions use the word "porter" as in 2 Samuel 18:26 (NIV "gatekeeper").

DOPHKAH (dŏf'kȧ). A station of the Israelites, between the Red Sea and Sinai (Num 33:12), about twenty-five miles (forty-two km.) NW of Mount Sinai.

DOR (dôr). A very ancient Canaanite city on the coast of Palestine, about eight miles (thirteen km.) north of Caesarea. Joshua 11:2 and 12:23 read "Naphoth Dor." Its ruler fought against Joshua, but he conquered it (Josh 11:1–8). In Judges 1:27 it is mentioned as one of the towns not occupied by the Israelites. Its place is now occupied by the village of Tantura.

DORCAS (Gr. *Dorkas, gazelle*). An early Christian disciple living at Joppa who was well known for her works of charity. When she died, her friends sent for Peter. He prayed, and she was raised from the dead. As a result, many believed (Acts 9:36–43).

DOTHAN (dō'thăn, Heb. *dōthān,* possibly *two wells*). A place in the boundaries between the tribes of Manasseh and Issachar, about thirteen miles (twenty-two km.) north of Shechem. If the suggestion is right that the name derives from a Chaldaic word meaning "two wells," it adds interest to the story of Joseph's brothers casting him into a dry well-pit there (Gen 37:24). Nearly a millennium after Joseph's experience, the prophet Elisha (2 Kings 6:13) was dwelling at Dothan when the king of Syria tried to capture him with an army, for he had learned that Elisha was able to tell his plans to the king of Israel, Joram. When Elisha's servant informed him that a great host surrounded Dothan, Elisha prayed that the Lord would open his servant's eyes, and the servant saw angelic hosts defending his master. The site, modern Tell Dotha, was excavated by J. P. Free from A.D. 1953 onward. It showed habitation as early as c. 3000 B.C. and in the next millennium was surrounded by a thick wall. At the time of Joseph (2200–1550), it had a well-built fortress and a strong wall. Occupation continued in varying degrees of intensity until the Byzantine period. ABF

DOUGH. The soft mass of moistened flour or meal that after baking becomes bread or cake. The word may apply before the mass has been raised by yeast, as in Exodus 12:34, 39, but generally after raising, as in Jeremiah 7:18 and Hosea 7:4.

DOVE (See BIRDS)

DOWRY (dou'rē). The price paid by the suitor to the parents of the prospective bride; also the portion that the bride brought to her husband. Genesis 30:20; 34:12; Exodus 22:17; and 1 Samuel 18:25 (KJV) illustrate various uses of the word. NIV renders "gift," "bride-price."

DRACHMA (See MONEY)

Remains of the ancient harbor at Dor, a coastal city southwest of Mount Carmel. Courtesy Seffie Ben-Yoseph.

DRAGON. The Hebrew words *tannîm* and *tannîn*, appearing thirteen and fourteen times respectively in the OT, are translated in different passages and versions as "dragon," "jackal," "sea-monster," "serpent," "whale," and "wolf." They were evidently large creatures and of frightening aspect. In the NT, Satan is referred to as a dragon (Rev 12:3, 4, 7, 9, 13, 16, 17; 13:2, 4, 11; 16:13; 20:2).

DRAM (See WEIGHTS AND MEASURES)

DRAWER OF WATER. Bringing water from a well or a spring to the house was generally relegated to the servants and was heavy work (Deut 29:11; Josh 9:23–27). Sometimes the daughters of a household did this chore (Gen 24:19–25).

Bedouin women, probably from Galilee, drawing water by means of lowering buckets tied to ropes. Photo from late nineteenth to early twentieth century. Courtesy University Library, Istanbul.

DREAM. In early patriarchal times, God often appeared in theophany to godly men, but from the time of Jacob onward his revelations were more often in dreams. (Contrast, e.g., the experience of Abraham in Gen 18 with that of Jacob in 28:10–17.) He could reveal his will in dreams today, but the written Word of God and the indwelling Holy Spirit have made dreams of this sort unnecessary for added revelation. (Contrast Num 12:6 with Jude 8.) Often in ancient times God spoke in dreams to persons outside the chosen family, e.g., to Abimelech of Gerar (Gen 20:3), to Laban (31:24), to the butler and baker of Pharaoh (40:8–19), to Pharaoh himself (41:36), then much later to Nebuchadnezzar (Dan 2:1–45; 4:5–33). In these dreams the meaning was clear enough to need no interpretation, as in those of Abimelech and Laban, or else God caused one of his servants to interpret the meaning, as in the latter cases. One principle of interpretation seems quite evident: When the symbol is in the natural realm, the interpretation is in the human realm; e.g., when Joseph dreamed of the sun, moon, and eleven stars bowing to him, his brothers immediately knew the meaning as referring to his father, mother, and brothers (Gen 37:9–11). When the symbol is in the human realm, as in Daniel 7:8, "Eyes like the eyes of a man and a mouth that spoke boastfully," the interpretation is in the spiritual realm. Dreams may lead men astray, but God's Word tells how to deal with this situation (Deut 13:1–3; cf. 1 John 4:1–6). Jeremiah 23:25–32 and other passages speak of lying prophets, perhaps akin to spiritists, and other deceivers of today. Notice the contrast between Mary, to whom God spoke directly through Gabriel (Luke 1:26–35), and Joseph, to whom the angel appeared in a dream (Matt 1:20–24). ABF

DREGS (See LEES)

DRESS. Our knowledge of the kind of clothing worn by the people of biblical times comes from biblical statements; from representations of the people and their clothing found on monuments, reliefs, seals, plaques, and tomb-paintings; and from graves and tomb remains.

All these, coupled with the traditions and usages extant among the present Bedouin Arab tribes, lead us to conclude that at a very early period people learned the art of spinning and weaving cloth of hair, wool, cotton, flax, and eventually silk (Gen 14:23; 31:18–19; 37:3; 38:28; Job 7:6; Ezek 16:10, 13). From these they established certain simple styles that were continued from generation to generation, then carried by Esau and Ishmael and their descendants into Arabia, where the Arab continued them through the centuries—always with a feeling that it was decidedly wrong to change.

When the Arabs overran the larger part of the Bible lands in the sixth century A.D., they returned with these patterns of clothing. In general they have so nearly continued the basic forms that in unspoiled areas much the same garments are worn today as were worn by Jacob of OT times and by Jesus of NT times.

The clothing worn by the Hebrew people of biblical times was graceful, modest, and exceedingly significant. They were considered so much a part of those who wore them that they not only told who and what they were, but were intended as external symbols of the individual's innermost feelings and deepest desires, and his moral urge to represent God aright. With certain kinds of cloth and with astonishingly vivid colors of white, purple, scarlet, blue, yellow, and black, they represented the state of their minds and emotions. When joyful and ready to enter into festive occasions, they donned their clothing of brightest array; and when they mourned or humbled themselves, they put on sackcloth—literally cloth from which sacks were made—which was considered the very poorest kind of dress, and quite indicative of their lowly feelings (1 Kings 20:31–32; Job 16:15; Isa 15:3; Jer 4:8; 6:26; Lam 2:10; Ezek 7:18; Dan 9:3; Joel 1:8).

When a person's heart was torn by grief, the inner emotions were given expression by "rending" or tearing the garments (Mark 14:63; Acts 11:14). To confirm an oath or seal a contract, a man plucked off his shoe and gave it to his neighbor (Ruth 4:8). When Jonathan made a

Officer wearing long dress-like tunic, on Lachish relief of Sennacherib, 701 B.C., from Kuyunjik. Reproduced by courtesy of the Trustees of the British Museum.

covenant with David, he went even farther and gave him his own garments (1 Sam 18:3–4).

There was variety in clothing characterizing the people from the various lands adjacent to Palestine, and within the narrow confines of the country itself there was a distinctive clothing that set off the Canaanite from the Philistine. Among the Hebrews there were slight differences in dress characterizing rank, trade, and profession. Yet it was little less than amazing how similar the general patterns were. The variety for the most part was in quality and in decoration. Clothing was colored, red, brown, yellow, etc., but white was much preferred. It denoted purity, cleanliness, and joy. Princes, priests, and kings of Near Eastern countries wore purple, except on special occasions when they often dressed in white garments. Others sometimes wore white on the occasions of joy and gladness. But in general the people wore darker colors, yet they tended toward the brighter side.

The basic garments used among the men of biblical times seem to have consisted of the *inner-tunic,* the *tunic-coat,* the *girdle,* and the *cloak.* Added to this was the *headdress* and the *shoes* or *sandals.*

1. The **inner-tunic** or undershirt, which in cooler weather the male members of the oriental family wore next to the body, was usually made of a long piece of plain cotton or linen cloth made into a short shirtlike undergarment. At times it was little more than a loincloth in length, and at other times it reached below the knees or even just above the ankles. It was not usually worn when the weather was warm. The KJV refers to such undergarments worn by priests as "breeches" (Exod 28:42).

2. The **tunic-coat,** or *ketonet,* was a close-fitting shirtlike garment that was the most frequently worn garment in the home and on the street. In ancient times it was often of one solid color, but at the present it is more often made of a gaily-colored striped cotton material that among the Arabs is often called "the cloth of seven colors" because of the narrow vertical stripes of green, red, yellow, blue, and white that alternate. It was lined with a white cotton material and worn over the undershirts when the weather was cool, but next to the body when it was warm. This garment usually had long sleeves and extended down to the ankles when worn as a dress coat and was held in place by a girdle. Hard-working men, slaves, and prisoners wore them more abbreviated—sometimes even to their knees and without sleeves—as shown on the Behistun Inscription.

On Sennacherib's Lachish relief (701 B.C.), the elders and important men of the city are shown wearing long dresslike white tunics that came down near the ankles. These garments were pure white, with no decorations, and no girdle to hold them. In this and other reliefs, however, the Hebrews had just been taken captive and were prisoners of war, therefore they could well have been divested of all but their basic garments.

3. The **girdle** was either a cloth or a leather belt, which was worn over the loose coatlike skirt or shirt. The *cloth girdle,* ordinarily worn by village and townspeople, was a square yard of woolen, linen, or even silk cloth first made into a triangle, then folded into a sashlike belt about five to eight inches (thirteen to twenty-one cm.) wide and some thirty-six inches (ninety-two cm.) long. When drawn about the waist and the tapering ends tied in the back, it not only formed a belt but its folds formed a pocket to carry a variety of articles such as nuts, loose change, and other small

objects or treasures. It was worn by both men and women and the model woman of Proverbs 31 made them to sell to the merchants. The girdle is not only a picturesque article of dress but also may indicate the position and office of the wearer. It is sometimes used to signify power and strength (2 Sam 22:40; Isa 11:5; Jer 13:1; Eph 6:14).

The **leather girdle** or belt was from two to six inches (five to fifteen cm.) wide and was often studded with iron, silver, or gold. It was worn by soldiers, by men of the desert, and by countrymen who tended cattle or engaged in the rougher pursuits of life. This type of girdle was sometimes supported by a shoulder strap and provided a means whereby various articles such as a scrip (a small bag or wallet for carrying small articles), sword, dagger, or other valuables could be carried. It was the kind of girdle worn by Elijah (2 Kings 1:8) and by John the Baptist (Matt 3:4). Today the laborer and the poorer classes use rawhide or rope for a girdle; the better classes use woolen or camel's hair sashes of different widths.

The girdle, whether made of cloth or leather, was a very useful article of clothing and often entered into many activities of everyday life. When one was to walk or run or enter into any type of service he "girded himself" for the journey or for the task at hand. Girded loins became a symbol of readiness for service or endeavor. Isaiah said of the Messiah that righteousness should be "his belt and faithfulness the sash around his waist" (Isa 11:5), and Paul spoke of the faithful Christian as having "the belt of truth buckled around your waist" (Eph 6:14).

4. The **cloak, mantle,** or **robe** was a large, loose-fitting garment, which for warmth and appearance was worn over all other articles of clothing as a completion of male attire. It was distinguished by its greater size and by the absence of the girdle. It existed in two varieties, which were usually known as the "me-il," and the "simlah."

The **me-il** was a long, loose-sleeved robe or public dress that was worn chiefly by men of official position and by ministers, educators, and the wealthy. It was the robe of the professions (1 Sam 2:18–19), a dress of dignity, culture, and distinction—the mark of high rank and station (24:11; 1 Chron 15:27). It was rich in appearance and could well have been the "coat of many colors" that Jacob gave to Joseph, or the like of which Hannah made and brought to Samuel from year to year as he ministered before the Lord at Shiloh (1 Sam 2:18–19). In its finest form, it must have been the high priest's robe of the ephod with its fringe of bells and pomegranates swaying and swinging and tinkling as he walked (Exod 28:31–38). It is generally understood that there were two kinds of ephods—one with its rich and elaborate insignia and paraphernalia peculiar to the office of high priest, and the other a more simple "linen ephod" worn by leaders of distinction other than the high priests (2 Sam 6:14).

The **simlah** was the large, loose-fitting, sleeveless cloak or mantle that, in general pattern, corresponds to the long and flowing garment that the Arab shepherd and peasant call an *abba* or *abayeh*. They wear it by day and wrap themselves in it by night, therefore it was not be to taken in pledge unless it was returned by sundown (Exod 22:26).

Limestone bas-relief from tomb of Horemheb picturing an Egyptian attendant wearing a pleated apron, leading a Syrian captive dressed in a long, sleeved robe extending to his ankles and encircled at his waist by a heavy girdle. From Memphis, second half of the fourteenth century B.C. Courtesy Rijksmuseum van Oudheden, Leiden, Netherlands.

These simple yet picturesque garments were usually made of wool, goat hair, or camel hair. Men of distinction often wore more colorful cloaks called "robes," which were made of linen, wool, velvet, or silk, elaborately bordered and lined with fur.

This long outer garment or topcoat was, in all probability, the "mantle" worn by Elijah and Elisha (2 Kings 2:8–14). It was the camel-hair garment worn by John the Baptist (Matt 3:4). It is frequently made of alternate strips of white, red, and brown, or is formed by sewing together two lengths of cloth so that the only seams required were those along the top of the shoulders. In unusual cases, however, the cloak is woven of one broad width, with no seam. Many believe that this was the garment Christ wore, and over which, at the Crucifixion, the Roman soldiers "cast lots" rather than tearing it, for it was "seamless, woven in one piece from top to bottom" (John 19:23–24).

On Shalmaneser's Black Obelisk (ninth century B.C.), the artist shows Israelite men wearing long cloaks or mantles with elaborate fringed borders both on the cutaway fronts and along the bottom. These were in keeping with the Mosaic injunction to make blue tassels on the borders of their garments to remind them to keep all the commandments and to be holy before God (Num 15:38–40; Deut 22:12).

The word "skirt," found several times in the KJV, usually refers to an article of male, not female, clothing, and has a number of meanings: "corner" (Ruth 3:9; 1 Sam 24:4ff.), "hem" (Exod 28:33), "collar" (Ps 133:2).

The **headdress** was worn chiefly as a protection against the sun and as a finish to a completed costume. It varied from time to time according to rank, sex, and nationality. In the main, however, there were three known types that were worn by the male members of the Hebrew and surrounding nations: the *cap,* the *turban,* and the *head-scarf.*

The ordinary brimless cotton or woolen cap, corresponding somewhat to our skullcap, was sometimes worn by men of poorer circumstances. Captives are seen wearing these on the Behistun Rock. The turban (hood, KJV; tiara, NIV—Isa 3:23) was made of thick linen material and formed by winding a scarf or sash about the head in artistic style and neatly concealing the ends. That of the high priest was called a *mitre* (Exod 28 KJV).

The head-scarf, known among the Arabs as the *kaffiyeh,* is usually made up of a square yard of white or colored cotton, wool, or silk cloth folded into a triangle and draped about the head. The apex of the triangle falls directly down the back, forming a V point, while the tapering ends are thrown back over the shoulders, or in cold weather they are wrapped about the neck. This graceful head-scarf is held in position by an *ajhal,* which is made of several soft woolen or silk twists bound by ornamental threads, and worn in coils about the head. An ornamental tassel falls to the side or down the back. When Ben-Hadad's shattered Syrian army realized the serious loss it had suffered, some of his men suggested to him that they go to the king of Israel "wearing sackcloth around their waists and ropes around their heads" (1 Kings 20:32), hoping that he would spare their lives.

Shoes and **sandals** were considered the lowliest articles that went to make up the wearing apparel of the people of Bible lands (Mark 1:7). In the Bible and in secular sources, they were mentioned at a very early period and are seen in considerable variety on the Egyptian, Babylonian, Assyrian, and Persian monuments. A pair of terra-cotta shoes, of the modern snowshoe variety, were found in an Athenian grave of about 900 B.C.

Shoes were of soft leather, while sandals were of a harder leather and were worn for rougher wear. According to some authorities, the sole was of wood, cane, or sometimes bark of the palm tree and was fastened to the leather by nails. They were tied about the feet with "thongs" (NIV), or "shoe-latchets" (Gen 14:23 KJV). It was customary to have two pairs, especially on a journey.

Shoes were usually removed at the doorway before entering a home, on approaching God (Exod 3:5), and during mourning (2 Sam 15:30). Property rights were secured by the seller pulling off his shoe and giving it to the purchaser (Ruth 4:7). The "clouts" referred to in Joshua 9:5 KJV are patched sandals (so NIV).

Women's Dress. Among the Hebrews neither sex was permitted by Mosaic law to wear the same form of clothing as was used by the other (Deut 22:5). A few articles of female clothing carried somewhat the same name and basic pattern, yet there was always sufficient difference in emboss-

Diorite statue from Ur, Abraham's city of origin, c. 2080 B.C., of the goddess Ningal, who is wearing a long flounced garment, over which is a short cape of the same material. Courtesy The University Museum, University of Pennsylvania.

ing, embroidery, and needlework so that in appearance the line of demarcation between men and women could be readily detected.

The women wore long garments reaching almost to the feet, with a girdle of silk or wool, many times having all the colors of the rainbow. Often such a garment would have a fringe hanging from the waist nearly to the ankles.

The ladies' headdress, for example, usually included some kind of a *kaffiyeh* or cloth for covering the head, yet the material that was in that covering was of different quality, kind, or color from that worn by the men. Also, it was often pinned over some kind of a cap made of stiff material and set with pearls, silver, gold, or spangled ornaments common to that day. If a woman was married, these or other more significant coins covered the entire front of her cap and constituted her dowry. Her undergarments would be made of cotton, linen, or silk, as might befit her wealth or station in life. She would probably wear a long gown with long, pointed sleeves. Over this was a small rather tightly fitted jacket or "petticoat"—meaning little coat. The small jacket was made of "scarlet" or other good material and was a thing of exquisite beauty because it was covered with "tapestry" or fine needlework, wrought with multicolored threads. A woman of even moderate circumstances could have beautiful clothing, for it was "the fruit of her own hands."

In the OT many articles of women's clothing are mentioned that cannot be exactly identified. Ezekiel 13:18, 21 KJV refers to a "kerchief." The Hebrew word is *mispahah,* a head-covering or veil (so NIV) of some sort, the exact nature of which is unknown. Isaiah 3:16–24 KJV speaks of "mufflers," probably two-piece veils (so NIV), one part covering the face below the eyes, the other the head, down over the neck; "wimples," is rendered "cloaks" in NIV; "stomachers" in English means that part of a woman's dress that covers the breast and the pit of the stomach—usually much ornamented—but the meaning of the Hebrew is unknown (NIV renders "fine clothing"); also "crisping pins" (NIV "purses"), and "cauls" (NIV "headbands"), cannot be certainly identified.

Women often added to their adornment by an elaborate braiding of the hair. Peter found it necessary to warn Christian women against relying on such adorning to make themselves attractive (1 Peter 3:3). In the OT there are a number of references to painting the eyes in order to enhance their beauty, but it is always spoken of as a showy and somewhat vulgar device, unworthy of good women. Jezebel painted her eyes (2 Kings 9:30).

In ancient times women especially were much given to various kinds of ornaments. Earrings and nose-rings were especially common. On account of their drop-like shape, earrings are called "chains" (Isa 3:19 KJV) and "pendants" (Judg 8:26). Men also wore such earrings (Gen 35:4; Judg 8:24). The nose-ring or nose-jewel made necessary the piercing of the nostrils. Rings were worn by both men and women. All ancient Israelites wore signet rings (Gen 38:18 KJV; NIV "seal"). Rings were often worn on the toes, anklets (spangles) on the ankles (Isa 3:18), bracelets on the arms and wrists (Gen 24:22; Ezek 16:11).

Beginning about the second century B.C., all male Jews were expected to wear at morning prayers, except on Sabbaths and festivals, two *phylacteries,* one on the forehead, called a *frontlet,* the other on the left arm. They consisted of small leather cases containing four passages of Scripture from the OT: Exodus 13:1–10, 11–16; Deuteronomy 6:4–9; 11:13–21. GFO and SB

DRINK. The most common beverage of the Jews was water. This was procured chiefly in two ways: by means of cisterns, which were possessed by every well-appointed house (2 Sam 17:18; Jer 38:6), and by means of wells, which were rare and were usually the possession of a clan or community.

Wine was also widely used, both in the form of new wine, called must, and fermented wine. In the heat of harvest, frequent use was made of a sour drink mixture of water and wine, and of a strong drink, called *shekhar*. How the latter was prepared is unknown. Wine was sometimes spiced to improve its taste. Wine was also made from pomegranates and possibly also from ripe dates and barley. The Mishna also speaks of honey-wine and cider.

Next to bread and vegetables, the most important food was milk, both of larger and smaller cattle, especially goat's milk. This was usually kept in skins. Because of the hot climate, fresh milk soon became sour, but it was very effective for quenching thirst. SB

DRINK OFFERING (See SACRIFICE AND OFFERINGS)

DROMEDARY (See ANIMALS)

DROPSY (See DISEASES)

DROSS. The refuse in impure metals that is generally separated by melting, when the dross rises to the top and may be skimmed off. It is used figuratively of what is worthless (Ps 119:119; Isa 1:22, 25; Ezek 22:18–19).

DRUNKENNESS. The Scriptures show that drunkenness was one of the major vices of antiquity, even among the Hebrews. Well-known cases of intoxication are Noah (Gen 9:21); Lot (19:33, 35); Nabal (1 Sam 25:36); Uriah (2 Sam 11:13); Ammon (13:28); Elah, king of Israel (1 Kings 16:9); and Ben-Hadad, king of Syria (20:16). The prophets often denounce drunkenness as a great social evil of the wealthy. Even the women were guilty (Amos 4:1). The symptoms and effects of strong drink are vividly pictured in the Bible (Job 12:25; Ps 107:27; Isa 28:7; Hos 4:11). While the writers of Scripture condemn intemperance in the strongest terms, they do not prescribe total abstinence as a formal and universal rule. Nevertheless, the principles laid down point in that direction. In ancient times the poor could not afford to drink to excess. The cheapening of alcoholic drinks has made drunkenness a much greater social problem in modern times. The following passages state principles pointing to voluntary abstinence from all intoxicants: Matthew 16:24–25; Mark 9:42–43; Romans 14:13–21; 1 Corinthians 8:8–13; Ephesians 5:18. Drunkenness is sometimes used figuratively (Isa 29:9). SB

DRUSILLA (drū-sĭl'ȧ, Gr. *Drousilla*). The youngest of the three daughters of Herod Agrippa I, her sisters being Bernice and Mariamme. At the age of fourteen she married Azizus, king of Emesa, but left him for Felix, procurator of Judea, who was captivated by her beauty and employed a Cyprian sorcerer to gain her for his wife. They had one son, Agrippa, who died in an eruption of Mount Vesuvius. When Paul unsparingly preached before Felix and Drusilla of righteousness, temperance, and judgment, Felix trembled (Acts 24:24–25). See also HEROD.

DUKE (Heb. *'allûph* and *nāsîkh*). These Hebrew words are sometimes rendered "duke" (especially when used of the leaders of the Edomites), "princes," "principal men," and "governor" in the KJV. In general, they mean a leader of a clan or a tribal chief. NIV usually translates "chief." See Genesis 36:15–16; Exodus 15:15; Joshua 13:21; 1 Chronicles 1:51–52.

DUMAH (dū'mȧ, Heb. *dûmâh, silence*). 1. One of the twelve sons of Ishmael (Gen 25:14–16) and apparently head of one of the twelve tribes of Ishmaelites in Arabia.

2. A place unknown but connected with Seir or Edom (Isa 21:11–12). The designation may be symbolic, applying to all Edom and indicating its coming destruction (cf. Obad 15–16).

3. A village in southern Judah and associated with Hebron in Joshua 15:52–54.

DUMBNESS (See DISEASES)

DUNG. The excrement of man or beast. NIV usually renders "offal," "refuse," "rubbish." In several of the offerings, under the Levitical priesthood the blood and the fat and the flesh were used, but the skins and the dung were discarded or burnt outside the camp (Exod 29:14; Lev 8:17 KJV; NIV "offal"). The ultimate disgrace was to have one's carcass treated as dung (2 Kings 9:37 KJV; NIV "refuse"). Dry dung was (and is) often used as fuel (see Ezek 4:12–15). Paul counted his natural advantages as dung (NIV "rubbish") compared with his blessings in Christ (Phil 3:8).

DUNG GATE. One of the eleven gates of Jerusalem in Nehemiah's time (see Neh 2:13; 3:13–14; 12:31). It was located near the SW corner of the wall and was used for the disposal of rubbish, garbage, and dung. It led out to the Valley of Hinnom.

DURA (dū'rȧ). A plain in the province of Babylon where Nebuchadnezzar set up his great image of gold to be worshiped (Dan 3:1).

DUST (Heb. *'avaq, dust; 'aphar, dust;* Gr. *koniortos, dust; chous, clay, earth*). In the warm and dry climate of the ancient Near East, dust was a reality that people had to face. Thus, such practices began as washing the feet on entering a home (John 13:1–17). Dust, however, also had a symbolic significance for Israel and the early church. (1) Throwing dust on the head as a sign of mourning or sorrow or repentance was common (Job 2:12; Rev 18:19). (2) Shaking off dust from the feet was a sign of having no further responsibility for the area where the dust was picked up, thus leaving that area to God's judgment (Matt 10:14; Luke 9:5; 10:11; Acts 13:51). (3) Paul described the first man (Adam) as a "man . . . of the dust" (Gr. *choikos*) in 1 Corinthians 15:47–49, meaning that he was created from the physical elements found in the earth (into which God breathed life—see Gen 1–2). Adam is to be contrasted with Jesus, the second Adam, for while he took his humanity from Mary he existed before his incarnation as the eternal Son of God. In referring to human beings as made of dust Paul was echoing a strong theme of the OT where man is said to be made from dust and to return to dust (Gen 2:7; 3:19; Job 4:19; 17:17).

DWARF (See DISEASES)

DYERS, DYEING (See OCCUPATIONS AND PROFESSIONS)

DYSENTERY (See DISEASES)

E

EAGLE (See BIRDS)

EAR (Heb. *'ōzen,* Gr. *ous, ōtion, the physical organ of hearing*). In biblical times people spoke to each other's ears; instead of listening they "inclined their ears." When they prayed, God "bowed down his ear" to hear them. The ear had a significant part in some Jewish ceremonies. It was sanctified by blood in the consecration of Aaron and his sons to the priesthood (Exod 29:20; Lev 8:24) and at the cleansing of a leper (Lev 14:14). The piercing of the ear of a slave denoted permanent servitude (Exod 21:6; Deut 15:17).

EARNEST (Gr. *arrabōn*). A legal term in English law denoting the payment of a sum of money to make a contract binding, guaranteeing a further payment to fulfill the contract. Thus the significance of the apostle Paul's use of this word in regard to the Holy Spirit in three passages may be understood (2 Cor 1:22; 5:5; Eph 1:14). The NIV renders "seal" in the first passage, "deposit" in the two others. The Holy Spirit's gift to believers is the assurance that their redemption will be fully carried out.

EARRING (Heb. *nezem, 'āghîl, hoop*). The ancient Hebrews had no specific word for earrings; these jewels were just rings or hoops made of gold (though sometimes the metal is not specified). They were worn by men and women either on the nose or on the ears: a nose-ring in some passages (Gen 24:47; Isa 3:21; Ezek 16:12) and an earring in others (Gen 35:4; Exod 32:2–3; Ezek 16:12). In the rest of the passages where such rings or hoops are mentioned, they may be either nose-rings or earrings (Exod 35:22; Num 31:50; Judg 8:24–26; Job 42:11; Prov 11:22; 25:12; Hos 2:13). When worn as earrings the ring was passed through a hole pierced in the lobe of the ear. Probably pendants were suspended from them. In Isaiah 3:20 the Hebrew term *lachash* is translated "amulets" (NASB, RSV), "charms" (MLB, NIV), and "earrings" (KJV).

EARTH (Heb. *'ădhāmâh, ground; 'erets, earth;* Gr. *gē, earth; oikoumenē, inhabited earth; kosmos, orderly arrangement*). The Hebrew word *'ădhāmâh* most commonly means the tilled reddish soil of Palestine. But it is also used to denote a piece of real estate (Gen 47:18ff.), earth as a material substance (2:7), a territory (28:15), the whole earth (Gen 12:3; Deut 14:2).

The word *'erets* denotes commonly the earth as opposed to the sky (Gen 1:1; Josh 2:11); also very frequently it means "land" in the sense of a country (Gen 13:10; 45:18). In the NT, *gē* means "ground," arable and otherwise (Matt 5:18; John 8:6); "the earth" as opposed to the heavens (Matt 6:10; Acts 2:19); "territory" or "region" (Luke 4:25; John 3:22). *Oikoumēnē* carries the meaning of the inhabited earth or the "world" (Matt 24:14; Luke 4:5), the Roman Empire (Luke 2:1), all the inhabitants of the earth (Acts 17:6; Rev 3:10). *Kosmos* in a derived sense is used to denote the earth, though it is always translated "world" in our Bibles. It has more to do with the inhabitants of the earth than with the actual planet.

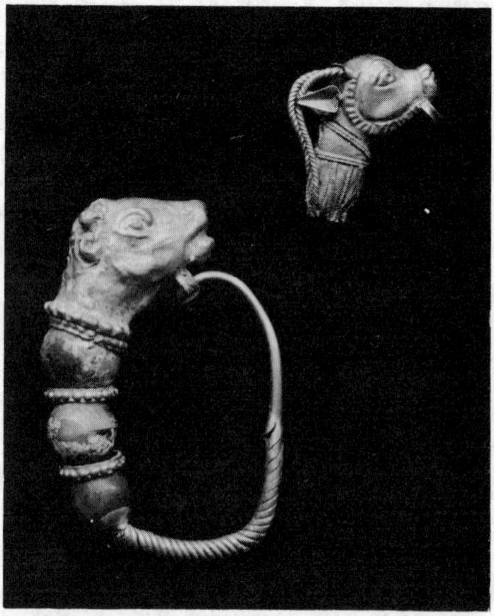

Gold earrings in shape of ram's head, from Ashdod (4th century B.C.). Courtesy Israel Museum, Jerusalem. Photo David Harris.

Sometimes it is difficult to tell whether the earth or the land is meant, particularly in the prophetic books. For example, in Isaiah 24:1, 3–5, the word "earth" may mean "land" instead. The ancient Hebrew had no idea of the shape or size of the earth, or that it was a planet. The earth was simply the area where men lived, moved, and had their being. But Job 26:7 is a scientifically correct statement, "He spreads out the northern skies over empty space; he suspends the earth over nothing."

EARTHQUAKE (Heb. *ra'ash, quaking;* Gr. *seismos, earthquake*). There are four actual earthquakes recorded in Scripture: the one that occurred at Mount Horeb for Elijah's benefit (1 Kings 19:11); the one referred to by Amos (1:1) and Zechariah (14:5) as occurring in the reign of Uzziah, king of Judah; the one that happened at the resurrection of Christ (Matt 28:2); and the one that freed Paul and Silas from prison (Acts 16:26). An earthquake is mentioned in Isaiah 29:6 as a form of judgment from the Lord on the enemies of his people, and this is in line with the steady biblical testimony that all natural phenomena—earthquake, wind, storm, rain, hail, and the rest—are under divine sovereign control and are part of his armory for ruling the world in righteousness.

EAST (Heb. *qedem* and other forms of this root, *front, aforetime, east; mizrâh, place of the sunrise, east;* Gr. *anatolē, rising, east*). East was a significant direction for the Hebrews. The gate of the tabernacle was on the east side (Exod 38:13–14). In the wilderness Moses and Aaron camped on the east side of the tabernacle, and this area was barred to strangers (Num 3:38). Judah camped on the east side of the camp (2:3). This same tribe was first in the line of march (10:14). Many scholars think the chief entrance of Solomon's temple was on the east side. In Herod's temple "the temple gate called Beautiful" (Acts 3:2) was the east gate. Ezekiel saw the glory of the Lord leave the doomed temple by the east gate (Ezek 10:19; 11:23). In this prophet's description of the Lord's temple, Ezekiel saw the glory of the Lord coming from the east and entering the temple by the east gate (43:2, 4).

The phrase "people of the East" occurs often in the OT. It refers to inhabitants of the lands east of Palestine on the edge of the desert. Job was such a one (Job 1:3). The Magi came from the east and said they had seen the star of the King of the Jews in the east (Matt 2:1–2). CEH

EASTER. The word "Easter" occurs only once in the Bible (Acts 12:4), the only time the KJV translates *pascha* (usually "Passover") in this way. It is the day on which most Christians celebrate the resurrection of Jesus Christ.

The annual Easter procession along the Mount of Olives in Jerusalem, marking Jesus' resurrection. Courtesy Zev Radovan.

There is no celebration of the Resurrection in the NT. The Jewish Christians linked it with the Passover, and so observed it on the fourteenth day of Nisan regardless of the day of the week. But Gentile believers celebrated the Resurrection on the Lord's Day, Sunday. This difference was settled by the Council of Nicea in A.D. 325, which ruled that Easter should be celebrated on the first Sunday after the full moon following the vernal equinox. This is the system followed today, the date of Easter varying between March 22 and April 25.

EAST SEA (See DEAD SEA)

EAST WIND (Heb. *qādîm*). Wind from the east came to Palestine over the desert; therefore it was a hot, dry wind (Jer 4:11). An east wind brought the plague of locusts on Egypt (Exod 10:13) and dried up the sea so that the Israelites could cross over on dry land (14:21). Many references mention the destructive results of the east wind: thin and withered heads of grain (Gen 41:6), broken ships (Ps 48:7; Ezek 27:26), withered plants (Ezek 17:10), dried fountains (Hos 13:15); Jonah's fainting spell (Jonah 4:8). The east wind was used as a means of judgment by God (Isa 27:8; Jer 18:17).

EBAL (ē'băl, Heb. *'êvāl,* meaning uncertain). 1. A son of Shobal (Gen 36:23; 1 Chron 1:40).

2. A mountain 3,077 feet (962 m.) high, one of the highest points in the land of Samaria. It stood opposite Mount Gerizim, across a valley through which ran an important route of travel. At its foot was Jacob's well (see John 4:20: "on this mountain"), and the city of Shechem was located nearby. When the Israelites first entered the land,

Mount Ebal, with the modern city of Shechem in the foreground, as viewed from Mount Gerizim. Courtesy Zev Radovan.

Moses commanded them to erect on Mount Ebal a monument of stones on which the law was inscribed and a stone altar for burnt offerings and peace offerings. The law, with its blessings and curses, was recited by the people antiphonally, the blessings from Mount Gerizim and the curses from Mount Ebal (Deut 27:4–26). Joshua renewed this procedure after the conquest of Ai (Josh 8:30–35). The central location of this mountain and its height made it valuable for military purposes. A ruined fortress is still visible on its summit.

3. In KJV one of the sons of Joktan; rendered Obal in NIV (1 Chron 1:22).

EBED (ē'bĕd, Heb., *'evedh, servant*). 1. Father of Gaal, the adversary of Ahimelech who unsuccessfully rebelled against this ruler in Shechem (Judg 9:26–45).

2. Son of Jonathan, one of the fifty men of the family of Adin that came from Babylon under Ezra (Ezra 8:6).

EBED-MELECH (ē'bĕd-mē-lĕk, Heb. *'evedh melekh, servant of the king*). An Ethiopian eunuch who, when he heard that Jeremiah had been cast into a muddy dungeon, was moved to go to the king and ask for permission to pull the prophet out. The king granted him thirty men, and with cords of rags and wornout garments they drew Jeremiah up out of that dungeon (Jer 38:7–13). The Lord gave Jeremiah a message for Ebed-Melech, assuring him of safety and protection in the coming destruction of the city (39:15–18).

EBENEZER (ĕb'ĕn-ē'zêr, Heb. *'even-'ezer, stone of help*). 1. A town of Ephraim near Aphek by which the Israelites camped before fighting a losing battle with the Philistines (1 Sam 4:1). The ark of God was captured by these enemies of Israel, and they brought it from Ebenezer to their city, Ashdod (5:1).

2. Later, God gave Israel victory over the Philistines. Samuel then took a stone and set it up as a memorial of the occasion, calling it *Eben-ezer,* "the stone of help," saying, "Thus far has the LORD helped us" (1 Sam 7:12).

EBER (ē'bêr, Heb. *'ēver*). This word means "a region across or beyond." The name of the Hebrew people may be derived from Eber, as its form is the same as the word *iberi* (meaning "Hebrew") without the gentilic ending. The Hebrews were a people who came from a region beyond the Euphrates River.

1. The son of Shelah, a grandson of Shem (Gen 10:24; 11:14; 1 Chron 1:18). He was the father of Peleg and Joktan (Gen 10:25; 11:16; 1 Chron 1:19–25).

2. The head of a family in the tribe of Gad (1 Chron 5:13).

3. The oldest son of Elpaal, a Benjamite (1 Chron 8:12).

4. A son of Shimei, a Benjamite (1 Chron 8:19).

5. Head of a priestly family that came from Babylon under Zerubbabel (Neh 12:20).

EBEZ (ē'bĕz). A town allotted to the tribe of Issachar (Josh 19:20; KJV "Abez"). Location unknown.

EBIASAPH (ē-bī'ā-săph, Heb. *'avî'āsāph* and *'ĕvî'āsāph, my father has gathered*). A son of Elkanah, a descendant of Kohath, son of Levi (Exod 6:24; 1 Chron 6:23; 9:19).

EBONY (See PLANTS)

EBRONAH (See ABRONAH)

ECBATANA (ĕk-băt'-ă-nȧ, Heb. *'ahmethā'*). The capital of Media and the summer residence of the Persian kings. It is found in the Behistun inscription of Darius I. It is mentioned in an inscription of Tiglath-Pileser I at a much earlier time. It was later the Parthian capital also. In Greek the name of this city became *Hagbatana* (Herodotus) or *Ecbatana* (2 Maccabees). It is mentioned in the Bible only in Ezra 6:2 (KJV Achmetha), denoting the location of the palace in which the decree of Cyrus authorizing the building of the Jewish temple was found. According to Herodotus, this city was founded by Deioces, a Median king. Cyrus captured it in 550 B.C., and Alexander the Great took it from the Persians in 330. The modern city of Hamadan is located on or near the same site. Very little remains of the ancient city.

ECCLESIASTES (ĕ-klē-zĭ-ăs'tēz, Gr. *Ekklēsiatēs,* Heb., *qōheleth,* meaning probably the official speaker in an assembly). Traditionally the book has been ascribed to Solomon. This ascription is based on several factors. The superscription introduces the book as "The words of the Teacher, son of David, king of Jerusalem" (Eccl 1:1). Several allusions in the book are appropriate to Solomonic authorship, such as the reference to the author's wisdom (1:16), his interest in proverbs (12:9; cf. 1 Kings 4:32), and his building projects (2:4–11).

From the time of Luther, however, a large number of scholars have questioned the Solomonic authorship of Ecclesiastes. The book does not actually name Solomon as its writer. The author says he *was* king of Jerusalem (Eccl 1:12), a statement difficult to apply to Solomon, and the language of the book may incline toward a time later than King Solomon. These observations have led many to hold that Solomon serves as a literary representation of the embodiment of wisdom.

The book presents a pessimistic view of life apart from God. The writer tells us that his observation of nature and human experience leads him to conclude that they, in and of themselves, do not impart purpose and meaning to life. He observes the endless cycles of nature (Eccl 1:2–11) and finds in them only tedium. They do not offer satisfaction, for the "eye never has enough of seeing" (1:8). Even wisdom (1:16–18; 2:12–17), pleasure (1:1–8), and toil (1:9–11; 2:18–23) are meaningless. There is no substance or satisfaction in them. They are a "chasing after the wind" (1:17).

In the history of its interpretation the book has been characterized as hedonistic because it concludes that "a man can do nothing better than to eat and drink and find satisfaction in his work" (Eccl 2:24). But this characterization of the book is rendered difficult by the fact that the writer concludes that pleasure does not lead to satisfaction either (2:1). The book is understood by some to be fatalistic in its approach to life. This is based on 3:16–22, which seems to conclude that man is not better off than the animal. This conclusion, however, is true only when men are viewed in and of themselves (Heb. *hemmah lahem,* 3:18), that is, apart from God.

There is a positive life view that emerges from the book that may be called a theology of contentment. In view of the lack of substance and meaning in life, Qoheleth urges his readers to enjoy life, for it is God who gives us that privilege (Eccl 2:24–25). This satisfaction does not belong to all mankind, for the work of the sinner ends in futility (2:26). Godly contentment, however, is not the ultimate good for mankind. Qoheleth reminds us of a future time when God will bring all things into judgment. This is the conclusion of his search for meaning in life (12:14). One is reminded of the counsel of the apostle Paul in view of the futility of life, for like Qoheleth, he looked away from life's meaninglessness to his future redemption (Rom 8:20; cf. vv. 22–25).

Qoheleth urges us to fear God and obey him. Only when God is taken into account (Eccl 12:1) and his will observed (12:13) does life impart purpose and satisfaction.

Bibliography: H. C. Leupold, *Exposition of Ecclesiastes,* 1952; Robert Gordis, *Koheleth—The Man and His World,* 1968; Derek Kidner, *A Time to Mourn and a Time to Dance,* 1976. TEM

ECCLESIASTICUS (See APOCRYPHA)

EDEN (Heb. *'ēden, delight*). 1. The district in which the Lord God planted a garden for the newly created man, Adam. In it grew every tree that was pleasant to see and good for food, including the tree of life and the tree of the knowledge of good and evil. A river flowed out of Eden and divided into four heads or streams: the Pishon, which went around the land of Havilah, where gold was found; the Gihon which flowed around the whole land of Cush; the Hiddekel (or Tigris), which flowed in front of Assyria; and the Euphrates (Gen 2:8–14). Adam and Eve lived there until they sinned by eating the forbidden fruit and were expelled from it (Gen 2–3). Later Scripture writers mention Eden as an illustration of a delightful place (Isa 51:3; Ezek 28:13; 31:9, 16, 18; 36:35; Joel 2:3).

The location of Eden has been much investigated in both ancient and modern times. The data given in Genesis, however, are not sufficient to fix its site because two of the rivers, the Pishon and Gihon, were unknown even to the ancients and still are to modern scholars. Attempts have been made to locate Eden in the mountains of Armenia in the area where the Tigris and Euphrates and several other rivers rise. But the sources of all these streams are not together but are separated by mountain ranges. Mesopotamia, where the Tigris and Euphrates rivers flow, is also within the Fertile Crescent where archaeology has found the oldest civilization. Some scholars suggest the district at the head of the Persian Gulf as the likely location. It has been widely believed that the silt brought down by the rivers has added over a hundred miles of land to the head of the gulf since 3000 B.C. But recent geological examination of this land has indicated that it may not have changed much during the ages. At the site of Eridu, situated near what was considered to be the ancient shoreline, clay tablets have been found that tell of a garden in the neighborhood in which grew a sacred palm tree. Further upstream, a short distance north of ancient Babylon, the Tigris and Euphrates flow close together so that canals connect them. Some consider this area to be the proper location of Eden.

2. An Eden mentioned by the Assyrians as conquered by them along with Gozan, Haran, and Rezeph (2 Kings 19:12; Isa 37:12). Ezekiel 27:23 also mentions this region. It is believed to be the *Bit-adini* of the Assyrian inscriptions. The house of Eden, or Beth Eden (Amos 1:5), was probably near Damascus, since it is mentioned in a Syrian context, but some scholars think it was the same place as *Bit-adini.*

3. A Gershonite who lived in Hezekiah's time and served under Kore, the porter of the east gate of the temple, in distributing the holy oblations (2 Chron 29:12; 31:15).

EDER (ē'dêr, Heb. *'edher, floods*). 1. A city in south Judah near Edom (Josh 15:21), possibly the same as Adar. Site unknown.

2. A son of Mushi, the son of Merari (1 Chron 23:23; 24:30). 3. A son of Beriah, grandson of Shaharaim, a Benjamite (1 Chron 8:15); KJV, Ader.

EDOM, EDOMITES (ē'dŏm, ē'dŏmīts, Heb. *'ĕdhōm, 'ădhômîn,* from *'ĕdhōm, red*). The nation and its people who were the descendants of Esau. He founded the country, so his name is equated with Edom (Gen 25:30; 36:1, 8). The country was also called Seir, or Mount Seir, the name of the territory in which the Edomites lived, the mountain and plateau area between the Dead Sea and the Gulf of Aqabah about 100 miles (167 km.) long and up to 40 miles (67 km.) wide. The original inhabitants of this land were the Horites or "cave dwellers" (14:6). When Esau departed from Canaan to find room for his cattle and came to Mount Seir (36:5–8), the Horites had some tribal chiefs reigning in the land (36:29–30). Esau took the daughter of one of these chiefs for a wife, Oholibamah, daughter of Anah (36:2, 25). Esau's sons and grandsons were also tribal chiefs (36:15–19, 40–43). Probably the Edomites gradually absorbed the Horites, until they disappeared (Deut 2:12, 22).

The kingdom of Edom was founded during the thirteenth century B.C., according to archaeological evidence. In the process of about four centuries the government of Edom changed from one under tribal chiefs to a monarchy. Eight of these kings reigned over Edom before the Israelites had any such ruler (Gen 36:31–39). One of these kings was on the throne at the time of Moses and refused to permit the Israelites to pass through his

The land of Edom, a region of rugged mountains and plateaus that extends from the southern end of the Dead Sea to the Gulf of Aqabah. Courtesy Studium Biblicum Franciscanum, Jerusalem.

country (Num 20:14–21). Other evidence of ancient Edom is the Papyrus Anastasi VI of Egypt, dated in the late thirteenth century, which mentions the passage of shepherd tribes from Edom to the richer pasture land of the Nile delta. The Amarna Letter No. 256 from about 1400, mentions Edom in the form *Udumu,* one of the enemies of a Jordan Valley prince.

Saul fought against the Edomites (1 Sam 14:47), but David conquered them and put garrisons throughout the whole land (2 Sam 8:14). The Israelite army spent six months cutting off all the men of the kingdom (1 Kings 11:15–16). Solomon made the Edomite cities Ezion Geber and Eloth, on the Gulf of Aqabah, seaports from which his ships sailed to Ophir

A series of rock-cut tombs at Umm el-Biyyara near Petra, identified as the Edomite stronghold Amaziah conquered; it was renamed Jokheel (2 Kings 14:7). Courtesy Israel Department of Antiquities and Museums.

(2 Chron 8:17–18). Judah lost Edom in the reign of Jehoram when she revolted against him about 847 B.C. (2 Kings 8:20, 22). About fifty years later, Amaziah, king of Judah, inflicted a severe defeat on the Edomites (14:7). About 735 B.C. Rezin, king of Syria, went to war with Judah, captured Eloth, and drove the Jews out (16:6). When Jerusalem was destroyed and Judah depopulated by the Babylonians in 586 B.C., the Edomites rejoiced over the affliction of the Judeans and began to take over the southern part of Palestine. Eventually they penetrated as far north as Hebron. This action intensified the already smoldering hatred between the Jews and Edomites (see Ps 137:7; Ezek 25:12–14; Amos 1:11; Obad 10–13).

The Edomites were subject also to Babylon. Under the Persian Empire, Edom became a province called Idumea, the Greek form of Edom. In 325 B.C. an Arab tribe known as the Nabateans conquered the eastern part of Edom's territory. In Maccabean times John Hyrcanus subdued the Idumeans and forced them to accept Judaism. When the Romans took over Palestine the Edomites also were included. From Idumea came Antipater, the father of Herod the Great. He became procurator of Judea. After the destruction of Jerusalem by the Romans in A.D. 70, the Idumeans disappeared from history. Thus the rather mournful career of the Edomites came to an end. Only in the early centuries of their kingdom, before the Israelites became powerful, did they enjoy freedom to any great extent.

The Assyrians came in contact with Edom as early as the seventh century B.C. When her kings began to penetrate as far south as Palestine, Edom, along with Judah and her other neighbors, paid tribute to Assyria for many years. She is mentioned many times in the inscription of the kings of Assyria, beginning with Adad-Nirari III (800) to Ashurbanipal (686–633).

Edom figures prominently in the prophetic Scriptures (Isa 11:14; 34:8ff.; 63:1ff.; Ezek 35:2ff.; Joel 3:19; Amos 9:12; Obadiah). The explanation of this often unexpected appearance of Edom finds its origin in the fact already noted that the conquest of Edom was a unique achievement of David; the overthrow of Edom therefore became a symbol of the reign of the Davidic Messiah.

EDREI (ĕd′rē-ī, Heb. *'edhre'î, strong*). 1. One of the chief sites of Og, king of Bashan (Deut 1:4; Josh 12:4) where he fought with the Israelites (Num 21:33; Deut 3:1). They defeated him and took his country with its cities, including Edrei (Deut 3:10). This town was assigned to the half-tribe of Manasseh (Josh 13:12, 31). It was located near the southern source of the Yarmuk river, about ten miles (seventeen km.) NE of Ramoth Gilead, and about thirty miles (fifty km.) east and a little south of the Sea of Galilee. In the temple of Ammon in Karnak, Egypt, is a list of the cities that Thutmose III (1490–1450 B.C.) claimed he conquered or exercised dominion over in Upper Retenu (Syria and Palestine). Edrei appears on this list. Its modern name is *Der'aa*, a town of about five thousand inhabitants in southern Syria.

2. A fortified city of Naphtali, location unknown (Josh 19:37).

EGG (Heb. *bêtsâ, whiteness*). This appears in the OT only in the plural form *bêtsîm:* birds' eggs (Deut 22:6); ostrich eggs (Job 39:14); any kind of eggs (Isa 10:14); snake eggs (59:5). Another word, *hallāmût* (Job 6:6) is translated "egg," but the meaning of the Hebrew is uncertain. An ASV marginal note has "purslain," a plant whose juice had an insipid taste.

EGLAH (ĕg′lȧh, Heb. *'eglâh, heifer*). The name of one of David's wives who was the mother of his sixth son, Ithream (2 Sam 3:5; 1 Chron 3:3).

EGLAIM (ĕg′lā-ĭm, Heb. *'eglayim*). A place in Moab (Isa 15:8). Site unknown.

EGLATH SHELISHIYAH (ĕg′lăth-shĭ-lĭsh′ĕ-yȧ, the third Eglath). A town near Zoar mentioned in prophecies against Moab (Isa 15:5; Jer 48:34).

EGLON (Heb. *'eghlôn*). 1. A city of Canaan located between Gaza and Lachish, whose king joined four others against Gibeon because this city had made a covenant with Joshua. Gibeon appealed to Joshua, who came with the Israelites and defeated and destroyed the five kings (Josh 10:3, 5, 23). Later Joshua captured the city (10:36–37; 12:12). It was assigned to Judah (15:39). Its modern site is believed to be *'Aglan* north of Tell el Hesey. Archaeologists have ascertained that it was destroyed by fire in the thirteenth century B.C., thus confirming Joshua's conquest of it. Remains of Solomon's building program have also been found there.

2. A king of Moab who, with the help of the Ammonites and Amalekites, captured Jericho, the city of palm trees (Judg 3:12–13). The Israelites served him for eighteen years (3:14). Then he was killed by Ehud, whom the Lord had raised up to save the children of Israel (3:21).

EGYPT (ē′jĭpt, Gr. *Aigyptos*).

I. Its Name. To the Israelites, Egypt was Mizraim (Heb. *mitsrayim*), a term of which the form and derivation are unknown. The Egyptians themselves had a number of names they used for their country; usually it was called "the Two Lands," which has reference to the origin of the nation in the union of Upper and Lower Egypt, just as the name "the United States of America" has historical derivation. Egypt was also Kemet, "the Black Land," the rich alluvial soil of the valley, as opposed to Desheret, "the Red Land," the barren waste of the desert.

II. The Nile. "Egypt," said Hecateus, echoed by Herodotus, "is the gift of the Nile." This is a reflection of actual circumstances and of the Egyptian appreciation of the great river. The Nile, which courses like a living vein through the desiccated hills and deserts of NE Africa, laid

Avenue of ram-headed sphinxes outside the great temple of Amon at Karnak. The ram was the sacred animal of the sun god (Amon). Courtesy Seffie Ben-Yoseph.

down the black alluvium of the delta and the entire river valley. In view of the almost complete absence of rain, the annual overflow of the Nile was of great importance to the land, for it watered the soil and provided it with new alluvium and some organic fertilizer. Its waters were used for drinking (Exod 7:18, 21, 24; Ps 78:44), for bathing (Exod 2:5), and for irrigation (Deut 11:10). Its stream (Heb. *ye'or*) was the main channel of commerce and travel, with a prevailing north wind to favor southbound sailing vessels against the current.

The regularity of the inundation afforded a practical agricultural calendar, and the coincidence of the rise of the Nile and the appearance of the Dog Star (Sirius; e.g., Sothis) on the horizon at daybreak around July 19 was the basis for a chronological unit of 1,460 years, which is termed a Sothic cycle. Since the Egyptian calendar of 365 days was one-fourth of a day short of the true year, the Egyptian New Year's Day worked its way through the calendar until it again coincided with the rising of Sothis and the inundation (365 x 4 = 1,460). The recognition of this cycle and several references to it in dates of historical records make some helpful checkpoints in Egyptian chronology.

The awareness of the dependence of land and people on the resources of the Nile led to the deification of the river. The longest river in the world, the Nile covers some 4,000 miles (6,667 km.) from its sources in equatorial Africa to its divided mouths that open into the Mediterranean. The White Nile is the principal stream, with tributaries joining it from their eastern points of origin in the Ethiopian hills. The Blue Nile enters at Khartoum. Farther north, the Atbara, the last consequential tributary, empties its periodic flow into the northbound stream. From this junction the Nile continues some 1,500 miles (2,500 km.) without tributary to the sea. Numbered from Aswan south, in order of their discovery by modern explorers, are six cataracts, areas in which hard rock resisted the erosive action of the rushing stream. To varying degrees these hindered river travel and served as barriers to military movement. From Aswan to Cairo is a stretch of somewhat less than 600 (1,000 km.) miles. Below Cairo spreads the fan of the delta, about 125 miles (208 km.) long and 125 miles (208 km.) wide.

III. Its Geography. The division of the land into Upper and Lower Egypt predates the union into one nation. Lower Egypt included the delta and a short section of the valley southward; the rest of the valley to Aswan was Upper Egypt. These areas were subdivided into administrative units that in Greek times were called "nomes," twenty in Lower Egypt and twenty-two in its southern counterpart. With the cataracts and the Nubian desert to the south and SE, the Libyan desert and the Sahara to the west, and the Arabian desert on the east, the valley was not subject to the frequent invasions that characterized less defensible lands. The biggest threat from outside was on the delta edges; even here the passage of armies was handicapped by terrain and climate. On the NE border, fronting Asia, the Egyptians made early use of fortresses and other checkpoints to control invasion from this direction. With such protection, the country was free to develop its culture in comparative security and still to retain a free exchange of goods and ideas with other peoples.

IV. Its Climate. The climate of the land, along with the particular beliefs of the people, has been of great advantage to archaeology, so that it may be said that Egypt is the archaeological area *par excellence*. Lack of rain and frost, plenty of dry sand to form a protective cover over remains, and abundant use of stone for monumental building are helpful environmental factors. The burial customs have been of much help to the cultural historian, for the relief sculpture, tomb furniture, models, and inscriptions tell much of the daily life of antiquity.

V. Its Religion. The religion of ancient Egypt is a vast and labyrinthine subject. Much of the religious literature appears as a hodgepodge of conflicting statements to the modern Western reader, to whom many of the allusions must remain obscure. In general, the religion may be described as a complex polytheism, with many local deities of varying importance. A list of these divinities would be impractical, but these may be singled out: Osiris and Isis, who are well known from their later adoption by the mystery religions of Greece and Rome; Ra (Re), a sun-god, who came into prominence in the Fifth Dynasty; Horus, another sun-god, the son of Osiris and Isis; Set, the rival of Osiris and Horus; Amon-Re, who became the god of empire; Ptah, the god of Memphis; Khnum, the god of Elephantine. The attempt of Akhenaton (Amenhotep IV) to reorient Egyptian religion with a primary emphasis on Aton, the sun-disc, has been widely discussed as a tendency toward monotheism. There is no evidence of possible Israelite influence on his beliefs. His innovations did not long survive him and the priests of Amon at Thebes scored a theological-political victory. Much of the religious literature has a mortuary interest; this preoccupation with death was a futile gesture to transfer

One of the world's best preserved edifices, the temple of the falcon deity (Horus), at Edfu, a prominent Upper Egyptian city during the period when the Macedonian dynasty governed Egypt. Construction began in 237 B.C. and was completed in 57 B.C. Courtesy Seffie Ben-Yoseph.

earthly life to an eternal dimension. There are no reflections of the Egyptian concept in the Bible, and the absence of any large body of OT teaching concerning life beyond the grave may be a divine avoidance of a possible snare to the Israelites. The influence of Egyptian religion on Israelite religious practice was largely negative. In several instances the Israelites were led into apostasy to worship Egyptian gods (see below), but even these occasions were rare.

VI. Its History. Preceding the historical or dynastic period are a number of prehistoric cultures that are known in general outline. In the late predynastic epoch there is interesting evidence of cultural influence from Mesopotamia. The rudiments of hieroglyphic writings also appear about this time and usher in the historical period. The materials for writing the political history of Egypt are lists of kings (such as those inscribed in temples of Abydos and Karnak, that of a tomb at Sakkarah, the Turin Papyrus, and the Palermo Stone) and numerous historical records, both of kings and of lesser persons active in history-making. The dynastic scheme is a historiographical convenience inherited from the priest-historian Manetho, who divided Egyptian history from Menes to Alexander into thirty-one dynasties. Egyptologists have used a somewhat standard arrangement of these dynasties into historical periods. A highly condensed outline follows.

A. **Protodynastic Period** (Dyn. 1–2; 3100–2700 B.C.). According to the tradition of Manetho, the first king of united Egypt was Menes, who came from Thinis in Upper Egypt, united the two lands, and established his capital at Memphis in about 3200–3100. Some scholars equate Menes with Narmer and/or Aha. Royal tombs of this period have been found at Sakkarah and Abydos.

B. **Old Kingdom** (Dyn. 3–6; 2700–2200). This is a high point in Egyptian history. The canons of art were firmly established in this period and perhaps the bases of the applied sciences were also laid. In the Third Dynasty, the step pyramid of Djoser, "the world's first monumental architecture in stone," was built at Sakkarah. Its architect, Imhotep, was also famed in other fields of accomplishment. The Fourth Dynasty was the time of the pyramid-builders *par excellence:* the pyramids of Khufu (Cheops), Khafre (Chephren), and Menkaure (Mycerions) were constructed at Giza. Kings of the Fifth and Sixth Dynasties had their pyramids at Sakkarah; in these were inscribed the religious writings known as the Pyramid Texts. The proverbs of Ptahhotep, a

The Great Pyramid at Giza, built during the reign of Khufu, 4th Dynasty (2575–2465 B.C.). The base area is 230 square meters; the original height was 146 meters. Courtesy Zev Radovan.

vizier of the Fifth Dynasty, are well-known.

C. **First Intermediate Period** (Dyn. 7–11; 2200–2050). This was a period of weakness and confusion. The Seventh and Eighth Dynasties were at Memphis, the Ninth and Tenth were at Herakleopolis, and the Eleventh was at Thebes. The literature is an outgrowth of the pessimism of the times; it includes the writings of Ipuwer, the dialogue of a Man Weary of Life; the Song of the Harper.

D. **Middle Kingdom** (Dyn. 12; 2050–1800) was another peak in Egyptian history. Art and architecture flourished. This is the time of the Eloquent Peasant and of the adventures of the courtier Sinuhe. In religious literature the Coffin Texts are found. There is a trend toward democratization of royal privileges, along with an emphasis on *ma'at*, "justice, right." The king is heralded as "the shepherd" of the people.

E. **Second Intermediate Period** (Dyn. 13–17; 1800–1580) was another dark age for Egypt. Insignificant rulers made up the Thirteenth and Fourteenth Dynasties. The Fifteenth and Sixteenth Dynasties are the Hyksos dynasties, which may be of greater importance than brief, derogatory Egyptian references lead us to think. The Seventeenth Dynasty was made up of Theban rulers who began the movement to expel the Hyksos.

F. **The New Kingdom or Empire** (Dyn. 18–20; 1580–1090) marked the height of Egyptian imperialistic ambitions, with some fluctuations. Outstanding rulers include: in the Eighteenth Dynasty, Hatshepsut, the woman-king who sponsored a voyage to Punt and built a fine mortuary temple at Deir el Bahri; Thutmose III, the energetic warrior and capable administrator; Amenhotep III, the Magnificent, a lavish spender who neglected the empire and with his successor Akhenaton, the religious innovator, ignored the pleas for help from Palestine-Syria (Amarna Tablets). In the Nineteenth Dynasty, the outstanding figure is Rameses II, the builder, renovator, and chiseler; in the Twentieth Dynasty, it is Rameses III, who defeated the Sea Peoples.

G. **The Post-Empire Period** or **Period of Decline** (Dyn. 21–25; 1150–663) finds Egypt a "broken reed."

H. **The Saite Period** (Dyn. 26; 663–525). There was a short restoration in this period, which includes Neco and Apries (biblical Hophra, Jer 44:30).

I. **Later Egypt.** In 525 B.C., Persia (under Cambyses) took over Egypt; what followed were two centuries of Persian domination, limited independence, and Egyptian rebellions (Dyn. 27–30; 525–332). With Alexander the Great came the end of the dynasties and of native rule. After the death of Alexander (323), Egypt was governed by the Ptolemies until the Romans made it a province in 31.

VII. Egypt and the Bible. To the Israelites, Egypt was somewhat of an enigma, a land of contrast, a country that they hated but respected. When a psalmist looked back to the days of the Exodus, he referred to the Egyptians as "a people of foreign tongue" (Ps 114:1), a description to which even many moderns may assent. Egypt was the iron furnace of affliction during the bondage, but Israelites were so impressed with the might of the Pharaonic kingdom that there were elements in Judah that looked to Egypt for help even after Egypt had become the broken reed of Assyrian contempt (cf. 2 Kings 18:21; Isa 36:6). An unreliable ally, Egypt was also a sanctuary for some of Israel's individual enemies. From Egypt, too, came some of the worst occasions for apostasy in Israel. Egypt appears in the Bible as a type of the transitory, earthbound system called "the world." In one instance it is an allegorical synonym for Sodom and for rebellious Jerusalem (Rev 11:8). Nevertheless, it was an abundant Near Eastern breadbasket and was for centuries the ranking world power. It afforded food for many a hungry Palestinian, and heat-smitten wandering tribes were permitted to cross its borders to graze their animals in the delta. Joseph realized that God's providence was in his being sold into Egypt (Gen 45:5–9), and Jacob was instructed by the Lord to go to Egypt (46:3–4).

Egypt appears early in biblical references, since Mizraim (Egypt) is found in the Table of Nations as a son of Ham (Gen 10:6). Abram's sojourn in Egypt is a well-known incident. It is evident from Genesis 12:10 that Egypt was the place to which Palestinians naturally looked in time of famine. The famous scene from the wallpaintings of the tomb of Khnumhotep II at Beni Hasan shows a

Columns of the great hypostyle hall at Karnak (Thebes). The relief decoration was done for Sethos I and Ramses II. Courtesy Seffie Ben-Yoseph.

group of Asiatics in Middle Egypt for purposes of trade and illustrates several facets of Abram's descent into Egypt. The fears of Abram concerning the king's interest in Sarai were real and perhaps well-founded, but there is no certain evidence for such royal behavior in Egyptian literature. The oft-cited Tale of Two Brothers relates a quite different sort of situation, for there the wife is anxious to be rid of her husband so that she may become a wife of Pharaoh.

The closest Egyptian-biblical relationships may be seen in the narrative of Joseph and the account of Israelite life in Egypt to the time of their Exodus (Gen 37, 39–50; Exod 1–15). A listing of some of the most intriguing elements includes: Joseph's coat (Gen 37); Potiphar, "an Egyptian" (ch. 39); Potiphar's wife (39:6–18), with interesting parallels in the Tale of Two Brothers, a not uncommon episode in many cultures; the prison for political offenders (39:20); the duties of butler and baker; dreams in Egypt; Egyptian viticulture (ch. 40); cattle and the Nile; grain-growing (ch. 41); shaving (41:14); east wind (41:27); taxes (41:34); the gold (41:42); chariots (41:43); the priest of On (Heliopolis) (41:45); Egyptian names; Egypt as a source of food (41:57); divination (44:5); the land of Goshen (ch. 47); the Egyptian priesthood (47:22); embalming, mummification, and burial rites (ch. 50).

In Exodus 1 there are references to brickmaking, field work, and obstetrical practices that are particularly Egyptian. In chapter 2 the references to the Nile are of interest. The account of the signs and the plagues shows an intimate knowledge of Egyptian life and provides a study in the relationship of natural and miraculous phenomena. In Exodus 11:2 the asking for jewelry of silver and gold is a reflection of the expert Egyptian work in metals. The Egyptian pursuit of the fleeing Israelites (14:10, 23) finds parallels in the battle reliefs of Egypt's chief monarchs. The ironic mention of graves in Egypt (14:11) reminds us of the vast necropolis that marks the desert fringe. Well into the wilderness, the refugees were outside of Egyptian concern and out of its effective reach; but, barely escaped from slavery, the Israelites were soon engrossed in worshiping the golden calf (ch. 32), a descendant of the bovine worship of Memphis and other Egyptian cities. There were also fond recollections of good eating in Egypt, with its fish, cucumbers, leeks, onions, and garlic, which the Israelites regarded as strength-giving fare (Num 11:5–6). During the period of the judges, the hill-country of Palestine saw little likelihood of antagonistic Egyptian interference. Egyptian power had declined; in about 1100 B.C. the royal emissary Wen-Amon found little respect for the might of Egypt along the Mediterranean coast.

With this weakness, the time was ripening for the rapid growth of a young and vigorous nation in the former Asiatic empire of Egypt. When the Israelite monarchy came into existence, neither Saul nor David recorded immediate dealings with the land of the Nile. Solomon, however, married

The island of Elephantine, a small island in the Nile opposite Aswan, place where Aramaic papyri were found from the archives of Jewish mercenaries who kept up correspondence with Palestine. Courtesy Seffie Ben-Yoseph.

a daughter of the current Pharaoh, who captured and destroyed Gezer and presented it to his daughter as dowry (1 Kings 9:16). It is stated that Solomon's wisdom excelled that of his commercial relations with Egypt (2 Chron 1:16–17). Late in Solomon's reign, an Edomite enemy, Hadad, who as a child had found asylum in Egypt after a raid by David into Edomite territory, left Egypt to become an active adversary of Solomon. Jeroboam fled to Egypt to escape Solomon; as first king of the northern tribes, this Jeroboam, "who made Israel to sin," set up calf images at Dan and Bethel (1 Kings 12:26–33), a religious importation influenced by his Egyptian exile. In the fifth year of Rehoboam (926 B.C.) the Egyptian King Sheshonk (biblical Shishak) carried out an expedition into Palestine that saw the temple stripped of its treasures to meet his demands (1 Kings 14:25, 26; 2 Chron 12:1–9).

Egypt was a strong influence in Judean politics in the days of Isaiah and Jeremiah, who were aware of the weakness of Egypt against the Assyrian threat. When the Assyrian remnant was making its dying stand and Egypt marched to aid them against the rampaging Babylonians, the Judean Josiah made a fatal effort to stop the Egyptian forces at Megiddo (2 Kings 23:29–30; 2 Chron 35:20–27). After the fall of Jerusalem in 586 B.C. and the subsequent murder of Gedaliah, the Judeans again looked to Egypt as a place of refuge in spite of the prophet's warning. Here they were scattered about, with a group as far south as Elephantine maintaining a temple and keeping up correspondence with Palestine, as revealed by the Aramaic papyri found at Elephantine.

In the NT most of the references to Egypt have to do with Israel's past. One important mention had current meaning, for Joseph was divinely directed to take the infant Jesus and Mary to Egypt to escape the wrath of Herod (Matt 2:13–15; cf. Exod 4:22; Hos 11:1).

VIII. Its Significance and Future. It is remarkable that Egypt so often was a place of refuge or a means of sustaining life. Though it is regarded by typological extremists as an invariable epitome of "the world," Egypt has the scriptural prediction of a wonderful future: "In that day Israel will be the third, along with Egypt and Assyria, a blessing on the earth. The LORD Almighty will bless them, saying, "Blessed be Egypt my people, Assyria my handiwork, and Israel my inheritance" (Isa 19:24–25; cf. 19:18–23). CEDV

EGYPT, RIVER OF. The dividing line between Canaan and Egypt (Gen 15:18; Num 34:5), the southern boundary of Judah (Josh 15:4, 47). In the four other occurrences it is coupled with the Euphrates River (Gen 15:18; 1 Kings 8:65; 2 Kings 24:7; 2 Chron 7:8) as marking the north and south limits of the land given to the Israelites. It is not really an Egyptian river, but a *wadi* (a stream and its valley that is dry except during a rainy period) of the desert near the border of Egypt. It is identified as the *Wadi el-Arish.*

EHI (e'hī, Heb. *'ēhî*). A son of Benjamin (Gen 46:21); in Numbers 26:38 spelled Ahiram; in 1 Chronicles 8:1 Aharah.

EHUD (ē'hŭd, Heb. *'ēhûdh, union*). 1. A descendant of Benjamin (1 Chron 7:10; 8:6).

2. A judge of the Israelites, a Benjamite, the son of Gera. The people were in distress because of the heavy hand of Eglon, the king of Moab, who had captured Jericho and extracted tribute from Israel. Ehud, a left-handed man, made a double-edged dagger that he carried on his right thigh. After he had delivered the tribute, he obtained an opportunity to speak with Eglon the king in private. He drew his dagger, thrust it through the king's body, and locked the doors of the room when he went out. The king's servants did not want to disturb him too quickly. During the delay, Ehud escaped. Back home he rallied the Israelites from Benjamin and Ephraim and led them against the Moabites. They subdued these enemies, and the land had peace for eighty years until Ehud died (Judg 3:15–30).

EKER (ē'kêr, Heb. *'ēqer, root*). A son of Ram, descendant of Judah (1 Chron 2:27).

EKRON (ĕk'rŏn, Heb. *'eqrôn, eradication*). The most northern of the five chief cities of the Philistines (see 1 Sam 6:17). It was located on the boundary between Judah and Dan (Josh 15:11; 19:43), but was assigned to Judah (15:45). After the Philistines returned the ark from Ekron to escape the wrath of God (1 Sam 6), the Israelites regained possession of Ekron and other cities (7:14). Following David's victory over Goliath, the Israelites drove the Philistines back to Ekron (17:52). The god of this city was Baal-Zebub (2 Kings 1:3). The prophets mention Ekron with other Philistine cities (Jer 25:20; Amos 1–8; Zeph 2:4; Zech 9:5, 7).

In the Assyrian inscriptions Ekron appears as *amquarruna.* Sennacherib assaulted it and killed its officials because they had been disloyal to Assyria. Esarhaddon called on twenty-two cities that paid tribute to him (Ekron was one) to help

Drawing of relief from Hall V of Sargon's palace at Khorsabad depicting Assyrian forces of Sargon II (722–705 B.C.) besieging the fortified town of Ekron. Courtesy Carta, Jerusalem.

transport building supplies for his palace. Ashurbanipal included Ekron in the list of cities that paid tribute to him. The Greek form of Ekron, *Accaron,* appears in 1 Maccabees 10:89 and in accounts of the Crusades. Its modern site is *'Agir* or *Catrah,* both on the Wadi *Surar.* CEH

EL (Heb. *'ēl, God*). The generic word for God in the Semitic languages: Aramaic *elah,* Arabic *ilah,* Akkadian *ilu.* In the OT, *el* is used over two hundred times for "God." In the prose books it often has a modifying term with it, but in the poetic books, Job and Psalms, it occurs alone many times. El was the chief, and somewhat vague, shadowy god of the Canaanite pantheon (see RAS SHAMRA) and the title is used in the OT to express the exalted transcendence of God. See ELOHIM. The Hebrews borrowed this word from the Canaanites. *El* has a plural, *elim,* occasionally *elhm* in Ugaritic; but the Hebrews needed no plural, though a plural term, *'elohim,* was their regular name for God.

The root from which *'ēl* was derived has been much discussed. Among the suggestions made by scholars: it came from *'wl,* "to be strong"; from an Arabic root *'ul,* "to be in front of" as a leader; from a Hebrew root *'lh* to which both *'el* and *'elohim* belonged, with the meaning "strong"; from the preposition *el,* "to be in front of"; and, using the same prepositions, as putting forth the idea of God as the goal for which all men seek. A truly satisfactory theory is impossible, because *'el* and the other terms for God, *'elohim* and *'eloha,* are all prehistoric in origin.

The Canaanite god El was the father of men and of gods. He is called *ab adm,* "father of mankind," or *ab snnm,* "father of years." He was an immoral and debased character. It is a tribute to the high morality of the OT understanding of God that a title that in Canaanite usage was so defiled could, without risk, be used to express the moral majesty of the God of Israel. CEH

ELA (ē'là, Heb. *'ēlā', terebinth*). The father of Solomon's commissary officer stationed in the tribe of Benjamin (1 Kings 4:18).

ELADAH (See ELEADAH)

ELAH (ē'lȧh, Heb. *'ēlâh, terebinth*). 1. A descendant of Esau who was a chief of Edom (Gen 36:41).

2. The valley in which David killed Goliath (1 Sam 17:2, 19; 21:9).

3. A king of Israel, the son of Baasha (1 Kings 16:8–14). He reigned two years and was assassinated by Zimri, a captain in his army, who destroyed all the rest of Baasha's descendants, thus fulfilling the prediction Jehu the prophet made in 1 Kings 16:1–4.

4. The father of Hoshea, the last king of Israel (2 Kings 15:30; 17:1; 18:1, 9).

5. A son of Caleb, the son of Jephunneh (1 Chron 4:15).

6. A Benjamite, one of the people who returned to Jerusalem from Babylon (1 Chron 9:8).

ELAM (ē'lăm, Heb. *'êlām*). 1. A son of Shem, thus making Elam a Semitic nation. The Hebrews looked at them as such, but neither in custom nor language were they Semitic (Gen 10:22; 1 Chron 1:17).

2. A son of Shashak, a descendant of Benjamin (1 Chron 8:24).

3. The fifth son of Meshelemiah, a doorkeeper of the Korahites (1 Chron 26:3).

4. The progenitor of a family of 1,254 members that returned from exile under Zerubbabel (Ezra 2:7; Neh 7:12).

5. Another forefather of a returned family with the same number of members (Ezra 2:31; Neh 7:34).

6. The father of two sons who returned from exile with Ezra (Ezra 8:7).

7. An ancestor of a man who confessed marriage to a foreign woman. Evidently this ancestor was either no. 4, 5, or 6 above (Ezra 10:2, 26).

8. A chief who sealed the covenant with Nehemiah (Neh 10:14).

9. One of the priests who took part in the dedication of the wall (Neh 12:42).

ELAM (ē'lăm, Heb. *'êlām*). A country situated on the east side of the Tigris River opposite Babylonia in a mountainous region. Its population was made up of a variety of tribes. Their language, different from the Sumerian, Semitic, and Indo-European tongues, was written in cuneiform script. It has not yet been deciphered to any great extent. Elam was one of the earliest civilizations. In Sumerian inscriptions it was called *Numma* (high mountain people), which became *Elamtu* in Akkadian texts; in classical literature it was known as *Susiana,* the Greek name for Susa, the capital city of Elam.

Sargon (2350 B.C.) claimed conquest of Elam in his day. Later on, about 2280, an Elamite king invaded Babylonia and took back much spoil. Gudea, a ruler of the city of Lagash, about 2100 mentions that the Elamites collected some of the timbers he used in constructing the temple of Ningirsu, the god of Lagash. Hammurabi (1728–1686) subdued the Elamites. In the time

Elamite soldier of the Persian guard holding a spear, on a glazed brick from Susa, fifth century B.C. He is carrying a quiver strapped over his back and an unsheathed bow on his shoulder. Courtesy Réunion des Musées Nationaux.

of Abraham, according to Genesis 14:1ff., an Elamite king, Kedorlaomer, made a raid on Palestine.

Elam figures prominently in Babylonian and Assyrian texts because it was situated so close to them. When Babylon became active against Assyrian supremacy, Elam became her chief ally. Assyria was not able to subdue Elam completely until the time of Ashurbanipal (668–626 B.C.), who sacked the country thoroughly in 640. This catastrophe practically finished Elam as a nation, but part of the country was not much affected by these intrusions of Semitic powers. This district called *Anzan* was, next to the capital at Susa, the most important part of the nation. From that area, Cyrus, the conqueror of Babylon, arose.

Isaiah cites Elam as one of the nations going up with Cyrus against Babylon (Isa 21:2) and joining the Assyrian army against Judah (22:6). Elam was one of the nations forced to drink the cup of God's wrath (Jer 25:25) and doomed to judgment (49:34–39). Ezra 4:9–10 refers to Elamites as among the peoples brought over to Samaria by the Assyrians. Acts 2:9 includes Elamite as one of the tongues being spoken by visitors at Jerusalem. CEH

ELASAH (ĕl'à-sàh, Heb. *'elʿāsâh, God has made*). 1. One of the sons of Pashhur who was guilty of marrying foreign women (Ezra 10:22).

2. Son of Shaphan, one of the men sent by Jeremiah from Jerusalem with a message of advice to the exiles in Babylon (Jer 29:3).

ELATH, ELOTH (Heb. *'êlâth,* or *'êlôth, lofty trees*). A town situated at the head of the Gulf of Aqabah in Edom. It was located very near to Ezion Geber, Solomon's seaport (1 Kings 9:26). The Israelites passed by the area on the way to the Promised Land (Deut 2:8). Azariah (767–740 B.C.) built it up, probably for use as a seaport, when he took it from Edom (2 Kings 14:22; 2 Chron 26:2). During the reign of Ahaz over Judah (736–716) Rezin, king of Syria, joined with Pekah, king of Israel, and threatened Jerusalem. Rezin captured Elath, and the Syrians (or more likely, the reading should be Edomites) occupied it (2 Kings 16:5–6). The Romans called it *Aelana* and made it a military post. After the Muslims conquered the Middle East a castle was erected there to protect the pilgrims going to Mecca from that port. In the tenth century A.D., according to reports, Elath was a great post of Palestine. Later it fell into decay. Turkey and Egypt both controlled it; after 1917 the Arabs took it over. Aqabah, or Eilat (its modern name) was in the territory allotted to the Jews in 1949. They have made it a port to bring in oil.

CEH

EL-BERITH (ĕl-bĕr-īth', God of the covenant). An alternate name for the god worshiped at Shechem (Judg 9:46). Some of the people of Shechem sought safety in his temple when Abimelech destroyed the city. Possibly to be identified with Baal-Berith of Judges 8:33; 9:4.

EL BETHEL (Heb. *'ēl bêth-'ēl, the God of the house of God*). The name Jacob gave to Luz because there God revealed himself to him (Gen 35:7).

ELDAAH (Heb. *'eldāʿâ, God has called*). A son of Midian (Gen 25:4).

ELDAD (Heb. *ʿelādh, God has loved*). A man who, along with another man, Medad, remained in camp when the seventy elders selected by Moses were gathered around the tabernacle to receive the gift of prophecy. The spirit of prophecy came to Eldad and Medad in camp, and they prophesied there. The news of this fact excited Joshua and he begged Moses to forbid them. But Moses said he wished that all God's people were prophets (Num 11:24–29).

ELDER (Heb. *zāqēn,* Gr. *presbyteros*). In ancient times the older men of a community were known as the elders. They governed the community and made all major decisions. Moses called the elders of Israel together to announce that the Lord had heard their cries for help and had appointed him to lead them out of Egypt (Exod 4:29). Later he called them out to institute the Passover (12:21). At Sinai, seventy of the elders went up the mountain with Moses and saw the God of Israel (24:9). In the wilderness, to relieve Moses, seventy elders shared his divine anointing (Num 11:25). After the Israelites had settled in Canaan and had a king over them, the elders still functioned. They were a separate group from the heads of the tribes and the princes of the fathers' houses (1 Kings 8:1). Each town had its group of elders, as Bethlehem did (1 Sam 16:4), "the elders . . . of each town" (Ezra 10:14). After the return from exile the elders made up the Sanhedrin, the governing council of the Jews.

This type of society continued into NT times. The elders joined the priests and scribes against Jesus (Matt 27:12). When churches came into being, elders were appointed for each congregation (Acts 14:23). The terms "elders" and "bishops" are used interchangeably in the NT. The "elders" of Acts 20:17 are called "bishops" in verse 28 (NIV "overseers"). In Titus 1:5, "elders" in the Cretan churches are mentioned; in listing qualifications for such an office, Paul calls them "bishops" in verse 7 (NIV "overseers"). These men were required to be blameless in their lives and obedient to the truth in their faith (1 Tim 3:1–7; Titus 1:6–9). Their duties involved spiritual oversight of the congregation and teaching the Word. Those who ruled well and also taught were worthy of "double honor" (1 Tim 5:17). Before the first century A.D. had elapsed, the term "bishop" had taken on a special meaning, denoting the one leader of a church. A biblical example of this (both in the Book of Acts and in Paul's letters) is James, the brother of Jesus, who was obviously the leader of the Jerusalem church.

Opinions vary regarding the twenty-four elders in heaven around the throne of God (as depicted in the Book of Revelation); probably they represent the heavenly priesthood of the church associated with Christ, the Great High Priest.

Bibliography: Leon Morris, *Ministers of God,* 1964; G. Berghoef and L. DeKoster, *The Elder's Handbook,* 1979; G. Bornkamm, TDNT, vol. 6, pp. 651–83. CEH

ELEAD (ĕ'lē-ăd, Heb. *'el 'ādh, God has testified*). An Ephraimite killed by men of Gath while making a raid to steal cattle (1 Chron 7:21).

ELEADAH (ē'lē-ā'dȧh, Heb. *'el 'ādhâh, God has adorned*). A descendant of Ephraim (1 Chron 7:20).

ELEALEH (ē'lē-ā'lĕ, Heb. *'el 'ālēh, God doth ascend*). A town always mentioned with Heshon, located about one mile (almost two km.) north of that place, in the tribe of Reuben (Num 32:3, 37). Isaiah and Jeremiah mention it in prophecies against Moab (Isa 15:4; 16:9; Jer 48:34). The modern site is marked by ruins and is called *El Ah.*

ELEASAH (ĕ'lē-ā-sȧh, Heb. *'el 'āsâh, God has made*). 1. A Hezronite (1 Chron 2:39–40).

2. A Benjamite, a descendant of Saul (1 Chron 8:37; 9:43).

ELEAZAR (ĕ-lē-ā'zȧr, Heb. *'el 'āzār, God has helped*). 1. The third son of Aaron (Exod 6:23). After the death of the two elder sons, Nadab and Abihu (Lev 10:1–2), Eleazar was designated to be chief priest (Num 3:32). He ministered before the Lord with Ithamar, his brother, helping his father. But the Lord assigned special tasks to Eleazar: gathering up the 250 censers offered to the Lord by rebellious men and hammering them into sheets to cover the altar (Num 16:36–39), and leading the ceremony involving a red heifer (19:3–4). When Aaron died, Eleazar became the chief priest (20:28). He assisted Moses in numbering the people (26:1–2), in dividing the spoil from the slaughter of the Midianites (31:13–54), and in assigning to two and a-half tribes their land east of the Jordan River (32:28). He was divinely appointed to help Joshua divide the Promised Land among the tribes (34:17) and carried out this task (Josh 14:1; 19:51). His only son was Phineas (1 Chron 6:4). Eleazar died soon after Joshua's death (Josh 24:33).

2. The son of Abinadab who was sanctified to keep the ark after it had been brought to his father's house (1 Sam 7:1).

3. Son of Dodai, one of the three mightiest men of David who gained a great victory over the Philistines (2 Sam 23:9–10; 1 Chron 11:12–14).

4. A childless son of Mahli (1 Chron 23:21–22; 24:28).

5. Son of Phineas, a Levite, one of the group to which Ezra delivered the temple treasures for tabulating and keeping for the temple (Ezra 8:32–34).

6. A priest who took part in the service dedicating the wall (Neh 12:42).

7. An ancestor of Joseph, the husband of Mary (Matt 1:15).

ELECTION AND PREDESTINATION. For God to predestinate (Gr. *proorizō*) is for him to decree or foreordain the circumstances and destiny of people according to his perfect will (Rom 8:29–30; Eph 1:11). It is, therefore, a particular aspect of the general providence of God that relates to God's superintendence of the whole cosmos and everything in it. For God to elect (Heb. *bachar,* Gr. *eklegomai*) is for him to choose for salvation and/or service a people or a person; the choice is based not on merit but on his free, sovereign love (Deut 4:37; 7:7; 14:2; Acts 13:17; 15:7; 1 Thess 1:4). Further, since predestination and election are both presented as acts of God, election cannot be on the basis of God's knowing in advance the reactions of people to his will. Election must be choice flowing only from God's own initiative. Believers were chosen in Christ before the foundation of the world (Eph 1:4).

Election is a prominent theme in the OT. There is the choice of Abraham and his "seed" that in him the nations of the world will be blessed (Gen 12:1ff.; 22:17–18); and there is the choice of (covenant with) the people Israel whom God led out of bondage into liberty (Exod 3:6–10; Deut 6:21–23). This nation was chosen by God as those to whom he could reveal himself and his will, and through whom he could exhibit and declare to the world his purposes and salvation (Deut 28:1–14; Isa 43:10–12, 20, 21). Further, there was the choice, from within the chosen people, of specific individuals—e.g., Aaron and David—for special roles and tasks (Deut 18:5; 1 Sam 10:24; Ps 105:26; 106:23).

In the NT, Jesus is the Elect One (Luke 9:35), in whom the election of Israel and of the church of God of the new covenant find their meaning and center. Jesus is the elect "cornerstone" of the new building that God is constructing, composed of both Jewish and Gentile believers (1 Peter 2:4–6). God destined us in love to be his sons through Jesus Christ (Eph 1:5). So the church of God is an elect race (1 Peter 2:9), replacing the old Israel in the purposes of God. And this new race is mostly composed of the poor and ordinary people (1 Cor 1:27ff.). God's election is never presented as a cause for speculation or controversy, but rather to celebrate the free grace of God that grants salvation and also to move believers to constant worship and lives of holiness and goodness. As in the OT there is in the NT the election of individuals for service (e.g., Acts 6:5; 15:22, 25). Further, the question as to whether the Jews are, as a people, still the elect of God is faced by Paul in Romans 9–11 in the light of the salvation of God in and through Jesus.

Bibliography: G. C. Berkouwer, *The Providence of God,* 1952, and *Divine Election,* 1960; D. A. Carson, *Divine Sovereignty and Human Responsibility,* 1982. PT

EL ELOHE ISRAEL (ĕl ē-lō'hĕ ĭz'rȧ-ĕl). An altar erected by Jacob when he settled near Shechem (Gen 33:20). The name means "the God [who is] the God of Israel." At the beginning of this pilgrimage, Jacob vowed that if the Lord would bring him safely back again then the Lord would be his God (Gen 28:20–21). He kept this vow, acknowledging his God and believingly incorporating his own new name.

ELEMENTS (Gr. *stoicheia, rows, series, alphabet, first principles of a science, physical elements, planets, personal cosmic powers*). In Hebrews 5:12 "elementary truths" (KJV "first principles") is clearly the meaning, as shown by Greek *archē,* "principles," (KJV) in Hebrews 6:1. Galatians 4:3, 9 refer to heathen deities and practices. Colossians 2:8, 20, translated "basic principles" (KJV "rudiments") indicate a more philosophical concept of the elements. Heavenly bodies or physical elements are referred to in 2 Peter 3:10, 12.

ELEPH. A place in the lot of Benjamin, near Jerusalem (Josh 18:28). The NIV renders Haeleph. Some suggest the name should be read in conjunction with the preceding word, as Zelah-eleph. The site is uncertain.

ELEPHANT (See ANIMALS)

ELEVEN, THE. The eleven apostles (Acts 1:26) or disciples (Matt 28:16) remaining after the death of Judas (Mark 16:14; Luke 24:9, 33; Acts 2:14).

ELHANAN. 1. A son of Jaare-Oregim (called also Jair), a Bethlehemite who killed Lahmi, the brother of Goliath (2 Sam 21:19; 1 Chron 20:5).

2. A son of Dodo of Bethlehem and one of David's thirty heroes (2 Sam 23:24; 1 Chron 11:26).

ELI (Heb. *'ēlî*). A member of the family of Ithamar, fourth son of Aaron, who acted as both judge and high priest in Israel. He lived at Shiloh in a dwelling adjoining the tabernacle (1 Sam 1–4; 14:3; 1 Kings 2:27). Little is known about him until he was well advanced in age, when Hannah came to pray for a son. The conduct of Eli's sons, Phinehas and Hophni, who, although lacking their father's character, were put into the priest's office, gave him grief in his declining years. Their conduct shocked the people, for they "were treating the LORD's offering with contempt" (1 Sam 2:17). While Eli warned them of their shameful ways, he did not rebuke with the severity their deeds merited. Instead, Eli mildly reasoned with his sons, saying, "Why do you do such things?" (2:23). But the sons no longer heeded their father, and he didn't restrain them. An old man of ninety, almost blind, Eli waited to hear the result of the battle between the Israelites and the Philistines. When the messenger came with the news of the slaughter of his sons and of the taking of the ark, Eli fell off his seat and died of a broken neck. Although a good and pure man, Eli was weak and indecisive.

ELI, ELI, LAMA SABACHTHANI (See ELOI, ELOI, LAMA SABACHTHANI)

ELIAB (ē-lī'ăb, Heb. *'ĕlî'āv*). 1. A son of Helon and leader of the tribe of Zebulun when the census was taken in the wilderness (Num 1:9; 2:7; 7:24, 29; 10:16).

2. A son of Pallu or Phallu, a Reubenite, and father of Nathan and Abiram (Num 16:1, 12; 26:8–9; Deut 11:6).

3. The eldest son of Jesse and brother of David (1 Sam 16:6; 17:13, 28). Of commanding appearance, he was serving with Saul's army when it was menaced by Goliath, and he resented his younger brother's interference. Eliab's daughter Abihail became one of Rehoboam's wives (2 Chron 11:18).

4. A Levite in David's time who was a tabernacle porter and musician (1 Chron 15:18, 20; 16:5).

5. A Gadite warrior who with others came over to David when David was hiding in the wilderness (1 Chron 12:9).

6. An ancestor of Samuel the prophet; a Kohathite Levite (1 Chron 6:27). Called Elihu (1 Sam 1:1) and Eliel (1 Chron 6:34).

ELIADA (ē-lī'à-dà, Heb. *'elyādhā'*). 1. One of David's sons (2 Sam 5:16; 1 Chron 3:8).

2. A Benjamite, a mighty warrior who led two hundred thousand of his tribe to the army of Jehoshaphat (2 Chron 17:17).

3. The father of Rezon, captain of a roving band that annoyed Solomon (1 Kings 11:23; KJV Eliadah).

ELIAHBA (ē-lī'à-bà). A Shaalbonite, and a member of David's famous guard (2 Sam 23:32; 1 Chron 11:33).

ELIAKIM (ē-lī'ă-kĭm, Heb. *'elyāqîm, God sets up*). 1. A son of Hilkiah, successor of Shebna as the master of Hezekiah's household. The manner of his displacing Shebna and the reasons for it, together with the responsibilities and honors of his office, are set forth in Isaiah 22:15–25. He was spokesman for the delegation from Hezekiah, king of Judah, which attempted to negotiate with the representatives of Sennacherib, king of Assyria, who was besieging Jerusalem (2 Kings 18:17–37; Isa 36:1–22). When these negotiations failed, Eliakim headed the delegation sent to implore the help of Isaiah the prophet (2 Kings 19:2; Isa 37:2).

2. The original name of King Jehoiakim (2 Kings 23:34; 2 Chron 36:4).

3. A priest who helped in the dedication of the rebuilt wall in Nehemiah's time (Neh 12:41).

4. A grandson of Zerubbabel and ancestor of Jesus (Matt 1:13).

5. Another earlier ancestor of Jesus (Luke 3:30).

ELIAM (ē-lī'ăm). 1. The father of Bathsheba, wife of David (2 Sam 11:3). Called Ammiel in 1 Chronicles 3:5.

2. The son of Ahithophel the Gilonite (2 Sam 23:34).

ELIAS (ē-lī'ăs). The Greek form of the name of

the prophet Elijah, used in KJV in all occurrences of the name in the NT.

ELIASAPH (ē-lī'á-săf). 1. The son of Deuel and head of the Gadites during the wandering in the wilderness (Num 1:14; 2:14; 7:42, 47; 10:20).

2. A son of Lael, a Levite and prince of the Gershonites during the wilderness wanderings (Num 3:24).

ELIASHIB (ē-lī'á-shĭb, Heb. *'elyāshîv, God restores*). 1. A priest in David's time from whom the eleventh priestly course took its name (1 Chron 24:12).

2. A son of Elioenai, descendant of Zerubbabel, a Judahite (1 Chron 3:24).

3. The high priest at the time of the rebuilding of the city wall (Neh 3:1, 20–21; 13:4, 7, 28).

4. A Levite and singer who put away his foreign wife (Ezra 10:24).

5. A son of Zattu who married a foreign wife (Ezra 10:27).

6. A son of Bani who also married a foreign wife (Ezra 10:36).

7. An ancestor of Johanan who helped Ezra in gathering together the foreign wives, and in other matters during the reign of Darius the Persian (Ezra 10:6; Neh 12:10, 22–23).

ELIATHAH (ē-lī'á-thá). A son of Heman and a musician in David's reign (1 Chron 25:4, 27).

ELIDAD (ē-lī'dăd). A prince of the tribe of Benjamin and a member of the commission in the division of Canaan (Num 34:21).

ELIEHOENAI (ĕl'ĭ-hō-ē'nī, *to Jehovah are my eyes*). 1. A descendant of Pahath-Moab who returned with Ezra in Artaxerxes's time (Ezra 8:4). Also called Elihoenai.

2. Perhaps also the seventh son of Meshelemiah the son of Kore of the sons of Asaph, a Korahite doorkeeper of the tabernacle in David's reign (1 Chron 26:3). See also ELIOENAI.

ELIEL (ē'lī-ĕl, ē-lī'ĕl, Heb. *'ĕlî'ēl, God is God*). A Levite of the family of Kohath and an ancestor of Samuel the prophet (1 Chron 6:34).

2. A chief man of the half tribe of Manasseh in Bashan (1 Chron 5:24).

3. A son of Shimei the Benjamite (1 Chron 8:20).

4. A son of Shashak, a Benjamite (1 Chron 8:22).

5. A Mahavite and a captain in David's army (1 Chron 11:46).

6. Another of David's heroes (1 Chron 11:47).

7. The seventh Gadite who joined David at Ziklag (1 Chron 12:11). Perhaps the same person as no. 5 or 6.

8. A chief of Judah, a man of Hebron, in David's time (1 Chron 15:9). Perhaps the same man as no. 5.

9. A chief Levite who helped in the return of the ark from the house of Obed-Edom (1 Chron 15:11).

10. A Levite overseer of tithes and offerings in Hezekiah's reign (2 Chron 31:13).

ELIENAI (ĕl'ĭ-ē'nī). A son of Shimei, a Benjamite (1 Chron 8:20).

ELIEZER (ĕl'ĭ-ē'zêr, Heb. *'ĕlî'ezer, God is help*). 1. Abraham's chief servant, and "son of his house," that is, one of his large household. He is named "Eliezer of Damascus" probably to distinguish him from others of the same name (Gen 15:2). Probably he is the unnamed servant Abraham sent to his own country and kindred to secure a bride for Isaac, his son of promise (Gen 24).

2. The second son of Moses and Zipporah to whom his father gave this name as a memento of his gratitude to God (Exod 18:4; 1 Chron 23:15, 17; 26:25).

3. A son of Beker and grandson of Benjamin (1 Chron 7:8).

4. A priest who assisted, by blowing a trumpet, in the return of the ark to Jerusalem (1 Chron 15:24).

5. Son of Zicri, a Reubenite ruler in David's time (1 Chron 27:16).

6. The prophet who rebuked Jehoshaphat for his alliance with Ahaziah in the expedition to Tarshish (2 Chron 20:37; see NIV footnote).

7. A chieftain sent with others to induce many of the Israelites to return with Ezra to Jerusalem (Ezra 8:16).

8. A priest who put away his foreign wife (Ezra 10:18).

9. A Levite who had done the same (Ezra 10:23).

10. One of the descendants of Harim who had done the same (Ezra 10:31).

11. An ancestor of Jesus in the intertestamental period (Luke 3:29).

ELIHOREPH (ĕl'ĭ-hō'rĕf). One of King Solomon's scribes (1 Kings 4:3).

ELIHU (ē-lī'hū, Heb. *'elîhû, he is my God*). 1. The father of Jeroham and great-grandfather of Samuel the prophet (1 Sam 1:1). Called also Eliel in 1 Chronicles 6:34.

2. A man of Manasseh who joined David at Ziklag (1 Chron 12:20).

3. A Kohathite of the family of Korah, and a tabernacle porter in David's time (1 Chron 26:7).

4. A brother of David; he became ruler over Judah (1 Chron 27:18). Also known as Eliab.

5. The youngest of Job's friends, the son of Barakel, a Buzite, that is, an Aramean (Job 32:2–6; 34:1; 35:1; 36:1).

ELIJAH (ē-lī'já, Heb. *'ēlîyāhû, Jehovah is God*). The name of four men in the Bible, of whom three are mentioned only once each.

1. A Benjamite and son of Jeroham, resident at Jerusalem (1 Chron 8:27).

2. A descendant of Harim who married a foreign wife during the Exile (Ezra 10:21).

3. An Israelite induced to put away his foreign wife (Ezra 10:26).

4. The prophet Elijah (1 Kings 17:1–2 Kings 2:12) whose ministry was set in the days of King Ahab (c. 874-852 B.C.) of the northern kingdom of Israel/Ephraim. Elijah was born in Tishbe and is described as one of the settlers in Gilead (1 Kings 17:1)—though some make a slight alteration in the Hebrew text (cf. NIV) that would permit the translation "from Tishbe in Gilead," thus distinguishing Elijah's birthplace from Tishbe in Naphtali. In either case, whether by emigration (as the Hebrew text says) or by birth (as the altered text says), Elijah appeared on the scene from east of Jordan.

In our ears his first message sounds like no more than a weather forecast, a drought (1 Kings 17:1) that would last over three years (18:1), but Ahab and all who heard knew that more was involved than a prediction of climatic hardship. The "forces of nature" are in the Lord's hands (see also EARTHQUAKE); he uses them to bless, to warn, and to judge his people (cf. Deut 28:1–2, 12, 15, 22–24). Elijah's commission therefore was to convey a stern message: All is not well between the Lord and his people, and they are about to suffer his judgments on their disobedience.

But, remarkably, the Lord did not leave Elijah there either to amplify the message or to seek to win the people back from the path of spiritual disaster. He took Elijah away into three hidden years of apprenticeship (1 Kings 17:3, "hide"). First, by the Lord's word, he returned to his own home area, for even though we do not know precisely where Kerith was, it was east of Jordan (17:2–5). There Elijah was marvelously provided for. In this way he began to learn that as long as he walked in obedience he would be safe (however unlikely the means of supply might be). The next test was more demanding: he had to go to Zarephath, which was only six miles (ten km.) south of Jezebel's hometown of Sidon. Elijah not only learned once again that the Lord cared for his obedient servant, but that the Lord's power is superior to all the power of man (18:10). The third story from the hidden years (17:17–24) was designed by the Lord to teach Elijah specifically the power of prayer to transform situations of death—a boy was restored to life (17:22) and his mother brought to spiritual faith and testimony (17:24).

Against this background the time came for the drought to be broken. Again the word of God came (1 Kings 18:1), and Elijah had learned in the apprentice years that when the word is obeyed all must be well. He therefore went without fear to meet Ahab, but it is in fact Ahab who had to come to meet Elijah (18:2–16). Another lesson learned in the hidden years now came to fruition: knowing that the Lord answers prayer (17:20–24), Elijah proposed a prayer contest (18:24) on Mount Carmel.

The behavior of the Baal prophets (1 Kings 18:26–29) was in accord with their beliefs (see also BAAL). According to a practice known as "imitative magic," the prophets sought to do on earth what they desired their god to do from heaven. First they limp (literally) or dance around the altar, trying to suggest flickering and dancing flames (18:26). When that failed, they resorted to the desperate expedient of slashing and cutting their bodies, in the hope that the down-pouring blood might prompt the down-pouring of fire. But it was all to no avail.

Elijah, on the contrary, began his appeal to the Lord by a deliberate disavowal of imitative magic. About to call for fire, he first demanded the pouring of water on the intended sacrifice. This was a direct denial of the whole Baal theology and tantamount to a denial of the reality of Baal. Then, with simplicity and dignity (1 Kings 18:36–37), he rested his case on the certainty that the Lord would answer prayer.

Why did Elijah demand the deliberate slaughter of the Baal entourage (1 Kings 18:40)? Perhaps we are repulsed by it because we have allowed our sense of moral and spiritual outrage to atrophy: we no longer feel any deep concern at the presence and threat of false religions; we are tolerant of error and of the menace it constitutes to the souls of people; we do not face up to the exclusiveness of the person and claims of the Lord. This is not to say that we should copy the methods of Elijah in this any more than we would build altars and sacrifice animals, but we must not criticize, much less scorn or look down on him for expressing in terms appropriate to his day a decisiveness of commitment, loyalty, and concern that we are failing to express in terms appropriate to ours.

Elijah had one more matter to occupy him on Mount Carmel. James (5:18) directs us to interpret Elijah's crouched attitude as one of prayer: he was praying for the fulfillment of what the Lord had promised (1 Kings 18:1). He was blessed with persistent faith, for, seven times he sent his servant to a lookout point, and as soon as even the slightest sign appeared, he responded in active faith to its message (18:43ff.).

The collapse of Elijah (1 Kings 19:1ff.) is not at all difficult to understand. The amount of sleep the Lord insisted on giving him (19:5–6) shows the extent to which he had neglected his physical well-being. He had allowed himself to become overtired and then he became overwrought (19:3) when he was faced, not with celebrations and triumphant crowds as he had hoped, but with Jezebel's undiminished influence. It seemed as though the victory on Mount Carmel had never happened. But the Lord was not defeated. First he gave his servant rest and nourishment (19:5–7); second, he brought him into his own presence (19:8–9); third, he renewed Elijah's sense of the power of the word of God. Elijah experienced the wind, earthquake, and fire—three notable instruments of divine purpose—but he had no sense of meeting the Lord in them (19:11–12). Yet when a "gentle whisper" came (19:12b), Elijah knew he was in the very presence of the Lord. How significant then the question is: What are you doing here? (19:13). In his hidden years, he did nothing without a word (17:2–3, 8–9; 18:1–2), but the Lord had not told him to flee from Jezebel! Understandably but tragically, in the crucial moment, Elijah forgot one of the central lessons of his apprenticeship: The servant of the Lord lives by the word of the Lord, and when he does so he is provided for and kept safe. Fourth, the Lord renewed Elijah's commission and gave him a word of encouragement (19:15–18). Perhaps we ought to note as a fifth element in the restorative work of the Lord that he left Elijah's prayer unanswered (19:4). He had it in mind to grant Elijah something far better than he would dare pray for. He would never die (2 Kings 2:11).

Elijah appears only once more in the reign of Ahab, when that weak king acquiesced in the murder of Naboth (1 Kings 21) and the violent seizure of his vineyard. In his response to this, Elijah is a true founder of the brilliant line of prophets that was to follow him in his concern for moral and social righteousness. In the reign of Ahab's son, Ahaziah (853–852 B.C.), he vigorously resisted the king's attempt to take him by force (2 Kings 1). Again we find ourselves affronted by the violence of Elijah's response, and we need to remind ourselves that he was acting in ways appropriate to his day with a decisiveness for God and a hatred and abhorrence of false religion that we might well covet for ourselves.

Elijah was a mighty man for God, but the Bible does not conceal his faults, but rather selects one for special mention. Elijah was what we call a "loner." He easily felt himself isolated and solitary (1 Kings 18:22), even when he knew that it was very far from the truth (cf. 18:13). It is true to character that when he most needed fellowship and help, he deliberately sought a solitary path (19:3–4), and when the Lord blessed him with the companionable and warm-hearted Elisha, he was unready to share with him the great experience that he knew was to be his (2 Kings 2:2, 4, 6). It is certain he would not have fled from Jezebel had he been willing to gather round him the supportive fellowship of Obadiah and his large prophetic group. Nevertheless the Lord gave Elijah, that man of like nature with ourselves (James 5:17), the glorious and unique honor of by-passing death and entering heaven in the whirlwind (2 Kings 2:11).

But though Elijah thus dramatically left the earthly scene, his story was not over. His prophecy regarding Jezebel (1 Kings 21:23) was fulfilled in 2 Kings 9:36, and his forecast regarding the dynasty of Ahab proved true in 2 Kings 10:10, 17. Furthermore, 2 Chronicles 21:12–15 records that Elijah also had a written ministry. Beyond that, too, his ministry continued. Malachi 4:5–6 foresaw the appearance of Elijah as the forerunner of the Messiah, and this was fulfilled in the ministry of John the Baptist (e.g., Matt 11:13–14; 17:9–13). Elijah's greatest privilege in the Bible story was to stand with the Son of God on the Mount of Transfiguration and speak with him of his coming death (Matt 17:3–4; Mark 9:4–5; Luke 9:30–33). JAM

ELIKA (ē-lī'kȧ). A Harodite, one of David's mighty men (2 Sam 23:25).

ELIM (ē'lĭm, Heb. *'êlīm, terebinths*). The second stopping-place of the Israelites after they crossed the Red Sea on their exodus from Egypt. It is on the west side of the Sinaitic peninsula, on the caravan route to the copper and turquoise mines of Sinai. In spite of its advantages, twelve springs of water and seventy palm trees, the Israelites seem not to have stayed there long, preferring to put a greater distance between themselves and the land of their bondage (Exod 15:27; 16:1; Num 33:9–10).

ELIMELECH (ē-lĭm'ĕ-lek̄, Heb. *'ĕlîmelekh, my God is king*). A man of Bethlehem-Judah who

Wadi Gharandel, a well-known watering spot with tamarisks and palms, located on the western side of the Sinai Peninsula and thought to be the probable site of Elim. Courtesy Ecole Biblique et Archéologique Française, Jerusalem.

emigrated to Moab during a famine in Judah in the time of the judges (Ruth 1:2–3; 2:1, 3; 4:3, 9). He and his sons died in Moab. He is remembered because his daughter-in-law Ruth was faithful to his widow Naomi.

ELIOENAI (ĕl'ĭ-ō-ē'nī, *to Jehovah are my eyes*). 1. A son of Neariah of the family of David (1 Chron 3:23–24).

2. The head of a family of Simeon (1 Chron 4:36).

3. The head of one of the families of the sons of Beker, son of Benjamin (1 Chron 7:8).

4. A son of Pashhur, a priest who put away his foreign wife (Ezra 10:22). Perhaps the same person as no. 6.

5. A son of Zattu who married a foreign wife (Ezra 10:27).

6. A priest, perhaps the same person as no. 4 (Neh 12:41).

See also ELIEHOENAI.

ELIPHAL (ē-lī'făl, ĕl'ĭ-făl, Heb. *'ĕlîphāl, God has judged*). Son of Ur, one of David's mighty men (1 Chron 11:35). Eliphal and Ur are thought to be Eliphelet and Ahasbai of 2 Samuel 23:34, for textual reasons.

ELIPHALET (See ELIPHELET)

ELIPHAZ (ĕl'ĭ-făz, Heb. *'ĕlîphaz,* possibly *God is fine gold*). 1. A son of Esau by Adah, daughter of Elon (Gen 36:4–16; 1 Chron 1:35–36).

2. The chief of Job's three friends (Job 2:11); from Teman, traditionally famous for its wise men (Jer 49:7). Eliphaz's speeches show clearer reasoning than those of the two other friends. In his first speech (Job 4–5), Eliphaz traces all affliction to sin, through the natural operation of cause and effect, and admonishes Job to make his peace with God. In his second address (ch. 15), Eliphaz shows irritation at Job's sarcasm, reiterates his arguments, and depicts strongly the fate of the wicked. In his third address (ch. 22), Eliphaz definitely charges Job with sin and points out to him the path of restoration. In Job 42:7–9 God addresses Eliphaz as the chief of Job's friends and commands him to make sacrifice in expiation for wrongly accusing Job, saying that Job will pray for them and they will be forgiven.

ELIPHELEHU (ē-lĭf'ĕ-lē'-hū). A Levite singer and harpist who had charge of the choral service when the ark was returned (1 Chron 15:18, 21). Also called Elipheleh.

ELIPHELET (ē-lĭf'ĕ-lĕt). 1. The last of David's sons born at Jerusalem (2 Sam 5:16; 1 Chron 14:7).

2. Another son of David born in Jerusalem (1 Chron 3:6). Also called Elpalet (1 Chron 14:5).

3. A son of Ahasbai, one of David's heroes (2 Sam 23:34).

4. A son of Eshek and descendant of Saul, a Benjamite (1 Chron 8:39).

5. A leader of the sons of Adonikam who returned from exile with Ezra (Ezra 8:13).

6. A son of Hashum who put away his foreign wife (Ezra 10:33).

ELISABETH (See ELIZABETH)

ELISHA (ē-lī'shȧ, called *Eliseus,* the Gr. form of Heb. *'ĕlîshā'*, in Luke 4:27 KJV; Elisha in NIV, ASV, RSV). At Horeb, God directed Elijah to anoint Elisha to be his successor (1 Kings 19:16–21), who was to aid Hazael, king of Syria, and Jehu, king of Israel, in taking vengeance on the enemies of God. Elijah left Horeb and on his way north found Elisha the son of Shaphat of Abel Meholah (19:16) plowing with the last of twelve yoke of oxen. The number of oxen indicates the wealth of the family. Elijah cast his mantle on Elisha, who understood the significance of the act as the choice of himself to succeed the older prophet. Elisha ran after Elijah, who had not tarried to explain his action, and begged for permission to kiss his parents farewell. Elijah's reply, "Go back. What have I done to you?" led Elisha to go home and make his own decision to accept the prophetic call. Elisha next appeared in connection with the translation of Elijah (2 Kings 2). He persisted in following Elijah till the latter was carried up to heaven. Because he saw him go, a double portion of Elijah's spirit was given him. Taking the mantle of Elijah, he used it to make a dry path over the Jordan, as his master had done, and tried to dissuade the sons of the prophets from a fruitless search for the body of Elijah.

Since Elisha thus comes into his ministry endowed with a double portion of Elijah's spirit we are on the alert to see what his first words or deeds will be. The narrative selects two immediate acts of the prophet: the healing of the waters at Jericho and the cursing of the rabble at Bethel, a curse removed (2 Kings 2:19–22) and a curse invoked (2:23–25).

Jericho had been put under a curse by Joshua (Josh 6:26) at the time of its destruction. It was, in its ruin, to be a perpetual memorial to the Lord's wrath against false religion and corrupt society. In the reign of Ahab, and within the era of Elijah and Elisha, Jericho had been rebuilt. Bible history (1 Kings 16:34) faithfully records the fulfillment of Joshua's prediction. The rebuilding of the cursed city is offered as plain evidence of the spiritually careless days of Ahab; the recording of the fulfillment of the curse is to assure us that though man may blithely assume power to disregard the word of God, the word remains in force. Those who had the temerity to live in the new city found this out to their cost. Every prospect was pleasing about Jericho, but nothing went right. The water was foul and the land (literally) "casts it young" (2 Kings 2:19). Animals were miscarrying, perhaps women too, and the meaning of the phrase has even been extended to crops: nothing came to full fruitage and term. Elisha's response was not "I could have warned you about that." He said nothing about their folly in disregarding divine wrath; rather he set about a work of grace. We see in Leviticus 2:13 and Numbers 18:19 that salt is linked with the covenant of God. Elisha's requirement that the salt be brought to him in a new bowl (2 Kings 2:20) was intended to safeguard the act as far as possible from the pollution of human use. The intention in pouring the salt into the spring was to bring the city and its life back within the covenant mercies of the Lord and (2:21–22) this is what in grace the Lord allowed to happen.

The case of Bethel was quite different. It was one of the centers of long-standing religious apostasy in the northern kingdom (1 Kings 12:26–29), and the arrival there of the new prophet of the Lord was bound to be an event of special significance. What follows is related in 2 Kings 2:23–25. Translations of *na'ar* (v. 23) vary: "little children" (KJV), "small boys" (JB, MOF, NEB, RSV), "young lads" (NASB), and "youths" (MLB, NIV). Some see here an irascible old man teased by playful children, losing his temper, and uttering a curse that is implemented by divine action; seemingly, the old man's God is as irascible and unattractive as he is himself. If this is the truth of the matter, then we have no recourse but to agree with those commentators who find the episode pointless and who say that it reflects no credit on either Elisha or his God. But is this what really occurred? First, Elisha was not an old man; rather, he was the young man who until recently was second in command to Elijah. Second, neither we nor the Bethelites would have any means of knowing whether he was bald or not, for custom kept the head well covered. Third, the Hebrew does not necessarily indicate toddlers or infants. In a suitable context the expression in verse 23 could mean youngsters of an early age (see the same expression in 2 Kings 5:14). But in 1 Samuel 20:35 we would more naturally think of a teen-age servant in the royal household. The noun in verse 23 is, by itself, indeterminate regarding age. It is used of Joseph aged seventeen (Gen 37:2) and of the trained men in Abram's private army (14:24). The different word in verse 24 leads to the same conclusions. It is used of Rehoboam and his contemporaries (1 Kings 12:8, 10, 14) at a time when 1 Kings 14:21 says Rehoboam was himself forty-one. In other words, the words in verses 23–24 derive their meaning from what suits the context, saving that the adjective in verse 23 means that they were less than adult. The word "kids" today is somewhat similar, covering a wide age-range short of adulthood.

The situation can be reconstructed, then, like this. Since succeeding Elijah, Elisha has stayed near Jericho, but he must soon return to their old prophetic center at Carmel. This road passes Bethel, and for the first time the new prophet and the old apostasy come face to face. The religious authorities at Bethel are determined not to let the chance pass; Elijah was too much for them, but they will strike at his successor before he consolidates his position. So they arrange a "reception committee" in the approved "rent-a-mob" fashion. Why they opened the proceedings with a taunt of baldness remains a mystery—though possibly, if Elisha was a Nazirite, they were, in fact, mocking the uncut and abundant hair flowing out from under his head covering. At all events, they are bent on a mischief that goes beyond verbal abuse. If the victory is to remain with Elisha, it can only be so if the Lord will come to his aid. Elisha expresses his need of the Lord, not in a "will he, won't he" wish for help but in a confident commanding of divine wrath. The Lord does not desert his beleaguered servant. We might well ask if we would want it to be otherwise.

Elisha had a long ministry during the reigns of Joram (KJV "Jehoram"), Jehu, Jehoahaz, and Jehoash (KJV "Joash"), kings of Israel. After the death of Ahab, Moab rebelled against his son Joram (2 Kings 3). When Joram secured the king of Edom and Jehoshaphat, king of Judah, as allies, Jehoshaphat insisted on consulting Elisha. Elisha referred Joram to the prophets of his parents, but out of regard to Jehoshaphat, counseled them to dig trenches to channel water from Edom to relieve their army, and predicted victory over the Moabites. Elisha saved a poor widow from financial distress by miraculous multiplication of her oil supply (4:1–7). He visited the home of a "well-to-do woman" and her husband in Shunem so often that she had a room built for him (4:8–37). Elisha sent his servant Gehazi to ask the woman what she would like to have him do for her in return for her hospitality. She asked for a son, and a son was given her. When the lad was old enough to go to the fields with his father, he suffered a fatal sunstroke. His mother herself went for Elisha, who, after sending Gehazi, whose efforts were fruitless, came himself, and after great effort the child came back to life. At Gilgal during a famine (4:38–41), Elisha saved a company of the prophets from death because of eating poisonous vegetables. When a present of food was given him, Elisha set it before a hundred men, and the Lord increased the supply to satisfy them (4:42–44). Elisha healed the Aramean (KJV "Syrian") captain Naaman of leprosy (ch. 5); Gehazi proved himself an unworthy servant. Elisha rescued a young prophet's borrowed axhead (6:1–7). He gave timely warning, repeatedly saving Israel from defeat by the Arameans (6:23). The Arameans came to Dothan, where Elisha was living with a servant, whom Elisha showed the armies of God protecting the city. The Arameans were stricken with blindness, and Elisha led them to Samaria and persuaded the king of Israel to feed them and release them. The Arameans invaded Israel no more for a time. When Aram finally besieged Samaria and the city was reduced to terrible straits, the king of Israel blamed Elisha (6:24–7:20). Elisha predicted relief the next day. Four lepers, considering their case hopeless, visited the Aramean camp and found it deserted. The spoils of the Arameans relieved the inhabitants of Samaria. Elisha advised the "well-to-do woman" of 2 Kings 4:8 to escape a coming famine by going to Philistia (8:1–6). When she returned and sought restoration of her property,

Gehazi, who had just been telling the king the deeds of Elisha, was the means by which the woman secured restitution.

Elisha visited Damascus and had an innocent part in Hazael's succeeding Ben-Hadad as king of Aram (2 Kings 8:7–15). Elisha sent a young prophet to anoint Jehu king of Israel (9:1–3). Before Elisha died (13:14–21), Jehoash, king of Israel, came to visit him and received an object lesson by means of arrows, with regard to his war against the Arameans (KJV "Syrians"). A man being hastily buried in Elisha's sepulcher touched Elisha's bones and revived (13:20–21). Elisha's ministry was filled with miracles, many relieving private needs, some related to affairs of state. Elisha's prophetic insight and wise counsel made him a valuable though not always appreciated adviser to kings. He finished the work of Elijah, destroying the system of Baal worship, completed the tasks assigned to Elijah of anointing Hazael and Jehu, and saw the final ruin of the house of Ahab and Jezebel. The mention of the cleansing of Naaman the Syrian from leprosy in Luke 4:27 perhaps indicates this as the crowning achievement of his career, giving Elisha an influence with the Syrian king that enabled him to help Israel. Elisha's story is told with vigor and vivid detail, making him live as few OT characters do. The incidents are not all told in chronological order, but they bear the marks of historical truth in the simplicity of their narration. ER and JAM

ELISHAH (ē-lī'shȧ, Heb. *'ĕlîshâh, God saves*). The eldest son of Javan, grandson of Noah and founder of a tribal family (Gen 10:4; 1 Chron 1:7). The land from which Tyre got its purple dye (Ezek 27:7); somewhere around the Mediterranean (South Italy, North Africa, or Greece), but not yet identified.

ELISHAMA (ē-lĭsh'ȧmȧ, Heb. *'ĕlîshāmā', God has heard*). 1. Grandfather of Joshua, son of Ammihud, prince of the Ephraimites at the outset of the wilderness journey (Num 1:10; 2:18; 7:48, 53; 10:22; 1 Chron 7:26).

2. A son of David born in Jerusalem (2 Sam 5:16; 1 Chron 3:8).

3. Another son of David, who is also called Elishua (1 Chron 3:6; cf. 2 Sam 5:15).

4. A son of Jekamiah, a Judahite (1 Chron 2:41).

5. Father of Nethaniah and grandfather of Ishmael "of royal blood" who lived at the time of the Exile (2 Kings 25:25; Jer 41:1). This may be the same as no. 4.

6. A scribe or secretary to Jehoiakim (Jer 36:12, 20–21).

7. A priest sent by Jehoshaphat to teach the people the law (2 Chron 17:8).

ELISHAPHAT (ē-lĭsh'ȧ-făt). One of the "commanders of units of a hundred" who supported Jehoiada in the revolt against Athaliah (2 Chron 23:1).

ELISHEBA (ē-lĭsh'ēbȧ). Amminadab's daughter, sister of Nahshon, captain of Judah (Num 2:3). By marrying Aaron (Exod 6:23) she connected the royal and priestly tribes.

ELISHUA (ĕl'ĭ-shū'ȧ, ē-lĭsh'wȧ). A son of David born in Jerusalem (2 Sam 5:15; 1 Chron 14:5). Also called Elishama in KJV (cf. NIV footnote) in 1 Chronicles 3:6.

ELIUD (ē-lī'ŭd). The son of Akim and father of Eleazar and ancestor of Christ (Matt 1:14–15).

ELIZABETH (Gr. *Elisabet, God is my oath,* KJV Elisabeth). The wife of the priest Zechariah, herself of the lineage of Aaron (Luke 1:5–57). In fulfillment of God's promise, in her old age she bore a son, John the Baptist. Her kinswoman (cousin), Mary of Nazareth in Galilee, having learned that she was to be the virgin mother of Jesus, visited Elizabeth in the hill country of Judea. Elizabeth's Spirit-filled greeting prompted Mary to reply in a song called *Magnificat*. After Mary returned home, Elizabeth's son was born. She was a woman of unusual piety, faith, and spiritual gifts, whose witness to Mary must have been an incomparable encouragement. Luke, who alone tells the story, appreciated the significant role of women in the history of redemption and emphasized the agency of the Holy Spirit in the life of Elizabeth.

ELIZAPHAN (ĕl'ĭ-zā'făn, ē-lĭz'ȧfăn, Heb., *'ĕlîtsāphān, God has concealed*). 1. The son of Uzziel, chief ruler of the Kohathites when the census was taken in Sinai (Num 3:30; 1 Chron 15:8; 2 Chron 29:13), called Elzaphan in Exodus 6:22 and Leviticus 10:4. In Chronicles his Levitical class is treated as coequal with the Kohathites.

2. The son of Parnach, prince of the tribe of Zebulun in the wilderness (Num 34:25).

ELIZUR (ē-lī'zĕr). The son of Shedeur, and prince of the Reubenites, who helped in the census Moses took (Num 1:5; 2:10; 7:30–35; 10:18).

ELKANAH (ĕl-kā'nȧ, Heb. *'elqānâh, God has possessed*). 1. The father of Samuel the prophet (1 Sam 1:1–2:21). His tender solicitude for his favorite wife Hannah and for their first son appears in the story. He is called an Ephraimite from Ramathaim-Zophim, in the hill country of Ephraim, but he appears to have been a Levite, descendant of Kohath (1 Chron 6:22–23, 27, 33–34), though the genealogical data are not clear.

2. A son of Korah, a Levite, descendant of Kohath (Exod 6:23–24; 1 Chron 6:24). The sons of Korah did not die with their father, who perished for rebellion against Moses and Aaron (Num 26:11).

3. The second in power to King Ahaz, killed by Pekah, king of Israel, when he invaded Judah (2 Chron 28:7).

4. One of the ambidextrous warriors who came to David at Ziklag (1 Chron 12:6).

5. In addition, several Levites bear the name Elkanah (1 Chron 6:22–28, 33–38; 9:16). It is impossible to distinguish them with certainty from one another. Elkanah was a favorite name in the Kohathite line.

ELKOSH, ELKOSHITE. Nahum is called the Elkoshite (Nah 1:1; RSV "of Elkosh"). Jerome says that a town in Galilee was shown him as Elkosh. The Nestorians locate the town and the tomb of the prophet near the Tigris, north of Mosul. Another tradition places Elkosh "beyond Jordan," but emendations of that text and other considerations lead some to believe that Elkosh was in southern Judah.

ELLASAR (ĕl-lā'sȧr, Heb. *'ellāsār*). One of the city-states whose king, Arioch (Eri-aku), invaded Palestine in the time of Abraham (Gen 14:1, 9). It is the ancient Babylonian Larsa (with the last three letters transposed in Heb.), modern Senkereh, SE of Babylon, between Erech and Ur. At first independent, it became subject to Hammurabi (Amraphel of Gen 14:1, 9) or to his successor. Ellasar was at this period a city of a high degree of civilization, a center of sun-god worship, with a temple tower (ziggurat) called "House of Light," which was a seat of mathematical, astronomical, and other learning. Ruins of city walls and of houses remain. Thus the four kings with whom Abraham fought (14:13–16) were no petty chieftains, but sovereigns of flourishing and cultured cities, from one of which Abraham himself had recently emigrated.

ELMADAM, ELMODAM (ĕl-mā'dăm). The son of Er, and ancestor of Joseph, Mary's husband (Luke 3:28).

ELNAAM (ĕl-nā'ăm). The father of David's guard, Jeribai and Joshaviah (1 Chron 11:46).

ELNATHAN (ĕl-nā'thăn, Heb. *'elnāthān, God has given*). 1. Father of Nehushta, the mother of Jehoiachin (2 Kings 24:8).

2. The son of Acbor, sent to Egypt by King Jehoiakim to bring back the prophet Uriah (Jer 26:22). He was one of those who urged King Jehoiakim not to burn the roll that Jeremiah had written (36:12, 25). He may be the same person as no. 1.

3. The name of three men listed among leaders and men of learning, Levites, sent on an embassy by Ezra (Ezra 8:16).

ELOHIM (ĕ-lō'hĭm). The most frequent Hebrew word for God (over 2,500 times in the OT). Several theories of the origin of the word have been proposed, some connecting it with Hebrew *'ēl* or *'ĕlôah,* others distinguishing them from *'ĕlōhîm.* The origin is prehistoric and therefore incapable of direct proof. Elohim is plural in form, but is singular in construction (used with a singular verb or adjective). When applied to the one true God, the plural is due to the Hebrew idiom of a plural of magnitude or majesty (Gen 1:1). When used of heathen gods (Gen 35:2; Exod 18:11; 20:3; Josh 24:20) or of angels (Job 1:6; Ps 8:5; 97:7) or judges (Exod 21:6; 1 Sam 2:25) as representatives of God, Elohim is plural in sense as well as form. Elohim is the earliest name of God in the OT, and persists along with other names to the latest period. Whatever its etymology, the most likely roots mean either "be strong," or "be in front," suiting the power and preeminence of God. Jesus is quoted as using a form of the name the cross (Matt 27:46; Mark 15:34). See next article. ER

ELOI, ELOI, LAMA SABACHTHANI (ā'lē, ā'lē, lă'mă sȧbăch'thănē). The English transliteration of a Greek phrase (Matt 27:46; Mark 15:34), which in turn is a transliteration of either the Hebrew or an Aramaic version of Psalm 22:1. The phrase as it appears in the best text of Matthew is closer to Aramaic; in Mark it is closer to Hebrew. The words are the central of the seven cries of Jesus from the cross, as gathered from all four Gospels. The fact that in both instances the words are first transliterated shows the deep impression they made on some of the hearers. Both evangelists then translated them for the benefit of readers unfamiliar with either Hebrew or Aramaic, and their translation is authoritative as to what Jesus meant when he uttered them, since during his resurrection ministry he explained to them the meaning of all that concerned his death (Luke 24:45–46). Conjecture connects *sabachthani* with an Aramaic verb meaning "deliverer," which would permit a rendering, "for this hast thou spared me," which is inconsistent with the evangelists' translation. Christ was forsaken by the Father when he bore our sins. ER

ELON (ē'lŏn). A Hittite whose daughter Basemath (Gen 26:34) or Adah (36:2) married Esau.

2. The second of Zebulon's three sons (Gen 46:14; Num 26:26).

3. The Zebulonite who judged Israel ten years (Judg 12:11–12).

ELON (place). 1. A town in the territory of Dan (Josh 19:43). Location unidentified.

2. Elon Bethhanan, a town in one of the districts that furnished provisions for Solomon's household (1 Kings 4:9).

ELOTH (See ELATH, ELOTH)

ELPAAL (ĕl-pā'ăl). Son of Shaharaim, a Benjamite and head of his father's house (1 Chron 8:11–12, 18).

ELPALET, ELPELET (See ELIPHELET)

EL PARAN (See PARAN)

EL SHADDAI (ĕl shăd'ȧ-ī, -shăd'ī). The name of God (translated "God Almighty") by which, according to Exodus 6:3, he appeared to Abraham, Isaac, and Jacob—recorded once to Abraham (Gen 17:1) and four times to Jacob (Gen 28:3; 35:11; 43:14; 48:3). Often "the Almighty" (*Shaddai* without *El*) is used as a name of God: in Jacob's deathbed words (Gen 49:25), in Balaam's prophecies (Num 24:4, 16), by Naomi (Ruth 1:20, 21), thirty times by Job and his friends (Job 5:17–37:23), by God himself (Job 40:2), and twice in the Psalms (Ps 68:14; 91:1). The name is rare in the prophets (Isa 13:6; Ezek 1:24; 10:5 ["Almighty God"]; Joel 1:15). "God (the) Almighty" (Gr. *pantokratōr*, "all-powerful") occurs nine times in the NT (2 Cor 6:18; eight times in Revelation). So this name for God, which was a favorite of the patriarchs, especially Jacob and Job, becomes prominent in the songs of heaven. The etymology of *El Shaddai* is in dispute, "Almighty God" being the widely accepted meaning; some who would derive the Hebrew religion from pagan cults favor "mountain god." ER

ELTEKEH (ĕl'tē-kē). A city in the territory given to Dan, on its southern border with Judah (Josh 19:44). With its pasturelands it was given to the Kohathite Levites (21:23). Probably Khirbet el-Muqenna, east of Ekron.

ELTEKON (ĕl'tē-kŏn). One of six cities in the hill country of Judah (Josh 15:59); site unknown; perhaps near Hebron because it is named with Beth Anoth, which is in that vicinity.

ELTOLAD (ĕl-tō'lăd). A city in the Negev of Judah toward Edom (Josh 15:30), but assigned to Simeon (19:4). Also (1 Chron 4:29) called Tolad.

ELUL (ĕ-lūl'). The sixth month of the Hebrew year, approximately August–September (Neh 6:15). See also CALENDAR.

ELUZAI (ē-lū'zā-ī). A Benjamite who joined David at Ziklag (1 Chron 12:15).

ELYMAS (ĕl'ĭmăs, Gr. *Elymas*). A Jew, Bar-Jesus (meaning *son of Jesus* or *Joshua*), a sorcerer who was with Sergius Paulus, the proconsul of Cyprus. He became blind following Paul's curse, causing the proconsul to believe in the Lord (Acts 13:4–13). His name, Elymas, is Greek in form but is not a Greek translation of Bar-Jesus or of "sorcerer" (Gr. *magos*); it may be the transliteration of an Aramaic or Arabic root meaning "wise," and equivalent to *magos;* hence the phrase "Elymas the sorcerer (for that is what his name means)" (13:8).

ELZABAD (ĕl-zā'băd, ĕl'zȧ-băd). 1. A Gadite who joined David at Ziklag (1 Chron 12:12).
2. The son of Shemaiah and a Korahite Levite (1 Chron 26:7).

ELZAPHAN (See ELIZAPHAN)

EMBALM (ĕm-bȧm). To prepare a dead body with oil and spices to preserve it from decay. Embalming was of Egyptian origin. The only clear instances of it in the Bible were in the cases of Jacob and Joseph. Joseph ordered his slaves, the physicians, to embalm his father (Gen 50:2–3; a process that took forty days); and later Joseph himself was embalmed (50:26). The purpose of the Egyptians in embalming was to preserve the body for the use of the soul in a future life. The purpose of the Hebrews was to preserve the bodies of Jacob and Joseph for a long journey to their resting place with Abraham (50:13). In the case of Joseph, centuries elapsed before burial in the ancestral tomb (Exod 13:19; Josh 24:32). The process of embalming is not described in the Bible. Body cavities were filled with asphalt, cedar oil, or spices, or all three. The body was wrapped tightly in linen cloths, the more perishable parts being stuffed with rolls of linen to maintain the shape of the human form. The Hebrew word for "embalm," *ḥānat,* means "to spice, to make spicy." The body of Asa is said to have been buried with spices, but is not said to have been embalmed (2 Chron 16:14). Jesus comments on the use of spices in burying (Matt 26:12; Mark 14:8; John 12:7); and his body was buried with a hundred pounds (forty-six kg.) of myrrh and spices, wrapped in a linen cloth (John 19:39–40). The women who watched the burial considered this inadequate, for they prepared and brought to the sepulcher more spices (Mark 16:1; Luke 23:35–36; 24:1). Martha thought the body of Lazarus was decaying, hence clearly he had not been embalmed (John 11:39); but he was so bound that he had to be loosened (11:44). The widow's son at Nain was simply being carried out for burial (Luke 7:11–17); Ananias (and presumably Sapphira) were merely wrapped up (Acts 5:6, 10). The biblical concept of the future life made embalming unnecessary. ER

EMBROIDERY, EMBROIDERER. The work and worker of ornamental needlework on cloth. Several Hebrew words are used in connection with this and with related skills. In Exodus 28:39, *shāvats* refers probably to a checkered weaving (ASV, RSV) or plaiting of the coat with

A wall painting from Sennedjem's tomb at Deir el-Medina, c. 1306–1290 B.C., of Anubis, the Egyptian god connected with mummification, preparing a body for burial. Courtesy Seffie Ben-Yoseph.

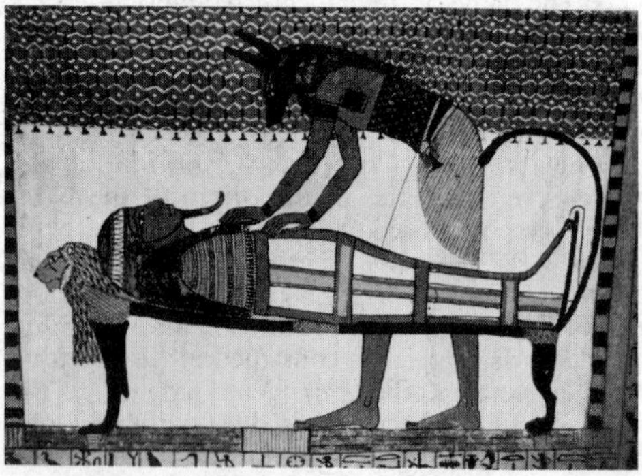

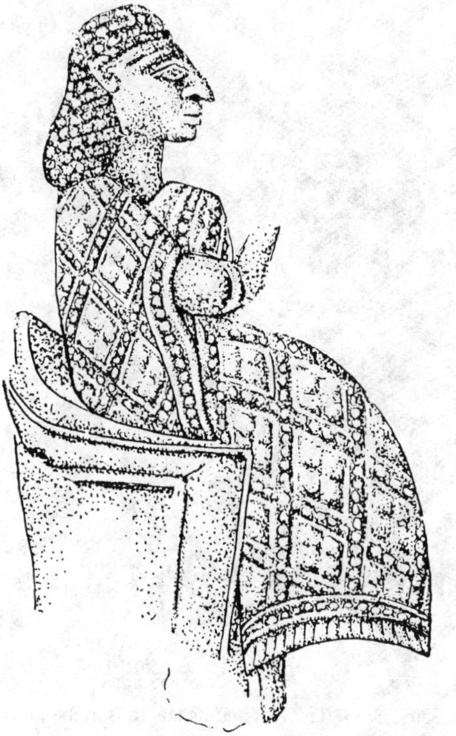

Goddess wearing a richly embroidered garment. Carved ivory from Phoenicia, ninth-eighth century B.C. Courtesy Carta, Jerusalem.

colored threads. Hebrew *rāqam* (Exod 35:35; 38:23) means "to variegate" or "to weave in colored threads." "Embroidered" (KJV "broidered") is used to translate Hebrew *riqmâh,* "variegated" (Ezek 16:10, 13, 18). In Exodus 28:4, Hebrew *tashbēts,* "tesselated stuff," is rendered by ASV and RSV as "checkerwork," and by NIV as "woven." Greek *plegma,* "twined, twisted, plaited," is used of hair (1 Tim 2:9; KJV "broided," ASV, RSV, NIV "braided"). *Riqmâh* is also translated "various colors" and "varied colors" (Ezek 17:3). Apart from the use of the Hebrew terms for the colors of gems and of feathers, they seem to have meant to weave into the cloth or draw in with a needle or applique colored threads to make checkered designs or the like, for hangings of the tabernacle; for the coats, girdles, and ephod of the priests; for royal garments; and for clothing of private persons. The details of such work given in the Bible impress us with the rich and gorgeously colorful character of needlework that may be called embroidery, but furnish no exact idea of its appearance or method of manufacture. ER

EMEK KEZIZ (ĕ'mĕk kēzĭz). A valley near Beth Hoglah in Benjamin (KJV), or a city (Josh 18:21, ASV, RSV, NIV). Emek means valley. The location is uncertain.

EMERALD (See MINERALS)

EMITES (ē'mīts, Heb. *'êmîm;* KJV, Emim). The original inhabitants of Moab (Deut 2:10–11). They were a great people—powerful, of advanced civilization, and numerous. They were also tall of stature, so that they were, like the Anakim, called giants. Out of harsh experience, the Moabites called them "Terrors," the meaning of Hebrew *'êmîm.* In Abraham's time they were defeated by the Mesopotamian invaders in Shaveh Kiriathaim (Gen 14:5), a plain east of the Dead Sea.

EMMANUEL (See IMMANUEL)

EMMAUS (ĕ-mā'ŭs). The village to which two disciples were going on the day of Jesus' resurrection, when he met and was recognized by them as he broke bread at supper (Luke 24:7–35). It was about seven miles (twelve km.) from Jerusalem, in what direction is not stated, though possibly to the NW. One site, *'Amwâs,* is 20 miles (33 km.) (some MSS read 160 stadia) from the city—too far to suit Luke's narrative. Kubeibeh, Kuloniyeh, and other sites have their partisans.

The ruins of Amwas, one of the possible sites for Emmaus, where Cleopas and his companion saw the risen Jesus, as told in the Gospel of Luke. Courtesy Zev Radovan.

EMMOR (See HAMOR)

EN EGLAIM (ĕn ĕg'lā-ĭm). A place by the Dead Sea. Between this site and En Gedi Ezekiel prophesied that fishermen would one day spread their nets (Ezek 47:10). The site is unknown.

EN GANNIM (ĕn găn'ĭm, Heb. *'ên gannîm, fountain, spring of gardens*). 1. A town in the foothills, valley, or Shephelah of Judah, mentioned with Eshtaol and Zanoah (Josh 15:34).

2. A town in the territory of Issachar, assigned to the Gershonite Levites (Josh 19:21; 21:29). The modern *Jenīn,* SW of Mount Gilboa, at the southern edge of the Plain of Esdraelon, on the main road through Samaria to Jerusalem; with beautiful gardens and fruitful orchards, well watered by local springs.

EN GEDI (ĕn gē'dī, Heb. *'ên gedhî, spring or fountain of the kid* or *wild goat*). An oasis on the

"And David . . . lived in the strongholds of En Gedi" (1 Sam 23:29). En Gedi and its environs in the Judean Wilderness with an oasis in the foreground. Courtesy Zev Radovan.

The oasis of En Gedi (place of refuge for David, 1 Sam 24:1), whose lush growth is due to the natural springs. Courtesy S. Zur Picture Library.

west coast of the Dead Sea about midway of its length, in the territory of Judah (Josh 15:62). Here David fortified a refuge from Saul (1 Sam 23:29; 24:1). Jehoshaphat defeated the Ammonites, Moabites, and Edomites from Mount Seir when they attacked by the narrow paths up the steep cliffs from the shore (2 Chron 20:2). En Gedi is there identified with Hazazon Tamar, occupied by Amorites, which Kedorlaomer invaded in the days of Abraham (Gen 14:7). Its luxurious vegetation, due to warm springs, was famous in the days of Solomon (Song of Songs 1:14). Ezekiel prophesied that fishermen would stand here, in the restored land (Ezek 47:10). Known then as Engaddi, it continued to be prominent through the NT period and until the time of Eusebius. It is the modern Ain Jidi, and the OT site is Tell ej-Jurn.

EN HADDAH (ĕn hăd'ȧ, Heb. *'ên haddâh, swift fountain*). A town on the border of Issachar (Josh 19:21).

EN HAKKORE (ĕn hăk'ō-rē, Heb. *'ên hakôrē', fountain of him who cried*). A spring that burst out from Ramath Lehi ("hill of the jawbone") at Samson's cry, when he was thirsty after killing a thousand Philistines with a jawbone (Judg 15:19).

EN HAZOR (ĕn hā'zôr, Heb. *'ên hātsôr, fountain of the village*). A fortified city in Naphtali named with Kedesh and Edrei (Josh 19:37). Probably modern Hasireh, west of Kedesh.

EN MISHPAT (ĕn mĭsh'păt, *fountain of judgment*). The older name for Kedesh (Gen 14:7).

EN RIMMON (ĕn rĭm'ŭn, Heb. *'ên-rimmôn, fountain of a pomegranate*). A place south of Jerusalem (Zech 14:10), eleven miles (eighteen km.) NE of Beersheba. Alternatively "Ain and Rimmon" in Joshua 15:32; 19:7; 1 Chron 4:32. En Rimmon was reinhabited after the Captivity (Neh 11:29).

EN ROGEL (ĕn rō'gel, Heb. *'ên rōghēl, fountain of feet*—so called because washermen trampled cloth with their feet there). It was on the border between Benjamin and Judah (Josh 15:7; 18:16), below Jerusalem near the junction of the Valley of Hinnom and the Valley of Jehoshaphat. Here Jonathan and Ahimaaz hid to receive intelligence for David from within the walls (2 Sam 17:17). Here also Adonijah held his sacrificial feast, expecting to seize the throne (1 Kings 1:9). Today it is a well 125 feet (39 m.) deep called Bir Aiyub or "well of Job." En Rogel is often mistaken for Gihon Spring (1:38) or "The Virgin's Fount," but this is too close to Jerusalem to be a hiding place (2 Sam 17:17).

EN SHEMESH (ĕn shĕm'ĭsh, *fountain of the sun*). Located about three miles (five km.) east of Jerusalem on the way to Jericho. It is mentioned in Joshua 15:7; 18:17; it served to mark Judah's northern border and Benjamin's southern border.

EN TAPPUAH (ĕn-tăp'ū-ȧ, Heb. *'ên tappûah, spring of apple*). A town on the eastern border of Manasseh in the land of Tappuah (Josh 17:7–8).

ENAIM, ENAM (ė-nā'ĭm, ē'năm, Heb. *'ênayim, place of a fountain*). One of fourteen cities in the Shephelah or foothills of Judah (Gen 38:14, 21). Enam is probably a variant that appears in the list of the towns of Judah and Simeon, between Adullam and Timnah (Josh 15:34).

ENAN (ē'năn). The father of Ahira, of the tribe of Naphtali, who assisted in the Sinai census (Num 1:15; 2:29; 7:78, 83; 10:27).

ENCAMPMENT (See CAMP, ENCAMPMENT)

ENDOR (ĕn'dôr, Heb. *'ên dor, spring of habitation*). A village about seven miles (twelve km.) SE of Nazareth, in Manasseh's territory in western Palestine. The hometown of the "witch of Endor," the spiritist medium Saul visited before his last battle with the Philistines (1 Sam 28:8–25).

ENGRAVER (See OCCUPATIONS AND PROFESSIONS)

ENOCH (ē'nŭk, Heb. *hănôkh, consecrated,* Gr. *Henoch*). 1. Cain's eldest son, for whom the first city was named (Gen 4:17–18).

2. Son of Jared (Gen 5:18) and father of Methuselah (Gen 5:21–22; Luke 3:37). Abram walked "before God" (Gen 17:1), but of Enoch and Noah alone it is written that they walked "*with* God" (5:24; 6:9). Walking with God is a relic of the first paradise when men walked and talked with God in holy familiarity; and it anticipates a new paradise (Rev 21:3; 22:3–4). The secret of Enoch's walk with God was faith—the ground of his pleasing God, and this was the ground of his being "taken from this life, so that he did not experience death" (Heb 11:5–6). After the monotonous repetition of the patriarchs who "lived . . . begat . . . and died" (Gen 5 KJV), the account of Enoch's walk with God and translation without death stands forth in bright relief. He, too, begat sons and daughters, yet family ties were no hindrance to his walking with God. Indeed, it was not until after he was sixty-five years old, when he begat Methuselah, that it is written, "Enoch walked with God." He typifies the saints living at Christ's coming who will be removed from mortality to immortality without passing through death (1 Cor 15:51–52). His translation out of a wicked world was an appropriate testimony to the truth ascribed to him in Jude 14–15, "See, the Lord is coming . . . to judge everyone."

ENOCH, BOOKS OF. A collection of apocalyptic literature written by various authors and circulated under the name of Enoch. First Enoch is an Ethiopic version made through the Greek from the original Hebrew text that was written by the Chasidim or by the Pharisees between 163–63 B.C. It is the best source for the development of Jewish doctrine in the last two pre-Christian centuries. Jude 14–15 may be an explicit quotation from it. Second Enoch was written A.D. 1–50. See also APOCALYPTIC LITERATURE.

ENOSH, ENOS (ē'nŏsh, ē'nŏs, Heb. *'ěnôsh, mortal,* Gr. *Enos*). Son of Seth and grandson of Adam (Gen 4:26; 5:6–11; Luke 3:38). Attached to his birth is an implication of godly fear. He lived 905 years.

ENVY. The Hebrew word *qin'a* is rendered in OT translations as both "envy" and "jealousy," though in English the two are not synonymous terms. Thus Saul "kept a jealous eye on David" (1 Sam 18:9), "jealousy arouses a husband's fury" (Prov 6:34), and "envy slays the simple" (Job 5:2). In Isaiah 26:11, NIV renders "zeal," and in Song of Songs 8:6 offers the marginal reading "ardor." The same Hebrew root is used with reference to the jealousy of the Lord or for his name (Exod 20:5; Ezek 39:25; Joel 2:18). In the NT two Greek words are found: *phthonos* and *zēlos*. The former always has a bad sense (e.g., Matt 27:18; Gal 5:21; Phil 1:29; James 4:5). While *zēlos* can be used similarly (Acts 13:45), it is more often translated "zeal" (e.g., John 2:17; Phil 3:6). The word is used by Paul in 2 Corinthians

11:2: "I am jealous for you with a godly jealousy."

EPAPHRAS (ĕp'à-frăs, Gr. *Epaphras*). A contraction of Epaphroditus, but not the same NT character. He was Paul's "dear fellow servant" and minister to the church at Colosse, perhaps its founder (Col 1:7). He brought to Paul a report of their state (1:4, 8) and sent back greetings to them from Rome (4:12). Commended by Paul for his ministry of intercession, he desired their perfect and complete stand in all the will of God—true pastoral concern that extended to other churches in the Lycus River Valley also (4:13). Paul also called him "my fellow prisoner." This may mean that he voluntarily shared the apostle's imprisonment, or he may have been apprehended for his zeal in the gospel.

EPAPHRODITUS (ē-păf-rō-dī'tŭs, Gr. *Epaphroditos, lovely*). The messenger sent by the Philippian church with gifts to the imprisoned Paul, which he gratefully received as a sweet-smelling sacrifice to God (Phil 4:18). On recovering from a serious illness, Epaphroditus longed to return to his concerned flock. Paul highly esteemed him as "brother, fellow worker and fellow soldier," and sent him back to Philippi with his letter (2:25–30).

EPENETUS (ēp-ē'nē-tŭs, Gr. *Epainetos, praised*). A Christian at Rome greeted by Paul as "my dear friend . . . the first convert to Christ in the province of Asia" (Rom 16:5). Nothing else is known of him.

EPHAH (See WEIGHTS AND MEASURES)

EPHAH (ē'fà, dark one). 1. A son of Midian in the line of Abraham through his concubine Keturah (Gen 25:4; 1 Chron 1:33). Isaiah speaks poetically of the "young camel of Midian and Ephah" (Isa 60:6).

2. A concubine of Caleb of the tribe of Judah (1 Chron 2:46).

3. A son of Jahdai of the tribe of Judah (1 Chron 2:47).

EPHAI (ē'fī, Heb. *'êphay, gloomy*). The Netophathite whose sons were among the captains of the forces left in Judah after the deportation to Babylon (Jer 40:8). They served under Gedaliah, the governor appointed by the Babylonians. After their warning of the plot against Gedaliah went unheeded (40:13–16), they were murdered with him by Ishmael, son of Nethaniah (41:3).

EPHER (ē'fĕr, Heb. *'ēpher, calf*). 1. Son of Midian and grandson of Abraham (Gen 25:4; 1 Chron 1:33).

2. Son of Ezra of the tribe of Judah (1 Chron 4:17).

3. A family head in the half-tribe of Manasseh east of Jordan (1 Chron 5:23–24).

EPHES DAMMIM (ē-fēs dăm'ĭm, Heb. *'ephes dammîm, boundary of blood*). A place so called from the bloody battles fought there between Israel and the Philistines. Lying between Soco and Azekah in Judah, it was the Philistine encampment when David killed Goliath (1 Sam 17:1). It is called Pas Dammim in 1 Chronicles 11:13. The modern Beit Fased ("house of bloodshed") may be over the ancient site.

EPHESIANS, LETTER TO THE. Generally acknowledged to be one of the richest and most profound of the NT letters. The depth and grandeur of its concepts, the richness and fullness of its message, and the majesty and dignity of its contents have made the Letter to the Ephesians precious to believers in all ages and in all places. Its profound truths and vivid imagery have deeply penetrated into the thought and literature of the Christian church.

Ephesians explicitly claims authorship by Paul (Eph 1:1; 3:1), and its entire tenor is eminently Pauline. The early Christian church uniformly received and treasured it as from Paul. Only within the modern era have liberal critics raised doubts as to its origin. The attacks are based solely on internal arguments drawn from the style, vocabulary, and theology of the letter. These arguments are subjective and inconclusive and offer no compelling reasons for rejecting the undeviating evidence of text and tradition. If Paul's authorship is rejected, the letter must be ascribed to someone who was fully Paul's equal, but the literature of the first two centuries reveals no traces of anyone capable of producing such a writing.

Ephesians was written while Paul was a prisoner (Eph 3:1; 4:1; 6:20). The prevailing view has been that it was written from Rome during his first Roman imprisonment (Acts 28:30–31). Some attempts have been made to shift the place of composition to Caesarea (24:27) or even to Ephesus during an unrecorded imprisonment there (19:10; 20:18–21, 31; 2 Cor 11:23), but the traditional Roman origin firmly holds the field.

Along with Colossians and Philemon (Col 4:7–8; Philem 9, 13, 17), the letter was transmitted to its destination by Tychicus (6:21–22). Thus all three were sent to the Roman province of Asia, but there is much scholarly disagreement as to the precise destination of Ephesians. The uncertainty arises from the fact that the words "at Ephesus" (*en Ephesō*) in Ephesians 1:1 are not found in three very ancient copies (the Chester Beatty Papyrus, the Uncials *Aleph* and *B*). Passages in the writings of Origen and Basil indicate that they also knew the enigmatic reading produced by the omission of "at Ephesus." But the words are found in all other manuscripts in their uncorrected form and in all ancient versions. With the exception of the heretical Marcion, whom Tertullian accused of tampering with the title, ecclesiastical tradition uniformly designates it as "to the Ephesians."

How are the phenomena to be accounted for? One widely accepted view is that the letter was really an encyclical sent to the various churches of Provincial Asia, of whom Ephesus was the most important. It is often further assumed that originally a blank was left for the insertion of the local place-name. The impersonal tone and contents of the letter are urged as confirmation.

The view is plausible, but it has its difficulties. If it was originally directed to a group of churches, would not Paul, in accordance with his known practice of including a direct address, rather have written "in Asia," or "in the churches of Asia"? In all other places where Paul uses the words "to those who are" he adds a local place-name. Then how is the uniform tradition of its Ephesian destination to be accounted for? Those who insist it was for Ephesus alone are confronted with the encyclical nature of its contents. A fair solution would seem to be that the letter was originally addressed to the saints "at Ephesus" but was intentionally cast into a form that would make it suitable to meet the needs of the Asian churches. As transcriptions of the original to the mother church were circulated, the place of destination might be omitted, though they were uniformly recognized as the letter originally addressed to the Ephesians.

Its contents offer no clear indication as to the occasion for the writing of Ephesians. Its affinity to Colossians in time of origin and contents suggests an occasion closely related to the writing of that letter. Ephesians seems to be the after-effect of the controversy that caused the writing of Colossians. Colossians has in it the intensity, rush, and roar of the battlefield, while Ephesians has a calm atmosphere suggestive of a survey of the field after the victory. With the theme of Colossians still fresh in mind Paul felt it desirable to declare the positive significance of the great truths set forth in refuting the Colossian heresy. A firm grasp of the truths here stated would provide an effective antidote to such philosophical speculations.

Ephesians sets forth the wealth of the believer in union with Christ. It portrays the glories of our salvation and emphasizes the nature of the church as the body of Christ. As indicated by the doxology in 3:20–21, its contents fall into two parts, the first doctrinal (1–3), the second practical and encouraging (4–6). An outline may suggest some of its riches.

I. The Salutation (1:1–2).
II. Doctrinal: The Believer's Standing in Christ (1:3–3:21).
  A. The thanksgiving for our redemption (1:3–14).
  B. The prayer for spiritual illumination (1:15–23).
  C. The power of God manifested in our salvation (2:1–10).
  D. The union of Jew and Gentile in one body in Christ (2:11–22).
  E. The apostle as the messenger of this mystery (3:1–13).
  F. The prayer for the realization of these blessings (3:14–19).
  G. The doxology of praise (3:20–21).
III. Practical: The Believers' Life in Christ (4:1–6:20).
  A. Their walk as God's saints (4:1–5:21).
    1. The worthy walk, in inward realization of Christian unity (4:1–16).
    2. The different walk, in outward manifestation of a changed position (4:17–32).
    3. The loving walk, in upward imitation of our Father (5:1–17).
    4. The summary of the Spirit-filled life (5:18–21).
  B. Their duties as God's family (5:22–6:9).
  C. Their warfare as God's soldiers (6:10–20).
IV. The Conclusion (6:21–24).

Bibliography: J. A. Robinson, *St. Paul's Epistle to the Ephesians* (on the Greek text), 1914; C. Hodge, *A Commentary on the Epistle to the Ephesians,* (1856; repr. 1950); F. F. Bruce, *The Epistle to the Ephesians,* 1961; Francis Foulkes, *The Epistle of Paul to the Ephesians* (TNTC), 1963; M. Barth, *Ephesians* (AB), 2 vols., 1974. DEH

EPHESUS (ĕf′ė-sŭs, Gr. *Ephesos, desirable*). An old Ionian foundation at the mouth of the

The library of Celsus, built in the time of Trajan (A.D. 98–117), the most remarkable building to be revealed from the extensive excavations at Ephesus. Below is the façade of the temple of Hadrian, located just southeast of the library and south of the famous theater. Courtesy Top: Duby Tal. Bottom: Dan Bahat.

The theater at Ephesus, magnificent memorial of Ephesus' greatness and locale for Acts 19 ("they rushed together into the theater" v. 29), overlooking the Arcadian Way, which led to the harbor. Courtesy Duby Tal.

Cayster. Greek colonies that surround the Mediterranean and Black Sea were primarily trading posts. Migrant communities of Greeks did not seek to dominate the hinterlands, but to secure an *emporion* or "way in," a bridgehead for commerce and enough surrounding coast and territory to support the community. Great cities grew from such foundations from Marseilles to Alexandria, some of them royal capitals. And in all cases colonies became centers or outposts of Hellenism, distinctive and civilizing.

Ephesus displaced Miletus as a trading port; but when its harbor, like that of Miletus, in turn silted up, Smyrna replaced both as the outlet and *emporion* of the Maeander Valley trade route. In the heyday of Asia Minor 230 separate communities, each proud of its individuality and wealth, issued their own coinage and managed their own affairs. The dominance of Persian despotism, wide deforestation, and the ravages of war on a natural bridge and highway between the continents slowly sapped this prosperity; but in early Roman times, as in the days of its Ionian independence, Ephesus was a proud, rich, busy port, the rival of Alexandria and Syrian Antioch.

Built near the shrine of an old Anatolian fertility goddess, Ephesus became the seat of an oriental cult. The Anatolian deity had been taken over by the Greeks under the name of Artemis, the Diana of the Romans. Grotesquely represented with turreted head and many breasts, the goddess and her cult found expression in the famous temple, served, like that of Aphrodite at Corinth, by a host of priestess courtesans.

Much trade clustered round the cult. Ephesus became a place of pilgrimage for tourist-worshipers, all eager to carry away talisman and souvenir, hence the prosperous guild of the silversmiths whose livelihood was the manufacture of silver shrines and images of the meteoric stone that was said to be Diana's image "fallen from heaven." Ephesus leaned more and more on the trade that followed the cult, and commerce declined in her silting harbor. Twenty miles (thirty-three km.) of reedy marshland now separate the old harbor works from the sea, and even in Paul's day the process was under way. Tacitus tells us that an attempt was made to improve the seaway in A.D. 65, but the task proved too great. Ephesus in the first century was a dying city, given to parasite pursuits, living, like Athens, on a reputation, a curious meeting place of old and new religions, of East and West. Acts 19 gives a peculiarly vivid picture of her unnatural life. The "lampstand" had gone from its place, for Ephesus's decline was mortal sickness, and it is possible to detect in the letter to Ephesus in the Apocalypse a touch of the lassitude that characterized the effete and declining community. The temple and part of the city have been extensively excavated. EMB

EPHLAL (ĕf'lăl, Heb. *'ephlāl, judge*). Son of Zabad of the tribe of Judah (1 Chron 2:37).

EPHOD (ē'fŏd, Heb. *'ēphōdh*). 1. A sacred vestment originally worn by the high priest and made of "gold, and of blue, purple and scarlet yarn, and of finely twisted linen—the work of a skilled craftsman" (Exod 28:6–14; 39:2–7). It was held together front and back by two shoulder pieces at the top and a girdle band around the waist. On each shoulderpiece was an onyx stone engraved with six names of the tribes of Israel. Attached to the ephod by chains of pure gold was a breastplate containing twelve precious stones. The blue robe of the ephod was worn underneath, having a hole for the head and extending to the feet, with a hem alternating with gold bells and pomegranates of blue, purple, and scarlet (28:31–35; 39:22–26).

Later, persons other than the high priest wore ephods. Samuel wore a linen ephod while ministering before the Lord (1 Sam 2:18), which was characteristic of the ordinary priests (2:28; 14:3; 22:18). David wore a linen ephod while he danced before the Lord after bringing the ark to Jerusalem (2 Sam 6:14). Abiathar carried off from Nob an ephod that represented to David the divine presence, for of it he inquired the will of the Lord (1 Sam 23:6, 9; 30:7–8).

The ephod was misused as an object of idolatrous worship by Gideon (Judg 8:27) and associated with images by Micah (17:5; 18:14).

2. Father of Hanniel who was the prince of the children of Manasseh (Num 34:23). AMR

EPHPHATHA (ĕf'à-thà, Gr. *Ephphatha* from Aram. *'etpătah,* passive imperative of the verb *petah, be opened*). A word occuring only in Mark 7:34. It was uttered by Jesus as he was healing a deaf man.

EPHRAIM (ē'frâ-ĭm, Heb. *'eprayim, double fruit*). The younger of two sons of Joseph and his Egyptian wife Asenath (Gen 41:50–52). The aged Jacob, when he blessed his grandsons Manasseh and Ephraim, adopted them as his own sons. Despite Joseph's protest, Jacob gave the preferential blessing (signified by the right hand) to Ephraim (48:1–22). When Jacob blessed his own sons, he did not mention Ephraim and Manasseh, but he did give a special blessing to their father, Joseph (49:22–26).

Ephraim was the progenitor of the tribe called by his name, as was also Manasseh. This brought the number of the Hebrew tribes to thirteen, but the original number twelve (derived from the twelve sons of Jacob, of whom Joseph was one) continued to be referred to. The separation of the tribe of Levi from the others for the tabernacle service, and its failure to receive a separate territory in which to live, helped to perpetuate the concept of "The Twelve Tribes of Israel."

Ephraim together with Manasseh and Benjamin camped on the west side of the tabernacle in the wilderness (Num 2:18–24). Joshua (Hoshea) the son of Nun, one of the spies and Moses' successor, was an Ephraimite (13:8). Ephraim and Manasseh were mentioned as making up the Joseph group in Moses' blessing (Deut 33:13–17).

At the division of the land among the tribes, the children of Joseph (except half of Manasseh, which settled east of the Jordan, Num 32:33, 39–42) received the central hill country of Palestine, sometimes called Mount Ephraim. This area is bounded on the north side by the Valley of Jezreel, on the east by the Jordan River, on the south by a "zone of movement" that runs from Joppa to Jericho (a series of valleys that invite travel across Palestine) and on the west by the Mediterranean. The Joseph tribes were not able to occupy this land completely for a long time, being forced up into the heavily wooded hill country (Josh 17:14–18) by the Canaanites and Philistines who occupied the good bottom lands and who by their superior civilization and power (Judg 1:27–29) kept the Hebrews subservient

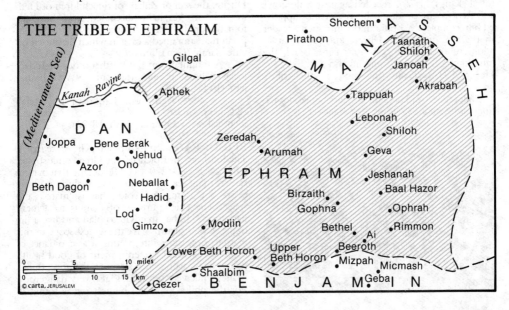

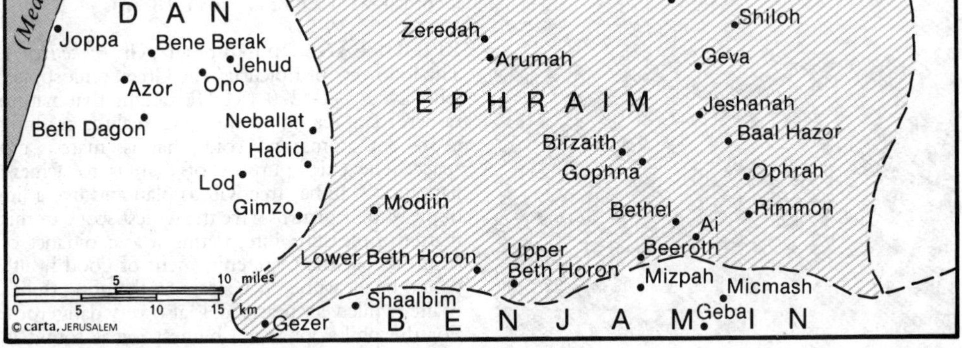

until the time of David. Ephraim and Manasseh seem to have been bitter rivals (Isa 9:20–21), Manasseh being the larger group (Gen 49:22), but Ephraim asserting the more vigorous leadership. Although they seem to have held their land in common for a time (Josh 17:14–18) it was presently divided between them. Ephraim's portion was well defined and very fruitful, its soil fertile and its rainfall more plentiful than Judah's to the south (Deut 33:13–16).

Ephraim's inheritance is described in Joshua 16:5–10. The territory was bounded on the south by the northern borders of Benjamin and Dan. Bethel was just across the line in Benjamin, the two Beth Horons were just in Ephraim, as was Gezer toward the sea. The western boundary seems ideally to have been the Mediterranean. On the north, the brook Kanah separated Ephraim from the half of Manasseh, as did the towns of Shechem (in Manasseh) and Taanath Shiloh. Then the line seems to have turned abruptly southward, through Ataroth, passing near Jericho and thence to the Jordan. References to the towns for Ephraimites within Manasseh (16:9; 17:9) suggest that the rivalry between these two tribes had resulted in some boundary changes.

At Shiloh, in the territory of Ephraim, Joshua pitched the tabernacle (Josh 18:1), and this town remained a religious center for the Hebrews (Josh 22:12; Judg 18:31; 21:19; 1 Sam 1:3, 9, 24; 2:14; 3:21) until it was destroyed by the Philistines after the battle of Ebenezer (1 Sam 4:1–11). Samuel was an Ephraimite (1:1). The Ephraimites contributed their share of the hatred and strife that divided the Hebrew tribes during the dark days of the judges (Judg 8:1–3; 12:1–6).

It would appear that Ephraim, in common with the rest of the central and northern tribes, was never completely reconciled to the rule of Judah that the Davidic dynasty brought (2 Sam 2:8–9; 1 Kings 12:16). When Jeroboam I, an Ephraimite (1 Kings 11:26), rebelled against Solomon's son Rehoboam, no doubt his own tribe supported him completely. Ephraim became such a leader in the new northern Hebrew kingdom that in addition to its more common name Israel, the kingdom is also called Ephraim (Isa 7:2, 5, 9, 17; Hos 9:3–16). From this time on the tribe's history is merged with that of this kingdom.

Ephraim is also the name of a city north of Jerusalem (2 Sam 13:23; John 11:54), identified with modern Et-Taiyibeh, a few miles NE of Bethel. The forest of Ephraim (2 Sam 18:6) was probably located in Transjordan near Mahanaim.

JBG

The hill country of Ephraim. The terrace-like formations are natural. Courtesy Zev Radovan.

EPHRAIM, FOREST OF (Heb. *ya'ar 'eprayim*). The term occurs only in 2 Samuel 18:6 ("wood" [KJV], "woods" [MLB] "of Ephraim"), where it denotes the place of the decisive battle in which David's soldiers defeated those of Absalom. The context indicates that this fighting took place in the land of Gilead east of the Jordan. The site has not been identified.

EPHRAIM, MOUNT OF (Heb. *har 'eprayim*). The mountainous part of the territory of the tribe of Ephraim (Josh 17:15) or "hill country," an inaccurate phrase, since all the hills are part of the same mountain range that runs through central Palestine.

EPHRAIMITE (Heb. *'ephrayim*, always in this plural form). A member of the tribe of Ephraim (Josh 16:10; Judg 12).

EPHRAIN (See EPHRON)

EPHRATAH, EPHRATH, EPHRATHAH (ĕf'răth-ȧ, Heb. *'ephrāth, fruitful land*). 1. The place where Rachel was buried (Gen 35:16).

2. Second wife of Caleb, son of Hezron. She was the mother of Hur (1 Chron 2:19–20).

3. The ancient name of Bethlehem or the district around it. This name is attached to that of Bethlehem in the great prophecy of the place of the birth of Christ (Mic 5:2).

EPHRON (ē'frôn, Heb. *'ephrôn, fawn*). 1. A Hittite, the son of Zohar, of the children of Heth in Hebron. Abraham purchased from him, for four hundred shekels of silver, the field of Machpelah that contained a cave in which he buried his wife Sarah (Gen 23:8–9).

2. A mountain on the north border of Judah, located about six miles (ten km.) NW of Jerusalem (Josh 15:9).

3. A city taken from Jeroboam by Abijah (2 Chron 13:19; KJV "Ephrain"). It is perhaps identical with Ophrah (Josh 18:23).

EPICUREANS (ĕp-ĭ-kū-rē'ănz, Gr. *Epikoureioi*). The followers of Epicurus, the Greek philosopher who lived 341–270 B.C. He taught that nature rather than reason is the true reality; nothing exists but atoms and void, that is, matter and space. The chief purpose of man is to achieve happiness. He has free will to plan and live a life of pleasure. Epicurus gave the widest scope to this matter of pleasure, interpreting it as avoidance of pain, so that the mere enjoyment of good health would be pleasure. Such stress on the good things of life, while very practical, is also very dangerous. For the philosopher the highest joy is found in

Epicurus, Greek philosopher (341–270 B.C.). From the Vatican Museum. Courtesy Carta, Jerusalem.

mental and intellectual pursuits, but for lesser souls lower goals of sensual satisfaction fulfill the greatest pleasure. Thus the high standards of the founder were not maintained, and the philosophy gained a bad reputation. Since such teaching appealed to the common man, this natural philosophy became widespread. It was widely held at the time of Christ. Paul met it at Athens when he encountered the philosophers of that city (Acts 17:16–33). They were not impressed by his teaching of creation, judgment, and resurrection, since all these doctrines were denied by the Epicurean philosophy.

EPILEPTIC (See DISEASES)

EPIPHANY. From a Greek word meaning "manifestation," the term originally marked a feast to celebrate the baptism of Christ (Matt 3:16–17)—and still does so in the churches of Eastern Orthodoxy. The Lord had similarly "revealed his glory" at his first miracle in Cana of Galilee (John 2:11). From the fourth century, however, Epiphany has been linked with Christ's manifestation of himself to the Magi, the first Gentiles who believed in him (Matt 2:1–12). In England, it has become customary for the monarch to offer gold, myrrh, and frankincense in the Chapel Royal every year on January 6, the day the feast is observed.

EPISTLE (ē-pis'l, Gr. *epistolē, letter, epistle*). Written correspondence, whether personal or official, has been common to all ages. The OT abounds with evidence of widespread written letters, among the best known being David's letter to Joab concerning Uriah (2 Sam 11:14–15), Jezebel's letter regarding Naboth (1 Kings 21:8–9), and Sennacherib's letter to Hezekiah (2 Kings 19:14); the NT also abounds (Acts 9:2; Rom 16:1ff.; 1 Cor 7:1).

The term is, however, almost a technical one, referring particularly to the twenty-one epistles of the NT. The NT epistles were written by five (possibly six) writers: James, John, Jude, Paul, Peter, and the author of Hebrews. Paul wrote thirteen (or fourteen, if Hebrews is by him); John, three; Peter, two; James, one; and Jude, one. According to the custom of the time, they usually began with the name or title of the writer and that of the addressee or addressees; then followed words of greeting, the message of the epistle; and at the end the author usually gave his name. It was Paul's usual practice to employ a secretary to write from dictation. The epistles were written to individual churches or groups of churches (almost always given by name) or to individuals. Seven are called General Epistles, because they were written to the church at large.

The epistles are not disguised doctrinal treatises. They were written in the way of ordinary correspondence and dealt with situations, whether doctrinal or practical, needing immediate attention. They were written in reply to letters or as the result of other information otherwise obtained. It is very apparent that the writers realized that what they wrote was authoritative and came from God. They all dealt with some aspect of the redemptive message and experience. Although written to deal with specific local situations, they set forth fundamental principles applicable to the individual and collective life of all believers. They were received from the beginning with the OT Scriptures (2 Peter 3:15–16).

The influence of the NT epistles on the literature of Christianity is seen in the writings of the next century, which were mostly epistolary in form. Indeed, heretics wrote epistles in the name of the apostles.

It is not to be supposed that all of the epistles of the apostles have survived. Paul in 1 Corinthians 5:9 refers to a letter he had written to the Corinthians prior to our 1 Corinthians; and in Colossians 4:6 he speaks of an epistle to the Laodicean church. SB

ER (Heb. *'ēr, watchful*). 1. Eldest son of Judah by the daughter of Shua the Canaanite. Judah took a wife for him named Tamar. He was so wicked the Lord put him to death (Gen 38:3, 6–7).

2. The third son of Shelah, the son of Judah (1 Chron 4:21).

3. An ancestor of Jesus in the maternal line (Luke 3:28).

ERAN (ē'răn, Heb. *'ērān, watcher*). The son of Shuthelah, who was the oldest son of Ephraim. His descendants were the Eranites (Num 26:36).

ERASTUS (ē-răs'tŭs, Gr. *Erastos, beloved*). A name that occurs three times, each time denoting a friend of Paul:

Part of the temple façade found in the temenos (sacred enclosure) of Eanna at Erech, ornamented with burnt brick reliefs depicting divinities. Kassite period, fifteenth century B.C. Courtesy Bildarchiv Foto, Marburg.

1. Acts 19:22, "He sent . . . Timothy and Erastus to Macedonia" while he stayed in Asia.

2. The treasurer of the city of Corinth whom Paul mentions as saluting the Christians at Rome (Rom 16:23).

3. Probably the same man is designated in 2 Timothy 4:20 as remaining at Corinth.

ERECH (ē′rĕk, Heb. *'erekh*). A city of ancient Babylonia mentioned in Genesis 10:10 as the second city founded by Nimrod. The Babylonian form of the name is *Uruk*. The modern site is called *Warka* and is located near the Euphrates River, forty miles (sixty-seven km.) NW of Ur. This city was mentioned much in ancient Mesopotamian literature. Erech was the home of Gilgamesh, the hero of the great Akkadian epic.

Archaeologists have found that this city was one of the oldest of Babylonia, founded before 4000 B.C. and continuing to flourish until after 300. One of the early dynasties of the Sumerians ruled from Erech. Culturally, it boasted the first ziggurat, or temple tower, and began the use of clay cylinder seals.

ERI (ē′rī, Heb. *'ērî, my watcher*). The fifth son of Gad (Gen 46:16).

ESAIAS (See ISAIAH)

ESARHADDON (ē′sar-hăd′ŏn, *Ashur has given a brother*). A younger son of Sennacherib, who obtained the throne of Assyria after his older brothers murdered their father (2 Kings 19:36–37; 2 Chron 32:21; Isa 37:37–38) . His reign (681–669 B.C.) saw important political developments. He restored the city of Babylon, which his father had destroyed, and fought campaigns against the Cimmerians and other barbaric hordes from beyond the Caucasus. His main achievement was the conquest of Egypt, Assyria's competitor for world domination.

In preparation for his Egyptian campaign, Esarhaddon subdued the Westlands. Sidon was destroyed, its inhabitants deported, its king beheaded, and a new city erected on its site. According to Ezra 4:2, Esarhaddon brought deportees into Samaria, which had already been colonized with pagans by Sargon when he destroyed it in 722 B.C. After Sidon's fall twelve kings along the Mediterranean seacoast submitted to the Assyrians and were forced to supply wood and stone for the king's palace in Nineveh. Among these was "Manasi king of Yaudi," the Manasseh of the Bible. Manasseh had little choice. The Assyrian Empire had now reached its greatest power; and it appears that most of the Judean citizenry preferred peaceful submission, even with the Assyrian pagan influences now imposed on them, to constant abortive rebellion. Manasseh's summons to appear before an Assyrian king, mentioned in 2 Chronicles 33:11–13, probably took place in the reign of Esarhaddon's successor, Ashurbanipal.

In 671 B.C. Egypt fell to Esarhaddon. He occupied Memphis and organized Egypt into districts under princes responsible to Assyrian governors. A later Egyptian rebellion necessitated a second Assyrian campaign there, during which Esarhaddon died and Ashurbanipal his son succeeded him.

Stele (3.22 meters high) of Esarhaddon, king of Assyria (680–669 B.C.), holding two royal captives, from Linjerli. His upraised right hand holds a cup, and his left hand holds a mace and ropes by which he secures his captives. Courtesy Staatliche Museen zu Berlin.

ESAU (ē'saw, Heb. *'ēsāw, hairy*). The first-born of the twin brothers, Esau and Jacob, sons of Isaac and Rebecca (Gen 25:24–25). Before their birth God had told their mother that the elder should serve the younger (25:23). Esau became a man of the fields. He apparently lived only for the present. This characteristic was demonstrated when he let Jacob have his birthright for a dinner of bread and stew because he was hungry (25:30–34).

At the age of forty he married two Hittite women (Gen 26:34). When the time came for Isaac to give his blessing to his son, he wanted to confer it on Esau, but, through trickery, Jacob obtained the blessing instead. This loss grieved Esau very much. He begged for another blessing, and when he received it he hated it because it made him the servant of his brother. He hated Jacob for cheating him and intended to kill him (Gen 27).

When Esau saw Jacob sent away to obtain a wife from his mother's relatives he understood that Canaanite wives did not please his father, so he went out and took for himself two additional wives of the Ishmaelites (Gen 28:6–9).

Years later, when he was living in Mount Seir, Esau heard that Jacob was returning to Canaan (Gen 32:3–5). With four hundred men he set out to meet his brother warmly (32:7–33:15). They soon parted company and Esau went back to Mount Seir (33:16).

In the providence of God, Esau was made subservient to Jacob. In Hebrews 12:16–17 he is described as a profane person. Long after Esau's death the Lord declared he had loved Jacob and hated Esau (Mal 1:2–3). The apostle Paul used this passage to illustrate how God carries out his purposes (Rom 9:10–13).

Sometimes in Scripture Esau is used as the name of the land of Edom in which his descendants lived (Gen 36:8). CEH

ESCHATOLOGY (ĕs-kȧ-tŏl'ō-gē, Gr. *eschatos,*

last and *logos, ordered statement*). The study of the last things to happen on this earth in this present age. The word is used to cover the study of such important events as the second coming/parousia of Jesus Christ, the judgment of the world, the resurrection of the dead, and the creation of the new heaven and earth. Related topics include the kingdom of God (the saving rule of God exhibited in Jesus Christ and experienced now through the Holy Spirit in anticipation of its fullness in the new heaven and earth of the age to come), the nature of the Millennium, the intermediate state, the concept of immortality, and the eternal destiny of the wicked. Since the article KINGDOM OF GOD treats that topic as well as the Millennium, only passing reference will be made to these two topics here.

Since the Lord is presented in Scripture as the Creator, Preserver, Redeemer, and King, that which will bring the present age to its end and inaugurate the new age is seen as being very much under his control. Thus, the believer is to have hope. However, it is helpful, in order to do justice to the tension within the NT between salvation already (but partially) experienced and salvation not yet (wholly) experienced, to speak of "inaugurated" eschatology and "fulfilled" eschatology. The people of God are living in the last days, but the Last Day has not yet arrived. The new age broke into this present evil age when Christ rose from the dead, but the new has not yet wholly replaced the old. The Spirit of Christ brings into the present age the life of the age to come; so what he makes available is "firstfruits" (Rom 8:23), and he is the "guarantee/guarantor" or "pledge" of the fullness of life to come (2 Cor 1:22; 5:5; Eph 1:14).

As the people of the new age yet living in the old world and age, the church is called to engage in mission and evangelism (Matt 24:14; 28:19–20) until Christ's return to earth. Signs of the times—i.e., that the end is sure and near—include the evangelization of the world, the conversion of Israel (Rom 11:25–26), the great apostasy (2 Thess 2:1–3—see also APOSTASY), the tribulation (Matt 24:21–30), and the revelation of Antichrist (2 Thess 2:1–12; see also ANTICHRIST). These signs are seen during the whole of the "last days," particularly in the last of the last days.

I. The Second Coming. Christ is now in heaven, seated at the right hand of the Father as our exalted Prophet, Priest, and King, waiting for the time appointed by the Father to return to earth. Three Greek words—*parousia* (presence, 1 Thess 3:13), *apokalypsis* (revelation, 2 Thess 1:7–8), and *epiphaneia* (appearance, 2:8)—are used of this event in the NT. This coming will be nothing less than the personal, visible, and glorious return of the same Jesus who ascended into heaven (Matt 24:30; Acts 1:11; 3:19–21; Phil 3:20). It will be an event of which everyone on earth will be abruptly aware, for it will mean the end of things as they are and the universal recognition of the true identity of Jesus of Nazareth. (Note: The position adopted here is the classic position, found in the ecumenical creeds—Apostles' and Nicene—but other scholars hold that Christ will come in two stages: first, secretly, to gather his faithful people, and then, seven years later, openly to be seen by all. This is part of the system of pretribulational dispensationalism and is expounded in the Scofield Reference Bible.)

II. The Resurrection of the Dead. Christ himself rose bodily from the dead. His body was a real, yet spiritual, body, and he is the "firstborn" from the dead (Rom 8:11, 29; Col 1:18) and the "firstfruits" of the resurrection of all believers (1 Cor 15:20). The resurrection (Gr. *anastasis*) of each and every person who has ever lived is part of God's plan for the human race (Dan 12:2; John 5:28–29; Acts 24:15); but the resurrection of the wicked will be the beginning of God's judgment on them, while the resurrection of the righteous will be the beginning of their life in Christ in the fullness of the kingdom of God. At the second coming of Christ, the dead will appear in their resurrection bodies; those who are alive will find that their bodies are marvelously changed, even though they remain the same individual persons. Little is taught in Scripture concerning the new bodies of the wicked; but we learn that the resurrection bodies of the righteous will be incorruptible, glorious, and spiritual (1 Cor 15:35ff.) and like Christ's glorious body (Phil 3:21). Life in the new age of the kingdom of God in the new heaven and earth will be everlasting, abundant life in an immortal body. The NT has no doctrine of the "immortality of the soul." (Note: Again, this is the classical tradition that there is one resurrection of the dead at Christ's coming. However, premillennialists maintain that there will be two resurrections—one of believers at the beginning of the one thousand years and one of unbelievers at the end of the Millennium. Those who adopt the dispensationalist premillennial approach specify two other groups that will be resurrected—saints from the Tribulation at the end of the seven years and saints from the Millennium at the end of the one thousand years.)

One should distinguish between (1) the resurrection to mortal life, that is, life that will involve death—as happened to the widow's son (1 Kings 17:17–24), the son of the Shunamite woman (2 Kings 4:32–37), the widow of Nain's son (Luke 7:11–17), the daughter of Jairus (Matt 9:18–26), and Lazarus (John 11:38ff.)—and (2) the resurrection to immortality, of which Jesus is the supreme example and the "prototype." The nature of the resurrected bodies of those who came to bodily life as Jesus expired on the cross (Matt 27:51–52) is difficult to determine.

III. The Last Judgment. Having returned to earth, Jesus Christ will be the judge of the nations and of every person who has ever lived. In the name of God the Father (Rom 14:10; 1 Peter 1:17), Jesus the Lord acts as universal judge (Acts 17:31). This judgment, however, is not to fix but to confirm the eternal destiny of human beings according to their acceptance or rejection of the gospel. Further, it is an examination of the motives and deeds of everyone, believer and unbeliever, together with judgment based on this evidence (Matt 11:20–22; 12:36; 25:35–40; 2 Cor 5:10) and on the human response to the known will of God (Matt 16:27; Rom 1:18–21; 2:12–16; Rev 20:12; 22:12). True believers will, in this judgment, be shown to be those in whom faith has manifested itself in love and deeds of mercy (Matt 7:21; 25:35ff.; James 2:18). Therefore, there are spiritual rewards in the age to come for those in this life who have faithfully served the Lord (Luke 19:12–27; 1 Cor 3:10–15; cf. Matt 5:11–12; 6:19–21). Those who hold to dispensationalism refer to several judgments—of the sins of believers (at Calvary), of the works of the believer (at the time of the Rapture), of individual Gentiles (before the Millennium), of the people Israel (before the Millennium), of fallen angels, and of the wicked (after the Millennium). After the second coming of Christ and the final judgment, those who are judged to be the righteous begin their life in the new heaven and earth, while those who are judged to be unrighteous are consigned to everlasting punishment.

IV. Eternal Happiness in the New Order of Existence (New Heaven and Earth). At or following the second coming of Christ, the old universe will be marvelously regenerated (Acts 3:19–21; Rom 8:19–21; 2 Peter 3:2) in order to be reborn as the "new heaven and earth," the new cosmos/universe. This is described in Isaiah 65:17–25; 66:22, 23; 2 Peter 2:13; and Revelation 21:1–4. In Revelation 21–22, God himself is presented as dwelling with his people in this new order of existence, and, thus, they are supremely happy with Christ as the center and light of all. It is fitting that those with resurrection bodies should dwell with their God in a regenerated universe, from which heaven—as God's place and sphere—is not separated but is rather present. This is the force of the picture of the descent of the heavenly Jerusalem in Revelation 21:2, to be the center of the new universe.

V. Eternal Misery and Punishment in Hell. Jesus himself had more to say about hell (see HELL) than any other person whose teaching is recorded in the NT (e.g., Matt 5:22, 29–30; 10:28; 13:41–42; 25:46). Through a variety of pictures and images, the NT presents a frightening portrayal of the everlasting suffering of those who have rejected the gospel. Since this is a difficult and hard teaching to accept, two alternatives have been proposed and remain popular. The first is universalism, which insists that God is love and that ultimately all people will receive God's salvation. This approach involves the denial of the commonsensical interpretation of many NT passages. The second is annihilation—the wicked cease to exist after the Last Judgment. This involves the view that human beings are mortal beings (like animals) who, unless they are given the gift of immortality through grace, return to nothingness.

VI. Immortality. God alone truly possesses immortality (*aphtharsia,* 1 Tim 6:16), for he is the eternal source of life. Human beings were created for immortality (rather than created with immortal souls); and this immortality, in the sense of receiving and enjoying God's life, is given to the righteous at the resurrection of the dead, in and through the gift of an imperishable and immortal new body (1 Cor 15:53–55). This immortal/eternal life, anticipated with the gift of the Spirit in new birth in this age, is fully given at the Resurrection. At all times the immortality of the redeemed sinner is dependent on the gift of God, the source of eternal life. Careless talk about the immortality of the soul can eclipse the biblical emphasis that immortality belongs to God alone and is given to believing human beings in and through a body (2 Cor 5:1–4). The wicked retain their personal existence but away from the holy love and immortal, abundant, eternal life of God. They are never said to have immortality or to exist eternally in immortal bodies, for the NT use of immortality is to denote the immunity from death and decay that results from sharing in the divine life.

VII. The Intermediate State. Those who are alive at the second coming of Christ will experience the transformation of their earthly, perishable bodies. But what of those who have died and will die before the end of the age and the resurrection of the dead? We know that their bodies return to dust. Since the emphasis of the NT is on the events that bring this age to an end and inaugurate the age of the kingdom of God, little is said about the existence of those who die before the Second Coming. This interim period when they await the resurrection is often called the Intermediate State. The parable of the rich man and Lazarus (Luke 16:19–31) suggests that there is conscious existence and that this can be of misery or of rest/happiness. Certainly the NT points to the comfort and security of those who die as disciples of Jesus (Luke 23:42–43; 2 Cor 5:6–8; Phil 1:21–23; 1 Thess 4:16; see also HADES; PARADISE; SHEOL). One of our problems in understanding this period is that it involves the great problem of the relation of time and eternity.

Bibliography: John Baillie, *And the Life Everlasting,* 1933; K. Hanhart, *The Intermediate State in the New Testament,* 1966; G. E. Ladd, *Presence of the Future,* 1974; R. G. Clouse (ed.), *Meaning of the Millennium: Four Views,* 1977; A. A. Hoekema, *The Bible and the Future,* 1978; M. J. Harris, *Raised Immortal,* 1984. PT

ESDRAELON (ĕs′drā-ē′lŏn, a Gr. modification of *Jezreel;* does not occur in Heb.; is Gr. in form; found only in Revelation). The great plain that breaks the central range of Palestine in two. In the OT it is known as the plain, or valley, of Jezreel. It affords a direct connection between the maritime plain and the Jordan Valley. It lies between Galilee on the north and Samaria on the south.

This plain is triangular in shape, and is fifteen by fifteen by twenty miles (twenty-five by twenty-five by thirty-three km.) in size. Several passes enter into it, making it easy of access and important commercially and in military operations. Many cities were situated in it, one of the

The Esdraelon (Jezreel) Valley with a view of the Hills of Mareh in the background. Naboth, the Jezreelite, had a vineyard in this area (1 Kings 21:1). Courtesy Zev Radovan.

most important being Megiddo, which guarded one of the main entrances. The Canaanites were strongly established in this region before the Israelites came into Palestine. The tribes of Issachar and Zebulun were assigned to this area, but the Israelites never gained complete control of it until the time of David.

Esdraelon was the scene of some of the most important battles in Bible history: The victory of Barak over Sisera (Judg 4) and of the Philistines over Saul and his sons (1 Sam 31). Here the Egyptians mortally wounded Josiah, king of Judah, when he went out to intercept the army of Pharaoh Neco (2 Kings 23:29).

This valley has always been very fertile. Today Jewish colonists find it a prosperous farming region. A great future conflict seems indicated for this area, according to Revelation 16:16. CEH

ESDRAS, BOOKS OF (See Apocrypha)

ESEK (ē'sĕk, Heb. *'ēseq, contention*). The name that Isaac gave to a well his servants dug in the Valley of Gerar and that the herdsmen of Gerar struggled for, claiming it belonged to them (Gen 26:20).

ESHAN (ĕsh'ăn, Heb. *'esh'ān*). A city in the territory assigned to the tribe of Judah (Josh 15:52). It was located in the Hebron area.

ESH-BAAL (ĕsh'-bā'ăl, Heb. *'esha'al, man of Baal*). The fourth son of Saul (1 Chron 8:33; 9:39). The same man is called Ishbosheth in 2 Samuel 2:8, 10, 12, et al. He was made king of Gilead by Abner after Saul's death. A few years later he was murdered.

ESHBAN (ĕsh'băn, Heb. *'eshvān, man of understanding*). A descendant of Seir the Horite (Gen 36:26; 1 Chron 1:41).

ESHCOL (ĕsh'kŏl, Heb. *'eshkōl, cluster*). 1. An Amorite who lived in Hebron and who helped Abram defeat King Kedorlaomer and his forces and bring back Lot and his family (Gen 14:13, 24).

2. A valley near Hebron. The men sent by Moses to spy out the land found a cluster of grapes here that they carried back to the people (Num 13:23–24).

ESHEAN (See Eshan)

ESHEK (ē'shĕk, Heb. *'ēsheq, oppression*). A descendant of Jonathan, son of Saul, and brother of Azel. His grandsons were mighty men of valor in the tribe of Benjamin (1 Chron 8:38–40).

ESHTAOL (ĕsh'tā-ŏl, Heb. *'eshtā'ōl*). A town in the lowlands of Judah on its border with Dan (Josh 15:33; 19:41). In the Book of Judges it is always mentioned with Zorah. Samson, as he grew up, began to be moved by the Spirit of the Lord at times in the camp of Dan between Zorah and Eshtaol (Judg 3:25). He was buried there

(16:31). The Danites sent out five brave men from Zorah and Eshtaol to look for an area where the tribe could have additional living space. After discovering the city of Laish, they returned to these cities and gave a favorable report. Then six hundred armed men set forth out of Zorah and Eshtaol to go and conquer Laish (18:2, 8, 11).

ESHTEMOA (ĕsh'tē-mō-ȧ, Heb. *eshte môa'*). 1. A city assigned to the Levites (Josh 21:14). It was located eight miles (thirteen km.) south of Hebron. This city, among others, received from David a share of the spoil of his victory over the Amalekites (1 Sam 30:28). The modern name of the site is *Es Semu.*

Remnants of a synagogue (4th–6th century, A.D.) at Eshtemoa. In a room alongside the synagogue a treasure of silver jewelry and ingots was discovered, believed to date from the period of David's kingdom. Courtesy Zev Radovan.

Ground plan of the Essene settlement at Qumran. Courtesy Carta, Jerusalem.

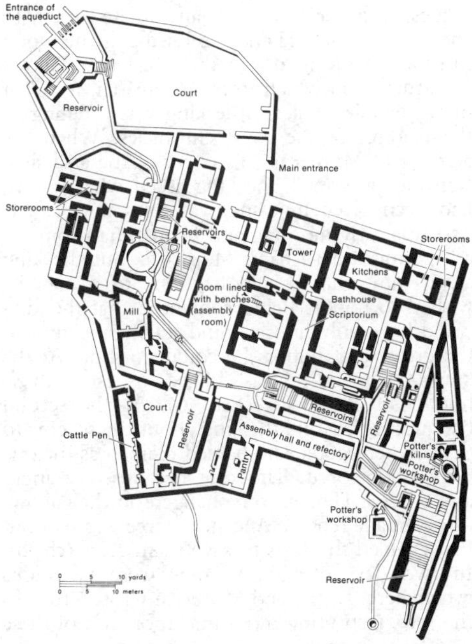

2. The son of Ishbah (1 Chron 4:17).

3. A Maacathite, a son of Hodiah (1 Chron 4:19).

ESHTEMOH (ĕsh'tē-mō). A city located in the hill country of Judah (Josh 15:50). The same as Eshtemoa above.

ESHTON (ĕsh'tŏn, Heb. *'eshtôn, perhaps effeminate*). A descendant of Judah (1 Chron 4:11–12).

ESLI (ĕs'lī, Gr. *Esli*). An ancestor of Christ (Luke 3:25).

ESROM (See HEZRON)

ESSENES (ĕ-sēnz', Gr. *Essenoi* or *Essaioi*). The meaning of the name is much debated; possibly it denotes "holy ones." They constituted a sect of the Jews in Palestine during the time of Christ but are not mentioned in the NT. Our principal sources of information regarding them are Josephus and Philo (first century) and Pliny the Elder and Hippolytus (second century).

The Essenes lived a simple life of sharing everything in common. They practiced strict rules of conduct. They were mostly unmarried. They were reported to number four thousand. The majority of them lived together in settlements, but some resided in the cities of the Jews. Apparently they kept their ranks filled by the adoption of other people's children. They did not participate in the temple worship but had their own purification rites. They observed the Sabbath day very strictly and greatly venerated Moses. They would take no oaths; but new members, after going through a three-year probationary period, were required to swear a series of strong oaths that they would cooperate in every way with the organization and would never reveal to outsiders any of the affairs or beliefs of the sect.

The Essenes have come into public attention in late years because of the study of the Dead Sea

The ruins and excavations at Qumran, off the northwestern shore of the Dead Sea, facing west. In foreground are remains of the "monastery" of the Essene community, first century B.C. Courtesy Israel Government Press Office.

Scrolls and the excavation of the monastery called Khirbet Qumran where the scrolls were written. This literature and building give evidence of an organization very similar to what is known about the Essenes. The structure was occupied from the end of the second century B.C. to A.D. 135. The Essenes are known to have flourished in this period. Also, the location of the building fits the description of the elder Pliny. The literature reveals that the people of the Qumran community were avid students of the Jewish Scriptures. Many scholars believe them to be the Essenes but so many religious groups were in existence during the last century B.C. that certainty in the matter has not yet been achieved.

Many of the Essenes perished in the wars against the Romans. Many of the survivors probably became Christians. CEH

ESTHER (Heb. *'estēr,* perhaps from Akkad. *Ishtar* [Venus], Gr. *astēr, star*). A Jewish orphan maiden in the city of Shushan who became queen of Persia. Her Hebrew name was Hadassah (*myrtle*). Her cousin Mordecai, who was a minor official of the palace, reared her as his own daughter. Xerxes (KJV Ahasuerus), the Persian king, had divorced his wife. When he sought a new queen from among the maidens of the realm he chose Esther. When the Jews in the empire were faced with destruction she was able to save them. In her honor the book that bears her name is read every year at the Feast of Purim.

ESTHER, BOOK OF. The last of the historical books of the OT. It was written after the death of King Xerxes (Esth 10:2; KJV "Ahasuerus"). Most scholars today agree that the KJV Ahasuerus was the Xerxes who reigned 486 B.C. to 465 B.C. Probably the book was written about 400. The author is unknown, but it is evident from the details of the record that he was well acquainted with the Persian court life. The Book of Esther has always been accepted as canonical by the Jews.

External proof of the career of Mordecai has been found in an undated cuneiform text that mentions a certain Mordecai (Marduka) who was a high official at the Persian court of Shushan during the reign of Xerxes and even before that under Darius I. This text came from Borsippa and is the first reference to Mordecai outside the Bible.

Outstanding peculiarities of the book are the complete absence of the name of God, the lack of any direct religious teaching, and no mention of prayer. These remarkable features can have occurred only by deliberate design. Probably the book was written for the Jews in the Persian Empire as an account that could be circulated without danger of offending the people of that land who ruled over many Jews.

The account contains many dramatic elements. King Xerxes gave a great feast for all the officials of his realm. Queen Vashti offended him when she refused to appear before the company at the command of the king. As a result he divorced her (Esth 1). Later, in order to procure another queen, he ordered all the beautiful maidens of the land brought together. Among them was Hadassah, who had been reared by her cousin Mordecai. Her name was changed to Esther by the Persians. This maiden was chosen by the king to be his queen. Mordecai discovered a plot against the king's life (ch. 2). The king made Haman his chief minister. Everybody bowed down to him except Mordecai. This disrespect infuriated the high official. Knowing Mordecai was a Jew, Haman decided to destroy all the Jews in revenge for his hurt feelings. Lots, called *Pur,* were cast to find an auspicious day for the destruction. The consent of the king was obtained, and an official decree was written and publicized throughout the empire, setting the date for the slaughter of the Jews (ch. 3). Mordecai sent word to Esther that she must plead for her people before the king (ch. 4). At the risk of her life she went in before the king. He received her favorably. Instead of pleading with him at once she invited him and Haman to a banquet. There the king asked her to state her request, but she put it off and invited them to another banquet. Haman, rejoicing in his good fortune but incensed at Mordecai, had a gallows constructed on which to hang him (ch. 5). That night, unable to sleep, the king was listening to the reading of the royal chronicles. When the account of Mordecai's discovery of the assassination plot was read, the king asked what reward had been given him and was told none at all.

The traditional tomb of Esther and Mordecai, at Ecbatana, modern Hamadan, Iran. Courtesy B. Brandl.

It was early morning and Haman had come to ask permission to hang Mordecai. But the king asked him what should be done to a man he wished to honor. Being convinced that the king could have only him in mind, Haman suggested the greatest of honors he could imagine. At the king's command he was obliged to bestow those honors on Mordecai (Esth 6). At the second banquet Esther told the king about the scheme to destroy her people and named Haman as the one responsible for it. The king became very angry and ordered Haman to be hanged on the gallows he had made (ch. 7). Another decree was sent out that enabled the Jews to save themselves (ch. 8). In two days of fighting they were victorious everywhere. Esther and Mordecai wrote letters to the Jews instituting the commemoration of these two days in an annual Feast of Purim (ch. 9). Mordecai, being next to the king, brought blessing to the people (ch. 10).

In the Septuagint, the Book of Esther contains several interpolations scattered through the account.

Bibliography: L. H. Brockington, *Ezra, Nehemiah and Esther* (NCB), 1969; A. M. Carey, *Esther* (AB), 1971. CEH

ESTHER, ADDITIONS TO (See APOCRYPHA)

ETAM (ē'tăm). 1. A town and clan in Judah between Bethlehem and Tekoa (1 Chron 4:3), Khirbet-el-Khokh, rebuilt by Rehoboam (2 Chron 11:6); also named in LXX of Joshua 15:59.

2. A village near En Rimmon in Simeon (1 Chron 4:32).

3. The rock where Samson lived after a slaughter of Philistines (Judg 15:8, 11). Perhaps the same as No. 1.

ETERNAL LIFE (See ESCHATOLOGY)

ETH KAZIN (ĕth kā'zĭn, Heb. *'ittah katsin*). A place on the border of Zebulun (Josh 19:13). The exact site is unknown.

ETHAM (ē'thăm, Heb. *'ēthām*). An uncertain site on Israel's journey out of Egypt, reached after leaving Succoth and before turning back to Pi Hahiroth. After crossing the Red Sea they traveled three days in the wilderness of Etham to reach Marah (Exod 13:20; Num 33:6–8). Thus Etham seems to have been a wilderness district on both sides of the north end of the Red Sea.

ETHAN (ē'thăn, Heb. *'êthan*). 1. An Ezrahite of Solomon's time, renowned for his wisdom (1 Kings 4:31; Ps 89 title).

2. A son of Zerah, son of Judah (1 Chron 2:6, 8).

3. A descendant of Gershon, son of Levi (1 Chron 6:39–43).

4. A singer, descendant of Merari, son of Levi (1 Chron 6:44; 15:17, 19).

ETHBAAL (ĕth'bā'ăl, Heb. *'ethbaal*). A king of Sidon whose daughter Jezebel became the wife of Ahab, king of Israel (1 Kings 16:31).

ETHER (ē'thêr, Heb. *'ether*). A town in Judah named in Joshua 15:42 (modern Khirbet Ater). Perhaps the same assigned to Simeon in Joshua 19:7, 9.

ETHIOPIA (ē'thĭ-ō'pĭ-à, Heb. *kûsh*, Gr. *Aithiopia*). A country extending south of Egypt from the first cataract of the Nile indefinitely, including Nubia, Sudan, and northern if not southern modern Ethiopia. The nation descended from Cush (Heb. *Kûsh*), son of Ham (Gen 10:6–8; 1 Chron 1:8–10), the most southern peoples known to the Hebrews, in Arabia and North Africa. Ethiopia, which may be anywhere in this general direction, is called Cush in the RSV and NIV (Gen 2:13). Job 28:19 mentions the topaz of Ethiopia (NIV Cush). Moses married an Ethiopian woman (Num 12:1). In the reign of Rehoboam, Ethiopians came against Judah with the king of Egypt (2 Chron 12:3); and in the reign of Asa (14:9–13; 16:7–9) Zerah the Ethiopian with a million men was defeated in Judah. "The Arabs who lived near the Cushites" (21:16) indicates the lands on both sides of the Red Sea, in the Arabian peninsula and in Africa, sometimes under the same rule.

The Ethiopians had skin of different appearance (Jer 13:23); the Greek name *Aithiops,* burnt-face, shows the color to have been dark. Pictures on monuments show that they were a mixed race, some Negro, some Semitic, some Caucasian. Ethiopia enters Bible history most prominently when Tirhakah, an Ethiopian king of a dynasty that had conquered Egypt, came against Judah in the days of Hezekiah and was only driven away by the superior force of Assyria (2 Kings 19:9; Isa 37:9). Henceforth the ultimate ruin of Ethiopia is a theme of prophecy (Isa 11:11; 18:1; 20:3–5; 43:3; 45:14; Jer 46:9; Ezek 29:10; 30:4–5; 38:5; Nah 3:9; Zeph 3:10). The English versions vary between "Ethiopia" and "Cush." Echoes are in Psalms 68:31; 87:4. Ethiopia is the western limit of the Persian Empire of Xerxes (Esth 1:1; 8:9). Ethiopia in NT times was ruled by a queen whose named or title was Candace (Acts 8:27). Ethiopia was a sparsely populated land traversed by the Blue and White Nile and their tributaries, a reservoir of hardy manpower for ambitious rulers (Isa 18:1–2).

ETHIOPIAN EUNUCH (ē'thĭ-ō'pĭ-ăn yū'-nŭk). Treasurer of Candace, queen of the Ethiopians (Acts 8:26–39). He was a mighty man (Gr. *dynastēs*) or nobleman. As a eunuch he could not be a full member of the Jewish community (Deut 23:1), but he had been worshiping in Jerusalem and was reading aloud the Book of Isaiah when Philip, sent by the Holy Spirit from Samaria to help him, met his chariot. From Isaiah 53, Philip led the African to faith in Christ, so that he asked

Drawing of a Roman carriage of the type probably used by the Ethiopian eunuch for interurban transportation (Acts 8:27). Courtesy Carta, Jerusalem.

for and received baptism and went on his way toward Gaza rejoicing.

ETHNAN (ēth'năn). A son of Helah, wife of Ashhur, a Judahite (1 Chron 4:7).

ETHNI (ĕth'nī). A Gershonite Levite and an ancestor of Asaph whom David set over the service of song (1 Chron 6:41). Likely the same person named Jeatherai in 1 Chronicles 6:21.

EUBULUS (yū-bū'lŭs). A Christian disciple at Rome who, with others, saluted Timothy (2 Tim 4:21).

EUERGETES (yū-ûr'jē-tēz). "Benefactors" (so RSV, NIV), a title of honor often voted by Greek states to public men. Our Lord alludes to the title (Luke 22:25).

EUNICE (yū'nĭs, yū-nī'sē, Gr. *Eunikē*). The Jewish wife of a Greek, daughter of Lois and mother of Timothy (Acts 16:1; 2 Tim 1:5). They lived at Lystra, where the two women and Timothy were converted, probably on Paul's first visit (Acts 14:6–20), since Timothy knew of Paul's persecution there (2 Tim 3:11). She brought up her son to know the OT Scriptures (3:15).

EUNUCH (yū'nŭk, Heb. *sārîs*, Gr. *eunouchos*). A castrated male. From the employment of such men as custodians of royal harems the term came to designate an officer, whether physically a eunuch or not. Heb. *sārîs* is translated variously *officer, chamberlain,* and *eunuch* (e.g., Gen 37:36; 2 Kings 23:1; Isa 56:3; Jer 29:2). The Mosaic Law forbade those blemished by castration to enter the congregation (Deut 23:1), but Isaiah prophesied of a day when this disability would be removed and their loss compensated (Isa 56:3–5). In English, eunuch is a transliteration of Greek *eunouchos.* The Ethiopian (Acts 8:27–39) was a queen's treasurer in whom Isaiah's prophecy may well have encouraged a new hope. Our Lord uses the term and its cognate verb four times in Matthew 19:12; those born eunuchs and those made eunuchs by men are physically incapable of begetting children; those who "have renounced marriage because of the kingdom of heaven" are those whom continence has kept chaste and celibate so they may concentrate their lives on promoting the kingdom of heaven (cf. Rev 14:4). The eminent though erratic Christian scholar Origen late in life regretted taking Matthew 19:12 literally.

EUODIA (yū-ō'dĭ-ȧ, Gr. *Euōdia, prosperous journey* or *fragrance*). A Christian woman at Philippi, also called Euodias. She is mentioned in Philippians 4:2 where Paul pleads with Euodia and Syntyche to "agree with each other in the Lord."

EUPHRATES (yū-frā'tēz, Heb. *perāth,* from a root meaning *to break forth,* Gr. *Euphratēs*). The longest and most important river of western Asia,

"The great river Euphrates" (Rev 16:12). Courtesy Studium Biblicum Franciscanum, Jerusalem.

The Euphrates River flowing past the small village of Halfeti in Turkey. View looking northward. Courtesy B. Brandl.

frequently in the OT called "the river," "the great river," as being the largest with which Israel was acquainted, in contrast to the soon dried up torrents of Palestine (Gen 15:18; Deut 1:7; Isa 8:7). It rises from two sources in the Armenian mountains, whose branches join after having run 400 (667 km.) and 270 miles (450 km.). The united river runs SW and south through the Taurus mountains toward the Mediterranean; but the ranges north of Lebanon prevent its reaching that sea; it turns SE and flows 1000 miles (1,667 km.) to the Persian Gulf. The whole course is 1,780 miles (2,967 km.); for 1,200 miles (2,000 km.) it is navigable for small vessels. The melting of the snows in the Armenian mountains causes the river to flood each spring. Nebuchadnezzar controlled the floods by turning the water through sluices into channels for distribution over the whole country. The promise to Abraham that his seed's inheritance should reach the Euphrates (Gen 15:18; Deut 1:7; Josh 1:4) received a partial fulfillment in Reuben's pastoral possessions (1 Chron 5:9–10); a fuller accomplishment under David and Solomon, when an annual tribute was paid by subject petty kingdoms in that area (2 Sam 8:3–8; 1 Kings 4:21; 1 Chron 18:3; 2 Chron 9:26). The Euphrates was the boundary between Assyria and the Hittite country after Solomon's time, according to inscriptions.

EUROCLYDON (yū-rŏk'lī-dŏn, Gr. *Euroklydōn,* from *euros, the east wind,* and *klydōn, a wave*). This term is found only in the KJV and MLB of Acts 27:14; it is translated as "Euraquilo" in NASB and RV and as "Northeaster" in NEB and NIV. It came down from the island of Crete, south of which Paul was sailing. It would be extremely dangerous to a ship with large sails, threatening either to capsize her or to drive her onto the sandbars (27:17).

EUTYCHUS (yū'tĭ-kŭs, Gr. *Eutychos, fortunate*). A young man of Troas mentioned in Acts 20:9 who, while listening to Paul preach, was overcome with sleep and fell out of the third story window to his death. Paul then went down and restored him to life.

EVANGELIST (Gr. *euangelistēs, one who announces good news*). Used in a general sense of anyone who proclaims the gospel of Jesus Christ. Sometimes in the NT, however, it designates a particular class of ministry, as in Ephesians 4:11: Christ "gave some to be apostles . . . prophets . . . evangelists . . . pastors and teachers." The evangelist founded the church; the pastor-teacher built it up in the faith. The evangelist was not confined in service to one spot but moved about in different localities, preaching the Good News concerning Jesus Christ to those who had not heard the message before. Once such had put their trust in the Lord, then the work of the pastor-teacher began. He would remain with them, training them further in the things pertaining to Christ and building them up in the faith. Apostles (Acts 8:25; 14:7; 1 Cor 1:17) did the work of an evangelist, as did also bishops (2 Tim 4:2–5). Philip, who had been set apart as one of the seven deacons (Acts 6:5), was also called "the evangelist" (21:8). The word refers to a *work* rather than to an *order*. Evangelist in the sense of "inspired writer of one of the four Gospels" was a later usage. BP

EVE (Heb. *hawwâh, life, living*). The first woman, formed by God out of Adam's side. Adam designated her (Gen 2:23) as woman (Heb. *'ishshâh*) for she was taken out of man (Heb. *'ish*). In these words there is suggested the close relationship between man and woman; a relationship the first man could not find in the animal creation (2:20). The way in which Eve was created and the designation "woman" emphasize also the intimacy, sacredness, and inseparability of the marital state, transcending even the relationship between children and parents (2:24). The name "Eve" was given to her after the Fall and implies both her being the mother of all living and the mother of the promised Seed who would give life to the human race now subjected to death. While the Scriptures uniformly trace the fall of the race to Adam's sin, the part Eve played in this tragedy is vividly portrayed in Genesis 3. Her greater weakness and susceptibility to temptation are juxtaposed with Adam's willful act of disobedience. Deceived by Satan, she ate of the fruit. Enamored of his wife, Adam chose to leave God for the one he had given him. Paul twice refers to Eve in his letters (2 Cor 11:3; 1 Tim 2:13). BP

EVI (ē'vī, Heb. *'ĕwî*). One of the five kings of Midian killed by the Israelites during their encampment in the plains of Moab (Num 31:8). His land was allotted to Reuben (Josh 13:21).

EVIL (Heb. *ra'*, Gr. *ponēros, kakos*). A term designating what is not in harmony with the divine order. In the Bible, evil is clearly depicted under two distinct aspects; moral and physical. The Hebrew word *ra'* has an immensely wide coverage, ranging from what tastes "nasty" right through to intrinsic moral and spiritual evil. Its two main "blocks" of meaning, spread evenly over some six thousand occurrences, cover meanings from "calamity," "disaster," and "downfall" to "wrong," "wicked," and "pernicious." For the precise meaning the context must always be consulted; for example, in Isaiah 45:7, KJV has the literal meaning of "evil," NIV interprets it as "disaster," JB and NASB choose "calamity," NEB has "trouble," and RSV takes it to mean "woe" (cf. Amos 3:6, where RSV has "evil").

The reconciliation of the existence of evil with the goodness and holiness of a God infinite in his wisdom and power is one of the great problems of theism. The Scriptures indicate that evil has been permitted by God in order that his justice might be manifested in its punishment and his grace in its forgiveness (Rom 9:22–23). Thus the existence of evil is a reminder of the manifold perfections of God. Moral evil, or sin, is any lack of conformity to the moral law of God. According to the Bible, it is the cause of the existence of physical or natural evil in this world. Adam and Eve, the first humans, enjoyed perfect fellowship with God in the Garden of Eden. The day they ate of the fruit of the tree that was in the midst of the Garden, disobeying God, they fell under his condemnation and were banished from the Garden. The ground was then cursed for man's sake, and from that time forward man has been forced to gain his sustenance through arduous, sorrowful toil, even as woman has borne children only through suffering and labor (Gen 3:16–19). In the NT the relationship between moral and natural evil is indicated by Paul in Romans 8:18–22.

Bibliography: C. R. Smith, *The Bible Doctrine of Sin,* 1953; O. F. Clarke, *God and Suffering,* 1964; J. Hick, *Evil and the God of Love,* 1966; J. W. Wenham, *The Goodness of God,* 1974; W. Grundmann, TDNT, 3:469–84. BP

EVIL-MERODACH (ē'vil-mĕ-rō'dăk). A king of Babylon who reigned two years (561–560

B.C.). His name (*Amelu-Marduk* is the Babylonian form) means "Man of Marduk." This is a theophorous name, Marduk being the chief god of Babylon (cf. Ish-Bosheth, Ish-Baal). The son and successor of Nebuchadnezzar, Evil-Merodach was murdered by his brother-in-law, Neriglissar (the Nergal-Sharezer of Jer 39:3), a prince who usurped the throne. References to him as lawless and indecent indicate the probable reasons for the coup that cut short his reign.

Evil-Merodach released Jehoiachin, king of Judah, from his thirty-seven-year Babylonian imprisonment and gave him a position of prominence among the captive kings and a daily allowance of food for the rest of his life (2 Kings 25:27–30; Jer 52:31–34); but he was not permitted to return home to Judah. Cuneiform tablets recovered from Babylon and assigned a date in Nebuchadnezzar's reign, refer to provisions supplied to Jehoiachin and other royal prisoners. The latest of these tablets is at least eight years earlier than the date of Jehoiachin's release referred to in Scripture. Evil-Merodach may have increased the king's allowance from the small amount mentioned in these tablets. JBG

EVIL SPIRITS (See DEMONS)

EWE (See ANIMALS)

EXALTATION. The term covers the sequence of events that begins with the resurrection of Christ and that includes his ascension and his coming again. The outcome of his humility and obedience, the "high exaltation" of Christ, will in turn lead to the bowing of every knee and the acknowledgment of his Lordship by every tongue (Phil 2:8–11; cf. Acts 2:33). The exaltation of Christ places him "at the right hand of God" (Rom 8:34), an expression used by Stephen (Acts 7:55–56), Paul (Eph 1:20), Peter (1 Peter 3:22), and the writer to the Hebrews (Heb 1:3; 10:12; 12:2). This firmly establishes the association of Christ with God in power and glory, a glorification noted by our Lord himself (John 17:5; cf. 12:32).

EXCOMMUNICATION. Disciplinary exclusion from church fellowship. The Jews had two forms of excommunication, apparently alluded to in Luke 6:22 by Christ: "Blessed are you . . . when they exclude you [the Jewish *middûy,* for thirty, sixty, or ninety days], and . . . reject your name as evil [the Jewish *hērem,* a formally pronounced, perpetual cutting off from the community], because of the Son of Man." Christian excommunication is commanded by Christ (Matt 18:15–18), and apostolic practice (1 Tim 1:20) and precept (1 Cor 5:11; Titus 3:10) are in agreement. "Hand this man over to Satan" (1 Cor 5:5; 1 Tim 1:20) seems to mean casting out of the church into the world that lies in the power of the wicked one (Eph 6:12; 1 John 5:19). The object of excommunication is the good of the offender (1 Cor 5:5) and the moral well-being of the sound members (2 Tim 2:17). Its subjects are those guilty of heresy or great immorality (1 Cor 5:1–5; 1 Tim 1:20). It is inflicted by the church and its representative ministers (1 Cor 5:1, 3–4; Titus 3:10). Paul's inspired words give no warrant for uninspired ministers claiming the same right to direct the church to excommunicate at will (2 Cor 2:7–9). BP

EXECUTIONER. An officer of high rank in the East, commander of the bodyguard who executed the king's sentence. Potiphar (Gen 37:36 ASV footnote) was the "chief of the executioners." Nebuzaradan (Jer 39:9 ASV footnote) and Arioch (Dan 2:14 ASV) held this office. In the Gospel record we are told that King Herod sent an executioner (Gr. *spekoulatōr,* originally a military watch or scout), i.e., one of his bodyguard, to behead John the Baptist (Mark 6:27).

EXILE. This usually refers to the period of time during which the southern kingdom (Judah) was forcibly detained in Babylon. It began with a series of deportations during the reigns of the Judean kings, Jehoiakim (609–598 B.C.), Jehoiachin (598), and Zedekiah (598–587). After the destruction of Jerusalem by Nebuchadnezzar (587) the kingdom of Judah ceased to exist as a political entity. Although there were settlements in Egypt, the exiles in Babylon were the ones who maintained the historic faith and provided the nucleus that returned to Judea after the decree of Cyrus (536). The northern kingdom (Israel) was earlier exiled to Assyria (722). It was the policy of the Assyrian conquerors to move the populations of captured cities, with the result that Israelites were scattered in various parts of the empire and other captives were brought to the region around Samaria (2 Kings 17:24). Subsequent history knows these people as the Samaritans. Although people from the northern kingdom doubtless returned with the Judean exiles, no organized return took place from the Assyrian captivity.

I. Causes. Both theological and political causes are mentioned in the biblical accounts of the Exile. The prophets noted the tendency of both Israel and Judah to forsake the Lord and adopt the customs of their heathen neighbors. These included the licentious worship associated with the Baal fertility cult and the Molech worship that required the offering of human beings in sacrifice to a heathen deity. Politically the Exile was the result of an anti-Babylonian policy adopted by the later kings of Judah. Egypt, the rival of Babylon, urged the Judean kings to refuse to pay tribute to Nebuchadnezzar. Although Jeremiah denounced this pro-Egyptian policy it was adopted with disastrous results. Egypt proved to be a "broken reed," and the kingdom of Judah was rendered impotent before the Babylonian armies. After a siege of eighteen months Nebuchadnezzar entered Jerusalem, destroyed the temple, and took captive the inhabitants of the city.

II. Social and Economic Conditions. The Exile worked great hardships on a people who were forcibly removed from their homeland and settled in new territory. The psalmist pictures the exiles weeping in Babylon, unable to sing the songs of Zion in a strange land (Ps 137:4). Among other hardships, they had to endure the failure of false prophecies of an exile that would only last two years (Jer 28:11). On the other hand, actual conditions of life in the Exile were not necessarily harsh. Jeremiah, knowing that a protracted period would be spent in Babylon, urged the exiles to settle down, build homes, marry, and pray for the peace of their new land. He predicted a seventy-year captivity (Jer 29:4–14). From Ezekiel, himself present among the exiles (Ezek 1:1–3), we gather that the exiles were organized in their own communities under their own elders (8:1). Ezekiel's own community was situated at Tel Abib (3:15), an otherwise unknown location on the river, or canal, Kebar.

III. Religious Conditions. The prophets Ezekiel and Daniel ministered in Babylon during the Exile. Jeremiah, who had urged Zedekiah to make peace with Nebuchadnezzar, was permitted to remain in Judah after the destruction of Jerusalem. The murder of Gedaliah, who had been appointed by Nebuchadnezzar as governor of Judah, precipitated a move on the part of the remaining Judeans to migrate to Egypt. Although tradition suggests that he subsequently went to Babylon, Jeremiah's actual prophetic ministry ends among those who had fled this way to Egypt.

Ezekiel was taken to Babylon at the time of the deportation of Jehoiachin. He prophesied to the exiles at Tel Abib, warning them of the impending destruction of Jerusalem. Subsequent to the fall of the city, Ezekiel held forth the hope of a return from exile and the reestablishment of the people of God in Palestine.

Daniel was one of the youths selected to be taken to Babylon at the time of the first deportation (under Jehoiakim). God-given abilities and a spirit of faithfulness enabled Daniel to rise to a position of influence in the Babylonian court—a position that he maintained through varying political regimes to the time of Cyrus the Persian, conqueror of Babylon. Like Ezekiel, Daniel spoke of the Exile as temporary in duration. He also depicted a succession of world powers, culminating in the reign of the Messiah as the goal of history.

Within preexilic Judaism, the center of worship was the Jerusalem temple where sacrifices were offered daily and where annual festive occasions were observed. With the destruction of the temple a new spiritual orientation took place. Jews came together for the purpose of prayer and the study of Scripture in gatherings that later were called synagogues. The emergence of the synagogue made possible the continuation of Jewish religious life during the period of absence from the temple. The synagogue persisted after the building of the second temple (516 B.C.) and is still an important factor in Jewish life.

The sacred books of the Jews assumed great importance during the period of the Exile. The law, which had been lost prior to Josiah's reign (2 Kings 22:8), became the subject of careful study. By the time of the return from Babylon, the institution of the scribe was established. Scribes not only made copies of the law, but they also served as interpreters. Ezra is regarded as the first scribe (Neh 8:1ff.). The Sabbath, a part of the Mosaic Law, assumed a new meaning to the displaced Jews of the Exile. It served as a weekly reminder of the fact that they had a definite covenant relationship to God, and became a marker to distinguish the Jew from his Babylonian neighbor. When Nehemiah led a group back to Palestine he insisted that the Sabbath be scrupulously observed (13:15–22).

IV. Political Conditions. The Exile began during the reign of the Neo-Babylonian king, Nebuchadnezzar and ended with the decree of the Persian king, Cyrus. Nebuchadnezzar defeated an Egyptian army that had joined forces with the Assyrians, who were retreating before the Babylonians, at Carchemish on the upper Euphrates (605 B.C.). The campaign against Egypt was deferred when Nebuchadnezzar, on receiving news of the death of his father, Nabopolassar, returned home to insure his succession to the kingdom. Judah was among the states of western Asia that Nebuchadnezzar claimed as heir to the Assyrians whom he had defeated in battle. Babylonian armies occupied Judah during the reign of Jehoiakim (c. 603) and took captive a number of its leading citizens, leaving only "the poorest of the people" in the land. Jehoiakim was allowed to retain his throne until he rebelled (2 Kings 24:12–16). In 598 the Babylonian king called on the vassal states (including Moab, Syria, and Ammon) to support his power in Judah by force of arms (24:2). When Jehoiakim was killed in battle his eighteen-year-old son, Jehoiachin, succeeded him. After a reign of but three months, Jehoiachin was deported to Babylon with ten thousand Jews, including Ezekiel. Jehoiachin's uncle, Zedekiah, the third son of Josiah, was made a puppet king in Jerusalem (24:17–19). In spite of the warnings of Jeremiah, Zedekiah yielded to the pro-Egyptian party and refused to pay tribute to Babylon. Thereupon Nebuchadnezzar laid siege to Jerusalem and, after eighteen months, entered the city, destroyed its temple, and deported its citizens (587). Following the murder of Gedaliah, whom Nebuchadnezzar had appointed to handle Judean affairs after the destruction of Jerusalem, the final deportation took place in about 581 (25:22).

Nebuchadnezzar reigned for more than forty years, but he left no able successor. Jehoiachin was given a place of honor among the exiles in Babylon by Evil-Merodach (561–560 B.C.), son and successor of Nebuchadnezzar. Neriglissar (559–556) and Labashi-Marduk (556) had brief, nonsignificant reigns. Nabonidus (Nabu-Na'id), with his son Belshazzar, served as the last ruler of the Neo-Babylonian Empire (556–539). Nabonidus had an interest in archaeology and religion but was inefficient as a ruler. He repaired the ziggurat to the moon god Sin at Ur where one of his daughters served as priestess. Another daughter is said to have maintained a small museum of archaeological finds. His diversified interests caused Nabonidus to name Belshazzar, his eldest son, as prince regent. It was during the reign of Belshazzar that the Neo-Babylonian Empire came to an end. Cyrus had made rapid conquests after his succession to the throne of the small Persian principality of Anshan (559). Successively unifying the Persians, conquering the neighboring Medes and the distant Lydians of Asia Minor, Cyrus marched against Babylon, which he defeated in 539. The governor of Babylon, Gubaru, is doubtless to be identified with "Darius the Mede" mentioned in Daniel 5 and 6. Cyrus issued the decree that permitted Jews to return to Jerusalem to rebuild the temple (Ezra 1:1–4). This may be regarded as the end of the Exile, although many Jews chose to remain in Babylon.

V. Results. Although the Exile ended the political independence of Judea, it served to emphasize the fact that God was in no sense confined to Palestine. He accompanied his people to Babylon and providentially cared for them there (cf. Ezek 11:16). The experience of life far away from the land, city, and house where the Lord had chosen to dwell, brought to the fore the monotheism that had always been part of the faith of the people of the Lord. At the same time, the teaching of the prophets that the Exile was the Lord's punishment on idolatry bore fruit. Their suffering, coupled with face-to-face contact with the realities of false religion, purged the people once and for all of idolatrous desire and, in time, gave rise to the fanatical and unthinking monotheism of the Jews of our Lord's day. Although many exiles returned to their homeland following the decree of Cyrus, others remained in the Persian Empire, with the result that in due time Judaism became international in scope.

Bibliography: J. B. Taylor, *Ezekiel* (TOTC), 1969, pp. 29–35; R. K. Harrison, *Old Testament Times,* 1971, pp. 255–69; C. F. Pfeiffer, *Old Testament History,* 1973, pp. 398ff., 414ff. CFP

EXODUS (Gr. *ex hodos, a going out*). The event that ended the sojourn of Israel in Egypt. The family of Jacob (Israel) voluntarily entered Egypt during a time of severe famine in Canaan. Joseph, who had been sold into slavery by jealous brothers, was then vizier of Egypt and his Israelite brothers were assigned suitable land in the NE section of Egypt known as Goshen (Gen 42–46). When a new dynasty arose "who did not know about Joseph" (Exod 1:8), i.e., forgot what he had done for Egypt, the Israelites were reduced to the status of slaves. Afraid that they might prove sympathetic with foreign invaders, Pharaoh ordered the male children destroyed. The infant Moses, however, was placed in an ark of bulrushes where he was rescued by Pharaoh's daughter (2:1–10). Raised in the royal court, Moses chose to turn his back on the possibilities of advancement in Egypt in order to lead his oppressed people into freedom.

I. Date of the Exodus. There has been a lack of unanimity among Bible students concerning the

Colossal statue of Ramses II, on the north side of the entrance to the great temple of Amon at Karnak (Thebes). Some scholars suggest that he may have been the Pharaoh of the Oppression or the Pharaoh of the Exodus. Courtesy Seffie Ben-Yoseph.

date of the Exodus, as well as the identity of the pharaohs who took part in the oppression of Israel. Later pharaohs are sometimes mentioned by name (e.g., Pharaoh Hophra, Pharaoh Neco), but only the title "Pharaoh" is given in the Exodus account. Some biblical scholars consider that 1 Kings 6:1 is decisive in furnishing the date of the Exodus. That verse states that Solomon began to build the temple "in the four hundred and eightieth year after the Israelites had come out of Egypt." Since we know the approximate dates of Solomon's reign, this information can be used in calculating the date of the Exodus. The date suggested by this method of computation, about 1441 B.C., falls within the reign of Amenhotep II, son of Thutmose III, one of the great empire builders of New Kingdom Egypt. Paintings from the tomb of Rekhmire, vizier of Thutmose III, depict Semites working as slave laborers on building projects.

Adherents of the "early date" of the Exodus (1441 B.C.) also find support for their position from the Amarna Letters (1400–1366). These cuneiform tablets discovered at the site of Akhnaton's capital contain correspondence from the kings of the city-states in Canaan, asking the help of the Pharaoh against a people known as Habiru. This, it is suggested, is a description of the battles fought after the Exodus by the armies of Israel when seeking to conquer Canaan.

There are, however, serious difficulties in accepting the early date. During the Eighteenth Dynasty of Egyptian history (when the early date would fall), the capital of Egypt was at Thebes, south of the delta, and the building operations of Thutmose III seem to have been centered there. Later, however (during the time of the Rameses), the pharaohs resided in the delta, where they engaged in extensive building activity. It is specifically in the delta region, adjacent to Goshen, that Moses met with Pharaoh, and it was in the city of Rameses (also known as Avaris and Tanis) in the eastern delta that the Israelites are reported to have labored (Exod 1:11). Advocates of the early date suggest that the name Rameses is a modernization of an older name.

Because of these problems in dating the Exodus as early as 1441 B.C., a number of biblical scholars have come to accept a date in the thirteenth century. Explorations in Transjordan by the archaeologist Nelson Glueck indicate a gap in the sedentary population of that region from about 1900 to 1300. The Bible, however, indicates that Israel met formidable opposition from Sihon and Og, kings in the East Jordan country, and that the Moabite king sought to bring a curse on Israel to prevent their progress into Canaan. The earlier suggestion of evidence that Jericho fell about 1400 has been questioned by recent expeditions there under the direction of Kathleen Kenyon. The excavations at Hazor by Yigael Yadin also tend to point toward a thirteenth-century date for the Exodus, as did earlier excavations at Lachish and Debir. The Stele of Merneptah (c. 1229) provides the first reference to Israel in the Egyptian monuments. Merneptah claims a decisive victory over the Israelite people. It may be significant that the ideogram for "nation" is not used. In any event, we know that Israelites were fighting in Canaan during the reign of Merneptah. Merneptah's predecessor was Rameses II, who reigned for sixty-seven years from his capital at Tanis (or Rameses) in the delta.

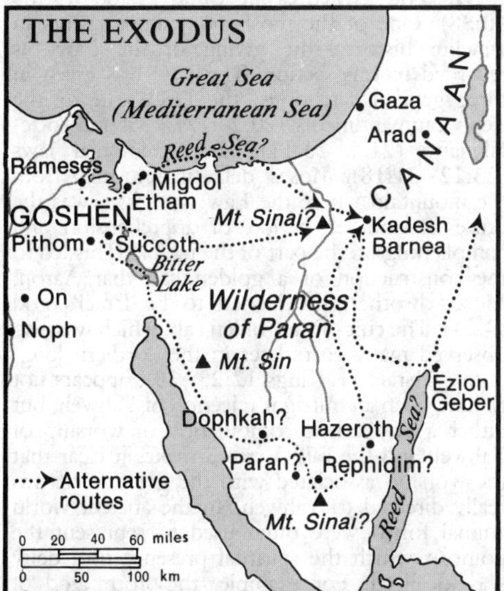

Some biblical scholars suggest that Seti I, father of Rameses, began the oppression, which was continued under Rameses, and that the Exodus took place during the reign of Rameses. Those who hold to this thirteenth-century date for the Exodus suggest that the 480 years of 1 Kings 6:1 be taken as a round number signifying twelve forty-year generations. Since generations are often much less than forty years apart, there may be a smaller time span between the Exodus and the building of Solomon's temple. This view is accepted by many who hold to the full inspiration of the scriptural text. In view of the fact that the non-Israelite characters in the account of the Exodus are not identified in Scripture, it is wise to avoid a dogmatic approach to the question. The evidence for the historicity of the Exodus account is decisive, but the evidence for specific dates is still inconclusive.

II. Route. The biblical record (Exod 13:17) states that Israel did not take the direct route through the Philistine country to Canaan. Had they done so, Israel would have had to pass the Egyptian wall (biblical Shur) that protected the NE highways out of Egypt. This wall was guarded and could be passed only with great difficulty. If they successfully crossed the border, further opposition could be anticipated from the Philistines. The discipline of the wilderness was a part of God's preparation for his people before they were to come into open conflict with formidable foes. Leaving Rameses (12:37) in the eastern delta, the Israelites journeyed SE to Succoth (Tell el-Mashkutah).

They then moved on to Etham "on the edge of the desert" where they were conscious of God's guidance in the pillar of cloud and pillar of fire (Exod 13:21–22). The word *etham* is derived from an Egyptian word meaning "wall" and was probably part of the series of fortifications built by the Egyptians to keep out the Asiatic nomads. From Etham they turned back and camped near Pi Hahiroth, described as "between Migdol and the sea" and near Baal Zephon. The location of these sites is not known with certainty. It is possible that Pi Hahiroth is Egyptian for "house of the marshes." Baal Zephon is the name of a Semitic deity who was worshiped in Egypt, doubtless at a shrine located at the town that bore his name.

After passing Pi Hahiroth, Israel arrived at the body of water designated in the English versions as the Red Sea, the Yam Suph of the Hebrew text. The geography of the Exodus suggests that Yam Suph, or Sea of Reeds, formed a natural barrier between Egypt and the Sinai Peninsula, the ultimate destination of the Israelites. The topography of this region has been altered since the construction of the Suez Canal, but the Yam Suph was probably north of Lake Timsah. An Egyptian document from the thirteenth century B.C. mentions a Papyrus Lake not far from Tanis—whose suggested location is the southern extension of the present Lake Menzaleh. The Exodus from

Egypt through the Yam Suph was made possible by the direct intervention of God who "drove the sea back with a strong east wind" (Exod 14:21). Israel was thus able to cross from Egypt to the Sinai Peninsula. When the armies of Pharaoh attempted to pursue the Israelites, the Egyptians were destroyed by the waters that returned to their normal course.

III. Number of Israelites. The Bible states that 600,000 men took part in the Exodus (Exod 12:37). A year later the number of male Israelites over the age of twenty was 603,550 (Num 1:46). During the years of Israel's sojourn in Egypt, the population multiplied to the point where Pharaoh was alarmed that Israel might side with an enemy during war (Exod 1:7–10). It was this very fear that brought about the oppression.

IV. Miracles. The Exodus period was one of the great epochs of biblical miracles. The first nine plagues may have been related to the natural phenomena of Egypt, but their timing and intensification were clearly supernatural. The last plague—the death of the first-born—signaled the beginning of the Exodus. Israel ate the Passover meal in haste, ready to depart from Egypt. The opening of the Red Sea by the "strong east wind" was the means by which God brought his people out of Egypt into the wilderness where, for a period of forty years, they were miraculously sustained.

Bibliography: C. de Wit, *The Date and Route of the Exodus,* 1960; D. Daube, *The Exodus Pattern in the Bible,* 1963; K. A. Kitchen, *Ancient Orient and Old Testament,* 1966, pp. 57–75; J. J. Bimson, *Redating the Exodus and Conquest,* 1978.

CFP

EXODUS, BOOK OF. The second book of the Bible. The title is a Latin term derived from the Greek word *Exodos,* "a going out." The book is called *Exodos* in the LXX. The title in the Hebrew tradition is comprised of the first several words of the book, "and these are the names." It refers to the names of the Israelites who came out of Egypt. Tradition ascribes the authorship of the book to Moses. It covers the history of the Israelites from the events surrounding the Exodus to the giving of the Law at Sinai.

I. The Israelites in Egypt (Exod 1:1–12:36). The historical events recorded in this section flow logically from the last chapters of the Book of Genesis where we are told how Jacob and his sons came to live in Egypt. The clan grew into a nation, but the lot of the Hebrew people changed when a pharaoh arose who did not remember the contributions of Jacob's son Joseph who had been elevated to prominence in the Egyptian government years before (1:8). This king forced the Hebrew people into hard servitude (1:13–14). The birth of Moses and his providential preservation, when the Pharaoh ordered the death of every male child born to the Hebrews (1:22), is recorded in chapter 2.

The account of Moses' call to lead the Hebrews out of Egypt (Exod 3:1–4:17) contains the classic statement of the Lord in which he depicts his divine character in the words, "I AM WHO I AM" (3:14) or "I am the one who is." While this statement has been understood in various ways, the context emphasizes the continuity of the promise made to the forefathers (3:13, 15–16). It is probably best to understand the words as connoting the continuity of God's dealings with his people—"I am the God who is," or "I am the God who continues to be," that is, the God who appeared to Moses was the same God who gave his gracious promises to their forefathers. The God of Moses was the God of Abraham.

The efforts of Moses to free his people met with no success until the first-born in Egypt were stricken by God. Only then were the Hebrews able to escape (see also EXODUS).

II. From Egypt to Sinai (Exod 12:37–19:2). Three important Hebrew traditions were formalized just after the flight from Egypt: the Passover (12:43–49), which commemorated the fact that the Lord had passed over the houses of the Israelites (12:27); the Feast of Unleavened Bread (13:3–10); and the consecration to God of every first-born male "whether man or animal" (13:2). When the Israelites had fled from Egypt the Pharaoh realized that he had lost a major source of manpower (14:5) and pursued them to the Red Sea, where God miraculously brought about their escape (14:21–31).

The period of Israelite history between the Exodus and the giving of the Law at Sinai was marked by frequent complaining by the people against God and their leader Moses. The complaints were often due to a lack of sustenance, but the deprivation was always met by miraculous displays of God's power. The bitter waters at Marah were made sweet (Exod 15:22–25), the hunger of the people was satisfied by the supply of manna (16:2–4) and quails (16:13), and their need for water on another occasion was met when God brought water out of a rock (17:2–7).

III. The Israelites at Sinai (Exod 19:3–40:38). One of the most momentous events in Israelite history—the giving of the Law—is recorded in this section. The Law was given in three general categories: the Decalogue or the Ten Commandments (20:2–17), civil and societal laws (21:1–23:11), and ceremonial laws (23:12–31:18). Moses' delay in returning from the mountain where the Law was given was the cause of another period of apprehension and complaining on the part of the people. This led to the construction of a golden calf that Aaron, Moses' brother, proclaimed to be Israel's god (32:4). The cult of the golden calf, which was also observed many years later in the northern kingdom of Israel (1 Kings 12:25–30), appears not to have been an outright rejection of Yahweh, but rather a syncretistic combination of worship of Yahweh and the calf. Verse 5 makes it clear that the worship associated with the golden calf was really directed to Yahweh. In the ancient world animal forms were often used to represent the point at which the spiritual presence of a deity was localized. For example, the storm god of Mesopotamia was prefigured as a lightning bolt set on the back of a bull. This is somewhat similar to the presence of Yahweh over the cherubim on the ark of the covenant.

The remainder of the Book of Exodus records the implementation of the ceremonial law in the construction of the tabernacle (Exod 35:4–38:31) and the fashioning of the priests' garments (39:1–43). When the tabernacle was completed it was filled with the glory of the Lord (40:34–38).

Bibliography: U. Cassuto, *A Commentary on the Book of Exodus,* 1951; J. P. Hyatt, *Commentary on Exodus* (NCB), 1971; R. E. Clements, *Exodus* (CBC), 1972; R. A. Cole, *Exodus: An Introduction and Commentary* (TOTC), 1973; B. C. Childs, *The Book of Exodus,* 1974. TEM

Fragment (7 cm. wide) from Assyria (late eighth century B.C.) of amulet designed to exorcise demons from the sick. Upper register contains seven demons, each with a different animal's head. The second register shows the horned demon Lamashtu holding a serpent in her hand. To the left is a bed for the sick; to the right is a smaller demon and demonic head. Courtesy Réunion des Musées Nationaux.

EXORCISM (Gr. *exorkizō, to adjure*). The expelling of demons by means of magic charms, spells, and incantations. It was a common practice among ancient heathen. In Acts 19:13–16 the profane use of Jesus' name as a mere spell was punished when the demon-possessed man turned on the would-be exorcists; these "vagabond Jews" were pretenders. Christ, however, implies that some Jews actually cast out demons (Matt 12:27)—some probably by demonical help, others (in the name of Jesus) without saving faith in him (7:22). He gave power to cast out demons to the twelve, the seventy, and to the other disciples after the Ascension (Matt 10:8; Mark 16:17; Luke 10:17–19; Acts 16:18). The Bible never mentions Christians "exorcising."

EXPANSE (See FIRMAMENT)

EXPIATION (See PROPITIATION AND EXPIATION)

EYE (Heb. *'ayin,* Gr. *ophthalmos*). The organ of sight. The literal sense is that which is most frequently found in the Scriptures, where the eye is recognized as among the most valued of the members of the body. In the Mosaic legislation, if a man hit a slave's eye so that it was blinded, the slave was to be released (Exod 21:26). One of the most cruel customs of the heathen nations was that of putting out the eyes of a defeated enemy (2 Kings 25:7).

The word is also used often in figurative expressions. Frequently "eye" speaks of spiritual perception and understanding. Thus the Word of God enlightens the eyes (Ps 19:8). Growth in spiritual knowledge comes through the "eyes of the heart being enlightened" (Eph 1:18). Other expressions speak of the eye as indicative of character. The good man has a "bountiful eye" (Prov 22:9 KJV). High or lofty eyes (Ps 131:1) describe the proud man. The envious man is one with an evil eye (Matt 20:15 KJV).

EYES, PAINTING OF. The ancient practice of painting the eyelids in order to enhance the beauty of the feminine face (Jer 4:30; Ezek 23:40). Jezebel "painted her eyes" (2 Kings 9:30). Oriental women still paint their eyelids with antimony or *kohl* (a black powder made of the smoke black from the burning of frankincense) to make them look full and sparkling, the blackened margin contrasting with the white of the eye.

EYESALVE (Gr. *kollourion*). A preparation compounded of various ingredients used either by simple application or by reduction to a powder to be smeared on the eye (Rev 3:18). When used figuratively it refers to the restoration of spiritual vision.

EZBAI (ĕz'bā-ī). The father of Naarai, one of David's valiant men (1 Chron 11:37).

EZBON (ĕz'bŏn). 1. One of the sons of Gad (Gen 46:16), also called Ozni (Num 26:16).

2. First named son of Bela, son of Benjamin (1 Chron 7:7).

EZEKIEL (ē-zēk'yĕl, Heb. *yehezqē'l, God strengthens*). A Hebrew prophet of the Exile. A play is made on this name in connection with the prophet's call (Ezek 3:7–8, 14). Of a priestly family (1:3), Ezekiel grew up in Judea during the last years of Hebrew independence and was deported to Babylon with Jehoiachin in 597 B.C., probably early in life. He was thus a younger contemporary of the prophet Jeremiah and of Daniel who, also as a young man, was taken to Babylon in 605. Ezekiel lived with the Jewish exiles by the irrigation canal Kebar (1:1, 3; 3:15) which connected the Tigris River with the Euphrates above Babylon; Daniel carried out his quite different work in the Babylonian court. We know little more about Ezekiel, except that he was married (24:18).

Ezekiel was called to be a prophet in the fifth year of his captivity (Ezek 1:1–2); the last date mentioned is the twenty-seventh year (29:17); his ministry therefore lasted at least twenty-two years, from about 593 to 571 B.C.

The "captivity" of the Jews consisted in their deportation to a foreign land. Once arrived in Babylon, however, the exiles seem to have been completely free to settle and live their lives as they pleased. At Nippur, located on the Kebar Canal, many records have been found of a Jewish business house, the Murashu Sons, indicating the possibilities open to the exiles. Many of the Jews became so settled in their adopted land that they refused to leave it at the end of the Exile, and from that time to this the majority of the Hebrews have lived outside of Palestine.

When Jerusalem was finally destroyed, some ten years after he arrived in Babylon, Ezekiel entered into the sufferings of his people. On the day on which the final siege began, the prophet's wife became suddenly sick and died. In this he became a sign to the people and was not allowed to go through the customary period of mourning, doubtless to emphasize to them the greater sorrow now coming on the nation.

In recent years a good deal of interest has been awakened regarding the unusual states of the prophets during the reception of their revelations. Some have diagnosed Ezekiel's condition as catalepsy, but the passages adduced (3:14–15, 26–27; 4:4–5; 24:27) hardly support such a theory. Rather it would seem that the occasional silence of the prophet and his lying on the ground were signs to gain the attention of the people and to act out his message.

Ezekiel was a powerful preacher. Possessing a deeply introspective and religious nature, he used allegory, vivid figures, and symbolic actions to clothe his message. His favorite expression to denote the divine inspiration, "the hand of the LORD was upon me" (1:3; 3:14, 22), shows how strongly he felt impelled to communicate the message given him. His preaching was directed to his Jewish brethren in exile; and, like Jeremiah's, it was often resented, for it held out little hope for the immediate future. No doubt his message was ultimately received, for the Exile became a time of religious purging. In Babylon the Jews were cured permanently of their idolatry; and Ezekiel, their major religious leader, must be given much credit for that.

The prophet's ministry was divided into two periods. The first ends with the siege of Jerusalem in 587 B.C. (24:1, 27). It was a message of approaching destruction for Jerusalem and of condemnation of her sin. The second period begins with the reception of the news of Jerusalem's fall, some two years later (33:21–22). Now the prophet's message emphasized comfort and looked forward to the coming of the kingdom of God. It would appear that during the two years between, Ezekiel ceased all public ministry.

Frequently in this book (more than seventy times), Ezekiel is referred to as "son of man." The term means a mortal, as in Psalm 8:4, and is used here to emphasize the prophet's weakness and dependence on God for his success. Later the term came to be a messianic designation. JBG

EZEKIEL, BOOK OF. Until quite recently universally accepted as written by Ezekiel. Some critics have denied the unity of the book and have attributed all or parts of it to later writers. There has been, however, no agreement among these critics. The arguments for both the unity of the book and its origin with Ezekiel are very strong. The book is autobiographical, that is, the author often uses the first person singular pronoun. The arrangement of the book shows its unity—all the parts fit together and, indeed, need each other to make the whole.

The locality of Ezekiel's ministry was Babylon, to which he had been deported in 597 B.C. Ezekiel 8–11 contains a unique vision of events that were transpiring in Jerusalem, made possible when "the Spirit lifted me up . . . and in visions of God he took me to Jerusalem" (8:3). Elsewhere in the book an intimate knowledge of events in faraway Jerusalem is implied (e.g., 24:1–2). It appears impossible that Ezekiel in Babylon could have known in such detail events in Jerusalem except by divine inspiration. Therefore many scholars are now of the opinion that Ezekiel really prophesied in Jerusalem until the city fell. The clear statements of the book, however, indicate his presence with the Jews in Babylon when he "saw" (8:6, 9–10) the events taking place at Jerusalem; and one who makes a serious attempt to understand the visions should grapple with these statements rather than deny them.

The book is divided into three parts: Denunciation of Judah and Israel (Ezek 1–24, dated 593–588 B.C.); oracles against foreign nations (chs. 25–32, dated 587–571); and the future restoration of Israel (chs. 33–48, dated 585–573).

The prophecies of the first section were uttered before the fall of Jerusalem. Ezekiel's call to the prophetic work is described in Ezekiel 1–3. Here occurs his vision of the divine glory—God's throne borne by an unearthly chariot of cherubim and wheels (1:4–21). The prophet eats the scroll on which his sad message is written (2:8–3:3); and he is commanded to be the Lord's watchman, his own life to be forfeited if he does not cry the alarm (3:16–21; cf. 33:1–9). Ezekiel then predicts the destruction of Jerusalem by symbolic acts (4:7), such as laying siege to a replica of the city (4:1–8) and by rationing food and drink (4:9–17). Next follows the famous vision of Jerusalem's iniquity, for which Ezekiel is raptured in spirit to Jerusalem (chs. 8–11), and sees all kinds of loathsome idolatry being practiced in the temple courts. While he watches the desecration of the house of the Lord, he beholds the divine glory, which had been manifested in the Most Holy Place (8:4), leave the temple and city (9:3; 10:4, 19; 11:22–23), symbolizing God's abandonment of his apostate people. At that moment

Ezekiel returns in spirit to Babylon. The rest of the first section (chs. 12–24) records symbolic actions and sermons of the prophet predicting the fall of Jerusalem. He enacts the departure into exile (12:1–7), preaches against false prophets (chs. 13), and in two deeply moving oracles (chs. 16, 23) depicts the ungrateful people's apostasy. His statement of the individual's responsibility before God (ch. 18) is famous. Finally he announces the beginning of the siege of Jerusalem, and in the evening of the same day his wife dies and he becomes dumb until the fall of the city (ch. 24).

After the prophecies of judgment against foreign nations (Ezek 25–32) comes the climax of the prophet's vision, written after the fall of Jerusalem—the restoration of Israel (chs. 33–48). God will bring back the people to their land, send the son of David to reign over them, and give them a new heart (chs. 34, 36). The vision of the valley of dry bones (ch. 37) is a figurative statement of this regathering of the nation. Then follows Israel's defeat of the Gentile powers, Gog and Magog (chs. 38–39). Finally a great restored temple is pictured (chs. 40–43), its holy services (chaps. 44–46), the river of life running from it (ch. 47), and the people of Israel living in their places around the city called "The Lord is there" (ch. 48), to which the glory of the Lord has returned (43:2, 4–5; 44:4).

Bibliography: H. L. Ellison, *Ezekiel: The Man and His Message,* 1956; C. L. Feinberg, *The Prophecy of Ezekiel,* 1969; J. B. Taylor, *Ezekiel: An Introduction and Commentary* (TOTC), 1969; J. W. Wevers, *Ezekiel* (NCB), 1969. JFG

EZEL (ē'zĕl, Heb. *hā'āzel, departure*). The stone near Saul's house that marked the final meeting place of David and Jonathan (1 Sam 20:19).

EZEM (ē'zĕm). A town near Edom assigned to Simeon (Josh 15:29; 19:3; 1 Chron 4:29). Sometimes rendered Azem.

EZER (ē'zêr, Heb. *'ēzer, help*). 1. One of the sons of Seir and a chief of the Horites (Gen 36:21; 1 Chron 1:38).

2. Descendant of Hur, of the tribe of Judah, and the father of Hushah (1 Chron 4:4).

3. An Ephraimite who was killed by men of Gath (1 Chron 7:21).

4. The first of the Gadite men of might who joined David in Ziklag when he was a fugitive from Saul (1 Chron 12:9).

5. The son of Jeshua, ruler of Mizpah. Under Nehemiah, Ezer repaired a section of the wall of Jerusalem (Neh 3:19).

6. One of the Levitical singers who participated in the dedication of the rebuilt walls of Jerusalem under Nehemiah (Neh 12:42).

EZION GEBER (ē'zĭ-ŏn gē'bêr, Heb. *'etsyôn gever*). A city near Elath on the Gulf of Aqabah. It was the last stopping place of the Israelites in their wilderness wanderings before Kadesh (Num 33:35–36). The city's period of greatest prosperity was in the time of Solomon, who there built a fleet of ships that sailed between Ezion Geber and Ophir, a source of gold (1 Kings 9:26ff.; 2 Chron 8:17–18). Similarly, Jehoshaphat joined with Ahaziah in building ships at Ezion Geber that were designed to sail to Ophir, but the fleet was destroyed before leaving port (2 Chron 20:35–36; 1 Kings 22:48–49). The site of Ezion Geber has been located at Tell Kheleifeh, and extensive excavations have been carried on there. The city was located between the hills of Edom on the east and the hills of Palestine on the west, where north winds blow strongly and steadily down the center of the Wadi el-Arabah. The location was chosen to take advantage of these winds, for the city was an industrial center as well as a seaport. The excavation uncovered an extensive industrial complex centered on the smelting and refining of copper (chiefly) and iron. The furnace rooms were so placed that they received the full benefit of the prevailing winds from the north, which were used to furnish the draft for the fires. Nearby mines were worked extensively in Solomon's day to supply the ore for these smelters. These operations were an important source of Solomon's wealth.

Early (1949) aerial photograph of Ezion Geber, looking northeast. The settlement is first mentioned as a stopping place during Israel's wilderness journeyings (Num 33:35–36). Courtesy Carta, Jerusalem.

Recent excavations at Jazirat Farun (Coral Island), seven and one-half miles (twelve and one-half km.) south of Elath with its port and shipyard have caused some to identify that site with Ezion Geber. It is the only natural anchorage in the Gulf. Ezion Geber is located in 1 Kings 9:26 "near Elath in Edom, on the shore of the Red Sea." The identification with Tell Kheleifeh remains most likely. BP

EZNITE (ĕz'nīt, Heb. *'etsnî*). Designation of Adino, one of David's chief captains (2 Sam 23:8 KJV, MLB, NASB). Some versions (NEB, NIV, RSV) are based on a conjecture that the statement about Adino the Eznite is a corruption of the Hebrew for "he lifted up his spear." A parallel passage (1 Chron 11:11) speaks of Jashobeam, a Hachmonite, who "raised his spear."

EZRA (ĕz'rà, Heb. *'ezrā', help*). 1. A man of

Judah mentioned in I Chronicles 4:17.

2. A leading priest who returned from Babylon to Jerusalem with Zerubbabel (Neh 12:1). In Nehemiah 10:2 the name is spelled in its full form, Azariah.

3. The famous Jewish priest and scribe who is the main character of the Book of Ezra and the co-worker of Nehemiah.

Ezra was a lineal descendant from Eleazar, the son of Aaron the high priest, and from Seraiah, the chief priest put to death at Riblah by order of Nebuchadnezzar (2 Kings 25:18–21). All that is really known of Ezra is what is told in Ezra 7–10 and Nehemiah 8–10. There are various traditions about him in Josephus, 2 Esdras, and the Talmud, but they are discrepant, and consequently no reliance can be put on anything they say unless it is also found in the canonical Scriptures.

In the seventh year of the reign of Artaxerxes Longimanus, king of Persia (458 B.C.), Ezra received permission from the king to return to Jerusalem to carry out a religious reform. Following the return from Babylonian captivity, the temple had been rebuilt in 516, in spite of much powerful and vexatious opposition from the Samaritans; but after a brief period of religious zeal, the nation drifted into apostasy once more. Many of the Jews intermarried with their heathen neighbors (Mal 2:11); the temple services and sacrifices were neglected (1:6–14); and oppression and immorality were prevalent (3:5). Just how Ezra acquired his influence over the king does not appear, but he received a royal edict granting him authority to carry out his purpose. He was given permission to take with him as many Israelites as cared to go; he was authorized to take from the king and the Jews offerings made for the temple; to draw on the royal treasury in Syria for further necessary supplies; to purchase animals for sacrifice; to exempt the priests, Levites, and other workers in the temple from the Persian tax; to appoint magistrates in Judea to enforce the law of God, with power of life and death over all offenders. Eighteen hundred Jews left Babylon with him. Nine days later, they halted at a place called Ahava, and when it was found that no Levites were in the caravan, thirty-eight were persuaded to join them. After fasting and praying three days for a safe journey, they set out. Four months later they reached the Holy City, having made a journey of nine hundred miles (fifteen hundred km.). The treasures were delivered into the custody of the Levites, burnt offerings were offered to the Lord, the king's commissions were handed to the governors and viceroys, and help was given to the people and the ministers of the temple.

When he had discharged the various trusts committed to him, Ezra entered on his great work of reform. The princes of the Jews came to him with the complaint that the Jewish people generally, and also the priests and Levites, but especially the rulers and princes, had not kept themselves religiously separate from the heathen around them, and had even married heathen wives. On hearing this report, Ezra expressed his horror and deep affliction of soul by tearing his garment and pulling out his hair. Those who still feared God and dreaded his wrath for the sin of the returned exiles gathered around him. At the evening sacrifice that day he made public prayer and confession of sin, entreating God not to remove his favor because of their awful guilt. The assembled congregation wept bitterly, and in the general grief, Shecaniah came forward to propose a covenant to put away their foreign wives and children. A proclamation was issued that all Jews were to assemble in Jerusalem three days later, under pain of excommunication and forfeiture of goods. At the time appointed, the people assembled, trembling on account of their sin and promising obedience. They requested that, since it was raining hard (it was the time of the winter rains in Palestine) and the number of transgressors was great, Ezra would appoint times for the guilty to come, accompanied by the judges and elders of each city, and have each case dealt with. A divorce court, consisting of Ezra and some others, was set up to attend to the matter; and after three months, in spite of some opposition, the work of the court was finished and the foreign wives were put away.

The Book of Ezra ends with this important transaction. Nothing more is heard of Ezra until thirteen years later in the twentieth year of Artaxerxes (446 B.C.), he appears again at Jerusalem, when Nehemiah, a Babylonian Jew and the favored cupbearer of Artaxerxes, returned to Jerusalem as governor of Palestine with the king's permission to repair the ruined walls of the city. It is uncertain whether Ezra remained in Jerusalem after he had effected the above-named reformation, or whether he had returned to the king of Persia and now came back with Nehemiah, or perhaps shortly after the arrival of the latter. Since he is not mentioned in Nehemiah's narrative until after the completion of the wall (Neh 8:1), it is probable that Nehemiah sent for him to aid in his work. Under Nehemiah's government his functions were entirely of a priestly and ecclesiastical character. He read and interpreted the law of Moses before the assembled congregation during the eight days of the Feast of Tabernacles, assisted at the dedication of the wall, and helped Nehemiah in bringing about a religious reformation. In all this he took a chief place. His name is repeatedly coupled with Nehemiah's, while the high priest is not mentioned as taking any part in the reformation at all.

Ezra is not again mentioned after Nehemiah's departure for Babylon. It may be that he himself returned to Babylon before that year.

Evidence points to Ezra's ministry taking place during the reign of Artaxerxes I (456–424 B.C.); but there are some modern critics who put Ezra after Nehemiah, holding that the sections dealing with them in the two books that bear their names have been transposed and that the chronicler (the supposed author of the two books and of 1 and 2 Chronicles) blundered in the few passages that associate the two.

According to Jewish tradition, Ezra is the

author of the Book of Ezra and of 1 and 2 Chronicles. Many modern scholars hold that he wrote the Book of Nehemiah as well. First Esdras, a part of the OT Apocrypha, reproduces the substance of the end of 2 Chronicles, the whole of Ezra, and a part of Nehemiah, and was written somewhere near the beginning of the first century A.D. There is also an apocalyptic book known as 2 Esdras, written about A.D. 100, describing some visions granted to Ezra in the Babylonian exile.

Ezra made a lasting impression on the Jewish people. His influence shaped Jewish life and thought in a way from which they never completely departed. SB

EZRA, BOOK OF. So named because Ezra is the principal person mentioned in it; possibly also because he may be its author. It does not in its entirety claim to be the work of Ezra, but Jewish tradition says it was written by him. Supporting this view is the fact that chapters 7–10 are written in the first person singular, while events in which he did not take part are described in the third person. The trustworthiness of the book does not, however, depend on the hypothesis that Ezra is the author. The majority of modern critics believe that the two books of Chronicles, Ezra, and Nehemiah constitute one large work, compiled and edited by someone designated the Chronicler, who has been dated from 400 to 300 B.C. Ezra's ministry is to be placed during the reign of Artaxerxes I (465–424 B.C.).

The Book of Ezra continues the narrative after Chronicles and records the return from Babylon and the rebuilding of the temple. The purpose of the author is to show how God fulfilled his promise given through prophets to restore his exiled people to their own land through heathen monarchs, and raised up such great men as Zerubbabel, Haggai, Zechariah, and Ezra to rebuild the temple, reestablish the old forms of worship, and put a stop to compromise with heathenism. All material that does not contribute to his purpose he stringently excludes.

As sources for the writing of the book, the author used genealogical lists, letters, royal edicts, memoirs, and chronicles. Some of these were official documents found in public records. This diversity of material accounts for the varied character of the style and for the fact that it is written in both Hebrew and Aramaic.

The order of the Persian kings of the period is Cyrus (538–529 B.C.), Darius (521–486), Xerxes (486–464), and Artaxerxes I (464–424). In view of this succession, Ezra 4:7–23 departs from the chronological order of events. The reason for this is probably that the author regarded a sequence of content more important than a chronological order. He brings together in one passage the successful attempts of the Samaritans to hinder the building of the temple and the city walls.

The period covered is from 536 B.C., when the Jews returned to Jerusalem, to 458, when Ezra

The Behistun Rock, northeast of Babylon, hewn by order of Darius I (521–486 B.C.), under whose authority the temple at Jerusalem was reconstructed after the Jewish return from exile in Babylonia, as recounted by Ezra. Here the king, followed by two attendants, stands before nine rebels roped together. Above is the figure of the Persian god Ahura Mazda. Accompanying the sculptures is a trilingual inscription in Old Persian, Elamite, and Akkadian. Courtesy B. Brandl.

came to Jerusalem to carry out his religious reforms. It thus covers a period of about seventy-eight years, although the fifteen years between 535 and 520 and the fifty-eight years between 516 and 458 are practically a blank. We have a description of selected incidents, not a continuous record of the period.

For an understanding and appreciation of the book, a few historical facts must be kept in mind. The last chapter of 2 Kings records the destruction of Jerusalem by Nebuchadnezzar and the deportation of many of its inhabitants into Babylonia. There they were settled in colonies and were not mistreated as long as they were quiet subjects. Many of them prospered so well that when, later, they had an opportunity to return to their homeland, they chose not to do so. Since the temple was destroyed, they could not carry on their sacrificial system; but they continued such religious ordinances as the Sabbath and circumcision, and gave great attention to the study of the Law. The chapter concludes by noting that Evil-Merodach, in the year he became king (561 B.C.) released Jehoichin from prison and allowed him to eat from then on at the king's table (2 Kings 25:27–30). This was about twenty-five years before the first events recorded in Ezra 1.

The Exile was brought to a close when the Babylonian Empire fell before Cyrus, king of Persia, in 538 B.C. The way in which the expectations of the Jews respecting Cyrus were fulfilled is told in the opening narrative of the Book of Ezra. The return from exile did not bring with it political freedom for the Jews. They remained subjects of the Persian Empire. Jerusalem and the surrounding districts were under the control of a governor, who sometimes was a Jew, but usually was not. Persian rule was in general not oppressive; but tribute was exacted for the royal treasury and the local governor. The hostile population surrounding them, especially the Samaritans, did all they could to make life miserable for them, especially by trying to bring them into disfavor with the Persian authorities. There were a few differences in the religious life of the Jews before and after the Exile. Idolatry no longer tempted them—and never did again. The external features distinctive of Jewish worship and the ceremonial requirements of the laws were stressed. Prophecy became less important, scribes gradually taking the place of the prophets.

The Book of Ezra consists of two parts. The first (chs. 1–6) is a narrative of the return of the Jews from Babylonia under Zerubbabel and the restoration of worship in the rebuilt temple; the second (chs. 7–10) tells the story of a second group of exiles returning with Ezra and of Ezra's religious reforms.

Bibliography: J. M. Meyers, *Ezra, Nehemiah* (AB), 1965; P. R. Ackroyd, *I & II Chronicles, Ezra, Nehemiah* (TBC), 1973; Derek Kidner, *Ezra and Nehemiah* (TOTC), 1979. SB

EZRAH (ĕz′rȧ). A man of Judah mentioned in 1 Chronicles 4:17 (KJV Ezra).

EZRAHITE (ĕz′rȧ-hīt, Heb. *'ezrāhî*). Designation of Ethan and Heman (1 Kings 4:31; titles of Pss 88–89).

EZRI (ĕz′rī, Heb. *'ezrî, my help*). Son of Kelub and overseer for David of those who tilled the ground (1 Chron 27:26).

F

FABLE. Usually defined as a narrative in which animals and inanimate objects of nature are made to act and speak as if they were human beings. The word "fable" is not found in the OT, but the OT has two fables: Judges 9:7–15 and 2 Kings 14:9. The word "fables" is found in the KJV as the translation of *mythos* in each of its five occurrences in the NT (1 Tim 1:4; 4:7; 2 Tim 4:4; Titus 1:14; 2 Peter 1:16). NIV has "cleverly invented stories" in 2 Peter 1:16, "myths" elsewhere; other versions variously use "fables," "legends," "myths," and "tales." The fables referred to in the pastoral letters may have to do with some form of Jewish-Gnostic speculation.

FACE. In the OT the translation of three Hebrew words: *'ayin,* "eye"; *'aph,* "nose"; *pānîm,* "face." In the NT the Greek is *prosōpon,* "face." The word is used literally, figuratively, and idiomatically. Often "my face" was nothing more than an oriental way of saying "I." Sometimes it meant "presence" and sometimes "favor." The hidden face was the equivalent of disapproval or rejection (Ps 13:1; 27:9). To spit in the face was an expression of contempt and aversion (Num 12:14). To harden the face meant to harden oneself against any sort of appeal (Prov 21:29 KJV). To have the face covered by another was a sign of doom (Esth 7:8). Falling on the face symbolized prostration before man or God (Ruth 2:10). Setting the face signified determination (Luke 9:51 KJV). To cover the face expressed mourning (Exod 3:6).

FAIR. A word translating more than a dozen Hebrew and Greek words, none of which has the modern sense of blond or fair-skinned. It has the meaning of beautiful, attractive (Hos 10:11; Acts 7:20 RSV; cf. NIV footnote); unspotted, free of defilement (Zech 3:5 KJV); plausible, persuasive (Prov 7:21 KJV); making a fine display (Gal 6:12 KJV); good weather (Job 37:22 KJV; Matt 16:12); honest, just (Judg 9:16; Prov 1:3).

FAIR HAVENS (Gr. *Kaloi Limenes*). A small bay on the south coast of Crete, about five miles (eight km.) east of Cape Matala. Paul stayed there for a time on his way to Rome (Acts 27:8–12). The harbor was not suitable to spend the winter in, so the captain decided to sail from there, with the hope of reaching Phoenix, a more secure harbor, also on the south coast of Crete.

FAITH (Heb. *'ēmûn,* Gr. *pistis*). Faith has a twofold sense in the Bible. On the one hand it means "trust," "reliance," and on the other it means "fidelity," "trustworthiness." An example of the first meaning is found in Romans 3:3, where "the faith of God" (KJV; NIV "God's faithfulness") means his fidelity to promise. In most other cases it has the second meaning.

In the OT the verb "to believe" occurs only thirty times, but this comparative infrequency does not adequately reflect the importance of the place of faith in the OT scheme of things. The NT draws all its examples of faith from the lives of OT believers (e.g., Rom 4:18ff.; Heb 11; James 2:14ff.), and Paul rests his doctrine of faith on the word of Habakkuk 2:4. It would thus be true to say that the OT demands faith more than it develops an explicit doctrine of faith. It looks for, and finds in its great individuals, a true commitment of self to God, an unwavering trust in his promises, and a persistent fidelity and obedience.

The foundation of Israel's faith was the Lord's revelation of himself to the patriarchs and to Moses, the covenant that he sealed at Sinai, and the conviction that God would keep his covenant promises. The observance of law and the life of faith were in no way incompatible because the law rested on the promises of God and obedience was motivated by a believing conviction that he would stand by what he had said. In connection, for example, with the sacrifices that the law commanded, we need to remind ourselves that the OT believer did not offer his sacrifice with any thought in mind of the perfect sacrifice of Christ that was yet to come. He did not (at that point) think of himself as doing something "pro tem" or as doing something that was allowed to be effective because the "real thing" was some day going to be done. He acted in simple faith in the promises of God. If asked how he knew his sins were forgiven, he would no doubt first reply that he was there and had seen the appropriate sacrifice offered. But if the question were pressed, why the sacrifice was effective, he would reply, "Because he said so." In this way personal faith—in exactly the same terms as Paul later developed in the doctrine of justification by faith—is the presupposition behind the provisions and prescriptions of the old covenant. Obedience to the Lord's law was the way of life incumbent on those who trusted him. OT faith is never a mere assent to a set of doctrines or the outward acceptance of a legal code, but utter confidence in the faithfulness of God and a consequent loving obedience to his will.

When used with a religious application, faith in the OT is sometimes in a specific word or work of God (Lam 4:12; Hab 1:5), or in the fact of God's revelation (Exod 4:5; Job 9:16), or in the words or commandments of God in general (Ps 119:66), or in God himself (Gen 15:6). Faith is put in the word of God's prophets because they speak for him, and he is absolutely trustworthy (Exod 19:9; 2 Chron 20:20). NT writers, especially Paul and the author of Hebrews, show that the faith manifested by OT saints was not different in kind from that expected of Christians.

In contrast with the extreme rarity with which the terms "faith" and "believe" are used in the OT, they occur with great frequency in the NT—almost five hundred times. A principal reason for this is that the NT makes the claim that the promised Messiah had finally come, and, to the bewilderment of many, the form of the fulfillment did not obviously correspond to the Messianic promise. It required a real act of faith to believe that Jesus of Nazareth was the promised Messiah. It was not long before "to believe" meant to become a Christian. In the NT, faith therefore becomes the supreme human act and experience.

In his miracles and teaching, Jesus aimed at creating in his disciples a complete trust in himself as the Messiah and Savior of men. Everywhere he offered himself as the object of faith and made it plain that faith in him is necessary for eternal life, that it is what God required of OT men, and that refusal to accept his claims will bring eternal ruin. His primary concern with his own disciples was to build up their faith in him.

The record in Acts shows that the first Christians called themselves "the believers" (Acts 2:44) and that they went everywhere persuading men and bringing them into obedience to the faith that is in Jesus (6:7; 17:4; 28:24). Before long, as communities of believers arose in various parts of the Mediterranean world, the apostolic leaders had to teach them more fully the meaning and implications of the Christian faith, and so the NT books appeared.

It is in Paul's letters that the meaning of faith is most clearly and fully set forth. Faith is trust in the person of Jesus, the truth of his teaching, and the redemptive work he accomplished at Calvary, and, as a result, a total submission to him and his message, which are accepted as from God. Faith in his person is faith in him as the eternal Son of God, the God-man, the second man Adam, who died in man's stead, making possible justification with God, adoption into his family, sanctification, and, ultimately, glorification. His death brings redemption from sin in all its aspects. The truth of his claims is attested by God's raising him from the dead. Some day he will judge the living and the dead. Faith is not to be confused with a mere intellectual assent to the doctrinal teachings of Christianity, though that is obviously necessary. It includes a radical and total commitment to Christ as the Lord of one's life.

Unbelief, or lack of faith in the Christian gospel, appears everywhere in the NT as the supreme evil. Not to make a decisive response to God's offer in Christ means that the individual remains in sin and is eternally lost. Faith alone can save him.

Bibliography: J. G. Machen, *What Is Faith?*, 1925; D. M. Baillie, *Faith in God*, 1927; G. Ebeling, *The Nature of Faith*, 1961; P. Helm, *The Varieties of Belief*, 1963; G. J. Wenham, *Faith in the Old Testament*, 1984. SB and JAM

FAITHFULNESS (Heb. *ĕmûnâh*). An attribute or quality applied in the Bible to both God and man. When used of God, it has in the OT a twofold emphasis, referring first to his absolute reliability, firm constancy, and complete freedom from arbitrariness or fickleness, and also to his steadfast love toward his people and his loyalty. God is constant and true in contrast to all that is not God. He is faithful in keeping his promises and is therefore worthy of trust. He is unchangeable in his ethical nature. God's faithfulness is usually connected with his gracious promises of salvation. Faithful men are dependable in fulfilling their responsibilities and in carrying out their word. In the NT there are frequent exhortations to faithfulness. It is one of the fruits of the Spirit in Galatians 5:22.

FALCON (See Birds)

FALL, THE. The Fall of man is narrated in Genesis 3 as a historical fact, not as a myth. It stands in a context of historical facts. Though not alluded to again in the OT, it is regarded as historical in the NT (Rom 5:12–13; 1 Cor 15:22; 1 Tim 2:14). Some philosophers and theologians think the account is an allegory describing the awakening of man from a brute state of self-consciousness and personality—a fall upward, rather than downward, but such an explanation conflicts radically with biblical teaching. There is no doubt that Paul takes the account literally and sees in the Fall the origin of sin in the human race. The scriptural view of sin and of redemption takes the Fall for granted.

The Scriptures teach us that man was created in the image of God, with a rational and moral nature like God's, with no inner impulse or drive to sin, and with a will free to do God's will. There was, moreover, nothing in his environment to compel him to sin or to make sin excusable. In these circumstances, solicitation to sin could come only from outside. The Bible does not allow us to probe the mystery of the presence of sin in God's fair universe; as in so many other things, it faces us with the practical reality, the voice of the Tempter coming to man from outside himself, the voice of the Serpent that the rest of the Bible recognizes as the voice of Satan.

The sin that constituted the Fall involved Adam and Eve in disobeying the word of God (Gen 3:1–4) and challenging the goodness of God by imputing to him an ill motive (3:5). But chiefly it consisted in disobeying the law of God. Such was the bounty of the Creator that the whole lavish richness of the Garden was open to man with only a single condition (2:16–17). The Fall was thus the breaking of the whole law of God. Equally involved in the Fall was the whole nature of man. Eve was first emotionally attracted to the forbidden fruit (3:6, "good for food and pleasing to the eye"); second, she was led into sin by the logic of her mind that contradicted the mind of God. He had said, "The tree of knowledge . . . you will surely die" (2:17). Eve appears to have said to herself that a tree of knowledge was bound to make those who partake wise. It was a question of God's logic or man's. Third, the Fall was an act of will: "she took . . . and ate it" (3:6). Emotions, mind, and will combined in the first sin. The whole law of God was broken by the whole nature of the sinner.

The effect of the Fall, as Genesis 4 and the remainder of the Bible explicitly and implicitly bring out, was not merely immediate alienation from God for Adam and Eve, but guilt and depravity for all their posterity and the cursing of the earth. Redemption from the Fall and its effects is accomplished through the Lord Jesus Christ (cf. Rom 5:12–21; 1 Cor 15:21–22, 45–49). SB and JAM

FALLOW DEER (See Animals)

FAMILIAR SPIRIT (Heb. *'ôv*, etymology and exact meaning unknown). Used in the KJV to refer to the spirit of a dead person that mediums claimed they could summon for consultation (Deut 18:11). The word "familiar" has in this phrase the sense of the Latin *familiaris*, belonging to one's family, and hence ready to serve one as a servant. Such a spirit was thought to be able to reveal the future (1 Sam 28:7; Isa 8:19). Since the voice seemed to come in a whisper from the ground, the medium was very likely a ventriloquist. Israelites were forbidden by the Lord to consult familiar spirits (Lev 19:31; Isa 8:19). This was regarded as apostasy so serious that those who consulted them were put to death (Lev 20:6). Saul put away mediums early in his reign, but consulted the witch of Endor when he became apostate just before his death (1 Sam 28:3–25; 1 Chron 10:13). Manasseh dealt with familiar spirits (2 Kings 21:6; 2 Chron 33:6), but his grandson Josiah carried out the Mosaic Law against them (2 Kings 23:24). The practice of consulting them probably prevailed more or less to the time of the Exile (Isa 8:19; 19:3). SB

FAMILY (Heb. *mišpāhāh, bayith, house*; Gk. *oikia, patria, house, clan*).

I. The General Nature of the Family. The Hebrew term *mišpāhāh*, having no exact equivalent in English, should be interpreted principally as "household." Another term for family, *bayith*, included all those living within the confines and jurisdiction of the dwelling. In a patriarchal setting the father was the head of the family, having authority over his wife, children, unmarried daughters, and sometimes married sons and their families, as well as cousins and their families and possibly grandparents and even great-grandparents (Gen 46:8–26). Additional members of the household also included in the designation of family would be concubines, servants, slaves, visitors, and occasionally prisoners of war. Some polygamy was practiced, and this also made the family unit more extensive.

In a wider sense, family could also mean clan, tribe, or village, and phrases such as "house of David" (Isa 7:13) or "house of Israel" (Ezek 9:9; 18:30) show that in broader terms the household could encompass the entire nation. Some families returning from exile in Babylon comprised several hundred members (Ezra 8:1–14).

A common bond of blood bound together the members of the larger family or clan, who referred to each other as "brothers" (1 Sam 20:29). Members of the clan accepted a communal responsibility for assistance, protection, the sharing of work, loyalty, and cooperation for the general well-being of the family. In places where the nomadic life gave way to a more settled existence, groups of villages (often interdependent and with intermarried members) formed a "family," as did the Danites at Zoreh and Eshtaol (Judg. 18:11). When arts and crafts developed, sons acquired skills from their fathers, and villages devoted to a particular type of production—such as wood or ironworking, linen or pottery (1 Chron 4:14; cf. 1 Chron 4:21, 23; Neh 11:35)—became common. With specialization, however, came a loss of the former self-sufficiency of the family and an increased interdependence on the producers of food and other goods.

Even as cities developed, evidence of relatives of the tribes of Benjamin and Judah living in particular areas is found, as in Nehemiah's census of Jerusalem (Neh 11:4–8). In general, however, city life tended to fragment the family, and the size of the houses excavated indicates that by this time the family unit consisted only of father, mother, and children. During the kingdom, as family ties loosened, so the absolute authority and responsibility of the father was transferred to the king. By the eighth century B.C., the individual, instead of working primarily for the good of the larger group, worked for his immediate family and for the ultimate benefit of the king or nation. Not surprisingly, as the focus of the family unit sharpened, the sense of communal responsibility lessened, and biblical reminders concerning obligations toward widows and orphans became more frequent (Isa 1:17; Jer 7:6). Family blood feuds declined as revenge for the honor of members of the wider family was no longer usual, though it was sometimes practiced and expected (2 Sam 3:27; 16:8; 2 Kings 9:26; Neh 4:14).

By virtue of marriage, the husband and wife were regarded as being akin, and their children were legitimate family members. Close kinship was an obstacle to marriage in the clan or tribe, and Leviticus 18:6–17 provided a list of degrees of relationship within which marriage was prohibited. One exception to this rule was the so-called levirate (i.e., husband's brother) marriage (Deut 25:5–10), in which a man was expected to marry the wife of a childless deceased brother so as to perpetuate his family name by means of children. Refusal to comply with this requirement brought shame upon the offender's house.

The family functioned as an essential unit of the religious community. the father was the spiritual head of the family and acted as the priest within the household. He was responsible for leading religious observances and for instructing the family in the religious and secular history of the Israelites, as well as in their manners and customs. The father maintained the family altar and ensured the religious observances and piety of the entire family. The religious observances and festivals were frequently family-oriented, particularly the Passover, which was observed as a religious family meal and thank offering (Exod 12:3–4, 46). In patriarchal times, before worship was centralized in the temple and the later synagogue, it was the fathers that offered sacrifice to God (Gen 31:54). The supreme position of religious and secular authority that the father had helps to clarify the subsequent reverence for his grave.

In the NT, little reference is made to the family, except to reinforce monogamous marriage and to denounce divorce (Matt 5:27–32; 19:3–12; Mark 10:2–12; Luke 16:18). While a child, Christ set an example of obedience to parents, with whom he evidently remained until the beginning of his ministry, his brothers not understanding him (Matt 10:36; John 7:1–8). It is Paul, however, who reinforces the duties of the family members (Eph 5:22–6:9; Col 3:18–22). He reiterates the financial responsibility of the members towards each other (1 Tim 5:4, 8) and the importance of teaching religion in the home (Eph 6:4). Also, in many of his epistles, Paul clearly insisted on the subordinate role of women in the family (1 Cor 11:3; Eph 5:22–24, 33; Col 3:18; cf. also 1 Peter 3:1–7). In Roman times, family ties loosened still further with the gradual disintegration of society. In the early church, however—where, in the absence of a church building, services took place in a private home—converts were often entire families (2 Tim 1:5) or all the members of the household (Acts 16:15, 31–34).

II. Roles of Family Members.

A. **Father: provider, procreator of children, master, teacher, priest.** In nomadic times the father, by means of his authority, held the family group together and became the symbol of their security in the encampment. His powers over the family members was awesome. His decisions could mean life or death; and as his status was unquestioned, he demanded respect and obedience. His responsibilities were extensive both within and beyond the family unit. In addition to providing for his own family security, he was expected from the time of the kingdom period to send his sons to defend the nation. Throughout biblical times the father was responsible for the economic well-being of those over whom he had authority. The entire family could be sold for falling into debt, and uncles and cousins would be expected to prevent family property from passing into outside hands (Lev 25:25; Jer 32:6–15). The father was also responsible for teaching his sons a trade, frequently his own, so that they would be productive members both of the family and society.

The teachings of Hebrew history, religion, law, and custom were passed on from father to son in the family setting (Exod 10:2; 12:26; Deut 4:9; 6:7) and reinforced by the many rites celebrated within the house, often associated with the family meal. All such occasions—whether in celebration of the Passover, some lesser feast, or an ordinary family meal—reinforced the faith, heritage, and nationalism of the family, as well as their own unity as a group. As the sons grew older it was the father's responsibility to find them suitable wives.

B. **Mother: child-bearer, household manager, teacher.** The list of a man's possessions included his wife, servants, slaves, goods, and animals (Exod 20:17; Deut 5:21). Even the phrase "to marry a wife" comes from a phrase that means "to become the master of a wife" (Deut 21:13; 24:1). Although she would even address the husband in subservient terms, the status of the wife was higher than that of the rest of the household.

The primary responsibility of the mother was to produce children, preferably sons. A large number of sons, who became workers from an early age, ensured the future economic prosperity and security of the family. The maximum number of children was normally seven. Babies were weaned at approximately three years of age, and husband and wife did not normally have sexual relations between the child's birth and the completion of the weaning process.

Throughout her life a woman was subject to the protecting authority of a male relative—as a daughter, that of her father, and as a wife, that of her husband. If she became a widow, her nearest male relative became her protector, and under the levirate marriage provisions he could also be her "redeemer." Under such conditions the woman was subject to the man's authority.

The bride-price paid by the betrothed male to his fiancée's father, though not directly a "purchase price," was intended to compensate the father for the loss of his daughter's services. Because of the exchange of money on most occasions, the bride was left with the stigma of having been sold to her future husband (cf. Gen 29:18, 27; Exod 22:16–17; 1 Sam 18:25; 2 Sam 3:14). After the wedding the bride normally went to live with her husband's family. Thus she became part of that extended family group and was subject to its authority. Aside from the primary duty of childbearing (Gen 1:28; 9:1), the wife's main responsibility was the organization of the household. This was her domain, and she was generally a respected manager. All aspects of food, from the collecting of olives and dates to the grinding of corn and cooking, were her responsibility, as well as the spinning and weaving of thread, the making of clothing, and the care of domestic animals.

The young children remained with their mother, and she was responsible for teaching the boys until they were about six years old, after which time they were likely to take on their own roles either as shepherds or goatherds. Some boys spent their days in the company of their father, whose skills they acquired by observation and practice.

The daughters remained with their mother, who trained them in the arts of cooking, spinning, weaving, and general household management, as well as schooling them in their future roles as wives and mothers. When the wife provided a son, her position was a little more secure. Prior to that it was somewhat precarious. She could be divorced for any apparent offense, whether related to her subservience, management of the household, or culinary skills (cf. Ecclus 25:26). In early times, when polygamy was still practiced, the wife could find herself replaced by a second wife or sometimes by a concubine. Nevertheless, despite the status of the mother, her role in actual fact was not as difficult as it might seem. In many families her opinion was sought in decision making, and her ideas were respected (Exod 20:12; Prov 19:26; 20:20; Ecclus 3:1–16).

By Persian times the status of the wife was showing definite improvement. She had her own position at games, the theaters, and religious festivals, often assisted her husband in business, and was known at times to manage her own property. In the New Testament one such woman, Lydia of Thyatira (Acts 16:24), operated a textile business out of her own home.

C. **Sons and daughters: status, childhood, education, and duties.** The law of primogeniture provided a double portion of the inheritance as the birthright of the eldest son (Deut 21:17). He always took precedence over his brothers and sisters (Gen 43:33), and the elder of twins, even if only by a few minutes, could also hold this premier position with all its attendant privileges (Gen 25:24–26; 38:27–30). The right to primogeniture could be forfeited as a result of a serious offense (Gen 35:22; 49:3–4; 1 Chron 5:1), surrendered voluntarily, or sold, as Esau did to his brother Jacob (Gen 25:29–34). David gave his kingdom to his youngest son, Solomon (1 Kings 2:15), despite a law protecting the eldest son from the favoritism of a father toward a younger brother (Deut 21:15–17). In a family that had no sons, property could be inherited by a daughter (Num 27:8).

The inferior status of a daughter in patriarchal society is depicted clearly. She could be sold into slavery or into concubinage and then possibly resold (Exod 21:7–11). Even her very life was at the disposition of her father. Both sons and daughters could be put to death for disobeying the head of the household. Abraham was prepared to sacrifice his son Isaac (Gen 22:1–14). Judah ordered the burning of Tamar on suspicion that she, a widow, was having sexual relations with a man who was not of her late husband's family (Gen 38:11–26), when she would normally have been expected to marry a relative of her husband and was, in fact, promised to his brother.

With the coming of the Mosaic Law, a father could no longer put his child to death without referring the case to the authorities. Thus the elders heard accusations of disobedience, gluttony, and drunkenness, which, on conviction, were punishable with death by stoning (Deut 21:20–21). Children, however, could no longer be held responsible for the crimes of their parents (Deut 24:16). By the time of king David, there was the right of ultimate appeal to the monarch himself (2 Sam 14:4–11).

Frequently, neither sons nor daughters were consulted when marriage partners were being selected for them. A marriage was often an alliance or contract between families, the wishes of the individual being regarded as unworthy of consideration. Although loved and valued, children were not pampered (Ecclus 30:9–12). As family disciplinarian, the father spared neither the rod nor the whip (Prov 13:24; 22:15; 29:15–17). In postexilic times, a son's more formal education took place within the precincts of the synagogue, and just prior to the time of Christ a form of general education was introduced into Palestine.

Childhood was brief, although boys and girls laughed, played, and sang. Some of them had whistles, rattles, and dolls, while the young ones sat on their mother's lap (Isa 66:12). In later Judaism a boy's coming of age was celebrated in a manner that reinforced his position within the home and also within the religious family of the synagogue. As soon as they were old enough, both boys and girls were expected to gather fuel (Jer 7:18), care for cattle, and tend the flocks.

Protecting sheep from wild beasts and from the danger of injuring themselves in the mountain crevices, finding them good pasture and water, and carrying them home when sick or injured, was neither a light task nor a small responsibility (Gen 29:6; Exod 2:16; 1 Sam 16:11). Young boys and girls would often follow their fathers to the fields to watch and help, but more often the girls would be learning the household skills from their mothers. One of the most menial and arduous tasks was that of fetching water, often from some considerable distance, and this was the responsibility of the mother or the daughter. Young girls were by no means secluded; rather, they were free to go about unveiled and visit with friends and neighbors (Gen 34:1).

Bearing in mind that all members of the household were subject to the strict authority of the head of the family, it is not surprising that as the household became smaller in postexilic times, it became the practice (where it was feasible practically and economically) for the married sons to move out of the patriarchal home and to set up their own family units.

III. Figurative Use. The concept of family in its broadest and most figurative sense is seen in the phrase "house of Israel" (Isa 5:7), meaning the entire nation. In the Old Testament, the relationship between God and Israel is seen in such family terms as "bride" (Jer 2:1), "daughter" (8:19; 31:22), "children" (3:14), or "betrothal" (Hos 2:19f.). In the New Testament, the bridal imagery describing the relationship between Christ and the church is continued (2 Cor 11:2; Eph 5:25–33; Rev 19:7; 21:9) and is given deep spiritual emphasis, and the church is referred to as the household of God (Gal 6:10; Eph 2:19; 3:15; 1 Peter 4:17).

Bibliography: T. G. Soares, *Social Institutions and Ideals of the Bible* (1915); E. D. Cross, *Hebrew Family* (1927); E. M. MacDonald, *The Position of Women as Reflected in Semitic Codes* (1931); M. I. Rostovtzeff, *The Social and Economic History of the Hellenistic World,* 3 vols. (1941); D. Jacobsen, *The Social Background of the Old Testament* (1942); E. Neufeld, *Ancient Hebrew Marriage Laws* (1944); J. Pederson, *Israel, Its Life and Culture* (1946), 1:2:46–60; I. Mendelsohn, "The Family in the Ancient Near East," *BA* 11 (1948): 25–40; idem., "On the Preferential Status of the Eldest Son," *ASOR* (1959) 145:38–40; E. A. Judge, *Social Pattern of the Christian Groups in the First Century* (1960); R. de Vaux, *Ancient Israel* (ET 1961), I, part one; A. N. S. White, *Roman Society and Roman Law in the New Testament* (1963). HWP

FAMINE (Heb. *rā'āv, hunger, famine,* Gr. *limos, want of good*). In ancient times in Palestine and Egypt, famines were not infrequent. They were produced by lack of rainfall in due season, destructive hail storms and rain out of season, destruction of crops by locusts and caterpillars, and the cutting off of food supplies by a siege. Pestilence often followed, and the suffering was great. Famines that were the result of natural causes are recorded as occurring in the time of Abraham (who left Canaan and stayed in Egypt, Gen 12:10), Joseph (when famine "had spread over the whole country," 41:56), the judges (Ruth 1:1), David (2 Sam 21:1), Ahab and Elijah (1 Kings 17:1; 18:2), and of Elisha (2 Kings 4:38; Luke 4:25). A famine produced by a siege is mentioned in 2 Kings 6:25—the siege of Jerusalem by Nebuchadnezzar. Nehemiah 5:3 tells of a famine after the return from the Babylonian captivity. The NT speaks of a famine "over the entire Roman world" (Acts 11:28) during the reign of Claudius. In the Olivet Discourse, Jesus predicted famines in various places (Matt 24:7; Mark 13:8; Luke 21:11), a prophecy believed to be partly fulfilled in the siege of Jerusalem by Titus, which is described with harrowing detail by Josephus, who says that "neither did any other city ever suffer such miseries" (*War* 5.10.5). Famines are sometimes said to be sent as punishments, and sometimes they are threatened as such (Lev 26:19–20; Deut 28:49–51; 2 Kings 8:1; Isa 14:30; 51:19; Jer 14:12, 15; Ezek 5:16). To be preserved in time of famine is a special mark of God's favor and power (Job 5:20; Ps 33:19; 37:19). Sometimes the word "famine" is used in a figurative sense, as when Amos says that God will send a famine, not of bread and water, but "a famine of hearing the words of the LORD" (Amos 8:11). SB

FAN (See WINNOWING FORK)

FARMING. The Israelites in the time of the patriarchs were a nomadic people. They first learned agriculture in Palestine after the conquest

Part of bas-relief on south wall at Meir (c. 1971–1928 B.C.) showing an emaciated herdsman, with ribs showing and clad only in a kilt, leading three oxen as a gift to Ukh-hotep. Courtesy Egypt Exploration Society.

Agricultural scenes in Theban tomb No. 1 at Deir el-Medina, belonging to Sennedjem, from the reign of Sethos I (1306–1290 B.C.). Sennedjem, accompanied by his wife, is shown reaping grain, plowing with a pair of cattle, and harvesting flax. Courtesy Seffie Ben-Yoseph.

of Canaan. After that a large proportion of the people were engaged in agrarian pursuits. The pages of the Bible have much to say about agricultural occupations.

Agriculture was the background for all the legislation of Israel. At the time of the conquest every family probably received a piece of land, marked off by stones that could not be removed lawfully (Deut 19:14; 27:17; Hos 5:10). The soil of Palestine was generally fertile. Fertilizing was almost unknown. To maintain the fertility of the land, the law required that farms, vineyards, and olive orchards were to lie fallow in the seventh year (Exod 23:10). On the year of Jubilee those who had lost their ancestral estates recovered possession of them. Terracing was necessary to make use of soil on the hillsides. Irrigation was not required, since there was usually sufficient rainfall.

Plowing to prepare the land for sowing was done in autumn, when the early rains softened the ground that had become stone-hard in the summer sun. This was done with a crude wooden plow drawn by oxen or, if the soil was thin, with a mattock. With such implements the surface of the ground was hardly more than scratched—perhaps three or four inches (eight or ten cm.). Little harrowing was done and was probably unknown in Palestine in early times.

The summer grain was sown between the end of January and the end of February. Usually the seed was scattered by hand from a basket, but careful farmers put it in furrows in rows (Isa 28:25). Between sowing and reaping, the crops were exposed to several dangers: The failure of the latter rain, which came in March and April; the hot, drying easterly winds that often came in March and April (Gen 41:6); hail storms (Hag 2:17); various kinds of weeds like tares and thorns (Jer 12:13; Matt 13:7, 25); injurious insects, especially the palmerworm, the cankerworm, the caterpillar, and the locust (Amos 7:2); the thefts of crows and sparrows (Matt 13:4); and fungus diseases, especially mildew (Deut 28:22). As the harvest season approached, particularly valuable crops were protected by watchmen (Jer 4:17); but the law permitted a hungry person to pick grain when passing by (Deut 23:25; Matt 12:1).

The time of harvest varied somewhat according to the climatic condition of each region, but usually began about the middle of April with the coming of the dry season. Barley was the first grain to be cut, and this was followed a few weeks later with wheat. The grain harvest generally lasted about seven weeks, from Passover to Pentecost. Whole families moved out of their village homes to live in the fields until the harvest was over. The grain was cut with a sickle and laid in swaths behind the reaper. It was then bound into sheaves and gathered into shocks (Exod 22:6). In the interest of the poor, the law forbade a field to be harvested to its limits.

The grain was threshed in the open air, a

custom made possible because the harvest season was free from rain (2 Kings 13:7). During the threshing time the grain was guarded by harvesters who spent the nights on the threshing floor (Ruth 3:6). The threshing floor was constructed in an exposed position in the fields, preferably on a slight elevation, so as to get the full benefit of the winds. It consisted of a circular area twenty-five to forty feet (eight to thirteen m.) in diameter, sloping slightly upward at the edges, and was usually surrounded with a border of stones to keep in the grain. The floor was level and hard. The sheaves of grain, brought in from the fields on the backs of men and animals, were heaped in the center. From this heap, sheaves were spread out on the floor; and then either several animals tied abreast were driven round and round the floor or two oxen were yoked together to a threshing machine, which they dragged in a circular path over the grain until the kernels of grain were separated from the stalks. The threshing machines were of two kinds, a board with the bottom studded with small stones or nails, or a kind of threshing wagon. While this was going on, the partly threshed grain was turned over with a fork. After that the grain was winnowed by tossing the grain and chaff into the air with a wooden fork or shovel so that the wind might blow away the chaff. This was usually done at night, to take advantage of the night breezes. The chaff was either burned or left to be scattered by the winds. The grain was then sifted with a sieve to remove stones and other impurities, and collected into pits or barns (Luke 12:18).

Of the large number of crops the Israelites cultivated, wheat and barley were the most important. They also raised rye, millet, flax, and a variety of vegetables. See also AGRICULTURE. SB

FARTHING (See MONEY)

FASTING (Heb. *tsûm,* Gr. *nēsteia, nēstis*). Fasting, meaning abstinence from food and drink for a long or short period, is frequently mentioned in the Scriptures. Sometimes, instead of the single word "fast," the descriptive phrase "to afflict the soul" is used, the reference being to physical fasting rather than to spiritual humiliation. This term is used in various parts of the OT in the KJV, but is the only one used to denote the religious observance of fasting in the Pentateuch (Lev 16:29–31; 23:27; Num 30:13; Isa 58:3, 5, 10). NIV generally renders "deny" oneself or "humble" oneself.

The only fast required by Moses was that of the Day of Atonement. Before the Babylonian captivity it was the one regular fast (Lev 16:29, 31; 23:27–32; Num 29:7; Jer 36:6). During this period there are many examples of fasts on special occasions, held because of transgression or to ward off present or impending calamity. Samuel called for such a fast (1 Sam 7:6); Jehoiakim proclaimed a fast after Baruch had read the condemnatory word of the Lord given through Jeremiah (Jer 36:9); Jezebel hypocritically called a fast when she sought to secure Naboth's vineyard (1 Kings 21:9, 12). We read of individuals who were moved to fast—for example, David, when his child became ill (2 Sam 12:16, 21–23), and Ahab on hearing his doom (1 Kings 21:27).

After the Captivity, four annual fasts were held in memory of the national calamities through which the nation had passed. They are mentioned only in Zechariah 7:1–7; 8:19. These fasts, established during the Captivity, were held in the fourth, fifth, seventh, and tenth months. The Mishna (*Taarith,* iv, 6) and Jerome (in *Zachariam,* viii) give information on the historical events that these fasts were intended to commemorate. By the time of Christ they had fallen into disuse and were not revived until after the destruction of Jerusalem by the Romans. In Rabbinic times the Feast of Purim, the origin of which is explained in Esther (9:31–32), was accompanied by a fast in commemoration of the fast of Esther, Mordecai, and the Jews (Esth 4:1–3, 15–17). The OT gives a number of instances of other fasts in which the whole people joined (Ezra 8:21–23; Neh 9:1). Examples of fasts by individuals are given in Nehemiah 1:4 and Daniel 9:3. A fast of great strictness was proclaimed by the heathen king of Nineveh to avert the destruction threatened by

Days of fasting in the Jewish sacred year. Both Isaiah (58:3–10) and Jesus (Matt 6:16–18) comment on this practice. Courtesy Carta, Jerusalem.

DAYS OF FASTING

17 Tammuz (Jun-Jul)	Breaking through the walls of Jerusalem (Second Temple).
9 Ab (Jul-Aug)	Destruction of the Temple.
3 Tishri (Sept-Oct)	Fast of Gedaliah.
10 Tishri	Day of Atonement.
10 Tebeth (Dec-Jan)	Beginning of the siege on Jerusalem (Second Temple)
13 Adar (Feb-Mar)	Fast of Esther.

the Lord through Jonah (Jonah 3:5).

Fasting among the Israelites was either partial or total, depending on the length of the fast. When Daniel mourned three full weeks, he ate no "choice food; no meat or wine touched my lips" (Dan 10:2–3). Another longer fast is mentioned in Nehemiah 1:4. The fast on the Day of Atonement was "from the evening . . . until the following evening" (Lev 23:32); and no food or drink was taken. Other daylong fasts were from morning till evening. The fasts of Moses and Elijah for forty days were exceptional (Exod 34:28; 1 Kings 19:8).

Religious fasting was observed as a sign of mourning for sin, with the object of deprecating divine wrath or winning divine compassion. The prophets often condemn the abuse of the custom, for Israelites superstitiously thought that it had value even when not accompanied by purity and righteousness of life (Isa 58:3–7; Jer 14:10–12; Zech 7–8). Fasts were not necessarily religious in nature. They were commonplace when someone near and dear died, as when the inhabitants of Jabesh fasted after they had buried Saul and Jonathan (1 Sam 31:13) and after the death of Abner (2 Sam 1:12).

There are few references to fasting in the Gospels, but what is said shows that frequent fasts were customary with those Jews who desired to lead a specially religious life. We are told that Anna "worshiped night and day, fasting and praying" (Luke 2:37). Again, the Pharisee in the parable says, "I fast twice a week" (Luke 18:12). Jesus fasted for forty days in the wilderness, but it is not clear whether this fast was voluntary or not. There is no reason to doubt that he observed the usual prescribed public fasts, but neither by practice nor by precept did he stress fasting. Jesus was so unascetic in his ordinary mode of life that he was reproached with being "a glutton and a drunkard" (Matt 11:19; Luke 7:34). In all his teaching he spoke of fasting only twice, in the following passages:

1. Matthew 6:16–18. In this passage voluntary fasting is presupposed as a religious exercise, but Jesus warns against making it an occasion for a parade of piety. The important thing is purity and honesty of intention. Fasting should be to God, not to impress men. Jesus approves of fasting if it is an expression of inner contrition and devotion. The externalism of the Pharisees had its own reward.

2. Matthew 9:14–17; Mark 2:18–22; Luke 5:33–39. Here the disciples of John and of the Pharisees ask Jesus, "How is it that we and the Pharisees fast, but your disciples do not fast?" Jesus replies that fasting, which is a sign of mourning, would be inconsistent with the joy that should characterize whose who know that the Messiah has finally come and is now with them. The time will come, however, when he will be taken away, and then his disciples will mourn. It is obvious that the reference to his being taken away is to his crucifixion, not his ascension, for the ascension, signifying the completion of his redemptive work, is no occasion for mourning. Jesus here sanctions fasting, as he does in the Sermon on the Mount; but he refuses to force it on his disciples. In the parables of the old wineskins and the old garment he shows that fasting belongs to the body of old observances and customs and is not congruous with the liberty of the gospel. The new era that he inaugurates must have new forms of its own.

The references to fasting in Matthew 17:21 and Mark 9:29 are regarded by textual scholars as corruptions of the text. The NIV includes them only as part of a footnote.

The Book of Acts has a few direct references to fasting. The church at Antioch fasted and prayed before sending out Paul and Barnabas as missionaries (Acts 13:2–3). On Paul's first missionary journey, elders were appointed in every church, with prayer and fasting (14:23). The reference to the fasting of Cornelius (Acts 10:30), found in KJV and many MSS, is omitted by many versions (e.g., NIV). The only other direct references to fasting in the NT are found in 2 Corinthians 6:5 and 11:27, where Paul describes his sufferings for Christ; and here, most likely, he has in mind involuntary fasting.

There are, therefore, in the NT only four indisputable references to voluntary fasting for religious purposes, two by our Lord in the Gospels, and two in the Acts of the Apostles. Jesus does not disapprove of the practice, but says nothing to commend it. The apostolic church practiced it, but perhaps only as a carry-over from Judaism, since most of the early disciples were Jews.

Bibliography: I. Abrahams, *Studies in Pharisaism and the Gospels,* 1917, I, pp. 121–28; D. E. Briggs, *Biblical Teaching on Fasting,* 1953; H. von Campenhausen, "Early Christian Asceticism," *Tradition and Life in the Church,* 1969, pp. 90–122; NIDNTT, I, pp. 611–13. SB

FAT (Heb. *ḥēlev, ḥelev*). 1. The subcutaneous layer of fat around the kidneys and other viscera, which, like the blood, was forbidden by the Mosaic law to be used for food, but was burned as an offering to the Lord, for a sweet aroma to him (Lev 4:31). This had to be done on the very day the animal was killed, apparently to remove temptation (Exod 23:18). The purpose of the law was to teach the Israelites that their best belonged to God. Long before the Mosaic Law was given, Abel brought the fat of the first-born of his flock to the Lord; and we read that the Lord looked with favor on Abel and his offering (Gen 4:4).

2. Sometimes used in the KJV to refer to a wine vat, a receptacle into which the grape juice flowed from the "press" above (Isa 63:2; Joel 2:24).

FATHER (Heb. *'āv*, Gr. *patēr*). The word has various meanings in the Bible. 1. Immediate male progenitor (Gen 42:13). In the Hebrew family the father had absolute rights over his children. He could sell them into slavery and have them put to death. Reverence and obedience by children is prescribed from the earliest times (Exod 20:12;

Lev 19:3; Deut 5:16). The Scriptures many times set forth the character and duties of an ideal father. See also FAMILY.

2. Ancestor, immediate or remote. Abraham is called Jacob's father (Gen 28:13), and God tells him he will be the "father of many nations" (17:4). The founders of the Hebrew race, the patriarchs (NIV) are referred to as its fathers (Rom 9:5 KJV); so also heads of clans (Exod 6:14; 1 Chron 27:1).

3. The word has many figurative and derived uses: A spiritual ancestor, whether good or bad, as Abraham, "the father of all who believe" (Rom 4:11); and the devil, "You belong to your father, the devil" (John 8:44); the originator of a mode of life ("Jabal . . . the father of those who live in tents and raise livestock," Gen 4:20); one who exhibits paternal kindness and wisdom to another: "Be my father and priest" (Judg 17:10); a revered superior, especially a prophet and an elderly and venerable man (1 Sam 10:12; 1 John 2:13); royal advisors and prime ministers: "God . . . made me father to Pharaoh" (Gen 45:8); early Christians who have died: "Ever since our fathers died" (2 Peter 3:4); a source: "Does the rain have a father?" (Job 38:28).

God is Father: As Creator of the universe, "the Father of the heavenly lights" (James 1:17); as Creator of the human race, "Have we not all one father?" (Mal 2:10); as one who begets and takes care of his spiritual children, "you received the Spirit of sonship. And by him we cry, '*Abba,* Father' " (Rom 8:15). In a special and unique sense, God is the Father of Jesus Christ (Matt 11:26; Mark 14:36; Luke 22:42). SB

FATHERLESS (See ORPHAN)

FATHOM (See WEIGHTS AND MEASURES)

FATLING (See ANIMALS)

FAWN (See ANIMALS)

FEAR (Heb. *yir'âh,* Gr. *phobos*). This word in English has two principal meanings: (1) that apprehension of evil that normally leads one either to flee or to fight and (2) that awe and reverence that a person of sense feels in the presence of God and, to a less extent, in the presence of a king or other dread authority. A child feels the first of these in the presence of a cruel parent and feels the second before one who is good but who must also be just. There are fifteen different Hebrew nouns that are rendered "fear" in KJV; the Greek word for "fear" *phobos.* The word "reverend," which occurs only in the KJV of Psalm 111:9 (NIV has "awesome"), means literally "to be feared" and is used only for God. ABF

FEASTS (Heb. *mô'ēdh, an assembling, hagh, dance, or pilgrimage*). The feasts, or sacred festivals, held an important place in Jewish religion. They were religious services accompanied by demonstrations of joy and gladness. In Leviticus 23, where they are described most fully, they are called "holy convocations." Their times, except for the two instituted after the Exile, were fixed by divine appointment. Their purpose was to promote spiritual interests of the community. The people met in holy fellowship for acts and purposes of sacred worship. They met before God in holy assemblies.

I. The Feast of the Weekly Sabbath (Lev 23:3). This stood at the head of the sacred seasons. The holy meetings by which the Sabbath was distinguished were quite local. Families and other small groups assembled under the guidance of Levites or elders and engaged in common acts of devotion, the forms and manner of which were not prescribed. Little is known of where or how the people met before the Captivity, but after it they met in synagogues and were led in worship by teachers learned in the Law.

II. The Passover, or the Feast of Unleavened Bread (Lev 23:4–8). The Passover was the first of all the annual feasts, and historically and religiously it was the most important of all. It was called both the Feast of the Passover and the Feast of Unleavened Bread, the two really forming a double festival. It was celebrated on the first month of the religious year, on the fourteenth of Nisan (our April), and commemorated the deliverance of the Jews from Egypt and the establishment of Israel as a nation by God's redemptive act. The Feast of Unleavened Bread began on the day after the Passover and lasted seven days (23:5–8). This combined feast was one of the three feasts that all male Jews who were physically able and ceremonially clean were required by Mosaic Law to attend (Exod 23:17; Deut 16:16). The other two were the Feast of Weeks, or Pentecost, and the Feast of Tabernacles. These were known as the pilgrimage festivals; on all of them special sacrifices were offered, varying according to the character of the festival (Num 28–29).

Theologically the Passover finds its heart in the doctrine of propitiation. The Lord entered Egypt bent on judgment (Exod 12:12); but, seeing the blood, he passed over that house completely at peace with those who were sheltering there. His wrath was assuaged by the blood of the lamb. See also SUBSTITUTION.

III. The Feast of Pentecost (Lev 23:15–21). Other names for this are the Feast of Weeks, the Day of the Firstfruits, and the Feast of Harvests. It was celebrated on the sixth day of the month of Sivan (our June), seven weeks after the offering of the wave sheaf after the Passover. The name "Pentecost," meaning "fiftieth," originated from the fact that there was an interval of fifty days between the two. The feast lasted a single day (Deut 16:9–12) and marked the completion of the wheat harvest. The characteristic ritual of this feast was the offering and waving of two loaves of leavened bread, made from ripe grain that had just been harvested. This was done by the priest in the name of the congregation. In addition to these wave offerings, the people were to give the Lord an offering of the first fruits of their produce. The amount of the offering was not designated.

IV. The Feast of Trumpets, or New Moon (Lev 23:23–25). This was held on the first day of the seventh month, Tishri (our October), which began the civil year of the Jews. It corresponded to our New Year's Day, and on it, from morning to evening, horns and trumpets were blown. After the Exile the day was observed by the public reading of the Law and by general rejoicing.

V. The Feast of the Day of Atonement (Lev 23:26–32). This was observed on the tenth day of Tishri. It was really less a feast than a fast, as the distinctive character and purpose of the day was to bring the collective sin of the whole year to remembrance, so that it might earnestly be dealt with and atoned for. On this day the high priest made confession of all the sins of the community and entered on their behalf into the Most Holy Place with the blood of reconciliation. It was a solemn occasion, when God's people through godly sorrow and atonement for sin entered into the rest of God's mercy and favor. In receiving his forgiveness, they could rejoice before him and carry out his commandments.

VI. The Feast of Tabernacles, or Booths, or Ingathering (Lev 23:33–43). This was the last of the sacred festivals under the old covenant in preexilic times. It began five days after the Day of Atonement (Lev 23:34; Deut 16:13) and lasted seven days. It marked the completion of the harvest and historically commemorated the wanderings in the wilderness. During this festival people lived in booths and tents in Jerusalem to remind themselves of how their forefathers wandered in the wilderness and lived in booths. The sacrifices of this feast were more numerous than at any other. The last day of the feast marked the conclusion of the ecclesiastical year. The whole feast was popular and joyous in nature.

Besides the above feasts, which were all preexilic and instituted by God, the Jews after the

THE JEWISH SACRED YEAR

MONTH		SPECIAL DAYS
Nisan	(April)	14 — Passover 15 — Unleavened Bread 21 — Close of Passover
Iyar	(May)	
Sivan	(June)	6 — Feast of Pentecost—seven weeks after the Passover (Anniversary of the giving of the Law on Mount Sinai)
Tammuz	(July)	
Ab	(August)	
Elul	(September)	
Tishri	(October)	1–2 — The Feast of Trumpets *Rosh Hashanah,* beginning of the civil year. 10 — Day of Atonement 15–21 — Feast of Tabernacles
Marchesvan	(November)	
Kislev	(December)	25 — Feast of Lights, *Hanukkah*
Tebeth	(January)	
Shebet	(February)	
Adar	(March)	14 — Feast of Purim

Captivity added two others, the Feast of Lights, or Dedication, and the Feast of Purim.

The Feast of Lights was observed for eight days beginning on the twenty-fifth day of Kislev (our December). It was instituted by Judas Maccabeus in 164 B.C. when the temple, which had been defiled by Antiochus Epiphanes, king of Syria, was cleansed and rededicated to the service of the Lord. During these days the Israelites met in their synagogues, carrying branches of trees in their hands, and held jubilant services. The children were told the brave and stirring deeds of the Maccabees so that they might emulate them.

The Feast of Purim was kept on the fourteenth and fifteenth days of Adar (our March), the last month of the religious year. It was instituted by Mordecai to commemorate the failure of Haman's plots against the Jews (Esth 9:20–22, 26–28). The word Purim means "lots." On the evening of the thirteenth the whole Book of Esther was read publicly in the synagogue. It was a joyous occasion.

See also CALENDAR.

Bibliography: H. Schauss, *The Jewish Festivals,* 1938; A. S. Herbert, *Worship in Ancient Israel,* 1959; H.-J. Kraus, *Worship in Israel,* 1966. SB

FELIX (Gr. *Phēlix, happy*). Born Antonius Claudius, a Greek subject, he was made a freedman by Claudius, the emperor from A.D. 41 to 54, and given the surname Felix, probably in congratulation. He and his brother Pallas were favorites of Claudius and later of Nero (54–68), and so Felix evidently thought that he could do as he pleased. Tacitus said of him that "he revelled in cruelty and lust, and wielded the power of a king with the mind of a slave." His very title of "procurator" hints at his fiscal duties of procuring funds for Rome, which he seems to have accomplished with all sorts of tyranny. He began his career as procurator of Judea by seducing Drusilla, the sister of Agrippa II and wife of the king of Emesa (modern Homs), and marrying her. Because she was Jewish (at least in part), he learned much of Jewish life and customs.

Felix appears in the biblical account only in Acts 23:24–25:14. He was susceptible to flattery, as the speech of Tertullus shows, and also to conviction of sin, as is shown by his terror when Paul reasoned before him about "righteousness, self-control and the judgment to come" (24:25). His conviction faded; he procrastinated; and he held Paul for about two years (c. 58–60), hoping that Paul "would offer him a bribe" for his freedom (24:26). He was then replaced by Festus, a far better man.

FELLOWSHIP (Gr. *koinōnia, that which is in common*). 1. Partnership or union with others in the bonds of a business partnership, a social or fraternal organization, or just proximity. Christians are told not to be unequally yoked together with unbelievers (2 Cor 6:14–18) because such a union, either in marriage, business, or society, is incompatible with fellowship with Christians and with God.

2. Membership in a local Christian church or in *the* church. From the very beginning of the church at Pentecost, "they devoted themselves to the apostles' teaching and to the fellowship, to the breaking of bread and to prayer" (Acts 2:42).

3. Partnership in the support of the gospel and in the charitable work of the church (2 Cor 8:4).

4. That heavenly love that fills (or should fill) the hearts of believers one for another and for God. For this love and fellowship, the Scriptures use a word, *agapē,* which seldom appears in classical Greek. This fellowship is deeper and more satisfying than any mere human love whether social, parental, conjugal, or other.

FERRET (See ANIMALS)

FERTILE CRESCENT. This term does not occur in Scripture but is a modern description of the territory that may roughly be described as reaching NW from the Persian Gulf through Mesopotamia, then west to the north of Syria, then SW through Syria and Palestine. In this crescent the land is mostly rich and fertile and is watered by the Tigris, the Euphrates, the Orontes, the Jordan, and numerous rivers descending the west side of Lebanon. In most of the region irrigation has also long been employed. Various grains such as wheat and barley, and fruits such as grapes, olives, figs, oranges, lemons, and pomegranates abound. A journey in a straight line across the crescent from one end to the other would go mostly through the great Syrian desert, with only an occasional oasis. This configuration of the land explains much of Bible history.

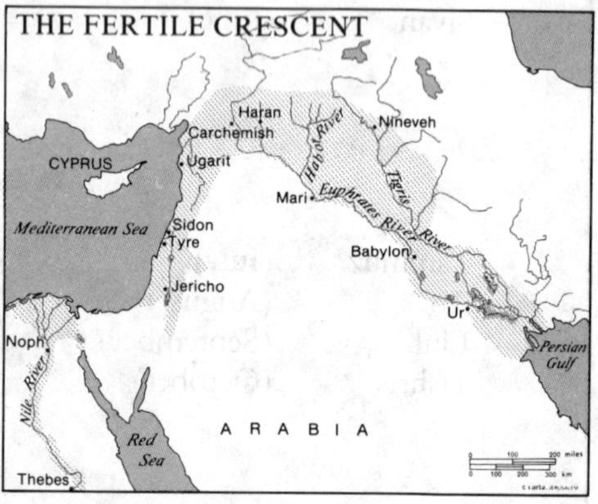

FESTIVALS (See FEASTS)

FESTUS PORCIUS (Gr. *Porkios Phēstos, festal, joyful*). The Roman governor who succeeded Felix in the province of Judea (Acts 24:27). The date of his accession is uncertain. Almost nothing is known of the life of Festus before his appointment by Nero as procurator of Judea. He appears in the Bible (24:27–26:32) principally in his relationship with his prisoner, the apostle Paul. Festus was apparently a far better and more efficient man than his predecessor. At the very beginning of his rule, he took up the case of Paul, and as King Agrippa said, Paul "could have been set free if he had not appealed to Caesar" (26:32). Paul had made this appeal when Festus, at the request of the Jews, was considering bringing Paul to Jerusalem for trial. Festus evidently knew that Paul was a good man (25:25), but he was unable to understand Paul's reasoning with King Agrippa and thought that Paul had gone mad with much study (26:24). Festus died at his post and was followed about A.D. 62 by Albinus.

FETTERS. (See SHACKLES)

FEVER (See DISEASES)

FIELD. The biblical "field" was usually not enclosed, but marked off from its neighbors by stone markers at the corners and sometimes one or two along the sides. Because they were unenclosed, and because of normally unsettled conditions, a watchman was often employed, especially when the crop was nearing maturity. Besides the danger of human intruders, there might be danger from straying cattle or even of cattle driven by rustlers (Exod 22:5), and of fire if a Samson (Judg 15:5) or an angry Absalom (2 Sam 14:30) were about. The word is used also in a larger sense for "territory," as in Genesis 36:35 (KJV), where "the country of Moab" (NIV) is intended; and as in the parable of the tares (Matt 13:38), where "the field is the world." Many of the ancient "fields" were the habitat of wild animals (Ps 80:13).

FIG (See PLANTS)

FIR (See PLANTS)

FIRE (Heb. *'ēsh,* Gr. *pyr*). Probably one of the earliest discoveries of man; perhaps first seen as a result of lightning, but man soon invented ways to use it and found it a most useful servant as well as a cruel master. The first use of the word "fire" in Scripture is in Genesis 19:24, which says that "fire from the LORD out of heaven" (KJV; NIV "burning sulfur . . . from the LORD out of the heavens") destroyed the cities of the plain; but the use of fire was far more ancient. Before the Flood, Tubal-Cain (4:22) was the father of smiths. In the account of the Abrahamic covenant (15:17) one reads of a smoking firepot and a flaming torch. Many students believe that God showed his acceptance of Abel's offering (4:4) by sending fire to consume it. In the institution of the Aaronic priestly ceremonies, God sent fire from heaven to consume the first offering (Lev 9:24) to show his acceptance. This fire was to be kept burning continually (6:9). When the two sons of Aaron, Nadab and Abihu, offered "unauthorized fire," probably when intoxicated (10:1, 9–10), God's fiery judgment descended on them and destroyed them. The final destiny of the enemies of God is the "fiery lake" (Rev 19:20; 20:10, 14). This world will some day be consumed by fire (2 Peter 3:7–12).

God uses "fire" not only for judgment but also for testing, and so we learn that the works of all believers will be tested as by fire (1 Cor 3:12–15). God's glory is accompanied by fire (Ezek 1:27). The seraphim are fiery creatures (Isa 6:2), as are the "venomous snakes" of Numbers 21:6 (from the same Hebrew verb *saraph,* "to burn"). Our Lord is pictured with eyes as a flame of fire, hinting at his work of judgment (Rev 1:14). Fire is used to refine gold and to cleanse us (Mal 3:2).

FIREBRAND. The KJV rendering of three Hebrew words, meaning: a stick for stirring fire (Isa 7:4; Amos 4:11); brands, sparks (Prov 26:18); and a torch, as in Judges 7:16 (see marginal note) and Judges 15:4.

FIREPAN (Heb. *mahtâh*). A vessel used for carrying live coals, as in Exodus 27:3. The Hebrew word is rendered "censer" many times, and "snuff dish" three times by KJV (e.g., Exod 25:38; Lev 10:1; NIV "wick trimmers"). The meaning is evident from the context. See also CENSER.

FIRKIN (See WEIGHTS AND MEASURES)

FIRMAMENT (Heb. *raqia'*). The expanse of sky surrounding the earth, made by God on the second day of creation to "separate water from water" (Gen 1:6). The Hebrews thought of the firmament as the apparent void above in which the clouds float and the lights of heaven are set by God. The Hebrew word suggests something stretched or spread out like a curtain (Isa 40:22). It corresponds to the "empty space" of Job 26:7. Our English word "firmament" does not correctly suggest the real meaning of the Hebrew word. NIV translates it as "expanse."

FIRSTBORN. (Heb. *bekhôr,* Gr. *prōtotokos*). The Hebrew word is used chiefly of men, but is used also of animals (Exod 11:5). It appears that man early felt that God had the first claim on animals (Gen 4:4). Among the ancestors of the Hebrews the first-born offspring of men and animals were sacrificed to the deity. Because the first-born of the Israelites were preserved at the time of the first Passover, every firstborn male of man and beast became consecrated to God (Exod 13:2; 34:19). The beasts were sacrificed, while the men were redeemed (Exod 13:13, 15; 34:20; cf. Lev 27:6). At Sinai the Levites were substituted for the Israelite firstborn (Num 3:12, 41, 46; 8:13–19). On the thirtieth day after birth the father brought his firstborn son to the priest and paid five shekels to redeem him from service in the temple (cf. Luke 2:27).

Among the Israelites the first-born son possessed special privileges. He succeeded his father as the head of the house and received as his share of the inheritance a double portion. Israel was the Lord's firstborn (Exod 4:22) and was thus entitled to special privileges, as compared with other peoples. Jesus Christ is described as the firstborn (Rom 8:29; Col 1:15; Heb 1:6), an application of the term that may be traced back to Psalm 89:27, where the Messiah is referred to as the firstborn of God. SB

FIRSTFRUITS (Heb. *rē'shîth, bikkûrîm,* Gr. *aparchē*). In acknowledgment of the fact that all the products of the land came from God, and to show thankfulness for his goodness, Israelites brought as an offering a portion of the fruits that ripened first. These were looked on as a pledge of the coming harvest. Such an offering was made both on behalf of the nation (Lev 23:10, 17) and by individuals (Exod 23:19; Deut 26:1–11). These firstfruits went for the support of the priesthood.

Jesus is the firstfruits of all who die in faith; that is, the resurrection of believers is made possible and is guaranateed by his resurrection (1 Cor 15:20). Believers, in turn, are "a kind of firstfruits" of all that God created (James 1:18); creation will share in the redemption of the children of God (Rom 8:19–21).

FISH (See ANIMALS)

FISH GATE. An ancient gate on the east side of the wall of Jerusalem, just west of Gihon, where in the days of Nehemiah, men of Tyre congregated to sell fish and various wares on the Sabbath (2 Chron 33:14; Neh 13:16). It is probably identical with the "Middle Gate" of Jeremiah 39:3.

FISHHOOK. Not only the means of catching fish as is done today, but also of keeping them, at least for a time (cf. Amos 4:2 with Job 41:1–2). Peter generally used a net, but see Matthew 17:27, where the Lord told him to cast a hook (KJV).

FISHING (See OCCUPATIONS AND PROFESSIONS)

FITCH (See PLANTS)

FLAG (See PLANTS)

FLAX (See PLANTS)

FLEA (See ANIMALS)

FLEECE. The shorn wool of a sheep. The first of the shearing was to be given to the priesthood, as a part of their means of support (Deut 18:4). Gideon's experience (Judg 6:37–40) has given rise to the custom of "putting out a fleece" in seeking God's guidance.

FLESH (Heb. *bāsār, shē'er,* Gr. *sarx*). 1. Literally, the soft part of the bodies of people and animals.

2. All animals, as in Genesis 6:19 (KJV); NIV "all living creatures."

3. Mankind in general, as in Numbers 16:22 KJV: "the God of the spirits of all flesh."

4. Our ordinary human constitution as opposed to our mental and moral qualities: "the spirit indeed is willing, but the flesh is weak" (Matt 26:41 KJV).

5. Human nature deprived of the Spirit of God and dominated by sin (Col 2:18; 1 John 2:16 KJV).

The believer's "sinful nature" (NIV), which is opposed to the life of the Spirit. Instead of being controlled by it, the believer ought to be controlled by the Spirit (Rom 8:12–17; Gal 5:16–23).

FLIES (See ANIMALS)

FLINT (See MINERALS)

FLOCK. A collection of sheep under the care of a shepherd, sometimes including goats also (Gen 27:9). The larger animals such as cattle, camels, asses, etc. were counted as herds, not flocks. Israel lived in OT times in a pastoral civilization, and a man's flocks made up most of his wealth, providing clothing, food, milk, and animals for sacrifice. Figuratively, Israel and the church are counted as flocks, and God is the Good Shepherd (Isa 40:11; Matt 26:31; Luke 12:32; 1 Peter 5:2–3).

Shepherds and their flock, roaming the open fields near Jerusalem. Courtesy Zev Radovan.

FLOG (See SCOURGE; STRIPES)

FLOOD, THE The Deluge, or world-wide destruction of man and beast, except for Noah, his family, and the animals in the ark.

I. Historical Background of Flood Interpretations. The Noahic flood has been a subject for discussion among scientists and theologians for many centuries. During the Middle Ages, the church was the authority in all areas of thought. Science as we know it today did not exist, for with its theological orientation the church looked with disfavor on observations that did not have theological explanations. It was only natural then that when the early geologists observed many thousands of feet of sedimentary rocks (formed from smaller particles of rocks or chemically precipitated from solution) in the mountains of Europe and the British Isles, they turned to the church for an explanation. The easiest answer for the layers of sediments was that they were laid down by the Flood.

As the sedimentary layers were studied further, problems arose when it was discovered that not all

Shepherdesses tending their flocks in the Negev—a timeless picture. Courtesy S. Zur Picture Library.

the layers were contemporaneous. It was also readily observed that some sediments had been deposited, hardened into rock, folded into mountain ranges, eroded off and then covered with new sediments. At some places the sedimentary rock layers were cut by formerly molten rock material, which indicated volcanic activity after the sediments were deposited. Sixteenth- and seventeenth-century scientists attempted to harmonize the interpretation of field observations with church tradition.

As a result, many interpretations of the meaning and physical characteristics of the Flood have been suggested, modified, abandoned, and sometimes reproposed. These interpretations have produced some highly improbable explanations of the events of the Deluge and have so confused the issue that it is difficult to separate the intelligent from the fanciful. The reality of the Flood can hardly be questioned, however, because of the many references to it in both the OT and NT (Gen 6–8; 9:11, 28; 10:1, 32; Matt 24:38–39; Luke 17:27; 2 Peter 2:5).

II. The Purpose of the Flood. An important aspect of the Deluge is that God preserved some men, for Noah and his family were saved from destruction by going into an ark that Noah made according to God's specifications, and in which he gathered animals and birds preserved to replenish the earth.

It is apparent from Genesis 6:5–7 and other passages such as 2 Peter 2:5–6 that the Flood was brought on the earth as a judgment on the sins of the people. Man had become so sinful that "the LORD was grieved that he had made man on the earth" (Gen 6:6). The Bible refers to the Flood in connection with the judgment at the second coming of the Lord (Matt 24:39) and with the destruction of Sodom and Gomorrah (Luke 17:27–29; 2 Peter 2:5–6).

The purpose of God, as stated in Genesis 6:7, indicates that the judgment was not against the inanimate rocks or against plants but against "men and animals, and creatures that move along the ground, and birds of the air."

III. The Phenomena of the Flood. In the following passage, however (Gen 6:11–13), the earth is included in the judgment. There is again difference of opinion as to the meaning of Genesis 6:13, in which God said, "I am going to put an end to all people, for the earth is filled with violence because of them. I am surely going to destroy both them and the earth." That the earth was not utterly destroyed as it will be in the last times (2 Peter 2:10) is apparent. Some writers would interpret Genesis 6:13 to mean that great geologic catastrophes overwhelmed the earth's surface, while others point out that Genesis 6:6–7, 12–13 all stress that it was the sin of living things that was to be punished and that the effect on the inanimate rocks of the world was only incidental to punishing the human race.

Despite all attempts at scientific explanation of the minute details of the Flood, there seems to be no doubt that God worked a miracle in causing it. In 2 Peter 3:5–6 the Flood is compared with the creation of the world and is a miracle of the same order. In the same passage, 2 Peter 3:7ff., the final destruction of the world is given the same miraculous explanation as the Noahic flood.

IV. The Source of the Flood. The biblical account of the accumulation and dispersal of the waters of the Flood is very brief. In Genesis 7:11 the source of the water is explained, ". . . all the springs of the great deep burst forth, and the floodgates of the heavens were opened."

The Hebrew word *tehom,* translated "great deep," is the same used in Genesis 1:2. That this does not necessarily include all the oceans is shown by its use in Isaiah 51:10 when it refers to the escape of the Israelites in "the depths of the sea" (the Red Sea). The Hebrew word *ma'yan* means literally *place of a spring*. This could mean that water rose from the ocean or from fresh water springs on the earth or both.

V. Suggested Causes of the Flood. Some would prefer to believe that the expression "the springs of the great deep burst forth" indicates that the ocean (actually the Persian Gulf, an arm of the ocean) invaded the land. Others have assumed this implies volcanic activity and that some of the water of the Flood is "juvenile water," which is formed from the oxygen and hydrogen that may occur as separate elements in the molten rock deep in the earth's crust. This school of thought would also attribute to this verse a great deal of diastrophism (movements of the solid crust that result in a relative change of position of the rock formations concerned). This could account for the sinking of the mountains of the earth so that they could be covered more easily by the waters of the Deluge.

To attribute volcanic activity to Genesis 7:11 is highly speculative, for at no place in the Genesis account of the Flood is any more specific description of conditions given. The fact that igneous rock (rock formed by the cooling of molten rock materials) is found between layers of sedimentary rock is not good evidence for volcanic activity at the time of the Flood. Sediments that have been laid down during historic time have been cut by lava from present-day volcanoes. It has also been observed that the oldest layers are also cut by igneous rocks. It seems apparent, therefore, that volcanic activity has gone on throughout the world's history. It is not possible to designate any particular rock body as being coincident with the Flood.

"The floodgates of the heavens were opened" has been accepted as a description of rain. Some have seen this as a torrential downpour greater than normally experienced on the earth today. A hypothesis has been proposed that the earth from the time of its creation (or at least man's creation) was surrounded by a canopy of water in some form until the time of the Flood. The canopy was supposedly made of water vapor, ice, or liquid water. It is proposed that the transfer of the canopy's water from around the earth to the earth would cause rain for many days.

The canopy idea, although firmly entrenched in literature, has doubtful biblical authority, though some cite older versions of Ezekiel 1:22 in support of it. Again it should be noted that if a miraculous explanation for the Flood is accepted, physical explanations are not necessary.

VI. The Duration of the Flood. The length of the Flood is generally agreed on within a few days. The Hebrews used a solar calendar in contrast to the Babylonian lunar month and the Egyptian arbitrary 365-day year. Most authorities would put the number of days from the time the rain started (Gen 7:11) to the time Noah left the ark (8:14) between 371 and 376 days.

VII. Traditions of the Flood. Traditions regarding a disastrous flood that occurred long ago are handed down by many peoples. Isolated tribes in all parts of the world have been found to have such traditions. This is not surprising, considering the destruction caused by present-day floods as well as hurricanes and tornadoes accompanied by great rains. A tribe occupying a limited area could be destroyed completely by one storm. Any survivors would date their civilization from such an event.

The Hebrews, Assyrians, and Babylonians who lived within the area of the Tigris-Euphrates basin, all had traditions of a great flood. These narratives stated the purpose of the Flood to be punishment because the world was full of violence, but the Hebrew account remained simple and credible, whereas the other accounts became complex and fanciful. Only the biblical account retained a monotheistic viewpoint. Although it is not possible to affirm dogmatically that all of these three histories had a common origin, it seems probable that they did.

VIII. The Universality of the Flood. One of the great differences of opinion in describing the Flood concerns its extent. Traditionally, most

Fragment of a clay tablet from the library of Ashurbanipal at Nineveh, with an Assyrian account of the Flood. Reproduced by courtesy of the Trustees of the British Museum.

biblical interpreters considered the submergence to be universal; that is, it covered the entire globe including the highest mountains. The reasons proposed to defend this viewpoint include the fact that universal terms are used in the Genesis account. "*All* the high mountains under the entire heavens were covered" (Gen 7:19), and "every living thing that moved on the earth perished" (7:21). It has been pointed out that if the Flood were local, there would be no need for an ark to preserve Noah, for God could have directed him to move with the animals to an area that was not to be submerged.

The fact that many civilizations have flood traditions has been cited as an evidence for a universal flood. The same evidence could be used to argue for a local flood because the accounts of floods in other parts of the world are less like the Hebrew tradition than those of the Assyrians and Babylonians, who lived in the same area as the Hebrews.

Today many conservative scholars defend a local flood. The crux of their argument seems to center in the covenant relation of God to man. He deals with certain groups, such as the children of Israel. The reasoning in regard to Noah is that Noah was not a preacher of righteousness to peoples of other areas but was concerned with the culture from which Abraham eventually came. Physical arguments have also been raised against a universal flood: origin and disposal of the amount of water necessary to make a layer six miles (ten km.) thick over the whole world, the effect on plant life of being covered for a year, the effect on fresh water life of a sea that contained salt from the ocean, and the fact that many topographic features of the earth (such as cinder cones) show no evidence of erosion by a flood and are thought to be much older than the Flood could possibly be.

IX. Chronology of the Flood. There is not any general agreement among conservative scholars concerning the actual date of the Deluge. Although Ussher in his chronology placed the Flood at 2348 B.C., most scholars today hold to an earlier date. Scholars who have advocated that the earth has developed to its present condition by a series of major calamities have been called catastrophists. These consider the Noahic flood as the greatest of these catastrophes and believe that the Pleistocene ice age was related to the Flood. Many catastrophists believe the Flood was associated in some way with the end of the Pleistocene ice age and so accept a date of about 10,000 B.C. The lack of consensus with regard to the details of the Flood should make all aware of the danger of placing so much importance on the interpretation of this event that the other lessons of the Bible are missed.

Bibliography: M. F. Unger, *Introductory Guide to the Old Testament,* 1951; A. Parrot, *The Flood and Noah's Ark,* 1955; J. C. Whitcomb and H. M. Morris, *The Genesis Flood,* 1961; F. A. Filby, *The Flood Reconsidered,* 1970. DCB

FLOUR. Fine-crushed and sifted grain, generally wheat or rye or barley (Judg 7:13). Eastern flour was not quite as fine or as white as ours, and thus the bread was more wholesome. The "meat" (it should be "meal") offerings were of flour (Lev 6:15 KJV).

FLOWER (See PLANTS)

FLUTE (See MUSIC AND MUSICAL INSTRUMENTS)

Tabulated Chronology of the Flood

1. The making of the ark (Gen 6:14)	
2. Collection of the animals (Gen 7:9)	seven days before the rain started
3. Springs of the great deep burst forth and the floodgates of heaven were opened (Gen 7:11)	Second month, seventeenth day in Noah's 600th year
4. Rain (Gen 7:12)	forty days and forty nights
5. All the high hills covered (Gen 7:19)	
6. Water flooded the earth (Gen 7:24)	150 days
7. Water receded from off the earth (Gen 8:3)	150 days
8. Ark rested on the mountains of Ararat (Gen 8:4)	Seventh month, seventeenth day
9. Waters decreased (Gen 8:4)	
10. Tops of mountains seen (Gen 8:5)	Tenth month, first day
11. Noah waited (Gen 8:6)	forty days
12. Noah sent out a raven and a dove; dove returned (Gen 8:7–9)	
13. Noah waited (Gen 8:10)	seven days
14. Noah sent forth dove again (Gen 8:10); dove returned with olive branch (Gen 8:11)	seven days
15. Noah waited (Gen 8:12)	seven days
16. Noah sent out a dove, which did not return (Gen 8:12)	seven days
17. Noah removed covering; face of the ground was dry (Gen 8:13)	first month, first day, Noah's 601st year
18. Earth dried; Noah left ark (Gen 8:14)	second month, twenty-seventh day

FLY (See ANIMALS)

FOAL (See ANIMALS)

FODDER. The mixed food of cattle, generally from several kinds of grain sown together (Job 6:5; 24:6; Isa 30:24).

FOOD. Nutritive material taken into a living organism to sustain life, to promote growth and the repair of the tissues, and to give energy for the vital processes. The Bible says little about food for animals. Bible animals for the most part are herbivorous, though carnivorous ones are mentioned. Some omnivorous animals, like pigs, are mentioned, but almost always in a contemptuous way (Matt 7:6). Pigs were forbidden as food (Isa 65:4).

At the very beginning of human history, Adam's food for his first day was probably some ripe fruit near him as he awoke to consciousness, and when he began to hunger, his nose as well as his eyes directed him to his first meal. Food and water would of course be necessary from that first day. Before sin had entered into human history, God apparently prescribed a vegetarian diet, both for man and beast (Gen 1:29–30), but one must not build too much on silence here as regarding the content of diet. By the time that Noah built the ark, there was a distinction between clean and unclean beasts (7:2–3) and when God made his covenant with Noah after the Flood (9:3–4), flesh was permitted as food. Blood was forbidden, and it seems that the reason for this prohibition was as much theological as sanitary for "the life [Hebrew *nephesh,* soul] of a creature is in the blood" (cf. Lev 17:11). Coming down now to the time of Moses, fat was also prohibited as food (3:16–17) and again, the reason given is religious, not hygienic. In the time of the Restoration (Neh 8:10) Nehemiah encouraged the people to "enjoy choice food" (KJV "eat the fat") while celebrating a national "Thanksgiving day." One might imagine here that Nehemiah had forgotten that "all the fat is the LORD's" (Lev 3:16) until one notices that the Hebrew word in Nehemiah could just as well be rendered "dainties" and refers probably to the various rich confections of which Eastern people are so fond.

The animals most frequently mentioned in the Bible are the domestic herbivorous animals, and these are divided sharply into two classes: the clean and the unclean (see Lev 11). The clean animals were to be used for food and for sacrifice and the four-footed ones were distinguished by their hoofs and by whether they chewed the cud. The camel chews the cud but does not have a split hoof and so was considered unclean, though its milk was and is used by desert-dwellers. Pigs have a split hoof but do not chew the cud and so were ceremonially unclean. They were perhaps prohibited as food because of the mischievous *trichina spiralis,* a worm that has long infested pigs, and from half-roasted pork can enter the human body and create great harm. Of the seafood that was reckoned unclean the principal ones were oysters and shrimps. One can easily realize how dangerous they would be in a land where climate was hot and there was no refrigeration. In other words, most of the distinctions between "clean" and "unclean" foods were clearly based on sanitary reasons.

In Palestine and Syria, fresh fruit can be obtained throughout the year. Oranges last in the spring until the very short season of apricots arrives. After the apricots come the plums, figs, pomegranates, etc., which last until the grapes appear; and they in turn remain until the oranges and lemons are again in season.

The preparation of food differs from Western custom. Generally meat is eaten not in steaks and roasts, but cut up and served with rice and often imbedded in "coosa" (a kind of squash) or wrapped in cabbage or grape leaves. The bread is not as white and fine as is ours but is far more healthful. A common laborer often takes as his lunch two hollow loaves of bread, one filled with cheese and the other with olives. There were several sorts of sweets, of which dried figs boiled in grape molasses (Gen 43:11) was one of the best known. Near the sea, fish were very commonly eaten. Various kinds of fruit and vegetables were used: beans, lentils, millet, melons, onions, gourds; also spices: cummin, mint, mustard, and salt; and honey.

Food is a figure of spiritual sustenance. Peter tells his readers to "crave pure spiritual milk, so that by it you may grow up in your salvation." Peter was writing to young Christians (1 Peter 2:2), but Paul clearly distinguishes between Scripture that can be likened to "milk for babes" and that which can be compared with "strong meat," or solid food (1 Cor 3:1–2). ABF

FOOLISHNESS, FOLLY. The opposite of wisdom, with which the OT often contrasts it (Eccl 2:13). The fool exhibits many characteristics ranging from simple stupidity (Prov 7:7, 22) and a hot temper (14:17) to wickedness (Gen 34:7), atheism (Ps 14:1), and rejection of God (Job 2:9–10). In the NT it can mean thoughtlessness (Gal 3:3) or lack of intelligence (Rom 1:21). In describing the "foolish" virgins, the adjective is from a Greek word on which we base the English noun "moron." The same word is used by Paul in saying that the preaching of the cross is "foolishness" to the lost (1 Cor 1:18). In Matthew 23:17 the Lord called the scribes and Pharisees fools, not implying intellectual stupidity but spiritual blindness. Men can be clever in mind, but at the same time be fools in spiritual matters.

FOOT. The foot of man, because it comes in contact with the earth, is thought to be less honorable than the hand or the head. But in the Christian church "the foot" (i.e., the lowest member) should not suffer a feeling of inferiority or of envy and say, "Because I am not a hand, I do not belong to the body" (1 Cor 12:15), nor should the more prominent directing member ("the head") say to the foot, "I don't need you!" (12:21). In the East shoes are ordinarily removed when entering a house, and the lowest servant is detailed to wash the feet of the visitor. The priests, before entering the tabernacle in divine service, washed their feet as well as their hands at the laver, just outside, so that no trace of defilement would accompany their service. (For spiritual application see John 13:10; Heb 10:22). In lands where irrigation is practiced, men use shovels to move the earth for the larger channels, but a foot will suffice for a small channel to water a furrow (Deut 11:10). To completely humiliate an enemy, one sometimes put his foot on the captives' necks as Joshua's captains did (Josh 10:24).

FOOTMAN. 1. A member of the infantry as distinguished from the cavalry—horsemen and charioteers. The bulk of ancient armies consisted of footmen.

2. A runner, one of the king's bodyguard (1 Sam 22:17 KJV).

FOOTSTOOL (Heb. *keves,* Gr. *hypopodion*). A word used in Scripture both literally (2 Chron 9:18) and figuratively: of the earth (Isa 66:1; Matt 5:35); of the temple (Lam 2:1); of the ark (Ps 99:5); and of subjection, especially of heathen enemies by the messianic King (Ps 110:1; Luke 20:43; Acts 2:35).

FORD (Heb. *ma'avar, mavarah*). A shallow place in a stream where men and animals can cross on foot. In the small streams of Palestine and Syria, fording places are quite frequent and can easily be found simply by following the main roads, which in many cases are mere bridle paths. Such probably were the fords of the Jabbok (Gen 32:22) where Jacob halted, and of the Arnon (Isa 16:2). The Jordan, however, is a strong and rapid stream, and its fording places are few and far between. When Israel crossed, God miraculously stopped the waters upstream by a landslide. John the Baptist baptized at Bethabara (John 1:28; NIV "Bethany"), the name indicating that a ford was there. Joshua's spies (Josh 2:7) evidently forded the Jordan, and Ehud (Judg 3:28) took the same place to prevent Moabites from crossing there. Farther up the river and about two hundred years after Ehud, Jephthah (12:5–6) made his famous "Shibboleth test" at a ford of the Jordan.

FOREHEAD. Because of its prominence, its appearance often determines our opinion of the person. In Ezekiel 16:12 KJV reads "I put a jewel on thy forehead," but NIV (more correctly) has "I put a ring on your nose." The forehead is used as a very dishonorable word where in the KJV we read of a "harlot's forehead" (Jer 3:3; NIV "brazen look of a prostitute") indicating utter shamelessness. At the same time it stands for courage, as when God told Ezekiel (Ezek 3:9) that he had made the prophet's forehead harder than flint against the foreheads of the people. The forehead is also the place for the front of a crown or mitre (Exod 28:38), where the emblem of holiness on Aaron's forehead would make the

Hittite period (eighth century B.C.?) basalt stele (1.24 m. high) from Marash in Turkey depicting two figures resting their feet on footstools as they sit before a table piled with offerings. They wear long, fringed garments with high cylindrical caps, and hold a cup and mirror in their raised hands. Courtesy Istanbul Museum. Photo B. Brandl.

gifts of the people acceptable before the Lord. A mark was put on the foreheads of the men of Jerusalem who mourned for its wickedness, and they were spared in a time of terrible judgment (Ezek 9:4). Similarly in Revelation 7 God's servants were sealed by an angel, and it seems that this seal not only saved the elect ones but showed forth their godly character. In the ages of glory that are to come, the name of God will be marked on the foreheads of his own people (Rev 22:4).
ABF

FOREIGNER (See STRANGER)

FOREKNOWLEDGE; FOREORDINATION (See ELECTION AND PREDESTINATION)

FORESKIN (Heb. *'orlâh,* Gr. *akrobystia*). The fold of skin that is cut off in the operation of circumcision. Just as the American Indians used scalps of enemies as signs of their prowess, so David presented two hundred foreskins of the Philistines (1 Sam 18:25–27). In Deuteronomy 10:16 (KJV) the word is used figuratively meaning submission to God's law. In Habakkuk 2:16 (KJV) it refers to the indecent exhibitionism of a drunken man.

FOREST (Heb. *ya'ar, sevakh, 'avîm*). A piece of land covered with trees naturally planted, as distinguished from a park where man's hand is more evident. In ancient times, most of the highlands of Canaan and Syria except the tops of the high mountains were covered with forests. Several forests are mentioned by name, those of Lebanon most often, for these were famous for the cedar and the fir trees. Hiram of Tyre (1 Kings 5:8–10) brought down cedar and fir trees from the forest of Lebanon, to the sea and floated them southward to the port that Solomon had constructed, from which his servants could transport the timbers to Jerusalem. Solomon's "Palace of the Forest of Lebanon" (7:2) was apparently his own house and was so named because of the prevalence of cedar in its structure. The crucial battle of Absalom's rebellion was fought in a wood or forest in Ephraim (2 Sam 18), and "the forest claimed more lives that day than the sword" (18:8).

FORGIVENESS (Heb. *kāphar, nāsā', sālach,* Gr. *apoluein, charizesthai, aphēsis, paresis*). In the OT, *pardon,* and in the NT, *remission,* are often used as the equivalents of *forgiveness.* The idea of forgiveness is found in either religious or social relations, and means giving up resentment or claim to requital on account of an offense. The offense may be a deprivation of a person's property, rights, or honor; or it may be a violation of moral law.

The normal conditions of forgiveness are repentance and the willingness to make reparation or atonement; and the effect of forgiveness is the restoration of both parties to the former state of relationship. Christ taught that forgiveness is a duty, and that no limit should be set to the extent of forgiveness (Luke 17:4). An unforgiving spirit is one of the most serious of sins (Matt 18:34–35; Luke 15:28–30). God forgives man's sins because of the atoning death of Christ. Jesus taught that the offended party is, when necessary, to go to the offender and try to bring him to repentance (Luke 17:3). God's forgiveness is conditional upon man's forgiveness of the wrongs done him (Matt 5:23–24; 6:12; Col 1:14; 3:13). Those forgiven by God before the Incarnation were forgiven because of Christ, whose death was foreordained from eternity. Christ's atonement was retroactive in its effect (Heb 11:40). God's forgiveness seems, however, to be limited. Christ speaks of the unpardonable sin (Matt 12:31–32), and John speaks of the sin unto death (1 John 5:16). The deity of Christ is evidenced by his claim to the power to forgive sins (Mark 2:7; Luke 5:21; 7:49).

Bibliography: H. R. Mackintosh, *The Christian Experience of Forgiveness,* 1927; F. H. Wales, *The Forgiveness of Sins,* 1940; V. Taylor, *Forgiveness and Reconciliation,* 1952; E. M. B. Green, *The Meaning of Salvation,* 1965; NIDNTT, I, pp. 697–703. SB

FORNICATION (Heb. zānâh, Gr. *porneia*). Used in the KJV for unlawful sexual intercourse of an unwed person. It is to be distinguished from adultery, which has to do with unfaithfulness on the part of a married person, and from rape, which is a crime of violence and without the consent of the person sinned against. When these sins are mentioned in the Bible, they are often figurative of disloyalty. Idolatry is practically adultery from God. This ugly sin ought not even to be a subject of conversation among Christians (Eph 5:3–4 KJV; NIV "sexual immorality") and is commonly associated with the obscene worship of the heathen. For the spiritualizing of this sin, see Jeremiah 2:20–36, Ezekiel 16, Hosea 1–3 (where it applied to Israel), and Revelation 17 (where it applied to Rome).

FORT, FORTRESS. Every major city in ancient times was fortified by a wall and its citadel. The KJV often speaks of such cities as "fenced," the NIV as "fortified." Even before the Israelites entered Canaan, they were terrified by the reports of cities "fortified and very large" (Num 13; Deut 1:28). Jerusalem was so well fortified that it was not until the time of David that the city was captured from the Jebusites. Usually the city was built on a hill, and the fortifications followed the natural contour of the hill. Many times there was both an inner and an outer wall. The walls were built of brick and stone and were many feet thick. After the Israelites entered the land they too built fortified cities (Deut 28:52; 2 Sam 20:6).

Herodium, a fortress built by Herod the Great in the first century B.C., located 4 miles southeast of Bethlehem. The fortress consists of a citadel with four round towers and retaining walls, inside of which stood Herod's palace. Courtesy Seffie Ben-Yoseph.

FORTUNATUS (fôr-tū-nā'tŭs, Gr. *Phortounatos, blessed, fortunate*). A Christian who came with two others to bring gifts from the Corinthian church to Paul when he was about to leave Ephesus in A.D. 59 (1 Cor 16:17).

FORUM APPII (See APPIUS, FORUM OF)

FOUNDATION (Heb. *yāsadh, to found,* Gr. *katabolē, themelios*). The word is used of the creation when God "laid the earth's foundation" (Job 38:4; Ps 78:69). In contrast with the disappearance of the wicked, the righteous are "an everlasting foundation" (Prov 10:25 KJV; NIV "stand firm forever"). This heightens the description of the Lord's anger as causing the foundations of earth to tremble (Isa 24:18), as well as mountains (Ps 18:7) and heaven (2 Sam 22:8). The NT speaks of the man who built his foundation on a rock (Luke 6:48). Christ is the foundation of the church (1 Cor 3:11); the apostles and prophets are the foundation on which Christians are built, with Christ as the chief cornerstone (Eph 2:20), and a good foundation can be built up by those "rich in this present world" by valuing more highly God's rich bounty (1 Tim 6:17–19). And God's "solid foundation" stands firm and immovable (2 Tim 2:19).

FOUNTAIN. A spring of water issuing from the earth. In a country near the desert, springs, pools, pits, cisterns, and fountains are of great importance. Many towns and other locations are named for the springs at their sites: e.g., Enaim, "two springs" (Gen 38:21); En Gedi, "the fountain of the kid" (Josh 15:62); and a dozen others, like the English "Springfield" or the French "Fontainebleau." In the story of the Flood, "the fountains of the great deep" were broken up, referring to the great convulsions of the earth's surface (Gen 7:11 KJV) that, with the rain, caused the Flood; and in the preparation of the earth for man, the Son of God (Wisdom personified) was with the Father before there were "springs abounding with water" (Prov 8:24). The word is used both literally and figuratively, both pleasantly and unpleasantly. Figuratively, it refers in the KJV to the source of hemorrhages (Lev 20:18; Mark 5:29). In Proverbs, compare "a muddied spring or a polluted well" (25:26) with "a fountain of life" (13:14; 14:27). In the bridegroom's praise of his pure bride (Song of Songs 4:15) she is "a garden fountain." In the curse of Ephraim (Hos 13:15), "his spring will fail" is a terrible punishment; but on the pleasant side, David speaks (Ps 36:9) of "the fountain of life," as being with the Lord. In the Lord's conversation with the woman at the well (John 4:14), he told her of "a spring of water welling up to eternal life." Among the delights of heaven will be "the spring of the water of life" (Rev 21:6). ABF

FOUNTAIN GATE. The gate at the SE corner of the walls of ancient Jerusalem, mentioned only in Nehemiah (2:14; 3:15; 12:37).

FOWL (See BIRDS)

FOWLER (Heb. *yōkēsh*). A bird-catcher. Because fowlers used snares, gins, bird-lime, etc. and caught their prey by trickery, "fowler" is used to describe those who try to ensnare the unwary and bring them to ruin (Ps 91:3; 124:7).

FOX (See ANIMALS)

FRANKINCENSE (See PLANTS)

FREEDMAN, FREE WOMAN. A rendering of two slightly different Greek words. *Apeleutheros,* 1 Corinthians 7:22, refers to a slave who has received his freedom, though this verse concerns one who has received spiritual freedom from the Lord. *Eleutheros,* is used in Galatians 4:22–23, 30 and Revelation 6:15, and refers to a free woman or man as opposed to a slave.

FREEDOM (See LIBERTY)

Copy of a tomb painting from Thebes (c. 1420 B.C.). Nakht and his wife (elaborately dressed standing on a papyrus boat) fowling and fishing in the marshes. Courtesy The Metropolitan Museum of Art (15.5.19e).

FRET (Heb. *hārâh, mā'ar*). To be vexed, chafed, irritated, angry. The godly man is not to fret (Ps 37:1, 7–8) but is to have his mind stayed on the Lord (Isa 26:3).

FRINGE (See TASSEL)

FROG (See ANIMALS)

FRONTLET (See DRESS)

FROST (Heb. *kephōr, hănāmāl*). Usual in winter on the hills and high plains in Bible lands. Frosts in the late spring do great damage to fruit. The manna in the wilderness is compared to frost (Exod 16:14). Frost is an evidence of God's power (Job 38:29).

FRUIT (Heb. *perî*, Gr. *karpos*). The fruits most often mentioned in Scripture are the grape, pomegranate, fig, olive, and apple; all of which are grown today; but the lemon, orange, plum, and apricot were unknown or at least unmentioned. The word "fruit" is often used metaphorically: "the fruit of your womb" (Deut 7:13), "the fruit of their schemes" (Prov 1:31). The fruit of the Holy Spirit consists of all the Christian virtues (Gal 5:22–23).

FUEL (Heb. *'ōkhlâh*, or *ma'ăkhōleth, food*). In ancient times, wood, charcoal, various kinds of thorn bushes, dried grass, and the dung of camels and cattle were used as fuel. There is no evidence that coal was used by the Hebrews as fuel; their houses had no chimneys (Isa 9:5, 19; Ezek 4:12; 15:4, 6; 21:32).

FULLER (See OCCUPATIONS AND PROFESSIONS)

FULLER'S FIELD (Heb. *sedhēh khôvēs*). A field just outside of Jerusalem where fullers or washermen washed the cloth material they were processing. A highway and a conduit for water passed through it (Isa 7:3; 36:2; NIV "Washerman's Field"). It was so near the city that the Assyrian Rabshakeh, standing and speaking in the field, could be heard by those on the city wall (2 Kings 18:17). Its exact site is in dispute.

FULLER'S SOAP. An alkali prepared from the ashes of certain plants and used for cleansing and fulling new cloth. The word is used figuratively in Malachi 3:2 (NIV "launderer's soap").

FUNERAL. The word does not occur in the KJV, and in NIV is found only twice, both times as an adjective (Jer 16:5; 34:5). Funeral rites differed with the place, the religion, and the times; except for royal burials in Egypt, the elaborate ceremonies we use today were not held.

Generally in Palestine there was no embalmment and the body was buried a few hours after death, sometimes in a tomb but more often in a cave. Coffins were unknown. The body was washed and often anointed with aromatic spices (John 12:7; 19:39). The procession of mourners, made up of relatives and friends of the deceased, was led by professional mourning women, whose shrieks and lamentations pierced the air. It was an insult to a man's reputation to be refused proper burial (Jer 22:19). The "Tombs of the Kings" on the east side of Jerusalem and the "garden tomb," where our Lord's body was laid, are evidences of the two types of burial. In Egypt the bodies were embalmed so skillfully that many of them are recognizable today after the lapse of thousands of years.

FURLONG (See WEIGHTS AND MEASURES)

Funeral procession showing men (dressed in short pleated skirts) carrying the deceased, his personal belongings (e.g., bed, chair, shoes), and offerings, on wall painting from the tomb of Ramose at Thebes, 12th Dynasty. Courtesy Egyptian Expedition, The Metropolitan Museum of Art (30.4.37).

FURNACE (Heb. *kivshān, kûr, attûn, 'ălîl, tannûr,* Gr. *kaminos*). Used to translate five Hebrew words, one Aramaic word, and one Greek word in Scripture. Furnaces for central heating are not mentioned in the Bible, nor are they much used today in Bible lands. The burning fiery furnace of Daniel 3 (Aram. *'attûn*, used ten times in the OT, all in Dan 3) was probably a smelting furnace and was used only incidentally for human punishment. Furnaces were used for melting—Proverbs 17:3 (gold), Ezekiel 22:22 (silver), 22:18 (copper, tin, iron, and lead)—and for baking bread (Neh 3:11 JB, KJV, MLB, NASB; "ovens" in NIV, RSV). The word "furnace" is sometimes used figuratively—e.g., to refer to Egypt (Deut 4:20) and to the punishment of the wicked at the end of the world (Matt 13:42, 50). Found in modern times, Solomon's ingenious smelting furnaces near Elath on the Gulf of Aqabah are arranged so that the constant north wind furnished a natural draft for melting the brass or copper. After being prepared there, the metal was taken to the plain of the Jordan for casting (1 Kings 7:46).

FURNISHINGS (Heb. *hār, kēlîm,* Gr. *skevē*). In the Bible the principal reference to furnishings is in the articles in and about the tabernacle and the temple. The main items were the large altar and the laver, outside; then the table of the bread of the Presence, the lampstand or "candlestick," and the altar of incense in the Holy Place; then in the Most Holy Place the ark of the covenant (Exod 25–40). Generally beds were mats, spread on the floor and rolled up during the day, though Og of Bashan is said to have had a bed of iron (Deut 3:11). The tables in OT times were generally very low and people sat on the floor to eat. Royal tables were often higher (Judg 1:7), as were those in NT times (Mark 7:28).

Furniture found at Thebes, including a painted pottery stand, table, seat, and low chair of acacia wood with a high back inlaid with ivory and ebony. About 1250 B.C. Reproduced by courtesy of the Trustees of the British Museum.

FUTURE LIFE (See ESCHATOLOGY)

G

GAAL (gā'ăl, Heb. *ga'al, loathing*). A son of Ebed (Judg 9:26–41), captain of a band of freebooters who incited the Shechemites to rebel against the rule of Abimelech. After the death of his father Gideon, Abimelech murdered all but one of his seventy brothers so that he might become king of Shechem (9:1–5). After gaining the confidence of the men of Shechem, Gaal boasted under intoxication that he could overcome Abimelech if made leader of the Shechemites. Zebul, the governor of Shechem, was jealous of Gaal and secretly relayed this information to Abimelech who set up an ambush by night with four companies against Shechem. In the morning when Gaal went out and stood in the gate of the city, Abimelech and his army rose up out of hiding and chased Gaal and his company into the city, but Zebul turned them out. Abimelech fought against the rebels, killed them, destroyed their city, and sowed it with salt (9:42–45). Nothing more is known of Gaal, but clearly Abimelech's weakness was foolhardy boasting, which he failed to make good in action.

GAASH (gā'ăsh, Heb. *ga'ash, quaking*). A hill near Mount Ephraim. On its north side was Timnath Serah, the city given to Joshua (Josh 19:49–50), where he was buried (Judg 2:9). The "ravines of Gaash" were Hiddai's native place (2 Sam 23:30).

GABA (See GEBA)

GABBAI (găb'ā-ī, Heb. *gabbay, collector*). A chief of Benjamin after the Captivity (Neh 11:8).

GABBATHA (găb'à-thà, Aram *gabbetha', height, ridge*). The place called "the Stone Pavement" (John 19:13). Here Pilate sat on the Bema, or judgment seat, and sentenced Jesus before the people. Josephus (*Antiq*. 15.8.5) states that the temple was near the castle of Antonia and implies that Herod's palace was near the castle (15.11.5). Therefore, if Pilate was residing in Herod's palace at Passover time in order to keep a watchful eye on the Jews, he was staying near the castle. An early pavement consisting of slabs of stones three feet (one m.) square and a foot (one-third m.) or more thick has been excavated near here. This may well have been the pavement where Jesus was brought from the judgment hall for sentencing.

GABRIEL (gā'brĭ-ĕl, Heb. *gavrî'ēl, man of God*, Gr. *Gabriēl*). An angel mentioned four times in Scripture, each time bringing a momentous message. He interpreted to Daniel the vision of the ram and the goat (Dan 8:16–17). In Daniel 9:21–22 he explained the vision of the seventy weeks. Gabriel announced to Zechariah the birth of John, forerunner of the Messiah (Luke 1:11–20); and he was sent to Mary with the unique message of Jesus' birth (1:26–38). His credentials are the ideal for every messenger of God: "I am Gabriel. I stand in the presence of God, and I have been sent to speak to you and to tell you this good news" (1:19). The Bible does not define his status as an angel, but he appears in the Book of Enoch (chs. 9, 20, 40) as an archangel.

GAD (Heb. *gādh, fortune*). 1. Jacob's seventh son, firstborn of Zilpah, Leah's handmaid (Gen 30:9–11). Of his personal life nothing is known except that he had seven sons at the time of the descent into Egypt (46:16).

The Gadites numbered 45,650 adult males at the census at Sinai (Num 1:24–25), but at the second census their number had fallen to 40,500 (26:18). Their position on the march was south of the tabernacle, next to Reuben. These two tribes and the half-tribe of Manasseh remained shepherds like their forefathers, and because of their "very large herds and flocks" (32:1) they requested of Moses the rich pasture lands east of Jordan for their possession. This was granted (Josh 18:7) on the condition that they accept their responsibility and accompany the nine and a half tribes across Jordan in warfare against the Canaanites. The warriors of these two and a half

Detail of the Gabbatha, or Pavement (see John 19:13), under the Convent of Our Lady of Sion in Jerusalem, showing marks of games cut in the flagstone, for the amusement of the Roman soldiers. Architectural remains in the area reveal an impressive courtyard with surrounding galleries. Courtesy Zev Radovan.

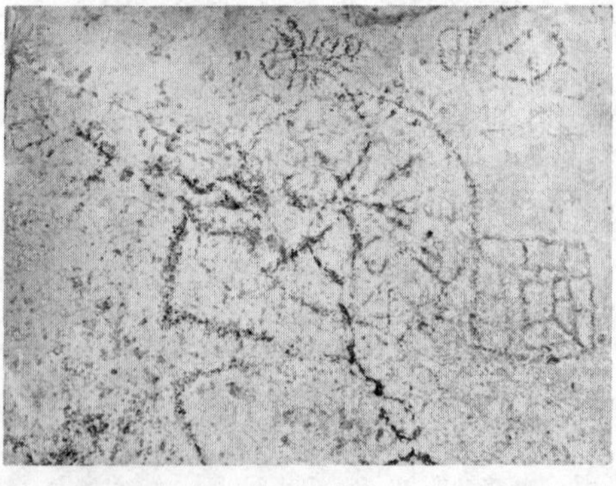

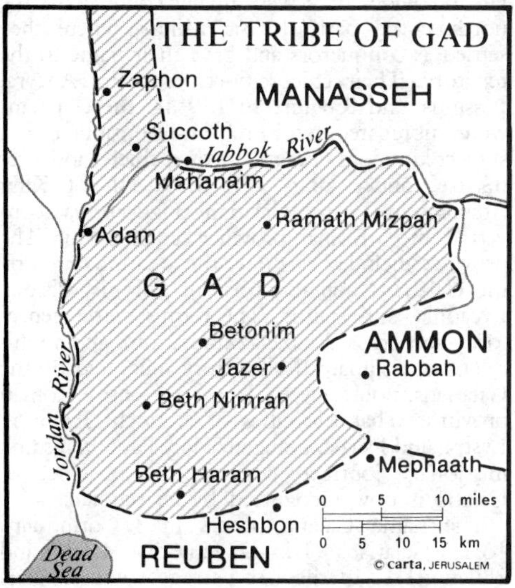

tribes took the lead in the conquest of western Palestine (1:12–18; 4:12) and returned to their families with Joshua's blessing (22:1–9). Fearing that the Jordan would alienate their children from the fellowship and faith of the western tribes, they erected a huge altar called "Ed" in the KJV ("witness") as evidence of their unity in race and faith (22:10–34). A satisfactory explanation removed the thought of war, which seemed inevitable at first over a schismatic religion.

The territory of Gad, difficult to define, was formerly ruled by Sihon, king of the Amorites. It lay chiefly in the center of the land east of Jordan, with the half-tribe of Manasseh on the north and Reuben to the south. The northern border reached as far as the Sea of Kinnereth (Josh 13:27); the southern border seems to have been just above Heshbon (13:26), though cities below this were built by Gad (Num 32:34). One of these is Dibon, where the famous Moabite Stone was found.

Genesis 49:19 seems to describe the military prowess of the Gadites. Moses said of them: "Blessed is he who enlarges Gad's domain! Gad lives there like a lion . . . " (Deut 33:20). Because they trusted in the Lord and cried to him for help, they totally defeated the Hagrites (1 Chron 5:18–22). It was natural for men of such faith and ability to extend their borders as far as Gilead (5:16). The Gadites who joined David were "brave warriors, ready for battle. . . . Their faces were the faces of lions, and they were as swift as gazelles in the mountains" (1 Chron 12:8). Other famous men of Gilead or Gad were Barzillai (2 Sam 17:27; 19:31–40) and Elijah. The land of Gad was along the battlefield between Syria and Israel (2 Kings 10:33). Gad finally was carried captive by Assyria (2 Kings 15:29; 1 Chron 5:26), and Ammon seized their land and cities (Jer 49:1).

2. The seer or prophet of King David. He advised David to get out of the stronghold and flee from Saul into Judah (1 Sam 22:5). Later he gave David his choice of punishment from the Lord for his sin in numbering the soldiers of Israel (2 Sam 24:11–17; 1 Chron 21:9–17) and told him to build an altar to the Lord on the threshing floor of Araunah (2 Sam 24:18). Gad assisted in arranging the musical services of the temple (2 Chron 29:25) and recorded the acts of David in a book (1 Chron 29:29).

3. A Canaanite god of fortune, seen in compound names such as Baal Gad (Josh 11:17; 12:7; 13:5) and Migdal Gad (15:37). AMR

GADARA, GADARENES (găd'à-rà, găd-à-rēnz', Gr. *Gadarēnoi, Gadara*). Gadara was a member of the Decapolis and is associated with "the country of the Gadarenes" in the Gospels (Matt 8:28; Mark 5:1; Luke 8:26, 37). NIV renders "Gerasenes" in the Mark and Luke references, but see footnote on each. Its ruins are identified with Um Keis today on a steep hill five miles (eight km.) SE of the Sea of Galilee and three miles (five km.) south of the Hieromax or Yarmuk River. At the foot of the hill to the north were hot springs and baths. When Christ came across the lake from Capernaum, he landed at the SE corner where the steep bank descends from the eastern highlands into the Jordan Valley. Two demoniacs met him, and Jesus cast many demons out of them. There were pigs feeding nearby, and when Jesus allowed the demons to enter them, they ran headlong down the steep slope into the lake and were drowned. In the cliffs around Gadara, or Um Keis, tombs have been excavated out of the limestone, some measuring twenty feet (six m.) square, with side recesses for bodies. Like the demoniacs, people still dwell in them today. Nearby there is a field of several acres strewn with stone coffins and their lids. This description would hardly fit Gerasa, a town some fifty miles (eighty-three km.) south of the Sea of Galilee, though it might be appropriate to refer generally to it as the "region of the Gerasenes," which is the reading of an important manuscript in Mark and Luke. Some texts of Matthew and Luke read

The country of the Gadarenes, with a view of the Yarmuk River, near the site of the Decapolis city of Gadara. This region, when visited by Jesus, saw the deliverance of two demon-possessed men (Matt 8:28). Courtesy Zev Radovan.

"region of the Gergesenes," which is identified with the present Khersa farther north on the eastern shore of the lake. This might not be improper if the town was under the jurisdiction of the larger Gadara. Khersa's steep hill rising from the water's edge with rock caves suitable for tombs does meet the narrative description of the Gospels. In Roman times Gadara was the best fortified city in Perea, and its remains are still impressive. A Roman street can be seen with its fallen colonnades on either side. AMR

GADDI (găd'ī, Heb. *gaddî*). The tribe of Manasseh's representative among the twelve spies (Num 13:11).

GADDIEL (găd'ĭ-ĕl, Heb. *gaddî 'al*). The tribe of Zebulun's representative among the twelve spies (Num 13:10).

GADFLY (See ANIMALS)

GADI (gā'dī). Father of Menahem, who usurped the throne of Israel from Shallum (2 Kings 15:14–20).

GAHAM (gā'hăm). A son of Nahor, brother of Abraham, by his concubine Reumah (Gen 22:24).

GAHAR (gā'hȧr). A family of temple servants (KJV Nethinim) who returned with Zerubbabel to Jerusalem (Ezra 2:47).

GAIUS (gā'yŭs, Gr. *Gaios*). 1. A Macedonian who traveled with Paul on his third missionary journey and was seized in the riot at Ephesus (Acts 19:29).

2. A man of Derbe who was one of those accompanying Paul from Macedonia to Asia (Acts 20:4).

3. A Corinthian whom Paul baptized (1 Cor 1:14). Since Paul wrote the Letter to the Romans from Corinth, this may be the same Gaius who was his host "whose hospitality I and the whole church here enjoy" (Rom 16:23)—either the Christians assembled in his house or they were given lodging there.

4. The addressee of 3 John. A convert of John, he is spoken of as "my dear friend" (3 John 1) and is commended for his love and hospitality to traveling preachers of the gospel (3 John 5–8).

GALAL (gā'lăl). The name of two Levites: 1. 1 Chronicles 9:15.

2. 1 Chronicles 9:16; Nehemiah 11:17.

GALATIA (gȧ-lā'shĭ-ȧ). The designation in NT times of a territory in north-central Asia Minor, also a Roman province in central Asia Minor. The name was derived from the people called Galatians (*Galatia*), a Greek modification of their original name *Keltoi* or *Keltai,* Celtic tribes from ancient Gaul. After having invaded Macedonia and Greece about 280 B.C., they crossed into Asia Minor on the invitation of Nikomedes I, king of Bithynia, to aid him in a civil war. After ravaging far and wide, they were finally confined to the north-central part of Asia Minor, where they settled as conquerors and gave their name to the territory. Their chief city-centers were Ancyra, Pessinus, and Ravium. In 189 B.C. the Galatians were subjugated by Rome and continued as a subject kingdom under their own chiefs, and after 63 B.C. under kings. On the death of King Amyntas in 25, the Galatian kingdom was converted into a Roman province called Galatia. The province included not only the area inhabited by the Galatians but also parts of Phrygia, Pisidia, Lycaonia, and Isauria. The term *Galatia* henceforth carried a double connotation: geographically, to designate the territory inhabited by the Galatians, politically to denote the entire Roman province. That the cities of Antioch, Iconium, Lystra, and Derbe, evangelized by Paul on his first missionary journey, were in the province of Galatia is now recognized by all scholars.

The name Galatia occurs in 1 Corinthians 16:1; Galatians 1:2; 2 Timothy 4:10; and 1 Peter 1:1. In the last passage some scholars think the reference may be to the European Gaul. In Acts 16:6 and 18:23 the name is an adjective (*Galatikē chōra*), the *Galatian country* or region. Luke apparently means the district, not the province, since in Acts, when speaking of Asia Minor, he uses the old ethnographic designations. The context in 1 Peter 1:1 seems clearly to indicate that the province is meant. Paul's general practice of using political designations points to that usage also in Galatians 1:1 and 1 Corinthians 16:1.

If *Galatia* in Galatians 1:2 refers to the Roman province, then the churches addressed were those founded on the first missionary journey (Acts 13–14); if it means the old ethnographic territory of Galatia, then the churches were established on the second missionary journey (16:6). DEH

GALATIANS, LETTER TO THE. A short but very important letter of Paul, containing his passionate polemic against the perversion or contamination of the gospel of God's grace. It has aptly been described as "the Magna Carta of spiritual emancipation," and it remains as the abiding monument of the liberation of Christianity from the trammels of legalism.

The contents of the letter so unmistakably reveal the traces of Paul's mind and style that its genuineness has never been seriously questioned even by the most radical NT critics. The testimony of the early church to its integrity and Pauline origin is strong and unambiguous.

Written to "the churches of Galatia," it is the only letter by Paul that is specifically addressed to a group of churches. They were all founded by Paul (Gal 1:8, 11; 4:19–20), were all the fruit of a single mission (3:1–3, 4:13–14), and were all affected by the same disturbance (1:6–7; 5:7–9). Paul had preached to them the gospel of the free grace of God through the death of Christ (1:6; 3:1–14). The Galatians warmly and affectionately received Paul and his message (4:12–15). The converts willingly endured persecution for their faith (3:4) and "were running a good race" when Paul left them (5:7).

The startling information received by Paul that a sudden and drastic change in attitude toward him and his gospel was taking place in the Galatian churches caused the writing of the letter. Certain Jewish teachers, who professed to be Christians and acknowledged Jesus as Messiah, were obscuring the simplicity of the gospel of free grace with their propaganda. They insisted that to faith in Christ must be added circumcision and obedience to the Mosaic Law (2:16; 3:2–3; 4:10, 21; 5:2–4; 6:12). Paul realized clearly that this teaching neutralized the truth of Christ's all-sufficiency for salvation and destroyed the message of justification by faith. By means of this letter Paul sought to save his converts from this fatal mixing of law and grace.

Because of the geographical and the political connotation of Galatia in NT times, two views concerning the location of the Galatian churches are advocated. The North-Galatian theory, which interprets the term in its old ethnographic sense to denote the territory inhabited by the Galatian tribes, locates the churches in north-central Asia Minor, holding that they were founded during the second missionary journey (Acts 16:6). The South-Galatian theory identifies these churches with those founded on the first missionary journey (Acts 13–14), located in the southern part of the Roman province of Galatia. The former was the unanimous view of the church fathers. They naturally adopted that meaning since in the second century the province was again restricted to ethnic Galatia and the double meaning of the term disappeared. The majority of the modern commentators support the latter view for the following reasons: It was Paul's habit to use provincial names in addressing his converts; it best explains the familiar reference to Barnabas in the letter; Acts 16:6 gives no hint of such a protracted mission as the older view demands; the older view cannot explain why the Judaizers would bypass the important churches in South Galatia; known conditions in these churches fit the picture in the letter.

Views concerning the place and date of composition are even more diverse. Advocates of the North-Galatian theory generally assign the letter to Ephesus during the third missionary journey, near the time of Romans. South-Galatian advocates vary considerably; some place it before the Jerusalem Conference (from Syrian Antioch), others place it on the second missionary journey (perhaps during the ministry at Corinth), and others place it as late as the third missionary journey.

The effort to date it before the Jerusalem Conference faces definite chronological difficulties. This early dating is not demanded by the silence of the letter concerning the conference decrees; the decrees were already known to the Galatians (Acts 16:4), and Paul, in writing the letter, would desire to establish his position on grounds independent of the Jerusalem church. Since he had apparently already visited the churches twice (Gal 1:9; 4:13), a date after Paul's second visit to the south-Galatian churches seems most probable (c. A.D. 52). During that second visit Paul had sought by warning and instructions to fortify his converts against the danger (1:9; 4:16; 5:3). The impact of the Judaizers on the Galatians threatened to destroy his work. The result was this bristling letter.

The contents of Galatians make evident Paul's purpose in writing. The first two chapters show that he was compelled to vindicate his apostolic authority. The Judaizers, in order to establish their own position, which contradicted Paul's teaching, had attempted to discredit his authority. Having vindicated his apostolic call and authority, Paul next sets forth the doctrine of justification to refute the teaching of the Judaizers. A reasoned, comprehensive exposition of the doctrine of justification by faith exposed the errors of legalism. Since the Judaizers asserted that to remove the believer from under the law opened the floodgates to immorality, Paul concluded his presentation with an elaboration of the true effect of liberty on the Christian life, showing that the truth of justification by faith logically leads to a life of good works. The letter may be outlined as follows:

- I. The Introduction (1:1–10).
  - A. The salutation (1:1–5).
  - B. The rebuke (1:6–10).
- II. The Vindication of His Apostolic Authority (1:11–2:21).
  - A. The reception of his gospel by revelation (1:11–24).
  - B. The confirmation of his gospel by the apostles at Jerusalem (2:1–10).
  - C. The illustration of his independence (2:11–21).
- III. The Exposition of Justification By Faith (3:1–4:31).
  - A. The elaboration of the doctrine (3:1–4:7).
    - 1. The nature of justification by faith (3:1–14).
    - 2. The limitations of the law and its relations to faith (3:15–4:7).
  - B. The appeal to drop all legalism (4:8–31).
- IV. The Nature of the Life of Christian Liberty (5:1–6:10).
  - A. The call to maintain their liberty (5:1).
  - B. The peril of Christian liberty (5:2–12).
  - C. The life of liberty (5:13–6:10).
- V. The Conclusion (6:11–17).
- VI. The Benediction (6:18).

Bibliography: J. B. Lightfoot, *Saint Paul's Epistle to the Galatians,* 1865 (on the Greek text); E. D. Burton, *The Epistle to the Galatians* (ICC), 1921 (on the Greek text); H. Ridderbos, *St. Paul's Epistle to the Churches of Galatia* (NIC), 1953; D. Guthrie, *Galatians* (NCB), 1969; H. D. Betz, *Galatians,* 1979; F. F. Bruce, *The Epistle of Paul to the Galatians,* 1982 (on the Greek text).

DEH

GALBANUM (See Plants)

GALEED (găl'ē-ĕd, Heb. *gal'ēdh, a heap of witnesses*). The name given by Jacob to the heap of stones that he and Laban raised on Mount Gilead as a memorial of their brotherly covenant (Gen 31:47–48). Sealing their compact of friendship with a common meal, Laban called the place *Jegarsahadutha,* the Aramaic or Chaldean equivalent, meaning "the heap of testimony."

GALILEAN (găl'ĭ-lē'ăn). A native or resident of Galilee (Matt 26:69; John 4:45; Acts 1:11; 5:37), often detected as such by his dialect (Mark 14:70).

GALILEE (găl'ĭ-lē, Heb. *hā-gālîl, the ring or circuit,* Gr. *Galilaia*). The most northerly of the three provinces of Palestine (Galilee, Samaria, Judea). Measuring approximately fifty miles (eighty-three km.) north to south and thirty miles (fifty km.) east to west, it was bounded on the west by the plain of Akka to the foot of Mount Carmel. The Jordan, the Sea of Galilee, Lake Huleh, and the spring at Dan marked off the eastern border. Its northern boundary went eastward from Phoenicia to Dan. The southern border ran in a southeasterly direction from the base of Mount Carmel and the Samaritan hills along the Valley of Jezreel (Plain of Esdraelon) to Mount Gilboa and Scythopolis (Beth Shan) to the Jordan. The Valley of Jezreel was a vital communications link between the coastal plain and the center of Palestine. For this reason, decisive battles were often fought here for possession of this desirable pass. The city of Megiddo was important for the control of the valley, and lends its name to *Har-Magedon,* the Hill of Megiddo, or Armageddon, where the conflict between Christ and the armies of the Antichrist is predicted to occur (Rev 16:16).

An imaginary line from the plain of Akka to the north end of the Sea of Galilee divided the country into Upper and Lower Galilee. "Galilee of the Gentiles" refers chiefly to Upper Galilee, which is separated from Lebanon by the Leontes River. It was the territory of Asher and Naphtali, where the ruins of Kedesh Naphtali, one of the cities of refuge can now be seen (Josh 20:7; 21–32). In this region lay the twenty towns given by Solomon to Hiram, King of Tyre, in payment for timber from Lebanon (1 Kings 9:11). The land was luxurious and productive, a rugged mountainous country of oaks and terebinths interrupted by fertile plains. It was said that Asher in the west would eat fat for bread and yield royal dainties and dip his feet in oil (Gen 49:20; Deut 33:24–25). The olive oil of Galilee has long been esteemed as of the highest quality. Lower Galilee was largely the heritage of Zebulun and Issachar. Less hilly and of a milder climate than Upper Galilee, it included the rich plain of Esdraelon (or Jezreel) and was a "pleasant" land (Gen 49:15) that would yield "treasures hidden in the sand" (Deut 33:19). The sand of these coasts was especially valuable for making glass. Important caravan trade routes carried their busy traffic through Galilee from Egypt and southern Palestine to Damascus in the NE as well as east and west from the Mediterranean to the Far East.

The northern part of Naphtali was inhabited by a mixed race of Jews and pagans (Judg 1:33). Its Israelite population was carried away captive to Assyria and was replaced by a colony of pagan immigrants (2 Kings 15:29; 17:24), hence called "Galilee of the nations" or "Gentiles" (Isa 9:1; Matt 4:13, 15–16). During and after the captivity, the predominant mixture of Gentile races impoverished the worship of Judaism. For the same reason the Galilean accent and dialect were noticeably peculiar (Matt 26:73). This caused the southern Jews of purer blood and orthodox tradition to despise them (John 7:52). Nathanael asked, rather contemptuously, "Nazareth! Can anything good come from there?" (1:46). Yet its very darkness was the Lord's reason for granting more of the light of his presence and ministry to Galilee than to self-satisfied and privileged Judea. He was sent for "a light for the Gentiles" (Isa 42:6) as well as to the "lost sheep of Israel" (Matt 15:24). Wherever he found faith and repentance, he bestowed his blessing, whereas unbelief often hindered his activity (13:58). He preached his first public sermon in the synagogue at Nazareth in Lower Galilee, where he had been brought up (Luke 4:16–30). His disciples came from Galilee (Matt 4:18; John 1:43–44; Acts 1:11; 2:7); in Cana of Galilee he performed his first miracle (John 2:11). Capernaum in Galilee, the home of his manhood (Matt 4:13; 9:1), is where the first three Gospels present his major ministry. Galilee's debasement made some of its people feel their need of the Savior. This and its comparative freedom from priestly and pharisaical prejudice may have been additional reasons for its receiving the larger share of the Lord's ministry.

After the death of Herod the Great in 4 B.C., Herod Antipas governed the tetrarchy of Galilee (Luke 3:1) until A.D. 39. Jesus referred to him as "that fox" (13:32). Sepphoris was his capital at first, three miles (five km.) north of Nazareth, but about A.D. 20 he built a new capital on the shore of the Sea of Galilee and named it Tiberias, after the reigning emperor. Herod Agrippa I succeeded him and took the title of "king." After his death in 44 (Acts 12:23) Galilee was joined for a while to the Roman province of Syria, after which it was given to Agrippa II. It became the land of Zealots and patriots who, in their hatred of foreign rule and in their longing for the Messiah, incited the populace to rebellion, and this led Rome to destroy Jerusalem in A.D. 70. After the fall of Jerusalem, Galilee became famous for its rabbis and schools of Jewish learning. The Sanhedrin or Great Council was moved to Sepphoris and then to Tiberias on the western shore of the Sea of Galilee. This is most interesting in light of the fact that when Herod Antipas built Tiberias on top of a cemetery, strict Jews utterly abhorred the place. The Mishna was compiled here, and the Gemara was added, forming the Palestinian Talmud. The remains of splendid synagogues in Galilee, such as those at Capernaum and Korazin, still attest to the prosperity of the Jews there from the second to the seventh century.

In 1925 the famous "Galilee skull" was found in a cave near the Sea of Galilee, and in 1932, in a cave near Mount Carmel, Dr. Theodore D. McCown discovered a Paleolithic skeleton resembling primitive Neanderthal man.

Bibliography: D. Baly, *Geography of the Bible,* 1957, pp. 184–92; S. Abramsky, *Ancient Towns in Israel,* 1963, pp. 174–250; Y. Aharoni, *The Land of the Bible,* 1967, pp. 41ff., 121–353.

AMR

GALILEE, SEA OF. So called from its location east of Galilee, it is also called "the Lake of Gennesaret" (Luke 5:1), since the fertile Plain of Gennesaret lies on the NW (Matt 14:34). The OT calls it "the Sea of Kinnereth" (Heb. "harp-shaped," Num 34:11; Deut 3:17; Josh 13:27), from the town so named on its shore (Josh 19:35), of which Gennesaret is probably the corruption. "The Sea of Tiberias" is another designation (John 6:1; 21:10); associated with Tiberias, the capital of Herod Antipas. All its names were derived from places on the western shore. Its present name is *Bahr Tabariyeh.*

Located some sixty miles (one hundred km.) north of Jerusalem, its bed is but a lower depression of the Jordan Valley. The surface of the water is 685 feet (214 m.) below the level of the Mediterranean and it varies in depth up to 150 feet (47 m.). As the Jordan River plunges southward on its course from Mount Hermon to the Dead Sea, it enters the Sea of Galilee at its northern end and flows out of its southern end, a distance of thirteen miles (twenty-two km.). The greatest width of the sea is eight miles (thirteen km.), at Magdala. The view from the Nazareth road to Tiberias is beautiful. The bare hills on the west, except at Khan Minyeh (present Capernaum) where there is a small cliff, are recessed from the shore. From the eastern side, the western hills appear to rise out of the water to a height of 2,000 feet (625 m.), while far to the north can be seen snowy Mount Hermon. The eastern hills rise from a coast of half a mile (one km.) in width and are flat along the summit. The whole basin betrays its volcanic origin, and this accounts for the cliffs of hard porous basalt and the hot springs at Tiberias, famous for their medicinal value. The warm climate produces tropical vegetation—the lotus thorn, palms, and indigo. The Plain of Gennesaret on the NW abounds with walnuts, figs, olives, grapes, and assorted wild flowers. The fresh water is sweet, sparkling, and transparent, with fish in abundance. The Gospel accounts picture fishing as a prosperous industry here in biblical times, but today, instead of fleets of fishing vessels, only a boat or two is seen. On these shores Jesus called his first disciples, four of whom were fishermen, and made them fishers of men (Matt 4:18; Luke 5:1–11).

The Sea of Galilee is noted for its sudden and violent storms caused by cold air sweeping down from the vast naked plateaus of Gaulanitis, the Hauran, and Mount Hermon through the ravines and gorges and converging at the head of the lake

A flock of sheep and goats along the shore of the Sea of Galilee. Courtesy Zev Radovan.

where it meets warm air. Jesus rebuked just such a storm (Mark 4:39). Here also Jesus walked on the tempestuous water (Matt 14:22–34; Mark 6:45–53; John 6:15–21).

The Sea of Galilee was the focus of Galilee's wealth. Nine cities of 15,000 or more stood on its shores. To the NW was Capernaum, the home of Peter and Andrew (Mark 1:29) and where Matthew collected taxes (Matt 9:9). It was the scene of much of Jesus' Galilean ministry. Below this, on the western side, was Magdala, home of Mary Magdalene; three miles (five km.) south was Tiberias, the magnificent capital of Galilee. On the NE corner was Bethsaida, the native town of Philip, Andrew, and Peter (John 1:44) and one-time capital of Philip the Tetrarch. Gergesa lay to the south. Of these towns—once thriving with dyeing, tanning, boat building, fishing, and fish curing—two are now inhabited, namely Magdala, consisting of a few mud huts, and Tiberias. AMR

GALL (See PLANTS)

GALLERY. Three terraced passageways or balconies running around the chambers in the temple of Ezekiel's vision (Ezek 41:15–16; 42:3, 5–6). The upper two stories were shorter because of the absence of supporting pillars.

GALLEY (See SHIPS)

GALLIM (găl'lĭm, Heb. *gallîm, heaps*). A town of Benjamin named with Laish and Anathoth (Isa 10:30). "Daughter of Gallim" refers to its inhabitants. It was the home of Phalti, the son of Laish (1 Sam 25:44). Site uncertain.

GALLIO (gal'ĭ-ō, *Gr. Galliōn*). Roman proconsul of Achaia when Paul was in Corinth (A.D. 51). Alarmed at the inroads that the gospel was making, the Jews in Corinth brought Paul before Gallio, of whom the Roman philosopher Seneca had said, "No mortal was ever so sweet to one as Gallio was to all." The Jews hoped to convince Gallio that Paul was guilty of an offense against a lawful religion, and hence against the Roman government itself (Acts 18:12–17), but Gallio rejected their argument. The Greeks then beat the chief ruler of the synagogue, but Gallio remained indifferent to the incident. A more stern governor might have arrested the violence at once, but in the providence of God, Gallio's action amounted to an authoritative decision that Paul's preaching was not subversive against Rome. This gave the apostle the protection he needed to continue his preaching there. Gallio did not become a Christian; he died by committing suicide.

GALLON (See WEIGHTS AND MEASURES)

GALLOWS. A pole for executing and exhibiting a victim by impalement. Made seventy-five feet (twenty-three m.) high by Haman for Mordecai (Esth 5:14; 6:4).

GAMALIEL (gȧ-mā'lĭ-ĕl, Heb. *gamlî'ēl, reward of God,* Gr. *Gamaliēl*). 1. Son of Pedahzur and

Inlaid game board (10.6 inches [27 cm.] long) and playing pieces from Ur (twenty-fifth century B.C.), made of shell, bone, red limestone, strips of lapis, set in bitumen. Reproduced by courtesy of the Trustees of the British Museum.

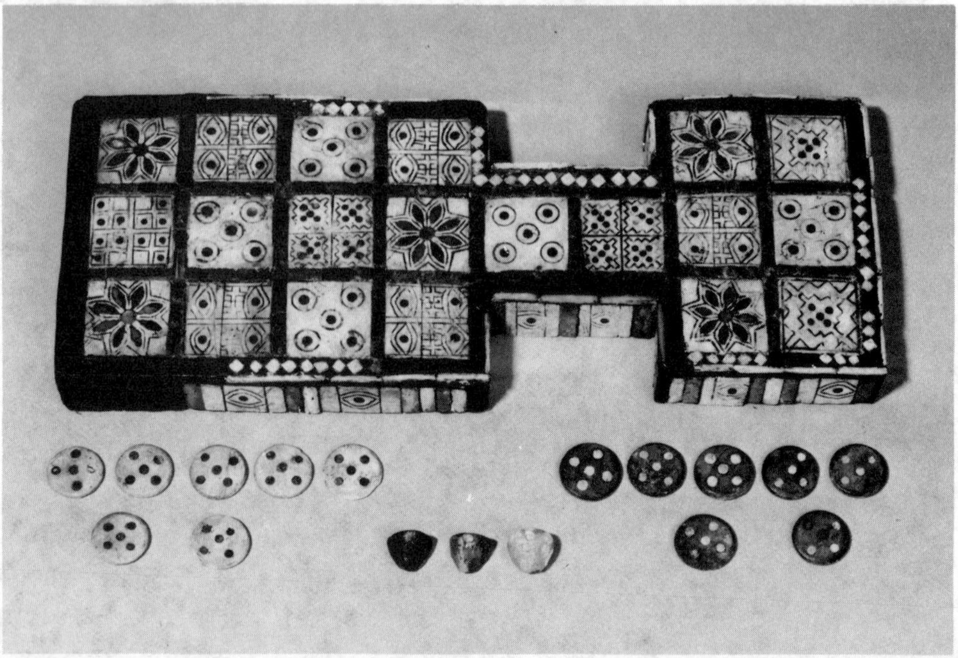

chief of the tribe of Manasseh (Num 1:10; 2:20; 7:54, 59; 10:23). He assisted Moses in numbering the people.

2. A Pharisee and eminent doctor of the law; grandson of Hillel and first of only seven rabbis to be given the title of Rabban. Paul was one of his pupils (Acts 22:3). When the enraged Sanhedrin sought to kill the apostles for their bold testimony to Christ, Gamaliel stood up in the council and urged judicious caution on the ground that if the new doctrine was of God they could not overthrow it, and if it were of man it would fail (5:34–39). Because he was held in esteem by all the people, his counsel was valued, and God used it to give a needed respite to the infant church. Inasmuch as Gamaliel believed in God's sovereign control, his advice was sound; but also underlying it was the premise of pragmatism that what succeeds is good and what fails is evil. On the contrary, the Scriptures point out that the wicked do often prosper (Ps 73:12) and the godly are often destitute (109:22–26). Truth must be tested by the standard of God's Word. The traditional belief that Gamaliel afterward became a Christian is incongruous with the high esteem accorded him in the Talmud: "Since Rabban Gamaliel died, the glory of the Law has ceased."

GAMES. Not much is known about the amusements of the ancient Israelites, partly because the earnestness of the Hebrew character did not give them prominence. Instead of public games, the great religious feasts gave them their occasions for national gatherings. There are references to dancing (Ps 30:11; Jer 31:13; Luke 15:25). The dance led by Jephthah's daughter (Judg 11:34) and the dances of the Israelite women mentioned in 1 Samuel 18:6; 21:11; 29:5 were public dances of rejoicing to celebrate a warrior's victory. Religious dancing was engaged in by Miriam and the women of Israel at the Red Sea (Exod 15:20), by the Israelites around the golden calf at Sinai (32:19), and by David before the ark (2 Sam 6:14, 16). (See also Ps 149:3; 150:4.) Of course, children of every race have their games. Zechariah prophesied that "the city streets will be filled with boys and girls playing there" (Zech 8:5). In the NT the only children's game mentioned is that of mimicking the wedding dance and the funeral wail to the music of the flute (Matt 11:16–17; Luke 7:32).

The public games of Greece and Rome were familiar to the Christians and non-Christians of the first century, providing the NT writers with rich source material to illustrate spiritual truths. Condemned criminals were thrown to lions in the arena as punishment and for sport. In 1 Corinthians 15:32 Paul alludes to fighting with beasts at Ephesus. When a Roman general returned home victorious, he led his army in a triumphal procession, at the end of which trailed the captives who were condemned to fight with beasts. Paul felt that in contrast to the proud Corinthians, the apostles had been put "on display, at the end of the procession, like men condemned to die in the arena." God had made them a spectacle to be gazed at and made sport of in the arena of the world (1 Cor 4:9). Nero used to clothe the Christians in beast skins when he exposed them to wild beasts. (Cf. 2 Tim 4:17, "I was delivered from the lion's mouth.")

In 1 Corinthians 9:24–25 the Isthmian games, celebrated every two years on the Isthmus of Corinth, are vividly alluded to. Held in honor of the Greek gods, the festival consisted of foot

Middle Bronze Age II (c. 1800–1500 B.C.) limestone game board from Beth Shemesh. Game pieces from Tell Beit Mirsim. Courtesy Israel Department of Antiquities and Museums. Exhibited and photographed by Israel Museum, Jerusalem.

Roman terracotta relief, made in Italy (last third of first century A.D.), illustrating a chariot race in which a four-horsed chariot approaches the three columns of the turning post. A *jubilator,* a rider who encourages the contestants, has already turned. Reproduced by courtesy of the Trustees of the British Museum.

races, horse races, chariot contests, jumping, wrestling, boxing, and throwing the discus and javelin. To the Greeks they were events of patriotic pride, a passion rather than a pastime, and thus made a suitable image of earnestness in the Christian race: "Do you not know that in a race all the runners run, but only one gets the prize? Run in such a way as to get the prize. Everyone who competes in the games goes into strict training. They do it to get a crown that will not last; but we do it to get a crown that will last forever." The coveted crown was a garland made of laurel, olive leaves, or pine needles; our crown is incorruptible (1 Peter 1:4) and therefore demands greater fidelity. If the competitor did not strive "according to the rules," he was not crowned (2 Tim 2:5). He had to keep to the bounds of the course, having previously trained himself for ten months with chastity, abstemious diet, the enduring of cold and heat, and extreme exercise. As in boxing, so in the Christian race, Paul beat his body and brought it under subjection, so that when he preached ("heralded"—the herald announced the name and country of each contestant and displayed the prizes) to others, he would not be rejected but receive the winner's crown (James 1:12). In view of the reward, Paul denied himself and became a servant of all in order to win more people to Jesus Christ. Christians do not beat the air, missing their opponent, but they fight certainly, with telling blows on the enemy (1 Cor 9:26–27). As the runner looks intently at the goal and discards every encumbrance, so Christians run, throwing aside not only sinful lusts but even harmless and otherwise useful things that would slow them down. They must run with "perseverance" the race set before them, fixing their eyes on Jesus, "the author and perfecter" of their faith (Heb 12:1–2). Paul used the same figure in addressing the Ephesians (Acts 20:24) and the Philippians (3:12–14). The Colossians were urged to let God's peace *rule as umpire* in their hearts, to restrain wrong passions so that they might attain the prize (Col 3:15). Other allusions to the language of games are in Ephesians 6:12, "our struggle is not against flesh and blood," and 2 Timothy 4:7, "I have fought the good fight, I have finished the race" (Gr. *I have struggled the good contest,* not merely a fight). See also 1 Timothy 6:12; Revelation 2:10. AMR

GAMMADIM (găm′á-dĭm, Heb. *gammādhîm*). Found only in Ezekiel 27:11 (KJV), the word is open to different interpretations. "Men of Gammad" (so NIV) were said to be in the towers of Tyre. ASV reads "valorous men," perhaps on the basis that foreigners would hardly be trusted to watch in those towers.

GAMUL (gā′mŭl, Heb. *gāmûl*). The head of the twenty-second course of priests (1 Chron 24:17).

GANGRENE (See DISEASES)

GARDEN (Heb. *gan, gannâh, a covered or hidden place;* Gr. *kēpos*). A cultivated piece of ground, usually in the suburbs, planted with flowers, vegetables, shrubs, or trees, fenced with a mud or stone wall (Prov 24:31) or thorny hedges (Isa

Tomb painting from Thebes, c. 1250 B.C., of an Egyptian gardener drawing water for his garden by means of a sweep or *shaduf,* a hand water-raising device consisting of a long pole pivoted to the top of a tall post and used to raise and lower the bucket. Courtesy The Metropolitan Museum of Art.

5:5), and guarded (whence "garden") by a watchman in a lodge (1:8) or tower (Mark 12:10) to drive away wild beasts and robbers.

The quince, citron, almond, and other fruits, herbs, and various vegetables and spices are mentioned as growing in gardens. A reservoir cistern, or still better a fountain of water, was essential to a good garden. See Song of Songs 4:15, "a garden fountain," i.e., a fountain sufficient to water many gardens.

The occurrence of no fewer than 250 botanical terms in the OT shows the Israelite fondness for flowers, fruits, and pleasant grounds. These are still a delight to the Oriental who lives in a hot, dry country. Every house court or yard generally had its shade tree. The vine that grew around the trellis or outside staircase was the emblem of the living and fruitful wife and happy home within (Ps 128:3). The "orchards" (Heb. *paradises*) were larger gardens especially for fruit trees. Solomon's gardens and fruit orchards with pools of water for irrigation (Eccl 2:4–6) very likely suggested the imagery of Song of Songs 4:12–15. The "king's garden" (2 Kings 25:4; Neh 3:15; Jer 39:4; 52:7) was near the pool of Siloam.

The Hebrews used gardens as burial places. The field of Machpelah, Abraham's burial ground, was a garden with trees in and around it (Gen 23:17). Manasseh and Amon were buried in Uzza's garden (2 Kings 21:18, 26). The Garden of Gethsemane was a favorite retreat of Jesus for meditation and prayer (Matt 26:36; John 18:1–2). In idolatrous periods gardens were the scenes of superstition and image worship, the awful counterpart of the primitive Eden (Isa 1:29; 65:3; 66:17). The new paradise regained by the people of God (Rev 22:1–5) suggests in a fuller way the old paradise planted by God but lost through sin (Gen 2:8).

The believer is a garden watered by the Holy Spirit (Jer 2:13; 17:7–8; John 4:13–14; 7:37–39). "A well-watered garden" expresses abundant happiness and prosperity (Isa 58:11; Jer 31:12) just as "a garden without water" (Isa 1:30) expresses spiritual, national, and individual barrenness and misery. AMR

GARDENER (See OCCUPATIONS AND PROFESSIONS: *Farmer*)

GAREB (gā′rĕb, Heb. *gārēv, scabby*). 1. An Ithrite, a member of one of the families of Kiriath Jearim (1 Chron 2:53) and one of David's mighty men (2 Sam 23:38; 1 Chron 11:40).

2. A hill near Jerusalem to which the city would expand, as foreseen by the prophet Jeremiah (31:39). The site is unknown.

GARLIC (See PLANTS)

GARMENTS (See DRESS)

GARMITE (gàr′mīt, Heb. *garmî*). A name applied to Keilah (1 Chron 4:19). Its meaning is obscure.

GARNER (See STOREHOUSE)

GARRISON (Heb. *matstsāv, netsîv*). Most of the OT occurrences of these words are translated "garrisons," but they also appear as "officer," "outpost," "pillar" (as when Lot's wife became a "pillar of salt," Gen 19:26), "place" (for the priests' feet in the crossing of the Jordan, Josh 4:3, 9), and "station." *Matstsāv* (ten OT occurrences) and netsîv (twelve OT occurrences) primarily refer to a military post for the occupation of a conquered country such as the Philistines had when they held the land of Israel (1 Sam 10:5; 13:3; 14:1, 6; 1 Chron 11:16). David put garrisons in Syria and Edom when he subjugated those people (2 Sam 8:6, 14; 1 Chron 18:13). Jehoshaphat put garrisons in "Judah and . . . Ephraim" to strengthen himself against Israel (2 Chron 17:2).

GASHMU (See GESHEM)

GATAM (gā′tăm, Heb. *ga'tām*). Grandson of Esau; an Edomite chief (Gen 36:11, 16; 1 Chron 1:36).

GATE (Heb. usually *sha'ar, opening,* Gr. *pylē*). The entrance to enclosed buildings, grounds, or cities. It was at the gates of a city that the people of the Middle East went for legal business, conversation, bargaining, and news. The usual gateway consisted of double doors plated with metal (Ps 107:16; Isa 45:2). Wooden doors without iron plating were easily set on fire (Judg 9:52; Neh 2:3, 17). Some gates were made of brass, as was the "gate called Beautiful" of Herod's temple (Acts 3:2), more costly than nine others of the outer court that had been "poured over" with gold and silver (Josephus, *War,* 5.5.3). Still others were of solid stone (Isa 54:12; Rev 21:21). Massive stone doors are found in ancient towns of Syria, single slabs several inches thick and ten feet (three m.) high, turning on pivots above and below. Gates ordinarily swung on projections that fitted into sockets on the post and were secured with bars of wood (Nah 3:13) or of metal (1 Kings 4:13; Ps 107:16; Isa 45:2).

As the weakest points in a city's walls, the gates were often the object of enemy attack (Judg 5:8; 1 Sam 23:7; Ezek 21:15, 22) and therefore were flanked by towers (2 Sam 18:24, 33; 2 Chron 14:7; 26:9). To "possess the gates" was to possess the city (Gen 24:60). Gates were shut at night and opened again in the morning (Deut 3:5; Josh 2:5, 7).

Markets were held at the gate, and the main item sold there often gave its name to the gate ("Sheep Gate," Neh 3:1; "Fish Gate," Neh 3:3; "Horse Gate," Neh 3:28). The gate was the place where people met to hear an important announcement (2 Chron 32:6; Jer 7:2; 17:19–27) or the reading of the law (Neh 8:1, 3) or where the elders transacted legal business (Deut 16:18; 21:18–20; Josh 20:4; Ruth 4:1–2, 11). "Those who sit at the gate mock me, and I am the song of the drunkards" (Ps 69:12)—i.e., he was an object of abusive language not only among the drunks but in the grave deliberations of the judges in the place of justice. The gate was also the king's or

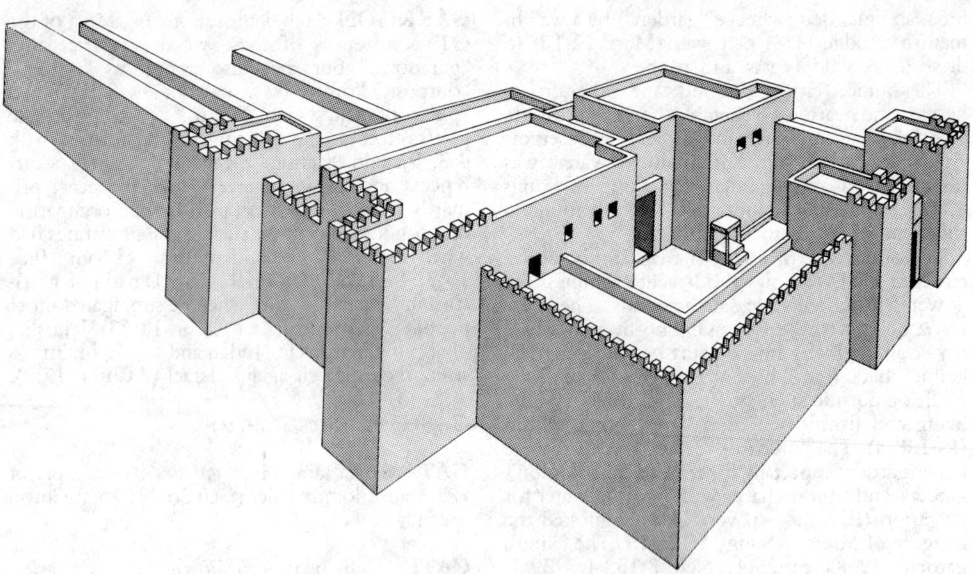

Reconstruction of the gate at Dan, tenth to ninth centuries B.C. Courtesy Carta, Jerusalem.

chief's place of audience (2 Sam 19:8; 1 Kings 22:10). Daniel sat in the gate of King Nebuchadnezzar as "ruler over the entire province of Babylon" (Dan 2:48–49 KJV; NIV "royal court"). Regarded as specially sacred, the threshold in Assyrian palaces bore cuneiform inscriptions and was guarded by human-headed bulls with eagles' wings. In Israel, sentences from the Law were inscribed on and above the posts and gates of private houses (Deut 6:9). Josiah destroyed the high places near the gates that were used for heathen sacrifices (2 Kings 23:8).

Figuratively, gates refer to the glory of a city (Isa 3:26; 14:31; Jer 14:2) or to the city itself (Ps 87:2; 122:2). In Matthew 16:18 the statement that the "gates of Hades" will not overcome the church is a reference either to the failure of the infernal powers to defeat the church or to the church's greater power to retain her members than the grave has over its victims. AMR

Reconstruction of the Israelite gate at Beersheba based on archaeological evidence. Tenth century B.C. Courtesy Carta, Jerusalem.

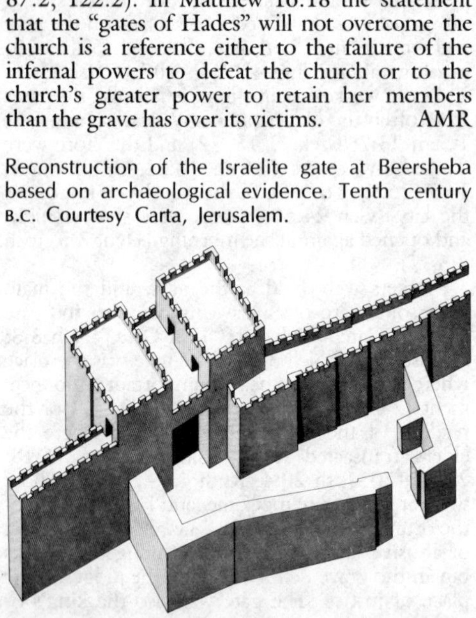

GATH (găth, Heb. *gath, winepress*). One of the five great Philistine cities (Ashdod, Gaza, Ashkelon, Gath, and Ekron [Josh 13:3; 1 Sam 6:17]). Its people were the Gittites, including Goliath and other giants (2 Sam 21:19–22). In harmony with this fact is the record of the Anakites' presence in Gath after Joshua had destroyed the neighboring territory (Josh 11:22). It was one of the five cities to which the Philistines carried the ark of God and whose people God afflicted with an outbreak of tumors (1 Sam 5:8–9). David fled from Saul to Gath, where he feigned madness to save his life (21:10–15). The second time he visited Gath, King Achish assigned him Ziklag as a residence (27:2–6). During his sixteen months there, he won the confidence of the king through subterfuge and intrigue (27:7–29:11). Some of David's six hundred followers were Gittites, one of whom was his loyal friend Ittai. They may have attached themselves to him at this time or when he defeated the Philistines (2 Sam 8:1; 15:18–21). Although David conquered it (1 Chron 18:1), Gath retained its own king (1 Kings 2:39). Rehoboam, Solomon's son, rebuilt and fortified the town (2 Chron 11:8). Later, Hazael, king of Syria, captured Gath from Jehoash, king of Judah (2 Kings 12:17), but Uzziah won it back (2 Chron 26:6). In a reference to the fall of this walled city Amos sounds a warning to those at ease in Zion (Amos 6:12). The omission of Gath from the later lists of the five cities (Amos 1:6, 8; Zeph 2:4–5; Zech 9:5–6) indicates it had lost its place among them by that time. Its site today is uncertain. Gath lay on the border between Judah and Philistia, between Socoh and Ekron (1 Sam 17:1, 52). Tell es-Safiyeh favors this description, lying on a hill at the foot of Judah's mountains, ten miles (seventeen km.) east of Ashdod and ten miles (seventeen km.) SE of Ekron.

GATH HEPHER (Heb. *gath ha-hēpher, winepress of the well*). A town on Zebulun's border (Josh 19:12–13). Birthplace of Jonah the prophet (2 Kings 14:25). Now El Meshed, where his supposed tomb is still shown, on a hill two miles (three km.) from Nazareth in Galilee.

GATH RIMMON (Heb. *gath rimmôn, winepress of Rimmon* or *pomegranates*). 1. A city of Dan on the Philistine plain, given to the Levites (Josh 19:45; 21:24; 1 Chron 6:69).

2. A town of Manasseh, west of the Jordan, assigned to the Levites (Josh 21:25). In 1 Chronicles 6:70 this is called Bileam, which is probably the true reading in Joshua 21:25, an error due to a copyist's eye catching "Gath Rimmon" in the previous verse.

GAULANITIS (See GOLAN)

GAZA (gā'zȧ, Heb. *'azzâh, strong*, Gr. *Gaza*). One of the five chief Philistine cities and the most southwesterly toward Egypt. Originally a seaport, the town moved to a hill three miles (five km.) inland on the great caravan route between Syria and Egypt. Here it became an important rest stop on the edge of the desert and a popular trading center. Its position and *strength* (the meaning of its name) made it the key of this line of communications. It is called by its Hebrew name *Azzah* in the KJV (Deut 2:23; 1 Kings 4:24; Jer 25:20).

Originally a Canaanite city (Gen 10:19), Gaza was assigned by Joshua to Judah (Josh 15:47) but was not occupied until after Judah had taken it (Judg 1:18), as the Anakites were still present (Josh 11:22; 13:3). The Philistines soon recovered it (Judg 13:1), and Samson perished there while destroying his captors (16:1, 21). Solomon ruled over it (1 Kings 4:24), but it was Hezekiah who gave the decisive blow to the Philistines (2 Kings 18:8). God through Amos threatened Gaza with destruction by fire for her transgressions (Amos 1:6). This was fulfilled by one of the pharaohs of Egypt (Jer 47:1). The predictions that Gaza would be forsaken (Zeph 2:4) and that its king would perish (Zech 9:5; i.e., its Persian satrap, or petty king subordinate to the great king of Persia) were fulfilled by Alexander the Great, who took the city in 332 B.C., after it had resisted his siege for two months. He bound Betis the satrap to a chariot and dragged him around the city; he killed ten thousand of Gath's inhabitants, selling the rest as slaves. The town was desolated again by fire and sword by the Maccabees in 96 B.C. In turn, Gaza passed under the control of Syria and Rome.

Philip met the Ethiopian eunuch on "the road—the desert road—that goes down from Jerusalem to Gaza" (Acts 8:26). Once Gaza was the seat of a Christian church and a bishop in the midst of Greek culture and temples, but most of its people turned to Islam in A.D. 634. Now, of its twenty thousand inhabitants, only a few hundred are Christians, the rest Muslims.

Modern Ghuzzeh is the metropolis of the Gaza Strip, which is crowded with Arab refugees today. North of Ghuzzeh lies an extensive olive grove whose fruit is used to make soap. The city's trade in corn is considerable, the corn still being ground by millstones such as Samson was forced to work at in his prison house at Gaza (Judg 16:21). The Tel el Muntar, or "hill of the watchman" (2 Kings 18:8), SE of Gaza, is the hill up which Samson carried the gates of the city (Judg 16:3). AMR

GAZELLE (See ANIMALS)

GAZER (See GEZER)

GAZEZ (gā'zĕz). 1. Son of Ephah.

2. Grandson of Ephah, Caleb's concubine (1 Chron 2:46).

GAZZAM (găz'ăm). One of the temple servants (Nethinim, KJV) whose posterity returned from exile (Ezra 2:48; Neh 7:51).

GE HARASHIM (gĕ hăr'ă-shĭm, Heb. *gê' hărāshîm, valley of craftsmen*). Located east of Joppa between Ono and Lod (Lydda), it was settled by one Joab, apparently of Judah (1 Chron 4:14). It received its name because artificers or craftsmen lived there (Neh 11:35).

GEBA (gē'bȧ, Heb. *geva', hill*). A town in the territory of Benjamin (Josh 18:24; KJV Gaba), assigned to the Levites (Josh 21:17; 1 Chron 6:60; 8:6). There Jonathan defeated the Philistines (1 Sam 13:3); he and Saul remained there (13:16; KJV Gibeah). Geba is SW of Wady Suweinit, opposite Micmash (14:5), where Jonathan and his armor-bearer by a bold stratagem won an outstanding victory. Geba should be Gibeon in 2 Samuel 5:25 and 1 Chronicles 14:16 (so NIV). Asa fortified Geba with the stones and timber that Baasha had gathered to build Ramah (1 Kings 15:22). In the time of Hezekiah, Geba was the northernmost city of the kingdom of Judah, as Beersheba was its southernmost (2 Kings 23:8; 2 Chron 16:6). The Assyrians, marching toward Jerusalem, stored their baggage at Micmash, crossed the pass to Geba, and camped for a night (Isa 10:28–29). Men from Geba returned after exile (Ezra 2:26; Neh 7:30). Levites from Geba helped in the rebuilding of Jerusalem (Neh 11:31; 12:29). Zechariah 14:10 prophesied that the land would be made a plain from Geba to Rimmon, except for lofty Jerusalem.

GEBAL (gē'băl, Heb. *geval, border*, Gr. *Byblos, Biblos*). 1. A seaport of Phoenicia, between Sidon and Tripolis; modern Jebeil, twenty-five miles (forty-two km.) north of Beirut. In the fifteenth century B.C. it was subject to Egypt. Its history included periods of independence alternating with subjection to successive empires. In Greek and Roman times it was called Byblos, from the manufacture of papyrus there. Joshua 13:5–6 refers to the land of the Giblites or Gebalites, the land of Lebanon at the foot of Mount Hermon, as

Sarcophagus of King Ahiram of Byblos (Gebal, between Beirut and Tripoli), thirteenth century B.C. The king is seated on a throne before a table of offerings approached by seven attendants. On the edge of the lid is a dedication inscription written in Phoenician, one of the earliest examples of Phoenician script to be found. Courtesy Studium Biblicum Franciscanum, Jerusalem. Photo Manoug.

part of the land God gave to the children of Israel; God promised to drive out its inhabitants if Joshua would divide it by lot to the Israelites; but we have no record of his accepting the offer, and the Israelites never controlled Gebal. Expert stonemasonry was a major industry of Gebal (cf. 1 Kings 5:17–18, KJV "stonesquarers"). Shipbuilding was another, for Ezekiel 27:9 tells us that caulkers from Gebal worked on ships at Tyre. Skilled technologies, paper making, fine stonework, and seaworthy shipbuilding distinguished Gebal in addition to its raw materials and mass production.

2. A land between the Dead Sea and Petra; modern Jibal in NE Edom. It was allied with Israel's enemies (Ps 83:6–8).

GEBER (gē'bêr). 1. One of Solomon's twelve purveyors for southern Gilead (1 Kings 4:13; NIV "Ben Geber").

2. The son of Uri. He was over great pasture lands east of the Jordan (1 Kings 4:19). The two Gebers are sometimes identified as the same person.

GEBIM (gē'bĭm). A place near Anathoth and Nob, whose inhabitants fled at the approach of the Assyrian invaders (Isa 10:31).

GECKO (See ANIMALS)

GEDALIAH (gĕd'á-lī'á, Heb. *gedhalyâh*). 1. A son of Shaphan, King Josiah's secretary and governor of Mizpah (2 Kings 25:22–25; Jer 39:14; 40:5–16; 41:1–18; 43:6). This Judean of high rank was the one who shared Jeremiah's views and protected him from the anti-Chaldeans. Nebuchadnezzar made him governor over "the poor people left in the land," but he ruled for only two months. The anniversary of his treacherous murder is observed as one of the four Jewish feasts (Zech 7:5; 8:19).

Decorative stone capital showing a figure in the doorway of a temple structure surmounted on the head of the goddess Hathor. From temple at Gebal (Byblos), a city of the N. Phoenician coast between Beirut and Tripoli, c. 500 B.C. Courtesy Réunion des Musées Nationaux.

2. Grandfather of the prophet Zephaniah (Zeph 1:1).

3. One of the six sons of Jeduthun, a harpist and head of the second of twenty-four companies, his consisting of twelve musicians (1 Chron 25:8–9).

4. A son of Pashhur, and the prince who caused Jeremiah to be imprisoned (Jer 38:1–6).

5. A priest, of the sons of Jeshua, who had taken a foreign wife during the Exile (Ezra 10:18).

GEDER (gē'dêr, Heb. *gedher*). A Canaanite royal city near Debir, taken by Joshua (Josh 12:13); perhaps Beth Gader (1 Chron 2:51) and the birthplace of Baal-Hanan the Gederite (27:28).

GEDERAH (gĕ-dē'rá, Heb. *gedhērâh, wall*). A town on the heights between the valleys of Sorek and Aijalon in the Shephelah of Judah (Josh 15:36, 41), also called Gedorothaim (two walls) and Gederoth (walls); modern Jedireh. Jozabad (1 Chron 12:4) was a Gederathite. For KJV "those that dwelt among plants and hedges"

(4:23), NIV has "who lived at Netaim and Gederah."

GEDEROTH (gĕ-dē'rŏth, Heb. *gedhēroth, walls*). A town named with Gederah and others as being "in the western foothills" of the area of the tribe of Judah (Josh 15:41).

GEDEROTHAIM (gĕ-dėrŏthā'ĭm, *two walls or two sheep pens*). Another name for Gederah (Josh 15:36).

GEDOR (gē'dôr, Heb. *gedhôr, wall*). 1. A city in the hill country of Judah (Josh 15:58); now Khirbet Jedur, a few miles north of Hebron.

2. The town where Jeroham lived, whose sons were among the Benjamites who came to David at Ziklag (1 Chron 12:7); location unknown.

3. A descendant of Benjamin who lived at Gibeon with his father Jehiel and brothers (1 Chron 8:31; 9:37).

4. Among the descendants of Judah, Penuel (1 Chron 4:4) and Jered (4:18) are both named as the "father" of Gedor. The genealogical tables are different, indicating two persons named Gedor.

5. In the time of Hezekiah, princes of Simeon went to Gedor to find pasture for their flocks; and finding it good, they drove out the inhabitants and settled there (1 Chron 4:38–41).

GEHAZI (gē-hā'zī, Heb. *gêhăzî, valley of vision*). The servant of Elisha. He first appeared when Elisha sought to reward the Shunamite woman for her hospitality (2 Kings 4:8–37). When she declined any reward, Gehazi said, "Well, she has no son and her husband is old." Elisha promised her that she would bear a child, and within a year the child was born. When the child had grown, he died of sunstroke, and the woman went with her sorrow to the prophet. He sent Gehazi with instructions to lay Elisha's staff on the face of the child, "but there was no sound or response." Elisha then came himself and restored the child to life. Elisha had Gehazi call the woman to receive her son. Gehazi is mentioned again when Naaman is healed (5:1–27). Elisha refused any reward from Naaman, but Gehazi ran after him and asked for something. Naaman gave him more than he asked. Gehazi hid his booty before he reached home, but Elisha knew what had happened and invoked on Gehazi the leprosy of which Naaman had been cured. Gehazi is last mentioned when he was telling the king of "all the great things Elisha has done" (8:4–6). When he told how the Shunamite woman's son was restored to life, the woman herself appeared and asked the king to restore to her the property she abandoned on the advice of Elisha during a seven-year famine. The king ordered her fully compensated. Because Gehazi appeared in the court of the king, it has been inferred that he had repented and had been healed of his leprosy, though 2 Kings 5:27 renders this doubtful. He showed no resentment against Elisha. Gehazi was an efficient servant, but weak enough to yield to greed. He lacked his master's clear moral insight and stamina, and he had no such relation with Elisha as Elisha had with Elijah.

GEHENNA (gē-hĕn'ȧ, Gr. *geenna,* a transliteration of the Aramaic form of Heb. *gê-ben-hinnôm, valley of the son of Hinnom*). In the OT it was referred to as the Valley of Ben Hinnom (NIV) or the valley of the son of Hinnom (KJV, RSV, ASV). A valley west and SW of Jerusalem that formed part of the border between Judah and Benjamin (Josh 15:8; cf. 18:16), it was still recognized as the border after the Exile (Neh 11:30–31) and is modern Wadi er-Rababi. Here Ahaz (2 Kings 16:3; 2 Chron 28:3) and Manasseh (2 Kings 21:6; 2 Chron 33:6) sacrificed their sons to Molech (Jer 32:35). For this reason Josiah defiled the place (2 Kings 23:10). After referring to

Gehenna, the Valley of Hinnom, notorious as the site where many of the Israelites worshiped false gods and sacrificed their children by burning them (2 Kings 23:10). In later times it became a place where rubbish was burned and a symbol for hell. Courtesy Duby Tal.

these idolatrous practices (Jer 7:31–32), Jeremiah prophesied a great slaughter of the people there and in Jerusalem (Jer 19:1–13).

After the OT period, Jewish apocalyptic writers began to call the Valley of Hinnom the entrance to hell, later hell itself. In Jewish usage of the first century A.D., Gehenna referred to the intermediate state of the godless dead, but there is no trace of this sense in the NT. The NT distinguishes sharply between Hades, the intermediate, bodiless state, and Gehenna, the state of final punishment after the resurrection of the body. Gehenna existed before the judgment (Matt 25:41). The word occurs twelve times in the NT, always translated "hell" (ASV, RSV margin "Gehenna"). Eleven times it is on the lips of Jesus: as the final punishment for calling one's brother a fool (5:22); for adultery, when the severest measures have not been taken to prevent commission of this offense (5:29–30); in a warning about whom to fear (Matt 10:28; Luke 12:5); and others (Matt 18:9; Mark 9:43, 45, 47). A hypocrite is called a "son of hell" (Matt 23:15) who cannot escape "being condemned to hell" (23:33). James 3:6 speaks of the "tongue" as "a fire . . . set on fire by hell." A fire was kept burning in the Valley of Hinnom to consume the garbage deposited there by the residents of Jerusalem. Terms parallel to Gehenna include "fiery furnace" (Matt 13:42, 50), "fiery lake" (Rev 19:20; 20:14–15), "lake of burning sulfur" (20:10), "eternal fire" (Jude 7); "hell" (2 Peter 2:4), where the Greek phrase "sent . . . to hell" means "cast down to Tartarus," a Greek name for the place of punishment of the wicked dead. Its use by our Savior Jesus Christ warns us of the destiny that even the love of God does not avert from those who finally refuse his forgiveness. See also HADES; HELL. ER

GELILOTH (gē-lī'lŏth). The name of a place on the border of Benjamin and Judah, east of Jerusalem (Josh 18:17); perhaps the same as the Gilgal of Joshua 15:7, whose name has a similar meaning ("circuit"). It cannot be the Gilgal near Jericho in the Jordan Valley.

GEM (See MINERALS)

GEMALLI (gē-măl'ī, *camel owner* or *rider*). The father of Ammiel, ruler of the tribe of Dan, and one of the twelve spies sent out to explore the land (Num 13:12).

GEMARIAH (gĕm'á-rī'á, *Jehovah has fulfilled,* or, *accomplishment of the Lord*). 1. A prince, son of Shaphan the scribe and brother of Ahikam (Jer 36:10–25). This scribe with others sought in vain to keep King Jehoiakim from burning the roll that Baruch had written at the dictation of Jeremiah.

2. A son of Hilkiah, sent by King Zedekiah as ambassador to Nebuchadnezzar at Babylon. He also carried a letter from Jeremiah to the captive Jews (Jer 29:3).

GENEALOGY (jĕn'ē-ăl'ō-jē, Heb. *yachas,* Gr. *genealogia*). A list of ancestors or descendants, descent from an ancestor, or the study of lines of descent. Genealogies are compiled to show biological descent, the right of inheritance, succession to an office, or ethnological and geographical relationships. The word occurs several times in the English Bible (1 Chron 4:33; 5:1, 7; 7:5, 7, 9, 40; 9:22; 2 Chron 12:15; 31:16–19; Ezra 2:62; 8:1; Neh 7:5, 64; 1 Tim 1:4; Titus 3:9), but most Bible genealogies are introduced by other words, such as "the book of the generations of," or "these are the generations of," or are given without titles.

Bible genealogies are not primarily concerned with mere biological descent. The earliest (Gen 4:1–2, 17–22) by its emphasis on occupations (Abel, shepherd; Cain, farmer and city-builder; Jabal, cattleman; Jubal, musician; Tubal-Cain, metal worker), in a family register of Cain's descendants, shows when new features of the culture were introduced. The genealogy of the line of Seth (4:25–26; 5:1–32), a list of long-lived individuals, contrasts with the genealogy in Genesis 10:1–32, which is clearly a table of nations descended from the three families of Shem, Ham, and Japheth. Many of the names are Hebrew plurals using the "-im" suffix signifying nations, tribes, cities, or towns rather than individuals. The scope of biblical genealogies narrows to the chosen people and their close relatives (Gen 11:10–22, Shem to Abraham; 22:20–24, Abraham's near kin). Next are the children of Abraham by Hagar (16:15; 25:12–18), by Sarah (21:1–3; 25:19–28), and by Keturah (25:1–4); then the children of Jacob (29:31–30:24; 35:16–26) and of his brother Esau (ch. 36). Jacob's posterity who came into Egypt are carefully enumerated (46:8–27), and part of them again (Exod 6:14–27) to bring the genealogy down to Moses and Aaron; the inclusion of brief mention of the sons of Reuben and Simeon before the fuller genealogy of the Levites may indicate that this list was taken from an earlier one. Numbers 26:1–56 records a census following genealogical relationships, for the purpose of equitable division of the land. The military organization of the Israelites for the wilderness journey was by genealogy (Num 1–3); this included the priests and Levites (3:11–39) and provided for a tax and offerings (7:11–89) for the support of religion (3:40–51), as well as the order of march in peace or war (ch. 10). Many other references to persons must be taken into account in attempting a complete genealogy. Ruth 4:17–22 picks up the genealogy of Judah from his son Pharez, to carry it down to David, whose children are listed: those born in Hebron (2 Sam 3:2–5) and in Jerusalem (5:13–16). David's "mighty men" are named, with brief notices of their descent (23:8–39); Solomon's princes and providers of food are also covered (2 Kings 4:1–19).

The major genealogical tables of the OT are in 1 Chronicles 1–9. They use most of the earlier genealogical material, but show differences that are puzzling to us today. Satisfactory solutions are not available for many of these. Mistakes in copying would account for some; differences in the purpose of the recorders for others. The books of Kings and Chronicles contain information about the family relationships of the kings of Judah and of Israel. Ezra 2:1–63; 8:1–20; and Nehemiah 7:7–63 name by families those who returned with Zerubbabel from Babylonian captivity, including many whose descent could not be traced. Ezra 7:1–6 gives Ezra's own line of descent from Aaron. Ezra 10:18–44 names those who had married foreign women. Nehemiah 3 names those who helped rebuild the walls of Jerusalem. There follow lists of those who helped Ezra proclaim the law of God (Neh 8:1–8); of those who sealed the covenant to keep the law (10:1–27); of the leading inhabitants in Jerusalem (11:1–10), in nearby Judah (11:20–24), and in more remote villages of Judah and Benjamin (11:25–36). Nehemiah 12 deals with the priests who accompanied Zerubbabel (12:1–9), the succession of high priests from Jeshua to Jaddua (12:10–11), the "heads of the priestly families" in the days of Joiakim (12:12–21), Levites in this period (12:22–26), princes and priests who took part in the dedication of the wall of Jerusalem (12:31–42). The prophets usually began their books with some indication of their genealogy (Isa 1:1; Jer 1:1; Ezek 1:3; Hos 1:1; Joel 1:1; Jonah 1:1; Zeph 1:1; Zech 1:1).

For the genealogies of Jesus Christ see GENEALOGY OF JESUS CHRIST. Other NT persons generally appear without indication of their descent. Occasionally the father is named (e.g., "James and John, the sons of Zebedee," Luke 5:10). Paul cherished his pure Hebrew descent (Phil 3:4–5). The genealogies of 1 Timothy 1:4 and Titus 3:9 are sometimes thought to refer to a pagan Gnostic series of beings intermediate between God and the created earth. However, it is more likely that the rabbinic overconcern with human genealogies is meant, because the false teachers seem to be Jewish and the term "genealogies" is not used by pagan authors of the pagan Gnostic series.

It is certain that the NT shows far less concern for the genealogy of human beings than does the OT. In the OT, God was bringing together a chosen people who would be a nation peculiarly devoted to preserving his revelation until, in the fullness of time, he sent his Son, who would draw to himself a new people, united not by descent from a common human ancestry but by a genealogy of one generation only: children of God by a new and spiritual birth.

Bibliography: J. Pedersen, *Israel, Its Life and Culture,* vol. 1, 1926, p. 257; J. O. Buswell, Jr., *A Systematic Theology of the Christian Religion,* vol. 1, 1962, pp. 325–43; M. D. Johnson, *The Purpose of Biblical Genealogies,* 1969; R. R. Wilson, *Genealogy and History in the Biblical World,* 1977. ER

GENEALOGY OF JESUS CHRIST. Two genealogies of Jesus are given in the NT: in Matthew 1:1–17 and in Luke 3:23–38. Matthew traces the descent of Jesus from Abraham and David, and divides it into three sets of fourteen generations each, probably to aid memorization. There are fourteen names from Abraham to and including David. From David to and including Josiah, and counting David a second time, there are fourteen names. (David is named twice in Matt 1:17.) From Jeconiah to Jesus there are fourteen names. Matthew omits three generations after Joram—namely Ahaziah, Joash, and Amaziah (1 Chron 3:11–12). Such an omission in Hebrew genealogies is not peculiar to Matthew. He names Zerah as well as Perez and mentions the brothers of Judah and of Jeconiah, which is unusual. Contrary to Hebrew practice, he names five women: Tamar, Rahab, Ruth, Bathsheba, and Mary, each name evoking associations, dark or bright, with the history of the chosen people. Matthew carefully excludes the physical paternity of Joseph by saying "Joseph, the husband of Mary, of whom was born Jesus" (1:16; the word "whom" is feminine singular in Greek). The sense of "begat" in Hebrew genealogies was not exact. It indicated immediate or remote descent, an adoptive relation, or legal heirship, as well as procreation.

Luke's genealogy moves from Jesus to Adam. Between Abraham and Adam it is the same as in 1 Chronicles 1:1–7, 24–28, or the more detailed genealogies in Genesis, making allowance for the different spelling of names in transliteration from Hebrew or Greek. From David to Abraham, Luke agrees with OT genealogies and with Matthew. Between Jesus and David, Luke's list differs from Matthew's, and there is no OT record to compare with Luke's, except for Nathan's being one of David's sons, and for the names of Shealtiel (KJV Salathiel) and Zerubbabel (KJV Zorobabel). At this point the two genealogies crossed, through adoption or otherwise.

As Matthew gave the line of the kings from David to Jeconiah, it is probable that from Shealtiel to Joseph he named those who were heirs to the Davidic throne. Luke's record then would be that of physical descent, though crossing the royal line at one point. In Luke 3:23 there is a question as to how much should be considered parenthetical. Some would include "of Joseph" in the parenthesis: "(as was supposed of Joseph)," making Heli in some sense the father of Jesus, perhaps his maternal grandfather. This construction is awkward. Another supposition is that Joseph is really the son-in-law of Heli, through his marriage to Mary, possibly Heli's daughter. If both genealogies are those of Joseph, his relationship to Heli must be different from his relationship to Jacob. Scholars have wrestled with the problems of the two genealogies from the second century, when pagan critics raised the difficulty. Many explanations have been more ingenious than convincing, involving complicated and uncertain inferences.

In a widely accepted view advanced by A. T. Robertson, Matthew gives the legal descent of heirship to the throne of David, through Joseph, while Luke gives the physical descent of Jesus through Mary. Matthew is concerned with the kingship of Jesus, Luke with his humanity. Both make plain his virgin birth, and therefore his deity. The agreement of Matthew and Luke on these facts is obvious, and their differences only accentuate their value as independent witnesses, whose testimony was prompted by the Holy Spirit, not by collaboration with each other. Matthew's genealogy establishes the legal claim to the throne of David through his foster-father Joseph; Luke's establishes his actual descent from David through Mary. Luke 1:32 says that Mary's child "will be called the Son of the Most High. The Lord God will give him the throne of his father David." Romans 1:3–4 agrees: Jesus "as to his human nature was a descendant of David," which could only be through Mary; and "declared with power to be the Son of God by his resurrection from the dead." See also 2 Timothy 2:8. Isaiah 11:1 indicates that the Messiah is to be physically a descendant of David's father Jesse. The genealogies must be seen in the light of this fact. See Matthew 22:41–46 and parallels with the answer in Romans 1:4.

Bibliography: J. G. Machen, *The Virgin Birth of Christ,* 1930, pp. 203–9; E. Stauffer, *Jesus and His Story,* pp. 22–25; NBD, pp. 410–11. ER

GENERATION. In the OT the translation of two Hebrew words: (1) *tôledhôth,* from a root *yalad,* to beget, used always in the plural, refers to lines of descent from an ancestor and occurs in the phrase "these are the generations of," introducing each of eleven sections of Genesis, from 2:4 to 37:2 (NIV "this is the account of"), and elsewhere. (2) *Dôr,* a period of time (e.g., Deut 32:7, past; Exod 3:15, future; Ps 102:24, both). It can signify also all the people living in a given period (e.g., Gen 7:1; Judg 3:2), a class of people characterized by a certain quality (e.g., Deut 32:5; Ps 14:5), and a dwelling place or habitation (Isa 58:12; Ps 49:19).

In the NT "generation" translates four Greek words, all having reference to descent: (1) *Genea,* most frequent in the Synoptic Gospels, signifying the lines of descent from an ancestor (e.g., Matt 1:17), all the people living in a given period (e.g., 11:16); or a class of people characterized by a certain quality (e.g., 12:39), or a period of time (Acts 13:36; Col 1:26). (2) *Genesis,* in Matthew 1:1, in a heading to verses 2–17, used to mean "genealogy." (3) *Gennēma,* in the phrase "brood of vipers" (Matt 3:7; 12:34; 23:33; Luke 3:7; KJV "generation," ASV "offspring"). (4) *Genos,* meaning "race" (1 Peter 2:9; KJV "generation," RSV "race," NIV "people"). Matthew 24:34 and parallels Mark 13:30 and Luke 21:32 present a special problem. If "this generation" (*genea*) refers to the people then living, these verses, despite their position, must relate to the destruction of Jerusalem and not to the second coming of Christ. But the meaning may be that the generation that sees the beginning of the special signs of the Second Coming will see the end of them. Another interpretation is that "generation" here refers to the Jewish nation. *Genea* may bear the sense of "nation" or "race." ER

GENESIS (jĕn′ĕ-sĭs). The first book of the Bible. In the Jewish tradition the book is named from its first word *berēshîth* ("in the beginning"). The name Genesis, which means "beginning," derives from the LXX and is found also in the Latin tradition (*Liber Genesis*). While much of the book is concerned with origins, the name Genesis does not reflect its total scope, for the larger portion of the book consists of the history of the patriarchs and concludes with the record of Joseph's life.

I. The Authorship of Genesis. The question of the authorship of Genesis has been the subject of debate for over two centuries. Tradition ascribes the book to Moses, but the application of source-critical methodology has partitioned Genesis into a number of sources attributed to various authors writing at widely diverse times in Israelite history. The identification of these sources (known simply as J, E, D, P, etc.) is based on several criteria such as style, usage of the divine name, alleged contradictions, linguistic peculiarities, and development of the Israelite religion. More recent trends have tended to modify this approach, putting less emphasis on traditional historicist methodology and more on literary or canonical concerns.

The concept of Mosaic authorship does not demand the belief that Moses was the first to write every word of each account in the Book of Genesis. It is generally understood today to mean that much of his work was compilation. Many historical accounts in Genesis predate Moses by great expanses of time. There is no reason why he could not have arranged these ancient accounts into the literary structure of the book.

Proponents of the Mosaic authorship of Genesis point to such evidence as the author's knowledge of Egypt (Gen 13:10) and the Egyptian language (41:43–45), archaisms in the language of Genesis (such as imprecision in the gender of certain nouns and pronouns), ancient customs recorded in Genesis that are paralleled in other cultures of the second millennium B.C., and the orderly and purposeful arrangement of the book (G. Archer, *A Survey of Old Testament Introduction,* 1964, pp. 101–9).

II. Archaeological Background of Genesis. Excavations at a number of sites in the ancient Near East have tended to support the antiquity and historical integrity of significant portions of the Book of Genesis. For example, excavations at Yorgan Tepe, the site of ancient Nuzi, have yielded thousands of tablets, most of which have been dated to the fifteenth century B.C. These tablets record several legal and societal practices that are strikingly similar to customs recorded in the patriarchal narratives. For example, Rachel's theft of the household gods of Laban (Gen 31:34) may be understood against the background of the Nuzi custom of determining inheritance rights by the possession of the family gods. Apparently Rachel wished to insure her husband's right to the property she felt was his (cf. 31:14–16). Also, the practice of taking a concubine to produce an heir when a married couple was childless is well known, both in Genesis (16:3; 30:4, 9) and the Nuzi material (R. K. Harrison, *The Archaeology of the Old Testament,* 1966, pp. 23–29). The similarity between the customs of Nuzi and those of the patriarchs gives strong support to the origin of the patriarchal accounts in a period very early in Hebrew history.

It has been asserted that the mention of camels in numerous passages in Genesis may be an anachronism, because evidence for the domestication of camels cannot be found before the end of the twelfth century B.C. (W. F. Albright, *The Archaeology of Palestine,* 1949, pp. 206–7). However, camel bones have been discovered at Mari (twenty-fifth/twenty-fourth centuries) and in Palestine (2000 to 1200) at various archaeological sites. Evidence for the domestication of the camel may be found in texts from the Old Babylonian period (c. 2000/1700) and a Sumerian text from Nippur (K. A. Kitchen, *Ancient Orient and Old Testament,* 1966, pp. 79–80).

III. Content of the Book of Genesis. The Book of Genesis may be divided roughly into three parts. Chapters 1–11 record events from the Creation to the death of Terah, the father of Abraham. Chapters 12–36 constitute a history of the patriarchs Abraham, Isaac, and Jacob. Chapters 37–50 present a sustained narrative that records the account of Joseph.

The first section begins with the account of creation. It is sometimes asserted that there are two creation narratives (Gen 1:1–2:4a; 2:4b–25) that give contradictory accounts of the order of the creative events. In the second account, which is attributed to the "J" writer, man appears to have been created before vegetation (2:5; cf. 2:7). This is different from the order of chapter 1, which is attributed to the "P" writer. However, the words for vegetation may connote "weeds" and "cultivated plants." The word translated "shrub" connotes weeds or brush in its other usages in the OT (Job 30:4, 7) and the word "plant" frequently refers to edible or cultivated grasses. The purpose of the account is to show that weeds and the need for cultivation were a result of the curse (cf. Gen 3:18–19). It is not necessary to understand the accounts to contradict one another.

There were other ancient cultures that produced creation accounts. For example, the Babylonian creation epic *Enuma Elish* depicts the origin of the physical phenomena. It is commonly held that the Genesis accounts are dependent on the Babylonian creation account. Yet an examination of the two accounts yields little evidence on which to base such an assertion.

Linguistic evidence for such dependence has been sought in the word *tehôm* ("deep"), which occurs in Gen 1:2 (B. S. Childs, *Myth and Reality in the Old Testament,* 1962, pp. 37–38). This word is said to find a counterpart in the word *Ti'âmat,* the name of a goddess in *Enuma Elish.* However, there is strong evidence against such a parallel. First, the word *Ti'âmat* does not contain the gutteral "h," which is present in the Hebrew word. One would expect the word to be spelled with an *aleph* in Hebrew, not a *hē*. Second, the Ugaritic material possesses the word *thm,* which is evidently the same word that appears in Hebrew as *tehôm.*

It may also be noted that the style and content of the two accounts are vastly different. The Babylonian account depicts the Creation as taking place as a result of the sexual union of the gods *Apsû* and *Ti'âmat*. It is patently mythical and pagan in its orientation.

However, similarities remain, particularly in the order of the creative events. A. Heidel says of this consonance between the accounts: "Our examination . . . shows quite plainly that the similarities are not so striking as we might expect. . . . In fact, the divergences are much more far-reaching and significant than are the resemblances, most of which are not any closer than what we should expect to find in any two more or less complete creation versions . . ." (A. Heidel, *The Babylonian Genesis,* 1963, p. 130).

The fall of the human race is recorded in Genesis 2–3. This event had profound significance, not only for man's relationship to God but for his relationships to others as well. No longer does an intimate relationship with God exist, as it did in the Garden. Murder (4:8, 23) and the lust for renown (4:17, 23–24; 6:1–4) now characterize the human race. These conditions led to the destruction of the race by a flood.

The question of the universality of the Flood (Gen 6:5–9:17) cannot be answered precisely from the biblical texts because of the ambiguity of the word "all" in the statement "all the high mountains . . . were covered" (7:19), which in Hebrew need not be understood in an absolute sense. Yet, it is difficult to conceive of the Noahic flood only as a local phenomenon in view of the fact that the waters apparently covered Mount Ararat (8:3–4). The presence of a flood account in many ethnological contexts, as well as the evidence of fossils found in various sites throughout the world are often appealed to as support for a universal flood (A. M. Rehwinkel, *The Flood,* 1951, pp. 127–52, 210–37). See also FLOOD, DELUGE.

The human race's effort to establish a name for itself culminated in the erection of the Tower of Babel (Gen 11:1–9). The destruction of the tower by divine intervention was accompanied by the confusion of language, which led to the geographical distribution of the race (11:8) and probably to the dialectical and linguistical differences that characterize human language today.

The patriarchal accounts that begin at Genesis 12:1 are of great importance to the theology of both Testaments, for they record the first formal statement of the promise to Abraham. The promise, which later was put into the form of a covenant (15:12–21), guaranteed an inheritance to the people of God in all ages.

The promise was placed in the form of a covenant in Genesis 15:7–21. It thus became a formalized statement that was invested with the authority of the divine oath. Among the elements of this covenant are the promise that Abraham's descendants would inherit the land of Canaan (12:7; 15:18–20), the promise that Abraham would be the father of a great nation (12:2; 17:2), and the promise of Gentile inclusion in the blessings of the covenant (12:3). When God gave the promise that Abraham would be the father of multitudes, that promise seemed unlikely to be fulfilled, because Abraham and his wife Sarah were well along in years (17:17–19). However, the integrity of the promise was maintained in the birth of Isaac (17:19; cf. 21:1–7).

The Genesis narratives set forth Abraham's faith as the central element in his relationship with God (Gen 15:6). His faith was given concrete expression in his willingness to sacrifice his son Isaac according to the word of God (22:1–9; cf. James 22:22–23).

The Genesis narratives give the least attention to the patriarch Isaac. But the promise is not absent from the account of his life (Gen 26:23–25). The narrative concerning Jacob also centers on the continuation of the promise-covenant in the patriarchal line. The elements of the promise were reiterated to him when he was forced to flee his home because he had deceived his father (27:18–45).

Jacob is the progenitor of the twelve tribes of Israel (Gen 35:22–23). When his name was changed from Jacob to Israel he gave a name to the Hebrew tribes (32:27–28).

A large portion of Genesis records the life of Joseph, Jacob's son by Rachel. Basic to this narrative is its recounting of the way in which the Hebrews came to reside in the land of Egypt. It was due to a famine that was apparently widespread in Egypt and Canaan. Joseph had wisely provided for such emergencies, and Jacob and his sons came to Egypt to pasture their flocks. Joseph recognized his family, from whom he had been separated for many years, and settled them in the land of Egypt (Gen 47:11–12).

The narratives concerning Joseph provide the historical background for the Book of Exodus, which records the bondage of the Israelites in Egypt and their subsequent exodus from that land. These narratives also look back to the period of Egyptian bondage mentioned in the Abrahamic covenant (Gen 15:13–14).

Bibliography: H. C. Leupold, *Exposition of Genesis,* 1950; Umberto Cassuto, *A Commentary on the Book of Genesis,* vol. 1, 1961; vol. 2, 1964; Derek Kidner, *Genesis: An Introduction and Commentary,* 1967; Walter Brueggemann, *Genesis: A Bible Commentary for Teaching and Preaching,* 1982. TEM

GENNESARET (gĕ-nĕs′à-rĕt). 1. Mentioned in Matthew 14:34 and Mark 6:53, this is a plain stretching about three miles (five km.) along the NW shore of the Sea of Galilee, extending about a mile (almost two km.) inland, the modern el-Ghuweir. With a rich, loamy, well-watered soil, today as in Bible times it is extraordinarily fertile, the only easily tillable land bordering the Sea of Galilee. The fig, olive, palm, and walnut trees, which ordinarily require diverse conditions, all grow well here.

The fertile Plain of Gennesaret along the northwest shore of the Sea of Galilee. The forbidding promontory to the left is Mount Arbel, associated with Beth Arbel (Hos 10:14). Courtesy Israel Government Press Office.

2. "The Lake of Gennesaret" (Luke 5:1), elsewhere in Luke simply "the lake"; the same as the Sea of Galilee (Matt 4:18; 15:29; Mark 1:16; 7:31; John 6:1) or the OT "Sea of Kinnereth" (Num 34:11; Josh 12:3).

GENTILES (Heb. *gôy,* plural *gôyîm, nation, people*). The KJV translates the Hebrew word as "Gentiles" 30 times, "people" 11 times, "heathen" 142 times, and "nation" 373 times (this being the usual translation also in ASV, RSV, NIV). Sometimes *gôy* refers to Israel (Gen 12:2; Deut 32:28; Josh 3:17; 4:1; 10:13; 2 Sam 7:23; Isa 1:4; Zeph 2:9; translated "nation" or "people" in KJV as well as in other versions). But *'âm* is the ordinary term for Israel. *Gôy* usually means a non-Israelite people. In the NT, Greek *ethnos* is a translation of *gôy,* while *laos* corresponds to Hebrew *'âm. Ethnos* is translated "Gentiles" in the NT. *Hellēnes* is translated "Gentiles" in KJV, "Greeks" in ASV, RSV (John 7:35; Rom 2:9–10; 3:9; 1 Cor 10:32; 12:13), and both ways in the NIV.

In times of peace, considerate treatment was accorded Gentiles under OT law (e.g., Num 35:15; Deut 10:19; 24:14–15; Ezek 47:22). Men of Israel often married Gentile women, of whom Rahab, Ruth, and Bathsheba are notable examples, but the practice was frowned on after the return from exile (Ezra 9:12; 10:2–44; Neh 10:30; 13:23–31). Separation between Jew and Gentile became more strict, until in the NT period the hostility was complete. Persecution embittered the Jew, and he retaliated by hatred of everything pertaining to Gentiles and by avoidance, so far as was possible, of contact with Gentiles. The intensity of this feeling varied and gave way before unusual kindness (Luke 7:4–5).

While the teachings of Jesus ultimately broke down "the middle wall of partition" between Jew and Gentile, as is seen in the writings of Paul (Rom 1:16; 1 Cor 1:24; Gal 3:28; Eph 2:14; Col 3:11) and in Acts, Jesus limited his ministry to Jews, with rare exceptions (the half-Jewish Samaritans, John 4:1–42; the Syrophoenician woman, Matt 15:21–28; Mark 7:24–30; the Greeks in John 12:20–36). He instructed his twelve disciples, "Do not go among the Gentiles or enter any town of the Samaritans" (Matt 10:5); but he did not repeat this injunction when he sent out the Seventy (Luke 10:1–16; NIV "seventy-two"). Jesus' mission was first to "his own" (John 1:11), the chosen people of God, but ultimately to "all who received him" (1:12). Limitations of time held his ministry on earth within the bounds of Israel; reaching the Gentiles was left to the activity of the Holy Spirit working through his disciples.

In Acts, from the appointment of Paul as the apostle to the Gentiles (9:15), the Gentiles become increasingly prominent. Even the letters addressed particularly to Jewish Christians (Rom 9–11; Hebrews; James; 1 Peter) are relevant to Gentiles also. The division of all mankind into two classes, Jew and Gentile, emphasizes the importance of the Jews as the people through whom God made salvation available to all people.

Bibliography: T. R. Glover, *The Conflict of Religions in the Roman Empire,* 1912; G. Murray, *Five Stages of Greek Religion,* 1925; G. H. C. MacGregor and A. C. Purdy, *Jew and Greek,* 1959; K. N. Clark, *The Gentile Bias and Other Essays,* 1980; M. L. Loane, *Grace and the Gentiles,* 1981. ER

GENTLENESS (Gr. *epieikeia* and *prautēs*). In English gentleness and meekness are closely related, and translations of these two Greek words make use of both. The adjective *epieikēs* occurs five times (Phil 4:5; 1 Tim 3:3; Titus 3:2; James 3:17; 1 Peter 2:18), and the noun *epieikeia* twice (Acts 24:4; 2 Cor 10:1). The basic idea behind this word-group is the attitude that rises above standing on one's rights in order to be conciliatory and to show forbearance: to be gentle and meek in the treatment of people.

The noun *prautēs* (2 Cor 10:1) and adjective *praus* (Matt 11:29; 21:5) are both used of Jesus. The noun is also used to describe one aspect of the fruit of the Spirit (Gal 5:23; cf. 1 Cor 4:21; Gal 6:1; Eph 4:2; Col 3:12; 2 Tim 2:25; James 1:21; 3:13; 1 Peter 3:15). KJV always translates this word as "meek" and "meekness," but other versions use "gentleness" and other words. The basic idea behind this Greek word-group is that of real strength under control—a gentleness that is truly strong. Thus, it derives from the character of God, whom KJV describes as "gentle" in 2 Samuel 22:36 and Psalm 18:35. See also MEEKNESS.

GENUBATH (gē-nū'băth, Heb. *genuvath, theft*). A son of Hadad the Edomite, the fugitive prince, by the sister of Queen Tahpenes, the wife of the pharaoh who governed Egypt toward the end of David's reign (1 Kings 11:20).

GERA (gē'rȧ, Heb. *gērā', grain*). A name common in the tribe of Benjamin:

1. A son of Benjamin (Gen 46:21).
2. A son of Bela and grandson of Benjamin (1 Chron 8:3, 5).
3. The father of Ehud (Judg 3:15).
4. A son of Ehud (1 Chron 8:7).
5. The father of Shimei (2 Sam 16:5; 19:16, 18; 1 Kings 2:8). Some of these are thought to be the same person, taking "father" to mean a remote ancestor and "son" a remote descendant.

GERAH (See WEIGHTS AND MEASURES)

GERAR (gē'rȧr, Heb. *gerār, circle, region*). A town in the Negev, near, but not on, the Mediterranean coast south of Gaza, in a valley running NW and SE, on a protected inland caravan route from Palestine to Egypt (Gen 10:19). Here Abraham stayed with its king, Abimelech (20:1–2); and later Isaac (26:1–33) had similar and more extended experiences with the king and people of the region. Here Asa and his army defeated the Ethiopians and plundered Gerar and the cities near it (2 Chron 14:13–14). Its site is thought to be the modern Tell ej-Jemmeh, which has been excavated, uncovering levels of occupation from the Late Bronze Age to the Byzantine period.

GERASA (gē-rȧ'sȧ). A city east of Jordan midway between the Sea of Galilee and the Dead Sea, in the Decapolis at the eastern edge of Perea;

Roman ruins at Gerasa showing the oval forum and main street. Gerasa was one of the leading cities of the Decapolis, today it is identified with Jerash in Jordan. Courtesy Garo Nalbandian.

View from the top of Mount Gerizim, in foreground, with remains of a Samaritan temple surrounded by trees. In the center right background is Mount Ebal. Courtesy Zev Radovan.

partially excavated; the modern Jerash. The name does not occur in the Bible, but the adjective Gerasenes occurs in Mark 5:1 and in some versions of Matthew 8:28 and Luke 8:26, 37. The MSS vary between Gadarenes, Gerasenes, and Gergesenes; and all the above occurrences relate to the region where Jesus healed a demoniac and permitted the demons that had possessed the man to enter some pigs, which thereupon rushed down a steep slope into the Sea of Galilee; hence this incident must have occurred on the shore. A possible location is at Kursi (Gergesa) on the eastern shore of the lake. Gadara (Muqeis) is SE of Lake Galilee. The place where the gospel incident occurred may have been referred to sometimes as the country of the Gergesenes, a purely local name; or of the Gadarenes, from the nearest city; or of the Gerasenes, from the most important city of the district. See also GADARENES.

GERGESA (See GERASA)

GERIZIM (gĕ-rī'zĭm, gĕr'ĭ-zĭm). A mountain of Samaria, Jebel et-Tôr, 2,849 feet (890 m.) high, SW of Mount Ebal. A main north-south road of Palestine runs through the valley, so that this pass is of strategic military importance. Moses commanded that when the Israelites came into the Promised Land, the blessing for keeping the law should be spoken from Mount Gerizim and the curse for not obeying it from Mount Ebal (Deut 11:29; 27:4–26), six tribes standing on the slopes of each peak (27:11–14). It is conjectured that Mount Gerizim was selected for the blessing because, from the point of view of one looking eastward, it would be on the right or "fortunate" side.

From the top of Mount Gerizim Jotham shouted his parable of the trees to the men of Shechem in the valley below, reminding them of all that his father Gideon had done for them (Judg 9:7–21). After the Israelites, returning from Babylonian exile, refused to let the mixed races of Samaria help rebuild Jerusalem (Ezra 4:1–4; Neh 2:19–20; 13:28), the Samaritans built themselves a temple on Mount Gerizim. "This mountain," referred to in John 4:20–21, is Gerizim, where the Samaritans worshiped in the open after their temple was destroyed by the Maccabees. The small Samaritan community of Nablus still celebrates the Passover on Mount Gerizim. Samaritan tradition maintains that Abraham attempted to sacrifice Isaac on this mountain (Gen 22:1–19), that at a nearby Salem he met Melchizedek (14:17–20), and that Jacob's dream (28:10–17) occurred at Khirbet Lanzah on Mount Gerizim. The ruins of a fortress built by the Emperor Justinian in A.D. 533 remain. A rock with a cup-shaped hollow that could have been used for libations, is the traditional altar of the Samaritan temple. The Nablus community also possesses an important MS of the Pentateuch.

GERSHOM (gûr'shŏm, from Heb. *gārash, to cast out,* but in popular etymology explained as from *gēr, stranger,* Exod 2:22; 18:3). 1. The firstborn son of Moses and Zipporah. He was born in Midian (Exod 2:22; 18:3; 1 Chron 23:15–16; 26:24). The unusual circumstances of his circumcision are told in Exodus 4:21–28.

2. The eldest son of Levi, according to 1 Chronicles 6:16–17, 20, 43, 62, 71; 15:7. Elsewhere called Gershon.

3. One of the family of Phinehas, and one of the "family heads" who returned with Ezra from Babylon (Ezra 8:2).

4. Father of Jonathan, the Levite who became priest to the Danites who settled in Laish (Judg 18:30). KJV and NASB call him "son of Manasseh," but ASV, RSV, NIV have "son of Moses," conjecturing that the "n" in the Hebrew text that converts "Moses" into "Manasseh" was inserted to disguise the fact that Moses had such a graceless descendant as this Jonathan.

GERSHON (See GERSHOM)

GERUTH KIMHAM (ğir'ūth kĭm'hăm). KJV "habitation of Chimham." An unidentified place near Bethlehem where Johanan and others stayed on their way to Egypt after the murder of Gedaliah (Jer 41:17–18).

GERZITES, GIZRITES, GERIZZITES (See GIRZITES)

Gethsemane, the place of Jesus' agony (Matt. 26:36), lying at the foot of the Mount of Olives outside the east wall of Jerusalem. Some of the present olive trees alongside the Church of All Nations (foreground) are believed to date back to the time of Jesus. Courtesy Zev Radovan.

GESHAN (gē'shăn). A son of Jahdai and descendant of Caleb (1 Chron 2:47). KJV Gesham.

GESHEM (gē'shĕm). The Arabian who, along with Sanballat and Tobiah, sought to oppose the building of the wall of the city of Jerusalem by Nehemiah (Neh 2:19; 6:1–2). The same as Gashmu in the KJV of Nehemiah 6:6.

GESHUR (gē'shûr, Heb. *geshûr, bridge*). 1. A country in Syria (2 Sam 15:8) on the western border of Og's kingdom of Bashan east of the Jordan (Josh 12:5). Jair of Manasseh conquered Bashan up to Geshur (Deut 3:14). Although in Israel's territory, the Geshurites were not fully driven out (Josh 13:11, 13). In fact, it may be that (as ASV, NIV, and RSV render it) Geshur and Aram took sixty towns from Jair (1 Chron 2:23), though perhaps (according to JB and KJV) Jair took the cities from Gilead. David made an alliance with Talmai, their King, by marrying his daughter Maacah (2 Sam 3:3; 1 Chron 3:2). Her son Absalom, after murdering Ammon, sought refuge with her father (2 Sam 13:37–38).

2. A district between southern Palestine and Sinai, near Philistine territory (Josh 13:2), unconquered at the close of Joshua's career. David made a raid against it when he was taking refuge from Saul among the Philistines (1 Sam 27:8). Whether these Geshurites were a branch of the same people as those of no. 1 is undetermined.

GETHER (gē'thêr, Heb. *gether*). Mentioned only twice in Scripture, once as one of Aram's four sons (Gen 10:23) and once as one Shem's nine sons (1 Chron 1:17).

GETHSEMANE (gĕth-sĕm'à-nē, probably from the Aramaic for "oil-press"). The place of Jesus' agony and arrest (Matt 26:36–56; Mark 14:32–52; Luke 22:39–54; John 18:1–12 [John tells of the arrest only]). In Matthew 26:36 and Mark 14:32 it is called "a place." Luke does not give the name but says that the place was one to which Jesus customarily went and that it was on the Mount of Olives. John 18:1, without naming it, explains that it was a garden across the Kidron Valley from Jerusalem. The traditional site, cared for by the Franciscans, is not far from the road, near the bridge over the Kidron, and is laid out in neat gardens. Within are eight large olive trees. If Emperor Titus destroyed all the trees around Jerusalem during the siege of A.D. 70, as Josephus asserts, these trees cannot be as old as the time of Jesus, but they are certainly ancient, and they add to the atmosphere of a place of Christian devotion. Armenian, Greek, and Russian churches claim other olive groves nearby as the correct site. It is without doubt in the vicinity. The sufferings of Christ as his hour approached—portrayed by Matthew, Mark, and Luke—and the humiliation of his arrest, told by all four evangelists, concentrate the reverent thought and feeling of believers, so that the very name Gethsemane evokes the love and adoration due the Savior who prayed there. ER

The garden of Gethsemane as it looked nearly a century ago. The olive trees, some thought to date back to Jesus' time, are still standing today. Courtesy University Library, Istanbul.

GEUEL (gē-ū'ĕl). A son of Maki, a prince of Gad and the representative of the Gadite tribe sent out to explore Canaan (Num 13:15).

GEZER (gē'zêr, Heb. *gezer, portion*). A fortified place, Tell-Jezer, eighteen miles (thirty km.) NW of Jerusalem, between the Valley of Sorek and the Valley of Aijalon. It lies south of the main road from Jerusalem to Jaffa (Haifa) and east of the railroad. The site was identified by M. Clermont-Ganneau in A.D. 1873. Its military importance, overlooking main routes through the country, has led to its occupation in many periods of history. The Egyptians captured Gezer about 1500 B.C., but their power decreased a century or so later. When Israel entered the land, Horam king of Gezer came to help Lachish, whose king had been killed in the battle of the day on which the sun stood still (Josh 10:1–34). Horam and his army were completely destroyed, but Gezer was not taken. The king of Gezer is listed (12:12) among those whom Joshua defeated. Gezer is on the southern boundary of Ephraim, near the Beth Horons (Josh 16:3–10; 1 Chron 7:28). The inhabitants of Gezer were not driven out (Josh 16:10; Judg 1:29) but later became slave labor. Gezer was one of the cities given to the Kohathite Levites (Josh 21:21; 1 Chron 6:67). David defeated the Philistines as far as Gezer (2 Sam 5:25, KJV "Gazer"; 1 Chron 14:16; 20:4), but it remained for Solomon to reduce the people of Gezer to forced labor and to rebuild the city, which the pharaoh of Egypt had taken and burned and later given to Solomon as a dowry with his daughter (1 Kings 9:15–17). Gezer was occupied in the Greek period. Though not mentioned in the NT, it was known in NT times as Gazara. The Crusaders fortified Gezer, and it has

Plan of Gezer. Courtesy Carta, Jerusalem.

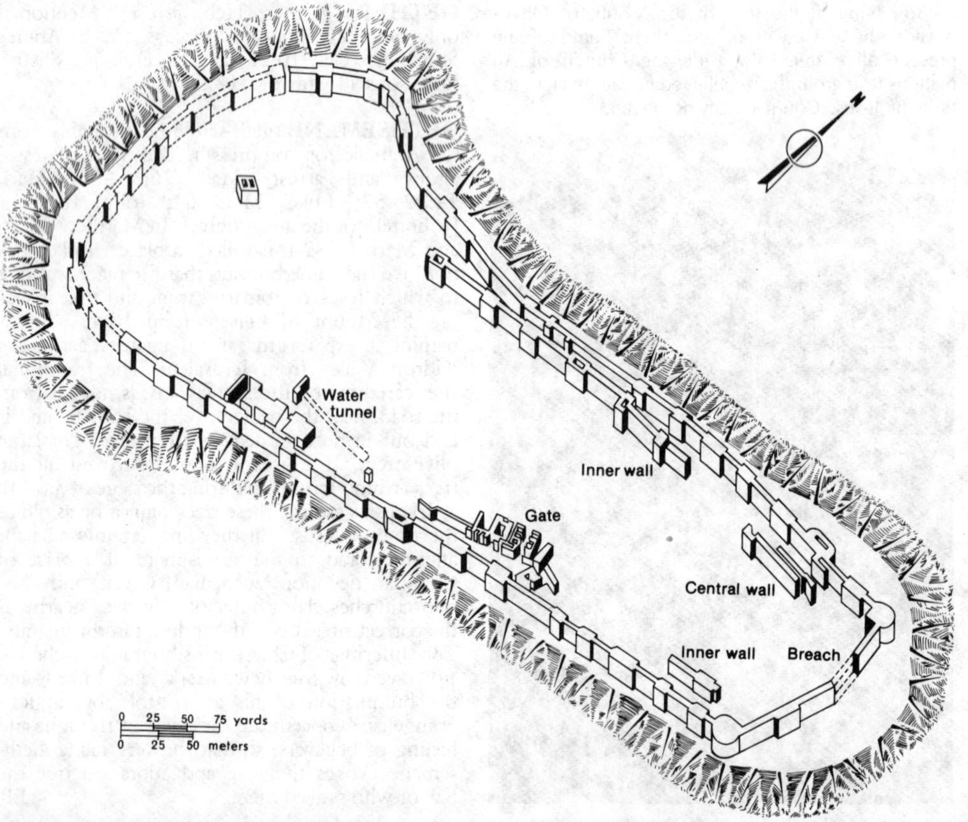

undergone several changes of ownership since then. Archaeological remains fully illustrate the life of the people.

Excavations here by R. A. S. Macalister in A.D. 1904–7; A. Rowe in 1934–35; G. E. Wright, William Dever, and others from 1964 to 1984 have revealed a stepped water tunnel 216 feet (68 m.) long (similar to tunnels found at Hazor, Megiddo, and Jerusalem), dating to the time of Solomon. City gates were also found from the time of Solomon matching those found at Hazor (cf. 1 Kings 9:15–16). A "high place" dating to

Remains of Solomonic gate (1) at Gezer facing south-southeast. Note the large drain running through the street. Courtesy Israel Government Press Office.

about 1600 B.C. was found here as well as a tenth-century calendar containing a Hebrew inscription of seven lines and citing an annual cycle of agricultural activities. It is one of the oldest-known pieces of Hebrew writing. The capture of Gezer is mentioned in the stele of Pharaoh Merneptah about 1220. ER

GHOST. The human spirit as distinguished from the body. Ghost translates Hebrew *nephesh,* "breath" (of life) in KJV, ASV of Job 11:20 (RSV "breathe their last"; NIV "a dying gasp"), and Jeremiah 15:9 (RSV "swooned away"; NIV "breathe her last"). For the Hebrew word *gāwaʿ* ("gasp out, expire"), RSV and NIV have "breathed his last" in connection with Abraham (Gen 25:8), Ishmael (25:17), Isaac (35:29), and Jacob (49:33). In some other passages (e.g., Job 3:11; 10:18; 13:19; 14:10) RSV uses varied expressions, whereas NIV has the simple verb "to die" in each case. In the NT "ghost" translates the Greek word *pneuma* ("breath, spirit") in Matthew 27:50 and John 19:30 of KJV; ASV, RSV, NIV have "spirit." In three verses (Mark 15:37, 39; Luke 23:46), RSV and NIV have "breathed his last" for the Greek word *ekpneō* ("breathe out"). These five verses in the Gospels all relate to Jesus. In Acts 5:5 (Ananias), 5:10 (Sapphira), and 12:23 (Herod), RSV and NIV have "died" for Greek *ekpsychō* ("lose consciousness, expire"). For "Holy Ghost," see HOLY SPIRIT.

GIAH (gī'ȧ). An unknown place near Gibeon, where Jacob overtook Abner (2 Sam 2:24).

GIANTS. The first mention of giants in the Bible is in Genesis 6:4, where ASV, RSV, NIV all have *Nephilim,* a Hebrew word of uncertain etymology. Nephilim were found in Canaan when the spies went through the land (Num 13:33; KJV giants). Beside these men of great stature, the spies felt like grasshoppers. Once (Job 16:14 KJV) "giant" is a translation of the Hebrew *gibbôr,* which RSV and NIV render "warrior." The ASV marginal note gives its usual meaning: "mighty men." The other Hebrew words sometimes translated "giant" are *rāphā', rāphâh,* and the plural *rephāîm,* of uncertain etymology. The giants whom the Israelites met when they tried to enter Canaan through Moab (Deut 2:11, 20) are called Rephaim in ASV, RSV, and Rephaites in NIV. They resembled the Anakim, and the Moabites called them Emims, while the Ammonites called them Zamzummims. They were tall, large-framed, and powerful. The last of this race was Og, king of Bashan, whose famous iron bedstead was nine cubits long (Deut 2:11; Josh 12:4; 13:12). The giant Rephaim were a vanishing race when the Israelites came out of Egypt. The land of the giants (Rephaites) is referred to in Joshua 17:15; the valley of the giants of Rephaim, located SW of Jerusalem, is mentioned in Joshua 15:8; 18:16. The Rephaim or Rephaites are named in Genesis 14:5; 15:20; the valley of Rephaim in 2 Samuel 5:18, 22; 23:13; 1 Chronicles 11:15; 14:9; Isaiah 17:5. So the memory of this fearsome race persisted in their ancient haunts. Second Samuel 21:15–22 records encounters of some of David's mighty men with descendants of the giant (Rapha). The best-known giant of all, Goliath of Gath, whom young David killed (1 Sam 17), is not called a giant but is only described as of a huge stature and great strength. It was not necessary to name the obvious. Thus giants terrorized the Israelites from their entry into Canaan until the time of David. Tall men like Saul were admired (1 Sam 10:23); the Lord had to remind Samuel not to consider height when choosing the next king (16:7). Isaiah 45:14 notes that the Sabeans were tall. The question, How tall is a giant? can be answered only in terms of the average height of the race that is using the term. Giants were abnormally strong, yet they had their weak points, as David's victory over Goliath proved.

GIBBAR (gĭb'ȧr). A man whose children returned from captivity with Zerubbabel (Ezra 2:20). Perhaps the Gibeon of Nehemiah 7:25.

GIBBETHON (gĭb'ē-thŏn). Tell el-Melât, west of Gezer in the territory of Dan (Josh 19:44), allotted to the Kohathite Levites (21:23). Baasha killed King Nadab at Gibbethon while Israel was besieging the city, which was now in the hands of the Philistines (1 Kings 15:27). A quarter century later, Israel again besieged Gibbethon, and Omri was made king there by the army, when they received the news that Zimri had killed King Baasha (16:15–17). The army then abandoned the siege.

GIBEA (gĭb'ē-à). A son of Sheva, and grandson of Caleb (1 Chron 2:49).

GIBEAH (gĭb'ē-à). 1. A city in the hill country of Judah; its site is unknown (Josh 15:57).

2. A city of Benjamin (Josh 18:28), modern Tell el-Fûl, in NT times Gabath Saul; on the east side of the north-south road about three miles (five km.) north of Jerusalem and on a height commanding a view of the latter; also called Gibeah of Saul, where excavation has uncovered the rustic but strong fortress-palace from which Saul ruled Israel. Here in the time of the judges a Levite's concubine was raped and abused, and this event brought war between Benjamin and the rest of Israel (Judg 19–20). The transactions at Gibeah during the reign of Saul are recorded in 1 Samuel 10:26; 11:4; 13:2, 15–16; 14:2 (ASV, RSV Geba); 14:16; 15:34; 22:6; 23:19; 26:1. When the ark of God was returned by the Philistines, the Israelite men put it in Abinadab's house on "the hill" (Gibeah; 1 Sam 7:1; cf. ASV footnote), where David went to get it and bring it into Jerusalem (2 Sam 6:3; cf. KJV). Here seven of Saul's descendants were hanged to satisfy the vengeance of the Gibeonites (21:6; RSV has Gibeon). One of David's mighty men was from Gibeah of Benjamin (2 Sam 23:29; 1 Chron 11:31). The people of Gibeah fled when the Assyrians marched toward them (Isa 10:29). Hosea called for a warning (Hos 5:8) at Gibeah because of the sins Israel had committed "as in the days of Gibeah" (9:9; 10:9); the sins of Saul's reign had been remembered for centuries.

GIBEATH HAARALOTH (gib'-ē-ăth hăr'à-lôth). The place where Joshua ordered the circumcision of all the male Israelites who had not been circumcised during the wandering in the desert (Josh 5:3); KJV "hill of the foreskins."

GIBEON (gĭb'ē-ŏn, Heb. *giv'ôn, pertaining to a hill*). A city of Benjamin (Josh 18:25) NW of Jerusalem; in NT times Gabao; modern ej-Jib. It was given to the priests (Josh 21:17). At the time of the Conquest, Joshua didn't consult the Lord and was deceived by the ambassadors of Gibeon into making a treaty with them (Josh 9), promising not to destroy them. When he discovered the deception, he spared their lives but made them woodcutters and water carriers. A coalition of Canaanite kings attacked Gibeon because they had made peace with Joshua (ch. 10). Joshua came to the aid of Gibeon, and in the battle that followed, Joshua called on the sun to stand still to give him time for more fighting (alluded to in Isa 28:21). No other city made peace with Israel (Josh 11:19). Gibeon was the chief of four Hivite cities (9:17). Abner of Israel and Joab of Judah met at a pool at Gibeon, the remains of which

The "pool of Gibeon" (2 Sam 2:13), with its spiral staircase of seventy-nine steps and measuring 36 feet (11 m.) in diameter and 30 feet (9 m.) in depth. Courtesy Zev Radovan.

may still be seen. Here, two groups of twelve men fought an indecisive contest, and the remaining forces joined in a disastrous battle (2 Sam 2:8–28; 3:30), following which Abner and Joab agreed to a cessation of the fighting. At a great stone in Gibeon Joab murdered Amasa (20:8–10). David defeated the Philistines from Gibeon on the north to Gezer on the south (1 Chron 14:16). Zadok the priest was assigned to minister at the high place in Gibeon (16:39–40; 21:29). Solomon, at the outset of his reign, came to Gibeon to sacrifice and there in a dream he chose wisdom above other gifts that God offered him (1 Kings 3:3–15; 2 Chron 1:2–13). Again Solomon received a message from the Lord here (1 Kings 9:1–9). In 1 Chronicles 8:29; 9:35 we read that the father of Gibeon, husband of Maacah, lived there. People from Gibeon returned to Jerusalem from the Captivity and helped rebuild the walls (Neh 3:7; 7:25). Jeremiah confronted a false prophet from Gibeon in the temple (Jer 28:1). Gibeon was the scene of a rescue of Israelites during the Assyrian occupation (41:11–16).

J. B. Pritchard excavated the site (A.D. 1957–62). All the remains are from the Iron Age (Israelite period) and later, except for a few traces of the Late Bronze Age. The main discoveries were two water tunnels, a large pool (mentioned in 2 Samuel 2:13) in which pottery vessels were found with the name Gibeon stamped on them in Hebrew, some houses, a wine cellar, and some fortifications.

GIBEONITES (gĭb'ē-ŏn-īts). The inhabitants of Gibeon; Hivites (Josh 9:3, 7), Hurrians, or Horites (Gen 36:20; Deut 2:12) who had formerly lived in Edom. Because of the deceitful manner in which they gained the favor of Joshua, they were made slave laborers for menial tasks such as chopping wood and drawing water (Josh 9). They were the peasants of the Mittannian Empire, which in 1500 B.C. reached from Media to the Mediterranean. Its rulers were Indo-Aryans, its peasants of another but non-Semitic race. The Gibeonites and their allies, at the time of the conquest by Joshua, controlled a tetrapolis—Berroth, Chephirah, Kiriath Baal, and Gibeon. During a prolonged famine, David inquired of the Lord and learned that the cause was blood-guilt because Saul had massacred the Gibeonites; therefore David turned over to them seven descendants of Saul for vengeance (2 Sam 21:1–9). A Gibeonite was leader of David's thirty mighty men (1 Chron 12:4). Gibeonites helped repair the walls of Jerusalem (Neh 3:7). ER

GIBLITES (See GEBAL)

GIDDALTI (gĭ-dăl'tī). A son of Heman, and one of the heads of music (1 Chron 25:4, 29).

GIDDEL (gĭd'ĕl). 1. A member of the family of temple servants (KJV Nethinims) who returned from exile with Zerubbabel (Ezra 2:47; Neh 7:58).

2. Also listed as coming up from exile with Zerubbabel are sons of Giddel, who was a servant of Solomon (Ezra 2:56; Neh 7:58).

GIDEON (gĭd'ē-ŏn, Heb. *Gidh'ôn, feller* or *hewer*). The son of Joash, an Abiezrite (Judg 6:11) who lived in Ophrah not far from Mount Gerizim (not the Ophrah of Benjamin listed in Josh 18:23). The record about Gideon is found in Judges 6:1–9:6. When he is first mentioned he was already a mature man. His firstborn, Jether, was a youth (8:20). Gideon had already become a noted warrior (6:12), perhaps by waging "underground" warfare against the marauding Midianites. The extent to which the people had been enslaved is shown by the fact that Gideon had to hide in a winepress to do the threshing (6:11). A supernatural fire that consumed Gideon's sacrifice (6:17–23) attested to the fact that the messenger who called Gideon to lead Israel was from God.

Gideon responded to the call and, with the help of some friends, overthrew the altar of Baal and cut down the sacred grove around it. He erected instead a new altar, naming it Jahveh-Shalom, "The LORD is Peace" (Judg 6:24). For his daring feat the followers of Baal wanted to kill him, but his father intervened. Instead of death he was given a new name, Jerub-Baal, or "contender with Baal" (6:28–32). Later the name was changed to Jerubbesheth, "contender with the Idol," evidently to eliminate any recognition of Baal (2 Sam 11:21). Gideon then issued a call to adjoining tribesmen to war against the Midianites. Having gathered a formidable host, he sought confirmation of his task and so put forth the famous test of the fleece (Judg 6:36–40). As further assurance, he was instructed to slip into the enemy's camp, and there he overheard one soldier tell another of a dream and interpret it to mean that Gideon's smaller army would win the battle (7:9–14). To prevent human boasting over victory, God instructed Gideon to reduce his force to three hundred picked men by (1) letting the faint-hearted go home and (2) choosing only those men who were cautious enough to dip their drinking water when they went down to a stream to drink (7:1–8).

By strategy involving psychological warfare, Gideon's small band surprised the enemy in a night attack. Three groups of one hundred each attacked from three directions. At the proper time a signal was given, shields for the lights were removed, and trumpets blared. The sleeping Midianites were terrified. So complete was their rout that they killed one another in their mad flight (Judg 7:15–22). Gideon then called on his allies to join in the chase. Ephraim captured two of the kings (8:1–3). Gideon pursued the other two northward and captured them near the junction of the Sea of Galilee and the Jordan (8:4–21). Thus the country was delivered all the way to the Jordan (7:22–23; 8:1–21). When his people wanted to make him king, Gideon refused and instead called for an offering of the golden trinkets that had been captured from the Midianites. With these he made a ephod, either an image of Jehovah, or a sacred vestment worn by a priest in the sanctuary. Because of its worth and beauty, it later became an object of worship (8:24–27). Gideon's ability and statesmanship are shown in his long and fruitful ministry of forty years as judge (8:28). During his life he had seventy-one sons (8:30)—one, Abimelech, by a concubine of Shechem (8:31). After Gideon's death idolatry returned (8:32–35), Abimelech seized an opportune time, engaged mercenaries, invaded the land of Gideon, and destroyed all the seventy sons except Jotham, who escaped by hiding (9:1–6). JDF

GIDEONI (gĭd'ē-ō'nī, *cutter down*). A prince of Benjamin's tribe (Num 7:60) whose son ruled them (10:24).

GIDOM (gī'dŏm, Heb. *gidh'ōm, desolation*). Mentioned only in Judges 20:45. An isolated place east of Bethel, to which the routed Benjamites fled from angry fellow Israelites.

GIER EAGLE (See BIRDS)

GIFTS, SPIRITUAL (Gr. *charismata*). A theological term meaning any endowment that comes through the grace of God (Rom 1:11). Paul discussed at length in 1 Corinthians 12 the spiritual gifts given for special tasks in and through the churches (Rom 12:6–8; 2 Cor 1:11; 1 Peter 4:10). They include the ability to speak an unlearned tongue (1 Cor 14:1–33), the interpretation of tongues (1 Cor 12:30; 14:27–28), power to drive out evil spirits (Matt 8:16; Acts 13:7–12), special ability in healing the sick (1 Cor 12:9), prophecy (Rom 12:6), keenness of wisdom (1 Cor 12:8), and special knowledge (1 Cor 12:8). Paul told the Corinthians to diligently seek these gifts (12:31), but he pointed out that "the most excellent way" (12:31) was an emphasis on faith, hope, and love, among which love is the greatest gift (13:13). The fruit of the Spirit is described in Galatians 5:22–23.

Everyone is accountable for any gift given to him or her (1 Cor 4:7; 1 Peter 4:10). Claims of having such gifts are to be tested by doctrine (1 Cor 12:2–3) and on moral grounds (Matt 7:15; Rom 8:9). The ability to preach is a spiritual gift (1 Cor 2:4; 2 Tim 1:6). To know the deep things of God requires spiritual insight (1 Cor 2:11–16). The gifts are distributed by the Holy Spirit (Heb 2:4). JDF

GIHON (gī'hŏn, Heb. *gîhôn, burst forth*). 1. One of the four rivers in Eden (Gen 2:8–14). The name indicates that it arose either from some large spring or from a cataract. Since it wound through "the whole land of Ethiopia" (KJV), it is thought to be the Nile. However, Ethiopia was the name given to the land occupied by the descendants of Cush and covered a vast area. Isaiah called it the land of Cush (11:11 as does the NIV of Gen 2:13). Cushan appears in Habakkuk 3:7. Since Eden was probably in the Tigris-Euphrates Valley, it is possible that Gihon was a small stream in that

Rock-cut entrance to the Gihon spring in Jerusalem, from which Hezekiah cut his conduit (2 Kings 20:20; 2 Chron 33:14), the famous Siloam tunnel to supply water to the pool of Siloam. Courtesy Israel Government Press Office.

region. Reliable evidence confirms the claim of some scholars that Cush refers to an area in NW India. *Kassi* (Cush) appears in some ancient records of the region.

2. Gihon is the name also of a noted spring near Jerusalem. Solomon was anointed there to succeed David (1 Kings 1:32–40). That the spring provided a good supply of water is shown by the fact that Hezekiah, during his prosperous reign, had its water diverted by a tunnel to serve the growing population of Jerusalem (2 Chron 32:27–30). Recent discoveries show that this tunnel was connected with the Pool of Siloam, where the people of the city went to draw water. Remains of an ancient canal have been found through which the water once entered and it may be of this that Isaiah wrote (8:6). This spring was originally controlled by the Jebusites (2 Sam 5:6), who cut a tunnel to bring it near enough to the wall for water to be drawn without exposing their women to raiders. JDF

GILALAI (gĭl'ȧ-lī). A member of a band of musicians who, under Ezra's direction, had part in the dedication of the wall of Jerusalem (Neh 12:36).

GILBOA (gĭl-bō'ȧ, Heb. *gilbō'a, bubbling*). It has been identified as Jabel Fuku'a, a range of barren hills on the eastern side of the Plain of Esdraelon, named from a noted spring. The mean elevation of the hills is about 1,600 feet (500 m.).

Partial west-southwest view of the Gilboa hills. The range is 11 miles (18 km.) long and 5½ miles (9 km.) wide, between the Jezreel and Beth Shean valleys. On these slopes occurred the defeat and death of Saul and his three sons (1 Sam 3:1). Courtesy Duby Tal.

Ain Jalud on the northern slope of the range has been identified as the location of the spring. Saul gathered his forces here to await an attack by the Philistines. Fear drove him to consult the witch of Endor (1 Sam 28:4–7). During the battle he was wounded, his forces were routed, and he committed suicide (1 Chron 10:1–8).

GILEAD (gĭl'ē-ăd, Heb. *gil'ādh, rugged*). The name is used to indicate Israel's possession east of the Jordan River. Josephus so understood it (*Antiq.* 12.8.3). It extended from the lower end of the Sea of Galilee to the northern end of the Dead Sea, and from the Jordan eastward to the desert, a plateau of some 2,000 feet (625 m.) elevation. In the time of Moses it was a lush region with good forests, rich grazing lands, and abundant moisture. A scenic gorge of the noted brook Jabbok divided it. Jacob camped at Gilead when fleeing from Laban (Gen 31:22–25). Overtaken there, he made a covenant with Laban that was confirmed by a pile of stones that Jacob named *Galeed,* "witness heap" (31:47; see footnote). During succeeding years the name came to be applied to the entire region, which included Mount Gilead (31:25), the land of Gilead (Num 32:1), and Gilead (Gen 37:25).

When Canaan was allocated to the Israelites, Gilead fell to the Reubenites, Gadites, and to half the tribe of Manasseh (Deut 3:13). An account of the conquest of the region is found in Deuteronomy 2 and 3. Moses was permitted to see the plain before his death (34:1). After the land was conquered a great altar was erected beside the Jordan so that true worship would not be forgotten (Josh 22:10).

Beside the Jabbok in Gilead Jacob had his reconciliation with Esau (Gen 32:22–33:15). Jair, a Gileadite, served for twenty years as judge over Israel (Judg 10:3). Jephthah, a great-grandson of Manasseh, was also a judge. Being the son of a concubine, he was banished by his brothers, but when Gilead was in dire distress, he was recalled by the elders (11:1–3). He defeated the Ephraimites and prevented fugitives from crossing the Jordan by resorting to the noted password "Shibboleth" (12:1–7). Absalom gathered his forces in Gilead when he rebelled against David (2 Sam 15:13–23). The Gileadites finally fell into gross idolatry (Hos 6:8; 12:11), were overcome by Hazael (2 Kings 10:32–34), and were led into captivity by Tiglath-Pileser (15:27–29).

Gilead became famous because of some of its products. Balm was exported to Tyre (Ezek 27:17); Jeremiah knew of its curative power (Jer 8:22; 46:11; 51:8). The Ishmaelites who bought Joseph carried balm to Egypt (Gen 37:25). JDF

GILGAL (gĭl'găl, Heb. *Gilgāl, circle of stones*). The first camp of Israel after they had crossed the Jordan (Josh 4:19–20). While they were camped there, Joshua restored the Hebrew rite of circumcision in response to God's promise to "roll away the reproach of Egypt" (5:2–9). The town that grew up was near the northern border of Judah (15:7). Most authorities agree that this is the town included in the judicial circuit of Samuel (1 Sam 7:16). The memorial altar of stones erected there became a pagan shrine of later years against which Hosea (4:15) and Amos (4:4) warned the people. According to Josephus, Gilgal was about ten miles (seventeen km.) from the Jordan and two miles (three km.) or more from Jericho.

Samuel sent Saul to Gilgal to be confirmed as king over Israel (1 Sam 11:15). There Saul later grew restless because of Samuel's delay in coming and offended the Lord by presuming to act as priest and make his own sacrifice (13:1–10). Judah gathered at Gilgal to meet David when he returned from defeating the rebels under Absalom (2 Sam 19).

Gilgal is not mentioned in the NT, and its location is not known. The town from which Elijah ascended to heaven was not this Gilgal (2 Kings 2:1). Gilgal furnished singers who had part in the dedication of the wall of Jerusalem (Neh 12:27–43). A large pool has been located at modern Jiljuliyeh, which may mark the site. Some authorities disagree with the idea that

The land of Gilead, southeast of the Sea of Galilee, showing the Yarmuk River in foreground. Courtesy S. Zur Picture Library.

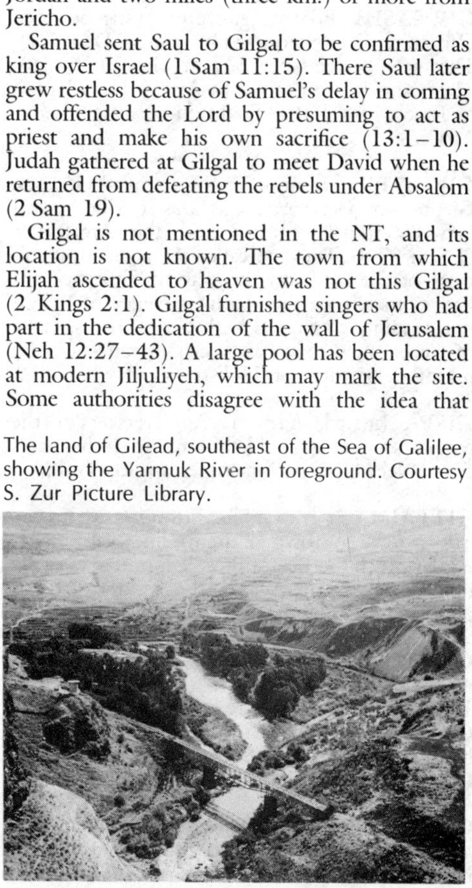

Gilgal near Jericho was the city in Samuel's circuit, and others claim that the Gilgal mentioned by Hosea and Amos was another city near Shechem. JDF

GILOH (gī'lō). Home of Ahithophel, one of David's counselors who rebelled with Absalom (2 Sam 15:12); also a town of Judah (Josh 15:51).

GIMZO (gĭm'zō, *place of lush sycamores*). A town some three miles (five km.) SW of Lydda, off the Jerusalem highway, captured by Philistines during the reign of Ahaz (2 Chron 28:18). Jimza is no doubt its modern location.

GIN (See SNARE)

GINATH (gī'năth, *protector*). The father of Tibni, a contender for the throne of Israel (1 Kings 16:21).

GINNETHON (gĭn'ā-thŏn). A priest who returned to Jerusalem with Zerubbabel (Neh 12:4) and signed the Levitical covenant (10:6, Gennetho in KJV).

GIRDLE (See DRESS; ARMS AND ARMOR)

GIRGASHITES (gûr'gȧ-shītes). One of seven Canaanite tribes conquered by Joshua (Deut 7:1). They were descendants of Ham (Gen 10:15–16). Their land was promised to Abram (15:21) and to Israel (Josh 3:10). Tradition says they fled to Africa.

GIRZITES (gûr'zīts). Variously called Gerzites, Gizrites, or Gerizzites, this was a tribe named between the Geshurites and the Amalekites (1 Sam 27:8). They are called the ancient inhabitants of the land, on the way to Shur, toward Egypt; that is, in the south or Negev of Judah; not certainly connected with Gezer. If originally of Gezer, they may have been driven south by invading Israelites or Philistines.

GISPA (gĭs'pȧ, *listener*). An overseer of the temple servants (KJV Nethinim), in Nehemiah's time (Neh 11:21). Sometimes spelled Gishpa.

GITTAIM (gĭt'ā-ĭm, Heb. *gittayim,* perhaps *two wine presses*). A town of Benjamin (Neh 11:31, 33) to which the Beerothites fled, probably at the time of Saul's cruelty (2 Sam 4:3), and lived as protected strangers. The exact site is unknown.

GITTITES (gĭt'īt, *of Gath*). Natives of Gath, unconquered at the time of Joshua's death (Josh 13:1–3). The ark was kept in a Gittite home (2 Sam 6:8–11). David's guard included six hundred men of Gath (15:18). Goliath was a Gittite (21:19).

GITTITH (gĭt'ĭth, Heb. *gittîth*). A word found in the titles of Psalms 8, 81, 84. Its meaning is uncertain. It may denote some musical instrument made in Gath, or a melody or march that was popular in Gath.

GIZONITE (gī'zō-nīt). Hashem, one of David's valiant men, was described as a Gizonite (1 Chron 11:34). Probably an error for Gunite. He was probably the same as Jashen the Gunite (2 Sam 23:32).

GLASS (See MINERALS)

GLEAN (Heb. lāqat, *'ālal*). The Hebrew custom of allowing the poor to follow the reapers and gather the grain that was left behind or the grapes that remained after the vintage (Judg 8:2; Ruth 2:2, 16; Isa 17:6). This custom was backed by one of the agricultural laws of Moses (Lev 19:9; 23:22; Deut 24:19–21). The word is also used figuratively to describe the utter destruction of Israel (Jer 6:9).

GLEDE (See BIRDS)

GLORY. The Hebrew word so translated, *kābôd,* means the "weight" and therefore the "worth" of something—as we speak of someone whose word "carries weight." The glory of God is the worthiness of God, more particularly, the presence of God in the fullness of his attributes in some place or everywhere. It is in this sense that Isaiah reports the words of the seraphim that "the whole earth is full of his glory" (Isa 6:3), meaning that the Lord in his full person, deity, and majesty is present in every place. Again, when the Lord says of the tabernacle that it "will be consecrated by [his] glory" (Exod 29:43), he means that without diluting or diminishing his full deity he will himself dwell in the great tent and make it holy by his presence. Moses asked that he might see the Lord's glory (33:18), and the Lord responded that he would himself proclaim his name to him, i.e., make Moses aware of all the glorious attributes and capacities that the one and only God possesses (33:19–34:8). Sometimes the Lord allowed his glory to become visible. Since the cloudy-fiery pillar was the place where he was present, there were occasions (e.g., 16:10) when (whatever form it took) there was a manifestation of his presence. Possibly the same was true in Exodus 40:34–35: Either there was an awesome manifestation of the Lord's presence or an overwhelming sense that God was there so that Moses dared not come near. Later thought defined this indwelling presence of God as the shekinah (or "indwelling").

NT references to the shekinah glory are seen in John 1:14 and Romans 9:4. Glory is both physical and spiritual, as is seen in Luke 2:9 ("the glory of the Lord shone around them") and John 17:22, where it refers to the glory of the Father that Jesus gave to his disciples. As for the saints, glory culminates in the changing of their bodies to the likeness of their glorified Lord (Phil 3:20).

Bibliography: I. Abrahams, *The Glory of God,* 1925; A. M. Ramsey, *The Glory of God and the Transfiguration of Christ,* 1949; G. Kittel, TDNT, 2:232–55. JAM

GNASH (Heb. *hāraq,* Gr. *brygmos*). In the OT the expression "to gnash with the teeth" most often represents rage, anger, or hatred (Job 16:9; Ps 35:16; 37:12; 112:10). In the NT it expresses disappointment and agony of spirit rather than anger (Matt 8:12; 13:42, 50; 22:13; 24:51; 25:30; Luke 13:28).

GNAT (See ANIMALS)

GNOSTICISM (Gr. *gnōsis, knowledge*). Though sometimes used of false teaching within the period when the NT was written, the word more accurately describes systems of knowledge in opposition to orthodox Christianity in the second and third centuries. It appears that some church members, embarrassed by the lowly origins of Christianity (birth in a stable, traveling teacher, death on a cross, etc.), linked aspects of traditional Christianity with attractive ideas taken from Greek philosophy and Eastern religion, magic, and astrology. We call the resulting systems Gnosticism, and they seem very complicated to modern people. Their main themes were as follows: The true God is pure spirit and dwells in the realm of pure light, totally separated from this dark world. This world is evil, for it is made of matter, and matter is evil. The true God will have nothing to do with it, for it was created by a lesser god and was a mistake. People in this world are normally made of body and mind, but in a few there is a spark of pure spirit. Such "spiritual" people need to be rescued from this evil world; thus there is need for a Savior. Jesus, who is pure spirit even though he appears to be body and mind, is the Savior who comes from the true God in light to bring knowledge (*gnōsis*) of the spiritual realm of light. Therefore those who have the spark of spirit can receive the knowledge and be reunited with the true God.

Within the NT there are references to claims to knowledge and wisdom (e.g., 1 Cor 1:17ff.; 8:1; 13:8;) that could be the roots of the growth that led to developed Gnosticism. There was a heresy in the church of Colosse (Col 2:8–23) and false teaching in the churches Timothy knew (1 Tim 1:4ff.; 4:3ff.; 2 Tim 2:18; 3:5–7) that may be termed a false *gnōsis* (1 Tim 6:20). Then in the Epistles of John there are references to false teaching about the reality of the humanity of Jesus (1 John 4:3; 2 John 7). But there is certainly nothing in the NT of the developed kind of false doctrines that the teachers of the church had to face a century or so later.

Bibliography: J. W. Drane, "Gnosticism and the New Testament," *Bulletin of the Theological Students Fellowship,* 68 and 69, 1974. PT

GOAD (gōd, Heb. *dōrevān, malmādh,* Gr. *kentron*). An eight-foot (two and one-half m.) wooden pole, having at one end a spade for removing mud from the plow and at the other a sharp point for prodding oxen. It was a formidable weapon in the hands of Shamgar (Judg 3:31). For oxen to "kick against the goads" (cf. Acts 26:14) pictures useless resistance to a greater power.

GOAH (gō'ă, Heb. *gō'âh*). A place of unknown location, but apparently west of Jerusalem. Mentioned only once (Jer 31:39) in connection with prophecy concerning the restoration of Jerusalem. Josephus refers to it as "the camp of the Assyrians."

GOAT (See ANIMALS)

GOATH (See GOAH)

GOB (gŏb, Heb. *gôv, pit, cistern*). A place mentioned in 2 Samuel 21:18 as the scene of two of David's battles with the Philistines. Here the brother of Goliath defied Israel but was killed by Jonathan, son of Shimei. The Septuagint calls it Gath, which is probably correct.

GOD (Heb. *'ĕlōhîm, ēl, 'elyôn, shaddāy, yahweh,* Gr. *theos*). The Bible does not contain a formal definition of the word "God," yet God's being and attributes are displayed on every page. The greatest definition of the word in the history of Christendom, that is, in the culture in which the Bible has been a prevailing influence, is the one found in the Westminster Shorter Catechism (Q.4): "God is a Spirit, infinite, eternal, and unchangeable, in his being, wisdom, power, holiness, justice, goodness, and truth." It is fair to say that this definition faithfully sets forth what the Bible constantly assumes and declares concerning God.

I. God Is a Spirit. These words mean that God is a nonmaterial personal being, self-conscious and self-determining.

The definition contains three adjectives, each modifying seven nouns. The descriptive units in which these words are combined are not logically separable but are inextricably woven together, and thus they delineate the unity and the integrated complexity of God's attributes. The analysis cannot be exhaustive but only descriptive.

II. God Is Infinite. The infinity of God is not an independent attribute. If we were to say, "God is the infinite," without specification, the meaning would be pantheistic, equal to saying, "God is everything." In using the word "infinite," we must always be specific:

A. **Infinite in his being.** This doctrine is intended to teach that God is everywhere. The omnipresence of God is vividly brought out in such Scriptures as Psalm 139. God is not physically, relatively, or measurably big. The word "immensity" is used by good theologians, but it conveys to some minds a false impression, as though God were partly here and partly there, like a giant, or an amorphous mass, or a fluid. The omnipresence of God means that wherever we are, even if we are like the fugitive Jacob at Bethel (Gen 28:16), God *himself* is there.

It is easier to conceive of God's omnipresence by saying, "Everything everywhere is immediately in his presence." Finite creatures can act instantaneously in a limited area. Everything within one's reach or sight is immediately in his presence, in the sense that distance is no problem. So in an absolutely perfect sense, everything in the universe is immediately in the presence of God.

B. **Infinite in his wisdom.** This phrase designates God's omniscience. The Bible throughout regards God's omniscience as all-inclusive, not dependent on a step-by-step process of reasoning. God's knowledge does not increase or diminish when the temporal events of his redemptive program take place. He eternally knows what he has known in the past and what he will know in the future.

C. **Infinite in his power.** These words point to his omnipotence, his ability to do with power all that power can do, his controlling all the power that is or can be.

D. **Infinite in his holiness, justice, and goodness.** These words signify God's moral attributes. Holiness is regarded in the Bible as his central ethical character. Basic ethical principles are revealed by the will of God and derived from and based on the character of God. "Be holy because I am holy" (Lev 11:44–45). Justice refers to his administration of rewards and punishments among the personal beings of the universe. Goodness in this context indicates his love, his common grace toward all, and his special grace in saving sinners.

E. **Infinite in his truth.** This is the attribute that designates the basis of all logic and rationality. The axioms of logic and mathematics, and all the laws of reason, are not laws apart from God to which God must be subject. They are attributes of his own character. When the Bible says that "it is impossible for God to lie" (Heb 6:18; Titus 1:2), it is not contradicting his omnipotence. How much power would it take to make two times two equal five? Truth is not an object of power.

There is no mere tautology in the Bible, as though the multiplication tables were true by mere divine fiat. As in ethics, so in rationality, the biblical writers constantly appeal to the truth of God's immutable character. "He cannot deny himself" (2 Tim 2:13 KJV).

Just as the adjective "infinite," in the definition we are considering, applies to all the specified attributes, so the words "eternal" and "unchangeable" similarly apply to all.

F. **Eternal.** This means without temporal beginning or ending, or in a figurative sense "eternal" may designate (as in the words "eternal life") a quality of being suitable for eternity.

That God existed eternally before the creation of the finite universe does not imply a personal subject with no object, for God is triune. (See TRINITY)

The idea that eternity means timelessness is nowhere suggested in the Bible. This false notion doubtless came into Christian theology under the influence of Aristotle's "Unmoved Mover," the influence of which is strong in Thomas Aquinas. That the Bible does not teach that God is timeless is an objective, verifiable fact.

G. **Unchangeable,** in Bible language, points to the perfect self-consistency of God's character throughout all eternity. This is not a static concept, but dynamic, in all his relations with his creatures. That God brings to pass, in time, the events of his redemptive program is not contradictory. The notion that God's immutability is static immobility (as in Thomism) is like the notion of timelessness and is contrary to the biblical view. The God of the Bible is intimately and actively concerned in all the actions of all his creatures.

III. God Is Known by His Acts. Supremely, "God . . . has spoken to us by his Son" (Heb 1:1ff.). Further, his "invisible" being, that is, his "eternal power and divine character" (*theiotēs* as distinguished from *theotēs*") are "known" and "clearly seen" by "what has been made" (Rom 1:20). "The heavens declare the glory of God" (Ps 19; Rom 10:18). It is customary to distinguish between "natural revelation," all that God has made, and "special revelation," the Bible.

IV. God Is Known in Fellowship. That God is known by faith, beyond the mere cognitive sense, in fellowship with his people, is one of the most prominent themes throughout the Bible. Moses, leading his people in the Exodus, was assured, "My Presence will go with you, and I will give you rest." And Moses replied, "If your Presence does not go with us, do not send us up from here" (Exod 33:13–14). The Bible abounds in invitations to seek and find fellowship with God. See Psalm 27, Isaiah 55, and many similar gracious invitations.

Other gods are referred to in the Bible as false gods (Judg 6:31; 1 Kings 18:27; 1 Cor 8:4–6) or as demonic (1 Cor 10:19–22).

GODLINESS (Gr. *eusebeia, theosebeia*). The piety toward God and the proper conduct that springs from a right relationship with him. It is not belief in itself, but the devotion toward God and love toward man that result from that belief. Religious faith is empty without godliness, for it is then but an empty form (2 Tim 3:5). The Greek *eusebeia* is found fifteen times in the NT. It is the sum total of religious character and actions, and it produces both a present and future state of happiness. It is not right action that is done from a sense of duty, but is the spontaneous virtue that comes from the indwelling Christ and reflects him.

GOG AND MAGOG (See MAGOG)

GOIIM (gŏy'ĭm). The territory, perhaps of a "mixed population," ruled by an otherwise unknown king named Tidal (Gen 14:1, 9), who was part of the confederacy defeated by Abraham when he rescued Lot from them. Also the name of the territory of an unnamed king defeated by Joshua (Josh 12:23, "Goyim"). (See also HAROSHETH; HAGGOYIM; HEATHEN, PAGAN)

GOLAN (gō'lăn, Heb. *gôlān*). A city in the territory of the half tribe of Manasseh in Bashan, east of the Jordan. It was one of the three cities of refuge and was assigned to the Gershonite Levites (Deut 4:43). Probably an important city in its day, it was destroyed by Alexander Janneus after his army had been ambushed there. The site cannot definitely be identified, but the archaeologist Schumacher believes it was seventeen miles (twenty-eight km.) east of the Sea of Galilee, in present Syria, located in Gaulanitis, one of the four provinces into which Bashan was divided after the Babylonian captivity. It is a fertile plateau, 1,000–3,000 feet (312–937 m.) in elevation.

GOLD (See MINERALS)

GOLDSMITH (See OCCUPATIONS AND PROFESSIONS)

GOLGOTHA (gŏl′gō-thȧ, Gr. *Golgotha,* from Aram. *gulgaltā*', *skull*). The place of our Lord's crucifixion. From the Hebrew *gulgoleth,* which implies a bald, round, skull-like mound or hillock. The Latin name, *Calvarius* ("bald skull"), has been retained in the form *Calvary* (Luke 23:33). In NIV, following RSV, it is simply, "The Skull." Two explanations of the name are found: (1) It was a place of execution and therefore abounded in skulls; (2) the place had the appearance of a skull when viewed from a short distance. The Gospels and tradition do not agree as to its location. Both Matthew (27:33) and Mark (15:22) locate it outside the city, but close to it (John 19:20) on the public highway, which was the type of location usually chosen by the Romans for executions. Tradition locates it within the present city.

GOLIATH (gō-lī′ăth, Heb. *golyāth*). A gigantic warrior of the Philistine army, probably one of the Anakites (Num 13:33; Josh 11:22). Goliath's size was extraordinary. If a cubit is twenty-one inches (fifty-four cm.), he was over eleven feet (three and one-half m.) in height; if about eighteen inches (forty-six cm.), he was over nine feet (almost three m.). The only mention made of Goliath is his appearance as a champion of the Philistines (1 Sam 17). The Philistines had ventured into Israel's territory and had taken a firm position on the slope of a hill, with Israel camped on the opposite hill. From the Philistine camp Goliath made daily challenges to personal combat, but after forty days no one had accepted. David had been sent to his brothers with provisions. When he heard Goliath's challenge, he inquired about its meaning. After being told, he went to face Goliath, armed only with a sling and five stones. Hit in the forehead, Goliath fell, and David cut off his head. When the Philistines saw that their champion was dead, they fled, pursued by victorious Israel. The Goliath of 2 Samuel 21:19 was probably the son of the giant whom David killed. He was killed by Elhanan, one of David's men. A discrepancy has been imagined, and some have thought that it was Elhanan who killed the giant Goliath of 1 Samuel 17.

GOMER (gō′mĕr, Heb. *gōmer,* possibly meaning *God accomplishes it* or *completion*). 1. Gomer was the oldest son of Japheth (Gen 10:2–3; 1 Chron 1:5–6) and the father/ancestor of a people (Ezek 38:6). The latter are probably to be equated with the Indo-European tribes, the Cimmerians (Gimirrai) of classical history who settled in Cappadocia.

2. Gomer was the wife of the prophet Hosea, and the daughter of Diblaim (Hos 1:3). She bore Jezreel, Lo-Ruhamah, and Lo-Ammi. God used the unfaithfulness of Gomer in her marriage to illustrate the unfaithfulness of Israel in their covenant relationship to himself. See also HOSEA, BOOK OF.

GOMORRAH (gō-mŏr′rȧ, Heb. *'ămōrâh,* Gr. *Gomorra, submersion*). One of the five "cities of the plain" located in the Vale of Siddim at the south end of the Dead Sea. Zoar alone escaped the destruction by fire from heaven in the time of Abraham and Lot. The district where the five cities were located was exceedingly productive and well-peopled, but today traces of the punitive catastrophe abound. There are great quantities of salt, with deposits of bitumen, sulphur, and niter on the shores of the Dead Sea. The location was long a contention, but it reportedly was established in A.D. 1924 by an archaeological expedition led by M. G. Kyle that placed it beneath the shallow waters of the Dead Sea south of the Lisan promontory. BPD

GOOD, GOODNESS (Heb. *tôbh,* Gr. *agathos, kalos*). The nonmoral (and nonreligious) use of "good" is common in the Bible (e.g., "good fruit," Matt 7:19; "good soil," "good seed," Matt 13:23–24). Apart from this general use the word "good" is used preeminently of God himself. Without any qualification it can be said that the Lord alone is truly good (Ps 136:1; Mark 10:18). Further, since Jesus is the Son of God (sharing deity with the Father), he is also good (John 10:11, 14, 32; Heb. 9:11); but, as Messiah and Servant of the Lord, he points to the unique goodness of God himself (Matt 19:17; Luke 18:19).

The Lord revealed his goodness in his relation to, and treatment of, Israel; and so the Levites and congregation are to confess that he is good (1 Chron 16:34, "Give thanks to the LORD, for he is good" (see also Ps 106:1; 107:1; 118:1). Further, in a derived but real sense, what God creates, gives, and commands is also good—and so is right response to what God says and requires.

The whole universe, the work of God's creative power, is good (Gen 1:4, 10, 12, 18, 31); Paul said that all God has created is good (1 Tim 4:4). God's self-revelation of his character and will, his word and his law as given to Israel and manifested in and through Jesus Christ, are good (Ps 119:39; Isa 61:1; Rom 7:12; Heb 10:1). The gospel is good tidings and good news. Further, the way God establishes and maintains relationships with people is good, as well as the gifts he gives to them and the providential care he exercises over them (Ps 145:9; Matt 7:11; Acts 14:17; Rom 8:28; James 1:17).

The land of Goshen, a rich and fertile land where Joseph settled his family (Gen 47:11), with an irrigation canal in the foreground and the pyramids of Giza in the distance. Courtesy Seffie Ben-Yoseph.

Although in themselves, because of their sin, human beings have no goodness that is acceptable in God's sight, they can receive and become channels of the goodness of God. When they respond positively to the grace, love, gifts, and providence of God, then what they do ("good works" [Gal 6:10; Eph 2:10; 1 Thess 5:15]), enjoy (having "a good conscience" [1 Tim 1:5, 19; Heb 13:18]), and become ("good" [Acts 11:24]) may be described as good. This is because in attitude, behavior, and deeds, true believers in Christ are reflecting the goodness of God and of Christ. This use of the word "good" is to be distinguished from the general use of the word with reference to behavior that is acceptable or commendable as a citizen of a country or member of a specific people (Rom 13:3–4).

Finally, the goodness of God that is experienced in this present age is only a foretaste of the fullness to be revealed and experienced in the age to come (Gal 6:9; Phil 1:6; Heb 9:11; 10:1).

Bibliography: J. W. Wenham, *The Goodness of God,* 1974; C. J. Orlebeke and L. B. Smedes, *God and the Good,* 1975; Donald Guthrie, *New Testament Theology,* 1981, pp. 896ff. PT

GOPHER WOOD (See PLANTS)

GOSHEN (gō'shĕn, Heb. *gōshen,* probably *mound of earth*). 1. The NE section of the Nile delta region is usually termed "the land of Goshen." The Israelites under Jacob settled here while Joseph was prime minister of Egypt (Gen 46). The district is not large, an area of some 900 square miles (2,368 sq. km.), but because of irrigation it is considered some of the best land of Egypt, excellent for grazing and for certain types of agriculture. The district had two principal cities, both built for the pharaohs by the Hebrews. The one of greater importance had, at various times, at least three and possibly four names. Zoan, Avaris, and Tanis were certainly its names, and archaeologists do not agree as to whether it also bore the name of Rameses. Some indicate a different location for Rameses. Under the name of Avaris, it was for five hundred years the capital of the Hyksos Empire. The other city, Pithom, is particularly interesting to the student of biblical archaeology because here is found a proof of Exodus 5:7–13. The labor overseers were told not to give the Hebrew workmen straw for making bricks, yet with no diminishing of the assigned quota. In a building at Pithom three types of bricks are found. At its foundation straw was used. After Pharaoh refused to supply straw any longer, the Hebrews desperately gathered all bits of straw and stubble they could find, and such bricks are found higher in the building. It was completed with bricks devoid of straw, as the uppermost bricks indicate.

2. A district of south Palestine, lying between Gaza and Gibeon, its name probably given in remembrance of Egypt (Josh 10:41).

3. A town mentioned with Debir, Socoh, and others, in the SW part of the mountains of Judah (Josh 15:51). BPD

GOSPEL (Gr. *euangelion, good news*). The English word *gospel* is derived from the Anglo-Saxon *godspell,* which meant "good tidings" and, later, the "story concerning God." As now used, the word describes the message of Christianity and the books in which the record of Christ's life and teaching is found. This message is the Good News that God has provided a way of redemption through his Son Jesus Christ. Through the gospel, the Holy Spirit works for the salvation of human beings (Rom 1:15–16). In the NT the word never means a book (one of the four Gospels); instead, it always refers to the good tidings that Christ and the apostles announced. It is called "the gospel of God" (Rom 1:1; 1 Thess 2:2, 9), "the gospel about Jesus Christ" (Mark 1:1; Rom 15:19); "the gospel of God's grace" (Acts 20:24); "the gospel of peace" (Eph 6:15); "the gospel of your salvation" (1:13); and "the gospel of the glory of Christ" (2 Cor 4:4). The gospel has to do entirely with Christ. It was preached by him (Matt 4:23; 11:5), by the apostles (Acts 16:10; Rom 1:15), and by the Evangelists (Acts 8:25). Not until about A.D. 150 was the word applied to the writings concerning the message of Christ. SB

GOSPEL: THE FOUR GOSPELS. The word *gospel* is derived from the Anglo-Saxon *godspell,* meaning "good tidings," and is a literal translation of the Greek *euangelion,* which meant originally a reward for bringing good news, and finally the good news itself. In the NT the term is applied to the revelation of God's plan for reconciling man to himself by forgiving his sin and by transforming his character. The gospel is the message of God's gift of salvation through the person and work of Christ that the church has been commissioned to proclaim (Mark 16:15; Acts 20:24; Eph 1:13). The impact of the life, death, and resurrection of Christ compelled his disciples to present his message to the public. By repeating the significant features of his ministry and his accompanying precepts, following the general order of his biography, they formulated a body of teaching that may have varied in detail with each recital, but that maintained the same general content.

The existence of this standardized message is confirmed by the NT itself. Paul, in the letter to the Galatians, mentioning a visit to Jerusalem that took place before A.D. 50, said: "I . . . set before them the gospel that I preach among the Gentiles" (Gal 2:2). In 1 Corinthians 15:1–5 he defined it clearly. A similar presentation is afforded by the report of Peter's address in the house of Cornelius, the Gentile centurion. After sketching the baptism, life, death, and resurrection of Jesus, Peter concluded: "[God] commanded us to preach to the people and to testify that he is the one whom God appointed as judge of the living and the dead. All the prophets testify about him that everyone who believes in him receives forgiveness of sins through his name" (Acts 10:42–43).

From such samples of apostolic preaching one may conclude that the facts of Jesus' life constituted the gospel, which was interpreted and applied to suit the occasion on which it was preached.

This gospel, which was initially proclaimed in oral form, has been transmitted through the writings called the "Gospels." Although Matthew, Mark, Luke, and John differ considerably in detail, they agree on the general outline of Jesus' career, on the supernatural character of his life, and on the high quality of his moral precepts. From the earliest period of the church they have been accepted as authoritative accounts of his life and teachings.

I. Character of the Gospels. Reduced to writing, the gospel message constitutes a new type of literature. Although it is framed in history, it is not pure history, for the allusions to contemporary events are incidental, and the Gospels do not attempt to develop them. They contain biographical material, but they cannot be called biography in the modern sense of the word, since they do not present a complete summary of the life of Jesus. The Gospels are not sufficiently didactic to be called opinions of their writers. The chief purpose of the Gospels is to create faith in Christ on the part of their readers, who may or may not be believers. Nothing exactly like them can be found either in the OT, to which their writers referred frequently, or in the Hellenic and Roman literature contemporary with them.

Of the numerous accounts and fragments that were composed to perpetuate the ministry and teaching of Jesus, only four are accorded a place in the NT: Matthew, written by Jesus' disciple Matthew Levi, the tax-gatherer; Mark, from the pen of John Mark, an inhabitant of Jerusalem and a companion of Barnabas and Paul; Luke, the first half of a history of Christianity in two volumes (Luke and Acts) by an associate of Paul; and John, a collection of select memoirs by John, the son of Zebedee. Although the traditional authorship of all four canonical Gospels has been disputed, there are strong arguments in their favor, even if, for one or two of them, the Evangelist's relation to the finished work may have been indirect rather than direct. Other Gospels, such as *The Gospel of Peter* or *The Gospel of Thomas*, are later productions of the second and third centuries and usually represent the peculiar theological prejudices of some minor sect.

II. Origin of the Gospels. The existence of the oral gospel is attested by Papias, bishop of Hierapolis in Phrygia, one of the earliest of the church fathers (c. A.D. 80–140). A quotation from the preface to his "Interpretation of our Lord's Declarations," preserved in a historical work by Eusebius, indicates that he still depended on the transmission of the gospel content by the living voice. "But if I met with any one who had been a follower of the elders anywhere, I made it a point to inquire what were the declarations of the elders . . . for I do not think that I derived so much benefit from books as from the living voice of those that were still surviving" (quoted in Eusebius, *Historia Ecclesiae,* 3.39). In the time of Papias, not more than two or three of the original band of Jesus' disciples would still be living, and he would be compelled to obtain his information from those who had heard the apostles. Nevertheless, he preferred the oral testimony to written record. Irrespective of the value of Papias's judgment, his words indicate that the contents of the apostolic preaching were still being transmitted by word of mouth two generations after the crucifixion, simultaneously with the use of whatever written records existed.

A clue to the transition from oral preaching to written record is provided by explanatory statements in the Gospels of Luke and John. In the introduction to his Gospel, Luke asserts that he was undertaking to confirm by manuscript what his friend Theophilus had already learned by word of mouth (Luke 1:1–4). He spoke of facts that were taken for granted among believers and indicated that there had already been numerous attempts to arrange them in orderly narratives. Since his use of the word "narrative" (Gr. *diēgēsis*) implies an extended account, there must have been a number of "gospels" in circulation that he considered to be either inaccessible or else unsatisfactory. If his use of language permits deductions by contrast, these rival gospels were the opposite of his own. They were partial in content, drawn from secondary sources, and perhaps were not organized by any consecutive line of thought. They may have been random collections of sayings or events that had no central theme, or they may not have contained enough biographical material to afford an adequate understanding of Jesus' life.

Luke affirmed on the contrary that he had derived his facts from those who "from the first were eyewitnesses and servants of the word" (Luke 1:2). Not only had his informants shared in the events of which they spoke, but also they had been so affected that they became propagandists of the new faith. Luke had been a contemporary of these witnesses and had investigated personally the truth of their claims, so that he might produce an orderly and accurate record of the work of Christ.

John also committed his Gospel to writing so that he might influence others to faith in Christ as the Son of God (John 20:30–31). He did not profess to give an exhaustive account of Jesus' activities, but took for granted that many of them would be familiar to his readers. The selective process that he used was determined by his evangelistic purpose and theological viewpoint.

Although Matthew and Mark are less explicit concerning their origins, the same general principles apply. The introduction of Matthew, "A record of the genealogy of Jesus Christ the son of David, the son of Abraham" (Matt 1:1), duplicates the phraseology of Genesis (Gen 5:1) to convey the impression that, like Genesis, it is giving a significant chapter in the history of God's dealing with the human race. Mark's terse opening line, "The beginning of the gospel about Jesus Christ, the Son of God" (Mark 1:1), is a title, labeling the following text as a summary of current preaching. Neither of these two offers any reason for its publication, but one may deduce fairly that all of the Gospels began in an attempt to preserve for posterity what had hitherto existed in the minds of the primitive witnesses and in their public addresses.

There has been some question whether the Gospels were first published in Aramaic (the language of Palestine, where the church began) or in Greek. Eusebius quoted Papias's statement that Matthew composed his history in the Hebrew dialect and everyone translated it as he was able (Eusebius, *Historia Ecclesiae,* 3.39). Without the original context, these words are ambiguous. Papias does not make clear whether by "Hebrew" he meant the speech of the OT, or whether he really meant Aramaic. He does not specify whether Matthew's contribution was simply collected notes of Matthew from which others composed a Gospel, or whether Matthew had already formed an organized narrative that was translated. He does imply that before the Gentile expansion had made the literature of the church Greek, there was a body of material written in Hebrew or Aramaic.

Papias's statement has aroused a great deal of controversy. There are Aramaisms in the Gospels such as *Ephphatha* (Mark 7:34); *Talitha koum* (5:41); and the cry from the cross, *Eloi, Eloi, lama sabachthani* (15:34). They reflect Jesus' use of his mother tongue and the perpetuation of his language in the memoirs of his followers. These, however, do not necessarily mean that the Gospels were originally written in Aramaic. C. C. Torrey (*Our Translated Gospels,* 1936) contended that all four Gospels were translations, but there is no agreement on the evidence. If they were translations, they must have been composed prior to the middle of the first century, when the churches were predominantly Palestinian. It is more likely that the Gospels originated in the evangelistic preaching to the Gentile world, and that they were written in Greek, though they contained an Aramaic background.

III. Composition of the Gospels. The personal reminiscences of the apostolic band, plus the fixed content of their preaching, constituted the materials from which the Gospels were constructed; and the purpose of the individual writers provided the method of organization. Both Luke (1:1–4) and John (20:30–31) pledge accuracy of historical fact before they proceed with interpretation, and the same may safely be assumed of Matthew and Mark. All the Gospels were composed for use in the growing movement of the church; they were not written solely for literary effect. Matthew obviously wished to identify Jesus with the Messiah of the OT by pointing out that he was the fulfillment of prophecy and that he was intimately related to the manifestation of the kingdom. Mark, by his terse descriptive paragraphs, depicted the Son of God in action among men. Luke used a smoother literary style and a larger stock of parables to interest a cultured and perhaps humanistic audience. John selected episodes and discourses that others had not used in order to promote belief in Jesus as the Son of God.

IV. The Publication of the Gospels. Where and when these documents were first given to the public is uncertain. The earliest quotations from the gospel material appear in the letters of Ignatius, the *Epistle of Barnabas*, the *Teaching of the Twelve Apostles,* and the *Epistle of Polycarp*. All of these are related to Antioch of Syria, and their quotations or allusions bear a stronger resemblance to the text of Matthew than to that of any other gospel. If, as Papias said, Matthew was first written for the Hebrew or Aramaic church in Jerusalem, it may have been the basis for a Greek edition issued from Antioch during the development of the Gentile church in that city. It would, therefore, have been put into circulation some time after A.D. 50 and before the destruction of Jerusalem in 70.

Clement of Alexandria (A.D. 200) described the writing of the Gospel of Mark: "When Peter had proclaimed the word publicly at Rome, and declared the gospel under the influence of the Spirit; as there was a great number present, they requested Mark, who had followed him from afar, and remembered well what he had said, to reduce these things to writing, and that after composing the Gospel he gave it to those who requested it of him. Which, when Peter understood, he directly neither hindered nor encouraged it" (Eusebius, *Historia Ecclesiae,* 6.14). Irenaeus (c. 100), Clement's contemporary, confirmed this tradition, adding that Mark handed down Peter's preaching in writing after his death. If Mark's Gospel represents the memoirs of Peter, it is possible that its content did not become fixed in literary form until A.D. 65 or later.

The Gospel of Luke may have been a private document, sent first of all to Luke's friend and patron, Theophilus. The adjective "most excellent" (Luke 1:3) implies that he probably belonged to the equestrian order (perhaps holding some official position) and that the dual work (Luke and Acts) that Luke wrote was calculated to remove any lingering doubts that he may have entertained concerning the historical and spiritual verities of the Christian faith. Luke can hardly have been written later than A.D. 62, since it must have preceded Acts, which was written about the end of Paul's first imprisonment.

The last chapter of John's Gospel tries to correct a rumor that he would never die. The rumor, begun by a misunderstanding of Jesus' remark to Peter about John, would have been strengthened by the fact that John had attained an advanced age at the time when the concluding chapter was written. It is possible that it can be dated before A.D. 50, but most conservative scholars place it about 85. Traditionally it has been ascribed to the apostle John, who ministered at Ephesus in the closing years of the first century.

V. The Synoptic Problem: The three Gospels of Matthew, Mark, and Luke are called *synoptic* from the Greek word *synoptikos,* which means "to see the whole together, to take a comprehensive view." They present similar views of the career and teaching of Christ and resemble each other closely in content and in phraseology.

The numerous agreements between these Gospels have raised the question whether the relationship between them can be traced to common literary sources. Almost the entire content of the Gospel of Mark can be found in both Matthew and Luke, while much material not found in Mark is common to the two other Gospels. On the other hand, each Gospel has a different emphasis and organization. The "Synoptic Problem," as it is called, may be stated as follows: If the three Gospels are absolutely independent of each other, how can one account for the minute verbal agreements in their text? If they are copied from each other, or compiled freely from common sources, how can they be original and authoritative? Are they, then, truly writings inspired by God, or are they merely combinations of anecdotes that may or may not be true?

Numerous theories have been propounded to account for these phenomena. The most popular in recent years has been the documentary theory, which assumes that the Gospels were derived from Mark and a hypothetical document called "Q" (from the German *Quelle,* meaning "source"), containing chiefly sayings of Jesus. According to this theory, Matthew and Luke were composed independently by combining Mark and "Q." B. H. Streeter (*The Four Gospels,* 1936) suggested also the addition of two special sources, *M* for Matthew, *L* for Luke, embodying the private knowledge or research of the two writers.

While this hypothesis seemingly solves the problem of the verbal resemblances, it is not entirely satisfactory. The existence of "Q" is at best only a probability; no copy of it has ever been found. R. M. Grant has pointed out that extant collections of the "Sayings of Jesus" dating from the second and third centuries should probably be assigned to the Gnostics, who in turn were dependent either on oral tradition or on the canonical Gospels for their text (*The Secret Sayings of Jesus,* 1960, pp. 29, 40–61). These documents, which have been considered analogous to "Q," and therefore as justifying the hypothesis of its existence, are themselves secondary. It is more likely that the common didactic passages of Matthew and Luke are drawn from utterances that Jesus repeated until they became fixed in the minds of his disciples and were reproduced later in the Gospels.

In recent years the discipline called "form criticism" has advanced another alternative. In an attempt to ascertain the development of the gospel before the Gospels, it has suggested that they were composed out of individual reminiscences of Jesus' deeds and bits of his teaching that were first preserved and circulated by his followers. Through repetition and selection these accounts took permanent shape and were incorporated into a general sequence that constituted the gospel narratives. Advocates of form criticism have separated the unitary sections of the Gospels into various classes: the *passion story* of Jesus' last days; the *paradigms,* accounts of Jesus' deeds that illustrate the message; *tales* of miraculous occurrences told to interest the public; morally edifying *legends* of saintly persons; *sayings* of Jesus that preserve his collected teachings in speeches or in parables.

This modification or oral tradition injects a greater uncertainty into the process of literary history. If the Synoptic Gospels are merely different arrangements of independent blocks of text, the problem of origins is multiplied. While sections of the Gospels may have been used for illustrative purposes, and while certain parts of them, like the Sermon on the Mount, might have once been a separate collection of sayings (or deeds, as the case may be), the fact that they were composed in the first century by trustworthy disciples of Jesus precludes fraud or unreliability.

Form criticism is one branch of the wider discipline of "tradition criticism" that, when applied to the Gospels, has its counterpart in "redaction criticism." Tradition criticism focuses attention on the Gospel material that each Evangelist received, whether it came to him orally or to some degree in written form; redaction criticism is concerned with the way in which each Evangelist handled the material he received. Redaction criticism reminds us that the Evangelists were no mere scissors-and-paste compilers, that each of them was an author in his own right, with his own interpretation and purpose.

Perhaps the best solution of the Synoptic Problem is the fact that all three Gospels are dealing with the life of the same Person, whose deeds and utterances were being continually preached as a public message. Constant repetition and frequent contact between the preachers tended toward fixing the content of the message. From the Day of Pentecost, the "apostle's teaching" possessed some definite form, for it was used in instructing inquirers (Acts 2:42). As the church expanded, the written accounts were created to meet the demand for instruction, and they reproduced the phraseology and content of the oral teaching. Each Gospel, however, was shaped to its own purpose and audience, so that the variations in wording reflected the differences of interest and environment. Matthew was written for Christians with a Jewish background; Mark, for active Gentiles, probably Romans; Luke, for a cultured and literary Greek. All three, however, bear united witness to the supernatural character and saving purpose of Jesus Christ.

VI. The Problem of John's Gospel: The Fourth Gospel differs markedly in character and in content from the Synoptics. Excluding the feeding of the five thousand and the Passion narrative, there are few points of agreement with the others. So radical are the differences that the veracity of the Gospel has been challenged on the grounds that if it is historical, it should coincide more nearly with the Synoptics.

For this reason some have held that the Fourth Gospel was written in the second century as the church's reflection on the person of Christ, phrased in terms of the Greek *Logos* doctrine. The discovery of the Rylands Fragment—a small scrap of papyrus on which a few verses of John were written—demonstrated that by the beginning of the second century the Gospel of John was circulated as far as southern Egypt. Since the handwriting of the fragment can be dated about A.D. 130, the Gospel must have been written earlier. It could not have been a late product of church tradition.

The language of the Gospel does not necessitate a Hellenistic origin. The existence of the concepts of light and of darkness, truth and falsehood, living waters, and others in the Dead Sea Scrolls show that John need not have drawn his vocabulary from Hellenism, but that many of his terms were a part of contemporary Judaism (William LaSor, *The Dead Sea Scrolls and the New Testament,* 1972, pp. 191–205). The Gospel of John is the account of an eyewitness writing in his later years and interpreting the person of Christ in the perspective of his Christian experience.

VII. Canonicity: The Gospels were among the first writings to be quoted as sacred and authoritative. Individual passages are quoted or alluded to in Ignatius of Antioch (c. A.D. 116), the *Epistle of Barnabas,* and the *Shepherd of Hermas,* which were written in the early part of the second century. Justin Martyr (c. 140) mentions the Gospels explicitly, calling them "Memoirs of the Apostles" (*First Apology,* 66). Marcion of Sinope (c. 140) included a mutilated edition of the Gospel of Luke in the canon of Scripture that he promulgated at Rome; he may have known the other Gospels but rejected them because of the presence of what he regarded as Jewish corruptions. Tatian (c. 170), an Assyrian who was converted in Rome under the ministry of Justin and later became an Encratite, produced the first harmony of the Gospels, called the *Diatessaron.* It included only the familiar four, weaving their text together into one continuous narrative. Only a few traces of the *Diatessaron* are still available in translations or in commentaries, but the existence of this work proves that Matthew, Mark, Luke, and John were already the chief sources of information concerning the life and works of Jesus in the first half of the second century.

Growing intercommunication between the churches and the need for strengthening their defenses against heresy and the attacks of pagan critics promoted the interest of the churches in a canon of the Gospels. By 170 the four Gospels were securely established as the sole authorities. According to Irenaeus's contention, "It is not possible that the Gospels can be either more or fewer in number than they are. For since there are four zones of the world in which we live and four principal winds . . . it is fitting that she [the church] should have four pillars, breathing out immortality on every side . . . " (*Against Heresies,* 3.11.8). Irenaeus's reasons are not cogent, but the fact that he acknowledged only four indicates the sentiment of his times. The Muratorian Canon, a fragmentary manuscript of the seventh or eighth century containing a list of accepted books earlier than 200, included in its original form the four Gospels; they were used by Tertullian of Carthage (c. 200), Clement of Alexandria (c. 200), Origen of Alexandria (c. 250), and Cyprian of Carthage (c. 250); and they appear in the manuscript texts of the Chester Beatty Papyri and of the Old Latin version, both in existence before 300. Eusebius (c. 350) and the fathers following him excluded all other Gospels from their official list, leaving these four the undisputed, supreme authorities for knowledge of the life and work of Jesus Christ. See also MATTHEW, GOSPEL OF; MARK, GOSPEL OF; LUKE, GOSPEL OF; JOHN, GOSPEL OF; CANONICITY.

Bibliography: Theodor Zahn, *Introduction to the New Testament* (ed. M. W. Jacobus), 1909, 2:307–617, 3:1–354; B. H. Streeter, *The Four Gospels* (revised), 1936; E. B. Redlich, *Form Criticism: Its Value and Limitations,* 1939; D. E. Nineham (ed.), *Studies in the Gospels,* 1955; R. M. Grant, *The Secret Sayings of Jesus,* 1960; N. B.

Sphinx and relief of a roaring lion from city gate at Gozan, one of the cities to which the Israelites were deported under the Assyrians (2 Kings 17:6, 18:11). Courtesy Bildarchiv Foto, Marburg.

Stonehouse, *Origins of the Synoptic Gospels,* 1963; X. Leon-Dufour, *The Gospels and the Jesus of History,* 1968; J. Rohde, *Rediscovering the Teaching of the Evangelists,* 1968; D. G. Buttrick et al. (eds.), *Jesus and Man's Hope,* 2 vols., 1970–71. MCT

GOURD (See PLANTS)

GOVERNOR. One who governs a land for a supreme ruler to whom he is subordinate. This word is the translation of a large variety of Hebrew and Greek words and is used as a title for someone who held one of a number of official governmental positions. For example, Joseph, the prime minister of Egypt, was called its governor (Gen 42:6); Gedaliah, left in Judah to rule the conquered Jews after the destruction of Jerusalem, was called governor (Jer 41:2). In the NT the term occurs chiefly in reference to the Roman procurators of Judea—Pilate, Felix, and Festus. In the first century A.D., Roman provinces were of two kinds: imperial and senatorial. The first were ruled by procurators appointed by the emperor; the second, by proconsuls appointed by the senate. Judea was an imperial province. Pontius Pilate was the fifth governor of Judea; Felix, the eleventh; and Festus, the twelfth. Procurators were directly responsible to the emperor for their actions and ruled for as long as he willed.

GOYIM (See GOIIM)

GOZAN (gō'zăn, Heb. *gôzān*). A city located in NE Mesopotamia, on the Habor River, a tributary of the Euphrates. Here the Israelites were deported by the Assyrians following the fall of Samaria, the capital of the northern kingdom (2 Kings 17:6; 18:11; 19:12; 1 Chron 5:26). The Assyrians called the city Guzanu (the Guzanitis of Ptolemy). In A.D. 1911 Baron von Oppenheim discovered a new culture at Tell Halaf, the modern name for Gozan. The relics of pottery are thought to date back to as far as 4000 B.C.

GRACE (Heb. *hēn,* Gr. *charis*). A term used by the biblical writers with a considerable variety of meaning: (1) Properly speaking, that which affords joy, pleasure, delight, charm, sweetness, loveliness; (2) good will, loving-kindness, mercy, etc.; (3) the kindness of a master toward a slave. Thus by analogy, grace has come to signify the kindness of God to man (Luke 1:30). The NT writers, at the end of their various letters, frequently invoke God's gracious favor on their readers (Rom 16:20; Phil 4:23; Col 1:19; 1 Thess 5:28). In addition, the word "grace" is often used to express the concept of kindness given to someone who doesn't deserve it: hence, undeserved favor, especially that kind or degree of favor bestowed on sinners through Jesus Christ (Eph 2:4–5). Grace, therefore, is that unmerited favor of God toward fallen man whereby, for the sake of Christ—the only begotten of the Father, full of grace and truth (John 1:14)—he has provided for man's redemption. He has from all eternity determined to extend favor toward all who have faith in Christ as Lord and Savior.

The relationship between law and grace is one of the major themes of Paul's writings (Rom 5:1,

15–17; 8:1–2; Gal 5:4–5; Eph 2:8–9). Grace is likewise without equivocation identified as the medium or instrument through which God has effected the salvation of all believers (Titus 2:11). Grace is also regarded as the sustaining influence enabling the believer to persevere in the Christian life (Acts 11:23; 20:32; 2 Cor 9:14). Thus, grace is not merely the initiatory act of God that secures the believers' eternal salvation, but also that which maintains it throughout all of the Christian's life. It is also used as a token or proof of salvation (2 Cor 1:5). A special gift of grace is imparted to the humble (James 4:6; 1 Peter 5:5). Grace can also refer to the capacity for the reception of divine life (1 Peter 1:10). There are also secondary senses in which "grace" is used: as a gift of knowledge (1 Cor 1:4) and also as thanksgiving or gratitude expressed for favor (1 Cor 10:30; 1 Tim 1:1–2).

Bibliography: N. P. Williams, *The Grace of God,* 1930; N. H. Snaith, *The Distinctive Ideas of the Old Testament,* 1944; C. R. Smith, *The Biblical Doctrine of Grace,* 1956; H. Conzelmann, TDNT, 9:372ff.

GRAFT. A horticultural process by which the branches of the wild olive tree in eastern lands are cut back so that branches from a cultivated olive may be inserted and grafting take place. Paul makes use of this practice in reverse (Rom 11:17–24) where the opposite process is envisioned; i.e., the wild branches, the Gentiles, are thought of as "grafted in" to the good stock of the parent tree, the children of Israel. This deliberate inversion, certainly not a foolish mistake, heightens rather than diminishes the picturesque figure of speech conveying the eternal truth of the rejection of Israel and the status of the church.

GRAIN (See PLANTS)

GRANARY (grăn'êrē, Heb. *māzû,* Gr. *apothēkē*). Derived from a Hebrew word meaning "to gather" (Ps 144:13) or Hebrew *ôtzār,* meaning "storehouse" (Joel 1:17). In the NT the term is sometimes rendered "barn," and sometimes "garner" (Matt 3:12; Luke 3:17 KJV). The Egyptians had storehouses for grain, liquor, armor, provisions, jewels, etc. Joseph, during the years of famine in Egypt, had authority over the storehouses (Gen 41:56).

GRAPE (See PLANTS)

GRASSHOPPER (See ANIMALS)

GRATING, GRATE (Heb. *resheth*). A copper network, moved by a copper ring at each corner and placed under the top of the great altar (Exod 27:4; 35:16; 38:4–5). It reached halfway up the altar and allowed a draft to enhance the burning of the sacrifices. It also allowed the ashes to fall to the ground below for easy removal.

GRAVE (Heb. *qĕvĕr, she'ôl,* Gr. *mnēmeion*). A place for the interment of the dead; a tomb, a

Tomb of Artaxerxes I (465–425 B.C.), king of Persia, cut in the rock at Nagsh-i-Rustam in Iran. One of three tombs (the other two belong to Darius I and Darius II) with identical façades. Lower part is imitation of an Achaemenian palace. Upper part shows a throne decorated by the king's vassals from various nations and, on top, the king is shown standing in worship before a fire altar. Courtesy B. Brandl.

sepulcher. Graves and accompanying burial customs differed in biblical times from country to country. Among the Hebrews, graves were sometimes mere holes in the earth (Gen 35:8; 1 Sam 31:13), natural caves or grottoes, or artificial tombs hewn out of the rock (Luke 7:12; John 11:30). In such a sepulcher, provided through the kindness of Joseph of Arimathea, the body of Jesus was laid. Flat stones were placed on the graves as markers to warn passers-by that they should not contract ceremonial defilement by unwittingly trespassing. These stones were whitewashed annually in the month of Adar. This was the underlying figure of speech behind Jesus' stinging rebuke of the Pharisees, "You are like whitewashed tombs" (Matt 23:27). Some traces of the idea of tombs as the dwelling places of demons were still extant in the days of Christ (8:28).

GRAVE CLOTHES (Gr. *keiria, winding sheet*). Before burial the body was washed, perhaps anointed with spices, wrapped in a linen winding sheet, with hands and feet bound with grave-bands, and the face covered with a napkin (John 11:44; 19:40).

GRAVEN IMAGE. An image of wood, stone, or metal, shaped with a sharp cutting instrument as distinguished from one cast in a mold (Isa 30:22; 44:16–17; 45:20 KJV; NIV "idols"). Images were, however, sometimes cast and then finished by the graver (40:19). Such images were used by the Canaanites (Deut 7:5), by the Babylonians, and by others (Jer 50:38; 51:47, 52). The Israelites were forbidden by the Decalogue to make them (Exod 20:4).

GREAT LIZARD (See ANIMALS)

GREAT OWL (See BIRDS)

GREAVES (See ARMS AND ARMOR)

GRECIA, GRECIANS. Grecia is Greece, the home of the Hellenes. Greeks and Grecians, however, are to be distinguished. Greeks are generally those of Hellenic race (e.g., Acts 16:1; 18:4; and probably John 12:20), but the word may be used to indicate non-Jews, foreigners, and aliens (Rom 1:16). Grecians were Greek-speaking Jews, people of the Dispersion, from areas predominantly Greek (Acts 6:1; 9:19).

Greece and its associated island groups form the SE end of southern Europe's mountain system, a rugged peninsula and archipelago, not rich in fertile or arable land. The southward movement of the Indo-European–speaking tribes, who became the Greek people, ended here. These tribes, or their predecessors, had established ordered life in the peninsula and islands by the twelfth century before Christ. Their civilization vanished before 1000 B.C., in a dark age of destruction and invasion occasioned by further waves of wandering tribes, just as Celt, Roman, Saxon, Dane, and Norman, ripples of the same folk-movement of related peoples, centuries later made a succession of construction and destruction in Britain. Out of four centuries of chaos emerged the complex of peoples on island and mainland who are called the Greeks. Their own generic name was Hellenes, but Grecia was a portion of the land that, lying in the NW, naturally came first to the attention of Rome. After the common fashion of popular nomenclature (see also PALESTINE), the name of the part that first became known was extended to include the whole. Mediated through Rome, the term Greece was applied to all Hellas, and all Hellenes were called Greeks by Western Europe.

Geography, as always, played a part in the history of the people. The formation of the city-state was a natural development in an isolated plain or in a river valley ringed by precipitous terrain. Seafaring naturally developed from the nearness of the sea. And from seafaring and the dearth of fertile land in a rugged peninsula, sprang colonization and the spread of Greek colonies that marked the first half of the pre-Christian millennium. As early as the eighth century before Christ, Greek ports and trading posts were scattered from the Crimea to Cadiz. In these same centuries the first flowering of Greek thought and poetry began. In Ionia the foundations of scientific and philosophical thought were laid. On Lesbos, in those same years, Sappho and Alcaeus wrote supreme lyric poetry. In short, the active, inquisitive, brilliant, inventive Greek race was visible in full promise around the eastern end of the Mediterranean before the bright flowering of fifth-century Athens. That century was one of the great golden ages of man. Greece, interpreted by the dynamic people of Attica, in one brief noontide of human spirit, made immortal contri-

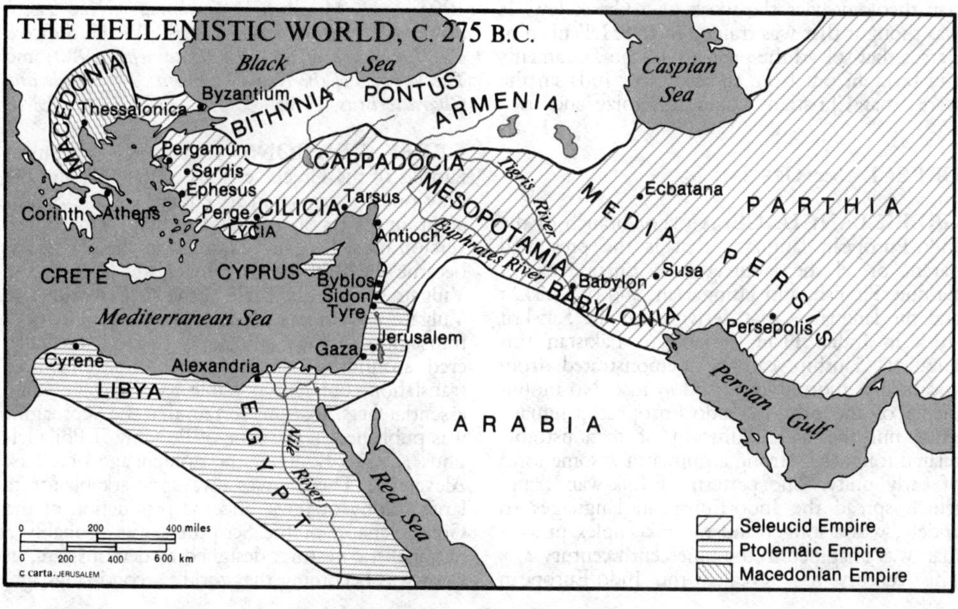

butions to literature, art, philosophy, and political thought. Everything Greek in all future centuries was deepened and colored by the achievement of Athens. Hellenism, which had centuries of dynamic life ahead of it, was shaped by Athens in the short years of its spiritual supremacy. The glory of Athens faded, and her strength was sapped in lamentable war with the dour and uncreative autocracy of Sparta.

On the ruins of a Greece fatally weakened from within, Philip of Macedon, in the mid-fourth century before Christ, built his empire. His son Alexander, in one of the strangest acts of conquest in all history, extended that empire to India, swept the vast state of Persia out of existence, and, as his father had unified Greece, brought under his single rule the great complex of states and kingdoms that lay between the Dardanelles and the Indus, the Caspian and the Nile. When Alexander died in Babylon at the age of thirty-three in 323 B.C., his generals divided the world; and out of the division arose the Oriental kingdoms that the Romans conquered when their empire rounded the Mediterranean Sea.

The Greek language, Greek thought, and Greek culture, in the wake of Alexander, provided a unifying element in all the Middle East. Without the vast flow of the Greek tide eastward, the NT could not have been born. Greece provided its language and fashion of thought. Hellenism was a stimulus to the human mind. To reason, question, and speculate, was a habit with the Greeks. Hence the logical mind of Greek-speaking Paul of Tarsus, heir of both Hellenism and Judaism. Hence the "Grecians" of the NT—Stephen, for example, and Philip—who sweep fresh, bold, and vigorous into the life of the early church, ready to reform and to rethink old concepts. Paul needed his Greek education, as he needed the Judaism of Gamaliel. Paul's synthesis of the covenants, so compelling in its logic, so fundamental in Christian theology, was the work of a Greek Jew. It was thought that was trained in the Hellenism of Tarsus that solved the problem of the Testaments and brought out from the stores of Judaism the wares that Christians could recognize and use.
EMB

GREECE (See GRECIA)

GREEK LANGUAGE. A major branch of the Indo-European language that is the presumed parent of all the languages of Europe except Basque, Finnish, and Hungarian, and of Sanskrit and the languages that derive from the Sanskrit stock in India. From Ireland to Pakistan this linguistic kinship can be demonstrated from vocabulary, morphology, and syntax. No monuments of the original Indo-European language exist, but the wide diffusion of demonstrably related tongues is strong argument for some form of early unity. The pattern of folk-wandering, which spread the Indo-European languages so widely, was a longer and more complex process than was imagined in the nineteenth century A.D. This century has revealed the Indo-European basis of Hittite, and in 1953 Michael Ventris showed that the language of the Pylos tablets was a primitive Greek, thus proving that the language was spoken in the Peloponnesus several centuries before the time once favored for the arrival in the area of the Hellenic tribes. The piecemeal nature of their southward infiltration, and the firm geographical subdivisions of the area they occupied, led to the survival into literary times of several dialects: *Attic-Ionic,* spoken in Attica and the Ionic areas of Asia Minor, with associated islands; *Achaean,* which included the Aeolic of Lesbos and the dialects of Thessaly and Boeotia, together with the undocumented dialect of the Arcado-Cyprian; and what L. R. Palmer calls *West Greek,* including under that name the dialects of Phocis, Locris, Elis, and Aetolia, together with the Doric of the Peloponnesus, the Peloponnesian colonies, and Magna Grecia. Of these dialects, Attic achieved the supreme position because of the worth and greatness of the literature in which it found expression. Attic Greek was one of the major achievements of the human mind. The richness and subtlety of its syntax, its flexibility, the delicacy of its particles—these and other linguistic features make Attic the most expressive medium ever developed for human thought. The dialects passed with passing of the city states and with the unification of Greece and were followed by a basic Greek that developed in the form of a simplified Attic. This, spread by Alexander's conquests throughout the eastern end of the Mediterranean, was called the *Koinē* or Common Dialect. It was the speech of the LXX and the NT, and the major influence in bringing the contributions of Palestine, Greece, and Rome into the partnership that determined the form and shape of the NT, the global gospel of Paul of Tarsus, the Christian church, and modern Europe.

Bibliography: G. A. Deissmann, *Bible Studies,* 1901; J. H. Moulton, *A Grammar of New Testament,* vol. 1 (*Prolegomena*), 1957; W. H. Simcox, *The Language of the New Testament,* 1980, and *The Writers of the New Testament: Their Style and Characteristics,* 1980. EMB

GREEK VERSIONS. 1. The first and most famous of the Greek versions of the OT, and the only one to survive in its entirety, is the Septuagint or "Version of the Seventy." This is the version most frequently quoted in the NT, for it became the Bible of the Hellenistic Jews, as the Vulgate became the Bible of the Latin world. The Vulgate was, in fact, in direct succession, being a translation of the Septuagint. Legend has gathered around so remarkable an achievement of translation, but it is possible to disengage some essential facts. It seems certain that the Septuagint was published in the time of Ptolemy II Philadelphus (295–247 B.C.), the golden age of Greek Alexandria. The city was always remarkable for its large colony of Jews, and the production of the Greek version of the Scriptures was probably a nationalistic gesture, designed to demonstrate, in what was becoming the world's second language, the worth of Jewish literature. It is doubtful whether the suggestion emanated from the king himself, interested though he was in all literature. The story of the seventy-two elders sent from Jerusalem, and the seventy-two days taken to complete the work, is legend. The Septuagint is written in the common dialect, but tinged by Hebraisms. The quality of the language and style varies, but on the whole the Greek is odd and undistinguished. It prompts knotty questions of criticism. The Dead Sea Scrolls have provided some solutions, as, for example, that the Septuagint followed an older Hebrew text than that which survived in the traditional OT.

2. The acceptance of the Septuagint as the Bible of Greek-speaking Christianity prompted orthodox Jewry to produce its own version distinct from it; hence the version of Aquila of Hadrian's day (A.D. 117–38). This version, of which only fragments exist, was in the worst "translation Greek," which followed slavishly the Hebrew forms and syntax.

3. Theodotian, an Ephesian of the second century and an Ebionite Christian, produced a version that could be described as a revision of the Septuagint. It found favor with the Christian community and was a freer translation than that of Aquila.

3. Symmachus produced, perhaps at the end of the second century, a Greek version that appears to have been the best of all the translations, a rendering into idiomatic Greek.

Bibliography: E. Nestle, *Introduction to the Textual Criticism of the Greek New Testament,* 1901; C. R. Gregory, *Canon and Text of the New Testament,* 1967; B. M. Metzger, *The Text of the New Testament,* 1968, and *Manuscripts of the Greek Bible,* 1981. EMB

GREYHOUND (See ANIMALS)

GRIND (Heb. *tāhan,* Gr. *alēthō, grind with a hand mill*). The grinding of grain into flour between two heavy stones was a domestic art usually performed by women; hence, the import of Christ's parable: "Two women will be grinding with a hand mill . . ." (Matt 24:41; Luke 17:35).

GROVE (Heb. *ăshērâh,* Gr. *alsos,* translated "grove" in the KJV following the LXX and the Vulgate). Although one gains a rather confused picture from the mere reading of the Scripture, there emerges a horrible panorama of iniquitous idolatry. The equipment for such worship, probably Phoenician in origin, was the "high place" (Heb. *bāmôth*), the altar crowning it, the standing pillars, and the images of the Asherah. The worship was interwoven with the concept of the fertility of the land, and so became a fertility cult. The chosen symbol of the cult was the trunk of a tree. This explains the prohibition against the planting of trees by the altar of the Lord (Deut 16:21; Judg 6:25, 28, 31). The goddess of the cult was Asherah, who also appears as mistress of the sea. The prophets of Israel roundly condemned the worship of Asherah and congratulated those kings who destroyed her shrines (1 Kings 15:13–14; 2 Kings 17:10; 21:3; 23:4). Allied with the idea of fertility, Asherah has her counterpart in the Babylonian Ishtar, the goddess of love, and as such the goddess of human reproduction.

GUARD. The translation of a number of Hebrew and Greek words. (1) *Tabbāh* ("slaughterer") is used in the title "captain of the guard," which was applied six times to Potiphar (Gen 37–41), nineteen times to Nebuzaradan (2 Kings 23; Jer 39–41, 43, 52), and once to Arioch (Dan 2:14). The term may refer to a member of the king's bodyguard, who also had the duty of "slaughtering" anyone who tried to harm the king. (2) *Rûts* ("runner") occurs fourteen times in the OT and refers to the trusted foot soldiers of a king, who performed various functions (1 Kings 14; 2 Kings 10–11; 2 Chron 12). (3) *Mishmār* ("watch") is a general term for one who guards (Neh 4:22, 23; Ezek 38:7). (4) *Mishma'ath* ("guard") is used twice of David's guard (2 Sam 23:23; 1 Chron 11:25). (5) *Spekoulatōr* ("guard, a spy, executioner" is used only to identify the one who beheaded John the Baptist (Mark 6:27). (6) *Koustōdia* ("watch") is used only of those assigned to guard Jesus' grave (Matt 27:65–66; 28:11). (7) *Stratopedarchō* ("captain of the guard") is used of the one to whom Paul and other prisoners were discharged in Rome (Acts 28:16 in some versions).

GUDGODAH (gŭd-gō'dȧ, Heb. *gudgōdhâh, cleft, division*). A place in the wilderness journeys of the children of Israel (Deut 10:7), corresponding to Hor Haggidgag of Numbers 33:32. Its identification is uncertain.

GUEST CHAMBER (Heb. *lishkâh,* Gr. *kataluma*). The *lishkâh* occurs forty-seven times in the OT and is usually translated "hall" in NIV and "chamber" in KJV, perhaps at times meaning a room in which sacrificial feasts were held. The Greek word occurs three times in the NT; once it means "inn" (Luke 2:7), and twice it is used to refer to the room in which the Last Supper took place (Mark 14:14; Luke 22:11).

GUILT. The deserving of punishment because of the violation of a law or a breach of conduct. In the OT, the concept of guilt is largely ritualistic and legalistic. A person could be guiltless before both God and the nation (Num 32:22); on the other hand, one could be guilty because of unwitting sin (Lev 5:17). Israel, moreover, was viewed as an organic whole: what one does affects all. There is collective responsibility for sin; when Achan sinned, all Israel suffered. The prophets stressed the ethical and personal aspects of sin and of guilt. God is less interested in ritual correctness than in moral obedience.

In the NT, Jesus stressed the importance of right heart attitude over against outwardly correct acts and taught that there are degrees of guilt, depending on a person's knowledge and motive

A view inside the tunnel built by King Hezekiah in the eighth century B.C., known as Hezekiah's Tunnel, or the Gutter (2 Kings 20:20). Courtesy Israel Department of Antiquities and Museums.

(Luke 11:29–32; 12:47–48; 23:34). Paul likewise recognized differences of degree in guilt (Acts 17:30; Eph 4:18), though also stating that the law makes everyone guilty before God (Rom 3:19). Theologians differ as to what Paul taught in Romans 5:12–21, both as to whether Adam's guilt was imputed to all his posterity and, if it was, as to just how it was done.

GUILT OFFERING (See SACRIFICE AND OFFERING)

GULL (See BIRDS)

GUNI (gū'nī). 1. A family clan of the tribe of Naphtali (Gen 46:24; Num 26:48; 1 Chron 7:13).

2. The head of a Gadite family (1 Chron 5:15).

GUR (gûr). A hill thought to be near Jenin, about twelve miles (twenty km.) NE of Samaria. Here Ahaziah received his mortal wound while fleeing from Jehu, after the slaughter of Joram (2 Kings 9:27).

GUR BAAL (*gûr' bā' āl, sojourn of Baal*). A small colony town of Arabs, against whom Uzziah of Judah was given divine aid (2 Chron 26:7); perhaps in the desert south of Beersheba.

GUTTER (Heb. *tsinnôr, pipe, spout, conduit*). The channel or tunnel (RSV, NIV "water shaft") through which David's soldiers are inferred to have marched to win the city of Jerusalem from Jebusite rule (2 Sam 5:8), at the fountain of Gihon, site of the later tunnel Hezekiah built (2 Kings 20:20) to connect the spring at Gihon with the pool of Siloam. It was 1,800 feet (563 m.) long and 6 feet (2 m.) high. It was dug out as a farsighted measure so that the city's water supply would not be in danger during the impending siege at the hands of Sennacherib of Assyria.

HAAHASHTARI, HAASHTARI (hā'ȧ-hăsh'tȧ-rī, hā-ăsh'tȧ-rī, *the Ahashtarite*). A man of Judah, mentioned in 1 Chronicles 4:6. He was probably a muleteer, son of Naarah.

HABAIAH (See HOBAIAH)

HABAKKUK (hȧ-băk'ŭk, Heb. *hăvaqqûq, embrace*). The name of a prophet and of the eighth book of the Minor Prophets, which is entitled "The oracle that Habakkuk the prophet received" (Hab 1:1). Of the man Habakkuk nothing is known outside of the book that bears his name. Legendary references to him (in the apocryphal *Bel and the Dragon* and elsewhere) appear to have no historical value. The musical references in chapter 3 have led some to believe that he was a member of a Levitical musical guild, but even this is uncertain.

Most traditional scholars believe the book to be a unity, the work of one author, Habakkuk, produced in Judah during the Chaldean period. The reasons for this view are found in the book itself. The temple still stands (Hab 2:20; 3:19) and the rise of the Chaldean power is predicted (1:5–6). The argument here depends on the understanding of the Hebrew word ***kasdîm,*** translated "Chaldeans." Some recent scholars emend the word to ***kittîm,*** meaning Cypriots, and understand it to refer to the Macedonian Greeks under Alexander the Great. They therefore date the book to this much later period. There is no good reason to make this emendation. *Kasdîm* clearly means Chaldeans.

The Neo-Babylonian or Chaldean empire first came to prominence when the Babylonian king Nebuchadnezzar defeated the Egyptians at the battle of Carchemish in 605 B.C. and reestablished Babylon as the seat of world power. The prophecy of Habakkuk could hardly have been given before 605. Jerusalem fell to Nebuchadnezzar in 587. The book must be placed somewhere between these dates, probably during the reign of the Judean king Jehoiakim. Some date the book earlier, believing that the Chaldeans were known to Judah before Carchemish and emphasizing the unexpectedness of the attack mentioned by Habakkuk (Hab 1:5). Still, a date soon after 605 seems to be preferred.

In modern times the unity of the book has been questioned. The psalm of chapter 3 is certainly somewhat different in style from the rest of the book, but this is hardly a sufficient reason to deny it to Habakkuk. The theory that all psalms were postexilic in Israel is now discredited. The theme of the prose part (Hab 1–2) is the same as that of

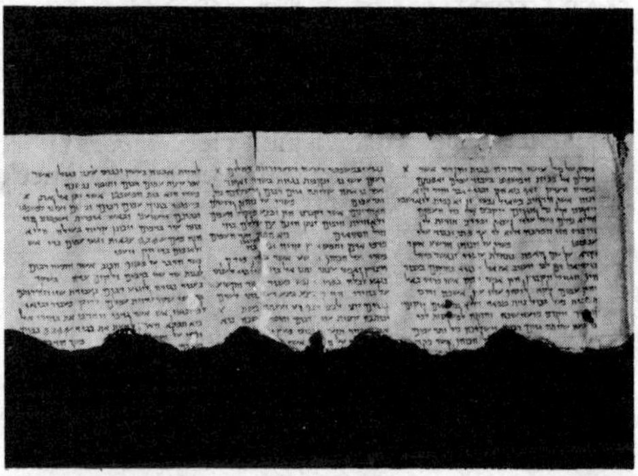

Part of a commentary on Habakkuk, beginning with 2:5, found in Cave 1 at Qumran near the Dead Sea. End of first century B.C. Courtesy Shrine of the Book, D. Samuel and Jeane H. Gottesman, Center for Biblical Manuscripts, Israel Museum, Jerusalem.

the psalm. And there are obvious similarities of language. Chapter 3 is specifically ascribed to Habakkuk (3:1), and there seems to be no good internal indication that he was not its author.

The first two chapters set forth Habakkuk's prophetic oracle, or burden. Twice the prophet is perplexed and asks for divine enlightenment; twice he is answered. First he is concerned over the violence and sin of his people, the Judeans. Why are these wicked men not punished (Hab 1:2–4)? God answers that he is about to send the Babylonians (Chaldeans) to judge Judah (1:5–11). This answer plunges Habakkuk into a greater perplexity: How can a righteous God use the wicked Babylonians to punish Judah, which, though it has become apostate, is still better than the Babylonians (1:12–17)? God's answer is that the proud conquerors will themselves be punished (2:2–20). The Babylonians are puffed up with self-sufficient pride, but in this hour of national calamity the righteous will live by his faithfulness, i.e., by his constancy. The prophet sees only two ways of looking at life: in faith or in unbelief. This statement naturally becomes important to the NT writers and is quoted in Romans 1:17; Galatians 3:11; and Hebrews 10:38. The second answer to Habakkuk concludes with a series of woes against the Babylonians (Hab 2:5–20).

Habakkuk 3 is called "a prayer of Habakkuk the prophet" (3:1). In a moving lyric poem the prophet records his final response to God's message of judgment. He describes the divine revelation in terms of a story theophany (3:2–15) but concludes that no matter what comes he will trust in God (3:16–19).

The commentary on chapters 1–2 found in the late 1940s at Qumran near the Dead Sea casts little light on the meaning of these chapters, though it gives us a glimpse of how the Essene community there in the first century B.C. understood the book.

Bibliography: D. M. Lloyd-Jones, *From Fear to Faith,* 1953; D. E. Gowan, *The Triumph of Faith in Habakkuk,* 1976. JBG

HABAZZINIAH (hab'ȧ-zĭ-nī'ȧ). Ancestor of the Recabites of the time of Jeremiah. Mentioned only in Jeremiah 35:3.

HABERGEON (hăb'êr-jŭn, Heb. *tahărā'*). A jacket of mail to protect the breast and neck (2 Chron 26:14; Neh 4:16). The NIV translates

Drawing from basalt stele, from Arslan Tash, c. 744–727 B.C., of Hadad, the Syrian storm god, standing on a bull and holding in each hand a double three-pronged fork that represents lightning. Courtesy Carta, Jerusalem.

this word "coat of armor" or simply "armor." Job 41:26 has "pointed shaft" (NIV "javelin") with "coat of mail" in the margin. Habergeon is used also to translate a different Hebrew word of uncertain meaning in Exodus 28:32; 39:23 (KJV).

HABIRU (hȧ-bī'rū). The name of a people first mentioned in the Amarna Tablets (fifteenth century B.C.) as among those who were intruders into Palestine. Since then the name has also appeared in Babylonian texts and documents from Mari (eighteenth century), the Hittite records from Boghaz-keui, and the Hurrian texts from Nuzi (fourteenth century). The same name appears in Egyptian records as *Apiru* as late as the twelfth century Abraham is the first person in the Bible to bear the name Hebrew, *'Ibri* (Gen 14:13). Some scholars equate the names Habiru and 'Ibri. The meaning of Habiru seems to be "wanderers." It is not an ethnic designation, for the Habiru of these various texts were of mixed racial origin, including both Semites and non-Semites. The name Habiru describes more than the Hebrews, therefore, but it came to be associated with them particularly. Even so, the connection, if there is any, of the Hebrews with the Habiru remains obscure.

HABOR (hā'bôr, Heb. *hāvōr*). A river of Gozan, the region in the northern part of Mesopotamia to which Shalmanezer, king of Assyria, banished the northern tribes of Israel after Hoshea, the last king, rebelled against him (2 Kings 17:6; 18:11). Tiglath-Pileser had carried the tribes east of Jordan to this same region (1 Chron 5:26).

HACALIAH, HACHALIAH (hăk'ȧ-lī'ȧ). The father of Nehemiah, governor of the Jews (Neh 1:1; 10:1).

HACHILAH (See HAKILAH)

HACMONI (hăk'mō-nī, Heb. *hakhmônî, wise*). The father of Jehiel, an associate of David's sons (1 Chron 27:32) and of Jashobeam, one of David's mighty men (11:11). "Tahkemonite" in 2 Samuel 23:8 is probably a variant of Hacmonite, but the text here is obscure.

HADAD (hā'dăd, *sharpness, fierceness*). 1. A grandson of Abraham through Ishmael (Gen 25:15; 1 Chron 1:30).

2. An early king of Edom, whose capital was at Pau or Pai (1 Chron 1:50). In Genesis 36:39 most manuscripts read "Hadar."

3. An earlier king of Edom, a son of Bedad, who defeated Midian in the country of Moab (Gen 36:35; 1 Chron 1:46).

4. An Edomite of royal descent whose life had been saved in his early childhood by flight from David's devastating attacks. Hadad went to Egypt, where Pharaoh received him and his men, gave him a house, and highly favored him. Hadad became brother-in-law to Tahpenes, queen of Egypt, but later when he learned that David's general, Joab, had died, he went back to Edom

and became an adversary to Solomon (1 Kings 11:14–25).

5. The supreme god of Syria, whose name is found in proper names like Ben-Hadad and Hadadezer. In Assyrian inscriptions he is identified with their air-god Ramman, i.e., Rimmon.

HADADEZER, HADAREZER (hăd'ăd-ē'zêr, hăd'ăr-ē'zêr, *Hadad is a help*). A king of Zobah, twice defeated in battle by David (2 Sam 8:3ff.; 10:15–19; 1 Chron 18:3ff.). Zobah was a kingdom lying NE of Damascus and between the valleys of the Orontes and the Euphrates.

HADAD RIMMON (hā'dăd rĭm'ŏn, *Hadad and Rimmon,* [two Syrian divinities]). A place in the Valley of Megiddo where Josiah, the last good king of Judah, was fatally wounded (2 Kings 23:29–30), and where later there was a memorable mourning for him as recorded in Zechariah 12:11. It is now called Rummaneh, i.e., "place of pomegranates."

HADAR (hā'dår). 1. According to Genesis 25:15 in KJV, a son of Ishmael, but the Hebrew, NIV, and ASV, supported by 1 Chronicles 1:30, call him Hadad.

2. The last of the ancient kings of Edom (Gen 36:39; NIV, Hadad), but in 1 Chronicles 1:50–51 he also is called Hadad. The two names are easily confused in Hebrew.

HADASHAH (hȧ-dăsh'ȧ, *new*). A town of Judah in the low plain in Joshua's time (Josh 15:37).

HADASSAH (hȧ-dăs'ȧ, *a myrtle*). Daughter of Abihail, who became Esther, queen of Xerxes, KJV, Ahasuerus (Esth 2:7, 15).

HADATTAH (See HAZOR)

HADES (hā'dēz, Gr. *Hadēs, haidēs, not to be seen*). The place or state of the dead, as contrasted with the final punishment of the wicked. In the NT Greek the word occurs ten times and is uniformly translated "hell" in KJV. In the TR, from which KJV was translated, the word occurs also in 1 Corinthians 15:55 and is rendered "grave"; but other manuscripts have the Greek *thanatē,* and both ASV and NIV render it "death." The NT word is taken over from Greek mythology, in which *Hades* was the god of the lower regions. Although the word was taken from pagan myths, the concept is from the OT word *Sheol. Sheol* occurs sixty-five times in the Hebrew OT and is rendered in KJV as "hell" thirty-one times, "the grave" thirty-one times, and "the pit" three times; but in ASV it is uniformly transliterated *Sheol,* even as *Hades* in the ASV is a transliteration rather than an attempt to translate the Greek. The word "hell" in English always has an unpleasant connotation and is properly thought of as the final destiny of the wicked when it translates *geenna,* which occurs twelve times and is always rendered "hell."

The NT generally does not give definite light on Hades. In Matthew 11:23 (cf. Luke 10:15) our Lord says that Capernaum will go down into Hades. The preposition "down" points to the OT teaching that Sheol is inside the earth (Ps 139:8; Amos 9:2), and the following verse (Matt 11:24) puts the day of judgment for both Sodom and Capernaum later than the stay in Hades. In the parable of the rich man and Lazarus (Luke 16:19–31) the rich man is pictured as being tormented in Hades but able to see in the distance Abraham with Lazarus by his side. He asks for a drop of water to cool his tongue and for a message to be sent to his five brothers who are still alive on earth, and in each case his request is denied. In the first Christian sermon, Peter quotes (Acts 2:25–31) from Psalm 16:8–11, proving from it that our Lord arose from the dead and was not left in Hades. In the Book of Revelation, death and Hades are four times associated (1:18; 6:8; 20:13–14), being treated as almost synonymous terms. In the last verse mentioned, death and Hades are to be cast into the lake of fire, i.e., doomed to utter destruction. See also GEHENNA.

ABF

HADID (hā'dĭd, Heb. *hādhîdh, sharp*). A village in Benjamin named with Lod and Ono (Ezra 2:33; Neh 7:37; 11:34). It was located about three miles (five km.) east of Lydda.

HADLAI (hăd'lī, *ceasing, forbearing*). The father of Amasa, an Ephraimite chief, mentioned only in 2 Chronicles 28:12.

HADORAM (hȧ-dō'răm, Heb. *hădhōrām*). 1. A son of Joktan (Gen 10:27; 1 Chron 1:21) and probably an Arab tribe of that name in Arabia Felix.

2. Son of the king of Hamath sent by his father to congratulate David on his victory over Hadadezer (1 Chron 18:9–11). In 2 Samuel 8:10 the name is written as Joram.

3. Rehoboam's superintendent of the men under forced labor (2 Chron 10:18; NIV "Adoniram," see footnote). The Israelites stoned him when Rehoboam sent him to them, presumably to collect taxes or to raise a levy of workers. Perhaps the same as Adoniram of 1 Kings 4:6.

HADRACH (hā'drăk, Heb. *hadhrākh*). A country associated with Damascus and Hamath and mentioned only in Zechariah 9:1. It may have been located east of Damascus.

HAELEPH (See ELEPH)

HAGAB (hā'găb, Heb. *hāghāv, locust*). Ancestor of some temple servants who returned with Zerubbabel (Ezra 2:46).

HAGABA (hăg'-ȧ-bė, Heb. *haghav, locust*). The head of a family of temple servants who returned from exile with Zerubbabel (Neh 7:48).

HAGABAH (hăg'ȧ-bȧ, Heb. *haghav, locust*). An

alternate form of Hagaba (Neh 7:48). It appears in Ezra 2:45.

HAGAR (hā′gȧr, Heb. *hāghār, emigration, flight*). An Egyptian handmaid to Sarai, wife of Abram. God had promised him a son and heir (15:4), but Sarai was barren. Following the marital customs of the times, she gave Hagar to her husband as her substitute (16:1–16). When Hagar saw that she had conceived, she despised her mistress, causing trouble in the household. Hagar was driven out, but the angel of the Lord appeared and sent her back to her mistress (16:7–14). When her son Ishmael was fourteen years old, his father one hundred, and Sarah ninety, Isaac was born. At a great feast held in connection with Isaac's weaning, Ishmael scoffed at the proceedings (21:9), so Sarah insisted that Hagar and her son be cast out, and Abraham unwillingly complied. God told Abraham that Ishmael's descendants would become a nation. Hagar is last seen taking a wife for her son out of the land of Egypt, her own land (21:1–21). Paul made Hagar's experience an allegory of the difference between law and grace (Gal 4:21–5:1).

HAGARENES, HAGARITES (See HAGRITES)

HAGGAI (hăg′ā-ī, Heb. *haggay, festal*). Prophet of the Lord to the Jews in 520 B.C. Little is known of his personal history. He lived soon after the Captivity and was contemporary with Zechariah (cf. Hag 1:1 with Zech 1:1).

After the return from the Captivity the Israelites set up the altar on its base, established daily worship, and laid the foundation for the second temple; then they were compelled to cease building for some years. However, although times were hard, the people were able to build finely paneled houses for themselves (Hag 1:4). Meanwhile kings succeeded one another in Persia. Cyrus, favored of God and friend of the Jews (2 Chron 36:22; Isa 44:28), passed away in 529 B.C.; his son Cambyses (the "Xerxes" of Ezra 4:6) reigned 529–522, followed for only seven months in 522 by the Pseudo-Smerdis (a usurper); then arose Darius Hystaspes (Ezra 4–6; Haggai; Zech 1–6), who helped and encouraged the Jews to go ahead and who allowed no opposition. In the second year of Darius (520) Haggai fulfilled his brilliant mission of rebuking and encouraging the Jews. The five short messages that make up his book are all dated, occupying only three months and twenty-three days; and in those few weeks the whole situation changed from defeat and discouragement to victory. Zechariah assisted Haggai in the last month of his recorded ministry (Zech 1:1–6).

In order to make the dates clearer to modern readers, we will give the months their approximately equivalent names in our calendar. On September 1, 520 B.C., the Lord spoke through Haggai, and instead of addressing the people at large, the prophet went straight to "headquarters," i.e., to Zerubbabel the prince and to Joshua the high priest. The people had stopped building the Lord's house though they were quite able to build their own, and God's message was "Give careful thought to your ways." The punishment for their neglect had been futility; they labored much but produced little. God used "weather judgments" to bring them to their senses. The leaders heeded the message and with the best of the people, they began immediately to build, and on September 24 God's short message was "I am with you" (Hag 1:13). A month later, the people were tempted to be discouraged when they contrasted their present effort with the former magnificent temple, and so God told them, "The glory of this present house will be greater than the glory of the former house" (2:9). This message was delivered on October 21, and it contained this notable statement: "The silver is mine and the gold is mine." The fourth and fifth messages came in one day, December 24, 520. In the fourth, Haggai said that holiness is not contagious, though evil is, and Israel's change in attitude would cause God to change chastening into blessing. In the last message (2:20–23), God predicts a shaking of the nations but at the same time a great reward to Zerubbabel. Perhaps his reward was inclusion as an ancestor of our Lord in both the royal line (Matt 1:13) and the line recorded in Luke (Luke 3:27).

Bibliography: F. E. Gaebelein, *Four Minor Prophets: Obadiah, Jonah, Habakkuk, and Haggai: Their Message for Today,* 1970; J. C. Baldwin, *Haggai, Zechariah, Malachi: An Introduction and Commentary,* 1972. ABF

HAGGEDOLIM (hăg′ė-dōlĭm). The father of Zabdiel, chief officer over the priests after the Exile (Neh 11:14). KJV has "one of the great men."

HAGGERI (See HAGRITES)

HAGGI (hăg′ī, *festal*). A son of Gad and grandson of Jacob (Gen 46:16); patriarch of the Haggites (Num 26:15).

HAGGIAH (hă-gī′ȧ, *a festival of Jehovah*). A Levite of the family of Merari, mentioned only in 1 Chronicles 6:30.

HAGGITES (See HAGGI)

HAGGITH (hăg′ĭth, *festal*). Wife of David (2 Sam 3:4) and mother of Adonijah (1 Kings 1:5–31).

HAGIOGRAPHA (hăg′ĭ-ŏg′rȧ-fȧ, *holy writings*). A name applied to the third division of the OT by the Jews, the other two being the Law and the Prophets. Sometimes they were called the "Writings." They are presented in the following order: Psalms, Proverbs, Job, Song of Songs, Ruth, Lamentations, Ecclesiastes, Esther, Daniel, Ezra, Nehemiah, 1 and 2 Chronicles.

HAGRITES (hăg′rīts). An Arab people with

whom, in the days of King Saul, the tribe of Reuben made war (1 Chron 5:19–20). The Hagrites were so strong that Reuben won the victory only by crying to God in the battle. Psalm 83 tells how the Hagrites were leagued not only with Moab and the Ammonites east of the Jordan, with Edom, the Ishmaelites, and Amalek to the south, but also with Begal, Tyre, and Philistia along the coast against Israel. Asaph prays that God for his own name's sake will defeat them utterly.

HAI (See Ai)

HAIL. 1. Hailstorms sometimes take place in the Near East in the spring and summer and do considerable damage to crops, sometimes even injuring property and endangering life. Plagues of hail are mentioned in Exodus 9:23–24 and Joshua 10:11. The prophets speak of hail as a means of punishing the wicked (Isa 28:2; Ezek 38:22; Rev 8:7; 11:19).

2. An interjection found only in the Gospels (Matt 27:29; Mark 15:18; John 19:3) as a translation of *chairē,* used as a greeting or salutation. A similar greeting is still to be heard in modern Greece.

HAIR. Hair varies in length, color, and structure among the different races and seems to be intended by God for protection, for beauty, and for identification. The peoples of the Bible lands were generally black-haired, though red-haired individuals are fairly common among the people of Israel. Hebrews and Arabs (cf. Rev 9:8) wore their beards long as a mark of dignity, but the Egyptians were clean-shaven (Gen 41:14).

The quick-whitening of hair was one of the symptoms of leprosy (Lev 13:3, 10), but if the leprosy and the white hairs covered the body and there was no raw flesh, the leprosy was no longer contagious (13:13). Thin yellow hair appearing in the head or beard was a symptom of an itch, related to leprosy (13:29–37).

Limestone relief of hairdressing scene, on the side of the sarcophagus of Princess Kawit, from Peir el-Bahri, 11th Dynasty (c. 2135–2000 B.C.). The princess sits holding a bowl in her right hand and a mirror in her left, as one female servant dresses her hair and the other pours milk from a flask. Courtesy Egyptian Expedition, The Metropolitan Museum of Art.

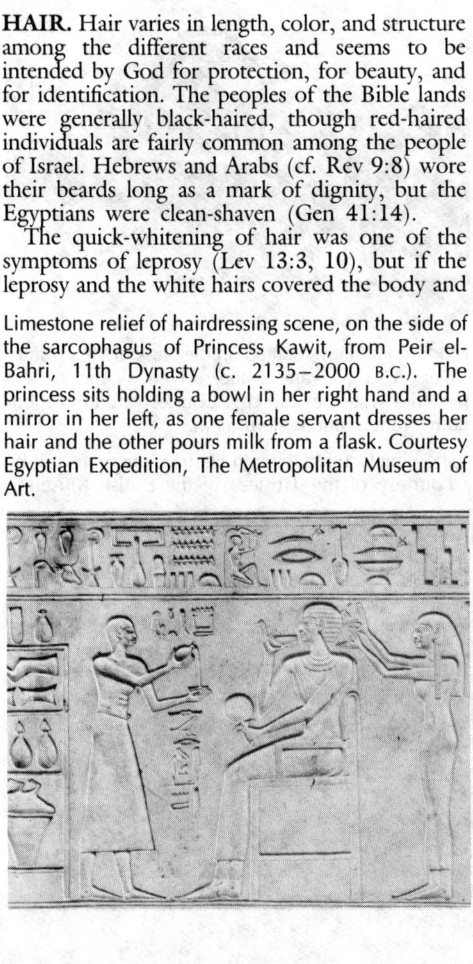

The men of Israel were not to clip off the edges of the beard (Lev 19:27), and this prohibition explains the "prayer-locks" in front of the ears of Orthodox Jewish men today.

The word "hair" is used in several figurative senses: e.g., in marksmanship some Benjamites could "sling a stone at a hair and not miss" (Judg 20:16); or in meaning complete safety—"not a hair of his head will fall to the ground" (1 Sam 14:45); or to indicate multiplicity—"my sins . . . are more than the hairs of my head" (Ps 40:12); or to show age or dignity—"the hair of his head was white like wool" (Dan 7:9).

Hair was a mark of beauty and sometimes of pride. Absalom's hair (2 Sam 14:26; 18:9), of which he was inordinately proud, caused his death. Samson's uncut hair was a symbol of his Naziritic dedication; and when he lost his hair, his strength went with it (Judg 13:7; 16:17–20). In NT times the length of the hair was one mark of distinction between the sexes, and Paul said that that disctinction should continue, pointing out that even nature teaches that long hair is a shame for a man but a glory for a woman (1 Cor 11:14–16). ABF

HAKILAH (hă-kī'lȧ). A hill in the wilderness SE of Hebron, near Siph and Maon (1 Sam 23:19; 26:1, 3). Here David hid from Saul but was discovered, and here Saul camped when he was seeking David.

HAKKATAN (hăk'ȧ-tăn, *the little one*). Father of the Johanan who returned with Ezra (Ezra 8:12).

HAKKOZ (hăk'ŏz, *the nimble;* KJV sometimes has Koz, once Coz). 1. A descendant of Aaron whose descendants returned with Zerubbabel from the Captivity (1 Chron 24:10; Ezra 2:61; Neh 3:4, 21).

2. A man of Judah (1 Chron 4:8 ASV; Koz in NIV, RSV, KJV).

HAKUPHA (hȧ-kū'fȧ, *bent, bowed*). Father of some of the temple servants (KJV Nethinim) who returned with Zerubbabel from Babylon (Ezra 2:51; Neh 7:53).

HALAH (hā'lȧ). A district in Media to which many of the captive Israelites were taken by Shalmanezer and by Tiglath-Pileser (2 Kings 17:6; 18:11; 1 Chron 5:26). It is about 80 miles (133 km.) west by north of the famous Behistun Rock on the road from Ecbatana to Babylon.

HALAK (hā'lăk, *smooth*). A mountain that marked the southern limit of the conquests of Joshua; perhaps the chalk cliffs crossing the Arabah about six miles (ten km.) south of the Dead Sea (Josh 11:17; 12:7).

HALHUL (hăl'hŭl). A town in the hill country of Judah (Josh 15:58) about four miles (seven km.) north of Hebron. It retains its ancient name and contains a mosque dedicated to the prophet Jonah.

HALI (hā'lī, *ornament*). A town on the southern boundary of the tribe of Asher (Josh 19:25).

HALL. In the KJV this denotes (1) the court of the high priest's palace (Luke 22:55) and (2) the official residence of a Roman provincial governor. It was called the praetorium (Matt 27:27; Mark 15:16).

HALLEL (hă-lāl, *praise*). Psalms 113–118, which were read on Passover Day, were called the "Egyptian Hallel"; Psalm 136 is an antiphonal psalm of praise and is sometimes called "The Hallel." Psalms 120–136 are often called "The Great Hallel."

HALLELUJAH (hăl'-lē-lū'yà, Heb. *halellû-yâh,* Gr. *allēlouia, praise ye Jehovah*). A word of praise found in most of the languages into which the Bible has been translated. The word is often translated "Praise the Lord" and is used by the writers of various psalms to invite all to join them in praising God (Ps 104:35; 105:45; 106:1, 48; 111:1; 112:1; 113:1, 9; 115:18; 116:19; 117:2; 135:1, 21; first and last verses of Pss 146 to 150). The term in Revelation 19:1, 3, 4, 6 is borrowed from these psalms.

HALLOHESH (hăl-lō'hĕsh, *the whisperer*). In Nehemiah 3:12 father of Shallum, a ruler, and in 10:24 one of the covenanters with Nehemiah; perhaps the same man.

HALLOW (hăl'ō, *to render or treat as holy*). The prime idea here, as in the kindred words "holy," "sanctify," is the setting apart of a person or thing for sacred use; to reverence as holy.

HAM (Heb. *hām,* perhaps *hot*). 1. The youngest son of Noah, born probably about ninety-six years before the Flood, and one of the eight persons to live through the Flood. He became the progenitor of the dark races—not the Blacks, but the Egyptians, Ethiopians, Libyans, and Canaanites (Gen 10:6–20). His indecency when his father lay drunk brought a curse on Canaan (Gen 9:20–27).

2. The descendants of Ham (Ps 78:51; 105:23; 106:22). In these passages "Ham" is used as another name for Egypt as representing Ham's principal descendants.

3. A city of the Zuzites, east of the Jordan (Gen 14:5).

HAMAN (hā'măn, Heb. *hāmān*). The great enemy of the Jews in the days of Esther. He is called "the Agagite," undoubtedly because he came from Agag, a territory adjacent to Media. Xerxes (KJV Ahasuerus) had promoted Haman to a high position in the court, but Mordecai, the noble Jew, refused to bow down to him. Therefore, Haman plotted to destroy the Jewish race, but God intervened. Esther foiled Haman's plot (Esth 7) and Haman died on the gallows he had made for Mordecai.

HAMATH (hā'măth, Heb. *hămāth, fortification*). One of the most ancient surviving cities on earth,

Modern Hamath, located on the bank of the Orontes River. A large water wheel driven by the current provides water for the city. Courtesy Studium Biblicum Franciscanum, Jerusalem.

Bronze relief from the gates of Balawat, c. 858–824 B.C. showing fortified town in Hamath under assault by the Assyrian army of Shalmaneser III. Reproduced by courtesy of the Trustees of the British Museum.

Sphinx orthostat (c. tenth to ninth centuries B.C.) found during excavations at Hamath in Syria. It is now in the Istanbul Museum. Photo: B. Brandl.

located in upper Syria on the Orontes River, from which it derives its water by means of immense undershot water wheels driven by the current. The "entrance to Hamath" (Num 34:8; NIV "Lebo Hamath," but see footnote) was to be the northern limit of Israel, but God left some of the Hivites in that neighborhood to be a test to the faithfulness of Israel (Judg 3:3–4). In the days of David, Hamath had a king of its own (2 Sam 8:9). Jeroboam II, the last powerful king of the northern tribes (2 Kings 14:23–28), recovered Hamath for Israel. The city has had a checkered history for thousands of years. For a time it was under the power of Assyria (18:34), later under the power of Babylonia (Jer 39:5). Still later Antiochus Epiphanes of Syria (c. 175–164 B.C.) renamed it Epiphaneia after himself. Today it is largely Muslim but has a large admixture of Christians. The city is dominated by its citadel hill, which no doubt contains layers of many different civilizations.

HAMATH ZOBAH (hā'măth zō'bȧ). Mentioned in 2 Chronicles 8:3, but the reference is uncertain. It could mean the neighbor kingdoms of Hamath and Zobah, or some place called Hamath, belonging to the kingdom of Zobah; or, to avoid confusion with the Zobah in the Hauran (2 Sam 23:36), Hamath may have been mentioned in connection with it.

HAMMATH (hăm'ăth, *hot spring*). 1. One of the fortified cities assigned by lot to the tribe of Naphtali in the division of the land under Joshua (Josh 19:35). It lay close to the shore of the Sea of Galilee, only a mile or so (about two km.) south of the city of Tiberias, and even today three of these hot springs send up sulphurous water at the southern extremity of the ancient ruins. It may have been the same as the Hammoth Dor of Joshua 21:32 and Hammon of 1 Chronicles 6:76.

2. The founder of the house of Recab (1 Chron 2:55; KJV Hemath).

HAMMEDATHA (hăm'ē-dā-thȧ). Father of Haman the Agagite, the villain in the Book of Esther (Esth 3:1).

HAMMER. The OT uses two chief words here: *pattish,* a tool for smoothing metals and for breaking rocks (Isa 41:7; Jer 23:29); and *maqqeveth,* a mallet to drive tent-pins into the ground (Judg 4:21; 1 Kings 6:7), for building, and for making idols (Isa 44:12; Jer 10:4). The word is also used figuratively for any crushing power, such as as Babylon (Jer 50:23) or God's word (23:29).

HAMMOLEKETH (hă-mŏl'ē-kĕth, *the queen*). A sister of Gilead (1 Chron 7:18; KJV Hammolecheth).

HAMMON (hăm'ŏn, *hot springs*). 1. A place in Asher about ten miles (seventeen km.) south of Tyre (Josh 19:28).

2. A city of Naphtali (1 Chron 6:76). Hammath (Josh 19:35) may be the same place.

HAMMOTH DOR (hăm'ŏth dôr, *warm springs of Dor*). A city in Naphtali, appointed as a city of refuge (Josh 21:32). See also HAMMATH.

HAMMUEL (hăm'ū-ĕl, *warmth of God*). A Simeonite mentioned only in 1 Chronicles 4:26; KJV Hamuel.

HAMMURABI (hȧm'ū-rȧ'bē). The king of the city of Babylon who brought that city to its century-and-a-half rule over southern Mesopotamia, known as the Old Babylonian Kingdom. He was an Amorite, the name given to a Semitic group that invaded the Fertile Crescent about 2000 B.C., destroying its civilization and establishing their own Semitic culture. There has been

Remains of an ancient Roman bathhouse at Hammath Tiberias (Hammath). The hot springs found here were famous in ancient times for their therapeutic properties and are still used today. Courtesy Seffie Ben-Yoseph.

Diorite statue found at Susa and thought to represent Hammurabi, the sixth and most famous king of the 1st Dynasty of Babylon (c. 1792–1750 B.C.). Courtesy Réunion des Musées Nationaux.

considerable difference of opinion about the date of his reign, recent scholars favoring 1728–1686.

Hammurabi made Babylon one of the great cities of the ancient world. Archaeologists have discovered that in his city the streets were laid out in straight lines that intersect approximately at right angles, an innovation that bears witness to city planning and strong central government, both little known in Babylon before this time. Marduk, the god of Babylon, now became the head of the pantheon, and his temple, Etemenanki, became one of the wonders of the ancient world. Many letters written by Hammurabi have been found. These show his close attention to the details of his realm and enable us to call him an energetic and benevolent ruler.

Hammurabi began the first golden age of Babylon—the second being that of Nebuchadnezzar, over a thousand years later. He systematically unified all of the old world of Sumer and Akkad (southern Mesopotamia) under his strongly centralized government. The prologue to his famous law code describes his administration: "Anu and Enlil [the sky and storm gods] named me to promote the welfare of the people, me, Hammurabi, the devout, god-fearing prince, to cause justice to prevail in the land, to destroy the wicked and the evil, that the strong might not oppress the weak, to rise like the sun over the black-headed [people], and to light up the land. Hammurabi the shepherd, called by Enlil, am I; the one who makes affluence and plenty abound . . . the one who revived Uruk, who supplied water in abundance to its people; the one who brings joy to Borsippa . . . who stores up grain for mighty Urash . . . the savior of his people from distress, who establishes in security their portion in the midst of Babylon . . . that justice might be dealt the orphan and the widow . . . I established the law and justice in the language of the land, thereby promoting the welfare of the people."

By far Hammurabi's most famous claim to fame is his law code. The code is inscribed on a magnificent stele of black diorite, eight feet (two and one-half m.) high, found at Susa in A.D. 1902. Formerly it had stood in Babylon, but the Elamites carried it off when they conquered Babylon in the twelfth century B.C. It is now in the Louvre in Paris. At the top of the stele is a finely sculptured scene showing Hammurabi standing before the sun god Shamash (the patron of law and justice), who is seated and is giving the laws to Hammurabi. Beneath the scene the laws are inscribed in beautiful cuneiform characters in fifty-one columns of text.

It is now known that Hammurabi's was not the first attempt to systematize the laws of Babylonia. Fragments of several previous law codes have been found. Ur-nammu of Ur and Lipit-Ishtar of Isin both promulgated earlier codes, and another was known in Eshnunna. But Hammurabi's code is the most complete expression of early Babylonian law, and undoubtedly incorporated many laws and customs that went back to far earlier times. Hammurabi did not invent these laws; he codified them.

The monument contains not only the code, but also a prologue and an epilogue, which narrated his glory (a portion of which was quoted above) and that of the gods whom he worshiped, blessed those who would respect his inscription, and cursed future vandals who might deface it. The entire inscription is translated in *Ancient Near Eastern Texts Relating to the OT* (edited by James B. Pritchard, 1950, pp. 163–80) and should be read by students interested in the subject.

The law code itself included nearly three hundred paragraphs of legal provisions concerning commercial, social, domestic, and moral life. There are regulations governing such matters as liability for (and exemption from) military service, control of trade in alcoholic drinks, banking and usury, and the responsibility of a man toward his wife and children, including the liability of a husband for the payment of his wife's debts. Hammurabi's code was harsher for upper-class offenders than on a commoner committing the same offense. Death was the penalty not only for homicide but also for theft, adultery, and bearing false witness in cases involving the accused's life. But the graded penalties show a great advance on primitive laws, and contemporary legal texts show that the harsher penalties were rarely exacted.

Women's rights were safeguarded. A neglected

Detail of upper part of the Hammurabi code, showing Hammurabi receiving the command to inscribe the laws from the sun-god Shamash. Diorite stele from Susa, 1728–1686 B.C. Courtesy Réunion des Musées Nationaux.

wife could obtain a divorce. A concubine who had become a mother was entitled to the restitution of whatever she had brought with her or a pecuniary indemnity appropriate to her social position. If a house fell on its owner or a doctor injured a patient, the one who built the house or treated the patient might suffer death, mutilation, or at least a heavy fine.

Students of the Bible are especially interested in the comparison of Hammurabi's code with the Mosaic legislation of the Bible. There are many similarities. In both a false witness is to be punished with the penalty he had thought to bring on the other person. Kidnapping and breaking into another person's house were capital offenses in both. The biblical law of divorce permits a man to put away his wife, but does not extend to her the same right as did Hammurabi. Both codes agree in prescribing the death penalty for adultery. The principle of retaliation, on which a number of Hammurabi's laws were based, is vividly stated in Exodus 21:23–25.

How are these similarities to be explained? It is obvious that Hammurabi could not have borrowed from Moses, for Moses lived several centuries after Hammurabi. Direct borrowing in the other direction also seems very unlikely. Most scholars today agree that the similarities are to be explained by the common background of the Hebrews and Babylonians. Both were Semitic peoples, inheriting their customs and laws from their common ancestors. At first this explanation seems to run counter to the biblical claim that Moses' law was given by divine revelation. A closer examination of the Pentateuch will show that the Hebrews, before they came to Sinai, followed many of the regulations set forth in the law (e.g., penalties against murder, adultery, fornication, Gen 9:6 and 38:24; the levirate law, 38:8; clean and unclean animals, 8:20; Sabbath, 2:3 and Exod 16:23, 25–29). Moses' law consisted of things both old and new. What was old (the customs the Hebrews received from their ancient Semitic ancestors) was here formally incorporated into the nation's constitution. Much is new, especially the high view of the nature of God and the idea that law is an expression of this nature (Lev 19:2).

Formerly many scholars identified the Amraphel, king of Shinar, whose invasion of Transjordan is described in Genesis 14:1–12, with Hammurabi, king of Babylon. Recently this identification has generally been given up. The two names are not the same and the chronological problems raised by the new late date for Hammurabi makes their equivalence very unlikely. JBG

HAMON GOG, VALLEY OF (hā'mŏn gŏg, *multitude of Gog*). A place east of the Dead Sea that will be set apart for the burial of the "multitude of Gog" (Ezek 39:11–15), after God's destruction of the northern host that will invade Israel in "the latter years" (Ezek 38:8 KJV).

HAMONAH (hȧ-mō'nȧ, *multitude*). Prophetic name of a city near the future burial place of Gog (Ezek 39:16).

HAMOR (hā'môr, Heb. *ḥămôr, an ass*). Father of the Shechem who criminally assaulted Dinah, a daughter of Jacob, as a result of which both father and son were killed in revenge by her brothers Simeon and Levi (Gen 34:1–31).

HAMSTRING (Hebrew *'āqar, to hamstring an animal*). The NIV of Genesis 49:6 reads, "They . . . hamstrung oxen," but KJV reads, "They digged down a wall." God commanded Joshua to hamstring (KJV, ASV "hough") the horses of the Canaanites, and Joshua obeyed (Josh 11:6, 9). David hamstrung the horses of Hadadezer, king of Zobah (2 Sam 8:4; 1 Chron 18:4). This was a cruel practice, justified only by extreme military necessity.

HAMUEL (See HAMMUEL)

HAMUL (hā'mŭl, *pitied, spared*). A grandson of Judah and son of Perez (Gen 46:12), head of the family of Hamulites.

HAMUTAL (hȧ-mū'tȧl, *father-in-law is dew*). Mother of two kings of Judah, Jehoahaz (2 Kings 23:31) and Zedekiah (24:18).

HANAMEL, HANAMEEL (hăn'ȧ-mĕl). Mentioned only in Jeremiah 32:7–12, he was a cousin of Jeremiah the prophet. While in prison Jeremiah bought a field from Hanamel when real estate values were low because of the Chaldean invasion. His purpose was to encourage the Jews to believe that the captivity would not be permanent and that restoration was certain.

HANAN (hā′năn, Heb. *hānān, gracious*). 1. A Benjamite of Jerusalem (1 Chron 8:23).

2. A son of Azel, a descendant of Jonathan (1 Chron 9:44).

3. One of David's mighty men, son of Maacah (1 Chron 11:43).

4. One of the Nethinim (KJV) or temple servants who returned with Zerubbabel (Ezra 2:46; Neh 7:49).

5. An interpreter of the Law (Neh 8:7).

6. Three covenanters with Nehemiah (Neh 10:10, 22, 26).

7. An influential Jew in Jerusalem (Jer 35:4).

HANANEL, HANANEEL (hȧ-năn′ĕl, hȧ-năn′ē-ĕl, Heb. *hănan'ēl, God is gracious*). A tower in the wall of Jerusalem (Jer 31:38; Zech 14:10) on the north side between the Sheep Gate and the Fish Gate (Neh 3:1; 12:39).

HANANI (hȧ-nā′nī, Heb. *hănānî, gracious*). 1. A son of Heman, David's seer who served in music (1 Chron 25:4, 25).

2. Seer in Asa's time who rebuked Asa and was imprisoned (2 Chron 16:7–10).

3. A priest who had married a foreigner (Ezra 10:20).

4. Brother of the great Nehemiah (Neh 1:2; 7:2). He brought to Nehemiah in Shushan the news of Jerusalem's sad state; and Nehemiah later gave to him and to Hananiah, governor of the castle, authority over Jerusalem.

5. One of the musical priests whom Nehemiah appointed for the celebration at the dedication of the wall of Jerusalem (Neh 12:36). Ezra was the leader of this band.

HANANIAH (hăn′ȧ-nī′ȧ, Heb. *hănanyâh, Jehovah is gracious*). 1. A son of Heman, David's seer (1 Chron 25:4, 23) who headed the sixteenth course of musical Levites.

2. A captain of Uzziah's army (2 Chron 26:11).

3. Father of Zedekiah, who was one of Jehoiakim's princes (Jer 36:12).

4. The grandfather of Irijah, who arrested Jeremiah for alleged treason (Jer 37:13).

5. Father of a Benjamite household who lived in Jerusalem (1 Chron 8:24).

6. The Hebrew name of Shadrach, one of the three who survived the furnace of fire (Dan 1:6–7).

7. A son of Zerubbabel (1 Chron 3:19, 21).

8. A priest who had married a foreign woman (Ezra 10:28).

9. A perfumer who repaired a section of the wall of Jerusalem in the time of Nehemiah (Neh 3:8).

10. Another repairer of the wall of Jerusalem (Neh 3:30).

11. A governor of the castle in Jerusalem, a faithful man who feared God (Neh 7:2).

12. One of the chief covenanters, perhaps the same as no. 11 (Neh 10:23).

13. Head of a priestly house in the days of the high priest Joiakim (Neh 12:12, 41).

14. A false prophet of Gibeon in the tribe of Benjamin in the days of Zedekiah, the last king of Judah (Jer 28). In the year 594 B.C. he stood up against Jeremiah, God's prophet who had been pronouncing the doom of Judah and Jerusalem. He prophesied that within two years Nebuchadnezzar would bring back the vessels of the temple; would restore to power Jehoiachin, who had reigned for three months in 597; and would bring back the Jewish captives. Jeremiah had been wearing a yoke of wood to symbolize the coming captivity. Hananiah broke it off and was told that a yoke of iron would take its place for the people of Judah. The Lord put Hananiah to death that year.

HAND. One of the most frequently used words in Scripture, occurring over sixteen hundred times. Besides its literal use, it occurs in many figurative senses as well. It very often stands for power, as in Genesis 9:2. "They are given into your hands" would make no sense if taken literally. To put one's hand under another's thigh as in Genesis 24:2, 9; 47:29 meant to take a solemn oath, evidently related to covenant obligations; to put one's hand on the head meant blessing, as in Genesis 48:14, and signified ordination, as in 1 Timothy 4:14 and 2 Timothy 1:6. To kiss the hand of another is one of the usual marks of respect in the East; however, this custom is not mentioned in Scripture.

In the OT the hand is also the symbol of personal agency. When the Lord stretches out his hand, it means that he is taking personal action in whatever case or situation is involved, and this usage carries over into the NT (e.g., 1 Sam 5:11; John 10:29; Acts 4:30). Correspondingly, for human beings the hand signifies a person in action (e.g., 1 Sam 26:23); and we should understand in this light the idiom by which the Hebrew expresses the consecration of priests to their holy duties: "to consecrate" is "to fill the hand" (e.g., Exod 29:9 KJV; see footnote), that is, to dedicate every capacity of personal action for the service and use of the Lord.

To be placed at the right hand of royalty is a high honor and, of course, at "the right hand" of God is incomparably higher. "The LORD says to my Lord: 'Sit at my right hand'" (Ps 110:1), showing the supreme position of the Son of God. When he judges the nations (Matt 25:31–46), separating "sheep" from "goats," "he will put the sheep on his right [hand] and the goats on his left," showing that the left hand is equally the place of dishonor. The Hebrew word for "north" is the same as for "the left hand" and for "south" the same as for "the right hand." In a trial the accuser stood at the right hand of the accused, as is shown in Zechariah 3:1, where Satan is the accuser; but our Advocate stands also at our right hand to defend us (Ps 16:8; 109:31). ABF

HANDKERCHIEF. The Gr. *soudarion* is a transliteration of the Latin word *sudarium,* which was a cloth intended to wipe sweat from the face. Handkerchiefs were brought from Paul's body for healing purposes (Acts 19:12); the wicked servant (Luke 19:20–23) kept his lord's money "in a piece of cloth"; the face of dead Lazarus was enclosed in a cloth (the same word) (John 11:44), as was also the face of our Lord (20:7).

HANDLE. The noun is found only in Song of Songs 5:5, referring to the doorknob. The Hebrew word has over a dozen meanings.

HANDMAID, HANDMAIDEN. In the KJV a female slave or servant. When used of oneself, it indicates humility, as in Ruth's speaking to Boaz (Ruth 3:9), Hannah's praying to the Lord (1 Sam 1:11) and speaking to Eli (1:16), and Mary's speaking to Gabriel (Luke 1:38) and singing (1:48).

HANDS, IMPOSITION OF (See LAYING ON OF HANDS)

HANES (hā'nēz). A place in Egypt mentioned only in Isaiah 30:4. From its association with Zoan and from the context, it would seem to have been in the Delta, though some associate it with Heracleopolis Magna, west of the Nile and far up the river.

HANGING. Death by strangulation was not a form of capital punishment used in Bible times. Where the word is found in Scripture, except in the two cases of suicide by hanging (Ahithophel, 2 Sam 17:23; Judas, Matt 27:5), it refers to the suspension of a body from a tree or post after the criminal had been put to death. This was practiced by the Egyptians (Gen 40:19, 22), the Israelites (Deut 21:22), and the Persians. Hanging added to the disgrace. The body was buried before nightfall (Deut 21:23; Josh 8:29; cf. 1 Sam 31:8–13).

Part of relief from central palace of Tiglath-Pileser III (744–727 B.C.) at Calah depicting three prisoners of war impaled on gallows. Reproduced by courtesy of the Trustees of the British Museum.

HANGINGS (Heb. *kelā'îm, māsākh*). The "curtains" (NIV) of the tabernacle and its court that preserved the privacy and the sacredness of what was within. Some were more or less permanent, but others could be removed to permit passage of a person. Of the first class were the "hangings" (KJV) of finely twined linen that enclosed the court (Exod 27:9–19) and the curtains of the tent itself (26:1–14); of the second class were the screen of the court (27:14–16), the curtain at the door of the tent (26:36), and the veil that did not allow anyone but the high priest to look into the Most Holy Place (26:31–35). This veil was the curtain that God tore from top to bottom at the crucifixion of our Lord (Matt 27:51; Heb 9:8; 10:19–20).

HANIEL (See HANNIEL)

HANNAH (Heb. *hannâh, grace, favor*). One of the two wives of Elkanah, a Levite who lived at Ramah (1 Sam 1:19), a village of Ephraim, otherwise known as Ramathaim (1:1). Peninnah, the other wife of Elkanah (1:2), had children; but Hannah was barren for a long time and, as is common in polygamous households, "her rival kept provoking her" (1:6). The fact that Elkanah loved Hannah and gave her a double portion (1:5) only increased the hatred and jealousy in Peninnah's heart. Hannah, however, was a godly woman, and she prayed for a son and vowed to give him to the Lord as a perpetual Nazirite (1:11). Eli saw Hannah's lips moving in silent prayer and rebuked her for what he thought was drunkenness. She replied very humbly and Eli apologized. The family returned home; Hannah conceived and became the mother of Samuel, the great prophet of Israel and the last of the judges. Hannah's praise (2:1–10) shows that she was a deeply spiritual woman. Mary's song, "the Magnificat," resembles Hannah's (Luke 1:46–55). Mary, like Hannah, praised God when she was expecting a baby by miraculous conception. Each woman rejoiced in the Lord; each expressed in marvelous fashion God's way of dealing with the proud and with the humble. See also Psalm 113:7–9. ABF

HANNATHON (hăn'nȧ-thŏn, Heb. *hannāthôn, gracious*). A city on the northern boundary of Zebulun (Josh 19:14). It is mentioned in the Amarna Letters.

HANNIEL (han'ĭ-ĕl, Heb. *hannî'ēl, the favor of God*). 1. Son of Ephod, the prince of the tribe of Manasseh, appointed by Moses to help in dividing the land (Num 34:23).

2. Son of Ulla, and a descendant of Asher (1 Chron 7:39).

HANOCH (hā'nŏk, Heb. *hănôkh, initiation*). 1. A grandson of Abraham and Keturah through their son Midian (Gen 25:4; 1 Chron 1:33; KJV Henoch).

2. Eldest son of Reuben (Gen 46:9; Exod 6:14; 1 Chron 5:3), he was the head of the family of the Hanochites (Num 26:5).

HANUKKAH (See FEASTS)

HANUN (hā'nŭn, Heb. *hănûn, favored*). 1. King of Ammon who, having mistaken David's friendly servants for spies, mistreated them, thus bringing on a war in which the Ammonites lost their independence (2 Sam 10; 1 Chron 19).

2. A man who, with the help of the inhabitants of Zanoah, built the Valley Gate, setting up the doors, locks, and bars of it in the wall of Jerusalem (Neh 3:13).

3. Son of Zalaph. He helped repair the wall of Jerusalem (Neh 3:30).

HAPHARAIM (hă-fà-rā'ĭm, Heb. *hăphāraîyim, two pits*). A city located near Shunem in Issachar (Josh 19:19). Modern Et-Taiyibeh.

HAPPIZZEZ (hăp'ė-zĕz). A Levite chief of the eighteenth of the twenty-four divisions for the service in the temple (1 Chron 24:15; KJV Aphses).

HARA (hă'rȧ, Heb. *hārā', mountain country*). A place named in 1 Chronicles 5:26, along with Halah, Habor, and the river of Gozan, as the destinations of the tribes of Reuben and Gad and the half-tribe of Manasseh when they were carried away by the Assyrians. But such a place as Hara is unknown. The LXX omits it in this verse, as also do 2 Kings 17:6 and 18:11 in naming the destinations of the captive nation Israel. Both these latter references add the phrase "in the cities of the Medes." The LXX has "mountains of the Medes." Some scholars think Hara should read Haran; others believe the text is a corruption.

HARADAH (hȧr-ā'dȧ, Heb. *hărādhâh, terror*). One of Israel's encampments in the wilderness wanderings where they stayed after leaving Mount Shepher (Num 33:24). The site is unknown, but its name suggests it was a mountain.

HARAN (hā'răn, Heb. *hārān, mountaineer*). 1. The youngest brother of Abram, and father of Lot, Abram's nephew. He died in Ur before his father Terah took his family from that city (Gen 11:27–28).

2. A son of Caleb by his concubine Ephah. This Haran had a son named Gazez (1 Chron 2:46).

3. A Gershonite Levite who lived in the time of David. He was the son of Shimei (1 Chron 23:9).

HARAN, CHARRAN (hā'răn, chă'răn, Heb. *hārān*, Gr. *charran*). A city located in northern Mesopotamia, on the Balikh River, a branch of the Euphrates, to which Abram's father Terah emigrated with his family (Gen 11:31). After his father's death, Abram left this city to go into the land of Canaan (12:4). His brother Nahor remained there. Abraham later sent his servant there to find a wife for his son Isaac among his relatives (24:4). Afterward Jacob, at the request of his father Isaac, came to this same area in search of a wife (29:4–5). In the time of Hezekiah, Rabshakeh, an officer of Sennacherib, when delivering a propaganda lecture to the people of Jerusalem, mentioned that Haran and other cities in the same area had been conquered by Assyria (2 Kings 19:12; Isa 37:12). Ezekiel mentions this city as one of those that carried on trade with Tyre (Ezek 27:23).

Basalt stele of Nabonidus, King of Babylon (559–539 B.C.), father of Belshazzar (Dan 5:29). His left hand holds a staff and his right is raised toward the symbols of Sin, Shamash, and Ishtar. Sin is the moon god. Courtesy The School of Oriental and African Studies (University of London).

Haran is often referred to in Assyrian and Babylonian records under the form of *harranu,* Anglicized as Harran. The term means "road," probably because this city was located at the intersection of the north-south trade route from Damascus and the east-west route between Carchemish and Nineveh. A center of worship of the moon-god Sin was established there in very early times. The city and temple were destroyed in the wars of the Assyrian kings. After the fall of Nineveh in 612 B.C., some Assyrian refugees fled to Haran and held out there until 610. Nabonidus, the king of Babylon, who delighted in restoring old temples, rebuilt the city and temple and reinstated the worship of the moon-god there about seventy-five years later. This city is mentioned in Mari documents in the form of Nakhur, probably from Nahor, Abram's brother. The Romans knew it as Carrhae, famous as the place where the Parthians defeated Crassus in 53 B.C. It is still in existence as Harran, near the original site in southern Turkey. The present-day Muslims who live in the area have many traditions concerning Abraham. CEH

HARARITE (hā'rȧ-rīte, Heb. *hărārî, mountain dweller*). An area in the hill country of either Judah or Ephraim. This term occurs only in the catalog of David's mighty men: Shammah, the son of Agee the Hararite (2 Sam 23:11, 33); Jonathan, the son of Shagee the Hararite (1 Chron 11:34); Ahiam, the son of Sacar the Hararite (11:35).

HARBONA, HARBONAH (hȧr-bō'nȧ, Heb. *harevônā', harevônâh, ass driver*). One of the seven chamberlains of Xerxes (KJV Ahasuerus), king of Persia (Esth 1:10; 7:9).

HARE (See ANIMALS)

HAREPH (hā'rēf, Heb. *hārēph, scornful*). Son of Caleb, and father of Beth Gader (1 Chron 2:51).

HARETH (See HERETH)

HARHAIAH (hȧr-hā'ja, Heb. *harhăyâh,* meaning unknown). Father of Uzziel, a goldsmith who repaired a portion of the wall of Jerusalem (Neh 3:8).

HARHAS (hăr'hăs, Heb. *harhas,* meaning uncertain). Grandfather of Shallum, husband of Huldah the prophetess (2 Kings 22:14). In 2 Chronicles 34:22 this name is Hasrah.

HARHUR (hăr'hûr, Heb. *harhūr, fever*). Head of one of the families who returned from exile with Zerubbabel (Ezra 2:51; Neh 7:53).

HARIM (hā'rĭm, Heb. *hārim, consecrated or slit-nosed*). 1. A priest assigned to the third division for temple service in David's time (1 Chron 24:8).

2. A family who returned from Babylon with Zerubbabel (Ezra 2:32; Neh 7:35).

3. A family of priests who returned from exile with Zerubbabel (Ezra 2:39; Neh 7:42; 12:15). Members of this family married foreign wives (Ezra 10:21).

4. Another family who married foreign wives (Ezra 10:31).

5. Father of Malkijah, a worker on the wall of Jerusalem (Neh 3:11). Perhaps the same as he who entered into a covenant with the Lord under Nehemiah (Neh 10:5).

6. Another man who covenanted with the Lord under Nehemiah (Neh 10:27).

HARIPH (hā'rĭf, Heb. *harîph, autumn*). A family who returned to Judah from Babylon with Zerubbabel (Neh 7:24). (Ezra 2:18 has Jorah.) A man of this name was among those who signed the covenant with God, according to Nehemiah 10:19.

HARLOT (See PROSTITUTE)

HARMON (hăr'mėn). Amos 4:3 names this as a place to which the people of Samaria would be exiled. No such place is known, and the text appears to be a corruption. Many suggestions have been made as to its meaning (e.g., KJV "cast them into the palace"), but scholars can reach no agreement.

HARNEPHER (hȧr'nĕ-fêr, Heb. *harnepher*). A son of Zophah in the tribe of Asher (1 Chron 7:36).

HAROD (hā'rŏd, Heb. *hârōdh, trembling*). A spring or well beside which Gideon and his men camped one morning. The Lord reduced his army there to three hundred men with whom he routed the Midianites that night (Judg 7:1). Harod was located in the Mount Gilboa area about four miles (seven km.) SE of the city of Jezreel. The modern name of the spring is Ain Jalud.

HARODITE (hā'rŏd-īt, Heb. *hărōdî, belonging to Harod*). The family name of two of David's mighty men, Shammah and Elika (2 Sam 23:25). In the parallel place in 1 Chronicles 11:27 this name is given as "Harorite"—a scribal error for "Harodite."

HAROEH (hȧ-rō'ĕ, Heb. *hārō'eh, the seer*). A son of Shobal and grandson of Caleb, son of Hur (1 Chron 2:52).

HAROSHETH HAGGOYIM (hā-rō'shĕth hă-gōyīm). A town near the Kishon River in northern Palestine. It was the home of Sisera, the captain of the army of Jabin, king of Canaan (Judg 4:2, 13, 16). The significance of the phrase "of the Gentiles" (see KJV) is unknown but suggests that mixed races lived there. It has been identified with modern Teil Amr in the Mount Carmel–Kishon area.

HARP (See MUSIC AND MUSICAL INSTRUMENTS)

HARROW (Heb. *sādhădh*). The Hebrew word occurs three times, always as a verb. In Job 39:10 it is translated "till" (KJV "harrow"). In Isaiah 28:24 it is translated by the phrase "breaking up and harrowing the ground" and in Hosea 10:11 by "break up the ground." From the root of the word it seems to mean dragging or leveling off a field.

HARROW (See PICKS)

HARSHA (hărshȧ, Heb. *harshā', dumb, silent*). The head of a family of temple servants (KJV Nethinim) who returned from exile under Zerubbabel (Ezra 2:52; Neh 7:54).

HART (See ANIMALS)

HARUM (hā'rŭm, Heb. *hārum, made high*). A descendant of Judah mentioned as the father of Aharhel (1 Chron 4:8).

HARUMAPH (hȧ-rū'maf, Heb. *hărûmaph,* perhaps *slit-nosed*). The father of Jedaiah, a worker who helped repair the wall of Jerusalem (Neh 3:10).

HARUPHITE (hȧ-rū'fīt, Heb. *harûphî,* or *hărîphî*). Shephatiah, one of the men who joined David's forces in Ziklag, was called the Haruphite or the Hariphite (1 Chron 12:5). If this latter form is the correct one, then this man may be connected with the Hariph clan (Neh 7:24).

HARUZ (hā'rŭz, Heb. *hārûts, diligent*). Father-in-law of Manasseh, king of Judah (2 Kings 21:19).

HARVEST. (hȧr-vĕst, Heb. *qātsîr,* Gr. *therismos*). The economy of the Israelites was strictly agricultural. Harvest time was a very significant event for them. They had three each year. The barley reaping (Ruth 1:22) came in April–May; the wheat harvest (Gen 30:14) was about six weeks later, in June–July; and the ingathering of the fruits of tree or vine took place in September–October.

Grain crops were reaped with sickles, and the cut stalks were laid in bunches that were carried to the threshing floor. Some laws governed these simple harvest operations. The corners of the fields were not to be reaped, and the scatterings of the cut grain were not to be picked up. The part of the crop thus left was for the poor people to use (Lev 23:22). The owner was required each year to present the firstfruits of the crop as an offering to God before he could take any of it for his own use (23:10, 14). Stalks of grain that grew up without being sown were not to be harvested (25:5). With a new orchard or vineyard the fruit was not to be gathered for three years, and the fourth year's crop had to be given entirely to the Lord. So the owner had to wait until the fifth year to get any fruit for himself (19:23–25).

The Lord fitted the three main religious feasts that he prescribed for the people into this agricultural economy. The Passover came in the season of the barley harvest (Exod 23:16). Seven weeks later at time of the wheat harvest the Feast of Pentecost occurred (34:22). The Feast of Tabernacles was observed in the seventh month, which was the period of the fruit harvest (34:22).

In the NT, most of the time the term "harvest" is used figuratively for the gathering in of the redeemed saints at the end of the age (Matt 13:39).

HASADIAH (hă-sȧ-dī'ȧ, Heb. *hăsadhyâh, Jehovah is kind*). A son of Zerubbabel (1 Chron 3:20).

HASENUAH (See HASSENUAH)

HASHABIAH (hăsh-ȧ-bī'ȧ, Heb. *hăshavyâh, whom Jehovah esteems*). 1. An ancestor of Ethan, a Levite and temple singer in David's time (1 Chron 6:45).

2. An ancestor of Shemaiah, a Levite who returned from Babylon (1 Chron 9:14) and lived in Jerusalem (Neh 11:15).

3. A son of Jeduthun, a musician in David's time (1 Chron 25:3).

4. A civil official in David's time (1 Chron 26:30).

5. Overseer of the tribe of Levi in David's time (1 Chron 27:17).

6. A chief of the Levites in Josiah's time (2 Chron 35:9).

7. A Levite teacher whom Ezra brought with him (Ezra 8:19).

8. A chief priest in Ezra's company (Ezra 8:24).

9. Ruler of half of the district of Keilah, a worker on the wall (Neh 3:17).

10. A priest, head of the family of Hilkiah (Neh 12:21).

11. An ancestor of Uzzi, the overseer of the Levites at Jerusalem in Nehemiah's time (Neh 11:22).

12. A chief of the Levites who sealed the covenant (Neh 3:17) and was appointed to praise God (12:24).

HASHABNAH (hȧ-shăb'ȧ, Heb. *hăshavnâh*). One of those who sealed the covenant with Nehemiah (Neh 10:25).

HASHABNEIAH (hăsh'ăb-nē-ī'ȧ, Heb. *hăshavneyâh*). 1. The father of Hattush, a worker on the wall (Neh 3:10).

2. One of the Levites who prayed at the confession of sin after Ezra had read from the "Book of the Law of God" (Neh 8:18–9:5).

HASHBADDANAH (hăsh-băd'ȧ-nȧ, Heb. *hashbaddānâh*). A man who stood on the left of Ezra as he read the Law to the people (Neh 8:4).

HASHEM (hā'shĕm, Heb. *hāshēm*). A man whose sons were among David's mighty men (1 Chron 11:34). The parallel passage (2 Sam 23:32) has Jashen.

HASHMONAH (hăsh-mō'nȧ, Heb. *hashmōnâh*). A station where the Israelites camped in the wilderness (Num 33:29–30). The site is unknown.

HASHUB (See HASSHUB)

HASHUBAH (hȧ-shū'bȧ, Heb. *hăshuvâh, consideration*). A son of Zerubbabel (1 Chron 3:20).

HASHUM (hā'shŭm, Heb. *hāshum*). 1. A family that returned from exile under Zerubbabel (Ezra 2:19; 10:33; Neh 7:22).

2. A priest who stood at the left of Ezra as he read the Law to the people (Neh 8:4).

3. A chief of the people who sealed the covenant (Neh 10:18). Perhaps the same as no. 2.

HASHUPHA (See HASUPHA)

HASMONEANS (See MACCABEES)

HASRAH (hăs'rȧ, Heb. *hasrâh,* meaning uncertain). Grandfather of Shallum, the husband of

Huldah the prophetess (2 Chron 34:22). In the parallel place (2 Kings 22:14) the name is given as Harhas.

HASSENAAH (hăs-ē-nā'-à. Heb. *hassenā'âh;* the word is *sena'ah* with the definite article prefixed, meaning *the hated one*). Father of the brothers who built the Fish Gate in the wall of Jerusalem (Neh 3:3).

HASSENUAH (hăs-ė-nū'à, Heb. *hassenūâh,* the word is *senuah,* with the definite article prefixed, meaning *the hated one*). 1. An ancestor of Sallu, a Benjamite who returned from exile (1 Chron 9:7).

2. The father of Judah, the assistant overseer of Jerusalem in Nehemiah's time (Neh 11:9). In KJV Senuah.

HASSHUB (hăsh'ŭb, Heb. *hashshûv, considerate*). 1. The father of Shemaiah, a Levite who returned from exile (1 Chron 9:14). He lived in Jerusalem (Neh 11:15, KJV Hashub).

2. A worker on the wall of Jerusalem (Neh 3:11).

3. Another such worker (Neh 3:23).

4. One who sealed the covenant (Neh 10:23). Perhaps identical with no. 2 or 3.

HASSOPHERETH (See SOPHERETH)

HASUPHA (hă-sūfà, Heb. *hasupha*). A family who returned from exile under Zerubbabel (Ezra 2:43; Neh 7:46).

HAT (See DRESS)

HATHACH (hā'-thăk, Heb. *hăthākh*). One of the eunuchs of King Xerxes (KJV Ahasuerus) assigned to attend Esther (Esth 4:5–6, 9). KJV and MLB have Hatach; Mof has Mothak.

HATHATH (hā'-thăth, Heb. *hăthath, terror*). A son of Othniel, the first judge of Israel (1 Chron 4:13).

HATIPHA (hȧ-ti'fà, Heb. *hătîphā',* meaning uncertain). Head of a family of temple servants (KJV Nethinim) who returned from exile under Zerubbabel (Ezra 2:54; Neh 7:56).

HATITA (hȧ-tī'tȧ, Heb. *hătîtā', exploring*). An ancestor of a family of Levitical porters who returned from exile under Zerubbabel (Ezra 2:42; Neh 7:45).

HATTIL (hăt'ĭl, Heb. *hattîl, waving*). A family who returned from exile under Zerubbabel (Ezra 2:57; Neh 7:59).

HATTUSH (hăt'ŭsh, Heb. *hattûsh,* meaning unknown). 1. A descendant in the royal line of Judah in the fifth generation from Zerubbabel (1 Chron 3:22).

2. A descendant of David who returned from Babylon with Ezra (Ezra 8:2).

3. A worker on the wall of Jerusalem (Neh 3:10); perhaps the same as no. 2.

4. One of those who sealed the covenant (Neh 10:4); perhaps the same as no. 2 or 3.

5. A priest who returned with Zerubbabel (Neh 12:2).

HAURAN (hȧ'ū-rȧn, Heb. *hawrān,* probably *black* or *black land*). The modern name of a great plain situated on a plateau 2,000 feet (625 m.) high east of the Jordan River and north of the land of Gilead. In ancient times it was called Bashan. Its soil is of volcanic origin and is very rich, making the region famous for its wheat crops. The name Hauran is mentioned only by Ezekiel in his description of the boundaries of the land of Israel in the millennial age (Ezek 47:16, 18).

The Israelites never had a very great hold on this area. Its openness to the east made it a frequent prey to robbers from the desert. Under the Romans Herod ruled over it as part of his realm, and he greatly encouraged settlement by stopping the robber raids. It was then known as Auranitis. Christianity flourished there from the second century A.D. until the seventh century, when it was overthrown by the Muslims. Today Hauran is an integral part of Syria.

HAVILAH (hăv'-ĭ-lȧ, Heb. *hăwîlâh, sand land*). 1. A son of Cush, a descendant of Ham (Gen 10:7; 1 Chron 1:9).

2. A son of Joktan, a descendant of Shem (Gen 10:29; 1 Chron 1:23). These names are generally taken to mean tribes or nations. If both references refer to the same area, they pertained to both Hamitic and Semitic peoples. It is generally thought to have been located in southern Arabia.

3. A land through which the Pishon River flowed from a source in the Garden of Eden; it contained gold and other minerals (Gen 2:11–12). It is probably located in Armenia or Mesopotamia, though its actual location is uncertain.

4. A land mentioned as one of the boundaries of the dwelling of the Ishmaelites "from Havilah to Shur, near the border of Egypt" (Gen 25:18). This Havilah is probably the same as the one mentioned in no. 2 above. Saul conquered the Amalekites in this same area "from Havilah to Shur, to the east of Egypt" (1 Sam 15:7).

HAVVOTH JAIR (hā-vŏth jā'îr, Heb. *hawwōth-yā'îr, villages of Jair*). A group of villages that Jair, son of Manasseh, took (Num 32:41). The word *hawwah* means a village of tents; it is used only in connection with these towns of Jair. This group consisted of thirty villages (Judg 10:4; 1 Chron 2:22–23). Jair captured both Gilead and Bashan; this latter district evidently contained thirty more towns (Deut 3:14; Josh 13:30; 1 Kings 4:13; 1 Chron 2:23). The phrase Havvoth Jair applied only to the villages in Gilead.

HAWK (See BIRDS)

HAZAEL (hăz′-ā-ĕl, Heb. *hăzā'ēl, God sees*). A high official of Ben-Hadad, king of Syria. When the king was sick, he sent Hazael to inquire of the prophet Elisha concerning his recovery from this illness. Elisha told Hazael to tell the king that he would certainly recover, but he would in fact die (2 Kings 8:7–15). Previously God had instructed Elijah to anoint Hazael king of Syria (1 Kings 19:15). Hazael pretended to be surprised by Elisha's statement that he would become king. He returned and suffocated Ben-Hadad and seized the throne for himself (2 Kings 8:7–15).

This usurpation is confirmed by an inscription of Shalmaneser III that states that Hadadezer of Damascus (that is, Ben-Hadad) perished and Hazael, a son of nobody, seized the throne. The phrase "a son of nobody" means he was not in the royal line of descent.

The date of Hazael's reign can be ascertained as at least forty-three years in length (841–798 B.C.); very likely it was a few years longer. Ahaziah, king of Judah, reigned only one year (2 Kings 8:26), namely, 841. During that year he fought with Joram, king of Israel, against Hazael (8:28). The annals of Shalmaneser III, king of Assyria (858–824), in his fourteenth year (844), record a battle against Hadadezer (Ben-Hadad) of Damascus. In his eighteenth year (840) Shalmaneser said he encountered Hazael at Damascus. So Hazael usurped the throne during the period 844–841. He reigned at least until 798, the date of the death of Jehoahaz, king of Israel, for Hazael oppressed Israel all the days of this king (13:22). He died shortly afterward (13:24).

Hazael greatly punished Israel, as Elisha had foreseen (2 Kings 8:12). He wounded Jehoram, son of Ahab, at Ramoth Gilead (8:19). During the reign of Jehu, Hazael took all the territory east of the Jordan Valley from Israel (10:32). While Joash was ruling in Judah, Hazael captured Gath and threatened Jerusalem, but Joash induced him to leave by giving him sacred objects and the gold from the temple and palace treasuries (12:17–18). Yet he continually raided Israel during the reign of Jehoahaz (13:3). As previously mentioned, he oppressed Israel all the days of this king (13:22). Shalmaneser III records two attacks on Hazael in which the Assyrian king claims great victories with severe damage to the Syrian countryside.

". . . He took the coverlet and dipped it in water and spread it over his face, till he died. And Hazael became king in his stead" (2 Kings 8:15). Ivory figure thought to represent Hazael, king of Damascus, from Arslan Tash, ninth century B.C. Courtesy Réunion des Musées Nationaux.

HAZAIAH (hȧ-zā′yȧ, *Jehovah sees*). A member of a family of Shiloh whose great-grandson lived in Jerusalem 444 B.C. (Neh 11:5).

HAZAR ADDAR (hā′zȧr ăd′ȧr). A place on the southern boundary of Judah, west of Kadesh Barnea and east of Azmon (Num 34:4). In Joshua 15:3 it is called simply Addar (KJV Adar).

HAZAR ENAN (hā′zȧr ē′năn, *village of fountains*). The NE corner of the land of Canaan as promised by the Lord to the people of Israel (Num 34:9–10; cf. Ezek 47:17).

HAZAR GADDAH (hā′zȧr găd′ȧ, *village of good fortune*). A town in the south of Judah, very close to the boundary of Simeon (Josh 15:27).

HAZAR SHUAL (hā′zȧr shū′ăl, *village of the jackal*). A town in southern Judah (Josh 15:28) later given to Simeon (19:3). After the Captivity it was held by Simeon (1 Chron 4:28) and Judah (Neh 11:27).

HAZAR SUSAH (hā'zȧr sū'sȧ, *village of a mare*). A town given to Simeon out of Judah (Josh 19:5), but called Hazar Susim, i.e., "village of horses" in 1 Chronicles 4:31. The site is uncertain.

HAZARMAVETH (hā'zȧr-mā'vĕth, *village of death*). Listed in the "Table of Nations" (Gen 10:26; 1 Chron 1:20), he was apparently a son of Joktan, but probably represented the people or the district of modern Hadramut.

HAZAZON TAMAR (hăz'ȧ-zŏn tā'mēr, *Hazazon of the palm trees*). The ancient name of a town on the west coast of the Dead Sea, occupied in Abraham's time by the Amorites (Gen 14:7) but conquered by the four great kings of the East. KJV has Hazezon-tamar.

HAZEL (See PLANTS)

HAZER HATTICON (hā'zer-hăt'ĭ-kŏn, *middle village*). Mentioned only in Ezekiel 47:16 as being near Damascus and on the border of Hauran. Its exact location is uncertain.

HAZEROTH (hȧ-zē'rŏth, *courts* or *villages*). A station on Israel's journeys in the wilderness, about forty-two (seventy km.) miles from Mount Sinai, northeastward toward the Gulf of Aqabah. The people seem to have stayed there for some time after the terrible plague at Kibroth Hattaavah (Num 11:35). Aaron and Miriam rebelled against Moses here (ch. 12). The identification of the place is uncertain.

HAZEZON TAMAR (See HAZAZON TAMAR)

HAZIEL (hā'zĭ-ĕl, *God sees*). A Gershonite Levite in the latter days of David (1 Chron 23:9).

HAZO (hā'zō). A son of Nahor and an uncle of Laban and Rebekah (Gen 22:22).

HAZOR (hā'zôr, Heb. *hātsôr, an enclosed place*).

Large building (ninth century B.C.) at Hazor, measuring 44.3 by 68 feet (13.5 by 20.75 m.) and having two rows of pillars. The building was probably used as a royal storehouse. Courtesy S. Zur Picture Library.

Ruins and excavations at Hazor (the name means "enclosure" or "settlement") of remains of a casement wall from the time of Solomon (1 Kings 9:15). Courtesy Israel Government Press Office.

The name of at least five towns mentioned in the Bible:

1. An important town in northern Palestine, ruled in the days of Joshua by Jabin (Josh 11:1, 10). Palestine at the time was a conglomeration of little city-states or kingdoms, and of various groups united by tribal ties. For the former, see Joshua 11:1; and for the latter, Joshua 11:3. This Hazor was reckoned as "the head of all those kingdoms" in Joshua's day, and Jabin led them against Joshua, who almost annihilated them. Nearly two centuries later, another Jabin (Judg 4) reigning at Hazor was reckoned as king of Canaan, but God used Deborah and Barak to subdue and destroy him. Hazor, having a strategic location in the hills about five miles (eight km.) west of the waters of Merom, was fortified by Solomon (1 Kings 9:15). Its Israelite inhabitants were carried away into captivity (2 Kings 15:29) in Assyria by Tiglath-Pileser about the middle of the eighth century B.C. The site is located almost nine miles (eighteen km.) due north of the Sea of Galilee, and is two hundred acres in its full extent (upper and lower areas). It was dug first by archaeologist J. Garstang in 1928 and more extensively by Y. Yadin in 1955–58, 1968–70. Yadin discovered twenty-two strata of occupation including what he believes to be clear evidence of Joshua's destruction. A unique water tunnel (like those at Gezer, Megiddo, and Jerusalem) was found, along with city gates similar to those at Gezer and Megiddo, dating to the time of Solomon (though some date them slightly later).

2. A town in the extreme south of Judah, mentioned only in Joshua 15:23.

3. Another town in the south of Judah (Josh 15:25). Its name, Hazor Hadattah, means simply New Hazor and indicates that some of the inhabitants of Hazor no. 2 had moved to a new location. KJV in Joshua 15:25 makes it seem that Hazor and Hadattah were separate places, but see NIV, ASV.

4. A town north of Jerusalem, inhabited by Benjamites in the restoration (Neh 11:33).

5. A region in southern Arabia against which Jeremiah pronounced a "doom" (Jer 49:28–33).

HAZOR HADATTAH (See HAZOR)

HAZZELELPONI, ZELELPONI (hăz'ĕ-lĕl-pō'nī, zĕlĕl-pō'nī). A Jewish woman mentioned only in 1 Chronicles 4:3.

HAZZOBEBAH (hăz-ōbĕ'bȧ). A Judahite, son of Koz (1 Chron 4:8).

HE (hā). The fifth letter of the Hebrew alphabet, pronounced like the English *h*. It was also used for the number 5.

HEAD (Heb. *rō'sh,* Gr. *kephalē*). The OT uses *rō'sh* 592 times, translated "chief," "leader," "top," "company," "beginning," "captain," and "hair" but most often "head," sometimes used figuratively: "the hoary head" (Prov 16:31 KJV, expressing old age), "heads over the people" (Exod 18:25 KJV), "round the corners of your heads" (Lev 19:27, KJV referring to a heathen custom of trimming the beard), "heads of the people" (Num 25:4, probably meaning "leaders," cf. ASV, NIV), "his blood will be on his own head" (Josh 2:19 NIV, meaning "we will not be responsible for his life"), "keeper of my head" (1 Sam 28:2 KJV; NIV "my bodyguard for life"), "Am I a dog's head?" (2 Sam 3:8 NIV, i.e., "Am I utterly contemptible?"), "I cannot lift my head" (Job 10:15 NIV, i.e., be proud), and "his head reached unto the clouds" (20:6 KJV).

Almost all the NT uses of kephalē refer to the upper part of the body, but eight verses use it figuratively for the God-ordained order of authority—(1) the husband as head of the wife (1 Cor 11:3; Eph 5:23), (2) Christ as head of the church (Eph 4:15; 5:22, 23; Col 1:18; 2:19), (3) Christ as head over all people and power (1 Cor 11:3; Col 2:10; 1 Peter 2:7), and (4) God the Father as head of Christ (1 Cor 11:3).

HEADBAND, HEADDRESS (See DRESS)

HEADSTONE (See CORNERSTONE)

HEART (Heb. *lēv, lēvāv,* Gr. *kardia*). Scripture uses the word *heart* more than nine hundred times, almost never literally; the principal exception is in Exodus 28:29–30, which speaks of the breastplate of decision over the heart of Aaron. The heart is regarded (as in the modern usage) as the seat of the affections (e.g., "comfort ye your hearts," 18:5 KJV; "though your riches increase, do not set your heart on them," Ps 62:10 NIV) but also as the seat of the intellect (e.g., "every inclination of the thoughts of his heart," Gen 6:5 NIV) and of the will ("seek him with all their heart," Ps 119:2 NIV). Often it signifies the innermost being (e.g., "his heart was filled with pain," Gen 6:6 NIV).

Both in ancient times and today, different parts of the body are used figuratively as the seat of different functions of the soul; and the ancient usage often differs from the modern. In expressing sympathy, we might say, "This touches my heart," where the ancients might say "My bowels were moved for him" (S of Sol 5:4 KJV; cf. Ps 7:9 in KJV ["the righteous God trieth the hearts and reins"] with NIV [". . . minds and hearts"]. This reflects a difference in common figurative usage; it is not a question of truth and error in ancient or modern psychology. The NT was written mostly by Jews and so is colored by Hebrew thinking and usage; for example, "they do always err in their heart" (Heb 3:10 KJV) may mean that they are wrong in both their thinking and their affections. Often the word *heart* implies the whole moral nature of fallen humanity (e.g., "The heart is deceitful above all things, and beyond cure," Jer 17:9; cf. 17:10, "search the heart . . . try the reins" KJV, "search the mind . . . try the heart" ASV, "search the heart and examine the mind" NIV).

Bibliography: A. R. Johnson, *The Vitality of the Individual in the Thought of Ancient Israel,* 1949; R. Bultmann, *Theology of the New Testament,* vol. 1, 1952, pp. 220–27; R. Jewett, *Paul's Anthropological Terms,* 1971; H. W. Holff, *Anthropology of the Old Testament,* 1974, pp. 40–58. ABF

HEARTH. In ancient times homes were heated very differently from today. In the houses of the poorer people the hearth consisted of a depression in the floor of a room in which a fire was kindled for cooking or for warmth. Chimneys were unknown; smoke escaped from the house as it could, or through a latticed opening for the purpose. The better houses were heated by means of a brazier of burning coals. The brazier was a wide, shallow pan that could also be used for cooking. (See Gen 18:6; Ps 102:3; Isa 30:14; Jer 36:22–23; Hos 13:3; Zech 12:6.)

HEATHEN, PAGAN (Heb. *gôy,* pl. *gôyim,* Gr. *ethnos, people, nation*). In the OT *gôy* is rendered "Gentiles," "heathen," and "nation," but it is usually used for a non-Israelitish people, and thus has the meaning of "Gentiles." Sometimes, however, it refers to the Israelites, as in Genesis 12:2; Deuteronomy 32:28, but the word ordinarily used for the people of God is *'ām.* In the NT *ethnos* is the equivalent of OT *gôy,* while *laos* corresponds to *'ām.* Sometimes in the KJV the Greek *Hellenes* is translated "Gentiles" (John 7:35; Rom 2:9–10).

The differentiation between Israelites and Gentiles was more sharply accentuated in NT times than in OT times, because the Jews had suffered so much from Gentile hands. Gentiles were looked on with aversion and hatred. This is evident in the NT (John 18:28; Acts 10:28; 11:3).

God's interest in and concern for the heathen is seen in the OT, especially in the Book of Jonah. In the NT Jesus commanded the apostles to preach the gospel to all the world; and we find them proclaiming it to Gentile nations throughout the Mediterranean world. SB

HEAVEN (Heb. *shāmayim,* Gr. *ouranos*). 1. Cosmologically, one of the two great divisions of the universe, the earth and the heavens (Gen

1:1; 14:19); or one of the three—heaven, earth, and the waters under the earth (Exod 20:4). In the visible heavens are the stars and planets (Gen 1:14–17; Ezek 32:7–8). Later Jews divided the heavens into seven strata, but there is no evidence for this in the Bible, though Paul spoke of being caught up into the third heaven (2 Cor 12:2). The term "heaven of heavens" (Deut 10:14; 1 Kings 8:27; Ps 148:4) is "highest heavens" in NIV.

2. The abode of God (Gen 28:17; Ps 80:14; Isa 66:1; Matt 5:12) and of the good angels (Matt 24:36). It is the place where the redeemed will someday be (Matt 5:12; 6:20; Eph 3:15), where the Redeemer has gone and intercedes for the saints, and from where he will someday come for his own (1 Thess 4:16).

3. The inhabitants of heaven (Luke 15:18; Rev 18:20).

HEBER (hē'bĕr, *associate*). 1. A great-grandson of Jacob through Asher and Beriah (Gen 46:17).

2. The Kenite whose wife Jael killed Sisera (Judg 4:11–21). He had been friendly with the Canaanites who had been oppressing Israel.

3. A son of Ezrah (KJV "Ezra") of the tribe of Judah and probably of the family of Caleb, the good spy (1 Chron 4:18).

4. A man of the tribe of Benjamin, and son of Elpaal (1 Chron 8:17).

5. The head of a family in the tribe of Gad (1 Chron 5:13 KJV; NIV "Eber").

6. A Benjamite, son of Shashak, mentioned only in 1 Chronicles 8:22 (KJV; NIV "Eber").

7. One mentioned in Christ's genealogy (Luke 3:35 KJV), father of Peleg and Joktan, properly called Eber in NIV and other versions (Gen 10:24–25; 11:12–16).

HEBREW, HEBREWS. These are traditionally considered designations for Abraham and his descendants, especially through Jacob, the equivalent of Israelite(s); 1 Samuel 14:21 may suggest that the terms are to be equated. Jews quite uniformly have used "Israel" and "the children of Israel" (later "Jews") in referring to themselves, finding in such terminology treasured religious and national associations. Foreigners thought of them as "Hebrews" (Exod 1:16; 2:6), and they so identified themselves in speaking to non-Jews (Gen 40:15; Exod 10:3; Jonah 1:9). Also, in contexts involving contrasts between Israelites and people of other nations, the same phenomenon appears (Gen 43:32; Exod 1:15; 2:11; 1 Sam 13:3; 14:21).

There is the possibility, however, that in OT times the names "Hebrews," "Habiru," "Khapiru," "Apiru," and "pr" were forms of the same word (equivalent to the Akkadian SA.GAZ), a designation without national significance. Rather, they indicated wandering peoples greatly restricted as regards financial means and without citizenship and social status. Ancient records show the "Habiru" to be scattered over western Asia for centuries until about 1100 B.C. Nomadic peoples, mostly Semitic—sometimes raiders, sometimes skilled artisans—they frequently offered themselves as mercenaries and slaves, with individuals occasionally rising to prominence. In Egypt, the Israelites were reduced to a lowly position and later moved about in the wilderness. Conceivably they could, therefore, have been known as "Hebrews." It is noteworthy that, in taking oaths, the Habiru swore by "the gods of the Habiru," whereas similar phraseology, "the God of the Hebrews," is found in Exodus 3:18; 5:3; 7:16. "Hebrews" and "Habiru" were terms used prior to the name "Israel," and both were discontinued generally about the time of the judges.

NT "Hebrews" references contrast people (Acts 6:1) and language (John 5:2; 19:13, 17, 20; 20:16) to differentiate between the Greeks and Hellenistic culture on the one hand and Jews and their traditional life and speech on the other. What is called "Hebrew language" may in John's Gospel refer to Aramaic, but in the Apocalypse to Hebrew proper (Rev 9:11; 16:16).

Etymologically, it has been debated whether "Hebrew" is to be traced to Eber, the father of Peleg and Joktan (Gen 10:24–25; 11:12–16) or is derived from the Hebrew root "to pass over" and has reference to "a land on the other side," as the dweller east of the Euphrates might think of Canaan. However, the possible equating of the Hebrews and the Habiru might suggest that the Hebrews were "those who crossed over" in the sense of trespassing, i.e., "trespassers." BLG

HEBREW LANGUAGE. With the exception of Aramaic in Ezra 4:8–6:18; 7:12–26; Daniel 2:4–7, 28; and Jeremiah 10:11, Hebrew is the language of the OT. The term "Hebrew" was first used as a designation for individuals or a people and only later denoted a language. The OT refers to the language not as "Hebrew" but as "the language of Canaan" (Isa 19:18) or "the Jews' language" (2 Kings 18:26, 28 KJV and parallel passages; also Neh 13:24). Josephus, Ecclesiasticus, and the NT (Rev 9:11; 16:16), however, speak of it as "Hebrew." With close affinity to Ugaritic, Phoenician, Moabitic, and the Canaan-

The Siloam Inscription, written in cursive Hebrew script, was found incised in the walls of Hezekiah's Tunnel in Jerusalem. Inscription reads ". . . while there were still 3 cubits to be cut through, (there was heard) the voice of a man calling to his fellow, for there was an excess in the rock on the right (and on the left). And, when the tunnel was driven through, the quarrymen hewed [the rock] each man toward his fellow, axe against axe; and the water flowed from the spring toward the reservoir for 1,200 cubits, and the height of the rock above the heads of the quarrymen was one hundred cubits." Courtesy Carta, Jerusalem.

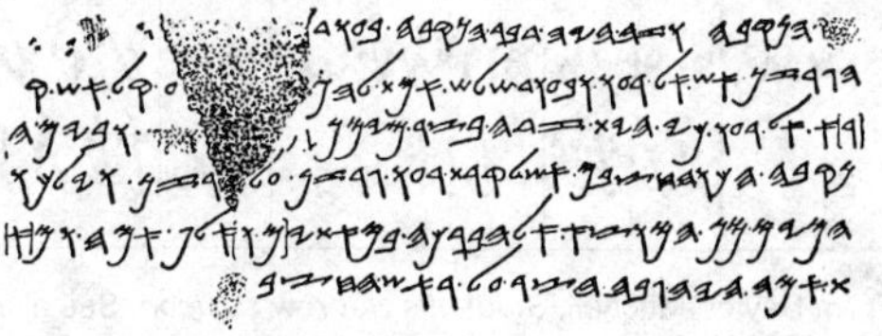

Ancient Semitic Alphabets

(With modern Hebrew, in column at right, for comparison)

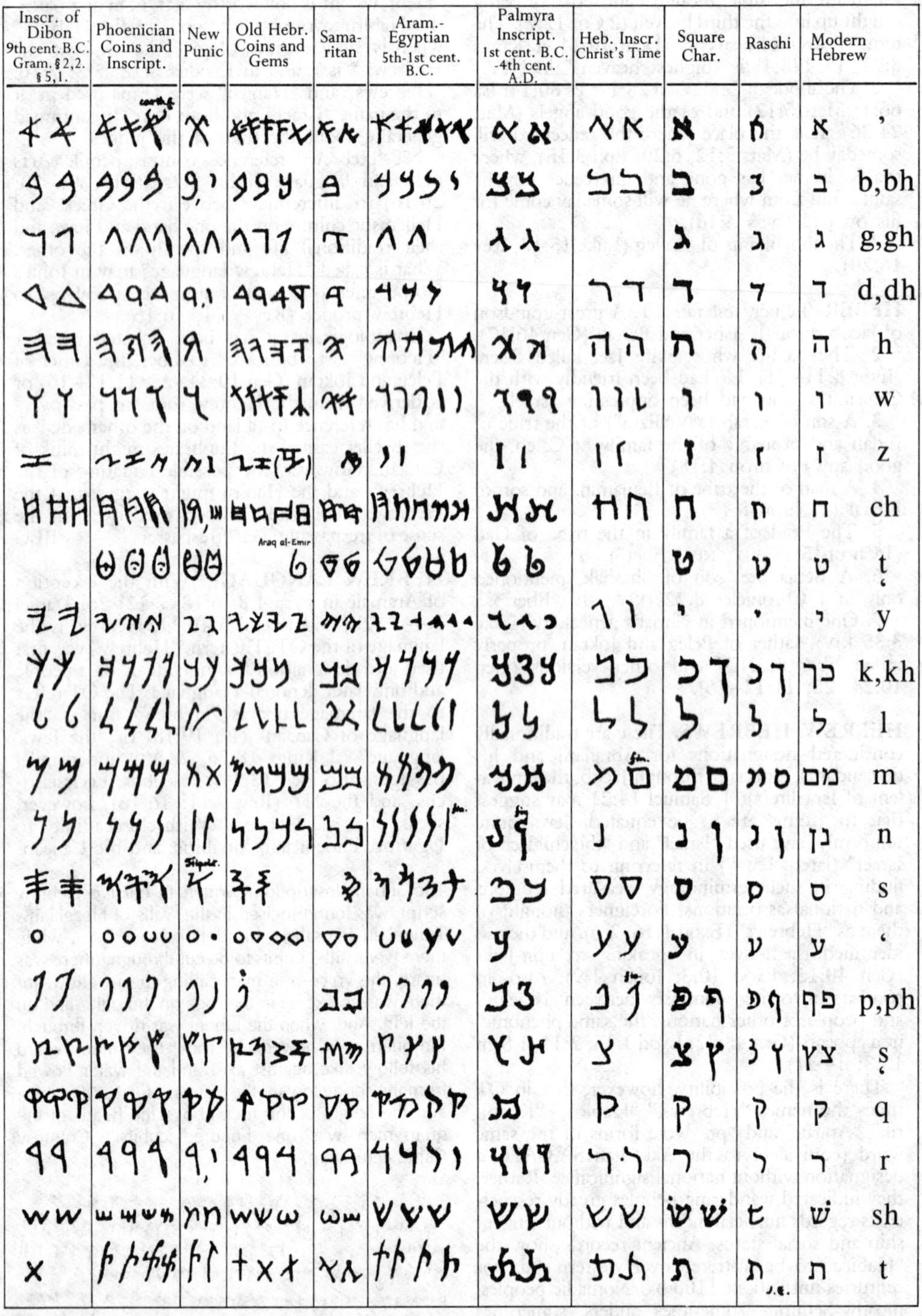
Inscr. of Dibon 9th cent. B.C. Gram. § 2,2. § 5,1.
Phoenician Coins and Inscript.
New Punic
Old Hebr. Coins and Gems
Samaritan
Aram.-Egyptian 5th-1st cent. B.C.
Palmyra Inscript. 1st cent. B.C.-4th cent. A.D.
Heb. Inscr. Christ's Time
Square Char.
Raschi
Modern Hebrew
Araq al-Emir
א ’
ב b,bh
ג g,gh
ד d,dh
ה h
ו w
ז z
ח ch
ט ṭ
י y
כך k,kh
ל l
מם m
נן n
ס s
ע ‘
פף p,ph
צץ ṣ
ק q
ר r
ש sh
ת t

From Davies-Mitchell, *Student's Hebrew Lexicon*. See also article on WRITING.

Samaritan ostracon with inscription in cursive Hebrew script, eighth century B.C. This inscription appears to be a letter giving instructions for distribution of barley. One of sixty-five ostraca discovered in the palace ruins at Samaria. Courtesy Israel Department of Antiquities and Museums.

ite dialects, Hebrew represents the northwest branch of the Semitic language family. Its sister languages include Arabic, Akkadian, and Aramaic. With few exceptions, extant texts of ancient Hebrew are those of the OT and certain of the apocryphal and pseudepigraphic works. Inscriptions employing the language include the Siloam Inscription from the eighth century B.C. and the Gezer Calendar from the tenth century.

In large measure, the OT Hebrew must be self-explanatory. However, the Ugaritic Ras Shamra Tablets shed much light on the meaning of the Hebrew Bible, and since the structure and vocabulary were so very similar in the various Semitic tongues, much cognate language help is available for the understanding of the language of the Israelites. The Greek translation of the OT, the LXX, is also of much value in interpretative study of biblical Hebrew.

Though Aramaic is itself a very ancient language and the presence of "Aramaisms" in the OT often indicates an early rather than a late date for the passages in which they occur, from the time of the Exile onward Hebrew was spoken less and less and correspondingly the use of Aramaic flourished. Some of the Dead Sea Scrolls were written in Hebrew. Hebrew was also the vehicle for the writing of such Jewish religious literature as the Mishna and the Midrashim in the early part of the Christian era and in medieval times for biblical commentaries and philosophical and literary works. In modern Israel, Hebrew has again become a living tongue.

The historical origins of the language are somewhat obscure but go back beyond 2000 B.C. The OT literature, written over a period of more than a thousand years, reveals a minimum of stylistic changes, though loan words and new ways of expression became more or less noticeable with the passing of years, especially after the Exile. It is also true that at a given time dialectical differences existed, a fact attested by the narrative in Judges 12, in which Ephraimites were unable to pronounce the "sh" of their neighbors to the south.

With its short sentences and simple coordinating conjunctions, ancient Hebrew lent itself well to the vivid expression of events. These features, together with parallelism and rhythm and special meanings and constructions, made Hebrew poetry, as found in the Psalms and to a large extent in the Prophets, most expressive and strikingly effective. BLG

HEBREW OF HEBREWS. When Paul in Philippians 3:15 so described himself, he meant that he was a pure-blooded Hebrew who had retained the language and customs of his fathers, in contrast to other Jews who had adopted Greek language and customs.

HEBREWS, LETTER TO THE.

I. Authorship. The writer of Hebrews does not attach his name to his letter. First John is the only other letter in the NT to which a name is not attached. Because of this fact, there has been much discussion since the first century as to who wrote Hebrews.

Early Christians held various opinions. Those on the eastern shore of the Mediterranean and around Alexandria associated the book with Paul. Origen (A.D. 185–254) held that the thoughts of the book were Paul's, but the language and composition were someone else's. In North Africa, Tertullian (155–225) thought that Barnabas wrote Hebrews. Although the letter was first known in Rome and the West (I Clement, dated around 95, cites Hebrews frequently), for two hundred years Christians in Rome and the West were unanimous in their opinion that Paul did not write Hebrews. These early Christians did not say who wrote it.

Present-day Christians should hardly be dogmatic about an issue that from the very beginning of the church has been surrounded with uncertainty. A careful study of the letter in the Greek text discloses some important things about the author: (1) The letter has a polished Greek style, like that of a master rhetorician. The continuous use of this style is unlike Paul's style: Paul frequently picked up a new stream of thought before he finished the one in which he was involved. (2) The vocabulary, figures of speech, and manner of argument show an Alexandrian and Philonic influence (Philo, 20 B.C. to A.D. 50 or 60). Paul, having come from Tarsus and having been educated in Jerusalem, did not have such a background. (3) Both Paul and the writer of Hebrews quote the OT frequently. But the way they introduce their quotations is quite different. Paul's formulas—"just as it has been written" (nineteen times), "it has been written" (ten times), "the Scripture says" (six times), "the Scripture proclaims good tidings beforehand" (one time)—never occur in Hebrews. Paul's manner of introducing quotations puts the reader's attention on the content quoted. The writer of Hebrews, as an orator, puts the stress on the one who speaks. For him the Father, Christ, or the Holy Spirit is speaking.

Along with many present-day scholars, this author favors Apollos as the possible writer of Hebrews. He was a Jew, born in Alexandria, a learned and cultured man, well-versed in the Scriptures (Acts 18:24). Being orally taught the way of the Lord, Apollos was teaching about Jesus even when he knew only John's baptism (18:25). He was a man of enthusiasm. Priscilla and Aquila, Paul's friends, led Apollos to a fuller knowledge of Christ (18:26). After he received this knowledge, he was a man of courage. He left Ephesus for Achaia to help the believers there (18:27). He consistently used the Scriptures in his public preaching (18:25). Paul testifies to Apollos's capability in 1 Corinthians 1–4. His polished rhetorical style may have been a contributing cause to the Apollos party that was found in Corinth (1 Cor 3:4–6). Apollos's modesty and desire to avoid friction are seen in 1 Corinthians 16:12. He was still an active coworker of Paul late in Paul's ministry (see Titus 3:13). In Apollos one can explain all of Hebrews' similarities with Paul as well as the distinct differences from Paul.

Assuming Apollos to be the author, one can best date the letter A.D. 68–70.

II. Original Readers. The letter was first known in Rome and the West. Its first readers were Jewish Christians who spoke and wrote Greek. The brief statement "Those from Italy send you their greetings" (Heb 13:24) certainly favors the readers' being located in Italy. If the writer had been in Italy, he would have named the precise place. A letter from any city in the United States would not say, "Those from the United States send greetings"; but if the letter came from an interior city of India or Brazil where Americans were present, such a greeting would be appropriate. Hence, it appears there were Italian Christians with the writer somewhere outside of Italy as he penned this letter. The writer knows the readers well. He refers to their spiritual dullness (5:11–14), their faithful ministering to the saints (6:9–10), and their experiences after their conversion (10:32–36). The term used for their spiritual leaders or rulers is *hoi hēgoumenoi* (13:7, 17, 24), a technical term not found elsewhere in the NT; but other writings coming from Rome and the West have this same term (cf. 1 Clement 1:3; 21:6; Shepherd of Hermas 2, 2:6; 9:7 [*proēgoumenoi*]). Their first leaders seem to have died (13:7), while their present leaders are continually engaged in the task of watching over the flock (13:17). To these the writer sends greetings (13:24).

Although we cannot be absolutely certain, it seems best to regard the original readers as being located somewhere in Italy. Many roads led to Rome. These believers may have been in one of the cities nearer or farther from the capital. Paul himself spent seven days with the brothers in Puteoli (Acts 28:13–14). They could have been in Rome or its suburbs. As the writer pens this letter, Timothy has departed from him and is absent (perfect tense)—very likely on some tour of churches. As soon as he appears (or if he comes soon), the writer and Timothy together will visit the readers (Heb 13:23).

III. Outline and Summary of Content—An outline shows the centrality of Jesus Christ in the Book of Hebrews.

I. *Prologue: Course and Climax of Divine Revelation* (1:1–3)
II. *Preeminence of Christ Himself* (1:4–4:13)
  A. Superiority of Christ to Angels (1:4–14)
  B. Warning: Peril of Indifference to These Truths (2:1–4)
  C. Reason Christ Became Human (2:5–18)
  D. Christ's Position Is Greater Than That of Moses (3:1–6)
  E. Warning: Unbelief Brings Temporal and Eternal Effects (3:7–4:13)
III. *Priesthood of Jesus Christ* (4:14–10:18)
  A. Importance of His Priesthood for a Believer's Conduct (4:14–16)
  B. Qualifications of a High Priest (5:1–10)
  C. Warning: Immaturity and Apostasy Are Conquered Only by Faith, Longsuffering, and Hope (5:11–6:20a)
  D. Melchizedek's Eternal Successor (6:20b–7:28)
  E. Heavenly Sanctuary and New Covenant (8:1–13)
  F. Priestly Service Under the Old Covenant and the New (9:1–28)
  G. Inadequacy of the Sacrifices Under the Law Contrasted With the Efficacy and Finality of Christ's Sacrifice (10:1–18)
IV. *Perseverance of Christians* (10:19–12:29)
  A. Attitudes to Be Sought and Attitudes to Be Shunned (10:19–39)
  B. Faith in Action—Illustrious Examples From the Past (11:1–40)
  C. Incentives for Action in the Present Scene and in the Future Goal (12:1–29)
V. *Postscript: Exhortations, Personal Concerns, Benediction* (13:1–25)

Although God spoke to the fathers by the prophets, he has now spoken by his Son. In the prologue we see the distinctiveness of the Son. He is before history, in history, above history, the goal of history, and the agent who brings about a cleansing of people from sins committed in history. He shares the essence of Deity and radiates the glory of Deity. He is the supreme revelation of God (Heb 1:1–3).

The writer's first main task is to make clear the preeminence of Christ (Heb 1:4–4:13). He is superior to angels. They assist those who will be heirs of salvation. Christ, by virtue of who he is, of God's appointment, and of what he has done, stands exalted far above them. It would be tragic to be careless of the great salvation that he proclaimed. He will achieve for man the promise that all things will be in harmonious subjection to man. He can do this because he is fully man and has provided the expiation for sins. He is superior to Moses, for Moses was a servant among the people of God, while Christ is a Son over the people of God. It would be tragic to cease trusting him. Unbelief kept one entire generation of Israelites from Canaan. Christians are warned of such unbelief. Faith is emphasized as well as zeal to enter into the eternal rest of God. Both the Gospel of God and God himself scrutinize people.

The second major emphasis in the letter falls on the priesthood of Christ (Heb 4:14–10:18). Qualifications, conditions, and experiences of the Aaronic priesthood are listed in comparison to Christ as a priest. Before further developing this theme, the writer warns his readers of their unpreparedness for advanced teaching. Only earnest diligence in things of God will bring them out of immaturity. Christ as a priest, like Melchizedek, is superior to the Levitical priesthood because his life is indestructible. He is both priest and sacrifice. His priesthood is eternal. His sanctuary is in heaven and his blood establishes the validity of the New Covenant, which is also an eternal covenant. His one offering on behalf of sins is final; i.e., it is for all time. Likewise he has made perfect for all time those who are in the process of being sanctified.

The last main section of Hebrews deals with the response of Christians (10:19–12:29). Perseverance on the part of Christians springs out of fellowship with God, activity for God, faith in God, and a consciousness of what lies ahead.

In concluding the letter the writer puts stress on the Cross as the Christian altar and the resurrection of the Shepherd of the sheep as the basis for God's action. Such redemptive-historical events move the believer to action (Heb 13:1–25).

IV. Teaching. Although more space is devoted to Christ, the letter has fully developed teaching about God the Father.

Much is said about Christ. He is fully God and fully man. He is active in creation. The atonement of Christ, as both priest and sacrificial victim, is developed in detail. In the role of a priest, he is a leader and guide. He also is the revealer of God. Great depth is achieved in all of these teachings about Christ's person and work.

Very little is said about the Holy Spirit in Hebrews. The Spirit is mentioned only seven times—three times in reference to the inspiration of the OT, once in regard to the work of Christ, once in regard to the apostate's rejection of Christianity, and twice in regard to the believer.

The old and new covenants are compared and reasons for the superiority of the new or eternal covenant are given.

The doctrine of sin in Hebrews focuses attention on unbelief and the failure to go on with God to the eternal city.

Shadow and reality are carefully contrasted. Heaven is the scene of reality. Earth is concerned with both shadow and reality. Christ is the bridge between the temporary and the eternal.

The people of God are looked on as migrating from a transitory setting to an abiding city. This migration involves God's Word; the matter of testing, discipline, or punishment; faithfulness; and God's activity in sanctifying or making holy. The Christian life is developed in the framework of this heavenly pilgrimage.

Eschatology or last things involves the obtaining of eternal rest, a final shaking of heaven and earth, the personal return of Christ, and glory belonging to God for ever and ever.

Bibliography: B. F. Westcott, *The Epistle to the Hebrews,* 1892 (on the Greek text); F. F. Bruce, *The Epistle to the Hebrews* (NIC), 1964; H. W. Montefiore, *The Epistle to the Hebrews* (HNTC), 1964; P. E. Hughes, *A Commentary on the Epistle to the Hebrews,* 1977; D. Guthrie, *The Letter to the Hebrews* (TNTC), 1983. ABM

HEBRON (hē′brŏn, Heb. *hevrôn, league, confederacy*). 1. One of the oldest cities of the world, and one that has had several names at different times. It is located nineteen miles (thirty-two km.) SW of Jerusalem on the main road to Beersheba and has one of the longest records of continuous occupation. Though lying in a shallow valley, it is about 3,000 feet (940 m.) above sea level and 4,300 feet (1,340 m.) above the Dead Sea, which lies a few miles east of Hebron. The hills about the city still bear choice grapes, and the Jewish people there make a fine wine. The Valley of Eshcol, from which the spies brought an immense cluster of grapes (Num 13:22–24), runs quite near Hebron. Hebron's original name was Kiriath Arba, i.e., "fourfold city" (Josh 14:15; 15:13).

Hebron is replete with historical interest. It was a camping place for Abram; here he moved his tent and lived by the "great trees of Mamre" (Gen 13:18, mistranslated in KJV "the plain of Mamre"). This was close to Hebron, and here Abram built an altar to the Lord. The only land that Abram owned, though God had promised him Canaan (15:18–21), was the field of Machpelah near Mamre, which he purchased from the Hittites as a burial place for Sarah (Gen 23:17–20; Heb 11:8–10). In this cave Sarah and Abraham, later Isaac and Rebekah, then Jacob and Leah, were buried. At the partition of Canaan after the partial conquest, Hebron and its environs were given to Caleb to conquer (Josh 14:6–15), and he did so (15:14–19); but later the city itself was given to the Kohathite Levites (1 Chron 6:55–56), though Caleb's descendants kept the suburban fields and villages. When David was king over Judah, but not yet over all Israel, his capital city was Hebron for seven and a half

General view of Hebron. The mosque in the center is built over the Cave of the Machpelah, traditional burial place of Abraham and Sarah. Courtesy Ecole Biblique et Archéologique Française, Jerusalem.

years. There the elders of Israel anointed him king over all Israel (2 Sam 5:3–5). Later he moved the capital to Jerusalem. When Absalom rebelled against his father, he made Hebron his headquarters and there prepared his coup d'etat (2 Sam 15:7–12).

2. Third son of Kohath, and so an uncle of Moses, Aaron, and Miriam (Exod 6:18). His descendants, 1,700 men of valor in the days of David, had the responsibility for the Lord's business and for the service of the king west of the Jordan (1 Chron 26:30).

3. A town in Asher (Josh 19:28 KJV). ASV, NASB, and RSV, as well as most Hebrew MSS, have "Ebron," but "Abdon" (21:30, copied in 1 Chron 6:74) is found in JB and NIV.

4. A descendant of Caleb, son of Hezron, son of Perez, son of Judah (1 Chron 2:42–43), not to be confused with Caleb, the good spy, who was a distant cousin.

HEDGE. Loose stone walls without mortar, or cut thorn branches or thorny bushes, common as "hedges" and "fences" in Palestine. The word can be translated "fence," "wall," or "hedge." The use of a hedge about a vine or tree was mainly for its protection (Ps 80:12). Figuratively, prophets should make up a hedge for the people's protection (Ezek 13:5), and God is pictured as doing so for his people (Mark 12:1). The very poor live in highways and hedges (Luke 14:23).

HEGAI, HEGE (hĕg'ā-ī, hē'gē). The eunuch employed by Xerxes (KJV Ahasuerus) as keeper of the women in the king's harem (Esth 2:3, 8, 15). Some think that "hegai" is not a proper name but means "eunuch."

HEIFER (See ANIMALS)

HEIFER, RED (See ANIMALS)

HEIR (See INHERITANCE)

HELAH (hē'là). One of the two wives of Ashhur, who was the posthumous son of Hezron (1 Chron 4:5, 7).

HELAM (hē'lăm, Heb. *hēlām*). A place in the Syrian desert east of the Jordan where David defeated the forces of Hadadezer, king of Zobah (2 Sam 10:16–17). The exact location is unknown.

HELBAH (hĕl'bà, *a fertile region*). A town of the tribe of Asher from which the men of Israel failed to expel the Canaanites. It is near the Leontes River in Lebanon (Judg 1:31).

HELBON (hĕl'bŏn, *fertile*). A city of northern Syria, celebrated in ancient times for its wine (Ezek 27:18). Some think that a village in Anti-Lebanon about thirteen miles (thirty-two km.) NW of Damascus is intended.

HELDAI (hĕl'dā-ī). 1. The army captain over twenty-four thousand men whose duties were in the twelfth month under David (1 Chron 27:15). Probably the same as Heled in 1 Chronicles 11:30 and as Heleb in 2 Samuel 23:29.

2. One of three noble Jews who brought gold and silver from Babylon, and who were to surrender the metal to Zechariah (Zech 6:9–15) that he might make a crown for Joshua the high priest. The name is Helem in 6:14 in KJV (cf. NIV footnote).

HELEB (hē'lĕb). One of David's valiant men of war (2 Sam 23:29 KJV; cf. NIV footnote). See also HELED and HELDAI.

HELED (hē'lĕd). A mighty man of David's army (2 Sam 23:29; 1 Chron 11:30). See also HELEB AND HELDAI.

HELEK (hē'lĕk). The second son of Gilead of the tribe of Manasseh and head of a family (Num 26:30; Josh 17:2).

HELEM (hē'lĕm, *health*). 1. A man of the tribe of Asher (1 Chron 7:35), called Hotham in verse 32.

2. An ambassador, mentioned only in Zechariah 6:14, but also certainly the same person as Heldai in Zechariah 6:10 (so NIV).

HELEPH (hē'lĕf, *change*). An ancient village on the border of Naphtali (Josh 19:33). It is perhaps on the site now called Beitlif in Galilee.

HELEZ (hē'lĕz). 1. A man of Judah, of the family of Hezron, but also of Egyptian descent (1 Chron 2:39).

2. One of David's mighty leaders, called a Paltite in 2 Samuel 23:26, but a Pelonite in 1 Chronicles 11:27; an Ephraimite (1 Chron 27:10).

HELI (hē'lī, Heb. *'ēlî*). The father of Joseph, the husband of Mary, in the genealogy of Jesus in Luke 3:23. According to another view, he is the father of Mary, the mother of Jesus, a view that is reached by punctuating the Greek differently. See also GENEALOGY OF JESUS CHRIST.

HELIOPOLIS (hē-lĭ-ŏp'ō-lĭs, Heb. *'ôn,* Gr. *Heliopolis, city of the sun*). A city near the south end of the Nile delta, the site of a temple to the sun built by Amenophis I. It is called "On" in most modern versions of Scripture. It was a very old and holy city, with a learned school of priests. Joseph's father-in-law belonged to the priests of the sun temple (Gen 41:45; 46:20). In the intertestamental period Onias built a Jewish temple there. The modern site is the village El-Matariye. See also ON.

HELKAI (hĕl'kā-ī, perhaps an abbreviation of *Helkiah*). A priest of the Jews in the days of Joiakim (Neh 12:15).

HELKATH (hĕl'kăth, Heb. *helqath, a field*). A town on the southern border of the tribe of Asher (Josh 19:25) that was given to the Gershonite Levites (21:31). It was later called Hukok (1 Chron 6:75). The site is uncertain.

HELKATH HAZZURIM (hĕl'kăth hăz'ū-rĭm, *the field of the sharp knives*). A piece of ground near the pool of Gibeon where twelve men of Joab fought with twelve men of Abner and all twenty-four died (2 Sam 2:12–16).

HELL. The real existence of hell is irrefutably taught in Scripture as both a *place* of the wicked dead and a *condition* of retribution for unredeemed man. It is plain that "to die in sin" is a dreadful thing (e.g., Ezek 3:18; NIV footnote). Sheol, which is in one sense the undifferentiated place of all the dead (cf. Job 3:13–22), is in another sense the special doom of the wicked (Ps 49:14). It is necessary to follow the NIV footnotes in such references, for if KJV was inaccurate in translating Sheol as "hell" (e.g., Ps 9:17), NIV is equally inaccurate in formalizing it as "the grave." Daniel 12:2 takes the matter as far as the OT will go, with its reference to "shame and everlasting contempt."

In the intertestamental period, both apocryphal literature and rabbinical teaching continued the development of the association of immortality and retribution until, during NT times, two words were used: Hades and Gehenna (see separate entry on each).

The *nature* of hell is indicated by the repeated reference to eternal punishment (Matt 25:46), eternal fire (Matt 18:8, Jude 7), everlasting chains (Jude 6), the pit of the Abyss (Rev 9:2, 11), outer darkness (Matt 8:12), the wrath of God (Rom 2:5), second death (Rev 21:8), eternal destruction from the face of God (2 Thess 1:9), and eternal sin (Mark 3:29). While many of these terms are symbolic and descriptive, they connote real entities, about whose existence there can be no doubt.

The *duration* is explicitly indicated in the NT. The word "eternal" (*aiōnios*) is derived from the verb *aiōn,* signifying an "age" or "duration." Scripture speaks of two *aeons,* or ages: the present age and the age to come (Matt 12:32; Mark 10:30; Luke 18:30; Eph 1:21). The present age—this world—is always contrasted with the age to come as temporal, while the future age will be endless. As the everlasting life of the believer is to be endless, just so the retributive aspect of hell refers to the future infinite age. In every reference in which *aiōnios* applies to the future punishment of the wicked, it indisputably denotes endless duration (Matt 18:8; 25:41, 46; Mark 3:29; 2 Thess 1:9; Heb 6:2; Jude 7).

Hell is, therefore, both a *condition* of retribution and a *place* in which the retribution occurs. In both of these aspects the three basic ideas associated with the concept of hell are reflected: absence of righteousness, separation from God, and judgment.

The absence of personal righteousness, with its correlative of the presence of personal unrighteousness, renders the individual unable to enter a right relationship with the holy God (Mark 3:29). The eternal state of the wicked, therefore, will involve a separation from the presence of God (John 3:36). The concept of judgment is heightened by the note of finality in the warnings against sin (Matt 8:12). It is a judgment, however, against man's sinful nature—still unredeemed though Christ died—(25:31–46) and is decisive and irreversible.

When all else has been said about hell, however,

there is still the inescapable fact taught by Scripture that it will be a retributive judgment on the *spirit* of man, the inner essence of his being. The severity of the judgment will be on the fixed character of a person's essential nature—his soul, which will involve eternal loss in exclusion from Christ's kingdom and fellowship with God.

Bibliography: J. A. Beet, *The Last Things,* 1905; J. S. Bonnell, *Heaven and Hell,* 1956; H. Buis, *The Doctrine of Eternal Punishment,* 1957; W. Eichrodt, *Theology of the Old Testament,* 1967, 2:210–28. CBB and JAM

HELLENISTS (See GRECIA, GRECIANS)

HELMET (See ARMS AND ARMOR)

HELON (hē'lôn, *valorous*). Father of Eliab, a leading man of Zebulun when the first census was taken (Num 1:9).

HELPMEET. Now often used as one word, meaning a helper (so NIV), generally a wife; but in Genesis 2:18 (KJV) it is two words. "I will make him a help meet for him," i.e., a helper suitable for or complementing him. It is often changed to "helpmate," which means the same.

HELPS. In the NT there are four lists of "gifts" that God has given to his church (Rom 12:6–8; 1 Cor 12:7–11, 28–31; Eph 4:11–12), and these are not to be confused with the officers who are listed elsewhere. "Helps" are mentioned only in 1 Corinthians 12:28, and the Greek word *antilēmpseis* occurs only there. It means protector or assistant and probably refers to the ability to perform helpful works in a gracious manner.

HEMAM (See HOMAM)

HEMAN (hē'măn, Heb. *hêmān, faithful*). 1. A grandson of Judah through Zerah (1 Chron 2:6) and listed as one of the most notable wise men.

2. The first of three Levites David appointed to lead music (1 Chron 6:33). He was "the king's seer," and his sons were "given him through the promises of God to exalt him" (25:5, Heb. "exalt the horn"). His fourteen sons and three daughters were in the choir (25:5–6).

3. Psalm 88 is attributed to Heman the Ezrahite, and if this means "Zerahite," as many think, he may be the same as no. 1 above.

HEMATH (See HAMATH; HAMMATH)

HEMDAN (hĕm'dăn, Heb. *hemdān, pleasant*). A son of Dishon and descendant of Seir, the Horite (Gen 36:26). NIV also has "Hemdan" in 1 Chronicles 1:41, but the Hebrew text, MLB, Mof, NASB, and RSV have "Hamran," and KJV and NEB have "Amram."

HEMLOCK (See PLANTS)

HEM OF A GARMENT. Fringes or tassels, with a blue thread in each, on the borders of the Jewish outer garment (Num 15:38–39). The word "hem" (Exod 28:33–34; 39:24–26) is translated "skirt" in ASV. To "touch the hem of his garment" (NIV "edge of his cloak," Matt 9:20–21; 14:36) denoted a reverent approach, not daring to lay hold of Jesus, but having faith in the efficacy of his miraculous power.

HEN (Heb. *hēn, favor*). 1. A son of Zephaniah (Zech 6:14). The NIV footnote has as an alternate reading "and the gracious one, the son of Zephaniah," in which the son's name disappears.

2. See BIRDS.

HENA (hēn'ȧ, Heb. *hēna'*). A city on the south bank of the Euphrates, about 180 miles (300 km.) NW of ancient Babylon. It was mentioned by Rabshakeh, along with four other cities whose gods could not save them from destruction by Sennacherib, as a proof that the Lord could not save Jerusalem (2 Kings 18:34; 19:13; Isa 37:13).

HENADAD (hĕn'ȧ-dăd, *favor of Hadad*). Head of a family of Levites who helped Zerubbabel (Ezra 3:9) and who in the next century helped Nehemiah in rebuilding the wall of Jerusalem (Neh 3:18, 24).

HENNA (See PLANTS)

HENOCH (See HANOCH)

HEPHER (hē'fēr, *pit, well*). 1. Head of the family of the Hepherites (Num 26:32). His son Zelophehad had five daughters who were commanded to marry within their tribe so as not to cause any of the tribal property of Manasseh to be deeded to another tribe (27:1–8; 36:1–9).

2. A son of Ashhur, the "father" of Tekoa (1 Chron 4:5–6).

3. One of David's mighty men (1 Chron 11:36) from Makerah, a place otherwise unmentioned and unknown.

4. A royal city in Canaan listed among the thirty-one that Joshua conquered (Josh 12:17). The land of Hepher (1 Kings 4:10) was SW of Jerusalem.

HEPHZIBAH (hĕf'zĭ-bȧ, Heb. *hephtsî-vâh, my delight is in her*). 1. Wife of King Hezekiah (2 Kings 21:1) and mother of Manasseh.

2. A symbolical name given to Zion (Isa 62:4).

HERB (See PLANTS)

HERD. Israel, before Joshua's time, like the Bedouins of today, were nomads. After the conquest of Canaan they continued to be a pastoral people for the most part. For the property of such a people, see Job 1:3 or 42:12. The herds consisted of the larger animals, as contrasted with the flocks of sheep, goats, etc. The cattle were used in plowing and threshing and for sacrifice but were not commonly fattened for food (though in contrast, see Ezek 39:18).

Hermon is a mountain range extending about 18 miles (29 km.), at the northern boundary of Palestine. The Psalmists sing of it (Ps 89:12; 133:3). Courtesy Zev Radovan.

HERDSMAN (See Occupations and Professions)

HERES (hē'rēz, *sun*). 1. A district around Aijalon from which the Amorites were not expelled (Judg 1:35). The meaning is uncertain.

2. A place east of the Jordan from which Gideon returned after his defeat of Zebah and Zalmunna (Judg 8:13).

3. An Egyptian city (Isa 19:18; see KJV margin). NIV translates it "City of Destruction," but cf. footnote.

HERESH (hē'rěsh, *dumb, silent*). A Levite who returned early from captivity (1 Chron 9:15).

HERESY (hâr'ĕ-sē, Gr. *hairēsis, sect, heretical group or opinion*, from *haireō, to choose*). A doctrine or group considered contrary to correct doctrine—from the Jewish (Acts 24:14; cf. 28:22) or Christian (2 Peter 2:1) perspective.

HERETH (hâr'-ĕth, Heb. *hereth*). The name of a forest in Judah where David stayed (1 Sam 22:5; KJV and NEB have "Hareth").

HERMAS (Gr. *Hermas*). A Roman Christian (Rom 16:14), not to be confused with the writer of *The Shepherd of Hermas* (second cent.).

HERMES (hûr'mēz, Gr. *Hermēs*). 1. One of the Greek mythological gods, a messenger of the gods (Acts 14:12); the Romans called him "Mercury" (as in ASV, KJV, and NEB).

2. One, otherwise unknown, to whom Paul sends greetings in Romans 16:14.

HERMOGENES (hûr'mŏj'ē-nēz, Gr. *Hermogenēs, born of Hermes*). One of the professed Christians in Asia (probably at Ephesus) who deserted Paul when he was in trouble (2 Tim 1:15).

HERMON (Heb. *hermôn, sacred mountain*). The mountain that marks the southern terminus of the Anti-Lebanon range. A line drawn from Damascus to Tyre will pass through Mount Hermon at its middle point and will practically coincide with the northern boundary of Palestine. The ridge of Hermon is about twenty miles (thirty-three km.) long. It has three peaks, two of them rising over 9,000 feet (2,813 m.). Hermon has had several names: the ancient Amorites called it "Shenir" or "Senir" (Deut 3:9; cf. Ps 29:6; Ezek 27:5, where it is called a source of fir trees for Tyre); the Sidonians called it "Sirion" (Deut 3:9, though Ps 29:6 would apparently separate them); and the Arabs call it "Jebel-esh-Sheikh" or "Mountain of the Old Man," perhaps because of its white head, but more likely because of its dignity.

Hermon is awe-inspiring whether seen from the NE at Damascus, the west from Lebanon back of Sidon, the SW from Nazareth, or the SE from Hauran. The Lord's transfiguration almost certainly occurred on its slopes, for he was at Caesarea Philippi just south of the mountain only a week before. Prior to the advent of modern refrigeration, both Damascus and the summer resorts on Mount Lebanon obtained ice from Hermon, and so it was often called "Jebel-et-telj," i.e., "Ice Mountain." Hermon is once called "Sion" (Deut 4:48; NIV "Siyon"), not to be confused with Zion in Jerusalem, which is "Sion" in the NT. ABF

HEROD (hĕr′ŭd). When the Roman ruler Pompey organized the East in 63 B.C., he appointed Hyrcanus, the second person of that name, to be the high-priestly ruler over Galilee, Samaria, Judea, and Perea. Antipater, an Idumean, was Hyrcanus's senior officer. Gabinius modified Pompey's arrangement in 57 by reducing Hyrcanus's authority and dividing the ethnarchy into autonomous communities. Notable services rendered at Alexandria to Julius Caesar in 48 led to the restoration of Hyrcanus's authority and the appointment (in 47) of Antipater to the procuratorship of Judea. Antipater had, in fact, been the leading spirit in the policy that won Caesar's favor, and Antipater used his advantage with an astuteness that foreshadowed the career of his son. He persuaded the now-aged Hyrcanus to appoint Phasael, Antipater's eldest son, to the prefecture of Jerusalem, and Herod, his second son, to the governorship of Galilee.

When Antipater was murdered in 43 B.C., his two sons succeeded to his position in Hyrcanus's court. It was the year after Julius Caesar's assassination. Jubilant that Caesar's plan for a decisive campaign on the vulnerable eastern frontier of Rome was shelved, the Parthians, the perennial military problem of the northeast, were restive. In 40 they penetrated Palestine, carried off Hyrcanus, and drove Phasael, also a captive, to suicide. Herod eluded both military action and Parthian treachery. He withdrew from Jerusalem, shook off pursuit by clever rearguard skirmishing near Bethlehem, and escaped to Egypt. Outwitting Cleopatra and reaching Rome through the perils of winter voyaging, Herod set his case before Octavian and Antony. It is a remarkable tribute to his charm, daring, political acumen, and consummate diplomacy that he won the support of both triumvirs who were so soon to divide in disastrous rivalry. The whole remarkable story is told dryly in Josephus's first book, *The Jewish War*.

The thirteen years that lay between the assassination of Caesar and the emergence of Octavian as the victorious Augustus, after Antony's defeat at Actium in 31 B.C., were a time of paralysis and uncertainty throughout the Roman world. Herod saw in such confusion the opportunity for decisive action. Landing at Acre in 39, with only the promise of Roman favor, Herod went to claim his kingdom and to unseat the Parthian puppet, Antigonus. Palestine's hill country, deserts, and walled cities called for a variety of military strategies. Herod showed himself the able master of varied types of war. The two years of tireless activity made him, by the age of thirty-six, the master of his inheritance and revealed all the facets of his amazing personality. He was a ruthless

The three Herodian towers, north of Herod's palace (from left to right—Phasael, Hippicus, and Mariamne), as seen in the scale model of Jerusalem in A.D. 66–70, located at the Holyland Hotel, Jerusalem. Courtesy Zev Radovan.

fighter but at the same time a cunning negotiator, a subtle diplomat, and an opportunist. He was able to restrain his Roman helpers and simultaneously circumvent the Jews. Between 39 and 37 Herod revealed those qualities, if they may be called qualities, that enabled him for thirty-four years to govern subjects who hated him, to work within the major framework of Roman imperial rule, to steer a safe course through political dilemma, and to pursue a dual policy without ruinous contradiction.

In 30 B.C. Herod succeeded in retaining the favor of Octavian, shared though that favor had been with the defeated rival Antony. He was confirmed in his kingdom, and for the rest of his life he never departed from the policy of supporting the emperor and in all ways promoting his honor. The restored town of Samaria was called Sebaste, the Greek rendering of Augustus; Caesarea was built to form a harbor on the difficult open coast of Palestine, providing Rome a base on the edge of a turbulent province, and forming a center of Caesar-worship in the land of the nationalistic and monotheistic Jews.

Herod followed a policy of Hellenization, establishing games at Jerusalem and adorning many of the Hellenistic cities of his domain. At the same time he sought to reconcile the Jews, who hated his pro-Roman and Hellenizing policies and who never forgave him for his Edomite blood. During the great famine of 25 B.C.in Judea and Samaria, Herod spared no trouble or private expense to import Egyptian corn. In the eighteenth year of his reign (20) he began to build the great Jerusalem temple, which was forty-three years under construction (John 2:20). However, nothing he did served to win metropolitan Jewry. It was Herod's policy to crush the old aristocracy, even though he was married to Mariamme, the heiress of the Hasmonean house. He built up a nobility of service, drawing on both Jews and Greeks. He sought subtly to channel messianic ambitions of the baser sort in his direction by encouraging the political party of the Herodians

Cone-shaped hill of Herodium, southeast of Bethlehem, a fortress built by Herod the Great in 40 B.C. and place of his burial (Matt 2:19). Courtesy Israel Government Press Office.

(Mark 3:6; 12:13), whose policy seems to have been the support of the royal house and a Hellenized society. Politically, this royalist group was descended from the old Hellenizing apostates whom Jason called Antiochians (2 Macc 9:9–14). They were probably Jews of the Dispersion, from whom Herod also recruited his subservient priesthood, and were Sadducees in religion. Such varied patronage and support produced checks and balances in the composite society of Herod's kingdom that made for stability of rule, but of course did nothing to reconcile the divided elements of the populace, metropolitan and Hellenistic Jews, Sadducees and Pharisees, people and hierarchy. It was only the common challenge of Christ that could draw together such dissidents as Sadducees and Pharisees, the Romans and the priests—just as it healed, according to a surprising side remark of Luke (23:12), a rift between Herod Antipas and Pilate.

To manage a situation so complex, and to survive, demanded uncommon ability and an ordered realm. Of Herod's ability there is no doubt, and with his foreign mercenaries, his system of fortresses, and the centralized bureaucracy that he built, he gave Palestine order and even opportunity for economic progress. At the same time Herod was a cruel and implacable tyrant. His family and private life were soiled and embittered by feuds, intrigue, and murder. The king's sister Salome and his son Antipater by Doris, his first consort, seem to have been in league against Mariamme, his favorite wife. Mariamme was put to death in 29 B.C. and her two sons, Alexander and Aristobulus, in 7. Antipater himself was put to death by Herod in the last days of Herod's reign. Herod died in 4. The murder of the innocent babies of Bethlehem (Luke 2) falls within the context of his final madness. Josephus's grim picture (*War* 1.33.5) of the physical and mental degeneration of the aging king is detailed enough for diagnosis. It is the picture of an arteriosclerotic who had once been athletic and vigorous but who became increasingly prone to delusions of persecution and uncontrollable outbursts of violence, the results of hypertension and a diseased brain.

Herod's will divided the kingdom. Archelaus, son of Malthace, a Samaritan woman, took Judea and Idumea—by far the choicest share. Herod Antipas, of the same mother, received Galilee and Perea; and Philip, son of a Jewess named Cleopatra, took Iturea, Trachonitis, and associated districts in the northeast. Archelaus, who inherited his father's vices without his ability, took the title of king and bloodily quelled the disorders that broke out in Jerusalem. The result was a wide uprising, which required the intervention of Varus, governor of Syria. It was at this time that the Holy Family returned from Egypt (Matt 2:22–23): "But when [Joseph] heard that Archelaus was reigning in Judea in place of his father Herod, he was afraid to go there . . . he withdrew to the district of Galilee, and he went and lived in a town called Nazareth."

It was imperative for Archelaus to reach Rome and secure from Augustus confirmation of his position before the situation in Palestine could be presented in too lurid a light by his enemies. Archelaus's petition was opposed in person by Herod Antipas and by a Jewish embassy. Somewhat surprisingly, Augustus declared in favor of Archelaus, though he denied him the royal title. The incident provided the background for the Parable of the Pounds, related by Luke (19:11–27). Archelaus was the "man of noble birth" who went "to have himself appointed king." The facts were no doubt brought to mind by the sight of the palace that Archelaus had built at Jericho, where the story was told (Josephus, *Antiq.* 17.13.1). Archelaus maintained his stupid and tyrannical reign for ten years. In A.D. 6 a Jewish embassy finally secured his deposition and banishment to Gaul. Judea fell under procuratorial rule. Coponius, a Roman knight, was appointed governor. A tax-census was the first administrative necessity, and this precipitated the revolt of Judas of Gamala and the emergence of the Zealots as a sinister force in Palestinian politics. Archelaus rebuilt and restored his father's palace at Jericho, as the palace had been burned down at Herod's death. It was discovered and excavated in 1951.

Herod Antipas (the word is an abbreviation for Antipater) equaled his father in having a long reign. "That fox," Christ called the ruler of Galilee (Luke 13:32), an epithet that has reference to the Herodian cunning, his subtle diplomacy, and his astute management of a difficult situation—qualities that enabled Antipas to retain his puppet position and petty royal power until A.D. 39. It was probably some time before 23 that Herod

Antipas met the evil genius of his later years, the dynamic Herodias, wife of his half-brother Philip. This brother, who is not to be confused with the tetrarch of Iturea mentioned earlier, was the son of an unnamed wife of Herod I. As the daughter of Aristobulus, son of Herod I and Mariamme, Herodias was Philip's niece as well as his wife. They lived quietly in Rome, and it was here that Antipas met Herodias.

It is difficult to say who was primarily to blame for the notorious liaison that took Herodias back to Palestine as the unlawful wife and queen of Antipas. She remained loyal to him in his later misfortunes, though offered release by Caligula, and the immoral partnership of the two seems to have been cemented by genuine physical attraction and community of temperament. But trouble dogged the union. According to Josephus, Herod Antipas's rightful queen, daughter of Aretas, king of the Nabateans, heard of the liaison before the couple reached Palestine and escaped first to the fortress of Machaerus and then to her father's capital of Petra, before her returning husband could detain her. Herod therefore came home to find a troublesome frontier war on his lands. He celebrated his birthday, the tragic feast described in Mark 6:14–29, at the stronghold of Machaerus. The death of John the Baptist occurred here also, for after his denunciation of Herod's sin the preacher of the wilderness had been imprisoned here. The crime so dramatically contrived was the final turning point in Herod's life. Until then, according to a strange remark in the Second Gospel (Mark 6:20), there had been some faint aspiration for good: "Herod feared John and protected him, knowing him to be a righteous and holy man. When Herod heard John, he was greatly puzzled; yet he liked to listen to him."

Antipas's campaign against his father-in-law Aretas ended disastrously. Antipas was forced to appeal to Rome for help, and the task was assigned to Vitellius, governor of Syria. The affair dragged on until A.D. 37 when Rome's ruler Tiberius died. A prey to the uncertainty that was increasingly to attend changes in the Roman principate, Vitellius hesitated, and Antipas never won revenge. Two years later Antipas fell. He had been trusted by Tiberius, who appreciated his continuation of his father's pro-Roman policy, to which the foundation of Tiberias on Galilee was a solid monument. Tiberius, in the last year of his principate (36), had even used Herod as a mediator between Rome and Parthia. Presuming on this notable imperial favor, and incited by Herodias, Herod petitioned Caius Caligula, Tiberius's successor, for the title of king. He was, however, deposed by that incalculable prince on a suspicion of treasonable conduct, a charge leveled by Herod Agrippa I, his nephew. Herodias accompanied the man she had ruined morally and politically into obscure exile. Salome her daughter, the dancer of the Machaerus feast, married her uncle Philip, tetrarch of Iturea, about 30. After Philip died in 34, she married her cousin Aristobulus, king of Chalcis, north of Abilene in the Anti-Lebanon hill country.

Philip of Iturea seems to have been the best of Herod's three surviving sons (Josephus, *Antiq.* 17.2.4). His remote province insulated him from some of the problems of Jewry, but he seems to have been a man of generous mold and notable justice. He beautified the town of Caesarea Philippi and marked his continuation of the Herodian pro-Roman policy by changing the name of the northern Bethsaida to Julias, after Augustus's unfortunate daughter.

The deceased Philip's vacant tetrarchy was the first foothold of the third Herod to be mentioned in the NT (Acts 12:1). Herod Agrippa I, grandson of Herod I, son of Aristobulus and brother of Herodias, had been brought up in Rome under the protection of Tiberius's favorite son, Drusus. He had all the Herodian charm and diplomatic subtlety, and this explains how, as the boon companion of the mad Caligula, he was able to deter that prince from the final folly of setting up his statue in the temple at Jerusalem (Josephus, *Antiq.* 18.8). Such an achievement demanded not only clever wits but also courage of no mean order. In A.D. 37, on Caligula's succession as emperor, Herod Agrippa was granted Philip's realm. Galilee and Perea were added when Antipas and Herodias were exiled. The malicious word in Rome had paid rich dividends. With his grandfather's subtlety, Agrippa knew how to survive a succession. When Caligula was assassinated in 41, Agrippa, who had played his cards with remarkable astuteness, remained in the favor of Claudius, Caligula's successor, who turned over to Agrippa's control the whole area of his grandfather's kingdom. He succeeded to such power, moreover, with the consent and the favor of the Jews. The old Jewish hostility to the Idumean dynasty had vanished, and even the Pharisees were reconciled. Luke's account (Acts 12:20–23) of the king's shocking death in his royal seat of Caesarea is substantiated by Josephus's longer narrative (*Antiq.* 19.8.2). Josephus looked on Herod with admiration as the last great Jewish monarch, and the correspondence between Josephus's and Luke's accounts is remarkable. In both accounts the pomp and circumstance of Agrippa's royal estate is notable. Agrippa died in 44, and his reign was therefore brief. Whether it would have long survived under a less indulgent emperor or under an imperial government that had already vetoed his proposal to fortify Jerusalem, is a matter that his early death left undecided. It is possible for modern medicine to diagnose the intestinal complaint described by Luke in the accepted terminology of his day. A symptom is a visible, violent, and agonizing peristalsis. Luke uses a single adjective, translated by the English phrase "eaten of worms," for the cause of Herod's death. Agrippa was only fifty-four years of age. After his death Palestine fell wholly under Roman rule, a takeover facilitated by the consolidation under Agrippa of the old Herodian domains. There was considerable disorder over the next four years.

Agrippa left a teen-age son, whom Claudius made king of Chalcis in A.D. 48. In 53 the territory of Philip the tetrarch and Lysanias were added to this realm, together with an area on the western side of Galilee, including Tiberias. The appointment carried the title of king, so in 53 Agrippa became Agrippa II, last of the Herodian line. He appears only in the brilliant account in Acts 25, where, as Festus's guest, he heard the defense of Paul. After the fashion of Eastern monarchies, Agrippa was married to his sister Bernice. Another sister was the wife of Antonius Felix, the procurator of Judea, whom Festus had succeeded.

In the account of the examination of Paul we see a vivid and revealing picture of the deference Rome was prepared to pay to a puppet king. Perhaps it is more accurate to say that here we see the respect that Rome undoubtedly owed to a remarkable royal house that had been a major bastion of Roman peace in the Middle East for three generations. In the king himself is seen a typical Herod of the better sort: royal, intelligent, pro-Roman, but vitally interested in Judaism, which, with unusual understanding, he saw to be the key to the history of his land.

With this event, which is difficult to date precisely, Agrippa and the Herodian line disappear from history. Festus died in A.D. 64. One brief reference in Josephus reveals that Agrippa lived on in the garrison town of Caesarea to see the vast ruin and destruction of his country in the Great Revolt of 66 to 70. So ended the Herods, an astonishingly able family, whose pro-Roman policy went far to postpone the inevitable clash between Rome and the Jews, and played, in consequence, an unwitting but significant part in holding the peace during the formative years of the Christian church in Palestine. EMB

HERODIANS (hĕ-rō'dĭ-ănz, Gr. *Hērōdianoi*). A party mentioned only three times (Matt 22:16; Mark 3:6; 12:13) as joining with the Pharisees to oppose Jesus. Nothing more is known about them than what the Gospels state. It appears that they were neither a religious sect nor a political party, but Jews who supported the dynasty of Herod and therefore the rule of Rome. The first time they are referred to they are seen joining with the Pharisees to destroy Jesus; the second time, trying to trap Jesus by asking him whether it is proper to pay tribute to Caesar.

HERODIAS (hĕ-rō'dĭ-ăs, Gr. *Hērōdias*). A wicked granddaughter of Herod the Great who married her uncle Philip; but his brother Antipas saw her at Rome, desired her, and married her. John the Baptist reproved Herod Antipas for his immoral action (Luke 3:19–20) and was put in prison for his temerity (Matt 14:3–12; Mark 6:14–29). This did not satisfy Herodias, so by a sordid scheme she secured his death. Later Antipas was banished to Spain. Herodias accompanied him and died there.

HERODION (hĕ-rō'dĭ-ŏn, Gr. *Hērōdiōn*). A Christian at Rome, kinsman of Paul and recipient of his greeting (Rom 16:11).

HERON (See BIRDS)

HESHBON (hĕsh'bŏn, Heb. *heshbôn, reckoning*). An ancient city of the Moabites lying nearly twenty miles (thirty-three km.) west of the Jordan. Sihon, king of the Amorites in the days of Moses, took this and the surrounding country from the Moabites, and Israel in turn took it from Sihon (Num 21:21–31). Sihon's territory, of which Heshbon was the capital, reached northward from the Arnon to the Jabbok, at the strong border of the Ammonites. The tribe of Reuben asked Moses for this land because it was suitable for cattle, and Moses granted their request; so, three hundred years later (1260 B.C.), when the Ammonites made war against Israel, Jephthah taunted them (Judg 11:12–28) with the fact that their god Chemosh was not able to stand against Israel for all those centuries. Heshbon and its suburbs were given to the Levites (1 Chron 6:81). Isaiah's prophecy of doom upon Moab (Isa 15:4; 16:8–9) describes the normal fertility of the land around Heshbon and the fact that it had gone back into the hands of Moab before Isaiah's time; and when Jeremiah, a century later, pronounced his dooms, Heshbon was still standing, though soon to be judged by the Lord (Jer 48:2–35; 49:3). The city still stands, but it is a ruin and is known as Hesban.

Ruins at Hesban, 20 miles (32 km.) east of the Jordan, marking the site of ancient Heshbon, the capital city of Sihon (Num 21:21–26). Viewed here are remnants of a Byzantine church built over earlier Roman remains. Studium Biblicum Franciscanum, Jerusalem.

HESHMON (hĕsh'mŏn). A town on the southern boundary of Judah (Josh 15:27).

HETH (Heb. *ḥēth*). Great-grandson of Noah through Ham and Canaan (Gen 10:15) and progenitor of the great Hittite people, sometimes called "sons" and "daughters" of Heth (23:3; 27:46). Rendered "Hittites" in each instance in the NIV. For many centuries their records, except as recorded in the Bible, were lost; but now the Hittites are well known to archaeologists and are reckoned with the Babylonians and the Egyptians as one of the great peoples of the time. See also HITTITES.

HETHLON (hĕth'lŏn, Heb. *hethlôn*). A place NE of Tripoli, Syria, just north of Mount Lebanon, from which one passes into the great plain of Coele Syria to the entrance of Hamath (Ezek 47:15; 48:1); mentioned as the beginning of the northern boundary of restored Israel. Its modern location is unknown.

HEXATEUCH (hĕk'sȧ-tūk). "The six-volumed book," a term invented to include the Book of Joshua with the Pentateuch in a literary unit, on the assumption that its component parts were combined by a common editor.

HEZEKI (See HIZKI)

HEZEKIAH (hĕz'ē-kī'ȧ, Heb. *hizqîyâh, Jehovah has strengthened*). 1. King of Judah for twenty-nine years, from c. 724 to 695 B.C. The record of his life is found in 2 Kings 18–20, 2 Chronicles 29–32, and Isaiah 36–39. He lived in one of the great periods of human history. The first Olympiad from which the Greeks dated their history occurred in 776; Rome was reputed to have been founded in 753; Assyria, though approaching its end, was still a mighty power; and Egypt, though weak, was still strong enough to oppose Assyria. Judah's position, on the main road between Egypt and Assyria, was a very precarious one. Hezekiah's grandfather Jotham reigned at Jerusalem (755–739) when Hezekiah was a child, and though he was in some ways a good king, he allowed the people to sacrifice and burn incense in the high places. Because of Judah's growing apostasy, the Lord permitted the Syrians and the northern kingdom to trouble Jerusalem. In Hezekiah's youth and early manhood, his weak and wicked father Ahaz was king. He went so far as to follow the abominable rites of the Moabites by burning children in the fire (2 Chron 28:3), in spite of the warnings of the prophets Hosea, Micah, and Isaiah. At this time, when Israel and Syria were threatening Judah, God gave through Isaiah the famous "virgin-birth" prophecy (Isa 7:14). For a while Hezekiah was associated in the government with his father, but because of his father's incapacitation he was made active ruler. He began his reign, at the age of twenty-five, in troubled and threatening times. Some counseled him to side with Egypt against Assyria; others favored surrender to Assyria to save themselves from Egypt. Isaiah warned against trusting in foreign alliances. One of the first acts of Hezekiah was the cleansing and reopening of the temple, which his father had left closed and desecrated. After this was accomplished, the Passover feast was celebrated (2 Chron 30). The idolatrous altars and high places were destroyed.

From the fourth to the sixth year of Hezekiah's reign the northern kingdom was in trouble. Sargon finally destroyed Samaria and deported the people to Assyria. Hezekiah became ill, probably from a carbuncle, and almost died; but God granted him a fifteen-year extension of life (2 Kings 20:1–11). After Hezekiah's recovery, Merodach-Baladan of Babylon sent an embassy

The tunnel constructed by King Hezekiah (2 Kings 20:20) that connected the Gihon Spring with the pool of Siloam, so that Jerusalem's water supply would not be imperiled by the impending siege by Sennacherib's army. Courtesy Zev Radovan.

ostensibly to congratulate him, but actually to persuade him to join a secret confederacy against the Assyrian power. This was the great crisis for Hezekiah, and indeed for Judah. During his illness he had received from God not only the promise of recovery, but also the pledge that the Lord would deliver Jerusalem from the Assyrians (Isa 38:6–7). The ambassadors of Merodach-Baladan were intent also on freeing Jerusalem from the Assyrians—but by force of arms and the power of a military alliance. The question facing Hezekiah was therefore whether to walk the way of faith that the Lord would keep his promise or to take the way of "works," setting out to liberate the city by his own abilities and clever policies. When Isaiah learned that Hezekiah had entertained the ambassadors and their suggestion, he knew that all was over for Judah and immediately (39:5–7) predicted the Babylonian captivity. Hezekiah paid a high price for dabbling in rebellion. Assyria compelled Judah to pay heavy tribute; and to obtain it, Hezekiah even had to strip the plating from the doors and pillars of the temple. Shortly after, Assyria decided to destroy Jerusalem, but God saved the city by sending a sudden plague that in one night killed 185,000 soldiers. After Hezekiah's death, his son Manasseh succeeded him (2 Kings 20:21).

2. One of the covenanters with Nehemiah (Neh 10:17; KJV Hizkijah). ABF

HEZION (hē'zē-ŏn, *vision*). Father of Tabrimmon and grandfather of Ben-Hadad, king of Aram (1 Kings 15:18).

HEZIR (hē'zir, *swine*). 1. A priest in the seventeenth course of Aaronic priests (1 Chron 24:15).

2. One of the covenanters with Nehemiah in the revival (Neh 10:20).

HEZRO, HEZRAI (hĕz'-rō, hĕz'ră-ē). A Carmelite, one of David's heroes (2 Sam 23:35; 1 Chron 11:37).

HEZRON (hĕz'rŏn, *enclosure*). 1. A grandson of Judah through Perez (Gen 46:12).

2. A son of Reuben (Gen 46:9).

3. A place on the southern border of Judah (Josh 15:3). See also HAZOR (no. 3), which is the same place.

HIDDAI (hĭd'ā-ī). One of David's heroes (2 Sam 23:30). The same as Hurai of 1 Chronicles 11:32.

HIDDEKEL (See TIGRIS)

HIEL (hī'ĕl, Heb. *hî 'ēl*, probably, *God liveth*). A man of Bethel during the reign of Ahab. He rebuilt Jericho and thereby brought on himself and his sons the curse that Joshua had pronounced half a millennium before (1 Kings 16:34; cf. Josh 6:26).

HIERAPOLIS (hī'ĕr-ăp'ō-lĭs, Gr. *Hierapolis, sacred city*). A city mentioned only in Colossians 4:13. It was in the territory of ancient Phrygia but in the NT period it became a part of the Roman province of Asia. It received its name from the fact that it was the seat of worship of important deities. The location was on the right bank of the Lycus about eight miles (thirteen km.) above its junction with the Maeander. Tradition connects the apostle Philip with the church; and Papias, notable disciple of John the beloved, was born there. Great ruins survive.

The city gate and Cardo, the main street of Hierapolis. Judging by its extensive remains, Hierapolis (mentioned along with Laodicea in Col 4:13) must have been a popular "spa" resort in Roman times. Courtesy Dan Bahat.

HIEROGLYPHICS (See WRITING)

HIGGAION (hĭ-gā'yŏn, Heb. *higgāyôn*). A musical term in Psalm 9:16, probably referring to the "solemn sound" (so 92:3 KJV) of harp music that was to be played at that point.

HIGH PLACES (Heb. *bāmâh, rāmâh, elevation*). It seems to be inherent in human nature to think of God as dwelling in the heights. From earliest times people have tended to choose high places for their worship, whether of the true God or of the false gods that man has invented. The reason for this is that the so-called gods were in fact the barely personified forces of nature; they were empty of moral character and therefore one could not appeal to them in the same sense as one could appeal to the God of Israel. They had made no promises and extended no covenant to their people. All, therefore, that the worshipers could do was choose an exposed site where the "god" was likely to see what they were doing and to perform there some act comparable to what they wished their god to do for them (see also BAAL). In Canaan the high places had become the scenes of orgies and human sacrifice connected with the idolatrous worship of these imaginary gods; and so, when Israel entered the Promised Land they were told, "Drive out all the inhabitants of the land before you. Destroy all their carved images and their cast idols, and demolish all their high places" (Num 33:52). Figured stones were covered with crude carvings, sometimes more or less like geometrical figures, or with talismans or other signs presumably understood by the priests and used to mystify or terrorize the worshipers. Israel partly obeyed but largely failed in this work. In Judges 1:19–35 we read of the failure of eight different tribes to drive out the people of the land, and though "Israel served the LORD throughout the lifetime of Joshua and of the elders who outlived him" (Josh 24:31; Judg 2:7), they soon relapsed into idolatry, used the high places for the worship of Baalim, and "provoked the LORD to anger."

Before God would use Gideon to drive out the

Unusual silica-draped terraces at Hierapolis (modern Pamukkale, Turkey), formed by limestone flowing from hot springs, for which the place was famous in Roman times. Courtesy Dan Bahat.

The "Great High Place" at Petra in Transjordan. The site is marked by two altars and a rectangular court, all hewn out of solid rock. It probably dates to the Nabatean period (second century B.C. to second century A.D.) and is built on a earlier Edomite site. Courtesy Garo Nalbandian.

Midianites (Judg 6:25), Gideon had to throw down his father's altar to Baal and the image ("Asherah pole") that was beside it. Before Solomon built the temple, there was a mixed condition of worship. The tent of meeting (i.e., the tabernacle) with most of its furniture was at the high place at Gibeon, several miles north of Jerusalem, though David had brought the ark to Jerusalem. Solomon went to the high place at Gibeon to offer sacrifice, and there God heard his prayer and granted him surpassing wisdom (2 Chron 1:1–13). Later some godly kings, including Hezekiah (31:1), destroyed the high places, whereas others, including Manasseh, relapsed and rebuilt them (33:3). After Manasseh had been punished and had repented, he was restored to his throne and resumed the temple worship; but the people "continued to sacrifice at the high places, but only to the LORD their God" (33:17). Through Manasseh's early influence, the people had gone so far into apostasy that they could not repent; but through the godliness of Josiah, especially after he had heard the law read (2 Kings 22:8–20), the judgment was delayed until after the death of Josiah. His great "housecleaning" is described in 2 Kings 23:1–25. God's attitude toward the godly kings and toward the wicked ones like Ahab in the north and Ahaz and Manasseh in the south depended largely on their attitude toward the high places. ABF

HIGH PRIEST (See PRIEST)

HILEN (hī'lĕn). A city of Judah assigned to the Levites (1 Chron 6:58). It is spelled Holon in Joshua 15:51; 21:15.

HILKIAH (hĭl-kī'ȧ, Heb. *hilqîyâh, the portion of Jehovah*). The name of seven persons, mostly priests, in Israel:

1. The father of Eliakim who was manager of Hezekiah's household (2 Kings 18:18).
2. A Merarite Levite (1 Chron 6:45).
3. Another Merarite, doorkeeper in David's time (1 Chron 26:11).
4. The high priest in the days of Josiah, king of Judah. He found the Book of the Law (thought by many to have been the Book of Deuteronomy) while cleaning the temple and sent it to Josiah (2 Kings 22; 2 Chron 34).
5. A priest who returned to Jerusalem with Zerubbabel, 536 B.C. (Neh 12:7).
6. The father of Jeremiah. He lived at Anathoth (Jer 1:1).
7. The father of Gemariah (Jer 29:3), a priest who stood with Ezra at the Bible reading (Neh 8:4).

HILL COUNTRY (Heb. *giv'âh, har, 'ōphel*). A term applied to any region of hills and valleys that could not quite be called mountainous. In Scripture it generally applies to the higher part of Judea (Luke 1:39, 65) and in the OT to the southern part of Lebanon east of Sidon (Josh 13:6; NIV "mountain region"). In Joshua 11:3, RSV and NIV have "hill country," JB has "highlands," and KJV and MLB have "mountains."

HILLEL (hĭl'ĕl, *he has praised*). The father of Abdon, who judged Israel. He was from Pirathon, a hill village of Ephraim.

HIN (See WEIGHTS AND MEASURES)

HIND (See ANIMALS)

HINGE. A contrivance that enables a movable part such as a door or window to swing in its place, often used figuratively for something of prime importance. Ancient heavy doors swung on "ball and socket" joints. KJV, MLB, Mof, and NASB have "hinges" in 1 Kings 7:50; NIV and RSV have "sockets," and NEB has "panels." In Proverbs 26:14 the word derives from a verb meaning to twist or to turn in pain or in laziness. The type of hinges we use today were unknown in ancient times.

HINNOM, VALLEY OF. More properly, "the valley of the son of Hinnom," running southward from the Jaffa Gate at the west side of Jerusalem, then turning eastward and running south of the city until it joined the valley of the Kidron. It was a part of the boundary between Judah on the south (Josh 15:8) and Benjamin on the north (18:16). Nothing is known of the "son of Hinnom" except that he lived before Joshua's time and presumably owned the valley. It seems to have been a dumping ground and a place for burning. Topheth was here (2 Kings 23:10), where human sacrifices had been offered to Molech, and so it was later to be called "the Valley of Slaughter" (Jer 19:6). The Hebrew name, transliterated into Greek as *geenna* (or *gehenna*), becomes the word for "hell." Jesus uses it in referring to the final destination of the wicked; and probably "the fiery lake of burning sulfur" (Rev 19:20; 20:10, 14–15; 21:8) is a description of the same terrible place. That the mythological name "Tartarus" was also used is implied in 2 Peter 2:4, where Peter uses a verb derived from "Tartarus" to mean "to cast down to hell." See also GEHENNA. ABF

The Valley of Hinnom (see Gehenna), looking southward from Mount Zion. The village of Siloam (John 9:7) is at the left. Courtesy Duby Tal.

The monument of King Hiram at Tyre, viewed from the southwest. Courtesy Ecole Biblique et Archéologique Française, Jerusalem.

HIP AND THIGH. Used only in Judges 15:8 (KJV, MLB, NEB, RSV) of Samson's thoroughness in killing Philistines (NIV "viciously").

HIPPOPOTAMUS (See ANIMALS)

HIRAH (hī'rȧ). A friend of Judah, living at Adullam (Gen 38:1, 12, 20), SW of Bethlehem.

HIRAM (hī'rām, Heb. *hîrām,* sometimes also *hûrām* and *hîrôm*). 1. King of Tyre in the reigns of David and Solomon, with both of whom he was on friendly terms. His father was Abibaal. Hiram is first mentioned in 2 Samuel 5:11, almost at the beginning of his reign, when he sent messengers to David with cedar logs, carpenters, and masons who built David a house. The wood was floated in rafts down the coast to Joppa and then brought overland to Jerusalem. Hiram, an admirer of David, sent an embassy to Solomon after David's death (1 Kings 5:1); and Solomon promptly took advantage of the situation and arranged for Hiram to send him cedar and fir timber from Lebanon. It is evident that Tyre was predominant over Phoenicia at the time, for the Sidonians (5:6) are spoken of as servants of Hiram, and the "stone-squarers" (5:18 KJV) were men of Gebal (modern Jebail) north of Beirut.

A century later, Sidon seems to have become more powerful, for Ethbaal, who is reckoned by the genealogists as a great-grandson of Hiram, is called "king of the Sidonians" (1 Kings 16:31).

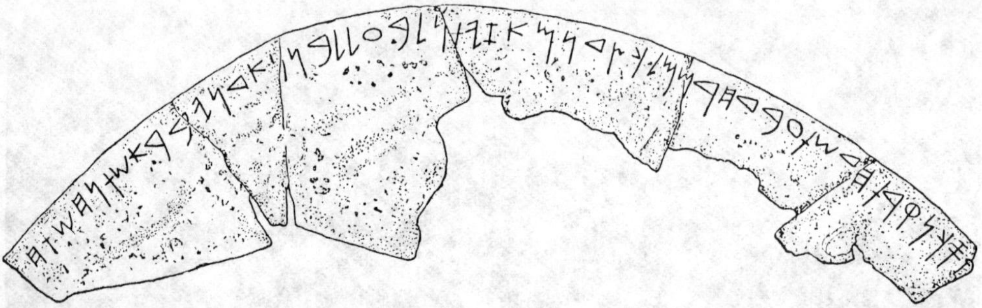

Inscription on a bronze bowl at Limassol in Cyprus: "merchant of Carthago, servant of Hiram, king of the Sidonians." On Hiram, see 2 Samuel 5:11 and 1 Kings 5:10, 11, 18. Courtesy Carta, Jerusalem.

Both Solomon and Hiram were Semites and were keen businessmen. Solomon not only supplied Hiram with vast quantities of wheat and olive oil annually for food (5:11), but he surrendered to Hiram twenty "towns" of Galilee (9:10–13). When Solomon had finished building the temple (seven years) and his own palace (thirteen years), Hiram journeyed to Galilee and was very dissatisfied when he saw the cities. He nicknamed them "Cabul," a term of uncertain origin that Josephus (*Antiq*. 8.5.3) says means "not pleasing" in the Phoenician tongue. Hiram and Solomon built a navy and supplied it with sailors on the Red Sea. They made expeditions from Ezion Geber at the head of the Gulf of Aqabah southward to Ophir, bringing back gold (9:28). They also had a "navy of Tarshish" (see NIV footnote) on the Mediterranean; this navy brought "gold, silver and ivory, and apes and baboons" (10:22). No definite record is found of Hiram's death. He had a daughter who became one of Solomon's "seven hundred wives" (11:1, 3).

2. A worker in brass whom Solomon brought from Tyre to help build the temple (1 Kings 7:13–14, 40–45 JB, KJV, MLB, MOF, NASB, RSV; "Huram" in 2 Chron 2:13–14; 4:11–16). See also HURAM.

HIRELING. A laborer who works for his wages. He was ordinarily to be paid at once: "Pay him his wages each day before sunset" (Deut 24:15); compare the parable of the eleventh-hour laborers (Matt 20:1–6). But service might be for a longer time, as when Jacob worked seven years for each of his wives and six years for his flocks and herds, all of which were his hire (Gen 29:15–20, 27–28; 30:28–36). A hireling from outside Israel could not eat the Passover (Exod 12:45).

HITTITES (hĭt'īts, Heb. *hittîm*). With the Mesopotamians and Egyptians (2 Kings 7:6), they were one of the three great powers confronting early Israel. The biblical portrayals of Hittite dominance, once held to be unreliable, were first substantiated by discoveries at Carchemish on the Euphrates in A.D. 1871 and then totally vindicated by Hugo Winckler's excavations at Khattusa (Boghaz-köy) in Turkey, 1906–7. Ten thousand tablets from this ancient Hittite capital served to confirm Joshua's description of the entire western Fertile Crescent as "all the Hittite country" (Josh 1:4).

The original Hittites, or "Hattians," sprang from Ham, through Canaan's second son Heth (Gen 10:15; 1 Chron 1:13), and became established by the mid-third millennium B.C. along the Halys River in what is now central Turkey. The Hittite dress of heavy coats and turned-up-toed shoes reflected the rugged cold of this Anatolian plateau. From some time after 2200 the Hattians were overrun by a vigorous, Indo-European speaking people from the north. They became Heth's ruling class, while adapting the older and often immoral Hittite culture.

Ancient monuments depict the Hittites as a stocky people with prominent noses, retreating foreheads, and thick lips. The Hittite strain became widely diffused throughout Palestine along with that of the Hurrians, whose Aryan rulers had assumed the leadership of upper Mesopotamia at about this same time. Scripture thus regularly lists "Hittites" among the peoples of Canaan (Gen 15:20; Exod 3:8, 17; Deut 7:1; 20:17). They were "the people of the land" (Gen 23:7), especially in the central hills (Num 13:29; Josh 11:3). At Hebron in 2029 B.C. Abraham purchased Machpelah from the Hittites (Gen 23:3–20; 49:29–32; 50:13); sixty years later, Esau married Hittite (or Hurrian-Hivite) wives

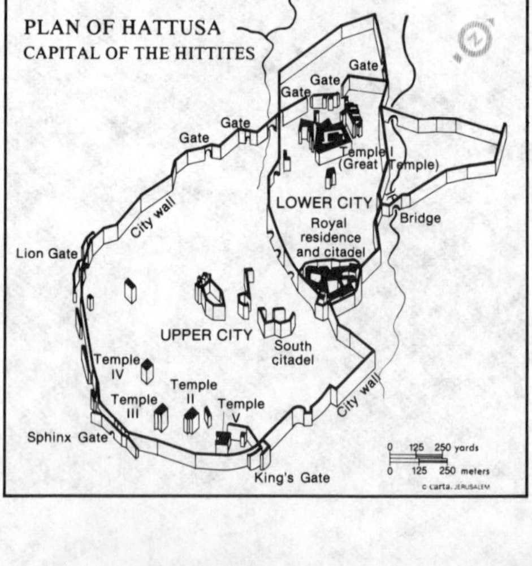

General view of the ruins of the Hittite capital, Hattusa, located about 100 miles (160 km.) east of Ankara in Turkey. Courtesy B. Brandl.

(26:34; 36:2), to the distress of Rebekah (27:46). With Israel's conquest of Canaan, despite the Mosaic ban (Deut 20:17), Hittite unions became common (Judg 3:5–6); and from Solomon to Ezra (1 Kings 11:1; Ezra 9:1) such intermarriage continued. Ezekiel thus condemned his people's morals and race by exclaiming, "Your mother was a Hittite and your father an Amorite" (Ezek 16:3, 45).

The history of the main body of Turkish Hittites embraces the Old Kingdom (1850–1550 B.C.) and the New Empire (1450–1200), though all Hittite dates are approximate, their hieroglyphic inscriptions furnishing no king lists with precise regnal years. Pitkhana of Kussara founded a major dynasty west of the Halys River about 1850. His son Anitta broke a rival coalition, took Khattusa itself, and subdued all Asia Minor. The dating of Anitta's son Tudkhaliya I at about 1750 makes improbable the proposed equating of him with Tidal, the opponent of Abraham (Gen 14). Detailed Hittite history begins with the Syrian raids of Labarna I (1650). His grandson Mursil I then succeeded in capturing Aleppo in 1570 and twenty years later sacked Babylon itself. After his assassination, however, traditional Hittite feudalism reasserted itself against weaker successors. During the early fifteenth century, Egypt swept north to the Euphrates; and on Egyptian withdrawal, the conquering Hebrews under Joshua overwhelmed the Palestinian Hittites (1406–1400; Josh 9:1; 11:3).

Meanwhile, Anatolia regained capable sovereigns (cf. Judg 1:26), who capitalized on the newly introduced horse-drawn war chariot (1 Kings 10:29). Suppiluliuma (1385–1345 B.C.), greatest of the New Empire monarchs, began his reign by instigating disorders within the nominally Egyptian states of Syro-Palestine (compare the contemporaneous raids of Cushan-Rishathaim of Mesopotamia; Judg 3:8). Eventually Suppiluliuma absorbed Hurrian Mitanni, extending his borders to Lebanon, and brought order to the entire west, securing Israel's forty years of peace under Othniel (3:11). His son Mursil II (1340–1310) inherited the most powerful monarchy of his time.

With the rise of the Nineteenth Dynasty in the 1320s B.C., a revived Egypt challenged Hittite supremacy, leaving Moab free to oppress Israel (Judg 3:12–14). But after defeating the Hittites on the Orontes, Pharaoh Seti I came to terms with Mursil. The famous treaty of 1315 divided the Near East into spheres of influence: Syria and the north to Heth; Phoenicia, Canaan, and the south to Egypt. The stability that resulted is then reflected in Israel's eighty years of peace following the victories of Ehud and Shamgar (3:30–31). A short time before the death of Muwatal (1310–1295), Rameses II aggressively broke his father's treaty. He survived a close but desperate struggle at Kadesh on the Orontes against superior Hittite tactics; but years of indecisive fighting followed, and in 1279 Khattusil III (1290–1260) achieved a renewal of the former treaty. Its terms were strictly enforced for the next half-century.

Drawing of a Hittite soldier, or relief from Carchemish, twelfth century B.C. He carries a shield on his back and a spear in his right hand, and a sword hangs from his left side. Courtesy Carta, Jerusalem.

Hittite decay ensued. The last significant monarch, Khattusil's grandson Arnuwanda III (1230–1200), suffered famine and civil revolt. Finally, invading "sea peoples" from the west, part of that general movement in which the Achaeans of Thessaly took Troy and Crete, overwhelmed Anatolia, burned Khattusa, and forever destroyed the Hittite Empire.

Hittite culture, however, survived for another half-millennium in the city states of Syria to the south. King Toi of Hamath, 1000 B.C., supported David (2 Sam 8:9–10); and Hittite warriors served among his heroes (1 Sam 28:6; 2 Sam 11:3; 23:39). Solomon reduced the Palestinian Hittites to bond service (1 Kings 9:20), but one of Ahab's major allies against Assyria at the battle of Qarqar in 853 was Irkhuleni of Hamath. The Hittite stronghold of Carchemish fell to the Assyrians only in 717 (cf. 2 Kings 19:13).

The spirit of independence continually plagued the Hittites, and their law codes exhibit mildness toward the feudal aristocracy. This produced a commendable humanitarianism that showed itself in restricted death penalties and in regard for womankind; but it also made serious moral laxity legitimate. In the service of their depraved mother-goddess of fertility, "Artemis of the Ephesians" (Acts 19:24–35), the Hittites became guilty of "a bestiality of which we would gladly think them innocent" and which corrupted God's people Israel (Ezek 16:44–45). JBP

HIVITES (hī'vīts, Heb. *hiwwî*). One of the seven nations of the land of Canaan that the Lord delivered into the hand of Joshua (Josh 24:11: "the Amorites, Perizzites, Canaanites, Hittites, Girgashites, Hivites and Jebusites"). They are generally named in conjunction with other tribes of the land. In the original table of the nations (Gen 10) they are listed with the Canaanite descendants of Ham, Noah's youngest son. All of these differed characteristically from the Japhethites who moved westward to the Mediterranean, northward into northern Europe, and eastward toward Persia and India. They differed also from the Semites who later occupied Mesopotamia, Palestine, and Arabia. The word "Hivite" probably comes from a word meaning "village of nomads"; and the Hivites seem to have been located in diverse places. In the time of Jacob, the city of Shechem, in the middle of Palestine, was ruled by the "son of Hamor the Hivite, the ruler of that area" (34:2). They seem to have been a peaceable commercial people (34:21), though with Canaanite morals.

Later in Joshua's time "the Hivites below Hermon in the region of Mizpah" are mentioned (Josh 11:3); thus they lived in the land east of the Sea of Galilee. Again, in Joshua 9:1, 7 the people of Gibeon just a few miles north of Jerusalem are classified as "Hivites." This indefiniteness of locality (or this variety of localities), plus the derivation of the word itself, seems to indicate that the Hivites were not a compact tribe, as the Jebusites of Jerusalem were (15:64); nor representatives of a great nation, as the Hittites were; nor descendants of one person, as the Moabites and the Ammonites (Gen 19:37–38) were, but villagers moving from place to place as business or politics dictated. The latest reference to them is in 2 Chronicles 8:7, an account of Solomon's conscripting some of the people as slave laborers. Some scholars doubt whether they ever had a separate existence. There is a possibility that they were the same as the Horites. ABF

HIZKI (hĭz'kē, Heb. *hizkî*). A Benjamite mentioned only in 1 Chronicles 8:17. KJV Hezeki.

HIZKIAH, HIZKIJAH (hĭz-kī'à, hĭz-kī'jà). 1. The great-great-grandfather of Zephaniah (Zeph 1:1), mentioned to show his relationship with King Josiah. The spelling should be Hezekiah, as in NIV.

2. One of the covenanters with Nehemiah (Neh 10:17). The spelling here also should be Hezekiah, as in NIV.

3. A son of Neariah, a member of the royal line after the Exile (1 Chron 3:23).

HOBAB (hō'băb, Heb. *hōvāv, beloved*). A person who is named only twice in the Bible. In Numbers 10:29 he is called "son of Reuel the Midianite, Moses' father-in-law"; this would seem to make him a brother of Moses' wife Zipporah (Exod 18:2) and thus Moses' brother-in-law. In Judges 4:11, most versions—e.g., KJV, JB, MLB, Mof, NASB, and RSV—speak of Hobab as the "father-in-law of Moses," while ASV, NEB, and NIV refer to him as "Moses' brother-in-law." The Hebrew word generally refers to one who gives his daughter in marriage. On the other hand, the people of the Middle East use words of relationship loosely; also, it has been argued that the aged Jethro (Reuel) could hardly have served with Moses as a guide to Israel in the wilderness, even if he desired to leave his work as the priest of Midian. In any case, Moses pleaded with Hobab to accompany Israel; after refusing at first, evidently he finally consented (Num 10:29; Judg 1:16; 4:11).

HOBAH (hō'bȧ). A place north of Damascus to which Abram pursued the captors of his nephew Lot (Gen 14:15).

HOBAIAH (hō-bā'yȧ, *Jehovah has hidden*). Ancestor of some priests in Zerubbabel's time (NIV, Ezra 2:61; Neh 7:63; "Habaiah" in other versions).

HOD (hŏd, *majesty*). A man of the tribe of Asher (1 Chron 7:37).

HODAVIAH, HODAIAH (hō'dȧ-vī'ȧ, hō-dā'yȧ). 1. A son of Elioenai, a descendant of the royal line of Judah (1 Chron 3:24).

2. A chief of the half-tribe of Manasseh, east of the Jordan (1 Chron 5:24).

3. The son of Hassenuah, a Benjamite (1 Chron 9:7).

4. A Levite, founder of the "line of Hodaviah" (Ezra 2:40). KJV, MLB, NASB, and RSV have "Hodevah" in Nehemiah 7:43 and "Judah" in Ezra 3:9 (NIV has "Hodaviah" in both).

HODESH (hō'dĕsh). A wife of Shaharaim, a Benjamite (1 Chron 8:9).

HODEVAH (See HODAVIAH)

HODIAH (hō-dī'ȧ). 1. Mentioned only in 1 Chronicles 4:19, either the sister of Naham (KJV, NEB) or the husband of the sister of Naham (ASV, NIV, RSV); in any case, a member of the tribe of Judah.

2. A Levite of the time of Ezra and Nehemiah (Neh 8:7; 9:5; 10:10, 13).

3. A chief of the people under Nehemiah (Neh 10:18).

HOGLAH (hŏg'lȧ). One of the five daughters of Zelophehad, a Manassite. Their father had no sons, so a new law was made that permitted daughters to inherit, provided they did not marry outside the tribe (Num 26:33; 27:1–11; 36:1–12; Josh 17:3–4).

HOHAM (hō'hăm). An Amorite king of Hebron who entered into league with other kings against Joshua; one of the five kings who were captured in the cave of Makkedah and put to death (Josh 10:3).

HOLINESS, HOLY. Usually translations of words derived from a Hebrew root *qadash* and Greek *hag-*. The basic meaning of *qadash* is "separateness, withdrawal." It is first applied to God and is early associated with ideas of purity and righteousness. Long before the prophetic period the ethical content is plain. Greek *hag-* is an equivalent of *qadash,* and its history is similar. Beginning as an attribute of deity, the *hag-* family of words developed two stems, one meaning "holy," the other "pure." The use of words of this family in the LXX to translate the *qadash* family resulted in a great development of their ethical sense, which was never clear in classical Greek. What became increasingly evident in the OT is overwhelmingly explicit in the NT: that holiness means the pure, loving nature of God, separate from evil, aggressively seeking to universalize itself; that this character is inherent in places, times, and institutions intimately associated with worship; and that holiness is to characterize human beings who have entered into personal relationship with God.

The words "holiness" and "holy" do not occur in Genesis, though they are implied in the dread that the presence of God inspires (Gen 28:16–17), but from Exodus 3:5 on, where God reveals his name and nature, holiness is constantly stressed. Only samples of the many biblical references will be given here. God is "majestic in holiness" (Exod 15:11); he acts with "his holy arm" (Isa 52:10); his words and promises are holy (Ps 105:42; Jer 23:9); his name is holy (Lev 20:3; 1 Chron 29:16); his Spirit is holy (Ps 51:10; Isa 63:10–11; see HOLY SPIRIT). Places are made holy by God's special presence: his dwelling in heaven (Deut 26:15), his manifestation on earth (Exod 3:5; Josh 5:15), the tabernacle (Exod 40:9), the temple (2 Chron 29:5, 7), Jerusalem (Isa 48:2), Zion (Obad 17). Anything set apart for sacred uses was holy: the altars and other furniture of the tabernacle (Exod 29:37; 30:10, 29), animal sacrifices (Num 18:17), food (Lev 21:22), the tithe (27:30), firstfruits (19:24; 23:20), anything consecrated (Exod 28:38), the anointing oil and incense (30:23–25, 34–38). Persons connected with holy places and holy services were holy: priests (Lev 21:1–6) and their garments (Exod 28:2, 4), Israel as a nation (Jer 2:3), Israel individually (Deut 33:3), many things connected with Israel (1 Chron 16:29). Times given to worship were holy (Exod 12:16; 16:23; 20:8; Isa 58:13).

In classical Greek *hagios* was first applied to sanctuaries; in Hellenistic times, to gods; then to the Mysteries (e.g., of Dionysos). *Hagios* came into frequent use from Middle Eastern religions in the occurrence in the LXX as the equivalent of *qdsh.* In the NT the holiness of things is less prominent than that of persons. What in Isaiah 6:3 was a personal revelation to the prophet is proclaimed to all from heaven in Revelation 4:8, with power and glory. God is holy and true (Rev 6:10). In one of his prayers, Jesus addressed God in this way: "Holy Father" (John 17:11). First Peter 1:15 repeats the assertion of Leviticus 19:2 that God is holy and his people are to be holy. Jesus' disciples are to pray that the name of God may be treated as holy (Matt 6:9; Luke 1:2). The holiness of Jesus Christ is specifically stressed. Evil spirits recognize him as "the Holy One of God" who has come to destroy them (Mark 1:24; Luke 4:34). Jesus is holy because of his wondrous birth

(Luke 1:35). The father set him apart "as his very own" and made him holy (John 10:36). He is "holy and true" (Rev 3:7). To the Jerusalem church Jesus is "the Holy and Righteous One" (Acts 3:14), the "holy servant Jesus" (4:27, 30), fulfilling the prophecy of Isaiah 42:1–4, quoted in Matthew 12:16–21. In Hebrews 9 Christ is the fulfillment of OT priesthood and sacrifice, in both of which capacities he had to be holy (Heb 2:11).

The holiness of the church is developed in the NT. As in the OT, Jerusalem is holy (Matt 4:5; 27:53; Rev 11:2), so is the temple (Matt 24:15; Acts 6:13) and the new temple, the church, collectively (Eph 2:21–22) and individually (1 Cor 3:16–17). Stephen refers to Mount Sinai as "holy ground" (Acts 7:33) and Peter to the Mount of Transfiguration as "the holy mount" (2 Peter 1:18 KJV; NIV "sacred mountain"). The Scriptures are holy (Rom 1:2; 2 Tim 3:15). The law is holy (Rom 7:12). Since the earthly holy place, priests, cult apparatus, sacrifices, and services were holy, much more are the heavenly (Heb 8:5). The church is a holy nation (1 Peter 2:9). The argument of Romans 11:11–32 rests the holiness of Gentile Christians on their growing out of the root (11:16) of Jesse (15:12). Christ died for the church in order to make it holy (1 Cor 1:2; sanctified in Christ Jesus, 1 Cor 6:11; Eph 5:26). The church as a whole, the local churches, and individual Christians are holy, "called . . . saints" (Rom 1:7; 1 Cor 1:2; 2 Cor 1:1; Eph 1:1; Phil 1:1; Col 1:2; "saints" being a translation of *hagioi,* holy). The life of the individual Christian is to be a living, holy sacrifice (Rom 12:1), not only through death (Phil 2:17), but through life itself (1:21–26). In the OT the sacrifice was a *thing,* separate from the offerer; in the NT it is the *offerer himself.* Holiness is equated with purity (Matt 5:8; 23:26; 1 Tim 1:5; 2 Tim 2:22; Titus 1:15; James 1:27), a purity that in Acts 18:6; 20:26 is innocence. The means of purification is the truth of the Word of God (John 17:17). The "holy kiss," in the early churches, was a seal of holy fellowship (1 Cor 16:20; 2 Cor 13:12; 1 Thess 5:26). Holiness is prominent in the Book of Revelation from 3:7 to 22:11.

Of other Hebrew and Greek words translated "holy," two must be mentioned. Hebrew *hāsîdh* and its Greek equivalent *hosios* mean "good, kind, pious." *Hāsîdh* has many translations, *hosios* a few. *Hāsîdh* is translated "holy" in five verses (Deut 33:8; Ps 16:10; 86:2; 89:19; 145:17). *Hosios* occurs seven times in the NT—once as a noun, the other six times being rendered "holy" (Acts 2:27; 13:35; 1 Tim 2:8; Titus 1:8; Heb 7:26; Rev 15:4); its derivatives appear in forms of the word "holy" (Luke 1:75; Eph 4:24; 1 Thess 2:10).

Summary: The idea of holiness originates in the revealed character of God and is communicated to things, places, times, and persons engaged in his service. The ethical nature of holiness grows clearer as revelation unfolds, until the holiness of God the Father, Son, and Holy Spirit; of the church as a body; and of individual members of that body fills the NT horizon. Holiness is interwoven with righteousness and purity. To seek holiness apart from the other qualities of a Christlike life is to wander from the way of holiness itself.

Bibliography: R. Otto, *The Idea of the Holy,* 1946; H. Ringgren, *The Prophetical Conception of Holiness,* 1948; S. Neill, *Christian Holiness,* 1960; O. R. Jones, *The Concept of Holiness,* 1961; O. Prochsch, TDNT, 1:88–115. ER

HOLON (hō'lŏn). 1. A city in the hill country of Judah (Josh 15:51; 21:15) assigned to the Levites (called Hilen in 1 Chron 6:58); Khirbet Alin.

2. A town probably in the Plain of Moab near Medeba (Jer 48:21). The site is unknown.

HOLY GHOST (See HOLY SPIRIT)

HOLY OF HOLIES (See TABERNACLE)

HOLY PLACE (See TABERNACLE)

HOLY SPIRIT (Gr. *pneuma hagion;* in KJV of NT, Holy Ghost). The third person of the triune Godhead (Matt 28:19; 2 Cor 13:14).

There is a rich revelation of the Spirit of the Lord in the OT, running along the same lines as that in the NT and directly preparatory to it. Customarily we think of the Spirit of God in the OT as powerfully endowing chosen individuals for great tasks, but actually his work ranges much more widely. First, we notice that the Spirit is God's agent in creation (e.g., Gen 1:1; Ps 33:6; 104:30). For animals (Isa 34:16) and man (Job 27:3) alike (cf. Isa 42:5), created life is the work of the Holy Spirit. Second, the Spirit is the agent in the providential work of God in the moral sphere, the areas of history and ethical relationships. Though the actual translation of Genesis 6:3 is uncertain, it is by his Spirit that God senses and reacts to wickedness on earth. In Ezekiel 1:14, 20 the Spirit is the power by which the sovereign God controls the complexities of life on earth (cf. Isa 4:4; 30:1; 63:14). The godly person knows that his sin offends the Holy One and he fears quenching the Spirit (Ps 51:11)—this is the form that the Lord's judgment on the disobedient Saul took (1 Sam 16:14). Third, the Spirit is known in the OT as a personal endowment. He indwells the people of God as a whole (Hag 2:5), just as he was among them at the Exodus (Isa 63:11). He endowed Bezalel for artistic skill (Exod 31:3) and many others for mighty deeds (Judg 3:10 and 6:34, literally "clothed himself with Gideon"; 11:29; 13:25; 1 Sam 11:6). These references correspond to what the NT speaks of as the "filling" of the Spirit, i.e., special endowment for a special task (cf. Acts 4:8); but there is also the constant endowment of individuals (Num 11:17, 29; 27:18; 1 Sam 16:13), especially those individuals who stood directly in the great messianic line (Isa 11:2; 42:1; 48:16; 61:1). The OT, indeed, looks forward to the messianic day as a time of special enjoyment of the Spirit of God (Isa 32:15; 44:3; 59:21; Ezek 36:27; 39:29; Joel 2:28–29). The verb "to pour out" is notable in these references and points to a hitherto unknown abundance. Fourth, the Spirit inspired the prophets (Num 11:29; 24:2; 1 Sam 10:6, 10; 2 Sam 23:2; 1 Kings 22:24; Neh 9:30; Hos 9:7; Joel 2:28–29; Mic 3:8; Zech 7:12). In all these references the personality of the Spirit is notable.

Moreover, the Spirit is wise (Isa 40:13; cf. 11:2; Dan 4:8–9, 18), he is vexed by sin and rebellion (Isa 63:10), and he is at rest when sin has been dealt with (Zech 6:8). He is holy (Ps 51:13; Isa 63:10) and good (Neh 9:20; Ps 143:10). We note that this is the same sort of evidence that we would adduce from the NT for holding that the Spirit of God is "He," not "it." But, like the NT, the OT goes further. Psalm 139:7 shows that the Spirit is the very presence of God himself in all the world. The Spirit of God is God himself actually present and in operation. In Isaiah 63:10, when the people vex the Spirit, God becomes their enemy; in 63:14 the work of the Spirit giving rest is parallel to the act of God leading his people. The ascription of holiness (e.g., Ps 51:13) accords to the Spirit the character and personality of God."

That the Holy Spirit has power and influence is plain from Acts 1:8; that he is a person, the NT makes clear in detail: he dwells with us (John 14:17), teaches and brings to remembrance (14:26), bears witness (15:26), convinces of sin (16:8), guides, speaks, declares (16:13, 15), inspires the Scriptures and speaks through them (Acts 1:16; 2 Peter 1:21), speaks to his servants, (Acts 8:29), calls ministers (13:2), sends out workers (13:4), forbids certain actions (16:6–7), and intercedes (Rom 8:26). He has the attributes of personality: love (Rom 15:30), will (1 Cor 12:11), mind (Rom 8:27), thought, knowledge, words (1 Cor 2:10–13). The Holy Spirit can be treated as one may treat a human person: he can be lied to and tempted (Acts 5:3–4, 9), resisted (7:51), grieved (Eph 4:30), outraged (Heb 10:29 RSV), blasphemed against (Matt 12:31). The Holy Spirit is God, equated with the Father and the Son (Matt 28:19; 2 Cor 13:14). Jesus speaks of him as of his other self (John 14:16–17), whose presence with the disciples will be of greater advantage than his own (16:7). To have the Spirit of God is to have Christ (Rom 8:9–12). God is spirit (John 4:24) in essential nature and sends his Holy Spirit to live and work in people (14:26; 16:7).

The Hebrew and Greek words that are translated "spirit" are *rûach* and *pneuma,* both meaning literally "wind, breath." Both came to be used for the unseen reality of living beings, especially God and man. Therefore, breath and wind are symbols of the Holy Spirit (Gen 2:7; Job 32:8; 33:4; Ezek 37:9–10; John 20:22). Other symbols are the dove (Matt 3:16; Mark 1:10; Luke 3:22; John 1:32), oil (Luke 4:18; Acts 10:38; 1 John 2:20), fire for purification (Matt 3:11; Luke 3:16; Acts 2:3–4), living water (Isa 44:3; John 4:14; 7:37–39) and earnest or guarantee of all that God has in store for us (2 Cor 1:22; Eph 1:13–14). In the OT the Spirit of God appears from the beginning (Gen 1:2); God calls him his Spirit (6:3); and the Spirit of God comes on certain men for special purposes (e.g., Bezalel, Exod 31:3; some judges, Judg 3:10; 6:34; 11:29; David, 1 Sam 16:13). This kind of endowment was temporary (e.g., Saul, 1 Sam 10:10; 16:14); so David, repentant, prayed, "Do not . . . take your Holy Spirit from me" (Ps 51:11). The Spirit of God came "upon" the Messiah (Isa 11:2; 42:1; 61:1). God acts by his Spirit (Zech 4:6). (For the meaning of "holy" see HOLINESS.)

In the Gospels, as in the OT, the Holy Spirit comes upon certain persons for special reasons: John the Baptist and his parents (Luke 1:15, 41, 67), Simeon (2:25–27), and Jesus as a man (Matt 1:18, 20; 3:16; 4:1; Mark 1:8, 10; Luke 1:35; 3:16, 22; 4:1, 14, 18; John 1:32–33). Jesus promises the Holy Spirit in a new way to those who believe in him (John 7:37–39; cf. 4:10–15); also as "what my Father has promised" in Luke 24:49; covered in fuller detail in Acts 1:1–8. Jesus taught the nature and work of the Holy Spirit in John 14:16, 26; 15:26; 16:7–15. This work is to dwell in the disciples as Comforter, Counselor, Advocate (Greek *paraklētos*); to teach all things; to help believers remember what Jesus said; to testify of Jesus; to reprove the world of sin, righteousness, and judgment; to guide the disciples into all truth; not to speak on his own initiative, but to speak only what he hears; to show the disciples things to come; and to glorify Jesus by showing the things of Jesus to the disciples. The evening of the Resurrection, Jesus "breathed on" the disciples (Thomas being absent) and said, "Receive the Holy Spirit" (John 20:22). This was not the complete enduement of the Holy Spirit that Jesus had taught and promised and that occurred at Pentecost, but it was provisional and enabled the disciples to persevere in prayer until the promised day.

At Pentecost a new phase of the revelation of God to people began (Acts 2)—as new as when the Word became flesh in the birth of Jesus. With the rushing of a mighty wind and what appeared to be tongues of fire, the disciples were all filled with the Holy Spirit and spoke in foreign languages (listed in 2:9–11). The excitement drew a crowd of visitors to the feast, to whom Peter explained that the prophecy of Joel 2:28–32 was being fulfilled in accordance with the salvation that Jesus of Nazareth had accomplished by dying on the cross. Another 3,000 souls were added by baptism to the 120 disciples, and thus began the fellowship of apostolic teaching, of breaking of bread and of prayer, the fellowship that is the church. When the first crisis that threatened the extinction of the early church was passed, again "they were all filled with the Holy Spirit" (Acts 4:31), binding them more closely together. When the first Gentiles were converted, the Holy Spirit was poured out on them and they spoke in tongues (10:44–48); likewise when Paul met a group of John the Baptist's disciples, the Holy Spirit came on them (19:1–7).

The NT is full of the work of the Holy Spirit in the lives of believers (Rom 8:1–27); e.g., he gives gifts (1 Cor 12:14), our "body is a temple of the Holy Spirit" (6:19), and he works in us "the fruit of the Spirit" (Gal 5:22–23). Being "filled with the Spirit" (Eph 5:18) means that one experiences Christ living within (Rom 8:9–10). As the heavenly Father is God and his Son Jesus Christ is God, so the Holy Spirit is God. The Holy Spirit as well as the Son was active in creation; he was active on certain occasions in his own person in OT times and more intensively in the Gospels; and in Acts and the Epistles he becomes the resident divine agent in the church and in its members. Teaching concerning the Holy Spirit has been both neglected and distorted, but the subject deserves careful attention as one reads the NT.

Bibliography: H. B. Swete, *The Holy Spirit in the New Testament,* 1909; R. B. Hoyle, *The Holy Spirit in Saint Paul,* 1928; H. W. Robinson, *The Christian Experience of the Holy Spirit,* 1928; G. S. Hendry, *The Holy Spirit in Christian Theology,* 1957; J. C. J. Waite, *The Activity of the Holy Spirit Within the Old Testament Period,* 1961; H. Berkhof, *The Doctrine of the Holy Spirit,* 1965; E. M. B. Green, *I Believe in the Holy Spirit,* 1975. ER

HOMAM (hō'măm). Seir's grandson (1 Chron 1:39). Genesis 36:22 has Hemam (JB, KJV, NASB, NEB), Heman (ASV, RSV), Homam (NIV).

HOMER (See WEIGHTS AND MEASURES)

HONEY (Heb. *devash,* Gr. *meli, honey*). Early regarded as among "the best products of the land" (Gen 43:11), it was found in clefts of the rocks (Deut 32:13; Ps 81:16) and in the comb on the ground (1 Sam 14:25–43). Job 20:17 speaks of brooks of honey and butter, indicating abundance due to the domestication of bees. Canaan was "a land flowing with milk and honey" (Exod 3:8; Ezek 20:15), Assyria "a land of olive trees and honey" (2 Kings 18:32). Honey was a product of Palestine (Jer 41:8; Ezek 27:17). Samson ate wild honey found in the carcass of a lion (Judg 14:8–18). Honey became a common food (2 Sam 17:29) even in times of scarcity (Isa 7:15, 22). It was never part of a sacrifice, but it was a firstfruits offering (Lev 2:11; 2 Chron 31:5). Strained honey was kept in a jar or cruse (1 Kings 14:3). Honey is a recommended food, but in moderation (Prov 24:13; 25:16, 27; 27:7; Ezek 16:13, 19). Honey is a standard of comparison for pleasant things, good or bad (Prov 16:24; 5:3; Song of Songs 4:11; 5:1; Ezek 3:3; Rev 10:9). John the Baptist ate honey (Matt 3:4; Mark 1:6).

HOOD (See DRESS)

HOOK. The translation of several Hebrew words: 1. *'aghmôn,* "reed" (Job 41:2, KJV where a rope of rushes is meant; NIV "cord").

2. *Wāw,* "hook" or "peg" of gold or silver, used to support the hangings of the tabernacle (Exod 26:32, 37; 27:10, 17; 36:36, 38; 38:10–19, 28).

3. *Had,* "hook, ring, fetter" (2 Kings 19:28; Isa 37:29; Ezek 29:4; 38:4).

4. *Hakkâh,* "angle, hook, fishhook" (Job 41:1 RSV, NIV).

5. *Tsinnâh,* "thorn, hook" (Amos 4:2).

6. *Shephattayîm,* "hook-shaped pegs, double hooks" (Ezek 40:43).

7. *Fleshhook, mazlēgh,* probably a small pitchfork with two or three tines (Exod 27:3; RSV "forks," NIV "meat forks").

8. "Pruning hook," *mazemērôth,* a sickle-shaped knife for pruning vines.

9. *Hôah,* "hook" (Job 41:2b RSV, NIV; KJV "thorn").

10. The Greek word, occurring only once in the NT, is *ankistron,* "fishing hook" (Matt 17:27 KJV; NIV "line").

HOOPOE (See BIRDS)

HOPE. A gift of the Holy Spirit that, with faith and love, is an essential characteristic of the Christian when prophecies, tongues, and knowledge pass away (1 Cor 13:8, 13). The Greek noun *elpis* and its related verb *elpizo,* usually rendered "hope," occur in the NT fifty-four and thirty-one times respectively. The biblical concept of hope is not mere expectation and desire, as in Greek literature, but includes trust, confidence, refuge in the God of hope (Rom 15:13). Christ in you is the hope of glory (Col 1:27). All creation hopes for redemption (Rom 8:19–25 RSV). Christ Jesus is our hope (1 Tim 1:1 RSV, NIV). Hope of eternal life is bound up with that "blessed hope—the glorious appearing of . . . Jesus Christ" (Titus 1:2; 2:13), which motivates purity (1 John 3:3). Hope is linked with faith (Heb 11:1). It depends on Jesus' resurrection (1 Cor 15:19). Hope is little spoken of in the Gospels, while Jesus was on earth, or in Revelation, where he will again be personally present. Acts and the Epistles are full of this Christ-centered hope. The hope that animated Paul (Acts 26:6–8) was "the hope of Israel" (28:20). NT hope has deep roots in the OT, where KJV "hope" translates a variety of Hebrew words, which mean "confidence," "trust," "safety," etc., sometimes so rendered in more modern versions. ER

HOPHNI (hŏf'nī, Heb. *hophnî*). A son of Eli, the high priest and judge who proved unworthy of his sacred offices (1 Sam 1:3; 2:34; 4:4, 17). Hophni is always associated with his brother Phinehas. The two were partners in evil practices and brought a curse on their heads (2:34; 3:14). Both were killed at the battle of Aphek, and their death, coupled with the loss of the ark, caused the death of Eli (4:17–18). Both sons disgraced their priestly office by claiming and appropriating more than their share of the sacrifices (2:13–17) and by their immoral actions in the tabernacle (1 Sam 2:22; Amos 2:6–8).

HOPHRA (See PHARAOH)

HOPPER (See ANIMALS)

HOPPING LOCUST (See ANIMALS)

Jebel Haroun, near Petra, long considered the site of Mount Hor. On the summit, a shrine was built in memory of Aaron's burial (Num 20:22–29). Courtesy Garo Nalbandian.

HOR (hôr, Heb. *hōr, mountain*). 1. A conspicuous mountain, probably a day's march north or NE of Kadesh Barnea, where Aaron died and was buried (Num 20:22–29; 33:37–41; Deut 32:50); perhaps Jebel Maderah, a prominent, steep-sided, white chalk hill. Israel marched south from here toward the Red Sea (Num 21:4), making possible the earlier identification with Jebel Neby Harun, SE of Kadesh Barnea, though this site is well within the borders of Edom in Mount Seir, a kingdom with which Israel had not yet made contact.

2. A mountain on the northern border of the land given to the Israelites, between the Great Sea (Mediterranean) and the entrance of Hamath (Num 34:7–8). It has been variously identified, with no certainty as yet possible.

HOR HAGGIDGAD (hôr'hă-gĭd'găd, *hollow* or *cavern of Gilgad*). An Israelite camp in the wilderness, between Bene Jaakan and Jotbathah (Num 33:32–33), called Gudgodah in Deuteronomy 10:7. See also GUDGODAH.

HORAM (hō'răm). A king of Gezer, defeated and killed by Joshua (Josh 10:33).

HOREB (hō'rĕb, *drought, desert*). The mountain where Moses received his commission (Exod 3:1); where he brought water out of the rock (17:6); and where the people stripped off their ornaments in token of repentance (33:6). It was eleven days' journey from Kadesh Barnea (Deut 1:2) and was mentioned also in Deuteronomy 1:6, 19; 4:10, 15; 5:2; 9:8; 18:16; 1 Kings 8:9; 2 Chronicles 5:10; Psalm 106:19; Malachi 4:4, in connection with the journeys of Israel, the giving of the Law, and events of the year in which the Israelites stayed nearby. Elijah fled here (1 Kings 19:8). It is geographically indistinguishable from Sinai.

HOREM (hō'rĕm, *consecrated*). A fortified city in Naphtali, near Iron (Josh 19:38), unidentified.

HORESH (hō'rĕsh, *forest*). A wood (so KJV) in the Desert of Ziph where David hid from Saul and where he made a covenant with Jonathan (1 Sam 23:15–19). It has been identified with Khirbet Khoreisa, about six miles (ten km.) south of Hebron.

HORI (hō'rī, *cave-dweller*). 1. A son of Seir, a Horite, and founder of the Horites (Gen 36:22, 29–30; 1 Chron 1:39).

2. A Simeonite whose son Shaphat was one of the twelve spies whom Joshua sent to investigate the land of Canaan (Num 13:5).

HORITE, HORIM (hō'rīt, hō'rĭm). A people found in Mount Seir as early as the time of Abraham and conquered by Kedorlaomer and his allies (Gen 14:6); the early inhabitants, before the Edomites dispossessed them and intermarried with them (Gen 36:20–30; Deut 2:12, 22). Esau married the daughter of one of their chieftains, also called a Hivite (Gen 36:2). The Hivites are thought to be identical with, or else confused with, the Horites (Gen 34:2; Josh 9:7), in which case the Horites lived as far north as Gibeon and Shechem in the time of Jacob's sons and until the conquest under Joshua. The LXX makes this identification. The Horites are now commonly thought to be Hurrians, from the highlands of Media, who before the middle of the second millennium B.C. overspread the region from Media to the Mediterranean, forming, or being merged in, the kingdom of Mitanni, subsequently destroyed by the Hittites. The Horites of Palestine, then, would be enclaves of this once-conquering race left behind when their empire receded before the Hittite advance. The Hurrian nobles appear to have been Aryans, the peasants

Cuneiform clay tablet (fifteenth to fourteenth centuries B.C.), one of the Nuzi documents, found to have preserved a remarkable record of Semite-Hurrian culture. From T. J. Meek, Excavations at Nuzi, 3.1935, Harvard Semitic Series. Courtesy Encyclopaedia Judaica Photo Archive, Jerusalem.

non-Aryans; whether they were Semites or other, perhaps Armenoids, is not settled. The Hurrian language is in the process of being deciphered, so that further investigation should clear up a picture that is confused at present. ER

HORMAH (hôr'mȧ, Heb. *hormâh, a devoted place*). Perhaps Tell-es Sheriah, north of the road between Gaza and Beersheba and about midway beteen the towns. Here the disobedient Israelites were defeated by Amalekites and Canaanites (Num 14:45; Deut 1:44). In the war with the king of Arad the place was taken by the Israelites and given the name Hormah, meaning "devoted," because it was devoted to destruction (Num 21:1–3). In the list of kings conquered by Joshua it appears with Arad (Josh 12:14). Hormah was originally given to' Judah (15:30), but shortly after was allotted to Simeon (19:4) because the portion of the tribe of Judah was too large for them. Judges 1:17 relates that it was Judah and Simeon who subdued Zephath and renamed it Hormah. David sent part of the spoil of Ziklag to Hormah, as one of the cities of Judah (1 Sam 30:26–30), but Hormah was reckoned among the cities of Simeon "until the reign of David" (1 Chron 4:30–31).

HORN (Heb. and Aram. *qeren,* Gr. *keras, an animal horn*). *Inkhorn* (Ezek 9:2–3, 11) is Hebrew *qeseth,* translated "writing case" in RSV, "writing kit" in NIV. In Joshua 6, Hebrew *yôvēl,* from a root meaning "ram," is a word that has puzzled interpreters. In the context here and elsewhere it appears to refer to the rams' horns that were blown on solemn occasions, and whose use gave rise to the term "Jubilee" for the fiftieth year of release, "the year of the ram's [horn]." *Qeren* referred to the horn on the animal (Gen 22:13); the horn used as a musical instrument (Josh 6:5; 1 Chron 25:5, but RSV and NIV have "to exalt him"); or a vessel to hold liquids (1 Sam 16:1, 13; 1 Kings 1:39). Tusks are meant in Ezekiel 27:15 (so RSV, NIV).

The "horns of the altar" were of one piece with the frame of the altar of burnt offering, made of acacia wood overlaid with bronze (Exod 27:2; cf. Ezek 43:15); likewise the altar of incense (Exod 30:2; 37:26; cf. Rev 9:13), but overlaid with gold. Blood of sacrificial animals was put on the horns of both altars on certain occasions (Exod 30:10; Lev 4:7, 18, 25, 30, 34; 16:18; cf. Ezek 43:20). To cut off its horns rendered an altar useless for religious purposes (Amos 3:14). A person seeking sanctuary might catch hold of the horns of the altar in the temple, but this did not save Adonijah (1 Kings 1:50–51; 2:28–34). Jeremiah felt that the sin of Judah was engraved on the horns of their altars (Jer 17:1). The purpose of altar horns is in doubt. For Psalm 118:27, NIV has: "Bind the festal sacrifice with ropes, and take it up to the horns of the altar" (contra JB, KJV, MLB, NASB, NEB, RSV).

Horns represent aggressive force (1 Kings 22:11; 2 Chron 18:10; Dan 8:7, symbolically; Deut 33:17; Ps 22:21; 92:10; Zech 1:18–21;

Horned incense altar from Megiddo, tenth-ninth century B.C. Courtesy Israel Department of Antiquities and Museums.

Luke 1:69, figuratively). Horns in Habakkuk 3:4 are translated "rays" in ASV, RSV, NIV, because of the context (light). Multiple horns on one animal denote successive nations or rulers (Dan 7:7–24; 8:3–22; Rev 13:1; 17:3–16); "seven" with "horns" (Rev 5:6; 12:3) indicates perfection of power, good or evil. The beast with two horns like a lamb, which spoke like a dragon (Rev 13:11), suggests outward lamblikeness and inward wickedness. ER

HORNED OWL (See BIRDS)

HORNET (See ANIMALS)

HORONAIM (hôr-ŏ-nā'ĭm, *two hollows, caves* or *ravines*). A place in Moab, location uncertain (Isa 15:5; Jer 48:3, 5, 34).

HORONITE (hôr'ō-nīt). A designation of Sanballat (Neh 2:10, 19; 13:28), probably indicating Moabite origin (from Beth Horon or Horonaim).

HORSE (See ANIMALS)

HORSE GATE. One of the gates of Jerusalem, between the Water Gate and the Sheep Gate; probably near the SE corner of the city (Neh 3:28–32; Jer 31:38–40). Here Athaliah was killed by order of Jehoiada the priest (2 Kings 11:16; 2 Chron 23:15).

HORSE LEECH (See ANIMALS)

HOSAH (hō'sà, Heb. *hōsâh, refuge*). 1. A town on the northern border of Asher, near Tyre (Josh 19:29). The site is uncertain.

2. A Levite porter selected by David to be one of the first doorkeepers to the ark after its return (1 Chron 16:38; 26:10–11, 16).

HOSANNA (hō-zăn'à, Heb. *hôsa'-nā'*, Gr. *hōsanna, save now*). Originally a prayer, "Save now, pray" (Ps 118:25), which had lost its primary meaning and become an exclamation of praise (Matt 21:9, 15; Mark 11:9–10; John 12:13). That it is transliterated instead of translated in three of the Gospels (Luke omits it) is evidence of the change of meaning. Not that the Hebrew word no longer had any connection with salvation: the context, which is a reminiscence of Psalm 118:25–26, if not a direct quotation from or allusion to it, shows that in its application to God the Father and to Jesus, hosanna was concerned with the messianic salvation.

HOSEA (Heb. *hôshēa', salvation*). Of all the prophetic material contained in the OT, the writings of Hosea were the only ones to come from the northern kingdom of Israel. This notable eighth-century B.C. prophet lived during a period of great national anxiety. He was born during the reign of Jeroboam II (c. 786–746), the last great king of Israel, and according to the superscription of his book (Hos 1:1) he exercised his prophetic ministry in Israel when Uzziah (c. 783–743), Jotham (c. 742–735), Ahaz (c. 735–715), and Hezekiah (c. 715–686) reigned in Judah. While Hosea did not mention the events referred to in Isaiah 7:1 and 2 Kings 16:5, in 733 he certainly experienced the raids of the Assyrian ruler Tiglath-Pileser III on Galilee and Transjordan.

First century B.C. Dead Sea Scroll of Hosea 2:8–9, 10–14 with commentary (4Qp Hos[a]), found in Qumran Cave 4. Courtesy Israel Museum, Jerusalem.

The time of Hosea was marked by great material prosperity. Under Jeroboam II the northern kingdom experienced a degree of economic and commercial development unknown since the early days of the united kingdom. The development of city life attracted many people from the agricultural pursuits that had formed the basis of the Israelite economy, and this presented serious problems at a later time. Characteristic of this period was the rise of successful middle-class businessmen, which was offset by the appearance of an urban proletariat or working class. The latter came into being because of the wanton demands made by the luxury-loving upper classes on the increasingly impoverished peasants and smallholders. As the latter succumbed to economic pressure, they were compelled to abandon their property and seek whatever employment was available in urban centers. Thus there resulted an ominous social gap between the upper and lower classes, a serious portent for the future of the national economy.

While there is no reference to the occupation of Beeri, father of Hosea, he may well have been a middle-class merchant, perhaps a baker. Hosea himself was an educated person and probably came from a town in Ephraim or Manasseh. A man of profound spiritual vision, he was gifted with intellectual qualities that enabled him to comprehend the significance of those unhappy events that marked his domestic life and interpret them as a timely reminder of divine love toward a wayward, sinful Israel.

Ever since the days of Joshua the religious life of the Israelites had been dominated by the influence of corrupt Canaanite worship. Archaeological discoveries in northern Syria have uncovered a great deal of information about the religion of the Canaanites, who had occupied Palestine from an early period (Gen 12:6). This seductive worship had already gained a firm foothold in Israelite religious life before the period of the judges, and by the time of Amos and Hosea Canaanite cult-worship had become the religion of the masses.

The deities chiefly venerated were the fertility god Baal (from a word meaning "lord," "master," or "husband") and his consort Anat (sometimes known as Asherah or Ashtoreth), a savage, sensual female. Both deities were often worshiped under the form of bulls and cows, so that when Jeroboam I set up two golden calves, one at Dan and the other at Bethel (1 Kings 12:28), he was encouraging the people to indulge in the fertility religion of Canaan.

The cultic rites were celebrated several times each year and were marked by drunkenness, ritual prostitution, acts of violence, and indulgence in pagan forms of worship at the shrines. The widespread prevalence of cultic prostitution is evident from the fact that in Jeremiah's day, a century after the time of Hosea, prostitution flourished in the temple precincts (2 Kings 23:7).

Hosea saw that this form of worship was the exact opposite of what God desired of his people. The Sinaitic covenant emphasized the exclusive worship of the Lord by a nation holy to him. However, the religious life of the covenant people had degenerated to the point of becoming identified with the shameless immoral worship of the pagan Canaanite deities. The emphasis on unbridled sexual activity coupled with excessive indulgence in alcohol was sapping the vitality not only of the Canaanites but also of Israel. All this, carried out against a background of magic and pagan mythology, was vastly removed from the purity of worship contemplated in the Sinai covenant.

It was Hosea's primary duty to recall wayward Israel to its obligations under the agreement made at Sinai. On that occasion Israel had voluntarily made a pact with God that involved surrender, loyalty, and obedience. As a result, Israel had become God's son (Hos 11:1; cf. Exod 4:22) by adoption and divine grace. Of necessity the initiative had come from God, but Hosea saw that it was important to emphasize the free cooperative acceptance of that relationship by the Israelites. Hence he stressed that Israel was really God's bride (Hos 2:7, 16, 19), and employed the marriage metaphor to demonstrate the voluntary association of the bride with her divine lover.

The catalyst of Hosea's prophetic message is his marriage to a woman named Gomer. There are two major views of this relationship. The proleptic view holds that Gomer was pure when she married Hosea but later proved unfaithful. Another major view holds that she was a harlot when the prophet married her. Either way, the shock effect of Hosea's marital difficulties would have had telling impact on the people of his community. The children born of this marriage were given symbolic names indicating divine displeasure with Israel. After Gomer had pursued her paramours, she was to be brought back and with patient love readmitted to Hosea's home, there to await in penitence and grief the time of restoration to full favor. This was a clear picture of wayward Israel in its relationship with God and showed the unending faithfulness of the Almighty.

The remainder of the prophecy (Hos 4–14) is an indictment of Israel, delivered at various times from the later days of Jeroboam II up to about 730 B.C. The style of this section is vigorous, though the Hebrew text has suffered in transmission, making for difficulties in translation. The first three chapters have been regarded by some as allegorical. Though the book is generally held to be a unity, critical writers have maintained that interpolations and editorial material occur throughout the work.

Analysis:

- 1–3 Hosea's unhappy marriage and its results.
- 4 The priests condone immorality.
- 5 Israel's sin will be punished unless she repents.
- 6 Israel's sin is thoroughgoing; her repentance half-hearted.
- 7 Inner depravity and outward decay.
- 8 The nearness of judgment.
- 9 The impending calamity.
- 10 Israel's guilt and punishment.
- 11 God pursues Israel with love.
- 12–14 An exhortation to repentance, with promised restoration.

Bibliography: W. R. Harper, *A Critical and Exegetical Commentary on Amos and Hosea* (ICC), 1905; D. A. Hubbard, *With Bands of Love,* 1968; F. I. Andersen and D. N. Freedman, *Hosea: A New Translation With Introduction and Commentary* (AB), 1980. RKH

HOSHAIAH (hō-shā'yȧ, Heb. *hôsha'yâh, Jehovah has saved*). 1. The man who led half the princes of Judah and walked behind the chorus at the dedication of the wall of the city of Jerusalem (Neh 12:32).

2. The father of Jezaniah (Jer 42:1) or Azariah (43:2), who opposed Jeremiah after the fall of Jerusalem (42:1–43:7). If Jaazaniah of 2 Kings 25:23 and Jeremiah 40:8 is the same Jezaniah, this Hoshaiah was a Maacathite.

HOSHAMA (hŏsh'ȧ-mȧ). A son of Jeconiah or Jehoiachin, captive king of Judah (1 Chron 3:18).

HOSHEA (hō-shē'ȧ, Heb. *hôshēa', salvation*). 1. Joshua's earlier name, changed by Moses (Num 13:8, 16 ASV, RSV, NIV; Deut 32:44 KJV).

2. The son of Azaziah and prince of Ephraim in David's reign (1 Chron 27:20).

3. A son of Elah; the last king of the northern kingdom (2 Kings 15:30; 17:1–6; 18:1–10).

4. A chief ruler under Nehemiah. With others he signed the covenant (Neh 10:23).

HOSPITALITY (Gr. *philoxenia, loving strangers*). Although the word occurs only a few times in the Bible (e.g., Rom 12:13; 16:23; 1 Tim 3:2; 5:10; Titus 1:8; 1 Peter 4:9; 3 John 8), the idea appears as early as Abraham (Gen 14:17–19). One might be entertaining angels unawares (Heb 13:2) as Abraham did (Gen 18), graciously inviting chance passers-by, washing their feet, preparing fresh meat and bread for them (18:1–8), and accompanying them when they left (18:16). Lot entertained the same angels (ch. 19). The extreme to which protection of a stranger might be carried is illustrated in Genesis 19:4–9. Rebekah showed kindness to Abraham's servant, giving him and his camels water and receiving various gold ornaments as a reward (24:15–28). Laban seconded her hospitality (24:29–31). Jacob fared well in the same household (29:1–14). Joseph's hospitality to his brothers had a purpose (43:15–34). As a refugee, Moses found welcome with Reuel, after helping his daughters water their flocks (Exod 2:15–22). Manoah entertained an angel (Judg 13:2–23), combining hospitality with a burnt offering. The plight of a stranger in a city where only one old man showed the ancient virtue of hospitality is told in Judges 19:11–28. Solomon entertained lavishly (1 Kings 4:22), as did Xerxes (Esth 1:2–8) and Vashti (1:9). Esther's dinners were private and purposeful (5:4–8; 7:1–10). Jezebel fed 850 false prophets (1 Kings 18:19). The common people continued to be hospitable (1 Sam 28:21–25; 2 Kings 4:8–10). Nehemiah regularly entertained 150 (Neh 5:17). The Law enjoined love and kindness to aliens (Lev 19:33–34). Jesus exercised hospitality when he fed five thousand (Matt 14:15–21; Mark 6:35–44; Luke 9:12–17; John 6:4–13), four thousand (Matt 15:32–38; Mark 8:1–9), and, after the Resurrection, his disciples (John 21:4–13). He received hospitality from grudging Pharisees (Luke 7:36–50; 14:1–14) and loving hospitality in a home at Bethany (Matt 21:17; 26:6–13; Mark 14:3–9; Luke 10:38–42; John 12:1–8). Jesus invited himself to Zacchaeus's house and was shown hospitality there (Luke 19:5–10). The owner of the Upper Room gladly gave Jesus and his disciples use of the room for the Last Supper (Matt 26:17–30; Mark 14:12–26; Luke 22:7–39; John 13:1–18:1). The disciples at Emmaus were hospitable to Jesus even when they did not recognize him (Luke 24:29–32). Jesus taught hospitality in Luke 10:30–37 by the parable of the Good Samaritan, and he told his disciples where they would and would not find it (Matt 10:11–15; Luke 10:5–12). The apostles were entertained and churches begun in hospitable homes (see especially Acts of the Apostles). Philemon and 2 and 3 John exhibit and exhort to hospitality. ER

HOST. In the OT: 1. Most often Hebrew *tsāvā'*, "army" (Gen 21:22, RSV "army," NIV "forces"); *angels* (Josh 5:14, RSV and NIV "army"; Dan 8:11); *heavenly bodies* (Deut 4:19, NIV "heavenly array"); *creation* (Gen 2:10); *God of hosts* (1 Sam 17:45, NIV "armies").

2. Hebrew *hayil*, "army" (Exod 14:4).

3. Twice Hebrew *hêl* (2 Kings 18:17, "army" in ASV, RSV, NIV; Obadiah 20, "army" in RSV and NIV).

4. Hebrew *mahanĕh*, more often translated "camp" (Exod 14:24; 32:27, RSV, NIV "army"). These references are only samples.

In the NT: 1. Greek *stratia*, "army" (Luke 2:13, "heavenly host"; Acts 7:42, "heavenly bodies" as objects of worship).

2. Greek *xenos*, "guest," also "host" (Rom 16:23).

3. Greek *pandocheus*, "one who receives all comers" (Luke 10:35, RSV and NIV "innkeeper"). ER

HOSTAGE (Heb. *ben-ta'ărûvôth, son of pledges*). Jehoash (Joash), king of Israel, took hostages after his victory over Judah, to ensure that King Amaziah would keep the peace (2 Chron 25:24).

HOTHAM, HOTHAN (hō'thăm, hō'thăn). 1. A son of Heber, of the family of Beriah. He was an Asherite (1 Chron 7:32). He is called "Helem" in 7:35.

2. An Aroerite, whose two sons Shama and Jeiel were among David's heroes (1 Chron 11:44).

HOTHIR (hō'thĕr). The thirteenth son of Heman, David's seer and singer. He was a Kohathite (1 Chron 25:4, 28).

HOUGH (See HAMSTRING)

HOUR. The word is found in the KJV OT only in Daniel as the translation of Aramaic *she'ā'*, "a brief time, a moment" (Dan 3:6, 15; 4:33; 5:5, where RSV, NIV have "immediately," except in 5:5, which has "suddenly"). In 4:19 ASV has "a while," NIV "a time," RSV "a long time." The day was divided into "degrees" (KJV, 2 Kings 20:9–11; Isa 38:8; "steps" in ASV, RSV, NIV) on the stairway of Ahaz. "Hour" is found in Ecclesiastes 9:12, "no man knows when his hour will come," a translation of Hebrew *'ēth*, "time."

In the NT, Greek *hōra*, "hour," is often used of a point of time (e.g., Matt 8:13). The day had twelve hours (John 11:9). The parable of the vineyard (Matt 20:1–16) names the third, sixth, ninth, and eleventh hours. As these are working hours, they obviously begin in the morning; this is the Palestinian mode of reckoning. So also in Acts 2:15, the third hour of the day; Acts 10:3, 9, the ninth and sixth hours; Acts 23:23, the third hour of the night. Elapsed time is indicated (Luke 22:39, an hour; Acts 5:7, three hours; Acts 19:34, two hours; Gal 2:5 RSV, NIV, a moment). Once Greek *arti*, "now," is translated "this hour" in KJV (1 Cor 8:7, NIV "still," ASV "now," RSV "hitherto"). In the accounts of the crucifixion, Mark 15:25 tells us that Jesus was crucified "the third hour." The supernatural darkness began at the sixth hour (Matt 27:45–46; Mark 15:33–34; Luke 23:44–46) and lasted until the ninth hour. John 19:14–16 says that it was about the sixth hour when Pilate brought Jesus out to the people and delivered him to be crucified. This raises the question whether John used the Palestinian reckoning of time. If so, he must have used "sixth hour" in a very general sense, for strictly speaking the sixth hour was noon. John, writing in Ephesus late in the first century, may well have adopted the then-current Roman reckoning that, like ours, numbers from midnight and from noon. John mentions the tenth hour (John 1:39), the sixth (4:6), and the seventh (4:52). In these cases 10 a.m., 6 p.m., and 7 p.m. respectively would be as appropriate as 4 p.m., noon, and 1 p.m. figured by Palestinian reckoning. References in Revelation—8:1 ("half an hour"); 9:15 ("this very hour"); 17:12; 18:10, 17, 19 ("one hour")—emphasize the brevity of a period of time. ER

HOUSE. In the OT it is most often Hebrew and Aramaic *bayith* ("a dwelling place"). It is used to refer to a "household," or "family" (Exod 2:1), the tabernacle (23:19; 34:26) or temple (1 Kings 5:3–7:1) as the house of God, and a temple of heathen gods (Judg 16:23–30; 1 Sam 31:9–10). It might be a nomad tent (Gen 14:13–14; cf. 18:1; 27:15) or a building (Gen 19:2–11) in a city. God contrasts tent with house in 2 Samuel 7:6. Jacob called a place outdoors marked by a stone "the house of God" (Gen 28:17–22). In

Psalm 83:12, KJV has "houses," ASV "habitations," RSV "pastures," NIV "pasturelands," for Hebrew *nā'âh.* In Job 1:3, Hebrew *'avudâh* ("service") is translated "household" in KJV and ASV, "servants" in RSV and NIV. In the NT, Greek *oikia* ("house") usually indicates a building; sometimes it refers to the inhabitants of a house (Matt 12:25; Mark 3:25; John 4:53; 1 Cor 16:15; Phil 4:22) or even to the human body (2 Cor 5:1). In Luke 2:49, the Greek words *tois tou patros mou* ("the [affairs] of my Father") are variously rendered: "my Father's affairs" (JB), "my Father's business" (KJV), and "my Father's house" (ASV, RSV, NIV). In 2 Corinthians 5:1 the first house (RSV, NIV "tent"; Greek "tent-house") is the physical body, the second house the resurrection body. The related Greek *oikos* also refers to a building (Matt 9:6–7, RSV, NIV "home"), but often to its inhabitants (Luke 19:9; Acts 11:14, RSV, NIV "household") or to descendants (Matt 10:6; Luke 1:33) or to the temple (Matt 12:4; 21:13; Mark 2:26; 11:17; Luke 6:4; 11:51; 19:46; John 2:16, 17; Acts 2:47, 49).

We read of no shelters in Eden, for probably none were needed in its mild climate; but Cain built a city (Gen 4:17), which could have been a tent-city or a cave-city. After the Flood, Nimrod is credited with the building of several cities (10:10–12), where archaeologists have uncovered the remains of early houses. In Mesopotamia burned bricks joined with bitumen were used in place of stone (11:3). Elaborate houses in Ur, of the period when Abraham lived there (11:31), have been excavated. He abandoned these luxurious surroundings to live in a tent (12:8) in the Land of Promise. Abraham found houses in Egypt (12:15), at least one for the pharaoh. When Lot separated from Abraham, at first Lot moved his tent to Sodom (13:12) but later lived in a house (19:2–11). Finally Lot took refuge in a cave (19:30). The house of Laban may well have been a tent (24:31–32, 29:13–14). When Joseph arrived in Egypt, there were houses there: Potiphar's (39:2–5), that of the captain of the guard in the prison (40:3), Joseph's own house (43:16–34; 44:14), and Pharaoh's (45:16). The law made provision in advance of the settlement in Canaan for the cleansing of a stone house in which there was leprosy (Lev 14:33–55). Israelite spies stayed in a house in Jericho (Josh 2:1) with a roof where stalks of flax were dried (2:6) and with a window (2:15); the house was built into the city wall (2:15).

After the conquest under Joshua, the Israelites came increasingly to live in houses in the cities and towns of Canaan; though some, like the Recabites (Jer 35:7, 10), continued to live in tents, and some took refuge in caves in times of uncertainty (1 Kings 19:9). House walls were often of rough stone as much as three feet (one m.) thick and often of unburned clay brick (Job 4:19), sometimes protected with a casing of stone slabs. In larger buildings the stones were squared, smoothed, and pointed. To enter the ordinary small house, from the street one first entered a forecourt, with a covered portion on one side.

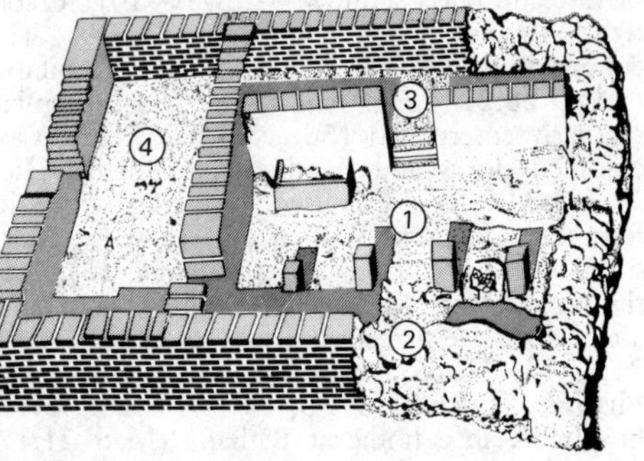

Reconstruction of a typical Israelite house, based on the excavations of Tell Qasila near Tel Aviv: (1) Central open courtyard, (2) and (3) kitchen and storerooms, and (4) living and sleeping rooms. Courtesy Carta, Jerusalem.

From the forecourt, doors opened into a living room, with two small bedchambers beyond. When sons married, additions were made as space permitted by using the court, complicating the design. Especially on a hilly site, a large boulder would be built into the corner to support the walls, the most necessary stone being called the cornerstone (Isa 28:16). The importance of dedicating a new house (in earliest times by sacrifices) was recognized by excusing a man from military duty until he had done so (Deut 20:5). The floor might be a leveled surface of stone, more often beaten clay. The rich often had a stone slab floor. Solomon's temple had a floor of cypress boards (1 Kings 6:15). For doors there were square openings in the wall with a stone or wood lintel, doorposts (Exod 12:22–23; 1 Kings 6:31), and a stone threshold. Doors might be of textiles, leather, or rushes, but wooden doors fastened by a bar were used early. Stone sill and head-sockets indicate pivot hinges, requiring sturdier construction of the door. A key is referred to as early as Judges 3:25. Locks (Song of Songs 5:5) may have been bolts. Hearths were provided, but no chimney, the smoke escaping through doors and windows. Braziers or firepots were also used (Jer 36:22). Windows were high, small openings with covers like the doors for protection; some had lattices. Roofs had beams with transverse rafters covered with brushwood and overlaid with mud mixed with chopped straw. They were flat and were beaten and rolled. The roof was used for worship (2 Kings 23:12; Jer 19:13; 32:29; Acts 10:9). Absalom pitched his tent on the roof for publicity (2 Sam 16:22). Three thousand Philistines used the roof of their temple as a grandstand (Judg 16:27), illustrating its strength, while its weakness was demonstrated when Samson pushed apart the middle pillars on which the structure depended. There were outside stairs leading to the roof of a house and its "upper chamber." In some cases the "upper room" may have been inside the house. In the living room a raised brick platform ran across one side of the room (in the Hellenistic period at least), sometimes with ducts to heat it, and on this the family spread their bedding by night or sat by day. In cold weather the cattle might be admitted to the lower part of the living room of a poor family.

Palaces were much more elaborate (1 Kings 7:1–12). There is a sharp contrast between the humble homes of the common people and the luxurious dwellings of kings and the very rich in Egypt, Mesopotamia, Palestine under the Hebrew monarchy and after, and in Greece and Rome of the Hellenistic period. A Christian community, many of whose members were slaves, would be familiar with the lavish contents of large houses (2 Tim 2:20). While Christians at first continued to worship in temple and synagogue, from the beginning they met also in private homes (Acts 1:13; 2:2, 46). Worship in homes was a well-established pattern in Paul's ministry (Rom 16:5; 1 Cor 16:19; Col 4:15; Philem 2). Special buildings for Christian churches do not appear in the NT. The family had been the religious unit from the beginning of creation; worship centered in the house, from tent to palace. Tabernacle and temple were "the house of God." In the NT the house where a Christian family lived was open to other Christian brothers and sisters to worship together; and when the temple was destroyed and the synagogue was closed to Christians, the church in the home became the sole refuge of the believer, until special buildings were erected. Thus the sanctifying influences of corporate worship were added to the human associations that made a house a home. ER

HUBBAH (hŭb'ȧ). Son of Shomer, an Asherite (1 Chron 7:34; KJV "Jehubbah").

HUKKOK (hŭk'ŏk). A border town of Naphtali, on the waters of Merom, west of Kinnereth and Capernaum at the northern end of the Sea of Galilee (Josh 19:34). Modern Yāqûq.

HUKOK (See HELKATH)

HUL (hŭl). The second son of Aram and grandson of Shem. A descendant of Noah (Gen 10:23). He is also called son of Shem (1 Chron 1:17).

HULDAH (hŭl'dȧ, Heb. *huldâh, weasel*). A prophetess in the reign of Josiah (2 Kings 22:14–20; 2 Chron 34:22–28). She was the wife of Shallum, keeper of the wardrobe, who lived in the second district of Jerusalem. When Hilkiah the priest found the Book of the Law in the temple, Josiah sent messengers to Huldah. She attested the genuineness of the book and prophesied ruin because of desertion of the Law. Her message, accepted as from God, greatly influenced the reforms carried out by Josiah.

HUMILITY (Heb. *'ănāwâh,* Gr. *tapeinophrosynē*). Humility and the related substantive and verb *humble,* translate several OT Hebrew words and the NT Greek *tapeinoō* family. The meaning shades off in various directions, but the central thought is freedom from pride—lowliness, meekness, modesty, mildness. There is a "false humility" (Col 2:18, 23) called "self-abasement" in RSV. God humbles people to bring them to obedience (Deut 8:2). To humble ourselves is a condition of God's favor (2 Chron 7:14) and his supreme requirement (Mic 6:8). God dwells with the humble (Isa 57:15). Humility is encouraged (Prov 15:33; 18:12; 22:4). To the Greeks humility was weak and despicable, but Jesus made it the cornerstone of character (Matt 5:3, 5; 18:4; 23:12; Luke 14:11; 18:14). Jesus by his humility drew people to himself (Matt 11:28–30; John 13:1–20; Rev 3:20). Paul emphasized the humility of Jesus (2 Cor 8:9; Phil 2:1–11); commanded us to be humble toward one another (Rom 12:10; 1 Cor 13:4–6; Phil 2:3–4), and spoke of himself as an example (Acts 20:19). Peter exhorted humility before the brethren and before God (1 Peter 5:5–6). The above and other passages show that humility is an effect of the action of God, circumstances, other people, ourselves, or of any or all of these on our lives. ER

HUMTAH (hŭm'tȧ). A town in the hill country of Judah near Hebron; unidentified (Josh 15:54).

HUNTER (See OCCUPATIONS AND PROFESSIONS)

HUPHAM (hū'făm). A son of Benjamin and founder of a tribal family known as the Huphamites (Num 26:39). Probably the same as Huppim in Genesis 46:21 and Huppites in 1 Chronicles 7:12, and as Huram in 1 Chronicles 8:5.

HUPPAH (hŭp'ȧ), a priest of the thirteenth course in David's time (1 Chron 24:13).

Ancient tomb on the Mount of Olives in Jerusalem, thought to be the tomb of Huldah, the prophetess from days of King Josiah (2 Kings 22:1–23:30). Courtesy Zev Radovan.

HUPPIM, HUPPITES (hŭp'ĭm, hŭp'īts, Heb. *huppîm, coast people*). Probably the same as Hupham, but the references leave his descent uncertain (Gen 46:21; 1 Chron 7:12, 15).

HUR (hûr, Heb. *hûr, whiteness*). 1. One who, with Aaron, held up Moses' hands during a battle against Amalek, bringing victory to Israel (Exod 17:10, 12). He was appointed magistrate while Moses was on the mountain (24:14).

2. Grandfather of Bezalel of the tribe of Judah, chief workman in the tabernacle (Exod 31:2; 35:30; 38:22; 2 Chron 1:5). According to 1 Chronicles 2:19–20, Caleb married Ephrath, who bore him Hur, grandfather of Bezalel. In verse 50, KJV and ASV say that Caleb the son of Hur was the firstborn of Ephrathah, but RSV and NIV divide the verse to remove the difficulty. In 1 Chronicles 4:1 Hur is named as a descendant of Judah, but in verse 4 he is called firstborn of Ephrathah, father of Bethlehem. Jewish tradition identifies nos. 1 and 2 as the same person and calls him the husband of Miriam, Moses' sister.

3. One of five Midianite kings killed with Balaam (Num 31:1–8). He was a leader of Midian and a prince of Sihon the Amorite king (Josh 13:21).

4. In KJV the father of one of twelve officers who supplied food for Solomon's household (1 Kings 4:8). ASV, RSV, NIV treat "son of" (Heb. *bēn*) as part of a proper name, Ben-hur.

5. Father of Rephaiah, who helped Nehemiah build the wall; ruler of half of Jerusalem (Neh 3:9).

HURAI (hū'rā-ī, hū'rī). One of David's heroes from the brooks of Gaash (1 Chron 11:32). He is also called Hiddai (2 Sam 23:30).

HURAM (hū'răm, Heb. *hûrām, noble-born*). 1. A Benjamite, son of Bela (1 Chron 8:5). See also HUPHAM.

2. The king of Tyre who aided Solomon (2 Chron 2:3, 11–12 in most versions). He is usually called Hiram (so NIV).

3. A Tyrian artificer sent to Solomon by Hiram king of Tyre (no. 2) (2 Chron 2:13–14; 4:11–16; called "Hiram" in most versions in 1 Kings 7:13–14, 40–45). His mother was a woman from the tribe of Dan who had married first into the tribe of Naphtali and then later a Tyrian man. "Of Huram, my father's" (KJV 2 Chron 2:13) and "Huram his father" (KJV 4:16) are also rendered "Huram-abi" (e.g., JB, NASB) and "my famed [honored, trusty] Huram (e.g., MLB, MOF).

HURI (hū'rī). The father of Abihail, a Gadite (1 Chron 5:14).

HURRIANS (See HORITE)

HUSBAND (See FAMILY; MARRIAGE)

HUSBANDMAN (See OCCUPATIONS AND PROFESSIONS)

HUSHAH (hū'shȧ). A son of Ezer, the son of Hur, a Judahite (1 Chron 4:4).

HUSHAI (hū'shī, hū'shā-ī). One of David's two leading men, an Arkite (2 Sam 15:32, 37; 16:16–18; 17:5–15; 1 Chron 27:33)—the friend and counselor of David who overthrew the counsels of Ahithophel. The Arkite clan occupied Ataroth, a border town of Ephraim (Josh 16:2, 7).

HUSHAM (hū'shăm). A king of Edom who succeeded Jobab. He came from the land of Teman (Gen 36:34–35; 1 Chron 1:45–46).

HUSHATHITE (hū'shăth-īt). The family name of Sibbecai, one of David's thirty heroes (2 Sam 21:18; 1 Chron 11:29; 20:4; 27:11). He is called Mebunnai in 2 Samuel 23:27.

HUSHIM, HUSHITES (hū'shĭm, hū'shīts). 1. The sons of Dan (Gen 46:23), called Shuham in Numbers 26:42.

2. The sons of Aher, a Benjamite (1 Chron 7:12); NIV "Hushites," KJV "Hushim."

3. One of the two wives of Shaharaim (1 Chron 8:8, 11).

HUSKS (See PLANTS)

HUZ (See UZ)

HUZZAB (hŭz'ăb, Heb. *hūtstsav*). It is disputed whether the word in Nahum 2:7 is to be taken as a noun or a verb. If a noun (KJV, RSV), it may be an epithet of Nineveh or of its queen. If a verb, it may be translated "it is decreed," as in ASV and NIV. Moffatt and the Jewish version have "the queen." Knox has "the warriors of Nineve(h)." Archaeology has as yet shed no light here.

HYACINTH (hī'ȧ-sĭnth, Gr. *hyakinthos*). The name of a color in ASV (Rev 9:17; RSV "sapphire," NIV "dark blue," KJV "jacinth").

HYENA (See ANIMALS)

HYMENAEUS (hī'mĕ-nē'ŭs, Gr. *Hymenaios, pertaining to Hymen,* the god of marriage). A professed Christian who had fallen into heresies, tried to shipwreck the faith of true believers, and was excommunicated by Paul (1 Tim 1:19–20; 2 Tim 2:16–18).

HYMN (See MUSIC AND MUSICAL INSTRUMENTS)

HYPOCRISY (hĭ-pŏk'rĭ-sē). From a Hebrew root *hnph,* "pollute," correctly translated "profane," "godless," "ungodly" in ASV, RSV, NIV (Job 8:13; 13:16; Ps 35:16; Prov 22:9; Isa 9:17; 10:6; 32:6; 33:14). The LXX used Greek *hypokrinomai,* "act a part in a play"; *hypokrisis,* "hypocrisy"; *hypokritēs,* "hypocrite," which occur in the NT and are taken over in English (Matt 6:2, 5, 16; 7:5; 23:27–28; Mark 7:6; 12:15; Luke 12:1,

56; 13:15). In Galatians 2:13 KJV, ASV have "dissimulated . . . dissimulation," RSV "acted insincerely . . . insincerity," but NIV retains the double use of "hypocrisy." The Greek word *anypokritos,* "without hypocrisy" (Rom 12:9; 2 Cor 6:6; 1 Tim 1:5; 2 Tim 1:5; 1 Peter 1:22), is usually rendered "sincere," "genuine" in RSV and NIV. In Luke 20:20 the verb is translated "feign themselves" (NIV "pretended"). The thought in the NT lies close to the literal meaning "play-acting," with special reference to religion: "having a form of godliness, but denying its power" (2 Tim 3:5), as Matthew 6:1–18 and 23:13–36 plainly show.

HYSSOP (See PLANTS)

I

IBEX (See ANIMALS)

IBHAR (ĭb'hàr, Heb. *yivhār, he chooses*). One of David's sons, born at Jerusalem (2 Sam 5:15; 1 Chron 14:5).

IBIS (See BIRDS)

IBLEAM (ĭb'lē-ăm, Heb. *yivle'ām*). A town in the territory of Issachar, given to the tribe of Manasseh (Josh 17:11). The inhabitants, however, were not driven out and continued to live in the land (Judg 1:27). Ahaziah, king of Judah, was killed near there when he fled from Jehu (2 Kings 9:27). Zechariah, king of Israel, was killed there (15:10, see NIV footnote). It is generally identified with Bileam, a town of Manasseh given to the Levites (1 Chron 6:70). Ruins of the town remain.

IBNEIAH (ĭb-nī'yà, Heb. *yivneyâh, Jehovah builds*). A son of Jeroham, a chief man in the tribe of Benjamin in the first settlement in Jerusalem (1 Chron 9:8).

IBNIJAH (ĭb-nī'jà, Heb. *yivnîyâh, Jehovah builds up*). A Benjamite, father of Reuel (1 Chron 9:8).

IBRI (ĭb'rī, Heb. *'ivrî, a Hebrew*). A Merarite Levite, son of Jaaziah (1 Chron 24:27).

IBSAM (ĭb'săm, Heb. *yivsām, fragrant*). A descendant of Issachar, family of Tola (1 Chron 7:2, KJV Jibsam).

IBZAN (ĭb'zăn, Heb. *'ivtsān*). The tenth judge of Israel, who ruled for seven years. He was a native of Bethlehem (whether of Judah or Zebulun is not stated). He had thirty sons and thirty daughters (Judg 12:8–10).

ICHABOD (ĭk'à-bŏd, Heb. *'îkhāvôdh, inglorious*). Son of Phinehas, Eli's son who was killed by the Philistines at the battle of Aphek when the ark was taken. Ichabod was born after his father's death and was given this name by his mother on her deathbed because, she said, "The glory has departed from Israel" (1 Sam 4:19–22). His nephew Ahijah was one of those who remained with Saul and his men at Gibeah just before Jonathan attacked the Philistines (14:2ff.).

ICONIUM (ī-cō'nĭ-ŭm, Gr. *Ikonion*). A city of Asia Minor that Paul and Barnabas visited on Paul's first missionary journey after they had been expelled from Antioch in Pisidia, which lay to the west. They revisited the city on their return journey to Antioch (Acts 13:51ff.). On his second missionary journey Paul with Silas stopped off at Iconium to read the letter sent out by the Jerusalem Council on the Judaizing question, and at nearby Lystra he took young Timothy with him as his associate (16:1–5). In 2 Timothy 3:11 Paul alludes to persecutions endured by him at Antioch, Iconium, and Lystra.

Modern Konya, site of Iconium in Asia Minor, visited by Paul on his first and second missionary journeys. Courtesy Dan Bahat.

In the first century it was one of the chief cities in the southern part of the Roman province of Galatia. It was a city of immemorial antiquity and was situated near the western end of a vast, level plain, with mountains a few miles toward the west, from which streams flowed that made it a veritable oasis. Two important trade routes passed through it, and it was on the road leading to Ephesus and Rome. Its geographical position makes it the natural capital of Lycaonia. Archaeological inscriptions found there in A.D. 1910 show that the Phrygian language was spoken there for two centuries after the time of Paul, though at neighboring Lystra the natives spoke "the Lycaonian language" (Acts 14:11). Hadrian made the city a Roman colony. The city has had a continuing history and is now known as Konia, still the main trading center of the Lycaonian plain.

IDALAH (ĭd'à-lă). A town assigned to the tribe of Zebulun (Josh 19:15). It is usually identified with Khirbet el-Hawarah, one mile (one and one-half km.) SW of Bethlehem.

IDBASH (ĭd'băsh, Heb. *yidbāsh, honey-sweet*). A man of Judah, one of the sons of the father of Etam (1 Chron 4:3).

IDDO (ĭd'ō). The English equivalent of several Jewish names:

1. Hebrew *yiddô.* (a) Son of Zechariah and a captain under David of the half-tribe of Manasseh east of the Jordan (1 Chron 27:21). (b) One who had taken a foreign wife at the time of Ezra (Ezra 10:43 ASV; NIV "Jaddai").

2. Hebrew *'iddô.* The head of a community of temple servants (KJV Nethinim) at Casiphia; they provided Ezra with Levites and temple servants (Ezra 8:17).

3. Hebrew *yiddô, ye'dô, ye'dî.* (a) A Levite descended from Gershom; ancestor of Asaph (1 Chron 6:21). (b) A seer and prophet who wrote a book that was the chronicler's source for the reigns of Solomon and Jeroboam (2 Chron 9:29); he also wrote books about the deeds of Rehoboam (12:15) and of King Abijah (13:22). (c) Father of Ahinadab, a district governor of Solomon at Mahanaim in Gilead (1 Kings 4:14). (d) Grandfather of the prophet Zechariah (Zech 1:1, 7; Ezra 5:1; 6:14).

IDOLATRY (ī-dŏl'à-trē, Gr. *eidōlolatria*). Idolatry in ancient times included two forms of departure from the true religion: the worship of false gods, whether by means of images or otherwise; and the worship of the Lord by means of images. All the nations surrounding ancient Israel were idolatrous, though their idolatry assumed different forms. The early Semites of Mesopotamia worshiped mountains, springs, trees, and blocks of stone—things in which the deity was supposed to be in some sense incarnate. A typical example of such wooden representations is the sacred pole or Asherah pole. This was the idol of Gideon's clan; Gideon destroyed it (Judg 6:25–32). The religion of the Egyptians centered mostly about the veneration of the sun and of the Nile as sources of life. They also had a number of sacred animals: the bull, cow, cat, baboon, crocodile, etc. Some of the deities were represented with human bodies and animal heads. Among the Canaanites, religion took on a very barbarous character. The chief gods were personifications of life and fertility. The gods had no moral character whatsoever, and worship of them carried with it demoralizing practices, including child sacrifice, prostitution, and snake worship. Human and animal images of the deities were worshiped. When the Israelites conquered the land they were commanded to destroy these idols (Exod 23:24; 34:13; Num 33:52; Deut 7:5).

The word "idolatry" has no exact Hebrew equivalent. There are, however, a number of Hebrew words that are translated "idol." They all give expression to the loathing, contempt, and dread excited in godly men by idolatry. The terms are as follows: (1) *Aven,* "emptiness, nothingness"; that is, a vain, false, wicked thing (Isa 66:3). (2) *Emah,* "an object of horror or terror," referring either to the hideousness of the idols or the shameful character of their worship (Jer 50:38). (3) *El,* the name of the supreme god of Canaan; used also as a neutral expression for any divinity (Isa 57:5). (4) *Elil,* "a thing of naught, a nonentity," resembling *aven* in meaning (Lev 19:4; 26:1; 1 Chron 16:26). (5) *Miphletseth,* "a fright, a horror" (1 Kings 15:12; 2 Chron 15:16). (6) *Semel,* "a likeness, semblance" (2 Chron 33:7, 15). (7) *Atsabh*, "a cause of grief" (1 Sam 31:9; 1 Chron 10:9). (8) *Etseb* "a cause of grief" (Jer 22:28 KJV). (9) *Otseb* "a cause of grief" (Isa 48:5). (10) *Tsir,* "a form," and hence an idol (45:16). Besides the above words there are a number of others that are not translated "idol" but refer to it, expressing the degradation associated with idolatry: *bosheth,* "shameful thing," applied to Baal and referring to the obscenity of his worship (Jer 11:13; Hos 9:10); *gillulim,* a term of contempt meaning "shapeless, dungy things" (Ezek 4:2; Zeph 1:17); and *shikkuts,* "filth," referring especially to the obscene rites associated with idolatry (Ezek 37:23; Nah 3:6). Theologically, idolaters thought of their gods as spiritual beings (or forces) of cosmic significance and, theoretically, to them the idol was as it were a focal point for worship. The OT insists, however, that the heathen worship idols and nothing more (cf. Ps 115:2–8; Isa 44:6–20). This is a straightforward contradiction of the theology held by the pagans and a demonstration of the rigorous monotheism of the OT.

Limestone stele from Egypt, c. 1350–1200 B.C., of the Syrian Goddess Qadesh standing on a lion, flanked by Min and Resheph. On lower part, three figures present offerings to the goddess Anat. Reproduced by courtesy of the Trustees of the British Museum.

Stele, c. 1900–1750 B.C., found in a sanctuary west of the great temple at Ugarit (Ras Shamra), picturing Baal, the Canaanite god of fertility and storms, with right hand uplifted and in his left hand a lance with a top stylized as forked lightning. Courtesy Réunion des Musées Nationaux.

The first clear case of idolatry in the Bible is the account of Rachel stealing her father's teraphim, which were images of household gods (Gen 31:19). Such images were used in Babylonia. Without Jacob's knowledge, Rachel stole them from Laban and carried them with her to Canaan. During their long sojourn in Egypt, the Israelites defiled themselves with the idols of the land (Josh 24:14; Ezek 20:7). Moses defied these gods by attacking their symbols in the plagues of Egypt (Num 33:4). In spite of the miracles of their redemption from Egypt, the Israelites insisted on having some visible shape with which to worship God; and at Sinai, while Moses was absent, they persuaded Aaron to make them a golden calf, an emblem of the productive power of nature with which they had become familiar in Egypt. The second commandment, forbidding people to make and bow down to images of any kind, was directed against idolatry (Exod 20:4–5; Deut 5:8–9). This sin seems to have been shunned until the period of the judges, when the nation was caught up in it again.

The whole of Judges tells of successive apostasies, judgments, and repentances. The narrative concerning Micah (Judg 17–18) is an illustration of how idolatry was often combined with outward worship of God. It is significant that Jonathan, a Levite and a grandson of Moses, assumed the office of priest to the images of Micah and that later he allowed himself to be persuaded by some Danites, who had stolen Micah's idol, to go with them as the priest of their tribe. He became the first of a line of priests to officiate at the shrine of the stolen idols all the time that the tabernacle was at Shiloh.

The prophet Samuel persuaded the people to repent of their sin and to renounce idolatry; but in Solomon's reign the king himself made compromises that affected disastrously the whole future of the kingdom. Solomon's wives brought their own heathen gods with them and openly worshiped them. Rehoboam, Solomon's son by an Ammonite mother, continued the worst features of his father's idolatry (1 Kings 14:22–24). Jeroboam, first king of the northern kingdom, effected a great and permanent schism in the religion of Israel when he erected golden calves at Bethel and at Dan and had his people worship there instead of in Jerusalem. The kings who followed Jeroboam in the northern kingdom differed little from him. One of them, Ahab, to please his Zidonian queen Jezebel, built a temple and an altar to Baal in Samaria (16:31–33), while she put to death as many prophets of the Lord as she could find (18:4–13). Baal worship came to be identified with the kingdom of Israel, and no king ever rose up against it.

Things went somewhat better in the southern kingdom. Hezekiah restored the temple services, which had been abandoned during his father's reign, but the change was only outward (2 Chron 28–29; Isa 29:13). Not long before the destruction of Jerusalem by Babylonia, Josiah made a final effort to bring about a purer worship, but it did not last (2 Chron 34). Not even the Captivity cured the Jews of their idolatrous tendencies. When Ezra went to Jerusalem from Babylon, he found to his dismay that many Jews had married foreign wives and that the land was filled with abominations (Ezra 9:11). More than two hundred years later, when Antiochus Epiphanes tried to eradicate Judaism and Hellenize the Jews, many of them obeyed his command to offer sacrifices to idols, although his action led to the Maccabean war.

God of war with shield and weapon, identified with the Canaanite god "Reshef" or "Baal." Bronze statuette from Megiddo, c. fourteenth century B.C. Courtesy Israel Department of Antiquities and Museums. Exhibited and photographed by Israel Museum, Jerusalem.

In the ritual of idol worship the chief elements were: offering burnt sacrifices (2 Kings 5:17), burning incense in honor of the idol (1 Kings 11:8), pouring out libations (Isa 57:6), presenting tithes and the firstfruits of the land (Hos 2:8), kissing the idol (1 Kings 19:18), stretching out the hands to it in adoration, prostrating oneself before it, and sometimes cutting oneself with knives (18:26, 28). Some of these practices were analogous to the worship of the Lord.

For an Israelite, idolatry was the most heinous of crimes. In the OT the relation between God and his covenant people is often represented as a marriage bond (Isa 54:5; Jer 3:14), and the worship of false gods was regarded as religious harlotry. The penalty was death (Exod 22:20). To attempt to seduce others to false worship was a crime of equal enormity (Deut 13:6–10). The God of Israel was a jealous God who brooked no rivals.

In the NT, references to idolatry are understandably few. The Maccabean war resulted in the Jews becoming fanatically opposed to the crass idolatry of OT times. The Jews were never again tempted to worship images or gods other than the Lord. Jesus, however, warned that to make possessions central in life is also idolatry, and said, "You cannot serve both God and Money" (Matt 6:24). Paul, in Romans 1:18–25, teaches that idolatry is not the first stage of religion, from which man by an evolutionary process emerges to monotheism, but it is the result of deliberate religious apostasy. When man sins against the light of nature and refuses to worship the Creator revealed by nature, God as a punishment withdraws the light, and man then descends into the shameful absurdities of idolatry. Christians in apostolic times, many of whom were converted from heathenism, are repeatedly warned in the letters of the NT to be on their guard against idolatry (e.g., 1 Cor 5:10; Gal 5:20). The OT conception of idolatry is widened to include anything that leads to the dethronement of God from the heart, as, for example, covetousness (Eph 5:5; Col 3:5).

A special problem arose for Christians in connection with meat offered to idols (Acts 15:29; 1 Cor 8–10). Some of the meat sold in butcher shops had been bought from heathen temples. Should a Christian make careful inquiry about the meat he purchased, and would he countenance or indirectly support idolatry if he bought meat that had been offered to an idol? Or should a Christian invited to dinner by a friend ask before accepting the invitation whether he would be eating meat that had been offered to an idol? Many Christians had real qualms about eating such meat, while others, feeling themselves "strong" spiritually, were convinced that there was no harm in it at all. Paul does not take sides in

Bronze stand (c. 10 cm. high) found at Megiddo and dating from Iron Age I (c. 1200–1000 B.C.), with square base and round top. On each side a figure is shown presenting a gift to, or standing in adoration before, a seated deity. Courtesy Israel Department of Antiquities and Museums.

the matter, but he urges against the latter that they should not be careless, for even though idols are nothing, they still are a tangible expression of demons who are back of them; and, moreover, Christians should never insist on their "rights," if such insistence will cause the weak to stumble. They should be governed by the law of love. In the last book of the Bible the apostle John predicts a time of idolatrous apostasy in the last days, when the Beast and his image will be accorded divine honors (Rev 9:20; 13:14).

Bibliography: W. R. Smith, *The Religion of the Semites,* 1927; E. Bevan, *Holy Images,* 1940; J. B. Payne, *The Theology of the Older Testament,* 1962; T. C. Vriezen, *The Religion of Ancient Israel,* 1963; H. Ringgren, *Israelite Religion,* 1966; J. M. Sasson, *The Worship of the Golden Calf,* 1973. SB

IDUMEA (ĭd'ū-mē̇ȧ, Gr. *pertaining to Edom*). The name used by the Greeks and Romans for the country of Edom (Mark 3:8). See also EDOM.

IEZER (See ABIEZER)

IGAL (ī'găl, Heb. *yigh'āl, God redeems*). 1. One of the twelve spies sent by Moses to search out the land of Canaan (Num 13:7).

2. One of David's heroes, the son of Nathan (2 Sam 23:36).

3. A son of Shemaiah, a descendant of King Jehoiachin (1 Chron 3:22).

IGDALIAH (ĭg'dȧ-lī'ȧ, Heb. *yighdalyāhû, Jehovah is great*). Father of the prophet Hanan (Jer 35:4).

IIM (See IYIM)

IJE-ABARIM (See IYE ABARIM)

IJON (ī'jŏn, Heb. *'iyôn, a ruin*). A town in the territory of Naphtali. It was captured by Ben-Hadad, king of Syria, at the instigation of Asa (1 Kings 15:20; 2 Chron 16:4). Its inhabitants were subsequently carried into captivity by Tiglath-Pileser in the reign of Pekah (2 Kings 15:29). The site is located about eight miles (thirteen km.) NW of Banias.

IKKESH (ĭk'ĕsh, Heb. *'iqqēsh, crooked*). A man from Tekoa, father of Ira, one of David's heroes (2 Sam 23:26; 1 Chron 11:28).

ILAI (ī'lā-ī, Heb. *'îlay*). One of David's mighty men (1 Chron 11:29); called Zalmon in 2 Samuel 23:28.

ILLYRICUM (ĭl-ĭr'ĭ-kŭm, Gr. *Illyrikon*). A province of the Roman Empire, bounded on the north by Pannonia, on the east by Moesia, on the south by Macedonia, and on the west by the Adriatic Sea. The Alps run through it. The inhabitants, wild mountaineers and pirates, were conquered by the Romans in the third century B.C. In Romans 15:19 Paul, emphasizing the extent of his missionary activities, says that "from Jerusalem all the way around to Illyricum, I have fully proclaimed the gospel of Christ." In this verse Illyricum probably means the Roman province, not the much wider area the name sometimes included. "To Illyricum" must mean up to the borders of Illyricum, though the preposition "to" may be either inclusive or exclusive. Paul's preaching tour to the Illyrian frontier must be assigned to his third missionary journey, as his movements on his first visit to Macedonia are too carefully recorded to allow for a trip to the borders of Illyricum.

IMAGE, IMAGE WORSHIP (See IDOLATRY)

IMAGE OF GOD. Two fundamental truths about man taught in Scripture are that he is created by God and that God made him in his own image. Man came into being as the result of special deliberation on the part of God. He is God's creature, and there is therefore an infinite qualitative difference between God and man; but man has been made like God in a way that the rest of creation has not. The passages in which it is expressly stated that man is made in God's image are Genesis 1:26–27; 5:1, 3; 9:6; 1 Corinthians 11:7; Ephesians 4:24; Colossians 3:10; and James 3:9. Psalm 8 should be added to these, although the phrase "image of God" is not used, for the creation narrative as it relates to man is given here in poetic form. Another passage where the idea is not directly stated but is implied is Acts 17:22–31—Paul's address on Mars Hill. The words "image" and "likeness," used together in Genesis 1:26–27, do not differ essentially in meaning, but strengthen the idea that man uniquely reflects God. They are, moreover, used interchangeably elsewhere. The Scriptures do not define precisely the nature of the image of God in man, and we should be careful not to single out any individual aspect or attribute of man as if it were in a special sense the "image." It is rather man in his entirety that is to be thought of as in the image of God. The primary meaning of the words "image" and "likeness" as shown by their use throughout the OT refers to outward, visible form (e.g., 1 Sam 6:5; 2 Kings 16:10), an actual copy.

Throughout the Bible the Lord manifests himself in human form—so much so that he is often at first simply described as "a man" (e.g., Judg 13:9–10). Often this is described as an accommodation, the Lord graciously taking the form that will make it easiest for us to understand him and communicate with him. God is spirit (Isa 31:3; John 4:24) and therefore essentially invisible and, though visible form is not part of the divine nature, yet there is an outward form that perfectly suits the invisible being of God. This is the form he takes when he wills to reveal himself visibly, and in this form he created man. The human body, therefore, has its own inalienable dignity and worth.

As we proceed through the opening chapters of Genesis, we see that there are other human distinctives that are specially mentioned. The union of the man and the woman in marriage (Gen 5:1ff.) is directly related to the image of God, a unity of two different but matching beings that constituted God's image. Likewise, when the Creator gives to the man and the woman their joint "dominion," this too is related to possession of the image of God (1:27–28). Archaeologists say that ancient kings set up statues of themselves (cf. 1 Sam 15:12) to mark areas in which their authority prevailed: so man is God's viceregent on earth. Furthermore, we note that a clear distinction is drawn between man and the rest of the animal creation in that God's command to be fruitful is *imposed* on the beasts (Gen 1:22, ". . . and said"), whereas the same command is *addressed* to man (1:28, ". . . and said to them"). This observation opens to us the unique spiritual nature of man: the supreme and unique creature with whom the Creator holds communion. In Genesis 2:15–17 the special moral nature of man is brought out. In contrast with the instinctive life of the beasts, man has been so created that he must order his life in terms of stated moral ends and in the light of the foreseeable good. Finally, man is seen in contrast with the beasts in terms of his rationality (2:19–20). Man has the capacity to discern both similarity and difference as he reviews his world, to frame definitions (give names) and to bring a variety of phenomena into categories and order. Here in essence is the work of both scientist and philosopher. In these six areas—physical, governmental, matrimonial, spiritual, moral, and intellectual—there is a summation of the nature of man and a view of this distinctive creature who alone was made in the image of God.

SB and JAM

IMLAH (ĭm'là, Heb. *yimlâh, fullness*). The father of Micaiah, a prophet of the Lord in the days of Ahab (1 Kings 22:8–9; 2 Chron 18:7–8).

IMMANUEL (ĭ-măn'ū-ĕl, Heb. *'immānû'ēl, God is with us*). The name of a child (occurring three times in the Bible—Isa 7:14; 8:8; Matt 1:23) whose birth was foretold by Isaiah and who was to be a sign to Ahaz during the Syro-Ephraimitic war (Isa 7). At this time, 735 B.C., Judah was threatened by the allied forces of Syria and Israel. They were trying to compel Judah to form an alliance with them against Assyria, whose king, Tiglath-Pileser, was attempting to bring the whole of Western Asia under his sway. The prophet directed Ahaz to remain confident and calm in the Lord and not to seek aid from Tiglath-Pileser. To overcome the king's incredulity, he offered him a sign of anything in heaven or earth; but when the king evasively refused the offer, Isaiah bitterly chided him for his lack of faith and gave him a sign, the sign of "Immanuel."

Isaiah's words have led to much controversy and have been variously interpreted, chiefly because of the indefinite terms of the prediction and the fact that there is no record of their fulfillment in any contemporary event.

1. The traditional Christian interpretation is that the emphasis should be laid on the virgin birth of our Immanuel, Jesus Christ, as Matthew does (Matt 1:22–23). See VIRGIN BIRTH.

2. Another explanation is that the event of the birth of the child is intended as a sign to Ahaz and nothing more. At the time of Judah's deliverance from Syria and Ephraim, some young mothers who give birth to sons will spontaneously name them "Immanuel." Children bearing this name will be a sign to Ahaz of the truth of Isaiah's words concerning deliverance and judgment.

3. A third view, somewhat similar to the preceding one, is that Isaiah has a certain child in mind, the *almah* being his own wife or one of Ahaz's wives or perhaps someone else. Before the child has emerged from infancy, Syria and Ephraim will be no more (Isa 7:16); and later in his life Judah will be a country fit only for the pastoral life (7:15).

4. There are semimessianic interpretations that apply the prophecy to a child of Isaiah's time and also to Jesus Christ.

5. Perhaps the most widely held view among Evangelicals is that Isaiah has in mind Israel's Messiah. When the prophet learns of the king's cowardice, God for the first time gives to him a revelation of the true King, who would share the poverty and affliction of his people and whose character and work would entitle him to the great names of Isaiah 9:6. In this interpretation the essential fact is that in the coming of Immanuel people will recognize the truth of the prophet's words. He would be Israel's deliverer, and the government would rest on his shoulders (9:6). The messianic idea was prevalent in Judah at this time (e.g., 2 Sam 7:12; Mic 5:3). SB

IMMER (ĭm'ĕr, Heb. *'immēr*). 1. The ancestral head of the sixteenth course of priests. He lived in David's time (1 Chron 24:14). Descendants of his are mentioned in Ezra 2:37; 10:20; Nehemiah 3:29; 7:40; 11:13.

2. A priest in Jeremiah's time; he was the father of Pashhur (Jer 20:1). It is possible that he was a descendant of the Immer mentioned in no. 1.

3. A place in Babylonia, the home of a priestly family (Ezra 2:59)

IMMORTALITY (See ESCHATOLOGY)

IMMUTABILITY (i-mū-tà-bĭl'ĭ-tē). The perfection of God by which he is devoid of all change in essence, attributes, consciousness, will, and promises. No change is possible in God, because all change must be to better or worse, and God is absolute perfection. No cause for change in God exists, either in himself or outside of him. The immutability of God is clearly taught in Scripture (Mal 3:6; Ps 102:26; James 1:17) and must not be confused with immobility, as if there were no movement in God. Immutability is consistent with constant activity and perfect freedom. God creates, performs miracles, sustains the universe, etc. When the Scriptures speak of his repenting, as in Jonah 3:10, one should remember that this is only an anthropomorphic way of speaking. God adapts his treatment of people to the variation of their actions and characters. When the righteous do wickedly, his holiness requires that his treatment of them must change.

IMNA (ĭm′nȧ, Heb. *yimnā'*, *He [God] keeps off*, i.e., *defends*). The ancestral head of a family of Asher (1 Chron 7:35).

IMNAH (ĭm′nȧ, Heb. *yimnâh, right hand,* or, *good fortune*). 1. Son of Asher and founder of a tribal family (Gen 46:17; Num 26:44; 1 Chron 7:30).

2. A Levite, father of Kore, in the reign of Hezekiah (2 Chron 31:14).

IMPRECATORY PSALMS. A number of OT psalms, especially Psalms 2, 37, 69, 79, 109, 139, and 143, contain expressions of an apparent vengeful attitude toward enemies. For some people, these expressions constitute one of the "moral difficulties" of the OT. We must note, however: (1) Imprecations are not confined to the OT, and, therefore, insofar as they constitute a moral problem, the problem pervades the Bible as a whole (cf. Luke 11:37–52; Gal 1:8ff.; Rev 6:10; 18:20; 19:1–6). We must be prepared to think, then, that what we find here is not a reprehensibly low morality but an aspect of the biblical view of the conflict between good and evil. (2) Many if not all of the imprecatory psalms contain (as well as the imprecation) theological and moral sentiments that we should wish to attain (e.g., Ps 139). We can hardly, therefore, dismiss these psalms under some blanket condemnation as "OT morality." (3) In fact, OT morality stoutly opposed a hostile and vindictive response to opponents (e.g., Lev 19:14–18). (4) All the imprecatory psalms except Psalm 137 are prayers. They are addressed to God about opponents, and there is no suggestion in any of them that the psalmist either said any of these things to his adversary or ever intended to take vengeance into his own hands. Even if, therefore, it should be decided that these are reprehensible as prayers, the way of the psalmist is to be preferred to the modern practice of killing, maiming, bombing, and destroying those whom we think are our enemies. (5) The imprecatory psalms are full of longing for the vindication of the Lord's good name. Over and over, the psalmist's desire is not personal relief but that the Lord should be seen in his goodness and holiness (e.g., Ps 58:11; 83:16–18). (6) Many of the actual imprecations do no more than ask God to do what he has at any rate said that he will do in such situations (e.g., 5:10; 54:5; 79:6–7). (7) The Bible teaches that there is a "pure anger." The fact that we do not feel it and cannot express it does not mean that God's people have never risen to such heights of holiness. Our problem may well be, also, that we have so allowed our sense of moral outrage to atrophy that we are incapable of identifying with a pure wrath. (8) The one imprecation that is not contained in a prayer is Psalm 137:8, and here the Bible translators continue to choose English renderings that in fact themselves create the problem (cf. NIV "happy"). The word concerned (*ashre*) can mean any of three things: (a) "blessed," i.e., under God's approval and blessing; (b) "happy," i.e., personally fulfilled and enjoying well-being; and (c) "right," i.e., matching exactly the moral norms that operate in such a situation. Psalm 137:8 would better read, "How right he is . . . ." The psalmist himself will not do it, for that would be an act of revenge, which the OT forbids, but he recognizes that in the outworking of moral providence this is what will happen. He does not rejoice in it but bows before its justice. JAM

IMPUTE (Heb. *hāshav*, Gr. *logizomai*). A word meaning to attribute something to another person, to reckon something to another's account. This sometimes takes place in a judicial manner, so that the thing imputed becomes grounds for reward or punishment. In some versions the Hebrew and Greek words are also translated "to account, to count, to esteem, to reckon, to think." The doctrine of imputation is mentioned throughout Scripture (Lev 7:18; 17:4; 2 Sam 19:19; Ps 32:2; Rom 4:3–25; 5:13; 2 Cor 5:19; Gal 3:6; James 2:23). It underlies the Scripture doctrines of original sin, atonement, and justification.

1. Imputation of Adam's sin to his posterity. The record of the Fall (Gen 2–3), taken in connection with the subsequent history of the human race as recorded in the rest of the OT, implies that Adam's sin not only affected but was imputed to his posterity. This doctrine is more fully developed in the NT, especially in Romans 5:12–21, where Paul shows that it was by Adam's sin that death and sin entered the world and passed to all men. All men were condemned and made sinners in Adam.

2. Imputation of the sin of man to Christ. This is not expressly stated in the Bible but is implied in those passages that affirm that Christ bore our sins and died in our place. Isaiah 53 teaches that the Servant of the Lord "took up our infirmities," and God laid on him the iniquity of us all. Peter had this passage in mind when he wrote that Christ "himself bore our sins in his body on the tree" (1 Peter 2:24). The same thought is expressed in 2 Corinthians 5:21 and in Galatians 3:13. This truth is basic to the doctrine of the atonement.

3. Imputation of Christ's righteousness to the believer. This is the basis of Paul's doctrine of justification, a judicial act of God by which he declares righteous, on the ground of Christ's expiatory work and imputed righteousness, those who put their faith in Christ as their Savior. The NT stresses that justification is absolutely free and unmerited so far as the sinner is concerned (Rom 3:24; 5:15; Gal 5:4; Titus 3:7). The merits of Christ's suffering and obedience are imputed to the sinner, and from then on he is viewed as just in God's sight. SB

IMRAH (ĭm′rȧ, Heb. *yimrâh, He [God] resists*). A

descendant of Asher; son of Zophah (1 Chron 7:36).

IMRI (îm'rī, Heb. *'imrî,* contraction of *Amariah*). 1. A man of Judah, son of Bani (1 Chron 9:4).

2. The father of Zaccur, who helped in the rebuilding of the wall of Jerusalem after the Captivity (Neh 3:2).

INCARNATION. The doctrine of the Incarnation is taught or assumed throughout the Bible and comes to explicit statement in such passages as John 1:14, "The Word became flesh and made his dwelling among us" (cf. 1 Tim 3:16; Rom 8:3). In NT usage "flesh" means "human nature." "Incarnation" is from the Latin meaning "becoming flesh," that is, "becoming human." The doctrine of the Incarnation teaches that the eternal Son of God (see TRINITY) became human, and that he did so without in any manner or degree diminishing his divine nature. A somewhat detailed statement of the Incarnation is found in Philippians 2:5–11. Christ Jesus, "remaining" (*hyparchōn*) in the "form" of God, i.e., with all the essential attributes of God, took the "form" of a servant and died on the cross.

The Virgin Birth is necessary for our understanding of the Incarnation. In the process of ordinary birth, a new personality begins. Jesus Christ did not begin to be when he was born. He is the eternal Son. The Virgin Birth was a miracle, wrought by the Holy Spirit, whereby the eternal Son of God "became flesh," i.e., took to himself a genuine human nature in addition to his eternal divine nature. It was a *virgin* birth, a miracle. The Holy Spirit has never been thought of as the father of Jesus. Jesus was not half man and half god like the Greek mythological heroes. He was fully God, the Second Person of the Trinity. "In Christ all the fullness of the Deity lives in bodily form" (Col 2:9). At the same time he became genuinely a man. To deny his genuine humanity is "the spirit of the antichrist" (1 John 4:2–3).

The biblical data on the Incarnation came to permanent doctrinal formulation at the council of Chalcedon, A.D. 451. That council declared that Christ was "born of the virgin Mary" and is "to be acknowledged in two natures, inconfusedly, unchangeably, indivisibly, inseparably . . . the property of each nature being preserved, and concurring in one Person. . . ." This doctrine is concisely stated in the Westminster Shorter Catechism, Question 21. "The only Redeemer of God's elect is the Lord Jesus Christ, who, being the eternal Son of God, became man, and so was, and continueth to be, God and man, in two distinct natures and one Person for ever."

The creed of Chalcedon was the culmination of more than three centuries of discussion in which the main stream of Christian thought eliminated a variety of false interpretations as follows: (1) The Gnostic Docetae, condemned in 1 John 4:2–3, denied the genuine humanity of Jesus and taught that he only appeared to suffer. (2) The Ebionites in the second century denied his deity. (3) The Arians, condemned at Nicea in A.D. 325, denied that his divine nature was equal with the Father's. (4) The Apollinarians, condemned at Constantinople, in 381, denied that he had a complete human nature. (5) The Nestorians, condemned at Ephesus in 431, admitted the two natures but taught that he was two personalities. (6) The Eutychians, condemned at Chalcedon, in 451, taught that the two natures were so united and so changed that he was neither genuinely divine nor genuinely human. (7) The biblical doctrine of the Incarnation formalized at Chalcedon, A.D. 451, as stated above, is the christology of the true historical church.

But we need an *understanding of the words* of our doctrine, not just a formula to repeat. First, the emphasis on the unity of his personality means that he was, in himself, in his *ego,* his nonmaterial self, the same numerical identity, the same person. The person who was God and with God "in the beginning" before the created universe is the same person who sat wearily at the well of Sychar, the same person who said, "Father, forgive them," on the cross. Second, the distinction of his natures means, and has always meant to the church, that Jesus is just as truly God as the Father and the Spirit are God, and at the same time, without confusion or contradiction, he is just as truly human as we are human. (His humanity as the "last Adam" is perfectly sinless, yet genuinely human, as was Adam before the Fall.)

In this second matter, we must remember that a "nature" in the biblical usage is not a substantive entity. A nature is not a personality in the sense in which we are speaking. *A nature is a complex of attributes.* Since man is made in the image of God (see Jesus' argument in John 10:34–38 as discussed in the article on TRINITY) it follows that for God the Son, without diminution of his divine attributes, to assume a genuine human complex of attributes, including a normal human body, involves no contradiction.

Bibliography: H. R. Mackintosh, *The Doctrine of the Person of Christ,* 1912; L. Hodgson, *And Was Made Man,* 1928; E. Brunner, *The Mediator,* 1934; L. Boettner, *The Person of Christ,* 1943; G. C. Berkouwer, *The Person of Christ,* 1954; A. M. Stibbs, *God Became Man,* 1957; L. Morris, *The Lord from Heaven,* 1958; D. M. Baillie, *God Was in Christ,* 1961; C. F. D. Moule, *The Origin of Christology,* 1977. JOB

INCENSE. The KJV translation of two Hebrew words that were distinct in meaning at first, although later the second came to have virtually the same meaning as the first: *levônâh,* "frankincense," and *qetōrâh,* "incense." Incense was an aromatic substance made of gums and spices to be burned, especially in religious worship. It was compounded according to a definite prescription of gum resin, onycha, galbanum, and pure frankincense in equal proportions, and was tempered with salt (Exod 30:34–35). It could not be made for ordinary purposes (Exod 30:34–38; Lev 10:1–7). Incense not properly compounded was rejected as "strange incense" (Exod 30:9 KJV).

The altar of incense was overlaid with pure gold and was set in the Holy Place, near the veil that concealed the Most Holy Place. Originally, to burn it was the prerogative of the high priest, and he did so each morning when he dressed the lamps (Exod 30:1–9). On the Day of Atonement he brought the incense within the veil and burned it in a censer in the Most Holy Place, so that the atonement cover of the ark was enveloped in a cloud of fragrant smoke (Lev 16:12–13). The Korahites were punished with death for presuming to take on themselves the right to burn incense (Num 16); the sons of Aaron died for offering it improperly (Lev 10). By the time of Christ, incense was offered by ordinary priests, from among whom one was chosen by lot each morning and evening (Luke 1:9). The offering of incense was regarded as a solemn privilege. In offering incense, fire was taken from the altar of burnt offering and brought into the temple, where it was placed on the altar of incense, and then the incense was emptied from a golden vessel onto the fire. When the priest entered the Holy Place with the incense, all the people were obliged to leave the temple. A profound silence was observed by them as they prayed outside (1:9–10). When the priest placed the incense on the fire, he bowed reverently toward the Most Holy Place and retired slowly backward, lest he alarm the congregation and cause them to fear that he had been struck dead for offering unworthily (Lev 16:13).

Vessel composed of a bowl, decorated with knobs, surmounting a stand. The stand has four windows and is decorated with a frieze portraying human heads, each molded separately and then attached. It was probably used for incense, and it is thought to originate in the Hebron hills. Late Israelite (Iron) period, c. 1000–586 B.C. Courtesy Reuben and Edith Hecht Museum, University of Haifa.

Incense spoon (Israelite period, provenance unknown) shaped in the form of a hand. It was also used as a jar stopper. Courtesy Reuben and Edith Hecht Museum, University of Haifa.

The use of incense in the temple may have been partly a sanitary measure, since the smell of blood from the many animal sacrifices must have polluted the atmosphere, and the air would have to be fumigated; but it is largely explained by the love of the Oriental for sweet odors. Incense was often offered to those one wished to honor. For example, when Alexander the Great marched against Babylon, incense was offered on altars erected to him. The offering of incense was common in the religious ceremonies of nearly all ancient nations (Egyptians, Babylonians, Assyrians, Phoenicians, etc.) and was extensively used in the ritual of Israel.

Incense was symbolic of the ascending prayer of the officiating high priest. The psalmist prayed, "May my prayer be set before you like incense" (Ps 141:2). In Revelation 8:3–5 an angel burns incense on the golden altar, and smoke ascends with the prayer of saints.

INDIA (Heb. *hōddû*). The name occurs only twice in the Bible (Esth 1:1; 8:9). This was the country that marked the eastern limit of the territory of Xerxes (KJV Ahasuerus). The Hebrew word comes from the name of the Indus, *Hondu,* and refers not to the peninsula of Hindustan, but to the country adjoining the Indus, i.e., the Punjab, and perhaps also Scinde. Some have thought that this country is the Havilah of Genesis 2:11 and that the Indus is the Pishon. Many characteristic Indian products were known to the Israelites.

INERRANCY (See INSPIRATION)

INFLAMMATION (See DISEASES)

INHERITANCE. The English word in the OT is a rendering of the Hebrew words *nahalâh, heleq, yerushshâh,* and *môrāshâh,* the latter two being rare. The first occurs most often—almost two hundred times—and is the common term for something inherited, an estate, a portion. A fundamental principle of Hebrew society was that real, as distinguished from personal, property belonged to the family rather than to the individual. This came from the idea that the land was given by God to his children, the people of Israel, and must remain in the family. The Mosaic Law directed that only the sons of a legal wife had the right of inheritance. The firstborn son possessed the birthright, i.e., the right to a double portion of the father's possession; and to him belonged the duty of maintaining the females of the family (Deut 21:15–17). The other sons received equal shares. If there were no sons, the property went to the daughters (Num 27:8), on the condition that they not marry outside of their own tribe (36:6ff) If the widow was left without children, the nearest of kin on her husband's side had the right to marry her; and if he refused, the next of kin (Ruth 3:12–13). If no one married her, the inheritance remained with her until her death, and then reverted to the next of kin (Num 27:9–11). An estate could not pass from one tribe to another. Since the land was so strictly tied up, testamentary dispositions or wills were not needed. This strong feeling regarding family hereditary privileges was chiefly responsible for the Jews' taking such care to preserve the family genealogies.

A deed of inheritance in which a father gives a house to his daughter. This Aramaic papyrus is from Elephantine, a small island in the Nile where a Jewish garrison was posted in the Persian period. Fifth century B.C. Courtesy The Brooklyn Museum, bequest of Miss Theodora Wilbour.

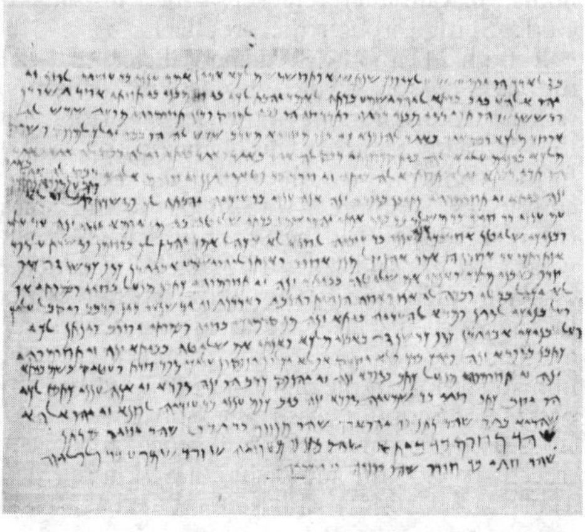

"Inheritance" is not used in Scripture only to refer to inherited property. It is used also with a definitely theological significance. In the OT at first it refers to the inheritance promised by God to Abraham and his descendants—the land of Canaan, "the land you gave your people for an inheritance" (1 Kings 8:36; cf. Num 34:2; Deut 4:21, 38; 12:9–10; 15:4; Ps 47:4; 105:9–11). The conquest of the land under the leadership of Joshua was by God's help, not by Israel's military prowess (Josh 21:43–45). God directed the partitioning of the land among the tribes (Num 26:52–56; Josh 14:1–5; 18:4–9). Israel could continue to possess the land only on condition of faithfulness to God (Deut 4:26ff.; 11:8–9). Disobedience to God would result in the loss of the land, which could be recovered only by repentance and a new wholehearted submission to God (Isa 57:13; 58:13–14).

The idea finds a further expansion and spiritualization in two other directions. Israelites came to learn that the Lord himself was the inheritance of his people (Jer 10:16) and of the individual believer (Ps 16:5–6; 73:26; 142:5), and that his inheritance is his elect, brought "out of Egypt, to be the people of his inheritance" (Deut 4:20; cf. 32:9). This conception was later broadened until the Lord's inheritance is seen to include the Gentiles also (Ps 2:8; Isa 19:25; 47:6; 63:17).

The conception of inheritance is very prominent in the NT too, but now it is connected with the person and work of Christ, who is the heir by virtue of being the Son (Mark 12:7; Heb 1:2). Through Christ's redemptive work believers are sons of God by adoption and fellow-heirs with Christ (Rom 8:17; Gal 4:7). As a guarantee of "the promised eternal inheritance" (Heb 9:15), Christ has given to them the Holy Spirit (Eph 1:14). The letter to the Hebrews shows that as Israel in the Old Covenant received her inheritance from God, so in the New Covenant the new Israel receives an inheritance, only a better one. This inheritance, moreover, is not for Jews alone but for all true believers, including Gentiles (3:6). The inheritance is the kingdom of God with all its blessings (Matt 25:34; 1 Cor 6:9; Gal 5:21), both present and eschatological (Rom 8:17–23; 1 Cor 15:50; Heb 11:13; 1 Peter 1:3–4). It is wholly the gift of God's sovereign grace. SB

INK (Heb. *deyô,* from a root meaning *slowly flowing,* Gr. *melan, black*). Any liquid used with pen or brush to form written characters. Mentioned once in the OT (Jer 36:18), where Baruch says he wrote Jeremiah's prophecies "in ink." Hebrew ink was probably lampblack and gum, as is suggested by the reference to "blot out" in Exodus 32:33 (cf. Num 6:23); but it is possible that in the course of Jewish history various inks were used. The word occurs three times in the NT (2 Cor 3:3; 2 John 12; 3 John 13). The NT books were written on papyrus, and the black ink used was made of vegetable soot mixed with gum and moistened as the writer needed it. The better black inks were made of nutgalls, sulphate of iron, and gum. The writing of MSS of the first century is remarkably well preserved.

INN (Heb. *mālôn,* Gr. *pandocheion, katalyma*). The Hebrew word means a "night resting-place" and can apply to any place where there is encampment for the night, whether by caravans, individuals, or even armies. The presence of a building is not implied. It was originally very probably only a piece of level ground near a spring where carriers of merchandise could, with their animals, pass the night. Inns in the modern sense were not very necessary in primitive times, since travelers found hospitality the rule (Exod 2:20; Judg 19:15–21; 2 Kings 4:8; Acts 28:7; Heb 13:2). We do not know when buildings were first used, but they would be needed early in the history of trade as a protection from inclement weather and in dangerous times and places. The "lodging place for travelers" (Jer 9:2) may have been such an establishment. An inn of the Middle East bore little resemblance to a modern hotel. It was a mere shelter for man and beast. Like the modern "khan" or "caravanserai," it was a large quadrangular court into which admission was gained by a strong gateway. The more elaborate ones were almost as strong as a fortress. In the center of the court there was a well, and around the sides there were rooms and stalls. An upper story was reached by stairways. Travelers usually brought food for themselves and their animals.

Innkeepers in ancient times had a very bad reputation; and this, together with the Semitic spirit of hospitality, led Jews and Christians to recommend hospitality for the entertainment of strangers. One of the best-known inns in Palestine was halfway between Jerusalem and Jericho (Luke 10:34). The Greek word *katalyma,* used of the Upper Room, where the Last Supper was held (Mark 14:14), and of the place in Bethlehem that turned away Joseph and Mary (Luke 2:7), was probably a room in a private house rather than in a public inn—corresponding to a spare room in a private house or in a village, probably that of a sheikh. The vast numbers who went to Jerusalem to attend the annual feasts were allowed to use such guest-chambers; and for this no payment was taken. SB

Ruins of an ancient caravanserai, or inn, from Byzantine period, on the Jerusalem-Jericho road, near the traditional site of the Inn of the Good Samaritan (Luke 10:34). Courtesy Zev Radovan.

INNOCENTS, SLAUGHTER OF (Matt 2:16). The murder by Herod the Great of all the male children in Bethlehem two years old and under, when the wise men failed to return and tell him where they found the infant Jesus.

I.N.R.I. The initials of the Latin superscription that Pilate had placed above the cross of Jesus in three languages (Greek, Hebrew, Latin). The Latin reads: *IESUS NAZARENUS, REX IUDAEORUM,* "Jesus of Nazareth, King of the Jews" (Matt 27:37; Mark 15:26; Luke 23:38; John 19:19).

INSECTS (See ANIMALS)

INSPIRATION. The word *inspiration* is used twice in the KJV—in Job 32:8 (NIV "breath"), to translate the Hebrew word *neshāmâh* ("to breathe"), and in 2 Timothy 3:16, where it translates the Greek word *theopneustos.* The latter passage has given its meaning to the word *inspiration* as commonly applied to Scripture. Literally translated, *theopneustos* means "God-breathed"(so NIV). The key to its meaning may be gleaned from the OT concept of the divine breathing as producing effects that God himself is immediately accomplishing by his own will and power (see Ps 33:6). By this word, therefore, Paul is asserting that the written documents, called Holy Scripture, are a divine product.

Precisely the same idea is set forth in 2 Peter 1:19–21. In this passage the prophetic Word (i.e., Scripture) is contrasted with mere fables devised by human cunning. Scripture is more sure and trustworthy than the testimony of any eyewitness. The explanation for its unique authority lies in its origin. It was produced not as a merely human private interpretation of the truth but by God's Spirit through the prophets.

In both 2 Timothy 3:16 and 2 Peter 1:19–21 the fact of the divine productivity (spiration rather than *in*spiration) of the "Holy Writings" is thus explicitly asserted. This divine (in)spiration is further confirmed by a host of NT passages. The authors of Scripture wrote in or by the Spirit (Mark 12:36). What the Scripture states is really what God has said (Acts 4:25; Heb 3:7; and see especially Heb 1:5ff.). This is true whether or not in the particular passage cited the words are ascribed to God or are the statements of the human author. In the mind of the NT writers any passage of Scripture was really "spoken" by God. Jesus used the same type of reference, attributing directly to God the authorship of Scripture (Matt 19:4–5).

Because of the character of the God of Truth who "inspired" (or produced) the Holy Scriptures, the result of "inspiration" is to constitute the Bible as fully trustworthy and authoritative. Indeed, this absolute divine authority of Scripture, rather than its inspiration, is the emphasis of scriptural teaching about its own nature (see Ps 19:7–14; 119:89, 97, 113, 160; Zech 7:12; Matt 5:17–19; Luke 16:17; John 10:34–35; 1 Thess 2–13). Besides those passages directly teaching the authority of Scripture, such phrases as "It is written" (Matt 21:13; Luke 4:4, 8, 10), "it [or he] says" (Rom 9:15; Gal 3:16), and "Scripture says" (Rom 9:17; Gal 3:8) all clearly imply an absolute authority for the OT Scriptures.

These passages teaching the authority of Scripture indicate also the extent of inspiration. If the authority and trustworthiness of Scripture are complete, inspiration itself must also extend to all of Scripture. This completeness of inspiration and consequent authority of all Scripture is made explicit in such passages as Luke 24:25: "How foolish you are, and how slow of heart to believe all that the prophets have spoken!" (see also Matt 5:17–19; Luke 16:17; John 10:34–35).

Inerrancy and *infallibility* as applied to the inspiration of Scripture, though not exactly synonymous terms, are nevertheless both correctly applied to Scripture in order to indicate that inspiration and authority are complete. The word *inerrant* suggests that the Scriptures do not wander from the truth. *Infallible* is stronger, suggesting an incapability of wandering from the truth. ("Are you not in error because you do not know the Scriptures?" Mark 12:24).

The completeness of inspiration is further established by the fact that Scripture lacks altogether any principle for distinguishing between (a) those parts of it that are inspired and thus possess binding authority and (b) supposedly uninspired parts that do not possess binding authority. The method of inspiration is never developed in the Scriptures, although the basic fact that Scripture is produced by the power of God working in and through such a writer as a prophet indicates the mutual interworking of the divine and human hand. By pointing to a human author of Scripture (e.g., "David himself, speaking by the Holy Spirit, declared"—Mark 12:36; "Moses wrote"—Mark 12:19; and "Isaiah says"—John 12:39), by stating his purpose in the writing of a book (e.g., Luke 1:1–4; John 20:30–31), and by acknowledging research in the preparation of the writing of Scripture (Luke 1:2–3), the biblical authors make completely plain that the divine method of inspiration was not always by a process of dictation.

At this point great caution should be taken not to read into the biblical idea of the origin of Scripture suggestions derived from the English word *inspiration* (or Latin *inspiratio*). The point of the biblical teaching is never a divine heightening of the human powers of the prophet (though the Bible does not deny that in certain instances such may have taken place). Rather, by all those inconceivable means at the disposal of a sovereign God, the Holy Spirit used the writers of Scripture to produce through them the message that he wished to communicate to us. God's Spirit obviously did not need in every case to "inspire" (i.e., to raise to greater heights than ordinary) a Micah or a Luke; rather, God produced the writing he wished by his sovereign preparation and control of a man who could and freely would write just what God desired to be his divinely authoritative message to his people.

In summary, biblical inspiration (as distinguished from illumination) may be defined as the work of the Holy Spirit by which, through the instrumentality of the personality and literary talents of its human authors, he constituted the words of the Bible in all of its several parts as his written word to the human race and, therefore, of divine authority and without error.

Bibliography: J. Orr, *Revelation and Inspiration,* 1927; N. B. Stonehouse and P. Woolley (eds.), *The Infallible Word,* 1946; R. L. Harris, *Inspiration and Canonicity of the Bible,* 1957; C. F. H. Henry (ed.), *Revelation and the Bible,* 1958; M. C. Tenney (ed.), *The Bible—The Living Word of Revelation,* 1968; J. W. Wenham, *Christ and the Bible,* 1972; G. C. Berkouwer, *Holy Scripture,* 1975. KSK

INTEREST (Heb. *neshekh, something bitten off; mashā', lending on interest,* Gr. *tokos, something produced by money*). In the OT there is no trace of any system of commercial credit. Large commercial loans were not made in ancient Israel. Only the poor borrowed, and they did it to obtain the necessities of life. The law of Moses forbade lending at interest to a fellow Israelite (Exod 22:25) but permitted charging interest to a foreigner (Deut 23:20). A needy Israelite might sell himself as a servant (Lev 25:39; 2 Kings 4:1). The prophets condemn the taking of interest as a heinous sin (Jer 15:10; Ezek 18:8, 13, 17). In the NT, references to the receiving of interest occur in two parables—of the Pounds (Luke 19:23) and of the Talents (Matt 25:27), and it is distinctly encouraged.

INTERMEDIATE STATE (See ESCHATOLOGY)

IPHDEIAH (ĭf-dē'yȧ, Heb. *yiphdeyâh, Jehovah redeems*). A descendant of Benjamin (1 Chron 8:25).

IPHTAH (ĭf'tȧ, Heb. *yiphtāh*). An unidentified town in the Shephelah of Judah. It is named with eight other towns (Josh 15:43, KJV Jiphtah).

IPHTAH EL (ĭf'tȧ-ĕl, Heb. *yiphtah'ēl*). The Valley of Iphtah El lay on the northern border of Zebulun (Josh 19:14, 27). It is probably to be identified with the modern Tell Jefat, nine miles (fifteen km.) NW of Nazareth.

IR (ĭr, Heb. *'îr, watcher*). The ancestral head of a clan of Benjamin (1 Chron 7:12). It is the same as Iri (7:7).

IR NAHASH (ĭr nā'hăsh, Heb. *'îr nāhāsh*). A town of Judah of which Tehinnah is called the "father," probably meaning "founder" (1 Chron 4:12). The site is uncertain.

IR SHEMESH (ĭr shē'mĕsh, Heb. *'îr shemesh, city of the sun*). A city of Dan (Josh 19:41), the same as Beth Shemesh.

IRA (ī'rȧ, Heb. *'îr'a*). 1. A chief minister or priest in the time of David (2 Sam 20:26).

2. A son of Ikkesh, a Tekoite, one of David's mighty men (2 Sam 23:26; 1 Chron 11:28).

3. An Ithrite, one of David's heroes (2 Sam 23:38; 1 Chron 11:40).

IRAD (ī'răd, Heb. *'îrādh*). Grandson of Cain and son of Enoch (Gen 4:18).

IRAM (ī'răm, Heb. *'îrām*). A chief of Edom (Gen 36:43; 1 Chron 1:54).

IRI (ī'rī, Heb. *îrî*). A Benjamite of the family of Bela (1 Chron 7:7). It is the same as Ir (7:12).

IRIJAH (ī-rī'jȧ, Heb. *yir'îyāyh, Jehovah sees*). A captain of the guard who arrested Jeremiah at the time of the Chaldean siege of Jerusalem. Jeremiah was leaving the city at the gate of Benjamin, and Irijah arrested him on suspicion of intending to desert to the enemy (Jer 37:13).

IRON (See MINERALS)

IRON (ĭ'rŏn, Heb. *yir'ôn*). A fortified city in the territory of Naphtali (Josh 19:38). It is probably the present village of Yarun, ten miles (seventeen km.) west of Lake Huleh.

IRPEEL (ĭr'pī-ĕl, Heb. *yirpe'ēl, God heals*). A city of Benjamin (Josh 18:27). The site is uncertain, but is it probably near the ancient Gibeon.

IRRIGATION. A word for which there is no Hebrew or Greek equivalent in the Bible, though the use of irrigation for watering plants and trees is frequently implied (Eccl 2:5–6; Isa 58:11). There was less need of irrigation in Palestine and Syria than in Egypt and Babylonia. In Palestine it was necessary only in the summer.

IRU (ī'rū, Heb. *'îrû*). Eldest son of Caleb (1 Chron 4:15), probably to be read Ir.

ISAAC (ī'zȧk, Heb. *yitshāk,* Gr. *Isaak, one laughs*). The only son of Abraham by Sarah, and the second of three Hebrew patriarchs (with Abraham and Jacob) who were the progenitors of the Jewish race. He was born in the south country, probably Beersheba (Gen 21:14, 31), when Abraham was a hundred and Sarah ninety years old (17:17; 21:5). He was named Isaac because both Abraham and Sarah had laughed incredulously at the thought of having a child at their age (17:17–19; 18:9–15; 21:6). His birth must be regarded as a miracle. Twenty-five years after God had promised the childless Abraham and Sarah a son, the promise was fulfilled. He is thus rightly called the child of promise, in contrast with Ishmael, who was born of Hagar,

Relief from the palace of Sennacherib, Kuyunjik (c. 704–681 B.C.) that depicts a man lifting water into an irrigation ditch by means of a sweep (*shaduf*), which consists of a long beam mounted on a stepped pillar acting as a fulcrum. Reproduced by courtesy of the Trustees of the British Museum.

Sarah's maid, and Abraham. When Isaac was eight days old, he was circumcised (21:4). Fearing future jealousy and strife between the two boys when she observed Ishmael mocking Isaac, Sarah tried to persuade Abraham to cast out Hagar and Ishmael. Abraham was loath to do this because he loved the boy and did so only when he received explicit direction from God, who said to him that his seed would be reckoned through Isaac, but he would also make a nation of Ishmael (21:9–13).

The next recorded event in the life of Isaac is connected with God's command to Abraham to offer him as a sacrifice on a mountain in the land of Moriah (Gen 22). His exact age then is not stated, but he is described as a "lad," able to carry the wood for the burnt offering up the mountainside. In this whole experience his unquestioning submission and obedience to his father stand out almost as remarkably as his father's faith. Bound on the altar and about to die, his life was spared when an angel of the Lord interposed and substituted for him a ram, which was offered up in his place. God's purpose in this great test of Abraham's faith is looked at in various ways, among the more important being the following: it is the last and culminating point in God's education of Abraham regarding the meaning of sacrificial obedience; it is a rebuke by God of the widespread heathen practice of sacrificing human beings; it is an object lesson to Abraham of the great sacrifice of the Messiah for the redemption of mankind.

Sarah died at Hebron when Isaac was thirty-six years old (Gen 23:1). At the age of forty Isaac married Rebekah, a kinswoman from Mesopotamia (ch. 24); but he and his wife were childless until, in answer to prayer, twin sons, Esau and Jacob, were born to them when he was sixty (25:20, 26). At a time of famine, God admonished him not to go down into Egypt, as he had thought of doing, but to remain in the Promised Land; and he pledged his word to be with him. He went to the Philistine city of Gerar, and there, fearing for his own life, he passed his wife off as his sister, as his father had done before him. He was justly rebuked by Abimelech the king for his duplicity (26:10). Isaac then pitched his camp in the Valley of Gerar and became so prosperous as a wheat-grower and herdsman that the envious Philistines began a systematic, petty harassment by stopping up the wells that his father had dug and he had opened again. Abimelech even advised him to leave the country in the interest of peace (ch. 26). Isaac subsequently returned to Beersheba. There the Lord appeared to him at night and promised to bless him for his father's sake. Realizing that God was with Isaac, Abimelech then came from Gerar to make overtures of peace, and the two men formally entered into a covenant (26:26–31). Probably at a considerably later period, Esau, at the age of forty, brought grief to Isaac and Rebekah by marrying two women of Canaan (26:34–35).

The last prominent event in the life of Isaac is the blessing of his sons (Gen 27). Esau, the elder,

The sacrifice of Isaac (Gen 22:2ff.), as depicted at Bet Alfa, a sixth century synagogue found in Kibbutz Heftzi Bah in the Jezreel Valley. Courtesy Zev Radovan.

was his father's favorite, even though God had told him that the elder would serve the younger. Rebekah's favorite was Jacob (25:28). When Isaac was over a hundred years old, and dim of sight, and perhaps thinking that his end was near, he wished to bestow his last blessing on his elder son; but through Rebekah's cunning and guile Jacob the younger supplanted his brother, and the blessing of the birthright was given to him. To save Jacob from the murderous wrath of Esau, who determined to kill him after his father's death, Rebekah induced Isaac to send Jacob into Mesopotamia, that, after his own example, his son might take a wife among his own kindred and not imitate Esau by marrying Canaanite women. Isaac invoked another blessing on Jacob and sent him away to Laban in Paddan Aram (27–28:5).

Isaac is mentioned only once more—twenty years later, when Jacob returned from his sojourn in Mesopotamia, having married into Laban's family. Jacob found his father at Mamre in Hebron. There Isaac died at 180 years of age, and his two sons, Esau and Jacob, buried him (Gen 35:27–29).

The NT refers to Isaac almost a score of times. His sacrifice by Abraham is twice mentioned, in Hebrews 11:17–18 and James 2:21; but while the submission of Isaac is referred to, the stress is on the triumph of Abraham's faith. Isaac is contrasted with Ishmael, as the child of promise and the progenitor of the children of promise (Rom 9:7, 10; Gal 4:28; Heb 11:18). In Jesus' argument with the Sadducees on the matter of resurrection, he represents Isaac, although dead in human terms, as still living to God (Luke 20:37). In the Sermon on the Mount Jesus proclaimed that many would come from the east and the west to sit down with Abraham, Isaac, and Jacob in the kingdom of heaven (Matt 8:11).

Of the three patriarchs, Isaac was the least conspicuous, traveled the least, had the fewest extraordinary adventures, but lived the longest. He was free from violent passions; quiet, gentle, dutiful; less a man of action than of thought and suffering. His name is always joined in equal honor with Abraham and Jacob. SB

ISAIAH. Little is known about the prophet

Isaiah except what his own words reveal. His name Isaiah (*Salvation of Jehovah*) is almost identical in meaning with Joshua (*Jehovah is Salvation*) which appears in the NT as Jesus, the name of the Messiah whom Isaiah heralded. That his name played a formative role in his life is not improbable, since it expresses the great theme of his prophetic ministry. His father Amoz may have been a person of prominence, since the prophet is so often called (thirteen times) "the son of Amoz"; but nothing is known about him. Isaiah was married and had two children to whom he gave significant names (Isa 7:3; 8:3).

I. Period. Isaiah prophesied during four reigns of kings of Judah, from Uzziah to Hezekiah (Isa 1:1). The first date given is the year of Uzziah's death (6:1), which probably occurred about 740 B.C. or several years later. The last historical event referred to is the death of Sennacherib (37:38), which occurred in 681. The most important events are the Syro-Ephraimitic war in the days of Ahaz (7:1–9), which Isaiah treated, despite its devastation (2 Chron 28:5–15), as almost insignificant compared with the far greater scourge from Assyria, which was so soon to follow (Isa 7:17–25). Assyria is the great enemy that much of chapters 7–39 deal with; and beyond it looms an even mightier foe, Babylon, whose downfall is foretold already in chapters 13–14 and who is the great theme of chapters 40–48. Over against these terrible instruments of divine judgment Isaiah pictures the messianic hope, first in counseling unbelieving Ahaz, and repeatedly thereafter.

II. Analysis. The structure of Isaiah is, in its broad outlines, a simple one, but in its details it raises many problems. It may be briefly analyzed as follows:

A. **Isaiah 1–5, Introduction.** Chapter 1 contains the "great arraignment." Like so many of Isaiah's utterances, it combines dire threatenings with urgent calls to repentance and gracious offers of forgiveness and blessing. It is followed by the promise of world redemption (2:1–5). Then comes a series of threatening passages, including a detailed description of the finery of the women of Jerusalem as illustrating the sinful frivolity of the people as a whole. The land is likened to an unfruitful vineyard, which will soon become desolate. It concludes with a series of six woes that end in gloom: "Even the light will be darkened by the clouds" (5:30).

B. **Isaiah 6, The Temple Vision.** Whether this represents the initial call of Isaiah has been much debated. If the woe pronounced on himself by the prophet is to be understood as the seventh woe,

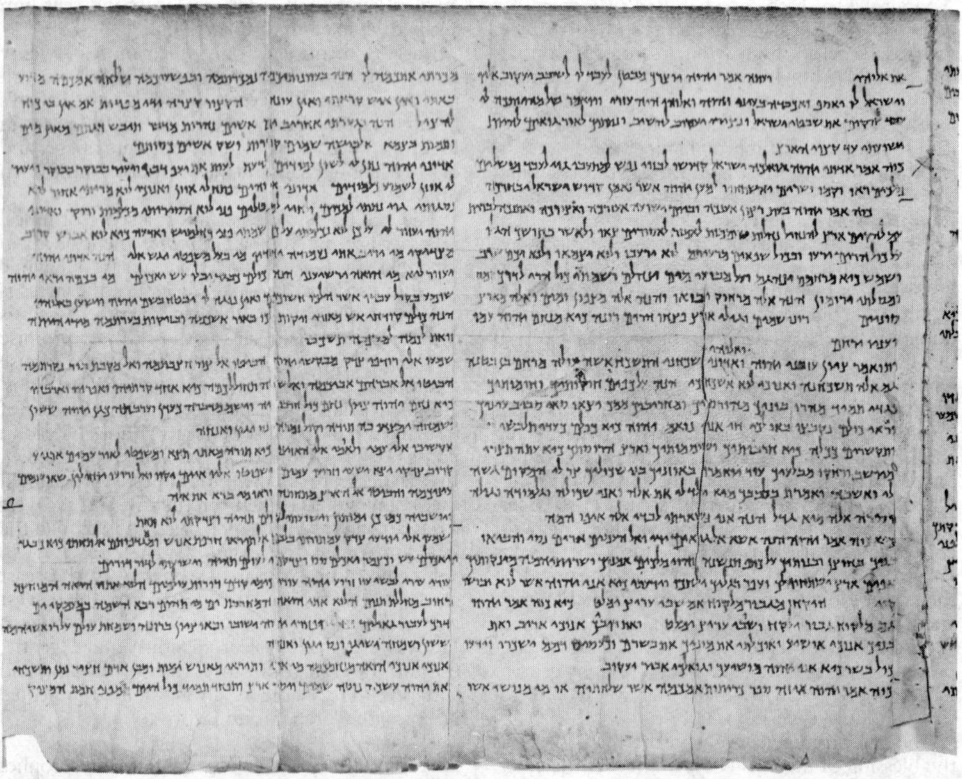

Part of the oldest surviving complete scroll of Isaiah in Hebrew found in Cave 1 at Qumran near the Dead Sea, dated c. 125–100 B.C. The entire scroll measures 24 feet (7 m.) in length. The passage shown is Isaiah 49:4–51:13. Courtesy The Shrine of the Book, D. Samuel and Jeane H. Gottesman, Center for Biblical Manuscripts, Israel Museum, Jerusalem.

intended to show that the prophet was as conscious of his own sin as of the sin of his people, we may assume that this chapter stands in its proper place chronologically and that this vision came to him some time after he began to prophesy. But the question must remain unsettled. It is a vision of the Holy God; and "Holy One of Israel" becomes one of Isaiah's favorite titles for the Deity in whose name he speaks.

C. **Isaiah 7–12, The Book of Immanuel.** This group of chapters belongs to the period of the Syro-Ephraimitic war (2 Kings 16:1–20; 1 Chron 28). In the midst of this time of peril, Isaiah utters the great prophecies regarding Immanuel (Isa 7:14–16; 9:6–7; 11:1–10); and he concludes with a song of triumphant faith that ends with the assurance, "Great is the Holy One of Israel among you" (12:6). Here again woe (10:1–4) and threatening (10:5–19) stand in vivid contrast with messianic blessing (11:1–16).

D. **Isaiah 13–23, Prophecies Against the Nations.** These are ten "oracles" (weighty, solemn, and grievous utterances; see Jer 23:33 and footnote) against nations that either were or would be a menace to God's people: Babylon (Isa 13–14:27), Philistia (14:28–32), Moab (15–16), Damascus (17–18), Egypt (19–20), Babylon (21:1–10), Dumah (21:11–12), Arabia (21:13–17), Jerusalem (22), Tyre (23). Here prophecies regarding the near future (16:14; 21:16; cf. 22:20 with 37:2) appear along with others that refer to a more distant (23:17) or a quite remote time. Thus the fall of Babylon is so certain that Israel is told the taunt that will be sung on the day that Babylon falls. Compare 21:6–20, which describes it as having already taken place, with 39:6, which speaks of the Babylonian captivity as still future—a method of prophetic description frequently found in Isaiah. This group of prophecies is chiefly threatening, but it also contains wonderful promises of blessing. Israel's mightiest foes will share with her in the future blessedness (19:23–25).

E. **Isaiah 24–35.** Isaiah 24 looks far into the future. It is world-embracing and may be called an *apocalypse*. The world judgment will be followed by songs of thanksgiving for divine blessing (25–26). A prophecy against Egypt follows (27). Then there are again six woes (28–34), the last being a frightful curse on Edom. This group also closes with a beautiful prophetic picture of future blessedness (35).

F. **Isaiah 36–39, Historical** (Compare parallel passages in Kings and Chronicles). These chapters describe the blasphemous threats of Sennacherib against Jerusalem, Hezekiah's appeal to Isaiah, who ridicules the invader, and the flight and death of the blasphemer (36–37)—one of the most thrilling episodes in the whole Bible. Probably Hezekiah's illness and the envoy of Merodach-Baladan (38–39) took place during the reign of Sargon king of Assyria and father of Sennacherib. If so, the arrangement is topical and intended to prepare for the prophecies of consolation that follow.

G. **Isaiah 40–66.** These chapters have been called the Book of Consolation. The words "Comfort, comfort my people" are clearly intended to give Israel a comfort and hope not to be gathered from Hezekiah's words, which they immediately follow. These chapters fall into three parts as is suggested by the refrain-like words, " 'There is no peace,' says the LORD, 'for the wicked' " (48:22; cf. 57:21), which have their terrible echo in Isaiah's final words (66:24).

1. *Isaiah 40–48* deals with the coming of Cyrus and the fall of Babylon as proof of the power of the God of Israel both to foretell and to fulfill, in amazing contrast to the idols of the heathen, which can do neither. The utter folly of idolatry is portrayed most vividly in 44:9–20 and 46:1–11. The last mention of Babylon, "Leave Babylon, flee from the Babylonians" (48:20), is clearly to be thought of as describing flight from a doomed city, like the flight of Lot from Sodom. In the two remaining parts of the book there is no mention of either Assyria or Babylon except by way of reminiscence (52:4).

2. *Isaiah 49–57* forms a logical and climactic sequel to the preceding group. The figure of the "servant" is common to both. The word occurs twenty times in chapters 40–53. Nine times he is called Israel, Jacob, or Jacob-Israel. Six times the Lord calls him "my servant." The title is used in three senses: of the servant as deaf and blind (42:18–19), sinful and needing redemption (44:22; cf. 43:25); of the servant as faithful and as having a mission to Israel and the Gentiles (42:1–7; 49:1–6; 50:6–9); and finally of One who, himself innocent, suffers for the sins of others (52:13–53:12). The first three of these four passages, which are often called the "Servant Songs," can refer to the pious in Israel as sharing with their Lord in his mission of salvation. In the last the reference to the Messiah is "predominant and exclusive" (Alexander). This is one of the most precious chapters in the Bible. It speaks both of the humiliation of the Savior and also of the glory that is to follow. The greatness of the salvation secured by the Servant is described in glowing terms and its world-wide scope is made clear in verses 10–12 and again and again in the chapters that follow, especially 61:1–3.

3. *Isaiah 58–66* continues the same general theme and reaches its height in 66:1–3, a passage that foretells that day of which Jesus spoke to the woman of Samaria, when the true worshiper will worship not in temples made with hands, but "in spirit and truth" (John 4:21–24). Yet here again as constantly elsewhere, warning and denunciation alternate with offers and assurances of blessing. Thus 65:17, which speaks of the "new heavens and a new earth" (cf. 66:22), follows a denunciation of those who practice abominations. And the book closes with a reference to the torments of the reprobate.

III. Principal Themes of Isaiah. Isaiah is preeminently the prophet of redemption. The greatness and majesty of God, his holiness and hatred of sin and the folly of idolatry, his grace and mercy and love, and the blessed rewards of obedience are constantly recurring themes. No wonder that the NT writers quote so often from Isaiah and that so much of Handel's *Messiah* is taken from it. *Redeemer* and *savior* (save, salvation) are among Isaiah's favorite words.The words that describe the character of the promised Messiah (9:6) are frequently on his lips: wonderful (25:1; 28:29; 29:14), counselor (19:17; 25:1; 28:29; 40:13–14, 16–17), mighty God (30:29; 33:13; 40:26–28; 49:20–26; 60:16), everlasting father (26:4; 40:28; 45:17; 55:3; 57:15; 60:19–20; 63:16; 64:8), prince of peace (26:12; 45:7; 52:7; 53:5; 55:12; 57:19; 66:12). Isaiah had a deep appreciation of beauty and wonder of the world of nature (e.g., ch. 35). A striking figure that he uses repeatedly is the "highway" (11:16; 19:23; 33:8; 35:8; 36:2; 40:3; 49:11; 57:14; 62:10). All the barriers that separate nation from nation and delay the coming of the King to his kingdom will be removed, and "the glory of the LORD will be revealed, and all mankind together will see it" (40:5).

IV. Importance. The importance of the book is indicated by how frequently it is quoted in the NT. Isaiah is quoted by name twenty-one times, slightly more than all the other writing prophets taken together; and there are many more allusions and quotations where his name is not given. He has been called the evangelist of the OT, and many of the most precious verses in the Bible come to us from his lips. The fact that the Lord began his public ministry at Nazareth by reading from Isaiah 61 and applying its prophetic words to himself is significant of the place that this book would come to hold in the Christian church.

V. Unity. An article on Isaiah written today must deal with the unity of the book, since this has been vigorously assailed for nearly two centuries. The attack is not due to any discoveries that have been made, but to the new theory regarding prophecy that is widely prevalent today and minimizes or denies prediction, declaring that the OT prophet spoke only to the people of his own time and not to future generations. This theory is refuted by the fact that the NT frequently quotes the words of the prophets, notably Isaiah, as fulfilled in the earthly life of Jesus Christ. In John 12:38–40 two quotations from Isaiah are brought together, the one from 53:1, the other from 6:9–10; and as if to make it quite clear that they have one and the same source, the evangelist adds: "Isaiah said this because he saw Jesus' glory and spoke about him."

The main argument for a second Isaiah is that Cyrus is referred to as one who has already entered on his career of conquest (e.g., Isa 41:1–2, 25); and it is claimed that the writer of all or part of chapters 40–66 must have lived at the close of the Babylonian captivity. We must note, therefore, that the prophets, notably Isaiah, often spoke as if they were eyewitnesses of the future events they described. The viewpoint or situation of the one who penned chapter 53 is Calvary. He describes the sufferings of the Servant as ended and depicts in glowing colors the glory that will follow, yet the prophet cannot have lived at that time. He must have lived many years, even centuries, before the advent of the One whose death he vividly portrays. Consequently, one must hold that the prophet, neither in chapters 7–12 nor in chapter 53, predicted the coming and work of the Messiah; or one must hold that he could and did speak of future events, of the coming of Cyrus, of One greater than Cyrus, as if he were living in the glorious days of which he spoke. For those who accept the testimony of the Bible and hold the conception of predictive prophecy that it sets forth, the unity of Isaiah is not a discredited tradition but a well-accredited fact.

Bibliography: J. A. Alexander, *Commentary on the Prophecies of Isaiah,* 1847; O. T. Allis, *The Unity of Isaiah: A Study in Prophecy,* 1950; H. C. Leupold, *Exposition of Isaiah,* 1968; E. J. Young, *The Book of Isaiah,* 2 vols., 1969–72; J. Ridderbos, *Isaiah* in *Bible Student's Commentary,* 1984.

OTA

ISCAH (īs'kȧ, Heb. *yiskâh*). A daughter of Haran and sister of Milcah (Gen 11:29). Identified by tradition with Sarah, Abraham's wife, but not with sufficient reason.

ISCARIOT (See JUDAS ISCARIOT)

ISHBAH (ĭsh'bă, Heb. *yishbah*). A member of the tribe of Judah, the ancestor or head of the inhabitants of Eshtemoa (1 Chron 4:17).

ISHBAK (ĭsh'băk, Heb. *yishbāq*). A name in the list of sons of Abraham by Keturah (Gen 25:2), the names probably representing tribes.

ISHBI-BENOB (ĭsh'bī-bē'nŏb, Heb. *yishbî venōv*). A giant who attacked David when he was exhausted in battle and was subsequently killed by Abishai (2 Sam 21:16–17).

ISH-BOSHETH (îsh'-bōshĕth, Heb. *'îsh-bōsheth, man of shame*). The fourth son of Saul (2 Sam 2:8), originally called Eshbaal, "man of Baal," but for some reason his name was subsequently changed. After the death of Saul and his three elder sons at the battle of Gilboa, where the Philistines won an overwhelming victory, he was proclaimed king over Israel by Abner, the captain of Saul's army, at Mahanaim (2:8ff.), while Judah proclaimed David its king. Ish-Bosheth was then about forty years old and reigned two years (2:8–10). He was not successful in the war he waged with David to rule over all twelve tribes, but the war did not come to a close until Abner transferred his allegiance to David because of a serious charge made against him by Ish-Bosheth (3:6ff.). Abner fulfilled David's condition to return to him Michal, his wife, before peace could be made. It was not, however, until Abner was murdered at Hebron that Ish-Bosheth lost heart and gave up hope of retaining his power (2 Sam 4). Soon after, Ish-Bosheth was murdered by his own captains, but David had the assassins put to death and buried Ish-Bosheth in the grave of Abner at Hebron. Ish-Bosheth's death ended the dynasty of Saul.

ISHHOD (ī'shŏd, Heb. *'îshehôdh, man of majesty*). A man from Manasseh whose mother was Hammoleketh (1 Chron 7:18).

ISHI (ĭsh'ī, Heb. *'îshî, my husband*). A symbolic term that expresses the ideal relation between the Lord and Israel (Hos 2:16 KJV, NASB), also rendered "my husband" (NIV, RSV).

ISHI (Heb. *yish'î, salutary*). 1. A man of Judah (1 Chron 2:31).

2. Another man of Judah (1 Chron 4:20).

3. A descendant of Simeon (1 Chron 4:42).

4. The head of a family of Manasseh (1 Chron 5:24).

ISHIAH (See ISSHIAH)

ISHIJAH (ī-shī'jȧ, Heb. *yishshîyâh*). A son of Harim, one of those induced by Ezra to send away their foreign wives (Ezra 10:31).

ISHMA (ĭsh'mȧ, Heb. *yishmā'*). The ancestral head of a clan of Judah; descended from Hur (1 Chron 4:3–4).

ISHMAEL (ĭsh'mā-ĕl, Heb. *yishmā'ēl, God hears,* Gr. *Ismaēl*). 1. The son of Abraham by Hagar, the Egyptian maid of his wife Sarah. Sarah was barren (Gen 16:1); and in accordance with the custom of the age she gave to Abraham her handmaid Hagar as his concubine, hoping that he might obtain a family by her. Abraham was then eighty-six years old and had been in Canaan for ten years (16:3). When Hagar saw that she had conceived, she began to despise her mistress, so that Sarah complained bitterly to Abraham, who told her that since Hagar was her slave, she could do anything she wanted with her. Sarah made things so difficult for Hagar that she fled, and somewhere on the road to Egypt the angel of the Lord met her and told her to return to her mistress and submit herself to her. He encouraged her with a promise of many descendants. Ishmael was circumcised when he was thirteen (17:25). Abraham loved him, and even after God had promised him a son by Sarah, he fervently exclaimed, "If only Ishmael might live under your blessing!" (17:18).

At the weaning of Isaac, the customary feast was held; and Sarah saw Ishmael, now a boy of sixteen, mocking Isaac. Jealous, and probably fearing future trouble if the boys were brought up together, Sarah urged Abraham to get rid of Ishmael and his slave mother, but he was unwilling until he was encouraged to do so by God. Sent away with bread and a bottle of water, Ishmael and his mother wandered about in the wilderness of Beersheba. When he became faint for thirst and was on the verge of death, she put him in the shade of a shrub and sat nearby, "for she thought, 'I cannot watch the boy die' " (21:16). For the second time in Hagar's life, the angel of the Lord appeared to her. He directed her to some water and renewed his former promise of Ishmael's future greatness (Gen 21:19–20). Ishmael grew up and became famous as an archer in the wilderness of Paran. His mother gave him in marriage to an Egyptian wife. When Abraham died, Ishmael returned from exile to help Isaac bury their father (25:9). He became the father of twelve sons and a daughter, whom Esau took for his wife. He died at the age of 137 (25:17). In Galatians 4:21–31 Paul uses the lives of Ishmael and Isaac allegorically. Hagar represents the old covenant, and Sarah, the new; the rivalry between Ishmael and Isaac foreshadows the conflict in the early church between those who would cling to the ordinances of the law, which must pass away, and those who realize that through the grace of Christ there is freedom from the law.

2. A descendant of Jonathan (1 Chron 8:38; 9:44).

3. The father of Zebadiah, a ruler in the house of Judah in the reign of Jehoshaphat (2 Chron 19:11).

4. The son of Jehohanan. He helped Jehoiada to restore Jehoash to the throne of Judah (2 Chron 23:1).

5. The son of Nethaniah, a member of the royal house of David. After the capture of Palestine, Nebuchadnezzar left behind as governor of Judah a Jew called Gedaliah, who promised to protect all those Jews who would put themselves under his care. Among those who came was Ishmael, who, instigated by the king of the Ammonites, intended to assassinate the governor. Gedaliah was warned of Ishmael's treachery by some loyal captains but paid no attention to the warning. About two months after the destruction of Jerusalem, Gedaliah and others with him were murdered at a banquet held in honor of Ishmael, who then attempted to flee to the Ammonite country with some captives he had with him, including the king's daughters. His pursuers overtook him at Gibeon. His captives were recovered, but Ishmael and a few of his men succeeded in escaping to the king of Ammon (2 Kings 25:25; Jer 40:7–41:18). SB

ISHMAELITE (ĭsh'mā-ĕl-īt, Heb. *yishme'ēlîm*). A descendant of Ishmael, the son of Abraham and Hagar, whom Abraham sent away into the desert after the birth of Isaac (Gen 21:14–21). The twelve sons of Ishmael and his Egyptian wife became princes and progenitors of as many tribes. They lived in camps in the desert of northern Arabia, though occasionally some of them, such as the Nabateans, settled down. Mostly, however, they lived like Ishmael, "a wild man" of the desert (16:12); also like him, they were famous for their skill with the bow. Joseph was sold by his brothers to some Ishmaelites (37:25–28).

The word is apparently used in the OT in a wider sense, referring to the nomadic tribes of northern Arabia generally (Gen 37:28, 36; Judg 8:24). All Arabs, following Muhammad's example, claim descent from Ishmael.

ISHMAIAH (ĭsh-mā'yȧ, Heb. *yishma'yâh, Jehovah hears*). 1. A Gibeonite who joined David at Ziklag (1 Chron 12:4).

2. Chief of the Zebulunites in David's reign (1 Chron 27:19).

ISHMERAI (ĭsh'mē-rī, Heb. *yishmeray, Jehovah keeps*). A Benjamite, son of Elpaal, resident of Jerusalem (1 Chron 8:18).

ISHOD (See ISHHOD)

ISHPAH (ĭsh'pȧ, Heb. *yishpâh, firm*). A Benjamite son of Beriah (1 Chron 8:16).

ISHPAN (ĭsh'păn, Heb. *yishpān, he will hide*). Son of Shashak, a Benjamite (1 Chron 8:22).

ISHTOB (See TOB)

ISHUI, ISHUAI (See ISHVI)

ISHVAH (ĭsh'vȧ, Heb. *yishwâh, he will level*). The second son of Asher (Gen 46:17; 1 Chron 7:30).

ISHVI (ĭsh'vī, Heb. *yishwi, level*). 1. The third son of Asher, and founder of a tribal family (Gen 46:17, KJV "Isui"; Num 26:44, KJV "Jesui"; 1 Chron 7:30, KJV "Ishuai").

2. A son of Saul (1 Sam 14:49; KJV Ishui).

ISLAND, ISLE. These words are translations of the Hebrew *i,* which has a much wider significance than the English words. Its root meaning is supposed to be "habitable land."

1. Dry land, as opposed to water (Isa 42:15).
2. An island as usually understood (Jer 2:10).
3. A coastland, whether belonging to continents or islands, as the coastland of Palestine and Phoenicia (Isa 20:6) and the coasts and islands of Asia Minor and Greece (Gen 10:5).
4. The farthest regions of the earth (Isa 41:5; Zeph 2:11). The Jews were not a maritime people, and so there are not many references to islands in the OT. Most of them are found in Isaiah, Jeremiah, and Ezekiel. In the NT a number of islands are mentioned in connection with the missionary journeys of the apostle Paul, viz., Cyprus, Crete, Lesbos, Samos, Samothrace, Chios, Melita, and Sicily. John was banished to the Isle of Patmos for the sake of the Word of God (Rev 1:9).

ISMAIAH (See ISHMAIAH)

ISMAKIAH (ĭs'mȧ-kī'ȧ, Heb. *yismakhyâhû, Jehovah sustains*). An overseer connected with the temple in the reign of Hezekiah (2 Chron 31:13).

ISPAH (See ISHPAH)

ISRAEL (ĭz'rā-ĕl). Used in Scripture to designate: (1) an individual man, the son of Isaac (see JACOB); or (2) his descendants, the twelve tribes of the Hebrews; or (3) the ten northern tribes, led by the tribe of Ephraim, as opposed to the southern, under the tribe of Judah.

Before the year 2100 B.C., the God who directs all history chose the patriarch Abraham and called him out of Ur of the Chaldees (Gen 11:31; Neh 9:7). The Lord's redemptive purpose was to bring Abraham and his descendants into a saving (covenant) relationship with himself (Gen 17:7) and also to make of Abraham's seed a nation in Palestine (17:8) and through them to some day bring salvation to the entire world (12:3; 22:18). God accordingly blessed Abraham's grandson Jacob with many children. Furthermore, when Jacob returned to Palestine in 1909 B.C., God "wrestled" with him and brought him to a point of total submission (32:25; Hos 12:4). By yielding his life to God's purpose, Jacob achieved victory; and God changed his name to Israel, Hebrew *Yisrā'ēl,* which means, "He strives with God and prevails" (Gen 32:28; 35:10). Jacob's twelve sons were, literally, the children of "Israel" (42:5; 45:21). Israel, however, was aware that God would build each of them into a large tribe (49:7, 16). The term "children of Israel" came to signify the whole body of God's chosen and saved people (32:32; 34:7). It included Jacob's grandchildren and all subsequent members of the household, as they proceeded to Egypt for a stay of 430 years, 1876–1446 (46:8; Exod 1:7).

I. Mosaic Period. In the space of approximately ten generations, God increased Israel from a clan of several hundred (Gen 14:14; 46:27) to a nation of almost 3 million souls (Exod 12:37; Num 1:46), equipped with all the material and cultural advantages of Egypt (Exod 2:10; 12:36; Acts 7:22). Their very increase, however, seems to have aroused the envy and fear, first of the land's foreign "Hyksos" rulers (Dynasties XV-XVI, about 1730–1580 B.C.) and then of the native Egyptian Empire that followed (Dynasty XVIII) (Exod 1:8–10). Israel was thus enslaved and compelled to erect certain Hyksos store-cities in the region of the eastern delta (1:11; cf. Gen 15:13) and was threatened with total national destruction under the anti-Semitic policy of the empire (Exod 1:16). Moses (born 1527) was befriended by an Egyptian princess, perhaps the one who was to become the famous queen, Hatshepsut; but even he was forced to flee Egypt during the reign of the great conqueror and oppressor Thothmes III (dated 1501–1447).

God, however, still remembered his covenant promises with Abraham (Exod 2:24–25). At the death of the great Pharaoh (2:23) God appeared to Moses in a burning bush at Mount Sinai and commissioned him to deliver the enslaved people (3:10). Moses accordingly returned to the Egyptian court, with the cry "This is what the LORD says: Israel is my firstborn son, and I told you, 'Let my son go, so he may worship me.' But you refused to let him go; so I will kill your firstborn son" (4:22–23). The new monarch, Amenhotep II (1447–1421 B.C.), had inherited the domineering qualities of his father; and he refused to heed the divine summons. Only after a series of ten miraculous plagues, climaxing in the death of all the first-born of Egypt (see PASSOVER), was the hardhearted Pharaoh compelled to yield to the Lord (12:31).

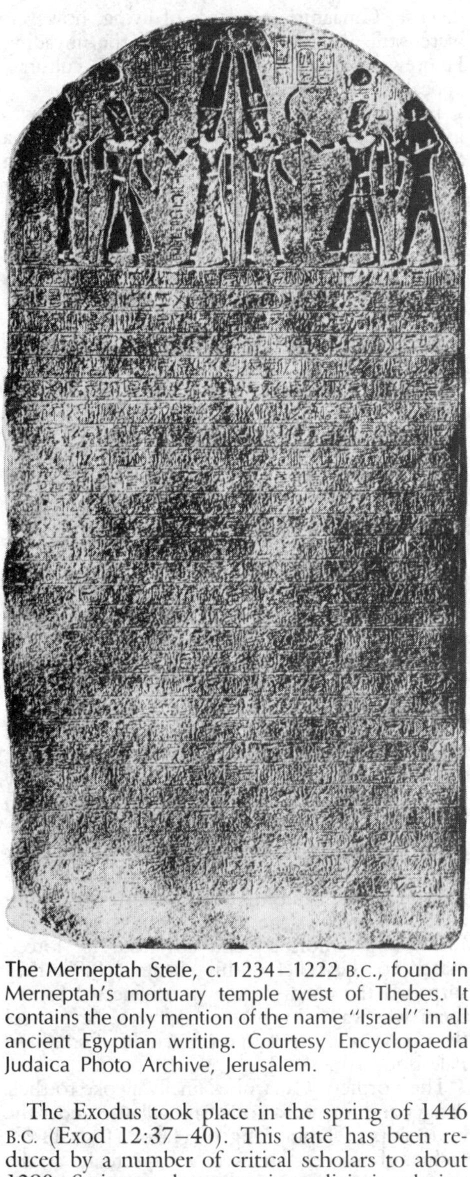
The Merneptah Stele, c. 1234–1222 B.C., found in Merneptah's mortuary temple west of Thebes. It contains the only mention of the name "Israel" in all ancient Egyptian writing. Courtesy Encyclopaedia Judaica Photo Archive, Jerusalem.

The Exodus took place in the spring of 1446 B.C. (Exod 12:37–40). This date has been reduced by a number of critical scholars to about 1290. Scripture, however, is explicit in placing the Exodus in the 480th year before the beginning of Solomon's temple in 966 (1 Kings 6:1); and the fifteenth-century date is then confirmed by other scriptural testimonies (cf. Judg 11:26; Acts 13:19 ASV). Israel marched eastward from Goshen toward the Red Sea. But when the perfidious Pharaoh pursued after the seemingly entrapped Hebrews (Exod 14:3), the Lord sent a strong east wind that blew back the waters of the sea (14:21). Israel crossed, and then the Lord caused the waters to return so that the Egyptians were destroyed to the last man (14:28; excepting Pharaoh, who is not mentioned after v. 10).

Israel reached Mount Sinai at the beginning of summer, 1446 B.C. (Exod 19:1). Here God extended the covenant offer of reconciliation that he had made with Abraham and Jacob (Gen 12:1–3; 28:13–15) so as to embrace the whole nation of the sons of Israel, promising, "Now if you obey me fully and keep my covenant, then out of all nations you will be my treasured possession. Although the whole earth is mine, you will be for me a kingdom of priests and a holy nation" (Exod 19:5–6). God, on his part, provided the objective way of salvation by officially "adopting" Israel as his own sons and daughters (cf. 4:22) on the basis of the atoning death that Jesus Christ, the unique Son of God, would someday suffer to redeem all of God's people (24:8; Heb 9:15–22). For Israel's choice involved a universal goal, that they would become a "kingdom of priests," to bring salvation to others (cf. Isa 56:6–7). Israel was required to fulfill certain subjective conditions, so as to share in this testamental inheritance: "*If* you keep my covenant, then . . . ." Basically, they must in faith commit themselves to God, to be his people. As Moses proclaimed, "Hear, O Israel: . . . Love the LORD your God with all your heart" (Deut 6:4–5). God provided Israel with his fundamental moral law, the Decalogue, or "Ten Commandments" (Exod 20:3–17), together with elaborations in the various other codes of the Pentateuch. God also furnished them with his ceremonial law, to depict Israel's reconciliation with their heavenly Father (e.g., Lev 23:39–40) and to provide a symbolical way of forgiveness, should they transgress his moral requirements (e.g., Lev 6:1–3, 6–7). The ceremonials, however, gained their true effectiveness because they foreshadowed the ultimate redemptive work of Jesus Christ (Heb 9:9–14, 23–24).

In May 1445 B.C. Israel broke up camp (Num 10:11) and marched northeast to Kadesh on the southern border of the Promised Land of Canaan. But after taking forty days to spy out the land, all the tribal representatives except Caleb and Joshua reported unfavorably on attempting any conquest of Canaan: "But the people who live there are powerful, and the cities are fortified and very large" (13:28). Impetuous Israel then refused to advance into the Promised Land and prayed for a return to Egypt (14:4). Moses' intercession did save them from immediate divine wrath; but the Lord still condemned them to wander for forty years in the wilderness, one year for each day of spying, until that entire generation died away (14:32–34).

Israel's route of march, after an extended stay at Kadesh (Deut 1:46), is described in Numbers 33; but the various camps cannot be identified, except that they are known to have passed through Ezion-Geber at the head of the Gulf of Aqabah before a final return to Kadesh (Num 33:35–36). This rough, nomadic existence forced the people into a life of dependence on God, who tested them and yet at the same time cared for them miraculously (Deut 2:7; 8:2–4). This training period was still marred by repeated "murmurings" and defections, such as the revolts of Korah, Dathan, and Abiram (Num 16–17). Even Moses, when producing water for the thirsty people, failed to credit God with the glory (20:10–11) and was therefore denied entrance into the Promised Land (20:12).

In the late summer of 1407 B.C. (Num 20:28; 33:38), the advance of the Hebrews on Canaan was resumed. However, the Edomites (a people descended from Israel's twin brother Esau) refused to allow kindred Israel to pass through their territories (20:21). The result was that the Israelites were compelled to double back to Ezion Geber on the Red Sea and go completely around the land of Edom, marching northward up "the king's highway" along the eastern border of Edom and Moab (21:4, 22). Opposite the midpoint of the Dead Sea, Israel reached the territory of the Canaanite kingdom of Sihon of Heshbon. Although Sihon refused to allow Israel further passage, it was actually God who had hardened the king's heart (Deut 2:30), whose very attack provided the occasion for his total overthrow and for Israel's occupation of the land of Gilead (Num 21:24). Similar aggression by Og, king of Bashan, resulted in Israel's acquisition of northern Transjordan as well (21:35). By the end of February 1406, Israel was able to set up camp on the Plains of Moab, across the Jordan from Jericho (Deut 1:3–5).

During the last month of Moses' life, God's great servant conducted a "numbering" or census of the people, which indicated a figure of over six hundred thousand fighting men, only slightly less than had taken part in the Exodus forty years before (Num 26:51; cf. 1:46). Moses then granted the request of the tribes of Reuben, Gad, and half of Manasseh to settle in the conquered lands of Transjordan (ch. 32); and he provided for the division of western Canaan among the remaining tribes (chs. 33–34). At this time Balaam, who had been employed by the Moabites to curse Israel, uttered his famous blessings. The seer climaxed his oracles by predicting the future messianic king, whose coming constituted the purpose of Israel: "I see him, but not now; I behold him, but not near. A star will come out of Jacob; a scepter will rise out of Israel. He will crush the foreheads of Moab, the skulls of all the sons of Sheth" (24:17). Moses then anointed Joshua as his successor (27:23), spoke the final two addresses that constitute most of the Book of Deuteronomy, chapters 1–4 and 5–30, and ascended Mount Pisgah to view the Promised Land. There Moses died and was buried by God's own hand (Deut 34:5–6). He had been the founder of the Hebrews as a nation. "Since then, no prophet has risen in Israel like Moses, whom the LORD knew face to face" (34:10).

II. The Conquest. At Joshua's accession, the land of Canaan lay providentially prepared for conquest by the Hebrews. Comprising nominally a part of the Egyptian Empire, Canaan suffered the neglect of Amenhotep III (c. 1412–1376 B.C.), called "the magnificent," whose rule was one of luxury, military inactivity, and decay. Political organization within Palestine was that of many small city-states, impoverished by a century of Egyptian misrule and deficient in cooperative defense. Canaanite standards of living, however, were still superior to those of the invading Hebrews, a fact that was later to lend "cultural" appeal to their debased religion.

In the spring of 1406 B.C. the Jordan River was in its annual flood stage (Josh 3:15). But Joshua anticipated a miracle of divine intervention (3:13), and the Lord did indeed open a gateway into Canaan. For "the water from upstream stopped flowing. It piled up in a heap a great distance away, at a town called Adam," some fifteen miles (twenty-five km.) north of Jericho (3:16). Israel marched across the dry riverbed, led by the ark of God's testament (3:13).

Joshua's war of conquest developed in three major campaigns: in central, southern, and northern Canaan. His first objective was the city of Jericho, to his immediate west in the Jordan Valley. "At the sound of the trumpet, when the people gave a loud shout" outside Jericho's walls, the Lord caused the walls to collapse (Josh 6:20), and Joshua proceeded to "devote" the city to God (6:21). Joshua ascended westward into Canaan's central ridge and, after an initial setback because of sin in the camp (7:20–21), seized the post of Ai. It seems to have served as an outer defense of the major city of Bethel (8:17), which surrendered without further resistance (12:16; cf. Judg 1:22). Joshua was thus able to assemble Israel at Shechem to reaffirm the Mosaic Law (Josh 8:33; according to Deut 27:11–26), having subdued all of central Canaan.

To the south, Gibeon next submitted and, by trickery, saved themselves from the destruction that God had decreed (Deut 7:2; Josh 9:15). Their action, however, provoked an alliance against them of five kings of the southern Amorites, under the headship of Jerusalem, who retaliated by laying siege to Gibeon (Josh 10:5). Joshua was informed and advanced by forced march to the relief of his clients (10:9); they surprised the enemy and with divine aid routed them westward down the Aijalon Valley. Israel then proceeded to ravage the whole of southern Palestine (10:28–42).

The northern Canaanites finally awoke to their danger and formed an offensive alliance under the leadership of Jabin, king of Hazor (Josh 11:5). Joshua, however, attacked unexpectedly at the Waters of Merom, NE of Galilee, and completely routed the allied forces (11:7–8). Only Hazor was actually destroyed (11:13), but this triumph meant that within six years of the fall of Jericho (cf. 14:10) all Canaan had come to lie at Joshua's feet (11:16). "So the LORD gave Israel all the land he had sworn to give their forefathers . . . every [promise] was fulfilled" (21:43, 45). The Canaanites had not yet lost their potential for resistance; and indeed, what the Lord had sworn to Israel had been a gradual occupation of the land (Exod 23:28–30; Deut 7:22). Much still remained to be possessed (Josh 13:1), but at this point Joshua was compelled by advancing age to divide the land among the twelve Hebrew tribes (Josh 13–22). He then charged his people with faithfulness to the Lord (24:15) and died.

III. Judges. Moses had ordered the "devotion" (extermination) of the Canaanites (Deut 7:2), both because of their longstanding immoralities (9:5; cf. Gen 9:22, 25; 15:16) and because of their debasing religious influence on God's people (Deut 7:4; 12:31). In the years immediately following Joshua's death, Judah accordingly accomplished an initial capture of Jerusalem (Judg 1:8; though the city was not held, 1:21); Ephraim and western Manasseh killed the men of Bethel (1:25) because the city had begun to reassert itself. But then came failure: Israel ceased to eradicate the Canaanites, no more cities were taken (1:27–34), and the tribe of Dan actually suffered eviction themselves (1:34). Israel's tolerance of evil had to be rectified by national chastening (2:3).

The next three and one-half centuries were used of God to impress on his people three major lessons: (1) The Lord's wrath because of sin. When Israel yielded to temptation God, "sold them to their enemies all around, whom they were no longer able to resist" (Judg 2:14). (2) God's mercy when people repented. The Lord would then raise "up a judge for them, he was with the judge and saved them out of the hands of their enemies" (2:18). (3) Man's total depravity. "When the judge died, the people returned to ways even more corrupt than those of their fathers" (2:19). The period of the fourteen judges (twelve in Judges, plus Eli and Samuel in 1 Samuel) demonstrates a repeated cycle of human sin, of servitude or supplication, and then of salvation.

From about 1400 to 1250 B.C. the chief external forces that God employed for the execution of his providential dealings were the rival empires of the Hittites north of Palestine and of the Egyptians to the south. Neither of these powers was conscious of the way God was using them; but still, the years in which either succeeded in maintaining Palestinian law and order proved to be just the period that God had chosen for granting "rest" to Israel. Suppiluliuma, for example, who took the throne of the Hittite New Kingdom in about 1385, fomented dissension among the Palestinian states that owed nominal allegiance to Egypt's Amenhotep III and Amenhotep IV; with this international intrigue coincides Israel's first oppression, by Cushan Rishathaim, an invader from Hittite-controlled Mesopotamia (Judg 3:8). The underlying cause, however, lay in Israel's sin against the moral requirements of God's Sinaitic covenant. (Compare the sordid events of Micah and the Danites and of the Benjamite outrage [Judg 17–21], which belong to this period, 18:1; Josh 19:47.) When they "cried out to the LORD, he raised up for them a deliverer, Othniel son of Kenaz, Caleb's younger brother" (Judg 3:9). The forty years of peace that then followed correspond to the time of undisputed Hittite sway over Palestine, until some years after the death of Suppiluliuma c. 1345.

Founded in the 1320s B.C., however, the Nineteenth Dynasty of Egypt began to reassert its territorial claims. Behind this international confusion lay the fact that "once again the Israelites did evil in the eyes of the LORD, and because they did this evil the LORD gave Eglon king of Moab power over Israel," for eighteen years (Judg 3:12, 14). Again the Israelites cried out to the Lord, and he gave them a deliverer—Ehud, a left-handed man, the son of Gera the Benjamite (3:15)—and granted them eighty years of peace. This was the time of the treaty of 1315 between Seti I of Egypt and Mursil II of Heth, who preserved order by dividing the Near East into separate spheres of influence. The treaty was then renewed in 1279, after a futile war of aggression by Rameses II, and was strictly enforced until the death of the last great Hittite king, c. 1250.

Against the oppressive Canaanite Jabin II of Hazor (Judg 4:2–3), God raised up the fourth of the judges, the woman Deborah. Her military commander, Barak, proceeded to muster the north-central tribes to the Valley of Esdraelon for war with Jabin's officer, Sisera. Then "the stars fought, from their courses they fought against Sisera" (5:20; cf. v. 21): a divinely sent cloudburst immobilized the powerful Canaanite chariotry, and Sisera himself was murdered in flight by a Kenite woman. The forty-year peace that followed Deborah's victory coincides with the strong rule of Rameses III at the turn of the century, the last great Pharaoh of the Nineteenth Dynasty.

Next came the nomadic Midianites and Amalekites out of the eastern desert to plunder sinful Israel (Judg 6:2–6). In about 1175 B.C., however, the Lord answered the repentant prayers of his people and raised up Gideon with his chosen band of three hundred. "A sword for the LORD and for Gideon" cleared Israel of the nomadic raiders (7:19–25; 8:10–12), as witnessed by the peaceful picture of Ruth 2–4 some twenty-five years later. The turmoil that resulted from the attempt of Gideon's son Abimelech to make himself king over Israel (Judg 9) was rectified by the sixth and seventh judges, Tola and Jair (who must have overlapped, for no separate deliverance is ascribed to the latter, 10:1–5). But with their deaths in 1110 and the apostasy that subsequently arose, God delivered up his land to two simultaneous oppressions: that of the Ammonites in the east, and that of the Philistines in the west (10:7). After eighteen years, eastern Israel was freed by Jephthah, the eighth judge (Judg 11), who was succeeded by three minor judges. Western Israel, however, remained subject to the rising power of the Philistines for a full forty years (13:1), until the advent of Samuel in 1070. This period must therefore embrace the activity of Eli, until about 1090 (1 Sam 4:18), as well as the spectacular but politically ineffective exploits of Samson, the twelfth and last judge of the Book of Judges, to about 1075 (Judg. 13–16; see 15:20).

These Philistines were a Hamitic people. But unlike the native Palestinians, who descended from Ham's son Canaan, they traced their descent from an elder brother, Mizraim (Egypt), through Casluhites (Cyrene, Gen 10:14) and Caphtor (Crete, Amos 9:7). Some of these "Minoan" peoples had settled along the Mediterranean coast of Palestine as early as 2100 B.C. (Gen 21:32; 26:14; cf. Deut 2:23; Josh 13:23). The very name Palestine, in fact, means the "Philistine land." But with the fall of Crete to a barbarian invasion in 1200, "the remnant from the coasts of Caphtor" (Jer 47:4) came to reinforce the older Minoan settlements. Although driven back from Egypt by a crushing defeat at the hands of Rameses III in about 1196, these "sea peoples," by reason of their superior discipline and equipment (cf. Judg 3:31; 1 Sam 13:22; 17:5–6), were able to mount three oppressions, commencing respectively in 1110, 1055, and 1010, and thereby to threaten the very existence of Israel.

Their opening oppression climaxed in the first battle of Ebenezer (1 Sam 4) and resulted in the deaths of Eli and his sons, in the capture of the ark, and in the destruction of the Lord's house at Shiloh (see Jer 7:14). God in his grace, however, raised up the prophet Samuel, who ended the oppression by a God-given victory at the second battle of Ebenezer in about 1070 B.C. (1 Sam 7). But later, as Samuel turned over many of his powers as judge to his corrupt sons (8:1–3), the Philistines returned with barbaric cruelty (cf. 31:8–10; Judg 16:25), seeking to crush disorganized Israel.

IV. The United Kingdom of Israel was precipitated by the demand of the people themselves. Despite God's directive that they be holy and separate (Lev 20:26), they still wished to be like "all the other nations" (1 Sam 8:5), with a human king to fight their battles (8:20), rather than having God acting through a theocratic judge (8:7). They conveniently forgot that it was faithlessness that brought them under attack in the first place. Still, their rebellion served to accomplish God's purpose (see Ps 76:10); for he had long before decreed a kingdom in Israel over which Jesus the Messiah would someday reign (Gen 49:10; Num 24:17). The Lord accordingly authorized Samuel to anoint a king (1 Sam 8:22) and directed him to Saul of Benjamin (ch. 9).

Saul's accession proceeded in three steps. He was first privately anointed by Samuel (1 Sam 10:1) and filled with God's Spirit (10:10), then publicly selected at Mizpah (10:24), and at last popularly confirmed at Gilgal, after having delivered the town of Jabesh Gilead from Ammonite attack (Judg 11). The primary concern of his forty-year reign (1050–1010 B.C., cf. Acts 13:21) was the Philistines. These oppressors had already occupied much of his territory, and open war was provoked when one of their garrisons was destroyed by Saul's son Jonathan (1 Sam 13:3). In the ensuing battle at Micmash, Jonathan's personal bravery (14:14), plus the Philistines' own superstitious reaction to a heaven-sent earthquake (14:15, 20), brought about their total defeat. Saul thus terminated the second oppression but, by his failure to submit to Samuel (13:8–9), suffered the rejection of his dynasty from the throne of Israel (13:14).

From his capital in Gibeah of Benjamin, Saul "fought valiantly" and pushed back the enemies of Israel on every hand (1 Sam 14:47–48). In about 1025 B.C., however, having been ordered to destroy Israel's implacable enemies the Amalekites (15:1–3; cf. Exod 17:14), Saul disobeyed and spared both the king and the best of the spoils, under pretext of making offerings to God (1 Sam 15:15). Samuel stated that "to obey is better than sacrifice" (15:22) and declared Saul's personal deposition from the kingship (15:23, 28). Samuel then privately anointed David, a son of Jesse of Judah, as king over Israel (16:13). David was about fifteen at the time (cf. 2 Sam 5:4); but by God's providence, he gained rapid promotion at court, first as a minstrel (1 Sam 16:21–23) and then by his victory over the Philistine champion Goliath (ch. 17). Even Saul's growing jealousy, which removed David from court to the dangers of battle, augmented the latter's popularity (18:27–30). Saul's overt hostility finally drove David and his followers into exile, first as outlaws in Judah (1 Sam 20–26) and then as vassals to the Philistine king of Gath (1 Sam 27–30). But while Saul was diverting his resources in the futile pursuit of David, the Philistines prepared for a third, all-out attack on Israel in 1010. David barely escaped engaging in war against his own people (29:4; cf. v. 8); and Saul, routed at Mount Gilboa, committed suicide rather than suffering capture (31:4). Israel's sinful demand for a king had brought about their own punishment.

Having learned of the death of Saul, David moved to Hebron and was there proclaimed king over his own tribe of Judah (2 Sam 2:4). But despite David's diplomacy, the supporters of Saul set up his son Ish-Bosheth over the northern and eastern tribes (2:8–9). Civil war followed, but David increasingly gained the upper hand (3:1). Finally, after the death of Ish-Bosheth, the tribal representatives assembled to Hebron and there anointed David as king over all Israel (5:3; 1003 B.C.). The Philistines now realized that their future depended on prompt action. David, however, after an initial flight to his former outlaw retreat (5:17), rallied his devoted forces (cf. 23:13–17) and, by two brilliant victories in the vicinity of Jerusalem (5:9–25), he not only terminated the last Philistine oppression but eventually incorporated Gath into his own territory and subdued the remaining Philistine states (1 Chron 18:1).

The time was ripe for the rise of a Hebrew empire. The Hittites had succumbed to barbarian invasion; the Twenty-first Dynasty of Egypt stagnated under the alternating rule of priests and merchants (1100 B.C. on); and Assyria, after having weakened others, was itself restrained by inactive kings. With Philistia broken, Israel remained free from foreign threat for 150 years. David's first strategic move was to capture Jerusalem from the Canaanites. Militarily, Mount Zion constituted a splendid fortress (2 Sam 5:6, 9); politically, the city afforded David a neutral capital between the recently hostile areas of Judah and northern Israel; and religiously, Zion's possession of the ark of God's testament (6:17) centered the people's spiritual hopes within its walls (Ps 87). From about 1002 to 995 David extended his power on every side, from the Euphrates River on the north (2 Sam 8:3) to the Red Sea on the south (8:14).

David sought to construct a "house," or temple, in Jerusalem that would be fitting for the Lord. This plan was denied him because of his excessive bloodshed (1 Chron 22:8; cf. 2 Sam 8:2); but God's prophet did inform him, "The LORD himself will establish a house for you" (2 Sam 7:11). He explained, "When your days are over and you rest with your fathers, I will raise up your offspring to succeed you, who will come from your own body; . . . he is the one who will build a house for my Name." God's promise, moreover, extended beyond Solomon and climaxed in that One in whom Israel's ultimate purpose would be fulfilled: "And I will establish the throne of his kingdom forever. I will be his [the Messiah's] father, and he will be my son" (7:13–14; Heb 1:5). The eternal Christ would indeed suffer a "testator's" death (Ps 22:16–18), but would rise in power to give everlasting life to his own (16:10–11; 22:22, 26). In the Lord's promises to him (89:3; 132:12) David experienced fundamental clarifications of God's former redemptive revelation on Mount Sinai. He exclaimed in his psalms and other inspired writings:

"Is not my house right with God?
  Has he not made with me an everlasting
    covenant,
  arranged and secured in every part?
Will he not bring to fruition my salvation
  and grant me my every desire?"
(2 Sam 23:5).

In his later life David became involved in sins of adultery and murder (2 Sam 11) and of failure to control his sons (ch. 13–14), and for this he received corresponding punishments (chs. 15–16; cf. 12:10–12). The revolt of Absalom served also to intensify the antagonism between northern Israel and southern Judah (19:41–43). But at his death in 970 B.C. David was able to commit to his son Solomon an empire that marked the peak of Israel's power.

Solomon, after a bloody accession (1 Kings 2:25, 34, 36), reigned in peace, culture, and luxury, experiencing only one military campaign in forty years (2 Chron 8:3). He was further able to consummate an alliance with the last pharaoh of the Twenty-first Dynasty (1 Kings 3:1). King Solomon is most famous, however, for his unexcelled wisdom (4:31), which was achieved by humility before God (3:7–12) and through which he composed the inspired Proverbs, Ecclesiastes, and Song of Songs, plus numerous other works (Pss 72, 127; cf. 1 Kings 4:32). His greatest undertaking was the building of the Jerusalem temple, erected from 966 to 959 B.C. (1 Kings 6) out of materials lavishly provided by David (1 Chron 22). Like the tabernacle before it, the temple symbolized the abiding presence of God with his people (1 Kings 8:11).

But Solomon also engaged in a number of luxurious building projects of his own (1 Kings 7:1–12), so that despite his great commercial revenues (9:26–28; 10:14–15) indebtedness forced him to surrender territory (9:11–12) and to engage in excessive taxation and labor conscription. Unrest grew throughout the empire; and, while the tribute continued during his lifetime (4:21), surrounding subject countries, such as Edom and Damascus, became increasingly independent (11:14, 23). More serious was Solomon's spiritual failure, induced by wanton polygamy (11:1–8). "The LORD became angry with Solomon because his heart had turned away from the LORD . . . . So the LORD said to Solomon 'Since this is your attitude and you have not kept my covenant, . . . I will most certainly tear the kingdom away from you and give it to one of your subordinates . . . . Yet I will not tear the whole kingdom from [your son], but will give him one tribe for the sake of David my servant and for the sake of Jerusalem, which I have chosen' " (11:9–12).

V. The Divided Kingdom. Early in 930 B.C. Solomon died, and his son Rehoboam went to Shechem to be confirmed as king. The people, however, were led by Jeroboam of Ephraim to demand relief from Solomon's tyranny (1 Kings 12:4), and when Rehoboam spurned their pleas, the ten northern tribes seceded to form an independent kingdom of Israel (or Ephraim). Underlying causes for the rupture include the geographical isolation of the tribes (compare the phrase "to your tents," 12:16) and their long-standing social tensions (2 Sam 2:7–9; 19:43). But the basic reason lay in God's decision to punish Israel for Solomon's apostasy (1 Kings 11:31; 12:15, 24). Furthermore, while northern Israel possessed the advantages of size, fertility of land, and foreign-trade contacts, these very features diminished their devotion to the Lord and his Word. Ephraim's spiritual laxness became immediately apparent when Jeroboam introduced two golden calves, with sanctuaries at Dan and Bethel to rival Jerusalem (12:28). He did attempt to associate these images with the historic God of the Exodus; but they were still idols, "other gods" (14:9), and not mere pedestals for the Lord's invisible presence. Each succeeding king of Israel likewise "walked in all the ways of Jeroboam, . . . and in his sin, which he had caused Israel to commit" (see e.g., 15:26; 16:19, 26). The division served ultimately to separate the sinful Hebrews from the two faithful tribes of Judah and Benjamin: "For not all who are descended from Israel [Jacob] are Israel" (Rom 9:6).

The relations between Ephraim and Judah passed through seven stages.

1. Hostility marked their course for the first two generations. Initially, both kingdoms suffered from raids by Shishak, the energetic founder of Egypt's Twenty-second Dynasty (2 Chron 12:1–9). Later, Jeroboam advanced against Rehoboam's son Abijah (913–910 B.C.); but God granted a great victory to outnumbered Judah (ch. 13), "because they relied on the LORD, the God of their fathers" (13:18). Pious Asa

(910–869) ended Twenty-second Dynasty threats by routing the hosts of Zerah the Cushite (Pharaoh Osorkon I?) at the turn of the century (14:9–15) and then led Judah in a revival of faith in God's covenant (15:12). But when faced by Ephraimite garrisons at Ramah, only six miles (ten km.) from Jerusalem, the king panicked and hired Ben-Hadad of Damascus to divert the energies of Israel (16:1–4). God's prophet condemned Asa because he "relied on the king of Aram and not on the LORD [his] God" (16:7); and the precedent of Syrian intervention had serious consequences. King Omri (885–874) founded Samaria as the new capital of Ephraim; but Ben-Hadad laid repeated siege to the city, and Omri's son Ahab was saved only by the grace of God (1 Kings 20).

2. Asa's son Jehoshaphat made peace with Ahab (1 Kings 22:44). The allies, together with Ben-Hadad, did manage to halt the westward advance of Shalmaneser III of Assyria at the bloody battle of Qarqar on the Orontes (853 B.C.). But Jehoshaphat had given his son in marriage to Athaliah, the Baal-worshiping daughter of Ahab and his Phoenician queen Jezebel, the persecutor of Elijah (19:2); and such compromise could never be honored by God (2 Chron 19:2). Jehoshaphat was almost killed at the side of Ahab at Ramoth Gilead (1 Kings 22:32–35). Their joint commercial projects met with disaster (2 Chron 20:35–37). Moab succeeded in revolting from Ephraim (2 Kings 1:1), and Edom from Judah (8:22); and when Jehu executed God's sentence against the house of Ahab in Israel (841), he killed Judah's young king with them (9:27). Athaliah then slaughtered her princely grandchildren and seized the throne in Jerusalem (11:1).

3. The years between 841 and 790 B.C. saw no major dealings between Israel and Judah because of Syrian domination over both kingdoms (see 2 Kings 8:12). Thus, even though Athaliah was killed in Jerusalem, the boy-king Joash suffered humiliating submission to Hazael of Damascus (12:17–18). Jehu fared even worse, rendering tribute to Shalmaneser in 841 and then, after Assyria's departure, forfeiting his entire Transjordanian territory to Hazael. Only an Assyrian victory over Damascus shortly before 800 brought relief to Israel (13:5).

4. By 790 B.C. Amaziah of Judah had recovered sufficiently to reconquer Edom (2 Kings 14:7), but his success deceived him. He dared to challenge Jehoash of Israel (14:10), and Jerusalem was rendered totally subservient to Ephraim until the death of Jehoash in 782.

5. Under the strong monarchs Jeroboam II in Israel and Uzziah in Judah the two kingdoms lived for thirty years in mutual respect and peace. It was their "Indian summer": Egypt slumbered on under the Twenty-third Dynasty; Syria was broken by Assyria; and Assyria herself, now without aggressive leadership, could be swayed even by the contemporary Hebrew prophet Jonah (2 Kings 14:25). But beneath the outward prosperity lay moral corruption. Amos proclaimed impending judgment on "the day of the LORD" (Amos 5:18). Hosea, too, warned of deportation to Assyria (Hos 10:6); but with the abolishment of God's old covenant with Israel, he anticipated a future, newer covenant in which people would "acknowledge the LORD" in truth, under "David [the Messiah] their king" (2:20; 3:5).

6. In 752 B.C. Jeroboam II's son was murdered, and Uzziah (Azariah) of Judah assumed the leadership of the western states against the rising power of Assyria. The general Pul, who became Tiglath-Pileser III, was able in 743 to chronicle his defeat of "Azariah the Yaudaean"; and while Judah apparently escaped with little damage, Damascus and Israel, being farther north, were laid under heavy tribute (2 Kings 15:19).

7. The Syrians and Ephraimites then united in reprisals against Ahaz, Judah's new but weak and faithless ruler (2 Kings 16:5; Isa 7:1–2). Isaiah admonished him to trust in God and in Immanuel, the virgin-born Messiah (Isa 7:3–14); but in 734 B.C. Ahaz submitted to Assyria for deliverance (2 Kings 16:7). Edom and Philistia continued to plunder Judah (2 Chron 28:17–18) and may thus provide the background to Obadiah (see Obad 10) and Joel (Joel 3:4, 19); but Ephraim's northern tribes were taken captive by Tiglath-Pileser in 733 (2 Kings 15:29), and Damascus was destroyed (16:9). Shortly after that the energetic Twenty-fifth (Cushite) Dynasty rose to power in Egypt, and So (Shabaka?) incited Israel to a final revolt (17:4). Samaria fell to the Assyrians in 722. Sargon II (722–705) proceeded to deport 27,290 Ephraimites (17:6) and replaced them with foreign colonists, who produced the half-breed Samaritans (17:24–33). "They . . . did not trust in the LORD their God. They rejected his decrees and the covenant. . . . So the LORD removed them from his presence. Only the tribe of Judah was left" (17:14–15, 18).

Hezekiah (725–696 B.C.) meanwhile seized the opportunity to purify the Jerusalem temple (2 Chron 29) and to destroy the corrupt high places, whether outrightly pagan or claiming the name of the Lord. His reform included even Israel, which was not helpless under Assyrian siege (31:1); and he invited Ephraimites and Judeans alike to the greatest Passover since Solomon (ch. 30). The name "Israel" came thus to be applied to God's faithful remnant, regardless of their previous citizenship (30:6; cf. Ezra 9:1; 10:5). Hezekiah was warned by both Isaiah (Isa 30:1–7; 31:1–3) and Micah (Mic 1:9) to take no part in Shabaka's disastrous battle against Sargon in 720; and he managed to withdraw from the equally unsuccessful revolt of Ashdod in 711, which was sponsored by Egypt and Babylon (Isa 20 and 39; cf. 36:1). But with the accession of Sennacherib in 705, Hezekiah attempted to throw off the Assyrian yoke. Egypt, however, proved again to be a "splintered reed" (2 Kings 18:21); Shabaka was defeated at Eltekeh near Ekron in 701, and Sennacherib claims to have taken over two hundred thousand Jews captive (cf. Isa 43:5, 14) and to have "shut up Hezekiah like a caged bird in Jerusalem." Hezekiah resubmitted (2 Kings 18:14–16), but the false Sennacherib made further demands (18:17). God then rose to the defense of his chastened people (Isa 37:6, 21–35), and, when a relief army arrived under Shabaka's brother Tirhaka, it found the Assyrians dead, for they had been killed by the angel of the Lord (2 Kings 19:9, 35; cf. the Egyptian legend of a plague of mice in the camp of Sennacherib, Herodotus, 2.141). The event ranks with the crossing of the Red Sea as one of the greatest examples of God's deliverance. Isaiah thus had a sound basis for comforting Israel (Isa 40:1–2) and directing their hope to that day when God would fulfill his redemptive purpose among them (53:6).

Manasseh's reign (696–641 B.C.) was the longest and worst in Judah's history. He gave up Hezekiah's dearly bought freedom by resubmitting to Assyria. He also rebuilt the high places, served Baal with human sacrifice, and mimicked Assyrian star worship (2 Kings 21:2–9). Through imprisonment (after the Babylonian revolts of 652–648?), he experienced personal conversion (2 Chron 33:11–16); but it was too late to reform the people as a whole (33:17; cf. 2 Kings 21:11, 15; 23:26). God, however, was yet to raise up Josiah (639–608), the greatest of Judah's reformers. While still in his teens (627), he responded to prophetic teaching such as Zephaniah's (Zeph 1:14–17) and began actively to eliminate idolatry (2 Chron 34:3–7). At this point the barbaric Scythians erupted over the Near East, and the terror they inspired seems to have turned men's hearts to God. (Compare Jeremiah's earliest sermons in Jeremiah 6:22–26.). The Scythians were finally driven back by the newly formed Twenty-sixth Dynasty in Egypt, but their devastations did serve to release Judah from foreign control for a full twenty years. Josiah used these last precious decades to establish the covenantal faith once and for all among the pious. His reforms climaxed in 621 with the discovery of "the Book of the Law of the LORD that had been given through Moses" (2 Chron 24:14), perhaps the chief sanctuary scroll of the Pentateuch (Deut 31:25–26) that had been misplaced under Manasseh (cf. 2 Chron 35:3). Josiah and his people reconsecrated themselves "to obey the words of the covenant written in this book" (34:31). He removed the high places (2 Kings 23:8–9), including even Jeroboam's original altar at Bethel (23:15), and kept the greatest Passover since the days of the judges (2 Chron 35). "Neither before nor after Josiah was there a king like him who turned to the LORD as he did—with all his heart and with all his soul and with all his strength, in accordance with all the Law of Moses" (2 Kings 23:25).

In 612 B.C. Nineveh fell to the Medes and Babylonians, just as Nahum had prophesied (Nah 3:18–19). The Medes then withdrew, but Egypt and Babylon arose to claim the spoils. Josiah intervened to oppose the advance of Pharaoh Neco II and was killed at Megiddo in 608 (2 Chron 35:20–24). Neco, however, was decisively defeated by the Babylonians at Carchemish in 605; and Nebuchadnezzar appropriated the former Assyrian territories (2 Kings 24:7). Josiah's son Jehoiakim (23:34) was threatened with deportation to Babylon (cf. 2 Chron 36:6 and 2 Kings 24:1–6), but only a few of the nobility, such as Daniel (Dan 1:3), were actually taken captive at this time. The date 605 marks the commencement of Judah's predicted seventy years of captivity (Jer 25:11–12). But while the prophet Habakkuk was admonishing his people to "live by . . . faith" (Hab 2:4), Jehoiakim reverted to the sins of his fathers (2 Kings 23:37). He also rebelled against Babylon (24:1), but he died in 598, and it was his son, with ten thousand of the leaders of Judah, who suffered the second deportation when Jerusalem surrendered on March 16, 597 (24:10–16). Finally, Jehoiakim's brother Zedekiah yielded to the inducements of Pharaoh Hophra of the Twenty-sixth Dynasty and defied Nebuchadnezzar (cf. Jer 37:11). The Babylonians advanced, Hophra withdrew, and Jerusalem fell in 586. The city and temple were burned (2 Kings 25:9), the walls were dismantled (25:10), and most of the people were carried into exile in Babylon (25:11). A small, fourth deportation in 582 removed even some of the poor that were left (25:12; Jer 52:30). Israel had "mocked God's messengers, despised his words and scoffed at his prophets until the wrath of the LORD was aroused against his people and there was no remedy" (2 Chron 36:16). But though the external kingdom of Israel ceased to exist, it did so because it had accomplished its divine purpose. A remnant, albeit small, had been nurtured to the point of profiting from the fiery trial of Babylon (see EXILE) so as to be ready for that ultimate day: " 'The time is coming,' declares the LORD, 'when I will make a new covenant with the house of Israel . . . I will put my law in their minds and write it on their hearts. I will be their God, and they will be my people. For I will forgive their wickedness and will remember their sins no more' " (Jer 31:31–34; Heb 8:6–13; 10:15–22).

Bibliography: H. M. Orlinsky, *Ancient Israel,* 1954; W. F. Albright, *From the Stone Age to Christianity,* 1957; M. Noth, *The History of Israel,* 1960; G. E. Wright, *Biblical Archaeology,* 1962; F. F. Bruce, *Israel and the Nations,* 1963; R. deVaux, *Ancient Israel,* 1965; R. K. Harrison, *Old Testament Times,* 1970; J. Bright, *A History of Israel,* 1972; J. H. Hayes and J. M. Miller (eds.), *Israelite and Judaean History,* 1977. JBP

ISSACHAR (ĭs'ȧ-kär, Heb. *yissākhār,* meaning uncertain). 1. The ninth son of Jacob and the fifth of Leah (Gen 30:17–18; 35:23). Almost nothing is known of his personal history beyond his share in the common actions of the sons of Jacob. He had four sons, who went with him into Egypt (46:13; Exod 1:3). There he died and was buried. His descendants formed a tribe, consisting of five great tribal families (Num 26:23–24).

Not much is known of the tribe. Its territory lay south of Zebulun and Naphtali and north of Manasseh. It was bounded on the east by the Jordan. It occupied the greater part of the very fertile plain of Esdraelon, which, however, was mostly held by the Canaanites. Along the southern edge of the plain there were fortresses held by Manasseh. At the first census in the wilderness the tribe numbered 54,400 fighting men (Num 1:28–29); at the second, 64,300 (26:25). In the days of David the figure reached 87,000 (1 Chron 7:5). Igal, son of Joseph, was the spy from Issachar (13:7). Deborah and Barak belonged to Issachar; and in Deborah's song (Judg 5:15) the tribe is mentioned as having taken part in the battle against Sisera. One of the judges, Tola, belonged to it (Judg 10:1), as did two kings, Baasha and his son (1 Kings 15:27). The princes of Issachar abandoned allegiance to Saul's family and accepted David as king of all Israel (1 Chron 12:32). Many men from the tribe attended Hezekiah's Passover, though they belonged to the northern kingdom (2 Chron 30:18). The tribe is mentioned in Revelation 7:7, where we are told that 12,000 from Issachar were sealed.

2. A Korahite doorkeeper in the reign of David (1 Chron 26:5).

ISSHIAH (ĭs′shī′ȧ, Heb. *yishshîyāhû, Jehovah exists*). 1. A man of Issachar (NIV 1 Chron 7:3; Izrachiah in JB, KJV, MLB, NASB, NEB, RSV).

2. One of those who came to David at Ziklag (1 Chron 12:6, Jesiah in KJV).

3. A Levite of the house of Rehabiah (1 Chron 24:21).

4. A Levite of the house of Uzziel (1 Chron 23:20; 24:25).

ISUAH (See ISHVAH)

ISUI (See ISHVI)

ITALIAN REGIMENT. A cohort of volunteer Roman soldiers recruited in Italy and stationed in Caesarea when Peter preached the gospel to Cornelius, who was a centurion in it (Acts 10:1). It consisted mostly of Italians who could not find service in the Praetorian Guard.

ITALY (Gr. *Italia*). The geographical term for the country of which Rome was the capital. Originally it applied only to the extreme south of what is now Italy, the region now called Calabria; but gradually the application of the name was extended, until in the first century of our era it began to be used in the current sense. It is referred to four times in the NT: (1) In Acts 18:2 Aquila and Priscilla had just come from Italy because Emperor Claudius had commanded that all Jews leave Rome. (2) It is mentioned in Acts 27:1, as Paul's destination when he had appealed to Caesar; and in verse 6 Paul is put on board a ship of Alexandria sailing for Italy. (3) In Hebrews 13:24 Christians from Italy send their greetings along with those of the author of the letter. (4) In Acts 10:1 it is mentioned as the country that gave its name to the cohort stationed at Caesarea, of which Cornelius was the centurion. Christianity was early introduced into Italy, but the time and circumstances are uncertain.

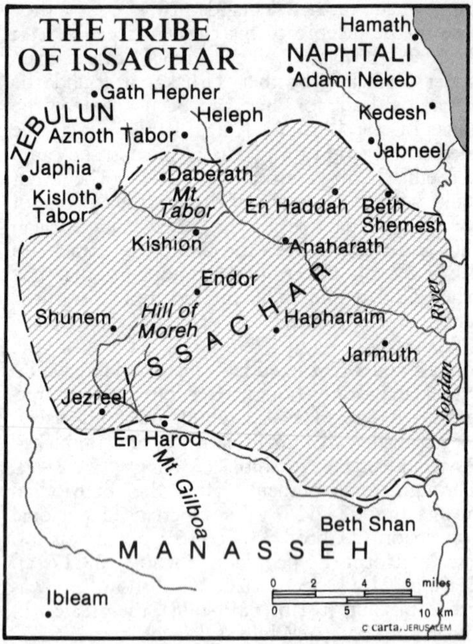

ITCH (See DISEASES)

ITHAI (îth′ā-ī, *'îthay*). A Benjamite, one of David's chief men (1 Chron 11:31); Ittai in 2 Samuel 23:29 (JB, KJV, MLB, NASB, NEB, RSV).

ITHAMAR (ĭth′ȧ-mȧr, Heb. *'îthāmār*). The youngest of the four sons of Aaron, the others being Eleazar, Nadab, and Abihu. Aaron and his sons were consecrated to the priesthood (Exod 28:1), but Nadab and Abihu were put to death for offering unauthorized fire (Lev 10). During the wilderness wanderings he was the treasurer of the offerings for the tabernacle (Exod 38:21) and superintendent of the Gershonites and Merarites (Num 4:28, 33). He founded the priestly family to which Eli and his descendants belonged, and this continued after the Captivity (1 Chron 24:4–6; Ezra 8:2).

ITHIEL (ĭth′ĭ-ĕl, *'îthî 'ēl, God is*). 1. One of two persons to whom Agur addressed his sayings (Prov 30:1).

2. A Benjamite (Neh 11:7).

ITHLAH (ĭth′lȧ, Heb. *yithlāh*). A town in the territory of the tribe of Dan (KJV "Jethlah"), near Aijalon (Josh 19:42). The site is unknown.

ITHMAH (ĭth′mȧ, Heb. *yithmâh, purity*). A Moabite, one of David's heroes (1 Chron 11:46).

ITHNAN (ĭth′năn, Heb. *yithnān*). A town in southern Judah (Josh 15:23). The place is not identified.

ITHRA (See JETHER)

ITHRAN (ĭth′răn, Heb. *yithrān, excellent*). 1. A

Horite, son of Dishon (Gen 36:26; 1 Chron 1:41).

2. A son of Zophah of the tribe of Asher (1 Chron 7:37).

ITHREAM (ĭth'rē-ăm, Heb. *yithre'ām*). The sixth son born to David at Hebron. His mother was Eglah (2 Sam 3:5; 1 Chron 3:3).

ITHRITE (ĭth'rīt, Heb. *yithrî, excellence*). A family that lived at Kiriath Jearim (1 Chron 2:53). Two of David's heroes belonged to this family: Ira and Gareb (2 Sam 23:28; 1 Chron 11:40).

ITTAH-KAZIN (See ETH KAZIN)

ITTAI (ĭt'ā-ī, Heb. *'ittay*). 1. A son of Ribai, a Benjamite, one of David's thirty mighty men (2 Sam 23:29 JB, KJV, MLB, NASB, NEB, RSV; but NIV has "Ithai," as in 1 Chron 11:31).

2. A native of Gath who left his Philistine city and joined David's army. He commanded six hundred men. He was loyal to David through all the ups and downs of his reign. When Absalom rebelled against David, Ittai fled with the king and refused to return to Jerusalem, where, David told him, his interests lay. David made him a commander of a third part of his army, with Joab and Abishai. In the battle that followed, Absalom was killed (2 Sam 15:18–22; 18:2, 5).

ITUREA (ĭt'ū-rē'ā, Gr. *Itouraia, pertaining to Jetur*). This word is found only once in Scripture, in the description of Philip's territory: "of Iturea and Traconitis" (Luke 3:1). It was a region NE of Palestine, beyond the Jordan, and cannot now be exactly located. The Itureans were descended from Ishmael (Gen 25:15), who had a son named Jetur, from whom the name Iturea is derived. The Itureans were seminomads and famous archers, a lawless and predatory people. According to an ancient writer, David warred against them. It is not known when they moved from the desert to the mountains in the north. Until the fourth century A.D. there was no defined territory called Iturea; only the ethnic name Itureans was used. In Luke 3:1, according to Ramsay, the word is an adjective. In 105 B.C. Aristobulus I conquered and annexed the kingdom to Judea. In 66 Pompey defeated its king, Ptolemaeus, who purchased immunity with a large sum of money. Lysanias, son of Ptolemaeus, was put to death by Antony, who thereupon gave the tetrarchy to Cleopatra (36). Later Augustus gave it to Herod the Great, and after his death it passed to his son Philip.

IVORY (Heb. *shēn*, Gr. *elephantinos*). The word *shen* means a "tooth," but it is also often used in the sense of "ivory." The context always makes clear how it should be translated. Ivory was brought to Palestine by both ship and caravan and came from India. Solomon's throne was made of ivory (1 Kings 10:18), and he imported large quantities of it. Amos denounced Israel for its luxuries, among them the use of ivory (Amos

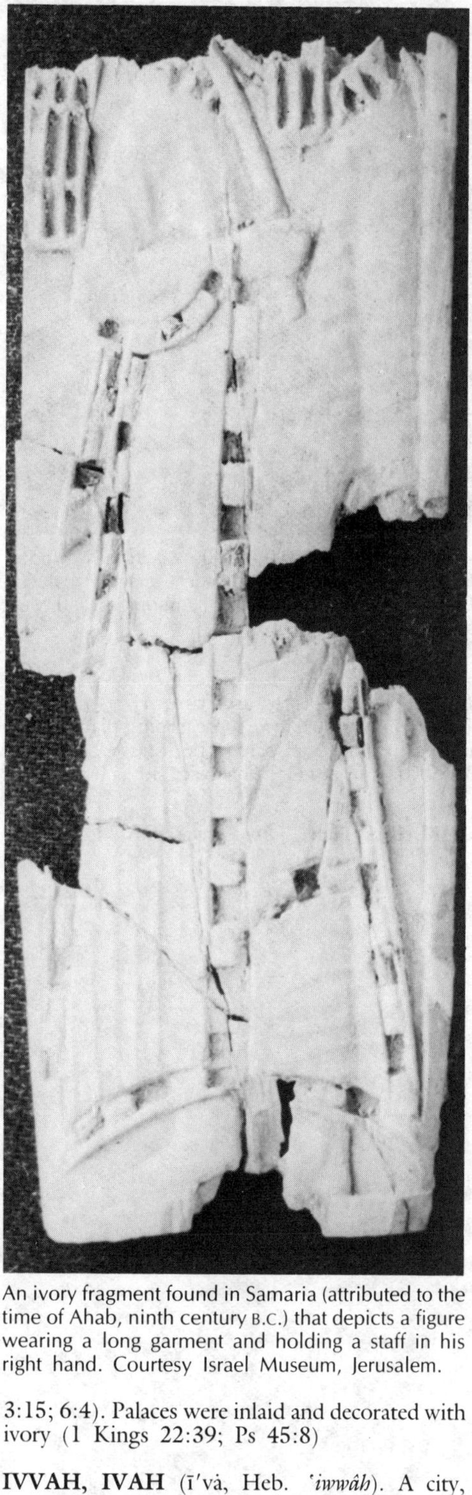

An ivory fragment found in Samaria (attributed to the time of Ahab, ninth century B.C.) that depicts a figure wearing a long garment and holding a staff in his right hand. Courtesy Israel Museum, Jerusalem.

3:15; 6:4). Palaces were inlaid and decorated with ivory (1 Kings 22:39; Ps 45:8)

IVVAH, IVAH (ī'vā, Heb. *'iwwâh*). A city, probably in Syria, captured by the Assyrians, according to the boast of Sennacherib's representative (2 Kings 18:34; 19:13; Isa 37:13)

Ivory carvings (c. 1350–1300 B.C.) from Megiddo, found in a treasury beneath the Canaanite palace. Courtesy Israel Department of Antiquities and Museums.

IYE ABARIM (ī'yĕ ăb'ȧ-rĭm, Heb. *'îyê hā-'ăvārîm, ruins of Abarim*). A camping place in the journeyings of Israel, said to be "on the border of Moab" (Num 33:44). The exact site is unknown.

IYIM (ī'ĭm, Heb. *'îyîm, heaps, ruins*). 1. A town in Judah near Edom (Josh 15:29; NIV Iim). The exact site is uncertain.

2. A town east of the Jordan River (Num 33:45), equated by NIV footnote with Iye Abarim.

IZHAR (ĭz'hȧr, Heb. *yitshār, the shining one*). 1. A Levite, son of Kohath, whose descendants formed a tribal family (Exod 6:18–19; Num 3:19; 1 Chron 6:18, 38).

2. In ASV and RSV a descendant of Judah, whose mother was Helah (1 Chron 4:7). NIV has "Zohar"; KJV and NEB have "Jezoar."

IZLIAH (ĭz-lī'ȧ, Heb. *îzlî 'āh*). A man of the tribe of Benjamin, son of Elpaal (1 Chron 8:18; KJV "Jezliah").

IZRAHIAH (ĭz'rȧ-hī'ȧ, Heb. *yizrahyâh, Jehovah arises* or *shines*). A chief of the tribe of Issachar (1 Chron 7:3).

IZRAHITE (ĭz'rȧ-hīt, Heb. *yizrâh, rising, shining*). Shamhuth, the captain of the fifth division of David's army, is called an Izrahite (1 Chron 27:8). The name may be a corruption of "Zerahite," a descendant of Zerah of Judah.

IZRI (ĭz'-rī, Heb. *yitsrî, creator, former*). A man of the sons of Jeduthun, chief of one of the Levitical choirs (1 Chron 25:11). Called Zeri in 25:3.

IZZIAH (ĭ-zī'ȧ, Heb. *yizzîyâh, Jehovah unites*). A Jew in Ezra's time who put away his foreign wife (Ezra 10:25; KJV "Jeziah").

J

JAAKAN (jā'ȧ-kăn, Heb.*ya'ăqān*). A descendant of Esau (1 Chron 1:35–42; NIV "Akan"; KJV "Jakan"). He was the son of Ezer, who was a Horite (Gen 36:20–27, "Akan"). Israel rested in the land of the Jaakanites, where there were wells, and Aaron was buried there (Deut 10:6–7). In the report of Israel's wanderings the camp is called *Bene* (sons of) *Jaakan* (Num 33:31–32).

JAAKOBAH (jā'ȧ-kō'bȧ). A Simeonite prince (1 Chron 4:36).

JAALA, JALLAH (jā'ȧ-lȧ). A servant of Solomon whose children returned from Babylon (Ezra 2:56).

JAALAM (See JALAM)

JAANAI (See JANAI; JANNAI)

JAAR (jā'ȧr, Heb. *ya'ăr, wood, forest*). KJV and ASV of Psalm 132:6 render the Hebrew word "the field of the wood," whereas NIV and RSV render it as a place-name, "Jaar." If it is a place, it can possibly be identified with Kiriath Jearim, where the ark was stored for twenty years before David brought it to Jerusalem.

JAARE-OREGIM (jā'ȧ-rē-ôr'ē-jĭm, Heb. *ya'ărê-ōreghīm*). The father of Elhanan, who killed the giant brother of Goliath (2 Sam 21:19; see footnote). The title *oregim* means weaver and seems to have been added by a scribe who confused the real name with the size of the giant's sword. Jaare also seems to be a scribal error, since the name is given in Chronicles as Jair (1 Chron 20:5). Most authorities agree that the name in Chronicles is correct.

JAARESHIAH (jā'ȧ-rē-sī'ȧ). A son of Jerohan (1 Chron 8:27), of the tribe Benjamin.

JAASIEL (jā-ā'sĭ-ĕl, Heb. *ya'ăsî'ēl, God makes*). A son of Abner, of the tribe of Benjamin, a leader of the Benjamites (1 Chron 27:21) and a valiant warrior (11:47).

JAASU (jā'ă-sū, Heb. *ya'ăsu*). One of a number of captives who married alien women but put them away when a council headed by Ezra demanded that they do so (Ezra 10:16–19, 37).

JAAZANIAH (jā-ăz'ȧ-nī'ȧ, Heb. *ya'ăzanyāhû, ya'ăzanyah, Jehovah hears*). 1. A soldier from Maacah whose land east of the Jordan was given to the tribe of Manasseh (Josh 13:7–11). He was captain under Gedaliah (2 Kings 25:23). Jeremiah calls him Jezaniah (Jer 42:1), Azariah (43:2), as well as Jaazaniah (40:8). He joined a group who killed Gedaliah and then, contrary to advice from Jeremiah, led a band of refugees into Egypt (43:1–7).

The seal of Jaazaniah (right) and its impression from Mizpah (Tell en-Nasbeh), late seventh century B.C. Inscription reads, "(Belonging) to Jaazaniah, servant of the king." Courtesy Palestine Institute of Pacific School of Religion, Berkeley, California.

2. The son of a Recabite named Jeremiah and was among a group of refugees who refused to drink wine that Jeremiah the prophet offered (Jer 35:1–11).

3. A leader in idolatrous worship that Ezekiel saw in a vision (Ezek 8:10, 12).

4. The son of Azzur, one of a band of twenty-five men who led in wickedness and idolatry in Israel (Ezek 11:1–3).

JAAZER (See JAZER)

JAAZIAH (jā'ȧz-ī'ȧ, Heb. *ya'ăzīyāhŭ, Jehovah strengthens*). A descendant of Levi; and a temple musician in David's time (1 Chron 24:26–27).

JAAZIEL (jā-ā'zĭ-ĕl, Heb. *ya'ăzî'ēl, God strengthens*). A temple musician (1 Chron 15:18), called Aziel in verse 20.

JABAL (jā'băl, Heb. *yāvāl*, meaning uncertain). A son of Lamech, who was the great-grandson of Cain (Gen 4:19–20). He and his brothers, Jubal and Tubal-Cain, are credited with the origin of civilized society (4:21–22).

JABBOK (jăb'ŏk, Heb. *yabbōq, flowing*). An important river east of the Jordan about halfway between the Dead Sea and the Sea of Galilee. It formed the northern border of the Amorite king Sihon (Josh 12:2) and was captured by the Hebrews after Sihon refused to let them cross his

The Jabbok River, modern Wadi Zerga, flows into the Jordan some 20 miles (32 km.) north of the Dead Sea. This is the river Jacob crossed with his wives, maids, and children (Gen 32:22) and that marked the boundaries between the territories of Ammon and Gad (Deut 3:16). Courtesy Garo Nalbandian.

land (Num 21:21–25). It was also the southern border of the kingdom of Og (Josh 12:5). At a ford on the Jabbok, Jacob had his encounter with the angel—the encounter that resulted in his being given a new name (Gen 32:22–30). The word for "wrestle" is *abbaq* and may have given the Hebrew name to the stream; or possibly an ancient fortress between Damascus and Mecca, Xarka, may have furnished the name. Its modern name is Ez-zerka, *river of blue*. It is shallow except during occasional rains, and its fords are easily crossed. Its basin is second in size of Jordan's eastern tributaries, only the Yarmuk to the north having a larger watershed. Its banks are covered with heavy vegetation, the portion near the Jordan being semitropical. The Jabbok rises within twenty miles (thirty-three km.) of the Jordan, but runs sixty miles (one hundred km.), at first NE, then nearly due west in a great arc before turning SW to the Jordan. This unusual course explains the statement in Numbers 21:24, the upper section being the boundary between Sihon and Ammon, and the arc the eastern boundary of Sihon's realm. JDF

JABESH (jā'bĕsh, Heb. *yavēsh, dry*). 1. Father of Shallum, who murdered Zachariah and reigned over Israel for a month (2 Kings 15:8–13).

2. A short term for Jabesh Gilead (1 Chron 10:12). See also JABESH GILEAD.

JABESH GILEAD (jā'bĕsh gĭl'ē-ăd, Heb. *yavēsh gil'ādh, dry*). The metropolis of the Gileadites (*Antiq.* 6.5.1). It lay a night's journey across the Jordan from Beth Shan (1 Sam 31:11–12). It was in the area given to the half-tribe of Manasseh (Num 32:33). When the citizens refused to attend the sacred assembly at Mizpah, an army was sent to destroy them (Judg 21:8–15). The city was not destroyed and grew again in power and wealth. During Saul's reign over Israel, Nahash, king of Ammon, besieged the city. When appealed to for a treaty, Nahash proposed to grant peace only if every able-bodied man would have his right eye put out. A seven-day truce was granted during which time Saul's help was enlisted. Saul killed a pair of oxen and sent the pieces throughout his land, indicating what would happen to those who refused to help in his battle for Jabesh. His army defeated Nahash; the city was saved and the nation reunited (1 Sam 11:1–15). One of the purposes behind this military aid was to secure wives for Benjamites, since Israel had sworn never to allow Benjamites to marry their daughters (Judg 21:1). Later, when Saul's forces had been routed by the Philistines and he and his sons had been killed, men of Jabesh Gilead rescued their bodies, cremated them, and buried the remains in Jabesh (1 Sam 31:1–13). After becoming king, David sent thanks for the act (2 Sam 2:4–6) and had the remains of Saul and Jonathan exhumed and interred in the tomb of Kish in the land of Benjamin (21:12–14).

It is probable that the stream Wady-Yabish received its name from the city. Al-Dair (ed Dair) is now thought to be the probable site of the ancient city. It was ten miles (seventeen km.) east of the Jordan and about twenty-five miles (forty-two km.) south of the Sea of Galilee. JDF

JABEZ (jā'bĕz, Heb. *ya'bēts, to grieve*). 1. The head of a family in Judah (1 Chron 4:9). His offspring are listed as scribes and as Kenites (2:55). He was more honorable than his brothers (4:9). He made an earnest appeal for a blessing and it was granted (4:10). Zobebah (4:8) is probably another title for him.

2. Jabez was also an unidentified town in Judah where scribes carried on their trade (1 Chron 2:55).

JABIN (jā'bĭn, Heb. *yāvîn, able to discern*). 1. A king of Hazor, the leading city in the northern part of Palestine (Josh 11:1). When Joshua had succeeded in conquering the neighboring provinces and had massed his forces at Gilgal (10:7), Jabin led in forming an alliance against him. These tribes occupied the area south of the Sea of Galilee (11:1–4). Joshua, faced by this great force gathered against him, was assured of God that he could defeat them (11:6). Joshua and his forces joined battle with Jabin at the waters of Merom. They chased the enemy all the way to the coast at Zidon, the leading city of Phoenicia (11:8). Hazor was taken, and Jabin killed (11:10).

2. A Canaanite who, after the death of Othniel,

enslaved Israel. Israel was rescued by the strategy of Deborah (Judg 4). Jabin seems to have been only a puppet of Sisera, since he is not mentioned in the Song of Deborah recorded in Judges 5.

JABNEEL (jăb'nē-ĕl, Heb. *yavne'ēl, God causes to build*). A town on the northern border of Judah, just south of Joppa (Josh 15:11), modern Jabna. It is called Jabneh in 2 Chronicles 26:6. It belonged to the tribe of Dan. Judas Maccabaeus captured it (2 Macc 12:8–9), but it was freed by Emperor Pompey in 62 B.C. Herod gave it to Salome, who in turn gave it to the wife of Augustus. Probably through her influence Augustus returned it to the Jews, A.D. 30 (Jos. *Antiq.* 13.2.2). After the fall of Jerusalem it became the seat of the Sanhedrin.

JABNEH (See JABNEEL)

JACAN (jā'kăn). A descendant of Gad (1 Chron 5:13).

JACHIN (See JAKIN)

JACINTH (See MINERALS)

JACKAL (See ANIMALS)

JACOB (jā'kŭb, Heb. *ya'ăqōv, supplanter*). One of the great names of history, a person about whom a multitude of traditions gathered and about whose record scholars have a wide diversity of opinion.

Jacob's name was an old one among the Semitic people. As early as 2000 B.C. it occurs among writings of Hammurabi as *Yakibula*. That it was a well-known name among the Canaanites of pre-Abraham days is attested by records in the temple at Karnak. Two cities captured by Thotmes III are similar to the Hebrew word: Joseph-el and Jakob-el.

Jacob and Esau were children of faith, as was their father (Heb 11:20). However, the continuing influence of Aramean paganism that Abraham had left behind is seen in Rachel's act of taking her father's idols when Jacob was leaving the home of Laban (Gen 31:19). From ancient Assyrian culture came the cunning and creative abilities that enabled Jacob to raise a family that shaped the destiny of the human race.

At the age of forty, Isaac married Rebekah, a sister of his uncle Laban (Gen 25:20). In answer to his prayer on behalf of his barren wife, she conceived twins (25:21). An unusual prenatal incident caused her to consult the Lord, who revealed to her that her children would become the founders of two great nations (25:23). An ominous rivalry, begun in the womb, became visible during the birth of the children. Esau came

Woodcut from the Bishops' Bible, 1568, that illustrates Jacob's Ladder Dream (Gen 28:10–15). Courtesy The British Library.

first; Jacob followed at once, holding Esau by the heel, giving Jacob the name "tripper" or "supplanter" (25:25–26). Nothing is revealed about the childhood of the boys. Because of the ancient law of primogeniture, Isaac naturally favored the older son; but, no doubt because of the revelation from God, Rebekah was partial to Jacob (25:28). Jacob's cunning was revealed in the way he induced Esau to sell his birthright (25:27–34).

Isaac became old and blind. Sensing that his end was near, he desired to impart the paternal blessing. Esau was still the favorite son, so Isaac asked him to prepare a favorite dish, saying that after eating it he would pronounce the blessing (Gen 27:1–4). Rebekah overheard the request and took advantage of Isaac's blindness to further her plan to make Jacob first in every way. Jacob, as ambitious as his mother, joined in the plot. A dramatic scene is given in Genesis 27:6–45. Jacob was dressed in his brother's robe, his mother having skillfully applied goat skins to make his hands and neck hairy like his brother's. Rebekah made a savory dish that Jacob presented to his father. He deliberately told falsehoods: (1) "I am Esau your firstborn," and, in reply to Isaac's question about how he had found the game so quickly, (2) "The Lord your God gave me success." Deceived by the odor of Esau's garments and pleased with the food, Isaac gave the firstborn's blessing to Jacob. Esau, on learning of his brother's treachery, wept and begged for another blessing, which was granted (27:34–40). Rebekah, knowing of Esau's vow to kill Jacob, induced Isaac to send Jacob to Haran to choose a wife from the family of Laban (27:42–28:5).

On the way to Haran, Jacob camped at Luz where he had a vision of a ladder, with angels ascending and descending. In his dream he had a promise from the Lord both to inherit the land about him and to have a numerous progeny (Gen 28:10–15). He recognized that God had been with him, and so he named the place Bethel, "House of God" (28:16–19), and made a vow to tithe all his further possessions (28:20–22). He met Rachel at a well in Haran, watered her flock, revealed himself to her, and was soon at home with Laban (29:1–14). His contract to serve seven years for Rachel ended after fourteen years of indentured servitude (29:15–30).

The conflict between Jacob and Esau had its counterpart in the conflict between Leah and Rachel. Leah won favor from God and bore Reuben (*See! a son!*), Simeon (*God hears*), Levi (*added*), and Judah (*praise,* Gen 29:31–35). Rachel was unable to conceive, and her desire for a son led her to give her maid to Jacob, and she bore Dan (*judge*) and Naphtali (*wrestling,* 30:1–8). Leah in turn gave her maid who bore Gad (*troop*) and Asher (*gladness*). She herself also bore Issachar (*pay for hire*), Zebulun (*abiding*), and finally Dinah (feminine for *Dan* or *judge*). Rachel then bore a son, Joseph (*adding,* 30:22–27). Then Jacob grew eager to return to his own land. After outwitting Laban in stockbreeding, he made his departure. Rachel, probably to insure her share in Laban's estate, stole the teraphim, or family gods (31:19). Laban, learning of Jacob's flight, pursued and overtook him at Mount Gilead where they settled their differences by a covenant, sealed on a memorial heap called Mizpah, or Watchtower (31:25–55).

At Mahanaim Jacob met God, then sent messengers to Esau in Edom. The messengers soon returned to report that Esau was near with a formidable force. Jacob went to the Lord in prayer and received assurance that all would be well. That night he wrestled with the angel of the Lord and secured a new name, Israel, or "Prince of God" (Gen 32:24–32). The meeting with Esau was emotion-packed (33:1–17). Jacob went to Shechem and bought land on which he erected an altar named *El Elohe Israel,* "God is God of Israel" (33:18–20). Dinah was raped at this place. The men of the city were deceived into thinking that by submitting to circumcision they would secure the marriage between Shechem and Dinah (34:1–24); but while they were incapacitated by the operation, Simeon and Levi killed them and pillaged the city (34:25–31). Jacob fled to Bethel. The twelfth son, Benjamin, *son of my right hand,* was born, and Rachel died in giving him birth (35:1–20). Jacob continued to live in Canaan, where Joseph incurred the ill will of his brothers, was sold to Egyptians, and became servant of Pharaoh's chief ruler. He saved the Hebrews (37:1–47:31). Jacob's final act was to call his twelve sons about him, prophesy regarding the future of each one's offspring, and bestow his parting blessing. When he died, he was embalmed, taken by Joseph and a troop of

Turn-of-the-century photograph of Jacob's Well near Shechem, where the Samaritan woman met Jesus (John 4). Courtesy University Library, Istanbul.

Egyptian soldiers to Canaan, and buried in the Cave of Machpelah (49:1–50:13). JDF

JACOB'S WELL. Modern *Bir Ya'kub* is doubtless the well mentioned in John 4:6 as the well of Jacob. For more than twenty-three centuries Samaritans and Jews have believed that this is true. The ground mentioned by John had been purchased by Jacob (Gen 33:19). The area was later wrested by force from the Amorites (48:22). The well is near the base of Mount Gerizim, whose bluffs may have been meant in Jesus' phrase "this mountain" (John 4:21). A narrow opening four feet (one and one-fourth m.) long led from the floor of the vault into the well, which was dug through limestone. The depth of the well has not been determined. One explorer in A.D. 670 claimed it was 240 feet (75 m.). Another reported in 1697 that it was 105 feet (33 m.). In 1861 a Major Anderson found it only 75 feet (23 m.) deep. For centuries, tourists cast pebbles into it until Greek Catholics bought the site and put it under guard.

JADA (jā'da, Heb. *yādhā', a wise one*). A son of Onam and grandson of Jerahmeel of Judah (1 Chron 2:26, 28).

JADAH (jā'da, *honeycomb*). A descendant of Saul (1 Chron 9:42, KJV Jarah; called Jehoaddah in 8:36).

JADDAI, JADAU (jăd'ā-ī, jā'dō, Heb. *yiddô*). An Israelite who married an alien woman during the Captivity (Ezra 10:43).

JADDUA (jā-dū'a, Heb. *yaddûa', known*). An Israelite prince who had part in making the covenant after the return from Babylon (Neh 10:21).

2. A priest who returned with Zerubbabel from Babylon (Neh 12:11, 22).

JADON (jā'dŏn, Heb. *yādhôn, he will plead*). One of the laborers who rebuilt the wall of Jerusalem under Nehemiah (Neh 3:7).

JAEL (jā'ĕl, Heb. *yā'ēl, wild goat*). The wife of Heber the Kenite (Judg 4:17). Sisera fled to Heber's tent when defeated by Barak (4:15, 17). The perfidy of Jael in ignoring the rules of Eastern hospitality becomes less heinous if seen in the light of the war's long record of brutality. Being a woman she could not meet Sisera in combat, so she resorted to cunning, killing him with a weapon she had long since learned to use, a tent peg. That Deborah approved of her act (5:24) only shows to what extremes a harassed people can be driven by a brutal foe. Jael's deed was considered an act of Israel, hence the manner in which Deborah gloated over it. The record raises no question about the moral nature of Jael's deed, nor is it attributed to divine leading, though the victory over Sisera was (5:20).

JAGUR (jā'gêr, Heb. *yâghûr*). A town in the extreme south of the territory of Judah (Josh 15:21). Its site is unknown.

JAH (Heb. *yāh*). A contraction of *Jahweh*. It is found in poetry, as in Psalms 68:4; 118:14 (RSV mg), and is seen in such compound words as Isaiah, *Jah is savior* and Abijah, *Jah is father*.

JAHATH (jā'hăth, Heb. *yahath,* perhaps *God will snatch up*). 1. A grandson of Judah (1 Chron 4:1–2).

2. A great-grandson of Levi (1 Chron 6:20, 43; NIV "Jeheth" in v. 20).

3. A chief among the Gershonite Levites (1 Chron 23:10–11).

4. Another Levite of the Izharite clan (1 Chron 24:22).

5. An overseer of construction during the restoration of the temple under Josiah (2 Chron 34:8–12). He was a Merarite.

JAHAZ (jāhăz). A city in Reuben's heritage (Josh 13:18) in the land given to the Merarites (21:34–36). Israel captured the city, conquered King Sihon, and took the region (Num 21:21–25). The Moabite Stone tells of a king of Israel who lived in Jahaz during a war with Mesha in which Mesha conquered. It was once a stronghold north of the Arnon River. Isaiah (15:4) and Jeremiah (48:20–21) call it a city of Moab.

JAHAZIAH (See JAHZEIAH)

JAHAZIEL (ja-hā'zĭ-ĕl, Heb. *yahăzî'ēl, God sees*). 1. One of a band of ambidextrous warriors who aided David at Ziklag (1 Chron 12:1–4).

2. A priest who sounded the trumpet before the ark (1 Chron 16:6).

3. A son of Hebron and one of a host called by David to help build the temple (1 Chron 23:2–20).

4. The chief bearer of the name was a descendant of Asaph. In a time of great peril he was led by the Holy Spirit to announce a victory when defeat seemed certain (2 Chron 20:14ff.). Psalm 83 may have been written by him to commemorate the victory.

5. An ancestor of one of the families of the restoration (Ezra 8:5).

JAHDAI (ja'dā-ī). Either a concubine or, more likely, a male descendant of Caleb (1 Chron 2:46–47).

JAHDIEL (ja'dĭ-ĕl, *God gives joy*). A mighty man, ancestral head of a Manassite clan (1 Chron 5:24).

JAHDO (ja'dō). A Gadite, a son of Buz and a Gileadite of Jotham's day (1 Chron 5:14).

JAHLEEL (ja'lē-ĕl). A son of Zebulun (Gen 46:14); founder of the Jahleelite clan (Num 26:26).

JAHMAI (jamā-ī). A grandson of Issachar, a chieftain in his tribe (1 Chron 7:1–2).

JAHWEH (See God; YHWH)

JAHZAH (jä'zȧ). A town given to Reuben (1 Chron 6:78; Jer 48:21). It is the same as Jahaz; see also Jahaz.

JAHZEEL (See Jahziel, Jahzeel)

JAHZEIAH (jȧ-zī'-ȧ, Heb. *yahzeyâh, God sees*). One of four who opposed Ezra's plan to rid Israel of alien wives married during the Captivity (Ezra 10:15).

JAHZERAH (jȧ'zĕ-rȧ). A priest of Israel (1 Chron 9:12), perhaps the same as Ahzai of Nehemiah 11:13.

JAHZIEL, JAHZEEL (jȧ'zĭ-ĕl, jȧ'zē-ĕl). A son of Naphtali (Gen 46:24; 1 Chron 7:13), founder of the Jahzeelite clan (Num 26:48).

JAIR (jā'ĕr, Heb. *yā'ir, he enlightens*). 1. A son of Manasseh and a leading warrior in the conquest of Gilead by Moses (Num 32:40–41).

2. One of the judges, a Gileadite who served twenty years (Judg 10:3–5).

3. A Bethlehemite and the father of Elhanan, who killed Lahmi, brother of Goliath the Gittite (1 Chron 20:5). The name is given as Jaare-Oregim in 2 Samuel 21:19 (niv).

4. The father of Mordecai (Esth 2:5).

JAIRUS (jā'ĭ-rŭs, Gr. *Iaeiros*). A synagogue ruler whose child Jesus raised from death (Mark 5:22; Luke 8:41). The Gospel accounts vary somewhat in details, but all agree that the miracle of rising from death occurred.

JAKAN (See Jaakan)

JAKEH (jā'kĕ, Heb. *yāqeh, very religious*). The father of Agur, a writer of proverbs (Prov 30:1–27). Nothing is known about either Jakeh or Agur. "Oracle" may mean prediction, burden, or prophecy. The Hebrew word *ha-massa* is believed to mean the *Massaite*. "Jakeh the Massaite" would be a natural reading (see footnote on 30:1; cf. Gen 25:14).

JAKIM (jā'kĭm, Heb. *yâkîm, God lifts*). 1. A son of Elpaal, a Benjamite (1 Chron 8:12, 19).

2. The head of the twelfth course of priests (1 Chron 24:12).

JAKIN (jā'kĭn, Heb. *yâkhîn, he will set up*). 1. The fourth son of Simeon (Gen 46:10; Jarib in 1 Chron 4:24). Founder of the clan of Jakinites (Num 26:12).

2. One of the priests in Jerusalem during the Captivity (Neh 11:10).

3. During David's reign a leader of the twenty-first course of priests (1 Chron 24:17).

JAKIN AND BOAZ (jā'kĭn, bō'ăz, Heb. *yākhîn, he will set up; bō'az, fleetness, strength*). The names of two symbolic pillars in the porch of Solomon's temple, Jakin on the south, Boaz on the north. They were designed by Hiram of Tyre (1 Kings 7:13–22), hence of Phoenician origin. They were at first ornamental but came to have a religious meaning, guarding the doors to the sacred halls.

Reconstruction of the palace entrance at Tell Ta'yinat in Syria. The two pillars are reminiscent of Jakin and Boaz, the two symbolic pillars in the porch of Solomon's temple (2 Chron 3:17). Courtesy Carta, Jerusalem.

JALAM (jā'lȧm). The second son of Esau by a Hivite woman. He became a chief in Edom (Gen 36:2, 5, 18).

JALON (jā'lŏn). A son of Ezra, of the tribe of Judah (1 Chron 4:17).

JAMBRES (See Jannes and Jambres)

JAMES (Gr. *Iakōbos*). The English form of Jacob. The name occurs thirty-eight times in the NT, mostly in the Synoptic Gospels. Apart from no. 1. below, the identities of those bearing this name have been much debated. They may have been as many as four in number, though some scholars argue for two or three. Jerome, with somewhat tortuous and question-begging argument, contrives the conclusion that the four are really only one. Much fascinating speculation has grown up around the problem, but in the absence of clear biblical connection between one and another, it is convenient to list the occurrence of the name in the maximum number of categories (five) as follows:

1. **James, the son of Zebedee.** He was a Galilean fisherman whose circumstances we can suppose to have been comfortable (Mark 1:20; cf. 15:41; Luke 8:3) and who was called to be one of the twelve apostles at the same time as his brother John (Matt 4:21; Mark 1:19–20). It is reasonable to assume that he was older than John, both

because he is nearly always mentioned first and because John is sometimes identified as "the brother of James" (Matt 10:2; 17:1; Mark 3:17; 5:37).

James, John, and Simon (Peter), who were part of a fishing partnership that included Andrew, Simon's brother (Luke 5:10), came to comprise also a trio that attained in some sense a place of primacy among the disciples. They are often found at the center of events; e.g., when Jairus's daughter was raised (Mark 5:37; Luke 8:51), at the Transfiguration (Matt 17:1; Mark 9:2; Luke 9:28), on the Mount of Olives (Mark 13:3), and in the Garden of Gethsemane (Matt 26:37; Mark 14:33). It was James and John, moreover, who had earlier accompanied Jesus to the home of Simon and Andrew (Mark 1:29).

James and John were given by Jesus the name "Boanerges" or "Sons of Thunder" (Mark 3:17), when they were rebuked by the Lord for impetuosity and for having totally misconceived the purpose of his coming. This may have been the result of a suggestion made by them that they should pray for the destruction of a Samaritan village, whose inhabitants had repulsed Jesus' messengers (Luke 9:54; cf. Mark 9:38; Luke 9:49–50).

Their presumption and ill-considered thinking were obvious also when James, after asking with his brother for a place of honor in the kingdom, was told that they would drink the cup their Master was to drink (Mark 10:35ff.; cf. Matt 20:20ff.). The two sons of Zebedee are also recorded as having been among those present when the risen Christ appeared to the disciples (John 21:1ff.), though it is curious to note that James's name is nowhere mentioned in the Fourth Gospel.

We know nothing about James's career after the Crucifixion until Jesus' prophecy was fulfilled when James was "put to death with the sword" by Herod Agrippa I about A.D. 44 (Acts 12:2). James thus became the first of the Twelve whose martyrdom was referred to in the NT.

The wife of Zebedee was Salome (Matt 27:56; cf. Mark 15:40) who appears to have been a sister of the Virgin Mary (cf. John 19:25). If this was so, James and John were cousins of Jesus and thus may have felt themselves in a privileged position.

An account attributed to Clement of Alexandria says that when James went on trial for his life, his steadfast testimony led to the conversion of his accuser, who was carried off with him to execution. A much less reliable tradition declares that he preached the gospel in Spain, of which country he is the patron saint.

2. **James, the son of Alphaeus.** Another of the apostles (Matt 10:3; Mark 3:18; Luke 6:15; Acts 1:13). Nothing is known for certain about him. Since Levi or Matthew is also described as "the son of Alphaeus" (Mark 2:14), he and James may have been brothers.

3. **James "the younger,"** the son of a Mary (Matt 27:56; Mark 15:40; Luke 24:10) who might have been the wife (or the daughter) of Clopas. Assuming that she was Clopas's wife, some go on to conclude from a superficial word resemblance that Clopas and Alphaeus are two forms of the same name. This in turn has led on to a suggested identification of James, son of Mary, with no. 2. above.

The description "the younger" seems to have been given to distinguish him from the son of Zebedee. The word could also signify that he was smaller than his namesake (the Greek word can cover both interpretations). About this James we know nothing more.

4. **James, the brother of Jesus.** The only two references to him in the Gospels mention him with his brothers Joses, Simon, and Judas (Matt 13:55; Mark 6:3). This James may have been, after Jesus, the oldest of the brothers.

Some scholars have raised the question whether these were indeed full brothers of Jesus by Mary, for such a situation has created difficulty for those who hold the view that Mary remained a virgin, but there seems no good reason to challenge the fact from Scripture. Like the other brothers, James apparently did not accept Jesus' authority during Jesus' earthly life (John 7:5).

There is no specific mention of his conversion; he may have been included in the group to which Jesus appeared after the Resurrection (1 Cor 15:7). He became head of the Jewish Christian church at Jerusalem (Acts 12:17; 21:18; Gal 2:9). Although Jesus had always taught the relative subordination of family ties (Matt 12:48–50; Mark 3:33–35; Luke 8:21), it is hard to believe that James's authority was not somehow strengthened because of his relationship to the Master.

This James was regarded as an apostle (Gal 1:19), although he was not one of the Twelve. Some suggest he was a replacement for the martyred son of Zebedee; others infer his apostleship by widening the scope of that term to embrace both the Twelve and "all the apostles" (see the two separate categories cited in 1 Cor 15:5, 7).

Tradition stated that James was appointed the first bishop of Jerusalem by the Lord himself and the apostles. What is certain is that he presided over the first Council of Jerusalem, called to consider the terms of admission of Gentiles into the Christian church, and he may have formulated the decree that met with the approval of all his colleagues and was circulated to the churches of Antioch, Syria, and Cilicia (Acts 15:19ff.).

James evidently regarded his own special ministry as being to the Jews, and his was a mediating role in the controversy that arose in the young church around the place of the law for those who had become Christians from both Gentile and Jewish origins. That he continued to have strong Jewish Christian sympathies is apparent from the request made to Paul when the latter visited Jerusalem for the last time (Acts 21:18ff.). This was also the last mention in Acts of James's career. His name occurs again in the NT as the traditional author of the Letter of James, where he describes himself as "a servant of God and of the Lord Jesus Christ" (James 1:1).

According to Hegesippus (c. A.D. 180), James's

faithful adherence to the Jewish law and his austere lifestyle led to the designation "the just." It seems clear that he suffered martyrdom; Josephus places his death in the year 61 when there was a Jewish uprising after the death of Festus the procurator and before his successor had been appointed.

Jerome refers to a passage in the Gospel of the Hebrews (the fragments of which appear in various patristic writings) that recounts the appearance of the risen Christ to James. In contrast to 1 Corinthians 15:7, this apocryphal work claims that this was the first appearance of the Lord after the Resurrection. The same writing is alleged to have noted James's vow to eat no bread from the time of the Last Supper until he had seen the risen Lord. This raises questions, not least about the assumption that James was present at the Last Supper.

5. **James, a relative of the apostle Judas.** This Judas (not Judas Iscariot, John 14:22) is called Thaddaeus in Matthew and Mark. The elliptical text in two passages ("Judas of James"—Luke 6:16; Acts 1:13) has been interpreted in two ways: Judas was the brother (KJV) or the son (most other versions) of James. JDD

JAMES, LETTER OF. This letter is among the last to become firmly established in the NT canon. While traces of it seem to be found in the writings of the apostolic fathers (A.D. 90–155), the oldest author to mention it by name is Origen (250), who considers it canonical, although he is aware that its canonicity is not universally acknowledged. Eusebius (323) lists it among the disputed books but says it is read in most churches. In the East the church accepted it from a very early period, but in the West it was not received into the canon until the end of the fourth century.

. The author of the letter refers to himself as "James, a servant of God and of the Lord Jesus Christ" (James 1:1). The NT mentions five who bore the name of James. See JAMES. Tradition attributes the authorship of the letter to James the brother of the Lord, who was probably favored with a special appearance of the risen Christ (1 Cor 15:7) and who from a very early date occupied a leading position in the church at Jerusalem (Acts 12:17; Gal 1:19). Paul names him first among the three pillars of the church in Jerusalem whom he saw on his second visit there after his conversion (Gal 2:9). In Acts 15 he is described as the leader and chief spokesman of the Apostolic Council. All that is known of him shows that he was highly esteemed not only by Christians but by unbelieving Jews. According to Josephus, he was put to death by the high priest in the interregnum between the death of Festus and the arrival of his successor Albinus in A.D. 62.

All the characteristics of the letter support the traditional attribution of it to James the brother of the Lord. The author speaks with the authority of one who knew he did not need to justify or defend his position. There is no more Jewish book in the NT than this letter; and this is to be expected from a man whom both tradition and the rest of the NT show was distinguished by a greater attachment to the law of Moses than Paul had. The whole of the letter, moreover, bears a striking resemblance to the Sermon on the Mount, both in the loftiness of its morality and in the simple grandeur of its expression.

The letter is addressed to "the twelve tribes scattered among the nations." This ambiguous expression may be interpreted in a number of ways: (1) The Jews of the Diaspora in general, who were living throughout the Mediterranean world outside Palestine. This meaning is impossible, for the writer is addressing Christians (James 1:18, 25; 2:1, 12; 5:7–9). (2) The Jewish Christians of the Diaspora. (3) The Christian church as the new people of God living far from their heavenly homeland. Early Christians regarded themselves as the true Israel (Gal 6:16), the true circumcision (Phil 3:3), and the seed of Abraham (Rom 4:16; Gal 3:29), so it would not be surprising if they also thought of themselves as "the twelve tribes." There is no doubt, however, that the letter is intended for Jewish Christians, although its message is applicable to all Christians. Those to whom the author writes worship in synagogues (James 2:2), and the faults he attacks were characteristic of Jews: misuse of the tongue (3:2–12; 4:2, 11), unkind judgments of one's neighbors (3:14; 4:11), the making of rash oaths (5:12), undue regard for wealth (2:1–13), etc. On the other hand, there is no mention of specifically pagan vices—e.g., idolatry, drunkenness, and impurity—against which Paul so often warns Gentile Christians. The object of the author was to rebuke and correct the error and sins into which his readers had fallen and to encourage them in the heavy trials through which they were going.

The scholars who consider this letter the work of James the brother of the Lord do not agree on the date when it was written. Two views are held, one that it was composed shortly before the death of James, in the early sixties; the other, that it appeared in the middle forties, before the Apostolic Council. In favor of the early date are the striking simplicity of church organization and discipline, the fact that Christians still met in the synagogue (James 2:2), and the general Judaic tone. All this is thought to suggest a time before Gentiles were admitted into the church in any large numbers. Scholars who prefer the later date say that the letter gives evidence of a considerable lapse of time in the history of the church, at least enough to allow for a decline in the spiritual fervor that characterized the church in early apostolic times. The readers are obviously not recent converts. The author has a position of long-established authority. The references to persecutions, moreover, fit a later date better than an early one.

The informal character of the letter makes a logical analysis difficult. It is not a formal treatise, but a loosely related series of exhortations, warnings, and instructions, all dealing with the moral and religious life. The author rules authoritatively on questions of church life and discipline that have been brought to his attention.

After the address (James 1:1), James first admonishes his readers on having a right attitude toward tribulations and temptations (1:2–18) and exhorts them to be doers and not merely hearers of the Word of God (1:19–25). He forbids them to slight the poor and favor the rich (2:1–13) and shows them the insufficiency of faith without works (2:14–26). He then warns them against the misuse of the tongue (3:1–12) and sets forth the nature of true and false wisdom (3:13–18). He rebukes them for their greed and lust (4:1–12) and for making foolhardy plans for the future in business (4:13–17). The letter closes with a warning to the godless rich (5:1–6), an exhortation to patience in suffering (5:7–12), a reminder of the power of prayer in every need (5:13–18), and a declaration of the joy of Christian service (5:19–20).

The section on faith and works (2:14–26) is not a polemic against Paul's doctrine of justification by faith, but a rebuke of the prevalent Jewish notion that saving faith is mere intellectual assent to a set of doctrinal propositions. James points out that saving faith manifests itself in works, and that if the works are not there, the genuineness of the faith may be questioned. Paul and James are in perfect harmony in their views of the relationship of faith and works to salvation.

Bibliography: J. B. Mayor, *The Epistle of St. James,* 1897 (on the Greek text); B. Reicke, *The Epistles of James, Peter and Jude* (AB), 1964; C. L. Mitton, *The Epistle of James,* 1966; J. B. Adamson, *The Epistle of James* (NIC), 1976; S. S. Laws, *The Epistle of James* (HNTC), 1980; P. H. Davids, *The Epistle of James* (NIGTC), 1982 (on the Greek text). SB

JAMIN (jā'mĭn, Heb. *yāmîn, right hand*). 1. A son of Simeon (Gen 46:10; 1 Chron 4:24), or a clan of Simeon (Num 26:12).

2. A son of Ram of the tribe of Judah (1 Chron 2:27).

3. A teacher of the law under Ezra (Neh 8:7).

JAMLECH (jăm'lĕk, Heb. *yamlēkh, whom God makes king*). A prince of the tribe of Simeon (1 Chron 4:34).

JANAI (jā'nī). A leader of the tribe of Gad (1 Chron 5:12).

JANIM (jā'nĭm). A town in the land of Judah, site unknown; part of the heritage of Judah (Josh 15:53).

JANNAI (jăn'ī, Gr. *Iannai*). An ancestor of Jesus, fifth in line before Joseph (Luke 3:23–24).

JANNES AND JAMBRES (jăn'ēz, jăm'brēz). Two magicians who withstood Moses and Aaron by duplicating some of their miracles. Paul, who was familiar with rabbinical traditions, named them as types of evil men of the last days (2 Tim 3:8).

JANOAH (jà-nō'à). 1. A town of Naphtali captured by Assyria (2 Kings 15:29).

2. A town on the boundary of Ephraim (Josh 16:6–7).

JANUM (See JANIM)

JAPHETH (jā'fĕth, Heb. *yepheth, God will enlarge,* Gen 9:27). A son of Noah. He was older than Shem (Gen 10:21), but comes third in some lists of the three sons (6:10; 9:18). Shem is usually named first (5:32; 11:10). Japheth and his wife were saved in the ark (7:7). Japheth aided Shem in covering the naked body of their drunken father (9:20–27). He is the progenitor of the more remote northern peoples of SE Europe. That he was to occupy the tents of Shem (9:27) is thought to refer to conquests of the Greeks, who were descendants of Japheth. This he did during the days of Assyrian power. He had seven sons whose descendants occupied the isles of the Gentiles, Hellenes or Greeks (10:5), an area including Asia Minor and upper Greece.

JAPHIA (jà-fī'à, Heb. *yāphîa', tall* or *may God make bright*). 1. A ruler of Lachish who joined a coalition against Joshua (Josh 10:1–5). In a momentous battle in the Valley of Aijalon (10:12–14), the allies were defeated. The five kings fled and sought refuge in a cave, which Joshua sealed up and left under guard while his forces pursued the enemy. Later he had the kings executed and buried in the cave (10:22–27).

2. A son of David born in Jerusalem (2 Sam 5:15; 1 Chron 3:7).

3. A small city on the eastern border of Zebulun (Josh 19:12). It has been identified with modern Yafa, a site not far from Nazareth.

JAPHLET (jăf'lĕt). A great-grandson of Asher, or the name of a clan descended from Asher (1 Chron 7:32).

JAPHLETITES, JAPHLETI (jăf'le'tīts, jăf'lē-tī). An ancient clan whose land was the western border of Joseph's heritage (Josh 16:1–3).

JAPHO (jā'fō). The Hebrew form of Joppa, a border town of Dan's inheritance (Josh 19:46 KJV). See also JOPPA.

JAR (See PITCHER)

JARAH (See JADAH)

JARED (jā'rĕd). The father of Enoch (Gen 5:18–20).

JARESIAH (See JAARESHIAH)

JARHA. (jär'hà). An Egyptian slave of Sheshan, a Jerahmeelite (1 Chron 2:34–35). Since Sheshan had no son, he gave Jarha his freedom so he could marry one of Sheshan's daughters. Jewish sources claim him as a proselyte. That Ahlai (2:31) was the wife seems probable, though the name is masculine. Another theory is that Ahlai is the name given Jarha when he was set free.

JARIB (jār′ĭb, *he strives*). 1. A son of Simeon (1 Chron 4:24), also called Jakin (Gen 46:10).

2. A chief of returning captives, sent by Ezra to secure Levites to carry on the temple worship (Ezra 8:15–20).

3. One of the priests who during the Captivity had married alien wives, whom Ezra ordered to be put away (Ezra 10:18).

JARMUTH (jar′mŭth, Heb. *yarmûth, height*). 1. One of the numerous places included in the heritage of Judah (Josh 15:35) that had been captured from its king, Piram, who was a member of the coalition called by the king of Jerusalem to oppose Joshua (10:1–5). Ruins of the city have been found sixteen miles (twenty-seven km.) WSW from Jerusalem. Walls and numerous wells show it to have been a stronghold—modern Khirbit el Yarmuk.

2. Another city of the name was given to the Gershonite Levites from the heritage of Issachar (Josh 21:27–29), also called Remeth (19:21) and Ramoth (1 Chron 6:73).

JAROAH (ja-rō′a). A chieftain of the tribe of Dan living in the land of Bashan (1 Chron 5:14).

JASHAR, BOOK OF (jā′shar). Quoted in Joshua 10:13; 2 Samuel 1:18; and in LXX of 1 Kings 8:53, this ancient book is thought to have been a collection of poetry, probably odes and psalms in praise of Israel's heroes and exploits. Many ideas about the book have been advanced: (1) It continued the Song of Deborah (Judg 5). (2) It contained the book of the law. (3) It vanished during the Babylonian captivity. It was certainly a well-known bit of Hebrew literature. KJV spells the name "Jasher."

JASHEN (jā′shĕn, *brilliant*). Father of some of David's heroes (2 Sam 23:32). Confusion arises from the fact that 1 Chronicles 11:33–34 calls him Hashem, the Gizonite (evidently another spelling); the LXX there has "the Gunite."

JASHER, BOOK OF (See JASHAR, BOOK OF)

JASHOBEAM (ja-shō′bē-ăm, Heb. *yāshōv'ām, the people return*). 1. One of the heroic men who went to Ziklag to aid David in his struggle against Saul (1 Chron 12:6). He was a Korahite.

2. One of David's chieftains who was a ruler of captains. He killed three hundred during one battle (1 Chron 11:11; or eight hundred, 2 Sam 23:8). The LXX usually gives the name as Ishbaal. He is called Josheb-Basshebeth in 2 Samuel 23:8 (but cf. footnote; KJV Adino). The difference in the report of the number killed has been explained by supposing that some scribe confused the words for three and eight when he copied the record in Samuel. Jashobeam is supposed to have been one of the three who brought David water from the well of Bethlehem (1 Chron 11:15–19).

3. One who commanded a division of twenty-four thousand men of Israel (1 Chron 27:2–3). This man may be the same as no. 2; if so, Hacmonite was an official title.

JASHUB, JASHUBITE (jā′shŭb, jā′shŭb-īt, Heb. *yāshûv, he returns*). 1. A son of Issachar (Num 26:24). Based on MT, Genesis 46:13 has "Job" (KJV, MLB) or "Iob" (NASB, NEB, RSV); LXX has "Jashub" (NIV).

2. One of those who had married foreign wives (Ezra 10:29).

JASHUBI LEHEM (ja-shū′bī-lē′hĕm, Heb. *yāshuvî-lehem*). A word of doubtful meaning (1 Chron 4:22). Either a place-name (NIV, RSV) or the name of a man, a member of the tribe of Judah (ASV, KJV, MLB, NASB).

JASIEL (See JAASIEL)

JASON (Gr. *Iason, to heal*). A believer who sheltered Paul and Silas in Thessalonica (Acts 17:5–9). He was among those who sent greetings from Corinth to Rome (Rom 16:21).

JASPER (See MINERALS)

JATHNIEL (jăth′nĭ-ĕl). A son of Meshelemiah, a Korahite Levite and a temple gatekeeper (1 Chron 26:2).

JATTIR (jă′têr). A large town in the hills of Judah (Josh 15:20, 48), given to the Levites (1 Chron 6:57). It was an important center (1 Sam 30:27). Modern Khirbet Attir is evidently its location.

JAVAN (jā′văn, Heb. *yāwān, Ionian*). 1. A son of Japheth (Gen 10:2, 4; 1 Chron 1:5, 7).

2. A region (perhaps settled by Javan), seen by Ezekiel (27:13, 19; cf. Isa 66:19) as an important trade center. Javan (Gr. *Iōnia*) came to be the name the Hebrews gave to Greece. From 700 to 630 B.C., the Ionians carried on extensive trade in the Near East; hence all people of Greece were called Javan. When the Phoenicians developed their commerce, they often sold captives from Judah to the Greeks (Joel 3:4–6). These later became the agents of God's vengeance against Greece (Zech 9:13); note the contrast of "your sons, O Zion" with "your sons, O Greece." Critics have suggested that Hebrews of preexilic days were not familiar with the Ionians, but discoveries prove that by Solomon's day the Hebrews had much trade with them.

JAVELIN (See ARMS, ARMOR)

JAZER (jā′zêr). A city, with dependent villages, in Gilead east of the Jordan (Num 21:31–32). Built by Gadites (32:34–35), it later became a Levitical city (Josh 21:34–39). David found mighty men among her citizens (1 Chron 26:31).

JAZIZ (jā′zĭz). An overseer of the flocks of David (1 Chron 27:31).

JEALOUSY, WATER OF. The name given

holy water used to determine the guilt or innocence of a wife accused by her husband of unfaithfulness (Num 5:11–28). The accuser brought his wife and made an offering; dust from the tabernacle floor was mixed with holy water, which the woman drank. If she was guilty, the curse pronounced would come true for her; if she was not, she would be cleared of guilt.

JEARIM (jē'à-rĭm). A hill on the northern border of Judah's heritage. The village of Kesalon was built on it (Josh 15:10).

JEATHERAI (jē-ăth'ē-rī). A Gershonite Levite, grandson of Iddo (1 Chron 6:21).

JEBEREKIAH (jē-bĕr'ē-kī'à). The father of Zechariah, a trusted scribe (Isa 8:2).

JEBUS (jē'bŭs, Heb. *yevûs*). The name by which Jerusalem was known while occupied by the Jebusites (Josh 15:63; Judg 19:10; 1 Chron 11:4). Small in area compared with the size of Jerusalem in Solomon's time, Jebus was taken from the Jebusites by David and made the capital of Israel (2 Sam 5:1–9). Its citadel was the stronghold of Zion (1 Chron 11:5).

JEBUSITES (jĕb'ū-zīts, Heb. *yebûsi*). A Canaanite tribe, descended from Canaan according to the table of nations in Genesis 10, and dwelling in the land before the Israelite conquest (Gen 10:15–16; Exod 3:8, 17; Deut 7:1; 20:17; Josh 3:10; 10:1–5; Judg 1:8). Their king, Adoni-Zedek, was one of the five who conspired against Gibeon and was killed by Joshua. The Jebusites lived many years at the site of Jerusalem (Jebus) and were not dislodged until David sent Joab and his men into the city (2 Sam 5:6–7). David then bought the threshing floor of Araunah (or Ornan) the Jebusite as a site for the temple (24:18ff.). This large flat rock where the altar of burnt offering stood is now said to be visible in the Dome of the Rock (Mount Moriah) at Jerusalem.

Eastern slope of Mt. Ophel, looking south, showing the site of the Jebusite citadel called "Zion" and the terracing believed to be the *millo* ("filling") referred to in 1 Kings 9:15, 24. Courtesy Encyclopaedia Judaica Photo Archive, Jerusalem. Photo David Eisenberg.

JECAMIAH (See JEKAMIAH)

JECOLIAH, JECHOLIAH (jĕk-ō-lī'à). Mother of King Uzziah (2 Kings 15:2; 2 Chron 26:3).

JECONIAH (jĕk'ō-nī'à, Gr. *Iechonias*). A variant of Jehoiachin (Matt 1:11–12), sometimes contracted to Coniah (Jer 22:24, 28; 37:1 JB, KJV, MLB, NASB, NEB; Koniah MOF; Jehoiachin NIV). A son of Jehoiakim and grandson of Josiah (1 Chron 3:15–17), he began to reign at age eighteen, but Nebuchadnezzar took him captive after only three months (Ezra 2:6; Jer 24:1; 27:20; 28:4; 29:2).

JEDAIAH (jĕ-dā'yà, Heb. *yedha'yâh, Jehovah knows*). A common name among the descendants of Aaron and Levi. To distinguish among those bearing it is difficult.

1. A descendant of Simeon and the father of a prince (1 Chron 4:37–38).
2. A priest who returned with Zerubbabel and aided in rebuilding the walls of Jerusalem (Neh 3:10; 12:6, 19).
3. One of the priests whose names were entered in the book of the kings that held the genealogy of the Hebrew captives in Babylon (1 Chron 9:1–10). He received the second lot when the order of temple service was set up (24:7). By the time of the return from Babylon his family had grown to be very large (Ezra 2:1, 36; Neh 7:39).

JEDIAEL (jĕ-dī'ā-ĕl, Heb. *yedhī'ă'ēl, known of God*). 1. A son of Benjamin who became head of a mighty clan (1 Chron 7:6, 11). Since the name does not appear among the three sons named in 1 Chronicles 8:1, it is assumed by some scholars that he and Ashbel are the same. Whether he is the same Jediael who joined David's forces at Ziklag and helped swell the host that supported him against Saul (1 Chron 19–22) is uncertain.

2. Another valiant man in David's band (1 Chron 11:45), probably the same as no. 1.

3. A temple doorkeeper, a descendant of Kore (1 Chron 26:1–2).

JEDIDAH (jĕ-dī'dà, *beloved*). Mother of King Josiah (2 Kings 22:1).

JEDIDIAH (jĕd'ĭ-dī'à, *beloved of Jehovah*). Either David or Bathsheba named their baby boy "Solomon," but because of God's love for the child the prophet Nathan gave him this name (2 Sam 12:24–25).

JEDUTHUN (jĕ-dū'thŭn, Heb. *yedhūthûn, praise*). A Levite whom, with Heman and others, David set over the service of praise in the tabernacle (1 Chron 25:1–3). They with their children were to give thanks and sing, with harps and cymbals accompanying. This Jeduthun must have been an old man in David's time, for his sons and their sons are mentioned as serving. In 1 Chronicles 25:3 he is credited with six sons, of whom five are named and the sixth was probably Shimei of verse 17. Psalm 39 by David is dedicated to Jeduthun and Psalms 62 and 77 are "after the manner of Jeduthun."

JEEZER (See ABIEZER)

JEGAR SAHADUTHA (jē'gȧrsā'hȧ-dū'thȧ, *heap of witness*). The name given by Laban to the "witness heap," called by Jacob *Galeed* (Gen 31:47).

JEHALLELEL (jĕ-hăl'ē-lĕl). 1. A descendant of Judah (1 Chron 4:16).

2. A Merarite Levite, father of one of the leaders in cleansing the temple in the days of Hezekiah (2 Chron 29:12).

JEHATH (See JAHATH)

JEHDEIAH (jĕ-dē'yȧ, *Jehovah will be glad*). 1. A descendant of Moses and contemporary of David (1 Chron 24:20). His father's name is Shubael here but Shebuel (JB, KJV, MLB, NASB, RSV; Shubael NEB, NIV) in 23:16, where he is called "the first" or "the chief" of his family.

2. A man of the tribe of Zebulun whom David appointed to have charge of the donkeys that belonged to the king (1 Chron 27:30).

JEHEZKEL (jē-hĕz'kĕl, *God will strengthen*). A priest in David's time (1 Chron 24:16).

JEHIAH (jē-hī'ȧ, *Jehovah lives*). One of the two doorkeepers for the ark in David's time (1 Chron 15:24).

JEHIEL (jē-hī'ĕl, *God lives*). 1. One of the players on psalteries set to high voices in David's time (1 Chron 15:18, 20; 16:5).

2. A Gershonite Levite treasurer for the Lord's house (1 Chron 23:8; 29:8).

3. A son of Hacmoni "the wise," who was with David's sons, probably as tutor (1 Chron 27:32).

4. A son of Jehoshaphat (2 Chron 21:2).

5. A descendant of Heman the singer in Hezekiah's time (2 Chron 29:14; ASV, RSV, Jehuel).

6. One of the overseers of the offerings brought to the temple under Hezekiah (2 Chron 31:13).

7. One of the rulers of the house of God in Josiah's time (2 Chron 35:8).

8. Father of Obadiah who came from captivity with 218 men in Ezra's day (Ezra 8:9).

9. Father of Shecaniah who in Ezra's time was the first to confess to having married a foreign wife and who proposed a covenant with God to put away these foreign wives and their children (Ezra 10:2).

10. One of the priests who confessed to having married a foreign woman (Ezra 10:21).

JEHIELI (jē-hī'ĕ-lī). A Gershonite Levite in David's day (1 Chron 26:21–22); cf. Jehiel (23:8).

JEHIZKIAH (jē'hĭz-kī'ȧ, *Jehovah strengthens*). A son of Shallum, an Israelite in the days of Ahaz king of Judah. He confronted the soldiers of Israel for bringing back as slaves their brothers of Judah (2 Chron 28:12).

JEHOADDAH (jē-hō'ȧ-dȧ). A descendant of King Saul through Jonathan (1 Chron 8:36). In 1 Chronicles 9:42 he is called Jadah (NIV) or Jarah (JB, KJV, MLB, NASB, NEB, RSV).

JEHOADDIN, JEHOADDAN (jē'hō-ăd'ĭn, jē'hō-ăd'ăn). Wife of King Joash of Judah and mother of Amaziah (2 Chron 25:1).

JEHOAHAZ (jē-hō'ȧ-hăz, Heb. *yehô'āhāz, Jehovah has grasped*). 1. The son and successor of Jehu, and eleventh king of Israel. He is said to have reigned seventeen years, c. 815–800 B.C. (2 Kings 10:35; 13:1). Like his father, he maintained the calf worship begun by Jeroboam; and as a result of his apostasy God permitted the Syrians to inflict heavy defeats on his armed forces, until he had almost none left. His kingdom became involved in such awful straits that he in desperation called on the Lord for help. God answered his prayers after his death in the persons of his two successors, Jehoash and Jeroboam II, through whom Israel's ancient boundaries were restored. The life of Elisha extended through his reign. When he died he was succeeded by his son Jehoash (13:2–9, 22–25).

2. King of Judah, 608 B.C. He was the third son of Josiah, and at his father's death he succeeded to the throne. However, he reigned only three months and was then deposed and taken in chains into Egypt by Pharaoh Neco, who had defeated Josiah in battle. The throne was given to Jehoahaz's elder brother (2 Kings 23:30–35). Two time he is called Shallum (1 Chron 3:15; Jer 22:10–12). He died in Egypt.

3. A variant form of the name of Ahaziah, king of Judah (2 Chron 21:17, see footnote; cf. 22:1).

4. The full name of Ahaz, king of Judah, according to an inscription of Tiglath-Pileser III.
SB

JEHOASH, JOASH (jē-hō'ăsh, Heb. *yehô'āsh;* jō'ăsh, Heb. *yô'āsh*). A word of uncertain meaning, perhaps *Jehovah supports* or *whom Jehovah gave*.

1. A son of Beker and grandson of Benjamin, probably born soon after the descent into Egypt (1 Chron 7:8).

2. An early descendant of Judah through Shelah, who with his brother Saraph ruled in Moab (1 Chron 4:22).

3. A descendant of Abiezer son of Manasseh (Josh 17:2; Judg 6:11). Evidently his family had become insignificant, for Gideon his son said, "My clan is the weakest in Manasseh, and I am the least in my family" (Judg 6:15); but in spite of that Gideon could call on ten of his servants for help (6:27). This Joash, though "Jehovah" was a part of his name, had succumbed to the polytheism around him and had built an altar to Baal; but when the men of his city demanded the death of Gideon for destroying the altar, Joash, truer to his family than to his god, stood by his son and said, "Jerubbaal," i.e., "Let Baal plead!" This exclamation became a nickname for Gideon, whom many called "Jerubbaal" thereafter (6:30–32). Gideon was later buried in Joash's sepulcher (8:32).

4. The keeper of David's cellars of oil (1 Chron 27:28).

5. One of the relatives of King Saul who fell away to David while he was in voluntary exile at Ziklag and became one of the commanders of his forces (1 Chron 12:3).

6. A son of King Ahab who was ordered to imprison Micaiah the prophet and to feed him "nothing but bread and water" till Ahab would return to deal with him—but Ahab never returned, and Joash presumably freed Micaiah (1 Kings 22:26; 2 Chron 18:25–26).

7. King of Judah from 884 to 848 B.C. (2 Kings 11–13; 2 Chron 24–25). As an infant he was rescued from Athaliah's massacre of the royal line after the death of Ahaziah in the revolt of Jehu (2 Chron 22:8–9). Jehosheba (2 Kings 11:2; 2 Chron 22:11–12), sister of King Ahaziah and wife of the priest Jehoiada, hid the baby Joash in the house of God for six years, after which Jehoiada showed him to the people and made a covenant with them. Joash became king, living a godly and useful life all the time that his uncle instructed him. See 2 Kings 12 and 2 Chronicles 24 for the details of his reign. He was succeeded by his son Amaziah.

8. The king of Israel from 848 to 832 B.C. (2 Kings 13:10–13; 14:8–16; 2 Chron 25:17–24). He was son of Jehoahaz, son of Jehu, and was father of Jeroboam II. These four comprised the dynasty of Jehu (2 Kings 10:30–31). Jehoash, like the other kings of the north, was an idolater.

JEHOHANAN (jē'hō-hā'năn, Heb. *yehôhānān, Jehovah is gracious*). 1. One of six brothers, doorkeepers of the tabernacle in David's time (1 Chron 26:3).

2. A military leader in Jehoshaphat's time (2 Chron 17:15).

3. The father of Ishmael, who assisted Jehoiada (2 Chron 23:1).

4. One who had married a foreigner in Ezra's time (Ezra 10:28).

5. A priest and head of a priestly family in the days of Joiakim the high priest (Neh 12:13).

6. A priestly singer at the dedication of the new wall of Jerusalem, rebuilt by Nehemiah (Neh 12:42).

7. An Ephraimite chief (NIV 2 Chron 28:12; JB, KJV, MLB, NEB, NASB, RSV Johanan).

8. One who married a foreign woman in Nehemiah's time (Neh 6:18; KJV Johanan).

9. Ezra used his room to fast or mourn for those who had taken foreign wives (Ezra 10:6; KJV Johanan). Jehohanan, or Johanan, is the origin of the name John.

JEHOIACHIN (jĕ-hoi'ȧ-kĭn, Heb. *yehôyākhîn, Jehovah establishes*). Next to the last king of Judah, reigning at Jerusalem three months and ten days (2 Chron 36:9) in the year 597 B.C. He is called Coniah three times (Jer 22:24, 28; 37:1 JB, KJV, MLB, NASB, NEB; Jehoiachin NIV), Jeconiah seven times, and Jechonias (the Hellenized name) once (Matt 1:11–12 lit., KJV).

Jehoiachin was born to Jehoiakim and his wife Nehushta during the reign of the godly Josiah, his grandfather. According to 2 Kings 24:8, he was eighteen when he came to the throne, but 2 Chronicles 36:9 (see NIV footnote) gives his age as eight. Probably an early scribe made a mistake of ten years in copying one of these two books. The evidence favors the record in 2 Kings, for 24:15 speaks of his wives, and he would hardly have been married at eight years of age. Jehoiakim displayed his contempt for the Word of God by cutting up and burning the prophecies of Jeremiah (Jer 36:23, 32), thereby adding to the curses that the Lord pronounced on Jerusalem.

In Ezekiel 19:5–9, Jehoiachin is characterized as "a strong lion. He learned to tear the prey and he devoured men." The prophet announced that the "strong lion" would be taken to Babylon, and this was literally fulfilled later. Although Jeremiah was prophesying with mighty power all through the youth of Jehoiachin, the influences of the palace were stronger than those of the prophet. Jehoiakim had been rapacious, violent, and oppressive. He had "the burial of a donkey—dragged away and thrown outside the gates of Jerusalem" (Jer 22:18–19). In these sad conditions and under the threatening shadow of Nebuchadnezzar, Jehoiachin became king; and in his three months of power "he did evil in the eyes of the LORD, just as his father had done" (2 Kings 24:9). "In the spring King Nebuchadnezzar sent for him and brought him to Babylon" (2 Chron 36:10), where he remained a captive the rest of his life, though apparently not under extremely hard conditions. Nebuchadnezzar died in 561 B.C., and his son Evil-Merodach, who succeeded almost immediately, took Jehoiachin from prison and "spoke kindly to him and gave him a seat of honor higher than those of the other kings who were with him in Babylon. So Jehoiachin put aside his prison clothes . . . ." and after thirty-seven years of captivity was given a daily allowance of food the rest of his life (2 Kings 25:27–30). ABF

JEHOIADA (jē-hoi'ȧ-dȧ, Heb. *yehôyādhā', Jeho-*

vah knows). 1. Father of Benaiah, one of David's most faithful officers. He is mentioned twenty times, but only as the father of his more notable son, who was over the mercenary troops of David. He came from Kabzeel in Judah (2 Sam 20:23; 23:20; 1 Kings 1:38).

2. Grandson of no. 1 (1 Chron 27:34). This Jehoiada was second counselor of David, immediately after Ahithophel, who later became a traitor.

3. A powerful descendant of Aaron who with 3,700 men came to David at Ziklag (1 Chron 12:27).

4. Son of Azariah and brother of Amariah whom he succeeded as high priest. Jehoiada was a high priest; a statesman; a man of God; by marriage a member of the royal family of Judah (2 Chron 22:11); and, humanly speaking, the preserver of the messianic line. He lived 130 years (24:15). He married Jehosheba (2 Kings 11:2), also called Jehoshebeath (2 Chron 22:11 KJV, MLB, MOF, NASB, RSV), and she bore him that Zechariah (24:20–22; Luke 11:51) who so denounced the wickedness of the people that they stoned him at Joash's command. He and his wife hid the child Joash from his evil grandmother (2 Kings 11). When Joash was seven years old, Jehoiada prepared his coup d'etat. He first revealed his plan to five of the captains of hundreds (11:4: 2 Chron 23:1) and showed them little Joash; then they went through Judah and gathered Levites and the heads of loyal houses to Jerusalem, where Jehoiada again exhibited little Joash and started the new reign by anointing him. Athaliah appeared and was killed; then Jehoiada made a covenant with the people to serve the Lord. During the early years of Joash's reign, when he was under the instruction and guidance of the godly Jehoiada, the temple was repaired and Judah began again to prosper. Jehoiada was buried among the kings (2 Chron 24:16). ABF

JEHOIAKIM (jē-hoi'ă-kĭm, Heb. *yehôyāqîm, Jehovah sets up*). Second son of the godly Josiah, king of Judah. He was originally named "Eliakim" (*whom God sets up*). In 607 B.C., Pharaoh Neco of Egypt marched northward, intending to fight the king of Assyria at the Euphrates River. Josiah imprudently intercepted him and was mortally wounded at Megiddo near Mount Carmel. The people of Judah passed by Eliakim and made his youngest brother, Shallum, or Jehoahaz, king after Josiah (1 Chron 3:15; 2 Chron 36:1). Jehoahaz reigned for three months in Jerusalem, when Neco in displeasure "put him in chains at Riblah" in the north of Syria, then sent him to Egypt, where he died (2 Kings 23:33–34). The king of Egypt next took Eliakim, elder half-brother of Jehoahaz, changed his name to Jehoiakim, put the land under heavy tribute, and made Jehoiakim king over Jerusalem, where he reigned from 607–597. Jehoiakim was an oppressive and thoroughly godless king (2 Kings 23:36–24:7; 2 Chron 36:4–8; cf. Jer 22–36).

The prophecies of Jeremiah 22:1–23 were uttered (if all at one time) soon after the death of Josiah and the taking away of Jehoahaz (22:10–12). They describe the wrongdoing and oppression by Jehoiakim (22:13–23). The prophet wrote about the dooms of Judah and the other nations at the direction of the Lord. When the princes heard these words, they let Jeremiah and his clerk Baruch hide themselves; then when the king heard the words of the book, he cut out the passages that displeased him and burned them, with the result that the Book of Jeremiah was rewritten and enlarged (Jer 36). Jehoiakim died in disgrace and had "the burial of a donkey" (22:19).

JEHOIARIB, JOIARIB (jē-hoi'ă-rĭb, joi'ă-rĭb, Heb. *yehôyārîv, Jehovah will contend*). 1. A priest in the days of David who drew first place in the divine service (1 Chron 24:7).

2. One of the first priests to return from exile with Zerubbabel (1 Chron 9:10).

3. A man Ezra sent back to Babylon to obtain Levites to assist the priests (Ezra 8:16–17).

4. The son of Zechariah, son of a man of Shiloh but of the tribe of Judah (Neh 11:5).

5. A priest who returned with Zerubbabel (Neh 11:10; 12:6).

Drawing of a stone window railing from palace of Jehoiakim, King of Judah (607–597 B.C.), at Ramat Rahel near Jerusalem. Courtesy Carta, Jerusalem.

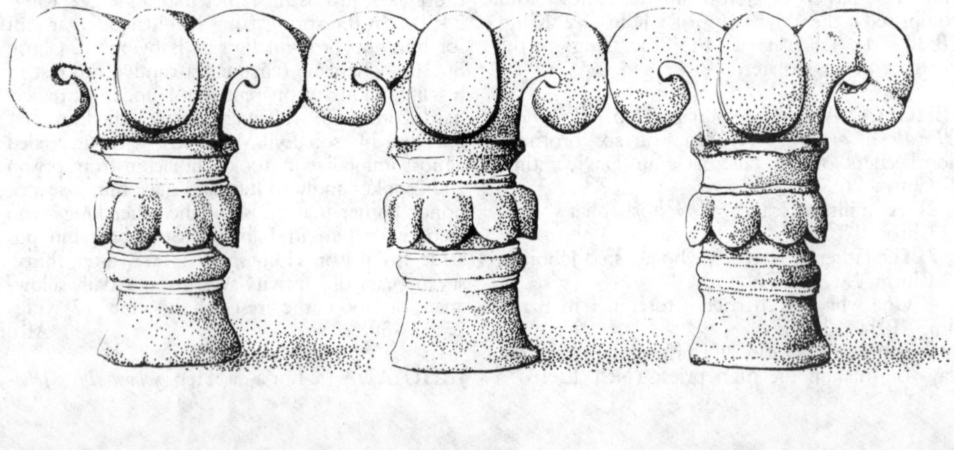

JEHONADAB (jē-hŏn'ā-dăb, Heb. *yehônādhāv, Jehovah is liberal*). Also appears as *Jonadab*. 1. Son of David's brother Shimeah (2 Sam 13:3; NIV "Jonadab").

2. Son of Recab, of the Kenite clan, who assisted Jehu in abolishing Baal worship in Samaria (2 Kings 10). In Jeremiah 35 he is called the forefather of the Recabites, who derived from him their primitive and simple manners.

JEHONATHAN (jē-hŏn'ā-thăn, Heb. *yehônāthān, Jehovah gave*). Variant form of *Jonathan*. 1. One of the administrators of the property of David (1 Chron 27:25). NIV shortens the name to Jonathan.

2. One of the teaching Levites appointed by the godly Jehoshaphat (2 Chron 17:8).

3. A priest in the days of Joiakim the high priest (Neh 12:18).

JEHORAM (jē-hō'răm, Heb. *yehôrām, Jehovah is exalted*). Often contracted to *Joram*. 1. Son of Jehoshaphat of Judah, Jehoram was associated with his father in the kingship for the last four or five years of Jehoshaphat's reign. He took complete charge at his father's death in 849 B.C. Jehoshaphat had seven sons, and in order that there might not be rivalry for the throne, he gave the younger ones great gifts of silver and gold and precious things, with fortified cities in the kingdom of Judah (2 Chron 21:2–3); but when Jehoram became the sole ruler, he murdered his own brothers with the sword. Just as we can charge a good deal of the abominable behavior of Ahab to his strong-minded but diabolical consort Jezebel, so we can guess that Athaliah, daughter of Ahab and Jezebel and wife of Jehoram, was behind most of Jehoram's wickedness. Jehoshaphat had been a godly man, but he had made one terrible error: political association with Ahab (1 Kings 22; 2 Chron 18). Through this league, Jehoram had married the wicked Athaliah. As soon as his father died (900) Jehoram began to slip into the idolatrous ways of the northern kingdom; but because of God's covenant with David (2 Kings 8:19) and no doubt because of Jehoshaphat's goodness, God did not remove the kingdom from Jehoram's hand but did cause him to have real troubles. Edom revolted from under the rule of Judah. Libnah in Judah, a Levitical city far enough from Jerusalem to be somewhat independent, showed its abhorrence of Jehoram's deeds by revolting at the same time (8:22). Meanwhile, the great prophet Elijah sent to Jehoram a letter of denunciation for his wickedness. God sent a plague on Judah, especially on the family of Jehoram. He suffered and died unlamented from a horrible disease (2 Chron 21:18–20). The Arabs or their associated forces killed all of Jehoram's sons (21:17) except Ahaziah, the youngest, who succeeded his father at his death.

2. Second son of Ahab and Jezebel, he succeeded his brother Ahaziah, who died childless, as king of Israel. He reigned for twelve years (853–840 B.C.).

Mesha, king of Moab, who had been paying tribute to Israel (2 Kings 3:4) rebelled after the death of Ahab, and Jehoram made war against him. Jehoram invited Jehoshaphat of Judah to assist him in the war (3:7) and Jehoshaphat accepted the invitation. Jehoram was not as evil as his father Ahab had been, but like all the other kings of the north he clung to the idolatry that Jeroboam had set up in order to keep the northern people from going to Jerusalem to worship at Solomon's temple. While Israel and Judah, with the help of Edom, where going against Mesha, they ran out of water and were in despair. Elisha, in deference to Jehoshaphat (3:14–16) told the kings to dig ditches; water came, and the Moabites seeing the reflection of the rising sun in the water, took it for blood and hastened to the prey, only to be badly defeated. Jehoram came to his end, with all his family, at the hand of Jehu (2 Kings 9). Jehu succeeded him to the throne.

3. A priest in the days of Jehoshaphat whom the king sent with a group of learned Levites to go through Judah and to teach the people the law of the Lord (2 Chron 17:8). ABF

JEHOSHABEATH (jē'hō-shăb'ē-ăth, Heb. *yehôshav'ath, the oath of Jehovah*). The name of Jehosheba as it is found in 2 Chronicles 22:11 (ASV, KJV, MLB, MOF, NASB, RSV).

JEHOSHAPHAT (jē-hŏsh'ā-făt, Heb. *yehôshāphat, Jehovah is judge*; shortened to *Joshaphat* in 1 Chron 15:24; Gr. *Jōsaphat* [Matt 1:8, KJV Josaphat]). 1. One of the seven priests who blew trumpets before the ark of the Lord in David's time (1 Chron 15:24, NIV Joshaphat).

2. Son of Ahilud, and recorder or chronicler in the time of David (2 Sam 8:16; 20:24).

3. Son of Paruah, appointed by Solomon as officer of the commissariat over the tribe of Issachar (1 Kings 4:17). He had to provide the household of the king with food one month of every year.

4. Son and successor of King Asa on the throne of Judah. He reigned for twenty-five years, including five years of rule with his father. He began to reign about 871 B.C. His mother was Azubah, the daughter of Shilhi. For the account of his reign, see 1 Kings 22; 2 Chronicles 17–20. Jehoshaphat was the second of the five kings of Judah who were outstanding for godliness, the later ones being Joash, Hezekiah, and Josiah. He took away the high places and Asherah poles from Judah (2 Chron 17:6), though he apparently was not able to keep the people from using certain high places in worshiping the Lord (1 Kings 22:43). One of the first men to sense the importance of religious education for the people, he sent out in the third year of his reign princes and priests and Levites to teach the people the law of the Lord. They went throughout the cities of Judah in doing this work (2 Chron 17:7–9). Because of Jehoshaphat's godliness, "the fear of the LORD" fell on the surrounding nations, and even the Philistines and the Arabs

brought him tribute. With all this godliness, he seems, however, to have been lacking in spiritual discernment, for he made the great and almost fatal mistake of associating with the wicked King Ahab of the northern kingdom; so much so that his son Jehoram married Athaliah, who was almost as wicked as her mother Jezebel.

Ahab made a great show of hospitality to Jehoshaphat during a visit to Samaria and then asked him if he would be his ally in a campaign to recover Ramoth Gilead. Jehoshaphat suggested that they first determine the will of God. Ahab agreed and asked his prophets for their advice, and they all prophesied good success for the venture. Jehoshaphat was not satisfied and asked if there were not a real prophet of the Lord present. They sent for Micaiah, a man of God, whom Ahab hated. He told them the truth, that God had put a spirit of delusion in the minds of all the prophets, so that Ahab might be doomed. Ahab partly believed this and arranged a trick, pretending to give Jehoshaphat the glory, but Ahab was killed. Jehoshaphat died at the age of sixty, about the year 850 B.C. His son Jehoram succeeded to the throne.

5. The son of Nimshi, and father of Jehu who destroyed the house of Ahab (2 Kings 9:2, 14).

JEHOSHAPHAT, VALLEY OF (jē-hŏsh'à-făt, Heb. *yehôshāphāt, Jehovah judges*). A name used in Joel 3:2, 12 as the scene where all nations will be gathered by the Lord for judgment. Since the fourth century the Kidron Valley has been named the Valley of Jehoshaphat, but there is no real reason for believing that this is the spot referred to by Joel. He may have spoken of an ideal spot only. There is no evidence that any valley ever actually bore this name.

JEHOSHEBA (jē-hŏsh'ē-bà, Heb. *yehôsheva', Jehovah is an oath*). Sister of Ahaziah (2 Kings 11:2), daughter of Jehoram and his wicked consort Athaliah (Jezebel's daughter), and wife of the high priest Jehoiada. When Athaliah usurped the throne and killed the royal line, Jehosheba (called Jehoshabeath in 2 Chron 22:11 ASV, KJV, MLB, MOF, NASB, RSV) rescued the baby Joash, hid him with his nurse in a bedchamber in the temple, and preserved the messianic line.

JEHOSHUA, JEHOSHUAH (See JOSHUA)

JEHOVAH. A misleading representation in English of the only name (as distinct from titles) of God in the OT. Since it is uncertain what vowels should be attached to the Hebrew consonants YHWH that make up the divine name, actual pronunciation must remain hypothetical, but there are reasonable grounds for thinking that the name was Yahweh. At a late date it became a matter of binding scruple not to pronounce the divine name, and Jews (in reading the Scriptures) customarily substituted the noun *adhonai,* which means "Lord." LXX followed this lead, using the Greek *kyrios,* "Lord," to stand for the divine name—a significant thing in the light of the usual NT designation of Jesus as *kyrios.* But the formulation "Jehovah" arose by inserting the vowels of *adhonai* into the consonants YHWH, thus producing a name that never was!

According to Exodus 6:2–3, the name YHWH had not been used prior to Moses as a meaningful understanding of the divine nature. When the patriarchs used the name, it was simply as a label and had not yet become a revelation of the nature of God. This is, in fact, an accurate statement of what we find in Genesis. For example, in Genesis 17:1 Yahweh appeared to Abram, but the revelation vouchsafed was not "I am Yahweh" but "I am El Shaddai." We must return to Exodus 3:13–15 for the moment when the theological significance of Yahweh was opened to Moses. We notice the following: (1) The name is related to the Hebrew verb "to be"; and it must be pointed out that while this verb cannot help meaning "to exist," its characteristic force is "to be actually present," "to be a present reality." (2) The form Yahweh, as a part of the verb "to be," could be translated either "I am actively present" or "I make to be actively present." Thus "I am who I am" means either "I am actively present as and when I choose" or "I bring to pass whatever I choose." In context Moses is made alert to the active presence of Yahweh in the coming events (the Passover-redemption and the Exodus) or to the fact that as sovereign God, he is bringing these events to pass by his own determination, volition, and power. Thus, in his very nature (as summed up in his name), the Lord identifies himself with redemption, the blood of the lamb, and the choosing out of his people for himself. It is important to note, though, that Moses is not left simply to watch unfolding events and make the best interpretation of them that he can. Exodus 3–4; 6:1–8 show that Yahweh is a God who speaks before he is a God who acts. Moses is made wise before the events, so that when they happen, they are a confirmation of the word that has preceded them, thus making the revelation of God doubly certain. Yahweh is thus, fundamentally, the covenant-Redeemer, the God who brought his people out of Egypt (Exod 20:1ff.).

Two further points must be mentioned. First, in the light of the total biblical revelation in the Old and New Testaments, the name Yahweh is not to be identified only with God the Father, but rather with the Holy Trinity. The way OT passages are made to refer alike to Father, Son, and Holy Spirit demonstrates this; and we should always beware of cramping our theological understanding by thinking of the God of the OT simply as God the Father—while at the same time recognizing that the doctrine of the Holy Trinity, while latent in the OT, is not discoverable there without the definitive revelation of the NT. Second, our English Bibles generally (the Jerusalem Bible is an exception) follow the scruple that avoids using the divine name. Printers have agreed on the convention that Yahweh is represented by the word "LORD"—in caps and small caps. When *adhonai* is used independently and in its own right in the OT as a divine title, it appears as "Lord." JAM

JEHOVAH-JIREH (jē-hō'vȧ-jī'rĕ, *Jehovah will provide*). The name Abraham gave to the place where God provided a ram in place of his son Isaac (Gen 22:14 KJV, MLB, MOF, NEB).

JEHOVAH-NISSI (jē-hō'vȧ-nĭs'ī, *Jehovah is my banner*). The name Moses gave to an altar he built as a memorial of Israel's victory over the Amalekites at Rephidim (Exod 17:15 JB, KJV, NEB).

JEHOVAH-SHALOM (jē-hō'vȧ-shā'lŏm, *Jehovah is peace*). The name Gideon gave to an altar he built at Ophra to commemorate the word spoken to him by the Lord, "The Lord is Peace" (Judg 6:24 KJV).

JEHOVAH-SHAMMAH (jē-hō'vȧ-shă'mȧ, *Jehovah is there*). The name of the heavenly Jerusalem as seen in the vision of Ezekiel (48:35 KJV, marginal note).

JEHOVAH-TSIDKENU (jē-hō'vȧ-tsĭd-kē'nū, *Jehovah is our righteousness*). The symbolic name given to the king who is to rule over restored Israel (Jer 23:6) and to the state or capital (33:16).

JEHOZABAD (jē-hŏz'ȧ-băd, Heb. *yehôzāvādh, Jehovah has bestowed*). 1. A son of Shimrith, a Moabitess. He conspired against King Joash (2 Chron 24:26).

2. One of the eight sons of Obed-Edom, a doorkeeper of the tabernacle in the days of David (1 Chron 26:4). He is not to be confused with the Obed-Edom of 2 Samuel 6:10–12.

3. A Benjamite in the days of King Jehoshaphat (2 Chron 17:18). He was commander of 180,000 soldiers prepared for war.

JEHOZADAK (jē-hŏz'ȧ-dăk, Heb. *yehôtsādhāk, Jehovah is righteous*). The high priest of Israel through most of the Babylonian captivity (1 Chron 6:14–15). His father, Seraiah, was killed by the Babylonians (2 Kings 25:18–21), and Jehozadak was taken into captivity. In Haggai and Zechariah, where he is six times referred to as father of Joshua, the high priest at the first return, KJV spells his name "Josedech"; and in Ezra and Nehemiah, KJV and ASV, referring to him in the same way five times, call him "Jozadak," a shortened form of Jehozadak.

JEHU (jē'hū, Heb. *yēhû'*, probably *Jehovah is he*). 1. Son of Obed and father of Azariah, mentioned only in the genealogy of Elishama (1 Chron 2:38).

2. A Simeonite mentioned only in 1 Chronicles 4:35.

3. A Benjamite of Anathoth who joined David at Ziklag (1 Chron 12:3).

4. Son of Hanani, and a prophet of Israel who pronounced the curse of the Lord on Baasha in almost the same words used against Jeroboam (cf. 1 Kings 14:11; 16:4). Several years later he went out to denounce Jehoshaphat (2 Chron 19:1–3) for helping Ahab. Jehu's account of the reign of Jehoshaphat was inserted in the lost "book of the kings of Israel" (20:34).

5. Tenth king of Israel and founder of its fourth dynasty. Son of Jehoshaphat, but more often

Detail of the "Black Obelisk of Shalmaneser III, set up at Nimrud (858–824 B.C.) that shows Jehu, king of Israel, bowing before that king of Assyria. Behind him are porters bringing in tribute. Reproduced by courtesy of the Trustees of the British Museum.

called "son of Nimshi," perhaps because Nimshi, his grandfather, was better known than Jehoshaphat. Jehu appears first as a soldier in the service of Ahab (2 Kings 9:25). Ahab and Jezebel were rejected for their crimes. God commanded Elijah to anoint Jehu king over Israel, a command that Elisha fulfilled. He sent a young prophet to Ramoth Gilead, where Jehu was with his army, to carry out the command. Jehu was commissioned to conquer the house of Ahab. When Jehu told his fellow officers that he had been so anointed, they proclaimed him king. Jehu sealed the city, that the news should not precede him, then he crossed the Jordan and drove impetuously as was his custom (9:20) to Jezreel, where King Joram of Israel had gone after being wounded in battle with Hazael of Syria. Jehu denounced Joram, killed him, and had his body thrown into the field of Naboth (9:24–26); then he caused Ahaziah, king of Judah, to be killed, and his servants carried him up to Jerusalem for burial. He also killed Jezebel and would have had her buried, but the dogs had eaten her. He executed God's judgments on the house of Ahab and thoroughly exterminated the worship of Baal, killing all its devotees who gathered together in response to Jehu's pretended interest in worshiping Baal with them; but he did not depart from the sins of Jeroboam. Jehu reigned in Samaria twenty-eight years (c. 842–814 B.C.). Because of his zeal for the Lord in the matter of Ahab's house, God allowed him to set up a dynasty that lasted just over one hundred years (Jehu, Jehoahaz, Joram, and Jeroboam II). ABF

JEHUBBAH (See HUBBAH)

JEHUCAL (jē-hūk'ăl, probably *Jehovah is able*). One whom King Zedekiah sent to Jeremiah, asking for prayers (Jer 37:3). Some versions of Jeremiah 38:1 have "Jucal."

JEHUD (jē'hŭd). A town in the tribe of Dan, about seven miles (twelve km.) nearly east of Joppa and near modern Tel Aviv (Josh 19:45).

JEHUDI (jē-hū'dī, Heb. *yehûdhî, a Jew*). One who sat with the princes in Jehoiakim's court and who secured from Baruch the prophecies of Jeremiah and read them to the king (Jer 36:14, 21).

JEHUSH (See JEUSH)

JEIEL (jē-ī'ĕl, Heb. *ye'î'ēl,* probably *God has gathered*). 1. A Reubenite (1 Chron 5:7).

2. A Benjamite of Gibeon (1 Chron 9:35).

3. Son of Hotham of Aroer. He was one of David's mighty men (1 Chron 11:44).

4. A harpist in the days of King David who also acted as gatekeeper of the tabernacle (1 Chron 15:18, 21).

5. A Levite of the sons of Asaph (2 Chron 20:14).

6. A scribe who acted as recorder of the military forces under Uzziah (2 Chron 26:11).

7. A Levite who took part in the reformation under Hezekiah (2 Chron 29:13).

8. A chief of the Levites in the days of Josiah (2 Chron 35:9).

9. A husband of a foreign wife in Ezra's time (Ezra 10:43).

JEKABZEEL (jē-kăb'zē-ĕl, Heb. *yeqavtse'ēl, God gathers*). One of the places resettled by the men of Judah (Neh 11:25).

JEKAMEAM (jĕkă-mē'-ăm, Heb. *yeqam' ām, the kinsman will raise up*). The head of a Levitical house (1 Chron 23:19; 24:23).

JEKAMIAH (jĕk'ȧ-mī'ȧ, Heb. *yekamyâh, may Jehovah establish*). 1. A man from Judah, son of Shallum (1 Chron 2:41).

2. A son of King Jeconiah (Jehoiachin); in KJV Jecamiah (1 Chron 3:18).

JEKUTHIEL (jē-kū'thĭ-ĕl, Heb. *yeqûthî'ēl, God will nourish*). A man of Judah, father of the inhabitants of Zanoah (1 Chron 4:18).

JEMIMAH (jē-mī'mȧ, Heb. *yemîmâh, a dove*). The first of the three daughters born to Job after his restoration from affliction (Job 42:14).

JEMUEL (jē-mū'ĕl, Heb. *yemû'ēl,* meaning unknown). A son of Simeon (Gen 46:10; Exod 6:15). He is called "Nemuel" in Numbers 26:12 and 1 Chronicles 4:24.

JEPHTHAH (jĕf'thȧ, Heb. *yiphtâh, opened* or *opener*). Eighth judge of the Israelites. His history is given in Judges 10:6–12:7. He was the son of Gilead, a Gileadite, and of a woman who was a harlot. Because of his illegitimacy, his brothers born in wedlock drove him from the paternal home and refused him any share in the inheritance. Their action was confirmed by the elders of Gilead. He fled to the land of Tob, probably a region in Syria or the Hauran. There he made a name for himself by his prowess and gathered about him a band of men without employment, like David's men (1 Sam 22:2). He must not be thought of as just a captain of a band of freebooters, for he was a God-fearing man, with a high sense of justice and of the sacredness of vows made to God. At the time of his expulsion by his brothers, Israel had been for many years under bondage to the Ammonites. In the course of time, when these oppressors of Israel were planning some new form of humiliation, the elders of Gilead offered to anyone who was willing to accept the office of captain the headship over all the inhabitants of Gilead. When no one volunteered, the elders in desperation went to Jephthah and urged him to become a captain of Israel's army. He accepted, and he and the elders made vows before the Lord to keep all promises. On assuming the headship of Gilead, Jephthah's first effort was to secure the cooperation of the tribe of Ephraim, one of the most influential of the tribes during the period of the judges; but they refused to help. He then sent messengers to the king of the Ammonites, asking for the grounds of his hostile action and requesting that he desist; but the king refused to listen to reason. Endued with the Spirit of the Lord, Jephthah prepared for war. Before going out to battle, he made a vow that if he was victorious he would offer to God as a burnt offering whatever first came to him out of his house. He defeated his enemies with a very great slaughter and recovered twenty cities from them. The Ephraimites then came to him with the complaint that he had slighted them in the preparation for the Ammonite campaign, but he answered their false accusation and defeated them in battle. Forty-two thousand Ephraimites were killed. Jephthah judged Israel for six years. Samuel cited him as one proof of God's faithfulness in raising up deliverers for Israel in time of need (1 Sam 12:11). He is listed among the heroes of faith in Hebrews 11 (v. 32).

The great point of interest in his history is his vow (Judg 11:29–40) and the way it was fulfilled. On his return home after the victory over the Ammonites, his own daughter was the first to meet him from his house. A man of the highest integrity, he knew that he could not go back on his vow to the Lord; and his daughter agreed with him. She asked only that she and her companions be allowed to go for two months to the mountains to bewail her virginity. When she returned to her father, he "did to her as he had vowed. And she was a virgin" (11:39). After that she was lamented by the daughters of Israel four days every year.

How was this vow fulfilled? Did he actually sacrifice his daughter as a burnt offering, or did he redeem her with money and doom her to perpetual celibacy? The ancient Jewish authorities and the early church fathers, as well as many in modern times, like Martin Luther, hold that she was actually sacrificed, as a first reading of the narrative suggests. It is said that Jephthah was either ignorant of the law against human sacrifices or that he flagrantly violated it. While his words and those of his daughter indicate knowledge of the Mosaic Law, his involvement in human sacrifice would be part of the revelation that Judges sets out to make of the fearful deterioration of the days and the need for the perfect king. Even the best men—Jephthah, for example—were tainted.

Leviticus 27:1–8 contemplates the possibility of a someone's vowing to give himself or some person of his household to the Lord and makes provision for the redemption of such a person by the payment of money. We know, too, from the experience of Samuel that sometimes persons coming under a vow were handed over for the service of the sanctuary (1 Sam 1:11). It is, therefore, thought by some that Jephthah redeemed his daughter with money and gave her up to the service of the Lord as a perpetual virgin. That may be the meaning of her request that she be allowed to bewail her virginity for two months, and of the statement that "she knew no man" (Judg 11:39 KJV). The fact is, however, that we cannot be absolutely certain of the mode of fulfillment of Jephthah's vow. SB

JEPHUNNEH (jē-fŭn'ĕ, Heb. *yephunneh, it will be prepared*). 1. The father of Caleb, one of the twelve spies. He was from the tribe of Judah (Num 13:6).

2. A son of Jether, an Asherite (1 Chron 7:38).

JERAH (jē'rȧ, Heb. *yerah, moon*). An Arabian tribe descended from Joktan (Gen 10:26; 1 Chron 1:20).

JERAHMEEL (jē-rȧ'mē-ĕl, Heb. *yerahme'ēl, may God have compassion,* or *God pities*). 1. A descendant of Judah through Perez and Hezron (1 Chron 2:9, 25–27, 33, 42).

2. A Merarite Levite, son of Kish, not Saul's father (1 Chron 24:29).

3. One of the three officers sent by King Jehoiakim to arrest Jeremiah and Baruch (Jer 36:26). He was probably a royal prince, though not necessarily the son of a ruling prince.

JERASH (See GERASA)

JERED (jē'rĕd, Heb. *yeredh, descent*). 1. Son of Mahalaleel (1 Chron 1:2 KJV; NIV "Jared").

2. A Judahite and father of the inhabitants of Gedor (1 Chron 4:18).

JEREMIAH (jĕr'ĕ-mī'ȧ, Heb. *yirmeyâhû, Jehovah founds,* or perhaps, *exalts*), in KJV of NT "Jeremy" and "Jeremias" (Matt 2:17; 16:14).

I. The Life of Jeremiah. Jeremiah was one of the greatest Hebrew prophets. He was born into a priestly family of Anathoth, a Benjamite town two and one-half miles (four km.) NE of Jerusalem. His father was Hilkiah (Jer 1:1), not to be confused with the high priest Hilkiah mentioned in 2 Kings 22–23. Because of the autobiographical nature of his book, it is possible to understand his life, character, and times better than those of any other Hebrew prophet.

Jeremiah was called to prophesy in the thirteenth year of King Josiah (626 B.C.), five years after the great revival of religion described in 2 Kings 23. This was a time of decision, a time filled with both hope and foreboding. Looking back, we can know it as the last religious awakening in a series that only slowed down the idolatry and apostasy of the Hebrews. Their apostasy finally plunged the nation into destruction. It was the time of the revival of the Babylonian Empire. After the fall of the city of Nineveh in 612, the Assyrian Empire disintegrated; and Babylon for a little while again ruled the world under her vigorous leader Nebuchadnezzar, who sought to subdue the whole Fertile Crescent to himself. Nebuchadnezzar's design on Egypt inevitably included control of Palestine, and Jeremiah's lifetime saw the fall of the Hebrew commonwealth to Babylon. This fall was preceded by a generation of unrest and decline in Judah. Many solutions to her troubles were proposed, and at court pro-Egyptian and pro-Babylonian parties vied for favor with the policy makers. A

The village of Anathoth, birthplace of Jeremiah, northeast of Jerusalem. Courtesy Ecole Biblique et Archéologique Française, Jerusalem.

knowledge of this situation of deepening crisis is necessary if we are to understand Jeremiah and his Book. Jeremiah's ministry continued through the reigns of five successive Judean kings, and Jeremiah saw the final destruction of Jerusalem in 587. The prophet died in Egypt, probably a few years after Jerusalem was destroyed.

Jeremiah's call is described in Jeremiah 1. The young priest pleads his youth (1:6), but God assures him that he will be given strength for his task. At this time the theme of destruction from the north (i.e., from Babylon) is already introduced (1:13–15). The prediction that Judah would inevitably fall because of its apostasy earned for the prophet the undying hostility of most of his contemporaries (even his fellow townsmen, 11:21) and led to his being charged with treason (38:1–6) and to frequent imprisonments. Jeremiah's faithfulness to his call under the most difficult circumstances makes him a prime example of devotion to God at greatest personal sacrifice.

Undoubtedly Jeremiah supported Josiah's reform (Jer 11:1–8; 17:19–27), but as time went on he realized its inadequacy to stave off national disaster (3:10). After Josiah's unhappy death (609 B.C.) Jeremiah mourned Judah's last good king (2 Chron 35:25), and life became more difficult for him. Jehoahaz, son of Josiah, reigned only three months before he was deported to Egypt. Jeremiah said that he would not return (Jer 22:10–12). Jehoiakim, the brother of Jehoahaz, succeeded him and reigned eleven years. A strong ruler and a very wicked man, he tried to do away with the prophet and, failing that, to silence him. In Jehoiakim's fourth year Jeremiah dictated the first edition of his prophecies to Baruch, but the king promptly destroyed it (ch. 36). During this reign Jeremiah preached the great temple discourse (chs. 7–10) that led to a plot to kill him; he was saved only by the intervention of friendly nobles who were a remnant of Josiah's administration (ch. 26). The battle of Carchemish (46:1–12) occurred at this time; in this battle Egypt was crushed (605) by the Babylonian crown prince Nebuchadnezzar, who soon afterward became king of Babylon. Egypt's star quickly set, and Babylon entered her brief period of greatness. Judah was brought into the Babylonian orbit when Jerusalem fell to Nebuchadnezzar in 605 and a few Hebrews (Daniel among them) were deported to Babylon. Jehoiakim later rebelled against Babylon. Jeremiah opposed the strong-willed Jehoiakim all his reign and predicted a violent death for him (22:13–19). It has been supposed that he fell in a palace coup.

Jehoiachin, son of Jehoiakim, succeeded him to the throne. Jeremiah called this king Coniah and Jeconiah (Jer 24:1; 27:20; 29:2 see NIV footnotes). After he had reigned only three months, the Babylonians attacked Jerusalem and carried Jehoiachin off to Babylon (597 B.C.), as Jeremiah had predicted (22:24–30), together with many artisans and other important Jews.

In Jehoiachin's place Nebuchadnezzar appointed Zedekiah, who maintained a precarious position on the throne for eleven years. Although a weak character, he protected Jeremiah and asked his advice, which he was never able to carry out. Jeremiah advised submission to Babylon, but, goaded by the nobles, Zedekiah rebelled and made an alliance with Egypt. Finally the Babylonians came again, determined to stamp out the rebellious Judean state. A long siege resulted, in which Jeremiah suffered greatly. He was accused of treason and thrown into a vile prison from which the king transferred him to the more pleasant court of the guard (Jer 37:11–21). Now that the judgment had come, the prophet spoke of a hopeful future for the nation (chs. 32–33). As the siege wore on, he was cast into a slimy cistern, where he would have perished had not Ebed-Melech, a courtier, rescued him (38:6–13). He was taken again to the court of the guard, until the city fell (38:28).

After a siege of a year and a half, Jerusalem was destroyed. Zedekiah was blinded and carried in chains to Babylon. For the events in Judah after the destruction of Jerusalem we are dependent almost exclusively on Jeremiah 40–45. The captors treated Jeremiah with kindness, giving him the choice of going to Babylon or remaining in Judah. He chose to stay behind with some of the common people who had been left in Judah when most of the Jews were deported. Gedaliah was made puppet governor over this little group. After civil unrest, in which Gedaliah was assassinated, the Jews fled to Egypt, forcing Jeremiah to accompany them. Jeremiah died in Egypt at an old age.

II. The Man and His Message. Jeremiah was called to be a prophet at a most unhappy time. With the failure of Josiah's revival, the final decline of the nation was under way. When God called Jeremiah, he intimated to him that his message would be one of condemnation rather than salvation (Jer 1:10, 18–19). Yet he was also given a message of hope (30:1–3, 18–22; 31:1–14, 23–40). Throughout his long ministry of more than forty years his preaching reflected this theme of judgment. God had risen early and sent his servants the prophets, but Israel would not hear (7:25; 44:4). Now the fate predicted for an apostate nation in Deuteronomy 28–30 was inevitable. Babylon would capture Judah, and it would be better for the people to surrender and so to save their lives.

This message, coming to people whose desperate nationalism was all they had to cling to, was completely rejected, and the bearer was rejected with his message. Jeremiah was regarded as a meddler and a traitor; and leaders, nobles, and kings tried to put him to death. Although he needed the love, sympathy, and encouragement of a wife, he was not permitted to marry; and in this prohibition he became a sign that normal life was soon to cease for Jerusalem (Jer 16:1–4). Because his book is full of autobiographical sections—Jeremiah's "Confessions"—Jeremiah's personality can be understood more clearly than that of any other prophet. These outpourings of the human spirit are some of the most poignant and pathetic statements of the tension of a man under divine imperative to be found anywhere in Scripture. The most important are listed below. They show us a Jeremiah who was retiring, sensitive, and afraid of people's "faces," a man we would consider singularly unfit for the work that was given him to do. That he tenaciously clung to his assigned task through the succeeding years of rejection and persecution is both a tribute to the mettle of the man and to the grace of God, without which his personality would surely have gone to pieces.

III. Jeremiah's Confessions.

10:23–24	17:9–11, 14–18
11:18–12:6	18:18–23
15:10–21	20:7–18

Jeremiah's penetrating understanding of the religious condition of his people is seen in his emphasis on the inner spiritual character of true religion. The external theocratic state will go, as will the temple and its ritual. Even Josiah's reform appears to have been a thing of the outward appearance—almost engineered by the king, an upsurge of nationalism more than a religious revival (Jer 3:10). The old covenant had failed; a new and better one will take its place and then God's law will be written on men's hearts (31:31–34). God will give his renewed people a heart to know him (24:7). In this doctrine of the "new heart" Jeremiah unfolds the depth of human sin and predicts the intervention of divine grace (Heb. 8:1–9:28).

IV. The Foe From the North. Throughout, Jeremiah's sermons refer to a foe from the *north* who would devastate Judah and take her captive. Chapter 4 is typical of these oracles: The foe will destroy like a lion or a whirlwind and leave the land in desolation like the primeval chaos. Who is this destroying enemy? The fulfillment indicates that the northern foe was Babylon. Although Babylon is on the same latitude as Samaria, her invasions of Palestine always came from the north, as the desert that separates the two was impassable. The view that the Scythians are referred to as the northern foe in some places of the book seems not to be held so widely today as it once was, and may be rejected.

Sometimes (Jer 50:3, 9, 41; 51:48) "north" may be a reference to the origin of the conquerors of Babylon. This use of the term is difficult to pinpoint. The Persians, who were the principal captors of Babylon, came from the east. Probably here north has become an expression for the source of any trouble, arrived at because Israel's troubles for so long a time had come from that direction.

IV. Other Jeremiahs. Six other Jeremiahs are briefly mentioned in the OT: a Benjamite and two Gadites who joined David at Ziklag (1 Chron 12:4, 10, 13); the head of a family in Manasseh (5:24); a native of Libnah and the father of

Hamutal, wife of King Josiah and mother of Jehoahaz (2 Kings 23:30–31); and the son of Habazziniah, a Recabite (Jer 35:3). JBG

JEREMIAH, BOOK OF.

I. The Composition of the Book. Jeremiah is a book of prophetic oracles or sermons, together with much autobiographical and historical material that gives the background of these oracles. Many modern scholars believe that the book contains substantial parts by later writers whose point of view differed markedly from the prophet's. Believing that the critics have failed to prove their case for later editors, this article takes the traditional position that the oracles are essentially Jeremiah's and that the narratives, if they were not dictated by the prophet (they are usually in the third person), were probably composed by Baruch.

Even though we may accept the fact that the book originated with Jeremiah, it is impossible to say how or when these materials were assembled in their present form. Plainly the book has gone through a number of editions, each succeeding one containing additional material. The account of the production of the first and second editions is told in Jeremiah 36. Baruch, the secretary of the prophet, wrote down certain judgment oracles of the prophet (we do not know the exact contents) at his dictation. This scroll was contemptuously burned by King Jehoiakim; the prophet, therefore, dictated again to Baruch "all the words of the scroll that Jehoiakim king of Judah had burned in the fire. And many similar words were added to them" (36:32); i.e., a new and enlarged edition was produced. Obviously this was not our present book, which carries the history on for at least twenty more years. This account is of great interest in that it gives the only detailed OT description of the writing of a prophetic book. That Jeremiah should dictate to a secretary was normal for the times. Writing was a specialized skill, often restricted to a professional class. Learned men might be able to read but (like executives today) scorned to write. The document was probably written on a blank papyrus scroll imported from Egypt.

It has long been noted that the Book of Jeremiah in the Greek translation of the OT called the Septuagint (done in Egypt before 132 B.C.) is about one-eighth shorter than the Hebrew book, from which our English translations have been made. Further, the Septuagint omits many of the repetitions that are contained in the Hebrew copy and rearranges the material somewhat. Some scholars believe that the Greek Jeremiah was made from a different edition of the Hebrew text from the one on which our present text is based. It is not now possible to arrive at any certain conclusion about the relationship of the Septuagint to the Hebrew text, nor to know how either version came to its present condition.

The material contained in Jeremiah's book is not arranged in chronological order. The outline given below indicates what seems to have been the purpose of the present arrangement—to set forth a group of oracles spoken against the Jewish nation, then to record selected events in the prophet's ministry, then to give certain discourses of Jeremiah against foreign nations, and finally to include an account of the fall of Jerusalem. The record of Jerusalem's fall had been given in Jeremiah 39; the somewhat different account at the end of the book (ch. 52) is practically identical to 2 Kings 24–25 and may have been added from that source to give a climactic conclusion to Jeremiah's oracles.

II. Outline

I. Jeremiah's Oracles Against the Theocracy, 1:1–25:38.
   A. The prophet's call, 1:1–19.
   B. Reproofs and admonitions, mostly from the time of Josiah, 2:1–20:18.
   C. Later prophecies, 21:1–25:38.
II. Events in the Life of Jeremiah, 26:1–45:5.
   A. The temple sermon and Jeremiah's arrest, 26:1–24.
   B. The yoke of Babylon, 27:1–29:32.
   C. The book of consolation, 30:1–33:26.
   D. Some of Jeremiah's experiences before Jerusalem fell, 34:1–36:32.
   E. Jeremiah during the siege and destruction of Jerusalem, 37:1–39:18.
   F. The last years of Jeremiah, 40:1–45:5.
III. Jeremiah's Oracles Against Foreign Nations, 46:1–51:64.
   A. Against Egypt, 46:1–28.
   B. Against the Philistines, 47:1–7.
   C. Against Moab, 48:1–47.
   D. Against the Ammonites, 49:1–6.
   E. Against Edom, 49:7–22.
   F. Against Damascus, 49:23–27.
   G. Against Kedar and Hazor, 49:28–33.
   H. Against Elam, 49:34–39.
   I. Against Babylon, 50:1–51:64.
IV. Appendix: The Fall of Jerusalem and Related Events, 52:1–34.

III. Chronological Order of the Book. In spite of the fact that the book is not at all in chronological order, it is possible to date many of its sections because they contain chronological notations. These sections are here listed with their dates.

1. In the Reign of Josiah.
   In the thirteenth year, ch. 1.
   Later in this reign, chs. 2–6.
   Possibly much of chs. 7–20 (except material specifically listed below) is to be dated to Josiah's reign.
2. In the Reign of Jehoahaz.
   None.
3. In the Reign of Jehoiakim.
   Early in this reign, ch. 26 and probably 7:1–8:3; 22:1–23.
   In the fourth year, chs. 25; 36; 45; 46:1–12.
   After the fourth year, ch. 35.

4. In the Reign of Jehoiachin.
   22:24–30; possibly ch. 14.
5. In the Reign of Zedekiah.
   In the beginning, chs. 24; 49:34–39.
   In the fourth year, chs. 27–28; 51:59–64.
   In unnoted years, chs. 21; 29.
   During the early part of the siege, ch. 34.
   During the interruption of the siege, ch. 37.
   During the resumption of the siege, chs. 32; 33; 38; 39:15–18.
6. In Judah After the Fall of Jerusalem.
   39:1–4; 40:1–43:7.
7. In Egypt After Jeremiah Was Taken There.
   43:8–44:30.

IV. Jeremiah and the Lachish Letters. Lachish, in the Judean foothills, was one of a series of fortresses for the defense of Jerusalem against attack from the Mediterranean Plain. It was one of the last cities to fall to the Babylonians prior to the final taking and destruction of Jerusalem (Jer 34:7). An interesting light has been shed on these last hectic days of Judah's history by a discovery in the ruins of ancient Lachish. When the city was excavated (in A.D. 1932–1938) twenty-one letters written on broken pieces of pottery were found in a guard room of the outer gate. They were written in the ancient Hebrew script with carbon iron ink at the time of Jeremiah, when Lachish was undergoing its final siege.

Reverse side of Lachish Letter No. III. The sender, Hoshaiah, writes to Yoash, apparently the military commander at Lachish, regarding the suspicion by the king that Hoshaiah has read one of the confidential royal letters sent by the king to Yoash. Courtesy Israel Department of Antiquities and Museums.

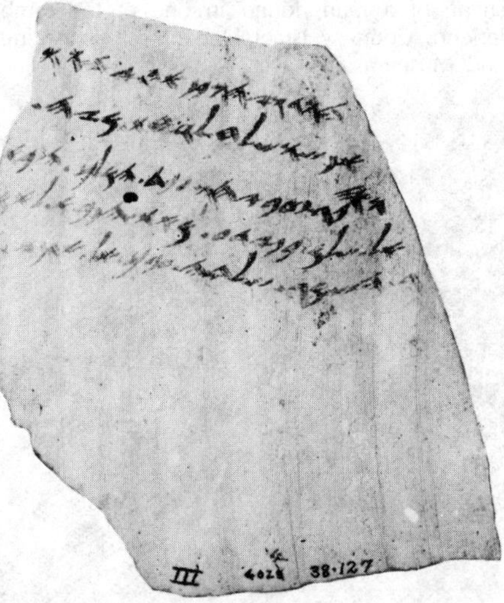

Many of these letters were written by a certain Hoshaiah, who was a military officer at some outpost near Lachish, to Yaosh, the commander of Lachish. Their language is very much like that of the Book of Jeremiah. Hoshaiah is constantly defending himself to his superior. Could it be that he was under suspicion of being ready to go over to the Babylonians? Once he describes one of the princes in words almost like those that the princes used against Jeremiah (Jer 38:4). There is mention of "the prophet" whose message is "Beware." Is this a reference to Jeremiah? We cannot be sure. According to the Book of Jeremiah, there were many prophets in that troubled time. Another letter mentions the inability of Hoshaiah to see the smoke signals of Azekah, although those of Lachish were still visible. Perhaps Azekah had already fallen (34:7). Although the specific meaning of many of the references of these letters eludes us, they do throw a vivid light on the disturbed and fearful days just prior to the fall of the Judean kingdom, the days of Jeremiah. A translation of these letters may be found in Pritchard.

Bibliography: James B. Pritchard, ed., *Ancient Near Eastern Texts Relating to the OT,* 1955; H. Cunliffe-Jones, *The Book of Jeremiah: Introduction and Commentary,* 1960; John Bright, *Jeremiah* (AB), 1965; R. K. Harrison, *Jeremiah and Lamentations* (TOTC), 1973; J. A. Thompson, *The Book of Jeremiah* (NIC), 1980. JBG

JEREMOTH (jĕr′ē-mŏth, Heb. *yerēmoth, swollen, thick*). 1. A Benjamite of the family of Beker (1 Chron 7:8).

2. Another Benjamite (1 Chron 8:14).

3. A Levite, family of Merari, house of Mushi (1 Chron 23:23). His name appears in 1 Chronicles 24:30 as Jerimoth.

4. Three men by this name who consented to put away their foreign wives in the time of Ezra (Ezra 10:26–27, 29).

JERIAH (jē-rī′à, Heb. *yerîyāhû, Jehovah sees*). Head of a Levitical house, the house of Hebron (1 Chron 23:19; 24:23; 26:31).

JERIBAI (jĕr′ĭ-bī, Heb. *yerîvay, Jehovah pleads*). A son of Elnaam, and one of David's mighty men (1 Chron 11:46).

JERICHO (jĕr′ĭ-kō, Heb. *yerēhô, yerîhô,* Gr. *Ierichō, moon city*).

I. The Site. Jericho, also called the City of Palms (Deut 34:3), is located five miles (eight km.) west of the Jordan and seven miles (twelve km.) north of the Dead Sea, some 800 feet (250 m.) below sea level. Its climate is tropical, with great heat during the summer. In the winter it becomes a resort for people fleeing the colder weather of the Palestinian hill country. In ancient times date palm trees flourished here; and balsam, from which medicine was extracted, was the source of great income. Today there are many banana groves here. The presence of springs of water makes the locality a green oasis in the

Excavations at Jericho revealing the pre-pottery Neolithic B levels at bottom and the defensive city walls. The "Mount of Temptation" is pictured in the background. Courtesy Studium Biblicum Franciscanum, Jerusalem.

middle of the dry Jordan rift area.

There are three Jerichos. The OT city was situated on a mound now called Tell es-Sultan, a mile NW of the modern town. NT Jericho is on a higher elevation nearby. Modern Jericho, called Er Riha by the Arabs, has a population of about ten thousand people of very mixed racial descent.

Jericho is probably the oldest city in the world. Its strategic site by a ford of the Jordan controlled the ancient trade routes from the East. After crossing the river these branched out, one going toward Bethel and Shechem in the north, another westward to Jerusalem, and a third to Hebron in the south. Thus Jericho controlled the access to the hill country of Palestine from Transjordan.

II. Jericho in the Bible. Jericho first entered the biblical record when it was captured by Joshua and the invading Hebrews as the opening wedge of their campaign to take Canaan (Josh 6). The city's location made its capture the key to the invasion of the central hill country. It was regarded as a formidable obstacle by the Hebrews. After the two spies had searched it (Josh 2), Joshua led the Hebrew forces against the city, marching around it daily for six days. On the seventh day they circled it seven times, then shouted and blew their trumpets, and "the wall collapsed; so every man charged straight in, and they took the city" (6:20). The city was devoted to God, totally destroyed and burned except for metal objects found in it (6:17–19). Only Rahab and her family, who had cared for the spies, was saved (6:22–23, 25). Joshua placed a curse on the place, that it might not be rebuilt (6:26). The site seems to have remained a ruin for centuries.

Jericho next became prominent when it was rebuilt by Hiel the Bethelite in the days of Ahab (c. 850 B.C.; 1 Kings 16:34). Evidently it again became an important place during the divided kingdom era. It is mentioned in connection with Elisha's ministry (2 Kings 2:5, 19; see also 2 Kings 25:5; 2 Chron 28:15; Ezra 2:34; Neh 3:2; 7:36; Jer 39:5).

In the time of Christ, Jericho was an important place yielding a large revenue to the royal family. Since the road from the fords of the Jordan to Jerusalem passed through it, it became a stopping place for Galilean pilgrims to Jerusalem, who came south through Perea to avoid defilement by contact with Samaritans. Thus Jesus passed through it on a number of occasions. Nearby are the supposed sites of his baptism (in the Jordan) and his temptation (the hill Quarantania, west of the city). Near the city Jesus healed Bartimaeus (Mark 10:46–52) and one or two other blind men (Matt 20:29–34). The conversion of Zacchaeus occurred here (Luke 19:1–10), one of the most graphic of the Gospel narratives. In the parable of the Good Samaritan (10:29–37) the traveler was attacked as he was going down from Jerusalem to Jericho, a winding road, often passing between crags, going through the desolate Judean wilderness, which was frequently a hiding place of criminals.

III. The Archaeology of Jericho. During the past fifty years there have been a number of excavations of Tell es-Sultan, OT Jericho. Between 1908 and 1910, the German scholars Sellin and Watzinger excavated there. A very important expedition, led by the British archaeologist John Garstang dug there from 1930 to 1936. The latest attempt to uncover ancient Jericho's secrets began in 1952, when the British School of Archaeology

Drinking vessel (rhyton), c. 2000–1750 B.C., in the shape of a man, found in one of the tombs at Jericho. Courtesy Israel Department of Antiquities and Museums.

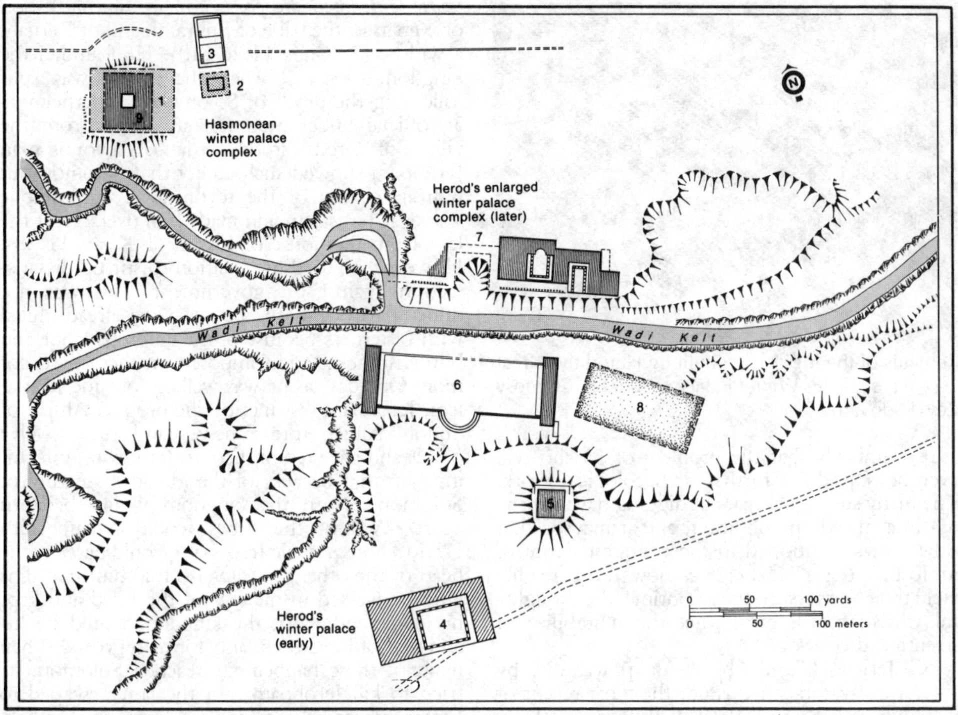

The general plan of ancient Jericho: (1) main palace, (2) pavilion(?), (3) pool surrounded by court, (4) palace (gymnasium), now covered over, (5) southern mound, (6) sunken garden, with the "Grand Façade" south of it, (7) northern wing, (8) pool, and (9) villa(?) built over Hasmonean palace. These ruins are located just west of the modern town and south of Tell es-Sultan. Courtesy Carta, Jerusalem.

and the American School of Oriental Research in Jerusalem, under the leadership of Dr. Kathleen Kenyon, excavated the tell. At the end of the 1957 season, this work was suspended.

The earliest evidence of settlement on this site is dated (by radiocarbon tests) to the seventh and sixth millennia B.C., when a prepottery Neolithic town was built there. A surprisingly strong city wall, mud-brick and stone houses, plastered floors with reed mats, and clay figurines of animals and the mother goddess show that the civilization was not crude. Of special interest from this period are several human skulls with the features modeled in clay and with shells for eyes, used possibly for cultic purposes. This is one of the oldest cities known to man—having existed some five thousand years before Abraham!

Of greatest interest to the Bible student is the archaeological evidence bearing on the overthrow of the city in the days of Joshua. About this Late-Bronze-Age city there has been dispute ever since Garstang's early excavations; and Kenyon's reports, which scholars had hoped would solve the mystery, only accentuated the problem. Garstang believed that he had found ample evidence of Joshua's destruction of the Late-Bronze-Age city, which he labeled "city D" and dated to the fifteenth century B.C. He found that this city had been surrounded by a double wall that encircled the summit of the mound, the inner wall twelve feet (four m.) thick, and the outer, six feet (two m.). These walls had been violently destroyed and had toppled down the slopes of the mound. Layers of ash and charcoal testified to the burning of the city by its captors, and great amounts of charred grain and other foodstuffs suggested the total destruction of which the Bible speaks. Not all of Garstang's fellow archaeologists accepted his reconstructions, and the world of scholarship awaited Kenyon's findings.

After seven seasons at Jericho, Kenyon reported that virtually nothing remains of the Jericho of the period of Joshua (1500–1200 B.C.). The mound has suffered such denudation that almost all remains later than the third millennium B.C. have disappeared. According to Kenyon, the two walls that Garstang connected with his "city D" should be dated about the third millennium, hundreds of years before the Exodus; only a bit of pottery and possibly one building remain from the Late Bronze Age. If there was once evidence of a great city of Jericho destroyed by Joshua, she believes that it has long since been eaten away by the elements. Much of the evidence on this subject that was written about prior to A.D. 1952—often written with the best intentions to "prove" the truth of the Bible—must now be reconsidered. A number of scholars now believe that the Jericho of Joshua's day was little more than a fort.

Remains of the frigidarium built by Herod the Great (37–4 B.C.), at his Winter Palace in Jericho. Courtesy Zev Radovan.

It is unlikely that the problem of Jericho will ever be solved by further archaeological work. The many successive years of digging have left the tell in a mixed-up condition, and it may be that other cities mentioned in the conquest narrative in Joshua (e.g., Hazor) will now more readily yield their answers. In the meantime, the thoughtful Christian will not forget the mutability of scientific theories.

NT Jericho (Tulul Abu el-Alaiq) was dug by several excavators since 1868, the most recent of which were J. Kelso (1950), J. Pritchard (1951), and E. Netzer (1973–74). Herod the Great's winter palace was found, containing a sunken garden, two large pools, a large Roman bath, two courtyards, a reception hall, and buildings with six private mikvehs (baptistries) dating to the second century B.C. Herod died here in 4 B.C. and was taken to Herodium for burial.

Bibliography: J. and J. B. E. Garstang, *The Story of Jericho,* 1948; K. M. Kenyon, *Digging Up Jericho,* 1957, and *Archaeology in the Holy Land,* 1960. JBG

JERIEL (jĕr'ĭ-ĕl). Head of a family in the tribe of Issachar (1 Chron 7:2).

JERIMOTH (jĕr'ĭ-mŏth, Heb. *yerēmôth, thick, swollen*). 1. A Benjamite (1 Chron 7:7).

2. A Benjamite who joined David at Ziklag (1 Chron 12:5).

3. A son of David and the father of Mahalath, the wife of Rehoboam (2 Chron 11:18).

4. A Levite, an overseer of the temple in the reign of Hezekiah (2 Chron 31:13).

5. A Levite musician in David's time (1 Chron 25:4; in 25:22 Jerimoth in NIV, Jeremoth in JB, MLB, KJV, NASB, NEB, RSV).

6. A son of Mushi, a Merarite (1 Chron 24:30); called Jeremoth in 1 Chronicles 23:23.

7. A prince of the tribe of Naphtali during David's reign (1 Chron 27:19).

JERIOTH (jĕr'ĭ-ŏth, Heb. *yerî'ôth, tent curtains*). One of Caleb's wives (1 Chron 2:18).

JEROBOAM I (jĕr'ō-bō'ăm, Heb. *yārov'ām, the people contend,* or *the people become numerous*). Son of Nebat, of the tribe of Ephraim, and of Zeruah, a widow (1 Kings 11:26–40). He founded the kingdom of Israel when the nation was split following the death of Solomon. His father was an official under Solomon and came from the village of Zeredah in the Jordan. As a young man Jeroboam showed such ability that Solomon put him in charge of the fortifications and public works at Jerusalem and made him overseer of the levy from the house of Joseph (1 Kings 11:28). However, he used his position to stir up dissatisfaction against the government. This was not difficult to do, as the people were already filled with bitterness because of the enforced labor and burdensome taxation imposed on them by Solomon. One day, as he was walking outside Jerusalem, Jeroboam was met by the prophet Ahijah of Shiloh. Ahijah tore a new mantle into twelve pieces and gave ten of them to Jeroboam, informing him that because of the idolatrous nature of Solomon's reign the kingdom would be torn apart. Two of the tribes would remain with David's house, while Jeroboam would become the head of the other ten. He also told him that if as king he walked in the fear of the Lord and kept his commandments, the kingdom would be his and that of his descendants for many years. When news of these happenings reached Solomon, he tried to kill Jeroboam; but the latter escaped to Egypt, where he was kindly received by Shishak, the pharaoh who had succeeded (and, it is thought, dethroned) the pharaoh whose daughter Solomon had married. As soon as Solomon died, Jeroboam returned from Egypt. When the people met at Shechem to proclaim Solomon's son Rehoboam king, they invited Jeroboam to come and take the lead in presenting their grievances. As spokesman of the people, he urged that their burdens be alleviated, but the protest was contemptuously rejected; therefore the ten tribes revolted from the house of David and made Jeroboam their king (12:1–16). In this way Ahijah's prophecy that the ten tribes would form a separate kingdom with Jeroboam as king was fulfilled (12:15).

Although he had been divinely set apart for his task, and although he had been raised to the throne with the full approval of the people, Jeroboam failed to rise to the greatness of his opportunities. The prophet had told him the conditions of success as a ruler, but it was not long before he began to depart from the counsels of the Lord. Afraid that if his people went annually to Jerusalem to worship it would not be long before they would be won back to the house of David, he decided to establish centers of worship at the two extremities of his kingdom—Dan in the north and Bethel in the south (1 Kings 12:26–30). This was at variance with the law of Moses, according to which there was to be but one altar of burnt offering and one place of meeting God. His disobedience became much greater when, in defiance of the commandment forbidding the worship of God by means of images, he set up a golden calf in each of the new sanctuaries and quoted to the people the words of Aaron, "Here are your gods, O Israel, who brought you up out of Egypt" (12:28; cf. Exod 32:4). These radical changes brought about other necessary changes. Since legitimate priests refused to serve at the new altars, Jeroboam had to find others to take their place "from all sorts of people" (1 Kings 12:31). Furthermore, he "built shrines on high places" (12:31) and ordained that the Feast of Tabernacles, which had been held in the seventh month, should now be observed in the eighth month. He even sometimes took it on himself to minister in the priests' office (12:33). The mass of people conformed to the new religious ways. This was the sin that Jeroboam "caused Israel to commit, so that they provoked the LORD . . . to anger by their worthless idols" (16:26). He sacrificed the higher interests of religion to politics. To establish his throne firmly, he led the people into the immoralities of heathenism, which led eventually to the destruction of the nation. The successive kings, with possibly one exception (Jehu), supported this idolatrous worship until Israel fell.

Although Jeroboam made Israel sin by introducing idolatrous religious customs, God gave him a solemn warning to give heed to his evil ways through an unnamed prophet who came to Bethel from Judah (1 Kings 13:1–6). One day—apparently the very day the altar was consecrated—as Jeroboam stood ministering at the altar, the man of God suddenly appeared before the king and foretold that the time would come when a member of the Davidic dynasty would desecrate that altar by burning men's bones on it, a prophecy that was fulfilled in the time of Josiah (2 Kings 23:15–16). When the king heard these words, he pointed to the prophet and cried out, "Seize him!" The hand that was extended instantly withered and became useless, and the altar was split in two so that the ashes spilled to the ground. The king then asked the prophet to pray that his hand might be restored. The prophet prayed, and the hand was restored. He refused the king's invitation to go home with him to dine, saying that it was against the will of God, and then left for home. In spite of this terrible warning from God, Jeroboam continued in his evil way, so that God decided to cut off and destroy his house.

At a later date, exactly when is not clear, Jeroboam's oldest son fell seriously ill. The distraught father thought of Ahijah, now old and blind, and sent his queen to him in disguise to find out whether the child would live. The prophet saw through her disguise and told her not only that the child would die, but that the house of Jeroboam would be utterly destroyed by someone whom the Lord would raise up to be king of Israel (1 Kings 14:1–18).

There was desultory warfare between Jeroboam and Rehoboam (1 Kings 15:6), and a great battle was fought between Jeroboam and Rehoboam's successor, Abijah (KJV Abijam). The army of Israel was thoroughly routed and was defeated with great slaughter, and Bethel, only a few miles from Jerusalem, was captured by Abijah (2 Chron 13). Jeroboam reigned for twenty-two years and was succeeded to the throne by his son Nadab (2 Kings 14:20).

For the people of Israel, the reign of Jeroboam was a supreme political and religious calamity. The warfare between the two kingdoms inevitably brought weakness to both, leaving them open to outside attack. The introduction of the golden calves led to the "baalization" of the religion of the Lord. In about two hundred years the moral and religious corruption of the people had gone so far that there was no more hope for them, and God brought in a heathen power to lead them into captivity.

Bibliography: J. Ellul, *The Politics of God and the Politics of Man,* 1966, pp. 121–26; C. F. Pfeiffer, *Old Testament History,* 1973, pp. 307–11. SB

JEROBOAM II (jĕr-ō-bō'ăm, Heb. *yārov'ām, the people contend,* or *the people become numerous*). The son and successor of Jehoash, king of Israel; fourth son of the dynasty of Jehu. He became king in Samaria c. 785 B.C. and reigned forty-one years. He followed the example of Jeroboam I in keeping up the idolatrous worship of the golden calves (2 Kings 14:23). In spite of this, his reign outwardly flourished. He ruled at the same time as Amaziah (14:23) and Uzziah (15:1), kings of Judah. He continued and brought to a successful conclusion the wars that his father had undertaken against Syria. He took their chief cities, Damascus and Hamath, which had once been subject to David, and restored to Israel territory east of the Jordan from Lebanon to the Dead Sea (14:25; Amos 6:14). Moab and Ammon, probably paying tribute to Syria, were reconquered (Amos 1:13; 2:1–3).

All these successful wars brought much tribute to Jeroboam and his nobles. The wealthy had both winter and summer homes; some lived in houses of ivory, others in houses of hewn stone. The prophet Amos, contemporary with Jeroboam in his later years, gives us a graphic description of a banqueting scene in which the perfumed guests lay on silken cushions, eating the flesh of lambs and stall-fed calves, drinking wine from bowls,

Cast of the Seal of Shema, Servant of Jeroboam (probably Jeroboam II), from Megiddo. Courtesy Israel Department of Antiquities and Museums.

and singing songs to the music of viols (Amos 6:4–6). But side by side with this luxury there was much poverty in the land. Twice the prophet says that the needy were sold for a pair of shoes (2:6; 8:6). No one was grieved for the afflictions of the poor or was distressed for the corruption that prevailed in the land. Drunkenness, licentiousness, and oppression went unchecked by the religious hierarchy.

Not that the land was devoid of religion. Worship went on not only at Dan and Bethel, but also at subsidiary temples and altars at Gilgal and Beersheba (Amos 4:4; 5:5; 8:14), places with long religious associations. Amos complained (5:21ff.) that ritual was substituted for righteousness, that devotees prostrated themselves before altars clothed in garments taken in cruel pledge, and that they drank sacrificial wine bought with the money of those who were condemned (2:8).

During the reign of Jeroboam the prophets Hosea, Joel, Jonah, and Amos ministered. Amos says that he was commanded by God to go to Bethel to testify against the whole proceedings there. He was to foretell the destruction of the sanctuaries of Israel and of the house of Jeroboam (Amos 7:9). When Amaziah, the high priest of Bethel, heard this denunciation, he sent a messenger to Jeroboam with a report of a "conspiracy" of Amos, saying that Amos had declared, "Jeroboam will die by the sword," which Amos had not done (7:10ff.). There are some who regard this as a prophecy that was not fulfilled, as there is no evidence that the king died other than a natural death, for he was buried with his ancestors in state (2 Kings 14:29). The probability, however, is that the high priest, in order to inflame Jeroboam against the prophet, gave his words an unwarranted twist.

In 2 Kings 14:25 we are told that a Jonah predicted the large extension of the territory of Israel by Jeroboam. This is the same Jonah, the son of Amittai, whose mission to Nineveh forms the subject of the Book of Jonah (1:1).

Jeroboam was succeeded on his death by his son Zechariah (2 Kings 14:29), a weak king with whom the dynasty ended. SB

JEROHAM (jē-rō'hăm, Heb. *jerōhām, may he be compassionate*, or *be pitied [by God]*). 1. A Levite, the father of Elkanah and grandfather of Samuel (1 Sam 1:1; 1 Chron 6:27, 34).

2. A Benjamite whose sons were chief men and lived at Jerusalem (1 Chron 8:27). Probably identical with no. 3.

3. A Benjamite, father of Ibneiah who lived at Jerusalem (1 Chron 9:8).

4. An ancestor of a priest in Jerusalem (1 Chron 9:12; Neh 11:12).

5. A Benjamite of Gedor, father of two of David's recruits at Ziklag (1 Chron 12:7).

6. The father of Azarel, chief of the tribe of Dan in the reign of David (1 Chron 27:22).

7. The father of Azariah, one of the captains who supported Jehoiada in overthrowing Queen Athaliah and putting Joash on the throne of Judah (2 Chron 23:1).

JERUB-BAAL (See GIDEON)

JERUB-BESHETH (See GIDEON)

JERUEL (jē-rū'ĕl, Heb. *jerû'ēl, founded by God*). A wilderness in Judah, "by the Pass of Ziz," in the vicinity of En Gedi. Its exact location is unknown. Jahaziel predicted that King Jehoshaphat would meet the armies of Moab and Ammon there (2 Chron 20:16).

JERUSALEM. The most important city on earth in the history of God's revelation to man in those divine acts by which redemption has been accomplished. It was the royal city, the capital of the only kingdom God has (thus far) established on earth. Here the temple was erected, and here, during the kingdom age, sacrifices were legitimately offered. This was the city of the prophets, as well as the kings of David's line. Here occurred the death, resurrection, and ascension of Jesus Christ, David's greatest Son. The Holy Spirit descended at Pentecost on an assembled group in this city, giving birth to the Christian church; and here the first great church council was held. Rightly did the chronicler refer to Jerusalem as "the city the LORD had chosen out of all the tribes of Israel in which to put his Name" (1 Kings 14:21). Even the first-century Roman historian Pliny referred to Jerusalem as "by far the most famous city of the ancient Orient." This city has been the preeminent objective of the pilgrimages of devout men and women for over two thousand years, and it was in an attempt to recover the Church of the Holy Sepulchre in Jerusalem that the Crusades were organized.

No site in all Scripture receives such constant and exalted praise as Jerusalem. Concerning no place in the world have such promises been made of ultimate glory and permanent peace.

I. Names of the City. While the word *Jerusalem* is Semitic, it apparently was not a name given to the city for the first time by the Hebrew people. Far back in the time of the Amarna Letters (1400 B.C.), it was called *U-ru-sa-lim,* that is, a city of Salim, generally taken to mean "city of peace." In the Hebrew Bible the word first appears in Joshua 10:1 where it is spelled *Yerushalayim.* In the Aramaic of Ezra 4:8, 20, 24; 5:1 it is *Jerushlem.* In the records of Sennacherib it is called *Ursalimu.* In the Syriac it is *Urishlem;* in the LXX, it is *Hierousalem.* The Romans, at the time of Hadrian, A.D. 135, changed the name to *Aelia Capitolina.* For some centuries now the Arabs have called the city *Al-Kuds al-Sharif,* which means "the Sanctuary." There is no reason for insisting that Salem is to be taken as the name of a Canaanitic deity, that is, the city of the god Salem. Salem was probably the earlier name for the city, the name given it in the memorable interview of Abraham with Melchizedek, the king of Salem (Gen 14:18; Ps 76:2). Because the very name of the city means *peace*, we are told that in this place God himself will give peace (Hag 2:9). The children of God are exhorted to pray for the peace of Jerusalem (Ps 122:6). Isaiah, at the end

Panorama of Jerusalem, as viewed from the Hill of Evil Council, south to northeast: (1) temple mount, (2) Ophel area, (3) Mount of Olives. Courtesy Israel Government Press Office.

of his great series of prophecies, returns to the theme, "For this is what the Lord says: 'I will extend peace to her like a river' " (Isa 66:12). This word "Salem" is the basis of the Arabic greeting "Salam," and the Jewish greeting "Shalom," both meaning "peace be with you."

The rabbis say there are sixty different names for Jerusalem in the Bible, a characteristic exaggeration, but truly there are a great number. The name Jerusalem itself occurs about six hundred times in the OT, though it is not found in Job, Hosea, Jonah, Nahum, Habakkuk, and Haggai.

Jerusalem appears in the NT after the close of the Book of Acts rather infrequently, four times near the conclusion of the Letter to the Romans (15:19, 25, 26, 31), once at the end of the First Letter to the Corinthians (16:3), and again in Galatians (1:17–18; 2:1). The name most often used for this city, apart from Jerusalem itself, is *Zion,* which occurs over one hundred times in the OT, beginning as early as 2 Kings 19:21 and found most often in the Book of Psalms and the prophecy of Isaiah (1:8; 4:4–5; 62:11). Zion appears in the NT in some interesting passages: twice on the lips of our Lord (Matt 21:5; John 12:15), twice in Romans (9:33; 11:36), and in 1 Peter 2:6 and Revelation 14:1. Jerusalem is often called "the city of David" (2 Sam 5:7, 9; 6:10–16; Neh 3:15; 12:37; Isa 22:9). This title is later applied to Bethlehem (Luke 2:4, 11).

The greatest group of titles for Jerusalem are those that identify it as *the city of God.* It is called this in the Psalms, as well as in the NT (Ps 46:4; 48:1, 8; 87:3; Heb 12:22; Rev 3:12). It is also called the city of the Lord (Isa 60:14), the mountain of the Lord (2:3; 30:29), the mountain of the Lord Almighty (Zech 8:3), Zion of the Holy One of Israel (Isa 60:14). The Lord himself refers to it, and to no other place, as "my city" (45:13), or more often, "my holy mountain" (11:9; 56:7; 57:13; 65:11, 25; 66:20). Because it is the city of God, where he has put his Name, it is often referred to as the Holy City (48:2; 52:1; Neh 11:1–18), a title used twice by Matthew (4:5; 27:53), once of a future event by John (Rev 11:2), and used also in referring to our eternal heavenly home at the close of the Scriptures (21:2; 22:19). Generally, the phrase "the holy mountain" refers to this city (e.g., Ps 48:1; Isa 11:9; 27:13; Dan 11:45). Once it is given the beautiful name of Hephzibah, meaning "My delight is in her" (Isa 62:4). Isaiah in one passage calls the city Ariel, the meaning of which is disputed (29:1, 2, 7), a word that in itself means "Lion of God." At the beginning of his prophecy Isaiah gives two titles to the city in most radical contrast. He designates it, because of its wickedness, as Sodom and Gomorrah (1:10); but in the same passage he promises that the day will come when it will be accurately called "the City of Righteousness" (1:26).

II. The Site. Unlike most cities that have witnessed great historical events over many centuries, Jerusalem has always remained on the same site. It is situated thirty-three (fifty-five km.) miles east of the Mediterranean and fourteen miles west of the Dead Sea, at an elevation of 2,550 feet (797 m.) above sea level. Geologically speaking, the city rests on three hills. The SE hill, the original city of the Jebusites, the city that David seized, later to be called Zion, occupied about eight to ten acres, and "was shaped somewhat like a gigantic human footprint about 1,250 feet [390 m.] long and 400 feet [125 m.] wide." The area of the fortress city of Megiddo in contrast was thirty acres. The northern hill was the one on which Solomon built the great temple and his own palace, called Ophel. It is probable that Millo (2 Sam 5:9; 1 Kings 9:15–16; see footnotes) was "either a fortress guarding the northern approach to Ophel or a fill of rocks and dirt to shore up the wall at its most vulnerable point" (Gottwald). On the east of these two hills was a deep valley known as the Kidron. To the south of the city was another deep valley called the Hinnom. Down through the middle of the city, running from north to south, was a third valley, now built over and discernible only by careful investigation of the contours of the rock level, called the Tyropoeon Valley. On the far side of the western hill was the Valley of Gehenna, a continuation of Hinnom. These valleys today give no idea of their original depth, for debris has filled them up in some places to a depth of fifty to sixty feet (sixteen to nineteen m.). The city never occupied what could be called a large area. Even in the time of Herod the Great, the area within the walls was not more than a mile (about one and one-half km.) in length, nor more than five-eighths of a mile (about one km.) in width. The city was off the beaten path of the great caravan routes and was not, as most larger world capitals, on a navigable river or on a large body of water. Its site, therefore, had an exclusiveness about it. On the other hand, being nineteen miles (thirty-two km.) north of Hebron and thirty miles (fifty km.) south of Samaria, it was centrally located to serve as the capital of the kingdom of Israel. Many travelers have testified to the fact that Jerusalem "from whatever direction it is approached, can be seen only when one has arrived in its immediate vicinity: a peculiarity which always brought a moment of pleasant surprise to travelers of by-gone days" (J. Simons).

III. Walls and Gates. The matter of Israel's gates and walls is complicated and has given rise to a great many technical disagreements; it can be discussed here only in a general way. Because of the deep valleys on the east, south, and west of the city, it was only the northern side that could be easily penetrated by an invading army. The walls on the east and west were built on the ridges of these valleys. There was probably in early days a southern wall extending far below the present southern wall structure. The first northern wall extended from what is called the Jaffa Gate to the middle of the great temple area. The second northern wall began at the Jaffa Gate, extended northward and then curved to the east to the Tower of Antonia, just beyond the northern end of the temple area. The modern wall extends north and then east from the northern end of the western wall to the northern end of the present eastern wall. There was a third north wall of which we have become aware only during the days of modern excavation. The walls of the city are more elaborately described in the Book of Nehemiah than in any other place in the Bible. Beginning at the SE end of the early wall is the Dung Gate; moving northward one comes to the Fountain Gate; and then, nearly in the middle of the wall of the old temple area, the famous now-closed Golden Gate. Above this is Stephen's Gate. Turning west on the northern modern wall, one comes to Herod's Gate, then the much-used Damascus Gate, and then toward the end of this northern wall, the New Gate. Turning left again at the western wall, one comes to the last of the gates now in use, the Jaffa Gate, from where the road proceeds to the Mediterranean. The present wall, though much of it is, no doubt, on the site of earlier walls, was built by Soliman II about A.D. 1540, extending for two and one-half miles (four km.), with an average height of thirty-eight feet (twelve m.).

IV. History. The early history of Jerusalem is wrapped in obscurity. Pottery from before 2000 B.C. has been found at Al Buqueia, SW of Jerusalem, though we do not know any names of individuals appearing at this site at such an early period. The first reference to Jerusalem in secular annals is in the famous Amarna Letters of the fourteenth century, in which is found some interesting correspondence from the governor of this city, Abd-Khiba, addressed to the pharaoh of Egypt, complaining that his city is being threatened and that the Egyptians are not giving him the support he needs and expected. There is, however, a reference to the Jebusites, who are the ones who inhabited the city of Jebus, that is, Jerusalem, as early as the great ethnological passage in Genesis 10:15–19. Actually, the first reference to Jerusalem as such is found in the account of Abraham's interview with Melchizedek, king of *Salem* (14:17–24). Here is the first occurrence of the word "priest" in the Bible, and because Melchizedek was the "priest of God Most High" we are compelled to believe that even before the nation Israel was founded, and perhaps eight hundred years before this site was taken by David, there was a witness to the true God at this place. While there is some difference of view on this point, many believe, and tradition is unanimous here, that the place where Abraham offered up Isaac at Mount Moriah (22:2; 2 Chron 3:1) is the exact site on which, centuries later, the temple of Solomon was built. Josephus himself affirms that Jerusalem was in existence during the days of Abraham (*Antiq*. 1.10.2; 7.11.3).

The actual name Jerusalem occurs for the first time in Joshua 10:5, where the king of the city confederated with four other kings in a futile attempt to defeat Joshua. In the same book it is frankly confessed that the Israelites were unable to drive out the Jebusites (15:8, 63; 18:28). At the beginning of the Book of Judges (1:7) it is stated, however, that the Israelites in an hour of victory overwhelmed a large opposing force including Adoni-Bezek and "brought him to Jerusalem," where he died. This seems to imply that for a brief

The gates of Jerusalem: (1) Jaffa Gate in the west, (2) Golden Gate in the east, (3) St. Stephen's Gate, or Lions' Gate, in the northeast, and (4) Zion Gate in the southwest. Most of the gates to be found today in the Old City wall were built after the Turkish conquest, c. 450 years ago. The gates shown here, a notable exception being the Zion Gate, were rebuilt on the foundations of the city gates from Roman times. The Zion Gate was altered to facilitate the approach to Mount Zion and the Tomb of David. Courtesy Israel Gov't. Press Office.

space the Israelites held part of this city but were not able to keep it (Judg 1:21).

Nothing is known of the history of Jerusalem either from biblical or nonbiblical writings from the time of Joshua's death until the capture of this city by David (2 Sam 5:6–10; probably 998 B.C.). No doubt the fortress that David took is that which later came to be called Zion, located on the SE hill, and outside of the present walls of the city. Kraeling estimates that the population of this city during David's time did not exceed 1,230 inhabitants. Later David purchased "the threshing floor of Araunah the Jebusite" (24:18; 1 Chron 21:18–28) where the great temple of Solomon was later erected. After finishing the temple, Solomon built a magnificent palace to the north of it, of which there is not a trace today.

With the death of Solomon, the glory of Israel and so also the glory of Jerusalem began to dim. In the fifth year of Rehoboam, 917 B.C., Shishak king of Egypt, without any struggle, came up to Jerusalem and "carried off the treasures of the temple of the LORD and the treasures of the royal palace. He took everything, including all the gold shields Solomon had made" (1 Kings 14:26; 2 Chron 12:9). This is the first of eight different plunderings of the Jerusalem temple, occurring within a little more than three hundred years. Not only must its wealth have been fabulously great, but also doubtless in times of national prosperity the more religiously inclined citizens of Judah would bestow new treasures on the temple. Only a short time later Asa (911–871) bribed Ben-Hadad king of Syria by taking "all the silver and gold that was left in the treasuries of the LORD's temple and of his own palace . . . and sent them to Ben-Hadad" (1 Kings 15:18). Twice, then, within a few years after Solomon's death, Judah's kings prevented an invasion of the city only by bribing her enemies with the treasures of the Lord's house. Again during the reign of Jehoram (850–843), in an episode about which we know very little, the Arabians and Philistines "carried off all the goods found in the king's palace, together with his sons and wives" (2 Chron 21:16–17). For the fourth time within a century and a half after the death of Solomon, the temple treasures were used for bribing a threatening enemy, by Joash (837–800), who "took all the sacred objects dedicated by his fathers . . . and the gifts he himself had dedicated and all the gold found in the treasuries of the temple of the LORD and of the royal palace, and he sent them to Hazael king of Aram, who then withdrew from Jerusalem" (2 Kings 12:18). Thus far it had been foreign kings that were bribed with these treasures, but the fifth occasion involved Jehoash, king of Israel (801–786). Coming up to Jerusalem, he broke down the western wall for a length of 600 feet (188 m.), and then "took all the gold and silver and all the articles found in the temple of the LORD and in the treasuries of the royal palace. He also took hostages and returned to Samaria" (2 Kings 14:13–14; 2 Chron 25:23).

One attack on the city of Jerusalem failed in the reign of Ahaz (733–714 B.C.), when Rezin king of Syria and Remaliah king of Israel were repulsed in their attempt to seize the temple (2 Kings 16:5). However, while Ahaz was still king, a

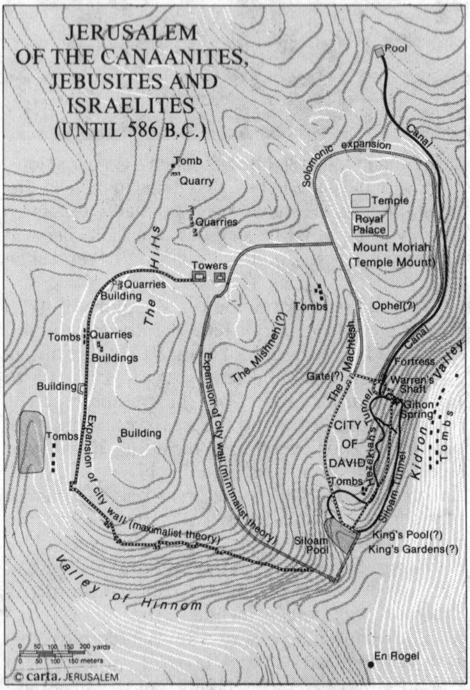

mighty king of Assyria, Tiglath-Pileser III (745–737) came up to Jerusalem. "Ahaz took some of the things from the temple of the LORD and from the royal palace and from the princes and presented them to the king of Assyria, but that did not help him" (2 Chron 28:20–21).

In 701 B.C. occurred an event to which the OT gives more space, with greater detail, than even to the destruction of Jerusalem by Nebuchadnezzar. Sennacherib threatened the city (704–681), casting one insult after another in the face of King Hezekiah (715–687), reminding him that he, Sennacherib, had already captured practically every city of Judah, and how could the king think Jerusalem would escape? But by divine intervention, with God's assurance that the king would this time be kept from invasion, Sennacherib's army suffered a mysterious destruction, and he returned to Assyria without fulfilling his threat (2 Kings 18–19; 2 Chron 32; Isa 36; for Sennacherib's own account of this episode, see ANET, pp. 287–88).

Another century passed during which we know very little of Jerusalem's history. In 605 B.C. Nebuchadnezzar king of Babylon forced Judah's king Jehoiakim into submission. After three years, the king of Judah foolishly revolted, and this brought Nebuchadnezzar back to the city for its final destruction in 597. It is estimated that some sixty thousand citizens were carried away to Babylon at this time, and the remaining treasures of the temple were also removed, to be restored again in the days of Ezra (2 Kings 24:1–25:21; 2 Chron 36:1–21; Jer 52). As Jeremiah vividly reminds us, "The kings of the earth did not believe, nor did any of the world's people, that enemies and foes could enter the gates of Jerusalem" (Lam 4:12).

Although the postexilic books of Ezra and Nehemiah are filled with details regarding Jerusalem, we mention only the two main events they record. Under Zerubbabel, the rebuilding of the temple by permission of Darius I was begun in 538 B.C., though due to many forms of opposition it was not finished until 516. Some sixty years later Nehemiah, cupbearer of the king of Persia, Artaxerxes I, successfully undertook the rebuilding of the walls of the city (Neh 1–6), followed by a great revival under the leadership of Ezra (Neh 8–9). The condition of the city, however, even under these great leaders, was not one marked by prosperity; somehow it had lost its attractiveness for the Jews, necessitating a vigorous effort to bring people from outlying areas into the city to live (11:1). For the next hundred years, we again know very little of Jerusalem's history.

On the death of Alexander the Great, the rulers of Egypt and the South were known as Ptolemies, and those of Syria and the North as the Seleucids. In 320 B.C. Jerusalem came under the rule of Ptolemy I Soter. One hundred years later the city passed from the Ptolemies to the Seleucids. In the year 199, but only for a year, Palestine and Jerusalem were recovered for Egypt by Scopas, the last time Egypt was to possess this city. In 198 the powerful Antiochus III (the Great) took the city. He was welcomed by the Jews, who were rewarded when the Syrian king presented treasures to the temple. Any hope, however, that this would be the beginning of happier days for them was soon seen to be unjustified. For in the next generation there appeared (169–168) the very type of Antichrist himself, Antiochus IV (Epiphanes), who desecrated the temple by sacrificing a pig on the altar; prohibited Jewish sacrifices, circumcision, and the observance of the Sabbath; and issued a decree that any Jew found possessing a copy of the Holy Scriptures should be killed; and great was the slaughter. (See the opening chapters of 1 Maccabees.)

The events that followed next must be referred to only briefly. In 165 B.C. Jerusalem was delivered from its bitter yoke by Judas Maccabaeus on the twenty-fifth of the month of Kislev (our month of December). Ever since, this time of deliverance has been celebrated by the Jews as Hanukkah, or the Feast of Lights. Two years later, Antiochus IV (Eupator) overthrew the walls and the temple, but soon after that the city again came into the hands of the Jewish authorities. But this did not mean peace. Jealousy and schism increased, until one of the Jewish leaders himself, Alexander Jannaeus, actually crucified eight hundred Pharisees.

The Romans now appeared on the scene. The city was besieged in 65 B.C. by a Roman general who, however, was ordered to desist, leaving the city open for the conquest by Pompey in 64, who destroyed Jerusalem's walls. The temple was again pillaged in 55 by Crassus. Fifteen years later the area was occupied by the Parthians. The hour had struck for the rise of that cruel but gifted ruler whose name will be prominent as the NT narrative opens, Herod the Great, made king of the Jews by Augustus in 40. He fought for the possession of the territory that had been given to him, but was not able to take Jerusalem until 37, after a siege of three months. Herod, like many other Romans, had a passion for erecting vast buildings, and out of this was born the determination to build what came to be known as Herod's temple, probably the most significant structure ever to stand on that holy site. He began its erection in 20. Herod died in 4, and not until A.D. 62 was the temple finished. In our Lord's day it presented a spectacle before which even the disciples seemed to stand in amazement (Matt 24:1).

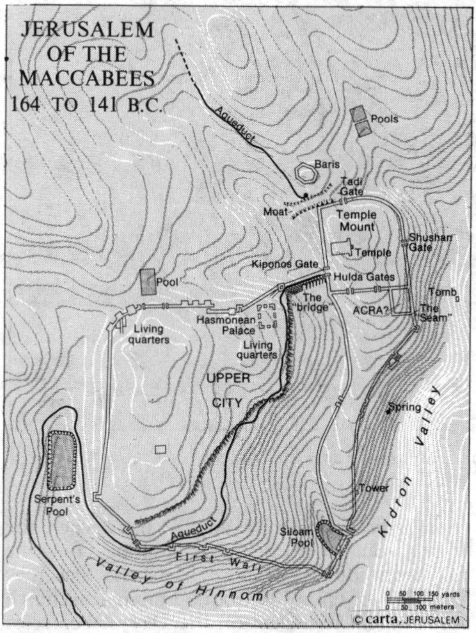

Entire books have been written on the single subject of Jesus and the city of Jerusalem. Here we can only summarize the relevant data. One is safe in saying that of the four Gospel writers, it is Luke who, though a Gentile, seems to have had the greatest interest in this city. The opening events of our Lord's life occurring here are exclusively in the Third Gospel, and many of the concluding events are recorded only here as well. We begin with the annunciation to Zacharias, a priest in the temple (Luke 1:5–22). When Jesus was a baby, he was taken up to Jerusalem for what is called his presentation (2:22–38). He then visited the city at the age of twelve (2:41–52). The principal episodes down to the last year of our Lord's life are given exclusively by John. If we place Jesus' death in A.D. 30, then the first cleansing of the temple occurred in April of the year 27 (John 2:13–25); in April in the year 28 the man at the Pool of Bethesda was healed (5:1–47); in October of 29, Jesus went up to Jerusalem at the time of the Feast of Tabernacles (7:2; 10:21); in December of 29, he was in Jerusalem for the Feast of Dedication (Luke 10:38–42). Of course, the final week of Jesus' life was spent in and near the city of Jerusalem (Matt 26:1–27:66; Mark 11:1–15:47; Luke 19:29–23:56; John 12:12–19:42). Of the five appearances of Jesus on Easter Sunday, four are found only in Luke's Gospel (Luke 24). The sixth appearance in Jerusalem a week later is recorded only by John (20:26–29). Jesus appeared in Jerusalem to all the disciples (Luke 24:49; Acts 1:1–8), and from the Mount of Olives nearby he ascended (Luke 24:50–53).

Our Lord made four principal statements about the city, all of them with a note of sadness. First, in stating that he must go up to Jerusalem, he declared, "Surely no prophet can die outside Jerusalem!" (Luke 13:33). On Tuesday of Holy Week he cried out, "O Jerusalem, Jerusalem, you who kill the prophets and stone those sent to you, how often I have longed to gather your children together, as a hen gathers her chicks under her wings, but you were not willing" (Matt 23:37). We are told by Luke that as Jesus wept over the city, he said sadly, "If you, even you, had only known on this day what would bring you peace—but now it is hidden from your eyes" (Luke 19:42). Finally, he declared that the buildings of that city and its very walls would be thrown

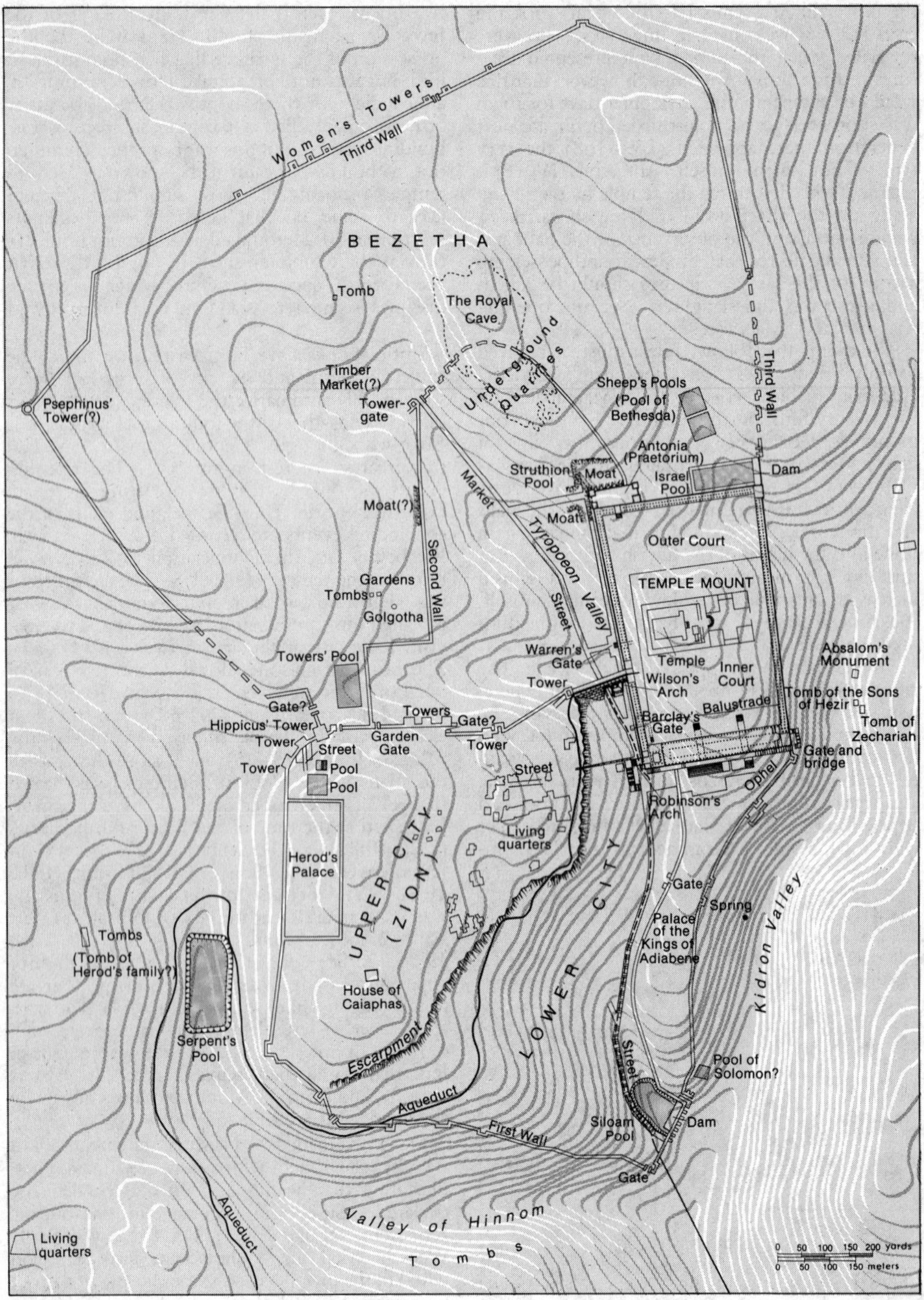

Jerusalem in the time of Jesus and the second temple. Courtesy Carta, Jerusalem.

down, adding, "Jerusalem will be trampled on by the Gentiles until the times of the Gentiles are fulfilled" (Matt 24:2; Mark 13:2; Luke 21:24).

The Book of Acts opens with a group of the followers of Jesus meeting together in an upper room in Jerusalem, probably the place where the Lord's Supper was held, waiting for the fulfillment of the promise of Christ that they would be given power from on high. The church was born in Jerusalem on the Day of Pentecost

(Acts 2). The early persecutions occurred in that city toward these initial believers, and the Sanhedrin that condemned Christ was now confronted with the phenomenon of a growing company of faithful followers of the crucified and risen Lord. In this city the first great crisis of the church was successfully faced in the first Council, deciding forever the fact that salvation is wholly by grace, apart from works (ch. 15). Years later in this same city, the apostle Paul was arrested, mobbed in the temple, and falsely accused (chs. 21–22).

The destruction of the city after a siege of 143 days by Roman armies under the leadership of Titus, though predicted in the Gospels, is not actually recorded anywhere in the NT. Before this dreadful event concluded, 600,000 Jews were killed and thousands more were led away into captivity. "Jerusalem has no history for 60 years after its destruction" (C. R. Conder). One futile and tragic attempt of the Jews to win freedom from the Romans was concentrated in the rebellion of A.D. 134, led by the false messiah Bar Kochba. This rebellion was overwhelmingly crushed, and what was left of the city was leveled to the ground, even the foundations being plowed up. Two years later the Romans began rebuilding the city, now to be called Aelia Capitolina. All Jews were strictly excluded from this new city for two centuries, until the reign of Constantine. In the early part of the fourth century, due to the fervent devotion of Helena, the mother of the emperor, concerning whom traditions soon multiplied regarding divine assistance given to her that led to the discovery of the true cross, the great Church of the Holy Sepulchre called Anastasis (the Greek word for resurrection) was built. From then on, Jerusalem became increasingly the object of pilgrimages and of rich gifts. Jerome says, "It would be a long task to try to enumerate chronologically from the day of the ascension of our Lord until our own time, the bishops, martyrs, and doctors of the Church who came to Jerusalem, believing themselves to be deficient in religion, in science, and to possess only an imperfect standard of virtue until they had worshiped Christ on the very spot where the Gospel first shone from the gibbet."

For Jerusalem's subsequent history, only the barest outline can be given here. In A.D. 614 a Persian general under King Chosroes II seized the city and slaughtered sixty thousand Christians, taking thirty-five thousand more into slavery. In 628 Heraclius made peace with the son of the invader Chosroes, entering Jerusalem in triumph through the Golden Gate. In 637 the city capitulated to Omar the Galiph, who entered its precincts without bloodshed. In 688 the first Dome of the Rock was erected.

Muhammad, more or less acquainted with both the OT and NT, felt it was necessary to be in some way identified with this city, holy to both Jews and Christians; and Islam soon interpreted a passage in the Koran as implying that Muhammad was miraculously carried to Jerusalem and was divinely consecrated there, but there is no real evidence for this journey. In A.D. 969 Jerusalem

Silver tetradrachma struck in the second year of the Bar-Kokhba War in A.D. 133. It depicts a temple façade symbolizing the temple of Jerusalem, which Bar-Kokhba wished to restore. The reverse depicts the four species of the Feast of Tabernacles. Hebrew inscriptions: obverse—"Year 2 of the freedom of Israel"; reverse—"Jerusalem." Courtesy Reuben and Edith Hecht Museum, University of Haifa.

fell under the power of the Shia'h Khalif of Egypt. In 1009 the Caliph Hakim, son of a Christian mother, began his devastating work in Jerusalem by ordering the destruction of the Church of the Holy Sepulchre. By 1014 some thirty thousand churches in Palestine had been burned or pillaged. In 1077 a general of the Seljuk Turks drove out the Egyptians, slaughtering some three thousand residing within the walls of the city.

A new era—pitiful, sad, and shameful—now dawned for Jerusalem. On June 7, A.D. 1099, the Christian army of the First Crusade camped before Jerusalem. The city was seized on July 14, and the awful slaughter pursued by these so-called Christian knights was something that the Muslim world has never forgotten or forgiven. For eighty years the city knew no other enemy at her gates. There then came on the stage of history the truly great Saladin who, after his overwhelming victory in his battle with the Crusaders at the Horns of Hattin, camped before the city on September 20, 1187. He entered it on October 2, enforcing strict orders that no violence or orgy of conquest should be engaged in by his soldiers such as the Christian Crusaders had participated in almost a century before. By this act of mercy he put the Christians to shame. But the city was not to know peace. In 1229, it was regained by Frederick II, through negotiations. In 1244 it fell before the Kharezmian Tartars. In 1247 it was seized again by the Egyptians. In 1260 it was recaptured by the Tartars. In 1517 it was taken by the Ottoman Turks, who held it for four centuries. On December 9, 1917, the British General Allenby entered the city on foot; on October 31, 1918, the armistice was signed, and four hundred years of Turkish misrule came to an end.

On April 24, A.D. 1920, the mandate for Palestine and Transjordan was assigned to Great Britain, and for nearly thirty years she suffered one reverse after another in attempting to rule the country. On May 14, 1948, the British mandate terminated, and the National Council at Tel-Aviv proclaimed the State of Israel. There followed the bitter, often brutal war for Palestine, as a result of which nearly a million Arabs were driven from their homes. By the spring of 1949, Israel was

At the entrance to the Citadel (Tower of David) inside the Jaffa Gate, the reading of General Allenby's address, ending four hundred years of Turkish rule, December 11, 1917. Courtesy Imperial War Museum.

recognized by forty-five governments. The struggle with the Arab bloc of nations has unhappily continued. One round of hostilities ended in 1967 with the end of Arab administration in the Old City, and the assumption of Israeli control over the whole city of Jerusalem. The city had been proclaimed the country's capital in 1950, but this was not recognized by the United Nations. The city's population at the 1980 census was 448,200.

V. Jerusalem in Prophecy. Although there are scores of prophecies in the Bible relating to cities, rivers, and nations, few reference works seem to handle such prophesies adequately. Here it is possible to give only a bare summary of those pertaining to Jerusalem.

1. In Deuteronomy 12, though no name is mentioned, six times reference is made to the future place of the sanctuary, "the place the LORD your God will choose" (see also 1 Kings 8:29, 48).
2. The promise that Sennacherib's attempt to capture the city would fail (2 Kings 19:32–34; Isa 29:7; 30:19; 31:4–5).
3. The destruction of the city by Nebuchadnezzar (2 Kings 22:16–17; 23:7; 2 Chron 34:24–25; Isa 4:3–5; 10:11–12; 22:9–11; Ezek 8:9; 24:1ff.).
4. The desecration of the city by Antiochus Epiphanes (Dan 8:11–14; 11:30–32).
5. The destruction of the city by the Romans under Titus (Dan 9:26; Matt 24:2; Mark 13:2; Luke 13:33–35; 19:41–44; 21:6, 20, 24).
6. A prophecy concerning this city during the present age (Dan 9:26; Zech 12:3; Luke 21:24).
7. The Jewish people at the end of this age will return to Palestine; sometimes Jerusalem is specifically designated (Joel 3:1). The erection of some kind of temple in the Holy City is also prophesied (Isa 55:11; 60:1–3; Jer 31:8–9; Dan 9:27; 12:11; Matt 24:15; Mark 13:14; 2 Thess 2:3–4).
8. The episode of the two witnesses to be martyred in this city (Rev 11).
9. A final assault on this city by the nations of the earth (Isa 29:1–7; 31–34; Joel 3:9–12; Zech 14:1–3).
10. A cleansing of the city of its spiritual uncleanness (Isa 1:25–26; 4:3–4; Joel 3:17; Zech 14:1–3).
11. A city that will ultimately and permanently know the presence of the glory of God (Isa 62:2; Ezek 43:1–2); peace (Ps 122:6–9; Isa 60:17; 66:12); and joy (Ps 53:6; Isa 5:11).
12. The city to which the nations of the earth will come for instruction and blessing (Ps 102:21–22; Isa 2:2–4).

VI. Recent Archaeology. Excavations from A.D. 1969 have revealed, among other things, that the temple stood about a hundred yards (ninety-four m.) north of the Dome of the Rock. An earlier gate (perhaps Solomonic) was detected beneath the present Golden Gate. A flight of thirty steps two hundred feet (sixty-three m.) wide, leading up to the southern gates of the temple mount, was found dating to the time of Christ. The Cardo Maximus (main street) of the Byzantine city was discovered along with foundations of Justinian's New Church dedicated to the Virgin Mary. The Essene gate mentioned by Josephus has probably been located in the SW wall south of the modern Holy Land Institute.

See also ARCHAEOLOGY.

Bibliography: C. R. Conder, *The City of Jerusalem,* 1909; G. A. Smith, *Jerusalem . . . from the Earliest Times to A.D. 70,* 1908; J. Simons, *Jerusalem in the Old Testament,* 1952 (this includes extensive bibliography); K. Kenyon, *Digging Up Jerusalem,* 1974; W. D. Davies, *The Gospel and the Land,* 1974; B. Mazar, *The Mountain of the Lord,* 1975; Y. Yadin (ed.), *Jerusalem Revealed,* 1975; J. Wilkinson, *Jerusalem as Jesus Knew It,* 1978; N. Avigad, *Discovering Jerusalem,* 1980; L. Levine (ed.), *The Jerusalem Cathedra,* 1981. WMS

JERUSALEM, NEW. A name found twice in the Bible (Rev 3:12; 21:2) where the new Jerusalem is described as coming down out of heaven from God. In Revelation 21:2 it is also called "the Holy City," and in Revelation 21:10 "the Holy City, Jerusalem." In Revelation 21:10–22:5 the city is described in material terms, as though it were literal. It is in the form of a cube, 1,500 miles (2,500 km.) square; its walls are of jasper; its streets, of gold; the foundations of the walls are precious stones; its twelve gates are of pearls. For light it needs neither moon nor sun. A pure river of water of life flows through it;

and in the midst of it there is the tree of life, whose leaves are for the healing of the nations.

Views on the nature of the city, whether it is literal or symbolic, and on when it comes into existence are legion. Hardly any two expositors fully agree, but in general there are two main views. Some hold that the city is a symbol of the ideal church as conceived in the purpose of God and to be fully realized in his own time. The church, allegorically depicted by the city, is of course already in existence, but God's ideal for it will not be reached until the new age has been ushered in by the Lord's return. The great size of the city denotes that the church is capable of holding almost countless numbers. The fact that the city descends "out of heaven from God" means that it is the product of God's supernatural workmanship in the historic process of redemption. In support of this view it is said that in Revelation 21:9–10, when John is told that he would be shown the bride, the Lamb's wife, he is actually shown the New Jerusalem; and, moreover, as Jerusalem and Zion often refer to the inhabitants and faithful worshipers of the Lord, so the new Jerusalem is symbolic of the church of God.

Those who consider the New Jerusalem a literal city usually regard it as the eternal dwelling place of God. Premillennialists believe see it as a special creation of God at the beginning of the Millennium, to be inhabited by the saints, first during the Millennium and then, after the creation of the new heaven and new earth, throughout eternity. It would seem, however, that the city will not be in sight during the Millennium but will be above the earthly Jerusalem. The saints in the city will have the privilege of seeing the face of God and of having his name on their foreheads. Some expositors hold that the New Jerusalem as a literal city does not appear above Jerusalem during the Millennium and that the description in Revelation 21:10–22:5 has reference to the eternal state. SB

JERUSHA, JERUSHAH (jē-rū'shȧ, Heb. *yerûsha', possessed,* i.e., *married*). The wife of Uzziah, king of Judah, and mother of Jotham, his successor (2 Kings 15:33; 2 Chron 27:1). Her father's name was Zadok (1 Chron 6:12).

JESARELAH (jĕ'sȧ-rē'-lȧ, Heb. *yesar'ēlâh,* meaning doubtful). The ancestral head of the seventh course of musicians (1 Chron 25:14).

JESHAIAH, JESAIAH (jē-shā'yȧ, jē-sā'yȧ, Heb. *yesha'yâhû, yesha'yâh, Jehovah saves*). 1. A son of Jeduthun, and a musician in David's reign; he became the ancestral head of one of the courses of musicians (1 Chron 25:3, 15).

2. A Levite, son of Rehabiah and ancestor of Shelomith, one of David's treasurers (1 Chron 26:25).

3. A son of Hananiah, and grandson of Zerubbabel (1 Chron 3:21).

4. A son of Athaliah and descendant of Elam. He returned from Babylon with Ezra (Ezra 8:7).

5. A descendant of Merari who returned with Ezra from Babylon (Ezra 8:19).

6. A Benjamite, the father of Ithiel (Neh 11:7).

JESHANAH (jĕsh'ȧ-nȧ or jē-shā'nȧ, Heb. *yeshānâh, old*). A town near Bethel, in Ephraim, captured by Abijah from the northern kingdom (2 Chron 13:19). It is probably the same as the Isanos of Josephus (*Antiq.* 14.15.12), and is represented by the modern Ain Sinia, 3¼ miles (5 km.) north of Bethel.

JESHARELAH (See JESARELAH)

JESHEBEAB (jē-shĕb'ē-ăb, Heb. *yeshev'āv,* meaning uncertain). The ancestral head of the fourteenth course of priests (1 Chron 24:13).

JESHER (jē'shēr, Heb. *yēsher, uprightness*). A son of Caleb (1 Chron 2:18).

JESHIMON (jē-shī'mŏn, Heb. *hayeshîmōn, a waste, a desert*). The word is often used as a common noun to refer to the desert of Sinai (e.g., Deut 32:10; Ps 78:40; 106:14; Isa 43:19) and is usually translated "desert." Sometimes it is used as a geographical term and probably refers to two different districts:

1. The "desert" in the Jordan Valley, NE of the Dead Sea, seen from the top of Pisgah (Num 21:20; 23:28 KJV; NIV "wasteland"). This is a bare, salty land without any vegetation.

2. The sterile plateau to which David went in fleeing from Saul. It was near Ziph and Maon, SE of Hebron. It refers to the eastern section of the Judean hills, which stretch toward the Dead Sea. For most of the year it is bare of vegetation. Its chalky hills have always been the home of outlaws (1 Sam 23:19, 24; 26:1, 3).

JESHISHAI (jē-shĭsh'ā-ī, Heb. *yeshîshay, aged*). A Gadite, descended from Buz (1 Chron 5:14).

JESHOHAIAH (jĕsh-ō-hā'yȧ, Heb. *yeshôhāyâh,* meaning unknown). A prince in Simeon (1 Chron 4:36).

JESHUA, JESHUAH (jĕsh'ū-ȧ, Heb. *yēshūa', another form of Joshua, Jehovah is salvation*). 1. A name used once for Joshua, the son of Nun (Neh 8:17 KJV; NIV retains "Joshua").

2. The name of the head of the ninth of the twenty-four courses of priests (1 Chron 24:11).

3. The name of a family of Pahath-Moab, who returned with Zerubbabel from Babylon to Jerusalem (Ezra 2:6; Neh 7:11).

4. A Levite in charge of the distribution of tithes in Hezekiah's time (2 Chron 31:15).

5. The high priest who returned with Zerubbabel (Ezra 2:2; Neh 7:7; called "Joshua" in Hag 1:1 and in Zech 3:1ff.). He helped to rebuild the altar (Ezra 3:2, 8) and the house of God (4:3; 5:2).

6. A Levite who supervised the workmen in the temple after the Exile (Ezra 2:40; 3:9; Neh 7:43). He also assisted in explaining the law to the people (Neh 8:7), in leading in worship (9:4),

and in sealing the covenant (10:9). From the last passage, it appears that Jeshua was the son of Azaniah.

7. A postexilic town in southern Judah (Neh 11:26). It is identified with Tell es-Sa'weh and may be the same as the Shema of Joshua 15:26.

JESHURUN (jĕsh'ū-rŭn, Heb. *yeshūrûn, upright one*). A poetical or ideal title of Israel. Except in Deuteronomy 32:15, where it is used of Israel in reproachful irony because they had departed from their moral ideal, it is always used as a title of honor (Deut 33:5, 26; Isa 44:2).

JESIAH (See ISSHIAH)

JESIMIEL (jē-sĭm'ĭ-ĕl, Heb. *yesîmi'ēl, God establishes*). A prince of Simeon (1 Chron 4:36).

JESSE (jĕs'ē, Heb. *yishay,* meaning uncertain). Son of Obed, of the family of Perez. He was descended from Nahshon, chief of the tribe of Judah in the days of Moses, and was the grandson of Boaz, whose wife was Ruth the Moabitess (Ruth 4:18–22). From his descent and from the fact that when Saul pursued David he entrusted his parents to the care of the king of Moab (1 Sam 22:3–4), we can assume that he was the chief man of his village. He had eight sons, of whom the youngest was David (17:12–14), and two daughters, the latter being by a different wife from David's mother (1 Chron 2:16; cf. 2 Sam 17:25). Jesse lived at Bethlehem and probably had land outside the town wall, as Boaz did. When Samuel went to Jesse to anoint a king from among his sons, neither of them at first discerned God's choice. Jesse had not even thought it worthwhile to call his youngest son to the feast (1 Sam 16:11). He is almost always mentioned in connection with his son David. After Saul had quarreled with David, he usually called him the son of Jesse (20:31; 22:7; 25:10), undoubtedly in derision of David's relatively humble origin. We are not told when Jesse died. The contrast between his small beginnings and future glory is brought out in Isaiah 11:1, 10; and Micah 5:2.

JESUI (See ISHVI)

JESUS, JESUS CHRIST (See CHRIST, JESUS)

JETHER (jē'thêr, Heb. *yether, abundance, excellence*). 1. In Exodus 4:18 another name for Jethro, father-in-law of Moses (see KJV marginal note).

2. Gideon's oldest son (Judg 8:20–21), who was asked by his father to kill the captives, Zebah and Zalmunna. Jether shrank from doing so, and thus the captives escaped the shame of dying at the hands of a boy.

3. The father of Amasa, Absalom's commander-in-chief (1 Kings 2:5). According to 1 Chronicles 2:17, he was an Ishmaelite.

4. A descendant of Judah through Jerahmeel (1 Chron 2:32).

5. A Judahite, the son of Ezrah (1 Chron 4:17).

6. A man of Asher, apparently the same as Ithran, son of Zophah (1 Chron 7:37; cf. v. 38).

JETHETH (jē'thĕth, Heb. *yethēth,* meaning unknown). A chief of Edom (Gen 36:40; 1 Chron 1:51).

JETHLAH (See ITHLAH)

JETHRO (jĕth'rō, Heb. *yithrô, excellence*). A priest of Midian and father-in-law of Moses

The Valley of Jethro, or Jethro's Pass, looking northwest. In the center is the monastery of St. Catherine, built at the foot of Mount Sinai in the mid-sixth century by the emperor Justinian. It was here that Codex Sinaiticus, the famous fourth-century Greek Bible manuscript, was discovered. The library, containing about 3,000 old manuscripts, historical documents, etc., is considered one of the most precious in the world. Courtesy Ecole Biblique et Archéologique Française, Jerusalem.

(Exod 3:1). Reuel, which means "friend of God," seems to have been his personal name (2:18; 3:1), and Jethro his honorary title. When Moses fled from Egypt to Midian, he was welcomed into the household of Jethro because of his kindness to the priest's seven daughters, whom he helped water their flocks. Moses married Zipporah, one of the daughters and kept his father-in-law's flocks for about forty years (3:1–2). After the Lord commanded Moses to return to Egypt to deliver the enslaved Israelites, Jethro gave him permission to depart. Moses took with him his wife Zipporah and their two sons (4:18–20), but later he sent the three back to stay with Jethro temporarily. After the deliverance from Egypt, before the Israelites reached Sinai, Jethro came to see Moses, bringing back to him his daughter and her two sons (18:1–7). We are told that "Jethro was delighted to hear about all the good things the LORD had done for Israel," and that he offered a burnt offering to the Lord. When he saw how occupied Moses was in deciding disputes among his people, he suggested the appointment of judges of various grades to help him decide cases of minor importance. Moses acted on his advice. Jethro then returned to his own country.

JETUR (jē'têr, Heb. *yetûr,* meaning uncertain). A people descended from Ishmael (Gen 25:15; 1 Chron 1:31). Reuben, Gad, and the half-tribe of Manasseh warred against this clan (1 Chron 5:18–19). They are the Itureans of NT times.

JEUEL (jē-ū'ĕl, Heb. *ye'û'ēl,* meaning unknown). 1. A man of Judah who with 690 of his clan lived at Jerusalem (1 Chron 9:6).

2. A leader of Ezra's company (Ezra 8:13, JB, KJV, NEB Jeiel).

JEUSH (jē'ŭsh, Heb. *ye'ûsh, he comes to help*). 1. A son of Esau by his wife Oholibamah (Gen 36:5).

2. A Benjamite, son of Bilhan (1 Chron 7:10).

3. A Gershonite Levite (1 Chron 23:10–11).

4. A descendant of Jonathan (1 Chron 8:39; Jehush KJV).

JEUZ (jē'ŭz, Heb. *ye'ûts, he counsels*). A Benjamite, son of Shaharaim by his wife Hodesh (1 Chron 8:10).

JEW (Heb. *yehûdî,* Gr. *Ioudaios,* Lat. *Judaeus*). This word does not occur before the period of Jeremiah in OT literature. Originally it denoted one belonging to the tribe of Judah or to the two tribes of the southern kingdom (2 Kings 16:6; 25:25). Later its meaning was extended, and it was applied to anyone of the Hebrew race who returned from the Captivity. As most of the exiles came from Judah, and as they were the main historical representatives of ancient Israel, the term *Jew* came finally to comprehend all of the Hebrew race throughout the world (Esth 2:5; Matt 2:2). As early as the days of Hezekiah the language of Judah was called Jewish (NIV Hebrew). In the OT the adjective applies only to the Jews' language or speech (2 Kings 18:26, 28; Neh 13:24; Isa 36:11, 13). In the Gospels, *Jews* (always plural, except for John 4:9; 18:35) is the usual term for Israelites; and in the NT, Jews (Israelites) and Gentiles are sometimes contrasted (Mark 7:3; John 2:6; Act 10:28). Paul warns against Jewish myths (Titus 1:14) and speaks of the Jews' religion (Gal 1:13–14, lit., KJV; Judaism NIV, RSV). SB

JEWEL, JEWELRY. Orientals are much more given to adorning themselves with jewelry than Occidentals are. This was true in ancient times as well as now. Consequently there are many allusions to jewelry in Scripture. Among the articles of jewelry in OT times were diadems, bracelets, necklaces, anklets, rings for the fingers, gold nets for the hair, pendants, gems for head attire, amulets and pendants with magical meanings, jeweled perfume and ointment boxes, and crescents for camels. Many were acquired as booty in war. Many were personal gifts, especially at betrothals. At the court of every king there were special quarters for goldsmiths, and silversmiths were a familiar sight in the silver markets of large cities. Jewelry was used not only for personal adornment and utility, but also for religious festivals. Custom required the use of rich, festal garments and a gorgeous display of jewelry when one approached the deity. When the worship was over, these items were taken off. What became of all these jewels? Many were buried in the ground for safekeeping in time of war and were never recovered; others were carried away as booty by conquerors. A surprisingly large number have been unearthed.

Among the oldest jewels discovered in Bible lands are those found in A.D. 1927 by the

Elaborate headdress and other twenty-fifth century B.C. jewelry of Queen Shub-ad on a model's head. The jewels, among the oldest discovered, were found with the crushed skull of the queen at Ur. The pieces include four gold diadems, nine yards of gold band, seven-pointed gold comb, lunate earrings, and a necklace of small gold and lapis beads with rosette-shaped pendant. Courtesy University Museum, University of Pennsylvania.

archaeologist Sir Leonard Woolley in the Sumerian city of Ur, the heathen city that Abraham left for the Promised Land. In his excavations he found a hoard of jeweled wealth in the royal tombs in which Queen Shub-ad, her husband, and her faithful court had been buried about 2500 B.C. Buried with the queen were sixty-eight court ladies, who in full regalia had walked alive into the tomb and had sat in orderly rows to die, thus showing their loyalty to her. In the royal tombs were found the queen's personal ornaments, including her diadem, a cape of polished gold and precious stones, rings, seals, earrings, amulets, and pins of gold. With the court ladies were found hair ribbons made of fine beaten gold. Ancient Sumerian artisans were capable of producing filigree work with gold at least equal in delicacy to the best done by goldsmiths today.

When the servant of Abraham went to Mesopotamia to find a bride for Isaac, he gave Rebekah an earring and two bracelets made of gold after she had watered his camels. At her betrothal to Isaac he gave her jewels of silver and of gold, and to others in the family he also gave precious things (Gen 24:22, 30, 53).

When the Israelites left Egypt with Moses, they "asked the Egyptians for articles of silver and gold" (Exod 12:35). Not much later, while Moses was on Mount Sinai receiving the law, they took the golden earrings worn by men and women and gave them to Aaron to make a golden calf (32:2–4). As evidence of their repentance, they were commanded by Moses to strip themselves of their ornaments (33:4–6). For the building of the first tabernacle, the people contributed, at Moses' request, bracelets, earrings, rings, tablets, and jewels of gold (35:22).

Exodus 39 gives a description of the official garments of the Jewish high priest, worn when discharging his peculiar duties. They were gorgeous in their jeweled splendor. The robe of the ephod, a long, blue sleeveless garment, was adorned with a fringe of alternate pomegranates and bells of gold. Over the robe the ephod was worn, a shorter, richly embroidered vestment intended for the front and back of the body. It was made of two parts clasped together at the shoulders by onyx stones. Over the ephod there was a breastpiece, described as square, made of gold thread and finely twisted linen, set with four rows of precious stones, three in a row, each inscribed with the name of a tribe of Israel. In the first row was a ruby, a topaz, and a beryl; in the second, an emerald, a sapphire, and a turquoise; in the third, a jacinth, an agate, and an amethyst; and in the fourth, a chrysolite, an onyx, and a jasper (but see footnote on 39:13 in NIV). Each stone was set in a gold mounting. Golden chains and rings fastened the breastpiece to the ephod of the priest at his shoulders and to the blue lacers of the woven bands. The "sacred diadem was made of pure gold, on which was engraved the words, "HOLY TO THE LORD."

In the period of the judges, Gideon, after turning down the offer of kingship, requested that every man cast into a spread garment all the gold earrings, crescents, necklaces, and camel chains captured from the Midianites. With these he made an ephod, which later became a snare to Israel when the people came to regard it idolatrously (Judg 8:24–27).

Until about 1000 B.C. gold and silver were not common in Palestine, and even iron was so scarce that jewelry was made of it for kings. Archaeology has uncovered comparatively little indigenous Palestinian art. Fragments of jewelry that have been found in excavated palaces of kings is the work of imported artists. Such finds have been made at Megiddo, a fortress-city guarding the Plain of Esdraelon that was destroyed in the period of the judges.

David accumulated a large mass of jewels, mostly won in conquests against Syrians, Moabites, Ammonites, Amalekites, and Philistines. All these he dedicated to the Lord (2 Sam 8:7–8) and passed on to Solomon for the building of the temple in Jerusalem. When his nobles saw what he was donating, they brought for the same purpose gold, silver, brass, and iron; and the common people added what they could (1 Chron 28). We are told that the Queen of Sheba brought to Solomon gold and precious stones. The throne of Solomon was overlaid with gold; the steps leading to it were of gold; his footstool was of gold; his drinking cups were all of gold; and "all the household articles in the Palace of the Forest of Lebanon were pure gold" (2 Chron 9:20). In the succeeding reigns of the kings of Judah and Israel both monarchs and people gave increasing regard to accumulations of jewelry. Repeatedly OT prophets warned the Israelites that apostasy would be punished with the loss of their gems (Ezek 23:26).

Gold jewelry from Tell el-Ajjul (Beth Eglaim), c. 1500–1400 B.C. Three toggle-pins, a mounted scarab, a ribbed earring, and a ring with a bar of lapis lazuli beads. Courtesy Israel Department of Antiquities and Museums. Photo David Harris.

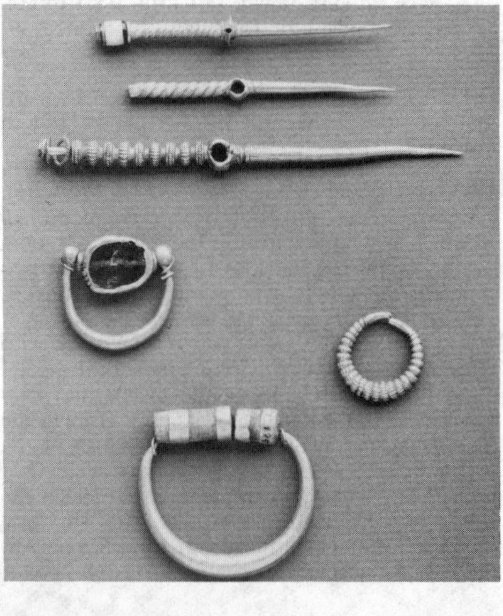

Not a great deal is said about jewelry in the NT, and what is said is mostly condemnatory. Jesus twice mentioned jewels, in the parable of the pearl merchant (Matt. 13:45–46) and in the saying about casting pearls before swine (7:6). Paul exhorts Christian women not to rely for adornment on "braided hair or gold or pearls or expensive clothes" (1 Tim 2:9). James warns his readers not to give preference to a man who comes into their assembly with a gold ring and fine apparel, as though he were better than a poor man (James 2:2). In the Revelation of Jesus to John the destruction of Babylon is described in terms of merchants who can no longer sell "cargoes of gold, silver, precious stones, and pearls" (Rev 18:12). The new Jerusalem is described in Revelation 21 as having a wall made of jasper, and the foundations of the walls decorated "with every kind of precious stone" (21:19)—jasper, sapphire, chalcedony, emerald, sardonyx, carnelian, chrysolite, beryl, topaz, chrysoprase, jacinth, and amethyst—a list recalling the list of precious stones in the breastpiece of the high priest.

See also MINERALS. SB

JEZANIAH (jĕz-à-nī'à, Heb. *yezanyāhû,* probably *Jehovah hears*). An army officer, son of Hoshaiah, a Maacathite. He lived at the time of the fall of Jerusalem (Jer 42:1; "Jaazaniah" in 2 Kings 25:23; Jer 40:7–8).

JEZEBEL (jĕz'ă-bĕl, Heb. *'îzevel,* meaning uncertain, perhaps *unexalted, unhusbanded*). 1. Daughter of Ethbaal, king of the Zidonians, and queen of Ahab, king of Israel (c. 874–853 B.C.). She had been brought up a zealous worshiper of Baal, and as the wife of Ahab she not only continued her ancestral religion but tried to impose it on the people of Israel. To please her, Ahab built a temple and an altar to Baal in Samaria (1 Kings 16:32). Four hundred fifty prophets of Baal ate at her table (18:19). She killed all the prophets of the Lord on whom she could lay her hands (18:4–13). When she was told of the slaughter of the prophets of Baal by Elijah, she threatened Elijah's life, and he was obliged to flee. In 2 Kings 9:7 we are told that the killing of Ahab's family was a punishment for the persecution of the prophets of the Lord by Jezebel. Later she secured Naboth's vineyard for Ahab by having its owner unjustly executed (1 Kings 21). When Elijah heard of this crime, he told Ahab that God's vengeance would fall on him and that dogs would eat Jezebel's body by the wall of Jezreel. The prophecy was fulfilled when, eleven years after the death of Ahab, Jehu executed pitiless vengeance on the royal household. Jezebel "painted her eyes and arranged her hair," looked out an open window, and taunted Jehu for being his master's murderer. Jehu asked those who were on his side to throw her down, and this was unhesitatingly done by some eunuchs. Jehu drove over her body with his chariot, and her blood spattered the horses and the wall. Later he gave directions that she be buried, but it was found that dogs had left nothing of her but the skull, the feet, and the hands (2 Kings 9:7, 30–37).

2. In Revelation 2:20, in the letter to Thyatira, we read of "that woman Jezebel, who calls herself a prophetess," and led some members of the Christian church there to commit spiritual fornication. This may be a symbolic name, given because of the resemblance between her and the idolatrous wife of Ahab. SB

JEZER (jē'zĕr, Heb. *yetser, form, purpose*). A son of Naphtali and founder of a tribal family (Gen 46:24; Num 26:49; 1 Chron 7:13).

JEZIAH (See IZZIAH)

JEZIEL (jē'zĭ-ĕl, Heb. *yezû'ēl,* meaning uncertain). A Benjamite, son of Azmaveth, who was one of David's recruits at Ziklag (1 Chron 12:3).

JEZLIAH (See IZLIAH)

JEZOAR (See ZOHAR)

JEZRAHIAH (jĕz-rà-hī'à, Heb. *yizrahyâh, Jehovah appears,* or *shines*). The leader of the singing at the purification of the people in the time of Nehemiah (Neh 12:42).

JEZREEL (jĕz'rē-ĕl, jĕz'rēl, Heb. *yizre'e'l, God sows*). 1. A city on the border of the territory of Issachar (Josh 19:18), not far from Mount Gilboa. The Israelites made their camp near it before the battle of Gilboa (1 Sam 29:1), its people remaining faithful to the house of Saul. Abner set Ish-Bosheth over it among other places (2 Sam 2:9). Ahab built a palace there (1 Kings 21:2), and his son Joram also lived there (2 Kings 8:29). Naboth was a Jezreelite, and he was stoned outside the city for refusing to give up his vineyard to Ahab (1 Kings 21). Jehu ordered that the heads of Ahab's seventy sons be placed in heaps at the gate of Jezreel (2 Kings 10:1–11). Jezebel met her death by being thrown from a window of the palace in Jezreel, and it was there that her body was eaten by dogs (9:30–35). Jezreel was the scene of the meetings between Elijah and Ahab (1 Kings 21:17ff.).

From the time of the Crusades the site of Jezreel has been identified with the modern village of Zer'in on the NW spur of Gilboa, but this identification is now questioned because excavations have failed to reveal any evidence of Israelite occupation in ancient times. From Jezreel there was a splendid view of the plain reaching toward the Jordan (Josh 17:16; Hos 1:5). Throughout history it has been a battlefield of nations. In the OT the term "valley of Jezreel" is applied to this valley, and not to the great plain immediately north of Carmel that is better known as the Plain of Esdraelon or the Plain of Megiddo.

2. A town in the hill country of Judah from which David obtained his wife Ahinoam the Jezreelitess (1 Sam 25:43; 27:3).

3. A descendant of Judah (1 Chron 4:3).

4. A son of the prophet Hosea, so called because God had declared that he would avenge the blood of Jezreel on the house of Jehu (Hos 1:4–5).

JIBSAM (See IBSAM)

JIDLAPH (jĭd'lăf, Heb. *yidhlāph,* perhaps *weeps*). A son of Nahor and Milcah, and the ancestral head of a Nahorite clan (Gen 22:22).

JIMNA (See IMNAH)

JIPHTAH (See IPHTAH)

JIPHTAH EL (See IPHTAH EL)

JOAB (jō'ăb, Heb. *yô'āv, Jehovah is father*). 1. The second of the three sons of Zeruiah, the half-sister of David, the two others being Abishai and Asahel (2 Sam 8:16; 1 Chron 2:16). He first appears in public life in the narrative of David's war with Ish-Bosheth for the throne left vacant by Saul's death. He was David's captain of the army, while Abner led the forces of Ish-Bosheth. When the two armies met, a tournament took place between twelve men from each side, followed by a general engagement in which, after Joab's men were routed, Asahel was killed in his pursuit of Abner (2 Sam 2:12–32). When Abner transferred his allegiance to David, Joab treacherously killed him, with the connivance of Abishai, for killing Asahel at the battle of Gibeon, though Abner had done so in self-defense. David declared himself innocent of this murder, and after composing a lament for Abner, commanded that there be a period of public mourning for the dead man (3:31). David pronounced a curse on Joab and his descendants, but he did not bring him to justice, perhaps because he was politically too weak to do so.

Joab was made the commander of all David's armies as a reward for being the first to enter the fortress on Mount Zion when that stronghold was assaulted. In the war against the Ammonites, which was declared when David's ambassadors to the king had been maltreated, Joab achieved a great victory, utterly routing the enemy (2 Sam 10:1–14; 1 Chron 19:1–15). After this war had been resumed he called for David to storm the town of Rabbah, which he himself had successfully besieged, in order that David might get credit for the victory (2 Sam 11:1; 12:26–29). It was during this war that David got Joab to put Uriah in the forefront of the battle so that he might be killed and David be free to marry Bathsheba (11:6–27).

Joab attempted to have Absalom restored to royal favor after a three-year banishment because of the murder of his brother Amnon. He arranged for a "wise woman" of Tekoa to bring to David an imaginary complaint about a son of hers who had killed his brother, and whose life was now sought, a story that paralleled David's own experience with Absalom. David saw in the story a rebuke of his own treatment of Absalom and gave permission to Absalom to return to Jerusalem, though he was to remain in his own house and was not allowed to see his father (2 Sam 14:1–24). Joab resisted Absalom's attempts to get him to intercede with his father for a complete restoration, until his barley field was set on fire by the prince (14:28–33). Joab then got David to receive his son back into the royal home.

When Absalom rebelled, he made Amasa, another nephew of David, general instead of Joab (2 Sam 17:24–25). Joab remained loyal to David, and when the king fled, pursued by Absalom, he led one of the three divisions of the royal forces and defeated the rebels. Informed that Absalom was caught in a tree by his hair, he first scolded his informer for not having killed him and then himself killed the prince by thrusting three darts through his heart. When David gave vent to extravagant grief at the death of his rebel son, Joab sternly rebuked him (19:1–8).

When David returned to Jerusalem, he replaced Joab as captain of his forces with Amasa. Shortly after this, Sheba, a Benjamite, led a revolt against David; and when Amasa took more time than was thought necessary to prepare to quell it, David asked Abishai to take the field. Joab seems to have gone with him. The two met Amasa at Gibeon, and there Joab, on pretense of kissing his rival, killed him. He then assumed command of Amasa's men, besieged Sheba in Abel Beth Maacah, and arranged with a woman of the city to deliver to him the head of Sheba. Thus ended the revolt (2 Sam 20:1–22).

Joab was opposed to David's suggestion of a census but eventually carried it out, though he intentionally did the work imperfectly (2 Sam 24:1–9; 1 Chron 21:1–6). He supported Adonijah in his claim to the throne, but deserted him on hearing that Solomon had been proclaimed king (1 Kings 1:7, 28–49). David on his deathbed made known that Joab should be brought to justice for the murders of Abner and of Amasa (2:5). At the order of Solomon, Joab was killed as he clung to the horns of the altar in the court of the tabernacle. His executioner was Benaiah, chief of the bodyguard, who became his successor as head of the army. He was buried in his own house in the wilderness (2:5–6, 28–34).

2. Son of Seraiah and descendant of Kenaz of the tribe of Judah. He was father of Ge Harashim (1 Chron 4:14).

3. Founder of a family of returned exiles (Ezra 2:6; 8:9; Neh 7:11).

4. A village, apparently in Judah (1 Chron 2:54 RV). KJV has the translation "Ataroth, the house of Joab"; and NIV, "Atroth Beth Joab." SB

JOAH (jō'à, Heb. *yô'āh, Jehovah is brother*). 1. A son of Obed-Edom (1 Chron 26:4).

2. A Levite, son of Zimmah and a descendant of Gershom (1 Chron 6:21). He may be the Levite who helped in the religious reformation under King Hezekiah (2 Chron 29:12).

3. Son of Asaph and recorder under King Hezekiah (2 Kings 18:18, 26; Isa 36:3, 11, 22). He was one of the three men sent by Hezekiah to

speak to the Assyrian envoys at the siege of Jerusalem.

4. Son of Joahaz and recorder under King Josiah (2 Chron 34:8).

JOAHAZ (jō'à-hăz, Heb. *yô'āḥāz, Jehovah has grasped*). Father of Joah, who was the recorder of King Josiah (2 Chron 34:8).

JOANAN (jō-ā'n-ăn). An ancestor of Christ (Luke 3:27; Joanna, lit., KJV).

JOANNA (Gr. *Iōana or Iōanna*). The wife of Cuza, Herod's steward. Along with other women whom Jesus healed, she traveled with him and financially supported his ministry (Luke 8:2–3). After preparing spices and ointments to embalm Jesus' body, she and other women went to the tomb and heard about the Resurrection (23:55–56; 24:10).

JOASH (See JEHOASH)

JOATHAM (See JOTHAM)

JOB (jōb, Heb. *'îyôv,* meaning uncertain). 1. The main character of the Book of Job (see JOB, BOOK OF; see also Ezek 14:14, 20; Jas 5:11).

2. A son of Issachar (Gen 46:13).

JOB, BOOK OF. This book has a definite kinship with eastern *chokmâ* (wisdom) literature. OT Wisdom books (cf. Prov, Eccl, and, in a sense, S of Sol) applied foundational Mosaic revelation to the problems of human existence and conduct as they were being formulated in the philosophical circles of the world of that day. A figure like Job, standing outside the Abrahamic and Mosaic covenants, was an ideal vehicle for biblical wisdom doctrine, concerned as it was with the common ways and demands of God rather than with his peculiarly theocratic government of Israel.

Even an approximate date for the anonymous author is uncertain. The events he narrates belong to the early patriarchal period, as is evident from features like Job's longevity, revelation by theophany (God visibly manifesting himself), the nomadic status of the Chaldeans, and early social and economic practices. But the question is, When was the tradition of Job transformed by the inspired author into the canonical Book of Job?

Modern discussions of authorship and date are perplexed by critical doubts concerning the unity of the book. Most widely suspected of being additions to an original poem are the prologue-epilogue, the wisdom hymn (ch. 28), the discourse of Elihu (chs. 32–37), and at least parts of the Lord's discourses (chs. 38–41). The LXX text of Job is about one-fifth shorter than the Massoretic, but the LXX omissions exhibit an editorial pattern of reduction. The argument for additions to the text, therefore, leans primarily on internal considerations—language, style, alleged inconsistencies of viewpoint. Conservative scholars, however, agree that the internal evidence points compellingly to the book's integrity, though they of course allow for corruption in textual details.

Dates have been assigned by twentieth-century critics all the way from the Mosaic to the Maccabean ages. The early extreme is eliminated by the nature of the development of the OT canon; the late extreme, by the discovery among the Dead Sea Scrolls of fragments of a manuscript of Job in old Hebrew script. The majority of negative critics favor exilic or postexilic date. Conservatives favor the preexilic era, especially the age of Solomon, because biblical *chokmâ* (Wisdom Literature) flourished then. There are close affinities in sentiment and expression between Job and parts of Psalms (see Pss 88–89) and Proverbs that were produced at that time. The same evidence indicates an Israelite identity for the anonymous author, conceivably one of Solomon's wisdom coterie (see 1 Kings 4:29–34). The theory that the author was an Edomite has found little support—that he was Egyptian, still less. **Outline:**

- I. Desolation: The Trial of Job's Wisdom (1:1–2:10)
- II. Complaint: The Way of Wisdom Lost (2:11–3:26)
- III. Judgment: The Way of Wisdom Darkened and Illuminated (4:1–41:34)
  - A. The verdicts of men (4:1–37:24)
    1. First cycle of debate (4:1–14:22)
    2. Second cycle of debate (15:1–21:34)
    3. Third cycle of debate (22:1–31:40)
    4. Ministry of Elihu (32:1–37:24)
  - B. The voice of God (38:1–41:34)
- IV. Confession: The Way of Wisdom Regained (42:1–6)
- V. Restoration: The Triumph of Job's Wisdom (42:7–17)

Stylistic comparison of other ancient wisdom writings with Job reveals similarities, but also reveals Job's uniqueness. The dialogue form of Job is paralleled to an extent in Egyptian and Babylonian wisdom poetry, and the various individual literary forms employed in Job (psalms of lament and thanksgiving, proverb, covenant oath, etc.) are not novelties. Nevertheless, as a masterly blend of a remarkably rich variety of forms, within a historical framework, with exquisite lyric and dramatic qualities, all devoted to didactic purpose, the Book of Job creates its own literary species. Of particular significance is the bracketing of the poetic dialogue within the prose (or better, semipoetic) prologue and epilogue. This A-B-A structure is found elsewhere (e.g., Code of Hammurabi, The Eloquent Peasant) and thus supports the book's integrity.

Job proclaims the fundamental stipulation of the covenant, a call for perfect consecration to our covenant head, the Lord. This call is issued through a dramatization of a crisis in redemptive history. God challenges Satan to behold in Job the triumph of divine grace. This faithful servant epitomizes the fulfillment of God's evangelical decree, which even at first took the form of an imprecatory challenge to the Tempter (Gen 3:15). By proving under fierce temptation the genuineness of his devotion to God, Job vindicates the veracity of his God as the author of redemptive promise and proves his sovereignty in putting enmity between his people and Satan. Prostrated by total grief, he praises God. While hopelessly despondent and protesting passionately against what he interprets as an unjust divine sentence on him, Job still turns and cries to no one but God. And he repentantly commits himself anew to his Lord, although the voice from the whirlwind has offered neither explanation of the mystery of his past sufferings nor promise of future restoration from his desolation. By following the covenant way, Job shows himself ready by God's grace, and contrary to Satan's insinuations, to serve his Lord "for nothing."

The particular purpose of the Book of Job as Wisdom Literature is to articulate and point the direction for a true apologetic for the faith. The doctrine of God as incomprehensible Creator and sovereign Lord is offered as the fundamental reality man must reckon with as a religious being serving God amid the historical tensions of life. It is also the presupposition with which a philosophical being bent on interpretative adventure must begin. This enterprise is illustrated by the debate of Job and his friends over the problem of theodicy (God's goodness versus evil). The folly of depending for answers on human observation and speculation is portrayed by the silencing of the trio who represent it. The Book of Job identifies the way of the covenant with the way of wisdom (cf. 28:28) and so brings philosophy under the authority of divine revelation.

No comprehensive answer is given to the problem of suffering since theodicy is not the book's major theme; nevertheless, considerable light is given. Elihu traces the mystery to the principle of divine grace: sufferings are a sovereign gift, calling to repentance and life. Moreover, impressive assurance is given that God, as a just and omnipotent covenant Lord, will ultimately visit both the curses and blessings of the covenant on his subjects according to righteousness. Especially significant are the insights Job himself attains into the role God will play as his heavenly vindicator, redeeming his name from all slander and his life from the king of terrors. Job utters in raw faith what is later revealed in the doctrines of eschatological theophany: resurrection of the dead and the final judgment. This vision does not reveal the why of the particular sufferings of Job or any other believer, but it does present the servants of God with a framework for hope.

Bibliography: M. H. Pope, *Job* (AB), 1965; E. P. Dhorme, *Commentary on the Book of Job,* 1967; F. I. Andersen, *Job: An Introduction and Commentary* (TOTC), 1976. MGK

JOBAB (jō'băb, Heb. *yôvāv, to call loudly, howl*). 1. An Arabian tribe descended from Joktan (Gen 10:29; 1 Chron 1:23).

2. The second king of Edom. He was the son of Zerah of Bozrah (Gen 36:33; 1 Chron 1:44–45).

3. A king of Madon. He joined the northern confederacy against Joshua, but he and his allies were thoroughly defeated at the waters of Merom (Josh 11:1; 12:19).

4. A Benjamite (1 Chron 8:9).

5. A Benjamite (1 Chron 8:18).

JOCHEBED (jŏk'ĕ-bĕd, Heb. *yôkhevedh, Jehovah is glory*). Daughter of Levi, wife of Amram and mother of Moses (Exod 6:20; Num 26:59). She was a sister of Kohtah, Amram's father (Exod 6:20).

JODA (jō'dȧ). An ancestor of Jesus (Luke 3:26; KJV "Juda").

JOED (jō'ĕd, Heb. *yô'ēdh, Jehovah is witness*). A Benjamite, descended from Jeshaiah (Neh 11:7).

JOEL (jō'ĕl, Heb. *yô'ēl, Jehovah is God*). 1. The prophet, son of Pethuel and author of the second book of the Minor Prophets. We know nothing of the man, his life, or times.

2. Samuel's firstborn son (1 Sam 8:2; 1 Chron 6:33).

3. A Simeonite prince (1 Chron 4:35).

4. A Reubenite chief (1 Chron 5:4, 8).

5. A Gadite chief (1 Chron 5:12).

6. An ancestor of Samuel, of the tribe of Levi (1 Chron 6:36).

7. A chief of Issachar (1 Chron 7:3).

8. One of David's mighty men (1 Chron 11:38).

9. A Levite (1 Chron 15:7, 11, 17), probably also mentioned in 1 Chronicles 23:8; 26:22.

10. David's officer over half of Manasseh (1 Chron 27:20).

11. A Levite of Hezekiah's time (2 Chron 29:12).

12. A Jew who had married a foreign wife (Ezra 10:43).

13. A Benjamite overseer (Neh 11:9).

JOEL, BOOK OF (jō'ĕl, Heb. *yô'ēl, Jehovah is God*). The Book of Joel is without the customary dating formula used by the prophets (Hos 1:1; Amos 1:1), and nowhere indicates the date either of the ministry of the prophet Joel or of the writing of the book. Indirect references throughout the book have been claimed in support of dates that have differed from each other by as much as half a millennium.

Scholars who follow the traditional viewpoint believe the book to be preexilic, written perhaps during the reign of the boy king Joash (837–800 B.C.), for the following reasons: (1) The enemies of Judah that are mentioned—the Philistines and Phoenicians (Joel 3:4), Egypt and Edom (3:19)—are those of the preexilic period (2 Kings 8:20–22; 2 Chron 21:16–17) rather than the Assyrians and Babylonians, who later troubled Judah. (2) Amos, a prophet during this time, seems to have been acquainted with Joel's prophecies (3:16; cf. Amos 1:2; 3:18; cf. 9:13). (3) The fact that the elders and priests are mentioned rather than the king would seem to point to the time of Joash's minority (2 Kings 11:21). (4) The location of the book between two early prophets and its style, quite different from that of the postexilic prophets, also argue for a preexilic date.

Many modern scholars believe the book to have been written much later, about 350 B.C. Others deny its unity and claim that the apocalyptic elements come from a time as late as 200. Thus it is claimed that Joel is the last OT prophetic book. Some arguments for the book's late date: (1) There is no reference to the northern kingdom, Israel. (2) The Greeks are mentioned in Joel 3:6. This is believed by some to be a reference to the Seleucid line that ruled Palestine in the second century. Even if the identification of the "Greeks" with the Seleucids is tenuous, it is felt that the Hebrews would hardly have known about the Greek people before the Exile. (3) References to the destruction of Jerusalem are detected in 3:1–3, 17. (4) Certain other arguments depend on a radical reconstruction of Israel's history and hardly need to be considered here.

The unity of the book may be taken for granted, since it is conceded by many radical critics today. The arguments for a late date are not strong. In such a short book there need be no reference to the northern kingdom, and it is quite possible that the Hebrews may have known the Greeks at a time well before the Exile. It should be added that since the book makes no claim as to its date, this matter is not of primary importance. Locust plagues are frequent in the Near East and almost any such visitations would provide a background for this book.

The occasion of the book was a devastating locust plague. Those who have not experienced such a calamity can hardly appreciate its destruction. An article, with convincing photographic illustrations, appeared in the *National Geographic Magazine* of December 1915, describing a locust attack on Jerusalem in that year. This description of a visitation similar to that which occasioned Joel's prophecy provides an excellent background for understanding the Book of Joel. The prophet, after describing the plague and its resulting chaos, urges the nation to repent of its sins and then goes on to predict a worse visitation, the future Day of the Lord. **Outline:**

- I. The Locust Plague and Its Removal (1:1–2:27).
  - A. The plague of locusts (1:1–20).
  - B. The people urged to repent (2:1–17).
  - C. God pities and promises relief (2:18–27).
- II. The Future Day of the Lord (2:28–3:21).
  - A. The Spirit of God to be poured out (2:28–32).
  - B. The judgment of the nations (3:1–17).
  - C. Blessing on Israel following judgment (3:18–21).

The book opens with a description of the locust plague in terms of a human army. The locusts are *like* soldiers (Joel 2:7) and horses and chariots (2:4–5). Once the figures of speech are understood to be such, the description is extremely vivid and entirely in keeping with OT figurative language. The locusts are called a "northern army" (2:20). Although locust plagues in Palestine do not ordinarily come from the north, invasions of these insects from that direction are not unknown, the last one having occurred in A.D. 1915. This calamity presages "the day of the LORD" (1:15; 2:1), for the prophet says, "the day of the LORD is near." The locust invasion provided Joel with a catalyst for his message that a greater day of judgment, known as the Day of the Lord, would come if God's people did not repent. The "Day of the Lord" is a designation given to any intervention of God in history for the purpose of judgment (Isa 2:12–3:5). It also designates the eschatological intervention of God when the ultimate punishment of evil will occur (Joel 2:10–11). Joel's message is that the present locust plague is a harbinger of greater woe if the people do not repent.

In the second chapter Joel continues to to describe the plague and to urge repentance. The verbs in 2:1–11 should be translated in the present tense, as in the RSV and NIV, for an event taking place in the prophet's own time is being described. Evidently the people responded to Joel's message, for a section full of comfort and promise of the renewal of the land follows (2:18–27).

The second major theme of Joel's prophecy is introduced in Joel 2:28: After the present trouble will come the future Day of the Lord, a time of great trouble for the nations when Israel will be vindicated and the messianic age of peace brought in. This frequent theme of OT prophecy is here presented with emphasis on the outpouring of the Spirit of God that will begin it (2:28–29). Then terrifying portents will appear (2:30–31), and Judah and Jerusalem will be delivered and the nations judged (3:1–21).

Joel's greatest contribution to Christian thought is his teaching about the outpouring of the Holy Spirit "on all people" (Joel 2:28). This prophecy is quoted by Peter in his Pentecostal sermon (Acts 2:14–21). The Holy Spirit came on people in OT times to enable them to serve God acceptably (Judg 6:34; 1 Sam 16:13) and certainly he was in the world and dwelling in the saints then as now, though they had very little consciousness of this fact. But in a special way the new age was to be one of the Spirit (Isa 32:15; Zech 12:10; John 7:39). All of God's people would now be priests and prophets, for the ideal stated when the law was given but never achieved would now become a reality (Exod 19:5–6; 1 Peter 2:9–10).

Bibliography: L. C. Allen, *The Books of Joel, Obadiah, Jonah and Micah* (NIC), 1976; H. W. Wolff, *Joel and Amos,* 1977. JBG

JOELAH (jō-ē′lȧ, Heb. *yô'ē'lâh,* perhaps *let him help*). A son of Jeroham of Gedor. He was one of David's recruits at Ziklag (1 Chron 12:7).

JOEZER (jō-ē'zēr, Heb. *yô'ezer, Jehovah is help*). One of David's recruits at Ziklag (1 Chron 12:6).

JOGBEHAH (jŏg'bē-à, Heb. *yoghbehâh, lofty*). A city in Gilead assigned to Gad (Num 32:35; Judg 8:11). It is represented today by Jubeihah, a village midway between Rabbath Ammon and es-Salt.

JOGLI (jŏg'lī, Heb. *yoghlî, led into exile*). Father of Bukki, of the tribe of Dan (Num 34:22).

JOHA (jō'hà, Heb. *yôhā', meaning unknown*). 1. A Benjamite, son of Beriah (1 Chron 8:16).

2. A Tizite, son of Shimri, and one of David's mighty men (1 Chron 11:45).

JOHANAN (jō-hā'năn, Heb. *yôhānān, Jehovah has been gracious*). 1. Son of Kareah, a captain who with his men submitted to Gedaliah, appointed by Nebuchadnezzar as governor over Judah (2 Kings 25:22–23; Jer 40:8–9). He warned Gedaliah of Ishmael's plot to murder him (Jer 40:13–14); and when the governor paid no heed and was assassinated, he tried to avenge his death (41:11–15). Against the advice of Jeremiah, he and other Jewish leaders led the remnant down into Egypt, taking Jeremiah with them.

2. The eldest son of King Josiah (1 Chron 3:15). He seems to have died young.

3. A son of Elioenai (1 Chron 3:24).

4. The father of the Azariah who was priest in Solomon's time (1 Chron 6:9–10).

5. A Benjamite recruit of David at Ziklag (1 Chron 12:4).

6. A Gadite recruit of David at Ziklag who was made captain in David's army (1 Chron 12:12, 14).

7. An Ephraimite chief (2 Chron 28:12 KJV, MLB, NASB, RSV; Jehohanan NEB, NIV).

8. A son of Hakkatan, of the clan of Azgad. He was one of the men who accompanied Ezra from Babylon (Ezra 8:12).

9. A son of Tobiah the Ammonite who married a Jewess in the days of Nehemiah (Neh 6:18 KJV; NIV "Jehohanan").

10. A son of Eliashib. Ezra went to his chamber and mourned there for the sin of those who had contracted foreign marriages (Ezra 10:6).

11. A high priest, grandson of Eliashib (Neh 12:22). The Jews at Elephantine appealed to him for help when their temple was destroyed in 411 B.C. (Elephantine Papyri). Josephus says that he killed his brother Jesus in the temple because he feared he might be superseded as high priest (*Antiq.* 11.7.1).

JOHN (Gr. *Iōannēs,* from Heb. *Yôhānān, Jehovah has been gracious*). 1. Father of Simon Peter (John 1:42; 21:15, 17, called Jonas in KJV).

2. A relative of Annas the high priest who took part with Annas, Caiaphas, Alexander, and other kindred of Annas in calling Peter and John to account for their preaching about Jesus (Acts 4:6).

See also JOHN, THE APOSTLE; JOHN THE BAPTIST; JOHN MARK.

JOHN, THE APOSTLE. The sources for the life of John are relatively meager. All that exists is what is found in the NT and what has been preserved by tradition. One can, therefore, give no more than a fragmentary account of his life. He was the son of Zebedee, and brother of James the apostle, who was put to death by Herod Agrippa I about A.D. 44 (Matt 4:21; Acts 12:1–2). It may be reasonably inferred that his mother was Salome (cf. Matt 27:56 with Mark 15:40) and that she was the sister of Mary the mother of Jesus. Jesus and John would then have been cousins. The family lived in Galilee, probably at Bethsaida. The father and the two sons were fishermen on the Sea of Galilee (Mark 1:19–20). There are reasons for thinking that the family was not poor. They had hired servants and thus belonged to the employer class. Salome was one of the women who ministered to Jesus of her own funds (Mark 15:40; Luke 8:3) and was also one of the women who bought spices and came to anoint the body of Jesus (Mark 16:1). In addition the fact that John knew the high priest well enough to gain entrance to the court where Jesus was tried and could get permission for Peter to enter also suggests that the family was not exactly poor.

John is first introduced as a disciple of John the Baptist (John 1:35). He had therefore heeded the Baptist's call to repentance and baptism in preparation for the coming of the Messiah. How long he had been a follower of the Baptist is not known. In his Gospel he tells how he first met Jesus and became his disciple (1:35–39). One day as he stood with Andrew and John the Baptist, he heard his master say, as Jesus walked by, "Look, the Lamb of God!" The two disciples of John immediately followed Jesus, and when they were asked what they wanted, they said they wanted to know where Jesus was staying. He invited them to come and see. Their stay changed their lives and was so memorable that many years later, when John recorded the account in his Gospel, he still remembered that it was about four o'clock in the afternoon. The next day he and some others accompanied Jesus to Galilee to attend a wedding feast at Cana (2:1–11). From Cana they went to Capernaum and then down to Jerusalem, where Jesus cleansed the temple and had an interview with Nicodemus (2:13–3:21). John was with Jesus during his seven-month sojourn in the country of Judea, calling the people to repentance and baptism. Since Jesus himself did not baptize, he undoubtedly helped in the administration of the baptismal rite (4:2). When Jesus heard of the Baptist's arrest, he decided to return to Galilee. A probable factor in his decision to leave Judea was his realization that the Jewish religious leaders were worried over the fact that he was acquiring an even larger following than the Baptist. On the way north, as they passed through Samaria, the incident with the Samaritan woman occurred, so fully described in John 4. For a time after Jesus returned to Galilee his disciples seem to have returned to their normal occupations, but one day Jesus appeared by the Sea of

Galilee and called Peter and Andrew, James and John from their fishing to be with him constantly so that they might be trained to become fishers of men (Matt 4:18–22; Mark 1:16–20; Luke 5:1–11). This was the second stage of discipleship in John's preparation for his life work. Some time later, he was chosen to the apostolate (Matt 10:2–4; Mark 3:13–19; Luke 6:12–19). The list of the Twelve given in Mark's Gospel states that Jesus surnamed James and John "Boanerges," that is, Sons of Thunder, evidently because of the impetuosity of their temperament.

During the course of the Lord's ministry the experiences of John were common to all the apostles. There are, however, a few scenes in which he takes an important part. The Gospels make clear that he was one of the most prominent of the apostles, and his own Gospel makes clear that he was greatly loved by Jesus. He was one of the three apostles who were closest to Jesus, the other two being Peter and James, John's brother. With the other two in the inner circle of the apostles, he was admitted to witness the raising of Jairus's daughter (Mark 5:37; Luke 8:51); the same three were chosen by Jesus to be present at the Transfiguration (Matt 17:1; Mark 9:2; Luke 9:28); and they were nearest to Jesus during his agony in Gethsemane (Matt 26:37; Mark 14:33). It was John who told Jesus that they had seen someone casting out devils in his name and that they had forbidden him because he was not of their company (Mark 9:38; Luke 9:49). The two brothers, James and John, gave evidence of their impetuosity when a Samaritan village refused to allow them to pass through on their way to Jerusalem; they said to Jesus, "Lord, do you want us to call fire down from heaven to destroy them?" (Luke 9:54). They showed tactlessness and presumptuous ambition when they went to Jesus with their mother and requested that in the coming kingdom they be given places of honor above the others (Mark 10:35). On Tuesday of Passion Week John was among those who asked Jesus on the Mount of Olives when his prediction about the destruction of the temple would be fulfilled (13:3). He and Peter were sent by Jesus to make preparations for the Passover (Luke 22:8), and at the Passover feast John lay close to the breast of Jesus and asked who his betrayer would be (John 13:25). When Jesus was arrested, John fled, as did the other apostles (Matt 26:56), but before long he recovered enough courage to be present at the trial of Jesus. Through his acquaintance with the high priest, he was able to have Peter come in too (John 18:16). He stood near the cross on which Jesus was nailed and there received Jesus' commission to look after his mother (19:26). On the morning of the Resurrection, when he and Peter were told by Mary Magdalene about the empty grave, they went together to see for themselves (20:2–3). In the account of the appearance of the risen Lord in Galilee the sons of Zebedee received special mention, and it is John who first recognized Jesus (21:1–7). In the scene that follows, the impression is corrected that John should not die before the Lord's return. At the end of the chapter the truthfulness of the gospel record is confirmed (21:20–24).

In the rest of the NT there are only a few scattered references to John. After the ascension of Jesus he remained in Jerusalem with the other apostles, praying and waiting for the coming of the Holy Spirit. In Acts he appears with Peter in two important scenes. Soon after Pentecost they healed a man who had been lame from his birth, and while explaining the miracle to the astonished crowd gathered around them, they were arrested. The next day they were brought before the Sanhedrin. After being warned not to preach about Jesus any more, they were released (Acts 4:1–22). Later, after the gospel had been preached to the people of Samaria by Philip, Peter and John were sent by the apostles to Samaria; and they prayed and laid hands on the new converts that they might receive the Holy Spirit (8:14–15). John's name is once mentioned in Paul's letters—in Galatians 2:9, where Paul says that on his second visit to Jerusalem after his conversion he met and consulted with James (undoubtedly the Lord's brother), Peter, and John, who were pillars of the church and who gave him the right hand of fellowship. The only other mention of John in the NT is in Revelation 1:1, 4, 9, where the authorship of the book is ascribed to him.

Five books of the NT are attributed to him—the Fourth Gospel, three letters, and Revelation. The only one in which his name actually appears is the last. According to tradition, he spent his last years in Ephesus. Very likely the seven churches of Asia enjoyed his ministry. The Book of Revelation was written on the island of Patmos, where he was exiled "because of the word of God and the testimony of Jesus" (Rev 1:9). Tradition says that he wrote the Gospel of John in Asia at the request of Christian friends and that he agreed to do so only after the church had fasted and prayed about the matter for three days. He apparently died in Ephesus about the end of the century.

It is evident from all we know of John that he was one of the greatest of the apostles. He is described as the disciple whom Jesus loved, no doubt because of his understanding of and love for his Lord. The defects of character with which he began his career as an apostle—an undue vehemence, intolerance, and selfish ambition—were in the course of time brought under control, until he became especially known for his gentleness and kindly love.

Bibliography: C. F. Nolloth, *The Fourth Evangelist,* 1925; J. Marsh, *Saint John,* 1968; S. S. Smalley, *John: Evangelist and Interpreter,* 1978.

SB

JOHN, GOSPEL OF.

I. Authorship, Date, Place. Never was there a book written that made higher claim for its "hero." To the Jesus of history its author gives the most exalted titles. In fact, in the very opening verse he calls him *God.* This becomes even more

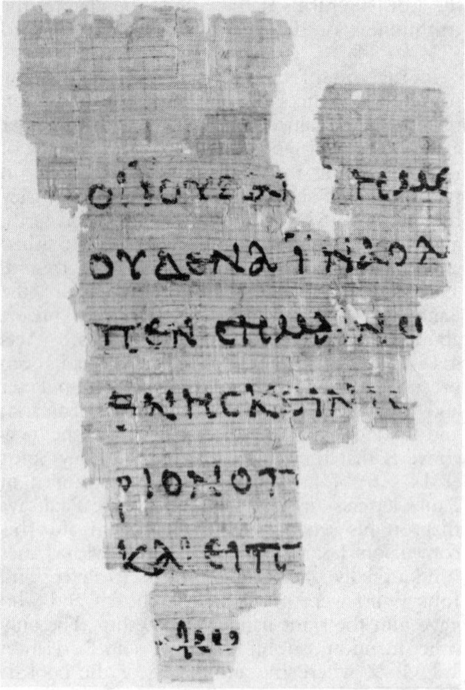

Papyrus fragment of John 18:31–33, the earliest extant copy of any New Testament book dated c. A.D. 150. Found in Egypt. Courtesy John Rylands Library, Manchester, England.

remarkable when we note that the author describes himself as one who belongs to the same race, stock, and family as Jesus, in fact as an eyewitness of the scenes that he so vividly portrays. No one knew Jesus better than he did. John walked with Jesus from day to day. He reclined on his bosom. He stood by his cross. He entered his tomb (John 13:25; 19:26; 20:8). Yet he does not shrink from proclaiming that this Jesus of history, whom he knew so well, was and is himself God.

Tradition holds the apostle John to be this author and that the date and place of authorship was sometime toward the close of the first century A.D., Asia Minor. This tradition can be traced back from Eusebius (the church historian) at the beginning of the fourth century to Theophilus, who flourished about 170–180. The major witnesses, besides Eusebius, are Origen, Clement of Alexandria, Tertullian, Irenaeus, the writer of the Muratorian Canon, and Theophilus. Irenaeus, one of the earliest of these witnesses, was a disciple of Polycarp, who, in turn, had been a disciple of the apostle John. The inference seems to be legitimate that this tradition can be traced back to the disciple whom Jesus loved. Moreover, because of his wide travels, the witness of Irenaeus may be called a representative testimony, the firm conviction of the early church this Greek church father knew so well. In fact, the early writers (mentioned above) show us that in the last quarter of the second century the Fourth Gospel was known and read throughout Christendom—in Africa, Asia Minor, Italy, Gaul, Syria—and that it was ascribed to the well-known apostle John.

Among even earlier witnesses, Justin Martyr (*Apology* I.61) quotes from John 3:3–5. He uses a number of expressions from this Gospel (see also his *Dialogue With Trypho,* chapter 105). His doctrine of the Logos presupposes acquaintance with the Fourth Gospel, which his pupil Tatian included in his *Diatessaron* or *Harmony*. Ignatius, who went to his martyrdom about the year A.D. 110, alludes to John's Gospel again and again (see *Epistles of Ignatius, Short Recension*). Very significant also is the testimonial of the elders of Ephesus (John 21:24). The traditional belief regarding the authorship and date of the Fourth Gospel has received strong confirmation in the discovery of a very early Gospel of John fragment of a papyrus codex, which seems to have originated in the Christian community of Middle Egypt. On the basis of solid evidence it has been established that this papyrus scrap belonged to a codex that circulated in that general region in the first part of the second century. This scrap contains part of John 18:31–33 and part of 18:37–38. Now if this Gospel was already circulating in Middle Egypt in the early part of the second century, it must have been *composed* even earlier. From Ephesus, where according to tradition this Gospel was written, to Middle Egypt, where this codex circulated, is a long distance. This means, therefore, that the traditional view with respect to the date and composition of the Fourth Gospel has at length been confirmed by archaeological evidence.

Internal evidence, moreover, is in line with tradition. The author was evidently a Jew, as his style (showing acquaintance with the OT) and intimate knowledge of Jewish religious beliefs and customs indicate (John 2:13, 17, 23; 4:9, 25; 5:1; 6:4, 15; 7:2, 27, 37–38, 42; 10:22–23, 34–35; 11:38, 44, 49; 12:40). He was probably a Palestinian Jew, for he has a detailed knowledge of Palestinian topography (1:28; 2:1, 12; 3:23; 4:11, 20; 11:1, 54; 12:21), particularly of Jerusalem and its immediate vicinity (5:2; 9:7; 11:18; 18:1; 19:17) and of the temple (2:14, 20; 8:2, 20; 10:22–23; 18:1, 20). Having been an eyewitness, he remembered the time and place where the events occurred (1:29, 35, 39; 2:1; 3:24; 4:6, 40, 52–53; 6:22; 7:14; 11:6; 12:1; 13:1–2; 19:14, 31; 20:1, 19, 26). He knew that Jesus was weary when he sat down by the well (4:6), remembered the very words spoken by the neighbors of the man born blind (9:8–10), saw the blood and water issuing from Jesus' pierced side (19:33–35), knew the servant of the high priest by name (18:10), and was acquainted with the high priest (18:15). So intimate and full is his knowledge of the actions, words, and feelings of the other disciples that he must have been one of the Twelve (1:35–42; 2:17, 22; 4:27; 6:19; 11:16; 13:22–28; 18:15–16; 20:2; 21:20–23). By a process of logical elimination it can easily be shown that the author was the apostle John and could not have been any one of the others who composed the Twelve, for though he does not mention himself by name but calls himself "the disciple whom Jesus loved," he distinguishes himself from others whom he does mention by name (Simon Peter, 1:40, 41–42, 44; Andrew 1:40, 44; 6:8; 12:22; Philip 1:43–46; Nathanael, 1:45–49; 21:2; Thomas, 11:16; 14:5; 20:24–29; 21:2; Judas (not Iscariot), 14:22; and Judas the Traitor, 6:71; 12:4; 13:2, 26, 29; 18:2–3, 5). Matthew's name can be eliminated for it is associated with another Gospel. So also the names of obscure disciples like James the Less and Simon the Zealot can be eliminated. This leaves only the sons of Zebedee: James and John. But James died an early death (Acts 12), while this Gospel's author survived even Peter (who survived James). It is clearly evident from 21:19–24 that John, "the disciple whom Jesus loved," was still alive and bearing witness when the Fourth Gospel first appeared (note present tense in 21:24), though Peter had already gained the martyr's crown (21:19). The reasonable conclusion would surely seem to be that the apostle John wrote the Fourth Gospel.

We are not saying that this external and internal evidence constitutes absolute proof. In the final analysis we accept it *by faith,* a faith that takes account of the facts, namely, that toward the close of the first century A.D. (probably sometime between 80 and 98), at or near Ephesus, the apostle John wrote the Fourth Gospel. Radical criticism has not been able to present any evidence whatever that demolishes this well-established position.

II. Purpose. The author states his purpose as follows: "Jesus did many other miraculous signs in the presence of his disciples, which are not recorded in this book. But these are written that you may believe that Jesus is the Christ, the Son of God, and that by believing you may have life in his name" (John 20:30–31). The faith of believers was being undermined by the errors of men like Cerinthus, who taught that Jesus was not really God and that Christ had not actually come into the flesh (i.e., had not adopted human nature). The apostle, seeing this danger and being guided by the Holy Spirit, wrote this Gospel in order that the church might abide in the true faith. Thus, Irenaeus definitely states that John sought by the proclamation of the gospel to remove the error that Cerinthus was trying to spread (*Against Heresies* 3.11.1). According to Cerinthus, at baptism the *Christ* in the form of a dove had descended on Jesus, but this same *Christ* had left him again on the eve of his (Jesus') suffering. Hence, it was not really Christ who suffered and died and rose again but Jesus (ibid., 1.26.1; 3.3.4). Over against this, John defended the thesis that Jesus Christ is *one,* and that this one divine and human Person came not only by water (baptism) but also by blood (suffering and death). For proof see John 19:34–37; cf. 1 John 5:6. From the very beginning, therefore, Jesus is himself God. He adopted human nature into personal union with his divine nature and will keep it ("the Word became flesh," John 1:1, 14). However, combating the error of Cerinthus was not John's *main* aim in writing this book. It was subsidiary to the aim already quoted from 20:30–31.

The readers for whom this gospel was primarily intended (though in the final analysis it was composed for the church of the entire NT period, cf. John 17:20–21) were living in Ephesus and surrounding areas. They were Gentile Christians mostly. This explains why the evangelist adds explanatory notes to some of his references to Jewish customs and conditions (2:6; 4:9; 7:2; 10:22; 18:28; 19:31, 41–42). It also explains the circumstantial manner in which he locates places that were situated in Palestine (4:5; 5:2; 6:1; 11:1, 18; 12:21).

III. Characteristics. In harmony with John's aim, as described above, this Gospel has the following characteristics:

1. It is emphatically the *spiritual* Gospel, whose aim is to show who Jesus is (and this with a definitely practical purpose, John 20:31). Hence, much of what is found in Matthew, Mark, and Luke (the Synoptics) is here omitted. On the other hand, much material is added, the type of material that brings into clear focus the glory of the Lord, his messianic office and deity. (See John 2:11; 3:16; 4:25–26, 29, 42; 5:17–18; 6:40; 7:37–38; 8:36, 46, 51; 9:38; 10:30; 11:40; 13:3; 14:6; 17:3, 5; 20:28.) The miracles here recorded also emphasize this same thought.

2. In close connection with the above paragraph is the fact that here it is not the kingdom (as in the other Gospels) but the King himself on whom the emphasis falls. This also accounts for the seven "I Ams" (John 6:35; 8:12; 10:9, 11; 11:25; 14:6; 15:50).

3. This Gospel, far more than the others, records Christ's work in Judea.

4. It is far more definite than are the others in indicating the time and place of the events that are related.

5. It abounds in nonparabolic teaching.

6. It dwells at great length on the events and discourses that belong to a period of less than twenty-four hours (chs. 13–19).

7. It records with special emphasis the promise of the coming and work of the Holy Spirit (John 14:16–17, 26; 15:26; 16:13–14).

8. Its style, especially in the prologue, is rhythmic. Both the manner in which the clauses are coordinated, so that often a truth is stated first positively, then negatively or vice versa (John 1:3; 14:6; 15:5–6; 14:18; 15:16) and the careful balancing of sentences so that antithesis is followed by synthesis, brief and pithy clauses by longer sentences all make this gospel a very beautiful book.

IV. Contents. The arrangement of John's Gospel is superb. First, we see the Word in his preincarnate glory, so that his condescending love in the salvation of sinners may be deeply appreciated. In his earthly ministry he reveals himself to ever-widening circles (to a few disciples; to his mother and friends at Cana; to Jerusalem; to Judea, Samaria, and Galilee), but he is rejected both in Jerusalem and in Galilee (John 1–6; especially 5:18; 6:66). Nevertheless, he makes his tender appeal to sinners, that they may accept him (chs. 7–10; especially 7:37–38; 8:12, 31–36; 10:7, 18, 27–28). Meanwhile opposition grows into bitter resistance (7:20, 49; 8:6, 40, 48–59, 9:22; 10:20, 31, 39). Next, by two mighty deeds—the raising of Lazarus and the triumphal entry into Jerusalem—Jesus manifests himself as the Messiah (chs. 11–12). But though the Greeks seek him (12:20–36), the Jews repulse him (12:37–50). By way of contrast this rejection causes the anointing at Bethany to stand out in all its beauty (12:1–8). So he turns—and this is indeed a *turning point* in this Gospel—to the inner circle and tenderly instructs the Twelve in the Upper Room, first mainly by means of example (washing the feet of his disciples, ch. 13), and then mainly by means of his Word (of comfort, ch. 14; of admonition, ch. 15; and of prediction, ch. 16). He commits himself, them, and all later generations of believers to his Father's care (ch. 17). In his very death (chs. 18–19) he overcomes the world and brings to completion the glorious work of redemption (19:30; cf. 12:30–31; 16:33). By means of his resurrection and loving manifestations (to Mary Magdalene, the eleven, the ten, the seven, particularly Peter and John) he proves his majestic claims and reveals himself as the proper object of abiding trust (chs. 20–21, especially 20:30–31).

V. Outline:

Jesus, the Christ, the Son of God

- I. During His Public Ministry
  - A. Revealing himself to ever-widening circles, *rejected* (chs. 1–6).
  - B. Making his tender appeal to sinners, *bitterly resisted* (chs. 7–10).
  - C. Manifesting himself as the Messiah by two mighty deeds, *repulsed* (chs. 11–12).
- II. During His Private Ministry
  - A. Issuing and illustrating his new commandment (ch. 13).
  - B. Tenderly instructing his disciples and committing them to the Father's care (chs. 14–17).
  - C. Dying as a substitute for his people (chs. 18–19).
  - D. Triumphing gloriously (chs. 20–21).

Bibliography: R. E. Brown, *The Gospel According to John* (AB), 2 vols., 1966–70; L. L. Morris, *Studies in the Fourth Gospel,* 1969, and *The Gospel According to John* (NIC), 1971; B. Lindars, *The Gospel of John* (NCB), 1972; C. K. Barrett, *The Gospel According to St. John,* 1978 (on the Greek text); S. S. Smalley, *John: Evangelist and Interpreter,* 1978; F. F. Bruce, *The Gospel of John,* 1983.

SB

JOHN, LETTERS OF

I. The First Letter of John is evidently written by the author of the Fourth Gospel. The author does not give his name in the letter or the gospel, but the early church attributed both works to the apostle John. This attribution is supported by internal evidence of both books. The writer of the letter speaks with authority, as an apostle would (1 John 1:2; 2:1; 4:6, 14). He claims to have firsthand knowledge of the facts that underlie the gospel message (1:1–3; 4:14). The tone and teaching of the letter are such as we would expect from the aged apostle, writing to his disciples a last message regarding the truths he had taught throughout his life. When the Gospel and the letter are compared, the conclusion is well-nigh irresistible that the two books are by the same person. There are striking resemblances in style, language, and thought. Among these resemblances are characteristic words used in a peculiar sense (e.g., *life, light, darkness,* and *world*), characteristic expressions (e.g., *eternal life, a new commandment,* and *abide in Christ*), and identical phrases (e.g., *walks in darkness* and *that your joy may be full*). The few divergencies are easily explainable on the basis of differences of purpose and of subject.

We cannot be sure whether the letter was written before or after the Gospel. Tradition says that the Gospel was written late in the life of John, toward the end of the first century. Evidences of a late date for the letter are that Christianity has been so long in existence that its precepts may be spoken of as an "old commandment" (1 John 2:7) and signs that the Gnostic movement had begun, though it had not yet grown to its developed form.

The purpose of the author is to warn the readers against false teachers who are trying to mislead them, and to exhort them to hold fast to the Christian faith they have received and to fulfill conscientiously the duties, especially brotherly love, that flow from it. Although he does not exactly describe the false doctrine he attacks, there is no doubt that he has in mind the heresy of Gnosticism, with its view that the person of Christ was only spiritual, not physical, and that Christians are free from moral law by virtue of grace. The false teachers are called antichrists (1 John 2:18, 22; 4:3). They claim a knowledge of God that is superior to that of ordinary Christians, but, John says, their claims are false (2:4). They deny that Jesus is the Christ (2:22), the Son of God (4:15; 5:5), and that Jesus Christ has come in the flesh (4:2). They also impugn the fundamental moral teachings of the church by their dualistic interpretation of existence, for, according to Gnosticism, sin is not moral opposition of the human personality to God, but the evil physical principle inherent in all matter.

Although 1 John does not have the usual characteristics of the ancient Graeco-Roman letters—salutation, final greetings, messages to individuals, etc.—there is no doubt that it is a genuine letter. Most likely it is a pastoral or circular letter addressed to the churches in the province of Asia, where the church was in danger of the errors that are warned against.

The plan of the letter is difficult to follow and has been differently understood. Some fail to recognize any regular plan at all. Thoughts that are repeated again and again throughout 1 John are the necessity of doing righteousness as an evidence of divine sonship, the necessity of love for the brethren by those who claim to love God, and believing that Jesus is the Christ come in the flesh.

II. The Second Letter of John. Both 2 and 3 John are similar in words, style, ideas, and character to 1 John, and must have been written by the same author, who refers to himself simply as "the elder" (2 John 1; 3 John 1). Both are very brief, containing just the number of words that could conveniently be written on one sheet of papyrus. Although written to different people and for different purposes, there are striking resemblances of wording in them. The opening address is almost identical, and in both letters the writer expresses joy in the spiritual progress of those to whom he writes, and does so in almost the same words. The conclusion of the letters is the same in both thought and words.

Second John is addressed to "the chosen lady and her children" (2 John 1). Many suppose that the reference is to a church and its spiritual children, while others hold that a particular individual named Kyria (Gr. for *lady*) is meant. The introductory greeting is followed by an exhortation to hold fast to the commandments they had received, especially brotherly love, a warning against false teachers who deny that Christ is come in the flesh, and a prohibition against receiving them. The author concludes with a promise to visit them soon.

III. The Third Letter of John. This is addressed to Gaius, "my dear friend" (3 John 1), who is eulogized for walking in the truth and being hospitable to evangelists sent, apparently by John, to the church of which Gaius is a member. The author then censures another member of the church, the talkative, overbearing Diotrephes, who for some unexplained reason, probably jealously, not only refused to receive the itinerant preachers but did all he could to get the whole church to follow his course, even to the length of threatening excommunication for those who took a different view of their duty. The elder adds that he had written a letter to the church also, but apparently he has little hope that it will overcome the headstrong opposition of Diotrephes. He threatens a speedy visit to the church, when he will call Diotrephes to account for his bad conduct. There is in this letter no suggestion of heretical tendency in the church.

Bibliography: F. F. Bruce, *The Epistles of John,* 1970; J. L. Houlden, *The Johannine Epistles* (HNTC), 1973; I. H. Marshall, *The Epistles of John* (NIC), 1978; R. E. Brown, *The Epistles of John* (AB), 1982; S. S. Smalley, *1, 2, and 3 John* (WBC), 1984. SB

JOHN THE BAPTIST. The immediate forerunner of Jesus, sent by God to prepare the way for the coming of the Messiah. John was of priestly descent on the side of both his parents. His father Zachariah (KJV Zacharias) was a priest of the course of Abijah, while his mother Elizabeth belonged to the family of Aaron. They are described as being "upright in the sight of God, observing all the Lord's commandments and regulations blamelessly" (Luke 1:6). John was born in a city of the hill country of southern Judea, about six months before the birth of Jesus. His parents were then old. His birth had been foretold by an angel to Zachariah while he was serving in the temple. The angel told him that his prayer for a child would be answered and that his wife would give birth to a son who was to be named John and who was to prepare the way for the coming of the Messiah. About his childhood and youth we know only that he lived as a Nazirite in the desert and that he was filled with the Holy Spirit even from birth (1:15). It is thought by some that he was a member of a Jewish sect of monks called the Essenes, but there is no clear evidence that this was so.

His first public appearance is carefully dated by Luke (3:1–2), according to the way time was then reckoned. This was somewhere about A.D. 26 or 27. His early ministry took place in the wilderness of Judea and in the Jordan Valley. The main theme of his preaching was the near approach of the messianic age and the need for adequate spiritual preparation to be ready for it. His mission was to prepare the people for the advent of the Messiah so that when he made his appearance, they would recognize and accept him. His message did not harmonize with what many of his hearers expected, for while they looked for deliverance from and judgment on the foreign oppressor, John said that the Messiah would separate the good from the bad and would cast into the fire any tree that did not bring forth good fruit. Many of the Jews, especially the Pharisees, thought that they would enter the kingdom of God automatically, simply because they were physically descended from Abraham; but John declared in no uncertain terms that this was not so at all. He called on them to repent sincerely of their sins and to be baptized. The baptism by water that he administered signified a break with and cleansing from sin. His baptism was not something utterly new to the Jews; it had its roots in practices already familiar to them: in the various washings required by the Levitical law (Lev 11–15), in the messianic cleansing foretold by the prophets (Jer 33:8; Ezek 36:25–26; Zech 13:1), and in the proselyte baptism of the Jewish church. His baptism, however, differed essentially from these in that while the Levitical washings brought restoration to a former condition, his baptism prepared for a new condition; the Jews baptized only Gentiles, but he called on Jews themselves to be baptized; and his baptism was a baptism of water only in preparation for the messianic baptism of the Spirit anticipated by the prophets.

While the multitudes of common people flocked to the Jordan, Jesus also came to be baptized. Although Jesus and John were cousins, it appears that John did not know that Jesus was the Messiah until he saw the Holy Spirit descend

The traditional birthplace of John the Baptist, Ein Karem, today within the southwest municipal boundary of Jerusalem. Courtesy Duby Tal.

on him at his baptism (John 1:32–34). When Jesus came to him for baptism, he saw that Jesus had no sin of which to repent, and John would have refused to baptize him, had Jesus not insisted, saying that it was necessary for him to fulfill all righteousness. Shortly after, John said to two of his disciples as they saw Jesus pass by, "Look, the Lamb of God, who takes away the sin of the world!" (1:29), and they left him to follow Jesus. He recognized the subordinate and temporary character of his own mission. For some unexplained reason, some of his disciples did not leave him to follow Jesus; and when some of them came to John with the complaint that all men were coming to Jesus, he said to them, "He must become greater; I must become less" (3:30), saying also that he was not the Messiah but only the forerunner of the Messiah. Little is known about John's training of his disciples beyond the fact that it included forms of prayer (Luke 11:1) and frequent fastings (Matt 9:14), but he must also have taught them much concerning the Messiah and his work. Their loyalty to him is shown in their concern about Jesus' overshadowing popularity, their refusal to abandon him in his imprisonment, the reverent care they gave his body after his death, and the fact that twenty years later there were disciples of his, including Apollos, the learned Alexandrian Jew, in faraway Ephesus (Acts 19:1–7).

The exact time of John's imprisonment or the length of time he was in prison is not known. It is clear, however, that Jesus began his ministry in Galilee after John was put in prison and that John was in prison approximately seven months when he sent two of his disciples to Jesus to inquire whether he really was the Messiah. This inquiry seems strange in view of his previous signal testimonies and is probably to be explained either in the interest of his disciples, who needed assurance that Jesus was really the Messiah; or in some misgivings of his own because the messianic kingdom was not being ushered in as suddenly and as cataclysmically as he had expected; or perhaps because he thought he was being forgotten while others were being helped. When the two disciples returned to John, Jesus expressed the frankest appreciation of John, declaring him to be more than a prophet, and that he was indeed God's messenger sent to prepare the way for him (Matt 11:10–19).

The Gospels tell that John met his death through the vindictiveness of Herodias, whom John had denounced for her sin of living in adultery with Herod. Josephus, on the other hand, attributes John's death to Herod's jealousy of his great influence with the people. He also says that the destruction of Herod's army, in the war with his spurned wife's father-in-law, was regarded by the Jews as God's punishment on him for the murder of John. Josephus undoubtedly gives, not the real reason, which he would not dare to give to the public, but the reason Herod chose that the public be given.

Bibliography: C. H. Kraeling, *John the Baptist*, 1951; J. Steinmann, *Saint John the Baptist and the*

Desert Tradition, 1958; C. H. H. Scobie, *John the Baptist,* 1964; W. Wink, *John the Baptist in the Gospel Tradition,* 1968. SB

JOHN MARK (See MARK, JOHN)

JOIADA (joi'ȧ-dȧ, Heb. *yôyādhā',* *Jehovah knows*). 1. A son of Paseah, one of those who repaired the walls of Jerusalem (Neh 3:6, KJV Jehoiada).

2. A son of Eliashib the high priest. One of his sons married the daughter of Sanballat, the governor of Samaria, and was therefore expelled from the priesthood by Nehemiah (Neh 12:10; 13:28).

JOIAKIM (joi'ȧ-kĭm, Heb. *yôyāqîm, Jehovah raises* up). Son of Jeshua and father of Eliashib, the high priest (Neh 12:10, 12, 26).

JOIARIB (See JEHOIARIB)

JOKDEAM (jŏk'dē-ăm, Heb. *yoqedh'ām*). A town in Judah, probably south of Hebron, named with Maon, Carmel, and Ziph (Josh 15:56).

JOKIM (jō'kĭm, Heb. *yôqîm, Jehovah raises up*). A man of Judah descended from Shelah (1 Chron 4:22).

JOKMEAM (jŏk'mē-ăm, Heb. *yoqme'ām, let the people arise*). A town of Ephraim (1 Chron 6:68). It was assigned to the Kohathite Levites. KJV in 1 Kings 4:12 wrongly has "Jokneam."

JOKNEAM (jŏk'nē-ăm, Heb. *yoqne'ām*). A town on or near Mount Carmel (Josh 12:22). It was assigned to the Merarite Levites (21:34). It was located on the southern margin of the Plain of Esdraelon, about fifteen miles (twenty-five km.) NW of Jezreel.

JOKSHAN (jŏk'shăn, Heb. *yoqshān,* meaning unknown). Son of Abraham and Keturah (Gen 25:2–3). Sheba and Dedan descended from him.

JOKTAN (jŏk'tăn, Heb. *yoqtān,* meaning unknown). A tribe descended from Shem through Eber and from whom thirteen tribes of Arabia subsequently descended (Gen 10:25–26, 29; 1 Chron 1:19–20, 23).

JOKTHEEL (jŏk'thē-ĕl, Heb. *yoqethe'ēl*). 1. A town in the lowland of Judah. The site is unknown (Josh 15:38).

2. A name given by Amaziah, king of Judah, to a place in Edom that he conquered (2 Kings 14:7). It is usually identified with Petra, the capital of Edom.

JONA (See JONAS)

JONADAB (jŏn'ȧ-dăb, Heb. *yehônādhāv, Jehovah is bounteous*). 1. Son of David's brother Shimeah (2 Sam 13:3). He planned for Amnon the sin against Tamar.

2. The son of Recab (2 Kings 10:15–16; NIV Jehonadab). After becoming head of his tribe, he taught them to live in tents, to live a nomadic life, and to refrain from wine. They kept these rules, so that their behavior became characteristic of the Recabites. He helped Jehu abolish Baal worship in Samaria.

JONAH (Heb. *yônâh, dove*). 1. A prophet of Israel. He was the son of Amittai and came from the town of Gath Hepher in the tribe of Zebulun (2 Kings 14:25). He predicted the restoration of the land of Israel to its ancient boundaries through the efforts of Jeroboam II. The exact words of the prophet are not given, nor are we told the specific time when the prophecy was uttered; but we may be certain that it was pronounced sometime before the conquests of Jeroboam, either about the start of Jeroboam's reign or toward the close of the preceding reign. Jeroboam ruled for a period of forty years (790–750 B.C.). When he ascended the throne, he found the kingdom weak because ever since the time of Jehu, his great-grandfather, the people had been forced to pay continual tribute to Assyria. He became the most powerful of all the monarchs who ever sat on the throne of Samaria, capturing Hamath and Damascus and restoring to Israel all the territory it used to have from Hamath to the Dead Sea. The prophet Hosea also prophesied in the time of Jeroboam, but it must have been only toward the very close of his reign, as his prophetic activity extended to the time of Hezekiah, sixty years later.

The identity of the prophet with the prophet of the Book of Jonah cannot reasonably be doubted. Jonah 1:1 reads, "The word of the Lord came to Jonah son of Amittai." It is extremely unlikely that there were two prophets with the same name. While the author of the Book of Jonah does not identify himself, the likelihood is that he is the same as the book bearing his name. It is sometimes objected that he writes in the third person; but this is true of the OT prophets in general. In all probability the book was written not long after the events took place, in the latter part of Jeroboam's reign.

The spirit and teaching of the Book of Jonah rank with the highest of the OT prophetical books. Not as much can be said for the prophet himself, who ranks low in the catalog of OT prophets. He was a proud, self-centered egotist: willful, pouting, jealous, bloodthirsty; a good patriot and lover of Israel, without proper respect for God or love for his enemies.

JONAH, BOOK OF. Fifth in the canonical order of the Minor Prophets. It differs from them in that while they for the most part contain prophetic discourses, with a minimum of narrative material, the Book of Jonah is mainly occupied with a narrative, and the prophetic message in it is almost incidental. The chapter divisions mark the natural divisions of the book: Chapter 1, Jonah's disobedience; chapter 2, Jonah's prayer; chapter 3, Jonah's preaching to the Ninevites;

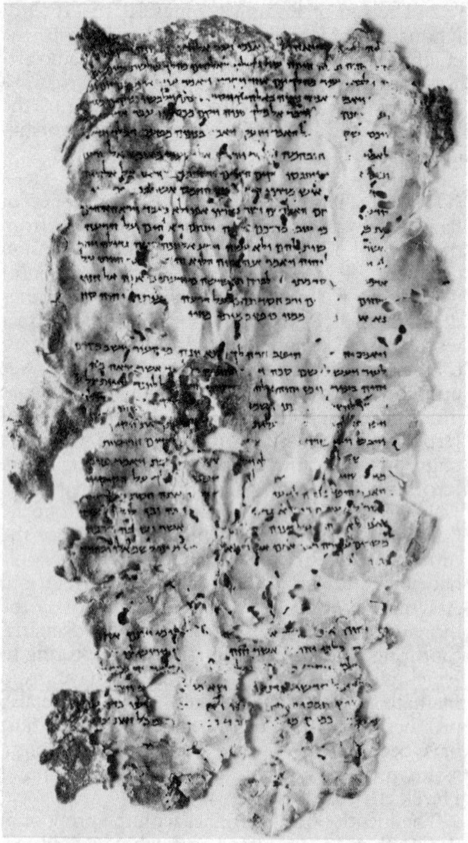

Jonah 3:2–4:1, part of the scroll of the Minor Prophets, found at Murabba'at, c. A.D. 100. Courtesy Israel Department of Antiquities and Museums.

chapter 4, Jonah's complaints. Chapter 1 records Jonah's call to preach at Nineveh because of its great wickedness. Instead of obeying, he took a ship in the opposite direction, to Tarshish, probably in SW Spain. His disobedience undoubtedly arose from his fear that the Ninevites would heed his message and repent, and that God would forgive the city that had for many years grievously oppressed his own land. He was a narrow-minded patriot who feared that Assyria would someday destroy his own people; and he did not want to do anything that might contribute to that event. He was unwilling to be a foreign missionary to a people for whom he could feel nothing but bitterness. In the sequel of the account he frankly gives his reason for refusing to obey God's command, "That is why I was so quick to flee to Tarshish. I knew that you are a gracious and compassionate God, slow to anger and abounding in love, a God who relents from sending calamity" (4:2). During a violent storm at sea, the heathen sailors prayed to their own gods who, they thought, must be offended with some person on board. They cast lots to discover the culprit, and when the lot fell on Jonah, he confessed that he was fleeing from the Lord and volunteered to be thrown overboard for their sakes. This was done, the storm subsided, and the sailors offered a sacrifice to God.

The Lord prepared a great fish to swallow Jonah. Surprised to find himself alive in the body of the fish, the prophet gave thanks to God and expressed the confident hope that he would ultimately be delivered. After three days and three nights the fish vomited him onto the dry land.

Commanded a second time to go to Nineveh, Jonah obeyed and delivered his message, "Forty more days and Nineveh will be overturned" (Jonah 3:4). The effect of his message was undoubtedly greatly heightened by the account of his deliverance, which had either preceded him or been told by himself. The people of Nineveh repented in sackcloth and ashes, and God spared the city.

When Jonah learned that Nineveh was to be spared, he broke out into loud and bitter complaint, not because he felt discredited as a prophet on account of the failure of his prediction, but because he was sure that the sparing of Nineveh sealed the doom of his own country. By the withering of a vine, the Lord taught the prophet that if a mean and perishable plant could come to have such value to him, how much greater should be the estimate put on the lives of thousands of children and cattle in the great city of Nineveh. These meant more to God than Jonah's vine could ever mean to Jonah.

The purpose of the book is primarily to teach that God's gracious purposes are not limited to Israel but extend to the Gentile world. The author wishes to enlarge the sympathies of Israel, so that as God's missionaries they will lead the Gentiles to repentance and to God. The ready response of the Ninevites shows that the heathen are capable of genuine repentance. The Book of Jonah may be regarded as a great work on foreign missions. It anticipates the catholicity of the gospel program of Jesus, and is the OT counterpart of John 3:16, "For God so loved the world."

The book is anonymous, and its authorship is in dispute. The traditional view is that the prophet Jonah is the author, and his book is a record of his own experiences. A more recent view is that the book was written long after Jonah's time by some anonymous author and that it is a work of fiction with a moral lesson. Among the chief arguments advanced for the second view are the following: (1) In the prayer ascribed to Jonah, there are quotations from postexilic psalms (cf. Jonah 2:3 with Ps 42:7; Jonah 2:5 with Ps 69:1; Jonah 2:9 with Ps 50:1). (2) The narrative is written throughout in the third person, with no indication that the prophet involved was the writer. (3) There are in the book Aramaic linguistic features that are found in later books. (4) From Jonah 3:3 it is inferred that Nineveh was a thing of the past (the city was destroyed in 612 B.C.). (5) The failure to give the name of the king of Assyria indicates that it was unknown to the author. These arguments, however, are debatable and therefore inconclusive.

The traditional view, that Jonah is the author

and the narrative is historically true, is supported by a number of considerations. (1) The book was written as a simple narrative, and it was so regarded by both Jews and Christians until about a century ago. (2) There seems no doubt that Jesus thought of the narrative as history and taught it as such. On three different occasions he referred to Jonah (Matt 12:38–41; 16:4; Luke 11:29–32), saying that as Jonah was three days and three nights in the body of the fish, so should the Son of Man be three days and three nights in the heart of the earth, and that the men of Nineveh repented at the preaching of Jonah, while his own contemporaries for the most part rejected his message. Some critics, taking refuge in the doctrine of the Kenosis (that Christ was somehow limited by his human nature; see Phil 2:5–8), set aside the teaching of Jesus on this point as erroneous; others, holding to a doctrine of accommodation, think that Jesus did not consider it worthwhile to correct the wrong views of his contemporaries. Neither of these explanations harmonizes with a biblical view of the person of Christ.

Most modern critical scholars in the last hundred years have regarded the book as a work of the imagination. Some call it a myth; others, an allegory; others, a parable; others, a didactic story, and so on. This interpretation avoids the miraculous elements in the narrative, which the critics find impossible to accept; but it does not do justice to the fact that our Lord very evidently held to the historicity of the book.

Bibliography: Hugh Martin, *The Prophet Jonah: His Character and Mission to Nineveh,* 1958; L. C. Allen, *The Books of Joel, Obadiah, Jonah and Micah* (NIC), 1976.

SB

JONAM (jō′năm, Gr. *Iōnam,* perhaps *Jehovah is gracious*). An ancestor of Jesus mentioned in the genealogy of Luke (Luke 3:30). He lived about two hundred years after David.

JONAS, JONA (jō′nȧs, jō′nȧ, Gr. *Iōnas, Iōna*). 1. The literal rendering, given in the KJV, of the Greek name of the prophet Jonah (Matt 12:39–41; 16:4; Luke 11:29, 30, 32.

2. The name given in John 21:15–17 (KJV) to the father of the apostle Peter; Jona in John 1:42; Bar-jona in Matthew 16:17.

JONATHAN (jŏn′ȧ-thăn, Heb. *yehônāthān, yônāthān, Jehovah has given*). A proper name common from the time of the judges onward.

1. A Levite, a son or more distant descendant of Gershom, son of Moses (Judg 18:30). For a time he lived in Bethlehem-Judah, but left to become the priest of Micah in Ephraim. Some Danites, after stealing idolatrous images from the house of Micah, induced him to go with them and be their priest. At Laish he founded a priesthood that officiated at the shrine of the stolen idols "until the time of the captivity of the land" (18:30).

2. Son of King Saul (see separate article below).

3. Son of the high priest Abiathar. He helped David during Absalom's rebellion and brought to Adonijah the news that Solomon had been crowned king (2 Sam 15:27, 36; 17:17, 20; 1 Kings 1:42–43).

4. A son of Shimeah, a nephew of David (2 Sam 21:21).

5. One of David's mighty men (2 Sam 23:32).

6. A Jerahmeelite (1 Chron 2:32–33).

7. A son of Uzziah, one of David's treasurers (1 Chron 27:25; Jehonathan, lit., KJV).

8. David's "uncle," a wise man and a scribe (1 Chron 27:32). He may be the same as no. 4 above.

9. The father of Ebed, a returned exile (Ezra 8:6).

10. A son of Asahel who opposed Ezra in the matter of foreign marriages (Ezra 10:15).

11. A priest, a son of Joiada, descended from Jeshua (Neh 12:11).

12. A priest in the days of the high priest Joiakim (Neh 12:14).

13. A Levite of the lineage of Asaph (Neh 12:35).

14. A scribe in whose house Jeremiah was imprisoned (Jer 37:15, 20).

15. A son of Kareah, probably the same as no. 14 above (Jer 40:8).

JONATHAN. The oldest son of Saul, the first king of Israel (1 Sam 14:49). He comes on the scene soon after his father was crowned king. He gained an important victory over the Ammonites, who had been harassing the Israelites. Saul's army numbered three thousand men (13:2), a third of whom he placed under the command of Jonathan at Gibeah, while the rest he retained at his headquarters at Micmash. In the valley midway between the two camps, at a place called Geba, the Philistines established an outpost and forced Saul to evacuate and fall back on Gibeah and Gilgal with a greatly reduced army, now numbering only six hundred men (13:15), the rest having fled in fear to hide in caves or having been pressed into the enemy's service. In spite of this, Jonathan, assisted only by his armor-bearer, surprised the Philistine outpost at Geba and killed twenty men (14:1–14). The resulting panic spread to the main camp, and when Saul came to attack, he found the Philistines confusedly attacking one another, and soon the whole Philistine army was in headlong flight. In this rout, the only weapons the Israelites had were farming implements (13:22), Saul and Jonathan alone being armed with swords and spears. The victory would have been even more complete had not Saul superstitiously ordered the people to refrain from eating until the day was over (14:24). Unaware of this prohibition, Jonathan, in his hot pursuit of the enemy, refreshed himself by eating wild honey. Saul would have had him put to death, but the people intervened. They recognized that, with the help of God, his energetic action had brought them a mighty victory.

But great as Jonathan's military qualities were, he is best remembered as the friend of David. He exemplified all that is noblest in friendship—

warmth of affection, unselfishness, helpfulness, and loyalty. His love for David began the day the two first met after the killing of Goliath (1 Sam 18:1–4), and it remained steadfast despite Saul's suggestion that David would someday be king in their stead (20:31). When Jonathan first realized his father's animosity toward David, he interceded for his friend (19:1–7); and later, more than once, he risked his life for him. Once Saul, angered by what he regarded as unfilial conduct, threw a javelin at him, as he had done several times at David. The last meeting of the two friends took place in the desert of Ziph, where Jonathan "helped his friend find strength in God" (23:16). He would not take part in the proceedings of his father against David, who was forced to live in hiding and from whom he was separated for many years. His disinterestedness and willingness to surrender all claims to the throne for the sake of his friend gives evidence of a character that is unsurpassed. While always holding to his own opinion of David, he conformed as much as he could to his father's views and wishes, and presents a noble example of filial piety. There was one temporary estrangement between Saul and Jonathan, provoked when Saul impugned the honor of Jonathan's mother (20:30). Jonathan died with Saul and his brothers on Mount Gilboa in battle against the Philistines (31:2). Their bodies were hung on the walls of Bethshan, but under cover of night the men of Jabesh Gilead, out of gratitude for what Saul had done for them at the beginning of his career (11:1–11), removed them and gave them honorable burial. One son, Mephibosheth, survived. David showed him kindness, and Saul's posterity through him may be traced for several generations. These descendants, like their ancestors, were famous soldiers, especially distinguished in the use of the bow (1 Chron 8:3ff.; 9:40ff.). SB

JOPPA (jŏp′pȧ, Heb. *yāphô*, Gr. *Ioppē*). Once in KJV Japho (Josh 19:46), an ancient walled town on the coast of Palestine, about thirty-five miles (fifty-eight km.) from Jerusalem. It was allotted to Dan, but there is no evidence that the Israelites ever possessed it in preexilic times. It is mentioned in the Amarna Letters. It was the seaport for Jerusalem. Timber from the forests of Lebanon was floated from Tyre to Joppa for the building of the temple of Solomon (2 Chron 2:16), and again when the temple was being rebuilt, after the return from the Babylonian captivity (Ezra 3:7). It was then under Phoenician control. Jonah boarded a ship there when he fled from the presence of the Lord (Jonah 1:3). In Maccabean times the city was garrisoned by Syrians, but when some two hundred Jews were treacherously drowned, after being induced to go aboard ships, Judas Maccabaeus in revenge set fire to the docks and the boats in the harbor and killed the fugitives. In NT times Peter raised Dorcas to life there (Acts 9:36–37), and on the roof of Simon the tanner's house he received the famous vision that taught him the gospel was intended for Jew and Gentile alike (10:1ff.; 11:5ff.). In the Jewish war of A.D. 66 the Romans killed 8,400 of its fanatical inhabitants. After that, pirates gained control of the city and preyed on the shipping in the surrounding waters. Vespasian then captured and destroyed the city. Joppa, now called Jaffa, is built on a rocky ledge 116 feet (36 m.) high, at

The modern city of Jaffa, ancient Joppa, on the Mediterranean coast. Courtesy Duby Tal.

the edge of the sea. The harbor is poor because of its many rocks. The city has a very picturesque setting. SB

JORAH (jō'rȧ, Heb. *yôrâh,* meaning uncertain). A family who returned with Zerubbabel (Ezra 2:18). It is called Hariph in Nehemiah 7:24.

JORAI (jō'rā-ī, Heb. *yôray, whom Jehovah teaches*). The ancestral head of a Gadite family (1 Chron 5:13).

JORAM (jō'răm, Heb. *yôrām, Jehovah is exalted*). 1. A son of Tou king of Hamath, who congratulated David on his victory over Hadadezer (2 Sam 8:10).

2. A Levite (1 Chron 26:25).

3. Son of Ahab king of Israel. He succeeded his brother Ahaziah on the throne. The name is the same as Jehoram (2 Kings 8:29).

4. Same as Jehoram king of Judah (2 Kings 8:21–24; 11:2; 1 Chron 3:11; Matt 1:8).

JORDAN RIVER. The only large flowing body of water in Palestine and, as such, it played a significant part in the history of Israel, as well as in the earlier days of our Lord's ministry. The word *Jordan* derives from a Hebrew word, *hay-yardēn,* meaning "flowing downward," or "the descender," and one with any knowledge of its course can easily see the appropriateness of the name. Four rivers in Syria are recognized as the source of what later becomes the Jordan River proper. They are the Bareighit; the Hasbany, at the western foot of Mount Hermon, twenty-four miles (forty km.) long; the Leddan; and, the most famous of all, though the shortest, the Banias, five and one-half miles (nine km.) long. On this last-named river once stood the city of Paneas, where the well-known grotto of the Greek god Pan was located. Later this was called Caesarea Philippi, and here the great confession of Simon Peter occurred (Matt 16:13). These rivers join and pour into Lake Huleh, twenty miles (thirty-three km.) long and five miles (eight km.) wide, the surface of which is seven feet (two m.) above sea level. In recent years this lake has been drained by Israeli settlers for farm land. The Jordan then descends for ten miles (seventeen km.) to the Sea of Galilee, a beautiful body of water. From the place where the Jordan makes its exit from the Sea of Galilee to the place where it enters the Dead Sea is, in a straight line, a length of 70 miles (117 km.). But the river itself, because of its serpentine curves, is 200 miles (333 km.) long. The surface of the Dead Sea is 1,292 feet (404 m.) below sea level. The Jordan River proper varies from ninety to one hundred feet (twenty-eight to thirty-one m.) in width, and from three to ten feet (one to three m.) in depth, but the gorge that it has cut out varies in width from four miles (seven km.) at the north to fourteen miles (twenty-three km.) near Jericho.

Though the largest river of Palestine, the Jordan differs from other great national rivers in that, because it has twenty-seven rapids between the Sea of Galilee and the Dead Sea, it carries no traffic; and because of the swampy condition of part of this valley, the terrific heat in many places, and the presence of many wild animals, especially during Israel's history, no large city was ever built directly on the banks of the Jordan.

An aerial view showing the winding course of the Jordan River, looking northward. This picture, which was taken near Jericho, just north of the Dead Sea, covers approximately 3 miles (5 km.). Courtesy Carta, Jerusalem.

Although the Jordan is never called by any other name in the Bible, it is once referred to as "the river of the wilderness" (Amos 6:14 KJV) and "the pride of the Jordan" (Jer 12:5; 49:19; 50:44; Zech 11:3, KJV).

The natural life found in the Jordan Valley has been carefully studied, some of it proving to be unique. Of the thirty species of fish found in this river, sixteen are said to be found nowhere else; of the forty-five species of birds observed in this tortuous valley, twenty-three are peculiar to this area. About 162 species of plants and trees have been identified, of which 135 are African. They include the castor oil plant, the tamarisk, willows, poplars, and, near Jericho, the oleander. Though no large city was actually ever built on the banks of the Jordan, there are some geographical terms that belong to this area. In the north at the time of our Lord's advent, there was an area called the Decapolis, a federation of ten Greek cities, nine on the eastern side of the Jordan, and mentioned once at the beginning of our Lord's ministry (Matt 4:25). Another city in this group was Pella, not mentioned in the Bible, but according to tradition the city to which the Christians fled at the time of the destruction of Jerusalem in A.D. 70.

A view of the Jordan, looking downstream, at the traditional site where John the Baptist preached and baptized. Courtesy Duby Tal.

Of the important rivers flowing into the Jordan, all are on the eastern side (no river emptying into the Jordan on the west is referred to in the OT). The first, four miles (seven km.) south of the Sea of Galilee, is the Yarmuk, not mentioned in the Bible. The great modern Rutenberg electric power plant is located here. Below this river was the city of Beth Shan, referred to in Joshua 17:16, the excavation of which has revealed a civilization going back to 3500 B.C. Later it was called Scythopolis. South of this site is Aenon where we are told that John the Baptist carried on some of his baptizing work (John 3:23). The Brook Kerith, referred to in 1 Kings 17:2–7, may have been located not far from here. The next important river, about midway between the Sea of Galilee and the Dead Sea, is the Jabbok, famous as the place where Jacob wrestled with the angel (Gen 32:22), later designated as a boundary (Num 21:24; Josh 12:2). At the confluence of this river with the Jordan was the site known as Adam, where the waters of the great river were held back at the time of Israel's crossing (Josh 3:16).

Near the Dead Sea on the western side of the river, one mile (one and one-half km.) east of Jericho, stood the city of Gilgal, where Israel set up twelve stones at the command of God (Josh 4:19–20), a place that later became an important religious center (1 Sam 7:16; 10:8).

By far the most significant single event relating to the Jordan River in the entire history of Israel is the crossing on the part of the Israelites after the death of Moses, a crossing anticipated by Moses in Deuteronomy 3:20, 25, 27. While the Jordan is now and then referred to as a boundary, it was not a boundary for Israel or even for the specific tribes, for Manasseh occupied a huge territory on both sides of the river. Nevertheless, Israel was told that until this river was crossed and the territory on the western side possessed, they would not be occupying the land flowing with milk and honey (Num 35:10; Deut 3:20; 11:31; 31:13; Josh 1:2). The Promised Land more generally refers to the territory on the western side of the Jordan than to all of the land occupied by Israel. The account of the crossing of the Jordan is given in detail in the third and fourth chapters of Joshua.

The Jordan is important in only one particular way in the NT. It was here that John the Baptist carried on his ministry (Matt 3:6; Mark 1:5; John 1:28; 3:26), and thus in this river Jesus himself was baptized (Matt 3:13; Mark 1:9; Luke 4:1). No other event occurs in the NT directly relating to the Jordan River. (References to the Lord's ministry on the far side of the Jordan—in Matt 19:1 and Mark 10:1—only imply that the Lord crossed the river.) In the statement relating to the closing days of Jesus' ministry, when escaping from those who wanted to make him king, he "went back across the Jordan to the place where John had been baptizing in the early days" (John 10:40). When the early church began its great missionary work, apart from the interview of Philip with the Ethiopian eunuch near Gaza, all the ministry of the apostles and early disciples, according to the NT, proceeded neither south into Egypt nor east toward Babylon, but north into Syria and Asia Minor, and then west to Greece, to Italy, and probably Spain. Nothing of any great historic importance has actually happened at the Jordan River since the baptism of Jesus. In fact, the Jordan Valley, from the Sea of Galilee to near Jericho, was practically unexplored until the nineteenth century.

The theme of the Jordan River is frequently found in the ritual of the church and in its hymnology and poetry. Comparing death for the Christian with the crossing of the Jordan by the Israelites cannot be regarded as a very accurate interpretation of Israel's history at this point. Israel did not enter into a time of peace when she crossed the Jordan but into a series of wars, many oppressions and defeats, followed by victories for a time, and ultimately ending in disaster and expulsion from the land. WMS

JORIM (jō'rĭm, Gr. *Iōrim,* from Heb. *yehôrām*). An ancestor of Jesus in the genealogy of Luke (3:29).

JORKEAM (jôr'kē-ăm, Heb. *yorqe'ām*). A place inhabited by members of the family of Hezron and house of Caleb (1 Chron 2:44). It may be identical with "Jokdeam" of Joshua 15:56.

JOSABAD (See JOZABAD)

JOSAPHAT (See JEHOSHAPHAT)

JOSE (jō'sė, Gr. *Iōse*; in some MSS *Iōsou*). In Luke's genealogy (3:29), an ancestor of Jesus.

JOSECH (jō'zėk, Gr. *Iōsēch*). An ancestor of Jesus according to Luke 3:26 (KJV "Joseph").

JOSEDECH (See JOZADAK)

JOSEPH (jō'zĕf, Heb. *yôsēph, may God add*). 1. The eleventh of Jacob's twelve sons, and the firstborn son of Rachel, who said when he was born, "May the LORD add to me another son," and therefore called his name Joseph (Gen 30:24). He became the ancestor of the two northern tribes, Manasseh and Ephraim. The account of his birth is told in Genesis 30:22–24, and the account of the rest of his life is found in Genesis 37–50. He was born in Paddan Aram when his father was ninety years old; he was his father's favorite child because he was Rachel's child and the son of his old age. The father's favoritism was shown in his getting for Joseph a coat of many colors, which was probably a token of rank indicating that it was his intention to make Joseph the head of the tribe. This favoritism naturally aroused the envy of Joseph's older brothers. Their ill will was increased when he somewhat imprudently told them two dreams he had that were suggestive of his future greatness and their subservience to him. When he was seventeen years old, his father sent him to see how his brothers were doing at Shechem, where they were feeding their flocks; but when he arrived, he found that they had gone on to Dothan, and he followed them there. When they saw him coming, they planned to kill him, and thus make impossible the fulfillment of his dreams. Reuben, however, persuaded them not to kill him but to throw him alive into a pit, intending to rescue him later and restore him to his father. When Reuben was absent for a short time, the brothers saw a caravan of Ishmaelites making their way to Egypt and decided that instead of allowing Joseph to die in the well, they would sell him to these merchantmen. They sold Joseph and then took his coat of many colors, smeared it with the blood of a goat they had killed, and took it to Jacob with the story that they had found the coat and assumed that their brother was dead, torn to pieces by some wild beast. The aged father, grief-stricken and disconsolate, mourned the loss of his son for many days.

In the meantime, Joseph was taken to Egypt by the Ishmaelites and sold in the slave market to an officer of Pharaoh, an Egyptian named Potiphar. The young slave proved himself to be so intelligent and trustworthy that his master soon entrusted to him all the affairs of his household, which prospered under Joseph's administration. But on the false accusations of Potiphar's wife, whose improper advances Joseph had rejected, he was cast into prison, where he remained for years. God was with him, however, and the providence that had previously saved his life now brought him to the favorable attention of the pharaoh. The prison keeper, finding he could put implicit confidence in Joseph, committed to his charge the other prisoners. Among these were two of the pharaoh's officers, his chief butler and chief baker, who had been imprisoned for offending the king. Joseph interpreted for them two dreams they had had; and three days later, on the king's birthday, as Joseph had foretold, the chief baker was hanged and the chief butler restored to his office (Gen 40:5–23).

After two years, during which Joseph's circumstances remained unchanged—the chief butler had forgotten his promise to mention him to the king—Pharaoh had two dreams that no one could interpret. They had to do with fat and lean cows and full and withered heads of grain. The chief butler now remembered Joseph and told the king of Joseph's skill in interpreting dreams. Joseph was sent for. He told Pharaoh that each dream had the same meaning: Seven years of plenty would be followed by seven years of famine. He then suggested that preparation be made for the years of famine by storing up the surplus produce during the seven years of plenty against the years of famine. Pharaoh immediately made Joseph head of the royal granaries and invested him with the authority necessary to carry out his proposals. As the head of the department of state, Joseph became one of the officials next in rank to the pharaoh (Gen 41:39–44), and as a further mark of royal favor, he was given an Egyptian name and was married to the daughter of the priest of the great national temple of On. Joseph was now thirty years old. During the seven years of plenty he amassed corn in the granaries of every city, and his wife bore him two sons, Manasseh and Ephraim.

The famine that Joseph predicted affected not only Egypt but all the known world, so that all countries came to Egypt to buy corn. Joseph's brothers came also. They did not recognize him, but he knew them; and when they prostrated themselves before him, he saw the fulfillment of the dreams that had aroused their intense jealousy years before. The climax of the episode is reached when Joseph, after testing their character in various ways, made himself known to them, told them that he bore no ill will for the wrong they had done him, and persuaded them and their father to settle in Egypt. The pharaohs reigning in Egypt during that era were probably members of the Hyksos dynasty and were Semites, like Joseph; and the present pharaoh consequently cordially welcomed Jacob and his family to Egypt.

In the years that followed, Joseph brought about a permanent change in the Egyptian system of land tenure because of the famine and the consequent poverty of the people, so that almost all the land became the property of the pharaoh, and the previous owners became his tenants. Jacob lived with Joseph in Egypt seventeen years. Before he died, he adopted Joseph's two sons, putting them on the same level as his own sons in the division of the inheritance. Joseph lived to the age of 110. Shortly before he died he expressed his confidence that God would some day bring the children of Israel back to Canaan, and solemnly directed that his bones be buried there. His wishes were carried out, and his bones were buried finally in Shechem, in the plot of ground bought there by Jacob (Josh 24:32). He became the ancestor of the two tribes Manasseh and Ephraim, the latter being the most powerful and important in northern Israel. Joseph presents a noble ideal of character, remarkable for his gentleness, faithfulness to duty, magnanimity, and forgiving spirit, so that he is often regarded as an OT type of Christ.

2. The father of Igal of Issachar, one of the twelve spies (Num 13:7).

3. A son of Asaph and head of a course of musicians in the reign of David (1 Chron 25:2, 9).

4. A son of Bani, who had married a foreign wife and was induced by Ezra to put her away (Ezra 10:42).

5. A priest of the family of Shecaniah in the days of the high priest Joiakim (Neh 12:14).

6. The name of three ancestors of Jesus, according to the KJV (Luke 3:24, 26, 30); the NIV reads "Josech" in 3:26.

7. The husband of Mary, the mother of Jesus (Matt 1:16; Luke 3:23). He was a carpenter (Matt 13:55) living in Nazareth (Luke 2:4). He was of Davidic descent (Matt 1:20; Luke 2:4), the son of Heli (Luke 3:23) or Jacob (Matt 1:16), and thought by many of that day to be the father of Jesus (Matt 13:55; Luke 3:23; 4:22; John 1:45; 6:42). After learning that Mary was pregnant before marriage, he had in mind to divorce her quietly, but an angel assured him in a dream that the child to be born had been conceived by the Holy Spirit, so he made her his wife (Matt 1:18–25). When the emperor Augustus decreed that a census should be taken of the entire Roman world, Joseph and Mary went to Bethlehem to enroll, and there Jesus was born. Joseph was with Mary when the shepherds came to do homage to Jesus (Luke 2:8–20) and when, forty days after his birth, Jesus was presented in the temple. Warned by the Lord in a dream that Herod was plotting the murder of the child, he fled with Mary and Jesus to Egypt (Matt 2:13–19), returning to Nazareth after the death of Herod. Every year Joseph attended the Passover Feast in Jerusalem (Luke 2:41); and when Jesus was twelve, he too went with Joseph and Mary. Joseph undoubtedly taught Jesus the carpenter trade (Mark 6:3). It is likely that he was alive after the ministry of Jesus had well begun (Matt 13:55), but as we do not hear of him in connection with the Crucifixion, and as Jesus commended Mary to John at the Crucifixion (John 19:26–27), it may be inferred that he had died prior to that event.

8. One of the brothers of Jesus (Matt 13:55). KJV has "Joses."

9. A Jew of Arimathea, a place probably to the NW of Jerusalem. He is described as a rich man, a member of the Sanhedrin (Matt 27:57; Mark 15:43), and a righteous man looking for the kingdom of God (Mark 15:43; Luke 23:50). A secret disciple of Jesus because of his fear of the Jews (John 19:38), he did not take part in the resolution of the Sanhedrin to put Jesus to death. After the Crucifixion he secured permission from Pilate to remove the body of Jesus from the cross, and he laid it in his own new tomb (Matt 27:57–60; Luke 23:50–53; John 19:38).

10. A Christian called Barsabbas, or son of Sabas, and surnamed Justus (Acts 1:23). He was one of those who had accompanied Jesus and the apostles from the time of Jesus' baptism and was one of the two candidates considered by the apostles as a replacement for Judas Iscariot. However, the lot fell to Matthias (1:21, 26).

11. The personal name of Barnabas (Acts 4:36; in KJV "Joses"). SB

JOSES (jō'sĕz, Gr. *Iōsēs,* Gr. form of *Joseph*). 1. One of Jesus' brothers (Mark 6:3 KJV). NIV and some MSS have *Joseph* in Matthew 13:55.

2. A name of Barnabas, for a time a co-worker of Paul (Acts 4:36 KJV). Here, too, some Greek MSS have *Joseph*, followed by the NIV.

JOSHAH (jō'shȧ, Heb. *yôshâh, Jehovah's gift*). A descendant of Simeon and the head of his family (1 Chron 4:34).

JOSHAPHAT (jŏsh'ȧ-făt, Heb. *yôshāphāt, Jehovah had judged*). 1. One of David's mighty men (1 Chron 11:43).

2. A priest and trumpeter in David's time (1 Chron 15:24; KJV Jehoshaphat).

JOSHAVIAH (jŏsh'ȧ-vī'ȧ, Heb. *yôshawyâh*). Son of Elnaam, one of David's mighty men (1 Chron 11:46).

JOSHBEKASHAH (jŏsh'bē-kā'shȧ). A son or descendant of Heman and a leader in music (1 Chron 25:4, 24).

JOSHEB-BASSHEBETH (jō'shĕb-bă'shē-bĕth, *he who sits on the seat,* 2 Sam 23:8). Probably a corruption of Jashobeam, as in 1 Chronicles 11:11. One of David's mighty men.

JOSHIBIAH (jŏsh'ĭ-bī'ȧ). A Simeonite mentioned only in 1 Chronicles 4:35.

JOSHUA (jŏsh'ū-ȧ). A son of Nun, an Ephraimite (1 Chron 7:22–27). Although born in Egyptian bondage c. 1500 B.C., he was named, significantly, Hoshea (Oshea), "salvation" (Num 13:8; Deut 32:44). Two months after Israel's exodus, he was appointed Moses' commander and successfully repulsed an Amalekite attack (Exod 17:9). Moses changed Hoshea's name to Jehoshua, *yehôshûa'*, "Jehovah is salvation" (Num 13:16; 1 Chron 7:27), or Joshua, later forms of which are Jeshua (*yēshûa'*, Neh 8:17) and, in Greek, Jesus (*Iēsous,* Acts 7:45; Heb. 4:8); compare Matthew 1:21. Joshua attended Moses on Sinai (Exod 24:13; 32:17) and guarded both his tent (33:11) and position (Num 11:28). Later he represented Ephraim in spying out Canaan. Joshua opposed the majority report, insisting that Israel, if faithful to God, could conquer Canaan. He almost suffered stoning for his trust in God (14:7–10). Subsequently, however, for having "followed the LORD wholeheartedly" (32:12), he not only escaped destruction (14:38) but also received assurance, unique to himself and Caleb (13:30; 14:24), of entering the Promised Land (14:30; 26:65).

About forty years later, east of the Jordan River, God designated Joshua as Moses' successor (Num 27:18). Moses charged him to be faithful (Num 27:23; Deut 31:23), committed the "song of admonition" and other writings to him (Exod 17:14; Deut 32:44), counseled him on procedures (Num 32:28; 34:17), and encouraged both new leader and people (Deut 3:21; 31:3, 7). God himself warned Joshua of coming apostasy (31:14) but promised that Joshua would be successful in the conquest of the Promised Land (1:38; 3:28; 31:23).

After Moses' death, Joshua, as the oldest man in Israel, must have been in his nineties (Caleb was eighty-five, Josh 13:1; 14:7–11). Yet God assured him of victory, as he relied on the inspired Book of Moses (1:6–9). From this point onward, Joshua's history is that of Israel's occupation of Canaan. His personal actions, however, include making preparations (1:10–18), sending spies against Jericho (2:1, 23–24), and then ordering Israel's advance across Jordan (3:1). His faith in crossing the Jordan inaugurated a life of undiminishing esteem, similar even to that of Moses (3:7; 4:14). West of Jordan, Joshua superintended Israel's rituals (5:2) and the construction of monuments for building the faith of children yet to come (4:4–7). The appearance of "the commander of the army of the LORD" (5:13–15) served as a dramatic sentence on Jericho but also as a visible confirmation of Joshua's divine call, similar to the appearance of the angel of the Lord to Moses at the burning bush (Exod 3:2–6). Joshua then executed the God-directed siege (Josh 6:2–6). He "devoted" (destroyed) Jericho (6:17), pronounced a curse on its rebuilding (6:26; 1 Kings 16:34), and achieved widespread recognition (Josh 6:27).

When the disobedience of Achan brought defeat at Ai, Joshua's prayer, his zeal for God's glory, and his enforcement of divine judgment (Josh 7:6–9, 19, 25) compare favorably with his subsequent faithfulness to God's orders and exemplary execution of Ai's king (8:2, 29; cf. 10:24–27, 40–41). With central Palestine subdued, Joshua personally wrote Moses' law on stone at Mount Ebal and then proclaimed this law to the whole Israelite assembly (8:30–35). Though guilty of rashness with the Gibeonites, he later condemned these pagans to bondage (9:15, 22–23, 26–27). The energy he displayed in forced marches and sudden attacks frustrated Canaanite counteroffensives in both south (10:9) and north (11:7). Basically it was the Lord who gave Israel her victories, especially evident in causing the sun to "stand still" during the battle at Beth Horon (10:12–14), on which compare Bernard Ramm, *The Christian View of Science and Scripture*, 1955, pp. 156–61, with J. Barton Payne, *BETS* 3:4 (1960), pp. 95–96. In six years (14:10) Joshua took the whole land; "he left nothing undone of all that the LORD commanded Moses" (11:15, 23).

Yet Moses had anticipated a gradual occupation (Exod 23:28–30). God had left in Canaan many nations, subdued but still powerful, to test his people (Josh 13:2–6; Judg 2:21–3:4); so Joshua could not achieve Israel's final "rest" (Heb 4:8). Thus, because of his advanced age, he divided Canaan among the tribes (Josh 13:6–7; 14:1; 19:51). At Gilgal he confirmed Moses' Transjordanian settlement of the two and one-half tribes and assigned territory to Judah, including Caleb's portion at Hebron (14:13; 15:13), and to Ephraim and Manasseh (cf. 17:4), encouraging them to more effective conquest even while refusing to show them partiality (17:14–18). Later, at Shiloh, he exhorted the seven hesitant tribes, dispatched a commission on apportionment, and thus allotted the remaining lands (18:3, 8–10), including cities of refuge and

Levitical assignments (Josh 20–21). He himself requested and built Timnath Serah in Ephraim (19:49–51).

As death approached, Joshua first summoned Israel's leaders, urging them to faithfulness in conquest (Josh 23), and then assembled the tribal heads to Shechem, charging them, "Choose for yourselves this day whom you will serve" (24:15). Having renewed their covenant with the Lord, he inserted it in the Book of the law (24:25–26) and died at the age of 110 (24:29–30; Judg 2:8–9). Throughout his days, and even afterward, his influence caused Israel to faithfulness to her Lord (Josh 24:31; Judg 1:1; 2:7). JBP

JOSHUA, BOOK OF. Standing sixth in Scripture, this book describes how Moses' successor, after whom the book is named, conquered Canaan (Josh 1:1; 24:31; see JOSHUA). But while Joshua is the first of "the historical books" in English (and Greek), it introduces "the prophets" in the original Hebrew canon of Law, Prophets, and Writings. These prophetic books include the "former prophets"—Joshua, Judges, Samuel, and Kings—since biblical prophets, as God's spokesmen (Exod 7:1–2), enforced their messages using the past as well as the future. Joshua exemplifies historical "prophetic" preaching, in respect of authorship as well as of content.

Joshua's prophetic author is not named; but his statements about the death of Joshua and his colleagues (Josh 24:29–31), plus his allusions to Othniel, the migration of the Danites (15:17; 19:47), and the name Hormah (12:14; 15:30; 19:4) indicate that he lived after the rise of Israel's judges, c. 1380 B.C. (Judg 1:12–13, 17). At the same time, his designation of Jerusalem as Jebusite (Josh 15:8, 63; 18:16, 28) and his writing before its choice as the site of God's temple (9:27), indicate that he wrote before the time of David, 1000 (1 Chron 11:4–6; 22:1). His references, moreover, to Sidon rather than to Tyre as Phoenicia's leading city (Josh 11:8; 13:4–6; 19:28) suggest a date prior to 1200. Indeed, the writer must have been an eyewitness of the events he describes. He speaks, for example, of the Lord's blocking Jordan "until *we* had crossed over" (5:1); he indentifies Israel's previous generation by saying, "they would not see the land that he had solemnly promised their fathers to give *us*" (5:6); he says of the harlot Rahab, "she lives among the Israelites to this day" (6:25); and after outlining their boundaries he addresses Judah directly, "This is [your] southern boundary" (15:4; cf. footnote). Compare also his detailed narratives (2:3–22; 7:16–26) and repeated use of preconquest place-names (15:9, 49, 54). Since the writer follows Moses' Deuteronomic style and seemingly had access to Joshua himself (cf. 5:13–15), a proposed author has been Phinehas, the son and successor of high priest Eleazar, the son of Aaron. He ministered at Peor in 1406 (Num 25:7–13; 31:6–8) and thereafter (Josh 22:13–20; Judg 20:28). Someone, then, of his standing composed the Book of Joshua about 1375 B.C.

Most modern critics, however, attribute Joshua to four mutually contradictory source documents, brought together over a millennium after the time of Phinehas—not such authenticated sources as Joshua's own writings (Josh 24:26) and the contemporary poetry (cf. 10:13), but JEDP documents, as alleged by Wellhausen for the Mosaic writings (see PENTATEUCH), thus making Genesis-Joshua into a "hexateuch." In particular, the "E" and "D" records of conquest under Joshua are rejected in favor of the earlier "J" records, purportedly teaching a gradual occupation of Palestine by independent tribes (cf. Judg 1). But while Joshua does fulfill God's former promises (Gen 13:14–17; 15:13–20), Scripture knows nothing of a hexateuch. The Pentateuchal books of Moses are unique (Josh 1:7–8; 2 Chron 34:14; cf. Christ's own testimony, Luke 24:44), while Joshua forms a sequel to the Law (Josh 24:26), though doubtless accepted on completion as a "prophet," and fully canonical in "the book" (1 Sam 10:25 ASV mg.).

The prophetical character of Joshua, moreover, affects the content in the book's two divisions: conquest (Josh 1–12) and settlement (chs. 13–24). The conquest embraces Israel's entrance into Canaan: Joshua's inauguration, the Jericho spies, crossing Jordan, and ceremonies (1–5:12); the conquest of the center: Jericho, Ai, and the assembly at Mount Ebal (5:13–8); of the south: Gibeon and the Jerusalem confederacy (chs. 9–10); and of the north: the Hazor confederacy, plus a summary (chs. 11–12). But since this took "a long time" (11:18; 1406–1400 B.C., 14:10), the biblical content limits itself to representative instances of rewarded faithfulness. Joshua was commanded to be strong and no one would be able to stand against him (1:5–6; cf. 11:23). Israel's settlement embraces Joshua's territorial apportionments at Gilgal (chs. 13–17) and Shiloh (chs. 18–19), including cities of refuge, Levitical towns, and Transjordan (chs. 20–22). The account demonstrates how God "gave Israel all the land he had sworn to give their forefathers" (21:43). Joshua's two farewell addresses follow, giving Israel that choice that every prophecy elicits: "We will serve the LORD our God and obey him" (24:24).

Bibliography: Carl Armerding, *The Fight for Palestine in the Days of Joshua,* 1949; I. Jensen, *Joshua: Rest-Land Won,* 1966; R. G. Boling, *Joshua* (AB), 1982. JBP

JOSIAH (jō-zī'à, Heb. *yō'shîyāhû, Jehovah supports him*). Son of Amon and Jedidah and the grandson of Manasseh, the son of Hezekiah (2 Kings 22:1). Josiah's reign on the Davidic throne for thirty-one years was the last surge of political independence and religious revival before the disintegration of the southern kingdom that ended with the destruction of Jerusalem in 586 B.C.

When palace officials murdered King Amon in 642 B.C. (2 Kings 21:23) the eight-year-old Josiah was crowned king of Judah. While the boy-king grew to manhood, the imposing international influence of Assyria declined rapidly. Insurrections and rebellions in the East and the death of Ashurbanipal (c. 633) provided an opportunity for a rising tide of nationalism in Judah. By 612 the coalition of Media under Cyaxares and Babylon under Nabopolassar converged on Nineveh to destroy Assyria's famous capital. Within three years the Babylonians had routed the last of the great Assyrian army. These decades gave Josiah the political advantage not only to assert Judah's independence but also to extend its influence into the northern tribes—perhaps even kindling fond hopes of claiming the boundaries as established by David and Solomon.

Josiah's religious leadership ranks him with Jehoshaphat and Hezekiah as an outstanding righteous ruler. Gross idolatry—Baal altars, Asherah poles, star and planetary worship, child sacrifice to Molech in the Valley of Ben Hinnom, astrology, occultism, altars for worshiping the host of heaven in the temple court, and the shedding of innocent blood—all these permeated the land of Judah during the reign of Manasseh (686–642 B.C.), whose personal penitence and reform (2 Chron 33:13) in all likelihood did not penetrate the kingdom of Judah sufficiently to reconstruct the religious pattern. Whatever reform had been accomplished by Manasseh after his release from captivity was countered by a reversion to idolatry under Amon. Josiah gradually reacted to these godless influences that permeated his kingdom (2 Chron 34). In the eighth year of his reign (c. 632) he began to seek after God and four years later initiated reforms. Images, altars, and all manner of idolatrous practices were destroyed not only in Jerusalem and Judah but in the cities of Manasseh, Ephraim, Simeon, and as far north as Naphtali. At the same time offerings and contributions were collected throughout the nation for the restoration of the temple in Jerusalem, which had been neglected for such a long period.

In the course of renovating the temple (622 B.C.) the Book of the Law was recovered. The reformation movement was now stimulated anew by the reading of this "Book of the Law . . . given through Moses" (2 Chron 34:15). Not only had the reading and observance of the law been neglected in preceding decades, but it is possible that Manasseh even destroyed existing copies that were in circulation throughout the land of Judah. Huldah the prophetess warned the people of impending judgment awaiting them for their neglect of the law (34:23–28). Stirred by these developments Josiah led his nation in the observance of the Passover in a manner unprecedented in Judah's history.

With the king himself leading the reformation movement, changes in personnel occurred. Priests serving by royal appointment of former kings and dedicated to idol worship were removed from office. Josiah, however, made temple revenues available for their support (2 Kings 23:8–9). The religious climate established by Josiah must have provided favorable conditions for Jeremiah during the first eighteen years of his ministry (627–609 B.C.), even though no references are made to the association of these great leaders in the historical records (2 Kings 22–23 and 2 Chron 34–35).

In 609 B.C. Josiah's leadership was abruptly ended. In an effort to interfere with Pharaoh Neco's plans to aid the Assyrians, Josiah was fatally wounded at Megiddo (2 Chron 35:20–24). National and religious hopes vanished with the funeral of this thirty-nine-year-old king so that all Judah had reason to join Jeremiah in lamenting for Josiah (35:25).

Bibliography: D. W. B. Robinson, *Josiah's Reform and the Book of the Law,* 1951; C. F. Pfeiffer, *Old Testament History,* 1973, pp. 371–74; J. A. Thompson, *The Book of Jeremiah,* 1980, pp. 59–67. SJS

JOSIBIAH (See JOSHIBIAH)

JOSIPHIAH (jŏs'ĭ-fī'ȧ, Heb. *yôsiphyâh, Jehovah will increase*). The ancestor of 160 men who returned with Ezra from Babylon (Ezra 8:10).

JOT. A corruption of *iote,* an English transliteration of *iota,* the ninth letter of the Greek alphabet and the nearest equivalent to Hebrew *yodh,* the smallest letter in the Hebrew alphabet and almost identical with our apostrophe sign ('). Used figuratively, the jot signifies something of apparently small moment. See Matthew 5:17–18; NIV "the smallest letter."

JOTBAH (jŏt'bȧ, Heb. *yotbâh, pleasantness*). A Levitical city in Judah, just south of Hebron, called Juttah in Joshua 15:55; 21:16. Mentioned in 2 Kings 21:19 as the home of the father-in-law of Jotham, king of Judah.

JOTBATHAH, JOTBATH (jôt'bȧ-thȧ, jŏt'-băth, Heb. *yotbāthâh, pleasantness*). A place in the Wilderness of Paran in the peninsula of Sinai where Israel camped (Num 33:33–34; Deut 10:7). Site unknown. In KJV once Jotbath (Deut 10:7).

JOTHAM (jō'thăm, Heb. *yôthām, Jehovah is perfect*). 1. The youngest of the seventy sons of Gideon, and the speaker of the first Bible parable (Judg 9:5–57). After the death of Gideon, Abimelech, an illegitimate son, got the men of Shechem behind him and desired to make himself a king over Israel. To that end he murdered his half-brothers, all but Jotham the youngest, who hid himself and so escaped. When the Shechemites had made Abimelech king, Jotham spoke his notable parable of the trees and the bramble and pronounced a curse on them and on Abimelech.

2. A man of the tribe of Judah (1 Chron 2:47).

3. King of Judah. He was born a son of Uzziah, king of Judah. Uzziah had been for the most part a good and powerful king, but his successes turned his head and he intruded into the priest's office (2 Chron 26:16). As a result, he was struck with leprosy, and Jotham acted as regent. Jotham began to reign just about the time Isaiah began

Drawing of an impression of a seal ring believed to be that of Jotham, King of Judah. The Seal, from Ezion Geber, depicts a ram; Hebrew inscription reads, "(Belonging) to Jotham." Jotham is described as one "who did right in the eyes of the Lord" (2 Kings 15–22ff; see also Isa 1:1). Courtesy Carta, Jerusalem.

his great ministry (Isa 6:1) and was probably influenced by that godly man, and perhaps by Hosea and Micah also. He had victory over the Ammonites, who were forced to pay him heavy tribute; he was a great builder, fortifying several places in Judah and building the upper gate of the temple. For the record of his life, see 2 Kings 15:32–38 and 2 Chronicles 27.

JOY. In the OT, joy is commonly a group expression, often associated with dancing (Ps 96:11) or the blessings of prosperity (Isa 60:15). God's praise is shouted or sung even in more formal public worship (Ezra 3:10–11; Ps 100:1–2). Linked with this concept also are musical instruments, clapping, leaping, or foot-stamping. Feasting or offering sacrifice (Deut 12:12; Isa 56:7), celebration of harvest or victory (1 Sam 18:6; Joel 1:16), enjoying prosperity or personal triumph (Ps 31:7; Isa 61:3ff.) are all occasions of joy.

In the NT, the word is often found in connection with salvation (1 Peter 1:6), or with eating, drinking, and feasting (Luke 12:19; Acts 7:41). Most often found in the NT, however, are the meanings "to boast, take pride, or rejoice in." Thus, Paul contrasts man's inclination to boast in himself (Rom 3:27) with his right to boast in Christ and his cross (Gal 6:14; Phil 3:3). The NT applies joy to suffering as well as to salvation. When reviled or persecuted or lied about, the Christian is to "rejoice and be glad," knowing that this is traditionally part of the believer's portion (Matt 5:11–12). Joy comes from the Holy Spirit (Gal 5:22).

JOZABAD (jŏz'à-băd, Heb. *yôzāvādh, Jehovah endows*). 1. A man from Gederah in Judah who joined David at Ziklag (1 Chron 12:4; "Josabad" in KJV).

2. Two men of the tribe of Manasseh who also joined David (1 Chron 12:20).

3. One of the Levites whom Hezekiah appointed to be overseers in the house of God (2 Chron 31:13).

4. A chief Levite in the time of Josiah who gave large offerings of cattle to the Levites for Passover offerings (2 Chron 35:9).

5. A Levite who assisted in the weighing of the gold and silver that Ezra and his companions had brought from Babylon as gifts for the house of God (Ezra 8:33).

6. A priest who had married a woman outside of Israel in the days of Ezra, and who gave his promise to put her away (Ezra 10:22).

7. A Levite who had committed the same offense (Ezra 10:23).

8. When the law was read during Nehemiah's reformation this Levite translated it from the Hebrew into the Aramaic so that the common people could understand (Neh 8:7).

9. A chief Levite in Nehemiah's time who helped oversee the "outside work" of the temple (Neh 11:16).

JOZACHAR (See ZABAD)

JOZADAK (jŏz'à-dăk, Heb. *yehôtsādhāq, Jehovah is righteous*). Father of Jeshua the priest who returned with Zerubbabel (Ezra 3:2, 8; 5:2; 10:18). He is called Josedech in Haggai and Zechariah.

JUBAL (jū'băl, Heb. *yûvāl*). Son of Lamech by his wife Adah. He was the inventor of the harp and pipe (Gen 4:21).

JUBILEE (Heb. *yôvēl, ram's horn, trumpet*). According to Leviticus 25, every fiftieth year in Israel was to be announced as a jubilee year. Three essential features characterized this year. First, liberty was proclaimed to all Israelites who were in bondage to any of their countrymen. The law provided that the price of slaves was to vary according to the proximity of the Jubilee Year. Second, there was to be a return of ancestral possessions to those who had been compelled to sell them because of poverty. This, of course, excluded the possibility of selling a piece of land permanently. This law applied to lands and houses outside of the walled cities and also to the houses owned by Levites, whether in walled cities or not. As in the case of the price of slaves, the law made provision that the price of real property was to vary according to the proximity of the Jubilee Year. The third feature of this year was that it was to be a year of rest for the land. The land was to remain fallow, even though it had been so in the previous sabbatical year. The people were to live simply, on what the fields had produced in the sixth year and whatever grew spontaneously. It is impossible to say whether the Jewish people ever really observed the Jubilee Year. SB

JUBILEES, BOOK OF. A Jewish apocalyptic book written in the intertestamental period. It gives a history of the world from the creation to the giving of the law, and defends Pharisaical views against liberal Hellenistic tendencies. See also APOCALYPTIC LITERATURE.

JUCAL (See JEHUCAL)

JUDA (See JODA)

JUDAEA (See JUDEA)

JUDAH (jū'dȧ, Heb. *yehûdhâh, praised*). 1. The fourth son of Jacob; his mother was Leah (Gen 29:35). Few details of his life are known. He saved Joseph's life by persuading his brothers to sell him to the Midianites at Dothan (37:26–28). His disgraceful actions recorded in Genesis 38 left a stain on his memory. He gradually appears to have achieved leadership among his brothers (43:3; 46:28; 49:8–12), and no doubt it was during his own lifetime there arose among them the rivalry that was much later to give rise to the division of the kingdom. Through his son Perez, Judah became an ancestor of David (Ruth 4:18–22) and of Jesus Christ (Matt 1:3–16). The blessing of dying Jacob to Judah (Gen 49:9–10) is usually understood as being a messianic prophecy.

2. The Hebrew tribe descended from the man Judah described above. In the wilderness the tribe camped to the east of the tabernacle, next to the tribe of Issachar (Num 2:3–5). Caleb, a hero among the Hebrew spies and captors of Canaan, was a member of this tribe (13:6; 34:19). Judah was one of the tribes that stood on Mount Gerizim to bless the people at the ceremony of covenant renewal at Shechem (Deut 27:12). After Joshua's death, this tribe seems to have been first in occupying its allotted territory in the southern hill country of Canaan, even to occupying temporarily the city of Jerusalem (Judg 1:1–20). The territory of the tribe of Judah extended from the extreme southern point of the Dead Sea eastward to the Mediterranean, lying south of Kadesh Barnea. Its western boundary was the Mediterranean. On the north, the boundary began at the northern end of the Dead Sea and continued westward in a crooked line, running south of Jericho and Jerusalem (the Valley of Hinnom, which was the southern boundary of this city, was also the Judeans' northern boundary); it continued to the Mediterranean through Beth Shemesh and Timnah. The Dead Sea was the eastern boundary (Josh 15).

Judah was one of the largest tribal territories. From east to west it measured some forty-five miles (seventy-five km.). The north-south dimension of the part fit for intensive habitation was about fifty miles (eighty-three km.), while if the Negev area, suited only for scattered dwelling, was included, the length was one hundred miles (one hundred sixty-seven km.). Judah's territory consisted of three north-south belts of land: (1) the Judean hill country (Josh 15:48), the eastern slopes of which were the wilderness of Judah; (2) the lowlands of Shephelah (15:33)—the low, rolling land where the hill country meets the plain—and (3) the plain near the Mediterranean Sea. The southern part, near and south of Beersheba, was called the Negev. Much of the tribe's land was hilly and rocky, but apart from the wilderness of Judah and the Negev, it was well suited for pasture and for the cultivation of grapes and olives (Gen 49:11–12). In ancient times the hills were terraced.

During the period of the rule of the judges, Judah tended to be separated from the rest of the Hebrew tribes, which were to the north, by the pagan people who lived between them (Gibeonites, Josh 9; Jebusites, Judg 19:10–13), and also by rough and wild land, with deep east-west valleys. The Simeonites, who lived in southern Judean cities, tended to become assimilated into Judah and thus to lose their tribal identity.

Othniel, the judge who delivered the people from the domination of Mesopotamia, was a Judean (Judg 3:8–11). The Philistine threat must have been especially troublesome to this tribe, for the Philistine plain, as it came to be called, was actually Judah's coastal plain land. The account of Ruth and Boaz, which centers in Bethlehem, occurred during the time of the judges and first brought the country town of Bethlehem into prominence in Hebrew history. Saul, whose reign brought the period of the judges to an end, ruled from Judah; and it was the Judeans who first anointed their fellow tribesman, David, king at Hebron (2 Sam 2:1–4).

3. Judah is also the name of five individuals who are mentioned in Ezra and Nehemiah. Three were Levites (Ezra 3:9 KJV; 10:23; Neh 12:8), one a Benjamite (Neh 11:9), and the fifth probably a prince of Judah (12:34). NIV has "Hodaviah" in Ezra 3:9 (cf. footnote). A Judah other than the son of Jacob is also named in Luke 3:30 as an ancestor of Jesus (KJV "Juda").

JUDAH, KINGDOM OF.

I. The United Hebrew Kingdom. Saul, a Benjamite, was Israel's first king (1 Sam 8–2 Sam 1). His reign was not a success, and when he died (about 1000 B.C.), a period of civil war broke out among the Hebrew tribes. Out of this chaos emerged David (2 Sam 1–1 Kings 2), a member of the tribe of Judah, who founded the dynasty that continued to rule in Jerusalem until the destruction of the capital city by the Babylonians (587). David and his son Solomon (1 Kings 2–11) succeeded in unifying the Hebrew tribes and imposing their rule on the whole nation. During their reigns the Hebrews achieved national greatness and their own empire. When Solomon died, all of this came to an end; the greater part of the nation seceded from the Judean rule to form the northern kingdom of Israel. The Davidic dynasty continued to rule at Jerusalem over a small remnant of the nation, the kingdom of Judah.

II. Background of the Divided Kingdom. It must not be thought that the mere ineptitude of Solomon's son Rehoboam (1 Kings 12) caused the split of the Hebrew kingdom. Ever since their settlement in Canaan after the Exodus from Egypt, the Israelite tribes had manifested a fierce independence from each other and a great reluctance to give up tribal sovereignty to a national head. On several occasions during the period of the judges (Judg 8:1–3; 12:1–6; 20:1–48), strife and even open war broke out among the tribes. It appears that the troubled period between the death of Saul and David's move of the capital to Jerusalem (2 Sam 2–4) produced a divided kingdom, with Judah (the southern center of power) adhering to David, and Israel (the Joseph tribes in central Palestine, and the northern tier of tribes) keeping aloof from David, seeking to establish Saul's son Ish-Bosheth as their king. Evidently they felt that accepting David's claims meant giving up too much local autonomy to the central government. After his capture of Jerusalem and the submission of all the tribes to him, David managed to keep the nation together by firm rule combined with a wise handling of explosive personalities. In the weakness of his old age, however, the centripetal forces again asserted themselves (2 Sam 20). Solomon clamped on the nation a firm rule, assessing heavy taxes and forced labor. We infer that Judah was exempt from his most objectionable requirements, a condition hardly likely to please the ever-restless Israelite tribes.

When Solomon died, there already existed an Israelite government in exile, headed by Jeroboam, son of Nebat (1 Kings 11:26–40). He returned to Palestine to confront Solomon's son Rehoboam with an ultimatum—"Lighten the harsh labor and the heavy yoke . . . and we will serve you" (12:1–11). Rehoboam, stubborn and inept, tried to assert force instead of making concessions, and Jeroboam split the kingdom by organizing a secession government in Israel, which ultimately (under Omri) was centered in the city of Samaria.

III. Resources and Organization of the Kingdom of Judah. Rehoboam continued to reign over a small southern region, mainly equal to the territory of Judah. Most of Benjamite territory appears to have gone with the northern rebels (1 Kings 12:20), but Jerusalem, in the extreme south of Benjamin, stayed with Judah because of the presence of Rehoboam's army there, and remained Judah's capital. Thus the boundary between Judah and Israel must have run a few miles north of Jerusalem. All of southern Palestine (much of it desert) was held by Rehoboam. Even so, his territory was not more than half the size of the northern kingdom; his arable land, less than one-fourth as much as Israel's. Judah claimed suzerainty over Edom and asserted it when they were able. Judah's population (estimated at 300,000) was about half that of Israel's. The northern kingdom had the best farm land and was favored with more rainfall than the south.

In spite of her small size Judah enjoyed certain advantages over Israel. She had control of Jerusalem, with its ancient heritage of the temple and its divinely ordained worship, together with the Davidic dynasty and the buildings and traditions of the strong Solomonic empire. Her location in the southern hill country removed her somewhat from the ever-increasing tempo of struggle for control of the road to Egypt by the Assyrians, a struggle that ended eventually in Israel's destruction. She tended to be a city-state (no other Judean city could begin to compete with Jerusalem) with a homogeneous population and strong centralization of authority, thus avoiding the weakness of decentralization that characterized the northern kingdom. The continuing Davidic dynasty (Israel had nine dynasties during the reigns of nineteen kings) and a Levitic priesthood (attached to the Jerusalem temple) were sources of continuing strength.

IV. The History of the Kingdom of Judah. It is difficult to isolate Judah's history. In the biblical sources (the books of Kings and Chronicles) the accounts of Israel and Judah are intertwined, with Israel predominating. One gets the impression that Israel's history is dynamic and attractive, while Judah's existence (except for certain great periods) was conservative—essentially a "holding operation."

This article will not attempt to detail the events of the reigns of each of Judah's nineteen kings. For such details, read the articles in this dictionary on each of these kings. The purpose of this article is to see the history as a whole. Judah's history from the death of Solomon to the fall of Jerusalem to the Babylonians may be divided into three periods:

A. **Judah from the death of Solomon to the mid-eighth century, 922–742 B.C.** During this period of nearly two centuries Judah and Israel lived side by side. For the first two generations the successive Judean kings fought against Israel, seeking to compel her to reunite with the South. Beginning with Jehoshaphat, however, they saw the impossibility of success in this attempt, for Israel was, if anything, more powerful than Judah. Jehoshaphat began a tradition of friendly cooperation with Israel, which, with few exceptions, characterized the Judean kings until the fall of Samaria left the South to carry on alone.

The split of the kingdom at the accession of Rehoboam has been described. Obviously, with this event the Hebrew empire raised by David and Solomon collapsed. Judah was now a second-rate power—a city-state in the hills. As if to prove its degradation, Shishak, a soldier turned king of Egypt, invaded Palestine, seeking to revive the Egyptian Empire. According to the Bible he badly looted Jerusalem (1 Kings 14:25–26); Shishak's own historical inscriptions at Karnak indicate that he sacked most of Palestine. Rehoboam's pathetic copper shields, a cheap imitation of the looted gold ones (14:27–28), symbolize the condition of post-Solomonic Judah—the grandeur had departed.

Rehoboam and his son Abijah (KJV Abijam) seem to have carried on Solomon's syncretistic tendencies; pagan rites flourished. Asa and Jehoshaphat instituted reforms aimed at purifying the worship of the Lord from pagan influence. Jehoshaphat is known for the marriage of his son Jehoram to Athaliah, daughter of Ahab and Jezebel of Israel, thus sealing his new policy of friendliness toward the northern kingdom. This policy seems to have brought great prosperity to Judah, but also the threat that the Baalism sponsored by Ahab in Israel might spread to the south.

Jehoram and Ahaziah were briefly succeeded by Athaliah, who was their wife and mother, respectively. She sought to stamp out all the Judean royal house and to make baalism the worship of Judah. A palace-temple coup resulted in her death (837 B.C.), the restoration of the Davidic line in the person of Joash, the boy king, and the revival of the worship of Yahweh sponsored by Jehoiada the high priest.

Amaziah and Uzziah reigned during a great burst of political and economic prosperity, just before the coming of the Assyrian invasions and Israel's captivity. Judah and Israel briefly occupied much of the land they had under Solomon's reign. Increased trade brought home great wealth. Luxury (especially in Israel) was unprecedented. It was to the spiritually careless people of this time, at ease in Zion, that the great eighth-century prophets—Amos, Hosea, Jonah, Isaiah, and Micah—came.

B. **Judah during the period of the Assyrian Ascendancy, 742–687 B.C.** In the third quarter of the eighth century an event occurred that was to influence all of succeeding history. The Assyrian Empire, with its capital at Nineveh, moved westward in its effort to capture the civilized world. Ultimately Israel, located as she was on the road to Egypt, was destroyed by Assyria (722), and Judah was severely damaged.

King Ahaz first brought Judah into the Assyrian orbit when he called on her to relieve him from the attack of an anti-Assyrian coalition, Syria and Israel (2 Kings 16:7). Judah was saved, Damascus destroyed, and part of Israel overrun by the Assyrians (733–732 B.C.), but at the cost of bringing Judah into the Assyrian orbit. There naturally followed spiritual subordination, and Ahaz introduced Assyrian religious practices into Jerusalem. This problem of imported paganism was to plague Judah until its fall. Late in Ahaz's reign the city of Samaria was destroyed and Israel's national existence brought to an end. Hezekiah, the pious son of Ahaz, sensing a weakening of Assyrian power, sought to throw off both the political and religious yoke of Assyria. Under him, Judah managed to survive the attacks of Sennacherib, although at fearful cost. Hezekiah reformed the national religion, purifying it of paganism. His treaty with the rising power of Babylon, a threat to Assyrian domination of Mesopotamia, although condemned by Isaiah, was another facet of his struggle to keep Judah free. The prophets Isaiah and Micah continued their ministry into this period. Certainly much of Hezekiah's success in religious reform was due to Isaiah's support.

C. **The Last Century of the Kingdom of Judah, 687–587 B.C.** During Judah's last century of national existence Palestine was the scene of intermittent warfare; empires clashed, fell, and rose around her until finally Judah fell to the last Semitic world empire—Babylon. The destruction of the city of Nineveh (612 B.C.) spelled the fall of the Assyrian Empire. It was replaced by the new Babylonian Empire, of which Nebuchadnezzar was the militant head. Egypt still tried to play a part in the political struggle, and her nearness to Palestine made her also a power to be reckoned with in Judah. Placed between great world powers, relying alternately on each but seldom (according to the prophets) on her God, Judah played a fateful, increasingly unsteady role until Jerusalem was destroyed and her people taken captive.

Manasseh, son of Hezekiah, through a long reign chose to submit again to Assyrian political and religious control. His grandson, Josiah, was the last good Hebrew king, and the last one whose reign saw anything like normal times in the Judean kingdom. Josiah's famous revival (621 B.C.), the most thoroughgoing in Judah's history, was aided by the rediscovery of the Mosaic Law (probably Deuteronomy) in the temple (2 Kings 22ff.). Josiah made a great effort to rid Judah of all paganism and to centralize all the worship of the Lord at the Jerusalem temple. This meant rebellion against Assyria, which Josiah was able to carry out; in fact, it was during his reign that the Assyrian Empire disintegrated. Josiah tragically lost his life trying to oppose the forces of the Egyptian Pharaoh Neco, who were crossing Palestine on their way to Syria to fight in the battles that marked the death throes of Assyria.

During Josiah's reign the young Jeremiah began his prophetic career, which extended into the period of the Captivity. A sad man with a depressing message, Jeremiah predicted the fall of the nation because of her sins. Evidently Josiah's revival had done little to stop the downward trend.

Unsettled, fearful times followed Josiah's death. King Jehoiakim, a puppet of Egypt, was unworthy to follow his father Josiah. Jeremiah steadily opposed his easy trust that the temple would bring security. The Babylonians raided Jerusalem during his reign (605 B.C.). Finally the proud, wicked king was killed in a coup, and his son Jehoiachin replaced him. After three months the Babylonians captured Jerusalem (597) and took captive to Babylon many important persons, including the king. This was the beginning of the end. Babylon, having replaced Nineveh as the center of world power, would dominate Judah until she destroyed her.

Zedekiah, another son of Josiah, was made regent in the place of captive Jehoiachin. He rebelled against Babylon, made a league with Egypt, and so incurred the wrath of the Babylonians that they decided to destroy Jerusalem. After a bitter siege of a year and a half the city fell to Nebuchadnezzar and was destroyed, Zedekiah was blinded and carried to Babylon, and the great bulk of the population taken there with him (587 B.C.). Archaeologists have found that all of the cities of Judah were completely destroyed at this time. Thus ended the glorious kingdom of David and Solomon. Observers would have said that the Hebrew nation was annihilated, and indeed, the other nations conquered by the Assyrians and Babylonians did cease to exist. But the prophets proclaimed a better hope for the chosen people. "A remnant will return" Isaiah had said (Isa 10:21), and in time this purged remnant returned and became the basis on which a new Israel would be built.

Bibliography: E. R. Thiele, *The Mysterious Numbers of the Hebrew Kings,* 1951; J. A. Thompson, *The Bible and Archaeology,* 1962; W. F. Albright, *The Biblical Period from Abraham to Ezra,* 1963; F. F. Bruce, *Israel and the Nations,* 1963; C. F. Pfeiffer, *Old Testament History,* 1973, pp. 245–397. JBG

JUDAISM. The religious system held by the Jews. Its teachings come from the OT, especially from the law of Moses as found from Exodus 20 through Deuteronomy; but also from the traditions of the elders (Mark 7:3–13), some of which our Lord condemned. The principal elements of Judaism include circumcision, a strict monotheism, an abhorrence of idolatry, and Sabbath-keeping.

JUDAS, JUDA (Heb. *yehûdhâh, praised,* Gr. *Ioudas*). 1. An ancestor of our Lord (Luke 3:30 KJV; NIV "Judah").

2. A Galilean insurrectionist (Acts 5:37). According to Gamaliel, this Judas perished and his followers were scattered.

3. One of the brothers of Jesus (Matt 13:55). This Judas is almost certainly the "Jude" who wrote the letter by that name. See also JUDE.

4. An apostle of Jesus called "Judas of James" (Luke 6:16), different versions rendering it either "brother of James" or "son of James."

5. One who apparently had a guest-house or hostel in the street called Straight in the city of Damascus and with whom Paul lodged (Acts 9:11).

6. One of the leading brethren at the Council of Jerusalem (Acts 15:6–35). His surname Barsabbas, i.e., "son of Saba," hints that he may have been a brother of Joseph Barsabbas (1:23), who was so highly regarded by the brethren before Pentecost that he was suggested as a replacement for Judas Iscariot. Judas Barsabbas was a preacher ("prophet," 15:32) and with Silas was entrusted with the decrees of the council for safe delivery to the Christians at Antioch. ABF

JUDAS ISCARIOT. The archtraitor, who betrayed the Lord. He and his father Simon were both surnamed "Iscariot" (John 6:71), a word thought to be from the Hebrew *Ish Kerioth,* i.e., "a man of Kerioth." Kerioth is almost certainly in southern Judah (Josh 15:25). Nothing is known of his early life. He may have joined the disciples of Jesus from pure motives and probably showed evidence of business acumen and so was appointed treasurer for the disciples (John 12:6; 13:29), but after his hopes for a high place in an earthly kingdom of Jesus were dashed (6:66), he became a thief. His indignation when Jesus was anointed at Bethany was hypocritical. His pretended zeal for the poor was really covetousness, and is so interpreted by John (12:6), though the disciples of Jesus apparently trusted him to the end (13:21–30). Jesus, however, was not deceived (6:64) but knew from the beginning who would betray him. It was only at the Last Supper that Jesus revealed that one of them "was later to betray him" (6:71). Then Satan entered into Judas; Jesus dismissed Judas; and Judas went out to do the dastardly deed that he had already planned (Mark 14:10). He sold the Lord for thirty pieces of silver, betrayed him with a kiss, then in remorse threw down the money before the chief priests and elders (Matt 27:3–10) and went out and committed suicide. Matthew (27:5) says he hanged himself, and Acts (1:18) says that "he fell headlong, his body burst open." He is always mentioned last among the apostles. ABF

JUDE (Gr. *Ioudas*). Writer of the last of the letters in the NT. Both James and Jude in the opening of their letters show their Christian humility and their faith in the deity of Jesus by referring to themselves as servants of Jesus Christ, rather than as his brothers in the flesh. Beyond this we know of Jude from Scripture only that, like his brothers, he did not believe in Jesus during his earthly ministry (John 7:5) but became his follower after the Resurrection (Acts 1:14). Hegesippus (c. A.D. 110–c. 180) says that two of his grandsons were brought before Domitian as descendants of David, but were dismissed as harmless peasants.

JUDE, LETTER OF. One of the General Epistles included in the earliest-known list (probably second century A.D.) of NT writings, although not otherwise cited or even mentioned by any of the early church fathers until Clement of Alexandria (c. 150–c. 215). It was regarded in the following generation by Origen as "of but few verses yet full of mighty words of heavenly wisdom."

I. Authorship and Date. The opening verse describes the author as "Jude, a servant of Jesus Christ and a brother of James." This may be the same person as "Judas," brother of James and Jesus (Matt 13:55; Mark 6:3; see BROTHERS OF THE LORD). Nothing more is known about him or about his place of writing, nor is precise dating of the letter possible. We do know that the problems it discusses were common during the last quarter of the first century when heresy was increasing.

II. Purpose. Here there is no doubt: The writer is directing to his readers an urgent appeal "to contend for the faith that was once for all entrusted to the saints" (Jude 3). The very basis of Christianity was in jeopardy.

III. Content. Jude goes on to deal with the new heresy threatening the churches from within. What it was, and who its supporters were, is not clear; but we are told something about their appalling lifestyle and its baneful influence on the church. Jude reminds Christians of the inevitability of opposition, of the need for compassion toward sinners, and of the ineffable attributes of God. As he denounces those who would under-

1. A flock of sheep and goats crossing "the great river Euphrates" (Rev 9:14). Courtesy B. Brandl.

2. The Nile at sunset, showing the typical sailboat of Egypt, the felucca. Courtesy D. Tal.

3. Possible site of Sela, in the rugged hills of Edom in Transjordan. Courtesy Garo Nalbandian.

4. The Judean desert, composed of hilly escarpments stretching from the eastern edge of the Judean hills to the Dead Sea. Courtesy Zev Radovan.

5. A view, looking northeast, of the southern end of the Sea of Galilee, with the Golan heights in background. Courtesy Zev Radovan.

6. The Judean hills west of Jerusalem. Historically, this region was the heart of the kingdom of Judah. Courtesy Zev Radovan.

7. The river Jordan, showing the traditional site where Jesus was baptized by John (Mark 1:9). Courtesy Garo Nalbandian.

8. Modern Bethlehem, with the Judean desert and the hills of Moab in background. Courtesy Garo Nalbandian.

9. Panoramic view of Nazareth, looking east. The Plain of Esdraelon is pictured in the background: the hills of Gilboa (right), the Hill of Moreh (center), and the area of Gilead (left). Courtesy Garo Nalbandian.

10. Aerial view of Jerusalem, looking west. The Mount of Olives can be seen in the foreground, the Temple Mount with the golden-domed Mosque of Omar in the center, and a complete view of the walled Old City. Beyond lies the "new" city of Jerusalem. Courtesy Zev Radovan.

11. The Acropolis at Athens, from Areopagus Hill (Mars Hill), as Paul must have seen it. Courtesy G. Nowotny.

12. Ruins along the Appian Way in Rome. The oldest of Roman roads, begun in 312 B.C., is now partly surfaced for modern travel. It must have been used by Paul on his way from Puteoli to Rome. Courtesy G. Nowotny.

13. Locusts (Matt 3:4).

14. Eagle (Rev 8:13).

15. Wild donkeys (Job 39:5).

16. Bird of prey (Job 28:7).

17. Vulture (Lev 11:13).

18. Wild goats (Ps 104:18).

Animals of the Bible. 13. Courtesy Dr. David Darom. 14–18. Courtesy Ofer Bahat.

19. Olive tree (Gen 8:11).

20. Almond blossoms (Eccl 12:5).

21. Pomegranates (S of Sol 4:13).

22. Papyrus (Job 8:11).

23. Hyssop (John 19:29).

24. Mandrakes (Gen 30:14).

Plants of the Bible. Photographs 19–24 courtesy Dr. David Darom.

Daily life in the Holy Land today. Photographs 25–28 courtesy Zev Radovan.
25. Threshing with a crude wooden sledge pulled over the grain by a horse.

26. Winnowing grain after it had been threshed, so that the chaff might be blown away.

27. Baking bread in a *taboon,* a clay-lined oven in which the dough, spread very thin, is placed on a layer of heated pebbles and almost immediately taken out, baked.

28. Shepherdess tending her flocks alongside a Bedouin camp in the Negev.

29

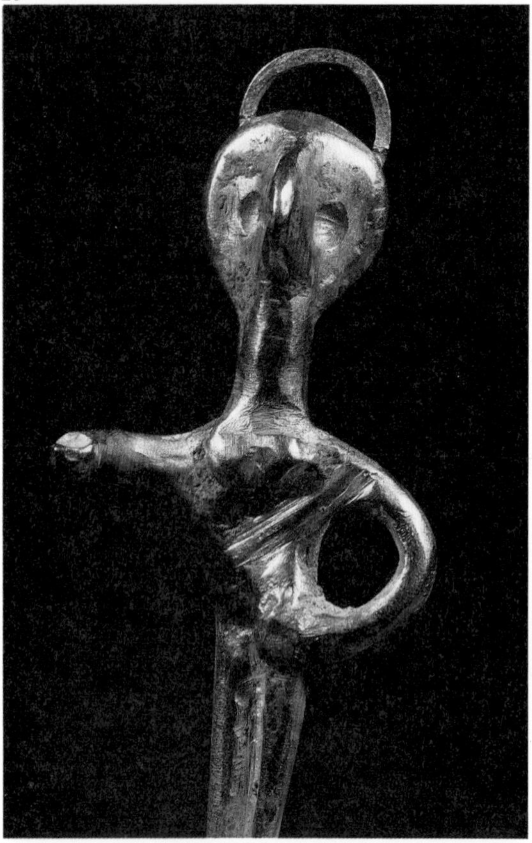

30

29. Rare figurine of solid gold, used as an amulet, 2000–1550 B.C. Photo: E. Lessing. 30. The Ephod, as worn by the high priest, carefully reconstructed according to Exod 28:31–35 and 39:22–26. From *The Tabernacle,* courtesy M. Levine, "Melechet Hamishkan." 31. LBA (1550–1200 B.C.) jewelry, made of carnelian and gold, apparently found in the anthropoid coffins from Deir el-Balah. Photo: E. Lessing. 32. Ivory cosmetic box shaped like a duck, LBA (1550–1200 B.C.). Photographs 29, 31, and 32 courtesy Edith and Reuben Hecht Museum, University of Haifa.

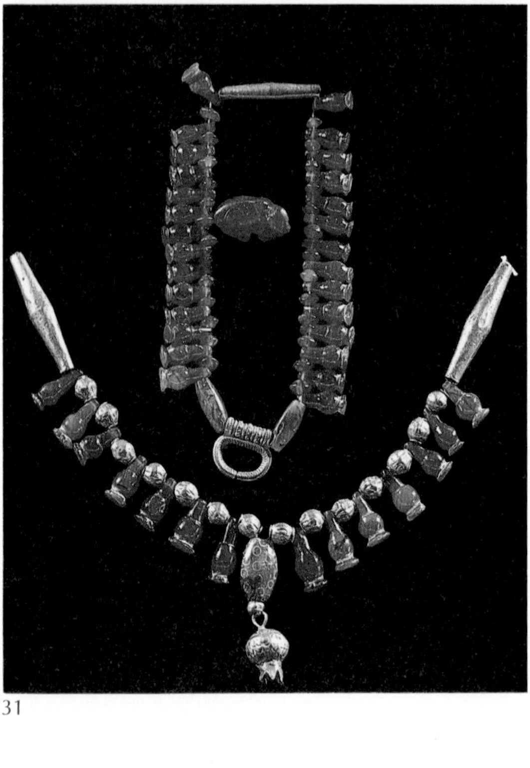

31

32

33. Egyptian.

34. Canaanite.

35. Assyrian.

36. Persian.

37. Greek.

38. Roman.

33–38. Artist's rendition of ancient peoples and their dress, based on scenes from history and monuments. Courtesy Carta, Jerusalem.

39. Scale model of Philistine ship (C. 1200 B.C.), based on wall relief from the temple of Rameses III at Medinet Habu. It depicts his battle against the "Sea Peoples." Collection of The National Maritime Museum, Haifa. Photo: Richard Cleave. Courtesy Carta, Jerusalem.

40. Phoenician warship, a bireme of C. 700 B.C., modeled after a bas-relief from the palace of King Sennacherib at Nineveh. Collection of The National Maritime Museum, Haifa. Photo: Richard Cleave. Courtesy Carta, Jerusalem.

One of Israel's most recent and exciting discoveries—the first ancient boat to be found in the Sea of Galilee, dated from the first century B.C. to second century A.D. and thus popularly called "the boat of Jesus."

41

41. Lifting the shipwrecked boat out of the Sea of Galilee soon after discovery and (42) placing it inside a pool that will be filled with special chemicals to prevent further erosions and to enable archaeological study. Courtesy The Israel Department of Antiquities and Museums.

42

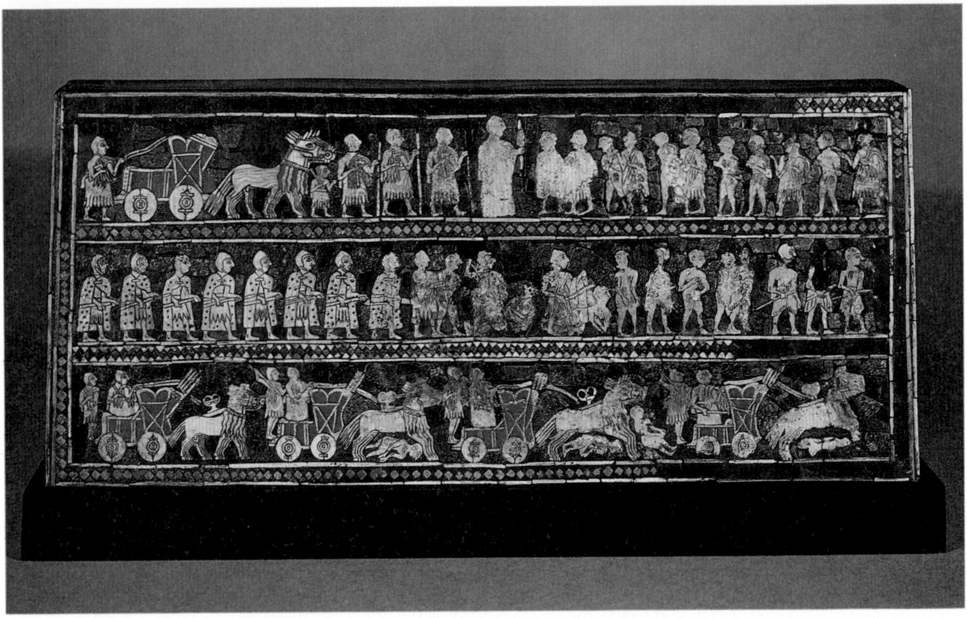

43. War panel from the "Standard of Ur," c. 2500 B.C., showing the triumph of a king over his enemies. Mosaic made of lapis làzuli, shell, and red limestone set in bitumen on wood. Height: 9 inches (23 cm.); length: 19 inches (48 cm.). Reproduced by courtesy of the Trustees of the British Museum.

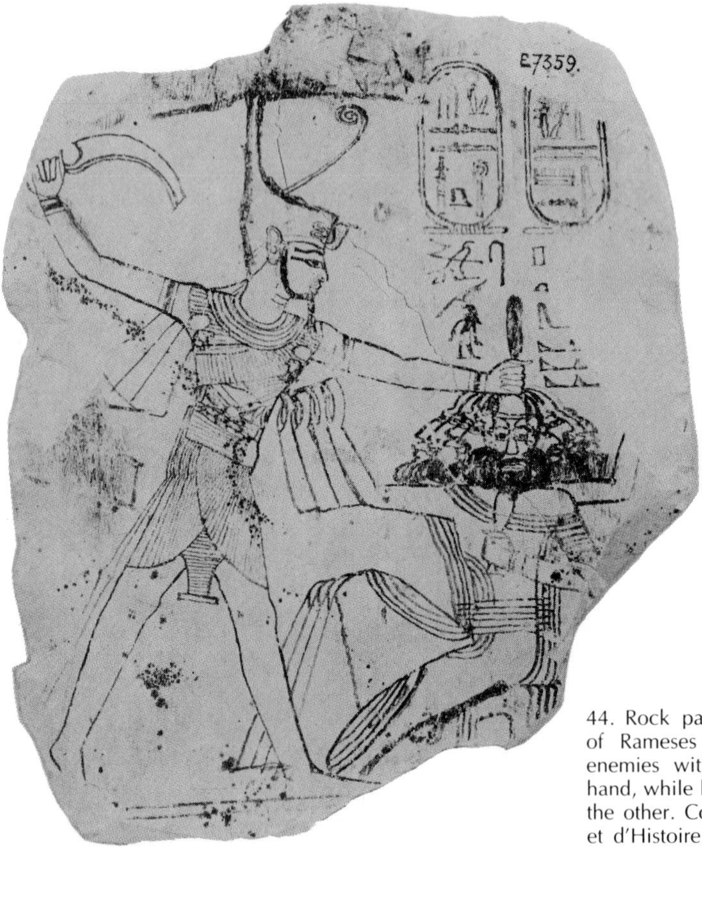

44. Rock painting (c. 1200–1150 B.C.) of Rameses III smiting his Canaanite enemies with a curved sword in one hand, while holding them by their hair in the other. Courtesy Musée Royaux d'Art et d'Histoire, Brussels.

mine the true faith, his voice seems to rise in righteous anger: this was a time for holy intolerance. There is no place in the church for those who divide the people of God (Jude 4–16). The Christian ranks had been infiltrated by "certain men" who held that those who became Christians were no longer under law and could behave as they wished (cf. Rom 6:1–2; 1 John 3:6). Gnostic heretics held that morals and religion were different things, but this teaching misunderstood the true nature of Christian liberty and degraded it to the level of pagan license (2 Peter 2:2). Using the most striking images (rainless clouds, blighted trees, wandering stars), Jude warns against those who pretend to piety but are rotten at heart and leave the trace of the mire behind them. Jude reminds his readers of God's punishment in the OT (Gen 6:1–4; 19:24; Num 14:29, 37) against people, angels, and cities that should have known better, and he leaves them in no doubt that God still punishes sin.

Jude 17–25 exhorts to continued perseverance. There is a reminder that the apostles had foretold the coming of the "scoffers" (cf. 2 Peter 3:3) who love worldly things and sow dissension among believers. Watchful, prayerful, expectant Christians had, however, nothing to fear from such renegades. Jude obviously knew too well the tensions and temptations, the awfulness of sin. He knew that some cases called for stern rebuke, others needed compassion and a right concern. The letter ends with a firm ascription of glory to the One to whom alone it belongs and who will bring his whole family at last, cleansed and complete, into his own presence forever.

Bibliography: R. Wolff, *A Commentary on the Epistle of Jude,* 1960; E. M. B. Green, *The Second Epistle General of Peter and the General Epistle of Jude,* 1968; J. N. D. Kelly, *The Epistles of Peter and of Jude* (HNTC), 1969; R. J. Bauckham, *2 Peter and Jude,* 1983 (on the Greek text). JDD

JUDEA, JUDAEA (jū-dē'á, Heb. *yehûdhâh,* Gr. *Ioudaia*). A geographical term that first appears in the Bible in Ezra 5:8 (KJV, NIV "district of Judah"), where it designates a province of the Persian Empire. The land of Judea is also mentioned in the apocryphal books 1 Esdras (1:30) and 1 Maccabees (5:45; 7:10). Since most of the exiles who returned from the Babylonian exile belonged to the tribe of Judah, they came to be called Jews, and their land Judea.

Under the Persian Empire, Judea was a district administered by a governor who was usually a Jew (Hag 1:14; 2:2). Under Rome, with the banishment of Herod's son Archelaus, Judea became annexed to the Roman province of Syria; but its governors were procurators appointed by the Roman emperor. Their immediate superior was the proconsul of Syria, who ruled from Antioch (Luke 3:1). The official residence of the procurators was Caesarea. This was true during the ministry of Christ. Geographically, Judea was about fifty-five miles (ninety-two km.) north to south and the same distance east to west, extending from the Mediterranean to the Dead Sea, with its northern boundary at Joppa and its southern boundary a few miles south of Gaza and the southern portion of the Dead Sea. Its exact boundary was, however, never fixed.

JUDGE (See OCCUPATIONS AND PROFESSIONS)

JUDGES, BOOK OF. The seventh book of the OT takes its name from the title of the men who ruled Israel during the period from Joshua to Samuel. They are called judges (*shōphetîm,* Judg 2:16), their principal function being that of military deliverers to the oppressed Hebrews.

The book makes no clear claim to authorship or date of composition. Much of it appears to be very old. The Jebusites are referred to as still dwelling in Jerusalem (Judg 1:21). David's capture of Jerusalem about 1000 B.C. (2 Sam 5:6–10) brought this situation to an end. The Canaanites still lived in Gezer (Judg 1:29), a city that first became a Hebrew city at the time of Solomon (1 Kings 9:16). On the other hand, there are also references that cannot be understood except as written at a time well after that of the judges. The thematic "In those days Israel had no king; everyone did as he saw fit" (Judg 17:6; 18:1; 19:1; 21:25) could not have been written before the reign of Saul; indeed, it would be unlikely until a time well after the institution of the monarchy, when the earlier chaotic days tended to be forgotten. The reference to the worship at Dan "until the time of the captivity of the land" (18:30) seems to be a reference to the conquest of Galilee by Tiglath-Pileser III in 733 B.C. It would seem, then, that the book contains very old material, which may well have been edited at a later date. It may be noted that recent scholarship, while holding to a later date for the final editing of the book, emphasizes the historicity of the narrative and its use as the major source for our understanding of the period of the judges.

It is difficult to date the historical period covered by the Book of Judges. It appears to have ended about a generation before Saul became king; thus we may place the end of the book at about 1020 B.C. The date of the death of Joshua, with which the book opens, depends on the date of the Exodus from Egypt, about which there is much dispute. Accordingly, some scholars date the beginning of the period of the judges at c. 1370–60; others, at c. 1220–10; still others, later. At first sight it appears that the book itself gives the answer, for it states the duration of the judgeships of the various judges. A close examination of the text, however, reveals that most of the judges were local, not national in their influence, and it appears likely that their periods overlapped. Further, the frequency of the number forty for the length of their office (Judg 3:11; 5:31; 8:28; 13:1; 1 Sam 4:18) makes it appear likely that this figure is a round number for a generation and not to be taken exactly.

The purposes of the Book of Judges are (1) to bridge in some manner the historical gap between the death of Joshua and the inauguration of the monarchy, (2) to show the moral and political degradation of a people who neglected their religious heritage and compromised their faith with the surrounding paganism, (3) to show the need of the people for the unity and leadership by a strong central government in the person of a king.

In its structure the book falls into three easily recognizable parts: (1) Introduction: the state of things at the death of Joshua, Judges 1:1–2:10; (2) Main body: the judges' cycles, Judges 2:11–16:31; (3) Appendix: life in Israel in the days of the judges, Judges 17–21.

I. Introduction (Judges 1:1–2:10). This section gives a description of the state of the conquest of Canaan when Joshua died. It is a record of incomplete success. The less desirable hill country had been taken, but the fertile plains and the cities were still largely in Canaanite hands. This description does not contradict the record of the conquest (found in the Book of Joshua), which only claims that the Hebrew armies had "blitzkrieged" the whole land, while plainly stating that not all had been possessed (Josh 13:1–6). It was one thing for the Hebrew armies to sweep through the land; it was quite another for the individuals and tribes of the Hebrews to dispossess the Canaanites from the land and settle there. They failed to dispossess them, and this failure meant that the Hebrews lived as neighbors with pagan Canaanites; thus, the way was prepared for the syncretism (combining worship of the Lord with worship of idols) that so characterized the Hebrews during this period. This culture and religion were often largely Canaanite and pagan. This is the reason for the moral and spiritual degradation of the Hebrew people during the period of the judges.

II. Main Body of the Book (Judges 2:11–16:31). Here occur the accounts of the judges, the cycles of failure, oppression, and relief by a judge. The cycle is set forth in the abstract in 2:11–3:6, and the accounts of the judges follow. It will be noted that these men were not principally civil magistrates. Rather, they were military deliverers, who led the people of Israel to freedom against their enemies, and seem frequently to have been singularly unfitted to be what we would today call *judges*. The judges and the part of Israel that they served (when that can be known) are listed here. For a discussion of the principal judges, see JUDGES, THE.

1. Othniel (3:7–11).
2. Ehud (3:12–30): Central Palestine and Transjordan.
3. Shamgar (3:31): Philistine plain.
4. Deborah and Barak (chs. 4–5): Central Palestine and Galilee.
5. Gideon (chs. 6–8): Central Palestine and Transjordan.
6. Abimelech (ch. 9): Central Palestine. Abimelech is considered by many as merely an outlaw and not a judge.
7. Tola (10:1–2): Central Palestine.
8. Jair (10:3–5): Transjordan.
9. Jephthah (10:6–12:7): Transjordan.
10. Ibzan (12:8–10): Southern Palestine.
11. Elon (12:11–12): Northern Palestine.
12. Abdon (12:13–15): Central Palestine.
13. Samson (chs. 13–16): Philistine plain.

III. Appendix (Judges 17–21). The events recorded here seem to have occurred, not after the judges mentioned in the main part of the book, but during their judgeships. They are relegated to the appendix probably because they are narratives in their own right and if inserted in the main body would have marred the symmetry of the judge cycles there. These narratives describe life during this turbulent near-pagan period and give a frank and unvarnished description of the brutality and paganism that Israel was contaminated with because of her close association with her pagan Canaanite neighbors.

The Levite (Judg 17–18) was a priest who could follow his religious practice anywhere. He was hired as a family chaplain and soothsayer, and his presence was certain to bring "good luck" (17:13). He evidently functioned with idols (18:20) and was quite willing to change situations if the change involved a better salary (18:19–20). All of this is in direct contrast to the divine command concerning the priesthood in the Mosaic Law.

The migration of the Danites (ch. 18) was necessitated by their failure to capture the territory assigned to them (Josh 19:40–48; Judg 1:34–36). They then traveled to a northern valley, remote and defenseless, captured it, and settled there. Thus originated the northern Dan, known in the expression, "from Dan to Beersheba" (e.g., 1 Sam 3:20; 2 Sam 3:10; 1 Kings 4:25).

The narrative of the Levite's concubine (Judg 19) casts a livid light on the brutality and bestiality of the times and introduces the war of the tribes against the Benjamites (chs. 20–21). This is not the only intertribal war of the period (8:1–3; 12:1–6). In fact, it is clear that the loyalty of the Hebrews at this time was a merely tribal one, as is the case with the Bedouin until today. There was no real Hebrew nation; Israel was at best a very loose confederation of tribes around a central sanctuary, the tabernacle at Shiloh (18:31).

The cruelty and paganism of the narratives of Judges are often a stumbling block to readers. It should not be imagined that the writer is approving of everything he records. Rather, the book should be viewed as a history of the tragic judgment of God on a people who failed to keep their heritage of true religious faith by assimilating far too much of their surrounding culture. The history of the judges has been called "the struggle between faith and culture." In this struggle, faith lost. And, of course, culture suffered also.

All this should not close our eyes to the beauty of the Book of Judges as literature. Many of the narratives would rank high in any collection of the short stories of the world. Even in the most brutal passages there is an austere dignity. Sin is never reveled in; it is always held up to the gaze of horror. In the pungent words of Jotham (Judg

9:7–15), Judges has preserved almost the only fable in ancient Hebrew literature. The song of Deborah, much studied by recent scholars, has a sonorous quality and vivid narrative power. The narratives of the book are amazingly brief. The Hebrew literary artist was at his best when he used only a few sentences to describe action- and emotion-packed events.

Bibliography: J. Garstang, *The Foundations of Bible History: Joshua-Judges,* 1931; A. E. Cundall and L. Morris, *Judges and Ruth,* 1967; L. Wood, *Distressing Days of the Judges,* 1975; J. A. Soggin, *Judges: A Commentary,* 1981.

JUDGES, THE.

I. The Civil Magistrate. In patriarchal times Hebrew life was organized around the family and the clan. Heads of families ("patriarchs") and elders of the tribes were the judges (Gen 38:24), and their authority was based on custom.

After the Exodus from Egypt, Moses (on the advice of Jethro; Exod 18:13–26), organized the nation into groups of thousands, hundreds, fifties, and tens, within each tribe. Over each unit a qualified man was placed as judge, and only the most important cases were brought before Moses (Deut 1:12–18; 21:2). After entering Canaan, a similar plan of local government was followed (Deut 16:18–20; 17:2–13; 19:15–20; Josh 8:33; 23:2; 24:1; 1 Sam 8:1). During the period of the judges the office assumed a very different character; this will be treated below.

When the monarchy was instituted, the king himself tried important cases (2 Sam 15:2; 1 Kings 3:9, 28; 7:7; Prov 20:8). David assigned Levites to the judicial office and appointed six thousand men as officers and judges (1 Chron 23:4; 26:29). According to 2 Chronicles 19:5–8, Jehoshaphat enlarged the judicial system of Judah with a kind of supreme court at Jerusalem, made up of Levites, priests, and heads of fathers' houses.

The prophets often complained bitterly that justice was corrupted by bribery and false witness (Isa 1:23; 5:23; 10:1; Amos 5:12; 6:12; Mic 3:11; 7:3). Kings were often unjust (1 Kings 22:26; 2 Kings 21:16; Jer 36:26). The case of Ahab's seizure of Naboth's vineyard (1 Kings 21:1–13) shows how far a king could go in getting his own way, in flagrant contradiction of law and custom, at least in the northern kingdom of Israel.

In OT times the judges' activities were not limited to what today would be considered judicial functions. Our present division of powers among the legislative, executive, and judicial branches is a modern innovation. The word *judge* is often parallel to *king* (Ps 2:10; 148:11; Isa 33:22; 40:23; Amos 2:3). In several Semitic languages the term used in the Hebrew Bible for judge (*shōphēt*) is used for rulers of various kinds. This breadth of meaning attached to the term judge in ancient times leads to its extended use in the Book of Judges.

II. The Leaders During the Period of the Judges. From the time of the death of Joshua to the reign of Saul, Israel's first king, the principal leaders of the people were called judges. These men and their times are described in the Book of Judges and in 1 Samuel 1–7. They were charismatic leaders; that is, they were raised up to be Israel's "saviors" by a special endowment of the Spirit of God. It is clear that they were judges only in the broadest sense of that term. In reality, they were principally military deliverers, raised up to save the people of Israel from oppressing foreign powers. Much general information about the period of the judges, together with a complete list of their names and the regions in which they ruled, is given in the article, JUDGES, BOOK OF.

This discussion will be restricted to a consideration of the careers and times of the most important of the judges. The times were most distressing. The period was cruel, barbarous, and bloody. The tribes, scattered in the hill country of Canaan, were divided into many separate enclaves. Even the tabernacle at Shiloh, which should have provided a religious unity, seems to have been generally neglected in favor of the local high places. Only an unusual crisis, such as the crime that brought on the Benjamite war (Judg 19:1–30; 20:1) could bring the tribes to united action. It appears that Judah in the south was unusually isolated from the other tribes.

The first judge mentioned in detail is Ehud, son of Gera (Judg 3:12–30). A Benjamite, he is said to have been lefthanded, a serious defect in those superstitious times. Few if any of the judges are pictured as ideal individuals. The occasion of God's raising up Ehud was the oppression by Eglon, king of Moab, who with the Ammonites and Amalekites (all Transjordanian herdsmen or nomads), occupied the region of Jericho ("the City of Palms," 3:13). After eighteen years of oppression, Ehud led a revolt by killing Eglon when he presented the tribute. The gory details of the deed fit well this violent period. With Ephraimite help Eglon took the fords of the Jordan and killed the Moabites as they sought to flee homeward. An eighty-year period of peace followed.

In the second detailed deliverance narrative (Judg 4–5), the scene shifts from the lower Jordan Valley to the Valley of Jezreel and the Galilee hill country in northern Palestine. The oppressor is Jabin, king of Canaan, who reigned in Hazor and whose nine hundred chariots of iron must have struck terror into the Hebrew tribes, for they had no such machines of war (1 Sam 13:19–22). The recent excavation of Hazor by Israeli scholars has underscored the importance of this Canaanite stronghold, probably the largest city in ancient Palestine. The deliverers were Deborah "a prophetess" (Judg 4:4), surely the actual leader of the uprising, and Barak, son of Abinoam, a fearful man (4:8) who led the Hebrew army at Deborah's urging. The tribes of the Galilee hill country united for this battle, which was fought in the Valley of Jezreel by the Brook Kishon. Evidently a cloudburst upstream caused the Kishon to overflow onto the plains through which it flows, thus immobilizing the chariots on which the Canaanites depended (4:15; 5:20–22). When the army of Jabin was defeated, his general Sisera fled, only to be killed ignominiously by the woman Jael (4:17–22). Deborah's warlike song of praise (ch. 5) is believed to be one of the oldest poems of the Bible and is noted for its rough, primitive vigor. A forty-year rest followed this deliverance.

The third great judge was Gideon (Judg 6–8), the location of whose village of Ophrah is a matter of uncertainty. It was located somewhere west of the Jordan, probably in the region between Beth Shan and Tabor. The oppressing Midianites, desert Bedouin from the Transjordan region, had crossed the Jordan and were raiding in Palestine proper. Gideon is commonly remembered for his doubt and reluctance to take action (6:15, 17, 36–40; 7:10), but it should be noted that once he assumed command he proved a steady and effective soldier (6:25–27; 7:15–24). His ruse, carried out by a mere three hundred companions, frightened the disorganized Bedouin from the Valley of Jezreel into full retreat across the Jordan. Gideon promptly called the Ephraimites to take the Jordan fords and thereby they destroyed the Midianites. Gideon appears to have established some form of regular rule over at least the region of the Jezreel Valley during his lifetime. His importance can be gauged by his rather large domestic establishment (8:30). Adhering to the ancient ideal of charismatic leadership, he rejected the idea of setting up a dynasty (8:22–23). His rule is said to have lasted forty years.

The account of Gideon's son Abimelech and his violent rule over the Shechem area in the central hill country is told in Judges 9. Abimelech is not called a judge, and he appears more as a brigand or political-military adventurer than as a deliverer of Israel from an oppressing enemy. He died as he lived—his skull was cracked by a millstone, and he was finally killed by his armorbearer. Probably his career is described solely to give a feeling of the violent, unsettled state of things during the times of the judges. If that is its purpose, it can be said to have succeeded.

Jephthah, a Transjordanian chieftain, appears next (Judg 11–12) as the deliverer of Gilead and Manasseh (northern Transjordan) from the oppression of the Ammonites—a pastoral people who pressured Manasseh from the south. He is chiefly remembered for his thoughtless vow (11:30–31). While authorities differ as to what was involved in it, it is not unlikely that the vow involved offering his daughter as a sacrifice to God in the event of victory over the Ammonites (11:34–39). If it be objected that this was completely out of keeping with Hebrew religious practice, it may be answered that this only emphasized the extent of the religious degradation of the Hebrews during this turbulent period.

The last of the great judges was Samson (Judg 13–16), with whom the scene shifts to a different part of Palestine—the Philistine plain. It is likely that Samson lived late in the judges period, at the time when a large invasion of the Palestinian seacoast was occurring. The invaders, sea peoples from the Aegean area, had been repulsed in their attempt to enter Egypt (by Rameses III) and had subsequently settled in what became known as the Philistine plain. Samson lived in the Shephelah area that bordered that plain. He was dedicated to a life of Nazirite obedience before his birth. His life was the tragedy of one whose great potential was vitiated through a lack of self-discipline.

Hardly a very religious person, Samson was known for his great strength. He thus became the Hebrews' champion against the Philistines, just as the Philistine Goliath later was against the Hebrews. His failure to discipline his sensuous nature led him into three liaisons with Philistine women. Doubtless each was an instrument of the Philistine lords in their effort to subdue Samson.

We do not read that Samson ever led a Hebrew army against the Philistines. Rather, he made single-handed exploits in Philistine territory, a number of which are described (Judg 14:19; 15:4–5, 8, 15; 16:3). The account of Samson's being subdued at the hand of Delilah is well-known. Killing in his death more Philistines than he killed in his life (16:30), he became at the last a tragic figure. He had judged Israel twenty years.

Eli (1 Sam 1–4) and Samuel (2:12) are also called judges. Although they did do some of the work of the judges described above, it would seem better to regard them as priest and prophet respectively—transitional figures preparing the way for the monarchy. JBG

JUDGMENT (Heb. *dhîn, mishpāt,* Gr. *krima, krisis*). A word found many times in Scripture. Sometimes it refers to the pronouncing of a formal opinion or decision by human beings, but more often it indicates either a calamity regarded as sent by God for punishment or a sentence of God as the Judge of all. Among the more important judgments of God prior to the Exodus are those on Adam, Eve, and the serpent after the Fall (Gen 3), the Flood (6:5), Sodom and Gomorrah (18:20), and the confusion of tongues (11:1–9). God brings judgment to his creatures when they rebel against his will.

In the OT, the relationship between the Lord and Israel is thought of under the form of a covenant. Of his own will, the Lord brought first Noah (Gen 6:17), then Abraham and his sons (15:18; 17:1ff.), into a close relationship with himself. He bound himself to them by covenant and looked in return for their responsive devotion. Similarly, with Israel in the time of Moses, grace reached out to redeem and restore (Exod 6:4) and looked for responsive, loving obedience (20:1ff.). Within the covenant, the Lord pledged blessing on obedience and judgment on disobedience (e.g., Deut 27:1–26; 28:1–68; cf. Lev 26:3–13ff.). The history of Israel, beginning with the Exodus, is the record of a succession of judgments on the enemies of God's people and on his covenant nation when they flouted his will. The "day of the LORD" becomes a day of punishment for all the unjust, even for those who boast of belonging to the people of the covenant

(Isa 2:12; Hos 5:8; Amos 5:18). The purpose of the judgment of God's people is not their total destruction but their purification. A remnant will survive, and this will be the nucleus of the new Israel (Amos 5:15). In the later prophets there are expressions of a hope of an ultimate victory of the divine Judge, of a final or last judgment. Here God's judgment is not thought of so much in terms of his intervention in history but of a last judgment of all human beings at the end of time. Perhaps the clearest expression of this is found in Daniel 12:1–3, where the dead are described as being raised, some for everlasting life, others for shame and everlasting contempt.

In the NT the idea of judgment appears in both human and divine contexts. Jesus warns against uncharitable judgments (Matt 7:1). Paul says that the spiritual man cannot be judged by unbelievers (1 Cor 2:15), and in Romans 14 and 1 Corinthians 8–10 he warns against judging those who are "weak" in the faith.

In the NT judgment is one of the aspects of the coming of the kingdom of God. God's judgment, says John the Baptist, will fall on those who do not make ready the way of the Lord (Luke 3:9). Jesus declares that someday he will come to judge both the living and the dead (Matt 25:31ff.).

In the NT, as in the OT, judgment is an aspect of the deliverance of believers (Luke 18:1–8; 2 Thess 1:5–10; Rev 6:10). God is long-suffering in meting out judgment so that people may be able to come to repentance (Luke 13:6–9; Rom 2:4; 2 Peter 3:9). The notion of judgment, when God will overthrow every resistance, both among evil spiritual powers (1 Cor 6:2–3) and also among people (Matt 25:31–46), will affect all people, because all are responsible to God according to the grace that has been granted them (Matt 11:20–24; Luke 12:17ff.; Rom 2:12–16). This present world will be shaken and destroyed (Matt 24:29, 35), and a new world will replace the present one (2 Peter 3:13; Rev 21:2). God will entrust the administration of this final judgment to his son at his appearance in glory (Matt 3:11–12; John 5:22; Rom 2:16).

See also ESCHATOLOGY. SB

JUDGMENT HALL (Gr. *praitōrion*). Originally the tent or building where the general or governor held council, it (or "hall of judgment") appears five times in KJV (John 18:28, 33; 19:9; Acts 23:35). The Greek term is used of (1) Pontius Pilate's palace in Jerusalem (Matt 27:27; Mark 15:16; John 18:28, 33; 19:9), (2) Herod's palace at Caesarea, used also as the official residence by the governors Felix and Festus (Acts 23:35), and (3) the imperial palace in Rome (Phil 1:13)—"in all the palace" (KJV), "throughout the whole palace guard" (NIV), "to all at headquarters here" (NEB). ASV and RSV use the Latin term *praetorium* or "praetorian guard." NIV has "palace" five times, "Praetorium" twice, and "palace guard" once.

JUDGMENT SEAT (Gr. *bēma, a raised place, platform, tribune*). The bench or seat where a judge sits to hear arguments and pleas and to deliver sentence. Although the word is used principally in the NT in connection with the trials of Christ (Matt 27:19; John 19:13) and of Paul (Acts 18:12), its main association is with the judgment seat of Christ before which all believers will stand (Rom 14:10; 2 Cor 5:10).

JUDGMENT SEAT OF CHRIST (See ESCHATOLOGY)

JUDGMENT, THE LAST (See ESCHATOLOGY)

JUDITH (Heb. fem. of *yehûdhî, Judean, Jew*). One of the wives of Esau (Gen 26:34) and daughter of Beeri the Hittite.

JUDITH, BOOK OF (See APOCRYPHA)

JULIA (Gr. *Ioulia*). An early Christian at Rome to whom Paul sent greetings (Rom 16:15), perhaps the wife of Philologus.

JULIUS (Gr. *Ioulios*). A Roman centurion of the Imperial Regiment (KJV "Augustan band") in whose care Paul was placed for the journey to Rome (Acts 27:1, 3). He trusted Paul to go to his friends at Sidon, and he and his soldiers saved Paul's life and their own lives by frustrating the sailors' plot near Malta.

JUNIAS, JUNIA (jū'nĭ-ăs, jū'nĭ-ȧ). A kinsman and fellow prisoner of Paul (Rom 16:7). He had become a Christian before Paul's conversion.

JUNIPER (See PLANTS)

JUPITER (See ZEUS)

JUSHAB-HESED (jū'shăb-hē'sĕd, Heb. *yûshav, hesedh, mercy has returned*). A son of Zerubbabel (1 Chron 3:20).

JUSTICE (See RIGHTEOUSNESS)

JUSTIFICATION (Heb. *tsedheq, tsādhēq;* Gr. *dikaioō, to make valid, to absolve, to vindicate, to set right*). Justification may be defined as "that judicial act of God by which, on the basis of the meritorious work of Christ, imputed to the sinner and received through faith, God declares the sinner absolved from sin, released from its penalty, and restored as righteous." Expressed simply, it is being placed by God in a right relationship with himself (see RIGHTEOUSNESS). The doctrine is found in Paul's letters, chiefly those to Galatia and Rome.

I. The Nature of Justification. As a reversal of God's attitude toward the sinner because of the sinner's new relation in Christ, justification is (1) a *declarative* act by which the sinner is declared to be free from guilt and the consequences of sin (Rom 4:6–8; 5:18–19; 8:33–34; 2 Cor 5:19–21); (2) a *judicial* act in which the idea of judgment and salvation are combined to represent Christ fulfilling the law on behalf of the sinner

(Matt 10:41; Rom 3:26; 8:3; 2 Cor 5:21; Gal 3:13; 1 Tim 1:9; 1 Peter 3:18); (3) a *remissive* act in which God actually remits sin in complete forgiveness (Rom 4:5; 6:7); and (4) a *restorative* act by which the forgiven sinner is restored to favor through the imputation of Christ's righteousness (Rom 5:11; 1 Cor 1:30; Gal 3:6).

The major emphasis in justification is that it is an *act* of God. It is an act, however, from three perspectives: (1) an act *in process of completion,* as a continuous operation of the work of Christ (Rom 4:25; 5:18); (2) an act *as already accomplished* in the completed work of Christ (Rom 5:16–18; 1 Tim 3:16); and, at the same time, (3) a *state in Christ* to which the justified sinner is elevated (Rom 8:10; 1 Cor 1:30).

Although an act of God, it necessarily leads in the life of the believer to a "walking in the Spirit," "bringing forth the fruit of the Spirit," and "serving righteousness," for the God who justifies also gives new birth and a call to wholehearted commitment. Saving faith leads to faithfulness to God in life, as Paul clearly shows in Galatians and Romans.

II. The Essentials of Justification. Four basic essentials in the act of justification are taught by Scripture. Justification involves:

A. **Remission of punishment,** in which the justified believer is declared to be free of the demands of the law since they have been satisfied in Christ (Rom 4:5) and is no longer exposed to the penalty of the law (6:7). It is more than a pardon from sin; it is a declaration by God that the sinner, though guilty, has had the fact of guilt remitted in Christ.

B. **Restoration to favor,** in which the justified believer is declared to be personally righteous in Christ, and therefore accepted as being in Christ's righteousness. Mere acquittal or remission would leave the sinner in the position of a discharged criminal. Justification goes further in that it implies that God's treatment of the sinner is as if that one had never sinned. The sinner is now regarded as being personally righteous in Christ (Gal 3:6). In this restoration there is not only acquittal, but also approval; not only pardon, but also promotion. Remission from sin is never separated from restoration to favor.

C. **Imputed righteousness of God,** which is granted the justified believer through Christ's presence. Salvation in Christ imparts the quality and character of Christ's righteousness to the believer (Rom 3:25–26). Christ is made the Justifier through whom a new life is inaugurated in the believer (1 Cor 1:30). Paul uses the word *righteousness* to mean both the righteousness that acquits the sinner and the life-force that breaks the bondage of sin. Salvation can never be separated from the participational act of the believer in Christ, in which that one is now regarded judicially as having righteousness because the actual effect of righteousness has indeed come by faith (Rom 3:22; Phil 3:9).

D. **New legal standing before God** in which, instead of being under the condemnation of sin, the justified believer stands before God in Christ. There has been an absolute interchange of position: Christ takes the place of the sinner, the place of curse (Gal 3:15), being made sin (2 Cor 5:21) and being judged for sin; the believer now stands in Christ's righteousness (Rom 3:25) and is viewed as a son (Gal 4:5).

III. The Grounds of Justification. The ground on which justification rests is the redeeming work of Christ's death. The inherent righteousness of Christ is the sole basis on which God can justify the sinner (Rom 3:24; 5:19; 8:1; 10:4; 1 Cor 1:8; 6:11; 2 Cor 5:1; Phil 3:9). It is this righteousness that, in being imputed to the justified believer, is the ground of justification. It declares the believer to have the same standing before God in personal holiness as Christ himself (Titus 3:7).

The instrumental cause of justification is faith, as the response of the soul to God's redeeming grace (Rom 3:28). Faith is the condition of justification not in that it is considered meritorious, but only as the condition by which the meritorious work of Christ is accepted by the sinner. The final ground of justification is the completed, finished, sufficient work of Christ atoning for the sinner in his redeeming work on the cross.

Bibliography: G. C. Berkouwer, *Faith and Justification,* 1954; H. Ridderbos, *Paul: An Outline of His Theology,* 1976; John Reumann, *Righteousness in the New Testament,* 1982; Peter Toon, *Justification and Sanctification,* 1983. CBB

JUSTUS (Gr. *Ioustos, just*). 1. The surname of Joseph Barsabbas, one of the two whom the "brethren" appointed as candidates for Judas' place among the Twelve (Acts 1:23–26).

2. The surname of Titius of Corinth, with whom Paul lodged for a time (Acts 18:7).

3. The surname of Jesus, an early Hebrew Christian at Rome, evidently known to the Christians at Colosse (Col 4:11).

JUTTAH (See JOTBAH)

K

KAB (See CAB; WEIGHTS AND MEASURES)

KABZEEL (kăb′zē-ĕl, Heb. *kavtse'ēl, [whom] God gathers*). A city in southern Judah near the border of Edom (Josh 15:21). It was the home of Benaiah (2 Sam 23:20), one of David's mighty men. In Nehemiah 11:25 it is called Jekabzeel. The site is unknown.

KADESH, KADESH BARNEA (kā′dĕsh bar′nē-a, Heb. *qādhēsh,* from *qādhôsh, be holy*). Also possibly Kedesh (Josh 15:23) and En Mishpat (Gen 14:7). Although there is some uncertainty about its modern identification, it is usually thought to be 'Ain Quedeis, discovered by J. Rowlands in 1842 and rediscovered by J. C. Trumbull in 1881, in the Negev (cf. Gen 20:1), about fifty miles (eighty-three km.) south of Beersheba. This Kadesh should not be confused with Kadesh on the Orontes, the site of the famous battle between Rameses III and the Hittites, presently identified as Tell Nebi Mend (this Kadesh is not mentioned in the Bible, with the possible exception of 2 Sam 24:6 LXX). The first biblical reference to Kadesh is Genesis 14:7, where it is equated with En Mishpat, one of the cities singled out in connection with the invasion by the four eastern kings. When Hagar fled from Sarah (16:7), she was met by the angel of the Lord at Beer Lahai Roi, which was located between Kadesh and Bered (16:14). Later Abraham went from Mamre toward the Negev and lived between Kadesh and Shur (20:1). The primary relationship of the Israelites to Kadesh centers in the period of time that they spent there during the Exodus (cf. Deut 1:46; Num 33:37–38; Deut 2:14). From Horeb (Sinai), via Seir, it was an eleven-day journey to Kadesh (Deut 1:2). Kadesh is described as being in the wilderness of Paran (Num 13:26); it is also said to be in the wilderness of Zin (33:36; cf. 20:1); Psalm 29:8 mentions "the Desert of Kadesh." These references illustrate the overlapping of geographic territories whose precise limits are

General view of the oasis at Kadesh Barnea, the most important place in the desert wanderings of the Israelites. It was also the departure point of the twelve spies (Deut 1:19–23). Courtesy Zev Radovan.

difficult to determine and indicate the character of Kadesh as a border location. When the Israelites reached this place, Moses sent the twelve spies to scout southern Canaan (Num 13:1, 17, 26; 32:8; Deut 1:19–25; Josh 14:6–7). Encouraged by the Lord to invade the land at that time, the people rebelled (Deut 9:23) and were sentenced to the delay in possessing the land (Num 14:34). At Kadesh, Miriam died and was buried (20:1). It was in this area also that the waters of Meribah ("quarreling") were located (Num 20:2–13, 24; Meribath-Kadesh, Num 27:14; Deut 32:51). It seems likely that while the Israelites were in this region they did not stay only at 'Ain Qedeis, which preserves the ancient name of Kadesh, but that they also availed themselves of nearby springs such as Ain Qudeirat and Ain Qoseimeh. Kadesh was also on the west border of Edom and it was from Kadesh that Moses sent emissaries to the king of Edom to request permission for Israel to pass through Edomite territory (Num 20:14–16, 22; cf. Judg 11:16–17). The conquest of the southern section of Palestine by Joshua refers to an area from Kadesh to Gaza (Josh 10:41). Kadesh also is named as marking the southern border of Judah (15:3, 23) and therefore the southern boundary of the land possessed by the Israelites (Num 34:4; Ezek 47:19; 48:28).
CEDV

Ruins of the Israelite fortress at Kadesh, or Kadesh Barnea, in the Negev (1200–600 B.C.). Courtesy Zev Radovan.

KADMIEL (kăd'mĭ-ĕl, Heb. *kadmî'ēl, God is in front*). Head of a family of Levites who returned with Zerubbabel (Ezra 2:40; Neh 7:43). He helped in the rebuilding of the temple (Ezra 3:9). One of his family sealed the covenant (Neh 10:9).

KADMONITES (kăd'mŏn-īts, Heb. *kadmōnî, children of the East*). A very ancient tribe, one of the ten whose possessions God gave to the descendants of Abraham. They lived somewhere between Egypt and the Euphrates (Gen 15:18–21).

KAIN (kān, Heb. *kāyin, smith*). 1. A town in Judah, in KJV spelled Cain (Josh 15:57).

2. In ASV and RSV a tribal name; NIV has "the Kenite" (Num 24:22; Judg 4:11). See also KENITES.

KALLAI (kăl'ā-ī, Heb. *qallai, swift*). A high priest in the days of Joiakim (Neh 12:20), of the family of Sallu.

KAMON (kā'mŏn). A town in Gilead mentioned in Judges 10:5 as the burial place of the judge Jair.

The brook of Nahal Kanah, viewed in foreground. Located south of Shechem, it flows westward to the Mediterranean Sea. Courtesy B. Brandl.

KANAH (kā'nȧ, Heb. *qānâh, reeds*). 1. A brook running from south of Shechem westward to the Mediterranean Sea. It formed a part of the boundary between the tribes of Ephraim and Manasseh (Josh 16:8; 17:9).

2. A city near the boundary of the tribes of Asher (Josh 19:28), probably modern Kana, about eight miles (thirteen km.) SE of Tyre.

KAREAH (kȧ-rē'ȧ, Heb. *qārēah, bald*). Father of Jonathan and Johanan, who warned Gedaliah, the Babylonian-appointed governor of Judah, of his danger (2 Kings 25:23, where KJV has Careah; Jer 40:8–43:5).

KARKA (kȧr'kȧ, Heb. *ha-qarqā'âh, ground*). A place on the southern boundary of Judah (Josh 15:3; KJV Karkaa).

KARKOR (kȧr'kôr, Heb. *qarqōr*). A place in the territory of the Ammonites where Zebah and Zalmunna were resting with the remains of the great army of the Midianites, and where Gideon overtook them and destroyed them (Judg 8:10). Its exact location is unknown.

KARTAH (kȧr'tȧ, Heb. *qartâh, city*). A city in Zebulun given to the Merarite Levites in the days of Joshua (Josh 21:34; also in NIV of 1 Chron 6:77, but see footnote).

KARTAN (kȧr'tăn, Heb. *qartān*). A city in Naphtali given to the Gershonite Levites in Joshua's time (Josh 21:32). Copied in 1 Chronicles 6:76 as Kiriathaim (KJV Kirjathaim), which means the same.

KATTATH (kăt'ăth, Heb. *kattah*). A town in Galilee given to Zebulun (Josh 19:15). Perhaps the same as Kitron in Judges 1:30.

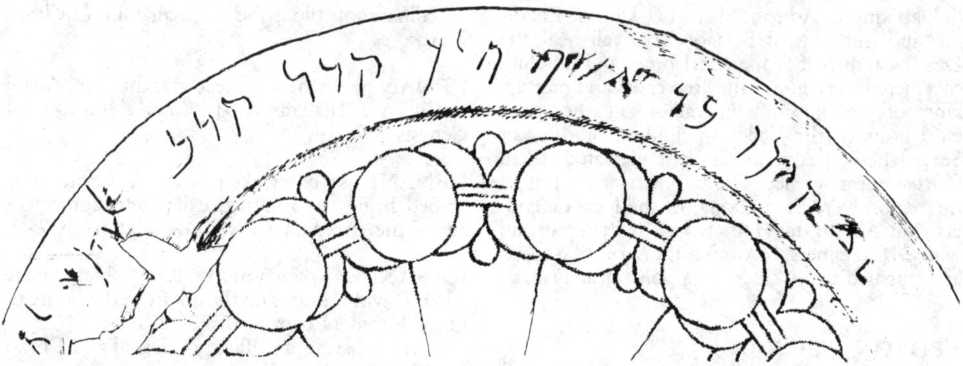

Aramaic inscription found on silver bowl from Tell el Maskhuta (Pithom?) in Egypt: "what Qaynu son of Geshem, king of Kedar, brought [as offering] to [the goddess] Han-Ilat." Late fifth century B.C. Courtesy Carta, Jerusalem.

KATYDID (See ANIMALS)

KEBAR (kē'bär). A river or canal beside which Ezekiel saw visions (Ezek 1:1; 3:23; 10:15, 20, 22; 43:3); in Babylonia (1:3), at Tel Aviv (3:15). It has not yet been identified.

KEDAR (kē'dêr, Heb. *kēdhār,* probably either *mighty* or *dark*). 1. One of the twelve sons of Ishmael, son of Abraham by Hagar (Gen 25:13). These sons were called "tribal rulers." They helped originate the Arab peoples.

2. The tribe that descended from Kedar and their territory. They were nomads for the most part (Ps 120:5; Song of Songs 1:5), raising sheep (Isa 60:7) but sometimes intruding into villages (42:11). The "doom of Kedar," declared in Jeremiah 49:28–33, tells us something of their desert civilization and also of their terror when they learned that Nebuchadnezzar was coming against them. Their territory was in the northern part of the Arabian Desert.

KEDEMAH (kĕd'ē-mä, Heb. *qēdhmâh, eastward*). One of the twelve sons of Ishmael, head of a clan (Gen 25:15).

KEDEMOTH (kĕd'ē-mŏth, Heb. *qedhēmôth, eastern parts*). A place east of the Jordan from which Moses sent a message to Sihon king of Heshbon asking for safe passage through his land (Deut 2:26). It was given to the tribe of Reuben (Josh 13:18) but was later set apart, with its suburbs, for Merarite Levites (21:37).

KEDESH (kē'dĕsh, Heb. *qedesh, sacred place*). 1. A city of the Canaanites conquered by Joshua in his northern campaign (Josh 12:22), later given to the tribe of Naphtali (19:37), appointed as a city of refuge (20:7; 21:32), and given to the Gershonite Levites. Here Barak and Deborah assembled the armies of Israel to fight against Sisera of the Canaanites (Judg 4:6–10); and about six hundred years later Tiglath-Pileser, king of Assyria, conquered the land of Naphtali, including Kedesh, and took their people to Assyria (2 Kings 15:29).

2. A city in the tribe of Issachar, given to the Gershonite Levites (1 Chron 6:72).

3. A city in the very southern part of Judah near the border of Edom (Josh 15:23). Perhaps it is the same as Kadesh Barnea.

KEDORLAOMER (kĕd'ŏr-lā-ō'mûr). He enters the biblical record in Genesis 14 because of his contact with Abram and Lot. Kedorlaomer was king (Gen 14) of Elam, south of Media and east of Babylonia. The nation was named by Semites (10:22) but was inhabited chiefly by Indo-Europeans; later it became part of Persia, modern Iran. Kedorlaomer (KJV Chedorlaomer), with Amraphel king of Shinar (Babylonia), Arioch king of Ellasar, and Tidal king of nations (KJV) or of Goiim (ASV, RSV, NIV), made war with Bera king of Sodom, Birsha king of Gomorrah,

Limestone incense altar, 1000–850 B.C., with four projecting horns, found at Kedesh (Tell Abu Qudeis) inside the chamber of a building that served as a cult place. Courtesy Israel Department of Antiquities and Museums.

Shinab king of Admah, Shemeber king of Zeboiim, and the king of Bela or Zoar, all near the Dead Sea, or Salt Sea. Kedorlaomer and his allies conquered the country they traversed and met the king of Sodom and his allies on the same battleground (the Valley of Siddim, or the Salt Sea) where Kedorlaomer had defeated them fourteen years earlier. The bitumen or tar pits of the region were the undoing of the local defenders. But Abram the Hebrew in a swift night raid with 318 retainers, recovered the spoil of Sodom and pursued the invaders to a point near Damascus.

KEDRON (SEE KIDRON)

KEHELATHAH (kē'hē-lā'thȧ, Heb. *kehēlāthāh, gathering*). A station in the wilderness of Paran where Israel camped (Num 33:22–23).

KEILAH (kē-ī'lȧ, Heb. *ke'îlâh*). 1. A city lying in the foothills of Judah (Josh 15:44). It was threatened by the Philistines, but David rescued it (1 Sam 23:1–13). Abiathar the priest joined him there. The people of Keilah, when faced with the threat of Saul's antagonism against David, would have betrayed David; therefore David had to leave.

2. A man of Judah, descended from Caleb, son of Jephunneh (1 Chron 4:19).

KELAIAH (kē-lā'yȧ, Heb. *kēlāyâh*). Also Kelita, a Levite who had taken a foreign wife in the days of Ezra and gave her up (Ezra 10:23).

KELAL (kē'lăl). A man of Pahath-Moab who put away his foreign wife (Ezra 10:30).

KELITA (See KELAIAH)

KELUB (ke'lŭb, Heb. *kelûv,* another form of *Caleb*). 1. A brother of Shuhah, a Judahite (1 Chron 4:11).

2. Father of Ezri, and superintendent of the field workers who farmed the land in David's time (1 Chron 27:26).

KELUHI (kĕl'ū-hī). One of the sons of Bani who married a foreign wife (Ezra 10:35).

KEMUEL (kĕm'ū-ĕl, Heb. *kemû'ēl*). 1. Son of Nahor and brother of Bethuel, therefore uncle of Laban and Rebekah (Gen 22:21). Nahor had married his niece Milcah, daughter of Terah's oldest son Haran (11:28) who had died before the family left Ur of the Chaldees. Kemuel had a son Aram.

2. A prince of the tribe of Ephraim appointed by Moses to help divide the land of Canaan (Num 34:24).

3. The father of Hashabiah, a leading Levite in the days of David (1 Chron 27:17).

KENAANAH (kē-nā'ȧ-nȧ). 1. The father of the false prophet Zedekiah, who slapped Micaiah (1 Kings 22:11, 24; 2 Chron 18:10, 23). 2. Son of Bilham of the tribe of Benjamin (1 Chron 7:10).

KENAN (kē'năn). A great-grandson of Adam (1 Chron 1:2). Translated "Cainan" in KJV of Genesis 5:9–14.

KENANI (kē-nā'nī, kĕn'ȧ-nī). A Levite who helped bring the returned exiles into agreement about the covenant worship of God (Neh 9:4).

KENANIAH (kĕn'ȧ-nī'ȧ). 1. A chief Levite when David brought up the ark from the house of Obed-Edom (1 Chron 15:22, 27).

2. An Izharite, an officer of David's (1 Chron 26:29). Some identify the two as one.

KENATH (kē'năth, Heb. *qenāth, possession*). A city of the Amorites in the region of Bashan in the kingdom of Og. In the last days of Moses, one Nobah, presumably of Manasseh, went and took it with its outlying villages and named it after himself (Num 32:42). Later the two little kingdoms of Geshur and Aram, near Mount Hermon, took Kenath along with Havvoth-Jair and the surrounding sixty cities in the land of Gilead (1 Chron 2:22–23).

KENAZ (kē'năz, *qenaz, hunting*). 1. A grandson of Esau through Eliphaz (Gen 36:11, 15). He and others are called "dukes" in KJV under the influence of English titles, and "chiefs" in ASV and NIV, but the Arab title "sheik" would give a truer picture.

2. Father of Othniel (Josh 15:17; Judg 1:13; 3:9–11).

3. A grandson of Caleb through his son Elah (1 Chron 4:15), though the Hebrew seems ambiguous here.

KENEZITE (See KENIZZITE)

KENITES (kē'nīts, Heb. *ha-qênî, smith*). 1. One of the ten tribes of Canaan in the time of Abraham (Gen 15:19), perhaps the same as those doomed by the prophecy of Balaam (Num 24:21–22).

2. The descendants of Hobab, the brother-in-law of Moses (Judg 4:11). Hobab visited Israel as they left Sinai, and Moses invited him to come along with Israel and to act as a pathfinder (Num 10:29–32), and he did so. His descendants were friendly with Israel; they went with Judah from Jericho (Judg 1:16) and amalgamated with the tribe of Judah. Later, Heber the Kenite (4:11) separated from the others, moved northward to Kedesh near the Sea of Galilee, and made peace with Jabin king of Hazor. Heber's wife Jael killed Sisera, the Canaanite general, and so fulfilled Deborah's prophecy to Barak that a woman would get the honor for his victory (see Judg 4). Later Saul, sent to destroy the Amalekites, gave friendly warning to the Kenites (1 Sam 15:6) to depart and save themselves, because of the kindness they had shown to Israel more than five hundred years before. David told Achish, king of

Gath (1 Sam 27:10), that he had raided the Kenites, but this was to deceive him.

KENIZZITE (kē'nĭz-īt, Heb. *qenizzî*). A family name derived from Kenaz. One of the ten tribes of Canaan in the days of Abram, mentioned only in Genesis 15:19. No one knows who was the "Kenaz" from whom these Kenizzites were descended; and the tribe disappears from history with this mention. Some think that the Edomite tribe descended from Kenaz, grandson of Esau (36:11, 15), united at least in part with Israel because Caleb of the tribe of Judah (Josh 14:6, 14) is called the "son" of Jephunneh the Kenizzite.

KEPHAR AMMONI (kē'fär ăm'ō-nī). An Ammonite town in the territory of Benjamin (Josh 18:24). The site is unknown.

KEPHIRAH (kē-fī'rȧ). A Hivite town that, with Gibeon, gained the protection of the Israelites by deceit (Josh 9:17). It was in the territory of Benjamin (18:26). Some of its citizens returned after the Exile (Ezra 2:25; Neh 7:29). It is identified with modern Tell Kefireh between Aijalon and Gibeon.

KERAN (kĕ'răn). Son of Dishon, the son of Seir the Horite (Gen 36:26; 1 Chron 1:41).

KEREN-HAPPUCH (kĕr'ĕn-hăp'ŭk, *horn of antimony,* i.e., *beautifier*). The youngest daughter of Job, born to him after his release from the torments of Satan (Job 42:14–15).

KERETHITES (kĕr'ĕ-thīts). A Philistine tribe in southern Palestine (1 Sam 30:14; Ezek 25:16; Zeph 2:5), from whom David drew his bodyguard, commanded by Benaiah (2 Sam 8:18; 15:18; 20:7, 23; 1 Kings 1:38, 44; 1 Chron 18:17). The Hebrew name may be from a root *kareth,* "to cut down," indicating that the Kerethite guards were executioners or at least swordsmen. Twice LXX translates "Cretans" (Ezek 25:16; Zeph 2:5), indicating their belief that the Kerethites came from Crete; and indeed the Philistines originated there. Elsewhere the LXX has *Cheleththi* or *Chereththi* (except 1 Sam 30:14, *Cholthi*). David's guard was probably recruited from foreign mercenaries.

KERIOTH (kēr'ĭ-ŏth, Heb. *qerîyôth, cities*). 1. Kerioth Hezron ("Kerioth and Hezron" KJV), a city in the south of Judah (Josh 15:25), elsewhere called "Hazor" and said to have been about ten miles (seventeen km.) south of Hebron.

2. A city of Moab and, judging from Amos 2:1–3, probably its capital in the eighth century B.C. In "the judgment of Moab" (Jer 48), Moab is pictured as ruined because of its idolatry (48:13) and its pride (48:29), and Kerioth is pictured as under judgment from God (48:24, 41). The city lay in what is now Jebel Druz, nearly south of Damascus and in high country.

KERITH (kē'rĭth). The brook where, at God's command, Elijah hid himself during the first part of the famine he had predicted (1 Kings 17:1–5). It was "before Jordan," "before" being a Hebrew expression (*'alpenê*) that means "toward the face of," of location, "in front of;" usually "east of" (so RSV, NIV), but not always so; hence it is no conclusive help in identifying the brook. Perhaps it was as obscure in Elijah's day as now and therefore a secure hiding place.

KEROS (kē'rŏs). One of the temple servants (KJV Nethinim), some of whose descendants returned with Zerubbabel (Ezra 2:44; Neh 7:47).

KERUB (kĕ'rŭb). An unidentified place in Babylonian territory from which exiles returned to Judea (Ezra 2:59; Neh 7:61).

KESALON (kĕs'ȧ-lŏn). A place identified (Josh 15:10) with Mount Jearim. It lay on the northern border of Judah, west of Jerusalem, NE of Beth Shemesh. It was on the site of modern Kesla.

KESED (kē'sĕd, kĕs'ĕd). The fourth son of Nahor, and a nephew of Abraham (Gen 22:22).

KESIL (kē'sĭl, kĕs'ĭl). A town in southern Judah, near Hormah and Ziklag (Josh 15:30). Its place in the lists is taken by Bethul in Joshua 19:4 and by Bethuel in 1 Chronicles 4:30.

KESULLOTH (kē-sŭl'ŏth). A town in Issachar (Josh 19:18). In NT times this was Exaloth or Xaloth, modern Iksal, SE of Nazareth.

KETTLE (Heb. *dûdh, a cooking vessel*). Mentioned with pan, pot, and caldron, and elsewhere translated by all these terms. Also a basket for carrying clay or bricks (1 Sam 2:14).

KETURAH (kĕ-tū'rȧ). Abraham's second wife (Gen 25:1), she was taken probably after the death of Sarah and the marriage of Isaac (24:67), but she was called his concubine (1 Chron 1:32; cf. Gen 25:6). She was the mother of six sons, ancestors of Arabian tribes (Gen 25:2–6; 1 Chron 1:33).

KEY (Heb. *maphtēah, opener*). An Oriental key was made of wood, with nails or wooden pegs to fit corresponding holes in the bolt holding the door fast (Judg 3:25). Figuratively, a symbol of authority, carried on the shoulder (Isa 22:20–22). Greek *kleis,* "something that shuts" (Luke 11:52); symbolic of the authority given to Peter (Matt 16:19), but which Jesus still retains (Rev 1:18; 3:7); the key that keeps destructive forces (9:1) and Satan (20:1) in the bottomless pit.

KEZIAH, KEZIA (kĕ-zī'ȧ). The second of three daughters of Job born after his great trial (Job 42:12). The name means "cassia."

KEZIB (kē'zĭb). The town where a son, Shelah, was born to Judah (Gen 38:5).

KEZIZ (See Emek Keziz)

KIBROTH HATTAAVAH (kĭb′rŏth hă-tā′ă-vă, *the graves of lust or greed*). The first encampment of the Israelites after they left the wilderness of Sinai. Here they longed for meat and gorged themselves on the quails God sent, dying of the resulting sickness. This explains the name (Num 11:34–35; 33:16–17; Deut 9:22).

KIBZAIM (kĭb-zā′ĭm). A town in Ephraim, assigned to the Kohathite Levites (Josh 21:22). Jokmean appears in its place in 1 Chronicles 6:68.

KID (See Animals)

KIDNEYS (Heb. always in the pl. *kelāyôth,* Gr. *nephroi*). This organ, being surrounded by pure fat, was adapted to burning in sacrifice, when the whole animal was not burned (Exod 29:13, 22; Lev 3:4, 10, 15; 4:9; 7:4; 8:16, 25; 9:10, 19). Slaughter in a war that was a judgment of God was a sacrifice in which the kidneys figured (Isa 34:6). "The finest kernels of wheat" were called "fat of kidneys of wheat" in Deuteronomy 32:14 KJV, ASV marginal note. From their inaccessible location in the body, the kidneys were regarded as the seat of the emotions; KJV, ASV marginal note, "reins"; usually "heart" in ASV, RSV, NIV (Job 19:27; Ps 7:9; Jer 11:20). Once RSV has "soul" (Prov 23:16); ASV, RSV "inward parts"; NIV "inmost being" (see also Ps 139:13). RSV has "kidneys" in Job 16:13, in a literal sense. In the NT, for KJV, ASV "reins," RSV and NIV have "mind," parallel with "heart" (Rev 2:23).

KIDON (kī′dŏn). The threshing floor where Uzzah died for touching the ark (1 Chron 13:9). It is called Nacon's in 2 Samuel 6:6. It was near Jerusalem, but its exact site is unknown.

KIDRON (kĭd′rŏn, kī′drŏn, Heb. *qidhrôn,* Gr. *Kedrōn*). The valley along the east side of Jerusalem, where the Pool of Gihon is located, whose water was brought by an aqueduct into the Pools of Siloam within the walls. South of the city the Kidron joins the Valley of Hinnom near the Pool of En Rogel, and the united valley, Wadi en-Nar, runs down to the Dead Sea. Through the Kidron Valley a winter torrent runs, the Brook Kidron, but the stream bed is dry much of the year. David's crossing of the Kidron (2 Sam 15:23) in his escape from his rebellious son Absalom marked the decisive abandonment of his throne. When Solomon spared Shimei, he warned him that to cross the Kidron would bring him death (1 Kings 2:37). Asa burned idols at the brook (1 Kings 15:13; 2 Chron 15:16), as did Josiah (2 Kings 23:4, 6, 12) and Hezekiah (2 Chron 29:16; 30:14). It is called "the stream" (32:4) that Hezekiah stopped, to deny the attacking Assyrians a water supply. Nehemiah went up it by night to view the state of the walls of Jerusalem (Neh 2:15 KJV, ASV "brook," RSV, NIV "valley"). Jeremiah mentions it in prophesying the permanent rebuilding of Jerusalem (Jer 31:38–40). After the Last Supper, Jesus and his disciples crossed it on their way out of the city to reach the Garden of Gethsemane on the slopes of the Mount of Olives (John 18:1, KJV Cedron). He must often have looked across this valley as he "was sitting on the Mount of Olives" (e.g., Matt

Section of the Kidron Valley in Jerusalem, facing northeast. The three tombs shown are from left to right: the Pillar of Absalom, the tomb of the priestly family of Hezir, and the tomb of Zechariah. All were built during the second temple period. Courtesy Zev Radovan.

24:3; Mark 13:3), and he must have crossed it on his triumphal entry into the city of Jerusalem (Matt 2:1–11; Mark 11:1–10; Luke 19:28–44; John 12:12–19). ER

KILEAB (kĭl'ē-ăb). The second son of David (the first by Abigail) born at Hebron (2 Sam 3:3). Called Daniel in 1 Chronicles 3:1.

KILION (kĭl'ĭ-ŏn). One of the two sons of Elimelech and Naomi, who married Orpah in Moab and died there (Ruth 1:2–5; 4:9–10).

KILMAD (kĭl'măd). A town whose merchants traded with Tyre. It is associated with Asshur (Ezek 27:23). The site is unknown, but perhaps it is modern Kalwadha near Baghdad.

KIMHAM (See GERUTH KIMHAM)

KIN (See KINSMAN)

KINAH (kī'nȧ). A city in the extreme south of Judah, near the border of Edom (Josh 15:21–22), perhaps near Arad (Judg 1:16). The site is uncertain.

KING. A male ruler, usually hereditary, of a city, tribe, or nation. Hebrew *melekh* may mean "possessor," stressing physical strength, or "counselor, decider," stressing intellectual superiority. Some combination of the two ideas probably was in the minds of most people, the latter predominating in better governed societies. Greek *basileus* is of obscure origin, but always denoted a ruler and leader of a people, city, or state. Kings often had priestly functions in the maintenance of the religion of the group, though most of these were separated from the kingly office in the Hebrew monarchy: the king was expected to further religion but not to act as its priest. In the Orient kings came to be regarded as divine beings. This was true of Egypt from the beginning. The idea was taken over by the Greek empire of Alexander and his successors, later by the Romans, after their empire came to include most of the East.

The earliest king mentioned in the Bible is Nimrod (Gen 10:8–12), whose Mesopotamian kingdom was extensive. From this region the kings who warred with kings of Canaan came and were driven off by Abraham (ch. 14). God promised Abraham (17:6) and Jacob (35:11) that kings would be among their descendants. There were city-kings such as Abimelech (20:2), called king of the Philistines (26:1, 8), and kings in Edom (36:31; 1 Chron 1:43) before Israel had kings. Later the Edomites called their rulers dukes, chiefs, or sheiks. Kings of Egypt, the pharaohs, figure in the Egyptian period of Israelite history (Gen 39–Exod 14; Deut 7:8, 11:3); they also appear later when Egyptian influence was strong in Judah. Israel contacted many kings in their wanderings (Num 20:14–33:40; Deut 1:4–4:47; 7:24; 29:7; 31:4) and in Canaan (Josh 2:2–24:12; Judg 1:7–11:25; 1 Sam 14:47; 15:8, 20, 32; 21:10, 12; 22:4). These varied in power from headmen of towns to rulers of large areas.

It is said several times that in the time of the judges there was no king in Israel (Judg 17:6; 18:1; 19:1; 21:25); everyone did what was right in his own eyes. Moses had foreseen that the people would demand a king as a strong human ruler (Deut 17:14–15; 28:36), not content with a theocracy, the direct rule of God as king over them (33:5). Hannah looked forward to a time when there would be a king of Israel who was appointed and anointed by God (1 Sam 2:10). Toward the end of Samuel's judgeship, however, Israel was unwilling to wait for a messianic king and demanded one "such as all the other nations have" (1 Sam 8:5, 22; 19:19, 24; 12:1–25; cf. Hos 13:10). Samuel duly warned the people what to expect of a king, then selected Saul, whose choice they ratified. The reigns of Israelite kings are recorded as follows: Saul (1 Sam 12–31; 1 Chron 10); David (2 Sam; 1 Kings 1; 1 Chron 11–29); Solomon (1 Kings 1–11; 1 Chron 28–2 Chron 9); later kings of Israel and Judah (1 Kings 12–2 Kings 25; 2 Chron 10–36). Ezra, Nehemiah, and Esther deal with kings of Persia.

The prophets (especially Isa 1–31; 36:1–39:7; Jer; Lam; Ezek; Dan) refer to kings of Judah and other nations. Job reflects that in death all are equal with kings (Job 3:14); that God debases kings (12:18); Eliphaz observes that trouble and anguish overwhelm a man like a king prepared for attack (15:24); Bildad says that the wicked are "marched off to the king of terrors" (18:14); Job remembers that in prosperity he was like a king (29:25); Elihu thinks of the fear inspired by a king (34:18) and says that God sets Leviathan as a "king over all that are proud" (41:34). Psalm 2 contrasts the messianic king (2:6) with kings of the earth (2:2, 10). Some references in Psalms are to human kings (Ps 20:9; 21:1, 7; 33:16; 63:11; 68:12, 14, 29; 72:10–11; 76:12; 89:27; 102:15; 105:14, 20, 30; 110:5; 119:46; 135:10–11; 136:17–20; 138:4; 144:10; 148:11; 149:8), some to God as king (Ps 5:2; 10:16; 18:50; 145:1; 149:2). Psalm 24 acclaims the Lord as king of glory. Psalm 45 may have been a marriage song for King Solomon, but its language well suits a messianic interpretation. Proverbs contains maxims for a king's conduct (e.g., Prov 31:1–9). Ecclesiastes and the Song of Songs view a king's life from the inside. Isaiah develops the concept of a messianic king (Isa 32:1; 33:17) identified with the Lord (33:22; 42:21; 43:15; 44:6). Jeremiah refers to God as king (Jer 8:19; 10:7, 10; 46:18; 48:15; 51:57) and to the messianic king (23:5). Ezekiel 37:22, 24 refers to the Davidic king of restored Israel whom the context shows to be messianic. The messianic king enters Jerusalem riding on a colt (Zech 9:9), and God is king (14:9, 16–17; Mal 1:14). Nebuchadnezzar praises the king of heaven (Dan 4:37).

The Gospels speak of kings in general (Matt 10:18; 11:8; 17:25; 18:23; 22:2, 7, 11, 13; Mark 13:9; Luke 10:24; 14:31; 21:12; 22:25) and in particular: Herod the Great (Matt 2:1, 3,

9; Luke 1:5); Herod Antipas (Matt 14:9; Mark 6:14, 22–27); David (Matt 1:6); the messianic king of the Jews (Matt 2:2; 21:5; 25:34, 40, 27:11, 29, 37, 42; Mark 15:2, 9, 12, 18, 26, 32; Luke 19:38; 23:2–3, 37–38; John 1:49; 6:15; 12:13, 15; 18:37, 39; 19:3–21); and God (Matt 5:35). References in Acts are to earthly kings except 17:7, which refers to Jesus. A few references in the epistles are to earthly kings; one is to God (1 Tim 1:17; cf. 6:15). In Revelation, besides earthly kings, reigning and prophesied, Jesus Christ is introduced as prince (ruler) of the kings of the earth (1:5), who made us kings (1:6; 5:10 KJV; ASV, NIV "a kingdom"; cf. 1 Peter 2:9). The king of the apocalyptic locusts (Rev 9:11) is the angel of the bottomless pit. God is king (15:3) and the Lamb is king of kings (17:4). A king sits on a throne, holds a scepter (Ps 45:6), wears a crown (2 Kings 11:12), lives in a palace (1 Chron 29:1), and rides in a royal chariot (1 Sam 8:11). From a few military and civil officers for city-kings and for Saul, the royal bureaucracy rapidly expanded (1 Sam 8:10–18) to the dimensions of David's (2 Sam 23:8–39; 1 Chron 11:10, 47) and Solomon's (1 Kings 9:22; 4:1–28; 2 Chron 8:9–10) establishments. Yet Solomon judged comparatively trivial cases (1 Kings 3:16–28); Ahab shared the personal oversight of his cattle (1 Kings 18:5–6). The Persian monarchy was a vast empire (Esth 1:1). Kings frequently met death by assassination. Among God's chosen people a rightful king was designated by God and anointed by his representative (1 Sam 9:15–16; 16:1–13) with the approval of the people. He ruled by virtue of a covenant between God and his people, to which the king was a party (2 Sam 7). This covenant was extended and renewed as the basis of the NT kingdom of God or of heaven, of which Jesus is sovereign until at the resurrection he delivers the kingdom to his Father (1 Cor 15:24–28). ER

KINGDOM OF GOD (Gr. *basileia tou theou*). The word *kingdom* is capable of three different meanings: (1) the realm over which a monarch reigns, (2) the people over whom he or she reigns, and (3) the actual reign or rule itself. In English the third use of the word is archaic and so is not always given its rightful place in discussion of the term; but in Greek and Hebrew, this is the primary meaning. All three meanings are found in the NT.

1. The kingdom of God is sometimes the people of the kingdom. In Revelation 5:10, the redeemed are a kingdom, not, however, because they are the people over whom God reigns, but because they will share his reign. The same usage appears in Revelation 1:6.

2. The kingdom of God is the realm in which God's reign is experienced. This realm is sometimes something present, sometimes future. It is a realm introduced after the ministry of John the Baptist; people enter it with violent determination (Luke 16:16). John did not stand within this new realm but only on its threshold; but so great are the blessings of God's kingdom that the least in it is greater than John (Matt 11:11). Jesus offered the kingdom to Israel, for they were its proper heirs (8:12); but the religious leaders, followed by most of the people, not only refused to enter its blessings but tried to prevent others from entering (23:13). Nevertheless, many tax collectors and prostitutes did enter the kingdom (21:31; see also Col 1:13). In all of these verses, the kingdom is a present realm where people may enjoy the blessings of God's rule.

Elsewhere the kingdom is a future realm inaugurated by the return of Christ. The righteous will inherit this kingdom (Matt 25:34) and will shine like the sun in God's kingdom (13:43). Entrance into this future kingdom is synonymous with entering the eternal life of the age to come (Matt 19:16, 23–30; Mark 10:30).

3. The kingdom is also God's reign or rule. *Basileia* is used of kings who have not received "royal power" (RSV) or authority to rule as kings (Rev 17:12). Later, these kings give their "kingdoms," i.e., their authority, to the beast (Rev 17:17). In Luke 19:12 a nobleman went into a distant country to receive the crown (*basileia*) that he might be king over his country.

This "abstract" meaning of kingdom is evident in many passages. Only those who "receive the kingdom of God," i.e., accept God's rule here and now, enter into the realm of its blessings in the future (Mark 10:15). When we seek God's kingdom and righteousness, we seek God's rule in our lives (Matt 6:33).

God's kingdom is, however, not merely an abstract rule. The kingdom is God's rule *dynamically* defeating evil and redeeming sinners. Christ must reign as King until he has destroyed (*katargeō*) all enemies, the last of which is death, and that he will then deliver the kingdom to God (1 Cor 15:24–26). Thus, the kingdom of God is the dynamic rule of God manifested in Christ to destroy his (spiritual) enemies and to bring to men and women the blessings of God's reign. Both death and Satan will be destroyed at Christ's second coming to raise the dead and to judge the world.

Jesus claimed that his ability to cast out demons was evidence that the kingdom of God had come among people (Matt 12:28). Furthermore, he said that no one could enter a strong man's house (Satan's realm) and take away his goods (deliver demon-possessed men and women) "unless he first ties up the strong man" (12:29). By this metaphor of binding, Jesus asserts that the kingdom of God has come among human beings to break Satan's power and deliver men and women from satanic bondage.

Thus, the kingdom of God—his redemptive rule—has come into history in the person of Christ to break the power of death and Satan; it will come in power and glory with the return of Christ to complete the destruction of these enemies. Because of this present victory of God's kingdom, we may enter the realm of its blessings in the present, yet look forward to greater blessings when Christ comes again.

We may now define the kingdom of God as the

sovereign rule of God manifested in Christ to defeat his enemies, creating a people over whom he reigns and issuing in a realm or realms in which the power of his reign is experienced.

The diversity of the NT data has led to diverse interpretations. 1. The **Old Liberal** interpretation of Harnack views the kingdom as the essence of ideal religion and altogether a present subjective and spiritual reality, having to do with the individual soul and its relation to God.

2. **Consistent Eschatology.** Albert Schweitzer held that the kingdom was in no sense a present spiritual reality. On the contrary, Jesus taught that (1) the kingdom of God was altogether a future eschatological reality that would come by a miraculous inbreaking of God to terminate human history and establish the kingdom; (2) this apocalyptic kingdom was to come immediately. Jesus' mission was to announce the imminent end of the world and to prepare people for the impending day of judgment.

3. **Realized Eschatology.** C. H. Dodd has reinterpreted eschatological terminology so that it no longer refers to the "last things" at the end of the age but to the "ultimate" realities experienced in Christ. The kingdom of God is the eternal that has broken into time in Christ.

4. **Inaugurated Eschatology** is a mediating view between Schweitzer and Dodd. The kingdom of God is indeed being realized in the present, but there must also be an eschatological consummation. Many scholars follow Schweitzer in holding that Jesus expected an immediate end of the world but modify Schweitzer's view by recognizing that in some sense the kingdom was also present in the person of Jesus. They hold that Jesus was right in the basic structure but wrong in the time of the coming of the kingdom.

Most schools of interpretation—liberal and conservative—believe that God's present reign through Christ in this world has implications for the poor—both the spiritually and the materially poor. This recognition has been a cause of the rise of Liberation Theology (which comes in various forms), which is often the expression of the belief that if God is truly king he must be concerned about the deprived and despised peoples of the world (see Luke 4:18–19).

The importance of the gospel of the kingdom of God for evangelism and social and political service is recognized in conservative circles. There is, however, a debate as to the meaning of the Millennium and its relation to the kingdom of God. Here are four approaches:

1. **Classical premillennialism** teaches that the kingdom of God has to do primarily with redemption. The kingdom was offered to Israel; but when it was rejected, its blessings were given to "a people who will produce its fruit" (Matt 21:43), the church (which is "a holy nation," 1 Peter 2:9). The kingdom now works in the world through the church, bringing to all who will receive it the blessings of God's rule. The return of Christ is necessary for the final defeat of the enemies of God's kingdom and will involve two stages: (1) the Millennium, or thousand-year period, when the glory of Christ's reign will be manifested in history and human society, and (2) the age to come with its new heavens and new earth (2 Peter 3:12–13; Rev 21:1). Israel, which is still a "holy people" (Rom 11:16), is yet to be saved and brought into the blessings of the kingdom, but that will occur in terms of NT redemption rather than the OT economy. This view accepts the basic premise that the OT prophecies are to be interpreted in terms of the NT teaching.

2. **Dispensational premillennialism** looks to the OT for its definition of the kingdom. The kingdom of God is theocratic, not soteriological. It is the earthly Davidic (millennial) kingdom destined primarily for Israel. It does not have to do chiefly with the church nor with the redemptive blessings brought into the world by Christ; rather, it concerns the earthly national blessings promised to Israel. This view believes that God has two plans that must be kept separate—an earthly national plan for Israel (theocratic) and a spiritual redemptive plan for the church (soteriological). The kingdom has to do with the former, not with the latter.

3. **Amillennialism** is a modification of classical premillennialism, accepting its basic definition and structure of the kingdom but omitting the millennial stage. The kingdom is God's redemptive rule in Christ working in the world through the church. It will come to its consummation with the second coming of Christ to inaugurate the age to come. Most amillennialists deny that Israel has any future but see the church as the new Israel, which has experienced the fulfillment of the OT prophecies in spiritual terms.

4. **Postmillennialism** sees the kingdom as the reign of God in Christ through the church, destined to conquer all the world and to establish God's reign in all human society through the triumphant preaching of the gospel. Only after this "Millennium" or Golden Age will Christ return for the final judgment and the resurrection of the dead to inaugurate the age to come.

Bibliography: J. Ridderbos, *The Coming of the Kingdom,* 1962; G. E. Ladd, *The Presence of the Future,* 1974; R. G. Clouse, ed., *The Meaning of the Millennium: Four Views,* 1977; John Bright, *The Kingdom of God,* 1978; John Gray, *The Biblical Doctrine of the Reign of God,* 1979; A. M. Hunter, *Christ and the Kingdom,* 1980; *Evangelism and Social Responsibility: The Grand Rapids Report,* 1982. GEL and PT

KINGDOM OF HEAVEN (See KINGDOM OF GOD)

KING JAMES VERSION (See BIBLE, ENGLISH VERSIONS)

KINGS, 1 AND 2, BOOKS OF. These are named in English, as in Hebrew, by subject matter: They cover four centuries of Israelite kings, from David (his death in 930 B.C.) to Jehoiachin (in Babylon, after 561). They thus provide a sequel to the books of Samuel, which cover the reigns of Saul and David. The LXX actually entitles 1 and 2 Samuel "Books A and B of the Kingdoms" (Latin Vulgate and KJV subtitle: "I and II Books of the Kings"), so that 1 and 2 Kings become, correspondingly, "III and IV King(dom)s." Like Samuel, Kings was written as a unit but was divided in two at the time of the LXX translation, about 200 B.C. In the original Hebrew canon (the Law, Prophets, and Writings), Kings preceded Isaiah-Malachi as the concluding volume of the "former prophets," following Joshua, Judges, and Samuel. For though listed among the "historical books" in English (and Greek), these four works possess an essentially prophetic character (contrast the priestly volumes of Chronicles), employing the events of past history as a vehicle for contemporary preaching (cf. Dan 9:6). Thus, even as Isaiah scanned the future to motivate his people's obedience (Isa 1:19–20), so the anonymous author of Kings drove home lessons, born of previous disasters, "because they had not obeyed the LORD their God" (2 Kings 18:12).

The date of composition is not specified; but the author refers repeatedly to conditions that continued to exist in his day (e.g., the presence of the ark within the temple, 1 Kings 8:8; cf. 9:21; 12:19), indicating that he wrote prior to the destruction of Judah in 586 B.C. (2 Kings 8:22; 16:6; 17:41 are less definite). Even had he drawn on earlier sources (see below), an exilic writer would hardly have penned such words. Threatening *predictions* of the Exile (1 Kings 9:7–9; 2 Kings 20:17–18; 21:14; 22:19–20) fail to invalidate this conclusion. First Kings 4:24 indeed speaks of the western Fertile Crescent as "west of the River," but this phrase had become stereotyped during Assyrian times and does not require Babylonian composition. Numerous stylistic parallels exist between the sermonic portions of 2 Kings 17 and 21 and the writings of Jeremiah. The whole book, moreover, breathes the spirit of Josiah's reform of 621 B.C. Thus, the prophet Jeremiah may well have composed 1 and 2 Kings, in his youthful enthusiasm for the Josianic reformation (Jer 11:8; cf. Isaiah's similar authorship of a biography of Uzziah, 2 Chron 26:22).

Yet the climactic eulogy of Josiah speaks of the fact that there was no king who turned to the Lord like Josiah, either before him or after him (2 Kings 23:25). Verse 26 goes on to assume the Exile (as does 24:3–4); 2 Kings: 25:6–7 describes the Captivity; and 25:27–30, though without awareness of the return in 538 B.C., speaks of events in Babylon from 561 down to the death of Jehoiachin (Jer 52:34). It would appear, therefore, that the final two and a half chapters of 2 Kings from 23:25b on, plus the total years of Josiah's reign in 22:1 must have been added, in Babylon, over half a century after the earlier writing. Talmudic tradition attributes the entire work to Jeremiah (*Baba Bathra* 15a); but Jeremiah seems to have died in Egypt, shortly after 586 (Jer 42–44). It has been suggested that Jeremiah in old age might have been taken to Babylon by Nebuchadnezzar, after his campaign against Egypt in 586 B.C. A more plausible approach, however, would be to suggest that a later Babylonian prophet, such as Ezekiel, supplemented Jeremiah's work (Ezekiel's dated prophecies extended only to 571 B.C., Ezek 29:17); but compare his known dependence on Jeremiah and the stylistic similarity of such sermons as 20:5–32).

In compiling the books of Kings, Jeremiah (?) and his successor utilized written sources: "The book of the annals of Solomon" (1 Kings 11:41) and "the book of the annals of the kings of Israel" (14:19; 15:31) and "Judah" (14:29; 15:7). These chronicles (not to be confused with the canonical books of Chronicles, written in postexilic days) were probably based on court annals, but their contents went beyond what would have appeared in the official records (2 Kings 15:15; 21:17). Second Chronicles 32:32 says that the events of Hezekiah's reign were recorded in both "the vision of the prophet Isaiah," and "the book of the kings of Judah and Israel" (cf. Isa 36–38:8; 38:21–39:8; with 2 Kings 18:13, 17–20:19). Other unidentified sources seemingly provided the detailed biographies of Elijah and Elisha (1 Kings 17–2 Kings 8:15), plus other prophetic narratives.

Recognition of this "two-stage" composition, however, in no way condones the current negative criticism of Kings, divided throughout into conflicting strata (cf. IB, III:10) similar to those of "JEDP" in the Pentateuch. The preexilic stratum, such views allege, was produced by the same prophetic group that "discovered" Deuteronomy in 621 B.C. and is said to be characterized by a tolerance of pre-Solomonic high places (1 Kings 3:4), by faith in the unconquerability of Judah (2 Kings 8:19), and by antagonism against northern Israel (17:21–23). The exilic stratum is then said to manifest opposite attitudes (1 Kings 3:3; 9:6–9; 12:24). But Solomon actually conducted legitimate worship at no high place or shrine outside of Jerusalem (1 Kings 3:15), other than at Gibeon, where rested the Mosaic tabernacle (1 Chron 16:39; 21:29); the northern kingdom obviously possessed both commendable and evil features; and the preservation of Judah never appears as more than temporary (2 Kings 20:19; 22:20).

The teachings of the books of Kings are, however, undeniably "deuteronomic." But since Deuteronomylike phrases appear as often in the quoted words of David as they do in the author's own comments, an unprejudiced explanation must be sought, not in theories of wholesale Josianic forgeries, but rather in the fact of the Mosaic authenticity of Deuteronomy, on which the lives and words of Judah's pious monarchs (cf. Josh 1:7–8) were consciously patterned. For Kings constitutes more than bare history (cf. its relative neglect of the politically significant reigns of Omri and Jeroboam II). A key to its theological aims appears in David's opening admonition: ". . . observe what the Lord your God requires . . . as written in the Law of Moses, so that you may prosper in all you do . . ." (1 Kings 2:3; cf.

3:14; 2 Sam 7:14). Divine retribution is then traced through the history of Solomon (1 Kings 1–11); the divided kingdoms (treated synchronously) (1 Kings 12–2 Kings 17; cf. *IB* 3:6, "a better scheme than most"); and through the history of surviving Judah (2 Kings 18–25). Accordingly, punishment is meted out to sinful Israel (2 Kings 17:7–23) and Judah (23:26–27; 24:1–4), but rewards are also given the righteous in both the northern (1 Kings 21:29) and southern (2 Kings 22:19–20) kingdoms. Hope is even extended into the Exile (25:27–30). Some may disparage the validity of this doctrine but, while admitting that many human acts do not find *immediate* retribution, particularly now when God deals less directly with his people, evangelical Christianity yet proclaims as fundamental to the gospel of redemption the holy theology of Kings, that "a man reaps what he sows" (Gal 6:7).

Bibliography: John Gray, *I & II Kings: A Commentary,* 1963; J. Robinson, *The First Book of Kings,* 1972, and *The Second Book of Kings,* 1976.

JBP

KINNERETH (kĭn'ē-rĕth). 1. A fortified city on the NW shore of the Sea of Galilee (Josh 19:35); modern Tel Oreimeh, meaning *Harp Hill.* Kinnereth means "harp," and the hill on which it stood is harp-shaped.

2. A district in Galilee: "All Kinnereth in addition to Naphtali" (1 Kings 15:20).

3. The sea later known as Gennesaret or Galilee (Num 34:11; Deut 3:17; Josh 11:2; 12:3; 13:27). The sea also is harp-shaped.

El Kerak, identified with Kir Hareseth, situated on a high rocky plateau east of the Dead Sea and south of the Arnon River. Today the hill is crowned by a medieval castle. Courtesy Studium Biblicum Franciscanum, Jerusalem.

KINSMAN (Heb. *gō'ēl, one who has the right to redeem*). Boaz exercised the right of redemption by marrying Ruth and purchasing the property of her first husband's father, a near relative (Ruth 2:20–4:14). In Ruth 2:1 the Hebrew *môdha',* "acquaintance," is used, the feminine form of which can also be used figuratively (Prov 7:4, RSV "intimate friend"). In Psalm 38:11 the Hebrew *qārôv,* is translated "neighbor." Hebrew *she'ēr* (its feminine form means "flesh") is used of an incestuous relationship (Lev 18:12–13, 17; also translated "kin" or "close relative" in 18:6; 20:19; 21:2). Once it is used of a relative who can inherit (Num 27:11). Once *gō'ēl* refers to one who can receive restitution for a wrong done to a dead relative (5:8). In the NT, Greek *syngenēs,* "of the same race," is usually translated "relative" (Mark 6:4; Luke 14:12; John 18:26; Acts 10:24; Rom 9:3; 16:7, 11, 21). The NT meaning is always the broad one of undefined relationship. In the OT, kinsman translates Hebrew words with three distinct ideas: one who has a right to redeem or avenge; one too closely related for marriage; a neighbor, friend, or acquaintance.

See also AVENGER.

KIOS (kī'ŏs). An island in the Mediterranean Sea twelve miles (twenty km.) west of Smyrna, past which (between Mitylene and Samos) Paul sailed on his voyage to Rome (Acts 20:15).

KIR (kûr, kĭr, Heb. *qîr, enclosure, wall*). A place to which the Assyrians carried captive the inhabitants of Damascus (2 Kings 16:9; Amos 1:5) and from which they were to be restored to Syria (Amos 9:7). In Isaiah 22:6 soldiers from Kir are associated with others from Elam, and this may indicate the general direction in which to look for Kir. In Isaiah 15:1, Kir Hareseth is called Kir of Moab, a different Kir. Hebrew *qir* means "wall," hence Kir may refer to a walled town or to an enclosure where prisoners were kept, and may not be a proper name at all.

KIR HARESETH (kĭr hăr'ĕ-sĕth). El-Kerak, east of the southern part of the Dead Sea. The name appears in various forms. It was formerly thought to mean "City of the Sun" but now is interpreted as "New City." It was the capital of Moab when Joram king of Israel made war on Mesha king of Moab (2 Kings 3:4–25) and devastated the country except for this city, which he besieged. When Mesha offered his son as a sacrifice on the wall, the siege was raised (3:26–27). Its later destruction is a subject for serious lamentation (Isa 15:1; 16:7, 11; Jer 48:31, 36).

KIRIATH, KIRJATH (kĭr'ĭ-ăth, kĭr'jăth, Heb. *qiryath, a city*). The word occurs alone (Josh 18:28) where Kiriath Jearim (so RSV) is meant, and as part of other names identified with the same (see Gen 23:2; Num 22:39; Josh 15:60; Ezra 2:25 for examples).

KIRIATHAIM (kĭr'ĭ-à-thā'ĭm, Heb. means *dou-*

Abu Ghosh, about 9 miles (15 km.) west of Jerusalem, the likely site of Kiriath Jearim, once a center of Baal worship, but perhaps best known as the place where the ark of the covenant remained for more than twenty years (1 Sam 7:1, 2). Courtesy Duby Tal.

ble city). 1. A city in the uplands of Moab, given to Reuben, who fortified it (Num 32:37; Josh 13:19). Later Israel lost it, and it became a Moabite town again (Jer 48:1, 23; Ezek 25:9). Around it were plains, Shaveh Kiriathaim (Gen 14:5). It is the modern el-Qereiyat, located east of the Dead Sea, a little south of Ataroth and east of Machaerus.

2. A city of the Gershonite Levites in Naphtali (1 Chron 6:76); Kartan in Joshua 21:32. In northern Galilee, SE of Tyre, el-Qureiyeh.

KIRIATH JEARIM (kĭr'ĭ-ăth jē'ȧ-rĭm, *city of woods*). With Gibeon, Kephirah, and Beeroth, one of four Gibeonite towns (Josh 9:17), same as Baalah (15:9) and Kiriath Baal (15:60); a Canaanite high place and center of Baal worship, first assigned to Judah (15:60); at the SW corner of the boundary with Benjamin, to which it was later assigned (18:14–15, 28). Men of Dan, seeking a new home, encamped west of it in Judah at Mahaneh Dan (Judg 18:12). Here the men of Beth Shemesh brought the ark when it was returned by the Philistines (1 Sam 6:21; 7:1–2); it remained here twenty years until David brought it up to Jerusalem (1 Chron 13:5–6; 2 Chron 1:4; it is called Baalah of Judah in 2 Sam 6:2). Men from Kiriath Jearim were among the returning exiles (Neh 7:29; Ezra 2:25). Men of Kiriath Jearim were listed in the genealogies (1 Chron 2:50–53). The prophet Uriah, son of Shemaiah, came from Kiriath Jearim (Jer 26:20). It is thought by some to be Tell-el-Azhar; by others, Abu Ghosh. Its location must be sought with reference to the other places mentioned, and it must be a high elevation. The name means "city of thickets or of forests," probably sacred groves.

KISH (kĭsh, Heb. *qîsh, bow, power*). 1. A Benjamite, a son of Abiel and father of Saul, Israel's first king (1 Sam 9:1, 3; 10:11, 21). Called Cis in KJV of Acts 13:21.

2. A son of Abi Gibeon, a Benjamite (1 Chron 8:30; 9:36).

3. A Levite in David's time, of the family of Merari and the house of Mahli (1 Chron 23:21–22; 24:29).

4. A Levite and a Merarite who assisted in the cleansing of the temple in Hezekiah's time (2 Chron 29:12).

5. A Benjamite, an ancestor of Mordecai, the cousin of Queen Esther (Esth 2:5).

KISHI (kĭsh'ĭ). A Merarite Levite, ancestor of Ethan (1 Chron 6:44); also called Kushaiah (15:17).

KISHION (kĭsh'ĭ-ŏn, kĭsh'yŏn). A city in the tribe of Issachar, given to the Gershonite Levites (Josh 19:20; 21:28 KJV Kishon; in 1 Chron 6:72 called Kedesh).

KISHON (kī'shŏn, kĭsh'ŏn, Heb. *qîshôn, curving*). A stream that flows from sources on Mount Tabor and Mount Gilboa westward through the

Plain of Esdraelon or Valley of Jezreel, and enters the Bay of Acre north of Mount Carmel. In winter it becomes a raging torrent, which subsides into pools that are soon drained off for irrigation, except that the last few miles are fed from the slopes of Mount Carmel and by tributaries from the north. It is treacherous to cross except at fords carefully chosen. It may be the brook (NIV ravine) east of Jokneam (Josh 19:11). Along the banks of the River Kishon, Deborah the prophetess and Barak led Israel to victory over the Canaanite hosts of Jabin, under their commander Sisera (Judg 4–5). The heavily armed soldiers and chariots that were not cut down by the pursuing Israelites were swept away by the raging Kishon (Judg 5:21; Ps 83:9, KJV Kison). After his contest with the priests of Baal on Mount Carmel, Elijah had the priests brought down to the brook Kishon and killed there (1 Kings 18:40). The stream is now known as the Nahr el-Muqatta.

KISLEV (kĭz'lĕv, KJV Chisleu). The ninth month of the Hebrew ritual year (Neh 11:1; Zech 7:1).

KISLON (kĭz'lŏn). The father of Elidad, the prince of Benjamin in Moses' time who assisted in the division of the land (Num 34:21).

KISLOTH TABOR (kĭs'lŏth tā'bêr). The same place as Kesulloth (Josh 19:12).

KISS (Heb. *nāshaq*, Gr. *phileō, philēma, kataphileō*). A common greeting among male relatives (Gen 29:13; 33:4; 45:15; Exod 4:27; 18:7; 2 Sam 14:33), male and female relatives (Gen 29:11; 31:28), in farewell (Gen 31:55; Ruth 1:9, 14), and before death (Gen 50:1). The kiss had a more formal character in connection with a blessing (Gen 27:26–27; 48:10) or the anointing of a king (1 Sam 10:1). Friends kissed (1 Sam 20:41; 2 Sam 19:39). The act might be a pretense (2 Sam 15:5; 20:9; Prov 27:6). Kissing was an act of worship toward heathen gods (1 Kings 19:18, 20; Job 31:27; Hos 13:2). Righteousness and peace will "kiss" each other; i.e., will unite to bless restored Israel (Ps 85:10). Kisses may be a lure to illicit love (Prov 7:13). The kiss in Psalm 2:12 is one of homage to the king's son. The same Hebrew word *nāshaq* is translated "brushing against" (Ezek 3:13) of the gentle contact of the wings of the living creatures. The kiss was generally given on the cheek, forehead, or beard, though a kiss on the lips is sometimes indicated (Prov 24:26) and is probable (in Song of Songs 1:2; 8:1). In the NT the Greek verb *phileō* is usually translated "love," but when associated with the strengthened form *kataphileō*, "kiss repeatedly, effusively," it is translated "kiss," and the noun *philēma* is always so translated. Once Jesus' host did not give him this customary greeting, but a sinful woman kissed his feet (Luke 7:38, 45). The father kissed the returning prodigal (15:20). Judas kissed Jesus as a sign to the temple police (Matt 26:48–49; Mark 14:44–45; Luke 22:47–48). The Ephesian elders kissed Paul in farewell (Acts 20:37). The kiss was adopted as a formal greeting among believers, the holy kiss (Rom 16:16; 1 Cor 16:20; 2 Cor 13:12; 1 Thess 5:26) or kiss of charity or love (1 Peter 5:14), given by men to men and by women to women.

KITE (See BIRDS)

KITLISH (kĭt'lĭsh). A town in the lowland of the territory of Judah (Josh 15:40). ASV and RSV have Chitlish. The site is unknown.

KITRON (kĭt'rŏn). A town in the territory of Zebulun, whose inhabitants that tribe did not drive out (Judg 1:30).

KITTIM (kĭt'ĭm, Heb. *kittîm*). 1. Descendants of Javan (Gen 10:4; 1 Chron 1:7).

2. The island of Cyprus is probably meant in Isaiah 23:1, 12; and Ezekiel 27:6 (see footnotes; KJV "Chittim"). Invasion from that direction was expected to help topple the Assyrian Empire. The word can characterize ships of Grecian pattern (Num 24:24), which roamed the Mediterranean very early (see also Dan 11:30 and footnote). Many think that the reference in Daniel is to the Roman fleet; even so, the Romans owed much to Greek naval architecture.

KNEADING TROUGH. A dish in which dough was prepared to be made into bread. The plague of frogs infested them in Egypt (Exod 8:3). The Israelites bound their kneeding troughs, dough and all, in the bundles of clothing on their backs, when they escaped from Egypt (12:34). They are called "kneading bowls" in RSV. KJV has "store" for the same Hebrew word where ASV, RSV, NIV have "kneading trough" (Deut 28:5, 17).

Clay figurine that shows the kneading of dough in a trough, from cemetery at Aczib (mentioned in Josh. 19:29–31), ninth-early sixth century B.C. Courtesy Israel Department of Antiquities and Museums.

KNEE (Heb. *berekh,* Gr. *gonu*). The first references are to taking on the knees in token of adoption (Gen 30:3 KJV; 48:12; 50:23). The knees are equivalent to the lap (Judg 16:19; 2 Kings 4:20; Job 3:12). Their strength or weakness is commented on (Job 4:14; Ps 109:24; Heb 12:12). Gideon rejected men who knelt to drink (Judg 7:5–6). Diseased knees follow disobedience (Deut 28:35). Knees knock and give way in fear (Dan 5:6; Nah 2:10). Daniel was set trembling on hands and knees (Dan 10:10). To bow the knee to Baal identified one as his worshiper (1 Kings 19:18; Rom 11:4). Kneeling expressed homage or worship (2 Kings 1:13, to Elisha; Matt 17:14; Mark 1:40; 10:17; Luke 5:8, to Jesus; 1 Kings 8:54; 2 Chron 6:13; Ezra 9:3; Rom 14:11 quoting Isa 45:23; Acts 7:60; 9:40; 20:36; 21:5; Eph 3:14; Phil 2:10, to God in prayer; notably Luke 22:41, Jesus in Gethsemane; Dan 6:10 shows that kneeling in prayer was already a customary practice). Kneeling in mockery is related in Mark 15:19.

Bronze statuette from Ashkelon (c. fourth century B.C.) of a kneeling priest with hands raised. Courtesy Israel Department of Antiquities and Museums.

KNIFE. 1. Hebrew *herev,* usually "sword," occasionally some other tool with a cutting edge. The "flint knives" used in circumcision (Josh 5:2–3) were kept for religious purposes long after bronze and iron were introduced; the priests of Baal cut themselves with "swords" (RSV, NIV) in their contest with Elijah (1 Kings 18:28). "A sharp sword" (ASV, RSV, NIV) was sometimes used as a razor (Ezek 5:1–2).

2. Hebrew *ma'ăkheleth,* a knife used to carve sacrifices (Gen 22:6, 10; Judg 19:29; figuratively, Prov 30:14).

3. Hebrew *sakkîn,* knife (Prov 23:2).

4. Hebrew *mahălāph* (Ezra 1:9); named among temple vessels taken from Jerusalem as spoils, and returned after the Exile, were twenty-nine knives (KJV, ASV), which RSV calls "censers" and NIV "silver pans." The meaning is uncertain. A "scribe's knive" (Jer 36:23) was used to sharpen reed pens. Knives were not used for eating. Meat was cut into small pieces before serving, and bread was broken at the table. The Philistines had metal knives long before they came into general use in Israel (see 1 Sam 13:19, 22).

KOA (kō'à). A people east of the Tigris, between Elam and Media, named with the Babylonians, Chaldeans, Assyrians, Pekod, and Shoa as about to invade Judah (Ezek 23:23).

KOHATH, KOHATHITES (kō'hăth, -īts). Second son of Levi (Gen 46:11), ancestor of Moses (Exod 6:16–20; Num 3:17, 19; 1 Chron 6:1–3). His descendants, the Kohathites, one of three divisions of the Levites, comprised four families (Num 3:17–20, 27–31). They camped south of the tabernacle. Numbering 8,600, on duty they cared for the ark, table, lampstand, altars, and vessels of the sanctuary. These they carried on foot, no wagons being assigned them (7:8–9). Joshua allotted them twenty-three cities (Josh 21:4–5). Under the monarchy they were prominent (1 Chron 23:13–20; 24:20–25), especially Heman in the service of song (6:33ff.; 16:41ff.; 25:1ff.). They took part in the religious service the day before Jehoshaphat's victory over his allied enemies (2 Chron 20:19); and they assisted in Hezekiah's cleansing of the temple (29:12–19).

KOLAIAH (kō-lā'yà, Heb. *qôlāyâh, voice of Jehovah*). 1. A Benjamite who settled in Jerusalem after the Captivity (Neh 11:7).

2. The father of the false prophet Ahab, who suffered death for his false prophecies (Jer 29:21).

KORAH, KORAHITE (kō'rà, -īt, Heb. *qōrah*). 1. A son of Esau (Gen 36:5, 14, 18; 1 Chron 1:35). One of his descendants.

2. A grandson of Esau, nephew of no. 1 (Gen 36:16).

3. A descendant of Caleb (1 Chron 2:43).

4. A son of Izhar, the son of Kohath, the son of Levi (Exod 6:21, 24; 1 Chron 6:37; 9:19). He led a rebellion, with two companions, resisting the civil authority of Moses (Num 16; 26:9–11;

Ruins of a 3rd–4th century A.D. synagogue at Korazin, similar in style to that found at Capernaum. Courtesy Zev Radovan.

27:3; Jude 11, KJV Core). For refusing to appear before him as commanded, Korah, Dathan, and Abiram and their followers were swallowed up by the earth, but the children of Korah were spared (Num 26:11). The two hundred fifty rebellious Levites were also consumed by fire from the Lord. From him descended the Korahites, who were doorkeepers and musicians in the tabernacle and temple (Exod 6:24; 1 Chron 6:22). The Korahites (KJV also Korhites, Korathites) are mentioned in several passages (Exod 6:24; Num 26:58; 1 Chron 9:19, 31, 12:6, 26:1; 2 Chron 20:19). The sons of Korah are named in the titles of Psalms 42, 44–49, 84, 85, 87, and 88.

KORAZIN (kō-rā'zĭn). Modern Khirbet Kerăzeh, ruins about two miles (three km.) north of Tell hŭm, the site of Capernaum. Korazin is mentioned only in the woes Christ pronounced on it (Matt. 11:21; Luke 10:13). His condemnation of this town, together with Bethsaida and Capernaum, indicates that it must have been an important center. It was no longer inhabited by the time of Eusebius (the latter half of the third century). Only a few carved stones remain today.

KORE (kō'rē). 1. A Korahite whose son, Shallum, was a tabernacle gatekeeper (1 Chron 9:19; 26:1, 19).

2. A Levite, son of Imnah, set over the freewill offerings in Hezekiah's time (2 Chron 31:14).

KOZ (kōz). A son of Helah of the tribe of Judah (1 Chron 4:8).

KUE (ku'ī). An ancient name for Cilicia. Solomon imported horses from this place (1 Kings 10:28; 2 Chron 1:16; cf. footnotes).

KUSHAIAH (kū-shā'yȧ). A Levite of the family of Merari (1 Chron 15:17). Called Kishi in 1 Chronicles 6:44.

L

LAADAH (lā′à-dà). A man of Judah of the family of Shelah (1 Chron 4:21), the progenitor of the inhabitants of Mareshah.

LAADAN (See LADAN)

LABAN (lā′băn, Heb. *lāvān, white*). 1. The nephew of Abraham who lived in Haran on a tributary of the Euphrates River in Mesopotamia. He belonged to that branch of the family of Terah (Abraham's father) that came from Abraham's brother Nahor and his niece Milcah (Gen 22:22–24), and is first mentioned as Rebekah's brother when she is introduced (24:29). In ancient Semitic custom, the brother was the guardian of the sister, and thus Laban takes a prominent place in the account of Rebekah's leaving for Canaan to be Isaac's bride. His grasping nature is hinted at in Genesis 24:30–31, where his invitation to Abraham's servant follows immediately after his appraisal of the servant's expensively equipped party.

Laban's later history is interwoven with Jacob's. When Jacob fled from the anger of his brother Esau, he settled in his uncle Laban's house in Haran and stayed there twenty years. The relationship between Laban and his nephew is an interesting one. Both appear to be resourceful, often grasping men, each eager to best the other in every transaction. Even in the circumstances surrounding the marriage of Jacob to Laban's daughters Rachel and Leah (Gen 29), this competition is evident. After Jacob had served fourteen years for his brides, there followed six more years in Haran during which, according to Jacob's testimony, Laban changed his wages ten times (31:41). The famous contract involving the speckled and spotted sheep (30:31–43) was evidently one of the ten.

At the end of the twenty years, Jacob quietly stole away from Laban, taking his now-large family with him to Canaan (Gen 31). Pursuing him, Laban overtook him in Gilead. After mutual protestations and incriminations, uncle and nephew parted, after erecting a "witness heap"—a kind of dividing line—between them. Laban is here called "the Aramean" (31:24), and he gives the heap an Aramaic name ("Jegar Sahadutha"), while Jacob calls it by its Hebrew equivalent "Galeed" (Gen 31:47–48), both meaning "witness heap."

These Aramaic references are interesting guides in the quest for better understanding of the origins of the patriarchs. In an old confession the Hebrews were taught to say, "My father was a wandering Aramean" (Deut 26:5). It seems likely that the patriarchal ancestors of the Hebrews sprang from a mixed Semitic stock in NE Mesopotamia, among which the Aramean was a prominent strain.

2. Laban is also the name of an unidentified place in the Plains of Moab, or perhaps in the Sinai peninsula (Deut 1:1). JBG

LABOR. The noun is today confined to the abstract use—the act of laboring (Gen 31:42; Rom 16:6). Formerly it expressed also the fruit of labor, as in Exodus 23:16, "When thou hast gathered in thy labours out of the field," or John 4:38, "Ye are entered into their labours" (both KJV). The word is used also of labor in childbirth (Gen 35:16 KJV).

In Bible times there was no class of men known as "labor" in contrast with "management." All but a favored few labored, and hard work was looked on as the common lot of man and a result of the curse (Gen 3:17–19), a bitter servitude. Slavery was commonly practiced in the Bible world; the conscription of freemen for labor on government building projects was practiced by Solomon (1 Kings 5:13–17) and Asa (15:22).

Although most workers in the simple culture of OT times were what we today would call "unskilled," there were certain skilled occupations. The potter (Jer 18) has left behind him unnumbered examples of his skill. Some technology in the working of metals was known. Remains of smelting furnaces have been found. Stone masons, scribes (Ezek 9:2; Jer 36:2, 4), dyers, weavers, and workers in precious stones and ivory carried on their work. But in general life was simple, work arduous, hours long, and wages small. "Then man goes out to his work, to his labor until evening" (Ps 104:23). "So I hated life, because the work that is done under the sun was grievous to me" (Eccl 2:17). By NT times things had changed, and the more complex civilization of the Roman world, with its skilled and more diversified occupations and better standards of living, had come to Palestine. See also OCCUPATIONS and PROFESSIONS. JBG

LACHISH (lā′kĭsh, Heb. *lākhîsh,* perhaps meaning *rough*). The name of a Canaanite royal city and Judean border fortress that occupied a strategic valley twenty-five miles (forty-two km.) SW of Jerusalem, the southernmost of the five that transect the Palestinian foothills and connect Judah's central ridge and the coastal highway leading into Egypt. First equated with Tell el-Hesy, Lachish has now been identified by written evidence (see below) with Tell ed-Duweir, a

Aerial view of Lachish, from the west: (1) approach road to gate, (2) outer gate, (3) inner gate, (4) outer wall, (5) inner wall, (6) Israelite palace, (7) Persian palace, (8) solar shrine, (9) Hellenistic structure, (10) shaft, (11) Fosse temple, (12) cemetery. Courtesy Carta, Jerusalem.

twenty-two-acre mound excavated by J. K. Starkey from A.D. 1932 until his death by violence in 1938.

Even before 3000 B.C. Lachish was inhabited by chalcolithic cave dwellers, but in about 2700 an Early-Bronze city was constructed on the virgin rock. Following a gap occasioned by invaders of calciform culture (c. 2300), Middle-Bronze Lachish arose, exhibiting cultural and political ties with Middle-Kingdom Egypt (2000–1780). This was succeeded by a Hyksos-type community, which provided Lachish with its first observable fortifications, including the characteristic dry moat, or fosse. An inscribed dagger, dated about 1650, furnishes one of the earliest examples of that acrophonic writing from which all modern alphabets derive, two centuries older than the Sinaitic or the five subsequent Lachish inscriptions. After the expulsion of the Hyksos from Egypt and their defeat in Palestine (c. 1578–1573), a Late-Bronze Canaanite citadel gave at least nominal allegiance to New-Empire Egypt. Its king, Japhia, joined with Adoni-Zedek of Jerusalem in a confederacy against Joshua in 1406 (Josh 10:3), only to be defeated and executed (10:23–26; 12:11). In Joshua's subsequent sweep through the southwest, Israel captured Lachish (reinforced by Gezer) and annihilated its inhabitants, in accordance with Moses' ban (Deut 7:2; Josh 10:31–33). Scripture contains no record, however, of its destruction (cf. Josh 11:13); and though assigned to Judah (15:39), Lachish must have suffered rapid Canaanite reoccupation, for a Late-Bronze temple constructed in the former fosse exhibits little interruption in its use. A generation later, the Amarna Letters criticize Lachish for furnishing supplies to the invaders and for overthrowing the Egyptian prefect Zimridi (Letters 287–288). Lachish was burned in about 1230. Some interpreters have tried to associate this conflagration with Joshua's campaign, but the excavators themselves attribute the fall of Lachish to the contemporaneous raids of Pharaoh Merneptah or to attacks by immigrating Philistines.

Lachish was fortified by Rehoboam shortly after the division of the Hebrew kingdom in 930 B.C. (2 Chron 11:9); and it was there that King Amaziah was murdered in 767 (25:27). The prophet Micah condemned Lachish's chariots as "the beginning of sin to the Daughter of Zion," perhaps because the city was used as a staging point for the extravagant importation of Egyptian horses (Mic 1:13; cf. Deut 17:16; 1 Kings

10:28–29). In any event, Lachish was successfully besieged by Sennacherib in 701 (2 Chron 32:9); Hezekiah sent a message of submission there (2 Kings 18:14); and from it Sennacherib's troops marched against Jerusalem (18:17; 19:8). Starkey's excavations demonstrate successive destructions of Lachish in 597 and 587, corresponding to Nebuchadnezzar's second and third attacks against Judah. From the final ashes twenty-one inscribed ostraca were recovered. Consisting primarily of communications from an outpost commander named Hoshaiah to his superior, Joash, at Lachish, they constitute our first truly personal, Palestinian documents. Letter IV mentions signal fires (cf. Jer 6:1) and establishes Jeremiah's assertion that Lachish and Azekah were the last cities, before Jerusalem, to fall to Nebuchadnezzar (34:7), and Letter VI speaks of a warning prophet (like Jeremiah himself) and of critics that "weakened the hands" of anti-Babylonian resistance (Jer 38:4). Finally, in Nehemiah's day, a resettled Lachish (Neh 11:30) achieved the construction of a palace and Persian sun temple that are among the finest of the period.

Recent archaeological work at Lachish (Y. Aharoni in 1966 and 1968; D. Ussishkin from 1973 to 1984 and continuing) has demonstrated that Level III represents the city destroyed by Sennacherib in 701 B.C. Ussishkin believes only one defensive wall surrounded the city and a lower revetment wall fortified an embankment between them. Four independent sources document the fall of Lachish: the Bible, Assyrian cuneiform texts, archaeological excavations, and pictorial reliefs found in Sennacherib's palace at Nineveh.

Bibliography: David Ussishkin, *The Conquest of Lachish by Sennacherib,* 1982; see detailed bibliography in ZPEB. JBP

Lachish Letter No. IV, one of twenty-one inscribed sherds discovered in the ruins of the last Israelite city of Lachish (588 B.C.). The inscription reads: ". . . And let (my lord) know that for the beacons of Lachish / we are watching, according to all the indications which / my lord hath given, for we cannot see / Azekah" (cf. Jer 34:7). Courtesy Israel Department of Antiquities and Museums.

LADAN (lā'dăn). 1. An Ephraimite, an ancestor of Joshua (1 Chron 7:26).

2. A Levite of the family of Gershon (1 Chron 23:7–9; 26:21), called Libni in 1 Chronicles 6:17.

LADDER (See STAIRS, STAIRWAY)

LAEL (lā'ĕl). A member of the family of Gershon, father of Eliasaph (Num 3:24). Meaning "belonging to God," the name is almost unique in the OT. It is formed by the addition of the divine name "el" to the preposition "la."

LAHAD (lā'hăd). A Judahite family name (1 Chron 4:2).

LAHMAS, LAHMAM (là'màs, là'măm, Heb. *laḥmām*). A town in the Judean foothills (Josh 15:40), possibly to be identified with modern el-Lahm, two and one-half miles (four km.) south of Beit Jibrin.

LAHMI (là'mī, Heb. *laḥmî*). According to 1 Chronicles 20:5, the brother of the giant from Gath who was killed by a certain Elhanan. In the parallel passage in 2 Samuel 21:9 the name Lahmi seems to have been corrupted to "Bethlehemite," Hebrew, *Beth Hallahmi.*

LAISH (lā'ĭsh, Heb. *layish*). 1. A city in the upper Jordan Valley. It was captured by the Danites and renamed Dan (Judg 18:7, 14, 27, 29). It is called Leshem in Joshua 19:47. Laish in the KJV and NEB of Isaiah 10:30 is Laishah in other versions (e.g., NASB, NIV). It is a town a short distance north of Jerusalem.

2. The father of Phalti or Phaltiel, a Benjamite, to whom Michal, David's wife, was given by Saul (1 Sam 25:44; 2 Sam 3:15).

LAISHAH (See LAISH)

LAKKUM, LAKUM (lăk'ŭm, lā'kŭm). A town of Naphtali (Josh 19:33). Its location is unknown.

LAMB. A translation of several Hebrew words in the English Bible, most of them referring to the young of the sheep. One, however (*sheh,* used in Exod 12:3–6), refers to the young of either sheep or goats (cf. 12:5) and seems to include adult specimens at times. The meat of lambs was considered a delicacy among the ancient Hebrews (Deut 32:14; 2 Sam 12:3–6; Amos 6:4). Meat was scarce among them, and the killing of a lamb would mark an important occasion. Lambs were used for sacrifices from the earliest times (Gen 4:4; 22:7).

The lamb was a staple in the Mosaic sacrificial system. A lamb was offered for the continual burnt offering each morning and evening (Exod 29:38–42), and on the Sabbath the number was doubled (Num 28:9). On the first day of each month (28:11), during the seven days of the Passover (28:16, 19), at the Feast of Weeks (28:26–27) and the Feast of Trumpets (29:1–2), on the Day of Atonement (29:7–8), and on the Feast of Tabernacles (29:13–36)

Stone statue of a man carrying a sacrificial lamb, from Susa, middle of third millennium B.C. Courtesy Réunion des Musées Nationaux.

lambs were offered. The lamb was one of the sacrifices accepted for the ceremonial cleansing of a woman after childbirth (Lev 12:6) or for the cleansing of a recovered leper (14:10–18). See also ANIMALS. JBG

LAMB OF GOD. Jesus was called the Lamb of God by John the Baptist (John 1:29, 36). The expression certainly emphasizes the redemptive character of the work of Christ. More than a score of times in the Book of Revelation the lamb is used as a symbol of Christ, and in Christian art of the succeeding centuries the motif is continued, as it is also in the communion service of many churches when they use these words: "Lamb of God, Son of the Father, that takest away the sins of the world, have mercy upon us."

The OT has numerous references to the lamb as a sacrificial victim (see LAMB). Of special interest is the Passover lamb (Exod 12:3–6) through whose sacrifice deliverance from Egypt was achieved. This deliverance became in time a picture of redemption from sin (Luke 9:31; 1 Cor 5:7). The substitutionary use of the unblemished lamb in sacrifice led to the idea of the Suffering Servant, who as a lamb died in the place of sinners (Isa 53:4–7).

LAME (See DISEASES)

LAMECH (lā'mĕk, Heb. *lemekh,* meaning undetermined). The name of two men in the antediluvian records.

1. A son of Methushael (Gen 4:18–24). This man, a descendant of Cain, had two wives, Adah and Zillah. Lamech's sons by Adah, Tubal and Jubal, founded the nomadic life and the musical arts. Lamech's son by Zillah, Tubal-Cain, invented metalcrafts and instruments of war. Lamech also had a daughter Naamah, by Zillah. As far as the record reveals, this man was the first poet. His song (4:23–24) expresses every feature of Hebrew poetry (alliteration, parallelism, poetic diction, etc.). It is addressed to his wives and has been interpreted variously. Some hold that it is nothing less than a bombastic boast of revenge on any man who will dare to attack him while he is armed with the weapons forged by his son Tubal-Cain. Others, with greater probability, maintain that Lamech, having already killed a man who attempted to murder him, is now claiming immunity on the ground that he acted in self-defense; thus, he logically asserts, his act will receive at the bar of justice a seventy-times-seven acquittal over Cain's cold-blooded murder of Abel.

2. The son of Methuselah (Gen 5:28–31). This man, a descendant of Seth, became the father of Noah. His faith is attested by the name he gave his son, Noah (meaning "rest"), and by the hope of "comfort" (5:29) that he anticipated in his son's life. Thus, basing his faith on the promised deliverance from the Adamic curse (3:14–19), he foresees, even if faintly, the coming of One of his seed (cf. 1 Chron 1:3; Luke 3:36) who will remove that curse (cf. Rom 8:18–25). He died at the age of 777. WB

LAMENTATIONS. This book, entitled in most English versions *The Lamentations of Jeremiah,* is placed between Jeremiah and Ezekiel in the LXX, Vulgate, and the English Bible. In the Hebrew text, however, it occurred in the Sacred Writings as one of the Megilloth or "five scrolls," of which it is the third. Its Hebrew title *êkhâh* ("Oh, how") is derived from the word with which the book commences. The Talmud renamed the book *Qinoth* ("Lamentations" or "elegies") as a more accurate designation of its true contents. This approach was adopted in the LXX title *Thrēnoi* ("Elegies") and the *Threni* ("Lamentations") of the Latin versions. The latter introduced the ascription of the work to Jeremiah, and this was followed by most English versions. Because of its position in the Megilloth, the Book of Lamentations is read in synagogue worship on the fast of the ninth of Ab, during the evening and morning services. This particular occasion commemorates the destruction of Jerusalem by Babylonian forces in 586 B.C., and again by the Roman armies under Titus in A.D. 70.

The book comprises five poems lamenting the desolation that had overtaken the Holy City in 586 B.C. The first four compositions are highly artificial in structure, consisting of acrostics based on the Hebrew alphabet. Each verse of chapters 1 and 2 commences with a word whose initial

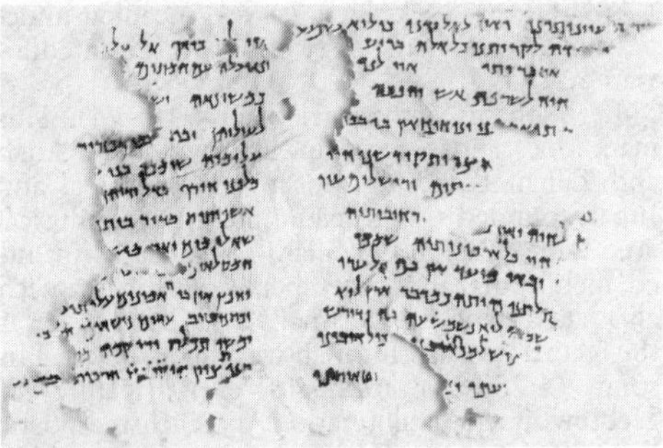

First century B.C. fragment of Lamentations, part of the Dead Sea Scrolls found in Cave 4 at Qumran (4Q Lam.). Courtesy Israel Department of Antiquities and Museums.

consonant is successively one of the twenty-two letters of the Hebrew alphabet. A slight variation of the regular order occurs in 2:16–17; 3:47–48; and 4:16–17. The third chapter is peculiar in that a triple alphabetical arrangement is followed, so that all three lines in each stanza commence with the same letter. The fifth chapter is not an acrostic, although like the others it contains twenty-two stanzas, and is a prayer rather than an elegy. Alphabetical forms of this kind probably served as a useful stimulus to memory at a time when manuscripts were rare and costly.

Some writers have regarded the mechanical structure of most of the book as incompatible with the grief and sincere penitence of the writer. These two ideas need not be inconsistent, however, particularly if the book was composed with a view to consistent liturgical usage. Judging from the manner in which it has survived among the Jews we may well believe that this was the intention of the author. The elegiac meter that characterizes the poems was occasionally employed in the writings of the eighth-century B.C. prophets in Jeremiah (9:19f.), Ezekiel (19), and some Psalms (e.g., 84, 119).

Although in the Hebrew no name was attached to the book, the authorship was uniformly ascribed by ancient authorities to Jeremiah. The LXX added an introductory note stating that "Jeremiah lamented this lamentation over Jerusalem," but the traditional view of the authorship appears to be rooted in the elegy composed for the mourning period of the deceased Josiah (c. 609 B.C.). Many modern critics have envisaged several authors at work in the book, or else have assumed that Baruch, Jeremiah's secretary, was responsible for the work in its final form. The reasons adduced include the fact that the physical circumstances of the prophet would make the work of composition rather difficult, that there are certain implicit contradictions between the prophecy of Jeremiah and the Book of Lamentations, and that some literary expressions characteristic of Jeremiah are lacking in Lamentations. Thus the thought of Lamentations 2:9 that God no longer reveals himself in his prophets is held to be inconsistent with the thought of Jeremiah. Similarly the reference in Lamentations 4:17 to the possibility of Egypt as a deliverer ill accords with the patriotism expressed by the prophet (Jer 42:15–17; 43:12–13).

On the other hand, most of the poems appear intimately connected with the calamity of the Exile. Chapters 2 and 4 indicate that the author personally witnessed the tragedy of 586 B.C., while the remainder of the book may have been written in Babylonia in the early captivity. It seems improbable that the final chapter was written in Jerusalem after the return from Exile, perhaps about 525 B.C., as has been suggested by some writers. The arguments for diversity of authorship do not seem particularly strong, though the possibility that the poems were recast in mnemonic form at a time subsequent to their original composition must not be overlooked. Until more decisive evidence is forthcoming, there seems little reason for questioning the substantial unity and traditional authorship of Lamentations.

The book bewails the siege and destruction of Jerusalem and sorrows over the sufferings of the inhabitants during this time. It makes poignant confession of sin on behalf of the people and their leaders, acknowledges complete submission to the divine will, and prays that God will once again favor and restore his people.

Analysis:

1. The fallen city admits its sin and the justice of divine judgment (chs. 1–2).
2. Lamentation; reassertion of divine mercy and judgment; prayer for divine intervention (chs. 3–4).
3. Further confession and prayers for mercy (ch. 5).

Bibliography: N. K. Gottwald, *Studies in the Book of Lamentations,* 1954; J. M. Meyers, *Ezra, Nehemiah* (AB), 1965; D. R. Hillers, *Lamentations* (AB), 1974. WB

LAMP. An instrument used for artificial lighting. Lamps are often mentioned in Scripture, but no description of their form and structure is given. Archaeology has recovered many specimens in a great variety of forms, from the early simple, shallow, saucerlike bowl (with one side slightly pointed for the lighted wick) to the later closed bowl (with only a hole on top to pour in the oil, a spout for the wick, and a handle to carry it). Lamps for domestic use were generally of terracotta or of bronze. KJV often has "candle" and "candlestick" and NEB has "standing lamp" where NIV has "lamp" and "lampstand."

The use of lamps is mentioned in connection with the golden lamps in the tabernacle and the ten golden lamps in the temple (Exod 25:37; 1 Kings 7:49; 2 Chron 4:20; 13:11; Zech 4:2). As shown from their usage, the "lamps" (KJV) of Gideon's soldiers (Judg 7:16) were doubtless torches (so NIV). The common NT mention of lamps is in connection with their household usage (Matt 5:15; Mark 4:21; Luke 8:16; 11:33; 15:8). Such lamps were generally placed on a

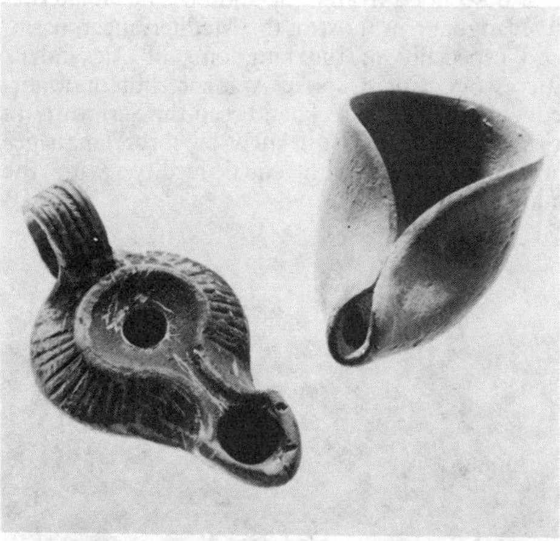

Two pottery lamps from the Hasmonean and Herodian period, c. 332 B.C.–A.D. 70. Courtesy Reuben and Edith Hecht Museum, University of Haifa.

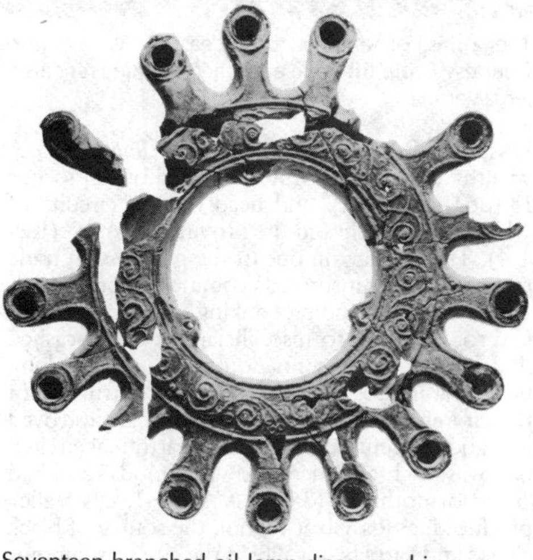

Seventeen-branched oil lamp discovered in excavations near Jericho, dating from the Roman period. Courtesy Zev Radovan.

"lampstand," usually a niche built into the wall. It appears that the Hebrews were accustomed to burning lamps overnight in their chambers, perhaps because of a dread of darkness, more likely to keep away prowlers. The use of oil-fed lamps in a marriage procession is mentioned in Matthew 25:1. Since such lamps contained only a few spoonfuls of oil, a reserve supply would be a necessity. The lighted lamp is also mentioned metaphorically to symbolize (1) God's Word (Ps 119:105), (2) God's guidance (2 Sam 22:29; Ps 18:28), (3) God's salvation (Isa 62:1 KJV), (4) man's spirit (Prov 20:27), (5) outward prosperity (Prov 13:9), (6) a son as successor (1 Kings 11:36; 15:4). DEH

LAMPSTAND. The Hebrew word *menôrâh,* always rendered "candlestick" in KJV, occurs

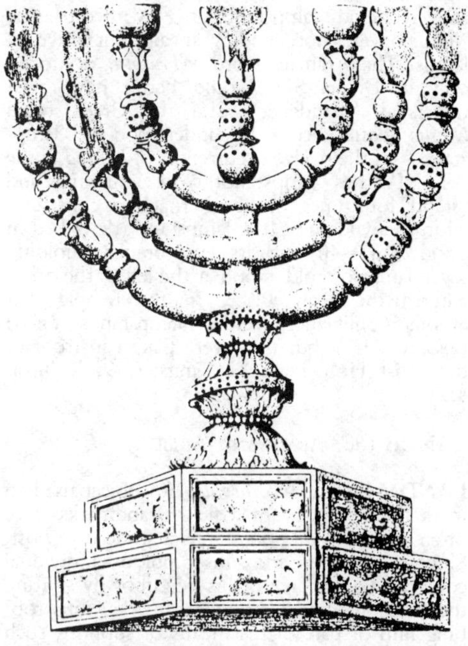

Seven-branched candlestick from relief on the Arch of Titus in Rome. Courtesy Carta, Jerusalem.

Fragments of the earliest known representation of the seven-branched lampstand (menorah) of the temple (c. 37 B.C.–A.D. 4). Found in 1969 excavations of the Old City of Jerusalem. Courtesy S. Zur Picture Library.

forty-three times in the OT, and is more accurately rendered "lampstand" in NIV, because the "lights" were not candles at all, but olive-oil lamps. The Aramaic word *nebrashta,* occurring only in Daniel 5:5, would better have been translated "chandelier"; and the Greek word *lychnia* would better be understood as "lampstand." Of the twelve occurrences of *lychnia* in the NT, NIV uses "lampstand(s)" in eight times and "stand" four times. In the tabernacle, as constructed in the wilderness, the lampstand (described in Exod 25:31–40) with its seven branches holding seven lamps of gold, stood at the left as the priest entered the Holy Place. In the temple that Solomon built, there were ten lampstands of gold (2 Chron 4:7), but they were placed in front of the Most Holy Place (1 Kings 7:49; 2 Chron 4:7).

LANCE (See ARMS AND ARMOR)

LANDMARK (Heb. *gevûl*). An object used to mark the boundary of a field. Landmarks were often such movable objects as a stone or a post. Since a cunning and unscrupulous individual could take advantage of his neighbor by shifting the location of such boundary marks, thus robbing him of part of his means of support, such removal of landmarks was prohibited by the Mosaic Law (Deut 19:14; 27:17). Hebrew piety denounced the act (Prov 22:28; 23:10), and it was considered equal to theft (Job 24:2).

LANE (Gr. *rhymē*). An alley of a city. The Greek word is usually translated "street" (Matt 6:2; Acts 9:11).

LANGUAGES. The first language spoken by the invading Israelite tribes in Palestine was Hebrew, a Semitic tongue related to Phoenician, to the Canaanite dialects of the tribes they dispossessed, and to the speech of Moab. The Tell-el-Amarna Letters and the inscription of Mesha are evidence of this. Hebrew, over the first centuries of the occupation of Palestine, was both the literary and colloquial language. It remained the literary language permanently. In colloquial use it was replaced by Aramaic. The date of this change is difficult to determine with precision. Eliakim's request to Sennacherib's field commander (2 Kings 18:26) to "speak to your servants in Aramaic," which, as a common eastern language of diplomacy the leaders understood, and not in Hebrew shows that the latter was still the Jewish vernacular in 713 B.C. Such was still the case as late as Nehemiah, two centuries later.

The next evidence is from the NT where phrases quoted in the Palestinian vernacular (e.g., *talitha koum,* in Mark 5:41 and the cry from the cross in Matt 27:46) are undoubtedly Aramaic. Before Aramaic replaced Hebrew, it had, of course, infiltrated its vocabulary. The other colloquial dialect of NT times was Greek, which also provided the literary language for the NT writings. It is the common dialect of Greek that is thus represented, that simplified and basic form that descended from Attic and became an alternative language in most of the Mediterranean basin, and especially in the kingdoms of Alexander's successors. Christ spoke Aramaic, but undoubtedly understood Greek, and read the Scriptures in classical Hebrew. Paul knew all three languages and used them with equal facility, with the addition of Latin. EMB

The ruins of ancient Laodicea in Asia Minor. Courtesy Ecole Biblique et Archéologique Française, Jerusalem.

LAODICEA (lā-ŏd'ĭ-sē'á, Gr. *Laodikia*). A wealthy city in Asia Minor founded by Antiochus II (261–246 B.C.), and head of the "circuit" of "the seven churches in the province of Asia" (Rev 1:4). The city lay on one of the great Asian trade routes, and this insured its commercial prosperity. Laodicea was a leading banking center. In 51 B.C. Cicero, en route to his Cilician province, cashed drafts there. It was no doubt the rich banking firms that in A.D. 60 financed the reconstruction of the city after the great earthquake that destroyed it. Laodicea refused the Senate's earthquake relief. She was "rich and increased with goods" and had "need of nothing" (3:17 KJV). The Lycus Valley produced a glossy black wool, the source of black cloaks and carpets, for which the city was famous. Laodicea was also the home of a medical school and the manufacture of collyrium, a famous eye salve. The scornful imagery of the apocalyptic letter to Laodicea is obviously based on these activities. It also has reference to the emetic qualities of the soda-laden warm water from nearby Hierapolis, whose thermal springs ran into the Maeander. Laodicea's water supply also came from Hierapolis, and Sir William Ramsay suggests that its vulnerability, together with the city's exposed position and its easy wealth caused the growth in the community of that spirit of compromise and worldly mindedness castigated in the Revelation. Under Diocletian, Laodicea, still prosperous, was made the chief city of the province of Phrygia. EMB

LAODICEANS, LETTER TO. Mentioned by Paul in Colossians 4:16 in urging the Colossians to exchange letters with the Laodiceans. A letter written by the Laodiceans to Paul is ruled out by the context: "from" (*ek*) here denotes present locality, not origin. There are three views of its identity: (1) The spurious "Letter to the Laodiceans" found among Paul's letters in some Latin MSS from the sixth to the fifteenth centuries. Its twenty verses, being phrases strung together from Philippians and Galatians, are a forgery with no heretical motive. (2) A Pauline letter to the Laodiceans now lost. This is not improbable; opponents hold it multiplies epistles unnecessarily. (3) Our Ephesians. This view is very probable if Ephesians is accepted as being encyclical, and it accounts for Marcion's title of Ephesians as "the epistle to the Laodiceans."

LAPIS LAZULI (See MINERALS)

LAPPIDOTH (lăp'ĭ-dŏth, Heb. *lappîdhôth, torches* or *lightning flashes*). The husband of Deborah the prophetess (Judg 4:4).

LAPWING (See BIRDS)

LASEA (lȧ-sē'ȧ). A small seaport town on the southern coast of Crete, about five miles (eight km.) east of Fair Havens, listed by Luke (Acts 27:8) in the log of Paul's voyage to Rome. No other ancient writer mentions the place.

LASH (See SCOURGE, STRIPES)

LASHA (lā'shȧ, Heb. *lāsha'*). A place near Sodom and Gomorrah mentioned in Genesis 10:19 to mark off the Canaanite territory. The historian Jerome, following Jewish sources, equates it with Callirrhoe, famous for its warm springs. The exact place has not yet been identified.

LASHARON (lă-shā'rŏn, Heb. *lashshārôn,* probably *to Sharon*). A royal Canaanite town whose king was killed by Joshua (Josh 12:18). Listed along with Aphek, it is probably identifiable with the ancient Sarona, located on the plateau six and one-half miles (eleven km.) SW of Tiberias.

LAST JUDGMENT (See ESCHATOLOGY)

LATIN. The language of the Romans and, in Palestine, used primarily by the Romans. The official superscription on the cross was written in Hebrew, Greek, and Latin (John 19:20). The NT contains about twenty-five administrative and military Latin words translated into Greek.

LATTICE. Latticework, made by crossing laths or other materials across an opening, served a threefold purpose: (1) privacy (so that one might look out without being seen), (2) ventilation (so that a breeze might flow in and the sun's hot rays kept out), and (3) decoration (so that a house or public building might be architecturally more attractive). Judges 5:28; 2 Kings 1:2; Proverbs 7:6; Song of Songs 2:9.

LAUGHTER. 1. Laughter's limitations: it cannot satisfy (Prov 14:13; Eccl 2:2; 7:3, 6; 10:19).

2. God's laughter: he laughs at his enemies (Ps 2:4; 37:13; 59:8).

3. The believers' laughter: they sometimes laugh incredulously (Gen 17:17; 18:12–15; 21:6), but they can laugh for real joy (Ps 126:2; Luke 6:21) and in derision of the wicked (Job 22:19; Ps 52:6; Isa 37:22).

4. The unbelievers' laughter: they laugh at Christ (Ps 22:7; Matt 9:24), at believers (Neh 2:19; Job 12:4; Ps 80:6), and at God's ordinances (2 Chron 30:10); but their laughter will vanish (Prov 1:26; Luke 6:25; James 4:9).

LAUNDERER'S SOAP (See FULLER'S SOAP)

LAW. I. The Terms of Scripture. Of Hebrew words, the one most often used, *tôrāh,* may refer to human instruction (Prov 1:8), to divine instruction (Isa 1:10), to a regulation (Lev 7:7), to the law of Moses (1 Kings 2:3), or to custom (2 Sam 7:19). Other words that may be so translated include *dāth, hôq, mitswâh, and mishpat.* The common Greek word *nomos* is occasionally used of law(s) in the most general sense (Rom 3:27) of a principle that governs one's actions (7:23), of the Pentateuch (Gal 3:10), and of the other portions of Holy Scripture (as John 10:34; 1 Cor 14:21), but most often for the Mosaic Law (Acts 15:5). English synonyms include *commandment, direction, judgment, ordinance, precept, statute,* and *testimony.*

II. The Moral Law. It is plain from the Decalogue (Exod 20:3–17; Deut 5:7–21) that morality is not to be derived from human standards and the verdict of society but from God and his declarations and one's relationship of subordination to him. Right and wrong are not deter-

Fragment of a leather scroll (first century B.C.) found at Qumran containing Deuteronomy 5, the Ten Commandments being shown in third column from the right. Courtesy Israel Department of Antiquities and Museums.

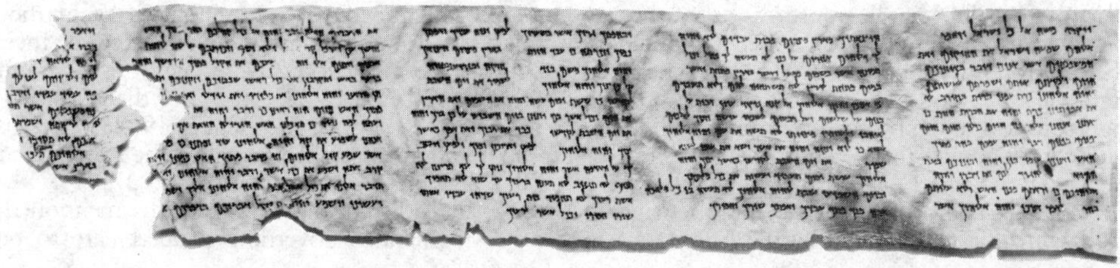

mined by the voice of society but by the voice of God.

The Ten Commandments declare the broad principles of God's moral law. We can find positive teaching as to the will of God for our lives in those commandments that are couched in the negative, and we can find admonition and prohibition in those framed as positive exhortations. The Commandments constitute the regulative core of revelation as to acceptable lines of human conduct.

The first table of the law was considered to express man's duty toward God (Exod 20:3–11), and the second his duty toward his fellow human beings (20:12–17). The NT seems to follow this division in summarizing the law, for Jesus said that it demands perfect love for God and love for one's neighbor comparable to the love that one has for oneself (Matt 22:35–40).

Rather than setting aside the moral law, the NT reiterates its commands, develops more fully the germinal truths contained in it, and focuses attention on the spirit of the law as over against merely the letter. So it is that Paul affirms there is but one God (Eph 4:6) and cautions against idolatry both directly and indirectly (Rom 1:21ff.; 1 Cor 10:14). While the NT suggests an attitude toward the Sabbath somewhat different from that of Jewish legalism (Mark 2:23–28) and comes to recognize the time of observance as the first day of the week (Acts 20:7; 1 Cor 16:2), it preserves the observance as of divine institution and enriches its significance by associating with it Christ's resurrection. So also, the NT emphasizes the law of love (Rom 13:8–10; Gal 5:14; James 2:8) and selflessness and humility as representative of the mind of Christ (Phil 2:3–8). Although the NT commandments are for the most part positive exhortations rather than warnings and prohibitions, the underlying principles are the same.

Scripture makes clear the function of the moral law. As the expression of the character and will of God, it sets forth the only standard of righteousness acceptable to him; but humans were without power to conform to that perfect standard. The law made them aware of their sinfulness (Rom 7:7, 13), condemned them as unrighteous (7:9–11; Gal 3:13; James 2:9), and, having removed any hope of salvation through their own righteousness, brought them to the place where they would cast themselves on the grace of God and trust only in the righteousness and merit of the atoning Savior, Jesus Christ (Gal 3:24).

Christians are free from the condemnation of the law (Rom 8:2) since the righteousness of him who kept the law perfectly and who vicariously paid the penalty for the transgression of the law on the part of his people has been imputed to them. More than that Christians are declared righteous by God (Rom 4:5–6), renewed in righteousness and progressively sanctified as the Holy Spirit applies the Word in their lives (2 Cor 5:21; Gal 5:16ff.; 1 Thess 5:23). The goal of the Christian is conformity to the moral image of God as manifested to them by the Incarnate Son (Eph 4:13). So it is that Christians are under obligation to keep the moral law (cf. Matt 5:19ff.; Eph 4:28; 5:3; 6:2; Col 3:9; 1 Peter 4:15), not as a condition of salvation, but that they may become more and more like their Father in heaven (Rom 8:1–9; Eph 4:13), and this because of love for the One who redeemed them (Rom 13:8–10; 1 John 5:2–3).

III. Social Legislation. In the giving of the law at Sinai, Moses first communicated to the people the body of principles, the Ten Words, and then the applicatory precepts. Careful study of the individual statutes shows the specific commands to be rooted in the basic principles set out in the Decalogue.

OT laws of judicial, civil, or political nature are to be found in the block of legislative material known as the Book of the Covenant (Exod 20:23–23:33), in the so-called Holiness Code (Lev 17–26), and here and there throughout most of the Book of Deuteronomy, especially chapters 21–25.

Since man is inherently sinful and lawless, social life must come under regulations. So it was that in the OT times both Jews and Gentiles found themselves subject to law. Nor was the civil legislation binding on Israel much different from that of the heathen nations. The Code of Hammurabi has much in common with the laws promulgated under Moses, and other ancient statutes are found among non-Jews as well as in Israel. Basic principles of right and wrong are the same everywhere and for all people, reflecting the work of the Holy Spirit in the realm of common grace. The difference was that in the Israelite theocracy the laws regulating society were recognized as declared through God's prophets and with divine authority, whereas in other nations the authority behind the codes was the voice of tradition or the voice of the state.

A basic institution ordained of God, the family was necessarily governed in its many relationships by various regulations that it might be preserved from corruption and dissolution. There were many prescriptions regarding marriage itself (Exod 21–22, 34; Lev 18, 21; Num 5, 25; Deut 7, 21–22, 24–25, 27). Within the family, children were to honor and obey their parents (Exod 20:12; Deut 5:16; 21:18–21; 27:16). And since the family circle might include servants, slaves, and strangers, there were laws pertaining to them also (Exod 12, 21–22; Lev 19, 22, 24–25; Num 9, 15, 35; Deut 1, 12, 14–16, 23–24, 27).

As might be expected, crimes against society were to be punished according to law. These might be of a moral nature, such as sexual violations or perversions (Exod 20–22; Lev 18–20; Num 5; Deut 5:22–25, 27). Again, they might be crimes against individuals, either their persons (Gen 9; Exod 20–23; Lev 19, 24; Num 35; Deut 5, 19, 21–22, 24, 27) or their property (Exod 20, 22; Lev 6, 19; Deut 5, 19, 23, 25, 27). Or the offenses might be against the state (Exod 20, 23; Lev 19; Deut 5, 16, 19, 27).

In addition to the laws already mentioned, other regulations governing property are to be found in Exodus 21–23; Leviticus 6, 24–25; Numbers 27, 36; and Deuteronomy 21–22, 25.

OT legislation contained numerous stipulations about the operation of the state. Certain aspects of political organization were outlined (Exod 22; Num 1, 3–4, 26, 33; Deut 17, 23). Specifications were made regarding the army (Num 1–2, 10, 26, 31; Deut 7, 11, 20–21, 23–24). Judicial prescriptions were set forth (Exod 18, 20–21, 23; Lev 5, 19; Num 35; Deut 1, 4–5, 16–17, 19, 25, 27), and provision was made for bringing to the people a knowledge of the law (Deut 6, 11, 27, 31; Josh 8).

Many Israelite laws were laws of kindness. Even the treatment of animals was subject to regulation (Exod 23, 34; Lev 22, 25; Deut 22, 25). The general commandment of love, whether for friends or strangers, was invoked (Exod 23; Lev 19; Deut 10). The poor, unfortunate, lowly, defenseless, and needy were to be treated humanely (Exod 21–23; Lev 19, 23, 25; Deut 14–16, 21–27).

The prescriptions of the law were to the end that there might be peace and order, whether in the operations of the state or the family or in other spheres of human interrelations. The dignity of the individual was to be preserved. A high premium was set on selflessness and consideration of others. God's wisdom and grace were manifest in the legislation given the Israelites through his servant Moses.

IV. Religious Legislation. Embodied in the OT are many laws governing the worship of God. Some are very general in nature, having to do with purity of worship. Large numbers of the laws concern the sanctuary, its priesthood, and the rites and ceremonies connected with it and the covenant relationship between the Israelites and their God. Some consist of prescriptions pertaining to special occasions of the religious year.

Basic principles of worship are outlined in the first table of the Decalogue (Exod 20:3–11). They are then worked out into detailed applicatory legislation. Because the Lord is the only true God, exalted and holy, other so-called gods are not to be worshiped (Exod 22–23, 34; Deut 5–6, 8, 11, 17, 30), apostasy is a sin (Deut 4:25–31; 31:16; cf. Lev 19, 26; Deut 27), and such occult arts as witchcraft, sorcery, and divination are not to be practiced (Exod 22; Lev 18–20; Deut 18). So also, blasphemy is not to be tolerated (Exod 22; Lev 18–19, 24), and God's Sabbath Day is to be kept inviolate (Exod 23, 31, 34–35; Lev 19, 26; Num 15).

Since the Lord is the only true God, his people are not only to study and keep his law (Lev 18–20, 25; Num 15; Deut 4–8, 10–11, 22, 26–27, 30), but are to separate themselves from the heathen and their religious practices (Exod 22–23, 34; Lev 18–20; Deut 6–7, 12, 14, 18). They are to be a holy nation (Exod 19, 22; Lev 19, 26; Deut 7, 14, 18, 26, 28), and they are to give to God the allegiance, love, gratitude, and obedient service due him (Exod 23, 34; Lev 19, 25; Deut 4–6, 8, 10–11, 13–14, 17, 30–31).

When Moses was on Mount Sinai, God delineated in detail the pattern for the sanctuary (Exod 25–27), and the tabernacle was built in conformity to that pattern (Exod 35–38). Later its essential features were reproduced in Solomon's temple (2 Chron 3–4). The sanctuary was in a special sense God's dwelling place among his people and spoke silently of his fellowship with them (Exod 25:8, 22). As the place where God drew nigh to the people and they to him, it was designed to remind them of him—his splendor, his magnificence, his glory, his transcendence, his holiness, his presence, his mercy and forgiveness, his requirements of Israel, and his covenant headship. Through its structure and the regulations as to who might enter each part, God's holiness was emphasized.

The brazen altar was for sacrifice and therefore implied the necessity of worship and atonement. As one approached the holy God, the laver was mute evidence of the fact that cleansing from defilement must first take place. The altar of incense pointed to the importance of adoration and praise (Ps 141:2: Isa 6:3–4). The table of showbread suggested the need for dedication, and the golden lampstand perhaps indicated that the worshiper should reflect in his life the light that comes from God and which is ever to be linked with him. These conclusions rest on the assumption that the sanctuary furnishings in the outer court and in the Holy Place were for the purpose of instructing the OT worshiper how they should draw near to God in worship.

On the other hand, the symbolism of the Most Holy Place may be thought of as speaking of God in his approach to people. Through the tables of law in the ark, through the ark's cover, and through the cherubim symbolizing the presence of God, the Lord said to his people, "I, God, am a spiritual Being here in your midst. My law accuses and condemns. Who can keep it? But I have provided a covering, a propitiation, an atonement. Despite sin, it is still possible for you to look forward to dwelling in my immediate presence." The veil testified that the time had not come, but the typology was unmistakable.

The worshiper might come only as far as the court. The ordinary priest could enter the Holy Place. Only the high priest might enter the Most Holy Place, and that but once a year. The symbolism was plain: it was not a light thing to seek acceptance in the presence of the holy God, but there was indeed a way of approach.

The OT worshiper learned that through the offering of sacrifice God dealt with sin and granted forgiveness (Lev 4:20), that through the shedding of blood there was atonement of sin (16:15–16), that the animal of the ceremony was reckoned as a substitute for the worshiper (16:20–22), that the sacrifices were perhaps not the full and final answer to the sin problem (since they must continue to be offered), that sacrifice without obedience to God's revelation was of no value (Isa 1:10–17), and that God's Suffering Servant was to be a guilt offering (53:10). The Mosaic legislation prescribes the kinds of sacrifices and the details governing them: the whole burnt offering (Exod 20; Lev 1, 6; Deut 12:27), the sin offering (Lev 4–6, 8–10; Num 15), the guilt offering (Lev 5–7, 19; Num 5), and the peace offering (Lev 3, 7, 19, 22). Also the law had much to say about other offerings and sacrificial dues (Exod 10, 13, 18, 22–23, 29–30, 34; Lev 2–3, 6, 14, 19, 22–23, 27; Num 3, 5–6, 8, 15, 18–19, 28, 30–31; Deut 12, 14–18, 23, 26).

Through the priesthood, people came to understand that the transcendent, holy God cannot be approached in a casual way by sinful people but only by a mediator representing both God and man, that the mediator must be emblematic of holiness and perfection, and that God deals with sin through the representative acts of the mediator. As to the concept of the priesthood, the focus of attention was narrowed from the whole nation (Exod 19:6) to the priests and Levites and finally to one man, the high priest, whose acts on behalf of the people brought reconciliation. Many passages contain laws pertaining to the priesthood (Exod 28–30, 39–40; Lev 2:5–8, 10, 16; 21–24, 27; Num 3–6, 15, 18, 31). The law codes regulated ceremonial cleanliness not only for the priests but also in reference to food (Exod 12, 22–23, 34; Lev 3, 7, 11, 17, 19–20, 22; Deut 12, 14–15) and purification (Lev 5:11–15:22; Num 6, 19, 31; Deut 21, 24).

The feasts and festivals had significance that was partly historical, partly merely symbolical, partly typical. The Passover was a reminder of physical deliverance from bondage in Egypt (Exod 12:17; Deut 16:1). Sacred history and prophecy often blend, and so the observance of the Passover might well have had this message: As God delivered, so he *will* deliver. The central sacrifice in this festival as in others pointed to a need for atonement just as did the daily and weekly sacrifices did, and the unleavened bread and the meat and drink offerings pointed to the importance of a holy, fruitful life before God. As a harvest festival, Pentecost signified rejoicing and the place of thanksgiving to God in the life of the covenant participant (Deut 16:9–10), especially in the light of deliverance from Egypt (Deut 16:12). Except for the significance of the extra sacrifices, the Feast of Tabernacles (Exod 23; Lev 23; Num 29; Deut 16) may have been to the Jews little more than a reminder of God's love and care during the period of the nation's youth when the Jews wandered in the wilderness and were tested by deprivation that they might learn to trust in God and his provision. On the other hand, the Day of Atonement emphasized the need for the expiation of sin, the atoning nature of the blood sacrifice, and the idea of substitution in relation to atonement.

The rite of circumcision symbolized the taking away of defilement that the individual might be rightly related to God and a partaker of the covenant of grace.

The NT spells out the antitypes involved. As God's dwelling among his people was symbolized in the OT through the Garden of Eden, the tabernacle, and the temple, so the New Covenant tells us that God as the Son "lived for a while among us" (John 1:14), that he indwells the individual believer (1 Cor 6:19) and the church (2 Cor 6:16), and that the final and everlasting dwelling place of God with man will be heaven itself (Heb 9:24; Rev 21:3).

In the new dispensation, that which was symbolized by the Passover celebration and circumcision came to be represented and defined more clearly in the Lord's Supper and Christian baptism. The types and shadows of the ceremonial law gave way to antitypes.

The cross replaced the brazen altar. There was no longer a sanctuary laver but a laver of regeneration, "a washing of rebirth" (Titus 3:5). "The prayers of the saints" (Rev 5:8) took the place of the altar of incense. Dedicated lives came to be offered (Rom 12:1–2) rather than symbolic showbread, and good works produced by children of the light made unnecessary the golden lampstand. Instead of the mercy seat as a "propitiatory covering" (LXX translation of 1 Chron 28:11), Christ became the propitiation for the sins of his people (Rom 3:25; 1 John 2:2; 4:10), and man redeemed and in fellowship with God became the prophetic fulfillment of the symbolic cherubim, which were basically human in form (Ezek 1:5; 10:21) and always associated with the presence of the Lord (Gen 3:24; Ps 18:10; Ezek 1, 10, 28). The Lord Jesus was seen to be God's Passover Lamb (1 Cor 5:7), a perfect, all-sufficient sacrifice (Eph 5:2; Heb 7:27; 9:11–14). As *the* High Priest, Christ made reconciliation (Heb 2:17) and lives to make intercession for his people (7:25).

A covenant child, our Lord was related to the ceremonial law as shown by his circumcision (Luke 2:21) and his presence at the temple at the Passover feast (2:42). He instructed lepers to carry out the provisions of the law (17:14). He drove from the temple those who defiled it (Matt 21:12–13). He and his disciples were accustomed to go to Jerusalem at feast time (John 7:37; 13:1, 29).

Christ spoke negatively regarding the traditions of the Jews but not of the ceremonial law as set forth in the OT. Yet he indicated that the time was coming when the ritual of the law would give place to spiritual worship (John 4:24).

In the transitional period after the Cross, the Resurrection, and the Ascension, conditions in each case determined whether the stipulations of the law should be observed. Paul might circumcise Timothy (Acts 16:3) but not Titus (Gal 2:3–4). He could assure the Corinthians that circumcision in the flesh was not essential for salvation (1 Cor 2:2; 7:18–19); and, in writing to the Galatians, he could argue strongly against the contentions of the Judaizers (Gal 2:4ff.; 5:1ff.) in line with the decisions of the Jerusalem Council (Acts 15:4ff.). The argument of the Book of Hebrews is that the types and shadows of the ceremonial law have passed away with the coming of Christ, the perfect High Priest, who as the Lamb of God offered himself on Golgotha that he might satisfy every demand of the law and purchase salvation for his people.

By means of the ceremonial law, God spoke in picture language of the salvation he was to effect through the life and death of the Incarnate Son. Therefore, it was necessarily imperfect and temporary. The social legislation governing Israel was designed for a particular culture at a given period of history, and so it, too, was only for a time; yet its principles are timeless and applicable to all generations. God's moral law is in force everywhere and at all times, for it is a reflection of his very being. It has never been abrogated, nor indeed can be.

Bibliography: H. H. Rowley, *From Joseph to Joshua,* 1950; J. A. Motyer, *The Revelation of the Divine Name,* 1959; J. Bright, *History of Israel,* 1960; G. A. F. Knight, *Law and Grace,* 1962; M. G. Kline, *Treaty of the Great King,* 1963; D. E. H. Whiteley, *The Theology of St. Paul,* 1964; G. A. Archer, *A Survey of Old Testament Introduction,* 1964; K. A. Kitchen, *Ancient Orient and Old Testament,* 1966; W. Elert, *Law and Gospel,* 1967; J. A. Motyer, *The Image of God, Law and Liberty in Biblical Ethics,* 1976, and *Law and Life: A Study of the Meaning of Law in the Old Testament,* 1978.

BLG

LAWGIVER (Heb. *mehōqēq,* Gen 49:10; Num 21:18; Deut 33:21; Ps 60:7; 108:8; Isa 33:22; Gr. *nomothetēs,* James 4:12). God is the only absolute lawgiver. Instrumentally, Moses bears this description (John 1:17; 7:19).

LAWYER (See OCCUPATIONS AND PROFESSIONS)

LAYING ON OF HANDS. An act pregnant with many implications. In the OT the act symbolizes (1) the parental bestowal of inheritance rights (Gen 48:14–20), (2) the gifts and rights of an office (Num 27:18, 23; Deut 34:9), and (3) substitution, of an animal for one's guilt (Exod 29:10, 15, 19; Lev 1:4; 3:2, 8, 13; 4:4, 15, 24, 29, 33; 8:14, 18, 22; 16:21; cf. Gen 22:9–13), of the Levites for the firstborn of the other tribes (Num 8:10–19), and of one's innocence for another's guilt (Lev 24:13–16; Deut 13:9; 17:7). In the NT the act symbolizes (1) the bestowal of blessings and benediction (Matt 19:13, 15; cf. Luke 24:50), (2) the restoration of health (Matt 9:18; Acts 9:12, 17), (3) the reception of the Holy Spirit in baptism (Acts 8:17, 19; 19:6), and (4) the gifts and rights of an office (Acts 6:6; 13:3; 1 Tim 4:14; 2 Tim 1:6).

LAZARUS (lăz'à-rŭs, Lat. from Gr., for Heb. *Eleazar*). 1. Lazarus, the brother of Martha and Mary, who lived in Bethany. Lazarus, during Christ's absence, became sick and died; Christ, after some delay, returned and raised him from death (John 11:1–12:19). The following factors enhance the importance of this miracle: (1) the number of days (four) between death and resurrection (11:39), (2) the number of witnesses involved (11:45; 12:17–18), (3) the evident health of Lazarus after the event (12:1, 2, 9), and (4) the significance of the event among the Jews (11:53; 12:10–11).

The traditional tomb of Lazarus at Bethany. "Then Jesus . . . came to the tomb; it was a cave, and a stone lay upon it" (John 11:38). Courtesy Studium Biblicum Franciscanum, Jerusalem.

This miracle (1) illustrates Christ's sympathy (John 11:5, 11, 34–35) and power (11:40ff.), (2) manifests the purposiveness of his miracles (11:4, 40; 20:31), (3) gives concrete backing to the truth of Luke 16:30–31, (4) affords opportunity for eschatological teaching (John 11:23–25), and (5) precipitates the Crucifixion (11:45–53; 12:9–19).

The silence of the Synoptic Gospels regarding this event is explainable: (1) the miracle was outside their scope; (2) it was not the leading accusation brought against Christ (cf. Matt 26:61–66); (3) it was indirectly confirmed by the "envy" they attribute to the Jews (27:18); and (4) it did not fit their purpose for writing as it did John's (John 20:31).

2. Lazarus, a beggar who died and went to Abraham's bosom (Luke 16:19–31). The passage illustrates these truths: (1) destiny is settled at death; (2) no purgatory awaits the righteous; and (3) man has sufficient warning now.

LEAD (See MINERALS)

LEAF. The word is used in three ways in the Bible. 1. The leaf of a tree (Ezek 17:6; Dan 4:12, 14, 21). As such it has semiphysical or semispiritual uses: (1) the insufficiency of man's righteousness (Gen 3:7), (2) the fruitfulness of the restored earth (8:11), (3) the sign of a distressed and nervous spirit (Lev 26:36; Job 13:25), (4) the spiritual productivity of the righteous (Ps 1:3; Prov 11:28; Jer 17:8), (5) the spiritual unproductivity of the wicked (Isa 1:30), (6) the completeness of God's judgment (Isa 34:4; Jer 8:13), (7) the frailty and evanescence of man (Isa 64:6), (8) the blessings of messianic times (Ezek 47:12), (9) the unfruitfulness of Israel (Ezek 17:9 KJV; Matt 21:19; Mark 11:13), (10) the nearness of the eschatological judgment (Matt 24:32; Mark 13:28), (11) the glory of an earthly kingdom (Dan 4:12, 14, 21), and (12) the glory and fruitfulness of the heavenly kingdom (Rev 22:2).

2. The leaf of a door. In 1 Kings 6:34, *tsēlā'* is thus used (= one of two swinging doors?); and

in Ezekiel 41:21 *deleth* can be translated both by "doors" and by "leaves."

3. The leaf of a book. So *deleth* in Jeremiah 36:23 KJV.

LEAH (lē'ȧ, Heb. *lē'âh,* meaning uncertain). Laban's daughter and Jacob's first wife (Gen 29:21–30); mother of Reuben, Simeon, Levi, Judah, Issachar, Zebulun, and Dinah (29:31–35; 30:17–21). Loyal to Jacob (31:14–16), she returned with him to Canaan, where, at her death, she was buried in Machpelah (49:31). Two of her sons (Levi and Judah) became progenitors of prominent tribes in Israel, and through Judah, Jesus Christ came (49:10; Mic 5:2; Matt 2:6; Heb 7:14; Rev 5:5; cf. Ruth 4:11).

LEATHER (Heb. *'ôr, skin,* Gr. *dermatinos, made of skin*). The skin of certain animals after it has been specially treated. Those who performed this work as a trade were called tanners (Acts 10:32). Leather was an article of clothing (Lev 13:48; Heb 11:37). However, John the Baptist (Matt 3:4) and his prototype, Elijah (2 Kings 1:8), are the only ones specifically mentioned as wearing "a leather belt." Leather was used also for armor, shoes, containers, and writing material.

LEAVEN (lĕv'ĕn, Heb. *se'ōr, hāmēts,* Gr. *zymē*). The answer to seven questions will cover most of the biblical material.

1. Why was leaven so rigorously excluded from meal offerings in the Sinaitic legislation (Exod 29:2, 23, 32; Lev 2:1–16; 6:14–23; 7:9–10; 8:2, 26, 31; 10:12; Num 15:1–9, 17–21; 18:9, cf. Exod 23:18; 34:15)? The answer seems to lie in the fact that leaven represented corruption and therefore symbolized evil.

2. Why was leaven permitted in certain other offerings (Exod 23:15–16; 34:22–23; Lev 2:11; 7:13–14; 23:17–18; Num 15:20)? The answer seems to be that leaven, a part of the daily food, is included in the offerings of thanks. Some hold that leaven here symbolizes the evil that still inheres in the worshiper.

3. Why was leaven excluded from the Passover (Exod 12:14–20; 23:15; 34:18; Deut 16:2–4)? The record indicates that Israel's haste in leaving Egypt prompted this exclusion (Exod 12:11, 29; Deut 16:3). However, the Passover as a type of Christ, who was wholly free of corruption, must be taken into account here (cf. 1 Cor 5:7–8).

4. Does Lot's use of unleavened bread (Gen 19:3) anticipate the symbolism of the Sinaitic legislation? Haste may have been the reason; but the latent symbolism of evil (as inconsistent with angels) cannot be entirely ruled out.

5. What does Amos 4:5 indicate? That the degenerate northern kingdom mixed the permitted (Lev 7:13; 23:17) with the forbidden (Exod 23:18; 34:25; Lev 2:11).

6. What about the NT significance of leaven? Apart from Matthew 13:33 (see below), leaven symbolizes either Jewish legalism (Matt 16:6, 12; Gal 5:9) or moral corruption (1 Cor 5:6ff.).

7. What, then, about Matthew 13:33? This is a much-disputed passage. Some interpret leaven as symbolizing the final apostasy of the professing church; others explain leaven as symbolizing the permeating effect of the gospel in Christianizing the world. WB

LEBANA (lĕbă'nȧ). The founder of a family of temple servants (KJV Nethinim) who returned from captivity with Zerubbabel (Neh 7:48).

LEBANAH (lĕ-bă'nȧ). His descendants were temple servants (KJV Nethinim) who returned with Zerubbabel from captivity (Ezra 2:45).

LEBANON (lĕb'ȧnŏn, Heb. *levānôn, white*). A snowclad mountain range extending in a NE direction for 100 miles (167 km.) along the Syrian coast, from Tyre to Arvad, and the country that bears its name. The name signifies the whiteness either of the fossil-bearing limestone cliffs or the snowy crests of this mountain system. Rising precipitously from the Mediterranean (Josh 9:1), Lebanon proper averages 6,000 feet (1,875 m.) above sea level (cf. the steep grades on the present Beirut-Damascus highway), with peaks rising to 10,200 feet (3,188 m.); but the elevation then drops to 2,300 feet (719 m.), for ten miles (seventeen km.) across the Orontes River Valley, known as Coele (hollow) Syria. East of this "Valley of Lebanon" (Josh 11:17; 12:7), however, rises the Anti-Lebanon range, the southernmost promontory of which is Mount Hermon, whose 9,383-foot (2,932 m.) peak remains visible as far south as Jericho. Scripture speaks of Lebanon and Sirion (Anti-Lebanon, Ps 29:6 = Senir, Deut 3:9; sometimes excluding Hermon, 1 Chron 5:23; Song of Songs 4:8), though "Lebanon" may designate both ranges, or even Anti-Lebanon alone (Josh 13:6), "Lebanon to the east" (13:5). The melting snow of these watersheds (Song of Songs 4:15; Jer 18:14) creates the Orontes, flowing northward; the Abana, watering Damascus to the east; the westward-flowing Leontes or Litany; and the Jordan, meandering southward through Palestine to the Dead Sea. Yet these same peaks desicate the moisture-laden western winds, causing desert farther east.

Lebanon's southern slopes grade into the foothills of Galilee, and the gorge of the Litany marks out a natural NW boundary for Israel (Deut 11:24; 2 Kings 19:23). Strictly speaking, Lebanon lies outside Palestine and, though included in God's promise, it was never totally occupied (Josh 13:5; though cf. its eschatological possession, Ezek 47:15–16). Its isolated crags, however, supported watchtowers (Song of Songs 7:4) and refuge points (Jer 22:20, 23) and came to symbolize the exalted status of Judah's royal house (Jer 22:6; Ezek 17:3).

Ancient Lebanon was heavily forested with varieties of budding foliage (Isa 29:17; Nah 1:4), including the Phoenician juniper, which resembles the cypress (1 Kings 5:8; 2 Kings 19:23) and other tall conifers (Ezek 27:5), but above all the great cedars of Lebanon (1 Kings 4:33).

The great cedars of Lebanon, used in biblical times in the construction of palaces and other major buildings. Felled intensively during many generations, only a few large trees remain. "The righteous . . . grow like a cedar in Lebanon" (Ps 92:12). Courtesy Studium Biblicum Franciscanum, Jerusalem. Photo Manoug.

Biblical poetry praises the motion of their massive branches (Ps 72:16 KJV), the fragrance of their wood (Song of Songs 3:6–9; cf. 4:11 and Hos 14:6 where Lebanon means trees, per Isa 10:34; 40:16), their height as symbolic of dignity or pride (Song of Songs 5:15; Isa 2:13), and their growth and resistance to decay (Ps 92:12). The psalmist's inspired thought thus advances to the corresponding greatness of the Creator, who both plants the cedars (Ps 104:16) and shatters them by his voice (29:5). The Lebanons were famous also for choice wine (Hos 14:7), for thorny plants, and for beasts such as the lion and leopard (2 Kings 14:9; Isa 40:16; Song of Songs 4:8). "The glory of Lebanon" climaxes Isaiah's prophetic descriptions (35:2; 60:13).

Coastal Lebanon was early inhabited by Phoenicians (Josh 13:5–6), skilled in the employment of its cedars for civil and marine construction (Ezek 27:4–5), while its sparser inland population was Hivite (Josh 11:3; Judg 3:3). The name Lebanon appears in ancient Ugaritic, Hittite, Egyptian, and Babylonian, its first biblical mention being Mosaic, 1406 B.C. (Deut 1:7). It was cited in Jotham's fable against Shechem, c. 1130 (Judg 9:15; cf. the reference to fire hazard), as well as in Jehoash's fable against Amaziah over three centuries later (2 Kings 14:9; 2 Chron 25:18). King Solomon contracted with Hiram of Tyre for the use of Lebanon's cedars in the Jerusalem temple, 966–959 (1 Kings 5:6–18; cf. Ezra 3:7, concerning the second temple also), ten thousand workers per month hewing the timbers and floating them in great rafts along the Mediterranean coast. Solomon likewise erected government buildings and palaces in his capital, including a hall and armory called "the Palace of the Forest of Lebanon" from its rows of cedar pillars and paneling (1 Kings 7:2–7; 10:17, 21; Isa 22:8). The king's Lebanese building projects (cf. 1 Kings 10:27) led him to construction work in Lebanon itself, at least portions of which came within his widespread domains (1 Kings 9:19; Song of Songs 4:8). Subsequent advances by the pagan empires of antiquity furthered both the conquest and ruthless exploitation of Lebanon's resources (Isa 33:9). Egyptians, Assyrians, and Greeks left their successive inscriptions at the mouth of the Dog River (Nahr el-Kelb); and Ezekiel compares the destruction of Assyria's king with the felling of cedars of Lebanon (Ezek 31:3, 15–16; cf. Zech 11:1). Habakkuk bewails the violence done also by Babylon in cutting down these forest giants (Hab 2:17; cf. Isa 14:8). By the days of Justinian (A.D. 527–565) the once-extensive groves had suffered heavy depletion, and most of the remainder were destroyed from 1914–19 to supply fuel for the Beirut-Damascus railway. Conservation projects, however, have in recent times attempted reforestation. JBP and WB

LEBAOTH (lĕ-bā'ŏthe, Heb. *levā'ôthe, lionesses*). A town in the southern part of Judah (Josh 15:32), also called Beth Lebaoth (Josh 19:6) and (probably) Beth Biri (1 Chron 4:31). Location otherwise unknown.

LEBBAEUS (See THADDAEUS)

LEB KAMAI (lĕb kăm'ī). A cryptogram for Chaldea, that is, Babylonia (Jer 51:1).

LEBO HAMATH (See HAMATH)

LEBONAH (lĕ-bō'nȧ, Heb. *levônâh, frankincense*). A town, mentioned only in Judges 21:19, north of Bethel on the highway between Shiloh and Shechem. It is now generally identified as the modern Lubban.

LECAH (lē'kȧ, Heb. *lēkhâh, walking*). A "son" of Er (1 Chron 4:21); probably the name of an unknown town.

LEECH (See ANIMALS)

LEEKS (See PLANTS)

LEES (Heb. *shemārîm,* pl. from *shemer, something preserved*). A word in the KJV that describes that undisturbed and thick portion of wine that naturally falls to the bottom of the vat. The word is used figuratively throughout to express (1) the blessings of messianic times (Isa 25:6; cf. 55:1), (2) the spiritual lethargy and decadence of Moab (Jer 48:11), (3) the indifference of Israelites to spiritual realities (Zeph 1:12), and (4) the bitterness and inevitability of God's wrath on the wicked (Ps 75:8, "dregs"). Usually translated "dregs" in NIV.

LEGION (Gr. *legiōn,* or *legeōn,* Lat. *legio*). The largest single unit in the Roman army, including infantry and cavalry. A division of infantry at full strength consisted of about six thousand Roman soldiers. Each division was divided into ten cohorts, and each cohort was further divided into six centuries. Each subdivision, as well as the large whole, had its own officers and its own standards. The term "legion" in the NT represents a vast number (Matt 26:53; Mark 5:9, 15; Luke 8:30).

LEHABITES, LEHABIM (lē'hȧ-bīts, lē-hăb'ĭm, Heb. *lehāvîm,* meaning uncertain). The descendants of the third son of Mizraim (Gen 10:13; 1 Chron 1:11). It is now generally believed that Libyans and Lehabites represent the same ethnic group (see 2 Chron 12:3; 16:8; Isa 66:19; Ezek 30:5; 38:5; Dan 11:43; Nah 3:9; Acts 2:10). Descendants of Ham, they occupied the north coast of Africa west of Egypt.

LEHI (lē'hī, Heb. *lehî, jawbone, cheek*). A place in Judah between the cliff Etam and Philistia, otherwise unknown, where Samson killed a thousand Philistines with a jawbone (Judg 15:9, 14). Samson's exploit changed its name to Ramath Lehi ("the hill of the jawbone")

LEMUEL (lĕm'ū-ĕl, Heb. *lemû'ēl, devoted to God*). A king, otherwise unknown, to whom his mother taught maxims in Proverbs 31:2–9. Though many identities have been proposed, the name undoubtedly describes Solomon (Prov 31:1).

LENTIL (See PLANTS)

LEOPARD (See ANIMALS)

LEPROSY, LEPER (See DISEASES)

LESHEM (lē'shĕm, Heb. *leshem, gem*). The original name of Dan (Josh 19:47), a city at the extreme north of Palestine (1 Sam 3:20). Variant of Laish.

LETHEK (See WEIGHTS AND MEASURES)

LETTER. This designates generally (1) an alphabetical symbol (Gal 6:11), (2) rudimentary education (John 7:15 KJV), (3) a written communication (see below), (4) the external (Rom 2:27, 29 KJV), or (5) Jewish legalism (2 Cor 3:6).

A letter as a means of communication for (1) information and instruction (2 Sam 11:14–15; Esth 1:22; 3:13, NIV "dispatches"; 9:20–30; Jer 29:1ff.) (2) a credential of authority (Ezra 7:11–28; Neh 2:7–9; Esth 8:5, 10ff., NIV "dispatches"; Acts 9:1ff.; 1 Cor 16:3; 2 Cor 3:1), (3) propaganda and strife (1 Kings 21:8–11; Ezra 4:7–24; Jer 29:24–32), (4) forged counter-instruction (1 Kings 21:8–11; 2 Thess 2:2), and (5) invitation (2 Chron 30:1–6). A letter could be a cause of misunderstanding (2 Kings 5:5–7; 2 Cor 10:9–11) and a cause for concern (2 Kings 19:14ff.).

LETUSHITES (lĕ-tū'shīts, Heb. *letûshîm, sharpened*). The descendants of the second son of Dedan, grandson of Abraham by Keturah (Gen 25:3). They probably settled in North Arabia.

LEUMMITES (lē-ŭm'īts, Heb. *le'ummîm, peoples, nations*). Mentioned only in Genesis 25:3 as descendants of the third son of Dedan, who was a grandson of Abraham by Keturah. They were possibly some tribe that settled in Arabia—otherwise unknown.

LEVI (lē'vī, Heb. *lēwî, joined*). 1. Jacob's third son by Leah (Gen 29:34; 35:23). Levi, born in Haran, accompanied his father on his return to Canaan. He joined his brothers in sinister plots against Joseph (37:4, 28); and, with them, eventually bowed before Joseph (42:6). A predicted famine caused Jacob's entire family to migrate to Egypt, where Levi died at age 137 (Exod 6:16). His three sons—Gershon, Kohath, and Merari (Gen 46:11)—later became heads of families. Three things deserve special attention. (1) His mother named him "Levi," hoping that Jacob, his father, would now be "attached" to her (29:34). (2) His part in the massacre of the Shechemites because of Shechem's raping of Dinah, his sister, showed two facets of his character: duplicity and righteous indignation (34:25–31). (3) Jacob, facing death, pronounced a curse on Simeon and Levi because of their iniquitous deed at Shechem (cf. 34:25–31 with 49:5–7); but because of holy zeal manifested at Sinai (Exod 32:25–29) and in his descendant Phinehas (Num 25:6–13), Levi's curse was turned into a blessing (Deut 33:8–11) for his descendants. See also LEVITES.

2. and 3. Ancestors of Jesus (Luke 3:24, 29).

4. See MATTHEW.

LEVIATHAN (See ANIMALS)

LEVIRATE MARRIAGE (lĕv'ĭ-rāt, lē'vĭ-rāt, from Lat. *levir, a husband's brother*). An ancient custom, sanctioned by practice (Gen 38:8ff.) and by law (Deut 25:5–10, which does not contradict Lev 18:16; 20:21, where the participants are all alive), whereby a deceased man's brother or nearest male kin was required to marry his brother's widow and raise up seed in his brother's name. To repudiate this obligation meant public infamy (Onan's sin was his refusal to fulfill his obligation to his dead brother (Gen 38:8–10). Ruth's marriage to Boaz recognized this law (Ruth 4:1–17). It also underlies the argument of the Sadducees in Matthew 22:23–33.

LEVITES (lē'vīts). The name given to the descendants of Levi.

I. Their Origin: Levi was the third son of Jacob by Leah (Gen 29:34; 35:22–26). The Genesis record gives no intimation regarding the later greatness of the tribe bearing Levi's name. Such silence bears indirect testimony to the fact that the Genesis account, contrary to the theories of negative criticism, must have been written prior to the noble event that took place at Mount Sinai (Exod 32:25–29) that caused Levi's descendants to receive special status in Israel. The Genesis record is thus free of any bias or hint of Levi's future greatness as a tribe in Israel. Furthermore, if the Genesis account had been written after the event on Mount Sinai, as claimed by modern criticism, it is difficult to understand why the record of Levi's notorious deed at Shechem (Gen 34:25–31) was still retained, especially if, as also claimed by modern criticism, the early "history" was written, subjectively, to reflect the later greatness of Israel. Let us remember also that Genesis closes with a curse on Levi for his participation in the crime at Shechem (49:5–7). This curse, pronounced by the dying Jacob, would be utterly inconsistent with the critical view that Genesis, written by multiple writers late in Israel's history, reflects the national prestige of later times. The conservative view, accepting the Bible history as a record of real events, is free of such problems.

II. Their Appointment. Several discernible factors undoubtedly influenced the selection of Levi's descendants for their special place in Israel's religion. (1) The divine selection of Moses and Aaron, who were descendants of Kohath, one of Levi's three sons (Exod 2:1–10; 6:14–27; Num 26:59), obviously conferred on the Levites an honor that was recognized by the other tribes. (2) However, an event of transcending importance at Mount Sinai (Exod 32:25–29) gave to the Levites as a tribe their place of privilege and responsibility in God's plan. The event just referred to transmuted the curse of Jacob's prophecy (Gen 49:5–7) into the blessing of Moses' prophecy (Deut 33:8–11). (3) Moreover, this choice was undoubtedly confirmed by a very similar event when an individual Levite, Phinehas by name, stayed the plague that was about to decimate the Israelites (Num 25:1–13). Thus the true record of history shows how the curse on Levi the ancestor became, by the wonders of God's providence, a blessing to his descendants.

Let us consider here some of the purposes served in the divine plan by the selection of the Levites for their special ministry in the worship of God's ancient people. (1) As just recounted, their selection and appointment were rewards for their faithfulness to the Lord in a time of moral declension (Exod 32:25–29). (2) The doctrine of substitution was illustrated by the selection of this tribe, for, although God claimed the firstborn males of all the tribes on the basis of the death of the firstborn among the Egyptians (13:11–16), God graciously allowed the Levites to become substitutes for their fellow tribesmen (Num 3:9, 11–13, 40–41, 45–51; 8:14–19). (3) The simplification of service would surely result from the selection of one tribe, for one such tribe closely knit by blood and by ancestral prestige, would be more manageable than uncertain detachments from many tribes. (4) The law of the tithe enhanced the selection of the Levites, for, in a sense, this tribe was a tithe of all the tribes; and it was to this tribe that the tithe was paid (Num 18:20–21; Deut 18:1–8; Neh 10:37–39; Heb 7:5, 9). (5) Israel's separation from the nations was further intensified by the selection of one tribe that was separated from all the other tribes and separated and purified to the Lord (Num 8:5–22). (6) Life as a sojourner without an inheritance here is illustrated by the fact that the Levites had no inheritance in Israel; the Lord alone was their inheritance (Num 18:20–24; 26:62; Deut 10:9; 12:12; 14:27). Nevertheless it is clear, in the light of Exodus 19:4–5, that humanly speaking the appointment of Levi as the priestly tribe to act on behalf of the whole people was an expedient arising from the fact that the people of God in their entirety could not yet attain to their privilege as priests of the Lord. This, however, has now been secured for us by Christ (cf. 1 Peter 2:9).

III. Their Organization. A threefold organization is discernible: (1) The top echelon was occupied by Aaron and his sons; these alone were priests in the restricted sense. The priests belonged to the family of Kohath. (2) The middle echelon included all the other Kohathites who were not of Aaron's family; to them were given certain privileges in carrying the most sacred parts of the tabernacle (Num 3:27–32; 4:4–15; 7:9). (3) The bottom echelon comprised all members of the families of Gershon and Merari; to them lesser duties were prescribed (3:21–26, 33–37).

IV. Priests and Levites. The Mosaic legislation

made a sharp distinction between the priests and nonpriests or ordinary Levites. (1) The priests must belong to Aaron's family; the Levites belonged to the larger family of Levi. A priest was a Levite; but a Levite was not necessarily a priest. (2) Priests were consecrated (Exod 29:1–37; Lev 8); Levites were purified (Num 8:5–22). (3) Levites were considered a gift to Aaron and his sons (3:5–13; 8:19; 18:1–7). (4) The fundamental difference consisted of this: only the priest had the right to minister at the altar and to enter the sanctuary (Exod 28:1; 29:9; Num 3:10, 38; 4:15, 19–20; 18:1–7; 25:10–13). The rebellion of Korah, a Kohathite (Num 16:1) against the uniqueness of Aaron's priesthood illustrated, in the way the rebellion was subdued, the heinous nature of attempting to enter the priesthood without the necessary prerequisites (Num 16). The choice of Aaron was further confirmed by the budding of his rod (Num 17:1–11; Heb 9:4).

V. Post-Mosaic Changes. NT typology (cf. Heb 8–10) considers the Sinaitic legislation the standard form. The post-Sinaitic activity of the Levites may be succinctly summarized in the following way:

1. In the settlement in Canaan the Levites were necessarily relieved of some of their duties; the tabernacle no longer needed transportation. It is doubtful if the Levites ever fully occupied all the forty-eight cities assigned to them and the priests. The episode in Judges 17:7–13 does not, as maintained by critics, represent the earliest information concerning the priesthood.

2. In David's time the neglect of the provision of Numbers 7:1–9 brought death to a Levite (1 Chron 13:7–10; 15:12–15). David introduced innovations in the age and service of the Levites (23:26). Certain Levites, particularly Asaph, became musicians and probably wrote some of the Psalms (1 Chron 6:39, 43; 15:16ff.; 16:4ff.; 25:1–9; Pss 50, 73–83).

3. In the disruption of the united kingdom many Levites from the northern kingdom sought political and religious asylum in Judah (2 Chron 11:13–16; 13:9–12; 15:9); but some Levites were evidently involved in the apostasy of the northern kingdom (Ezek 44:10–15). The Levites during this period were still considered teachers (2 Chron 17:8ff.; 19:8; cf. Deut 33:10).

4. The exilic period brings before us the symbolism of Ezekiel: only the true Levites, sons of Zadok, ministered in the temple (Ezek 43:19; 44:10–16; 48:11–12).

5. In the postexilic period Levites did not return from Babylon in the same proportion as the priests (Ezra 2:36–42; Neh 7:39–45). Later, a special effort was required to get the Levites to return (Ezra 8:15–19). They were still considered to be teachers (8:15ff.) and musicians (2:40–41; 3:10ff.; Neh 7:43–44).

6. Only a few references to the Levites are found in the NT (Luke 10:32; John 1:19; Acts 4:36; Heb 7:11). Two points merit a final word: first, Levi, through his ancestor Abraham, paid tithes to Melchizedek (Gen 14:17–20), thus proving the superiority of Melchizedek's (i.e., Christ's) priesthood to Aaron's (Heb 7:4–10); second, since the Levitical priesthood could not bring perfection, it was required that another priest, from a different tribe and a different order, arise (Heb 7:11–17; cf. Gen 49:10; Ps 110).

WB

LEVITICAL CITIES. The plan set out in Numbers 35:1–8 (fulfilled in Joshua 21) gave the Levites forty-eight cities. This plan involved a threefold purpose: (1) Such cities caused the Levites to be "scattered" in Israel and thus fulfilled Jacob's dying prophecy (Gen 49:7). (2) Thus "scattered," they could carry out their teaching ministry better (Deut 33:10). (3) Since six of their cities were to be "cities of refuge" (Num 35:6), they would thereby become more accessible to those seeking legal protection (Deut 19:1–3, 7–10, 17ff.). Negative criticism finds three problems: (1) The Levites were given "no inheritance" in Israel (Num 18:20). However, although these cities were not an inheritance, they were a gift from the other tribes (35:2, 4, 6–8). (2) No substantial evidence exists in preexilic history for such cities. True, but Israel also failed to carry out fully other Mosaic legislation (cf. 2 Chron 35:18; 36:21). (3) Numbers 35:2–8 is only an ideal theory never realized until Ezekiel

48:8–14. Not so; Ezekiel's symbolic idealization is based on Numbers 35:1–8 (and Josh 21), though not literally confined to the earlier legislation.

LEVITICUS (lĕ-vĭt'ĭ-kŭs, Gr. *Levitikon, relating to the Levites*). The designation in the English Bible of the third book of the Pentateuch, derived from the Latin rendering (*Liber Leviticus*) of the Greek title *Levitikon*. The Hebrew title merely consists of the first word of the text (*wayyiqrā'*), "and he called." The book is closely associated with Exodus and Numbers in historical continuity, but differs from them in that the purely historical element is subordinate to legal and ritual considerations. Although the emphasis in Leviticus is more on priests than on Levites, the English title is not inappropriate, since the Jewish priesthood was essentially Levitical (cf. Heb 7:11).

Leviticus enshrines the laws by which the religious and civil organization of the primitive theocracy in Canaan was to be regulated. At Sinai the Israelites had been incorporated into a special relationship with God, had been given the covenant laws, and had been provided with a tabernacle for worship. Leviticus contains much that is technical in nature and meant for the direction of the priesthood in the conduct of worship and the regulating of social life. Thus it is distinct from Deuteronomy, which is in effect a popular exposition of Levitical law.

The composition of the book was universally ascribed by ancient tradition, both Jewish and Gentile, to Moses the lawgiver of Israel. During the Middle Ages a number of writers denied certain aspects of Mosaic authorship to the Pentateuch, but it was only during the eighteenth century that literary criticism seriously challenged the traditional view. The movement grew in the following century and reached its classic formulation under Wellhausen in 1887. Using a background of Hegelian evolutionary philosophy, he reconstructed Israelite history, and on the basis of a documentary hypothesis for Pentateuchal origins he assigned Leviticus to a postexilic date along with other elements of the so-called priestly code.

This view has been widely espoused by liberal scholars, and in its developed forms holds that Leviticus was compiled by temple priests between 500 and 450 B.C., using earlier legislation such as the "holiness code" (Lev 17–26), which is regarded as dating from about 650. Most critical writers, however, concede that Leviticus contains much older material, such as the Azazel or scapegoat ritual in chapter 16 and traditional historical narratives including the punishment of Aaron's sons (10:1–7) and the stoning of the blasphemer (24:10–14).

The literary criteria used in assigning a late date to the bulk of Leviticus have been criticized continuously since the time of Wellhausen, and the number of scholars who find them very difficult to sustain is increasing gradually. This arises in part from a wider knowledge of the media of communication in antiquity and also from historical and archaeological considerations. It is now known that if the techniques of compilation alleged by Wellhausen had actually been employed in the composition of Leviticus and the rest of the Pentateuch, it would have been unique in the literary annals of the ancient Near East. Archaeological discoveries have shown that in actual fact the Hebrews used much the same literary methods as their neighbors, and that significant areas of biblical literature are closely related in language and style to other writings of that day.

The historical evidence furnished by the canon of the Samaritan Pentateuch indicates a date for Leviticus much in advance of that suggested by critical scholars. According to 2 Kings 17:24–28, organized Samaritan worship began in the time of Esarhaddon (c. 681–669 B.C.). Since the Samaritans used only the Pentateuch as their basis for doctrine and worship, it is reasonable to assume that it was in its final form by about the eighth century B.C. Archaeological discoveries in the Dead Sea caves uncovered a fragment of Leviticus written in the Phoenician script current in the seventh century B.C. If this is a genuine product of that period, it alone will compel careful reexamination of the entire Wellhausen theory. Other fragments of Leviticus dated c. 100 were also found in the caves and appeared to have come from a Samaritan manuscript.

Analysis: The first seven chapters of Leviticus give the detailed sacrificial procedures showing how the various kinds of burnt offerings, the meal offering, the sin and guilt offerings, and other sacrifices avail for the removal of sin and defilement under the covenant. A subsequent liturgical section (8:1–10:20) describes the consecration of Aaron and the priesthood, followed by the designation of clean and unclean beasts and certain rules of hygiene (11:1–15:33). The ritual of the Day of Atonement occurs in chapter 16, followed by a section (17:1–20:27) treating sacrificial blood, ethical laws, and penalties for transgressors. The theme of 21:1–24:23 is priestly holiness and the consecration of seasons, while the following chapter deals with the legislation surrounding the sabbatical and jubilee years. A concluding chapter outlines promises and threats (26:1–46), and an appendix (27:1–34) covers vows. Man as sinner, substitutionary atonement, and divine holiness are prominent throughout Leviticus.

Bibliography: J. L. Mays, *The Book of Leviticus, The Book of Numbers* (LBC), 1963; Martin Noth, *Leviticus: A Commentary,* 1977; G. J. Wenham, *The Book of Leviticus* (NIC), 1979. RKH

LEVY (lĕv'ē, Heb. *mas, tribute*). A tax or tribute, often to be rendered in service. It is used in reference to the thirty thousand free Israelites conscripted by Solomon for four months' service a year in Lebanon (1 Kings 5:13–14 KJV); also of the tribute labor imposed on the surviving Canaanites (1 Kings 9:21 KJV). It is also used in

Relief from Nineveh (668–633 B.C.) in which King Ashurbanipal is shown holding in his right hand a shallow bowl, from which he pours a libation over the four dead lions at his feet. In front of the king are an offering table and incense stand, and two musicians playing lyres. Reproduced by courtesy of the Trustees of the British Museum.

the NIV for the tribute of gold and silver imposed by Pharaoh Neco on Judah (2 Kings 23:33; 2 Chron 36:3).

LIBATION. Usually referred to as a "drink offering"; the pouring out of liquids, such as wine, water, oil, etc., but generally wine, as an offering to a deity. Libations were common among the heathen nations (Deut 32:38). Drink offerings accompanied many OT sacrifices (Exod 29:40–41; Lev 23:13, 18, 37; Num 15:4–10, 24; 28:7–10). In 2 Timothy 4:6 and Philippians 2:17, Paul pictures his death as a drink offering. See also SACRIFICE AND OFFERINGS.

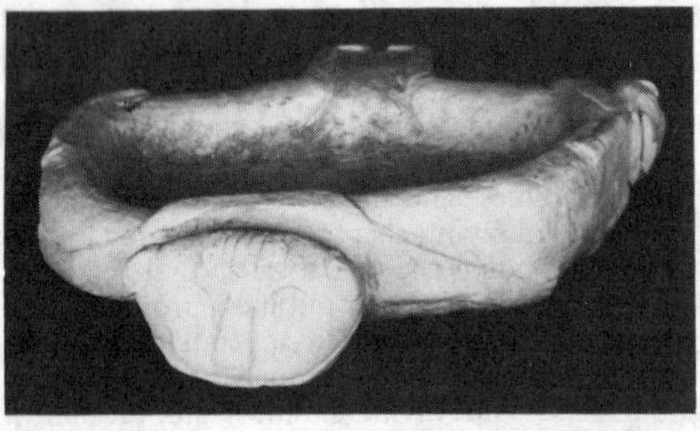
Stone libation tray decorated with a carved lion's head, from Tell Beit Mirsim (Debir), c. 1400–1200 B.C. Courtesy Israel Department of Antiquities and Museums.

LIBERTINES (Gr. *Libertinoi*). Probably originally captive Jews brought to Rome by Pompey in 63 B.C., liberated subsequently, and repatriated to Palestine, where, presumably, they built a synagogue still occupied by their descendants a century after Pompey's Palestinian campaign (Acts 6:9). These people were Roman citizens. There seems to be some evidence for a synagogue of Libertines at Pompeii. There is no substance in the conjectural alternative explanation that the Libertines were natives of "Libertum" near Carthage. The place is unknown to history or geography. The explanation adopted goes back to Chrysostom.

LIBERTY. Freedom, the opposite of servitude or bondage, whether physical, moral, or spiritual. The term is used of slaves or captives being set free from physical servitude or imprisonment (Lev 25:10; Jer 34:8, 15–17; Acts 26:23; Heb 13:23), or the granting of certain privileges while imprisoned (Acts 24:23; 27:3). In Ezekiel 46:17 reference is made to "the year of freedom," which is the Year of Jubilee. The term has a legal and moral tone in 1 Corinthians 7:39 in asserting the right of a widow to remarry. The special concern of Christianity is the spiritual liberty of believers in Christ. Found in union with Christ, it carries with it freedom from the ceremonial law (Gal 5:1; 2:4) and must be valued and guarded. The essence of Christian liberty lies not in external freedom but in deliverance from the bondage of sin and its consequent inner corruption (John 8:34–36; Rom 6:20–22).

Spiritual liberty is the result of the Spirit's regenerating work, for his presence and work within produces liberty (2 Cor 3:17), giving a sense of freedom through a filial relation with God (Rom 8:15–16). Godly men of the OT knew a measure of this spiritual liberty (Ps 119:45), but the gospel reveals and offers it in its fullness. Using the picture of Isaiah 61:1, Christ proclaimed this liberty to be the goal of his mission (Luke 4:18). Intimately related to practical holiness of life (Rom 6:18–22), spiritual liberty never condones license. Believers are warned against abuse of this liberty in sinful indulgence (Gal 5:13; 1 Peter 2:16; 2 Peter

2:19); and speech and conduct are to be judged by "the law of liberty" (James 2:12), which has taken the place of the ancient law. In regard to things not expressly commanded or forbidden, Christian liberty must be granted, allowing for the exercise of individual judgment and Christian conscience before God (1 Cor 10:29–31); but its use must be limited by considerations of love, expediency, and self-preservation, lest that liberty become a stumbling block to the weak (8:9). Romans 8:21 points to creation's future "liberation" from decay and imperfection when God's children are glorified.

Bibliography: Peter Richardson, *Paul's Ethic of Freedom,* 1979; NIDNTT, 1:715–20.

DEH

LIBNAH (lĭb′nȧ, Heb. *livnâh, whiteness*). 1. A desert camp of Israel, the fifth station after leaving Sinai (Num 33:20–21). It is perhaps the same as Laban (Deut 1:1). Its location is unknown.

2. A Canaanite city, near Lachish, captured by Joshua (Josh 10:29–32; 12:15) and named at the head of a group of nine cities in the lowland (15:42–44). It was designated a Levitical city in Judah (Josh 21:13; 1 Chron 6:57). Simultaneously with Edom it revolted from Jehoram (2 Kings 8:22; 2 Chron 21:10). As a strong fortified center it sustained the siege of Sennacherib for some time (2 Kings 19:8; Isa 37:8). It was the native city of Hamutal, the wife of King Josiah and mother of Jehoahaz and Zedekiah (2 Kings 23:31; 24:18; Jer 52:1). Archaeology has identified it with modern Tell es Safi, at the head of the Valley of Elah.

LIBNI (lĭb′nī, Heb. *livnî, white*). 1. The first-named of the two sons of Gershon, the son of Levi (Exod 6:17; Num 3:18; 1 Chron 6:17, 20). He is also called Ladan (1 Chron 23:7; 26:21). His descendants are called Libnites (Num 3:21; 26:58).

2. A Levite, son of Mahli, son of Merari (1 Chron 6:29).

LIBYA (lĭb′ĭ-ȧ). The ancient Greek name for northern Africa west of Egypt. The Hebrew is *Put* (Jer 46:9; Ezek 30:5; 38:5; Dan 11:43), and is so rendered by ASV and NIV, except Daniel 11:43. It was the country of the Lubim, descendants of Ham (Gen 10:13). Cyrene was one of its cities (Acts 2:10).

LICE (See ANIMALS)

LIE, LYING (Heb. *seqer,* Gr. *pseudos*). Since God is truth and truthful, he cannot lie as humans do (Num 23:19). Because Israel is not in a harmonious relation to God and because the people have rejected his truth, they have fallen prey to a lie—a false view of life often including idolatry. Thus they have become liars. They have eaten the fruit of lies ("deception") (Hos 10:13), allowed lies to become their refuge (Isa 28:15), and been led astray by lies (Amos 2:4). But God will make an end of all liars (Ps 5:6). In contrast to those who live a life of lies, the righteous remnant of Israel "do no wrong . . . speak no lies" (Zeph 3:13). In the law of Moses there are laws against bearing false witness (Exod 20:16) and perjury (Lev 19:12) and there is the general command, "Do not lie" (19:11).

The NT also presents the picture of people of the world who prefer a lie to truth (Rom 1:25—exchanging the truth about God for a lie). Within the churches there are those who make God a liar by claiming they are not sinners (1 John 1:10) and those who preach a lie—that Jesus is not the Christ (1 John 2:22; Rev 2:2). The source of lies is the devil (John 8:44; Acts 5:3). Christians must not lie to one another (Eph 4:25; Col 3:9), for Christ is the truth and those who lie are not one with him. Therefore those who are redeemed by the Lamb are those with no lie on their lips (Rev 14:5).

Connected with the idea of a lie are those who live a lie or convey a lie—a false brother (2 Cor 11:26), a false apostle (11:13), a false teacher (2 Peter 2:1), a false witness (Matt 26:60), a false prophet (7:15), and a false Christ (24:24). In each of these cases the Greek word begins with *pseudo* ("lying" or "false"). PT

LIEUTENANT (See SATRAP)

LIFE. A complex concept with varied shades of meaning, rendering several Hebrew and Greek terms. It may denote *physical* or natural life, whether animal (Gen 1:20; 6:17; Rev 8:9) or human (Lev 17:14; Matt 2:20; Luke 12:22). It is the vital principle or breath of life, which God

Painting from the tomb of the Vizier Ramose at Thebes (fourteenth century B.C.) showing a Libyan, distinguished by a sidelock of hair ending in a curl below the neck (far right), standing—together with the other traditional enemies of Egypt (the Nubians and Asiatics)—in homage to the king. Courtesy B. Brandl.

imparted to man, making him a living soul (Gen 2:7). This life is a precious gift, and the taking of life is prohibited (Gen 9:5; Exod 20:13; Lev 24:17). It is propagated through physical generation and is subject to physical death. It may signify the period of one's earthly existence, one's lifetime (Gen 23:1; 25:7; Luke 16:25), or the relations, activities, and experiences that make up life (Exod 1:14; Deut 32:47; Job 10:1; Luke 12:15). Occasionally it means one's manner of life (1 Tim 2:2; 1 John 2:16) or the means for sustaining life (Deut 24:6; 1 John 3:17). But the primary concern of the Scriptures is *spiritual* or *eternal* life for the human race. It is the gift of God, mediated through faith in Jesus Christ (John 3:36; 5:24; Rom 5:10; 6:23; 1 John 5:12). It is not synonymous with endless existence, which is also true of the unsaved. It is qualitative, involving the impartation of a new nature (2 Peter 1:3–4). It is communicated to the believer in this life, resulting in fellowship with God in Christ, and is not interrupted by physical death (1 Thess 5:10). It will find its perfection and full reality of blessedness with God in the life to come (Rom 2:7; 2 Cor 5:4). As "the living God" (Deut 5:26; Ps 42:2; 1 Thess 1:9; 1 Tim 3:15), the eternal and self-existent One, God has *absolute* life in himself (John 5:26) and is the source of all life (Ps 36:9; John 1:4; 17:3; 1 John 1:1–2; 5:20). DEH

LIFE, THE BOOK OF. A figurative expression denoting God's record of those who inherit eternal life (Phil 4:3; Rev 3:5; 21:27). From man's point of view individuals may be blotted out of that book (Ps 69:28; Matt 25:29); but from God's point of view it contains only the names of the elect, which will not be blotted out (Rev 3:5; 13:8; 17:8; 20:15).

LIGHT. The first recorded utterance of God in the Bible is "Let there be light" (Gen 1:3), the first sign of divine operation in the world of chaos and darkness. Dawn indicates the sure dispelling of darkness, the essence of all God's gifts. God is the creator of both light and darkness (Isa 45:6–7) and watches over their orderly succession (Ps 104:20; Amos 4:13), yet light is superior (Eccl 2:13). It is virtually impossible to distinguish between natural and metaphorical uses of light in the Bible. Light is above all the source of life (11:7). The word is often used in synonyms for being alive (Job 3:20) or being born (3:16) or for the pleasures of life (Ps 97:11) or for good days for the righteous (112:4) or for an essential in man's happiness (36:9). Light brings order to the world. Light and truth are coupled biblically (Ps 43:3; cf. Ps 19; Prov 6:23; Isa 51:4). Truth and law give knowledge (Ps 19:8; 139:11–12) and guidance (Deut 28:29; Job 22:28; Prov 4:18; cf. Mic 7:8). The recipient of light himself becomes a light, shining outwardly (Ps 34:5; Eccl 8:1) and inwardly (Prov 20:27; Dan 5:11). The manifestations of light are the work of "the Father of the heavenly lights" (James 1:17), he who dwells in light (Exod 13:21; Ps 104:2; 1 Tim 6:16) and who imparts light as a divine gift. The OT concept of Scripture as a lamp or a light is taken over in the NT (2 Peter 1:19). Conversion is spoken of as illumination (Heb 6:4; 10:32). Believers are "people of the light" (Luke 16:8; 1 Thess 5:5) and the "light of the world" (Matt 5:14). Because the gift may be lost through inactivity (John 5:35; 1 Thess 5:5–6), the heavenly light must be used as armor or a weapon (Eph 6:12; Rom 13:12) in the fight against darkness. The light is permanently present in Christ (John 1:7–9; Heb 1:3) and in the gospel (Acts 26:23; 2 Cor 4:4). In the new age there will be no more night (Rev 21:23). John stresses that "God is light" (1 John 1:5), and he who hates his brother is in darkness (2:11).

See also DARKNESS.

Bibliography: C. H. Dodd, *The Bible and the Greeks,* 1955; B. Vassady, *Light Against Darkness,* 1961; L. Sibum, *The Bible on Light,* 1966; H. Conzelmann, TDNT, 9:310–58. JDD

LIGHTNING (Heb. *bārāq,* Gr. *astrapē*). A visible electric discharge between rain clouds or between a rain cloud and the earth, producing a thunderclap. In Palestine and Syria lightning is common during the heavy fall and spring rains. Lightning is generally accompanied by heavy rain, and at times by hail (Exod 9:23–24). The Scriptures mention lightning as a manifestation of God's power, symbolizing his command of the forces of nature (Job 28:26; 38:35; Ps 135:7; Zech 10:1). Lightnings are his instruments in bringing about the destruction of his opponents (Ps 18:14; 144:6; Zech 9:14–15). Lightning is a symbol of speed (Ezek 1:14; Nah 2:4; Zech 9:14) and of dazzling brightness (Dan 10:6; Matt 28:3). In Matthew 24:27 and Luke 17:24 Jesus uses the figure of lightning to indicate the unmistakable certainty of the fact that he will come again. In Luke 10:18 Jesus speaks of beholding Satan fallen as lightning, symbolic of a definite and terrific defeat.

LIKHI (lĭk'hī). A Manassite of the family of Gilead, mentioned in 1 Chronicles 7:19 as the third son of Shemida.

LILY (See PLANTS)

LINE. A translation of six different Hebrew words and one Greek word. Usually the meaning is *a measuring line* (Jer 31:39; Ezek 47:3; Zech 1:16; 2:1) or a cord or thread (Josh 2:18, 21; Ezek 40:3). In Isaiah 44:13 it means either "pencil" (ASV) or a cutting instrument (NIV, however, retains "line"). In Psalm 16:6 it means "portion" as fixed by measurement (NIV "boundary lines"); in 19:4 it signifies the sound made by a musical chord (cf. Rom 10:18). In Isaiah 28:10 "line upon line" (NIV "rule on rule"), is the drunkard's sneer at the childishness of Isaiah's ceaseless chidings. In 2 Corinthians 10:16 "line" means a "province" or sphere worked by another (NIV "another man's territory").

LINEN. Thread or cloth, prepared from the fiber

of flax. The use of flax fiber for cloth and other purposes is very ancient, being traceable as far back as the Stone Age. Flax was cultivated in Mesopotamia, Assyria, and Egypt, and linen was well known in the ancient biblical world. Ancient Egypt was noted for its fine linen and carried on a thriving export with neighboring nations. Flax was being cultivated in the tropical climate around Jericho at the time of the conquest (Josh 2:6). Having learned the art in Egypt (Exod 35:25), Hebrew women practiced the spinning and weaving of flax (Prov 31:13, 19). The clans of Beth Ashbea attained eminence as workers in linen (1 Chron 4:21).

Linen is the translation of several different Hebrew and Greek words. The Hebrew *pīshteh* denotes the flax plant (Josh 2:6; Judg 15:14; Prov 31:13; Isa 19:9) or the material made from it (Lev 13:47; Deut 22:11; Jer 13:1; Ezek 44:17), as opposed to woolen material. *Shaatnēz* is used twice to signify a garment made of two sorts of thread, linen and woolen, which the Israelites were forbidden to wear (Lev 19:19; Deut 22:11). The term *badh,* used twenty-three times (e.g, Exod 28:42; Lev 6:10; 1 Sam 2:18; Ezek 9:2), means "linen cloth," with the subordinate ideas of white and fine. *Shēsh,* like the later term *bûts,* means "fine linen," the adjective "fine" being coupled with it by the translators to denote a finer quality of linen (Prov 31:22). Since its meaning is "whiteness," it may have included other materials besides linen. It is equivalent to the Greek *byssos,* "fine linen." The Hebrew *sādhîn* denotes an undergarment of linen worn next to the body (Prov 31:24; Isa 3:23; "sheet" in Judg 14:12–13, KJV) and is synonymous with the Greek *sindon,* the term for the linen sheet in which the body of Jesus was wrapped (Matt 27:59; Mark 15:46; Luke 23:53). In John 19:40; 20:5ff.; Luke 24:12, "linen clothes" (NIV "strips of linen") is *othonion,* linen bands, linen cloth torn into strips. In Revelation 15:6 the word used is *linon,* a linen garment.

The biblical references show varied uses of linen. For clothing it was preferred to cotton material in warm climates because of the sensation of coolness given by linen garments. Its use is frequently mentioned in connection with the garments of the Aaronic priests (Exod 28:42; Lev 6:10; 1 Sam 22:18), their tunics, undergarments, and headdresses being exclusively of linen, and the girdle largely of it (Exod 28:39; 39:27–29). It was also preferred by others for dress in religious services; it was worn by the child Samuel (1 Sam 2:18), by the Levitical singers in the temple (2 Chron 5:12), and even by royal personages (2 Sam 6:14; 1 Chron 15:27). Angels are described as dressed in it (Ezek 9:2; 10:2; Dan 10:5; 12:6), as also the host of the redeemed returning with Christ from heaven (Rev 19:14). In Revelation 19:8 linen is used figuratively of the moral purity of the saints. Linen was used also for garments of distinction (Gen 41:41; Esth 8:15). Apparently linen garments of a coarser material were worn by men (Judg 14:12–13) and women (Prov 31:22). But the use of fine linen for ordinary purposes was apparently a sign of luxury and extravagance (Isa 3:23; Ezek 16:10; Luke 16:19; Rev 18:12, 16). Linen was used also for nets (Isa 19:9), measuring lines (Ezek 40:3), girdles (Jer 13:1), and for fine hangings (Esth 1:6). In NT times at least, linen was extensively used by the Jews for burial shrouds, as at the burial of Jesus (Matt 27:59; Mark 15:46; Luke 23:53; John 19:40; 20:5ff.). Egyptian mummies were wrapped exclusively in linen sheets of vast proportions.

LINUS (lī'nŭs). A Christian in Rome joining Paul in sending salutations to Timothy in 2 Timothy 4:21. According to Irenaeus and Eusebius, he became the first bishop of Rome.

LION (See ANIMALS)

LITTLE OWL (See BIRDS)

LIVER (Heb. *kāvēdh, heavy*). The heaviest of the viscera, both in weight and importance, mentioned fourteen times in the OT. Usually the reference is to the bodily organ in connection with sacrificial instructions (e.g., Exod 29:13, 22; Lev 3:4, 10, 15; 4:9; 7:4). Its use for purposes of divination was common among heathen nations (Ezek 21:21), but the practice is not verified among the Jews. Being closely identified with the source and center of life, it is mentioned in depicting profound sorrow (Lam 2:11 KJV), and piercing it was fatal (Prov 7:22–23).

LIVING CREATURES. A term (often "beasts" in KJV) that apparently sometimes indicates the cherubim (Ezek 1:5–22; 3:13; 10:15–20; Rev 4:6–9). In the Creation account "living creatures" designates aquatic animals (Gen 1:21), mammals (1:24), or any animals (2:19).

Clay liver model inscribed with omens and magical formulae for the use of diviners From Babylonia, c. 1830–1530 B.C. Reproduced by courtesy of the Trustees of the British Museum.

LIZARD (See ANIMALS)

LO-AMMI (lō-ăm'ī, Heb. *lō'-'ammî, not my people*). The symbolic name given to Hosea's third child; it is transliterated "Lo-Ammi" in Hosea 1:9a, but translated "not my people" in Hosea 1:9b–10; 2:23. Originally applied to express the rejection of the northern kingdom in contrast to the election of Judah (Hos 1:6–7), the name prophetically and paradoxically (1:11; 2:23) becomes the designation of the rejected Gentiles now, during Israel's present blindness (Rom 11:25–26), incorporated into the true Israel of God (Rom 9:24–26; cf. Deut 32:21; Isa 65:1; Rom 2:28–29; 9:6ff.; 10:19–20; 1 Peter 2:9–10).

LOCK, LOCKS. 1. A mechanical device for fastening a city gate or a door. The primitive locks used to fasten city gates consisted simply of heavy beams of wood, the ends of which were dropped into slots cut into the masonry of the gate (Neh 3:3–15; cf. Deut 3:5; 1 Sam 23:7). Used figuratively, their strengthening spoke of divine protection (Ps 147:13), their burning of a country's invasion (Jer 51:30; Nah 3:13). To strengthen them, iron bars were used (1 Kings 4:13; Isa 45:2). When used to lock house doors (Judg 3:23–24) they were smaller and were flat bolts. Usually several sliding pins dropped into corresponding holes in the bar, requiring a key to release them. Keys varied in size, often being large enough to be carried on the shoulder (Isa 22:22). To open the door from outside, the key was inserted through the hole in the door; the hole might be big enough to admit the hand with the key (Song of Songs 5:5). Fear of the Jews caused the disciples to lock the door of the room where they were staying (John 20:19, 26).

2. In reference to the hair of the head, "lock(s)" is a translation of several different Hebrew words. The term indicates the unshorn and disheveled locks of the Nazirite (Num 6:5), the braided locks of the Nazirite Samson (Judg 16:13, 19), a forelock of the prophet's hair (Ezek 8:3), and the luxuriant locks of the Hebrew youth (S of Sol 5:2, 11). In three verses (S of Sol 4:1; 6:7; Isa 47:2) some versions have "veil" or "tresses" instead of "locks."

LOCUST (See ANIMALS)

LOD (Heb. *lôdh*). A town built by Shemed, a Benjamite (1 Chron 8:12), located in the Shephelah or low hills in SW Palestine. This is the Lydda of the NT.

LO DEBAR (lō' dē'bär, Heb. *lô dhevār,* probably *without pasture*). A town in Gilead east of Jordan, where Mephibosheth, Saul's grandson, lived in the house of Machir until summoned by David to eat at his table (2 Sam 9:1–13). Machir also supplied David's needs when David fled from Absalom to eastern Jordan (17:27ff.). The town is otherwise unknown.

LODGE. A temporary shelter erected in a garden for a watchman guarding the ripening fruit (Isa 1:8, KJV; NIV "hut"). It is of a more temporary nature than a watchtower. In relation to travelers, "a lodging" is a temporary place of sojourn for strangers (Acts 28:23; Philem 22 KJV).

LOGIA. The Greek word for "sententious sayings" or "epigrams," employed in reference to the nonbiblical sayings of Christ, the latest collection of which is the so-called Gospel of Thomas discovered in A.D. 1945 and first made public in 1959. The church has always been aware of sayings of Christ not included in the Gospels. Paul speaks of "the words the Lord Jesus himself said: 'It is more blessed to give than to receive' " (Acts 20:35). The Muslims have retained some such sayings. An ode of the poet Nizami tells the story of the dead dog in the marketplace in whom none could find aught but horror and ugliness. "Pearls," said one standing nearby, "cannot rival the whiteness of his teeth." A mosque near Agra contains another Muslim memory of Christ. Among the arabesques is woven the logion: "Jesus, on whom be peace, said, The world is merely a bridge; ye are to pass over it, and not build your dwellings upon it." This saying may descend from Thomas, who according to tradition carried the gospel to India. Its imagery may be based on the causeway of Tyre. The Codex Bezae inserts a logion after Luke 6:5, "On the same day, seeing someone working on the sabbath, he said to him, Man if you know what you are doing, blessed you are. If you do not know, you are accursed, and a transgressor of the law." Luke speaks of "many who have taken in hand to draw up a narrative," and tradition has it that Matthew, before he wrote his Gospel, made a collection of sayings of Christ. Many such collections were probably current, of which the Gospel of Thomas is one. De Joinville, the medieval French crusader and historian, tells of another. In his account of the Third Crusade, De Joinville tells of the visit of a monk on an embassy to the Lebanese sheik, "the Old Man of the Mountain." The monk reported that his host had a book called *The Words of the Lord unto Peter.* This was in 1248. In the closing years of the nineteenth century a sheet of such sayings was discovered among the papyri. It included two new and now well-known logia: "Thou hearest with one ear but the other thou hast closed"; "Whenever there are two they are not without God, and if one be alone anywhere I say that I am with him. Raise the stone, there thou shalt find me. Cleave the wood, and there I am." A second sheet was discovered in 1904. It contained the logion reminiscent of a saying of Plato: "Let him who seeks cease not till he finds, and when he finds he shall be astonished. Astonished he shall reach the Kingdom, and having reached the Kingdom he shall rest." See also AGRAPHA.

LOGOS (Gr. *logos*). A philosophical and theological term and concept that goes back to the Ionian philosopher Heraclitus (c. 500 B.C.), to whom it meant the universal reason permeating the world and finding self-consciousness in the mind of the philosophers. Stoicism adopted the term for a dynamic principle of reason operating in the world and forming a medium of communion between God and man. The latter function becomes prominent in Philo, with whom the Logos is at once the Stoics' active, intelligent, world-principle, the thought in the divine mind, which was identical with sum-total of Plato's "Forms" or "Ideas," and a mediator between God and the matter of his creation. For Philo, as indeed for his predecessors, the Logos is neither personal nor impersonal. It was vaguely equated with God's utterance (Gen 1:3; Ps 33:9), his "word" in such passages as Psalms 107:20; 147:15, 18, and such expressions as "the angel of the covenant," and with "wisdom" in such personifications as those of Proverbs 8 and Wisdom of Solomon 9:15ff. It is possible that the Qumran community fused the same Hebrew and Hellenistic concepts into their doctrine of the spirit of truth, which, like the spirit of error, was a creature of God. The relevant passages in the "Rule of the Community" document do not admit of dogmatism.

In the New Testament the Logos appears principally in John's writings (John 1:1ff.; 1 John 1:1; Rev 19:13), though references from Paul's writings and the Epistle to the Hebrews might be added. Logos is imperfectly translated "Word," and it is not easy to comprehend the full context of the idea in its Judeo-Hellenistic context. There can be no doubt that both John and Paul saw value in expressing Christian thought in the terminology of the day, a point appreciated by the early church fathers in their sometimes perilous development of the Logos doctrine. Significantly enough, John wrote his prologues at the end of the first century when the first signs of Gnostic error were discernible. In John's use of "Logos" we must certainly see that blending of Judaic and Hellenistic concepts that appeared in Philo's use of the term. From its Greek ancestry, etymological and philosophical, the Johannine word would contain not only the notion of reason, but also the active expression of reason on a divine and perfect plane. Hence the conception of the visible universe as an expression of God's reason, that reason being the force and agency of creation, the Word who said: "Let there be . . . ." But John becomes entirely original and creative when he boldly equates this reason with God himself, and simultaneously sees its incarnation in Christ. It seems likely that John, in this bold thought, brought to firmer expression in the terminology of Hellenistic thought a concept already expressed in 1 Corinthians 8:6, Colossians 1:15–17, and Hebrews 1:2–3. In view of the Colossian heresy of angelic mediatorship the last context is significant.

EMB

LOIN. Used in the KJV to describe the part of the body between the ribs and the hip bones. It is the place where the girdle was worn (Exod 12:11; 2 Kings 1:8; Jer 13:1; Matt 3:4) and the sword was fastened (2 Sam 20:8). Pain and terror were reflected in weakness and shaking of the loins (Ps 38:7; 66:11; 69:23; Jer 30:6). Girding the loins with sackcloth was a sign of mourning (1 Kings 20:32; Isa 32:11; Jer 48:37). As the place of the reproductive organs the loins are euphemistically named for the generative function (Gen 35:11; 1 Kings 8:19; Acts 2:30; Heb 7:5). Since Oriental garments were worn ungirded about the house, to gird up the loins signified preparation for vigorous action (Exod 12:11; 1 Kings 18:46; Job 38:3; Prov 31:17; Luke 12:35; 1 Peter 1:13). To have the loins girded with truth signified strength in attachment to truth (Eph 6:14; cf. Isa 11:5).

LOIS (lō'ĭs, Gr. *Lōis*). The maternal grandmother of Timothy. Commended by Paul for her faith (2 Tim 1:5), she apparently was associated with Eunice in the religious training of Timothy.

LONGSUFFERING (Heb. *'erekh, 'appayim, slow to anger,* Gr. *makrothymia*). The noun preferred by KJV (other versions use "forbearance") to account for the delay of the Lord in inflicting punishment or exercising his anger/wrath. The idea is that God delays his exercise of wrath to give time for repentance and amendment of life (Exod 34:6; Num 14:18; Ps 86:15; Jer 15:15; Rom 2:4; 2 Peter 3:9). In a similar manner, Christ is said to be longsuffering (1 Tim 1:16; 2 Peter 3:15).

KJV also uses the noun to describe human beings (other versions use "patience" and "forbearance"). As so used, it refers to being patient especially when being faced with evil. It is one of the aspects of the fruit of the Spirit (Gal 5:22), for the Lord's servants must be longsuffering (2 Tim 2:24). The relation between divine and human longsuffering/forbearance/patience is conveyed by the parable of the unforgiving servant told by Jesus in Matthew 18:21–35 (where the verb *makrothymeō,* "to have patience," is used in vv. 26 and 29).

PT

LORD. The KJV translation for a variety of Hebrew and Greek terms. It is applied to both men and God and expresses varied degrees of honor, dignity, and majesty. In the Aramaic portion of Daniel (2:4–7:28) three words are translated "lord": *rab* (2:10), "a chief, leader, or captain"; *rabrevān,* "magnate or prince," of certain Babylonian nobles (4:36; 5:1, 9–10, 23; 6:17); *mārē',* "an exalted one," of the king (4:19, 24) and of God (2:47; 5:23). *Seren*—used only in the plural and only Joshua, Judges, 1 Samuel, and 1 Chronicles—always designates the *lords* of the Philistines. *Sar* (Ezra 8:25), a title of nobility, means "a prince," while *shālîsh* (2 Kings 7:2, 17, 19) indicates an "officer of the third rank" (NIV "officer"). The familiar term *Baal* (Heb. *ba'al,* "master or owner") is applied to heathen deities or to a man as husband; in Isaiah 16:8 "the *lords* of the heathen" (NIV "the rulers of the nations") denotes heathen princes invading Moab. The Hebrew *'ădhōnay,* often translated "lord" or "master," may be a term of respect (Gen 23:11;

24:18), but its meaning of *owner* indicates one who has absolute control, as an owner of slaves, or a king. When applied to God, it denotes the owner and governor of the whole earth (Ps 97:5; 114:7; Isa 1:24). The term *'adōnai*, perhaps the plural of *'ādhôn* ("the Lord"), is always used where God is submissively and reverently addressed (Exod 4:10; Josh 7:8; Neh 1:11). In the KJV, *'ădhōnay* is given as "Lord," and Jehovah (Heb. *Yahweh,* "the self-existent One") is printed "LORD." The Jews, due to their interpretation of Leviticus 24:16, read *'ădhōnay* to avoid pronouncing *Yahweh* (the supreme name of God alone). In the ASV it is given as "Jehovah," which the KJV has only four times (Exod 6:3; Ps 83:18; Isa 12:2; 26:4) and the NIV never.

Of the four Greek terms rendered "lord," *megistanēs* is used in Mark 6:21 and means (pl.) "great men, courtiers." *Rabbouni,* "my Lord" (heightened form of Heb. *rab*), occurs in Mark 10:51 KJV and John 20:16 (transliterated). *Despotēs,* implying absolute ownership or power, is rendered "Lord" in Luke 2:29; Acts 4:24; 2 Peter 2:1; Jude 4; Revelation 6:10. The prevailing Greek term rendered "lord" is *kyrios,* "master or owner," one who has power or authority over some property (Matt 20:8; Luke 10:2), animals (Luke 19:34), or persons (Matt 13:27). It may be used as a term of respect (Matt 21:30; John 4:15; 12:21). It is frequently used of God (Matt 1:22; Mark 5:19; Acts 7:33) as well as of Jesus as Messiah, who by his resurrection and ascension was exalted to lordship (Acts 2:36; Rom 1:4; 14:8; Phil 2:9–11). At times it is difficult to determine whether by "the Lord" the Father or the Son is meant (Acts 1:24; 9:31; 16:14; Rom 14:11; 1 Cor 4:19; 2 Thess 3:16).

DEH

LORD'S DAY. The day especially associated with the Lord Jesus Christ. The expression occurs in the NT only in Revelation 1:10. The adjective *kyriakos,* translated "the Lord's," is a possessive and means "belonging to the Lord"—to Christ. It denotes a day consecrated to the Lord (cf. the parallel expression "the Lord's Supper," 1 Cor 11:20). Some would equate it with the OT prophetic "day of the Lord," but clearly John is not speaking of that prophetic day. The form of his expression marks a distinction between the prophetic "day of the Lord" (1 Cor 5:5; 2 Cor 1:14; 1 Thess 5:2) and the first day of the week, on which Christ arose. It was the resurrection victory on that day that marked it as distinct and sacred to the Christian church. The gospel emphasis on "the first day of the week" as the day of resurrection stresses its distinctiveness. On that day the risen Christ repeatedly appeared to his disciples (Luke 24:13–49; John 20:1–25), and again a week later (John 20:26). The Pentecostal outpouring apparently also came on that day. Acts 20:7 and 1 Corinthians 16:1–2 show that the early church consecrated the day to worship and almsgiving (but not to earning). Sunday (the name is of pagan origin) as the day of special worship is a Christian institution and must be sharply distinguished from the Sabbath. Nor were the OT Sabbath regulations transferred to the Lord's Day as a "Christian Sabbath." The Sabbath related to the old creation (Exod 20:8–11; 31:12–17; Heb 4:4), whereas the Lord's Day commemorates the new creation in Christ Jesus. No "Sabbath" observance was stipulated in the demands on Gentile Christians in Acts 15:28–29. Some Jewish Christians continued to observe the Sabbath and Jewish festivals, while some members of the primitive church made no distinction between days (Rom 14:5–6), but it was held to be a matter of liberty (Rom 14:1), as long as the observance of a special day was not regarded as necessary for salvation (Gal 4:10; Col 2:16–17).

DEH

LORD'S PRAYER. Properly, "the Disciples' Prayer," since it was not prayed with but taught to them by Jesus (Matt 6:9–13; Luke 11:2–4). In Luke, Jesus, at the request of a disciple, gave a modified form of his earlier spontaneous presentation in the Sermon on the Mount. The earlier form is fuller and is commonly used. As a pattern prayer it is unsurpassed for conciseness and fullness, delineating the proper approach and order in prayer. It directs the disciples, as members of God's family reverently to pray to a personal heavenly Father. The petitions are divided into two parts, the first three relating to God's interests. They are arranged in a descending scale, from himself, through the manifestation of himself in his kingdom (the coming messianic kingdom), to the complete doing of his will by his subjects. Placing God's interest first, the disciple can pray for his own needs. The petitions, whether counted as three or four, are arranged in an ascending scale—from the supply of daily material needs to the ultimate deliverance from all evil. The doxology in Matthew, which constitutes an affirmation of faith, is lacking in the leading MSS and is generally regarded as a scribal addition derived from ancient liturgical usage.

DEH

LORD'S SUPPER (Gr. *kyriakon deipnon*). This expression occurs once in the NT (1 Cor 11:20), but there is a related expression, "Lord's table" (1 Cor 10:21). However, the institution of that which Paul called "the Lord's Supper" is described in four passages (Matt 26:26–29; Mark 14:22–25; Luke 22:15–20; 1 Cor 11:23–25). On the night before the Crucifixion, Jesus adopted the position of head of a household and ate the Passover meal with his disciples in a room within the city limits of Jerusalem. It is interesting to note that he did not give new and special significance to the special parts of that meal (e.g., lamb and bitter herbs) but to the bread and wine, common to many meals. Distributing the bread he had broken for his disciples, he said, "I am myself this bread." Later in the meal, passing to them the third cup of the four cups of the meal, he said of the wine, "This is my blood of the covenant, which is poured out for many." Then at the end of the meal Jesus refused to drink from

Traditional room of the Last Supper, or Coenaculum, on Mount Zion in Jerusalem. The Basilica of Zion built over the Cenacle, is believed to have been the first Christian church. Courtesy Zev Radovan.

the fourth cup, saying that he would not drink again of the fruit of the vine until he drank it anew in the kingdom of God.

There are two important themes in the words of Jesus. First he was telling them that the cup of red wine represented his own blood, shed to inaugurate a new covenant between God and "the many" (see Isa 52:15; 53:12). He was to offer himself to God as a sacrifice for sin so that a new relationship could be created by God between himself and the redeemed community of believers. Second, he was pointing toward the full realization and consummation of the kingdom of God at the end of the age, when the meal would be resumed in the "messianic banquet." Thus, it may be said that the Lord's Supper is eaten in remembrance of his atoning death by which comes redemption and in expectation of the arrival of the kingdom of God in its fullness.

Paul's teaching is found in 1 Corinthians 10–11. He stressed the spiritual communion between Christ and his body (disciples) and within the body. Even as Israelites were miraculously fed by manna and water in the wilderness, so in communion with Christ believers are spiritually nourished by heavenly food. Therefore, those who eat the body and drink the blood of Christ are not to participate in Jewish or pagan sacrifices (10:16–22), and they are to ensure that when they partake of the Supper, they partake worthily, being in genuine fellowship with fellow believers.

The actual services of the Lord's Supper began in the church after the coming of the Spirit on the Day of Pentecost: Acts 2:42 refers to the table fellowship as "breaking of bread" (cf. Acts 20:7). These acts of worship and fellowship are to be seen as the result of the fusion of various strands of experience enjoyed by the disciples with Jesus. They had fellowship with Jesus in eating (Matt 14:13–21; 15:23–39—and note that according to John 6:33–34, when he fed the five thousand Jesus taught that he was the true heavenly food). These times of miraculous feeding and the Last Supper itself (within the Passover meal) belong to the time before the Crucifixion; then the table fellowship with the risen Lord (Luke 24:30–35; John 21:13; Acts 10:41) in the "forty days" belongs to the post-Resurrection period. Thus, when the disciples came together on that Day of Pentecost and on subsequent occasions, their breaking of bread was the continuation of a rich tradition of fellowship already established by Jesus and into which they incorporated the actual Lord's Supper. At first the Supper was a part of a larger meal (see 1 Cor 11:17ff.); but, being a special part, it could be separated and, as the years went by, it was in fact separated. It became the second half of the Sunday worship of the local church, the first part being the ministry of the Word, prayers, singing of psalms, and intercessions.

Nowhere in the NT is the Lord's Supper called a sacrifice. However, the believers are said to be offering spiritual sacrifices to God when God is worshiped, served, and obeyed (Rom 12:1; Heb 13:15–16; 1 Peter 2:5). The Lord's Supper as a part of the worship and service offered to God is thus a sacrifice of praise and thanksgiving. Regrettably the Eucharist (ministry of Word and Lord's Supper as one service) has often been referred to in sacrificial terms as though it were a sacrifice in a unique sense—an unbloody sacrifice. While the Supper is the memorial of a sacrifice, and is a sacrifice of praise offered to God, it is neither a repetition of the sacrifice of Christ made at Calvary nor a participation in the self-offering that Christ is perpetually making to the Father in heaven as the heavenly Priest. It is a proclamation of the Lord's death sacramentally until he returns to earth.

Bibliography: A. J. B. Higgins, *The Lord's Supper in the New Testament,* 1952; O. Cullmann, *Early Christian Worship,* 1953; A. M. Stibbs, *Sacrament, Sacrifice and Eucharist: The Meaning, Function and Use of the Lord's Supper,* 1961; J. Jeremias, *The Eucharistic Words of Jesus,* 1966.

PT

LO-RUHAMAH (lō-rū-hă'mă, Heb. *lô'-rūḥā-māh, not pitied*). The symbolic name given to Hosea's daughter—transliterated "Lo-Ruhamah" in Hosea 1:6, 8, but translated "not my loved one" in Hosea 2:23. It would seem to be a lesser description of the people described in Hosea as Lo-Ammi.

LOT 1. A means of deciding an issue or of determining the divine will in a matter. The use of the lot to determine doubtful matters is very old, and the practice of casting lots was common among the nations of antiquity: Haman's efforts to determine a lucky day to exterminate the Jews (Esth 3:7), the detection of guilty Jonah by the pagan mariners (Jonah 1:7), the gambling of the Roman soldiers for the garments of Jesus (Matt 27:35). See also Joel 3:3; Nahum 3:10; Obadiah

11. Its use among the Jews, generally with religious intent, is mentioned in determining the scapegoat (Lev 16:8), assigning the land of Palestine among the tribes (Num 26:55; Josh 18:10; Acts 13:19), selecting men for an expedition (Judg 1:1–3; 20:9), detecting a guilty person (Josh 7:14; 1 Sam 14:40–42), selecting the first king (1 Sam 10:20–21), dividing the returned priests into twenty-four divisions (1 Chron 24:3–19), and determining the service of the priests in the temple worship (Luke 1:5–9). In none of these instances is there a direct statement of the method or methods used in casting lots (but cf. Prov 16:33). It was held in religious esteem by the covenant people, and its use to determine God's will was usually accompanied by prayer (Judg 1:1–3; Acts 1:24–26). Many scholars think that Urim and Thummim were used as lots. Only in the choice of a successor to Judas (Acts 1:26) is the use of lots by Christ's followers mentioned. As a distinctly Jewish mode of seeking divine direction, its use was appropriate for the occasion. After the coming of the Spirit at Pentecost to take direction of the affairs of the church its use is never mentioned again.

2. That which is assigned by lot, as a *portion, share,* or *inheritance* (Deut 32:9; Josh 15:1; Ps 105:11; 125:3; Isa 17:14; Acts 8:21). DEH

LOT (Heb. *lôt, envelope, covering*). Haran's son and Abraham's nephew (Gen 11:31; 12:5). His life may be summarized under the following heads: (1) *Departure and dependence.* Lot's father died and left him his possessions; Lot now was willing to follow Abraham from Mesopotamia to Canaan, thence to Egypt, and back again to Canaan (11:27–32; 12:5, 10; 13:1). During this period there was unity and fellowship between uncle and nephew. (2) *Decision and destiny.* Because of a conflict between their herdsmen, Abraham suggested that his nephew choose another place. Lot, prompted by selfishness, chose the country in the environs of Sodom, a city that had already become notorious because of its wickedness (13:5–13). This fatal choice determined his subsequent destiny. It was Abraham now who maintained the greater spiritual status (13:14–18). (3) *Devastation and deportation.* Lot, then in Sodom, was taken captive when Kedorlaomer and his confederates conquered the king of Sodom and his four allies (14:1–12). Abraham, the separated and faithful servant, pursued the enemies and rescued his nephew (14:13–16). (4) *Depravity and degeneration.* Angels then visited Lot in Sodom to hasten his departure from the imminent doom decreed on the wicked city. Although originally only a sojourner (19:9), Lot acted like a citizen; he had imbibed their mores and standards. Look at his willingness to sacrifice his daughters' chastity (19:8), his utter ineffectiveness in dealing with his sons-in-law (19:14), his hesitation in leaving the doomed city (19:15–16), and his unwillingness to leave the comforts of a city (19:17–22). In spite of all these adverse things, Lot was, as the NT plainly declares, "a righteous man" (2 Peter 2:7–8); and, furthermore, his righteous soul was daily vexed with the lawless deeds (2:8) of Sodom's inhabitants. By implication, it seems that the term "godly" is also applied to Lot (2:9). (5) *Dénouement and disgrace.* Lot, because of fear, left Zoar and lived in a cave with his two daughters (Gen 19:30), his wife already having become, because of unbelief, "a pillar of salt" (19:17, 26; Luke 17:29). In this cave one of the most unseemly scenes recorded in the Bible took place (Gen 19:31–38). Made drunk by his daughters, Lot became the unwitting father of their sons, Moab and Ben-Ammi, the progenitors of the Moabites and the Ammonites (Deut 2:9, 19; Ps 83:8). Entirely unsupported is the critical view that maintains that this infamous incident in the cave was "created" by a later writer to justify the inferior position of the Moabites and the Ammonites in their relationship with Israel. The almost buried faith of Lot reappeared in Ruth, a Moabitess, the great-grandmother of David and thus a member of the messianic line (Ruth 1:16–18; 4:13–21).

Pillars of salt on the western shore of the Dead Sea, reminiscent of the fate of Lot's wife (Gen 19:26). Courtesy Seffie Ben-Yoseph.

Lot's life illustrates spiritual truths: (1) The degenerating influence of a selfish choice (Gen 13:11–12); (2) the effect of a wicked environment on one's family (Gen 19); (3) retribution in one's children (Gen 19:8, 31ff.); (4) God as the only true judge of a man's real state (2 Peter 2:7ff.). WB

LOTAN (lō'tăn, Heb. *lôtān, a wrapping up*). Son of Seir and father of Hori and Homam (1 Chron 1:38–39; in Gen 36:20, 22, 29 NIV has Homam; JB, KJV, MLB, MOF, NASB, NEB have Hemam).

LOVE (Heb. *'ahăvâh,* Gr. *agapē*). This is presented in Scripture as the very nature of God (1 John 4:8, 16) and the greatest of the Christian virtues (1 Cor 13:13). It receives definition in Scripture only by a listing of its attributes

(13:4–7). It lies at the very heart of Christianity, being essential to man's relations to God and man (Matt 22:37–40; Mark 12:28–31; John 13:34–35). Jesus taught that on it hang all the law and the prophets (Matt 22:40). It is the fulfillment of the law, for its sense of obligation and desire for the welfare of the one loved impels it to carry out the demands of the law (Rom 13:8–10). Love found its supreme expression in the self-sacrifice on Calvary (1 John 4:10).

The Bible makes the unique revelation that God in his very nature and essence is love (1 John 4:8, 16), Christianity being the only religion thus to present the Supreme Being. God not only loves, he *is* love. In this supreme attribute all the other attributes are harmonized. His own Son, Jesus Christ, is the unique object of this eternal love (Isa 42:1; Matt 3:17; 17:5; John 17:24). God loves the world as a whole (John 3:16), as well as individuals in it (Gal 2:20), in spite of the sinfulness and corruption of the human race (Rom 5:8–10; Eph 2:4–5). God's love for his creatures manifests itself not only in supplying all their needs (Acts 14:17) but supremely in the redemption wrought for sinners (Rom 5:8; 1 John 4:9–10). Believers in Christ are the objects of his special love (John 16:27; 17:23), causing him to deal in chastisement with them (Heb 12:6–11), but they are assured that nothing can separate them from his unfathomable love in Christ (Rom 8:31–39).

All human love, whether Godward or manward, has its source in God. Love in its true reality and power is seen only in the light of Calvary (1 John 4:7–10). It is created in the believer by the Holy Spirit (Rom 5:5; Gal 5:22), prompting him to love both God and man (2 Cor 5:14–15; 1 John 4:20–21). Love finds its expression in service to our fellowmen (Gal 5:13) and is the chief test of Christian discipleship (Luke 14:26; John 13:35; 1 John 3:14). Love is vitally related to faith; faith is basic (John 6:29; Heb 11:6), but a faith that does not manifest itself in love both toward God and man is dead and worthless (Gal 5:6, 13; James 2:17–26). The Christian must love God supremely and his neighbor as himself (Matt 22:37–39). He must love his enemy as well as his brother (Matt 5:43–48; Rom 12:19–20; 1 John 3:14). Our love must be "without hypocrisy" (Rom 12:9 ASV) and be "with actions and in truth" (1 John 3:18). Love is the bond uniting all the Christian virtues (Col 3:14).

See also LOVING-KINDNESS.

Bibliography: R. B. Girdlestone, *Synonyms of the Old Testament,* 1897, pp. 107ff.; N. H. Snaith, *The Distinctive Ideas of the Old Testament,* 1944, pp. 94–142; G. A. F. Knight, *A Christian Theology of the Old Testament,* 1959, pp. 224–29; G. L. Carr, *The Song of Solomon* (TOTC), 1984, pp. 60–67. DEH

LOVE FEAST (Gr. *agapē*). A common meal eaten by early Christians in connection with the Lord's Supper to express and deepen brotherly love. Although often mentioned in postcanonical literature, these feasts are spoken of in the NT only in Jude 12 and the dubious footnote to 2 Peter 2:13. But the situation in 1 Corinthians 11:20–22, 33–34 makes it clear that they were observed in the early Jerusalem church (Acts 2:42–47; 4:35; 6:1). As implied by the situation in 1 Corinthians 11, these love feasts were observed before, but in connection with, the Lord's Supper (perhaps after the close relation between the first Lord's Supper and the Passover). Because of abuses, which already appeared in apostolic churches (1 Cor 11:23–29; Jude 12), they were separated from the Lord's Supper. They subsequently fell into disfavor and were ultimately forbidden to be held in churches, largely due to the growth of the sacerdotal view of the Eucharist—a view that regarded the union of the two as sacrilegious. A few smaller Christian groups today observe them. DEH

LOVING-KINDNESS. The Hebrew word *hesedh* is one of the most important in the OT and lies at the center of the Lord's self-revelation of his attitude toward his people. Throughout the OT the meaning remains unchanged from that found in the first examples: as the Lord looks on us, his *hesedh* is rooted in his grace (Gen 19:19; it combines the ideas of love, commitment, duty, and care). It is explicitly linked with "truth"—i.e., being true to oneself, truthfulness, reliability—and so there is a stress on the loyalty with which love acts (Gen 32:10; Exod 34:6). The Lord's *hesedh* leads him to redeem his people (Exod 15:13); it is a patient (Num 14:18) and inexhaustible (Ps 118:1–3) attribute, rooted in the divine nature (62:12). The word *hesedh* has the same "triangularity" as the word "love" (*agapē*) in the NT. It is how the Lord feels and acts toward his people; in consequence, it is how the Lord's people, following his example, should act toward others (Josh 2:12; 2 Sam 9:1) and how they should respond to the Lord himself (e.g., Isa 57:1; Jer 2:2; Hos 6:6). Taking the whole evidence of the OT, *hesedh* holds together the ideas of love and loyalty with a strong emphasis on the practical more than the emotional sides of these ideas. It is the loyal love that is displayed when there is no other motive to action except love and loyalty.

For bibliography see LOVE. JAM

LUBIM (See LIBYA)

LUCIFER (See DEVIL; SATAN)

LUCIUS (lū'shĭ-ŭs, Gr. *Loukios*). 1. A Christian from Cyrene ministering in the church at Antioch (Acts 13:1). 2. A kinsman of Paul who evidently was with him in Corinth when he wrote his letter to Rome (Rom 16:21).

LUD, LUDITES (lŭd, lŭ'dīts, Heb. *lûdh, lûdhîm*). Either one or two nations of antiquity. Lud was the son of Shem (Gen 10:22; 1 Chron 1:17). It is generally agreed that Lud was the kingdom of Lydia in Asia Minor. Ludites were the sons of Mizraim (Egypt) (Gen 10:13; 1 Chron 1:11), indicating an African country. Other Bible references are Isaiah 66:19, which suggests Lud was in the Mediterranean area; Jeremiah 46:9, in a prophecy against Egypt, showing an African location for Ludites; Ezekiel 27:10, in a prophecy against Tyre, suggesting that Lud might be in Asia or Africa; and Ezekiel 30:5, in a prophecy against Egypt, again indicating an African setting for Lud. This interchanging of Ludites (KJV Ludim) for Lud has caused some scholars to think they are the same people. If the Ludites were a different people in Africa, it has not been established just what nation they were.

LUHITH (lū'hĭth, Heb. *lûhîth*). A town of Moab located on a slope (Isa 15:5; Jer 48:5).

LUKE (Gr. *Loukas*). According to the oldest extant list of NT writings, known from the name of its discoverer as the Muratorian Fragment, and dating from the latter half of the second century A.D., Luke was the writer of the Third Gospel and the Acts of the Apostles. From the latter book his association with Paul is established. In four passages of varying length the author of Acts writes in the first person (16:10–17; 20:5–15; 21:1–18; 27:1–28:16). These so-called "we sections" constitute the major portion of the extant biographical material on Luke. Apart from this he is mentioned three times in the NT (Col 4:14; Philem 24; 2 Tim 4:11). From the first reference it is evident that Luke was a physician; from the last, that he was with Paul some time after he disappears from view at the end of the Acts of the Apostles. The context of the Colossians reference also suggests that Luke was a Gentile and a proselyte.

It appears from Luke's own writings that he was a man of education and culture. He begins his Gospel with an elaborate paragraph, showing that he could write in the sophisticated tradition of the Hellenistic historians, and then lapses into a polished vernacular. He uses this speech with vigor and effectiveness. He is an accurate and able historian and has left some of the most powerful descriptive writing in the NT. His medical knowledge and his interest in seafaring are apparent from his writings. Whatever is said beyond this is tradition and conjecture. Luke was not "Lucius of Cyrene" (Acts 13:1), for Lucas is an abbreviation of Lucanus, as Silas for Silvanus, and Annas for Annanus. There is no solid support for the conjecture that Luke was one of "the Seventy" (Luke 10:1; NIV "seventy-two"), one of the Greeks of John 12:20, or one of the two disciples of Emmaus (Luke 24:13). More certain evidence supports other conjectures and traditions. That he knew Mary is fairly clear from the earlier chapters of his Gospel, and the period of acquaintance may have been during Paul's incarceration at Caesarea. Eusebius and Jerome say that Luke was a Syrian of Antioch, and he does seem to have a close knowledge of the church there. On the other hand, certain features of the account of Paul's visit to Philippi suggest that Luke had an intimate knowledge of that city and no little loyalty toward it. Here, too, on two occasions, he appears to have joined Paul's party. This has given grounds for the contention that Luke was a Macedonian. Tradition and conjecture could be reconciled if Luke was an Antiochene of Macedonian origin, who had studied at the medical school of Philippi and spent significant years in Macedonia. Luke must have been a person of singular sweetness of character to earn the apostle's adjective "beloved" (Col 4:14 KJV; NIV "dear"). He was obviously a man of outstanding loyalty, of unusual capacity for research, and with the scholar's ability to strip away the irrelevant and dispensable detail. A bare tradition states that he suffered martyrdom in Greece. EMB

LUKE, GOSPEL OF.

I. Authenticity. The authenticity of the Third Gospel has not been successfully challenged. References are frequent in the second century A.D.

Luke 16:16–21 in Greek, from a Bodmer papyrus codex, found in Upper Eygpt (c. A.D. 180). Courtesy Fondation Martin Bodmer.

(Justin, Polycarp, Papias, Hegesippus, Marcion, Heracleon, the Clementine Homilies, Theophilus of Antioch). It is probable that Clement alludes to it (95). It is mentioned as the work of Luke by the Muratorian Fragment (170) and by Irenaeus (180). Such testimony continues into the third century (Clement of Alexandria, Tertullian, Origen). Such a mass of evidence is quite decisive.

II. Date. Although uncertain, the date can be confined to fairly narrow limits. The abrupt termination of the Acts of the Apostles suggests that the author did not long survive his friend and associate Paul. Nor is it likely to have been written after the fall of Jerusalem in A.D. 70. The period of Paul's imprisonment in Caesarea saw Luke in Palestine, and this period (conjecturally 58–59) would presumably give abundant opportunity for the research that is evident in the record. Luke's Gospel is thus the latest of the Synoptic Gospels.

III. Historiography. W. M. Ramsay's work on the Acts of the Apostles has established the right of Luke to rank as a first-rate historian in his own capacity. He was demonstrated to have maintained a consistent level of accuracy wherever detail could be objectively tested, and the vividness of narration so evident in the second work is visible also in the Gospel.

IV. Style. Luke's preface is in the elaborate style of ancient historians and demonstrates that Luke could write with facility in the literary tradition of his time. At Luke 1:5 he moves into an easy vernacular, which he employs for his whole narrative. His language is the common dialect, but used with grace and vigor and with an educated man's skill in composition.

V. Unique Features. Many incidents and much teaching are found only in Luke's Gospel:

1. The Nativity section is fresh and different and seems to point to direct contact with Mary herself. The record of the birth of John the Baptist is especially noteworthy, as are the four psalms (Luke 1:46–55, 68–79; 2:14, 29–32) that form a striking link between the hymnology of the OT and that of the NT.

2. The human genealogy (3:23–38) of Christ, traced to Adam, is chosen in accordance with the cosmopolitan flavor of the Gospel and the writer's conception of his writing as the first movement of the great historical process that took the faith from Bethlehem to Rome.

3. The childhood of Jesus is recorded in Jesus' visit to the temple (2:41–52). Found only in Luke, this account also points to the probability that Mary was the chief authority.

4. Some of Jesus' discourses and sayings, together with their associated incidents, Luke alone records, especially those contained in the unique section (9:51 to 18:14). Matthew and Mark report some of the sayings from this section in different connections. No revision, correction, or contradiction is involved, for preachers and teachers inevitably repeat their words on different occasions. The Beatitudes (6:21–23) are an illustration. In Luke they were uttered "on a plain" (6:17) and were not associated with the discourse that contained the Lord's Prayer. The latter is associated with other teaching (11:6–28), which may have been omitted by Matthew from the discourse "on the mount." Chapters 7, 9–10 contain much that is found only in Luke (the rejection by the Samaritans, the sending out of the Seventy). The discourses of 14:25–35; 17:1–10 are similarly unique. So is the visit to Zacchaeus (Luke 19) and important parabolic teaching (see 5 below). An interesting illustration of Luke's management of an incident similarly reported in the other three Gospels is the account of the banquet in the house of Simon the Pharisee and its associated sayings and incidents (7:36–50; cf. Matt 26:6–13; Mark 14:3–9; John 11:2–12:8).

5. Parables and illustrative anecdotes that only Luke records are those of the two debtors (7:41–43), the good Samaritan (10:30–37), the persistent friend at night (11:5–8), the rich fool (12:16–21), the barren fig tree (13:6–9), the lost coin and the prodigal son (15:3–32), the unrighteous steward and the rich fool and Lazarus (16:1–12, 19–31), the wicked judge and the Pharisee and the tax collector (18:2–14), the ten minas (KJV "pounds"; 19:13–27).

6. Only Luke records the following miracles: the large catch of fish (5:1–11), the widow's son (7:11–14), the sick woman (13:11–13), the sick man (14:2–6), the ten lepers (17:12–19), the healing of Malchus in Gethsemane (22:51).

7. In the closing chapters of the Gospel, the prayer on the cross (23:34), the penitent thief (23:39–43), the walk to Emmaus (24:13–35), and much of the Ascension narrative are recorded only by Luke.

VI. Special Characteristics. Apart from material content there are special characteristics of Luke's approach that should be noted: (1) As in the Acts of the Apostles, he exalts womanhood, an emphasis natural enough if Luke was a Macedonian. Apart from the Nativity narratives, see, for examples, Luke 7:11–17; 8:1–3, 48; 10:38–42; 13:16; 23:28. Luke alone mentions Anna and records the intimate account of Martha and Mary (10:38–42). He alone mentions the tender phraseology of 8:48; 13:16; and 23:28. (2) It is perhaps part of the universality of Luke's conception of the Christian message that he stresses the Lord's attitude toward the poor. See 6:20–25; 8:2–3; 12:16–21; 14:12–15; 16:13; 18:25. (3) The same notion of a universal evangel, natural in an associate of Paul, is found as vividly in Luke's completion of John's Isaian quotation ("And all mankind will see God's salvation," 3:6), as in Acts 17:27. Note in the same connection the strain of racial tolerance. The tale of the good Samaritan and the word of praise for the grateful Samaritan leper illustrate this, as also do the rebukes of Luke 9:49–56. (4) Luke also gives prominence to prayer. He speaks of the Lord's prayer at his baptism, after cleansing the leper, before calling the Twelve, on the Mount of Transfiguration, on the cross, and at death. See also 11:8; 18:1; 21:36 and the parables in 11:5–13 and 18:1–8. (5) A kindliness of judgment pervades Luke's Gospel as was proper in one who was not himself an associate of the Twelve. Note his milder version of Peter's denial. The faults of the apostles are touched with gentle hand, for Luke was, after all, writing of the leaders of the church. Note how the conversation on the leaven of the Pharisees and the ambitious request of James and John are, for example, omitted. Similarly the disciples in the garden slept "from sorrow" (22:45), and their flight in the hour of danger is not recorded. This tact throws light on the reserve that marks the educated and wise man. Others had a right to record such things, and properly did so. With equal propriety Luke ordered his narrative differently.

VII. Sources. Beyond the writer's own statement that he collected his material from eyewitnesses (Luke 1:2), it is impossible to be dogmatic. From the first words of the Gospel it is evident that Luke had both written accounts and living witnesses to draw from. In parts he appears to have followed Mark or Mark's authorities and tradition. Mary could have supplied information regarding the Nativity, and the unique material on the Passion and Resurrection had apostolic authority.

Bibliography: I. H. Marshall, *Luke: Historian and Theologian,* 1970; E. E. Ellis, *The Gospel of Luke* (NCB), 1974; L. L. Morris, *The Gospel According to St. Luke* (TNTC), 1974; I. H. Marshall, *The Gospel of Luke* (NIGTC), 1978 (on the Greek text); J. A. Fitzmyer, *The Gospel According to Luke* (AB), 2 vols., 1985–. EMB

LUNATIC (See DISEASES)

LUTE (See MUSICAL INSTRUMENTS)

LUZ (lŭz, Heb. *lûz, turning aside*). 1. A town located on the northern boundary of the area of the tribe of Benjamin (Josh 16:2; 18:13). Jacob came here when fleeing from home. He slept here, and God appeared to him in a dream. To commemorate the occasion Jacob changed the name of the town to Bethel ("house of God," Gen 28:19). But the place continued to be called Luz down to the time of the judges.

2. A town in the land of the Hittites built by a man from Luz in Canaan (Judg 1:26).

LYCAONIA (lĭk'ā-ō'nĭ-à, Gr. *Lykaonia*). A district in the central plain of Asia north of the Taurus range, in early Roman days a division (or *conuentus*) of the province of Cilicia. Trajan transferred it to Galatia, but it reverted largely to Cilicia under the boundary adjustments of Antoninus Pius. Iconium, an ancient city rich in history, was the administrative capital. The province generally was backward, the inhabitants still speaking a vernacular language in the first century A.D. In Acts 14:6 it is implied that one crossed a frontier in passing from Iconium to Lystra, an implication once set down as an error of the historian. W. M. Ramsay demonstrated the accuracy of the passage from local inscriptions.

LYCIA (lĭsh'ĭ-à, Gr. *Lykia*). A district on the coast of the southern bulge of western Asia Minor, forming the western shore of the Gulf of Adalia. A mountainous area, Lycia successfully maintained its independence against Croesus of Lydia and was granted a measure of independence under the Persians. The Athenians established a brief foothold there in Cimon's day (468–446 B.C.), but Lycia reverted to Persian rule. Under Alexander's successors the area was part of Syria, but the Ptolemies of Egypt exercised brief authority in the third century. After the Roman overthrow of Syria, Lycia was placed briefly under Rhodes, a situation its people bitterly resented. Freed in 169, the region enjoyed comparative independence in the imperial system until Vespasian. Even then the forms of local administration were retained (see 1 Macc 15:23; Acts 21:1–2; 27:5).

LYDDA (lĭd'à, Heb. *lôdh,* Gr. *Lydda*). Lydda, or Lod, lies some thirty miles (fifty km.) NW of Jerusalem at the mouth of the Valley of Aijalon and at the head of the valley that runs down to Joppa, an old highway called the Valley of the Smiths in recollection of ancient Philistine supremacy in iron (1 Sam 13:19). On the edge of the Maritime Plain, Lydda was of some commercial importance, "a village not less than a city," according to Josephus. After the Exile, the settlements of the returning Jews reached this point before meeting the resistance of the occupants of the plain (Ezra 2:33; Neh 7:37, "Lod"). Sir George Adam Smith demonstrated that the local cult of St. George, venerated by both Christian and Muslim, may have mythological links with the fish god Dagon once worshiped in this area by the Philistines. The incident of Peter and Aeneas took place at Lydda (Acts 9:32–38).

LYDIA (lĭd'ĭ-à, Gr. *Lydia*). Paul's first convert in Europe. She resided in Philippi as a seller of the purple garments for which Thyatira, her native city, was famous. She was evidently well-to-do, as she owned her house and had servants. She was "a worshiper of God," meaning a proselyte. She and other women, probably also proselytes, resorted to a place by a river for prayer. She came into contact with the gospel when Paul and his company came there and spoke to the women, and she became a believer. After she and her household had been baptized, she invited the group to come to her home to stay, and they did so (Acts 16:14–15). Her home thus became the first church in Philippi (16:40).

As Lydia was from a city in the kingdom of Lydia, and her name was the common term to denote a woman from Lydia, some scholars have suggested that her personal name was unknown, or that she may be either Euodia or Syntyche mentioned in Philippians 4:2 by Paul as women who labored with him in the gospel.

LYING (See LIE, LYING)

LYRE (See MUSIC AND MUSICAL INSTRUMENTS)

LYSANIAS (lī-sā'nĭ-ăs, Gr. *Lysanias*). Tetrarch of Abilene mentioned by Luke (3:1). The tetrarchy is a small region in Lebanon. There is no satisfactory explanation of the inclusion of this obscure non-Jewish ruler in the dating list. Epigraphical evidence frees the historian from the old allegation that he confused the tetrarch with an earlier ruler.

LYSIAS (lĭs'ī-ăs, Gr. *Lysias*). Claudius Lysias, of the Jerusalem garrison, tribune by rank, was probably one of the career men of the days of Pallas and Narcissus, the powerful freedmen and executive officers of the Emperor Claudius. Lysias was a Greek, as the name Lycias shows. His first name was assumed when he secured Roman citizenship at "a big price" (Acts 22:28), no doubt by bribing one of the freedmen of the court. Paul was fortunate in encountering this officer. Lysias was a vigorous and capable soldier.

LYSTRA (lĭs'trȧ, Gr. *Lystra*). A Roman colony founded by Augustus. It had an aristocratic core of citizens with franchise, a group likely to honor the similar status of Paul. The community at large was not culturally advanced. In Lystra W. M. Ramsay discovered an inscription dedicating a statue to Zeus and Hermes, two deities who were linked in a local cult explained by Ovid.

Philemon and Baucis, the legend ran, entertained the two gods unawares with hospitality the rest of the community churlishly withheld. Hence the identification of Paul and Barnabas with the same two deities (Latinized by Vulgate and KJV into Jupiter and Mercury). At Isauria, not far away, an inscription has been found to "Zeus before the gate," hence it was probably the location of the proposed ceremony mentioned in Acts 14:13. Timothy was a native of Lystra (Acts 16:1). Its ruins are near the modern village of Katyn Serai.
EMB

M

MAACAH, MAACHAH (mā'ȧ-kȧ, Heb. *ma'ăkhâh, oppression*). 1. Son of Nahor, brother of Abraham, by his concubine Reumah (Gen 22:24).

2. A wife of David and the daughter of Talmai, king of Geshur; she became the mother of Absalom (2 Sam 3:3; 1 Chron 3:2).

3. The father of Achish, king of Gath, in Solomon's time (1 Kings 2:39).

4. The favorite wife of Rehoboam, and the mother of Abijam (2 Chron 11:20–22). She is said to be the daughter of Absalom (11:20; 1 Kings 15:2), but Absalom had only one daughter, whose name was Tamar (2 Sam 14:27). The mother of Abijam, Micaiah (Maacah), is said to be the daughter of Uriel of Gibeah (2 Chron 13:2); probably she was the granddaughter of Absalom. She outlived Abijam and was queen during the reign of her grandson Asa, until he deposed her for making an idol (1 Kings 15:10, 13; 2 Chron 15:16).

5. A concubine of Caleb, son of Hezron (1 Chron 2:48).

6. Sister of Huppim and Shuppim, and wife of Machir, the son of Manasseh (1 Chron 7:14–16).

7. The wife of Jeiel, the founder of Gibeon (1 Chron 8:29; 9:35).

8. The father of Hanan, one of David's mighty men (1 Chron 11:43).

9. The father of Shephatiah, the overseer of the tribe of Simeon in David's reign (1 Chron 27:16).

10. A small country on the edge of the Syrian desert north of Gilead. The Ammonites hired a thousand men of the king of this nation to assist them in fighting against David. In the battle, the Ammonites and their helpers were put to rout and the Arameans fled (2 Sam 10:6–14; Aram Maacah in 1 Chron 19:6). David defeated them and they became subservient to him (2 Sam 10:18–19).

MAACATHITES (mā-ăk'ȧ-thīts, Heb. *ma'ăkhāthî*). The people of the nation of Maacah, residing near the Geshurites in the region of Bashan. They were in the area taken by Jair, the son of Manasseh (Deut 3:14), situated on the border of the kingdom of Og king of Bashan (Josh 12:5). The half-tribe of Manasseh and the tribes of Reuben and Gad were assigned among other adjacent areas, "Gilead, the territory of the people of Geshur and Maacah, all of Mount Hermon and all Bashan" (13:11). The Israelites did not drive out the Maacathites or Geshurites but lived with them (13:13). The grandfather of Eliphelet, one of David's mighty men, was a Maacathite (2 Sam 23:34). After the fall of Jerusalem, among the men who came to Gedaliah, the Babylonian governor at Mizpeh, was Jaazaniah, the son of a Maacathite (2 Kings 25:23; Jer 40:8). Eshtemoa, the son of Hodiah, a descendant of Judah, was a Maacathite (1 Chron 4:19). These Maacathites were descendants of the people not expelled by the Israelites.

MAADAI (mā'ȧ-dā'ī, Heb. *ma'ădhay, ornaments*). A son of Bani. He was one of the Israelites who married foreign women (Ezra 10:34).

MAADIAH (mā-ȧ-dī'ȧ, Heb. *ma'adhyâh, the* LORD *is ornament*). One of the chiefs of the priests who returned from exile with Zerubbabel (Neh 12:5).

MAAI (mā-ā'ī, Heb. *mā'ay, to be compassionate*). One of the sons of the priests who blew trumpets at the dedication of the wall of Jerusalem (Neh 12:36).

MAALEH-ACRABBIM (See AKRABIM)

MAARATH (mā'a-răth, Heb. *ma'ărāth, a place naked of trees*). One of the cities in the territory of Judah, located near Hebron (Josh 15:59).

MAASAI (mā'ȧsī, Heb. *ma'say, work of the* LORD). A priestly family that lived in Jerusalem after returning from exile (1 Chron 9:12).

MAASEIAH (mā'ȧ-sē'yȧ, Heb. *ma'ăsēyāhû, work of the* LORD). 1. One of the Levites appointed to play a psaltery in praise of God while the ark was brought up to Jerusalem (1 Chron 15:18, 20).

2. One of the captains of hundreds, the son of Adaiah. Jehoiada the priest made a covenant with him to resist the usurpation by Athaliah of the throne of Judah (2 Chron 23:1).

3. An officer in the army of Uzziah king of Judah (2 Chron 26:11).

4. A son of Ahaz king of Judah. He was killed by Zicri, a mighty man of Ephraim, during a war with Israel (2 Chron 28:7).

5. The governor of Jerusalem in Josiah's reign, one of the officials whom the king put in charge of repairing the temple (2 Chron 34:8).

6. One of the priests who had married a foreign woman (Ezra 10:18).

7. A priest of the family of Harim who took a foreign wife (Ezra 10:21).

8. A priest of the family of Pashhur who took a foreign wife (Ezra 10:22).

9. A man of Israel of the family of Pahath-

Moab who took a foreign wife (Ezra 10:30).

10. The father of Azariah, a man who worked on the wall of Jerusalem near his house (Neh 3:23).

11. One of the men who stood on the right side of Ezra as he read the Law to the people (Neh 8:4).

12. One of the men who explained the Law to the people (Neh 8:7).

13. One of the chiefs of the people who sealed the covenant with Nehemiah (Neh 10:25). May be the same as no. 12.

14. One of the descendants of the son of Baruch of Perez who lived in Jerusalem (Neh 11:5).

15. A Benjamite whose descendants lived in Jerusalem (Neh 11:7).

16. A priest who blew a trumpet at the dedication of the wall of Jerusalem (Neh 12:41).

17. Another priest who took part in the dedication of the wall (Neh 12:42).

18. A priest whose son Zephaniah was one of the two men whom Zedekiah king of Judah sent to Jeremiah to ask him to inquire of the Lord for him (Jer 21:1; 37:3).

19. The father of Zedekiah, a false prophet whom Jeremiah condemned (Jer 29:21).

20. The doorkeeper of the temple in Jeremiah's time (Jer 35:4).

21. An ancestor of Baruch (Jer 32:12; ASV, NIV Mahseiah).

MAATH (mā'ăth, Gr. *maath, to be small*). An ancestor of Christ (Luke 3:26).

MAAZ (mā'ăz, Heb. *ma'ats, wrath*). Son of Ram, the firstborn son of Jerahmeel (1 Chron 2:27).

MAAZIAH (mā-à-zī'à, Heb. *ma'azyâhû, consolation of the LORD*). 1. A priest of the twenty-four sons of Eleazar and Ithamar, sons of Aaron, to whom was assigned the twenty-fourth division to serve in the tabernacle (1 Chron 24:18).

2. A priest who sealed the covenant with Nehemiah (Neh 10:8).

MACBANNAI (măk'bà-nī, Heb. *makhbannay, clad with a cloak*). A Gadite who joined David's forces at Ziklag (1 Chron 12:13).

MACBENAH (măk-bē'nà, Heb. *makhbēnâh, bond*). The name of a place in Judah that occurs in the genealogical list of Caleb. It is from the same root as Cabban (1 Chron 2:49).

MACCABEES (măk'à-bēs, Gr. *Makkabaioi*). The name given to a Jewish family of Modin in the Shephelah. They initiated the Jewish revolt against Antiochus Epiphanes, the Seleucid Syrian king who was forcing his Hellenizing policies on Palestine.

The story is told in the two books of the Maccabees in the Apocrypha. The uprising began in 168 B.C., when Mattathias, an aged priest, struck down a royal commissioner and an apostate

Remains of the tombs of the Maccabees at Modi'in. "Maccabees" is the name given to the brothers and associates of Judas Maccabaeus, the Jewish liberator (d. 160 B.C.). The mausoleum that Simon, last survivor of the brothers, built for his family remained a notable monument for several centuries. Courtesy Zev Radovan.

Jew who were about to offer pagan sacrifice in the town. Mattathias leveled the altar and fled to the hills with his sons. To his standard rallied the Chasidim ("the Pious," Gr. *Hasidaioi*). The old priest died after a few months of guerrilla warfare, and the same early fighting claimed two of his sons, Eleazar and John. The remaining three sons—Judas, Jonathan, and Simon—each in turn led the insurrection; and all left a deep mark on Jewish history.

Judas won the name of Maccabee, or "the Hammerer," and he was the only member of the family to whom the term was applied in the Apocrypha. It was later history that used it as a surname for all three brothers. Judas was a fine soldier and patriot, with a clear policy of Jewish independence and religious reconstruction. Raising and organizing a fighting force of Galileans, Judas defeated major military expeditions sent against him in 166 and 165 B.C. In December of the latter year, Judas formally cleansed the temple of Syrian pollution and celebrated the occasion with a great festival. This festival became a permanent fixture, falling on December 25 and lasting eight days (1 Macc 4:52–59; 2 Macc 10:6; John 10:22).

For the next eighteen months, Judas campaigned east of Jordan, while his brother Simon collected the Jews who were scattered through Galilee into the comparative safety of Judea. Judas at this point lost some of the support of the Chasidim, whose ambitions were largely fulfilled by the reestablishment of the temple service. Religious division, the perennial problem of all the Jewish struggles for independence, was thus responsible for a weakening of Judas's position. Lysias, the Syrian general whom Judas had signally defeated at Beth Zur in the autumn of 165 B.C., gained his revenge at Beth Zacharias. Judas was routed, and the Syrian garrison still holding out in the citadel of Jerusalem was relieved. Lysias was in control of Syria during the brief reign of the minor, Antiochus Eupator, who

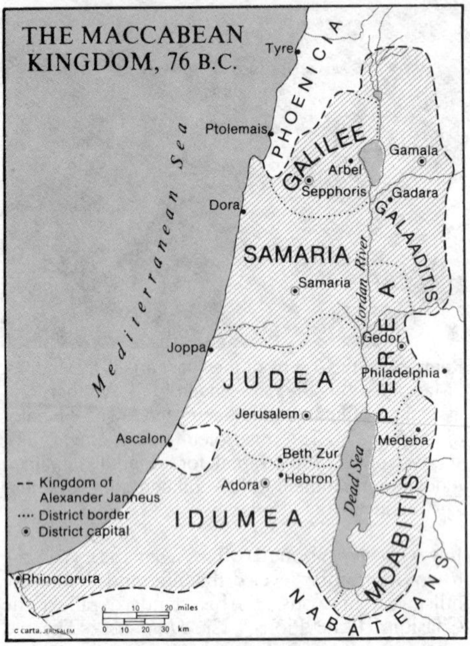

succeeded Epiphanes in 163, and he was sensible enough to abandon Epiphanes' attack on the religion of the Jews for the much more effective political policy of patronage. He set up a puppet high priest, Alcimus, who was accepted by the Chasidim. Judas was thus isolated but on Lysias's withdrawal, marched against Alcimus. Demetrius I, the able and decisive ruler who succeeded Eupator in 162, sent a force under Nicanor to put down this new rebellion. Defeated by Judas, Nicanor retired to Jerusalem, but foolishly drove "the Pious" into renewed support of Judas by threatening reprisals against the temple. With the country again behind him, Judas defeated the Syrians at Adasa. Judas was now in control of the land and negotiated a treaty with Rome, in the terms of which Rome ordered Demetrius I to withdraw from Palestine. Judas's move was a shrewd one, for since the Peace of Apamea (188) Syria had existed by Rome's sufferance, and Demetrius had spent his youth as a hostage in Rome. Time was against Judas, for before the Senate's prohibition was delivered to the king, Judas was defeated and killed by the general Bacchides at Elasa (1 Macc 3–9:22). The international policy, illustrated by the approach to Rome, had again alienated the fickle Chasidim; and the withdrawal of support fatally weakened Judas's power of resistance and led directly to his military defeat.

Jonathan succeeded his brother in 161 B.C., and the Maccabean revolt reverted to the guerrilla warfare with which it had begun. Dynastic troubles in Syria, however, played into Jonathan's hands. Alexander Balas, supported by Pergamum and Egypt, aspired to the Syrian throne; and both Demetrius and Alexander thought it expedient to secure the support of so determined a fighter as the second Maccabee. Demetrius offered the control of all military forces in Palestine and the governorship of Jerusalem. Alexander added an offer of the high priesthood. Jonathan chose Alexander and thus became the founder of the Hasmonean priesthood. By skillful support of Demetrius II, who dethroned Alexander, Jonathan maintained and strengthened his position. The difficulties of the later Seleucid Empire served his purposes well. Jonathan was even able to extend his power over the maritime plain, to fortify Jerusalem and other strong points in Judea, and to enter into treaty relationships with Rome. An army revolt in 143 unseated Demetrius II, and the young son of Alexander was enthroned as Antiochus VI. Power was in the hands of the generals, one of whom, Tryphon, laid hold of Jonathan by treachery and executed him (1 Macc 9:23–12:54).

Simon, the third brother, inherited this critical situation. Simon was an able diplomat, who carried on his brother's policy of profiting with some success by Syria's internal troubles. In 143 and 142 B.C. he succeeded in establishing the virtual political independence of Judea. In 141, at a great assembly of princes, priests, and elders of the land, Simon was elected to be high priest, military commander, and civil governor of the Jews, "for ever until there should arise a faithful prophet." The high priesthood was thus rendered hereditary in the family of Simon. Simon reestablished the treaty with Rome, which had proved a useful diplomatic advantage over Syria, whom Rome watched with some care and was not sorry to see embarrassed by her petty imperialism. Simon was murdered by his son-in-law at a banquet (1 Macc 13–16:16). His son, the celebrated John Hyrcanus, succeeded him and held the inherited authority for thirty years before passing it on to his son Aristobulus, who assumed the royal title. The Hasmoneans continued their dynasty until 34, when Herod and the Romans put down Antigonus, the last of Mattathias's line; but the Maccabees proper ended with Simon in 134.

The story as above outlined is told in two independent narratives written by authors of different emphases and abilities, the First and Second Books of the Maccabees. The first book is an honest piece of historical writing, detailing without adornment the events of a stirring struggle for freedom. The second book covers much of the same material but slants the account in the direction of religious instruction and admonition. "By way of briefly characterizing the two authors of 1 and 2 Maccabees," writes Bruce M. Metzger, "it may be said that the former was a sober historian who wished to glorify Israel and its heroic Maccabaean leaders and that the latter was a moralizing theologian who wished to emphasize the immeasurable superiority of Judaism over heathenism" (*An Introduction to the Apocrypha*, p. 130). EMB

MACCABEES, 1 AND 2 (See APOCRYPHA)

MACEDONIA (măs′ē-dō′nĭ-ȧ, Gr. *Makedōnia*). The term is of varied import. Lying geographically between the Balkan highlands and the Greek peninsula, Macedonia was both a Greek kingdom and a Roman province. The kingdom, in its early centuries, occupied a quadrangle of territory that formed only the eastern half of the Roman provincial unit. The province extended from the Aegean to the Adriatic, with Illyricum to the NW, Thrace to the NE, and Achaia to the south. Culturally, Macedonia came under strong Athenian influence in the latter years of the fifth century before Christ and in the first half of the fourth century, the period between Euripides, who emigrated to Macedonia in 408 or 407 B.C., and Aristotle, who came to Macedonia as tutor to Alexander in 343 or 342 after the death of Plato. The population was Indo-European but of mixed tribal elements, of which the Dorian stock was probably a strong ingredient.

The history of the early kingdom is confused, and the tradition that Perdiccas I conquered the Macedonian plain in 640 B.C. probably marks the emergence of one dominant clan among an agglomeration of mountain tribes striving for the mastery of a significant area on an ancient invasion route. Until the reign of Philip II (359 to 336), the kingdom was insignificant in Aegean history and was preoccupied with the continual tension of tribal war. By consolidation, conquest, pacification, and an enlightened policy of Hellenization, carried out with the speed, precision, ruthlessness, and clear-headed determination that marked the man, Philip unified Macedonia and finally conquered all Greece. The orations of Demosthenes, directed against the Macedonian menace, are poignant documents of this day of the democratic decadence of Athens and the upsurge of Macedonian power that was to extend Greek rule to the east. It was the army created by Philip that followed Alexander, his son, to the Ganges and overthrew the Persian Empire.

The history of Macedonia from Hellenistic times to the Roman conquest and annexation (167 B.C.) is undistinguished. Macedonia was the first part of Europe to receive Christianity (Phil 4:15). The "man from Macedonia" of Paul's dream may have been Luke, who, if not a native of Philippi in Macedonia, was certainly long a resident there (Acts 16:9ff.). Paul was more than once in the province (Acts 19:21; 20:1–3; 1 Cor 16:5; 2 Cor 1:16). Macedonians were close to the apostle; for example, Gaius and Aristarchus, Secundus, Sopater, and Epaphroditus (Acts 17:11; 20:4; Phil 4:10–19; 1 Thess 2:8, 17–20; 3:10). EMB

MACHAERUS (mă-kē′rŭs, Gr. *Machairous*). Herod's southernmost stronghold east of the Dead Sea, built by Alexander Janneus (90 B.C.?) and called by Pliny "the second citadel of Judea." The fort was on the border of Perea, the tetrarchy of Herod Antipas. To the south lay the domains of Aretas, Herod's father-in-law, king of the Nabateans. Herod's wife escaped from Machaerus to her father in the Arnon Valley, twelve miles

Machaerus, dubbed the Masada of Transjordan, was one of Herod's fortresses. According to Josephus, John the Baptist was imprisoned and beheaded here. Courtesy Studium Biblicum Franciscanum, Jerusalem.

(twenty km.) to the south, when Herod tried to replace her with Herodias. In the subsequent troubles Herod occupied Machaerus with Herodias and Salome, and here John the Baptist died (Matt 14:3ff). In the Great Rebellion Jewish zealots were starved out of Machaerus by the Romans and the fort was razed.

MACHBANAI (See MACBANNAI)

MACHBENAH (See MACBENAH)

MACHI (See MAKI)

MACHIR (See MAKIR)

MACHPELAH (măk-pē'là, Heb. *makhpēlâh, a doubling*). A field near Hebron that Abraham purchased from Ephron the Hittite for four hundred shekels of silver in order to use a cave in it as a place of burial for Sarah (Gen 23:19–20). Abraham, Isaac, Rebekah, Leah, and Jacob were also buried there (25:9; 49:31; 50:13). Its name may mean it was a double cave. A Muslim mosque stands over the cave of Machpelah today, and entrance into it is forbidden.

MACNADEBAI (măk-năd'ē-bī). One of the men who married a foreign wife (Ezra 10:40).

MADAI (măd'ā-ī, Heb. *mādhay, Media*). A people descended from Japheth (Gen 10:2; 1 Chron 1:5). They occupied the same area that Persia, modern Iran, does today. They were called the Medes.

MADMANNAH (măd-măn'nà, Heb. *madhmannâh, dunghill*). 1. A town in southern Judah located about eight miles (thirteen km.) south of Kiriath Sepher (Josh 15:31).

2. A grandson of Caleb (1 Chron 2:48–49).

MADMENAH (măd-mē'nà, Heb. *madhmēnâh, dunghill*). A town in the tribe of Benjamin, evidently a little north of Jerusalem, but its location is uncertain (Isa 10:31).

MADON (mā'dŏn, Heb. *mādhôn, contention*). A royal city of the Canaanites, whose king Jobab was defeated by Joshua (Josh 11:1; 12:19). It was located near modern Hattin, about five miles (eight km.) east of the Sea of Galilee.

MAGADAN (See MAGDALA)

MAGBISH (măg'bĭsh, Heb. *maghbîsh, congregating*). The name of either a man, the head of a family of which 156 persons returned with Zerubbabel from exile, or of a place to which these people belonged. The list contains names of both towns and persons (Ezra 2:30). It is listed in some atlases as a town, location unknown.

MAGDALA (măg'dà-là, Gr. *Magdala*). A town on the NW shore of the Sea of Galilee, three miles (five km.) north of Tiberias (Matt 15:39; ASV and NIV have Magadan; Mark 8:10, Dalmanutha). Identified mainly by the modern village of El Mejdel, it may be Taricheae, one of the lost fishing towns of the lake. The town was the home or birthplace of Mary Magdalene (Matt 27:56, 61; 28:1; Mark 15:40, 47; 16:1, 9; Luke 8:2; 24:10; John 19:25; 20:1, 18).

MAGDALENE (See MARY)

MAGDIEL (mag'dĭ-ĕl, Heb. *maghdî'ēl, God is noble*). One of the chiefs of Edom (Gen 36:43; 1 Chron 1:54).

MAGGOT (See ANIMALS)

MAGI (mā'jī, Gr. *magoi*). Originally a religious caste among the Persians. Their devotion to astrology, divination, and the interpretation of dreams led to an extension in the meaning of the word, and by the first century B.C. the terms "magi" and "Chaldean" were applied generally to fortune tellers and the exponents of esoteric religious cults throughout the Mediterranean world. Magus or "sorcerer" is the name given to Simon in Acts 8:9, to Bar-Jesus in 13:6, and to Elymas in 13:8. The "wise men from the East" in Matthew 2 are often referred to as "the Magi." Nothing is known of their land of origin, but it is a likely theory that they came from Arabia Felix (Southern Arabia). Astrology was practiced there, and a tradition of Israelite messianic expectation may have survived in the region since the days of the Queen of Sheba. Much early legend connects Southern Arabia with Solomon's Israel. Ancient report, linked to later astrological study, may have prompted the famous journey. This, of course, can be no more than speculation. The legend of "the Three Kings" is late and medieval. The old Arabian caravan routes enter Palestine "from the East." See also WISE MEN. EMB

MAGIC. Originally the word meant the science or art of the Magi, the Persian priestly caste, who, like the Levites, were devoted to the practice of religion. With the wide extension of the term "magus," the word magic, too, acquired broader significance. It came to mean all occult rituals or processes designed to influence or control the course of nature; to dominate men or circumstances by the alliance, aid, or use of supernatural powers; and generally to tap and to employ the forces of an unseen world. Divination, the art of forecasting the future with a view to avoiding its perils and pitfalls, might be included under the same classification. Its methods were frequently "magic." In lands ethnologically stratified, magic was often associated with the religion of a conquered or depressed class, or with imported faiths. Therefore magic was found frequently in the hands of foreign elements, was secret in its practice, and was often under official ban as antisocial and illicit. For this reason the Bible gives stern prohibitions against all forms of "wizardry" and "sorcery" (Exod 22:18; Lev 19:26; 20:27; Deut 18:10–11), causing security

Clay figurine of bound prisoner, inscribed with magical formulae (execration text) intended to place a curse upon the enemies of Egypt. Saqqara, c. eighteenth century B.C. Courtesy Carta, Jerusalem.

precautions like those surrounding the royal visit to "the witch of Endor" (1 Sam 28).

In the Mosaic Law, contact with magic and its practitioners was strictly forbidden (e.g., Deut 18:9–14). This is not only because it was typical of the abominations of the heathen that the people of God were to avoid and, indeed, destroy, but more particularly because it was a denial of the true function of prophecy and therefore of the way of faith. In a word, magic is man's attempt to make the future secure, whether by trying to find out about it in advance or by casting spells so as to make things happen in a predetermined and favorable way. The Lord's desire for his people is that they should recognize that his sovereignty has planned the future already, and that their part is, therefore, to walk trustfully into it. Furthermore, the voice of prophecy brings them all the immediate guidance and future knowledge that God thinks they need, and their task is to trust his trustworthiness.

Magic was widely practiced in Egypt (Exod 7:11; 8:7, 18–19; 9:11) and in Babylon (Dan 1:20; 2:2). In both empires the craft and ritual of magic came long before the Persian religious caste whose practices provided the later name. Nonetheless, both before and after Moses, the intrusion of such unhealthy beliefs may be detected in Hebrew history. The incident of the mandrakes found by Reuben (Gen 30:14) is a clear example, and perhaps also the obscure incident of Jacob's trickery with the rods at the waterhole (30:37). It is not claimed in the record that the magic manipulation was the prime cause of the result. It is fairly evident that Jacob's believed his knowledge of animal genetics was determining the breeding trend, but God revealed to him in a dream that it was the Lord, not his own manipulations, that caused the favorable results (30:10–12). Jacob's family was remote from the lofty monotheism of Abraham, and the Euphrates Valley towns were devoted to magic, hence the "teraphim," or "household gods," later in the account (Gen 31:19; see also Judg 17:5; 1 Sam 19:13; Ezek 21:21–26; Zech 10:2). These were household deities, crudely carved, like the Roman Lares and Penates. In popular religion their worship was a base addition to, or substitute for, the worship of the Lord. Similar in concept was the cult of the "baals" of the fields, whose corrupt worship in fertility rituals and sympathetic magic was fiercely castigated by the prophets for the obscene thing it was. In every revival of pure worship the teraphim were swept away with other forms of vicious paganism (e.g., 2 Kings 23:24).

References to magic practices are also found in the NT. The reference to the pagans' "vain repetitions" (Matt 6:7 KJV; e.g., see 1 Kings 18:26 and Acts 19:28) may allude to the belief in the magic repetition of set formulas such as the Tibetan's meaningless *"om mani padme hum"* ("Hail to the jewel in the lotus flower"). Simon (Acts 8:9) and Elymas (Acts 13:8) are spoken of as practicing "sorcery." There is evidence that this tribe of charlatans was widespread and often Jewish in origin (e.g., "the Sons of Sceva" in Ephesus, Acts 19:14). The Emperor Tiberius had given much encouragement to "the Chaldeans and soothsayers" by his belief in magic. Juvenal pictures the old prince in retirement on Capri "with his wizard mob" (*cum grege Chaldaeo*). The Senate, indeed, had more than once banished them, but a Roman weakness for the caster of horoscopes and the purveyors of superstition always ensured the return of the magicians, whom Tacitus bitterly describes as "a tribe faithless to the powerful, deceitful to those who hope, which will ever be banned among us—and ever tolerated." Sergius Paulus, the governor of Cyprus, seems to have held his Jewish soothsayer with a light hand and to have been quite convinced by the apostle's exposure of him. The record of the first Christian impact on the city of Ephesus reveals the tremendous influence of magic among the populace at large. With the spread of Christian doctrine, those who practiced "curious arts" brought their books of incantations of magic formulas to burn. The estimated price was "fifty thousand drachmas." The reference is probably to a silver coin, one of which was the standard wage for a day's labor in the Palestine of the Gospels. The early church in general did not dismiss magic as a delusion, but attributed its results to the work of malign and evil beings who were without power against a Christian. The Council of Ancyra (A.D. 315) first legislated against magic.

Bibliography: M. F. Unger, *Biblical Demonology,* 1952, pp. 107–64; A. L. Oppenheim, *The Interpretation of Dreams in the Ancient Near East,* 1956; D. Basham, *Deliver Us From Evil,* 1972.

EMB

MAGISTRATE (măg'ĭs-trāt, Heb. *shephat, judge,* Gr. *archōn, ruler, stratēgos, commander*). The word *shephat* is found only once (Ezra 7:25), when it is translated "magistrates." The term *archōn* is only once rendered magistrate (Luke 12:58). The word *stratēgos* is translated "magistrates" five times (Acts 16:20, 22, 35, 36, 38), where it denotes the rulers of the city of Philippi, a Roman colony. These authorities were called *praetors* in Latin. They were the highest officials in the government of a colony and had the power of administration of justice in less important cases.

MAGNIFICAT (măg-nĭf'ĭ-kăt). The song of praise by Mary recorded in Luke 1:46–55. This name comes from its first word in the Vulgate version, *Magnificat mea anima* ("My soul doth magnify"). Mary spoke this song in response to the assurance from Elizabeth that God would surely fulfill the words of the angel Gabriel that she would be the woman chosen to bring the Son of God into the world. The song resembles closely the poetry of the OT; its similarity to Hannah's prayer in 1 Samuel 2:1–10 is very striking. There can be no doubt that Mary said these words; all the Greek manuscripts ascribe it to her, but three Latin manuscripts read Elizabeth instead of Mary in verse 46.

MAGOG (mā'gŏg, Heb. *māghôgh, land of God?*). A son of Japheth (Gen 10:2; 1 Chron 1:5) Josephus and Greek writers generally applied this name to the Scythians. Some modern Christian writers indicate the Tartars of Russia and of southern Europe. The names of King Gog, "prince of Rosh, Meshech and Tubal" (Ezek 38:2; see NIV footnote) resemble the modern Russia, Moscow, and Tobolsk. "The nations in the four corners of the earth—Gog and Magog" (Rev 20:8) means all the ungodly nations of the earth who oppose the people of God.

MAGOR-MISSABIB (mā'gôr-mĭs'à-bĭb, *terror on every side*). The symbolic name that Jeremiah gave to Pashhur, the son of the priest Immer, who struck him (Jer 20:3).

MAGPIASH (măg'pĭ-ăsh, Heb. *magpi'osh, moth killer*). A chief who sealed the covenant with Nehemiah (Neh 10:20).

MAGUS, SIMON (See SIMON)

MAHALAH (See MAHLAH)

MAHALALEL (mà-hā'là-lĕl, Heb. *mahălal'ēl, praise of God*). The son of Kenan, who lived 895 years, and was the father of Jared (Gen 5:12–13, 15–17; 1 Chron 1:2; Luke 3:37). In Luke 3:37 NIV has "Mahalaleel."

MAHALATH (mā'hà-lăth, Heb. *mahălath, sickness*). 1. A daughter of Ishmael whom Esau took for his third wife (Gen 28:9).

2. The first wife of Rehoboam; she was a granddaughter of David (2 Chron 11:18).

3. A musical term in the heading of Psalms 53 and 88.

MAHALI (See MAHLI)

MAHANAIM (mā'hà-nā'ĭm, Heb. *mahănayim, two hosts*). A town so named by Jacob when he was met there by angels as he was returning from Paddan Aram to Canaan (Gen 32:2). This town was appointed a city of refuge and was assigned to the Levites (Josh 21:38; 1 Chron 6:80). It was situated in Gilead east of the Jordan, on the boundary between Gad and Manasseh (Josh 13:26, 30). After the death of Saul, Mahanaim was made the capital of Israel for a short time (2 Sam 2:8). David, fleeing from Absalom, came to this place (19:32). Solomon's officer Abinadab was stationed in this city (1 Kings 4:14).

Mahanaim is mentioned in an Egyptian inscription as one of the cities conquered by Sheshonk I (Shishak of the Bible). This occurred on his raid into Palestine (1 Kings 14:25–26; 2 Chron 12:2–3). The exact location of Mahanaim, though much discussed, remains uncertain.

Song of Songs 6:13 refers to a dance called Mahanaim. CEH

MAHANEH DAN (mā'hà-nĕ dăn, Heb. *mahănēh-dhān, camp of Dan*). 1. A place where Samson grew up and first began to be moved by the Spirit of the Lord. It was situated between Zorah and Eshtaol (Judg 13:25).

2. A place behind Kiriath Jearim where six hundred men of war of the tribe of Dan encamped on their way to conquer Laish (Judg 18:12). This may be the same place as no. 1, though they seem to be several miles apart.

MAHARAI (mà-hăr'ā-ī, Heb. *mahăray, impetuous*). One of David's mighty men (2 Sam 23:28; 1 Chron 11:30). He was the captain over 24,000 men who served the king during the tenth month of the year. He was a Zerahite living in Netoph (1 Chron 27:13).

MAHATH (mā'hăth, Heb. *mahath, seizing*). 1. A Kohathite, an ancestor of Heman the singer (1 Chron 6:35).

2. One of the Levites who cleansed the temple in Hezekiah's reign (2 Chron 29:12). He was appointed one of the overseers of the dedicated things (2 Chron 31:13).

MAHAVITE (mā'hȧ-vīt, Heb. *mahăwîm*). The family name of Eliel, one of David's warriors (1 Chron 11:46).

MAHAZIOTH (mȧ-hā'zĭ-ŏth, Heb. *mahăzî'-ôth, visions*). A son of Heman who praised God in the temple in song and with instruments (1 Chron 25:4). He was given the twenty-third lot to serve in music (25:30).

MAHER-SHALAL-HASH-BAZ (mā'hēr-shăl'ăl-hăsh'băz, *the spoil speeds, the prey hastens*). This phrase was written down by Isaiah and officially recorded by witnesses according to God's direction. Later when the prophet's second son was born the Lord told Isaiah to give him this phrase as a name. It was a sign that Samaria would be carried away before the child would be old enough to talk (Isa 8:1, 3).

MAHLAH (mȧ'lȧ, Heb. *mahlâh, disease*). 1. Oldest daughter of Zelophehad of the tribe of Manasseh. This man had no sons but seven daughters, who obtained permission to inherit land as if they were sons, provided they married within the tribe (Num 26:33; 27:1ff.; 36:1ff.; Josh 17:3ff.).

2. Daughter of Hammoleketh, the sister of Makir, son of Manasseh (1 Chron 7:18).

MAHLI (mȧh'lī, Heb. *mahlî, sick*). 1. Son of Merari, son of Levi, ancestor of the Mahlites (Exod 6:19; Num 3:20; Ezra 8:18).

2. Son of Mushi (1 Chron 6:47; 23:23; 24:30).

MAHLITE (mȧh'līt, Heb. *mahlî*). A descendant of Mahli, son of Merari (Num 3:33; 26:58). There was one case among them of a family of daughters who married cousins (1 Chron 23:22).

MAHLON (mȧ'lŏn, Heb. *mahlôn, sick*). Son of Elimelech. He married Ruth in Moab, leaving her a widow about ten years later (Ruth 1:2, 5; 4:9–10).

MAHOL (mā'hŏl, Heb. *māhôl, dance*). Father of Calcol and Darda, men famous for their wisdom but not as wise as Solomon (1 Kings 4:31).

MAHSEIAH (See MAASEIAH)

MAID, MAIDEN. 1. Hebrew *'āmâh, handmaiden, or female slave,* the property of her owners (Exod 2:5; 21:20, 26) and often a bondmaid (Lev 25:44).

2. Hebrew *bethûlâh, virgin,* a girl secluded and separated from intercourse with men. Often used with this meaning (Exod 22:16; Judg 19:24; Ps 78:63; 148:12).

3. Hebrew *har'ărâh, girl, maiden* (Exod 2:5; Ruth 2:8, 22–23; 3:2).

4. Hebrew *'almâh, a girl of marriageable age,* occurs only seven times (Gen 24:43; Exod 2:8; Ps 68:25; Prov 30:19; Song of Songs 1:3; 6:8; Isa 7:14).

5. Heb. *shiphhâh, maid servant,* a synonym of *amah, maid* (Gen 16:2–3, 5–6, 8; 29:24, 29; 30:9ff.), *bondmaid* (Lev 19:20), *bond woman* (Deut 28:68; 2 Chron 28:10; Esth 7:4), *handmaid* (Gen 16:1; 25:12; 29:24, 29), *maidservant* (Gen 12:16; 24:35; 30:43).

MAIL, COAT OF (See ARMS AND ARMOR)

MAIMED (See DISEASES)

MAKAZ (mā'kăz, Heb. *māqats*). A town near Beth Shemesh where Solomon's supply officer, Ben-Deker, was stationed (1 Kings 4:9).

MAKHELOTH (măk-hē'lŏth, Heb. *maqhēlōth*). A station where Israel encamped in the wilderness (Num 33:25–26).

MAKI (mā'kī, Heb. *mākhî*). The father of Geuel, who was appointed from the tribe of Gad to be one of those who spied out the Promised Land (Num 13:15).

MAKIR (mā'kĭr, Heb. *mākhîr, sold*). 1. The oldest son of Manasseh, son of Joseph. He married and had a family before the Israelites left Egypt (Gen 50:23). By the time of the dividing up of the Promised Land, his descendants, the Makirites, were numerous and powerful. They conquered Gilead and settled there (Num 32:39–40), except the family of Hepher, who settled in Canaan (Josh 17:3). So Makir is called the father of Gilead several times, and he is even said to have begotten Gilead (Num 26:29). In Judges 5:14 Makir stands for Manasseh.

2. The son of Ammiel. David took Mephibosheth out of his house (2 Sam 9:4–5). This Makir was one of the men who brought refreshments to David as he fled from Absalom (17:27).

MAKKEDAH (măk-kē'dȧ, Heb. *maqqēdhâh, a place of shepherds*). A town near Libnah and Azekah conquered by Joshua. Five kings hid in a cave in this town and were killed and buried there (Josh 10:16ff.). The city was assigned to Judah (15:41).

MALACHI (măl'ȧ-kī, Heb. *mal'ākhî, messenger of the* LORD or *my messenger*). The name given to the last book of the OT, and probably also the name of the prophet whose oracles the book contains. The book's title reads: "An Oracle: The word of the LORD to Israel through Malachi" (Mal 1:1). Thus it would seem that the prophet's name was Malachi. *Malachi* is the Hebrew expression meaning "my messenger," and it is so translated in 3:1, where there is an obvious play on the author's name. For this reason, some have supposed Malachi to be a title for the prophet, not his proper name. But since the other prophetic books of the OT always begin by stating the prophet's name, it seems more likely that here, too, the name of the prophet is given. It is not unusual to have word-plays on the names of real people (Ezek 3:8–9). Nothing more is known about the author of this book.

The Book of Malachi is believed to be one of the latest of the OT books. Since no statement as to its date is made in the book, one must seek to determine this by the nature of its contents. It is clearly postexilic. The temple had been completed and sacrifices were being offered (Mal 1:7–10; 3:8). A Persian governor (the word for governor in 1:8 is a borrowed word, used for the Persian governors in Palestine in postexilic times) was ruling in Jerusalem. This indicates a date later than that of Haggai and Zechariah.

It is also clear that the early zeal for the rebuilding of the temple had died out, and a situation of moral and religious declension had set in. The mixed marriages (Mal 2:10–12), failure to pay tithes (3:8–10), and offering of blemished sacrifices (1:6–14) are conditions not unlike those referred to in the times of Ezra and Nehemiah (Ezra 7–Neh 13); and it would seem that Malachi's prophecy was given at about that time, or possibly shortly thereafter—about the middle or end of the fifth century B.C.

There are two principal themes in the book: (1) The sin and apostasy of the people of Israel, emphasized in Malachi 1–2; and (2) the judgment that will come on the faithless and the blessing in store for those who repent, predominating in chapters 3–4. A more detailed analysis follows:

I. Contents

1. Title, 1:1.
2. An argument for the love of God toward Israel as shown in the contrasted experiences of Edom and Israel, 1:2–5.
3. A protest against the negligence of the priests in worship, 1:6–2:9.
4. A condemnation of those who divorce their wives and marry foreign women, 2:10–16.
5. An answer to those who complain that God is indifferent to injustice: a day of judgment is at hand, 2:17–3:5.
6. A rebuke for the neglect of tithes and offerings, 3:6–12.
7. A reply to doubters and a promise to the faithful, 3:13–4:3.
8. A recall to the law and prophecy of the coming of Elijah, 4:4–6.

II. Unique Features

1. The use of the rhetorical question and answer as a method of communication. This device begins most of the eight sections referred to above. It anticipates the later catechetical method of teaching.

2. Malachi contains prophetic and priestly interests. It has been called "prophecy within the law." Generally the prophets exhibit little interest in sacrifices and ceremonial laws, preferring to stress the more inward aspects of religious life. Malachi, however, sees the people's apostasy manifested by their carelessness in the sacrificial offerings (Mal 1:6–14), the priests' neglect of their duties (2:1–9), and the failure of the people to pay their tithes and other offerings (3:7–12). This book is thus an antidote to the view commonly held today that the prophets did not believe in the necessity of the ritual law. They accepted the sacrificial system but often protested against its abuse that resulted from the people's failure to apprehend the necessity of inward faith and outward moral righteousness in addition to ritual cleanness.

3. The growing OT messianic expectation is witnessed to in the announcement of God's "messenger of the covenant," by whose coming Israel will be purified and judged (Mal 3:1–5; cf. Matt 11:10), and of the prophet Elijah who will announce the Day of the Lord (Mal 4:5–6; cf. Matt 17:9–13).

Bibliography: J. G. Baldwin, *Haggai, Zechariah, Malachi* (TOTC), 1972; Rex Mason, *The Books of Haggai, Zechariah and Malachi,* 1977.

JBG

MALCHAM, MALCAM (See MOLECH)

MALCHIAH (See MALKIJAH)

MALCHIEL (See MALKIEL)

MALCHIJAH (See MALKIJAH)

MALCHIRAM (See MALKIRAM)

MALCHI-SHUA (See MALKI-SHUA)

MALCHUS (măl'kŭs, Gr. *Malchos*). A servant of the high priest whose ear Peter cut off with a sword during Christ's arrest (John 18:10).

MALELEEL (See MAHALALEL)

MALICE (Gr. *kakia*). An evil desire to do harm to or act wickedly toward someone. The adjective *kakos,* which means "bad," "evil," occurs fifty times in the NT, while the noun *kakia* is less common. KJV translates *kakia* as "malice" in Romans 1:29; 1 Corinthians 5:8; 14:20; Ephesians 4:31; Colossians 3:8; Titus 3:3; 1 Peter 2:1, 16, and in most cases so do RSV and NIV. It is obviously an internal feeling or attitude that Christians must put away (Eph 4:31; 1 Peter 2:1), for it is wholly opposed to the life in, and the fruit of, the indwelling Spirit of God. It belongs to the old nature, the "flesh" that is under the domination of sin. See also EVIL.

MALKI-SHUA (măl-kĭ-shū'â, Heb. *malkîshûa'*, *king of aid*). Third son of King Saul (1 Sam 14:49; 31:2; 1 Chron 8:33; 9:39). He was killed by the Philistines (1 Sam 31:2; 1 Chron 10:2).

MALKIEL (măl'kĭ-ĕl, Heb. *malkî'ēl, God is my king*). Son of Beriah, son of Asher (Gen 46:17; Num 26:45; 1 Chron 7:31).

MALKIJAH, MALCHIAH (măl-kī'jà, măl-kī'à, Heb. *malkîyâh, malkîâ, my king is the* LORD). 1. A Gershonite, the ancestor of Asaph, the singer in David's time (1 Chron 6:40).

2. An ancestor of the priest Adaiah who returned from exile and lived in Jerusalem (1 Chron 9:12; Neh 11:12).

3. A priest in David's time to whom was assigned the fifth lot of service (1 Chron 24:9).

4. An Israelite in the family of Parosh who had married a foreign woman (Ezra 10:25).

5. Another in the same family who did the same (Ezra 10:25).

6. A member of the family of Harim who was guilty of the same practice (Ezra 10:31).

7. A son of Harim who worked on the wall (Neh 3:11), possibly the same as no. 6.

8. The son of Recab who repaired the Dung Gate of the wall (Neh 3:14).

9. A goldsmith who worked on the wall (Neh 3:31).

10. One of the men who stood on the left side of Ezra as he read the law to the people (Neh 8:4).

11. One of those who sealed the covenant with Nehemiah (Neh 10:3).

12. A priest who took part in the dedication of the wall (Neh 12:42). Perhaps the same as no. 11.

13. Father of Pashhur, messenger of King Zedekiah to Jeremiah (Jer 21:1). Pashhur helped arrest the prophet (38:1).

14. The son of King Zedekiah and the owner of the dungeon into which Jeremiah was put (Jer 38:6).

MALKIRAM (măl-kī'răm, Heb. *malkîrām, my king is high*). Son of Jehoiachin (1 Chron 3:18).

MALLOTHI (măl'ō-thī, Heb. *mallôthî, I have uttered*). One of the sons of Heman, who with their father praised God with musical instruments. To him fell the nineteenth lot (1 Chron 25:4, 26).

MALLOW (See PLANTS)

MALLUCH (măl'ŭk, Heb. *mallûkh, counselor*). 1. Ancestor of Ethan, a Levite, son of Merari (1 Chron 6:44).

2. A son of Bani. He was one of the men who married foreign women (Ezra 10:29).

3. A son of Harim. He was another man who took a foreign wife (Ezra 10:32).

4. A priest who sealed the covenant (Neh 10:4). He had come from Babylon under Zerubbabel (12:2).

5. A chief of the people who sealed the covenant (Neh 10:27).

MALTA (Gr. *Melitē*). An island situated in a strategically important position some sixty miles (one hundred km.) south of Sicily. It was colonized by the Phoenicians about 1000 B.C. and became part of the empire of Carthage some four centuries later. Rome acquired the island in 218, but the Carthaginian language continued to be spoken. Hence Luke's phrase "the barbarous people" (Acts 28:2 KJV), "barbarous" used in the Greek sense of "foreign-speaking." Malta was the scene of Paul's shipwreck (27:27ff.). Acts 28:3 speaks of a snake on Malta; there are none there today. EMB

MAMMON (Gr. *mamōnas, riches*). The Aramaic word for "riches." Christ used it as a life goal opposed to God (Matt 6:24; Luke 16:13 KJV; NIV "Money"). Jesus also used the word in the phrase "mammon of unrighteousness" (NIV "worldly wealth") in commenting on his parable on the unjust steward (Luke 16:11, 13 KJV).

MAMRE (măm'rē, Heb. *mamrē', strength*). 1. An Amorite who was allied with Abram (Gen 14:13, 24).

2. A place a few miles north of Hebron where oak trees grew. Abram lived by the "great trees of Mamre" (Gen 13:18; 18:1). This place apparently derived its name from the Amorite above who lived there. The burial cave in the field of Machpelah is described as located before Mamre (23:17, 19; 25:9; 35:27; 49:30; 50:13). The modern name of the site is Ramet el-Khalil.

View of Herodian ruins at Mamre (Ramat el-Khalil), near Hebron. Courtesy Duby Tal.

MAN (Heb. *'ādhām, 'îsh*, Gr. *anthrōpos*). In the Bible "man" (see ADAM) refers both to the human species and to the male member. Thus the doctrine of man is the teaching concerning human beings in their relation to God and his creation. It includes the following truths: (1) As Creator, God made the human species, first the male and then the female (Gen 1–2). Human beings are a part of the created order as a single species (Acts 17:26), but they are also separate from the animal world with a special relationship both to God and to the created order. (2) God made man in the image and likeness of himself (Gen 1:26–27; Ps 8:5). This points to that which separates man from the animals in terms of his moral conscience, self-knowledge, and capacity for a spiritual communion with his Creator. All human beings thus have two aspects, a bodily and a spiritual (body and soul, or body and mind, or body and spirit), and so have the capacity to relate fully both to the created order and to their Creator. (3) This capacity has been seriously restricted, misdirected, and abused because of sin. Adam and Eve, the first pair of human beings, freely chose to disobey the divine command and to assert their will against that of their Creator. They lost their personal communion with God, and this had repercussions for the whole of their lives and relationships. It also had an effect on their children and their children's children (Gen 3; Rom 6:12ff.). (4) Whatever their historical and social context, human beings have found themselves capable, on the one hand, of great heroism, public service, personal kindness and goodness; and, on the other hand, of self-centeredness, pride, self-pity, and cruelty (Mark 7:20–23). They show signs both of being God's special creation and of being sinful creatures (Rom 7:14–25). (5) The eternal Son of God became Man in order to provide salvation from sin and a new, permanent relationship with God both in this world and, more fully, in the world to come (Rom 5:12ff.). As such, Jesus Christ is called the "last Adam" (1 Cor 15:45), and the world to come is "the new heaven and earth" (Rev 21:1). (6) Thus in Christ human beings are restored to their right and proper relationship both with their Creator and with his created order (Col 1:15–20). (7) Either as unbeliever or believer, each human being is held by God to be a responsible creature, and so each person will be judged at the Last Judgment (Rom 2:16).

See also WOMAN.

Bibliography: J. G. Machen, *The Christian View of Man,* 1937; G. L. Carey, *I Believe in Man,* 1977; H. D. McDonald, *The Christian View of Man,* 1981. PT

MAN, SON OF (See SON OF MAN)

MANAEN (măn'à-ĕn, Gr. *manaēn,* the Gr. form of the Heb. *menahem, comforter*). A leader in the church of Antioch (Acts 13:1). He is designated as the foster-brother of Herod the Tetrarch (Herod Antipas).

MANAHATH (măn'à-hăth, Heb. *mānahath, resting place*). 1. An Edomite, the son of Shobal (Gen 36:23; 1 Chron 1:40).

2. A town in Edom, site unknown (1 Chron 8:6).

MANAHATHITES (mà-nā'hăth-īts, Heb. *mānahtî*). 1. Half of the Manahathites, a Judean clan, were descendants of Shobal, son of Caleb, the son of Hur (1 Chron 2:52).

2. Another group, "half the Manahathites," descended from Salma, son of Caleb, the son of Hur (1 Chron 2:54).

MANASSEH (mă-năs'sĕ, Heb. *menashsheh, one who forgets*). 1. The older son of Joseph, born in Egypt (Gen 41:51). Jacob claimed him and his younger brother Ephraim for his own sons, and when he blessed them he predicted Ephraim would be greater than Manasseh (48:5, 19). Manasseh had a son named Makir, and his descendants made up the tribe of Manasseh. According to 1 Chronicles 7:14 Manasseh also had another son, Asriel. But in Numbers 26:30 Asriel and his descendants are listed with the sons of Gilead, son of Makir. So probably 1 Chronicles 7:14 means Asriel was Manasseh's grandson.

2. King of Judah and son of Hezekiah. He was only twelve years old when he came to the throne in 687 B.C. Evidently after the death of his father the orthodox party was considerably weakened. The group in power around the new king were doing away with the religious reforms Hezekiah had made. Manasseh was too young to hinder them. He went along with them. No doubt the people had resented being deprived of the high places, and they rebuilt them the first chance they had after Hezekiah's death. But Manasseh went way beyond this restoration. Judah was a vassal of Assyria and paid tribute every year. The young king must have been much more impressed by the power of Assyria than by the power of God. He became a fanatical idolater, bringing a whole host of heathen practices into his realm. He built altars to Baal and made an Asherah pole. He worshiped and served the host of heaven—sun, moon, stars, and planets. He built altars to them in the courts of the temple. He also put a heathen altar in the temple and later moved the Asherah pole into this building, which had been dedicated to the true God of Israel (2 Kings 21:1–7). He also had horses and chariots dedicated to the sun (23:11).

Much of this idolatry came from Assyria and Babylon, where there was widespread worship of the heavenly bodies. Heathen practices expressly forbidden were introduced into Judah by Manasseh. He made his son pass through the fire, which probably means he sacrificed him to Molech the god of the Ammonites; he practiced soothsaying; he used enchantments or observed omens; he indulged in sorcery; he sponsored ghosts and familiar spirits, that is, persons in touch with the spirit world (2 Kings 21:6; 2 Chron 33:6). He persecuted the pious people who were faithful to the Lord, the true God (2 Kings 21:6). Jewish tradition says he sawed the prophet Isaiah in two. All this evil influence set loose in Judah sealed her fate. The subsequent reformation of Josiah could not bring the people back to true worship. Manasseh brought his country to ruin (Jer 15:4).

As a vassal of Assyria this king must have been suspected of disloyalty because he was taken captive by the king of Assyria and carried to Babylon. After a time he repented of his sins and was returned to his throne in Jerusalem, where he tried to undo his evil work (2 Chron 33:10–13, 15–17). He also did some building (33:14).

Many critics refuse to believe that this episode in the life of Manasseh could be true. If he actually had been taken captive to Babylon, he would never have been sent back, and someone else would have reigned in his place. But in the Assyrian records is a report of Neco, an Egyptian king who was carried captive to Nineveh and later sent back to his throne by Ashurbanipal. This incident, which all critics accept, is almost a parallel case to Manasseh's experience. The Assyrian king could find no one else to take his place and made him swear to remain loyal to Assyria. Other Assyrian inscriptions prove Judah paid tribute to Assyria during Manasseh's reign. He is mentioned by name in them. All these inscriptions mentioned are translated in *Ancient Near Eastern Texts Relating to the Old Testament*.

3. A priest of an idol at Dan (Judg 18:30 KJV, NASB; NIV and RSV read "Moses"). The difference in Hebrew between *Manasseh* and *Moses* is one letter between the first two consonants of *Moses*. Some say that since it was thought a disgrace for one with so honored a name as Moses to be guilty of such sacrilege, someone changed the name to Manasseh.

4. One of those who married a foreign woman (Ezra 10:30).

5. Another of those who married a foreign woman (Ezra 10:33).

MANASSEH, PRAYER OF (See APOCRYPHA)

MANASSEH, TRIBE OF. The descendants of Manasseh. This tribe contained 32,200 men of war, those over twenty years old (Num 1:34), before the Israelites marched from Sinai. When the tabernacle was finished and dedicated, each tribe through its leader presented an offering. Gamaliel, the son of Pedahzur, offered on the eighth day for Manasseh (7:54). In the order of march Manasseh came in the eleventh place (10:23). In the layout of the camp Manasseh was on the west side in the third division (2:20). Forty years later the new generation in Manasseh numbered 52,700 men of war (26:34). Before the Israelites crossed over the Jordan River into Canaan, half the tribe of Manasseh along with the tribes of Reuben and Gad chose land east of the river, and Moses assigned it to them (32:33). The descendants of Makir, son of Manasseh, conquered Gilead and lived there. Jair also captured other towns (32:39–41). The half-tribe of Manasseh was given the north half of Gilead, all of Bashan, and the region of Argob (Deut 3:13). This territory included sixty cities, among which were Gilead, Ashtaroth, and Edrei (Josh 13:31). The rest of the tribe was given ten parts of land in Canaan including areas for Zelophehad's daughters (17:1–6). This territory was situated between Ephraim on the south and Asher, Zebulun, and Issachar on the north. Its eastern border was the Jordan River and on the west was the Mediterranean Sea (17:7–10). Golan, in the territory of the half-tribe east of the Jordan, was selected as one of the cities of refuge (20:8). East of the river thirteen cities of Manasseh were assigned to the Gershonite clan of the Levites, and west Manasseh furnished ten cities to the

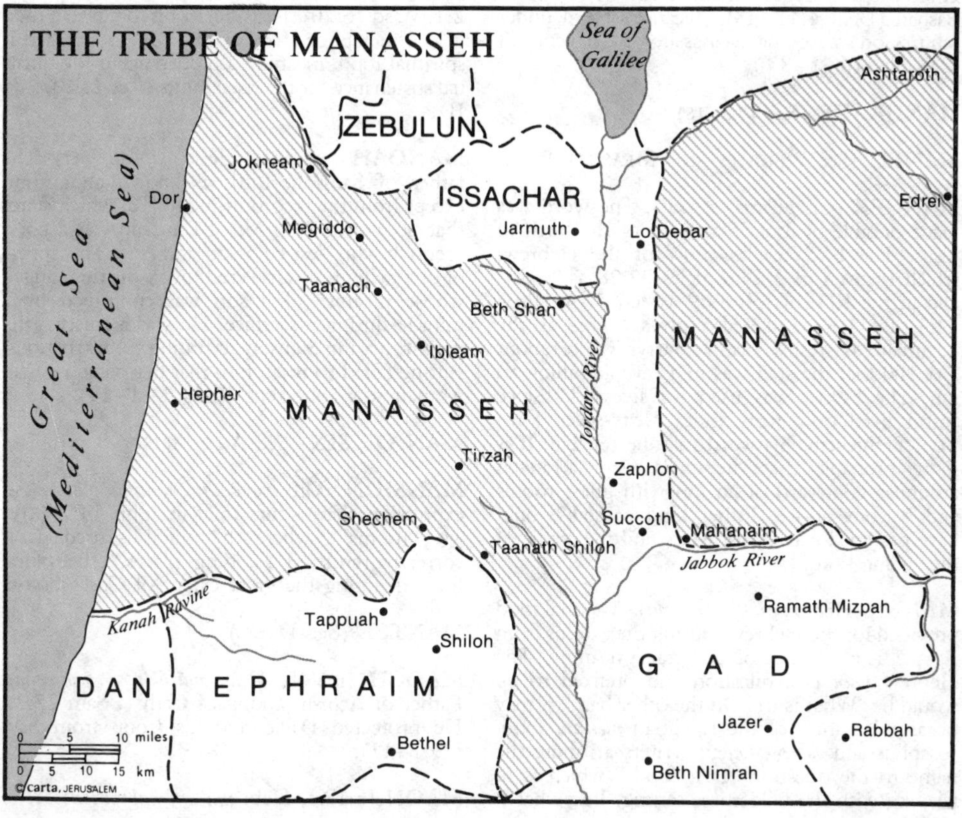

Kohathites of the Levites (21:5–6). West Manasseh failed to drive the Canaanites out of the towns (Judg 1:27). Gideon was of the tribe of Manasseh (6:15), so was Jair the Gileadite, who judged Israel twenty-two years (10:3). Jephthah came from Gilead in east Manasseh (11:1). This half-tribe, with Reuben and Gad, fell into idolatry and was later carried away into captivity by Assyria (1 Chron 5:25–26) during Pekah's reign over Israel (2 Kings 15:29).

Manasseh joined David while he was a fugitive from Saul (1 Chron 12:19–22). When David was made king at Hebron, west Manasseh furnished 18,000 soldiers, and east Manasseh with Reuben and Gad 120,000 (12:31, 37). People from Manasseh and Ephraim joined with Judah in making a covenant to seek the Lord during the reign of Asa king of Judah (15:9–15). Certain pious souls from west Manasseh joined in the Passover during Hezekiah's reign (2 Chron 30:10–22). When Josiah was king, he destroyed idols and purged altars in Manasseh's territory as well as elsewhere (34:6). The people of Manasseh contributed to an offering for the repairing of the temple in Josiah's time (34:9). CEH

MANASSITES (mȧ-năs'īts, Heb. *menashshî, forgetting*). Descendants of the oldest son of Joseph (Gen 41:51). This was a tribe of noble standing, which Gilead, under Jephthah, delivered from the Ephraimites by the password "Shibboleth" (Judg 12:4–6). Moses gave them a city of refuge in Bashan (Deut 4:41–43). Because of evil under Jehu, God cause the Manassites to be cut off (2 Kings 10:31–33).

MANDRAKE (See PLANTS)

MANEH (See WEIGHTS AND MEASURES)

MANGER (Gr. *phatnē, a stall*). The word was made notable by Luke's account of the birth of Jesus. The LXX used *phatnē* for the Hebrew, which is given in 2 Chronicles 32:28 as "stalls" and in the KJV of Job 39:9 as "crib" (see Prov 14:4; Isa 1:3). Luke also gives *phatnē* as the birthplace of Jesus. Justin Martyr wrote about A.D. 100 that the stall was in a cave adjoining an inn. The cavern was used for livestock. Since Justin lived only forty miles (sixty-seven km.) from Bethlehem, his word may be reliable. It is more probable that the stalls were arranged around a courtyard of an inn with guest rooms and balcony above. Either kind of stall would have provided privacy for Mary and the cradle of the infant Lord.

MANNA (Heb. *mān*, Gr. *manna*). A special food provided for the Hebrews during the exodus from Egypt. The name is of uncertain meaning. The Hebrew *mān* is a question and prefixed to *hu* would be "What is it?" On the other hand, it may be an adaptation of the Egyptian *mennu,* food. Josephus and other ancient writers attribute the name to the question "Is it food?" which is in keeping with the wilderness setting. Just what it was has puzzled naturalists for ages. It came at night, resembling hoarfrost, coming with the dew (Num 11:9), and may have collected in dewdrops (Exod 16:4). It was white, of delicious flavor, and resembled seed of the coriander, a plant of the eastern Mediterranean area that was both tasty and nourishing (16:31). That it came by miraculous means is shown by its nature, its time of coming, and its preservation over the Sabbath (Exod 16:20–26; Deut 8:3). Being seedlike in form it had to be ground (Num 11:7–8). As soon as other food was available, the manna ceased (Josh 5:12).

Although many attempts have been made to explain the manna as a natural phenomenon, ancient Hebrew scholars knew it to be of supernatural origin (Wisd 17:20). No known substance meets the description of this food. A tamarisk plant that grows along the route of the Hebrews from Sinai exudes a sweet liquid, which collects at night on twigs and falls to the ground. After sunrise it disappears unless protected. But this plant produces the food for only a brief period each year. Other naturalists would identify manna with a peculiar mossy plant that at maturity is round and is eaten with honey. But neither is it available for the entire year.

The Bible makes it certain that manna came as a temporary provision for the chosen people. The poet Asaph called it "corn from heaven" (Ps 78:24). It was also bread from heaven (105:40). Hebrew writers called it "angels' bread" (2 Esd 2:1; Wisd 16:20). Jesus, referring to himself, used it as a metaphor (John 6:31–58). John called it spiritual food, meaning a hidden agent for spiritual sustenance for the risen saints (Rev 2:17). JDF

MANOAH (mȧ-nō'ȧ, Heb. *mānôah, rest*). The father of Samson. Little is known about him except from the record in Judges 13, which states that he was of the tribe of Dan and was a good Hebrew who desired a son and heir. The appeal of his wife was answered by a visiting angel, whose promise of a son was confirmed by a miracle during a sacrifice. He was a trustworthy parent, rearing Samson according to instructions. But he failed to teach him that marrying a pagan woman was abhorrent (Judg 14:1–11).

MAN OF SIN (See ANTICHRIST)

MANSION (Gr. *monē, an abiding place*). An expression that occurs only in John 14:2 (KJV; NIV "rooms"), where the plural is used. It is correctly rendered "abiding places," the plural form denoting the great extent of God's house.

MANTLE (See DRESS)

MAOCH (mā'ŏk, Heb. *mā'ôkh, a poor one*). Father of Achish, a king of Gath (1 Sam 27:2). He protected David and his troop from Saul (29:1–11).

MAON (mā'ŏn, Heb. *mā'ôn, habitation*). 1. A

Above, general view of Tell Sandahannah, identified with Mareshah, and, below, the interior of a painted tomb (196–119 B.C.) that was found at the site. Courtesy Ecole Biblique et Archéologique Française, Jerusalem.

descendant of Caleb and father of Beth Zur, or perhaps the founder of this fortress near Bethlehem (1 Chron 2:42–45).

2. A town on an elevated plain south of Hebron. Around it lay an unpopulated region where David found refuge from Saul until the Philistines forced the king to cease pursuit. Because of this rescue, the hill was called Rock of Separation (1 Sam 23:24–28 mg; NIV "Sela Hammahlekoth," "rock of parting"). It was the home of Nabal and Abigail (25:1–3).

MAONITES (mā'ŏn-īts). There is confusion about these enemies of Israel. They are named with others who were defeated by the Lord (Judg 10:11–12). They were called Mehunim and may have been from Arabia. Their descendants were among the temple servants of Ezra's day (Ezra 2:50). Doubtless they came from the Arabian peninsula and were called Maonites because they grew strong on the Maon Plain.

MARA (mà'rà, Heb. *mārâh, bitter*). A name adopted by Naomi instead of her own, which meant pleasant or delightful (Ruth 1:20).

MARAH (mā'rà, Heb. *mārâh, bitterness*). A place about three days' journey from the Red Sea crossing, where the Hebrews found bitter water. When they complained, God showed Moses a plant whose foliage sweetened the water (Exod 15:23–26).

MARALAH (măr'à-là, Heb. *mar'ălâh*). A city on the border of Zebulun's heritage (Josh 19:10–11). It was about four miles (seven km.) from Nazareth, though its exact location is not known.

MARANATHA (mār'à-năth'à, Aramaic, *mārā-nā' 'āthāh, our Lord comes!*). An expression of greeting and encouragement as well as of triumphant faith, such as is shown in 1 Corinthians 16:22, RSV mg. That is to say, "Our Lord comes, regardless of man's enmity!" Paul put this word over against *anathema,* the curse that befalls idolaters.

MARBLE (See MINERALS)

MARCUS (See MARK, JOHN)

MARDUK (mår'dūk, Heb. *merōdhākh,* Akkad. *Marduk*). A Babylonian god (Jer 50:2; KJV "Merodach").

MARESHAH (mà-rē'shà, Heb. *mārēshâh, a possession*). 1. The father of Hebron (1 Chron 2:42).

2. A grandson of Judah, more probably a town (1 Chron 4:21).

3. An important city of Judah, SW of Jerusalem

Marduk, chief god in the Babylonian pantheon, as depicted on a cylinder seal from Babylon, mid-ninth century B.C.
"Babylon will be captured;
Bel will be put to shame,
Marduk filled with terror" (Jer 50:2).
Courtesy Carta, Jerusalem.

(Josh 15:44), which Rehoboam considered strategic and which he fortified (2 Chron 11:5–12). King Asa met a big Ethiopian army at Mareshah in the Valley of Zephathah and with divine aid overwhelmed it (14:9–15). Eliezer, a native of Mareshah, delivered a warning from God to wicked King Jehoshaphat for an unholy alliance with Ahaziah (20:35–37). It was a good city in Micah's day and he promised its people an heir (Mic 1:15). Little of its record is found in the Bible, but Josephus tells how the city was ravished during the Maccabean period by Judas Maccabeus; that Hyrcanus, high priest about 130 B.C., captured it and compelled its citizens to adopt Jewish laws and customs; and that it was strong enough to win favors from Pompey. When the Parthians invaded Judea in 40, the city fell and was destroyed. Discovery of some elaborate tombs about one mile (one and one-half km.) south of modern Beit Jibrin confirmed the belief that El Sandahannah is its location.

MARK. A word used to translate words of varied meanings: (1) *'Ôth,* a special sign or brand. The *'ôth* of Cain (Gen 4:15) is considered a brand of infamy, but was more probably a sign of the covenant to be protected against avengers. The marks Paul bore were scars (*stigmata*) caused by the beatings he had suffered (Gal 6:17). (2) *Tāu'*, a seal or sign of ownership. Ezekiel saw this symbol put on the foreheads of a special people (Ezek 9:4, 6). In a similar way, the redeemed are to be protected in the last days (Rev 7:2–8). *Tāw* appears in Job 31:35 and is rendered "signature" by RSV. The illiterate man still makes his "mark" as a signature. (3) *Mattārā'*, a target. Jonathan pretended to be shooting at *mattārā'* (1 Sam 20:20). Job felt himself such a mark (Job 16:12) and so did Jeremiah (Lam 3:12) (4) *Qa'aqa'*, a form of tattooing banned by the Lord (Lev 19:28). (5) *Skopos,* a goal or end to be attained. Paul set his heart on such a mark (Phil 3:14). (6) *Charagma,* a particular brand or characteristic, denoting the nature and rank of people. The mark of the beast is physical (Rev 13:16). JDF

MARK, GOSPEL OF. The shortest of the four Gospels. In comparison with Matthew and Luke, it contains relatively little of the teachings of Jesus and nothing at all about his birth and childhood. Starting with the ministry of John the Baptist, it comes immediately to the public ministry of Christ, ending with his death and resurrection.

I. Authorship. On two points the tradition of the early church is unanimous: the Second Gospel was written by Mark and presents the preaching of Peter. Papias (c. A.D. 140) is quoted by Eusebius as saying, "And John the presbyter also said this, Mark being the interpreter of Peter, whatsoever he recorded he wrote with great accuracy . . . he was in company with Peter, who gave him such instruction as was necessary, but not to give a history of our Lord's discourses" (*Eccl. Hist.,* 3.39). This suggests that Mark has given us a summary of the message of Peter.

Justin Martyr (c. A.D. 150) quotes Mark 3:17 as from "Peter's Memoirs." Irenaeus (c. 185) writes that after the departure (*exodus*) of Peter and Paul from Rome, "Mark the disciple and interpreter of Peter, also transmitted to us in writing what had been preached by Peter" (Eusebius, *Eccl. Hist.,* 5.8). Most scholars hold that "departure" means "death." Clement of Alexandria, however, affirms that the Gospel was written during Peter's lifetime. Here is his statement: "When Peter had proclaimed the word publicly at Rome, and declared the Gospel under the influence of the Spirit; as there was a great number present, they requested Mark . . . to reduce these things to writing, and that after composing the Gospel he gave it to those who requested it of him. Which when Peter understood, he directly neither hindered nor encouraged it" (ibid., 6.14). In spite of this minor confusion, the early church fathers, including specifically Tertullian (c. 200) and Origen (c. 230), unite in affirming that Mark's Gospel gives us the preaching of Peter. Such strong tradition can hardly be discounted, though some recent scholars have sought to do so. The traditional authorship of the Second Gospel is accepted more universally today than is the case with any of the other three Gospels.

II. Date. Most scholars today place the writing of Mark between A.D. 65 and 70, shortly before the destruction of Jerusalem in the latter year. Conservatives commonly hold to a date in the 50s. Of course, if one accepts the tradition that Mark wrote after Peter's death, the later dates would have to be adopted.

III. Place of Writing. About this there is little question. From the early church—with the exception of Chrysostom—to the present it has been held that Mark's Gospel was written at Rome. Several distinctive features point in this direction. Mark uses ten Latin words, some of which do not occur elsewhere in the NT. He explains Jewish customs because he is writing to Gentiles. To his Roman readers he presents Jesus as the mighty conqueror and the suffering servant of the Lord. Because of this purpose no genealogy nor infancy narratives are given. These are found only in Matthew and Luke.

IV. Character. In addition to those just mentioned, there are three main characteristics of this Gospel. The first is *rapidity of action.* The narrative moves quickly from one event to the next. This probably reflects the impulsive personality of Peter. Over forty times we find the Greek word *euthys,* translated (KJV) "immediately," "straightway," "forthwith." As Vincent aptly says, "His narrative runs" (*Word Studies,* I, 160). The second characteristic is *vividness of detail.* Mark often includes details omitted by the other Synoptics that make the narrative more alive. He gives special attention to the looks and gestures of Jesus. The third characteristic is *picturesqueness of description.* Mark's is preeminently the pictorial Gospel. He describes, for instance, the five thousand sitting on the green grass in "groups" (literally, "flower beds"). Peter evidently was impressed with the striking scene of the groups of people in brightly colored Oriental garments of red and yellow sitting on the green hillside, and Mark has preserved the picture for us.

Mark's is the Gospel of action. Only one long message of Jesus is recorded, the Olivet Discourse (Mark 13). Mark includes eighteen miracles of Jesus, about the same number as Matthew or Luke. In contrast he has only four of the parables, compared with eighteen in Matthew and nineteen in Luke.

V. Content. The period of preparation (Mark 1:1–13) for Jesus' public ministry is described very briefly. It consists of three items: the ministry of John the Baptist (1:1–8), the baptism of Jesus (1:9–11), and the temptation of Jesus (1:12–13). After an introduction of only 13 verses—in contrast to 76 in Matthew and 183 in Luke—Mark plunges immediately into the public ministry of the Master.

First comes the great Galilean ministry (Mark 1:14–9:50). This is commonly thought to have lasted about a year and a half. It may be divided into three sections. The first period (1:4–3:12) was a time of immense popularity. Jesus called four fishermen to follow him—and later Levi—and engaged in a vigorous healing ministry. This was the time when large crowds thronged about him.

In the second period (Mark 3:13–7:23) he appointed the twelve apostles, and opposition began to show itself. The Pharisees clashed with Jesus over questions about Sabbath observance and ceremonial cleansing. He healed the Gerasene demoniac and the woman with the issue of blood and raised Jairus's daughter. He sent out the Twelve and fed the five thousand.

In the third period (Mark 7:24–9:50) Jesus gave more attention to his disciples. Three times he is described as withdrawing from the crowd to teach the disciples. After Peter's confession at Caesarea Philippi he began a new phase of teaching: predicting his passion.

The great Galilean ministry was followed by the briefer Perean ministry (Mark 10:1–52), and then by Passion Week (11:1–15:47) and the Resurrection (Mark 16).

VI. Ending. A word must be said about the last twelve verses of Mark (16:9–20). The two oldest Greek manuscripts, Vaticanus and Sinaiticus (both fourth century A.D.), and the Sinaitic Syriac end the Gospel at 16:8. The majority of scholars now believe that these last twelve verses are not a part of the original Gospel of Mark, although the matter is not settled conclusively.

VII. Priority. Most scholars today favor the theory that Mark's Gospel was written first and was used by Matthew and Luke when they composed their Gospels. The fact is that about 95 percent of Mark is found in Matthew and or Luke. The freshness and vividness of Mark's language suggest it was written first. It should be noted, however, that this position is still being challenged.

VIII. Evaluation. In the early church the Gospel of Mark received the least attention of any of the four. This is not true today. The importance of Mark as giving us the basic message of the primitive church (cf. Acts 1:22; 2:22–24, 36) is increasingly recognized. The theological as well as historical value of this Gospel is widely appreciated. It is the logical place to start one's study of the four Gospels.

Bibliography: Vincent Taylor, *The Gospel According to St. Mark,* 1952 (on the Greek text); C. E. B. Cranfield, *The Gospel According to Saint Mark* (CGTC), 1959 (on the Greek text); C. F. D. Moule, *The Gospel According to Mark* (CBC), 1965; E. Schweizer, *The Good News According to Mark,* 1970; R. P. Martin, *Mark: Evangelist and Theologian,* 1972; W. L. Lane, *The Gospel According to Mark* (NIC), 1974. RE

MARK, JOHN (Gr. *Markos,* from Lat. *Marcus, a large hammer,* Gr. *Iōannēs,* from Heb. *Yôhānān, the* LORD *is gracious*). Mentioned by name ten times in the NT. John was his Jewish name, Mark (Marcus) his Roman. In Acts he is twice (13:5, 13) referred to simply as John, once (15:39) as Mark, and three times (12:12, 25; 15:37) as "John, also called Mark." In the Epistles he is uniformly (four times) called simply Mark (KJV calling him Marcus three times).

The first allusion to John Mark may be in Mark 14:51–52. The most reasonable explanation for the passing mention of this incident is that it was a vivid personal memory in the mind of the author of the second Gospel. The first definite reference to John Mark is Acts 12:12. Peter, when delivered from prison, went to the home of John Mark's mother, where many believers were praying for him. When Barnabas and Saul returned to Antioch from their famine visit at Jerusalem (Acts 11:27–30), they took along John Mark (12:25). This opened the opportunity for him to accompany them on their missionary journey as "their helper" (13:5).

The missionaries first evangelized the island of Cyprus. When they reached Perga in Pamphylia, John returned home to Jerusalem. This decision was probably due to a mixture of homesickness, fear of perils in the mountainous country ahead, and displeasure that Paul had become the leader of the expedition (Acts 13:13, "Paul and his companions"). Whatever his motive, Paul distrusted him and refused to take him on the second journey (15:37–38). The result was that two missionary parties were formed. Barnabas took Mark and revisited Cyprus, while Paul chose a new associate, Silas, and went overland to Asia Minor.

Mark next appears in Rome, where he is a fellow worker with Paul (Philem 24). Paul recommended him to the church at Colosse (Col 4:10). Here he was called "the cousin of Barnabas." That John Mark had fully reinstated himself with Paul is shown by the latter's statement in 2 Timothy 4:11. Peter refers to him as "my son Mark" (1 Peter 5:13). This may be a mere expression of affection, or it may indicate that Mark was converted under Peter's ministry.

An early tradition says that Mark founded the church in Alexandria, Egypt, but this is uncertain.

RE

View of the Roman ruins at Palmyra, ancient Tadmor, a city about 120 miles (193 km.) northeast of Damascus. The agora, or market place, is shown in foreground. Courtesy Studium Biblicum Franciscanum, Jerusalem.

MARKET (Heb. *ma'ărāv, a place for trade*). The term also means things traded, hence the "market" of Ezekiel 27:13, 17, 19 is more correctly rendered "merchandise" in NIV. The NT word is *agora,* the civic center where people gathered for recreation (Matt 11:16–17), where the unemployed loafed (20:3, 6), and where the proud paraded (Mark 12:38; Luke 11:43). It was a courtroom (Acts 16:19) and also a forum (17:17). From a corner shop the market developed into a great urban multipurpose center.

MAROTH (mā'rŏth, Heb. *mārôth*). A town probably in the plain west of Jerusalem. Its citizens waited for relief when disaster had come on God's people (Mic 1:12).

MARRIAGE. The formalization and sanctification of the union of man and woman for the procreation of children. The common Hebrew term *lāqah,* "to take in marriage," should be seen in association with the verb *bā'al,* "to be master, rule, or possess in marriage," as well as with the noun *ba'al,* "master, lord, husband." A comparable NT verb would be *gameō,* "to marry, take to wife," along with its cognate forms *gamizō* and *gamiskō,* both meaning "to give in marriage."

Historically, as Hebrew society developed from nomadic to village settlement, more complex customs and feasts became associated with the ceremony of marriage, and in the Christian era it became regarded as a sacrament. Normally the bride left her family at marriage, and from that time she, and subsequently her children, became part of her husband's family or clan (Gen 24:58–61) and, as such, part of their responsibility also.

There are some well-known instances in the Old Testament of the bride continuing to live with her own family. After Jacob had worked for the agreed period of fourteen years in order to pay his father-in-law Laban the required bride price for his daughters Leah and Rachel, he remained voluntarily with Laban for a further six years (Gen 31:41). Laban considered that the children of the union belonged to him and were a part of his family (31:43). Similarly, Gideon's concubine and her son lived with her family (Judg 14:8; 15:1–2). These examples, however, are few, and neither Gideon, visiting a concubine rather than a wife, nor Samson, whose bride was a foreigner, was ever considered a part of the woman's family.

Marriage contracts appear to have originated with the Sumerians and soon became common features of life in Mesopotamia and beyond. Indeed, according to the Code of Hammurabi (128), they were essential to a marriage, since they constituted the public attestation of the event. From Ugarit, evidence contained in contacts shows that marriages could be temporary or permanent, while tablets from Nuzu mention a childless wife forced to secure a concubine for her husband, in order to safeguard the future of the family (cf. Code of Hammurabi, 146). Egyptian marriages were often documented by means of contracts, and some contracts recovered from Elephantine, near Aswan, stated the terms of the union and made provision for divorce and the disposal of property in the event of the death of either partner.

Marriage was often a means of strengthening and promoting the fortunes of the family, quite aside from the prospect of producing children. A bride was more likely to be chosen because of the desirability of union with her family, or for her healthy physique and suitability for family life, rather than for other considerations. The father was responsible for finding a suitable bride for his son, and the wishes and feelings of the young people were largely irrelevant to this decision. On some occasions the bride's consent was asked for after the actual marriage arrangements had been made. Thus Isaac's marriage was arranged between his father's servant and his future wife's brother. She was then consulted (Gen 24:33–53, 57–58), though perhaps only because her father was no longer living. On rare occasions, parental advice was either ignored, rejected, or not sought (26:34–35), and, in a most unusual initiative, Michal, daughter of Saul, expressed her love for David (1 Sam 18:20).

In general, marriages were arranged with relatives or with those of the same clan. One might marry a member of the same tribe or possibly move outside this circle to marry within another Israelite tribe. Marriage to a foreigner was generally discouraged, though some Hebrews took wives from among those women captured in war, while others, such as Samson, received permission from their parents to marry a foreigner, Samson marrying a Philistine woman (Judg 14:2–3). Concern was always expressed that marriage with a non-Israelite would dilute the covental faith by the introduction of ideas and practices concerning strange gods (1 Kings 11:4).

Because marriages with close relatives were common, limits of consanguinity are recorded for the Israelites to follow (Lev 18:6–18). Formerly, a man could marry his half-sister on his father's side (Gen 20:12; cf. 2 Sam 13:13), though this is forbidden in Leviticus 20:17. Cousins—such as

Isaac and Rebekah, as well as Jacob, Rachel, and Leah—frequently married, though a simultaneous marriage with two sisters was specifically forbidden (Lev 18:18). The union between an aunt and her nephew produced Moses (Exod 6:20; Num 26:59), though a marriage between such relatives was subsequently forbidden by the Mosaic Law.

In the ancient world the primary purpose of marriage was procreation rather than companionship, and, as a result, large numbers of offspring were regarded as an asset. But an important secondary objective of marriage was the maintaining or increasing of family property, and in royal circles many marriages constituted the seal to what in fact were really political alliances. From the time of the patriarchs, wealthy and powerful people were able to indulge in polygamy, but because of the bride-price there were comparatively few men who could afford more than two wives. One way of circumventing this problem, however, was for a man to have several concubines, and this custom seems to have had quasi-legal sanction in cases where the legitimate wife was barren. Thus the childless Sarah provided her handmaid Hagar for her husband Abraham (Gen 16:3), as a woman in these circumstances would also have been required to do under the law code of Hammurabi (146). Jacob, already married to the two sisters Rachel and Leah, was also provided with the maid of each of his wives (Gen 30:3–9), while his brother Esau had three wives (26:34; 28:9; 36:1–5).

Marriage contract between Ananiah ben Haggai and Yehoyishma on Aramaic papyrus from Elephantine, Egypt, c 450 B.C. Courtesy The Brooklyn Museum, Bequest of Miss Theodora Wilbour.

Less mention is made of polygamy after the patriarchal period ended, though Gideon is described as having "many wives" (Judg 8:30–31), and the practice was still popular in royal circles, where vast polygamous marriages for political reasons were common. Solomon is described as having had "seven hundred wives of royal birth and three hundred concubines" (1 Kings 11:1–3). Individual preferences gave rise to strong rivalries between wives and children in such polygamous households (1 Sam 1:6). Nevertheless, the law codes of Assyria (about 2000 B.C.) and Hammurabi (about 1760 B.C.) both protected the rights of the wife, concubine, and children, and this precedent continued to be followed by the Israelites.

Despite these examples of polygamy, the most general and acceptable form of marriage was monogamy, which received the sanction of the Mosaic Law (cf. Exod 20:17; 21:5; Deut 5:21, et al.). This followed the tradition of the instruction to Adam and his descendants that "a man . . . shall cleave to his wife" (Gen 2:24), and Adam's fidelity to the one mate. In the postexilic period the emphasis that Ezra laid on the purity and integrity of the Jewish national stock reinforced the ideals of monogamy, against which the marital encounters of Herod the Great stood out as a glaring exception. The teaching of Jesus on marriage stressed the lifetime nature of the commitment, and while recognizing that Moses had regularized an already existing practice of divorce "because of the hardness of your hearts" (Mark 10:4–5), He taught the traditional Hebrew monogamy and added that the remarriage of a divorced person while the spouse was still alive constituted adultery (Mark 10:11–12).

The importance of maintaining and protecting the family name and property led to the institution of levirate marriage, from the Latin *levir* ("husband's brother"). Where a man died without issue, it was the responsibility of the closest male relative, usually his brother, to marry the widow. The first baby born of this union would then be regarded as the child of the dead man and would be entitled to his name and the entire rights of his property. Even if the widow already had children, the male relative would still be expected to marry and support her on the theory that women needed to live under a protector all their lives.

Before marriage, a woman was a member of her father's household, and as such she was subject to his authority. At marriage, her husband became her protector, and on his death, through her levirate marriage, she found her new "redeemer." Like many other Hebrew traditions, the levirate marriage was also known to the Canaanites,

Assyrians, and Hittites. The best-known levirate marriage in the Old Testament is that of Ruth the Moabitess, who married Boaz after the next of kin refused to undertake the responsibility (Deut 25:5–10; Ruth 4:1–12). See also KINSMAN.

In addition to finding a bride who was healthy and suitable for the family alliance, parents also had to be aware of the bride price that was payable to the girl's father. However this is viewed, whether as a payment for the loss of her services to her own parents or simply as a gift, it still retains something of a stigma by implying that the exchange of gifts or money meant that, in fact, the bride had been sold by the father to her future husband. Under the Mosaic Law a man's wife, children, slaves, and animals were listed as his possessions (Exod 20:17).

The sum of money payable for the bride price varied according to the "value" of the bride and the social position of the family (1 Sam 18:23–25). Where it was thought desirable, jewelry, animals, goods, or service could be substituted for gold or silver (Gen 34:12; 1 Sam 18:25). In Leviticus 27:4–5, ten to thirty shekels is mentioned as a price when people made special vows to the Lord, but whether the thirty shekels mentioned in connection with a woman was the same as the bride price is unknown. There seems some reason for thinking that by the time of the second temple a sum of about fifty shekels was more usual as a bride price for a virgin, whereas a widow or a divorced woman was worth only half that amount. It was during this period that a marriage with a virgin bride normally took place in the middle of the week, so that if she were found not to be a virgin, her husband had time to take proof to court the following day, which was still prior to the Sabbath.

Traditions concerning the bride price show some variation. Often the bride price came to the daughter on the death of her father. Under Assyrian law it was paid directly to the bride, while the Code of Hammurabi specified that the sum had to be paid to the bride's parents, with a penalty clause of double the amount if the engagement was broken off (160–61). The Babylonian tradition was for the bride's father to bring gifts to the husband, similar to a dowry, for his use but not his ownership, since they reverted to the bride on the death of her husband. It was customary for the Hebrew groom to bring gifts for other members of the bride's family, but these would rarely have been as valuable as those that Rebekah and her family received (Gen 24:53).

The betrothal (Deut 28:30; 2 Sam 3:14) had a particular legal status attached to it that made it almost identical to marriage. The law required that a man committing adultery with a betrothed virgin should be stoned for violating his neighbor's wife (Deut 22:23–24). A one-year betrothal was considered normal, and it constituted a part of the permanent marriage relationship (Matt 1:18; Luke 1:27; 2:5). For one year after being married the groom was exempt from military service (Deut 24:5) so that the marriage might be established on a proper footing. The bride's father already used the term "son-in-law" from the time of the betrothal (Gen 19:14), a custom that enhanced the concept of family solidarity.

There remained a distinction between betrothal and marriage, however, especially in the later periods of Jewish history; and although Mary and Joseph were betrothed, and in all other respects she was considered his wife, intercourse would not have taken place until after the marriage, and in this particular situation not until after the birth of Jesus. Following normal Hebrew practice, sexual relations were not resumed until after the baby was weaned, at approximately three years of age.

Circumcision as an initiation rite before marriage was practiced from about 1500 B.C. in Palestine and Syria. The Hebrew tradition of circumcision was of an independent kind, however, since it signified the admission of the baby to the fellowship of the covenant nation. It was in this connection that God legislated for that event to occur for male children on the eighth day (Lev 12:3). The events in Genesis 34:14–19 and Exodus 4:24–26 are of a different category, however, the former relating to adult males who, as uncircumcised persons, wished to enter the Hebrew community by marriage, while in the latter the child was uncircumcised, perhaps according to local custom.

The wedding ceremony itself was usually brief, but from early days it became surrounded by an elaborate tradition of ceremony and feasting that was very much in vogue in the time of Christ. Both bride and groom were attired in the finest, colorful clothing, the bride being especially resplendent in an elaborate dress. She had previously been washed, perfumed, and decked out with the gold and jewels of her family, together with any personal gifts that she had received. Toward sunset of the marriage day the groom would set out in procession with his friends, attendants, and musicians for the home of the bride's parents, where she would be waiting with her procession of friends and handmaidens. Then the marriage procession, with the attendant torchbearers, would pass through the village or town streets, to the accompaniment of shouts and singing. At the house where the groom's family lived the feasting, dancing, and entertainment would normally last for seven days, or occasionally for fourteen (Gen 29:27; Judg 14:12; Tob 8:20). The crowning of the bride and groom as king and queen of the nuptials dates from the Solomonic period and, with other accretions, also became part of the wedding tradition.

In the pre-Christian period, divorce was an option that was always available to the husband and sometimes also to the wife. After the return from exile, wholesale divorce was required of those Hebrews who had married foreign wives. This provision was to ensure that the purity of the Hebrew religion would not be tainted by the influence of those who had grown up with the tradition of strange gods and idolatrous practices. Normally, however, there was a distinct tendency in Jewish tradition to discourage divorce, and, following Egyptian custom, a substantial fine of "divorce money" was levied as a deterrent. The status of the wife was not very high, however, and the bill of divorce could take the form of a simple repudiation by the husband in some such expression as, "She is not my wife, and I am not her husband" (Hos 2:2). In the early Christian period, divorce could be considered only when there was a mixed marriage (between a Christian and a pagan), and even then the Christian was not permitted to remarry while the spouse was alive. It was even thought that the early church was exercising leniency when it first permitted widows to remarry.

The role of the wife was always subservient to that of her husband. He was the provider, decision-maker, protector, and master. The wife was the legal mother of his sons and manager of his household. She obeyed his instructions, was his helper, and became his confidante. By Roman times the status of the wife had improved, particularly at the higher levels of society. In those households where menial tasks were performed by slaves, the Roman matron occupied a position of respect and was able to indulge in her own special way of life.

Bibliography: D. S. Bailey, *The Mystery of Home and Marriage* (1952); H. A. Bowman, *A Christian Interpretation of Marriage* (1959); M. Burrows, "Levirate Marriage in Israel," *JBL* 59 (1940); M. Burrows, *The Basis of Israelite Marriage* (1938); P. H. Goodman, *The Jewish Marriage Anthology* (1965); L. Köhler, *Hebrew Man* (1956); W. Lacey, *The Family in Classical Greece* (1968); B. Malinowski, *Sex, Culture and Myth* (1963); E. Neufeld, *Ancient Hebrew Marriage Laws* (1944); A. van Selms, *Marriage and Family Life in Ugaritic Literature* (1954); D. H. Small, *Design for Christian Marriage* (1959); W. R. Smith, *Kinship and Marriage in Early Arabia* (1903); E. Westermarck, *History of Human Marriage*, 1–3 (1922). HWP

MARROW. The soft tissue in the cavities of bones (Job 21:24; Heb 4:12). It is used figuratively of richness (Ps 63:5 KJV) and good things (Isa 25:6 KJV).

MARSENA (mär-sē′nȧ, Heb. *marsenāʾ*). One of the counselors who advised King Xerxes (KJV Ahasuerus) to banish Queen Vashti for disobeying the imperial command (Esth 1:10–14).

MARS HILL (Gr. *Areios pagos, Hill of Ares*). A barren hill, 370 feet (116 m.) high, NW of the famous Acropolis in Athens. It was dedicated to Ares, the god of war. The elevated place became the seat of the Greek council, the Areopagus. Because of the Athenians' sudden interest in his message, Paul was taken there to clarify his mysterious teachings (Acts 17:16–34).

MARSH. Swamplands near the mouths of some rivers and at various places along the banks of the Jordan and of the Dead Sea. Cf. Ezekiel 47:11.

MARTHA (Aram. *lady, mistress*). Sister of Lazarus and Mary of Bethany. Luke mentions a visit of Jesus to the home of Martha at a certain village (Luke 10:38). It is inferred from this that the beloved friends of Jesus had resided in Galilee before going to Bethany. Another problem grows out of the connection between the name of Martha and that of Simon the leper. Was Martha the widow of Simon? It is quite possible that she was, and that the Bethany home had been inherited from him on his death. Matthew 26:6–12 and Mark 14:3 may indicate this. It seems more natural to think of Martha as a near relative of Simon for whom she acted as hostess. The scriptural narrative reveals that Jesus was an intimate friend of Martha, Mary, and Lazarus. The sisters knew of his ability to work miracles (John 11:3, 5). He, no doubt, was a guest in their home during his last fateful days on earth (Matt 21:17; Mark 11:1, 11). Martha was a careful hostess and was familiar enough with Jesus to complain to him about her sister's conduct (Luke 10:38–42) and about his delay in coming when Lazarus was ill (John 11:1–3, 21). She gave the Master an occasion for presenting the great statement about the resurrection (11:25). JDF

MARTYR (Gr. *martys, martyr, witness*). Because of its use in connection with Stephen (Acts 22:20) and others who died for Christ, the word came to mean one who paid the extreme price for fidelity to Christ. Antipas was a faithful witness (Rev 2:13). The harlot, Babylon, was drunk with the blood of martyrs (17:6).

MARY (Gr. *Maria, Mariam,* from Heb. *miryām*). The name of several women in the NT.

1. Mary of Rome. A diligent worker in the church at Rome to whom Paul sent special greetings (Rom 16:6).

2. The mother of John Mark. She lived in Jerusalem, where she had a house in which Christians met for prayer. It was to her home that Peter immediately went when he was miraculously released from prison by an angel (Acts 12:1–16). She may have been a woman of some means, as she had at least one servant, a girl named Rhoda (16:13). John Mark is described as being the cousin of Barnabas (Col 4:10), but the exact relationship of Barnabas to Mary is unknown. Some scholars think the Upper Room in which Jesus observed the Lord's Supper was in her home, but there is no proof of this.

3. Mary of Bethany, the sister of Lazarus and Martha. She lived in Bethany (John 11:1), about one mile (one and one-half km.) east of the Mount of Olives. Jesus commended her for being more interested in hearing him than in providing a bounteous dinner (Luke 10:42). John relates that she joined with Martha in saying to Jesus after the death of Lazarus, "Lord, . . . if you had been here, my brother would not have died" (John 11:21). Afterward, a week before the last Passover, when Jesus was a guest in the house of Simon the Leper (Mark 14:3), she showed her devotion to Jesus by anointing his head and feet

Majdal, a ruin on the northwest shore of the Sea of Galilee, identified with Magdala, birthplace of Mary Magdalene. The domed structure in foreground is the tomb of the Moslem Sheikh Mohammed Raslan. Courtesy Zev Radovan.

with costly ointment and wiping his feet with her hair (John 12:3). To those who complained of this as being wasteful, Jesus said that her act would always be remembered (Matt 26:6–13; Mark 14:3–9). Jesus looked on what she did as an act of love and as a preparation, though perhaps unintentional, for his coming death (John 12:7–8).

4. Mary the mother of James and Joses. There is uncertainty regarding this Mary. There is reason for thinking that she (Matt 27:56), the "other Mary" (Matt 27:61), and Mary the wife of Clopas (John 19:25) were the same person. Little is known about her except that she was very probably among the company of women who served Jesus in Galilee (Luke 8:2–3). She was at the cross when Jesus died (Matt 27:56; Mark 15:40). She witnessed the burial of her Lord (Mark 15:47), came to the tomb to anoint his body (16:1), and fled when told by the angel that Jesus was not in the tomb (16:8). A comparison of Matthew 28:1; Mark 16:1; and Luke 24:10 seems to make it certain that the mother of James and Joses was also the wife of Clopas. That Clopas (Cleopas, Luke 24:18) and Alphaeus (Matt 10:3) were the same has not been proved.

5. Mary Magdalene. Her name probably indicates that she came from Magdala, on the SW coast of the Sea of Galilee. After Jesus cast seven demons out of her (Mark 16:9; Luke 8:2), she became one of his devoted followers. There is no real ground for thinking that she had been a woman of immoral life before Jesus healed her. The only ground for so thinking is that fact that the first mention of her (Luke 8:2) comes immediately after the account of the sinful woman who anointed Jesus (7:36–50). She followed the body of Jesus to the grave (Matt 27:61) and was the first to learn of the Resurrection (Matt 28:1–8; Mark 16:9; Luke 24:1, 10). Nothing is known of her life after Christ's resurrection. JDF

MARY, THE MOTHER OF JESUS. All the authentic information we have about the Virgin Mary is found in the NT. In the opinion of many scholars she was descended from David, because she was told that her Son would receive the throne of his father David, also because Christ "as to his human nature was a descendant of David" (Rom 1:3; Acts 2:30; 2 Tim 2:8); and again because it is thought by many that Luke's genealogy of Christ is through his mother. She appears in several passages:

I. Mary in the Infancy Narratives (Matt 1–2; Luke 1–2). The source of these narratives is not known, but it is more than likely that they came from Mary herself. She lived into the apostolic period, whereas Joseph seems to have died before the crucifixion of Jesus, for there is no mention of him after the incident of Jesus in the temple when he was twelve. Mary could very well have told this to the early leaders of the church, including Luke. She was a "relative" of Elizabeth, the mother of John the Baptist (Luke 1:36), but the exact nature of this relationship is uncertain. Luke writes about Jesus' birth from Mary's standpoint, describing her maidenly fears (1:26–27), her humble submission to the will of God (1:38), and her hymn of praise to God for the favor accorded her in being the mother of the Messiah (1:39–55). Matthew, on the other hand, writes from the standpoint of Joseph, describing his reaction when he found she was with child, his determination to protect her from shame and insult as much as possible, his obedience to God's command that he marry Mary, and his taking her and Jesus to Egypt to escape the wrath of Herod. The two accounts harmonize and dovetail perfectly.

Mary shows herself to be a woman with a quiet spirit, humble piety, self-control, and knowledge of the OT. She was not given to talking with others about the mysteries of her experience, but kept all these things hidden in her heart (Luke 2:51). It is apparent that neither she nor Joseph fully understood her Son (2:50). In spite of their experiences with the supernatural in relation to him, he was something of an enigma to them.

II. Mary at Cana in Galilee (John 2:1–11). In this episode Mary seems to have some intimation that Jesus had more than natural powers. She may have needed some correction from him regarding her notion about the use of those powers, but it is wrong to think that Jesus sharply rebuked her. It must be kept in mind that he actually did exercise his power by relieving an embarrassing situation, as she had suggested, and the word "woman" (NIV "dear woman") is the same word he used when on the cross he tenderly commended her to the beloved disciple (19:26). His words to her were a gentle suggestion that it was not for her or any other human being to determine the course of action, for that was entirely in the Father's hands.

III. The Episode of Matthew 12:46; Mark 3:21, 31ff.; Luke 8:19–21. In this incident Jesus is informed, while teaching the multitudes, that his mother and brothers desire to see him. The reason for this desire is not stated; but it appears from the context in Mark's account that they were concerned for his safety because of the bitter opposition of the authorities, who were accusing him of casting out demons in the power of Beelzebub; and they wanted to induce him to go into retirement for a time, until it was a safe to teach in public again. Jesus' words "For whoever does the will of my Father in heaven is my brother and sister and mother" are meant to teach that physical relationship to him conveys no special privilege, no right of interference with him—the same lesson he taught on a later occasion (Luke 11:27).

IV. Mary at the Cross (John 19:25ff.). In this incident we find Mary, who had come to Jerusalem for the Passover, watching the Crucifixion with agony. Jesus shows his appreciation of the earthly filial relation by committing her to the trustworthy keeping of the apostle who was closest to him.

V. The Scene in the Upper Room (Acts 1:14). After the resurrection and ascension of Jesus, Mary appears in the midst of the Christian community, engaged with them in prayer for the baptism of the Holy Spirit, but without any discernible preeminence among them. This is the last mention of her in Scripture. It is not known how or when she died.

After Mary's death, many legends grew up around her name, but none of them are trustworthy. The keen desire to know further particulars about her was partly satisfied by the writers of apocryphal gospels. There is no direct evidence of prayer being offered to Mary during the first four centuries. Augustine was among the earliest of the church fathers who thought it possible that she had never committed actual sins, though he agreed that she shared the common corruption of humanity. This led eventually to the promulgation by the pope of the dogma of the Immaculate Conception of Mary (A.D. 1854). About the middle of the fifth century some Christian leaders, wishing to exalt her, began to invent new phrases in her honor. With the development of the idea that the celibate and virgin state is morally superior to the married state, it was suggested that she was a perpetual virgin and that the "brothers" and "sisters" of Jesus mentioned in the Gospels were not her children at all, but were either Joseph's children by a prior marriage or were the cousins of Jesus. In 1950 Pope Pius XII declared the dogma of the Assumption of Mary; that is, that Mary's body did not decompose in the grave but was reunited by God to her soul soon after she died. Roman Catholic theologians now openly refer to Mary as the "Co-creator" and the "Co-redemptrix" of the human race. None of these postapostolic developments has any support in Scripture. SB

MASH (Heb. *mash*). A son of Aram and grandson of Shem (Gen 10:22–23 JB, KJV, MLB, MOF, NASB, NEB, RSV; NIV has Meshech). He is called Meshech in 1 Chronicles 1:17.

MASHAL (mā'shăl). A village of the tribe of Asher (1 Chron 6:74), assigned to the Gershonite Levites. It is called "Mishal" (KJV "Misheal") in Joshua 19:26; 21:30. It was probably located in the plain south of Acre, but its exact location is uncertain.

MASKIL, MASCHIL (mȧs'kĭl, Heb. *maskîl, attentive, intelligent*). A Hebrew word found in the titles of Psalms 32, 42, 44, 45, 52–55, 74, 78, 88, 89, and 142. The meaning of the word is not certain, but it is usually taken to mean an instructive or meditative ode.

MASON (See OCCUPATIONS AND PROFESSIONS)

MASREKAH (măs'rē-kȧ, Heb. *masrēqâh,* perhaps, *vineyard*). A place mentioned in the list of kings who reigned in Edom "before any Israelite king reigned" (Gen 36:31). It was the royal city of Samlah, son of Hadad (Gen 36:36; 1 Chron 1:47). Its locality is unknown.

MASSA (măs'ȧ, *burden*). A tribe descended from Ishmael (Gen 25:14; 1 Chron 1:30). The marginal reading of the heading to Proverbs 31 refers to Lemuel as king of Massa, but the reading is doubtful. The tribe lived in the Arabian desert near the Persian Gulf.

MASSAH (măs'ȧ, *strife*). A name given to the site of the rock in Horeb from which Moses drew water for the rebellious Hebrews (Exod 17:1–17; Deut 6:16; 9:22). The name is connected with Meribah (Deut 33:8).

MASTER. A term used for five Hebrew and seven Greek words in the Bible: (1) *'ādhôn*, "lord, master, ruler," often denoting the master of a servant or slave (Gen 24:9; 39:2), in the plural usually used only of God; (2) *sar*, "captain, chief, prince, ruler" (1 Chron 15:27); (3) *ba'al*, "husband, owner" (Exod 22:8; Isa 1:3); (4) *'ûr*, "to awake, stir up" (Mal 2:12); (5) *rav*, "elder, great, mighty" (Dan 1:3; Jonah 1:6); (6) *didaskalos*, "teacher" (Matt 8:19; 9:11); (7) *despotēs*, "sovereign master" (1 Tim 6:1); (8) *epistatēs*, "overseer" (Luke 5:5; 8:24); (9) *kathēgētēs*, "guide, leader" (Matt 23:10); (10) *kyrios*, "lord," used often of God or of Christ (1:20, 24); (11) *kybernētēs*, "steersman, shipmaster" (Acts 27:11); (12) *rhabbi*, "teacher" (Matt 26:25, 49).

MATRED (mā'trĕd, Heb. *matredh, expulsion*). The mother of Mehetabel, wife of King Hadar (Gen 36:39, KJV, MLB, MOF, NASB, RSV; Hadad JB, NIV) or Hadad (1 Chron 1:50) of Edom.

MATRI (mā'trī, Heb. *matrî, rainy*). Head of a family of Benjamites from which Saul, son of Kish, was chosen by Samuel to be king of Israel (1 Sam 10:21).

MATTAN (măt'ăn, Heb. *mattān, a gift*). 1. A priest of Baal. He was among those who were killed during Jehoiada's purge after Queen Athaliah had supplanted the worship of the Lord with Baal worship (2 Kings 11:1–18). Following the slaughter of Athaliah, a new order was begun (2 Chron 23:16–17).

2. Another man named Mattan was among the conspirators who, incensed by Jeremiah's prophecies, cast the prophet into a filthy dungeon, from which he was rescued by order of King Zedekiah (Jer 38:1–28).

MATTANAH (măt'à-nȧ, Heb. *mattānâh, a gift*). The name of one of the camps of Israel while they were en route to Canaan, probably the site of a good well (Num 21:18).

MATTANIAH (măt'à-nī'à, Heb. *mattanyāhû, gift from the LORD*). This was a common name among the Hebrews; ten men who bore it are found in the OT record:

1. A brother of Jehoiachin's father whom Nebuchadnezzar set up in Jehoiachin's place as king, changing his name to Zedekiah, which means "the LORD is mighty" (2 Kings 24:17).

2. A descendant of Asaph and chief choir leader (Neh 11:17; 12:8). He was also a watchman over the storehouse (12:25).

3. A son of Heman. He was one of the musicians whom David appointed to prophesy with instruments of music. He became head of the ninth group of Levites to whom this duty was assigned. There were 288 of these musicians, all skilled men (1 Chron 25:4–5, 7, 16).

4. A Levite whose descendant, Jehaziel, was inspired to help King Jehoshaphat battle against invaders from Moab (2 Chron 20:14).

5. A descendant of Asaph and one who helped Hezekiah restore the temple worship (2 Chron 29:13).

6. Son of Elam who put away his foreign wife (Ezra 10:26).

7. A son of Zattu who divorced his foreign wife (Ezra 10:27).

8. A son of Pahath-Moab who did the same (Ezra 10:30).

9. A son of Bani. He also put away his alien wife (Ezra 10:37).

10. A grandfather of Hanan, one of the Levites whom Nehemiah placed in charge of the Levitical storehouse (Neh 13:10–13).

MATTATHA (măt'à-thȧ). An ancestor of Jesus. He was a son of Nathan and a grandson of King David (Luke 3:31).

MATTATHAH (măt'à-thȧ, Heb. *mattattâh, gift of the LORD*). A son of Hasum who was among the Israelites who put away pagan wives under Ezra (Ezra 10:33).

MATTATHIAS (măt'à-thī'ăs, Gr. *Mattathias, gift of the LORD*). The name borne by two ancestors of Christ (Luke 3:25–26).

MATTENAI (măt'ē-nā'ī, Heb. *mattenay, a gift from the LORD*). 1. A priest of the Restoration who was among a special class called "heads of the priestly families" (Neh 12:12–19).

2. Two priests under Ezra who were among the many who put away alien wives (Ezra 10:33, 37).

MATTHAN (mătt'hăn, Gr. *Maththan, gift of God*). Grandfather of Joseph, Mary's husband (Matt 1:15).

MATTHAT (măt'thăt, Gr. *Matthat* and *Maththat, gift of God*). Two men in the ancestry of Jesus mentioned in the genealogy of Luke (Luke 3:24, 29).

MATTHEW (Gr. *Maththaios*). Son of Alphaeus (Mark 2:14), a tax collector (*telōnēs*), also called Levi (Mark 2:14; Luke 5:27), whom Jesus met at the tax office and called to be one of his disciples (Matt 9:9; Mark 2:14; Luke 5:27). Since double names were common among the Jews (e.g., Simon became Peter, Thomas was called Didymus, Bartholomew was probably also named Nathanael, and Saul became Paul), there can be little doubt that Levi and Matthew were one and the same person. Levi probably changed his name to Matthew ("gift of Yahweh," or if a later form of Amittai, "true") when he became a disciple of Jesus.

The readiness with which Matthew responded to Jesus' call seems to indicate that he had previously come into contact with Jesus and his teachings and had already decided to dedicate his life to Jesus' cause. That Jesus should have chosen as his disciple a Jewish tax collector who was in the employ of the Roman government is indeed remarkable. Tax collectors were bitterly hated by their own countrymen and regarded as little more than traitors. However, Matthew's background and talents must have been of great value to Jesus. As a tax collector he was skilled at writing and keeping records. In addition, he must have been a man of deep spiritual convictions. This is revealed by his concern for his former colleagues whom he invited to a dinner at his own house (Luke's account alone in 5:29–32 makes it clear that it was Matthew's house, not Jesus'), Jesus being the honored guest. No doubt Matthew's purpose was to win these men to Christ. Apart from the mention of Matthew in the lists of the apostles (Matt 10:3; Mark 3:18; Acts 1:13), no further notices of him are found in the NT. WWW

MATTHEW, GOSPEL OF. In the early church Matthew was the most highly valued and widely read of the four Gospels. This is revealed both by its position in the canon—it is found in first place in all the known lists of the Gospels except two—and by its widespread citation, for it is by far the most often quoted Gospel in the Christian literature before A.D. 180. Among the reasons for this popularity two are particularly important:

1. The Gospel's apostolic authority. Matthew's name was associated with it from at least the early second century A.D.

2. Its emphasis on Christ's teaching. A growing church needed the authoritative word of Christ both to instruct converts and to refute heresy.

I. Authorship. The First Gospel, as is the case with the other three, is anonymous. Nevertheless, the church, from the early second century until the rise of modern critical studies, unanimously ascribed it to Matthew, one of the Twelve (Matt 9:9; 10:3; Mark 3:18; Acts 1:13), also called Levi (Mark 2:14; Luke 5:27), a tax collector by occupation. The results of source criticism, in particular the evident dependence of Matthew on Mark's Gospel, have led many, but by no means all, biblical scholars (of the older school the German Protestants T. Zahn and A. Schlatter, and more recently the Roman Catholic scholars B. C. Butler and L. Vaganay, in addition to the Episcopalian, P. Parker, have defended the traditional view) to abandon Matthew's authorship. Why would an eyewitness to the life of Christ, as Matthew most certainly was, depend so heavily on Mark's account? On the other hand, how does one account for the early and unanimous tradition of Matthew's authorship? The answer of the consensus of modern biblical scholarship is that the First Gospel was ascribed to Matthew, not because he wrote it, but because he was the author of one of its sources—viz., a sayings source, usually referred to as Q (from the German, *Quelle,* "source").

Despite the results of source criticism, strong arguments persist for the traditional view:

1. Matthew's occupation as a tax collector qualified him to be the official recorder of the words and works of Jesus. His job accustomed him to note-taking and the keeping of records. Since shorthand was widely known in the ancient Hellenistic world, perhaps he kept a shorthand notebook record of Jesus' activities and teachings. E. J. Goodspeed suggests that Jesus, after the practice of the prophets (cf. Isa 8:16–17), may have called Matthew to become a disciple for the specific purpose of preserving for posterity a written account of his teachings (*Matthew: Apostle and Evangelist,* 1959, pp. 50–56).

2. There is a good historical tradition that Matthew actually wrote Gospel material. This comes from Papias of Hierapolis as quoted by the church historian Eusebius: "Matthew wrote down the Logia in the Hebrew [i.e., Aramaic] language and everyone translated them as best he could" (*Eccl. Hist.,* 3.39.16). Much uncertainty exists as to the meaning of this famous statement, but one of two explanations seems most likely: (1) the reference is to an Aramaic Gospel, written by Matthew prior to the Greek Gospel, for the Jewish-Christian community in Palestine, or (2) Papias's statement refers to an Aramaic compilation of the sayings of our Lord made by Matthew for the instruction of Jewish converts.

In either case, the authorship by Matthew of our present Greek Gospel is not excluded. If an Aramaic Gospel preceded our Matthew, the publication of the Greek edition completely superseded the Aramaic, since no fragment of an Aramaic Matthew remains. A Greek edition is more likely than a Greek translation, since the Greek Gospel does not, on the whole, give evidence of being a translation. If the second alternative is accepted, viz., that the *Logia* were a collection of our Lord's sayings, then it is possible that Matthew expanded these into a Greek Gospel. It is a significant fact that the so-called Q material, with which Matthew's Logia is most often associated, shows signs of being a translation from Aramaic.

Further, the authorship by Matthew of the first Gospel does not necessarily rule out its dependence on Mark. Dr. G. E. Ladd well remarks: "If Matthew wrote a first edition of his Gospel in Aramaic for the Jewish-Christian community in Antioch and Mark wrote a Gospel in Rome embodying the Petrine tradition, it is entirely credible that when Matthew later produced a second edition in Greek, he made free use of the Petrine Gospel, thereby adding his own testimony to its authority and proving that the apostolic witness to Christ was not divided" ("More Light on the Synoptics," *Christianity Today,* March 2, 1959, p. 16).

3. It is more likely that the Gospel would have taken its name from the person who put it in its Greek dress than from the author of one of its sources. Dr. Goodspeed makes a strong case for this point (*Matthew,* passim). The Greeks were not interested so much in who was the authority behind the sources of a book as in who made the book available in the Greek language. In this respect it is significant that although Peter is certainly the source of Mark's Gospel, it was not called the Gospel of Peter but of Mark.

4. The unanimous Christian tradition is that Matthew wrote it.

Thus, although certainty eludes us, there are cogent reasons for holding the traditional view that Matthew, the apostle and eyewitness to the events of Christ's life, wrote the First Gospel. If he used other sources, in particular Mark, he added his own apostolic witness to that of Peter's, and by so doing may have contributed to the alleviation of tensions between Gentile and Jewish Christianity.

II. Date and Place of Origin. We do not know precisely when Matthew was written. Its dependence on Mark and its failure to mention the destruction of Jerusalem (especially in connection with Jesus' prediction of that event in ch. 24) suggest a date shortly before A.D. 70.

Antioch is the most likely place of origin. Early in the second century Ignatius of that city refers to Matthew as "the Gospel." Also, the Gentile-Jewish character of the Antioch church accords well with the contents of the book.

Characteristics:

1. Matthew is the teaching Gospel par excellence. In this respect it greatly supplements Mark, which is more interested in what Jesus did than in what he said.

2. Matthew is the Gospel of the *church.* Matthew is the only Evangelist who uses the word "church" at all (Matt 16:18; 18:17). The first occurrence is in Jesus' response to Peter's confession. Here its use is clearly anticipatory. In 18:17 the context is church discipline and seems to indicate not only the existence of a church, but also the emergence of problems within it.

3. Matthew is the Gospel of *fulfillment.* It is

especially concerned with showing that Christianity is the fulfillment of the OT revelation. The many OT proof texts cited by the use of the formula "that it might be fulfilled," the emphasis on the messiahship of Jesus, and the presentation of Christianity as a new "law," all reveal this basic concern of the author. F. F. Bruce has pointed out that "in places he even implies that the experiences of Jesus recapitulate the experiences of the people of Israel in OT times. Thus, just as the children of Israel went down into Egypt in their national infancy and came out of it at the Exodus, so Jesus in his infancy had also to go down to Egypt and come out of it, that the words spoken of them in Hosea 11:1 might be fulfilled in his experience, too: 'Out of Egypt have I called my son' (Matt 2:15)" (*The New Testament Documents,* 1960, p. 41).

4. Matthew is the Gospel of the King. The genealogy of chapter 1 traces Jesus' lineage back to David: at his birth the Magi come asking, "Where is the one who has been born king of the Jews?" (Matt 2:2); eight times the regal title "Son of David" is ascribed to Christ (1:1; 9:27; 12:23; 15:22; 20:30–31; 21:9, 15); the Triumphal Entry clearly has kingly significance (21:1–11); in the Olivet Discourse Jesus prophesied his future kingly reign (25:31); To Pilate's question "Are you the king of the Jews?" Jesus gave the tacit assent, "Yes, it is as you say" (27:11); and over the cross were written these words: "This is Jesus the king of the Jews" (27:37). The climax comes at the very end of the Gospel, where Jesus in the Great Commission declared: "All authority in heaven and on earth has been given to me" (28:18). There can be no doubt that the author of this Gospel deliberately presents Jesus as the King.

III. Structure. The arrangement of the material reveals an artistic touch. The whole of the Gospel is woven around five great discourses: (1) Matthew 5–7; (2) Matthew 10; (3) Matthew 13; (4) Matthew 18; (5) Matthew 24–25, each of which concludes with the refrain, "And it came to pass when Jesus ended these sayings . . . ." In each case the narrative portions appropriately lead up to the discourses. The Gospel has a fitting prologue (Matt 1–2) and a challenging epilogue (28:16–20).

IV. Outline:

1. Prologue: The birth of the King (Matt 1–2).
2. Narrative: The preparation of the King (Matt 3–4).
3. First discourse: The law of the kingdom (Matt 5–7).
4. Narrative: The power of the King (Matt 8–9).
5. Second discourse: The proclamation of the kingdom (Matt 10).
6. Narrative: The rejection of the King (Matt 11–12).
7. Third discourse: The growth of the kingdom (Matt 13).
8. Narrative: The mission of the King (Matt 14–17).
9. Fourth discourse: The fellowship of the kingdom (Matt 18).
10. Narrative: The King goes to Jerusalem (Matt 19–23).
11. Fifth discourse: The consummation of the kingdom (Matt 24–25).
12. Narrative: The death and resurrection of the King (26:1–28:15).
13. Epilogue: The great challenge of the Kingdom (28:16–20).

Bibliography: D. Hill, *The Gospel of Matthew* (NCB), 1972; E. Schweizer, *The Good News According to Matthew,* 1975; F. W. Beare, *The Gospel According to Matthew,* 1981; R. H. Gundry, *Matthew: A Commentary on His Literary and Theological Art,* 1982. WWW

MATTHIAS (mă-thī'ăs, Gr. *Matthias* or *Maththias, gift of the* LORD). The one chosen by lot after the death of Judas Iscariot to take his place among the twelve apostles (Acts 1:15–26). He had been numbered among the followers of Christ (1:21–22). Some number him among the Seventy, as, for instance, Clement of Alexandria and Eusebius. Nothing certain is known of him after his appointment.

MATTITHIAH (măt'ĭ-thī'à, Heb. *mattithyâh, gift of the* LORD). At least four men bear this name in the OT; scholars differ about their identification.

1. A Korahite Levite, born of Shallum, put in charge of the baked offerings of the temple after the Exile (1 Chron 9:31).
2. A Levite, the sixth son of Jeduthun, appointed by David to minister before the ark in music and thanksgiving (1 Chron 15:18, 21; 16:5; 25:3, 21). Some consider the man in 16:5 a different person, but this is probably unwarranted.
3. One of the sons of Nebo who after the Exile put away his Gentile wife (Ezra 10:43).
4. One who stood at Ezra's right hand as he read the Law to the people (Neh 8:4). Possibly same as no. 1.

MATTOCK (Heb. *mahărēshâh* in 1 Sam 13:20–21; *herob* in 2 Chron 34:6 RV mg; *ma'dēr* in Isa 7:25). A single-headed pickax with a point on one side and a broad edge on the other for digging and cutting.

MAUL (Heb. *mēphîts, a breaker*). Originally a hammer such as used by coppersmiths. Today it refers to any smashing weapon like those carried by shepherds (Prov 25:18 KJV; NIV "club").

ME JARKON (mē jár'kŏn). A town assigned to the tribe of Dan.

MEADOW (Heb. *'āhû* in Gen 41:2, 18; *ma'ărēh* in Judg 20:33). The first word, meaning "reeds," would make meadow to be a place where reeds grow. The word comes from an Egyptian word meaning "marshy ground." The second word implies a portion of land without trees.

MEAL (Heb. *qemah* in Gen 18:6; *sōleth* in Lev 2:1; Gr. *aleuron* in Matt 13:33). The ground grain used for both food and sacrificial offerings. It typified Christ in his perfect humanity. It has a remote figurative use in such passages as Isaiah 47:2 and Hosea 8:7. NIV generally reads "flour."

MEAL OFFERING (See SACRIFICE AND OFFERINGS)

MEALS. In Bible times meals varied greatly in terms of eating, diet, and table customs. Two meals were generally served daily, though three were not uncommon. The time of these meals was not set as ours are today. The first meal of the day could be served at any time from early morning until noon (Prov 31:15; John 21:12, 15). The rank and occupation of a person caused the time of the noon meal to vary. It came after the work of the morning was completed (Mark 7:4) or when the noonday heat made work too difficult (Ruth 2:14). The evening meal was not served at any set time, but came when the day's work ended. This was usually the principal meal of the Hebrews (3:7), whereas the Egyptians served their main meal at noon (Gen 43:16). Jesus fed the multitudes at the end of the day (Matt 14:15; Mark 6:35; Luke 9:12).

The food of the Eastern peoples generally may be classified into four groups: grains, vegetables, fruits, and animal foods. Wheat, barley, millet, spelt, lentils, beans, cucumbers, onions, leeks, garlic, saltwort, pods of the carob tree referred to as "husks," and wild gourds were all eaten. The corn referred to in the Bible (KJV) was wheat. The grain was often picked in the field, rubbed in the hands to separate it from the chaff, and eaten raw (Luke 6:1). Sometimes it was crushed with mortar and pestle and made into a porridge or cakes (Num 11:8; Prov 27:22). More often the grain was ground between two stones. The grinding was usually done by women (Matt 24:41) or by servants (Exod 11:5; Judg 16:21).

No meal was considered complete without bread. Edersheim points out that the blessing was spoken over the bread and was presumed to cover all of the food that followed. Bread was both leavened and unleavened. Sometimes honey and oil were mixed into the dough as it was being made in the kneading troughs or wooden bowls. In times of poverty bread was made from beans, millet, and spelt (Ezek 4:9). Bread was usually eaten warm and seldom by itself, but was served with sour wine or meat gravy (John 13:26; 21:13).

Spices, used freely as flavors, consisted of cummin or dill, mustard or mint. Salt also became an important item in the diet of these people.

Fruits grew in great abundance in Palestine and consisted of grapes, figs, olives, mulberries, pomegranates, oranges, lemons, melons, dates, almonds, and walnuts. Grapes were eaten as fresh food and dried as raisins. They were the chief source of the wines, which were used both sweet and fermented. Olives were eaten as food as well as used to make olive oil. There were two kinds of figs, early (Isa 28:4) and late (Jer 8:13). The late figs were dried and pressed into cakes. Dates were used both raw and dried.

The bulk of the meat came from sheep, lambs, kids, and fatted calves. Pork was eaten, but not by the Hebrews. Some game such as the hart, gazelle, goat, antelope, and deer, as well as doves, turtledoves, and quails, formed part of the meat diet. Some eggs were used for food (Isa 10:14). Locusts and fish were also eaten. The Hebrews used milk from cattle and goats for drinking. From this they made cheese and butter. Arabs

Cross section of an Assyrian officer's tent where a meal and couch are being prepared for him. In the adjoining tent a butcher prepares a carcass. Relief from Nineveh. Courtesy Bildarchiv Foto, Marburg.

Ancient sixth-century mosaic map of Palestine, discovered in 1884 in the Greek Orthodox church at Medeba. It shows Jerusalem as an oval, walled city. It is now incorporated in the pavement of the church. Courtesy Studium Biblicum Franciscanum, Jerusalem.

drank camels' milk. Cheese was made from curdled milk, and after being salted and formed into small units was placed in the sun to dry. Some of this was later mixed with water to make a sour but cooling drink.

Knives, forks, and spoons were not used in eating. The hands were usually washed and a prayer was offered before the meal. Meat was cooked and placed with its gravy in a large dish on the table. The contents were taken either with the fingers or placed on bread and carried to the mouth. The Egyptians sat at a small round table for their meals. The early Hebrews sat, knelt, or squatted as they ate, but later they evidently reclined at meals. The custom of reclining, probably derived from the Persians, became the NT practice. Women were sometimes included and sometimes excluded at mealtime. Three generally lay on one couch, thus the head of one was on the bosom of another (John 13:23–25). They reclined at the three sides of a rectangular table leaving the fourth side free for the servants to use in serving.

Food was cooked in a variety of ways over a fire made from charcoal (Prov 26:21), sticks (1 Kings 17:10), thorns (Isa 33:12), or grass (Luke 12:28). Archaeology is throwing light increasingly on the variety of utensils used in preparing food. HZC

MEASURES (See WEIGHTS AND MEASURES)

MEAT (See FOOD)

MEAT OFFERING (See SACRIFICE AND OFFERINGS)

MEBUNNAI (mē-bŭn'ī, Heb. *mevunnay, well-built*). One of David's bodyguards (2 Sam 23:27) who killed a Philistine giant (21:18, Sibbecai). Due to a scribal error the spelling of this name is quite varied.

MECHERATHITE (See MEKERATHITE)

MECONAH (mĕ-kō'na', Heb. *mekhonah*). A town in the southern part of Judah near Ziklag and inhabited after the Exile (Neh 11:28).

MEDAD (mē'dăd, Heb. *mēdhādh, affectionate*). One of the seventy elders appointed to assist Moses in the government of the people (Num 11:24–30). He, together with Eldad, empowered by the Spirit, remained in the camp and prophesied. Joshua attempted to hinder them, but they were defended by Moses.

MEDAN (mē'dăn, Heb. *medhān, strife*). A son of Abraham by Keturah (Gen 25:2; 1 Chron 1:32). He as a brother of Midian and by some writers mistaken for him.

MEDEBA (mĕd'ē-bȧ, Heb. *mêdhevā', uncertain*). A city lying high in the grazing section of Moab east of the Jordan. It was first referred to in Numbers 21:30. It is part of the section of land assigned to the tribe of Reuben (Josh 13:9) and is remarkably level. The claim to this land was often disputed by Reubenites (who soon vanished from the scene), Ammonites, and Moabites. The Ammonites united with the Syrians in a campaign against Joab and were successfully defeated (1 Chron 19:7). The biblical records together with the testimony of the Moabite Stone show that the city was constantly changing hands (cf. 1 Chron 19:7 with Isa 15:2). From 1 Maccabees 9:36–42 we read how John, the son of Mattathias, was murdered by Jambri of Medeba. Jonathan and Simon avenged this death by lying in ambush in a cave and slaughtering a marriage party of the Jambri that was passing by. Josephus relates that later the city was taken by Hyrcanus after the death of Antiochus. Later on in Roman history it became the seat of one of the early bishops. Today the modern Arab village of Madeba occupies the general area, but the ruins of the old civilization are much in evidence. Some archaeological work has been carried on here. In A.D. 1896 an ancient mosaic map of Palestine was discovered and, though badly damaged, has proved to be of real value.

MEDES, MEDIA (mēdz, mē'dĭ-à, Heb. *mādhî, mādhay*). The inhabitants of the land of Media. The boundaries of this land have varied from time to time, but generally it was regarded as that land to the west and south of the Caspian Sea. It was bounded on the west by the Zagros Mountains, on the north by the Araxes and Cyrus rivers, on the east by Hyrcania and the great Salt Desert, and on the south by Susiana or Elam. Josephus feels its name was derived from Madai, the son of Japhet. It is shaped like a parallelogram with its longest portion extending 600 miles (1,000 km.) and its greatest width about 250 miles (417 km.), thus making it a territory of some 150,000 square miles (384,615 sq. km.). It had many natural barriers, making its defense easy. Its water supply was scant, thus making much of the land arid and sterile, though some of its valleys were abundantly productive. Irrigation for the most part was impractical, for some of its rivers were salty while others had worn such deep canyons as to make their waters useless for this purpose. Its few towns were scattered, since its people preferred to live in small groups. Its climate was varied, with some extreme temperatures in both directions. Minerals were many and animals and birds were plentiful. Eventually these factors led to luxurious living, spelling the downfall of the empire. It became famous for its horses, and at one time paid yearly tribute of 3,000 horses, plus 4,000 mules and almost 100,000 sheep.

The people of Media were warlike and skilled in their use of the bow. They were linked very closely in their background, linguistically and religiously, to the Persians, whom they antedate by several centuries and with whom they eventually united. While their early worship was polytheistic, there were some monotheistic leanings that were very significant. Their worship was conducted by priests and consisted of hymns, sacrifices—bloody and unbloody—and a ceremony in which the priests offer an intoxicating liquor to the gods and then consume it until they are drunken. Their religion was a revolt against the nature worship about them. They believed in real spiritual intelligence divided into good and bad. At the head of the good beings was one supreme intelligence who was worshiped as supreme creator, preserver, and governor of the universe. He was called Ahura-Mazda and was the source of all good. Later, along with Zoroastrian dualism, there developed a worship of heavenly bodies.

The people were for a long period a strong power. Shalmaneser plundered several of their more important cities, evidently with the sole purpose of exacting tribute. They continued strong and were a menace to Assyria's last king, Ashurbanipal, after whose death the Median king Cyaxares carried on an extensive campaign.

Relief (cf. 521–465 B.C.), on stairway from Persepolis, that shows the head of a Mede. He wears a high rounded cap with neck flap, and earring that protrudes from elaborately curled hair and beard. Courtesy Oriental Institute, University of Chicago.

The more than twenty references to these people or their land in the Scriptures show their importance. Their cities are referred to in 2 Kings 17:8; 18:11. Esther tells of the binding character of their laws (Esth 1:19); Isaiah and Daniel speak of their power against Babylon (Isa 13:17; Dan 5:28). The last scriptural reference to them is in Acts 2:9, where representatives are in Jerusalem at the time of Pentecost. HZC

MEDIATOR (Gr. *mesitēs, a middle man*). One who brings about friendly relations between two or more estranged people. He corresponds to the "umpire" ("daysman" KJV) of Job 9:33. The NT uses *mesitēs* twice in connection with Moses as the mediator of the law (Gal 3:19–20) and four times regarding Jesus. Jesus is the *mesitēs*, or peacemaker, between God and human beings (1 Tim 2:5). He is the agent by whom the new covenant between God and the redeemed is made efficacious (Heb 8:6; 9:15; 12:24). Three facts regarding this divine ministry should be noted:

I. The Grounds of Mediation. Throughout the Bible the estrangement between man and God is repeatedly set forth. God is the moral ruler;

man, his natural subject, has violated his laws, hence has gone away from God. All people are thus alienated (Rom 3:23) because they refused to be led by the revelation that God made of himself (1:18–26). Three inescapable moral facts never cease to be realized by man—namely, the fact of a moral order, the fact of sin, and the fact that atonement must be provided to bring release from guilt. Since man cannot keep the law perfectly from birth until death, it is evident that he cannot be saved from the curse of sin by the law (John 7:19; Acts 13:39; Rom 3:20; 8:3). The law, therefore, is the pedagogue, the servant of God, who, by making sinners aware of their estrangement from God, causes them to turn to Christ as mediator (Gal 3:24–25).

II. Examples of Mediatorial Work. These can be found in the OT. Jonathan was intercessor for David before Saul (1 Sam 19:4). Abraham made intercession on behalf of Abimelech (Gen 20) and Sodom (18:23–33). Moses was mediator on behalf of Pharaoh (Exod 8:8–13; 9:28–33) and for Israel (33:12–17). Samuel was middleman when Israel was given a king (1 Sam 9:15–27) and when she became wicked (12:19).

III. Other Agents of Mediation. In addition to the intercessory work of such individuals as Moses, God dealt with Israel through other agents. There were angels who acted as media through whom God's will was made known to man (Gen 22:15; 24:40; 32:1; Judg 6:11). Because of the tendency of unthinking worshipers to put the mediating angel in the place of the promised Messiah, later Jewish scholars refused to recognize angels as mediators. At times God appeared in human form (Gen 12:7; 17:1; 35:7, 9; Dan 8:17). In some cases the "angel of the Lord" seems to have been a manifestation of God, perhaps a temporary appearance of Messiah (Gen 16:7–13). As the revelation from God came to be more fully understood and the results of it more clearly seen, there came the priestly class between man and God (Lev 1–7). With the development of this class there arose the elaborate ritualistic rules for worship whereby God set forth the requirements for making atonement. Leviticus 9–24 gives rules for special events, for healing diseases, and for making atonement; chapter 25 establishes the holy days and seasons; and chapter 27 lists penalties for violation of the laws. From this elaborate ritual the priests and rabbis slowly developed a system of rules that separated man from God and made him feel wholly dependent on the prelates for contact with God. So, as the priests degenerated, the people likewise became more wicked. During days of captivity, when priests were not always at hand to serve, the longing of the people for the Promised One increased. And when Jesus did come, he broke down the middle wall of partition between sinful man and the offended God (Eph 2:14).

Bibliography: E. Brunner, *The Mediator,* 1934; W. Mason, *Jesus the Messiah,* 1943; G. S. Duncan, *Jesus Son of Man,* 1948; A. R. Johnson, *Sacral Kingship,* 1955; A. Oeoke, TDNT, 4:598–624. JDF

The Mediterranean shore as viewed from the southern tip of the "Ladder of Tyre" at Rosh Hanikra. Courtesy Zev Radovan.

MEDITERRANEAN SEA. Because this body of water was the largest known to the Hebrews, it became known as *The Sea.* The Canaanites occupied the land from Jordan to the Sea (Num 13:29). It marked the end of the Promised Land (34:5). Joshua located it as "the Great Sea on the west" (Josh 1:4). It was the utmost sea (Deut 11:24) or western sea (34:2). It was known also as the Sea of the Philistines (Exod 23:31). Cedar for the temple was shipped from Tyre to Joppa (2 Chron 2:16). This sea played a big part in NT days. On one occasion Jesus may have seen its waters (Mark 7:24). Paul's missionary tours took him across the eastern half. If he did set foot in Spain, he saw most of this inland sea.

The sea was known and used by many early civilized people, and they had commercial dealings across Palestine with civilizations of the Tigris-Euphrates Valley. At one time it had been an open channel to the Red Sea. Drifting sands from the African desert and silt from the Nile River closed this and made a land route from Asia to Africa. The sea is 2,300 miles (3,833 km.) long and more than 1,000 miles (1,667 km.) across at its widest point. An elevated underwater area once reached from upper Tunisia in Africa east to Sicily. This shallow area divides the sea into the Eastern, or Levant, and the western sea. Its northern shore is broken by the Grecian and the Italian peninsulas. Crete and Cyprus made havens for shippers of ancient times. Paul was on both islands during his journeys (Acts 13:4; 27:7). JDF

MEEKNESS (Heb. *'ănāwâh, suffering,* Gr. *praütēs*). A quality often commended in Scripture. The meek (oppressed) are assured of divine help and ultimate victory (Ps 22:26; 25:9; 37:11). Jesus was sent to minister to the oppressed (Ps 45:4; Isa 11:4; 29:19; Zeph 2:3). Meekness is a fruit of the Spirit (Gal 5:23). It is characteristic of Jesus (Matt 11:29; 2 Cor 10:1). Believers are commanded to be meek and to show a lowly spirit one to another (Eph 4:2; Col 3:12; Titus 3:2). A teacher should be meek (2 Tim 2:25). Meekness is a mark of true discipleship (1 Peter 3:15). The word does not imply a weak, vacillating, or a supine nature.

MEGIDDO, MEGIDDON (mĕ-gĭd'ō, Heb. *meghiddô, meghiddôn*). A city situated on the Great Road, which linked Gaza and Damascus. It controlled the principal pass through the Carmel Range, connecting the coastal plain and the Plain of Esdraelon. The road was the channel for the flow of peaceful commerce and also the route by which the armies of antiquity marched. One of the best recorded and most interesting military operations of ancient times took place at Megiddo when Thutmose III defeated an Asiatic coalition headed by the king of Kadesh. The importance of the city is reflected in the statement of the Egyptian king that the capture of Megiddo was the capture of a thousand towns. The continuing practicality of the Megiddo pass for the movement of troops is seen from its effective use in A.D. 1918 by Allenby, whose cavalry thus took the Turks by surprise. The first mention of Megiddo in the Bible is in the list of kings defeated by Joshua west of the Jordan (Josh 12:21). In the tribal allotments, Megiddo was in the territory of Manasseh, but this tribe was unable to conquer Megiddo and the other fortress cities that rimmed the plains of Esdraelon and Jezreel (Josh 17:11; Judg 1:27).

During the period of the judges, Israelite forces under Deborah and Barak annihilated the army of Sisera in a battle that raged in part "by the waters of Megiddo" (Judg 5:19), the sources of the Kishon. Though the biblical record does not relate the circumstances under which Israel finally took the city, there are indications of the greatness of Megiddo during the Solomonic period. Megiddo is listed among the cities in the charge of Baana, one of the twelve officers responsible in rotation for the monthly provisions of the king and his court (1 Kings 4:12). It is also singled out as one of the cities to which Solomon assigned forced labor for construction (9:15); the text speaks of store cities and cities for chariots and horsemen (1 Kings 9:19; cf. 2 Chron 1:14; see below). In the coup of Jehu against Joram king of Israel, the hard-driving Jehu killed Joram with an arrow, as that king fled in his chariot, and ordered the shooting of the Judean Ahaziah, who also was attempting to escape. Mortally wounded, Ahaziah went as far as Megiddo and died there (2 Kings 9:27). In 609 B.C. Neco of Egypt marched north to aid the Assyrian remnant at Carchemish; on his way he was opposed by Josiah king of Judah. In the brief battle that ensued in the Plain of Megiddo, Josiah was hit by Egyptian archers and soon died (2 Kings 23:29–30; 2 Chron 35:20–27).

The OT has only one reference to Megiddo in the prophetical writings: Zechariah mentions a heathen mourning that took place in the Plain of Esdraelon: "On that day the weeping in Jerusalem

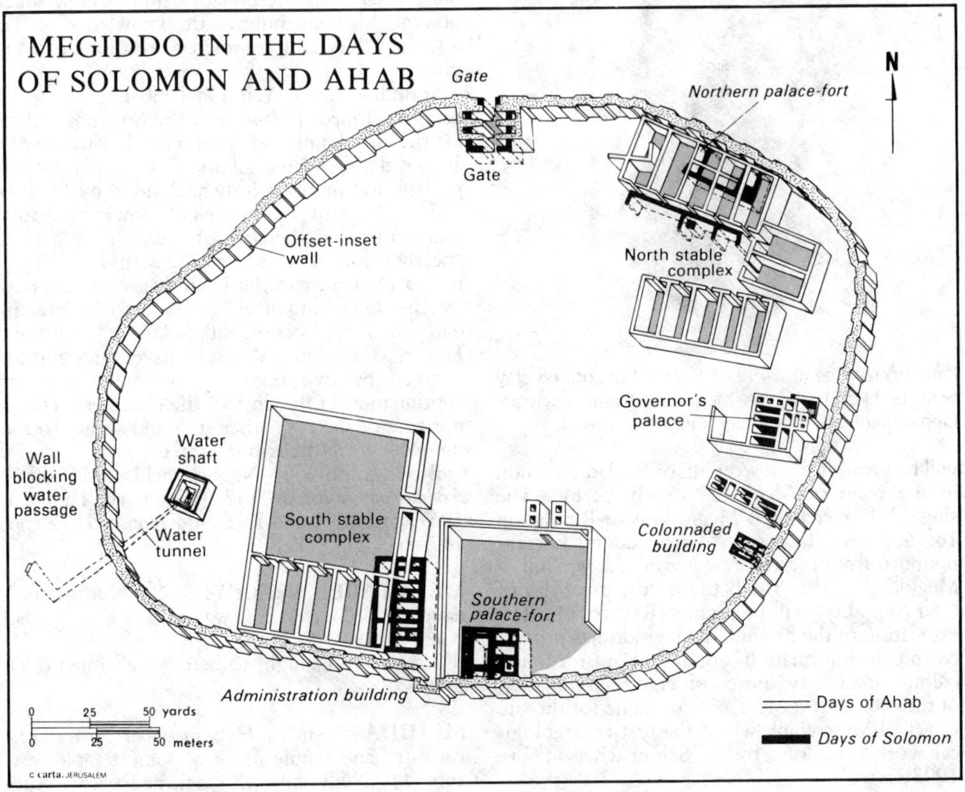

Late Bronze Age (c. 1450–1300 B.C.) decorated clay wall bracket found at Megiddo. Courtesy Israel Department of Antiquities and Museums.

will be great, like the weeping of Hadad Rimmon in the plain of Megiddo" (Zech 12:11). The single NT reference to Megiddo is in Revelation 16:16, where the word "Armageddon" is compounded from the Hebrew *har megiddôn,* "hill of Megiddo," where "the battle on the great day of God Almighty" will be fought (Rev 16:14). The excavation of the mound of Megiddo has provided much information about the history and culture of the city and considerable illumination of the biblical text. The modern name for the site is Tell el-Mutesellim, where the first archaeological work was done by G. Schumacher in A.D. 1903–5.

In A.D. 1925 the Oriental Institute of the University of Chicago began a large-scale stratigraphic clearance of the entire mound and continued until 1939. When the work was halted, soundings had revealed twenty strata and the clearance had reached Stratum V. The more important discoveries include the city gate and wall, the governor's residence, and the stables of Stratum IV; the water system, the temples and palaces of earlier levels; and a remarkable find of ivories (early twelfth century B.C., Stratum VII). Though there are questions concerning the date of Stratum IV, it is usually assigned to Solomonic times. The stables for at least 450 horses illustrate the statements of 1 Kings 9:15–19 and 2 Chronicles 1:14. Evidence of similar structures had been found at Tell el-Hesi, Taanach, Gezer, and Tell el-Far'ah. (Megiddo and Gezer are included among the cities in which Solomon engaged in building activities, 1 Kings 9:15, 17.) An interesting feature of Stratum IV is the use of the three courses of hewn stone and a course of cedar beams, as described in the building process of Solomon at Jerusalem (7:12). The temples and shrines of the earlier levels and numerous cult objects from various periods shed light on the religious life of the city. Inscriptional material includes some Egyptian cartouches and titles; e.g., a fragment of a stele of Shishak (Sheshonk) appeared early in the work of the Oriental Institute. Schumacher found two seals with Hebrew inscriptions, one reading "[Belonging] to Shema, servant of Jeroboam." Innumerable small objects also contribute to the knowledge of the art, daily life, and commercial relations of Megiddo.

Soundings by Y. Yadin in 1960 and later years have confirmed, in his view, the Solomonic date of the six-chambered gate (D. Ussishkin has argued that it is later; he notes two similar "later" gates found more recently at Ashdod by Dothan and at Lachish by himself). However, Yadin points out that the date of the Ashdod gate is "nearly identical" to that of the Megiddo according to Dothan, and the Lachish gate is reported by Ussishkin himself as "seeming to be later in date than the period of Solomon." Further, Hazor, Gezer, and Megiddo have gates further fortified by two outer towers built in direct continuation of the lines of the chambers. This is not true of the two other sites and speaks to the uniqueness of the former three.

Bibliography: J. N. Schofield, "Megiddo," *Archaeology and OT Study* (ed. D. W. Thomas), 1967, pp. 309–28; Y. Yadin, *Hazor,* 1972, pp. 147–64.

CEDV

MEHETABEL (mě-hět'á-běl, *God benefits*). 1. A daughter of Matred. She was wife of King Hadad (Gen 36:39).

2. One who sought to betray Nehemiah (Neh 6:10–13).

MEHIDA (mē-hī'dá, Heb. *mehîdhā',* *renowned*). Ancestor and family name of some temple servants (KJV Nethinim) who returned with Zerubbabel from Babylonia to Judah (Ezra 2:52; Neh 7:54).

MEHIR (mē'hîr, Heb. *mehîr, price, hire*). A son of Kelub (1 Chron 4:11) and a descendant of Judah.

MEHOLAH, MEHOLATHITE (mē-hō'là-thīt, Heb. *mehôlāthî*). The Gentile designation of Adriel to whom Saul gave his daughter Merab as a wife (1 Sam 18:19; 2 Sam 21:8). The place Abel Meholah was probably located in the Jordan Valley near Beth Shan, the native place of Elisha (1 Kings 19:16). See also ABEL MEHOLAH.

MEHUJAEL (mē-hū'jā-ĕl, Heb. *mehûyā'ēl*). A descendant of Cain through Enoch and Irad. He was the father of Methushael (Gen 4:18).

MEHUMAN (mē-hū'măn, Heb. *mehûmān*). One of the eunuchs of Xerxes (KJV Ahasuerus), king of Persia (Esth 1:10).

MEKERATHITE (mē-kē'răth-īt, Heb. *mekhērāthî, dweller in Mekarah*). A description of Hepher, one of David's mighty men (1 Chron 11:36). Perhaps the name should read Maacathite (2 Sam 23:34).

MEKONAH (See MECONAH)

MELATIAH (mĕl-à-tī'àh, Heb. *melatyâh*). A Gibeonite who helped to repair the walls of Jerusalem in the days of Nehemiah (Neh 3:7).

MELCHI (See MELKI)

MELCHIAH (See MALKIJAH)

MELCHI-SHUA (See MALKI-SHUA)

MELCHIZEDEK, MELCHISEDEK (mĕl-kĭz'ĕ-dĕk, Heb. *malkî-tsedhek, king of righteousness*). A priest and king of Salem, a city identified with Jerusalem. The reference in Genesis 14:18–20 is the first mention of Salem in the OT.

Melchizedek went out to meet Abram after his return from the slaughter of Kedorlaomer and the kings who were with him in the Valley of Siddim. He presented Abram with bread and wine and blessed him in the name of "God Most High, Creator of heaven and earth." Abram gave him "a tenth of everything." The Hebrew word for God in this instance is the same as in such phrases as "God Almighty" (Gen 17:1), "the Eternal God" (21:33), and "God of Bethel" (35:7) and is the oldest Semitic designation for God. Melchizedek was thus a monotheist and worshiped essentially the same God as Abram, who recognized him as a priest.

He appears next in Psalm 110:4: "You are a priest forever, in the order of Melchizedek." This psalm is of special interest because Jesus referred to it (Matt 22:41–42; Mark 12:35–36; Luke 20:41–42), and it is regarded as one of the messianic psalms. The ideal ruler of the Hebrew nation would be one who combined in his person the role of both priest and king.

The author of the Letter to the Hebrews uses Melchizedek (Heb 5–7) in his great argument showing Jesus Christ as the final and perfect revelation of God because in his person he is Son and in his work he is Priest (1:2–10:18). The author cites Psalm 110:4, indicating that Jesus' priesthood is of a different order from the Levitical: it is "in the order of Melchizedek."

The author of Hebrews, looking back on the history of his people, comes to the conclusion that the Levitical priesthood proved to be a failure. It was incapable of securing victory over sin and full communion with God.

And so the author cites Psalm 110. The ideal priest must belong to "the order of Melchizedek." To the author, Christ was the fulfillment of this prophecy, for he came out of Judah, a tribe with no connection to the Levitical priesthood. While the claims of the old priesthood were based on genealogy, Christ's were displayed in his power of an endless life. The claim of Jesus to be the real fulfillment of the psalmist's prophecy rested on the fact of his resurrection and the proof it gave that his life was indestructible. The psalmist had declared that the ideal high priest would be forever—and only one whose life could not be destroyed by death could be said to answer to the psalmist's ideal, a priest "in the order of Melchizedek." JGJ

MELEA (mē'lē-à, Gr. *melea*). An ancestor of Jesus through Mary, in Luke's genealogy (Luke 3:31).

MELECH (mē'lĕk, Heb. *melekh, king*). A son of Micah, a grandson of Mephibosheth, or Merib-Baal, and a great-grandson of Jonathan, mentioned in the genealogy of Benjamin (1 Chron 8:35; 9:41).

MELICU (See MALLUCH)

MELITA (See MALTA)

MELKI (mĕl'kī, Gr. *Melchi*). The name of two ancestors of Jesus through Mary, according to Luke's genealogy:

1. The son of Addi and the father of Neri (Luke 3:28).

2. The son of Janna and the father of Levi, fourth from Mary (Luke 3:24).

MELON (See PLANTS)

MEMBER (Heb. *yātsur,* Gr. *melos*). A word usually denoting any feature or part of the body (Job 17:7; James 3:5 KJV, MOF, NEB, RSV), "the members" meaning "the body" (Ps 139:16). The word is used for members of the body of Christ (1 Cor 6:15; 12:12–27; Eph 4:25; 5:30).

MEMPHIS (mĕm'fĭs, Heb. *nōph, mōph,* Copt. *menphe, memphi,* Gr. *Memphis*). The first capital of

The famous alabaster sphinx. "The word . . . concerning all the Jews . . . in . . . Memphis . . ." (Jer 44:1). This is what they could see every day. Courtesy Seffie Ben-Yoseph.

united Egypt (c. 3200 B.C.), situated on the west bank of the Nile, about twenty miles (thirty-three km.) south of modern Cairo. Legend ascribes the founding of the city to Menes, the traditional first king. The original name of the city was "The White Wall." Later it was called Men-nefer-Pepi, after the name of the pyramid of Pepi I of the Sixth Dynasty; it is from this name that "Memphis" is derived. The chief god of Memphis was Ptah; also prominent at Memphis was the worship of the Apis bull, whose famous burial place, the Serapeum, is located just to the west in the necropolis of Sakkarah. All of the biblical references to Memphis are in the Prophets. Hosea foretold a return of Israelites to Egypt and refers to Memphis (Hos 9:6). After the murder of Gedaliah, a number of Jews fled from Palestine to Egypt (cf. Jer 41:16–18), and Memphis is mentioned as a place of their residence (44:1). Both Isaiah and Jeremiah had seen the results of an Egyptian-Judean alliance and refer to Memphis (Isa 19:13; Jer 2:16). Jeremiah prophesied that Memphis would become a ruin (cf. Jer 46:13, 19). Ezekiel declared that the Lord would "destroy the idols and put an end to the images in Memphis" (Ezek 30:13) and spoke of coming distresses in that city (30:16). Today there is little for the casual visitor to see in the ruins of Memphis, and only the colossus of Ramses II and the alabaster sphinx attract tourist attention.
CEDV

MEMUCAN (mē-mū'căn, Heb. *memûkhān*). One of the seven wise men at the Persian court who advised King Xerxes (KJV Ahasuerus) to punish Queen Vashti for her refusal to appear at the court festival (Esth 1:13–22).

MENAHEM (mĕn'á-hēm, Heb. *menahēm, comforted*). Son of Gadi and king of Israel (2 Kings 15:13–22). His reign of ten years began by his killing his predecessor Shallum. "He did evil in the eyes of the Lord." Through gifts collected from his subjects, he bribed the Assyrian king Pul (Tiglath-Pileser III) and was thereby able to retain his throne. In this restless period of the northern kingdom, with sinful men usurping the throne time and again, Menahem was the only king who died a natural death. His son Pekahiah inherited the kingdom.

MENAN (See MENNA)

MENE, MENE, TEKEL, PARSIN (mē'nē, mē'nē, tē'kĕl, ū-pàr'sĭn). Four Aramaic words that suddenly appeared on the wall of Belshazzar's banquet hall where the king "gave a great banquet for a thousand of his nobles and drank wine with them" (Dan 5:1) out of the golden vessels taken by Nebuchadnezzar from the temple at Jerusalem after its capture in 586 B.C. (2 Kings 25:14–15). The king became terrified when he saw the writing. "All the king's wise men" failed to interpret the words, and Daniel, at the suggestion of the queen, was called in to decipher the message.

There has been much discussion about the original form of the inscription and about its interpretation. The words seem to refer to three weights in common use: the "mina," the "shekel," and the "half-mina." Or they may be terms used in Mesopotamian counting houses: "numbered, numbered, weighed, and divisions." *Upharsin* (KJV, MLB, NASB, NEB; *parsin* NIV, RSV) in the inscription (Dan 5:25) is *peres* in the interpretation (5:28). The *u* is the connecting participle "and"; *pharsin* is the plural of *peres*, a word that naturally suggests the Persians.

What Daniel had to deliver as the message by the mysterious writer was the fact that "God had numbered" the days of the kingdom; the king had "been weighed on the scales and found wanting"; his "kingdom is divided and given to the Medes and Persians." There was not much time between interpretation and fulfillment, for "that very night Belshazzar, king of the Babylonians, was slain."

See J. G. Baldwin, *Daniel* (TOTC), 1978. JGJ

MENNA (mĕn'á, Gr. *mainan, menna*). An ancestor of Jesus through Mary in Luke's genealogy (Luke 3:31; KJV Menan).

MEONOTHAI (mē-ŏn'ō-thī, Heb. *me'ônōthay, my dwelling*). A son of Othniel and the father of Ophrah (1 Chron 4:13–14). He was a descendant of Judah though Caleb.

MEPHAATH (mĕf'ā-ăth, Heb. *mēpha'ath,*

splendor). A town in the territory of Reuben (Josh 13:18) and given to the Levitical family of Merari (21:37). At the time of Eusebius and Jerome a Roman garrison was stationed in this place.

MEPHIBOSHETH (mē-fĭb'ō-shĕth, Heb. *mephîvōsheth*). 1. A son of King Saul and his concubine Rizpah. Together with his brother and other men, Mephibosheth was delivered to the Gibeonites to be hanged, with David's consent (2 Sam 21:8).

2. A son of Jonathan and grandson of Saul. His name appears as Merib-Baal in 1 Chronicles 8:34; 9:40. After the disaster at Mount Gilboa, where both Saul and Jonathan were killed in the battle against the Philistines (2 Sam 1:4; 1 Chron 10:1–8), Mephibosheth as a child of five was carried by his nurse to Lo Debar east of the Jordan, where they took refuge in the house of Makir, the son of Ammiel (2 Sam 9:4).

On David's accession to the throne, Mephibosheth was called back to Jerusalem, given his father's inheritance, and allowed to eat at the king's table for the rest of his life. Saul's servant Ziba was commanded to serve him. The servant, however, tried to ingratiate himself with David at the expense of his master by representing Mephibosheth as a traitor (2 Sam 16:1–4). David did not fully believe the servant's story, for later he received Mephibosheth in a friendly manner (19:24–30).

Mephibosheth was the father of Mica (2 Sam 9:12), or Micah in 1 Chronicles 8:35.

MERAB (mē'răb, Heb. *mērav,* perhaps *increase*). The older daughter of King Saul, her sister being Michal. After David killed Goliath, the women sang his praises (1 Sam 18:7) and aroused Saul's jealousy. Saul sought to have David killed by the Philistines and so promised him Merab as wife if he would fight valiantly; however, he then gave Merab to another man; but Michal loved David, and to win her David killed two hundred Philistines. In 2 Samuel 21:8 by an early copyist's error "Michal" is written for "Merab," as the context clearly shows. NIV follows the context and uses "Merab." Merab's five sons were killed by the men of Gibeon.

MERAIAH (mē-rā'yȧ, *rebellious*). A priest of Israel in the time of Joiakim (Neh 12:12).

MERAIOTH (mē-rā'yŏth, Heb. *merāyôth, rebellious*). 1. A high priest of Israel in the seventh generation from Aaron (1 Chron 6:6–7).

2. Another in the priestly line and ancestor of the great Hilkiah (1 Chron 9:11).

3. Ancestor of Helkai, a priest in the days of Joiakim the high priest (Neh 12:15 KJV, MLB, MOF, NASB, NEB, RSV). The NIV has "Meremoth" (as in Neh 12:3). In the very ancient Hebrew script the names are quite similar.

MERARI (mē-ra'rī, Heb. *merārî, bitter*). The youngest son of Levi, patriarch of the tribe of that name. The high priesthood descended through Aaron, and the other Levites assisted in the divine service. The "Merarites" had the responsibility for the wood framing of the tabernacle in its journeys (Num 3:17, 33–37). Later they had twelve cities in Reuben, Gad, and Zebulun (Josh 21:7, 34–40).

MERATHAIM (mĕr-ȧ-thā'ĭm, *repeated rebellion*). A symbolic name for Babylon, used by Jeremiah (50:21) in his "doom of Babylon" in chapters 50–51.

MERCURY, MERCURIUS (See HERMES)

MERCY (Heb. *hesedh, kindness, raham, bowels, hānan, gracious, Gr. eleos, kindness, oiktirmos, compassion*). 1. Forbearance from inflicting punishment on an adversary or a lawbreaker.

2. The compassion that causes one to help the weak, the sick, or the poor. Showing mercy is one of the cardinal virtues of a true Christian (James 2:1–13) and is one of the determinants of God's treatment of us. Christian mercy is a "fruit of the Spirit" (Gal 5:22–23), made up in part of love, longsuffering, kindness, gentleness, and goodness. God's mercy toward sinful man was shown most clearly and fully in his giving of his beloved Son to die in our stead; and our Lord's mercy enabled him to make willingly the awful sacrifice (Rom 5:8). The Hebrew word *raham* is the most emotional of the terms used to describe the Lord's love for his people (Ps 103:13), rightly meriting the translation "compassion." It is related to the word for "womb" and is well exemplified in the upsurging of motherly emotions in 1 Kings 3:26.

See also LOVING-KINDNESS.

MERCY SEAT (See TABERNACLE)

MERED (mē'rĕd, *rebellion*). A descendant of Judah who married a daughter of one of the pharaohs (1 Chron 4:17–18).

MEREMOTH (mĕr'ē-mŏth, Heb. *merēmôth, elevations*). 1. A priest who returned from Babylon with Zerubbabel (Neh 12:3).

2. One who returned with Ezra in 457 B.C. and who weighed silver and gold that had been brought back. He was the son of Uriah, a priest of Israel (Ezra 8:33). He helped Nehemiah to rebuild the wall (Neh 3:4, 21). (This may possibly be two persons.)

3. One who had taken a foreign wife (Ezra 10:36).

4. A priest who signed the covenant with Nehemiah (Neh 10:5).

MERES (mē'rez, *worthy*). A Persian prince (Esth 1:14) under Xerxes (KJV Ahasuerus).

MERIBAH (mĕr'ĭ-bȧ, Heb. *merîbâh, contention*). 1. A place near and to the NW of Sinai where Moses, at the Lord's command, struck the rock and water gushed out for the refreshment of the people (Exod 17:1–7). Moses named the place

"Massah," i.e., "tempting," and "Meribah," because of the quarreling of the children of Israel and because they tempted the Lord.

2. A place near Kadesh Barnea where the people again thirsted and where the Lord commanded Moses to speak to the rock. Moses exceeded his instructions and, apparently wanting some credit for the miracle, struck the rock, and water came forth (Num 20:1–13). For this arrogance, Moses was forbidden to enter the Promised Land.

MERIBAH KADESH (See MERIBAH)

MERIB-BAAL (mĕr'ĭb-bā'ăl, *Baal contends*). Son of Jonathan, the son of King Saul (1 Chron 8:34; 9:40). Possibly the same as Mephibosheth.

MERODACH (See MARDUK)

MERODACH-BALADAN (mē-rō'dăk-băl'ă-dăn, *Marduk has given a son*). A king of Babylon called Merodach-Baladan in some versions of 2 Kings 20:12. He was a strong, courageous leader, known outside the OT as Marduk-apla-iddina II. He was by far the most successful rebel against the then dominant power of Assyria. In spite of Assyrian counterattack, he maintained his kingship in Babylon from 721 B.C., when he captured the city from Assyria, until 720 when Sargon first subdued the Elamites and then entered Babylon without meeting resistance. On the death of Sargon in 705, Merodach-Baladan supposed that he was released from any duty he owed to Assyria and worked again for an independent Babylonian kingdom. He enjoyed a brief, final reign in Babylon until defeated and driven out by Sennacherib in 703.

Below the emblems of four deities of Babylonia, Merodach-Baladan investing an official with a grant of patronage and land. Black marble, seventh century B.C. Courtesy Bildarchiv Foto, Marburg.

It is understandable that Hezekiah, in his tiny and far-off kingdom of Judah, should be flattered and indeed lose his head when he was the recipient of a special delegation from this front runner among the anti-Assyrian rebels (Isa 39). It would be at some point in his second bid for power (705 B.C.) that Merodach-Baladan tried to encourage diversionary rebellions in western Palestine. Isaiah's prophecy prevented Hezekiah's revolt. However, it could not annul the divine edict of eventual captivity, and it may well have contributed to the weakening of the cause of Merodach-Baladan and therefore to his failure to establish his Babylonian kingdom. We do need to realize, however, in order to keep a correct perspective on the ancient world, that, politically speaking, Assyrian dominance was in the balance. Merodach-Baladan was no minor threat; he could have brought about, there and then, the end of the Assyrian Empire. It was part of the political reality of the time that, within Isaiah's lifetime, Judah could have gone into captivity to Babylon, though, in divine mercy, the date of the disaster was postponed.

Bibliography: S. Elandsson, *The Burden of Babylon*, 1970, pp. 86–92. JAM

MEROM (mē'rŏm, Heb. *mērôm, a high place*). A district near the headwaters of the Jordan River, north of the Sea of Galilee. Most of it is high in comparison with the "waters of Merom" through which the Jordan flows and which is just about at sea level. In Bible times the waters of Merom formed a small lake, but for a long time since then it was only a marsh that has recently been drained. Its only mention in Scripture is in Joshua 11:5, 7 as the site of the great battle of Joshua's northern campaign in which he, with the help of God, defeated Jabin king of Hazor and his Canaanite allies. The men of the tribe of Dan, when searching for a more commodious land for the tribe (Judg 18), passed through this region and described it as "very good" and said that "the land is large."

MERONOTHITE (mē-rŏn'ă-thīt). An inhabitant of Meronoth, a region in Galilee that was given to the tribe of Naphtali. Its principal town was Shimron Meron, which Joshua conquered (Josh 11:1; 12:20). For two Meronothites see 1 Chronicles 27:30; Nehemiah 3:7.

MEROZ (mē'roz, Heb. *mērôz*). A place in Galilee not far from Nazareth. It is infamous because its inhabitants "did not come to help the Lord" when Deborah and Barak needed help against Jabin, king of Canaan. Judges 5:23 attributes its being cursed to the angel of the Lord.

MESECH (See MESHECH)

MESHA (mē'shȧ, Heb. *mēshā', mēshā'*). 1. A place in southern Arabia that marks a boundary of the lands of the early Semitic Arabs (Gen 10:30).

2. A Benjamite mentioned only in 1 Chronicles 8:9. He was probably born in Moab.

Nos. 1 and 2 seem to have the root meaning "retreat," whereas nos. 3 and 4 are spelled differently in Hebrew and mean "welfare."

3. A fourth-generation descendant of Judah through Perez, Hezron, and Caleb (1 Chron 2:42).

4. A king of Moab in the days of Ahab and his two sons who succeeded him, Ahaziah and Jehoram. From David's time (2 Sam 8:2) Moab had been more or less subject to Israel; and Mesha, who was a sheepmaster, had been obliged to pay a tremendous tribute (2 Kings 3:4). But when he rebelled against Ahaziah. Jehoram, with the help of Jehoshaphat of Judah, attacked and defeated him (3:4–27). Mesha in desperation sacrificed his own son. For Mesha's account of the episode see MOABITE STONE.

MESHACH (mē'shăk, Heb. *mēshakh*). A pagan name given to Mishael, one of the four princes of Judah taken by Nebuchadnezzar to be trained in his palace as counselors to the king. These four had Hebrew names containing the syllable "el" for "God" or "iah" for "the LORD," but the names were changed to honor gods of Babylon (Dan 1:3–7).

MESHECH (mē'shĕk, Heb. *meshekh, tall*). 1. A son of Japheth in the "Table of the Nations" (Gen 10:2) associated with Magog and Tubal, and thought by many to have been progenitors of Russians and other Slavic peoples.

2. A grandson of Shem (1 Chron 1:17); called Mash in Genesis 10:23 (except NIV).

3. The people descended from the preceding. They are noted for their merchandizing with Tyre in slaves as well as articles of bronze (Ezek 27:13). Ezekiel prophesied that they would join in a northern confederation against Israel and would be destroyed on the mountains of Israel (Ezek 38–39). The leader of this northern group is called "Gog."

4. A tribe mentioned in Psalm 120:5 with (or probably contrasted with) the tents of Kedar. Probably the same as No. 3 above.

MESHELEMIAH (mē-shĕl'ē-mī'ȧ). Father of Zechariah, leading gatekeeper of the tent of meeting. He had seven sons (1 Chron 9:21; 26:1–2, 9). This man is called "Shelemiah" in 1 Chronicles 26:14.

MESHEZABEL (mē-shĕz'ȧ-bēl, *God delivers*). 1. Ancestor of Meshullam (Neh 3:4).

2. A covenanter with Nehemiah (Neh 10:21).

3. A descendant of Judah through Zerah (Neh 11:24).

MESHILLEMITH, MESHILLEMOTH (mē-shĭl'ē-mith, mē-shĭl'ē-moth, *recompense*). 1. Father of Berekiah, a noble Ephraimite who helped to clothe and feed the captives from Judah and to restore them to their homes (2 Chron 28:12).

2. Priestly ancestor of Amashsai, who lived at Jerusalem in the Restoration (Neh 11:13). Meshillemith (1 Chron 9:12) is another spelling of the same name.

MESHOBAB (mē-shō'băb, *restored*). A Simeonite in the days of Hezekiah, who with others defeated the Meunites at Gedor near Hebron and took their pasture land (1 Chron 4:34).

MESHULLAM (mē-shŭl'ăm, Heb. *meshullām, reconciled*). A very common name in the OT.

1. A gandfather of Shaphan, trusted scribe of Josiah (2 Kings 22:3).

2. A son of Zerubbabel in the Jewish royal family (1 Chron 3:19).

3. A leading Gadite in the days of Jeroboam II (1 Chron 5:13).

4. A chief Benjamite in Jerusalem (1 Chron 8:17).

5. The father of Sallu, a Benjamite of Jerusalem after the Captivity (1 Chron 9:7).

6. Another Benjamite of Jerusalem (1 Chron 9:8).

7. A priest in the high-priestly lines whose descendants lived at Jerusalem (1 Chron 9:11; Neh 11:11).

8. An ancestor of another priest (1 Chron 9:12).

9. A Kohathite, overseer of repairing the temple in the days of Josiah (2 Chron 34:12).

10. A chief man who returned with Ezra in 457 B.C. (Ezra 8:16).

11. One appointed by Ezra in the matter of doing away with foreign marriages (Ezra 10:15).

12. One of the offenders in this matter (Ezra 10:29).

13. One who rebuilt two portions of the wall but was connected by marriage with Tobiah, who hindered the rebuilding (Neh 3:4, 30; 6:18).

14. Another repairer (Neh 3:6).

15. One who stood with Ezra in the revival (Neh 8:4).

16. A priest who signed the covenant with Nehemiah (Neh 10:7).

17. Another covenanter (Neh 10:20).

18. A man of Benjamin whose descendants lived in Jerusalem about 444 B.C. (Neh 11:7).

19. A priest c. 470 B.C. (Neh 12:13).

20. Possibly the same man as no. 19 (Neh 12:33).

21. Another priest c. 470 B.C. (Neh 12:16).

22. A Levite gatekeeper at the same time (Neh 12:25).

MESHULLEMETH (mē-shŭl'ē-mĕth, fem. of *Meshullam*). Daughter of Haruz of Jotbah, who married King Manasseh of Judah and was mother of Amon, who succeeded to the throne (2 Kings 21:19).

MESOBAITE (See MEZOBAITE)

MESOPOTAMIA (mĕs′ō-pō-tā′mĭ-à, from Gr. *mesos, middle,* and *potamos, river*). The name applied in particular to the area between the Tigris and Euphrates rivers, a region that in Hebrew is called Aram, Aram Naharaim, or Paddan Aram, along with various other names for localities or peoples of this region. In present-day application the term is used of a territory practically coextensive with modern Iraq. There are indications of the latter usage in the NT, such as Acts 7:2 and possibly Acts 2:9. The KJV frequently translates *'aram naharayim,* "Aram of the two rivers," as "Mesopotamia," while NIV transliterates as "Aram Naharaim." Genesis 24:10 states that the servant of Abraham "set out for Aram Naharaim and made his way to the town of Nahor." This is in the vicinity of the Khabur River, and attempts have been made to localize Aram Naharaim between the Euphrates and the Khabur. Balaam, the soothsayer hired by Balak, king of Moab, to curse the Israelites, came from Pethor "in Aram Naharaim" (Deut 23:4; cf. Num 22:5). In Judges 3:8, 10 the oppressor of the Israelites, Cushan-Rishathaim, is called "king of Aram Naharaim." This geographic reference indicates the area east of the Euphrates, and some commentators have regarded this king as a foreign conqueror of this territory.

Early in the reign of David, Hanum king of the Ammonites insulted the ambassadors whom David sent to bring condolences to the new Ammonite king after the death of his father. Fearing reprisals on David's part, the Ammonites hired "chariots and charioteers from Aram Naharaim, Aram Maacah and Zobah" (1 Chron 19:6). In the descriptions of the ensuing events, the hired allies are lumped together under the term "Arameans" (KJV "Syrians"). Aram (Gen 10:22–23; 1 Chron 1:17) was the progenitor of the Arameans, or Syrians. Bethuel and Laban are called Arameans in NIV, Syrians in KJV (Gen 25:20; 31:20), and even Jacob is referred to as "a wandering Aramean" (Deut 26:5) from his stay in Paddan Aram, a term used in the Bible only in connection with Jacob and which the LXX gives as Mesopotamia or Mesopotamia-Syria. There is some uncertainty about the meaning of the word Paddan; it has been suggested that it means "garden," "field," or "plain." There can be no doubt about the location of Paddan Aram, for it is associated with Haran (Gen 28:10; 29:4), and therefore is in the same general area as Aram Naharaim. The most important cities in the region were Haran, on the Balikh River, and Gozan (2 Kings 17:6, probably modern Tell Halaf) on the Khabur. Both of these rivers are tributaries of the Euphrates. It was in this district that relatives of Abraham lived, and it is of more than passing interest that the names of a number of individuals mentioned in the biblical text are preserved in place-names from this very area.

Several significant archaeological and historical features are associated with this Mesopotamian region. Tell Halaf is the type site for the period of beautifully painted pottery that appears from Assyria to Syria and the Mediterranean coast. To the SE on the Euphrates was Mari (Tell Hariri), which was an important state of the Hammurabi era. Its king, Zimri Lim, had a palace of almost three hundred rooms and also a library and archives of more than twenty thousand clay tablets. A royal concern for divination is attested by the presence of clay liver models found in one of the palace rooms; hepatoscopy was an important Mesopotamian practice, and its appearance here is instructive in relation to the determined effort made by the king of Moab to procure Balaam to curse the Israelites (Num 22ff.). Just before the time of the Amarna Letters, this area was the seat of Mitanni, a powerful Hurrian (Horite) kingdom ruled by an Indo-European aristocracy. The king of Mitanni was involved in the official correspondence with Egypt found at el-Amarna, and shortly thereafter Mitanni was overwhelmed by the Hittite Subbiluliuma.

In the NT the mention of Mesopotamia as one of the regions from which the Jews of the Diaspora had come to Jerusalem (Acts 2:9, "residents of Mesopotamia") probably has reference to that part of the Near East included in modern Iraq and may refer more particularly to the area near ancient Babylon. Stephen's allusion to the fact that the call of God came to Abraham "while he was still in Mesopotamia, before he lived in Haran" (7:2), definitely puts southern Iraq in Mesopotamia, for Abraham was then in the city of Ur (Gen 11:31). The southern part of Mesopotamia, including Ur and a number of other city-states, was known as Sumer; the central section was called Akkad and later was named Babylonia, after the city of Babylon gained the ascendancy; the northern division along the Tigris was Assyria, the land of Asshur. CEDV

MESSIAH. A word that represents the Hebrew *māshîah,* the Aramaic *meshîhā'*, and the Greek *Messias.* "Messias" (John 1:41, 4:25 KJV) is a transcription of the Greek word. Thus "Messiah" is a modification of the Greek form according to the Hebrew. The basic meaning of the word is "anointed one." "Christ" is the English form of the Greek *Christos,* which means "anointed." The Septuagint uses *Christos* forty times to translate the Hebrew *māshîah.* In ancient Israel both persons and things consecrated to sacred purposes were anointed by having oil poured over them. When the tabernacle was dedicated, the building, its various parts, and the holy vessels were anointed (Exod 30:26–30; 40:9–11). Official persons were consecrated with oil. Sometimes prophets were anointed when they were consecrated (1 Kings 19:16). The statement in Isaiah 61:1 "The LORD has anointed me to preach good news to the poor" is an allusion to this practice. Priests were also anointed with oil for their office (Exod 29:21; Lev 8:30). The kings apparently were anointed regularly (1 Sam 9:16; 16:3; 2 Sam 12:7; 1 Kings 1:34). The king was "the Lord's anointed" in a special sense. In the OT the primary significance of the expression "the Lord's anointed" refers to the earthly king who is reigning over the Lord's people. It is a reference to the king's close relationship to the Lord and to the sacral character of his position and person. The Israelites did not think of crowning a king but of anointing him when he was enthroned. The fact that he was anointed was the essential characteristic of the ruler.

Where the expressions "the Lord's anointed," "my anointed," "your anointed," etc., occur in the OT, the reference is not used as a technical designation of the Messiah, but refers to the king of the line of David, ruling in Jerusalem, and anointed by the Lord through the priest. Isaiah uses the term only once, and then of the Persian Cyrus (Isa 45:1). Later the expression "Son of David" was a synonym for "Messiah" (Matt 21:9; Mark 10:47–48). It is obvious that there must be some historical connection between the designations "the Lord's anointed," "my anointed," "your anointed," "the anointed one," and the title "Messiah." The latter term apparently is a later expression and is an abbreviation of the fuller title "the Lord's anointed." It shows that the Messiah of Israel's messianic hope derived his name from the sacral title of the kings of David's line. With the possible exception of Daniel 9:25–26 the title "Messiah" as a reference to Israel's eschatological king does not occur in the OT. It appears in this sense later in the NT and in the literature of Judaism. In the NT the Messiah is "the Christ," the Greek equivalent of the Hebrew *māšîaḥ*.

Closely related to the eschatological character of the Messiah is his political significance. He will destroy the world powers in an act of judgment, deliver Israel from her enemies, and restore her as a nation. The Messiah is the king of this future kingdom to whose political and religious domination the other nations will yield. His mission is the redemption of Israel and his dominion is universal. This is the clear picture of the Messiah in practically all of the OT passages that refer to him. The Messiah will put an end to war, for he is the Prince of Peace, and he will rule righteously over his people. He himself is righteous and is called the righteous Messiah or the Messiah of righteousness (Jer 23:6). But this implies more than just a judgment and government of his people. The term "righteousness" when used in connection with the Messiah is inseparably related to salvation. The Messiah will establish the right of his people against any foe from without or within. He will establish this salvation and maintain it in the face of all opposing forces. Righteousness and salvation are the same because the Messiah's righteousness is declared in his saving acts. Jewish writers have made much of this with reference to Malachi 4:2. At the same time it is often emphasized that by his righteousness the Messiah will establish justice and righteousness, in the ethical sense, in the land. Sin will be rooted out, and Israel will become a holy people.

Perhaps the most profound spiritual work of the Messiah is seen in his position as the intermediary between God and the people by interceding for them. This is the Targum's interpretation of Isaiah 53, but this chapter is much more profound than the Jewish exegetes seemed to realize. It is true that the Targum on Isaiah identifies the Servant of the Lord with the Messiah and that it uses this expression as a title of the Messiah, but his suffering is interpreted merely as the danger and anxiety that are his lot in the war with the ungodly. There is no real distinction here between the suffering of the Servant and the suffering the prophets of Israel experienced in fulfilling their mission. But what Isaiah said of the suffering of the Servant of the Lord is infinitely more significant than this. In the Suffering Servant the Messiah is seen making vicarious atonement through his passion and death, which has a positive purpose in the plan of God for the salvation of sinful men. The Messiah as the Suffering Servant sums up the entire prophetic movement and constitutes a climax in OT prophecy.

The progress of prophetic revelation in history leads up to the idea of the innocent Suffering Servant of God, who in the redemptive purpose of his death reconciles men to God. In the Messiah's sacrifice of himself as an expiation for sin his priestly office is revealed and combined with his work as prophet and king. The redemptive work of the Messiah includes the restoration of the paradise that existed in the beginning but was lost through the fall of Adam. Through the Messiah the kingdom of the end time will be established, the kingdom of God on earth, the restoration of Israel. As the Messiah was present from the first in the creation so he is also present as the central figure of the last events. He is declared to be the firstborn of creation and also the end and goal of creation (John 1:1; Col 1:15–17; Rev 3:14).

The NT conception of the Messiah is developed directly from the teaching of the OT. The essential features of the OT picture of the Messiah are in the person of Jesus. The suffering, dying, and glorified Servant of the Lord of the OT is that same NT Son of Man who will return on the clouds of heaven. The Messiah, as the Son of Man, will suffer, die, and rise again on the third day, "according to the Scriptures." But even though Jesus was victorious over death in his resurrection and ascension, he did not yet reign in his full messiahship in his righteous kingdom. His ultimate victory is revealed to be in the future, and consequently he must come again in power to establish his messianic throne and kingdom. Jesus often used the phrase "the Son of Man" to express his interpretation of his nature and his part in the coming of God's kingdom. It seems that Jesus preferred this title in referring to himself. He did not use it primarily to express his humanity; on the contrary, it was a proclamation of the paradox that he, who appeared as an ordinary man, was at the same time the One in whom there are supernatural powers of the kingdom of God. He who took on himself the form of a man will some day be revealed as "the Son of Man" with power and glory. The title, then, is an expression for the triumphant Messiah who comes on the clouds in the majesty of his exaltation.

The expression "the Son of Man" used of the

Messiah reflects the general picture in the NT of a more profound view of his person. The Messiah as the Son of Man is a preexistent heavenly being. Long before Abraham, Jesus said, the Son of Man *was* (John 8:58; cf. John 17:5; Col 1:17). The origin of creation is linked with the Messiah Jesus in various Scriptures (1 Cor 8:6; 2 Cor 8:9; Col 1:15–17). It is also as preexistent that Jesus is called "elect" (1 Peter 2:6; NIV "chosen"). God has prepared him to carry out his purpose in redemption and eschatological judgment. Furthermore, the Messiah is revealed to be the Son of Man in a unique sense (John 1:1; Rom 1:4). Jesus affirmed this in his conversation with the priests and elders. Jesus was asked to declare if he was "the Messiah, the Son of God" (Matt 26:63–64; Mark 14:61; Luke 22:67–70), and his claim is clear. As the Son of God, the Messiah possesses the power of God's authority. It is as the Son of God that the divine nature of the Messiah is supremely revealed.

Bibliography: W. Manson, *Jesus the Messiah,* 1943; H. Frankfort, *Kingship and the Gods,* 1948; H. H. Rowley, *The Servant of the Lord,* 1952; T. W. Manson, *The Servant Messiah,* 1953; H. L. Ellison, *The Centrality of the Messianic Idea for the Old Testament,* 1953; H. Ringgren, *The Messiah in the Old Testament,* 1956; F. F. Bruce, *This Is That,* 1968; G. E. Ladd, *A Theology of the New Testament,* 1974; R. T. France, "Messiah," IDB, pp. 763–72. ACS

METALS (See MINERALS)

METHEG AMMAH (mē'thĕg ăm'à, *the bridle of the metropolis*). A town David took from the hands of the Philistines (2 Sam 8:1).

METHU SHAEL (mē-thū'shā'ĕl). Father of Lamech in the line of Cain before the Flood (Gen 4:18).

METHUSELAH (mē-thū'zĕ-là, Heb. *methûshelah, man of the javelin*). A descendant of Seth before the Flood. He died at 969 years of age, in the very year of the Flood (Gen 5:22–27). He was the son of Enoch and the father of Lamech (5:21, 25).

MEUNIM, MEUNITES (mē-ū'nĭm, mē-ū'nīts, Heb. *me'ûnîm, the people of Maon*). The people of an Arab city still existing south of the Dead Sea not far from the more famous Petra. They are listed among the tribes that Uzziah of Judah conquered. Ezra 2:50, repeated in Nehemiah 7:52, speaks of their descendants. The Masoretes say that the word rendered by some versions as "habitations" (1 Chron 4:41) should read "Meunim." Ezra counts them among the Nethinim (temple servants) at the return from exile (Ezra 2:50, KJV Mehunim; in 2 Chron 26:7, KJV Mehunims).

ME-ZAHAB (mĕz'ā-hăb, Heb. *mêzāhāv*). Grandfather of Mehetabel, who married Hadad, an Edomite king (Gen 36:39; 1 Chron 1:50).

MEZOBAITE (mē-zō'bà-īt, perhaps *from Zobah*). A family name referring to a place otherwise unknown and unheard of (1 Chron 11:47).

MIAMIN (See MIJAMIN)

MIBHAR (mĭb'hàr, Heb. *mivhār, choice*). One of David's mighty men, the son of Hagri (1 Chron 11:38).

MIBSAM (mĭb'săm, Heb. *mivsām, sweet odor,* related to *balsam*). 1. One of the twelve Ishmaelite patriarchs, corresponding to the twelve sons of Jacob (Gen 25:13).

2. A grandson or great-grandson of Simeon, perhaps named after the preceding (1 Chron 4:25).

MIBZAR (mĭb'zàr, Heb. *mivtsār, a fortress*). One of the eleven "sheiks" or chiefs descended from Esau (Gen 36:42).

MICA, MICHA (mī'cà, Heb. *mîkhā'*, evidently, like Micah, an abbrev. of Micaiah, *Who is like Jehovah?*).

1. A grandson of Jonathan (2 Sam 9:12).
2. A Levite covenanter (Neh 10:11).
3. Another Levite (Neh 11:17).
4. Another Levite (1 Chron 9:15; Neh 11:22).

MICAH (mī'kà, Heb. *mîkkâh*). Short form of the name *Micaiah* (or Michael), meaning "Who is like God?") The name is applied to six individuals in the OT:

1. An Ephraimite mentioned in Judges 17–18. See explanation below.
2. A Reubenite listed in 1 Chronicles 5:5.
3. A grandson of Jonathan (1 Chron 8:34; 9:40).
4. A Levite (1 Chron 23:20).
5. The father of Abdon, one sent by Josiah to the prophetess Huldah (2 Chron 34:20); called "Acbor son of Micaiah" in 2 Kings 22:12.
6. The canonical prophet Micah from Moresheth (Mic 1:1; Jer 26:18).

Of these men, only no. 1, the Ephraimite, calls for special comment. The sixth, Micah the prophet, is unknown to us apart from the book that bears his name (See MICAH, BOOK OF).

Micah, the name of the Ephraimite, may indeed be a shortened form of Michael, as names compounded with *El,* "God," are more common in the early times before the monarchy. The record of Micah is a sad tale of apostasy in the days of the judges. It forms a kind of appendix to the history of the twelve judges (Judg 1–16), a place that it occupies along with the narrative of the Benjamite war (Judg 19–21) and, in old Hebrew lists, the Book of Ruth, which was at one time appended to Judges and, like the two other accounts, concerns Bethlehem-Judah.

Micah had stolen some money from his mother but confessed and restored it. She declared she had already dedicated it for an idol for her son and proceeded to use two hundred shekels of it (a little over five pounds) to make such an image.

Micah set up a private sanctuary and ordained one of his sons as priest. Later he ordained a wandering Levite of Bethlehem-Judah. His idolatry, though far from the Mosaic prescriptions, was in the name of the Lord, and he evidently felt that a Levite would win greater sanctity for his idol shrine.

This incident is linked with the Danite migration. The tribe of Dan first inherited in southern Palestine. Feeling restricted, they later moved to the far north where they appear later (Josh 19:47; 1 Kings 12:29). On the way, their spies noticed Micah's sanctuary and later the Danite army pillaged Micah's shrine, abducted his priest, and set up the sanctuary for their own—all this while the tabernacle was in Shiloh. The name of Micah's priest was Jonathan, a descendant of Moses (called *Manasseh* in most versions in Judg 18:30 by courtesy of the Jewish scribes to protect the reputation of Moses). RLH

MICAH, BOOK OF. The fifth of the Minor Prophets, dating from the late 700s B.C. The book predicts the fall of Samaria, which occurred in 722, but concerns more especially the sins and dangers of Jerusalem in the days of Hezekiah around 700. As an outline will show, the message varies between condemnation for the present sins and God's purpose of ultimate blessing for his people:

Outline:

I. Predicted Desolation of Samaria and Jerusalem (1:1–3:12)
II. Eventual Blessings for Zion (4:1–8)
III. Invasion and Deliverance by Davidic Ruler (4:9–5:15)
IV. Condemnations for Sins (6:1–7:6)
V. Eventual Help From God (7:7–20)

In the opening portion of the book, Micah 1:1–3:12, God's judgment is first announced on Samaria for her idolatry. Micah's interest seems to lie chiefly in Jerusalem, however, whose desolation is announced in 3:12 in very similar terms. Chapters 2 and 3 are a catalogue of Judah's sins. Oppression of the poor was a characteristic, but another basic factor was the refusal to hear God's prophets. As in Jeremiah's day, they preferred prophets who predicted peace (cf. 3:5 with Jer 8:10–11; Ezek 13:10). It is not improbable that Jeremiah and Ezekiel took their texts on this subject from Micah. At least Micah's warnings of 3:12 were well known in Jeremiah's day (Jer 26:18). Jeremiah's friends quote these words verbatim, ascribing them to the Micah of Hezekiah's time. Negative critics point out that Jeremiah quotes Micah as a prophet of *doom,* and they conclude that no prediction of hope in Micah is genuine. The conclusion seems far-fetched. Jeremiah's friends quoted only that part of the book that was applicable to their situation. This argument need not be extended to the rest of the book.

The second section, Micah 4:1–8, includes a passage that is practically identical with Isaiah 2:1–4. Many have questioned whether Micah quoted Isaiah or vice versa, or whether both quoted a common oracle. But Isaiah 2:1 calls this passage the word of Isaiah, which should decide the matter. Micah evidently uses Isaiah's promise and skillfully weaves it into his own composition.

The third section, Micah 4:9–5:15, comes against the background of the wars of Hezekiah's day. The Assyrians carried captive forty cities of Judah and received tribute from Hezekiah as Sennacherib himself tells us (cf. also 2 Kings 18:13–16). But God delivered Jerusalem (18:35). The "seven shepherds, even eight leaders of men" of Micah 5:5 probably is merely a symbolic numerical way of saying "one great deliverer"—a numerical device that can be paralleled in old Canaanite literature.

Yet in this section the Captivity and return from Babylon are also predicted. Negative critics insist that similar passages in Isaiah (e.g., 48:20) are late and actually written after the events described. In their denial of supernatural prediction, they must also say that Micah 4:10 is late. But according to Isaiah 39:6 and also by Assyrian testimony, Babylon was a menace in Micah's own day; so these verses are quite appropriate.

Against these dangers to Judah, God holds out that messianic hope of Micah 5:2. The mention of Bethlehem Ephrathah identifies the Messiah as of David's line (cf. Isa 11:1; Jer 23:5; Ezek 37:24). The "clans of Judah" is read the "rulers of Judah" in Matthew 2:6 by using different (and probably correct) vowels on the Hebrew consonants. "You, Bethlehem," is masculine and therefore is probably a direct reference to the Messiah from Bethlehem, for the gender would be feminine if only the city were addressed.

The condemnations of the fourth section (Mic 6:1–7:6) include several references to the Pentateuch and other historical books (Mic 6:4–5, 16; cf. also 5:6 with Gen 10:8–9). The response of Micah 6:8 is famous. Some have argued that it teaches salvation apart from sacrifice. Actually, it alludes to Deuteronomy 10:12 and involves Israel's duty to obey *all* the Mosaic injunctions. Christ probably refers to this verse in his condemnation of the formalistic Pharisees (Matt 23:23).

The book closes with the prophet's declaration of faith in the ultimate fulfillment of God's covenant of blessing for Abraham.

Bibliography: L. C. Allen, *The Books of Joel, Obadiah, Jonah and Micah* (NIC), 1976; J. L. Mays, *Micah: A Commentary,* 1976. RLH

MICAIAH (mī-kā'yȧ, Heb. *mîkhāyāhû, Who is like Jehovah?*). 1. A true prophet of God, residing at Samaria, the capital of the northern tribes of Israel c. 900 B.C., in the last days of Ahab king of Israel and of Jehoshaphat king of Judah. Jehoshaphat, though a man of God, made the mistake of associating with Ahab, the worst of all the kings of Israel. (Contrast 2 Chron 17:3–6 with 1 Kings 16:30–33.) Ahab took advantage of Jehoshaphat's visit by asking his assistance in taking Ramoth Gilead from the Syrians, whose king Ben-Hadad I had taken it from Ahab's father Omri. Jehoshaphat, letting his courtesy overcome his good judgment, consented, asking only that the prophets be consulted. Four hundred of Ahab's false prophets said, "Go, for the Lord will give it into the king's hand" 1 Kings 22:6 (see 1 Kings 22; 2 Chron 18).

When Jehoshaphat showed his distrust in the prophets and asked if there was not a prophet of the Lord also, Ahab replied, "There is still one man through whom we can inquire of the LORD, but I hate him because he never prophesies anything good about me, but always bad. He is Micaiah son of Imlah" (1 Kings 22:8). A messenger was sent to bring Micaiah, who was told to prophesy favorably, but Micaiah replied that he could speak only what God would give him. After replying frivolously to Ahab's question, the king demanded the truth, and Micaiah told him how the hosts of heaven had planned to ruin Ahab by putting a false spirit in the mouth of all his prophets. Micaiah, after being insulted by the false prophet Zedekiah, was sent back to the city to be imprisoned and fed only bread and water until the king returned to deal with him. Micaiah boldly told Ahab that if he returned at all, he, Micaiah, was a false prophet. Since Ahab partly believed this prophecy, he contrived a clever trick to get Jehoshaphat killed in his place. With a show of generosity he proposed that Jehoshaphat wear his kingly robes in the battle, but Ahab would disguise himself like a common soldier. The outcome was that Jehoshaphat cried out and escaped, but a Syrian drew his bow at random and the arrow killed Ahab.

2. Father of Acbor, whom King Josiah sent with others to Huldah the prophetess to inquire about the prophecy that had been read to him (2 Kings 22:12–14); "Abdon son of Micah" in 2 Chronicles 34:20.

3. A daughter of Uriel of Gibeah (2 Chron 13:2, JB, KJV, MLB, NASB, RSV; Maacah NEB, NIV), who had married Tamar, daughter of Absalom. She was the wife of King Rehoboam of Judah and the mother of Abijah, the next king. The name is given as Maacah in 1 Kings 15:2.

4. A prince of Judah whom Jehoshaphat sent to teach the people (2 Chron 17:7).

5. An ancestor of a priest in Nehemiah's time (Neh 12:35).

6. A priest in Nehemiah's time (Neh 12:41).

7. Grandson of Shaphan the scribe in Josiah's day who brought the book of the Law of the Lord to the king (Jer 36:11–13). ABF

MICHA (See MICA, MICHA)

MICHAEL (mī'kĕl, Heb. *mîkhā'ēl, Who is like God?*).

1. Father of Sethur, a spy from the tribe of Asher (Num 13:13).

2. Two Gadites who lived in Bashan (1 Chron 5:13–14).

3. A Gershonite of the eleventh generation, great-grandfather of Asaph, the singer (1 Chron 6:40).

4. A chief man of Issachar (1 Chron 7:3).

5. A Benjamite (1 Chron 8:16).

6. A captain of a thousand of the tribe of Manasseh who joined David in Ziklag (1 Chron 12:20).

7. The father of Omri of Issachar, one of David's mighty men (1 Chron 27:18).

8. A prince of Judah, son of Jehoshaphat and brother of Jehoram, kings of Judah (2 Chron 21:2).

9. Father of Zebadiah, a chief Jew who returned with Ezra (Ezra 8:8).

10. The archangel whose chief responsibility seems to have been the care of the Jewish people (Dan 12:1). Michael had a dispute with Satan himself (Jude 9).

MICHAIAH (See MICAIAH)

MICHAL (mī'kăl, Heb. *mîkhāl,* a contraction of *mîkhā'ēl, Michael*). The younger daughter of King Saul of Israel (1 Sam 14:49). Saul, insanely jealous of David, desired to kill him but, finding it impossible to do so by his own hands (18:11), he tried trickery. He offered David his elder daughter Merab for his service against the Philistines, but changed his mind and gave her to another; then he learned that Michal loved David, so he offered her to David if he would give evidence of having killed a hundred Philistines. David killed two hundred and married Michal; but Saul hated him all the more. Once, when Saul sent some men to kill David, Michal helped him to escape (19:11–17), deceiving Saul's officers by putting an idol in his bed. Though Michal truly loved David, she could not comprehend him, and so scoffed at him for rejoicing before the Lord (2 Sam 6:16–23). As a result, she never had a child.

MICMASH, MICHMASH (mĭk'măsh, Heb. *mĭk'hmash, a hidden place*). A place in the ancient tribe of Benjamin about eight miles (thirteen km.) NE of Jerusalem. A notable battle occurred here between Israel and the Philistines in the reign of Saul (1 Sam 13–14). Micmash lay in the pass that goes eastward from Bethel and Ai down to Jericho, and at one place the pass was contained between two cliffs, "Bozez and Seneh" (14:4). There Jonathan and his armor-bearer clambered up and started the victory over the Philistines, and

The village of Mukhmas, built over the biblical site of Michmash, on the border between the Judean hills and desert. Courtesy Ecole Biblique et Archéologique Française, Jerusalem.

there the British forces under General Allenby used the same strategy and won victory over the Turks. In Isaiah 10:28, where the prophet is picturing with dramatic detail an advance of the Assyrian forces against Jerusalem, he mentions Micmash as the place where the invaders stored their baggage, hoping no doubt to gather it on their return (37:36). In the return from the Captivity under Zerubbabel (Ezra 2:27; Neh 7:31) 122 men of this place are mentioned, indicating that it was a fair-sized community at the time. Jonathan Maccabaeus made his governmental headquarters here for a time (1 Macc 9:73).

MICMETHATH (mĭk'mē-thăth, Heb. *mikhmethâh*). A landmark on the borders of Ephraim and Manasseh (Josh 16:6; 17:7). It was east of, but quite close to Shechem; and instead of being a town, it may have been, as its name implies, merely a "lurking place."

MICRI (mĭk'rī, Heb. *mikhrî*). Grandfather of Elah, a Benjamite in Jerusalem after the Captivity (1 Chron 9:8).

MIDDIN (mĭd'ĭn, Heb. *middîn*). One of the six cities of Judah lying in the wilderness just west of the Dead Sea (Josh 15:61).

MIDIAN, MIDIANITES (mĭd'ĭ-ăn, -īts, Heb. *midhyān, midhānîm*). 1. A son of Abraham by Keturah (Gen 25:1–6).

2. Midian's descendants and the land they claimed, lying mostly east of the Jordan and the Dead Sea, then southward through the Arabah and (in the time of Moses) including the southern and eastern parts of the Sinai peninsula. Traders in a caravan are called "Ishmaelites" (Gen 37:25), then "Midianites" (37:36), the former referring to their descent from Ishmael (Gen 25:12–18) and the latter to their abode in the land of Midian. When Moses fled from Egypt forty years before the Exodus (Exod 2:15–21), he helped the daughters of Reuel (or Jethro) the priest of Midian, was invited to their encampment, and married Zipporah, the priest's daughter. Thus the descendants of Moses had Midianite as well as Levite ancestry. Jethro, though priest of Midian, acknowledged the God of Israel as supreme (18:11); but neither he nor his son Hobab, though very friendly to Moses, could bring himself to join Israel (Num 10:29).

Toward the end of the life of Moses, Midian had apparently become confederate with Moab (Num 22:4). Through the counsel of Balaam, the Midianite women and girls wrought much harm in Israel, and God commanded Moses to conquer the nation (25:16–18). Two hundred years later, in the days of Gideon, God delivered Israel into the hand of Midian for seven years (Judg 6:1–6). They allowed the Israelites to plow and to sow the seed, but they (the Midianites) did the reaping. Gideon defeated them and killed their two kings Zebah and Zalmunna (8:21). The names of these kings and of the princes of Midian, Oreb and Zeeb (7:25), give us a picture of their civilization. Zebah means "a slaying" or "a sacrifice"; Zalmunna, "deprived of shade"; Oreb, "raven"; and Zeeb, "a wolf."

Though the Midianites were nomads, they had great wealth in the time of Moses. They had not only 675,000 sheep, 72,000 oxen, and 61,000 donkeys, but also gold, silver, brass, iron, tin, and lead; all of which are mentioned in the booty taken by the men of Israel (Num 31:22, 32–34). The Midianites have long since disappeared from the earth. ABF

MIGDAL EDER (mĭg'dăl ē'dêr). A place between Bethlehem and Hebron where Jacob stayed after Rachel's death. Here Reuben lay with his father's concubine (NEB, NIV Gen 35:21–22; tower of Edar [Eder] KJV, MLB, NASB, RSV).

MIGDAL EL (mĭg'dăl ĕl, *tower of God*). One of the nineteen fortified cities of Naphtali (Josh 19:38); thought by some to be the Magadan (KJV "Magdala") of Matthew 15:39.

MIGDAL GAD (miğ'dăl găd, *tower of Gad*). A city of Judah when Joshua divided the land (Josh 15:37). Now probably Mejdal about twenty-four miles (forty km.) west of Hebron.

MIGDOL (mĭg'dŏl, Heb. *mighdôl*). 1. A place just west of the former shallow bay at the north end of the Gulf of Suez, the westward arm of the Red Sea (Exod 14:2; Num 33:7). Near here the Israelites made their last encampment in Egypt, and here Pharaoh thought he had them trapped.

2. A place in northern Egypt where many Jews went in the days of Jeremiah, and where they even practiced idolatry in spite of the prophet's warnings (Jer 44:1–14; 46:14).

MIGRON (mĭg'rŏn, Heb. mighrôn, *precipice*). A locality near Gibeah of Saul about seven miles (twelve km.) NE of Jerusalem, in the tribe of Benjamin. Saul sat (1 Sam 14:2) here under a pomegranate tree and made the place the headquarters of his little troop of about six hundred men. In Isaiah 10:28 the prophet pictures the Assyrians passing Migron as they approached to attack Jerusalem.

MIJAMIN (mĭj'à-mĭn, Heb. *mîyāmîn, from the right hand*). 1. A priest in David's time (1 Chron 24:9).

2. A priest who covenanted with Nehemiah (Neh 10:7).

3. A priest who returned with Zerubbabel from Babylon (Neh 12:5).

4. A man who put away his foreign wife (Ezra 10:25).

MIKLOTH (mĭk'lŏth, Heb. *miqlôth, rods*). 1. A Benjamite in Jerusalem after the Exile (1 Chron 8:32; 9:37–38).

2. A ruler of twenty-four thousand men in the time of David (1 Chron 27:4).

MIKNEIAH (mĭk-nē′yȧ). A Levite harp player in David's time (1 Chron 15:18, 21).

MILALAI (mĭ-ȧ-lā′ī). A priest with a musical instrument in Nehemiah's celebration (Neh 12:36).

MILCAH (mĭl′kȧ, Heb. *milkâh, counsel*). 1. A daughter of Haran, Abram's youngest brother, who died at Ur of the Chaldees, and sister of Lot. She married her uncle Nahor and bore him eight children, of whom one was Bethuel, father of Rebekah and Laban (Gen 11:27–29; 22:20–23; 24:24).

2. One of the five daughters, co-heiresses of Zelophehad, the Manassite. They had to marry within their tribe (Num 36).

MILCOM (See Molech)

MILDEW. A pale fungus growth that discolors and spoils grains and fruits in warm, damp weather. In Scripture it is always associated with "blight" (Deut 28:22; 1 Kings 8:37; Amos 4:9; Hag 2:17). Leviticus contains many laws regarding contamination by mildew in clothing and houses (e.g., Lev 13:47, 55–56; 14:35, 39, 44). It is called leprosy in the KJV.

MILE (See Weights and Measures)

MILETUS (mī-lē′tŭs, Gr. *Milētos*). In KJV once Miletum (2 Tim 4:20). Pausanias says Miletus, southernmost of the Greek cities of Asia Minor, had Cretan origins. According to Homer, it was occupied by "foreign-speaking" Carians who fought in the Trojan confederation. Perhaps shortly after the Trojan War (twelfth cent. B.C.) Ionians seized the city. In the great age of Greek colonization (eighth to sixth cent.) Miletus planted many commercial centers around the Black Sea, and their wealth points to vigorous, expansive life in the metropolis (shown also by her exerting of pressure on Egypt and her maintenance of contact with Sybaris in Italy until the fall of that town in 510). Miletus must have exercised strong sea-power during these active centuries, and her military might is shown by the resistance she offered to the Lydian kings and the privileged position accorded her even by the greatest of those rulers, Croesus. When Croesus' kingdom fell to the Persians in 546, no attempt was made to reduce Miletus' independence. In 499 Miletus (with help from Athens, not Sparta) took the lead in precipitating the Ionian Revolt. In a naval engagement at Lade she suffered defeat, and the city was occupied by the Persians in 494.

The disaster ended Miletus' long prosperity, until then damaged only by the factional strife that was endemic in all ancient Greek cities. In the sixth century Milesian scholars flourished—savants like Thales (statesman, philosopher, physicist, and astronomer), Anaximander and Anaximenes (physicists and astronomers), and Hecataeus (geographer). Industry flourished, and Milesian woolen goods were famous. After Persia's defeat at Mycale in 479, Miletus regained her freedom and joined the Delian League, Athens' security organization, leaving it in 412 in the day of Athens' decline and disaster, only to fall under Persia again. In the fourth century the city was under Caria, from which her first founders had come. Aspasia (blue-stocking mistress of Pericles), Hippodamus (who planned the Piraeus), and Timotheus (the poet) belong to this second period of Milesian vigor.

The ancient harbor at Miletus, now silted up and deserted, with remains of the city's bathhouse and theater in the background. Miletus was visited by Paul on his third missionary journey, and here he said farewell to the Ephesian elders (Acts 20:15–17). Courtesy Dan Bahat.

The rest of her history was undistinguished. A silting harbor, the common bane of that coast, ended her sea power and sea-borne commerce. At the time of Paul's visit (Acts 20:15, 17) Miletus was a city of no great standing in the Roman province of Asia. The sea is now ten miles (seventeen km.) from the ancient site. EMB

MILK (See Food)

MILL (Heb. *rēḥeh*, Gr. *mylos, mylōn*). An apparatus used to grind any edible grain—wheat, barley, oats, rye, etc.—into flour. It consists of two circular stones, the lower one having a slightly convex upper surface to help the drifting of the broken grain toward the outer edge from which it drops. It is made of a hard stone, which after being shaped is scratched with curved furrows so as to multiply the cutting and grinding effect. The lower stone has a stout stick standing at its center, and the upper one (called the rider) has a hole at its center so that it can rotate around the stick, and a handle eight or ten inches from the center by which it is turned. Generally it is worked by two women, facing each other, and each grasping the handle to turn the rider. One woman feeds the grain in at the center of the rider and the other guides and brushes the products into a little pile. The process is very ancient, for we read of "the slave girl, who is at her hand mill" in the days of Moses (Exod 11:5), and the process was no doubt old at that remote time. Even the manna that fell in the wilderness was hard enough or tough enough so that the people used to grind it in mills or beat it in mortars before cooking it (Num 11:7–8).

It is altogether probable that people pounded grain before they thought of grinding it, and so the mortar is probably more ancient even than the mill. Because people depended on flour as their "staff of life" and because they generally ground it only as needed, it was forbidden to take a millstone in pledge (Deut 24:6). In Jeremiah 25:10 "the sound of millstones" is mentioned as a sign of happy prosperous life, but in Isaiah 47:2 the prophet taunted the proud and delicate women of Babylon with the thought that they would have to become slaves and labor at the mill. When the Philistines blinded Samson (Judg 16:21), he had to grind in the prison, and this mill was probably a large one ordinarily turned by a blinded ox or donkey. Abimelech, usurping "king" of Israel, was killed by a woman who dropped a millstone on his head (9:53). Our Lord prophesied that at his coming "two women will be grinding with a hand mill; one will be taken and the other left" (Matt 24:41). A millstone cast into the sea is a symbol of absolute destruction (Rev 18:21). ABF

MILLENNIUM (See Kingdom of God)

MILLET (See Plants)

MILLO (mĭl'ō, Heb. *millô', fullness*). A mound or rampart built up and filled in with earth and stones to raise the level.

1. An ancient fortification in or near Shechem. In Judges 9:6, 20 "Beth Millo" mentioned three times probably means the inhabitants of this tower or fortification.

2. A place just north of Mount Zion and outside the city of David, though it was inside the city of Jerusalem from Hezekiah's time onward. NIV refers to it as "the supporting terraces," but see footnote (2 Sam 5:9). When David had taken Zion (5:7–9), he began to fill up Millo and to build inward toward Zion. Solomon later strengthened Millo (1 Kings 9:15, 24; 11:27). Hezekiah, three hundred years later, again strengthened it, this time against the Assyrians (2 Chron 32:5). The "Beth Millo" where the godly Joash, king of Judah, was killed by his own officials was probably this same fortification. (2 Kings 12:20–21).

MINA (See Weights and Measures)

MIND. A word for a number of Hebrew and Greek nouns in Scripture. Among the more important are the Hebrew *lebh,* "heart"; *nephesh,* "soul"; and the Greek *nous* and *dianoia,* the former denoting the faculty of reflective consciousness, of moral thinking and knowing, while the latter means "meditation, reflection." None of these words is used with any precision of meaning. In the NT the word "mind" frequently occurs in an ethical sense, as in Romans 7:25 and Colossians 2:18.

MINERALS. The present science of mineralogy with its names and exact terminology is a young science, younger even than physics, chemistry, astronomy, or mathematics. Mineralogy as a science certainly did not exist at the time the Bible was written. It is impossible to be certain in all cases that when a mineral is named in the Bible it is the same mineral designated by that name in modern mineralogy. The gemstones or precious stones of the Bible are minerals with identities that are presently in a state of uncertainty and confusion. There are, of course, a number of minerals that present no problems. Water is a mineral whose identity we have always been certain about. No one questions the meaning of gold, silver, or iron.

Mineralogists find it somewhat difficult to define the word "mineral," but its scientific meaning can be clarified by the use of specific examples. A granite boulder belongs to the mineral kingdom as contrasted to the animal or vegetable kingdoms, but it is a rock and not a mineral. It is composed of a number of minerals most of which are of microscopic size. The minerals in granite, visible to the naked eye, are the clear, glassy particles of quartz, one or more of the white or pink feldspars, and the darker biotite or hornblende. Quartz is classified as a mineral for a number of reasons: it is formed in nature, it is not formed by plant or animal, it has a uniform composition throughout the particle, and it always crystallizes in a hexagonal system of crystals. Quartz is always composed of 46.7 percent silicon and 53.3 percent oxygen. Slight amounts of impurities may impart a wide variety of colors. This results in precious stones with different names, such as yellow quartz, which is false topaz or citrine, and purple quartz, which is amethyst. Pure water-clear quartz is rock crystal. Yet these precious stones crystallize into identical hexagonal forms. The chemist may make silicon dioxide in the laboratory, which has the same percentage of silicon and oxygen as that of natural quartz, but it is not a mineral. It does not pass the test of having been formed in nature unattended by man. It is referred to as a synthetic. Alcohol in dilute form was certainly known by the ancients, but it cannot be considered a mineral, since it can be traced back to the sugar present in grapes. Quartz has a definite composition, but this is not a rigorous requirement for all minerals. The biotite or black mica of granite is a mineral that varies somewhat in composition. This mineral contains chiefly the elements hydrogen, potassium, magnesium, iron, aluminum, silicon, and oxygen. Hydrogen and potassium may replace each other in the crystal pattern; they may also interchange. The shape of the crystal remains essentially the same as does the general appearance.

The minerals will be grouped as follows:

I. Precious stones.

II. Metals.

III. Common minerals such as salt, sulfur, and water.

I. Precious Stones. The reaction of the human race to beauty and to the things that endure does not change. We share certain criteria with the ancients for evaluating precious stones. There must be beauty of color, transparency, luster, and brilliance. There must be some degree of durability, at least if the gem is to be worn or handled. Selenite, a clear crystalline variety of gypsum, may be beautiful, but it is so soft that it can easily be scratched by the thumbnail. We now use a scale of hardness called the Mohs scale which rates the hardness of gems on the basis of the ease or difficulty of scratching. On this scale the hardness of thumbnail is 2½.

The Mohs Scale of Hardness (H)

1. Talc	5. Apatite	9. Corundum
2. Gypsum	6. Orthoclase	10. Diamond
3. Calcite	7. Quartz	
4. Fluorite	8. Topaz	

The most precious stones are those that have a hardness of 7, 8, 9, and 10. All of these could easily scratch glass, which has a hardness of 5½ to 6. Many of the precious stones of the Bible belong to the quartz or chalcedony family with a hardness of 7. Emerald is a green beryl (H 7½ to 8); topaz has a hardness of 8; the ruby and sapphire, both forms of the mineral corundum, have a hardness of 9.

There are four principal lists of minerals recorded in the Scriptures. They are as follows:

1. The twelve precious stones of Aaron's breastplate. Each stone represented one of the tribes of Israel (Exod 28:17–20; 39:10–13).

2. The wisdom of Job (Job 28:16–19). Listed are onyx, sapphire, crystal, coral, jaspar, ruby, and topaz.

3. The gems of the king of Tyre (Ezek 28:13). Listed are ruby, topaz, emerald, chrysolite, onyx, jaspar, sapphire, turquoise, and beryl.

4. The precious stones of the Holy City (Rev 21:18–21). There is a precious stone for each of twelve foundations.

The precious stones of the Bible are as follows:

A. **Agate** (ăg′ăt) (Exod 28:19; 39:12). This member of the chalcedony family is described under *Chalcedony*. It was the second stone in the third row of the priest's breastplate.

B. **Amethyst** (ăm′ė-thĭst) (Exod 28:19; 39:12; Rev 21:20). A purple to blue-violet form of quartz. This is one of the loveliest forms of quartz, and there is general agreement that the amethyst of the Bible is our present amethyst. The LXX translates the term by *amethystos* (amethyst). Natural cubic crystals of fluorite in transparent blues and purples match amethyst for beauty, but this mineral has a hardness of only 4 and is easily split by the tap of a knife blade. Amethyst was the third stone of the third row of the priest's breastplate and will be the twelfth of the foundation stones of the Holy City.

C. **Beryl** (bĕr′yl) (Exod 28:17; 39:10; Ezek 28:13; Rev 21:20). A beryllium aluminum silicate. It is now mined and valued as a source of beryllium, a light metal unknown until A.D. 1828. A single crystal taken from the Black Hills of South Dakota weighed as much as seventy-five tons. Gem varieties include yellow or golden beryl; emerald, which is a highly prized translucent to transparent sea-green stone; aquamarine, which is blue; and morganite, a rose-red variety. Beryl was the third stone in the top row of the priest's breastplate, and will be the eighth of the foundation stones of the Holy City.

D. **Carnelian** (kär-nēl′yăn) (Rev 4:3; 21:20). (See carnelian under *Chalcedony*.) Carnelian is also known as sard or sardius. (See *Sardius*.) It is to be the sixth foundation stone of the Holy City.

E. **Chalcedony** (kăl-sĕd′ō-nĭ) (Rev 21:19). The third foundation stone of the Holy City. Quartz and chalcedony are both composed of silicon dioxide, but chalcedony does not crystallize into the bold hexagonal forms taken by quartz. Any crystalline character that the various forms of chalcedony have is of microscopic size. The lighter colored varieties are named chalcedony in contrast to such names as carnelian and jaspar.

The following are some of the varieties of chalcedony.

1. **Agate.** Agate is chalcedony with colors unevenly distributed, often banded, with the bands curved. Petrified wood is often a form of agate in which the silicon dioxide has replaced the original wood. Agates are very common and many varieties exist. They have become one of the most popular minerals for cutting and polishing. The moss agates found along the Yellowstone River from Glendive, Montana, to Yellowstone Park are particularly well known. The "thunder eggs" of Idaho and Oregon may look like drab gray stones, but when sawed in two with a diamond saw, they may reveal a center of lovely agate.

2. **Carnelian, sard,** or **sardius.** Carnelian is chalcedony with colors usually clear red to brownish red. Iron oxide imparts the color.

3. **Chrysoprase.** This is an apple-green variety of chalcedony, sometimes called green jaspar. A small percentage of nickel may account for the green color. Beads of genuine chrysoprase dating to 1500 B.C. have been taken from an Egyptian grave.

4. **Flint.** This is usually a dull gray to black form, not prized or classified as a precious stone, but highly prized by primitive peoples for arrowheads, spear points, skinning knives, etc.

5. **Jaspar.** Jaspar pebbles may be found in many gravel deposits. The petrified wood of Arizona is largely jaspar. Jaspar is hard, opaque, and takes a beautiful polish. It is sufficiently abundant so that it must have been used by ancient man as a gem stone. Although this gem has many shades, the chief colors are red, yellow, brown, and green. Green jaspar is also known as chrysoprase. The colors largely result from the presence of iron oxide.

6. **Onyx.** Onyx is similar to banded agates, except that the bands are flat. Specimens are usually cut and polished parallel to the layers. This enables cameo production. Objects of Mexican onyx, beautifully cut and polished and available in a number of Mexican border cities, are really not onyx at all. The composition is calcium carbonate

instead of silicon dioxide. A little hydrochloride acid added to Mexican onyx will cause effervescence, whereas all forms of silica react to this negatively.

7. **Sardonyx.** Sardonyx is merely onyx that includes layers of carnelian or sard.

F. **Chrysolyte** (krĭs′ō-līt) (Exod 28:20; 39:13; Song of Songs 5:14; Ezek 1:16; 10:9; 28:13; Dan 10:6; Rev 21:20). Chrysolite is a yellow to greenish-yellow form of olivine. A green olivine is known as peridot. The mineral is a silicate of magnesium and iron. In Revelation 21:20 it is the seventh foundation stone of the Holy City, and in Exodus it is the first gem in the fourth row of the priest's breastpiece.

G. **Chrysoprase** (krĭs′ō-prāz) (Rev 21:20). (See under *Chalcedony.*) The tenth foundation stone of the Holy City.

H. **Coral.** (Job 28:18; Ezek 27:16). Although coral has its origin in the animal world, it is considered here because it is included along with gem stones in the Bible, and gem coral is used in the production of jewelry today.

When the writer of Job speaks of the priceless value of wisdom, he compares it to a number of precious stones and metals. One of these is coral. The inclusion of coral, which grows in the sea, is difficult to understand on the basis of modern classifications of precious stones. This indicates that in the ancient world other factors were taken into account in the classification of gem stones. Factors that contributed to the value of coral probably included its beauty; its use in the production of jewelry, creating an economic demand for it; and its workability.

In Ezekiel, coral is associated with turquoise and ruby.

I. **Crystal** (Job 28:17; Rev 4:6; 21:11; 22:1). In the OT the word "crystal" is derived from a verb that means "bright," "pure." In the NT it is derived from the word for "ice" and thus connotes a mineral that is bright and transparent. It is generally understood to refer to glass or clear quartz. This type of quartz is remarkably brilliant and beautifully shaped, even as it is found in nature. However, the word could connote other brilliant colorless minerals. The Book of Job says that wisdom cannot compare with it. It is used in Revelation to depict the brilliance of the objects with which it is compared, such as the "sea" of glass (Rev 4:6), the Holy City (21:11), and the water of life (22:1).

J. **Emerald** (Exod 28:18; 39:11; Ezek 28:13; Rev 4:3; 21:19). The emerald is a transparent to translucent deep green form of beryl (beryllium aluminum silicate). The meaning of the Hebrew word is uncertain. It is probably derived from a root that means "to hammer" and may refer to the hardness of this gem. The Greek word connotes a light green gem and is almost certainly the emerald. The emerald was the last stone in the second row of the priest's breastplate and is listed as the fourth foundation stone of the Holy City.

K. **Flint** (Exod 4:25; Josh 5:2–3; Isa 5:28; 50:7; Jer 17:1; Ezek 3:9; Zech 7:12). (See under *Chalcedony.*) In all its occurrences in the Bible the emphasis is on its hardness and its ability to hold a sharp edge.

L. **Jacinth** (jā′sĭnth) (Exod 28:19; 39:12; Rev 21:20). In modern mineralogy the jacinth is the transparent red, yellow, orange, or brown form of the mineral zircon (zirconium orthosilicate). The meaning of the word in Hebrew is uncertain. However, in the Greek the word connotes a dark blue stone. It is possible that it is the sapphire; if so, the NIV renderings of "sapphire" may represent the lapis lazuli (see *Sapphire*). The jacinth was the first stone in the third row of the priest's breastplate and will be the eleventh foundation stone of the Holy City.

M. **Jaspar** (Exod 28:20; 39:13; Job 28:18; Ezek 28:13; Rev 4:3; 21:11, 18–19). (See under *Chalcedony.*) The jaspar was the third stone in the fourth row of the priest's breastplate and is listed as the first foundation stone of the Holy City.

N. **Lapis lazuli** (lăp′ĭs lăz′ū-lī). (NIV margin for sapphire in OT.) The lapis lazuli is a gem of deep azure-blue. It is a soft stone composed of sodium aluminum silicate. It was fashioned by the ancients into various types of ornaments (see *Sapphire*).

O. **Onyx** (ŏn′ĭks) (Gen 2:12; Exod 25:7; 28:9, 20; 35:9, 27; 39:6, 13; 1 Chron 29:2; Job 28:16; Ezek 28:13). (See under *Chalcedony.*) The onyx was the second stone in the fourth row of the priest's breastplate.

P. **Pearl** (Gen 2:12 mg.; Matt 7:6; 13:45; 1 Tim 2:9; Rev 17:4; 18:12, 16; 21:21). Pearls, like coral, develop in the sea by the abstraction of calcium carbonate from sea water. The pearl develops around a bit of foreign matter within the shell of oysters or mussels. Like coral, it cannot be classed with the hard enduring precious stones. It is easily destroyed. A small amount of acid would convert it to nearly worthless calcium chloride, a water-soluble salt, and the gas carbon dioxide. The reference in Matthew 7:6 implies a fragile structure. Swine might step on rubies without harming them, but pearls would be crushed. They are not much harder than a fingernail. The references to pearls are found almost exclusively in the NT, and there is no reason to doubt the identity of this precious stone.

Q. **Ruby** (Exod 28:17; 39:10; Job 28:18; Prov 3:15; 8:11; 20:15; 31:10; Isa 54:12; Lam 4:7; Ezek 27:16; 28:13). Corundum as a mineral usually occurs as a dull, unattractive but hard form of aluminum oxide, often crystallized in hexagonal forms. Corundum of a rich, clear, red variety is the ruby, whereas the other colors of gem-quality corundum account for the sapphires. The best source for the good rubies is Burma. The ruby was the first stone in the priest's breastplate.

R. **Sapphire** (săf′īr) (Exod 24:10; 28:18; 39:11; Job 28:6, 16; Song of Songs 5:14; Isa 54:11; Lam 4:7; Ezek 1:26; 10:1; 28:13; Rev 21:19). Sapphires, like rubies, belong to the corundum or aluminum-oxide family, with a hardness of 9, or next to diamond. True sapphires are blue; others are colorless, yellow, or pink. The sapphire is listed as the second of the foundation stones of the Holy City, and the second stone in the second row of the priest's breastplate. It is generally agreed that our modern lazurite (lapis lazuli) was called sapphire by the ancients. But we must remember that is is entirely possible that a variety of blue stones were termed sapphire. Lazurite does not seem to belong to the elite company of the most precious stones. For the greater part these most precious stones are noted for a rich purity of color, which lazurite does not have. Lazurite is beautiful but usually consists of a considerable mixture of minerals, including pyrite, calcite, muscovite, and pyroxene. In hardness it is softer than glass (H 5 to 5½).

In three of the references given above, there is a strong implication that the mineral referred to was blue (Exod 24:10; Ezek 1:26; 10:1).

In Lamentations sapphire is linked to ruby, the other highly prized form of corundum.

S. **Sardonyx** (sȧr-dŏn'ĭks) (Rev 21:20). The sardonyx is an onyx layered with red sard or carnelian. It is the fifth foundation stone in the Holy City.

T. **Topaz** (tō'păz) (Exod 28:17; 39:10; Job 28:19; Ezek 28:13; Rev 21:20). The modern topaz is an aluminum fluoro hydroxy silicate with a hardness of 8, thus harder than the quartz and chalcedony groups. The most highly prized is the yellow topaz; but colorless, pink, blue, and green varieties occur as well.

The topaz was the second stone of the first row of the priest's breastplate and is listed as the ninth foundation stone of the Holy City.

U. **Turquoise** (tûr'koiz) (Exod 28:18; 39:11; 1 Chron 29:2; Isa 54:11; Ezek 27:16; 28:13). A blue to bluish-green mineral which is a hydrous phosphate of aluminum and copper. It has a hardness of 5 to 6. The stone polishes well and is commonly fashioned into beads. It was the first stone in the second row of the priest's breastplate.

II. Metals. Of the 103 elements now known to man, 78 are metals. Of these only gold, silver, iron, copper, lead, tin, and mercury were known to the ancients. A metal is an element with a metallic luster; it is usually a good conductor of heat and electricity. Metals such as gold, silver, and copper may occur in nature as the free recognizable metal, or as is true of most metals, they may occur in compound form, chemically united with other elements in such a way that the ore appears dull and nonmetallic.

A second century B.C. bronze bowl (bottom and full view) and ladle found at Tell Anafa, an ancient mound in the Upper Galilee region. Courtesy Museum of Art and Archaeology, University of Missouri.

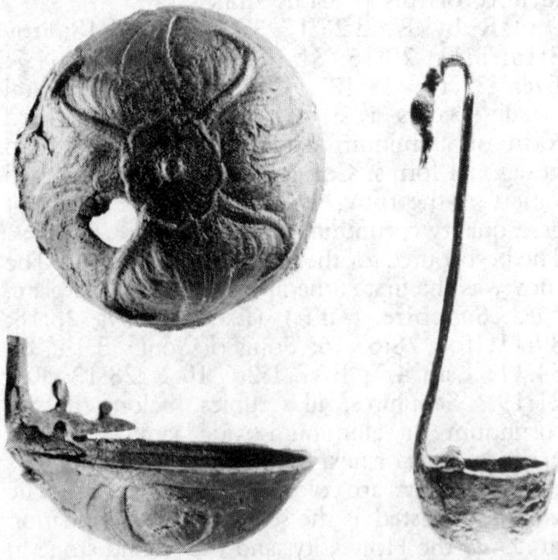

Metallurgy is the science of separating the metal from its ore and the subsequent refining and treating for adapting it to its many and varied uses. The earliest reference to a man skilled in iron and bronze work is to Tubal-Cain in Genesis 4:22.

Human progress in metal working has provided anthropologists and archaeologists with a chronological structure for dating various periods in ancient history. This structure includes the Chalcolithic, or Copper Age (4000–3000 B.C.), the Bronze Age (3000–1200), and the Iron Age (1200–586). There is, of course, much overlapping, and none of these ages has really ended. In fact, when one considers the tonnages used, it should be apparent that we are still living in the Iron or Steel Age.

The metals mentioned in the Bible are as follows:

A. **Bronze.** A metal alloy composed of varying amounts of copper and tin. It is generally believed that bronze had its origin in Mesopotamia. The discovery and production of bronze marked a turning point in human history because of its degree of hardness. The softer copper, which continued to be used for some purposes, was replaced to a great extent by bronze in the production of utilitarian objects. However, nails, knives, statuettes, and other objects continued to be made of pure copper far into the Bronze Age. Cyprus bronze usually contained from 2 to 4 percent tin, while a cup from Nineveh, dated about 1000 B.C., tested over 18 percent tin.

In the Bible bronze was used in ornamental construction (Exod 25:3; 26:11; 27:2), and the manufacture of such utilitarian objects as pots (Lev 6:28) and mirrors (Job 37:18). Cymbals of bronze were used in the temple for worship (1 Chron 15:19). The use of bronze weaponry is found in the reference to the armament of the Philistine warrior Goliath (1 Sam 17:5–38) and the shields made under the direction of Rehoboam (2 Chron 12:10). However, the latter appear to have been primarily objects of decoration or value rather than weapons of war. Job 20:24 speaks of arrows tipped with bronze.

In Hebrew the same word refers to both bronze and pure copper, doubtless because of their similarity. The KJV uses the word *brass,* which at the time of its writing denoted any alloy of copper.

B. **Copper.** Copper is a heavy, reddish-yellow metal. It is frequently found on or near the surface of the ground. Its malleability and accessibility account for its being one of the first metals to be used by early man.

Gold dagger and sheath found attached to a belt in a grave at Ur, twenty-fifth century B.C. Ur, Abraham's city of origin, had one of the most advanced cultures of the world. Courtesy The University Museum, University of Pennsylvania.

Pliny claimed that copper was found first on the island of Cyprus. He also indicated that it was sometimes alloyed with silver and gold.

In the Bible the presence of copper ore in Canaan is cited as one of the benefits of that land (Deut 8:9). The process of smelting copper and other metals is used illustratively in its other references in the OT (Job 28:2; Ezek 22:18, 20; 24:11). In the NT reference is made to the use of copper only in coinage (Matt 10:9; Mark 12:42; Luke 21:2).

C. **Gold.** Gold was used freely and skillfully in the oldest of civilizations. A multitude of gold ornaments in the museums of the world verify this. The earliest evidence of gold mining may be found in rock carvings of Egypt, depicting the washing of gold sands and the melting of gold in a small furnace. This went back to at least 2500 B.C. Strabo describes the country of the Iberians (Spain) as full of metal such as gold, silver, copper, and iron. He tells of mining gold by digging for it in the usual way and also by washing for it (hydraulic mining). Pliny the Elder accurately described the occurrence of placer gold in stream beds, including the finding of nuggets. He also described the process of hydraulic mining. He claimed that a river was brought from a distance and from the heights, with enough fall to wash away whole mountain sides, leaving the gold in sluice baffles. Most surprising of all, Pliny described in some detail the use of mercury to capture the gold from the ore by amalgamation.

Gold is mentioned very early in the Bible (Gen 2:11–12). We are told that in the land of Havilah, in the vicinity of the Garden of Eden, there was gold, and that the gold was good.

Why has man valued gold so highly? Why is gold good? Gold is good and highly prized because it is warmly beautiful. It is enduring, for it never rusts or dissolves away. It retains its beauty. Of the common acids, only a mixture of concentrated nitric and hydrochloric acids (*aqua regia*) will dissolve it. Strong acid alone will have no effect. Pliny mentions gold as the only metal unharmed by fire. In fact Pliny said each time it went through a fire it came out better or more refined than before. Gold is good because it is so adaptable to shaping. It can be melted without harm; it can be hammered into thin leaves because it is extremely malleable. It may easily overlay large objects thus imparting beauty and protection to the whole. It may readily be alloyed with other metals with an improvement of the degree of hardness while still retaining the beauty of gold. In fact Pliny noted correctly that gold comes naturally alloyed with silver. Finally gold has been valued because of its scarcity. It seems reasonable to presume that if the core of the earth is largely iron, the free metals such as gold, platinum, and even cobalt and nickel have been depleted to a great extent because they have dissolved in this core.

Gold is also mentioned at the end of the Bible in Revelation 21:15, 18, 21. Here the most precious of metals is envisioned as constituting the Holy City and its streets. The rod used to measure the city was a gold rod.

There are so many references to gold in the Bible that one must use a concordance to find them all. Exodus 37 describes the construction of the ark of the covenant and other appointments of the tabernacle, all made of gold or overlaid with gold.

When the writer of Job asks where wisdom can be found (Job 28:12), he responds by observing that wisdom is so priceless that gold, silver, and precious stones cannot buy it (28:15–19). It is worthy to note that gold is mentioned five times in this passage, whereas each of the other precious items is mentioned only once.

D. **Iron.** In spite of advances in the use of light metals such as aluminum, magnesium, and beryllium, we are still living in the Iron Age. No other metal rivals iron in the amount produced. The reason for this is that iron ores, chiefly the oxides and carbonates, are abundant in concentrated deposits, the metal is easily won from the ore and varies over a wide range in its properties. By removing impurities, by heat treatment, and by alloying, the strength, hardness, ductility, malleability, resistance to corrosion, appearance, and retention of temper may be varied.

Iron does not occur free in nature. When it is so found it is on such a minute scale that it may be considered a curiosity. Terrestrial-free iron is very likely secondary, having been formed from regular ores by hot carbon or carbon-containing materials, a process that is carried out in blast furnaces today. It is clear that ancient man found meteoric iron and shaped it for utilitarian purposes. Iron beds taken from a grave in Egypt dating from about 4000 B.C. contain a nickel analysis corresponding favorably to that of meteorites. In fact, the Egyptians and people of other cultures referred to iron as the metal from heaven. In ancient religious literature the Egyptians claimed that the firmament of heaven was made of iron. An iron object dating to about 3000 was blasted out of the masonry at the top of the Great Pyramid of Gizeh and is now in the British Museum. No one knows who first discovered the way to reduce iron from ore in a furnace. Evidently the discovery was made in the undetermined past. Egyptian frescoes dated at about 1500 depict small furnaces with men operating bellows or mouth blowpipes. This is the essential principle of the modern blast furnace. The first reference to iron in the Bible is found in Genesis 4:22 where Tubal-Cain is cited as a worker of iron. In Deuteronomy 4:20; 1 Kings 8:51; and Jeremiah 11:4 there is evidence that the Hebrews were familiar with furnaces for the making of iron. There is evidence that as slaves in Egypt they had to work at these furnaces. Their lot must have been difficult. The smith and his forge were well known to Isaiah (44:12 and 54:16). The Philistines hindered the Hebrew occupation of the whole of Canaan because they were skilled in iron working. They prevented the Hebrews from making and maintaining their own tools and weapons by refusing to allow a single smith in all the land. The Israelites were forced to go to the Philistines to sharpen their plowshares, mattocks, axes, and sickles (1 Sam 13:19–20). But the great victories of David ended all this. When David came to power, iron was used freely by the Israelites. Additional items of iron not previously mentioned are as follows:

The bed of Og, the Amorite king of Bashan, was made of iron (Deut 3:11). Og was a giant and needed a large strong bed. It was about thirteen feet (four m.) long and six feet (two m.) wide.

The Israelites feared the Canaanites because they had iron chariots (Josh 17:16, 18).

The spear shaft of Goliath weighed six hundred shekels (roughly fifteen pounds) (1 Sam 17:7).

There is ample evidence that many types of fetters and other implements for binding captives and slaves were made of iron. In addition to these references the term is used in a figurative sense (Ps 2:9; 107:10; Jer 28:13–14).

Pliny in his thirty-fifth book of natural history discusses the working of iron at considerable length. He introduces his discussion with this comment: "Iron serves as the best and the worst of the apparatus of life, inasmuch as with it we plough the ground, plant trees, trim the trees . . . with it we build houses and quarry rocks, and we employ it for all other useful purposes, but we likewise use it for wars and slaughter and brigandage." His further discourses are reminiscent of Isaiah 2:4 concerning beating swords into plowshares and spears into pruning hooks.

E. **Lead.** Free metallic lead is extremely rare. The chief ore is lead sulfide (galena), which often occurs as bright glistening clusters of cubic crystals. The metal is readily obtained from the ore and was known long before it came into common usage. The British Museum had a lead figure of Egyptian origin dated at about 3000 B.C. Lead plates and statuettes have been found in Egyptian tombs of 1200.

References to lead in the Scriptures are as follows:

The high density of lead is noted in Exodus 15:10. In Numbers 31:22 lead is listed along with gold, silver, bronze, iron, and tin. Its use for lettering in rock is noted in Job 19:24. Jeremiah 6:29 speaks of the use of bellows in the processing of the metal. Lead is listed with copper, tin, and iron as metals melted in a furnace (Ezek 22:18, 20) and again with silver, iron, and tin as metals used for monetary exchange (Ezek 27:12). See also Zechariah 5:7–8.

F. **Silver.** At the present time much more silver is obtained as a by-product of the refining of copper and lead than by mining native silver or silver ore. The methods used in this refining were not available to the Hebrews, since it requires the extensive use of electricity, cyanide, zinc, and aluminum. However, silver is ten times as abundant in the crust of the earth as is gold, and much of it was mined by the ancients. Pliny says, "Silver is only found in deep shafts, and raises no hopes of its existence by any signs, giving off no shining sparkles such as are seen in the case of gold." He describes its use for making mirrors and notes that, "the property of reflecting is marvelous; it is generally agreed that it takes place owing to the repercussion of the air which is thrown back into the eyes."

The shekel and talent of silver were used as mediums of exchange. At first this was done by

Two bull figurines, one of solid silver, the other of solid bronze. Early Israelite (Iron) period (c. 1200–1000 B.C.). Courtesy Reuben and Edith Hecht Museum, University of Haifa. Photo Zev Radovan.

weighing out the silver pieces. This is apparent in Job 28:15: ". . . nor can its price be weighed in silver."

Silver was used in conjunction with gold because of its beauty. A great many references to silver and gold are found in the Bible. Only occasionally are the terms reversed as in Esther 1:6, which refers to couches made of gold and silver. When Christ sent out the Twelve, he commanded them to carry neither gold nor silver nor brass in their purses (Matt 10:9).

Many objects made of silver are referred to in the Scriptures. The cup that Joseph had hidden in Benjamin's sack of food was a silver cup (Gen 44:2). Demetrius, the silversmith of Ephesus, made silver shrines for Diana (Acts 19:24).

III. The Common Minerals.

A. **Alabaster** (Matt 26:7; Mark 14:3; Luke 7:37). These passages refer to an alabaster box or jar used to contain a precious ointment. Modern alabaster is a form of gypsum (hydrated calcium sulfate). It is soft, with a hardness of 2, and may be scratched by the thumbnail. It is easily carved and many larger decorative articles like book ends, vases, and paper weights are made of this material. It is usually very light in color, but may be mottled or veined with various colors. The ancients may have used a calcite or aragonite mineral resembling our modern alabaster in its general appearance. A simple test with the thumbnail will distinguish between the two varieties. Calcite has a hardness of 3 and cannot be scratched with the thumbnail. Alabaster is usually formed by the process of water deposition in caves.

Alabaster bottle shaped like a flower. Found in Israel but originates in Egypt. Middle Bronze II (c. 1800–1500 B.C.). Courtesy Reuben and Edith Hecht Museum, University of Haifa.

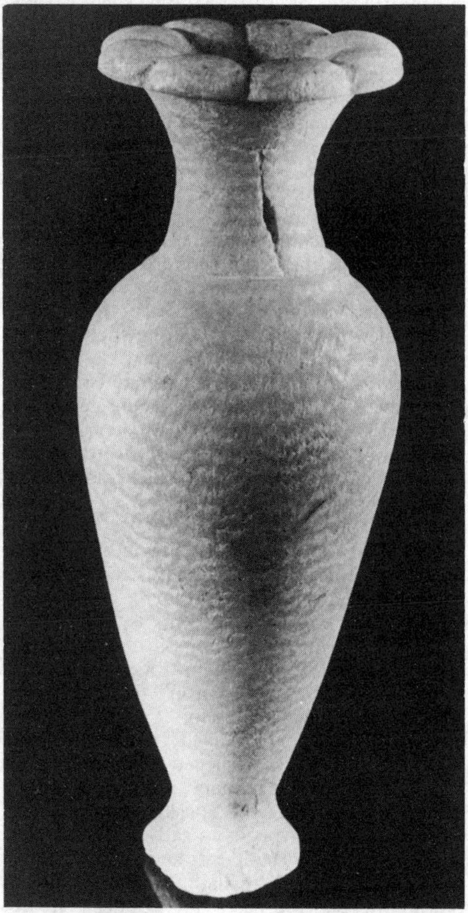

B. **Glass** (Rev 4:6; 15:2; 21:18, 21). Glass is a product of the fusion of silicates, borates, or phosphates. Although its use appears to have been widespread in the ancient world, its place of origin is unknown. The ancient Egyptians were, to the best of our knowledge, the first to make small vessels of glass. It appears in the Bible only in the Book of Revelation where it describes the appearance of the "sea" before the throne, and the purity and transparency of the gold of which the street and wall of the Holy City are made.

C. **Marble** (1 Chron 29:2; Esth 1:6; Song of Songs 5:15; Rev 18:12). Marble is recrystallized limestone, capable of receiving a high polish. Limestone is somewhat impure calcium carbonate. Dolomitic marble contains a considerable

Late Bronze Age (late fifteenth century B.C.) Egyptian glass vessel, with two handles and painted design, found in a cave at Gezer. Courtesy Israel Department of Antiquities and Museums.

Sculptured marble columns of the temple of Artemis at Jerash, ancient Gerasa, in Transjordan. Courtesy Studium Biblicum Franciscanum, Jerusalem.

amount of magnesium carbonate as well as the calcium compound. Marble is used for decorative purposes such as statuary, pillars, and walls of buildings. There is no reason to think that the marble of the Bible was different from the marble of modern times, except in the sense that marble from different quarries varies in color and texture.

D. **Salt.** Salt is extremely abundant. The evaporation of one cubic mile of sea water would leave approximately 140 million tons of salts, most of which would be sodium chloride or common salt. The "salt sea" of the Bible was no doubt the Dead Sea. In most of the many references to salt, either the preservative property or else the savor it adds to food is the point of interest. Jesus states that the children of the kingdom are the salt of the earth (Matt 5:13). He uses the analogy of salt losing its "saltiness." The implication is that Christians must not lose that which makes them distinctive. How could salt lose its "saltiness"? It has been suggested by some that as salt was stored it would eventually react chemically and be salt no more. Under any conditions salt would remain salt. But if stored salt was contaminated with other salts, such as magnesium chloride or sulfate, these salts would attract moisture. In due time enough salt might leach away to leave behind the less soluble contaminants, and this would result in a salt of much poorer quality. The container might then be emptied on a foot path to inhibit the growth of weeds.

E. **Soda** (Job 9:30; Prov 25:20; Jer 2:22). Soda is a term applied today to several forms of sodium. In the Bible it probably refers only to sodium carbonate. This forms a gas with vinegar and effervesces freely. It thus fits the description of the process described in Proverbs 25:20 where it speaks of vinegar poured on soda. In Job 9:30 and Jeremiah 2:22 it is associated with soap. Sodium carbonate would be useful in washing with soap because it acts as a softener of water. It is used today in the making of soap. It is found either in solution in salty seas or in the mud that surrounds such seas.

F. **Sulphur** (Gen 19:24; Deut 29:23; Job 18:15; Ps 11:6; Isa 30:33; 34:9; Ezek 38:22; Luke 17:29; Rev 9:17–18; 14:10; 19:20; 20:10; 21:8). In modern times most sulfur comes from deep deposits and is brought to the surface by hot water and compressed air. Sulfur deposits also may be found in the vicinity of volcanoes. Hot gases such as sulfur dioxide and hydrogen sulfide are emitted and deposit sulfur in the surrounding rock by chemical reaction. Sulfur deposits may also be found in the vicinity of some hot springs that are the relics of previous volcanic action. When sulfur is burned, it gives off a blue flame that forms a gas (sulfur dioxide). This gas is used as a bleaching agent.

In the Bible sulphur is nearly always associated with fire and metaphorically with punishment or devastation. No natural product readily available to the ancients would so completely symbolize the awful punishment to be meted out to the wicked. The flame of burning sulphur is very hot, and the sulfur dioxide gas has a suffocating stench. Hot sulfur eventually turns to a bubbling, dark red, sticky liquid.

G. **Water.** This is the most marvelous and exciting mineral of the Bible. Every modern textbook of mineralogy includes a section on the oxides of nature such as those of silicon, copper, iron, aluminum, etc., but hydrogen oxide heads the list. This extremely abundant mineral is found either in liquid or in solid forms, such as snow and ice. There are more references to this mineral in the Bible than to any other.

As a chemical it is an unusual compound with unusual properties. When it freezes to ice it expands so that it floats. The chemist accounts for most of its odd properties by explaining that hydrogen bonds form between oxygen atoms holding particles together in a framework. Were it not for these hydrogen bonds water would boil away at 150 degrees Fahrenheit *below* zero.

In the Bible the chaotic condition that existed before God formed the earth is described as a watery mass. Water was important for various ceremonies of washing found in Leviticus. Elaborate cisterns and water systems may be found at the sites of certain ancient cities in Israel. The importance of water for life is reflected in its metaphorical usage, such as the water of life in Revelation 21:6. Cleansing with water is also used to depict the process of regeneration (Eph 5:26). TEM

MINES, MINING. An occupation of man that is very ancient, for we read in the description of Eden and its surroundings before the Flood of the "land of Havilah, where there is gold" (Gen 2:11–12); and in the account of the antediluvian Cainite patriarchs, Tubal-Cain "forged all kinds of tools out of bronze and iron" (4:22). In Job 28:1–11 there is mention of "a mine for silver and place where gold is refined. Iron is taken from the earth, and copper is smelted from ore." This is followed by a poetic account of a man digging a mine. In Sinai are very ancient copper mines, worked by the Egyptians as early as Dynasty IV (the great pyramid builders); and, at the head of the Gulf of Aqabah, at Elath, are the remains of Solomon's blast furnaces for copper. At this

One of the ancient copper mines popularly known as "King Solomon's Mines," in the Arabah, north of Elath. The abandoned mine is filled with water from a flood. Archaeological finds indicate that the mines operated chiefly in the Late Bronze and Iron Age. Courtesy Duby Tal.

locality there is a constant strong north wind, and through openings and conduits this wind was used to form a draft for the furnaces. The great development of metalworking in Israel must have come between the time of Saul and the time of Solomon. Compare 1 Samuel 13:19–22, where the Philistines are in the Iron Age, which the Israelites had not yet reached, with the accomplishments of Solomon's time (1 Kings 7:13–50) only about a century later.

The Greeks and the Romans considered mining and metalworking as very ancient, for they pictured Hephaestus or Vulcan, son of Zeus or Jupiter, as a metalworker, a sort of mythological

Relief of an Assyrian minister standing behind King Tiglath-pileser III (745–727 B.C.). Reproduced by courtesy of the Trustees of the British Museum.

"Tubal-Cain." In the time of Moses, the Midianites had gold, silver, brass, iron, tin, and lead (Num 31:22); and the Israelites knew how to cleanse them by fire. Moses described the Promised Land as "a land where the rocks are iron and you can dig copper out of the hills" (Deut 8:9). Although shafts have been found in the "valley of the cave" in Sinai, they do not penetrate far, the reason probably being the inability of the ancients to ventilate their mines. The fact that the Midianites had tin in the days of Moses probably points to a very ancient penetration of the Phoenician ships through the Mediterranean and across to the southern shore of Britain. ABF

MINGLED PEOPLE (Heb. *'ērev,* from *' ărav, to mix*). The same Hebrew word is translated "mixed multitude," "other people," and "all . . . of foreign descent" in some versions of Exodus 12:38 and Nehemiah 13:3. In the former passage the reference is to non-Israelite people who left Egypt with the Israelites. In Jeremiah 25:20 and 50:37 the term is used as an expression of contempt for the mixed blood of certain of Israel's enemies. In Numbers 11:4 such a motley body seduced Israel to sin.

MINIAMIN (mĭn'yà-mĭn, *from the right hand*).
1. A Levite in Hezekiah's time (2 Chron 31:15).
2. Head of a family of priests in Nehemiah's time (Neh 12:17).
3. A priest in the time of Nehemiah (Neh 12:41).

MINISTER (Heb. *shārath, shārēth,* Gr. *diakonos, leitourgos, hypēretēs*). Originally a servant, though distinguished from a slave who may work against his will, and a hireling, who works for wages. Joshua, as a young man, was "minister" to Moses (Exod 24:13 KJV; NIV "aide"), though in rank he was a prince of the tribe of Ephraim (Num 13:8). As minister of Moses, he led the army of Israel against Amalek (Exod 17:8–16) and was permitted to ascend Mount Sinai with Moses. The queen of Sheba, visiting King Solomon, was amazed at the attendance (Hebrew "standing") of his ministers (1 Kings 10:5 KJV). In the NT certain governmental offices are called "God's ministers" (Rom 13:6 KJV). The word *hypēretēs,* which originally meant "an under-rower," is also used for "minister": "And he closed the book and gave it back to the minister [most modern versions have "attendant"] and sat down" (Luke 4:20 KJV). The same word is used of John Mark (Acts 13:5) as an attendant of Paul and Barnabas. God himself has his ministers, the angels (Ps 103:21; 104:4 KJV; NIV "his servants"), who praise him and go about as his messengers. In Jeremiah 33:21–22 God calls the priests of Israel his ministers, and this usage of the word for priests or religious leaders has come over into the Christian church. The Christian minister is not only a servant of God, but he should also make it his business to serve the local church to which he is attached; and lest this be thought to be a degradation of dignity, even our Lord declared,

"For even the Son of Man did not come to be served, but to serve, and to give his life as a ransom for many" (Mark 10:45). The NT word *diakonos,* i.e., "deacon," means "minister" and indicates the duty as well as the privilege of the office. "Deacon" should not be confused with "elder" or "presbyter." ABF

MINNI (mĭn'ī, Heb. *minnî*). Mentioned only in Jeremiah 51:27 as a kingdom associated with Ararat and Ashkenaz as instruments or agents for the destruction of wicked Babylon. It was in what was later called Armenia, and some think that the word "Armenia" is from *har-minni,* i.e., the mountain of Minni. In 719 B.C., Sargon king of Assyria defeated the Minni. The kingdom is little known, and the known references to it are very scarce.

MINNITH (mĭn'ĭth, Heb. *minnîth*). A city of the Ammonites that Jephthah defeated while overcoming this nation. It and Abel Keramim were the easternmost limit of Jephthah's victories (Judg 11:33). It lay four miles (seven km.) north of Heshbon in the tribe of Reuben. It was a source of wheat for the markets of Tyre (Ezek 27:17).

MINT (See PLANTS)

MIRACLES. The word "miracle" (Latin *miraculum*) literally means a marvelous event or an event that causes wonder. Some of the more important biblical words designating miracles are *thauma,* "wonder"; *pele'* and *teras,* "portent"; *gêvhurâh* and *dynamis,* "display of power"; *'ôth* and *sēmeion,* "sign."

The use of "miracle" in Christian theology includes, but goes beyond, the meanings of the ancient words. A miracle is (1) an extraordinary event, inexplicable in terms of ordinary natural forces, (2) an event that causes the observers to postulate a superhuman personal cause, or (3) an event that constitutes evidence (a "sign") of implications much wider than the event itself.

Negatively, miracles should be distinguished in the following ways:

1. Miracles should be distinguished from works of providence. We must recognize that in good use "miracle" has a metaphorical or hyperbolical meaning, such as when we say that every sunrise, every tree, every blade of grass is a "miracle." But works of providence are, for Christians, the ordinary works of God through secondary causes. Unbelievers generally deny the supernatural cause of such events.

However, in the biblical events strictly regarded as miracles, the adversaries of faith acknowledged the supernatural character of what took place. After the healing of the man "crippled from birth . . . , the rulers, elders, and teachers . . . since they could see the man who had been healed standing there with them, there was nothing they could say." But they said, "Everybody living in Jerusalem knows they have done an outstanding miracle, and we cannot deny it" (Acts 3:1–4:22). In the case of the miracle at Lystra (14:8–23) the pagans said, "The gods have come down to us in human form!" With reference to the resurrection of Christ, Paul could ask a Roman court of law to take cognizance of an indisputable, publicly attested fact, for, he said, "it was not done in a corner" (26:26).

2. Miracles are further to be distinguished from the type of answers to prayer that do not constitute "signs" or demonstrative evidence for unbelievers. When Elijah prayed for fire on the altar of the Lord (1 Kings 18:17–46), God answered with a demonstrative miracle that convicted the priests of Baal. In the experience of Christians, however, there are numberless events, constantly recurring, in which those who know the Lord can see the hand of God at work, but in which there is not the demonstrative "sign" element. It is a great mistake for Christians to distort their reports of answered prayer so as to make out "sign" miracles where nothing comparable to the biblical "signs" has occurred. God gives abundant evidence of his love and care without any exaggeration on our part.

3. Miracles of God should also be distinguished from works of magic. In magic the wonder-worker himself possesses a formula that causes the result. The alleged supernatural power is controlled by the performer. Compare Exodus 7:11; 8:7. In miracles of God the results depend wholly on the divine will, and the one who works the miracle is simply an agent for the Lord.

4. Miracles of God must be distinguished from miracles of Satanic or demonic origin. Christ warned in his Olivet Discourse: "For false Christs and false prophets will appear and perform great signs and miracles to deceive even the elect—if that were possible" (Matt 24:24). Paul foretells of the Man of Sin "in accordance with the work of Satan displayed in all kinds of counterfeit miracles, signs and wonders" (2 Thess 2:9; cf. Rev 13:14; 16:14; 19:20).

5. Miracles must also be distinguished from mere exotic occurrences. There are many events in nature that excite wonder, but such matters are evidences of nothing but oddity. Genuine miracles are always "signs" that teach a lesson. Every miracle of God is a part of God's great integrated system of revealed truth.

I. Epochs. The majority of the miracles recorded in the Bible fall into three great epochs. First came the miracles of the Exodus: the burning bush, the ten plagues of Egypt, the numerous miracles between the parting of the Red Sea and the crossing of the Jordan, the fall of Jericho, and the battle of Gibeon. The *first epoch of miracles* came at a time of great spiritual depression. The people in slavery in Egypt had forgotten the name of the Lord their God. Wholly by his grace God brought them out, amalgamated them into a nation at Sinai, and brought them into the Promised Land. In all subsequent history, God's people have looked back to the miracles of the Exodus as a type of divine salvation.

There followed, after the first epoch of miracles, a long period of decline under the judges, and then a revival of godly faith under David and Solomon. During all this time miracles were very few. God did not leave himself without a witness, but the working of miracles was not his chosen method.

Then came a period of idolatrous compromise and "inclusive" religion. The names of the Lord and Baal were hyphenated, and even the good king Jehoshaphat was badly mixed up with idolatrous Ahab (1 Kings 21:25–26; 22:1–50). So God gave the *second epoch of miracles,* centering in the ministry of Elijah and Elisha. By mighty "signs" and works of his grace, God restored and confirmed his pure worship.

The miracle of Jonah and two notable miracles at the time of Isaiah (2 Kings 19:35; 20:9-11) were of outstanding significance, as were two or three special miracles in the experience of Daniel. But from the epoch of miracles in the time of Elijah and Elisha until the time of Christ and the apostles, miracles were again very few. God worked through the prophets, through the providential discipline of the Babylonian captivity, and in other ways. Enough revelation had been given by the time of Malachi for the spiritual life of God's people until the time of the coming of Christ. God's faithful servants were sustained without demonstrative "sign" miracles.

The *third epoch of miracles,* the greatest in all recorded history, occurred in the ministry of Christ and his apostles. It was, in a way, a time of the lowest ebb of spirituality. At the Exodus God's people had forgotten his name. At the time of Elijah and Elisha they had hyphenated his name with the name of Baal. But at the time of Christ and his apostles God's people had made the divinely prescribed system of worship an idolatrous object to such an extent that they were steeped in self-righteousness and hypocrisy. They read the Torah diligently, but they read with a dark veil of hardness over their eyes and hearts. They were so "religious" in their pride that they crucified the Lord of glory. It was to this kind of world that God sent his Son.

Nearly forty demonstrative "sign" miracles wrought by Christ are recorded in the Gospels; but these are selected by the writers from among a much larger number. John says, "Jesus did many other miraculous signs in the presence of his disciples, which are not recorded in this book" (John 20:30).

The ministry of the apostles after Christ's ascension began with the miracle of "languages" on the Day of Pentecost. This miracle recurred until the church organization for this age was well established, and probably until the NT books were all put into circulation. There were numerous other demonstrative miracles. As the author of the Letter to the Hebrews puts it, this "salvation, which was first announced by the Lord, was confirmed to us by those who heard him. God also testified to it by signs, wonders and various miracles, and gifts of the Holy Spirit distributed according to his will" (Heb 2:3–4).

II. Purpose. The purpose of miracles is revelation and edification. After saying that there were many unrecorded miracles of Christ, John adds, "But these are written that you may believe that Jesus is the Christ, the son of God, and that by believing you may have life in his name" (John 20:31). Christ several times expressed his purpose in working miracles. He rebuffed those who had only a desire to see the spectacular. "A wicked and adulterous generation asks for a miraculous sign!" This was not a complete rejection even of idle curiosity, for he followed his rebuke with a powerful reference to Jonah as a type of his own resurrection (Matt 12:39–40; cf. also Luke 23:8). To seek to see miracles is better than merely to seek free food (John 6:26). His miracles were evidence of the genuineness of his message. "For the very work that the Father has given me to finish, and which I am doing, testifies that the Father has sent me" (5:36). He preferred that people would accept his message for its intrinsic worth, but to believe him because of his miracles was not wrong. "Do not believe me unless I do what my Father does. But if I do it, even though you do not believe me, believe the miracles, that you may know and understand that the Father is in me, and I in the Father (10:37–38).

III. The Question of Miracles Today. This is a disturbing question to many. In the ancient church the Montanist party insisted that miracles and predictive prophecy must be perpetual gifts. Christ pointed out that miracles do not occur with any uniform regularity (Luke 4:25–27). In fact, if miracles were regular occurrences, they would cease to be regarded as miracles. Paul's rules for the restriction of the use of foreign languages (1 Cor 14) might be applied by analogy to all miracles. Evidently the miracle of language that occurred on the Day of Pentecost had been confused, in the minds of devout people in Corinth, with mere ecstatic meaningless utterances. Paul points out, "Tongues, then, are a sign, not for believers but for unbelievers" (14:22). And he commands that in Christian assemblies not more than two or, at the most, three, in turn, should be allowed to speak in a foreign language, and "if there is no interpreter, the speaker should keep quiet in the church and speak to himself and God" (14:27–28). At the same time Paul does not forbid the language of untranslatable utterances in private (14:2–5).

If Paul's restrictions were literally carried out in the modern church, making sure that the translator (*diermēneutēs*) is a genuine translator, following known rules of grammar and syntax and vocabulary, the actual miracle of languages as it occurred on the Day of Pentecost would never be interfered with. Rather it would be the better attested; but the counterfeit "miracle" would be eliminated.

If analogous methods were used in examining reports of alleged miracles, genuine miracles would never be hindered, but would be the better attested. At the same time delusions and exaggerations would be prevented.

Some have sought to account for the occurrence or nonoccurrence of miracles on "dispensational" grounds. Accordingly, God's dealings with and his gifts to his people have varied throughout history. Thus, perhaps God used miracles to initiate the present "age of grace" but has withdrawn any such special "gift" that some early believers possessed. It must be recalled, however, that the period of time between Sinai and Calvary is recognized with general unanimity by dispensationalists as one uniform age of "law." Yet this "dispensation" included the epoch of miracles under Elijah and Elisha, as well as long periods during which no miracles were recorded.

From Bible history, and history since Bible times, the fact stands out that God does not choose to reveal himself by demonstrative miracles at all times. On the contrary, there have been long periods of history, even in Bible times, when God did not use miracles (except the "miracle of grace") in his dealings with his people.

The Bible does not specifically say that God cannot or that God will not work demonstrative "sign" miracles in our day. It is, however, a reasonable opinion, not controvertible by any clearly attested facts, that God generally ceased to work through "sign" miracles when the NT was finished; and that it is his will that the "miracle of grace," the witness of the Spirit, answered prayer, and, supremely, the written Word shall be the chief sources of knowledge of himself for his people during this age. It should be clear to all that, except on extremely rare occasions, even the most godly, sacrificial, competent ministers, missionaries, and laymen today do not experience demonstrative "sign" miracles.

A healthy mind, full of faith in God's power and in God's wisdom, without denying that "sign" miracles may occur when God chooses to use them, expects to learn foreign languages by regular processes of study and hard work. A healthy Christian mind expects to observe the ordinary principles of bodily health and sanitation, using such physical provisions of food, shelter, and medicine as divine providence may make available. In spreading the gospel one does expect the convicting ministry of the Spirit and the evidence of transformed lives, but one does not expect, unless God should so choose, that the sudden healing of a man born with twisted feet and ankle bones will gather a crowd to hear the Word preached. One is prepared to serve the Lord, to experience wonderful answers to prayer, and to find that the Word does not return void, regardless of "signs and wonders."

IV. Essential to Christianity. Miracles are an absolutely essential element in Christianity. If Jesus Christ is not God manifest in the flesh, our faith is a silly myth. If he did not arise from the dead in bodily form, the grave being empty and his appearance being recognizable, then we are yet in our sins and of all people most miserable. If the miracle of grace is not verifiable in the transformation of the life of the one who puts his faith in Jesus as his Lord and Savior, then our Christian gospel is a miserable fraud.

V. Rational. The rational nature of miracles has been misconstrued by David Hume and those who follow his positivistic methods. Miracles are not violations of natural law as Hume supposed; they are intelligent acts of a personal God. They are not erratic or exotic occurrences; they are reasonable parts and phases of a cosmic program of revelation and redemption. There is no greater logical problem in the act of God in raising the dead than there is in the act of a person in lifting his hand. We speak or signal to our children and our neighbors with appropriate gestures, and God reveals himself and his plan for us by "signs" or by other means according to his will.

Christianity is indeed a "supernatural" faith, but the distinction between the natural and the supernatural is only a convenient classification of events. From the point of view of the biblical writers it was perfectly natural for God to wrestle with Jacob or to roll back the Red Sea or to raise his Son from the dead.

Consistent, miracle-believing, Christian theism is just as unified in rational thought, just as scientific in its attitude toward evidence and verification, as any laboratory technician who believes that natural law does not exclude intelligent, purposeful, personal causation.

Bibliography: R. C. Trench, *Notes on the Miracles of Our Lord,* 1846, repr. 1949; A. B. Bruce, *The Miraculous Element in the Gospels,* 1886, repr. 1929; B. B. Warfield, *Counterfeit Miracles,* 1918; J. O. Buswell, Jr., *Behold Him,* 1936; C. S. Lewis, *Miracles,* 1947; G. H. Clark, *The Philosophy of Science and Belief in God,* 1964; C. F. D. Moule (ed.), *Miracles,* 1965; E. and M. L. Keller, *Miracles in Dispute—A Continuing Debate,* 1969. JOB

MIRIAM (mĭr'ĭ-ăm, Heb. *miryām,* various suggested meanings). The daughter of Amram and Jochebed and the sister of Moses and Aaron (Num 26:59; 1 Chron 6:3). She showed concern and wisdom in behalf of her infant brother Moses when he was discovered in the Nile by the Egyptian princess (Exod 2:4, 7–8). Miriam first appears by name in Exodus 15:20, where she is called a prophetess and is identified as the sister of Aaron. After passing through the Red Sea, she led the Israelite women in dancing and instrumental accompaniment while she sang the song of praise and victory (15:20–21). In Numbers 12:1 Miriam and Aaron criticized Moses for his marriage to a Cushite woman. Because of this criticism, Miriam was punished by the Lord with leprosy (12:9), but on the protest of Aaron and the prayer of Moses (12:11, 13) she was restored after a period of seven days, during which she was isolated from the camp and the march was delayed. Her case of leprosy is cited in Deuteronomy 24:9. Miriam died at Kadesh and was buried there (Num 20:1). Micah refers to her along with her brothers as leaders whom the Lord provided to bring Israel out of the Egyptian bondage (Mic 6:4). CEDV

MIRMAH (mûr'mȧ, *fraud*). Head of a father's house in Benjamin after the Captivity (1 Chron 8:10).

Bronze mirror from Egypt, New Kingdom, c. 1550–1350 B.C. Courtesy The University Museum, University of Pennsylvania.

MIRROR. Any smooth or polished surface as of glass or of metal that forms images by reflecting light. The mirrors of the serving women were made of brass (Exod 38:8) and so could be used as material for the laver. Elihu in Job 37:18 speaks of the sky as resembling "a mirror of cast bronze." He was, no doubt, thinking of the brightness of the sky as like that of polished metal. Of the inadequacy of these ancient mirrors Paul says (1 Cor 13:12) that "now we see but a poor reflection." James compares a hearer of the word who is not also a doer to "a man who looks at his face in a mirror" (James 1:23–24) and then forgets what he looks like. "Mirror" is a better translation than "glass" or "looking glass," because the material was metal, not glass.

MISGAB (mĭs′găb, Heb. *ha-misgāv, a lofty place*). A town in the high hills of Moab, possibly another name for Moab's capital (Jer 48:1). Thus the NIV rendering, "the stronghold."

MISHAEL (mĭsh′ā-ĕl, Heb. *mîshā'ēl, Who is what God is?*). 1. A cousin of Moses and Aaron, being son of Uzziel, son of Kohath (Exod 6:22; Lev 10:4). He helped dispose of the bodies of Nadab and Abihu, whom the Lord had killed.

2. A man, presumably a Levite, who stood with Ezra at the reading of the Law (Neh 8:4).

3. A prince of Judah, taken captive by Nebuchadnezzar. A chief official of Babylon changed his name to Meshach, a name of disputed, though undoubtedly heathen meaning. Mishael and his companions, Hananiah and Azariah, were thrown into a blazing furnace (Dan 3:19–30) but came out unharmed, having had the fellowship of One who looked like "a son of the gods."

MISHAL (mī′shăl, Heb. *mish'āl*). A Levitical city (Gershonite) in the tribe of Asher (Josh 21:30), called also "Misheal" (19:26 KJV) and "Mashal" (1 Chron 6:74).

MISHAM (mī′shăm). A Benjamite builder of cities (1 Chron 8:12), son of Elpaal.

MISHEAL (See MISHAL)

MISHMA (mĭsh′mȧ, Heb. *mishmā'*). 1. A son of Ishmael and a prince of the Ishmaelites (Gen 25:14; 1 Chron 1:30).

2. Progenitor of a large family of Simeonites through his descendant Shimei (1 Chron 4:25ff.). They held their cities until David's time.

MISHMANNAH (mĭsh-măn′ȧ, *fatness*). A mighty man of Gad, who joined David at Ziklag (1 Chron 12:10).

MISHRAITES (mĭsh′rā-īts). A family of Kiriath Jearim in Judah (1 Chron 2:53).

MISPAR (See MISPERETH)

MISPERETH (mĭs′pē-reth). One who returned with Zerubbabel (Neh 7:7), called "Mispar" in Ezra 2:2.

MISREPHOTH MAIM (mĭs′rē-fŏth mā′ĭm, *hot springs*). A town or a region near Sidon to which Joshua chased the kings of the north who had joined against him (Josh 11:8; 13:6). Perhaps the same as Zarephath where Elijah lodged (1 Kings 17:9–10; Luke 4:26). It is on the coast between Sidon and Tyre.

MIST. 1. Steamy vapor rising from warm, damp ground into a humid atmosphere (Gen 2:6 KJV; NIV "streams").

2. A blinding dimness of vision like that caused by cataracts (Acts 13:11).

3. A part of the description of false teachers in 2 Peter 2:17.

MITE (See MONEY)

MITHCAH (mĭth′kȧ, *sweetness*). Probably a sweet fountain in Arabia Petrea (Num 33:28–29). ASV "Mithkah."

MITHNITE (mĭth′nīt). The family name of

Joshaphat, a mighty man of David (1 Chron 11:43).

MITHRAISM. The cult of Mithras, a Persian sun god, the worship of which reached Rome in or about A.D. 69, by the agency of the eastern legions who set up Vespasian as emperor. It is possible that the cult was known in the capital a century before, but it was the latter half of the first century of the Christian era that saw its strong dissemination in the West, and indeed its notable challenge to Christianity. Based on the trials, sufferings, and exploits of Mithras, the cult appealed to soldiers; and two shrines of Mithraism on Hadrian's wall, one excavated in 1948 at Carrawburgh, and another still covered at Housesteads, reveal the popularity of Mithraism with the British legions. Professor Ian Richmond has established a sequence of destruction and rebuilding at Carrawburgh that he interprets as indicative of the practice of Mithraism or Christianity at local headquarters. The same shrine has a place of ordeal under the altar, for the initiate advanced through various grades by way of physical suffering and endurance. At that site archaeologists were able to establish the fact that chickens and geese were eaten at the ritual feasts and that pine cones provided aromatic altar fuel. December 25 was the chief feast of Mithras, and in fixing on that date for Christmas, the early church sought to overlay both the Mithraic festival and the Saturnalia. Christianity triumphed over Mithraism because of its written records of a historic Christ, and its associated body of doctrine adapted for preaching, evangelism, and the needs of every day. Christianity, too, was universal, excluding neither woman, child, nor slave. It preached salvation by faith and demanded no stern ordeals. EMB

MITHREDATH (mĭth′rē-dăth, Heb. *mithredhāth, given by Mithras,* i.e., by the sun). The Persian name of two men. 1. The treasurer of Cyrus, king of Persia, who had charge of the vessels from the temple (Ezra 1:8).

2. An enemy of the Jews in the days of Artaxerxes, son of Cyrus (Ezra 4:7). He and others slandered the Jews and stopped their work for a time.

MITRE (See DRESS; PRIEST, PRIESTHOOD)

MITYLENE (mĭt-ĭ-lē′nē, Gr. *Mitylēnē*). The name is more properly spelled Mytilene. It was the chief city of Lesbos, a splendid port with a double harbor (Acts 20:14), and a center of Greek culture. It was the home of Sappho and Alcaeus, the early lyric poets, and a considerable maritime and colonizing power. Sigeum and Assos were Mitylene's foundations. Mitylene's history forms the usual checkered story of a Greek state too weak for independence and torn between the demands of rival imperialists—Persia, Athens, and Rome.

MIXED MULTITUDE (See MINGLED PEOPLE)

Ninth century B.C. city gate at Tell en-Nasbeh, identified with Mizpah of Benjamin, viewed from the north. Courtesy Israel Department of Antiquities and Museums.

MIZAR (mī′zȧr, Heb. har *mits'ār, small*). A small peak in the neighborhood of the great Mount Hermon (Ps 42:6). The word may be a common noun, "a little hill."

MIZPAH (mĭz′pȧ, Heb. *mitspâh, mitspēh, watchtower, lookout-post*). As a common noun meaning "watchtower, guardpost" (*mitspēh*), the Hebrew word is found in 2 Chronicles 20:24 and Isaiah 21:8. As a proper noun, it is used of the following:

1. An unidentified town in the territory of Judah (Josh 15:38), in the vicinity of Lachish.

2. An unknown city in Moab (1 Sam 22:3), to which David went to confer with the king of Moab concerning a place of refuge for his parents while he was dodging the armies of Saul.

3. An unidentified region or valley mentioned in Joshua 11:3 (*mitspâh*), and 11:8.

4. A town in Gilead (Judg 11:29; cf. Ramath Mizpah, Josh 13:26).

5. A town in Benjamin (Josh 18:26), tentatively identified as Tell en-Nasbeh (see below).

Mizpah is: (1) A town in Gilead (see no. 4 above and Josh 10:17), which may be associated with Genesis 31:49, where the name is given to a heap of stones set up as a memorial or witness between Jacob and Laban. This town was also the home of Jephthah (Judg 11:34). (2) Most frequently Mizpah refers to the town of Benjamin (no. 5 above).

At Mizpah the Israelites gathered to consider the steps to be taken against Gibeah in the case of the atrocity related in Judges 19 (cf. Judg 20:1, 3; 21:1, 5, 8). Mizpah was one of the cities closely associated with Samuel, for he made the circuit of Bethel, Gilgal, and Mizpah and judged Israel in those places (1 Sam 7:16). At Mizpah, Israel came to meet with Samuel in repentance (7:5–16) and from there they went out to meet the attacking Philistines and to gain the victory that was celebrated by the setting up of the Ebenezer memorial "between Mizpah and Shen." Asa king of Judah fortified Mizpah with stones transported from the building venture of Baasha king of Israel at Ramah (1 Kings 15:22; 2 Chron 16:6). After the destruction of Jerusalem by Nebuchadnezzar in 587/6 B.C., Gedaliah was appointed governor of Judah. He located his headquarters at Mizpah (2 Kings 25:22–23; Jer 40:5–12), and the Jews who remained in the land gathered to him there. Johanan the son of Kareah and the other military leaders came to Mizpah and warned Gedaliah of a plot against his life by Ishmael, son of Nethaniah. Johanan volunteered to kill Ishmael, but Gedaliah rejected the offer (Jer 40:16) and ignored the warning. Ishmael carried out his plot successfully, killing not only Gedaliah but also other Jews and Babylonian soldiers who were there (2 Kings 25:25; Jer 41:1–3). The following day a group of eighty men on a religious pilgrimage arrived from Shechem, Shiloh, and Samaria. Ishmael deceived the men, killed them, and threw them into a cistern, except for ten men who were able to buy their lives. The cistern that Ishmael filled with the dead was part of the defense system that Asa had made against Baasha of Israel (Jer 41:9). Ishmael took captive the remainder of the people of Mizpah, but the captives made their escape when Johanan and others gave pursuit. The survivors then went to Egypt, contrary to the command of the Lord (41:17–42:22). Mizpah also appears in the lists of rebuilders of the walls of Jerusalem (Neh 3:7, 15, 19) and is mentioned by Hosea (5:1) in his rebuke of Israel. Identified with Tell en-Nasbeh about eight miles (thirteen km.) north of Jerusalem, Mizpah was excavated by W. F. Bade (A.D. 1926–36), revealing the main period of occupation as Israelite. Many houses with four rooms typical of the time were found, as well as a ninth-century wall and gate built apparently by Rehoboam. Numerous Hebrew seals and seal impressions were found, one inscribed with "Jaazaniah servant of the king" (probably the Jezaniah who met with Gedaliah at Mizpah, Jer 40:8; 42:1).

Bibliography: C. C. McCowan, *Excavations at Tell En-Nasbeh,* 2 vols., 1947. CFP

MIZPEH (See MIZPAH)

MIZRAIM (mĭz′rā-ĭm, Heb. *mitsrayim,* form and derivation uncertain). 1. The second son of Ham (Gen 10:6; 1 Chron 1:8) is associated with NE Africa, possibly along with his brothers, Cush and Put. Some of the descendants of Mizraim (Gen 10:13–14; 1 Chron 1:11–12) probably are also to be linked with this area.

2. The usual Hebrew word for "Egypt" and always so translated in the RSV.

MIZZAH (mĭz′ȧ, Heb. *mizzâh, terror*). A grandson of Esau through his wife Basemath and their son Reuel. He was reckoned as one of the chiefs of Edom (Gen 36:13, 17).

MNASON (nā′sŏn, Gr. *Mnason*). A well-to-do Cypriot who had a house in Jerusalem, and who furnished hospitality for Paul and those with him on their return from the third missionary journey. He had been a Christian from the early days of the church (Acts 21:16).

MOAB (mō′ăb, Heb. *mô'āv, seed*). 1. Grandson of Lot by incest with his elder daughter (Gen 19:30–38).

2. The nation or people descended from Moab. They settled first at Ar, just east of the southern part of the Dead Sea and quite close to the site of the destroyed cities of the plain. The Lord commanded Moses not to vex them when Israel passed through their vicinity on their way to the Promised Land. However, when Israel had almost reached their destination and were camped in the plains of Moab (Num 22–24), Balak, sensing that he could not save himself from Israel by force of arms, hired Balaam to come and curse Israel. Balaam went to do so; but after being rebuked by the voice of a donkey for his sin, God permitted him to proceed, but on the condition that he would speak only the words God gave him to speak. As a result he prophetically gave blessing to Israel four times. However, he evidently told Balak and the Moabites and Midianites, "Though you cannot conquer Israel by force of arms, you can seduce them." Thus the Moabite girls entered the camp of Israel (Num 31:16) and seduced the

Stele of a Moabite warrior, eighth century B.C. He is clothed in a short kilt held by a belt at the waist, and he holds a spear in his left hand. Found east of the Dead Sea at Rujm el-'Abd. Courtesy Réunion des Musées Nationaux.

The Balu'ah Stele found in Moab and dating from the thirteenth or twelfth century B.C. To the left is a god, clothed in a kilt, wearing the crown of Upper and Lower Egypt and holding a *was* scepter. Before him is a suppliant standing with upraised hands and, to the right, a goddess wearing a long garment and headdress composed of the high crown and feathers. The inscription above is illegible. Courtesy Studium Biblicum Franciscanum, Jerusalem.

men (25:1–9). As a result God sent a plague that killed twenty-four thousand men.

It was on Mount Pisgah in the land of Moab that Moses died.

Nearly a century after the conquest of Canaan, Israel was "subject to Eglon king of Moab for eighteen years" (Judg 3:12–14). Moab was able to gather the Ammonites and the Amalekites against Israel, but when the children of Israel repented and prayed, God raised up Ehud, who killed Eglon and so subdued Moab (3:30). There seems to have been considerable travel between Moab and Judah, for in the days of the judges Elimelech of Bethlehem took his family to Moab to stay during a famine; there his two sons married and died, and Ruth the Moabitess returned with Naomi, married Boaz and became an ancestress of David. David, when in difficulty with King Saul, took his father and mother to the king of Moab for their protection (1 Sam 22:3–4). Later Mesha king of Moab paid heavy tribute to Ahab king of Israel (2 Kings 3:4). After the death of Ahab, he rebelled, but Joram king of Israel with Jehoshaphat of Judah thoroughly defeated him and, so far as possible, ruined his land. From that time on, Moab gradually declined in accordance with the word of the Lord through his prophets. Amos 2:1–3 pronounces the death sentence on Moab; Isaiah 15–16, "the prophecy against Moab," gives in much detail the coming destruction of Moab, and this was fulfilled by Shalmanezer of Assyria or by his successor Sargon. Isaiah points out the prevailing sin of Moab aside from their idolatry: "We have heard of Moab's pride—her overweening pride and conceit, her pride and her insolence" (16:6); and Ezekiel and Jeremiah, a century and a half later, completed the picture. Moab and Seir were to be punished for likening the house of Judah to the other nations (Ezek 25:8–11). Jeremiah 48 depicts both past and future judgments on Moab, and Zephaniah 2:8–11 foretells utter destruction on Moab for their wicked pride.

3. The land of the Moabites. Moab was bounded on the west by the Dead Sea, on the east by the desert, on the north by the Arnon, and on the south by Edom. It is about 3,200 feet (1,000 m.) above sea level and is chiefly rolling country, well adapted for pasturage. Machaerus, the place where John the Baptist was imprisoned and lost his life, was in Moab. ABF

MOABITE STONE, THE. An inscribed stone found in Moab and recording Moabite history. In 1868 F. A. Klein, a German missionary employed by the Church Missionary Society (Church of England), while traveling through the territory formerly occupied by the tribe of Reuben east of the Dead Sea, was informed by an Arab sheik of a remarkable stone inscribed with writing and lying at Dibon, near Klein's route. The stone was bluish basalt, neatly cut into a monument about four by two feet (about one by one-half m.), with its upper end curved and a raised rim enclosing an inscription. Klein informed the authorities of the Berlin Museum, and meanwhile M. Ganneau of the French Consulate at Jerusalem and a Captain Warren made "squeezes" and so secured roughly the material of the inscription. While the French and the Germans were bargaining with the Turks for the stone, the Arabs, with Oriental astuteness, argued that if the stone as a whole was of value it would be far more valuable if cut to pieces, so they built a fire around it, poured cold water over it, and well-nigh destroyed it. However, their purpose was largely thwarted because the inscription had already been ascertained. The fragments of the stone were purchased and pieced together and are now in the Louvre in Paris. The writing consisted of thirty-four lines, in the Moabite language (practically a dialect of the Hebrew) by Mesha, king of the Moabites in the time of Ahaziah and Joram, the sons of Ahab. It gives his side of the account found in 2 Kings 3. It reads, in part: "I, Mesha, king of Moab, made this monument to Chemosh to commemorate deliverance from Israel. My father reigned over Moab thirty years, and I reigned after my father. Omri, king of Israel, oppressed Moab many days and his son after him. But I warred against the king of Israel, and drove him out, and took his cities, Medeba, Ataroth, Nebo and Jahaz, which he built while he waged war against me. I destroyed his cities, and devoted the spoil to Chemosh, and the women and girls to Ashtar. I built Qorhah with prisoners from Israel. In Beth-Diblathaim, I placed sheep-raisers." It seems strange that though Mesha names Omri who had long since died, he does not name his son Ahab, who reigned almost twice as long, and to whom Mesha had paid heavy tribute (2 Kings 3:4). Perhaps he hated his very name. Neither does he mention the sons of Ahab, Ahaziah and Joram, though he warred against them. Probably he had the monument made before the time of his defeat by Joram and Jehoshaphat.

Although the inscription is almost in pure Hebrew, it was written in the old "round" letters, which were later superseded (some say in Ezra's time) by the "square" letters in which Hebrew is printed today. Very ancient Hebrew, and Arabic as well, were written practically without signs for vowel sounds, but the Moabite Stone used the *aleph, waw,* and *yodh* as both consonants and vowels, and also used the silent *he* at the end of the words, just as in the OT. Some have called the Moabite Stone "the earliest important Hebrew inscription" though written in Moabite. Since Moab and Jacob were both descendants of Terah, it is not strange that their tongues should resemble one another. ABF

The Moabite stone, erected by Mesha, king of Moab, and dating back to c. 850 B.C. The basalt slab carries over thirty lines of writing in ancient Moabite. The name of Yahweh is mentioned in line 18. The stone is significant for the language and syntax of Moabite. Courtesy Carta, Jerusalem.

MOADIAH (See MAADIAH)

MOLADAH (mŏl'à-dà, Heb. *môlādhâh, birth*). One of the cities mentioned in Joshua 15 and 19 in the lists both of Judah and of Simeon. It lies about ten miles (seventeen km.) east of Beersheba. Now called Khirbet-el-Milh. At the Restoration, Judah occupied it (Neh 11:26).

MOLE (See ANIMALS)

MOLECH, MOLOCH (mō'lĕk, mō'lŏk, Heb. *ha-mōlekh*). A heathen god, especially of the Ammonites, who was worshiped with gruesome orgies in which children were sacrificed. At least in some places an image of the god was heated and the bodies of children who had just been slain were placed in its arms. The worship of Molech was known to Israel before they entered Canaan, for Moses very sternly forbade its worship (Lev 18:21; 20:1–5). In spite of this prohibition, King Solomon, to please his numerous heathen wives, set up high places for Chemosh and for Molech on Mount Olivet (1 Kings 11:7), though Molech's principal place of worship in and after Manasseh's time was the valley of Ben Hinnom (2 Chron 33:6), a place of such ill repute that Gehenna "the valley of Hinnom") became a type for hell (Matt 5:29–30). The words *Malcham* (Zeph 1:5 KJV), *Milcom* (1 Kings 11:5 KJV), *Molech*, and *Moloch* are all variants of Hebrew words meaning "the reigning one." Later Jews, after making sacrifices to Molech, would often go to worship in the house of the Lord (Ezek 23:37–39), and this impiety was particularly offensive to the Lord (see Jer 7:9–11; 19:4–13). Because of this heathen worship by Israel, God allowed her enemies to rule over her for many years (Ps 106:35–42). ABF

MOLID (mō'lid, *begetter*). An early member of the tribe of Judah, mentioned only in 1 Chronicles 2:29.

MOLTEN SEA (See TABERNACLE)

MONEY. While "the love of money is a root of all kinds of evil" (1 Tim 6:10), the study of money, particularly of money mentioned in the Bible, is rich and rewarding. Jesus and the apostles taught Christians about the proper attitude toward and use of money. The early Christians used money in their daily lives just as Christians and churches do today. Translators of the Bible, however, have always had difficulty finding terms for the various kinds of money in the Bible that indicate their value or purchasing power in Bible times. Therefore, a knowledge of the nature and value of ancient money is very helpful to the Bible reader in understanding the Word today.

I. A Brief History of Money. Money in the sense of stamped coins did not exist in Israel, so far as is known, until after the Exile. Before this time exchange of values took place by bartering; i.e., trading one thing for another without the exchange of money. This method was followed by the weight system, later by minted coins and still later by paper money, until today we have the credit system by which one may live, buy, and sell without the physical transfer of money at all. Wealth is first mentioned in the Bible in connection with Abraham (Gen 12:5): "He took his wife Sarai, his nephew Lot, *all the possessions they had accumulated*" (cf. 12:16, 20). The three main items of wealth in the ancient world are listed in Genesis 13:2, and Abraham had all three: "Abram had become very wealthy in *livestock* and in *silver* and *gold*." Among the Romans the word for money was *pecunia*, which is derived from *pecus*, the Latin word for cow or cattle. Perfumes and ointments also had great value. Besides gold, the Magi brought frankincense and myrrh to worship the newborn King.

II. The Shekel. The first metal exchange was crude, often shapeless, and heavy so as to approximate the value of the item purchased in actual weight. The buyer usually weighed his "money" to the seller. The Jewish shekel was such a weight (*shekel* means "weight"). It was based on the Babylonian weight of exchange, generally of gold, silver, bronze, and even iron. Among the Jews the shekel was used for the temple tax, the poll tax, and redemption from the priesthood (Exod 30:11–16; 13:13; Num 3:44–51). Since Jesus was a firstborn son not of the tribe of Levi, his parents redeemed him from the priesthood (Luke 2:21ff.) by payment of a shekel, worth about a day's wages at the time. The redemption shekel, we know from the discovery of a piece believed to be from the days of the Maccabees (175–140 B.C.), has on the obverse (front) a pot of manna (Exod 16:33) with the legend (writing or inscription) "Shekel Israel." On the reverse is Aaron's budding rod (Num 17:8) with the legend in Hebrew letters, "Jerusalem the Holy." Other weights mentioned in the Bible are: *talent* (circle), *māneh* (part), *gērâh* (grain), and *beqa'* (half shekel). It required three thousand shekels to equal one talent of silver, which reveals that the ten thousand talents the unmerciful servant owed his master (Matt 18:23–25) was an overwhelming debt. The *pound* (Luke 19:13) is a translation of the old weight *mina* or *māneh* (Greek: *mna*). Since a talent was sixty minas, a mina equaled fifty shekels in Attic weight and one hundred shekels in OT weight, which means that in the parable the gift of the Lord to his people is a most precious gift, namely, the gospel.

Silver shekel struck in A.D. 68. The obverse (right) depicts the Omer cup of the temple surrounded by ancient Hebrew inscription: "Shekel of Israel"; above the cup is a date: "Year 3." The reverse (left) has a branch with three pomegranates; the inscription is: "Jerusalem the Holy." Courtesy Reuben and Edith Hecht Museum, University of Haifa.

III. Beginning of the Coin System. The Hebrews were not the first people to use minted coins. Except for a few brief periods of independence, they were compelled to use the coinage of their pagan conquerors. Thus in the Bible we find a wide variety of coins—mainly Greek, Roman, and Jewish—all used by the same people. Most historians believe that the earliest money pieces were struck about 700 B.C. in the small kingdom of Lydia in Asia Minor. These early Lydian "coins" were simply crude pieces of metal cut into small lumps of a standard weight and stamped with official marks to guarantee the value. The Egyptians also developed such a system. Later the quality of the metal and the image on the coin indicated the worth in buying power, much like today. It is believed that the Jews first became acquainted with the coinage of the Babylonians and Persians during the Captivity and that they

A hoard of ancient Tyrian and Jewish shekels and the vessel in which they were found, dated A.D. 68. On loan from the Reifenberg family. Courtesy Israel Museum, Jerusalem.

carried these coins with them when they returned to Palestine.

IV. The Drachma. After 330 B.C. the world-conquering Greeks developed the Persian and Babylonian coinage, and their own, into something of a fixed world system. Animals, natural objects, and the Greek gods were used as symbols on the coins. Each coin was made individually with hammer, punch, and die. The Greeks called these coins drachmas (*drachma* means "handful") of which there was a variety with about the same value. Later the terms *drachma* and *shekel* were used more or less interchangeably. The "lost coin" (Luke 15:8) was a silver drachma equivalent to a Roman denarius, a day's wages. The temple or half-shekel tax (Matt 17:24) was a didrachma. Another drachma was the tridrachma of Corinth, a silver coin about the size of our quarter with the head of Athena on one side and the winged horse Pegasus on the other. It was worth a day's pay and no doubt Paul earned it making tents and used it for payment of passage on ships during his journeys. A Greek coin Paul also may have "spent" is the now-famous "bee coin," a silver tetradrachma of Ephesus dating back to 350 B.C. All these drachmas were about equal in value to the Jewish shekel.

Drawing of silver tridrachma of Corinth, c. 300 B.C. Obverse: winged horse Pegasus. Reverse: the goddess Athena. Courtesy Carta, Jerusalem.

V. The Stater. The coin Peter found in the fish's mouth was the Greek stater (Matt 17:27). Since the temple tax was a half-shekel, the stater would pay for two. Many authorities believe that the stater really was the tetradrachma of Antioch or Tyre since these coins were accepted at the temple. It is believed that the thirty pieces of silver (Matt 26:15; 27:3–5) that bought the greatest betrayal in history were these large silver coins, tetradrachmas of either Tyre or Antioch from about 125 B.C. In Exodus 21:32 we read that thirty shekels was the price of a slave.

VI. The Assarion. The Greek assarion is mentioned twice in the NT (Matt 10:29; Luke 12:6): "Are not two sparrows sold for a penny?" (see "assarion" in NIV footnote). In the Roman Empire this Greek coin was small in both size and value, and the English translators simply translated "penny" as a similar small coin with which the English people would be familiar.

VII. Lepton and Kodrantes (Widow's Mite). During pre-Roman times under the Maccabees (175–140 B.C.) the Jews for the first time were allowed to issue money of their own. One such piece, as we have seen, was the shekel. Another piece was the lepton, a tiny bronze or copper coin, which we know as the "widow's mite," from the famous incident in Mark 12:42 and Luke 21:2. *Lepton* was translated "mite" in the KJV because it was the coin of least value among coins, as is clearly implied in Luke 12:59; NIV has "penny" there but "two very small copper coins" in the other two passages, adding that they were worth "only a fraction of a penny." Even the metal was inferior and deteriorated easily. This coin should really be the "penny" of the Bible, not the denarius. The coins, in contrast to those of pagan rulers, had pictures from their religious history and agriculture instead of gods and men, obeying the command, "You shall not make for yourself an idol in the form of anything" (Exod 20:4). A farthing (Gr. *kodrantēs*, Matt 5:26; Mark

Silver tetradrachma of Ephesus, drawn from coin minted c. 350 B.C. Obverse: bee. Reverse: stag, and palm tree. Both creatures were symbols of the goddess Diana of the Ephesians. Courtesy Carta, Jerusalem.

12:42), twice the value of a mite, was like a two-cent piece.

VIII. The Denarius. The most interesting coin of the Bible is the Roman denarius (Gr. *denarion*), known by collectors as the "penny" of the Bible because of this translation in KJV. This silver coin, which looks like our dime, was the most common Roman coin during the days of Jesus and the apostles. Collectors have been able to obtain originals of all twelve Roman emperors (Augustus to Nerva) who reigned during the NT period, 4 B.C. to A.D. 100. There were also gold denarii, but these were generally special issues and not nearly so numerous. The Romans as well as the Greeks struck mainly silver coins (alloys) and kept large government-owned silver mines throughout the empire, e.g., at Antioch and Ephesus. When Paul writes, "The love of money is a root of all kinds of evil," he really says in Greek, "The love of *silver* (*philargyria*) . . ." (cf. Luke 16:14; 2 Tim 3:2).

The true value of the denarius may be seen in our Lord's parable of the laborers in the vineyard: "He agreed to pay them a denarius for the day and sent them into his vineyard" (Matt 20:2, 10). This was the normal rate, the equivalent of what a Roman soldier also received. When the Samaritan (Luke 10:35) gave the innkeeper two days' wages and was willing to pay anything more above that amount to aid an unknown stranger, he showed how great his love for his neighbor was.

The denarius is mentioned in the miracle of feeding the five thousand (John 6) when Philip declared (6:7), "Eight months' wages would not buy enough bread for each one to have a bite!" Similar light is thrown on the generous act of Mary, who anointed Jesus with perfume that, according to Judas, was "worth a year's wages" (12:3–5). See also the reference in Revelation 6:6.

The denarius was also the "tribute money" imposed by the Romans on the Jewish people. The "image" on the denarius handed our Lord in Matthew 22:19 was the head of either Caesar Augustus (43 B.C. to A.D. 14) or that of Tiberius Caesar (A.D. 14–39). On it Caesar's name was spelled out entirely to the right of the head, as in the case of a coin that has survived: CAESARAVGVSTVS. To the left of the head are the following Latin abbreviations, all run together: DIVIMPPATERPATRIAE. DIV means "divine," IMP is "imperator," PATER PATRIAE is Latin for "Father of His Country." On the reverse one sees the figures of two Caesars, and above and around the figures the Latin abbreviations: AVGVSPONCOSTRPGER. AVGVS is "Augustus"; PON is "Pontifex Maximus" (religious ruler or "Highest Priest"); COS is "consulship"; TRP is "Tribuncia Potestate," tribune power, civil head of the state. Below the images is the word CAESARES, Latin for "Caesars." From this coin alone one can discern that the Roman emperor was an absolute monarch, head of both state and religion.

To study and handle these coins, some over two thousand years old, makes one feel close to the people who lived in Bible days, and helps us understand the times in which they lived. A study of the denarius reveals that this coin was not only a medium of exchange, but a disseminator of information and propaganda for the emperor. This was an age without newspapers! The Roman emperors believed the people read the legends on the coins and went to much trouble to change them often, sometimes every year. The coins also yield much historical data, i.e., the dates of the emperors, and help to establish the historicity of the Bible.

The value of coins fluctuated much in ancient times, making it difficult to state the exact value of each coin. The government issued money through moneychangers, and often the rate of exchange varied according to what a changer was willing to give on a certain day. The denarius became much less valuable after the second century.

To give the value of Bible coins in modern terms can be misleading. Many modern translators simply transliterate the Greek and Latin names (denarius, shekel, assarion, etc.), and allow the Bible reader to interpret for himself the value of the coins.

Bibliography: E. Rodgers, *A Handy Guide to Jewish Coins,* 1914; A. Reifenbery, *Israel's History in Coins from the Maccabees to the Roman Conquest,* 1953; F. A. Banks, *Coins of Bible Days,* 1955; L. Kadman et al., *The Dating and Meaning of Ancient Jewish Coins,* 1958; E. W. Klenowsky, *On Ancient Palestinian and Other Coins,* 1974. LMP

MONEYCHANGER (See CHANGERS OF MONEY)

MONOTHEISM (mŏn′ō-thē-ĭzm, from Gr. *monos, one, theos, god*). The doctrine or belief that there is but one God. Atheism is the belief that there is no god; polytheism, that there is more than one god; monolatry, the worship of one god as supreme, without denying there are other gods; and henotheism, belief in one god, though not to the exclusion of belief in others. There are three great monotheistic religions: Judaism, Christianity, and Islam, the latter two having their origin in the first. According to the Bible, man was originally a monotheist. This has been denied by the school of comparative religion, which teaches that monotheism was a late development in human religious experience. It holds that the religion of Israel was not originally monotheistic but that it gradually became so through the influence of the prophets. W. Schmidt, S. M. Zwemer, and others have shown, on the contrary, that polytheism was a late development. The Christian doctrine of the Trinity does not conflict with the monotheism of the OT. Rather, the manifold revelation of God contained in the OT is crystallized in the NT into the supreme doctrine of the Three Persons. See also JEHOVAH. SB

MONSTERS (See ANIMALS)

MONTH (See CALENDAR; TIME)

MOON (See ASTRONOMY)

MORASTHITE (See MORESHETH GATH)

MORDECAI (môr′dē-kī, Heb. *mordekhay,* from *Marduk,* chief god of Babylon). 1. A leader of the people of Judah during the return of Zerubbabel from exile (Ezra 2:2; Neh 7:7).

2. The deliverer of the Jews in the Book of Esther. He was a Benjamite who had been deported during the reign of Jehoiachin (Esth 2:5–6). He lived in Susa (KJV "Shushan"), the Persian capital, and brought up his cousin Esther, whose parents were dead (2:7). When Esther was taken into the royal harem, Mordecai forbade her to reveal her nationality (2:20); yet he remained in close connection with her. Mordecai discovered at the palace gate a plot against the king. By informing Esther of the plot, he secured the execution of the two eunuchs responsible (2:19–23). When Haman was made chief minister, Mordecai aroused his wrath by refusing to bow before him. To avenge the slight, Haman procured from the king a decree to destroy the Jews (ch. 3). Mordecai then sent Esther to the king to seek protection for her people (ch. 4). Haman meanwhile prepared a high gallows on which he planned to hang Mordecai (ch. 5). By a singular, highly dramatic series of events, Haman fell from favor and was hanged on the gallows he had prepared for Mordecai (ch. 7). Mordecai

succeeded him as chief minister of the king (ch. 8). Thus the Persian officials everywhere assisted the Jews, who killed their enemies and instituted the feast of Purim to celebrate their deliverance (ch. 9). The Book of Esther ends with an account of the fame and dignity of Mordecai (ch. 10). In the apocryphal additions to Esther, Mordecai is glorified still more. He is a favorite character in the rabbinical literature also. JBG

MOREH, HILL OF (mōr'ĕ, Heb. *môreh, teacher*). Mentioned only in Judges 7:1. Near this hill the Midianites were camped when Gideon attacked them. Although it cannot certainly be identified, most scholars believe the Hill of Moreh to be present-day Jebel Nabi Dahi, sometimes called the Little Hermon, to the NW of the Plain of Jezreel, about eight miles (thirteen km.) NW of Mount Gilboa and one mile (one and one-half km.) south of Nain.

MOREH, TREE OF (NIV tree; NASB, RSVoak ; KJV plain). Mentioned in Genesis 12:6 as a place near Shechem where Abraham camped and erected an altar to the Lord. It was probably the tree under which Jacob later buried the amulets and idols his family had brought from Haran (Gen 35:4). In Deuteronomy 11:30 there is mention of "the great trees of Moreh" as a landmark near Ebal and Gerizim. Sacred oaks have been known in Palestine from early times. Probably believed to be the abode of ancestral spirits by the Canaanites, they were thought to have oracular powers and may have been tended by priests, as are cedars of Lebanon today.

MORESHETH GATH (mō'rĕsh-ĕth găth, *possession of Gath*). A town mentioned only in Micah 1:14 in a group of places in the Judah-Philistine border area. Micah calls himself an inhabitant of Moresheth (Mic 1:1; Jer 26:18)—probably the same place. Gath may have been added to the name to indicate that this was the Moresheth that is near Gath. It may be identified with Tell ej-Judeideh, about five miles (eight km.) west of Gath in the Shephelah.

MORIAH (mō-rī'ȧ, Heb. *mōrîyâh*). A land or district where Abraham was told to offer up Isaac (Gen 22:2). It was about a three day's journey from Beersheba where Abraham was living when given the command. Its location is not given. Jewish tradition has identified it with Jerusalem; Samaritan tradition identifies it with Mount Gerizim. According to 2 Chronicles 3:1, Solomon built the temple on Mount Moriah, where God had appeared to David (1 Chron 21:15–22:1). Whether this is the same Mount Moriah mentioned in the account of Abraham is not certain.

MORNING SACRIFICE (See OFFERINGS)

MORNING STAR (See DAYSTAR)

MORTAL, MORTALITY. In the OT (only in Job 4:17) this represents the Hebrew *'ĕnôsh* (lit. "man"), translated "mortal man." In the NT it is the translation of *thnētos*—subject to death (Rom 8:11; 1 Cor 15:53–54). "Mortality" occurs only in 2 Corinthians 5:4 and is a translation of the same Greek word.

MORTAR. 1. A bowl-shaped vessel of stone or basalt rock in which grain, spices, etc., were crushed with the use of a pestle. The manna was so ground before cooking (Num 11:8; cf. Prov 27:22).

2. A substance used to bind bricks or stones together in a wall. Mud or clay was often used (Nah 3:14); for better houses, mortar made of sand and lime was used. Some have thought that Ezekiel 13:10–11, 14–15, refers to poorly mixed mortar (KJV "untempered morter"). Recent scholars, however, believe the passage to refer to whitewash (NIV, RSV) applied over a poorly made wall to disguise its weakness. In Babylon, bitumen was used for mortar (Gen 11:3 RSV). Many walls in Palestine were made by piling up large stones, using smaller stones, without mortar, to fill in the spaces between (cyclopean walls).

Mortar and pestle on the right from En Gev, Upper Paleolithic period. Mortar on the left dates from Late Mesolithic and was found in excavations at Eynan in Upper Galilee. Courtesy Israel Department of Antiquities and Museums.

MOSAIC. A picture or design made by setting tiny squares or cones of varicolored marble, limestone, or semiprecious stones in some medium such as bitumen or plaster to tell a story or to form a decoration. Mosaics are one of the most durable parts of ancient structures and often are the only surviving part. Mosaics have survived from ancient Sumer from as early as 2900 B.C. They were widely used in the early Christian and Byzantine buildings in Palestine, and remaining examples throw considerable light on ancient biblical customs and afford insight into early Christian beliefs and symbols.

Very famous is the fine mosaic picture-map of Jerusalem from the floor of a church in Madaba, probably from the sixth century A.D. This is one of the earliest maps known from Palestine. The mosaics from the Arab palace at Khirbet al-Mafjar (near Jericho) are among the most beautiful known. Ancient Palestinian synagogues have yielded interesting designs and even pictorial art, as, e.g., the Beth Alpha synagogue, with its large circular representation of the zodiac, and the scene of Abraham sacrificing Isaac. JBG

MOSERAH (mō-sē'rȧ, *bond*). An encampment of the Israelites in the wilderness near Bene Jaakan (Deut 10:6). In KJV it is Mosera. In Numbers 33:30 the plural form Moseroth is used as the name of the place. The site is unknown, but it was near Mount Hor, by the border of Edom.

MOSES (Heb. *mōseheh*, Egyp. *mēs, drawn out, born*). The national hero who delivered the Israelites from Egyptian slavery, established them as an independent nation, and prepared them for entrance into Canaan. Exact dates for the life of Moses are dependent on the date of the Exodus. On the basis of an early date for the Exodus, c. 1440 B.C., Moses was born about 1520. Some scholars date the Exodus as late as 1225. (For a brief discussion and bibliography on various dates, see Samuel J. Schultz, *The Old Testament Speaks,* 1960, pp. 47–49.)

Moses was born of Israelite parents in the land of Egypt (Exod 2:1–10). Perilous times prevailed. Not only were the Israelites enslaved, but a royal edict designed to keep them in subjection ordered the execution of all Israelite male children at birth. Hidden among the reeds near the river's bank, Moses was discovered by Pharaoh's daughter. So favorably was she disposed toward this Hebrew babe that she requested Moses' mother to nurse him until he was old enough to be taken to the royal court, where he spent the first forty years of his life.

Little is narrated in the Book of Exodus regarding the early period of the life of Moses. Stephen in his address to the Sanhedrin (Acts 7:22) asserts that Moses was not only instructed in the science and learning of the Egyptians but also was endowed with oratorical ability and distinctive leadership qualities. The court of Egypt provided educational facilities for royal heirs of tributary princes from city-states of the Syro-Palestinian territory subject to the Egyptian rulers. Consequently Moses may have had classmates from as far north as the Euphrates River in his educational experiences in the Egyptian court.

Moses' first valiant attempt to aid his own people ended in failure. While trying to pacify two fellow Israelites, he was reminded that he had killed an Egyptian (Exod 2:11–25). Fearing the

Drawing of Moses and the burning bush, from a wall painting in the synagogue at Dura-Europos, Syria, third century. Courtesy Carta, Jerusalem.

vengeful hand of Pharaoh, Moses escaped to Midian, where he spent a forty-year period in seclusion.

In the land of Midian Moses found favor in the home of a priest named Jethro (also known as *Reuel* in Hebrew or *Reguel* in Greek). In the course of time he married Jethro's daughter Zipporah. As shepherd of his father-in-law's flocks Moses gained firsthand geographical knowledge of the territory surrounding the Gulf of Aqabah. Little did he realize that through this area he would one day lead the great nation of Israel!

The call of Moses was indeed significant. Confronted with a bush afire, he was given a revelation from God, who commissioned him to deliver his people Israel from Egyptian bondage (Exod 3). Fully acquainted with Pharaoh's power, Moses was assured of divine support in contesting the authority of the ruler of Egypt. He furthermore anticipated the lack of confidence and the reluctance of the Israelites to accept him as a leader. To counter this, God assured him that the great *I AM* was about to fulfill his promise made to the patriarchs to redeem Israel from bondage and settle them in the land of Canaan (Gen 15:12–21). In addition two miraculous signs—Moses' staff changed to a serpent and his hand became leprous and later was healed—were provided as evidence for the verification of divine authority (Exod 4:1–17). Finally, Moses was assured of Aaron's support in his divine commission to deliver the Israelites from the powerful clutch of Pharaoh. Accompanied by his wife Zipporah and their two sons, Moses returned to the land of Egypt.

In a series of ten plagues Moses and Aaron countered Pharaoh's attempt to retain Israel in bondage (Exod 7–11). As a whole these plagues were directed against the gods of Egypt, demonstrating God's power to the Egyptians as well as to the Israelites. Pharaoh immediately expressed his attitude of resistance, retorting, "Who is the LORD, that I should obey him and let Israel go? I do not know the LORD, and I will not let Israel go" (5:2). As Pharaoh continued to resist, his heart hardened. Finally the last plague brought judgment on all the gods of Egypt, as the firstborn sons were killed throughout the land. Then Pharaoh complied with Moses' demand and allowed the Israelites to leave.

On the eve of Israel's dramatic departure the Passover Feast was initially observed (Exod 12). Each family unit that followed the simple instructions of killing a year-old male lamb or goat and applying the blood to the doorposts and lintel of their home was passed by in the execution of divine judgment. The directions given (Exod 12:3–4) for the choice of the Passover lamb stressed the equivalence that was to be made between the lambs and the people who would find shelter beneath the shed blood. This accords with the word spoken to Moses even before he entered Egypt: "Israel is my firstborn son" (4:22). Passover night saw the climax of the context of the firstborn sons. All the firstborn of Egypt died (12:29), but the Lord's firstborn was redeemed by the blood of the lamb. In a special sense it was the actual firstborn of every Israelite household that was spared this dreadful but still only token divine judgment. Therefore, the firstborn son of every Israelite family belonged to God. Immediately after the partaking of this Passover meal consisting of meat, unleavened bread, and bitter herbs, the Israelites left Egypt. The annual observance of the Passover on the fourteenth day of Abib (later known as Nisan) was to remind each Israelite of the miraculous deliverance under Moses.

The exact route by which Moses led the Israelites, who numbered some 600,000 men, plus women and children, is difficult to ascertain. Succoth, Etham, Pi Hahiroth, Migdol, and Baal Zephon are place-names with imprecise meanings and whose geographical identifications are uncertain. When the Israelites reached the Red Sea (Sea of Reeds) they were threatened by the Egyptian armies from the rear (Exod 14). As they appealed to Moses, divine protection was provided in the pillar of cloud that barred the Egyptians from overtaking them. In due time a strong east wind parted the waters for Israel's passage. When the Egyptian forces attempted to follow they were engulfed in a watery grave. Miriam, Moses' sister, led the Israelites in a song of victory (15:1–21).

Under divine direction Moses led Israel southward through the Desert of Shur (Exod 15:22–27). At Marah bitter waters were sweetened, at Elim the Israelites were refreshed by twelve springs of water and seventy palm trees, and in the wilderness of Sin daily manna was supplied, solving the food problem for this great multitude throughout their years of desert wanderings until they reached the land of Canaan (Exod 16). At Rephidim Moses was commanded to strike the rock, which brought forth a gushing water supply for his people (17:1–7). Confronted by an Amalekite attack, Moses prevailed in intercessory prayer with the support of Aaron and Hur, while Joshua led the armies of Israel in a victorious battle (17:8–16). In his administrative duties Moses appointed seventy elders to serve under him in accordance with Jethro's advice. In less than a three months' journey from Egypt the Israelites settled in the environs of Mount Sinai (Horeb), where they remained for approximately one year (Exod 18–19).

In this wilderness encampment Moses became the great lawgiver through whom Israel's religion was revealed. As a representative for his people Moses received the law from God. This law constituted God's covenant with his newly delivered nation. In turn the congregation ratified this covenant (Exod 20–24), which included the Ten Commandments, also known as the Decalogue. To enable the Israelites to worship their God properly Moses was given detailed instructions for the building and erection of the tabernacle. These plans were carefully executed under Moses' supervision. At the same time the Aaronic family, supported by the Levites, was designated for their priestly service and carefully equipped for their ministration (Exod 25–40). Details concerning various sacrifices, laws for holy living, and the observance of feasts and seasons were set forth through Moses as God's prescription for his people Israel (Lev 1–27). In this manner the Israelites were distinctively set apart from the religious and cultural pattern of Egypt and Canaan.

Moses also supervised the military census and organization of the Israelites during this encampment in the Sinaitic peninsula. The tabernacle with its court occupied the central position. Since the firstborn of every Israelite family belonged to God by virtue of being spared during the last plague in Egypt, provision was now made for a Levite as a substitute. Consequently the Levites were placed immediately around the court, with Moses and the Aaronic family located at the east end before the entrance to the tabernacle. The other tribes were divided into four camps—each camp composed of three tribes—with the camp of Judah taking the place of leadership ahead of the priestly family.

Guidance and protection were provided for Moses and his people throughout this wilderness journey in the pillar of cloud and fire that was visible day and night. Representing the presence of God with his people, this cloud first made its appearance in preventing the Egyptians from overtaking them (Exod 13:21–22; 14:19–20).

Mount Sinai (Jebel Mousa), the traditional site where Moses received the law from God (Exod 19:16–19). Courtesy Israel Government Press Office.

During Israel's encampment the cloud hovered over the tabernacle. Efficient human organization and responsible leadership provided the counterpart to the divine guidance conveyed by the cloud. Silver trumpets were used to assemble the leaders as well as to alert the people whenever divine indication was given en route. An efficient organization was in evidence whether Israel was encamped or journeying. Law and order prevailed throughout (Num 1:1–10:10).

In an eleven-day march northward from the Sinaitic peninsula of Kadesh, which was only about forty miles (sixty-seven km.) SW of Beersheba, Moses not only encountered the murmurings of the multitude but was also severely criticized by Miriam and Aaron (Num 11–12). The grumbling crowds who hungered for the meat they had eaten in Egypt were satiated to the point of sickness when quails were supplied in excessive abundance. Aaron and Miriam were likewise humiliated when the latter was temporarily subjected to leprosy.

While at Kadesh, Moses sent out twelve representatives to spy out the land of Canaan (Num 13–14). The majority report, given by ten spies, influenced the Israelites to demonstrate their unbelief. In open rebellion they threatened to stone Joshua and Caleb, the two spies who exercised faith and recommended that they should conquer and occupy the land promised to them. When God proposed to destroy the rebellious and unbelieving Israelites, Moses magnanimously responded with intercession in behalf of his people. The final verdict involved all of the people who had been twenty years of age and older at the time of the Exodus: they were doomed to die in the wilderness. Joshua and Caleb were the only exceptions.

Relatively little is recorded about Moses' leadership during the thirty-eight years of wilderness wandering (Num 15–20). Not only was the political leadership of Moses challenged by Dathan and Abiram, but Korah and his supporters contested the ecclesiastical position of Aaron and his family. In the course of these rebellions fourteen thousand people perished in divine judgment. Furthermore all Israel was given a miraculous sign when, among the twelve rods representing the tribes of Israel, Levi's rod produced buds, blossoms, and almonds. With Aaron's name inscribed on this rod the Aaronic priesthood was securely established.

The Israelites, denied permission to use the highway through the land of Edom, were led from Kadesh to the Plains of Moab by way of the Gulf of Aqabah. En route Moses himself forfeited entrance into the Promised Land when he struck the rock that he should have commanded to supply water for his people (Exod 20). When a scourge of serpents caused many murmuring Israelites to die, Moses erected a bronze snake, which offered healing to all who turned to it in obedience (21:4–9). This incident was used by Jesus in explaining his own death on the cross and the simple principle of salvation involved (John 3:14–16).

When Moses bypassed Moab and led the Israelites into the Arnon Valley, he was confronted by two Amorite rulers—Sihon, king of the Amorites, and Og, king of Bashan. Israel defeated both kings and as a result claimed the territory east of the Jordan River, which was later allotted to Reuben, Gad, and half of the tribe of Manasseh. With this Amorite threat removed, the Israelites settled temporarily in the Plains of Moab, north of the Arnon River (Exod 21:10–35).

Balak king of Moab was so disturbed about Israel's encampment near his people that he chose a subtle way to bring about the ruin of God's covenant people (Num 22–25). He enticed Balaam, a prophet from Mesopotamia, with rewards of riches and honor, to curse Israel. Balaam accepted Balak's invitation. While en route he was vividly reminded by his donkey that he was limited in his oracles to speak only God's message. Although the Moabite leaders prepared offerings to provide an atmosphere for cursing, Balaam was restricted to pronounce blessings for Israel each time he spoke. God did not allow his chosen people to be cursed. When Balaam was dismissed, his parting advice to the Moabites and Midianites was to seduce the Israelites into immorality and idolatry. Incurring divine wrath by accepting invitations to these heathen festivities, thousands of Israelites died in a plague and many guilty leaders were executed. Moses led his people in a punitive war against the Midianites. In this battle Balaam, the son of Beor, was killed (31:16).

Moses once more ordered a military census. This was supervised by Eleazer, Aaron's son, who had served as high priest since his father's death. The total count of Israel's military manpower was actually somewhat lower than it had been when they left Egypt (Num 26). Joshua was appointed and consecrated as the successor to Moses. Inheritance problems and additional instructions for regular offerings, festivals, and vows were carefully delineated (Num 27–30). Reluctantly Moses granted permission to the Reubenites, Gadites, and some of the Manasseh tribe to settle east of the Jordan, exacting from them the promise to aid the rest of the nation in the conquest of the land beyond the river (Num 32).

Anticipating Israel's successful occupation of the land of Canaan, Moses admonished them to destroy the idolatrous inhabitants. He appointed twelve tribal leaders to divide the land among the tribes and instructed them to provide forty-eight cities throughout Canaan for the Levites with adequate pasture area adjoining each city. Six of these Levitical cities were to be designed as cities of refuge where people might flee for safety in case of accidental bloodshed (Num 34–35). Moses also provided solutions to inheritance problems when daughters inherited the family possessions (Num 36).

The magnitude of Moses' character is clearly set forth in his farewell speeches to his beloved people. Even though he himself was denied participation in the conquest and occupation of the land, he coveted the best for the Israelites as they entered Canaan. His admonition to them is summed up in his addresses as given in the Book of Deuteronomy. He reviewed the journey, beginning from Mount Horeb, where God had made a covenant with Israel. He pointed out especially the places where the Israelites had murmured, reminding them of their disobedience. Because of this attitude the generation that Moses had led out of Egypt had been denied entrance into the land that God had promised them for a possession. With that as the background Moses warned them to be obedient. For their encouragement he pointed to the recent victories God had given them over the Amorites. This experience provided a reasonable basis for the hope of victory under the leadership of Joshua as they actually entered the land of Canaan (Deut 1:1–4:43).

In his second speech (Deut 4:44–28:68) Moses emphasized that love as well as obedience is essential for a wholesome relationship with God. The Decalogue at Mount Sinai was repeated. Wholehearted love for God in daily life represented the basis for maintaining this covenant relationship in such a way that they could enjoy God's blessing. Consequently each generation was responsible for teaching the fear of the Lord their God to the next generation by precept and obedience. In this pattern of living they would be God's holy people in practice. Faithfully Moses delineated many of the laws already given, admonishing the people to be true to God, warning them against idolatry, advising them in the administration of justice, and adding various civil and religious regulations. He concluded this speech with a list of curses and blessings that were to be read publicly to the entire congregation after they crossed the Jordan. In this manner he set before the Israelites the way of life and death. Moses provided a written record of the law as a guide for Israel.

At the close of Moses' career, Joshua, who had already been designated as Israel's leader, was ordained as successor to Moses. In a song (Deut 32) Moses expressed his praise to God, recounting how God had delivered Israel and provided for them through the wilderness journey. Then, with the pronouncement of the blessing on each tribe, Moses departed for Mount Nebo, where he was privileged to view the Promised Land before he died.

Bibliography: Martin Buber, *Moses,* 1944; H. H. Rowley, *From Moses to Qumran,* 1963, ch. 2, and *Men of God,* 1963, ch. 1; R. A. Cole, *Exodus* (TOTC), 1973, pp. 16–46; E. H. Merrill, *An Historical Survey of the Old Testament,* 1966, pp. 96–129; C. F. Pfeiffer, *Old Testament History,* 1973, pp. 125–90. SJS

MOSES, ASSUMPTION OF (See APOCALYPTIC LITERATURE)

MOST HIGH. A name applied to God. It represents the Hebrew word *el-elyon* (Gen 14:18, 20, 22; Ps 7:17), which is translated "God Most High." The expression comes into the Greek of the NT as a part of the Semitic background inherited from the OT (Mark 5:7; Acts 7:48).

MOST HOLY PLACE (See TABERNACLE)

MOTE. A particle of dust or chaff, or a splinter of wood that might enter the eye. Rendered as "speck" by NIV, the word is used by Jesus (Matt 7:3–5; Luke 6:41–42) in contrast with "beam" (KJV), "log" (RSV), or "plank" (NIV) to rebuke self-righteousness in correcting small faults in others, while cherishing greater ones of our own.

MOTH (See ANIMALS)

MOTHER (See FAMILY; MARRIAGE)

MOUNT, MOUNTAIN. *Hill, mount,* and *mountain* are terms roughly synonymous in the English Bible. Much of Palestine is hilly or mountainous. These elevations are not dramatically high but are old worn-down hills. A central hill country stretches from north to south in Palestine, attaining its greatest elevations in Galilee (nearly 4,000 feet [1,250 m.] above sea level) and finally ending in the Negev in the south. Much of Transjordan is high plateau land, although in Syria north of Palestine this section reaches a great height in Mount Hermon (c. 9,000 feet [2,813 m.] above sea level), which is snow-covered throughout the year.

Many ancient peoples considered mountains holy places. Mount Sinai (Deut 33:2; Judg 5:4–5) and Mount Zion (Ps 68:16) were specially honored by the Hebrews as the places of God's revelation and abode. Mountains in Scripture are symbolic of eternity (Gen 49:26) and of strength and stability, but God is infinitely strong and stable (Ps 97:5; 121:1–2 RSV; Isa 40:12). They also portray the difficult obstacles of life, but God will overcome these mountains for his people (Isa 49:11; Matt 21:21).

"Mount" in several places in the KJV refers to the mounds raised against the wall of a besieged city by an attacking army (Jer 6:6; Ezek 26:8).

JBG

MOUNT OF BEATITUDES. The site of the Sermon on the Mount (Matt 5–7; Luke 6:20–49), which contains the Beatitudes, is not identified in the Gospels. Tradition has identified it with Karn Hattin, near Capernaum, but with very little factual basis. Like many of the sites of Jesus' ministry, its exact location is unknown.

MOURN, MOURNING. The ancient Hebrews placed a much greater emphasis on external symbolic acts than do modern Western people; people in the East today still carry on this respect for symbolic actions. Ceremonies for expressing grief at the death of a relative or on any unhappy occasion are referred to frequently in the Bible. One reared in the modern West must be careful not to view these public expressions as hypocritical; they were a natural valid manifestation of grief in that culture.

The OT contains warnings against pagan mourning rites (Lev 19:27–28; Deut 14:1–2). Israelite priests were not allowed to take part in any mourning or other funeral ceremonies (Lev 21:1–4, 10–11).

When bad news was received or when sudden calamity came, it was customary to tear the clothes (2 Sam 1:2) and to sprinkle earth or ashes on the head (Josh 7:6). Hair cloth ("sackcloth") was adopted as clothing in times of grief (Isa 22:12). We read of covering the head in mourning (Jer 14:3), and also the lower part of the face (Ezek 24:17, 22). Among those who habitually wore some covering on the head it was a sign of mourning to let the hair go loose (Lev 10:6), which normally (like that of a Greek Orthodox priest in the Near East) would be coiled up.

A death in the household set in motion an elaborate ceremony of mourning that lasted a week or more. The members of the family and their friends gathered around the corpse and indulged in lamentations bordering on hysteria. The rites mentioned above were observed, but in a more abandoned form than for other mourning. During the last century, W. M. Thomson saw a ceremony of mourning carried out by the Arabs of Palestine. He described the three concentric circles of mourners, slowly marching, clapping their hands, and chanting a funeral dirge. At times they stopped and, flinging their arms and handkerchiefs about in wild frenzy, screamed and wailed like maniacs.

Professional mourners were often called in for a funeral (Jer 9:17–22; Amos 5:16; Matt 9:23). In the earliest times these were probably to protect the living from the spirits of the departed, who were greatly feared. By Bible times, however, the mourning women served merely as another manifestation of grief for the departed.

Painting from the tomb of Ramose at Thebes, 12th Dynasty. Women and girls stand with raised hands mourning for the deceased. One small girl is shown nude; others wear long, flowing garments that extend to the feet. Indication of tears can be seen on the faces. Courtesy Egyptian Expedition, The Metropolitan Museum of Art (30.4.37).

Female mourners, from the sarcophagus of King Ahiram of Byblos, thirteenth century B.C. The first two women are shown holding or beating their breasts; the other two have their hands raised in a gesture of grief. Courtesy Ecole Biblique et Archéologique Française, Jerusalem.

Jeremiah, the weeping prophet, made many references to mourning. He taught the mourning women their dirge (Jer 9:17–22), heard the land lament because of the destruction by the Babylonians (9:10; 12:4, 11; 14:2; 23:10), and mentioned Rachel's mourning (31:15–16). He urged Israel to mourn for its sins (4:8; 6:26; 7:29) and secretly mourned for the nation himself (9:1; 13:17). JBG

MOUSE (See ANIMALS)

MOUTH. The principal Hebrew words are *peh,* translated "mouth," but also "language," "corner," "edge," "skirt," and any opening, such as of a well (Gen 29:2), of a sack (Gen 42:27), of a cave (Josh 10:22), or of a grave (Ps 141:7); and *hēkh,* translated "mouth" and "roof of the mouth" (Job 29:10). In the NT *stōma* is translated "mouth" except in the idiomatic "face to face" (lit., "mouth to mouth," 2 John 12; 3 John 14), and "edge [lit., mouth] of the sword" (Heb. 11:34).

The way in which the Bible constantly uses the organ of speech in the sense of "language" is a good example of the employment of the concrete for the abstract. Silence is the laying of the hand on the mouth (Job 40:4), freedom of speech is the enlarged mouth (Eph 6:19). So to receive a message is to have words put into the mouth (Jer 1:9). Humiliation is the mouth laid in the dust (Lam 3:29; NIV "bury his face in the dust").

Finally, the mouth is personified; it is an independent agent. It brings freewill offerings (Ps 119:108). God sets a watch before it (141:3); it selects food (Prov 15:14), uses a rod (14:3), and has a sword (Rev 19:15). This personification helped to contribute to the Jewish idea of the Angel of the Lord and the voice of the Lord and prepared the way for the "word made flesh" (John 1:14). JBG

MOWING. In early Bible times, mowing of the ripe grain was done with a short sickle made of pieces of sharp flint set in wood or even bone. As the Hebrews became more technologically advanced, they made sickles made of metal—bronze and then iron. The farmer grasped the grain with his left hand and lopped off the stalks fairly high up. They were then bound into sheaves and taken to the threshing floor. The king's mowings (Amos 7:1) were the portion of the spring harvest taken by the king as taxes. Only after the king's agents had taken the tax-grain could the owner mow the rest of his field. See also AGRICULTURE.

MOZA (mō'zȧ, Heb. *môtsâh, sunrise*). 1. A man of Judah, of the family of Hezron, the house of Caleb (1 Chron 2:46).

2. A descendant of Jonathan (1 Chron 8:36–37).

MOZAH (mō'zȧ, Heb. *môtsâh*). A town of Benjamin (Josh 18:26). Its site is not certain: Qaloniyeh, about four and two-thirds miles (eight km.) NW of Jerusalem on the road to Jaffa, has been suggested.

MUFFLER (See DRESS)

MULBERRY TREE (See PLANTS)

MULE (See ANIMALS)

MUPPIM (mŭp'ĭm, Heb. *muppîm*). A son or descendant of Benjamin (Gen 46:21). He is also called Shupham (Num 26:39) and Shuppim (1 Chron 7:12, 15). Possibly the Shephuphan of 1 Chronicles 8:5 is the same person.

MURDER. From the days of Noah the biblical penalty for murder was death; "Whoever sheds the blood of man, by man shall his blood be shed" (Gen 9:6). Throughout the OT times, the ancient Semitic custom of the avenger of blood was followed: a murdered man's nearest relative (the *goel*) had the duty to pursue the murderer and kill him (Num 35:19). Since in the practice of avenging blood in this fashion men failed to distinguish between murder and manslaughter, and vicious blood feuds would frequently arise, the Mosaic Law provided for cities of refuge (Num 35). To these cities a person pursued by the avenger of blood could flee. He would be admitted and tried; if judged guilty of murder, he would be turned over to the avenger; if judged innocent, he was afforded protection in this city from the avenger. It appears likely that the advent of the monarchy began a trend away from the ancient *goel* custom, for we find the king putting a murderer to death (1 Kings 2:34) and pardoning another (2 Sam 14:6–8).

In a murder trial, the agreeing testimony of at least two persons was necessary for conviction (Num 35:30; Deut 17:6). An animal known to be vicious had to be confined, and if it caused the death of anyone, it was destroyed and the owner held guilty of murder (Exod 21:29, 31).

The right of asylum in a holy place was not granted a murderer; he was dragged away even from the horns of the altar (Exod 21:14; 1 Kings 2:28–34). No ransom could be accepted for a murderer (Num 35:21). When a murder had been committed and the killer could not be found, the people of the community nearest the place where the corpse was found were reckoned guilty. To clear them of guilt, the elders of that community would kill a heifer, wash their hands over it, state their innocence, and thus be judged clean (Deut 21:1–9). JBG

MUSHI, MUSHITES (mū'shī, mū'shīts). A Levite, son of Merari, and the founder of the tribal family, or house, called the Mushites (Exod 6:19; Num 3:20; 26:58; 1 Chron 6:19, 47; 23:21, 23; 24:26, 30).

MUSIC AND MUSICAL INSTRUMENTS.

I. Musical Instruments.

A. **The Bell** (Heb. *pa'amôn*). In Exodus 28:33–35, where the Lord prescribes the high priest's garments, he states: "Make pomegranates of blue, purple and scarlet yarn around the hem of the robe, with gold bells between them. The gold bells and the pomegranates are to alternate around the hem of the robe. Aaron must wear it when he ministers. The sound of the bells will be heard when he enters the Holy Place before the LORD and when he comes out, so that he will not die." The little bells (*pa'amônîm*) were either small bells or jingles. This custom typifies the ringing of the bell during the Roman Mass to call the attention of the worshipers to the sacred function in the sanctuary. Bells and jingles on the hem of garments not only were found in Israel but also are used by many primitive tribes in worship.

B. **The Cymbals** (Heb. *tseltselîm* and *metsiltayim*). The only permanent percussive instrument in the temple orchestra was the cymbal. In the Holy Scriptures, the use of cymbals is solely confined to religious ceremonies—bringing back the ark from Kiriath Jearim (1 Chron 15:16, 19, 28), at the dedication of Solomon's temple (2 Chron 5:13), at the restoration of worship by Hezekiah (29:25), at the laying of the foundation of the second temple (Ezra 3:10), and the dedication of the wall of Jerusalem (Neh 12:27).

In Psalm 150 two types of cymbals are pointed out: "Praise him with the clash of cymbals, praise him with resounding cymbals." The "clashing cymbals were of a larger diameter than the "resounding" cymbals, and were two-handed cymbals. The resounding cymbals were much smaller and were played by one hand—the cymbals being attached to the thumb and the middle finger.

In the time of David and Solomon, much stress was laid on the cymbal and percussive instruments. The chief singer of David, Asaph, was a cymbal player (1 Chron 16:5). However, in the last century of the second temple the percussive instruments were restricted to one cymbal, which was used to mark pauses only, not to be played while the singing and the playing were going on.

Although these temple instruments were definitely rhythmical in character, it is interesting to note that the rhythm of the melody was largely dependent on the innate rhythm of the words sung, for the content and the spirit of the words dominated the music. The singing and the playing of the instruments was not to perform or entertain or to elevate a lover of refined art, but rather to serve as a highly exalted form of speech. Rhythm proved important only in nonreligious music, and the Jews also made a distinction between what they called spiritual music of the highly educated and the popular music of the masses.

C. **The Harp** (Heb. *nēbhel*). In 1 Samuel 10:5 Samuel the prophet tells the newly anointed King Saul that he would meet "a procession of prophets coming down from the high place with lyres, tambourines, flutes and harps being played before them, and they [would] be prophesying." This is the first time the *nēbhel* is mentioned in the Bible. This large harp, like the lyre, was made of berosh and almugwood, but the harp had a resonant body. According to Josephus, the harp was played with the fingers and had twelve strings, in contrast to ten strings of the lyre, which was played with a plectrum.

These two instruments were the most important ones in the temple orchestra, without which no public religious ceremony could be held. The harp seems to have been a vertical, angular instrument, larger in size, louder, and lower in

Four musicians (a harper, a lute players, and two flute players) on limestone relief from the tomb of Paatenemheb, near Saqqara, Egypt, c. 1350 B.C. Courtesy Rijksmuseum van Oudheden, Leiden, Netherlands.

Wall painting from Theban tomb of Djeserkaraseneb, time of Thutmose IV (c. 1421–1413 B.C.). Egyptian musicians with (left to right) harp, lute, double-pipe, and lyre. In center, a small girl dances with clenched fists. Courtesy Egyptian Expedition, The Metropolitan Museum of Art (30.4.9).

pitch than the lyre. The harp is mentioned frequently in the Book of Psalms: 33:2; 57:8; 71:22; 81:2; 92:3; 108:2; 144:9; 150:3.

The harp was often used at secular festivities. Isaiah the prophet complains, "They have harps and lyres at their banquets, tambourines and flutes and wine, but they have no regard for the deeds of the LORD, no respect for the work of his hands" (Isa 5:12). Amos the prophet writes of God's protest: "Away with the noise of your songs! I will not listen to the music of your harps" (Amos 5:23). And in Amos 6:1, 5 he prophesies woe to Israel, complaining, "You strum away on your harps like David and improvise on musical instruments."

D. **The Lyre** (Heb. *kinnôr*). Jewish historians ascribe the first use of musical instruments to the seventh generation after the creation of the world. Genesis 4:21 states that Jubal, son of Adah and Lamech, offspring of Methushael, son of Mehujael, son of Irad, son of Enoch, son of Cain, Adam and Eve's firstborn "was the father of all who play the harp [*kinnôr*] and flute." The *kinnôr* was the famous instrument on which, later on, King David excelled, and which has erroneously been called "King David's harp." The *kinnôr* was a stringed instrument, but it had no resonant body like the harp. It was a lyre, and whether its original form was square or triangular is not known due to the ancient commandment to refrain from the creation of images. No representation of musical instruments and no original biblical melodies have come down to us. The *kinnôr* was made of wood—David made it of *berôsh,* but in 1 Kings 10:12 it is recorded that Solomon made some of almugwood for use in the temple. According to Josephus, the Jewish historian, the *kinnôr* had ten strings that were plucked with a plectrum, and they were probably tuned pentatonically, without semitones, through two octaves.

The *kinnôr* was used on joyous occasions; for instance, it is stated in Genesis 31:26–27: "Then Laban said to Jacob, 'What have you done? You've deceived me, and you've carried off my daughters like captives in war. Why did you run

Reconstructed lyre consisting of a wooden soundbox with a gold head of a bearded bull at its end, from the graves at Ur, c. 2500 B.C. Mosaic decoration was made of shell, lapis, and red limestone, separated by bands of sheet gold. Courtesy University Museum, University of Pennsylvania.

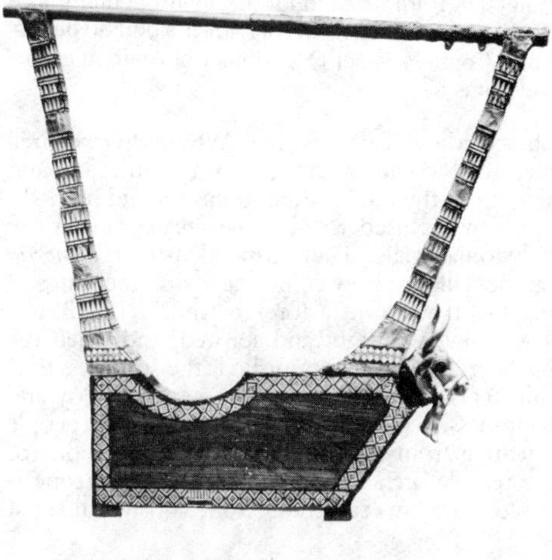

Cult stand from Ashdod, c. tenth century B.C., decorated with musicians playing the double pipe or horn. Courtesy Israel Department of Antiquities and Museums.

off secretly and deceive me? Why didn't you tell me, so I could send you away with joy and singing to the music of tambourines and harps?'" The Jews refused to play the *kinnôr* during the Babylonian exile. They suspended their *kinnôrîm* on the willows; how could they "sing the songs of the LORD while in a foreign land?" (Ps 137:4). The *kinnôr* was light and spirited, and when the prophets of old admonished the people, they threatened that the *kinnôr*, the symbol of joy and happiness, would be silenced unless the people repented from their sins. The *kinnôr* was one of the temple orchestra instruments, and its tone is described as sweet, tender, soft, and lyrical. First Chronicles 25:3 states that Jeduthun and his sons prophesied with a *kinnôr;* and 1 Samuel 16:23 says about David and Saul: "David would take his harp and play. Then relief would come to Saul; he would feel better, and the evil spirit would leave him." The *kinnôr* was also a popular instrument among the more cultured classes in Israel.

E. **The Oboe** (Heb. *chālîl*). In 1 Kings 1:40 it is stated that after Zadok the priest had anointed Solomon, "all the people went up after him, playing flutes and rejoicing greatly, so that the ground shook with the sound." The pipe (*chālîl*) was a double-reed instrument and is the biblical equivalent of the modern oboe. It was probably also a double-pipe instrument, whose pipes could be blown individually as well as simultaneously. There is no mention of this instrument as having been used in the services of the first temple. In the second temple two to twelve oboes (*chalîlîm*) were used on twelve days of the year—at first and second Passover sacrifice, on the first day of Passover, at the Feast of Weeks, and in the eight days of the Feast of Tabernacles. The oboes were played at joyous festivities as well as mourning ceremonies. When Christ entered Jairus's home to restore life to his dead daughter, he found the funeral oboes in action. In Israel even the poorest men hired at least two oboes for the funeral of their wives.

F. **The Pipe** (Heb. *'ûgabh*). The shepherd's pipe (NASB, NEB, RSV), flute (MLB, NIV), or organ (KJV) is the other musical instrument mentioned in Genesis 4:21. It is not mentioned in the list of the musical instruments that were used in the temple. There are only three other OT references to *'ûgabh* (Job 21:12; 30:31; Ps 150:4).

G. **The Psaltery** (Heb. *'āsôr*, from the Hebrew word for ten). The harp (*nēbhel*) is often associated with the psaltery. The psaltery is mentioned twice in the Psalms in connection with the harp (Ps 33:2; 144:9) and with both harp and lyre (*kinnôr*) in Psalm 92:3.

It is generally accepted that this was a ten-stringed, rectangular zither. To the early church fathers this psaltery was symbolical: the ten strings, the Ten Commandments; and the four sides, the Gospels.

H. **The *Shālîsh*.** The word *shālîsh* has been the most disputed musical term in Hebrew. Clearly connected with the Hebrew word meaning "three," the word has been translated many times as triangles, triangular harps, three-stringed instruments, and three-stringed lutes (even three-stringed fiddles and a kind of pipe). Of its twenty-one OT occurrences, only once is it perhaps a musical term (1 Sam 18:6), and there it is translated "lutes" in the NIV (instruments of music KJV, RSV; musical instruments NASB; lyre JB): "When the men were returning home after David had killed the Philistine, the women came out from all the towns of Israel to meet King Saul with singing and dancing, with joyful songs and with tambourines and lutes."

I. **The Sistrum, or Rattle** (Heb. *mena'an'im*). This term occurs only in 2 Samuel 6:5, where NIV translates it "sistrum" (cornets KJV; castanets

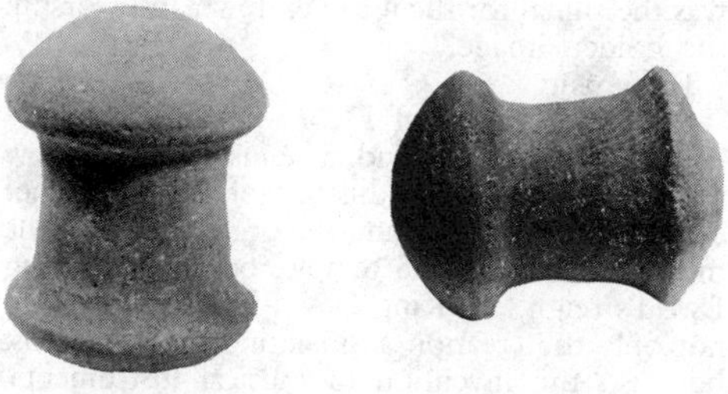

Cylinder shaped rattles made of clay, with small stones inside. Iron Age (c. 1200–1000 B.C.). Courtesy Reuben and Edith Hecht Museum, University of Haifa. Photo Hanna Ophir-Rosenstein.

JB, NASB, NEB, RSV): "David and the whole house of Israel were celebrating with all their might before the LORD, with songs and with harps, lyres, tambourines, sistrums and cymbals." This seems to refer to an instrument that is to be shaken, perhaps the sistrum, a rattle of Sumerian origin, which consisted of a handle and a frame with jingling crossbars.

J. **The Tambourine** (Heb. *tōph*). The *tōph* was a small drum made of a wooden hoop and probably two skins, without any jingling contrivance like the modern tambourine. It was a rhythm-indicator and was used for dances and joyous occasions as well as religious celebrations. Second Samuel 6:5 states that David employed the *tōph* at the installation of the ark in Jerusalem. It is not listed among the musical instruments either of the first or second temple, despite its being mentioned three times in the Psalms: 81:2; 149:3; 150:4. The *tōph* was played primarily by women: "Then Miriam the prophetess, Aaron's sister, took a tambourine in her hand, and all the women followed her, with tambourines and dancing" (Exod 15:20); Jephthah's unfortunate daughter came out to meet him "dancing to the sound of tambourines" (Judg 11:34); and the women of Israel, coming to greet King Saul after David had killed Goliath, came "singing and dancing . . . with tambourines and lutes" (1 Sam 18:6).

K. **The Trumpet** (Heb. *shôphār* or *qeren*). The only temple instrument still being used today in the synagogue is the *shôphār* or *qeren*. Originally, it was a ram's horn without a mouthpiece. It was used chiefly as a signal instrument in religious as well as in secular ceremonies. One single incident stands out in conjunction with the blowing of the *shôphār*. This is recorded in Joshua 6:20: "When the trumpets sounded, the people shouted, and at the sound of the trumpet, when the people gave a loud shout, the wall collapsed; so every man charged straight in, and they took the city." Gideon the judge frightened his enemies, the Midianites, by the sound of the Lord's horns blown by three hundred of his men (Judg 7:16–22). The blowing of the *shôphār* was even attributed to the Lord himself, in order to frighten his enemies and to gather the scattered remnant of Israel to his sanctuary. Thus Zechariah says, "The Sovereign LORD will sound the trumpet . . . the LORD Almighty will shield them" (Zech 9:14–15).

During the latter part of the period of the second temple, two types of *shôphār* were in use: the curved ram's horn and the straight (female) mountain goat's horn. The Talmudian tractate *Rosh-hoshana* 3:2–6 gives a detailed description of the *shôphār:* "All *shofars* are valid save that of the cow. The *shofar* blown in the temple at the New Year was made from the horn of the mountain goat, straight, with its mouthpiece overlaid with gold. At the sides of them that blew the *shofar* were two priests that blew upon the silver trumpets. The *shofar* blew a long note and the trumpets a short note, since the duty of the day fell on the *shofar.* The *shofar* blown on New Year's Day was to remind God of his promise to Abraham, Isaac, and Jacob, and especially of Isaac's sacrifice and of the ram that was substituted for him (Gen 22:13).

"The *shofars* blown on days of fasting were ram's horns, curved, with mouthpieces overlaid with silver. Between them were two priests who blew upon silver trumpets. The *shofar* blew a short note and the trumpets a long note, since the duty of the day fell on the trumpets. The Year of Jubilee is like to the New Year in the blowing of the *shofar.* Today, the sound of the *shofar* is to stir the hearts of the Jewish people to awe and reverence and to remind them of their duties to God. As a matter of fact, the Shofar Song is a simple but beautiful call to worship."

L. **The Trumpet** (Heb. *chatzōtzerâ*). "The LORD said to Moses: 'Make two trumpets of hammered silver, and use them for calling the community together and for having the camps set out. . . . When you go into battle in your own land against an enemy who is oppressing you, sound a blast on the trumpets. Then you will be remembered by the LORD your God and rescued from your enemies. Also at your times of rejoicing—your appointed feasts and New Moon festivals—you are to sound the trumpets over your burnt offerings and fellowship offerings, and they will be a memorial for you before your God. I am the LORD your God' " (Num 10:1–2, 9–10).

Both the trumpets and the *shôphār* were blown by the priests and not by the Levites, who were, so to speak, the professional musicians of the temple. Both these instruments served the same function of signaling.

Jewish historian Josephus has described the trumpet as a straight tube, "a little less than a cubit long," its mouthpiece wide and its body expanding into a bell-like ending. The form of the trumpet is still preserved on the Jewish coins of the latter part of the period of the second temple. When, in A.D. 70 the Romans erected an arch for Emperor Titus after his conquest of Jerusalem, they depicted on it his triumphant return to Rome with the holy objects robbed from the temple, among them a trumpet, which corresponds exactly to the description of Josephus.

Two of these silver trumpets were the minimum requirement for the temple service; the

Zither player seated on a folding stool. On terracotta relief from Tell Asmar, early second millennium B.C. Courtesy Réunion des Musées Nationaux.

maximum, 120. Second Chronicles 5:12 states: "All the Levites who were musicians—Asaph, Heman, Jeduthun and their sons and relatives, stood on the east side of the altar, dressed in fine linen and playing cymbals, harps and lyres. They were accompanied by 120 priests sounding trumpets."

M. **Nebuchadnezzar's Orchestral Instruments.** Finally, a word about the orchestral instruments of Nebuchadnezzar king of Babylon, as described by Daniel: "As soon as you hear the sound of the horn, flute, zither, lyre, harp, pipes and all kinds of music, you must fall down and worship the image of gold that King Nebuchadnezzar has set up" (Dan 3:5). The Hebrew words for the above mentioned instruments would be the *qeren* (horn or trumpet), the *mashrôqîthâ* (a pipe or a whistle), the *qathrōs* (a lyre), the *sabbekhâ* (a kind of harp), the *pesantērîn* (a psaltery, a stringed instrument that was used to accompany the Psalms), the *symphonia,* which means a combination of sounds, or just orchestra. "If we accept the Aramaic text of the book of Daniel," says Curt Sachs, "the King's subjects heard the various instruments first singly and then all together, a performing custom of the orchestras of the East. The addition, 'all kinds of music,' may refer to drums and other percussion instruments. The people were thus instructed to wait for the horn signal, followed by solos of pipe, lyre, harp, and psaltery, after which the 'all kinds of music' (percussion instruments) would join the solo instruments in a *sumphonia* of sounds, which was the signal for them to fall down and worship the golden image."

II. Music

A. **The History of Hebrew Music.**

1. **The Time of David.** The history of Hebrew music, as well as the history of Israel's higher civilization in general and the organization of the musical service in the temple, began with King David's reign. To King David has been ascribed not only the creation and singing of the psalms, but also the invention of musical instruments. Second Chronicles 7:6 mentions "the LORD's musical instruments, which King David had made for praising the LORD"; and according to 1 Chronicles 23:5, David himself said to the princes of Israel, to the priests, and Levites, "Four thousand are to praise the LORD with the musical instruments I have provided for that purpose."

King David chose the Levites to supply musicians for the holy temple. Out of the thirty thousand who were employed at this time, the impressive number of four thousand was selected for the musical service. First Chronicles 15:16 states, "David told the leaders of the Levites to appoint their brothers as singers to sing joyful songs, accompanied by musical instruments: lyres, harps and cymbals."

Solomon's Temple. Years later, when King Solomon had finished all work for the temple and brought in all the things David his father had dedicated, the priest and the congregation of Israel assembled before the ark, and the musical service was begun by the Levites. First Chronicles 25:6–7 relates that the number of them who were instructed in the songs of the Lord was 288, divided into twenty-four classes. On the day of the dedication of the temple, "all the Levites who were musicians—Asaph, Heman, Jeduthun and their sons and relatives—stood on the east side of the altar, dressed in fine linen and playing cymbals, harps and lyres. They were accompanied by 120 priests sounding trumpets. The trumpeters and singers joined in unison, as with one voice, to give praise and thanks to the LORD. Accompanied by trumpets, cymbals and other instruments, they raised their voices in praise to the LORD and sang: 'He is good; his love endures forever.' Then the temple of the LORD was filled with a cloud, and the priests could not perform their service because of the cloud, for the glory of the LORD filled the temple of God" (2 Chron 5:12–14). When the king and the people had offered their sacrifices, the Levites began to play, "the priests blew their trumpets, and all the Israelites were standing" (7:6).

In Solomon's temple the choir formed a distinct body. They were furnished homes and were on salary. Ezekiel says they had chambers between the walls and windows with southern views (Ezek 40:44). The choir numbered two thousand singers and was divided into two choirs. The Psalms, according to the Mishna, were sung antiphonally. The first examples in the Bible of antiphonal or responsive singing are the songs of Moses and Miriam after the passage through the Red Sea (Exod 15).

There were three forms after which the Psalms and the prayers were rendered in the temple. First, the leader intoned the first half verse, whereupon the congregation repeated it. Then the leader sang each succeeding half line, the congregation always repeating the same first half line, which thus became a refrain throughout the entire psalm. Second, the leader sang a half line at a time, and the congregation repeated what he had last sung. The third form was responsive in the real sense of the word—the leader would sing the whole first line, whereupon the congregation would respond with the second line of the verse. In ancient times the people, primitive as yet, would respond with but one word as a refrain to tributes and praise. Refrains such as *Amen, Halleluyah, Hoshiannah* ("Oh, help!"), *Anenu* ("Answer us!") were mostly used in public worship. In later times a higher musical development of the people is shown in their response with phrases rather than single words as in Psalm 118:1–3 and Psalm 136.

3. **The Second Temple.** The orchestra and the choir personnel were greatly reduced in the second temple. The orchestra consisted of a minimum of two harps and a maximum of six; a minimum of nine lyres, maximum limitless; a minimum of two oboes and a maximum of twelve; and one cymbal. The second temple choir consisted of a minimum of twelve adult singers, maximum limitless. The singers, all male, were between thirty and fifty years of age. Five years of musical training was a prerequisite to membership in the second temple choir. In addition to the male adults, sons of the Levites were permitted to participate in the choir "in order to add sweetness to the song."

4. **The Time of Christ.** The musical service in the temple at the time of Christ was essentially the same as that in King Solomon's temple, with the exception of a few minor changes in certain forms of singing. There were two daily services in the temple—the morning and evening sacrifices. The morning sacrifice began with burning incense on the golden altar within the Holy Place. The offering of incense took place before daybreak, and the priest on whom the lot had fallen for the most honorable service in the daily ministry was alone in the Holy Place while burning the incense; the congregation was praying outside the gates of the temple at the time of incense offering. The morning sacrifice followed. The president would direct one of the priests to ascend some pinnacle to see if it was time to kill the daily sacrifice. If the priest reported, "The morning shineth already," he was asked again, "Is the sky lit up as far as Hebron?" If so, the president would order the lamb, which had been kept in readiness for four days, brought in. The elders who carried the keys now gave the order to open the gates of the temple. As the last great gate opened, a signal was given to the priests to blow three blasts on their silver trumpets, calling the Levites and the representatives of the people to their duties, and announcing to the city that the morning sacrifice was about to be offered. Immediately after this the gates to the Holy Place were opened to admit the priests who were to cleanse the candlestick and the altar of incense. The opening of these great gates was actually the signal for the slaughter of the lamb without blemish. Following a prayer, the Ten Commandments were recited, and this was followed by the Jewish Creed "Shema": "Hear, O Israel: The LORD our God, the LORD is one" (Deut 6:4–9).

After the priestly benediction, found in Numbers 6:24–26, the meal offering was brought, and oil added to it. Having been previously salted, it was laid on the fire. Now the high priest's daily meal offering was presented, which consisted of twelve cakes broken in halves. Twelve halves were presented for the morning sacrifice and the other twelve for the evening sacrifice. Finally came the drink offering, which consisted of wine poured at the foot of the altar.

With the sacrificial acts over, the *'ûgabh* was sounded, which was the signal for the priests to prostrate themselves, but for the Levites it marked the beginning of the musical service. Two priests would now take their stand at the right and left of the altar and blow their silver trumpets. After this, these two priests would approach the cymbal player and take their stand beside him, one on the right and one on the left. When given a sign with a flag by the president, this Levite sounded his cymbal, and this was the sign for the Levites to begin singing a part of the daily psalm accompanied by instrumental music. Whenever they stopped singing, the priests would again blow their trumpets, and the people would prostrate themselves. Not only psalms were sung but also parts of the Pentateuch. The psalm of the day was sung in three sections and at the close of each the priests would blow three fanfares on their silver trumpets, a signal for the congregation to bow down and to worship the Lord.

B. **Music in the Psalms.** The order of the Psalms in the daily service of the temple was as follows: On the first day of the week, Psalm 24: "The earth is the LORD's" in commemoration of the first day of creation. On the second day they sang Psalm 48: "Great is the LORD, and most worthy of praise." On the third day, Psalm 82: "God presides in the great assembly." On the fourth day, Psalm 94: "O LORD, the God who avenges." On the fifth day, Psalm 81: "Sing for joy to God our strength." On the sixth day, Psalm 93: "The LORD reigns." On the seventh day they sang Psalm 92: "It is good to praise the LORD."

With the singing of the daily psalm, the morning sacrifice came to a close. The evening sacrifice was identical to the morning sacrifice, with the exception that the incense offering followed the evening sacrifice, at sunset. Thus they began and ended the day with prayer and praise, of which the burning of incense was symbolical.

The real meaning of the headings of the various psalms is still veiled in darkness. Whether they indicate the names of the instruments employed in accompanying the psalms, or whether they refer to the tune to which they were sung, is still a

General view of the ancient port city of Myra, looking westward. It was here that Paul boarded an Alexandrian ship sailing for Italy (Acts 27:5–6). Courtesy Duby Tal.

problem for the musicologist. Curt Sachs made a comparison of moods of psalms that have similar headings and found that the six *negînôth* psalms (4, 54, 55, 61, 67, 76) are all prayers for escape, and that the three *gittîth* psalms (8, 81, 84) are joyful in character, and that the three Jeduthun psalms (39, 62, 77) express a mood of resignation.

The word *selâh,* which is found so frequently in the Psalms, is another word that has not been satisfactorily explained. Whether it means an interlude, a pause, or a cadence, is not known. Many scholars believe it indicates a musical interlude by the temple orchestra.

C. **The Dance** (Heb. *māchôl*). Dance was considered an integral part of the religious ceremonies in ancient Israel. This Hebrew word is found in the Holy Scriptures associated with the word *tōph* or timbrel: "Then Miriam the prophetess, Aaron's sister, took a tambourine in her hand, and all the women followed her, with tambourines and dancing" (Exod 15:20); and again, "When Jephthah returned to his home in Mizpah, who should come out to meet him but his daughter, dancing to the sound of tambourines!" (Judg 11:34). "David, wearing a linen ephod, danced before the LORD with all his might . . . " (2 Sam 6:14). Religious dancing fell into disuse in the Jerusalem temple, and it is mentioned only twice in Psalms (149:3; 150:4). On the Feast of Tabernacles, at the celebration of "water libation," prominent men would dance, displaying their artistic skill in throwing and catching burning torches. The custom, however, of a procession around the sanctuary or around the altar on the Feast of Tabernacles was retained in the temple, accompanied with singing.

MUSTARD (See PLANTS)

MUTE See DISEASES: *Dumbness*)

MUTHLABBEN (mŭth'lăb'ĕn). An expression of uncertain meaning, occurring only in the title of Psalm 9 (KJV, MLB, NASB, RSV). Probably it indicates the name of the tune (NIV; cf. Christian hymnals) or the instruments of accompaniment (JB) to which the psalm was sung.

MUZZLE. The Mosaic Law forbade the muzzling of oxen when they were treading out the grain, i.e., threshing (Deut 25:4). This was a simple, humane command, in accordance with the kindly spirit of much of the law. Paul makes a curious use of the injunction in 1 Corinthians 9:9 and 1 Timothy 5:18 where he quotes the command in support of his thesis: "The worker deserves his wages" (NIV).

MYRA (mī'rȧ, Gr. *Myra*). Now Dembre, one of the southernmost ports of Asia Minor, and once the chief haven of Lycia. Paul came here on a ship from Adramyttium (Acts 27:2, 5), the seaport on the Aegean opposite Lesbos. There was an Alexandrian ship in port, and they transferred to it. The vessel had chosen this northerly coasting route because of the lateness of the season. Some are, however, of the opinion that the Lycian coast was the regular shipping route from Egypt.

MYRRH (See PLANTS)

MYRTLE (See PLANTS)

MYSIA (mĭsh'ĭ-ȧ, Gr. *Mysia*). A district occupying the NW end of Asia Minor bounded (proceeding clockwise from the west) by the Aegean, the Hellespont (i.e., the Dardanelles), the Propontis (i.e., the Sea of Marmora), Bithynia, Phrygia, and Lydia. There were five areas: (1) Mysia Minor along the northern coast. (2) Mysia Major, the SE hinterland, with Pergamum as its chief city. (3) Troas, a geographical unit in the NW angle between Mount Ida and the sea, the name deriving from the legend that it was under the rule of Troy, whose stronghold was a few miles inland at the entrance to the strait. It was a strategic area, a fact that no doubt accounted for the Achaean assault on Troy. It was also the scene of Alexander's first clash with the Persians (on the Granicus River). (4) Aeolis or Aeolia. This was the southern part of the western coast, a linguistic and ethnological, rather than a geographical, unit. Near the end of the second millennium before Christ, Aeolian Greeks from Boeotia and Thessaly had migrated to this area by way of Lesbos and Tenedos. (Troas was not occupied by Greeks until much later.) Until the Persian conquest the political organization of this Hellenized district was a league of small city-states. (5) Teuthrania was the SW angle between Temnus and the Lydian frontier. The aboriginal or early inhabitants of Mysia, the Mysi, had Tracian affinities and were probably, like the Trojans and the Hittites, an early wave of Indo-European invaders. The Hellespont made no fundamental racial division in early times.

From 280 B.C. Mysia formed part of the kingdom of Pergamum and fell to the Romans in 133 by the will and testament of Attalus III. It thereafter formed part of the province of Asia. The area was traversed by Paul on his second missionary journey (Acts 16:7–8), but no work was done. There is, however, evidence of very early church foundations. EMB

MYSTERY (Gr. *mystērion*). The Greek word occurs twenty-eight times in the NT (including 1 Cor 2:1 where it appears in the better MSS; see NIV footnote). Neither the word nor the idea is found in the OT. Rather, they came into the NT world from Greek paganism. Among the Greeks, *mystery* meant not something obscure or incomprehensible, but a secret imparted only to the initiated, what is unknown until it is revealed. This word is connected with the mystery religions of Hellenistic times (see separate article). The mysteries appealed to the emotions rather than the intellect and offered to their devotees a mystical union with the deity, through death to life, thus securing for them a blessed immortality. Great symbolism characterized their secret ritual, climaxing in the initiation into the full secret of the cult.

The chief use of mystery in the NT is by Paul. He, as an educated man of his day, knew well the thought world of the pagans and accepted this term to indicate the fact that "his gospel" had been revealed to him by the risen Christ. This fact could best be made clear to his contemporaries by adopting the pagan term they all understood, pouring into it a special Christian meaning.

In a few passages the term refers to a symbol, allegory, or parable, which conceals its meaning from those who look only at the literal sense, but is the medium of revelation to those who have the key to its interpretation. See Revelation 1:20; 17:5, 7; Mark 4:11 (NIV "secret"); and Ephesians 5:32, where marriage is a mystery or symbol of Christ and the church.

The more common meaning of mystery in the NT, Paul's usual use of the word, is that of a divine truth once hidden but now revealed in the gospel. A characteristic usage is Romans 16:25–26: ". . . my gospel and the proclamation of Jesus Christ, according to the revelation of the mystery hidden for long ages past, but now revealed and made known through the prophetic writings by the command of the eternal God, so that all nations might believe and obey him" (cf. Col 1:26; Eph 3:3–6). A mystery is thus *now* a revelation: Christian mysteries are revealed doctrines (Rom 16:26; Eph 1:9; 3:3, 5, 10; 6:19; Col 4:3–4; 1 Tim 3:16). Christianity, therefore, has no secret doctrines, as did the ancient mystery religions. To the worldly wise and prudent the gospel is foolishness (Matt 11:25; 1 Cor 2:6–9); it is not uncommunicated to them, but they do not have the capacity to understand it (2 Cor 4:2–4). The Christian mystery, then, is God's world-embracing purpose of redemption through Christ (Rom 16:25). JBG

MYSTERY RELIGIONS. A term applied in the Greek, the Hellenistic, and the Roman world to the cult of certain deities that involved a private initiation ceremony and a reserved and secret ritual. They were probably vestiges of earlier religions, maintaining themselves as secret societies after the introduction of the Olympian and other Indo-European deities, and ending after what seems a common social pattern, by winning their way with the conquering people. The deities with whose worship the Greek "mysteries" were principally connected were Demeter, whose cult was organized into the ceremonials of Eleusis, and Dionysus, a predominantly female cult. The worship of Demeter and Dionysus appears to have been in origin a nature worship, with a ritual symbolizing death and resurrection in a seasonal sequence, and a spiritual reference of this natural pattern to the experience of the soul.

Little is known about the rites of worship and initiation, for the initiates seem to have been faithful in the keeping of their vows of secrecy; but it is fairly certain that the worship had to do with notions of sin, ritual uncleanness, purification, regeneration, and spiritual preparation for another life. It is probable that their influence was widespread, and, on the whole, salutary in tranquility of spirit and uprightness of conduct. Besides the worship of the goddess and the god already named in connection with metropolitan Greece, there were other ancient deities whose cults can be properly named "mystery religions," for example, the worship of Orpheus, Adonis or Tammuz, Isis, and especially Mithras. S. Angus (*The Mystery Religions and Christianity*, London, 1925) is of the opinion that the triumph of Christianity over the powerful rivalry of the mystery cults, and especially Mithraism, was due principally to its possession of a historic Person as the center of its faith. Paul adapted some of the vocabulary of the mystery cults to a Christian purpose, and his use of the word "mystery" for a truth revealed but comprehended only by the "initiated," is a clear reference to them. EMB

N

NAAM (nā'ăm, Heb. *na'am, pleasant*). A son of Caleb, and thus a descendant of Judah (1 Chron 4:15).

NAAMAH (nā'ȧ-mȧ, Heb. *na'ămâh, pleasant*). The feminine of Naam and the name of:

1. A daughter of Lamech and Zillah (Gen 4:22). She was a sister of Tubal-Cain, who "forged all kinds of tools out of bronze and iron."

2. A woman of Ammon, wife of Solomon, and mother of Rehoboam (1 Kings 14:21, 31) and as such the chief lady of the court.

3. A town mentioned in Joshua 15:41 as an inheritance of Judah. It was situated in the lowland, probably near Makkedah, though the site has not been identified. Some believe it was located where the modern Na'anah now is. There is no other mention of this place.

4. Possibly a town in north Arabia. In Job 2:11 Zophar is called the Naamathite and may have been from this town.

NAAMAN (nā'ȧ-măn, Heb. *na'ămân, pleasant*). 1. A son of Bela and grandson of Benjamin (Gen 46:21), and the head of the clan called the Naamites (Num 26:40).

2. The "commander of the army of the king of Aram" (2 Kings 5:1). He was a courageous general in the continuous warfare existing in those days. To the successful record of his life, the Scriptures, however, add the pathetic phrase, "but he had leprosy." This was a most dreadful disease at the time and meant ostracism and an untimely death.

A young girl, who had been taken captive in one of the Syrian raids into Israelite territory, served Naaman's wife. One day she said to her mistress, "If only my master would see the prophet who is in Samaria! He would cure him of his leprosy" (2 Kings 5:3).

After a fruitless visit at the court of the king of Israel, Naaman finally went to the prophet Elisha and was told to wash himself seven times in the River Jordan, a suggestion that Naaman met with anger and contempt as he recalled the clear waters of the rivers of Damascus (2 Kings 5:12). Prevailed on, however, by his servants to heed the prophet, Naaman followed the prophet's instructions, "and his flesh was restored and became clean like that of a young boy" (5:14). Naaman's cure led to his acceptance of the God of Israel as the only God "in all the world."

The rest of the account (as told in 2 Kings 5:15–19) shows how the people believed in henotheism—the belief that nations had their individual gods. Naaman wanted some of Israel's soil to take home so that he could worship Israel's God even if it was in "the temple of Rimmon" where his official duties required him to be with his king. (Rimmon was the thundergod of the Assyrians.)

The great Omaiyid Mosque at Damascus, today the city's most magnificent structure is, according to tradition, built on the site of the temple of Rimmon where Naaman deposited his load of soil from Israel.

In Luke 4:27 Jesus referred to this incident "in the time of Elisha the prophet" when he spoke in the synagogue at Nazareth. JGJ

NAAMATHITE (nā'ȧ-mȧ-thīt, Heb. *na'ămāthî, a dweller in Naamah*). A gentilic noun with an article, applied to Zophar, one of Job's friends (Job 2:11; 11:1; 20:1; 42:9). The place was probably in north Arabia. See NAAMAH.

NAAMITES (nā'ȧ-mīts, Heb. *ha-na'ămî*). Family name of those descended from Naaman, Benjamin's grandson (Num 26:40).

NAARAH (nā'ȧ-rȧ, Heb. *na'ărâh, girl*). 1. One of the wives of Ashhur, the father of Tekoa (1 Chron 4:5–6).

2. A place on the border of Ephraim (Josh 16:7).

NAARAI (nā'ȧ-rī, Heb. *na'ăray*). The son of Ezbai (1 Chron 11:37), one of "the mighty men" of the armies in David's time.

NAARAN (nā'ȧ-răn, Heb. *na'ărān*). One of the towns in the possession of the sons of Ephraim (1 Chron 7:28). In Joshua 16:7 it is called Naarah.

NAASHON, NAASSON (See NAHSHON).

NABAL (nā'băl, Heb. *nāvāl, fool*). A rich sheepmaster of Maon in the southern highland of Judah. The vivid narrative in 1 Samuel 25:1–42 tells how he insulted David when the latter asked for food for his men, who had protected Nabal's men and flocks, how his wife Abigail averted David's vengeance by her gifts and by wise words and so won David's esteem. Abigail returned home to find Nabal feasting like a king. After he sobered she told him, and his heart died within him, and he became as a stone, dying ten days later. Then David sought and won Abigail as his wife.

NABATEA, NABATEANS (năb'ȧ-tē'ăn, Gr.

Nabataioi). An Arabian tribe named in the Apocrypha but not in the Bible, and important to Bible history. Between the sixth and fourth centuries B.C. they moved to Edom and Moab (as alluded to in Obad 1–7; Mal 1:1–7). In Hellenistic times they were a formidable foe to the Greek successors of Alexander the Great, their capital, Petra, being inaccessible and impregnable. While their king Aretas I befriended the early Maccabees, they were in conflict with the later Maccabees. By NT times their territory stretched from the Mediterranean Sea south of Gaza and the Red Sea, to the Euphrates, including Damascus. They lost Damascus when the Romans came to the aid of the Jews against them, but later recovered it, so that their king Aretas IV controlled it when Paul was there (2 Cor 11:32). Aretas IV fought with the Romans against the Jews, and was victorious over Herod Antipas, who had divorced Aretas's daughter to marry Herodias. Nabatea was absorbed into the Roman province of Arabia in A.D. 106. The Nabateans, a nomadic people, influenced by Aramean, Hellenistic, and Roman culture, developed skill in pottery, fine specimens of which have been recovered. The architecture of Petra, "the rose-red city," is remarkable; its religious high places, pillars and figures carved out of sandstone cliffs of a canyon, are accessible only on foot or muleback. By 100 B.C. the Nabateans developed water storage and irrigation systems in the highlands of Transjordan, the remains of which are still impressive. Yet the Nabateans in the Sinai peninsula and other outlying districts remained nomadic. They were traders between

Ed-Deir, an elaborately carved tomb (second century A.D.) built into the rose-red rock of the Nabatean capital of Petra. Courtesy Ecole Biblique et Archéologique Française, Jerusalem.

Khaznet Far'un (treasury) at the Nabatean capital city of Petra. The most magnificent monument at Petra, this columned façade probably dates from the second century A.D. Courtesy Ecole Biblique et Archéologique Française, Jerusalem.

Egypt and Mesopotamia, dealing also in wares from India and China, both by caravan overland and by sea from a port on the Aqabah.

NABOPOLASSAR (năb'ō-pō-lăs'âr). First ruler of the Neo-Babylonian Empire, 626–605 B.C. Allied with Medes and Scythians, he overthrew the Assyrian Empire, destroying Nineveh in 612, as prophesied by Nahum 2:1–3:9 and Zephaniah 2:13–15. The destruction earlier prophesied by Jonah was averted by Nineveh's repentance (Jonah 3). When Pharaoh Neco came to aid the Assyrians, Josiah (king of Judah) opposed him and was killed at Megiddo (2 Kings 23:29; 2 Chron 35:20–27). Nabopolassar died in Babylon about the time his son Nebuchadnezzar II was engaged in the battle of Carchemish.

NABOTH (nā'bŏth, Heb. *nāvôth*). The Israelite who owned a vineyard beside the palace of King Ahab in Jezreel. The king coveted this land for a garden, but Naboth's refusal to sell his inheritance made Ahab angry and sullen (1 Kings 21:1–4). His wife Jezebel undertook to get it for him by having Naboth falsely accused of blasphemy and stoned to death (21:7–14). When Ahab went to take possession of the vineyard, Elijah met him and pronounced judgment on him and his family. Ahab repented and a temporary stay was granted (21:27–29), but after further warning by Micaiah the prophet, punishment fell on Ahab (22:24–40) and on his son Joram and wife

Jezebel (2 Kings 9:25–37, where the vineyard is called "property, field, plot of ground"—see KJV, ASV, RSV, NIV—showing that its use had been changed as Ahab had planned, 1 Kings 21:2).

NACHOR (See NAHOR)

NACON, NACHON (nā'kŏn, Heb. *nākhôn*). A Benjamite at whose threshing floor Uzzah was struck dead for touching the ark (2 Sam 6:6). He is called Kidon in 1 Chronicles 13:9.

NADAB (nā'dăb, Heb. *nādhāv*). Firstborn son of Aaron and Elisheba (Exod 6:23; Num 3:2; 26:60; 1 Chron 6:3; 24:1). He accompanied Moses, Aaron, the seventy elders, and his brother Abihu up Mount Sinai, where they saw the God of Israel (Exod 24:1–2, 9–15). He and his father and brothers were appointed priests (28:1). Nadab and Abihu offered unauthorized (NIV; unholy RSV; strange KJV, NASB) fire in burning incense before the Lord. Fire from the Lord devoured them; they were buried, and mourning was forbidden (Lev 10:1–7; Num 3:4; 26:61).

2. A great-grandson of Jerahmeel (1 Chron 2:26, 28, 30).

3. A son of Jeiel the "father" of Gibeon (1 Chron 8:30; 9:36).

4. A son of Jeroboam I and king of Israel for two years (1 Kings 14:20; 15:25–31). His evil reign was ended by his assassination at the hands of Baasha of Issachar, ending the dynasty of Jeroboam and fulfilling Ahijah's prophecy (14:1–20).

NAGGAI, NAGGE (năg'ī, nāg'ā-ī, năg'ē). An ancestor of Jesus Christ (Luke 3:25). KJV has Nagge, modern versions Naggai. Both are Greek forms of Hebrew *Nogah*.

NAHALAL, NAHALOL (nā'hȧ-lăl, nā'hȧ-lŏl). A town in Zeubulun whose inhabitants were not driven out but were subjected to forced labor. Perhaps this is Tell en-Nahal, north of the River Kishon, NE of Mount Carmel. In Joshua 19:15 KJV has Nahallal, but it follows other versions by having Nahalal in Joshua 21:35, Nahalol in Judges 1:30.

NAHALIEL (nȧ-hā'lĭ-ĕl, nȧ-hăl'ī-ĕl). A valley between Mattanah and Bamoth where the Israelites camped on their way from the Arnon to Jericho (Num 21:19). Perhaps Wadi Zerqâ Mā'in, which flows into the Dead Sea midway along its eastern side.

NAHAM (nā'hăm, Heb. *naham, comfort*). A descendant of Judah through Caleb, he is mentioned only in 1 Chronicles 4:19. He was either Hodiah's brother (KJV, NEB) or the brother of Hodiah's wife (ASV, NIV, RSV).

NAHAMANI (nā'hȧ-mā'nī, nȧ-hăm'ȧ-nī). One of the leaders of the people who returned from captivity with Zerubbabel (Neh 7:6–7).

NAHARAI, NAHARI (nā'hȧ-rī). A Beerothite, Joab's armorbearer (2 Sam 23:37; 1 Chron 11:39).

NAHASH (nā'hăsh, Heb. *nāhāsh*, probably from a root meaning *serpent* rather than from one meaning *oracle* or one meaning *copper*). 1. An Ammonite king whose harsh demands on the men of Jabesh Gilead led Saul to rally the Israelites against him and to defeat him. This victory proved decisive in making Saul king (1 Sam 11:1–2; 12:12).

2. An Ammonite king whose son Hanun David befriended. Mistaking David's intentions, Hanun insulted David's messengers. David avenged the insult and had no more trouble with the Ammonites (2 Sam 10; 1 Chron 19). His son Shobi brought provisions to David during his flight from Absalom (2 Sam 17:27–29). This Nahash may be the same as no. 1, though the length of time between the beginning of Saul's reign and the rebellion of Absalom in David's reign favors the view that no. 2 was a descendant of no. 1.

3. A parent of Abigail and Zeruiah (2 Sam 17:25). The state of the Hebrew text is unclear about whether this Nahash was a man or a woman. First Chronicles 2:16 calls Jesse father of Abigail and Zeruiah. Either Nahash was their mother, or Nahash was an alternative name for Jesse, or Nahash was the former husband of Jesse's wife. Nahash is a masculine name.

NAHATH (nā'hăth, Heb. *nahath*). 1. A son of Reuel, son of Esau (Gen 36:13, 17; 1 Chron 1:37).

2. A descendant of Levi, ancestor of Samuel (1 Chron 6:26); perhaps the same as Toah (6:34) and Tohu (1 Sam 1:1).

3. A Levite, overseer of offerings in the days of Hezekiah (2 Chron 31:13).

NAHBI (nȧ'bi). The representative from Naphtali among the spies sent out by Moses (Num 13:14).

NAHOR (nā'hôr, Heb. *nāhôr*). 1. Son of Serug, father of Terah, grandfather of Abraham (Gen 11:22–26; 1 Chron 1:26–27).

2. Son of Terah and brother of Abraham (Gen 11:26–29; 22:20–23; 24:15, 24, 47; 29:5; Josh 24:2). The city of Nahor is in Mesopotamia (Gen 24:10). Nahor's God is the same God as Abraham's God (31:53). KJV has Nachor (lit. translation) in Joshua 24:2 and Luke 3:34.

NAHSHON (nȧ'shŏn, Heb. *nahshôn*). The son of Amminadab (1 Chron 2:10–11); ancestor of David (Ruth 4:20); leader of the tribe of Judah on the march through the wilderness (Num 1:7; 2:3; 10:14) and in presenting offerings at the dedication of the tabernacle (7:12, 17). His sister Elisheba married Aaron (Exod 6:23, KJV Naashon). He is named Naasson in Jesus' genealogies (lit. translation, KJV in each—Matt 1:4; Luke 3:32).

NAHUM (nā'hŭm, Heb. *nahûm, compassionate*).

Quotations from Nahum 3:1–6, with commentary. Dead Sea Scroll from Qumran Cave 4, late first century B.C. Courtesy The Shrine of the Book, D. Samuel and Jeane H. Gottesman Center for Biblical Manuscripts, Israel Museum, Jerusalem.

The name is a shortened form of *Nehemiah.*

1. Nahum the Elkoshite. Of this prophet and his city of Elkosh nothing is known outside of the book that bears his name (Nah 1:1). See NAHUM, BOOK OF.

2. One of the ancestors of Christ mentioned in Luke 3:25 (KJV "Naum").

NAHUM, BOOK OF. The short Book of Nahum is largely a poem, a literary masterpiece, predicting the downfall of Nineveh, the capital of Assyria. Nineveh was conquered by the Babylonians, Medes, and Scythians in 612 B.C. Nahum declared that Nineveh would fall as did Thebes, which the Assyrians themselves had conquered in 663. The book therefore was written between 663 and 612—in turbulent times. In 633 Ashurbanipal, the last great king of Assyria, died. Soon Babylon rebelled, and the Assyrian power rapidly dwindled. In Judah the wicked Manasseh reigned until about 641, followed by Amon's two-year reign and then the long reign of the good King Josiah (639–608). Perhaps it was in Josiah's day that Nahum prophesied the overthrow of the mighty nation that had so oppressed the Jews. Zephaniah also predicted in Josiah's time the overthrow of Nineveh (Zeph 1:1; 2:13).

The Book of Nahum is in two parts: First, a poem concerning the greatness of God (Nah 1:2–15), then another and longer poem detailing the overthrow of Nineveh (2:1–3:19). The impassioned expressions of Nahum can be better understood when we remember how Assyria had overthrown the northern kingdom of Israel in 722 B.C. and had later taken forty cities of Judah captive, deporting over 200,000 people—according to Sennacherib's own boast in his royal annals (cf. 2 Kings 18:13). The cruelty of the Assyrians is almost beyond belief. Their policy seems to have been one of calculated terror. Their own pictures show captives staked to the ground and being skinned alive. No wonder Nahum exulted at the overthrow of the proud, rich, cruel empire of Assyria.

Some modern critics take issue with Nahum's theology, saying that such vengeful expressions are far from the spirit of the gospel. Such views are usually based on a one-sided conception of NT teaching. In truth, Nahum declares, God is merciful, a statement similar to that found in Exodus 34:6 (Nah 1:3). Nahum also quotes from Isaiah the promise of good tidings of peace for his own (Nah 1:15; cf. Isa 52:7). But for Nineveh the cup of iniquity was full. A century and a quarter earlier, Nineveh had repented at the preaching of Jonah. But the repentance was temporary, and now a hundred years of savage cruelty and oppression of God's people must be paid for. Assyria, the pride of Tiglath-Pileser, Sargon, Sennacherib, and Ashurbanipal, must be laid in the graveyard of nations.

The poem of Nineveh's doom (Nah 2:1–3:19) is really quite remarkable. The figures of speech are bold and depict in staccato fashion the strokes of war. The glamour of the attack with whip and prancing horses and flashing swords suddenly gives way to the picture of the innumerable corpses that mark Nineveh's defeat (3:2–3). If it was wrong for Nahum to rejoice at Nineveh's fall, what shall be said of the heavenly throng of Revelation 19:1–6? Inveterate sin must at last bring well-deserved punishment. The death knell of all opposition to the gospel is here: "'I am against you,' declares the LORD Almighty" (Nah 2:13; 3:5).

Bibliography: A. Haldar, *Studies in the Book of Nahum,* 1947; W. A. Maier, *The Book of Nahum: A Commentary,* 1959; J. D. W. Watts, *Joel, Obadiah, Jonah, Nahum,* et al. (CBC), 1975.

RLH

NAIN (nā'ĭn, Gr. *Nain*). Modern Nein, a village

of Galilee. Though unwalled, it had gates, near which Jesus raised a widow's son from death (Luke 7:11–17). The situation is beautiful, on the NW slope of the Hill of Moreh, known as Little Hermon. Eastward are ancient rock-hewn tombs. The view is wide, across the plains NW to Mount Carmel; north to the hills behind Nazareth, six miles (ten km.) away; and NE past Mount Tabor to the snowy heights of Mount Hermon. To the south is Mount Gilboa.

NAIOTH (nā'ŏth, ōth, Heb. *nāyôth*). A place in or near Ramah of Benjamin, not far north of Jerusalem, where David stayed with Samuel during an early flight from Saul (1 Sam 19:18–20:1). It was the home of a band of prophets. When Saul pursued David there, Saul himself was seized with the spirit of prophecy, giving rise to the saying, "Is Saul also among the prophets?" David fled from Saul and went to Jonathan, Saul's son.

NAME (Heb. *shem,* Gr. *onoma*). In Bible times the notion of "name" had a significance it does not have today, when it is usually an unmeaning personal label. A name was given only by a person in a position of authority (Gen 2:19; 2 Kings 23:34) and signified that the person named was appointed to a particular position, function, or relationship (Gen 35:18; 2 Sam 12:25). The name given was often determined by some circumstance at the time of birth (Gen 19:22); sometimes the name expressed a hope or a prophecy (Isa 8:1–4; Hos 1:4). When a person gave his own name to another, it signified the joining of the two in very close unity, as when God gave his name to Israel (Deut 28:9–10). To be baptized into someone's name therefore meant to pass into new ownership (Matt 28:19; Acts 8:16; 1 Cor 1:13, 15). In the Scriptures there is the closest possible relationship between a person and his name, the two being practically equivalent, so that to remove the name was to extinguish the person (Num 27:4; Deut 7:24). To forget God's name is to depart from him (Jer 23:27). The name, moreover, was the person as he had been revealed; for example, the "name of the LORD" signified the Lord in the attributes he had manifested—holiness, power, love, etc. Often in the Bible the name signified the presence of the person in the character revealed (1 Kings 18:24). To be sent or to speak in someone's name meant to carry that person's authority (Jer 11:21; 2 Cor 5:20). In later Jewish usage the name *Jehovah* was not pronounced in reading the Scriptures (cf. Wisdom 14:21), the name *Adhonai* ("my Lord") being substituted for it. To pray in the name of Jesus is to pray as his representatives on earth—in his Spirit and with his aim—and implies the closest union with Christ. SB

NAMES. When God named what he had made, he described for man the essence of the thing (Gen 1:5, 8, 10; 2:11–14). By allowing Adam to give names, God enabled him to express relationships to his fellow creatures: Adam named the beasts (2:19–20) and woman (2:23). Eve's personal name is from her function as mother of all living (human) beings (3:20). Cain's name is a play on two Hebrew words (4:1). Seth is a reminder that God "appointed" him instead of Abel (4:25). "Men began to call on the name of the LORD" (4:26); did they possibly already at this time begin to recognize him by his revealed name, Jehovah (Yahweh)? God changed the name of Abram to Abraham in view of his destiny (17:5). Names in Genesis 10 are of individuals (e.g., Nimrod) or nations (e.g., Egypt [=Mizraim], Jebusites, Canaanites), or eponymous ancestors or tribes descended from them. People were named for animals (Caleb, dog; Tabitha and Dorcas, gazelle), plants (Tamar, palm tree), precious things (Penninah, coral or pearl), qualities (Hannah, grace; Ikkesh, perverse; Ira, watchful), historical circumstances (Ichabod, inglorious), or for relatives (Absalom named a daughter after his sister Tamar).

The significance of the names of the tribes of Israel is brought out in Genesis 48–49. Men were distinguished as sons (ben, bar), women as daughters (bath) of their fathers (Benzoheth, Simon bar-Jona, Bathsheba). Names compounded with El (God) or Jeho-, -iah (Jehovah) became common. Jacob (Gen 32:24–32) received the name Israel, prince of God, for Jacob, supplanter, and recognized God without learning his secret name. Prophets gave their children symbolic names (Isa 8:1–4; Hos 1:4–11). The Messiah was given significant names: Immanuel, God with us; Jesus, Savior (Isa 7:14; Matt 1:21, 23; Luke 1:31). In his name (Acts 3:16) miracles were wrought, as he promised (John 14:13–14). When we act in Jesus' name, we represent him (Matt 10:42). Place-names are for natural features (Lebanon, white, because it is snow-capped; Bethsaida and Sidon from their fishing; Tirzah, pleasantness, for its beauty). By NT times both personal and family names were common (Simon bar-Jona) or descriptive phrases were added, as for the several Marys. Hybrid or duplicate names occur in a bilingual culture: Bar (Heb.), -timeus (Gr.); Saul (Heb.) = Paul (Gr.); John (Heb.), Mark (Rom.). Patriarchal times saw names as indicators of character, function, or destiny. Soon names began to be given more hopefully than discriminatingly, until finally we are not sure whether the name tells us anything about the nature: Was Philip a "lover of horses," or could Archippus ride them? The many genealogical tables in the Bible follow the practice of ancient historians, showing the importance of descent and of the relations thus established between individuals. ER

NAOMI (nā'ō-mī, nā-ō'mĭ, Heb. *nā'ŏmî*). Wife of Elimelech of Bethlehem. Left without husband or sons, she returned from a sojourn in Moab with her Moabite daughter-in-law Ruth. In her depression she said she should no longer be called Naomi, "pleasantness," but now more appropriately Mara, "bitterness." She advised Ruth in the steps that led to Ruth's marriage to Boaz (Ruth 3:1–6), and she nursed Ruth's child (4:16–17).

NAPHISH (nā'fish, Heb. *nāphîsh*). A son of Ishmael whose clan was subdued by Reuben, Gad, and Manasseh (Gen 25:15; 1 Chron 1:31; 5:19). His descendants, temple servants (KJV Nethinim), returned with Zerubbabel from exile (Ezra 2:50; Neh 7:52; NIV Nephussim).

NAPHOTH DOR (See DOR)

NAPHTALI (năf'tà-lī, Heb. *naphtālî*). 1. A son of Jacob. Naphtali was the second son of Bilhah, Rachel's handmaid. The name is a play on the word *pāthal,* "fight" or "struggle." Of the patriarch himself practically nothing is known. He had four sons (Gen 46:24). Jacob's blessing for Naphtali was brief and noncommittal (49:21).

2. The tribe of Naphtali. Naphtali appears in the lists of Numbers as a tribe of moderate size. It furnished 53,400 soldiers at Kadesh Barnea (Num 1:43) and 45,000 at the mustering of the troops across from Jericho (26:50). In the wilderness organization, Naphtali was supposed to camp on the north side of the tabernacle under the standard of Dan, and this group of tribes brought up the rear in marching. Interestingly, they settled together in Canaan. Naphtali's prince

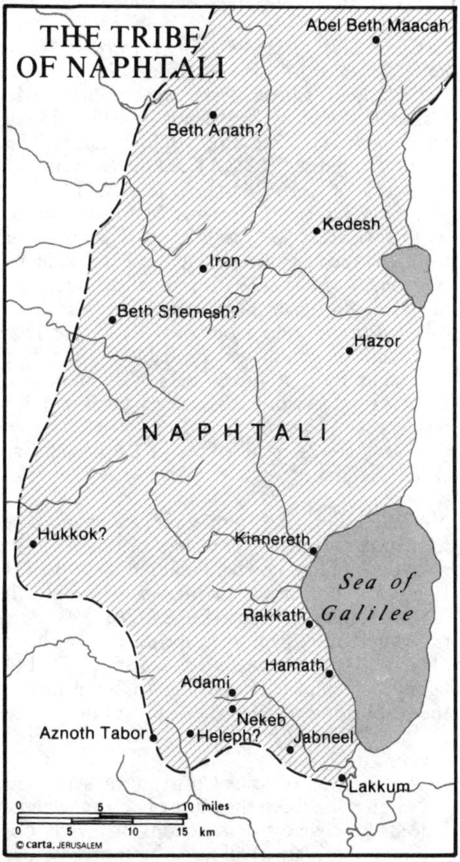

Ahira gave the last offering for the dedication of the altar (7:78). Naphtali received the next to the last lot in the final division of the land (Josh 19:32–39), but in many ways its inheritance was the best.

The territory of Naphtali, as nearly as we can tell, included the fertile scenic area just west of the Sea of Galilee and the sources of the Jordan. It reached from the lower limits of the Sea of Galilee almost up to a point opposite Mount Hermon. On the west it reached halfway to the Mediterranean, being bounded by the tribe of Asher. The chief cities of Naphtali were Hazor, Kinnereth at the north end of the Sea of Galilee, and Kadesh Naphtali. The latter was the northernmost city of refuge in western Palestine.

Kadesh Naphtali was the home of Barak, and Naphtali figured largely in Deborah's conquest of Hazor (Judg 5:18). Men from this tribe also assisted Gideon (7:23). Naphtali is mentioned as one of Solomon's revenue districts (1 Kings 4:15), and the collector was a son-in-law of the king.

Naphtali, lying exposed in the north, was conquered by Ben-Hadad (1 Kings 15:20), and the tribe was later deported after the first invasion of Tiglath-Pileser about 733 B.C. (2 Kings 15:29), who settled Gentiles in the territory. This event is mentioned in Isaiah 9:1 with a prediction of the Messiah, who preached, as Matthew (4:12–16) reminds us, in this same region of Galilee of the Gentiles in fulfillment of the ancient prophecy.

RLH

NAPHTUHITES, NAPHTUHIM (năf'tū-hīts, năf'tū-hĭm, Heb. *naphtūhîm*). A "son" of Mizraim or of Egypt (Gen 10:13; 1 Chron 1:11). Naphtuhites being plural in form denotes a people. Their location has been sought inconclusively in various parts of Egypt.

NAPKIN (See HANDKERCHIEF)

NARCISSUS (nar-cĭs'ŭs, Gr. *Narkissos*). A Roman whose household Paul greeted. The apostle's salutation is not addressed to Narcissus himself but to the members of his household. He may have been the favorite freedman of Claudius the emperor (Rom 16:11).

NARD (See PLANTS)

NATHAN (nā'thăn, Heb. *nāthān, God has given*). 1. The prophet at the royal court in Jerusalem during the reign of David and the early years of Solomon. David consulted him regarding the building of the temple (2 Sam 7; 1 Chron 17). Nathan at first approved, but that same night he had a vision directing him to advise David to leave the building of the temple to the son who would succeed him. David humbly obeyed, expressing gratitude to God for blessings bestowed and others promised. Later Nathan rebuked David for adultery with Bathsheba (2 Sam 12:1–25). David earnestly repented. The title of

Psalm 51 links it with this incident. When Adonijah sought to supplant his aged father David as king, Nathan intervened through Bathsheba to secure the succession for her son Solomon (1 Kings 1:8–53). Nathan wrote chronicles of the reign of David (1 Chron 29:29) and shared in writing the history of the reign of Solomon (2 Chron 9:29). He was associated with David and Gad the seer in arranging the musical services for the house of God (29:25).

2. A son of David, born to him after he began to reign in Jerusalem (2 Sam 5:14; 1 Chron 14:4). His mother was Bathshua, daughter of Ammiel (1 Chron 3:5). He is named in the genealogy of Jesus Christ as son of David and father of Mattatha (Luke 3:31).

3. Nathan of Zobah, father of Igal, one of David's mighty men (2 Sam 23:36). He may be the same as Nathan the brother of Joel (1 Chron 11:38).

4. The two Nathans mentioned in 1 Kings 4:5 as fathers of Azariah and Zabud may be the same man, and identified with no. 1, the prophet. If Zabad (1 Chron 2:36) is the same as Zabud, his father Nathan may also be the prophet. In that case we know that the prophet's father was Attai, a descendant of Jerahmeel (2:25).

5. One of the leading men among those who returned from exile, whom Ezra sent on a mission (Ezra 8:16)

6. One of the returning exiles who had married a foreign wife and who put her away (Ezra 10:39).

Zechariah 12:12 prophesies that the house of Nathan will join on the Day of the Lord in mourning "the one they have pierced." It is probable that the descendants of the prophet (no. 1) are meant (12:10–14); but it is possible that the descendants of David's son (no. 2) are meant.

NATHANAEL (nȧ-thăn'ā-ĕl, Heb. *nethan'ēl, God has given*). One of the apostles introduced to Christ by Philip (John 1:45ff.; 21:2). Nathanael was presumably of Cana in Galilee. The circumstances surrounding his calling are somewhat striking, since Christ praises his integrity at their initial encounter and demonstrates to Nathanael his own foreknowledge by reference to the fig tree. Evidently Nathanael's knowledge of the Scripture was considerable because of the remarkable theological repartee that occurred between Christ and him (1:47–51). Nathanael is commonly identified as Bartholomew. The two names are used interchangeably by the church fathers.

NATHAN-MELECH (nā'thăn-mē'lek, Heb. *nethan melekh, king's gift*). An officer to whom King Josiah remanded the horses "dedicated to the sun" after burning the chariots in the fire (2 Kings 23:11). The LXX identifies him as "Nathan, the king's eunuch."

NATIONS (See GENTILES; HEATHEN)

NATURAL. 1. The word is used once (Deut 34:7) for Moses' physical ability (natural force KJV, RSV; strength NIV). The Hebrew word is *lēah* ("moist," "full of sap").

2. In the NT the word translates four Greek words: *physis*, "nature" (Rom 11:21, 24 natural branches; 2 Peter 2:12 natural brute beasts [NIV brute beasts, creatures of instinct]), *physikos*, "belonging to nature" (Rom 1:26–27 natural relations [KJV natural use]), *psychikos*, "animal, sensuous" (1 Cor 2:14, natural man [NIV man without the Spirit]; 1 Cor 15:44, natural body), and *genesis*, "origin, birth" (James 1:23, natural face [NIV face]).

NATURE. A word that in KJV is found only in the NT, where it is a translation of *genesis* once (James 3:6, course of nature; RSV cycle of nature; NIV course of . . . life) and *physis* ten times—the inherent character of a person or thing (Rom 1:26; 2:14; 11:24; 1 Cor 11:14; Gal 4:8), birth (Rom 2:27; Gal 2:15; Eph 2:3), or disposition (2 Peter 1:4).

NAUM (See NAHUM)

NAVEL (nā'vĕl, Heb. *shōr*). Following the LXX, a different reading has been suggested in Proverbs 3:8: *she'ēr*, "muscle, body" (so NIV). In Ezekiel 16:4 the reading "navel" has been retained in the sense of the umbilical cord (so NIV) not being cut; a picture of an unwanted, untended baby.

NAZARENE (năz'ȧ-rēn, Gr. *Nazarēnos, Nazōraios*). 1. A word derived from Nazareth, the birthplace of Christ. Jesus was often called a Nazarene. Used by his friends, it had a friendly meaning (Acts 2:22; 3:6; 10:38). Jesus applied the title to himself (22:8). Used by his enemies, it was a title of scorn (Matt 26:71; Mark 14:67). It is not altogether certain what Matthew intended in the words, "So was fulfilled what was said through the prophets: 'He will be called a Nazarene'" (Matt 2:23). It is usually thought that he refers to Isaiah 11:1, where the Messiah is called *netser,* or shoot out of the roots of Jesse. The name Nazareth was probably derived from the same root. Matthew sees a fulfillment of Isaiah's prophecy in Jesus' parents' taking up their residence in Nazareth.

2. In Acts 24:5 adherents of Christianity are called Nazarenes.

NAZARETH (năz'ȧ-rĕth, Gr. *Nazaret* and other forms). A town in lower Galilee belonging to the tribe of Zebulun, nowhere referred to in the OT. It was the hometown of Mary and Joseph, the human parents of Jesus (Luke 1:26; 2:4). After their flight into Egypt to escape the ruthless hands of Herod the Great (Matt 2:13ff.), the holy family contemplated returning to Bethlehem of Judea. Hearing that Herod's son was now reigning in Judea, they withdrew to Nazareth in Galilee.

The rejection of Jesus Christ in the synagogue of Nazareth has been the cause of debate, whether indeed there were two rejections or merely one. Although the matter will never be entirely settled,

Looking west, a general view of Nazareth, situated on the southernmost ranges of Galilee. Courtesy Ecole Biblique et Archéologique Française, Jerusalem.

it seems as if there were two such experiences in the life of Christ. (Cf. Luke 4:16–30 with Mark 6:1–6 and Matt 13:54–58.) The first occurred at the beginning of the ministry of Jesus (Luke 4:14), the second on Christ's final visit to Nazareth (Matt 13:54ff.). The very exegetical structures of the accounts appear to make their own demands for two incidents, as in the first account (in Luke) there arose such great hostility that the congregation actually attempted to take his life. In the second instance a spirit of faithless apathy was the only noticeable reaction to his words. (Cf. Luke 4:29–31 with Matt 13:57–58.)

In regard to the city of Nazareth itself, the ancient site is located by the modern en-Natzirah, a Muslim village of about ten thousand inhabitants, on the most southern ranges of lower Galilee. Nazareth itself lies in a geographical basin so that not much of the surrounding countryside is in plain view. However, when one scales the edge of the basin, Esdraelon with its twenty battlefields and the place of Naboth's vineyard come into view. One can see for a distance of thirty miles (fifty km.) in three directions. Unfortunately, however, the people of Nazareth had established a rather poor reputation in morals and religion. This is seen in Nathaniel's question: "Nazareth! Can anything good come from there?" (John 1:46).

NAZARETH DECREE. An inscription cut on a slab of white marble, sent in 1878 from Nazareth for the private collection of a German antiquarian named Froehner. It was not until 1930, when, on Froehner's death, the inscription found a place in the Cabinet de Medailles of the Louvre, that the historian Michel Rostovtzeff noticed its significance. The Abbe Cumont published the first description in 1932.

The decree states: "Ordinance of Caesar. It is my pleasure that graves and tombs remain undisturbed in perpetuity for those who have made them for the cult of their ancestors, or children or members of their house. If, however, any may lay information that another has either demolished them, or has in any other way extracted the buried, or has maliciously transferred them to other places in order to wrong them, or has displaced the sealing or other stones, against such a one I order that a trial be instituted, as in respect of the gods, so in regard to the cult of mortals. For it shall be much more obligatory to honor the buried. Let it be absolutely forbidden for anyone to disturb them. In the case of contravention I desire that the offender be sentenced to capital punishment on the charge of violation of sepulchure."

Evidence suggests that the inscription falls within the decade that closed in A.D. 50. The central Roman government did not take over the administration of Galilee until the death of Agrippa in 44. This limits the date, in the opinion of competent scholarship, to five years under Claudius. It is possible to date the inscription rather more precisely. The Book of Acts, confirmed by Orosius and Suetonius, the Roman historians, says that Claudius expelled the Jews from Rome (Acts 18:2). This occurred in 49. Suetonius adds that this was done "at the instigation of one Chrestos." The reference is obviously to Christ, and Suetonius's garbled account confuses two Greek words, *christos* and *chrestos*.

Claudius was a learned man, misjudged by his contemporaries because of physical defects due to the effects of what may possibly have been Parkinson's disease. His interest in continuing

Stone slab from Nazareth, known as the Nazareth Decree, inscribed with an ordinance of Caesar, (c. A.D. 50). Courtesy Photograph Bibliothèque Nationale, Paris.

Augustus's religious policy led to a wide knowledge of the religions of the Empire and prompted investigation in the courts of any case involving cults or religious beliefs. Suetonius's phrase and the act of expulsion probably reflect the first impact of Christianity in Rome, disturbance in the ghetto, proceedings in the courts, and a review of the rabbis' complaints and the Christian apologia in reply before the court with the Emperor on the bench. He hears the Pharisaic explanation of the empty tomb (Matt 28:13), and, Nazareth having recently fallen under central control, he proceeds to deal with the trouble on the spot. Inquiries are made in Palestine, and the local authority asks for directions. The result is a "rescript" or imperial ruling. Claudius wrote more than one long letter on religious matters (e.g., a notable letter to the Jews of Alexandria in A.D. 41). The decree set up at Nazareth was a quotation from such a communication, verbatim or adapted from a larger text.

NAZIRITE, NAZARITE (năz'ĭ-rīt, năz'ă-rīt, Heb. *nāzîr;* connected with *nadhar, to vow,* hence, *people of the vow,* i.e., *dedicated* or *consecrated*). An Israelite who consecrated himself or herself and took a vow of separation and self-imposed abstinence for the purpose of some special service.

I. Origin. The question whether the concept of the Nazirite was indigenous to Israel has often been asked. It would appear that the practice of separation for religious purposes is very ancient and is shared by a number of peoples. In Israel, however, it assumed unique proportions. Its regulatory laws are laid down in Numbers 6:1–23. There were two different types of Naziritism, the temporary and the perpetual, of which the first type was far more common. In fact, we know of only three of the latter class: Samson, Samuel, and John the Baptist.

II. Distinguishing Traits. The three principal marks that distinguished the Nazirite were (1) a renunciation of wine and all products of the vine, including grapes; (2) prohibition of the use of the razor; and (3) avoidance of contact with a dead body. The OT nowhere explains why these three areas of prohibition were chosen as giving expression to the Nazirites' positive "separation to the LORD" (Num 6:2), but there are some fairly obvious, even if speculative, lines of thought. Abstention from wine could point to the renunciation of earthly joys in order to find all joy in the Lord. Allowing the hair to grow must surely symbolize the dedication of personal strength and vitality to the Lord—at the end of the period of the vow the hair was shaved and cast into the fire of sacrifice (6:18); not, however, the fire of the burnt offering (that is, dedication holding nothing back), but of the fellowship (or peace) offering, for he has been walking in fellowship with the Lord with all his strength all the days of the separation. The avoidance of contact with the dead symbolizes the primacy of his relationship to the Lord: no duty to mankind can take its place. It should be noted that he was not expected to withdraw from society, that is, to live a monastic type of life, nor to become a celibate. The question has been raised whether the Recabites of Jeremiah 35 were included within the Nazirite classification. It appears, however, that the Recabites had more the status of a (Hebrew) nomadic group, since they were not merely forbidden to drink wine but also to refrain from owning real estate. They lived in tents (Jer 35:7, 10).

III. Nazirites in the NT. John the Baptist, the forerunner of Christ, was a Nazirite from birth (Luke 1:15). The connection between John the Baptist and the Qumran community is rather tenuous, nor can it be proved that the men of Qumran were all Nazirites. The case of Paul and Naziritism has frequently elicited discussion. Although it cannot be established that the apostle assumed such vow, it is certain that he did assume the expenses of those who did (Acts 21:23f.). The court of Herod Agrippa supported a large number of Nazirites, according to Josephus.

IV. Reason for Assuming the Vow. The reasons for taking a Nazirite vow were numerous. A vow might be assumed by a parent before the birth of a child; by one in some sort of distress or trouble; or by a woman suspected by her husband of unfaithfulness in their marriage relationship until the suspicion could be removed. Women and slaves could take vows only if sanctioned by their husbands or masters.

The period of time for the Nazirite vow was anywhere from thirty days to a whole lifetime. During the Maccabean days, a number of Jews became Nazirites as a matter of protest against the Hellenistic practices and demands of Antiochus Epiphanes.

V. Nazirites and the Prophets. There is only one clear-cut mention of the Nazirites by the prophets. The prophet Amos (2:11–12) voices a complaint of the Lord against the children of Israel that he had given to Israel the prophets and the Nazirites as spiritual instructors and examples, but that the people had given wine to the Nazirites and had offered inducements to the prophets to refrain from prophesying. JFG

NEAH (nē'à, Heb. *hanē'âh*). A town given by lot to the tribe of Zebulun (Josh 19:13), possibly the same as the "Neiel" of 19:27. Its exact location is unknown.

NEAPOLIS (nē-ăp'ō-lĭs, Gr. *Neapolis*). A town on the north shore of the Aegean Sea: the seaport of Philippi where Paul and his party sailed after seeing the "Man of Macedonia" at Troas (Acts 16:11–12). Paul may have revisited Neapolis on his return trip to Jerusalem (20:3–5). The exact location of Neapolis is yet uncertain. However, on the basis of literary and archaeological evidences, it would appear that it is near Kavalla.

NEARIAH (nē'à-rī'à). 1. A descendant of David (1 Chron 3:22).

2. A descendant of Simeon (1 Chron 4:42).

The LXX translates both occurrences as "Noadiah."

NEBAI (nē'bī). One of the signers of the covenant in the days of Nehemiah (Neh 10:19).

NEBAIOTH, NEBAJOTH (nē-bā'yŏth, nē-bā'jŏth, Heb. *nevāyôth*). 1. The firstborn son of Ishmael, son of Abraham (Gen 25:13; 28:9; 36:3; 1 Chron 1:29).

2. Isaiah mentions Nebaioth as a tribe (Isa 60:7). Some scholars regard Nebaioth as identical with the Nabateans.

NEBALLAT (nē-băl'ăt). A Benjamite town occupied after the Exile, named along with Lod and Ono (Neh 11:34). It is now Beit Nabala, four miles (seven km.) NE of Lydda.

NEBAT (nē'băt). The father of Jeroboam I, the first king of the northern confederacy after the great schism (1 Kings 12:15).

NEBO (nē'bō, Heb. *nevô*, Assyr. *Nabu*). 1. A god of Babylonian mythology. The special seat of his worship was the Babylonian city of Borsippa. He receives mention by Isaiah (Isa 46:1). Nebo was the god of science and learning. The thrust of Isaiah the prophet against him seems to be that Nebo himself, the imagined writer of the fate of all, is destined to go into captivity.

2. The name of the mountain from which

Mount Nebo, the mountain in Transjordan from which Moses saw the Promised Land, as viewed from the Springs of Moses. Courtesy Studium Biblicum Franciscanum, Jerusalem.

Moses viewed the Promised Land (Deut 34:1ff.). See also PISGAH.

3. A Moabite town near or on Mount Nebo (Num 32:3).

4. A town mentioned immediately after Bethel and Ai (Ezra 2:29; Neh 7:33).

NEBO-SARSEKIM (nē'bō-săr-sē'kĭm). An official of Nebuchadnezzar when Jerusalem was conquered (Jer 39:3; but cf. footnote).

NEBUCHADNEZZAR, NEBUCHADREZZAR (nĕb'ū-kăd-nĕz'êr, nĕb'ū-kăd-rĕz'êr). The great king of the Neo-Babylonian Empire who reigned from 605 to 562 B.C. It was he who carried away Judah in the seventy-year Babylonian captivity. He figures prominently in the books of Jeremiah, Ezekiel, Daniel, and the later chapters of Kings and Chronicles. Until recently, not many of Nebuchadnezzar's historical records had been found, though his building inscriptions are numerous. Now the publication by Wiseman of Nebuchadnezzar's chronicle fills in some of the gaps.

The name Nebuchadnezzar means "Nebo protect the boundary." The form Nebuchadrezzar is probably a minor variant. Cf. the variations Tiglath-Pilneser (1 Chron 5:26; 2 Chron 28:20 KJV) and Tiglath-Pileser (2 Kings 15:29). The appearance of the "n" in Nebuchadnezzar may be an inner Hebrew phenomenon, perhaps a rendition of the name assuming a variant etymology, "Nebo protect the servant."

Nebuchadnezzar's father, Nabopolassar, seems to have been a general appointed by the Assyrian king. However, in the later years of Assyria he rebelled and established himself as king of Babylon in 626 B.C. The rebellion increased and finally Nabopolassar with the Medes and Scythians conquered Nineveh, the Assyrian capital, in 612. The Medes and Babylonians divided the Assyrian Empire, and a treaty was probably sealed by the marriage of the Median princess to the Babylonian prince, Nebuchadnezzar. In 607 the crown prince Nebuchadnezzar joined his father in the battle against the remnants of the Assyrian power and their allies, the Egyptians. In 605, when his father was in his last illness, he decisively defeated the Egyptians at Carchemish. At this time Nebuchadnezzar took over all Syria and Palestine.

Sixth century B.C. cuneiform tablet, inscribed with a listing of the events from the last year of Nabopolassar to the eleventh year of Nebuchadnezzar II, including the account of the taking of Jerusalem. Reproduced by courtesy of the Trustees of the British Museum.

Apparently Jehoiakim, king of Judah, who had been vassal to Egypt, quickly did homage to Babylon and gave hostages (Dan 1:1). Nebuchadnezzar at this time got news of his father's death, and with a picked bodyguard he hastened home to secure his throne. On repeated occasions thereafter he struck toward the west. In about 602 Jehoiakim revolted (2 Kings 24:1), probably with promise of Egyptian help, but was forced to submit. In 601 Nebuchadnezzar attacked Egypt itself but was defeated, as he frankly admits. Later, Pharaoh Hophra submitted to him. In 597 Jehoiakim rebelled again, and Nebuchadnezzar called out his troops for another western expedition. Jehoiakim died either in a siege or by treachery (Jer 22:18–19), and his son Jehoiachin ascended the throne. But he lasted only three months until the campaign was over; he was taken as a hostage to Babylon, where he lived and finally was given relative freedom. Here the biblical account (2 Kings 25:27–30) is confirmed by discovery of the Weidner Tablets.

Nebuchadnezzar installed Jehoiachin's uncle as puppet king, taking heavy tribute from Jerusalem. Ezekiel was among the captives of that expedition. Nebuchadnezzar's chronicle agrees with the biblical account, telling how (in 597 B.C.) he "encamped against the city of Judah and on the second day of the month Adar [Mar. 15/16] he seized the city and captured the king. He appointed there a king of his own choice, received its heavy tribute and sent them to Babylon" (D. Wiseman, *Chronicles of the Chaldean Kings,* 1956, p. 73). This discovery gives about the best authenticated date in the OT.

In later years the Chronicle tells of repeated expeditions of Nebuchadnezzar toward the west to collect tribute and keep the satellite kingdoms in line. Unfortunately, the present tablets do not go beyond 593, so they give no record of the final and brutal devastation of Jerusalem in 586 when Zedekiah revolted. The historical gap extends to 556 except for a brief account of a campaign to southern Asia Minor by Neriglissar in 557.

Nebuchadnezzar is celebrated by the historians of antiquity for the splendor of his building operations as well as for the brilliance of his military exploits. Koldewey's excavations in Babylon illustrate the histories. Still impressive are the remains of the Ishtar Gate and the processional street lined with façades of enameled brick bearing pictures of griffins (fabled monsters with eagle head and wings and lion body). The temple of Esagila was famous, as were also the ziggurat, or temple tower, and the hanging gardens. These were regarded by the Greeks as one of the wonders of the world, though nothing certain of them has been excavated. According to legend, they were built for Nebuchadnezzar's wife, the Median princess Amytis, who was homesick for her mountains. Parrot, in a study of the ziggurat, reconstructs it as a pyramidal tower, 298 feet (93 m.) square and rising in seven stages to a height of 300 feet (94 m.).

Historical records are brief and could hardly be expected to mention the incidents of Nebuchad-

Reconstruction of the palace of Nebuchadnezzar II at Babylon: (1) Ishtar Gate, (2) Nebuchadnezzar's throne room, perhaps the scene of Belshazzar's feast, and (3) the temple dedicated to Ninmah, located to the east of Ishtar Gate and the Processional Way. After Koldewey. Courtesy Carta, Jerusalem.

nezzar's life detailed by Daniel. But there is nothing false about the dream of the vision of chapter 2 nor in the incident of the idol and the fiery furnace. A similar practice seems to be referred to in Jeremiah 29:22. It has been pointed out that this incident is more suited to the Babylonian period than the later Persian time, for the Persians worshiped fire and would be less apt to use it for execution.

As to the madness of Nebuchadnezzar in Daniel 4, there is no historical account remaining for us, but it must be remembered that much of Nebuchadnezzar's reign is a historical blank. Anything could have happened. Among the Dead Sea Scrolls a fragment has been found, the *Prayer of Nabonidus,* that refers to an illness of the king for seven years that was healed by God after the testimony of a Jewish magician. Some now say that this is the source of the legend that in Daniel is misapplied to Nebuchadnezzar. This can hardly be proved or denied from historical evidence. It seems equally possible that the canonical record

Glazed reliefs (now in the Istanbul Museum) of roaring lions, which lined the Processional Way at Babylon during the time of Nebuchadnezzar II (605–562 B.C.). Photo: B. Brandl.

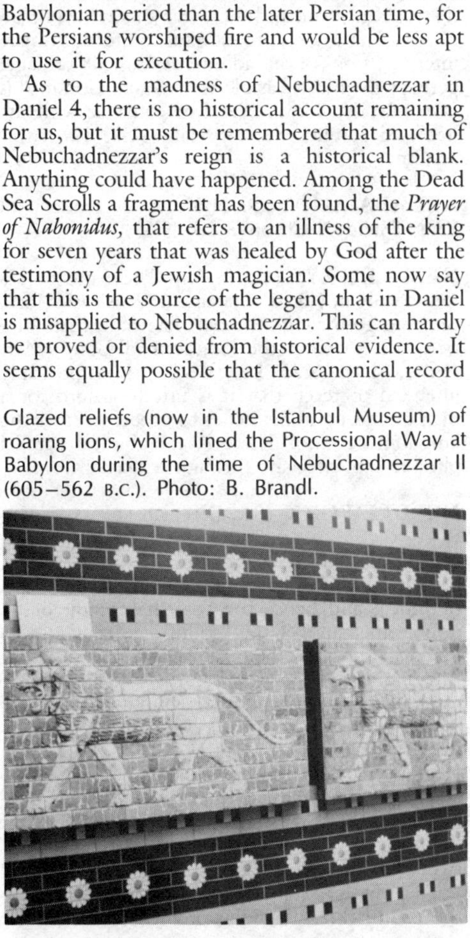

was duplicated and applied to the later king. Indeed, more than one king suffered from illness and from mental distress—Ashurbanipal and Cambyses may be mentioned. If truth is stranger than fiction, both Nebuchadnezzar and Nabonidus may have suffered in a somewhat similar way—the similarities being emphasized in the latter's prayer. There is perhaps a bare possibility that the names are confused. Two rebels after the reign of Cambyses apparently took the name of Nebuchadnezzar. There is uncertainty as to the name of Labynetus, who mediated the Median-Lydian treaty of 585 B.C. Some think he was Nabonidus, some say Nebuchadnezzar. Is it out of the question that Nabonidus also on occasion adopted the name Nebuchadnezzar? He had abundant precedent, but we have no positive evidence.

Of the death of Nebuchadnezzar we have no knowledge. He was succeeded by his son Evil-Merodach (Amil-Marduk), then by his son-in-law Nergal-Sharezer (Neriglissar), for brief reigns. Nabonidus, who followed after the short reign of Labashi-Marduk, was perhaps related. There is some evidence that Nabonidus's mother was the daughter of Nebuchadnezzar by a second wife, Nitocris. With the passing of the brilliant Nebuchadnezzar, however, the Neo-Babylonian Empire soon crumbled and fell an easy prey to the Persians under Cyrus. RLH

NEBUSHAZBAN (nĕb'ū-shăs'băn, Akkad. *Nebo, save me*). An important officer in the army of Nebuchadnezzar at the time of the Babylonian siege of Jerusalem in 586 B.C. To his care another Babylonian official delivered the prophet Jeremiah (Jer 39:11–14).

NEBUZARADAN (nĕb'ū-zȧr-ā'dăn, Akkad. *Nebo has given seed*). Nebuchadnezzar's general when the Babylonians besieged Jerusalem (2 Kings 25:8, 11–12, 20; Jer 52:12ff.). The prophet Jeremiah was made the special charge and responsibility of Nebuzaradan (Jer 39:11–14). Nebuzaradan bore the title "commander of the

Green stone drawing of a statuette (12 cm., c. 594–588 B.C.) of Psamtik II, king of the 26th Dynasty, to which belonged the Egyptian king mentioned in the Bible under the name of Neco (e.g., 2 Kings 23:29). Courtesy Carta, Jerusalem.

imperial guard." After the fall of the city of Jerusalem in 586–85 B.C., Nebuzaradan was commissioned by Nebuchadnezzar to conduct the captives to Babylon. Before the appointment of Gedaliah (40:5) Nebuzaradan was provisional governor of Palestine for the Babylonians. Nebuzaradan presented the option to Jeremiah to travel with him to Babylon or to remain in his own land (40:1–6). The prophet chose to remain.

NECK (Heb. *tsawwār, tsawwā'râh*, Gr. *nōtos, back*). A term often used in Scripture with literal and figurative meanings. The bowed neck is often used as a symbol of submission, while the unbowed or "stiff neck" represents insubordination and disobedience (Exod 32:9; Deut 9:13; Ps 75:5; Acts 7:51). It was a military custom for the conqueror to place his foot on the neck of the vanquished (Josh 10:24; Ps 110:1; Rom 16:20). "To shake off" or "to break the yoke" signifies to gain freedom. "To fall upon the neck" of (NIV to embrace, or throw one's arms around) a person is a common mode of salutation in the East and sometimes portrays great emotional stress (Gen 46:29; Luke 15:20; Acts 20:37).

NECKLACE (Heb. *ravidh*). A chain worn as an ornament around the neck, and to which might be attached pendants (Isa 3:19) or rings (Gen 38:25). The word is not found in the KJV but is used in the NIV, and such ornaments were very popular in ancient times.

NECO, NECHO, NECHOH (*nē'kō*, Heb. *par'ōh nekhōh* or *nechoh*). Ruler of Egypt (609–595 B.C.), son of Psamtik I, famous in Greek history. Neco began his rule at a propitious time: the Assyrian Empire was falling, and the Neo-Babylonian Empire was emerging. He thus was able to gain and retain control over Syria until his humiliating defeat at the hands of Nebuchadnezzar at the battle of Carchemish. Of particular interest to the reader of the Bible is Josiah's defeat by Neco at the battle of Megiddo (2 Kings 23:29; 2 Chron 35:20ff.). When Josiah died, Jehoahaz was made king, but Neco dethroned him and set up in his stead Jehoahaz's brother Jehoiakim (2 Kings 23:29–34; 2 Chron 35:20–36:4). In 605 he was badly defeated by Nebuchadnezzar at the battle of Carchemish and lost all of his Asiatic possessions (2 Kings 24:7).

NECROMANCER, NECROMANCY (něk'-rō-măn-sẽr, něk'rō-măn-sē). Necromancy was a form of witchcraft and was considered one of the "black" or diabolical arts. Etymologically, the term signifies conversing with the dead for purposes of consultation or divination. The Mosaic Law sternly forbade such a practice (Deut 18:10–11). The most familiar case in the Bible is that of King Saul and the witch of Endor (1 Sam 28:7–25). There are several quite legitimate interpretations of this admittedly difficult passage; perhaps the most feasible view is that God for his own purpose allowed Saul to converse with the deceased Samuel. See especially verse 12 of this account.

NEDABAIAH (něd'à-bī'à). A descendant of King David (1 Chron 3:18).

NEEDLE'S EYE (Gr. *raphis*). The expression is found only in Christ's statement "It is easier for a camel to go through the eye of a needle than for a rich man to enter the kingdom of God" (Matt 19:24; Mark 10:25; Luke 18:25). Jesus probably intended to teach that it is utterly absurd for a man bound up in his riches to expect to enter the kingdom of God. There is a rabbinical parallel phrase: "an elephant through a needle's eye."

NEEDLEWORK (See EMBROIDERY)

NEGEV, NEGEB (něg'ěv, Něg'ěb, Heb. *neghev, dry*). The desert region lying to the south of Judea, and hence the term has acquired the double meaning of the "south" (usually so rendered in the KJV), because of its direction from Judah, and the "desert," because of its aridity. It came to refer to a definite geographical region, as when we read concerning Abraham that he journeyed "into the south" (KJV; NIV "to the Negev") to Bethel (Gen 13:1). Numbers 13:22 represents the twelve spies as spying out the land by way of the Negev (KJV "south"). The Negev is the probable site of Debir, a city of Judah about twelve miles (twenty km.) SW of Hebron.

The physical characteristics of the Negeb are the rolling hills that abruptly terminate in the

Bedouin camp in the Negev. Courtesy S. Zur Picture Library.

desert region. This region is bounded on the east by the Dead Sea and on the west by the Mediterranean Sea. It is a land where the water supply is scarce because of a very meager amount of rainfall in the summer months. At other seasons of the year, however, it is used by the nomads for pasturage. In this territory Hagar encountered the angel when she fled from the face of her mistress Sarah (Gen 16:7, 14; NIV "desert," KJV "wilderness"). Here both Isaac and Jacob lived (24:62; 37:1). This territory was part of the original land of the Amalekites (Num 13:29). On the basis of Joshua 19:1–9, the Negev was allotted to the tribe of Simeon. However, according to Joshua 15:20–31, it was given to the tribe of Judah. Many of David's exploits during the reign of Saul are described as happening in the Negev, centering around Ziklag (1 Sam 27:5ff.). After Nebuchadnezzar sacked Jerusalem in 586–585 B.C., a group of Jews retreated to the Negev, where they were harassed by the Edomites who sided with the Babylonians. Judas Maccabaeus expelled the Edomites in 164. John Hyrcanus compelled them to become Jews in 109.

NEHELAMITE (nē-hĕl'à-mīt, Heb. *hanĕhelāmî*). Shemaiah, a false prophet, an adversary of Jeremiah, is styled a Nehelamite (Jer 29:24, 31–32). The place-name Nehelam is not found in the OT.

Aerial view of southern Negev. Courtesy Duby Tal.

NEHEMIAH (nē'hĕ-mī'à, Heb. *nehemyâh, Jehovah has comforted*). 1. One of the leaders of the returning exiles under Zerubbabel (Ezra 2:2; Neh 7:7).

2. The son of Azbuk, a prince of Beth Zur who helped repair the wall of Jerusalem (Neh 3:16).

3. The son of Hacaliah and governor of the Persian province of Judah after 444 B.C. Of Nehemiah the son of Hacaliah little is known aside from what is in the book that bears his name. His times, however, are illuminated by the rather considerable material found in the Elephantine Papyri from Egypt, which were written in the fifth century. These papyri come from a military colony of Jews residing on an island far up the Nile, opposite Aswan, and are written in Hebrew. They include copies of letters to and from Jerusalem and Samaria. They name several men who are also mentioned in the Book of Nehemiah.

Nehemiah was a "cupbearer" to King Artaxerxes (Neh 1:11; 2:1). Inasmuch as some of the Elephantine Papyri that are contemporary with Nehemiah are dated, we know that this Artaxerxes must be the first, called Longimanus, who ruled 465–423 B.C. The title "cupbearer" clearly indicates a responsible office—not merely a servile position—for the king speaks to Nehemiah as an intimate and also indicates that he regards Nehemiah's journey to Jerusalem only as a kind of vacation from official duties (2:6). Furthermore, the credentials given Nehemiah by the king and also the office of governor entrusted to him show that the king looked on him as a man of ability. That a captive Jew should attain to such an office need not surprise us when we remember the examples of Daniel, Esther, and others. Indeed some ancient courts made it a practice to train captive noble youths for service in the government (Dan 1:4–5).

Nehemiah was an officer of the palace at Susa, but his heart was in Jerusalem. Word came to him from Hanani, one of his brothers, of the ruined condition of Jerusalem. Overcome with grief, Nehemiah sought the refuge of prayer—and God answered abundantly.

Hanani is called Nehemiah's brother in Nehemiah 1:2. In 7:2 a Hanani and Hananiah are both mentioned. It is possible that this verse means to equate the two forms of the name Hanani, calling Nehemiah's brother ruler of the palace at Jerusalem. It has been suggested that this Hanani is the same man mentioned in the Elephantine Papyri as an official who seems to have come into Egypt on a government mission. It was probably on another official trip that Hanani told Nehemiah of the sad state of affairs in Jerusalem.

Only about twelve years earlier, in Artaxerxes's seventh year (457 B.C.), Ezra had gone back to Jerusalem with about 1,750 men, besides women and children (Ezra 8:1–20) and treasure worth a king's ransom (8:26–27). But if we refer Ezra 4:6–23 to the days of Ezra himself, it appears that his adversaries had persuaded the king to stop Ezra's efforts at rebuilding. The city, therefore, lay unrepaired, needing a new decree from the king. This permission Nehemiah providentially secured, thanks to his position at the court. Nehemiah therefore appeared at Jerusalem with a royal commission to continue the work that Ezra had begun.

Nehemiah was a man of ability, courage, and action. Arriving at Jerusalem, he first privately surveyed the scene of rubble (Neh 2:1–16), and he encouraged the rulers at Jerusalem with his report of answered prayer and the granting of the king's new decree (2:18). Then he organized the community to carry out the effort of rebuilding the broken-down wall. Courageously and squarely he met the opposition of men like Sanballat, Tobiah, and Geshem (who are all now known from nonbiblical documents); and at last he saw the wall completed in the brief span of fifty-two days (6:15).

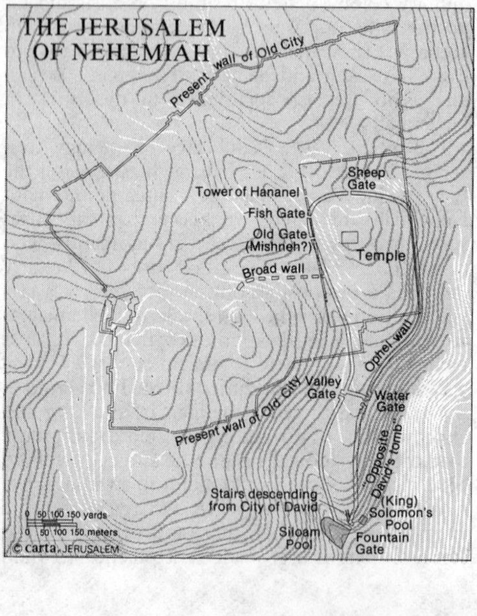

Nehemiah cooperated with Ezra in numerous reforms and especially in the public instruction in the law (Neh 8). However, he left for Persia, probably on official business, in 431 B.C. (13:6). Later he returned to Jerusalem, but for how long we do not know. Of the end of his life we know nothing. The Elephantine Papyri indicate that a different man, Bagohi, was governor by 407 B.C.

RLH

NEHEMIAH, BOOK OF. The Book of Nehemiah closes the history of the biblical period. Closely allied to the Book of Ezra, it was attached to it in the old Jewish reckoning. It gives the history and reforms of Nehemiah the governor from 444 to about 420 B.C.

Outline:

I. Nehemiah Returns to Jerusalem (1:1–2:20).
II. Building Despite Opposition (3:1–7:4).
III. Genealogy of the First Returning Exiles (7:5–73 [= Ezra 2:2–70]).
IV. The Revival and Covenant Sealing (8:1–10:39).
V. Dwellers at Jerusalem and Genealogies (11:1–12:26).
VI. Final Reforms (13:1–31).

Nehemiah's great work of restoring the wall of Jerusalem depended basically on securing permission from the king. Ezra had returned to Jerusalem with a sizable group of people and much gold and silver only a dozen years previously (see NEHEMIAH), but had been hindered in his work by adverse royal decrees secured by his enemies. In God's providence Nehemiah secured the restoration of royal favor.

The actual building of the wall was parceled out among different leaders. Various cities of the province of Judea sent contingents of workers, and we can here learn something of the extent of Nehemiah's domain. The rapidity of building may have been due to preliminary work that Ezra might have accomplished. Most of the gates and sections of the wall mentioned in chapter 3 cannot be identified with certainty. Perhaps the wall enclosed only the eastern hill of Jerusalem.

The opposition to Nehemiah by Sanballat and others combined ridicule, threat, and craft. Sanballat is called the governor of Samaria in the Elephantine Papyri. He was apparently not anxious to see a rival province strengthened, and there was religious antagonism as well to Nehemiah's strict reform program.

Internal difficulties also developed. The rich charged interest of one percent (per month, apparently, Neh 5:10), whereas the Mosaic Law required outright charity to the poor. But against all opposition the wall was built by men who used both sword and trowel in the work of the Lord.

The genealogy of Nehemiah 7, which is a duplicate of the list in Ezra 2, is of interest. There are unimportant differences between the lists such as might be expected in the copying of detailed data like this. It is instructive to note that the record of Zerubbabel's returnees that Nehemiah used was a *written* record—not preserved by oral tradition as many have suggested was the method used for the passing on of Israel's histories.

Nehemiah's reform involved the teaching of Moses' Law by Ezra and others at the Feast of Tabernacles (as commanded in Deut 31:10). This led to the great prayer of confession of Nehemiah 9, redolent with quotations from and allusions to the Pentateuch. A covenant was solemnly sealed to walk in the Law of the Lord as given by Moses (10:29).

Nehemiah's final reform included the removal of Tobiah from the temple precincts. Tobiah had entered through friendship with Eliashib the high priest while Nehemiah was back in Persia. Also a grandson of Eliashib had married Sanballat's daughter (Neh 13:28). Evidently Eliashib was followed by his son Johanan in the reign of Darius II (423–404 B.C.). This Johanan is mentioned in the Elephantine Papyri as high priest in Jerusalem. The mention of him seems to indicate that Nehemiah's history continued until at least 423 B.C.

Bibliography: J. M. Myers, *Ezra, Nehemiah* (AB), 1965; D. Kidner, *Ezra and Nehemiah* (TOTC), 1979; F. C. Fensham, *The Books of Ezra and Nehemiah* (NIC), 1982. RLH

NEHILOTH (nē'hĭ-lŏth). A musical term found in the title to Psalm 5 (KJV). NIV has the phrase "For flutes."

NEHUM (nē'hŭm, Heb. *nehûm*). One of the twelve heads of Judah returning with Zerubbabel, also called Rehum (Ezra 2:2; Neh 7:7).

NEHUSHTA (nē-hŭsh'tȧ, Heb. *nehushtā'*). The mother of King Jehoiachin of Judah. She was the daughter of Elnathan of Jerusalem (2 Kings 24:8). She was exiled with her son to Babylon (2 Kings 24:12; Jer 29:2).

NEHUSHTAN (nĕ-hŭsh'tăn, Heb. *nehushtān*, perhaps *brass serpent*). The name given to the serpent of brass surviving from the times of Moses but destroyed by Hezekiah during his reforms because the Israelites had been making it an object of worship (2 Kings 18:4).

NEIEL (nē-ī'ĕl). A boundary town between Zebulun and Asher (Josh 19:27), may be the same as Neah (19:13).

NEIGHBOR (Heb. *rēa', 'āmîth, friend, qārôv, shākhēn*, Gr. *plēsion, nearby, geitōn, inhabitant*). The duties and responsibilities towards one's neighbor are varied. In the OT, injunctions are given more in the negative than in the positive. The tenth commandment is directed toward the protection of the neighbor's property (Exod 20:17); the commandment immediately preceding, toward the protection of a neighbor's reputation (20:16). Cities of refuge were appointed for one who killed his neighbor accidentally (Deut 19:4). The Book of Proverbs is replete with admonitions concerning one's neighbor, of which the following may be regarded as the epitome: "He who despises his neighbor sins" (Prov. 14:21). Due regard for one's neighbor is expressed in the great OT and NT precept, "Love your neighbor as yourself" (Lev 19:18; Matt 19:19). The parable of the Good Samaritan (Luke 10:30–37) was given in answer to the question, "And who is my neighbor?" (10:29).

NEKEB (See ADAMI NEKEB)

NEKODA (nē-kō'dȧ). The head of a family of temple servants (KJV Nethinim) who could not prove their Israelite descent at the return from Babylon (Ezra 2:48, 60; Neh 7:50, 62).

NEMUEL (nĕm'ū-ĕl, Heb. *nemû'ēl*). 1. A Reubenite, brother of Dathan and Abiram who led the insurrection against Moses and Aaron (Num 26:9).

2. A son of Simeon (Num 26:12; 1 Chron 4:24); also Genesis 46:10, where the variant "Jemuel" is used.

NEPHEG (nē'fĕg, Heb. *nephegh, sprout, shoot*). 1. Son of Izhar, brother of Korah, Dathan, and Abiram (Exod 6:21).

2. A son of David (2 Sam 5:15; 1 Chron 3:7; 14:6).

NEPHEW (Heb. *nekēdh*, Gr. *ekgonon*). A term found in the KJV four times, meaning grandson (Judg 12:14), descendant (Job 18:19; Isa 14:22), grandchild (1 Tim 5:4). NIV uses it three times, all with today's common meaning of the son of one's sister or brother (Gen 12:5; 14:12; Ezra 8:19).

NEPHILIM (See GIANTS)

NEPHISH (See NAPHISH)

NEPHISHESIM (See NEPHUSSIM)

NEPHTHALIM (See NAPHTALI)

NEPHTOAH (nĕf-tō'ȧ, Heb. *nephtôah, an opening*). A spring between Judah's and Benjamin's border (Josh 15:9; 18:15). Identified as modern Lifta, a village two miles (three km.) NW of Jerusalem.

NEPHUSSIM, NEPHISHESIM (nĕ-fūs'ĭm, nē-fĭsh'ĕ-sĭm). A family of temple servants (KJV Nethinim), perhaps originally from the tribe Naphish (Ezra 2:50; Neh 7:52).

NER (nûr, Heb. *nēr, a lamp*). 1. Father of Abner (1 Sam 14:50; 26:14).

2. The grandfather of King Saul (1 Chron 8:33; see 2 Sam 8:12; 1 Kings 2:5, 32).

NEREUS (nē'rūs, Gr. *Nēreus*). A Roman Christian to whom the apostle Paul extended greetings (Rom 16:15). The name has been discovered in an inscription containing a listing of the emperor's servants. Whether this is the same Nereus is uncertain.

NERGAL (nûr'gȧl, Heb. *nereghal*). A Babylonian deity of destruction and disaster, associated with the planet Mars (2 Kings 17:30).

Cylinder seal from Larsa, an ancient Sumerian city, c. 2360–2180 B.C., that shows the god Nergal standing with one foot upon the body of an enemy. Courtesy Carta, Jerusalem.

NERGAL-SHAREZER (nûr'găl-shȧ-rē'zêr, Assyr. *nerghal sar-usar, may Nergal protect the prince*). The son-in-law of Nebuchadnezzar. He is also called Neriglissar. Evil-Merodach (Amil—Marduk), who succeeded Nebuchadnezzar as king, was assassinated by Nergal-Sharezer, who then became king (Jer 39:3–13).

NERI (nē'rī, Gr. *Nēri*). A name listed in the ancestry of Jesus Christ, the grandfather of Zerubbabel (Luke 3:27). See NERIAH.

NERIAH (nē-rī'ȧ, Heb. *nērîyâh, whose lamp is Jehovah*). The father of Seraiah and Baruch, the latter being the scribe of Jeremiah (Jer 32:12, 16; 36:4; 43:3). In the apocryphal book Baruch 1:1, the Greek form is given, *Nērias,* which Luke uses in abbreviated fashion as Neri (Luke 3:27).

NERIGLISSAR (See NERGAL-SHAREZER)

NERO (nē'rō, Gr. *Nērōn*). The fifth Roman emperor, born A.D. 37, commenced reign 54, died June 9, 68. The original family name of Nero was Lucius Domitius Ahenobarbus, but after he was adopted into the Claudian family line by the Emperor Claudius, he assumed the name of Nero Claudius Caesar Germanicus. Nero's father was Enaeus Domitus Ahenobarbus, a man given to viciousness and vice. His mother was Agrippina, who cared little for her son's morals but was interested only in his temporal advancement.

The first years of Nero's reign were quite peaceful and gave promise of good things to come. Nero himself could boast that not a single person had been unjustly executed throughout his extensive empire. During these "rational years" of Nero's administration, the apostle Paul, in compliance with Paul's own expressed appeal (Acts 25:10–11), was brought before him as the reigning Caesar (c. A.D. 63). We can hardly do otherwise than infer that Paul was freed of all charges to continue his labors of evangelization.

Nero's marriage to Poppaea opened the second period of his reign. He killed his mother, his chief advisers Seneca and Burrus, and many of the nobility to secure their fortunes.

In A.D. 64 a large part of Rome was destroyed by fire. Whether or not Nero actually ordered the burning of the city is very controversial. However, justly or not, the finger of suspicion was pointed in Nero's direction. A scapegoat was provided in the Christians. Even the Roman historian Tacitus, who certainly cannot be given the name "Christian," bears testimony as to the severity of the sufferings inflicted on them. "Their death was made a matter of sport; they were covered in wild beast's skins and torn to pieces by dogs or were fastened to crosses and set on fire in order to serve as torches by night. . . . Nero had

The Roman Emperor Nero (A.D. 54–68). Courtesy Carta, Jerusalem.

offered his gardens for the spectacle and gave an exhibition in his circus, mingling with the crowd in the guise of a charioteer or mounted on his chariot. Hence, . . . there arose a feeling of pity, because it was felt that they were being sacrificed not for the common good, but to gratify the savagery of one man" (Tacitus, *Annals* 15, 44).

Nero's private life was a scandal. Surrendering himself to the basest of appetites, he indulged himself in the most evil forms of pleasure. Conspiracies and plots dogged his latter years. He was advised to destroy himself, but could not find the courage to do so. Learning that the Senate had decreed his death, Nero's last cruel act was to put many of the Senate members to death. He finally died by his own hand in the summer of A.D. 68. Thus perished the last of the line of Julius Caesar. Both Paul and Peter suffered martyrdom under Nero. JFG

NEST (Heb. *qēn,* Gr. *nossia* or *kataskēnōsis*). The nests of birds differ from species to species (Ps 104:17; Jer 22:23; 48:28; Ezek 31:6). Many nests are built high (Job 39:27; Jer 49:16; Obad 4; Hab 2:9). Mosaic law forbade one who found a bird's nest with the mother and her brood from harming the mother bird (Deut 22:6). Semite people in general view with extreme disfavor anyone who willfully disturbs a bird in the nest. Isaiah compares the despoiling of Israel by the Assyrians to the robbing of a bird's nest (Isa 10:14). Jesus contrasts birds having nests with his having no home (Matt 8:20; Luke 9:58).

NETAIM (nĭ-tā'ĕm, plantings). A town of Judah where potters lived and worked for the king (1 Chron 4:23).

NETHANEL, NETHANEEL (nē-thăn'ĕl, nē-thăn'ē-ĕl, Heb. *nethan'ēl, God has given*). The name of ten OT men:

1. The prince of Issachar just after the Exodus (Num 1:8; 2:5).
2. Son of Jesse and older brother of David (1 Chron 2:14).
3. One of the priests who played trumpets before the ark (1 Chron 15:24).
4. A Levitical scribe whose son Shemaiah was a recorder under David (1 Chron 24:6).
5. Fifth son of Obed-Edom, appointed as one of the doorkeepers of the tabernacle (1 Chron 26:4).
6. A prince of Judah whom Jehoshaphat appointed to teach in Israel (2 Chron 17:7).
7. A wealthy Levite in Josiah's time (2 Chron 35:9).
8. A priest in Ezra's time who had taken a foreign wife (Ezra 10:22).
9. A priest and head of a household in the days of Joiakim c. 470 B.C. (Neh 12:21).
10. A priestly musician in the days of Nehemiah (Neh. 12:36).

Nathanael of Cana of Galilee in the days of Jesus (John 1:45–49) had the same name, though in the Greek it is slightly changed.

NETHANIAH (nĕth'à-nī'a, Heb. *nethanyāhû, whom Jehovah gave*). 1. Father of Ishmael the assassin of Gedaliah (Jer 40:8–41:18).
2. A chief singer (1 Chron 25:2, 12).
3. A teaching Levite (2 Chron 17:8).
4. Father of Jehudi whom the princes sent to Baruch for Jeremiah's book (Jer 36:14).

NETHINIM (nĕth'ĭ-nĭm, Heb. *nethînîm, given ones*). A large group of temple servants, mentioned only in the later books of the OT. In a sense, all the Levites were Nethinim (Num 8:19), for they were given by the Lord as a gift to Aaron and his sons for the divine service. At the conquest of Midian (Num 31) the plunder was divided between the warriors and the congregation, and a fixed proportion was "given" for the Lord's service (31:40, 42, 47), of which 32 were "nethinim" to the priests and 320 to the Levites in general. Later, when the men of Gibeon deceived Israel by claiming to have come a great distance (Josh 9), they were allowed to live but were made "hewers of wood and drawers of water." The 392 descendants of these two groups, called Nethinim eighteen times in the KJV (1 Chron 9:2; Ezra; Neh), came back with Israel after the Babylonian captivity (Ezra 2:43–58). At Ezra's return he lists 220 Nethinim (Ezra 8:20) and explains that David had appointed these for the service of the Levites.

NETOPHAH, NETOPHATHITES (nē-tō'fà, nē-tŏ'fa-thīts). A village of Judah and its inhabitants. It lies about three miles (five km.) south of Jerusalem and three and a half miles (almost six km.) south of Bethlehem. The "villages of the Netophathites" (1 Chron 9:16; Neh 12:28) were apparently given to, or inhabited by, Levites, although Netophah is not mentioned in the earlier books. Several of David's men are named as from this place (2 Sam 23:28–29; 1 Chron 2:54). Seraiah, the son of Tanhumeth the Netophathite, is mentioned (2 Kings 25:23) among the murderers of Gedaliah, the governor.

NETTLE (See PLANTS)

NETWORK. This represents three distinct words in the Hebrew:
1. Networks (Isa 19:9 KJV; white cloth JB, NASB; white cotton RSV; fine linen NIV).
2. An ornamental carving or bas-relief on the pillars of Solomon's temple (1 Kings 7:18–42).
3. A network of brass that served as a grate for the great altar of burnt offering at the tabernacle (Exod 27:4; 38:4).

NEW BIRTH (See REGENERATION)

NEW MOON (See CALENDAR; FEASTS)

NEW TESTAMENT. A collection of twenty-seven documents, the second part of the sacred Scriptures of the Christian church, the first part being called by contrast the "Old Testament." In the name "New Testament," apparently first given to the collection in the latter half of the second century, the word "testament" represents Greek *diathēkē,* variously translated "testament," "settlement," "covenant" (the last of these being on the whole the most satisfactory equivalent). The new covenant is the new order or dispensation inaugurated by the death of Jesus (compare his own designation: "the new covenant in my blood" in Luke 22:20; 1 Cor 11:25). It was so called because it fulfilled the promise made by God to his people in Jeremiah 31:31–34 that he would "make a new covenant" with them whereby the desire and power to do his will would be implanted within them and all their past sins would be wiped out (cf. Heb 8:6–12). By contrast with this covenant the earlier covenant established by God with Israel in Moses' day came to be known as the "old covenant" (cf. 2 Cor 3:14; Heb 8:13). The foundation documents of the covenant instituted by Jesus are accordingly known as "the books of the new covenant (testament)," while the earlier Scriptures, which trace the course of the old dispensation, were known as "the books of the old covenant [testament]" from the time of Melito of Sardis (A.D. 170) onward.

I. Contents. In speaking of the books of the NT we must be clear whether we refer to the individual documents or to the whole collection as such. The individual documents naturally existed before the collection, and some of them were grouped in smaller collections before they were ultimately gathered together in the complete NT. All, or nearly all, of the individual documents belong to the first century A.D.; the NT as a collection makes its appearance in the second century.

The order in which the twenty-seven documents appear in our NT today is an order of subject-matter rather than a chronological order. First come the four Gospels—or rather the four records of the one and only gospel—narrating Jesus' ministry, death, and resurrection. These are followed by the Acts of the Apostles, which begins by mentioning Jesus' appearances to the disciples following the Resurrection; from then on we are told how, over the next thirty years, Christianity spread along the road from Jerusalem to Rome. This book was originally written as the continuation of the Gospel of Luke. These five constitute the narrative section of the NT.

The next twenty-one documents take the form of letters written to communities or individuals. Thirteen of these bear the name of Paul as writer, one the name of James, two of Peter, and one of Jude (Judas). The others are anonymous. One of these, the Letter to the Hebrews, is more properly described as a homily with an epistolary ending; its authorship remains a matter of conjecture to this day. The three that we know as the letters of John are so called, not because they bear John's name, but because it is plain from their contents that they are closely associated with the fourth Gospel (which, though itself anonymous, has from early times been known as John's). First John is an exhortation in which the writer impresses on his readers (whom he calls his "dear children") the practical implications of some of the leading themes of John's Gospel. In 2 and 3 John the writer refers to himself as "the elder."

The last book of the NT bears some features of the epistolary style in that it is introduced by seven covering letters addressed to churches in the Roman province of Asia; but for the most part it belongs to the class of literature to which it has given its own name ("apocalyptic," from "Apocalypse" or "Revelation"). In apocalyptic literature the out-working of God's purpose on earth is disclosed in the form of symbolical visions. Written probably between A.D. 69 and 96, when the Flavian dynasty ruled the Roman Empire, Revelation aims to encourage persecuted Christians with the assurance that they are on the winning side; that Jesus, and not the Roman emperor, has won the victory that entitles him to exercise sovereignty over the world and control its destiny.

II. Order of Writing. Although the four Gospels deal with events of the first thirty years of the Christian era and the NT letters belong to the remaining two-thirds of the first century, several of the letters were in existence before even the earliest of the Gospels. With the possible exception of James, the earliest NT documents are those letters that Paul composed before his two years' detention in Rome (A.D. 60–62). Therefore, when one of Paul's earlier letters mentions an action or saying of Jesus, that mention is our first written account of it. For example, Paul's account of the institution of Holy Communion (1 Cor 11:23–25) is earlier by several years than the account of it given in our oldest Gospel (Mark 14:22–25).

Jesus himself wrote no book, but he gave his teaching to his disciples in forms that could be easily memorized and enjoined them to teach others what they had learned from him. There is good reason to believe that one of the earliest Christian writings was a compilation of his teaching, arranged according to the chief subjects he treated, though this document has not been preserved in its original form but has been incorporated into some of the existing NT books.

The necessity for a written account of the life of Jesus was not felt acutely in the earlier years of the Christian mission. In those years, when there were so many eyewitnesses of the saving events who could testify to what they had seen and heard, their testimony was regarded as sufficient, and the Gospel material circulated far and wide by word of mouth. But even in those early years the necessity arose for an apostle to give instruction in writing to people from whom he was separated at the time. While ministering in Ephesus, Paul heard disturbing news of the state of affairs in the church he had founded three or four years previously in Corinth. He was unable just then to visit Corinth in person but sent his converts in that city a letter conveying much the same message as he would have given them orally had he been with them. Again, a few years later, he proposed to visit Rome and thought it wise, during a brief stay in Corinth, to prepare the Roman Christians for his coming, especially as he had never been in their city before. So he sent them a letter in which he took the opportunity of making a full-length statement of the gospel as he understood and preached it. In such "occasional" circumstances the NT letters were first written. Yet Paul and the other writers were conscious of the fact that they expressed the mind of Christ, under the guidance of his Spirit. Their letters are therefore full of teaching, imparted to the first readers by apostolic authority, which retains its validity to the present day, and have by divine providence been preserved for our instruction.

The Gospels began to appear about the end of the first generation following the death and resurrection of Jesus. By that time the eyewitnesses were being removed by death, one by one, and before long none of them would be left. It was desirable, therefore, that their testimony should be placed on permanent record, so that those who came after would not be at a disadvantage as compared with Christians of the first generation. About the middle sixties, then, we find gospel writing first undertaken. Mark provided the Roman church with an account of Jesus' ministry, from his baptism to his resurrection, which is said by Papias and other second-century writers to have been based in large measure on the preaching of Peter. In the following years Matthew provided the Christians of Antioch and the neighborhood with an expanded version of the life of Jesus, including a systematic presentation of his teaching. Luke, Paul's companion and dear physician, having traced the course of events accurately from the beginning, set himself to supply the "most excellent Theophilus" with an ordered narrative of Christian origins that not only related "all that Jesus began to do and to teach until the day he was taken up" (Acts 1:1–2), but went on to tell what he continued to do after that, working by his Spirit in his apostles. Then, toward the end of the century, John recorded Jesus' life in a different way, bringing out its abiding and universal significance, so that his readers might apprehend the glory of Jesus as the Word that became flesh, and by believing in him might have life in his name. These four records are not biographies in the ordinary sense of the term; they are concerned rather to perpetuate the apostolic witness to Jesus as Son of God and Savior of the world.

III. Early Collections of Writings. For some time these four evangelic records circulated independently and locally, being valued, no doubt, by those for whom they were primarily written. But by the early years of the second century they were gathered together and began to circulate as a fourfold record throughout the Christian world. When this happened, Acts was detached from Luke's Gospel, to which it originally formed the sequel, and set out on a new, but not insignificant, career of its own.

Paul's letters were preserved at first by those to whom they were sent. At least, all that have come down to us were so preserved, for here and there in his surviving correspondence we find reference to a letter that may have been lost at a very early date (cf. 1 Cor 5:9; Col 4:16). But by the last decade of the first century there is evidence of a move to bring his available letters together and circulate them as a collection among the churches. Thus Clement of Rome, writing as foreign secretary of his church to the church of Corinth about A.D. 96, was able to quote freely, not only from Paul's letter to the Romans (which would naturally be accessible to him) but also from 1 Corinthians and possibly from one or two of his other letters. What provided the stimulus for this move to collect Paul's letters, or who began to collect them, can only be a matter of speculation. Paul himself had encouraged some interchange of his letters (cf. Col. 4:16), and one or two of them may have been from the start general or circular letters, not to be confined to one single group of recipients.

By the first or second decade of the second century, at any rate, a Pauline collection was in circulation—first a shorter collection of ten letters, and then a longer collection of thirteen (including the three "pastoral letters," those addressed to Timothy and Titus).

From the time when the first collection of Paul's letters began to circulate, the letters appear to have been arranged mainly in descending order of length. That principle is still apparent in the arrangement most familiar today: Paul's letters to churches come before his letters to individuals, but within these two groups the letters are arranged so that the longest comes first and the shortest comes last. (There is one inconspicuous exception to this rule: Galatians, which is slightly shorter than Ephesians, comes before it, and has had this position since the second century. There may have been some special reason for this.)

IV. Canon of the New Testament. The circulation of two collections—the fourfold gospel and the Pauline corpus—did not constitute a NT, but it marked a stage toward that goal. About A.D. 140 the Gnostic leader Valentinus, according to Tertullian, accepted practically the whole NT as it was recognized toward the end of the second century. It is not certain, however, whether Valentinus knew the NT as a closed canon or simply quoted as authoritative most of the documents that Tertullian acknowledged as making up the NT.

The church was stimulated to define the NT limits more precisely, not by the main Gnostic groups, but by Marcion. Marcion came to Rome about A.D. 140 from Asia Minor, where he had tried unsuccessfully to press his views on leading churchmen. He rejected the OT altogether, as reflecting the worship of a different God from the God whom Jesus revealed as Father, and he held that the writings of all the apostles except Paul had been corrupted by an admixture of Judaism. He promulgated a Christian canon comprising (1) "The Gospel" (an edition of Luke's Gospel edited in accordance with his own viewpoint) and (2) "The Apostle" (ten letters of Paul, excluding the Pastorals, similarly edited). Paul, in Marcion's

The last three verses of Luke and the beginning of John (1:1–16) from the Bodmer XIV–XV papyrus (early third century A.D.) found in Upper Egypt. Courtesy Fondation Martin Bodmer.

eyes, was the only faithful apostle of Christ, all the others having Judaized; but even Paul's letters had been tampered with by Judaizing scribes or editors and required correction back to their original form.

The publication of Marcion's NT, with its restricted number of documents, was a challenge to the leaders of Christian orthodoxy. If they refused Marcion's canon, it was incumbent on them to define the canon they accepted. They replied to his challenge by saying, in effect, that they did not reject the OT. They accepted it as Holy Scripture, following the example of Christ and the apostles. Along with it they accepted the NT writings—not one Gospel only, but four (one of the four being the authentic text of the Gospel that Marcion issued in a mutilated form); not ten letters only of Paul, but thirteen; not letters of Paul only, but of other apostolic men as well. They also accepted the Acts of the Apostles and appreciated as never before its crucial importance as the "hinge" of the NT. Acts links the fourfold Gospel with the apostolic letters because it provides the sequel to the former and supplies a historical background for much of the latter. Moreover, it provides irrefutable independent evidence of the sound basis for the authority that Paul claims in his letters. Tertullian and others were not slow to expose the folly of those Marcionites who asserted the exclusive authority of Paul while rejecting the one document that supplied objective testimony to his authority. The Marcionites, indeed, had no option but to reject Acts, as it also bore witness to the authority of Peter and the other apostles, whom they repudiated. But the very fact that Acts attested the authority both of Paul and of Peter and his colleagues gave it all the greater value in the eyes of orthodox churchmen. From this time on it was called "The Acts of the Apostles." Indeed, toward the end of the second century one zealously anti-Marcionite work, the Muratorian list, goes so far as to call it "The Acts of *All* the Apostles." That was a great exaggeration, but Acts does at least record something about most of the apostles or apostolic men to whom are ascribed the letters the catholic church came to acknowledge as canonical.

Another factor that made it advisable to define what was, and what was not, the Word of God was the rise of the Montanists from the mid-second century onward. They claimed to announce further revelations by the Spirit of prophecy; it was helpful, therefore, to appeal to a recognized standard by which such claims might be evaluated; and such a standard was provided by the canon of Scripture.

From the second half of the second century, then, the church came to acknowledge a NT of the same general dimensions as ours. For a considerable time there was some questioning about a few of the books at the end of our NT, and arguments were occasionally put forward for the recognition of books that did not ultimately maintain their place within the collection. But after some generations of debate about the few "disputed" books in relation to the majority of "acknowledged" books, we find the twenty-seven books that make up our NT today listed by Athanasius of Alexandria in A.D. 367, and not long after by Jerome and Augustine in the West. These leaders did not impose decisions of their own but published what was generally recognized. It is unhistorical to represent the limits of the NT as being fixed by the verdict of any church council. When first a church council did make a pronouncement on this subject (A.D. 393), it did no more than record the consensus of the church in East and West.

The invention of the codex, or leaf-form of book, made it a practicable matter to bind the NT writings, or indeed the whole Bible, together in one volume—something that could not have been done with the older scroll-form of book. The earliest comprehensive codices known to us belong to the fourth century, but already in the third century, and possibly even in the second, groups of NT books were bound together in smaller codices. The Chester Beatty biblical papyri (early third century) include one codex of the four Gospels and Acts, one of ten Pauline letters and Hebrews.

V. Authority of the New Testament. The authority of the NT is not based on archaeological evidence or on any other line of comparative study. By such means we can confirm the historical setting of the record in the first century and provide ourselves with an illuminating commentary on it. The value of this should not be underestimated, but the essential authority of the NT derives from the authority of Christ, whether exercised in his own person or delegated to his apostles. The NT documents are the written deposit of the apostles' witness to Christ and of the teaching they imparted in his name. When we emerge from the "tunnel" period, which separates the apostolic age from the last quarter of the second century, we find the church still attaching high importance to apostolic authority. The apostles are no longer there, but the apostolic faith is confessed, the apostolic fellowship is maintained, and apostolic church order is observed. We find too, that the apostolic writings, whether penned directly by apostles or indirectly by their associates ("apostolic men"), are available in the NT canon to serve as the church's rule of faith and life—the criterion by which it may be determined whether doctrine or fellowship or anything else that claims to be apostolic really is so. And from those days to our own, it is the NT that, from time to time, has called Christians back to the ways of apostolic purity, to the truth as it is in Jesus. Reformation is not something that the church needed once for all in the sixteenth century; true "reformation according to the word of God" is an abiding need of the church. And where the NT is given its proper place in the church's belief and practice, true reformation goes on continually.

Not only in his works and words during his earthly ministry, but also in the continuing ministry that he has exercised since his exaltation, Jesus reveals God to human beings. Therefore not only the Gospels, which record the revelation given in the days of his flesh, but also the other NT books, which record the further outworking of that revelation, are accepted by the church as her normative documents. The Holy Spirit, who came to make the significance of Jesus plain to his followers and to lead them into all the truth, still performs these services for his people; and the NT writings are his primary instrument for their performance. How else could the Spirit take the things of Christ and declare them to men and women today if these writings were not available as a basis for him to work on? The Spirit who was imparted in fullness to Jesus and who worked through the apostles is the Spirit under whose direction the Christians of the earliest centuries were enabled to distinguish so clearly the documents that bore authoritative witness to Jesus. He is also the Spirit by whose illumination we today may appropriate that witness for our own and others' good.

In all this the place of the OT as an integral part of the Christian Scriptures is not ignored. The two Testaments are so organically interwoven that the authority of the one carries with it the authority of the other. If the OT records the divine promise, the New records its fulfillment; if the OT tells how preparation was made over many centuries for the coming of Christ, the New tells how he came and what his coming brought about. If even the OT writings are able to make the readers "wise for salvation through faith in Christ Jesus" and equip them thoroughly for the service of God (2 Tim 3:15–17), how much more is this true of the NT writings! Our Lord's statement of the highest function of the earlier Scriptures applies with at least equal force to those of the NT: "These are the Scriptures that testify about me" (John 5:39).

Bibliography: D. Guthrie, *New Testament Introduction,* 1970; F. F. Bruce, *New Testament History,* 1971; G. E. Ladd, *A Theology of the New Testament,* 1974; R. P. Martin, *New Testament Foundations,* 2 vols., 1975–78; I. H. Marshall, ed., *New Testament Interpretation,* 1977; R. F. Collins, *Introduction to the New Testament,* 1983; M. C. Tenney, *New Testament Survey Revised,* 1985. FFB

NEW YEAR (See FEASTS)

NEZIAH (nē-zī'á, *sincere*). One of the temple servants (KJV Nethinim) whose descendants returned from captivity with Zerubbabel (Ezra 2:54; Neh 7:56).

NEZIB (nē'zĭb, Heb. *netsîv*). A village mentioned only in Joshua 15:43, belonging to Judah and lying about ten miles (seventeen km.) NW of Hebron. The word means "something set" and thus a "garrison." It still retains its name "Beit Nusib," i.e., "House of the Garrison."

NIBHAZ (nĭb'hăz, Heb. *nivhaz*). A god whose image in the form of a dog was made and worshiped by the Avvites when the Samaritan race was being formed (2 Kings 17:31).

NIBSHAN (nĭb'shăn, Heb. *nivshān*). A town in southern Judah between Beersheba and the Dead Sea (Josh 15:62).

NICANOR (nī-kā'nôr, Gr. *Nikanōr*). One of the seven chosen by the church at Jerusalem to administer alms (Acts 6:5).

NICODEMUS (nĭk'ō-dē'mŭs, Gr. *Nikodēmos, victor over the people*). A leading Pharisee, "a ruler of the Jews," and a member of the Sanhedrin. Perhaps from curiosity, and possibly under conviction, but certainly led of God, he came to Jesus by night (John 3:1–14). He must have thought of himself as quite condescending to address Jesus, the young man from Galilee, as "Rabbi," but Jesus, instead of being puffed up by the recognition, quickly made Nicodemus aware of his need by announcing the necessity of a new

The Nile River, with the typical sailboat, the felucca. Courtesy Seffie Ben-Yoseph.

birth in order "to see the kingdom of God." Nicodemus did not then understand but was deeply touched, though he had not yet the courage to stand out for the Lord. Later, when at the Feast of Tabernacles (7:25–44) the Jewish leaders were planning to kill Jesus, Nicodemus spoke up, though timidly, in the Sanhedrin, suggesting their injustice in condemning a man without a fair trial. After the death of Jesus, however, Nicodemus came boldly with Joseph of Arimathea (19:38–42), provided a rich store of spices for the embalmment, and assisted in the burial of the body. After that he is not mentioned in Scripture.

NICOLAITANS (nĭk′ō-lā′ĭ-tănz, Gr. *Nikolaitai*). A group of persons whose works both the church at Ephesus and our Lord hated (Rev 2:6) and whose doctrine was held by some in the Pergamum church (2:15). Nothing else is surely known about them, but some have guessed that they were the followers of Nicolas of Antioch, one of the first so-called deacons (Acts 6:5), but there is no evidence for this. Their doctrine was similar to that of Balaam, through whose influence the Israelites ate things sacrificed to idols and committed fornication (Rev 2:14–15). A sect of Nicolaitans existed among the Gnostics in the third century, as is known from church fathers of the time (Irenaeus, Clement of Alexandria, and Tertullian). It probably had its origin in the group condemned in Revelation.

NICOLAS, NICOLAUS (nĭk′ō-lȧs, nĭk′ō-lā′ŭs, Gr. *Nikolaos, conqueror of the people*). A man from Antioch, a "convert to Judaism" mentioned only in Acts 6:5, whom the church at Jerusalem very early chose to administer alms as one of the seven original "deacons." Confusing him with the "Nicolaitans," many writers even in early times have accused him of originating this sect.

NICOPOLIS (nĭ-cŏp′ō-lĭs, Gr. *Nikopolis, city of victory*). An ancient city of Epirus situated on the Gulf of Actium and founded by Augustus Caesar to celebrate his decisive victory over Mark Antony, 31 B.C. (In modern terms this city is "on the Gulf of Arta" on the west coast of Greece.) When Paul wrote his letter to Titus, in the interval between his first and his final imprisonment under Nero at Rome, he had determined to winter there (Titus 3:12).

NIGER (nī′jêr, Gr. *Niger, black*). A surname of Simeon, one of the five "prophets and teachers" of the church at Antioch who were led of the Lord to send Paul and Barnabas on the first missionary journey (Acts 13:1–3). Probably a Hebrew Christian from North Africa.

NIGHT (See TIME)

NIGHT CREATURE, NIGHT HAG (See BIRDS)

NIGHT HAWK (See BIRDS)

NILE (nīl, Gr. *Neilos,* meaning not certainly known). The main river, not only of Egypt, but of Africa as well, being exceeded in all the earth in length only by the Amazon and the Missouri-Mississippi rivers; and in the extent of the territory that it drains, ranking sixth among the river systems of the world. The word *Nile* does not appear in the Hebrew OT or in the KJV, strange to say. When we find in Scripture the words *the River*, we can generally judge by the context whether the Nile (e.g., Gen 41:1 NIV) or the Euphrates (e.g., 31:21) is intended, though there is uncertainty about Psalm 72:8. The common Bible name for the Nile is *ye'ôr,* an Egyptian word meaning "river" and almost always referring to the Nile, except in Daniel 12:5–7, where it clearly refers to the Tigris (cf. Dan 10:4). In Isaiah 23:3 the word *Shihor* (NEB, RSV; KJV Sihor; NIV Nile), its root meaning "turbid," refers to the Nile. But where it marks the SW border of Canaan, it refers to the Wadi el Arish, a little channel that enters the Mediterranean about halfway from the present Suez Canal to the southern end of the Dead Sea. The same stream is meant by the phrase "the river of Egypt" (Gen 15:18).

The Nile issues forth from Lake Victoria on the equator and flows northward nearly 2,500 miles (4,167 km.) to the Mediterranean. Of this, the northernmost 500 miles can be said to be in Egypt, from Aswan northward. The "White" Nile rises as above at the equator and has a fairly even flow northward till it is joined by the "Blue" Nile at modern Khartoum in the Sudan. This stream and the other affluents that join the Nile from the east, rise in the mountains of Ethiopia and are fed by the torrential rains of the springtime. They fluctuate greatly and provide the annual inundation that for thousands of years has flooded and fertilized lower Egypt. The ancient mythological belief was that the goddess Isis annually shed a tear into the upper Nile, thus causing the flood that is so great a blessing that Egypt has been called, from the time of Herodotus onward, "the Gift of the Nile."

Near the end of June the water at Cairo and onward takes on a greenish tinge and an unpleasant taste because of the vast multiplication of the algae; then about the beginning of July the life-giving inundation begins so that the delta region overflows and the stream deposits the rich gift of sediment brought down from the mountains. During an average year, the vast delta seems almost like a sea with islands protruding here and there. If the inundation is unusually deep, many houses are destroyed and loss ensues, while if it is much below the average level, famine follows. A failure of this inundation for seven successive years (Gen 41) was used by God to work a great but peaceful revolution in Egypt in which Joseph bought up for the pharaoh practically all private property except that of the priests and brought the Israelites into Egypt for a stay of several hundred years.

In Upper Egypt the Nile flows for many miles through high walls of sand and rock, with the desert encroaching on both sides, so that only by great efforts could the people irrigate a narrow strip of land; but from a point a few miles south of Cairo, the Nile divides. The delta begins, and Lower Egypt (i.e., Northern Egypt) has long been one of the most fertile regions in the world.

From the days of Abraham, who as Abram went down into Egypt (Gen 12:10), until the infancy of our Lord Jesus Christ (Matt 2:14), Egypt and the Nile were well known by Israel and exerted a strong effect on the civilization of Israel. In describing the Promised Land, Moses (Deut 11:10–12) emphasized its difference from Egypt "where you planted your seed and irrigated it by foot" (i.e., by irrigating furrows manipulated, and then altered from time to time, by foot power); and the prosperity or poverty of Egypt at various periods was in proportion to the ingenuity and faithfulness of the people in spreading the water of the Nile on their plants. The rise and fall of the Nile is very regular, but there have been times (e.g., A.D. 1877) when an unusually feeble flood led to widespread famine and many deaths. It was, no doubt, a series of these dry years in the days of Joseph that caused the seven years of famine (Gen 41) and that led, under God, to the descent of Israel into Egypt.

Hundreds of years later we find various references to the rivers of Egypt in the prophets; e.g., in Isaiah 7:18 we read that "the LORD will whistle for flies from the distant streams of Egypt," hinting at the prevalence of flies there. Even today the land seems full of them. In Isaiah 19:5 KJV "the waters shall fail from the sea, and the river shall be wasted and dried up"—"the sea" is a common title given to the Nile, which during the annual inundation must resemble a sea from parts of the delta. Isaiah 19:7 says that the plants and the sown fields of the Nile will become dry and will be blown away—and this has come to pass literally when the irrigating works have been neglected for a time. Three times in this verse *ye'ôr* (KJV brooks; MLB river; NASB, RSV Nile; NIV Nile twice, river once) refers to the Nile. ABF

NIMRAH (nĭm'rȧ, Heb. *nimrâh, limpid* or *flowing water*). A city in Gilead, assigned by Moses to the tribe of Gad (Num 32:3). Cf. 32:36, where it is called "Beth Nimrah," i.e., "house of limpid water." It lies about ten miles (seventeen km.) NE of Jericho. In Joshua 13:27 it is described as being "in the valley" and a part of the former kingdom of Sihon, king of the Amorites, whose capital was Heshbon.

NIMRIM (nĭm'rĭm, Heb. *nimrîm*). A place in Moab noted for its waters (Isa 15:6; Jer 48:34). It was probably SE of the Dead Sea.

NIMROD (nĭm'rŏd, Heb. *nimrōdh*). In the "Table of the Nations" (Gen 10) many of the names seem to be those of cities, e.g., Sidon (10:15); countries, e.g., Canaan (10:6, 15); or tribes, e.g., "Heth and the Jebusites" (10:15–18); but Nimrod stands out clearly as an individual man and a very interesting character. The beginning of his kingdom was in Babylonia, whence he moved northward and became the founder of Nineveh and other cities in or near

Assyria. He became distinguished as a hunter, ruler, and builder. Many legends have grown up around the name of Nimrod, some claiming that he was identical with "Ninus," an early Babylonian king or god. Again, some have associated Nimrod with the building of the Tower of Babel (11:1–9). Others have identified him with the ancient king of Babylonia, Gilgamesh, but there is no proof that the two were identical.

NIMRUD (nĭm'rŭd). Ancient Calah in Assyria, founded by Nimrod, and scene of extensive excavations. See also CALAH.

NIMSHI (nĭm'shī). The grandfather of Jehu whose coup d'état ended the rule of the house of Ahab (2 Kings 9:2, 14). Elsewhere Jehu is called "son of Nimshi" (1 Kings 19:16).

NINEVEH, NINEVE (nĭn'ĕ-vĕ, Heb. *nînewēh*). One of the most ancient cities of the world, founded by Nimrod (Gen 10:11–12), a great-grandson of Noah, and enduring till 612 B.C. Nineveh lay on the banks of the Tigris above its confluence with the Greater Zab, one of its chief tributaries, and nearly opposite the site of the modern Mosul in Iraq. It was for many years the

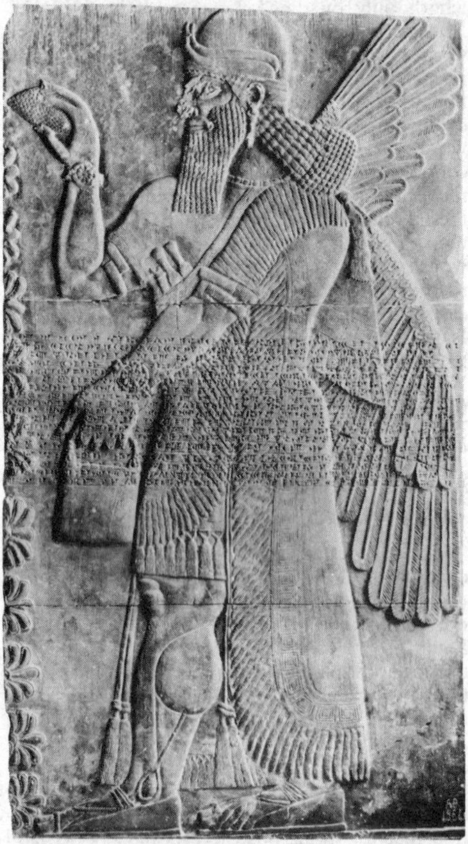

Relief from the palace of Ashurnasirpal II, 883–859 B.C., at Nimrud, that shows a winged worshipper carrying out a fertilization rite at the sacred tree. Courtesy Réunion des Musées Nationaux.

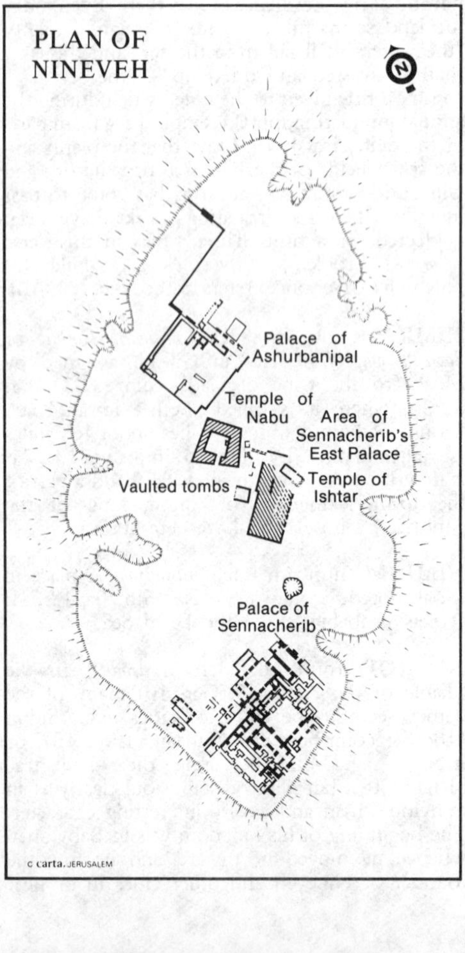

capital of the great Assyrian Empire, and its fortunes ebbed and flowed with the long strife between Babylonia and Assyria. Of the two kingdoms, or empires, Babylonia was the more cultured, but Assyria the more warlike. The kingdom over which Nineveh and its kings long ruled was north of Babylon and in the hills, and these facts made more for warlikeness than the more sedentary culture of a warmer climate. Babylon was the more important from Abraham's time to David's; then from David's time to that of Hezekiah and Manasseh, Nineveh and its kings were paramount; then still later, from the time of King Josiah and the prophets Jeremiah, Ezekiel, Habakkuk, and Daniel, Babylon was again at the head.

Among the great rulers of Assyria may be mentioned Tiglath-Pileser I, who made conquests about 1100 B.C., and Ashurnasirpal and Shalmaneser III, who inaugurated a system of ruthless conquest and deportation of whole populations, which greatly increased the power of Assyria and the influence of Nineveh. It was this latter king (sometimes numbered as II instead of III) who defeated Hazael of Syria and boasted of receiving tribute from Jehu of Israel. The Assyrians, instead of numbering their years, named them from certain rulers; and lists of these "eponyms" have been found, but with a gap of fifty-one years around the beginning of the eighth century, due no doubt to some great calamity and/or the weakness of her kings. It was in this space of time that Jonah was sent of the Lord to warn the people of Nineveh: "Forty more days and Nineveh will be overturned" (Jonah 3:4), but God gave Nineveh a respite for nearly two hundred years. Esarhaddon, the great king of Assyria from 680–668, united Babylonia to Assyria and conquered lands as far away as Egypt (Isa 19:4) and North Arabia. He was succeeded by his greater son Ashurbanipal (called by the Greeks "Sardanapalus"), who presided over Assyria in its brief climax of power and culture; but Nabopolassar of Babylon, who reigned from 625 to 605, freed it from Assyria and helped to bring about the destruction of Nineveh in 612 (some date this destruction 606). About 623 Cyaxares, king of the Medes, made his first attack on Nineveh, and this was probably the occasion of Nahum's prophecy. His book is undated, but 3:8 speaks of Thebes (Heb., *No Amon*) in the past tense (it was destroyed in 663) and of Nineveh's destruction as future, so it must have been written about this time.

One of the stelae on the site of the royal road at Nineveh, it depicts the Assyrian king Sennacherib (705–681 B.C.) worshiping the divine emblems. Courtesy Istanbul Museum. Photo: B. Brandl.

For many centuries the very location of Nineveh was forgotten, but it has been discovered and excavated (largely by Botta and Layard from A.D. 1843–45), and among its buried ruins the great palace of Sargon, with its wonderful library of cuneiform inscriptions and its still-striking wall ornamentation, has been exhumed. Because the name Sargon was omitted in some of the ancient lists of kings, some of the scholars scoffed (around 1840) at Isaiah 20:1, "sent by Sargon king of Assyria," saying in effect, "This is one of the errors of Isaiah, for we know that Sargon never did exist." It is said that when Botta sent to Berlin some ancient bricks with the name Sargon baked into them, the "scholars" claimed that he forged the bricks! Nahum's reference (2:4) to chariots raging in the streets and rushing to and fro in the broadways of Nineveh does not prophesy automobile traffic, as some have tried to make out, but refers to the broad streets that distinguished Nineveh. ABF

NISAN (See CALENDAR)

NISROCH (nĭs'rŏk, Heb. *nisrōkh*). A god who was worshiped at Nineveh. In the temple of this god Sennacherib was killed by his two sons Adrammelech and Sharezer after his return from his disastrous experience near Jerusalem (Isa 37:36–38 repeated in 2 Kings 19:35–37). The name is not found elsewhere.

NITER (nī'têr, Heb. *nether*). Not the same as our present niter, but an impure mixture of washing and baking sodas found in deposits around the alkali lakes of Egypt. The references in Scripture are to its fizzing with vinegar and its use in cleansing (Prov 25:20; Jer 2:22; "soda" in NIV, "nitre" in KJV).

NO (Heb. *nō' 'āmôn, the city of the god Amon*). The great city and capital of Upper Egypt, lying on both sides of the Nile at the great semicircular curve of the river about 400 miles (667 km.) south of Cairo. Egypt's capital as early as the eleventh century, its tremendous ruins at Luxor and Karnak are among the world's wonders. Its fuller name was No Amon (Amon from a local

A view, looking west, of the rear part of the Great Temple of Amon, at Karnak (Thebes), with the standing obelisk at far left and the hypostyle hall in the center. Courtesy B. Brandl.

god). KJV translates *Nō' 'āmôn* in Jeremiah 46:25 as "multitude of No," but NIV has "Amon god of Thebes"; in 46:25 KJV again translates *'āmôn* by "multitude," but NIV has "craftsmen." In Nahum 3:8, however, KJV translates *Nō' 'āmôn* as "populace No"; NIV has simply "Thebes," the name known to the classical writers. Its site is now occupied by small villages on both sides of the Nile.

NOADIAH (nō'à-dī'à, Heb. *nô'adhyâh, with whom Jehovah meets*). 1. One of the Levites before whom the gold and silver vessels were weighed on the return to Jerusalem (Ezra 8:33).

2. A false prophetess, associated with Sanballat and Tobiah, who tried to terrorize Nehemiah, and against whom Nehemiah prayed (Neh 6:14).

NOAH (nō'à, Heb. *nōah, rest*). 1. The son of Lamech and tenth in descent from Adam in the line of Seth (Gen 5:28–29). He received this name because Lamech foresaw that through him God would comfort (Heb. *nāham,* same root as "Noah") the race and partially alleviate the effects of the Edenic curse. Noah was uniquely righteous (6:1–13). When he was 480 years old, 120 years before the Flood (6:3), he was warned of God that the world would be destroyed by water (Heb 11:7). He was then given exact instructions for building the ark (Gen 6:14–16). While engaged in this colossal task, he warned men of the coming catastrophe, as a "preacher of righteousness" (2 Peter 2:5), while God in longsuffering waited for men to repent (1 Peter 3:20). Noah's three sons—Shem, Ham, and Japheth—were not born until he was 500 years old (Gen 5:32). One week before the Flood God led Noah and his family into the ark and supernaturally directed the animals also to enter. When all were safely inside, God shut the door (7:16).

The Flood came in Noah's six-hundredth year, increased steadily for 40 days, maintained its mountain-covering depth for 110 more days, and then subsided sufficiently for Noah to disembark in the mountains of Ararat after another 221 days (see FLOOD). During all this time, "God remembered Noah and all the wild animals . . . in the ark" (Gen 8:1), implying that God did not leave the task of caring for these creatures entirely to Noah. To determine whether it was safe to disembark, Noah sent forth first a raven and then a dove at regular intervals (8:6–10). The freshly plucked olive leaf proved to him that such sturdy plants had already begun to grow on the mountain heights. God commanded him to disembark, and Noah built an altar and offered clean beasts as burnt offerings to God. The Lord then promised never to send another universal flood, confirming it with the rainbow sign (8:21–22; 9:9–17). God blessed Noah and his family and commanded them to multiply and fill the earth (9:1). From now on animals would fear man, and they were given to be food for man, except the blood (9:2–4). Human government was instituted by the provision of capital punishment for murderers (9:5–6).

Among the things preserved in the ark was sinful human nature. Noah became a husbandman, planted a vineyard, drank himself into a drunken stupor, and shamefully exposed himself in his tent (9:20–21). Ham, presumably led by his son Canaan, made fun of Noah. For this foul deed, Canaan was cursed and Ham received no blessing (9:25–27). On the other hand, Shem and Japheth showed due respect to their father (9:23) and received rich blessings for their descendants. Noah lived 350 years after the Flood, dying at the age of 950 (9:29).

In the Babylonian flood account (the Gilgamesh Epic), Noah's counterpart is Utnapishtim. He likewise received divine warnings of the Flood, built a huge ark, preserved human and animal life, sent out birds, and offered sacrifices. However, the gross polytheism and absurdities of the Babylonian account demonstrate that it suffered from a long oral transmission and that it did not influence Genesis in any way (cf. Merrill Unger, *Archaeology and the Old Testament,* 1954, pp. 46–71).

2. One of the five daughters of Zelophehad, of the tribe of Manasseh (Num 26:33; 27:1; 36:11; Josh 17:3), who received an inheritance in the land in their father's name, in spite of having no brothers. JCW

NOB (nōb, Heb. *nōv*). A town of the priests in the tribe of Benjamin just north of the city of Jerusalem. The language of Isaiah 10:32 indicates that it was within sight of Jerusalem. In the time of King Saul the tabernacle stood here for a time, and David's visit to Ahimelech the priest (1 Sam 21) was the cause or at least the occasion for the complete destruction of the city by Saul (22:19). David, fleeing from Saul, asked for provision for his young men and for a sword, all of which the priest granted; but a mischief-maker, Doeg the Edomite, was a witness to the transaction and reported it to Saul who, in his insane hatred and jealousy of David, had the priests murdered and their city destroyed.

NOBAH (nō'bà, Heb. *nōvâh, barking*). 1. A man of Manasseh in the days of Moses, who in the conquest of the land of Bashan took the city of Kenath from the Amorites (Num 32:42).

2. A town in the neighborhood of which Gideon finally defeated the Midianites and took their kings (Judg 8:11).

NOBAI (See NEBAI)

NOBLEMAN. One belonging to a king, *basilikos,* as in John 4:46–53 (NIV "royal official"), or one well-born, *eugenēs,* as in the parable of the pounds (Luke 19:12–27).

NOD (nŏd, Heb. *nôdh, wandering*). A district eastward from Eden to which Cain went in his wandering (Gen 4:16). (Cf. Ps 56:8 KJV, "my wanderings.")

NODAB (nō'dăb, Heb. *nôdhāv*). A tribe of

Arabs, probably Ishmaelites east of the Jordan, early conquered by the two-and-a-half tribes (1 Chron 5:19). Probably a family name from an ancestor by that name. The name means "noble."

NOE (See NOAH)

NOGAH (nō'gȧ, Heb. *nōghah, brilliance*). A son of David born in Jerusalem (1 Chron 3:7; 14:6).

NOHAH (nō'hȧ, Heb. *nôhâh, rest*). The fourth among the ten sons of Benjamin (1 Chron 8:2) but not mentioned in Genesis 46:21.

NON (See NUN)

NOON (See TIME)

NOPH (nŏf, Heb. *nōph*). Better known as Memphis, a city on the west side of the Nile south of Cairo (Isa 19:13; Jer 2:16; 46:19).

NOPHAH (nō'fȧ, Heb. *nōphâh*). A city of Moab (Num 21:30), site unknown.

NORTH. The word often occurs merely as a point of the compass, but there are many passages, especially in the prophets, where it refers to a particular country, usually Assyria or Babylonia (Jer 3:18; 46:6; Ezek 26:7; Zeph 2:13). Although Nineveh and Babylon were east of Jerusalem, they are usually referred to as "the north" because armies from there could not come across the desert, but had first to go north to Syria and then south. It is uncertain what country Ezekiel 38:6 refers to by "the north."

NOSE, NOSTRILS (Heb. *'aph, nehîrayim*). Because the nostrils quiver in anger, the word for nostril is rendered "anger," almost akin to "snorting" in 171 places; and this is used not only of Jacob (Gen 27:45) but also of Moses (Exod 32:19) and even of the Lord (Num 11:1, 10). A tempestuous wind is described poetically as "the blast of your nostrils" (Exod 15:8; 2 Sam 22:16), referring of course to God. A long nose was counted an element of beauty (Song of Songs 7:4), and the nose was often decorated with a ring (Ezek 16:12 NIV, cf. Isa 3:21). A hook in the nose however was a means of subjection (Isa 37:29).

NOSE JEWEL (See DRESS)

NOVICE (nŏv'ĭs, Gr. *neophytos, newly planted*). Used only in 1 Timothy 3:6 (KJV; MLB, NASB new convert; NIV recent convert) concerning the requirements for being a bishop. This is the Greek term from which we get *neophyte*.

NUMBERS. The Hebrews in ancient times used the common decimal system as a method of counting. There is no evidence that they used figures to denote numbers. Before the Exile they spelled the numbers out in full, as is seen in the present text of the Hebrew Scriptures, in the Siloam Inscription, and on the Moabite Stone. After the Exile some of the Jews employed such signs as were used among the Egyptians, the Arameans, and the Phoenicians—an upright line for 1, two such lines for 2, three for 3, etc., and special signs for 10, 20, 100. At least as far back as the reign of Simon Maccabaeus (143–135 B.C.), they numbered the chapters and verses of the Hebrew Bible and expressed dates by using the consonants of the Hebrew alphabet: aleph for 1, beth for 2, etc. The letters of the Greek alphabet were used in the same way.

Numbers were used conventionally and symbolically. Certain numbers and their multiples had sacred or symbolic significance: 3, 4, 7, 10, 12, 40, 70. For example, three expressed emphasis, as in "A ruin! A ruin! I will make it a ruin!" (Ezek 21:27). From early times seven was a sacred number among the Semites (Gen 2:2; 4:24; 21:28). Ten was regarded as a complete number. Forty was often used as a round number (Exod 24:18; 1 Kings 19:8; Jonah 3:4). Some of the higher numbers also seem sometimes to have been used as round numbers: 100 (e.g., Gen 26:12; Lev 26:8; 2 Sam 24:3), 10,000 (e.g., Lev 26:8; Deut 32:30).

The later rabbis developed the theory that all numbers have secret meanings and all objects their fundamental numbers, and elaborate mathematical rules were devised to carry out these concepts. The system came to be known as gematria (a corruption of geometria). Some Bible students think that an example of this is found in Revelation 13:18, where the number of the Beast is 666. It is thought that the context shows that the number was intended to be recognized as a definite person by those who knew how to interpret the book, while outsiders were left in the dark regarding his identity. SB

NUMBERS, BOOK OF. The fourth book of the Pentateuch, called *In the Wilderness* by the Jews after its first significant word. The Hebrew title is more meaningful than the English, for the book picks up the account of the wilderness wandering after the arrival at Sinai (Exod 19), and records the Bedouinlike travels of Israel through all the forty years of wandering.

The name *Numbers* comes from the Greek translation, which gives a misleading impression of one of the features of the book. Both at the beginning (1:2–46) and near the end (26:2–51) the number of the Israelites is given—a little over 600,000 males above twenty years of age. The procedure sounds familiar to us. We call it a census. But the biblical censuses were not just that. Israel was not merely interested in vital statistics. This was a count of the fighting forces. Indeed, it probably was an actual mustering and organizing of the army. It is for this reason that the women, children, and Levites were not included. The numbering occurs twice because the army was called up twice for battle—first at the abortive attempt to invade the land at Kadesh Barnea, and second at the end of the forty years of wandering just before the conquest of Canaan.

Exception has been taken to the large number

of Israelites—totaling an estimated two million. Some say the territory could not sustain so many people. This is true if the Israelites traveled as a closely knit group seeking forage in a limited radius. But if they fanned out with their flocks over a wide area, they could sustain themselves as did the large Nabatean kingdom in the same area in Roman times. Furthermore, God specially and miraculously fed and sustained Israel. The size of the Israelite nation was surely great or Joshua would never have been able to conquer and occupy the land of Palestine as he clearly did. Large and well-fortified cities were conquered in the area from Lachish in the south to Hazor 120 miles (200 km.) to the north, as well as the territory in all Transjordan. Six hundred thousand men, not all active, would not have been too large a force to accomplish such a feat. David in later days of prosperity called up an army of 1,300,000 (2 Sam 24:9). David's numbers support the size of Joshua's army. Joshua's action explains the sinfulness of David's act. Like Joshua, he was not merely taking a census; he apparently was starting an unwarranted aggressive war.

The body of Numbers up to 10:11 gives additional legislation and the organization of the host. From 10:11 to 12:16 is recorded the march from Sinai to Kadesh Barnea. Then comes the debacle at Kadesh recorded in chapters 13 and 14. The three leaders of this occasion—Joshua and Caleb, the believing spies, and Moses the intercessor—are forever memorialized as among God's great men. Chapters 15 to 21:11 record the repeated faithlessness on the part of the people. Apparently during much of the forty years, according to Amos 5:25–26 and Joshua 5:2ff., the people wandered far away from God, and even their national unity may have lapsed temporarily. The forty years are treated very briefly.

From Numbers 21:11 on, the accounts of the conquest of Transjordan and the preparations to enter the land are given. Sihon and Og of the northern territory were conquered in swift moves detailed more extensively in Deuteronomy. Then Numbers portrays the very interesting activity of Balaam, the hireling prophet who was supernaturally restrained from cursing Israel (chs. 22–24). These chapters are now studied with new interest because they appear to show a very early type of Hebrew. Final material includes Joshua's installation (ch. 27), the summary of the journeys (ch. 33), and the provision of cities of refuge (ch. 35).

Bibliography: Martin Noth, *Numbers: A Commentary,* 1968; John Sturdy, *Numbers* (CBC), 1976; G. J. Wenham, *Numbers: An Introduction and Commentary* (TOTC), 1981. RLH

NUN (nŭn, Heb. *nûn*). A man of Ephraim and the father of Joshua (Exod 33:11; Neh 8:17). His descent is given in 1 Chronicles 7:25–27.

NURSE (See OCCUPATIONS AND PROFESSIONS)

NUT (See PLANTS)

NYMPHA, NYMPHAS (nĭm'fā, nĭm'făs, Gr. *nympha*). A believer in Laodicea or Colossae in whose house the church met and to whom Paul sent greetings (Col 4:15).

O

OAK (See PLANTS)

OATH (ōth, Heb. *shevûʿâh,* *ʾālâh,* Gr. *horkos*). An appeal to God to witness the truth of a statement or of the binding character of a promise (Gen 21:23; 31:53; Gal 1:20; Heb 6:16). Two varieties of the oath are found in the OT—a simple one for common use and a more solemn one for cases of greater solemnity. Oaths played a very important part not only in legal and state affairs, but in the dealings of everyday life. A number of formulas were used in taking an oath, such as "the LORD is witness between you and me forever" (1 Sam 20:23) and "as the LORD who rescues Israel lives" (14:39). Certain ceremonies were observed in taking an oath—in ordinary cases the raising of the hand toward heaven (Gen 14:22; Deut 32:40), in exceptional cases the putting of the hand under the thigh of the one to whom the oath was made (Gen 24:2; 47:29). Sometimes one taking an oath killed an animal, divided it into two parts, and passed between the pieces (15:8–18). Swearing was done by the life of the person addressed (1 Sam 1:26), by the life of the king (17:55), by one's own head (Matt 5:36), by the angels, by the temple (23:16), by Jerusalem (5:35), and by God. It was forbidden to swear by a false god (Josh 23:7). A virgin could take an oath if her father did not disallow it; and a married woman, if her husband permitted it. By the time of Christ the OT law regarding oaths (Exod 22:11) was much perverted by the scribes, and our Lord therefore condemned indiscriminate and light taking of oaths, saying that people should be so transparently honest that oaths between them are unnecessary. The lawfulness of oaths is recognized by the apostles, who called on God to witness to the truth of what they said (2 Cor 11:31; Gal 1:20).

OBADIAH (ō'bà-dī'à, Heb. *ʿōvadhyâh, servant of Jehovah*). The name of several men in the OT:

1. The governor of Ahab's household (1 Kings 18:3–16) who "feared the LORD greatly" (KJV), but who seemed to fear Ahab even more.

2. The head of a household of David's descendants (1 Chron 3:21).

3. A chief man of Issachar in David's time (1 Chron 7:3).

4. One of the six sons of Azel, a Benjamite (1 Chron 8:38 copied in 9:44).

5. A Levite who returned early from captivity (1 Chron 9:16). He is called "Abda" in Nehemiah 11:17.

6. One of the martial Gadites who joined David in the wilderness (1 Chron 12:9).

7. Father of Ishmaiah, a prince of Zebulun in the days of David (1 Chron 27:19).

8. One of five princes of Judah whom Jehoshaphat sent out to teach the people of Judah the Law of the Lord (2 Chron 17:7).

9. A Levite of the Merarite family, whom Josiah made an overseer of repairing the temple (2 Chron 34:12).

10. A Jew who led back 218 men in Ezra's return from captivity (Ezra 8:9).

11. A priestly covenanter with Nehemiah (Neh 10:5).

12. A gatekeeper of Jerusalem in Nehemiah's time (Neh 12:25).

13. The prophet who wrote the Book of Obadiah.

OBADIAH, BOOK OF. The subject of the book is the destruction of Edom (Obad 1). From time immemorial Edom and the Edomites were hostile to Israel.

The book, like others of the Minor Prophets, is undated. The principal clue to the date of its writing is in verses 11, 14. If "the day you stood aloof" (v. 11) alludes to the events of 2 Kings 8:20–22 and 2 Chronicles 21:16–18, when the Edomites and others rebelled against King Jehoram early in the ninth century B.C., the book probably would be dated quite early; but if the reference is to Psalm 137:7; 2 Chronicles 36:20; and Ezekiel 25:13–14, the prophecy would be late, later than 586. The more likely view is that 2 Chronicles 28:16–18 is the apposite reference and that the time was late in the eighth century, during the reign of Ahaz of Judah. At that time Edom and the Philistines were associated in warfare against Judah, and the names of the two nations are again coupled in Obadiah 19.

Obadiah 1–9 pronounces punishment on Edom. (cf. Jer 49:7–22). Apparently either Jeremiah or Obadiah made use of the other, or both made use of a common source that is no longer available.

In Obadiah 10–14 Edom is arraigned for its guilt in standing with the enemies of Israel in the time when Judah and Jerusalem were in deep distress. In verses 12–14 the prophet exhorts Edom to quit its evil association with the enemies of Jerusalem. In verses 15–16 "the day of the LORD," i.e., a time of awful judgment, is proclaimed as being "near for all nations," and national annihilation is predicted for those peoples who fight against the Lord—they will "be as if they had never been." To this point in Obadiah, the Lord has been addressing Edom in the second person singular, but in the closing paragraph, he speaks of a coming restoration of Israel when Zion will be holy and God will use Israel as a flame to destroy Esau. The people of the Negev (the southern part of Judah) are to possess the land of Edom; Israel will greatly enlarge its borders (vv. 19–21). The principal message of Obadiah to the peoples of today seems to be the proclamation, not only of the danger of fighting against God, but also of the peril of fighting his people.

Bibliography: F. E. Gaebelein, *Four Minor Prophets: Obadiah, Jonah, Habakkuk, and Haggai: Their Message for Today,* 1970; L. C. Allen, *The Books of Joel, Obadiah, Jonah and Micah,* 1976.

ABF

OBAL (ō'băl). An early Arab, son of Joktan (Gen 10:28), called Ebal in the Hebrew and most versions of 1 Chronicles 1:22 (JB, KJV, MLB, MOF, NASB, NEB, RSV; Obal NIV).

OBED (ō'bĕd, Heb. *'ōvēdh,* worshiper). The name of five OT men:

1. If no names are omitted in the messianic genealogy, the son of Boaz and Ruth and grandfather of David the king (Ruth 4:21–22, copied in 1 Chron 2:12; Matt 1:5; Luke 3:32).

2. An early man of Judah, descended through Hezron and Jerahmeel (1 Chron 2:37–38).

3. One of the mighty men of David's army (1 Chron 11:47).

4. A Levitical gatekeeper of the tabernacle in David's time (1 Chron 26:7).

5. The father of one of the captains whom Jehoiada chose to help make Joash king (2 Chron 23:1).

OBED-EDOM (ō'bĕd-ē'dŏm, Heb. *'ōvēdh-'ĕdhôm, one who serves Edom*). 1. A man of Gath into whose house David had the ark of God carried after "Perez Uzzah," when God struck Uzzah dead for touching the ark when the oxen stumbled (2 Sam 6:10–12; 1 Chron 13:9–13). Obed-Edom and his family revered the ark, and God blessed them greatly. He probably is the same Obed-Edom as the one in 1 Chronicles 26:4–8 who had eight sons and seventy-two early descendants.

2. One of the musical Levites (1 Chron 15:18–24) who played a harp.

3. A son of Jeduthun who was a gatekeeper of the tabernacle (1 Chron 16:38).

4. Perhaps the same as no. 3, appointed with his sons over the treasury (1 Chron 26:15).

5. A descendant of no. 4 who kept the treasury in Amaziah's time (2 Chron 25:24).

OBEDIENCE (Heb. *shāma'*, Gr. *hypakoē*). The Bible, by exhortation and commandment, requires submission and obedience to six principal authorities: (1) parents (Eph 6:1; Col 3:20; 1 Tim 3:4), (2) teachers (Prov 5:12–13), (3) husbands (Eph 5:21-22, 24; Col 3:18; Titus 2:5; 1 Peter 3:1, 5, 6), (4) masters—today, employers—(Eph 6:4; Col 3:22; Titus 2:9; 1 Peter 2:18), (5) government (Rom 13:1–2, 5; Titus 3:1; 1 Peter 2:13), and (6) God (Gen 26:5; Eph 5:24; Heb 5:9; 12:9; James 4:7). When there is a clear conflict regarding obedience to authority, Christians are to obey God, not human beings (Acts 5:29). The supreme test of faith in God is obedience (1 Sam 28:18); the Bible often links obedience to faith (Gen 22:18; Rom 1:5; 1 Peter 1:14). Jesus' obedience to the Father (Phil 2:8) is the supreme example for Christians, who are to be "obedient children" (1 Peter 1:14).

OBEISANCE (ō-bā'săns, Heb. *shāhâh*). The act of bowing low or of prostrating oneself—before (1) God (Mic 6:6), (2) a god (2 Kings 5:18), (3) an earthly ruler (Gen 42:6), or (4) one's equals in a gesture of courtesy (23:12). Courteous obeisance is a mark of culture; worshipful obeisance is a dreadful sin if directed to any other than the true God (Exod 20:4–6).

OBIL (ō'bĭl, *camel driver*). An Ishmaelite in the days of David who was put in charge of the king's camels (1 Chron 27:30).

OBLATION (See SACRIFICE AND OFFERINGS)

OBOTH (ō'bŏth, Heb. *'ōvōth, water-bags*). A place east of Moab, where Israel set up camp (Num 21:10–11; 33:43).

OCCUPATIONS AND PROFESSIONS.

Apothecary. See *Perfumer.*

Artificer. See *Craftsman.*

Author. The composer of a literary production; an authority on a statement or fact. Agur and Lemuel are referred to as having recorded "words" or "sayings" in the form of prophecy and wisdom (Prov 30:1; 31:1).

Baker. A trade that occupied a special street in Jerusalem (Jer 37:21). The baking of bread is one of the chief household duties. But in the towns and principal villages, the larger oven of the regular baker is required (1 Sam 8:13). The superiority of this bread is implied in the Arabic proverb, "Send your bread to the oven of the baker, though he should eat the half of it."

The modern Oriental baker does not, as a rule,

Limestone statue, from Giza, c. 2494–2345 B.C. (height: 0.282 m.; length: 0.45 m.), that shows a servant figure using a quern and muller for grinding grain. Courtesy Museum of Fine Arts, Boston.

Lower register (on the left) shows a brewer pouring water into a vat containing the fermented bread and (on the right) workers pouring beer into jars. Relief from Saqqara, Old (Egyptian) kingdom (2700–2200 B.C.) that portrays the process of making bread and beer. Top register shows a man mixing dough in a vessel (left), two men kneading the dough into loaves, and another man tending the oven on which the loaves are being baked. Courtesy of Rijksmuseum van Oudheden, Leiden, Netherlands.

prepare the dough, but bakes what is sent to him. A common sight is the baker's boy carrying on his head a tray of fresh bread for one house, and on his side a similar tray for another house. The dough is prepared by the house baker and sent to the public baker, who kneads it into flat cakes for his oven.

The Oriental oven is a long, low stone vault, with a stone pavement down the middle and a long narrow strip at each side for the firewood.

In addition to the home baker and the public baker, there was the royal baker, who baked for the king (Gen 40:1–22; 41:10).

The Hebrews used large stone jars, open at the mouth, about three feet (one m.) high, with a fire inside for baking bread and cakes. As soon as the sides were sufficiently heated, the thin dough was applied to the outside, and the opening at the top was closed. Sometimes wood was used for heating, but more often thorns and occasionally dry dung were used (Ezek 4:12).

There were various kinds of ovens: (1) The bowl oven, the simplest form of oven, was used by ancients, and was made of clay, with a movable lid. The bowl was placed inverted on small stones, and thus heated with dry dung heaped over and around it. (2) The jar oven, heated by grass or stubble, dry twigs or thorns (see above). (3) The pit oven, partly in the ground and partly built up of clay and plastered throughout, narrowed toward the top. The fire was kindled inside the oven.

Barber. One whose trade possibly originated in connection with the shaving of the head as part of a vow (Num 6:18–19). The instruments of his work were probably the razor, the basin, the mirror, and perhaps the scissors. He usually plied his trade in the open, on the street.

The word *barber* occurs only once in Scripture (Ezek 5:1). However, great attention was paid to the hair and beard among the ancients. The barber must have been a well-known tradesman.

Beggar. The beggar as a professional class was unknown during Mosaic times. The law of Moses made ample provision for the poor of the land. In imprecatory fashion, Psalm 109:10 sets forth begging as the fate and punishment of the children of the wicked. As cities developed, begging became more prevalent. In the NT beggars appear with some frequency: the blind beggar (John 9:8–9); blind Bartimaeus (Mark 10:46–52); the beggar by the "Beautiful" gate of the temple (Acts 3:1–11); and perhaps most famous of all, Lazarus, the godly beggar who is presented in opposition to the ungodly rich man (Luke 16:19–31).

Begging is sometimes only a simple statement of poverty: "I am poor," "I want a loaf of bread," or "Give me the price of a loaf." But occasionally the expressive gesture of bringing the forefinger across the teeth and holding it up was used as proof that absolutely no trace of food was there. Hunger brought "cleanness of teeth" (Amos 4:6; see NIV footnote).

Some of the beggars posed as sent of God. "I am your guest! I am God's guest! God will direct you! God will recompense you! God will preserve your children! God will prolong your days!" The beggars are thus the street-preachers of the East. Sometimes entire families beg for a meager living.

Butler. See *Cupbearer*.

Carpenter. A worker in wood; a builder. Joseph, the legal or foster father of Jesus, was a carpenter (Matt 13:55); so also was Jesus (Mark 6:3). The work of carpenters is often mentioned in the Bible (Gen 6:14; Exod 37; Isa 44:13). David employed Phoenician carpenters in building his palace (2 Sam 5:11; 1 Chron 14:1).

The chief work of the carpenter was making roofs, doors, window-shutters, lattice-squares, and divan frames for the houses; plows; and yokes. Hence, Jesus knew yokes, as well as the various aspects of farm life, and could say, "My yoke is easy and my burden is light" (Matt 11:30).

Some of the tools used by the ancient Egyptians were the adze, saw, square, awl, hammer, and glue-pot (Exod 21:6; Jer 10:4). The adze was their favorite implement. In ripping a board with the saw, the carpenter sat on the board and sawed away from himself (Isa 44:13). In its broadest sense, carpentry included crafting in stone and metal, as well as in wood.

Chamberlain. An officer employed to look after the personal affairs of a sovereign. Potiphar seems to have had such an officer (Gen 39:1). A chamberlain was introduced into the court by Solomon and was sometimes referred to as "steward" (1 Kings 4:6; 16:9; 18:3) or "governor."

His duties seem to have been to superintend the palace and attend to royal etiquette. This post later became one of special increased influence, including the right of introduction to the king. He thus became the chief minister.

Erastus, the "chamberlain" of the city of Corinth, was named by Paul in his salutation to the Roman Christians (Rom 16:23). His office was apparently that of director of public works.

Clerk. The clerk or "city clerk" (Acts 19:35) was likely the city recorder. He was probably a magistrate of considerable authority and influence. He may have been mayor or the chief sovereign of the city. The clerk is often mentioned in Ephesian inscriptions.

The clerk may have been literally a temple-keeper. This term, found on Ephesian coins struck about the time of Paul, originally signified a temple servant whose business it was to sweep out and decorate the temple. Ultimately this office grew to be an honorary title of towns in Asia Minor that were especially devoted to the service of any divinity and possessed a temple consecrated to that divinity.

Confectioner. A perfumer or apothecary. When the orange trees, violets, and roses were in bloom, the women, who performed this function in the OT, made scented waters that they kept in large, tightly sealed bottles for use in the summer as cooling syrup drinks. These were presented to guests in tumblers of brass on silver trays. The king's confectioners (NIV "perfumers") would be occupied with the preparation and mixing of such flavoring essences (1 Sam 8:13).

Coppersmith. More generally thought of as a worker in any kind of metal (2 Tim 4:14). The coppersmiths had a particular way of smelting copper and iron. Their smelters were located so as to face the wind currents, thus using the natural winds to fan their fires sufficiently for smelting. King Solomon not only mined copper in the Arabah (south of the Dead Sea) and had it smelted at Ezion Geber, but he also enjoyed a thriving trade in this very useful metal (1 Kings 7:45).

Counselor. An adviser in any matter, particularly as the king's state adviser (2 Sam 15:12; 1 Chron 27:33). His position usually ranked him among the chief men of the government (Ezra 4:5; Job 3:14; 12:17; Isa 19:11). In the NT the name probably refers to a member of the Sanhedrin (Mark 15:43; Luke 23:50).

Craftsman. A fabricator of any material, as carpenter, smith, engraver, etc. (Gen 4:22; Isa 3:3). Also called artisans and artificers (KJV), these workers were skilled in metals, carving wood and plating it with gold, setting precious stones, and designing embroideries (2 Kings 24:14, 16; Jer 24:1; Acts 19:24). From "artificers" comes "artifacts," an archaeological term, meaning anything that was made or modified by human art or workmanship. Solomon procured many craftsmen from Hiram, king of Tyre, when building the temple (1 Chron 29:5; 2 Chron 34:11).

Cupbearer. An officer of considerable responsibility who attended Eastern monarchs. This office is of very great antiquity, being mentioned in connection with the Egyptians, the Persians, the Assyrians, and the Jewish rulers. The cupbearer (sometimes called the butler in KJV) was required to taste of the foods and wines before serving them, as a pledge that they were not poisoned (Gen 40:1; Neh 1:11). The butlers enjoyed the esteem and confidence of their royal masters (1 Kings 10:5; 2 Chron 9:4).

Diviner. One who obtains or seems to obtain secret knowledge, particularly of the future. He stands in contrast to the prophet of the Lord, since he was believed to be inspired by demon

A Palestinian farmer plowing his land with a primitive, one-handled wooden plow. Courtesy S. Zur Picture Library.

power, and the Lord's prophet by the Spirit of God (Zech 10:2). Balaam was a heathen diviner but temporarily rose to the status of a bona-fide prophet of the Lord. He later advised Balak on a plan to destroy Israel (Num 22–25; 31:15–16). Though the diviner is classed with the prophet, this does not mean an endorsement of divination (1 Sam 6:2; Jer 27:9; Dan 4:7).

Dyer. The practice of dyeing textiles was in existence even before the time of Abraham. Dyeing vats and clay looms that were used as weights have been found in Lachish.

The dyer obtained his dye from various sources. The crimson was obtained from a worm or grub that fed on the oak or other plants. Indigo was made from the rind of the pomegranate. Purple was made from the murex shellfish found on the beach at the city of Acre. It was also found along the Phoenician coast north of Acre. Luke tells of Lydia, "a dealer in purple cloth from the city of Thyatira" (Acts 16:14). Excavations have revealed that "a guild of dyers" existed in the vicinity of Thyatira.

Elder. Men of Israel who formed one of the three classes represented in the Sanhedrin. The scribes and priests formed the two other classes (Acts 5:21). The elders were considered chief men or magistrates (Ps 105:22). See Numbers 11:16–30; Mark 14:43.

Engraver The OT and archaeology reveal a knowledge of engraving or carving among the Israelites. However, their knowledge was not developed as extensively nor as skillfully as among some of the neighboring countries, perhaps because of the command against worshiping graven images (Exod 20:4). Signet rings, engraved with a man's seal or sign, were common (Gen 38:18; Esth 3:12: Jer 22:24). Each of the two onyx stones on the high priest's shoulders was engraved with the names of six tribes, and his breatplate bore twelve stones, each engraved with the name of a tribe (Exod 28:9–21). Bezaleel and Aholiab were craftsmen in gold, silver, brass, stones, and wood (31:1–9; 38:22–23). God gave them the skills to make the furnishings of the tabernacle. Not only did they carve and engrave, but they also taught these skills to others (35:30–35).

Farmer. Farming had its beginning with the first man, Adam. Cain tilled the soil, and Abel was a livestock farmer, perhaps a shepherd (Gen 4). The early farm implements were very crude. The plow was a simple affair, being made of wood and having an iron share, small and shaped like a sword. Donkeys and oxen were used to pull the light plow, which had only one handle, except in cases where human beings were used in place of oxen. See also *Plowman*.

When Israel entered the land of Canaan, farming took on a new aspect. Every seventh year, the farmers allowed the ground to remain idle. Whatever grew of itself was left to the poor, the stranger, and the beasts of the field (Lev 25:1–7). To the Hebrews, the terms "grain" and "corn" included almost every object of field culture. The farmers cultivated millet, spelt, various species of beans and peas, pepperwort, cummin, cucumbers, melons, flax, and perhaps cotton. Farming was practiced by Cain, Noah, Elisha, David, Uzziah, and Solomon. Farmers were also called husbandmen, tillers of the ground, and laborers, and they were subject to certain laws (Isa 28:24; Jer 14:4; Matt 13:3; Mark 12:1; James 5:7).

Fisher. The frequent allusions to the art of fishing in Scripture are in connection with the Sea of Galilee (Matt 4:18; 13:48; Mark 1:16; Luke 5:2). Several methods of fishing were practiced. (1) The casting net was a common method used. The fisherman stood on the bank or waded breast-deep into the water, and skillfully threw the net, which he had arranged on his arm, into the water in front of him. It fell in the shape of a ring, and as the weights dragged it down, the net took the shape of a dome or cone and enclosed the fish. (2) The dragnet was used in herring and salmon fishing, with floats marking the location of the submerged nets. It was usually operated from boats. (3) Hooks or angles were occasionally used. Fish were speared on the Mediterranean coast, being attracted to the surface by a moving torch. Night fishing was very common, especially on the Sea of Galilee. In modern times Jewish fishing fleets operate along the Mediterranean coast and on the Sea of Galilee. Schools of fish are sometimes seen on the Sea of Galilee from the shore when the fishermen in the boat cannot see them (John 21:4–6).

Fuller. One who washes or bleaches clothing. This is one of the oldest arts and at an early period was comparatively perfect. Both men and women engaged in cleaning clothes and other materials. The work of the fuller may have been a subdivision of the dyers' trade. However, it consisted chiefly in cleaning and bleaching garments. The cleansing was done by treading or stamping the garments with the feet or with rods or sticks in containers of water. Alkaline, potash, soda (KJV niter), and herbs were used in the washing and bleaching process.

The fullers discovered a singular art of bleaching cloth white by the aid of alkali, soap, putrid urine, fumes of sulphur, and the ashes of certain desert plants. Therefore, the fuller's shop was located usually outside the city where offensive odors could be avoided, the cloth could be trampled clean in a running stream, and then spread out for drying. In Jerusalem the "fuller's field" or the "washerman's field" was located near the conduit of the upper pool, which was in all probability in the Kidron Valley between Gihon (the present Virgin's Fountain) and the well En Rogel (2 Kings 18:17; Isa 7:3; 36:2).

Gatekeeper. Often translated "porter" in KJV. The biblical porter was a gatekeeper and not a burden-bearer (2 Sam 18:26; 1 Chron 9:22). The Levites who had charge of the various entrances to the temple were called gatekeepers (1 Chron 9:17; 15:18; 2 Chron 23:19). In some versions the word used is "doorkeeper" (1 Chron 15:23–24). A gatekeeper was stationed at the city gates and among the shepherds, where he was responsible for guarding the doors of the sheepfold. In David's time, the gatekeepers of the temple, who were also guards, numbered four thousand (23:5).

Goldsmith. An artisan who works in gold. The furnishings of the tabernacle and the temple that were constructed of gold or overlaid with gold required skilled workmen (see, e.g., Exodus 25). Goldsmiths were not above helping out in the reconstruction of the wall of Jerusalem after the Exile (Neh 3:8, 31–32). Most often the word "goldsmith" in the NIV is used of those who craft idols from gold (Isa 40:19; 41:7; 46:6; Jer 10:9 et al.).

Herdsman. A tender of oxen, sheep, goats, and camels. The patriarchs were great herdsmen. The occupation was not inconsistent with state honors. David's herdsmen were among his chief officers of state. In general, however, the herdsman was seldom the owner of the flock or herd that he tended (Gen 13:7; 26:20; 1 Sam 21:7; Amos 1:1; 7:14).

The rich owners placed the herdsmen in charge of their herds. The herdsmen's duty was to protect the herd from wild beasts, to keep them from straying, and to lead them to suitable pasture. The herdsmen usually carried a sharpened or metal-pointed goad and a small bag, or scrip, for provisions. Their dress consisted of a long cloak. Their food was very simple, and they usually lived on what they could find. Their wages were given them in products taken from the herd.

Alabaster relief from Nimrud, c. 883–859 B.C., of Ashurbanipal, king of Assyria, standing in his chariot hunting lions as two footmen (armed with bows, shields and dirks) assist in the hunt. Reproduced by courtesy of the Trustees of the British Museum.

Relief from the palace of Sargon II at Khorsabad (721–705 B.C.) that shows Assyrian hunters in a wood shooting birds and other game. Reproduced by courtesy of the Trustees of the British Museum.

Hunter. The work of hunter or fowler was one of the earliest occupations. It was originally a means of support, but later became a source of recreation. It was held in very high repute and was engaged in by all classes, but more often by royalty (Gen 10:9; 27:3, 5; 1 Sam 26:20; Job 38:39; Prov 6:5).

Three principal methods of hunting are mentioned in the Bible: (1) Shooting with bow and arrows (Exod 27:3). (2) Snaring by spring net and cage, especially for birds such as quail, partridge, and duck (Jer 5:27; Amos 3:5). (3) Pits covered with a net and brushwood for deer, foxes, wolves, bears, lions, etc. (Ps 35:7; Isa 24:18; 42:22).

Husbandman. See *Farmer.*

Judge. The head of the house was considered the judge over his own household. With the enlargement of the human family, this power quite naturally passed to the heads of tribes and clans. After Israel came into the wilderness beyond Sinai, Moses found the responsibility of handling all the judicial matters too great. Taking the advice of his father-in-law Jethro, he was advised to choose "men who who fear God, trustworthy men who hate dishonest gain" to handle these matters. There were to be judges over thousands and hundreds and fifties (Exod 18:19–26; Deut 1:16). After coming into Canaan, judges sat at the gates of the cities (Deut 16:18).

Lawyer. One who is conversant with the law. There were court lawyers and synagogue lawyers (Matt 22:35; Luke 7:30; 10:25; 11:45–46, 52; 14:3; Titus 3:13). The scribe functioned in the capacity of a lawyer in the pronouncement of legal decisions. (See *Teacher of the Law.*)

Magician. One who practices superstitious ceremonies to hurt or to benefit mankind. The Hebrews were forbidden to consult magicians (Gen 41:8; Exod 7:11, 22; Dan 1:20; 2:2; 5:11; Acts 13:6, 8). Magic is of two kinds—(1) natural, or scientific, and (2) supernatural, or spiritual. The first attributes its power to a deep, practical acquaintance with the power of nature. The second attributes its power to an acquaintance with celestial or infernal agencies.

There are many accounts of the use of magical art in the Scriptures. Before Israel left Egypt the magicians were called by Pharaoh to duplicate the works of God in changing a rod into a serpent and turning water into blood. They were sometimes classified with the "wise men." In the interpretation of dreams and visions, the magicians and soothsayers were called. The Chaldeans were particularly famous as magicians.

Mason. A worker in stone. Certain villages were famous for their masons. The farmers were usually skillful in building low terrace walls of undressed stone for the fields and vineyards. But most buildings required a master mason.

The mason was acquainted with the proper kind of foundation. He knew how to lay the cornerstone. He knew how to select and lay the stones in the wall. His equipment consisted of the plumb line, the measuring reed, the leveling line, the hammer with the toothed edge for shaping stones, and a small basket for carrying off earth (2 Kings 12:12; 22:6; 1 Chron 22:15; 2 Chron 24:12; Ezra 3:7).

A stone mason at work with chisel and hammer. Courtesy Zev Radovan.

Merchant. A dealer in merchandise. Merchants bought goods from distant lands or from caravans and sold them to traders in the marketplaces. Many became wealthy. Sometimes merchants are spoken of appreciatively (2 Chron 9:13–14; Song of Songs 3:6), but sometimes merchants were dishonest (Hos 12:7), and, especially in the Book of Revelation, they are condemned for seeking only material gain (18:3, 11, 15, 13).

Musician. Since music was a very prominent art in biblical, especially OT, times and played

Relief (1.13 m. high) from Zinjerli, c. eighth century B.C., depicting four musicians playing upon hand drums and lyres. Each musician is dressed in a full-length robe, fringed at the bottom, and contained at the waist by a broad belt with three-pronged tassels. Courtesy Istanbul Museum. Photo: B. Brandl.

such an important part in the life of Israel and in their religious exercises and festivities, there was a demand for those who were adept at playing instruments and in singing hymns and psalms (Ps 68:25). Hebrew music was primarily vocal, yet many of the psalms have signs indicating that they were to be accompanied by musical instruments (1 Kings 10:12; 2 Chron 9:11; Rev 18:12). The "chief musician" occurs in the titles of fifty-four psalms. Asaph and his brothers were apparently the first to hold this position, and the office was probably hereditary in the family (1 Chron 15:19; 2 Chron 35:15). Among the instruments used by the Hebrews were the cymbal, harp, organ, pipe, psaltery, and trumpet. See separate article MUSIC AND MUSICAL INSTRUMENTS.

Nurse. One who looks after, tutors, or guides another, as in a period of inexperience or sickness. In ancient times the nurse had an honored position in a home, often as a nursemaid, or nanny (2 Sam 4:4; 2 Kings 11:2). Most patriarchal families had a nurse or nurses. Rebekah's nurse went with her to Canaan and was buried with great mourning (Gen 24:59; 35:8). Foster fathers or mothers were sometimes referred to as nurses (Ruth 4:16; Isa 49:23).

Perfumer. A compounder of drugs, oils, and perfumes. KJV translates the word as "apothecary." All large oriental towns had their perfumers' street. Their stock included anything fragrant in the form of loose powder, compressed cake, or essences in spirit, oil, or fat, as well as seeds, leaves, and bark.

Perfumes were used in connection with the holy oil and incense of the tabernacle (Exod 30:25, 33, 35; 37:29; 2 Chron 16:14; Neh 3:8). The ritual of Baal-worshipers (Isa 57:9) and the embalming of the dead and rites of burial (2 Chron 16:14; Mark 16:1; Luke 23:56) all used perfume. The apothecary compounded and sold these sweet spices and anointing oils (Eccl 10:1).

The frequent references in the OT to physicians and perfumers indicate the high esteem in which the professions were held (Gen 50:2; Jer 8:22; Luke 4:23).

Physician. One who understands and practices medicine in the art of healing. The priests and prophets were expected to have some knowledge of medicine. In the days of Moses there were midwives and regular physicians who attended the Israelites (Exod 1:19). They brought some knowledge of medicine with them from Egypt, whose physicians were renowned for their healing arts. In the early stages of medical practice, attention was more often confined to surgical aid and external applications. Even down to a comparatively late period, outward maladies appear to have been the chief subjects of medical treatment among the Hebrews, though they were not entirely without remedies for internal and even mental disorders.

The medicines prescribed were salves, particular balms, plaster and poultices, oil baths, mineral baths, etc. In Egypt the physicians also aided in carrying out the elaborate preparations connected with embalming a body (Gen 50:2). See also DISEASES.

Plowman. The terms *husbandmen* and *plowmen* were used synonymously in the Scriptures. The plowman was a farmer in general. Where primitive methods of farming are still used in Palestine today the plow is lightly built, with the least possible skill or expense, and consists of two poles, which cross each other near the ground; the pole nearer the oxen is fastened to the yoke, while the other serves one end as the handle, the other as the plowshare (1 Sam 13:20–21; Isa 2:4). It is drawn by oxen, camels, cows, or heifers.

Porter. See *Gatekeeper.*

Potter. Although regarded as an inferior trade, the work of pottery making supplied a universal need. In antiquity, potters lived in settlements in the lower city of Jerusalem (Jer 18:2–4), in the neighborhood of Hebron and Beit Jibrin, where clay was plentiful and where the royal potteries probably were situated (1 Chron 4:23).

There is a great demand for potters in the Middle East because copper vessels are expensive and leather bottles are not suitable for some purposes.

The maker of earthenware was one of the first manufacturers. The potter found the right kind of clay, prepared it by removing stones and other rough substances, shaped and made it into the vessel desired, baked it, and marketed it. If the vessel became marred in the shaping process, it was made over again into another vessel. When one broke after baking, it was discarded and thrown into the "potter's field" (Matt 27:7, 10). The Hebrew potter, sitting at his work, turned the clay, which had first been kneaded with his feet, into various kinds of vessels on his potting wheels, which were generally made of wood (Lam 4:2). See also POTTERY.

Late Bronze Age (1550–1200 B.C.) Basalt potter's wheel from Hazor. With his feet, the potter turned the two stones, one pivoted upon the other. Courtesy Israel Department of Antiquities and Museums.

Preacher. One who heralds or proclaims, usually by delivering a discourse on a text of Scripture. This method of presenting messages from God to man is as old as the human family. Noah is referred to as "a preacher of righteousness" (2 Peter 2:5). The prophets were given the responsibility of delivering messages of truth in song and action, in accusation and rebuke, with pleading and exhortation, by prophecy and promise. The temple, the synagogue, and the church were designed chiefly as places where the profession of preaching was practiced, where human beings became the conveyors of God's message.

Since the completion of the Bible, preaching has come to mean the exposition of the Word of God to believers or the declaration of the gospel message to unbelievers.

Priest. See separate article PRIEST, PRIESTHOOD.

Publican. See *Tax Collector.*

Rabbi. A title given by the Jews to the teachers of their law. It was also applied to Christ by his disciples and others (Matt 23:7–8; John 1:38, 49). The term *rabbi* means "master" or "teacher" (John 20:16). The use of the term cannot be verified before the time of Christ.

Recorder. An officer of high rank in the Jewish state, exercising the functions not simply of an annalist, but of chancellor or president of the privy council (Isa 36:3, 22). He was not only the grand custodian of the public records, but he also kept the responsible registry of the current transactions of government (2 Sam 8:16; 20:24; 2 Kings 18:18).

In David's court, the recorder appears among the high officers of his household (2 Sam 8:16; 20:24). In Solomon's court, the recorder is associated with the three secretaries and is mentioned last, probably as being their president (1 Kings 4:3).

Robber. One who engages in theft and plunder. Ishmael, the Bedouin, became a "wild donkey of a man" and a robber by trade (Gen 16:12). Among the nomad tribes of the East, it was considered a most worthy profession.

The Mosaic Law strictly forbids robbery; it is denounced in Proverbs and by the prophets. The prophet Hosea compares the apostate priests to robbers, bandits, and marauders (Hos 6:9, 7:1). Robbery is often mentioned in the Bible, but never is it commended (Isa 61:8; Ezek 22:29; Luke 18:16; John 10:8).

Ruler. One who governs or assists in carrying on government. An honor often bestowed by kings on their subjects. Daniel was made ruler over the whole province of Babylon by Nebuchadnezzar for interpreting a dream, and again made third ruler of the kingdom after interpreting the writing on the wall at the time of Belshazzar's great feast (Dan 2:10, 38; 5:7, 16, 29).

There was the ruler of the synagogue, the ruler of the treasures, or the chief treasurer, and the high priest who was considered the "ruler of the house of God" (1 Chron 9:11; Mic 3:1, 9; Luke 8:49).

Sailor. One whose occupation is navigation, or the operation of ships, particularly one who manipulates a ship with sails (1 Kings 9:27; John 1:5, 7; Rev 18:17).

Saleswoman. A woman who sells merchandise. Lydia, the "dealer in purple cloth" from Thyatira was a convert of the apostle Paul at Philippi (Acts 16:14–15, 40).

Schoolmaster. One who exercises careful supervision over scholars, educating them, forming their manners, etc. Such a person was considered stern and severe. The Mosaic Law, likened to a "schoolmaster *to bring us* unto Christ" (Gal 3:24 KJV), awakens a consciousness of sin and prepares a person to accept Christ.

Scribe. A person employed to handle correspondence and to keep accounts. They were given a high place alongside the high priest. Hezekiah set up a body of men whose work it was to transcribe old records, or to put in writing what had been handed down orally (Prov 25:1). The scribe became known as a student and an inter-

Painted limestone statue of an Eygptian scribe holding a partly opened roll of papyrus. The eyes are inlaid with quartz, crystal, and ebony wood. From Saqqara, 5th Dynasty (2500–2350 B.C.). Courtesy Réunion des Musées Nationaux.

preter of the law (Neh 8:1–13; Jer 36:26).

In the time of Christ, the scribes had attained great influence and power as a class and were regarded with much respect. They were given the best places at feasts and the chief seats in the synagogues (Matt 23:5; Luke 14:7).

Seer. One who is considered able to foresee things or events; a prophet (1 Sam 9:9). Samuel identified himself as a seer (10:19). Often kings and rulers had their own personal seers to assist them in decision making, especially when the future seemed unclear (2 Sam 24:11; 2 Chron 29:25; 35:15).

Senator. See *Elder.*

Sergeant. A Roman lictor or officer who attended the chief magistrates when they appeared in public, and who inflicted the punishment that had been pronounced (Acts 16:35, 38 KJV; NIV "officers"). They were literally "rod-holders."

Servant. Applied to anyone under the authority of another, implying that not all servants were domestics or slaves. In some passages of Scripture, the word properly means "young man" or "minister." It is applied to the relation of men to others occupying high position, as Eliezer, whose place in the household of Abraham compared with that of a prime minister (Gen 15:2; 24:2; Prov 14:35; John 18:20).

Sheepmaster. One who is both a shepherd and the owner of the sheep (2 Kings 3:4 KJV, MOF; NIV raised sheep). In some areas, the sheepmaster is one who owns a superior kind of sheep.

Sheepshearer. When the wool of the sheep is long and ready to "harvest," a sheep-shearing time is announced, and it is a great time of rejoicing (Gen 38:12; 2 Sam 13:23–24). This festival is usually marked by revelry and merry-making (Gen 31:19).

Shepherd. One employed in tending, feeding, and guarding the sheep. Abel, Rachel, and David were all keepers of sheep. The shepherd's equipment consisted of a bag made of goat's skin with legs tied, in which food and other articles were placed; a sling for protection against wild animals; a rod (stick) about thirty inches (seventy-seven cm.) in length with a knob on one end; a staff, usually with a crook on one end; a flute made of reeds for entertainment and for calming the

Limestone statue (1.77 m. high)—found in the temple of Nabu at Nimrud (810–783 B.C.)—of a divine servant, bearded and standing with folded hands, ready to serve. Reproduced by courtesy of the Trustees of the British Museum.

Shepherds leading their flock along an ancient colonnaded road that was built Roman times in Samaria. Courtesy Zev Radovan.

sheep; and a cloak to use as bedding at night. Sheep would learn to recognize the voice of their master (Gen 46:32; 1 Sam 17:20; John 10:3–4). Metaphorically, God is pictured as the shepherd of his flock (Gen 48:15; John 10; Rev 7:17).

Silversmith. A worker in silver, the most famous example of which was Demetrius the silversmith, whose business was interfered with by the evangelistic work of the apostle Paul (Judg 17:4; Prov 25:4; Acts 19:24).

Singer. A trained or professional vocalist. Hebrew music was primarily vocal. Barzillai mentioned the "voices of men and women singers" (2 Sam 19:35). Solomon was a composer of songs (1 Kings 4:32). David's trained choir numbered 288 members (1 Chron 25:7).

Slave. A person held in bondage to another, having no freedom of action, his person and service being wholly under the control of his master or owner. Jewish slaves were of two classes—Hebrew and non-Hebrew—and both were protected by law. Hebrew slaves became such through poverty or debt, through theft and inability to repay, or in case of females, through being sold by their parents as maidservants. The slavery of Hebrews was the mildest form of bondservice (Exod 21:20–32; Deut 21:14; Jer 34:8–16).

At the time of Christ, slavery was established throughout the world and considered even by the wisest people as a normal state of society. But Christianity, by teaching the common creation and redemption of mankind and enjoining the law of kindness and love to all, instructed believers how to live under slavery and then provided principles that have been used as the basis for emancipation and the ultimate extinction of the whole institution (1 Cor 12:13; Gal 3:28; Col 3:11; Rev 19:18).

Slave Driver. One whose duty is to assign tasks; an overseer or bond master. Pharaoh appointed slave drivers over the Hebrews to make their work hard and wearisome. He hoped by such oppression to break down their physical strength and thereby to reduce their numerical growth and also to crush their hope of ever gaining their liberty (Exod 1:11; 3:7; 5:6, 10, 13–14).

Smith. A workman in stone, wood, or metal. The first smith mentioned in Scripture is Tubal-Cain (Gen 4:22). So necessary was the trade of the smith in ancient warfare that conquerors removed the smiths from a vanquished nation to more certainly disable it (Isa 44:12; 54:16; Jer 24:1).

Soldier. One who engages in military service and receives pay for his services. In the earlier times, every man above the age of twenty was a soldier (Num 1:3); and each tribe formed a regiment, with its own banner and its own leader (2:2; 10:14). Up until the time of David, the army consisted entirely of infantry (1 Sam 4:10; 15:4), the use of horses having been restrained by divine command (Deut 17:16).

The Jews had experienced the great advantages found in the use of chariots, both in their contests with the Canaanites and at a later period with the Syrians, and hence they eventually attached much importance to them (1 Kings 22; 2 Kings 9; 1 Chron 19:6–7).

Soothsayer. See *Magician.*

Sorcerer. One who practices the arts of the magicians and astrologers, by which he pretends to foretell events with the assistance of evil spirits (Isa 47:9, 12; Acts 8:9, 11). In its broader sense, a sorcerer is one who practices in the whole field of divinatory occultism (Exod 7:11: 22:18; Jer 27:9).

Spinner. A person who uses the distaff and the spindle in the making of thread from wool, flax, or cotton (Prov 31:19; Matt 6:28).

Steward. One to whose care is committed the management of the household (Gen 43:19; Luke 16:1). The term is also applied to ministers (1 Cor 4:1 KJV) and to Christians (1 Peter 4:10 KJV). The meaning of the word is different in Genesis 15:2, where NIV has this description: "the one who will inherit my estate."

Tanner. One who is skilled in dressing and preserving hides or skins of animals. Among the ancient Jews, ceremonial uncleanness was attached to the occupation of the tanner, and hence he was obliged to do his work outside the town. The tanneries of Joppa are now on the shore south of the city, where possibly the "house of Simon" was located (Acts 9:43; 10:6, 32).

Taskmaster. See *Slave Driver.*

Tax Collector. A tax collector of Roman revenue. Of these there appear to have been two classes: (1) the "chief tax collector," of whom Zacchaeus is an example (Luke 19:2), and (2) the ordinary publican, the lowest class of the servants engaged in the collecting of revenue and of whom Levi (later the apostle Matthew) is an example (Matt 9:11).

The publicans or tax collectors were hated for being the instruments through which the subjection of the Jews to the Roman emperor was perpetuated. They looked at the paying of tribute as a virtual acknowledgment of the emperor's sovereignty. Tax collectors were noted for imposing more taxes than were required so that they might more quickly enrich themselves. The publicans of the NT were regarded as traitors and apostates, defiled by their frequent contacts with pagans, and willing tools of the oppressor. Hence, they were classed with sinners, harlots, and pagans (Matt 9:11; 21:31; Mark 2:16; Luke 5:27–30).

Teacher. One who imparts instruction, and communicates knowledge of religious truth or other matters. "Teachers" are mentioned among the those having divine gifts in Ephesians 4:11, where Paul seems to reckon teaching among the extraordinary gifts of God and uses no mark of distinction or separation between "apostles," with which he begins, and "teachers" with which he ends. "Teacher" doubtlessly refers to the well-informed persons to whom inquiring Christian converts might have recourse for removing their doubts and difficulties concerning Christian observances, the sacraments, and other rituals, and for receiving from Scripture and demonstration that "this is the very Christ," that the things relating to the Messiah have been accomplished in Jesus (Ezra 7; Matt 23; Heb 5:12).

Teacher of the Law. Gamaliel was such a person (Acts 5:34). As teacher of the law, he kept and handed down the sacred laws as received from Mount Sinai. He was the thirty-fifth receiver of the traditions. This term may also have applied to the scribe in his practical administration of the law in the pronouncement of legal decisions.

Tentmaker. One skilled in making tents from hair, wool, or skins. The early patriarchs largely lived in tents and were skilled in the art of tentmaking. In NT times it was the custom to teach every Jewish boy some trade. Jesus was a carpenter, and Paul was a tentmaker. Paul practiced his trade in company with Aquila at Corinth (Acts 18:1–3).

Tetrarch. A ruler over a fourth part of a kingdom or province in the Roman Empire. Locally, his authority was similar to that of a king, and the title of king was often given to him (Matt 14:1; Luke 3:1; Acts 13:1).

Tiller. See *Farmer; Plowman.*

Treasurer. An important officer in Middle East courts, probably having charge of the receipts and disbursements of the public treasury (Ezra 1:8; 7:21; Isa 22:15; Dan 3:2–3). This title was given to the officer of state, was considered superior to all others, and was sometimes filled by the heir to the throne (2 Chron 26:21).

Watchman. One whose duty was to stand in the tower on the walls or at the gates of the city. He also patrolled the streets, and, besides protecting the city and its inhabitants from violence, he was required to call out the hours of the night (2 Sam 18:24–27; Song of Songs 5:7; Isa 21:11–12). God's prophets were also his "watchmen" to warn his people (Isa 21:6 KJV; NIV "lookout").

Weaver. One who is skilled in the making of cloth or rugs from spun thread or string. The Israelites probably perfected the art of weaving while in Egypt, though they no doubt made progress in it from their own resources, even before they entered Egypt. Weaving, for the most part, was done by women. The fibrous materials woven were usually linen, flax, and wool (Exod 35:35; Lev 13:48; 1 Chron 11:23; Isa 38:12).

Witch. A "knowing or wise one." Witch was the name given to the woman and wizard the name given to the man who practiced "witchcraft." There was an apparent communication with demons and a pretended conversation with the spirits of the dead by means of which future events were revealed, diseases cured, and evil spirits driven away. The woman of Endor to whom Saul went for help is called a medium in NIV (1 Sam 28). Witchcraft was severely denounced (Lev 20:6; 2 Kings 9:22; Gal 5:20). See also *Sorcerer.*

Writer. The knowledge of writing was possessed by the Hebrews at a very early period. The materials on which they wrote were of various kinds. Tables of stone, metal, plaster, skins, paper made from bulrushes, and fine parchment were used. The pens were also different, to correspond with the writing material (Judg 5:14; Ps 45:1; Ezek 9:2). The prophets were often told by the

Lord to write and may be considered writers (Rev 1:11; 21:5). HPH

OCRAN, OCHRAN (ŏk'răn, Heb. *'ōkhrān*). Father of Pagiel, prince of the tribe of Asher, appointed to assist in the first census of Israel (Num 1:13, 7:72).

ODED (ō'dĕd, Heb. *'ôdhēdh, he was restored,* or *prophet*). 1. The father of Azariah the prophet (2 Chron 15:1).

2. A prophet in Samaria in the days of Ahaz, king of Judah (2 Chron 28:9–15). Pekah, king of the northern tribes, had taken captive 200,000 Jews, after killing 120,000 valiant men of Judah. As the captives and the spoil were being brought into Samaria, Oded rebuked them and persuaded them to feed and clothe the captives and to return them to Judah. Oded strongly emphasized that the wrath of God had brought ruin to the men of Judah and would ruin Israel also.

ODOR (ō'dêr, Heb. *besem,* Gr. *osmē*). That which affects the sense of smell. In ASV the word refers to a pleasant or sweet odor, while an unpleasant one is called "ill savor" or "stench." The Levitical offerings that did not deal with sin were called offerings of sweet savor; and the incense also (Mal 1:11) with its perfumed odor was acceptable to the Lord. The prayers of the saints (figuratively) are offerings of a sweet savor to the Lord (Rev 5:8). Hypocrisy stinks (Amos 5:21).

OFFAL (See DUNG)

OFFENSE (ŏ-fĕns', Heb. *'āsham, hāṭā',* Gr. *skandalon*). The word is used in a variety of ways in Scripture, as it is in English: injury, hurt, damage, occasion of sin, a stumbling block, an infraction of law, sin, transgression, state of being offended. In the NT it is often used in the sense of stumbling block (Matt 5:30; 11:6; 18:6; 1 Cor 8:13). Throughout the NT there is warning by Christ and the apostles against doing anything that would turn anyone away from the faith.

OFFERINGS (See SACRIFICE AND OFFERINGS)

OFFICER. A holder of an official position. The word is used in a variety of senses: (1) one who has been set up over others (e.g., 1 Kings 4:27); (2) a eunuch, such as Eastern kings set in charge of their women and also of much of the routine business of the court (e.g., Esth 1:10); (3) a writer or clerk (e.g., Deut 20:9); (4) a police officer or bailiff (Luke 12:58); (5) originally an assistant or underruler (Matt 5:25).

OFFSCOURING (Heb. *sehî, refuse,* Gr. *peripsēma, dirt*). A contemptuous word in the KJV for sweepings, scrapings, filth, dung. "Thou hast made us as the offscouring" (Lam 3:45); "the filth of the world . . . the offscouring of all things" (1 Cor 4:13).

OG (ŏg, Heb. *'ôgh*). Amorite king of Bashan (Deut 31:4; Josh 2:10; 13:12; 1 Kings 4:19). He was a man of gigantic stature, a physical characteristic of which there is strong evidence among the Canaanite tribes. He held sway over sixty separate communities. Og's defeat before the invading Hebrews (Deut 3:1–13) became proverbial, for it dispelled a legend of invincibility based on the daunting appearance of some of the Canaanite giants (1:28). The tradition was long-lived (Ps 135:11; 136:20). Og's territory was assigned in the partition of Palestine to Reuben, Gad, and the half-tribe of Manasseh (Num 32:33). The "bed . . . of iron" preserved as a museum piece at Rabbah among the Amorites (Deut 3:11) was possibly a sarcophagus cut from black basaltic rock. Iron was not common in Palestine at the time, the Iron Age having been introduced by the Philistines. To prepare a sarcophagus was common aristocratic practice.

OHAD (ō'hăd, Heb. *'ōhadh,* meaning unknown). The third son of Simeon (Gen 46:10) and head of a clan in that tribe (Exod 6:15).

OHEL (ō'hĕl, Heb. *ōhel, tent*). A son of Zerubbabel, a descendant of King Jehoiakim (1 Chron 3:20).

OHOLAH, OHOLIBAH (ō-hō'là, ō-hŏl'ĭ-bà, Heb. *'ohŏlâh, 'ohŏlîvâh, tent-woman, my tent is in her*). A woman is mentioned in Ezekiel 23 who represents Samaria, capital of the northern kingdom, whose worship was self-devised (John 4:9, 20–22). Her sister Oholibah is a symbol of Jerusalem (Ezek 23:4), capital of Judah, whose worship was appointed by God. These "women"

Relief from his palace at Khorsabad that shows King Sargon II, 722–705 B.C., receiving an Assyrian officer. Reproduced by courtesy of the Trustees of the British Museum.

had been unfaithful to the Lord, their true husband (Isa 54:5). Later, Oholah (Israel) was spiritually adulterous by her coalition with Egypt and Assyria. For these whoredoms God punished her with captivity by the very agent of her sin (Ezek 23:9–10). Oholibah (Judah) yielded to Babylonian culture (23:11–22), for which God promised her a similar captivity by the very agent of her sin (23:22–49).

OHOLIAB (ō-hō'lĭ-ăb, Heb. *'ohŏlîav, father's tent*). A man who was divinely endowed with artistic skill to construct the tabernacle (Exod 31:6).

OHOLIBAMAH (ō-hōl'ĭ-bă'mȧ, Heb. *'ohŏlîvamâh, tent of the high place*). 1. One of Esau's three wives (Gen 36:2, 14, 18), called also Judith, perhaps her personal name (Gen 26:34), Oholibamah being her married name.

2. A chief descended from Esau (Gen 36:41; 1 Chron 1:52), probably so named from the district of his possession.

OIL (Heb. *shemen,* Gr. *elaion*). In the Bible almost always olive oil, perhaps the only exception being Esther 2:12, where it is oil of myrrh. The olives were sometimes beaten (Lev 24:2), sometimes trodden (Mic 6:15), but generally crushed in a mill designed for that purpose. The upper stone, instead of rubbing against the lower as in a flour mill, rolled on it and so pressed out the oil. The wheel usually was turned by ox-power or donkey-power, the animal being blindfolded. Olive oil was not only a prime article of food, bread being dipped in it, but it was also used for cooking, for anointing, and for lighting. Oil was one of the principal ingredients in making soap (Jer 2:22).

Anointing with oil was for three diverse purposes: wounded animals were anointed for the soothing and curative effects of the oil (Ps 23:5); people anointed themselves with oil for its cosmetic value (104:15); but most notably men were anointed as an official inauguration into high office. Priests (Exod 28:41; 29:7), prophets, and kings (1 Kings 19:15–16) were anointed and were called "messiahs," i.e., "anointed ones" (Lev 4:3, 5, 16; 1 Sam 2:10; 1 Chron 16:22). Anointing the head of a guest with oil was a mark of high courtesy (Luke 7:46). Oil is used also as a symbol for the Holy Spirit. Jesus' messiahship was not bestowed with the use of literal oil but was confirmed when the Holy Spirit came down on him in the form of a dove at his baptism (3:22). Oil was also the prime source of light in homes and in the tabernacle. Home lamps were little clay vessels having a wick lying in the oil and supported at one end, where the oil burned and furnished just about "one candlepower" of light.

OIL TREE (See PLANTS)

OINTMENTS AND PERFUMES. The use of perfume in the form of ointment or impregnated oil was a Middle Eastern practice long before it spread to the Mediterranean world. In all probability it was originally used for ceremonial purposes, first religious then secular, and became a personal habit with the growing sophistication of society and the need for deodorants in hot lands (Esth 2:12; Prov 7:17; 27:9; Isa 57:9). So universal was the practice that its suspension was an accepted sign of mourning (Deut 28:40; Ruth 3:3; 2 Sam 14:2; Dan 10:3; Amos 6:6; Mic 6:15). The skin as well as the hair was perfumed and anointed (Ps 104:15); and, especially on high occasions, the scented unguent was used with profusion (133:2). Anointing an honored guest was a courtesy a host performed (Luke 7:46). Among the directions listed for the service of the tabernacle are two prescribed "recipes," possibly Egyptian in form (Exod 30:23–25, 34–36). One recipe prescribes 750 ounces of solids in six quarts of oil. It is possible that the oil was pressed off when the scent of the aromatic gums was absorbed. The liquid would then be used as anointing oil, while the solid residue provided an incense. The process of manufacture is not clear, and the account takes for granted that "the work of a perfumer" is commonly familiar to the reader (Exod 30:25, 35; Neh 3:8; Eccl 10:1). It is clear, however, that the compound was based on the aromatic gum of Arabian plants (indigenous especially in Arabia Felix in the south of the peninsula) and that the medium or base was some form of fat or oil (probably calves' fat and olive oil). In its later trade form perfume was sometimes packed in alabaster boxes or flasks (Luke 7:37). Such ointment was heavily scented (John 12:3) and costly (12:5). EMB

OLD GATE. The KJV name of the gate at the NW corner of the city of Jerusalem in Nehemiah's time, near the present site of the Holy Sepulcher

An ancient oil press found among the ruins at Capernaum. There were three stages in producing oil. First, the hard olives were crushed into a soft paste. This was then squeezed, the crude oil flowing out, as a result of the pressure, into the vat shown here. Finally, the crude oil was stored in vessels or vats for some time, in which the sediments and water from the olives settled and the pure oil rose to the surface. The oil was then collected for storage or use. Courtesy Zev Radovan.

A cosmetic flask (1500–1200 B.C.), found at Lachish and made from an ivory tusk. In lands where water was very scarce, ointments and perfumes were often used in lieu of bathing and for self-enhancement. Courtesy Israel Department of Antiquities and Museums.

(Neh 3:6). NIV reads "Jeshanah Gate" (see footnote). See also Nehemiah 12:39 for the celebration.

OLD TESTAMENT. The OT is composed of thirty-nine books—five of law, twelve of history, five of poetry, five of major prophets, and twelve of minor prophets. The classification of the present Hebrew Bible is different—five of law, eight of prophets, and eleven of miscellaneous writings. These twenty-four in various combinations contain all of our thirty-nine books. Neither of these classifications exhibits the fact that much of the Pentateuch is history, nor do they show the chronological relation of the books. A logical survey of the OT literature may approach the subject chronologically.

I. Before Abraham. The first eleven chapters of Genesis give a brief outline of major events from the creation to the origin of the Jewish people in Abraham. Genesis 1 is a majestic revelation of God creating all the material and organic universe, climaxing in man. This picture is not given in the categories of modern science and yet is in general agreement with much modern scientific theory. A prominent contemporary theory declares that all matter had a beginning in the distant but measurable past with a vast nuclear explosion, from which the universes have been differentiated. Creation of the universe or of man is not dated in Genesis. The creation of plants, animals, and human beings is spread over six "days." Genesis 2 and 3 detail the special creation of human beings and God's dealing with them in Eden. Adam and Eve on probation fell into sin, and the race was involved in sin and misery. God, however, promised a Redeemer (3:15) and instituted sacrifice as a type that redemption.

II. The Flood. As people multiplied, sin increased, and God sent a flood to destroy all mankind (Gen 6–8). Evidence is accumulating that about 8000 B.C. some catastrophe associated with increased sedimentation on ocean floors occurred, perhaps having to do with glacial formation and with the change of polar climates, resulting in the destruction and freezing of great numbers of mammoths, notably in Siberia, and other animals. Many widely separated cultures, including the old Babylonian, preserve legends of a great flood.

III. Early Genealogies. Preflood and postflood genealogies seem to be schematic and incomplete, as are other biblical genealogies. If Genesis 11:10–26 has no gaps, Shem outlived Abraham, but no other hint of this is given in the biblical picture.

IV. Abraham and the Patriarchs. As sin again increased, God chose Abraham to found a new nation, which God would protect, isolate to a degree, and through whom he would reveal himself at last as Savior. Abraham left polytheistic Mesopotamia and lived in Canaan, where God instructed and blessed him, his son Isaac, and grandson Jacob. From Jacob came the twelve sons who fathered the tribes of Israel. The midpoint of Genesis, chapter 25, records the death of Abraham, who lived in the Middle Bronze Age, about 1900 B.C. His main characteristic was faith. To the sacrifices God now added infant circumcision as a sign of his covenant. Although circumcision was practiced elsewhere in antiquity, infant circumcision seems to have been unique. It was to be a sign both of the material and spiritual aspects of the covenant.

V. Bondage and Exodus (Exod 1–19). Through providential circumstances of famine and through Joseph's exaltation, God took Jacob's family to Egypt for a period of growth. At first it was sheltered under Joseph's viziership. Later Israel was enslaved. God saw their bitter bondage and through Moses delivered Israel by an outstretched hand. Ever since, Israel has remembered the deliverance from Pharaoh's army when the Lord brought them through the Red Sea (actually, one of the lakes through which the Suez Canal now passes). God led Israel to Mount Sinai, where the company of slaves became a nation under Moses, the great lawgiver, and where the

Ten Commandments and other legislation were received.

The date of the Exodus has been much discussed. The biblical data (1 Kings 6:1; Judg 11:26; Acts 13:20) appears to favor a date of 1440 or 1400 B.C. (LXX) and a conquest of Palestine in the Amarna Age. Some of the archaeological evidence favors this, but some is interpreted to favor an invasion at about 1230. There was indeed a general desolation of Palestinian cities at that time, but was it by Joshua's conquest or because of other conflicts in the troubled period at the beginning of the Iron Age? The cities of Palestine also changed hands in the Amarna Age—about 1360—and this date for Joshua's conquest is preferable.

VI. Israel's Law (Exod 20–Num 10). At Sinai Israel encamped for one year. Here God revealed himself and his commandments in majestic miracles. The Ten Commandments of Exodus 20 and Deuteronomy 5 summarize the eternal principles of man's duty to God and to his fellow men. The last twenty chapters of Exodus, except for the apostasy of the golden calf, which took place while Moses was on the mount, concern the building of the tabernacle. Leviticus mainly concerns the ceremonial worship of Israel—the offerings, feasts, and cleansings. The section Leviticus 18–22, however, also includes regulations for civil conduct of the nation, as does Exodus 21–23. Leviticus 11–15 includes laws of cleanliness, which have significance as types. Their main purpose, however, seems to have been to protect Israel's food sources and storage, to protect from vermin by requiring strict cleanliness, and to protect from contagion by instituting certain quarantines.

VII. The Wilderness (Numbers 11–36). Numbers adds some laws to Leviticus but mainly records the abortive attempt to invade Canaan from the south and the experiences during the forty years of wilderness wanderings. The first numbering is not a mere census but a mustering of the ranks for the invasion. In Numbers 14 Israel at Kadesh Barnea hears the reports of the spies and, in little faith, fails to conquer. Condemned to wander, they live as nomads at the edge of the arable land in Sinai until the "generation of wrath" dies. Several of the rebellions of these years are given in Numbers. At the end of the book a new mustering of the people provides 600,000 fighting men for Joshua's army. These numbers seem large, but in those days they allowed for no exemptions from the army for physical or other reasons. The numbers compare favorably with David's manpower of 1,300,000 and Saul's army of 330,000 and the figures in Judges 20:2, 15 of 426,000.

VIII. Deuteronomy. Moses conquered Transjordan and allowed two and a half tribes to settle there. In Deuteronomy Moses records this campaign and recounts much of the history and regulations of Exodus, Leviticus, and Numbers.

IX. Job. The date of Job is uncertain. As it seems to speak of a time before the Levitical legislation and names descendants of Uz, Buz, and others of Abraham's kin, it may be placed in the general time of Moses and in the area east of Palestine. It poses the problem of the suffering of the righteous and answers that the sovereign God has his own purposes, for which he is not answerable to people. It suggests a further answer that apparent injustices in the treatment of people are to be adjusted in a future life.

X. The Conquest. Joshua's invasion of Canaan is detailed in the first half of his book, Joshua 1–12. In a whirlwind campaign, after the miracles of the crossing of Jordan and the fall of Jericho, he gained possession of the middle of the country. At Aijalon he conquered the army of the southern confederacy and, thanks to the extended day of the battle, demolished the enemy before it took refuge in its cities. The deserted cities were then easily taken. Shortly, he turned north to Hazor and its confederates and won a signal victory, burning it to the ground. But Israel did not at once effectively occupy the area. The Canaanites reestablished themselves in many cities. Key fortresses like Beth Shan, Megiddo, and Jerusalem were not subdued. The land was allocated to the tribes in the last half of the Book of Joshua, but the period of the judges witnessed various battles, with the Israelites restricted mainly to the central mountain section.

XI. The Judges and Ruth. For some 350 years the Israelites lived disorganized and to an extent disunited. Frequently falling into apostasy, they were punished by God. Then a leader arose for military deliverance and often for spiritual reviving as well. Sketches of six of these twelve judgeships are given. The rest are barely named. The beautiful account of Ruth, the Moabite convert, belongs in this time.

XII. The Early Monarchy. The last judge was Samuel. In his days Philistine expansion became a great threat to Israel. The sanctuary at Shiloh was destroyed, as excavations also attest, at about 1050 B.C. The nation was laid low. Yet under the leadership of four great men, Israel in one hundred years attained its peak of greatness. Samuel, the first of these men, was a prophet of power. His preaching, prayers, and policies led to an evangelical revival that was the basis for much of Israel's later successes. He was followed by Saul, who was capable but not good. Condemned in the records for his disobedience, he nevertheless seems to have made a real military contribution to Israel's unity. His army numbered 330,000 men. He gained important victories in the south and east and had some limited successes against the Philistines. His strength was sapped by disobedience to God and insane jealousy of David. He made a pitiable spectacle at the house of the witch of Endor before his final failure, in which he dragged down his fine son Jonathan and all Israel with him to defeat.

XIII. The Golden Age. David's history as king begins in 2 Samuel, which parallels 1 Chronicles after the first nine chapters of genealogies in the latter book. God had schooled David the hard way. Highly emotional, and consecrated to God as a child, he had gone through deep waters.

Military lessons had been learned in repeated dangers when he was exiled by Saul. Faith was begotten and tested in adversity. Eventually God used this background to make David Israel's greatest conqueror and best-loved poet, the founder of the royal house and reestablisher of the Lord's worship. Family troubles resulting from David's grievous sin with Bathsheba marred his later days, but the greatness of the man was shown in the depth of his repentance. He was a man after God's own heart.

In David's day people would probably have honored him mostly for his military successes, his power, and his wealth; but actually, his greatest blessing to mankind has doubtless been his work in the establishing of psalmody. David composed at least half of the psalms and arranged for the temple choirs and for Israel's liturgy. First Chronicles 15–16 and 25 tell something of this work. Amos 6:5 mentions his lasting fame as an inventor of musical instruments. David's psalms of praise have lifted up the hearts of millions in godly worship. His psalms of trust in the midst of trouble have for centuries comforted those in sorrow and in despair. Psalm 23 is perhaps the best-loved of the OT. In the hour of death and in times of deliverance alike, it has expressed the faith of untold multitudes of God's people. Associated with David in song were the prophets Asaph, Heman, Jeduthun, and others.

Solomon inherited David's vast kingdom, which reached from the Euphrates in Syria to the border of Egypt and from the desert to the sea. To these large possessions Solomon added the natural resources of the copper mines south of the Dead Sea. He built a famous foundry at Ezion Geber, using the force of the prevailing winds to increase the temperature of his fires. For the first time people had harnessed the forces of nature in industrial processes. The products of his industry he exported in lucrative trade that drenched Jerusalem in opulence. His building program was extensive and is illustrated by many excavations, especially at Megiddo. It is best remembered in his construction of the temple, described in 1 Kings and 2 Chronicles. This remarkable building was so engineered that the stones were cut at a distance and the sound of a hammer was not heard on the spot. It was double the dimensions of the wilderness tabernacle and more lavishly adorned. Its two rooms repeated the tabernacle plan with the inner shrine, a suitable type of the holiness of God, who is unapproachable except through atoning blood. In the outer room the priests maintained the light of the seven-branched candelabra, symbolic of the Holy Spirit; the bread of the Presence, typical of the communion of persons with God; and the altar of incense, representing the prayers of saints. The building was about thirty feet (nine m.) high and wide, and ninety feet (twenty-eight m.) long. A porch in front was also thirty feet (nine m.) high (according to some texts), and the building was flanked on each side with three stories of rooms for priests' quarters and storage. In the front court was the great altar where Israel declared its faith that there is remission of sin through the blood of a substitute. Nearer the temple was the large and ornate laver or "sea" for the cleansing of the priests. Near the end of his reign Solomon and his kingdom decayed. Solomon probably did not marry his many women because of lust, but because of his extensive political alliances. They proved his undoing, however. He had married these foreign women ("outlandish women," Neh 13:26 KJV) and joined them to some extent in their heathen worship. For this compromise he was rejected.

XIV. Divided Monarchy to Ahab. Solomon's sins bore bitter fruit. Rehoboam attempted to maintain the old glory without returning to the old sources of power. God punished him and all Israel by allowing division. Jeroboam I took ten tribes and established the northern kingdom about 920 B.C. Ahijah promised him God's blessing if he would do God's will, but for political reasons he at once broke with the worship of the Lord at Jerusalem. He set up golden calves at Dan and Bethel in the north and south of his realm, instituted a new priesthood and counterfeit feasts. He thus sealed his doom. Following kings did not depart from Jeroboam's sins. In the next two hundred years of its existence the northern kingdom had nine dynasties and many revolutions, and they sank deeply into idolatry. The southern kingdom, Judah, had its troubles, but many of its kings, such as Asa, Jehoshaphat, Hezekiah, and Josiah were great and good men.

The north fell most deeply into the worship of Baal of Phoenicia in the reign of Ahab. He was faced with the threat of the Assyrian Empire expanding to the west. His policy was to form a western coalition. Thus he married Jezebel, daughter of the king of Tyre. He united with Jehoshaphat of Judah, marrying his daughter to Jehoshaphat's son. Politically he was successful, and his coalition at the battle of Qarqar in 854 B.C. stopped the Assyrians. The Assyrian records tells us that Ahab was their principal opponent.

Religiously, Ahab was a failure. The Bible, being more interested in character than in conquest, shows the unvarnished sins of Ahab and his queen, Jezebel. At this time the great prophets Elijah and Elisha ministered in the north. Their deeds are graphically told (1 Kings 17–2 Kings 13). Only a passing reference is made to them in Chronicles, which is a book more interested in Judah. Elijah, the fearless prophet who stood alone on Mount Carmel, was one of two men in all history taken to heaven without death. Encouraged by Elisha, Jehu revolted, exterminated the dynasty of Ahab, slaughtered the devotees of Baal, and even killed Ahaziah of Jerusalem who was in Samaria at the time.

XV. The Kingdoms to Hezekiah. For the chronology of the kingdoms, a reliable guide is E. R. Thiele, *Mysterious Numbers of the Hebrew Kings* (rev. ed., 1983). The dynasty of Jehu began about 840 B.C. and lasted a century, its chief king being Jeroboam II, 793 to 753. The kings of Judah included some good men, but from about 740 to 722 both kingdoms were evil and felt the scourge of the great Assyrian monarchs—Tiglath-Pileser, Shalmaneser, Sargon, and Sennacherib. This was the time of Isaiah and the first six minor prophets. Their messages in the north went unheeded, and Samaria was destroyed in 722. In Judah there was a revival under Hezekiah, and God wonderfully delivered him.

XVI. Isaiah and His Contemporaries. Hosea, Amos, and Micah prophesied especially to Israel; Obadiah and Joel preached to the southern kingdom; Jonah, the disobedient prophet, finally ministered in Nineveh. His experiences in the fish's belly—miraculous, of course—may well have affected his skin and compelled attention from the Ninevites. And quite likely the repentance of the Ninevites may well have delayed their invasion of Israel for a generation. However, their repentance did not have lasting results in the Assyrian Empire. Amos and Micah forthrightly denounced the sins of the court and of the rich men of Israel. At the same time, Amos and Hosea, especially, denounced the idolatry of Bethel and of Samaria. Against the background of rebuke, these prophets announced Israel's and Judah's hope—the coming of the child from David's city, Bethlehem, and the reestablishing of the fallen tabernacle of David. To Isaiah, the evangelical prophet, it was given to condemn Ahaz for his idolatry, to encourage Hezekiah in his reforms, and to see beyond his day the threat of Babylon, the liberation of the exiles by Cyrus, and the coming of the Messiah in future suffering and glory. We think instinctively of the prediction of the virgin birth of Christ in Isaiah 7:14, of the atonement in chapter 53, and of the portrayal of the new Jerusalem in chapter 60.

XVII. Judah's Fall. The reforms of Hezekiah were engulfed in the long and wicked reign of his son Manasseh. Further decline followed in Amon's two years. Then in 640 B.C. the good king Josiah came to the throne. In Josiah's thirteenth year, Jeremiah began his ministry; and in five more years Josiah, in a real revival, invited all Judah and the remnant of Israel to a great Passover. But, as a reading of Jeremiah shows, the mass of the people were not changed. Josiah's successors again did evil.

In 612 B.C. Babylon conquered Nineveh, and the Assyrian government fled west. Egypt assisted Assyria, attempting to keep the old balance of power. On Egypt's first march north against Babylon, Josiah attempted to prevent Pharaoh Neco's passage at Megiddo and was killed. His son Jehoahaz succeeded him, but when Neco returned southward in three months, he took Jehoahaz to Egypt as a hostage and set his brother Jehoiakim on the throne. In 605 Nebuchadnezzar in his first year conquered the Assyrian and Egyptian forces at Carchemish on the Euphrates and proceeded south to Judah. He received Jehoiakim's submission and carried Daniel and others into captivity. In 597 Jehoiakim died, perhaps by assassination, and his son Jehoiachin took the throne, revolting against Babylon. Nebuchadnezzar came and on March 15, 597 (see tablets published by D. J. Wiseman, *Chronicles of Chaldean Kings*, 1956, p. 33), destroyed Jerusalem and took Ezekiel and others captive. He put a third son of Josiah, Zedekiah, on the throne. Zedekiah continued the wicked policies of the others. In 586 he too rebelled, and Nebuchadnezzar returned in a final thrust, devastating Jerusalem and the cities of Judah. Palestine never fully recovered.

Nahum, Habakkuk, and Zephaniah were early contemporaries of Jeremiah. Nahum predicted the downfall of Nineveh. Habakkuk is famous for contrasting the wicked Babylonian invader with the just person who lives by faith.

In Jeremiah's ministry to his people, he rebuked them for sin and idolatry. The Assyrian and Babylonian gods had filtered into Judah until Judah's idols were as numerous as the streets in Jerusalem. When some Jews had gone to Babylon, Jeremiah counseled the later kings to submit. Resistance was futile and would make it hard for those Jews already in exile. God would care for Israel in captivity and in seventy years would bring them back (Jer 25:11–12).

XVIII. The Exile. For seventy years, from about 605 B.C. to about 538, the Jews were slaves in Babylon. Some Jews were left in Judah, and Jeremiah at first ministered to them. Many Jews had fled to Egypt, and finally Jeremiah was taken to Egypt by some of these men. In Babylon God blessed the Jews and kept them in the faith through the witness of Ezekiel, Daniel, and others.

Ezekiel prophesied to his people in exile, being still greatly concerned with Jerusalem before its final fall. Like Jeremiah, he used many object lessons in his preaching. Finally came the word that the city had fallen (Ezek 33). Thereafter Ezekiel emphasized more the coming of the Davidic king, the Messiah. His final chapters picture in schematic form the reestablishment of the temple, a prophecy held by many to apply to millennial times. Daniel was a towering figure of those days. Beloved of God and granted many remarkable visions of the future times, he maintained his faith while he held an important position at court. His prophecies accurately depict the future kingdoms of Medo-Persia, Greece, and Rome and tell of both Christ's first coming and his return. Christ's own designation for himself, "Son of Man," likely comes from this book. The book has been heavily attacked by criticism, but there is no good reason to deny the authorship by Daniel.

XIX. Postexilic Times. When Cyrus the Persian conquered Babylon, his policy was to allow captive peoples to go home. Thus he befriended the Jews. Ezra and Nehemiah tell about these returns. Haggai, Zechariah, and Malachi prophesied in this period. Zerubbabel led back the first contingent of about 50,000 men shortly after Cyrus gave them permission. His work is detailed in Ezra 1–6. He laid the foundation of the temple at once, but did not finish the temple until 516 B.C. under the prophesying of Haggai and Zechariah. A second contingent returned in 456 under Ezra, as is related in Ezra 7–10. Nehemiah

Panoramic view of the Mount of Olives in Jerusalem, facing east. Note the Basilica of the Agony at the foot of the mount. The onion-shaped domes of the Russian Church of Mary Magdalene are in the center. Courtesy Israel Government Press Office.

returned with various royal pledges in 444, and these two together did much work in restoring Jerusalem. Nehemiah organized the work and carried through the rebuilding of the wall. Ezra, a knowledgeable scribe in the law of Moses, instructed the people in the faith. Malachi, the final book of the OT, was written around 400. It reveals the problems of the day caused by insincerity among some of the priests themselves. But it also, like so many of the other prophets, pointed forward to messianic times. The OT closes with the annunciation of the rise of a new and greater prophet in the spirit and power of Elijah who would precede the Messiah of Israel. RLH

OLIVE (See PLANTS)

OLIVES, MOUNT OF (called Olivet twice in the KJV—2 Sam 15:30; Acts 1:12).

I. Geographical. The Mount of Olives is a flattened, rounded ridge with four identifiable summits. Its name is derived from the olive groves that covered it in ancient times. It is of cretaceous limestone formation, something over a mile (almost two km.) in length, and forms the highest level of the range of hills to the east of Jerusalem (Ezek 11:23; Zech 14:4), rising 250 feet (78 m.) higher than the temple mount, and to 2,600 feet (813 m.) above sea level. Hence the supreme tactical significance of the Mount of Olives, demonstrated in the Roman siege of Jerusalem under Titus in A.D. 70. The Romans seem to have named the northern extension of the ridge "the Lookout," or Mount Scopus, for this very reason. It gave "a plain view of the great temple," according to Josephus (*Wars* 5.2.2). The legions had a large camp on the mount itself, which, as Josephus describes it in the same context, "lies over against the city on the east side, and is parted from it by a deep valley interposed between them." The valley is the so-called Valley of Jehoshaphat, through which flows the Kidron stream, encompassing the city in a slight curve to the east, before turning SE to flow down the long valley to the Dead Sea.

Near the foot of the Mount of Olives, on the western slope above the Kidron, is the likely site of the Garden of Gethsemane. In NT times the whole area seems to have been a place of resort for those who sought relief from the heat of the crowded city streets. Dean Stanley called it the "park" of Jerusalem. In much earlier times it must have been heavily wooded, for when the Feast of the Tabernacles was restored in 445 B.C., Nehemiah commanded the people to "go out into the hill country and bring back branches from olive and wild olive trees, and from myrtles, palms and shade trees, to make booths" (Neh 8:15). The palm fronds of Palm Sunday were also gathered there. Four summits are traditionally distinguished. Scopus has already been mentioned.

R. A. S. Macalister (HDB, p. 668) considers it erroneously named, and not the vantagepoint to which Josephus refers. Second, there is the "Viri Galilaei," the Latin invocation of Acts 1:11 ("Men of Galilee"), and the reputed site of the Ascension. To the south, above the village of Silwan (old Siloam) is the so-called Mount of Offense. This vantage-point is separated from the rest of the mount by a deep cleft. It faces west along the line of Jerusalem's second valley, the Valley of the Sons of Hinnom or Gehenna. The eminence derives its name from the tradition that Solomon here built his altars to Chemosh, "the detestable god of Moab," and to Molech, "the detestable god of the Ammonites" (1 Kings 11:7). The "offense" of this blatant paganism was purged by Josiah four and a half centuries later (2 Kings 23:13). The Josian context adds Ashtoreth to the "abominations" on the site.

II. Historical. Historical associations have found incidental reference above, where their significance is inseparable from topography. The following points should be added. The ridge, besides being a tactical vantage point in war, was a peacetime highway into Jerusalem. It was the route of David's flight from Absalom in the time of the palace rebellion (2 Sam 15:30; 16:1, 13) and, significantly, was the route of Christ's approach for the triumphal entry on Palm Sunday, for it was there that the acclaiming multitude met him. Hence, too, the prominence of the mount in Josephus's account of the "Egyptian false prophet" and his thirty thousand dupes (*Wars* 2.13.5). "These he led round from the wilderness," the account runs, "to the mount which is called the Mount of Olives, and was ready to break into Jerusalem by force from that place." Here, it would appear, Felix met the rebels with his legionary force and broke the revolt. The remaining OT reference to the Mount of Olives is the scene of the theophany of Zechariah 14:4, an obscure apocalyptic portion that awaits a clear explanation.

Historically the Mount of Olives finds its chief interest in NT times, where it is a locality intimately connected with the Jerusalem ministry of Christ. It is important here to distinguish authentic history from the thick accretions of legend and tradition. Christ's first sight of the city was from the summit of the Mount of Olives (Luke 19:41), and his visits to the home of Mary, Martha, and Lazarus in Bethany must have frequently taken him that way (21:37). The barren fig tree of his striking object lesson on fruitless profession was probably on the slopes (Matt 21:19). The mount was also the scene of his apocalyptic utterance, inspired no doubt by the prospect of doomed Jerusalem from the mountainside (chs. 24–25). Gethsemane has already been mentioned as a place somewhere on the Mount of Olives. The rest is wavering ecclesiastical tradition. Macalister remarks (HDB, p. 668) that "the places pointed out have by no means remained unaltered through the Christian centuries, as becomes evident from a study of the writings of the pilgrims." He lists among the spurious sites the Tomb of the Virgin; the Grotto of the Agony; one or both of the sites of the Garden, admitted though it is that it was somewhere on the mount; the "footprint of Christ" in the Chapel of the Ascension; the Tomb of Huldah, the impossible site for Christ's lament over Jerusalem; the place where he taught the Lord's Prayer, and where the Apostles' Creed was composed. This does not exhaust the list of legends. It has been the fate of Jerusalem to suffer thus from the pious but not too scrupulous imagination of men. More authentic are a few archaeological remains, some Jewish and Christian tombs, and an interesting catacomb known as "the Tombs of the Prophets." EMB

OLYMPAS (ō-lĭm'păs, Gr. *Olympas*). A Christian in Rome to whom Paul sent greetings (Rom 16:15).

OMAR (ō'mar, Heb. *'ômār*). A grandson of Esau through his oldest son Eliphaz (Gen 36:11, 15).

OMEGA (ō-mē'gȧ). Literally, large "O," the last letter of the Greek alphabet, long "o." In three contexts (Rev 1:8; 21:6; 22:13) it is used as a symbol of inclusiveness: ". . . the Alpha and the Omega, the First and the Last, the Beginning and the End."

OMER (See WEIGHTS AND MEASURES)

OMNIPOTENCE (ŏm-nĭp'ō-tĕns). The attribute of God that describes his ability to do whatever he wills. God's will is limited by his nature, and he therefore cannot do anything contrary to his nature as God, such as to ignore sin, to sin, or to do something absurd or self-contradictory. God is not controlled by his power, but has complete control over it: otherwise he would not be a free being. To a certain extent, he has voluntarily limited himself by the free will of his rational creatures. Although the word "omnipotence" is not found in the Bible, the Scriptures clearly teach the omnipotence of God (Job 42:2; Jer 32:17; Matt 19:26; Luke 1:37; Rev 19:6).

OMNIPRESENCE (ŏm'nĭ-prĕz'ĕns). The attribute of God by virtue of which he fills the universe in all its parts and is present everywhere at once. Not a part, but the whole of God is present in every place. The Bible teaches the omnipresence of God (Ps 139:7–12; Jer 23:23–24; Acts 17:27–28). This is true of all three members of the Trinity. They are so closely related that where one is the others can be said to be also (John 14:9–11).

OMNISCIENCE (ŏm-nĭsh'ĕns). The attribute by which God perfectly and eternally knows all things that can be known—past, present, and future. God knows how best to attain to his desired ends. God's omniscience is clearly taught in Scripture (Ps 147:5; Prov 15:11; Isa 46:10).

OMRI (ŏm'rē, Heb. *'omrî*). 1. The sixth king of Israel, whose reign may be tentatively dated from 886 to 874 B.C. Omri, an able if unscrupulous soldier and founder of a dynasty, is the first Hebrew monarch to be mentioned in nonbiblical records, and the fact may be some measure of his contemporary importance. It was not until 847 that Mesha included Omri's name in the inscription of the Moabite Stone, but it is a fact that Omri subdued Moab. It is of more significance that the Assyrian records after Omri's day frequently refer to northern Palestine as "the land of Humri" (the Assyrians spelled the name with an initial aspirate).

The brief but vivid account of Omri's military coup d'état and his extremely wicked reign is told in 1 Kings 16:15–28. Omri was the commander-in-chief under Elah, son of Baasha. When Elah was murdered by Zimri, Omri was proclaimed king by the army in the field, a pattern of events that was to become grimly familiar in the imperial history of Rome. The army was engaged at the time in siege of the stronghold of Gibbethon, a Levite town (Josh 21:23) in the tribal territory of Dan (19:44), which the Philistines appear to have held for a considerable period (1 Kings 15:27; 16:15). Omri immediately raised the siege, marched on the royal capital of Tirzah, which does not appear to have been vigorously defended against him. Zimri committed suicide by burning the palace over his head. There was some opposition to the dominance of the military, for four years of civil war ensued, with half the populace supporting Tibni, son of Ginath, as king. Omri prevailed, and after a six-year reign at Tirzah, transferred the capital to Samaria, an eminently sensible move from the point of view of military security. Here Omri reigned for at least another six years. Samaria was named after Shemer, from whom Omri bought the hill site (1 Kings 16:24).

Omri is dismissed by the Hebrew historian as an evil influence (1 Kings 16:25–26). Indeed, the marriage of his son Ahab to Jezebel, princess of Tyre, probably to cement a trade alliance, was fraught with most disastrous consequences, even though it was a continuation of Solomon and David's Tyrian policy. The calf worship of Jeroboam (1 Kings 12:32) was continued at Bethel throughout Omri's reign; and 140 years after Omri's death, Micah is found denouncing "the statutes of Omri" (Mic 6:16). The palace of Omri has been excavated at Samaria, a series of open courts with rooms ranged round them. Omri died opportunely, one year before the first tentative thrust of the Assyrians toward the Mediterranean and Palestine. It was in 874 B.C. that Ashurnasirpal marched to "the Great Sea of the land of Amurru," and received tribute from the peoples of the coast. The Assyrian action was the preface to much misery.

2. A Benjamite, family of Beker (1 Chron 7:8).

3. A man of Judah, family of Perez (1 Chron 9:4).

4. A prince of the tribe of Issachar in David's reign (1 Chron 27:18).

ON (ŏn, Heb. *'ôn*). 1. A delta city of Egypt, called by the Greeks Heliopolis (City of the Sun) and so translated in the Septuagint (Gen 41:45, 50; 46:20; cf. Jer 43:13; Ezek 30:17, both NIV). On is an Egyptian word signifying "light" or "sun," so the Greek and Hebrew names are fair translations. "Cleopatra's Needle" of Thames Embankment fame was originally one of the obelisks before the temple of the Sun at On, erected by Thothmes II (1503–1449 B.C.). On was founded at a very early date and was an important city long before the unification of Egypt. Herodotus's description of Egypt in his second book gives On (or Heliopolis) great attention. It was a center of communication and a terminus of numerous caravan routes. In consequence it was the major center of commerce in northern Egypt. The priest of On, whose daughter Asenath became Joseph's wife, was thus a person of considerable importance. The worship of the sun god, which was centered there, had peculiar features that suggest Syrian influence. Ra was identified with Baal by Semites and with Apollo by the Greeks. There must therefore have been a cosmopolitan element in the temple cult to match the atmosphere of a center of international trade. It is perhaps significant that On is named as the place of sojourn of the holy family after the flight into Egypt. Strabo the geographer describes the site as almost deserted in early Roman times. His account was written just before the Christian era. On is still a ruin, the site of the famous temple being marked by one conspicuous obelisk, a monument set up by Sesostris I about 2000 B.C.

2. A Reubenite chief who took part in the rebellion of Korah (Num 16:1). EMB

ONAM (ō'năm, Heb. *'ônām, strong*). 1. Fifth son of Shobal, son of Seir the Horite (Gen 36:23).

2. Great-great-grandson of Judah (1 Chron 2:26, 28).

ONAN (ō'năn, Heb. *'ônān, strong*). Second son of Judah by a Canaanite wife who was a daughter of Shua. He refused to consummate a levirate marriage with Tamar, widow of his elder brother Er, who had been wicked, and so the Lord put him to death also, leaving Tamar twice a widow (Gen 38:4–10).

ONESIMUS (ō-nĕs'ĭ-mŭs, Gr. *Onesimos, profitable*). Probably a common nickname for a slave. Paul plays on the word *onesimos* in Philemon 11 and again in verse 20. A plain reading of the letters to Philemon and the Colossian church leads to the conclusion that Onesimus was a slave of Philemon of Colosse. He robbed his master and made his way to Rome, the frequent goal of such fugitives, the "common cesspool of the world," as the aristocratic historian Sallust called the city. Some Ephesian or Colossian person in Rome, perhaps Aristarchus (Acts 27:2; Col 4:10–14; Philem 24), or Epaphras (Col 1:7; 4:12–13; Philem 23) seems to have recognized the man and brought him to Paul in his captivity.

Onesimus became a Christian and was persuaded to return to his master. From that incident came the exquisite letter of Paul to Philemon, which demonstrates so vividly the social solvent that Christianity had brought into the world. It appears that Onesimus left Rome in company with Tychicus, carrying the letter to Philemon and also Paul's letters to the Ephesian and Colossian churches. Nothing more is known about Onesimus. The tradition that Onesimus became the martyr bishop of Berea is of doubtful authenticity. EMB

ONESIPHORUS (ŏn'ĕ-sĭf'ō-rŭs, Gr. *Onēsiphoros, profit-bringer*). An Ephesian who ministered fearlessly to Paul at the time of the apostle's second captivity in Rome (2 Tim 1:16–18; 4:19). Paul's warm gratitude and, in the midst of his own distress, his thoughtfulness in greeting the Ephesian family, shed light on his generous character and give further evidence of his capacity for commanding devotion. There are no valid grounds for concluding, as some scholars do, that Onesiphorus was dead at the time Paul wrote, much less to base on the passage a doctrine of prayers for the dead. (See Guthrie, *The Pastoral Epistles* [TNTC], pp. 135–36). In the apocryphal *Acts of Paul and Thecla* an Onesiphorus appears as a man of Iconium. A man of the same name was martyred in Mysia sometime between A.D. 102 and 114.

ONION (See PLANTS)

ONLY-BEGOTTEN. A title that appears six times in the KJV of the NT. Five times it is applied to Jesus (John 1:14, 18; 3:16, 18; 1 John 4:9; cf. NIV footnotes), connected with the doctrine of the "eternal generation of the Son of God" (cf. Ps 2:7 with Acts 13:33; Heb 1:5; 5:5), and once to Isaac (Heb 11:17).

ONO (ō'nō, Heb. *'ônô, strong*). A town ascribed to Benjamin in 1 Chronicles 8:12 because it was built by Shemed, a Benjamite, though it was in the territory originally assigned to the tribe of Dan. It lay in the plain, near the Valley of the Craftsmen (Neh 11:35) and was about six miles (ten km.) SE of Joppa. Many of its men returned from captivity with Zerubbabel (Ezra 2:33), and the town was later inhabited by men of Benjamin (Neh 11:35). Nehemiah refused an invitation to go there (6:2).

ONYCHA (See PLANTS)

ONYX (See MINERALS)

OPHEL (ō'fĕl, Heb. *ha-'ōphel, hill*). Properly a hill, but when used with the definite article in Hebrew, it is translated "Ophel" and refers to a part of Jerusalem. In 2 Kings 5:24 the word is translated "tower" in the KJV and "hill" in the NIV, but no one knows the exact location. In Micah 4:8 it is translated "stronghold" in the KJV and NIV, but the ASV has "the hill of the daughter of Zion," and probably refers to *the* Ophel of Jerusalem. In Isaiah 32:14, the KJV has "forts," and the NIV "citadel," but the ASV, more accurately, reads "hill," probably referring to Ophel. Ophel lies outside the wall of modern Jerusalem just south of the Mosque "el Aksa" and above the junction of the valleys of the Kidron and of the "son of Hinnom." Jotham, king of Judah, built much on the wall of Ophel (2 Chron 27:3), and his great-grandson Manasseh further improved it (33:14), so that from then on it was inside the ancient city. In the restoration period it was principally a place of residence for the temple servants (KJV Nethinim; Neh 11:21).

The Hill of Ophel, at the southeast corner of the Jerusalem city wall, beyond which is the temple area (6); (1) the lower, outer city wall of the Bronze and Iron Ages; (2) the lower city of the Israelite period; (3) southeast corner of the Ophel stepped stone structure; (4) the "Millo" area; (5) the Gihon spring; (7) to the Siloam Pool. Courtesy Zev Radovan.

OPHIR (ō'fêr, Heb. *'ôphîr*). 1. A son of Joktan, son of Eber (Gen 10:29). Of Eber's two sons, Peleg became ancestor of the "Hebrews" thus named from Eber, but Joktan and his progeny moved into Arabia. The names in "the table of nations" (Gen 10) often indicate locations, and Ophir is placed between Sheba and Havilah, both in southern Arabia.

2. The land occupied by the descendants of Ophir. In 1 Kings 9:28 it is mentioned as the source of much gold (cf. Gen 2:11–12, where Ophir's neighbor Havilah is cited for its good

gold). Ophir in Arabia was not only the source of gold, but it may have been a way-station for the "ships of Tarshish" coming westward from India—that is, if the apes, ivory, and baboons (1 Kings 10:22), as well as the almugwood (10:11–12), had to come from India. These large ships, which made the round trip once in three years (10:22), could have voyaged from the neighborhood of Goa on the west coast of India to Ophir, and thence up the Red Sea and the Gulf of Aqabah to Ezion Geber (1 Kings 9:26), keeping in sight or nearly in sight of land all of the way. Although many of the ancients, including Josephus (*Antiq.* 8.6.4), thought of Ophir as being in India, the consensus of opinion today places it, as indicated above, in Arabia. Although gold is not mined there today, Ophir was famous for its gold from very early days (Job 22:24; 28:16).

OPHNI (ŏf'nī, Heb. *hā-'ophnî*). A city in the northern part of Benjamin, mentioned only in Joshua 18:24. It lay about two and a half miles (four km.) NW of Bethel on one of the two main roads northward from Jerusalem to Samaria. Now called Jifneh.

OPHRAH (ŏf'rȧ, Heb. *'ophrâh, hind*). 1. A town in Benjamin (Josh 18:23). Now called *Et-Taiyibah.* It lies on a conical hill about three miles (five km.) NE of Bethel and probably is the "Ephraim" (John 11:54) to which our Lord retired when under persecution.

2. A town in the tribe of Manasseh (Judg 6:24) pertaining to the Abiezrites, a family of that tribe. Here the angel of God appeared, sitting under an oak tree, and talked with Gideon, commissioning him to deliver Israel from the Midianites. Gideon placed in Ophrah the ephod that the children of Israel worshiped (8:27).

3. A son of Meonothai, an early member of the tribe of Judah (1 Chron 4:14).

ORACLE (ŏr'ȧ-k'l, Heb. *dāvar,* Gr. *logion*). 1. An utterance supposedly coming from a deity and generally through an inspired medium. This is the classical usage (cf. "Sibylline Oracles").

2. In the Bible, an utterance from God. In the KJV of 2 Samuel 16:23 we read that Ahithophel was so highly regarded before he turned traitor to David that his words were considered oracles from God.

3. The OT was referred to as "living [KJV "lively"] oracles" or "words" (Acts 7:38). NIV has "elementary truths" in Hebrews 5:12 and "the very words of God" in 1 Peter 4:11.

ORATOR. 1. In Isaiah 3:3, KJV has "eloquent orator," but other versions more accurately have "soothsayer" (JB), "clever enchanter" (NIV), or "expert in charms" (RSV).

2. A public speaker, especially an advocate. Acts 24:1 mentions "a lawyer named Tertullus" whom the Jews engaged to speak against Paul before Felix, not that they lacked eloquence, but because Tertullus, a Roman, could make the accusation in Latin, the language of the Roman courts.

ORCHARD (See GARDEN)

ORDAIN, ORDINATION. In the KJV *ordain* is the translation of about thirty-five different Hebrew and Greek words. The word has many shades of meaning, chiefly four: (1) set in order, arrange (Ps 132:17; Isa 30:33); (2) bring into being (1 Kings 12:32; Num 28:6; Ps 8:2–3); (3) decree (Esth 9:27; Acts 16:4; Rom 7:10); (4) set apart for an office or duty (Jer 1:5; Mark 3:14; John 15:16; Acts 14:23; 1 Tim 2:7; Titus 1:5; Heb 5:1; 8:3).

Ordination in the sense of setting aside officers of the church for a certain work by the laying on of hands was practiced in apostolic times (1 Tim 4:14; 2 Tim 1:6), but it is nowhere described or enjoined. No great emphasis was placed on this rite.

OREB AND ZEEB (ō'rĕb, zē'ĕb, Heb. *'ōrēv, se'ēv, raven* and *wolf*). Two princes of the Midianites in the days of Gideon. After Gideon's notable defeat of the Midianites, the Midianites who survived fled; and Gideon called on the men of Manasseh to cut off the retreat at the crossings of the Jordan. Here they captured the two princes and beheaded them. The places of their deaths were named in their memory: Oreb died at the rock of Oreb and Zeeb at the winepress of Zeeb (Judg 7:24–25). Asaph, hundreds of years later, recalls these events in Psalm 83:11. The exact location of the killing is unknown.

OREB, ROCK OF (See OREB AND ZEEB)

OREN (ō'rĕn, Heb. *'ōren, cedar*). Son of Jerahmeel, son of Hezron, son of Perez, son of Judah (1 Chron 2:25).

ORGAN (See MUSIC AND MUSICAL INSTRUMENTS: *Pipe*)

ORION (See ASTRONOMY)

ORNAMENT (See DRESS)

ORNAN (See ARAUNAH)

ORONTES (ō-rŏn'tēz). The chief river in Aram (Syria), almost 400 miles (640 km.) long, begins in the Anti-Lebanon range, at the height of almost 4,000 feet (1,250 m.), and flows north for the major portion of its course. It turns west around the northern end of its range at Antioch, and then bends SW to the sea. Its fertile valley forms the only extensive area in Syria-Palestine not broken by mountains where a powerful political unit might take shape. The Orontes valley was the scene of the campaign of Rameses II against the Hittites in 1288 B.C. The campaign and the culminating battle of Kadesh on the river constitute the most publicized feat of ancient Egyptian armed conflict. The Roman satirist Juvenal, writing of the undesirable Syrian immi-

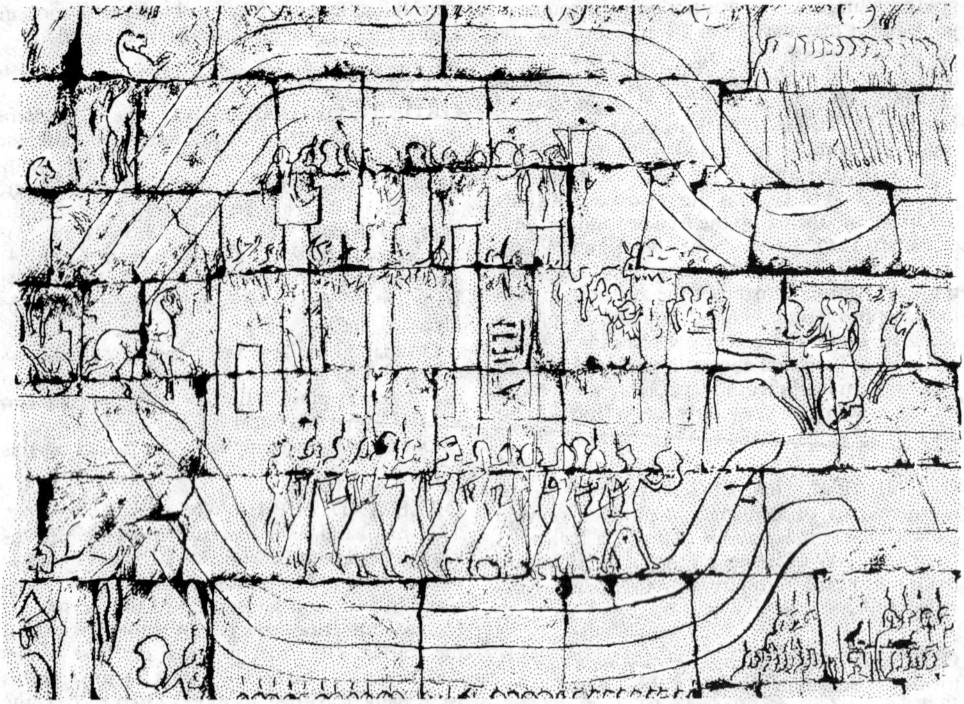

The fortified town of Kadesh on the Orontes, surrounded by a moat, scene of the culminating battle of Rameses II against the Hittites in 1288 B.C. Drawing from relief on east tower at Luxor. Courtesy Carta, Jerusalem.

grants in Rome, uses the river as a metaphor for the whole province: "Long since has Syrian Orontes been a tributary of the Tiber."

ORPAH (ôr'pȧ, Heb. *'orpâh, neck,* i.e. *stubbornness*). A Moabite woman whom Kilion, son of Elimelech and Naomi, married. She loved her mother-in-law, but kissed her good-by and remained in Moab, while Ruth, Naomi's other daughter-in-law, stayed with her (Ruth 1:4, 14; 4:9–10).

OSNAPPER (See ASHURBANIPAL)

OSPREY (See BIRDS)

OSSIFRAGE (See BIRDS)

OSTRACA (ŏs'trȧ-kȧ). Inscribed fragments of pottery (sing., *ostracon*). In the ancient world handy writing material was rare, but potsherds, or broken pieces of earthenware, were abundant, hence the habit of writing brief memoranda or communications on such ready material. The surface holds the inscription well and some important ancient documents have come down to us in this form (e.g., the Lachish Letters). In ancient Athens the use of potsherds, or straka, for voting tablets in the peculiar Athenian process of relegation, led to the term "ostracize." The verb originally meant the writing on an ostracon of the name of the person the voter wished thus to exile. Most of the ostraca from early Ptolemaic Egypt are tax receipts. Later, orders, lists, brief letters, school exercises, magic formulas, and religious texts, both pagan and Christian, appear. A good deal about Egyptian Christianity has been deduced from this source. The material is scattered, most ostraca being recovered casually from rubbish mounds or house ruins.

OSTRICH (See BIRDS)

Lachish Letter No. IV (obverse side). This is one of twenty-one ostraka found at Lachish dating from the last days of the Judean Monarchy (c. 586 B.C.). The Lachish Letters represent correspondence between the military commander of Lachish and outpost commanders in the days when Nebuchadnezzar was closing in on Jerusalem. Courtesy Israel Department of Antiquities and Museums.

OTHNI (ŏth'nī, Heb. *'othnî,* abbrev. of Othniel). Son of Shemaiah, a doorkeeper of the tabernacle under David (1 Chron 26:7).

OTHNIEL (ŏth'nĭ-ĕl, Heb. *'othnî'ēl*). A son of Kenaz, brother of Caleb, the spy who with Joshua had brought back a good report of the land of Canaan. Caleb, in his old age at the division of the land, offered his daughter to any one who would take Debir, about ten miles (seventeen km.) to the SW of Hebron. His nephew Othniel took Debir and so acquired Acsah as wife (Josh 15:13–19; Judg 1:11–15). Within fifteen years after the death of Joshua, Israel fell into apostasy, and God delivered them into the hand of Cushan-Rishathaim (Judg 3:8–11), king of Mesopotamia. In their distress they prayed to the Lord who raised up Othniel to deliver them. He was thus the first of the seven "judges" to deliver Israel from foreign oppression. He so restored Israel that a period of forty years of peace set in. His son was Hathath (1 Chron 4:13).

OUCHES (ouch'ĕz, Heb. *mishbetsôth*). Settings for precious stones on the high priest's ephod (Exod 28:11 KJV). NIV reads "filigree settings."

OUTPOST (See GARRISON)

OVEN. A chamber that is heated so as to roast or to bake the food materials placed inside. There were three principal types. In Egypt there was in nearly every house a structure of clay built on the house floor. In this, or on it, baking was done. In Palestine and Syria, a barrel-shaped hole in the ground was coated with clay and a quick hot fire of brambles or dry dung mixed with straw heated it. The dough, beaten very thin, was spread on the inside and almost immediately taken out, fully baked. In some places, a curved plate of iron is put over the sunken oven; but in cities the oven is a chamber of stone, from which the fire is raked when the oven is very hot and into which the unbaked loaves are then placed (Hos 7:4–7). See also BREAD; OCCUPATIONS AND PROFESSIONS: *Baker.*

OVERSEER. The translation of several Hebrew and Greek words, each with its distinctive meaning: Heb. *pāqadh,* "inspector, overseer" (Gen 39:4–5; 2 Chron 34:12, 17); *menatstsehîm,* "foreman" (2 Chron 2:18; 34:13); *shōtēr,* almost always "officer"; Greek *episkopos,* "bishop, overseer" (Acts 20:28).

OWL (See BIRDS)

OX (See ANIMALS)

OXGOAD (See GOAD)

OZEM (ō'zĕm, Heb. *'ōtsem*). 1. The sixth son of Jesse (1 Chron 2:15).

2. A son of Jerahmeel (1 Chron 2:25).

OZIAS (See UZZIAH)

OZNI (ŏz'nī, Heb. *'oznî*). Son of Gad and father of the Oznites (Num 26:16).

P

PAARAI (pā′à-rī, Heb. *pa'ăray, devotee of Peor*). One of David's mighty men called "the Arbite" (2 Sam 23:35). He is called Naarai in 1 Chronicles 11:37.

PADDAN ARAM (pā′dăn-ā′răm, *plain of Aram*). The word originally, as shown by the cuneiform contract tablets, signified a unit of measuring. It is the home of Jacob's exile (Gen 31:18), the home of Laban. It is almost certainly to be identified with Haran of the upper Euphrates Valley. It is also sometimes translated simply as "Mesopotamia." In Genesis 48:7 it is given as Paddan only.

PADON (pā′dŏn, Heb. *pādhôn, redemption*). The name of one of the temple servants (KJV Nethinim) who returned with Zerubbabel from Babylon (Ezra 2:44; Neh 7:47).

PAGIEL (pā′gĭ-ĕl, Heb. *pagh'î'ēl, a meeting with God*). The son of Ocran who was over the tribe of Asher (Num 7:72).

PAHATH-MOAB (pā′hăth-mō′ăb, Heb. *pahath-mô'ăv, governor of Moab*). A head of one of the chief houses of Judah. Part of the descendants of this man returned from Babylon with Zerubbabel (Ezra 2:6; Neh 7:11) and another part returned with Ezra (Ezra 8:4). A son of Pahath-Moab, Hasshub, aided in repairing both the wall and the Tower of the Ovens (Neh 3:11). He is one of the lay princes who signed the covenant with Nehemiah (9:38; 10:14). His place (second) in this list speaks of his importance. Eight of the sons of this man put away their foreign wives (Ezra 10:30).

PAI (See PAU)

PALACE (Heb. *'armôn, bîrâh, hēkhāl*, Gr. *aulē*). The dwelling place of an important official. Palaces are found all over the biblical world. The science of archaeology has given much light on these ancient structures. Israel built many palaces, and one finds frequent mention of them in Scripture. At Gezer the remains of a palace belonging to the period of Joshua's conquest have been found. It is thought to be the palace of Horam, king of Gezer, whom Joshua conquered (Josh 10:33). This palace belongs to the group of palaces known as fortress palaces. Many of these old palaces were made of stone. They were sometimes the entrances to great tunnels. Some were constructed over important wells or springs of water, which they controlled.

The ruins of another palace at this site stem from a much later period. It is the Maccabean palace and is thought to be the private headquarters of John Hyrcanus, the military governor.

W. F. Albright has excavated Saul's palace-fortress at Gibeah. Not much remains in order here, but there is enough to reveal the massive walls that once made up this structure.

David had two palaces at different times in his reign. The first was a simple one located at Hebron, but the second one was much more elaborate, built of cedar trees furnished by Hiram of Tyre and erected by workmen that Hiram supplied (2 Sam 5:11). Solomon's palace, which was built later, was a much more lavish structure, judging from its description given in 1 Kings 7. It was about 150 feet (47 m.) by 75 feet (23 m.) in size, constructed mostly of cedar in the interior and of hand-hewn stones for the exterior. Some of the foundation stones were 15 feet (4.6 m.) long. Solomon's wealth and the skill of the Phoenician craftsmen must have produced a magnificent building. Nothing remains of this building today.

Remains of a palace have been found at Megiddo. Another palace has been discovered at Samaria and identified as belonging to Omri. The foundation of this palace is in the bedrock common in that area. Most of these palaces are similar in style—a series of open courts with rooms grouped around them.

An ivory palace belonging to Ahab is mentioned in 1 Kings 22:39. For a long time scholars denied the truthfulness of this record, but archaeologists have confirmed the report. It was a large edifice 300 feet (94 m.) long from north to south. Many of its walls were faced with white

Two ivory panels from Samaria, probably decorative pieces from the ivory palace of King Ahab (1 Kings 22:39). Courtesy Israel Department of Antiquities and Museums.

Herod's Palace, as shown in the model of Jerusalem in A.D. 66, located at the Holyland Hotel, Jerusalem. Courtesy Israel Government Press Office.

marble. Wall paneling, plaques, and furniture made of or adorned with ivory have been uncovered.

Later on in the history of Israel material prosperity produced a very great wickedness that led to murder even in these royal palaces of splendor. This was especially true in the time of Jeroboam II.

Probably the most famous palace in the NT period was the one belonging to Herod the Great. Josephus informs us that this structure was built in Jerusalem. Its rooms were of a very great height and were adorned with all kinds of costly furniture.

Besides these palaces of Palestine, there were many splendid structures in Mesopotamia in the Assyrian and Babylonian period. The remains of the great temple of Sargon II have been found at Khorsabad, twelve miles (twenty km.) north of the site of old Nineveh. It was a mammoth structure covering twenty-five acres. Some of its walls were from nine to sixteen feet (three to five m.) thick. In the Oriental Institute Museum in Chicago one may see one of the stone bulls that once stood at the entrance of this palace. It is sixteen feet (five m.) long and sixteen feet (five m.) high, weighing forty tons (thirty-six metric tons).

There are many other important palaces in Mesopotamia. One was built by Nebuchadnezzar at Babylon, elaborately decorated. Another has been found on the Euphrates at Mari. This one has been quite well preserved and reveals paint-

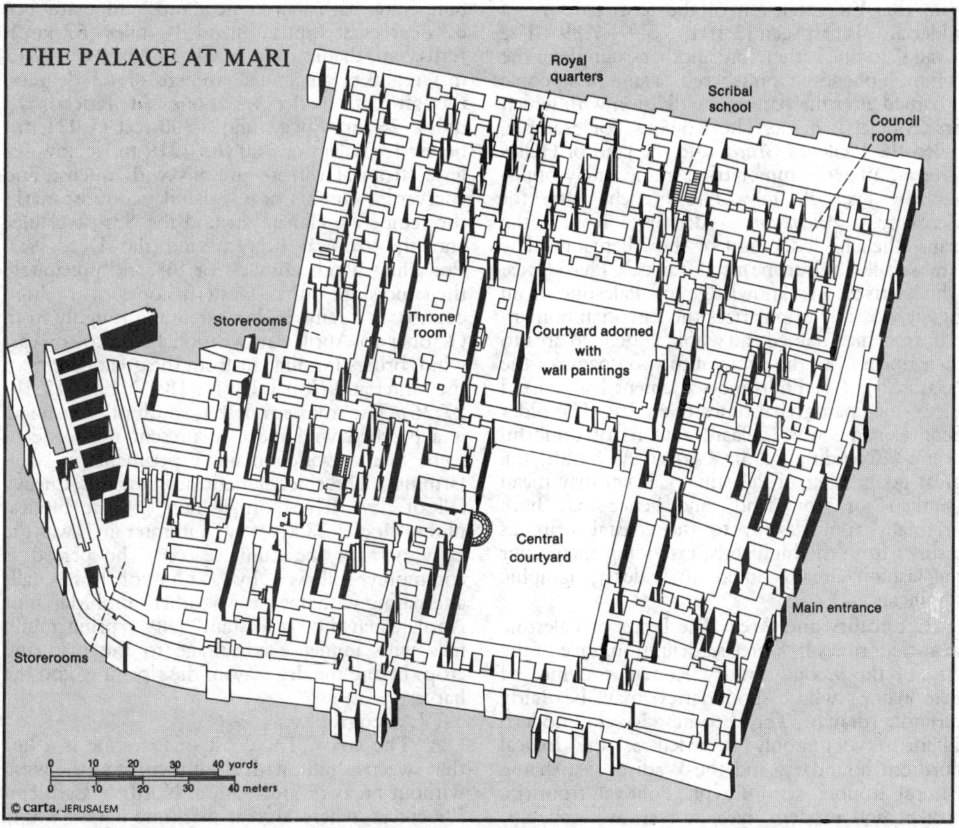

ings, offices, apartments, and even a scribal school. Albright refers to it as one of the "show places of the world." This discovery was important for many reasons, but especially because it "revolutionized our idea of the development of Near-Eastern art in the early second millennium B.C." (Albright).

Many famous palaces belonging to the pharaohs have also been found in Egypt. Perhaps the best known of these is the palace of Merneptah, from about 1230 B.C. Many of these were very elaborate structures. HZC

PALAL (pā'lăl, Heb. *pālāl, he judges*). Son of Uzai. He helped in repairing the Jerusalem walls (Neh 3:25).

PALESTINE (păl'ĕs-tīn, Heb. *pelesheth*).

I. Name. The term *Palestine* is not used in the NIV; it occurs four times in the KJV (Exod 15:14; Isa 14:29, 31; Joel 3:4). In all four contexts it refers to Philistia (so NIV), the SE coastal strip of the Mediterranean; this was an area that was occupied by the Philistines, an Indo-European people from Crete. *Philistia* derives from the Hebrew term for the region, *eres Pelistim* ("the land of the Philistines"), and *Philistine* was a native term of unknown origin and significance. Josephus used *Palaistinē* in the same restricted geographical sense (e.g., *Antiq*. 1.6.2; 13.5.10). It is in Herodotus, the fifth-century Greek historian, that the extension of the term to cover a wider area is first seen (2.104; 3.5; 91.7.89). The name Palestine is therefore another example of the common phenomenon whereby a land or a people is named after the part or the division with which first contact is made. The Romans, for example, called the Hellenes *Graeci,* and the land of Hellas *Graecia,* after the minor tribe immediately opposite the heel of Italy. The French name for Germany, *Allemagne,* derives from the trans-Rhenane federation of the Allemanni. The Arabs call all Europeans "Franks." Herodotus, who derived his knowledge of Palestine from Egypt, possibly popularizes the Egyptian nomenclature, which named the whole ill-defined area to their north from the name of the occupants of the "Gaza Strip." A Philistine settlement had existed there since patriarchal times (Gen 26). The older Semitic name was Canaan, a word of doubtful origin. According to Sir George A. Smith, the great geographer of Palestine, Canaan may mean "sunken" or "low land" and hence may have originally applied only to the coastal strip, as distinct from the highlands, extending then, after the fashion already noted, to wider geographic significance.

II. Locality and Area. The limits of Palestine in ancient times lack precise definition, save in the case of the second-century Roman province of that name, whose boundaries may be fairly certainly drawn. The Leontes River (modern Litani) is commonly regarded as the logical northern boundary, and the Wadi el 'Arish the natural frontier with Egypt. Political frontiers, ancient and modern, have not always respected these ideal boundaries. Even the limits of Israel poetically marked in the phrase "from Dan to Beersheba" do not correspond (Judg 20:1). Dan was Laish, 30 miles (50 km.) due east of Tyre on the sources of the Jordan. Beersheba lay 150 miles (250 km.) to the south, as the crow flies, just where Palestine merges into the desert of the Negev. The "Promised Land" of Joshua 1:4 is geographically much more inclusive. The seacoast formed a definite enough western boundary, though alien powers, from ancient Philistine to modern Egyptian, have always disputed the possession of these fertile lowlands behind the coast. The deepening desert made a firm, though changing boundary line to the east. West of a line drawn down the Jordan Valley, Palestine measures 6,000 square miles (15,385 sq. km.). If areas east of the Jordan, from time to time counted part of Palestine, are also included, the total area is nearer 10,000 square miles (25,640 sq. km.). It is thus a little larger than the state of Vermont. Again, the distance from Dan to Beersheba is 150 miles (250 km.). From west to east the distances are smaller still. In the north, from Acco to the Sea of Galilee, the distance is 28 miles (47 km.). From Gaza to the Dead Sea in the south the distance is 54 miles (90 km.).

III. Climate. In spite of its narrow limits, the varied configuration of Palestine produces a great variety of climates. Thanks to the adjacent sea, the coastal plain, lying between latitudes 31 and 33, is temperate, with an average annual temperature of 57 degrees at Joppa. Inland 34 miles (57 km.), Jerusalem, thanks to its height of 2,600 feet (813 m.) registers an annual average of 63 degrees, though with wider variations. At Jericho, 15 miles (25 km.) away, and 3,300 feet (1,031 m.) below Jerusalem or 700 feet (219 m.) below sea level, tropical climate prevails with intense and enervating summer heat. A similar contrast marks the temperate climate around the Sea of Galilee and the tropical heat around the Dead Sea. Prevailing winds are west or SW and precipitate their moisture on the western slopes of the high country in a rainy season extending roughly from October to April. An occasional sirocco, or east wind, brings burning air from the great deserts of the hinterland (Job 1:19; Jer 18:17; Ezek 17:10; 27:26). The southern desert, south of Beersheba, is a parched wilderness, at present the scene of some of the world's major experiments in "dry-farming." The chief climatic advantage is a heavy fall of dew. The "former rain" of the biblical phrase (Joel 2:23 KJV; NIV "autumn rain") was the early part of the rainy season. The period is commonly followed by a time of heavy falls alternating with fine clear weather, until March or April, when the "latter rain" (NIV "spring rain") falls with immense advantage to the maturing crops before the dry season, the ripening, and the harvest.

IV. Geography.

A. **The coast.** The coast of Palestine is a line that sweeps south, with a slight curve to the west, without break or indentation. North of Carmel is Phoenicia, where a great maritime nation found

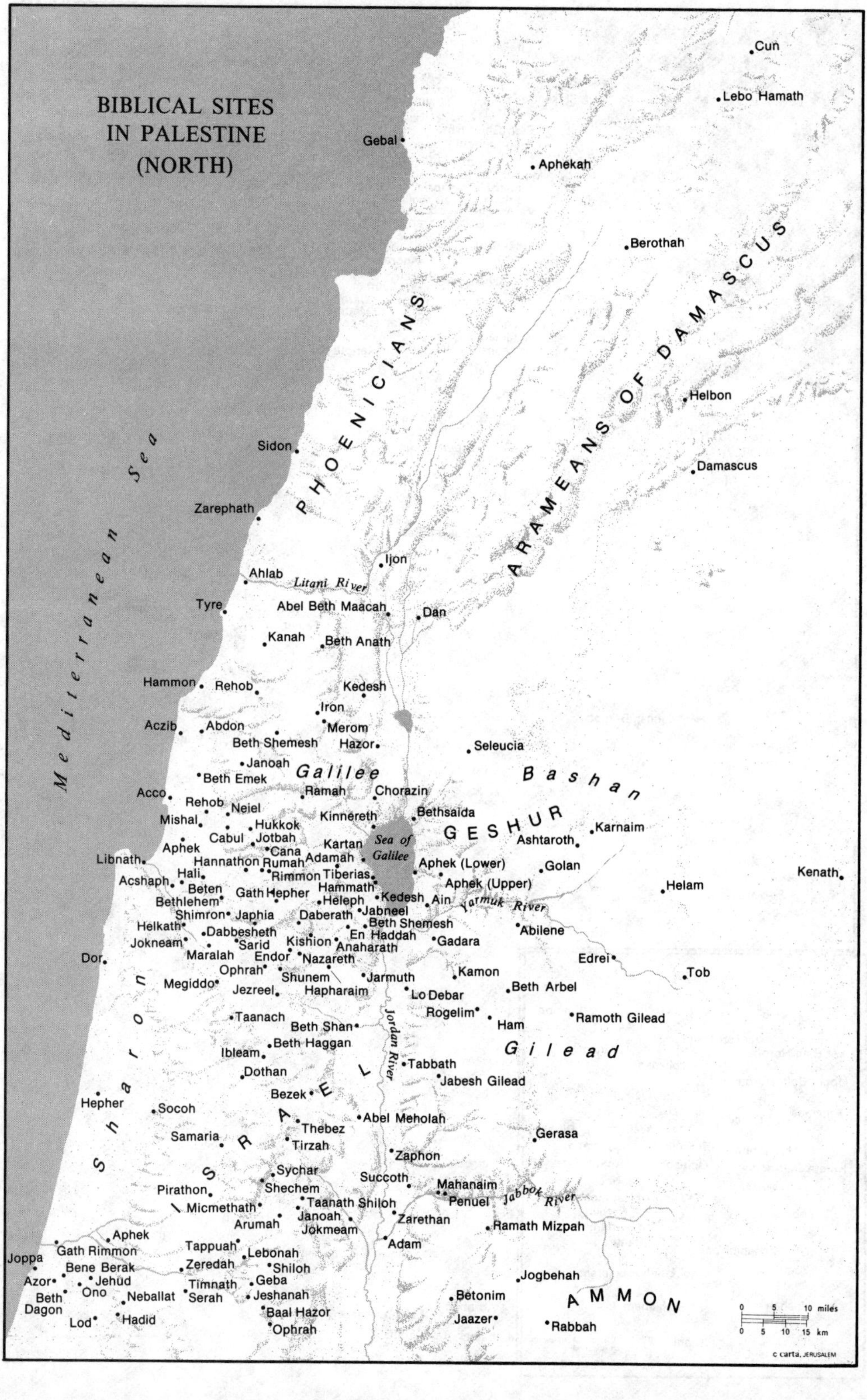
BIBLICAL SITES IN PALESTINE (NORTH)
Mediterranean Sea
PHOENICIANS
ARAMEANS OF DAMASCUS
Cun
Lebo Hamath
Gebal
Aphekah
Berothah
Helbon
Damascus
Sidon
Zarephath
Ijon
Ahlab
Litani River
Tyre
Abel Beth Maacah
Dan
Kanah
Beth Anath
Hammon
Rehob
Kedesh
Iron
Aczib
Abdon
Merom
Beth Shemesh
Hazor
Seleucia
Janoah
Galilee
Beth Emek
Bashan
Acco
Rehob
Ramah
Chorazin
Mishal
Neiel
Kinnereth
Bethsaida
Hukkok
GESHUR
Karnaim
Cabul
Jotbah
Ashtaroth
Aphek
Cana
Kartan
Sea of Galilee
Libnath
Hannathon
Rumah
Adamah
Aphek (Lower)
Golan
Hali
Rimmon
Tiberias
Kenath
Acshaph
Beten
Hammath
Aphek (Upper)
Helam
Bethlehem
Gath Hepher
Heleph
Kedesh
Ain
Yarmuk River
Shimron
Japhia
Daberath
Jabneel
Helkath
Beth Shemesh
Abilene
Dabbesheth
En Haddah
Jokneam
Sarid
Kishion
Anaharath
Gadara
Maralah
Endor
Nazareth
Edrei
Dor
Ophrah
Shunem
Jarmuth
Kamon
Tob
Megiddo
Jezreel
Hapharaim
Lo Debar
Beth Arbel
Rogelim
Taanach
Ham
Ramoth Gilead
Beth Shan
Beth Haggan
Jordan River
Gilead
Ibleam
Tabbath
Dothan
Jabesh Gilead
Bezek
Hepher
Socoh
Abel Meholah
Thebez
Samaria
Gerasa
Tirzah
ISRAEL
Sharon
Zaphon
Sychar
Shechem
Succoth
Mahanaim
Pirathon
Penuel
Jabbok River
Micmethath
Taanath Shiloh
Janoah
Zarethan
Arumah
Jokmeam
Ramath Mizpah
Aphek
Gath Rimmon
Tappuah
Adam
Joppa
Lebonah
Bene Berak
Zeredah
Shiloh
Jogbehah
Azor
Jehud
Timnath Serah
Geba
Beth Dagon
Ono
Neballat
Jeshanah
Betonim
AMMON
Baal Hazor
Lod
Hadid
Ophrah
Jaazer
Rabbah
0 5 10 miles
0 5 10 15 km
c carta, JERUSALEM

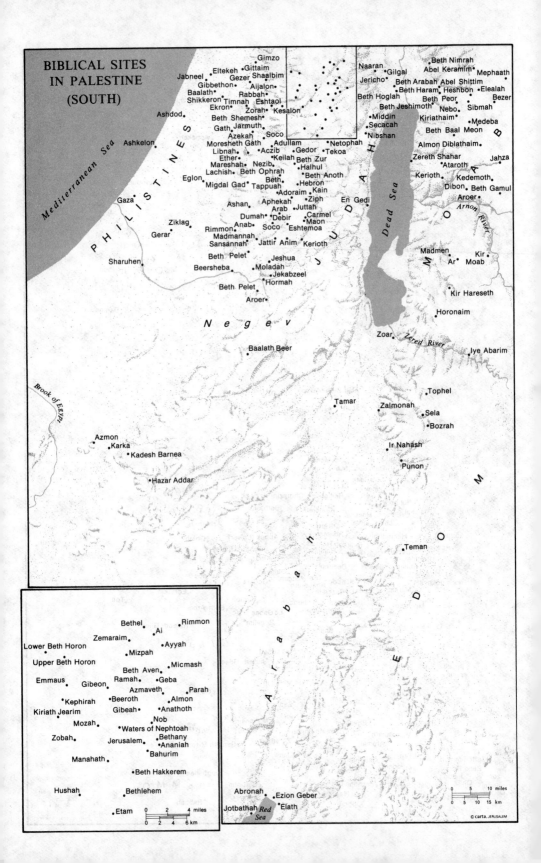

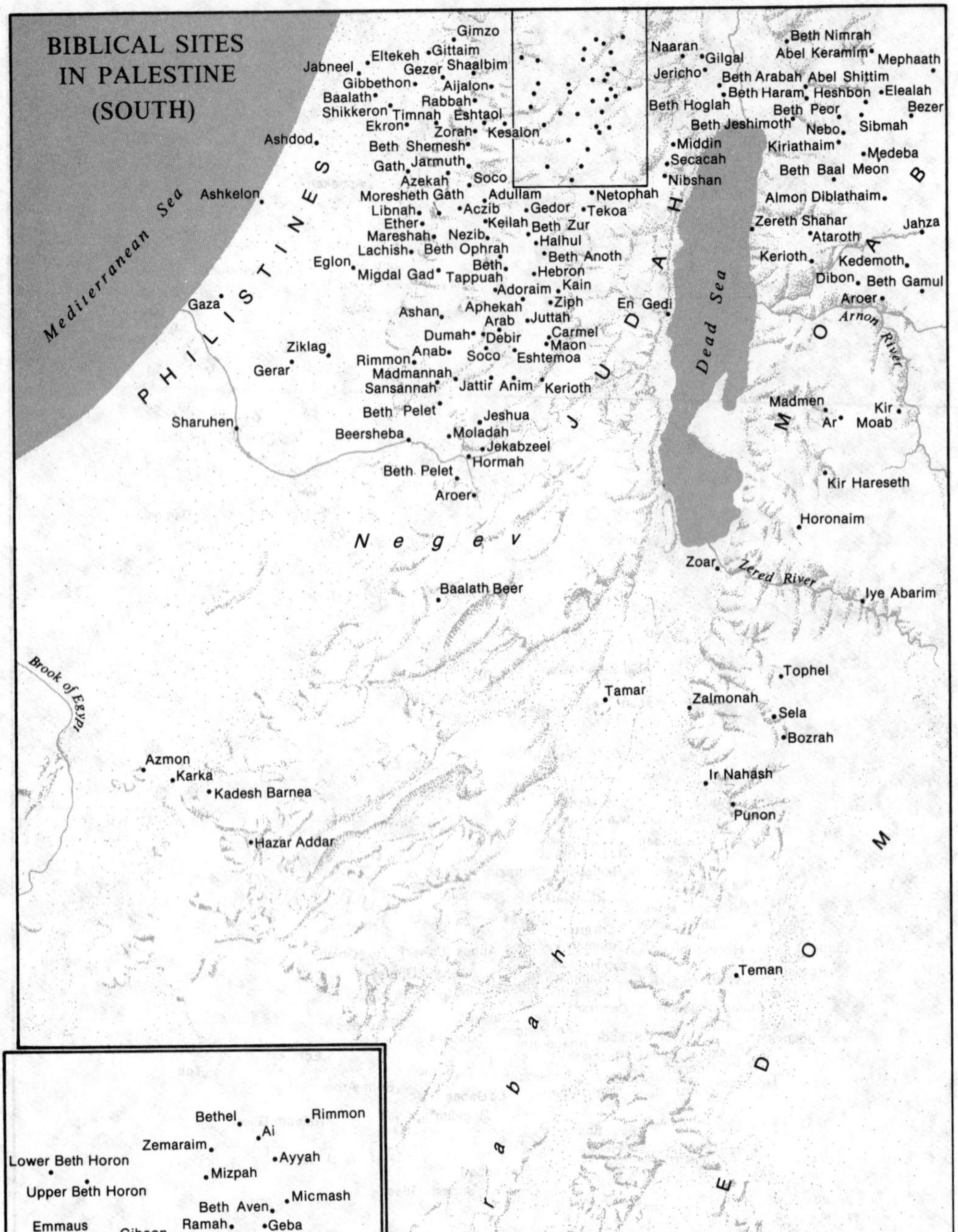
BIBLICAL SITES
IN PALESTINE
(SOUTH)
Mediterranean Sea
PHILISTINES
JUDAH
MOAB
EDOM
Negev
Arabah
Dead Sea
Arnon River
Zered River
Brook of Egypt
Red Sea
Gimzo
Eltekeh
Gittaim
Jabneel
Gezer
Shaalbim
Gibbethon
Aijalon
Baalath
Rabbah
Shikkeron
Timnah
Eshtaol
Ekron
Zorah
Kesalon
Ashdod
Beth Shemesh
Gath
Jarmuth
Azekah
Soco
Ashkelon
Moresheth Gath
Adullam
Netophah
Libnah
Aczib
Gedor
Tekoa
Ether
Keilah
Beth Zur
Mareshah
Nezib
Halhul
Lachish
Beth Ophrah
Beth Anoth
Eglon
Beth Tappuah
Hebron
Migdal Gad
Adoraim
Kain
Gaza
Ashan
Aphekah
Ziph
En Gedi
Arab
Juttah
Dumah
Debir
Carmel
Ziklag
Maon
Rimmon
Anab
Soco
Eshtemoa
Gerar
Madmannah
Sansannah
Jattir
Anim
Kerioth
Beth Pelet
Jeshua
Sharuhen
Moladah
Beersheba
Jekabzeel
Hormah
Beth Pelet
Aroer
Naaran
Gilgal
Jericho
Beth Hoglah
Beth Nimrah
Abel Keramim
Mephaath
Beth Arabah
Abel Shittim
Beth Haram
Heshbon
Elealah
Beth Peor
Bezer
Beth Jeshimoth
Nebo
Sibmah
Middin
Kiriathaim
Medeba
Secacah
Beth Baal Meon
Nibshan
Almon Diblathaim
Zereth Shahar
Jahza
Ataroth
Kerioth
Kedemoth
Dibon
Beth Gamul
Aroer
Madmen
Ar
Kir Moab
Kir Hareseth
Horonaim
Zoar
Iye Abarim
Baalath Beer
Tophel
Tamar
Zalmonah
Sela
Bozrah
Azmon
Karka
Kadesh Barnea
Ir Nahash
Punon
Hazar Addar
Teman
Abronah
Ezion Geber
Jotbathah
Elath
0 5 10 miles
0 5 10 15 km
© carta, JERUSALEM
Bethel
Rimmon
Ai
Zemaraim
Ayyah
Lower Beth Horon
Mizpah
Upper Beth Horon
Micmash
Beth Aven
Emmaus
Ramah
Geba
Gibeon
Azmaveth
Parah
Kephirah
Beeroth
Almon
Kiriath Jearim
Gibeah
Anathoth
Nob
Mozah
Waters of Nephtoah
Zobah
Jerusalem
Bethany
Ananiah
Bahurim
Manahath
Beth Hakkerem
Hushah
Bethlehem
Etam
0 2 4 miles
0 2 4 6 km

the means to use and tame the sea; in this area, significantly, the coast is more hospitable, and offers hope of haven for ships. Those who lived behind the stern, flat coast of Palestine necessarily found the sea a barrier (Josh 1:4) and an image of violence and restlessness (Isa 17:12–13). By the same token, they were agricultural rather than maritime. From Carmel south to the Nile Delta, the coastline is built of sandhills and low cliffs, without a sheltering offshore island to form a roadstead, or a river mouth to give minimum protection from the sea. It is "a shelf for the casting of wreckage and the roosting of sea-birds" (G. A. Smith: *Historical Geography of the Holy Land,* p. 128). The currents are parallel with the coast, and still bear the silt of the Nile. The prevailing wind beats on the shore with ceaseless surf. No intruder, with the possible exception of the Philistines themselves, has ever landed there. Palestine's invaders have followed the open roads of her north-south plains and valleys. For the same reason, artificial harbors anciently built on the coast, even Herod's fine port of Caesarea, have always been difficult to maintain: on the first relaxation of human effort, the sea has overwhelmed them. A recent survey of the coast has indicated that the lost ports of Palestine are likely to prove a fruitful field of underwater archaeological exploration. The makeshift or artificial ports on the Mediterranean coast may be listed as follows: Dor was used as a port, but it was an open roadstead, and never in firm control of the Israelite authorities. Joppa was little better, save that some offshore reefs broke the force of the Mediterranean swell and offered a fair-weather port. First under Philistine and later under Syrian control, Joppa fell to the Jews as a conquest of Simon Maccabaeus in 148 B.C. "To add to his reputation," runs the account, "he took Joppa for a harbor, and provided an access for the islands of the sea" (1 Macc 14:5). Simon found a considerable Greek population in the port and had some trouble in occupying and fortifying it. After eighty-five years, during which the Syrians twice reoccupied the port, Pompey allotted it to Syria in his organization of the East (63). In 47 Caesar returned it to the Jews, and Augustus made it part of the domains of Herod the Great. These historical vicissitudes illustrate the disadvantages of a coastline that is geographically so disadvantageous. Ashkelon, the only Philistine city actually on the coast, and a foundation old enough to find mention in the Tell-el-Amarna Letters, served also as a port, and archaeology may establish the presence of harbor works. Caesarea, Herod's ambitious foundation twenty miles (thirty-three km.) south of modern Haifa, was an efficient port. Herod spent twelve years building, not only a harbor, but also a city of some magnificence. Enormous blocks of stone formed a breakwater, two hundred feet (sixty-two m.) wide in twenty fathoms (thirty-eight m.) of water, and made the only real harbor on the coast. Hence the Hebrew name *Leminah,* a Hebraic rendering of Greek *limen,* "a harbor." Associated harbor buildings, navigational aids, and a well-equipped town made Caesarea the natural seat for Roman authority in Palestine.

B. **The Maritime Plain.** A coastal plain shaped like a long spear point, with its tip where Carmel thrusts to the sea, is the main western geographical feature of Palestine. North of Carmel, the small plain of Acco or Acre, a detached section of the coastal plain, should be mentioned. South of Carmel, widening from eight miles (thirteen km.) to twelve miles (twenty km.), and extending for forty-four miles (seventy-three km.), is the Plain of Sharon, once an extensive oak forest, well-watered, and bounded to the south by low hills. South again of this inconsiderable barrier, and similarly widening over the course of its forty miles (sixty-seven km.) to the borders of Egypt, is the famous Plain of Philistia, after which the entire land was named. Marshes—the "Serbonian Bog" of Strabo, Diodorus, and Pliny—were found at the southern end of the Philistine plain. These were salt marshes behind the coastal dunes and are mentioned because they were a breeding ground of disease, which has played its part in history. Somewhere near here Sennacherib's army was destroyed, perhaps by some devastating plague, sent, as Scripture says, by the angel of the Lord (2 Kings 19:35–36). Historical records, extending even to Napoleon, refer to similar decimating attacks of pestilence among large bodies of men traversing this area. However, in spite of the unhealthiness of the marshy strip, the coastal plain has always been a highway of commerce or aggression. By this path traveled the Egyptian conquerors Thothmes III, Ramses II, and Seti I, seeking out their northern foes, the Hittites. By this same path, and thence into the Plain of Esdraelon, traveled Cambyses, Alexander, Pompey, Saladin, Napoleon, and Allenby. The plain forms the western blade of the Fertile Crescent, the grand highway between Africa, Asia, and Europe.

C. **The Uplands.** The tumbled hill-country that forms the core or backbone of the land, is a continuation of the more clearly defined Lebanon ranges to the north of Palestine. This extended mountain chain breaks up into confused hills in the desert of the south. Three divisions are to be distinguished: Galilee, Samaria, and Judah. Galilee is rugged, especially to the north, where a height of 4,000 feet (1,250 km.) above sea level is reached near Merom. The southern portion is less hilly and might even be described as rolling land, arable, fertile, and temperate in climate. South of Galilee, the Valley of Jezreel, or the Plain of Esdraelon, cuts the range, the location of many important ancient towns and an open highway to the north. The town of Megiddo controlled the pass into the Plain of Sharon. Since Mount Carmel dominated the road along the coast, Megiddo was a place of paramount strategic importance. From the strife that, through the centuries, necessarily gathered around it, Armageddon, or "the Hill of Megiddo" became a symbol of the struggle of nations (Rev 16:16). Two valleys from Esdraelon give access to the Jordan. One passes between Tabor and Moreh,

A view of the hills and plains of Samaria. Courtesy Zev Radovan.

the other between Moreh and Gilboa. Here lay the best east-west travel routes of the land.

The Samaria hill-country forms the geographical heart of Palestine. The uplands rise in the north to 1,640 feet (513 m.) in Mount Gilboa, and cast up two conspicuous peaks: Ebal (3,077 ft.–962 m. above sea level) and Gerizim, a lower eminence. Fertile valleys intersect these high masses, and since the valley floors are themselves of considerable altitude, the higher country has not the visible height or prominence that the sea level figures appear to indicate.

The third division of the hill country is Judah. Here the summits are lower than in the region of Samaria, falling to 2,600 feet (813 m.) in Jerusalem and touching their highest point, 3,370 feet (1,053 m.), near Hebron. This country forms a watershed that strains the moisture from the Mediterranean sea breezes. The eastern slopes, in consequence, deteriorate into the barren "wilderness of Judah," deeply intersected by the arid ravines that converge on the Dead Sea. This barren wasteland was the refuge of David in his outlaw days. Ordered life and agriculture was concentrated on the west in the so-called "Shephelah," the sloping foothills and valley tongues that led up from the coastal plain into the Judean hills. In sheltered folds of the hills, agriculture flourished, and fertility seeped down from the higher land. The Shephelah was disputed territory. In days of strength the Hebrew highlanders pressed down toward the plain. When their strength wavered or flagged, the Philistine lowlanders thrust up into the foothills. The Shephelah saw a pressure front between the Semitic claimants from the desert and the east, and those from the west. Fortresses such as Lachish, Debir, Libnah, Azekah, and Beth Shemesh were located in the Shephelah. To the south the Judean hill-country breaks up into the arid wilderness of the Negev. There is strong archaeological evidence for a considerable population in this area in the early centuries of the Christian era, made possible by efficient water conservation, irrigation systems,

"At that time Mary got ready and hurried to a town in the hill country of Judah where she . . . greeted Elizabeth." (Luke 1:39). A view of the Judean hill country, looking westward. Courtesy Israel Government Press Office.

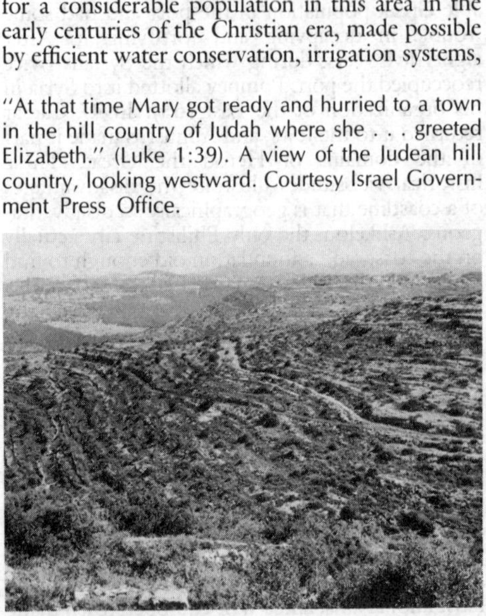

and the effective use, through rock-mulching, of the heavy fall of dew.

D. **The Jordan Valley.** This depression, which contains the Jordan River and its associated bodies of water, is part of a huge split in the crust of the globe, a geological fault that extends north to form the valley between the two Lebanon ranges, and south of the Dead Sea, to form the arid valley of the Arabah, the Gulf of Aqabah, and the African chain of lakes. The Jordan rises from multiple sources on the western slopes of Hermon and becomes a distinctive stream a few miles north of the shallow reedy lake called Huleh today, Semechonitis by Josephus, and "the Waters of Merom" in Joshua 11:5. The Canaanite stronghold of Hazor lay a few miles to the SW. From its sources to Huleh, the Jordan drops 1,000 feet (313 m.) over a distance of 12 miles (20 km.), and enters the lake 7 feet (2 m.) above sea level. Over the 11 miles (18 km.) to the Sea of Galilee, it drops to 682 feet (213 m.) below sea level. From Galilee to the Dead Sea there is a further drop of 600 feet (188 m.). Galilee is the OT *Kinnereth* or *Kinneroth* (Num 34:11; Josh 12:3), names echoed in the NT Gennesaret. John, writing for Gentile readers, calls the lake "the Sea of Tiberias" from the name of the town founded by Herod Antipas on the shore. Some of Palestine's most fertile soil is found around the shores,

The farmlands of the Jordan Valley near Beth Shan, facing east. Beth Shan is located at the junction of the Jordan and Jezreel valleys. Courtesy Zev Radovan.

and the lake itself was the center of an extensive and vigorous fishing industry. Capernaum, Bethsaida, and perhaps Korazin, were lakeside towns. So were Tiberias and Tarichea, neither of which is mentioned in the Gospels, unless the latter town is, in fact, Magdala. Bethsaida means "fishing place," and Tarichea derives its name from a Greek word meaning "preserved fish." Both names therefore point to the lake's fishing industry. It is clear that the first disciples were called from an active and prosperous stratum of Galilean society. Flowing south from Galilee, through a wide-floored valley walled by cliffs, the Jordan follows a fantastically meandering course, taking 200 miles (333 km.) of winding stream to cover 65 miles (108 km.) measured in a straight line. Much of the valley floor is tangled vegetation, fed lushly by the periodic floodwaters of the river. It is this wilderness that Jeremiah calls "the swelling" (KJV) or "the thickets" (NIV) of Jordan (Jer 12:5; 49:19). Fords are numerous. The river enters the Dead Sea near Jericho. This lake has no outflow and its water is therefore 25 percent salt deposits, the raw material of a flourishing chemical industry recently established in the region of the lake. Two-thirds of the way down the eastern coast, west of Kir Hareseth in Moab, an irregular peninsula known as "the Tongue" projects into the sea. South of this peninsula the water is only a few feet deep, forming a large bay known anciently as "the Valley of Siddim" (Gen 14:3). Here, it is thought, were situated the "cities of the Plain," Sodom, Gomorrah, Admah, Zeboiim, and Zoar. About 2000 B.C. a great catastrophe overwhelmed the area and depressed the ground level. Underwater archaeological exploration seems to confirm that Sodom and its associated towns perished in this cataclysm.

E. **The Plateau of Transjordan.** This is not part of modern Palestine and was alien territory over much of ancient history. It was, however, intimately connected with biblical history, and its geography is relevant in consequence. North of the Yarmuk, a tributary of the Jordan south of the Sea of Galilee, is Bashan. Through this region in NT times curved the eastern members of the federation of ten cities known as the Decapolis. In its eastern quarter lay the Trachonitis of the Greeks (Luke 3:1), a tumbled waste of ancient volcanic stone, a natural defensive area, and part of the principality of Og of Bashan (Deut 3:4). South of Bashan, and extending to the river, is Gilead. The Jabbok, whose banks were the scene of Jacob's contest (Gen 33), rose near Rabbath Ammon, the Philadelphia of the Decapolis, and irrigated a considerable territory. In the tribal settlement recorded in Numbers 32 and Joshua 12, Manasseh was allotted all Bashan in the north, Reuben the Moabite highlands in the south, and Gad the central land of Gilead. Hence the identification of Gad with Gilead in Judges 5:17. In Gilead was the Kerith, scene of Elijah's retreat, and David's refuge of Mahanaim. It was well watered and wooded. South of Jabbok, down to the Arnon, which joins the Dead Sea halfway down its eastern coast, the plateau becomes increasingly arid and desolate. This area contains the height of Nebo, the old land of Ammon. South of Arnon is Moab, a high plateau seldom controlled by Israel; and further south still is Edom, a region valuable for its mineral deposits and first controlled and exploited by David and Solomon. It was possibly the iron of Edom, smelted in the considerable industrial district that had been developed just north of the Gulf of Aqabah, that enabled Israel to emerge from the Bronze Age and meet the iron-using Philistines on their own terms. Petra, the strange rock of the desert trade routes, was originally an Edomite stronghold.

V. Animal Life. Besides the common domesticated animals of the ancient Middle East (horse, ox, sheep, goat, camel, ass, mule), Palestine was the habitat of numerous predatory beasts, principally the lion, leopard, wolf, jackal, and fox. The hare, the coney (a species of rabbit), the wild boar, and the deer were also found. A concordance, under any of these heads, will show the variety of metaphor and imagery based on animal life, both tame animals and the "beasts of the field." The dog was considered almost a wild creature and provided a term for uncleanness, treachery, and contempt. The dog of Palestine was a pariah and scavenger; no mention is made of its being used in hunting nor shepherding, except Job 30:1 (see ANIMALS). The cryptic reference to dogs in Deuteronomy 23:18 (JB, KJV, MLB, NASB, RSV) probably has to do with homosexual prostitution (NEB, NIV). Song birds are rare, but scavenger and predatory fowl included the eagle, vulture, owl, hawk, and kite. The heron, bittern, osprey, partridge, peacock, dove, pigeon, quail, raven, stork, and sparrow were common and find frequent reference in both Testaments (see BIRDS). Fish were plentiful, especially in Galilee, where the shoals were dense. The chief edible fish seem to have been carp. Bees, grasshoppers, and locusts were among the insects (see ANIMALS). Palestine lies in the belt of territory subject to locust invasion, and the Book of Joel is striking evidence for the destructive visitation of such insect swarms.

VI. Plant life. Flowers are abundant in spring, giving brilliant display for a brief period only; hence their use as a symbol of the ephemeral nature of life (Job 14:2; Ps 103:15). The "lilies of the field" (Matt 6:28) may have been a comprehensive term covering anemones, irises, and other blooms. The rose was probably the crocus (Song of Songs 2:1; Isa 35:1). Trees grow vigorously in Palestine under proper cultivation, but the forest coverage in ancient times is a matter for conjecture. It may be safely assumed that parts of Palestine must have been more heavily wooded in ancient times than today. Invasion and the Turkish tax on trees combined over the centuries to destroy the arboreal flora of Palestine. On the other hand, Palestine is not an ideal region for major forest growth. The chief kinds of trees were the oak, including the evergreen ilex, the terebinth, the carob, and the box, which attains a height of twenty feet (six m.); some pines; cypresses; and plane trees by the water. The plane is probably the tree of Psalm 1, "planted by streams of water." Josephus mentions the walnut, and the sycamore-fig is mentioned in Amos (7:14), Isaiah (9:9–10; NIV "fig"), and Luke (19:4). Smaller growth is formed of dwarf or scrub oak, dwarf wild olive, wild vine, juniper, and thorn. Such scrub often marks the abandoned sites of ancient cultivation. Oleanders sometimes line riverbeds. The olive, the vine, the fig, and the date palm were the chief fruit-bearing trees or plants of ancient Palestine, and balsam groves were farmed at Jericho. Grain crops were barley, wheat, and millet. Wheat grew in the broader valleys and plains, the best areas for its cultivation being Philistia and Esdraelon. Barley grew on the higher slopes, a less-valued crop. It is significant that the apprehensive Midianite soldier saw Israel in his dream in the symbol of a barley cake rolling disastrously from the hills (Judg 7:13). Beans and lentils were the chief vegetables. Jacob's "red stew" (Gen 25:30) was probably a variety of red beans or lentil. The land was poor in grass; pasturage, as Western countries know it, was unknown. Hence the imagery of grass in reference to the brevity of life (Ps 90:5–7; 103:15; Isa 40:6). (See also PLANTS.) EMB

PALLU, PALLUITE (păl'ū, păl'ū-īt, Heb. *pallû', distinguished, a descendant of Pallu*). Reuben's second son (Gen 46:9; see also Exod 6:14; Num 26:5, 8; 1 Chron 5:3). He was the founder of the Palluites (Num 26:5).

PALMER WORM (See ANIMALS)

PALM TREE (See PLANTS)

PALMYRA (See TADMOR)

PALSY (See DISEASES)

PALTI (păl'tī, Heb. *paltî, delivered*). One of the twelve spies, from the tribe of Benjamin (Num 13:9).

PALTIEL (păl'tī-ĕl, Heb. *paltî 'ēl, God delivers*). 1. The son of Azzan from the tribe of Issachar, he helped in the division of the Promised Land (Num 34:26).

2. The man to whom Saul gave Michal, David's wife (KJV has lit., Phalti, in 1 Sam 25:44 and lit., Phaltiel, in 2 Sam 3:15).

PALTITE (păl'tīt, Heb. *paltî, delivered*). The Gentile name of Helez, one of David's valiant men. Called the Pelonite (1 Chron 11:27; 27:10). Same as Palti.

PAMPHYLIA (păm-fĭl'ĭ-à, Gr. *Pamphylia*). At the time of Paul, Pamphylia was a small Roman province of southern Asia Minor, extending 75 miles (125 km.) along the Mediterranean coast and 30 miles (50 km.) inland to the Taurus Mountains. It was surrounded by Pisidia on the north, Cilicia to the east, and Lycia to the SW. It never became an important province, and its boundaries were often changed by sudden and arbitrary political decisions. The Emperor Claudius brought it into the Roman provincial system in the first century A.D.

The tiny country is first mentioned in the NT in Acts 2:10, where it is said that some people at Pentecost were from Phrygia and Pamphylia. Paul visited the territory on his first missionary journey when he preached at Perga, its chief city (Acts 13:13; 14:24). It was at this point that John Mark left the party and returned to Jerusalem (13:13; 15:38). Later, when Paul as a prisoner sailed near Pamphylia (27:5), he evidently crossed the Pamphylian Gulf. It is said that most of the inhabitants of Pamphylia were backward and illiterate. Christianity never flourished there as in other places of Asia Minor.

PANNAG (See PLANTS)

PAP (Heb. *shadh*, Gr. *mastos, bulging*). An English word, now obsolete, that has been replaced by the word "breast," e.g., in RSV (Luke 11:27; Rev 1:13, NIV "chest").

PAPER (See PAPYRUS; WRITING)

PAPHOS (pā'fŏs, Gr. *Paphos*). The capital city of Roman Cyprus, located at the extreme western end of this large island. The Paphos of the Bible is really New Paphos, a Roman city rebuilt by Augustus; the old Greek city of Paphos, dedicated to the worship of Aphrodite, lay ten miles (seventeen km.) to the south. In New Paphos, Paul and Barnabas encountered the wiles of the Jewish sorcerer Elymas in the court of Sergius Paulus, the Roman governor. Paul's miracle of blinding the magician led to the conversion of Paulus (Acts 13:6–13). New Paphos is now known as Baffa.

PAPYRUS (pȧ-pī'rŭs, Gr. *papyros*). A plantlike reed or rush that grows in swamps and along rivers or lakes, often to the height of twelve feet (almost four m.) with beautiful flowers at the top. The stalk is triangular in shape, something like a giant celery stalk. In ancient times it was found mainly along the Nile in Egypt but was also known in Palestine. For commercial use the stalk was cut into sections about one foot (one-third m.) long, and these pieces were then sliced lengthwise into thin strips, which were shaped and squared and laid edge to edge to form a larger piece. Other strips were laid horizontally over these strips and both were pressed together, dried in the sun, scraped, and rubbed until there emerged a smooth yellowish sheet much like our heavy wrapping paper, only thicker and heavier. The juice of the pith served as the glue, but sometimes other paste was added.

The manufacture of papyrus was a flourishing

Papyrus growing in the Huleh reservoir (Nov. 1958). The papyrus is a perennial, growing to a height of up to 15 feet. Courtesy Israel Government Press Office.

Detail of a papyrus plant. Papyrus farming was big business in Egypt in ancient times. Courtesy P. Schlesinger.

business in Egypt, where baskets, sandals, boats, and other articles were made of it. It was not unknown among the Hebrews (Job 8:11), and some believe that the ark that held baby Moses was made of papyrus (Exod 2:3). But the most common use of the product was for writing material, so much so that *papyrus* became the name for writing paper. The art of making papyrus goes back to 2000 B.C., and it was the common writing material in the Greek and Roman worlds from 500 B.C. until A.D. 400, when vellum largely replaced it. There is little doubt that the NT books were written on papyrus (pl. *papyri*). The material was also called *chartēs* in Greek, and John no doubt wrote his second letter on such paper (2 John 12). For long books (rolls or scrolls) many pieces of papyrus were glued together and rolled up. Such a roll was called *biblos* or *biblion,* from which our word *Bible* is derived (cf. Ezek 2:9–10; 2 Tim 4:13; Rev 10:2, 8, 9–10). The width of the roll varied from three to twelve inches (eight to thirty-one cm.), and sometimes the roll got to be as long as twenty-five

An Aramaic papyrus letter, rolled and tied with a cord from Elephantine. Under the Persian Empire, a mercenary garrison including Aramaic-writing Jews was posted on the island. Courtesy The Brooklyn Museum, Bequest of Miss Theodora Wilbour.

feet (eight m.). Luke's Gospel is estimated to have been thirty feet (nine and one-half m.) long, 2 Thessalonians may have been only eighteen inches (forty-six cm.) long, and short letters like Jude or Philemon were perhaps written on a single small sheet. The writer wrote in columns evenly spaced along the length of the roll, and the reader read one column at a time, unrolling with one hand and rolling up with the other.

Papyrus, however, becomes brittle with age and easily decays, especially when damp. This is why the autographs of the NT writings have perished. They may also have been literally read to pieces and during persecution were deliberately destroyed. But thousands of ancient papyri have been found in the dry sands of Egypt and elsewhere. Our libraries contain large collections of both biblical and secular papyri—Bible texts, legal documents, marriage contracts, letters, etc. Many of the NT papyri antedate all other codices. Examples are the Rylands Papyrus, the famous Chester Beatty Papyri, and the more recent Bodmer Papyrus of the Gospel of John. They have added much to our knowledge of the Greek language and the text of the NT. LMP

PARABLE (păr'á-b'l, Gr. *parabolē, likeness*). Derived from the Greek verb *paraballō,* composed of the preposition *para* meaning "beside" and the verb *ballō,* "to cast." A parable is thus a comparison of two objects for the purpose of teaching.

Although the word properly belongs to the NT and is used frequently there, it does occur several times in the OT. There it is the translation of the Hebrew *māshāl,* used in the OT in several senses: In Numbers it is seen more as a prophetic figurative discourse (Num 23:7, 18 KJV). Ezekiel uses the word much as one would today with the idea of similitude or parable (Ezek 17:2; 24:3). A writer in Psalms treats the word as a poem (Ps 78:2). Finally it is associated with the riddle or "dark saying" (Ps 49:4; Ezek 17:2; 20:49). Five times the NT uses the Greek word *paroimia* for parable. This may be synonymous with *parabolē* or, as found in John's writings, it may refer to a didactic, symbolic, or figurative utterance (John 10:6 KJV).

There are a number of English words similar in meaning to parable. R. Trench says: "The parable differs from the fable, moving as it does in a spiritual world, and never transgressing the actual order of things natural" (*Notes on the Parables of Our Lord,* 1841, pp. 15–16). The importance of definition is shown by Moulton when he says that because of varied definitions of a parable, scholars have counted seventy-nine, seventy-one, fifty-nine, thirty-nine, thirty-seven, and thirty-three parables in the NT (W. J. Moulton, "Parable" in HDCG). See also Herbert Lockyer, *All the Parables of the Bible,* 1963.

In comparing the parable with the similar figures of speech, one must bear in mind that often the parable contains elements of these other figures. For instance, there are often elements in the parable that must be treated as allegorical interpretation.

While Christ did not invent the parable, it is significant that he is the only one who used it in the NT. At one time in his ministry it was his only method of speaking to the masses (Matt 13:34). It is interesting to note when Christ began to use this methodology. So abrupt was the change in his form of teaching that his disciples asked him why he did this (13:10). In his reply one notes the value of this method of instruction. It was an effective method of revealing truth to the spiritual and ready mind and at the same time of concealing it from others (13:11). Christ came as Israel's King and only after they had rejected him did he employ this form of imparting spiritual truth. Those who had rejected him were not to know the "secrets of the kingdom of heaven" (13:11).

In the discussion of the parable there is probably no area fraught with greater disagreement than the principles of interpretation. Ramm, in discussing the rules for interpreting the parables, notes four principles: "Perspective, cultural, exegetical and doctrinal" (Bernard Ramm, *Protestant Biblical Interpretation,* 1956, p. 257). Perspectively, one must understand the parables in their relation to christology and God's kingdom. Culturally, one must not overlook the background in which our Lord lived and worked. Ramm shows four things that are involved in the exegetical principle: "(1) Determine the one central truth the parable is attempting to teach. . . . (2) Determine how much of the parable is interpreted by the Lord himself. . . . (3) Determine whether there are any clues in the context concerning the parable's meaning. . . . (4) The comparative rule" (Ibid., pp. 258–67).

The following classification of parables is adapted from A. B. Bruce, *The Parabolic Teaching of Christ,* 1904, pp. 8ff.:

I. Didactic Parables

- A. Nature and Development of the Kingdom
  1. The Sower (Matt 13:3–8; Mark 4:4–8; Luke 8:5–8)
  2. The Tares (Matt 13:24–30)
  3. The Mustard Seed (Matt 13:31–32; Mark 4:30–32; Luke 13:18–19)
  4. The Leaven (Matt 13:33; Luke 13:20–21)
  5. The Hidden Treasure (Matt 13:44)
  6. The Pearl of Great Price (Matt 13:45–46)
  7. The Drag Net (Matt 13:47–50)
  8. The Blade, the Ear, and the Full Corn (Mark 4:26–29)
- B. Service and Rewards
  1. The Laborers in the Vineyard (Matt 20:1–16)
  2. The Talents (Matt 25:14–30)
  3. The Pounds (Luke 19:11–27)
  4. The Unprofitable Servants (Luke 17:7–10)
- C. Prayer
  1. The Friend at Midnight (Luke 11:5–8)
  2. The Unjust Judge (Luke 18:1–8)

D. Love for Neighbor: The Good Samaritan (Luke 10:30–37)
E. Humility
1. The Lowest Seat at the Feast (Luke 14:7–11)
2. The Pharisee and the Publican (Luke 18:9–14)
F. Worldly Wealth
1. The Unjust Steward (Luke 16:1–9)
2. The Rich Fool (Luke 12:16–21)
3. The Great Supper (Luke 14:15–24)

II. Evangelic Parables
A. God's Love for the Lost
1. The Lost Sheep (Matt 18:12–14; Luke 15:3–7)
2. The Lost Coin (Luke 15:8–10)
3. The Lost Son (Luke 15:11–32)
B. Gratitude of the Redeemed: The Two Debtors (Luke 7:41–43)

III. Prophetic and Judicial Parables
A. Watchfulness for Christ's Return
1. The Ten Virgins (Matt 25:1–13)
2. The Faithful and Unfaithful Servants (Matt 24:45–51; Luke 12:42–48)
3. The Watchful Porter (Mark 13:34–37)
B. Judgment on Israel and Within the Kingdom
1. The Two Sons (Matt 21:28–32)
2. The Wicked Husbandmen (Matt 21:33–34; Mark 12:1–12; Luke 20:9–18)
3. The Barren Fig Tree (Luke 13:6–9)
4. The Marriage Feast of the King's Son (Matt 22:1–14)
5. The Unforgiving Servant (Matt 18:23–25)

Bibliography: T. W. Manson, *The Teaching of Jesus,* 1935; C. H. Dodd, *The Parables of the Kingdom,* 1936; A. M. Hunter, *Interpreting the Parables,* 1960; J. Jeremias, *The Parables of Jesus,* 1963; J. D. Crossan, *In Parables: The Challenge of the Historical Jesus,* 1973. HZC

PARACLETE (See HOLY SPIRIT)

PARADISE (Gr. *paradeisos, park*). A word of Persian origin, found only three times in Scripture (Luke 23:43; 2 Cor 12:4; Rev 2:7), referring in each case to heaven. There was a similar word in the Hebrew OT, *pardēs,* translated "forest" or "orchard" or "park" (Neh 2:8; Eccl 2:5; Song of Songs 4:13). Scholars feel it was introduced into the Greek language very early and popularized by Xenophon.

The LXX uses the Greek word forty-six times, applying it to quite a wide category of places. It is used of the Adamic Eden (Gen 2:15; 3:23) and of the well-watered plains of the Jordan that Lot viewed (13:10). Since it was used to describe gardens of beauty and splendor, one is not surprised to see the NT begin to use the term to refer to the place of spiritual bliss (Luke 23:43).

An oasis in Wadi Faran in the central Sinai Peninsula, thought to be the wilderness area of Paran. This is the region settle by Ishmael (Gen 21:21) and crossed by the Israelites at the Exodus (Num 10:12; 12:16). Courtesy Israel Government Press Office.

The exact location of paradise is uncertain. Paul uses it in 2 Corinthians 12:4, identifying it with the third heaven. Ecclesiasticus 44:16 identifies paradise with heaven into which Enoch was translated. Christ's single use of the term seems to establish its location best for the believer, for he uses it in reassuring the dying thief (Luke 23:43).

PARAH (pā'rȧ, Heb. *pārāh, heifer*). A city in Benjamin's territory (Josh 18:23), now identified as Farah, a short distance NE of Jerusalem.

PARALYSIS, PARALYTIC (See DISEASES)

PARAMOUR (păr'ȧ-mūr, Heb. *pileghesh, a concubine*). KJV (Ezek 23:20, NIV lovers; elsewhere [36 times] KJV, NIV concubine) for a Hebrew term that only here means "male lover."

PARAN (pā'răn, Heb. *pā'rān, ornamental*). A wilderness area first referred to in Genesis 14:6 as "El Paran." Its boundaries seem uncertain; according to some scholars it may include the wilderness of Shur; others think the two have separate boundaries. It lies in the central area of the Sinaitic Peninsula. The four eastern kings passed through this region in trying to suppress the rebellion of their subjects (Gen 14:6). It was the area in which Ishmael lived (21:21). Twice after the Israelites left Mount Sinai they camped in this wilderness (Num 10:12; 12:16). When Moses commanded the spies to search the land of

Canaan as God had ordered, they went up from the wilderness of Paran (13:3) and later returned to it (13:26). When David was grieved at the loss of Samuel, he resorted to Paran (1 Sam 25:1). One of the main trade routes of that day ran through Paran, so that Hadad after revolting from Solomon traversed it in his flight to Egypt.

Twice in the Scriptures (Deut 33:2; Hab 3:3) Mount Paran is mentioned. Two mountains are suggested as being identified as Mount Paran, but the rugged range of mountains west of the Gulf of Aqabah seems to be the most logical site.

PARAPET. A term applied to battlements with open spaces, surmounting ancient fortified buildings and city walls. Stones, lances, and arrows were hurled from the openings upon attacking forces below. Deuteronomy 22:8 enjoins the construction of parapets around the roofs of houses to keep people from falling to the ground below. Roofs were often used for evening recreation.

PARCHED GROUND (Heb. *shārāv, a mirage*). The ERV uses "glowing" instead of "parched" in this phrase in Isaiah 35:7, referring doubtless to the strange movement of air just above dry, hot earth accompanied by mirages. The word here may be rendered "looming sandwaste," which is the Arabic name for mirage, but NIV prefers "thirsty ground."

PARCHMENT (See WRITING)

PARDON (See FORGIVENESS)

PARENT (Gr. *goneus*). A distinctly NT word, occurring only in the plural (*goneis, parents*). Although this English word does not occur in the OT in the KJV and only infrequently in the NIV, there is much instruction there about the parent-child relationship. Children were to honor their parents (Exod 20:12) and obey and reverence them (Lev 19:3; Deut 5:16). Failure here on the child's part could be punished by death (Deut 21:18–21). The same high regard for parents is expected of children in the NT (Eph 6:1; Col 3:20). Parents were expected to love their children, care and provide for them, and not to provoke them to wrath (2 Cor 12:14; Eph 6:4; Col 3:21).

PARMASHTA (pȧr-măsh'tȧ, Heb. *parmashtā', the very first*). One of the sons of Haman. He is listed as one of those killed by the Jews (Esth 9:9).

PARMENAS (pȧr'mē-năs, Gr. *Parmenas, constant*). One of the seven chosen to care for the daily distribution to the poor (Acts 6:5). Tradition tells of his martyrdom at Philippi.

PARNACH (pȧr'năk, Heb. *parnākh*, meaning uncertain). The father of Elizaphan the prince of Zebulun (Num 34:25).

PAROSH (pā'rŏsh, Heb. *par'ōsh, a flea*). One whose descendants returned to Babylon under Zerubbabel (Ezra 2:3; Neh 7:8) and under Ezra (Ezra 8:3, *Pharosh* in KJV). One of their number, Pedaiah, helped rebuild the walls (Neh 3:25).

PAROUSIA (See ESCHATOLOGY)

PARSHANDATHA (pȧr'shăn-dā'thȧ, Heb. *parshandātha', inquisitive*). The oldest of Haman's sons (Esth 9:7).

PARTHIANS (pȧr'thĭ-ănz, Gr. *Parthoi*). Luke's geographical list of the people who were in Jerusalem on the Day of Pentecost (Acts 2:9) is headed by "Parthians and Medes." By "Parthians" Luke no doubt meant all the Jews and proselytes who lived in the old Parthian Empire to the east, known today as Iran. The earliest dispersion of the ten tribes took place in the eastern countries. Later they were augmented by immigration and colonization so that by the first century A.D. the number of Jews in the eastern territories ran into millions.

There is only scant information about the early history of Parthia, a small country, 120 by 300 miles (200 by 500 km.), NW of old Persia and south of the Caspian Sea. Alexander subdued the people, and after the breakdown of his far-flung empire they fell under the rule of the Seleucids. After a successful revolt they soon became a rival power of Rome. Proud Roman Crassus was defeated and killed by them in 53 B.C. In 40 they seized Jerusalem. At one time their empire extended from the Tigris to India. Rome and Parthia learned to respect each other's power and there were many years of somewhat peaceful coexistence extending through the first century A.D. The Parthians' success was due mainly to their unusual way of fighting. Almost all of their soldiers were mounted on horseback. They were excellent with the bow and arrow so that they have been described as "archers fighting on horseback." Known for their prowess in war, instead of the arts and sciences, they never developed a literature of their own. But it is certain that the apostles of our Lord preached the gospel among them.

PARTITION, MIDDLE WALL OF. In Ephesians 2:14 (KJV) Paul asserts that Christ has broken down the "middle wall of partition" (NIV "dividing wall of hostility") that divided Jews and Gentiles, and has made of the two one new people. Paul probably has in mind a literal wall as a tangible symbol of the division between Jews and Gentiles—the wall in the temple area in Jerusalem separating the court of the Gentiles from the courts into which only Jews might enter. On this wall was a notice in Greek and Latin, warning Gentiles to keep out on pain of death. In A.D. 1871 archaeologists who were excavating the site of the temple found a pillar with this inscription, "No man of another nation is to enter within the fence and enclosure around the temple, and whoever is caught will have himself to blame that his death ensues." Paul himself almost lost his life in the temple enclosure when at the end of his third missionary journey his Jewish enemies accused him of bringing Trophimus the Ephesian past this barrier in the temple (Acts 21:29).

PARTRIDGE (See BIRDS)

PARUAH (pȧ-rū'ȧ, Heb. *pārûah, blooming*). The father of Jehoshaphat employed by Solomon (1 Kings 4:17).

PARVAIM (pȧr-vā'ĭm, Heb. *parwāyim,* meaning uncertain). A place mentioned in 2 Chronicles 3:6 from which Solomon obtained gold for the temple.

PAS DAMMIM (pās'dăm'ĭm, Heb. *pasdamîm, place of bloodshed*). A place of encounter between David and the Philistines in Judah (1 Chron 11:13; also in 2 Sam 23:9 in NIV). It is called also Ephes Dammim (1 Sam 17:1).

PASACH (pā'săk, Heb. *pāsakh, to divide*). The son of Japhet who descended from Asher (1 Chron 7:33).

PASEAH (pȧ-sē'ȧ, Heb. *pāsēah, lame*). 1. A son of Eshton (1 Chron 4:12).

2. The head of a family of temple servants (KJV Nethinim) (Ezra 2:49; Neh 7:51), one of whose descendants helped in the restoration of one of the gates of Jerusalem (Neh 3:6).

PASHHUR (păsh'hėr, Heb. *pashhûr*). A priest, the son of Immer (Jer 20:1), the "chief officer" in the Lord's house. Angered by Jeremiah's prophecies, he placed him in stocks located near the house of the Lord. When released, Jeremiah told him that the Lord had changed his name to Magor-Missabib, meaning "terror on every side." Jeremiah also foretold Judah's future captivity by Babylon.

2. The priestly son of Malkijah, who was one of the chief court princes during Zedekiah's reign (Jer 21:1). When Nebuchadnezzar was preparing for one of his attacks on Jerusalem, he was sent by the king to Jeremiah. Later he joined others in seeking to have Jeremiah put to death. Probably he is the same person referred to in 1 Chronicles 9:12; Ezra 2:38; Nehemiah 7:41; 10:3; 11:12.

3. The father of Gedaliah, who aided in Jeremiah's imprisonment (Jer 38:1).

PASS (Heb. *ma'avar, ford*). This may refer to a mountain pass (1 Sam 13:23).

PASSION OF CHRIST (See CHRIST, JESUS)

PASSOVER, FEAST OF (See FEASTS)

PASTORAL LETTERS.

I. Authorship. The term "Pastoral Letters," as a common title for 1 and 2 Timothy and Titus, dates from the early part of the eighteenth century. It is not exact. Though these letters do furnish worthwhile directions for pastors, the addressees were not pastors in the usual, present-day sense of that term. Rather, they were Paul's special envoys sent by him on specific missions and entrusted with concrete assignments according to the need of the hour. For biographical articles see TIMOTHY and TITUS.

In the nineteenth century F. Schleiermacher rejected the authorship by Paul of one of these letters (1 Timothy), and F. C. Baur of all three. Baur had many followers, and today this rejection is rather common. The grounds on which it is based are as follows:

A. **Vocabulary.** Difference in vocabulary between these three (1 and 2 Timothy and Titus) and ten other of Paul's letters (Romans, 1 and 2 Corinthians, etc.) must be admitted, but it has often been exaggerated. Of words found in the three but not found in the ten, only nine are common to the three. Detailed study, moreover, has shown that the Pastoral Letters contain not one single word that was foreign to the age in which Paul lived and could not have been used by him. Besides, vocabulary always varies with the specific subject that is being discussed. Thus, in addressing Timothy and Titus, who were in need of good counsel with respect to their own task of imparting instruction, the frequent use of words belonging to the word-family of *teaching* is certainly not surprising. Other factors that may have influenced the choice of words are the character of the addressees, the apostle's age and environment, the progress of the church with its ever-expanding vocabulary, and the not improbable use of secretaries.

B. **Style.** This argument is self-defeating, for candid examination of the actual facts clearly points to Paul as the author of these letters. The three and the ten picture the same kind of person: one who is deeply interested in those whom he addresses, ascribing to God's sovereign grace whatever is good in himself and/or in the addressees, and showing wonderful tact in counseling. Again, both the three and the ten were written by a person who is fond of litotes or understatements (cf. "not ashamed of the gospel" [Rom 1:16], with "do not be ashamed to testify about our Lord" [2 Tim 1:8]), of enumerations (1 Tim 3:1–12; cf. Rom 1:29–32), of plays on words (1 Tim 6:17; cf. Philem 10–11), of appositional phrases (1 Tim 1:17; cf. Rom 12:1), of expressions of personal unworthiness (1 Tim 1:13, 15; cf. 1 Cor 15:9), and of doxologies (1 Tim 1:17; cf. Rom 11:36). When the three are compared with similar parts of the ten, it is clear that their style is definitely Pauline. Hence, many critics now grant that Paul wrote some but not all of their contents. But this theory does not go far enough in the right direction, for those who hold it are unable to show where the genuine material begins and the spurious ends. The acceptance, in some real sense, of Paul's authorship for the entire contents is the only theory that fits the facts.

C. **Theology.** It is claimed that grace is no longer in the center, and that there is here an overemphasis on good works. The facts contradict this judgment. Is not grace the heart and center of such passages as 1 Timothy 1:14; 2 Timothy 1:9; Titus 2:11–14; 3:5? It is true that in these three letters the fruit (good works) of faith is emphasized, but the reason is that the nature of faith and its necessity over against law-works had been fully set forth in the letters that preceded. The tree is first; then comes the fruit.

D. **Marcionism.** It is said that the Pastorals controvert second-century Marcionism (a heresy with erroneous views of Christ's person), hence they cannot have been written by first-century Paul. The question is asked, "Does not 1 Timothy 6:20 refer to the very title of Marcion's book *Antitheses*?" This is shallow reasoning. Surely a merely verbal coincidence cannot prove any relationship between Marcion and the author of this verse. What the author has in mind is not Marcion's contrast between Christianity and Judaism but the conflicting opinions of those who speculated in Jewish genealogies. Other supposed allusions to second-century -isms are equally farfetched.

E. **Ecclesiastical Organization.** Do not the Pastorals reveal a marked advance in church government, far beyond the time of Paul? Some critics reason that the three letters evidence the beginning of pyramidal organization, where one bishop (1 Tim 3:1–2; Titus 1:7) rules over several presbyters (Titus 1:5). In the Pastorals the terms *bishop* (overseer) and *presbyter* (elder) refer to the same individual, as is proved by 1 Timothy 1:5–7 (cf. 1 Tim 3:1–7; Phil 1:1; 1 Peter 5:1–2). With respect to age and dignity these men were called presbyters; with respect to the nature of their task they were called overseers. From very early times the church had its elders (Acts 11:30; 14:23; cf. 1 Thess 5:12–13). It is also very natural that Paul, about to depart from the earth, should specify certain qualifications for office, so that the church might be guarded against the ravages of error, both doctrinal and moral.

F. **Chronology.** It is maintained that the Book of Acts, which records Paul's life from his conversion to a Roman imprisonment that terminated in the apostle's execution, leaves no room for the Pastorals, which presuppose journeys not recorded in Acts. However, Acts points toward Paul's release, not his execution (Acts 23:12–35; 28:21, 30–31); so do Paul's Prison Letters (Phil 1:25–27; 2:24; Philem 22). Early writers—Clement of Rome, Eusebius—as well as later ones—Chrysostom, Jerome—bear witness to two Roman imprisonments with ample room for the writings of the Pastorals after the first of these two.

As to internal evidence, not only does the writer call himself "Paul, an apostle" (1 Tim 1:1; 2 Tim 1:1), but he also *describes* himself, and this description agrees with that of Paul in Acts. The letter-plan of the three, moreover, is similar to that of the ten. All the evidence, accordingly, favors Paul's authorship of the Pastorals.

II. Background and Purpose.

A. **Common to Timothy and Titus.** Released from his first Roman imprisonment, Paul, perhaps while on his way to Asia Minor, left Titus on the island of Crete to bring to completion the organization of its church(es) (Acts 2:11; Titus 1:5). At Ephesus Paul was joined by Timothy (back from Philippi? cf. Phil 2:19–23). On leaving for Macedonia, Paul instructed Timothy to remain in Ephesus, which was sorely in need of his ministry (1 Tim 1:3–4). From Macedonia Paul wrote a letter to Timothy in Ephesus (1 Tim) and one to Titus in Crete (Titus).

B. **Further Background and Purpose of 1 Timothy.** At Ephesus Judaizers were spreading strange and dangerous doctrines (1:4, 7; 4:7). Both men and women attended worship spiritually unprepared (ch. 2). To cope with that situation there was Timothy—*timid* Timothy. The letter's aim:

1. To impart guidance against error (cf. 1:3–11, 18–20; chs. 4, 6). With this in mind proper organization is stressed: choosing the right kind of leaders (chs. 3, 5).
2. To stress the need of proper preparation and conduct (for both men and women) with respect to public worship (ch. 2).
3. To bolster Timothy's spirit (4:14; 6:12, 20).

C. **Further Background and Purpose of Titus.** The reputation of the Cretans was poor. True sanctification was needed (2:11–14; 3:10). Gospel workers (such as Zenas and Apollos, whose itinerary included Crete and who probably carried with them Paul's letter) had to receive every assistance. As to Paul himself, having recently met Timothy, and the situation in Crete being critical, it is natural that he wished to have a face-to-face conference with Titus also.

Purpose of Paul's letter to Titus:

1. To stress the need of thorough sanctification.
2. To speed on their way Zenas the law-expert and Apollos the evangelist (3:13).
3. To urge Titus to meet Paul at Nicopolis (3:12).

D. **Background and Purpose of 2 Timothy.** Emperor Nero, blamed for Rome's fearful conflagration (July, A.D. 64), in turn blamed Christians, who suffered frightful persecution. Paul was imprisoned (second Roman imprisonment). He faced death (2 Tim 1:16–17; 2:9); Luke alone was with him. Others had left him, either on legitimate missions (Crescens, Titus) or because they had become enamored of the present world (Demas; 4:6–11). Meanwhile, soul-destroying error continued in Timothy's Ephesus (1:8; 2:3, 12, 14–18, 23; 3:8–13). The letter's purpose was, accordingly:

1. To urge Timothy to come to Rome as soon as possible in view of the apostle's impending departure from this life, and to bring Mark with him, as well as Paul's cloak and books (2 Tim 4:6–22).
2. To admonish Timothy to cling to sound doctrine, defending it against all error (2 Tim 2; 4:1–5).

III. Contents.

1 Timothy

Theme: The apostle Paul, writing to Timothy,

gives directions for the administration of the church.

Chapter 1

Paul salutes Timothy and repeats his order that Timothy remain at Ephesus to combat the error of those who refuse to see their own sinful condition in the light of God's holy law, while pretending to be law experts. By contrast, Paul thanks God for having made him, who regards himself as "chief of sinners," a minister of the gospel.

Chapter 2

Paul gives directions with respect to public worship. Prayers must be made in behalf of all men. Both the men and the women must come spiritually prepared.

Chapter 3

The apostle gives directions with respect to the offices and functions in the church.

Chapter 4

He warns against apostasy and instructs Timothy how to deal with it.

Chapters 5 and 6

He gives directions with respect to certain definite groups and individuals: old(er) men, young(er) men, old(er) women, young(er) women, etc.

Titus

Theme: The apostle Paul, writing to Titus, gives directions for the promotion of the spirit of sanctification.

Chapter 1

In congregational life. Well-qualified elders must be appointed in every town. Reason: Crete is not lacking in disreputable people who must be sternly rebuked.

Chapter 2

In family and individual life. All classes of individuals who compose the home-circle must conduct themselves so that by their life they adorn their doctrine. Reason: the grace of God has appeared to all for sanctification and joyful expectation of the coming of "our great God and Savior, Jesus Christ."

Chapter 3

In social (i.e., public) life. Believers should be obedient to the authorities and kind to all people. Foolish questions should be shunned and persistently factious people should be rejected. Concluding directions are given with respect to kingdom travelers and believers in general.

2 Timothy

Theme: Sound Doctrine.

Chapter 1

Hold on to it, as did Lois and Eunice, as I (Paul) do, and as did Onesiphorus.

Chapter 2

Teach it. This brings great reward, for the gospel is glorious in its contents. Vain disputes serve no useful purpose.

Chapter 3

Abide in it, knowing that enemies will arise, and that it is based on the sacred writings.

Chapter 4

Preach it, in season, out of season. Remain faithful in view of the fact that I, Paul, am about to set sail.

Bibliography: P. N. Harrison, *The Problem of the Pastoral Epistles,* 1921; E. K. Simpson, *The Pastoral Epistles,* 1954 (on the Greek text); D. Guthrie, *The Pastoral Epistles* (TNTC), 1957; J. N. D. Kelly, *The Pastoral Epistles* (HNTC), 1963; A. T. Hanson, *Studies in the Pastoral Epistles,* 1968; M. Dibelius and H. Conzelmann, *The Pastoral Epistles,* 1972; A. T. Hanson, *The Pastoral Epistles,* 1981; B. Van Elderen, *The Pastoral Epistles* (NIC), 1984. WH

PATARA (păt'à-rȧ, Gr. *Patara*). An ancient seaport of Lycia near the mouth of the Xanthus. Coins date from 440 B.C. There was an old shrine of Apollo situated in the town. Hence the poetic title for the god "Patareus." The trade of the river valley and its position on the Asia Minor coast gave the port its importance. It was convenient for ships running east before the prevailing autumn wind for Phoenicia or Egypt. Paul, for example, made for Tyre in one stage from Patara (Acts 21:1–2).

PATHROS (păth'rŏs, Heb. *pathrôs*). Mentioned twice in the OT—in Ezekiel 29:14; 30:14—in connection with the repatriation of Jewish remnants. The KJV also uses the name in Isaiah 11:11 and Jeremiah 44:1, 15 where NIV has "Upper Egypt." Pathros was Upper Egypt, the Egyptian "Pteres" or "Southland," extending from south of Memphis to the first cataract. The division corresponds to two ancient kingdoms. There is papyrological evidence for settlements of Jews at Syene at the southern extremity of Pathros as early as 525 B.C. The "Pathrusites" of Genesis 10:14 seem to have been the inhabitants of this territory.

PATHRUSITES, PATHRUSIM (Heb. *pathrūsî, an inhabitant of Pathros*). Egyptians who, it is believed, came from Pathros, Egypt (see PATHROS). They are descended from Mizraim (Gen 10:13–14; 1 Chron 1:11–12).

PATIENCE (Gr. *hypomonē* and *makrothymia*). Both of these Greek words are translated by our English word *patience,* but they are not exactly synonymous in meaning. *Hypomonē* is the quality of endurance under trials. Those possessing this virtue are free from cowardice or despondency. It is mainly an attitude of heart with respect to things. *Makrothymia* ("longsuffering") is an attitude with respect to people. Patience is a fruit of the Spirit (Gal 5:22, KJV longsuffering); it is a virtue that God prizes highly in human beings and seems to be best developed under trials (Rom 5:3–4; James 1:3–4; 5:11 KJV; NIV perseverance). Both terms are used of God (Rom 2:4; 1 Peter 3:20), apparently always in relation to persons. See also LONGSUFFERING.

PATMOS (Gr. *Patmos*). A tiny wind-swept island of the Sporades group, lying off the coast of Asia Minor in the Aegean Sea about twenty-eight miles (forty-seven km.) south of Samos. It is only ten miles (seventeen km.) long and six miles (ten km.) wide at the broadest point, and its coastline is so irregular that it is only twenty-five square miles (sixty-four sq. km.) in area. Being of volcanic origin, it is rocky and almost treeless, with many volcanic hills rising as high as 800 feet (250 m.). The harbor of Scala, the chief city, divides the islet, which is shaped like a horse's head, into two parts.

Few people would know of the island if it were not mentioned in the Bible. It was one of the many isolated places to which the Romans banished their exiles, and according to tradition the Emperor Domitian banished the apostle John to this lonely place from Ephesus in A.D. 95 (Rev 1:9). During the estimated eighteen months spent there, he received the visions of the Lord now recorded in the Book of Revelation. The cave or grotto near Scala in which John lived is still pointed out to travelers, as well as the Monastery of St. John above the city. During the Middle Ages the island was all but deserted, but today it has a population of a little over two thousand. It was under Turkish rule until 1912, when it passed into the hands of the Italians. It was ceded to Greece in 1947. LMP

PATRIARCH (Gr. *patriarchēs, the father of a family, tribe,* or *race*). A title given in the NT to those who founded the Hebrew race and nation. In the NT it is applied to Abraham (Heb 7:4), the sons of Jacob (Acts 7:8–9), and David (2:29). The term is now commonly used to refer to the persons whose names appear in the genealogies and covenant histories before the time of Moses (Gen 5 and 11, histories of Noah, Abraham, Isaac, Jacob, et al.). In the patriarchal system the government of a clan was the right of the oldest lineal male. The patriarchal head was the priest of his own household.

While past scholars have often tended to regard the biblical accounts in the patriarchal dispensation as legendary, recent archaeological discoveries have confirmed the truthfulness of the narratives and have thrown much light on puzzling customs of the time, such as Abraham's taking Sarah's slave Hagar as a concubine, his making his steward Eliezer his heir, and Rachel's carrying away her father's household gods. Excavations at Ur, where Abraham lived, reveal it to have been a rich commercial center, whose inhabitants were people of education and culture.

See also ABRAHAM; ISAAC; JACOB; JOSEPH.

PATROBAS (păt′rō-bȧs, Gr. *Patrobas*). A Roman Christian to whom Paul sent greetings (Rom 16:14).

PAU (pā′ū, Heb. *pāʿû, bleating*). The capital city of King Hadar of Edom (Gen 36:39). Also called Pai (1 Chron 1:50 most versions; Pau NIV), it remains unidentified.

PAUL (Gr. *Paulos,* from Latin *Paulis, little*). The great apostle to the Gentiles. The main biblical source for information on the life of Paul is the Acts of the Apostles, with important supplemental information from Paul's own letters. Allusions in the letters make it clear that many events in his checkered and stirring career are unrecorded (cf. 2 Cor 11:24–28).

I. Names. His Hebrew name was Saul (Gr. *Saulos*) and he is always so designated in Acts until his clash with Bar-Jesus at Paphos, where Luke writes, "Then Saul, who was also called Paul . . ." (Acts 13:9). Thereafter in Acts he is always called Paul. In his letters the apostle always calls himself Paul. As a Roman citizen he doubtless bore both names from his youth. His double name is implied in Luke's statement "Saul, the one also Paul" (*Saulos ho kai Paulos*). It was a common practice among Jews of the Dispersion. The change to the use of the Greek name was peculiarly appropriate when he began his position of leadership in bringing the gospel to the Gentile world.

II. Background. Providentially, three elements of the world's life of that day—Greek culture, Roman citizenship, and Hebrew religion—met in the apostle to the Gentiles. Paul was born near the beginning of the first century in the busy Greco-Roman city of Tarsus, located at the NE corner of the Mediterranean Sea. A noted trading center, it was known for its manufacture of goats' hair cloth, and here the young Saul learned his trade of tentmaking (Acts 18:3). Tarsus had a famous university; although there is no evidence that Paul attended it, its influence must have made a definite impact on him, enabling him to better understand prevailing life and views in the Roman Empire. He had the further privilege of being born a Roman citizen (22:28), though how his father had come to possess the coveted status is not known. Proud of the distinction and advantages thus conferred on him, Paul knew how to use that citizenship as a shield against injustice from local magistrates and to enhance the status of the Christian faith. His Gentile connections greatly aided him in bridging the chasm between the Gentile and the Jew. But of central significance was his strong Jewish heritage, which was fundamental to all he was and became. He was never ashamed to acknowledge himself a Jew (21:39; 22:3), was justly proud of his Jewish background (2 Cor 11:22), and retained a deep and abiding love for his brethren according to the flesh (Rom 9:1–2; 10:1). Becoming a Christian meant no conscious departure on his part from the religious hopes of his people as embodied in the OT Scriptures (Acts 24:14–16; 26:6–7). This racial affinity with the Jews enabled Paul with great profit to begin his missionary labors in each city in the synagogue, for there he had the best-prepared audience.

Born of purest Jewish blood (Phil 3:5), the son of a Pharisee (Acts 23:6), Saul was cradled in orthodox Judaism. At the proper age, perhaps thirteen, he was sent to Jerusalem and completed his studies under the famous Gamaliel (22:3; 26:4–5). Being a superior, zealous student (Gal 1:14), he absorbed not only the teaching of the OT but also the rabbinical learning of the scholars.

At his first appearance in Acts as "a young man" (Acts 7:58), probably at least thirty years old, he was already an acknowledged leader in Judaism. His active opposition to Christianity marked him as the natural leader of the persecution that arose after the death of Stephen (7:58–8:3; 9:1–2). The persecutions described in 26:10–11 indicate his fanatical devotion to Judaism. He was convinced that Christians were heretics and that the honor of the Lord demanded their extermination (26:9). He acted in confirmed unbelief (1 Tim 1:13).

III. Conversion. The persecution was doubtless repugnant to his finer inner sensitivities, but Saul did not doubt the rightness of his course. The spread of Christians to foreign cities only increased his fury against them, causing him to extend the scope of his activities. As he approached Damascus, armed with authority from the high priest, the transforming crisis in his life occurred. Only an acknowledgment of divine intervention can explain it. Repeatedly in his letters Paul refers to it as the work of divine grace and power, transforming him and commissioning him as Christ's messenger (1 Cor 9:16–17; 15:10; Gal 1:15–16; Eph 3:7–9; 1 Tim 1:12–16). The three accounts in Acts of the conversion vary according to the immediate purpose of the narrator and supplement each other. Luke's own account (Acts 9) is historical, relating the event objectively, while the two accounts by Paul (Acts 22, 26) stress those aspects appropriate to his immediate endeavor.

When the supernatural Being arresting him identified himself as "Jesus, whom you are persecuting," Saul at once saw the error of his way and surrendered instantaneously and completely. The three days of fasting in blindness were days of agonizing heart-searching and further dealing with the Lord. The ministry of Ananias of Damascus consummated the conversion experience, unfolded to Saul the divine commission, and opened the door to him to the Christian fellowship at Damascus. Later in reviewing his former life Paul clearly recognized how God had been preparing him for his future work (Gal 1:15–16).

IV. Early Activities. The new convert at once proclaimed the deity and messiahship of Jesus in the Jewish synagogues of Damascus, truths that had seized his soul (Acts 9:20–22). Since the purpose of his coming was no secret, this action caused consternation among the Jews. Paul's visit to Arabia, mentioned in Galatians 1:17, seems best placed between Acts 9:22 and 23. There is no hint that its purpose was to preach; rather it seems that he felt it necessary to retire to rethink his beliefs in the light of the new revelation that had come to him. The length of the stay is not certain, but Paul came out of Arabia with the essentials of his theology fixed.

After returning to Damascus, his aggressive preaching forced him to flee the murderous fury of the Jews (Acts 9:23–25; Gal 1:17; 2 Cor 11:32–33). Three years after his conversion Saul returned to Jerusalem with the intention of becoming acquainted with Peter (Gal 1:18). The Jerusalem believers regarded him with cold suspicion, but with the help of Barnabas became accepted among them (Acts 9:26–28). His bold witness to the Hellenistic Jews aroused bitter hostility and cut the visit to fifteen days (Gal 1:18). Instructed by the Lord in a vision to leave (Acts 22:17–21), he agreed to be sent home to Tarsus (9:30), where he remained in obscurity for some years. Galatians 1:21–23 implies that he did some evangelistic work there, but we have no further details. Some think that many of the events of 2 Corinthians 11:24–26 must be placed here.

After the opening of the door of the gospel to the Gentiles in the house of Cornelius, a Gentile church was soon established in Syrian Antioch. Barnabas, who had been sent to superintend the revival, saw the need for assistance, remembered Saul's commission to the Gentiles, and brought him to Antioch. An aggressive teaching ministry "for a whole year" produced a profound impact on the city, resulting in the designation of the disciples as "Christians" (Acts 11:20–26). Informed by visiting prophets of an impending famine, the Antioch church raised a collection and sent it to the Jerusalem elders by Barnabas and Saul (11:27–30), marking Saul's second visit to Jerusalem since his conversion. Some scholars equate this visit with that of Galatians 2:1–10, but Acts 11–12 reveals no traces as yet of such a serious conflict in the church about circumcision.

V. Missionary Journeys. The work of Gentile foreign missions was inaugurated by the church at Antioch under the direction of the Holy Spirit in the sending forth of "Barnabas and Saul" (Acts 13:1–3).

The first missionary journey, begun apparently in the spring of A.D. 48, began with work among the Jews on Cyprus. Efforts at Paphos to gain the attention of the proconsul Sergius Paulus encountered the determined opposition of the sorcerer Elymas. Saul publicly exposed Elymas's diabolical character, and the swift judgment that fell on Elymas caused the amazed proconsul to believe (13:4–12). It was a signal victory of the gospel.

After the events at Paphos, Saul, henceforth called Paul in Acts, emerged as the recognized leader of the missionary party. Steps to carry the gospel to new regions were taken when the party sailed to Perga in Pamphylia on the southern shores of Asia Minor. Here their attendant, John Mark, cousin of Barnabas (Col 4:10), deserted them and returned to Jerusalem, an act that Paul regarded as unjustified. Arriving at Pisidian Antioch, located in the province of Galatia, the missionaries found a ready opening in the Jewish synagogue. Paul's address to an audience composed of Jews and God-fearing Gentiles, his first recorded address in Acts, is reported at length by Luke as representative of his synagogue ministry (Acts 13:16–41). The message made a deep impression, and the people requested that he preach again the next Sabbath. The large crowd, mainly of Gentiles, who flocked to the synagogue the following Sabbath aroused the jealousy and fierce opposition of the Jewish leaders. In consequence Paul announced a turning to the Gentiles with their message. Gentiles formed the core of the church established in Pisidian Antioch (13:42–52). Jewish-inspired opposition forced the missionaries to depart for Iconium, SE of Antioch, where the results were duplicated and a flourishing church begun. Compelled to flee a threatened stoning at Iconium, the missionaries crossed into the ethnographic territory of Lycaonia, still within the province of Galatia, and began work at Lystra, which was apparently without a synagogue. The healing of a congenital cripple caused a pagan attempt to offer sacrifices to the missionaries as gods in human form. Paul's horrified protest (14:15–17), arresting the attempt, reveals his dealings with pagans who did not have the OT revelation. Timothy apparently was converted at this time. Fanatical agitators from Antioch and Iconium turned the disillusioned pagans against the missionaries, and in the uproar Paul was stoned. Dragged out of the city, the unconscious apostle was left for dead, but as the disciples stood around him, he regained consciousness, and reentered the city. The next day he was able to go on to neighboring Derbe. After a fruitful and unmolested ministry there, the missionaries retraced their steps to instruct their converts and organize them into churches with responsible leaders (14:1–23). They returned to Syrian Antioch and reported how God "had opened the door of faith to the Gentiles" (14:27). That is a summary of Paul's message to the Gentiles: salvation is solely through faith in Christ.

The Jerusalem Conference (Acts 15; Gal 2:1–10) arose out of the tension produced by the mass influx of Gentiles into the church. This movement evoked the anxiety and opposition of the Pharisaic party in the church. Certain men from Judea came to Antioch and taught the brothers that unless they received circumcision they could not be saved. This demand, contrary to Paul's doctrine of justification by faith, aroused sharp controversy and resulted in the sending of Paul, Barnabas, and certain others to Jerusalem concerning this matter.

Although some scholars reject the identification, it seems best to equate Galatians 2:1–10 with Acts 15. The differences are due to the differing standpoint of the two writers, Luke's account being historical, whereas Paul's was personal. In Acts there are apparently two public sessions, 15:4 and 5–6, while Paul speaks of a private meeting with the Jerusalem leaders. After ample discussion of the problem, the conference repudiated the view of the Judaizers and refused to impose the law on Gentile believers, only requesting them to abstain from specific offensive practices. The decision was formulated in a letter and was sent to Antioch through Judas and Silas as official delegates.

Their position vindicated, Paul and Barnabas continued their ministry at Antioch. Apparently during this time the incident of Galatians 2:11–21 occurred. The Jerusalem conference left unmentioned the problem of the relation of Jewish believers to the law. As represented by James, Judaic Christians continued to observe the Mosaic Law, not for salvation, but as a way of life, because they were *Jewish* believers. Peter's withdrawal from table fellowship with Gentiles, lest he offend those of the circumcision, led him into inconsistency, which Paul recognized as undermining the status of the Gentile believer.

For the second missionary journey Paul and Barnabas separated because of their "sharp disagreement" concerning John Mark. Barnabas sailed to Cyprus with Mark, while Paul chose Silas and revisited the churches in Galatia (Acts 15:36–41). At Lystra Paul added young Timothy to the missionary party, having circumcised him to make him acceptable for work among the Jews. Negative leadings closed the door to missionary work in Asia and Bithynia, but at Troas Paul received the positive call to Macedonia (16:1–9). The use of "we" (16:10) reveals Luke's presence with the group that sailed for Macedonia. The accounts of Lydia's conversion, the deliverance of the demon-possessed slave girl, the subtle charges against and imprisonment of Paul and Silas, and the startling events that followed (16:11–40) are so vivid they must be the work of an eyewitness. Paul's demands of the magistrates the next morning established the dignity of the preachers and safeguarded the status of the young church.

Leaving Luke at Philippi, the missionaries next began an expository ministry in the synagogue at Thessalonica. With the synagogue soon closed to him, Paul apparently carried on a successful Gentile ministry there. A Jewish-instigated riot forced the missionaries to flee to Berea, where a fruitful ministry resulted among the "noble" Bereans. When the work there was interrupted by agitators from Thessalonica, Silas and Timothy remained, but Paul, the leader of the work, was brought to Athens by some brothers (17:1–15). From 1 Thessalonians 3:1–2 it appears that Timothy and Silas came to Athens as requested; Timothy was sent back to Thessalonica, and Silas apparently went back to Philippi (Phil 4:15; 2 Cor 11:9).

Distressed by the Athenian idolatry, Paul preached in the synagogue and daily in the marketplace. Drawing the attention of the Athenian philosophers, he was requested to give a formal exposition of his teaching. His appearance at the Areopagus was not a formal trial. His memorable speech before the pagan philosophers (Acts 17:22–31) is a masterpiece of tact, insight, and condensation; but the people's contemptuous interruption at the mention of the Resurrection kept him from elaborating the essentials of the gospel. A few converts were made, but Paul regarded the mission at cultured, philosophical, sophisticated Athens with keen disappointment.

By contrast, the work at Corinth—a city of commerce, wealth, squalor, and gross immorality—proved to be a definite success, lasting eighteen months (Acts 18:1–17). After finding employment at his trade with Aquila and Priscilla, recently expelled from Rome, Paul preached in the Corinthian synagogue. Apparently he was depressed from his experience at Athens, but the coming of Silas and Timothy lifted his spirits and a vigorous witness was begun (18:5). Timothy's report concerning the Thessalonians caused the writing of 1 Thessalonians. A few months later, because of further information about them, 2 Thessalonians was written. Unable to return to Thessalonica, Paul wrote both letters to meet the needs of his converts. Some would also place the writing of Galatians at Corinth, but Galatians is capable of a wide range of dating within the Acts framework. A successful work among the Gentiles resulted in the formation of a large church, the majority of the members being from the lower levels of society (1 Cor 1:26). With the arrival of the new proconsul, Gallio, perhaps in May A.D. 52, the Jews accused Paul of teaching an illegal religion, but the governor, declaring a religious controversy outside his jurisdiction, refused to judge the matter. His action in effect gave tacit governmental recognition to Christianity.

When he left Corinth, Paul took Aquila and Priscilla with him as far as Ephesus, intending on his return to continue the profitable partnership with them there. Refusing an invitation for further ministry in the Ephesian synagogue, Paul hurried to Judea. He apparently visited Jerusalem and then spent some time at Antioch (Acts 18:18–22).

Paul's departure from Antioch traditionally marks the beginning of the third missionary journey. It is convenient to retain the traditional designation, but we should remember that with the second journey Antioch ceased to be the center for Paul's activities.

Having strengthened the disciples in "the region of Galatia and Phrygia," Paul commenced a fruitful ministry at Ephesus that lasted nearly three years (Acts 19:1–41; 20:31). His work at Ephesus, one of the most influential cities of the east, placed Paul at the heart of Greco-Roman civilization. After three months of work in the synagogue, Paul launched an independent Gentile work, centering his daily preaching in the school of Tyrannus for a two-year period. The Ephesian ministry was marked by systematic teaching (20:18–21), extraordinary miracles (19:11–12), a signal victory over the magical arts (19:13–19), and devastating inroads on the worship of Diana (19:23–27). Streams of people came to Ephesus for purposes of commerce, religion, or pleasure. Many of them came into contact with the gospel, were converted, and spread the message throughout the province (19:10). But the work was marked by constant and fierce opposition (20:19; 1 Cor 15:32). The financially prompted riot led by Demetrius brought the work of Paul at Ephesus to a close (Acts 19:23–20:1).

At Ephesus Paul had inaugurated a collection among the Gentile churches for the saints in Judea (1 Cor 16:1–4). Since its delivery was to mark the close of his work in the east, Paul was making plans to visit Rome (Acts 19:21), intending to go from there to Spain (Rom 15:22–29).

While at Ephesus Paul experienced anxieties because of difficulties in the Corinthian church. In a letter, now lost (1 Cor 5:9), he counseled them about their relations to pagan society. Perhaps he also made a brief visit to Corinth (2 Cor 12:14). The arrival of a delegation from Corinth with a letter from the church was the immediate occasion for the writing of 1 Corinthians (1 Cor 16:17–18; 7:1), in which Paul dealt with the evils plaguing that church. Titus was sent to Corinth with plans for him to come to Paul at Troas. Paul found an open door at Troas, but anxiety because of the continued absence of Titus caused him to leave for Macedonia. The report of Titus, whom he met in Macedonia, relieved Paul's anxiety, and it was the immediate occasion for his writing of 2 Corinthians (2 Cor 2:12–13; 7:5–16), which he sent back to Corinth with Titus (8:6, 16–18). After speaking "many words of encouragement" in Macedonia, Paul spent the three winter months in Corinth (Acts 20:2–3), where he wrote the Letter to the Romans to prepare them for his coming visit and to secure their support for his contemplated work in Spain (Rom 15:22–29; 16:1, 23).

Paul's plan to take the collection to Jerusalem directly from Corinth was canceled because of a plot on his life; instead he went by way of Macedonia, leaving Philippi with Luke after the Passover (Acts 20:3–6). Their church-elected travel companions waited for them at Troas, where they spent a busy and eventful night (20:7–12). Hoping to reach Jerusalem for Pentecost, Paul called the Ephesian elders to meet him at Miletus. His farewell to them is marked by tender memories, earnest instructions, and searching premonitions concerning the future (20:17–35). The journey to Jerusalem was marked by repeated warnings to Paul of what awaited him there (21:1–16). Some interpreters hold that Paul blundered in persisting on going to Jerusalem in the face of these clear warnings, thus cutting short his missionary labors. Paul apparently interpreted the warnings not as prohibitions but as tests of his willingness to suffer for the cause of his Lord and the church.

VI. Paul the Prisoner. Although cordially received at Jerusalem by James and the elders, Paul's presence created tension in the church because of reports that he taught Jews in the Dispersion to forsake Moses. To neutralize these reports, the elders suggested to Paul a plan to prove that he had no aversion to a voluntary keeping of the law (Acts 21:17–25). Always anxious to avoid offense, Paul agreed to their proposal. The act of conciliation apparently satisfied the Judean believers, but it caused Paul's arrest. Certain Jews from Asia, seeing him in the temple, created a tumult by falsely charging him with defiling the temple. Rescued from death at the hands of the Jewish mob by the Roman commander and some soldiers, Paul secured permission to address the Jews from the steps of the barracks. They gave silent attention until he mentioned his commission to the Gentiles, when the riot broke out anew (21:37–22:29). A scourging, ordered to force information out of him, was avoided by Paul's mention of his Roman citizenship. The commander's efforts the next day before the Sanhedrin to gain further information about Paul proved futile. That night the Lord appeared to the discouraged apostle, commended his efforts at witnessing, and assured him that he would go to Rome. Informed of a plot to murder Paul, the commander sent Paul to Caesarea under a large protective guard (23:17–35).

The trial before Felix at Caesarea made it clear to the governor that the charges against Paul were spurious, but, unwilling to antagonize the Jews, he simply postponed a decision. Asked to expound the Christian faith before Felix and his Jewish wife Drusilla, Paul courageously probed their consciences by preaching "on righteousness, self-control and the judgment to come." Terrified, Felix dismissed the preacher but later sent for him frequently, hoping Paul would try to use bribery to secure his release. After two years Felix was summoned to Rome and left Paul an uncondemned prisoner (Acts 24:1–27).

With the coming of the new governor, Festus, the Jewish leaders renewed their efforts to have Paul condemned. When it became clear to Paul that he could not expect justice from the new governor, he used his right as a Roman citizen and appealed his case to Caesar, thereby removing it from the jurisdiction of the lower courts (Acts 25:1–12). When Herod Agrippa II and his sister Bernice came to visit the new governor, Festus discussed Paul's case with Agrippa, an acknowledged expert in Jewish affairs. The next day before his royal audience Paul delivered a masterly exposition of his position and used the occasion to seek to win Agrippa to Christ. Uncomfortable under Paul's efforts, Agrippa terminated the meeting but frankly declared Paul's innocence to the governor (25:13–26:32).

Paul was sent to Rome, perhaps in the autumn of A.D. 60, under the escort of a centurion named Julius. Luke and Aristarchus accompanied him. Luke's detailed account of the voyage has the minuteness, picturesqueness, and accuracy of an alert eyewitness. Adverse weather delayed the progress of the ship. At Myra they transferred to an Alexandrian grain ship bound for Italy. Futile efforts to reach commodious winter quarters at Phoenix caused the ship to be caught in a hurricane-force storm for fourteen days, ending in shipwreck on the island of Malta. After spending three months on Malta, the travelers journeyed to Rome in another Alexandrian grain ship. Paul's treatment in Rome was lenient; he lived in his own hired house with a soldier guarding him. Permitted to receive all who came, he was able to exercise an important ministry in Rome (Acts 27-28). The Prison Letters—Colossians, Philemon, Ephesians, and Philippians—are lasting fruit of this period, which afforded him opportunity to meditate and to write.

VII. Closing Years. Acts leaves the question of Paul's release unanswered, but there is strong evidence for believing that he was released at the end of two years. The amicable attitude of the Roman government in Acts favors it, the Prison Letters expect it, the Pastoral Letters demand it, and tradition asserts it. Paul's subsequent activities must be inferred from scant references in the Pastorals. From their contents it seems clear that 1 Timothy and Titus were written before the outbreak of the persecution under Nero. After his release, perhaps in the spring of A.D. 63, Paul went east, visited Ephesus, stationing Timothy there when he left for Macedonia (1 Tim 1:3). He left Titus to complete the missionary work on Crete, and in writing to him mentions plans to spend the winter at Nicopolis (Titus 1:5; 3:12). From Nicopolis he may have made the traditional visit to Spain, working there at the outbreak of the persecution by Nero in the autumn of 64. Second Timothy makes it clear that Paul is again a prisoner in Rome, kept in close confinement as a malefactor (2 Timothy 1:16–17; 2:9). At his first appearance before the court he escaped immediate condemnation (4:16–18), but to Timothy he writes of no hope for release (4:6–8). He was executed at Rome in late 66 or early 67. Tradition says he was beheaded on the Ostian Way.

VIII. Achievement and Character. Paul's achievements proclaim him an unexcelled missionary statesman. His labors firmly planted churches in the strategic centers of Galatia, Asia, Macedonia, and Achaia, while his plans for work at Rome and in Spain reveal his imperial missionary strategy. His foresight led him to select and train strong young workers to carry on the work after him. Paul was supremely the interpreter of the gospel of Jesus Christ, interpreted to the Gentile world through his labors and letters. It was primarily through his work that the worldwide destiny of Christianity was established and liberated from the yoke of legalism. His letters to various churches—formulating, interpreting, and applying the essence of Christianity—are vital to Christian theology and practice. His theology was rooted in his own revolutionary experience in Christ. Paul saw the human race's inability to attain to righteousness through their own efforts, but realized that God had provided a way of salvation, wholly out of grace and love, in Christ Jesus, available through faith alone. He also saw that the gospel made strenuous ethical demands on the life and conduct of the believer. The essence of the Christian life for Paul was union with Christ, whom he loved and served and for whose imminent return he yearned.

Physically, Paul did not present an imposing appearance, as is evident from 2 Corinthians 10:10. Tradition pictures him as small of stature, having a decidedly Jewish physiognomy. That he had a rugged physical constitution seems plain from all the hardships and sufferings he underwent (2 Cor 11:23–27) and from his ability, amid his spiritual anxieties, to earn his own living through manual labor. He endured more than most men could endure, yet he keenly felt the frailty of his body. He was especially afflicted by "a thorn in [his] flesh" (12:7). The exact nature of the affliction can only be conjectured; attempts at identification have varied widely. Whatever its precise nature, his feelings of weakness made him constantly dependent on divine empowerment (2 Cor 12:10; Phil 4:12–13).

The many-sided personality of Paul is difficult to gather into one picture. He seems to embody polar extremes: bodily weakness and tremendous power, a keen intellect and profound mysticism, strongly attracting and furiously repelling people. Intellectually he was a man of outstanding ability, one of the world's great thinkers. He grasped truth at its full value and logically worked out its implications. But his subtlety of intellect was combined with practical good sense. He was a man of strict integrity, ever careful to maintain a good conscience. His life was characterized by a love of the truth that allowed no temporizing for the sake of expediency. Having understood his duty, he followed it unflinchingly, undeterred by possible consequences to himself. He was characterized by native zeal and ardor, giving himself wholly to his work. He was warm-hearted and affectionate, longing for and making strong friendships. He was humble, sincere, and sympathetic. He was by nature a religious man, and, already as a Jew but much more as a Christian, his faith dominated his life and activities. The secret of his unique career lay in his fervent nature as possessed and empowered by the living Christ.

Bibliography: W. Barclay, *The Mind of St. Paul,* 1958; G. Bornkamm, *Paul,* 1971; F. F. Bruce, *Paul, Apostle of the Heart Set Free,* 1977; J. C. Baker, *Paul the Apostle,* 1980; Michael Grant, *St. Paul,* 1982. DEH

PAULUS, SERGIUS (pô'lŭs, sûr'jĭ-ŭs, Gr. *Paulos Sergios*). When Paul and Barnabas visited Paphos, the capital of Cyprus, on their first missionary journey, they were called before Sergius Paulus, the Roman proconsul, because this man of understanding "wanted to hear the word of God" (Acts 13:6–12). When Elymas, his court magician, attempted to turn him against the gospel, Paul through a miracle struck him with blindness. The incident so affected Sergius Paulus that he "believed, for he was amazed at the teaching about the Lord" (13:12). It is often said that Paul, then known as Saul of Tarsus, took his name from this first Gentile convert, but this may be only coincidence.

PAVEMENT (See GABBATHA)

PAVILION (pȧ-vĭl'yŭn, Heb. *sōkh* in Ps 27:5, *sukkâh* in 31:20, *booth, tent*). Used in KJV to refer to a covered place in which a person may be kept hidden. NIV usually has "dwelling." It is used chiefly to symbolize God's favor and protection provided for his children (18:11). It grows out of the fact that no one has access to the eastern king's inner court or pavilion except those to whom he gives permission.

PEACE (Heb. *shālôm, peace,* Gr. *eirēnē, concord*). The word used in the OT and still found today among Semitic peoples basically means "completeness" or "soundness." It can denote neighborliness (Ps 28:3 KJV) or well-being and security (Eccl 3:8) or the reward of a mind stayed on God (Isa 26:3). It is linked with honest dealing and true justice (Zech 8:16 KJV), and is a prominent feature of the coming Messiah (Isa 9:6).

According to the NT, peace results from God's forgiveness (Phil 4:7) and is the ideal relation with one's brother (2 Cor 13:11; cf. Matt 5:23–24). Peace is a mark of serenity (John 14:27) to be sought after (Heb 12:14), and it summarizes the gospel message (Acts 10:36). It is a fruit of the Spirit (Gal 5:22), will benefit those who practice it both now (James 3:18) and at the Second Coming (Rom 2:10), and is the opposite of disorder or confusion (1 Cor 14:33). Peace is the presence of God, not the absence of conflict. The Christian who knows peace is charged to tell others so that it may come for them, too, through Christ, who brought, preached, and is our peace (Eph 2:14ff.).

PEACE OFFERING (See SACRIFICE AND OFFERINGS)

PEACOCK (See ANIMALS; BIRDS)

PEARL (See MINERALS)

PEDAHEL (pĕd'ȧ-hĕl, Heb. *pedhah'ēl, God delivers*). A prince of Naphtali appointed by Moses to apportion Palestine (Num 34:28).

PEDAHZUR (pē-dȧ'zêr, Heb. *pedhāhtsûr, the rock*). A prince of the tribe of Manasseh, father of Gamaliel whom Moses appointed to aid in numbering the people (Num 1:10; 2:20).

PEDAIAH (pē-dā'yȧ, Heb. *pedhāyāhû, Jehovah redeems*). 1. One from Rumah, father of Zebidah who was Josiah's wife and Jehoiakim's mother (2 Kings 23:36).

2. Father of Zerubbabel, son of Jeconiah (1 Chron 3:18).

3. The father of Joel and ruler of western Manasseh under David (1 Chron 27:20).

4. One from the family of Parosh who aided in repairing the wall of Jerusalem (Neh 3:25).

5. A Benjamite, father of Joed, Kolaiah's son (Neh 11:7).

6. A Levite appointed by Nehemiah as one of the treasurers over the Lord's house (Neh 13:13).

PEG (See PIN)

PEKAH (pē'kȧ, Heb. *peqah, to open*). The son of Remaliah and eighteenth king of Israel. In the fifty-second year of Uzziah, he usurped the throne by murdering his predecessor, Pekahiah. He began to reign about 734 B.C. and reigned twenty years (2 Kings 15:27). Incensed by the weakening of Israel under the leadership before him, caused by internal trouble and the heavy tribute paid to Assyria, he formed a league with the Gileadites to resist the encroachments of Assyria. To strengthen his position further and accomplish his purposes, he allied himself with Rezin of Damascus against Jotham king of Judah (15:37–38). The godly character of Jotham (2 Chron 27) probably delayed the realization of this plot until Jotham's son Ahaz was on the throne. The details of this campaign are recorded in two places in the OT (2 Kings 16; 2 Chron 28). Perhaps the most important thing about this struggle was that it occasioned the important prophecies of Isaiah 7–9. Finally Pekah became subject to the Assyrians (2 Kings 15:29) and a short time later was murdered by Hoshea. His sad epitaph is summarized in 2 Kings 15:28: "He did evil in the eyes of the LORD."

PEKAHIAH (pěk'ȧ-hī'ȧ, Heb. *peqahyâh, Jehovah has opened*). Israel's seventeenth king, the son of Menahem. He was a wicked king, following the practices of idolatry formulated by Jeroboam (2 Kings 15:24). Regarding the date of his reign, there are some problems caused by this phrase in 2 Kings 15:23: "in the fiftieth year of Azariah." By dating the beginning of his reign 735 B.C., most of the date problem dissolves. After a brief reign of only two years, he was brutally murdered by Pekah and the fifty Gileadites associated with him.

PEKOD (pē'kŏd, Heb. *peqôdh, visitation*). A name applied to an Aramean tribe living east of, and near the mouth of, the Tigris River and forming part of the Chaldean Empire in Ezekiel's day (Jer 50:21; Ezek 23:23).

PELAIAH (pē-lā'yȧ, Heb. *pelā'yâh, Jehovah is wonderful*). 1. Elioenai's son from Judah's royal house (1 Chron 3:24).

2. The Levite who aided Ezra in explaining the law (Neh 8:7) and later sealed the covenant with Nehemiah (10:10).

PELALIAH (pěl'ȧ-lī'ȧ, Heb. *pelalyâh, Jehovah has judged*). The priestly father of Jeroham and son of Amzi who was a worker in the Lord's house (Neh 11:12).

PELATIAH (pěl'ȧ-tī'ȧ, Heb. *pelatyâh, Jehovah has delivered*). 1. Hananiah's son who descended from Shealtiel from the family of David (1 Chron 3:21). He was the grandson of Zerubbabel.

2. Ishi's son who headed a Simeonite group that helped rid the area of the Amalekites (1 Chron 4:42) in Hezekiah's reign.

3. One of those who sealed the covenant with Nehemiah (Neh 10:22).

4. One of the princes of the people, son of Benaiah (Ezek 11:1). He along with others plotted evil and gave wicked advice in Jerusalem (11:2). Ezekiel was instructed to prophesy against them, and while he was doing so Pelatiah fell dead (11:13).

PELEG (pē'lěg, Heb. *pelegh, division*). One of the sons of Eber, brother of Joktan and the father of Reu (Gen 10:25; 11:16–19; 1 Chron 1:25). The reason for his being named Peleg is that "in his time the earth was divided." This probably refers to the confounding of the language and the consequent scattering of the descendants of Noah (Gen 11:1–9).

PELET (pē'lět, Heb. *pelet, deliverance*). 1. Jahdai's son (1 Chron 2:47).

2. One of Azmaveth's sons from the tribe of Benjamin. He joined David at Ziklag while David hid from Saul (1 Chron 12:3).

PELETH (pē'lěth, Heb. *peleth, swiftness*). 1. The father of On, from the tribe of Reuben, who became a part of the conspiracy against Moses and Aaron (Num 16:1).

2. A descendant of Jerahmeel through Onan (1 Chron 2:33).

PELETHITES (pěl'ē-thīts, Heb. *pelēthî, courier*). A group who along with the Kerethites formed David's bodyguard (2 Sam 8:18; 20:17; 1 Kings 1:38, 44; 1 Chron 18:17). Perhaps, as the meaning of their name suggests, they were the ones who conveyed the king's messages to distant places.

PELICAN (See BIRDS)

PELONITE (pěl'ō-nīt, Heb. *pelônî, separates*). The title of two of David's mighty men, Helez and Ahijah (1 Chron 11:27, 36). It is thought that this designation originated from their place of birth because of the reference in 1 Chronicles 27:10 that Helez was from Ephraim's tribe.

PELUSIUM (See SIN)

PEN (See WRITING)

PENCE (See MONEY)

PENDANT (See DRESS)

PENIEL (pē-nī'ěl, Heb. *penî 'ēl, face of God*). The place where Jacob wrestled with the angel of God (Gen 32:24–32). The exact location is not known, though it was not far from Succoth and east of the Jordan.

PENINNAH (pē-nĭn'ȧ, Heb. *penninâh, coral*). One of Elkanah's wives. She bore children and taunted Hannah (1 Sam 1:2–7) because Hannah was childless.

PENNY (See MONEY)

PENTATEUCH, THE (pĕn'tà-tūk, Heb. *tôrâh, law or teaching*). The first five books of the Bible: Genesis, Exodus, Leviticus, Numbers, and Deuteronomy. These books, whose canonicity has never been called into question by the Jews, Protestants, or Catholics, head the list of the OT canon. As a literary unit they provide the background for the OT as well as the NT.

Chronologically the Pentateuch covers the period of time from the creation to the end of the Mosaic era. Since the date for the creation of the universe is not given, it is impossible to ascertain the length of this entire era.

Genesis begins with an account of creation but soon narrows its interest to the human race. Adam and Eve were entrusted with the responsibility of caring for the world about them, but forfeited their privilege through disobedience and sin. In subsequent generations all mankind became so wicked that the entire human race, except Noah and his family, was destroyed. When the new civilization degenerated, God chose to fulfill his promises of redemption through Abraham. From Adam to Abraham represents a long period of time, for which the genealogical lists in Genesis 5 and 10 hardly serve as a timetable.

The patriarchal era (Gen 12–50) narrates the events of approximately four generations—namely, those of Abraham, Isaac, Jacob, and Joseph. Scholars generally agree that Abraham lived during the nineteenth or eighteenth century B.C., some dating him a century earlier and some considerably later. The contemporary culture of this period is much better known to us today through recent archaeological discoveries. In A.D. 1933 a French archaeologist, André Parrot, discovered the ruins of Mari, a city located on the Euphrates River. Here he found numerous temples, palaces, and statues and some twenty thousand tablets—all of which reflected the culture of the patriarchal era. Nuzi, a site east of Nineveh, excavated about 1925–41, yielded several thousand documents that likewise provide numerous illustrations of customs that reflect the patriarchal pattern of living as portrayed in the Genesis record.

After the opening verses of Exodus the rest of the Pentateuch is chronologically confined to the lifetime of Moses. Consequently the deliverance of Israel from Egypt and their preparation for entrance into the land of Canaan is the prevailing theme. The historical core of these books is briefly outlined as follows:

Exodus 1–19, from Egypt to Mount Sinai.

Exodus 19–Numbers 10, encampment at Mount Sinai (approximately one year).

Numbers 10–21, wilderness wanderings (approximately thirty-eight years).

Numbers 22–Deuteronomy 34, encampment before Canaan (approximately one year).

The Mosaic Law was given at Mount Sinai. As God's covenant people the Israelites were not to conform to the idolatrous practices of the Egyptians nor to the customs of the Canaanites whose land they were to conquer and possess. Israel's religion was a revealed religion. For nearly a year they were carefully instructed in the Law and the covenant. A tabernacle was erected as the central place for the worship of God. Offerings and sacrifices were instituted to make atonement for their sins and for expression of their gratitude and devotion to God. The Aaronic family, supported by the Levites, was ordained to serve at the tabernacle in the ministration of divine worship. Feasts and seasons likewise were carefully prescribed for the Israelites so that they might worship and serve God as his distinctive people. After the entrance into Canaan was delayed for almost forty years because of the unbelief of the Israelites, Moses reviewed the law for the younger generation. This review, plus timely instructions for the occupation of Palestine, is summarized in the Book of Deuteronomy.

For study purposes the Pentateuch lends itself to the following analysis:

- I. The Era of Beginnings (Gen 1:1–11:32)
  - A. The account of creation (1:1–2:25)
  - B. Man's fall and its consequences (3:1–6:10)
  - C. The Flood: God's judgment on man (6:11–8:19)
  - D. Man's new beginning (8:20–11:32)
- II. The Patriarchal Period (Gen 12:1–50:26)
  - A. The life of Abraham (12:1–25:18)
  - B. Isaac and Jacob (25:19–36:43)
  - C. Joseph (37:1–50:26)
- III. Emancipation of Israel (Exod 1:1–19:2)
  - A. Israel freed from slavery (1:1–13:19)
  - B. From Egypt to Mount Sinai (13:20–19:2)
- IV. The Religion of Israel (Exod 19:3–Lev 27:34)
  - A. God's covenant with Israel (Exod 19:3–24:8)
  - B. The place of worship (24:9–40:38)
  - C. Instructions for holy living (Lev 1:1–27:34)
    1. The offerings (1:1–7:38)
    2. The priesthood (8:1–10:20)
    3. Laws of purification (11:1–15:33)
    4. Day of atonement (16:1–34)
    5. Heathen customs forbidden (17:1–18:30)
    6. Laws of holiness (19:1–22:33)
    7. Feasts and seasons (23:1–25:55)
    8. Conditions of God's blessings (26:1–27:34)
- V. Organization of Israel (Num 1:1–12:10)
  - A. The numbering of Israel (1:1–4:49)
  - B. Camp regulations (5:1–6:21)
  - C. Religious life of Israel (6:22–9:14)
  - D. Provisions for guidance (9:15–10:10)
- VI. Wilderness Wanderings (Num 10:11–22:1)
  - A. From Mount Sinai to Kadesh (10:11–12:16)
  - B. The Kadesh crisis (13:1–14:45)
  - C. The years of wandering (15:1–19:22)

D. From Kadesh to the Plains of Moab (20:1–22:1)

VII. Instructions for Entering Canaan (Num 22:2–36:13)
  A. Preservation of God's chosen people (22:2–25:18)
  B. Preparation for conquest (26:1–33:49)
  C. Anticipation of occupation (33:50–36:13)

VIII. Retrospect and Prospect (Deut 1:1–34:12)
  A. History and its significance (1:1–4:43)
  B. The law and its significance (4:44–28:68)
  C. Final preparation and farewell (29:1–34:12)

The authorship of the Pentateuch has been a major concern of OT scholars for the last two centuries. According to the consensus of scholarship as developed since A.D. 1750, the Pentateuch was composed of four major documents, which actually reflected the historical conditions between Davidic and exilic times. These documents were then combined into one literary unit about 400 B.C. or even later. This is called the Graf-Wellhausen theory. It originated in the observation that Exodus 6:2–3 appears to teach that the divine name, Yahweh, was not revealed until the time of Moses, whereas the Book of Genesis as we have it allows the knowledge of the name from Genesis 4:26 onward. Since it is unreasonable that a single author would use the name virtually from the start and then say that it was not known until much later, it became fashionable to divide sections Genesis and Exodus into originally separate documents depending on whether the divine name was used or not. This process of sifting out original documents was then extended to the rest of the Pentateuch. In its classical form the Graf-Wellhausen theory held to four basic documents, for convenience named J (a document using the divine name Yahweh), E (a document using Elohim to refer to God), P (a document specializing in priestly material, genealogies, sacrifices, etc.), and D (the Book of Deuteronomy). Of these, J and E were the earliest (900 onward), D was the product of the reform of Josiah (650 onward), and P was postexilic (400 onward). This theory has been modified in specialist circles by the pressures of archaeology, which has shown that there is no need to count as late in time even the most advanced theological ideas (such as monotheism or God the Creator) found in the Pentateuch; and now it is more fashionable to think of streams of tradition, many of them reaching back to Mosaic times.

The Pentateuch itself, from Exodus to Deuteronomy, registers a pervasive claim to be Mosaic, not necessarily in that Moses wrote every word of it, but in the sense that by far most of the material claims to come directly from Moses, however it was written down. Like all leaders of the ancient world, Moses must have had his own secretary, and it would be taken for granted that written records would be kept. Moses was himself a highly educated man, brought up in the most advanced and sophisticated society of his day. For the interpretation of Exodus 6:2–3, from which the Graf-Wellhausen theory developed, see JEHOVAH.

The Book of Genesis, unlike Exodus-Deuteronomy, registers no authorship claim, though it should be considered a reasonable understanding of the evidence that whoever is responsible for Exodus onward is also responsible for Genesis. Genesis gives evidence of quoting source documents, and Moses would have been better placed than anyone else to have access to the archives of his people.

Bibliography: O. T. Allis, *The Five Books of Moses,* 1943; G. C. Aalders, *A Short Introduction to the Pentateuch,* 1949; E. J. Young, *Introduction to the Old Testament,* 1949, pp. 47–153; J. A. Motyer, *The Revelation of the Divine Name,* 1959; M. H. Segal, *The Pentateuch,* 1967; R. K. Harrison, *Introduction to the Old Testament,* 1970, pp. 19–82, 495–541; J. W. Wenham, "Moses and the Pentateuch," NBC rev., 1970, pp. 41–43.

SJS and JAM

PENTECOST (pĕn'tĕ-kŏst, Gr. *pentēcostē*). The word derives from the Greek for "the fiftieth day." It was the Jewish Feast of Weeks (Exod 34:22; Deut 16:9–11), variously called the Feast of Harvest (Exod 23:16) or the Day of Firstfruits (Num 28:26), which fell on the fiftieth day after the Feast of the Passover. The exact method by which the date was computed is a matter of some controversy.

Originally, the festival was the time when, with appropriate ritual and ceremony, the firstfruits of the corn harvest, the last Palestinian crop to ripen, were formally dedicated. The festival cannot therefore have antedated the settlement in Palestine. Leviticus 23 prescribes the sacred nature of the holiday and lists the appropriate sacrifices. Numbers 28 appears to be a supplementary list, prescribing offerings apart from those connected with the preservation of the ritual loaves. In later Jewish times, the feast developed into a commemoration of the giving of the Mosaic Law. To reinforce this function, the rabbis taught that the Law was given fifty days after the Exodus, a tradition of which there is no trace in the OT nor in the Jewish authorities, Philo and Josephus. It was the events of Acts 2 that transformed the Jewish festival into a Christian one. Some have seen a symbolic connection between the first fruits of the ancient festival and the firstfruits of the Christian dispensation. "Whitsunday" is therefore the fiftieth day after Easter Sunday. The name derives from the wearing of white garments by those seeking baptism at this festival, a practice of very ancient origin.

Of the events of Pentecost recorded in Acts 2, we must consider the "gift of tongues," for the claim to such a supernatural manifestation became, in the early decades of the twentieth century, the most characteristic mark of religious groups that may be generally termed "Pentecostal." The nature of the "tongues" (Acts 2:4) is difficult to determine. The following points must be taken into account. First, those listed in Acts 2:9–11 were Jewish pilgrims from the synagogues of the Dispersion among the peoples named. They would all readily understand the two tongues of Palestine—Aramaic and Greek. The few foreign proselytes, who were no doubt of their number, would also be conversant with Greek, if not with Aramaic. No multiple "gift of tongues" in the literal sense of the phrase was therefore necessary; nor, if such an endowment was indeed given, as most commentators imply, did it long endure. Paul and Barnabas were clearly without knowledge of the tongue of Lystra (Acts 14:11–14), in spite of the fact that Paul says he had "spoken with tongues" after the fashion discussed in 1 Corinthians 12 and 14 (cf. also Acts 10:46 and 19:6). It is generally assumed that the latter manifestation was a species of ecstatic utterance, which Paul tries to tone down, tolerate it though he does as a passing phase because, without specific direction, he hesitates to quench ardent spirits in the church. Commentators vary strikingly. R. B. Rackham (*Acts of the Apostles,* p. 21) holds that Pentecost saw the glossolalia of Corinth, but that it was worship, not proclamation, that formed the subject of the message. Peter alone preached. Rackham admits that according to Acts 2:8 and 11 some of the utterances were clothed in foreign words. In a polyglot world it is to be expected that such emotional and ecstatic speech would contain intrusions of alien vocabulary. F. F. Bruce (*The Acts of the Apostles,* p. 82) regards the phenomenon of Pentecost as a deliverance, under the urge of ecstatic emotion, from the peculiarities of Galilean speech and something different from the Corinthian experience, a purified or exalted utterance that removed dialectical barriers to understanding.

It seems reasonable, therefore, in view of the fact that in a Greek and Aramaic-speaking audience no practical purpose can be seen for a multiple use of languages, to reject the view that unknown tongues were used for the preaching of the new faith at Pentecost. The lack of any need for "interpreters" also makes it difficult to identify the situation in Acts with the one Paul sought to regulate in the Corinthian church. The "tongues" made for clarity; they did not destroy clarity for those who listened with sympathy. EMB

PENUEL (pē-nū'ĕl, Heb. *penî 'ēl, face of God*). 1. Hur's son, the father of Gedor (1 Chron 4:4).

2. One of Shashak's sons (1 Chron 8:25).

PEOR (pē'ôr, Heb. *pe'ôr, opening*). 1. The name given to the mountain in Moab where King Balak led Balaam that he might see and curse Israel (Num 23:28). It was a high peak near the town of Beth Peor opposite the valley in which Israel camped (Deut 3:29).

2. In Numbers 25:18, 31:16, and Joshua 22:17, Peor is used four times as a contraction for Baal Peor.

3. Moses uses the term in two places (Num 25:18; 31:16) to refer to the god of Baal Peor.

PERAEA (See PEREA)

PERATH. The Hebrew name for the Euphrates River (a Greek word). Used in Jeremiah 13:4–7 to refer to the place where Jeremiah was instructed to hide a linen belt. See also EUPHRATES.

PERAZIM, MOUNT (pĕr'à-zĭm, Heb. *har perātsîm, mount of breaches*). Usually identified with Baal Perazim, where David obtained a victory over the Philistines (2 Sam 5:20; 1 Chron 14:11).

PERDITION (pêr-dĭ'shun, Gr. *apōleia, perishing, destruction*). The idea of a loss or destruction predominates in the use of this word. Each of the eight uses of perdition in the KJV (John 17:12; Phil 1:28; 2 Thess 2:3; 1 Tim 6:9; Heb 10:39; 2 Peter 3:7; Rev 17:8, 11; NIV destruction, destroyed; RSV perdition, destruction [each four times]) refers to the final state of the wicked. In popular usage this word is a synonym for hell (eternal punishment).

PERDITION, SON OF (Gr. *huios tēs apōleias*). A phrase used to designate two men in the NT. Christ uses it in referring to Judas Iscariot (John 17:12 KJV, NASB, RSV; NIV one doomed to destruction). Paul uses it in 2 Thessalonians 2:3, applying it to the "man of lawlessness" (the Antichrist). The phrase comes from the Hebrew custom of of noting a certain trait or characteristic in a person and then referring to him as the son of that trait. The term therefore would designate these two men as being the complete devotees of all that "perdition" signified.

PEREA (pĕ-rē'à, Gr. *Peraia, Peraios, Peraites*). A word that does not occur in the Bible but was used by Josephus and others to designate the small territory on the east side of the Jordan opposite old Judea and Samaria; known in the Gospels as the land "beyond the Jordan." For example, the words in Matthew 4:25 *apo tēs Galilaias kai . . . Ioudaias kai peran tou Iordanou* should be understood as "from Galilee and Judea *and Perea,"* and is so listed on Bible maps (cf. Matt 4:15; Mark 3:7–8). The curious statement in Matthew 19:1 that says that Jesus "left Galilee" and came into "the region of Judea to the other side of the Jordan," must mean that Jesus went from Galilee to Judea by way of Perea, the usual road the Jews took in order to avoid going through Samaria.

In the days of Jesus, Herod Antipas ruled the unfertile desert country together with Galilee; but after the Herods, at the time the Gospels were written, Perea belonged to the larger province of Judea. It stretched from Pella in the north to Machaerus in the south. In the days of the Maccabees it was inhabited chiefly by Gentiles, but at the time of Christ it had a heavy Jewish population. Gadara may have been the capital. John baptized in Bethabara "on the other side of

Jordan," or in Perea (John 1:28). Jesus did much of his teaching in Perea (Mark 10:1–33) and made his final journey to Jerusalem from there (John 10:40; 11:54). Today it is part of the modern kingdom of Jordan with the capital at Amman.

PERES (pē'rĕs, Aram. *peras, to split*). A word in Daniel's interpretation of what was written by the hand on the wall for Belshazzar (Dan 5:28). It is the singular of *upharsin* (Dan 5:25 KJV, MLB, NASB, NEB; *parsin* NIV, RSV). See MENE, MENE, TEKEL, PARSIN.

PERESH (pē'rĕsh, Heb. *peresh, dung*). Makir's son by his concubine (1 Chron 7:16).

PEREZ (pē'rĕz, Heb. *perets, pherets, breach*; Gr. *phares*). Twin son of Judah (Gen 38:29), often called *Pherez* (e.g., 1 Chron 2:4, 5; *Pharez* KJV 10 of 13 times), three times called *Phares* (KJV Matt 1:3; Luke 3:33).

PEREZ UZZAH (pē'rez ŭz'ȧ, Heb. *perets-'uzâh, the breach of Uzzah*). Uzzah was one who accompanied the ark on its journey from Kiriath Jearim. When the oxen stumbled, Uzzah, contrary to the command of God, took hold of the ark and died immediately. David, therefore, named the spot Perez Uzzah (2 Sam 6:8; 1 Chron 13:11). It is perhaps to be identified with Khirbet el-Uz, "the ruins of Uzzah," located a short distance from Kiriath Jearim.

PERFECTION, PERFECT (Heb. *shālēm, tāmîm*, Gr. *teleios, teleiotēs*). In the Bible, God alone, who lacks nothing in terms of goodness or excellence, is presented as truly perfect. Everything he is, thinks, and does has the character of perfection (Deut 32:4; 2 Sam 22:31; Job 37:16; Ps 18:30; 19:7; Matt 5:48). When human beings are called perfect in the OT, it means that they are "upright" or "blameless" (Gen 6:9; Job 1:1; Ps 37:37). Sacrificial animals were deemed perfect if they were without spot or blemish and thus wholesome or sound (Lev 3:1, 6; 4:3; 14:10).

The Greek *teleios* conveys the idea of reaching the point of full growth or maturity. This meaning is intended in 1 Corinthians 14:20 and Hebrews 5:14 where there is a contrast between immaturity and maturity; but it is also present in 1 Corinthians 2:6; 14:20; Ephesians 4:13; Philippians 3:15; Colossians 1:28; 4:12. The word of Jesus in Matthew 5:48 concerning the perfection of God and the perfection of the disciple of the kingdom suggests that there is a perfection appropriate to God (who is eternal) and to a disciple (who is a fallen creature in the process of being saved). The latter perfection is the highest possible maturity within the conditions of fallenness and finitude.

The theme of perfection is found in the letter to the Hebrews. Here Christ is presented as perfected (totally prepared and fitted for his priestly ministry in heaven) through suffering (Heb 2:10) and then as perfect (in his divine and human natures, 7:28) as he sits at the right hand of the Father in the perfect heavenly sanctuary (9:11). By his unique sacrifice for sin he has made perfect forever those who are set apart as Christians for the service of God (10:14); here the idea is that Christ has perfectly consecrated those for whom he died on the cross, for there is nothing lacking in his meritorious atonement.

See also CONSECRATION; SANCTIFICATION.

Bibliography: R. N. Flew, *The Idea of Perfection in Christian Theology,* 1934; J. du Plessis, *The Idea of Perfection in the New Testament,* 1959. PT

PERFUME (See OINTMENTS AND PERFUMES)

PERFUMER (See OCCUPATIONS AND PROFESSIONS)

PERGA (pûr'gȧ, Gr. *pergē*). The chief city of old Pamphylia of Asia Minor located about twelve miles (twenty km.) from Attalia on the River Cestris, which formed an inland port. Paul and Barnabas passed through the city twice on the first missionary journey, both going and returning (Acts 13:13–14; 14:24–25). Here John Mark

Remains of the city gate and colonnaded street at ancient Perga. Courtesy Studium Biblicum Franciscanum, Jerusalem.

A view of the well-preserved walls of Perga, behind which is the theater. Paul and Barnabas began their first missionary journey there (Acts 13:13). Little is known of the city before Alexander the Great, and the visible remains belong mostly to the Roman period. Courtesy Dan Bahat.

Ancient Pergamum, situated on a hill 1,000 feet high, looking north over the Caicus valley. Most extant remains date from the third to second centuries B.C. Shown here are the city walls, the theater in foreground, and the temple of Dionysus at lower left. "I know where you live—where Satan has his throne" (Rev 2:12–13). Courtesy Dan Bahat.

left the party and returned to Jerusalem. During Greek times a celebrated temple of Artemis or Diana was located in the vicinity, which perhaps was the reason Christianity never flourished there as in other cities of Asia Minor. Today it is known as Murtana and the well-preserved ruins still reveal an immense theater holding about thirteen thousand people.

PERGAMUM, PERGAMOS (pûr′gȧ-mŭm, Gr. *Pergamos*). A city of Mysia in the Caicus Valley, fifteen miles (twenty-five km.) inland; in KJV, Pergamos (Rev 1:11; 2:12). Royally situated in a commanding position, Pergamum was the capital until the last of the Pergamenian kings bequeathed his realm to Rome in 133 B.C. Pergamum became the chief town of the new province of Asia and was the site of the first temple of the Caesar cult, erected to Rome and Augustus in 29 B.C. A second shrine was later dedicated to Trajan, and the multiplication of such honor marks the prestige of Pergamum in pagan Asia. The worship of Asklepios and Zeus were also endemic. The symbol of the former was a serpent, and Pausanias describes his cult image "with a staff in one hand and the other on the head of a serpent." Pergamenian coins illustrate the importance that the community attached to this cult. Caracalla is shown on one coin, saluting a serpent twined round a bending sapling. On the crag above Pergamum was a thronelike altar to Zeus (cf. Rev. 2:13) now in the Berlin Museum. It commemorated a defeat of a Gallic inroad and was decorated with a representation of the conflict of the gods and the giants, the latter shown as monsters with snakelike tails. To deepen Christian horror at Pergamum's obsession with the serpent-image, Zeus was called in this connection "Zeus the Savior." It is natural that "Nicolaitanism" should flourish in a place where politics and paganism were so closely allied (2:15), and where pressure on Christians to compromise must have been heavy.

Pergamum was an ancient seat of culture and possessed a library that rivaled Alexandria's. Parchment (*charta Pergamena*) was invented at Pergamum to free the library from Egypt's jealous ban on the export of papyrus. EMB

PERIDA (pē-rī′dȧ, Heb. *perîdhā'*, *divided*). One of Solomon's servants (Neh 7:57). It is spelled "Peruda" in Ezra 2:55.

PERIZZITE (pâr′ĭ-zīt, Heb. *perizzî*). References in the Pentateuch, Joshua, and Judges make it clear that the Perizzites were a pre-Israelite tribe or racial group of Palestine (Gen 13:7; 34:30; Exod 3:8, 17; 23:23; 33:2; 34:11; Deut 20:17; Josh 3:10; 24:11; Judg 1:4). Apart from these well-defined biblical references, the Perizzites seem to have left no other marks on history. No nonbiblical document mentions them. There is an etymological similarity between the word and the term for "dweller in an unwalled village," hence the suggestion that the Perizzites were Canaanite agriculturists (or nomads) who were not a part of the ordered town and village communities of Palestine, but were not racially distinct. The suggestion is reasonable but cannot at this stage be proved.

PERJURY. A word rarely found in our English Bible (but see Mal 3:5; Jer 7:9; 1 Tim 1:10) but closely related to several biblical words such as *oath* or *punishment*. Oaths were considered to be binding promises, so that to break an oath was regarded as perjury as well as using falsehood under oath (Lev 19:12; Ezek 16:59).

PERSECUTION. In its most common sense, this signifies a particular course or period of systematic infliction of punishment or penalty for adherence to a particular religious belief. Oppression is to be distinguished from it. Pharaoh oppressed the Hebrews; so did Nebuchadnezzar. Daniel and Jeremiah were persecuted. Systematic persecution began with the Roman imperial government. Notably tolerant toward alien religious beliefs in general, the Romans clashed with the Christians over the formalities of Caesar worship. In that fact, according to W. M. Ramsay, lies the prime significance of the persecutions. Persecution began as a social reaction and became political later, a process that can be detected in the surviving documents (Acts of the Apostles; Tacitus's *Annals;* Pliny, *Epistles* 10). The state's policy of repression was intermittent and, as the evidence of Tertullian shows, was visibly daunted by the growing numbers of the Christians. A considerable body of literature has gathered around the difficult theme of the legal basis on which the authorities pursued their policy and on the incidence and severity of the persecutions themselves. Disregarding Claudius's anti-Semitism of A.D. 49 (Acts 18:2), in which the Christians were not distinguished from Jews, Nero must be regarded as the first persecutor. In 64 (Tactitus, *Annals* 15:38–44) this emperor used the small Christian community as a scapegoat for a disastrous fire in Rome, placing on the Christians the charge of arson that was popularly leveled against him. Domitian's execution of Glabrio and Flavius Clemens in 95 and the exile of Domitilla for "atheism" and "going astray after the customs of the Jews" (Dio Cassius 67:44) was probably anti-Christian action, incidents that strikingly reveals the spread of Christianity to prominent Roman citizens by the end of the first century. Pliny's famous correspondence with Trajan in 112 (Pliny, *Epistles* 10.96–97) reveals the state more moderate but still uncompromising in its action against Christians. Trajan's policy, laid down for Pliny in Bithynia, was followed by Hadrian and Antonius Pius (117–161). Marcus Aurelius was guilty of a sharp persecution at Lyons (117). At the close of the second century, with the death of Septimius Severus, a long period of peace followed, broken by Maximinus Thrax, Decius, and Valerian, but without widespread action or much determination. Diocletian continued a now-established policy of toleration until 303, when, under the influence of Galerius, he initiated the last short but savage period of persecution, described by Lactantius and Eusebius. (The historical questions involved are dealt with in W. M. Ramsay, *The Church in the Roman Empire before A.D. 170;* E. G. Hardy, *Christianity and the Roman Government.* More briefly, the social background and historical significance are dealt with in Tyndale Lectures 1951 and 1959 by E. M. Blaiklock: *The Christian in Pagan Society* and *Rome in the New Testament*). EMB

PERSEVERANCE (Gr. *proskarterēsis*). This word occurs only once in the NT (Eph 6:18 KJV, RSV) and means there persistence and steadfastness in prayer. The word, however, has become an "umbrella term," especially in the expression "the perseverance of the saints." It is used to cover the biblical theme that, because God's gift of salvation is an eternal gift, believers are to persist in their Christian commitment and life, whatever their circumstances, knowing that God is on their side (Rom 8:31). As Paul told the Philippians, "Continue to work out your salvation with fear and trembling, for it is God who works in you to will and to act according to his good purpose" (Phil 2:12–13). At all stages a believer confesses, "By the grace of God I am what I am" (1 Cor 15:10; see also Phil 1:6; 2 Thess 3:3; 1 Peter 1:5). PT

PERSIA (pûr'zhȧ, Heb. *pāras,* Gr. *Persis*). As a geographical term Persia may be taken to mean the Iranian plateau, bounded by the Tigris Valley on the west and south, the Indus Valley on the east, and by the Armenian ranges and the Caspian Sea to the north, comprising in all something near one million square miles (2.5 million sq. km.). The plateau is high and saucer-shaped, rimmed by mountains rich in mineral wealth, but with wide tracts of arid desert in the interior. The land lies across the old road communications of Europe and Asia, a fact that has done much to determine Persia's ethnology and history. It is seldom possible to separate history and geography, and the term Persia has signified both less and more than the geographical and general meaning just given. The original Persia was a small area north of the Persian Gulf, known as Persis, the modern Fars. It was a rugged area with desert on its maritime borders, its chief town known to the Greeks as Persepolis. The Medes lay to the north, Elam was on the west, and Carmania to the east. This small province was the original home of the Iranian tribe that finally dominated the whole country and founded the vast Persian Empire, which at the time of its widest extent stretched from the Aegean Sea, the Dardanelles, and the Bosporus to the Indus River, and from north to south extended from the Black Sea, the Caucasus, the Caspian Sea, the Oxus, and the Jaxartes to the Persian Gulf, the Indian Ocean, and the cataracts of the Nile. This was the imperial power, de-

The ruins of Persepolis, royal seat of the Achaemenid kings of Persia. Construction was begun by Darius I in 518 B.C. and completed in 460 B.C. Courtesy B. Brandl.

scribed by Herodotus, that clashed with the Greeks at the beginning of the fifth century before Christ and that Alexander overthrew a century and a half later. This, too, was the imperial Persia of the OT, which rose on the ruins of Babylon, which is seen in the life of Esther, and which formed the background of the events described in the books of Ezra and Nehemiah.

The Persians belonged to the race or group of nations that speaking hypothetical Indo-European language, so called and conjectured because most of the languages of Europe together with the Indic languages descended from it. The Iranian dialects formed a southern group. A common linguistic ancestry, and therefore, in all probability, a common homeland, can be demonstrated for all this group. Migrations during the third and second millennia before Christ—mainly west, east, and south—appear to have spread tribal groups who spoke a common language through the European peninsulas, into India, and into the northern Middle East. The picture is complex. Britain itself, for example, experienced three waves of invasion—Celtic (itself multiple), Roman, and Teutonic (Angles, Saxons, Danes). Infiltration into the Middle East was just as tangled a process. Just as the inhabitants of an enclave by the Tiber, speaking a minor Italic dialect, imposed their will on the whole of Italy and began the process of historical evolution that produced the Roman Empire, so the Persians emerged to dominate the whole complex of the Iranian tribes, twelve in number according to Xenophon, ten according to Herodotus. A ninth-century Assyrian inscription mentions Parsua as a northern country adjoining Media. This may be the first historical reference to the Persians before their movement south into Anshan and Parsa, the Persis mentioned above. The Assyrian reference may catch the Iranian tribe in the process of its migration. In Persis, the Persians were at first subject to the power of their northern neighbors, the Medes, although Elam, encroaching from the west, tended to form a buffer state between them. If reasons are sought for historical processes, it could have been the stimulus of Elam that caused Persian expansion.

Through Elam, Persis had contact with the developed civilizations of the Euphrates Valley. On the other hand, it may have needed no more than the emergence of a masterful personality to initiate the process. Such a person was Cyrus, second of that name from the ruling family of the Achaemenids. Cyrus is the Latinized form of Greek *Kyros,* Persian *Kurash*. According to tradition, Cyrus was related to Astyages, king of Medea. Rising against his relative, Cyrus threw off the Median hegemony and established the Persians as the dominant tribe in 549 B.C. Some form of governmental partnership appears to have been established, for Medes held privileged posts in the new administration. Cyrus then moved west to defeat the Lydian Empire of Croesus in 545, and south to defeat Nabonidus of Babylon in 538. The conquest of Lydia gave Cyrus Asia Minor; the overthrow of Babylon made him master of the Euphrates River plain, Assyria, Syria, and Palestine. Thus arose the greatest West

Wall relief from east wall of the Treasury at Persepolis showing King Darius I seated on his throne. Courtesy B. Brandl.

Asian Empire of ancient times. It was indeed the first of the world's great imperial organizations, a foreshadowing of the system of Rome, beneficent and humane when compared with the Assyrian Empire, but too loosely held and geographically divided to survive. The conflict between Samaria and Jerusalem, depicted in the life of Nehemiah, is an illustration of the indiscipline that could reign in remoter corners. Nehemiah was working by royal decree and yet found his work hampered by armed interference. Ezra's fear (Ezra 8:22) suggests similar pockets of anarchy.

Cyrus's great empire was organized by him and by Darius (Dariavaush, 521–486 B.C.), who succeeded him, after a period of revolt and dynastic trouble. Coming to terms with geography, Cyrus and Darius sought to combine a measure of local autonomy with centralization in a supreme controlling power, a difficult task even where communications are swift and efficient. The empire was cut into provinces, each under the rule of a satrap, who might be a local ruler or a Persian noble. With the satrap were military and civil officials directly responsible to the king, who was also kept informed on local matters by means of his "eyes," or his itinerant inspectors. This was an attempt to check maladministration in the satrapies and to anticipate such challenges to the royal power as that described by Xenophon in his *Anabasis.* All provinces were assessed for monetary and manpower contributions to the central treasury and armed forces. An attempt was wisely made to preserve efficient forms of local government, and Greek city-states on the Ionian seaboard still functioned, with religion, language, and civic government intact. Inscriptions suggest that there were three official languages—Persian, Elamitic, and Babylonian. Darius further unified his empire by an efficient gold coinage, state highways, and a postal system, arrangements that became famous for their usefulness. The four books of the OT in which Persia forms a background (Ezra, Esther, Ezekiel, and Daniel) all illustrate the royal tendency to delegate special authority to individuals for specific tasks.

Cyrus and the Achaemenid kings were Zoroastrians, worshipers of Ahura Mazda, "the Wise Lord." The Magi of the Medes appear to have been reorganized by Cyrus into a Mazdaist priesthood. Zoroaster taught that Ahura Mazda, together with his holy spirit, warred against an evil spirit, Ahriman. There was an element of messianism in the cult, for it taught that after the earthly life of a future savior, God will finally triumph over evil, and that all souls pass over the "bridge of decision" and enjoy eternal bliss, though some must first go through a purgatory of fire. Zoroaster stressed truth and mercy. Isaiah 45:7 is supposed by some to be a reference to Zoroastrian religion. The context is a tribute to Cyrus, and in contrast with the crude paganism of other peoples, the Persian monotheism may have appeared to the Hebrews to contain elements of divine insight. The notable favor shown to the religion of the Lord in the books of Ezra and Nehemiah may illustrate the same affinity from the other side. It will be useful in conclusion to list the Persian kings whose reigns have significance in OT history:

1. Cyrus, 538–529 B.C. 2 Chronicles 36:22–23; Ezra 1 to 5 passim; Isaiah 44:28; 45:1; Daniel 1:21; 6:28; 10:1.
2. Cambyses, 529–522 B.C. Some have suggested that Cambyses is the mysterious Darius the Mede of Daniel 5:31; 6:9, 25; 9:1; 11:1. Others think this obscure person was Gobryas, governor of Media, who exercised authority for Cyrus in Babylon.
3. Gaumata, a usurper, who held brief royal authority until put down by Darius, 522–521 B.C.
4. Darius I (Hystaspis), 521–486 B.C., the great imperialist, whose seaborne attack on Greece was defeated at Marathon in 490. He is known for his trilingual inscription at Behistun, famous in linguistic studies. This is the Darius mentioned by Ezra under whose protection permission was given for the temple to be built.
5. Xerxes I (Ahasuerus), 486–465 B.C. This is the mad king who in a mighty combined opera-

tion sought to avenge Marathon and whom the Greeks defeated at Salamis (480) and Plataea (479). The feast and assembly of Esther 1:3 is plausibly equated with Herodotus 7:8, while Esther 2:16 is a reference to the events of Herodotus 9:108–9.

6. Artaxerxes I (Longimanus), 464–424 B.C. It was this monarch who permitted Ezra to go to Jerusalem to restore the affairs of the Jewish community (Ezra 7–8), and who promoted the mission of his cupbearer Nehemiah, thirteen years later. (In Ezra 4 chronology is broken and it is a matter of some difficulty to identify and arrange events. The IVF Commentary [in loco] deals with the matter well.) See Nehemiah 2:1; 5:14; 13:6. Note: Darius the Persian (Neh 12:22) is Codomannus, the last king of Persia, overthrown by Alexander in 330.

Bibliography: A. T. Olmstead, *History of the Persian Empire,* 1948; E. Porada, *Ancient Iran,* 1965; B. Porten, *Archives from Elephantine,* 1968; R. N. Frye, *The Heritage of Persia,* 1975. EMB

PERSIS (pûr′sĭs, Gr. *Persis, Persian*). A Christian woman at Rome greeted by Paul as his "dear friend . . . who has worked very hard in the Lord" (Rom 16:12).

PERUDA (See PERIDA)

PESHITTA (pĕ-shēt′tà). Often called "simple" version, it is the common name for the ancient Syriac (Aramaic) translation of the Bible. The OT was translated before the Christian era, no doubt by Jews who spoke Aramaic and lived in the countries east of Palestine. Syriac Christians translated the NT during the early centuries of the church, the standard version being that of Rabbula, bishop of Edessa in the fifth century. The Syriac Bible played an important role in the Christian missionary thrust into the countries of the Far East, including India.

PEST (See ANIMALS)

PESTILENCE (pĕs′tĭlĕns, Heb. *dever,* Gr. *loimos*). In the OT (KJV 47 vv.; NIV 4 vv.), any fatal epidemic, often the result of divine judgment (Exod 5:3 KJV, MLB, MOF, NASB, NEB, RSV; plague(s) JB, NIV); NT usage is only by Jesus (Matt 24:7; Luke 21:11).

PESTLE (pĕs″l, Heb. *'ĕlî, lifted*). An instrument either of wood or of stone, rounded at the ends and used to grind material in a mortar (Prov 27:22).

PETER (pētêr, Gr. *Petros, rock*). The most prominent of the twelve apostles in the Gospels and an outstanding leader in the early days of the Christian church. His original name was Simon, a common Greek name, or more properly Symeon (Acts 15:14), a popular Hebrew name.

I. Background. He was a native of Bethsaida (John 1:44), the son of a certain John (1:42; 21:15–17), apparently an abbreviation for Jonah

Two rock-hewn cuneiform inscriptions found at Ganj Nameh, southwest of Ecbatana—of Darius I (522–485 B.C.), left, and Xerxes I (485–465 B.C.). The trilingual inscriptions (in Old Persian, Neo-Elamite, and Neo-Babylonian) pay homage to the Persian god Ahura Mazda and list the lineage and conquests of the two rulers. Courtesy B. Brandl.

(Matt 16:17). As a Jewish lad he received a normal elementary education. As a native of "Galilee of the Gentiles" he was able to converse in Greek, while his native Aramaic was marked with provincialisms of pronunciation and diction (26:73). The evaluation by the Sanhedrin of Peter and John as "unschooled, ordinary men" (Acts 4:13) simply meant that they were unschooled in the rabbinical lore and were laymen. He and his brother Andrew followed the hardy occupation of fishermen on the Sea of Galilee, being partners with Zebedee's sons, James and John (Luke 5:7). He was a married man (Mark 1:30; 1 Cor 9:5) and at the time of Christ's Galilean ministry lived in Capernaum (Mark 1:21, 29).

II. The Gospel Period. Of the second period of his life, from his first encounter with Jesus until the Ascension, the Gospels give a vivid picture. Simon attended the preaching ministry of John the Baptist at the Jordan and, like Andrew, probably became a personal disciple of John. When he was personally introduced to Jesus by his brother Andrew, Jesus remarked, "You are Simon son of John. You will be called Cephas" (John 1:42). That John translated the Aramaic *Kēphās* into Greek *Petros,* both meaning "rock," indicates that it was not a proper name but rather a descriptive title (cf. "Sons of Thunder," Mark 3:17). The designation, afterward more fully explained in its prophetic import (Matt 16:18; Mark 3:16), came to be regarded as his personal name. (No other man in the NT bears the name Peter.) After a period of companionship with Jesus during his early Judean ministry (John 1:42–4:43), Peter resumed his ordinary occupation.

With the commencement of Christ's Galilean ministry, Peter and Andrew, with James and John, were called by Jesus to full-time association with him to be trained as "fishers of men" (Mark 1:16–20; Luke 5:1–11). With the growth of the work, Jesus selected twelve of his followers to be his nearest companions for special training (Mark 3:13–19; Luke 6:12–16). In the lists of these twelve designated apostles (Luke 6:13), Peter is always named first (Matt 10:2–4; Mark 3:16–19; Luke 6:14–16; Acts 1:13–14). His eminence among them was due to his being among the first chosen as well as his native aggressiveness as a natural leader. But the other disciples did not concede to Peter any authority over them, as is evident from their repeated arguments about greatness (Matt 20:20–28; Mark 9:33–34; Luke 22:24–27). While he was with them, Jesus alone was recognized as their leader.

The development of an inner circle among the disciples is first seen when Jesus took Peter, James, and John with him into the house of Jairus (Mark 5:37; Luke 8:51). The three were further privileged to witness the Transfiguration (Matt 17:1; Mark 9:2; Luke 9:28) and the agony in the Garden (Matt 26:37; Mark 14:33). Even in this inner circle Peter usually stands in the foreground, but the fourth Gospel indicates that his position of eminence was not exclusive.

Peter was the natural spokesman of the twelve. When Christ's sermon on the Bread of Life produced a general defection among his followers, Peter spoke for the twelve in asserting their loyalty to him (John 6:66–69). Again, at Caesarea Philippi, when Jesus asked the twelve their view of him, Peter promptly replied, "You are the Christ, the Son of the living God" (Matt 16:16). His confession of the messiahship and deity of our Lord expressed a divinely given insight higher than the current view, which regarded the Messiah only as a man exalted to the messianic office (cf. 22:41–46). His confession elicited Christ's prompt commendation and the further assertion, "You are Peter, and on this rock I will build my church" (16:18). By his believing confession Peter has identified himself with Christ the true Rock (Isa 28:16; 1 Cor 3:11; 1 Peter 2:4–5), thus fulfilling Christ's prediction concerning him (John 1:42). He has thus become a rock (*petros*); and on "this rock" (*petra*), composed of Peter and the other apostles, joined by faith in Christ the chief cornerstone (Eph 2:20), Jesus announces that he will build his triumphant church.

The account in Acts historically interprets Peter's use of the keys in opening the doors of Christian opportunity at Pentecost (Acts 2), in Samaria (ch. 8), and to the Gentiles (ch. 10). The power of binding and loosing was not limited to Peter (Matt 18:18; John 20:3). But Peter was also the spokesman in attempting to dissuade Jesus from his announced path of suffering, thus proving himself a "stumbling block" (Matt 16:23; Mark 8:33).

Peter came into prominence in the Gospels also in connection with the matter of the payment of the temple tax (Matt 17:24–27), his inquiry as to the limits on forgiveness (18:21), and his reminder to Jesus that they had left all to follow him (19:27; Mark 10:28). During Passion Week his activities were prominent. He called Jesus' attention to the withered fig tree (Mark 11:21), and with three others he asked Jesus concerning his prediction about the temple (13:3). With John he was commissioned to prepare for the Passover (Luke 22:8). Peter objected to the Lord's washing his feet in the Upper Room, but impulsively swung to the opposite extreme when informed of the implications of his denial (John 13:1–11). He beckoned to John to ask the identity of the betrayer (13:23–24) and stoutly contradicted Jesus when warned of his impending denials (Matt 26:33–35; Mark 14:29–31; Luke 22:31–34; John 13:37–38). In the Garden of Gethsemene, when chosen with James and John to watch with Jesus, he slept (Matt 26:37–46; Mark 14:33–42). In fleshly zeal he sought to defend Jesus, and Jesus rebuked him for it (John 18:10–11). He fled with the other disciples when Jesus was bound; but, anxious to see the end, he followed afar, was admitted (through John's action) into the court of the high priest, and there shamefully denied his Lord three times (Matt 26:58, 69–75; Mark 14:66–72; Luke 22:54–62; John 18:15–18, 25–27). The look of Jesus broke his heart, and he went out and wept bitterly (Luke 22:61–62). That Peter witnessed the Crucifixion is not stated (but cf. 1 Peter 5:1).

On the Resurrection morning he and John ran to the tomb of Jesus to investigate the report of Mary Magdalene (John 20:1–10). Somewhere during that day the risen Lord appeared to Peter (1 Cor 15:5). At his postresurrection manifestation to seven at the Sea of Galilee, John was the first to recognize the Lord; but, typically, Peter was the first to act. Following the group breakfast, Christ tested Peter's love and formally restored him by the threefold commission to feed his sheep (John 21:1–23).

III. The Early Church. The third period in Peter's life began with the ascension of Jesus. In the early days of the church (Acts 1–12), Peter appeared as the spokesman of the apostolic group, but there is no hint that he assumed any authority not also exercised by the other apostles. He suggested the choice of another to fill the place of Judas (1:15–26), preached the Spirit-empowered sermon on Pentecost to the assembled Jews (2:14–40), and with John healed the lame man, the first apostolic miracle to arouse persecution (3:1–4:21). He was used to expose the sin of Ananias and Sapphira (5:1–12), was held in high esteem by the people during the miracle ministry in the church that followed (5:12–16), and spoke for the Twelve when arraigned before the Sanhedrin (5:27–41). With John he was sent to Samaria, where, through the laying on of hands, the Holy Spirit fell on the Samaritan believers and Peter exposed the unworthy motives of Simon (8:14–24). While on a tour through Judea, Peter healed Aeneas and raised Dorcas from the dead (9:32–43). Through a divinely given vision at Joppa, Peter was prepared and commissioned to preach the gospel to Cornelius at Caesarea, thus opening the door to the Gentiles (10:1–48). This brought on him the criticism of the circumcision party in Jerusalem (11:1–18). During the persecution of the church by Agrippa I in A.D. 44, Peter escaped death by a miraculous deliverance from prison (12:1–19).

IV. His Later Life. With the opening of the door to the Gentiles and the spread of Christianity, Peter receded into the background and Paul became prominent as the apostle to the Gentiles. In the Acts narrative Peter is last mentioned in connection with the Jerusalem conference, where he championed the liberty of the Gentiles (15:6–11, 14). The remaining NT references to Peter are scanty. Galatians 2:11–21 records a visit to Syrian Antioch, where his inconsistent conduct evoked a public rebuke from Paul. From 1 Corinthians 9:5 it appears that Peter traveled widely, taking his wife with him, doubtless in Jewish evangelism (Gal 2:9).

Nothing further is heard of Peter until the writing of the two letters that bear his name, apparently written from Rome. In the first letter, addressed to believers in five provinces in Asia Minor, the shepherd-heart of Peter sought to fortify the saints in their sufferings for Christ, while in the second he warns against dangers from within. A final NT reference to the closing years of Peter's life is found in John 21:18–19. John's interpretation of Christ's prediction makes it clear that the reference is to Peter's violent death. Beyond this the NT is silent about him.

Tradition uniformily asserts that Peter went to Rome, that he labored there, and there in his old age suffered martyrdom under Nero. The embellished tradition that he was bishop of Rome for twenty-five years is contrary to all NT evidence. He apparently came to Rome shortly after Paul's release from his first imprisonment there.

V. His Character. The character of Peter is one of the most vividly drawn and charming in the NT. His sheer humanness has made him one of the most beloved and winsome members of the apostolic band. He was eager, impulsive, energetic, self-confident, aggressive, and daring, but also unstable, fickle, weak, and cowardly. He was guided more by quick impulse than logical reasoning, and he readily swayed from one extreme to the other. He was preeminently a man of action. His life exhibits the defects of his character as well as his tremendous capacities for good. He was forward and often rash, liable to instability and inconsistency, but his love for and associations with Christ molded him into a man of stability, humility, and courageous service for God. In the power of the Holy Spirit he became one of the noble pillars (Gal 2:9) of the church.

DEH

PETER, FIRST LETTER OF. The keynote of the First Letter of Peter is suffering and the Christian method of meeting it. The writer endeavored to convey a message of hope to Christians who had been undergoing persecution and who were succumbing to discouragement because they could find no redress. He brings an exhortation of Christian truth calculated to strengthen believers.

I. Authorship. Of the two letters that bear the name of Peter, the first is better attested. Echoes of its phraseology appear as early as the Letter of Polycarp to the Philippians (c. A.D. 125), the Letter of Barnabas (c. 135), and the writings of Justin Martyr (c. 150). The Second Letter of Peter refers to a former letter, probably meaning this one (2 Peter 3:1). It was unanimously accepted as a letter of Peter by all of the church fathers, who mention it by name, beginning with Irenaeus (c. 170).

The internal structure reflects Peter's mind and life. The first main paragraph, "Praise be to the God and Father of our Lord Jesus Christ! In his great mercy he has given us new birth into a living hope through the resurrection of Jesus Christ from the dead" (1 Peter 1:3), expresses the joy that Peter felt after the risen Christ forgave him for his denial. The injunction to "be shepherds of God's flock" (5:2) is almost identical in language with Jesus' commission to him at the lake of Galilee (John 21:16). "Clothe yourselves with humility" may be a reminiscence of the Last Supper, when Jesus wrapped a towel around his waist and washed the disciples' feet (John 13:4–5).

There are also some remarkable agreements between the vocabulary of 1 Peter and the speeches of Peter in Acts—1 Peter 1:17, Acts 10:34; 1 Peter 1:21, Acts 2:32, 10:40–41; 1 Peter 2:7–8, Acts 4:10–11).

II. Destination. The letter was directed to members of the Dispersion located in the northern Roman provinces of Asia Minor, which Paul did not visit and which may have been evangelized by Peter between the Council of Jerusalem (A.D. 48) and the Neronian persecution at Rome (64). There is some question whether the "Dispersion" should be taken literally as applying strictly to Jews or whether it may be used figuratively of Gentile Christians who were scattered abroad. In favor of the former conclusion are one or two passages that seemingly indicate that the recipients were Jews (1 Peter 2:12; 3:6); on the other hand, "Gentiles" may be equivalent to "brethren," and the references to the ungodly past of these people (1:14; 4:3) do not seem to agree with the hypotheses that they were of Jewish descent. If Peter wrote this letter from Rome, he may have been writing to refugees from the Neronian persecution who were converts from Judaism or proselytes who turned from Judaism to Christianity.

III. Date and Place. If Silas (KJV Silvanus, 5:12) and Mark (5:13) were the same persons mentioned in Paul's letters (2 Cor 1:19; 1 Thess 1:1; Col 4:10; 2 Tim 4:11), 1 Peter must have been written subsequent to Silas's departure from Paul and prior to Mark's rejoining him. Silas was with Paul in Corinth in the early fifties, and Mark probably rejoined him just before his death, which took place about A.D. 65–67. Furthermore, 1 Peter bears traces of the influence of Paul's Letter to the Romans and to the Ephesians in its structure and thought (compare the following: 1 Peter 2:13, Rom 13:1–4; 1 Peter 2:18, Eph 6:5; 1 Peter 3:9, Rom 12:17; 1 Peter 5:5, Eph 5:21), implying that it was written after 60. Probably 1 Peter was written about the year 64, when the status of Christians in the empire was very uncertain and when persecution had already begun in Rome.

The place of writing is closely connected with the date. "Babylon" (1 Peter 5:13) may refer to the ancient city on the Euphrates, where there was a large Jewish settlement in Peter's day, or to a town in Egypt near Alexandria, where Mark traditionally ministered, or figuratively to Rome as the center of the pagan world (Rev 17:5; 18:10). The second alternative need not be considered seriously, for the Egyptian Babylon was only a border fort. Opinion among commentators is divided between the other two opinions. In the absence of any strong tradition that Peter ever visited in the literal Babylon, it seems more likely that he wrote this letter from Rome shortly before his martyrdom. He would have had opportunity to find some of Paul's writings there and to have met Silas and Mark, both of whom were familiar to Paul.

Those who deny Peter's authorship place the letter in the early second century under the reign of Trajan (A.D. 96–117). Sir William Ramsay assigned it to the time of Domitian (87–96), conceding that Peter might have been executed in the time of Vespasian or Domitian (c. 80).

IV. Structure and Content. In general arrangement 1 Peter closely resembles the letters of Paul, with a salutation, body, and conclusion. Its main subject is the Christian's behavior under the pressure of suffering. Its key is the salvation that is to be revealed at the last time (1:5). The letter may be outlined as follows:

I. Introduction (1:1–2)
II. The Nature of Salvation (1:3–12)
III. The Experience of Salvation (1:13–25)
IV. The Obligations of Salvation (2:1–10)
V. The Ethics of Salvation (2:11–3:12)
VI. The Confidence of Salvation (3:13–4:11)
VII. The Behavior of the Saved Under Suffering (4:12–5:11)
VIII. Concluding Salutations (5:12–14)

Bibliography: E. G. Selwyn, *The First Epistle of Peter,* 1946 (on the Greek text); F. W. Beare, *The First Epistle of Peter,* 1959 (on the Greek text); B. Reicke, *The Epistles of James, Peter and Jude* (AB), 1964; J. N. D. Kelly, *The Epistles of Peter and of Jude* (HNTC), 1969; E. Best, *The First Epistle of Peter* (NCB), 1971. MCT

PETER, SECOND LETTER OF. A general treatise, written to warn its readers of threatening apostasy. It purports to have been written by Simon Peter and contains a definite allusion to a preceding letter (2 Peter 3:1).

I. Authorship. Second Peter has the poorest external attestation of any book in the canon of the NT. It is not quoted directly by any of the church fathers before Origen (c. A.D. 250), who affirms Peter's authorship of the first letter, but who seemed uncertain about the second, although he did not repudiate it. Eusebius, to whom we are indebted for quoting Origen's testimony, placed 2 Peter in the list of disputed writings. Its literary style and vocabulary differ from that of 1 Peter, and its close resemblance to the Book of Jude has led some scholars to believe that it is a late copy or adaptation of that work. Numerous scholars have pronounced it spurious and have relegated it to the middle of the second century.

On the other hand, the internal evidence favors authorship by Peter. If a forger knew 1 Peter, it seems he could have been more careful to follow its style exactly. The allusions to Peter's career agree with the existing records and can best be explained as the testimony of an eyewitness. They include the Transfiguration (2 Peter 1:17–18), at which Peter was present (Matt 17:1–18), and the Lord's prediction of his death (2 Peter 1:14; John 21:18–19). The Greek of the second letter is more labored than that of the first, but if Peter did not have the aid of Silas in this work, as he did in the first letter (1 Peter 5:12), he may have been forced to rely on his own writing. Doubtlessly he knew Greek, as most Galileans did, but he may not have been able to write it easily. Second Peter reads more like a book that has been composed with the aid of a dictionary rather than by a man whose native tongue was Greek.

The allusion to the writings of "our dear brother Paul" (2 Peter 3:15) confirms the impression that 2 Peter was written by someone who knew Paul personally and who treated him as an equal. A writer of the second century would have been more likely to say "the blessed apostle," for he would have regarded Paul with a greater veneration and would thus have used a more elevated title.

Reasons exist, therefore, for accepting the letter as Peter's. The relative silence of the early church may be explained by the brevity of the letter, which could have made it more susceptible to being overlooked or lost.

II. Date and Place. Second Peter must have been written subsequent to the publication of at least some of Paul's letters, if not of the entire collection. It cannot, therefore, have been written before A.D. 60; but if Paul was living and was still well known to the existing generation, it could not have been later than 70. Probably 67 is as satisfactory a date as can be established. The writer was anticipating a speedy death (2 Peter 1:14), and this may mean that the letter was sent from Rome during the tense days of the Neronian persecution. There is no indication, however, that Peter had spent a long time in Rome. He may have labored there only at the conclusion of Paul's life (between 63 and 67).

III. Destination and Occasion. The reference to a previous letter sent to the same group (2 Peter 3:1) connects the document with 1 Peter, which was written to the Christians of northern Asia Minor. Whereas the first letter was an attempt to encourage a church threatened with official persecution and repression, the second letter dealt with the peril of apostasy, which was an even greater threat. An influx of conscienceless agitators who repudiated the lordship of Christ (2:1) and whose attitude was haughty (2:10), licentious (2:13), adulterous (2:14), greedy (2:14), bombastic (2:18), and libertine (2:19) seemed imminent. Knowing that he would not be spared to keep control of the situation, Peter was writing to forestall this calamity and to warn the church of its danger.

IV. Content and Outline. The key to this letter is the word "know" or "knowledge," which occurs frequently in the three chapters, often referring to the knowledge of Christ. This knowledge is not primarily academic, but spiritual, arising from a growing experience of Christ (2 Peter 3:18). It produces peace and grace (1:2) and fruitfulness (1:8), is the secret of freedom from defilement (2:20), and is the sphere of Christian growth (3:18). It may be that the false teachers were Gnostics, who stressed knowledge as the means to salvation, and that Peter sought to counteract their falsehoods by a positive presentation of true knowledge.

Second Peter teaches definitely the inspiration of Scripture (2 Peter 1:19–21) and stresses the doctrine of the personal return of Christ, which was ridiculed by the false teachers (3:1–7). It concludes with an appeal for holy living and with the promise of the new heavens and the new earth.

The following is a brief outline of the Epistle:

I. Salutation (1:1)
II. The Character of Spiritual Knowledge (1:2–21)
III. The Nature and Perils of Apostasy (2:1–22)
IV. The Doom of the Ungodly (3:1–7)
V. The Hope of Believers (3:8–13)
VI. Concluding Exhortation (3:14–18)

Bibliography: E. M. B. Green, *Second Peter Reconsidered,* 1961, and *The Second Epistle General of Peter and the General Epistle of Jude* (TNTC), 1968; J. N. D. Kelly, *The Epistles of Peter and of Jude* (HNTC), 1969; R. J. Bauckham, *2 Peter and Jude* (Word Biblical Commentary), 1983 (on the Greek text). MCT

PETHAHIAH (pĕth'ȧ-hī'ȧ, Heb. *pethahyâh, Jehovah opens up*). 1. The head priest of the nineteenth course of priests during David's reign (1 Chron 24:16).

2. A disobedient Levite who, in Ezra's time, married a foreign woman (Ezra 10:23). Most scholars identify him with the one named in Nehemiah 9:5.

3. Meshezabel's son who descended from Zerah from the tribe of Judah. He was the counselor for King Artaxerxes "in all affairs relating to the people" (Neh 11:24).

PETHOR (pē'thôr, Heb. *pethôr*). Mentioned twice in connection with the hireling prophet Balaam (Num 22:5; Deut 23:4). Both passages place Pethor in Mesopotamia on the Euphrates. There is a reference in an Assyrian inscription of Shalmaneser II to a place called Pitru on the Sagur near its confluence with the Euphrates. It cannot be proved that Pitru is Pethor, but if such a reasonable inference is true, Pethor would be just west of Carchemish on the west bank of the Euphrates.

PETHUEL (pē-thū'ĕl, Heb. *pethû'ēl, God's opening*). Father of the prophet Joel (Joel 1:1).

PETRA (pē'trȧ). Translates *sela',* meaning *rock, cliff,* or *crag,* and, as a proper noun, seems to refer to one or two places in the OT (Judg 1:36; 2 Kings 14:7; Isa 16:1; NIV "Sela"). No certain geographical identification is possible, though the second reference may be to the Petra of later history, the "rose-red city half as old as time," of Dean Burgon's sonnet, and capital city of the Nabateans from the close of the fourth century B.C. until A.D. 105, when it became part of the Roman Empire. The town lies in a basin surrounded by mountains. The town's considerable ruins are not impressive, even though Burgon's eulogy is often quoted. The main curiosities of Petra are the narrow canyons that form its approaches, and the rock-hewn temples and tombs in the surrounding cliffs. Nothing is

The *sik* (or gorge), on the way to Petra, east of the Jordan. Courtesy University Library, Istanbul.

The tomb of ed-Deir at Petra. Elaborately carved in the mountainside, the façade measures 132 feet (40 m.) in height and 154 feet (47 m.) in width, being the largest surviving monument of the Nabatean site. Courtesy Garo Nalbandian.

known of Petra's history before the Nabateans took over in 312 B.C.

PEULLETHAI (pē-ŭl'ē-thī, *Jehovah is a reward*). A Levite who was Obed-Edom's eighth son. He was a porter of the tabernacle in the time of David (1 Chron 26:5).

PHALEC (See PELEG)

PHALLU (See PALLU)

PHALTI (See PALTIEL)

PHALTIEL (See PALTIEL)

PHANUEL (fā-nū'ĕl, Heb. *penû'ēl, face of God*, Gr. *Phanouēl*). The father of Anna the prophetess (Luke 2:36).

PHARAOH (fâr'ō, Heb. *par'ōh*). The government of Egypt, and ultimately the supreme monarch in whom all its powers were vested, was known as the "Great House," in Egyptian "Per-o," whence comes the term *pharaoh*. The recorded rulers of Egypt, twenty-six separate dynasties, extend from Menes, 3400 B.C. to Psamtik III, deposed at the Persian conquest in 525. The term pharaoh can be traced back to the Twenty-second Dynasty (945–745), since when it was commonly attached to the monarch's name. Thus "Pharaoh Neco" and "Pharaoh Hophra" are exact Hebrew translations of the Egyptian title.

Pharaohs of Egypt are mentioned in the following OT contexts: 1. Genesis 12:10–20. The date of Abram's descent into Egypt must be in the early years of the second millennium B.C. Amenemhet I, according to Breasted's dating, was Pharaoh from 2000 to 1970. There is no strong evidence that northern Egypt was already under the power of the Hyksos intruders at this time, plausible though it may seem to connect the patriarch's sojourn with the presence of racially related rulers. On the tomb of Khnumhotep at Beni Hassan, dating from the twentieth century B.C., the visit of such a Semitic party is vividly portrayed.

2. Genesis 39 to 50 passim. It is reasonable to place the period of Joseph's (and Israel's) favor in Egypt in the times of the Hyksos invaders. These foreigners, who included Canaanite and Semitic elements from Palestine, supplanted the weak rulers of the Thirteenth and Fourteenth Dynasties and settled in the Delta and Lower Egypt, where they maintained their power for some two centuries. They were driven out in 1580 B.C.

3. Exodus 1 to 15 passim. Controversy surrounds the identity of the Pharaoh of the Oppression and the date of the Hebrew exodus. One, to some extent, depends on the other. John Garstang's excavations at Jericho in the early 1930s seemed to establish a date for the Hebrew storming of the city around the turn of the fourteenth century B.C. This would postulate a date for the Exodus around 1440, and would identify Thutmose III as the Pharaoh of the Oppression and the famous princess Hatshepsut as Moses' protectress. The theory produces a neat pattern of dates, and the events of the Oppression through to the infiltration of the tribes into Palestine correspond very well with events of

Two of four colossal seated statues of Pharaoh Ramses II, part of the façade of the great temple at Abu Simbel. The temple is located between the first and second cataracts of the Nile. Courtesy Seffie Ben-Yoseph.

Egyptian history during the years 1580 to 1350, the period of the great Eighteenth Dynasty. Ahmose I would thus be the Pharaoh "who did not know about Joseph." Indeed, as the first native ruler after the expulsion of the hated Hyksos, he would be naturally hostile to the shepherd proteges of the old regime. The breakdown of Egyptian control in Palestine under Amenhotep IV (Ikhnaton) would also account for the comparative ease of the Hebrew conquest and explain the "Habiru" references of the Tell-el-Amarna Letters.

Competent orthodox scholarship, however, not without backing from more recent work at Jericho, still argues for the older dating, under which Seti I (1313–1292 B.C.) is regarded as the Pharaoh of Exodus 1:8. Ramses II (1292–1225), in whose reign the store cities of Pitham and Rameses were completed, would thus fill the role of Pharaoh of the Oppression, and perhaps of the Exodus (Exod 1:11; 12:40). Rameses was the fort from which the great militarist Ramses II sought to control his Asiatic empire, and the war base from which he marched to his great battle with the Hittites at Kadesh on the Orontes, the conflict depicted on the walls of the Ramesseum at Thebes. Those who thus identify the Pharaoh of the Oppression, point out that the Egyptian hold over Palestine slackened after Ramses' treaty with the Hittites, and that this weakening of policy allowed the fragmentation of the country from which the Hebrew incursion profited. Some more precisely date the Exodus in the reign of Ramses' son, Merneptah, mainly on the strength of the "Israel Stele," discovered by Flinders Petrie in 1896. This inscription, self-dated in "the third year of Merneptah" (1223 B.C.), tells of the Pharaoh's victories in Canaan. One line runs: "Israel is devastated. Her seed is not" (or "Her crops are destroyed"). A natural reference from this statement might, however, be that Israel was already in settled possession of large tracts of Palestine. At this point the matter must be left.

4. First Chronicles 4:18 speaks of "the children of Pharaoh's daughter Bithia, whom Mered had married." No identification of this Pharaoh is possible, and the name of the princess appears to be Hebraized.

5. First Kings 3:1; 9:16, 24; 11:1. Solomon's reign may be reliably dated 961 to 922 B.C., a period that corresponds with the reign of Pharaoh Sheshonk I (945 to 924), the founder of the Twenty-second Dynasty. Under this Pharaoh, Egypt's foreign policy again took on an aggressive character, and at all such times it was Egypt's custom (not without illustration in recent events) to establish the safety of the northern approaches, virtually her only invasion route. Hence the policy of Thutmose III, Ramses II, Seti I, and Sheshonk. The dynastic alliance with Solomon and the handing of the city of Gezer to his authority were part of the recurrent Egyptian plan to create a defensive buffer in Palestine. The ruler who acted with such foresight and energy can hardly have been one of the feeble monarchs of the earlier dynasty. A further facet of the same policy is revealed by Pharaoh's befriending of Hadad of Edom (1 Kings 11:14–22). Hadad was a useful

weapon for possible employment against a recalcitrant Solomon or against a hostile Palestine.

6. Second Kings 18:21 and Isaiah 36:6 both mention the Pharaoh of Sennacherib's day. He is "that splintered reed of a staff, which pierces a man's hand and wounds him if he leans on it," says the field commander to the people of Jerusalem. The date is 701 B.C. Egypt was in the state of political disintegration and weakness pictured in Isaiah 19. Shabaka was Pharaoh, the first monarch of the feeble Twenty-fifth Dynasty. The army scraped together to face the Assyrian threat was a motley horde of mercenaries and ill-armed levies. Egyptian contingents had served in the past against Assyria, but this was the first time the two empires, that of the Tigris and that of the Nile, actually confronted each other. Sennacherib led in person. Shabaka entrusted his force to his nephew Taharka who, some thirteen or fourteen years later, became king of Ethiopia. Hence the title given in 2 Kings 19:9 by anticipation of events. The Assyrian rapidly dealt with Taharka's force, and was proceeding to overthrow Palestine and the strong pocket of resistance in Jerusalem, when the famous plague that decimated his army fell on him. This overwhelming catastrophe was the cause of the Assyrian retreat and deliverance for both Palestine and Egypt.

7. Second Kings 23:20–35. Pharaoh Neco was the last Pharaoh to endeavor to reestablish Egyptian authority in the northern approaches. He succeeded Psametik I, founder of the Twenty-sixth Dynasty, in 609 B.C., and reigned until 593. Immediately after his accession, taking advantage of the collapse of Nineveh, Neco drove north into Philistia. On the Plain of Megiddo, where Egypt had won control of the land nine hundred years before, Neco routed and killed Josiah. He moved on to the Euphrates, unopposed by Nineveh, but not feeling strong enough to go against that stronghold. From Ribleh on the Orontes, three months after the battle at Megiddo, Neco deposed Jehoahaz and sent him to die in Egypt. He placed Jehoiakim on the throne of Judah and fixed a tribute for the conquered land. Two years later Neco's new empire fell before the attack of Babylon. Jeremiah refers to the event (Jer 37:7; 46:2).

8. Ezekiel 29:1. The date is 587 B.C., and the Pharaoh referred to must therefore be Hophra, or Apries, in the first year of his rule. He reigned from 588 to 569. This was the Pharaoh whose troops failed to relieve Jerusalem in 586 and whose weak action against Nebuchadnezzar's Babylon brilliantly vindicated the advice of Jeremiah. Egypt escaped the calamity that befell Palestine by prudent modification of her challenge. Preoccupied with Tyre, Nebuchadnezzar did not press the war against Egypt, and Hophra brought his country its last flourish of prosperity before the land fell in the Persian conquest. Jeremiah (44:30, the sole biblical reference to Hophra by name) prophesied his end. See EGYPT.

EMB

PHARISEES (fâr'ĭ-sēz, Heb. *perûshîn,* Gr. *Pharisaioi*). Of the three prominent parties of Judaism at the time of Christ—Pharisees, Sadducees, and Essenes—the Pharisees were by far the most influential. The origin of this most strict sect of the Jews (Acts 26:5) is shrouded in some obscurity, but it is believed the organization came out of the Maccabean Revolt (165 B.C.). There was, however, a group of Jews resembling the Pharisees as far back as the Babylonian captivity.

The name "Pharisee," which in its Semitic form means "the separated ones, separatists," first appears during the reign of John Hyrcanus (135 B.C.). Generally, the term is in the plural rather than in the singular. They were also known as *chasidim,* meaning "loved of God" or "loyal to God." They were found everywhere in Palestine, not only in Jerusalem, and even wore a distinguishing garb so as to be easily recognized. According to Josephus, their number at the zenith of their popularity was more than six thousand. Because of the significant role the Pharisees played in the life of the Lord and the apostles, knowledge of the character and teachings of this group is of great importance for the understanding of the NT. They are mentioned dozens of times, especially in the Gospels, and often form the background for the works and words of Jesus.

Three facets, or characteristics, of the Jewish nation contributed to the development of the Pharisees, or, paradoxically, it may be said that the Pharisees made these contributions to Judaism, so that ultimately Pharisaism and Judaism became almost synonymous. The first of these is Jewish legalism, which began in earnest after the Babylonian captivity. Temple worship and sacrifices had ceased, and Judaism began to center its activities in Jewish Law and the synagogue. The Pharisees studied the traditional exegesis of the Law and made it a part of Jewish thought. The rise of the Jewish scribes, who were closely associated with the Pharisees, also gave great impetus to Jewish legalism. The Pharisees—more of a fraternal order or religious society than a sect—were the organized followers of these experts in interpreting the Scriptures; they formalized the religion of the scribes and put it into practice. This is why the NT mentions the scribes and Pharisees together nineteen times, all in the Gospels (e.g, Matt 5:20; 15:1; 23:2, 13, 14, 15, 23, 25, 27, 29; Luke 11:39, 42, 43, 44, 53). The Pharisees were the religious leaders of the Jews, not the practical politicians (like the more liberal Sadducees). The highest qualification for membership was strict adherence to the Law, oral or written. Josephus, a contemporary Jewish historian, aptly describes them as "a certain sect of Jews that appear more religious than others, and seem to interpret the laws more accurately" (*War* 1.5.2). A modern authority on Judaism, C. F. Moore, says, "The Pharisees were a party whose endeavor it was to live in strict accordance with the Law thus interpreted and amplified by the study and exposition of the Scribes, and the tradition of interpretation which they had established, and to bring the people to a similar conformity" (*Judaism in the First Centuries of the*

Christian Era, p. 66). This familiar characteristic of the Pharisees is well exemplified in the NT concerning the Sabbath (e.g., John 9:16).

A concomitant and blood brother of Jewish legalism was Jewish nationalism. Continued persecution and isolation crystallized this narrow spirit. During the Captivity the Jews were a small minority in a strange nation. The fierce persecution of Antiochus Epiphanes (175–164 B.C.), who made a bold attempt to Hellenize and assimilate the Jews, only drew the Jewish people closer together. The Pharisees took the occasion to cultivate a national and religious consciousness that has hardly been equaled.

A third contributing factor to Pharisaism was the development and organization of the Jewish religion itself after the Captivity and the revolt. Formulation and adaptation of Mosaic Law by scribe and rabbi, increased tradition, and a more rabid separatism from almost everything resulted in an almost new religion, much the opposite from that handed down in the covenant by the prophets. Pharisaism epitomized this spirit. Especially did they vehemently oppose all secularization of Judaism by the pagan Greek thought that penetrated Jewish life after the Alexandrian conquest. They ferreted out and sought the death of any liberal or antinomian person, especially if he was a fellow Jew. The Jewish ability to die for their "religion" made the people all the more proud of their traditions and law. This pride even developed into a feeling of superiority over the other nations and people. The extreme separatism from the Samaritans, for example (John 4:9), which went far beyond intermarriage and social intercourse, came from a superior feeling as well as religious emotion and found its most extreme expression among the Pharisees. They became a closely organized group, very loyal to the society and to each other, but separate from others, even their own people. They pledged themselves to obey all facets of the traditions to the minutest detail and were sticklers for ceremonial purity. They even vowed to pay tithes of everything they possessed in addition to the temple tax. They would not touch the carcass of a dead animal or those who had come into contact with such things. They had no association with people who had been defiled through sickness. In truth, they made life difficult for themselves and bitter for others. They despised those whom they did not consider their equals and were haughty and arrogant because they believed they were the only interpreters of God and his Word. It is only natural that ultimately such a religion became only a matter of externals and not of the heart, and that God's grace was thought to come only from doing the Law.

The doctrines of the Pharisees included predestination, or, as some have termed it, a teaching of special divine providence. They also laid much stress on the immortality of the soul and had a fundamental belief in spirit life, teachings that usually caused much controversy when they met the Sadducees, who just as emphatically denied them (Acts 23:6–9). Being people of the Law, they believed in final reward for good works and that the souls of the wicked were detained forever under the earth, while those of the virtuous rose again and even migrated into other bodies (Josephus, *Antiq.* 18.1.3; Acts 23:8). They accepted the OT Scriptures and fostered the usual Jewish messianic hope, which they gave a material and nationalistic twist.

It was inevitable, in view of these factors, that the Pharisees bitterly opposed Jesus and his teachings. If they despised the Herods and the Romans, they hated Jesus' doctrine of equality and claims of messiahship with equal fervor (John 9:16, 22). He in turn condemned both their theology and life of legalism. They often became a fertile background against which he taught God's free salvation by grace through his own death and resurrection. Clashes between Jesus and the Pharisees were frequent and bitter, as examples in the Gospels reveal: he called them a generation of vipers and condemns them for impenitence (Matt 3:7), condemned their work-righteousness (5:20), upbraided their pride against others (9:12; Luke 19:10), scorned their lovelessness on the Sabbath (12:2), rebuked them for not being baptized (Luke 7:30), taught them regarding divorce (Matt 19:3) and taxes (Mark 12:17), and condemned them for their covetousness (Luke 16:14). The Pharisees, in turn, accused Jesus of blasphemy (5:21), of being in league with the devil (Matt 9:34), and of breaking the Law (12:2). They often planned to destroy him (12:14). Jesus' longest and most scathing rebuke of the Pharisees is found in Matthew 23: "Woe to you, teachers of the law and Pharisees, you hypocrites! You are like whitewashed tombs, which look beautiful on the outside but on the inside are full of dead men's bones and everything unclean" (23:27).

The picture of the Pharisees painted by the NT is almost entirely negative, but the discriminating Bible student should bear in mind that not everything about every Pharisee was bad. It is perhaps not just to say that all Pharisees were self-righteous and hypocritical. Many Pharisees actually tried to promote true piety. What we know as Pharisaism from the NT was to some degree a degeneration of Pharisaism. Jesus condemned especially the Pharisees' ostentation, their hypocrisy, their salvation by works, their impenitence and lovelessness, but not always Pharisees as such. Some of the Pharisees were members of the Christian movement in the beginning (Acts 6:7). Some of the great men of the NT were Pharisees—Nicodemus (John 3:1), Gamaliel (Acts 5:34), and Paul (Acts 26:5; Phil 3:5). Paul does not speak the name "Pharisee" with great reproach but as a title of honor, for the Pharisees were highly respected by the masses of the Jewish people. When Paul says he was, "in regard to the law, a Pharisee" (Phil 3:5), he did not think of himself as a hypocrite but claimed the highest degree of faithfulness to the law. In similar manner, church leaders today might say, "We are the Pharisees." Much of modern scholarship, however, has cast the Pharisees into too favorable a light; when one reads our Lord's heated denunciation of Pharisaism in Matthew 23, where he specifically lists their sins, one has not only a true but also a dark picture of Pharisaism as it was at the time of Christ.

Bibliography: R. T. T. Herford, *The Pharisees,* 1924; J. Finkelstein, *The Pharisees,* 2 vols., 1938; W. D. Davies, *Introduction to Pharisaism,* 1967; Marcel Simon, *Jewish Sects at the Time of Jesus,* 1967; Martin Hengel, *Judaism and Hellenism,* 2 vols., 1974. LMP

PHAROSH (See PAROSH)

PHARPAR (fär'pär, Heb. *parpar*). The scornful Naaman contrasted the silt-laden waters of the Jordan with "Abana and Pharpar, the rivers of Damascus" (2 Kings 5:12). Abana is identified with the Barada. Pharpar is possibly the Awaj, a stream that rises east of Hermon, and one of whose sources is the Wadi Barbar. Naaman's remark does not necessarily mean that the river is close to Damascus.

PHARZITE (See PEREZ)

PHASEAH (See PASEAH)

PHEBE (See PHOEBE)

PHENICE (See PHOENIX)

PHICOL (fī'kŏl, Heb. *pîkhōl*). The army captain belonging to Abimelech, who was the Philistine king of Gerah (Gen 21:22, 32; 26:26).

PHILADELPHIA (Gr. *Philadelphia, brotherly love*). A Lydian city founded by Attalus II Philadelphus (159–138 B.C.). The king was so named from his devotion to his brother Eumenes, and the city perpetuated his title. Philadelphia was an outpost of Hellenism in native Anatolia. It lies under Mount Tmolus, in a wide vale that opens into the Hermus Valley, and along which the post road ran. It is on a broad, low, easily defended hill, and this explains Philadelphia's long stand against the Turks. The district is disastrously seismic, and the great earthquake of A.D. 17 ruined it completely. Placed right above the fault, Philadelphia was tormented by twenty years of recurrent quakes after the disaster of 17. Hence, says Ramsay, is derived the imagery of Revelation 3:12 ("Him who overcomes I will make a pillar in the temple of my God. Never again will he leave it."). The new name is certainly a reference to the proposal to rename the city Neocaesarea in gratitude for Tiberius's generous earthquake relief. The district was an area of vine growing and wine production, and therefore was a center for the worship of Dionysus, god of wine and fertility. A Christian witness, in spite of Muslim invasion and pressure, was maintained in Philadelphia through medieval and into modern times.

PHILEMON, LETTER TO (fī-lē'mŏn, Gr. Philēmōn, *loving*). Paul's letter to Philemon dates, in all probability, from the period of his Roman imprisonment. Paul's authorship is not seriously disputed. The letter is addressed: "To Philemon . . . Apphia . . . Archippus . . . and to the church that meets in your home." Apphia was Philemon's wife, and Archippus, not improbably, his son. Archippus appears to have been a person of some standing, but perhaps not notable for stability of character (Col 4:17). The Christian community was organized around a home, a practice of the early church. Many ancient churches were no doubt founded on the sites of homes where early Christians met. There is no evidence of church building of any sort before the third century. The fourth-century Christian chapel, recently discovered in the Roman villa of Lullingstone, Kent, England, is an illustration of the earlier practice. Justin Martyr provides similar evidence.

The occasion of the letter was the return of the runaway slave Onesimus to his master. There is a celebrated letter of the Roman writer Pliny on a similar subject, written perhaps forty years later. It is interesting to compare Pliny's language of humane generosity with Paul's language of brotherly affection. Pliny puts the plea for forgiveness on humanitarian and philosophical grounds; Paul founds all he has to say on Christian fellowship. He writes with exquisite tact and with words of praise before referring to obligation. The word "brother" comes like a friendly handclasp at the end of verse 7; "for my son Onesimus" adds a curiously poignant appeal at the end of verse 10. He is Paul the ambassador and as such might speak of duty. An imperial legate had a right to speak for the emperor, and the analogy would not be lost on Philemon. Paul reminds Philemon that, in respect to bondage, his own position did not vary from that of the man for whom he pleaded. Onesimus was a fellow bondsman and a son. The Talmud said, "If one teaches the son of his neighbor the Law, this is the same as if he had begotten him." Paul has the rabbinical saying in mind. "Onesimus" means "useful," and the writer makes a play on the word in verse 11, proceeding immediately to point to the sacrifice he himself was making. Onesimus was "briefly" parted from Philemon, says Paul, and he proceeds strongly to hint that manumission might be the truest mark of brotherliness. With a closing touch of humor Paul offers to pay Philemon back for anything the runaway owes, discounting, as he returns to seriousness, Philemon's own deep debt.

"I do wish, brother," Paul concludes, "that I may have some benefit from you in the Lord." He puns once more on Onesimus's name (*onaimēn* is the verb). The remark is a further appeal for Onesimus's freedom. The approach is characteristic of early Christianity. Slavery is never directly attacked as such, but principles that must prove fatal to the institution are steadily inculcated. To speak of brotherly love between master and slave ultimately renders slavery meaningless.

The letter ends on notes of intimacy. There was something truly Greek about Paul. The great Greek orators seldom placed the climax of their speech in the closing words, ending on a minor note designed to bring the excited audience back to normalcy and rest. So Paul ends here.

Bibliography: See Bruce, Lightfoot, Lohse, Martin (No. 2), Moule, O'Brien in bibliography to COLOSSIANS; also J. Knox, *Philemon Among the Letters to Paul,* 1960. EMB

PHILETUS (fī-lē'tŭs, Gr. *Philētos, worthy of love*). Like several other men named in the Scriptures—Judas Iscariot, Alexander, Demas, and Hymenaeus, for example—Philetus is remembered only for the evil he did. Paul alone mentions him as a false teacher in the church of Ephesus who, together with Hymenaeus, held that "the resurrection has already taken place" (2 Tim 2:18); that is, he did not radically deny a doctrine of the resurrection but allegorized it into a spiritual awakening or conversion and not a bodily resurrection as Paul taught in 1 Corinthians 15.

PHILIP (See HEROD)

PHILIP THE APOSTLE (Gr. *Philippos, lover of horses*). In the lists of the apostles (cf. Matt 10:3) the fifth in the list is called simply Philip, but the church has always called him "the apostle" to distinguish him from Philip the evangelist or Philip the deacon (Acts 6:8). His hometown was Bethsaida of Galilee, and no doubt he was a close friend of Andrew and Peter who lived in the same fishing village (John 1:44). It is almost certain that he was first a disciple of John the Baptist, because Jesus called him directly near Bethany beyond the Jordan, where John was preaching (1:43). He is often characterized as being timid and retiring, but nonetheless he brought Nathanael to Jesus (1:43). A more apt description appears to be that he was reluctant to believe wholeheartedly in the kingdom, and at times he seems to have had difficulty in grasping its meaning (14:8–14). This no doubt is why Jesus asked him the unusual question to arouse and test his faith before feeding the five thousand: "Where shall we buy bread for these people to eat?" (6:5–6). He served as something of a contact man for the Greeks and is familiarly known for bringing Gentiles to Jesus (12:20–23). The last information regarding Philip in the NT is found in Acts 1:13 where we are told that he was among the number of disciples in the upper chamber before Pentecost. His days after this are shrouded in legend and mystery, but the best tradition says he did mission work in Asia Minor. The historian Eusebius says that he was a "great light of Asia," and that he was buried at Hierapolis. LMP

PHILIP THE EVANGELIST (Gr. *Philippos, lover of horses*). Although the church, beginning with the second century, often confused him with Philip the apostle, this Philip's name does not occur in the Gospels. He appears in the Book of Acts as one of the famous seven deacons, said to be men "known to be full of the Spirit and wisdom" (Acts 6:3). He is second in the list, following Stephen, the first Christian martyr (6:5), so he must have been well known in the early church. Since he was a Hellenist (a Greek-speaking Jew), as a deacon he was to serve under the apostles (6:6) by taking care of the neglected Hellenist widows and the poor in general in the Jerusalem church. But after the death of Stephen the persecutions scattered the Christians abroad and, because of the great need, the deacons became evangelists or Christian missionaries. They even performed signs and wonders among the people (8:39; 6:8). In Acts 8 it is said that Philip preached in Samaria with great success: "When the crowds heard Philip and saw the miraculous signs he did, they all paid close attention to what he said." He cast out devils and healed the paralytics and the lame just as the apostles did. Some of his converts were Simon the sorcerer of Samaria (8:9–13) and the Ethiopian eunuch (8:26–40). Thus perhaps Philip was instrumental in introducing Christianity into Africa. Most of his labors seem to have been centered along the Mediterranean seaboard, where, following the Lord's command, he preached to the Gentiles. It can easily be seen, therefore, why Paul stayed at his home (21:8–9), since they had much in common. Philip was a forerunner of Paul in preaching to the Gentiles. In Acts 21 it is said that Philip had four unmarried daughters who were prophets. Little else is known of his later life.

PHILIPPI (fĭ-lĭp'ī, Gr. *Philippoi*). A Macedonian town in the plain east of Mount Pangaeus. It was a strategic foundation of Philip II, father of Alexander, in 358/7 B.C. The position dominated the road system of northern Greece; hence it became the center for the battle of 42 B.C., in which Antony defeated Brutus and Cassius. After Actium (31), Octavian (the future Augustus) constituted the place a Roman colony, housing partisans of Antony whose presence was undesirable in Italy. Philippi had a school of medicine connected with one of those guilds of physicians that the followers of early Greek medicine scattered through the Hellenistic world. This adds point to the suggestion that Luke was a Philippian. There is a touch of pride in Luke's description of Philippi as "the leading city of that district" (Acts 16:12), though Amphipolis was the capital. Philippi was the first European city to hear a Christian missionary, as far as the records go. Paul's choice of the locality throws light on the strategy of his evangelism. LMP

PHILIPPIANS, LETTER TO THE (fĭ-lĭp'ĭ-ănz). One of the most personal of all the apostle Paul's letters. It was written to "all the saints in Christ Jesus at Philippi" (Phil 1:1).

The church at Philippi in ancient Macedonia was the first European church founded by Paul and thus represents the first major penetration of the gospel into Gentile territory (cf. Phil 4:14–15). The events leading to the founding of the congregation are related in Acts 16:9–40. The great apostle, accompanied by his co-workers Silas, Timothy, and Luke, was on his second missionary journey through Asia Minor. Forbidden by the Holy Spirit to preach in Asia and in

Bithynia to the north, they made their way to Troas, farthest port of Asia on the Aegean Sea. In Troas Paul received a vision from the Lord to take the gospel to Europe. A man stood before him, a Greek of Macedonia, begging him, "Come over to Macedonia and help us" (Acts 16:9). Paul and his companions immediately answered this divine call and set sail for the nearest port—Neopolis of Philippi, named for Philip II of Macedon, the father of Alexander the Great.

Philippi had been thoroughly colonized by the Romans after 30 B.C., but the city was still more Greek in culture than Roman. Also the city was the first station on the Egnation Way and was the gateway to the East. Luke describes the city as follows: "From there we traveled to Philippi, a Roman colony and the leading city of that district of Macedonia. And we stayed there several days" (Acts 16:12). It is not unusual, therefore, that Paul's first convert there was a merchant woman named Lydia, a seller of purple. Her whole household was baptized and became the nucleus of the new church (16:15). The remarkable conversion of the jailer with its accompanying miraculous events also took place in Philippi (16:25–34). There was, therefore, a very intimate relationship between the apostle and this church. No doubt this was true also because the congregation consisted mainly of Gentiles and Paul saw in them the real future of the church. They were poor, but the fruits of faith were abundant. On several occasions they collected funds for Paul and also aided him while he was in prison (Phil 4:10–16). He had visited this favorite congregation whenever possible. He has no rebuke for it in this letter. The members are his "joy and crown" (4:1).

Before 1900 it was universally accepted that the Letter to the Philippians was written at Rome where Paul was in prison after his third missionary journey. In recent years, however, scholars have developed the hypothesis that it was written during Paul's imprisonment in Caesarea, but still more recently from the prison in Ephesus. The main reason for their hypotheses is that the old arguments for Roman authorship no longer fit the Roman situation alone. The problem of distance; the travels mentioned in Philippians itself; and the similarity to the earlier letters to Thessalonica, Galatia, and Corinth make us believe it is more likely that the letter was written from Ephesus. Although no specific imprisonment of Paul is mentioned in Ephesians, it is possible Paul was in prison in Ephesus (cf. 1 Cor 9:23; 15:32).

Very few scholars—mostly extreme radicals—have said Paul did not write the letter. Today it is almost universally believed that the apostle Paul is the author. Some scholars also believe the letter is made up of two or three smaller letters of Paul, but the best scholars now proclaim that Philippians is a single document, written wholly on one occasion.

The letter was occasioned by the gift of funds and clothing that Epaphroditus brought to Paul in prison. Paul took the opportunity to thank the Philippians for this and other favors. In doing so, as was his custom, Paul added practical Christian admonition to humility, joy, and steadfastness, which a reading of the letter will reveal. The main emphasis is joy; the concept "rejoice" appears no fewer than sixteen times in the letter. It also is a theological letter. The doctrines of the person and work of Christ, justification by faith, and the second coming of Christ are found among the practical admonitions.

General outline of contents of Philippians:

I. Chapter 1
- Greetings and thanksgiving (1:1–11).
- Progress of the gospel (1:11–20).
- On remaining in the world and working and suffering for Christ (1:21–30).

II. Chapter 2
- Exhortation to humility based on the humiliation and exaltation of Christ (2:1–13).
- Exhortation to the Christian life (2:14–18).
- Personal remarks involving Timothy and Epaphroditus (2:19–30).

III. Chapter 3
- Warning against false teachers (3:1–3).
- Paul's mighty confession of his faith (3:4–14).
- The Christian's hope of heaven (3:15–21).

IV. Chapter 4
- "Rejoice in the Lord always" (4:1–7).
- Admonition to Christian virtues (4:8–13).
- Paul's confidence in divine providence (4:14–19).
- Final greeting (4:20–22).

Bibliography: J. B. Lightfoot, *Saint Paul's Epistle to the Philippians,* 1881 (on the Greek text); F. W. Beare, *The Epistle to the Philippians* (HNTC), 1959; R. P. Martin, *Philippians* (NCB), 1976, and *Carmen Christi: Philippians 2:5–11 in Recent Interpretation and in the Setting of Early Christian Worship,* 1983; F. F. Bruce, *Philippians* (GNC), 1983. LMP

PHILISTINES (fĭ-lĭs′tēnz, Heb. *pelishtîm*). The name given to the people who inhabited the Philistine plain of Palestine during the greater part of OT times. The five cities of the Philistines were Ashdod, Gaza, Ashkelon, Gath, and Ekron (Josh 13:3; 1 Sam 6:17). They were situated in the broad coastal plain of southern Palestine, except for Gath, which is in the Shephelah or hill country. Our word "Palestine" is derived from the term "Philistine."

I. Origins. The origin of the Philistines is not completely known. They are said to have come from Caphtor (Jer 47:4; Amos 9:7), which is believed to be a name for Crete, or perhaps for the island world of the Aegean area. It is clear that they had migrated to Canaan within historical

The great battle of Ramses III against the Sea Peoples (Philistines), as depicted on a relief from temple of Ramses III at Medinet Habu, Thebes, c. 1182—1151 B.C. Courtesy Seffie Ben-Yoseph.

times and that this migration was remembered by the Hebrews.

Most authorities connect the coming of the Philistines with certain political and ethnic movements in the eastern Mediterranean area in the late thirteenth and early twelfth centuries B.C. Five groups of sea peoples left their homeland and moved southeastward at this time. They destroyed Ugarit (an ancient city-state in what is now Syria) and sought to invade Egypt, where they were repulsed by Ramses III in a great naval and land battle about 1191. On his monuments Ramses pictures these peoples as Europeans. Their pottery indicated that they came from the Greek islands, particularly Crete. The Philistines were one of these groups, and the Thekels another. After their repulse by the Egyptians, they invaded Canaan, the Philistines settling in what is now called the Philistine Plain, and the Thekels settling farther north, in the Sharon Plain.

What caused these people to leave their Aegean homeland and come to Canaan? There appears to have taken place at this time a great torrent of migration out of Europe, which swept through the Aegean world, Anatolia, and northern Syria, destroying the Hittite Empire and creating a situation of movement and folk wandering that was destined to change the ethnic make-up of the eastern Mediterranean world.

II. Civilization. The Philistines had a unique political organization. Their five city-states were ruled by five "lords of the Philistines" (Josh 13:3; Judg 16:5 KJV). The term "lord" is *seren* (always used in the plural, *seranim*), a non-Semitic word probably to be equated with *tyrannos,* the Greek word denoting the ruler of a city-state. The Philistine city-states were certainly united in some sort of a confederation.

It is clear that the Philistines were more wealthy and more advanced in technology than their Hebrew neighbors. According to 1 Samuel 13:19–22 they had the knowledge of metallurgy, whereas the Hebrews did not. This monopoly the Philistines jealously guarded, forcing the Hebrews to come to them even for agricultural implements, which they repaired at exorbitant cost (13:21). This situation has been confirmed by archaeology; the Philistines were in the Iron Age when they came to Palestine; the Hebrews attained to this level of advance only in the time of David. This technological superiority (the Philistines even had chariots, 13:5) is the reason for the Philistines' military domination of the Hebrews so evident toward the end of the period of the judges and in Saul's reign.

While the Philistines seem to have taught the Hebrews technology, the Hebrews and Canaanites influenced their Philistine neighbors in other ways. Soon after migrating to Canaan the Philistines seem to have adopted the Canaanite language and Semitic names. The Philistines worshiped the Semitic gods Dagon (Judg 16:23; 1 Sam 5:1–7), Ashtoreth (1 Sam 31:10), and Baal-Zebub (2 Kings 1:2, 6, 16). On the other hand, their non-Semitic origin is recalled in the epithet "uncircumcised" (Judg 14:3), so frequently used of them in the Bible.

III. History. The Book of Judges mentions the

Ancient sea ramparts of Ashdod, one of the five cities of the Philistines, on the Mediterranean shore. Courtesy Seffie Ben-Yoseph.

Philistines as a major contender against the Hebrews for the possession of Palestine. No doubt the tribes of Judah, Simeon, and Dan felt the pressure most, for their lands were adjacent to the Philistines. The judge Shamgar fought them (Judg 3:31). A Philistine oppression is briefly mentioned in Judges 10:6–7. The life of Samson, the last of the deliverers mentioned in the Book of Judges, is set in a violent struggle with the Philistines (Judg 13–16; note 14:4c; 15:11). Samson, a man of great strength but little self-discipline, was finally snared by a Philistine spy, Delilah (16:4–21). No doubt the Danite migration (Judg 18) was occasioned by the Philistine pressure that kept the Danites from occupying the territory assigned them and forced them to seek a more easily taken area. The Book of 1 Samuel opens with the theme of Philistine oppression with which Judges closes. Eli's judgeship seems to have been characterized by Philistine domination (1 Sam 4–6). Samuel was able to see a measure of victory when he defeated them at the battle of Mizpah and forced them to return certain cities they had taken from Israel (7:7–14). Saul's reign, although it began well, ended in complete defeat for the Hebrews; and the Philistines seem to have overrun most of Palestine west of the Jordan, even occupying Beth Shan at the eastern end of the Valley of Jezreel (13:5; 14:1–52; 17:1–58; 31:1–13).

During the latter part of the reign of Saul, David, the contender for the throne, fled for safety to the Philistines (1 Sam 21:10–15; 27:1–28:2; 29:1–11), who gladly protected him, thinking thus to contribute to the weakness of the Hebrews. No doubt David learned from the Philistines many things he later used to advantage when he became king, including perhaps the technique for working iron.

Probably David remained a Philistine vassal during the seven and a half years he reigned at Hebron (2 Sam 2:1–4). When at the end of this time he asserted his independence and united all Israel under his rule, he was immediately opposed by them, but he decisively defeated them in two battles (5:17–25). From this time on, the Philistine grip was broken. In later campaigns (21:15–22; 23:9–17) David consistently bested them, and it seems clear that from this time on the

Ruins of Ashkelon, one of the five principal cities of the Philistines, who made it a seat of one of their princes. Protruding pillars are lodged in the ruins. The heavy-handed occupation of the Crusaders ravaged the site. Courtesy Seffie Ben-Yoseph.

Philistines were confined to their own territory and were no longer a threat. David must have had peaceful relations with them at times, for his bodyguards, the Kerethites and Pelethites, appear to have been recruited from them (8:18; 15:18).

After the death of Solomon and the division of the Hebrew kingdom, the Philistines reasserted the independence they had lost to David and Solomon. Their cities appear to have engaged in commerce, for which their location certainly was ideal (Joel 3:4–8; Amos 1:6–8). Some of them paid tribute to Jehoshaphat, after whose death they raided Judah (2 Chron 17:11; 21:16–17). When the Assyrians later sought to control the road to Egypt, it is quite natural that the Philistines were frequently mentioned in their inscriptions, along with Israel and the other "Westlands" countries. Sargon (722–705 B.C.) captured the Philistine cities, deported some of the inhabitants, and set an Assyrian governor over them. In the days of Hezekiah the Philistines played a great part in the revolt against Sennacherib. It appears that among them, as in Jerusalem, there were two political parties, one recommending submission to the world conquerors, the other urging a stubborn fight for freedom in union with their neighbors the Judeans.

Esarhaddon and Ashurbanipal name Philistine tributaries as well as the Judean king Manasseh. The later struggles between Egypt and Assyria were the cause of great suffering to the Philistine cities, and practically close their history as strictly Philistinian. The cities did continue as predominantly non-Jewish centers, becoming Hellenistic cities in the Greek period.

IV. Early Biblical Mention. Before the times of the judges certain Philistines are mentioned in Genesis (10:14; 26:14). The Philistine land is referred to (21:32, 34). Abimelech king of Gerar is called "king of the Philistines" (26:1; cf. 26:14–15). These references have often been regarded as anachronisms, since the Philistines appear not to have entered Canaan before the period of the judges. A more generous judgment has seen here a later revision of the text, bringing the proper names up to date. It is possible that a later editor, perhaps during the Hebrew kingdom, may have revised the proper names to make them meaningful in his time, thus introducing the name Philistine into Genesis (cf. also Exod 13:17; 23:31; Josh 13:2–3).

On the other hand, recent studies of the problem suggest another approach. Folk movements are never completed in one generation. It is not impossible that the great Philistine movement that entered Canaan during the judges period may have had a small precursor as early as the patriarchal age. The army of Ramses III, which repulsed the invading Philistines in 1191 B.C., itself contained soldiers who are portrayed on the Egyptian monuments as Philistines. Evidently these had joined the Egyptian army as mercenaries at an earlier date. Further, pottery identified as Philistine has turned up in Palestinian excavations recently in layers earlier than those of the judges period. It also seems that the sea peoples invading Egypt came from land as well as sea, and Ramses III refers to "The Peleset [i.e., Philistines] who are hung up in their towns," implying that some of these troublesome people had already settled nearby.

It therefore seems possible that some Philistines were settled in Gerar by the time of Isaac. They were not a large hostile group (as later), but a small settlement with which the patriarch had more or less friendly relations. JBG

PHILO JUDAEUS (fī'lō jū-dē'ŭs). Jewish scholar and philosopher, born in Alexandria about 20 B.C. Alexandria had an old tradition of Jewish scholarship, and Philo sprang from a rich and priestly family. Few details are known of his life, save that in A.D. 39 he took part in an embassy to Rome to plead the case of the Jews whose religious privileges, previously wisely recognized by Rome, were menaced by the mad Caligula. Philo lived until 50 and was a prolific author. His writings include philosophical works, commentaries on the Pentateuch, and historical and apologetic works in the cosmopolitan tradition of Alexandrian Jewry, which had long sought to commend its literature to the Gentile world. Hence Philo's development of an allegorical interpretation of the OT. His aim was to show that much of the philosophy of the Greeks had been anticipated by the Jews. He was also, like Paul of Tarsus, a citizen of two worlds and sought to synthesize his own Hellenistic and Hebraic traditions. His doctrine of God most notably reveals this synthesis. His doctrine of the Logos is discussed earlier (see LOGOS). The Logos, in Philo's rendering of the Greek doctrine, was simultaneously the creative power that orders the universe and also a species of mediator through whom people know God. John seems therefore to have had Philo's philosophy in mind when he wrote the first eighteen verses of the fourth Gospel, sharply personal though John's interpretation is. Others, too, were influenced by Philo's mysticism and principles of exegesis. Clement and Origen used his works; and the Latin fathers, generally following his methods of allegorical interpretation, established a tradition of exegesis that still finds favor in some quarters. EMB

PHILOLOGUS (fī-lŏl'ō-gŭs, Gr. *Philologos, fond of learning*). A believer in Rome to whom Paul sent a salutation (Rom 16:15).

PHILOSOPHY. The word with its cognate terms is usually found in a derogatory sense in the Bible. It is not a genuine love of wisdom that Paul deprecates in Colossians 2:8, but "hollow and deceptive philosophy, which depends on human tradition and the basic principles of this world rather than on Christ."

The same thought is expressed in the discussion of "wisdom" in 1 Corinthians (1:18–2:16; 3:18–21), where Paul not only emphasizes the inadequacy of worldly wisdom, but says, "We . . . speak a message of wisdom among the mature" (2:6), a wisdom based on revelation. This is similar to the "wisdom" doctrine of Job, Ecclesiastes, certain psalms, and especially Proverbs. The Book of Ecclesiastes, which teaches that "all is vanity under the sun," may be regarded as an answer to modern philosophical naturalism. For the "philosophers" of Acts 17:18, see EPICUREANS and STOICS.

PHINEHAS (fĭn'ē-ăs, Heb. *pînehās, mouth of brass*). 1. A son of Eleazar and grandson of Aaron (Exod 6:25; 1 Chron 6:4, 50; 9:20; Ezra 7:5; 8:2). He killed Zimri and Cozbi at God's command (Num 25:6–15; Ps 106:30). He conducted a successful embassy to the Transjordan tribes regarding the altar they had built (Josh 22:13–34). These incidents evidence his great zeal and faithful service.

2. A son of Eli, unfaithful in his ministration of the priest's office (1 Sam 1:3; 2:12–17, 22–25, 27–36; 3:11–13). He and his brother Hophni brought the ark into the camp of Israel, hoping its presence would bring victory against the Philistines, but the ark was taken and Hophni and Phinehas killed (ch. 4).

3. Father of Eleazar who with other priests accounted for the valuables brought back to Jerusalem with the exiles returning from the Babylonian captivity (Ezra 8:33).

PHLEGON (flē'gŏn, Gr. *Phlegōn, burning*). A believer in Rome to whom Paul sent a loving greeting (Rom 16:14).

PHOEBE (fē'bē, Gr. *Phoibē, pure*). A woman mentioned in the Scriptures only in Romans 16:1–2. She was one of the first deaconesses, if not the first, of the Christian church and was highly recommended by Paul. In a single sentence he speaks of her Christian status ("sister"), of her position or office (*diakonos,* "servant"), of her service record ("she has been a great help to many people, including me"), and of the importance of her work ("give her any help she may need from you"). Phoebe was serving as deaconess of the church at Cenchrea, port of Corinth, when Paul arrived there at the end of his third journey, and where he wrote his letter to the Romans. Either she was on her way to Rome to serve that church or Paul sent her with this important letter to the Roman Christians.

PHOENICIA, PHENICIA (fē-nĭsh'ĭ-â, Gr. *Phoinikē*). A strip of coastal territory between the Lebanon range, the uplands of Galilee, and the Mediterranean Sea, containing the trading ports of the great maritime people that bore its name. Exact definition of boundaries is not possible, for the Phoenicians were associated with their cities rather than with their hinterland, after the fashion of the Greek colonies. It can be said, however, that to the north Phoenicia never extended beyond Arvad or Arados on the modern island of Ruad, eighty miles (one hundred thirty-three km.) north of Sidon. The southern limits were Acco, modern Acre, just north of Carmel, and, according to the Egyptian papyrus that tells the

A general view of the excavated ruins at Gebal (Byblos), that shows remnants of a temple dedicated to the Canaanite god, Reshef, c. thirteenth century B.C. Courtesy Studium Biblicum Franciscanum, Jerusalem. Photo Manoug.

story of Wen-Amon, Dor, just south of Carmel. The Semitic name for the land was Canaan, the "Kinachchi" or "Kinachna" of the Tell-el-Amarna Letters, and the "Chua" of Phoenician coins. The name is of doubtful significance, but may mean "lowland," as distinct from the uplands parallel with the coast, which are a geographical feature of the eastern end of the Mediterranean. The term Phoenicia is from a Greek work meaning "dark red," but there is no clear reason why this was applied to the land. "Phoenix," in fact, may mean "dark red" because the Phoenicians were the discoverers of the crimson-purple dye derived from the murex shellfish. "Phoenix" also means a date palm, and there may be a clue in the fact that the palm is a symbol on Phoenician coins.

The Phoenicians were Semites who came to the Mediterranean as one ripple of the series of Semitic migrations that moved west and south round the Fertile Crescent during the second millennium B.C. Abraham was part of this historical process, but the movement brought major tribal elements, the Amorites, for example, to Palestine, the Kassite dynasty to Babylon, and the Hyksos to Egypt. The tribes who occupied the coastal strip turned their attention to the sea because of the pressure on the agricultural lands in the narrow lowland strip, never more than twenty miles (thirty-three km.) wide, behind them. A tradition of seafaring may have accompanied the immigrants from the Persian Gulf, itself the first scene of human navigation and seaborne trade. Such was the challenge and stimulus that made the Phoenicians the most notable sailors of the ancient world and led to their feats of colonization, which spread their trading posts around the African coast from Carthage westward and established them in Spain and Sicily.

It is not known whether they built the towns that formed the centers of their power and trade, or whether, descending to the sea, they found the towns awaiting their occupation. According to Herodotus, who visited Tyre, the city was founded in 2755 B.C. He did not name the founders. Like that of the Greeks, the Phoenician civilization was organized around the city. That is why Phoenicia had no place in history as a political unit. It is Tyre and Sidon, and less frequently other cities, such as Acco and Dor, that appear in the record as units. Sidon was the most powerful and influential of the Phoenician cities. To the Greek poet Homer, Phoenicians were commonly Sidonians. He referred to "Phaedimus" as "the king of the Sidonians." The OT uses the same nomenclature. "The gods of Sidon," Baal and Ashtaroth (Judg 10:6), were the gods of the Phoenicians generally (also Judg 18:7; 1 Kings 5:6; 11:5, 33; 16:31; 2 Kings 23:13). The reference to "Jezebel daughter of Ethbaal king of the Sidonians" (1 Kings 16:31) is at first sight strange, for Ethbaal was king of Tyre. As stated above, however, "Sidonian" had become a generic term for "Phoenician." The fact is further established by Vergil, the Roman poet, who called Dido queen of Carthage and daughter of Belus (Ethbaal) king of Tyre, "Sidonia Dido."

Phoenicia first appears in recorded history in the Egyptian account of the northern campaigns of Thutmose III. In his campaign against the Hittites of 1471 B.C., the pharaoh found it necessary to secure the Phoenician coastal strip as an essential avenue of communications. He punished severely the revolt of Arvad, the northernmost town of the Phoenicians, and went to considerable pains to organize the series of Phoenician ports as supply depots. Sporadically, as with the rest of the lands to the north, Egypt asserted or relaxed her authority. The Tell-el-Amarna Letters show Phoenicia in the same state of disunity and internal rivalry as Palestine during the weak reign of the mystic Amenhotep IV. Seti I (1373–1292) pushed his conquests as far as Acco and Tyre, Ramses II (1292–1225) as far as Biruta (modern Beirut). The whole coast revolted in the reign of Merneptah (1225–1215), including Philistia, for Pharaoh boasts, "Plundered is Canaan with every evil."

Egyptian influence fluctuated over the next century, and when Ramses XII (1118–1090 B.C.) sent the priest Wen-Amon to buy cedar for his funeral barge, the Egyptian envoy was treated with the scantest courtesy in Dor and Tyre. An entertaining papyrus tells his story. A century later found Hiram, king of Tyre, in alliance with David, a partnership that developed into a trade alliance in the days of Solomon. Solomon's fleet of "ships of Tarshish" at Ezion Geber on the Gulf

The god Shadrafa standing on a lion above mountains and swinging a small lion in his hand. Limestone stele from Amrit in Phoenicia, c. 550 B.C. Courtesy Réunion des Musées Nationaux.

of Aqabah seems to have been part of a combined trading venture whereby the Phoenicians used Solomon's port and piloted Solomon's ships to southern Arabia and India (1 Kings 10:22; 2 Chron 9:21). If indeed "ivory, and apes and baboons" are Tamil words (a language of India), Tarshish in these passages must be sought in East rather than the West. The cargoes are certainly not Spanish.

With the division of Israel, Phoenicia became the neighbor and partner of the northern kingdom, while Judah lay along the communication route with the Gulf of Aqabah and the Red Sea. Hence Ahab's alliance with Jezebel, the prosperity of the north (Ahab's "Ivory House"), and the sequence of events that led to Elijah's protest and the contest on Carmel. The Assyrians had dealings with Phoenicia. Ashurnasirpal (884–860 B.C.) imposed tribute on Tyre and Sidon after his thrust to the sea. Shalmaneser II added Arvad. Tiglath-Pileser (745–727) reasserted the Assyrian authority, which had lapsed. Shalmaneser IV (727–722) unsuccessfully besieged Tyre for five years. Sennacherib (705–681) besieged Sidon, took tribute from Sidon and Acco, but left Tyre undisturbed. Tyre was a formidable task for a besieger. Ashurbanipal (668–626) claimed to have reduced Tyre and Arvad, but by the end of his reign Phoenicia was free again, as Assyria lapsed into one of her phases of fatigue. Nebuchadnezzar (604–562) beseiged Tyre for thirteen years and seems to have captured the city (Ezek 26–29) or received its surrender on terms. Hence, probably, the preeminence of Sidon in Persian times. According to historians Diodorus and Herodotus, Sidon provided Xerxes with his best ships for the great raid on Greece. All the Phoenician cities submitted to Alexander after Issus (333), except Tyre, which Alexander took after a vigorous siege of seven months. Under the successors, the power of the Ptolemies of Egypt first extended far up the Phoenician coast, but after 197 the Seleucids of Syria controlled the land, until the whole area passed into Roman hands in 65. The reference to a woman "born in Syrian Phoenicia" in Mark 7:26 reflects the fact of the century and a half of Syrian rule.

The Phoenician stock must by this time have been heavily diluted by immigrant blood, principally Greek. The whole area figured largely in the early evangelism of the church (Acts 11:19; 15:3; 21:2). Phoenicia's achievement was principally in the realm of trade and in her simplification and diffusion of the alphabet, as a tool and means, no doubt, of commerce. Ezekiel 27 and 28 give some notion of the extent and variety of Phoenician trade, but the Phoenicians did nothing to spread or communicate the knowledge, geographical and social, that their voyaging won. Tyre's colony at Carthage blockaded the Straits of Gibraltar for many generations in an attempt to guard the western and Atlantic trade routes, and this secrecy was a Phoenician principle. The land made no contribution to art and literature, and its religious influence, heavily infected with the cruder fertility cults, was pernicious. EMB

PHOENIX (fē'nĭks, Gr. *Phoinix*). A town and harbor on the south coast of Crete (Acts 27:12). It has been identified with Loutro, the only harbor west of Fair Havens large enough to accommodate a galley as large as the vessel in the account. Some difficulty in this identification arises from the fact that Luke speaks of the harbor as "facing both southwest and northwest." Loutro faces east, and the ERV resolves the difficulty by taking the text to mean "in the direction in which the south-west and north-west winds blow." There is no proof for this assumption.

PHRYGIA (frĭj'ĭ-ȧ, Gr. *Phrygia*). In Bible times an inland province of SW Asia Minor. Its tablelands, which rose to 4,000 feet (1,250 m.), contained many cities and towns considerable in size and wealth. Most historians agree that the province included greater or lesser territory at different times, and there is no common agreement on the boundaries, as they shifted almost every generation. It seems that at one time it included a greater part of western Asia Minor. Then it was divided into Phrygia Major and Phrygia Minor; later the Romans even divided it into three parts. Some Bible students believe the term "Phrygia" is used loosely in the NT, as in the Book of Acts, and that it even included small provinces like Pisidia. In these days "Phrygia" meant an extensive territory, which at times contributed area to a number of different Roman provinces. It is thought to have this broader meaning in Acts 2:10, which speaks of devout Jews from Phrygia at Pentecost.

Whatever the exact extent of the province, it receives its renown mainly from Paul's missionary journeys. Paul and his co-workers visited the fertile territory, which contained rich pastures for cattle and sheep and a heavy population in need of the gospel, during all three missionary journeys. If Phrygia is understood in its broader sense, Paul and Barnabas introduced Christianity into the province during the first journey (Acts 13:13; 14:24). Acts 16:6 briefly describes the visit of Paul and Silas on the second journey in these words: "Paul and his companions traveled throughout the region of Phrygia and Galatia, having been kept by the Holy Spirit from preaching the word in the province of Asia." On his third journey Paul quickly revisited the province on his way to Ephesus and Corinth (18:23): "After spending some time in Antioch, Paul set out from there and traveled from place to place throughout the region of Galatia and Phrygia, strengthening all the disciples." Although a great deal of Christian activity took place in ancient Phrygia, with this reference it passes from the biblical record. LMP

PHURAH (See PURAH)

PHUT (See PUT)

PHUVAH (See PUAH)

PHYGELUS, PHYGELLUS (fī-jĕl'ŭs, Gr. *Phy-*

gelos). In his second letter to Timothy (1:15) Paul mentions Phygelus and Hermogenes by name as being among those Christians of Asia (western province of Asia Minor) who had turned away from the apostle. From the context (2 Tim 1:13–14) it may be assumed that the apostasy included the repudiation of Paul's doctrine. If we connect Phygelus with 2 Timothy 4:16 ("at my first defense, no one came to my support"), we may infer that he, being in Rome, forsook Paul's personal cause in the Roman courts at a crucial time when his testimony could have meant much for the future of the church. Some scholars feel that Phygelus may also have been one of the leaders of a group of wayward Christians in Rome (Phil 1:15–16).

PHYLACTERY (See DRESS)

PHYSICIAN (See OCCUPATIONS AND PROFESSIONS)

PI BESETH (See BUBASTIS)

PICKS (Heb. *hārîts*). A sharp instrument made of iron. David consigned conquered peoples to hard labor with "saws . . . picks and axes" (2 Sam 12:31; 1 Chron 20:3). The KJV rendering of "harrow" in these verses has no connection with the verb "harrow" used elsewhere.

PICTURES. The word occurs three times in the KJV. In Numbers 33:52, ASV and RSV have "figured stones," NIV "carved images." In Proverbs 25:11, ASV has "network," RSV and NIV "setting," an apparent reference to pleasing inlaid work in gold and silver. In Isaiah 2:16 another word from the same Hebrew root is translated "imagery" in ASV. RSV has "beautiful craft." NIV reads "stately vessel." The carved figureheads of ships, usually idolatrous symbols, may be intended. The Hebrew root suggests something conspicuous or showy.

PIETY. The word occurs only once in KJV and ASV (1 Tim 5:4): "Let them learn first to show piety at home." RSV uses "religious duty," NIV "put their religion into practice." NIV has "piety" three times in Job (4:6; 15:4; 22:4), where others use "fear" (of God) or (once in RSV) "integrity."

PIG (See ANIMALS)

PIGEON (See BIRDS)

PI HAHIROTH (pī hà-hī'rŏth, Heb. *pî-haḥîrôth*). The place in NE Egypt where the Israelites last camped before crossing the Red Sea. Here the Egyptian army overtook them (Exod 14:2, 9; Num 33:7). Exact location unknown.

PILATE (pī'lăt, Gr. *Pilatos*). The fifth procurator, or governmental representative, of imperial Rome in Palestine at the time of Christ, holding this office A.D. 26 to 36. Whether it be considered an honor or a disgrace, he is the one man of all Roman officialdom who is named in the Apostles' Creed—"suffered under Pontius Pilate." To Christians, therefore, he is known almost entirely for his cowardly weakness in the condemnation of Jesus to Roman crucifixion in 30. The four Gospels relate the sad but glorious events fully, especially the Gospel of John. Pilate is also mentioned in the Acts of the Apostles (3:13; 4:27; 13:28) and in 1 Timothy 6:13, where we are told that Jesus "before Pontius Pilate made the good confession." *Pontius* was his family name, showing that he was descended from the Roman family, or *gens,* of *pontii. Pilate* no doubt came from the Latin *pilatus,* meaning "one armed with a *pilum,* or javelin."

Beyond this, little is known of his early or later years, since most of the secular references may be only legend and tradition, such as the story that he was an illegitimate son of Tyrus, king of Mayence, who sent him to Rome as a hostage. In Rome, so a story goes, he committed murder and was then sent to Pontus of Asia Minor where he subdued a rebellious people, regained favor with Rome, and was awarded the governorship of Judea. It is more probable that, like the sons of many prominent Romans, he was trained for governmental service; and either because of his political astuteness or as a political plum the Emperor Tiberius gave him the hard task of governing the troublesome Jews. The Romans had many such governors throughout the provinces, which was part of their success in local government. Judea had a succession of these smaller rulers before and after Pilate. Generally they were in charge of tax and financial matters, but governing Palestine was so difficult that the procurator there was directly responsible to the emperor and also had supreme judicial authority such as Pilate used regarding Christ. His territory included Judea, Samaria, and old Idumea.

Most procurators disliked being stationed in a distant, difficult, dry outpost such as Judea. Pilate, however, seemed to enjoy tormenting the Jews, although, as it turned out, he was seldom a match for them. He never really understood them, as his frequent rash and capricious acts reveal. The Jewish historian Josephus tells us that he immediately offended the Jews by bringing the "outrageous" Roman standards into the Holy City. At another time he hung golden shields inscribed with the names and images of Roman deities in the temple itself. Once he even appropriated some of the temple tax to build an aqueduct. To this must be added the horrible incident mentioned in Luke 13:1 about "the Galileans whose blood Pilate had mixed with their sacrifices," meaning no doubt that Roman soldiers killed these men while they were sacrificing in the Holy Place. These fearful events seem to disagree with the role Pilate played in the trial of Jesus, where he was as clay in the hands of the Jews, but this may be explained by the fact that his fear of the Jews increased because of their frequent complaints to Rome.

According to his custom, Pilate was in Jerusalem at the time to keep order during the Passover

Early photograph of the Ecce Homo Arch in Jerusalem. This is the traditional site of Pilate's famous declaration "Behold the man!" Courtesy University Library, Istanbul.

Feast. His usual headquarters were in Caesarea. After the Jews had condemned Jesus in their own courts, they brought him early in the morning to Pilate, who was no doubt residing in Herod's palace near the temple. It is surprising he gave them a hearing so early in the day (John 18:28). From the beginning of the hearing he was torn between offending the Jews and condemning an innocent person, and, apart from simply acquitting him, he tried every device to set Jesus free. He declared Jesus innocent after private interrogation; he sent him to Herod; he had Jesus scourged, hoping this would suffice; finally he offered the Jews a choice between Jesus and a coarse insurrectionist. When he heard the words, "If you let this man go, you are no friend of Caesar," and "We have no king but Caesar!" he thought of politics rather than justice and condemned an innocent man to crucifixion. Washing his hands only enhanced his guilt. Pilate is to be judged in the light of his times when one lived by the philosophy of self-aggrandizement and expediency.

Scripture is silent regarding the end of Pilate. According to Josephus, his political career came to an end six years later when he sent soldiers to Samaria to suppress a small harmless religious rebellion, and in that suppression innocent men were killed. The Samaritans complained to Vitellius, legate of Syria, who sent Pilate to Rome. His friend Tiberius the emperor died while Pilate was on his way to Rome, and Pilate's name disappears from the official history of Rome. The historian Eusebius says that soon afterward, "wearied with misfortunes," he took his own life. Various traditions conflict as to how and where Pilate killed himself. One familiar legend states that he was banished to Vienna; another that he sought solitude from politics on the mountain by Lake Lucerne, now known at Mount Pilatus. After some years of despair and depression, he is said to have plunged into the lake from a precipice. LMP

PILDASH (pĭl'dăsh, Heb. *pildash*). Sixth son of Nahor, Abraham's brother (Gen 22:22).

PILEHA (See PILHA)

PILGRIM (Gr. *parepidēmos, a sojourner in a strange place*). Hebrews 11:13–16 (KJV) shows that the faithful sought a heavenly city and did not consider themselves permanently attached to earth. First Peter 2:11 exhorts Christians to purity because of this status. Pilgrims might be exiles (RSV) or voluntary sojourners in a foreign country. NIV uses the terms "aliens" and "strangers."

PILGRIMAGE (Heb. *māghôr, a place of sojourning,* or *the act of sojourning;* see Exod 6:4, NIV "lived as aliens;" Ps 119:54). In Genesis 47:9 a lifetime is meant. The Hebrew root *ghûr* means "to dwell as a foreigner, newly come into a land in which he has no citizens' rights, such as the original inhabitants possess." The biblical usage, whether the word is translated "pilgrimage" or otherwise, began with the wanderings of Abraham and his descendants, and later was applied to the status of a believer in the one true God, living on an earth unfriendly to God and to his people.

PILHA (Heb. *pilhā'*). One of those who, with Nehemiah, sealed the covenant (Neh 10:24).

PILLAR. Several Hebrew words are so translated in the OT. Hezekiah's pillars (2 Kings 18:16 KJV) are called doorposts in RSV and NIV; Hebrew *'ōmenôth* from a root meaning "to stand firm." The pillars for the house of the Lord (1 Kings 10:12) are called supports in RSV and NIV; Hebrew *mīse'ādh.* More frequent are derivatives from the root *ntsb,* "to stand." There is a religious element in the purpose and use of such pillars: stones were set erect as memorials of a divine appearance in connection with the worship of the one true God (Gen 28:18–22; 31:13; 35:14; Exod 24:4; Isa 19:19; Hos 3:4; 10:1–2). Lot's wife, looking back at the ruin of Sodom, became a pillar of salt (Gen 19:26). In addition to heaping up stones, people set up stone pillars to signify an agreement with religious conditions between them (31:43–52). Rachel's grave was marked by a pillar (35:20). Absalom in his lifetime erected a pillar to be his memorial (2 Sam 18:18). In Judges 9:6 the ASV footnote has "garrison," but other versions agree on "pillar." Abimelech was made king either at a military stronghold or by a religious ceremony at a consecrated pillar.

Standing stones used in idolatrous worship are

A Canaanite shrine with a series of basalt stelae representing sacred pillars, ranged round an offering table, at Hazor, thirteenth century B.C. Courtesy Israel Department of Antiquities and Museums.

referred to (Deut 12:3) and are usually called images in KJV (NIV "sacred stones"), where ASV and RSV read "pillars" (Exod 23:24; 34:13; Lev 26:1; Deut 7:5; 12:3; 16:22; 1 Kings 14:23; 2 Kings 17:10; 18:4; 23:14; 2 Chron 14:3; 31:1; Mic 5:13). In Ezekiel 26:11 KJV reads "garrisons," ASV, RSV, NIV "pillars."

Another common Hebrew word for pillar, *amudh,* from a root "to stand," refers to (1) the pillar of cloud and fire (see next article) that guided Israel in the wilderness, (2) tabernacle pillars either of shittim wood (KJV; acacia ASV, NIV, RSV) or of bronze or material not named (Exod 26:32, 37; 27:10–17; 36:36, 38; 38:10–17, 28; 39:33, 40; 40:18; Num 3:36–37; 4:31–32), (3) the pillars of Solomon's temple (1 Kings 7:2–42; 2 Kings 25:13–17; 1 Chron 18:8; 2 Chron 3:15, 17; 4:12–13; Jer 27:19; 52:17–22), (4) the pillars of the new temple that Ezekiel saw in a vision (Ezek 40:49; 42:6), (5) the supporting pillars that Samson pushed apart in the Philistine temple (Judg 16:25–29), (6) the marble pillars of the Persian king's palace (Esth 1:6), and (7) the pillars (KJV, MLB; posts NIV, RSV) of silver Solomon's litter or carriage (S of Sol 3:10).

Figuratively, Scripture speaks of "columns of smoke" (Judg 20:20), "a column of smoke" (S of Sol 3:6), and "billows of smoke" (Joel 2:30), but the Hebrew word is *timeroth* ("palm trees"), referring to their spreading tops. God promised to make Jeremiah an iron pillar (Jer 1:18). A man's legs are compared to pillars of marble (S of Sol 5:15). The seven pillars of wisdom are mentioned but not defined (Prov 9:1). The pillars of the earth (Job 9:6; Ps 75:3) and of heaven (Job 26:11) refer to the fixed order in the heavens; God "suspends the earth over nothing" (Job 26:7). In Hannah's song (1 Sam 2:8 KJV, MLB, MOF, NASB, RSV; foundations NEB, NIV) the Hebrew is *mātsûq,* "molten pillars." The four NT uses of *stylos* ("pillar") are figurative: a victorious Christian (Rev 3:12), the church (1 Tim 3:15), apostles (Gal 2:9), and an angel (Rev 10:1). ER

PILLAR OF CLOUD AND FIRE. God guided Israel out of Egypt and through the wilderness by a pillar of cloud by day. This became a pillar of fire by night that they might travel by night in escaping from the Egyptian army (Exod 13:21–22). When the Egyptians overtook the Israelites, the angel of the Lord removed this cloudy, fiery pillar from before them and placed it behind them as an effective barrier (14:19–20, 24). The pillar of cloud stood over the tent of meeting outside the camp whenever the Lord met Moses there (33:7–11). The Lord came down for judgment in the cloud (Num 12; 14:13–35), and God met Moses and Joshua in the cloud at the tent of meeting to make arrangements for the succession when Moses was near death (Deut 31:14–23). Psalm 99:7 reminds the people that God spoke to them in the pillar of cloud. When Ezra prayed in the presence of the returning exiles at Jerusalem, he reviewed the way God had led the people by the pillar of cloud and fire (Neh 9:12, 19). First Corinthians 10:1–2 speaks of the Israelite forefathers being under the cloud, baptized into Moses in the cloud. No natural phenomenon fits the biblical description. The cloud and fire were divine manifestations, in a form sufficiently well-defined to be called a pillar. ER

PILLOW. In Genesis 28:11, 18, Heb. *mera-'ăshōth,* "at the head," refers to the stones Jacob set up, either under his head (ASV, RSV, NIV) or at his head when sleeping outdoors. The same Hebrew word is translated "bolster" in 1 Samuel 19:13, 16 (KJV) in connection with *kevîr,* a "quilt" (ASV footnote). NIV prefers to say simply "at the head." In Ezekiel 13:18, 20 the Hebrew word is *kesāthôth,* "fillet, arm-band," from a root "to bind, take captive." In modern Hebrew it means "pillow, bolster, cushion." RSV translates this as "bands," in conformity with the belief that women sewed magic amulets on their arms (NIV "wrists" and "arms"). Only in Mark 4:38, Greek *proskephalaion,* "cushion for the head," or any cushion (ASV, RSV, NIV), do we have an approach to the modern meaning. This is probably the pad on which a rower sat.

PILTAI (pĭl'tī, Heb. *piltāy*). A priest, head of his father's house of Moadiah in the days of Joiakim (Neh 12:17).

PIM (See WEIGHTS AND MEASURES)

PIN (Heb. *yāthēdh*). A tent peg, usually of wood, sharpened at one end, shaped at the other for attaching the tent cord (Judg 4:20, 21; 5:26 nail KJV, tent pin ASV, tent peg NIV, RSV). The tent pins or pegs of the tabernacle (Exod 35:18; 38:31; 39:40; Num 3:37; 4:32) were of bronze (Exod 27:19; 38:20). The pin of Judges 16:14 was a stick used for beating up the woof in the loom. Pins were used to hang things on (Ezek 15:3 KJV, peg NIV), and this meaning occurs figuratively (Isa 22:23, 25 nail ASV, KJV, peg NIV, RSV; Ezra 9:8 nail ASV, KJV, secure hold RSV, firm place NIV). The word *stakes* (Isa 33:20; 54:2) is found where Zion is compared to a tent. In Deuteronomy 23:13 the word may refer to a paddle (KJV), spade (MLB, NASB), stick (RSV), trowel (NEB), or (generally) something to dig with (NIV). The tent peg, like the cornerstone, assures support (Zech 10:4). The crisping pins (Heb. *hărîtîm* KJV, satchels ASV, handbags RSV, purses NIV) of Isaiah 3:22 were probably bags or purses.

PINE (See PLANTS)

PINNACLE (pĭn'à-k'l, pĭn'ĭ-k'l, Gr. *pterygion*). Anything shaped like a wing; a turret, battlement, pointed roof, or peak of a building. The temple pinnacle (Matt 4:5; Luke 4:9 KJV, MOF, NASB, RSV; highest point NIV) is the spot to which Satan brought Jesus, tempting him to jump off. Many reasons have been advanced for various locations, but none is certain.

PINON (pī'nŏn, Heb. *pînōn*). A duke or chief of Edom, of the family of Esau (Gen 36:40–41; 1 Chron 1:52).

PIPES (See MUSIC AND MUSICAL INSTRUMENTS)

PIRAM (pī'răm, Heb. *pir'ām*). The Canaanite king of Jarmuth, one of those who joined Adoni-Zedek against Gibeon and who was killed there, either by Joshua or by hailstones (Josh 10:1–11).

PIRATHON (pĭr'à-thŏn, Heb. *pir'āthôn*). A town of Ephraim in the hill country of the Amalekites, where Abdon, one of the judges, lived and was buried (Judg 12:13–15). Benaiah was from Pirathon (2 Sam 23:30; 1 Chron 11:31; 27:14). Perhaps to be identified with Pharathon, now Far'atā, west of Mount Gerizim, south of Samaria.

PISGAH (pĭz'ga, Heb. *ha-pisgâh*). A mountain on the NE shore of the Dead Sea; Ras es-Siaghah, slightly NW of Mount Nebo. First mentioned in Numbers 21:20 as a peak in Moab looking down on Jeshimon (KJV) or the desert (ASV, RSV; NIV "the wasteland"), or the route of the Israelites toward the Promised Land. Balak brought Balaam into the field of Zophim, to the top of Pisgah, where he built seven altars and tried to persuade Balaam to curse Israel (Num 23:14).

Râs es-Siâghah, identified with Pisgah, the mountain on the northeastern shore of the Dead Sea from which Moses viewed the Land of Promise. Courtesy Ecole Biblique et Archéologique Française, Jerusalem.

Ashdoth Pisgah (KJV) or the slopes of Pisgah (ASV, RSV, NIV) helps define the territory of the tribes settled east of the Jordan (Deut 3:17). The springs or slopes of Pisgah are named in bounding the same territory, as taken from the kings of the Amorites (4:49). From the top of Mount Pisgah Moses viewed the Land of Promise, which he was not permitted to enter (3:27; 34:1). The latter verse either identifies or closely associates Mount Pisgah with Mount Nebo. The two peaks are near to each other, and the Hebrew name, from a root meaning "pass through," means "cleft," probably referring to the shape of the mountain, either as sharply cut out, or as split into two peaks. The peak (head or top) of the mountain, its slopes, its springs, and a field near the top figure in the Bible references. ER

PISHON, PISON (pī'shŏn, Heb. *pîshôn*). First of the four rivers of Eden, flowing around the whole land of Havilah (Gen 2:11). Conjectures as to its identification are almost as numerous as the rivers of SW Asia, and include the Persian Gulf thought of as a river, and even the Nile.

PISIDIA (pĭ-sĭd'ĭ-à, Gr. *Pisidia*). One of the small Roman provinces in southern Asia Minor, just north of Pamphylia and lying along the coast. It was mountainous but more densely populated than the rough coastal areas, especially because it contained the important city of Antioch. Because of this, Paul visited the city twice. On his first journey (Acts 13:14–50; NIV "Pisidian Antioch") he preached a lengthy sermon in the synagogue, testifying of Christ. A week later "almost the whole city gathered to hear the word of the Lord" (13:44). Then the jealous Jews stirred up both the honorable women and the chief men of the city (13:50), and Paul and Barnabas were forced out of this greatest Pisidian city. On his second journey Paul revisited Pisidia and Antioch, "strengthening the disciples and encouraging them to remain true to faith" (14:21–24).

PISPAH, PISPA (Heb. *pispā'*). An Asherite, a son of Jether (1 Chron 7:38).

PISTACHIO (See PLANTS)

PIT. This represents several Hebrew and two Greek words whose usages are not sharply distinguished. A pit may be a bitumen deposit (Gen 14:10, so RSV; NIV "tar pit"); a deep place, natural or manmade (Gen 37:20–29; Exod 21:33–34; 2 Sam 17:9; Matt 12:11); often a well (Luke 14:5) or cistern (Isa 30:14; Jer 14:3; Lev 11:33 ASV, "earthen vessel," NIV "clay pot"). "Pit" also stands for death, the grave, or Sheol (Num 16:30, 33; Job 33:18; Isa 14:15; Rev 9:1–2).

PITCH (Heb. *zepheth, kōpher, pitch*). 1. Either bitumen or a viscous, inflammable liquid associated with it. It was found in Mesopotamia and around the Dead Sea (Gen 14:10; RSV; NIV "tar") and was used to make vessels watertight (Gen 6:14 [*kōpher* and cognate verb]; Exod 2:3 [*zepheth*]). Also used as a destructive agent (Isa 34:9; cf. Gen 19:24).

2. "Pitch" is a translation of several Hebrew words also translated "encamp, set up" and refers to placing tents or the tabernacle (Gen 12:8; 31:25; Exod 17:1; Num 1:51; Josh 8:11) or other objects (Josh 4:20).

PITCHER (Heb. *kadh*). An earthenware jar with one or two handles, ordinarily borne on the head or shoulder for carrying water (Gen 24:14–20, 43–46 KJV; jar ASV, NIV, RSV). Pitchers empty of water once held lamps (Judg 7:16–20 KJV; jars NIV, RSV). To break one was so serious as to be a figure for death (Eccl 12:6). It was a container (barrel KJV, bowl NASB, jar NIV) for meal (1 Kings 17:12–16) or for water (1 Kings 18:33). Once *nevel* ("earthen jar") refers to pitchers (Lam 4:2 KJV; pots of clay NIV). The NT uses *keramion* ("earthenware vessel") twice (Mark 14:13; Luke 22:10).

PITHOM (pī'thŏm, Heb. *pithōm*). A city in Egypt in the valley between the Nile and Lake Timsah; perhaps Tell er-Retabah; dedicated to the sun-god Atum; with Rameses to the north, one of the store cities built by the slave labor of the Israelites (Exod 1:11), probably in the reign of Seti I or Ramses II (1319–1234 B.C.). Recent excavations at Tell Mashkutah near Succoth have uncovered bricks made without straw in the upper layers; made with stubble and weeds pulled up by the roots on the middle level; and made with good, clean straw at the bottom of the walls. An inscription at Rameses relates that it was built with Semitic slave labor from Asia. Whether Pithom is at Tell Mashkutah or Tell er-Retabah, it must be in the neighborhood; and the archaeological evidence mentioned above illustrates its construction by Israelite slaves. As a store city on the frontier it held supplies of grain for military forces operating there.

PITHON (pī'thŏn, Heb. *pîthôn*). A son of Micah and descendant of King Saul (1 Chron 8:35; 9:41).

PITY. A tender, considerate feeling for others, ranging from judicial clemency (Deut 7:16) through kindness (Job 6:14; Prov 19:17; 28:8) and mercy (Matt 18:33) to compassion (Lam 4:10). Pity may be mere concern for a thing (Jonah 4:10) or for a thing deeply desired (Ezek 24:21). It may also be the concern of God for his holy name (36:21). Pity for one's children is of the essence of fatherhood, human or divine (Ps 103:13 KJV), inherent in the redemptive activity of God (72:13). The several Hebrew words are translated variously in all versions, the translators being guided by the meaning in context rather than by the particular word used, for each has a wide range of connotation. In the NT the word *esplangnizō* is used to express pity: "A Samaritan . . . took pity on him" (Luke 10:33). Three Greek words occur once each: *eleeō*, "have mercy" (Matt 18:33); *eusplangchnos,* "sympathetic" (1 Peter 3:8); *polysplangchnos,* "full of compassion" (James 5:11 KJV), referring to God.

PLAGUE (See DISEASES)

PLAGUES OF EGYPT. Ten in number, these were the means by which God induced Pharaoh to let the Israelites leave Egypt. A series chiefly of natural phenomena, they were unusual (1) in their severity, (2) in that all occurred within one year, (3) in their accurate timing, (4) in that Goshen and its people were spared some of them, and (5) in the evidence of God's control over them. The plagues overcame the opposition of Pharaoh, discredited the gods of Egypt (the Nile and the sun), and defiled their temples.

1. **Water Became Blood** (Exod 7:14–25). When the Nile is at flood in June, its water turns red from soil brought down from Ethiopia, but is still fit to drink, nor do fish die. But when the river is at its lowest, in May, the water is sometimes red, not fit to drink, and fish die. The

Egyptians had to dig wells, into which river water would filter through sand. God directed Moses to lift up his rod at the right time. Once the time was disclosed, the Egyptian magicians could do likewise.

2. **Frogs** (Exod 8:1–15). When the flood waters recede, frogs spawn in the marshes and invade the dry land. God directed Moses to lift up his rod at such a time. This sign the Egyptian magicians also claimed to produce.

3. **Lice** (Exod 8:16–19). What insect is meant is uncertain; RSV and NIV have "gnats"; ASV footnote, "sand flies or fleas." So many biting, stinging pests abound in Egypt that people might not be discriminating in naming them. The magicians failed, by their own admission, to reproduce this plague and recognized in it "the finger of God"; but Pharaoh would not listen to them.

4. **Flies** (Exod 8:20–31). The rod is no longer mentioned. Swarms of flies came over Egypt in unusual density to feed on dead frogs. God directed Moses as to the time. The magicians no longer competed with Moses. Now there was a differentiation between Goshen and the rest of Egypt. Pharaoh tentatively offered to let the people go to sacrifice to their God, only in the land of Egypt (8:25). Moses protested that their sacrifice would be an animal that the Egyptians think it improper to sacrifice and insisted that they must go three days' journey into the wilderness. Pharaoh assented, provided they did not go far, and the plague was stayed at the intercession of Moses. When the plague was removed, Pharaoh again refused to let Israel go.

5. **The plague** (RSV, NIV) **of murrain** (KJV) **on cattle** (Exod 9:1–7). This was announced with a set time (tomorrow) for its occurrence. There is no record of its removal. Presumably it wore itself out. The Israelite cattle were spared, evidence of God's favor and power.

6. **Boils** (KJV, NIV), **blains** (ASV), **or sores** (RSV) **on man and beast** (Exod 9:8–12). Moses was told to take soot (KJV "ashes") from a furnace and sprinkle it in the air. The air over Egypt was filled with dust, and it became boils breaking out on man and beast. The magicians, still watching Moses, could not stand because of the boils. From the specific mention that the plague was on "all the Egyptians" we may infer that the Israelites were not attacked. This plague was not recalled. Presumably it also wore itself out.

7. **Hail** (Exod 9:13–35). God directed Moses to stretch forth his hand, and hail (which rarely occurs in Egypt) descended in unusual violence. Egyptians who feared the word of the Lord—and after such displays of power there may have been many—brought their cattle in out of the coming storm. Those who did not, lost them to the violent hail. Only in Goshen was there no hail. The hand of God directed its local incidence. The season must have been January or February, for the flax was in the ear and the barley in bud or bloom.

8. **Locusts** (Exod 10:1–20). After seven plagues, even a frequently recurring one such as locusts, was so dreaded that Pharaoh's servants used bold language in advising that the Israelites be let go (10:7). Goshen was not spared the locusts' visitation. Still Pharaoh was obdurate.

9. **Darkness** (Exod 10:21–29). A sandstorm, accentuated by the dust-bowl condition of the land and borne on the west wind that drove off the locusts, brought a tawny, choking darkness. The patience of God was at an end: Pharaoh would see the face of Moses no more. The darkness lasted three days, but the children of Israel had light where they lived.

10. **Death of the firstborn** (Exod 11:1–12:36). This final and convincing demonstration of God's power broke down the resistance of Pharaoh long enough for the Israelites to escape. The Israelites were directed to protect their firstborn with the blood of the Passover lamb, that they might not be killed along with the firstborn of the Egyptians. They "borrowed" valuables of the Egyptians and, amid the lamentations of the latter, were allowed to leave. Egypt had had enough. Even if the deaths were due to bubonic plague, as many think, the incidence on the firstborn alone is not thereby explained. Bubonic plague is said to take the strongest, but this does not explain why all the firstborn and only the firstborn died. The character of this plague is clearly that of divine judgment on incurable obstinacy.

The memory of the plagues was cultivated as a warning to Israel for generations to come (Ps 78:43–51; 105:26–36; 135:8–9; Acts 7:36; 13:17; Heb 11:28). ER

PLAIN. 1. Hebrew *'āvēl,* "meadow" (Judg 11:33 KJV; rendered by NIV as a place name: see ABEL KERAMIN).

2. Hebrew *'ēlôn,* "terebinth" (Gen 13:18 KJV; ASV "oaks," NIV "great trees").

3. Hebrew *biq'āh,* "broad valley, plain" (Gen 11:2; Ezek 3:22).

4. Hebrew *kikkār,* "a round thing"; the Plain of Jordan (Gen 13:10–12; RSV "valley"); the Valley of Jericho (Deut 34:3); the plain around Jerusalem (Neh 12:28 KJV; RSV "circuit," NIV "region").

5. Hebrew *mîshôr,* "a level place, the tableland" east of Jordan (Deut 3:10 KJV; NIV "plateau"); a plain as opposed to the hills (1 Kings 20:23); tableland as distinguished from the low country or Shephelah (2 Chron 26:10); a plain path (Ps 27:11 KJV; RSV "level," NIV, "straight").

6. Hebrew *'ărāvāh,* "desert-plain, steppe"; of Moab (Num 22:1); of Jordan near Jericho (31:12); the Arabah, the deep valley from the upper Jordan to the Persian Gulf (Deut 1:1). By another reading of the text, ASV, NIV, and RSV have "fords" twice (2 Sam 15:28; 17:16) where JB and KJV have "plain."

7. Hebrew *shephēlâh,* "lowland"; usually the strip west of the mountains of Judea (1 Chron 27:28 KJV; NIV "western foothills").

8. Greek *topos pedinos,* "a level, flat place" (Luke 6:17), which may have been on a mountain (Matt 5:1) or elsewhere.

9. An adjective and adverb: Hebrew *nākôah*

(Prov 8:9 KJV; RSV "straight," NIV "right"). Hebrew *tam* (Gen 25:27 KJV; NIV"quiet"); Greek *orthos,* "straight, correct" (Mark 7:35 KJV; RSV and NIV "plainly").

10. As verb, Hebrew *bāʿar* (Hab 2:2); Hebrew *shavâh* (Isa 28:25 KJV; NIV "leveled"); Hebrew *sālal* (Prov 15:19, KJV; NIV "highway," RSV "level highway").

PLAITING (See DRESS)

PLANE. A scraping tool used by carpenters, called a chisel in NIV. It was used in shaping idol images (Isa 44:13 KJV).

PLANE TREE (See PLANTS)

PLANK (See BEAM)

PLANTS. Plants mentioned in the Bible present a fascinating study of various shrubs, herbs, trees, and vines that far outweighs the perplexing problems that have arisen. Such difficulties surfaced because of a lack of information about the botany of ancient Palestine, exegetical hardships, and faulty translations. Better translations, along with more accurate botanical analyses, have helped to remove some of the confusion regarding the identification of plant names included in such categories, for example, as spices, gums, fruits, and thorns.

"The almond tree blossoms" (Eccl 12:5). The tree blooms in Israel in January or February; the fruit only ripens in late summer. Courtesy Seffie Ben-Yoseph.

"I will put in the desert . . . the acacia" (Isa 41:19). Courtesy Seffie Ben-Yoseph.

The names of most plants growing in the Holy Land during Bible times present little or no difficulty for the translator, for they clearly refer to the plants or the close relatives of species that are growing in our own day; however, the origins of some are lost in antiquity.

Acacia. A genus of trees and shrubs of the mimosa family native to warmer climates. The gnarled, rough-barked, thorny acacia or shittah trees (Isa 41:19) of the OT are most likely the *Acacia seya L. Delile.* The acacia or shittim wood is a durable, close-grained wood, orange when cut, turning darker with age. The tabernacle and the ark of the covenant were constructed from this sturdy wood (Exod 25–27, 35–38; Deut 10:3). The acacia tree yields gum arabic and gum senegal used in adhesives, pharmaceuticals, dyes, and confections. Thorny acacia bushes, such as the *acacia nilotica,* thickly covered the land of Palestine in early times.

Algum Tree. Known as the *Grecian juniper,* it reaches a height of sixty-five feet (twenty m.) and is pyramidal in shape. Growing abundantly in the mountains of Lebanon and Gilead, its wood is popular for building. King Solomon used algumwood in the construction of the temple (2 Chron 2:8; 9:10–11).

The algum tree is a red sandalwood (*Pterocarpus santalinus L.*) native to India. Algumwood is black on the outside and ruby red on the inside. Taking a high polish, this sweet-scented timber is suitable for building purposes. King Solomon's builders undoubtedly selected algumwood for the pillars of the temple because of its specific qualities of strength, beauty, and long life (1 Kings 10:11–12).

Almond. This tree (Heb. *shāqed*) belongs to the rose family (*Prunus amygdalus*) and blooms late in January in Palestine. Its pink blossoms and young fruit resemble those of the peach until it reaches maturity. Budded almond branches will blossom prematurely when placed in water in a warm place. Under normal conditions its blossoms will appear before its leaves. As the fruit ripens, it will discharge the nut through its leathery covering. In antiquity, the almond nut was used as a confectionary, a source of almond oil, and for food (Gen 43:11; cf. Num 17:8; Eccl 12:5; Jer 1:11). The Israelites adopted the buds and blossoms of the almond flower (Exod 25:33–36; 37:19–20) for the ornamentation of the cups of the golden lampstand. The word *luz* appears only once in the OT (Gen 30:37 hazel KJV; almond rod NIV).

Almug Tree. See *Algum Tree.*

Aloe. A genus of the lily family (*Aloe succatrina Lam.*) with thick fleshy basal leaves containing aloin. The OT references to aloes (Num 24:6 lign aloes KJV; Ps 45:8; Prov 7:17; S of Sol 4:14) are more likely referring to a large and spreading tree known as the eaglewood (*Aquilaria agallocha Roxb.*). When decaying, the inner wood gives off a fragrant resin used in making perfumes. John 19:39 is probably the only biblical reference to true aloe, a shrubby succulent plant containing juices that were used by the ancients for embalming and as a purgative.

Anise. See *Dill.*

Apple. See *Apricot.*

Apricot. A shade tree that reaches nearly thirty feet (nine m.) in height. It yields orange-colored fruit and grows abundantly in Palestine. Traditionally this fruit has been translated "apple" (Song of Songs 2:3, 5; 7:8; 8:5; Joel 1:12; Zech 2:8). However, the western apple, introduced recently into Palestine, does not grow well in its soils. Existing in Mesopotamia prior to the patriarchal period, the apricot (*Prunus armeniaca*) meets all the requirements of the OT contexts, possibly being the "forbidden" fruit of the Garden of Eden (Gen 3:3–13).

Ash. See *Pine Tree.*

Aspen. See *Willow.*

Balm of Gilead. See *Balsam.*

Balsam. An aromatic resinous substance flowing from a plant, used as a healing ointment, and rendered "balm" in most translations. This substance is difficult to identify. It was taken by Ishmaelites of Gilead to Egypt (Gen 37:25); Jacob sent it to the king of Egypt as a gift (43:11); Jeremiah refers to the therapeutic balm of Gilead (Jer 8:22; 46:11; 51:8); and Ezekiel mentions it as an item of export from Palestine (Ezek 27:17). The balm of Gilead, otherwise known as *Commiphora opobalasmum Engl.*, comes from a small tree indigenous to Arabia, but not found in Gilead. The healing balsam of Jeremiah might refer to a small bush (*Balanites aegyptiaca [L.] Delile*), native to North Africa, growing in abundance around the Dead Sea. The balsam tree is also mentioned by NIV in 2 Samuel 5:23–24 and 1 Chronicles 14:14–15 (KJV "mulberry trees").

Barley. A grain cultivated for man and beast in ancient Mesopotamia as early as 3500 B.C. Barley (*Hordcum distichon L.*) was the main staple bread plant of the Hebrews (Deut 8:8) and the main food of the poor (Ruth 1:22; 2 Kings 4:42; John 6:9, 13). Its adaptability to a variety of climate conditions and its short growing season make it an excellent foodstuff. Barley straw served also for bedding and feed for livestock. Barleycorn was used by the Hebrews as a measure of length (one-third in.—one cm.).

Bay Tree. The Hebrew term for bay, meaning "native," is found only in Psalm 37:35, where it describes a tree symbolic of wealth and wickedness. It is translated in various ways: cedar of Lebanon (JB, RSV), green bay tree (KJV), green tree (NIV), luxuriant tree (NASB), native green tree (MLB), and spreading tree (NEB).

Bean. The broad bean, *Faba vulgaris, L.,* is extensively cultivated in Palestine. The bean is sown in the fall and harvested after barley and wheat in the spring. A staple article of diet for the poor of Palestine (2 Sam 17:28), the dried ground beans were mixed in with grain flour to make bread (Ezek 4:9).

Bitter Herb. See *Herb.*

Bramble. A fast-growing rough, prickly shrub (*Rubus ulmifolius Scott*) of the rose family, usually associated with thorns or nettles (Isa 34:13; Luke 6:44 KJV; NIV "thorns") or representing the rabble of society (Judg 9:14–15 KJV; NIV "thornbush").

Brier, Briar. A plant with a woody or prickly stem (Judg 8:7, 16; Ezek 28:24). A sure identification of the exact Hebrew and Greek words that mean brier is next to impossible. Fifteen Hebrew and four Greek terms are interchangeably

"When the almond tree blossoms and the grasshopper drags himself along . . . then man goes to his eternal home" (Eccl 12:5). (1) Almond branch in bloom; (2) barley; (3) box tree branch; (4) broom tree branch. Courtesy Carta, Jerusalem.

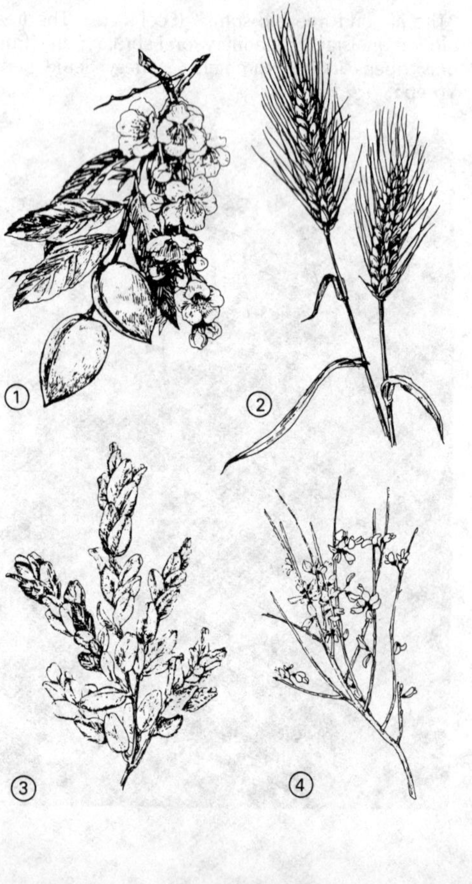

translated as bramble, brier, thistle, or thorn, among the different English translations.

Broom. A small flowering shrub or tree, reaching a height of twelve feet (almost four m.), with long slender branches and small leaves. The OT passages refer to the white broom, *Retama raetam (Forsk.) Webb. and Berth.* The white broom's scant foliage provides little relief from the desert sun (1 Kings 19:4); its burning quality makes good firewood (Ps 120:4); and its mildly poisonous roots supply little gratification to hungry people (Job 30:4).

Bulrush. A tall, slender reedlike plant that formerly grew prolifically in and along the banks of the Nile (Exod 2:3; KJV "ark of bulrushes"; NIV "papyrus basket"). Papyrus (*Cyperus papyrus L.*) provided the earliest known material for the making of paper, which receives its name from the plant (Exod 2:3; Job 8:11; Isa 18:2). Flag, of the iris family, is a generic term used for a variety of marshal plants (KJV; Exod 2:3, 5; Job 8:11). An orderly alignment of the six Hebrew words referring to marsh plants with their English translations is difficult since they are interchangeably translated as bulrush, flag, papyrus, reed, and rush.

Bush, Burning Bush. See *Acacia.*

Calamus. A fragrant ginger-grass (*Andropogon aromaticus Roxb.*) from NW and central India. Its bruised leaves give off a strong, spicy, aromatic scent and their pungent taste is like ginger. The sweet calamus is a valuable import item in Palestine (Song of Songs 4:14; Jer 6:20; Ezek 27:19). In some translations (e.g., KJV, RSV) the calamus of Isaiah 43:24 is rendered sweetcane or sugar cane (*saccharum officinarum L.*), a stout perennial, growing to a height of fifteen feet (almost five m.). The juice of the sugar cane, though not used at that time for sugar making, was highly esteemed for sweetening foods and drinks, and the pithy sweet stalks for chewing. Cane (KJV "calamus") was an ingredient mixed in the sacred ointment used in the tabernacle (Exod 30:23).

Camphire. See *Henna.*

Cane. See *Calamus.*

Caper. A small prickly shrub (*capparis spinosa L.*), common to the Mediterranean. A supposed aphrodisiac, this plant also acts as an appetite stimulant for the aged. It is the young pickled buds that give the "desire" or relish to the food. The fruit is inedible. Translated "desire" (NIV, KJV, RSV) or "caperberry" (NASB) (Eccl 12:5).

Caraway. See *Dill.*

Carob. *Ceratoria Siliqua L.*, a member of the pea family, native to the eastern Mediterranean, about fifty feet (sixteen m.) tall, with shiny evergreen leaves and red flowers. These red flowers form into pods in which seeds are embedded in a flavorful, sweet, and nutritious pulp. Called "St. John's bread" from a belief that carob pods rather than insects were the locusts that John the Baptist ate (Matt 3:4; Mark 1:6). Doubtless the pods of the carob tree were the "pods" (KJV "husks") eaten by the prodigal son in Jesus' parable (Luke 15:16).

The cedars of Lebanon. ". . . and grow like a cedar in Lebanon" (Ps. 92:12). Courtesy Studium Biblicum Franciscanum, Jerusalem.

Cassia. An aromatic bark of the *Cinnonomum cassia Blume,* related to cinnamon, though its bark is less delicate in taste and perfume. Its buds are used as a substitute for cloves in cooking. Cassia was mixed into the holy anointing oil of the tabernacle (Exod 30:24) and was a valuable trade product (Ezek 27:19).

Cedar. Derived from an old Arabic root meaning a firmly rooted, strong tree, the word denotes a magnificent evergreen, often 120 feet (38 m.) high and 40 feet (13 m.) wide. It exudes a fragrant gum or balsam used as a preservative for fabric and parchment. The wood does not quickly decay and is insect-repellent. Cedarwood is of a warm red tone, durable, light, and free from knots. The stately *Cedrus libani Loud* is the cedar of Lebanon to which the OT often refers (1 Kings 6:9; Job 40:17; Ps 92:12; Ezek 27:5). Though the cedar of Lebanon was once abundant in the Mediterranean region, it is now scarce.

Chestnut. See *Plane Tree.*

Cinnamon. A bushy evergreen tree (*Cinnamomum zeylanicum Nees*), about twenty feet (six m.) high, with spreading branches, native to Sri Lanka (Ceylon). Commercial cinnamon is obtained from the inner bark of the young branches. A cinnamon oil is also distilled from the branches for use in food, perfume, and drugs. The sweet, light brown aromatic spice was as precious as gold to the ancients. It was used for embalming and witchcraft in Egypt, the anointing oil of the tabernacle (Exod 30:23), perfume (Prov 7:17), spice (Song of Songs 4:14), and trade merchandise (Rev 18:13).

Citron, Citrus Tree. A small shrubby evergreen tree (*Citrus medica*) growing to a height of eleven feet (three and one-half m.) with irregular spreading branches, cultivated in the Mediterranean. The fruit of the Etrog citron or "Holy Citron" is used in the Jewish Feast of Tabernacles. The Greek word occurs once in the NT (Rev 18:12), translated "citron" (NASB, NIV) or "thyine" (KJV). The thyine tree (*Tetraclinis articulata [Vahl] Masers*) is a small, slow-growing evergreen tree, native to Africa. Its reddish-brown, fine-grained, durable wood takes a high polish and is almost indestructible. This highly valued wood, commonly said to be "worth its weight in gold," yields a resin known as "sandarac," which is used in making varnish and as an incense.

The "goodly tree" mentioned in Leviticus 23:40 (KJV) derives its name from a Hebrew word meaning beautiful, magnificent, ornamental in reference to the tree or to its fruit.

Cockle. An annual sturdy noxious weed (*Agrostemma githago L.*) with purplish red flowers found in abundance in Palestinian grain fields. The only place in Scripture that cockle is mentioned (KJV, MLB; stinkweed NASB; weed NIV, RSV) is in Job 31:40.

Coriander. A herb (*Coriandrum sativum L.*) of the carrot family, native to the Mediterranean region; it bears small yellowish-brown fruit that gives off a mild, fragrant aroma. The coriander seed is used for culinary and medicinal purposes. In the OT it was comparable in color and size to manna (Exod 16:31; Num 11:7).

Corn. See *Grain.*

Cotton. *Gossypium herbaceum L.* was imported into Palestine from Persia shortly after the Captivity. The Egyptians spun cotton into a fabric in which they wrapped their mummies. The RSV translation of "cotton" in Esther 1:6 and Isaiah 19:9 is perhaps more accurately "linen" (so NIV)—the material made from cotton fibers.

Crocus. *Crocus biflorus L.* is a spring-flowering herb with a long yellow floral tube tinged with purple specks or stripes, indigenous to the Mediterranean region (Isa 35:1).

Cucumber. A succulent vegetable cultivated from an annual vine plant with rough trailing stems and hairy leaves. Several varieties were known to the ancient Egyptians; *Cucumis sativus L.* was probably the most common. The refreshing fruit of the cucumber vine was one delicacy the children of Israel longed for in the hot wilderness after leaving Egypt (Num 11:5). The "lodge in a garden of cucumbers," mentioned in Isaiah 1:8 (KJV; NIV "hut in a field of melons"), was a frail temporary construction of four poles and walls of woven leaves, meant to house the watchman who guarded the garden during the growing season.

Cummin. This small, slender plant (*Cuminum cyminum L.*) is not found wild. It is the only specie of its genus and is native to western Asia. The strong-smelling, warm-tasting cummin seeds were used as culinary spices and served medicinal functions (Matt 23:23). The seeds are still threshed with a rod as described in Isaiah 28:25–27.

Cypress. A tall, pyramidal-shaped tree with hard, durable, reddish-hued wood (Isa 41:19; 60:13; box JB, KJV, NEB). NIV says cypress (*Cupressus sempervirens*) was used in the ark (Gen 6:14; gopher wood KJV, NASB, RSV). KJV has *cypress* once, the one OT use of *tirzah* (Isa 44:14).

Date Palm. See *Palm.*

Desire. See *Caper.*

Dill. An annual or biennial weedy umbellifer that grows like parsley and fennel. Native to Mediterranean countries, dill (*Anethum graveolens*) is used as a culinary seasoning and for medicinal purposes. This plant was cultivated for its aromatic seeds, which were subject to tithe. The one verse that mentions it (Matt 23:23 KJV anise) refers to the Pharisees tithing it.

The Hebrew word has been variously translated as "dill" (RSV, NASB), "fitch" (KJV), and "caraway" (NIV). The fitch (*Nigella sativa L.*) belongs to the buttercup family and is called the "nutmeg flower" (unrelated to cultivated nutmeg). Its tiny, hot, and easily removed seeds are sprinkled on food like pepper and also serve as a carminative. In like fashion, caraway (*Carum carvi*) faintly resembles dill, both being of the carrot family; it yields a pungent fruit used for similar purposes.

Dove's Dung. This is mentioned only once (2 Kings 6:25 KJV; cf. NIV footnote), as a food that the famished people of Samaria were reduced to eating. Josephus and others believe this food substance to be the literal excrement of pigeons that may have contained food or mineral value. Others think that the original text meant to read "seed pods" (NIV), "carob pods" or "locust beans" (NEB), or "wild onion" (NAB). A final conjecture is that dove's dung is *Ornithogalum umbellatum L.*, the bulb of the spring-blooming "Star of Bethlehem." Dug up and dried, it can be eaten roasted or ground to flour and mixed with meal to make bread.

Ebony. A hard, heavy, durable, close-grained wood (*Diospyros ebenaster Retz.*) that takes a glistening polish. Because of its excellent woodworking qualities, this black heartwood, native to Sri Lanka (Ceylon) and southern India, has long been a valuable trade item (Ezek 27:15).

Eelgrass. A type of marine eelgrass from the *Zosteraceae* family, it thrives in tidal waters and may grow out to a depth of thirty-five feet (eleven m.). Its slimy, ribbonlike leaves, three to four feet (one to one and one-fourth m.) long, lie in submerged masses, a menace to the offshore diver who may become fouled in their coils. The "weed" (KJV, RSV) and "seaweed" (NIV) of Jonah 2:5 is most likely a reference to some type of marine eelgrass.

Elm. See *Terebinth.*

Fig. A versatile, bushlike tree (*Fiscus carica L.*), ranging from three to thirty-nine feet (one to twelve m.) high and producing pear-shaped fruit, excellent for eating (1 Sam 25:18). Because of its natural abundance in most Mediterranean countries and its good food qualities, it has become known as "the poor man's food." The fig was the first plant to be mentioned in the Bible (Gen 3:7); it represented peace and prosperity (1 Kings 4:25; Mic 4:4; Zech 3:10). A fig tree was the object of Jesus' curse (Matt 21; Mark 11).

Fir Tree. A member of the pine family, the fir tree was an emblem of nobility and great stature. It is mentioned in Isaiah 41:19; 60:13. Native to western Asia, there was throughout the time of the Crusades an entire forest of these pines between Jerusalem and Bethlehem. The fir tree yields turpentine, paper pulp, and oleoresins. The Hebrew word has been variously translated as pine, juniper, cypress, and fir.

Fitch. See *Dill.*

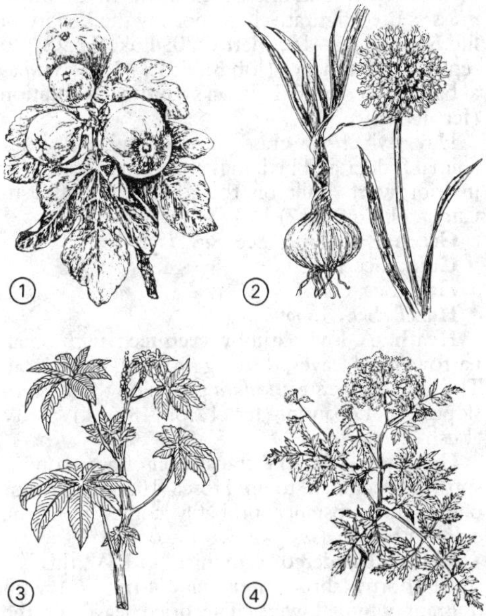

"See! The winter is past, the rains are over and gone. Flowers appear on the earth . . . the fig tree forms its early fruit. The blossoming vines spread their fragrance" (S of Sol 2:11–13). (1) Fig branch; (2) garlic; (3) gourd; (4) hemlock. Courtesy Carta, Jerusalem.

Flag. See *Bulrush.*

Flax. A slender-stalked, blue flowering plant (*Linum usitatissimum*), cultivated to make linen and linseed oil. The fibers from the stem of the plant are the most ancient of the textile fibers (Exod 9:31; Josh 2:6), manufactured into various grades of linen for clothing and other articles where material requiring strength and resistance to moisture is necessary (Prov 31:13; Isa 19:9). The cooling effect that linen has on the wearer makes it a useful garment to be worn under the hot Mediterranean sun.

Frankincense. A clear yellow resin obtained from certain trees of the *Boswellia* genus, family Burseraceae, native to northern India and Arabia. To obtain frankincense, an incision is made through the bark of the tree deep into the trunk, from which flows a milklike juice that hardens in the air. When sold, frankincense is in the form of teardrops or irregular lumps. It is used in perfumes, as a medicine, and as incense in religious rites. Incense is spoken of as coming from Sheba (Isa 60:6; Jer 6:20; Matt 2:11, 15). It was an ingredient in the perfume used in the Most Holy Place (Exod 30:34–38). Frankincense (NIV "incense") was mingled with the flour in the meal offering (Lev 2:1, 15–16) but was excluded from the sin offering (5:11), which was far from being an offering of a sweet savor. Soon after the birth of Jesus, the wise men presented to him gifts of gold, frankincense (NIV "incense"), and myrrh; and these precious gifts, presented in worship, may well have helped to finance his family's sojourn in Egypt (Matt 2:11, 15).

Galbanum. A brownish yellow aromatic, bitter gum excreted from the incised lower part of the stem of the Persian *Ferula galbaniflua*. It has a pungent, disagreeable odor but when mixed with other ingredients in the sacred incense the fragrance of the incense was increased and lasted longer (See Exod 30:34). Galbanum also functions as an antispasmodic.

Gall. The translation of two Hebrew words and one Greek word. One Hebrew term probably refers to colocynth (*Citrullus colocynthis L.*), an African vine bearing orange-colored fruit used as a cathartic (Deut 29:18; Jer 8:14; 9:15 KJV; NIV "poison, poisoned"). A less favored notion is that it refers to the opium poppy, which induces a sleep so heavy that a person becomes insensible. The other Hebrew word means "bitter" and refers to human gall (Job 16:13; 20:25) and to the venom of the serpent (KJV). The Greek word, found in Matthew 27:34 (cf. Ps 69:21) correlates with the myrrh of Mark 15:23. It was a bitter resin added to the analgesic potion given to criminals before crucifixion to deaden their pain. Jesus refused the drink, choosing to bear the full agony of death.

Garlic. A bulbous perennial plant (*Allium sativum L.*) with a strong, onionlike aroma used for flavoring foods and as an ingredient of many medicines. Small edible bulblets grow within the main bulb. Garlic grew in great abundance in Egypt. The only reference to it in the Bible (Num 11:5) mentions Israel's longing for the garlic of Egypt while they were traveling through the wilderness.

Goodly Tree. See *Citron, Citrus Tree.*

Gopher Wood. See *Cypress.*

Gourd. Better described as the castor-oil plant (*Ricinus communis L.*), this is a fast-growing, shady bush fifteen feet (almost five m.) high, which produces the poisonous castor bean. Extracted from the bean, castor oil was used as fuel for lamps and oil for ceremonial rites. All true gourds are indigenous to tropical America and Mexico and were thus unknown to Jonah in biblical times (Jonah 4:5–7 KJV; NIV "vine").

The wild gourd or "wild vine" (NIV) in all probability is the colocynth (*Citrullus colocynthis [L.] Schrad.*), a trailing vine resembling the cucumber, growing wild over large areas in the Holy Land. When the orange-sized fruit is ripe, it bursts. The dry, powdery, poisonous pulp, when used as a medicine, acts as a violent purgative (2 Kings 4:39).

Grain. Edible, starchy, kerneled fruits from the grasses, including corn, wheat, and rice varieties. Grain is a staple food in most diets, providing calorie and protein content. Fifteen Hebrew words and four Greek terms are variously translated as grain in the Bible, suggesting the importance of it in ancient times. The most common kinds of grain were barley, millet, spelt, and wheat. The translation "corn" for grain by KJV (Gen 27:28, 32; Deut 7:13; and Josh 5:11–12; Luke 6:1; 1 Tim 5:18) was an old English term meant to describe generically these kerneled fruits,

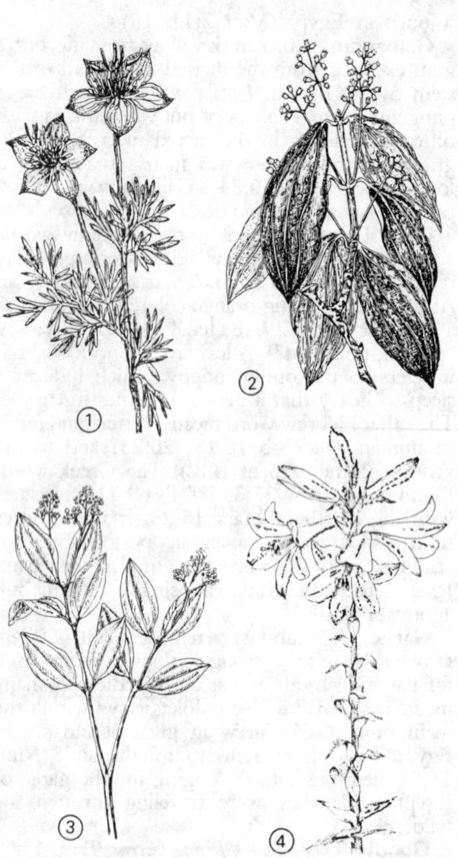

"And why do you worry about clothes? See how the lilies of the field grow" (Matt 6:28). (1) Caraway; (2) cassia; (3) cinnamon branch; (4) lily. Courtesy Carta, Jerusalem.

better translated "grain" (Lev 2; Amos 9:9).

Grape. A small, climbing, woody vine or an erect shrub from the genus, *vitis,* that produces leaves and small green flowers that mature into grapes. Grapes may be eaten fresh or dried as raisins or drunk as grape juice or wine. The grapevine is the first plant to be recorded as cultivated in biblical history (Gen 9:20). The grape, its origin lost in antiquity, grew first on the ground, over walls, or on crude supports. Later it was trained on a trellis and finally cultivated in vineyards. It was a symbol of fruitfulness, and the grape harvest was a time of joyous festivity (Gen 40:9–11; Deut 8:8; Ps 105:33; Zech 3:10). The wild grape mentioned in Isaiah 5:2–4 and Jeremiah 2:21 refers to a wild variety of grapes that closely resembles the cultivated grape; it could deceive the owner of the vineyard.

Grass. A low, green, nonwoody plant serving a multitude of functions for the soil, beast, and man. There are a great many species of grasses in Palestine, but actual turf is virtually unknown. In English the word "grass" is used in a more comprehensive sense and is the rendering of eight Hebrew terms and one Greek word. In the Bible, grass is used figuratively to portray the brevity of life (Ps 103:15–16; Matt 6:30; Luke 12:28), to represent abundance (Job 5:25; Ps 72:16), and as a barometer for OT Israel's spiritual condition (Jer 12:4).

Hay, which is grass mowed and cured for animal fodder and bedding, represented useless or inferior work built on the foundation of Jesus Christ (1 Cor 3:12).

Green Bay Tree. See *Bay Tree.*

Gum. See *Spice.*

Hay. See *Grass.*

Hazel. See *Almond.*

Heath. A low shrubby evergreen with small narrow, rigid leaves, thriving on open, barren soil. The species *Erica verticillata* grows on the western slopes of Lebanon (Jer 17:6; 48:6 KJV; NIV "bush").

Hemlock. The KJV translation of a poisonous substance alluded to in Hosea 10:4 and Amos 6:12. The substance probably comes from the colocynth (see *Gall*) or wormwood.

Henna. Rendered "camphire" in KJV, this is a small thorny shrub (*Lawsonia inermis L.*) with fragrant white flowers. The dried leaves of the henna, crushed and made into a paste, provided a gaudy yellow stain for the hair and beard. This use of it, common among the Egyptians, was cautioned against in Deuteronomy 21:11–14. King Solomon lauded its fragrance (Song of Songs 1:14; 4:13). Henna still grows by the Dead Sea at En Gedi.

Herb. A seed-producing plant that does not develop woody fibers and dries up after its growing season (2 Kings 4:39; Luke 11:42). Bitter herbs were gathered fresh and eaten as a salad at the time of the Passover (Exod 12:8; Num 9:11). These include endive, common chicory, garden lettuce, watercress, sorrel, and dandelion. At the Passover the bitter herbs were symbolic of the bitterness of Israel's servitude to the Egyptians.

Holm Tree. The RSV translation of a word in Isaiah 44:14, where the designation of cypress (so NIV) or plane tree would better fit the context. The holm tree is a southern European evergreen oak.

Husks. See *Carob.*

Hyssop. Probably the Egyptian marjoram (*Origanum maru. var. aegypticum [L.] Dismn.*) in OT occurrences of the term. This is a member of the mint family. The hairy stem of the multi-branched inflorescence holds water externally very well; thus it was a suitable instrument for sprinkling blood during the Passover rites (Exod 12:22; Lev 14; Heb 9:19).

The hyssop of the NT probably refers to the sorghum cane (*Sorghum vulgare var. durra [Forsk.] Dinsm.*), which reaches a height of over six feet (two m.). The seed is ground for meal and is known in Palestine as "Jerusalem corn." This is thought to be the hyssop of John 19:29.

Incense. A combination of gums and spices used to emit a fragrant odor when burned. The incense of the Levitical practice was composed of equal amounts of gum resin (KJV "stacte"), onycha, galbanum, and pure frankincense (Exod 30:34–35; Num 7; Heb 9:4). Strict Levitical laws governed its mixture and use. Burning incense was a common practice in most Middle Eastern countries. The imagery of the incense offering was used by John in symbolically representing the prayers of the saints (Rev 5:8; 8:3–4).

Juniper. A shrub (not *Juniperus*, the true juniper) that shades and whose poisonous roots make excellent charcoal. KJV mentions it (Heb. rōthem; broom NIV) four times (1 Kings 19:4–5; Job 30:4; Ps 120:4). See *Broom*.

Leek. A robust, bulbous biennial plant (*Alium porrum L.*) of the lily family, with succulent broad leaves, the bases of which are edible. Its much-desired small bulbs, growing above ground, native to the Mediterranean region, were used in seasoning along with onions and garlic (Num 11:5).

Lentil. A small, trailing leguminous plant (*Lens esculenta Moench.*) of the pea family. When soaked and cooked, its seeds make a nourishing meal known as "pottage," and the rest of the plant serves as fodder for the animals. The red pottage or stew for which Esau exchanged his birthright was probably the red Egyptian lentil (Gen 25:30–34). A favorite food in antiquity, lentils still appear on many tables in the East (2 Sam 17:28; Ezek 4:9).

Lign. See *Aloe*.

Lily. A standing, leafy-stemmed bulbous perennial. Blooming from a bulb after the spring rains, the lilies of the field, possibly the sword lily, carpeted the plains and roadsides of Palestine with its colorful blossoms (Matt 6:28; Luke 12:27). The lily flower served as a pattern in ornamental design for Solomon's temple (1 Kings 7:19–26; 2 Chron 4:5). In the Song of Songs, it was a symbol of loveliness (2:16; 4:5; 6:3). The lily of Song of Songs 5:13 might be related to the chalcedonicum lily (*Lilium chalcedonicum L.*), which produces a lovely red flower.

Locust. See *Carob*.

Mallow. Because the Hebrew word *malluah* implies saltiness, many believe that this plant is a species of salt herb or saltwort known as the "sea orache" (*Atriplex halimus L.*), a robust bushy shrub eaten as a vegetable but supplying little nutritional value. Mallows are mentioned only once in Scripture (Job 30:4 JB, KJV, MLB, NASB, RSV; salt herbs NIV ; saltwort NEB), where it is seen as a food of the poor.

Mandrake. A member of the nightshade family, native to the Mediterranean, with ovate (egg-shaped) leaves, white or purple flowers, and a forked root. Its root is large, sometimes resembling the human body in shape. The mandrake (*Mandragora offinarum L.*), also called the "love apple," was believed to possess magical powers. Although insipid tasting and a slightly poisonous narcotic, it was used for medicinal purposes, as a charm against the evil spirits, and, as indicated by the account of Rachel and Leah, it was credited with aphrodisiac qualities (Gen 30:14–16; Song of Songs 7:13). It is no longer used in medicine.

Melon. A generic term referring to annual vine-trailing watermelons (*Citrullus vulgaris Schrad.*) and muskmelons (*Cucumis melo*), both of which were familiar to ancient Palestinian and Egyptian cultures. The muskmelon varieties include the casuba, honeydew, and cantaloupe. Watermelons originated in Africa, while muskmelons began in Asia. These luscious fruits grew in abundance in Egypt and were used by rich and poor alike for food, drink, and medicine. Their seeds were roasted and eaten. Traveling under a hot desert sun, the weary Israelites remembered with longing the melons of Egypt (Num 11:5; Isa 1:8; Jer 10:5).

Millet. Various grasses bearing small edible seeds from which a good grade of flour can be made. One stalk may carry a thousand grains. Millet (*Panicum miliaceum L.*) is still a main food staple in Asia. The common people ate a mixture of wheat, barley, beans, lentils, and millet moistened with camel's milk and oil (Ezek 4:9).

Mint. An aromatic plant with hairy leaves and dense white or pink flower spikes, extensively cultivated in the eastern Mediterranean for its food-flavoring value. This pungent garden mint, along with the sharp-scented pennyroyal mint and peppermint, were used to make the meat dishes of the Jews more palatable. Mint was a tithable herb according to Jewish tradition (Matt 23:23; Luke 11:42) and one of the bitter herbs used in the paschal supper of the Passover.

Mulberry Tree. A fruit-bearing ornamental, genus *Morus*, indigenous to Palestine and western Asia. The "mulberry tree" of KJV (2 Sam 5:23–24; 1 Chron 14:14–15) is better explained as "balsam tree" (NIV) or "baka shrub" (NASB mg). The black mulberry or sycamine tree (*Morus nigra L.*) was cultivated throughout Palestine for its delectable fruit (Luke 17:6).

Mustard. Thick-stemmed plants (*Brassica hirta* and *Brassica nigra*), reaching a height of fifteen feet (almost five m.) under suitable growing conditions, native to the Mediterranean region. For over two thousand years the mustard plant has been an important economic plant of the Holy Land. Its seeds were either powdered or made into paste for medicinal and culinary purposes. The mustard tree and seed were used by Jesus to illustrate and explain faith (Matt 13:31; 17:20; Mark 4:31; Luke 13:19; 17:6).

Myrrh. A yellow to reddish-brown gum resin obtained from a number of small, thorny trees. One of the most valuable of these gum resins is collected from the shrub-like tree *Commiphora myrrha (Nees.) Engl.* (or *Balsamodendron myrrha*). The pale yellow liquid gradually solidifies and turns dark red or even black, and is marketed as a spice, medicine, or cosmetic (Song of Songs 5; Matt 2:11; Mark 15:23; John 19:39).

The Hebrew word *lōt* in Genesis 37:25 and 43:11 has been generally translated "myrrh." However, it is questionable whether *Commiphora myrrha*, native to Arabia and east Africa, was known in Palestine during the patriarchal period. A better translation for this word would be "labdanum," a gummy resin produced by the small labdanum shrub (*Cistus creticus L.*), growing abundantly in the rocks and sand in Palestine.

Myrtle. A small, evergreen shrub (*Myrtus comminis L.*) with fragrant flowers, blackberries, and spicy-sweet scented leaves. This aromatic plant was considered a symbol of peace and prosperity (Isa 55:13). Highly valued by the Jews, myrtle boughs were used in constructing the booths for the Feast of Tabernacles (Neh 8:15; Zech 1:7–8).

Nard. See *Spikenard.*

Nettle. A little scrubby plant of the *Urticaceae* family, covered with tiny prickly hairs containing poison that when touched produce a painful, stinging sensation. The nettly and its companions—such as briers, thorns, thistles, brambles, underbrush, and weeds—form the low, scrubby rabble of plant life in Palestine that thrive in neglected areas (Job 30:7; Prov 24:31; Isa 34:13; Hos 9:6; Zeph 2:9).

Nut. See *Pistachio; Walnut.*

Oak. A durable, long-lived tree or shrub of the beech family, with green deciduous or evergreen leaves and round, thin-shelled acorns, many varieties native to the Mediterranean area. At least six species of the *Quercus* genus grow in Palestine: holly oak, Valonia oak, Aleppo oak, cork oak, kermes oak, and the Lebanon oak. The Jerusalem oak is not considered a true oak. Five Hebrew words are translated "oak," referring most likely to one of the six varieties mentioned above. The oak is rich in resources, providing tannin, dyes, cork, and durable hardwood timber. In the OT the oak of Bashan was the religious symbol of strength and long life (Gen 35:8; Isa 2:13; Ezek 27:6; Zech 11:2).

Oil Tree. See *Olive Tree; Pine Tree.*

Olive Tree. A broad-leaved evergreen tree (*Olea europaea L.*), ranging from ten to forty feet (three to thirteen m.) in height, yielding edible fruit from which oil is obtained. Indigenous to the Near Eastern area, the olive tree was cultivated by Semitic groups as early as 3000 B.C. The olive tree is named or alluded to nearly eighty times throughout the Bible in reference to the tree itself (Isa 24:13; Rom 11), its wood (1 Kings 6:23–33), its oil (Exod 30:24; Rev 18:13), or to a geographical location named for its olive groves (Matt 24:3; John 8:1). It flourishes near the sea and under proper cultivation. The olives were beaten down with poles when ripe (black) and crushed by an upright stone wheel. The oil thus obtained was stored in vats. Olive oil was used for the lights of the temple (Exod 27:20). Heated in lye to remove the bitter taste and soaked in brine, green olives were eaten with coarse brown bread (Hos 14:6).

The oil tree, sometimes called "Jerusalem willow," or "Oleaster," produces a fruit like a small olive from which an inferior grade of medicinal oil may be pressed. Its fruits are edible but slightly bitter. Translated "oil tree" by KJV (Isa 41:19), it is "olive" in NASB and NIV (NASB mg "Oleaster").

Onion. A bulbous plant (*Allium cepa L.*), originating in the eastern Mediterranean and parts of Asia. Both its inflated leaves and its bulbous underground base were universally used for culinary purposes. The onion has been cultivated since time immemorial. Mentioned only in Numbers 11:5, the onion was one of a list of foods in Egypt, regrettably unavailable to the disgruntled journeying Israelites.

Onycha. There are different opinions about the exact identification of the spice to which the Hebrew word *shehēleth* refers. One conjecture is that onycha is of the rockrose family of plants from which a spicy, aromatic gum, known as labdanum, is produced. Others suppose that onycha is the horny shield of a certain mussel found in India, that when burned emits an odor resembling musk. Both substances were evidently known to the ancients. In either case, onycha was an element added to the sacred mixture specified in Exodus 30:34–36 for incense used in the tabernacle.

Palm Tree. This is more accurately identified as the date palm (*Phoenix dactylifera L.*). The crown of the date palm may reach seventy-five feet (twenty-three m.) above the ground. Its cultivation goes back at least five thousand years. The fruit hangs in clusters below the leaves. Every part of the palm has some economic use. The leaves are woven into mats and the fibers provide thread and rigging for boats. Syrup, vinegar, and liquor are derived from its sap. Its trunk provides timber, and its seeds can be ground into a grain

Ancient olive tree. An olive tree, the most sacred of all biblical trees, can live 1,000 years or longer. Courtesy Israel Government Press Office.

Palm trees on the Sinai coast. "The righteous flourish like the palm tree" (Ps 92:12). Courtesy Seffie Ben-Yoseph.

meal for livestock. This ornamental palm was a welcome sight to the travel-weary Israelites (Exod 15:27; Num 33:9). Palm branches were used in the Jewish celebration of the Feast of Tabernacles (Lev 23:40; Neh 8:15); were laid at Jesus' feet on his triumphal entry into Jerusalem, which Christians celebrate as Palm Sunday (John 12:13); and came to signify victory (Rev 7:9).

Pannag. See *Millet.*

Papyrus. See *Bulrush.*

Pine Tree. The exact species of tree to which the Hebrew points is not firmly established. In the context of Isaiah 41:19; 60:13 it can reasonably be assumed that these trees were either those of the pine or fir. The pine exemplifies peace, prosperity, and reconciliation to God.

Pistachio. An oval nut containing two green edible halves covered by a reddish outer shell, from a small but wide-spreading tree with pinnate (featherlike) leaflets. Also known as the green almond, the pistachio nut has been cultivated in Palestine for nearly four thousand years. It is used for food and food coloring. Considered a good product of the land, it was carried by Jacob's sons to Egypt (Gen 43:11).

Plane Tree. A stately tree, thriving along the lowland streams and rivers of the Holy Land. Each year the bark peels off, leaving the trunk and older branches smooth and yellowish-white (Gen 30:37). The plane tree can attain a height of one hundred feet (thirty-one m.), comparable to the cedars of Lebanon (Ezek 31:8). KJV translates both occurrences of the Hebrew word (*'armô*) "chesnut." Chestnuts grow in the Near East but are not native to Palestine.

Pomegranate. A small bush or tree, common to Palestine, yielding leathery-skinned fruit. Its hard, orange-shaped fruits with thin rinds contain many seeds, each in a pulp sack filled with a tangy, sweet amethyst-colored juice. Although a small tree giving little shade, its refreshing fruit more than compensated the tired traveler who rested under it (1 Sam 14:2). The fruit of the pomegranate was used as a decorative model in building (1 Kings 7:18, 20, 42) and as an ornament on the vestment of the Levitical high priest (Exod 28:33–34). The tree grew in the hanging gardens of Babylon, and King Solomon possessed an orchard of them (Song of Songs 4:13).

Poplar. A tall, straight, quick-growing tree found in the hills of Palestine. However, the exact identification is not certain. Some hold that the word comes from an Arabic term meaning "white tree" or the "storax" (RV), a shrub (*Storax officinale L.*), twenty feet (six and one-fourth m.) tall, with hairy leaves and large white flowers. Both trees, native-grown in Palestine, would be feasible possibilities for Genesis 30:37 and Hosea 4:13. See also *Willow.*

Poppy. See *Gall.*

Reed. A plumed, hollow-stemmed water plant (*Phragmutes communis Trin.*) found in the Near East by the sides of rivers and in standing waters (Job 40:21; Matt 11:7). It grows in clumps, its stalks reaching twelve feet (almost four m.) in height, from which animal pens are constructed. The reed metaphorically represents Israel as weak and overcome with sin, leaving her like a "reed swaying in the water" (1 Kings 14:15).

Resin, Gum Resin. See *Stacte.*

Rolling Thing. See *Tumbleweed.*

Rose. A prickly shrub, with pinnate (feather-

"Finally all the trees said to the thorn bush, 'Come and be our king' " (Judg. 9:14). (1) Reed; (2) sweet cane; (3) thorn branch. Courtesy Carta, Jerusalem.

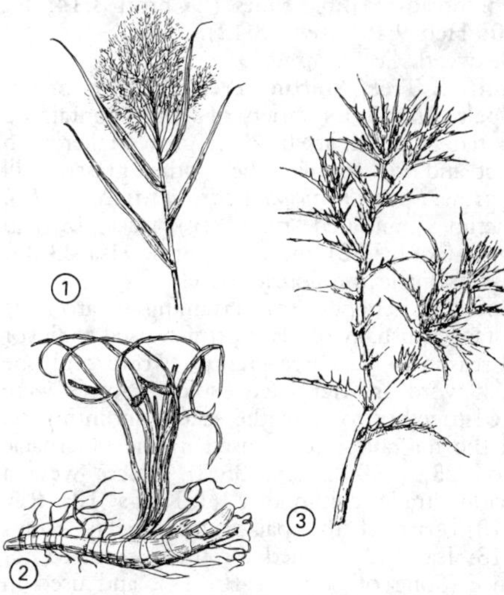

like) leaves and showy flowers; seven species are extant in Palestine. Trying to decide what plant the Hebrew mentions in Song of Songs 2:1 and Isaiah 35:1 is a dubious affair. Some suggest that it is the bulbous-rooted yellow narcissus (*Narcissus tazetta L.* or *N. scrotinas L.*) that grows wild and in abundance on the Plain of Sharon. Another conjecture is the *Tulipa sharonensis Dinsm.*, the Sharon tulip, found on the sandy soils of the coastal Plain of Sharon. The rose of Sharon or the *Hibiscus syriacus,* a little Asiatic tree with rose-colored, bell-shaped flowers, offers another possibility. Finally, the theory supported by most is that the rose of Sharon is the purple-flowered, bulbous, perennial autumn crocus or meadow saffron (*Crocus sativas L.*) also native to this region.

Rue. A small, woody, perennial shrub (*Ruta graveolens L.*), noted for its pungent, bitter leaves and yellow flowers. Of the four varieties grown, the species *graveolens,* meaning "strong smelling," is the most common, indigenous to the eastern Mediterranean coast. It was relished for its peculiar strong taste and used as a culinary spice and for medicinal reasons. It was a customary tithable garden plant (Luke 11:42).

Rush. A cylindrical, hollow-stalked plant of the *Juneus* genus. There are twenty varieties of this grasslike plant growing in and along the water courses of Palestine. Where NASB and KJV have "rush" (Job 8:11; 41:20; Isa 19:6; 35:7), NIV has "papyrus" or "reed." See also *Bulrush.*

Rye, Rie. See *Spelt.*

Saffron. A purple-flowered, bulbous plant (*Crocus sativas L.*), called the autumn crocus. The stigmas of the autumn crocus are highly valued for their aromatic odor and deep orange color, used for food flavoring and coloring, and as a dye (Song of Songs 4:14).

Scarlet. A lasting and rich red dye produced by the kermes insect (*Chermes ilicis*), which breeds in the soft, milky down on the twigs of the kermes oak tree (*Quercus coccifers L.*). This dye was used for a scarlet and crimson coloring of wool and linen thread in Bible times (2 Chron 3:14; Jer 4:30; Heb 9:19; Rev 18:12).

Seaweed. See *Eelgrass.*

Shittah Tree, Shittim Tree. See *Acacia.*

Spelt. An inferior variety of wheat, containing two red grains in its head. It grows taller than wheat and will survive where other grasses will not grow. Spelt (*Triticum aestivum var. Spilta L.*), sometimes translated "rye" (KJV), was grown in Egypt (Exod 9:32) and in Palestine (Isa 28:25) and was made into bread (Ezek 4:9).

Spice. A generic term pertaining to aromatic substances, usually of plant extract, used to flavor and season food. Three Hebrew words and one Greek word are translated "spice." Spices were mixed together to form the sacred anointing oil and the fragrant incense used in the tabernacle (Exod 25:6; 30:23–25; 35:8). Spices were a precious trade commodity (1 Kings 10; Rev 18:13), part of the palace treasury (2 Kings 20:13; Isa 39:2), valued for their aromatic fragrance (Song of Songs 4:10, 14), and used in preparing Jesus' body for burial (Luke 23:56; John 19:40).

In Genesis 37:25; 43:11, the reference is to the gum exuded from the thorny astragal (*Astragalus tragacantha L.*).

Spikenard. A costly perennial herb (*Nardostachys jatamansi [Wall.] D.C.*), with an aromatic root, native to East India and presently cultivated on the Himalayas. The rose-red fragrance ointment made from its dried roots and woolly stems was a favorite perfume of the ancients (Song of Songs 1:12; 4:13–14 KJV; NIV "perfume, nard"). The ointment is stored in an alabaster jar to preserve its fragrance. Mary's anointing of Jesus with the precious nard was an act of real sacrifice (Mark 14:3; John 12:3).

Stacte. A strongly perfumed gum resin that drains from the incised bark of the small, shrubby storax tree (*Styrax officinalis L.*), used in biblical days as a component of the perfume formulated for use in the tabernacle (Exod 30:34). NIV has "gum resin."

Sweet Cane. See *Calamus.*

Sycamine. See *Mulberry Tree.*

Sycamore. A large spreading tree, producing sweet, edible fruit, native-grown in Egypt and Asia Minor. The sycamore-fig tree (*Ficus sycomorus*) bears fruit, like the ordinary fig, directly on the stem, but its fruit is of inferior quality. Its

A sycamore tree growing wild on the coastal plain of Israel. In biblical times the sycamore was one of the most valuable trees, its wood being used as building timber. Amos states that besides being a shepherd he also took care of sycamore-fig trees (Amos 7:14). Courtesy Seffie Ben-Yoseph.

wood is light, durable, and good for carpentry. The Egyptians made their mummy cases of this wood (1 Kings 10:27; Amos 7:14; Luke 19:4).

Tamarisk. A small, shrubby tree (*Tamarix mannifera*), with narrow, evergreen leaves and bunches of little pink-and-white flowers, native to the semiarid regions of the Mediterranean. Nine species are known to exist in Palestine (Gen 21:33; 1 Sam 22:6; 31:13).

Tare. An annual weedy grass, probably the bearded darnel (*Lolium temulentum L.*), that flourishes in grain fields. It is difficult to distinguish domesticated grains from the wild darnel until their heads mature. At harvest time the grain is fanned and put through a sieve. The smaller darnel seeds left after fanning pass through the sieve, leaving behind the desired fruit. The darnel is host to an ergot-like smut fungus, which infects the seeds and is poisonous to man and herbivorous animals but not to poultry. The word is translated "weed" by NIV (Matt 13:24–30, 36–43).

Teil Tree. See *Terebinth.*

Terebinth. A thick-trunked, spreading tree (*Pistacia terebinthus var. palaestine [Boiss.] Post.*) of hot, dry places. Usually a solitary tree, it provides a dense, cooling shade. When the bark is cut, a perfumed oily resin (the cyprus turpentine of commerce) flows out (so called the turpentine tree). NIV has terebinth in two of sixteen OT uses of *'ēlāh* (Isa 6:13 teil tree KJV; Hos 4:13).

Thistle. A prickly plant, often with pink or purple-flowered heads. Generic in character, it is represented in nineteen Hebrew and Greek words interchangeably translated bramble, brier, thistle, and thorn (2 Kings 14:9; 2 Chron 25:18; Hos 10:8; Matt 7:16; 13:7; Heb 6:8). Of the more than two hundred species of thistles that grow in Palestine, Mary's thistle (*Silybum marianum [L.] Gaerth.*) and the true star-thistle (*Centaurea calcitrapa L.*) are the most common. Thistles originated at the time of God's curse on Adam because of his sin (Gen 3:18) and are found in every part of Palestine.

Thorn. The generic term includes small, spiny shrubs and vines. The *Zizyphus spina-christi L.* and the Palestine buckthorn, *Rhamnus palastine Boiss.*, are the two thorny shrubs most widespread and well known in biblical times in Palestine. Both were planted as hedges and the latter was used as firewood (Judg 9:14–15; Prov 26:9; Isa 55:13; Matt 7:16; Luke 6:44).

The crown of thorns placed on Jesus' head at the time of his crucifixion might have been the Christ's-thorn (*Paliurus spina-christi Mill.*), a straggling shrub, growing from three to nine feet (one to three m.) tall. Its pliable branches, with their uneven stiff thorns, lent themselves to the braiding of the "crown" or "wreath" made by the soldiers (Matt 27:29; Mark 15:17; John 19:2, 5). However, since the Christ's-thorn was not readily accessible in Jerusalem, the *Zizyphus* or *Rhamnus* might have been the thornbush used.

Thyine. See *Citron, Citrus Tree.*

Tumbleweed. The translations "whirling dust" (RSV, ASV), "wheel" and "rolling thing" (KJV) (Ps 83:13; Isa 17:13) probably refer to the "tumbleweed" (NIV), long known as the "holy resurrection flower." A member of the mustard family, the six-inch (fifteen-cm.) stems of the tumbleweed lie in a circle flat on the ground until the seeds are mature; then the stems become dry and curved in, forming a globe. The wind eventually breaks the dry taproot at ground level; then the plant rolls over and over, spreading its seeds as it goes.

Notobasis, a common thorn or thistle that grows wild in Palestine. Courtesy S. Zur Picture Library.

Turpentine Tree. See *Terebinth.*

Vine. See *Grape.*

Vine of Sodom. Mentioned in Deuteronomy 32:32, this plant cannot be clearly identified. Possible fruit plants have been suggested, but each one has problems in fully satisfying the requirements of the text. It is generally accepted that the vine of Sodom is an example of Hebrew poetry, epitomizing the utter wickedness of Sodom, from which comes toxic fruit and fatal drink.

Walnut. A large, ornamental, spreading shade tree (*Juglans regia L.*), with long leaves and woody edible fruit, native to Iran. Also named the "English walnut" or the "Persian walnut," this tree provides edible fruit; dark, close-grained hardwood for woodworking; and dye. The "nut trees" of Song of Solomon 6:11 are most likely walnut trees.

Weed. See *Cockle; Eelgrass; Tare.*

Wheat. A common cereal grain (*Triticum compositum L.*) that yields fine flour. Wheat is sown in the winter and harvested in late spring or early summer in Palestine. Egypt, Babylonia, Syria, and Palestine were renowned for their quality wheat. Wheat is first noted in Genesis 30:14. Certain varieties of wheat still yield sixty to a hundred grains per head as they did in Jesus' day (Matt 13:3–8). Heads roasted over fire consti-

A limestone relief of a wheat field, from Tell-el Amarna, c. 1350 B.C. Courtesy Israel Museum, Jerusalem.

tuted the "parched corn" (KJV) of the OT (Lev 23:14; Ruth 2:14; 1 Sam 17:17; 25:18). Straw and stubble are the dried stalks and remnants of wheat and other cereal grains (Exod 5:12; 1 Cor 3:12).

Wild Gourd. See *Gourd.*

Willow. A fast-growing shade tree (*Salix alba L.*) with narrow leaves and catkins. It is found in moist places and on the margins of rivers and shallow streams. The willows of Job 40:22; Isaiah 15:7; 44:4 (KJV; NIV "poplars"); and Ezekiel 17:5 are thought to belong to one of four Palestinian species of willow. The willows of Psalm 137:2 (KJV; NIV "poplars") inhabit the river and stream banks from Syria to Palestine, especially along the Jordan Valley. They are considered either the Euphrates aspen (*Populus euphratica Oliv.*) or the weeping willow (*Salix Babylonica, L.*), one from which, tradition has it, the Israelites hung their harps.

Wormwood. A bitter, aromatic herb (*Artemisia judaica L.*) with clusters of small, greenish yellow flowers and alternating greenish gray leaves, growing in desert areas. Related to our sagebrush, the wormwood is the source of an essential oil obtained from the dried leaves and the tops of the plant. Five species are known to exist in Palestine. The plant was a symbol of bitterness, embodying the hardships and evils of life (Prov 5:4; Lam 3:15, 19; Amos 5:7 (KJV; NIV "gall, bitterness"; Rev 8:11).

Bibliography: H. N. and A. L. Moldenke, *Plants of the Bible,* 1952; W. Walker, *All the Plants of the Bible,* 1957; M. Zohary, *Plant-Life of Palestine,* 1962; R. K. Harrison, *Healing Herbs of the Bible,* 1966; A. Goor and M. Nurock, *Fruits of the Holy Land,* 1968; A. Alon, *The Natural History of the Land of the Bible,* 1969. JLL

PLASTER. The Egyptians plastered their stone buildings, even the finest granite, inside and out, to make a smooth surface for decoration. The poor used a mixture of clay and straw. On better buildings the first coat was gypsum and red clay or ashes, the finish coat slaked lime and white sand, sometimes including chopped straw. In Palestine and Syria, an outside clay coating had to be renewed after the rainy reason. Mortar was usually made with limestone, the process of its manufacture otherwise similar to that in Egypt. The Arabic word for mortar means "clay." Hebrew *sîdh* (Deut 27:2, 4) means "to boil up," because of the action when water is poured on unslaked lime. Hebrew *gîr* (Dan 5:5) means "burned in a kiln" (either lime or gypsum). *Tûah* (Lev 14:42–48) means "to daub, smear."

PLATTER (See CHARGER)

PLEDGE. Personal property of a debtor held to secure a payment (Gen 38:17–18, 20). It translates several Hebrew words. Mosaic Law protected the poor. An outer garment, taken as a pledge, had to be restored at sunset for a bed covering (Exod 22:26–27; Deut 24:12–13). The creditor was forbidden to enter his neighbor's house to take the pledge (24:10–11). A handmill or its upper millstone might not be taken (24:6), nor a widow's clothing (24:17–18). Abuses of the pledge were censured (Job 22:6; 24:3, 9; Amos 2:8; Hab 2:6, the Hebrew word in Hab 2:6 [*'avṭîṭ*, thick clay KJV] occurring only here in the OT). In two passages (2 Kings 18:23; Isa 36:8) a wager (JB, RSV; bargain NIV) seems to be meant. The person who puts up security for strangers ought to be taken in pledge (Prov 20:16; 27:13). The pledge David was to take from his brothers in exchange for cheeses may be a prearranged token (JB, NEB, RSV) or assurance (NIV) of their welfare (1 Sam 17:18). The pledge (Gr. *pistis,* "faith"; faith KJV) in 1 Timothy 5:12 is the marriage vow.

PLEIADES (See ASTRONOMY)

PLOWMAN (See OCCUPATIONS AND PROFESSIONS)

PLOW, PLOUGH. A farming tool used to break up the ground for sowing. An ancient plow, as Hebrew *harash* indicates, scratched the surface but did not turn over the soil. It consisted of a branched stick, the larger branch, usually the trunk of a small tree, hitched to the animals that pulled it, the branch braced and terminating in the share, which was at first simply the sharpened end of the branch, later a metal point. It was ordinarily drawn by a yoke of oxen (Job 1:14; Amos 6:12). Plowing with an ox and an ass yoked together was forbidden (Deut 22:10), but this prohibition is not observed today. A man guided the plow with his left hand, goading the oxen and from time to time cleaning the share with the goad in his right, keeping his eyes forward in order to make the furrow straight (Luke 9:62). Plowing done, the farmer sowed (Isa 28:24–26 RSV, NIV). He who does not plow in autumn will have no harvest (Prov 20:4 RSV, NIV). Amos 9:13 foretells a time when the soil will be so fertile that there will not need to be a fallow interval between harvest and the next plowing. Then foreigners will plow for Israel (Isa 61:5). Plowing may indicate destruction (Jer 26:18; Mic 3:12). Hosea 10:11–13 contrasts plowing for righteous and for evil ends (Job 4:8; Ps 129:3). Servants plowed (Luke 17:7). The plowman should plow in hope of a share of the crop (1 Cor 9:10). Elisha plowing with twelve yoke of oxen indicates his ability and the magnitude of his farming operations (1 Kings 19:19). Samson calls the Philistines' badgering of his betrothed to tell his riddle plowing "with his heifer" (Judg 14:18).

One of the clearest representations of a Babylonian plow with seed-drill, shown in lower register on black (21.6 cm. high) basalt stele of Esarhaddon (680–669 B.C.). To the left, a stylized ear of grain or hill, and to the right, a plam tree. Top register shows the king (?) standing before an altar surmounted by a horned crown. Reproduced by courtesy of the Trustees of the British Museum.

PLOWSHARE (Heb. *'ēth, the blade of a plow*). To beat swords into plowshares was symbolic of an age of peace (Isa 2:4; Mic 4:3); to beat plowshares into swords portended coming war (Joel 3:10).

PLUMB LINE (Heb. *'anāk*). A cord with a stone or metal weight, the plummet, tied to one end; used by builders to keep a wall perpendicular. Plumb line and plummet are used figuratively of God's action in testing the uprightness of his people (2 Kings 21:13; Isa 28:17; Amos 7:7–9).

POCHERETH (See POKERETH-HAZZEBAIM)

PODS (See PLANTS)

POET (Gr. *poiētēs, a maker*). In Acts 17:28 Paul quotes from *Phaenomena,* 5, by the Greek poet Aratus (c. 270 B.C.) of Soli in Cilicia. A similar phrase occurs in the *Hymn to Zeus,* by the Stoic philosopher Cleanthes (300–220), who taught at Athens. First Corinthians 15:32 may contain a quotation from Menander; Titus 1:12, from Epimenides. The poetic quality of many OT and NT passages entitles their authors to be called poets.

POETRY. The recent versions of the Bible have happily tried to differentiate poetry from prose in the OT (RSV, NIV). The fact that they do not always agree what is poetry and what is prose arises from the distinctive nature of Hebrew poetry, which is very different from its Greek, Latin, or English counterparts. While it is certainly not lacking in rhythm, rhyme, alliteration, and other literary features such as we accept in classical and English poetry, in OT poetry everything is subservient to meaning, and in consequence lines of Hebrew poetry are not to be "scanned" by marking off long and short syllables (as though the "form" were the primary consideration), but marking off significant words or groups of words (because the message is primary). Thus (as, for example, in the so-called "dirge" rhythm) a line of three significant words is followed by a line with two (usually written 3:2). Another frequent "rhythm" in Hebrew poetry is 3:3.

But the most familiar feature of Hebrew poetry arises from the balance between successive lines. This feature is called parallelism. Many varieties have been distinguished, of which the three principal ones are *synonymous,* in which the meaning of both members is similar (e.g., 1 Sam 18:7; Ps 15:1; 24:1–3); *antithetic,* in which the meanings of the members are opposed (Ps 37:9; Prov 10:1; 11:3); and *synthetic,* in which noun corresponds to noun, verb to verb, and member to member, and each member adds something new (e.g., Ps 19:8–9). Quite a number of poems are alphabetical acrostics; that is to say, the successive lines of the poem begin with the successive letters of the Hebrew alphabet (e.g., Pss 34, 37; Lam 1–4). In Psalm 119 each group of eight verses begins with the same letter. This literary device of the alphabetical acrostic was not chosen for arbitrary factors of form but, just as we say, "That's the whole thing, from A to Z," so the poet alerts us to the fact that a total coverage of the chosen theme is intended. Thus in Psalm 119 we have a total statement about the Word of God.

Short poems (usually so printed in NIV) are embedded in the historical books as follows: Adam to Eve (Gen 2:23); God to the serpent, Adam, and Eve (3:14–19); Lamech to his wives (4:23–24); Noah about his sons (9:25–27); Melchizedek's blessing (14:19–20); God to Rebekah (25:23); Isaac's blessing on Jacob (27:27–29) and Esau (27:39–40); Jacob in blessing Joseph (48:15–16) and in prophecies concerning his sons (49:2–27); the victory song of Moses (Exod 15:1–18, 21); the priestly blessing (Num 6:24–26); a quotation from the Book of the Wars of the Lord (21:14–15); the song of the well (21:17–18); a ballad (21:27–30); Balaam's prophecies (23:7–10, 18–24; 24:3–9, 15–24); Moses' song (Deut 32:1–43) and blessing of the people (33:2–29); the curse on a future rebuilder of Jericho (Josh 6:26b); a quotation from the Book of Jasher (1:12b–13a); the song of Deborah and Barak (Judg 5); Samson's riddle, solution, and answer (14:14, 18); his victory song (15:16); Hannah's song (1 Sam 2:1–10); a poem by Samuel (15:22–23); a women's song (18:7); David's lament over Jonathan (2 Sam 1:19–27) and over Abner (3:33–34); his psalm (Ps 18:2–50; 22:5–31); his last words (2 Sam 23:1–7); a quatrain by Solomon (1 Kings 8:12–13); a popular song (12:16; 2 Chron 10:16); a prophetic poem by Isaiah (2 Kings 19:21–28); a soldiers' song (1 Chron 12:18); a refrain (2 Chron 5:13; 7:3b, "He is good; his love endures for ever"); a snatch of song by Solomon (6:1b–2, 41–42).

In the NT, easily recognizable poems are all in Luke: The Magnificat of Mary (1:46b–55), adapted from Hannah's song (1 Sam 2:1–10); the prophecy of Zachariah (Luke 1:68–79); the angels' Gloria in Excelsis (2:14); and the Nunc Dimittis of Simeon (2:29–32). All these are echoes of Hebrew poetry, sung by Hebrews. Snatches of Christian hymns are thought to be found in some of the letters (Eph 5:14; 1 Tim 1:17; 3:16; 6:16; 2 Tim 4:18). Paul rises to heights of poetic eloquence (e.g., Rom 8; 11:33–12:2; 1 Cor 13; 15:25–57). James's letter is lyrical. The language of Jesus is poetic in the highest degree. The NT contains many quotations of OT poetry. But it is the elevated thought of the NT as of the OT, and not the technical form, that gives us the feeling of poetry. Thus Bible language has lent itself admirably to the use of hymn writers, in many languages and to their own native poetic forms.

Bibliography: R. K. Harrison, *Introduction to the Old Testament,* 1970, pp. 965–75; F. F. Bruce, *The Poetry of the Old Testament,* (NBCrev), 1970, pp. 44–47; F. D. Kidner, *Psalms* (TOTC), 1973, pp. 1–4. ER and JAM

POISON (Heb. *hēmâh, rō'sh,* Gr. *thymos, ios*). The venom of reptiles (Deut 32:24, 33; Job 20:16; Ps 58:4; Rom 3:13). James 3:8 may reflect a belief that the tongue conveyed the poison. Job 6:4 refers to poisoned arrows. Vegetable poisons also were known (Hos 10:4, KJV hemlock; RSV and NIV poisonous weeds; 2 Kings 4:39–40, gourds). The "deadly thing" of Mark 16:18 was a poisoned drink (cf. NIV).

POKERETH-HAZZEBAIM (pŏk'ē-rĕth-hăz'à-bā'ĭm). The head of a postexilic family; a servant of Solomon (Ezra 2:57; Neh 7:59). KJV has "Pochereth of Zebaim."

POLLUTION (Heb. *gā'al,* Gr. *alisgēma*). This may be regarded as from menstruation (Ezek 22:10 KJV; NIV "ceremonially unclean"), from food sacrificed to idols (Acts 15:20, 29), or from the evil in the world (2 Peter 2:20 KJV; RSV "defilements," NIV "corruption"). Imperfect offerings, brought with a wrong motive, were polluted (Mal 1:7–9 KJV; NIV "defiled"). An altar was to be of unhewn stone: to cut the stone was to pollute it (Exod 20:25 KJV; RSV "profane," NIV "defile"). Several Hebrew and Greek words translated "pollute" refer to ceremonial or moral defilement, profanation, and uncleanness.

POLLUX (See CASTOR AND POLLUX)

POLYGAMY (See MARRIAGE)

POMEGRANATE (See PLANTS)

PONTIUS PILATE (See PILATE)

PONTUS (Gr. *Pontos, sea*). A large province of northern Asia Minor that lay along the Black Sea (Pontus Euxinius). All the references to Pontus in the NT indicate that there were many Jews in the province. Jews from Pontus were in Jerusalem at the first Pentecost (Acts 2:9). Luke mentions in Acts 18:2 that a certain Christian Jew named Aquila was born in Pontus. So far as we know, Pontus and the other northern provinces were not evangelized by Paul. The Holy Spirit did not permit him to preach in Bithynia (16:7). However, Peter addresses his first letter to "strangers in the world, scattered throughout Pontus" and other regions (1 Peter 1:1), lending credence to the tradition that Peter preached in northern Asia Minor rather than in Rome after Pentecost. In secular history, Pontus is noted for the dynasty of kings, headed by the great Mithridates, that ruled from 337 to 63 B.C.

POOL. A pocket of water, natural or artificial.

Hebrew *'ăgham,* "a marshy, reedy pond," refers to a natural depression with water (Exod 7:19; 8:5, "ponds"). Pools tell of a restored wilderness (Ps 107:35; 114:8; Isa 35:7; 41:18). Dried-up pools speak of judgment (42:15). For the sluices and ponds of the KJV of Isaiah 19:10, ASV, RSV, and NIV adopt entirely different readings of the text. Hebrew *berēkhâh,* "pool," from the root "bless," refers to an artificial pool to conserve water for irrigation or drinking. Large ones were made by damming streams. Smaller ones were rectangular, wider than they were deep, to collect rain from the roofs or from the surface of the ground; similar to cylindrical pits or cisterns that served the same purpose. Water from springs was collected in masonry pools. All these were necessary in a dry land. We read of the following pools: of Gibeon (2 Sam 2:13), of Hebron (4:12), of Samaria (1 Kings 22:38), of Heshbon (Song of Songs 7:4), of Siloah or Siloam (Neh 3:15), the Upper Pool (2 Kings 18:17; Isa 7:3; 36:2), the pool Hezekiah made (2 Kings 20:20), the Lower Pool (Isa 22:9), the Old Pool (22:11); the King's Pool (Neh 2:14), and the artificial pool (3:16). Solomon made pools to water his forest nursery (Eccl 2:6 KJV; NIV "reservoirs"). Psalm 84:6 speaks of the rain filling the pools (ASV has "blessings" here). Nineveh was once being destroyed, like a pool whose waters are running out (Nah 2:8). Greek *kolymbēthra,* "pool, place for diving, swimming-bath"; the pool of Bethesda (John 5:2, 4, 7) and of Siloam (9:7, 11).

POOR (Heb. *'evyôn, dal, 'ānî, rûsh,* Gr. *ptochos*). God's love and care for the poor are central to his providence (Ps 34:6; 68:10; Eccl 5:8). He encourages us to do the same (Exod 22:23). The Mosaic Law has specific provisions for the benefit of the poor (Exod 22:25–27; 23:11; Lev 19:9–10, 13, 15; 25:6, 25–30; Deut 14:28–29; 15:12–13; 16:11–14; Ruth 2:1–7; Neh 8:10).

Coin of Mithridates, king of Pontus. Pontus was a region in northern Asia Minor occupying a considerable part of the southern coast of the Black Sea. Courtesy Carta, Jerusalem.

Israel as a nation was born out of deep poverty (Exod 1:8–14; 2:7–10) and was never allowed to forget it (e.g., 1 Kings 8:50–53). If Israel met the conditions of God's covenant, there would be no poor among them; but God knew this would never be realized (Deut 15:4–11). Willful neglect leading to poverty is not condoned (Prov 13:4–18). National disasters caused the poor to become almost synonymous with the pious (e.g., Ps 68:10; Isa 41:17). Even in the early nomadic and later agricultural economy there were slaves and poor freemen, but there were many more in the urban and commercial economy of the monarchy. The wrongs done to the poor concerned the prophets (e.g., Isa 1:23; 10:1–2; Ezek 34; Amos 2:6; 5:7; 8:6; Mic 2:1–2; Hab 3:14; Mal 3:5).

At the outset of his ministry, Jesus, taking for his text Isaiah 61:1–2, presents as his first aim, "to preach good news to the poor." That physical poverty is meant is shown by the contrasts in Luke 6:20–26. In Matthew 5:3 Jesus commends the poor in spirit, the humble ones. Jesus moved among the poor and humble. He associated himself with them in his manner of living and his freedom from the encumbering cares of property (8:20). He understood and appreciated the sacrificial giving of a poor widow (Mark 12:41–44). He recognized the continuing obligation toward the poor and at the same time appreciated a unique expression of love toward himself (14:7). The early church moved among the poor, who were not too poor to be concerned for one another's welfare (2 Cor 8:2–5, 9–15), drawing inspiration from Christ's leaving heavenly riches for earthly poverty. The origin of the diaconate is linked with a special need (Acts 6:1–6). Those with property contributed to the common fund (2:45; 4:32–37). The Jerusalem Council asked Paul and Barnabas to remember the poor (Gal 2:10). James has some sharp words about the relations of rich and poor (James 1:9–11; 2:1–13; 5:1–6).

POPLAR (SEE PLANTS)

PORATHA (pō-rā'thȧ, pŏr'ȧ-thȧ). One of the sons of Haman the Agagite. He died with his brothers (Esth 9:8).

PORCH (Heb. *'êlām, 'ūlām, porch*). In Solomon's temple (1 Kings 6:3); in Solomon's palace (7:6ff.), in Ezekiel's new temple (Ezek 40:7ff.). RSV has "vestibule"; NIV "portico." Hebrew *misderôn,* "porch, colonnade" (Judg 3:23, RSV "vestibule"), before an upper room. Greek *proaulion,* "place before a court, vestibule" (Mark 14:68, NIV entryway). Greek *pylōn,* "gateway" (Matt 26:71). Greek *stoa,* "roofed colonnade" (John 5:2); five porches at the pool of Bethesda (John 10:23; Acts 3:11; 5:12; RSV "portico," NIV "colonnade"). In every case an area with a roof supported by columns appears to be meant.

PORCIUS (See FESTUS)

PORPHYRY (See MINERALS)

PORTER (See OCCUPATIONS AND PROFESSIONS)

PORTION. A part—that is, less than the whole; a share (Num 31:30, 47 KJV), of food served to one person (Neh 8:10, 12; Dan 1:5–16; 11:26 KJV; NIV "amount, provision"; Deut 18:8 KJV) or of property acquired by gift (1 Sam 1:4–5) or by inheritance (Gen 31:14 KJV; Josh 17:14). It can also refer to a plot of ground (2 Kings 9:10, 36–37 KJV) or one's destiny (Job 20:29 KJV; Ps 142:5; Lam 3:24). Several Hebrew and Greek words are translated "portion" in the KJV, sometimes otherwise in ASV, RSV, NIV. The shades of meaning are determined by the context. The most significant meaning appears in passages like Psalm 119:57, where one's relation to God and eternal well-being are involved.

POST (Heb. *mezûzâh, doorpost; rûts, to run; 'ayil, strength*). The first word represented the parts to the doorway of a building (1 Kings 6:33 KJV; NIV "jams"). The last word is a post also, but has a wider meaning as well; that is, anything strong (Ezek 40:14, 16 KJV). One of the most common uses of the word *post* is its designation of anyone who conveyed a message speedily. These were very early means of communication (Job 9:25 KJV; NIV "runner"). The first went by foot and later by horses. Royal messages were conveyed in this way (2 Chron 30:6, 10 KJV; NIV "couriers").

POT. The translation of more than a dozen Hebrew and Greek words. Most of them referred to utensils for holding liquids and solid substances such as grain or ashes. The Hebrew *sîr* was the most common pot used in cooking (2 Kings 4:38; Jer 1:13). It was also the vessel that held ashes (Exod 27:3). Some of these vessels were made of metal and others of clay, and there were a great variety of sizes and shapes. Their chief NT use was for water or wine (Mark 7:4; John 2:6 KJV; NIV "pitchers, jars").

POTENTATE (pō'tĕn-tāt, Gr. *dynastēs, mighty one*). Used in Luke 1:52 (NIV "rulers") and Acts 8:27 (NIV "important official").

POTIPHAR (pŏt'ĭ-fêr, Heb. *pôtîphara', whom Re has given*). One of the pharaoh's officers mentioned in Genesis in connection with Joseph's sojourn in that land. He purchased Joseph from the Midianites and made him head overseer over his house. When Joseph was falsely accused by the wife of Potiphar, he threw Joseph into prison (Gen 39:1–20).

POTIPHERA, POTIPHERAH (pō-tĭf'êr-ȧ, Heb. *potiphera, the one given by the sun-god*). The Egyptian priest of On whose daughter Asenath was given to Joseph for a wife (Gen 41:45, 50; 46:20).

POTSHERD (pot shurd, Heb. *heres*). A piece of earthenware. Job used a potsherd to scrape his body in his affliction (Job 2:8 KJV; NIV "broken piece of pottery"). Potsherds are referred to in other places (Ps 22:15; Isa 45:9). There are many inscribed potsherds known as "ostraca" that furnish valuable data for the archaeologist. See OSTRACA.

POTSHERD GATE (See POTTER'S GATE)

POTTAGE (Heb. *nāzîdh, boiled*). A kind of thick broth made with vegetables and meat or suet. Jacob bought Esau's birthright for a mess of pottage (Gen 25:29–30, 34 KJV; NIV "red [or lentil] stew"; see also 2 Kings 4:38–39).

POTTER (See OCCUPATIONS AND PROFESSIONS: *Pottery*)

POTTER'S FIELD (See AKELDAMA)

POTTER'S GATE. A gate in the wall of Jerusalem that is thought to be referred to by Jeremiah (Jer 19:2 KJV). NIV reads "Potsherd Gate." It may be the same gate that led to the Valley of Hinnom—i.e., the Dung Gate.

POTTERY. Pottery making is one of the oldest crafts in Bible lands. James L. Kelso and J. Palin Thorley have termed pottery "the first synthetic to be discovered by mankind . . . an artificial stone produced by firing clay shapes to a temperature sufficiently high to change the physical and chemical properties of the original clay into a new substance with many of the characteristics of stone" ("Palestinian Pottery in Bible Times," BA, 8, 1945, p. 82). References, both literal and figurative, to the potter and his products occur throughout the Scriptures.

I. Pottery Production in Palestine. Let us follow Jeremiah down to the potter's house (Jer 18:1–6). This "factory" was in the Valley of Hinnom near the Potsherd Gate (19:2) and near the tower of the furnaces or pottery kilns (Neh 3:11; 12:38). In addition to his workshop the potter (Heb. *yôtsēr*) needed a field (Matt 27:7) for weathering the dry native clay-dust (*'āphār*) or wet stream-bank clay (*tît*, Nah 3:14) and for mixing it with water and treading it by foot into potter's clay (*hōmer*), as in Isaiah 41:25. For cooking vessels, sand or crushed stone was added to temper the clay. In his house the potter kneaded the clay for several hours to remove all air bubbles. He could either build up a large vessel freehand, using long sausagelike rolls of clay; or he could "throw" a ball of soft clay on the center of a pivoted disc or dual stone wheel (*'obnāyim*) that was spun counterclockwise by his hand or by his apprentice. By thrusting his forearm into the mass of wet clay, he hollowed out the interior. The centrifugal force imparted to the spinning lump enabled the potter in a matter of minutes to form a vessel with only light pressure from his fingers. In mass production he pinched off (*qātsar*, Job 33:6b) the completed jug from the cone of clay spinning on the wheel. Impurities in the clay or insufficient treading could mar the vessel on the wheel. The potter

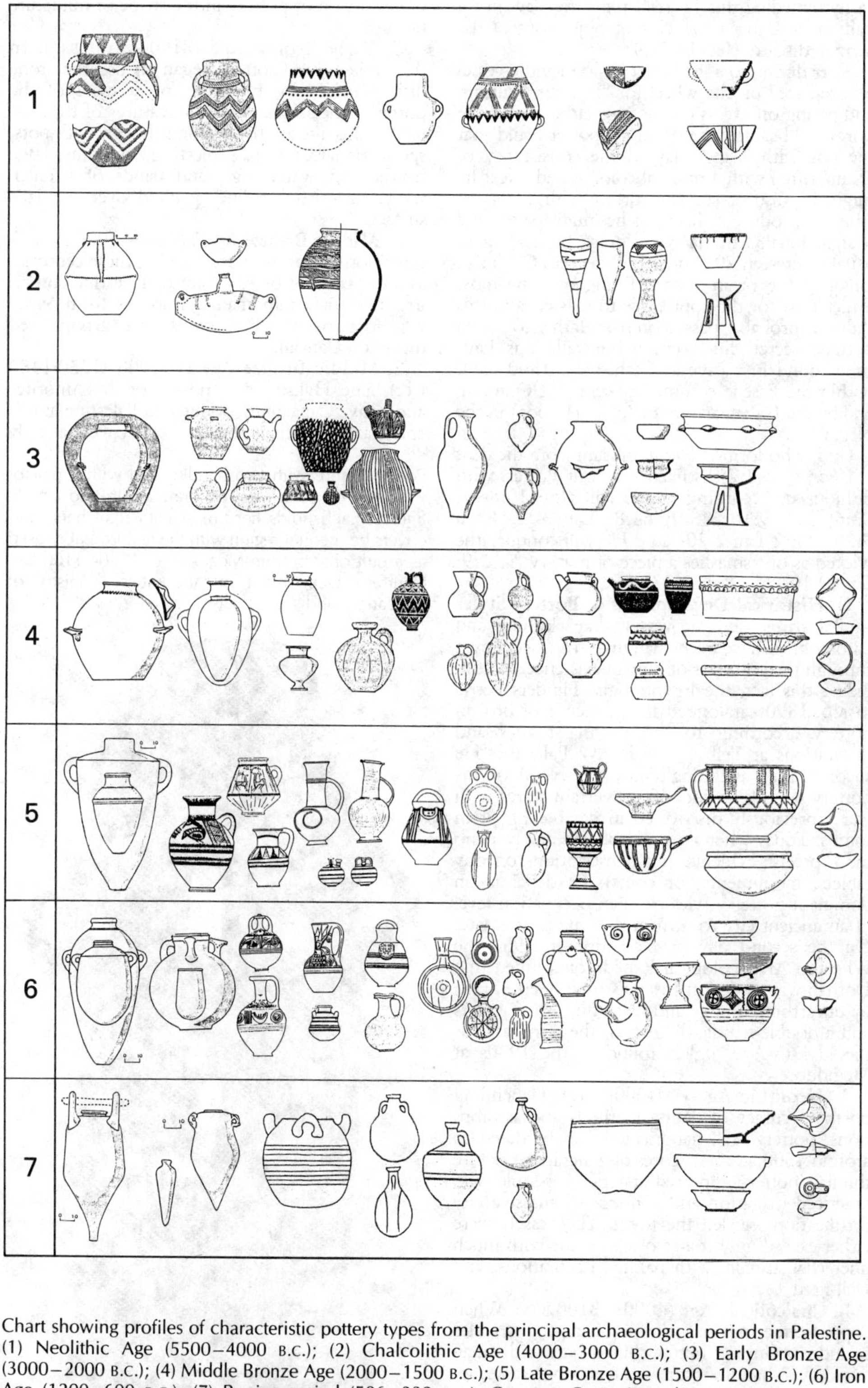

Chart showing profiles of characteristic pottery types from the principal archaeological periods in Palestine. (1) Neolithic Age (5500–4000 B.C.); (2) Chalcolithic Age (4000–3000 B.C.); (3) Early Bronze Age (3000–2000 B.C.); (4) Middle Bronze Age (2000–1500 B.C.); (5) Late Bronze Age (1500–1200 B.C.); (6) Iron Age (1200–600 B.C.); (7) Persian period (586–332 B.C.). Courtesy Carta, Jerusalem.

easily remedied this by reshaping the clay into a ball and making a less elegant object out of the former discard (Jer 18:3–4).

After drying to a leathery consistency the vessel was replaced on the wheel for "turning," cutting and paring off excess clay as on a lathe. To fill the pores and beautify the vessel the potter could coat the pot with "slip," clay of the consistency of cream, often with a mineral color added. Next he might burnish or rub the surface with a smooth stone to produce a sheen, or he might paint on a design. Finally, the jar was "fired" by heating it, usually between 700 and 1,050 degrees Celsius in an open fire or in a kiln. Firing was the most difficult art for the apprentice to master, and this skill was probably passed on from father to son as a trade secret. Such potters' installations have been found in a cave at Lachish (c. 1500 B.C.), within the Essene community center at Qumran, and by the Nabatean city of Avdat (Eboda) in the Negev.

God, who formed (*yāṭsar*) Adam from the dust (*ʿāphār*, Gen 2:7), is likened to our Potter, who fashions us according to his will (Job 10:8–9; 33:6; Isa 29:16; 45:9; 64:8; Lam 4:2; Rom 9:20–23; 2 Tim 2:20–21). He will conquer the wicked as one smashes a piece of pottery (Ps 2:9; Jer 19:10–11; Rev 2:27).

II. Historical Development of Pottery Styles in Palestine. Ceramic vessels, like clothing and automobiles, have been changing in fashion down through the centuries of human existence. Recognizing this fact, the Egyptologist Flinders Petrie in A.D. 1890 catalogued the sequence of broken pottery according to the varying shapes and decorations at Tell el-Hesi in SW Palestine. He succeeded in assigning dates to several of his pottery periods by identifying certain wares with wares previously discovered in datable Egyptian tombs. Today when an archaeologist uncovers no more precise evidence (e.g., inscriptions on clay tablets, monuments, or coins), he depends on dominant pottery styles from an occupation level of an ancient city to furnish the clue to the date. On the second day of excavation in 1953 the Wheaton Archaeological Expedition verified that Dothan was settled in Joseph's time (Gen 37:17) by unearthing orange and black burnished juglets and a double-handled juglet, of the same style as the Hyksos-Age juglets found in the 1930s at Megiddo.

A. **Neolithic Age** (?–4000? B.C.). Depending on the accuracy of dating methods and assumptions, pottery—all handmade—can be dated to around 4500 B.C. But scores of generations before the first pottery appeared at Jericho, people who practiced irrigation and constructed massive city fortifications settled the town. The vessels were either exceedingly coarse or else made with much finer clay, usually with painted decorations, and well-fired.

B. **Chalcolithic Age** (4000?–3100 B.C.). When copper came into use, the peculiar pottery styles included swinging butter churns; jars with small "cord-eye" handles; cups with a long, tapering, spikelike "cornet" base; and ossuaries for human bones, made of pottery in the shape of miniature houses.

C. **Early Bronze Age** (3100–2100 B.C.). In this millennium potters began to use the stone disc tournette or turntable, predecessor of the potter's wheel. Characteristic features of the pottery of this age are flat bottoms, hole-mouth pots, spouts on jars, inward-projecting bowl rims, ledge handles on water jugs, and bands of parallel, wavy, or crisscross lines painted over the jar's surface.

D. **Middle Bronze Age I** (2100–1900 B.C.). A transition period in pottery styles, these centuries saw the coming of Abraham to Palestine and an irruption of seminomadic Amorites from Syria, who destroyed many towns and depopulated much of Canaan.

E. **Middle Bronze Age II** (1900–1550/1480 B.C.). The Hyksos, descendants of the Amorites and native Canaanites, dominated Palestine in this era. Hazor was their chief city. They were already

Pottery stand, with two handles and with a pair of windows on each side, decorated with two female figures. Each holds her breast with right hand and covers her genital region with the left. Probably used as a cult object, from Megiddo, c. 1150–1100 B.C. Courtesy Department of Antiquities, Ministry of Education and Culture, Israel.

Decorated Philistine jug with typical design, from Gezer, c. tenth century B.C. Courtesy Zev Radovan.

entering Egypt as merchants or Egyptian slaves in the nineteenth century when Jacob came to Goshen. Later they ruled in Egypt, 1730–1570. In the nineteenth century the fast-spinning potter's wheel revolutionized the industry in the Near East. Virtually all Middle Bronze II pottery was wheel-made. Distinctively Hyksos were the pear-shaped juglets with "button" base, double- or triple-strand handles, chalk-filled pinprick designs, and highly burnished vessels with orange or black coating. Bowls and jars with ring or disc bases were introduced in Palestine, as well as dipper flasks and chalices. Hyksos cities in southern Palestine fell before the pursuing Egyptians about 1550, whereas cities in northern Palestine remained in Hyksos hands until the campaigns of Thutmose III (c. 1480).

F. **Late Bronze Age** (1500–1230 B.C.). With the Hyksos's power broken, numerous petty kings ruled in Canaan. The native pottery declined in gracefulness and technique as the prosperity slumped. Thus, imported vessels from Cyprus are all the more striking: milk bowls with wishbone handles, and "bilbils," jugs with a metallic ring when tapped. From 1400 to 1230 B.C. Mycenean pottery imports were common: stirrup vases, squat pyxis (cylinder-shaped) jars, and large craters with horizontal loop handles. While the nomadic Israelites invaded Canaan about 1400, they continued using wooden bowls, goatskins, and cloth sacks (Lev 11:32) and produced little pottery until they could conquer a town and discard tents for more permanent houses.

G. **Iron Age I** (1230–925 B.C.). In the latter time of the judges Israel was more settled, and iron came into common use. Typical pottery objects were the traveler's water canteen, many-handled wine craters, and lamps with a thick, disclike base. The decorative features are the most distinctive: hand burnishing and gaudy, painted designs, even on rims and handles. After 1150 Philistine painted-ware, very similar to late Mycenean pottery elsewhere, is outstanding with its designs of swans pluming themselves, dolphins, spirals, loops, and maltese crosses. In Israel the period ended when Pharaoh Shishak destroyed many towns on his Palestinian campaign.

H. **Iron Age II** (925–586 B.C.). During the divided monarchy the cities of Israel prospered materially, and their potters excelled. Most helpful for dating a town to this period are the ring-burnished water decanters; wheel burnishing on banquet bowls; twisted, ridged handles on storage jars; black perfume juglets; and the beautiful red, highly burnished Samaria ware. Archaeologists have unearthed Hebrew writings in ink on potsherds, such as the seventy-odd Samaria ostraca from the palace of Jeroboam II and the twenty-one Lachish Letters dated to 589/8. From Isaiah's time onward in Judah belong many inscribed handles of jars for wine, olive oil, or grain. In some cases, as on those found at Gibeon, the name of the owner of a vineyard was inscribed. On others the letters *lmlk* ("belonging to the king") appear together with the name of one of four cities, probably where royal potteries were established to make jars of the correct capacity for the payment of taxes in produce (cf. 1 Chron 4:23). Nebuchadnezzar's devastating invasion produced a cultural void in Palestine for fifty years.

I. **Iron Age II** (538–333 B.C.). During this Persian period locally made storage jars had pointed bases rather than the earlier rounded style. The lip of the lamp evolved into an elongated spout. The most distinctive pottery in the sixth century was imported Greek black-figured ware, and in the fifth, Greek red-figured ware. Coins, which began to appear in Palestine in the fifth century, aid the archaeologist in dating.

J. **Hellenistic Age** (333–63 B.C.). Alexander's conquest began the Hellenization of Palestine. The double potter's wheel, with a large footpower wheel to turn the thrower's wheel (Ecclus 38:29–30), was a Greek improvement. The ubiquitous Rhodian wine-jar handles, each stamped with the name of the potter or of the annual magistrate in Rhodes, immediately classify a stratum of an ancient town as Hellenistic.

K. **Roman Age** (63 B.C.–A.D. 325). Pompey's capture of Jerusalem in 63 B.C. brought Palestine under Roman domination. Significant pottery styles are the beautiful red-glazed (*terra sigillata*) bowls and plates, jugs and pots with horizontally corrugated surfaces, and the exquisitely painted, extremely thin Nabatean pottery from about 50 B.C. to A.D. 150.

III. Identification of Biblical Terms for Pottery Objects. The Hebrew and Greek words,

Pottery of the Roman period found at Masada: two plates, a jug, and a bowl. Courtesy Zev Radovan.

about which there is some degree of understanding, are classified under several main groups:

A. **Bowls, basins, and cups.** The "cups" of biblical times were usually small bowls without handles. Flat dinner plates were unknown, shallow bowls serving as platters and dishes.

1. *Kôs, potērion.* This was a "cup," a small individual drinking bowl for water (2 Sam 12:3; Ps 23:5; Matt 10:42) or for wine (Prov 23:31; Jer 35:5; Matt 26:27). Figuratively a cup might be symbolic of one's destiny, whether it be of salvation (Ps 16:5; 116:13) or of judgment and suffering (Isa 51:17, 22; Jer 49:12; Matt 20:22; 26:39; Rev 14:10).

2. *Tselōḥîth.* Only in 2 Kings 2:20, this vessel must have been an open, shallow bowl (NIV "new bowl") to hold salt, for salt would cake up in a cruse.

3. *Tsallaḥath.* Similar to no. 2, this must have been the well-known ring-burnished bowl of Iron Age II. It had no handles to hang it up, hence it was turned over to dry (2 Kings 21:13). It could be used by a sluggard both for cooking and to contain his food (Prov 19:24; 26:15).

4. *'Aggān.* A banquet bowl, ring- or spiral-burnished on the interior, with two or four handles, similar in size and purpose to our punch bowls (Song of Songs 7:2). The "lesser vessels" in Isaiah 22:24 were hung from a nail or peg in the tent-pole but were large enough to sometimes cause the peg to give way (see also *nevel* on this verse).

5. *Sēphel.* Probably an earlier style of no. 4, since the Arabic word for a large four-handled bowl in Palestinian villages today is *sifl.* Since it was called a "bowl fit for nobles," Jael may have offered Sisera curdled milk in one imported from Mycenae or Cyprus, decorated with painted designs and having pushed-up horizontal loop handles, holding from four to ten pints (nineteen to forty-seven dl.) (Judg 5:25). Or it may have been smaller and of the variety known as the Cypriote milk bowl with a wishbone handle, typical of the Late Bronze Age, and holding from one to three pints (five to fourteen dl.). Gideon squeezed the dew from his fleece into a similar bowl (6:38).

6. *Tryblion.* A large deep dish or bowl, either of metal or fine Roman sigillata pottery, from which all could take out food (Matt 26:23).

7. *Niptēr.* A basin or vessel for washing the hands and feet (John 13:5). In Iron Age II the Israelites had oval ceramic footbaths, about two feet (about one-half m.) long, with a raised footrest in the middle and drain hole at the bottom of one side.

B. **Cooking pots.** Sherds of these common vessels are very numerous in excavated cities since every household needed several such pots. Because these vessels broke or cracked easily, they were often "despised," considered the lowliest type of pottery; hence they are seldom found in tombs.

1. *Sîr.* The wide-mouth, broad, round-bottom cooking pot, in Iron Age I handleless, in Iron Age II and later with two handles. The large diameter of its mouth permitted it to be used as a washbasin (Ps 60:8). It could be of great size, large enough to boil vegetables for all the sons of the prophets at Gilgal (2 Kings 4:38). It was used by the Israelite slaves in Egypt (Exod 16:3) and by the poor family whose only fuel was the thorn bush (Eccl 7:6; the word for "thorns" is *sîrîm,* thus a play on words).

2. *Pārûr.* A one- or two-handled cooking pot, deeper and with a narrower mouth than the *sîr.* With one hand Gideon carried a *pārûr* containing broth, in the other hand a basket containing bread and meat (Judg 6:19). The Israelites boiled manna in a *pārûr* (Num 11:8).

3. *Marhesheth.* A ceramic kettle used for deep-fat frying (Lev 2:7; 7:9); the meal-offering cakes made in this vessel would be of the texture of our doughnuts.

4. *'Etsev.* The despised vessel of Jeremiah 22:28 was probably a cooking pot (so NIV), not an idol (KJV). Thus Coniah was a "big pot," about to be broken.

C. **Jars.** These include the large stationary jars for water (Arabic *zîr*), apparently not mentioned in the Bible, as well as the smaller jars for carrying water from well to house and for the storage of grain, of olive oil, and of wine.

1. *Kadh, hydria.* A jar thirteen to twenty inches (thirty-three to fifty-one cm.) tall, with two handles, an egg-shaped bottom, and a small mouth used for carrying water on one's shoulder (1 Kings 18:33; Eccl 12:6; John 4:28). In Rebekah's day the flat-bottom, folded ledge-handle jar was in use in Palestine. When the purpose was to store grain or meal, the jar was often more cylindrical, with or without handles (1 Kings 17:12, 14, 16; barrel KJV; bowl NASB; jug NIV). The Late-Bronze jars used by Gideon's three hundred to conceal their torches must have had handles and must have been common and easily obtainable (Judg 7:16ff.).

2. *Nēvel.* Originally a wineskin (1 Sam 1:24; 10:3; 25:18; 2 Sam 16:1; Jer 13:12). A prepared goatskin held five to twelve gallons (nineteen to forty-six l.). In ceramics the *nēvel* was the storage jar used especially for wine, olive oil, and grain. It held approximately a *bath,* or about six gallons (twenty-three l.) and stood about two feet (one-half m.) high. Since the *nēvel* had two handles, one could hang it from a peg, but its weight might break the peg (Isa 22:24). The men of Judah, recipients and containers of the Lord's blessings as well as of his judgments, are likened to the *nēvel:* the breaking of a storage jar with its valued contents would be a household disaster (Isa 30:14; Jer 13:12; 48:12; Lam 4:2).

3. *'Asûk.* In 2 Kings 4:2 the *'āsûk* was the typical Iron Age II jar for olive oil. It had three handles arranged at ninety degrees around the mouth; the fourth quadrant has a funnel or spout

Storage jar with Phoenician inscription, "(Belonging) to Shalmai," from tomb at Azor, late seventh to mid-sixth centuries B.C. The name was incised prior to firing. Courtesy Israel Department of Antiquities and Museums.

probably "intended to hold the small dipper juglet used for taking oil from the jar. . . . Any drippings of oil from the juglet would go through the pierced spout back into the jar, or, in the unpierced variety, would be caught in the funnel" (J. W. Crowfoot, G. M. Crowfoot, Kathleen M. Kenyon, *The Objects from Samaria,* 1957, p. 193). Various sizes stand from six to sixteen inches (fifteen to forty-one cm.) in height.

D. **Decanters, flasks, and juglets.**

1. *Baqbûq.* The handsome ring-burnished water decanter of Iron II. Its narrow neck caused a gurgling sound when the water was poured; hence its name. It came in graduated sizes from four to ten inches (ten to twenty-six cm.) high. James L. Kelso says, "It is the most artistic and expensive member of the pitcher family. It was thus well-fitted to typify Jerusalem in Jeremiah's illustrated sermon (19:1–15). Its use was doubly significant since it had the narrowest neck of all pitchers and therefore could never be mended (19:11)" (*The Ceramic Vocabulary of the Old Testament,* 1948, p. 17). Jeroboam I sent to the prophet Ahijah a gift of honey in the *baqbûq* with other foods, a trifling gift from a king (1 Kings 14:3).

2. *Tsappahath.* The two-handled traveler's flask or canteen so popular from the Late Bronze Age until the middle of Iron Age II. "It was made of a lightly baked clay, which gives a certain porosity to the jar so that the air blowing on the moist surface of the canteen cools the water within [by evaporation]. The mouth of the canteen is shaped both for drinking and for easy stoppering" (Ibid., p. 30). See 1 Samuel 26:11ff.; 1 Kings 19:6. In 1 Kings 17:12–16 this word is used for the oil jar of the widow of Zarephath. While the porous clay of the canteen is ill-suited to contain oil, the widow was very poor and may have had to put her few vessels to unwonted uses; probably also she never had had a large supply of oil before this.

3. *Pak.* A small juglet for holding perfumed anointing oil (1 Sam 10:1; 2 Kings 9:1, 3). In one or both of these cases the "vial" or "box" of KJV may have been a lovely Cypro-Phoenician juglet. Or it may have been the local blue-black hand-burnished juglet found in such quantities at Megiddo and Tell Beit Mirsim. NIV has "flask" in all three cases.

4. *Keramion.* The one-handled ribbed water jug, eight to twelve inches (twenty-one to thirty-one cm.) high, by which Jesus' disciples were to identify the owner of the house with the Upper Room (Mark 14:13; Luke 22:10). Ordinarily only a woman would be seen carrying a jug of water into the city from the fountain.

E. **Other vessels**

1. *Nēr.* The common pottery lamp that burned olive oil. Basically the *nēr* in OT times was a small bowl or saucer; while the molded clay was still soft, the potter pinched in the rim at one section to hold the linen or flax wick (Isa 42:3). Never more than a few inches in diameter, the lamp was suitable for carrying in the palm of the hand when walking (Ps 119:105; Zeph 1:12) or for placing in a niche in the wall of the house or cave-home. The Oriental feared darkness and left a lamp burning all night (Prov 31:18); thus it was just as essential as the millstones for grinding grain (Jer 25:10). The presence of a burning lamp with its light symbolized joy and peace (2 Sam 22:29), whereas the extinguishing of the lamp suggested utter gloom and desolation (Job 18:5–6; 21:17; Prov 13:9; 20:20; 24:20). Since the ancient considered his life to be continued through his sons, his "light" was not put out if he had a son; thus the lamp also symbolized posterity (1 Kings 11:36; 15:4; 2 Kings 8:19). In patriarchal times (Middle Bronze I) the lamp sometimes had its rim pinched in four places. Some Israelite lamps had seven such pinched "wick-holders," undoubtedly reminiscent of the seven-branched golden candlestick or lampstand of the tabernacle and temple.

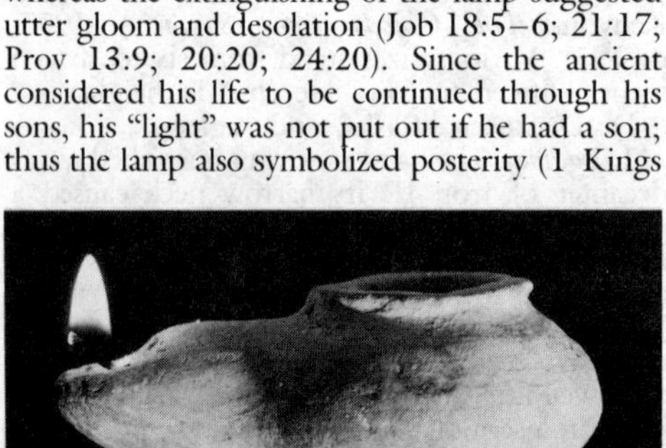

The common slipper-type earthenware oil lamp of biblical times. ". . . keep your lamps burning" (Luke 12:35). Courtesy Zev Radovan.

2. *Lampas.* Also a hand-sized clay lamp but with considerable change in shape from the OT lamps. By the first century A.D. the pinched rim had given way to a nozzle for the wick. This type was carried by the ten virgins (Matt 25:1–8), by the band led by Judas (John 18:3 BV), and by the Christians congregating in an upper room in Troas (Acts 20:8). See also LAMP.

3. *Lychnos.* The lamp placed on a lampstand (*lychnia*) (Matt 5:15; Luke 11:33–36).

4. *Menôrâh.* Usually a reference to the golden lampstand in the tabernacle and temple. But in 2 Kings 4:10 it probably refers to a pottery lamp of a different style from the *nēr*. Often discovered in Palestinian sites are "cup-and-saucer" lamps, a high cup in the center of a small bowl all made in one piece by the potter. Sometimes this style has been found in connection with shrines, serving a ritual purpose. Since the Shunammite couple considered Elisha a holy man of God, they chose a type of lamp appropriate for him.

5. *Tannûr, klibanos.* Chiefly, the common oven in every home, for baking flat bread (Lev 2:4; 7:9a; Hos 7:4–8). Like a hollow truncated cone, the *tannûr* was made of clay nearly an inch thick. The household oven varied from one-and-a-half to two-and-a-half feet (50–85 cm.) in diameter, and often was plastered over with additional mud and potsherds on the outer surface. Placed over a depression in the courtyard floor, the oven was preheated by a smoky fire of grass, thorns, twigs, or stubble kindled inside it (Mal 4:1; Matt 6:30). The soot was then wiped off (Lam 5:10), and the thin sheets of dough were slapped onto the concave inner surface of the oven and baked in a few seconds. A large cooking pot could be placed over the top opening, making the *tannûr* serve also as a stove (Lev 11:35). When ten women could bake their pitifully small loaves in a single oven, then there was severe famine in the land (26:26).

6. *'Ah.* The small brazier for holding burning coals. King Jehoiakim's winter house may have had a metal or a ceramic brazier or firepot (Jer 36:22–23).

7. *Mahăvath.* Probably the nearly flat disclike baking tray or griddle mentioned in Leviticus 2:5; 6:14; 7:9; 1 Chronicles 23:29. Such pans, twelve to fourteen inches (thirty-one to thirty-six cm.) in diameter, had holes punched or notched on the concave surface, which was placed over the fire.

8. *Paropsis.* The side dish for relishes and other delicacies. Jesus accused the scribes and Pharisees of cleaning the outside of this dish but filling the inside with greed and self-indulgence (Matt 23:25–26). JR

POULTRY (See BIRDS)

POUND (See WEIGHTS AND MEASURES)

POVERTY (See POOR)

POWER (See AUTHORITY)

POWER OF THE KEYS (Gr. *kleis, key*). A phrase whose origin lies in the words of Jesus to Peter, "I will give you the keys of the kingdom of heaven; whatever you bind on earth will be bound in heaven, and whatever you loose on earth will be loosed in heaven" (Matt 16:19). It has also been connected with the binding and loosing of Matthew 18:18 and the authority to forgive or not to forgive of John 20:22–23. Moreover, Jesus is presented in Revelation 3:7 as having the key to open and shut the door into the church and kingdom of God. The possession of keys—not as a doorkeeper but as chief steward in a household—was a symbol of rule and authority conferred by the master. So the Father conferred such authority on the Messiah, and the Messiah conferred that authority on Peter and the other apostles. They had authority to preach the gospel and perform the deeds of the gospel, and in so doing to admit into God's household those who responded in repentance and faith. They were not to be like the Pharisees whose word and example actually only shut the kingdom of heaven (Matt 23:13). The "power of the keys" has also been understood as the authority to make binding rules for the young and developing church in the earliest period and/or as the power to exercise discipline within the church through the use of the power of excommunication. Further, the words of Jesus to Peter (16:17–19) seem to establish a particular role for Peter in the creation and early growth of the church. To claim that this role is repeated in the bishops of Rome is hardly a legitimate deduction from the text. PT

PRAETORIUM (prē-tō′rĭ-ŭm). Sometimes spelled Pretorium, the Latin term for the Greek *praitōrion,* which among the Romans could refer to a number of things. Originally it meant the general's tent in the camp of an army station. Sometimes it referred to the military headquarters in Rome itself or in the provincial capitals. It also meant the staff of men in such an establishment or even the session of a planning council. In the Gospels (Matt 27:27; Mark 15:16; John 18:28, 33) it refers to the temporary palace or headquarters ("judgment hall") of the Roman governor or procurator while he was in Jerusalem, which was actually Herod's palace adjacent to the temple (cf. Acts 23:35). It was the scene of the trial of Jesus before Pontius Pilate. No doubt the debated reference in Philippians 1:13 (cf. 4:22, "Caesar's household") means the headquarters of the emperor's bodyguard, which modern research has shown could have been either in Rome or in some of the provincial capitals.

PRAISE. A general term for words or deeds that exalt or honor men (Prov 27:21), women (31:30), heathen gods (Judg 16:24), or God, especially in song (Exod 15:11 KJV, NASB, NEB; glorious deeds RSV; glory NIV). Some of the Hebrew and Greek words mean "thanksgiving," "blessing," or "glory," and are often so translated (2 Chron 7:3, 6; Luke 1:64; John 9:24). *Aretē* ("virtue") is translated "praises," or "excellencies," in 1 Peter 2:9. We are to be the praise of God's glory (Eph 1:6, 12, 14). Praise fills the Book of Psalms, increasing in intensity toward the end (Pss 145–50). Psalms 113–18 are called the Hallel, the praises. Praise for redemption dominates the NT (Luke 2:13–14; Rev 19:5–7).

PRAYER. In the Bible prayer is the spiritual response (spoken and unspoken) to God, who is known not merely to exist but to have revealed himself and to have invited his creatures into communion with himself. Thus prayer covers a wide spectrum of addressing and hearing God, interceding with and waiting for the Lord, and contemplating and petitioning our Father in heaven. What prayer is may best be seen in the example and teaching of Jesus. This information can then be supplemented by the apostolic practice of, and teaching on, prayer as well as examples of prayer from the OT.

I. Jesus at Prayer. In the Gospels there are seventeen references to Jesus at prayer. These may be divided into four groupings. (1) Prayers at critical moments in his life: (a) his baptism (Luke 3:21), (b) the choice of the apostles (6:12–13), (c) the confession of his being the Messiah (9:18), (d) his Transfiguration (9:29), (e) before the cross in Gethsemane (22:39–40), and (f) on the cross (23:46). (2) Prayers during his ministry: (a) before the conflict with the Jewish leaders (5:16), (b) before providing the "Lord's Prayer" (11:1), (c) when Greeks came to him (John 12:7–8), and (d) after feeding the five thousand (Mark 6:46). (3) Prayers at his miracles: (a) healing the multitudes (1:35), (b) before feeding the five thousand (6:41), (c) healing a deaf-mute (7:34), and (d) raising Lazarus from death (John 11:41). (4) Prayers for others: (a) for the Eleven (17:6–19), (b) for the whole church (17:20–26), (c) for those who nailed him to the cross (Luke 23:34), and (d) for Peter (22:32). We are to understand these as pointing to a rich prayer life rather than considering them the only times when Jesus prayed. As the letter to the Hebrews put it, "In the days of Jesus' life on earth, he offered up prayers and petitions with loud cries and tears . . . and he was heard because of his reverent submission" (Heb 5:7).

II. Jesus' Teaching on Prayer. It was seeing the prayer life of Jesus (so different from the usual way of prayer in Judaism) that led the disciples to say, "Lord, teach us to pray" (Luke 11:1). In response, Jesus provided them with what we now call the Lord's Prayer (11:2–4; Matt 6:9–13). This prayer has three parts: (1) Invocation: "Our Father, who art in heaven." (2) Petition: there are six requests—for God's name to be hallowed, for God's kingdom to come, for God's will to be done, for daily bread to be provided, for forgiveness of our debts (sins), and for deliverance from temptation (testing) and evil (the evil one). (3) Doxology: "Thine is the kingdom, the power and the glory . . . ."

From the rest of the teaching of Jesus we note that he taught that prayer may be characterized by (1) importunity (Luke 11:5–8)—a laying hold of God's willingness to bless; (2) tenacity (18:1–8)—a persistence and certainty in praying; (3) humility (18:10–14)—penitence and a sense of unworthiness; (4) compassion (Matt 18:21–35); (5) simplicity (6:5–6; 23:14; Mark 12:38–40); (6) intensity and watchfulness (Mark 13:33; 14:38); (7) unity of heart and mind in the community of prayer (Matt 18:19ff.); and (8) expectancy (Mark 11:24).

Jesus also indicated some of the themes for intercession in prayer. (1) The casting out of evil forces from the hearts of those in darkness and despair (Mark 9:14–29). (2) The extension of the kingdom of God in the hearts and minds of people everywhere (Matt 9:35ff.; Luke 10:2). (3) The true good of enemies (Matt 5:44; Luke 6:28).

A major new departure in the method of prayer introduced by Jesus was that disciples should ask the Father in the name of Jesus (John 14:13; 16:23–24). To pray in this manner is not to use a magic formula but rather represents the new ground on which the worshiper stands, a new plea for the success of his petitions, and a new mind within which the prayer is conceived. Thus the aim of prayer is not to make God change his will but to enable disciples of Jesus to change their minds and dispositions as they are molded by his Spirit.

III. The Apostles' Teaching on Prayer. The letters of Paul are saturated with references to prayer; these range from praise to petition, from celebration of God's grace and benevolence to urgent requests for the needs of the churches. Conscious at all times that the exalted Jesus is making intercession for his church (Rom 8:34), Paul saw prayer as arising through the presence and activity of the Spirit (sent from Christ) within the body of Christ and within the individual believer (8:15–16), and being offered to the Father in and through the Lord Jesus.

A variety of verbs are used to cover the spectrum of prayer; e.g., (1) *doxazō,* to glorify God the Father (Rom 15:6, 9); (2) *exomologeuomai,* to praise God the Father (Eph 1:6, 12, 14); (3) *eulogeomai,* to bless (or give thanks to) God (1 Cor 14:16; 2 Cor 1:3); (4) *proskyneō,* to worship God the Father (John 4:20–24; 1 Cor 14:25); (5) *eucharisteō,* to offer thanksgiving to God the Father (Phil 1:3; Col 1:3); (6) *deomai* and *proseuchomai,* to ask God for personal things (Rom 1:10; 1 Cor 14:13; 2 Cor 12:8); (7) *hyperentynchanō,* to ask God on behalf of others (Gal 1:3; 6:16; 1 Thess 3:10–13; 5:23). The most obvious feature of Paul's prayers and references to prayer is that they arise within and are motivated by the gospel concerning Jesus Christ.

James also saw the Christian life as a life of prayer. "Is any one of you in trouble? He should pray. Is anyone happy? Let him sing songs of praise. Is any one of you sick? He should call the elders of the church to pray over him . . . and pray for each other . . ." (James 5:13–16). Then

A votive statue of a man from Mari, with hands clasped and wearing a long, fleece-like woolen skirt. White stone. Mid-third millennium B.C. Courtesy Studium Biblicum Franciscanum, Jerusalem.

James pointed to the example of Elijah, "who prayed earnestly . . ." (5:17–18). He was well aware that the Hebrew Scriptures supply many examples of prayer and provide guidelines (especially in the Psalms) on the content and nature of prayer.

IV. Examples of Prayers and Ways to Pray. Most of the recorded prayers of leaders of Israel are intercessions; see the prayers of Moses (Exod 32:11–13, 31–32; 33:12–16; Num 11:11–15; 14:13–19; Deut 9:18–21), Aaron (Num 6:22–27), Samuel (1 Sam 7:5–13), Solomon (1 Kings 8:22–53), and Hezekiah (2 Kings 19:14–19). God always answered the prayers of his people, but sometimes his answer was no (Exod 32:30–35). Once Jeremiah was commanded not to intercede (Jer 7:16; 11:14; 14:11). We are to assume that the prophets were constantly engaged in prayer in order to be the recipients of the word of the Lord (see Isa 6; Dan 9:20ff.; Hab 2:1–3).

In the five books of the Psalter many types of prayers are found. There are communal hymns (Pss 33, 145–150), communal laments (44, 74, 79), royal psalms (2, 18, 20, 21), laments of the individual Israelite (3, 5–7, 13), thanksgivings of the individual Israelite (30, 32, 138), songs for pilgrimage (84, 122), thanksgivings of the community (67, 124), wisdom poems (1, 37, 73, 112), and liturgies (15, 24, 60, 75).

Obviously the emphasis in the whole Bible is not on the right posture or the correct position, but on the right attitude in prayer. Thus people pray kneeling (1 Kings 8:54; Ezra 9:5; Dan 6:10; Acts 20:36), standing (Jer 18:20), sitting (2 Sam 7:18), or even lying prostrate (Matt 26:39). They pray sometimes with hands uplifted (1 Kings 8:22; Ps 28:2; 134:2; 1 Tim 2:8). They pray silently (1 Sam 1:13); they pray aloud (Ezek 11:13); they pray alone (Matt 6:6; Mark 1:35); they pray together (Ps 35:18; Matt 18:19; Acts 4:31); they pray at fixed times (Ps 55:17; Dan 6:10) or at any time (Luke 18:1). They pray everywhere (1 Tim 2:8)—in bed (Ps 63:6), in an open field (Gen 24:11–12), in the temple (2 Kings 19:14), at the riverside (Acts 16:13), on the seashore (21:5), on the battlefield (1 Sam 7:5). They pray spontaneously (Matt 6:7); they pray liturgically (e.g., Pss 120–126); they pray, as we have observed, quite literally for everything (Gen 24:12–14; Phil 4:6; 1 Tim 2:1–4).

See also WORSHIP.

Bibliography: A. R. George, *Communion with God in the New Testament,* 1953; L. Kohler, *Old Testament Theology,* 1957; J. G. S. S. Thomson, *The Praying Christ,* 1959; B. Martin, *Prayer in Judaism,* 1968; G. P. Wiles, *Paul's Intercessory Prayers,* 1974. PT

PREACHER, PREACHING (See OCCUPATIONS AND PROFESSIONS)

PRECIOUS STONES (See MINERALS)

PREDESTINATION (See ELECTION)

PREFECT (prē'fĕct). A person appointed to a position of responsibility in the Babylonian government. Mentioned only in Daniel 3:2–3, 27; 6:7. KJV has "governor."

PRESBYTERY (prĕz'bĭ-têr-ē, Gr. *presbyterion*). The Christian elders who formally recognized Timothy's spiritual gift (1 Tim 4:14 KJV, NASB; JB, NIV body of elders). The same word occurs in Luke 22:66 (elders KJV, MLB, NEB; council of the elders NIV) and Acts 22:5 for the organized body of Jewish elders in Jerusalem.

PRESIDENTS (Heb. *sārekhîn, chief*). Administrative officers whose duties are not clearly defined. Three were placed by Darius over the 120 satraps in his kingdom, and Daniel was one of the three (Dan 6:2–7). NIV translates this word as "administrators."

PRESS (for oil or wine). A rendering of several Hebrew and Greek words that refer to a device used for extracting liquids from certain fruits from which wines and oils were made. Some of these were small handmills while others were made of two large stones. One turned on the other by horses or mules so that the fruit was crushed between them.

PRIDE. One of the worst forms of sin, regarded, indeed, by many as the basis of all sin. The various Hebrew words reflect the deep-seated and far-reaching nature of pride, for they are associated with terms such as presumption, vanity, vain boasting, haughtiness, and arrogance. Pride makes impossible a right perspective toward both God and man. It deceives the heart (Jer 49:16) and hardens it (Dan 5:20). It brings contention (Prov 13:10; 28:25) and destruction (16:18). It was a fundamental fault of the wandering Israelites that brought a stern warning from God (Lev 26:19) and was associated with the punishment on King Uzziah (2 Chron 26:16ff.), Moab (Isa 25:11), Judah and Jerusalem (Jer 13:9), Jacob (Amos 6:8), and Edom (Obad 3), among others. Nebuchadnezzar testified of the "King of heaven" that "those who walk in pride he is able to humble" (Dan 4:37). The Greek words used also convey the idea of empty display, glorying, and arrogance. James quotes Proverbs 3:34 in pointing out God's opposition to the proud (James 4:6). Paul made it clear that no one has any grounds for boasting in God's sight, but he does also speak of "pride" as a legitimate attribute (e.g., 2 Cor 5:12; 7:4).

PRIEST, PRIESTHOOD. The English word *priest* is derived from the Greek *presbyteros,* which means "elder" and suggests the priestly function of counsel. The NT word for "priest," *hiereus,* related to *hieros,* "holy," indicates one who is consecrated to and engaged in holy matters.

The Hebrew *kōhēn,* "priest," is of uncertain origin. For practical Bible study we may say simply that a priest is a minister of any religion, whether pagan (Gen 41:45; Acts 14:13) or biblical (Matt 8:4; 1 Peter 2:5, 9).

I. The History of the Formal Priesthood.

The formal priesthood in Israel began with the time of the Exodus. In the patriarchal times the heads of families offered sacrifices and intercessory prayers and performed general religious functions, but there seems to have been no specialization and no separate priestly office, as there was among the Egyptians (Gen 47:22, 26) and in the instance of Melchizedek (14:18–20).

We read in Exodus 24:5 that Moses sent young men of Israel to offer the burnt offerings at the covenant ceremony at Mount Sinai. Presumably these must be linked with the command in Exodus 13:1 that the Lord's claim to all the firstborn males among the people be honored. Was it, then, the divine intention at this point that the priestly officiants should be taken from all the people, in this way reflecting the Lord's desire that his people should be a kingdom of priests? (Exod 19:4–5). Note too that Aaron is described in Exodus 4:14 as "the Levite." Was there, even then, some particular significance attaching to the tribe of Levi? Furthermore, the appointment of Aaron and his sons as priests (Exod 28–29) precedes the events at Sinai (Exod 32) that led to the special appointment of the tribe of Levi to officiate before the Lord, and to do so instead of the firstborn (Num 8:16). It looks, therefore, as if the Lord intended a "priestly people" who would exercise their priesthood through their firstborn sons under the rule of the house of Aaron, but that this became, through the failure of the people, the Aaronic-Levitical system familiar throughout the OT period. Yet, in the background, the vision of the priest-people remains, waiting to become the "priesthood of all believers" under the one and only New Testament Priest, the Lord Jesus Christ.

In Exodus 28–29 and Leviticus 8 is the record of the founding of the Aaronic order of priests. The choice of the tribe of Levi as the priestly tribe to serve as assistants to the Aaronic priests is recorded in Numbers 3 (see Exod 32:26–29; Num 8:16ff.).

It is not possible in this article to go into technical historical and critical questions related to the OT priesthood. The reader who is interested in those matters will find extended discussions from a relatively conservative point of view in ZPEB, ISBE, HBD, and in Oehler's *Old Testament Theology* (see his index). The common critical view is given in R. H. Pfeiffer's *Introduction to the Old Testament,* 1941 (see "Priesthood," "Priestly Cities," and "Priestly Code" in the index, p. 913). Current critical opinion on the historical priesthood is reflected in the *Journal of Biblical Literature* for March 1961 in an article by Professor R. B. Y. Scott of Princeton University discussing the relationships between the priests, the prophets, and the wise men; and in the first article of a series by Professor Menahem Horan of the Hebrew University of Jerusalem on the ancient *Levitical Cities.*

Major attention must here be confined to the theological, devotional, and ethical implications of the biblical idea of the priest and the priesthood.

II. Christ's Priesthood. The priesthood of Christ is the principal theme of the Letter to the Hebrews. "Christ as our redeemer executeth the offices of a prophet, of a priest, and of a king, both in his estate of humiliation and exaltation" (*Westminster Shorter Catechism,* p. 23). The three offices of Christ are the subject of chapter 15 of Book II of Calvin's *Institutes.* The distinction of the offices, particularly that of priest, is not to be made rigidly, as though there were no overlapping; nevertheless the distinction has been found illuminating and profitable for an understanding of the Bible.

That Christ combines in himself the three offices is a matter of special significance. After the establishment of the Aaronic priesthood, it was considered an offense in Israel for anyone not officially consecrated as a priest to offer formal ritual sacrifices. The rebellion of Korah (Num 16) involved intrusion into the priesthood, even though he and his associates were Levites (16:8–9). King Saul was most severely rebuked for a similar intrusion (1 Sam 13:18ff.), and King Uzziah was struck with leprosy for this offense (2 Chron 26:16ff.).

The offices of prophet and priest might be combined in one person (John 11:49–52). Jeremiah was a member of a priestly family (Jer 1:1). The offices of king and prophet might also be combined (Acts 2:29–31), but the kingly line of David was of the nonpriestly tribe of Judah, and therefore no king of David's line could have been also a priest according to the Levitical law.

The NT writers made much of the fact that Jesus belonged to the house and line of David (Luke 2:4–5; cf. Matt 21:9; Mark 11:10). How then could he be also a priest? The author of the Letter to the Hebrews finds the scriptural answer in the priestly order of Melchizedek (Heb 6:10, 20–7:17), who was Abraham's superior and both king and priest. This amplifies Zechariah's prophecy (6:13) that "the Branch" (cf. Isa 4:2; Jer 23:5–6) will be "a priest on his throne."

A. **The atonement of Christ** was just as effective before the event as afterward. The high priestly office of Christ did not begin at his incarnation; it was a fact known to David (Ps 110:4) along with his sovereign lordship (110:1). His priesthood with reference to fallen humanity was established in the eternal decrees of God and has been exercised in every age on behalf of God's elect. The Bible presents Christ, our Prophet, Priest, and King, as a figure of cosmic proportions, whose work as our Redeemer has "neither beginning of day nor end of life."

B. The priestly ministry of Christ is introduced in Hebrews 1:3 in the words "after he had provided purification for sins." This is, of course, a reference to his death on the cross, regarded as an atoning sacrifice. But this act of sacrifice was not a mere symbol, as were all of the Aaronic priestly acts; it was of infinite intrinsic worth. He was "crowned with glory and honor because he suffered death, so that by the grace of God he might taste death [sufficiently for the offer of salvation] for everyone" (2:9).

Christ's priesthood was in no sense contrary to the Aaronic order. It fulfilled all the soteriological significance of it. But the priesthood of Christ furnished the *substance* of which the Aaronic priesthood was only the shadow (Col 2:17; Heb 8:5) and symbol.

Examination of the wealth of detail in which the priesthood of Christ is said to complete and supersede the Aaronic priesthood, especially in Hebrews 5–10, would require an elaborate and extended thesis. All that is possible here is an attempt to clarify certain points of misunderstanding.

C. The tabernacle of which Christ is the High Priest is the entire cosmic scene of the redemption of God's elect. This was the "pattern" that Moses saw (Heb 8:5)—God's plan of salvation. It includes all the spiritual and temporal furniture of heaven and earth. The cross of Christ was the altar of sacrifice on which he offered himself. When he gave up his life on the cross, the atonement was "finished" (John 19:30) once and for all (Heb 7:27; 9:26) with absolutely nothing more for God or man to add to it. The meaning of Romans 4:25 is not that his resurrection added anything to our justification but that, having died "for our sins," which we had committed, he was raised from the dead "for our justification," which he had fully accomplished in his death. His resurrection does not add to the atonement, but of course death could not keep him, and for us it is a proof that his death was a victory.

On the Day of Atonement in Levitical ritual (Lev 16) the high priest had to go in and out past the curtain that separated the Most Holy Place from the Holy Place. By this symbolism the Holy Spirit (Heb 9:8–9) signified that "the way into the Most Holy Place had not yet been disclosed" while the Levitical mode of worship still had its proper standing. But when Jesus' body was broken on the cross, this symbolized the tearing of the curtain (10:19–22) and the clear revealing of the way into the very presence of God (Matt 27:51; Mark 15:38; Luke 23:45).

The notion that the atonement was not finished until Jesus presented his blood in some far-distant sanctuary is entirely unscriptural. The atonement was finished on the cross in the immediate presence of God the Father. The "way of the sanctuaries" is now fully revealed. The curtain has been torn from top to bottom and no longer hides the "place of mercy."

True, the curtain is once spoken of as though it still cuts off our view (Heb 6:18–20; see also 4:14), but this is a different metaphor. It is not the "mercy seat" that is hidden in Hebrews 6:18–20, but the "hope offered to us," the "kingdom that cannot be shaken" (9:28; 12:14–29).

D. **The present intercession of Christ** is taught in Romans 8:34; Hebrews 7:25. (Cf. Rom 8:26–27 for the intercession of the Holy Spirit.) But there is nothing in the Scripture to indicate an unfinished atonement or an unfinished case in court. (The Adventist doctrine of "investigative judgment" is particularly erroneous. See Walter Martin's discussion of this doctrine in his valuable book on *Seventh Day Adventism,* 1960.) The NT word for intercession does not necessarily indicate any plea being offered. It suggests conferring over, or brooding over. Similarly the word "advocate" in 1 John 2:1 (KJV) does not mean that our case is not completely settled. "Who will bring any charge against those whom God has chosen?" (Rom 8:33). Satan accuses, but he has no standing in court. The case is settled, the verdict has been given. We are justified in Christ. Now our "Advocate," our great High Priest, broods over us and counsels and guides.

The comparisons of different priesthoods in the Letter to the Hebrews are *not* between the religion of the OT and the "Churchianity" of this age. The comparisons are between the *outward form* of Judaism and the *reality* in Christ. Every argument against Judaism could be turned with equal logic against the outward forms of the church, if Christ is not the center of it all.

III. The Priesthood of Believers. This can be but briefly mentioned. Our church sacraments conducted by ordained ministers are analogous to those of the OT. They are but shadows, as worthless as "the blood of goats and bulls and the ashes of a heifer sprinkled on those who are ceremonially unclean" (Heb 9:13), unless they are received by genuine faith in the atonement of Christ. No act of any human being in any age could do more than shadow the atonement of Christ. "No man can redeem the life of another or give to God a ransom for him" (Ps 49:7).

The nation of Israel was called a "a kingdom of priests" (Exod 19:6), and the church (1 Peter 2:5, 9 priesthood KJV; Rev 1:6; 5:10) and all who have part in the first resurrection (Rev 20:6) are called priests. Paul uses symbols of priestly ritual with reference to his own ministry (Rom 15:16; Phil 2:17; and 2 Tim 4:6). Neither the apostles (Matt 19:28; Luke 22:18, 28–30) nor believers in general (Rev 20:6; cf. 1 Cor 4:8) reign with Christ—i.e., are "kings"—until he comes to reign; but we are priests as we bring the gospel to human beings and human beings to Christ. It is significant that the priestly function of believers continues through the millennial reign of Christ (Rev 20:6) but is not mentioned as being part of the perfection of the new heavens and new earth, when mortality will have ended, and sin will have been completely eliminated. There will be no need for the priesthood of believers after the the Great White Throne judgment; "today" is the day of salvation (Heb 3:13).

Bibliography: E. O. James, *The Nature and Function of Priesthood,* 1955; T. W. Manson, *Ministry and Priesthood,* 1959; T. J. Meek, *Hebrews Origins,* 1960; C. C. Eastwood, *The Royal Priesthood of the Faithful,* 1963; J. H. Elliott, *The Elect and the Holy,* 1966; H.-J. Kraus, *Worship in Israel,* 1966; J. Jeremias, *Jerusalem in the Time of Jesus,* 1969; NIDNTT, 3:32–44.

JOB

PRINCE, PRINCESS. A prince is a leader, an exalted person clothed with authority. A princess is the daughter or wife of a chief or king. Several Hebrew and Greek words occur, the meaning varying with the context. KJV quite consistently reads "prince[s]" in all cases, whereas NIV, RSV, and to some extent ASV have "ruler," "leader," or "officer," depending on the context. There were princes of various nations (Matt 20:25), of (part of) the land of Canaan (Gen 34:2), of Ishmael's descendants (17:20; 25:16), of the Hittites (23:6), of Egypt (12:15), of the Philistines (1 Sam 18:30), of Persia (Esth 1:3; called "satraps" in Dan 3:2), of Babylon (Jer 39:13), of Tyre (Ezek 32:30), and of Meshech and Tubal (38:2). There were merchant princes in Tyre (Isa 23:8). The heads of the tribes or of the congregation of Israel were princes (Num 1:16; Josh 9:15). Jeroboam is called "leader" or "prince" (1 Kings 14:7), and David eulogized Abner as a prince (2 Sam 3:38). The enemies of Jesus called him Beelzebub, prince of the demons (Mark 3:22). The devil is the prince of this world (John 12:31). The personal spiritual powers of evil are princes (1 Cor 2:6; Eph 2:2). Messiah is the Prince (Dan 9:25): of Peace (Isa 9:6), of Life (Acts 3:15), of the kings of the earth (Rev 1:5). Bethlehem is called one of the princes of Judah (Matt 2:6) because the Davidic dynasty had its origin there.

Of princesses far less is said. Solomon had seven hundred princesses or women "of royal birth" as wives, in contrast with three hundred concubines (1 Kings 11:3). Jerusalem is called a princess or queen (Lam 1:1). A king's daughter (Ps 45:9–13), a prince's daughter (Song of Songs 7:1), and daughter of a leader of Midian (Num 25:18) are mentioned. The new name of Abraham's wife, Sarah, means "princess" (Gen 17:15).

PRINCIPALITIES (Heb. *mera'ă-shôth, headparts,* Gr. *archē, first*). The Hebrew word is found only in Jeremiah 13:18. The KJV several times uses the word in the NT with reference to powerful angels and demons (e.g., Rom 8:38; Eph 6:12; Col 2:15).

PRISCILLA, PRISCA (prĭ-sĭl'á, prĭs'ká, Gr. *Priskilla, Priska*). Priscilla (diminutive of *Prisca,* Rom 16:3, see NIV footnote) was the wife of the Jewish Christian, Aquila, with whom she is always mentioned in the NT. They were tentmakers who seem to have migrated about the Mediterranean world, teaching the gospel wherever they went. Paul met them in Corinth (Acts 18:2); they instructed Apollos in Ephesus (18:24–26); Paul sent them greetings in Rome (Rom 16:3); and in 1 Corinthians 16:19 Paul spoke of their being in Ephesus again, where they had a church in their house. In Romans 16:3–4 Paul lauded not only their service but also their courage ("they risked their lives for me"), and plainly stated that all the churches owed them a debt of gratitude. From all the scriptural references one may easily see that Priscilla was a well-known and effective worker in the early church. ER

PRISON. A place where persons suspected, accused, or convicted of crime are kept. Most Hebrew and Greek words used have the idea of restraint. Joseph was thrown into a pit, while his brothers decided how to dispose of him (Gen 37:22–28), and into the Egyptian king's prison, in the house of the captain of the guard (39:20–40:7). Samson was confined in a Philistine prison at Gaza (Judg 16:21, 25). Prisoners taken in war were usually killed or enslaved (Num 21:1; Isa 20:4). Under the monarchy Micaiah the prophet was put into prison (1 Kings 22:27; 2 Chron 18:26), where his food was bread and water. Jeremiah was threatened with prison (Jer 29:26), including the stocks and shackles or collar (ASV, RSV) or neck irons (NIV), and subjected to long imprisonment (32:2; 33:1) in the court of the guard in the king's house. He was also kept in a dungeon before being transferred to the house of Jonathan the scribe, which had been made a prison (37:14–21); then he was held in a dungeon or cistern (RSV, NIV) in the prison (38:2–28), from which Ebed-Melech rescued him. He was restored to the court of the guard and finally released (39:14). Kings were imprisoned by conquerors (2 Kings 17:4; 25:27, 29; Eccl 4:14; Jer 52:11, 33).

The pitiable state of those in prison is spoken of (Ps 79:11; Isa 14:17; 42:22; Lam 3:34; Zech 9:11), and sometimes their hope in God is declared (Ps 69:33; 102:20; 142:7; 146:7; Isa 42:7). John the Baptist was imprisoned for criticizing a king's marriage (Matt 4:12; 11:2; 14:3, 10), Peter and John were imprisoned for preaching about Jesus (Acts 4:3; 5:18–25); Peter was delivered by an angel (12:3–19). Paul led Christians to prison (8:3; 22:4; 26:10) and was himself often in prison (2 Cor 11:23): with Silas at Philippi (Acts 16:23–40), in Jerusalem (23:18), in Caesarea (25:27), and on shipboard (27:1, 42). He was under house arrest in his own rented dwelling (28:16–17, 30). He refers to his imprisonment as for the Lord (Eph 3:1; 4:1; Phil 1:14; 17; 2 Tim 1:8; Philem 9), and he mentions his fellow prisoners (Rom 16:7; Col 4:10). Barabbas was released from prison in place of Jesus (Matt 27:15–16). Jesus refers to imprisonment for debt (Matt 5:25; 18:30; Luke 12:58) and to visiting those in prison (Matt 25:36, 39, 43–44). He predicts that his followers will be put in prison during persecution (Luke 21:12; Rev 2:10). Peter expresses willingness to go to prison with Jesus (Luke 22:33). Disobedient spirits are now in prison (1 Peter 3:19–20); Satan will be imprisoned during the Millennium (Rev 20:1–7). ER

PROCONSUL (prō'kŏn-sŭl, Gr. *anthypatos*). A Roman official, generally of praetorian or consular rank, who served as deputy consul in the Roman provinces. The term of office was one year, though it could be longer in special instances, but the powers of the proconsul were unlimited in both the military and civil areas. Sergius Paulus, Paul's famous convert (Acts 13:7), and Gallio (18:12) were such officials mentioned in the Bible. They are often called "deputy" in the English Bible.

PROCORUS, PROCHORUS (prŏk'ō-rŭs). The third in the list of the first deacons (Acts 6:5) who were elected to take care of the Greek-speaking widows and probably the Christians living in poverty in Jerusalem.

PROCURATOR (prŏ'kū-rā'têr). The Latin term for the Greek *hēgemōn,* translated "governor" in KJV. Pilate, Felix, and Festus were such governors in Palestine with headquarters in Caesarea. Generally the procurators were appointed directly by the emperor to govern the Roman provinces and were often subject to the imperial legate of a large political area. It should be noted that Quirinius, "governor of Syria" (Luke 2:2), was really not a procurator but an imperial legate of the larger province of Syria.

PROFANE (Heb. *hālal, to open* and Gr. *bebēloō, to desecrate*). The basic idea seems to be to desecrate or defile. For one to do what he was not allowed to do in connection with holy things or places was to profane them. Such things as the altar, the Sabbath, the sanctuary, and God's name could all be profaned. Esau was called a profane person (KJV; NIV "godless") because he despised his birthright (Heb 12:16). The profane persons mentioned in 1 Timothy 1:9 are called irreligious in NIV.

PROFESSIONS (See OCCUPATIONS AND PROFESSIONS)

PROMISE (Heb. *dāvār, speaking, speech; dāvar, to speak; 'āmar, to say; 'ōmer, speech;* Gr. *epaggelia, promise*). In the OT there is no Hebrew word corresponding to "promise"; the words "word," "speak," and "say" are used instead. In the NT, however, the word "promise" is often used, usually in the technical sense of God's design to visit his people redemptively in the person of his Son. This promise was first given in the *protoevangelium* (Gen 3:15) and was repeated to Abraham (12:2, 7). It was given also to David when God declared that his house would continue on his throne (2 Sam 7:12–13, 28). It is found repeatedly in the OT (Isa 2:2–5; 4:2; 55:5). In the NT all these promises are regarded as having their fulfillment in Christ and his disciples (2 Cor 1:20; Eph 3:6). Jesus' promise of the Spirit was fulfilled at Pentecost. Paul makes clear that God's promises to Abraham's seed were meant not only for the circumcision but for all who have Abraham's faith (Rom 4:13–16). In the NT there are many promises of blessing to believers, among them the kingdom (James 2:5), eternal life (1 Tim 4:8), and Christ's coming (2 Peter 3:9).

PROPHETESS (Heb. *nevî'âh,* Gr. *prophētis*). A woman who exercised the prophetic gift in ancient Israel or in the early Christian church. In general she would possess the charismatic gifts and powers characterizing the prophets themselves. There are at least five women bearing this designation in the OT: (1) Miriam, sister of Moses (Exod 15:20); (2) Deborah (Judg 4:4); (3) Huldah (2 Kings 22:14); (4) Noadiah (Neh 6:14); and (5) the unnamed wife of Isaiah, who bore him children to whom he gave prophetic names (Isa 8:3). In the NT there was Anna (Luke 2:36), and Philip the evangelist is said to have had "four unmarried daughters who prophesied" (Acts 21:8–9). After Pentecost the differentiation between sexes regarding prophetic gifts was removed (Acts 2:19; cf. Joel 2:28). See also PROPHETS.

PROPHETS. Three Hebrew words are used in the OT to designate the prophets, namely *nāvî',* *rō'eh* and *hōzeh.* The last two words are participles and may be rendered "seer." They are practically synonymous in meaning. The first term, *nāvî',* is difficult to explain etymologically, although various attempts have been made. The significance of these words, however, may be learned from their usage.

Each of the words designates one who is spokesman for God. The usage of *nāvi'* is illustrated by Exodus 4:15–16 and 7:1. In these passages it is clearly taught that Moses stood in relation to the pharaoh as God. Between them was an intermediary, Aaron. Aaron was to speak to Pharaoh the words that Moses gave to him. "He [Aaron] will speak to the people for you, and it will be as if he were your mouth and as if you were God to him" (Exod 4:16). The man who can be designated a *nāvi',* then, is one who speaks forth for God.

The two words *rō'eh* and *hōzeh* perhaps have primary reference to the fact that the person so designated sees the message God gives him. This seeing may mean that the message first came through a vision and in some instances it did, but overall the use of these two words is as broad as the English words *perceive* and *perception.* They may refer to sight, but they usually refer to insight. Thus the words designate one who, whether by vision or otherwise, is given insight into the mind of God, and who declares what he has "seen" as a message to the people. The biblical emphasis throughout is practical. It is not the mysterious mode of reception of the prophetic revelation that is emphasized, but rather the deliverance of the message itself for God.

The biblical prophet must be distinguished from the *prophētēs* of the Greeks. The latter really acted as an *interpreter* for the muses and the oracles of the gods. The prophets, however, were not interpreters. They uttered the actual words that God had given to them, without any modification or interpretation on their part. The Bible itself gives an accurate description of the function of the true prophet: "I will put my words in his mouth, and he will tell them everything I command him" (Deut 18:18). The words were placed in the prophet's mouth by God; i.e., they were revealed to the prophet, and then the prophet spoke to the nation precisely what God had commanded him.

I. The Position of the Prophet in the Old Testament Administration. The establishment of the prophetic institution was necessitated by the settlement of the nation Israel in the Land of Promise. Israel entered Canaan with the precious possession of the law. This law, revealed by God at Mount Sinai, laid the broad basis on which the life of the people of God was to be built. The basic principles of divinely revealed ethics and morality are found in the Ten Commandments, and sundry rules for particular situations are expressed in the other laws. On this basis the life of the people of God was to be conducted.

At the same time this law was not adequate to meet all the situations that would arise when the period of Israel's nomadic wanderings came to an end. This inadequacy was not due to any inherent weakness in the law itself, but simply to the fact that the law did not speak in detail on every possible situation that could arise in Israel's life. There would be occasions when a specific revelation of God would be needed in order to show the nation the course it should pursue. This needed revelation God would give to the people by means of his servants, the prophets.

When Israel entered Canaan, it would find a people that sought to learn the future and the will of the gods by the practice of various superstitions, which the Bible calls "abominations" or "detestable ways" (Deut 18:9). These abominations were being regularly and continually practiced by the inhabitants of Canaan, and there was a danger that the Israelites would be influenced by them and would themselves learn to do them. To offset this danger the Lord declared that he would raise up the prophets and that the Israelites were to listen to the prophets and to obey them (18:15). In this passage, Scripture points both to a great individual prophet, one who would be as significant and central to the people as was Moses at Sinai, and also to what we, with hindsight, would call the successive line of prophets. Note that in verses 21–22 a test was given whereby the true might be distinguished from the false. Just as later the people would wonder if the next Davidic king in line would be the promised Greater David, so also from the time of Moses onward there was expectation of the coming Mosaic prophet (cf. Deut 34:10), and each prophet who arose would be scrutinized (cf. John 1:21) to see if he were the one Moses predicted. By the order of prophets, the Lord enabled his people to walk into the unknown future with faith and obedience, trusting in the sovereign God, not, as the pagan, trying to secure and control the future by magic rites. (See MAGIC.)

The prophet whom the Lord would raise was to be like Moses; just as Moses was a mediator between God and the nation, so that prophet would serve as a mediator. At Horeb, when God appeared to the nation, the people trembled and asked that Moses alone should speak to them. God commended Israel for their request and announced that there would be a mediator, even the prophets. The prophets, then, served as mediators between God and the nation. Just as the priests represented the people before God, so the prophets represented God to the people.

In ancient Greece we have the god, the oracle, the prophet, and the people. The same seems to have been the case in the Mesopotamian countries. In Israel, however, there was only one intermediary between God and the people, namely, the prophet. This arrangement was truly unique. One who heard the words of the prophet heard the very words of God himself, and these words required implicit obedience.

In many nations of antiquity there were soothsayers or people who had visions. They represented a part of that web of superstition that covered the ancient world. The prophetic institution of Israel, however, according to the testimony of the Bible, was of divine origination. God himself raised up this institution (Deut 18:15–18), and it is this fact that distinguished the prophets from the soothsayers of the Homeric world and from the so-called prophets of antiquity.

II. The Relation of the Prophets to Moses. Unique as was the prophetical body, it can properly be understood only as having served under Moses. Moses occupied a position of preeminence in the OT economy. He was faithful *in* all God's house as a servant, and so pointed forward to Christ who as a Son is faithful *over* God's house (Heb 3:1–6). To the prophets God made himself known in dreams and visions and probably also in dark, enigmatic sayings. To Moses, however, God spoke clearly and distinctly, mouth to mouth, as a man speaks to his friend (Num 12:1–8). A distinction in the method or manner of revelation thus appears with respect to Moses and the prophets. Moses was the leading figure of the OT administration, and the prophets served under him. The revelations made to them were sometimes obscure and ambiguous, in that they were given in dreams and visions. It would follow therefore, that when the prophets spoke, they spoke in terms and forms of thought that were current in and that characterized the OT dispensation.

The entire Mosaic administration must be understood as a witness of the later-to-be-revealed NT administration. Moses and the prophets therefore were types of Christ and of his blessings. They witnessed, not to themselves, but to the "things to be spoken of" (Heb 3:1–6). In speaking of the future salvation under Christ the prophets spoke sometimes in language that was not free of ambiguity, and the interpretation of their prophecies depended on a further revelation and in particular on the NT.

It is sometimes said that the prophets were forth-tellers and not foretellers. Such a disjunction, however, is not warranted. It is true that the prophets were forth-tellers, speaking forth the message of the Lord. That message, however, sometimes had to do with past occurrences, as when the prophets often reminded the people of how God had brought them out of the land of Egypt and given them Canaan for a possession. They also spoke of contemporary events, as witness the words of Isaiah with respect to the situation that confronted Ahaz (Isa 7). At the same time it must not be forgotten that the prophets also spoke of the future. They predicted future calamity to come on the nation because of the people's refusal to repent of their sins, and they spoke also in language beautiful and mysterious of the coming of One who would save his people from their sins. The prophets truly were forth-tellers, but they were foretellers as well; and the predictive element is extremely important for a proper understanding of the true nature of the prophets.

III. Classification of the Prophets. In the arrangement of the books of the Hebrew OT there are three parts—the Law, the Prophets, and the Writings. The division known as the Prophets is further subdivided into the former and the latter prophets. Under the first heading are included Joshua, Judges, 1–2 Samuel, and 1–2 Kings. These books are anonymous, their authors are not known. These books are rightly classified as "former prophets" because the history they contain conforms to the biblical definition of prophecy as a declaration of the wonderful works of God (Acts 2:11, 18). This does not mean they are less than true history, but that the process of selection of things to record was performed to show how God was at work in and for his people and how the moral principles of divine providence worked out over the centuries. Against this background of interpretative history we are to understand the work of the great prophets. The former prophets cover the period from Israel's entrance into the Land of Promise until the destruction of the theocracy under Nebuchadnezzar.

The latter prophets are also called writing prophets. They are the prophets who exercised so great a ministry in Israel—Isaiah, Jeremiah, Ezekiel, and the Twelve. The designation "latter" does not necessarily have reference to historical chronology, but is simply a designation of those prophetical books that follow the "former" prophets in the Hebrew arrangement of the OT.

The "later" or "writing" prophets were not anonymous. The reason for this is that they were entrusted by God with the task and responsibility of addressing prophetical messages not only to the people of their own day but also to posterity. They must be accredited to their audience as genuine prophets, and for that reason their name is known to us. There were some prophets whose names we do not know, as, for example, the man who approached Eli and announced to him the downfall of his house. It is not necessary that we know the name of this man; it is enough that it was known to Eli. Those who received the messages of the prophets had sufficient evidence of their accreditation; they knew who spoke to them. The writing prophets, however, have uttered messages that are more relevant to us; they have spoken, for example, of the coming of the Messiah, and it is essential that we be assured that those who uttered such messages were truly accredited spokesmen of the Lord.

Note, however, that the former and the latter prophets complemented one another. The "former" prophets set forth the history of a particular period in Israel's life; the "latter" or "writing" prophets interpreted particular phases of that history. The one is necessary for the proper understanding of the other.

The Scripture does not say much as to the methods used by the great "writing" prophets in preparing their messages. The theory has been advanced by Herman Gunkel that the prophets were first of all oral preachers, and that they did not write their messages. The written books that we now possess, Gunkel argued, were the work of disciples of the prophets. From the example of Jeremiah, however, it appears that the prophets did write down their messages. It may be impossible for us fully to know what is the precise relationship between their spoken word and their written messages. It could very well be that the prophets often spoke far more than they have written down. It could be that in many instances they enlarged on their messages when they were delivering them orally and that they made digests of these messages for writing.

With respect to the last twenty-seven chapters of the Book of Isaiah, for example, it may well be that these messages were never delivered orally. It is quite likely that the prophet, after retirement from active preaching and prophesying, went into solitude during the latter days of Hezekiah and wrote down the wondrous messages that concern the future destinies of the people of God and their deliverance from sin by the Servant of the Lord. It is quite possible also that some of the prophecies of Jeremiah are the results of intense polishing and reworking. These written messages need not in every instance have been identical with what had been delivered orally. What we have in the Scriptures is what the Spirit of God intended us to have.

IV. Schools of the Prophets. After the people had entered the Promised Land, there came a time when "everyone did as he saw fit" (Judg 21:25). It was evident that the nation had to have a king, but the first requests for a king were made in a spirit and for a purpose that conflicted with what God intended the theocracy to be. The first king was not a man after God's own heart, but one who often did his own desires. This was a time when there was danger not only from the idolatry of Canaan but also from the incursions of the Philistines. For the encouragement and spiritual welfare of the nation, bands (*hevel*) of prophets were raised up.

It is difficult to say what is intended by the word *band*. Whether the groups of prophets so designated had a formal organization or not, one cannot tell. It may be that such groups were more or less loosely knit together, and that they served under Samuel. For that matter it cannot be positively asserted that Samuel was the founder of such groups, although such a supposition seems to have much in its favor.

Following Samuel's death these prophetical bodies seem to have disbanded. We hear no more of them until the times of Elijah and Elisha. During the days of these men groups of prophets again appear, though most likely they are not to be thought of as hereditary descendants of the bodies that existed under Samuel. The reason for this is that in Elijah's day they appear only in the northern kingdom. The theocracy had become divided because of the schism introduced by Jeroboam the son of Nebat. There was now need for support against the worship of the Tyrian Baal as well as the calf worship at Dan and Bethel. Both Elijah and Elisha exercised a vigorous ministry in the north, but the government was opposed to them. They needed particular assistance, and this was found in the companies that now bear the designation "sons of the prophets." The phrase reveals the close and intimate association in which these men stood to the great prophets Elijah and Elisha. After this period, however, they seem to die out, and we hear no more of them.

V. The Prophets and the Temple. The regular worship by ancient Israel after the establishment of the monarchy was conducted in the temple located in Jerusalem. This worship was in the hands of priests, men who represented the nation before God. What was the relation in which the prophets stood to the temple worship? It used to be held, particularly by the school of Wellhausen, that the prophets and the priests were working in opposition to one another, that the priests represented a sacrificial type of worship, whereas the prophets were more concerned about ethics and behavior. It was even held that the prophets denied that God had ever required sacrifices. This supposition was used to support the position of Wellhausen that the books of the Pentateuch in which sacrifices were commanded were not composed until late in Israel's history, when the priestly religion had triumphed over the prophetical.

This reconstruction of Israel's history, once so dominant, is more and more losing ground. It is now being recognized, even by those who are very sympathetic to Wellhausen, that there was not, after all, such an antagonism between prophet and priest. In fact, some of the prophets, such as Jeremiah and Ezekiel, were themselves priests. Indeed, what the prophets were condemning, as a more careful and sober exegesis has shown, was not the sacrifices themselves, but the manner in which the sacrifices were offered (cf. Isa 1:9–15). The sacrifices were truly an approach to God, but the worshiper must come with clean hands and a pure heart. Otherwise the sacrifices in themselves, divorced from a proper attitude of humility and repentance on the part of the worshiper, were nothing but vain oblations and were not acceptable to the Lord.

If, then, the prophets were not condemning sacrifice in itself, what was the relation in which they actually stood to the worship of the temple? In recent years the opinion has become more and more widespread that the prophets were servants of the temple, and that they may even have received a salary and been in the employ of the temple. It is perhaps safest to say that this question cannot be answered positively one way or the other. The prophets at times may have been officially connected with the temple; at times they may have been more or less "on their own" in being special spokesmen of the Lord. It is difficult to say how they did earn their livelihood. The servant of Saul had suggested the giving of a small gift to Samuel in return for information as to the whereabouts of the lost donkeys of Saul's father (1 Sam 9:8). Possibly the prophets at times were dependent on such small gifts and on donations they obtained for services rendered. That they were actually officials in the employ of the temple is a matter on which it is wisest not to speak dogmatically.

VI. True and False Prophets. True religion has always been plagued by imitators. Alongside the faithful and true prophets of the Lord there were others, men who had not received a revelation from God. Jeremiah refused to have anything to do with these men. They were not true prophets, but men who deceived. There were those who claimed to have received messages from God, who as a matter of fact had not received such messages.

In the OT there were three tests the people could apply in order to discern between the true and the false prophet. First, the theological test (Deut 13). Through Moses there had been a revelation of the Lord who brought his people out of Egypt. Even if the prophet performed some sign to give validation to what he was saying, if his message contradicted Mosaic theology—the truth known about the Lord who brought his people out—the prophet was false. Second, the practical test (18:20ff.). The prediction that is not fulfilled has not come from the Lord. We ought to notice that this is a negative test. It does not say that fulfillment is proof that the Lord has spoken, for that might in fact be the evidence offered by a false prophet to validate his word. What is not fulfilled is not from the Lord. Third, the moral test (Jer 23:9ff.). This is a test first to be applied to the lives of the prophets themselves (23:13–14) and then to the tendency of the message they preach. Do they in fact strengthen the hands of evildoers, assuring them that they need not fear judgment to come (23:17)? This is a sure sign they have not stood before the Lord to hear his word (23:18–19). The prophet who comes fresh from the Lord's presence has a message turning people from evil (23:22).

VII. Messianic Prophecy. Any proper estimation of the prophetic movement must take into account the following three factors. Prophecy was a continuous movement, extending over several centuries in Israel's history. There was nothing essentially similar to it anywhere in the ancient world. The prophets, during so many centuries, all claimed to be recipients of messages from Yahweh, the God of Israel, and to speak the messages that he had given to them. Lastly, in all these messages there ran a teleological element: the prophets spoke of future deliverance to be wrought by the Messiah. It is this element of prophecy that we call "messianic prophecy."

The word *Messiah* is itself not frequently used in the OT. It means "one who is anointed," and this anointing possesses an abiding character. The Messiah is a human individual who came to earth to perform a work of deliverance for God. He is also himself a divine person, as appears from passages such as Isaiah 9:5–6. His coming to earth reveals the coming of the Lord, and so it was a supernatural coming. Furthermore, his coming represents the end of the age. It occurred in the "last days," and hence was eschatological. He came as a king, a descendant of David, and is to reign on David's throne. Lastly, the purpose of his coming is to save his people from their sins. He is a Savior and is to bear the sins of his own that they may stand in right relation with God.

Messianic prophecy must be understood against the dark background of human sin. Man's disobedience in the Garden of Eden had involved man in corruption of the heart and also in guilt before God. Man could not of his own efforts make himself right with God, and hence it was necessary that God take the initiative. This God did in announcing that he would place enmity between the woman Eve and the serpent. God also announced the outcome of that enmity, in that the seed (NIV "offspring") of the woman would bruise the serpent's head (Gen 3:15). Though the point is debated, this seems to be the first definite announcement that the Messiah would come and that his work would be victorious.

All subsequent messianic prophecy is based on this Edenic prediction. To Noah it was announced that the blessing of God would be with Shem, and hence among the descendants of Shem one must look for the Messiah. The promise is then narrowed down to Abraham and after him to Isaac. For a time it seemed that Abraham would have no son, and then Ishmael was born to Abraham's concubine. Yet the promise was not to be fulfilled through Ishmael, but through Isaac. After Isaac had been born, however, Abraham was commanded to sacrifice him. Finally, when Abraham's faith was sufficiently tested, it was made clear that Isaac was after all the one through whom the Messiah was to come.

Of Isaac's two sons, Jacob was chosen and Esau rejected. Finally, Jacob called his twelve sons about him and announced to them what would take place in the "days to come" (Gen 49:1). In his prophecy he clearly pointed to the fact that redemption would come in Judah. Later Balaam, a heathen soothsayer, also prophesied, "A star will come out of Jacob; a scepter will rise out of Israel" (Num 24:17). In Deuteronomy, in the passage in which the divine origin of the prophetic movement is revealed, we learn also of the prophet to come, who was to be like Moses. Whereas in a certain sense the entire prophetic body was like Moses, there was really only one who followed Moses, and that one was the Messiah.

In the books of Samuel it is revealed that the throne of David was to be established permanently, and that a ruler on that throne would rule over an eternal kingdom (2 Sam 7). On the basis of this prophecy we are to understand many of the Psalms that speak of a king (e.g., Pss 2, 45, 72, 110) and also many of the prophecies. The Messiah was to be the king of a kingdom that will never perish. This is taught by Isaiah, for example, who announced the supernatural birth of the Messiah and the government over which he is to rule. He was to be born of a virgin, and his supernatural birth was to be a sign to the people that God was truly with them. They did not have to fear before the growing power of Assyria. The Assyrian king would not destroy them nor render void the promises of God. They were to look to the king whom God would present to them. This king is the Messiah. His kingdom is to be eternal; it is to be built up in righteousness and justice and is to be the hope of the people.

Daniel also spoke of this kingdom as eternal. He contrasted it with the kingdoms of this world, which are both temporal and local. These kingdoms, great and powerful as they are, would nevertheless pass away; and there would be erected a kingdom that would belong to a heavenly figure, the one like a Son of Man. His kingdom alone would be universal and eternal, for he is the true Messiah. Stressing, as they do, the kingly work of the Messiah, many of these prophecies do not lay their emphasis on the actual saving work the Messiah was to perform.

There was a danger that the eyes of the people would be so attracted to the Messiah as a king that they might tend to think of him only as a political figure. This danger became very real, and the Jews more and more conceived of him as merely one who was political, who would deliver them from the yoke of foreign oppressors.

To offset this danger it was necessary that the people know full well that the Messiah's work was truly to be spiritual in nature. Hence, in the latter portion of his book, Isaiah with remarkable lucidity speaks of what the Messiah would do to save his people. It is in these great "Servant" passages that we learn that the Messiah was to be a Savior. He is set forth as one laden with griefs and sorrows, but they were not his own. They belonged to his people, and he bore them in order that people might be free and have the peace of God. The Messiah suffers and dies vicariously; that is the nature of his saving work, and Isaiah presents it with great vividness.

All the prophets were under Moses, and just as Moses was a type of Christ, so it may be said that the prophetical body as such, being under Moses, was also typical of the great prophet to come. Although they did not understand the full depth of their messages, yet they were speaking of the coming salvation and so of Jesus Christ. Through them God spoke in "divers manners" to the children of Israel. What is so remarkable is that, when their messages are taken as a whole and in their entirety, they form such a unified picture of the work of the Messiah.

We must guard against the view that there is merely a correspondence between what the prophets said and what occurred in the life of Jesus Christ. There was of course a correspondence, but to say no more than this is not to do

CHRONOLOGICAL CHART OF THE PROPHETS

Northern Kingdom Prophet	King		Southern Kingdom Prophet	King	
	Jeroboam	933–912			
	Nadab	912–911			
	Baasha	911–888			
	Elah	888–887			
	Zimri	887			
	Tibni	887–863			
	Omri	887–877			
ELIJAH	Ahab	876–854		Jehoshaphat	873–849
	Ahaziah	854–853		Jehoram	849–842
ELISHA	Jehoram	853–842		Ahaziah	842
	Jehu	842–815		Athaliah	842–836
	Jehoahaz	814–798	JOEL?	Jehoash	836–797
	Jehoash	798–793		Amaziah	797–779
JONAH	Jeroboam II	793–743	ISAIAH	Uzziah	779–740
AMOS	Zachariah	743	MICAH		
HOSEA	Shallum	743	OBADIAH?		
	Menahem	743–737			
	Pekahiah	737–736		Jotham	740–736
	Pekah	736–730		Ahaz	736–728
	Hoshea	730–722		Hezekiah	727–699
Fall of the Northern Kingdom					
			NAHUM?	Manasseh	695–642
				Amon	642–640
			JEREMIAH	Josiah	640–609
			HABAKKUK?		
			ZEPHANIAH?		
The Exile					
			DANIEL	Jehoiakim	609–597
				Jehoiachin	597
			EZEKIEL	Zedekiah	597–586
The Restoration					
			ZECHARIAH 520		
			HAGGAI 520		
			MALACHI 432?		

justice to the situation. Jesus Christ did not merely find a correspondence between the utterances of prophets and the events of his own life. Rather, the events of his life constituted the fulfillment of what the prophets had declared. It is this point on which we must insist if we are to understand them properly. As was said of Isaiah, so we may say of the entire prophetic body: they saw Christ's day and spoke of him.

Bibliography: E. J. Young, *My Servants the Prophets,* 1952; W. McKane, *Prophets and Wise Men,* 1965; H. E. Freeman, *An Introduction to the Old Prophets,* 1960; S. J. Schultz, *The Prophets Speak,* 1968; R. K. Harrison, *Introduction to the Old Testament,* 1970, pp. 741–63; J. A. Motyer, "Prophecy" (IBD), 1980, vol. 3, pp. 1276–84.

EJY

PROPITIATION AND EXPIATION (Gr. *hilastērion, hilasmos*). KJV uses the word *propitiation* three times—"God set forth [Christ] to be a propitiation" (*hilastērion*, Rom 3:25); "[Christ] is the propitiation for our sins" (*hilasmos*, 1 John 2:2); "God . . . sent his Son to be the propitiation for our sins" (*hilasmos*, 4:10)—and NASB uses it a fourth time—"[Christ became a man] to make propitiation for the sins of the people" (*hilaskomai*, Heb 2:17)—in all of which RSV and NEB use *expiation* and NIV has either *sacrifice of atonement* or *atoning sacrifice*.

Propitiation and *expiation* are very different in meaning. Propitiation is something done to a person: Christ propitiated God in the sense that he turned God's wrath away from guilty sinners by enduring that wrath himself at Calvary. Expiation is what is done to crimes or sins or evil deeds: Jesus provided the means to cancel, or cleanse, them. The NT clearly affirms that Jesus' death provided an expiation for the sins of the world; but was it necessary for Jesus to provide a propitiation (to avert God's wrath against guilty sinners) in order to provide expiation (cleansing, forgiveness, and pardon)? Scholars who hold that the biblical portrayal of God's wrath describes a real, perfect attitude of God toward sin (of which genuine human righteous indignation would be an imperfect analogy) recognize that propitiation was necessary and that Christ's death was such.

Scholars who hold that God's wrath is not his personal attitude toward sin and sinners but rather only a way of describing the results of evil and sin in the world, prefer to think of Christ's death as only an expiation. Yet, even when it is accepted that *hilastērion* and *hilasmos* point to God's genuine active anger toward sin being appeased by Christ's death, the translation "propitiation" is not always used.

Bibliography: Leon Morris, *The Atonement*, 1983. PT

PROSELYTE (prŏs'ĕ-līt). The Greek word *prosēlytos* (from the verb *proserchomai*, "to come to") is the common LXX translation of the Hebrew word *gēr*, which means a "foreign resident." It is often rendered "stranger," as in "thy stranger that is within thy gates" (Exod 20:10; Deut 5:14 KJV). Before NT times the word had come to apply to a more limited group religiously and a more extended group geographically. In the NT and the writings of Philo and Josephus the word designates a person of Gentile origin who had accepted the Jewish religion, whether living in Palestine or elsewhere.

The word occurs only four times in the KJV of the NT: (1) in Jesus' denunciatory discourse (Matt 23:1–39, in which hypocritical Pharisaism is condemned); (2) in the list of places and people represented in Jerusalem on the Day of Pentecost (Acts 2:10), "Jews and proselytes" (NIV "Jews and converts to Judaism") are mentioned; (3) in the selection of the first diaconate (6:1–6) one of the seven was "Nicolas, a proselyte from Antioch" (NIV renders "a convert to Judaism"); (4) after Paul's great sermon in the synagogue at Pisidian Antioch (13:14–41), "many of the Jews and devout converts to Judaism" (KJV "religious proselytes") followed Paul and Barnabas.

There has been much scholarly debate over whether all proselytes were fully initiated Jews or whether the term included also Gentile believers in God who had not accepted the initiatory rites, but who were associated with synagogue worship in varying degrees of fellowship. The probability is that the first-century Jews had no very fixed or rigid use of the term and that they differed among themselves. Judaism up to the time of Christ was not the narrow racial national religion it is sometimes made out to be. There were evidently many Gentiles in the synagogue at Pisidian Antioch (Acts 13:16, 26, 43, 50). See also the references to those who "worshiped," or "feared" God (10:2, 7; 16:14; 18:7), and study the instance of Cornelius (10:1–11:18) and Jesus' relations with the Roman centurion (Matt 8:5–13; Luke 7:1–10).

Among the non-Israelite worshipers of the true God in the OT are Melchizedek, Job, Ruth, Rahab, Naaman, Uriah the Hittite, the Ninevites at the time of Jonah's preaching, and the converts at the time of Esther (Esth 8:17). The "magi from the east" (Matt 2:1) are in the same category.

The subject of Israel's ancient mission among the Gentiles would require a far more extended study than is possible here. Psalm 15; Isaiah 2:2–4; 44:5; Jeremiah 3:17; 4:2; 12:16; Zephaniah 3:9–10; Zechariah 8:20–23 are only a few of the OT passages indicating an evangelistic attitude toward the Gentiles. JOB

PROSTITUTE. A word that, with "whore" and "harlot," is designated by four terms in the OT: (1) *zonah*, the most frequently used; (2) *qedēshâh*, a religious harlot, a priestess of a heathen religion in which fornication was part of worship (Gen 38:21–22; Deut 23:17); (3) *ishshah zarah*, or *zarah* alone, a "strange woman" (so KJV; NIV usually "wayward wife" or "adulteress"), a term found only in the Book of Proverbs; (4) *nokhriyah*, "stranger," "foreigner," a word also used in Proverbs, evidently also meaning "harlot." The NT word is *pornē* ("one sold," "fornicator").

Legal measures were in force concerning prostitutes. Parents were not to force their daughters into the practice (Lev 19:29; 21:7, 14), priests were not to marry harlots (19:29), and the wages of prostitution were not to be brought into the temple to pay a vow (Deut 23:18). These prohibitions were necessary to keep the worship of the Lord free from the impurities of the sin of harlotry.

The actual punishment of prostitutes was severe when enforced. In Genesis 38:24 Judah ordered Tamar to be burned for being a prostitute (until he came to see his own sin as worse than hers, v. 26). Leviticus 21:9 commanded burning for a priest's daughter who became a harlot. Deuteronomy 22:21 ordered stoning for a bride who was found not to be a virgin.

Such a common sin needed to be guarded against. The Book of Proverbs, which mentions every term for harlot except *qedēshâh*, teaches about and warns against prostitutes by admonition and illustrations. The situation in the Corinthian church was such that Paul had to give the Christians there special warnings against fornication with prostitutes (1 Cor 6:15–16).

The words harlot or prostitute, harlotry or prostitution, are used very often, especially in the prophetic books, to describe idolatry. This figurative use was evidently based on the idea that the Lord was the husband of the nation of Israel (Jer 3:20). When the people took their allegiance from God and gave it to idols instead, he called it "prostituting themselves to their gods" (NIV). This expression occurs often in the prophetic books in this or similar forms, a few times in other books, and several times in Revelation 17. CEH

PROVERB. A pithy saying, comparison, or question; in the OT usually Heb. *māshāl*, from a root meaning "represent," or "be like"; notably of Solomon's proverbs (1 Kings 4:32; Prov 1:1, 6; 10:1; 25:1; Eccl 12:9) and others (1 Sam 10:12; 24:13; Ezek 12:22–23; 16:44; 18:2–3). A person or a nation might become a proverb or a byword (Deut 28:37; 1 Kings 9:7; 2 Chron 7:20). ASV and RSV, have "byword" in Psalm 69:11; RSV and NIV in Jeremiah 24:9; ASV "parable," RSV and NIV "taunt" in Isaiah 14:4. Numbers 21:27 is a short poem (quoted in Jer

48:45–46) that RSV ascribes to "ballad singers," NIV to "poets." *Māshāl* is also translated "parable"; a few times "utter, speak," "be like, compare." Hebrew *hîdhâh*—"riddle, perplexing saying," or "question"—is translated "proverb" once in KJV (Hab 2:6, RSV and NIV "taunt"). It is also translated "riddle, dark saying, hard saying," "sentence, speech." In the NT, Greek *parabolē,* whose basic meaning is "comparison, placing side by side," is once translated "proverb" (Luke 4:23). Usually it is translated "parable"; a few times "comparison or figure." Greek *paroimia,* also equivalent to Hebrew *māshāl* and to *mîdhâh,* means a saying of popular origin, ancient and widely known, accepted as obviously true (2 Peter 2:22). In John 16:25, 29, ASV has "dark sayings," RSV "figures," NIV "speaking figuratively." A proverb is thought of as a short saying, a parable a somewhat longer saying, but the distinction is relative and is not always observed by Bible writers. Comparison, using the concrete facts of life to represent its abstract principles, is the essential characteristic of both. A proverb may be a snatch of poetry with parallel structure, a sharp question, a pithy sentence, or a very brief story. Felicity of expression insures its long preservation and wide currency through oral transmission, even after it is fixed in literary, written form. ER

PROVERBS, BOOK OF. The best representative of the so-called Wisdom Literature of ancient Israel, the Book of Proverbs comprises thirty-one chapters of pithy statements on moral matters. Its text is "The fear of the LORD is the beginning of knowledge" (Prov 1:7).

The headings in Proverbs 1:1 and 10:1 claim a Solomonic authorship for the bulk of the book; and this claim, though often denied in recent days, has no objective evidence against it. Chapters 25–29 are said to be by Solomon, copied by the men of Hezekiah. This obscure reference may refer to later collecting or editing of other Solomonic material. Of the authors Agur (ch. 30) and King Lemuel (ch. 31) we know nothing. They may be poetic references to Solomon himself. Proverbs is mentioned in the apocryphal book of Ecclesiasticus (47:17), written about 180 B.C. Although the canonicity of Proverbs, Ezekiel, and a few other books was questioned by individual rabbis as late as in the Council of Jamnia, A.D. 90, still it had long been accepted as authoritative Scripture, as the quotation in the Zadokite Document shows (col. 11, 1.19ff.). It is quoted and alluded to several times in the NT.

An outline of the book should accord with the material and style of the composition. Damage has been done by some who find in the book merely a collection of ancient maxims for success—a kind of *Poor Richard's Almanac.* Actually the book is a compendium of moral instruction. It deals with sin and holiness. And the vehicle of instruction is a favorite Semitic device—teaching by contrast. The style of Proverbs with its trenchant contrasts or more extended climactic poems can be paralleled in ancient literature in Egypt and Mesopotamia. The Hebrew author, however, has given instruction on life and holiness in proverbial form. The case is similar in Christian hymnody. There are countless examples of secular poetry and melody combined in ordinary song. But Christian hymns use the vehicles of poetry and song to express distinctively Christian thought and experience.

Outline:

I. Introduction (1:1–9)
II. Sin and Righteousness Personified and Contrasted (1:10–9:18)
III. Single-Verse Contrasts of Sin and Righteousness (10:1–22:16)
IV. Miscellaneous and Longer Contrasts (22:17–29:27)
V. Righteousness in Poems of Climax (30:1–33:31)

The first section of the book begins (Prov 1:7) and ends (9:10) with the statement that "the fear of the LORD is the beginning of knowledge" and "wisdom." Thus the wisdom extolled in Proverbs is not just a high degree of intelligence but a moral virtue. This is made plain in the first section by the contrasts involved. Wisdom is personified as a righteous woman (8:1). This is natural because *wisdom* is a feminine noun in Hebrew. The foolish woman is depicted as using words similar to those of wisdom, to invite men into her house (9:4, 16), but she invites them to sin. The harlot, who is given prominence in this section, represents all sin. Murder and theft are the opposite of wisdom in chapter 1, but usually the harlot, also called the strange woman, the simple woman, or the foolish woman, is held up as the opposite of personified righteousness. Some find Christ personified in the wisdom cited in Proverbs 8:22, but this is not certain. This word is not so used in the NT.

In the major section, Proverbs 10:1–22:16, the same contrast appears in single-verse aphorisms. Here the personification of sin and righteousness does not appear, but the same synonyms for virtue and vice are repeatedly used and should be understood as such. Perhaps the greatest error in interpreting the book comes from the tendency to quote these Proverbs as mere secular maxims instead of godly instruction. "Folly" here does not mean stupidity, just as "the woman of folly" (9:13) does not refer to an ignoramus. Both terms refer to sin. Through this whole section the terms *wisdom, understanding, integrity,* and *knowledge* are synonymous terms referring to holiness. Their opposites, *fool, folly, simple, mocker, quarrelsome,* etc., refer to wickedness. In short, a "foolish son" is not a dullard, but a scoundrel. A "mocker" is not just supercilious, but is a rebel against wisdom. The lack of context sometimes clouds the interpretation. But occasionally a verse is partially repeated elsewhere, where the variant form clarifies the meaning (cf. 27:15 with 21:19).

Section IV, Proverbs 22:19–29:27, is more general but uses the same vocabulary of morality. In this part are some special parallels with an Egyptian work entitled *The Wisdom of Amen-em-Opet.* The correspondence, however, does not invalidate the above claim that the author of Proverbs gives distinctive treatment to his theme.

The last section, Proverbs 30:1–31:31, includes several climactic proverbs that apparently emphasize the fourth point (cf. 6:16–19, where among seven things the seventh is the climax). Here also is the famous final poem—an alphabetical poem—extolling the wife of noble character.

Bibliography: Derek Kidner, *The Proverbs: An Introduction and Commentary* (TOTC), 1964; J. C. Rylaarsdam, *The Proverbs, Ecclesiastes, The Song of Solomon* (LBC), 1964. RLH

PROVIDENCE. The universal providence of God is the basic assumption of all Scripture. As in English, the corresponding Hebrew and Greek words such as *rā'âh* (Gen 22:8; 1 Sam 16:1) and *problepō* (Heb 11:40) in their contexts mean far more than mere foresight or foreknowledge. The meaning is "prearrangement." As used historically the theological term "providence" means nothing short of "the universal sovereign rule of God."

The definition of the answer to Question 11 of the Westminster Shorter Catechism expresses the view of all Bible-believing Christians: "God's works of providence are his most holy, wise and powerful preserving and governing all his creatures, and all their actions." Divine providence is the outworking of the divine decrees, which are "the plan of him who works out everything in conformity with the purpose of his will (Eph 1:11).

The biblical doctrine of divine providence does not imply a mechanistic or fatalistic view of the processes of the world or of human life. In a more extended treatise on this subject, secondary causes, and the relation between human responsibility and divine sovereignty would have to be canvassed. For the present purposes it must suffice to quote what are possibly the best available brief creedal statements on these matters:

"Although, in relation to the foreknowledge and decree of God, the first cause, all things come to pass immutably and infallibly, yet, by the same providence, he ordereth them to fall out according to the nature of second causes, either necessarily, freely, or contingently.

"God's providence includes the permission of all . . . sins of angels and men, and that not a bare permission, but such permission as hath joined with it a most wise and powerful bounding, and otherwise ordering and governing of them, in a manifold dispensation, to his holy ends; yet so as the sinfulness thereof proceedeth only from the creature, and not from God; who, being most holy and righteous, neither is nor can be the author or approver of sin" (Westminster Confession, ch. V., paragraphs II and IV).

"Second causes" are the ordinary forces and events of nature that God usually employs to accomplish his purposes.

That God's providence includes his decree to permit sin should not seem strange or paradoxical. One of the good features of so-called progressive education is *learning by experience,* and this is based on the assumption that what *ought not to be* is *not* the same as what *ought not to be permitted.* One of the clearest biblical illustrations of this principle is found in Joseph's words to his brothers, who had sold him into slavery: "You intended to harm me, but God intended it for good to accomplish what is now being done, the saving of many lives" (Gen 50:20).

It is customary to distinguish *special* providence from *general* providence. The former term refers to God's particular care over the life and activity of the believer. "We know that, in reference to those who love God, God works all things together for good" (Rom 8:28, author's tr.). "If the LORD delights in a man's way, he makes his steps firm" (Ps 37:23; see Phil 1:28). "But seek first his kingdom and his righteousness, and all these things [daily needs] will be given to you as well" (Matt 6:33). The entire Book of Job is devoted to the temporal sufferings of a godly man under divine providence. Hebrews 11:40 teaches that providence, for men of faith, includes something far better than experiences of this life.

General providence includes the government of the entire universe, but especially of the affairs of men. "To the LORD your God belong the heavens, even the highest heavens, the earth and everything in it" (Deut 10:14). "The Most High gave the nations their inheritance, when he divided all mankind, he set up boundaries for the peoples . . ." (Deut 32:8; see also Neh 9:6; Dan 4:35).

God by his providence is revealed as "sustaining all things by his powerful word" (Heb 1:3); "He causes his sun to rise on the evil and the good, and sends the rain on the righteous and the unrighteous" (Matt 5:45, see Ps 68:9; Acts 14:15–17; Rom 1:20).

Although God's grace is always offered to all people (Acts 10:34–35), yet the *main stream* of historical revelation and blessing for the world, through the instrumentality of Israel and the church, is a principal theme of all Scripture (see Acts 7:1–60; 13:16–43; Rom 3:1–2; 9:3–6; 11:1; 1 Tim 3:15; cf. Heb 11:38a). To this end God sometimes moves in unrecognized events and processes (Isa 40:1–5; 44:28–45:4).

Not only is the general course of nature sustained by God's providence, but the moral order and its logical consequences are as well: "A man reaps what he sows. The one who sows to please his sinful nature, from that nature will reap destruction; the one who sows to please the Spirit, from the Spirit will reap eternal life" (Gal 6:7–8). Divine providence sustaining the moral order is the principal theme of the Book of Proverbs.

The distinction between God's immanent or natural action and his transcendent or supernatural action is of supreme importance in the understanding of the doctrine of providence. See the article on MIRACLES. The case of Christianity depends entirely on the miracles of the incarnation and the resurrection of Christ. Nevertheless, as the article on miracles shows, godly faith has always existed in a world in which there are long periods of time, even in Bible history, in which

God does not choose to give "signs" or display miracles as evidences. It is imperative that we learn to see the glory of God in the regular works of providence as well as in the miraculous.

Christians who are scientists sometimes complain that some Fundamentalists tend to invoke the supernatural whenever there are gaps in scientific knowledge. The latter are, of course, embarrassed when scientists fill in the gaps with well-accredited facts. A mere "God of the Gaps" idea may be as harmful as mechanistic pantheism. The genuinely miraculous in Christianity is not dimmed but rather magnified by recognition of God's providential faithfulness in the regular processes of nature. JOB

PROVINCE. A word of doubtful etymology, it signifies the sphere of duty of a magistrate. The "roads and forest of Italy" for example, were a *province,* supervised by the appropriate commissioner. With the empire's gradual acquisition of new lands, spheres of magisterial duty signified increasingly the defense, organization, and government of distant territories; and the word *province* acquired the geographical significance that became its prime Latin meaning and its exclusive derived meaning. The provinces of Rome in this sense of the word were acquired over a period of more than three centuries. The first was Sicily (241 B.C.). The last were Britain, organized by Claudius, and Dacia, acquired by Trajan. Marcus Aurelius made a province out of Mesopotamia. Under the settlement of 27 B.C., all provinces were divided into two categories. First there were the imperial provinces, those that required a frontier army and that, in consequence, were kept under the control of the emperor, who was commander-in-chief of all armed forces. Second there were the senatorial provinces, those that presented no major problems of military occupation or defense and that were left in the control of the Senate. Imperial provinces were governed by the emperor's *legati* or, in the case of smaller units like Judea or Thrace, by procurators. The senatorial provinces were under a "proconsul" (NIV) or "deputy" (KJV); see Acts 13:7. Cyprus became a senatorial province in 22. Egypt, a special case, was governed by a prefect. EMB

PROVOCATION (prŏv'ō-kā'shŭn, Heb. *ka'as, mārâh,* Gr. *parazēloō, parorgizō*). Any cause of God's anger at sin; the deeds of evil kings (1 Kings 15:30; 21:22; 2 Kings 23:26), of Israel (Ezek 20:28), or mockers (Job 17:2). In their prayer of repentance the returned exiles mentioned the disobedience, rebellion, and idolatry of Israel and pleaded for mercy (Neh 9:18, 26, 36–37). In Psalm 95:8 ASV, RSV, and NIV transliterate instead of translating Hebrew *Meribah,* the geographical location named for the provocation when the Israelites demanded water, which Moses brought out of the rock (Exod 17:1–7; Num 20:13, 24; 27:14; Deut 32:51; 33:8; Ps 81:7), the waters of Meribah. The one NT passage in which (in KJV) *provocation* occurs (Heb 3:8, 15–16 NIV "rebellion") relates to this incident. The verb *provoke* occasionally has a good sense, "to stir up" (Heb 10:24).

PRUNING HOOK (Heb. *mazmerôth*). An agricultural tool used in the cultivation of the vine, with a sharp knifelike end for pruning (Isa 2:4; Joel 3:10; Mic 4:3).

PSALMS, BOOK OF. The longest book in the Bible follows "the Law" and "the Prophets" in the Hebrew OT (Luke 24:44) and inaugurates the final division of the OT, called "the Writings" (see CANON). The majority of its chapters, moreover, are antedated only by Genesis–Ruth. But the basic reason why Psalms is more often quoted by the NT and more revered by Christians than any other OT book is found in its inspiring subject matter. Both for public worship—"the hymnbook of Solomon's temple"—and for individual devotional guidance, its 150 poems constitute the height of God-given literature.

I. Name. The Hebrew designation of Psalms is *Tehillîm,* meaning "praises," a term that reflects much of the book's content (cf. Ps 145, title). Its name in Latin and English Bibles, however, comes from the Greek, *Psalmoi,* which means "twangings [of harp strings]," and then, as a result, songs sung to the accompaniment of harps. This latter name originated in the LXX (cf. its NT authentication, Luke 20:42) and reflects the form of the book's poetry. The same is true of its alternate title, *Psalterion,* meaning "psaltery," a collection of harp songs, from which comes the English term "Psalter."

II. Authorship. The individual psalms, naturally enough, make no attempt within their respective poetic framework to reveal the circumstances under which they were written. But, as might be expected, many of them do prefix explanatory titles in prose, indicating their authorship and occasion for writing, often giving poetic and musical direction as well (see below, Sections V and VI). The phrase, Psalm of Moses (David, etc.), appears most commonly. The Hebrew preposition rendered by the word "of" expresses authorship (cf. Hab 3:1, "of Habakkuk the prophet") or dedication (e.g., Ps 4, "For the director of music"). But while "Psalm of David" has sometimes been interpreted to mean merely "a Psalm of Davidic character," or ". . . belonging to a collection entitled *David,*" its actual usage in Scripture clearly indicates Davidic authorship (cf. Pss 7, 18). The Book of Psalms thus assigns seventy-three of its chapters to David, two to Solomon (Pss 72, 127), one each to the wise men Heman and Ethan (Pss 88, 89; cf. 1 Kings 4:31), one to Moses (Ps 90), and twenty-three to Levitical singing clans of Asaph (Pss 50, 73–83) and Korah (Pss 42–49, 84–85, 87–88). Forty-nine remain anonymous.

Modern biblical criticism consistently rejects the psalm titles as of little value (IB, 4:8). One suspects, however, that such denials spring from evolutionary bias, which refuses to admit as genuinely Davidic the advanced spiritual conceptions that Scripture thus assigns to an era one thousand years before the birth of Christ. From the viewpoint of lower criticism there is no reason for denying their authenticity within the text of the OT: all Hebrew manuscripts contain these titles; the earliest versions (such as the LXX) not only exhibit their translation but even misrepresent certain of their meanings, which had been lost in antiquity; and Hebrew Bibles regularly include them in the numbered verses of the inspired text (thus raising the verse numbers of many of the psalms by one or two). From the viewpoint of higher criticism, the exhaustive analysis of R. D. Wilson has demonstrated the compatibility of David's authorship with the content of each psalm attributed to him (cf. Ps 44, once considered Maccabean, but equally comprehensible as from David's era, under military duress). Archaeological research in Babylonia and Egypt has brought to light advanced hymnody centuries before Abraham; and the recovery of Canaanite literature at Ugarit has furnished significant parallels to the Psalms, from the time of Moses. David himself is known to have had certain musical and literary endowments (1 Sam 16:16–18; Amos 6:5; cf. his acknowledged composition of 2 Sam 1:19–27), exercised leadership in the development of Israel's liturgy (2 Sam 6:5, 13; 1 Chron 15–16, 25; 2 Chron 7:6; 29:30), and realized Spirit-born empowerment as "Israel's singer of songs" (2 Sam 23:1–2; Mark 12:36; Acts 1:16; 2:30–31; 4:25; see DAVID).

The NT repeatedly authenticates ascriptions to David: Psalms 16 (Acts 2:25), 32 (Rom 4:6), 69 (Acts 1:16; Rom 11:9), 110 (Luke 20:42; Acts 2:34). Some of the anonymously titled psalms are also recognized as of Davidic composition: Psalms 2 (Acts 4:25), 95 (Heb 4:7), 96, 105, 106 (underlying David's words in 1 Chron 16:8–36, though cf. HDB, IV:148). But it is significant that no psalm that claims *other* authorship, or contains later historical allusions (as Ps 137, exilic) is ever attributed in Scripture to him.

III. Occasions. The titles of fourteen of the Davidic psalms designate specific occasions of composition and contribute to a historical understanding of Scripture as follows (chronologically):

Psalm 59 (= 1 Sam 19:11) sheds light on David's envious associates (59:12).

Psalm 56 (1 Sam 21:11) shows how David's fear at Gath led to faith (56:3).

Psalm 34 (1 Sam 21:13) illuminates God's subsequent goodness (34:6–8).

Psalm 142 (1 Sam 22:1) depicts David at Adullam, persecuted (142:6).

Psalm 52 (1 Sam 22:9) emphasizes Saul's wickedness (52:1).

Psalm 54 (1 Sam 23:19) judges the Ziphites (54:3).

Psalm 57 (1 Sam 24:3) concerns En Gedi, when Saul was caught in his own trap (57:6).

Psalm 7 (1 Sam 24:9) introduces slanderous Cush (7:3, 8 correspond to 1 Sam 24:11–12).

Psalm 18 (2 Sam 7:1) is repeated in 2 Samuel 22.

Psalm 60 (2 Sam 8:13–14) illumines the dangerous Edomitic campaign (60:10; 1 Kings 11:15).

Psalm 51 (2 Sam 12:13–14) elaborates on David's guilt with Bathsheba.

Psalm 3 (2 Sam 15:16) depicts David's faith versus Absalom's treachery (3:5).

Psalm 63 (2 Sam 16:2) illumines the king's eastward flight (63:11).

Psalm 30 (2 Sam 24:25; cf. 1 Chron 22:1) reviews David's sin prior to his dedication of the temple area (30:5–6).

Among the remaining psalms that ascribe authorship, the twenty-three composed by Israel's singers exhibit widely separated backgrounds, since these Levitical clans continued active in postexilic times (Ezra 2:41). Most of them concern the Davidic or Solomonic periods. Psalm 83, however, suits the ministry of the Asaphite Jahaziel in 852 B.C. (cf. 83:5–8 with 2 Chron 20:1–2, 14), while Psalms 74, 79, and the concluding strophe of Psalms 88, 89 were produced by Asaphites and Korahites who survived the destruction of Jerusalem in 586. (74:3, 8–9; 79:1; 89:44). A few anonymous psalms stem from the Exile (Ps 137), from the return to Judah in 537 (107:2–3; 126:1), or from Nehemiah's rebuilding of Jerusalem's walls in 444 (147:13). Yet others that depict tragedy could as easily relate to the disorders of Absalom's revolt or to similar Davidic calamities (cf. Ps 102:13–22; 106:41–47). Liberal scholars once spoke confidently of numerous Maccabean psalms (second century B.C.) ; but the discovery of the Dead Sea Scrolls, which date from this very period and contain manuscripts of both the canonical psalms and secondary psalmodic compositions, establishes the Persian era as the latest possible point for inspired psalmody. It reinforces the evangelical hypothesis of Ezra as the writer of 1–2 Chronicles (the last book in the Hebrew Bible) and as compiler of the entire Jewish canon, shortly after 424 (Darius II, mentioned in Neh 12:22).

IV. Compilation. Psalms is organized into five books: 1–41, 42–72, 73–89, 90–106, and 107–150; and, since the same psalm appears in more than one collection—e.g., Pss 14 and part of 40 (Book I) as 53 and 70 (Book II), and the latter halves of 57 and 60 (Book II) as 108 (Book V)—it seems likely that each compilation originally experienced independent existence. Furthermore, since the last psalm of each collection was composed with terminal ascriptions that were designed for the book as a whole (41:13; 72:18–20; 89:52; 106:48; and the entire 150th Psalm for Book V), it appears that the origins of these five concluding psalms provide clues for the compilation of their respective books. Psalm 41 was written by David; and, since the remaining psalms of Book I are also attributed to him (except for Ps 1, which constitutes the book's introduction; Ps 10, which combines with 9 to form one continuous acrostic; and Ps 33, which has no title), it appears that David himself brought together this first collection. He further composed Psalm 106 (cf. 1 Chron 16:34–36), so

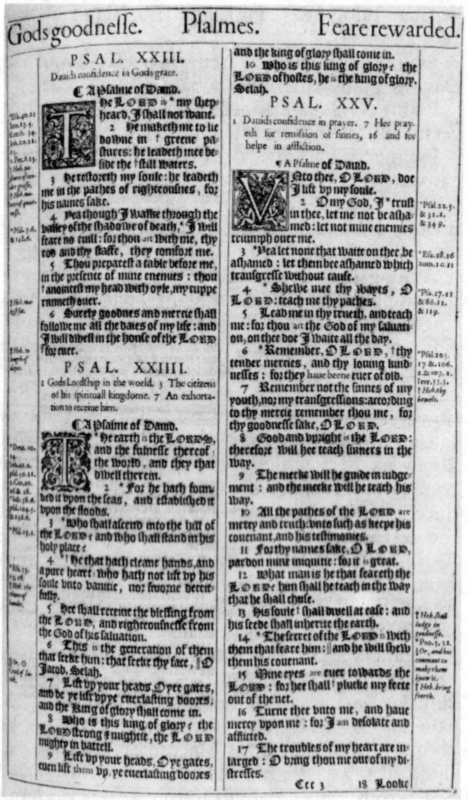
Gods goodnesse. Psalmes. Feare rewarded.

PSAL. XXIII.

Dauids confidence in Gods grace.

¶ A Psalme of Dauid.

The LORD is my shepheard, I shall not want.
2 He maketh me to lie downe in greene pastures: he leadeth mee beside the still waters.
3 He restoreth my soule: he leadeth me in the pathes of righteousnes, for his names sake.
4 Yea though I walke through the valley of the shadowe of death, I will feare no euill: for thou art with me, thy rod and thy staffe, they comfort me.
5 Thou preparest a table before me, in the presence of mine enemies: thou anointest my head with oyle, my cuppe runneth ouer.
6 Surely goodnes and mercie shall followe me all the daies of my life: and I will dwell in the house of the LORD for euer.

PSAL. XXIIII.

1 Gods Lordship in the world. 3 The citizens of his spirituall kingdome. 7 An exhortation to receiue him.

¶ A Psalme of Dauid.

The earth is the LORDS, and the fulnesse thereof: the world, and they that dwell therein.
2 For he hath founded it vpon the seas, and established it vpon the floods.
3 Who shall ascend into the hill of the LORD? and who shall stand in his holy place?
4 He that hath cleane hands, and a pure heart: who hath not lift vp his soule vnto vanitie, nor sworne deceitfully.
5 Hee shall receiue the blessing from the LORD, and righteousnesse from the God of his saluation.
6 This is the generation of them that seeke him: that seeke thy face, O Iacob. Selah.
7 Lift vp your heads, O yee gates, and be ye lift vp ye euerlasting doores; and the King of glory shall come in.
8 Who is this king of glory? the LORD strong & mightie, the LORD mighty in battell.
9 Lift vp your heads, O ye gates, euen lift them vp, ye euerlasting doores: and the king of glory shall come in.
10 Who is this king of glory? the LORD of hostes, he is the king of glory. Selah.

PSAL. XXV.

1 Dauids confidence in prayer. 7 Hee prayeth for remission of sinnes, 16 and for helpe in affliction.

¶ A Psalme of Dauid.

Vnto thee, O LORD, doe I lift vp my soule.
2 O my God, I trust in thee, let me not be ashamed: let not mine enemies triumph ouer me.
3 Yea let none that waite on thee, be ashamed: let them bee ashamed which transgresse without cause.
4 Shewe mee thy wayes, O LORD: teach me thy pathes.
5 Lead me in thy trueth, and teach me: for thou art the God of my saluation, on thee doe I waite all the day.
6 Remember, O LORD, thy tender mercies, and thy louing kindnesses: for they haue beene euer of old.
7 Remember not the sinnes of my youth, nor my transgressions: according to thy mercie remember thou me, for thy goodnesse sake, O LORD.
8 Good and vpright is the LORD: therefore will hee teach sinners in the way.
9 The meeke will he guide in iudgement: and the meeke will he teach his way.
10 All the pathes of the LORD are mercy and trueth: vnto such as keepe his couenant, and his testimonies.
11 For thy names sake, O LORD, pardon mine iniquitie: for it is great.
12 What man is he that feareth the LORD? him shall he teach in the way that he shall chuse.
13 His soule shall dwell at ease: and his seede shall inherite the earth.
14 The secret of the LORD is with them that feare him: and he will shew them his couenant.
15 Mine eyes are euer towards the LORD: for hee shall plucke my feete out of the net.
16 Turne thee vnto me, and haue mercy vpon me: for I am desolate and afflicted.
17 The troubles of my heart are inlarged: O bring thou me out of my distresses.

Ccc 3 18 Looke

A page of Psalms, beginning with the 23rd, from the King James Version 1611. Courtesy The British Library.

that Book IV, with its liturgical nature (contrast the more personal character of Pss 1–41), must likewise be traced to David's own hand, prior to 970 B.C., the year of his death. Books II–III exhibit more of a national interest (cf. their stress on Elohim, God transcendent, rather than on the Lord's personal name, Jehovah). King Solomon (died 930), who was responsible for the doxology of 72:18–20, thus becomes the historical compiler of Book II (his reference to "the prayers of David," 72:20, seems to be due to his father's having composed over half of the chapters that make up Pss 42–72). Book III, however, was completed and collected by unnamed Korahites soon after 586 (see above); for though the body of Psalms 88–89 was written by Solomon's Ezrahites, the title that is prefixed to both designates the sons of Korah as its ultimate compilers (cf. its terminal strophe, 89:38–52, which they seem to have suffixed in the spirit of Ps 88). Indeed, this third book includes several post-Solomonic and sixth-century compositions; and, when combined with Books I–II, it constituted Israel's psalter of the Exile. Finally Book V, which parallels David's Book IV in liturgical interest but includes several postexilic (as well as early Davidic) psalms, came into being shortly after 537. It then remained for a Spirit-led scribe to bring Books IV and V into union with I–III, adding his own inspired composition of Psalms 146–150 as a grand hallelujah for the entire Psalter. Since this last writing occurred in 444 (Ps 147:13) at the time of Ezra's proclamation of the written law and reform of the temple worship (Neh 8–10), it may well be that Ezra himself executed the final compilation of the book (cf. Ezra 7:10).

V. Contents. Each of the 150 psalms exhibits the formal character of Hebrew poetry. This consists, not primarily in rhyme, or even rhythmic balance, but rather in a parallelism of thought, whereby succeeding phrases either repeat or in some way elaborate the previous line. The poems vary in content. Hermann Gunkel has proposed a number of categories, not all of which appear valid (see Section VI); but the following psalm-types do distinguish themselves, by subject or by their Hebrew titles. Certain portions (e.g., Ps 34:11–16) exhibit a marked gnomic or wisdom character, much akin to Proverbs (cf. Pss 37, 49, 73, 128, 133, and especially Solomon's Ps 127). The title *maskill*, "instructive" (?), which suggests a didactic or at least meditative quality, appears in thirteen of the superscriptions. Included is the historical 78th Psalm (cf. the recited histories of Pss 81, 105, 106). The title *miktam* "atoning" (?), introduces Psalms 16, 56–60, perhaps because of reference to covered sins; and among David's most famous penitential psalms are 32 and 51 (cf. Pss 38, 130, 143).

Most of the poems possess a lyric, singing quality and are entitled "psalm" (*mizmôr,* stringed accompaniment; fifty-seven times) or "song" (*shîr,* joyful melody; thirty times). Their praises may be general (Ps 145) or specific (e.g., Pss 19, 119, concerning God's revelation). The term *shiggaion* (Ps 7; Hab 3:1), "dirge," suggests the emotion of grief and validates Gunkel's categories of both national and individual laments. Of related character are the imprecatory psalms (see IMPRECATORY PALMS). Particularly significant are the seventeen specifically messianic psalms, in the whole or in parts of which Christ either is referred to in the third person (8:4–8; 72:6–17; 89:3–4, 28–29, 34–36; 109:6–19; 118:22; 132:11–12), is addressed in the second person (45:6–7; 68:18; 102:25–27; 110), or speaks himself in the first person (2; 16:10, 22; 40:6–8; 41:9; 69:4, 21, 25; 78:2).

VI. Use. Psalm titles in Books I–III contain a number of musical terms in Hebrew. Some of these designate ancient melodies, to which the poems may have been sung: "The Doe of the Morning" (Ps 22); "Do Not Destroy," probably a vintage song (Pss 57–59, 75; cf. Isa 65:8); "A Dove on Distant Oaks" (Ps 56); "The Death of the Son" (Ps 9); "Lilies" (Pss 45, 69); and "The Lily of the Covenant" (Pss 60, 80). Others preserve musical instructions, much of the significance of which is now uncertain: *alamoth,* "maidens, treble" (?) (Ps 46), perhaps contrasted with *sheminith,* "[lower] octave" (Pss 6, 12); *gittith,* "the instrument from Gath"(?) (Pss 8, 81, 84); *mahalath* (*leannoth*), "grief" (for afflicting)

(Pss 53, 88); *neginoth,* "stringed instruments" (seven times, plus Hab 3:19); *nehiloth,* "for flutes" (Ps 5); and Selah (seventy-one times, not in titles but at the end of strophes; cf. 3:2, 4, 8), perhaps indicating a dramatic pause for musical effects (cf. *Higgaion, Selah,* "meditation pause" (?) in 9:16). A number of Israel's psalms had specific liturgical usage. The "songs of ascents" (Pss 120–134) may have been chanted by pilgrims ascending to Jerusalem (cf. 121:1; 122:4). Psalm 92 was composed for Sabbath use. The "Hallel" ("praise") psalms (113–118) accompanied the Passover (cf. Matt 26:30), and the psalms that begin, "The Lord reigns" (Pss 93–100) constitute a liturgical series magnifying God's sovereignty. Gunkel, accordingly, proposes a category of "psalms for the enthronement of Yahweh." Sigmund Mowinckel even postulates an elaborate Hebrew new year's festival based on Babylonian analogies: the king, as the Lord's "son," is said to have participated in various cult-dramas and processions, with a climactic reestablishment of God's kingship for another season. But while verses such as 24:7, "Lift up your heads, O you gates . . . that the King of glory may come in," probably do preserve references to David's historic procession to bring the ark of God into Jerusalem (2 Sam 6; cf. 1 Kings 8:6), Mowinckel's enthronement theory is both theologically unacceptable and historically unsupported (IB, 4:7).

Paralleling Mowinckel's stress on cultic origins is a modern emphasis on a collective rather than individualistic understanding and use of Psalms. Yet while certain of its poems do exhibit group expression (particularly among the pilgrim songs, 124, 126, even when using "I," 129), others manifest distinctly individualistic consciousness (Pss 1, 21, 112, 127). The compilation embraces not simply the congregational hymnbook of Solomon's temple, but also the devotional heartbeat of men like David, who "found strength in the LORD his God" (1 Sam 30:6). The richest blessings of the Psalms flow from their affirmations of personal faith—"The LORD is my shepherd, I shall not be in want" (Ps 23:1).

Bibliography: W. S. Plumber, *Psalms,* 1867; John Paterson, *The Praises of Israel,* 1950; H. C. Leupold, *Exposition of the Psalms,* 1959; R. L. Harris, "Psalms," *The Biblical Expositor* (ed. C. F. H. Henry), 1960, 2:34–70; Arthur Weiser, *The Psalms: A Commentary,* 1962; C. Westermann, *The Praise of God in the Psalms,* 1965; A. A. Anderson, *Psalms (1–72)* (NCB), 1972; Derek Kidner, *Psalms,* (TOTC) 1973, 1975. JBP

PSALMODY, PSALTER, PSALTERY (See MUSIC AND MUSICAL INSTRUMENTS; PSALMS, BOOK OF)

PSEUDEPIGRAPHA (sū'dē-pĭg'rá-fá). Intertestamental books not in the Hebrew canon or the Apocrypha, ascribed to earlier authors. They include The Ascension of Isaiah, Assumption of Moses, Book of Enoch, Book of Jubilees, Greek Apocalypse of Baruch, Letters of Aristeas, 3 and 4 Maccabees, Psalms of Solomon, Secrets of Enoch, Sibylline Oracles, Syriac Apocalypse of Baruch, Epistle of Baruch, and Testament of the Twelve Patriarchs. They are important for their disclosure of Jewish ideas in the intertestamental period.

PTOLEMAIS (See ACCO)

PTOLEMY (tŏl'ĕ-mē, Gr. *Ptolemaios*). The common name of the fifteen Macedonian kings of Egypt whose dynasty extended from the death of Alexander the Great in 323 B.C. to the murder of the young Caesarion, son of Julius Caesar and Cleopatra, at Octavian's orders in 30. The first Ptolemy, surnamed Soter, 367 to 282, was a distinguished officer of Alexander. He became satrap of Egypt in 323, but converted his command into a kingdom in 305. As a successor of the pharaohs, Ptolemy I took over the ancient administration of Egypt, and especially the theory glimpsed in the OT record of Joseph's life, the ownership of the land. His vast and highly centralized bureaucracy, which became a permanent feature of Ptolemaic rule, prepared the way for the Roman imperial administration of Egypt and contrasted with the Hellenistic policies of the rival Seleucid regime in Syria.

A mass of papyrological evidence provides a detailed picture of state control in the Ptolemaic system. In passing, it may be mentioned that Ptolemy I wrote a history of Alexander, which is most unfortunately lost. The second Ptolemy, surnamed Philadelphus, 308 to 246 B.C., consolidated the organization of the land. He was responsible for much of his government's remarkable financial system, including the most highly developed banking system of ancient times; a rigid machinery of control in commerce and industry; and a nationalized, planned, and budgeted economy.

In the reign of Ptolemy II there first erupted the long rivalry with the Seleucids of Syria over the Palestinian frontier. Ptolemy II also instituted the cult of the divine ruler, a simple enough graft on old indigenous beliefs, a preparatory factor for Caesar worship. The great city of Alexandria grew apace during this reign. Ptolemy II built the amazing Pharos lighthouse outside the twin harbors, and the Museum, the most notable center of culture and literature in the ancient world. He established the famous library of Alexandria and cut a canal from the Red Sea to the Nile. This was the Golden Age of Ptolemaic Egypt.

The next reign, that of Ptolemy III, surnamed Euergetes I, 288 to 221 B.C., saw the high tide of expansion and the first symptoms of decline. These symptoms were in full view under the fourth Ptolemy, surnamed Philopator, 244 to 205, whose reign saw some significant native uprisings and the loss of Nubia for a generation. There followed a century of dynastic strife, palace intrigue, anarchic minorities, and decline, during which Egypt survived through the strength of its natural defenses and its strategic isolation rather than through the worth and enlightenment of its

Ptolemy I (323–282 B.C.), drawn from a silver tetradrachma of the period. Courtesy Carta, Jerusalem.

leadership. Ptolemy XI, surnamed Alexander II, 100 to 80 B.C., was the last of the male line of Ptolemy I. He was killed by rioting Alexandrians, notoriously an unruly populace.

Ptolemy XII, surnamed Auletes or the Fluteplayer, 116 to 51 B.C., fled to Rome in the face of Alexandrian lawlessness. His restoration to his tottering throne by Gabinius, at the Senate's orders, was Rome's first significant intervention in the land, which the Republic (no less than Napoleon nearly nineteen centuries later) saw to be the strategic key to the Middle East. The wife of Ptolemy XIII was Cleopatra VII, the famous bearer of the name. Domestic, and consequently political and dynastic, strife between husband and wife led to Caesar's intervention, after his rival Pompey had met his death in Egypt. Ptolemy XIV was an insignificant brother of Cleopatra, and Ptolemy XV was her ill-fated son by Caesar.

The great achievement of the Ptolemies was Alexandria, with all that its immense cultural institutions signified in the ancient world. Alexandria was creative and conservative. It preserved much of the literature of Greece and, but for the plague of Islam that engulfed the land, would have preserved more. It produced great writers and scientists. It fathered the Septuagint. It created "Alexandrianism," which means much in the literature of Rome. Alexandria always stood apart from Egypt. It was a Greek city, and its peculiar contribution to Hellenism was the gift to history and civilization of the first Ptolemies.

EMB

PUAH (pū'ȧ, Heb. *pû'âh*). 1. A member of the clan of Tola, of the tribe of Issachar (Num 26:23; Judg 10:1).

2. One of the Hebrew midwives who refused to obey the edict of Pharaoh to destroy the infant sons born of Hebrew women (Exod 1:15–20).

PUBLICAN (See OCCUPATIONS AND PROFESSIONS)

PUBLIUS (pŭb'lĭ-ŭs, Gr. *Poplios*). The chief person on the island of Malta in the Mediterranean. He gave lodging and food to Paul and his companions after their shipwreck on the island's rocky coast. Paul healed the man's father and many others (Acts 27:27–44; 28:7–10).

PUDENS (pū'dĕnz, Gr. *Poudēs, modest*). A Christian in the city of Rome who sent greetings to Timothy in Paul's last letter (2 Tim 4:21)

PUHITES (See PUTHITES)

PUITES (pū'īts, Heb. *pûnî*). Descendants of Puah, of the tribe of Issachar (Gen 46:13; Num 26:23; 1 Chron 7:1). KJV "Punites."

PUL (pŭl, pūl). 1. A king of Assyria, Tiglath-Pileser III, who invaded Israel in the days of Menahem and was bribed to depart (2 Kings 15:19), though he carried off captives (1 Chron 5:26).

2. A tribe or place in Africa, named between Tarshish and Lud (Isa 66:19 KJV), some Septuagint manuscripts read Put (Libyans, so NIV). See also PUT.

PUNISHMENT. Death was the punishment for the following sins: striking or even reviling a parent (Exod 21:15–17), blasphemy (Lev 24:14, 16, 23), Sabbath-breaking (Num 15:32–36), witchcraft (Exod 22:18), adultery (Lev 20:10), rape (Deut 22:25), incestuous or unnatural connection (Lev 20:11, 14, 16), kidnapping (Exod 21:16), and idolatry (Lev 20:2). Being cut off from the people was ipso facto excommunication or outlawry; it meant forfeiture of the privileges of the covenant people (18:29). The hand of God executed the sentence in some cases (Gen 17:14; Lev 23:30; 20:3; Num 4:15, 18, 20). Capital punishment was by stoning (Deut 22:24), burning (Lev 20:14), the sword (Exod 32:27), hanging (the hanged were accounted accursed, so were buried at evening, as the hanging body defiled the land [2 Sam 21:6, 9; Gal 3:13]), and strangulation (not in Scripture, but in rabbinical writings). Other cruel treatment, including torturous methods of killing, were sawing people in two (Heb 11:37); consigning to hard labor (2 Sam 12:31); throwing people from a cliff (2 Chron 25:12; Luke 4:29); flogging, only forty lashes were allowed (Deut 25:2–3), therefore only thirty-nine given (2 Cor 11:24). The convict who was to be flogged was stripped to the waist and received lashes them from a three-thonged whip, either lying on the ground (Deut 25:2) or tied to a pillar in a bent position. If the one flogging exceeded the allowed or prescribed number of lashes, he was punished. People who committed crimes against others were often punished in kind (*lex talionis*—Exod 21:23–25), including also the recompense of time or restitution of an article or its equivalent (21:19, 30). Slander of a wife's honor was punished by a fine and flogging (Deut 22:18–19). Crucifixion was not practiced until Roman times. Punishment for sin is widely recognized in the Bible and is in the hands of God (directly, Gen 4:1–16; Lam 3:37–39; 4:6; Zech 14:19; indirectly, 1 Peter 2:14; in everlasting punishment, Matt 25:46). ER

PUNISHMENT, EVERLASTING (See ESCHATOLOGY)

PUNITES (See PUITES)

PUNON (pū'nŏn, Heb. *pûnōn*). A desert encampment of the Israelites marking the second stop after leaving Sinai (Num 33:42–43). Eusebius identified it as being north of Petra, a penal colony where convicts were sent to mine copper, also called Phinon or Phainon. Eusebius is probably correct in this identification.

PUR (See PURIM)

PURAH (pū'rȧ, Heb. *purâh, branch*). A servant of Gideon who went down with him to spy on the army of Midian (Judg 7:10–11).

PURE (See CLEAN)

PURIFICATION. That the conception of purity was deep within the religio-social structure of the children of Israel since very early times is well known to the student of the Bible. The attitude of the Jews as a whole, and of the Pharisees as a class, is expressed in Mark 7:3–4. Religious purity was both ceremonial and ethical. Under the Mosaic Law, ceremonial purification was required for four acts: (1) the birth of a child, removed through circumcision (if male) and through the isolation of the mother for a varying period (Lev 12:2ff.); (2) contact with a corpse, the offering of a red heifer being prescribed for sacrifice of purification (Num 19:1–10); (3) certain diseases, such as leprosy (Lev 13:8); and (4) uncleanness due to a running sore (Lev 15). Family purity was guarded through strict regulations concerning sex (Lev 20:1–21; Deut 22:20–21). In the NT, though there is a transference from the outward to the inner, there is no relaxing of the basic requirements for purity itself (Matt 5:27–28; 19:3–9; Mark 10:2–11; 1 Cor 5:9–13; 6:18–20; 7:8ff.).

PURIM (pūr'ĭm, Heb. *pûrîm, lots*). A Jewish festival celebrated on the fourteenth and fifteenth of the month Adar (February-March), commemorating the deliverance of the Hebrews from the murderous plans of the wicked Haman in the postexilic period (Esth 3:7; 9:26). This festival is named from the casting of the lot to determine the most expeditious time for the mass murder of the Jews.

PURITY (See CLEAN; PURIFICATION)

PURPLE (Heb. *'argāmān*, Gr. *porphyra*). (Exod 25:4; 26:36; 28:15; Judg 8:26; 2 Chron 2:14; 3:14; Esth 1:6; 8:15; Song of Songs 3:10; Mark 15:17–20; Luke 16:19; Acts 16:14.) Purple was a very costly dye extracted from the *marine mulex trunculus,* a marine mollusk, from which the Phoenicians were able to manufacture the dye. The shell was broken so that a small gland in the neck of the mollusk might be removed and crushed. The crushed gland gave out a milklike fluid that turned purple or scarlet on contact with the air. The shells of the mollusk from which purple is obtained can still be seen strewn along the shore of Tyre and near the ancient dye-works of Athens and Pompeii. The Book of Exodus lists extensive use of purple in the tabernacle and for the priests' garments. Because of its extreme costliness, it became a mark of distinction to wear a robe of purple. In later times ecclesiastical officials arrayed themselves in purple robes. In early times royalty was so dressed. In very ancient times the common people of Sumerian civilization were forbidden on pain of punishment to wear purple. The Savior was dressed in mockery at his trial in a robe of purple (Mark 15:17). Lydia, Paul's first European convert, was a seller of purple (Acts 16:14), i.e., the purple dye.

PURSE (Gr. *ballantion*). A rather finely finished leather pouch or bag that served as a "purse" in ancient times. The term translated "purse" in Matthew 10:9 KJV (NIV "belts") is Greek word *zōnē* and refers to the Middle Eastern girdle made of crude leather or woven camel's hair worn around the waist. Sometimes these "girdles" were finely tooled and contained "slots" in which gold and silver coins could be kept. If the "girdle" was made of cloth, then the money was placed within the folds themselves (cf. Luke 10:4; 12:34).

PUT (pŭt, Heb. *pût*). The third son of Ham (Gen 10:6; 1 Chron 1:8). His descendants are not named. A comparison of translations of Hebrew *pût* in KJV, ASV, RSV, and NIV reveals the difficulty of locating Put (Isa 66:19; Jer 46:9; Ezek 27:10; 30:5; 38:5; Nah 3:9). The question is partly textual, whether there is confusion between Put and Pul (Isa 66:19), between Ludim and Lubim; partly etymological, whether the word is of Egyptian origin; partly involved in the location of lands with which Put is associated. Some locate Put west of Egypt on the North African coast; some in Nubia; others east of Somaliland, on both sides of the Red Sea, in both Africa and Asia. Genesis 10:6, which names Put between two African lands, Cush (Ethiopia) and Mizraim (Egypt), and Asian Canaan, suggests the ambiguity, and no other reference removes it. The men of Put were valued mercenary soldiers of Tyre (Ezek 27:10) and Egypt (Jer 46:9). They used shield (Jer 46:9) and helmet (Ezek 38:5), probably also the bow (Isa 66:19). Possibly there were settlements of them in widely scattered places. Certainly they traveled far to fight. See also PUL. ER

PUTEOLI (pū-tē'ō-lē, Gr. *Potioloi, little wells* or *springs*). A well-known seaport of Italy located in the Bay of Naples; it was the nearest harbor to Rome. It was the natural landing place for travelers from the East to Rome. In Acts 28:13–14 Luke reports that Paul landed there with the other prisoners when he was taken to Rome for trial. Paul and Luke and their party found Christian brothers there and enjoyed their hospitality for seven days before going on to Rome. The old ruins may still be seen in the northern part of the bay, including part of a pier Paul is supposed to have used. The modern name is Pozzuoli.

PUTHITES (pū'thīts, Heb. *pûthî, simple*). A family descended from Caleb, residing in Kiriath Jearim (1 Chron 2:50, 53).

PUTIEL (pū'tĭ-ĕl, Heb. *pûtî'ēl*). The father-in-law of Eleizer, Aaron's son (Exod 6:25).

PUVAH (See PUAH)

PYGARG (See ANIMALS)

PYRRHUS (pĭr'ŭs, Gr. Pyrros, *fiery red*). The father of Sopater (Acts 20:4).

PYTHON (See ANIMALS)

Q

QUAIL (See Birds)

QUARRIES (Heb. *pesîlîm, graven images*). The "quarries" are mentioned in a doubtful passage in Judges 3:19, 26 KJV. The marginal readings in KJV and ASV suggest "graven images," a rendering supported by the authority of LXX and Vulgate. RSV has "sculptured stones," NIV "idols." Some piece of local nomenclature and a lost tradition are no doubt involved. Perhaps the place was a dump for discarded and roughly broken idols. Perhaps the reference is to Joshua's stones of commemoration by Jordan. The word "quarry" occurs in another disputed passage at 1 Kings 6:7. RSV and NIV say that the stones or blocks were dressed "at the quarry." NIV uses the English word in a less doubtful context elsewhere (e.g., Eccl 10:9; Isa 51:1).

QUARTUS (kwôr'tŭs, Gr. *Kouartos*). A Christian man of Corinth whose greetings Paul sent to the church at Rome together with those of Gaius and Erastus (Rom 16:23). No doubt he was a friend and assistant of Paul and a worker in the Corinthian church. There is an old tradition that he was originally one of the seventy disciples or missionaries Jesus sent out in Palestine (Luke 10:1).

QUATERNION (kwȧ-tĕr'nĭ-ŭn, Gr. *tetradion*). A detachment of four men (Acts 12:4). The "four quaternions" (KJV; NIV "four squads of four soldiers each"), to whom the prisoner was committed, were the four patrols who took the four watches of the night. Two, no doubt, watched inside and two outside the guardhouse.

QUEEN. Dowager queens, or mothers of the monarch, are those who appear in the most influential roles in the biblical records: (1) Jezebel, princess of Tyre who, during the twenty-two years of her husband Ahab's reign and during the thirteen years of the reigns of her sons Ahaziah and Joram, exercised a strong influence in favor of Phoenician pagan cults (1 Kings 16:28–2 Kings 9:37, passim). (2) Athaliah, daughter of Jezebel and of similar character, was the wife of Jehoram of Judah, son of Jehoshaphat. On the accession of her son Ahaziah (not to be confused with Ahaziah of Israel, his uncle), Athaliah exercised a dominant authority and after Ahaziah's assassination held the throne alone, securing her position by dynastic massacre (2 Kings 11). (3) Bathsheba, mother of Solomon, widow of David and Uriah, demonstrated her decisive character as her husband David lay dying (1 Kings 1).

The foreign queens mentioned in the OT are (1) Vashti, the queen that Xerxes (KJV Ahasuerus) of Persia deposed (Esth 1), (2) Esther, the Jewess, Vashti's successor, a brave woman whose situation, nonetheless, violated the tenets of the law and demonstrated the compromised position of those who took no part in the movements of restoration headed by Ezra and Nehemiah, (3) Balkis, legendary name of the Queen of Sheba (1 Kings 10), and (4) unnamed queens referred to in Nehemiah 2:6 and Daniel 5:10.

In the NT are (1) Bernice, or Berenice, sister of Agrippa II and wife of her uncle, Herod, king of Chalcis (Acts 25–26), and (2) Drusilla, wife of Azizus, king of Emesa, whom she deserted to become the third wife of Felix, procurator of Judea (Acts 24). EMB

QUEEN OF HEAVEN (Heb. *melekheth ha-shāmayim*). Some controversy surrounds the philology and significance of this title, but it seems best to regard it as the female deity to whom, with their families' aid and connivance, Hebrew women made offerings (Jer 7:18; 44:17–25). The most likely identification is with Ashtoreth, goddess of love and fertility, synonymous with the Assyrian and Babylonian Ishtar and the Roman Venus. The "mourning for Tammuz" was associated with her cult (Ezek 8:14). Its ritual was the license and obscenity characteristic of the eastern fertility cults, ever a temptation to the Hebrews and the chief objective of the prophets' attack on paganism.

QUICKSANDS (See Syrtis)

QUIET, QUIETNESS. These and related words, as well as "silence and "silent," are found in Scripture (mostly in the OT) as the translation of about thirty different Hebrew and Greek words. Most uses are in the prophetic (e.g., Isa 53:7) or historical (e.g., Matt 26:63) portions of Scripture, but several are involved with apostolic instructions to Christians. Followers of Christ are encouraged to live (1 Thess 4:11) and work quietly (2 Thess 3:12), those who speak in tongues should remain silent if there is no interpreter present (1 Cor 14:28), a prophet speaking in church is to stop speaking if another prophet gets a revelation (1 Cor 14:30), and women are to have a quiet spirit (1 Peter 3:4) and to remain silent in church (1 Cor 14:34; 1 Tim 2:11, 12).

QUIRINIUS (kwĭ-rĭn'ĭ-ŭs, Gr. *Kyrēnios*). The reference to this Roman governor in Luke 2:2 has raised some historical difficulties. If Luke wrote the words, and he probably did, a historian of such proved accuracy is not likely to have made a major mistake. The task falls on the commentator to sort out the facts with due consciousness of the gaps in our historical material. It is known that Quirinius was governor of Syria A.D. 6–9, that Judea was incorporated at the time, and that a census was taken that caused the rebellion of Judas (Acts 5:37). Abundant papyrological evidence from Egypt has established the fourteen-year cycle of the census in that province, and fixes A.D. 20 as a census year. This fixes Quirinius' census in A.D. 6 and demands 9 or 8 B.C. for an earlier occasion, or at least 7 or 6 B.C., if account be taken of political and practical impediments not apparent today. The difficulty then arises that Sentius Saturninus, and not Quirinius, was governing Syria from 9 to 7 B.C., and Quinctilius Varus from 6 to 4 B.C. A clue to a solution lies in an inscription that states that P. Sulpicius Quirinius governed Syria twice. W. M. Ramsay offers the best solution to this puzzle. He suggests that Quirinius was in control of the foreign relations of Syria during the war with the Cilician hill tribe of the Homonadenses in 6 B.C. This is consistent with the term used and with Roman policy. An enrollment in Herod's kingdom would thus be supervised by him. The enrollment could have taken place in the autumn of 5 B.C., postponed by the dying Herod's devices of obstruction and procrastination. EMB

QUIVER (Heb. *'ashpāh, telî*). As a case for carrying arrows, a quiver was used by soldiers (Job 39:23; Isa 22:6; Jer 5:16; Lam 3:13) and by hunters (Gen 27:3). The man who has many children is like the quiver that is full of arrows (Ps 127:4–5), and the servant of Jehovah says that he has been hidden in Jehovah's quiver (Isa 49:2).

QUMRAN (See DEAD SEA SCROLLS)

R

RA (See Egypt)

RAAMAH (rā′ȧ-mȧ, Heb. *ra'mā'*). A son of Cush and grandson of Ham (1 Chron 1:9); the father of Sheba and Dedan (Gen 10:7; cf. 1 Chron 1:9). The prophet Ezekiel identifies Raamah as one of the merchant tribes that traded in spices, gold, and precious stones with Tyre (Ezek 27:22).

RAAMIAH (rā′ȧ-mī′ȧ, Heb. *ra'amyâh, Jehovah has thundered*). One of the companions of Zerubbabel who returned with him to Jerusalem from captivity (Neh 7:7); called Reelaiah by Ezra (Ezra 2:2). The text may be corrupt at this point.

RAAMSES (See Rameses)

RABBAH, RABBATH (răb′ȧ, Heb. *rabbâh*; in KJV twice "Rabbath" [Deut 3:11; Ezek 21:20]). The full name is *rabbath benê 'ammôn,* "Rabbah of the children of Ammon." The only city of the Ammonites to receive mention in Scripture; therefore we may conclude its importance. It is first mentioned in connection with the "bed" or sarcophagus of Og, king of Bashan (Deut 3:11). Rabbath lay east of the Jordan and was not assigned to the tribe of Gad at the time of the division of the land (Josh 13:2–5). It disappears from history following the days of Joshua until the days of David who sent an embassage of consolation to Hanun king of the Ammonites because of the death of his father. The Ammonite monarch grossly insulted the messengers of David (2 Sam 10:1–6). The next spring Rabbah was besieged by the army of David. The city capitulated when Joab captured its water supply. The prophetic utterances against Rabbah of the Ammonites are of interest. Jeremiah utters imprecatory judgment against Molech, the chief Ammonite deity (Jer 49:2–3). Ezekiel pictures Nebuchadnezzar as pausing at Rabbah to decide his further course of action (Ezek 21:20–21). Amos predicts, "I will set fire to the walls of Rabbah" (Amos 1:14). It seems to have been at Rabbah that Baalis, king of the Ammonites, concocted the

A view of present-day Amman, capital of Transjordan, showing the old Roman theater in center. In ancient times the city was called Rabbath-Amon and served as capital of the Ammonites (2 Sam 11–12; 1 Chron 20). Courtesy Studium Biblicum Franciscanum, Jerusalem.

Stone statue of a king, from Amman, c. eighth century B.C. He wears a heavy crown and long garment with short sleeves. A shawl around his waist and over his shoulder ends in a tassel. Courtesy Studium Biblicum Franciscanum, Jerusalem.

plot that was to cost Gedaliah, the provisional governor for the Babylonians, his life (Jer 40:14–15). Subsequently, Rabbah was captured by Ptolemy Philadelphus (285–247 B.C.), who changed its name to Philadelphia. It later became the seat of Christian bishops. It is now known as Amman, the capital of the kingdom of Jordan.

Excavations by J. B. Hennessy revealed a Late-Bronze (1550–1200 B.C.) temple. Remains exist from the Roman period on the citadel above Philadelphia (the name of the city in the Roman times) and in the city below. These include a beautifully preserved, six-thousand-seat theater, a smaller odeum (music hall), and a nymphaeum. These all date to the second century A.D. The principal remains are on Citadel Hill, which contained all the public buildings, temples, churches, etc.

RABBI (See OCCUPATIONS AND PROFESSIONS)

RABBIT (See ANIMALS)

RABBITH (răb′ĭth, Heb. *hārabbîth*). A town in the tribe of Issachar (Josh 19:20). Identified by Knobel as Arabonheh at the southern tip of Mount Gilboa, and by Conder as Rama, eight miles (thirteen km.) south of Gilboa.

RABBONI (răb-bō′nī). A variant of *Rabbi,* the Hebrew word for "Teacher." The title used by Mary Magdalene to Jesus on resurrection morning (John 20:16). See OCCUPATIONS AND PROFESSIONS: *Rabbi.*

RAB-MAG (răb′măg, Heb. *rav māgh*). One of the Babylonian princes present at the capitulation of Jerusalem (Jer 39:3 KJV). Same as Nergal-Sharezer (39:3)

RABSARIS (răb′sȧ-rĭs, Heb. *rav-sārîs*). The title of an Assyrian and Babylonian official usually taken to be "chief eunuch," though Assyriologists have produced evidence for the reading "chief of the 'heads' [leaders, leading men]." The title appears in the Bible only in 2 Kings 18:17 (KJV; NIV "chief officer"), where it is related that Sennacherib "sent his supreme commander, his chief officer and his field commander with a large army, from Lachish to King Hezekiah at Jerusalem" to effect the capitulation of that city to the Assyrians. The mission was unsuccessful but was followed by another, which also conveyed a letter to Hezekiah. Hezekiah took the matter to God in prayer and was encouraged by the word of the Lord as spoken by Isaiah. The angel of the Lord struck the Assyrian forces, and Sennacherib returned to Nineveh (19:35–36).

RABSHAKEH (răb′shȧ-kĕ, Heb. *ravshāqēh*). The title of an Assyrian official, with the meaning "chief cup-bearer" or "chief of the officers[?]" (2 Kings 18:17, 19, 26–28, 37; 19:4, 8, and parallel; Isa 36:2, 4, 11–13, 22; 37:4, 8). While Sennacherib was besieging Lachish, he sent his Rabshakeh (KJV; NIV "field commander") to Jerusalem to deliver an ultimatum to that city. When representatives of Hezekiah protested that he should speak in Aramaic so that the people on the wall could not understand, he deliberately addressed his challenge to those onlookers and then left to join the Assyrian forces at Libnah.

RACA (rȧ′kȧ, Gr. *rhaka, empty, vain,* or *worthless fellow*). A term of contempt, signifying a derogatory estimate of someone's intellectual ability (Matt 5:22).

RACAL (rā'căl, Heb. *rākhāl*). A place in the Negev of Judah where David and his men roamed as fugitives from the relentless Saul (1 Sam 30:29). David sent spoil from Ziklag to some of its leading men.

RACE (Heb. *ōrah, mērôts,* Gr. *agōn, stadion,* most frequently, *a foot race*). The clearest uses of these words are in 1 Corinthians 9:24; 2 Timothy 4:7; and Hebrews 12:1. Other passages may well allude to it (Rom 9:16; Gal 5:7; Phil 2:16). The Greek race was one of a series of highly competitive games. It consisted of (1) the goal, a square pillar opposite the entrance to the course, marking the end of the track; (2) the herald, whose duty it was to announce the name and the country of each competitor, as well as the name and family of the victor; (3) the prize, the crown or wreath that was awarded the winner (cf. 1 Cor 9:25; 2 Tim 2:5); and (4) the judges (2 Tim 4:8). The Lord is viewed as the righteous Judge who bestows the wreath on those who have truly run well.

RACHEL (rā'chĕl, Heb. *rāhēl, ewe,* Gr. *Rhachēl*). The wife of Jacob, the mother of Joseph and Benjamin (Gen 29:6, 16, 18, 31; 30:1–9; cf. Jer 31:15; Matt 2:18). Rachel was the younger daughter of Laban, the Aramean (ASV "Syrian"), the brother of Rebekah, Jacob's mother (Gen 28:2); thus Jacob and Rachel were full cousins. The circumstances under which Jacob met Rachel are interesting. Jacob had quarreled bitterly with his brother Esau over the stolen blessing (27:35ff.). Accordingly, Jacob's mother, Rebekah, suggested that her son Jacob leave for a time, which she hopefully imagined would be brief, and go to the house of her brother Laban in Haran (Paddan Aram) (27:43–45). On his arrival, struck by Rachel's beauty, Jacob immediately fell in love with her (29:17–18). He signed a contract with Laban for seven years of labor (the usual period of indentured servants), at the expiration of which Rachel was to be his wife. In the light of the Nuzi tablets, many of the transactions between the two men become easier to understand, if not entirely justifiable by Christian mores. It appears that according to Nuzian customs, Jacob became male heir, Laban at this time having no male heir of his own. He thus adopted Jacob as his son, giving him both Leah and her sister Rachel as his wives. After becoming prosperous, Jacob took his departure from the house of Laban (31:21). One reason "Laban's attitude toward him was not what it had been," is that Laban by now apparently had sons, and they regarded Jacob as an interloper (31:1). Thus arose the dispute over the right of the possession of the teraphim, the household gods that Rachel concealed in the baggage as she, together with Jacob her husband, fled away (31:30–31). These household deities, about the size of miniature dolls, were regarded as indisputable evidence of the rights and privileges of family ownership and inheritance. Cf. Laban's indignant query, "But why did you steal my gods?" (31:30).

For some time, Rachel remained barren, bearing no children. The two children that Rachel finally had were Joseph (30:22), while yet in the house of Laban, and Benjamin after the return home. Rachel, however, died in childbirth with Benjamin (35:16–19). This may partially show why Jacob favored the sons of his beloved Rachel above the sons of Leah. The character of Rachel varies between very attractive and unattractive. She inherited her family's traits of scheming and duplicity (31:34). A believer in monotheism, she yet clung to the forms of polytheism. Jeremiah pictures her as rising from her grave to weep over the children who are being carried to Babylon, never to return (Jer 31:15). Matthew cites this in connection with Herod's murder of the children in Bethlehem (Matt 2:18). JFG

RADDAI (răd'ā-ī, Heb. *radday*). The fifth of the seven sons of Jesse, the father of David (1 Chron 2:14).

RAGAU (rā'gô, Gr. *Rhagau*). The Greek form of Reu, an ancestor of Christ (Luke 3:35).

RAGUEL (See REUEL)

RAHAB (rā'hăb, Heb. *rāhāv, broad,* Gr. *Rhachab*). 1. A woman best known for her prominent role in the capture of Jericho during the days of Joshua (Josh 2:1ff.; Matt 1:5; Heb 11:31; James 2:25). The spies sent by Joshua were received into the house of Rahab prior to the siege of the city by the army of Israel. When the king of Jericho sent a posse of men in search of the spies, Rahab refused to betray their whereabouts. As a reward for her fidelity in this affair, she was promised by the two spies her own safety and the protection of her family, on condition of her continued loyalty and secrecy (Josh 2:14–20). True to the promise that the spies had made to her, Joshua and his men spared Rahab and her family after they captured the city (6:17). Jewish tradition has held Rahab in high honor, one tradition making her the wife of Joshua himself.

According to Matthew's genealogy, she is not only one of the four women mentioned in the family tree of the Savior, but also the mother of Boaz, the husband of Ruth, and the great-grandmother of King David (Ruth 4:18–21; Matt 1:5). The author of Hebrews speaks of her as a shining example of faith (Heb 11:31). James shows his appreciation of her as a person in whom faith was not merely "theological" but also practical (James 2:5).

2. A mythical monster of the deep. In such passages as Job 9:13 and Psalm 89:10 the motif of the slaying of the dragon appears. In Isaiah 51:9 the Lord's victory is complete because he has cut Rahab, the monster, to ribbons. This poetic symbolism has much in common with the Ras Shamra literature and may be the prototype of

legends like St. George and the Dragon. The *Rahab Yashab* ("Rahab the Do-Nothing") of Isaiah 30:7 portrays the impotency of the monster of Egypt (symbolized by the crocodile) in the day of invasion.

RAHAM (rā'hăm, Heb. *raham, pity, love*). Son of Shema, father of Jorkeam (1 Chron 2:44).

RAHEL (See RACHEL)

RAIMENT (See DRESS)

RAIN (Heb. *māṭār, geshem, heavy rain, yôreh, former rain, malkôsh, latter rain,* Gr. *brechō, hyetos*). The word in the Scriptures is used in both a literal and a figurative sense. The amount of rainfall in biblical countries varies greatly. In Egypt, for example, there is very little rainfall, the land being dependent on the Nile for water. In Syria and the land of Israel, however, the rainfall normally is abundant. The contrast between Egypt and Palestine in rainfall is brought out in Deuteronomy 11:10–12. Since the summer is very dry in Israel, the rainy seasons come in the spring (the "latter rains") and in the fall (the "former rains"). One can be almost certain that from about May 1 to about October 15, no rain will fall. "The winter is past; the rains are over and gone" (Song of Songs 2:11). Many people thus sleep on the roofs of the houses to escape the heat and to enjoy the cooling night breezes. The greatest amount of rain falls between November and February, tapering off until the coming of summer, and beginning again the next autumn. The latter or spring rains are considered such a natural blessing that they assume an eschatological significance (Joel 2:23; Zech 10:1). The withholding of the rain at the proper season, particularly in the spring, was regarded as a most severe punishment (Deut 28:23–24; 1 Kings 17:1–16; 18:18), and conversely, the abundance of rain denoted the rich blessing of the Lord on his people (Deut 28:12). Famine, one of the more tragic effects of the lack of rain, was therefore seen as an indication of divine displeasure (2 Sam 21:1–14). In pagan concepts, Baal was conceived of as the god of rain. This aids in explaining the immoral practices of the fertility cults, which believed that their sexual orgies would induce Baal to send rain. Elijah's contest on Carmel was to prove the superiority of the God of Israel in the realm of the forces of nature.

RAINBOW (Heb. *qesheth, bow*). The biblical interpretation of the rainbow is found in the record of Noah's life. God's covenant with Noah declared that he would never again send a universal flood to destroy the whole inhabited earth (Gen 9:8–17). This feature of the flood account is unique in that none of the accounts from Babylon, as the well-known Gilgamesh Epic, makes mention of the rainbow as the covenantal sign. In the Bible the rainbow is the first of the covenant signs and provides the key to understanding all of them, including the signs of baptism and the Lord's Supper in the new covenant. The rainbow in the clouds speaks to man from God. God allowed Noah to understand what the bow means to him: a visible declaration that the Lord will never again destroy the earth by flood. The rainbow is the Lord's promise made visible. Thus covenant signs express covenant promises to covenant people. Ezekiel compares the glory of God to that of a rainbow (Ezek 1:28). John, as a prisoner on Patmos, beheld the throne of God encircled by the rainbow (Rev 4:3).

RAISINS (See FOOD)

RAKEM (rā'kĕm, Heb. *raqem*). A man of the tribe of Manasseh, son of Sheresh (1 Chron 7:16).

RAKKATH (răk'ăth, Heb. *raqqath*). One of the fortified cities assigned to the tribe of Naphthali (Josh 19:35). It is near the Sea of Galilee. There is some evidence that Tiberias was built on the ruins of Rakkath.

RAKKON (răk'ŏn, Heb. *raqqōn*). One of the cities in the inheritance of Dan (Josh 19:46). Thought to be about fifteen miles (twenty-five km.) north of Joppa.

RAM (See ANIMALS)

RAMAH, RAMA (rā'mȧ, Heb. *hārāmâh, height*). 1. Ramah Arael, a city assigned by lot to the tribe of Naphtali, probably to be identified with the modern er-Rama, a large Christian village on the southern tier of the mountains of upper Galilee (Josh 19:36).

2. Rhama-Ramah, a territory mentioned as forming the boundary of Asher (Josh 19:29). It has been identified with Ramiyeh, a village some thirteen miles (twenty-two km.) SE of Tyre, and twelve miles (twenty km.) east of the "Ladder of Tyre."

3. Ramah Iamah (or Ramah of Benjamin, and various other orthographic forms), a city assigned to the tribe of Benjamin, mentioned along with Gibeon and Beeroth; the headquarters of Deborah, judge of Israel during the days of the oppression of Sisera (Judg 4:5). The Levite whose concubine's flight and killing brought about intertribal warfare (Judg 19–20) could have spent the night here, but stayed in Gibeah instead. At the time of the division of the kingdom, Ramah of Benjamin was destroyed, for we read that Baasha of Israel built it again to ward off his rival, Asa king of Judah (1 Kings 15:16–17). Ramah of Benjamin is mentioned in the "catalogue of doom" listing the cities about to be punished by the Assyrian king (Isa 10:28–32). This is probably the Ramah that is referred to in Jeremiah 37:15 and Matthew 2:18.

4. Ramah Aramathaim, the hometown of Elkanah and Hannah, and the birthplace of the prophet Samuel (1 Sam 1:19; 2:11). The text at this point bears evidence of having been corrupt-

ed, and various readings have been suggested, as Ramathaim Zophim (KJV) and Ramathaim (NIV). Later Samuel made it the center of his circuit (7:16–17). Here Israel demanded a king (8:4), and here Samuel first became acquainted with King Saul (9:6ff.). Samuel retired here after his final break with Saul (15:34). This is the place where David found refuge from the crazed king (19:18) and where Samuel was buried (25:1; 28:3). Its present site seems to be Er-Ram, NW of Jerusalem.

5. Ramah in the Negev, Ramah of the South. A city in the southern sector of Judah that was allotted to the tribe of Simeon (Josh 19:8; KJV "Ramath of the South"). It is understood to be the same as Baalath Beer by many, as well as identified with the Ramoth (pl.) to whose inhabitants David sent gifts that he had taken as spoil from the Amalekites (1 Sam 30:27). All proposed identification is tenuous.

RAMATH LEHI (rā'măth lē'hī, Heb. *rāmath lehî*, the *hill* or *height of Lehi*). The place where Samson threw away the jawbone of a donkey after the slaughter of the Philistines (Judg 15:17). The hill may have received its name because of its real or fancied resemblance to a jawbone. It is sometimes identified with the Wady-es Sarrar, not far from Timnath and Zorah, Samson's area of operation (13:25; 14:1).

RAMATH MIZPEH (rā'măth mĭz'pĕ, Heb. *rāmath-mitspeh, the heights,* or *the watchtower*). The northern boundary line of the tribe of Gad (Josh 13:26). It is probably the same place that marked the early sanctuary erected by Jacob and Laban as a witness (Gen 31:46–48). It has the triple names of Mizpeh, Galeed, and Jegar Sahadutha. Mizpeh implies the idea of watching, while the other two names convey the thought of a heap of stones set up as a witness between two contending parties. Probably Mizpeh is the same as Ramoth Gilead, so famous in the subsequent history of Israel.

RAMATH OF THE SOUTH (See RAMAH, no. 5)

RAMATHAIM (See RAMAH)

RAMATHAIM ZOPHIM (See RAMAH)

RAMATHITE (See RAMAH)

RAMESES, RAAMSES (râ-ăm'sēz). A Hebrew place-name derived from the Egyptian royal name Ramses. In the OT it appears first as the name of the district of the Delta in which Jacob and his sons were settled by Joseph (Gen 47:11). (The LXX also reads *Ramessē* for the second "Goshen" of the Hebrew and English text of Gen 46:28.) Rameses and Pithom are the names given in Exodus 1:11 for the two store cities the Israelites were forced to build for the Pharaoh of the Oppression. From Rameses the Israelites began their exodus from Egypt (Exod 12:37; Num 33:3, 5). At present there is fairly general agreement that Rameses is to be identified with Avaris-Tanis-Zoan, the modern San el Hagar in the NE part of the Delta, an identification that has considerable bearing on the interpretation of the Exodus. CEDV

RAMIAH (rà-mī'à, Heb. *ramyâh, God is set on high*). A descendant of Parosh, mentioned in the list of those who renounced their foreign wives at the request of Ezra (Ezra 10:25).

RAMOTH (rāmoth, Heb. *rāmôth, height*). 1. One of the cities of refuge in the tribe of Gad, elsewhere called Ramoth Gilead (Josh 20:8; 21:38). It formed one of the administrative districts of Solomon, over which Ben Geber was stationed (1 Kings 4:13). It is perhaps best known as the scene of the last battle of King Ahab. It is identified as Tell Ramith in north Jordan (22:1–37).

2. Ramoth Negev. See RAMAH, no. 5.

3. An Israelite who after the Exile divorced his Gentile wife at the urging of Ezra (Ezra 10:29 KJV; NIV "Jeremoth").

RAMSES, RAMESSES (râ-ăm'sēz). The most common royal Egyptian name in the Nineteenth and Twentieth dynasties. Ramses I was the founder of the Nineteenth Dynasty, but the most illustrious of the bearers of this name was his

Colossal statue of Ramses II, part of the rock-cut façade of the great temple at Abu Simbel, measuring about 69 feet (21 m.) high. Courtesy Seffie Ben-Yoseph.

grandson, Ramses II. He was ambitious and imperious. He made a determined effort to recover the Asiatic Empire, but his errors in judgment in the Hittite encounter at Kadesh on the Orontes brought about a stalemate, which later produced an Egyptian-Hittite treaty. Ramses established his capital at Tanis, in the Delta, but his building and rebuilding activities extended throughout the land and even beyond Egypt proper. Among his impressive constructions are the completion of the hypostyle hall at Karnak, his father's funerary temple at Abydos, his own temple at Abydos, the forecourt and pylon of the Luxor temple, the Ramesseum at the Theban necropolis, and Abu Simbel in Nubia. Extensive building operations were supplemented by his usurpations of monuments of his predecessors, a practice that enhanced his reputation beyond his merits. This, plus the presence in the OT of the name Rameses for a city and district in the Delta, brought about the acclamation of Ramses II as the Pharaoh of the Oppression, in spite of chronological complications with OT data. Among the varying interpretations of the Exodus, this identification of Ramses II is not widely held at present. Ramses III was the second king of the Twentieth Dynasty; perhaps his most outstanding accomplishment was the repelling of an invasion of the Delta by the Sea Peoples. His best-known construction is his mortuary temple at Medinet Habu, not far from the Ramesseum. At the end of his reign a serious harem conspiracy occurred. The other eight kings of this name, who followed in Dynasty Twenty, are relatively unimportant, though documents relating to the tomb robberies in the Theban necropolis in the reign of Ramses IX are of interest. Although certain of these kings, such as Ramses II and III, must have had at least indirect influence on Israelite life, none of them is mentioned in the OT. CEDV

RAMS' HORNS (See MUSIC AND MUSICAL INSTRUMENTS)

RAM SKINS. The skins of the sheep tanned with oil used for outer clothing by the shepherds of the Near East. They were also used as the exterior covering for the tabernacle (Exod 25:5).

RANSOM (răn'sŭm, Heb. *kōpher, pidhyôn, gā'al,* Gr. *lytron, antilytron*). The price paid for the redemption of a slave (Lev 19:20); a reparation paid for injury or damages (Exod 22:10–12); a fee, fine, or heavy assessment laid on a person as a substitute for his own life (21:30). There was no ransom provided for the willful murderer (Num 35:31). In the NT the term signifies the redemptive price offered by Christ on the cross for the salvation of his people (Mark 10:45; 1 Tim 2:6).

RAPHA (rā'fa, Heb. *rāphā'*). 1. The last son of Benjamin (1 Chron 8:2).

2. Four enemy warriors of David are listed as descendants of Rapha, probably to identify them as giants (so KJV) (2 Sam 21:15–22; 1 Chron 20:6, 8).

RAPHAH (rā'fa, Heb. *rapha*). A descendant of Saul through Jonathan (1 Chron 8:37). KJV "Rapha."

RAPHU (rā'fū, Heb. *rāphû'*). Father of Palti, one of the spies sent out to investigate the land of Canaan (Num 13:9).

RAS SHAMRA (ràs shàm'rà, Arab. *Fennel Head*). The modern name of the mound that marks the site of the ancient city of Ugarit, located on the Syrian coast opposite the island of Cyprus. The city, with its port Minet el Beida (White Harbor), was an important commercial center through which passed the trade of Syria and Mesopotamia with Egypt, Cyprus, and the Aegean area. Occasionally antiquities had been found here by local people, but in A.D. 1928 a peasant struck the roof of a buried tomb with his plow and made a discovery that attracted the attention of the authorities. In 1929 the French archaeologist C. F. A. Schaeffer began a series of excavations that have revealed much of the history of the site. Test shafts showed that there were five major strata, the earliest dating to the Neolithic period.

Ugarit was swept from the historical scene in about 1200 B.C., when the Sea Peoples overran the area. The city is mentioned in Egyptian historical inscriptions, in the Amarna Tablets (Akkadian), and in Hittite records. Its relations with Egypt were quite close during the Twelfth Dynasty and again in the time of Ramses II. Ugarit was at the peak of its prosperity in the fifteenth–fourteenth centuries B.C. but was destroyed by an earthquake in the mid-fourteenth century. It recovered from this catastrophe but was under Hittite and then Egyptian domination. Although the excavation of the mound has resulted in many significant finds, the most striking was that of a scribal school and library of clay tablets, adjoining the temple of Baal and dating from the Amarna Age. Various Near Eastern languages and scripts appeared at Ugarit, but the majority of the tablets used an unknown cuneiform script, which study showed to have an alphabet of some thirty signs. Credit for the work of deciphering the script must go to H. Bauer, E. Dhorme, and C. Virolleaud. The language, now called Ugaritic, was found to be of the Semitic family and closely related to Hebrew. The texts contain various types of writings: syllabaries and vocabularies; personal and diplomatic correspondence; business, legal, and governmental records; veterinary texts dealing with diagnosis and treatment of ailments of horses; and, most important, religious literature.

The myths and legends of Ugarit have provided valuable primary sources for the knowledge of Canaanite religion. These stories have been given modern titles, e.g., "The Loves and Wars of Baal and Anat," "The Birth of the Gods," "The Wedding of Nikkal and the Moon," "The Legend of Keret," "The Legend of Aqhat." At the head of the Ugaritic pantheon was El, who was also known as Father of Man, Creator of Creators,

Statue (24.8 cm. high) from Ras Shamra, nineteenth to seventeenth century B.C., of a seated goddess. She wears a long garment with a rolled edge or cord at the bottom. A similar cord wound about the upper part of the body may represent a serpent. Courtesy Réunion des Musées Nationaux.

Bull El. His consort was Asherah, a fertility goddess who was a stumbling block to Israel. Ahab (1 Kings 16:33) and Jezebel (18:19) promoted her worship, and Manasseh even put her image in the temple (2 Kings 21:7). Among the many offspring of El and Asherah was Dagon (Judg 16:23; 1 Sam 5), a grain god, whose son Baal was of great prominence. A god of rain and storm, Baal, whose proper name was Hadad (Thunderer), also figured in the fertility cycle. Baal was also called Aliyan Baal, Dagon's Son, Servant of El, Rider of Clouds, and Baal-Zebub (cf. 2 Kings 1; Matt 12:24). In Israel the priests of Baal lost an important contest with the prophet of God on Mount Carmel (1 Kings 18). Baal's sister and wife, the virgin Anat, goddess of love and fertility and goddess of war, is known in the OT as Astarte or Ashtoreth. In addition to these, numerous lesser divinities are named. The deities of Ugarit are often quite ungodly: El ordinarily is easygoing and easily influenced, but sometimes is rash and even immoral, as in his seduction and expulsion of two women. Baal mates with his sister and also with a heifer. Anat slaughters people and wades in blood and gore. This aspect of Canaanite religion occasioned the stern warning of the Lord to Israel concerning such worship.

The texts provide information concerning ritual and sacrifice and the temple plan, and recovered objects also contribute to an understanding of the religion and culture. The tablets and the OT elucidate each other; the Ugaritic texts have been used in OT textual criticism and have been helpful in Hebrew lexicography. Many interesting suggested relationships may be cited. Ugaritic practice illuminates the biblical prohibition against boiling a kid in its mother's milk (Exod 23:19; 34:26; Deut 14:21). A veterinary text refers to a poultice that has been cited as a parallel to Isaiah's prescription for King Hezekiah (2 Kings 20:7; Isa 38:21). The legend of Aqhat tells of a good and just king named Dan'el, whom some have sought to equate with the Daniel of Ezekiel (14:14, 20; 12:3). The system of weights used at Ugarit was like that of Israel. These examples illustrate the type of information provided and discussion aroused by the investigation of the remains of this long-dead city. CEDV

RAT (See ANIMALS)

RAVEN (See BIRDS)

RAVENOUS BIRD (See BIRDS)

RAZOR, RASOR (rā'zêr, Heb. *ta'ar, môrâh*). The earliest razors were made of flint. Later they were made of bronze and finally of steel. Joseph is said to have shaved himself before he was liberated from prison to stand before Pharaoh (Gen 41:14). This was no doubt in deference to Egyptian custom, as the priests of Egypt shaved daily. The cutting of the beard by a priest of Israel was forbidden, presumably because of its affinity to pagan practices (Lev 21:5). The Nazirite was

Two ancient razor blades made of bronze. Upper blade has three holes for attaching to handle, similar to that of fractured blade underneath. From Nubia, Egypt, c. 1550–1350 B.C. Courtesy The University Museum, University of Pennsylvania.

likewise forbidden the use of a razor as long as his vows were valid (Num 6:5).

RE, RA (rā). A masculine deity in the pantheon of the gods of Egypt, identified with the sun-god. He stands within the circle of the "creation-myths." Creation is viewed as a procreation on the part of the male and his female. The ancients, unlike the nation of Israel, drew no line of differentiation between the brute forces of nature and their deities. In fact, the elemental forces of nature were the deities, to whom were assigned personalized names. Re was thought to have engaged in a fierce battle against the dragon of chaos and darkness. The struggle was repeated yearly, sometimes even daily, in the ceremonial liturgy of Egypt. Yet life was not regarded in such tragic fashion as it was in Mesopotamia. Victory was always assured in the fullness and glory of the present order. The primeval hill on which Re held sway emerged from the floor of the ocean of chaos. Creation came from the sun. In later times, Re came to be referred to as Amen-Re, Osiris, and other such names. In the mystery religions, he was designated as Soter-Theos, a "savior-god," a deity who rescued his people from death. The center of the worship of Re was Heliopolis, the ancient On. The ninth plague was in reality a judgment on Re, the sun god (Exod 12:21–23). Joseph, after being made food administrator of the land, married the daughter of the priest of On of the cult of Re (Gen 41:45).

REAIAH, REAIA (rē-ā'yȧ, Heb. *re'āyâh, God has seen*). 1. The eponym of a Calebite family (1 Chron 4:2).

2. A Reubenite (1 Chron 5:5).

3. The family name of a company of temple servants (KJV Nethinim) (Ezra 2:47; Neh 7:50).

REAPING (Heb. *qātsar*, Gr. *therizō*). Reaping in ancient times consisted in either pulling up the grain by the roots, or cutting it with a sickle. The stalks were then bound into bundles and taken to the threshing floor. In Bible lands cutting and binding are still practiced. The reaper sometimes wears pieces of cane on his fingers to prevent the sharp spears of wheat or the sickle from cutting him. Strict laws for reaping were imposed on Israel (Lev 19:9; 23:10; 25:11; Deut 16:9). Samuel mentions that reaping will be a duty that the nation's newly chosen king, Saul, will demand of them (1 Sam 8:12). The figurative usage of the term speaks of deeds that produce their own harvest (Prov 22:8; Hos 8:7; 1 Cor 9:11; Gal 6:7–8).

REBA (rē'bȧ, Heb. *reva'*). One of the five chieftains of Midian killed by Israel at the command of Moses (Num 31:8; Josh 13:21).

REBEKAH, REBECCA (rĕ-bĕk'ȧ, Heb. *rivqâh*, Gr. *Rhebekka*). The daughter of Bethuel. Her mother's name is unrecorded. Her grandparents were Nahor and Milcah. She was the sister of Laban, the wife of Isaac, mother of Esau and Jacob, and first is mentioned in the genealogy of Nahor, the brother of Abraham (Gen 22:20–24).

It is in Haran, "the city of Nahor," where we are first introduced to Rebekah (Gen 24). In that incident Eliezer, the servant of Abraham, was sent out to seek a bride for Isaac. After listening to the urgings of the servant, Rebekah decided to marry Isaac. In this narrative the delineation of her character is winsome and attractive. In the narrative that follows, however, she is not only ambitious but grasping and rapacious. Rebekah was loved by Isaac (24:67), but she bore him no children for twenty years. It was only after special intercession on the part of Isaac that God gave her twins—Esau and Jacob. Esau was reckoned as the firstborn. However, God told Rebekah, "The older will serve the younger" (25:23). Whether she was directly influenced by this statement or not, Jacob became her favorite. This led her to perpetrate a cruel ruse on the aged and blind Isaac. Disguised as his brother Esau, Jacob obtained the blessing (27:5–17). When it became evident that Jacob and Esau could no longer live under the same roof, at her suggestion, Jacob fled from home to her relatives in Aram (27:42–46). Rebekah never saw her son again. Outside of Genesis there is only one reference to her (Rom 9:10–12).

RECAB (rē'kăb, Heb. *rēkhāv, horseman*). 1. One of the assassins of Ish-Bosheth, a son of Saul. He and his brother Baanah entered the home of Ish-Bosheth while he was taking a rest at noon and killed him in his own bed. They then decapitated him and carried his head to David expecting to receive a reward, as the murder of Ish-Bosheth left David without a rival on the throne of Israel. However, the reaction of the king was quite different from what they had anticipated: he commanded them both to be executed (2 Sam

4:5–11). They were Benjamites from Beeroth (4:5).

2. An early ancestor of the Kenite clan, which later became identified with the tribe of Judah (1 Chron 2:55). Recab was the founder of the order of the Recabites. It was Jehonadab, a son of Recab, who rode with Jehu on the penal mission against the house of Ahab (2 Kings 10:15ff.). Jeremiah used the example of the Recabites and their obedience to their father to drink no wine as a method of sharply berating the nation for their lack of obedience to God (Jer 35:1–19). The Recabites, though thirsty, had refused to partake of the wine rather than break faith; the Israelites, though partakers of the divine blessings, had indeed broken the covenant (35:12–16).

RECAH, RECA (rē'kȧ, Heb. *rēchâh*). An unknown place in the tribe of Judah (1 Chron 4:12).

RECONCILIATION (rĕk'ŏn-sĭl-ĭ-ā'shŭn, Gr. *katallagē*). Reconciliation is a change of relationship between God and man based on the changed status of man through the redemptive work of Christ. Three aspects of this change are suggested by three words used for it in the NT.

1. A reconciliation of *persons* between whom there has existed a state of enmity. The Greek *katallassō* denotes an "exchange" which, when applied to persons, suggests an exchange from enmity to fellowship. Reconciliation is, therefore, God's exercise of grace toward man who is in enmity because of sin, establishing in Christ's redemptive work the basis of this changed relationship of persons (2 Cor 5:19). That this reconciliation is the burden of God is shown by Romans 5:10 where it is suggested that even while we were enemies, God reconciled *us* to himself through the death of his son.

This changed relationship, however, is possible only because of the changed status of man, not of God. God is never said to be reconciled to man, but man to God, since it is man's sinfulness that creates the enmity (Rom 8:7; Col 1:21). This enmity precipitates God's wrath (Eph 2:3, 5) and judgment (2 Cor 5:10), which is allayed only through the reconciliation brought about through the death of Christ (Rom 5:10), who knew no sin but became sin for us that we might receive his righteousness as the basis of reconciliation.

2. A reconciliation of *condition* so that all basis of the enmity relationship is removed and a complete basis of fellowship is established (2 Cor 5:18–20; Eph 2:16). *Apokatallassō* denotes a "movement out of" and suggests that since man is redeemed through the righteousness of Christ he is redeemed out of his condition of unrighteousness and thus reconciled to God in this new relationship. The grace of God assures the reconciled person that the grace basis replaces the sin basis and that he or she is established before God in a new relationship.

3. A reconciliation arising out of the change in man *induced by the action of God*. *Katallagē* suggests that man is not reconciled merely because his relationship has changed, but because *God* has changed him through Christ so that he can be reconciled (Rom 5:11; 11:15; 2 Cor 5:18; Eph 2:5). Reconciliation arises, therefore, out of God, through Christ, to man, so that not only may the barriers to fellowship existing in sinful person be removed, but the positive basis for fellowship may be established through the righteousness of Christ imputed to man.

The definitive basis for reconciliation rests both in what God does in annulling the effects of sin in a person so that no enmity exists and in what he does in creating a redeemed nature in that person so that there can be fellowship between God and the redeemed one. Reconciliation is always preeminently God working in man to change the basis of relationship. Yet people are (1) given the ministry of reconciliation (2 Cor 5:18) and (2) invited to be reconciled to God (5:20). From his position of being reconciled, as accomplished as fact, man is to turn to God to respond to the new relationship in faith and obedience.

Even though the sufficient ground of reconciliation is established in the completed redemptive work of Christ, reconciliation is the basis on which the continued fellowship is established, "For if, when we were God's enemies, we were reconciled to him through the death of his Son, how much more, having been reconciled, shall we be saved through his life!" (Rom 5:10). CBB

RECORDER (See OCCUPATIONS AND PROFESSIONS)

RED (Heb. *ādhōm*, Gr. *erythos*). The Hebrew word is a derivative of *dam* signifying "blood"; hence, a bloodlike or a blood-red color. The adjective "red" is applied to the following items: (1) the dyed ram skins that formed the outward covering for the tabernacle (Exod 25:5; 26:14; 35:7), (2) the color of certain animals (Num 19:2; Zech 1:8; 6:2; Rev 6:4; 12:3), (3) the color of the human skin (Gen 25:25; 1 Sam 16:12), (4) redness of eyes (Gen 49:12; Prov 23:29), (5) certain sores (Num 12:10), (6) wine (Prov 23:31; Isa 27:2 AV), (7) water (2 Kings 3:22), (8) pavement (Esth 1:6), (9) the color of sin (Isa 1:18), (10) the shields of the foe advancing against the city of Nineveh (Nah 2:3) and (11) the Red Sea (Acts 7:36; Heb 11:29). See also RED SEA.

REDEEMER (See REDEMPTION)

REDEMPTION (Heb. *ge'ullâh*, Gr. *lytrōsis*, *apolytrōsis*). A metaphor used in both OT and NT to describe God's merciful and costly action on behalf of his people (sinful human beings). The basic meaning of the word is release or freedom on payment of a price, deliverance by a costly method. When used of God it does not suggest that he paid a price to anyone, but rather that his mercy required his almighty power and involved the greatest possible depth of suffering. Thus God redeemed Israel from Egypt by delivering the people from bondage and placing them in a new land (Exod 6:6; 15:13; Ps 77:14–15), and he did this by his "mighty hand."

Two virtually synonymous verbs are used in the OT doctrine of redemption: *gā'al,* usually translated "to redeem," and *pādhāh,* usually translated "to ransom." The basic meaning of the former is fixed in the secular example of Boaz and Ruth. In a word, Naomi and Ruth were in need, and it was the right of the next-of-kin to take their needs on himself. The dramatic tension in the Book of Ruth centers on the desire of Boaz to play the part of the *gō'el* (a participle of the verb *gā'al,* "one who acts as redeemer"), and Ruth's wish that he should do so (see RUTH, BOOK OF). Ruth 4:4 uses the verb *qānāh,* "to acquire by purchase," as a parallel to *gā'al,* showing how the price-paying concept lies at the heart of redemption. When the *gā'al/gō'el* word group is used of the Lord, it is pervasively of the Exodus (cf. Exod 6:6; 15:3; Isa 43:1ff.; 51:10–11; Ps 77:15ff.). The Exodus was itself an act of redemption (e.g., Ps 74:2; 106:10) and a model for such acts, as well as the basis on which appeal is made to the Lord to redeem (Isa 43:14–16; 48:20; 63:16; Jer 31:11). Isaiah 43:3 brings to the fore the price-paying concept: at the Exodus the Lord redeemed Israel at the expense of Egypt. Since it was a case either that Israel perish at Egypt's hand or that Egypt perish in order that Israel go free, the Lord did not hesitate, nor, says Isaiah, would he ever hesitate to pay whatever price Israel's redemption demanded: *at all costs* he will redeem a people for himself.

The verb *pādhāh* is virtually synonymous. In its secular use it is entirely given over to express ransom-price (e.g., Lev 27:27; Num 18:15–17; Ps 49:7). When it is used of the Lord's ransoming work, thirteen out of the thirty-nine references allude to the Exodus (e.g., Deut 9:26; 2 Sam 7:23; Neh 1:10). Three references speak specifically of the forgiveness of sins (Deut 21:8; Ps 130:8; Isa 1:27). Insofar, then, as the two verbs cover the same area of meaning, it is that redemption demands the payment of an equivalent price; insofar as they differ, *pādhāh* concentrates on price and payment, while *gā'al* also points with emphasis to the person of the redeemer as the closest of kin.

To appreciate the NT theme of redemption, the position of human beings as slaves of sin must be assumed (John 8:33–34). Thus they must be set free in order to become the liberated servants of the Lord. "For even the Son of Man did not come to be served, but to serve, and to give his life as a ransom for many" (Mark 10:45). Here again the use of the metaphor of ransom does not require that the question, "To whom was the ransom paid?" be answered. The emphasis is on costly sacrifice, the giving of a life.

Paul wrote of "the redemption that came by Christ Jesus" (Rom 3:24) and claimed that in Christ "we have redemption through his blood" (Eph 1:7). Peter wrote that "it was not with perishable things . . . that you were redeemed . . . but with the precious blood of Christ" (1 Peter 1:18–19; cf. Heb 9:12, 15; Rev 5:9–10). This redemption paid for by the costly sacrifice of the life of Jesus is a completed act as far as God is concerned. But the results of the redemption as far as we are concerned are experienced in part now and in full at the beginning of the new age, following the Last Judgment. There is real freedom from the guilt and power of sin now as well as a freedom to love and serve God (Gal 5:1, 13); but the final freedom from this mortal body and the principle of sin within it will only be known at the resurrection of the dead (Luke 21:27–28; Rom 8:23; Eph 4:30).

Bibliography: R. B. Girdlestone, *Old Testament Synonyms,* 1897, pp. 117–26; N. H. Snaith, *Distinctive Ideas of the Old Testament,* 1944, pp. 79ff.; A. M. Stibbs, *The Finished Work of Christ,* 1954; Leon Morris, *The Apostolic Preaching of the Cross,* 1955; John Murray, *Redemption Accomplished and Applied,* 1961; D. A. Leggett, *The Levirate and Goel Institutions in the Old Testament,* 1974. JAM and PT

RED HEIFER. The ashes of the red heifer were used for the removal of certain types of ceremonial uncleanness, such as purification of the leper, or defilement incurred through contact with the dead (Num 19:2). See also ANIMALS.

RED SEA (Heb. *yam sûph*). On the occasion of the Exodus of the Israelites from Egypt, "God did not lead them on the road through the Philistine country, though that was shorter. . . . God led the people around by desert road toward the Red Sea" (Exod 13:17–18). With Rameses as their point of departure (12:37), the nation of liberated slaves marched across the eastern boundaries of the land of Goshen toward a body of water, traditionally translated the "Red Sea." The site of Israel's encampment, however, previous to their crossing, is recorded as Pi Hahiroth, between Migdol and the Sea. Hence, Israel took a southeasterly course to Succoth, about thirty-two miles (fifty-three km.) away, and from there a road to Sinai, which they most easily followed. Often the target of critics, the route of the Exodus has now been fairly well established, since a long series of Egyptian fortifications along the route has actually been described by Pharaoh Seti I in his Karnak inscriptions in Upper Egypt. The "store chambers" of which the biblical record speaks were actually discovered by Naville, not at Pithom, but at Succoth, about nine miles (fifteen km.) east in the Wady Tumilat.

It is now quite evident that the "Red Sea" rendering is erroneous, as *Yam Sûph* should be rendered "Reed Sea" or "Marsh Sea." It is highly improbable that the northern arm of the Red Sea (the Gulf of Suez) is meant. There are no reeds in the Red Sea. In addition, the text implies that the *Yam Sûph* formed the barrier between the land of Egypt and the desert. If the Red Sea were intended, then Israel would have been obliged to cross a far greater territory in a far shorter span of time than the account actually indicates. Near the city of Rameses-Tanis (in Goshen, where the Israelite slaves lived) there were two bodies of water, the "Waters of Horus," which is the same as Shihor (Isa 23:3; Jer 2:18), and a body of

View of the Red Sea, just south of Elath, looking west. Courtesy S. Zur Picture Library.

water that the Egyptians themselves referred to as "Suph," called also the "papyrus marsh." This last-mentioned "Sea of Reeds," or Lake Timsah, is beyond reasonable doubt the body of water crossed by the fleeing Israelites, with the Egyptians in hot pursuit. This newer identification in no way mitigates or militates against the miraculous deliverance by God, nor does it dissipate the awful judgment that overtook Pharaoh's armies.
JFG

REED (Heb. *qāneh, 'ăghammîm, 'ādhû,* Gr. *kalamos*). A reed stalk was used as a measuring rod. In Babylonia six cubits made a reed or *qāneh*. Among the Israelites a reed came to denote a fixed length of six long cubits (Ezek 40:5; 41:8). In Revelation 11:1; 21:15–16, a reed is used to measure the temple and the Holy City.

REED SEA (See RED SEA)

REELAIAH (rē'ăl-ā'yȧ, Heb. *re'ēlyâh*). One of the twelve heads of families returning with Zerubbabel after the Captivity (Ezra 2:2; Neh 7:7). Nehemiah renders the name "Raamiah," but "Reelaiah" seems to be the preferred form.

REFINER (See OCCUPATIONS AND PROFESSIONS: *Coppersmith, Craftsman, Goldsmith, Silversmith*)

REFUGE, CITIES OF (See CITIES OF REFUGE)

REGEM (rē'gĕm, Heb. *reghem*). A descendant of the house or clan of Caleb, son of Jadhai (1 Chron 2:47).

REGEM-MELECH (rēg'ĕm mĕlĕk, Heb. *reghem melekh*). One of a delegation sent to inquire of Zechariah concerning the propriety of the act of fasting (Zech 7:2).

REGENERATION (rē-jĕn-êr-ā'shun, Gr. *palingenesia*). Regeneration has as its basic idea "to be born again" or "to be restored." Though the word is actually used only twice in the NT (Matt 19:28; Titus 3:5), many synonymous passages suggest its basic meaning. Related terms are "born again" (John 3:3, 5, 7), "born of God" (1:13; 1 John 3:9), "quickened" (Eph 2:1, 5), and "renewed" (Rom 12:2; Titus 3:5).

Regeneration is, therefore, the spiritual change wrought in people's hearts by an act of God in which their inherently sinful nature is changed and by which they are enabled to respond to God in faith. This definition grows out of the nature of man's sinfulness. As long as man is in sin, he cannot believe in God. If he is to believe, he will do so only after God has initiated a change by which he may be released from the bondage of his will to sin. Regeneration is that act of God by which a person is thus released and by which he may exercise the dispositions of a freed nature.

Regeneration is, therefore, an act of God through the immediate agency of the Holy Spirit operative in man (Col 2:13), originating in him a new dimension of moral life, a resurrection to new life in Christ. This new life is not merely a neutral state arising out of forgiveness of sin, but a positive implantation of Christ's righteousness in man, by which he is quickened (John 5:21), begotten (1 John 5:1), made a new creation (2 Cor 5:17), and given a new life (Rom 6:4).

Regeneration involves an illumination of the mind, a change in the will, and a renewed nature. It extends to the total nature of man, irrevocably altering his governing disposition, and restoring him to a true experiential knowledge in Christ. It is a partaking of the divine nature (2 Peter 1:4), a principle of spiritual life having been implanted in the heart.

The efficient cause of regeneration is God (1 John 3:9) acting in love through mercy (Eph 2:4–5) to secure the new life in man through the instrument of his Word (1 Peter 1:23).

In regeneration, the soul is both passive and active: passive while it is still in bondage to sin and active when it is released. The regenerating work of the Holy Spirit is not conditioned by a prior acquiescence of the soul, but when the soul is released from sin, regenerated, it voluntarily and spontaneously turns toward God in fellowship. CBB

REHABIAH (rē'hă-bī'ă, Heb. *rehavyâh, rehavāhû, God is wide*). Son of Eliezer, and a grandson of Moses (1 Chron 23:17; 24:21; 26:25).

REHOB (rē'hōb, Heb. *rehōv, broad*). 1. The northern limit to which the spies came as they searched out the land (Num 13:21). It is mentioned in the wars of David against the Arameans (2 Sam 10:8). On the basis of 2 Samuel 10:6, 8, Rehob and Beth Rehob appear to be identical.

2. Two separate towns belonging to the tribe of Asher (Josh 19:28, 30).

3. The father of Hadadezer, king of Aram, whose capital appears to have been Zobah, which David conquered in the battle on the banks of the Euphrates (2 Sam 8:3, 12).

4. A Levite who was one of the cosigners of the covenant of Nehemiah (Neh 10:11).

REHOBOAM (rē'hō-bō'ăm, Heb. *rehav'ām*). A son of Solomon, and his successor on the throne of Israel. His mother was Naamah, an Ammonitess (1 Kings 14:21). He was born about 975 B.C. and was forty-one when he began to reign. He chose Shechem as the site of his inauguration. Solomon's wild extravagances and his vain ambition to make Israel the world power of his day led him to set up a tremendously expensive capital and a very elaborate harem. The importation of so many pagan women for his harem resulted in a spiritual debacle in Israel. The luxuries of his palace and the expenses of his diplomatic corps and of his vast building program resulted in burdensome taxation. The northern tribes turned for leadership to Jeroboam, to whom God had revealed that he was to rule ten of the tribes (11:26–40). When the coronation had been set, Jeroboam was called home from Egypt, and through him an appeal was made to Rehoboam for easier taxes. The latter, however, heeding the advice of young men, refused to heed the appeal, with the result that Israel rebelled against him. When Adoram was sent to collect the tribute, he was killed, and Rehoboam fled to Jerusalem (12:16–19). Jeroboam was then made king of the ten tribes. Rehoboam raised an army from Judah and Benjamin, but was forbidden by God to attack (12:20–24). Jeroboam then fortified Shechem and Peniel, instituted pagan rites, and waged a relentless struggle against Rehoboam (12:25–28; 14:29–30).

Rehoboam set to work to make his realm strong. Pagan high places were set up and shrines throughout the land allowed abominable practices to be observed among the people (1 Kings 14:22–24). After being dissuaded from attacking Israel, Rehoboam began to strengthen his land. He fortified Bethlehem, Gath, Lachish, Hebron, and other cities and made them ready to endure a siege by enemy forces. He gave refuge to priests and Levites whom Jeroboam had driven from Israel, and they brought wisdom and strength to his realm (2 Chron 11:5–17). The fortified cities were captured by King Shishak of Egypt. It is possible that Shishak's invasion resulted from Jeroboam's influence in Egypt, where he had fled to escape Solomon's wrath (1 Kings 11:40). Inscriptions in the temple at Karnak name 180 towns captured by Shishak, many of them in the northern kingdom.

Rehoboam seems to have inherited his father's love for luxury and show, for he gathered a substantial harem and reared a large family (2 Chron 11:18–23). He had eighteen wives and sixty concubines (thirty according to Josephus, *Antiq.* 5.8.1; 10.1). He was not content with fortifying his land but spent large sums on ornate places of worship. He made Abijah, his son, his successor.

REHOBOTH (rē-hō'bŏth, Heb. *rehōvôth, broad places*). 1. The name of a city built in Assyria by Asshur (KJV; NIV "Nimrod") (Gen 10:11 KJV; NIV "Rehoboth Ir"). The home of Saul (Shaul in 1 Chron 1:48), a king of Edom prior to the coming of a Hebrew monarch (Gen 36:31–37). Its location is not known.

2. A well dug by Isaac in the Valley of Gerar after Abimelech had driven him from the land of the Philistines (Gen 26:9–22). Ruhaibah, near Beersheba, is the probable site, its ruins with numerous cisterns cut into solid rock indicating an ancient stronghold.

REHUM (rē'hŭm, Heb. *rehûm, beloved*). 1. A Hebrew who returned from captivity with Ezra (Ezra 2:2). Called "Nehum" in Nehemiah 7:7.

2. An officer of Artaxerxes's court who helped frame a report to his king, accusing the Jews of rebelling and warning him that to permit the completion of the job of restoring Jerusalem would result in the loss of these vassal people (Ezra 4:7–24).

3. A son of Bani. He helped repair the walls of Jerusalem (Neh 3:17).

4. One who signed the covenant with God after

Israel had returned from captivity and had been so signally blessed (Neh 10:25).

5. A priest among those who returned to Palestine with Zerubbabel (Neh 12:3).

REI (rē'ī, Heb. *rē'î, friendly*). One who did not join Adonijah in rebelling against David (1 Kings 1:8).

REINS (Heb. *kilyâh,* Gr. *nephros*). A word used in the KJV to designate the inward parts. The reins (kidneys) were thought by the Israelites to be the seat of the emotions (Job 19:27; Ps 7:9; 26:2; Jer 17:10). NIV usually translates this word as "mind." See also KIDNEYS.

REKEM (rĕ'kĕm, Heb. *reqem, friendship*). 1. A king of Midian who was executed by order of the Lord (Num 31:1–8). He is called a prince in Joshua 13:21.

2. A city belonging to Benjamin (Josh 18:27), the location now unknown.

3. A son of Hebron, and the father of Shammai of the tribe of Judah (1 Chron 2:42–44).

RELIGION (Gr. *thrēskeia, outward expression of spiritual devotion*). The Latin *religare* means to hold back or restrain. It came to be applied to the services and ritual and rules by which faith in and devotion to deity were expressed. In the OT there is no word for religion. Fear (Ps 2:11; Prov 1:7) and worship (Deut 4:19; 29:26; Ps 5:7; 29:2) of God refer primarily to attitudes of the mind and acts of adoration, rather than to a ritual. *Thrēskeia* in the NT means outward expression of religion and the content of faith. James makes a distinction between the sham and the reality of religious expression (James 1:26–27). Paul was loyal to his Hebrew religion before being converted (Acts 26:1–5). *Religious* in James 1:26 (*thrēskos*) implies superstition.

REMALIAH (rĕm'ȧ-lī'ȧ, Heb. *remalyāhû, Jehovah adorns*). The father of King Pekah (2 Kings 15:25).

REMETH (rĕ'mĕth, Heb. *remeth, height*). A city in the tribe of Issachar (Josh 19:17–21); probably Ramoth of 1 Chronicles 6:73 and Jarmuth of Joshua 21:29.

REMMON (See RIMMON)

REMNANT. A translation of different Hebrew words: *yether,* "what is left" (Deut 3:11; 28:54); *she'ār,* "the remainder" (Ezra 3:8; Isa 10:20; 11:16); *she'ērîth,* "residue" (2 Kings 19:31; Isa 14:30). At first the word denoted a part of a family or clan left from slaughter, and later it came to be applied to the spiritual kernel of the nation who would survive God's judgment and become the germ of the new people of God. Thus Micah saw the returning glory of Israel (Mic 2:12; 5:7). Zephaniah saw the triumph of this remnant (Zeph 2:4–7), and so did Zechariah (Zech 8:1–8). Isaiah named a son *She'ār-Jashub,* which means "a remnant returns" (Isa 7:3).

REMON METHOAR (See RIMMON)

REMPHAN (See REPHAN)

REPENTANCE (Heb. *nāham, shûbh,* Gr. *metanoia*). The process of changing one's mind. In the KJV of the OT God himself is described as repenting (Exod 32:14; 1 Sam 15:11; Jonah 3:9–10; 4:2—using *nāham*), in the sense that he changed his attitude to a people because of a change within the people. God as perfect Deity does not change in his essential nature; but because he is in relationship with people who do change, he himself changes his relation and attitude from wrath to mercy and from blessing to judgment, as the occasion requires. His change of mind is his repentance, but there is no suggestion of change from worse to better or bad to good. In contrast, human repentance is a change for the better and is a conscious turning from evil or disobedience or sin or idolatry to the living God (2 Kings 17:13; Isa 19:22; Jer 3:12, 14, 22; Jonah 3:10—using *shûbh*).

In the NT repentance and faith are the two sides of one coin (Acts 20:21). They are a response to grace. Jesus preached the need for the Jews to repent (Matt 4:17), and required his apostles/disciples to preach repentance to Jews and Gentiles (Luke 24:47; Acts 2:38; 17:30). Repentance is a profound change of mind involving the changing of the direction of life from that of self-centeredness or sin-centeredness to God- or Christ-centeredness. God's forgiveness is available only to those who are repentant, for only they can receive it.

The positive side of repentance is conversion, the actual turning to God or Christ for grace. This is conveyed in the NT by the noun *epistrophē* (once only, in Acts 15:3) and the verb *epistrephō* (e.g., Acts 15:19; 2 Cor 3:16). The difference between *metanoia* and *epistrophē* and *metanoeō* and *epistrephō* is only one of emphasis, for a full repentance is truly a conversion. See also CONVERSION.

Bibliography: "The Biblical Doctrine of Conversion," SJT, vol. 5, 1952; E. M. B. Green, *Evangelism in the Early Church,* 1970. PT

REPHAEL (rē'fā-ĕl, Heb. *rephā'ēl, God heals*). A son of Shamaiah. He served as a tabernacle gatekeeper (1 Chron 26:7–12).

REPHAH (rē'fā, Heb. *rephah, a prop*). A grandson of Ephraim, and a resident of Bethel (1 Chron 7:23–25).

REPHAIAH (rē-fā'yȧ, Heb. *rephayah, Jehovah heals*). 1. Descendant of David (1 Chron 3:21, "Rhesa" of Luke 3:27).

2. A son of Ishi. He helped defeat the Amalekites (1 Chron 4:42–43).

3. A grandson of Issachar and head of a clan (1 Chron 7:2).

4. A descendant of Jonathan (1 Chron 9:40–43).

5. Son of Hur, a builder (Neh 3:9).

REPHAIM, VALLEY OF (rĕf'ā-ĭm, *vale of giants*). This was a fertile plain south of Jerusalem, three miles (five km.) from Bethlehem. It was a productive area (Isa 17:4–5) and thus was a prize for which the Philistines often fought. David twice defeated the Philistines in this valley (1 Chron 14:8–16).

REPHAITES, REPHAIM (rĕf'ā-īts, rĕf'ā-ĭm, Heb. *rephā'îm, mighty*). The name of a giant people, called also Rephainer (Gen 14:5; 15:20 KJV), who lived in Canaan even before the time of Abraham. They are listed among Canaanites who were to be dispossessed (15:20). They were like the Anakim in Deuteronomy 2:11, 20. Og, king of Bashan, was a descendant of the Rephaites (Josh 12:4; 13:12).

REPHAN (rē'făn). A pagan deity worshiped by the Israelites in the wilderness (Acts 7:37–50). It is probably a name for Chiun or Saturn (Amos 5:26; see NIV footnote), a view supported by the LXX.

REPHIDIM (rĕf'ĭ-dĭm, Heb. *rephîdhîm, plains*). A camping site of the Hebrews in the wilderness before they reached Sinai. There Moses struck a rock to secure water (Exod 17:1–7; 19:2). At this place also occurred the battle with the Amalekites (17:8–16). The camp of the Hebrews is supposed to have been at the present Wady Feiren. If so, it afforded ample protection against a surprise attack, its gateway into the vale being between rocky cliffs from one of which the water came. Archaeologists have found at this place evidence of a once-fertile valley in which a strong city had been built.

REPROBATE (rĕp'rō-bāt, Gr. *adokimos*). The basic idea in reprobation is that of failing "to stand the test." *Adokimos,* the negative of *dokimos* ("to approve") connotes disapproval or rejection. When applied to humanity's relation to God, it suggests moral corruption, unfitness, disqualification—all arising out of a lack of positive holiness. The KJV uses it of a reprobate [disapproved] mind (Rom 1:28) and of a sinful nature (2 Cor 13:5, 6, 7). Its other NT uses (2 Tim 3:8; Titus 1:16) bear the same disapproval quality. Human beings in sin are reprobate, disqualified, disapproved, and rejected because they cannot "stand the test" of holiness. Approval comes only in Jesus' righteousness.

REPTILE (See ANIMALS)

RESEN (rē'sĕn, Heb. *resen, fortified place*). A town founded by Nimrod (Gen 10:8–12) between Nineveh and Calah. Xenophon reports that Larissa was a strongly fortified city in this section, and this may be the Resen of Scripture.

RESERVOIR (Heb. *miqwâh, a source of water*). Because most of western Asia was subject to periodic droughts, and because of frequent sieges, cities set great store by their waterworks. Some of the reservoirs and many private cisterns were hewn into solid rock. Some provided for abundant storage (Neh 9:25). Uzziah helped his land by having many cisterns built (2 Chron 26:10). Elisha bade Israel provide many special reservoirs (ditches) near Jerusalem (2 Kings 3:12–17). It was considered wise for each home to have its own cistern (18:31). Among the most famous reservoirs of Palestine were the pools of Solomon, thirteen miles (twenty-two km.) from the city (Eccl 2:6). Water from these was conveyed to the city by aqueducts, some of which remain today.

RESHEPH (rē'shĕf, *a flame*). A descendant of Ephraim (1 Chron 7:25). Nothing else is known about him.

RESIN, GUM RESIN (See PLANTS)

REST (Heb. *nûah, menûhâh, peace, quiet,* Gr. *anapausis, katapausis*). A word of frequent occurrence in the Bible, in both Testaments. It is used of God as resting from his work (Gen 2:2), and as having his rest in the temple (1 Chron 28:2). God commanded that the seventh day was to be one of rest (Exod 16:23; 31:15) and that the land was to have its rest every seventh year (Lev 25:4). God promised rest to the Israelites in the land of Canaan (Deut 12:9). The word is sometimes used in the sense of trust and reliance (2 Chron 14:11). Christ offers rest of soul to those who come to him (Matt 11:28). Hebrews 4 says that God offers to his people a rest not enjoyed by those who died in the wilderness.

RESURRECTION (Gr. *anastasis, arising, egersis, a raising*). A return to life subsequent to death. "The Bible . . . knows nothing of an abstract immortality of the soul, as the schools speak of it," observes James Orr, "nor is its Redemption a Redemption of the soul only, but of the body as well. It is a Redemption of man in his whole complex personality—body and soul together" (p. 196). This distinctive fact has been noted by many other competent exegetes and commentators. To deny the Resurrection is, in biblical thought, to deny any immortality worthy of the character of our faith in God (Matt 22:31–32; Mark 12:26–27; Luke 20:37–38). It is not that the soul does not exist in a disembodied state between death and resurrection, but in the biblical view, man in the intermediate state is incomplete and awaits "the redemption of our bodies" (Rom 8:23; cf. 2 Cor 5:3ff.; Rev 6:9–11).

In the OT the most explicit passage on the resurrection is Daniel 12:2, which clearly predicts the resurrection and eternal judgment of those who have died. Almost equally explicit is Isaiah 26:19. In its context, this verse is parallel to verses 11–15. In them the voice of God's people is heard, repeating his promises and looking forward to their fulfillment; in verse 19 the voice of the Lord responds, affirming the hope that lies before his distressed people, confirming the conviction that they will rise again. The reference to "dew" is added by way of explanation: dew had a wide metaphorical use, picturing the heavenly contribution to earthly well-being. The dead wait in the dust until God's life-giving, reviving dew falls on them and brings them to life. Again, Isaiah 25:8 is explicit in its affirmation that in the Lord's Day, even death itself will disappear to be seen no more. The meaning of Job 19:23–27 is much disputed and the Hebrew text is not at all easy to translate, yet a case can undoubtedly be made out for an interpretative translation along the following lines: "Though, after my skin (i.e., my present life, wasting away with disease), they destroy this (body), yet from (the vantage point of) my flesh I shall see God."

In the providence of God, revelation is a matter of progress rather than full clarity all at once. The Lord educated his people from truth to truth, as any careful teacher does. Each age was given sufficient light for its own needs so as to enjoy spiritual life and fellowship with God. The full revelation of immortality awaited the advent of our Lord and Savior who "brought life and immortality to light through the gospel" (2 Tim 1:10).

In the NT the word *anastasis,* "resurrection," signifies the arising to life of dead bodies, or a dead body. There is one possible exception, Luke 2:34, though probably "resurrection" is the meaning here, too. In secular Greek the word may refer to any act of rising up or sitting up; but the theological interpretation of the word in the NT does not depend only on its literal meaning but on the contexts in which it is found.

The doctrine of resurrection is stated clearly in its simplest form in Paul's words before the Roman law court presided over by Felix: "There will be a resurrection of both the righteous and the wicked" (Acts 24:15). The most detailed statement of the doctrine of twofold resurrection is found in Revelation 20:4–15.

In the words of Jesus, the only clear allusion to a twofold resurrection is found in John 5:25, 28–29. It must be remembered that John shares the cosmic perspective from which the eschatological complex began with the Incarnation (see 1 John 2:18). In John 5:25 Jesus refers to the fact that he "now" exercises his power to raise the dead selectively, "those who hear will live." (Compare the resurrection of Lazarus, John 11, and of the son of the widow of Nain, Luke 7:11–17, as well as Matt 27:50–53). John 5:28–29 refers to the future and alludes to the distinction made in Daniel 12:2, which John develops in Revelation 20:4–15.

Some see in 1 Thessalonians 4:16–17 an implication that the dead who are not "in Christ" will not be raised at the same time as the redeemed. This is possibly also the implication of 1 Corinthians 15:20–28. John 5:28–29 bases the resurrection of the dead firmly on the power of Christ as exhibited in his own resurrection (see RESURRECTION OF JESUS CHRIST), and state the substance of the later pronouncement before Felix (Acts 24:15). By the power of Christ all the dead will be raised.

With 1 Corinthians 15:23 Paul begins an enumeration of three "orders" of resurrection, one of which, the resurrection of Christ, is past. (1) Christ the firstfruits. (2) "Those who belong to him." This second "order" of resurrection is said to take place "when he comes." (3) "Then the end." The "end" in this context follows the resurrection of those who are Christ's. It includes the time when Christ "reigns" and subdues all his enemies. The last enemy, death itself, is to be subdued. This must be regarded as taking place when all the rest of the dead without exception stand before the Great White Throne (Rev 20:12ff.). This final subduing of death is Paul's third "order" of resurrection.

Since Paul's first "order" is the resurrection of Christ, it is obvious that Paul's second and third "orders" of resurrection coincide with John's future "first resurrection" and his resurrection of "the rest of the dead" (Rev 20:4–15).

For further discussion see ESCHATOLOGY.

Bibliography: R. Martin-Achard, *From Death to Life,* 1960; J. A. Motyer, *After Death,* 1965; W. Zimmerli, *Man and His Hope in the Old Testament,* 1971; J. Orr, *The Christian View of God and the World,* 1983. JOB and JAM

RESURRECTION OF JESUS CHRIST (Gr. *anastasis, egeirō, anistēmi*). There were no witnesses of the resurrection of Jesus of Nazareth. What the disciples witnessed was the appearance of the resurrected Jesus. They saw also the empty tomb. In fact, only disciples were witnesses of the appearances of Jesus; but both disciples and others saw the empty sepulcher.

In the NT there are six accounts of what followed the resurrection of Jesus. Each of the four Gospels contains an account (Matt 28; Mark 16; Luke 24; John 20–21), and there are two others (Acts 1:1–11; 1 Cor 15:1–11). It is not easy to provide a systematic and chronological account of the appearances of Jesus to his apostles and disciples in the forty days before his final departure, but a creditable effort has been made by John Wenham, *The Easter Enigma,* 1984.

I. The Narratives. The brief accounts of the Resurrection appearances contrast with the lengthy narratives of the passion and death of

The entrance to the Garden Tomb. The Garden Tomb is one of two different sites vying for recognition as the burial place of Jesus. Courtesy Duby Tal.

Entrance to the Garden Tomb enclosure, one of two different sites vying for recognition as the burial place of Jesus. The tomb is located some distance to the right of the bridge. See: "The Garden Tomb—Was Jesus buried here?" Biblical Archeological Review 12:2 (March/April 1986), pp. 40ff. Courtesy Duby Tal.

Jesus. The reason for this is as follows. Concerning the death of Jesus, Jews asked, "How could Jesus be the true Messiah and die on a cross when the Law of Moses teaches that to die such a death is to be under God's curse?" And Gentiles asked, "If Jesus was the true King of the Jews, why was he rejected by his own people?" Thus long accounts were necessary to provide answers. But the questions concerning the Resurrection were basically concerning proof. So the six accounts provide the testimony of eyewitnesses who claimed to have seen not only the empty tomb but also the resurrected Jesus. There was no need for lengthy descriptions.

II. Within and Beyond History. On the basis of the NT, Christians usually make two parallel claims concerning the resurrection of Jesus. First, it was a definite historical event and as such is open to historical investigation. Second, it was more than a historical event, for it involved a major dimension that is not open to historical investigation.

The evidence for the Resurrection as an event within history may be listed as follows:

1. *The tomb of Jesus was found empty some thirty-six hours after his burial.* Despite efforts by Jews to prove that the body was stolen and buried elsewhere, the body was never located or produced by those who allegedly stole it or by anyone else. Further, the suggestion that Jesus only swooned on the cross and then revived in the cool tomb is impossible to substantiate.

2. *The disciples claimed that Jesus actually appeared.* They saw Jesus when they were fully awake and when they doubted that he was alive. What they saw was neither a subjective vision (in their imagination, a kind of hallucination) nor an objective vision (provided by God to show that the true and essential *spirit* of Jesus was alive). They actually saw Jesus on earth; they were witnesses of resurrection.

3. *The sober nature of the narratives describing the Resurrection appearances.* There is no attempt to describe the Resurrection itself, and there is no obvious collusion between the various writers to doctor or adorn their material. The most amazing event in human history is described with reverential reserve.

4. *The transformation of the disciples and the existence of the church.* Men who were cowards became fearless preachers and founded the church for one reason and one alone—they believed with all their hearts that Jesus had risen from the dead and was alive forevermore. And when they preached the gospel that Jesus who was crucified now lives as Lord and Savior, they saw lives changed by that living Lord.

This century there has been a readiness within the church to discount or hold loosely to the fact of the resurrection of Jesus as an event within history. This tendency must be resisted, for if his resurrection is not an event within history (within the same physical universe and space and time in which we live), then what the NT claims that God accomplished in Jesus Christ on the cross for salvation is not applicable to us in history. The bodily resurrection of Jesus (as Paul insists in 1 Cor 15) is of fundamental importance and cannot be ignored or set aside.

As a real event in history, the Resurrection cannot, however, be wholly explained in terms of historical causation. There is both continuity and discontinuity with history. The continuity is seen in the kind of information listed above as evidence. The discontinuity is in terms of what the believing church receives and accepts concerning that Resurrection—e.g., that it is the disclosure of the kingdom of God; that it is the incursion of the new creation into the old creation; and that it is the foundation of a new humanity in Jesus, the second and last Adam. These "theological truths" are beyond historical investigation, for they are claims that can be verified only at the end of the age.

III. What Kind of Body? There were both differences and similarities in the pre- and postresurrection body of Jesus. Yet there was a basic identity so that one may speak of "identity-in-transformation." For Jesus, bodily resurrection meant resuscitation with transformation—that is, not only resuscitation (as with Lazarus in John 11), but also the metamorphosis of the body so

The Garden Tomb, the traditional site of the crucifixion, near Gordon's Calvary. "At the place where Jesus was crucified, there was a garden, and in the garden a new tomb in which no one had ever been laid" (John 19:41). Courtesy Zev Radovan.

that what was a physical and mortal body became a spiritual and immortal body, transformed by the power of God, Creator of life and bodies. Apart from isolated incidents (e.g., walking on the water), the pre-Easter Jesus was subject to material, physical, and spatial limitations. He walked from one place to another, passed through doors to enter rooms, and climbed steps to get onto the roofs of houses. Yet after his resurrection he was no longer bound by these limitations. He passed through a sealed tomb, through locked doors, and appeared and disappeared without notice. He became visible here and there and from time to time. This suggests that his true or essential state as a transformed person was that of invisibility and immateriality, with the ability to be localized at will.

IV. A Theology of Resurrection. There are various ways of stating a theology of resurrection, but perhaps that which best reflects the NT evidence is the theme of vindication.

1. *God raised Jesus from the dead and thereby vindicated him as the true Messiah.* The manner of Jesus' death gave the impression that God had rejected him, for to hang on a tree was to be under the divine curse (Deut 21:23; Gal 3:13). In resurrection, Jesus was vindicated. He was no longer implicitly claiming to be the Messiah by his teaching and deeds: he was now demonstrated to be Messiah in fact and in truth. Peter, over a year before the crucifixion, had asserted, "You are the Christ" (Matt 16:16), and fifty days after the Resurrection he told the crowd in Jerusalem: "Therefore, let all Israel be assured of this: God has made this Jesus, whom you crucified, both Lord and Christ" (Acts 2:36). Later, by means of a quotation from Psalm 118, Peter explained to the Jewish leaders the vindication of Jesus; he claimed that Jesus is "the stone you builders rejected, which has become the capstone" (Acts 4:11). Then Paul wrote that Jesus "as to his human nature was a descendant of David, and who through the Spirit of holiness was declared

Interior of the Garden Tomb, the traditional site of Christ's burial. Courtesy Ecole Biblique et Archéologique Française, Jerusalem.

with power to be the Son of God by his resurrection from the dead" (Rom 1:3–4). Jesus was always Son of God, but the Resurrection was the actual vindication of this Sonship.

2. *God raised Jesus from the dead and thereby vindicated his teaching and work of atonement.* The Resurrection is God's "Amen" to the cry of Jesus, "It is finished." The Resurrection is God's "Yes" to the ministry and teaching of Jesus. Jesus was "delivered over to death for our sins and was

raised to life for our justification" (Rom 4:25). In the light of the Resurrection Paul could "boast . . . in the cross of our Lord Jesus Christ" (Gal 6:14) because it revealed the eternal love of God for human sinners.

3. *God caused the new age to dawn in the Resurrection.* With the raising of Jesus from death and the transformation of his body, there began a new order of existence. What belongs to the future kingdom of God, the glorious age to come, has made its appearance in this present evil age. Paul deliberately spoke of the resurrected Jesus as the "firstfruits" of the harvest of the age to come (1 Cor 15:20, 23).

In the NT the theology of the Resurrection cannot be separated from the theology of the Ascension or the theology of exaltation. Often in the NT the word "resurrection" includes the idea of ascension, while the word "exaltation" takes in both resurrection and ascension.

Bibliography: Walter Kunneth, *The Theology of Resurrection,* 1965; G. E. Ladd, *I Believe in the Resurrection of Jesus,* 1975; J. M. Harris, *Raised Immortal,* 1984; John Wenham, *The Easter Enigma,* 1984. PT

RETRIBUTION. The word is not found in Scripture, but the idea is expressed in reference to the wrath of God, vengeance, punishment, and judgment when God "will give to each person according to what he has done" (Rom 2:6). The concept reminds us not to be so fully engrossed in the grace of the gospel that we overlook God's judgment on the impenitent sinner (1:18). Retribution is the natural outcome of sin (Gal 6:7–8), the thought of which was reflected in John the Baptist's warning to "flee from the coming wrath" (Matt 3:7; Luke 3:7; cf. 1 Thess 1:10). One of the NT's most terrible references is to "the wrath of the Lamb" (Rev 6:16).

REU (rē'ū, Heb. *re'û, friendship*). The son of Peleg and a fifth-generation son of Shem (Gen 11:10–19). In the KJV Peleg is called Phalec in Luke 3:35, and Reu is called Ragau.

REUBEN (rū'bĕn, Heb. *re'ûvēn*). The oldest son of Jacob, born to him by Leah in Paddan Aram (Gen 29:32). Nothing is known about his early life, except that he brought his mother mandrakes, which she used in getting Jacob to give her another son (30:14–15). Reuben committed incest at Eder (35:22). Either because of this sin or out of innate weakness (49:4) his tribe never rose to power. He delivered Joseph from death by warning his brothers against the results of such an act (37:19–22; 42:22) and later offered his sons as surety for Benjamin (42:37). He took four sons into Egypt (46:9). When Israel went from Egypt, he had 46,500 descendants (Num 1:21; 2:10). The Reubenites made a covenant with Moses in order to occupy the rich grazing lands of Gilead (32:1–33). That they kept the covenant is attested by the monument to Bohan, a descendant of Reuben (Josh 15:6). When the other tribes were settled in Canaan,

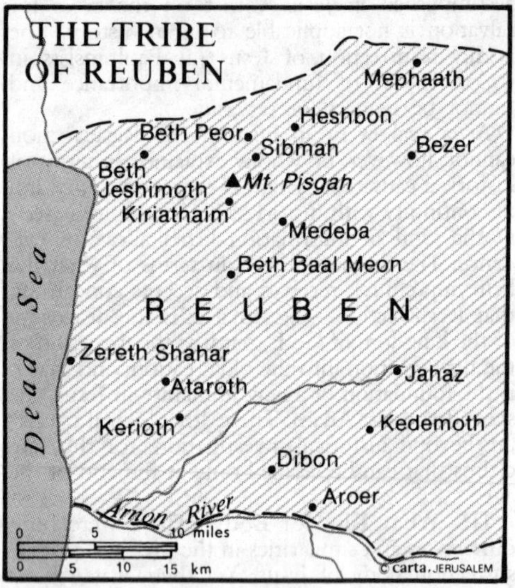

Reuben, Gad, and half of Manasseh returned to Gilead and set up a great monument as a reminder of the unity of the Israelites (Josh 22). In protecting their flocks against marauding nomads they became a bold and skilled warlike people (1 Chron 5:1–19). Along with Gad and the half-tribe of Manasseh, they sent 120,000 men to support King David (12:37). They were oppressed during Jehu's reign (2 Kings 10:32–33). They were taken into captivity by Tiglath-Pileser of Assyria (1 Chron 5:25–26).

REUBENITES (rū'bĕn-īts). Descendants of Reuben, son of Jacob. When Moses took the census in Midian, Reuben numbered 43,730 men of military age (Num 26:1–7). They were joint possessors of Gilead and Bashan (Deut 3:12; 29:8), and were praised by Moses for their fidelity (Josh 22:1–6). They supported David against the Philistines (1 Chron 11:42; 12:37). Tiglath-Pileser took them into the Assyrian captivity.

REUEL (rū'ĕl, Heb. *re'û'ēl, God is friend*). 1. A son of Esau by Basemath (Gen 36:4, 10).

2. A priest in Midian who gave Moses a daughter as wife (Exod 2:16–22), probably the same as Jethro (3:1).

3. The father of Eliasaph in the KJV of Numbers 2:14. Called Deuel in Numbers 1:14; 7:42. NIV retains Deuel in Numbers 2:14.

4. A Benjamite (1 Chron 9:8).

REUMAH (rū'mȧ). A concubine of Nahor who was a brother of Abraham (Gen 22:20–24).

REVELATION. A theme central to the idea of Christianity, it may be studied in two ways. First, it may be used as a summary or umbrella word and as a theological concept to refer to the trustworthy account of God's self-revelation in word and deed contained in the Scriptures. To call the Bible the Word of God is to claim that it is the unique and faithful statement of God's self-revelation to mankind. When used in this way, it usually is supplemented by the concept of *inspiration* (the work of the Holy Spirit in guiding the writers of the Bible to put down what God wanted them to write), and by *illumination* (the work of the Holy Spirit on the hearts and minds of readers and hearers of the contents of the Bible). The equation of the Bible with revelation derives from such texts as John 10:34–35; 2 Timothy 3:15–16; Hebrews 3:7–11; 2 Peter 1:19–21. Second, revelation may be studied as an actual theme within the Bible by noticing how the cluster of words that convey the idea of God's self-disclosure in word and deed are used. This article will deal with the latter theme.

In the NT such words as the verbs *apokalyptō, phaneroō, epiphainō,* and *chrēmatizō,* and the nouns *apokalypsis, phanerōsis, epiphaneia,* and *chrēmatismos,* together with related words, convey the whole spectrum of ways and means through which God discloses himself, his will, and his purposes to his people. And God reveals himself in order that his people might know, love, trust, serve, and obey him as Lord.

At the center of God's self-unveiling or revelation is Jesus, the Messiah and Incarnate Son. In the past God spoke to the patriarchs and prophets in many and varied ways, but his complete and final word is given in and through Jesus, the Logos (John 1:1; Heb 1:1). The presence, words, deeds, and exaltation of Jesus constitute revelation. He is the Light for revelation (*apokalypsis*) to the Gentiles (Luke 2:32), and it is he who reveals (*apokalyptō*) the Father to the disciples (Matt 11:27). The Incarnate Son is the embodiment of revelation: "The grace of God that brings salvation has appeared (*epihainō*) to all men" (Titus 2:11); and with the Incarnation "the kindness and love of God our Savior appeared" (*epiphainō*) for men to see (Titus 3:4).

Before the ascension of Jesus the apostles were the recipients of revelation, even though their hearts and minds were not always open or able to receive it. After the sending of the Holy Spirit, who came from the Father through the exalted, Incarnate Son, and who came to represent the Son within the apostolic group and within the church they created, the apostles were very conscious of having witnessed revelation in and by Jesus before his ascension, and of receiving revelation from the exalted Jesus through the Spirit since Pentecost. In fact, the Spirit shared with them the mind of the exalted Christ so that they were able to see his ministry, death, resurrection, and exaltation in the way in which he, as Messiah, saw them (John 14:26; 15:26; 16:13). Thus to hear them preach the Good News was the same as hearing Jesus himself proclaim the kingdom of God (Matt 10:40; Luke 10:16; John 12:44). Paul was conscious that Christ was working and speaking through him (Rom 15:18; 2 Cor 13:3). Therefore what the apostles preached and taught, and what eventually they wrote in the books of the NT, constitutes God's revelation given to and through them. In fact they refer to the receiving of revelation not only in terms of the central realities of the faith, but also in the form of personal instructions and guidance for their own lives and ministry (e.g., 2 Cor 12:1–10; Gal 2:2).

Christ revealed God in ancient Galilee and Judea, and Christ will reveal God when he returns to earth to judge the living and the dead. The last book of the Bible, which tells of the last days, is called Revelation (*apocalypsis*). Paul taught that Christians should look for the glorious appearing (*epiphaneia*) of their Savior (2 Thess 2:8; 1 Tim 6:14; 2 Tim 4:1).

Bibliography: G. C. Berkouwer, *General Revelation,* 1955; G. Moran, *Theology of Revelation,* 1967; L. L. Morris, *I Believe in Revelation,* 1976; W. Mundle, NIDNTT, 3:309ff.

REVELATION, BOOK OF THE (Gr. *apokalypsis, an unveiling*). Sometimes called *The Apocalypse.* This is the last book of the Bible and the only book of the NT that is exclusively prophetic in character. It belongs to the class of apocalyptic literature in which the divine message is conveyed by visions and dreams. The title that the book itself assumes (Rev 1:1) may mean either "the revelation that Christ possesses and imparts," or "the unveiling of the person of Christ." Grammatically, the former is preferable, for this text states that God gave this disclosure to Christ that he might impart it to his servants.

I. The Author. Unlike many apocalyptic books that are either anonymous or published under a false name, Revelation is ascribed to John, evidently a well-known person among the churches of Asia Minor. He identified himself as a brother of those who were suffering persecution (Rev 1:9).

The earliest definite historical reference to this Apocalypse appears in the works of Justin Martyr (c. A.D. 135), who, in alluding to the twentieth chapter, said that John, one of the apostles of Christ, prophesied that those who believed in Christ would dwell in Jerusalem a thousand years. Irenaeus (180) quoted Revelation five times and named John as the author. Clement of Alexandria (c. 200) received the book as authentic Scripture, and the Muratorian Fragment (c. 170) lists it as a part of the accepted canon by the end of the second century.

Its relation to John, the son of Zebedee, was questioned by Dionysius of Alexandria (A.D. 231–265) on the grounds that the writer unhesitatingly declared his name, whereas the author of the Fourth Gospel did not do so, and that the vocabulary and style were utterly different from John's Gospel and Letters. He admitted that the Apocalypse was undoubtedly written by a man called John, but not by the beloved disciple. Eusebius, who quotes Dionysius at length, mentions both in the quotation and in a discussion of his own that there were hints of two Johns in Ephesus, and intimates that one wrote the Gospel, and the other wrote Revelation. This view is not generally supported by the church fathers, nor does the internal evidence make it necessary. The second "John" is a shadowy figure and cannot be identified with any of the known disciples of Jesus mentioned in the Gospels. The so-called grammatical mistakes are chiefly unidiomatic translations of Hebrew or Aramaic expressions, which would be impossible to render literally into Greek. The very nature of the visions made smooth writing difficult, for the seer was attempting to describe the indescribable. There are some positive likenesses to the accepted writings of John, such as the application of the term "Word of God" to Christ (Rev 19:13), the reference to the "water of life" (22:17), and the concept of the "Lamb" (5:6). It is possible that John had the aid of a secretary in writing the Gospel and his Letters, but that he was forced to transcribe immediately the visions without the opportunity to reflect on them or to polish his expression.

II. Date and Place. There are two prevailing views regarding the date of the Apocalypse. The earlier date in the reign of Nero is favored by some because of the allusion to the temple in Revelation 11:1–2, which obviously refers to an early structure. Had the Apocalypse been written after A.D. 70, the temple in Jerusalem would not have been standing. The number 666 in Revelation 13:18 has also been applied to Nero, for the total numerical value of the consonants of his name, if spelled NERON KESAR, will add up to 666 exactly. In chapter 18 the allusion to the five kings that are fallen, one existing, and one yet to come, could refer to the fact that five emperors—Augustus, Tiberius, Caligula, Claudius, and Nero—had already passed away; another, perhaps Galba, was reigning, and would be followed shortly by still another (17:9–11). By this reasoning the Revelation would have occurred at the end of Nero's reign, when his mysterious suicide had given rise to the belief that he had merely quit the empire to join the Parthians, with whom he would come to resume his throne later.

A second view, better substantiated by the early interpreters of the book, places it in the reign of Domitian (A.D. 81–96), almost at the close of the first century. Irenaeus (c. 180), Victorinus (c. 270), Eusebius (c. 328), and Jerome (c. 370) all agree on this date. It allows time for the decline that is presupposed by the letters to the churches, and it fits better with the historical conditions of the Roman Empire depicted in the symbolism.

The place of writing was the island of Patmos, where John had been exiled for his faith. Patmos was the site of a penal colony, where political prisoners were condemned to hard labor in the mines.

III. Destination. Revelation was addressed to seven churches of the Roman province of Asia, which occupied the western third of what is now Turkey. The cities where these churches were located were on the main roads running north and south, so that a messenger carrying these letters could move in a direct circuit from one to the other. There were other churches in Asia at the time when Revelation was written, but these seven seem to have been selected because they were representative of various types of need and of Christian experience. They have been interpreted (1) as representing successive periods in the life of the church or (2) as seven aspects of the total character of the church. Undoubtedly they were actual historical groups known to the author.

IV. Occasion. Revelation was written for the express purpose of declaring "what must soon take place" (Rev 1:1), in order that the evils in the churches might be corrected and that they might be prepared for the events that were about to confront them. The moral and social conditions of the empire were deteriorating, and Christians had already begun to feel the increasing pressure of paganism and the threat of persecution. The Book of Revelation provided a new perspective on history by showing that the kingdom of Christ was eternal, and that it would ultimately be victorious over the kingdoms of the world.

V. Methods of Interpretation. There are four main schools of interpretation. The *preterist* holds that Revelation is simply a picture of the conditions prevalent in the Roman Empire in the late first century, cast in the form of vision and prophecy to conceal its meaning from hostile pagans. The *historical* view contends that the book represents in symbolic form the entire course of church history from the time of its writing to the final consummation, and that the mystical figures and actions described in it can be identified with human events in history. The *futurist,* on the basis of the threefold division given in Revelation 1:19, suggests that "what you have seen" refers to the immediate environment of the seer and the vision of Christ (1:9–19), "what is now" denotes the churches of Asia or the church age they symbolize (2:1–3:22), and "what will take place later" relates to those events that will attend the return of Christ and the establishment of the city of God. The *idealist* or *symbolic* school treats Revelation as purely a dramatic picture of the conflict of good and evil, which persists in every age but which cannot be applied exclusively to any particular historical period.

Structure and Content. Revelation contains four great visions, each of which is introduced by the phrase "in the Spirit" (Rev 1:10; 4:2; 17:3; 21:10). Each of these visions locates the seer in a different place, each contains a distinctive picture of Christ, and each advances the action significantly toward its goal. The first vision (1:9–3:22) pictures Christ as the critic of the churches, who commends their virtues and condemns their vices in the light of his virtues. The second vision (4:1–16:21) deals with the progressive series of seals, trumpets, and bowls, which mark the judgment of God on a world dominated by evil. The third vision (17:21–1:8) depicts the overthrow of evil society, religion, and government in the destruction of Babylon and the defeat of the beast and his armies by this victorious Christ. The last vision (21:9–22:5) is the establishment of the city of God, the eternal destiny of his people. The book closes with an exhortation to readiness for the return of Christ.

Outline:

I. Introduction: The Return of Christ (1:1–8)
II. Christ, the Critic of the Churches (1:9–3:22)
III. Christ, the Controller of Destiny (4:1–16:21)
IV. Christ, the Conqueror of Evil (17:1–21:8)
V. Christ, the Consummator of Hope (21:9–22:5)
VI. Epilogue: Appeal and Invitation (22:6–21)

Bibliography: H. B. Swete, *The Apocalypse of St. John,* 1906 (on the Greek text); G. B. Caird, *The Revelation of St. John the Divine* (HNTC), 1966; I. T. Beckwith, *The Apocalypse of John,* 1967 (1919) (on the Greek text); G. E. Ladd, *A Commentary on the Revelation of John,* 1972; G. R. Beasley-Murray, *The Book of Revelation* (NCB), 1974; R. H. Mounce, *The Book of Revelation* (NIC), 1977. MCT

REVELING, REVELLINGS (Gr. *kōmos, orgy*). Any extreme intemperance and lustful indulgence, usually accompanying pagan worship. Paul lists it with murder as barring the way into the kingdom of God (Gal 5:21), and Peter denounces it (1 Peter 4:3). *Kōmos* occurs a third time (Rom 13:13, rioting KJV; orgies NIV). NIV translates another Greek word this way in 2 Peter 2:13.

REVILE (Heb. *qālal,* Gr. *antiloidoreō, blasphēmeō, loidoreō, oneidizō*). A word meaning "to address with abusive or insulting language," "to reproach." Israelites were forbidden to revile their parents on pain of death (Exod 21:17 KJV; NIV "curses"). Israel was reviled by Moab and Ammon (Zeph 2:8 KJV; NIV "taunts"). Jesus endured reviling on the cross (Mark 15:32 KJV). Revilers will have no part in the kingdom of God (1 Cor 6:10 KJV). The NIV uses the word when speaking of those who insult or blaspheme God (Ps 10:13; 44:16; 74:10, 18).

REVISED VERSIONS (See BIBLE, ENGLISH VERSIONS)

REWARD. A word representing at least a dozen different Hebrew and Greek words with similar meanings. In modern English the word means something given in recognition of a good act. In the ERV, however, it generally refers to something given, whether for a good or a bad act (Ps 91:8; Jer 40:5; Mic 7:3; 1 Tim 5:18). The rich meaning of the reward of faith as it is promised throughout Scripture can be seen in the beginning of the covenant of grace when God said to Abram: "I am your . . . very great reward" (Gen 15:1), and in the final chapter of Revelation, when Jesus says, "Behold, I am coming soon! My reward is with me, and I will give to everyone according to what he has done" (Rev 22:12).

REZEPH (rē'zĕf, Heb. *retseph, stronghold*). An important caravan center in ancient times. It was ravaged by Assyria during Hezekiah's reign (2 Kings 19:8–12; Isa 37:12). It may be the modern Rusafah, a few miles west of the Euphrates River.

REZIA (See RIZIA)

REZIN (rē'zĭn, Heb. *retsîn*). 1. The last king of Syria to reign in Damascus. He was used to chasten Judah (2 Kings 15:37). He recaptured Syrian cities from Judah (16:6). The siege that he and Pekah, the king of Israel, undertook against Jerusalem led Isaiah to assure Judah by issuing the prophecy about the virgin birth of the Messiah (Isa 7:4–16). To escape Rezin, Ahaz king of Judah made an alliance with Tiglath-Pileser, who invaded Israel, captured Damascus, killed Rezin, and carried the Syrians into captivity (2 Kings 16:9). Tiglath left many records of his conquests, some of which show Rezin (Rasuni in the tablets) to have been an important ruler. One tablet contains an account of his death, but it was lost after the English scholar Sir Henry Rawlinson had read it. After Rezin's death Syria never recovered her prestige.

2. The founder of a family of temple servants (KJV Nethinim) who are mentioned in Ezra 2:43–48.

REZON (rē'zŏn, Heb. *rezôn, nobleman*). A citizen of Zobah, a small country NW of Damascus. Evidently a rebel, he took advantage of an invasion of Zobah by David and led a band of guerrillas to Damascus where he made himself king. Hadadezer, the rightful king, was overthrown by David, and Rezon met little opposition (1 Kings 11:23–25). He must have been a wise ruler, for Syria soon became a strong nation. He made an alliance with Hadad of Edom and began to harass Israel whom he hated (11:25). He is almost certainly the same as Hezion mentioned in 1 Kings 15:18, though Hezion could have been his son. In either case, he founded a dynasty of strong Syrian rulers, among them the noted Ben-Hadad I and his son Ben-Hadad II.

RHEGIUM (rē'jĭ-ŭm, Gr. *Rhēgion*). A Greek colony on the toe of Italy, founded in 712 B.C.; modern Reggio. Opposite Messana in Sicily, where the strait is only six miles (ten km.) wide, Rhegium was an important strategic point. As such it was the special object of Rome's care, and in consequence a loyal ally. The port was also a haven in extremely difficult water. The captain of the ship Paul was on, having tacked widely to make Rhegium, waited in the protection of the port for a favorable southerly wind to drive his ship through the currents of the strait on the course to Puteoli (Acts 28:13).

RHESA (rē'sȧ, Gr. *Rhēsa*). A son of Zerubbabel, hence a descendant of Solomon (Luke 3:27).

RHODA (rō'dȧ, Gr. *Rhodē, rose*). The name of the girl who answered the door in the very human

Lindus (Gr. Lindos), on the eastern coast, was one of the three city-states of ancient Rhodes before their union (408 B.C.). Excavated remains include the Doric temple of Athena Lindia on the acropolis and stoa (colonnade) of the fourth century B.C. Rhodes, an island off the SW coast of Asia Minor, is mentioned in Acts 21:2. Courtesy Gerald Nowotny.

narrative of Acts 12:13. She was a servant, probably a slave of Mary, John Mark's mother.

RHODES (rōdz, Gr. *Rhodos, rose*). A large island off the mainland of Caria, some 420 square miles (1,077 sq. km.) in extent. Three city-states originally shared the island, but after internal tension and conflict with Athens, which lasted from 411 to 407 B.C., a federal capital with the same name as the island was founded. Rhodes controlled a rich carrying trade, and after the opening of the east by Alexander, became the richest of all Greek communities. It was able to maintain its independence under the Diadochi, or "Successors," of Alexander. Rhodes, over this period, became a center of exchange and capital and successfully policed the seas. Coming to terms with the rising power of Rome, Rhodes cooperated with the Republic against Philip V of Macedon, and Antiochus of Syria (201–197). In the third Macedonian war Rhodes adopted a less helpful attitude, and in spite of the protest of Cato, preserved in one of the earliest samples of Latin oratory, the state was punished by economic reprisals. Rome in fact was seeking an excuse to cripple a rival to her growing eastern trade. The amputation of Rhodes's Carian and Lycian dependents, and the declaration of Delos as a free port ruined the community (166 B.C.) . Loyalty to Rome in the war with Mithridates won back some of the mainland possessions, but Rhodes's glory was past; and when Paul stopped on his way from Troas to Caesarea (Acts 21:1), Rhodes was only a station on the trade routes, a free city, but little more than a provincial town. Rhodes was the center of a sun cult, the famous colossus being a statue of Helios. See also RODANIM. EMB

Mandrakion Harbor at Rhodes, site of the famous colossal statue of Helios, 100 feet (30 m.) or more in height. The bronze statue, erected c. 290 B.C., was toppled during a severe earthquake and never rebuilt. It has been immortalized as one of the Seven Wonders of the World. Courtesy Gerald Nowotny.

RIBAI (rī'bī). A Benjamite of Gibeah, father of Ithai (2 Sam 23:29), a mighty man (1 Chron 11:26, 31).

RIBLAH (rĭb'lȧ, Heb. *rivlâh*). The city at the

head waters of the Orontes River was a stronghold for both Egyptians and Assyrians. Copious water ran from its springs; fertile lands, east and west, and timber lands in nearby Lebanon made it a coveted prize of war. When Pharaoh Neco captured Jerusalem about 600 B.C. he took King Jehoahaz, put Judah under tribute to Egypt, and led the king to Egypt, where he died (2 Kings 23:31–34). A few years later, Nebuchadnezzar, then at war with Egypt, captured Jeremiah and took King Zedekiah to Riblah as a captive. There Zedekiah's sons were killed before him, his eyes were put out, and he was taken in chains to Babylon (25:6–7). Nebuchadnezzar then destroyed Jerusalem, and the chief priests and temple guards were led to Riblah, where, before the Jews were taken into captivity, they were executed (25:21). Riblah was on the east side of Ain, probably near Mount Hermon (Num 34:11).

RICHES (See WEALTH)

RIDDLE (Heb. *hîdhâh,* from a root meaning *to bend* or *twist*, hence any artifice in speech, *a hidden saying, a proverb*). This form of language has long been used. The queen of Sheba propounded to Solomon "hard questions," or riddles (1 Kings 10:1; 2 Chron 9:1). A classic example of the riddle is that propounded by Samson to entrap his enemies (Judg 14:14), as is his noted retort to the Philistines (14:18). Solomon became famous as an author of proverbs and riddles (1 Kings 4:32); Ezekiel was told to speak a riddle to Israel (Ezek 17:2). To know dark sayings is a mark of wisdom (Prov 1:6). Riddle also refers to words of indefinite meaning (Num 12:8; Ps 49:4; Dan 5:12). One NT riddle appears in Revelation 13:18; it has been suggested that "through a glass darkly" in another (1 Cor 13:12 KJV) be translated "by means of an enigmatic word."

RIGHTEOUSNESS (Heb. *sadîq, saddîq,* Gr. *dikaiosynē*). The Lord God always acts in righteousness (Ps 89:4; Jer 9:24). That is, he always has a right relationship with people, and his action is to maintain that relationship. As regards Israel, God's righteousness involved treating the people according to the terms of the covenant that he had graciously made with them. This involved acting both in judgment (chastisement) and in deliverance (Ps 68; 103:6; Lam 1:18). The latter activity is often therefore equated with salvation (see Isa 46:12–13; 51:5). The picture behind the word "righteousness" is from the law court (forensic). This comes to the surface in passages from the Prophets (e.g., Isa 1:2–9; Jer 2:4–13; Mic 6:1–8); there the Lord is presented as the Judge, and Israel as the accused party, with the covenant supplying the terms of reference.

As God acts in righteousness (because he is righteous), so he called Israel to be righteous as his chosen people. They were placed in his covenant, in right relationship with him through faith (Gen 15:6; Hab 2:4), and were expected to live in right relationship with others. The king as the head and representative of the people was called by God to be righteous—to be in a right relationship with God, his people, and the surrounding nations (Ps 72:1–4; 146:7–9). So we see that righteousness begins as a forensic term but easily becomes an ethical term in the OT. Much the same is found in the NT.

In the teaching of Jesus, righteousness means a right relationship with God (see the parable of the Pharisee and tax collector, Luke 18:14), as well as the quality of life that involved a right relationship both with God and one's fellow human beings (Matt 5:6, 17–20). But it is Paul who uses the word to the greatest effect in the NT with his creation of the doctrine of justification by faith (that is, being placed by God in a right relationship with himself in and through Christ by faith). His great statement is found in Romans 1:16–17. The gospel is the power of God for salvation because "a righteousness from God is revealed, a righteousness that is by faith from first to last." That is, the gospel is effective because, along with the proclamation, a righteousness goes forth—a righteousness that God delights to see and accept. This righteousness is the provision of a right relationship with himself through the saving work of Jesus, substitute and representative Man. To receive this gift of righteousness is to be justified by faith. And those who receive the gift then are to live as righteous people, devoted to the service of what God declares to be right.

Bibliography: J. A. Zeisler, *The Meaning of Righteousness in Paul,* 1970; E. P. Sanders, *Paul and Palestinian Judaism,* 1977; John Reumann, *Righteousness in the NT,* 1983. PT

RIMMON (rĭm'ŏn, Heb. *rimmôn, pomegranate*). 1. A city near Edom in the southern part of Judah's heritage (Josh 15:32). It was often associated with Ain. Nehemiah called it En Rimmon (Neh 11:29).

2. A noted rocky fortress not far from Gibeah was named Sela Rimmon, or the rock of Rimmon (Judg 20:45–47).

3. A Benjamite of the clan of the Beerothites. He had two sons who murdered Ish-Bosheth, Saul's son, and took his head to David in anticipation of receiving praise. But David, in great anger, had them killed (2 Sam 4:2–12).

4. A Syrian god was named Rimmon. After Naaman had been healed of his leprosy, he asked God's prophet for permission to accompany his king when he went to the temple of Rimmon to worship (2 Kings 5:15–19).

5. A village of Simeon's heritage. It is listed next to Ain (1 Chron 4:32).

6. A city of Zebulun's heritage. It was made a Levitical possession, going to the children of Merari (1 Chron 6:77 KJV; NIV "Rimmono").

RIMMONO (See RIMMON)

RIMMON PEREZ (rĭm'ŏn pĕ'rĕz, *Parez* in KJV). This was the fourth camp of Israel after Sinai (Num 33:16–19). Rimmon was a common place-name, due to the abundance of pomegranates (Heb. for *Rimmon*) in the Near East then. Perez ("cleft") was no doubt a valley into which entrance was made between cliffs.

RING (Heb. *tabba'ath, to sink* or *stamp,* Gr. *daktylios, pertaining to a finger*). This article of jewelry derived its name from its use as a signet. It became the symbol of authority. The pharaoh gave a *tabba'ah* to Joseph (Gen 41:42–43). King Xerxes (KJV Ahasuerus) gave one to Haman, the enemy of the Jews (Esth 3:10). The prodigal's father placed a ring on the hand of his son (Luke 15:22). This was more than an ornament: it restored the son to authority in the household. The ring early became very valuable, as is shown by Isaiah's lament (3:18–23). Originally the signet was worn on a chain or wire about the neck, but the need to safeguard it led to its being put on the hand. Earrings and nose rings were not called *tabba'ath*. The seal was an engraved stone, fastened to the ring (Exod 28:11). Such rings have been found among Egyptian artifacts. That they were common during apostolic days is seen from James 2:2, where the Greek word *chrysodaktylios* means "ringed with gold" or "wearing many rings." See also DRESS and TABERNACLE.

RINGLEADER (Gr. *prōtostatēs*). Accusatory term used once, against Paul (Acts 24:5).

RINNAH (rĭn'à, Heb. *rinnâh*). A son of Shimon of Judah, called son of Hanan in LXX (1 Chron 4:20).

RIPHATH (rī'făth, Heb. *rîphath*). A son of Gomer (Gen 10:3; 1 Chron 1:6).

RISSAH (rĭs'à, Heb. *rissâh, ruins*). Israel's sixth camp after leaving Sinai (Num 33:21). Its site is not known, but it was some 200 miles (333 km.) south of Jerusalem.

RITHMAH (rĭth'mà, Heb. *rithmâh, juniper*). The third camp of Israel from Sinai (Num 33:18). Some authorities think this is an error for Ramah of the Negev (Josh 19:8).

RIVER. Of the dozen or so words translated "river" in the Bible, only three need be mentioned. 1. *Nāhār* (Gr. *potamos*) is used of the largest rivers known to the Israelites—the Tigris and Euphrates (Gen 2:14), the Abana and Pharpar (2 Kings 5:12), the Jordan (Mark 1:5), and the rivers of Ethiopia (Zeph 3:10). The river or the great river usually refers to the Euphrates (Gen 15:18; 31:21).

2. *Nahal* usually means a winter torrent, the bed of which is dry in summer, but may refer to a perennial stream like the Jabbok (Deut 2:37).

3. *Ye'ôr,* "a stream," usually refers to the Nile and its mouths (Gen 41:1; 2 Kings 19:24). Once it denotes the Tigris (Dan 12:5–7).

RIVER OF EGYPT (See EGYPT, RIVER OF)

RIZIA (rĭ-zī'à). A descendant of Asher (1 Chron 7:39).

RIZPAH (rĭz'pà, Heb. *ritspâh, hot stone*). A daughter of Aiah, a Horite (1 Chron 1:40, called Ajah in Gen 36:24). Saul took her as a concubine (2 Sam 3:7). Ish-Bosheth, a son of Saul, accused Abner, a cousin, of committing incest with her (3:7). The accusation enraged Abner, who transferred his allegiance from Saul to David (3:8–21). In his zeal to establish Israel, Saul had killed a host of Gibeonites, and as a result a serious famine had come to Israel. On consulting Gibeonites about restitution for the evil, David learned that only the death of Saul's sons would atone. Among those turned over to Gibeon were two sons by Rizpah (21:1–8). Because of Rizpah's devotion to her sons, David had the bones of her sons and those of Saul and Jonathan buried in the tomb of Saul's father, Kish (21:14).

ROADS. In Palestine the chief south-to-north traverse is the road via Pelusium, Rafia, and Gaza, up the Maritime Plain, the ancient invasion route used by Thutmose, Ramses, Sennacherib, Cambyses, Alexander, Pompey, Titus, Saladin, Napoleon, and Allenby. Carmel closes the northern end. Passage was possible by a rough and exposed route on the seaward side, a path used by Richard I of England and by Napoleon on his withdrawal, and known as *Les Detroits* by the Crusaders. On the landward side Esdraelon and Phoenicia were reached by several low passes, chiefly those that run through Megiddo, and the route through the Valley of Dothan (Gen 37:35). The latter route was used by those traveling to Jordan and Damascus.

A more easterly route from Damascus south lay through the arid deserts and mountains east of the Jordan Valley, through the tribal territories of Manasseh, Reuben, and Gad, into Moab, and down the desert valley of the Arabah (Deut 8:15). This was the so-called King's Highway.

Lateral roads from the high country joined the north-south communications of the Maritime Plain and provided alternative routes across Palestine to Syria and Damascus. One road ran from Gaza to Hebron. Another from Jerusalem ran through Lydda (Lod) to Joppa, with a loop to Emmaus, if that town may be properly located west of Jerusalem (Luke 24). This road was probably Paul's route to Caesarea (Acts 23), branching north at Lydda and passing through Antipatris.

North-south routes inland were naturally not so numerous as those on the easy Maritime Plain. However, a road ran up to Jerusalem from Hebron through Bethlehem and continued north from Jerusalem to Samaria, forking at Sychar (John 4).

The roads from the east into Judea crossed miles of arid and difficult wilderness. There were roads from Jericho NW to Ai and Bethel, SW to Jerusalem, and SSW to the lower Kidron and Bethlehem. The first was Israel's invasion route, the second the road of Jesus' last journey to Jerusalem, the third probably the route of Naomi and Ruth. There were numerous minor roads west from En Gedi and Masada.

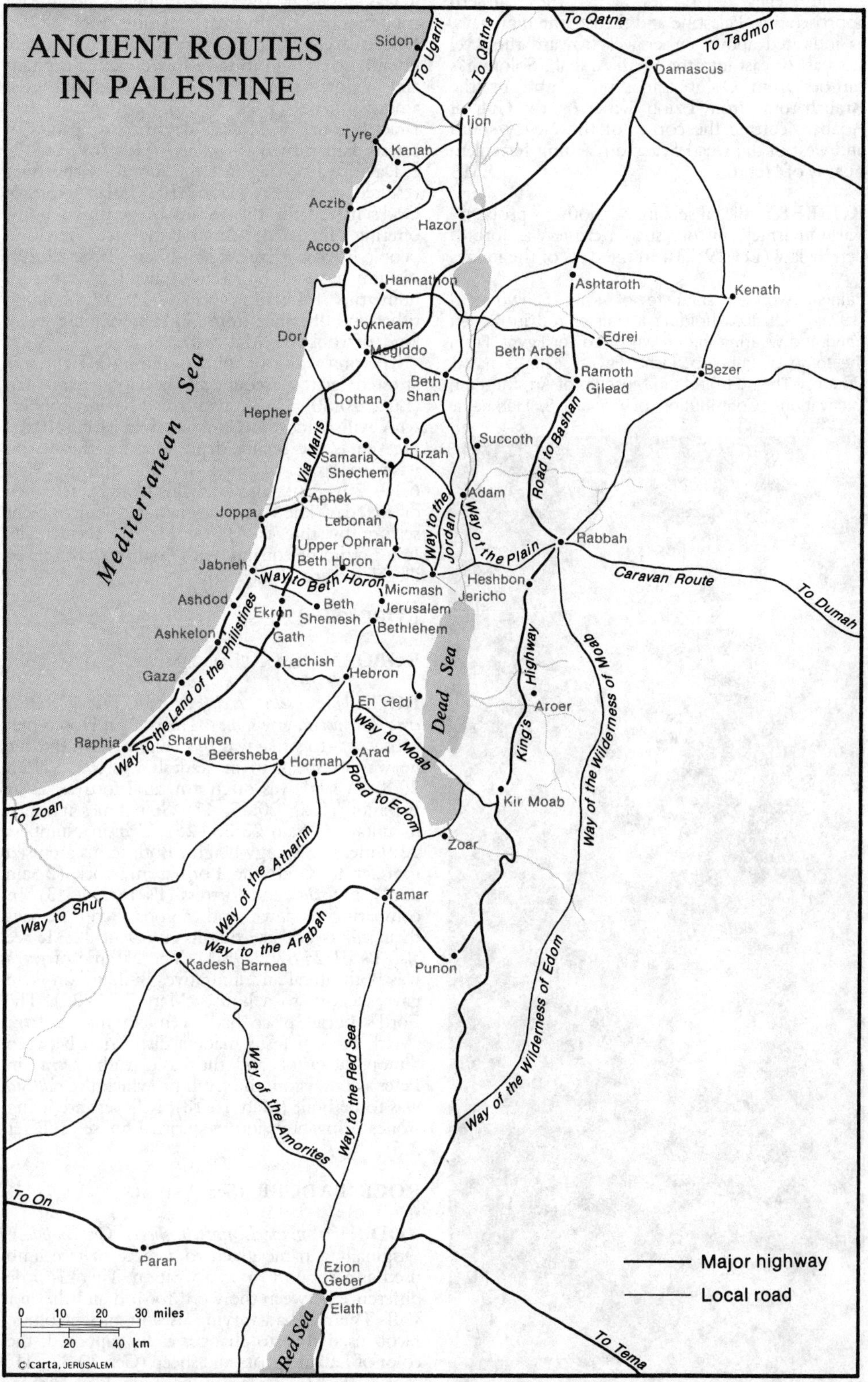

ANCIENT ROUTES
IN PALESTINE
Mediterranean Sea
Sidon
To Ugarit
To Qatna
To Qatna
To Tadmor
Damascus
Ijon
Tyre
Kanah
Aczib
Hazor
Acco
Hannathon
Ashtaroth
Kenath
Jokneam
Dor
Megiddo
Edrei
Beth Arbel
Ramoth
Gilead
Bezer
Beth
Shan
Dothan
Hepher
Succoth
Road to Bashan
Via Maris
Tirzah
Samaria
Shechem
Adam
Aphek
Joppa
Lebonah
Way to the Jordan
Way of the Plain
Rabbah
Upper
Beth Horon
Ophrah
Jabneh
Way to Beth Horon
Micmash
Heshbon
Jericho
Caravan Route
To Dumah
Ashdod
Ekron
Beth
Shemesh
Jerusalem
Bethlehem
Ashkelon
Gath
Lachish
Hebron
Gaza
Dead Sea
King's Highway
Way of the Wilderness of Moab
En Gedi
Aroer
Way to the Land of the Philistines
Way to Moab
Raphia
Sharuhen
Beersheba
Hormah
Arad
Road to Edom
Kir Moab
To Zoan
Zoar
Way of the Atharim
Tamar
Way to Shur
Way to the Arabah
Kadesh Barnea
Punon
Way of the Wilderness of Edom
Way of the Amorites
Way to the Red Sea
To On
Paran
Ezion
Geber
Elath
Red Sea
To Tema
Major highway
Local road
0 10 20 30 miles
0 20 40 km
© carta, JERUSALEM

The Negev desert lies across the southern approaches to Palestine and thrusts the highways, as indicated above, either west toward the level seacoast or east into the Wadi Arabah. Solomon's cargoes from Ophir came, no doubt, by the Arabah route from Ezion Geber on the Gulf of Aqabah, cutting the corner of the Negev south and west of the Dead Sea and reaching Jerusalem by way of Hebron. EMB

ROBBERY. Illegal seizure of another's property. Early in Israel's history such a crime was forbidden by law (Lev 19:13). In the days of the judges it was unsafe to travel the highways because of robberies by highwaymen (Judg 5:6; 9:25). Houses were built to resist robbers, who were often base enough to seize the money of orphans and widows (Isa 10:2). Honor did not exist among thieves (Ezek 39:10). So depraved had Israel become by Hosea's day that companies of priests had turned to pillage (Hos 6:9).

Painted wooden statuette of King Senwosret I (1971–1926 B.C.) holding a staff or rod in his left hand and wearing the crown of Lower Egypt. From the tomb of Imhotep, Lisht, Egypt, 12th Dynasty. Courtesy The Metropolitan Museum of Art, Museum Excavations, Contribution of Edward S. Harkness.

David warned against the lust for riches that resulted in robbery (Ps 62:10). Isaiah wrote of God's hatred for this means of getting a burnt offering (Isa 61:8). Among the vices of God's people listed by Ezekiel is robbery (Ezek 22:29). Nahum accused Nineveh of being a center of numerous robberies (Nah 3:1). Withholding tithes and offerings from God's storehouse was a kind of robbery (Mal 3:8).

The prevalence of robbery during NT times is attested by the account of the Good Samaritan (Luke 10:30–37). Jesus warned against robbers who will enter the Christian fold (John 10:1). Heaven is the secure depository for those who wish to store treasures for the future (Matt 6:19–20). Paul, who knew his world as few men of his day knew it, was familiar with violent seizure by thieves (2 Cor 11:26). Incidentally Jesus' claim to equality with God was not one of illegal seizure (Phil 2:6).

ROBE (See DRESS)

ROBOAM (See REHOBOAM)

ROCK (Heb. *sela'*, *a cliff* or *mass of stone, tsûr, a crag,* Gr. *petra,* any *stone*). The rock in Horeb that Moses was to strike was *tsûr* (Exod 17:6), the one he was to speak to in Kadesh was *sela'* (Num 20:8). A *sela'* was often a natural fortress, as at Rimmon (Judg 20:45, 47). Sometimes it was a mountain (1 Sam 23:25–26). *Tsûr* in Numbers 23:9 means a craggy height. Both terms are used to refer to God: the Lord is my rock (2 Sam 22:2), my *sela'* and fortress (Ps 18:2; 71:3). In comparing God with other gods, Scripture says their *tsûr* is not like our Rock (Deut 32:31; see also Ps 61:2; 62:2; 95:1). The NT use of *petra* was both literal and figurative. Building on *petra* gave security to a house (Matt 7:24–25). The Lord's burial place had been cut into a *petra* (Mark 15:46). Jesus made a distinction between Simon the *petros* and the basic truth (*petra*) in Peter's confession, the truth on which the *ekklēsia* was to be built (Matt 16:18). Believers are living stones being built into a spiritual house (1 Peter 2:5).

ROCK BADGER (See ANIMALS)

ROD (Heb. *maqqēl, matteh, shēvet,* Gr. *rhabdos*). Originally a name given to a piece of tree limb used as a support or as a weapon. There is little difference between the word for rod and that for staff. The rod had varying uses in ancient times. Jacob used rods to change, as he supposed, the color of Laban's goats and sheep (Gen 30:37–41; cf. 31:10–12). Rods became symbols of authority (Jer 48:17). Moses carried a rod when he returned to Egypt (Exod 4:2, 17, 20; 7:9–20). Aaron's rod was used to bring gnats on Egypt (8:16–17). Moses' rod, upheld, brought hail and lightning (9:23) and locusts (10:13). It caused the sea to divide (14:16). He struck the rock at Horeb (17:5–7) with a rod, and at Kadesh (Num 20). It was held aloft in Rephidim (17:9–13). The rod, used at first as a weapon, came to be a sign of authority, hence a scepter. To kill a servant with the rod was illegal (21:20). The shepherd's rod was used in counting sheep (Lev 27:32). God's anger was for Job a rod (Job 9:34). Chastisement was symbolized by the rod (Ps 89:32; 125:3; Prov 13:24; 22:15; 29:15). The coming of Christ was to be preceded by the rod (Mic 5:1). Jesus is to win with a rod (scepter, Ps 2:9). Paul would use a rod if forced to do so (1 Cor 4:21). Aaron's budding rod was symbolic of Christ's eternal reign (Heb 9:1–28). The victorious believer will rule with a scepter or rod (Rev 2:27). The temple of God was measured with a rodlike reed (11:1).

RODANIM (rŏd'ȧ-nĭm). A tribe descended from Javan, a son of Japheth (1 Chron 1:7). Both here and in Genesis 10:4, RSV has "Dodanim," but the LXX gives "Rodanim" or "Rodians," which rendering is supported by RSV "men of Rhodes" (Ezek 27:15), a reading followed by NIV. Ezekiel's account of the trade by Dedan (KJV) would link the city with Rhodes. Records of trade between Rhodes and western Mediterranean ports date back to 700 B.C.

RODENT (See ANIMALS)

ROE, ROEBUCK (See ANIMALS)

ROGELIM (rō'gē-lĭm). A thrifty community near Mahanaim. Its citizens took supplies to David's army (2 Sam 17:27, 29) and led him across the Jordan (19:31).

ROHGAH (rō'gȧ). A descendant of Asher (1 Chron 7:34).

ROLL. A scroll, a literary work on papyrus or parchment rolled around a core or spool. The decree of Cyrus to restore the temple was a roll (Ezra 1:1), and Jeremiah wrote on such a roll (Jer 36:2). Books with pages did not come into use until the second century A.D. See also PAPYRUS and WRITING.

ROMAMTI-EZER (rō-măm'tĭ-ē'zẽr, *highest help*). One of the twelve sons of Heman who were set by David as temple musicians (1 Chron 25:4, 31).

ROMAN EMPIRE. 1. *Territorial.* Considered as a territorial phenomenon, the Roman Empire was the result of a process of expansion that began in the sixth and seventh centuries before Christ. The process was initiated by the pressure of a rapidly filling and not overfertile peninsula on a Latin-speaking community that occupied a strategically advantageous position on some low hills by the major ford over the Tiber. The main fortress and federation of this group of associated settlements was called Rome, probably an Etruscan name. The origin of the population was an amalgam of tribal elements welded into a dynamic unity by the pressure of the Etruscans to the north and the Italic hill-tribes of the hinterland. Casting off the domination of Etruria in 509 B.C., Rome early began the search for a stable frontier that was to form the guiding motive of her history. That quest took her step by step to the subjugation of the Italian peninsula and the domination of its peoples—the Etruscans, whose culture and empire, Asiatic in origin, opportunely decayed in the fourth century before Christ; the Italic tribes who occupied the highland spine of the peninsula with its associated plains; the Greeks, whose colonies, since the eighth century, had dotted the coastline from Cumae to Tarentum; and finally the Celtic Gauls of northern Italy and the Po Plain.

Italy was Roman to the Alps by the middle of the third century before Christ. This metropolitan empire was no sooner achieved than Rome clashed with Carthage, the great Phoenician commercial empire of the north African coast.

Memorial tablet found near Jaffa Gate in Jerusalem, second to third century A.D. with inscription commemorating the Tenth Roman Legion commander, Marcus Junius. It reads: "(Belonging) to Marcus Junius Maximus, Legate of Augustus Caesar, Legate of the Tenth Legion Fretensis [Antoniana]. From Cius Domitius Sergius and Julius Honoratus and His officers." Courtesy Zev Radovan.

The island of Sicily, half Greek, half Carthaginian, lay between the continents and became the scene of the first collision between two powers, for whom the Western Mediterranean was proving too small a common sphere. Sixty years of intermittent war followed, from which Rome emerged victorious with her first provinces, Sicily, Sardinia, and Spain. An overseas empire thus visibly began, but defense and security were still the motives as Rome moved into the sister peninsulas, first Spain and then Greece. Despite such later leaders as Caesar and Pompey, originally and generally Roman imperialism owed no inspiration to an Alexander seeking conquest for motives of personal glory and mysticism, no Sennacherib or Nebuchadnezzar systematically building empires and concentrating the world's wealth in mighty capitals, no Cortes or Pizzaro in frank search of loot. Even in the second and first centuries before Christ, when the material advantages of the Empire were corrupting the Republic's ruling class, expansion and conquest were still associated with the search for a defensible frontier and military security.

The eastward movement through Greece, Asia Minor, and the Middle East began because of Macedon's support of Carthage in the Second Punic War. It continued in the clash with imperial Syria and found uneasy pause with Pompey's pacification and organization of the eastern Mediterranean, completed in 63 B.C. The historic process of expansion was associated with the emergence of successive perils, and Rome's attempts to meet them. The northward expansion through Gaul, which paused finally on the Rhine and the fortification lines of Northern Britain, was a process similarly motivated. If Pompey was the architect of the eastern Empire, Julius Caesar was the builder of the western. Although the personal ambitions of army commanders is an element the historian cannot discount, it remains a fact that it was the uneasy memory in Italy of barbarian inroads from the unpacified northern hinterlands that provided the stimulus for the conquest of Gaul and the associated islands across the English Channel.

By the beginning of the Christian era the Roman Empire was reaching the limits of its expansion. It was the policy of Augustus to consolidate, but that policy was based on a shrewd realization that the physical limit of Roman expansion was in sight. It is true that the stable frontier long sought for was still elusive. A major military disaster in A.D. 9 caused Augustus to choose the Rhine as a northern frontier. The Danube formed its logical eastward continuation. The Rhine-Danube line in general remained the limit of the Empire. Extensions beyond it were never completely integrated, and safer and more defensible alternatives were beyond physical reach. History was to demonstrate how difficult the Rhine-Danube line was to defend. Spain, Gaul, and Britain formed stable enough buttresses in the west, while the southern marches rested on the Sahara, a desert frontier, and strategically the most stable of all. The east was never totally secured, and some of the imagery of the Apocalypse reflects the fear felt in the Middle East of the archer cavalry from over the Euphrates.

Portrait head from a statue of Titus, who captured Jerusalem in A.D. 70 and succeeded his father, Vespasian, to the throne in A.D. 79, ruling the Roman Empire until his death in A.D. 81. Reproduced by courtesy of the Trustees of the British Museum.

The NT came into being, and the early church was established in an Empire that had organized and pacified a deep belt of territory around the Mediterranean basin and western Europe. That area owed its security to Rome, a security achieved against notable dangers and grave disadvantages and destined to endure for a vital three centuries. The same complex of territories owed to Rome a more stable government than much of it had ever known, and a community of life that went far to produce the fusion of Greece, Rome, and Palestine that formed the background and climate for the NT and subsequent Christendom.

2. *Politically,* the term Roman Empire must be distinguished from the Roman Republic. The Empire describes the system of rule and government known as the principate. The year 31 B.C., the date of the Battle of Actium, is arbitrarily chosen as the dividing line, when Republic became Empire. The observer of that day was conscious of no change or transition. Such an observer saw the passing of danger, and the prospect of peace after another violent bout of civil strife and constitutional crises. Octavian, Julius Caesar's adoptive nephew, had defeated Antony. When the victor drew into his hands the powers of the republican magistrates and the ancient constitutional executives, adding the

marks of prestige that accompanied the titles of "princeps," "imperator," and "Augustus," no one at the time, who observed merely the surface of events, saw anything but a continuation and an intensification of a policy that for fifty years had made a mockery of constitutional government. Extraordinary commands and special powers had long since prepared the way for the autocracy that emerged full-fledged with Augustus.

The constitutional breakdown from which the principate arose can be traced back for over a century. The Senate had ruled Rome, more by prestige than by a clearly defined legal right to do so, in the great days of Rome's struggle with Carthage. A tight oligarchy, the great families whose members gave Rome her generals and administrators, ruled with a strength and a decisiveness the times demanded, and the land had no reason to regret their leadership. Rome emerged from the wars with Carthage, shaken but victorious, at the beginning of the second century before Christ. At the end of that century the ills that broke the Republic and led to the principate were in full view. The Senate, whose leadership had sufficed for a compact city-state and for Italy, proved unequal to the task of governing an empire. Three problems were beyond their solution: the city mob, tool and instrument of a new breed of demagogues; the corruption arising from the temptations of rule in conquered lands; and the power of the generals. All three were problems of empire. The urban working class had been built out of a decayed farming class ruined by changes in Italian land utilization when vast amounts of capital from subjugated territories began to come in. The generals owed their power to the needs of distant defense and the military forces that new frontiers demanded. Commander and soldier alike had a vested interest in these new frontiers. Rome, throughout the next four centuries, was never to hear the last of it. The only answer would have been the creation of a strong, free middle class, which the early acceptance of Christianity would have provided. Julius Caesar was the most notable of the military dynasts, and he died under the daggers of a frustrated Senate because he drove too ruthlessly toward the autocratic solution of the Senate's corruption and the Republic's breakdown. His adoptive nephew, Octavius, was a more suitable person. By a mixture of good fortune, astute diplomacy, and a flair for picking colleagues, Octavius won power; but it was always power with a flavor of constitutional legality. Octavius, later called by the honorary title Augustus, was emperor only in the sense that, as supreme commander, he alone had the right to the title "imperator," with which victorious generals had ever been saluted by their troops. To most men he was simply "princeps," or "prince," which meant simply "first citizen." His varied powers, functions, and privileges nevertheless added up to autocracy. The system gave peace, and the world, especially the provinces, was prepared to barter a pretense of liberty for peace.

The Roman Empire, using the word in the political sense of the term, was the governmental framework of the Roman Peace, that era of centralized government that kept comparative peace in the Mediterranean world for significant centuries. No wonder the Eastern provinces, accustomed since ancient days to the deification of rulers, early established the custom of worshiping the emperor. The notion gained currency through the writings of poets such as Horace and Vergil, who genuinely believed in the divine call of Augustus and who, without a higher view of deity, saw no incongruity in ascribing divine attributes to a mere man of destiny. Such were the sinister beginnings of a cult that Rome chose as a cement of empire, and which led to the clash with the church, the early acceptance of which might have provided a more noble and effective bond.

EMB

ROMANS, LETTER TO THE. The genuineness of the letter has never been seriously questioned by competent critics familiar with first-century history. Although other NT letters have been wrongly attacked as forgeries not written by the alleged authors, this letter stands with Galatians and 1 and 2 Corinthians as one of the unassailable documents of early church history.

There can be no doubt that the author, Paul, formerly Saul of Tarsus (Acts 13:9), was a highly intellectual, rabbinically educated Jew (Acts 22:3; Gal 1:14) who had been intensely hostile to the Christian movement and had sought to destroy it (Acts 8:1–3; 9:1–2; 1 Cor 15:9; Gal 1:13). Even the critics who reject the supernatural cannot deny the extraordinary nature of the fact that this able enemy became the greatest exponent of the Christian faith and wrote the most powerful statements of Christian doctrine. The accounts of his conversion are given in Acts 9:3–19; 22:1–16; 26:9–18, and the event is alluded to in his writings (1 Cor 15:8–10; Gal 1:15).

I. Literary Unity. The literary unity of the last two chapters with the body of the letter has been questioned. There are manuscripts that have the doxology of Romans 16:25–27 at the end of chapter 14; some have it in both places. Yet none of the manuscripts lacks chapters 15 and 16, and there is no evidence that the letter was ever circulated without its last two chapters. It is not difficult for anyone who is familiar with letters of a theological and missionary nature to imagine how this inspiring doxology might appear out of its intended place in some copies.

This is a letter, not a treatise. It was not intended to be a formal literary product. In the midst of greetings from friends who were with the author as he wrote (Rom 16:21–23), Tertius, the scribe to whom the letter was dictated, puts in his own personal greeting (16:22). Perhaps Paul was interrupted at verse 21. As he stepped away, he may have said, "Tertius, put in your greeting while I attend to so and so." He returned in a moment and resumed his dictating. The people of the Bible were human beings under human circumstances, and the letter means more to us because this is so.

Perhaps Paul composed this segment, Romans

16:25–27, at the end of his discussion of "judging and scandalizing" (chap. 14). This little doxology is a compact paragraph, a unit in itself. It would fit appropriately in a number of places.

The opening verses of Romans 15, on "the strong and the weak," are obviously related to the material in chapter 14. One can picture Paul resuming his work at 15:1 after an interruption. Tertius takes up his pen, and Paul says, "I must say more about the treatment of the weaker brother. The little paragraph of praise to God that we did last, is to go at the very end, after we have finished everything else." Tertius draws a line through it, and later faithfully copies it at the end.

The prayer at the end of Romans 15 is not to be taken as the conclusion of a letter. It is only the appropriate conclusion of a particular topic. Paul had been telling of his itinerary. He was deeply moved as he contemplated the perils of his impending visit to Jerusalem, and he strongly implored the prayers of the saints in Rome in respect to this matter (15:30–32). Quite naturally and spontaneously at this point he broke into a prayer for them. The conclusions of Paul's letters always contain some striking use of the word "grace" (see 2 Thess 3:17–18), a word not found here. Therefore the prayer of 15:33 should not be construed as a conclusion of a letter.

The main body of the letter ends at Romans 16:20 with the words "The grace of our Lord Jesus be with you." Verses 21 to 24 are intentionally a postscript. He has finished the personal greetings to people in Rome. Phoebe, who is to take the letter to Rome, is nearly ready to begin her journey. Greetings from friends in Corinth, who may have assembled for a farewell, belong by themselves in a postscript, followed by another benediction (16:24). Then finally comes the exalted doxology (16:25–27).

The peculiarities, which have caused some to question the literary unity of the last two chapters with the main body of the letter, give no ground whatever for questioning the letter's genuineness. No forger or redactor would have left such matters open to question. The only reasonable explanation of the data is that the letter is exactly what it purports to be, a personal letter from the apostle Paul to the church at Rome, which he was planning to visit.

II. The Time of writing This cannot here be discussed in detail. Suffice it to say that the letter clearly places itself in the three-month period (Acts 20:3) that Paul spent in Corinth just before going to Jerusalem. According to the best authorities in NT chronology this three-month period was about December A.D. 56 to February 57.

III. The Reason for Writing. It is not difficult to know why this epistle was written. In the first place Paul was emphatic in his claim to be "the apostle of the Gentiles" (Rom 11:13; 15:16; see also Acts 9:15; 22:15–21; 26:17–20, 23; Gal 2:7–9; Eph 3:2–8), and Rome was the capital of the Gentile world. Paul was a Roman citizen, and a visit to Rome was consistent with his regular mode of operation. He established churches in strategic centers and worked in major cities.

There was this difference, however. There was a church already existing at Rome, probably founded by local people who had heard the gospel in their travels. It was Paul's peculiar policy to preach in hitherto unevangelized areas (Rom 15:17–24; cf. also 2 Cor 10:14–16). His proposed visit to Rome was not inconsistent, however, for (1) he had a contribution to make to their spiritual welfare (Rom 1:11–13) and (2) he planned to visit Rome on his way to evangelize Spain (15:24). He was asking the church in Rome to help him in this project. The structure of the letter is built around Paul's travel plans.

There was a great theological reason for the writing of this letter, a problem that had demanded the Letter to the Galatians at an earlier juncture in Paul's ministry. It concerned the relation of (1) the OT Scriptures, (2) contemporaneous pharisaic Judaism, and (3) the gospel implemented by the earthly work of Christ. It had been difficult for Peter to orient himself to the new day (Gal 2:6–14ff.), but he had made the transition (Acts 15:7–12; see also 2 Peter 3:15–16). We may well marvel at Peter's humility and true vision when, in calling Paul's letters "scripture," he certainly included Galatians, in which his own short-sightedness is recalled.

It has been said that if Galatians is the "Magna Charta" of the gospel, Romans is the "Constitution." The theological substance of this letter had to be presented to the NT church, whether addressed to Rome or not, but there were circumstances in Rome that made it appropriate for Paul, in a relatively calm frame of mind, with time for fuller elaboration, and without having become personally involved in local affairs, as he had in Galatia, to expand the central doctrine of the Letter to the Galatians. Thus he explained his purpose in coming to Rome and the main purpose of his life ministry and message. There was friction and misunderstanding between Jewish and Gentile Christians in the Roman church. We know from the personal greetings at the end that it was a mixed church. The problem is reflected in almost every section of the letter, but especially in chapters 3, 4, 9, 10, and 11. Both sides were stubborn. There was a moment, probably brief, even after Paul had reached Rome, when Mark and a certain Jesus Justus were the only Christian Jews in Rome who would cooperate with Paul (Col 4:10–11). A clarification of the gospel and its implications was needed.

IV. The Content and Outline. These must be understood from the point of view of Paul's total ministry and his particular travel plans. True, the greatest theme in the work is *justification by faith.* But this is not an essay on that subject. Much of the material simply does not fall under any subheading of that theme. This is a letter from the apostle to the Gentiles of the church in Rome, and the subject is "Why I am Coming to Visit You." Outlines that fail to see this viewpoint and seek to force the material into formal divisions as though this were an essay, are very likely to assign subtopics and secondary subheadings that do not fit. Some outlines are almost like "zoning" laws, forbidding the reader to find in certain sections material that certainly is there.

The following very simple outline is suggested. (The great doctrinal themes are discussed in articles on doctrinal topics.)

I. The Apostle Paul to the Christians in Rome.
I am entrusted with a message that I must deliver to you; i.e., the gospel in all its implications (1:1–17).

II. The World Is Lost
A. The Gentile world is wretchedly lost (1:18–32) in spite of God's justice for attempted morality (2:1–16).
B. The Jewish world is equally lost, in spite of all their privileges (2:17–3:20).

III. Justification by Faith Is My Great Message (3:21–5:21).
There is no space for the wealth of subtopics.

IV. Holy Living in Principle (6:1–8:39).

V. God Has Not Forgotten the Jews (9:1–11:36).

VI. Details of Christian Conduct (12:1–15:13).

VII. Miscellaneous Notes
A. Travel plans (15:14–33).
B. Personal to people in Rome (16:1–20).
C. Personal from people in Corinth (16:21–23).
D. Doxology (16:24–27).

Bibliography: C. K. Barrett, *The Epistle to the Romans* (HNTC), 1957; F. F. Bruce, *The Epistle to the Romans* (TNTC), 1963; M. Black, *Romans* (NCB), 1973; C. E. B. Cranfield, *The Epistle to the Romans* (ICC), 2 vols., 1975–79; E. Käsemann, *Commentary on Romans,* 1980. JOB

ROME. Of the Indo-European tribes who entered Italy, the Latins formed a separate branch, occupying an enclave round the mouth of the Tiber and the Latium Plain. They were surrounded, and indeed constricted, by the Etruscan Empire in the north, the Greek maritime colonies in the south, and by related but hostile Italic tribes who held the rest of the peninsula and the arc of hill-country, which fenced off the Latin plain. Therefore, a sense of unity arose in the Latin speaking communities, and their scattered groups were linked into leagues and confederacies. The lowlanders built defendable stockaded retreats to which the plainsmen could retire with flocks and families, and located such forts on hills and outcrops of higher land. In this way Rome came into being. Vergil's idyllic picture of primitive Rome in the Eighth Book of his *Aeneid* is not far from the truth. The most ancient acropolis could have been the Palatine hill, where the stockade of one shepherd community was built.

But the Palatine was not the only hill of Rome. The Tiber River cut into the soft limestone of the area, and the valley thus formed was further eroded by tributary streams, forming the famous group of hills with which the future city of Rome

Part of the remains of the Roman Forum. The temple of Antoninus and Faustina (in the background) was built by Antoninus Pius in A.D. 141. It was later converted into a church. Courtesy Gerald Nowotny.

was always associated. They were the Capitol, the Palatine, and the Aventine, with the Caelian, Oppian, Esquiline, Viminal, and Quirinal as flat-topped spurs. Through the area the river forms an S-shaped curve. In the course of this curve the river grows shallow and forms an island. This point is the one practicable ford on the river between the sea and a very distant locality upstream. The Tiber tends to run narrow and deep. Geography thus played a dominant role in history. The group of hills and spurs were ultimately occupied by separate communities such as those whose ninth-century B.C. traces have been discovered on the Esquiline and the Quirinal. The old habit of Latin federation gave them a sense of unity, which was finally translated into common institutions and defense. Traffic across the Tiber ford necessarily concentrated at this point. Indeed all the trade between the Etruscan north and the Greek and Italian south had to cross the river here. The river valley was also a highway of commerce between the sea and the hills. Salt may have been the principal commodity carried on that route. The group of hill settlements thus straddled central Italy's main communications, and those who have held such positions of advantage have always grown rich and powerful. Perhaps a faint memory of the significance of the Tiber ford is embedded in the Latin name *pontifex,* which appears to mean etymologically "bridgemaker."

Archaeological evidence suggests that the settlements had joined to form the original city of Rome by the sixth century B.C., for burials from the Palatine and Capitoline cemeteries on the edge of the marshy bottom (which was to be the Forum) cease at that time. The Cloaca Maxima, which drained these hollows, may have been built about this date. Synoecism, therefore, took place under the kings whose rule in early Rome, encrusted though it is with legend, is established fact. The Wall of Servius made Rome into a considerable fortress. Over the period of the kings, and especially the Etruscan kings, whose rule closes the regal period of early Roman history, the city built the Pons Sublicius to replace the Tiber ford, developed the Campus Martius as

Exterior and interior view of the Colosseum, or Amphitheatrum Flarium, in Rome, built by Vespasian and Titus and completed A.D. 82. The scene of gladiator fights and other contests, the structure measures 620 by 513 feet (190 by 155 m.) overall and seats c. 50,000 spectators. Courtesy Gerald Nowotny.

a training-ground, concentrated business activities in the Forum, and began to crowd the hills and hollows with houses and temples. Rome was probably a large populous city by the fourth century B.C. Valleys formed an irregular pattern for roads—a pattern that remained a feature through all history, and by the third century there is evidence of the great "insulae" or tenement houses that were to become another characteristic feature of Rome and that suggest the overcrowding, squalor, and slums of the early capital. It is difficult to obtain a clear picture of a city that has always been occupied, and whose accumulated buildings have limited archaeological investigation. Aqueducts, bridges, quays, temples, porticoes, the monuments of civic and of family pride, followed over the centuries. It is possible to trace great bursts of building activity at certain periods. At the end of the second century B.C., the influx of capital from the beginnings of provincial exploitation promoted expansion. Sulla endeavored to bring order to some of the central urban tangle, Pompey did much to adorn the city, and Augustus boasted that he had "found the city built of brick and left it built of marble." Augustus set the fashion for two imperial centuries, and it is from the first and second centuries after Christ that most of the surviving ruins date: the great baths of Caracalla, Diocletian, and Constantine, for example, and, most famous of all, the Flavian Amphitheater, called still by the medieval name of Colosseum.

A vivid picture of the perils and inconveniences of life in the great city at the turn of the first century of our era is found in the *Third Satire of Juvenal,* a rhetorical poem. In population the city of Rome probably passed the million mark at the beginning of the Christian era, and during the first century may have risen somewhat above this figure. It was a motley and cosmopolitan population. Early in the second century Juvenal numbers the foreign rabble as one of the chief annoyances of urban life, to be ranked with traffic dangers, fire, and falling houses. In the third and fourth centuries, a time of urban decay all over the Empire, the city declined, and the population probably fell to something near half a million by the last days of the Western Empire.

It is possible roughly to estimate the proportion of Christians over the imperial centuries. In the Catacombs, ten generations of Christians are buried. It is difficult to reach an accurate estimate of the extent of these galleries in the limestone rock or of the number of graves they contain. The lowest estimate of the length is 350 miles (583 km.), the highest 600 miles (1,000 km.). The lowest estimate of the burials is 1,175,000, the highest 4,000,000. Given a population averaging one million over the ten generations of the church's witness, and this is rather high in view of the third- and fourth-century decline, we have on the first figure a Christian population averaging 175,000 per generation, and on the higher figure one averaging 400,000 per generation. Such averaging is obviously inaccurate, for the number of the Christian population would be smaller in the earlier and larger in the later centuries. But if the figure of 175,000 is taken to represent a middle point in the period, say about the middle of the third century after Christ, it becomes clear that Gibbon's well-known estimate is hopelessly awry. Gibbon suggested that, at this time, probably one-twentieth of the population of the city were Christians. The most conservative estimate from the evidence of the Catacomb burials is that at least one-fifth were Christians, and that probably the proportion was much larger.

Orr pointed out in his Morgan Lectures some eight-five years ago (*Neglected Factors in the History of the Early Church*) that the Catacombs also provide evidence of the vertical spread of Christianity in the imperial society of the capital. He likewise refuted Gibbon's statement that the church was "almost entirely composed of the dregs of the populace." The case of Pomponia Graecina, for example, reported by Tacitus (*Ann.,* 13.32), may be traced to the Catacombs. De Rossi established the fact that the Crypt of Lucina was connected with the Pomponian family and suggested plausibly that Lucina may have been the Christian or baptismal name of Pomponia herself. From Tacitus's report, she appears to have faced a domestic tribunal because of a Christian faith. If Pomponia was, in fact, a Christian, since she lived on into the principate of Domitian, she

Remains of the Forum of Augustus at Rome, first inaugurated in 2 B.C. Courtesy Gerald Nowotny.

may have had part in two aristocratic conversions of which there is evidence—those of Flavius Clemens the consul and of Domitilla, his wife. The former was the cousin and the latter was the niece of Domitian himself. Dio Cassius (67:44) informs us that these two were accused of "atheism," a common allegation against Christians, and of "going astray after the custom of the Jews." Flavius Clemens was put to death and his wife banished. De Rossi appears to have established the fact that the illustrious pair were Christians. He discovered the crypt of Domitilla and also an elegantly constructed "crypt of the Flavians." Harnack's contention that "an entire branch of the Flavian family embraced Christianity" thus seems established. Next to Domitian, Flavius Clemens and Domitilla held the highest rank in the Empire. Their two sons had even been designated by Domitian as his heirs. It seems, as James Orr remarked (ibid., pp. 117ff.), "almost as if, ere the last Apostle had quitted the scene of his labors, Christianity was about to mount the seat of Empire."

Rome, like Babylon, became a symbol of organized paganism and opposition to Christianity in the Bible. In the lurid imagery of Revelation, John mingles Empire and City in his symbolism of sin. Chapters 17 and 18 of the Apocalypse envisage the fall of Rome. Chapter 17, passionate, indeed shocking in its imagery, shows Rome like a woman of sin astride the seven hills, polluting the world with her vice. The second of the two chapters reads like a Hebrew "taunt-song." It pictures, in imagery reminiscent of Ezekiel on Tyre, the galleys loading for Rome in some Eastern port. There were "cargoes of gold, silver, precious stones, and pearls; fine linen, purple, silk and scarlet cloth, . . . ivory, costly wood, bronze, iron and marble, . . . cinnamon and spice, . . . cattle and sheep; horses and carriages; and bodies and souls of men." The climax is bitter, as John pictures Rome under the smoke of her burning, the voice of gladness stilled.

The city appears several times in a historical context, the most notable being Paul's enforced stay there. Paul landed at Puteoli; and alerted by the little church there (Acts 28:14–15), members of Rome's Christian community met Paul at two stopping-places. On the evidence of the Nazareth Decree, it appears that a group of believers had been established in Rome since the principate of Claudius in the late forties of the first century. Paul probably entered Rome by the Capena Gate. His "rented house" (28:30) would be in some block of flats, an "insula." EMB

ROOM. 1. A chamber in a house (Acts 1:13).
2. In KJV the word also always translates *prōtoklisia*, place of honor at a dinner (Matt 23:6; Mark 12:39; Luke 14:7–8; 20:46).

ROOSTER (See BIRDS)

ROOT (Heb. *shōresh*, Gr. *rhiza*). Usually used in a figurative sense. Judah was promised new roots after the Captivity (2 Kings 19:30; Isa 37:31; see Rom 15:12). The roots of the wicked shall not

The Rosetta Stone, which takes its name from the Egyptian village 30 miles (48 km.) from Alexandria, is one of the most important archaeological finds in history, with a trilingual inscription in hieroglyphic, demotic, and Greek scripts. Reproduced by courtesy of the Trustees of the British Museum.

endure (Isa 5:24). Jesus was the root of David (11:1, 10). The Messiah was to come from an unexpected root (53:2). Daniel used the word in writing about Nebuchadnezzar, whose roots (the remnant of his kingdom) would remain during his period of suffering for sin (Dan 4:8–23). In the parable of the sower, the roots did not develop on or among stones (Matt 13:20). The fig tree and its roots died (Mark 11:20). The source of spiritual life is in the roots (Rom 11:17–18), even as the love of money is a root of all kinds of evil (1 Tim 6:10).

ROPE (Heb. *hevel, line* or *cord, 'ăvōth, a woven band,* Gr. *schoinion, a cable*). Hushai counseled Absalom to have Israel bring *hevel* (strong cables) with which to pull into the river the city where David might take refuge (2 Sam 17:7–13). Sackcloth on the body and a *hevel* about the head (a woven band) were symbols of deep servility (1 Kings 20:31–32). In 2 Samuel 8:2, *hevel* is a cord, a small linear measure. Rahab used a *hevel* (rope) to let the spies over the wall of Jericho (Josh 2:1–16). *'Ăvōth* was used for binding Samson (Judg 16:11–12). Isaiah used it in deriding Israel's efforts to pile up iniquity (Isa 5:18–19). Small ropes or cords were used to fasten the sacrificial animal to the altar (Ps 118:27 KJV; see NIV footnote). In the NT *schoinion* means either a rope made of bulrushes (Acts 27:32) or small cords used to lead or drive cattle (John 2:15).

ROSE, ROSE OF SHARON (See PLANTS)

ROSETTA STONE. A damaged inscribed basalt slab, found accidentally at Fort St. Julien on the Rosetta branch of the Nile, near the city of Rosetta, by a French army work crew in A.D. 1799. Terms of the French surrender to the British gave the French finds to the victors, and the Rosetta Stone was placed in the British Museum. The monument was originally set up in 196 B.C. as a formal decree of the Egyptian priesthood in honor of Ptolemy V (Epiphanes) with an identical text in three parts: hieroglyphic, demotic, and Greek. The parallel texts furnished the key for the decipherment of the Egyptian, with the proper names providing the basic clues for the achievement. Decipherment of the hieroglyphs was accomplished by Jean François Champollion in A.D.1822.

ROSH (rŏsh, Heb. *rō'sh, head*). 1. A son of Benjamin who went to Egypt with Jacob and his sons (Gen 46:21). He probably died without any descendants.

2. In ASV (cf. NIV footnote) head of three nations that are to invade Israel during the latter days (Ezek 38:2, 8). Gog is chief of Magog, Meshech, and Tubal. These tribes were from the far north, hence Rosh could possibly be Russia.

ROW, ROWERS (See SHIPS)

RUBY (See MINERALS)

RUDIMENTS (rū'di-mĕnts, Gr. *stoicheia, the first principles or elements of anything*). Stoicheia is found in the NT seven times, and KJV translates it in three different ways: "elements" (Gal 4:3, 9; 2 Peter 3:10, 12), "rudiments" (Col 2:8, 20), and "first principles" (Heb 5:12). NIV also translates it three ways. In 2 Peter it probably means the physical "elements" of the world. NIV has "elementary truths" in Hebrews 5:12; NEB imaginatively reads "the ABC." The other four verses refer to rudimentary religious teachings, in this instance the ceremonial precepts of the worship of the Jews—RSV "elemental spirits," NIV "basic principles."

RUE (See PLANTS)

RUFUS (rū'fŭs, Gr. *Rhouphos*). The brother of Alexander and the son of Simon of Cyrene who bore the cross (Mark 15:21). A Rufus is also greeted by Paul in Romans 16:13: "Rufus, chosen in the Lord, and his mother, who has been a mother to me, too," is the apostle's affectionate wording. If the two references are to one man, it may be conjectured that Simon or Simon's widow became a Christian and emigrated from Cyrene to Rome, this being the reason for Mark's cryptic reference. Mark was probably writing in Rome.

RUHAMAH (See LO-RUHAMAH)

RULER (See OCCUPATIONS AND PROFESSIONS: *Prince, Princess*)

RUMAH (rū'mȧ, Heb. *rûmâh, tall place*). The home of Pedaiah, whose daughter, Zebudah, bore Jehoiakim to Josiah of Judah. It is probably Arumah of Judges 9:41, Dumah in Joshua 15:52 LXX.

RUSH (See PLANTS)

RUTH, BOOK OF. The author of this book is unknown. The historical setting is the period of the judges (Ruth 1:1), but there are certain indications that it was composed, or at least worked into its final form, at a much later time. For example, the opening words, "In the days when the judges ruled" looks back to that period; the "gloss" in 4:7 explains an ancient custom for later readers; and 4:22 mentions David. Thus the final editorial process could not have ended before the time of David. It is best to place its final shaping in, or immediately following, the reign of David.

The book records the circumstances that led to the marriage of Ruth, a Moabitess, to Boaz, an Israelite. A famine forced Naomi and her husband to move to Moab, where her sons married Moabite women, one of whom was Ruth. Naomi and her daughter-in-law became widows, and Ruth and Naomi settled in Bethlehem. In the course of providing food for herself and her mother-in-law, Ruth met Boaz, a prosperous farmer and a relative of Naomi. With Naomi's encouragement, Ruth tenderly reminded Boaz of the levirate obligation (Ruth 3:1–9), a Deuteronomic law that required a man to marry his brother's widow if she was childless, the purpose being that the dead man have an heir (Deut 25:5–10). However, Boaz was not the nearest of kin. When the closest relative learned that there was a levirate obligation attached to the redemption of Naomi's land, he rejected it (Ruth 4:1–6), and Boaz was free to marry Ruth.

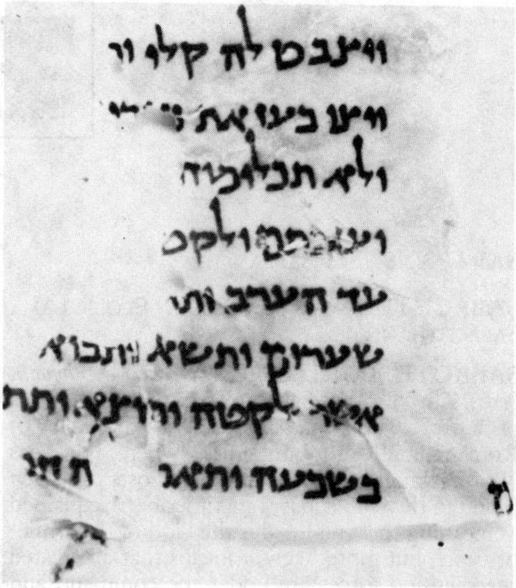

Part of a leather scroll (c. A.D. 150) from Qumran (2Q16) that includes Ruth 2:13–19. Courtesy Israel Department of Antiquities and Museums.

The Book of Ruth demonstrates the providence of God at work in the life of an individual, and it exalts family loyalty. It shows how a Gentile became part of the Davidic ancestry (4:17–21); thus Ruth is cited in the genealogy of Christ in Matthew 1:5.

Bibliography: E. C. Rust, *The Book of Judges, The Book of Ruth, The First and Second Books of Samuel* (LBC), 1961; A. E. Cundall and Leon Morris, *Judges and Ruth* (TOTC), 1968. TEM

RYE (See PLANTS)

S

SABAEANS (See SABEANS)

SABACHTHANI (See ELOI, ELOI, LAMA SABACHTHANI)

SABAOTH, LORD OF (săb'ă-ōth, Gr. *sabaoth, hosts*). The "Lord of Sabaoth" is the same as "Lord of hosts." The phrase is used in the KJV of Romans 9:29 and James 5:4, where NIV has "Lord Almighty." The "Lord of hosts" is often found in the OT. It has sometimes been explained as meaning that the Lord is the God of the armies of Israel, but more likely it means that all created agencies and forces are under the command and leadership of the Lord. The title expresses his great power.

SABBATH (săb'ath, Heb. *shabbāth,* Gr. *Sabbaton, to desist, cease, rest*). The weekly day of rest and worship of the Jews. The Sabbath was instituted at creation. The record of creation (Gen 1:1–2:3) closes with an account of God's hallowing of the seventh day, because on it he rested from his creative labors. We read, "And God blessed the seventh day and made it holy, because on it he rested from all the work of creating that he had done" (2:3). There is no distinct mention of the Sabbath in Genesis, but a seven-day period is mentioned several times in connection with the Flood (7:4, 10; 8:10, 12) and once in connection with Jacob's years at Haran (29:27–28), showing that the division of time into sevens must have been known then.

There is no express mention of the Sabbath before Exodus 16:21–30. In the Desert of Sin, before the Israelites reached Mount Sinai, God gave them manna, a double supply being given on the sixth day of the week, in order that the seventh day might be kept as a day of rest from labor. Moses said to the people, "This is what the LORD commanded: 'Tomorrow is to be a day of rest, a holy Sabbath to the LORD. So bake what you want to bake. . . . Save whatever is left and keep it until morning'" (Exod 16:23). Shortly afterward the Ten Commandments were given by the Lord at Sinai (20:1–17; 34:1–5). The fourth commandment enjoined Israel to observe the seventh day as a holy day on which no work should be done by man or beast. Everyone, including even the stranger within the gates, was to desist from all work and to keep the day holy. The reason given is that the Lord rested on the seventh day and blessed and hallowed it. It is clear that God intended the day to be a blessing to man, both physically and spiritually. The Sabbath is frequently mentioned in the Levitical legislation. It was to be kept holy for the worship of the Lord (Lev 23:3) and was to remind the Israelites that God had sanctified them (Exod 31:13). Forty years later, Moses reminded the Israelites of God's command to observe the Sabbath and told them that they were under special obligation to keep it because God had delivered them from bondage in Egypt (Deut 5:15).

Various attempts have been made by OT critics to find a Babylonian origin for the Jewish Sabbath. There is evidence that among the Babylonians certain things were to be avoided on the seventh, fourteenth, nineteenth, twenty-first, and twenty-eighth days of the month; but the nineteenth day breaks the sequence of sevens; and there is no question that the Hebrew Sabbath is much older than this Babylonian observance. Among the Hebrews, moreover, the Sabbath was associated with the idea of rest, worship, and divine favor, not certain taboos.

After the time of Moses the Sabbath is mentioned sometimes in connection with the festival of the new moon (2 Kings 4:23; Isa 1:13; Ezek 46:3; Hos 2:11; Amos 8:5). The prophets always exalted the Sabbath and found fault with the Israelites for the perfunctory observance of it. They made confession of Israel's sin in profaning the Sabbath (Isa 56:2, 4; 58:13; Jer 17:21–27; Ezek 20:12–24).

The sanctity of the Sabbath is shown by the offering on it of two lambs, in addition to the regular burnt offering (Num 28:9–10). The twelve loaves of showbread were also presented on that day (Lev 24:5–9; 1 Chron 9:32). A willful Sabbath-breaker was put to death (Num 15:32–36). The Israelite was not permitted even to light a fire in his home on the Sabbath. Psalm 92, expressing delight in the worship and works of the Lord, was composed for the Sabbath day. In the Persian period Nehemiah rebuked and took strong measures against those who disregarded the law of the Sabbath by doing business on it (Neh 10:31; 13:15–22).

With the development of the synagogue during the Exile, the Sabbath became a day for worship and the study of the Law, as well as a day of rest. There are not many references to the Sabbath in the apocryphal books. Antiochus Epiphanes tried to abolish it, along with other distinctively Jewish institutions (168 B.C.) . At the beginning of the Maccabean war, Jewish soldiers allowed themselves to be massacred rather than profane the Sabbath by fighting, even in self-defense. After one thousand Jews were slaughtered in this way, they decided that in the future it would be permissible to defend themselves if attacked on the sacred day, but not to engage in offensive operations (1 Macc 2:31–41). It was not, however, considered allowable to destroy siege-works on the Sabbath; and so Pompey was permitted to raise his mound and mount his battering rams against Jerusalem without interference from the Jews (Josephus, *Antiq.* 14.4.2 and 3).

During the period between Ezra and the Christian era the scribes formulated innumerable legal restrictions for the conduct of life under the law. Two whole treatises in the Talmud are devoted to the details of Sabbath observance. One of these, the *Shabbath,* enumerates the following thirty-nine principal classes of prohibited actions: sowing, plowing, reaping, gathering into sheaves, threshing, winnowing, cleansing, grinding, sifting, kneading, baking; shearing wool, washing it, beating it, dyeing it, spinning it, making a warp of it; making two cords, weaving two threads, separating two threads, making a knot, untying a knot, sewing two stitches, tearing to sew two stitches; catching a deer, killing, skinning, salting it, preparing its hide, scraping off its hair, cutting it up; writing two letters, blotting out for the purpose of writing two letters, building, pulling down, extinguishing, lighting a fire, beating with a hammer, and carrying from one property to another. Each of these chief enactments was further discussed and elaborated, so that actually there were several hundred things a conscientious, law-abiding Jew could not do on the Sabbath. For example, the prohibition about tying a knot was much too general, and so it became necessary to state what kinds of knots were prohibited and what kind not. It was accordingly laid down that allowable knots were those that could be untied with one hand. A woman could tie up her undergarment, and the strings of her cap, those of her girdle, the straps of her shoes and sandals, of skins of wine and oil, of a pot with meat. She could tie a pail over the well with a girdle, but not with a rope. The prohibition regarding writing on the Sabbath was further defined as follows: "He who writes two letters with his right or his left hand, whether of one kind or of two kinds, as also if they are written with different ink or are of different languages, is guilty. He even who should from forgetfulness write two letters is guilty, whether he has written them with ink or with paint, red chalk, India rubber, vitriol, or anything which makes permanent marks. Also he who writes on two walls which form an angle, or on the two tablets of his account book, so that they can be read together, is guilty. He who writes upon his body is guilty. If any one writes with dark fluid, with fruit juice, or in the dust on the road, in sand, or in anything in which writing does not remain, he is free. If any one writes with the wrong hand, with the foot, with the mouth, with the elbow; also if any one writes upon a letter of another piece of writing, or covers other writing" (*Shabbath,* xii. 3–5). Jesus had things like this in mind when he said, "And you experts in the law, woe to you, because you load people down with burdens they can hardly carry, and you yourselves will not lift one finger to help them" (Luke 11:46).

Jesus came into conflict with the religious leaders of the Jews especially on two points: His claim to be the Messiah, and on the matter of Sabbath observance. The rabbis regarded the Sabbath as an end in itself, whereas Jesus taught that the Sabbath was made for man's benefit, and that man's needs must take precedence over the law of the Sabbath (Matt 12:1–14; Mark 2:23–3:6; Luke 6:1–11; John 5:1–18). He himself regularly attended worship in the synagogue on the Sabbath (Luke 4:16).

The early Christians, most of whom were Jews, kept the seventh day as a Sabbath, but since the resurrection of their Lord was the most blessed day in their lives, they began very early also to meet for worship on the first day of the week (Acts 2:1) and designated it as the Lord's Day. Paul directed the Corinthian Christians to bring their weekly offering to the charities of the church on the first day of the week (1 Cor 16:1–2). As the split between the Jews and Christians widened, the Christians came gradually to meet for worship only on the Lord's Day and gave up the observance of the seventh day.

Bibliography: A. A. Hodge, *The Day Changed and the Sabbath Preserved,* 1916; P. Cotton, *From Sabbath to Sunday,* 1933; A. E. Millgram, *Sabbath: The Day of Delight,* 1944; J. Daniélou, *The Bible and the Liturgy,* 1960; R. T. Beckwith and W. Scott, *This Is the Day,* 1977; S. Bacchiocchi, *From Sabbath to Sunday,* 1977. SB

SABBATH DAY'S WALK. Used only in Acts 1:12 (KJV "sabbath day's journey"), where it designates the distance between Mount Olivet and Jerusalem. A Sabbath day's walk was a journey of limited extent that the scribes thought a Jew might travel on the Sabbath without breaking the law. Such a journey was 2,000 cubits (3,000 ft.–938 m.) from one's house, a distance derived from the statement found in Joshua 3:4 that there was to be that much distance between the ark and the people on their march. The rabbis, however, devised a way of increasing this distance without infringing the law by depositing some food at the 2,000-cubit limit before the Sabbath, and declaring that spot a temporary residence.

SABBATICAL YEAR (See FEASTS)

SABEANS (să-bē'ănz, Heb. *sevā'îm*). The name Seba is mentioned in Genesis 10:7 and 1 Chronicles 1:9 as a son of Cush. In Isaiah 43:3 the name is coupled with Ethiopia, and in Psalm 72:10 with Sheba. In Isaiah 45:14 God says to Israel, "The products of Egypt and the merchandise of Cush, and those tall Sabeans—they will come over to you and will be yours." "Sabeans . . . brought from the desert" are referred to in Ezekiel 23:42. Saba was situated between the Nile and the Atbara. It is a region about 400 miles (667 km.) long and 200 miles (333 km.) broad and was known to the Hebrews as Cush. Strabo says a harbor named Saba was on the west coast of the Red Sea. Josephus identifies the Sabeans with the people of Saba in Upper Egypt, which he says

Moses besieged and captured when in the service of the Egyptians. Another Sabean race, mentioned in Genesis 10:28 and 25:3, was located in Arabia. They built a unique civilization and great empire. The queen of Sheba, who made a visit of state to the court of Solomon, came from there.

SABTA, SABTAH (săb'tȧ, Heb. *savtā', savtâh*). The third son of Cush (Gen 10:7; 1 Chron 1:9). There was probably a place named Sabta in South Arabia, but its exact location is uncertain.

SABTECA, SABTECAH (săb'tē-kȧ, Heb. *savtekhā'*). The fifth-named of the sons of Cush in the genealogy of Genesis 10:5–7 and 1 Chronicles 1:9. His descendants probably lived in South Arabia.

SACAR (sā'kȧr, Heb. *sākhār, wages*). 1. Father of Ahiam, a follower of David. He was a Hararite (1 Chron 11:35). In 2 Samuel 23:33 the name is spelled "Sharar."

2. A son of Obed-Edom (1 Chron 26:4).

SACKCLOTH. The English word is derived from the Hebrew *sak,* a coarse cloth, dark in color, usually made of goat's hair. It was worn by mourners (2 Sam 3:31; 2 Kings 19:1–2), often by prophets (Isa 20:2; Rev 11:3), and by captives (1 Kings 20:31). Its exact shape is not known. Some think that originally it was a loincloth that was the only article of clothing worn by Israel's ancestors and then later was worn only as a religious duty. Others think it was like a corn sack, with openings for the neck and arms. It was usually worn over another garment, but sometimes next to the skin (1 Kings 21:27; 2 Kings 6:30; Job 16:15; Isa 32:11; Jonah 3:6).

SACRAMENT (săk'rȧ-mĕnt). Derived from the Latin *sacramentum,* which in classical times was used in two chief senses: As a technical legal term to denote the sum of money that the two parties to a suit deposited in a temple, of which the winner had his part returned, while the loser forfeited his to the temple treasury; as a technical military term to designate the oath of obedience of a soldier to his commander. In the Greek NT there is no word corresponding to "sacrament," nor do we find the word used in the earliest history of Christianity to refer to certain rites of the church. Pliny the Younger (c. A.D. 112) uses the word in connection with Christianity in a famous letter in which he says that the Christians of Bithynia bound themselves "by a sacramentum to commit no kind of crime," but it is doubtful whether he uses the word with any special Christian meaning. The word *sacramentum* was used with a distinctively Christian meaning for the first time in the Old Latin Bible and in Tertullian (end of the second century). In the Old Latin and in the Vulgate it was employed to translate the Greek *mystērion,* "mystery" (e.g., Eph 5:32; 1 Tim 3:16; Rev 1:20; 17:7). For a long time it was used not only to refer to religious rites but to doctrines and facts.

Sabean grave stele from South Arabia. In upper register is a figure seated before an offering table with attendants standing alongside. In lower register are two camels and a rider. The Sabeans were known for the extent of their trade (Job 6:19; Isa 60:6; Jer 6:20). Second or third century A.D. Courtesy Réunion des Musées Nationaux.

Because of the absence of any defined sacramental concept in the early history of the church, the number of sacraments was not regarded as fixed. Baptism and the Lord's Supper were the chief. In the twelfth century Hugo of St. Victor listed thirty sacraments that had been recognized by the church, while Gregory of Bergamo and Peter Lombard listed only seven: baptism, confirmation, the Eucharist, penance, extreme unction, orders, and matrimony—a list adopted by Thomas Aquinas and later by the Council of Trent. The number seven was supported by many fanciful arguments that seven is a sacred number. There is no NT authority for it, and it is a purely arbitrary figure. It is hard to see on what principle baptism and the Lord's Supper, which were instituted by Christ, can be put in the same category with marriage, which is as old as the human race.

The Reformers saw in the NT sacraments three distinguishing marks: (1) they were instituted by

Christ, (2) Christ commanded that they be observed by his followers, and (3) they are visible symbols of divine acts. Since baptism and the Lord's Supper are the only rites for which such marks can be claimed, there can be only two sacraments. There is justification for classifying them under a common name because they are associated together in the NT (Acts 2:41–42; 1 Cor 10:1–4).

Some modern critics challenge the claim that baptism and the Lord's Supper owe their origin to Christ, but a fair reading of the NT shows that these sacramental rites were universal in the apostolic church and that the apostles observed them because they were convinced that Christ had instituted them. They taught the church to observe the things that Christ commanded (Matt 28:20). Circumstances of great solemnity surrounded the institution of the sacraments by Christ. He appointed the Lord's Supper on the eve of his redemptive sacrifice and commanded baptism in the Great Commission at the time of his ascension.

These rites were regarded as ritual acts of faith and obedience toward God (Matt 28:19–20; Acts 2:38; Rom 6:3–5; 1 Cor 11:23–27; Col 2:11–12). They are symbolic rites setting forth the central truths of the Christian faith: death and resurrection with Christ and participation in the redemptive benefits of Christ's mediatorial death. They are visible enactments of the gospel message that Christ lived, died, was raised from the dead, ascended to heaven, and will some day return, and that all this is for man's salvation. In the NT the idea of baptism is intimately connected with the following: the forgiveness of sin (Acts 2:38; 22:16; Eph 5:26; Titus 3:5), the gift of the Holy Spirit (Acts 2:38; 1 Cor 12:13), union with Christ in his death and resurrection (Rom 6:3–6; Col 2:12), regeneration (John 3:5; Titus 3:5), entering into the relationship of sonship with God (Gal 3:26–27), belonging to the church (Acts 2:41), and the gift of salvation (Mark 16:16). The Lord's Supper symbolizes Christ's death for the remission of sins (Matt 26:28). It is a seal of the New Covenant in Christ's blood, an assurance of eternal life now, a promise of the Second Coming, a pledge of the eventual messianic triumph.

See also BAPTISM; LORD'S SUPPER; MYSTERY.

Bibliography: A. M. Stibbs, *Sacrament, Sacrifice and Eucharist,* 1961; Bernard Cooke, *Ministry to Word and Sacrament,* 1975. SB

SACRIFICE AND OFFERINGS (Heb. *zevah,* Gr. *thysia*). A religious act belonging to worship in which offering is made to God of some material object belonging to the offerer—this offering being consumed in the ceremony, in order to attain, restore, maintain, or celebrate friendly relations with the deity. The motives actuating the offerer may vary, worthy or unworthy, and may express faith, repentance, adoration, or all of these together; but the main purpose of the sacrifice is to please the deity and to secure his favor.

I. Origin of Sacrifice. The origin of sacrifice is a matter of dispute. The question is, Did sacrifice arise from the natural religious instinct of man, whether guided by the Spirit of God or not, or did it originate in a distinct divine appointment? Genesis records the first sacrifice, by Cain and Abel, but gives no account of the origin of the idea. The custom is clearly approved by God, and in the Mosaic Law it is adopted and elaborately developed. The view that the rite was initiated by an express command of God is based mainly on Genesis 4:4–5, which states that Abel offered to God an acceptable sacrifice, and on Hebrews 11:4, where it is said that Abel's sacrifice was

Twelfth century B.C. bronze model from Susa (60 cm. long, 40 cm. wide) representing the ritual of the dawn. Equipment includes altars of sacrifice, libation bowls or jars, sacred trees, and other cult objects. Two nude persons squat, one holding out his hands while the other offers ablutions. At the ends are stepped temples (ziggurats). Courtesy Réunion des Musées Nationaux.

acceptable to God because of his faith. It is argued that Abel's faith was based on a specific command of God in the past and that without such a divine command his sacrifice would have been mere superstition. Many who hold this view also say that the garments provided by God to hide the nakedness of Adam and Eve must have come from an animal that had been sacrificed and that in this sacrifice we have a type of the sacrifice of Christ to cover man's spiritual nakedness before God. While all this possibly may be deduced from Scripture, it is obviously not a necessary deduction.

Those who hold that sacrifice was devised by man, with or without direction by God's Spirit, as a means of satisfying the wants of his spiritual nature, have advanced several theories. (1) The *gift* theory holds that sacrifices were originally presents to God that the offerer hoped would be received with pleasure and gratitude by the deity, who would then grant him favors. (2) The *table-bond* theory suggests that sacrifices were originally meals shared by the worshipers and the deity, with the purpose of knitting them together in a firmer bond of fellowship. (3) The *sacramental-communion* theory is a modification of the table-bond theory. The basis of it is the belief among some primitive peoples that animals share along with man in the divine nature. The worshiper actually eats the god, thus acquiring the physical, intellectual, and moral qualities that characterized the animal. (4) The *homage* theory holds that sacrifice originates not in man's sense of guilt, but in man's desire of expressing his homage to and dependence on the deity. (5) The *expiatory* theory says that sacrifices are fundamentally piacular or atoning for sin. Conscious of his sin and of the punishment that it deserves, man substitutes an animal to endure the penalty due to himself, and so makes his peace with the deity.

Offering plaque (19 cm. high), 2500–1500 B.C., from Nippur, the chief religious center of Sumer. In the upper register is a duplicate scene: a nude priest is offering libations to a seated god. The bottom register shows a sheep and a goat driven by two figures, one bearing a container on his head, the other carrying a stick. Courtesy Istanbul Museum. Photo: B. Brandl.

II. Classification of Sacrifices. Sacrifices have been classified in a variety of ways, chiefly the following: (1) Those on behalf of the whole congregation and those on behalf of the individual. (2) Animal or bleeding sacrifices and bloodless offerings. (3) Sacrifices assuming an undisturbed covenant relationship and those intended to restore a relationship that has been disturbed. (4) Animal sacrifices, vegetable sacrifices, liquid and incense offerings. (5) Sacrifices made without the help of a priest, those made by a priest alone, and those made by a layman with the help of a priest. (6) Sacrifices that express homage to the deity; those designed to make atonement for sin; and peace offerings, to express or promote peaceful relations with the deity. (7) Self-dedicatory sacrifices, eucharistic sacrifices, and expiatory sacrifices. (8) Sacrifices in which the offering was wholly devoted to God, and sacrifices in which God received a portion and the worshiper feasted on the remainder.

III. History of Sacrifice in OT Times. The sacrifices of Cain and Abel (Gen 4:4–5) show that the rite goes back almost to the beginnings of the human race. No priest was needed in their sacrifices, which were eucharistic and possibly expiatory. The sacrifice of Noah after the Flood (8:20–21) is called a burnt offering and is closely connected with the covenant of God described in Genesis 9:8–17. In the sacrifices of Abraham, several of which are mentioned (12:7–8; 13:4, 18; 15:4ff.), he acted as his own priest and made offerings to express his adoration of God and probably to atone for sin. In Genesis 22 God reveals to him that he does not desire human sacrifices, a common practice in those days. The patriarchs Isaac and Jacob regularly offered sacrifices (26:25; 28:18; 31:54; 33:20; 35:7; 46:1). Job and his friends offered sacrifices (Job 1:5; 42:7–9), probably to atone for sin. The Israelites during their sojourn in Egypt no doubt were accustomed to animal sacrifices. It was to some such feast that Moses asked the pharaoh for permission to go into the wilderness (Exod 3:18; 5:3ff.; 7:16); and he requested herds and flocks for the feast to offer burnt offerings and sacrifices (10:24–25). The sacrifice of the Passover (12:3–11) brings out forcibly the idea of salvation from death. Jethro, Moses' father-in-law, a priest, offered sacrifices on meeting Moses and the people (18:12).

The establishment of the covenant between Israel and the Lord was accompanied by solemn sacrifices. The foundation principle of this covenant was *obedience*, not sacrifices (Exod 19:4–8). Sacrifices were incidental—aids to obedience, but valueless without it. The common altars were not abolished with the giving of the covenant Code (20:24ff.) but continued to be used for centuries by Joshua, Gideon, Jephthah, Samuel, Saul, David, Elijah, and many others. They were perfectly legitimate and even necessary at least until the building of the temple in Jerusalem.

Sacrificial animals, possibly gazelles, carried by a procession of offering bearers. Basalt relief from Carchemish, ninth-eighth century B.C. Reproduced by courtesy of the Trustees of the British Museum.

At the division of the kingdom in 931 B.C. golden-calf worship was established at Dan and Bethel, with priests, altars, and ritual (1 Kings 12:27–28). High places, most of them very corrupt, were in use in both kingdoms until the time of the Exile, although occasionally attempts were made in the southern kingdom to remove them. With the destruction of the temple in Jerusalem in 586 B.C. the entire cultus was suspended, but on the return from the Captivity an altar was built and sacrifices resumed. At the time of Nehemiah there existed a temple at Elephantine in Egypt, built by Jews, where a system of sacrifices was observed. Sacrifices were made in the temple in Jerusalem until its destruction by the Romans in A.D. 70. The Jews have offered none since then.

IV. The Mosaic Sacrifices. Every offering had to be the honestly acquired property of the offerer (2 Sam 24:24). Sacrifices had value in the eyes of the Lord only when they were made in acknowledgment of his sovereign majesty, expressed in obedience to him, and with a sincere desire to enjoy his favor. The only animals allowed for sacrifice were oxen, sheep, goats, and pigeons. Wild animals and fish could not be offered. The produce of the field allowed for offerings was wine, oil, grain, either in the ear or in the form of meal, dough, or cakes. Sacrifices were of two kinds: animal (with the shedding of blood) and vegetable or bloodless.

A. **Animal Sacrifices.** Both sexes were accepted for sacrifice, although for some sacrifices the male was prescribed. With one exception (Lev 22:23), no animal with any sort of wound or defect could be offered (22:21–24). The law commanded that animals be at least eight days old (22:27); and in some cases the age of the animal is specified (9:3; 12:6; Num 28:3, 9, 11). According to the later rabbis, animals more than three years old could not be sacrificed. There was no prescription of age or sex with regard to pigeons or turtle doves, but they were offered only by the poor as substitutes for other animals.

1. **The Sin Offering** (Lev 4:1–35; 6:24–30). This was for sins unconsciously or unintentionally committed; sins committed intentionally, but with mitigating circumstances (5:2–3; 12:6–8); certain kinds of ceremonial defilements (5:2–3; 12:6–8); and sins deliberately committed but afterwards voluntarily confessed. For conscious and deliberate violations of the law no atonement was possible, with some exceptions, for which provision was made in the guilt offerings. Capital crimes: the breaking of the law of the Sabbath (Num 15:32), adultery (Deut 22:22–23), murder (Exod 21:12), and sacrilege (Josh 7:15) were punished with death. Sin offerings were made for the whole congregation on all the feast days and especially on the Day of Atonement. They were also offered on the occasion of the consecration of priests and Levites (Exod 29:10–14, 36). Every year, on the great Day of Atonement, sin offerings were offered for the high priest. With the exception of these important national occasions, the sin offerings were presented only on occasions of special circumstances that demanded expiation of sin.

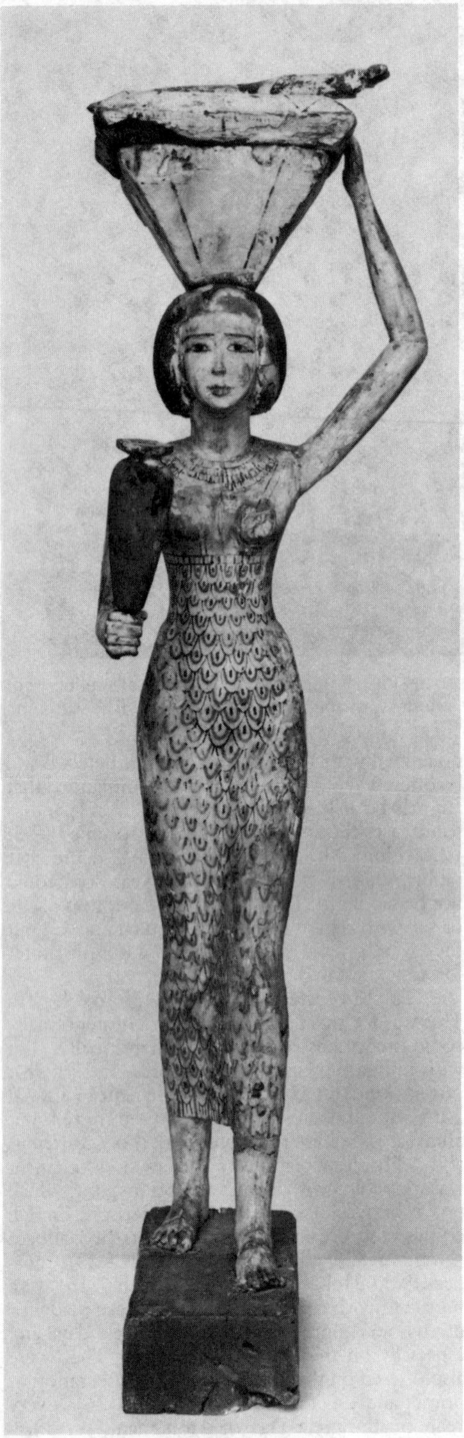

Middle Kingdom (twentieth to nineteenth century B.C.) wooden statue of Egyptian woman bearing offerings for the dead. In her hand is a vessel for water and, on her head, a chest surmounted by a leg of beef. Courtesy Réunion des Musées Nationaux.

The costliness of the offering and the procedure to be followed depended on the theocratic importance of the offender. For the high priest a young bullock was the appointed offering (Lev 4:3); for a prince it was a male goat (4:23); in ordinary cases a female goat or a sheep was sufficient. The poor could offer two pigeons, and where even these were too much, a small portion of fine flour was substituted (5:7, 11).

In all other blood sacrifices the blood was simply poured around the altar; in this one the blood was sprinkled. If a member of the congregation made the offering, the blood was smeared on the horns of the altar in the forecourt (Lev 4:7, 18, 25, 30). When a sin offering was for a priest or the whole congregation, the officiating priest took some of the blood of the sacrifice into the Holy Place and sprinkled it seven times before the veil of the sanctuary and then smeared it on the horns of the altar of incense. The blood that was left had to be poured out at the base of the altar. After the blood was sprinkled, the fat portions of the animal were burned on the altar. The remainder of the flesh was disposed of in two ways: in the case of sin offerings of any of the congregation the flesh was eaten in the forecourt by the officiating priest and his sons; in the case of sin offerings for a priest or for the whole congregation, the whole animal was burned outside the camp in a clean place.

2. **The Guilt Offering** (Lev 5:14–6:7). (In the KJV the "trespass offering.") This was a special kind of sin offering and was offered for transgressions where restitution or other legal satisfaction could be made, or was made. When the rights of God or men were violated, the wrong had to be righted, the broken law honored, and the sin expiated by a guilt offering. The offering, which was always a lamb, with one exception (14:12), was given after the required satisfaction had been made. The ritual was the same as in the sin offering, except that the blood was not sprinkled but poured over the surface of the altar. Its main purpose was to make expiation for dues withheld from God, like neglect to pay at the proper time what was due to the sanctuary; and from man, like robbery, failure to return a deposit, swearing falsely regarding anything lost, and seduction of a betrothed slave girl. The sin offering of a lamb made atonement to God. Restitution, with an additional one-fifth, made reparation to man.

3. **The Burnt Offering** (Lev 1). The distinguishing mark of this offering was that it was wholly consumed on the altar, while in other animal sacrifices only the fat portions were burned. The purpose of the offering was propitiation; but with this idea was united another, the entire consecration of the worshiper to the Lord. Because of the regularity and frequency with which it was offered, it was called the "continual" burnt offering (Exod 29:42); and because no part was left for human consumption, it was also called the "whole burnt offering" (Ps 51:19). This was the normal sacrifice of the Israelite in proper covenant relationship with God and was the only sacrifice regularly appointed for the sanctuary

service. It was offered every day, in the morning and in the evening. On ordinary days a yearling lamb was sacrificed; on the Sabbath day two lambs were offered at morning and evening sacrifice (Num 28:9–10). On other special feast days a larger number of animals was offered. There were also private burnt offerings when a Nazirite fulfilled his vow or defiled himself (Num 6), at the consecration of priests (Exod 29:15), at the cleansing of lepers (Lev 14:9), at the purification of women (12:6), and for other ceremonial uncleanness (15:15, 30). This was the only sacrifice that a non-Israelite was permitted to offer (17:8; 22:18, 25).

4. **The Fellowship Offering** (Lev 3). (In the KJV the "peace offering.") These were called fellowship offerings because they were offered by those who were at peace with God, to express gratitude and obligation to God, and fellowship with him. They were not commanded to be offered at any set time except Pentecost (23:20) and were presented spontaneously as the feelings of the worshiper prompted (19:5).

The ritual was the same as for the sin offering, except that the blood was wholly poured on the altar, as in the guilt offering and burnt offering. The fat was burned; the breast and thigh were kept by the priests; and the rest of the flesh was

Seti I giving offerings to his god, Osiris, who is seated on a throne, wearing the *atef*-crown, ceremonial beard, broad collar, and holding the flail and crook. The king wears the blue crown, broad collar, arm bands, and pleated collar. Wall painting inside the tomb of Seti I at Thebes, c. 1300 B.C. Courtesy Seffie Ben-Yoseph.

eaten at the sanctuary by the sacrificer and his friends (Lev 7:15–16, 30–34; Deut 12:1, 17–18). A meat and drink offering always accompanied this sacrifice. This meal denoted the fellowship that existed between the worshiper and God and was a symbol and pledge of friendship and peace with him. There were three kinds of fellowship offerings: praise offerings, votive offerings, and freewill offerings. For all three classes oxen, sheep, and goats of either sex could be offered (Lev 3:1, 6, 12). The animals had to be without blemish, except for the freewill offerings, where animals with too short or too long a limb were allowed (22:23). Fellowship offerings were also offered on occasions of great public solemnity or rejoicing.

B. **Vegetable or Bloodless Sacrifices.** These were of two kinds, the grain offerings (called "meat offerings" in the KJV and "meal-offerings" in the ASV) and the drink offerings. They were offered on the altar of the forecourt.

1. **The Grain Offerings** (Lev 2:1–16; 6:14–18) were not animal offerings as the name in the KJV suggests, but offerings of fine flour or of unleavened bread, cakes, wafers, or of ears of grain toasted, always with salt and, except in the sin offering, with olive oil (2:1, 4, 13–14; 5:11). They were sometimes accompanied by frankincense. Only a portion was consumed by fire on the altar; the rest was kept by the priests, who ate it in a holy place (6:16; 10:12–13). The grain offering accompanied the other offerings, except the sin offering, on all important occasions (7:11ff.; Num 15). It always followed the morning and evening burnt offerings. The idea behind the grain offering seems to have been that since people would not ordinarily eat meals consisting only of flesh, it would be wrong to offer only flesh to God.

2. **The Drink Offerings** were not independent offerings under the law but were made only in connection with the grain offering that accompanied all burnt offerings and all fellowship offerings that were Nazirite, votive, or freewill (Num 6:17; 15:1–2). They did not accompany sin and guilt offerings. The drink offering consisted of wine, which was poured out on the altar, probably on the flesh of the sacrifice.

Besides the above, three offerings were regularly made in the Holy Place: the twelve loaves of showbread, renewed every Sabbath; the oil for the seven-branched lampstand, which was filled every morning; and the incense for the altar of incense, which was renewed every morning and evening.

Bibliography: G. B. Gray, *Sacrifice in the Old Testament,* 1925; E. O. James, *The Origins of Sacrifice,* 1933; W. O. E. Oesterley, *Sacrifices in Ancient Israel,* 1938; F. D. Kidner, *Sacrifice in the Old Testament,* 1952; R. K. Yerkes, *Sacrifice in Greek and Roman Religion and in Early Judaism,* 1952; H. Ringgren, *Sacrifice in the Bible,* 1962; B. A. Levine, *In the Presence of the Lord,* 1974. SB

SACRILEGE (săk′rĭ-lĕj). The expression *commit sacrilege,* used once (Rom 2:22 KJV, MLB), translates *hierosyleō* in the NT; *hierosylos*, a related term, may generally mean one who commits irreverent acts against a holy place.

SADDLE (Heb. *mercāv, a riding seat*). The verb *habhash,* "to bind on," is used of getting a beast (always a donkey) ready for riding (Gen 22:3; Num 22:21; Judg 19:10; 2 Sam 16:1; 17:23; 19:26; 1 Kings 2:40; 2 Kings 4:24). Donkeys were not ridden with saddles. A donkey carrying a heavy burden had a thick cushion on its back to relieve the pressure.

SADDUCEES (săd′yū-sēz, Gr. *Saddoukaioi*). One of the religious parties that existed among the Jews in the days of Christ and the early church, but exercised comparatively little influence among the people. They resisted the truth of the gospel. Their origin is uncertain, but it is to be sought in the period in Jewish history between the restoration of the Jews to their own land (536 B.C.) and the Christian era. No evidence of Sadduceeism is to be found in Israel before the Captivity.

The origin of the name of the sect is obscure. The root of the word means "to be righteous," and the word has sometimes been taken to be an adjective ("the righteous ones"); but since the Sadducees were not particularly distinguished for their righteousness, it is unlikely that they got their name from this word. Probably the name is derived from someone named Zadok. The best-known Zadok in history was the Davidic high priest (2 Sam 8:17), from whom succeeding high priests claimed to descend. He himself was descended from Aaron through the line of Eleazar (1 Chron 24:3) and was instrumental in the return of the ark (2 Sam 15:24–29). The prophet Ezekiel, in his description of the restored temple, says that because the sons of Zadok remained loyal to the Lord when the Israelites went astray, they would be ministers in the new sanctuary (Ezek 40:46; 44:15). Some scholars hold that the Sadducees trace their origin to this Zadok. Others, however, think that the name comes from another Zadok, a disciple of Antigonus of Socho (c. 250 B.C.), who taught that obedience to God should be absolutely disinterested, without expectation of future reward. This view goes back to an apocryphal legend in the Abot-de-Rabbi Nathan (c. A.D. 1000). There is also the possibility that the name may be derived from some Zadok unknown to us.

The chief authorities for our knowledge of this sect are the Jewish historian Josephus, the NT, and the Talmud. Josephus lays great stress on the aristocratic nature of the Sadducees. He says, "They only gain the well-to-do; they have not the people on their side." They were the political party of the Jewish aristocratic priesthood from the time of the Maccabees to the final fall of the Jewish state. The Sadducees were priests, but not all priests were Sadducees. Josephus, for example, was a priest and a Pharisee. The likelihood is that the priestly party only gradually crystallized into the sect of the Sadducees. From the time of the Exile, the priesthood in general constituted the nobility of the Jewish people, and the high priest became an increasingly powerful figure. The priestly aristocracy became leaders in the Hellenizing movement that began with Alexander the Great. Because of their sympathy with the policy of Antiochus Epiphanes, they took no part in the Maccabean struggle, which was supported mainly by the Pharisees, a group of religious enthusiasts who opposed what they regarded as the religious deterioration of the Jewish nation. The high priesthood and the throne were united in a single person when, c. 143 B.C., Simon was recognized as both high priest and ruler of the Jews. This centralization of power led to a number of forms of reaction, especially from the Pharisees. Probably not theological at first, the Sadducees became so in order to defend their policies against the attacks of the Pharisees. Under the Romans they become the party favorable to the government. As aristocrats they were naturally very conservative and were more interested in maintaining the political status quo than in the religious purity of the nation. Since they were satisfied with the present, they did not look forward to a future messianic age. Not popular with the people, they nevertheless sometimes found it necessary to adopt the pharisaic policy in order to win the popular support.

The Sadducees had a number of distinctive beliefs, contrasting strongly with those of the Pharisees:

1. They held only to the written law and rejected the traditions of the Pharisees. Josephus says, "The Pharisees have delivered to the people a great many observances by succession from their fathers, which are not written in the law of Moses; and for that reason it is that Sadducees reject them, and say that we are to esteem those observances to be obligatory which are in the written Word, but are not to observe what are derived from the tradition of our forefathers. And concerning these things it is that great disputes and differences have risen among them" (*Antiq.* 13.10.6). In other words, the Sadducees believed that the Word of God alone was the seat of religious authority. The Pharisees, on the contrary, believed that just as binding as the Law itself was the supposed oral tradition of the teachings of Moses and the rulings on the law made by the scribes over the years. Some of the church fathers, notably Hippolytus, Origen, Jerome, and Tertullian, credited the Sadducees with regarding the Pentateuch as alone canonical; but this is apparently an error, since Josephus does not mention this, and in the Talmud the Sadducees are introduced as drawing arguments from the other books of the OT in their own defense. It is unlikely, moreover, that the Sadducees would have been admitted to the Sanhedrin had this been true.

2. A second distinctive belief of the Sadducees was their denial of the resurrection of the body, personal immortality, and retribution in a future life. "The doctrine of the Sadducees," says Josephus, "is this, that souls die with the bodies"

(*Antiq*. 18.1.4); and again, "They also take away the belief of the immortal duration of the soul, and the punishments and rewards in Hades" (*War* 2.1.14). According to the NT, the Sadducees denied the resurrection of the body (Matt 22:23; Mark 12:18; Luke 20:27; Acts 23:8; cf. Acts 4:1–2), but the NT says nothing about their denial of personal immortality and future retribution.

3. According to Acts 23:8,- the Sadducees denied the existence of angels and spirits. Seeing that they accepted the OT, in which spirits often appear, it is hard to understand their position on this subject. A number of factors may have been responsible for this: Their general indifference to religion, their rationalistic temper, and the wild extravagances of the angelology and demonology of the Pharisees.

4. The Sadducees differed from both the Pharisees and the Essenes on the matter of divine predestination and the freedom of the human will. According to Josephus, the Essenes held that all things are fixed by God's unalterable decree; the Pharisees tried to combine predestination and free will; and the Sadducees threw aside all ideas of divine interposition in the government of the world. "They take away fate," says Josephus, "and say there is no such thing, and that events of human affairs are not at its disposal, but they suppose that all our actions are in our own power, so that we are ourselves the causes of what is good, and receive what is evil from our own folly" (*Antiq*. 13.5.9; cf. also *War* 2.8.14). They felt no need of a divine providence to order their lives. They thought human beings were entirely the master of their own destinies and that the doing of good or evil was entirely a matter of free choice.

The Sadducees are mentioned by name in the NT only about a dozen times (Matt 3:7; 16:1, 6, 11–12; 22:23, 34; Mark 12:18; Luke 20:27; Acts 4:1; 5:17; 23:6–8); but it must be remembered that when mention is made of the chief priests, practically the same persons are referred to. They seem mostly to have ignored Jesus, at least in the early part of his ministry. Jesus directed his criticism against the Pharisees, although once he warned his disciples against the "yeast" of the Sadducees (Matt 16:6, 11). With the Pharisees, the Sadducees asked Jesus to show them a sign from heaven (16:1). They resented his action in cleansing the temple (Matt 21:12; Mark 11:15–16; Luke 19:45–46) and were filled with indignation at his claim of the messianic title "son of David" (Matt 21:15–16). They tried to discredit him in the eyes of the people and get him into trouble with the Roman power by their questions as to his authority (21:23), as to the resurrection (22:23), and as to the lawfulness of paying tribute to Caesar (Luke 20:22). They joined the scribes and Pharisees in their attempt to destroy him (Mark 11:18; Luke 19:47). They sat in the Sanhedrin, which condemned him; and the chief priest who presided was a member of their party. In their opposition they were probably most influenced by their fear that a messianic movement led by him would bring political ruin (John 11:49).

After the Day of Pentecost the Sadducees were very active against the infant church. Along with the priests and the captain of the temple they arrested Peter and John and put them in prison. A little later they arrested all the apostles and made plans to kill them (Acts 5:17, 33). Their hostile attitude persisted throughout the apostolic times. There is no record of a Sadducee being admitted into the Christian church. According to Josephus (*Antiq*. 20.9.1), they were responsible for the death of James, the brother of the Lord. With the destruction of Jerusalem in A.D. 70, the Sadducean party disappeared.

Bibliography: W. O. E. Oesterley, *The Jews and Judaism during the Greek Period,* 1941; T. W. Manson, *The Servant-Messiah,* 1953; L. Finkelstein, *The Pharisees,* 2 vols., 1962; J. Jeremias, *Jerusalem in the Time of Jesus,* 1969. SB

SAFFRON (See PLANTS)

SAIL (See SHIPS)

SAILOR (See OCCUPATIONS AND PROFESSIONS)

SAINT. In KJV the word "saint" is used to translate two Hebrew words: *qādôsh* and *hasîdh*. The root idea of the first is separation. In a religious sense it means that which is separated or dedicated to God, and therefore removed from secular use. The word is applied to people, places, and things; for example, the temple, vessels, garments, the city of Jerusalem, priests. The root of the second word is personal holiness. The emphasis is on character. It has a strong ethical connotation. These words are used either in the plural or with a collective noun. The reason for this is that a person's standing before God is regarded as a matter of his belonging to a larger whole—the nation Israel or the Christian church—this larger whole standing in covenant relationship to God. In the LXX the word *hagioi* is used to refer to God's covenant people Israel.

In the NT the word *hagioi* is applied to OT (Matt 27:52) and NT believers (e.g., Acts 26:10; Rom 8:27; 13:12; 16:2; 2 Cor 1:1; Eph 1:1; 1 Thess 1:13; Jude 3; Rev 13:,7 10). The church is made up of people called out of the world (Rom 1:7; 1 Cor 1:2) by God's electing grace to be his own people. All who are in covenant relation with him through repentance and faith in his Son are regarded as saints. Objectively, the saints are God's chosen and peculiar people, belonging exclusively to him. Subjectively, they are separated from all defilement and sin and partake of God's holiness. Throughout the Bible, but especially in the NT Epistles, the saints are urged to live lives befitting their position (Eph 4:1, 12; 5:3; Col 1:10; cf. 2 Cor 8:4). SB

SAKIA (sà-kī'à, Heb. *sakheyah,* probably *Jehovah has hedged about*). Son of Shaharaim, a Benjamite (1 Chron 8:10).

SALA, SALAH (See SHELAH)

SALAMIS (săl'ȧ-mĭs Gr. *Salamis*). A town on the east coast of Cyprus, founded, according to tradition, by Teucer, who was from the island of Salamis off the coast of Greece. It possessed a good harbor and was a populous and flourishing town in the Hellenic and Roman periods. Paul and Barnabas preached the gospel there in the synagogues of the Jews (Acts 13:5), showing that there was a large Jewish community in Salamis. Nothing is said of the duration or success of the visit. Paul did not return to Salamis, but Barnabas doubtless did on his second missionary journey (15:39). According to tradition he was martyred there in the reign of Nero.

SALATHIEL (See SHEALTIEL)

SALECAH, SALCAH (Heb. *salekhâh*). A city on the extreme NE boundary of the kingdom of Bashan, near Edrei (Deut 3:10; Josh 12:5; 13:11). Og, king of Bashan, once ruled it; and undoubtedly it was included in the portion given to the half-tribe of Manasseh. It later became the northern limit of the Gadites (1 Chron 5:11). It is now known as Salkhad.

SALEM (sā'lĕm, Heb. *shālēm, peace*). The name of the city of which Melchizedek was king (Gen 14:18; Heb 7:1–2). Josephus says that Jewish writers generally regarded it as a synonym of Jerusalem. It is apparently so regarded in Psalm 76:2.

SALIM (sā'lĭm, Gr. *Saleim*). A place referred to in John 3:23 as near Aenon, where John was baptizing. A comparison of John 1:28; 3:26; 10:40 shows that it must have been west of the Jordan, but its exact location is unknown.

SALLAI (săl'ā-ī, Heb. *sallay*). Chief of a family of Benjamites who lived at Jerusalem (Neh 11:8).

SALLU (săl'ū, Heb. *Sallay*). 1. The head of a family of Benjamin who settled in Jerusalem after the Exile (1 Chron 9:7; Neh 11:7).

2. The head of a family of priests who returned with Zerubbabel after the Exile (Neh 12:7, 20; KJV has "Sallai" in 12:20).

SALMA (săl'mȧ, Heb. *salmā', strength*). A son of Caleb, son of Hur, and father of Bethlehem (1 Chron 2:51, 54).

SALMON (săl'mŏn, Heb. *salmôn, clothing*). The father of Boaz the husband of Ruth. He was the grandfather of Jesse, father of David (Ruth 4:20–21; 1 Chron 2:11; Matt 1:4–5; Luke 3:32).

SALMONE (săl-mō'nē, Gr. *Salmōnē*). A promontory forming the eastern extremity of the island of Crete. Paul sailed near it on his way to Rome (Acts 27:7). It is now know as Cape Sidero.

SALOME (sȧ-lō'mē, Gr. *Salōmē,* fem. of Solomon). 1. The wife of Zebedee, and mother of James and John (cf. Matt 27:56 with Mark 15:40; 16:1). She was one of the women who accompanied Jesus in Galilee to care for his needs (Mark 15:40–41). She was present at the crucifixion of Jesus and was among those who at Easter morning came to the tomb to anoint the dead body of their Lord (16:1).

2. The daughter of Herodias, and the grandniece of Herod Antipas. Her dancing before Herod pleased him so much that as a reward she was given the head of John the Baptist (Matt 14:3–11; Mark 6:17–28). Her name is not given in the Gospels (but see Josephus, *Antiq.* 17.5.4).

SALT (See MINERALS)

SALT, CITY OF. A city in the wilderness of Judah, not far from the Dead Sea. It is mentioned as being between Nibshan and En Gedi (Josh 15:62). Its exact site is uncertain.

SALT, COVENANT OF. A covenant of permanent and perpetual obligation. Since salt is a necessary part of the daily diet, and salt was always used in sacrifices to the Lord (Lev 2:13), it was not long before people saw a connection between salt and covenant making. To "eat salt with" a person meant to share his hospitality. When covenants were made, they were usually confirmed with sacrificial meals, and salt was always present. Numbers 18:19 says that offerings to the Lord were to be "an everlasting covenant of salt before the LORD."

SALT SEA (See DEAD SEA)

SALT, VALLEY OF. A valley in which great victories were won over the Edomites, first by the army of David (2 Sam 8:13), and later by Amaziah king of Judah (2 Kings 14:7; 2 Chron 25:11). It was between Jerusalem and Edom, but its exact site is uncertain.

SALU (sā'lū, Heb. *sālû'*). A prince of the tribe of Simeon. He was the father of Zimri who was killed by Phinehas (Num 25:14).

SALUTATION (săl-ū-tā'shŭn, Gr. *aspasmos*). A greeting given either orally (Luke 1:29, 41, 44) or in writing (1 Cor 16:21; Col 4:18; 2 Thess 3:17). Greetings in the Bible sometimes included acts as well as words: a profound obeisance or prostration, a kissing of the hand, kneeling, falling on the neck of another, or embracing. Every situation in life had its own salutation: the return of a friend from a journey, the birth of a son, a marriage, wearing new clothes, dining, and the appeals of a beggar. Among the more common salutations on meetings were the following: "God be gracious to you" (Gen 43:29); "The LORD be with you" (Ruth 2:4); "Peace be with you" (Luke 24:36); "Greetings" (Matt 26:49). Monarchs were saluted with the words "May the king live forever" (Neh 2:3; 1 Kings 1:31). The Pharisees especially liked salutations in public places (Matt

23:7; Mark 12:38). Because salutations were usually time-consuming, when Jesus sent out the Seventy, he forbade salutations by the way (Luke 10:4). Salutations were given at partings as well as at meetings. "Go in peace," or "Farewell" (1 Sam 1:17; 20:42; 2 Sam 15:9; Mark 5:34). Salutations in letters were more brief and direct. The salutations of Paul's letters are usually elaborate and of rich spiritual fullness. SB

SALVATION (Heb. *yeshû'âh,* Gr. *sōtēria*). What God in mercy does for his sinful, finite human creatures is presented in the Bible through a variety of metaphors, images, and models (e.g., redemption and justification). Of these, none is more important or significant than salvation: thus God is called "Savior" (Hos 13:4; Luke 1:47) and portrayed as the "God of salvation" (Ps 68:19–20; Luke 3:6; Acts 28:28).

In the OT, salvation refers both to everyday, regular types of deliverance—as from enemies, disease, and danger (see 1 Sam 10:24; Ps 72:4)—and to those major deliverances that are specifically interpreted as being a definite part of God's unique and special involvement in human history as well as special revelations of his character and will. The supreme example of the latter is the Exodus (Exod 14:13, 30–31; 15:1–2, 13; 18:8), which involved deliverance from the bondage of Egypt, safe travel to the Land of Promise, and settlement there as a new people in a new relationship with God (Deut 6:21–23; 26:2–10; 33:29).

There are two further aspects to salvation in the OT. First, salvation refers to the future action of God when he will deliver Israel from all her enemies and ills and create a new order of existence ("a new heaven and a new earth") in which she and all people will worship the Lord and live in peace and harmony (see Isa 49:5–13; 65:17ff.; 66:22–23; Hag 2:4–9; Zech 2:7–13). Second, intimately related to the future salvation of God is the hope of the Messiah, who will deliver his people from their sins, and will act for the Lord, who alone is Savior (Isa 43:11; 52:13; 53:12).

Further, in the OT the theme of salvation is closely related to the themes of God's righteousness and God's creation. God is righteous when he acts to preserve his side of the covenant he made with the people of Israel. Thus when he acts to deliver his people, he acts in righteousness, and his act is also one of salvation (Isa 45:21; 46:12–13). God's future salvation involves a new creation, the remaking and renewing of the old created order (9:2–7; 11:1–9; 65:17ff.).

In the NT, Jesus is portrayed as the Savior of sinners (Luke 2:11; John 4:42; Acts 5:31; 13:23; Phil 3:20; 2 Peter 1:1, 11; 1 John 4:14). The title reserved for God in the OT is transferred to Jesus as Incarnate Son in the NT. He is the Savior or Deliverer from sin and its consequences as well as from Satan and his power. Jesus preached the arrival of the kingdom of God—the kingly, fatherly rule of God in human lives. When a person repented and believed, that person received salvation—"Today salvation has come to this house" (Luke 19:9–10), said Jesus to Zacchaeus. To others who believed and received God's kingdom/salvation Jesus said, "Your sins are forgiven" or "Your faith has saved you" (Mark 2:5; Luke 7:50). And since healing of the body was not separated by Jesus from healing of the person, to be healed by Jesus was to receive God's salvation. In fact the verb *sōzein* means both "to heal" and "to save" (Mark 1:40–45; 5:33–34).

Peter preached that "salvation is found in no one else, for there is no other name under heaven given to men by which we must be saved" (Acts 4:12). Paul wrote, "Now is the day of salvation" (2 Cor 6:2). The writer of Hebrews asked, "How shall we escape if we ignore such a great salvation?" (Heb 2:3). Because of the life, death, and exaltation of Jesus, salvation is a present reality and the gospel is the declaration that salvation is now accomplished and available in and through Jesus. It is deliverance from the dominion of sin and Satan; it is freedom to love and serve God now. Salvation is also, however, a future hope, for we will "be saved from God's wrath through him" at the Last Judgment (Rom 5:9), and Peter wrote of the salvation "that is ready to be revealed in the last time" (1 Peter 1:5). Salvation, which belongs to our God (Rev 19:1), includes everything that God will do for and to his people as he brings them to fullness of life in the new heaven and the new earth of the age to come.

See also JUSTIFICATION; KINGDOM OF GOD; RECONCILIATION; REDEMPTION.

Bibliography: C. R. Smith, *The Bible Doctrine of Salvation,* 1946; E. M. B. Green, *The Meaning of Salvation,* 1965; O. Cullmann, *Salvation in History,* 1967; J. D. Douglas (ed.), *Let the Earth Hear His Voice,* 1975; J. R. W. Stott, *Christian Mission in the Modern World,* 1975; H. D. McDonald, *Salvation,* 1982. PT

SALVE (See EYESALVE)

SAMARIA (sȧ-mâr'ĭ-ȧ, Heb. *shōmerôn,* Gr. *Samareia*). The country of Samaria occupied a rough square of some forty miles (sixty-seven km.) north and south by thirty-five miles (fifty-eight km.) east and west. It was the territory occupied by the ten tribes led by Jeroboam, extending roughly from Bethel to Dan and from the Mediterranean to Syria and Ammon. The political and geographical frontiers are somewhat blurred. Sir George Adam Smith, after careful geographical and historical analysis, concludes: "The southern frontier . . . gradually receded from the Vale of Aijalon to the Wady Isher and 'Akrabbeh. The northern . . . lay from the Mediterranean to Jordan, along the southern edge of Esdraelon, by the foot of Carmel and Gilboa. If Carmel is shut off, the edge of Sharon may be taken as the western boundary; the eastern was Jordan. . ." (*Historical Geography of the Holy Land,* pp. 324–25; for detailed description see pp. 249–56). The earliest name for this section of the Palestinian uplands was Mount Ephraim (Josh 17:15; 19:50; Judg 3:27; 4:5).

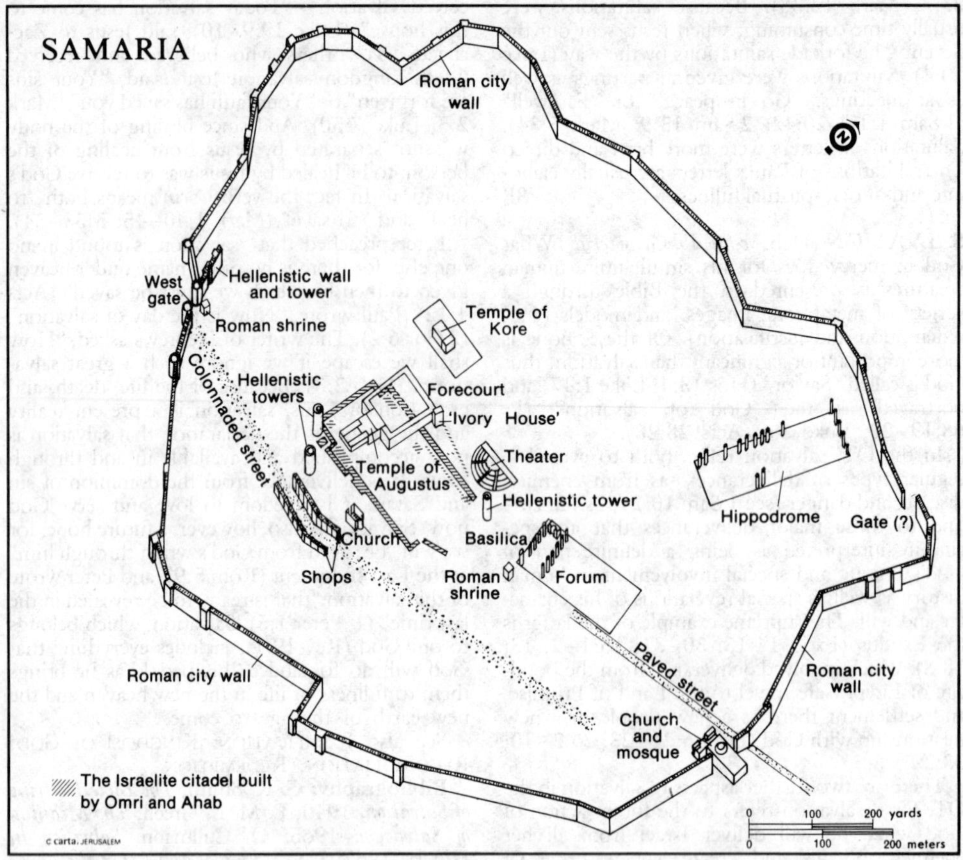

Viewed from the sea, the area does, in fact, seem to be a unity. The western flank, generally poor country, falls away from the summits in a slope more gradual than that of the Judean highlands. Access is easy, and little history gathered around slopes that were so indefensible and sterile. Over the divide, the one conspicuous pass is that in which Shechem lies, between mounts Ebal and Gerizim. It crosses the range and merges into a valley swinging south to Jordan, dividing the eastern flank of Mount Ephraim into two portions, a bulwark of high country to the south and an open series of broad valleys to the north. "Plains, meadows, and spacious vales," according to Sir G. A. Smith, were a remarkable feature within this highland mass, providing both gentle access and secluded pasturelands within. Hence the trend of Samaria's history. The country was too open for successful defense. Hence, too, the chariot is mentioned frequently in the annals of the northern kingdom, and the surrounding paganism poured almost unrestricted into the life of the northern kingdom.

Extensive excavations were carried out here by G. Reisner, C. S. Fisher, and D. H. Lyon in 1908 and 1910–1911, and later by J. W. Crowfoot, K. Kenyon, and others in 1931–1935. Impressive remains of a palace from the time of Omri and Ahab have been found on the acropolis. Ostraca written in ancient Hebrew were found dating to the reign of Jeroboam II or Menahem, as well as numerous ivory plaques reminiscent of the "house of ivory" that Ahab built (1 Kings 22:39; Amos 3:15; 6:4).

From the Hellenistic and Roman periods there were revealed large round towers in the city wall (one measuring sixty-three feet [twenty m.] in diameter). In the second century B.C. a new wall with square towers was built around the acropolis. In the Roman period the entire 170-acre city was surrounded by a wall, whose western gate with its two round towers forty-six feet (fourteen m.) in diameter still stand on the square bases of the Hellenistic period. A temple of Augustus, a hippodrome, and a forum, built by Herod the Great, and a small theater from the third century A.D. were found on the mound

For further details on Samaria, see BETHEL; SHECHEM; SHILOH; SYCHAR. EMB

SAMARITANS (sȧ-măr'ĭ-tăns, Heb. *shōmerōnîm,* Gr. *Samareitai*). The word may signify, according to context, (1) the inhabitants of Samaria (the region rather than the town; e.g., 2 Kings 17:26; Matt 10:5; Luke 9:52; 10:33; 17:16; John 4:9, 30, 40; Acts 8:25); (2) the sect that derived its name from Samaria, a term of contempt with the Jews (John 8:48); (3) since the seventeenth century A.D., "a good Samaritan" (Luke 10:33) has signified a generous and self-forgetful person.

Racially, the Samaritans are difficult to identify. In 721 B.C. Sargon of Assyria destroyed Samaria. He recorded the fact on the walls of the royal palace at Dur-Sarraku (Khorsabad), as well as his subsequent policy of depopulation, deportation, and reestablishment: "In my first year of reign . . . the people of Samaria . . . to the number of 27,290 I carried away. . . . The city I rebuilt—I made it greater than it was before. People of the lands which I had conquered I settled therein. My tartan I place over them as governor." It seems clear that the policy of deportation applied particularly to Samaria as a city and not as a region. Jeremiah 41:5, for example, seems to imply that a remnant of true Israelites remained in Shechem, Shiloh, and Samaria a century later; so a substratum, or admixture of the Hebrew stock in the later total population must be assumed. The newcomers from the north may be presumed to have intermarried with the Israelite remnant, and ultimately the population took the general name of Samaritans.

The completeness of the devastation left by the Assyrian invasion is evident from the infestation by wild beasts of which the immigrants complained (2 Kings 17). Superstitiously, the intruders concluded that "the god of the land" was angry at their presence and their ignorance of his propitiatory rites. They sent to the Assyrian monarch and asked him to select a priest from among the deportees to instruct them in the necessary ritual of worship. The king (Esarhaddon) acceded to the request, and some instruction in the faith of the true God penetrated the stricken district. A mixed religion resulted. "They worshiped the LORD," we read, "but they also served their own gods" (17:33). Josiah's reforms crossed the border at Bethel and seem to have extended into the northern districts. There was

A Samaritan priest with an ancient scroll, traditionally dating from the thirteenth year of the Israelite settlement in Canaan. "Samaritan" in the NT refers to an Israelite sect whose central sanctuary was on Mount Gerizim (John 4:19). Courtesy Encyclopaedia Judaica Photo Archive, Jerusalem. Photo David Harris.

Remains of the Roman theater at Samaria. Courtesy Zev Radovan.

little, indeed, to prevent their infiltration. Religious revival was not the sort of military penetration that invited Assyrian attention (2 Kings 23:15; 2 Chron 34:6–7). The measure of purification, which may be presumed to have taken place in the Samaritan religion about this time, did not, however, reconcile the Samaritan and the Jew racially.

After the return from Captivity, enmity became inveterate between the Samaritans and the Jewish remnant of Ezra and Nehemiah. On the strength of their worship of the LORD "since the time of Esarhaddon" (Ezra 4:2), the Samaritans sought a share in the rebuilding of the temple in Jerusalem, but were firmly rebuffed; hence the policy of obstruction from Sanballat of Samaria, which was a serious hindrance to Nehemiah's work (Neh 2:10, 19; 4:6–7). Sanballat's son-in-law was Manasseh, grandson of the Jewish high priest; and Nehemiah's drive for racial purity led to the expulsion of this young man from Jerusalem. By his emigration with a considerable band of dissident Jews to Samaria, the rift between the peoples, politically and religiously, was made permanent. Manasseh persuaded the Samaritans, according to tradition, to abandon many of their idolatrous practices; and with Sanballat's building on Mount Gerizim of a schismatic temple for his son-in-law, the sect of the Samaritans was established. It was from this time too that Samaria became a refuge for malcontent Jews, with the consequent use of "Samaritan" as a term of abuse

Samaritans congregating in prayer during a Samaritan Passover feast on Mount Gerizim. Courtesy S. Zur Picture Library.

for a dissident rebel (John 8:48). John Hyrcanus destroyed the temple on Gerizim along with the city in 109 B.C. When Herod provided another temple in 25 B.C., the Samaritans refused to use it, continuing to worship on the mount (John 4:20–21).

Founded as it was before the rise of the great prophetic tradition, the religion of the Samaritans was based on the Pentateuch alone. Their position was held with some firmness, and Josephus mentions a disputation before Ptolemy Philometor on the question that the Samaritan woman poses in John 4:20, the answer to which resulted in the death, according to the rules of the debate, of the defeated Samaritan advocates. Christ's firm answer (4:21–23) stressed the incompleteness of the Samaritan tradition, its inadequate revelation, and the common transience of the cherished beliefs of both Samaritan and Jew. The greatness of Christ is shown in the passage, for at no time had the bitterness between Samaritan and Jew been greater. At one Passover during the governorship of Coponius (A.D. 6–9), when, according to annual custom, the gates of the temple were opened at midnight, some Samaritans had intruded and polluted the Holy Place by scattering human bones in the porches. Samaritans were thereafter excluded from the services (Josephus, *Antiq.* 18.2.2). They were cursed in the temple. Their food was considered unclean, even as swine's flesh. The whole situation narrated in John 4 is therefore remarkable, the buying of food in Sychar, the conversation at Jacob's Well, and the subsequent evangelization of the area. (See also Acts 8:5–25.) It is a magnificent illustration of the emancipation that Christianity was to bring to those grown immobile in the bondage of Judaistic prejudice. EMB

SAMGAR, SAMGARNEBO (See NEBO-SARSEKIM; SARSECHIM)

SAMLAH (Heb. *samlâh, a garment*). One of the kings of Edom. He was a native of Masrekah and reigned before the Israelites had kings (Gen 36:36–37; 1 Chron 1:47–48).

SAMOS (sā'mŏs, Gr. *Samos, height*). An island off western Asia Minor colonized by Ionians in the eleventh century B.C.. It was notable for metalwork, woolen products, and probably utility pottery, though it is not certain that "Samian ware" necessarily implied a large native industry of this sort. Samos joined the Ionian revolt but was treated generously by the Persians, fought for Xerxes at Salamis, but later joined the Athenian confederacy. With typical fickleness she deserted this union also, and her revolt was crushed by Pericles himself (441). After this she was loyal to Athens, and the Samians were given citizenship by a grateful Athens after Aegospotami, the last battle of the Peloponnesian War in 405. Samos was accepted by Lysander in 404 and regained by Athens only in 365. Samos produced the moralists and poets Aesop, Ibycus, and Anacreon, and the astronomer Conon. Paul touched at Samos on his last voyage to Jerusalem (Acts 20:15).

SAMOTHRACE (săm'ō-thrās, Gr. *Samothrakē, Samos of Thrake*). An island in the NE Aegean, mountainous and rising to over 5,000 feet (1,563 m.). Its population was Samian, and it was associated with the Athenian maritime confederacies. Samothrace was the home of the mystery cult of the Cabiri, twin gods of Phrygian or Phoenician origin, which was in wide vogue during the Hellenistic age and included Roman notables among its initiates. Paul called here on his first voyage to Europe (Acts 16:11).

SAMSON (săm'sŭn, Heb. *shimshôn,* probably *little sun,* Gr. *Sampsōn,* Lat. and Eng. *Samson*). One of the judges of Israel, perhaps the last before Samuel. The record of his life is found in Judges 13–16. He was an Israelite of the tribe of Dan, the son of Manoah.

Zorah, where he was born, was about halfway between Jerusalem and the Mediterranean, along the coast of which the Philistines lived. His birth was announced by the angel of the Lord beforehand to his mother, who was barren. The angel told her that she would have a son, that this son should be a Nazirite from his birth, and that the Lord would begin to use him to deliver Israel out of the hand of the Philistines. Nazirites were under a special vow to God to restrain their carnal nature, thus showing the people generally that if they would receive God's blessing, they must deny and govern themselves and be faithful to their vows of consecration as God's covenant people. The preternatural strength that Samson exhibited at various times in his career was not his because he was a natural giant, but because the Spirit of the Lord came on him to accomplish great deeds.

At the time of his birth the Israelites had been in bondage to the Philistines for forty years because they had done evil in the sight of the Lord. After his birth "he grew and the LORD blessed him, and the Spirit of the LORD began to stir him while he was in Mahaneh Dan, between Zorah and Eshtaol" (Judg 13:24–25). But almost from the beginning of his career he showed one conspicuous weakness, which was ultimately to wreck him: he was a slave to passion. He insisted, against the objections of his parents, on marrying a Philistine woman of Timnath, which was not far from Zorah. At the wedding feast he challenged the guests with a riddle, making a wager with them for thirty changes of clothing. By threatening the life of his bride, the Philistines compelled her to obtain the answer from him. When he found he had been tricked, he killed thirty Philistines of Ashkelon in revenge and gave his guests their garments, thus fulfilling his wager. He went home without his wife, giving the impression that he had forsaken her. When he returned later, he found that her father had given her in marriage to someone else, and he was offered her sister in her stead. In revenge Samson caught three hundred foxes and sent them into the Philistine grain fields in pairs, with burning torches tied between their tails. The Philistines retaliated by burning his wife and her father to death.

This act of vengeance only provoked another and a greater vengeance from Samson. He "attacked them viciously and slaughtered many of them" and went to a cave in a rock called Etam. The Philistines invaded Judah and demanded the surrender of their archenemy. Samson agreed to allow the Israelites to deliver him into the hands of the Philistines; but on the way he broke the cords that bound him and, seizing the jawbone of a donkey, killed one thousand men with it. With this great feat Samson clearly established his title to the position of a judge in Israel. The historian says in this connection, "Samson led Israel for twenty years in the days of the Philistines" (Judg 15:20). The expression "in the days of the Philistines" implies that the ascendancy of the Philistines was not destroyed but only kept in check by the prowess of Samson.

Samson next went down to Gaza, a Philistine stronghold, and yielded to the solicitations of a harlot. When it became known that he was in the city, the Philistines laid a trap for him; but at midnight Samson got up, took the doors of the gate of the city and the two posts, and carried them a quarter of a mile to the top of the hill before Hebron. God in his mercy continued to give him supernatural strength in spite of his evil actions.

Continuing his life of self-indulgence, Samson before long became enamored of a Philistine woman named Delilah, through whom he lost his physical power. The Philistine leaders bribed her with a large sum of money to betray him into their hands. By their direction she begged him to tell her in what his great strength lay. Three times he gave her deceitful answers, but at last he gave in to her importunities and revealed that if only his hair were cut he would be like other men. She lulled him into a profound sleep, his hair was cut, and when he awoke and heard her derisive cry, "Samson, the Philistines are upon you!" he found that not merely his strength but also God had departed from him. Now at the mercy of his enemies, he was bound with chains, his eyes were put out, and he was sent to grind in the prison of Gaza.

How long Samson continued in this state of shameful bondage is unknown—perhaps some weeks or even months. On the occasion of a great feast to the god Dagon, his captors resolved to make sport of him before the assembled multitude. The temple of Dagon was filled with people—with three thousand on the roof to watch the sport. Meanwhile, his hair had grown again, and with his returning strength he longed for revenge on his enemies for his two blinded eyes (Judg 16:28). He asked the servant who attended him to allow him to rest between the two pillars on which the building was supported. Taking hold of them, he prayed that God would help him once more; and with a mighty effort he moved the pillars from their position and brought down the roof, burying with himself a large number of Philistines in its ruins. In dying he killed more than he had killed in his life.

With all of his failings he is listed with the heroes of faith in Hebrews 11:32. By faith in God's gift and calling, he received strength to do the wonders he performed. Too often animal passion ruled him. He was without real self-control, and accordingly he wrought no permanent deliverance for Israel. SB

SAMUEL (săm'ū-ĕl, Heb. *shemû'ēl, name of God,* or *his name is El;* some grammarians prefer a derivation from *yishma'' Ēl, God hears;* others associate the name with *sha'al, to ask,* on the basis of 1 Sam 1:20). Samuel is often called the last of the judges (cf. 1 Sam 7:6, 15–17) and the first of the prophets (3:20; Acts 3:24; 13:20). He was the son of Elkanah, a Zuphite, and Hannah, of Ramathaim in the hill country of Ephraim. The account of the events associated with the birth of Samuel indicates that his parents were a devoted and devout couple. Hannah's childlessness led her to pour out her complaint and supplication to God in bitterness of heart; but she trusted God to provide the answer and promised to give to the Lord the son she had requested. When Samuel was born, she kept her promise; as soon as the child was weaned she took him to Shiloh and presented him to Eli. Then she praised the Lord in prayer (usually called her "Song," 1 Sam 2:1–10). Samuel grew up in the Lord's house and ministered before the Lord (2:11; 3:1), and each year when his parents came to sacrifice at Shiloh, his mother brought a little robe for him (2:19). Spiritually and morally, the times were bad. The sons of Eli were unworthy representatives of the priestly office. In their greed they violated the laws of offering (2:12–17); they also engaged in immoral acts with the women who served at the entrance to the tent of meeting (2:22). Though Eli remonstrated with them, he was not firm enough, and the Lord declared that he would punish him (2:27–36).

Under such circumstances there was little communion with God, but the Lord called to Samuel in the night and revealed to him the impending doom of Eli's house. The Lord blessed Samuel and "let none of his words fall to the ground" (1 Sam 3:19), so that all Israel knew that Samuel was a prophet of the Lord. Eli died when he received the news of the death of his sons and the capture of the ark of the covenant in a Philistine victory over Israel. Some time after the return of the ark to Israel, Samuel challenged the people to put away foreign gods and to serve the Lord only (7:3). When the Philistines threatened the Israelite gathering at Mizpah, Samuel interceded for Israel and the Lord answered with thunder against the enemy. The Philistines were routed and Samuel set up a memorial stone, which he called Ebenezer ("stone of help," 7:12).

Samuel, judge and priest, made his home at Ramah, where he administered justice and also built an altar. He went on circuit to Bethel, Gilgal, and Mizpah (1 Sam 7:15). In his old age he appointed his sons, Joel and Abijah (cf. 1 Chron 6:28), as judges in Beersheba, but the people protested that his sons did not walk in his ways but took bribes and perverted justice. The people requested a king to rule them, "such as all the other nations have" (1 Sam 8:5–6). Samuel was displeased by their demand, but the Lord told him to grant their request and to warn them concerning the way of a king. Samuel was now brought into acquaintance with Saul the son of Kish, who was searching for his father's lost donkeys. About to give up, Saul was encouraged by his servant to confer with Samuel, of whom he said, "Look, in this town there is a man of God; he is highly respected, and everything he says comes true" (9:6). In 1 Samuel 9, Samuel is called a "seer" (*ro'eh*) rather than a "prophet" (*nabi'*), "because the prophet of today used to be called a seer" (9:9). God had revealed to Samuel that Saul was to come to see him, and at the conclusion of this first meeting, Samuel secretly anointed Saul as king (10:1) and foretold some confirmatory signs, which came to pass as predicted (10:1–13). Samuel then called an assembly of Israel at Mizpah, and the choice of Saul was confirmed by lot. Samuel related to the people the rights and duties of a king and wrote these in a scroll, which was placed in the sanctuary "before the LORD" (10:25). After Saul's victory over the Ammonites, Samuel again convened Israel and Saul's kingship was confirmed at Gilgal. Samuel was now advanced in years and retired from public life in favor of the king. In his address to Israel he reviewed the Lord's dealings with them and reminded them of their duty to serve God. He called on the Lord to give witness to the words of his prophet by sending a thunderstorm, though it was the season of wheat harvest. The Lord sent the storm, and "all the people stood in awe of the LORD and of Samuel" (12:18). They requested Samuel to intercede for them, and he replied with a significant statement on responsibility and intercession (12:19–25).

Samuel next appears in conflict with Saul; a national crisis had arisen with a Philistine threat and Saul summoned the people to Gilgal. When Samuel was late in coming to make offerings, Saul presumed to make them himself. Samuel accused Saul of foolishness and disobedience and said that Saul's kingdom would not continue. Samuel then went to Gibeah and Saul engaged in a victorious battle with the Philistines. After Saul's success, Samuel commissioned him to annihilate the Amalekites (1 Sam 15). In this expedition Saul again showed incomplete obedience; Samuel reminded him of the necessity of absolute obedience and told him God had rejected him as king. This was the last official meeting of Samuel and Saul (15:35). Samuel returned to Ramah and grieved over Saul.

The Lord appointed Samuel to serve again as "kingmaker" and sent him to Bethlehem to anoint the young shepherd David as Saul's successor (cf. 1 Chron 11:3). Later, in flight from Saul, David took refuge on one occasion with Samuel in Naioth of Ramah (1 Sam 19:18), where Samuel was head of a group of prophets. When Saul came after David, the Spirit of God came on Saul, and he prophesied before Samuel (19:23–24). Second Chronicles provides additional information concerning Samuel's part in the organization and conduct of the service of God. David and Samuel installed the gatekeepers of the tent of meeting (1 Chron 9:22). Samuel also dedicated gifts for the house of the Lord (26:28). Samuel was diligent in the Lord's service and kept the Passover faithfully (2 Chron 35:18). Samuel was also a writer (cf. 1 Sam 10:25); he is credited with "the records of Samuel the seer" (1 Chron 29:29). Jewish tradition also ascribed to him the writing of the biblical books that bear his name. Samuel died while Saul was still king; he was buried by solemn assembly of the people at Ramah (1 Sam 25:1).

Samuel's last message to Saul came when Saul consulted the medium of Endor on the eve of his death on Mount Gilboa. Samuel is mentioned in several other OT books and is recognized as a man of prayer. In Psalm 99:6 it is said that he was "among those who called on [God's] name." The intercession of Samuel is cited in Jeremiah 15:1. In the NT he is referred to by Peter (Acts 3:24) as one who foretold the events of NT times. Paul mentions him in a sermon at Antioch of Pisidia (Acts 13:20). In Hebrews 11:32 he is listed among those whose faith pleased God.

From the standpoint of modern research, a number of places named in the OT in connection with Samuel have been identified and some have been excavated. Among those at which archaeological work has been done are Shiloh (Tell Seilun), Mizpah (Tell en-Nasbeh?), Gibeah (Tell el Ful), and Bethel (Beitin). Tradition also associates with Samuel the site called Nebi Samwil ("prophet Samuel"), which has also been suggested as the site of Mizpah. CEDV

SAMUEL, BOOKS OF. The books are named after Samuel, the outstanding figure of the early section. Originally there was only one book of Samuel, but the LXX divided it into two. This division was followed by the Latin versions and made its appearance in the Hebrew text in Daniel Bomberg's first edition (A.D. 1516–1517). In the LXX the Books of Samuel and the Books of Kings are called Books of Kingdoms (I–IV); the Vulgate numbers them similarly but names them Books of Kings. The title "Samuel," which appears in Hebrew manuscripts, is followed in most English translations.

I. Authorship and Date. There is little external or internal evidence about the authorship of Samuel. Jewish tradition ascribes the work to the

An extra-canonical edition to Samuel following 1 Sam. 10:27. Dead Sea Scroll from Qumran, 4Q Sama, Column 10, Lines 6–9, late first century B.C. Courtesy The Shrine of the Book, D. Samuel and Jeane H. Gottesman Center for Biblical Manuscripts, Israel Museum, Jerusalem.

prophet Samuel: "Samuel wrote the book that bears his name and the Book of Judges and Ruth" (*Baba Bathra,* 14b); it also raised the problem relating to Samuel's death, which is recorded in 1 Samuel 25:1. All of the events of 1 Samuel 25–31 and 2 Samuel occurred after Samuel's death. The statement of 1 Samuel 27:6, "Ziklag . . . has belonged to the kings of Judah ever since," is taken by some to refer to a date in the divided kingdom; others insist that this need not be later than the end of the reign of David. Samuel was a writer, and certainly his writing was used in the composition of these books. First Chronicles 29:29 refers to "the records of Samuel the seer, the records of Nathan the prophet and the records of Gad the seer." Since David's death is not included in our books of Samuel, it has been thought probable that they were written before that event. Another suggestion is that some Judean prophet wrote the books shortly after the division of the kingdom, writing by inspiration and using sources such as those mentioned above. Liberal scholars regard Samuel as a composite of at least two sources, early and late, similar to the so-called J and E sources of the Pentateuch. The earlier is dated to Solomonic times and centers around Saul and David; the later, dated to the eighth century B.C., deals with Samuel; their union is assigned to a date about a century after that. O. Eissfeldt isolates three sources, which he labels, L, J, and E. This division into "documents" stands on traditional liberal bases: duplicates, contradictions, and differences in style and viewpoint. For detailed discussion, one must refer to the commentaries. In general it may be noted that alleged duplicates are records either of separate but similar events, of the same incident from different viewpoints, or of references to previously recorded happenings. Supposed contradictions may often be harmonized by close examination of the text and context. Differences in style and point of view need not indicate multiple authorship but may reflect various purposes in the writing of a single author. As usual in theories of composite authorship, the redactor or editor must bear a heavy load of mixed credit and blame. Positively, the unity of Samuel is attested by the following: (1) the orderly and consistent plan of the work; (2) the interrelations of parts of the books, as noted by Driver; and (3) uniformity of language throughout. The unity of 2 Samuel is generally recognized. Additional light on the text of Samuel may be supplied by the Qumran materials.

II. Content (Outline after Pfeiffer)

A. Shiloh and Samuel (1 Sam 1:1–7:1)
B. Samuel and Saul (1 Sam 7:2–15:35)
C. Saul and David (1 Sam 16–31; 2 Sam 1)
D. David as King of Judah (2 Sam 2–4)
E. David as King of All Israel (2 Sam 5–24)

1. The book begins with Hannah's distress, her supplication, and the answer in the form of Samuel's birth. The song of Hannah shows relationships to both the Magnificat (Luke 1:46–55) and the prophecy of Zechariah (1:68–79). Samuel's childhood was spent at Shiloh; here the Lord spoke to him and revealed the future of the priestly line of Eli. The battle with the Philistines resulted in a Philistine victory, the capture of the ark, and the death of Eli. A source of trouble in Philistia, the ark was sent back to Israel.

2. When the people requested a king, Samuel remonstrated with them but was directed by the Lord to grant their request. Saul was brought to Samuel and was secretly anointed as king. This selection was later confirmed by lot at an assembly of all Israel at Mizpah. Saul's first impressive act, the rescue of Jabesh Gilead from the besieging Ammonites, led to his confirmation as king at Gilgal. Samuel now retired from active public life (1 Sam 12) though he continued to serve as adviser to the king. Saul's incomplete obedience brought about his rejection from the kingship.

3. God designated the youthful David as Saul's successor and Samuel secretly anointed him. David became Saul's court musician and later served king and country well by killing Goliath in single combat. On this occasion Saul inquired concerning David's family, so that Jesse too could be rewarded (cf. 1 Sam 17:24). David now became a close friend of Jonathan, Saul's son, but Saul was now both jealous and afraid of David, and his hostility soon produced open attempts on David's life. David was forced to flee, and the pursuit by Saul, though intermittent, was not concluded until the Philistines swept the Israelites before them on Mount Gilboa and Saul and his sons perished. David mourned their passing in an eloquent elegy (2 Sam 1).

4. David reigned as king of Judah in Hebron for seven and a half years. Overtures were made to unite all Israel under his leadership.

5. These efforts were crowned with success, and David wisely took Jerusalem and made it his new capital, for since the time it had been in Jebusite hands it had had no definite affiliation with Judah or the northern tribes. David continued to build the kingdom and the Lord announced to him the perpetuity of his dynasty (2 Sam 7). Though David conquered his enemies and was gracious to Jonathan's son, he was overcome by temptation in the idleness of semiretirement. The affair with Bathsheba led to bitter heartache and also to sincere repentance on the part of the king. Circumstances in the royal family brought about the rebellion of Absalom, which again saw David in flight for his life. The killing of Absalom ended the revolt but increased David's sorrow. Restored to Jerusalem, David had to deal promptly with the short-lived revolt of Sheba. Second Samuel ends with a summary of battles with the Philistines, David's praise of the Lord (1 Sam 22; 23:2–7), the listing of his mighty men, and the catastrophe of the census (ch. 24).

III. Purpose. The purpose of all OT history is clearly stated in the NT (Rom 15:4; 1 Cor 10:11): to serve as warning, instruction, and encouragement. More specifically, the books of Samuel present the establishment of the kingship in Israel. In preserving the account of Samuel, the judge and prophet, the books mark the transition from judgeship to monarchy, since Samuel filled the prophetic office and administered the divine induction into office of Israel's first two kings.

Bibliography: W. G. Blaikie, *The Second Book of Samuel,* 1887, and *The First Book of Samuel,* 1893; R. D. Gehrke, *1 and 2 Samuel,* 1968; P. K. McCarter, Jr., *I Samuel* (AB), 1980. CEDV

SANBALLAT (săn-băl'ăt, Heb. *sanvallat,* Assyr, *Sin-uballit, the god Sin has given life*). A Horite, that is, a man of Beth Horon. He was a very influential Samaritan who tried unsuccessfully to defeat Nehemiah's plans for rebuilding the walls of Jerusalem (Neh 4:1ff.). He then plotted with others to invite Nehemiah to a conference at Ono in order to assassinate him, but Nehemiah saw through his stratagem and refused to come. When this device failed, he tried vainly to intimidate the Jewish governor (6:5–14). Sanballat's daughter married into the family of Eliashib, the high priest at the time of the annulment of the mixed marriages forbidden by the law (13:28); but her husband refused to forsake her and went with her to Shechem, where he became the high priest of a new temple built by his father-in-law on Mount Gerizim. Sanballat's name is mentioned in some interesting papyri letters found at the end of the nineteenth century A.D. in Egypt. He was then the governor of Samaria.

SANCTIFICATION (Gr. *hagiasmos* from the verb *hagiazō*). The process or result of being made holy. As the article on HOLINESS makes clear, holiness when applied to things, places, and people means that they are consecrated and set apart for the use of God, who is utterly pure and apart from all imperfection and evil. When used of people, it can refer also to the practical realization within them of consecration to God: that is, it can have a moral dimension. Thus in the NT, believers are described as already (objectively) sanctified in Christ—"your life in Christ Jesus, whom God made our sanctification" (1 Cor 1:30 RSV), and "those sanctified in Christ Jesus" (1:2). Also, though set apart in Christ for God and seen as holy by God because they are in Christ, believers are called to show that consecration in their lives—"It is God's will that you should be sanctified" (1 Thess 4:3), and "May . . .

the God of peace sanctify you" (5:23). The same emphasis is found in Hebrews (2:11; 9:13; 10:10, 14, 29; 13:12). Because believers are holy in Christ (set apart for God by his sacrificial, atoning blood), they are to be holy in practice in the power of the Holy Spirit. They are to be sanctified because they are already sanctified.

See also HOLINESS; HOLY SPIRIT.

SANCTUARY (Heb. *miqdāsh,* Gr. *hagion, holy place*). This refers almost exclusively to the tabernacle or temple. God's sanctuary was his established earthly abode, the place where he chose to dwell among his people. Psalm 114:2 says that "Judah became God's sanctuary, Israel his dominion." God himself is a sanctuary for his people (Isa 8:14; Ezek 11:19). The word is used particularly of the Most Holy Place, whether of the tabernacle or of the temple. When it is used in the plural, it usually denotes idolatrous shrines, or high places, which Israelites who compromised with heathenism sometimes built (Amos 7:9). A sanctuary was also a place of asylum, the horns of the altar especially being regarded as inviolable (cf. 1 Kings 2:28–29). In the NT the word is used in the Letter to the Hebrews (8:2; 9:1–2; 13:11), where the author makes clear that the earthly sanctuary was only a type of the true sanctuary, which is in heaven, of which Christ is the High Priest and in which he offers himself as a sacrifice (10:1–18).

SAND (Heb. *hôl,* Gr. *ammos*). A rock material made up of loose grains of small size formed as the result of weathering and decomposition of various kinds of rocks. It is found in abundance in deserts, in the sea, and on the shores of large bodies of water. The writers of the Bible were very familiar with it, and they often referred to it as a symbol of (1) numberlessness, vastness, (2) weight, (3) instability. The descendants of Abraham were numberless (Gen 22:17; Jer 33:22; Rom 9:27; Heb 11:12); as were also the enemies of Israel (Josh 11:4; Judg 7:12; 1 Sam 13:5). Joseph accumulated grain as measureless as the sand of the sea (Gen 41:49). God gave to Solomon understanding and largeness of heart as the sand on the seashore (1 Kings 4:29). The thoughts of God, says the psalmist, "outnumber the grains of sand" (Ps 139:18). Job says that if his grief were weighed, it would be heavier than the sand of the sea (Job 6:3). A house built on sand symbolizes a life not built on hearing the teachings of Jesus (Matt 7:26).

SAND LIZARD (See ANIMALS)

SAND REPTILE (See ANIMALS)

SANDAL (See DRESS)

SANHEDRIN (săn′hē-drĭn, Talmudic Heb. transcription of the Gr. *synedrion, a council*). The highest Jewish tribunal during the Greek and Roman periods, often mentioned in the NT, where the KJV always has "council" for the Greek

Top view showing the entrance to the tombs of the Sanhedrin in north. Jerusalem and below, the interior. The caves were cut during the second temple period and are believed to be the tombs of the Sanhedrin court of judges. At least three of the members of the Sanhedrin—Nicodemus (John 3:1), Joseph of Arimathea (John 19:38), and Gamaliel (Acts 5:34)—are mentioned in the New Testament. Courtesy Zev Radovan.

name. The Talmud connects the Sanhedrin with Moses' seventy elders, then with the alleged Great Synagogue of Ezra's time; but the truth is that the origin of the Sanhedrin is unknown, and there is no historical evidence for its existence before the Greek period. During the reign of the Hellenistic kings Palestine was practically under home rule and was governed by an aristocratic council of elders, which was presided over by the hereditary high priest. The council was called *gerousia,* which always signifies an aristocratic body. This later developed into the Sanhedrin. During most of the Roman period the internal government of the country was practically in its hands, and its influence was recognized even in the Diaspora (Acts 9:2; 22:5; 26:12). After the death of Herod the Great, however, during the reign of Archelaus and the Roman procurators, the civil authority of the Sanhedrin was probably restricted to Judea, and this is very likely the reason why it had no judicial authority over the Lord so long as he remained in Galilee. The Sanhedrin was abolished after the destruction of Jerusalem (A.D. 70). A new court was established bearing the name

"Sanhedrin," but it differed in essential features from the older body: it had no political authority and was composed exclusively of rabbis, whose decisions had only a theoretical importance.

The Sanhedrin was composed of seventy members, plus the president, who was the high priest. Nothing is known as to the way in which vacancies were filled. The members probably held office for life, and successors were likely appointed either by the existing members themselves or by the supreme political authorities (Herod and the Romans). Since only pure-blooded Jews were eligible for the office of judge in a criminal court, the same principle was probably followed in the case of the Sanhedrin. New members were formally admitted by the ceremony of the laying on of hands.

The members of the Sanhedrin were drawn from the three classes named in Matthew 16:21; 27:41; Mark 8:31; 11:27; 14:43, 53; 15:1; Luke 9:22; 22:26: "the elders, the chief priests and the teachers of the law." By the chief priests is meant the acting high priest, those who had been high priests, and members of the privileged families from which the high priests were taken. The priestly aristocracy comprised the leading persons in the community, and they were the chief members of the Sanhedrin. The teachers of the law (KJV scribes) formed the Pharisaic element in the Sanhedrin, though not all Pharisees were professional scribes. The elders were the tribal and family heads of the people and priesthood. They were, for the most part, the secular nobility of Jerusalem. The president bore the honorable title of "prince." Besides the president, there were also a vice-president, called the "head or father of the house of judgment," and another important official, whose business it was, in all probability, to assist in the declaration of the law. There were also two or three secretaries and other subordinate officials, of which "officer" (Matt 5:25) and "servant of the high priest" (Matt 26:51; Mark 14:47; John 18:10) are mentioned in the NT. According to Josephus, in the time of Christ the Sanhedrin was formally led by the Sadducean high priests, but practically ruled by the Pharisees, who were immensely popular with the people (*Antiq.* 18.1.4). The Pharisees were more and more represented in the Sanhedrin as they grew in importance.

In the time of Christ the Sanhedrin exercised not only civil jurisdiction, according to Jewish law, but also, in some degree, criminal. It could deal with all those judicial matters and measures of an administrative character that could not be competently handled by lower courts, or that the Roman procurator had not specially reserved for himself. It was the final court of appeal for all questions connected with the Mosaic Law. It could order arrests by its own officers of justice (Matt 26:47; Mark 14:43; Acts 4:3; 5:17–18; 9:2). It was also the final court of appeal from all inferior courts. It alone had the right of judging in matters affecting a whole tribe, of determining questions of peace or war, of trying the high priest or one of its own body. It pronounced on the claims of prophets and on charges of blasphemy. The king himself could be summoned to its bar; and Josephus relates that even Herod did not dare to disobey its summons (*Antiq.* 14.9.4). It had the right of capital punishment until about forty years before the destruction of Jerusalem. After that it could still pass, but not execute, a sentence of death without the confirmation of the Roman procurator. That is why Jesus had to be tried not only before the Sanhedrin but also before Pilate (John 18:31–32). But for this, he would have been put to death in some other way than by crucifixion, for crucifixion was not a Jewish mode of punishment. The stoning of Stephen (Acts 7:57–58) without the approval of the procurator was an illegal act—a lynching. In the case of one certain offense the Sanhedrin could put to death, on its own authority, even a Roman citizen, namely, when a Gentile passed the gate of the temple that divided the court of the Jews from that of the Gentiles (cf. 21:28), but even this was subject to the procurator's revision of the capital sentence. The Roman authority was, however, always absolute, and the procurator or the tribune of the garrison could direct the Sanhedrin to investigate some matter and could remove a prisoner from its jurisdiction, as was done in the case of Paul (22:30; 23:23–24).

The Sanhedrin at first met in "the hall of hewn stones," one of the buildings connected with the temple. Later, the place of meeting was somewhere in the court of the Gentiles, although they were not confined to it. They could meet on any day except the Sabbath and holy days, and they met from the time of the offering of the daily morning sacrifice until that of the evening sacrifice. The meetings were conducted according to strict rules and were enlivened by stirring debates. Twenty-three members formed a quorum. While a bare majority might acquit, a majority of two was necessary to secure condemnation, although if all seventy-one members were present, a majority of one was decisive on either side. To avoid any hasty condemnation where life was involved, judgment was passed the same day only when it was a judgment of acquittal. If it was a judgment of condemnation, it could not be passed until the day after. For this reason, cases involving capital punishment were not tried on a Friday or on any day before a feast. A herald went before the condemned one as he was led to execution and cried out: "So-and-so has been found worthy of death. If anyone knows anything to clear him, let him come forward and declare it." SB

SANSANNAH (săn-săn'à, Heb. *sansannâh, a palm branch*). A town in the south of Judah (Josh 15:31), identical with Hazar Susah, a town of Simeon (19:5), and almost certainly the same as Hazar Susim (1 Chron 4:31). The site is not exactly identified.

SAPH (Heb. *saph, a basin, threshold*). A Philistine giant, one of the four champions of the race of Rapha who was killed by one of David's heroes (2 Sam 21:18; "Sippai" in 1 Chron 20:4).

Remains of the great temple of Artemis at Sardis, a city with a church (Rev 3:1). Courtesy Dan Bahat.

SAPHIR (See SHAPHIR)

SAPPHIRA (să-fī'rȧ, Aramaic *shappîrā', beautiful*). The wife of Ananias who with her husband was struck dead because they lied to God (Acts 5:1–10).

SAPPHIRE (See MINERALS)

SARAH, SARA, SARAI (sâ'rȧ, Heb. *sārâh, sāray,* Gr. *Sara.* Sarah means *princess;* the meaning of Sarai is doubtful). The wife of Abraham, first mentioned in Genesis 11:29. She was ten years younger than Abraham and was married to him in Ur of the Chaldees (11:29–31). According to Genesis 20:12, she was Abraham's half-sister, the daughter of his father but not of his mother. Marriage with half-sisters was not uncommon in ancient times. Her name was originally Sarai. She was about sixty-five years old when Abraham left Ur for Haran. Later she accompanied Abraham into Egypt and was there passed off by him as his sister because he feared the Egyptians might kill him if they knew she was his wife. Years later Abraham did the same thing at the court of Abimelech king of Gerar (20:1–18). In each instance, grievous wrong was averted only by God's intervention, and Abraham was rebuked by the pagan rulers for his lack of candor. Still childless at the age of seventy-five, Sarah induced Abraham to take her handmaid Hagar as a concubine. According to the laws of the time, a son born of this woman would be regarded as the son and heir of Abraham and Sarah. When Hagar conceived, she treated her mistress with such insolence that Sarah drove her from the house. Hagar, however, returned at God's direction, submitted herself to her mistress, and gave birth to Ishmael. Afterward, when Sarah was about ninety, God promised her a son; her name was changed; and a year later Isaac, the child of promise, was born (17:15–27; 21:1–3). It was during this period that Abraham almost brought on himself dishonor and ruin by lying about Sarah to Abimelech king of Gerar. A few years later, at a great feast celebrating the weaning of Isaac, Sarah observed Ishmael mocking her son, and demanded the expulsion of Hagar and Ishmael (ch. 21). Abraham reluctantly acceded, after God had instructed him to do so. Sarah died at Kiriath Arba (Hebron) at the age of 127 and was buried in the cave of Machpelah, which Abraham purchased as a family sepulcher (23:1–2). Sarah is mentioned again in the OT only in Isaiah 51:2, as the mother of the chosen race. She is mentioned several times in the NT (Rom 4:19; 9:9; Gal 4:21–5:1; Heb 11:11; 1 Pet 3:6). SB

SARAPH (sā'răf, Heb. *sārāph, noble one*). A descendant of Judah. At one time he was ruler in Moab (1 Chron 4:22).

SARDINE (See MINERALS)

SARDIS (sȧr'dĭs, Gr. *Sardeis*). The chief city of Lydia, under a fortified spur of Mount Tmolus in the Hermus Valley; near the junction of the roads from central Asia Minor, Ephesus, Smyrna, and Pergamum; capital of Lydia under Croesus; and seat of the governor after the Persian conquest.

Sardis was famous for arts and crafts and was the first center to mint gold and silver coins. So wealthy were the Lydian kings that Croesus became a legend for riches, and it was said that the sands of the Pactolus were golden. Croesus also became a legend for pride and presumptuous arrogance, when his attack on Persia led to the fall of Sardis and the eclipse of his kingdom. The capture of the great citadel by surprise attack by Cyrus and his Persians in 549 B.C., and three centuries later by the Romans, may have provided the imagery for John's warning in Revelation 3:3. The great earthquake of A.D. 17 ruined Sardis physically and financially. The Romans contributed ten million sesterces in relief, an indication of the damage done, but the city never recovered.

Relief portrait of Sargon II, King of Assyria (722–705 B.C.), from palace at Khorsabad. Sargon is mentioned in Isaiah 20:1. Reproduced by courtesy of the Trustees of the British Museum.

SARDITE (See SEREDITE)

SARDONYX, SARDIUS (See MINERALS)

SAREPTA (See ZAREPHATH)

SARGON (sȧr'gŏn, Heb. *sargôn, the constituted king*). 1. Sargon I was a famous king of early Babylon who founded an empire that extended to the Mediterranean (2400 B.C.). He is not referred to in the Bible. The story is told that he (like Moses) had been put by his mother into an ark of bulrushes in the river, there to be rescued—by Akki the irrigator.

2. Sargon II (722–705 B.C.) was an Assyrian king who is mentioned by name in the Bible only in Isaiah 20:1. He was a usurper, perhaps of royal blood. Shalmaneser V, his predecessor, besieged Samaria in 724. During the siege Shalmaneser died (722), and in 721 the city fell to Sargon. It is strange that the Bible does not mention him in the record of Samaria's fall (2 Kings 17:1–6). Some authorities believe that Sargon did not become king until after the city fell. However, Sargon claims to have captured Samaria, and a certain ambiguity in 2 Kings 17:6 allows for a new, although unnamed, Assyrian monarch there.

Soon after Sargon came to the throne, the Babylonians, assisted by the Elamites, revolted against him and were subdued with difficulty. According to Sargon's inscriptions the remnant of the Israelites at Samaria, who had been put under an Assyrian governor, revolted, along with other Syrian and Palestinian provinces (720 B.C.). This revolt Sargon quickly suppressed. At this time he also defeated the Egyptian ruler So, who had come to the aid of rebelling Gaza (2 Kings 17:4).

Later Sargon captured Carchemish, the great Hittite city (717 B.C.), thus precipitating the fall of the Hittite Empire. He also mentions placing Arab tribes as colonists in Samaria. Sargon claims on his inscriptions to have subdued Judah. Evidently Judah became more or less involved in a rebellion against Assyria, led by Ashdod. This Philistine city was captured by the Assyrians and reorganized as an Assyrian province (711; cf. Isa 20:1), and Judah was subdued but not harmed. Hezekiah was later to revolt against Sargon's son Sennacherib.

Sargon built a new palace and royal city ten miles (seventeen km.) NE of Nineveh, which he called Dur-sharrukin (Sargonsburg), the ruins of which are called Khorsabad. He was murdered in 705 B.C. and succeeded by his son Sennacherib.

JBG

SARID (sā'rĭd, Heb. *sārîdh, survivor*). A village on the boundary of Zebulun (Josh 19:10, 12), probably modern Tell Shadud, north of Megiddo.

SARON (See SHARON)

SARSECHIM (sȧr'sē-kĭm, Heb. *sarsekhîm*). In

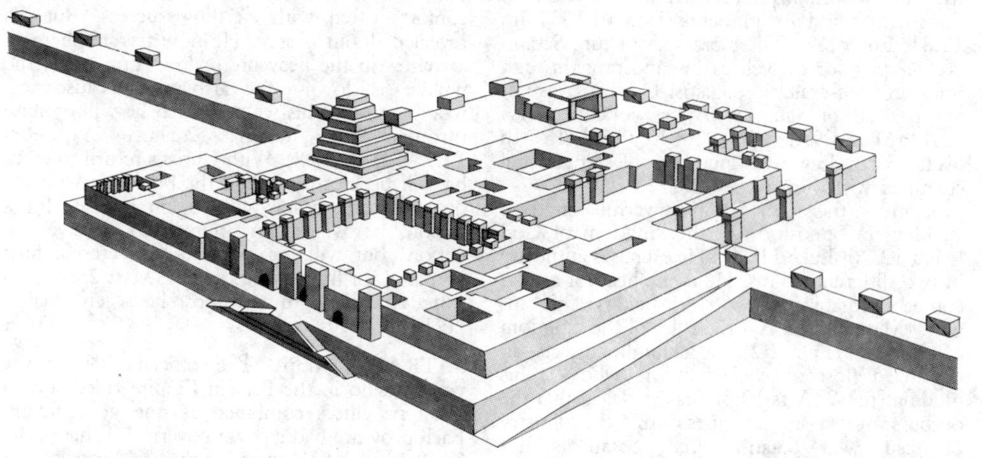

Reconstruction of the palace of Sargon II (722–705 B.C.) at Khorsabad, distinguished by several courtyards, a ziggurat, and a temple. He is mentioned in Isaiah 20:1. After V. Place. Courtesy Carta, Jerusalem.

the KJV one of Nebuchadnezzar's princes who entered Jerusalem when it fell (Jer 39:3). The name is difficult to identify. Many scholars believe that it (together with the Nebo of the previous word—i.e., Nebo-Sarsekim, as in NIV)—represents Nebushazban (cf. Jer 39:13), a good Babylonian name. This person's title was Rabmag (i.e., a court official).

SARUCH (See SERUG)

SATAN (sā'tăn, Heb. *sātān,* Gr. *Satan* or *Satanas, an adversary*). The chief of the fallen spirits, the grand adversary of God and man. Without the article, the Hebrew word is used in a general sense to denote someone who is an opponent, an adversary—e.g., the angel who stood in Balaam's way (Num 22:22), David as a possible opponent in battle (1 Sam 29:4), and a political adversary (1 Kings 11:14). With the definite article prefixed, it is a proper noun (Job 1–2; Zech 3:1–2), designating Satan as a personality. In Psalm 109:6 the article is lacking, and reference may be to a human adversary (cf. NIV "an accuser"), but it is generally conceded that in 1 Chronicles 21:1 the word is a proper name without the article. The teaching concerning evil and a personal devil finds its full presentation only in the NT. There the term *Satan,* transliterated from the Hebrew, always designates the personal Satan (but cf. Matt 16:23; Mark 8:33). This malignant foe is known in the NT by a number of other names and descriptive designations. He is often called the devil (Gr. *diabolos*), meaning "the slanderer" (Matt 4:1; Luke 4:2; John 8:44; Eph 6:11; Rev 12:12). ("Devils" in KJV and ERV is properly "demons.") Other titles or descriptive designations applied to him are "Abaddon" or "Apollyon" (Rev 9:11); "Accuser of our brothers" (12:10); "enemy," Greek *antidikos* (1 Peter 5:8); "Beelzebub" (Matt 12:24); "Belial" (2 Cor 6:15); the one who "leads the whole world astray" (Rev 12:9); "the evil one" (Matt 13:19, 38; 1 John 2:13; 5:19); "the father of lies" (John 8:44); "the god of this age" (2 Cor 4:4); "a murderer" (John 8:44); "that ancient serpent" (Rev 12:9); "the prince of this world" (John 12:31; 14:30); "the ruler of the kingdom of the air" (Eph 2:2); "the tempter" (Matt 4:5; 1 Thess 3:5).

These varied designations indicate the dignity and character of Satan. In the Book of Job he is pictured as mixing with the sons of God (angels) in their appearing before God, though by his moral nature not one of them. Jude 9 pictures him as a formidable foe to Michael the archangel. While clearly very powerful and clever, he is not an independent rival of God but is definitely subordinate, able to go only as far as God permits (Job 1:12; 2:6; Luke 22:31). Christ gives a fundamental description of his moral nature in calling him the evil one (Matt 13:19, 38). Moral evil is his basic attribute; he is the very embodiment of evil. Christ's words in John 8:44 give the fullest statement of Satan's moral character: "He was a murderer from the beginning, not holding to the truth, for there is no truth in him. When he lies, he speaks his native language, for he is a liar and the father of lies." First John 3:8 asserts that "the devil has been sinning from the beginning." Because he is a murderer, liar, and sinner, evil is the very environment and inherent nature of the devil.

The origin of Satan is not explicitly asserted in Scripture, but the statement that he did not hold to the truth (John 8:44) implies that he is a fallen being, while 1 Timothy 3:6 indicates that he fell under God's condemnation because of ambitious pride. While many theologians refuse to apply the far-reaching prophecies in Isaiah 14:12–14 and Ezekiel 28:12–15 to Satan, contending that these passages are strictly addressed to the kings of Babylon and Tyre, conservative scholars generally hold that they contain a clear revelation of Satan's origin. These profound prophecies seem clearly to go much beyond any earthly ruler and harmonize with the scriptural picture of Satan's close relations with world governments (Dan 10:13; John 12:31; Eph 6:12). These passages picture Satan's prefall splendor as well as his apostasy through pride and self-exaltation against God. A consuming passion of Satan is to be worshiped (Isa 14:14; Matt 4:9; 1 Cor 10:20; Rev 13:4, 15). In his fall Satan drew a vast number of lesser celestial creatures with him (Rev 12:4).

Satan is the ruler of a powerful kingdom standing in opposition to the kingdom of God (Matt 12:26; Luke 11:18). He exercises authority in two different realms. He is the head of a vast, compact organization of spirit-beings, "his angels" (Matt 25:41). As "the ruler of the kingdom of the air" (Eph 2:2), he skillfully directs an organized host of wicked spirits who do his bidding (6:12). Acts 10:38 makes it clear that the outburst of demonic activities during the ministry of Jesus was Satan-inspired. Satan is not omnipresent, but through his subordinates he makes his influence practically world-wide. He also exercises domination over the world of lost humanity. He is "the prince of this world" (John 12:31, 14:30, 16:11), the evil world system that he has organized on his own principles (2 Cor 4:3–4; Col 1:13; 1 John 2:15–17). That "the whole world is under the control of the evil one" (1 John 5:19) indicates that the world is in the grip of and passively yielded to the power of the devil. This power over people he holds by virtue of usurpation.

Animated by an unrelenting hatred against God and all goodness, Satan is engaged in a world-wide and agelong struggle against God, ever seeking to defeat the divine plans of grace toward mankind and to seduce people to evil and ruin. As he who "leads the whole world astray" (Rev 12:9), his primary method is that of deception—about himself, his purpose, his activities, and his coming defeat. Satan was the seducer of Adam and Eve (Gen 3:1–7; 2 Cor 11:3); he insinuated to God that Job served him only for what he got out of it (Job 1:9); and he stood up against Israel (1 Chron 21:1) and God's high priest (Zech 3:1–2). Under divinely imposed limitations he may be instrumental in causing physical affliction or financial loss (Job 1:11–22; 2:4–7; Luke 13:16; 2 Cor 12:7). He snatches away the Word of God sown in the hearts of the unsaved (Matt 13:19), sows his counterfeit Christians among the children of the kingdom (13:25, 38–39), blinds the minds of people to the gospel (2 Cor 4:3–4), and induces them to accept his lie (2 Thess 2:9–10). Often he transforms himself into "an angel of light" by presenting his apostles of falsehood as messengers of truth (2 Cor 11:13–15). He clashes in fierce conflict with the saints (Eph 6:11–18), is ever alert to try to destroy them (1 Peter 5:8), and hinders the work of God's servants (1 Thess 2:18). Certain members of the church who were expelled are said to have been delivered to Satan, but with the design to produce their reformation, not their destruction (1 Cor 5:5; 1 Tim 1:20).

Although Satan was judged in the Cross (John 13:31–33), he is still permitted to carry on the conflict, often with startling success. But his revealed doom is sure. He now has a sphere of activities in the heavenly realms (Eph 6:12); he will be cast down to the earth and will cause great woe because of his wrath, which he will exercise through "the dragon" (2 Thess 2:9; Rev 12:7–12; 13:2–8). With Christ's return to earth he will be incarcerated in the bottomless pit for one thousand years; when again released for a season, he will again attempt to deceive the nations but will be cast into "the eternal fire" prepared for him and his angels (Matt 25:41), to suffer eternal doom with those he deceived (Rev 20:1–3, 7–10). DEH

SATRAP (sā'trăp). The official title of the viceroy who in the Persian Empire ruled several small provinces combined as one government. Each province had its own governor. Where NIV has "satrap," KJV consistently has "princes" for the Aramaic term (nine verses) and "lieutenants" for the Hebrew term (four verses).

SATYR (săt'êr). A word used (Isa 13:21; 34:14; JB, KJV, RSV; goat NIV; he-goat NEB; shaggy goat MLB) to translate the the two OT uses of the Hebrew word *sā'ir*, in one passage (13:21) describing the wild animals or demons that would dance among the ruins of Babylon.

SAUL (sôl, Heb. *shā'ûl, asked of God*, Gr. *Saulos*).
1. A king of Edom (see SHAUL, SHAULITES).

2. A son of Simeon (see SHAUL, SHAULITES).

3. An ancestor of Samuel and descendant of Levi (see SHAUL, SHAULITES).

4. A prominent apostle (see PAUL).

5. The first king of Israel, a son of Kish (Acts 13:21), of the tribe of Benjamin, a handsome man a head taller than his fellow Israelites. He is introduced in 1 Samuel 9, after the people had asked Samuel for a king (1 Sam 8). Saul and Samuel met for the first time when Saul was searching for some lost donkeys of his father. Greeted by Samuel with compliments, Saul replied with becoming humility (9:21; cf. Judg 6:15), but, sadly, before the record of Saul's life is concluded we are to find that he suffered, to a chronic degree, the disability that matches his virtue: he was diffident and personally insecure more than most, making him both attractively unassuming and also (in later days) pathologically defensive and highly overreactive. Before Saul left, Samuel secretly anointed him as king of Israel, as the Lord had directed. God gave Saul a changed heart (1 Sam 10:9), and Saul prophesied among a group of prophets who met him on his way home. We must not diminish the significance of Saul's new heart. It corresponds to the blessing of regeneration—Saul became a child of God. In the light of this the remainder of his life is deeply sad and pointedly relevant.

The choice of Saul as king was confirmed by lot at an assembly of Israel convened by Samuel at Mizpah, but the bashful young man was in hiding and had to be brought before the people. In spite of his manly appearance he was ridiculed by some riffraff, "but Saul kept silent" (1 Sam 10:27). His forbearance was supplemented by compassion and decision in his rescue of Jabesh Gilead from the threat of the Ammonites (1 Sam 11). The lowly nature of the young kingdom is demonstrated by the fact that the king earned his livelihood as a farmer. When the message arrived from the besieged city, Saul was returning from the field behind his oxen (11:5). The king's summons to the people, in the form of pieces of a dismembered yoke of oxen, galvanized Israel into a unified response (11:7; cf. Judg 19:29).

After the deliverance of the city, Saul showed his generosity by insisting that his earlier detractors should not be punished. A military crisis with the Philistines revealed flaws in the character of Saul. When Samuel delayed in coming to make offering before battle, Saul presumed to present the offering himself. He found himself in the sort of situation that imposed the severest pressures on a man of his temperament. No leader easily accepts the criticism of inaction nor is any leader always aware when the moment of action has come. Those who, like Saul, are temperamentally hesitant, are often betrayed into hasty responses to crises lest they be thought inadequate. For such, as for Saul, the solution is a resolute determination to obey such commands of God as touch the situation. Saul had a command (cf. 1 Sam 10:8), and his sin was that he listened to the voice of his own insecurity rather than to the plain word of God. For this the privilege of founding a dynasty was withdrawn from him (13:13–14).

On the human side we are reminded of the pressure of the situation: the great superiority of the Philistines in number (1 Sam 13:5), attitude (13:6–7), and equipment (13:19–23). The Philistines had a monopoly on the metal industry; they limited smiths to the Philistine territory and charged the Israelites high rates for the sharpening of tools. At the time of battle only Saul and Jonathan among the Israelites had sword or spear. The Philistines were routed in spite of Saul's bad judgment in denying food to the Israelites at a time when they most needed strength. Saul fought valiantly and successfully against all the enemies of Israel (14:47–48); though he was a brave leader he was not a good soldier, for he was not aware of the necessity of absolute obedience. The affair of the Amalekites, though a military success, was a spiritual failure. We have no ground for accepting the excuse Saul made for his incomplete obedience (1 Sam 15:21). It is consistent with Saul's deep-seated inner insecurity that popular pressure, coupled with his genuine religious feeling, made him a compromiser in such a situation: the people were bent on a religious festival that would have been as much a party for them as a thanksgiving to the Lord. We can share Saul's tossings and turnings until he gives way. Once more obedience has been sacrificed on the altar of temperament, and this time (15:27–28) the continuance of his own period of reign and indeed the validity of his kingship itself comes under judgment.

David enters the narrative in 1 Samuel 16; he was anointed by Samuel as future king and was introduced to court life by appointment as court musician to play the lyre for Saul when the king was tormented by an evil spirit. After David defeated Goliath, David was again presented before Saul and was heralded by the women of Israel as a greater hero than Saul. Jealousy, hatred, and fear led Saul to direct and indirect attempts against David's life (18:10–11, 21; 19:1, 11) and resulted in the hide-and-seek chase that twice drove David into Philistine territory (21:10; 27:1ff.). The unsuspecting aid given to David by the priests of Nob moved Saul to slaughter the priests and to annihilate the city (22:17–19). Saul's life was spared by David on two occasions—at En Gedi (24:1–7) and in the wilderness of Ziph (26:6–12).

The eve of what proved to be Saul's final battle brought the king under desperate pressure. He was so far gone in the disintegration of his personality that he did not know how to get right with God, and in a final and tragic way his temperamental insecurity again triumphed. He yielded to advice that affronted all that his life had held dear and all that his considerably successful period as king had achieved—he turned to the forces of darkness, those same forces he had earlier banished from the land (1 Sam 28:3). The heartrending tragedy of his life reached its climax in the darkened room of a spiritist medium. Samuel could give him no earthly comfort, but we may wonder if Saul was too far gone in mental disintegration to notice the word of compassionate divine grace that the message included: "Tomorrow you and your sons will be with me" (28:19). The Lord never gives up on his own. The next day Saul and his sons died in the battle on Mount Gilboa. The Philistines decapitated Saul and took his remains to Beth Shan, where they placed his armor in the temple of the Ashtoreths (31:10), his head in the temple of Dagon (1 Chron 10:10), and his body on the city wall. The men of Jabesh Gilead remembered Saul's concern for them; in gratitude they recovered his body and the bodies of his sons from the walls of Beth Shan, gave them honorable burial at Jabesh, and fasted in mourning. David also, when he heard the report, went into mourning and expressed his grief in the elegy of 2 Samuel 1:19–27.

Bibliography: H. W. Hertzberg, *I and II Samuel*, 1964, pp. 75–234. CEDV and JAM

SAVIOR (sāv'yôr, Gr. *sōtēr, savior, deliverer, preserver*). One who saves, delivers, or preserves from any evil or danger, whether physical or spiritual, temporal, or eternal. A basic OT concept is that God is the Deliverer of his people; it is emphatically declared that man cannot save himself and that the Lord alone is the Savior (Ps 44:3, 7; Isa 43:11; 45:21; 60:16; Jer 14:8; Hos 13:4). The Hebrew term rendered "savior" is a participle rather than a noun, indicating that the Hebrews did not think of this as an official title of God but rather as a descriptive term of his activity. In the OT the term is not applied to the Messiah; he received salvation from God (2 Sam 22:51; Ps 28:8; 144:10); but he came to offer salvation to all (Isa 49:6, 8; Zech 9:9). The term is also applied to people who are used as the instruments of God's deliverance (Judg 3:9, 15 ASV; 2 Kings 13:5; Neh 9:27; Obad 21).

The Greeks applied the title *sōtēr* (Savior) to their gods; it was also used of philosophers (e.g., Epicurus) or rulers (e.g., Ptolemy I, Nero) or men who had brought notable benefits on their country. But in the NT it is a strictly religious term and is never applied to a mere man. It is used of both God the Father and Christ the Son. God the Father is Savior, for he is the author of our salvation, which he provided through Christ (Luke 1:47; 1 Tim 1:1; 2:3; 4:10; Titus 1:3; 2:10; 3:4; Jude 25). Savior is preeminently the title of the Son (2 Tim 1:10; Titus 1:4; 2:13; 3:6; 2 Peter 1:1, 11; 2:20; 3:2, 18; 1 John 4:10). At his birth the angel announced him as "a Savior . . . he is Christ the Lord" (Luke 2:11). His mission to save his people from their sins was announced before his birth (Matt 1:21) and was stated by Jesus as the aim of his coming (Luke 19:10). The salvation that he wrought is for all mankind; he is "the Savior of the world" (John 4:42; 1 John 4:14). Those who are saved are brought into a spiritual union with Christ as members of his body; hence he is called "the Savior" of "the body [the church]" (Eph 5:23). In Titus 2:10 it is implied that Christian salvation extends also to the ethical sphere, since "the teaching about God our Savior" is urged as an incentive to holy living. Believers await a future work of Christ as Savior when he will come again to consummate our salvation in the transformation of our bodies (Phil 3:20).

SAVOUR (sā'vôr, Heb. *rēah,* Gr. *osmē*). The KJV translation of words meaning "taste" (Matt 5:13; Luke 14:34) or, more often, "smell." In the latter case it is in the OT usually qualified by the word "sweet" and is used to refer to a sacrifice that that pleased God. Thus "the Lord smelled the pleasing aroma" or, as in KJV, "a sweet savour" (Gen 8:21; cf. Num 15:3). *Osmē* refers to the scent of Mary's ointment (John 12:3) and (metaphorically) the incense burned in a victor's triumphal procession (2 Cor 2:14), a Christian's influence (2 Cor 2:16), Christ's obedience to God (Eph 5:2), and a Christian's sacrifice of obedience to God (Phil 4:18).

SAW (Heb. *megerah*). Probably the earliest saws were made of flint, with serrated edges, mounted in a frame. Other saws were like knives, of bronze or iron. Small handsaws were like ours today, but the teeth were shaped in the other direction, so that the worker did not shove but pulled against the wood. Large handsaws were unknown in Bible times. Palestinian carpenters probably sat on the floor and held the wood between their toes, which became as skillful as extra hands.

Stone was sawed as well as wood (1 Kings 7:9). Saws used in the construction of the pyramids and other great buildings of Egypt were made of bronze and had one handle. The Assyrians used a double-handled saw. When Scripture says that David put his war captives under saws (2 Sam 12:31 KJV, NASB; cf. 1 Chron 20:3), it probably means that he made them labor with saws (NIV, RSV).

Hebrews 11:37 speaks of martyrs who were sawn asunder (sawn in two NIV). Jewish tradition (in the *Martyrdom of Isaiah,* a pseudepigraphical book) states that the prophet Isaiah was sawn asunder with a wooden saw by Manasseh. Perhaps the reference in Hebrews is to this event.

SCAB (See DISEASES)

SCAFFOLD (Heb. *kiyyôr*). Solomon knelt on a "brazen scaffold" when he dedicated the temple (2 Chron 6:13 KJV). RSV and NIV translate the expression "a bronze platform."

SCALE. 1. Only fish having fins and scales were permitted as food for the Hebrews (Lev 11:9–12).

2. The Greek word *lepis* means "rind, husk, flake," and is used to describe Saul's recovery from temporary blindness—"something like scales fell from Saul's eyes, and he could see again" (Acts 9:18). See also DISEASES.

3. Scales as an instrument for weighing are referred to in Isaiah 40:12 and Proverbs 16:11 (balance, KJV). A simple balance is here meant. The weights used in these scales were obviously handmade and never uniform, hence the constant temptation to use "differing weights and dishonest scales" (Prov 20:23).

SCALE INSECT (See ANIMALS)

SCALL (See DISEASES)

SCAPEGOAT (Heb. *'ăzā'zēl*). A term that occurs only in Leviticus 16:8, 10, 26 and has been interpreted variously. It is used to refer to the second of two goats for which lots were cast on the Day of Atonement. The first was sacrificed as a sin offering (16:9), but the second scapegoat (16:26) had the people's sins transferred to it by prayer and the laying on of hands and was then taken into the wilderness.

The Hebrew term translated "scapegoat" is thought to be related to an Arabic word meaning "remove"; thus it is often translated "removal" (i.e., scapegoat). The actual meaning of the term and its use in the context of Leviticus 16 are very uncertain.

Some authorities regard the term to be the name of a solitary place to which the goat was taken. This does not seem very likely. Others (as KJV) regard it as a qualifying word for goat—i.e., the goat that removes the guilt of the people, the scapegoat. Some scholars see in the word the name of a personal being—a demon of the wilderness or a fallen angel who seduces people to evil (as in the *Book of Enoch*), or an epithet applied to the devil.

A parallel to the scapegoat may be seen in the Scriptures. In the ritual for a recovered leper, a living bird was released in the country to carry the evil away, and the leper was declared clean (Lev 14:6). In the Babylonian new year's day festival a similar rite was practiced, when a slain sheep was taken and thrown into the rivers, its bearers being regarded as unclean (cf. 16:26). Certainly the general idea of the scapegoat is clear: guilty Israel's sin had been removed and forgotten by God.

Bibliography: G. J. Wenham, *The Book of Leviticus,* 1979, pp. 233–35. JBG

SCARLET. The Hebrew and Greek words usually translated "scarlet" in the Bible are *shānî* and *kokkinos,* from the latter of which is derived the English cochineal. In Daniel 5:7, 16, 29 the Aramaic word for purple has been translated "scarlet" in some older versions (RSV, NIV retain "purple"). The color was probably a bright rich crimson, obtained from the eggs of an insect (see PLANTS: *Scarlet*). Scarlet cloth was used for the hangings of the tabernacle (Exod 25:4; Num 4:8) and for the high priest's garments (Exod 39:1). Scarlet yarn was used for the cleansing of the recovered leper (Lev 14:4) and in other ceremonies of purification (Num 19:6). Its significance in this connection is unknown. Royal or expensive apparel was of scarlet (2 Sam 1:24; Prov 31:21; Lam 4:5; Matt 27:28; Rev 17:4). Scarlet thread or rope appears to have been used to mark things (Gen 38:28, 30; Josh 2:18, 21), and the lips of the bride in Song of Songs are likened to scarlet ribbon (4:3). Sins are "like scarlet" (Isa 1:18); this may be the origin of the custom of using the term red or scarlet to denote things sinful, still in use today.

SCEPTER (sĕp'têr, Heb. *shēvet,* Gr. *rhabdos*). A rod held in the hands of kings as a token of authority. The Hebrew *shēvet* is the word for "rod" or "club," and is used of an ordinary rod (2 Sam 7:14), a shepherd's crook (Ps 23:4), or the staff of a commander (as NIV translates Judg 5:14; KJV "writer") who evidently mustered the troops, as well as of the symbol of authority.

This staff-scepter might be used for protection (2 Sam 23:21; Ps 23:4) or for punishment (Isa 10:24; 30:31). When dying Jacob blessed his son Judah and promised him the royal leadership in words that Christians understand as a messianic prediction, it was the scepter that denoted the royal prerogative (Gen 49:10). Thus, frequently the scepter indicates sovereignty in general, perhaps even conquest (Num 24:17; Isa 14:5; Amos 1:5, 8; Zech 10:11). God's kingship is also represented thus (Ps 45:6).

The use of the scepter by an oriental monarch is illustrated by the account of King Xerxes (KJV Ahasuerus), who held his scepter out to Esther as a mark of favor. She touched the top of it, perhaps as an act of homage or possibly to

Sandstone statue (1.02 m. high) from Nimrud, 883–859 B.C., of King Ashurnasirpal II of Assyria holding a royal scepter in his right hand and a mace in his left. Reproduced by courtesy of the Trustees of the British Museum.

Goddess holding in her left hand a *was* scepter, on a gold pendant from a Canaanite temple at Beth Shan, fourteenth century B.C. Courtesy Israel Department of Antiquities and Museums.

indicate a desire to be heard (Esth 5:1–2). The scepter of Xerxes was of gold; Ezekiel refers to scepters made from vine branches (Ezek 19:11, 14). When Christ was mocked as a king, a reed or staff was placed in his hand for a scepter (Matt 27:29). JBG

SCEVA (sē′vȧ, Gr. *Skeua*). A Jew, who was a chief priest living in Ephesus, whose seven sons were exorcists (Acts 19:14–17). There were only synagogues in Asia Minor, so he could not have been an officiating high priest. The Jews, although scattered throughout the Roman world, remembered their ancestry; and priests were probably then as now singled out for honor in the synagogue. A demon-possessed man overpowered the sons of Sceva, and they fled the house naked and wounded.

SCHISM (sĭz′m, Gr. *schisma, a rent or division*). Used once (1 Cor 12:25 KJV; discord RSV; division NIV) to translate *schisma*, referring to dissensions that threaten disruption, not always involving doctrinal heresy (the more modern meaning). *Schisma* is also used of a garment (Matt 9:16; Mark 2:21 rent KJV; tear NIV), of a crowd (John 7:43; 9:16; 10:19 division), and again of divisions among Christians (1 Cor 1:10; 11:18).

SCHOOL. A place or institution devoted to teaching and learning. The word "school" occurs in the English Bible only in Acts 19:9 (KJV) where the reference is to the lecture hall (so NIV) of Tyrannus, apparently a Greek teacher of rhetoric or philosophy. But the references to teachers and teaching are numerous in both Testaments. The OT stresses the duty and importance of religious teaching and training. Hebrew appreciation of the nature and value of the teaching function is evident from the fact that ten different Hebrew verbs are translated "teach" in KJV. Yet significantly the Mosaic legislation contains no commands requiring the establishment of schools for formal religious instruction. Hebrew education was mainly domestic and continued to be so until after the return from the Babylonian captivity.

The home was the first and most effective agency for religious training. During the nomadic life of the patriarchs, education was purely a domestic activity, and the parents were the teachers. God called Abraham as the father of the chosen people and put on him the responsibility to train his children and his household to walk in the ways of the Lord (Gen 18:19; cf. Ps 78:5–7). The reference in Genesis 14:14 to Abram's "trained men" implies a definite training program supervised by him. The varied commands in Deuteronomy to teach the children, clearly imply domestic education (Deut 4:9; 6:7–9; 11:19; 32:46). Proverbs 22:6 is an exhortation extolling the importance of parental instruction. The training was imparted primarily through conversation, example, and imitation; it utilized effectively the interest aroused by actual life situations, such as the Passover, the redemption of the firstborn, and family rites (Exod 12:26–27; 13:14–16). The well-known talent of the East for storytelling would also be used in the vital transmission of religious truth and faith to the children. Although all teaching was religiously oriented, reading, writing, and elementary arithmetic were taught. The command to the Israelites to write the precepts of the law on their doorposts and gates (Deut 6:9; 11:20) and on great plastered stones in the land (27:2–8) implies a general ability among the people at the time to read and write.

The older people had opportunity to receive religious instruction from the priests and Levites (Lev 10:10–11), who could be found at the sanctuary or in Levitical cities. Every seventh year, at the Feast of Tabernacles, the law was read publicly for the instruction of the assembled people (Deut 31:10–13). The priests and Levites, supported by the offerings of the people, were to be the religious teachers of the nation, but it seems clear that this aspect of their work was not consistently maintained. Only during the revival under King Jehoshaphat does one read of the priests and Levites fulfilling their calling to teach the people all the ordinances of the law (2 Chron 17:7–9). The ineffective teaching ministry of a corrupt priesthood was supplemented by the service of the prophets, the first of whom was Samuel. To make his reform permanent and effective, Samuel instituted a school of the prophets at Ramah (1 Sam 19:19–20). Later such schools flourished at Bethel (2 Kings 2:3), Jericho (2:5), Gilgal (4:38), and elsewhere (6:1). Living in colonies under a leader, these "sons of the prophets" formed a religious training center, their chief study being the law and its interpretation. They became teachers and preachers who denounced national, family, and personal sins (1 Kings 20:35–42; 2 Kings 17:13). Not all the students in these schools possessed the predictive gift, nor were all the prophets of Israel students in such schools (Amos 7:14–15). The preaching of God's prophets—rebuking, instructing, and announcing the future purposes of God—spread religious knowledge and stimulated spiritual life. Professional teachers were employed in the homes of the wealthy (2 Sam 12:25; 2 Kings 10:5; Isa 49:23). The sages, or "men of wisdom," were apparently informal, self-appointed teachers, instructors in practical philosophy, the spiritual descendants of the great Solomon (Ps 119:99; Prov 5:13; 13:20). But there is no positive evidence that special rooms or buildings for school purposes were yet used, although the thought is not excluded.

With the return of the Jews from Babylonian captivity there came a renewed emphasis on religious instruction. Regular teaching was carried on during the days of Ezra and Nehemiah, the Levites being the teachers of the people (Ezra 7:10; Neh 8:7–9). Ezra the priest, described as "a teacher well versed in the Law of Moses" (Ezra 7:6), made the study and teaching of the law his chief concern. With the cessation of prophecy in Israel the study of the law became a matter of scholastic learning. Gradually there arose a class of men who came to be known as the scribes or teachers of the law, men whose chief employment was the study and interpretation of the law and its application to the practical duties of life. At first the scribes restricted their educational activities to adults, and the education of the children remained in the home.

The synagogue, which has a prominent place in postexile Jewish life, apparently had its origin during the Babylonian captivity. When the exiled people were deprived of their temple and its services, they found it helpful to gather for the reading of the Scriptures and prayer. On their return to the Land of Promise the synagogue spread rapidly and developed into an important education agency. The synagogue services with their readings from the Law and the Prophets and the sermonic "exhortation" (Luke 4:17–21; Acts 13:15–16; 15:21) made their educational contribution to the religious life of the people. Regarded chiefly as places of teaching (never of sacrifice), they became associated with the development of an elementary school system among the Jews. Even before the days of Jesus, synagogues with schools for the young were to be found in every important Jewish community. The synagogue "attendant" (Luke 4:20) generally served as teacher; if there were more than twenty-five students, an assistant was provided. Reading, writing, and arithmetic were taught as a means to an end. Since the primary aim of education was religious, the OT furnished the subject matter of instruction. Memorization had a prominent place, with emphasis on catechizing, drill, and review. Discipline was strict, the cane was kept available, but undue severity was not condoned. Students seeking training beyond that given in the synagogue schools turned to eminent scribes for further instruction. This was given partly in their homes and partly in the synagogues or the temple porticoes. The instruction was devoted to the rabbinical interpretation of the law and its applications to life. Such advanced theological training Saul of Tarsus received in Jerusalem "under Gamaliel" (Acts 22:3).

Jesus was much more than a teacher, but he was first of all a teacher and was recognized as such by his contemporaries. Although unauthorized by the Jewish authorities, as a God-sent teacher he was constantly engaged in teaching the people. He generally used the methods of the rabbis but poured into his teachings an authority that challenged and held his audiences. In selecting and training the Twelve he became a teacher of teachers. He commissioned his followers to carry out a world-wide teaching ministry (Matt 28:19–20). Teaching was an important phase of the work of the early church in Jerusalem (Acts 2:42; 4:1–2; 5:21, 28). The work of Barnabas and Saul at Antioch was essentially a teaching ministry (11:26). Paul the apostle, preeminent as missionary and evangelist, was an itinerant teacher, teaching in public assemblies, by personal contact, and by his letters. He thought of himself as "a teacher of the true faith to the Gentiles" (1 Tim 2:7). The NT places emphasis on the teaching function in the Christian church. "Pastors and teachers" (Eph 4:11) were recognized as Christ's gift to his church. Teaching, or discipleship training, was regarded as an essential function of the pastor (1 Tim 3:2). Unofficial or volunteer teachers also had an important part in the work of the church (Rom 12:7; James 3:1). The author of Hebrews insisted that all believers should mature spiritually so that they could become teachers (Heb 5:12). Much unofficial Christian teaching was carried on by members in their homes (Acts 18:26; Titus 2:3–4). In NT times the Christian churches assembled in the homes of members (Rom 16:3–5; 1 Cor 16:19;

A Jewish scribe penning a manuscript from the Book of Esther. Courtesy Zev Radovan.

Col 4:15; Philem 2). By the end of the first century the educational work of the church came to be systematically developed. The church fathers were foremost in all educational matters and did much to develop and promote education, the chief handmaid of the church. DEH

SCHOOLMASTER (See OCCUPATIONS AND PROFESSIONS)

SCIENCE. The KJV translation of Hebrew *maddā'* in Daniel 1:4 and Greek *gnōsis* in 1 Timothy 6:20, both meaning "knowledge." Daniel 1:4 is literally "understanding knowledge or thought." In 1 Timothy 6:20 the reference is to that professed knowledge that sets itself up in contradiction to the truth of the gospel. As used here the word does not have its modern connotation.

SCORPION (See ANIMALS)

SCORPION PASS (See AKRABIM)

SCOURGE (skûrj, Heb. generally *shut, to whip, lash, scourge; shôt, a whip, scourge,* Gr. *mastigoō, to whip, flog, scourge; mastix, a whip, lash; phragelloō, to flog, scourge,* as a public punishment of the condemned). The act or the instrument used to inflict severe pain by beating. Scourging, well known in the East, was familiar to the Hebrews from Egypt. The Mosaic Law authorized the beating of a culprit, apparently with a rod, but limited to forty the strokes given the prostrate victim (Deut 25:3). Leviticus 19:20 does not impose true scourging (*biqqoreth,* translated "due punishment" in NIV, expresses an investigation). First Kings 12:11, 14 apparently refers to true scourging. It was later legalized among the Jews, and a three-thonged whip was used, but the legal limitation was observed (2 Cor 11:24). It was administered by local synagogue authorities (Matt 10:17; Acts 22:19) or by the Sanhedrin (Acts 5:40).

Among the Romans either rods were used (Acts 16:22; 2 Cor 11:25) or whips, the thongs of which were weighted with jagged pieces of bone or metal to make the blow more effective (Matt 27:26; Mark 15:15; John 19:1). It was used to wrest confessions and secrets from its victims (Acts 22:24). The number of blows was left to the whim of the commanding officer. Its victims, tied to a stake with back bared to the tormentors, generally fainted from the resulting lacerations, some even died. It was forbidden to scourge Roman citizens (22:25), that punishment generally reserved for slaves or those condemned to death.

"Scourge" is used figuratively for "affliction" in Job 9:23; Isaiah 28:15, 18. Note the mixed metaphors in Isaiah 28:15. DEH

SCREECH OWL (See BIRDS)

SCRIBE (See OCCUPATIONS AND PROFESSIONS)

SCRIBES, JEWISH. A class of learned men who made the systematic study of the law and its exposition their professional occupation. In the NT they are generally called "teachers of the law" (Gr. *grammateis,* "experts versed in the law"; KJV "scribes"), corresponding to the Hebrew *sopherim.* They are also called "experts in the law," or in KJV "lawyers" (Gr. *nomikoi,* "legal experts, jurists"; Matt 22:35; Luke 7:30; 10:25; 11:45; 14:3) and "teachers of the law," KJV "doctors of the law" (Gr. *nomodidaskaloi,* "teachers of the law"; Luke 5:17; Acts 5:34). They are prominent in the Gospels, often associated with the Pharisees (Matt 5:20; 12:38; 15:1; 23:2, 13; Mark 7:5; Luke 5:21, 30; 6:7; 11:53; 15:2; John 8:3). But they are also mentioned alone and were not necessarily Pharisees (Matt 9:3; Mark 2:6; 3:22; 9:14; Luke 20:39). The Pharisees were a religious party, while the scribes held an office. The double designation distinguishes them from the Pharisees, but the majority of the scribes belonged to the Pharisee party, which recognized the legal interpretations of the scribes. Certain expressions (e.g., "the Pharisees and the teachers of the law who belonged to their sect") imply that the Sadducees also had their scribes (Mark 2:16; Luke 5:30; Acts 23:9).

The powerful position of the scribes in the NT was the result of a long development. The scribes of preexilic days were public writers, governmental secretaries, and copiers of the law and other documents (2 Sam 8:17; 20:25; 1 Kings 4:3; 2 Kings 12:10; Prov 25:1; Jer 8:8; 36:18). The distinctive nature of the office of the scribe first comes into view with Ezra, who set himself to the task of teaching the law to the returning exiles (Ezra 7:6, 10–11, 21). At first this naturally fell to the priests (Neh 8), but gradually there arose a separate group of professional students who devoted themselves to the preservation, transcription, and exposition of the law. When during the Hellenistic period the leading priests became largely tainted with paganism, the scribes became the zealous defenders of the law and the true teachers of the common people. By NT times they held undisputed sway as the recognized exponents of the law and the revered representatives of Judaism. They received the deep respect of the people, as indicated in the honorable term *rabbi,* meaning "my master [or teacher]." Proudly they claimed the positions of first rank, sought the acclaim of the masses, and dressed in long robes like the nobility (Matt 23:5–7; Mark 12:38–39; Luke 11:43; 20:46). They demanded from their disciples utmost reverence, claiming an honor surpassing that due to parents. To facilitate discussion and the exchange of opinions, the scribes lived in communities, the main seat of their activity being Jerusalem (Matt 15:1; Mark 3:22), but they were also found in Galilee (Luke 5:17) and even in the Dispersion.

Accepting the law as the basis for the regulation of all of life, they made it their primary task to study, interpret, and expound that law as the rule for daily life. The lack of details in the law they filled up through the gradual development of an extensive and complicated system of teaching intended to safeguard the sanctity of the law. By their practice of making "a fence about the law" they added to its actual requirements, loading the people with "burdens they can hardly carry" (Matt 23:4; Luke 11:46). They felt that their diligent search of the OT for profound meanings was meritorious and entitled them to eternal life (John 5:39). This vast and complicated mass of scribal teaching, known as "the tradition of the elders" (Matt 15:2–6; Mark 7:1–13), was orally transmitted and required prolonged study to master. In their desire to know the law the common people readily turned to the legal experts as teachers. They taught in the synagogues and trained their pupils in their scribal lore. All higher instruction, if not all instruction of the day, was in their hands. Because of their legal knowledge the scribes were often called on to serve as judges in Jewish courts. They constituted an important element in the membership of the Sanhedrin (Matt 26:57; Mark 14:43; 15:1; Luke 22:66; Acts 4:5). Since the scribes functioned as judges and the law prohibited judges from receiving presents or bribes (Exod 23:8; Deut 16:19), they were obliged to make their living some other way. Most of them, like Paul (Acts 18:3), followed some trade even though their activity as scribe was primary. But apparently this no-fee principle was strictly observed only in connection with their judicial, not their instructional, activities. Christ's denunciation of their greed makes it obvious that while they professed to offer instruction gratuitously they had indirect ways of secur-

A Samaritan high priest displaying an ancient scroll. Courtesy Zev Radovan.

ing their fees (Mark 12:40; Luke 20:47).

Because Jesus refused to be bound by the scribal additions to the law (Mark 7:1–13; John 5:10–18), the scribes soon fiercely opposed him. Throughout his ministry they were his most watchful and determined opponents (Mark 2:16; Luke 5:30; 15:2). Their hypocrisy and unrelenting hatred drew forth Christ's devastating denunciation of them, as recorded in Matthew 23. They played an important part in the death of Jesus (Matt 26:57; 27:41; Mark 15:1, 31; Luke 22:66; 23:10) and in the persecution of the early church (Acts 4:5; 6:12). Not all the scribes were wholly bad, for Nicodemus and Gamaliel were scribes; but as a whole they were marked by spiritual corruption, and their thoughts and actions were the very essence of Pharisaism. DEH

SCRIP (See DRESS)

SCRIPTS (See WRITING)

SCRIPTURE (See BIBLE; CANON; NEW TESTAMENT; OLD TESTAMENT)

SCROLL. The scroll, or roll, was the usual form of a book in Bible times. It had been used in Egypt from very early times, the early ones being made of papyrus, the paperlike tissue taken from the reeds growing along the Nile. As the successive columns (Jer 36:23 leaves KJV, MOF) of Jeremiah's scroll were read, the king cut them off and burned them. Since the burning of skins in an open fire pot would have produced an intolerably bad smell, the roll of a book, mentioned three times in the OT (KJV *megillath-sephĕr*, Jer 36:2, 4; Ezek 2:9; scroll for [of] a book NIV; *megillath* ["roll, scroll"] appears by itself another eighteen times, twelve in Jer 36 alone), was probably made of papyrus. The papyrus was imported from Egypt. Several sheets, glued together to the desired length, were rolled on rods so that the beginning of the scroll was on the right and the end on the left (the Hebrews wrote from right to left).

A library or royal archives is called a house of rolls (Ezra 6:1 KJV). Ezekiel was commanded to eat a scroll (Ezek 2:9–3:3), no doubt in a vision.

As time went on, perhaps after the Exile, the Hebrews began to write important works on scrolls of smoothed skins of animals. Such rolls would last much longer than those of paper. The first scroll of Isaiah from Qumran (the Dead Sea Scrolls) was written on seventeen pieces of skin of different sizes, sewn together at their edges, and in one place glued together as well. This scroll is a little more than ten inches (twenty-six cm.) wide and when unrolled is twenty-four feet (forty m.) long. It contains fifty-four columns of text. Some skins were leather, but in later times the skins were treated in a special way and were called parchment, which was whiter and in general had a more attractive appearance than did regularly tanned leather.

The Jews were extremely careful in the preparation of scrolls of the Scriptures. Only the skins of clean animals could be used. To the present day the scroll is the form of the book used in the reading of the Scriptures in the synagogue.

The book form, or codex, was introduced for private MSS in the second century A.D., and soon took over as a far more convenient form, except in the synagogue. The famous fourth-century MSS of the Greek Bible (Sinaiticus, Vaticanus) are in the codex form.

There were different ways of dividing the books of the Bible on the scrolls; either a separate scroll was taken for each book or several books were written on one scroll. "The Twelve" is the Hebrew name for the twelve Minor Prophets, since all were written on one scroll. To write the whole OT on one scroll would be almost impossible.

Among the awful portents of the Day of Judgment, it is said that "the heavens will be dissolved and the sky rolled up like a scroll" (Isa 34:4). JBG

SCROLLS, DEAD SEA (See DEAD SEA SCROLLS)

SCULPTURE (See ART)

SCUM (See OFFSCOURING)

SCURVY (See DISEASES)

SCYTHIAN (sĭth'ē-ăn, Gr. *hoi Skythai*). The name is used by classical writers as a general term for the barbarians of the steppes. In common parlance it was a term for the savage and uncivilized (Col 3:11). Scythia was the name given by the Greeks to an ill-defined area between the Carpathians and the Don, the western portion of which included the black earth wheatlands of the modern Ukraine. The steppe land was wide open to nomadic invasion, and the Indo-European tribes who occupied it in the seventh century B.C.

A relief from stairway of the apadana at Persepolis (c. 485–465 B.C.) showing Scythians, with pointed hats and armed with sheaths and daggers, bringing offerings of bracelets, folded coats, trousers, and a horse. Courtesy B. Brandl.

Cylinder seal and its impression from Mesopotamia, picturing the liberation of the sun-god from between two mountains. Akkadian period, c. 2360–2180 B.C. Reproduced by courtesy of the Trustees of the British Museum.

are those to whom most properly the term "Scythian" is applied. There must have been a considerable "folk-wandering" about this time, because Scythians appeared in upper Mesopotamia and Syria between 650 and 620 B.C. and another force reached the middle Danube. South Russia, to speak in modern geographical terms, was firmly occupied. The nomads were formidable soldiers, swift archer cavalry versed in the tactics of desert warfare and mobile strategy. By a "scorched-earth" policy and by their elusive defense they frustrated an attack of Darius in 512 and similarly beat off Alexander's general Zopyrion in 325. They exploited the labor of the earlier inhabitants and were exporters of large quantities of wheat to the Greek Black Sea colonies. Greek pottery and metal work were taken in exchange, and the tombs of the chiefs have produced a rich profusion of such articles. The Celts and Samaritans seem to have displaced the Scythians in the last three centuries before Christ. EMB

SEA (Heb. *yām*, Gr. *thalassa*). In the Bible the term is used in several ways.

1. The ocean, the gathering of the waters at the creation, is called sea (Gen 1:10; Ps 8:8; 24:2).

2. Almost any body of water, salt or fresh, is called sea. The Mediterranean (Acts 10:6), the Sea of Galilee (Num 34:11; Matt 4:18), the Dead Sea (Deut 3:17), and the Red Sea (Exod 13:18; 14:2) are referred to in Scripture. Obviously, not all of these would be called seas by us. Galilee is a lake, being only about twelve and a half by seven and a half miles (twenty-one by thirteen km.) in size, but it is often called a sea.

3. Even rivers may, in poetic language, be called a sea: the Nile (Isa 18:2; 19:5) and the Euphrates (21:1).

4. The basin in Solomon's temple was called a sea (see BRONZE SEA).

The ancient Hebrews were not a sea people. The sea in the Bible becomes a symbol of restlessness, instability, and sin (Isa 57:20; Jer 49:23; James 1:6; Jude 13; Rev 13:1).

SEA, BRAZEN (See BRONZE SEA)

SEA MEW (See BIRDS)

SEA OF GLASS. In the vision of heaven in the Revelation, a glassy sea is seen before the throne of God (Rev 4:6; 15:2). It is translucent, "clear as crystal." Nearby stand the victorious singing saints. The sea symbolizes God's purity and holiness and also the victory of the redeemed hosts who have crossed it.

SEAH (See WEIGHTS AND MEASURES)

SEAL (Heb. *hôthām, seal, signet, tabbʿath, signet ring, hātham, to seal*, Gr. *sphragizō, katasphragizomai, to seal*). 1. Literal sense. A device bearing a design or a name made so that it can impart an impression in relief on a soft substance like clay or wax. When the clay or wax hardens, it permanently bears the impression of the seal. The discovery by archaeologists of thousands of seals reveals that their use goes back to the fourth millennium B.C. and that they were used throughout the ancient civilized world from Mesopotamia to Rome. They were made of a variety of hard substances like limestone, metal, and all kinds of precious stones. Originally they took the form of a cylinder with a hole from end to end for a cord to pass through, but this was gradually superseded by the scarab (beetle-shaped). Some were carried by cords hung from the neck or waist; many were cone-shaped and were kept in boxes; but most were made into finger rings. Every person of any standing had a seal. The best ones were engraved by skilled seal cutters and were works of art. The designs were of a great variety of objects—deities, people, animals, birds, fish, plants, and combinations of these. Many of the seals bore inscriptions giving the name of the owner or of his overlord and his profession or office. Many seals with biblical names have been found—among them Hananiah, Azariah, Menahem, Micaiah, Jotham, Nehemiah, and Gedaliah. Excavations in Palestine have produced hundreds of jar handles bearing seal impressions, some with the place of manufacture and personal names (perhaps of the potter).

Seals were used for a various purposes: (1) as a mark of authenticity and authority to letters, royal commands, etc. (1 Kings 21:8; Esth 3:12; 8:8, 10); (2) as a mark of the formal ratification of a

Cylinder seal and its impression in Syro-Mitanni Style, from Late Bronze Age tomb near Acco c. 1550–1400 B.C. Courtesy Israel Department of Antiquities and Museums.

Limestone scarab seal inscribed with hieroglyphs from Lachish, eighteenth century B.C. Courtesy Israel Department of Antiquities and Museums.

Impression of a Hebrew Royal Seal, which reads "(Belonging to) Géaliahu, son of the king." From Beth Zur, late seventh-early sixth century B.C. Courtesy Israel Department of Antiquities and Museums.

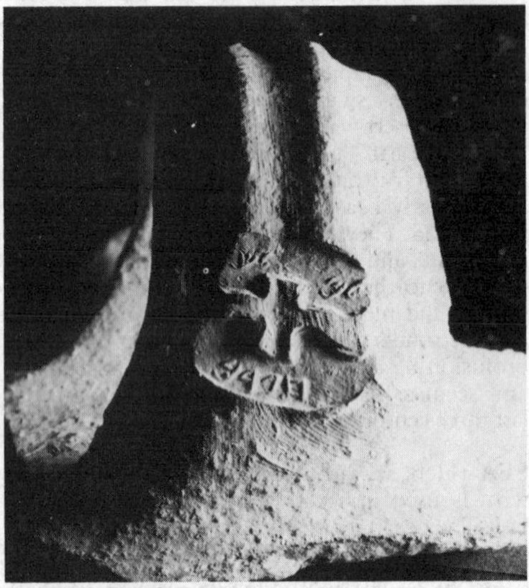

Typical Hebrew royal seal on a jar handle, from Lachish, late seventh century B.C. Inscription reads "(Belonging) to the king . . . Hebron." Courtesy Israel Department of Antiquities and Museums.

transaction or covenant, as when Jeremiah's friends witnessed his purchase of a piece of property (Jer 32:11–14) or when the chief men of Jerusalem set their seal to a written covenant to keep its laws (Neh 9:38; 10:1); (3) as a means of protecting books and other documents so that they would not be tampered with (Jer 32:14; Rev 5:2, 5, 9; 6:1, 3); (4) as a proof of delegated authority and power (Gen 41:42; Esth 3:10; 8:2); (5) as a means of sealing closed doors so as to keep out unauthorized persons (Dan 6:17; Matt 27:66; Rev 20:3)—usually by stretching a cord across them and then sealing the cord; and (6) as an official mark of ownership, as, for example, on jar handles and jar stoppers.

2. Figurative sense. Scripture often uses the term metaphorically to indicate authentication, confirmation, ownership, evidence, or security. God does not forget sin, but stores it up against the sinner, under a seal (Deut 32:34; Job 14:17). Prophecies that are intended to be kept secret for a time are bound with a seal (Dan 12:4, 9; Rev 5:1ff.; 10:4). Paul speaks of having sealed the offering of the Gentiles for the saints in Jerusalem (Rom 15:28 KJV). This may have been literal, thus guaranteeing his honesty, or it may denote Paul's approval of the Gentile gift. The word has the sense of authentication in 1 Corinthians 9:2, where Paul describes his converts at Corinth as the "seal" placed by Christ on his work—the proof or vindication of his apostleship. The circumcision of Abraham is described as an outward ratification by God of the righteousness of faith that he had already received before he was circumcised (Rom 4:11). Believers are said to be "marked in him with a seal, the promised Holy Spirit" (Eph 1:13), as an owner sets his seal on his property; and the same thought is conveyed in the words, "with whom you were sealed for the day of redemption" (4:30). God marks off his own by putting his seal on their foreheads (Rev 7:2–4). SB

SEASONS (See CALENDAR; TIME)

SEAT (Heb. *môshāv, sheveth, kissē', tekhûnâh,* Gr. *kathēdra, thronos*). A place or thing on which one sits, as a chair or stool (Judg 3:20; 1 Sam 20:18). Often (especially when it represents the Greek word *thronos*) it means "throne" (Luke 1:52; Rev 2:13; 4:4; 11:16; 13:2; 16:10). It is used also of the exalted position occupied by men of rank or influence (Ps 1:1; Matt 23:2). Jesus reproached some of the men of his day for preferring the chief seats in the synagogue (Matt 23:6; Mark 12:39; Luke 11:43; 20:46). These were special seats set in front of the reader's platform, facing the congregation, reserved for those held in honor. The great synagogue in Alexandria had seventy-one such seats, which were occupied by members of the great council of that city.

SEBA (sē'bȧ, Heb. *sevā'*). A people descended from Cush (Gen 10:7) who lived in southern Arabia. Seba is a dialectical variation of Sheba. The people of Seba were called Sabeans. See SHEBA, nos. 4–6.

SEBAM (See SIBMAH)

SEBAT (See CALENDAR)

SECACAH (sē-kā'kȧ, Heb. *sekhākhâh*). A village in the wilderness of Judah (Josh 15:61), whose location is unknown.

SECHU (See SECU)

SECOND COMING (See ESCHATOLOGY)

SECT (Gr. *hairesis, sect*). Pertaining to schools of philosophy—Sadducees (Acts 5:17), Pharisees (15:5; 26:5), and Christians (24:5; 28:22). *Hairesis* also refers to heresy (KJV; Acts 24:14 sect NIV; 1 Cor 11:19 differences NIV; Gal 5:20 factions NIV; 2 Peter 2:1 heresies NIV).

SECU (sē'kū, Heb. *sēkhû*). A village near Samuel's town of Ramah (1 Sam 19:22), probably in the direction of Gibeah (19:9). The name is spelled Sechu in KJV.

SECUNDUS (sē-kŭn'dŭs, Gr. *Sekoundos,* a name of Latin origin meaning *second*). A Thessalonian Christian, otherwise unknown, who with several others had preceded Paul to Troas (Acts 20:4). If he was one of the delegates entrusted with the collection, he probably accompanied Paul to Jerusalem (Acts 24:17; Rom 15:25–26; 2 Cor 8:23).

SEED (Heb. *zera',* Gr. *sperma, sporos*). There is a threefold use of this word in Scripture.

1. *Agricultural.* The farmer held his seed in his upturned garment, casting it out as he walked. Grain was sown in the early winter, after the first rains. Christ's parable of the sower is well known (Mark 4:1–20; Luke 8:5–15). Land was measured by the amount of seed that could be sown on it (Lev 27:16). The wilderness was "land not sown" (Jer 2:2).

Drawings of Palestinian seats from Tell el-Far 'ah (right) and Megiddo (center, left). Courtesy Carta, Jerusalem.

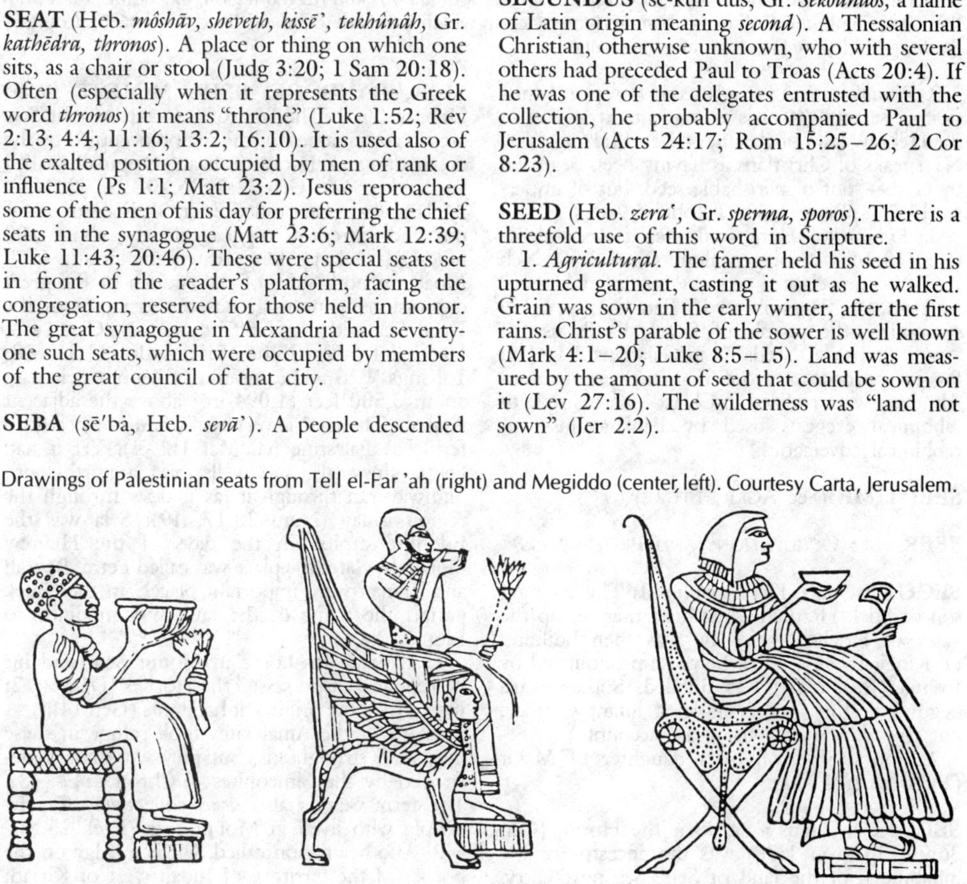

General view of the land of Seir, looking east. It is a mountainous and rugged region, extending south from the Dead Sea to the Gulf of Aqabah, and the place in which Esau's descendants lived (Gen 36:8). Courtesy Studium Biblicum Franciscanum, Jerusalem.

2. *Physiological.* A "man's seed" (KJV) or "emission of semen" (NIV) is a frequent expression in the Hebrew laws of cleanness (Lev 15:16ff.). The NT speaks of Christians as having been begotten by God—"not of perishable seed, but of imperishable" (1 Peter 1:23; 1 John 3:9).

3. *Figurative.* Here seed means descendants (Gen 13:16 KJV) or genealogy (Ezra 2:59; Neh 7:61 KJV) or a class of people ("seed of evildoers," Isa 1:4 KJV). "The holy seed" (Ezra 9:2; Isa 6:13) symbolizes the people of Israel. Paul's use of "seed" ("not . . . 'seeds' ") in Galatians 3:16 had for its purpose a proof that the promises to Abraham were realized in Christ—an example of rabbinical exegesis used by Paul against his rabbinical adversaries.

SEEDTIME (See AGRICULTURE)

SEER (See OCCUPATIONS AND PROFESSIONS)

SEGUB (sē'gŭb, Heb. *seghûv*). 1. The younger son of Hiel. He died when his father set up the gates of Jericho, which he was then building (1 Kings 16:34). Thus the curse pronounced by Joshua (Josh 6:26) was fulfilled. Some regard Segub's death as an example of infant sacrifice, but this is not clear from the account.

2. Son of Hezron by a daughter of Makir (1 Chron 2:21–22).

SEIR (sē'ēr, Heb. *sē'îr*). Seir the Horite (Gen 36:20; 1 Chron 1:38) was the ancestor of the inhabitants of the land of Seir. See next entry.

SEIR, LAND OF; SEIR, MOUNT (sē'ēr, Heb. *sē'îr*). 1. The land of Seir and Mount Seir are alternate names for the region occupied by the descendants of Edom or Esau. Originally called the land of Seir (Gen 32:3; 36:20–21, 30; Num 24:18), it was later called Edom. It is a mountainous and extremely rugged country, about 100 miles (167 km.) long, extending south from Moab on both sides of the Arabah or the great depression connecting the southern part of the Dead Sea with the Gulf of Aqabah (Gen 14:6; Deut 2:1, 12; Josh 15:1; Judg 11:17–18; 1 Kings 9:26). The summit of Mount Seir rises about 3,500 feet (1,094 m.) above the adjacent Arabah. The land is very rocky and not nearly so fertile as Palestine (cf. Mal 1:2–4). Yet it had fields, vineyards, and wells, and a north-south highway ran through it, as it does through the region today (Num 20:17, 19). Sela was the Edomite capital in the days of the Hebrew monarchy; later the place was called Petra. Bozrah and Teman were important places. In the Greek period the name of the land was modified to Idumea.

Esau made his home in Mount Seir, and his descendants dispossessed the Horites (Deut 2:12; Josh 24:4), the original inhabitants (Gen 14:6). A remnant of the Amalekites took refuge in these mountain strongholds, but they were finally destroyed by the Simeonites (1 Chron 4:42–43). The term Seir is also used collectively for the people who lived in Mount Seir (Ezek 25:8).

2. Another region called Seir is a ridge on the border of the territory of Judah west of Kiriath

Jearim (Josh 15:10), generally identified with the rocky point on which the village of Saris stands, SW of Kiriath Jearim. JBG

SEIRAH, SEIRATH (sē-ī'rȧ, sē-ā'răth). A place in Mount Ephraim, probably in the SE part, to which Ehud escaped after murdering Eglon (Judg 3:26).

SELA (sē'lȧ, Heb. *sela'*, Gr. *petra*). A place in Edom taken by King Ahaziah (2 Kings 14:7). It may also be referred to in three passages (of the sixty OT uses of *sela'*) where the KJV has "rock" (2 Chron 25:12, cliff NIV, rock RSV; Isa 42:11, Sela NIV, RSV; Obad 3, rock RSV, rocks NIV, Sela NIV footnote). It seems to be the place made famous in Greek times by the name Petra, the Nabateans' capital.

SELA HAMMAHLEKOTH (sē'la hȧ-mă'lē-kōth, "rock of divisions or escapes"). A cliff in the wilderness of Maon. It was so called because there David eluded Saul (1 Sam 23:28). About eight miles (thirteen km.) NE of Maon there is a great gorge called Wadi Malaki, impassable except by making a detour of many miles; this is probably the place.

SELAH (sē'lȧ, Heb. *sālal, to lift up*). A term occurring seventy-one times in the Psalms and also in Habakkuk 3:3, 9, 13. The meaning of selah is unknown. It is generally believed that its usage was that of a musical or liturgical sign. The LXX seems to understand it as a direction to the orchestra—"lift up"; i.e., play the instruments while the singers are silent. The Jewish Targums and Jerome translate it "for ever," but there is no support for this. Jacob of Edessa (A.D. 640–708) compared it to the Amen sung by the Christians after the Gloria. Perhaps selah was used in a similar way, as a signal for the singing of some sort of doxology or benediction after psalms or parts of psalms divided for liturgical use. The word usually occurs at a place where a very significant statement has been made, making that a good place for a break or pause. It is believed that "selah" was introduced during the late Persian period.

SELED (sē'lĕd, Heb. *seledh*). A man of Judah of the family of Jarahmeel (1 Chron 2:30).

SELEUCIA (sē-lū'shĭ-ȧ, Gr. *Seleukia*). The Seleucia of the NT was founded in 300 B.C. by Seleucus I Nicator, to provide a seaport for Syrian Antioch, which lay some sixteen miles (twenty-seven km.) inland. It lay near the mouth of the Orontes and was a naval base in Roman imperial times. It was the port of departure for Paul and Barnabas on their first journey (Acts 13:4). This city is to be distinguished from the Seleucia on the Tigris founded by the same monarch twelve years earlier.

SELEUCIDS (sĕ-lū'sĭds, Gr. *Seleukos*). The Seleucids took their name from Seleucus, a cavalry officer of Alexander. He was one of the Diadochi, or "Successors," the name given to those remarkable military personalities who successfully divided Alexander's empire after his death. By 312 B.C. Seleucus had established himself in command of Babylonia, Susiana, and Media, and from this date his dynasty and era can be conveniently reckoned. By 301 he was master of Syria, founding Antioch and Seleucia to express the westward expansion of his kingdom and to balance Seleucia on the Tigris, its eastern bastion.

The Seleucids were the true heirs of the kingdom of Alexander. Their borders fluctuated, but for over two centuries of independent rule the Seleucids held the major portion of Alexander's realms. Their empire was frequently called Syria from their holdings on the NE corner of the Mediterranean, where their major centers were located and where they sought to establish an eastern Macedonia. In many ways they followed Alexander's policies. They sought to Hellenize their domains, to mingle immigrant Greeks with Asiatics. In so doing they set the stage for Paul of Tarsus, heir of two cultures, and for the Greek NT. The clash between the Seleucids and the Jews that brought on the Maccabean revolt inhibited to a great extent Hellenizing influences in Israel. The Greek cities, which the Seleucids founded all over their empire, were in general a civilizing force that prepared the way for the fruitful mingling of Palestine, Greece, and Rome, and hence for the development of Europe in the West. Greek life and thought took root in the Middle East and penetrated far into Asia. Royal authority, in spite of its Greek democratic foundations, was shaped by the Seleucids on the autocratic model favored by Alexander. The Seleucid monarchy, therefore, prepared the eastern half of the Roman Empire for the later deification of the emperor. This imperial cult helped to precipitate the damaging contest between the Christians and the Roman State in NT times. EMB

SEM (See SHEM)

SEMAKIAH (sĕm'ȧ-kī'ȧ, *the* LORD *has sustained*). A Levite, a descendant of the gatekeeper Obed-Edom (1 Chron 26:7).

SEMEIN, SEMEI (sĕm'ē-īn, sĕm'ē-ī, Gr. *Semein, Semei*). An ancestor of Christ. He lived after the time of Zerubbabel (Luke 3:26).

SEMITES (sĕm'īts). The term *Semite* is derived from Noah's son Shem (Gen 9:18–19; 10:21–31) and is used to identify a diverse group of ancient peoples whose languages are related, belonging to the Semitic family of languages. It is not certain that since these Semitic peoples spoke related languages, they themselves were related in blood. But since it is impossible now to gain a more accurate knowledge of the relationship of ancient peoples, this obvious connection in language is of some use.

The world of the Semites, in ancient historical times, was the Fertile Crescent, the green land that begins in southern Babylonia in the east and includes Mesopotamia, Syria, and Palestine, ending at the border of Egypt in the west. It is hemmed in by mountains, seas, and deserts. Strangely enough, one of the latter, the great Arabian desert, appears to have been the original homeland of the Semites. From earliest times there have been irruptions from this desert into the Fertile Crescent, bringing new strength to the Semitic civilizations. We can name some of the principal invasions: the Amorites, the Canaanites, the Arameans, the Nabateans, and the Arabs. The last of these, under Muhammad's leadership, brought a new religion and later a great empire to a large part of the Asia-Africa-Europe continent.

The principal Semitic peoples of ancient times were:

I. The Akkadians. The Babylonians and Assyrians who lived in Mesopotamia spoke a common language. From c. 2350 B.C. to 538 these gifted, vigorous people dominated Mesopotamia. Several times they produced empires that ruled the ancient world. Their Akkadian language, written on clay by means of cuneiform signs, was for more than a millennium the lingua franca of the world of that time. The cities of Ur, Babylon, and Nineveh and rulers such as Sargon I, Shalmaneser III and V, Sennacherib, Hammurabi the law codifier (who though an Amorite ruled a Babylonian Empire), and Ashurbanipal the library builder testify to the greatness of the Akkadian civilization.

II. The Arameans. Principally traders and catalysts of culture rather than its creators, the Aramean-speaking people lived in Syria from c. 1700 B.C. to the time of Christ, though their political power ceased some centuries earlier. Damascus, Aleppo, Hama, and Zobah were their cities. Their language supplanted Akkadian as the world language and was adopted by the Jews after their return from exile. It became the language of much of the Talmud, and half of the Book of Daniel was written in Aramaic. It was through the Aramaic language that the Semitic civilization was given to the Greeks and Romans. Syriac (a form of Aramaic) was an important language in the early church. Today there are still a few Aramaic-speaking islands of culture in the Middle East.

Part of relief showing the figure of a Semite, from the temple of Ramses II at Abu Simbel, on the Nile in Nubia. Courtesy Bildarchiv Foto, Marburg.

III. The Canaanites. This term is used to designate a number of peoples who lived in southern Syria (including Palestine) in ancient times. Even the Hebrews can be considered a Canaanite group. Although we still know very little about the Canaanites before the coming of the Hebrews, the recent finds at Ugarit are shedding light on their culture. The Edomites, Ammonites, and Moabites were Canaanites. It appears that the Canaanites invented the alphabet. The Hebrews seem to have borrowed the Canaanite language and culture and made it their own. The Phoenicians were a Canaanite people who took to the sea and became the first people to dominate the Mediterranean and make it their common highway (1200–400 B.C.).

IV. The Arabs. Little is known about the inhabitants of Arabia prior to Muhammad. The great contributions of the Arabs after the coming of Islam lie beyond the scope of this work.

V. The Ethiopians. Across the Red Sea from southern Arabia, the Ethiopians had a flourishing Semitic civilization from 500 B.C. to the time of Mohammed. JBG

SENAAH (sē-nā'à, Heb. *senā'âh*). The descendants of Senaah (sometimes called Hassenaah, with the Hebrew definite article attached). These people were a part of the company returning from captivity under Zerubbabel (Ezra 2:35; Neh 7:38). They rebuilt the Fish Gate of Jerusalem (Neh 3:3). The name may also refer to a place (unknown).

SENATE (Gr. *gerousia, a council of elders*). Mentioned in Acts 5:21, in KJV, RSV, NEB (NIV "assembly of the elders"); not a body different from the "council" (Sanhedrin), but a more precise designation indicating its dignity as composed of old men.

SENATOR (See OCCUPATIONS AND PROFESSIONS)

SENEH (sē'nĕ, Heb. *seneh*). The name of the southern of two great cliffs between which ran the gorge of Micmash. Jonathan and his armor-bearer passed here on their way to surprise the Philistine garrison (1 Sam 14:4–5). Located three and a half miles (six km.) SE of Micmash.

SENIR (sē'nĭr, Heb. *senîr*). The Amorite name

of Mount Hermon (Deut 3:9; Song of Songs 4:8), a source of fir timber (Ezek 27:5). Twice spelled Shenir in KJV.

SENNACHERIB (sĕ-năk'ĕr-ĭb, Heb. *sanhērîv, Assyr. Sin-ahe-irba, Sin* [moon-god] *multiplied brothers*). An Assyrian king (705–681 B.C.), the son and successor of Sargon II (722–705). He restored the capital to Nineveh, on the east bank of the Tigris, opposite the present city of Mosul. It is represented today by the mounds Kuyunjik and Nebi Yunus ("prophet Jonah"); Kuyunjik was dug in part by Layard and the palace of Sennacherib was found. Sennacherib constructed palaces, temples, city walls, and a water system, including the aqueduct of Jerwan (cf. building inscriptions, D. D. Luckenbill, *Ancient Records of Assyria and Babylonia,* 1927, 2:362–483; hereafter ARAB). He was an able soldier, and it is in this capacity that he is best remembered. On his succession to the throne he found it necessary to deal with revolts throughout the empire. Exasperated by the repeated intrigues of Babylon and its king, Merodach-Baladan, he finally reduced the city to ruins in 689. In the west there was also rebellion; among the rebels was Hezekiah of Judah. On his third campaign in 701, Sennacherib marched west to settle those difficulties. The accounts of his campaigns were recorded on clay prisms, among which are the Taylor Prism (British Museum) and the Oriental Institute Prism, which include the Assyrian version of the conflict with Hezekiah. Sennacherib took Sidon and moved south, receiving tribute and capturing Ashkelon, Beth Dagon, Joppa, and other Palestinian cities (ARAB, 2:239). At Eltekeh (cf. Josh 19:44; 21:23) he defeated a coalition of Palestinians, plus some Egyptian forces. Hezekiah had taken Padi, king of Ekron, who was allied with Sennacherib, and made him a captive (ARAB, 2:240). Sennacherib now seized Ekron and restored Padi to his throne. He did not take Jerusalem, but he boasted that he shut up Hezekiah "like a bird in a cage." The OT gives three records of this invasion and its results (2 Kings 18:13–19:17; 2 Chron 32:1–22; Isa 36:1–37:38).

It was in the fourteenth year of Hezekiah that Sennacherib came against Judah and took all of its fortified cities. Hezekiah offered to pay tribute and had to strip the temple of its treasures to make payment. The Assyrian sent his officers to Jerusalem to deliver an ultimatum concerning capitulation. At this time Sennacherib was besieging Lachish, which he took and then moved against Libnah. The reliefs of the palace of Sennacherib at Kuyunjik depicted the capture of Lachish. When Sennacherib heard that Tirhakah king of Egypt was coming against him, he sent a second message to Hezekiah. Hezekiah made this a matter for prayer, and the prophet Isaiah brought him God's assurance of deliverance. Tirhakah was involved in the coalition defeated by Sennacherib; Egypt of that period was correctly evaluated by the Assyrian spokesman as "that splintered reed" (2 Kings 18:21; Isa 36:6). The Bible relates that Jerusalem was delivered by the Lord, who sent his angel to strike the Assyrian armies and force Sennacherib to retire to his homeland (2 Kings 19:35–36; 2 Chron 32:21; Isa 37:36–37). Various naturalistic explanations of this incident have been attempted. Herodotus preserves a story of an Assyrian defeat occasioned by a plague of mice, which consumed the equipment of the armies and left them helpless before their enemies; some have associated the mice with the carrying of some disease or plague.

The famous Taylor Prism, a hexagonal cylinder bearing an account of Sennacherib's raid into Judah, dated 701 B.C. (cf. 2 Kings 18:13). Reproduced by courtesy of the Trustees of the British Museum.

Back in Nineveh, Sennacherib was assassinated by two of his sons in 681 B.C. (2 Kings 19:37; Isa 37:38) in an effort to upset the succession that he had decreed for Esarhaddon, but Esarhaddon was equal to the situation and gained the throne. The Assyrian account of the Judean campaign follows: "As to Hezekiah, the Jew, he did not submit to my yoke, I laid siege to forty-six of his strong cities, walled forts and to the countless small villages in their vicinity, and conquered (them) by means of well-stamped (earth-) ramps, and battering-rams brought (thus) near (to the walls) (combined with) the attack by foot-soldiers, (using) mines, breeches (sic) as well as sapper work. I drove out (of them) 200,150 people, young and old, male and female, horses, mules, donkeys, camels, big and small cattle, beyond counting, and considered (them) booty. Himself I made a prisoner in Jerusalem, his royal residence, like a bird in a cage. I surrounded him with earthwork in order to molest those who were leaving his city's gate. . . . Hezekiah himself . . . did send me later, to Nineveh, my lordly city, together with thirty talents of gold, 800 talents of silver . . . his (own) daughter to deliver the tribute and to do obeisance as a slave he sent his (personal) messenger" (ANET, p. 288; cf. ARAB, 2:240). CEDV

SENSUAL (Gr. *psychikos, pertaining to the soul*). Used twice in the KJV to denote the unspiritual nature and characteristics of the soul, the natural life that human beings have in common with brutes (James 3:15; Jude 19). It is also used twice in the NIV (Col 2:23; 1 Tim 5:11). *Psychikos* is used six times (1 Cor 2:14; 15:44 [twice], 46; James 3:15; Jude 19).

SENUAH (See HASSENUAH)

SEORIM (sē-ō'rĭm, Heb. *se'ōrîm*). A descendant of Aaron; head of one of the courses or subdivisions of the priests in the time of David (1 Chron 24:1–8).

SEPHAR (sē'făr, Heb. *sephārâh*). The eastern limit of the territory of the sons of Joktan (Gen 10:30). This may be equated with the Arabic Zafar, the name of two towns in southern Arabia.

SEPHARAD (sē-fā'răd, Heb. *sephārādh*). The place of captivity of certain people of Jerusalem (Obad 20). Its location is uncertain; perhaps it is to be identified with Shaparda, which Sargon II, who exiled Israelites to the cities of the Medes and claims to have conquered Judah, mentions as a district of SW Media. Among the Jews of the postbiblical period the term was used to refer to Spain.

SEPHARVAIM, SEPHARVITE (sĕf'ár-vā'ĭm, sē'făr-vīt). The place from which the Assyrians brought colonists to live in Samaria (2 Kings 17:24, 31). The inhabitants of the place were called Sepharvites. The place is also referred to in the Assyrian commander's threatening speech to Jerusalem (18:34; 19:13) as a place conquered by the Assyrian armies. Formerly Sepharvaim was identified with Sippar in Babylonia, but recently scholars have tended to reject that theory and have identified it with the Sibraim of Ezekiel 47:16, a place located in the region of Hamath.

SEPTUAGINT (sĕp'tū-á-jĭnt). The first and most important of a number of ancient translations of the Hebrew OT into Greek. Little is certainly known about it, for our information is frequently based on ancient traditions of doubtful authenticity; and scholars are divided in their judgments concerning both its origin and its usefulness in textual criticism.

The story of the origin of the Septuagint is told in the *Letter of Aristeas,* a pseudepigraphical book written in the second half of the second century B.C. It states that Ptolemy II (called Philadelphus, the king of Egypt, 285–247) wished to have a translation of the Jewish law for his famous library in Alexandria. At his request the high priest Eleazer of Jerusalem sent seventy-two men, six from each tribe, to Egypt with a scroll of the Law. In seventy-two days they translated one section each from this scroll and afterward decided on the wording together. So the version was called the Septuagint (the translation of the seventy, abbreviated LXX). Later writers elaborated on this story to the effect that the seventy-two had translated the whole OT (not the Pentateuch only), each independently of the other, in seclusion. The exact agreement of the seventy-two copies proved the work's inspiration.

What is the truth of this story? It is generally agreed that the Pentateuch was translated from Hebrew into Greek in Egypt around the time of Ptolemy II, ca. 280 B.C. The rest of the OT was done at a later date. Most scholars believe the whole to have been finished by 180, although some scholars (notably Kahle) disagree, believing that the LXX never contained more than the Pentateuch until the Christians took it over and added the rest of the OT books much later.

It seems most likely that the LXX originated not by the desire of Ptolemy II (although the project may have had his approval), but out of the need of the Alexandrian Jews. Alexandria of the third century B.C. was a large city with a great Jewish population. These Jews were Greek-speaking, having long since forgotten their own language. The vigorous Jewish intellectual life of Alexandria (exemplified by Philo Judaeus in a later century) would demand the Torah in Greek, just as an earlier generation of Jews made Targums of the OT in the Aramaic language.

The fact that the LXX was not made all at once is plain by the unevenness of its character. Some parts, e.g., the Pentateuch, are a rather literal and accurate translation of the Hebrew text. Other books, such as 1 and 2 Samuel, differ greatly from the Masoretic Text (our present Hebrew Bible). Recent finds at Qumran ("The Dead Sea Scrolls") include a Hebrew MS of Samuel whose text seems very close to the LXX of this book. The LXX Daniel was such a free paraphrase that it was set aside in favor of a later translation made by Theodotion. The LXX Jeremiah is one-seventh, and the LXX Job is about one-fourth shorter than the Masoretic Text. The LXX, then, is not one book, but a collection of translations of the OT produced by Jews of the Dispersion.

The LXX came to have great authority among the non-Palestinian Jews. Its use in the synagogues of the Dispersion made it one of the most important missionary aids. Probably it was the first work of substantial size ever to be translated into another language. Now the Greeks could read the divine revelation in their own tongue. When the NT quotes from the OT, as it frequently does, the form of the quotation often follows the LXX.

The early Christian church, built largely on converts from the synagogues of the Greek-speaking world, took over the LXX as their Bible. Their use of it, to prove to the Jews that Jesus was the Messiah, caused a change in the Jews' attitude toward it. Soon after A.D. 100 the Jews completely gave up the LXX, and it became a Christian book. The Jews sponsored new translations of the OT, those by Aquila, Symmachus, and Theodotion being best known.

Our oldest copies of the LXX today are from the three great Greek MSS of the Bible from the fourth and fifth centuries A.D.—Sinaiticus, Vaticanus, and Alexandrinus. It is quite plain that these represent a LXX that has had a long textual history, and that it is now impossible to say to what extent these copies agree with the original translation made some six or seven hundred years before. Origen (died c. A.D. 250) sensed the problem of many divergent readings in the MSS in his day and sought to produce a resultant text in his *Hexapla*. The textual criticism of the LXX is a difficult task, on which the last word remains to be said.

The LXX is of use in two ways to biblical studies today:

1. It is a valuable witness to the understanding of the OT in pre-Christian days. As such it is frequently the originator of an exegetical tradition still followed. When, e.g., the majority of English Old Testaments render the covenant name for God (in Hebrew YHWH) by "LORD," they are merely following the lead of the LXX, which rendered the word by the Greek *kyrios*—"Lord." Another example of the LXX's influence on subsequent translations is its rendering of the Hebrew *'ĕlōhîm* (God) by *angeloi*, "angels," e.g., in Psalm 8:5 (KJV; NIV "heavenly beings"). The writer of the Letter to the Hebrews (2:7) followed the LXX here, as did the NIV and the KJV: "a little lower than the angels."

2. The LXX is a very important tool for use in the science of textual criticism—the attempt to bring to light the original text of the Bible. In quite a few cases the Masoretic Text and the LXX do not agree. A person knowing neither of the original languages can sense the difference by comparing Amos 9:11–12 with Acts 15:16–17. James quotes Amos, and his quotation agrees in general with the LXX, which is quite different from the Masoretic Text. Of course, the great majority of the differences between the two are inconsequential; the Amos-Acts passage was cited because the difference there is of some consequence for the meaning of the passage. Another example is Psalm 22:16, where the Hebrew Bible's "like a lion my hands and my feet" is rendered "they pierced my hands and my feet" in the English Bibles, following the LXX. Often when the Hebrew text is difficult (as in the last example) modern translators correct the text by using the easier-to-explain readings of the LXX. To what extent this adherence to the easier reading is justified is not easy to say. A recent trend of thought among biblical scholars is to question the correctness of these easier LXX readings and to seek by etymological study to make sense of the more difficult reading in the Masoretic Text. In spite of these problems, it can be said that the LXX is an eloquent witness to the accuracy with which the OT has come down to us from ancient days. JBG

SEPULCHER (See TOMB)

SERAH (sē'rȧ, Heb. *serah*). A daughter of Asher (Gen 46:17; Num 26:46; 1 Chron 7:30).

SERAIAH (sē-rā'yȧ, Heb. *serāyāhû*). 1. A son of Kenaz (1 Chron 4:13).

2. A scribe who held office under David (2 Sam 8:17).

3. A Simeonite, son of Asiel (1 Chron 4:35).

4. One of the men sent to arrest Jeremiah and Baruch (Jer 36:26).

5. The high priest when Nebuchadnezzar captured Jerusalem. He was put to death by Nebuchadnezzar at Riblah (2 Kings 25:18–21; Jer 52:24–27). He was the father of Jehozadak, who was taken into captivity, and the grandfather of Jeshua, the high priest under Zerubbabel at the return from exile. He may also be the Seraiah named as an ancestor of Ezra (1 Chron 6:14–15; Ezra 3:2; 7:1).

6. The son of Neriah, a quartermaster (RSV; NIV "staff officer") carried to Babylon when Jerusalem fell (Jer 51:59–64).

7. The son of Tanhumeth, from the town of Netophah (2 Kings 25:23; Jer 40:8).

8. A priest, the third in the list of those who returned from Babylon to Jerusalem with Zerubbabel (Ezra 2:2; Neh 7:7, where he is called Azariah; 12:1), and third also in the record of those who sealed the covenant binding all Jews not to take foreign wives (Neh 10:2). He became governor of the temple when it was rebuilt (Neh 11:11). He is mentioned (as Azariah) also in 1 Chronicles 9:11.

SERAPHS, SERAPHIM (sĕr'ȧ-fĭm, Heb. *serāphîm*). Called seraphs (JB, NIV), seraphim (MLB, NASB, NEB, RSV, *-im* being the Hebrew plural ending), and seraphims (KJV). They were celestial beings whom Isaiah, when he was called to the prophetic ministry, saw standing before the enthroned Lord (Isa 6:2–3, 6–7). This is the only mention of these creatures in the Bible.

Six-winged figure on basalt relief from Tell Halaf, reminiscent of the creature Isaiah saw standing before the enthroned Lord (Isa 6:2). The figure, perhaps a woman, wears a long fringed robe and six wings, two springing from her shoulders, two from her hips, and two emerging from her knees. She wears an elaborate crown, perhaps intended to represent horns. Courtesy Carta, Jerusalem.

The word *seraphim* means "burning ones." The same word is used to describe the snakes in the wilderness (Num 21:6, 8; cf. Deut 8:15; Isa 14:29; 30:6); some commentators think that the seraphim of Isaiah's vision were serpentine in form. This cannot be correct, because it conflicts with the evidence given in Isaiah 6. Like the cherubim and the living creatures, they belong to an order of unearthly beings attending the throne of God. Isaiah saw that they were standing upright with three pairs of wings and human hands, faces, and voices. The designation "burning ones" matches the context. Its focus on God's holiness makes the emphasis on fire a suitable one, as does also the fact that a seraph performed a burning ministry toward Isaiah himself (Isa 6:6–7). The seraphim are in a particular sense, therefore, the guardians of the holiness of the Lord and the ministers of his holy purposes by means of a just, substitutionary salvation. See also FIRE.

SERED (sē'rĕd, Heb. *seredh*). A son of Zebulun (Gen 46:14; Num 26:26), and founder of a tribal family.

SEREDITE (sĕr'ē-dīt). A name given to the descendants of Sered (Gen 46:14; Num 26:26). KJV has "Sardite."

SERGEANT (See OCCUPATIONS AND PROFESSIONS)

SERGIUS PAULUS (See PAULUS, SERGIUS)

SERMON ON THE MOUNT. The first of six extended discourses of Jesus given in the Gospel of Matthew, covering chapters 5–7. The other discourses are (2) the mission of the Twelve (Matt 9:35–11:1), (3) the parables by the sea (13:1–52), (4) humility (ch. 18), (5) denunciation hypocrisy (ch. 23), and (6) eschatology (ch. 24–25).

Some of these discourses are given in Mark and Luke in the same situations as in Matthew, but always in shorter form. Much of the teaching material that Matthew gives in these long discourses is given also by Mark and Luke, with close verbal similarity, but in fragments in other settings than Matthew's.

These facts have caused critical students to question, in greater or lesser degree, the integrity of Matthew's record of the Lord's teaching ministry. Some relatively conservative scholars have held that Matthew's six great discourses of Jesus were built up by Matthew from scattered materials.

It is obviously impossible in this short article to give an answer in detail, but it can be stated that there is no sound reason to doubt that Matthew's account of the discourses of Jesus is true and reliable.

The nature of Jesus' itinerant ministry to shifting crowds was such that he must have repeated similar material a great many times under a great variety of circumstances. Moreover, in any one extended session of his teaching, there were interruptions, questions, arguments, digressions.

The word "sermon" is misleading to the modern mind. Matthew does not say that Jesus arose, entered the pulpit, and delivered a sermon that he had formally prepared in a quiet library. The crowds were following him (Matt 5:1; Luke 6:17) to see his miracles. He went up the mountain a little way so that his immediate followers would be nearer than the rest (Matt 5:1); and then he came down with them to a level place (Luke 6:17), still in "the mountain." Presently he sat down and began to teach, with special attention to the disciples who were near.

The biblical writers, of course, used no quotation marks, and the modern reader must understand that they do not claim to give quotations word for word. Neither do they claim to give all that was said on any occasion. They do claim that their words are a true presentation of the substance quoted.

Let the reader allow his imagination to picture the giving of the first beatitude, for example. Jesus says, "Blessed are you poor people." A dull person interrupts, "How can that be? We're in want." Jesus replies, "God's kingdom is yours [if you will have it], but more important, Blessed are they who feel their spiritual poverty, for the kingdom of heaven is theirs" (Matt 5:3; Luke 6:20).

The "sermon," then, is a student's (Matthew's) report of a class lecture and discussion and should be studied in that light. Luke's account is to be understood as based on another student's notebook (see Luke 1:1–4 for Luke's sources of information). The fact that there are digressions from a formal outline (Matt 5:25–26, 29–30) is evidence of the genuineness of the record. What teacher in touch with the minds of his class is ever able to avoid digressions from his basic outline?

This mode of regarding the matter does not in any way contradict the inspired truthfulness of the Gospel record as it stands.

It is remarkable what unity and order of thought is evident in the Sermon on the Mount. There is no space for a detailed analytical outline, which the careful reader can profitably make for himself. Is the teaching of Jesus literally applicable to human beings in this world? The meek do not now inherit the earth (Matt 5:5), and public or national nonresistance leads to slavery.

If we take the teaching of Jesus in the same reasonably flexible way that it seems he interpreted the Ten Commandments (Matt 12:4–5, 11–12), the way of the heart rather than of mere outward conduct (5:22, 28), there is not a word that we need not heed today. We should be willing to take a slap in the face. This is not to say that we must stand by and see the innocent suffer lawless injury. Jesus did not contradict the principle that those responsible for law enforcement must bear "the sword" (Rom 13:1–5) and that "not for nothing." The Sermon on the Mount is Christ's instruction to us for godly living in the present world.

Bibliography: H. Marriott, *The Sermon on the Mount,* 1925; M. Dibelius, *The Sermon on the Mount,* 1940; D. M. Lloyd-Jones, *Studies in the Sermon on the Mount,* 2 vols., 1959–60; T. W. Manson, *The Sayings of Jesus,* 1957; R. A. Guelich, *The Sermon on the Mount,* 1982. JOB

SERPENT (See ANIMALS)

SERUG (sē'rŭg, Heb. *serûgh,* meaning uncertain). A descendant of Shem; son of Reu and great-grandfather of Abraham (Gen 11:20, 22–23; 1 Chron 1:26). In KJV of Luke 3:35 he is called Saruch (NIV retains Serug). He is thus in the messianic line. *Saurgi,* a city of the district of Harran mentioned in Assyrian texts, was probably named after him. He lived 230 years.

SERVANT (See OCCUPATIONS AND PROFESSIONS)

SERVANT OF JEHOVAH. A term applied in the KJV of the OT to the patriarchs (Exod 32:13), Moses (Num 12:7–8), Joshua (Judg 2:8), David (2 Sam 7:5–29), the prophets (Zech 1:6), and others. It is chiefly used, however, as a title for the Messiah (Isa 42:1–4; 49:1–6; 50:4–9; 52:13–53:12). NIV generally has "a servant of the LORD" or "my servant."

The interpretation of these passages has been contested. Some contend that the prophet was speaking of himself, a view that can sustain itself only by the unwarranted removal of 49:3 (in whole or part) from the text of Isaiah and by the most tortuous and unlikely interpretation of chapter 53. A much more prevalent view is that Isaiah was speaking of the mission, suffering, and marvelous continuance of Israel, the nation. This view accords with 49:3 but makes difficult an explanation of chapter 53 in credible terms; for in what possible sense can the national sufferings be understood as vicarious when the prophet himself says (e.g., 42:18–25) that it was all their own fault? Besides, though Israel is spoken of as the servant (e.g., 43:10), the portrait of the servant-nation outside the key passages and of the Servant in the passages is dramatically different. The only interpretation capable of sustaining itself through all the details of the four passages is that which sees Isaiah as looking forward to the perfect Servant and his perfect act of service.

On this understanding the passages fit perfectly into their context and offer a developing portrait of the Lord Jesus Christ. The plight of the Gentile world (41:28–29) prepares for the Servant, who will bring "judgment," i.e., the revelation of the Lord and of his will, to the Gentiles (42:1–4). Following this, Isaiah becomes increasingly aware of the plight of national Israel (e.g., 42:18ff.) until, by chapter 48, he is ready to say that the people no longer have any right to their privileged name as "Israel" (48:1) and that, though mercy may redeem them from slavery in Babylon (48:20–21), yet they know nothing of peace with God (48:22). This prepares us for the lesson that the Servant's task (49:1–6) is first to Israel and then to the whole world and that he is himself the only one deserving the name Israel (49:3). Unlike the nation (49:13–50:4), the Servant is obedient, resolute, and filled with buoyant faith, notwithstanding that his obedience will involve him in dreadful suffering (50:4–9), but as we obey the call to "behold" (52:13 KJV) we see that these sufferings, arising from perfect obedience, are in fact the sufferings of a holy sin-bearer (53:1–12), and that as soon as he has suffered, the call to enter and enjoy a free salvation can go out alike to Israel (ch. 54) and to the whole world (ch. 55).

Earlier in Isaiah (7:14; 9:6–7; 11:1–5) the Servant had been described. He is also identified as "the Branch" (cf. Isa 4:2; 11:1; 53:2 with Jer 23:5–6; 33:15; Zech 3:8; 6:12–13).

The NT applies Isaiah's Servant passages to Christ (Isa 42:1–4 is quoted as fulfilled in Matt 12:18–21; and Isa 52:13–53:12 is quoted in Matt 8:17; Luke 22:37; John 12:38; Acts 8:32–33; Rom 10:16; cf. also John 1:29; Rom 8:34; Heb 9:28; 1 Peter 2:21–25). The Servant's mission is fulfilled only in Christ: election

(Isa 42:1; 49:7; 1 Peter 2:4, 6), birth (Isa 49:1; 53:2; Luke 1:31–35), anointing (Isa 42:1; 48:16; 59:21; 61:1; Matt 3:16; Luke 4:18–19), ministry (Isa 49:8–13; Acts 3:13–18), obedience (Isa 50:4–7; Phil 2:7–8), new covenant (Isa 42:6; 49:8; 55:3; Matt 26:26–29), vicarious death (Isa 53:4–12; 1 Peter 2:22–25), resurrection (Isa 53:10–12; Acts 2:24–36), offer of salvation (Isa 49:8; 6:1–2; Luke 24:46–49), mission to Gentiles (Isa 42:1, 6–7; 49:6, 12; 60:3, 9; Matt 28:18–20), glorification and intercession (Isa 49:3; 53:12; Acts 2:33–36; Phil 2:6–11; Heb 7:24–25).

Bibliography: H. C. Leupold, *Exposition of Isaiah,* 1968; E. J. Young, *The Book of Isaiah,* 3 vols., 1972; H. Blocher, *The Songs of the Servant,* 1975; E. J. Hamlin, *A Guide to Isaiah 40–66,* 1979; J. A. Motyer, "Messiah," IDB, pp. 987–94.
JAM and WB

SETH (Heb. *shēth*, "appointed," i.e., "substituted") Adam's third son; father of Enosh (Gen 4:25–26; 5:3–8). His name signifies that he was considered a "substitute" for Abel (4:25). His birth recalled man's tragic loss of the divine image (5:1–2). He became the founder of the line of faith (Gen 4:26; Luke 3:38).

SETHUR (sē'thēr, Heb. *sethûr, hidden*). Son of Michael, a representative prince of the tribe of Asher sent by Moses, at the Lord's command, to spy out Canaan (Num 13:2–3, 13).

SEVENEH (See ASWAN)

SEVENTY, THE. Disciples of our Lord. The mission of the Seventy (mentioned only in Luke 10:1–20 KJV, MLB, MOF, NASB, RSV; seventy-two JB, NEB, NIV) has parallels—in both the disciples' responsibilities and the conditions they would meet—with the work of the early church: (1) the mission of others than the Twelve (Luke 10:1; Acts 8:1, 4), (2) the inclusion of the Gentiles (Luke 10:8; Acts 10:17), (3) the kingdom of God proclaimed (Luke 10:9, 11; Acts 8:22), (4) the reception (Luke 10:5–9; Acts 2:41–42) and rejection (Luke 10:10ff.; Acts 7:54–60) of the gospel, (5) triumph over demons (Luke 10:17ff.; Acts 16:16ff.), and (6) the joy of discipleship (Luke 10:17; Acts 5:41). Between this mission and Pentecost, however, Jesus radically altered the guidelines for the disciples' equipment (Luke 22:35–39).

SEVENTY WEEKS, THE. A name applied to Daniel 9:24–27, a prophecy that presumably, in contrast to the general prophecies in Daniel 2 and 7, pinpoints the exact time within the fourth kingdom when the Messiah will appear. Almost all agree that the "weeks" designate 490 years. The prophecy is (1) divided: the successive periods are described as 7, 62, 1; (2) dated: its *terminus a quo* ("from"—9:25) and its *terminus ad quem* ("until"—9:25); (3) determinative: its purposes regard Israel (9:24), redemption (9:24), the Messiah (9:24, 26–27), the sacrifices (9:27), and Jerusalem (9:25–27); and (4) debated (see below).

Three main views are held. (1) The *critical view* says that the "prophecy" was written by a pseudo-Daniel in 165 B.C. and synchronizes (inaccurately) with the history between 586 B.C. (Jerusalem's fall) and 164 B.C. (Antiochus). (2) The *dispensational view* has the sixty-ninth week terminating before the Crucifixion, leaving the seventieth (the present age being a "great parenthesis") to be fulfilled in the Great Tribulation. (3) The *conservative*, or *traditional, view* says the seventieth week was introduced by Christ's baptism and bisected (three and a half years) by his death, thus causing the sacrifices to cease (9:27).

SEVEN WORDS FROM THE CROSS. These words of Christ were probably uttered in the following order: (1) Before the darkness: "Father, forgive them . . ." (Luke 23:34), "Today you will be with me . . ." (23:43), "Dear woman, here is your son . . ." (John 19:26); (2) During the darkness: "My God, my God . . ." (Matt 27:46; Mark 15:34); (3) After the darkness: "I am thirsty" (John 19:28, fulfilling Ps 69:21), "It is finished" (19:30), "Father, into your hands . . ." (Luke 23:46, quoting Ps 31:5).

These seven words may be designated as follows: (1) propitiatory—"Father, forgive"; (2) promissory—"Today you will be with me in paradise"; (3) provisionary—"Dear woman, here is your son"; (4) protestatory—"My God, my God, why have you forsaken me?"; (5) preemptory—"I am thirsty"; (6) proclamatory—"It is finished"; (7) pacificatory—"Father, into your hands I commit my spirit." Theologically, these words, in the order given above, illustrate (1) divine forgiveness, (2) assurance of immortality, (3) good works, (4) the awfulness of Christ's death, (5) the true humanity of Christ, (6) the perfection of Christ's atonement, and (7) the divine complacency.

SHAALABBIN (shā'ȧ-lăb'ĭn, Heb. *sha'alabbîn,* probably *haunt of foxes;* cf. Judg 15:4). A town listed in Joshua 19:42 between Ir Shemesh and Aijalon as assigned to the Danites. See next entry.

SHAALBIM (shā-ăl'bĭm, Heb. *sha'albîm*). A town won by the Danites from the Amorites with the help of the Ephraimites (Judg 1:35). In Solomon's time a representative from this town was appointed as commissary officer (1 Kings 4:9). "Eliahba the Shaalbonite" (2 Sam 23:32; 1 Chron 11:33), one of David's special guards, came from this town (Shaalbon = Shaalbim). Some have identified Shaalbim with modern Selbit, a town in central Palestine.

SHAALBONITE (See SHAALBIM)

SHAALIM (shā'lĭm, Heb. *sha'alîm, district of foxes*). A region, probably near the northern boundary of Benjamin's territory, traversed by Saul in search of his father's donkeys (1 Sam 9:4).

SHAAPH (shā'ăf, Heb. *sha'aph,* meaning uncertain). 1. The sixth in a list of sons of Jahdai (1 Chron 2:47).

2. A descendant scion of Caleb by Maachah, a concubine. This man became the progenitor of the inhabitants of Madmannah (1 Chron 2:49; cf. Josh 15:31).

SHAARAIM (shā'a-rā'ĭm, Heb. *sha'ărayim, two gates,* so rendered in LXX of 1 Sam 17:52; KJV [incorrectly] Sharaim in Josh 15:36). 1. A town belonging to Judah in the Shephelah or "low country" (Josh 15:36; 1 Sam 17:52).

2. A town belonging to Simeon (1 Chron 4:31). It is listed as Sharuhen in Joshua 19:6 and Shilhim in Joshua 15:32.

SHAASHGAZ (shā-ăsh'găz, Heb. *sha'ashgāz*). A chamberlain or eunuch in charge of "the second house" of concubines belonging to King Xerxes (KJV Ahasuerus). Esther was entrusted to his care (Esth 2:14).

SHABBETHAI (shăb'ē-thī, Heb. *shabbethay, Sabbath-born*). A Levite of Ezra's time who is mentioned as a participant in the foreign-wives controversy (Ezra 10:15), as an interpreter of the Law (Neh 8:7–8), and as a chief Levite over the temple (11:16).

SHACHIA (See SAKIA)

SHACKLES Bonds, chains, or fetters, generally for the feet of prisoners, and made of bronze or of iron (Judg 16:21; Ps 105:18; 149:8). The NT word (Mark 5:4; Luke 8:29) indicates that the shackles were for the feet.

SHADDAI (See EL SHADDAI)

SHADOW. A word used literally, figuratively, and theologically. Literally, a shadow of a mountain (Judg 9:36), of a tree (Hos 4:13; Mark 4:32), of a dial (2 Kings 20:9–11), of a booth (Jonah 4:5), of a gourd (4:6), of a person (Acts 5:15). Figuratively, it signifies life's shortness (1 Chron 29:15; Job 8:9; Ps 102:11), protection (either good, as in Ps 17:8; 36:7; 91:1; or evil, as in Isa 30:3; Jer 48:45), the Messiah's blessings (Isa 4:6; 32:2; 49:2; 51:16), and death (either physical, as in Job 10:21–22; Ps 23:4; or spiritual as in Isa 9:2; Matt 4:16; Luke 1:79). Theologically it is used (1) of God's unchangeableness (James 1:17); (2) of the typical nature of the OT (Col 2:17; Heb 8:5; 10:1), illustrated in these facts: the OT prefigures in outline the NT substance; the OT represents externally (in rites and ceremonies) what the NT fulfills internally; the OT saints, nevertheless, could by faith comprehend the inner reality of the shadow; the NT, therefore, fulfills and abolishes the OT shadow; the NT saints, however, can still draw spiritual instruction from the shadow; and, finally, even NT saints, with the shadow and the substance, await the full day of spiritual understanding (1 Cor 13:12).

SHADRACH (shā'drăk, Heb. *shadhrakh,* meaning uncertain). The Babylonian name given to Hananiah; Meshach and Abednego are mentioned in all fifteen places his name appears (Dan 1:7; 2:49; 3:12–30). They were captives with Daniel.

SHAGEE, SHAGE (shā'gē, shā'ge, Heb. *shāghē', wandering*). A Hararite ("the mountaineer"), father of Jonathan and one of David's mighty men (1 Chron 11:34; however, the text here is uncertain; cf. 2 Sam 23:11, 33).

SHAHARAIM (shā'ha-rā'ĭm, Heb. *shaḥărayim, double dawn*). A Benjamite who, in the land of Moab, had three wives (Hushim, Baara, Hodesh) and nine sons, who became heads of families (1 Chron 8:8–11). The text of verse 8 is uncertain.

SHAHAZUMAH, SHAHAZIMAH (shā'ha-zū'ma, shā'ha-zī'ma, Heb. *shaḥătsûmâh, toward the heights*). A town in Issachar between Tabor and the Jordan (Josh 19:22).

SHALIM, LAND OF (See SHAALIM)

SHALISHA, SHALISHAH (sha-lī'sha, Heb. *shālishâh, a third part*). A district through which Saul went in search of his father's lost donkeys (1 Sam 9:4); identified by some with Baal Shalishah (2 Kings 4:42).

SHALLEKETH GATE (shăl'ĕ-kĕth). The name of the west gate of Solomon's temple assigned by lots to Shuppim and Hosah, Levitical porters (1 Chron 26:13–16). Some suppose that the offal of the temple was "cast" through this gate.

SHALLUM, SHALLUN (shăl'ŭm, shăl'ŭn, Heb. *shallûm,* or *shallûn, recompense*). A name (*Shallum*) applied to all of the following except the last (*Shallun*). 1. The youngest son of Naphtali (1 Chron 7:13 KJV; NIV retains the Shillem of Gen 46:24 and Num 26:48–49).

2. The son of Shaul and grandson of Simeon (1 Chron 4:25; cf. Gen 46:10; Exod 6:15; Num 26:12–13).

3. The son of Sismai and father of Jekamiah (1 Chron 2:40–41).

4. Son of Kore and chief of the gatekeepers (1 Chron 9:17, 19, 31; Ezra 2:42; 10:24; Neh 7:45; Meshelemiah in 1 Chron 26:1 and Shelemiah in 1 Chron 26:14).

5. Son of Zadok and father of Hilkiah (1 Chron 6:12–13); ancestor of Ezra (Ezra 7:1–2; Meshullam in 1 Chron 9:11 and Neh 11:11).

6. A king of Israel who, having murdered Zechariah, reigned in his place for one month; then he himself was killed by Menahem (2 Kings 15:10–15).

7. The father of Jehizkiah and an Ephraimite chief (2 Chron 28:12).

8. Son of Tikvah and husband of the prophetess Huldah; custodian of the priests' wardrobe (2 Kings 22:14; 2 Chron 34:22; perhaps also Jer 32:7, Jeremiah's uncle; see No. 10).

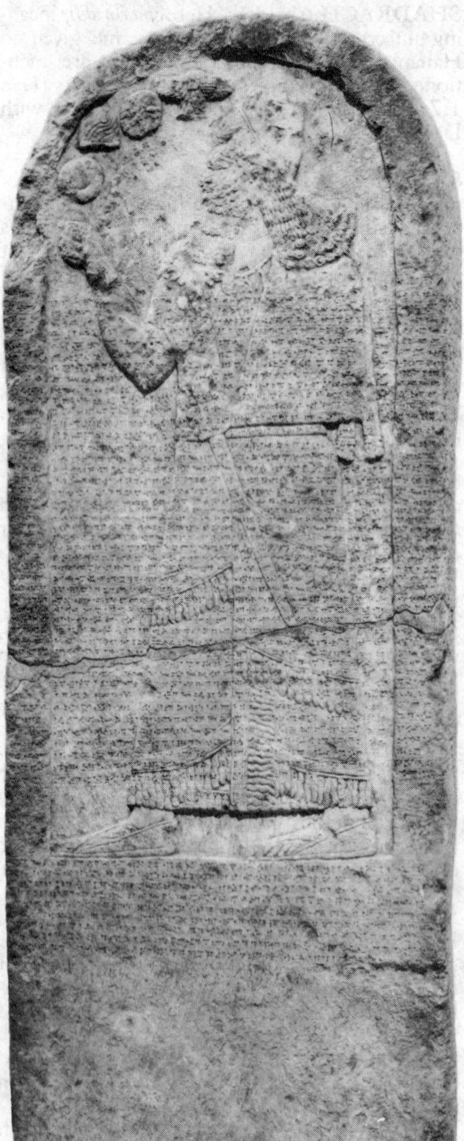

Stele (2.20 m. high) of Shalmaneser III, King of Assyria (858–824 B.C.). In front of the king are carved the symbols of four of the Assyrian gods. The inscription describes the events of the first six years of his reign. From Kurkh, southeast Turkey, c. 850 B.C. Reproduced by courtesy of the Trustees of the British Museum.

9. A king of Judah, son of Josiah (1 Chron 3:15; Jer 22:11); better known as Jehoahaz II (2 Kings 23:30–31, 34; 2 Chron 36:1).

10. An uncle of Jeremiah (Jer 32:7; see No. 8).

11. The father of Maaseiah (Jer 35:4; cf. 52:24).

12. One of the Levitical porters who was compelled to divorce his foreign wife (Ezra 10:24).

13. A son of Bani who was compelled to divorce his foreign wife (Ezra 10:42).

14. The son of Hallohesh; a ruler who, with his daughters, helped to build the walls of Jerusalem (Neh 3:12).

15. Shallun, son of Col-Hozeh; ruler of the Mizpah district; a builder of the walls of Jerusalem (Neh 3:15 Shallum RSV).

SHALMAI (shăl'mī, Heb. *shalmay* in Ezra 2:46; *salmay* in Neh 7:48, Salmai ASV, RSV, Shalmai KJV, NIV). The ancestral head of the family of temple servants (Nethinim KJV) that returned with Zerubbabel.

SHALMAN (shăl'măn, Heb. *shalman*). Mentioned only in Hosea 10:14. The person (Shalman) and the place (Beth Arbel) are now unknown. The ancient versions differ considerably. The two most likely theories: (1) a contraction of Shalmaneser; (2) the Moabite king Salmanu, mentioned in the inscriptions of Tiglath-Pileser.

SHALMANESER (shăl'măn-ē'zêr, Heb. *shalman'-eser,* Assyr. *Sulman-asaridu, Sulman [the god] is chief*). The title of five Assyrian kings, only one of whom is directly mentioned in the OT; another one is important because he refers to an Israelite king.

1. Shalmaneser III (859–824 B.C.), son of Ashurnasirpal; the first Assyrian king who, as far as the records reveal, had political and military contacts with a king of the northern kingdom of Israel. Although Shalmaneser III is not mentioned as such in the biblical narrative (1 Kings 16:29–22:40; 2 Chron 18:1–34), yet his Monolith Inscription in the British Museum recounts a coalition composed principally of Syria (Hadadezer = Ben-Hadad) and of Israel ("Ahab, the Israelite"), which he met and presumably defeated at Karkar, north of Hamath in the Orontes Valley, in 853. Ahab, according to this inscription, contributed two thousand chariots and ten thousand troops in the battle against Shalmaneser. As indicated above, no record of this event is found in the contemporary biblical data. The reference to Ahab in a nonbiblical archaeological source adds substantial weight to the trustworthiness of the OT record.

2. Shalmaneser V (726–722 B.C.), son of Tiglath-Pileser (who died in 727); the only Assyrian king named Shalmaneser in the OT history (unless Shalman, in Hos 10:14, is a contraction of Shalmaneser). There are two references to him: (1) 2 Kings 17:3–5, which recounts how Shalmaneser received tribute from Hoshea, the last king of the northern kingdom; then, after Hoshea had formed an alliance with So, king of Egypt, Shalmaneser returned to Palestine in a more extensive campaign, imprisoned Hoshea, and besieged the city of Samaria for three years. The prophet Hosea, a contemporary of Hoshea's turbulent reign, speaks out against entanglements with either Assyria or Egypt (Hos 5:13; 7:11; 8:9; 12:1); (2) 2 Kings 18:9–11, which agrees in essential details with the previous

passage (17:3–5), but also synchronizes the siege and fall of Samaria with the ruling house of Jerusalem (Hezekiah). Since not Shalmaneser, but Sargon, was, according to his own testimony, the conqueror of Samaria (in 722/721), the biblical record can be understood to agree, for it says that (a) "the king of Assyria took Samaria" (2 Kings 17:6) and (b) "the Assyrians took it" (2 Kings 18:10)—in neither case actually affirming that Shalmaneser was the one who took the city. (See SARGON.) There is a possible allusion to Shalmaneser V in "King Jareb" (KJV; NIV "the great king"), which Hosea uses as a humorous or sarcastic reference to some Assyrian king (Hos 5:13; 10:6). WB

SHAMA (shā'mȧ, Heb. *shāmā', He [God] has heard*). A son of Hotham, the Aroerite; one of David's mighty men (1 Chron 11:44).

SHAMARIAH (See SHEMARIAH)

SHAMBLES (Gr. *makellon,* from Lat. *macellum, meat market,* which latter meaning is followed by RSV and NIV). Paul, answering a question of conscience regarding meat sold in the *makellon,* instructed the Corinthian Christians to eat such meat without further inquiry as to its use in pagan sacrifices. The essential nature of the meat as food had not been affected (cf. 1 Tim 4:4); but this liberty was not to endanger a weaker brother's conscience (1 Cor 10:23–33).

SHAME, SHAMEFACEDNESS (Heb. *bosheth,* Gr. *aischynē,* Gr. *aidos*). This subject has many aspects: subjective (Gen 2:25; 3:7) and objective (Jer 11:13; Hos 9:10); positive (Prov 19:26; 28:7) and negative (Prov 10:5; Rom 1:16; 1 John 2:28); literal (Exod 32:25) and figurative (Rev 3:18; 16:15); individual (Gen 38:23) and national (Judg 18:7; Isa 30:3–5); removable (Isa 54:4) and unremovable (Jer 23:40); loved (Hos 4:18 ASV) and hated (Eph 5:12); punitive (Isa 47:3; Ezek 16:51–54; 44:12) and commendatory (1 Sam 20:30–34; 2 Sam 6:20; 13:11–14); now (Heb 6:6) and future (Ezek 32:24–25; Dan 12:2); human (Ps 119:31) and divine (Ps 69:7–9; 89:45; Isa 50:6; Heb 12:2); due to something natural (2 Sam 19:1–5; 1 Cor 11:6, 14) and due to something unnatural (2 Sam 13:11–14; Phil 3:19). "Shamefacedness" in 1 Timothy 2:9 KJV denotes sexual modesty (NIV "decency and propriety").

SHAMED (See SHEMED)

SHAMER (See SHEMER)

SHAMGAR (shăm'gȧr, Heb. *shamgar*). A son of Anath; slayer of six hundred Philistines (Judg 3:31; cf. 1 Sam 13:19–22). He is listed as a judge between Ehud and Deborah; but no definite years are assigned to his judgeship. Since Beth Anath belonged to the tribe of Naphtali (Josh 19:38; Judg 1:33), and since this tribe was prominent in the contemporary struggle against the Canaanite king Jabin (Judg 4:6, 10; 5:18), it is probable that Shamgar was also a member of this tribe. Israel had been commanded to exterminate the inhabitants of Canaan completely (Exod 23:31–33; Deut 7:1–5; 20:16–18) but had disobeyed this divine command (Judg 1:27–36); therefore, these unsubdued Canaanites had now become a snare to the Israelites. In fact, the situation was now somewhat reversed: Israel was cowed and disarmed, surreptitiously using the "winding paths" rather than the roads (5:5–6). In this chaotic condition Shamgar killed six hundred Philistines, using only an oxgoad as his weapon. He thus prepared the way for the greater deliverance of Israel under Deborah and Barak.

SHAMHUTH (shăm'hŭth, Heb. *shamhûth, desolation*). An Izrahite. He was the fifth divisional commander, for the fifth month of the year, in David's organization of his army (1 Chron 27:8); probably the same person as Shammah the Harodite (2 Sam 23:25) and Shammoth the Harorite (1 Chron 11:27).

SHAMIR (shā'mêr, Heb. *shāmîr, a sharp point*). 1. A town allotted to Judah (Josh 15:48); now usually identified with the ruin Somerak, about thirteen miles (twenty-two km.) SW of Hebron.

2. A town in Mount Ephraim; the residence and burial place of Tola, one of the judges (Judg 10:1–2). Its identification is still uncertain. The residence of Tola, of the tribe of Issachar, in a city of Ephraim has been explained as due either to the turbulent condition of Issachar's territory or to the fact that Issachar had cities within Ephraim.

3. A Levite, son of Micah; a temple attendant (1 Chron 24:24).

SHAMMA (shăm'ȧ, Heb. *shammā', astonishment* or *desolation*). One of the eleven sons of Zophah; a descendant of Asher (1 Chron 7:37).

SHAMMAH (shăm'ȧ, Heb. *shammâ, waste*). 1. Son of Reuel and grandson of Esau; an Edomite chief (Gen 36:13, 17; 1 Chron 1:37).

2. The third son of Jesse and brother of David (1 Sam 16:9; 17:13); also called Shimea (1 Chron 20:7), Shimeah (2 Sam 13:3, 32), and Shimei (21:21). He was one of the seven sons of Jesse rejected before the choice of David as king (1 Sam 16:1–13). With his two older brothers he fought against the Philistines (17:13–19, 22–23). He was the father of Jonadab (2 Sam 13:3, 32) and the Jonathan whose victory over the Philistine giant is especially noted (21:21–22).

3. One of David's three mightiest men, the son of Agee (2 Sam 23:11; Shagee in 1 Chron 11:34). His single-handed victory over the Philistines (2 Sam 23:11–12), his loyalty to David in the cave of Adullam (23:13), and his heroic deed in David's behalf (23:15–17) are especially noted concerning him. A comparison of 1 Chronicles 11:12 with 2 Samuel 23:11, 33 suggests that Shammah's name is accidentally omitted from the former passage.

4. One of David's mighty men (2 Sam 23:33); also called Shammoth (plural of Shammah) (1 Chron 11:27) and Shamhuth (27:8). Perhaps the same as no. 3.

SHAMMAI (shăm'ā-ī, Heb. *shammay,* contraction of *shema' yâ, Jehovah has heard*). The name of three descendants of Judah:

1. A son of Onam, who was the son of Jerahmeel by Atarah; father of Nadab and Abishur (1 Chron 2:28, 32).

2. A son of Rekem and father of Maon (1 Chron 2:44–45); a descendant of "Caleb the brother of Jerahmeel" (2:42).

3. A descendant of Ezrah (1 Chron 4:17–18). The text here is very ambiguous and uncertain; probably, by a transposition, Shammai was the son of Mered by Bithiah, Pharaoh's daughter (4:18).

SHAMMOTH (shăm'ōth, Heb. *shammôth, desolation*). One of David's mighty men of war (1 Chron 11:27); apparently the same as Shammah (2 Sam 23:25) and Shamhuth (1 Chron 27:8).

SHAMMUA, SHAMMUAH (shă-mū'à, Heb. *shammû' a, heard* or *renowned*). 1. A son of Zaccur. He was sent to spy out the land of Canaan as the representative of the tribe of Reuben (Num 13:4).

2. A son of David by Bathsheba; brother of Solomon (2 Sam 5:14, KJV has Shammuah; 1 Chron 3:5, KJV has Shimea; 14:4).

3. A Levite, father of Abda (or Obadiah) (Neh 11:17; Shemaiah in 1 Chron 9:16).

4. The representative of the priestly family of Bilgah (Neh 12:18). He was a priest whose father returned with Zerubbabel (12:1–7); he officiated in the high priesthood of Joiakim (12:12).

SHAMSHERAI (shăm'shē-rī, Heb. *shamsheray*). First named of six sons of Jeroham; a Benjamite (1 Chron 8:26).

SHAPHAM (shā'făm, Heb. *shāphām*). A Gadite who lived in Bashan, second in authority in the time of Jotham (1 Chron 5:12).

SHAPHAN (shā'făn, Heb. *shāphān, hyrax* or *rock rabbit*). The faithful scribe during Josiah's reign (2 Kings 22:3–20; 2 Chron 34:8–28). The record cites four responsibilities faithfully performed: (1) his oversight of the finances of the temple repairs (2 Chron 34:8–13, 16–17); (2) his transmission of the newly discovered law book to Josiah (34:14–15); (3) his reading of this book before Josiah (34:18); and (4) his mission, with others, to carry Josiah's message to the prophetess Huldah (34:20–28). Shaphan's faith is seen in the names he gave his sons: Ahikam (*my brother has risen up*); Gemariah (*The LORD has accomplished*); Elasah (*God has made*); Jaazaniah (*The LORD hearkens*). Shaphan's faith is seen in his sons' lives: Ahikim accompanied his father on the mission to Huldah (34:20ff.) and later became Jeremiah's protector (Jer 26:24); Elasah, with others, transmitted Jeremiah's message to exiles in Babylon (29:1–3); Gemariah resisted destructive attempts against Jeremiah's writings (36:10, 12, 25); but Jaazaniah did not possess his father's faith (Ezek 8:11). Two sons of Ahikam, however, continued their grandfather's faith: Micaiah (Jer 36:11–13) and Gedaliah (39:14; 40:5–12; 43:6).

SHAPHAT (shā'făt, Heb. *shāphāt, he has judged*). 1. The son of Hori, chosen from the tribe of Simeon to spy out the land of Canaan (Num 13:5).

2. The father of Elisha the prophet (1 Kings 19:16, 19; 2 Kings 3:11; 6:31).

3. A Gadite chief in Bashan (1 Chron 5:12).

4. A son of Adlai, one of David's herdsmen (1 Chron 27:29).

5. The last-named son of Shemaiah, a descendant of the royal line of David (1 Chron 3:22). Shemaiah's is said here to have had six sons, but the fact that only five are actually named shows that one name has probably been lost in the process of the transmission of the text. Or possibly Shemaiah is to be understood as the sixth brother, rather than the father of the five listed.

SHAPHER (See SHEPHER)

SHAPHIR (shā'fĕr, Heb. *shāphîr, glittering*). One of a group of towns mentioned in Micah 1:10–15. Because of its association with Gath, Aczib (of Judah), and Mareshah it seems likely that it was located in SW Palestine.

SHARAI (shà-rā'ī, Heb. *shāray*). A "son" of Bani, mentioned in a list of men who, at Ezra's command, divorced their foreign wives (Ezra 10:10, 40, 44).

SHARAIM (See SHAARAIM)

SHARAR (shā'rêr, Aram. *shārār, firm*). The father of Ahiam the Hararite; one of David's mighty men (2 Sam 23:33; Sacar in 1 Chron 11:35).

SHARE (Heb. *maharesheth, plowshare*). An agricultural instrument mentioned only in 1 Samuel 13:20 (NIV "plowshares"). LXX has "a reaping-hook," and other versions differ considerably.

SHAREZER (shà-rē'zêr, Heb. *sar'etser,* Assyr. *Shar-usur, protect the king*). 1. A son of the Assyrian king Sennacherib who, with his brother Adrammelech, murdered his father (2 Kings 19:37; Isa 37:38).

2. A contemporary of Zechariah the prophet and member of a delegation sent from Bethel to Jerusalem (Zech 7:2; Sherezer in KJV).

SHARON (shăr'ŭn, Heb. *shārôn, plain*). 1. The coastal plain between Joppa and Mount Carmel, a place proverbial in ancient times for its fertility, pasturage, and beauty (1 Chron 27:29; Song of

Songs 2:1; Isa 35:2); the location of such towns as Dor, Lydda (Acts 9:35), Joppa, Caesarea, and Antipatris.

2. The suburban pasturelands of Sharon possessed by the tribe of Gad (1 Chron 5:16).

3. Figuratively, it may mean (1) a person's state of regeneracy—of fruitfulness and glory (Isa 35:2) or (2) a person's eternal state—of peace forevermore (65:10, 17).

SHARONITE (shăr'ŭn-īt, Heb. *shārônî, of Sharon*). A description applied to Shitrai, David's chief herdsman in the Plain of Sharon; the only Sharonite mentioned in the Bible (1 Chron 27:29).

SHARUHEN (shȧ-rū'hĕn, Heb. *shārûhen*). An ancient town in SW Palestine, south of Gaza and west of Beersheba. It was assigned to the tribe of Simeon within Judah's territory (Josh 19:6; cf. Gen 49:7); apparently the same as Shilhim (Josh 15:32) and Shaaraim (1 Chron 4:31). It has now been identified with Tell el-Fār'ah.

SHASHAI (shā'shī, Heb. *shāshay, whitish* or *noble*). A descendant of Binnui. He is listed among those men who, at Ezra's command, divorced their foreign wives (Ezra 10:40).

SHASHAK (shā'shăk, Heb. *shāshaq*). A Benjamite, son of Beriah (1 Chron 8:14–15). He had eleven sons (8:22–25).

SHAUL, SHAULITES (shā'ŭl, shā'ŭ-līts, Heb. *shā'ûl, asked* [of the LORD], *shā'ûlî, of Shaul*). 1. The sixth in a list of eight kings who ruled over Edom (Gen 36:37–38 [Saul in KJV]; 1 Chron 1:48–49).

2. A son of Simeon (Gen 46:10; Exod 6:15; Num 26:13; 1 Chron 4:24). He is called "the son of a Canaanite woman" (Gen 46:10; Exod 6:15). Thus the Shaulites (Num 26:13), who descended from him, were of mixed blood.

3. A descendant of Levi, son of Uzziah (1 Chron 6:24). An ancestor of Samuel (6:27).

SHAVEH, VALLEY OF (shā'vĕ, Heb. *shāwēh, a plain*). Also called "the king's dale"; a place near Salem (i.e., Jerusalem, Ps 76:2), where, after rescuing his nephew Lot, Abraham met the king of Sodom (Gen 14:17). It is identified by some as the same place where Absalom erected a memorial to himself (2 Sam 18:18).

SHAVEH KIRIATHAIM (shā'vĕ kĭ'r-yȧ-thā'ĭm, Heb. *shāwēh qiryāthayim, the Plain of Kiriathaim,* i.e., "twin cities"). A plain where Kedorlaomer conquered the Emites (Gen 14:5), probably located east of the Dead Sea (cf. Num 32:37).

SHAVING. The act of shaving is represented by the Hebrew words *gāzaz,* "to shear." Used of animals except in Job 1:20 (of man's head); Jeremiah 7:29 (fig. of Jerusalem); Micah 1:16 (of a woman's, i.e., Jerusalem's, hair); Nahum 1:12 ("cut down," destruction by the Assyrians; cf. Isa 7:20 below). The Hebrew *gālaḥ* is used only of human shaving (in KJV "poll," 2 Sam 14:26), meaning "to shave, shave off, be shaven." *'Avar ta'ar,* is a Hebrew word meaning "to cause a razor to pass over" (Num 6:5; 8:7). The Greek word *xyraō* is used only in Acts 21:24 and 1 Corinthians 11:5–6 in the NT. The priests (Lev 21:5; Ezek 44:20) and the Nazirites (Num 6:5; cf. 1 Sam 1:11) among the Israelites were prohibited from shaving; furthermore, the Hebrews as a people, in contrast to surrounding nations, generally accepted the beard as a sign of dignity (cf. 2 Sam 10:4–5). Shaving had these connotations: it was (1) an act of contrition (Job 1:20), (2) an accommodation to a custom (Gen 41:14; cf. 1 Cor 11:5–6), (3) an act of consecration for Levites (Num 6:9; 8:7), (4) an act of cleansing for lepers (Lev 14:8–9; 13:32ff.), (5) an act that completes a vow (Num 6:18; Acts 18:18; 21:24), (6) an act of commitment to a captive woman (Deut 21:12), (7) an act of conspiracy against a man's Nazirite vow (Judg 16:19), (8) an act of contempt (2 Sam 10:4; 1 Chron 19:4), and (9) an act expressing the cleansing of a corrupt nation (Isa 7:20; cf. 1:16; 6:5; and 2 Kings 18:13ff.).

SHAVSHA (shăv'shȧ, Heb. *shawshā'*). David's secretary of state (1 Chron 18:16; Shisha in 1 Kings 4:3; Seraiah in 2 Sam 8:17; Sheva in 2 Sam 20:25).

SHEAF (Heb. *'ălummâh, 'ōmer, 'āmîr*). The sheaf was a handful of grain left behind the reaper (Jer 9:22 RSV), gathered and bound usually by children or women (Ruth 2:7, 15) in a joyous mood (Ps 126:6; 129:7–8). Thus stacked the sheaves became dry and inflammable (Zech 12:6; cf. Judg 15:1–5 ASV); but they made a beautiful sight (Song of Songs 7:2). A donkey (Neh 13:15) or a heavily loaded cart (Amos 2:13) bore these bundles to the threshing floor (Ruth 3:6–7; Mic 4:12). Some sheaves, however, were left behind for the poor (Deut 24:19; cf. Ruth 2:7, 15; Job 24:10). The sheaf of the firstfruit (Lev 23:10–15; cf. 2 Chron 31:5–10) typically represents (1) Christians, as representatives of a larger harvest (Rom 16:5; 1 Cor 16:15; James 1:18), possessed by the Spirit (Rom 8:23), and dedicated to God (Rev 14:1–5) or (2) Christ, as an evidence of believers' later resurrection (1 Cor 15:20, 23).

SHEAL (shē'ăl, Heb. *she'āl, asking*). A descendant of Bani. He is listed among those who divorced their foreign wives (Ezra 10:29).

SHEALTIEL (shē-ăl'tĭel, Gr. *Salathiel, I have asked God;* KJV "Salathiel"). The son of Jeconiah, king of Judah, and father of Zerubbabel, according to the genealogy in Matthew 1:12. In Luke's genealogy he appears as father of Zerubbabel, but as the son of Neri (Luke 3:27). The apparent discrepancy in the genealogies is probably explicable on the principal that Matthew gives the genealogy of Jesus according to the legal succession, while Luke gives it according to the actual succession or right of consanguinity. If the direct line failed in Jeconiah because he had no son to succeed him, the right of succession went to Shealtiel, a descendant of Nathan and the son of Neri who, as the legal heir of Jeconiah, was reckoned his son by Matthew.

SHEARIAH (shē'á-rī'á, Heb. *she'aryâh, the* LORD *esteems*). One of the sons of Azel. He was a descendant of Jonathan (1 Chron 8:38; 9:44).

SHEARING HOUSE (Heb *bêth 'ēqedh hārō'îm, house of binding of the shepherds,* i.e., *binding-house of the shepherds*). "Shearing house" in KJV is "Beth Eked of the Shepherds" in NIV. The place between Jezreel and Samaria where Jehu met and killed forty-two unsuspecting members of the royal house of Ahaziah, king of Judah. They were on their way, apparently ignorant of Jehu's revolt, to Ahaziah, who was visiting Joram, the wounded king of Israel (2 Kings 10:12–14). The corpses were cast into a pit (Heb. *bôr* ; cf. its use in Gen 37:24; Jer 41:7, 9). A possible identification of Beth-Eked of the Shepherds is *Kufr Ra'i,* the *Ra'i* supposedly preserving the Hebrew word for "shepherds" (*rô'îm*).

SHEAR-JASHUB (shē'ār-já'shŭb, Heb. *she'ār yāshûv, a remnant shall return*). The symbolic name of Isaiah's oldest son (Isa 7:3). The symbolism is reflected in the historic return from Babylon and is fulfilled in the spiritual return to the Lord at Messiah's advent (Isa 1:9; 4:3–4; 10:20–23; 65:8–9; Rom 11:5–6, 16–29).

SHEBA (shē'bá, Heb. *shevā', seven, an oath*). 1. A chief of a Gadite family (1 Chron 5:13).

2. A town allotted to Simeon (Josh 19:2). Some suppose the name to be a corruption of Shema (cf. LXX and Josh 15:26); others, in view of its absence in 1 Chronicles 4:28, which gives a similar summation (cf. Josh 19:2–6), suppose either that it is a variant form of Beersheba (see ASV) or that it has been accidentally introduced by the process known as dittography.

3. A son of Bicri, a Benjamite. Motivated by jealousy over the rising power of the tribe of Judah, as represented by David, Sheba inspired a short-lived insurrection against the kingship of David. Finally cornered by Joab in Abel Beth Maacah, Sheba met an unexpected end when the town's inhabitants, at the urging of a wise woman, threw Sheba's head over the town's wall and thus pacified the wrath of Joab and brought the rebellion to an inglorious end. As a result, David's rule over all Israel was considerably strengthened.

4. A son of Raamah, who was a son of Cush (Gen 10:7; 1 Chron 1:9).

5. A son of Joktan; grandson of Eber (Gen 10:28; 1 Chron 1:22); the probable founder of the kingdom of the Sabeans (Sheba) in southern Arabia (see no. 6).

6. The oldest son of Jokshan, Abraham's son by Keturah (Gen 25:3; 1 Chron 1:32). It is probable that this man's descendants, by intermarriage or otherwise, finally became identified with the descendants of no. 4 and no. 5; together they constitute what is called the kingdom of Sheba or the Sabeans. These people, known particularly through the Queen of Sheba and her illustrious visit to King Solomon (1 Kings 10:1–13; 2 Chron 9:1–12; Matt 12:42), are pictured in the Bible as traders in precious stones and incense (Isa 60:6; Jer 6:20; Ezek 27:22; 38:13) and in slaves (Job 1:15; Joel 3:8).

SHEBAH (shē'bá, Heb. *shiv'âh, seven* or *oath*). The name of a well that the servants of Isaac dug. The town Beersheba, i.e., "well of the oath," is so called from this well (Gen 26:31–33; but cf. 21:28–31). NIV renders "Shibah."

SHEBAM (See SIBMAH)

SHEBANIAH (shĕb'á-nī'á, Heb. *shevanyâh,* meaning uncertain). 1. One of the seven priests appointed to blow trumpets before the ark of the covenant when it was brought to Jerusalem (1 Chron 15:24).

2. One of the Levites who led the people in praising God in Nehemiah's time and later signed the covenant with him (Neh 9:4–5; 10:10).

3. Another Levite who was among the covenanters (Neh 10:12).

4. A priest who was among the covenanters (Neh 10:4).

5. The head of a family of priests who served in the days of the high priest Joiakim (Neh 12:14 JB, KJV, MLB, NASB, NEB, RSV; Shecaniah NIV).

SHEBAT (See CALENDAR)

SHEBER (shē'bêr, Heb. *shever*). Son of Caleb (not the famous spy) by his concubine Maachah (1 Chron 2:48).

SHEBNA (shĕb'ná, Heb. *shevnā'*). 1. Steward of Hezekiah (Isa 22:15–21) who, in pride, had made a grave for himself. For his pride, the Lord predicted that he would toss him like a ball into a far country where he would die, and his place would be taken by the godly Eliakim (Isa 22:22).

2. A scribe, also in Hezekiah's time, who went out with others to face the Assyrian field commander, the emissary of Sennacherib (2 Kings 18; Isa 36:3–37:2).

SHEBUEL (See SHUBAEL)

SHECANIAH, SHECHANIAH (shĕk-ă-nī'á, Heb. *shekhanyâh, dweller with the* LORD). 1. Head of the tenth of the twenty-four courses of priests in the days of David. The priests had so multiplied that David divided them thus, giving two-thirds of the courses to descendants of Eleazar and one-third to descendants of Ithamar, the sons of Aaron (1 Chron 24:11).

2. A priest in the time of Hezekiah. He faithfully assisted in distributing the freewill

Hebrew inscription (c. 700 B.C.) found on a lintel of a tomb from the first temple period at Siloam (Silwan). Inscription reads: "This is [the sepulcher of Shebna]yahu, who was (steward) over the (kings) house. There is no silver and gold here . . . cursed be the man who opens this." This may be Shebna, the royal steward rebuked by Isaiah (22:15–16). Reproduced by courtesy of the Trustees of the British Museum.

offerings of the people to the priests (2 Chron 31:15).

3. A descendant of David in the time of the Restoration, head of a house (1 Chron 3:21–22).

4. A descendant of Parosh, whose descendant Zechariah returned with Ezra, leading 150 men (Ezra 8:3).

5. A son of Jehaziel (Ezra 8:5). He led back three hundred men.

6. A son of Jehiel. He admitted that some had married foreign women, then proposed a covenant be made and the foreign wives and children be put away (Ezra 10:2–4).

7. The keeper of the East Gate of Jerusalem in the time of Nehemiah. His son Shemaiah was one who helped repair the wall (Neh 3:29).

8. Son of Arah and father-in-law to Tobiah, the notorious foe of Nehemiah at the time of the rebuilding of the walls of Jerusalem (Neh 6:18). The fact that he had given his daughter to Tobiah the Ammonite was proof of his unworthiness.

9. One of the chiefs of the priests who returned with Zerubbabel (Neh 12:3).

10. Head of a priestly family in the days of Joiakim (Neh 12:14 NIV; Shebaniah JB, KJV, MLB, MOF, NASB, NEB, RSV).

SHECHEM (shē'kĕm, Heb. *shekhem, shoulder*). A personal name and the name of a district and city in the hill country of Ephraim in north-central Palestine. The city makes its initial appearance in biblical history as the first place in Canaan to be mentioned in connection with Abram's arrival in the land. Here the Lord appeared to Abram and promised the land to his descendants; Abram responded by building an altar (Gen 12:6–7). When Jacob returned from Paddan Aram, he settled down at Shechem and purchased land from the sons of Hamor (33:18–19; Josh 24:32). In Genesis 33–34 it is seen that Shechem was the name of the city and also of the prince of the city. It appears that the names Shechem and Hamor are hereditary names or perhaps a kind of title (cf. Judg 9:28). While Jacob was at Shechem the unfortunate incident of Dinah occurred; and Simeon and Levi, her full brothers, exacted drastic revenge on the city (Gen 34). Later the brothers of Joseph were herding Jacob's flock at Shechem when Joseph was sent to check on their welfare (37:12–14). The city is not referred to again until the listing of the tribal divisions of the land after the Conquest (Josh 17:7); Shechem was in the territory allotted to Ephraim. It was selected by Joshua as one of the cities of refuge (Josh 20:7; 21:21; 1 Chron 6:67). Joshua gave his farewell address here (Josh 24:1) and made a covenant with the people (24:25). Joseph was buried in the plot of ground that his father Jacob had purchased here (Josh 24:32).

One of the interesting personages in the kalei-

A view of modern Shechem, which lies in a valley between Mount Ebal and Mount Gerizim. Viewed from Mount Gerizim, facing northwest. Courtesy Zev Radovan.

General view from Mount Ebal of ancient Shechem, Tell Balata, located just east of Nablus. Courtesy Ecole Biblique et Archéologique Française, Jerusalem.

doscopic history of Judges, Abimelech, the son of Gideon and a concubine, is closely associated with Shechem. Abimelech conspired with his mother's relatives to kill all the other sons of Gideon and to have himself made king of Shechem (Judg 9:6). Trouble developed between Abimelech and the people of Shechem; a conspiracy against Abimelech was revealed to him by the ruler of the city. In the fighting that followed, Abimelech took the city and completely destroyed it. When a number of people took final refuge in the stronghold of the temple of Baal-Berith or El-berith, Abimelech gathered fuel and fired the stronghold, so that about one thousand persons perished in the conflagration (9:46–49).

After the death of Solomon, his son Rehoboam went to Shechem to be made king by all Israel (1 Kings 12:1; 2 Chron 10:1); when the principles of his prospective administration were challenged by Jeroboam, Rehoboam followed the disastrous advice of his impetuous, youthful counselors and thus caused the rupture of the kingdom. Jeroboam became king of ten tribes and "fortified Shechem in the hill country of Ephraim" (1 Kings 12:25) as his capital. The city is mentioned in parallel passages in the Psalms (Ps 60:6; 108:7) and is named in a list of prophetic condemnations against Israel (Hos 6:9). After the destruction of Jerusalem, men from Shechem and other cities came to Mizpah to be under the protection of Gedaliah and there were deceived and murdered by Ishmael (Jer 41:5ff.). The city is not certainly mentioned again in the Bible, but the conversation of Jesus and the Samaritan woman (John 4) occurred in this vicinity. It has been suggested that the Sychar (usually identified as modern Askar) of John 4:5 should be read Sychem (Shechem; cf. Acts 7:16), with the Old Syriac Gospels. In A.D. 72 the city was rebuilt as Flavia Neapolis, from which the name of the present village of Nablus is derived.

The name Shechem occurs in historical records and other sources outside Palestine. It is mentioned as a city captured by Senusert III of Egypt (nineteenth century B.C.) and appears in the Egyptian cursing texts of about the same time. "The mountain of Shechem" is referred to incidentally in a satirical letter of the Nineteenth Dynasty of Egypt. Shechem also figures in the Amarna Letters; its ruler, Lab'ayu, and his sons are accused of acting against Egypt, though the ruler protests that he is devotedly loyal to the pharaoh. The site of the ancient city is Tell Balatah, just east of Nablus. The tell has a mixed archaeological history: E. Sellin began work here in A.D. 1913 and resumed it in 1926. In 1928 G. Welter succeeded him as director; in 1934 the seventh and final campaign of the German archaeologists was in charge of H. Steckeweh, whose labors are of particular value because the previous work had shown inadequate handling of both pottery, chronology, and stratigraphy. In spite of limitations, the work produced some important results. In the first campaign a triple gate of Middle Bronze date was found in the NW section of the city; nearby, unearthed in 1926, was a large temple that has been identified as the temple of Baal-Berith. In 1926 the eastern gate of the city was found, along with part of the city wall. Middle Bronze Shechem had a fine battered (sloping) wall of large, undressed stones, found standing to a maximum height of thirty-two feet (ten m.), with some of its stones over six and one-half feet (two m.) long. Hyksos-type fortifications also occur at Shechem, with ramparts of beaten earth. Several cuneiform tablets of the Amarna Age add to the store of written materials from Palestine. In 1934 a limestone plaque bearing a representation of a serpent goddess and an inscription in alphabetic script was found. The most recent work at Balatah is that of the Drew-McCormick Expedition, with G. Ernest Wright as director. The first two seasons (1956, 1957) were devoted to a study of the fortifications and of the temple area. In 1960 work was continued on the temple and the palace underlying it, and the expedition set for its objective the recovering of the stratigraphy of the city in a residential complex. It is of great interest that the excavators conclude that the temple of Baal-Berith (Judges 9:4), "Beth Millo" (9:6), and the "tower" (9:46ff.) are designations of the same temple-citadel structure. It is significant for the chronology of Judges that it appears that the events of Judges 9 are to be dated to the first half of the twelfth century B.C. Considerable work for the future is outlined by staff members of the expedition. CEDV

SHECHINAH (See SHEKINAH)

SHEDEUR (shĕd'ē-êr, Heb. *shedhê'ûr, caster forth of light*). A Reubenite, the father of Elizur, prince of Reuben (Num 1:5; 2:10; 7:30; 10:18).

SHEEP (See ANIMALS)

SHEEPCOTE (See SHEEP PEN)

SHEEP GATE (Heb. *sha'ar ha-tsō'n*). A gate of Jerusalem mentioned in Nehemiah 3:1, 32; 12:39. It was probably near the NE corner of the wall as Nehemiah built it, but about one-fourth mile (about one-half km.) inward from the present NE corner of the wall.

SHEEP MARKET. Not mentioned in the Greek NT but possibly implied in John 5:2. The Greek simply means something that pertains to the sheep.

SHEEPMASTER (See OCCUPATIONS AND PROFESSIONS)

SHEEP PEN, SHEEPFOLD (Heb. *gedhērâh, mikhlâh, mishpethayin, nāweh,* Gr. *aulē*). An enclosure intended for the protection of sheep and also to keep them from wandering out and getting lost. These folds were simple walled enclosures, usually without roofs, with the walls covered with thorns to keep out robbers. Several flocks would usually pass the night in one fold under the care of a shepherd who guarded the door. Each shepherd knew his own sheep and was known by them. (See John 10:1–6.)

SHEEPSHEARER (See OCCUPATIONS AND PROFESSIONS)

SHEERAH (shē'ra, Heb. *she'ĕrâh*). A daughter or granddaughter of Ephraim and apparently a powerful woman, for she built or fortified three villages (1 Chron 7:24; cf. 2 Chron 8:5).

SHEET. A large piece of linen (Acts 10:11; 11:5). The word used indicates the material rather than its use. In Judges 14:12–13 "sheets" in KJV probably means "linen undergarments," though NIV has merely "linen garments" (cf. Prov 31:24).

SHEHARIAH (shē-ha-rī'a, Heb. *shehar yâh*). One of the sons of Jeroham, a Benjamite. He and his brothers were listed among the early inhabitants of Jerusalem after the Captivity (1 Chron 8:26).

SHEKEL (See MONEY)

SHEKINAH (she-kī'na, Heb. *shekhînâh, dwelling of God*). A word, though not occurring in the Bible, that is employed by some Jews and by Christians to describe the visible presence of the Lord. It is alluded to in such places as Isaiah 60:2 by the phrase "his glory" and in Romans 9:4 by the phrase "the glory." Moses calls this the "cloud" in Exodus 14:19. Its first appearance occurred for a twofold purpose when Israel was being led by Moses out of Egypt. It hid the Israelites from the pursuing Egyptians and lighted the way at night for Israel (Exod 13:21; 14:19–20). To the Egyptians it was a cloud of darkness, but to Israel a cloud of light. It later covered Sinai when God spoke with Moses (24:15–18), filled the tabernacle (40:34–35), guided Israel (40:36–38), filled Solomon's temple (2 Chron 7:1), and was frequently seen in connection with Christ's ministry in the NT (Matt 17:5; Acts 1:9).

SHELAH, SHELANITE (shē'la, Heb. *shēlâh,* Gr. *Sala,* Heb. *shē'la-nīt, sprout*). 1. A son of Arphaxad and the father of Eber, he was one of the early Semites (Gen 10:24 Salah KJV; Luke 3:35 Sala KJV).

2. From another root meaning "a petition," the third son of Judah (Gen 38:5–26). The Shelanites were named after him (Num 26:20).

SHELEMIAH (shĕl-ē-mī'a, Heb. *shelemyâh, friend of the LORD*). 1. Doorkeeper at the east side of the house of God in David's time (1 Chron 26:14). In the previous verses of this chapter he is called Meshelemiah.

2. The son of Cushi and grandfather of Jehudi whom the princes of Jehoiakim sent to Baruch, Jeremiah's secretary (Jer 36:14).

3. The son of Abdeel, and one of the three whom Jehoiakim sent to arrest Baruch and Jeremiah the prophet (Jer 36:26).

4. The father of Jehucal or Jucal whom Zedekiah sent to Jeremiah to ask his prayers (Jer 37:3; cf. 38:1).

5. Son of Hananiah and father of Irijah, a captain of the ward who arrested Jeremiah on a false charge as Jeremiah was about to leave Jerusalem (Jer 37:13).

6. Two men of the family of Bani in the days of Ezra who had taken foreign wives and were compelled to give them up in order to purify Israel (Ezra 10:39, 41).

7. The father of Hananiah, a repairer of the wall (Neh 3:30).

8. A priestly treasurer in Nehemiah's day (Neh 13:13).

SHELEPH (shē'lĕf, Heb. *shālepn*). A son of Joktan and head of an Arab tribe named for him (Gen 10:26).

SHELESH (shē'lĕsh, Heb. *shēlesh*). A son of Helem, an early descendant of Asher, son of Jacob (1 Chron 7:35).

SHELOMI (shē-lō'mī, Heb. *shelōmî, at peace*). Father of Ahihud, a prince of the tribe of Asher whom the Lord appointed to help divide the land (Num 34:27).

SHELOMITH, SHELOMOTH (shē-lō'mĭth, shēlō'mōth, Heb. *shelōmîth, shelōmôth, peaceful*). 1. A daughter of Dibri of the tribe of Dan, in the days of Moses. She had married an Egyptian, and their son was executed for blasphemy (Lev 24:10–12, 23).

2. A chief Kohathite Levite and a cousin of Miriam, Aaron, and Moses (1 Chron 23:18, Shelomith; 24:22, Shelomoth).

3. A leading Gershonite Levite in David's time (1 Chron 23:9).

4. A descendant of Moses through his son Eliezer (1 Chron 26:25). David set him and his relatives over the treasuries that were dedicated to the Lord to maintain his house.

5. A son or daughter of Rehoboam, king of Judah (2 Chron 11:20), and therefore brother or sister of King Abijah of Judah.

6. A daughter of Zerubbabel (not the Zerubbabel who led back the Jews at the request of Cyrus, but his cousin, both named "Zerubbabel," i.e., "born in Babylon") and sister of Meshullam and Hannaniah (1 Chron 3:19).

7. An ancestor of a family of 160 men who returned with Ezra in 457 B.C. (Ezra 8:10). LXX has "of the sons of Bani, Shelomith, the son of Josiphiah," while the Hebrew text followed by the English is obscure.

SHELUMIEL (shē-lū'mĭ-ĕl, Heb. *shelumî'ēl, God is peace*). A chief Simeonite in the days of Moses. He helped take the census and presented an offering for his tribe when the tabernacle was dedicated (Num 1:6; 7:36).

SHEM (shĕm, Heb. *shēm*, Gr. *Sēm, name, fame*). This second son of Noah and progenitor of the Semitic race was born ninety-eight years before the Flood (Gen 11:10). He lived six hundred years, outliving his descendants for nine generations (except for Eber and Abraham). In the racial prophecy that Noah made after the episode of his drunkenness (9:25–27), he mentioned "the LORD, the God of Shem." The three great monotheistic religions—Judaism, Christianity, and Islam—all had Semitic origins. Noah added that Japheth's descendants would "live in the tents of Shem," indicating that the Aryan peoples to a large extent have derived their civilization from the Semites. In the "Table of the nations" (Gen 10) Shem had five sons, of whom Arphaxad (10:22) was clearly an individual and the others were peoples or progenitors of peoples: e.g., "Lud" refers to the Lydians in Asia Minor, "Elam" points to the Elamites who lived east of the Tigris River; "Aram" means Arameans or Syrians who lived in Syria and Mesopotamia, and "Asshur" is Assyria. Critics pointed out a century ago that "Asshur" is mentioned also in the Hamite list (10:11), but archaeologists have found Hamitic artifacts under Semitic ruins of Assyrian cities. Shem, Ham, and Japheth probably differed only as brothers do, but their descendants are quite distinct.

SHEMA (shē'mȧ, Heb. *shemā', fame, rumor*). 1. A town in the southern part of Judah (Josh 15:26).

2. A son of Hebron of the descendants of Caleb in Judah, and the father of Raham (1 Chron 2:44).

3. A son of Joel, and the father of Azaz in the genealogy of the Reubenites (1 Chron 5:8). He is possibly the same as Shemaiah no. 2 below (5:4).

4. A Benjamite, head of a family who lived at Aijalon and drove out the inhabitants of Gath (1 Chron 8:13).

5. One who stood at the right hand of Ezra in the revival in Jerusalem when Ezra read the Book of the Law to the people (Neh 8:4).

6. "Shema" is the Hebrew name for Deuteronomy 6:4, probably the most often quoted verse in the Bible, as every good Jew repeats it several times every day—"Hear, O Israel: The LORD our God, the LORD is one."

SHEMAAH (shē-mā'ȧ, *shemā'âh, fame*). A man of Gibeah of Benjamin whose two sons helped David at Ziklag (1 Chron 12:3).

SHEMAIAH (shē-mā'yȧ, Heb. *shem'yâh, The LORD has heard*). 1. A prince among the families of the tribe of Simeon (1 Chron 4:37).

2. A Reubenite, son of Joel (1 Chron 5:4), possibly the same as Shema (no. 3) of verse 8.

3. A chief Levite of the sons of Elizaphan in the days of David (1 Chron 15:8, 11).

4. A Levite scribe in the days of David; son of Nethanel, who recorded the courses of the priests (1 Chron 24:6).

5. Also in David's time, the firstborn son of Obed-Edom and father of the mighty men among the doorkeepers of the house of God (1 Chron 26:4, 6–7).

6. A brave prophet of God who forbade Rehoboam king of Judah to go against the house of Israel in the north (1 Kings 12:22–24).

Shemaiah later wrote a biography of Rehoboam, but it has been lost (2 Chron 12:15).

7. A descendant of David, related to the messianic line (1 Chron 3:22) and the father of five or six sons.

8. A Merarite Levite in the days of Nehemiah. He lived in Jerusalem (1 Chron 9:14; Neh 12:18)

9. A Levite, son of Galal and a descendant of Elkanah, mentioned among the first inhabitants who returned from exile (1 Chron 9:16). In Nehemiah 11:17 he is called "Shammua."

10. A Levite whom King Jehoshaphat sent to teach in the towns of Judah (2 Chron 17:8).

11. One of the Levites who cleansed the temple in the days of Hezekiah (2 Chron 29:14).

12. A Levite who was appointed to assist in the distribution of food to the cities of the priests in the days of Hezekiah (2 Chron 31:15).

13. A chief Levite in the days of Josiah. He assisted in the great Passover (2 Chron 35:9).

14. A leader of the Levites who returned with Ezra (Ezra 8:13).

15. One whom Ezra sent back for additional Levites (Ezra 8:16), possibly the same as no. 14.

16. A descendant of the priests; he had married a foreign wife (Ezra 10:21).

17. Another man who was guilty of marrying a foreign wife (Ezra 10:31).

18. Son of Shecaniah, keeper of the East Gate of Jerusalem. He helped rebuild the wall (Neh 3:29).

19. One who tried to intimidate Nehemiah (Neh 6:10).

20. A priest who signed the covenant (Neh 10:8).

21. A priest or Levite who returned with Zerubbabel (Neh 12:6).

22. A musical priest in the days of Nehemiah (Neh 12:36).

23. A priest who assisted in the celebration of the completing of the wall of Jerusalem, possibly the same as no. 22 (Neh 12:42).

24. The father of Uriah the prophet, whom Jehoiakim king of Judah killed for prophesying against the sins of Jerusalem (Jer 26:20).

25. A false prophet who fought against Jeremiah to his own hurt and therefore was not to see God's blessing nor to have any offspring (Jer 29:24–32).

26. The father of Delaiah, one of the princes in the days of Jehoiakim, who heard the words of the prophet (Jer 36:12).

SHEMARIAH (shĕm-à-rī'à, Heb. *shemaryâh, The* LORD *keeps*). 1. One of the mighty men of Benjamin who joined David while he was at Ziklag (1 Chron 12:5).

2. A son of Rehoboam king of Judah by his cousin Mahalath, a granddaughter of David (2 Chron 11:19). KJV has "Shamariah."

3. One of the family of Harim who had married a foreign woman and was compelled by Ezra to put her away (Ezra 10:32).

4. One of the sons of Bani or Binnui; he had been likewise guilty of marrying a foreign woman (Ezra 10:41).

SHEMEBER (shĕm-ē'bẽr, Heb. *shem' ever*). King of Zeboiim, a city in the vicinity of the Dead Sea in the time of Abraham (Gen 14:2). He rebelled against Kedorlaomer of Elam.

SHEMED (shē'mĕd, Heb. *shamedh, destruction;* however, some MSS have *shamer, watcher*). The third-named son of Elpaal. He built Ono and Lod (1 Chron 8:12).

SHEMER (shē'mẽr, Heb. *shemer, guard*). Owner of a hill in central Palestine that Omri king of Israel bought, fortified, and named Samaria after its former owner (1 Kings 16:24; 1 Chron 6:46). This man's name is Shamar in KJV of Chronicles.

SHEMIDA, SHEMIDAH (shē-mī'dà, Heb. *shemîdhā'*). An early member of the tribe of Manasseh through Gilead, and therefore inheriting land east of the Jordan (Num 26:32; Josh 17:2). He had four sons (1 Chron 7:19).

SHEMIDAITES (shē-mī'dà-īts, Heb. *shemîdhā'*). The family descended from Shemida (Num 26:32; Josh 17:2), belonging to the half-tribe of Manasseh.

SHEMINITH (shĕm'ĭ-nĭth, *eighth,* i.e., the octave, and meaning the lower octave). A musical term. The harps tuned to the "sheminith" were to be used with men's voices (1 Chron 15:21, titles for Pss 6 and 12).

SHEMIRAMOTH (shē-mĭr'à-mŏth, Heb. *shemîrāmôth*). 1. One of the second rank of Levites whom David selected for making music at the return of the ark of the covenant to Jerusalem. His part, with seven others, was to play the lyre (1 Chron 15:18, 20).

2. One of the teaching Levites appointed by King Jehoshaphat to teach in Judah (2 Chron 17:8).

SHEMUEL (shĕ-mū'ĕl, Heb. *shemû'ēl, name of God*). The same as Samuel in Hebrew.

1. A Simeonite, divider of Canaan under Joshua (Num 34:20).

2. A Kohathite Levite in charge of music in the temple (1 Chron 6:33; Samuel NIV).

3. The head of a house in Issachar (1 Chron 7:2; Samuel NIV).

SHEN (shĕn, Heb. *ha-shēn, tooth* or *pointed rock*). A sharp rock a short distance west of Jerusalem near which Samuel set up the monument of victory that he called "Ebenezer" (1 Sam 7:12).

SHENAZZAR (shē-năz'ar, Heb. *shen' atsar*). A son of Jeconiah, i.e., Jehoiachin, son of Jehoiakim. He was born in captivity (1 Chron 3:18; Shenazar KJV).

SHENIR (See SENIR)

SHEOL (shē'ōl, Heb. *she'ôl*). In the OT the place to which all the dead go, immediately upon death. Sometimes KJV translates it "grave," sometimes "hell," depending on whether or not the individuals in the particular passage were viewed as righteous, but this procedure involves importing distinctions into the OT that were not clarified until Jesus' ministry. NIV prefers to translate *she'ôl* as "grave" (in all but eight passages) and place the name itself in a footnote, a procedure that is neither helpful nor justifiable. It seems best—as in ASV, NASB, and (except for Ps 49:14) RSV—to not translate *she'ôl*, because it is a name.

The OT makes three main points about Sheol: (1) All the dead alike go there (e.g., Gen 37:35; Isa 14:9ff.). (2) Sheol is in some unspecified sense the lot of the wicked. References such as Psalms 6:5; 30:3, 9; 88:3–6 (cf. Job 17:13–16; Isa 38:18) are often quoted as allegedly showing that the OT knew of no hope after death, that the dead are cut off from the Lord and he from them. In all these references, however, the speakers believe themselves to be facing death under the wrath of God, estranged from him, without any indication of divine favor. The OT takes the matter no further; there is some undefined sense in which Sheol involves those who die under wrath in separation from God—the God their wickedness has offended. (3) On the other hand, there are those who can confidently look forward to glory (Ps 73:23–24), and this is seen as redemption from Sheol (49:14–15). But again we are not aided by further OT revelation on the point. We must wait for the One who brought life and immortality to light in the gospel (2 Tim 1:10).

Bibliography: J. A. Motyer, *After Death,* 1965.

SHEPHAM (shē'făm, Heb. *shephām, nakedness*). A place in the NE of Canaan, near the Sea of Galilee (Num 34:10–11).

SHEPHATIAH (shĕf'à-tī'à, Heb. *shephatyâh, the* LORD *is judge*). 1. The fifth son of David. He was born at Hebron to his wife Abital (2 Sam 3:4).

2. A son of Reuel and father of Meshullam. He lived in Jerusalem soon after the return from captivity (1 Chron 9:8).

3. One of the mighty men who joined David at Ziklag (1 Chron 12:5).

4. A son of Maacah. He was a Simeonite officer ruling his tribe in the days of David (1 Chron 27:16).

5. One of the seven sons of Jehoshaphat king of Judah (2 Chron 21:2).

6. The founder of a family with 372 descendants who returned with Zerubbabel (Ezra 2:4).

7. One of the children of Solomon's servants whose descendants returned with Zerubbabel (Ezra 2:57).

8. One whose descendant Zebadiah returned with Ezra (Ezra 8:8). Perhaps this is the same as no. 7.

9. A son of Mahalalel. His descendant Athaiah lived in Jerusalem soon after the walls had been rebuilt (Neh 11:4).

10. One of the men of Zedekiah who desired that Jeremiah be put to death for prophesying (Jer 38:1).

SHEPHELAH, THE (shē-fē'là, Heb. *ha-shephēlâh, low country*). The word is not in the English Bible. KJV translates the Hebrew word "low country" or "low plain" four times, "plain" three times, "vale" five times, and "valley" eight times; NIV has "foothills" seven times and "western foothills" thirteen times; ASV always has "lowland." It represents the undulating country between the mountains of Judah and the maritime plain south of the Plain of Sharon, extending through the country of Philistia along the Mediterranean. One of the Promised Land's six geographical sections west of Jordan (Josh 12:8), it had many sycamore trees (1 Kings 10:27). Its limestone hills were 500 to 800 feet (156–250 m.) high. Good crops, especially grapes, grew in the valleys. Samson's exploits took place there, and David hid there from Saul.

SHEPHER (shā'fĕr, Heb. *shepher*). The name of a mountain between Kehelathah and Haradah where the Israelites encamped in their wilderness wanderings (Num 33:23). It is otherwise unknown and unidentified. KJV has "Shapher."

SHEPHERD (See OCCUPATIONS AND PROFESSIONS)

SHEPHO (shē'fō, *barrenness*). One of the early descendants of Seir the Horite (Gen 36:23; 1 Chron 1:40). KJV has "Shephi" in 1 Chronicles.

SHEPHUPHAN (shē-fū'făm, Heb. *shephûphān*). A grandson of Benjamin through Bela his firstborn (1 Chron 8:5). The name appears in Genesis 46:21 as "Muppim"; in 1 Chronicles 7:12, 15 as Shuppites; and in 26:16 as "Shuppim."

SHERAH (See SHEERAH)

SHEREBIAH (shĕr-ē-bī'à, Heb. *sherēvyâh*). 1. One of the chief priests who were brought from Casiphia to join Ezra on his return to Jerusalem, to whom Ezra entrusted treasures for the temple (Ezra 8:18, 24). These men translated the reading of the law into Aramaic for the people (Neh 8:7) and confessed the sins of Israel (9:4).

2. A covenanter with Nehemiah (Neh 10:12).

3. A Levite who returned with Zerubbabel (Neh 12:8).

4. A chief Levite in the days of Eliashib (Neh 12:24).

SHERESH (shē'rĕsh, Heb. *shāresh*). A grandson of Manasseh through Machir (1 Chron 7:16) and the ancestor of Manassites living in Gilead.

SHEREZER (See SHAREZER)

SHESHACH (shē'shăk, Heb. *shēshakh*). In the opinion of many, a cryptogram from "Babel" formed by reversing the letters of the alphabet. When the prophet first used this device (Jer 25:26), it was the first year of Nebuchadnezzar, and it would have been folly openly to predict the doom of Babylon. When he later used it (51:41), Israel was in captivity, Jerusalem had long been in ruins, and the use of the word with its explanation as Babylon could do no harm.

SHESHAI (shē'shī, Heb. *shēshay*). One of the sons of Anak, giants whom the spies feared (Num 13:22) but whom Caleb drove out (Josh 15:14) and Judah destroyed (Judg 1:10).

SHESHAN (shē'shăn, Heb *shē'shān*). An early descendant of Judah through Perez, Hezron, and Jerahmeel (1 Chron 2:31, 34). He gave his daughter as wife to an Egyptian servant, Jarha (2:35–41).

SHESHBAZZAR (shĕsh-bāz'êr, Heb. *sheshbatstsar*). A prince of the Jews when Cyrus made a decree permitting the Jews to go back to Jerusalem to rebuild the house of God. He was made governor, was given the sacred vessels of the temple that had been taken at the Captivity, and helped lay the foundation of the temple (Ezra 1:8, 11; 5:14, 16). He may be the same as Zerubbabel.

SHETH (shĕth, Heb. *shēth, compensation*). 1. In the KJV the name of Eve's third son (1 Chron 1:1, lit. trans.), elsewhere called Seth.

2. "The sons of Sheth" in Numbers 24:17 refers to the Moabites, whom Balaam predicted would be conquered by an Israelite ruler. ASV here reads "sons of tumult," but compare the footnote.

SHETHAR (shē'thȧr, Heb. *shēthar*). One of the seven princes of Persia and Media who "saw the king's face" in the days of Xerxes (Esth 1:14).

SHETHAR-BOZENAI, SHETHAR-BOZNAI (shē'thȧr-bŏz'ē-nī, shē'thȧr-bŏz'nī). A Persian official who tried to prevent the Jews from building the temple and complained to the king (Ezra 5:3, 6).

SHEVA (shē'vȧ, Heb. *shewā'*). 1. David's scribe or secretary (2 Sam 20:25), perhaps the same as "Seraiah" in 8:17.

2. A son of Caleb (probably not the famous spy) by his concubine Maacah (1 Chron 2:49).

SHEWBREAD (See TABERNACLE)

SHIBAH (See SHEBAH)

SHIBBOLETH (shĭb'bō-lĕth, Heb. *shibbōleth, an ear of grain* or *a stream*). A word that was differently pronounced on the two sides of the Jordan, and so was used by the men of Gilead under Jephthah as a test to determine whether the speaker was of Ephraim or not (Judg 12:5–6). This word is used proverbially today; e.g., "That was his Shibboleth."

SHIBMAH (See SIBMAH)

SHICRON (See SHIKKERON)

SHIELD (See ARMS AND ARMOR)

SHIGGAION (shĭ-gā'yŏn, Heb. *shiggāyôn*). A musical term found in the heading of Psalm 7. It may refer to a dithyramb or rhapsody.

SHIGIONOTH (shĭg-ĭ-ō'nŏth). Plural of Shiggaion. It is the heading (Hab 3:1) of Habakkuk's lovely psalm (3:2–19).

SHIHON (See SHION)

SHIHOR, SIHOR (shī'hôr, Heb. *shîhôr*). At least three views have been held regarding Shihor (usually Sihor in KJV): (1) it refers to the Nile; (2) it refers to a stream that separated Egypt from Palestine; (3) it refers to a canal, with water drawn from the Nile, on the border between Egypt and Palestine. See Joshua 13:3; 1 Chronicles 13:5; Isaiah 23:3; Jeremiah 2:18.

SHIHOR LIBNATH (shī'hôr lĭb'năth, Heb. *shîhôr livnāth*). A smali stream flowing into the Mediterranean Sea on the southern border of Asher (Josh 19:26). Perhaps the Belus near Acre, from the sand of which glass was made.

SHIKKERON (shĭk'rŏn, Heb. *shikkerôn*). A town west of Jerusalem on the northern border of Judah (Josh 15:11). KJV has "Shicron."

SHILHI (shĭl'hī, Heb. *shilhî*). The father-in-law of Jehoshaphat king of Judah (1 Kings 22:42).

SHILHIM (shĭl'hĭm, Heb. *shilhîm*). A town in southern Judah in Joshua's time (Josh 15:32).

SHILLEM, SHILLEMITES (shĭl'ĕm, shĭl'ĕm-īts). The fourth son of Naphtali (Gen 46:24); the family descended from him (Num 26:49). He is also called Shallum (1 Chron 7:13 except NIV).

SHILOAH (See SILOAM)

SHILOH (shī'lō, Heb. *shīlōh*). 1. The person referred to in the prophecy of Jacob in Genesis 49:10: "The scepter will not depart from Judah, nor the ruler's staff from between his feet, until he comes to whom it belongs," or as the footnote reads, "until Shiloh comes." This has been interpreted in many different ways. The ASV footnote has "Till he come to Shiloh, having the obedience of the peoples." Or, according to the Syrian, "Till he come whose it is." The NIV has "until he comes to whom it belongs and the obedience of the nations is his." The principal interpretations are the following:

a. The passage is messianic. The difficulty of this interpretation is that nowhere else in the OT is Shiloh found as a personal name, and none of the ancient MSS apply the word personally to the Messiah. This application is not older than the sixteenth century (apart from the fanciful passage in the Talmud).

b. Shiloh was the town in central Palestine where Joshua placed the tabernacle after the conquest of Canaan (Josh 18:1). The reading, "Till he comes to Shiloh," is favored.

c. Shiloh is not regarded as a proper name at all. It is thought to be a compound word meaning "whose it is." This is apparently the reading presupposed in the LXX, the Peshitta, and the Jewish Targums, and seems to be alluded to in Ezekiel 21:27, "until he comes to whom it rightfully belongs." The passage has a messianic reference if this reading is adopted.

2. A city in the tribe of Ephraim, about twelve miles (twenty km.) north and east of Bethel and about the same distance south of Sychar where Jacob's well was, just east of the highway from Bethel to Shechem (Judg 21:19). It stood on an isolated hill that could easily be defended either against the Canaanites from the north or the Philistines from the SW. Here the children of Israel under Joshua assembled after the first phases of the conquest of Canaan and set up the tabernacle, thus making Shiloh the capital city of Canaan under the theocracy. Here the tabernacle remained until in the days of Samuel, about four hundred years later, when the ark was removed in a battle with the Philistines (1 Sam 4:3) and was not returned to its place until shortly before the days of Solomon's temple. From Shiloh the men of Benjamin, by Israel's permission, kidnapped wives after the Benjamite war under the priesthood of Phinehas, the grandson of Aaron (Judg 21). The godly Elkanah and his wife went to Shiloh before the birth of Samuel (1 Sam 1:3). Here the boy Samuel received his call from God (3:20–21).

From the time of the removal of the ark, Shiloh gradually lost its importance, especially when David made Jerusalem the capital of the kingdom of Israel. This loss of importance was principally because God "abandoned the tabernacle of Shiloh, the tent he had set up among men" (Ps 78:60). During the reign of King Saul and especially during his war with the Philistines, Ahijah, great-grandson of Eli, was high priest of Israel, wearing the sacred ephod at Shiloh (1 Sam 14:3). After the division of the kingdom, though the ark and the temple were at Jerusalem, and though Jeroboam, the apostate king, had set up centers of worship at Dan and at Bethel, another Ahijah, prophet of the Lord, was still at Shiloh, representing God before the true people of God in the northern kingdom. To him Jeroboam sent to inquire about his sick son (1 Kings 14), and here Ahijah pronounced the doom of Jeroboam's house (14:13).

In the days of Jeremiah, Shiloh was a ruin (Jer 7:12, 14), though there were some men there after the destruction of Jerusalem (41:5).

The city, identified with Tell Seilun about thirty miles (fifty km.) north of Jerusalem, was excavated by a Danish expedition in 1926, 1929, 1932, and 1963, directed by H. Kjaer and others. Basically the results confirm the biblical data.

The site of Shiloh, about 18½ miles (30 km.) north of Jerusalem. The structure viewed here is thought to have been built on Israelite foundations. "Go now to my place that was in Shiloh, where I made my name to dwell at first, and see what I did to it . . ." (Jer 7:12). Courtesy Duby Tal.

Shiloh was prosperous in the period of the judges (twelfth to tenth centuries B.C.) when it was fortified. It was destroyed and burned, probably by the Philistine invasion, and revived in the Israelite period. It reached its height in the Roman period from which a villa with a bath and a city wall were uncovered. A Byzantine basilica with a mosaic pavement from the fifth century A.D. was found there. SB and ABF

SHILONITE, SHILONI (shī'lō-nīt, shī-lō'nī, Heb. *shîlōnî*). 1. An inhabitant of Shiloh, such as Ahijah the Shilonite (1 Kings 12:15; 2 Chron 9:29).

2. An ancestor of Maaseiah, one of the Jewish princes who lived in Jerusalem under Nehemiah (Neh 11:5 KJV; NIV "a descendant of Shelah").

SHILSHAH (shĭl'shȧ, Heb. *shilshâh*). One of the eleven sons of Zophah, an early member of the tribe of Asher (1 Chron 7:37).

SHIMEA (shĭm'ē-ȧ, Heb. *shim' ā'*). 1. A brother of David whose son killed a giant of Gath (1 Chron 20:7).

2. A son of David and Bathshua (Bathsheba), born in Jerusalem (1 Chron 3:5 JB, KJV, MLB, MOF, NASB, NEB, RSV; Shammua NIV).

3. A Merarite Levite (1 Chron 6:30).

4. A Gershonite Levite, grandfather of the Asaph, who stood with Heman in the service of sacred song under David (1 Chron 6:39).

No. 1 is probably the same as Shimma (1 Chron 2:13 KJV), Shammah (1 Sam 16:9), Shimeah (2 Sam 21:21), and Shimei (21:21). The name is spelled three ways in Hebrew, five ways in English.

SHIMEAH (shĭm'ē-ȧ, Heb. *shim' ā'*). 1. A brother of David (2 Sam 13:3).

2. A son of Mikloth a Benjamite (1 Chron 8:32) who lived at Jerusalem. In 9:38 his name is Shimeam.

SHIMEAM (See SHIMEAH)

SHIMEATH (shĭm'ē-ăth, Heb. *shim' ath, fame*). An Ammonitess whose son Zabad (2 Chron 24:26) or Jozabad (2 Kings 12:21) helped to assassinate King Joash of Judah.

SHIMEATHITES (shĭm'ē-ăth-īts, Heb. *shim-'āthîm*). One of the three families of scribes who lived at Jabez in Judah (1 Chron 2:55). They were Kenites related to the Recabites.

SHIMEI (shĭm'ē-ī, Heb. *shim' î, famous*). 1. A son of Gershon and head of a Levite family. His name is spelled Shimi in KJV (Exod 6:17).

2. A Gershonite Levite in the days of David, and head of one of the courses of Levites (1 Chron 23:7–10).

3. One of David's mighty men who remained faithful during Adonijah's rebellion (1 Kings 1:8).

4. One of Solomon's district governors, in charge of food provisions from Benjamin (1 Kings 4:18).

5. The grandson of Jehoiachin, or, as he was later called, Jeconiah (1 Chron 3:19).

6. A Simeonite, father of twenty-two children (1 Chron 4:26–27).

7. An early Reubenite, son of Gog and father of Micah (1 Chron 5:4).

8. An early Merarite Levite, cousin once removed of Moses and Aaron (1 Chron 6:29).

9. The head of a family in Benjamin (1 Chron 8:21), spelled Shimhi in KJV.

10. The head of one of the twenty-four courses of musical Levites, who with his twelve sons and brothers made up the tenth course (1 Chron 25:17).

11. A man of Ramah, whom David set over the vineyards (1 Chron 27:27).

12. A Benjamite of the house of Saul and son of Gera. He cursed David and threw stones at him when David was fleeing from his son Absalom. David refused to let his cousin Abishai kill him (2 Sam 16:5–14). When David was returning victorious, Shimei prayed for forgiveness, and David pardoned him (19:16–23); but Solomon, upon ascending the throne, first confined him to Jerusalem, then executed him for disobedience (1 Kings 2:36–46).

13. One of the descendants of Heman the singer. He helped in the cleaning of the temple under Hezekiah (2 Chron 29:14).

14. A Levite, treasurer over the freewill offerings and tithes in Hezekiah's time (2 Chron 31:12–13).

15. One of the Levites who had married a foreign woman in Ezra's time (Ezra 10:23).

16. One of the family of Hashum who had married a foreign woman in Ezra's time (Ezra 10:33).

17. One of the family of Bani who had also married a foreign woman (Ezra 10:38).

18. A son of Kish and grandfather of Mordecai the Jew who brought up Esther (Esth 2:5).

19. A representative of a leading family who in the final restoration of Israel will mourn when they look on the One they have pierced (Zech 12:13).

SHIMEON (shĭm'ē-ŭn, Heb. *shim' ôn, hearing*). One of the family of Harim in Ezra's time. He had married a foreign woman (Ezra 10:31).

SHIMHI, SHIMI (See SHIMEI)

SHIMITE (shĭm'īt). A member of the family descended from Shimei (Num 3:21 KJV; ASV and NIV "Shimeites").

SHIMMA (See SHIMEA)

SHIMON (shī'mŏn, Heb. *shîmôn*). The head of a family in the tribe of Judah (1 Chron 4:20).

SHIMRATH (shĭm'răth, Heb. *shimrăth, watch*). One of the sons of Shimei in the tribe of Benjamin (1 Chron 8:21).

SHIMRI (shĭm'rī, Heb. *shimrî*). 1. A son of Shemaiah and the head of a family in the tribe of Simeon (1 Chron 4:37).

2. The father of Jediael and Joha, two of David's mighty men (1 Chron 11:45).

3. A son of Hosah of the Merarite Levites, whom, though he was not the firstborn, Hosah made chief of his thirteen kinsmen. Spelled Simri in KJV (1 Chron 26:10).

4. A Levite who assisted in cleansing the temple (2 Chron 29:13).

SHIMRITH (shĭm'rĭth, Heb. *shimrîth, watchful*). A Moabitess, mother of Jehozabad, who helped to kill Joash king of Judah (2 Chron 24:26); also called Shomer (2 Kings 12:21).

SHIMRON, SHIMROM (shĭm'rŏn, shĭm'rŏm, Heb. *shimrôn, a guard*). 1. The fourth son of Issachar, son of Jacob (Gen 46:13; 1 Chron 7:1). In 1 Chronicles KJV has "Shimrom."

2. A town in the northern part of Canaan whose king united with Jabin, king of Hazor, to fight against Joshua and the Israelites (Josh 11:1ff.). In Joshua 19:15 it is mentioned among the cities given in the division of the land to the tribe of Zebulun. In Joshua 12:20, among the conquests of Joshua, it is called Shimron Meron.

SHIMRON MERON (shĭm'rŏn mē'rŏn). A town listed among the thirty-four that Joshua conquered in the conquest of Canaan (Josh 12:20).

SHIMSHAI (shĭm'shī, Heb. *shimshay, sunny*). A scribe among the enemies of the Jews who had been hindering the attempts to rebuild the temple (Ezra 4:8).

SHINAB (shī'năb, Heb. *shin'āv*). King of Admah, one of the Canaanite cities destroyed with Sodom (Gen 14:2).

SHINAR (shī'nar, Heb. *shin'ār*). The region

containing the cities of Babel, Erech (cf. modern Iraq), Akkad, and Calneh (Gen 10:10), the locations of which, except Akkad, are unknown. Akkad may have been the Agade known to archaeologists as the capital chosen by Sargon I, ancient king of Babylon. Shinar lay on the alluvial plain of Babylonia, and for many centuries was perhaps the most fertile region on earth. Herodotus speaks of two-hundredfold yields of grain there. Genesis 11:1–9 speaks of the early postdiluvians traveling east and finding a plain in the land of Shinar, where they started to build a tower. Amraphel, king of Shinar, invaded Canaan in the days of Abraham (Gen 14:1). Nebuchadnezzar was ruler of the land of Shinar (Dan 1:2 JB, KJV, MLB, MOF, NASB, NEB, RSV; Babylonia NIV), and it is mentioned in two prophecies (Isa 11:11; Zech 5:11), where NIV again has Babylonia in the text and Shinar in a footnote to each.

SHION (shī'ŏn, Heb. *shî'ôn, overturning*). A town in Issachar, perhaps about three miles (five km.) NW of Mount Tabor (Josh 19:19; KJV Shihon).

SHIPHI (shī'fī, Heb. *shiph'î*). Father of Ziza, a prince in one of the families of Simeon (1 Chron 4:37).

SHIPHMITE (shĭf'mīt, Heb. *shephām*). The family name of Zabdi, who was over the produce of the vineyards under David (1 Chron 27:27). The name is probably from Shepham in Judah.

SHIPHRAH (shĭf'rȧ, Heb. *shiphrâh, beauty*). One of the Hebrew midwives who risked their lives to save the Hebrew boy babies (Exod 1:15–21).

SHIPHTAN (shĭf'tăn, Heb. *shiphtān, judicial*). Father of Kemuel, a prince of Ephraim, whom Joshua appointed to help divide the land (Num 34:24).

SHIPS (Heb. *'ŏnîyâh, tsî, sephînâh*, Gr. *ploion, ploiarion, naus, skaphē*). Ships and navigation find only a small place in the OT. The Hebrews were an agricultural people, and the Phoenicians and Philistines, over long periods, separated them from a coastline that was itself harborless and difficult. In Judges 5:17 there is cryptic reference to some experience of ships in the case of the two tribes of Asher and Dan, but Hebrew seafaring in general was secondhand. The Phoenicians, confined to their coastal strip, and with the timber resources of the Lebanon range in their hinterland, were prompted by geography to exploit the sea, and became, in the process, the great navigators of the ancient world; hence the symbolic vessel with ivory benches and embroidered purple sails of Ezekiel's metaphor in his denunciation of Tyre (Ezek 27:4–11). Solomon's fleet at Ezion Geber (1 Kings 9–10) consisted of Phoenician ships manned by Phoenicians. Jehoshaphat's later attempt to revive the trade ended in shipwreck, due, no doubt, to Hebrews' inexperienced handling of the ships. The ships of Tarshish mentioned in this connection and elsewhere (e.g., Isa 2:16 JB, KJV, MLB, MOF, NASB, NEB, RSV; trading ship NIV) were probably sturdy vessels built at first for commerce with Tartessus in Spain, the term later being applied, like "China clipper" and "East Indiamen," to vessels generally used for arduous and distant voyaging. Solomon's southern fleet, for example, traded to Ophir, and, if the cargoes are an indication, to southern India as well (1 Kings 10:22).

It is certain that the Phoenicians penetrated to Cornwall for tin and to the Canary Islands. They probably used the trireme, the useful vessel with three banks of oars, which was a Phoenician invention. Remaining OT references are few and commonly poetic. Psalm 107:23–27 speaks of the terrors of a storm at sea, and Psalm 104:26 briefly mentions ships. Isaiah 18:2 speaks of the boats or rafts built of bound bundles of papyrus; these are sometimes depicted in Egyptian murals. Daniel 11:30 refers to warships from the western coastlands or Cyprus (Chittim or Kittim). In NT times the shipping of the Mediterranean was principally Greek and Roman. The Romans maintained war fleets of triremes and quinqueremes (ships with three and with five banks of oars). How the rowers on these vessels were arranged has been much debated, and the view that there were three (or five) banks of benches is now

Silver boat model with leaf-blade paddles, from the Royal Cemetery at Ur, twenty-fifth century B.C. Courtesy University Museum, University of Pennsylvania.

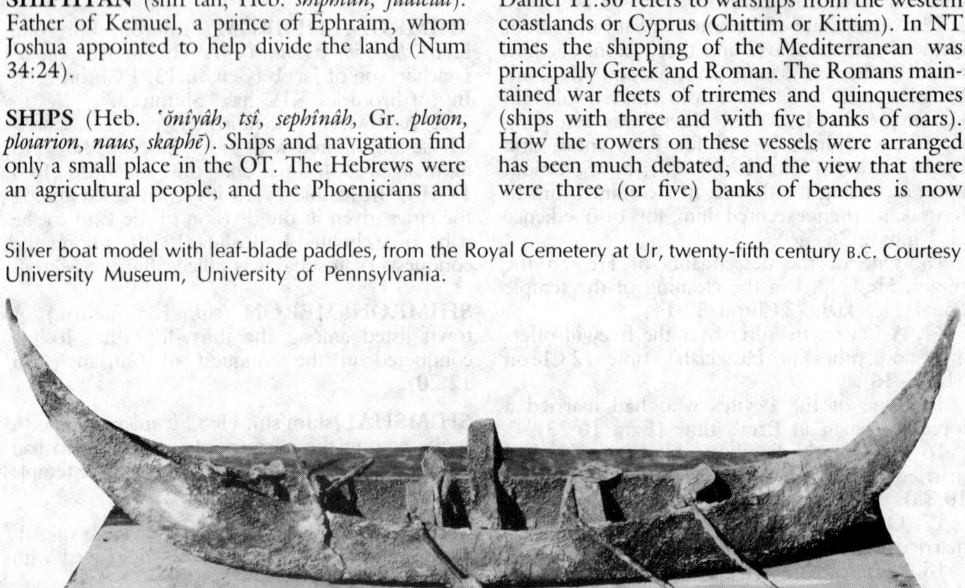

Reconstructed model of a warship manned by the Sea Peoples (the "foreigners of the sea," among whom were Philistines), from the days of Ramses III (1182–1151 B.C.), based on a temple relief at Medinet Habu, a modern name applied to a group of ruined temples and a later settlement near the south end of west Thebes. Courtesy The Maritime Museum, Haifa.

generally rejected. It is probable that the benches had a forward slant, and that each rower pulled an individual oar sitting three (or five) to a bench. The warship (or "long ship," as it was sometimes called) was not designed for heavy loads but for speed and maneuverability. Hence the frequency of shipwreck, and sometimes mass disaster, in Roman naval history. The great artists in the naval use of the trireme were the Athenians, whose admiral Phormion (c. 440–428 B.C.) developed the tactics that kept the Athenians supreme at sea until the Syracusans invented the ramming device, which struck Athenian naval power a fatal blow in the Great Harbor (413 B.C.). Merchant ships were more heavily built and were designed to stay at sea for long periods in all weathers, carrying considerable cargoes.

The classic passage is Acts 27, which contains Luke's brilliant account of the voyage and wreck of the Alexandrian grain ship. These vessels were of considerable size. There were 276 people aboard the ship on which Paul and Luke traveled (27:37). Josephus states that he traveled to Rome on a ship with no fewer than 600 aboard (*Life* 3). The Alexandrian grain ship, Isis, of the second century A.D., measured 140 by 36 feet (44 by 11 m.), and would be rated at 3,250 tons (2,955 metric tons) burden. No doubt these were exceptional vessels, and the average merchant ship was probably in the vicinity of 100 tons (90 metric tons). Paul's ship may have been on a northern route because of the lateness of the season (27:6), though Ramsay is of the opinion that this was the regular route from Egypt to Rome (*St. Paul the Traveller,* p. 319). According to Vegetius, from mid-September to mid-November was a particularly dangerous period for autumn navigation. Paul's voyage fell within this period.

The account illustrates the difficulty of handling the ancient sailing ship in adverse winds. From Myra, on the extreme southern point of Asia Minor, the ship was proceeding west to Cnidus, a port at the SW extremity of Asia Minor. A wind off the shore drove the vessel south, and the shipmaster was compelled to seek shelter under the lee of the island of Crete (27:7), which was 140 miles (233 km.) long. Fair Havens, where the ship found refuge was (and is) a little more than halfway along this coast, just east of the part where the island rises into a group of lofty mountains. Funneled down from these highlands (27:14), the NE wind drove them south from the

A Roman warship (bireme) with two banks of oars, as depicted on a relief dating from c. 30 B.C. Courtesy Photo Sadeh.

"more commodious" harbor of Phenice, over 23 miles (38 km.) of turbulent sea, to the off-shore island of Clauda. The brief advantage of the island's protection was used to haul in the boat, which was being towed waterlogged behind (27:16). To the south lay the Syrtes, ancient graveyard of ships, as modern underwater archaeology has strikingly revealed. Hence the battle to maintain a westerly course, aided by a veering of the wind to the east, as the cyclonic disturbance shifted its center.

At this point (27:17) they "passed ropes under the ship itself." These tautened cables, used to bind the straining timbers against the stress of the sea and the leverage of the loaded mast, are mentioned elsewhere in ancient literature. "See you not," says Horace, writing metaphorically of the laboring ship of state (*Odes* 1:14), "that the side is stripped of oars, the masts crippled by the rushing southwest wind, the yard-arms groaning, and that without ropes the hull can scarcely bear the too preemptory sea." (See also Plato, *Republic* 10:616c.) It is possible that the hull was "undergirded" by strong ropes, but that an extension of the cables above deck formed a network that could be twisted to tautness. It is probable that the "tackling," which was thrown overboard, was the rigging and the long spar on which the mainsail depended, a device likely to become unmanageable during a storm.

The ship on which Paul continued his voyage from Malta to the grain port of Puteoli had "the sign" of Castor and Pollux (28:11). In Greek mythology, the Great Twin Brethren were the patrons of shipmen and had special charge of storm-bound ships (Horace, *Odes* 1:12:27–32). The account in Acts 27 also tells of soundings for depth (27:28) and the bracing of the ship by a system of compensatory anchors (27:29). This is the purport of the metaphor in Hebrews 6:19. James 3:4 refers to the rudder paddles.

The boats of the Sea of Galilee, mentioned in the Gospels, were sturdy fishermen's craft or the barges of local lakeside trade. They comfortably held a dozen men, but even two of them could not hold all that Jesus' miracle produced (Luke 5:7). It is not known what wood was used for these boats, but Theophrastus says that seagoing ships were made of larch, cypress, and fir.

EMB

SHIPWRIGHT (See OCCUPATIONS AND PROFESSIONS)

SHISHA (shī'shȧ, Heb. *shîshā'*). The father of two of Solomon's secretaries, Elihoreph and Ahijah (1 Kings 4:3). He is thought by some to be identical with Seraiah (2 Sam 8:17), Sheva (20:25), and Shavsha (1 Chron 18:16).

SHISHAK (shī'shăk, Heb. *shîshaq,* Egyp. *Sheshonk*). An Egyptian king, the founder of the Twenty-second or Libyan Dynasty. He was from a Libyan family that for some generations had been situated at Herakleopolis in the Fayyum. Libyan mercenaries were common in the Egyptian army in the Twenty-first Dynasty, and some of them rose to positions of rank. The weakness of Egypt during much of the Twentieth and Twenty-first Dynasties ironically permitted the Libyan-Egyptian Sheshonk to seize control of Egypt some two centuries after Ramses III had decisively defeated the Libyans. Shishak I located his capital at Bubastis (Pi Beseth, Ezek 30:17) in the eastern Delta. To secure the succession of his newly founded dynasty he married his son to the daughter of the last king of the Twenty-first Dynasty. Shishak was a vigorous leader, who inaugurated an aggressive foreign policy and attempted to recover the lost Asiatic Empire by force of arms. In the fifth year of Rehoboam king of Judah, c. 926 B.C., he marched on Palestine, reaching as far north as Megiddo and Beth Shan and east into Transjordan.

List of Palestinian and Syrian towns conquered by Shishak (Sheshonk I), on south wall of Amon temple at Karnak. The names (originally about 180) shed important light on the Egyptian invasion of Palestine (1 Kings 14:25–26; 2 Chron 12:2–4). In the center is a large figure of Amon, and at the bottom right are the massed enemies with upraised hands. Courtesy Seffie Ben-Yoseph.

Earlier in his reign he had provided asylum to the Israelite Jeroboam, who had fled to Egypt to escape the wrath of Solomon (1 Kings 11:40). With Jeroboam on the northern throne, Shishak showed no favoritism but impartially overran both Judah and Israel. Jerusalem was a victim of this campaign, and the temple was looted of its treasures (1 Kings 14:25–26; 2 Chron 12:1–9). At Megiddo a badly damaged stela of Shishak was found by the Oriental Institute of the University of Chicago. In Egypt the record of the campaign was carved on the south exterior wall of the temple of Karnak, just east of the Bubasite Portal. Shishak is depicted in the traditional attitude of conquering his enemies, here Asiatics, and the god Amon is shown leading before the king a total of 156 captives in ten lines, each prisoner representing a conquered Palestinian town. The captives are portrayed in stylized form, an oval containing the name of the city surmounted by the head, shoulders, and pinioned arms of the victim. Many of the names that can be read and identified occur in the OT. Among them are Megiddo, Taanach, Shunem, Beth Shan, Aijalon, Beth Horon, Gibeon, and Socoh. The interesting place name, "Field of Abraham," appears in this list. The undisturbed burial of Shishak I was found at Bubastis (Tanis) by P. Montet in 1938–39. Although his dynasty endured for roughly two hundred years, internal conflict, stagnation, and incapability kept it at, or below, the level of mediocrity. CEDV

SHITRAI (shĭt'rī, Heb. *shitray*). A Sharonite, placed by David over the flocks that fed in Sharon (1 Chron 27:29).

SHITTAH TREE (See Plants)

SHITTIM (shĭt'ĭm, Heb. *ha-shittîm*). A contraction of Abel Shittim, i.e., "meadow of acacias," the last stop of Israel in the wilderness before crossing the Jordan into the Promised Land (Num 25:1; 33:49). There Balaam tried to curse Israel but had to bless instead, and there he told Balak how to seduce the men of Israel (Num 25:1–3; Mic 6:5). From there Joshua sent the two spies to Jericho (Josh 2:1), and Israel departed to cross the Jordan from Shittim (3:1). Used perhaps symbolically for a place that, in the future, the Lord will richly bless (Joel 3:18 KJV; NIV "valley of acacias").

SHITTIM WOOD (See Plants: *Acacia*)

SHIZA (shī'zà, Heb. *shîzā'*). A man of Reuben, father of Adina, one of David's mighty men (1 Chron 11:42).

SHOA (shō'à, Heb. *shōa', rich*). Although written in the English versions as though a country or province, it is probably (with Pekod and Koa) to be taken as a description of Israel's great enemy, the Chaldeans (Ezek 23:23).

SHOBAB (shō'bab, Heb. *shôvāv*). 1. A grandson of Hezron of Judah through Caleb (1 Chron 2:18).

2. A son of David born in Jerusalem (1 Chron 3:5).

SHOBACH (shō'bak, Heb. *shôvakh*). The general of the Syrian army under Hadadezer king of Zobah. He was defeated by David (2 Sam 10:16–18). In 1 Chronicles 19:16 the name is given as "Shophach."

SHOBAI (shō'bī, Heb. *shovāy*). A gatekeeper of the temple, some of whose descendants returned with Zerubbabel (Ezra 2:42; Neh 7:45).

SHOBAL (shō'băl, Heb. *shôvāl*). 1. One of the sons of Seir the Horite, a very early inhabitant of what was later Edom (Gen 36:20, 23). These Horites, or Hurrians, were expelled and destroyed by the Edomites, descendants of Esau (Deut 2:12). Shobal is listed as one of the chiefs of the Horites (Gen 36:29).

2. An early Ephrathite of the sons of Caleb (not the spy), an ancestor or founder of Kiriath Jearim (1 Chron 2:50, 52).

3. A grandson of Judah and father of Reaiah (1 Chron 4:1–2).

SHOBEK (shō'bĕk, Heb. *shôvēq*). One of the forty-four chiefs of the Jewish people who covenanted with Nehemiah to keep the law of the Lord (Neh 10:24).

SHOBI (shō'bī, Heb. *shōvî*). A prince of the Ammonites, son of Nahash and probably brother of Hanun (2 Sam 17:27).

SHOCHO (See Soco)

SHOE (See Dress)

SHOE LATCHET (See Dress)

SHOFAR (See Music and Musical Instruments)

SHOHAM (shō'hăm, Heb. *shōham*). A Merarite Levite in the days of David (1 Chron 24:27).

SHOMER (shō'mêr, Heb. *shōmēr, keeper, watcher*). 1. The father of Jehozabad, one of the conspirators against Joash of Judah. Jehozabad killed Joash because he had murdered the son of Jehoiada the priest (2 Kings 12:20–21; 2 Chron 24:25–26).

2. A great-grandson of Asher, through Beriah and Heber (1 Chron 7:32). In verse 34 he is called Shemer (ASV) and Shamer (KJV).

SHOPHACH (shō'făk, Heb. *shôvakh*). A Syrian general whom David killed (1 Chron 19:16, 18). In 2 Samuel 10:16 he is called Shobach.

SHOPHAR (See Music and Musical Instruments)

SHORE. The land where it meets the sea, represented by five words in Scripture—three Hebrew and two Greek:

1. *Hôph,* that which is washed by the sea (Judg 5:17; Jer 47:7).
2. *Qātseh,* the end or extremity (Josh 15:2), referring to the Dead Sea.
3. *Sāphâh,* the lip or edge (Gen 22:17), the sand that is on the seashore.
4. *Cheilos,* the same idea as no. 3 (Heb 11:12).
5. *Aigialos,* the beach. In the ministry of our

Terracotta model shrine consisting of a high façade with two columns surmounted by leaf capitals and carrying high square geisons supporting an entablature, and decorated with geometric patterns. A small cubicle niche is attached to the back of the façade, and a dove perches above the entrance. Imitating temple architecture and probably used in small sanctuaries or in homes, model shrines were connected with Astarte religion, one of whose symbols was the dove. Israelite (Iron) period, ninth-eighth century B.C. Courtesy Reuben and Edith Hecht Museum, University of Haifa. Photo Zev Radovan.

Lord in Galilee, the multitude stood on the shore and Jesus sat in a boat so that all could see and hear without crowding him (Matt 13:2). After his resurrection, Jesus stood on the shore while the disciples were fruitlessly fishing to hide their sorrow and perplexity (John 21:4). In Acts 27:39 (KJV) the bank of a wide creek is called a shore.

SHOSHANNIM (shō-shăn'ĭm, *lilies*). Found in the titles of Psalms 45, 69, and 80 and in Psalm 60 in the singular. Perhaps lily-shaped musical instruments, perhaps the name of spring songs. NIV has "To [the tune of] 'Lilies'" (or "To the tune of 'The Lily [or Lilies] of the Covenant'").

SHOULDER (Heb. *shekkem, kathēph, serôa' shôq*, Gr. *ōmos, brachion*). A word often used in both a literal and a figurative sense. When a man of Israel offered an ox or a sheep as a sacrifice, the shoulder went to the officiating priest as a part of his portion (Deut 18:3). The shoulder pieces of the ephod, the sacred garment of the high priest, were to bear onyx stones on which were engraved the names of the tribes (Exod 28:1–12), thus indicating that the priest bore a heavy responsibility for the people; and, similarly, a ruler bears on his shoulders the weight of the government (Isa 9:6). Although in traveling, the sections of the tabernacle could be carried in wagons, the priests had to carry the sacred furniture on their shoulders (Num 7:6–9), much as the Lord is pictured as bearing his beloved on his shoulders (Deut 33:12), and as the good shepherd carries the lost sheep when he finds it (Luke 15:5). In much of the East, the maidservants went to wells to draw water, carrying it on their shoulders (Gen 21:14) in large jars; and even well-born maidens carried water in this way (24:15). To "pull away the shoulder" (Zech 7:11 KJV) is to refuse to obey, and to "shove with flank and shoulder" (Ezek 34:21) is insolence.

SHOULDER PIECE (Heb. *kathēph*). 1. That part of the ephod where the front and the back were joined together, making the garment to be of one piece (Exod 28:7–8).

2. The piece of meat that is taken from the shoulder of the animal (Ezek 24:4).

SHOVEL (Heb. *rahath, ya', yāthēdh*). A tool used for clearing out ashes from the altar (Exod 27:3; 2 Chron 4:11), for sanitary purposes (Deut 23:13), or for winnowing (Isa 30:24).

SHOWBREAD (See TABERNACLE)

SHRINE (Gr. *naos*). A dwelling for a god (Acts 19:24), used only once in the English versions; but the same Greek word *naos* is translated "temple" in its other forty-five NT occurrences (e.g., Acts 17:24; 1 Cor 3:16).

SHROUD (Heb. *hōresh*). Generally the dress for the dead. Also can refer to a bough or branch in Ezekiel 31:3, where KJV has "a shadowing shroud" and NIV "overshadowing the forest."

SHRUB (See PLANTS)

SHUA (shū'à, Heb. *shua', prosperity*). 1. A Canaanite whose daughter became Judah's wife (Gen 38:2, 12 JB, MLB, NASB, NIV, RSV; Shuah KJV; Bathshua MOF, NEB).

2. The daughter of Heber, who was the grandson of Asher (1 Chron 7:32).

SHUAH (*shū'ah*, Heb. *shûah, depression*). 1. A son of Abraham by Keturah (Gen 25:2; 1 Chron 1:32).

2. See SHUA.

3. Kelub's brother (1 Chron 4:11 KJV; NIV "Shuhah"). Some MSS read "son of." This name is another form of "Caleb" and is doubtless used to distinguish him from Caleb, the son of Hezron, and from Caleb, the son of Jephunneh.

SHUAL (shū'al, Heb. *shû'āl, fox*). 1. One of the eleven sons of Zophah from the tribe of Asher (1 Chron 7:36).

2. First Samuel 13:17 refers to the "Land of Shual." It is named as one of the places invaded by one of the marauding tribes of Philistines. It probably lies a few miles NE of Bethel.

SHUBAEL (shū-bā'ĕl, Heb. *shevū'ēl*). 1. A chief Levite in the time of David, descended from Moses through Gershom (1 Chron 24:20), placed over "the treasuries of the house of God and the treasuries for the dedicated things" (26:20). He is also called Shebuel (1 Chron 23:16; 26:24 JB, KJV, NASB, MLB, RSV; Shubael MOF, NEB, NIV).

2. One of the sons of Heman, chief musician in David's service of praise (1 Chron 25:20. He is also called Shebuel (1 Chron 25:4 JB, KJV, NASB, MLB, RSV; Shubael MOF, NEB, NIV).

SHUHAH (See SHUAH)

SHUHAM, SHUHAMITE (shū'hăm, shū'-hăm-īt, Heb. *shûhām*). The son of Dan (Num 26:42), also called "Hushim" (Gen 46:33). Dan's descendants are called "Shuhamites."

SHUHITE (shū'hīt, Heb. *shûhî, a native of Shuah*). A term describing Job's friend Bildad (Job 2:11; 8:1; 18:1; 25:1; 42:9). It is very likely that this term refers back to Abraham's son by Keturah named Shuah. From him came a tribe of Arabs that lived near Uz, the birthplace of Job (1:1; 2:11). The exact location of this tribe is not certainly known, but it is likely that these people lived in the far northern area west of the Euphrates. If they were near Uz, as Job 2:11 indicates, this would place Uz farther north than is commonly thought.

SHULAMMITE (shū'lăm-īt, Heb. *shûlammîth, peaceful*). A title applied to a young woman in the Song of Songs 6:13. There is some difference of opinion as to the origin of this term. It is not unlikely that it is a feminine form of Solomon. If this word is the same word as "Shunammite," as the LXX rendering would imply, then it could be derived from the town of Shunem. See also SHUNAMMITE; SHUNEM.

SHUMATHITES (shū'măth-īts, Heb. *shumāthî, garlic*). A family of Kiriath Jearim (1 Chron 2:53).

SHUNAMMITE (shū'năm-īt, Heb. *shûnammîth, a native of Shunem*). 1. An unnamed woman whose son the prophet Elisha raised from the dead (2 Kings 4:12). This woman had made her home available to the prophet when he was in that area. Later God used Elisha to save her from death during a famine (8:1–6).

2. This word is applied also to David's nurse Abishag (1 Kings 1:3; 2:17–22).

SHUNEM (shū'-nĕm, Heb. *shûnēm*). A place belonging to the tribe of Issachar (Josh 19:18). Here the Philistines encamped before they fought at Gilboa (1 Sam 28:4). David's nurse, Abishag, lived here (1 Kings 1:3). Shunem was also the home of the woman who befriended Elisha and whose son Elisha restored (2 Kings 4:8–37). It lies in a very rich section of Palestine a short distance north of Jezreel at the foot of "Little Hermon." A valuable spring of water doubtlessly attracted the Philistines to choose it as a campsite.

SHUNI, SHUNITE (shū'nī, shū'nīt, Heb. *shûnî*). The son of Gad who founded a group known as Shunites (Gen 46:16; Num 26:15).

SHUPHAM (shū'fam, Heb. *shûphām*). A son of Benjamin and founder of the group known as "Shuphamites" (Num 26:39). He is probably to be identified with the person "Shephuphan" (1 Chron 8:5).

SHUPPIM (shŭ'pĭm, Heb. *shuppîm*). One of the two who had charge of the Shalleketh Gate of the temple (1 Chron 26:16), a Levite.

SHUPPITES. A Benjamite (1 Chron 7:12, 15 NIV; Shuppim JB, KJV, MLB, MOF, NASB, RSV).

SHUR (shūr, Heb. *shûr, wall*). A locality south of Palestine and east of Egypt. It was in this region that the angel of the Lord found Hagar when she fled from Sarah (Gen 16:7–14). Abraham too lived in this territory at one time (20:1).

SHUSHAN (See SUSA)

SHUTHELAH, SHUTHELAHITE (shū-thē'là, shū-thē'là-hīt, Heb. *shûthalhî*). 1. One of the three sons of Ephraim (Num 26:35–36). His descendants are called "Shuthelahites" and are named in 1 Chronicles 7:20–21.

2. The sixth person descending from Shuthelah is also called by his name. First Chronicles 7:21 mentions his father as Zabad and reveals that he is the father of Ezer and Elead.

SHUTTLE (shŭ't'l, Heb. *'eregh*). A word used as a figure of the quick passing of life (Job 7:6). Job says that his days pass as swiftly as the rapidly moving shuttle of the weaver.

SIA, SIAHA (sī'à, sī'a+-hà, Heb. *sî'ā', assembly*). A leader of the temple servants (KJV Nethinim) whose descendants returned with Zerubbabel (Neh 7:47). He is called Siaha in Ezra 2:44.

SIBBECAI, SIBBECHAI (sĭb'ē-kī, sĭb'ē-kī, Heb. *sibbekhay*). A captain of several thousand men in David's army. He is usually designated as "the Hushathite" (2 Sam 21:18; 1 Chron 11:29; 20:4; 27:11). He found a place among the mighty men of David chiefly for his victory over the Philistine Saph (2 Sam 21:18).

SIBBOLETH (See SHIBBOLETH)

SIBMAH (sĭb'mà, Heb. *sevām*). A town located east of the Jordan and belonging originally to Moab. It was finally taken by the Amorites led by King Sihon (Num 21:26). Later it was captured by and given to the tribe of Reuben (Josh 13:19). Most scholars feel it is to be identified with Sebam (Num 32:3) or Shibmah (32:38 KJV). It was famous for its luxurious vines and fruits (Isa 16:8; Jer 48:32).

SIBRAIM (sĭb-rā'ĭm, Heb. *sivrayim*). A point marking Palestine's northern boundary between Damascus and Hamath (Ezek 47:16).

SIBYLLINE ORACLES (See APOCALYPTIC LITERATURE)

SICHEM (sī'kĕm, Heb. *shekhem*). The same as Shechem.

SICILY (sĭs'ĭ-lē). The triangular island lying off the toe of Italy was colonized by a tribe closely related to those from the region of the Tiber who became the Roman people. The west and south of the island was colonized from the eighth century B.C. onward by the Carthaginians (themselves Phoenician colonists from Tyre), and the east and north by the Greeks. Colonization in both cases was by the building of "emporia," or seacoast towns, designed to exploit the hinterland. Centuries of tension and strife between the Greeks and Carthaginians ended with the intervention of Rome in the middle of the third century B.C. The western Mediterranean was too small for two first-class powers, and Rome and Carthage both looked on Sicily as a bridgehead. Hence the firmness with which Rome took advantage of factional strife at Messana to invade the island. The end of the Punic wars saw Sicily a Roman province.

SICKLE (sĭk'l, Heb. *hermēsh, a reaping hook, maggāl, a reaping hook*, Gr. *drepanon, a tool used for cutting grain*). The earlier sickles varied in size, shape, and the material from which they were made. The earliest type seems to have been constructed of wood. It resembled our modern scythes, though smaller, and its cutting edge was made of flint. Later sickles were constructed of metal. These were used mostly for cutting grain, but on occasion they were used for pruning. Mark and John use the sickle in a figurative sense as the instrument of God's judgment (Mark 4:29; Rev 14:14–20).

Black basalt sarcophagus of Eshmunazar, King of Sidon, inscribed with a well-preserved Phoenician inscription. Fifth century B.C. Courtesy Réunion des Musées Nationaux.

SICKNESS (See DISEASES)

SIDDIM, VALLEY OF (sĭd'ĭm, Heb. *'ēmeq hasiddîm, the valley of the fields*). A place mentioned in Genesis 14:3–8 as the battleground where Kedorlaomer and his allies met the kings of Sodom and other nearby cities. In the time of Abraham it must have been a place of great fertility, since it was chosen by Lot because of its productivity (13:10). From Genesis 14:3, 10 it seems to have been near to the Dead Sea and full of slime pits. In the past some scholars have placed it at the north end of the Dead Sea. The general view today, however, is that Siddim was located at the southern end of the Dead Sea. Because of the wickedness of the inhabitants of this area, God judged the locality in the days of Abraham. Its cities were completely destroyed and probably much of this territory was inundated by the waters of the Dead Sea.

SIDON (sī'dŏn, Heb. *tsîdhôn*, Gr. *Sidōn*). A Phoenician city midway between Berytus (Beirut) and Tyre. Small offshore islands made an excellent port; in ancient times they seem to have been linked by piers. Sidon appears in the OT as the chief city of Phoenicia, and the name was applied frequently to the whole nation (Gen 10:15; Judg 10:12). The city seems to have been a center of trade and enterprise. Homer, whose text dates from the eighth century before Christ, speaks of Sidon's artistic metal work ("A mixing bowl of silver, chased; six measures it held, and in beauty it was far the best in all the earth, for artificers of Sidon wrought it cunningly, and men of the Phoenicians brought it over the misty sea" (*Iliad* 23.743–748). The *Odyssey* 4.613–619 speaks of a similar cup "lipped with gold." Purple dyeing and glass blowing were also Sidonian industries. By an odd chance the crimson dye, which Sidonian inventors found how to extract from the murex shellfish, was called after the name of the other great Phoenician town, "Tyrian purple."

The art of glass blowing was discovered in the first century B.C. at Sidon, and the names of a number of Sidonian glass blowers have been recovered from surviving samples of their art. Sidon shared fully in the seafaring, commercial, and colonizing enterprises of the Phoenician people. The colonization extended, according to tradition, as far as Malta. Outside the OT, Sidon finds its first mention in ancient documents in the Amarna Letters, which reveal Prince Zimrida of Sidon contesting Egyptian lordship of the coastal strip, the main area that the Phoenicians aspired to rule. Similar advantage was taken of a period of Egyptian withdrawal and decline, in the period

A view of the old harbor at Sidon, with remains of a Crusader fortress. Courtesy Duby Tal.

of Sidonian expansion that followed the death of Ramses II. It was at this time that Sidon came into conflict over Dor with the other occupants of coastal Palestine, the Philistines. Israel suffered from the same burst of activity (Judg 1:31; 10:12). By and large, the history of Sidon followed the course of that of all Phoenicia. In common with the rest of the lands of the Middle East, Sidon fell under the power in turn of Assyria, Babylon, Persia, Greece, and Rome. Brief-lived patterns of alliance (Jer 27:3) and periods of independence, parley, subjection, ill-advised revolt, destruction, and renaissance were the common lot of the smaller lands of the region amid the rise and fall of the great empires. Sidon had a bad name in Scripture as a hotbed of Phoenician idolatry (Isa 23; Ezek 28) and of Gentile materialism (Matt 11:21–22). The neighborhood of Sidon, not more than fifty miles (eighty-three km.) from Nazareth, was visited by Christ (Matt 15:21; Mark 7:24–31), and Sidonians came to him (Mark 3:8; Luke 6:17). Sidon was a residence of Christian disciples and one of Paul's ports of call (Acts 27:3). EMB

SIEGE (See WAR)

SIEVE (sĭv, Heb. *kevārâh, netted, nāphâh, a sieve*). A utensil used by the eastern people to sift grains. Some of the Egyptian sieves were made of strings or reeds. Those constructed of string were used for finer work whereas those made from reeds were used for sifting coarser material. The word is used in the Bible in a figurative sense in both passages where it occurs (Isa 30:28; Amos 9:9).

SIGN (Heb. *'ôth, a signal, môphēth, a miracle, omen,* Gr. *sēmeion, an indication*). In Scripture this word generally refers to something addressed to the senses to attest the existence of a divine power. Miracles in the OT were often signs (Exod 4:8; 8:23). Several specific things were given as signs, such as the rainbow (Gen 9:12–13), some of the feasts (Exod 13:9), the Sabbath (Exod 31:13), and circumcision (Rom 4:11). Often extraordinary events were given as a sign to insure faith or demonstrate authority. When Moses would not believe God, his rod was turned into a serpent and his hand became leprous as signs of God's divine commission (Exod 4:1–8). Sometimes future events were given as signs, as in the case of Ahaz (Isa 7:14). When Christ was born, the place of his birth and his dress were to be signs of his identity to the shepherds. When the scribes and the Pharisees asked Jesus for a sign, he assured them that no sign was to be given them except the sign of Jonah, whose experience in the fish portrayed Christ's burial and resurrection. Revelation tells that before Christ returns there will be signs in the heavens, in the stars, moon, and sun. See also CIRCUMCISION; COVENANT; MIRACLE; RAINBOW.

SIGNET (See SEAL)

SIHON (sī'hŏn, Heb. *sîhôn*). A king of the Amorites who became prominent chiefly because of his opposition to Israel on their journey from Egypt to Palestine. His capital in the land east of the Jordan River was Heshbon. Prior to Israel's journey the Amorites under his leadership had driven out the Moabites from this section of land and had taken over this territory. God permitted him to dispossess the Moabites, but when he led the attack against Israel, he was killed and his forces scattered (Num 21:21–24; Deut 1:4, 20, 24–30). His capital was taken and the territory given to Israel. This episode is often referred to as a reminder to Israel of what God had done for them and became a source of encouragement to them (Deut 3:2). When the Moabites came and demanded that Israel return this land to them (Judg 11:12–13), Jephthah reminded them that Sihon had seized this property and God had given it to Israel. Therefore, neither they nor the Ammonites had any right to it.

SIHOR (See SHIHOR)

SILAS (sī'làs, probably the Aramaic form of Saul, *asked*). A name identifying a prominent member of the Jerusalem church (Acts 15:22, 32) and a Roman citizen (16:38) who was sent by the church with Paul and Barnabas to deliver the letter which was formulated by the Jerusalem Council to the church at Antioch (15:22–23). After spending some time at Antioch, Silas returned to Jerusalem. When Paul fell out with Barnabas, he turned for help on his second missionary journey to Silas, whose ministry he no doubt had closely observed at Antioch. Little is said of Silas in Luke's account. He was with Paul at Philippi and shared both in the beating and imprisonment there. When Paul left Berea for Athens, Silas and Timothy were left behind. Apparently Timothy rejoined Paul at Athens, while Silas stayed on in Macedonia. He, along with Timothy, who had returned to Thessalonica, rejoined Paul at Corinth (18:5). The NT calls him *Silouanos* four times (2 Cor 1:19; 1 Thess 1:1; 2 Thess 1:1; 1 Peter 5:12; Silvanus JB, KJV, MLB, MOF, NASB, NEB, RSV; Silas NIV).

SILENCE (See QUIET, QUIETNESS)

SILK (Heb. *meshî, drawn,* Gr. *sērikon, silken*). The word "silk" is mentioned four times in the KJV of the OT (Prov 31:22; Ezek 16:10, 13). It is doubtful if the passages refer to silk as we know it. The NIV translations "fine linen," "costly garments," and "costly fabric" are probably more accurate. But Revelation 18:12 does refer to actual silk. The Greek word is *sēr,* the Greek name for China, from which silk came.

SILLA (sĭl'à, Heb. *sillā',* *embankment*). An unknown place in the valley below Beth Millo (2 Kings 12:20).

SILOAM (sĭ-lō'ăm, Gr. *Silōam*). A reservoir located within the city walls of Jerusalem at the southern end of the Tyropoean Valley. Second Kings 20:20 states that Hezekiah "made the pool and the tunnel by which he brought water into the city," and 2 Chronicles 32:30 says that he "blocked the upper outlet of the Gihon spring and channeled the water down to the west side of the City of David." These words undoubtedly refer to the conduit leading from the intermittent Spring of Gihon (Jerusalem's most important water supply) through the rock Ophel to the reservoir called the Pool of Siloam. The earliest knowledge of this tunnel dates back to A.D. 1838 when it was explored by the American traveler and scholar Edward Robinson and his missionary friend Eli

The Pool of Siloam at the southern end of Hezekiah's Tunnel. The tunnel, discovered in 1880, was cut from both ends through solid rock for 1700 feet (518 m.). It was built by Hezekiah (c. 715–686) to bring water from the Spring of Gihon into Jerusalem. Referred to in 2 Kings 20:20. Courtesy Israel Government Press Office.

The Siloam inscription, in cursive Hebrew script, c. 700 B.C. It describes the completion of Hezekiah's Tunnel on the day when workmen cutting from the two sides met. Discovered in 1880. Courtesy Israel Department o. Antiquities and Museums.

Smith. They first attempted to crawl through the tunnel from the Siloam end, but soon found that they were not suitably dressed to crawl through the narrow passage. Three days later, dressed only in a wide pair of Arab drawers, they entered the tunnel from the Spring of Gihon end and, advancing much of the way on their hands and knees and sometimes flat on their stomachs, went the full distance. They measured the tunnel and found it to be 1,750 feet (547 m.) in length.

The tunnel has many twists and turns. The straight line distance from the Spring of Gihon to the Pool of Siloam is only 762 feet (238 m.), less than half the length of the tunnel. Why it follows such a circuitous route has never been adequately explained. Grollenberg suggests that it may have been "to avoid at all costs any interference with the royal tombs, which were quite deeply hewn into the rock on the eastern slope of Ophel" (*Atlas of the Bible,* 1956, p. 93).

In A.D. 1867 Captain Charles Warren also explored the tunnel, but neither he nor Robinson and Smith before him, noticed the inscription on the wall of the tunnel near the Siloam end. This was discovered in 1880 by a native boy who, while wading in the tunnel, slipped and fell into the water. When he looked he noticed the inscription. The boy reported his discovery to his teacher, Herr Conrad Schick, who made the information available to scholars. The inscription was deciphered by A. H. Sayce, with the help of others. It consists of six lines written in Old Hebrew (Canaanite) with pronglike characters. The first half of the inscription is missing, but what remains reads as follows: "[. . . when] (the tunnel) was driven through:—while [. . .] (were) still [. . .] axe(s), each man toward his fellow, and while there were still three cubits to be cut through, [there was heard] the voice of a man calling to his fellow, for there was an *overlap* in the rock on the right [and on the left]. And when the tunnel was driven through, the quarrymen hewed (the rock), each man toward his fellow, axe against axe; and the water flowed from the spring toward the reservoir for 1,200 cubits, and the height of the rock above the head(s) of the quarrymen was 100 cubits" (ANET, p. 321).

The importance of the Siloam inscription can scarcely be overestimated. Not only does it give a fascinating account of the building of the tunnel, but as G. Ernest Wright says, it "has for many years been the most important monumental piece of writing in Israelite Palestine, and other Hebrew inscriptions have been dated by comparing the shapes of letters with it" (*Biblical Archaeology*, 1957, p. 169).

In A.D. 1890 a vandal entered the tunnel and cut the inscription out of the rock. It was subsequently found in several pieces in the possession of a Greek in Jerusalem who claimed he had purchased it from an Arab. The Turkish officials seized the pieces and removed them to Istanbul where they are today.

The Siloam tunnel was not the only conduit that had been built to bring water from the Spring of Gihon into Jerusalem. At least two others preceded it, but neither was adequately protected against enemy attack. It was probably to one of these former conduits that Isaiah referred in the words "the flowing waters of Shiloah" (Isa 8:6).

It was to the Pool of Siloam that Jesus sent the blind man with the command, "Go, . . . wash" (John 9:7). He obeyed and came back seeing.
WWW

SILOAM, TOWER IN (sĭ-lō'ăm). A tower that was probably part of the ancient system of fortifications on the walls of the city of Jerusalem near the Pool of Siloam. The collapse of this tower and the resulting death of eighteen persons (Were they workmen employed on the aqueduct that Pilate was building? Cf. Josephus, *War* 2.9.4) is cited by Jesus (Luke 13:4). Apparently the accident was well known to his hearers, but it is not mentioned elsewhere.

SILOAM, VILLAGE OF (sĭ-lō'ăm). There is no mention of a village by this name in the Bible. However, across the valley east of the Spring of Gihon (see SILOAM above) is a rocky slope on which is situated the modern village of Silwan (Siloam). At this site an inscription over the door of a tomb, discovered at the end of the nineteenth century A.D. but only recently deciphered by Professor N. Avigad, indicates that the tomb may have belonged to Shebna, an official during Hezekiah's time (cf. Isa 22:15–16).

SILVANUS (See SILAS)

SILVER (See MINERALS)

SILVERSMITH (See OCCUPATIONS AND PROFESSIONS)

SIMEON (sĭm'ē-ŭn, Heb. *shim' ôn,* Gr. *Symeōn*). 1. The second son of Jacob by Leah (Gen 29:33). He and his brother Levi massacred the Hivites living in Shechem because Shechem the son of Hamor had raped their sister Dinah (34:24–31).

2. The tribe of which Simeon, the son of Jacob, became the founder. He had six sons, all but one of whom founded tribal families. At the distribution of the land of Canaan the extreme south of Canaan was assigned to this tribe. Eventually most of the tribe disappeared.

3. An ancestor of Jesus (Luke 3:30).

4. A righteous and devout man to whom the Holy Spirit revealed that he would not die until he had seen the Messiah. When the infant Jesus was brought into the temple, Simeon took him into his arms and praised God (Luke 2:25, 34).

5. Simon Peter (Acts 15:14). See PETER.

6. The man whose surname was Niger. He was one of the Christian leaders in the church of Antioch who set apart Paul and Barnabas for their missionary work (Acts 13:1–2). Nothing more is known of him.

SIMEONITE. A member of the tribe of Simeon; see SIMEON.

SIMON (sī'mŭn, Gr. *Simōn, hearing*). 1. The son of Jonas, and brother of Andrew, a fisherman who became a disciple and apostle of Christ. He was surnamed Peter, "stone," and Cephas, Aramaic for "rock" (Matt 4:18; 16:17–18). See PETER.

2. Another disciple of Jesus called the "Canaanite" in the KJV, a member of the party later called "the Zealots" (so NIV, Matt 10:4; Mark 3:18). The word does not mean "inhabitant of Cana." Luke properly translates the Hebrew by *Zealot* (Luke 6:15; Acts 1:13).

3. A leper of Bethany in whose house Jesus' head was anointed (Matt 26:6; Mark 14:3).

4. A brother of the Lord (Matt 13:55; Mark 6:3).

5. A man from Cyrene, father of Alexander and Rufus, who was compelled to carry the cross of Jesus (Matt 27:32; Mark 15:21; Luke 23:26).

6. A Pharisee in whose house Jesus' feet were anointed by the sinful woman (Luke 7:40, 43–44).

7. Judas Iscariot's father (John 6:71; 13:2, 26).

8. Simon Magus, a sorcerer at Samaria and a man of great power and influence among the people (Acts 8:9–13). He "believed" as the result of Philip's preaching there, though the real nature of his faith is not clear, as his subsequent action reveals. He undoubtedly was especially impressed by the operation of divine power in Philip, a power that exceeded his own. After being baptized he continued with Philip, hoping, no doubt, to learn more of this power. Subsequently Peter and John were sent from the Jerusalem church to Samaria to pray for the new converts and lay hands on them with a view to their receiving the Holy Spirit. When Simon saw that the Spirit was given by the laying of hands, he wanted to buy this power for himself from the apostles. His request called forth a blistering rebuke by Peter (8:14–24).

Simon Magus plays a prominent role in postapostolic Christian literature. Irenaeus (*Against Heresies* 1.23) viewed him as the founder of Gnosticism and the leader the sect of Simonians was named after. According to Justin Martyr (*Apology* 1.26), he went to Rome during the reign of Claudius, and the *Acts of Peter* relates how he led Roman Christians astray by his false teachings.

In the pseudo-Clementine *Recognitions* and *Homilies* he is particularly prominent, appearing as Peter's chief opponent. The relationship between this Simon and the one in Acts is not clear. The actual founder of the sect of the Simonians may have been confused early in the church with the Simon in Acts 8.

9. A tanner who lived at Joppa. Peter stayed with him for a period of time (Acts 9:43; 10:6, 17, 32).

SIMON MACCABEUS (sī′mŭn măk′ȧ-bē-ŭs). The second son of the priest Mattathias. He was surnamed Thassi and was the older brother of Judas Maccabeus. With his father and brothers he fought against the Syrians. At his father's death, he was made the adviser of the family. Eventually, as the last surviving member of the family, he succeeded in defeating the Syrians. He was acknowledged by the Jews as high priest, captain, and leader, and was authorized to wear the purple. In 135 B.C. he was murdered by his son-in-law while visiting the cities of his dominion.

SIMON MAGUS (See SIMON)

SIMON PETER (See PETER)

SIMPLE (Heb. *pethî, silly*, Gr. *akakos, akeraios, harmless*). The basic idea of the word in the OT is "easily influenced" (Ps 19:7; 119:130; Prov 7:7). The two uses of the word in the KJV of the NT (Rom 16:18–19) are rendered "naïve" and "innocent" in the NIV.

SIMRI (See SHIMRI)

SIN (Heb. *ḥāttā'the, 'awôn, pesha', ra'*, Gr. *adikia, hamartia, hamartēma, parabasis, paraptōma, ponēria*). The biblical writers portray sin in such a variety of terms because they have such a powerful sense of the living Lord, who is utterly pure and holy. For sin is that condition and activity of human beings that is offensive to God, their Creator. However, it is only as they are conscious of his holiness that they are truly aware of their sin (1 Kings 17:18; Ps 51:4–6; Isa 6).

The first book of the OT reveals how human beings were created by God without sin but chose to act contrary to his revealed will and thereby caused sin to become an endemic feature of human existence (Gen 3; Ps 14:1–3). Sin is revolt against holiness and sovereign will of God. Therefore, it is both a condition of the heart/mind/will/affections (Isa 29:13; Jer 17:9) and the practical outworking of that condition in thoughts, words, and deeds that offend God and transgress his holy law (Gen 6:5; Isa 59:12–13). For Israel, sin was a failure to keep the conditions of the covenant that the Lord graciously made with the people at Sinai (Exod 19ff.).

There is no person in Israel or the whole world who is not a sinner. However, those who have a right relationship with God, receive his forgiveness, and walk in his ways are sometimes described as righteous (Gen 6:9) and blameless (Job 1:1; Ps 18:20–24). This is not because they are free from sin, but because the true direction of their lives is to serve and please God in the way he requires.

Since Israel is the one people of God and thus a solidarity, the sins of the fathers have repercussions for their children and their children's children (Isa 1:4; Lam 5:7). Yet it is also true that individual Israelites are personally responsible to God for their own sins (Jer 31:19–20; Ezek 18:1ff.; 33:10–20). Sin was punished by God in various ways—e.g., exile from the Promised Land (2 Kings 17:6ff.)—but the final punishment for individual sin and wickedness was death—"You shall die" (Gen 2:17; Ps 73:27; Ezek 18:4). This is certainly physical death but is also spiritual death, being cut off from communion with the living God.

The reality of sin and the need for atonement to be made (and confession of it offered to God) are clearly presupposed by the sacrifices offered to God in the temple—e.g., the regular guilt (or trespass) offering and sin offering, as well as the special annual sacrifice of the Day of Atonement (Lev 4; 6:24ff.; 7:1ff.; 16:1ff.). They are also presupposed in the prophecy of the vicarious suffering of the Servant of the Lord who acts as a "guilt offering" and bears the sin of many (Isa 53:10, 12).

The NT strengthens the OT portrayal of sin by viewing it in the light of Jesus and his atonement, which is a victory over sin. Jesus was sinless and taught that the root of sin is in the human heart: "For from within, out of men's hearts, come . . . evils" (Mark 7:20–23). The outward life is determined by the inner (Matt 7:15–17), and thus an outward conformity to laws and rules is not in itself a true righteousness if the heart is impure (5:17ff.). The law of God, rightly understood, requires inner as well as outer comformity to its standards. But sin is more than failure to keep the law: it is also the rejection of the Messiah and the kingdom he proclaims and personifies. The work of the Holy Spirit, said Jesus, is to convict "the world of . . . sin . . . because men do not believe in me" (John 16:8–9; 15:22). Further, to live without the light of God from Jesus, the Messiah, is to live in darkness and to be in the grip of evil forces (1:5; 3:19–21; 8:31–34). And to call the light darkness and the Spirit of the Messiah unclean is to commit the unforgivable sin (Matt 12:24, 31).

Paul has much to say about sin. He believed that sin is revealed by the law of God, but it is only as the Holy Spirit enlightens the mind that a person truly sees what righteousness the law demands of us (Rom 3:20; 5:20; 7:7–20; Gal 3:19–24). Thus for Paul a person could be a devout keeper of the law (externally) and yet be a slave of sin (internally) because he knew, as Jesus also said, that sin begins in the heart (or flesh)—see Romans 6:15–23. The origin of sin can be traced back to the first human beings, Adam and Eve, and to their revolt against the Lord (Rom 5:12–19; 2 Cor 11:3; 1 Tim 2:14).

There is a positive message in all this. In a

Gathering at one of a number of ancient church remains found among the rugged slopes of the Sinai mountains. Courtesy Zev Radovan.

dream Joseph was told that Mary's baby "will save his people from their sins" (Matt 1:21), and John the Baptist proclaimed that Jesus was the Lamb of God who takes away the sin of the world (John 1:29)—referring to Jesus as the fulfillment of the atoning sacrifices of the temple. Paul declared that God sent his only Son to be a sin offering (Rom 8:3). Jesus made himself to be the friend of sinners (Luke 7:34), and he understood that his ministry leading to death was the fulfillment of the ministry of the Suffering Servant who gives his life as a ransom for many (Mark 10:45). See also EVIL; FLESH; HEART.

Bibliography: C. R. Smith, *The Bible Doctrine of Sin,* 1953; F. Greeves, *The Meaning of Sin,* 1956; J. Murray, *The Imputation of Adam's Sin,* 1959; G. C. Berkouwer, *Sin,* 1971; H. W. Wolff, *The Anthropology of the Old Testament,* 1974. PT

SIN (Heb. *sîn, clay*). An Egyptian city mentioned only in the KJV of Ezekiel 30:15–16, called by the Greeks "Pelusium" (so NIV), lying on the eastern arm of the Nile River. Ezekiel refers to it as "the stronghold of Egypt" (Ezek 30:15). A wall was built on the south, and with the sea on the north and impassable swamps on the other sides, the city was practically impregnable. Since Thebes and Sin were at the opposite ends of Egypt, mentioning these two cities as Ezekiel does implies God's judgment falling on the entire land of Egypt.

SIN, DESERT OF. A wilderness through which the Israelites passed on their journey from Elim and Mount Sinai (Exod 16:1; 17:1; Num 33:11–12). KJV reads "wilderness of Sin." It is probably to be identified with Debbet er-Ramleh, a sandy tract in the interior of the peninsula of Sinai at the foot of Jebel et-Tih; but the coastal plain of el-Markhah has also been suggested. The fixing of its position depends on the location of Mount Sinai, about which scholars are in disagreement. See also SINAI.

SINAI (sī′nī, Heb. *sînay,* meaning uncertain). A word used in three senses in the OT.

1. It is applied to a peninsula that lay to the south of the Wilderness of Paran between the Gulf of Aqabah on the east and Suez on the west. This peninsula has a triangular shape and is 150 miles (250 km.) wide at the north and 250 miles (417 km.) long. Some of the Egyptian dynasties claimed this region as part of their most valued area. They carried on mining operations for

Passing through a stone gate on the way to Mount Sinai (Jebel Musa), which is seen in background. Courtesy S. Zur Picture Library.

turquoise, iron, and copper; and much of their red granite and pink gneiss came from this locality.

2. It is applied to a wilderness, the "Desert of Sinai" (Exod 19:1). It is the place where Israel came in the third month after they left Egypt. It may be used loosely as a synonym for the Sinaitic Peninsula but probably technically does not embrace as much territory.

3. Finally, there is a mountain often referred to as Mount Sinai (Exod 19:20), or Horeb. It was there that God met and talked with Moses and gave him the law (19:3). There has been much debate over the exact location of Mount Sinai. There are four possible sites: (1) Mount Serbal, on Wadi Feiran. A serious objection to this identification, however, is that there is no plain large enough in the neighborhood to offer camping ground for a large group of people. (2) Jebel Musa (Mountain of Moses) and Ras Safsaf, a short ridge with two peaks, one with an altitude of 6,540 feet (2,044 m.) and the other 7,363 feet (2,501 m.). St. Catherine's Monastery, a monastery of Greek monks, is located at the foot of Jebel Musa. (3) Jebel Hellal, a 2,000-foot (625-m.) elevation thirty miles (fifty km.) south of El-a'Arish. (4) Mount Seir, on the edge of the Arabah. The only later visit to the mount recorded in Scripture is Elijah's when he fled from Jezebel (1 Kings 19:8).

SINEW (sĭ'nū, Heb. *gîdh, sinew*). The tendons and sinews of the body (Job 40:17; Ezek 37:6–9 KJV; NIV "tendons"). The word is used also in a figurative sense (Isa 48:4).

SINGER (See OCCUPATIONS AND PROFESSIONS)

SINGING (See MUSIC AND MUSICAL INSTRUMENTS; SONG)

SINGLE EYE (Gr. *ophthalmos haplous, a healthy eye*). Used in the KJV for an eye that is clear, sound, and healthy, with the connotation "generous" (Matt 6:22; Luke 11:34). NIV has "eyes are good."

SINIM (sī'nĭm, Heb. *sînîm*). A country cited in a prophecy by Isaiah (49:12) to illustrate God's promise that the dispersed Israelites would some day be gathered from the farthest regions of the earth. It is obviously not west or north, since both are mentioned in the prophecy. It must, therefore, be south or east, and apparently very far away. The most widely held view is that China is meant, either because some Israelites were already living there, or would live there. There is evidence that the Jews traded with the Chinese as early as the third century B.C.

SINITES (sī'nīts, Heb. *sînî*). A tribe descended from Canaan (Gen 10:17; 1 Chron 1:15). No definite identification is possible.

SIN OFFERING (See SACRIFICE AND OFFERINGS)

SION, MOUNT (See HERMON)

SIPHMOTH (sĭf'mŏth, Heb. *siphmôth*). A place in the southern part of Judah to which David often came (1 Sam 30:28). The site has not been positively identified.

SIPPAI (sĭp'ī, Heb. *saph*). A man, known also as Saph, descended from the giants. He was slain at Gezer by Sibbecai (1 Chron 20:4).

SIRAH (sī'rȧ, Heb. *sirâh*). A well mentioned in 2 Samuel 3:26. It is probably Ain Sarah which is located about one mile (one and one-half km.) north of old Hebron.

SIRION (sĭr'ĭ-ŏn, Heb. *siryôn, coat of mail*). A name given to Mount Hermon by the Zidonians (Deut 3:9).

SISERA (sĭs'êr-ȧ, Heb. *sîserā'*). 1. A man employed by Jabin, king of Hazor, as the captain in his army. In Judges 4–5 we have the account of the battle that was carried on between Sisera and Israel's Barak. Sisera oppressed Israel for twenty years, waging war against them with nine hundred iron chariots (4:2–3). Finally, Deborah the prophetess, who judged Israel at that time, urged Barak under the direction of God to unite his forces and go against Sisera. She assured Barak that God would deliver Sisera into his hands. He agreed, if Deborah would go with him, and she gave her consent. These two armies met in battle on the plain at the foot of Mount Tabor (4:14). The forces of Sisera were killed or scattered, and Sisera fled on foot, taking refuge in the tent of Jael, the wife of Heber the Kenite. Here he was killed by Jael while he slept in her tent. The remarkable victory was celebrated by the Song of Deborah. See also BARAK; DEBORAH.

2. The name Sisera is found again in the names of the temple servants (KJV Nethinim) who returned from captivity under Zerubbabel's leadership (Ezra 2:53; Neh 7:55).

SISMAI, SISAMAI (sĭs'mī, sĭs'ă-mī, Heb. *sismay*). A son of Eleasah from the tribe of Judah. One who descended from Sheshan's daughter (1 Chron 2:40).

SISTER (Heb. *'āhôth*, Gr. *adelphē*). A word used in both Hebrew and Greek with varying ideas. In the OT it is used of females having the same parents, having but one parent in common, a female relative, or a woman of the same country (Gen 20:12; Num 25:18; Lev 18:18; Job 42:11). In the NT it is used of girls belonging to the same family or just to blood relatives (Matt 13:56; Mark 6:3; Luke 10:39). It is also used figuratively (Ezek 16:45; 23:11; Rom 16:1; 2 John 13).

SISTRUMS (See MUSIC AND MUSICAL INSTRUMENTS)

SITHRI (sĭth'rī, Heb. *sithri, my protection*). A Kohathite Levite, first cousin of Aaron and Moses (Exod 6:22).

SITNAH (sĭt'nà, Heb. *sitnâh, hostility*). The name given to the second well dug by Isaac (Gen 26:21), suggesting a contest between the Israelites and the people of Gerar.

SIVAN (sē-vàn', Heb. *sîwān*). The name given to the third month of the Hebrew sacred year; this is the ninth month of the civil year (Esth 8:9). See also CALENDAR.

SIYON (See HERMON)

Detail of Philistine prisoners of war, bound and tied together by a rope that encircles the neck of each. Wall relief from the great temple of Ramses III at Medinet Habu. Courtesy B. Brandl.

SKIN (Heb. *'ôr, naked, geledh, smooth, bāsār, flesh*, Gr. *derma, skin, dermatinos, of a skin*). A very common word in the OT, *'ôr* used of both animal skin (Gen 3:21; 27:16; Jer 13:23) and human skin (Exod 34:35 KJV; Lev 13:2; Job 7:5). *Geledh* is found only once in the Bible (Job 16:15), describing the action of Job putting sackcloth on his body. This was a tight-fitting garment expressive of mourning and perhaps suggesting the sad condition of Job's physical appearance. *Bāsār* is the most common word used for human flesh (Gen 2:21; 2 Kings 4:34; Prov 14:30 KJV; NIV "flesh, body").

Skins of animals were used as bottles both for water and for wine. They formed many useful articles for clothing. Various kinds formed the protection for the tabernacle in the wilderness. Ezekiel tells of shoes being made from skins (Ezek 16:10 KJV; NIV "leather").

The word is also used figuratively in several places (Job 2:4; 19:20). The two Greek words are used only three times in the NT (Matt 3:4; Mark 1:6; Heb 11:37) and in each case speak of articles of clothing.

SKINK (See ANIMALS)

SKIRT (See DRESS)

SKULL (See GOLGOTHA)

SKY (Heb. *shahaq, vapor*). A word found only in the plural in the Bible (Ps 18:11; Isa 45:8). The word refers sometimes to the clouds and other times to the firmament. At least once it is used figuratively (Deut 33:26).

SLANDER (Heb. *dibbâh, slander*, Gr. *diabolos, slanderer*). A malicious utterance designed to hurt or defame the person about whom it is uttered. The Scriptures often warn against it (Lev 19:16; Ezek 22:9; Eph 4:31; Col 3:8; James 4:11).

SLAVE, SLAVERY (Heb. *'evedh, servant, slave*, Gr. *doulos, bondslave, servant*). While the Hebrew and Greek words are very common in the Bible, the English word *slave* is found only twice (Jer 2:14; Rev 18:13), and the word *slavery* does not occur at all in KJV, because both the Hebrew and the Greek word involved are more often rendered "servant."

Among the Hebrews, slaves could be acquired in a number of ways: as prisoners of war (Num 31:7–9), by purchase (Lev 25:44), by gift (Gen 29:24), by accepting a person in lieu of a debt (Lev 25:39), by birth from slaves already possessed (Exod 21:4), by arrest if the thief had nothing to pay for the object stolen (22:2–3), and by the voluntary decision of the person wanting to be a slave (21:6). Slaves among the Hebrews were more kindly treated than slaves among other nations, since the Mosaic Law laid down rules governing their treatment. They could gain their freedom in a number of ways (Exod 21:2–27; Lev 25:25ff.; Deut 15:12–23). Slavery continued in NT times, but the love of Christ

Catching wildfowl by means of a clap-net snare. Man hiding behind a papyrus thicket signals to close net. Two men to the left clean and prepare fowl for use. Many Egyptian paintings exhibit scenes of fowling. Tomb painting from Thebes, c. 1400 B.C. Courtesy The Metropolitan Museum of Art (15.5.19e).

seemed to militate against its continued existence (Eph 6:5–9; Gal 3:28).

SLEEP (Heb. *shēnâh, yāshēn, shākhav*, Gr. *hypnos*). A word used in a number of ways in the Bible. Its most natural use is to refer to physical rest (1 Sam 26:7; Jonah 1:5–6). Most cases of physical sleep were natural ones, but some were supernaturally imposed to accomplish a divine purpose (Gen 2:21; 15:12). Believers' rest in sleep is considered a gift from God (Ps 127:2).

Methods of sleep varied usually with the social status of the people. The most common bed was simply a mat (Matt 9:6). No special bed clothes were provided in this case, but those worn during the day were used (Exod 22:26–27). Wealthy people had more elaborate beds variously constructed (Deut 3:11; 1 Sam 19:13).

In the NT, KJV translates *hypnos* "sleep" all six times it occurs, NIV only in John 11:13 and Acts 20:9. Sometimes "sleep" indicates the spiritually indolent (e.g., Rom 13:11, the only figurative use of *hypnos*) or believers who have died (e.g., 1 Cor 11:30; 15:51; 1 Thess 4:13).

SLIME (Heb. *hēmār, boiling up, zepheth, flowing*). Where KJV has *slime* (Gen 11:3; Exod 2:3; slimepits, Gen 14:10), NIV has *tar*. Probably it resembled asphalt, and perhaps it was used most often in waterproofing and as a cement for bricks. It may be derived of oxidation from natural gas and petroleum. In early biblical history it seems to have been plentiful in the area around the Dead Sea.

SLING (See ARMS AND ARMOR)

SLOW (Heb. *kāvēdh, heavy, 'erekh, to make long*, Gr. *bradys, dull, argos, inactive*). Moses said he was slow of speech (Exod 4:10). This does not refer to any particular defect but simply to the fact that his words did not come readily. "Longsuffering" would almost be a synonym of *'erekh* as seen in many OT passages (Neh 9:17; Ps 103:8; 145:8). It always refers to the passions in the OT. The Greek words are found only three times in the NT (Luke 24:25; Titus 1:12; James 1:19).

SLUG (See ANIMALS)

SMITH (See OCCUPATIONS AND PROFESSIONS)

SMYRNA (smîr'nȧ, Gr. *Smyrna*). A port on the west coast of Asia Minor at the head of the gulf into which the Hermus River flows, a well-protected harbor and the natural terminal of a great inland trade-route up the Hermus Valley. Smyrna's early history was checkered. It was destroyed by the Lydians in 627 B.C. and for three centuries was little more than a village. It was refounded in the middle of the fourth century before Christ, after Alexander's capture of Sardis, and rapidly became the chief city of Asia. Smyrna was shrewd enough to mark the rising star of Rome. A common danger, the aggression of Antiochus the Great of Syria, united Smyrna with Rome at the end of the third century before Christ, and the bond formed remained unbroken. Smyrna was, indeed, the handiest of the bridgeheads, balancing the naval power of Rhodes in the Aegean Sea. Smyrna referred to their ancient alliance with Rome when, in A.D. 26, they petitioned Tiberius to allow the community to build a temple to his deity. The permission was granted, and Smyrna built the second Asian temple to the emperor. The city had worshiped Rome as a spiritual power since 195 B.C., hence Smyrna's historical pride in her Caesar cult. Smyrna was famous for science, medicine, and the majesty of its buildings. Apollonius of Tyana referred to her "crown of porticoes," a circle of beautiful public buildings that ringed the summit of Mount Pagos like a diadem; hence John's reference (Rev 2:10). Polycarp, Smyrna's martyred bishop of A.D. 155, had been a disciple of John. EMB

SNAIL (See ANIMALS)

SNAKE (See ANIMALS)

SNARE (Heb. *pah, a spring net*, Gr. *pagis, trap, brochos, a noose*). A device for catching both birds (Ps 124:7) and animals. The word is used often in the Bible in a figurative sense, to imply anything that might destroy (Ps 91:3; 141:9). The word is used also in a variety of ways to point out things God's people should avoid: heathen gods (Deut 7:16), the ephod Gideon made (Judg 8:27), false prophets (Hos 9:8), and riches (1 Tim 6:9 KJV; NIV "trap").

SNOW (Heb. *shelegh, white, telagh, white,* Gr. *chiōn*). Snow is common in the hill country of Palestine. It never gets very deep, and it is not uncommon to have winters without any. The tops of the high mountains are covered with snow most of the year, and this becomes the source of much of the water there. It is stored in caves in the mountains in the winter for cooling beverages and for refrigeration purposes in the summer.

The Bible often refers to snow figuratively. "Time of snow" (KJV) represents a winter's day (2 Sam 23:20 NIV "snowy day"). Fear of snow is a similar phrase representing cold (Prov 31:21). Snow is a symbol of the highest purity and stands for the condition of the redeemed soul (Ps 51:7; Isa 1:18). It symbolizes whiteness and purity (Matt 28:3; Rev 1:14) and describes the whiteness of the leper (2 Kings 5:27).

SNUFF (Heb. *sha'aph, to inhale, naphah, to blow at*). The first Hebrew word expresses the practice of wild donkeys who pant for wind like jackals because of the heat (Jer 14:6 KJV; NIV "pant"). Malachi uses the second Hebrew word symbolically to express contempt for God's sacrifices (Mal 1:13 KJV; NIV "sniff").

SO (Heb. *sô'*). The name of a king of Egypt, mentioned in 2 Kings 17:4 as king in the days of Ahaz king of Judah and Hoshea king of Israel. Hoshea made an alliance with So, bringing down the wrath of Assyria on Israel (17:5). It is difficult to identify him. He is either the king mentioned in Herodotus by the name of *Sabaeo,* or he is to be identified with *Sib'e* who in 720 B.C., because of his alliance with the king of Gaza, had to fight with Sargon, by whom he was defeated.

SOAP (Heb. *bōrîth*). Soap in a modern sense was unknown in OT times. Even until recent time it was not used in some parts of Syria. Clothes, cooking utensils, and even the body were cleansed with the ashes of certain plants containing alkali (e.g., soapwort, glasswort, and saltwort). This cleansing material is referred to in Jeremiah 2:22 and Malachi 3:2.

SOCKET (See TABERNACLE)

SOCO, SOCOH (sō'kō, Heb. *sōkhōh, branches*). 1. One of the cities given to the tribe of Judah (Josh 15:35). Later, King Rehoboam strengthened this city after the northern tribes had revolted (2 Chron 11:7). From this city Solomon drew his supplies (1 Kings 4:10). It is identified with Khirbet Shuweikeh.

2. About ten miles (seventeen km.) SW of Hebron lies another city by this name (Josh 15:48).

The site of Socoh, identified with Khirbet Shuweikeh, located in the Shephelah and scene of the Philistine defeat (1 Sam 17). Courtesy Ecole Biblique et Archéologique Française, Jerusalem.

SODA (See MINERALS)

SODI (sō'dī, Heb. *sôdhî*). The father of the Israelite spy representing the tribe of Zebulun (Num 13:10).

SODOM, SODOMA (sŏd'ŭm, sŏ-dō'mȧ, Heb. *sedhōm,* Gr. *Sodoma*). One of the so-called "Cities of the Plain," along with Admah, Gomorrah, Zeboiim, and Zoar. The site of "the Plain" has been variously conjectured. Sir George Adam Smith pointed out that "no authentic trace" remains, but recently the suggestion has been revived that "the Plain" is the shallow southern end of the Dead Sea, and that the waters cover the remains. Underwater archaeology may or may not confirm this assertion, which appears first to have been made by Thomson in his nineteenth-century classic, *The Land and the Book.*

An area around the northern end of the Dead Sea was later favored, mainly on the grounds that only this region is fully within the range of vision from Bethel, from which vantage point Lot made his fatal choice (Gen 13:10–12). The southern end is shut off by the high country around En Gedi. Abraham's field of view from a point east of Hebron, from which he looked in the morning toward Sodom and Gomorrah (19:28), may lead to the same conclusion. But what the patriarch saw was the column of smoke from whatever form of catastrophe destroyed the whole area. Attempts have been made to pinpoint the site by a reconstruction of the invasion route of the raid described in Genesis 14. According to 2 Chronicles 20:2, Hazazon Tamar is En Gedi, halfway up the western shore of the Dead Sea. If the invaders, circling the sea from the south, clashed with the Amorites here, they must then have continued north to capture Sodom, and not returned on their tracks. But could not the Hazazon Tamar of Genesis 14 be the Tamar of Ezekiel 47:19 to the SW of the water? Zoar can be located on the Moabite shore from Isaiah 15:5 and Jeremiah 48:34 and at the southern end of the sea from Josephus (*War* 4.8.4), but Deuteronomy 34:3

The southern end of the Dead Sea, now largely dried up with salt deposits, is the area in which Sodom is probably located. Courtesy Duby Tal.

assumes that the town was visible from Pisgah. Perhaps there were two towns of the name. Failing conclusive archaeological evidence, the Cities of the Plain must be listed as lost. Sodom, because of the episode of Genesis 19, became a name for vice, infamy, and judgment (Isa 1:9–10; 3:9; Jer 23:14; Lam 4:6; Ezek 16:46; Amos 4:11; Zeph 2:9; Matt 10:15; Luke 17:29; Rom 9:29; 2 Peter 2:6; Jude 7; Rev 11:8; cf. Sodomites [KJV]—Deut 23:17; 1 Kings 14:24; 15:12; 22:46; 2 Kings 23:7). The idea of judgment on iniquity was no doubt in mind when a Jew or Christian, some time before the eruption of A.D. 79, scribbled "SODOMA GOMORRA" on a wall in Pompeii. EMB

SODOMY (sŏd'ŭm-ĕ, Heb. *qādhēsh, a male temple prostitute*). A sodomite was one who practiced that unnatural vice for which Sodom became noted (Gen 19:5). Though not named as such it is referred to in Romans 1:27. God strictly forbade this practice (Deut 23:17). Usually the practice was in connection with heathen worship, and its presence was a sign of departure from the Lord (1 Kings 14:24). Both Asa (15:12) and Jehoshaphat took measures against this sin (22:46), but its practice continued, until in the days of Josiah it was being practiced in the Lord's house (2 Kings 23:7).

SOLDIER (See OCCUPATIONS AND PROFESSIONS; WAR)

SOLOMON (sŏl'ō-mŭn, Heb. *shelōmōh, peaceable*). The third and last king of united Israel. He built the kingdom to its greatest geographical extension and material prosperity. Though a very intelligent man, Solomon in his later years lost his spiritual discernment and for the sake of political advantage and voluptuous living succumbed to apostasy. His policies of oppression and luxury brought the kingdom to the verge of dissolution, and when his son Rehoboam came to the throne the actual split of the kingdom occurred. Solomon was the second son of David and Bathsheba, the former wife of Uriah the Hittite. When he was born, the Lord loved him, so that the child was also called Jedidiah, "because the LORD loved him" (2 Sam 12:24–25). He did not enter the history of Israel until David's old age, when a conspiracy attempted to crown as king Adonijah, the son of David and Haggith. Nathan and Bathsheba quickly collaborated to persuade David of the seriousness of the situation, and David had Solomon anointed king at Gihon by Zadok the priest while the conspirators were still gathered at En Rogel. As David's death drew near, he gave Solomon practical advice as to faithfulness to God, the building of the temple, and the stability of the dynasty. Solomon had to deal harshly with Adonijah and his followers when they continued to plot against him. Adonijah and Joab were put to death, and Abiathar the priest was expelled from the priesthood. Solomon made Benaiah head of the army, and Zadok became priest in Abiathar's stead. David had also told Solomon to kill Shimei, who had cursed David at the time of Absalom's revolt; this was done by Solomon after Shimei violated the probation Solomon had ordered.

Solomon then began a series of marriage alliances that were his eventual undoing. He married the daughter of the king of Egypt, who had sufficient power to capture Gezer and to present it as a dowry to his daughter. Early in Solomon's reign he loved the Lord; he sacrificed at the great high place of Gibeon, where the tabernacle was located; here he offered a thousand burnt offerings. The night he was at Gibeon the Lord appeared to him in a dream and told him to request of him of whatever he desired. Solomon chose above all else understanding and discernment. God was pleased with this choice, granted his request, and also gave him riches and honor. A demonstration of this gift came when he returned to Jerusalem, where his decision in the case of two harlots caused the people to see that God's wisdom was in the king. He was an efficient administrator: Each department had its appointed officers and the country was divided into twelve districts, different from the tribal divisions, each responsible for the provisions of the royal household for a month of the year. With taxation and conscription Israel began to see some of the evils of monarchy against which Samuel had warned (1 Sam 8:11ff.), though during the reign of Solomon "Judah and Israel were as numerous as the sand on the seashore; they ate, they drank and they were happy" (1 Kings 4:20). The kingdom extended from the Euphrates in the north to the border of Egypt in the SW.

Solomon was a wise and learned man; it is stated that his wisdom was greater than that of the wise men of the East and of Egypt. Expert in botany and zoology, he was also a writer, credited with three thousand proverbs and one thousand songs (1 Kings 4:32) and named the author of two psalms (titles, Pss 72, 127) and of the books of Proverbs (Prov 1:1), Ecclesiastes (Eccl 1:1, 12), and Song of Solomon, his greatest song (S of Sol 1:1). His fame was widespread, and people came from afar to hear him.

He made an alliance with Hiram king of Tyre, who had been a friend of David. This relationship was of great advantage to Solomon, as he undertook an immense building program, particularly that of the temple in Jerusalem on Mount Moriah. He contracted with Hiram for the supply of cedar and cypress wood and arranged for Phoenician builders to supplement the Israelite conscription of workers. A chronological reference is supplied in 1 Kings 6:1, which states that the year that construction of the temple was begun numbered the 4th year of Solomon and the 480th year after the exodus from Egypt. David had wanted to build the temple, but the Lord reserved that privilege for Solomon (2 Sam 7:13; 1 Chron 17:4–6, 12; 22:6–11; 28:6); nevertheless, Solomon got the complete plan of the structure from his father (1 Chron 28:11–19). David had also gathered much building material, especially precious metals and other costly commodities, and had taken freewill offerings for the building of the temple (1 Kings 7:51; 1 Chron 22:2–5; 29:1–19). A description of the temple is given in some detail (1 Kings 6:2–36). It is said incidentally that "he built the inner courtyard of three courses of dressed stone and one course of trimmed cedar beams" (6:36; cf. 7:12). The archaeologists of the Oriental Institute of the University of Chicago found at Megiddo evidence of the use of this technique in the Solomonic level.

The temple was finished in seven years, and Solomon's palace was thirteen years in building. The latter consisted of various houses or halls: the House of the Forest of Lebanon, the Hall of Pillars, the Hall of the Throne (also the Hall of Judgment), his royal quarters, and a palace for his Egyptian wife. A great amount of bronze was used for ornamental work, for architectural features such as the two large pillars of the temple vestibule, and for decorative and functional articles, such as the altar, the molten sea, and all sorts of utensils and implements used in the temple service. This part of the project was the responsibility of a craftsman, Huram of Tyre (1 Kings 7:14; KJV "Hiram"; cf. 2 Chron 2:13–14). Much of the copper used for these purposes probably came from mines worked by the Israelites. It is only in comparatively recent years that the great mining and smelting enterprises of Solomon have become known, for they are not referred to in the

Inside Solomon's Quarries, 656 feet (200 m.) long, under the old city of Jerusalem between Damascus and Herod's gates. Legend has it that the stones for the temple were quarried from here. Courtesy Duby Tal.

Bible. In his explorations in the Negev, Glueck found that the area was of much importance in Solomonic times. Many towns were built and fortified, a number of copper mines were worked, and the preliminary processing done nearby. Exploration led to the identification of Tell al Kheleifeh as Ezion Geber (proposed earlier by F. Frank). Excavation here brought to light the remains of an industrial town, with blast furnaces utilizing the prevailing winds to operate on the modern principle of the Bessemer forced-air draft.

When the temple was completed, an impressive dedication service was held. The ark of the covenant was brought up from Zion by the priests and was placed in the Most Holy Place (1 Kings 8). Solomon blessed the people and made a heartfelt prayer of dedication. Sacrifices were made, and fire from heaven consumed them. Finally, a great feast was held. The Lord appeared to Solomon again, as at Gibeon; he had heard his supplication and now promised to establish his heirs as he had promised to do for David, if he and his descendants would remain faithful to the Lord. After the celebration of the dedication, Solomon settled accounts with Hiram king of Tyre. Solomon gave him twenty cities in the land of Galilee, but when Hiram inspected them and was not satisfied, he also paid him 120 talents of gold. Solomon's work of building extended throughout the land, with labor provided by a forced levy of the descendants of the people Israel did not annihilate at the time of the conquest. He built at Gezer, Hazor, Megiddo, Upper Beth Horon, Lower Beth Horon, Baalath, Tadmor in the desert, and in Lebanon. He did additional building at Jerusalem. He made store cities throughout the domain.

And now Israel no longer had a lack of armaments. Solomon had 1,400 chariots and 12,000 horsemen (2 Chron 1:14); he also had 4,000 stalls for horses (9:25). He built cities for his chariots and cavalry. Stables for at least 450 horses were found at Megiddo. Similar stables were excavated at Gezer, Taanach, Tell el Hesi, and Tell el Far'ah. He also engaged in a profitable trade in chariots and horses between Egypt and the Hittites. His commercial interests led him to the sea; since the Mediterranean coast afforded no good harborage in the area held by him, he made his port at Ezion Geber near Eloth on the Gulf of Aqabah of the Red Sea. Again he was assisted by Hiram, who provided Phoenician seamen (8:18).

The rulers were enriched by this trade with the East. Ophir was a source of gold, almugwood (algumwood), and precious stones. Solomon's ships also went to Tarshish with the Phoenician fleet and brought back all sorts of exotic things. Immense wealth thus came to Solomon by commerce, mining, tribute (1 Kings 4:21), and gifts from visitors (10:25). Among the most distinguished of these visitors was the queen of Sheba. Women were a serious weakness of Solomon; not only did he make many political alliances through marriage, but he "loved many foreign women" (11:1) and "held fast to them in love" (11:2). God had warned that such marriages would lead to apostasy. The harem of Solomon held a collection of some seven hundred wives and three hundred concubines; and "his wives turned his heart after other gods, and his heart was not fully devoted to the LORD his God" (11:4). He built places of worship for the false gods to satisfy his heathen wives. The Lord was angered at Solomon's failure to keep his explicit commands and announced to him the rift in the kingdom that was to take place in the reign of his son.

Solomon's Stables at Megiddo, which consisted of five units, each accommodating about 24 horses. Shown here are remains of the hitching posts and mangers. Solomon at one time kept as many as twelve thousand horses (2 Chron 1:14; 9:25). Courtesy Oriental Institute, University of Chicago.

The rule of Solomon had been quite peaceful, but trouble was brewing. Hadad the Edomite, who as a child had survived a raid by David and had escaped to Egypt, now returned to plague him. In Syria, Rezon was made king at Damascus and became an enemy of Israel. In Israel a capable young man, Jeroboam the son of Nebat, was informed by the prophet Ahijah that he would become ruler of ten tribes of Israel. Solomon attempted to kill Jeroboam, but Jeroboam took refuge in Egypt until the death of Solomon. The signs of the impending division of the kingdom were evident; when he died in 930 B.C. and his son Rehoboam became king, the break soon became a reality. Other historical records of Solomon's reign cited in the Bible include "the book of the annals of Solomon" (1 Kings 11:41), "the records of Nathan the prophet," "the prophecy of Ahijah the Shilonite," and "the visions of Iddo the seer concerning Jeroboam the son of Nebat" (2 Chron 9:29). A great temporal ruler, possessing every natural advantage, almost inconceivably wealthy in material splendor, learning, and experience, Solomon was nevertheless a disappointment. Although he began extremely well, the tragedy of his gradual apostasy had more disastrous results than the infamous scandal of his father, who sincerely repented and was a man after the Lord's own heart. CEDV

SOLOMON, SONG OF (See SONG OF SONGS)

SOLOMON, WISDOM OF (See APOCRYPHA)

SOLOMON'S COLONNADE. A magnificent porch built by Solomon on the east side of the temple area. Christ and the apostles walked in it (John 10:23; Acts 3:11; 5:12).

SOLOMON'S POOLS. Three in number, these were located a short distance from Jerusalem and were fed by two chief sources—surface water and springs. Cleverly engineered aqueducts carried water from the desired spring to the pools. From these pools the water was conveyed by the same means to the wells under the temple area (Eccl 2:6).

In the summer of A.D. 1962, Solomon's Pools were again in the news, when a severe drought made necessary an emergency pipeline from a big new well at Hebron, to alleviate Jerusalem's water shortage. The eighteen miles (thirty km.) of pipe, furnished by the United States Agency for International Development, was laid within days; and the water was pumped into the ancient reservoirs, Solomon's Pools, eight miles (thirteen km.) south of Jerusalem. See *Time* magazine, August 17, 1962.

SOLOMON'S SERVANTS (Heb. *'avedhê shelōmōh*). The descendants of Solomon's servants are named among those returning from Babylon to Jerusalem under Zerubbabel (Ezra 2:55, 58; Neh 7:57, 60; 11:3). In the days of Solomon some were appointed to care for certain temple duties, and the descendants of these servants presumably carried on the same kind of duties. Whether they were Levites or non-Israelites is not known.

SOLOMON'S TEMPLE (See TEMPLE)

SON (Heb. *bēn,* Gr. *huios*). A word with a variety of meanings in the Bible. Genetically the Hebrew word expresses any human offspring regardless of sex (Gen 3:16). In genealogical records the word "son" is often a general term expressing descendants (Dan 5:22). Many times, of course, the word means a person, usually a male, who was the direct child of a given father (Gen 9:19; 16:15).

Another very common biblical use of this word is in connection with another following word to express something about the individual or individuals described. Perhaps the most familiar usage of this kind is as a title for our Lord (see SON OF MAN and SON OF GOD). "Son of perdition" is used of Judas. Sometimes groups are thus designated (1 Thess 5:5). Genesis 6:4 speaks of sons of God, Deuteronomy 13:13 of children of Belial (KJV; wicked men NIV).

Closely allied to this use is still another in which the word *son* indicates relationship in a certain group. Believers in the OT are called children

One of the three pools of Solomon, south of Jerusalem. The three pools are on separate levels and connected by conduits. They were part of Jerusalem's water supply in Roman times. Courtesy Seffie Ben-Yoseph.

(sons) of God (e.g., Deut 14:1), and believers in the NT have the same designation (e.g., 1 John 3:2). The word sometimes indicates a person is a member of a guild or of a profession (KJV—2 Kings 2:3, 5; Neh 3:8). HZC

SONG (Heb. *shîr, shîrâh*). Singing played a prominent part in the worship and national life of the Hebrews. The first song in the Bible was sung by Lamech (Gen 4:23–24). It was not uncommon for the Jews to compose a song celebrating some special victory or religious experience that was significant (Exod 15). The Psalter has been designated "The Song Book of Israel," and it contains many kinds of songs. The music to which these songs were sung has been lost, but it was undoubtedly similar to that of the Jews and Arabs today—plaintive, limited in compass, and marked by emphasis in rhythm.

Paul urges believers to sing (Eph 5:19; Col 3:16). The Book of Revelation speaks often of heavenly singing (Rev 5:9; 14:3).

SONG OF SONGS, SONG OF SOLOMON (Heb. *shîr ha-shîrîm*). This is unique among biblical books, for it centers in the joys and distresses of the love relationship between a man and a woman.

I. Name. The Hebrew name, "Song of Songs," is taken from 1:1, which introduces the book as "the song of songs which is Solomon's." This use of the Hebrew superlative declares the book the best of the 1,005 songs of Solomon (1 Kings 4:32), or perhaps the greatest of all songs. It also provides the basis for the older title of the book in English versions, "Song of Solomon," as well as for the title in the NIV, "Song of Songs."

II. Authorship and Date. There is considerable range of opinion as to the authorship and date of the book. R. H. Pfeiffer concludes that the Song of Songs is "an anthology of erotic poems," of about 250 B.C., using the language as the sole criterion for the date. The frequent use of Aramaic forms and words, the presence of names of foreign products, a Persian word, and a Greek word are taken as evidence for a late date. On the other hand, it has been pointed out that these usages are not inconsistent with authorship by Solomon. In view of the extensive commerce and widespread diplomatic relations of Solomon, the presence of foreign terms, especially for articles imparted or imitated from foreign sources, is to be expected. The use of Aramaic is not a valid indication of date and may be accounted for by the northern origin of the Shulammite (Song of Songs 6:13). The book ascribes its authorship to Solomon, and there are lines of evidence that agree with this ascription. The book has affinities with other writings attributed to Solomon. The author's acquaintance with plants and animals is reminiscent of Solomon (1 Kings 4:33). The mention of "a mare harnessed to one of the chariots of Pharaoh" (Song of Songs 1:9) accords with Solomon's involvement in horse trading with Egypt and with his being married to a daughter of the pharaoh. The lover is called "the king" (1:4), and there are other indications of his royal interests, in addition to references to Solomon by name. The place-names range throughout Palestine and thus fit well with an origin predating the divided kingdom.

III. Content. Though the book is difficult to analyze, the divisions of Delitzsch are often followed: (1) the mutual admiration of the lovers (1:2–2:7); (2) growth in love (2:8–3:5); (3) the marriage (3:6–5:1); (4) longing of the wife for her absent husband (5:2–6:9); (5) the beauty of the Shulammite bride (6:10–8:4); (6) the wonder of love (8:5–8:14).

IV. Interpretation. There is great diversity and much overlapping among interpretations of the Song of Songs. Various views are: (1) allegorical, (2) typical, (3) literal, (4) dramatic, (5) erotic-literary, (6) liturgical, and (7) didactic-moral.

1. The *allegorical* view may be Jewish, Christian, or a combination of these. The first regards the Song as descriptive of the love of God and his people Israel; the second discerns the love of Christ and the church or the individual believer. Usually this view denies or ignores the historicity of the events described. Hippolytus and Origen introduced this interpretation into the church, and this has been the popular or prevailing position, along with the typical view. There are two major arguments in its favor: (1) It explains the inclusion of the book in the canon. (2) It harmonizes with the biblical use of marriage as an illustration of the Lord's relationship to his people. Opposing arguments include the following: (1) Other reasons may be advanced for its presence among the canonical books. (2) Elsewhere the figure of the marriage relationship is made the basis for specific teaching. (3) Nothing in the book itself invalidates its historicity. (4) The necessity of interpreting details leads to fanciful and absurd interpretations.

2. The *typical* interpretation combines literal and allegorical views, maintaining both the historicity and the spiritualizing of the book. In support of this view: (1) The superlative of the title connotes spiritual meaning. (2) Solomon is a type of Christ. (3) Marriage also is a type (cf. above). Against this view: (1) Spiritual value does not demand typology. (2) The definition and application of "type" are debatable.

3. The *literal* view is that the book presents actual history and nothing more.

4. The *dramatic* interpretation regards the Song as a drama based on the marriage of Solomon to a Shulammite girl. Here may be included the Shepherd hypothesis (Jacobi, Ewald, et al.), which proposes a triangle of Solomon, the girl, and her shepherd-betrothed. On this hypothesis, the girl refuses the blandishments of the king and remains true to her shepherd. The book is not labeled drama, which was not a widely used Hebrew literary form. If the book were merely a drama, its presence in the canon is not explained.

5. The *erotic-literary* view (Eissfeldt, Pfeiffer) is that the book is simply a collection of love songs.

6. The *liturgical* view regards the Song as borrowed pagan liturgy associated with fertility

cults. It is inconceivable that a work of such an origin should be in the canon.

7. The *didactic-moral* interpretation holds that the book presents the purity and wonder of true love. It regards the book as history and also agrees that the love portrayed does direct us to the greater love of Christ, in accordance with the history of Christian interpretation. The purpose of the Song of Songs, therefore, is to teach the holiness and beauty of the marriage-love relationship that God ordained.

Bibliography: L. Waterman, *The Song of Songs,* 1948; R. Gordis, *The Song of Songs,* 1954; W. J. Fuerst, *Ruth, Esther, Ecclesiastes, The Song of Songs, Lamentations,* 1975; D. F. Kinlaw, "Song of Solomon," EBC, vol. 5, 1985. CEDV

SONG OF THE THREE HOLY CHILDREN (See APOCRYPHA)

SONGS OF DEGREES (See ASCENTS, SONGS OF)

SON OF GOD. One of the primary titles of Jesus in the NT. His claim to this title was the principal charge that the Jewish leaders made against him. "Tell us if you are the Christ, the Son of God," the high priest taunted (Matt 26:63–64; Mark 14:61–62; cf. John 5:17–18; 19:7). Further, the confession that Jesus is the Son of God was basic to the teaching of the apostles and the faith of the early church (2 Cor 1:19; Gal 2:20; 1 John 4:15; 5:5, 13). The title is to be understood both as a synonym for Messiah (Ps 2:7; Matt 16:16; 26:63; 27:40) and as implying deity through a unique relation with the Father (John 5:18). Sometimes the latter implication is obvious (as in the Gospel of John), and sometimes it is hidden (as often in the three other Gospels).

Jesus became conscious of his special relation with the Father as a boy and expressed it when he was twelve years old (Luke 2:49). At his baptism, the voice from heaven confirmed what he already knew—that he had a unique spiritual and moral union with the Father and that he was called to be the Messiah and to do the work of God's Chosen Servant (Matt 3:13–17; Mark 1:9–12; Luke 3:21–22). This consciousness was severely tested in the temptations (Matt 4; Luke 4). Throughout his ministry Jesus was sustained and inspired by the knowledge that he was the Father's Son, doing his will (Matt 17:5; 21:33–44). In Gethsemane and on the cross this consciousness remained his possession (Matt 26:36–42; Luke 22:39–44; 23:46).

The filial consciousness of Jesus and his unique relationship with the Father are particularly emphasized in John's Gospel. Jesus is God's only Son (John 1:18), one with the Father (10:30), always doing the Father's will (4:34; 5:30; 6:38), and being in the Father as the Father is in him (10:38). He speaks what he hears from the Father (12:50), has unique knowledge of the Father (10:15; cf. Matt 11:27), and possesses the authority of the Father (John 3:35; 5:22; 13:3; 16:15). Thus, only in and through the Son is God's salvation given (3:36; 5:26; 6:40). However, Scripture indicates limitations on the Son—both incarnationally and positionally (Mark 13:32; John 14:28).

Outside the Gospels, God is called "the God and Father of our Lord Jesus Christ," suggesting a particular intimacy between Father and Son (Rom 15:6; 2 Cor 1:3; Eph 1:3; Col 1:3; 1 Peter 1:3; Rev 1:6). By his resurrection and ascension Jesus is designated Son of God (Rom 1:3) and preached to be so (Acts 8:37; 9:20; 13:33; 2 Cor 1:19). The distinction and difference between Jesus and the great prophets of Israel is that Jesus is the unique Son of God (Heb 1; 3:6). True unity in the church and true spiritual maturity involves growing into "the knowledge of the Son of God" (Eph 4:13). The people of God wait for the Son to return to earth from heaven (1 Thess 1:10).

Finally, there is the trinitarian formula in Matthew 28:19—". . . baptizing them in the name of the Father and of the Son and of the Holy Spirit."

See also SONS OF GOD, CHILDREN OF GOD.

Bibliography: O. Cullmann, *The Christology of the New Testament,* 1963; F. Hahn, *The Titles of Jesus in Christology,* 1969; M. Hengel, *Jesus, the Son of God,* 1976. PT

SON OF MAN. (Heb. ben *'ādhām,* Gr. *ho huios tou anthrōpou*). An expression found in the OT and used as a self-description of Jesus in the NT. In Hebrew, "son of man" means an individual man, a man from the genus man (Num 23:19; Ps 8:4–5. "Adam" is "mankind"). This phrase was used once by the Lord in addressing Daniel (Dan 8:17) and over eighty times in addressing Ezekiel. There must have been a special reason for its use with them. Both of them were privileged to see visions of God. Probably the Lord wanted to emphasize to them that they were, after all, only men of the earth, in spite of this privilege of receiving the divine word. In Psalm 80:17 the king of Israel is called "the son of man" whom God has raised up for himself.

Daniel used this phrase to describe a personage whom he saw in a night vision. He saw one "like a son of man" (that is, a member of the genus man) coming with the clouds of heaven and approaching God (the "Ancient of Days") to be given authority, glory, and an everlasting kingdom (Dan 7:13–14). While opinions differ about the interpretation of this vision, and many hold the "son of man" to be a personification of "the saints of the most high" (see 7:22) to whom the dominion is given, it is on the whole entirely in accord with the evidence to see here a messianic figure predictive of the Lord Jesus Christ. In the extrabiblical *Similitudes of Enoch* the presentation of the Son of Man in the terms found in Daniel's prophecy is continued.

Why Jesus decided to call himself "Son of Man" (eighty-two times in the Gospels; see also Acts 7:56; Rev 1:13; 14:14) is not known, despite much scholarly study of the question. Often he put his statements about himself in the third person to give his teachings more force. Whenever he did this he used this phrase as a name for himself. No doubt he took it from Daniel's prophecy. The Jews must have been familiar with this prophecy. Jesus, in assuming this title, was saying to the Jews, "I am the Son of man in that prophecy." This title emphasized his union with mankind. It was also a name no one would criticize. Jesus could not call himself the Son of God or the Messiah. The Jews would not accept him as such. But they did not object to the term, the Son of Man. But no one else ever called him by that name.

Jesus certainly used the title in a variety of contexts: (1) As a substitute for "I" (e.g., Matt 11:19; 16:13; Luke 9:58). (2) When making his important declarations and claims (e.g., Matt 20:28; Mark 10:45; Luke 9:56; 11:30; 19:10). These relate to his saving role. (3) Once this phrase occurs without the definite article: "a son of man" (John 5:27 ASV). Jesus made the statement that he had been given authority to execute judgment because he was a son of man. That is, because of his experience as man, living among men, he was qualified to judge man. See also MESSIAH. (4) Concerning his resurrection: "Don't tell anyone what you have seen, until the Son of Man has been raised from the dead" (Matt 17:9). (5) Concerning the glorious state into which as the exalted Son of Man he would enter (Matt 19:28; 24:30; 26:64; Mark 13:26; 14:62; Luke 17:26, 30; 22:69). These verses relate to his reign with the Father in and from heaven. (6) Concerning the return to earth in a glorious manner (Matt 24:27, 30, 44; Luke 17:24; 18:8). (7) Concerning his role in judgment (Matt 13:41; 25:31–32; Luke 9:56; 21:36). (8) Most important of all, concerning his passion and violent death (Matt 17:12, 22; 26:2, 24, 45; Mark 9:12, 31; 10:33; 14:21, 41; Luke 9:44; 18:31–32; 22:22, 48). In view of the usage of "son of man" in Daniel 7:13, this emphasis by Jesus that he as Son of Man must, of necessity, suffer, is quite remarkable.

See also ADAM.

Bibliography: E. J. Young, *Daniel's Vision of the Son of Man,* 1958; O. Cullmann, *The Christology of the New Testament,* 1963; M. D. Hooker, *The Son of Man in Mark,* 1967; F. Hahn, *The Titles of Jesus in Christology,* 1967; J. G. Baldwin, *Daniel* (TOTC), 1978. CEH and PT

SONS OF GOD, CHILDREN OF GOD. A description of those who are in a special or intimate relationship with God. In the OT the Lord chose the people Israel and made a holy covenant with them. As a result, the people as a unit (and thus each member) were described as the son(s) of God. Moses told Pharaoh that the Israelite nation was God's "firstborn son," and that this "son" must be released in order to offer worship to his "Father" (Exod 4:22). Later the description was "children of God" and "a people holy to the Lord" (Deut 14:1). Further, the Davidic king-Messiah was described as the Son of God (see 2 Sam 7:14; 23:5; Ps 2:7; 89:27–28). This usage is continued in the NT, where the ancient people of Israel are said to possess the "sonship" (Rom 9:4) and be God's children (John 11:52) and the Messiah is seen as God's "Son" (Heb 1:5; citing Ps 2:7 and 2 Sam 7:14).

Building on this OT usage, members of the new covenant are also described as sons/children of God. Paul declared that "you are all sons of God through faith in Christ Jesus" (Gal 3:26), and he used the image of adoption to convey the idea of being taken into God's family, of receiving forgiveness and the gift of the indwelling Spirit (Rom 8:14ff.). John taught that by spiritual birth believers become the children of God and are thereby in an intimate spiritual/moral union with God their heavenly Father. ("How great is the love the Father has lavished on us, that we should be called children of God!" [1 John 3:1]). Both Paul and John insisted that to be called son or child meant living in a way that reflects this relationship (Rom 8:17, 29; 1 John 3:9). Jesus himself made a similar point (Matt 5:9, 44–45; 12:48–50). Again this continues the OT emphasis that to be the son or child of God means being godlike in behavior (Deut 32:6; Isa 1:2; Hos 1:10).

Within the OT there is at least one other way in which "sons of God" is used. That is, a few passages appear to refer to angels (Job 1:6; 2:1; 38:7; Ps 89:6). Genesis 6:1–2 may likewise involve angels (in this case they are fallen ones) or they may be demon-possessed individuals, but others view these "sons of God" as kings/rulers/princes. PT

SONS OF THE PROPHETS. A title given to members of prophetic guilds or schools. Samuel was the head of a company of prophets at Ramah (1 Sam 7:17; 28:3), and two hundred years later Elijah and Elisha were leaders of similar groups. They were men endowed with the prophetic gift (10:10; 19:20–23), who gathered around God's great leader for common worship, united prayer, religious fellowship, and instruction of the people (10:5, 10; 2 Kings 4:38, 40; 6:1–7; 9:1). In the times of Elijah and Elisha they formed a comparatively large company (2 Kings 2:7, 16) and lived together at Bethel, Jericho, and Gilgal (2:3, 5; 4:38).

SOOTHSAYER. (See OCCUPATIONS AND PROFESSIONS)

SOP (Gr. *psōmion, a morsel of bread*). The word is used in the KJV and describes a thin wafer used to dip food from a common platter (John 13:26). Using the sop had long been common among the Hebrews (Ruth 2:14; Prov 17:1).

SOPATER (sō'pá-têr, Gr. *Sōpatros*). Son of Pyrrhus who accompanied the apostle Paul on his last journey from Corinth to Jerusalem (Acts 20:4). He was a Christian from the church at Berea and is the same as Sosipater who joined with Timothy, Lucius, and Jason in sending greetings to the church at Rome (Rom 16:21).

SOPHERETH, SOPHORETH (sō'fĕr-ĕth, Heb. *sōphereth*). One of Solomon's servants who was among the captives to return to Jerusalem with Zerubbabel listed in Ezra 2:55 (KJV; NIV "Hassophereth") and Nehemiah 7:57.

SORCERER, SORCERY (See MAGIC; OCCUPATIONS AND PROFESSIONS)

SORE (See DISEASES)

SOREK (sō'rĕk, Heb. *sôrēq, vineyard*). A valley that extends from near Jerusalem to the Mediterranean Sea about eight and one-half miles (fourteen km.) south of Joppa. It was in this valley that Samson found Delilah (Judg 16:4). It was a fertile area where vineyards flourished. Today it produces rich harvests of grain. A modern railroad follows the valley to Jerusalem. In OT times a highway ran along the same route. It was over this road that the ark was conveyed after it had been taken from the Philistines (1 Sam 6:10–14). There the Philistines suffered a great defeat at the hands of the Israelites (7:3–14). It is doubtless Wadi es-Sarar.

SOSIPATER (See SOPATER)

SOSTHENES (sŏs'thĕ-nēz, Gr. *Sōsthenēs*). The apparent successor of Crispus, the ruler of the synagogue at Corinth. During Paul's first visit in that city, Sosthenes was beaten by the crowd in the presence of Gallio, the Roman proconsul of Achaia (Acts 18:17). No reason is given for this action, but it is likely that they took "advantage of the snub that the proconsul had administered to the leaders of the Jewish community" to vent their anti-Semitic sentiment (F. F. Bruce, *The Book of Acts,* 1956, p. 375). It is quite possible that he subsequently became a Christian, for a Sosthenes joins Paul in the salutation of 1 Corinthians 1:1. If this is not the Sosthenes of Acts 18, he is otherwise unknown in the NT.

SOTAI (sō'tī, Heb. *sōtay*). One of the servants of Solomon who returned from captivity under Zerubbabel (Ezra 2:55; Neh 7:57).

SOUL (Heb. *nephesh,* Gr. *psychē*). The word commonly used in the Bible to designate the nonmaterial ego of man in its ordinary relationships with earthly and physical things. It is one of a number of psychological nouns, all designating the same nonmaterial self, but each in a different functional relationship. Thus, the "mind" (*nous*) is the self in its rational functions. Again "mind" (*phronēma*) is the self as deeply comtemplating. "Heart" (*kardia*) is the self as manifesting a complex of attitudes. "Will" (*thelēsis*) is the self as choosing and deciding. "Spirit" (*pneuma*) is the self when thought of apart from earthly connections. When the blessed dead in heaven are spoken of as having been put to a martyr's death, they are called "souls" (Rev 6:9). When there is no reference to their former bodily experience, they are called "spirits" (Heb 12:23).

These functional names of the ego are not used with technical discrimination. They often overlap. The difference between man and beast is not that man has a soul or spirit (Gen 1:20; 7:15; Eccl 3:21), but that man is created in the image of God, whereas the beast is not.

The above remarks assume dichotomy, that is, that there are only two substantive entities that make up the whole person: (1) the body, which at death returns to dust, awaiting the resurrection, and (2) the nonmaterial self, which if regenerate goes to paradise or heaven; if not, to the abode of the wicked dead. There are many, however, who hold to a trichotomous view, arguing that "soul" and "spirit" are two distinct substantive entities, and the body, a third. They cite 1 Corinthians 15:44; 1 Thessalonians 5:23; Hebrews 4:12 for evidence.

Modern non-Christian psychology ignores or denies the existence of the soul as a substantive entity. The "self" is usually spoken of as a mere behavior pattern, a conscious*ness,* but not a being that is conscious.

It is reasonable to see that, in this created world, whenever movement in space occurs, there is something that moves; and similarly, whenever consciousness occurs, there is something, the soul or mind, that is conscious. JOB

SOUTH. The translation of various Hebrew words in the KJV. They refer to a compass point, a country, or a general direction. The most common word (*neghev, a dry region*) refers primarily to an indefinite area lying between Palestine and Egypt. Abram journeyed toward the south (Gen 12:9) and went to the south when returning from Egypt (13:1). David conquered the south (1 Sam 27:8–12), and so did the Philistines (2 Chron 28:18). Ramoth was in this area (1 Sam 30:27). Isaac lived here when he met Rebekah (Gen 24:62–67). Israel was commanded to conquer the area (Deut 1:7). Judah's heritage extended from the Dead Sea, across the south, to the confluence of the River of Egypt and the Great Sea (Josh 15:1–47). Caleb gave a portion of the south to his daughter Acsah as her dowry when she was married to Othniel (Judg 1:15). In all these passages the NIV reads "Negev."

The Negev or southern region extended from the lower end of the Dead Sea SW to Kadesh Barnea, NW along the River of Egypt to the Mediterranean, its boundaries being somewhat indefinite in the semidesert regions. Its name, "a dry region," does not indicate a desert; it probably arose because it had a less ample supply of water than Judah had. In it the Hebrews found Amalekites (Num 13:29), Jerahmeelites (1 Sam 27:10), and other tribes whom they either exterminated or absorbed. JOB

SOVEREIGNTY OF GOD. The word "sovereign," although it does not occur in any form in the English Bible, conveys the oft-repeated scriptural thought of the supreme authority of God. He is called *Pantokratōr* "Almighty" (2 Cor 6:18

and nine times in Revelation); "the blessed and only Ruler, the King of kings and Lord of lords" (1 Tim 6:15). He "works out everything in conformity with the purpose of his will" (Eph 1:11). His sovereignty follows logically from the doctrine that he is God, Creator, and Ruler of the universe.

The sovereignty of God is sometimes presented in the Bible as an unanalyzed ultimate. "But who are you, O man, to talk back to God? Shall what is formed say to him who formed it, 'Why did you make me like this?' Does not the potter have the right to make out of the same lump of clay some pottery for noble purposes and some for common use?" (Rom 9:20–21; see Isa 45:9; cf. Ps 115:3; Dan 4:35; and many similar passages). God is not subject to any power or any abstract rule or law that could be conceived as superior to or other than himself.

Yet the Scripture is equally emphatic that God's character is immutably holy and just and good. "He cannot disown himself" (2 Tim 2:13). "It is impossible for God to lie" (Heb 6:18; cf. Titus 1:2). A man of faith may rightly stand before the Lord and plead, "Will not the Judge of all the earth do right?" (Gen 18:25). "His love endures forever" is an oft-recurring phrase (Ps 136). He assures his people of his eternal self-consistency: "I the LORD do not change. So you, O descendants of Jacob, are not destroyed" (Mal 3:6).

The inscrutable sovereignty of God is manifested, not so much in the punishment of the reprobate as in the salvation of his people. In his holy character he must logically punish moral evil (see SIN). But his sovereignty is most marvelously revealed in that he has graciously elected to save a people from their sin and from its consequences. JOB

SOWER, SOWING (See AGRICULTURE)

SPAIN (Gr. *Spania*). The westernmost peninsula of Europe, populated basically by an Indo-European stock allied to the Celts. The land was early noticed by the Phoenicians who established a major center of trade at Tartessus. The Carthaginians inherited the Phoenician interest in Spain, and New Carthage (Cartagena) was developed by Hannibal as his base against Italy in the Second Punic War. Spain, in consequence, became a theater of conflict in this clash of nations, and with the victory of Rome remained in Roman hands. It was not until the time of Augustus that the peninsula was finally pacified and organized. It was rapidly Romanized. Trajan, Hadrian, and Theodosius I, among the emperors, were Spaniards; among men of letters the two Senecas, Lucan, Columella, Quintillian, Martial, and Prudentius came from Spain. Paul's projected visit (Rom 15:24) was clearly in line with his evident policy to capture for the church the principal centers of the empire. EMB

SPAN (See WEIGHTS AND MEASURES)

SPARROW (See BIRDS)

SPEAR (See ARMS AND ARMOR)

SPECKLED (Heb. *nāqōdh, mottled in color*). A word used to denote varied colors of beasts. The most familiar example of its use is in Genesis 30:25–43 where Jacob applied his knowledge of selective breeding of livestock in order to collect from Laban what he considered a fair wage. However, God revealed to him in a dream that it was not his doings, but God's, that effected the selective breeding (31:10–12).

SPICE (Heb. *besem, bōsem, sammîn, nekhō'th, reqah*, Gr. *arōma, amōmon*). Anything having a pleasant odor, usually herbs. The principal Hebrew word (*besem*, "sweet-scented") refers to any aromatic vegetable compound, such as myrrh, cinnamon, cassia, and so forth (Exod 30:23–24). Spices were often mixed with oil to make them more durable and easily applied (30:25; 35:8). Spices played an important part in worship throughout the Near East (25:1–6). In the temple the Levites were keepers of spices (1 Chron 9:29). A rare spice (*bōsem*, "creating desire") is indicated in the Song of Songs 5:13; 6:2. In Genesis 37:25 and 43:11 spices, or spicery, mean treasure. Hezekiah revealed to spies of Babylon the temple treasures, including rich spices and was rebuked by Isaiah (2 Kings 20:12–18). Spices were used in preparing the body of Jesus for burial (John 19:40). Some were brought to the tomb after Jesus had risen (Mark 16:1). See also PLANTS: *Spice*.

SPIDER (See ANIMALS)

SPIES (Heb. *rāgal, to travel by foot*). The custom of sending secret agents to discover facts about an enemy is age-old. The Hebrew word for a spy is suggested by the secrecy with which he did his work—he went stealthily. Joseph accused his brothers of being spies (Gen 42). Joshua sent spies to Jericho (Josh 6:23). David sent them to see if Saul was with his army at Hakilah (1 Sam 26:1–4). Absalom put secret agents throughout Israel to seize power when they were notified he had become king (2 Sam 15:7–10). Priests and scribes sent spies to entrap Jesus (Luke 20:20).

SPIKENARD (See PLANTS)

SPINDLE (Heb. *kîshôr, shaft*). An implement, eight to twelve inches (twenty-one to thirty-one cm.) long, used in spinning. The rope of carded fiber or wool was attached to one end and the spindle rotated by hand. Thus the thread was twisted. In Egypt both men and women did spinning, but among the Hebrews only women did the work (Exod 35:25; Prov 31:19).

SPINNING (See OCCUPATIONS AND PROFESSIONS)

SPIRIT (Heb. *rûach, breath, spirit*, Gr. *pneuma, wind, spirit*). One of the biblical nouns (see the list of such nouns and also the trichotomist view in

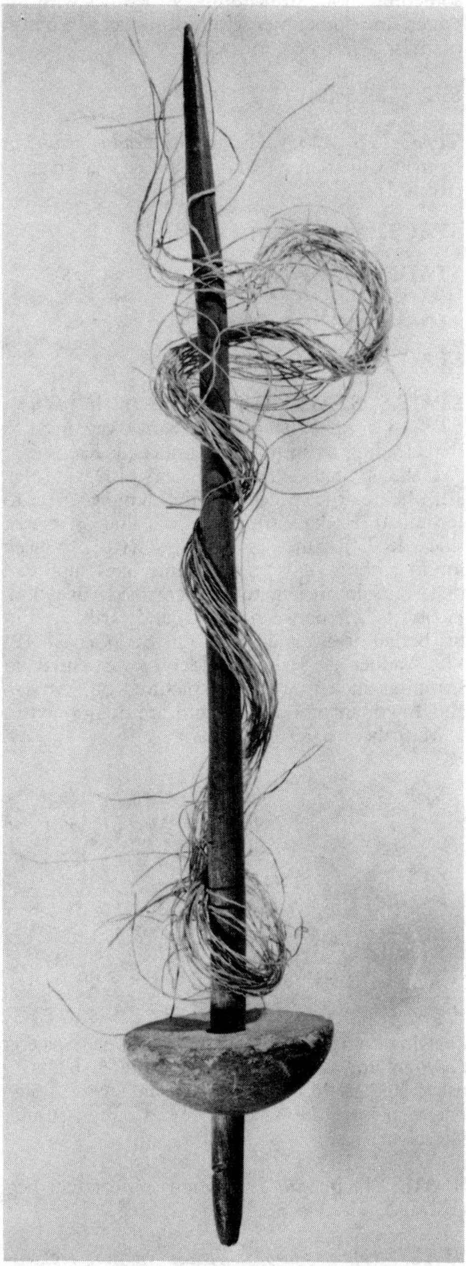

Wooden spindle from Thebes, New Kingdom (c. 1300 B.C.), with a limestone whorl and ancient flaxen thread. An owner's mark is scratched on the underside of the whorl. Reproduced by courtesy of the Trustees of the British Museum.

the article on SOUL) denoting the nonmaterial ego in special relationships. The self is generally called "spirit" in contexts where its bodily, emotional, and intellectual aspects are not prominent, but where the direct relationship of the individual to God is the point of emphasis.

A typical instance is Romans 8:15b–16, "By him we cry, . . . 'Father.' The Spirit himself testifies with *our spirit* that we are God's children." The martyrs in heaven are called "souls" when there is special reference to the brutal form of their death (Rev 6:9). But in the exalted description of the heavenly goal that lies before the church (Heb 12:22–24), the blessed dead are referred to as "the spirits of righteous men made perfect."

In modern non-Christian culture the biblical personal meaning of "spirit" is commonly denied. The biblical word "spirit" can have an impersonal meaning in both Hebrew and Greek, as it can in English. See the expression "a spirit of stupor" in Romans 11:8 and "the spirit of deep sleep" in Isaiah 29:10 KJV. The context must show whether the meaning is personal or impersonal. Usually there is no doubt.

The same Hebrew and Greek words translated "spirit" can also mean "wind" or "breath." In at least one passage (John 3:8) the interpretation is doubtful, but this verse would much better be translated, "The Spirit breathes where he chooses. You hear his voice, but you do not know where he comes from nor where he goes. So everyone is born who is born from the Spirit." This brings out the sovereign grace of God in regeneration. In the context the word *pneuma* clearly designates the Holy Spirit, who is a nonmaterial person. (See John 4:24, "God is spirit"; see also GOD.) JOB

SPIRIT, HOLY (See HOLY SPIRIT)

SPIRITS IN PRISON. The words under consideration occur in 1 Peter 3:18–20, and the same thought is suggested in 1 Peter 4:6. Some use these and other verses to support a doctrine of a *limbus patrum,* or borderland place of confinement of the patriarchs who died before the time of Christ. They see Ephesians 4:8ff. as teaching that, at his ascension, Christ took the patriarchs from this limbus to heaven. Matthew 27:52–53 is sometimes referred to as well, and the phrase "He descended into Hades" in the Apostles' Creed is also brought in.

Another view has been held (though not in every detail) by such students of Scripture as John Calvin (*Institutes* 2.16.9), Charles Hodge (*Systematic Theology*, 2:616–25), A. T. Robertson (*Word Pictures*, 6:115ff.), and B. B. Warfield (quoted by Robertson). According to them, (1) "made alive by the Spirit" (1 Peter 3:18) refers to Christ's resurrection (Rom 8:11), not to his disembodied state. (2) The time when Christ, in the Spirit, "went and preached" (1 Peter 3:19) was "when God waited patiently in the days of Noah" (3:20; cf. 1:11; 2 Peter 2:5). (3) The "spirits in prison" (3:19–20) are those who, in the days of Noah, refused Noah's message and are now, as Peter writes, in the Tartarus (2 Peter 2:4, see footnote), part of Hades. (4) Thus, 1 Peter 4:6 means "this is why the gospel was preached [of old (cf. Gal 3:8)] to [those who are now] dead, so that they might be judged as men [now] in the flesh [are to be judged], and might live according to God by the Spirit."

Scripture does not warrant the idea that people will hear the gospel after death. JOB

SPIRITUAL GIFTS (See GIFTS, SPIRITUAL)

SPIT, SPITTLE, SPITTING (Heb. *yāraq, rōq,* Gr. *ptuō*). Spitting in the face indicated gross insult (Num 12:14; Deut 25:9). Allowing spittle to run on the beard made one appear foolish or even "insane" (1 Sam 21:13). The Greek word for spit evidently arose because of the peculiar sound made in spitting, *ptuō*. Jesus used spittle in curing blind eyes in Bethsaida (Mark 8:23) and put spittle on a mute tongue in the Decapolis (7:33). Jesus was insulted during his trial by being spit on (Matt 26:67; Mark 14:65).

SPOIL (Heb. *bizzâh, meshissâh, shōd, shālāl,* Gr. *harpagē, skylon*). The plunder taken from the enemy in war—pillage, booty, loot. The spoils of war were divided equally between those who went into battle and those who were left behind in camp (Num 31:27; Josh 22:8; 1 Sam 30:24). Parts were given to the Levites and to the Lord (Num 31:28, 30). Under the monarchy, the king received part of the spoils (2 Kings 14:14; 1 Chron 18:7, 11).

SPOKES (Heb. *hishshūrîm*). Rods connecting the rim of a wheel with the hub. In the temple there were ten lavers or basins made of bronze (1 Kings 7:27–33), apparently for the washing of sacrifices. They were set on bases of elaborate design moving on wheels. The spokes were part of these wheels.

SPONGE (See ANIMALS)

SPOT (Heb. *mûm,* Gr. *spilos*). The Hebrew word denotes a blemish or "flaw" on the face (Song of Songs 4:7). It is also rendered "blemish" (Lev 24:19 KJV) and "blot" (Prov 9:7 KJV). The Greek word is used figuratively of a stain of sin (2 Peter 3:14; Jude 23).

SPOUSE (See MARRIAGE)

SPREAD, SPREADING (Heb. *pāras, to disperse,* Gr. *strōnnymi*). To scatter, strew, or disperse, as in "spread abroad" (Isa 21:5; Matt 21:8; Mark 1:28).

SPRING (See FOUNTAIN)

SPRINKLING (Heb. *zāraq, nāzâh,* Gr. *rhantizein*). Sprinkling of blood, water, and oil formed a very important part of the act of sacrifice. In the account of the forming of the covenant between the Lord and Israel (Exod 24:6–8), half of the blood was sprinkled on the altar and the rest on the people. When Aaron and his sons were consecrated, some blood was sprinkled on the altar and some on Aaron and his sons and on their garments. In the various offerings—burnt, peace, sin—blood was always sprinkled. Sprinkling was sometimes done in handfuls, sometimes with the finger, and sometimes with a sprinkler—a bunch of hyssop fastened to a cedar rod.

SPY (See SPIES)

STACHYS (stā'kĭs, Gr. *Stachys, head of grain*). A Roman Christian to whom Paul sent a greeting (Rom 16:9).

STACTE (See PLANTS)

STADIA (See WEIGHTS AND MEASURES)

STAFF, STAVES (See ROD)

STAG (See ANIMALS)

STAIRS, STAIRWAY, STEPS (Heb. *maălâh, sullam,* Gr. *anabathmos*). The name was given to steps leading to an upper chamber (1 Kings 6:8; Acts 9:37). Stairs led up to the city of David (Neh 12:37), to the porch of the temple gate to Jerusalem (Ezek 40:6), and to the altar on its east side (43:17). Since stone steps have not been found among ruins in Palestine, it is supposed that stairs in ancient times were made of wood. Jacob's ladder between heaven and earth, seen in his Bethel dream is called a stairway (Gen 28:12; KJV "ladder"). Scaling ladders, often used in storming ancient cities, are pictured on Assyrian and Egyptian monuments and are mentioned in 1 Maccabees 5:30.

Drawing from relief on palace at Nineveh depicting Assyrian army of King Ashurbanipal (668–633 B.C.) using ladders to storm an Egyptian town as prisoners, below, are taken away. Courtesy Carta, Jerusalem.

STAKE (Heb. *yāthēdh*). A tent pin or tent peg (Exod 27:19; Isa 33:20; 54:2).

STALL (Heb. *marbēq, 'āvas, 'urvâh, repheth, ēvūs,* Gr. *phatnē*). A place for the care of livestock. One kind was not enclosed, often being a thatched or tented shelter, at times a fattening place (Amos 6:4 KJV, cf. NIV; Mal 4:2). In winter horses were kept in barns in which each had its fenced enclosure. Solomon's barns provided stalls for four thousand horses (2 Chron 9:25; forty thousand in 1 Kings 4:26). The stall where Christ was born was a feeding place, usually connected with an inn (Luke 13:15).

STALLION (See ANIMALS)

STANDARD (See WEIGHTS AND MEASURES)

STAR (See ASTRONOMY)

STAR OF THE WISE MEN (See ASTRONOMY)

STATURE (Heb. *middâh, measure,* and *qômâh, standing up,* Gr. *hēlikia, greatness*). Used primarily in the KJV, referring to great size, tallness, height (so NIV). The giant of Gath was of great stature (2 Sam 21:20), as were the sons of Anak (Num 13:32–33) and the Sabeans (Isa 45:14). God does not regard stature in size as a primary asset for leadership (1 Sam 16:7; Isa 10:33). Jesus grew in stature (Luke 2:52), as did Samuel (1 Sam 2:26). Zacchaeus was short in stature (Luke 19:3). One's height cannot be increased by wishing (Matt 6:27; Luke 12:25; see NIV footnote).

STEED (See ANIMALS)

STEEL (See MINERALS)

STEER (See ANIMALS)

STELE (stē'lē, Gr. *stele, an erect block or shaft*). The custom of erecting stone markers, usually upright narrow slabs, prevailed among ancient Egyptians. They were placed in tombs and public buildings where they honored people of high estate. The Hebrews do not seem to have adopted the custom, probably because it was felt they violated the fourth commandment (Exod 20:4). A noted stele showing a Moabite victory over Israel was found in Beth Shan in A.D. 1868. The Grecian stele was the forerunner of modern gravestones.

STEPHANAS (stĕf'ă-năs, Gr. *Stephanas, crown*). A Christian at Corinth, whose household were Paul's first converts in Achaia (1 Cor 16:15). Paul had not only won them to Christ, but they also were among the few at Corinth whom he had personally baptized (1:16). Subsequently, they had rendered invaluable service to the church (16:15). Stephanas himself had come to Paul at Ephesus along with Fortunatus and Achaicus (16:17). It is thought that they may have delivered the letter that was sent by the Corinthian church to Paul.

STEPHEN (stē'vĕn, Gr. *Stephanos, crown*). One of the seven appointed to look after the daily distribution to the poor in the early church (Acts 6:1–6). The need for such men arose out of the complaint of the Hellenists (i.e., Greek-speaking Jews) that their widows were not receiving a fair share of this relief. Stephen, described as "a man full of faith and of the Holy Spirit" (6:5), and six others were selected by the church and consecrated by the apostles in order to insure an equitable distribution.

Stephen's ministry was not, however, limited to providing for the poor. He did "great wonders

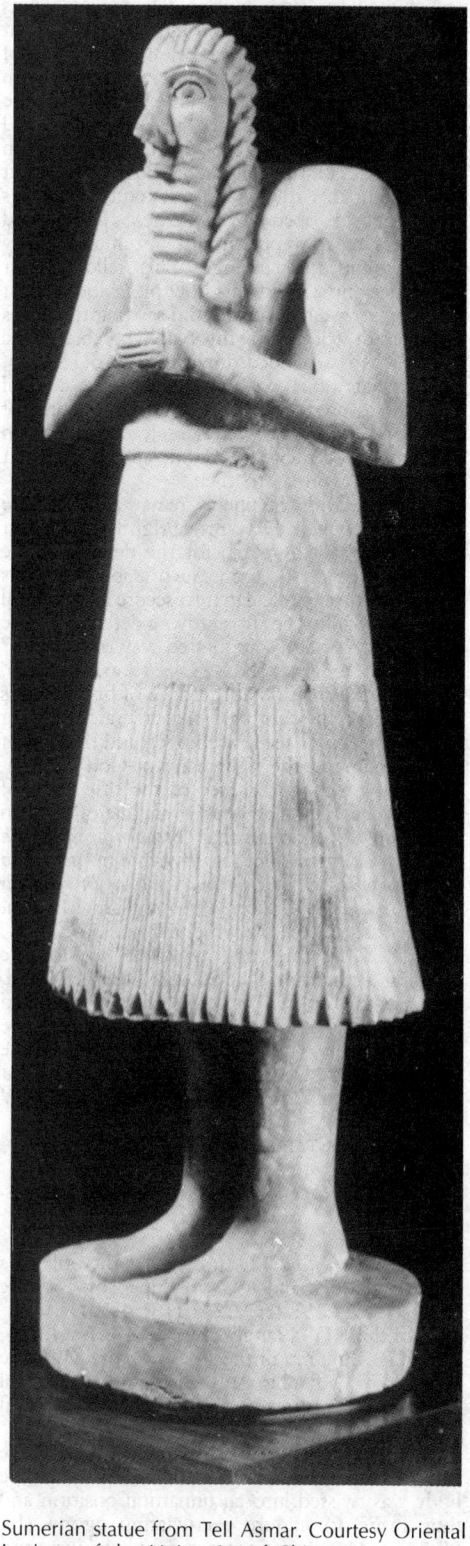

Sumerian statue from Tell Asmar. Courtesy Oriental Institute of the University of Chicago

and miraculous signs among the people" (Acts 6:8). While this probably brought him into great favor with the people generally, another aspect of his ministry engaged him in bitterest conflict with the adherents of Judaism. He taught in the synagogue of the Libertines (i.e., freedmen) and there debated with Jews of the Dispersion from Cyrene, Alexandria, Cilicia, and Asia. When it was evident that they could not refute Stephen's arguments in open debate, these Jews hired informers to misrepresent his arguments. They went around proclaiming, "This fellow never stops speaking against this holy place and against the law. For we have heard him say that this Jesus of Nazareth will destroy this place and change the customs Moses handed down to us" (6:13–14). These accusations were such that the council could be assured of the support of the people of Jerusalem. Since they were largely dependent on the temple for their livelihood, any threat to it constituted a threat to them.

Acts 7 records Stephen's remarkable *apologia* before the council. F. F. Bruce rightly points out that it was "not a speech for the defense in the forensic sense of the term. Such a speech as this was by no means calculated to secure an acquittal before the Sanhedrin. It is rather a defense of pure Christianity as God's appointed way of worship" (*The Book of Acts* [NINTC], 1956, p. 141). Stephen's exclamation at the close of his speech is particularly important to a proper understanding of it: "Look . . . I see heaven open and the Son of Man standing at the right hand of God" (7:56). This is the only occurrence of the title "Son of Man" in the NT on the lips of anyone other than Jesus himself. It reveals that *"Stephen grasped and asserted the more-than-Jewish-Messianic sense in which the office and significance of Jesus in religious history were to be understood,"* (William Manson, *The Epistle to the Hebrews,* 1951, p. 31).

Such radical thinking was too much for the listening Sanhedrin. "They covered their ears and, yelling at the top of their voices, they . . . dragged him out of the city and began to stone him." The witnesses, whose responsibility it was to cast the first stones (cf. Deut 17:7), laid their clothes at Saul's feet (Acts 7:57–58). WWW

STEPS (See STAIRS)

STEWARD (See OCCUPATIONS AND PROFESSIONS)

STOCK, STOCKS. 1. In the KJV the bole of a tree was a stock and was worshiped by apostate Israel (Isa 44:19; Jer 2:27; Hos 4:12).

2. In the KJV a family (Lev 25:47; Isa 40:24; Phil 3:5). Children of the stock of Abraham were appealed to by Paul in Antioch (Acts 13:26). Paul was proud of being of the Hebrew stock (Phil 3:5).

3. An instrument of punishment. There were various kinds. One was a mechanism by which the body was twisted into an unnatural position and thus made to endure excruciating agony (Jer 20:2–3). Madmen, posing as prophets, were put on the rack (29:26). Paul and Silas were put in stocks to make sure they did not escape from prison in Philippi (Acts 16:24).

STOICISM (stō'ĭ-sĭzm). Although the influence of Stoicism on the NT writers was apparently next to negligible (cf. Morton Scott Enslin, *The Ethics of Paul,* pp. 14–44), this school of philosophy is of interest to Bible readers because Paul encountered it in Athens (Acts 17:18). Boasting a galaxy of distinguished exponents, both Greek and Roman—e.g., Zeno, Cleanthes, Seneca, Cicero, Epictetus, and Marcus Aurelius—Stoicism was a system of pantheistic monism. It held that fire is the ultimate substance with God, the active principle of the cosmos, permeating everything as a sort of soul. Nature, it taught, is a hierarchical unity controlled by the universal Logos, an impersonal reason at once immanent and divine. As participant in the Logos, man is also participant in deity. Indeed, the true essence of humanity is *nous* or mind, the capacity to understand the rational order veiled by phenomena. As a logos-being, man can perceive and assent to the determinism that makes all events necessary and therefore reduces evil to mere appearance. By assenting to this determinism—indifferently called fate or providence—man is able to live in harmony with nature. Hence the Stoic ethic is egocentrically negative. Nothing lies within man's power except imagination, desire, and emotion; thus by cultivating not only detachment from the world outside him but also mastery over his reactions to the world's impingement on himself, the philosopher achieves freedom, happiness, and self-sufficiency. Impressively noble and lofty when practiced by, say, a Marcus Aurelius, Stoicism was aristocratic and austere, rigorously excluding pity, denying pardon, and suppressing genuine feeling. Its view of sin was hopelessly shallow, since it did not think in terms of obedience to a personal God. Sin was simply an error of judgment, easily rectified by a change of opinion. But among its virtues were cosmopolitanism and egalitarianism. Whatever his position or handicap, any man, Stoicism affirmed, even a slave like Epictetus, can be inwardly free. Moreover, as partakers of a common rational nature, people everywhere are subject to the same law. Implicit in Stoicism, accordingly, was the idea of a universal morality rooted in the universal Logos. VCG

STONE (Heb. *'even,* Gr. *lithos*). When entering Canaan, the Hebrews, who had made bricks in Egypt (Exod 5:7), readily turned to the abundant supply of stones, both from quarries and from stream beds. Limestone (Isa 27:9), gravel (Lam 3:16), and stones rounded by water in streams (1 Sam 17:40; Job 14:19) were abundant.

Large flat slabs were used as covers for wells (Gen 29:2–10), doors for caves (Josh 10:18), and for burial caves (Matt 27:60). Stones were also used as landmarks (2 Sam 20:8). The stones mentioned in Deuteronomy 19:14; 27:17; and Proverbs 22:28 were boundary stones (see Josh 15:16; 1 Kings 1:9). Great stones were used in

A well-preserved buried cave in the Adullam region, with a rolling stone at the entrance, second-third century. The city of Adullam figures prominently in the history of Israel from the days of Joshua, when it was a Canaanite royal city-state, to at least the time of Judas Maccabaeus, who retired to the city in 163 B.C. Courtesy Zev Radovan.

the foundation of the temple (1 Kings 6:7). The palace for the pharaoh's daughter was of high-grade stone (7:8–12). One may today see samples of Israelite stonework in the Wailing Wall of Jerusalem. A stone from the city wall is fourteen feet (four and one-half m.) long and three and three-quarter feet (over one m.) high and wide. Remains of quarries in many places of the land show how widespread the use of stone was in ancient times.

Stones were used in setting up altars and memorials. These objects were of various kinds: monuments, tables, steles or upright slabs, and circular areas enclosed by rocks. After Joshua had led the Hebrews over Jordan he set up a monument composed of twelve stones taken from the river's bed by representatives of the twelve tribes (Josh 4:1–9). Jacob set up a monument to commemorate his experience at Bethel (Gen 28:18). His contract with Laban was sealed by a stele (31:45–46). The miraculous victory over the Philistines called for a memorial (1 Sam 7:5–12). A heap of stones was placed over one who was executed by stoning, as over the king of Ai (Josh 8:29) and over Absalom (2 Sam 18:17–18). Joshua's last official act was to erect a memorial to Israel's covenant with God (Josh 24:26–28).

Stone weapons were frequently used by the Israelites. The familiar account of David's victory over the giant of Gath reveals the skill of one who had mastered the use of the sling (1 Sam 17). Among David's warriors were some who could sling stones (1 Chron 12:2). King Uzziah included in his arsenal stones for slingers and for catapults (2 Chron 26:14–15). Stones were used in individual conflict (Exod 21:18; Num 35:17–23). Certain crimes were punished by stoning (Lev 20:2, 27; 24:23).

The transition from using an object *in* worship to making it an object *of* worship is never difficult. So Israel was prone to worship stones. Among other pagan evils Isaiah found libations being offered to river stones (Isa 57:3–7). The law prohibited any such use of stones (Lev 26:1).

Figurative uses of the word *stone* are frequent in Hebrew writings: Egyptians sank like stones (Exod 15:5); God's arm could make his enemies still as stones (15:16); Nabal's fear petrified him (1 Sam 25:37); Job spoke of ice as stone (Job 38:30). The hard heart is like stone (Ezek 11:19), but God has power to change stony hearts into hearts of flesh (Matt 3:9). Jesus gave a new name to Simon (*Petros,* "a little stone") as an indication of the character that this apostle would have in the days ahead (John 1:42). God is the stone of Israel (Gen 49:24; Dan 2:34). The messianic kingdom is a stone that will crush the kingdoms of men (Dan 2:34; Matt 21:44). Jesus Christ is the stone the builders rejected (Ps 118:22; Matt 21:42). Paul presented Jesus as the chief cornerstone of the new dispensation (Eph 2:20–22).

Remains of storehouses at Tell Beersheba from the Israelite period. They contained an abundance of pottery of various types including cooking pots, bowls and other vessels. Courtesy Zev Radovan.

Believers are living stones in God's temple (1 Peter 2:5–8). JDF

STONES, PRECIOUS (See MINERALS)

STONING. The ordinary form of capital punishment prescribed by Hebrew law. Stoning was the penalty for blasphemy (Lev 24:16), idolatry (Deut 13:6–10), desecration of the Sabbath (Num 15:32–36), human sacrifice (Lev 20:2), and occultism (20:27). Achan and his family were stoned because of his treachery to Israel (Josh 7:16–26). Jesus rebuked Jerusalem for stoning prophets (Matt 23:37; Luke 13:34). Stephen was stoned (Acts 7:58–59). Executions by stoning took place outside the city (Lev 24:14; 1 Kings 21:10, 13; Acts 7:58).

STOOL. A three or four-legged seat, used already in ancient times. The Shunammite woman put one in Elisha's room (2 Kings 4:10 KJV; NIV "chair"). A stool of peculiar form was used in Egypt for women in childbirth (Exod 1:16).

STORE CITIES. Supply depots for provisions and arms. Solomon built some in a region given to his Egyptian wife by Pharaoh (1 Kings 9:15–19; 2 Chron 8:4–6). Some were captured by Ben-Hadad (2 Chron 16:4) and restored by Jehoshaphat (17:12).

STOREHOUSE. A place for keeping treasures, supplies, and equipment. Obedience to the Lord was rewarded with full storehouses (Deut 28:8 KJV). Joseph stored grain in storehouses in Egypt against the coming famine (Gen 41:56). Hezekiah had many treasures in his storehouses and willingly showed them to visitors (2 Kings 20:13). The temple storehouse was a vital link in Hebrew worship and was always guarded (1 Chron 26:15–17; Mal 3:10).

STORK (See BIRDS)

STOVE. In Palestine the stove was usually made of clay. Some were small portable fireplaces, burning charcoal. Others were built outside the house and were heated with dry sticks, grass, and even dung. The hearth or firepot mentioned in Jeremiah 36:22 was a bronze heater. Only the well-to-do could afford a brazier. For cooking, the stove was molded so as to hold the pot or pan above the fire bowl through which air passed from vents at the bottom. The fire by which Peter warmed himself during the trial of Jesus was probably in a brazier (Mark 14:67).

STRAIGHT STREET. A name given to any route extending in a straight course across a city. Most streets were narrow and crooked. The avenue that ran through Damascus, one hundred feet (thirty-one m.) wide with a walk along each side, was called Straight (Acts 9:11).

STRANGER (Heb. *gēr, sojourner, stranger, tôshāv, sojourner, nokhrî, ben nēkhar, foreigner, zār,* *stranger*). A *gēr* or *tôshāv* was a foreigner who put himself under the protection of Israel and of Israel's God. He submitted to many requirements of the law of Israel and was therefore given certain privileges not accorded to the *nokhrî* and the *zār*, who were also called strangers. The *gēr* was allowed to rest on the Sabbath and was supposed to be treated kindly (Exod 20:10; 22:21; 23:9, 12). He was classed with the Levite, the fatherless, and the widow (Deut 14:21, 29; 16:11; 26:11–13). He offered sacrifices to the Lord and was expected to observe various ceremonial and other requirements (Lev 17:10ff.; 18:26; 20:2; 24:16–22). The *nokhrî* was a foreigner who did not have religious fellowship with Israel, since his allegiance was claimed by another people and another deity. He was forbidden to enter the sanctuary (Ezek 44:7–9), and interest could be exacted from him (Deut 15:3; 23:20). The *zār* was not necessarily a foreigner. Its meaning may be determined from the context. It is often used of foreigners as people entirely different from, or even hostile to, Israel (Isa 1:7; Ezek 11:9).

STRANGLE (Heb. *hānaq*, Gr. *pnigō, to choke*). To deprive of life by choking, and so without bloodshed. Israelites were forbidden to eat flesh from strangled animals because it contained the blood of the animals (Lev 17:12). At the Jerusalem Council even Jewish Christians were forbidden to eat such meat (Acts 15:20). The prohibition against eating any meat with the blood still in it is a part of the covenant God made with Noah and has not been invalidated in the New Testament (Gen 9:3–5).

STREAM OF EGYPT (See EGYPT, RIVER OF)

STRINGED INSTRUMENTS (See MUSIC AND MUSICAL INSTRUMENTS)

STRIPES (Heb. *nākâh*, Gr. *plēgē*). Scourging by lashing was a common form of punishment in ancient times. The Jewish law authorized it for certain ecclesiastical offenses (Deut 25:2–3). Among the Jews a scourge consisting of three thongs was used, and the number of stripes varied from a few up to thirty-nine (to make sure that the law's limit of forty was not exceeded). When scourging took place in the synagogue, it was done by the overseer, but the Sanhedrin also administered such punishment (Acts 5:40). Roman scourges had pieces of metal or bones attached to the lashes. The victim was stripped to the waist and bound in a stooping position. The body was horribly lacerated so that often even the entrails were exposed.

STRONG DRINK (See WINE)

STRONGHOLD A place of refuge, a fortress. This can be a literal place, as in time of distress (Judg 6:2; 1 Sam 24:22), and figuratively, as in Psalm 27:1: "The LORD is the stronghold of my life."

STUBBLE (Heb. *qāsh, teven*, Gr. *kalamē*). The stalks of grain, usually about half of the stem, left standing after reaping. When the Hebrews made brick in Egypt, they had to gather this rather than use the straw from threshing floors that had previously been provided (Exod 5:10–14). The word became a simile for wayward Israel (Isa 47:14).

STUMBLING BLOCK (Heb. *mikshôl*, Gr. *skandalon*). Anything that causes a person to trip or fall or, figuratively, causes material or spiritual ruin. Israel's iniquity and idolatry were a stumbling block to her (Jer 18:15; Ezek 14:3–4). Paul forbade putting a stumbling block in a Christian's way (Rom 14:13; 1 Cor 8:9). Jesus, as preached by Paul (Rom 9:32), was a stumbling block to the Jews (1 Cor 1:23).

SUAH (sū'à, Heb. *sûah*). One of the descendants of Asher (1 Chron 7:36).

SUBMISSION (See OBEDIENCE)

SUBURB (Heb. *migrāsh, open land*). Used in the KJV for lands near cities used for pasturage of animals (e.g, Josh 21:2–42; Ezek 45:2). NIV reads "open land" or "pasturelands."

SUCATHITES (sū'kăth-īts). A native or inhabitant of Sucah, or Socah (1 Chron 2:55).

SUCCOTH (sŭk'ŏth, Heb. *sukkôth, booths* or *huts*). 1. A place east of the Jordan at which Jacob built a house for himself and shelters for his animals after his return from Mesopotamia (Gen 33:17). It was in the Jordan Valley, near Zarethan (1 Kings 7:46), and was assigned to the Gadites (Josh 13:27). Gideon punished the town severely for its refusal to assist him when he pursued Zebah and Zalmunna (Judg 8:5–16). It is probably to be identified with Tell Deir Alla, excavated by H. J. Franken between A.D. 1960 and 1964, but the identification is not certain. A number of sanctuaries were found of the Late Bronze period (1550–1200 B.C.), but no defensive walls. Three clay tablets in an unknown script were also found.

2. The first station of the Hebrews on leaving Rameses (Exod 12:37; 13:20; Num 33:5). The city is tentatively identified with a place near Jebel Mariyam on the west bank of Lake Timsah.

SUCCOTH BENOTH (sŭk'ŏth bē'nŏth, Heb. *sukkōth benôth*). A pagan god whose image was worshiped in Samaria after Assyria had captured it and put foreign rulers over it (2 Kings 17:24–30). It may be a title of Marduk, the guardian deity of Babylon.

SUKKITES, SUKKIIM (sŭk'īts, sŭk'ī-ĭm, Heb. *sukkîyîm*). A tribe of people whose warriors joined Shishak of Egypt when he invaded Judah (2 Chron 12:3). Their identity is uncertain.

SUKKOTH (See FEASTS)

SULFUR, SULPHUR (See BRIMSTONE; MINERALS)

Gold dagger and sheath found with belt in a grave at Ur in Sumer. The gold blade is inscribed with the mark of a craftsman or the owner. The hilt is of lapis lazuli studded with gold and the sheath of gold filigree work imitates an earlier reed pattern. C. 2500 B.C. Courtesy Iraq Museum.

SUMER (sū'mêr). One of the two political divisions, Sumer and Akkad, originally comprising Babylonia. Its principal cities were Nippur, Adab, Lagash, Umma, Larsa, Erech, Ur, and Eridu, most of which were on or near the Euphrates.

SUN (Heb. *shemesh, server, ôr, luminary, hammâh, hot body, heres, blistering,* Gr. *hēlios, sun*). The beneficent nature of the sun was known among the Hebrews. Sun, moon, and stars determine times and seasons (Gen 1:14; Jer 31:35). Night and day were "caused" by the sun (Gen 1:5). Since the location of the sun determined the extent of heat and light, the day was divided accordingly. Mid-morning was when the sun grew hot (1 Sam 11:9); noon was when it was brightest (Gen 43:16); beyond noon the heat waned and it was the cool of the day (3:8). Times and seasons were controlled by the "laws of the heavens" (Job 38:33; Ps 119:91). The sun also determined directions. The direction of the rising of the sun became east (Isa 45:6); the direction of its going down (Ps 50:1) became west. The left hand or darker quarter was north, and the right hand or brighter quarter south (Gen 13:14; Job 37:17; Ezek 40:24). The sun also made it possible for man to survive, for it produced fruits (Deut 33:14). Poetic fancies arose about the sun. It is like a bridegroom (Ps 19:4–5), stands in his house (Hab 3:11), is ever watchful (Ps 19:6), dependable (72:5), and tells of God's continuing care (84:11). The problem of astronomy created by the standing sun (Josh 10:13) and the returning sundial (2 Kings 20:11; Isa 38:8) may be answered, at least in part, by scientists' recent discoveries of these extra segments of time in the history of the universe. JDF

SUNDAY. The name Sunday is derived from pagan sources. Dividing the calendar into seven-day weeks was the work of Babylonian astrologers. From them the plan went into Egypt, where the days were named for planets, one for the sun. By 250 A.D. this method of reckoning time had become well established throughout the civilized world (Cassius, *Hist. of Rome,* 37:18). After Christianity had been planted in northern Europe, the Teutonic people substituted the names of their gods for Egyptian titles, so we have Tiwes-day (Tuesday), Woden's Day (Wednesday) and Thor's Day (Thursday). But the first day continued to be called Sun's Day, largely because Emperor Constantine by royal decree in 321 made it *Solis Day,* day of the sun.

No doubt Abraham learned about the seven-day week while in Ur. The revelation given to Moses about the order followed in creation (Gen 1) confirmed the teachings of Abraham. The

Sumerian cuneiform writing. Courtesy Trustees of the British Museum.

Sabbath thus became a vital part of the seven-day week. Jesus, by his example, led the Jewish converts to continue to observe the Sabbath (Matt 12:9; 13:54; Mark 6:2; Luke 4:16; John 6:59). But he also distinguished between the ritual-bound Sabbath of the Jews and the day God had sanctified for the welfare of man. He said he is the Lord of the Sabbath (Matt 12:1–8). He healed the sick on the Sabbath (12:10–13). Slavery to sabbatical regulations is not the will of God (Mark 2:27–28). In places where the Jews were numerous, their refusal to concede that one can be saved apart from observance of the Hebrew ritual led to grave controversy within the ranks of Christians, especially those in Antioch. From A.D. 200 on we find no mention by the church fathers of the observance of the seventh day as the time for Christian worship.

After the Resurrection (Luke 24:1; John 20:1), to celebrate the event. some of Jesus' appearances occurred on the first day of the week (Mark 16:9; John 20:19). The disciples in Troas worshiped on the first day (Acts 20:7). In his First Letter to the Corinthians, Paul admonished the Christians in Corinth to lay in store as God had prospered them, doing it week by week on the first day (1 Cor 16:2). Since the Greeks had no seven-day week at the time, one must infer that Paul had already let the Corinthians know that the first day is the Christian Sabbath. That he nowhere mentions the seventh day as a day for worship is evidence that it had been supplanted by the first day. The term *Lord's Day* occurs only in Revelation 1:10 and is a natural adaptation of a Roman custom of calling the first day of the month "Emperor's Day." By A.D. 150 the designation had been accepted throughout the Christian world. As the stronger Hebrew Christian churches declined in influence, the tendency to observe the Hebrew Sabbath slowly passed.

The early Christian writers confirm that the first day was taken as the Christian day of worship, and subsequent history proves that it supplanted the Hebrew Sabbath, even among the converts from Judaism. Justin Martyr, who lived during the second century A.D., wrote of the Lord's Day services. Ignatius, bishop of Antioch about 110, claimed that the day had supplanted the Jewish Sabbath. The Epistle of Barnabas, written in the second century, likewise supports the view that the Lord's Day had become the day for stated worship of Christians. The Roman historian Pliny wrote in 112 to Emperor Trajan, telling him how Christians in Bithynia met on a certain day before dawn to sing hymns to Christ as God. The Didache, or "The Teaching of the Lord to the Gentiles through the Twelve Apostles," gives a command for believers to come together on the Lord's Day. Undoubtedly Jewish persecution caused Christian Jews to abandon meeting in the synagogues on the Sabbath. Eventually, they met only on the Lord's Day to worship their Lord.

See also LORD'S DAY. JDF

SUPERSCRIPTION (sū'pêr-skrĭp'shŭn, Gr. *epigraphē, an inscription*—so RSV, NIV). 1. The wording on coins (Matt 22:20; Mark 12:16; Luke 20:24).

2. The words inscribed on a board attached to the cross (Mark 15:26; Luke 23:38). The Roman custom was to have such a board, naming the crime involved, carried before the condemned person to the place of execution. John 19:19–20 calls it a title (KJV, Gr. *titlos*; notice, sign NIV); according to Matthew 27:37, the written charge was placed above Jesus' head. Each Evangelist gives the wording as it impressed him, John the most fully, or perhaps it appeared in a slightly different form in each of the three languages in which it was written.

SUPERSTITIOUS (sū'pêr-stĭsh'ŭs). In Acts 17:22 Paul calls the Athenians *deisidaimonesterous* (extremely [uncommonly] scrupulous JB, NEB; too superstitious KJV; very religious ASV, NIV, RSV). Found only here in the NT, the Greek word is neutral, applying to any religion, good or bad. Paul used it in the comparative form ("more religious than most people"); he would not deliberately antagonize his hearers.

SUPH, SUPHAH (sūf, Heb. *sûph*). KJV has "the Red Sea" for both names. Suph (Deut 1:1, ASV, RSV, NIV) is the place in front of which Moses repeated the law to Israel. The sea (*yam sûph*) that the Israelites crossed in their flight from Egypt should be called the Reed Sea rather than the Red Sea. See RED SEA. Suphah (Num 21:14, ASV, RSV, NIV) is also east of Jordan. Neither place can be identified.

SUPPER, LORD'S (See LORD'S SUPPER)

SUPPLICATION (See PRAYER)

SURETY. 1. In the phrase "of a surety" meaning "surely," as the translation of various words (Gen 15:13; 18:13; 26:9; Acts 12:11, all KJV).

2. Also in the KJV relating to the giving of a pledge and a promise to give or do something if another fails; signified by "striking hands." Thus Judah remained in prison as surety that Benjamin would come to Joseph (Gen 43:9). Becoming surety for either a foreigner or a neighbor is consistently condemned in Proverbs (6:1–5; 11:15; 17:18; 20:16; 22:26; 27:13) as imperiling the assets and the peace of mind of the surety. Job, unable to find any human being to give him the needed assurance, asks God to be his surety (Job 17:3). Jesus, by his incarnation, life, death, resurrection, and ascension became the surety for the performance of all the promises of God relating to salvation and assurance in the new and better covenant (Heb 7:22). ER

SURFEITING (sûr'fĕt-ĭng, Gr. *kraipalē, a drinking-bout*). Overindulgence in eating or drinking, intoxication, a drunken headache (Luke 21:34 KJV). "Dissipation" (RSV, NIV) is a good translation.

SUSA (sū'sȧ, Heb. *shûshan*). A city of the

Babylonians probably named from the lilies that grow in this region in large numbers. It was famous in biblical history as one of the capitals of the Persian Empire (Neh 1:1; Esth 1:2; Dan 8:2) during the time of Darius the Great. Here also Persian kings came to reside for the winter, and here Daniel had a vision (Dan 8:1–14; see v. 2). The Hebrews called this place "Shushan" (so KJV). It was located in the fertile valley on the left bank of the Choaspes River called the Ulai Canal in Daniel 8:2, 16. It enjoyed a very delightful climate. Many Jews lived here and became prominent in the affairs of the city as the Books of Esther and Nehemiah show. From this city was sent the group who replaced those removed from Samaria (Ezra 4:9).

In the last part of the nineteenth century the French carried on extensive excavations at Susa directed by Dieulafoy. This archaeological effort uncovered the great palace of King Xerxes (KJV Ahasuerus, 486–465 B.C.) in which Queen Esther lived.

SUSANNA (Heb. *shôshannâh*, Gr. *Sousanna, lily*). One of the women who went with Jesus and the Twelve on their missionary journeys and supported them out of their own means (Luke 8:1–3).

SUSANNA, THE HISTORY OF (See APOCRYPHA)

SUSI (sū'sī, Heb. *sûsî*). A Manassite, father of Gaddi, one of the twelve men sent to spy out the land (Num 13:11).

SWADDLING BAND (Heb. *hăthullâh*, Gr. *spargana*). Strips of cloth (so NIV) in which a newborn baby was wrapped. The child was placed diagonally on a square piece of cloth, which was folded over the infant's feet and sides. Around this bundle bands of cloth were wound. Mary herself wrapped the baby Jesus in swaddling bands (Luke 2:7, 12 KJV). For a figurative use, see Job 38:9.

SWALLOW (See BIRDS)

SWAN (See BIRDS)

SWARMING THING (See ANIMALS)

SWEAR (See OATH)

SWEAT (Heb. *zē'âh*, Gr. *hidrōs*). After the Fall, God told Adam that he would have to work hard enough to cause sweat in order to get his food (Gen 3:19). Priests in the future temple are not to wear anything that causes them to perspire (Ezek 44:18).

SWEAT, BLOODY. A physical manifestation of the agony of Jesus in Gethsemane (Luke 22:44). Ancient and modern medicine has documented cases of blood extravasated from the capillaries mingling with and coloring the sweat, under severe stress of emotion. See under DISEASES.

Glazed relief of a winged bull from the palace of King Xerxes at Susa (Shushan), Archaemenid period, fourth century B.C. Queen Esther lived in this palace. Courtesy Réunion des Musées Nationaux.

SWIFT (See BIRDS)

SWINE (See ANIMALS)

SWORD (See ARMS AND ARMOR)

SYCAMINE (See PLANTS)

SYCAMORE, SYCOMORE (See PLANTS)

SYCHAR (sī'kår, Gr. *Sychar*). A village of Samaria located near Jacob's well, where Jesus met the Samaritan woman (John 4:5). It was situated on the main road that led from Jerusalem through Samaria to Galilee. No mention is made of it in the OT, but there is a Suchar or Sichar referred to in the rabbinical writings. Sychar is most often identified with the modern Askar, though the identification is not certain. It is situated close to Shechem (with which it has often been incorrectly identified) and on the eastern slope of Mount Ebal. The site, which by continuous tradition has been identified with Jacob's well, lies about half a mile (about one km.) to the south. In Jesus' day Sychar was only a small village.

SYCHEM (See SHECHEM)

SYENE (See ASWAN)

SYMBOL. That which stands for or represents something else; a visible sign or representation of an idea or quality or of another object. Symbolism in its religious application means that an object, action, form, or words or whatever else is involved has a deeper spiritual meaning than a simple literal interpretation might suggest. A symbol, unlike a type, is usually not prefigurative but rather represents something that already exists. The Passover, however, was both symbolical and typical, and the symbolic actions of the OT prophets were often predictive in nature.

I. Interpretation of Symbols. The literature of

all the peoples of the world contains symbols. Symbolism was particularly attractive to the Oriental mind. Thus the Bible contains many symbols. Some parts of Scripture, of course, contain more (e.g., the prophetic literature and apocalyptic books) than others. The interpretation of these symbols presents a formidable problem to the student of the Word of God.

Symbols and their meanings arise out of the culture of the peoples that use them. The more remote and obscure the culture, the more difficult the interpretation of the symbols. Bernard Ramm (*Protestant Biblical Interpretation,* 1956, pp. 214–15) suggests the following general rules for the interpretation of symbols:

1. *Those symbols interpreted by the Scriptures are the foundation for all further studies in symbolism.* The Book of Revelation interprets many of its symbols, e.g., the bowls of incense are the prayers of the saints (Rev 5:8), the great dragon is Satan (12:9), the waters are peoples, multitudes, nations, and tongues (17:15). When the Bible interprets its own symbols, we are on sure ground and can often find the same symbols used elsewhere in Scripture in the same or at least similar ways.

2. *If the symbol is not interpreted:* (1) We should investigate the context thoroughly. (2) By means of a concordance we can check other passages that use the same symbol and see if such cross references will give the clue. (3) Sometimes we may find that the nature of the symbol is a clue to its meaning (although the temptation to read the meanings of our culture into these symbols must be resisted). (4) Sometimes we will find that comparative studies of Semitic culture reveal the meaning of a symbol.

3. *Beware of double imagery in symbols.* Not all symbols in the Bible have one and only one meaning. The lion is a symbol both for Christ ("the Lion of the tribe of Judah") and for the devil (1 Peter 5:8). Some entities or persons have more than one symbol to represent them—e.g., Christ (the lion, the lamb, and the branch) and the Holy Spirit (water, oil, wind, and the dove).

II. Symbolism of Numbers. It is evident that certain numbers in the Bible have symbolical significance, some being particularly important. *Seven,* probably the most important number in Scripture (it occurs about six hundred times), has been called the sacred number par excellence. In the literature of ancient Babylonia it is the number of totality or completeness. To speak of the seven gods is to speak of all the gods. This seems to be its primary symbolical meaning in Scripture (cf. the seven creative days in Gen 1), although M. S. Terry thinks that it symbolizes "some mystical union of God with the world, and accordingly, may be called the sacred number of the covenant between God and his creation" (*Biblical Hermeneutics,* 2d ed., n.d., p. 382). The Book of Revelation makes frequent use of the number seven. There are seven churches (Rev 1:4), spirits (1:4), lampstands (1:12–13), stars (1:16), lamps (4:5), seals (5:1; 8:1), horns and eyes (5:6), trumpets (8:2), thunders (10:3), heads of the great dragon (12:3), angels with plagues (15:1), vials (15:7), heads of the beast (13:1), mountains (17:9), and kings (17:10). *Three* appears to be symbolical of "several," "a few," "some," although at times it means "many" or "enough." Terry thinks that it is the number of divine fullness in unity (ibid., p. 381). The three persons of the Trinity particularly suggest this symbolical meaning. *Four* in the Bible seems to stand for completeness, especially in relation to range or extent. Thus there are four winds (Jer 49:36; Ezek 37:9); four directions; four corners of a house (Job 1:19), of the land of Israel (Ezek 7:2), and of the whole earth (Isa 11:12). *Ten,* since it is the basis of the decimal system, is also a significant number. In the Bible it is often a round number of indefinite magnitude. *Twelve* seems to be the mystical number of the people of God. The twelve tribes, twelve apostles, and the twelve thousand times twelve thousand sealed in the Book of Revelation bear out this symbolical meaning. *Forty* is the round number for a generation and also appears to be symbolical of a period of judgment (cf. the forty days of the Flood, the forty years of wilderness wandering, and the forty days and nights of Jesus' temptation).

Of special interest is the mysterious number 666 in the Book of Revelation (13:18). This may be an example of Jewish *Gematria,* i.e., the art of attaching values to names according to the combined numerical value of the letters composing them. The numerical value of *Neron Kaesar* in Hebrew is 666. However, M. Tenney points out that "the usual spelling of Caesar must be changed in order to fit the explanation—a device which makes the interpretation dependent upon it at least suspicious" (*Interpreting Revelation,* 1957, p. 19).

III. Symbolism of Colors. Since color differentiations were not as exact in the ancient world as they are in modern times, it is difficult to identify biblical colors precisely. As an example, Ramm cites the use of the Latin word *purpureus,* which "was used to describe snow, the swan, the foam of the sea, a rose, a beautiful human eye, and purple objects" (*Protestant Biblical Interpretation*, p. 218). Particularly difficult are the Hebrew words translated blue, purple, and scarlet. No unanimity of opinion exists among biblical scholars with regard to the symbolical meaning of colors. Much care must be taken, therefore, in seeking to assign symbolic meanings to colors. The following are suggestions: *White,* the color of light, is a symbol of purity, holiness, and righteousness (Rev 7:14). *Blue* is difficult, but perhaps Terry is right when he says that "blue, as the color of the heaven, reflected in the sea, would naturally suggest that which is heavenly, holy and divine" (*Biblical Hermeneutics*, p. 393). *Scarlet,* since it was most often the dress of kings, is regarded as symbolic of royalty. *Black,* the opposite of white, would naturally be associated with evil, such as famine (Rev 6:5–6) or mourning (Jer 14:2). *Red* is symbolic of bloodshed and war (Rev 6:4; 12:3).

IV. Symbolic Actions. Not only objects,

names, numbers, and colors are symbolic in Scripture, but actions too may be symbolic. Symbolic actions often are prefigurative and are especially associated with the OT prophets. H. L. Ellison points out that "behind these actions lie the deep convictions of more primitive men that words and actions are significant, and that by doing something similar to what you prophesy, you are helping forward the fulfilment and making it more certain" (*Ezekiel, the Man and His Message,* 1956, p. 32). Ellison does not mean that the prophets necessarily believed this but that it made their message more impressive. Such symbolical actions by the prophets are found as early as Samuel's day. When Saul took hold of Samuel's robe and tore it, this was understood by Samuel to be symbolic of the tearing away of Saul's kingdom (1 Sam 15:27–28). By tearing his own garment into twelve pieces Ahijah symbolized the breakup of the kingdom of Solomon (1 Kings 11:29–30; cf. also 2 Kings 13:14–19; 22:11). Symbolic action is especially frequent in the prophecies of Jeremiah and Ezekiel. Jeremiah's smashing of the pot before the elders of the people and the senior priests in the Valley of Ben Hinnom was clearly understood by the people, as their subsequent reaction shows (Jer 19). Symbolic action was involved in Ezekiel's call to the prophetic office when the Lord commanded him to eat the scroll, inscribed on the front and back with words of lamentation and mourning and woe (Ezek 2:9–10). Ezekiel was not only thereby informed of the content of his message but also made aware of the importance of assimilating it. Many of Ezekiel's symbolic actions were calculated to gain a hearing for the message God had given him to proclaim. This was particularly true of his drawing on a clay tablet the siege of Jerusalem (Ezek 4:1–4). Ellison pointedly remarks, "We can easily understand . . . the excitement in Tel-Abib as the news went round that Ezekiel, who had not been seen outside the house for days, was acting in a way calculated to bring disaster to Jerusalem" (ibid., p. 33).

Jesus also used symbolical actions to convey spiritual truth. While all the Gospels attest to our Lord's symbolical actions, the author of the fourth Gospel places special stress on them. He calls Jesus' miracles "signs" (*sēmeia*). Tenney has pointed out that the verb form of this word (*sēmainein*) "evidently meant a kind of communication that is neither plain statement nor an attempt at concealment. It is figurative, symbolic, or imaginative, and is intended to convey truth by picture rather than definition" (*Interpreting Revelation*, p. 186). When in the fourth Gospel Jesus multiplies the loaves, this is symbolic of the fact that he is himself the Bread of Life (John 6). The blind man healed is symbolic of Christ as the Light of the world (John 9), and Lazarus's being raised from the dead is symbolic of Jesus as the Resurrection and the Life (John 11).

Bibliography: In addition to the books cited in the above article, see G. Cope, *Symbolism in the Bible and the Church,* 1955; and F. W. Dillistone, *Christianity and Symbolism,* 1955. WWW

SYNAGOGUE (Gr. *synagōgē, place of assembly*). A Jewish institution for the reading and exposition of the Holy Scriptures. It originated perhaps as early as the Babylonian exile. It is supposed that the synagogue had its precursor in the spontaneous gatherings of the Jewish people in the lands of their exile on their day of rest and also on special feast days. Since religion stood at the very center of Jewish existence, these gatherings naturally took on a religious significance. The Jews of the Exile needed mutual encouragement in the faithful practice of their religion and in the hope of a restoration to the land. These they sought and found in spontaneous assemblies, which proved to be of such religious value that they quickly spread throughout the lands of the Dispersion. G. F. Moore thinks that elements of the later synagogue service originated in the things that would have been most natural for the people to do and say under such circumstances (*Judaism,* 1927, 1:283).

No specific mention of a synagogue occurs in pre-Christian writings, with the possible exception of Psalm 74:8: "They burned every place where God was worshiped ['meeting places' RSV] in the land." This is a late psalm, possibly belonging to the Persian era.

From about the second century B.C. onward, the sect of the Pharisees assumed a leading role in the synagogues. It was an institution peculiarly adapted to achieve their ends. Moore says that "through it, more perhaps than by any other means, they gained the hold upon the mass of the people which enabled them to come out victorious from their conflicts with John Hyrcanus and Alexander Jannaeus and to establish such power as Josephus ascribes to them" (ibid., 2:287).

By NT times the synagogue was a firmly established institution among the Jews, who considered it to be an ancient institution, as the words of James in Acts 15:21 show: "For Moses has been preached in every city from the earliest times and is read in the synagogues on every Sabbath." Josephus, Philo, and later Judaism traced the synagogue back to Moses. While this, of course, has no historical validity, it does reveal that Judaism regarded the synagogue as one of its basic institutions.

In the first Christian century synagogues could be found everywhere in the Hellenistic world where there were sufficient Jews to maintain one. In large Jewish centers there might be numbers of them. However, the 480 synagogues claimed by the Jerusalem Talmud (*Megillah* 73 d) for Jerusalem must be taken with a grain of salt!

I. Purpose. The chief purpose of the synagogue was not public worship, but instruction in the Holy Scriptures. The very nature of Judaism, a religion of revelation, demanded such an institution to survive. For the Jews "it was not to be imagined that a man or a people could be righteous without knowing God's holy character, and what was right in his eyes and what was wrong. And if God had revealed these things, plainly revelation was the place to go to learn them" (ibid., 1:282). All of the rabbis emphasized

Ruins of the ancient synagogue at Capernaum, with a row of Corinthian capitals shown in foreground. Below, a reconstruction of the synagogue façade. Courtesy Zev Radovan (photo) and Carta, Jerusalem (drawing).

the importance of knowing the law. Hillel taught: "An ignorant man cannot be truly pious" (*Aboth* 2.5) and, "The more teaching of the law, the more life; the more school, the more wisdom; the more counsel, the more reasonable action. He who gains a knowledge of the law gains life in the world to come" (*Aboth* 2.14). The destiny of both the nation and the individual was dependent on the knowledge of the law. It was the explicit purpose of the synagogue to educate the whole people in the law.

How effectively the synagogue, along with the school, fulfilled this purpose is to be seen (1) from the survival of Judaism, especially in the Dispersion despite the pressures of pagan influences; (2) from the thorough Judaistic nature of Galilee in the first century, which in the time of Simon Maccabeus was largely pagan; and (3) from the knowledge of the Scriptures, which the apostle Paul assumes of his hearers in the Hellenistic synagogues.

II. Officials. Although there might be more in some of the larger synagogues, there were always at least two officials. The Ruler of the Synagogue (Heb. *ro'sh ha-keneseth,* Gr. *archisynagōgos*) was probably elected by the elders of the congregation. He was responsible for (1) the building and property; (2) the general oversight of the public worship, including the maintenance of order (cf. Luke 13:14); (3) the appointing of persons to read the Scriptures and to pray; and (4) the inviting of strangers to address the congregation (Acts 13:15). Generally there was only one ruler for each synagogue, but some synagogues had more (13:15).

The minister or attendant (Heb. *ḥazzān,* Gr. *hypēretēs,* cf. Luke 4:20) was a paid officer whose special duty was the care of the synagogue building and its furniture, in particular the rolls of Scripture. During the worship it was the *ḥazzān* who brought forth the roll from the chest and handed it to the appointed reader. He also returned it to its proper place at the conclusion of the reading (4:20). He had numerous other duties, which included the instruction of children in reading, the administration of scourgings, and the blowing of three blasts on the trumpet from the roof of the synagogue to announce the beginning and end of the Sabbath. Since his work was closely associated with the synagogue building and its equipment, he sometimes lived under its roof.

III. Building and Furniture. Synagogue buildings varied greatly. They were usually built of stone and lay north and south, with the entrance at the south end. Their size and elegance were largely determined by the numerical strength and prosperity of the Jewish communities in which they were built. The principal items of furniture were (1) a chest in which the rolls of Scripture were kept, wrapped in linen cloth; (2) a platform or elevated place on which a reading desk stood; (3) lamps and candelabra, trombones and trumpets; and (4) benches on which the worshipers sat.

IV. Worship. The congregation was separated, the men on one side and the women on the other. The more prominent members took the front seats. The service began with the recitation of the Jewish confession of faith, the *Shema'*: "Hear, O Israel: The LORD our God, the LORD is one. Love the LORD your God with all your heart and with all your soul and with all your strength" (Deut 6:4–5). This was both preceded and followed by thanksgivings, two before and one after the morning *Shema'*, and two both before and after the evening *Shema'*. The first of the two that preceded both morning and evening *Shema'* reads: "Blessed art thou, O Lord our God, King of the world, former of light and creator of darkness, author of welfare (peace), and creator of all things."

After the *Shema'* came the prayer (*Tefillah*). The Ruler of the Synagogue could call on any adult male of the congregation to say this prayer. The person praying usually stood before the chest of the rolls of Scriptures. The oldest form of the *Tefillah* consisted of a series of ascriptions or petitions, each of which ended in the benedictory response: "Blessed art thou, O Lord." About the close of the first century an arrangement was made in which there were eighteen of these

Reconstruction of the façade of the third century synagogue at Korazin (Chorazin). The structure, made of basalt, is similar in style to that found at Capernaum, with the façade characteristically on the side nearest Jerusalem. Courtesy L. Ritmeyer.

prayers, from which the name "The Eighteen" (*Shemoneh 'Esreh*) was derived, a name that was maintained even when a nineteenth prayer was added. Prayers 1–3 were in praise of God; 4–16 were petitions; and 17–19 were thanksgivings. On Sabbaths and festival days only the first three and last three were recited. A single prayer was substituted for the intervening thirteen petitions, so that the total prayer consisted of seven parts. On New Year's, however, three prayers were substituted for the thirteen.

The Scripture lesson that followed the *Tefillah* could be read by any member of the congregation, even children. The only exception was that at the Feast of Purim a minor was not allowed to read the Book of Esther. If priests or Levites were present in the worship service, they were given precedence. The readers usually stood while reading (cf. Luke 4:16).

Prescribed lessons out of the Pentateuch for special Sabbaths were established early. For other Sabbaths the reader himself chose the passage, but subsequently all the Pentateuchal readings became fixed. Sections, called *sedarim,* were established in order to complete the reading of the Pentateuch within a prescribed time. Babylonian Jews divided the Pentateuch into 154 sections and thus completed reading it in three years, whereas Palestinian Jews read it through once every year.

A lesson from the Prophets immediately followed the reading from the Pentateuch. This custom is mentioned as early as the Mishnah and was practiced in NT times. When Jesus came to his hometown of Nazareth and entered the synagogue, he stood up to read (Luke 4:16ff.). The book of the prophet Isaiah was given to him, and when he opened the book, he read. It is not clear from this account whether or not Jesus himself chose the portion. He may have, because the readings from the Prophets were not fixed, and either the ruler of the synagogue or the reader could choose them. The prophetical lessons were usually considerably shorter than those from the Pentateuch and have been likened to texts rather than Scripture lessons. Translations often accompanied both readings. In Palestine the Scriptures were read in Hebrew, accompanied by an extemporaneous and free translation in Aramaic, one verse at a time for the Law, three at a time for the Prophets.

The sermon followed the reading from the Prophets (cf. Acts 13:15 where it is called a "message of encouragement," *logos paraklēseōs*). That this was an important part of the synagogue service is revealed by the many references to teaching in the synagogue in the NT (Matt 4:23; Mark 1:21; 6:2; Luke 4:15; 6:6; 13:10; John 6:59; 18:20). The preacher usually sat (Luke 4:20), but the Acts account has Paul standing (Acts 13:16). No single individual was appointed to do the preaching. Any competent worshiper might be invited by the ruler to bring the sermon for the day (Luke 4:16–17; Acts 13:15). The importance of the "freedom of the synagogue," as this custom was called, to the propagation of the gospel can scarcely be overemphasized. Jesus constantly went into the synagogues to teach, and everywhere Paul went he searched out the synagogue. This was not only that he might preach the Good News to his fellow countrymen but also to reach the God-fearers (*hoi sebomenoi, hoi phoboumenoi*). These were Gentiles who had become disillusioned with the old pagan religions and were attracted to Judaism because of its high ethical morality and its monotheistic faith. They were not proselytes. Certain requirements in order to attain that status, particularly circumcision, kept them out. But they were interested observers. Some even kept the Jewish holy days, observed eating regulations, and were tolerably conversant with the synagogue prayers and Scripture lessons. These God-fearers proved to be ready recipients of the gospel, and it was primarily to reach them that Paul often used the "freedom of the synagogue" to preach Christ.

The worship in the synagogue closed with a blessing that had to be pronounced by a priest and to which the congregation responded with an "Amen." If no priest was present, a prayer was substituted for the blessing.

The form of worship of the synagogue was adopted by both the Christian and Muslim religions, and that form in its general outline is to be found today in Jewish places of worship.

Bibliography: I. Abrahams, *Studies in Pharisaism and the Gospels,* vol. 1, 1917; E. L. Sukenik, *Ancient Synagogues in Palestine and Greece,* 1934; G. F. Moore, *Judaism,* 1937, 1:281–307; C. W. Dugmore, *The Influence of the Synagogue Upon the Divine Office,* 1944; I. Levy, *The Synagogue,* 1963.
WWW

SYNOPTICS (See GOSPELS)

SYNTYCHE (sĭn′tĭ-chē, Gr. *Syntychē,* fortunate). A prominent woman member of the church at Philippi who was having a disagreement with a fellow female Christian, Euodias. Paul, in his letter to that church, entreats these two women to "agree with each other in the Lord" (Phil 4:2).

SYRACUSE (sĭr′ȧ-kūs, Gr. *Syrakousai*). A town on the east coast of Sicily, Syracuse was the most important and prosperous Greek city on the island. It boasted two splendid harbors, which contributed substantially to its material prosperity. Corinthian and Dorian Greeks, led by Archias, founded the city in 734 B.C. The Athenians, at the height of their power (413), tried to take the city but were completely routed. In 212 Syracuse came under the control of Rome.

The Alexandrian ship in which Paul sailed from Malta to Puteoli put in at Syracuse for three days (Acts 28:12). Whether or not Paul went ashore during this time is not stated in the Acts account.

The Roman amphitheater at Syracuse. Partly rock-cut and partly built, it measures about 460 × 390 feet (140 × 119 m.) overall; the arena is 227 × 129 feet (69 × 39 m.). The amphitheater is situated southeast of the famous Greek theater. Courtesy Gerald Nowotny.

SYRIA (Heb. *'ărām,* Gr. *Syria*). An abbreviation of Assyria or possibly from the Babylonian *Suri,* the name of a district in northern Mesopotamia. Herodotus first applied the name Syria to the territory occupied by the Arameans, but this name was not popularized until the Hellenistic period. In the Hebrew Bible it is called *Aram,* after the Arameans, nomads from the Syro-Arabian desert who occupied the area in the twelfth century B.C.

I. Location and Area. The territory of Syria varied considerably, often had vague boundaries, and really never constituted a political unit. Generally speaking, it included the area south of the Taurus Mountains, north of Galilee and Bashan, west of the Arabian Desert, and east of the Mediterranean. This was a territory approximately 300 miles (500 km.) north to south and 50 to 150 miles (82 to 250 km.) east to west. The chief cities were Damascus, Antioch, Hama, Biblos, Aleppo, Palmyra, and Carchemish.

II. Topography. Two mountain ranges, both running north and south, constitute the most prominent topographical features. The eastern range includes Mount Hermon (over 9,000 ft. [2,813 m.] high); the western, Mount Casius and the Lebanon. Between these two ranges is the high plain called Coele Syria watered by the Jordan, Leontes, and Orontes rivers. To the east of Hermon flow the Abana and the Pharpar, while in the north of Syria there are tributaries of the Euphrates. The many rivers and good soil made Syria generally more prosperous than her neighbor to the south.

III. History. In the earliest period of its history Syria was dominated by Amorites, Hittites, Mitanni, and especially Egyptians. When, however, the sea peoples invaded Syria from the north in the twelfth century B.C., an opportunity was afforded the Semitic Aramean tribesmen of the desert to abandon their nomadic way of life and settle in the best areas of Syria. They had actually begun to infiltrate this area before the twelfth century, but had not had the chance to establish themselves.

The Arameans at the time of David and Solomon were divided into a number of small kingdoms, the principal ones being Aram of Damascus, Aram of Zobah, Aram Maacah, Aram of Beth Rehob, and Aram Naharaim. The strongest of these was Zobah, whose king Hadadezer David defeated in battle along with the Syrians of Damascus who came to Hadadezer's aid (2 Sam 8:3–7). David also subdued Aram Maacah (1 Chron 19:6–19), Aram of Beth Rehob (2 Sam 10:6), and Aram Naharaim ("Aram of the two rivers," translated "Mesopotamia" in RSV and "Northwest Mesopotamia" in the NIV footnote, 1 Chron 19:6).

Solomon was unable to hold David's gains in Syria, and the political and military weakness in Israel caused by the disruption afforded the Syrian kingdoms, particularly Damascus, opportunity to further strengthen themselves.

Asa king of Judah (911–876 B.C.) appealed to Syria for help against Baasha king of Israel (909–886). This resulted in an invasion of the

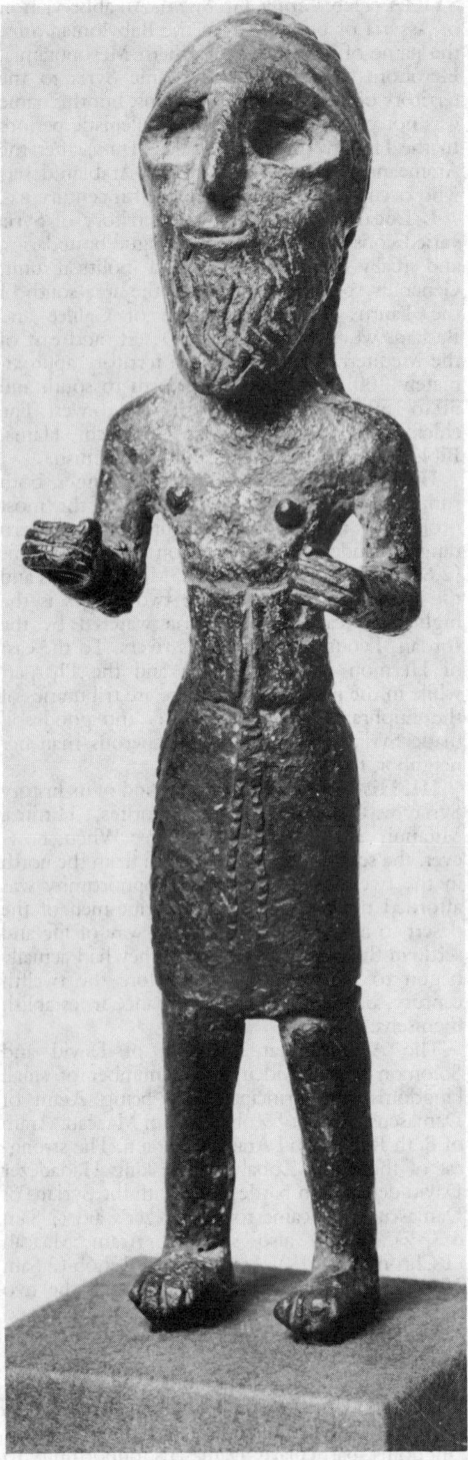

Sixteenth to fifteenth century B.C. bronze statuette from Sidon of a Syrian with full beard and wearing a simple kilt held by a broad belt at the waist. Courtesy Réunion des Musées Nationaux.

northern kingdom by Ben-Hadad I king of Damascus (1 Kings 15:16–21).

Omri (885–874 B.C.) of Israel, being faced with the growing power of Syria, strategically consummated an alliance with the Phoenicians by the marriage of his son Ahab to Jezebel, daughter of Ethbaal king of the Sidonians (1 Kings 16:31). Twice during Ahab's reign (874–853) the Syrians under Ben-Hadad I tried to invade Israel but were put to flight first at Samaria (20:1–21) and the following year at Aphek (20:26–34). Three years of peace with Syria followed. Then Ahab, in alliance with Jehoshaphat of Judah, made an attempt to recover Ramoth Gilead but was killed on the field of battle.

Jehoram of Israel (852–841 B.C.) allied himself with Ahaziah of Judah (852) to war against Ben-Hadad's successor, Hazael, and was wounded in battle at Ramoth Gilead (2 Kings 8:28–29).

During Jehu's reign (841–814 B.C.) Hazael captured the area east of the Jordan (2 Kings 10:32–33), and during the reign of Jehu's son Jehoahaz (814–798) he completely overran Israel and took numbers of its cities. These were retaken by Jehoash (798–782) from Hazael's successor, Ben-Hadad II (13:25). The successes of Jehoash were continued by his son Jeroboam II (782–753), who recovered all of the cities that had been taken by the Syrians from Israel over the years. He even successfully reduced Damascus (2 Kings 14:25–28).

Nothing is known of Syria from about 773 B.C. until the accession of Rezin in 750. During this time the Assyrian threat, which had been present already for a considerable time, was becoming progressively more real. To meet it, Rezin of Damascus and Pekah of Israel (740–732) formed a military alliance. In 735 or 736 they attacked Jerusalem (2 Kings 16:5; Isa 7:1), either to eliminate Judah as a possible foe or to force her into their coalition. Judah's king, Ahaz (735–715), had just come to the throne. He panicked and, despite the prophet Isaiah's warnings, sent for help from Assyria (Isa 7:1, 25). This apparently was just the excuse Tiglath-Pileser III needed to invade Syria-Palestine. He captured the Israelite cities in the territories of Dan and Naphtali (2 Kings 15:29) and took the people captive to Assyria. He then turned his attention to Damascus and in 732 subdued the city and brought an end to the Aramean state, something his predecessors had tried vainly to accomplish for over fifty years.

In subsequent years the Chaldeans and Egyptians fought over Syria and with the rise of the Persians it passed into their hands. The Battle of Issus (331 B.C.) brought Syria under the control of Alexander the Great. At his death it became the most important part of the Seleucid kingdom, which included large areas to the east, including Babylon. By the close of the second century, Syria, with Antioch as its capital, was all that was left of the kingdom of the Seleucids. In 64 the Romans made it a province and increased its area to include all the territory from Egypt to the

Taurus Mountains, and from the Mediterranean to the Euphrates.

Syria played a prominent part in the early church. It was at Antioch that the followers of Jesus were first called Christians (Acts 11:26). Paul was converted in Syria on the road to Damascus (9:1–9) and was commissioned with Barnabas by the Antioch church to take the gospel to the Gentiles.

Bibliography: R. T. O'Callaghan, *Aram Naharaim,* 1948; M. F. Unger, *Israel and the Arameans of Damascus,* 1957. WWW

SYRIAC, SYRIAK. The Syrian language. Once in KJV *'ărāmîth* is translated Syriak (Dan 2:4; Aramaic NIV), four times Syrian (2 Kings 18:26; Ezra 4:7; Isa 36:11; Aramaic NIV). Syriac is Eastern Aramaic, the literary language of the Christian Syrians. Early Syriac versions of the Bible are important for textual study (see TEXTS AND VERSIONS).

SYRIAN, SYRIANS (Heb. *'ărām,* Gr. *Syroi*). 1. The language of Syria (see SYRIAC).

2. The people of Syria (2 Sam 8:5); in earlier times, broadly the Arameans (Gen 25:20; 28:5; Deut 26:5). See also SYRIA.

SYROPHOENICIAN (sī'rō-fē-nĭsh'ăn, Gr. *Syrophoinikissa*). An inhabitant of the region near Tyre and Sidon, modern Lebanon. A Greek woman, born in Syrian Phoenicia, by persistence and humility won from Jesus healing for her daughter (Mark 7:26; cf. Matt 15:22).

SYRTIS (sûr'tĭs, Gr. *Syrtis*). The Syrtes (pl.) were the sandbars off the coast of Libya. The Greater Syrtis was located west of the Cyrene. When the northeaster hit the ship on which Paul was traveling, the sailors feared that they would be run aground on these sandbars (Acts 27:17).

T

Looking southward, a view of the ruin mound of Taanach, an important Canaanite stronghold situated in the Plain of Esdraelon. Courtesy Ecole Biblique et Archéologique Française, Jerusalem.

TAANACH (tā'á-năk, Heb. *ta' anak*). A fortified city of Canaan. Its king was defeated by Joshua, but the city was not occupied by the Israelites until later, when it was held by Manasseh (Josh 12:21; 17:11; Judg 1:27; 5:19; 1 Chron 7:29). Mentioned in the Amarna Letters and other Egyptian records. A ruin mound remains.

TAANATH SHILOH (tā'á-năth-shī'lō, Heb. *ta' ănath shilōh, approach to Shiloh*). A town on the NE border of the heritage of Ephraim (Josh 16:6). It was about ten miles (seventeen km.) east of Shechem and the same distance west of the Jordan River. Several large cisterns and ruins SE of Nablus are supposed to mark the site of the town.

TABALIAH (tăb-ă-lī'á, Heb. *tevalyahu*). A son of Hosah, a Merarite Levite, a gatekeeper of the tabernacle under David (1 Chron 26:11).

TABBAOTH (tă-bā'ŏth, Heb. *tabbā' ôth, rings*). A family of temple servants (KJV Nethinim) who returned to Jerusalem under Zerubbabel (Ezra 2:43; Neh 7:46).

TABBATH (tăb'áth, Heb. *tabbāth*). A place named in tracing the route of flight of the Midianites and their allies after Gideon's three hundred defeated them (Judg 7:22). If the current identification with a site east of the Jordan between Jabesh Gilead and Succoth is correct, the army must have crossed the Jordan in their flight.

TABEEL, TABEAL (tā'bē-ĕl, tā'bē-ăl). 1. The father of one of the allied kings whom Rezin of Damascus and Pekah of Israel attempted to make their puppet king of Judah (Isa 7:6).

2. An official in Samaria who complained to Artaxerxes about the activity of the Jews (Ezra 4:7).

TABERAH (tăb'ĕ-rá, Heb. *tav' ērâh, burning*). A place in the wilderness where the fire of the Lord burned some outlying parts of the camp of Israel

The mound of Taanach, showing excavated areas. Taanach remained an important Canaanite stronghold until the reign of Solomon. Courtesy Carta, Jerusalem.

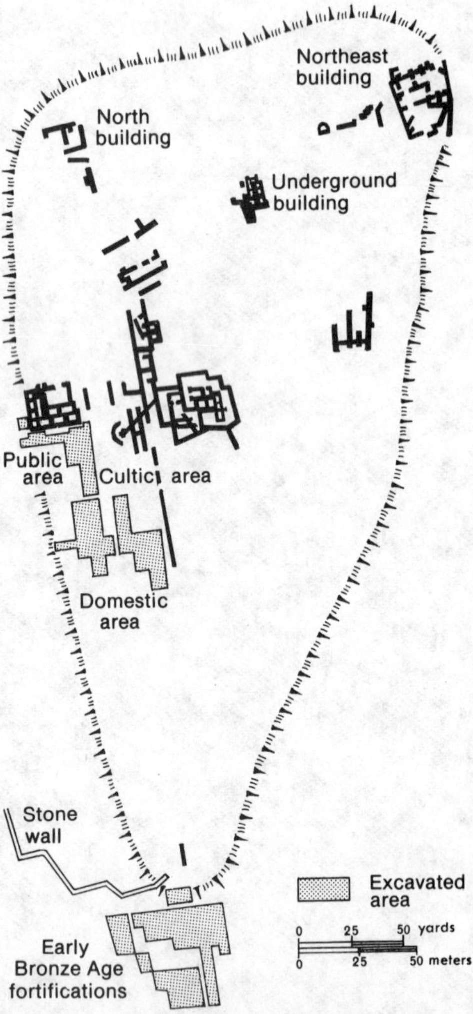

as punishment for their complaining (Num 11:1–3; Deut 9:22). It was probably three day's journey from Sinai (Num 10:33), but its site is unidentified.

TABERNACLE (Heb. *'ōhel, mô'ēdh, tent of meeting, mishkān, dwelling,* Gr. *skēnē, tent*). The religious vitality of the Hebrews and the resilience of their social and political organization in the time of Joshua would indicate that the period of the wilderness wanderings was the truly creative era from which all that was best in subsequent Israelite history and religion took its rise. Under the dynamic spiritual leadership of Moses the children of Israel came to worship a cosmic deity whose vitality contrasted sharply with the capricious, decadent gods of ancient Near Eastern religion. The God of Sinai revealed himself as a supremely moral being whose leadership extended over the whole earth. He was the only true God, and he desired to enter into a special spiritual relationship with Israel as a means of his self-expression in the world.

Elaborately decorated cult stand from Taanach, tenth century B.C., comprised of lion and human faces, with winged leonine bodies in relief along the side panels. On the top register, a calf and a winged sun disk are flanked by columns with voluted decoration. Courtesy Israel Department of Antiquities and Museums. Exhibited and photographed at Israel Museum, Jerusalem.

Since this relationship demanded the undivided worship of the Israelites, it was of supreme importance for a ritual tradition to be established in the wilderness so that Israel could engage in regular spiritual communion with God. The nomadic nature of the sojourn in the Sinai Peninsula precluded the building of a permanent shrine for worship. The only alternative was a portable sanctuary that would embody all that was necessary for the worship of the Lord under nomadic conditions and could also serve as a prototype of a subsequent permanent building.

Such tent-shrines were by no means unknown in the ancient world. An early writer (c. 700 B.C.) spoke of a primitive Phoenician structure that was apparently placed on a cart and pulled by oxen. In pre-Islamic times the *qubbah* or miniature red leather tent with a dome-shaped top was used for carrying the idols and cultic objects of the tribe. Some *qubbahs* were large enough to erect on the ground, while others were smaller and were mounted on the backs of camels. Such tents were credited with the power of guiding the tribe in its journeys, and in time of war were particularly valuable for the degree of protection they afforded. The *qubbah* possessed an innate sanctity that was only slightly inferior to that of the sacred cultic objects it housed. It was used as a rallying point, a place of worship, and a locale for the giving of oracles. Since the majority of tents in antiquity were dark in color, the fact that the sacred shrine was a conspicuous red (cf. Exod 25:5) indicates a religious tradition that reaches back to remote antiquity. Other forms of portable tent-shrines have been preserved on bas-reliefs, notably one from the time of Ramses II (c. 1301–1234 B.C.) that shows the tent of the divine king placed in the center of the Egyptian military camp. Another from the Roman period at Palmyra in Syria depicts a small domed tent erected on the back of a camel.

At Sinai Moses was given a divine revelation concerning the nature, construction, and furnishings of the tabernacle (Exod 25:40). The work was carried out by Bezaleel, Oholiab, and their workmen; and when the task was accomplished, the tent was covered by a cloud and was filled with the divine glory (40:34).

The descriptions of the tabernacle in Exodus 26–27 and 35–38 make it clear that the structure was a portable shrine. Particularly characteristic of its desert origins are the tent curtains, the covering of red leather, and the acacia wood used during the construction. While it is possible to be reasonably certain about the ground plan of the Mosaic tabernacle, there are a number of problems connected with the terminology used in relation to the structure itself. The tabernacle stood in an outer enclosure or court, described in Exodus 27:9–18 and 38:9–20. Taking the ancient Hebrew cubit to indicate a linear measure of eighteen inches (forty-six cm.), the dimensions of the enclosure were one hundred fifty feet (forty-seven m.) in length and seventy-five feet (twenty-three m.) in width. The sides were covered with curtains made from finely woven linen. They were about seven feet (two m.) long and were fastened at the top by hooks and at the bottom by silver clasps to sixty supporting pillars of bronze, placed at intervals of some seven feet (two m.). The enclosure thus formed was uninterrupted apart from an opening in the east wall that was screened by linen curtains embroidered in red, purple, and blue. These hangings were about thirty feet (nine m.) wide, while those at either side of the entrance were a little over twenty feet (six m.) wide. The pillars had capitals (KJV "chapiters") overlaid with silver and were set in bases (KJV "sockets") of bronze. They were held in position by bronze pins (27:19; 38:20).

Within this open court the various types of sacrificial offerings were presented and the public acts of worship took place. Near the center was situated the great altar of burnt offering made from acacia wood overlaid with bronze (Exod 27:1–8). This alter measured nearly eight feet (two and one-half m.) square and about five feet (one and one-half m.) in height. Its corner projections were known as the "horns" of the altar. The various sacrificial implements associated with this altar were also made of bronze. A fire that had been miraculously kindled burned continuously on the altar and was tended by the priests (Lev 6:12; 9:24). Almost in the center of the court was the bronze laver, used by the priests for ritual ablutions (Exod 30:17–21).

To the west end of the enclosure, parallel to the long walls, stood the tabernacle itself. A rectangular structure about forty-five feet by fifteen feet (fourteen by five m.), it was divided into two parts, a Holy Place and a Most Holy Place. The basic constructional material was acacia wood, easily obtainable in the Sinai Peninsula, fashioned into forty-eight "boards" some fifteen feet (five m.) in height and a little over two feet (one-half m.) in width, overlaid with gold. The Hebrew word *qerashim* (board KJV, NASB; frame JB, MLB, NIV, RSV; plank NEB) is found on a Canaanite tablet describing the "throne room" (i.e., a trellis pavilion) of the deity El. When the vertical arms (*yadhoth*) were joined to the acacia frames, the same general effect would be produced. The resulting structure would be light in weight yet sufficiently sturdy for ritual purposes. The base of the trellis was set in a silver fixture, and the whole was held together by horizontal bars at the top, middle, and bottom.

The completed tabernacle was divided into two compartments by a curtain on which cherubim were embroidered in red, purple, and blue, and which was suspended on four acacia supports. The outermost of these two areas was known as the Holy Place and was about thirty feet by fifteen feet (nine by five m.) in area. The innermost part of the tabernacle, the Holy of Holies or the Most Holy Place was fifteen feet (five m.) square. The entrance to the tabernacle was screened by embroidered curtains supported by five acacia pillars overlaid with gold.

The wooden framework of the tabernacle was adorned by ten linen curtains (Exod 26:1–7) that were embroidered and decorated with figures of cherubim. It measured about forty feet (twelve and one-half m.) in length and six feet (two m.) in width, being joined in groups of five to make two large curtains. These were then fastened together by means of loops and golden clasps (KJV "taches") to form one long curtain sixty feet (eighteen m.) long and forty-two feet (thirteen m.) wide. This was draped over the tabernacle proper in such a way that the embroidery was visible from the inside only through the apertures of the trellis work. Three protective coverings were placed over these curtains. The first was made of goat's hair and measured forty-five feet (fourteen m.) long and six feet (two m.) wide; the second consisted of red-dyed rams' hides, while the third was made of *tahash* leather (KJV "badger's skins," NIV "hides of sea cows"). Much speculation has centered on the latter term, and it appears to be connected etymologically with an early Egyptian word *tj-h-s,* used technically of treating or processing leather. Thus the Hebrew would imply a specially finished covering of leather.

The information furnished in Exodus makes it difficult to decide whether the tabernacle proper had a flat, somewhat sagging drapery roof, or one that was tentlike in shape with a ridgepole and a sloping roof. Present-day models of the tabernacle vary in their interpretation of this question. Historically speaking, if the influence of the desert tent was predominant, there may well have been some peak or apex to the structure. If, however, the tabernacle had anything in common with the design of contemporary Phoenician shrines, it probably had a flat roof.

Exodus 25:10–40 describes the furniture of the sanctuary. The Holy Place, or outer chamber of the tabernacle, contained a table for the bread of the Presence (KJV "shewbread"), a small acacia-wood structure overlaid with gold, measuring three feet (one m.) in length, eighteen inches (forty-six cm.) in breadth and a little over two feet (one-half m.) in height. According to Leviticus 24:5–9, twelve cakes were placed on this table along with dishes, incense bowls, and pitchers of gold. The bread was renewed each week and was placed in two heaps on the table. Nearby stood the elaborately wrought *menorah* or seven-branched lampstand of pure gold. A carefully executed floral motif was a feature of its design, and associated with the lampstand were gold wick trimmers and trays (KJV "snuffers"). The furnishings of the Holy Place were completed by the addition of a gold-covered altar of incense, about eighteen inches (forty-six cm.) square and three feet (one m.) in height. Like the great bronze altar, it had projections on each corner, and like the table of the bread of the Presence, it had golden rings and gold-covered staves to enable it to be moved readily.

The furniture of the innermost shrine, the Most Holy Place, consisted only of the ark of the covenant. This was a small, boxlike structure of

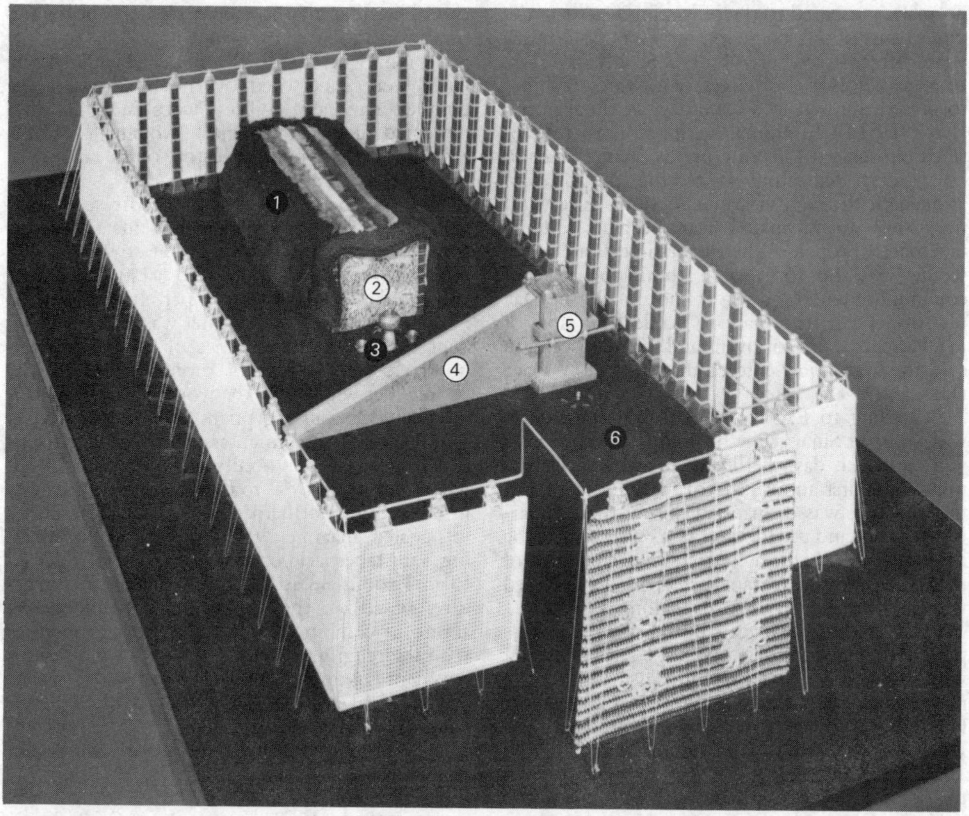

Model of the tabernacle: (1) ram skin covering for the sanctuary, (2) screen, (3) laver, (4) sloped ramp, (5) bronze altar (for burnt offering), (6) and court. Of the 60 pillars of the court, all of acacia wood, 20 stood on the south side, 20 on the north, 10 in the west, and 10 in the east. The pillars were connected to each other by a rod going through the top of the capitals, thus forming a frame. Each pillar was fastened to the ground by ropes stretching from the capital to copper pegs in the ground. Courtesy *The Tabernacle*, M. Levine, "Melechet Hamishkan," Tel Aviv, 1969.

acacia wood, whose length was just under four feet (one and one-fourth m.), while the breadth and height were slightly above two feet (one-half m.). It was covered on the inside and outside with sheet gold and had golden rings and staves like the table of the bread of the Presence and the altar of incense. The lid of the ark, the "mercy seat," was covered with solid gold. On each end was a golden cherub whose wings stretched toward the center of the lid. The precise appearance of the cherubim is a matter of some uncertainty, but in the OT they were generally represented as winged creatures having feet and hands. Some ivory panels unearthed at Samaria depict a composite figure having a human face, a four-legged animal body, and two elaborate, conspicuous wings.

The ark was the meeting place of God and his people through Moses, and contained the tablets of the law (Exod 25:16, 22). According to Hebrews 9:4 a pot of manna and Aaron's rod were also placed in the ark. An elaborately worked veil separated the Most Holy Place from the outer compartment of the tabernacle, and when the Israelites journeyed from place to place, the sacred ark was secluded from view by being wrapped in this curtain. Consequently the ark was normally seen only by the high priest, and that on very special ceremonial occasions.

In the tabernacle all the sacrifices and acts of public worship commanded by the law took place. A wealth of detail surrounds the legislation for sacrificial offerings in the Mosaic code, but for practical purposes they could be divided into two groups, animal and vegetable. Flour, cakes, parched corn, and libations of wine for the drink offerings constituted the normal vegetable sacrifices and were frequently offered in conjunction with the thanksgivings made by fire (Lev 4:10–21; Num 15:11; 28:7–15). Acceptable animals were unblemished oxen, sheep, and goats, not under eight days old and normally not older than three years (cf. Judg 6:25). People who were poor were allowed to offer doves as sacrifices (Exod 12:5; Lev 5:7; 9:3–4), but fish were not acceptable. Human sacrifice was explicitly prohibited (Lev 18:21; 20:25). Salt, an emblem of purity, was used in conjunction with both the vegetable and animal offerings. The sacrifices were normally presented to the officiating priests in the outer court of the sanctuary, but on occasion they were offered elsewhere (Judg 2:5; 1 Sam 7:17). In all sacrifices it was necessary for the worshiper to present himself in a condition of ritual purity (Exod 19:14). In animal sacrifices he then identified himself with his offering by laying his hand on it and dedicating it to the purposes of atonement through vicarious sacrifice. Afterward the blood was sprinkled near the altar and the tabernacle proper. When worshipers ate of a sacrifice in the form of a meal, the idea of communion with God was enhanced. On the Day of Atonement the nation's collective sins of inadvertence were forgiven, and on that occasion only the high priest entered the Most Holy Place (Lev 16).

According to Exodus 40:2, 17 the tabernacle was set up at Sinai at the beginning of the second year, fourteen days before the Passover celebration of the first anniversary of the Exodus. When the structure was dismantled during the wanderings, the ark and the the two altars were carried by the sons of Kohath, a Levite. The remainder of the tabernacle was transported in six covered wagons drawn by two oxen (Num 7:3ff.).

For over thirty-five years during the wilderness period the tabernacle stood at Kadesh, during which time the ordinary sacrifices were apparently not offered consistently (cf. Amos 5:25). Apart from the comment that the ark preceded the Israelites when they were on the march (Num 10:33–36), little is said of the tabernacle during the sojourn in the Sinai Peninsula.

Under Joshua the first site of the tabernacle in Canaan was probably at Gilgal (Josh 4:19), though this is not directly mentioned. Probably an early location was at Shechem, where the desert covenant was renewed (8:30–35). During Joshua's lifetime, the tabernacle was settled in Shiloh, in Ephraimite territory, to avoid disputes and jealousy on the part of the tribes. Perhaps the degree of permanence associated with this site led to the designation of the structure by the term "temple" (1 Sam 1:9; 3:3). This may indicate that the fabric of the original tabernacle had become worn out and that it had been replaced by a more substantial building. Whatever may have been the case, Shiloh was the central sanctuary until the ark was captured by the victorious Philistines after the battle of Ebenezer (c. 1050 B.C.).

The subsequent history of the tabernacle is somewhat obscure. Saul established it at Nob, close to his home in Gibeah; but after he massacred the priests there (1 Sam 22:11ff.), the tabernacle was transferred to Gibeon (1 Chron 16:39; 21:29), perhaps by Saul himself.

When David wished to institute tabernacle religion in his capital city of Jerusalem, he prepared a place for the ark and pitched a tent in the tradition of the Gibeon tabernacle (2 Sam 6:17ff.). The ark was brought from Kiriath Jearim and subsequently lodged in the Davidic tabernacle with due ceremony. This act climaxed David's plan to give the security and legitimacy of religious sanction to his newly established monarchy. The altar of the tabernacle at Gibeon was used for sacrificial worship until the time of Solomon, when both it and the Davidic tabernacle were superseded by the building of the temple. The new edifice incorporated all that remained of earlier tabernacle worship (1 Kings 8:4) and at that point the history of the tabernacle terminated.

Some of the archaic technical terms associated with the tabernacle call for comment. The designation *'ōhĕl mō'ēdh* (Exod 33:7 et al.) or "tent of meeting" was first applied to a structure that antedated the tabernacle proper. It was pitched outside the camp, and Joshua was its sole attendant (33:11) in the absence of a formal priesthood. It was a place of revelation, where the people met with God. The word *mō'ēdh* has been discovered in an Egyptian document dated c. 1100 B.C. referring to an assembly of the citizens of Byblus. The term occurs again in Isaiah 14:13, where the reference is to the assembly of the gods in the remote northern regions, a popular theme in pagan Canaanite writings. The "tent of meeting" or "tabernacle of the congregation" referred to in Exodus 33 is apparently an interim structure, based on the pattern of a simple desert shrine. It combined political and social functions with the religious revelations given by God to his covenant assembly.

The word *mishkan,* commonly used to designate the tabernacle, is related to the ordinary Canaanite word for "dwelling place" and meant originally a tent, thus reflecting the nomadic background of tabernacle worship. A related verb, *shakhan* (KJV "dwell"), is used of God's being "tabernacled" with his people (Exod 25:8; 29:45; et al.). This usage is found in a number of ancient Semitic writings and means "to encamp." The sense is that of God revealing himself on earth in the midst of his chosen people. This is clearly distinguished from the use of the verb *yashav,* "to dwell," "to inhabit," which is only used of God as dwelling in heaven. This subtle distinction was noted by the apostle John when he recorded that the word became flesh (i.e., a body) and dwelt (*eskēnōsen,* literally, was "tabernacled") among us (John 1:14). The doctrine of the *shekinah* glory, which developed in the intertestamental period, was also related to the words *shakhan* and *mishkan,* denoting a local manifestation of divine glory.

A degree of symbolism was naturally attached by the Hebrews to various aspects of the tabernacle. The structure typified God's living with his people (Exod 25:8), while the ark of the covenant spoke particularly of his presence and forgiving love. The twelve loaves of the bread of the Presence represented the twelve tribes dedicated to divine service. The *menorah* typified Israel as a people called to be the children of light (cf. Matt 5:14ff.), and the ascending incense symbolized the act of prayer (cf. Rev 5:8; 8:3). The writer of Hebrews interpreted the tabernacle proper in terms of its twofold division typifying the earthly and heavenly aspects of Christ's ministry. The old tabernacle was but a shadow of the true ideal

(Heb 8:5; 10:1), the latter being pitched by God, not man (8:2). The language of Ephesians 5:2 is distinctly reminiscent of Levitical sacrificial terminology, and the Evangelists were sufficiently impressed by the symbolism of the torn veil to point out that Christ had opened up for all a way into the Most Holy Place (Matt 27:51; Mark 15:38; Luke 23:45). In the early church and in later times more elaborate, sometimes even fanciful, interpretations were imposed on the structure and ritual of the tabernacle.

Bibliography: F. H. White, *Christ in the Tabernacle,* 1875; D. W. Gooding, *The Account of the Tabernacle,* 1959; A. Jacob, *God's Tent,* 1961; A. H. Hillyard, *The Tabernacle in the Wilderness,* 1965; U. Cassuto, *A Commentary on the Book of Exodus,* 1967; R. K. Harrison, *Introduction to the Old Testament,* 1970, pp. 430ff. RKH

TABERNACLES, FEAST OF (See FEASTS)

TABITHA (tăb'ĭ-thȧ, Aram *Tabeitha,* Gr. *Dorcas,* meaning, in Greece, *a roe;* in Syria and Africa, *a gazelle*). The name of a Christian woman disciple who lived in Joppa and made clothing to give to poor widows. When she died, Peter was summoned, and he raised her from death (Acts 9:36–43).

TABLE (Heb. *lûah,* Gr. *plax, writing tablet*). The law was engraved on stone tablets (Exod 24:12; 2 Cor 3:3; Heb 9:4) of undefined material (Isa 30:8; Luke 1:63; Heb 2:2; Gr. *pinakidion*). The law is also engraved figuratively, on the tablet of the heart (Prov 3:3; 7:3; Jer 17:1). Hebrew *mēsav* (Song of Songs 1:12) and Greek *klinē* (Mark 7:4) mean "couch." Hebrew *shulehan* was originally a leather mat spread on the ground (Ps 23:5; 78:19); the table of the bread of the Presence (Exod 25:23, et al.; Heb 9:2, Gr. *trapeza*) was made of acacia wood overlaid with gold. Kings, queens, and governors had dining tables (1 Sam 20:29; 1 Kings 18:19; Neh 5:17); sometimes private persons also did (1 Kings 4:10; Job 36:16). Psalm 128:5 is an attractive picture of a family table. Greek *trapeza,* a four-legged table, is used of dining tables (Luke 22:21; Acts 6:2). To eat under the table was for dogs and the despised (Judg 1:7; Matt 15:27; Luke 16:21). Moneychangers used tables (Matt 21:12). Communion is served from the Lord's table (1 Cor 10:21).

TABLETS OF THE LAW. Stone tablets on which God, with his own finger, engraved the Ten Commandments (Exod 24:3–4, 12; 31:18; Deut 4:13; 5:22). When Moses came down from the mountain and saw the worship of the golden calf, he threw down the tablets, breaking them (Exod 32:15–16, 19; Deut 9:9–17; 10:1–5). At God's command, Moses again went up the mountain with two new tablets and God wrote the law anew (Exod 34:1–4, 27–29). God gave Moses words in addition to the Ten Commandments and told him to write them down (34:10–27). Moses put the two tablets in the ark (Deut 10:5), where they were in the time of Solomon (1 Kings 8:9; 2 Chron 5:10). They are referred to in the NT (2 Cor 3:3; Heb 9:4).

See also COMMANDMENTS, TEN.

Funerary stele from Marash, Hittite period (c. eighth century B.C.) depicting a small table, with bull's feet, laden with offerings for the dead. On each side sits a figure clothed in long garments. The one on the left holds a cup (?) in her upraised hand; the other holds a pomegranate. Courtesy Istanbul Museum. Photo: B. Brandl.

TABOR (tā'bêr). 1. A mountain in Galilee where the borders of Issachar, Zebulun, and Naphtali meet (Josh 19:22). On its slopes Barak gathered ten thousand men of Naphtali and Zebulun (Judg 4:6, 12, 14; 5:18), including contingents from some other tribes (5:13–15), to fight against Sisera and the Canaanite army at Megiddo. Here Zebah and Zalmunna, kings of Midian, killed Gideon's brothers (8:18–19). This commanding height was long a sanctuary of idolatrous orgies (Hos 5:1). Mount Tabor is east of Nazareth, SW of the Sea of Galilee, NE of the Plain of Esdraelon. From its summit, 1,843 feet (576 m.) above sea level, the Hill of Moreh rises to the south with Mount Gilboa beyond. To the north beyond the north Galilean hills rises Mount Hermon, with which Tabor is linked in Psalm 89:12. With Mount Carmel it is compared to the might of Nebuchadnezzar's advance against Egypt (Jer 46:18). Ancient tradition places the Transfiguration here, though it is far from Caesarea Philippi and can be called "exceeding high" only because of the extensive view. But six days would have sufficed to make the journey from Caesarea Philippi to Mount Tabor (Matt 16:13; 17:1; and parallels), hence the identification is not impossible. A Franciscan church, monastery, and hostel, perpetuating the tradition, crown the summit.

2. In the KJV the plain of Tabor (ASV, RSV, "oak of Tabor"; NIV "great tree of Tabor," 1 Sam 10:3). Samuel told Saul he would meet men bearing gifts here, as a sign of God's favor.

Mount Tabor with the Jezreel Valley in background Mount Tabor is situated some 6 miles (97 km.) southeast of Nazareth. Courtesy Israel Government Press Office.

Geographical notes in the context of 1 Samuel 9:5–10:10 have led to the opinion that this oak cannot have been on Mount Tabor, in which case its site is uncertain. Anciently and until recently, Mount Tabor was heavily forested. The oak or terebinth (ASV footnote) might have been a well-known sacred tree or grove.

3. A Levite city of the sons of Merari in Zebulun (1 Chron 6:77). Some identify it with the village of Dabareh or Dabrittha, modern Deburiyeh, on the western slope of Mount Tabor, whose name may perpetuate the memory of the prophetess and judge Deborah of Judges 4–5. ER

TABRET (See MUSIC AND MUSICAL INSTRUMENTS)

TABRIMMON (tăb-rĭm'ŏn). A son of Jezion and the father of Ben-Hadad king of Syria (1 Kings 15:18).

TACHEMONITE (See TAHKEMONITE)

TACHMONITE (See TAHKEMONITE)

TACKLE (Heb. *hevel, rope,* Gr. *skeuē, equipment, ship's tackle*). This refers either to the rigging (Isa 33:23) or furniture (Acts 27:19) of a ship.

TADMOR (tăd'môr, Heb. *tadhmōr*). A city in the desert NE of Damascus. In patriarchal times a much-traveled road ran through it from Damascus north to Haran. When Israel was in Egypt, a caravan route already ran eastward from Qatna to the Euphrates. Solomon either built a new city close by or rebuilt the old, after his conquest of Hamath Zobah (2 Chron 8:4). The context (8:3–6) mentions Solomon's building projects in various parts of his dominion. In the parallel passage in 1 Kings 9:18 KJV, Tadmor is spoken of as "in the wilderness, in the land," with which NIV substantially agrees, with a footnote indicating that the Hebrew may also be read as "Tamar" (so ASV). RSV has "Tamir." The Hebrew consonantal text has *tmr,* which should represent Tamar; but it is pointed with the vowel signs of Tadmor, and so it was traditionally read. The context in 1 Kings 9:15–19 also speaks of many places throughout Solomon's kingdom, though in a different order (from 2 Chron 8:3–6), so that it is possible that the two Tadmors are identical. If so, the added "of Judah" in RSV must be rejected. There are textual variants that would yield either "in the wilderness of Aram [Syria]" or "in the wilderness of the South [Negev]" instead of "in the wilderness, in the land" (1 Kings 9:18 KJV). In NT times the later Tadmor or Tudmur became Palmyra, city of palm trees, magnificent and wealthy, on the caravan route eastward from Emesa to Babylon and to Dura. Excavations reveal impressive Roman ruins. Palmyra enjoyed its greatest fame and prosperity under its Roman-appointed king Odenatus and his widow Zenobia, who made herself queen and defied the Romans. The ruins include Corinthian columns and a temple to the sun. ER

TAHAN, TAHANITE (tā'hăn-īt, Heb. *tahan*). 1. A son of Ephraim, and a founder of a tribal family (Num 26:35).

2. A descendant of the same family in the fourth generation (1 Chron 7:25).

TAHASH (tā'hăsh, Heb. *tahash*). A son of Reumah, concubine of Nahor, Abraham's brother (Gen 22:24).

TAHATH (tā'hăth, Heb. *tahath, below*). 1. A Kohathite Levite, son of Assir and father of Uriel (1 Chron 6:24, 37).

2. A son of Bered and a grandson of Shuthelah, a descendant of Ephraim (1 Chron 7:20).

3. A grandson of no. 2 (1 Chron. 7:20).

4. The name of the twenty-fourth station of Israel from Egypt, and the eleventh from Sinai (Num 33:26–27).

TAHKEMONITE (tăk'mō-nīt, Heb. *tahkemōnî*). The family of David's chief captain (2 Sam 23:8), who sat in the seat (KJV); his name was Josheb-basshebeth (ASV, NIV, RSV). He is the same as Jashobeam, a Hacmonite (1 Chron 11:11). The text of both verses is difficult.

TAHPANHES, TAHAPANES (tăp'á-nēz, tă-hăp'á-nēz, Heb. *tahpanhēs*). A fortress city at the eastern edge of the Nile Delta, on the eastern border of Egypt, on an old caravan road to Palestine and beyond. Early it became a Greek settlement, the Greeks naming it Daphnae, perpetuated in the modern Tell Defenneh. Jeremiah saw it as powerful enough to break "the crown of Judah." Jews fled here after the fall of Jerusalem (Jer 2:16; 43:1–7). Here Jeremiah prophesied its destruction (43:8–11; 44:1; 46:14); Ezekiel also (30:18). During their century it was a city of trade and the manufacture of pottery and jewelry. Excavations have uncovered ruins of this period.

TAHPENES (tá'pēn-ēz, Heb. *tahpenês*). The Egyptian queen who brought up Genubath, the son of her sister and of Hadad, the Edomite adversary of David and Solomon (1 Kings 11:14–22).

TAHREA (tá'rē-á, Heb. *tahrēa'*). A grandson of Mephibosheth, son of Micah, and so a descendant of Saul through Jonathan (1 Chron 9:41; called Tarea in 8:35).

TAHTIM HODSHI (tá'tĭm hŏd'shī). A town at the northern limit of David's census (2 Sam 24:6).

TALE. The word in KJV renders several Hebrew and Greek words that modern versions translate according to their different meanings. Thus, for example, NIV gives the connotations of a moan (Ps 90:9), a quota (Exod 5:8, 18), a count (1 Chron (9:28), slander (Ezek 22:9), and nonsense (Luke 24:11).

The magnificent Roman remains of Palmyra, or biblical Tadmor, showing the monumental arch, behind which is the Grand Colonnade. The city of Palmyra was about 120 miles (193 km.) northeast of Damascus. Courtesy Studium Biblicum Franciscanum, Jerusalem.

TALEBEARING. This is forbidden (Heb. *rākîl*—Lev 19:16 KJV; gossiper MLB; slanderer RSV) and denounced (Heb. *rākîl*—Prov 11:13; 20:19 KJV, MLB; gossip NEB, NIV; Heb. *nirgān*—Prov 18:8; 26:20, 22 JB, KJV; gossip NIV).

TALENT (See MONEY; WEIGHTS AND MEASURES)

TALITHA KOUM (tä-lē'thȧ kūm). The Aramaic words that Jesus spoke when he raised Jairus's twelve-year-old daughter from death (Mark 5:41). They are intimate and endearing and might be translated, "Little lamb, get up."

TALMAI (tăl'mī, Heb. *talmay*). 1. A son of Anak in Hebron and probably the founder of the family of the Anakim, driven from Hebron by Caleb (Num 13:22; Josh 15:14; Judg 1:10).

2. A king of Geshur, whose daughter Maacah was one of David's wives and Absalom's mother (2 Sam 3:3; 13:37; 1 Chron 3:2).

TALMON (tăl'mŏn, Heb *talmôn*). A Levite porter and founder of a tribal family, members of which returned with Zerubbabel and served as porters in the new temple (1 Chron 9:17; Ezra 2:42; Neh 7:45; 11:19; 12:25).

TALMUD (tăl'mŭd). A collection of Jewish writings of the early Christian centuries. There is a Palestinian Talmud and a later, more authoritative, much longer Babylonian Talmud. Each consists of Mishnah and Gemara. Mishnah grew out of oral tradition, whose origin is obscure. The Mosaic Law did not cover all the needs of a developing society, and the defect was supplied by oral rabbinical decisions. When the Jewish leaders felt the need to preserve them, they wrote them down; later they felt a need for a commentary on them. This function the Gemara fulfills. The scope of the Talmud may be seen in the titles of the six parts of the Mishnah: Seeds, Relating to Agriculture; Feasts; Women and Marriage; Civil and Criminal Law; Sacrifices; Clean and Unclean Things and Their Purification.

TAMAH (See TEMAH)

TAMAR (tā'mêr, Heb. *tāmār, palm tree*). 1. The wife of Er, then becoming the levirate wife of Onan. After the death of Onan, her father-in-law Judah had twin sons by her, Perez and Zerah (Gen 38). She is remembered in Ruth 4:12, in the genealogy in 1 Chronicles 2:4, and her name is recorded in the ancestral line of Jesus (Matt 1:3; KJV "Thamar").

2. A daughter of David and sister of Absalom, whom her half-brother Amon violated (2 Sam 13:1–33).

3. The daughter of Absalom (2 Sam 14:27).

4. A place at the SE corner of the boundary of the future Holy Land as described in Ezekiel's vision (Ezek 47:18–19; 48:28).

5. A city in Syria, more commonly known as Tadmor, later Palmyra. See TADMOR.

TAMARISK (See PLANTS)

TAMBOURINE (See MUSIC AND MUSICAL INSTRUMENTS)

TAMMUZ (tăm'ŭz, Heb. *tammûz*). A fertility god widely worshiped in Mesopotamia, Syria, and Palestine; equivalent to Osiris in Egypt and Adonis of the Greeks. His consort was the goddess Ishtar (Astarte or Ashtoreth). Their cult involved licentious rites. Tammuz was supposed to have been killed by a wild boar while shepherding his flocks. His wife rescued him from the underworld. His death was taken to represent the onset of winter. The long dry season was broken by spring rains when he came to life again. The fourth month of the Babylonian and later Jewish calendar was named for him (June–July). The only mention of him in the Bible occurs in connection with the custom of women mourning for him (Ezek 8:14), which, being observed at the very gate of the temple of the true God, seemed to the prophet one of the most abominable idolatries. His Greek name, Adonis, is derived from the Phoenician and Hebrew word for "Lord."

Cylinder seal from Erech, end of the fourth century B.C., depicting the god Tammuz (a fertility god widely worshipped in Mesopotamia, Syria, and Palestine) feeding the cattle of the temple. Ezekiel (8:14) was horrified to see women mourning for Tammuz at the very gate of the temple of the Lord. Courtesy Carta, Jerusalem.

TANACH (See TAANACH)

TANHUMETH (tăn-hū'mĕth, Heb. *tanhūmeth*). A Netophathite and father of Seraiah, one of the Hebrew captains who joined Gedaliah at Mizpah (2 Kings 25:23; Jer 40:8).

TANIS (See ZOAR)

TANNER, TANNING (See OCCUPATIONS AND PROFESSIONS)

TAPHATH (tā'făth, Heb. *tāphath*). Solomon's daughter, wife of the son of Abinadab, Solomon's commissariat office in Dor (1 Kings 4:11).

TAPPUAH (tă-pū'ȧ, Heb. *tappûah*). 1. A city whose king Joshua conquered (Josh 12:17). It was in the lowland or shephelah of Judah (15:34), but its exact location is uncertain.

2. A town on the boundary of Ephraim (Josh 16:8). "Manasseh had the land of Tappuah, but Tappuah itself, on the boundary of Manasseh, belonged to the Ephraimites" (17:8). Its spring,

Sheikh Abu Zarad, site of biblical Tappuah (Josh 16:8). The structure shown in background is the sheikh's tomb. Courtesy B. Brandl.

En Tappuah, was on the boundary of Manasseh (17:7). It is the modern Sheikh Abu Zarad.

3. One of the sons or descendants of Hebron (1 Chron 2:43). Beth Tappuah in the hill country of Judah (Josh 15:53) may have been his home.

TAR (See SLIME)

TARAH (See TERAH)

TARALAH (tăr'á-lȧ, Heb. *tar'ălâh*). A city of Benjamin between Irpeel and Zelah (Josh 18:27). Its exact location is unknown.

TAREA (tā'rē-ȧ, Heb. *ta'ărēa'*). A descendant of King Saul (1 Chron 8:35), written Tahrea in 1 Chronicles 9:41.

TARES (See PLANTS)

TARPELITES (tȧr'pĕl-īts, Heb. *tarpelāyē'*). These people were transported into the region around Samaria by Ashurbanipal (Ezra 4:9–10 NIV; Asnappar NEB; Asnapper KJV, MLB; Osnappar NASB, RSV). He was probably Esarhaddon (Ezra 4:2) or a general under him.

TARSHISH (tȧr'shĭsh, Heb. *tarshîsh*). 1. A son of Javan, great-grandson of Noah (Gen 10:4), and presumably progenitor of a Mediterranean people, as most of these names in the "Table of the Nations" refer not only to individuals but also to the people descended from them.

2. A place, presumably in the western Mediterranean region, conjecturally identified by many with Tartessus, an ancient city located on the Atlantic coast of Spain but long since lost. Jonah fled to it (Jonah 1:3).

3. "Ships of Tarshish" seems to refer to large ships of the kind and size that were used in the Tarshish trade, for Solomon had "ships of Tarshish" going from Ezion Geber through the Red Sea and on to India, making the round trip in three years (1 Kings 10:22; see NIV footnote). See SHIPS.

4. A great-grandson of Benjamin (1 Chron 7:10).

5. One of the seven princes of Persia and Media who stood in the presence of Xerxes (Esth 1:14).

TARSUS (tȧr'sŭs, Gr. *Tarsos*). A city of Cilicia, the capital of the province from A.D. 72. It was the birthplace and early residence of the apostle Paul, a fact that he himself notes with civic pride in Acts 21:39, echoing a line of Euripides applied to Athens, which the Tarsians appear to have appropriated. The city stood on the Cilician Plain, a little above sea level and some ten miles (seventeen km.) inland. The Cydnus River provided an exit to the sea, and in ancient times the river course was equipped with dock and harbor facilities. Tarsus was an ancient city, the seat of a provincial governor when Persia ruled, and, in the days of the Greek Syrian kings, the center of a lumbering and linen industry. During the first century before Christ the city was the home of a philosophical school, a university town, where the intellectual atmosphere was colored by Greek thought.

Tarsus stood, like Alexandria, at the confluence of East and West. The wisdom of the Greeks and the world order of Rome, mingled with the good

The city of Tarsus, birthplace of Paul, in Asia Minor, showing the "Gate of St. Paul." Courtesy Ecole Biblique et Archéologique Française, Jerusalem.

and ill of Oriental mysticism, were deep in its consciousness. A keen-minded Jew, born and bred at Tarsus, would draw the best from more than one world. The Jews had been in Tarsus since Antiochus Epiphanes' refoundation in 171 B.C., and Paul belonged to a minority that had held Roman citizenship probably since Pompey's organization of the East (66–62). EMB

TARTAK (tȧr'tăk, Heb. *tartāq*). A god worshiped by the Avvites, a people who were transplanted from their land to Samaria after its fall to Assyria (2 Kings 17:31).

TARTAN (tȧr'tăn, Heb. *tartān*). In the KJV a commander-in-chief of the Assyrian army (2 Kings 18:17; Isa 20:1). A title, not a proper name.

TASKMASTERS (See OCCUPATIONS AND PROFESSIONS)

TASSEL (Heb. *tsîtsith, tassel, lock*). The fringe of twisted cords fastened to the outer garments of Israelites to remind them of their obligations to be loyal to the Lord (Num 15:38–39; Deut 22:12). Later they became distinct badges of Judaism (cf. Zech 8:23). They were common in NT times (Matt 23:5).

TATTENAI, TATNAI (tăt'ĕ-nī, tăt'nī, Heb. *tat-tenay*). A Persian governor of the territory west of the Jordan who was ordered to assist the Jews in the rebuilding of the temple (Ezra 5:3, 6; 6:6, 13).

TAVERN (See INN)

TAVERNS, THREE (See THREE TAVERNS)

TAX COLLECTOR (See OCCUPATIONS AND PROFESSIONS)

TAXES. Charges imposed by governments, either political or ecclesiastical, on the persons or the properties of their members or subjects. In the nomadic period taxes were unknown to the Hebrews. Voluntary presents were given to chieftains in return for protection. The conquered Canaanites were forced to render labor (Josh 16:10; 17:13; Judg 1:28–35). Under the theocracy of Israel every man paid a poll tax of a half-shekel for the support of the tabernacle worship (Exod 30:13; 38:25–26), and this was the only fixed tax. It was equal for rich and poor (30:15). Under the kings, as Samuel had warned the people (1 Sam 8:11–18), heavy taxes were im-

Statue (found at Babylon, Ur III period, c. 2060–1955 B.C.) of Puzur-Ishtar, governor of Mari, wearing a heavily fringed and tasseled mantle wrapped over his left shoulder and arm. Courtesy Staatliche Museen zu Berlin.

posed. They amounted to a tithe of the crops and of the flocks besides the forced military service and other services that were imposed. In the days of Solomon, because of his great building program (the magnificent temple, the king's palaces, thousands of stables for chariot horses, the navy, etc.), the burden of taxes was made so oppressive that the northern tribes rebelled against his successor, who had threatened even heavier taxation and oppression (1 Kings 12).

During the days of the divided kingdom Menahem (2 Kings 15:19–20) bribed the Assyrian king with a thousand talents of silver to support him, raising the amount from the rich men of his kingdom. Similarly Hoshea (17:3) paid heavy tribute to Assyria, and when he refused to pay further, he lost his kingdom. Later, Pharaoh Neco of Egypt put Judah under heavy tribute, and Jehoiakim oppressively taxed Judah (23:33, 35). Under the Persian domination, "taxes, tribute or duty" (Ezra 4:13) were forms of taxation, though Artaxerxes exempted "priests, Levites," etc. (7:23–24). The Ptolemies, the Seleucids, and later the Romans, all adopted the very cruel but efficient method of "farming out the taxes," each officer extorting more than his share from those under him, and thus adding to the Jewish hatred of the tax collectors, among whom were at one time Matthew and Zaccaeus, both converts later.
ABF

TEACHER, TEACHING (See OCCUPATIONS AND PROFESSIONS; SCHOOL; SYNAGOGUE)

TEACHERS OF THE LAW (See SCRIBES, JEWISH)

TEBAH (tē'bȧ, Heb. *tevah*). 1. A nephew of Abraham, born to Nahor by his concubine Reumah (Gen 22:24).

2. A city that David captured from Hadadezer. Most versions (JB, KJV, MLB, NASB, NEB, RSV) call it Betah (2 Sam 8:8; Tebah NIV) or Tibhath (2 Chron 18:8; Tebah NIV).

TEBALIAH (See TABALIAH)

TEBETH (See CALENDAR)

TEETH (Heb. *shēn*, Gr. *odous*). Isaiah 41:15 tells of "a threshing sledge, new and sharp, with many teeth," literally "possessor of sharp edges," a figure referring to Israel as God's instrument of judgment on the nations. In Psalm 58:6 "teeth," literally "biters," could refer either to teeth or jaws. In Proverbs 30:14 "jaws are set with knives" is clearly figurative, referring to the oppressors of the poor, and the same word in Joel 1:6, "the teeth of a lion," is hyperbole, describing the very destructive habits of the locust. In none of the preceding instances is the ordinary word for tooth used. Some of the more frequent uses of the common words are illustrated in the following passages: In Genesis 49:12 "his teeth whiter than milk" probably refers to the purity and holiness of the Messiah; "tooth for tooth" (Exod 21:24) is of

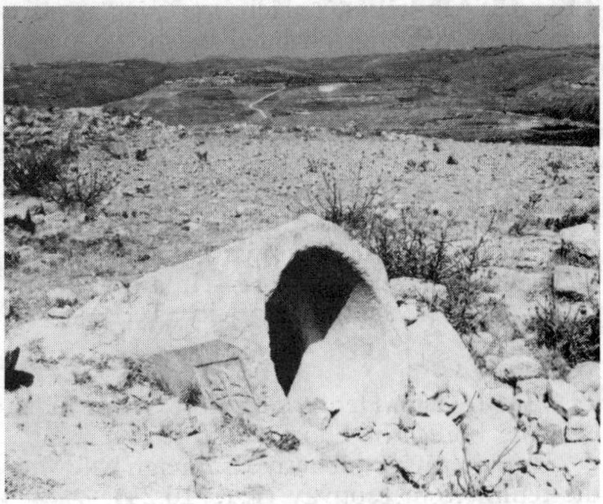

The site of Tekoa, birthplace of the prophet Amos, located 4 miles (7 km.) south of Bethlehem. Courtesy B. Brandl.

course literal; gnashing with the teeth can be a token of anger (Job 16:9) or of remorse (Matt 8:12 and several other references to the suffering of the wicked after death) or of contemptuous rage (Lam 2:16; Acts 7:54). Proverbs 10:26 provides a hint, if one is needed, that the ancients did not have good dental care. Song of Songs 4:2 speaks of the beauty of teeth.

TEHINNAH (tē-hĭn'ȧ, Heb. *tehinnâh, entreaty*). Son of Eshton of Judah, "father of Ir Nahash" (1 Chron 4:12).

TEIL TREE (See PLANTS)

TEKEL (tĕ'kĕl, Heb. *teqēl*). Part of the curse of Belshazzar, who was weighed in the balances and found wanting (Dan 5:25). It means "weighed," from the same root as "shekel," which was a weight long before it was a coin.

TEKOA, TEKOAH, TEKOITE (tĕ-kō'ȧ, tĕ-kō'āīt, Heb. *teqôa', tekô'âh*). A city of Judah, an inhabitant of it. Tekoa lay twelve miles (twenty km.) south of Jerusalem and the same distance NE of Hebron. It was fortified by Rehoboam (2 Chron 11:6). Previous to this, Joab, David's cousin and general, had sent to Tekoa for a "wise woman" and plotted with her to persuade David to bring back Absalom. The prophet Amos describes himself as one of the shepherds of Tekoa (Amos 1:1) and later as one who cared for sycamore-fig trees (7:14), giving us a hint as to the civilization of the city and surrounding country. Jeremiah warned Judah of the approaching danger from the north (Jer 6:1). Ruins of the place survive in Takua.

TELAH (tē'lȧ, Heb. *telah, fracture*). An early Ephraimite (1 Chron 7:25).

TELAIM (tē-lā'ĭm, Heb. *ha-telā'îm, lambs*). The place where Saul mustered his army against Amalek (1 Sam 15:4); possibly the same as Telem (Josh 15:24) in Judah.

TEL ASSAR (tĕl ăs'ẽr, Heb. *tela'ssār*). A place mentioned as being inhabited by the people of Eden, whose gods could not deliver them from the Assyrian kings (Isa 37:12). It has not been identified.

TEL AVIV, TEL ABIB (tĕl' ā'vĭv, tĕl' ā'bĭb, Heb. *tēl 'āvîv*). A place by the river Kebar in Babylonia where Ezekiel visited and ministered to the Jewish exiles (Ezek 3:15). It is not to be confused with the modern city Tel Aviv in Palestine.

TELEM (tē'lĕm, Heb. *telem*). 1. A city of Judah near the border of Edom (Josh 15:24).

2. A porter who put away his foreign wife after the return from captivity (Ezra 10:24).

TEL HARSHA (tĕl har'sha, Heb. *tēl-harshā'*). A place in Babylonia. Returnees from here had difficulty proving they were Israelites (Ezra 2:59; Neh 7:61).

TELL (Arabic, Heb. *tēl*). A mound or heap of ruins that marks the site of an ancient city and is composed of accumulated occupational debris, usually covering a number of archaeological or historical periods and showing numerous building levels or strata. Ordinarily, city sites were selected in association with certain natural features, such as a spring or other convenient water supply, a hill or similar defense advantage, or trade routes determined by local geography. In the course of the history of a town, many reconstructions would be necessary because of destruction by war, earthquake, fire, neglect, or like causes. In the Bible the fact that a city had become only a mound is often regarded as a result of judgment. Deuteronomy 13:16 prescribes that an apostatizing city should be destroyed and reduced to a tell. Joshua executed judgment on Ai when he burned it and "made it a permanent heap of ruins" (Josh 8:28). Jeremiah prophesied that Rabbah of the Ammonites would become "a mound of ruins" (Jer 49:2). In harmony with this is the declaration of Jeremiah that in the restoration of the land of Israel "the city will be rebuilt on her ruins" (30:18). According to Joshua 11:13, in the northern campaign Joshua did not burn any of the cities built on their mounds (the cities that stood still in their strength KJV) except Hazor. In addition to these five OT occurrences, the Hebrew term *tel* also appears as an element in place-names of living towns (e.g., Ezra 2:59; Neh 7:61; Ezek 3:15). CEDV

TELL EL AMARNA (See AMARNA, TELL EL)

TEL MELAH (tĕl mē'la, Heb. tēl-melah, *hill of salt*). A Babylonian town, probably on the low salty district not far north of the Persian Gulf (Ezra 2:59; Neh 7:61).

TEMA (tē'ma, Heb. *têmā'*). 1. One of the twelve sons of Ishmael and progenitor of a tribe (Gen 25:12–16).

2. A place at the northern edge of the Arabian Desert where the above tribe lived (Job 6:18–20; Isa 21:14; Jer 25:23).

TEMAH (tē'ma, Heb. *temah*). The children of Temah were temple servants (KJV Nethinim) who returned from exile with Zerubbabel (Ezra 2:53; Neh 7:55).

TEMAN (tē'măn, Heb. *têmān, on the right,* i.e., *toward the south*). 1. A grandson of Esau through Eliphaz (Gen 36:11, 15).

2. An Edomite chief, probably not the same as no. 1 above (Gen 36:42).

3. A city in the NE part of Edom, noted at one time for the wisdom of its people (Jer 49:7).

TEMANI, TEMANITES (tĕm'a-nī, tĕm'a-nīts). Inhabitants of Teman (Gen 36:34).

TEMENI (tĕm'ĕ-nī, Heb. *têmenî*). A son of Ashhur (1 Chron 4:6).

TEMPERANCE (Gr. *enkrateia, sōphrosynē*). The prime meaning is self-control (Acts 24:25; 1 Cor 9:25; Gal 5:23; 2 Peter 1:6). It is not limited to abstinence from liquor. In Acts 24:25 the reference is to chastity. In 1 Timothy 3:2, 11; Titus 2:2 it is the opposite of "drunken."

TEMPLE (Heb. *hêkhāl, bayith,* Gr. *hieron, naos*). The name given to the complex of buildings in Jerusalem that was the center of the sacrificial cult for the Hebrews. This ritual of sacrifices was the central external service of the ancient people of God and the unifying factor of their religion, at least in OT times. By the time of Christ, the importance of the temple was somewhat lessened because of the place of the local synagogue in Jewish life. See SYNAGOGUE.

Three temples stood successively on Mount Moriah (2 Chron 3:1) in Jerusalem. This site is today called the Haram esh-Sherif and is a Muslim holy place. The first temple was built by Solomon, the second by Zerubbabel and the Jews who returned from the Babylonian exile. The third temple, which was in use in the days of Jesus, was begun and largely built by Herod the Great.

Most ancient religions had temples. Indeed the Canaanite temples found at Megiddo and Hazor are not unlike that of the Hebrews in ground plan. The Jerusalem temple was distinctive in that it contained no idol in the inner sanctum, but only a box (called the ark) containing the two tablets of the law, with the symbolic worshiping cherubim above.

The central place of the temple in the religious life of ancient Israel is reflected throughout the Bible. The Psalms abound in references to it (42:4; 66:13; 84:1–4; 122:1, 9; 132:5, 7–8, 13–17). The temple was the object of religious aspiration (23:6; 27:4–5). Pilgrimage to the temple brought the people of Israel from the ends of the earth (Ps 122:1–4; Acts 2:5–11). The visit of Jesus to the temple at the age of twelve is

General view of the temple mount in Jerusalem. The Dome of the Rock Mosque now stands over the site of the temple itself (center). Courtesy Zev Radovan.

well-known (Luke 2:41–51). Later he exercised some of his ministry there (Matt 26:55; Luke 19:45; John 7:28, 37; 10:23). The early Jerusalem Christians also worshiped there until the break between Israel and the church became final (Acts 3:1; 5:12, 42; 21:26–34).

I. Solomon's Temple. The great economic and cultural development of the Hebrews during the reigns of David and Solomon led to David's desire to build a temple. The tabernacle, the previous sacrificial center (Exod 35–40), was a simple and impermanent structure brought to Palestine by the Hebrews from their desert wanderings. It was natural enough that David should wish God's house to be as grand as his own (2 Sam 7:2). David, however, was not permitted to undertake the construction of this "house" (2 Sam 7:5–7; 1 Chron 22:8). He did prepare for it, however, both in plans and materials (1 Chron 22:1–19; 28:1–29:9) and more especially by arranging its liturgical service (23:1–26:19).

There are no known remains of Solomon's temple. It is clear that it was patterned after the tabernacle, but it was much more complex and ornate. The Phoenicians, who were more advanced culturally than the Hebrews, played a great part in the design and construction of the temple. Recently archaeologists have discovered remains in Phoenicia and Syria that have increased our understanding of the details and motifs of the temple of Jerusalem. Especially useful is the temple found at Tell Tainat in Syria, which was built at about the same time as Solomon's. Its architectural details are believed to be the best guide extant today in reconstructing the details of Solomon's temple. Much of this information is to be found in an article by Paul L. Garber, "Reconstructing Solomon's Temple" (BA, 14:1, May 1951), and in a model of the temple made by E. G. Howland (based on Garber's research). This model is probably a much more authentic reconstruction than the famous one made by Schick in the previous century.

The temple was noted for lavish beauty of detail

Ground plan of the temple at Tell Taiyinat in northern Syria, which resembles that of Solomon's temple. Courtesy Carta, Jerusalem.

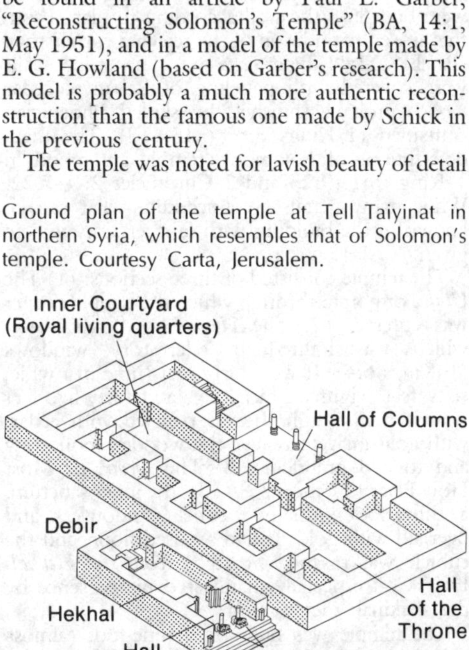

Artist's reconstruction of Solomon's temple, based on biblical sources and the archaeological finds from Tell Taiyinat in Syria, whose temple plan is similar to that of the temple of Solomon. Construction of the temple began in the fourth year of Solomon's reign and continued for seven years. Courtesy Carta, Jerusalem.

rather than for great size. It was accessible only to the priests; the lay Israelites came to it but never entered it. Seven years were required to complete the temple. It was dedicated in Solomon's eleventh year, c. 950 B.C. (1 Kings 6:38), and was destroyed when the Babylonians burned Jerusalem in 587 B.C.

The temple was a prefabricated building. It was made of limestone finished at the quarries (1 Kings 6:7) in or near Jerusalem. When the stones were brought to the building site, they were built into the wall according to plan. From this arose the tradition of the rejected cornerstone (Ps 118:22; 1 Peter 2:6–8). The stone walls were covered with paneling of Lebanese cedar wood, probably finished by skilled Phoenician craftsmen (1 Kings 5:6; 6:15, 18). The main descriptions of Solomon's temple are found in 1 Kings 5:1–9:25 and 2 Chronicles 2:1–7:22. While many details are uncertain, what can be known of the building with fair certainty is here given.

The temple consisted of three sections: (1) The *Ulam*, or porch, through which the temple proper was entered. (2) The *Hekhal*, or Holy Place, which was lighted by clerestory windows (1 Kings 6:4). It was thirty feet (nine m.) wide, sixty feet (eighteen m.) long, and forty-five feet (fourteen m.) high. It was paneled with cedar, with gold inlay to relieve the wooden monotony and to add grandeur. (3) The *Devir*, or Most Holy Place (2 Chron 3:8–13), the inner sanctum, a thirty-foot (nine-m.) cube, windowless and overlaid with gold. It had a raised floor, and the cubicle was reached by steps from the *Hekhal*. Here God especially manifested his presence by the shekinah glory cloud.

The temple was built on a nine-foot (almost three-m.) high platform, which was reached by ten steps, a dramatic approach for religious processions. On this platform, before the entrance to the *Ulam*, stood two pillars, called Jakin and Boaz (1 Kings 7:15–22). Possibly these names are the first words of inscriptions carved on the pillars. Just behind them, doors led to the *Ulam* or porch, a kind of antechamber to the *Hekhal*. The cypress doors were carved with cherubim, palm trees, and open flowers inlaid with gold (6:18, 32, 35). These motifs are frequently found in ancient Near Eastern temple structures.

The *Hekhal* contained ten golden lampstands (1 Kings 7:49; candlesticks KJV). A lampstand from Herod's temple is pictured on the Arch of Titus in Rome, where it is being carried away by the Roman soldiers after the destruction of Jerusalem in A.D. 70. Twelve tables held the twelve loaves of the bread of the Presence (showbread KJV, MLB). The incense altar (7:48), with horns, stood near the entrance of the *Devir*.

The *Devir* contained two guardian cherubim, made of olive wood and adorned with gold. A number of archaeological remains have led to the conclusion that these were winged sphinxes, with a lion's body, human face, and great wings. They symbolized the majestic presence of God. On the floor beneath them stood the ark of the covenant, the box overlaid with gold, its lid called the mercy seat, on which the atoning blood was sprinkled on the Day of Atonement (Lev 16:14–15).

At both sides and at the rear of the temple were built three-storied rooms. They were not as high as the central structure and thus the light from the clerestory windows supplied illumination for the *Hekhal*. This clerestory feature was perhaps an ancestor of the same window arrangement of the medieval cathedrals (recessed window-walls rising above the lower wings or aisle portions). In the chambers around the sanctuary the immense

The Rock of Moriah, traditional site of the altar of burnt offering in Solomon's Temple, as seen from the dome in the Dome of the Rock mosque, shown below, at the Temple Mount in Jerusalem. Courtesy Ecole Biblique et Archéologique Française, Jerusalem.

temple treasury was kept (1 Kings 7:51).

In the courtyard before the temple stood two objects intimately connected with the temple worship: the sacrificial altar and the laver, or molten sea. The altar of burnt offering was the central object in the sacrificial service. It was made of brass (2 Chron 4:1) and probably stood on the great rock that is today covered by the Dome of the Rock on the Haram esh-Sherif.

South of the altar stood the copper alloy laver, or molten sea (1 Kings 7:22–26; 2 Kings 16:17; 2 Chron 4:2–6). This mammoth cast "Sea" was made in the Jordan Valley where clay suitable for molding the metal was to be found. It was three and one-half inches (nine cm.) thick, about fifteen feet (four and one-half m.) in diameter and seven and one-half feet (two m.) high, and stood on the backs of twelve bulls, three facing in each direction. Similar animal supports for thrones are known to have existed among Israel's neighbors. The bull was the Canaanite symbol of fertility and was associated with Baal (Hadad), the god of rain. The presence of this motif in Solomon's temple suggests that more syncretism may have taken place in the Hebrew religion than is at first evident when one reads the Bible. Some scholars have doubted whether this immense reservoir with a capacity estimated at 10,000 gallons (38,000 l.) could have practicably been used for the ceremonial washing, especially since ten small lavers are mentioned (2 Chron 4:6). They think that its main purpose was to symbolize that water or the sea is the source of life. The Babylonians broke up and carried off this amazing example of ancient metal casting (2 Kings 25:13).

The temple did not stand alone; it was one of a number of royal buildings constructed by Solomon in the new section of Jerusalem, just north of the old city of David. Solomon's own palace, another for the Pharaoh's daughter, the House of the Forest of Lebanon, the Hall of Pillars, and the Hall of the Throne (1 Kings 7:1–8) were other buildings in this government quarter. Viewed in this context, the temple appears like a royal chapel. The temple was dedicated by Solomon himself. His prayer on that occasion (8:22–61) shows a great religious spirit reaching out to include even the pagan nations in the worship of Yahweh.

Certain changes doubtless took place in the temple during the Hebrew kingdom. Pagan idolatry was occasionally introduced (2 Kings 16:10–18; 21:4–9; Ezek 8:3–18). Pious kings reformed, refurbished, and rededicated the temple (2 Chron 29:3–31:21; 34:8–33). Foreign kings raided it (1 Kings 14:25–26; 2 Kings 12:18; 14:14; 18:15–16). When Jerusalem finally fell to the Babylonians in 587 B.C., the temple along with the rest of the city was destroyed and its valuable contents carried to Babylon (2 Kings 25:8–9, 13–17).

II. Ezekiel's Temple. Ezekiel the prophet was also a priest. In the early part of his book he predicts that God will judge his idolatrous people by withdrawing his presence from Jerusalem, leaving it to the Gentiles to desolate. But the latter part of the book predicts the reversal of this. Judah and Israel reunited will be regathered. The climax of this vision is the prophet's description of the restored temple of God, with the living waters proceeding from it and the people of God dwelling around it (Ezek 40–48). *Yahweh Shammah* ("The Lord is there") is the key to this vision; God will yet again live among his people. The temple here described is an ideal construction, both like and unlike Solomon's; none like it ever existed, and it is difficult to see how any such temple could ever be built.

Differing views have been held concerning the meaning of this temple vision. Those interpreters who look for a very literal fulfillment of the prophecies believe that this temple will be a part of the millennial kingdom, a great world center of the worship of God, located at Jerusalem. The sacrifices mentioned (Ezek 43:18–27) are regarded as commemorative in nature—looking back to Christ's perfect sacrifice rather than forward to it, as did the OT sacrifices.

Other scholars argue that this description can hardly be taken literally. They maintain that the Letter to the Hebrews states that the sacrificial system prefigured Christ, and now that his perfect sacrifice has been made, the imperfect types are

Plan of the temple as seen by Ezekiel (chs. 40–44). Courtesy "Treasures of the Bible," Dwir-Mikra Co., Berlin.

done away (Heb 7:11–10:39). John in the Revelation (21:9–22:5) appears to use Ezekiel's temple vision, but he writes, not of a millennial temple, but of the eternal glory of the church. Thus these interpreters understand Ezekiel's temple as a highly figurative foreshadowing of the new and holy temple of the Lord, which is the body of Christ (Eph 2:11–3:6).

III. The Restoration Temple of Zerubbabel. The return from Babylonian exile (in 538 B.C.), made possible by the decree of Cyrus, was a small and unpromising one. The returnees were few in number, and their resources were so meager as to need frequent strengthening from the Jews who remained in Babylon. The temple they built is a good example of this. When the foundation was laid, the old men, who had seen the "first house" (Solomon's temple), wept for sorrow (Hag 2:3), but the young men, who had been born in exile, shouted for joy (Ezra 3:12). Like most of the reconstruction in that first century of the Second Commonwealth, the temple must have been modest indeed.

Soon after the return, the community began to rebuild the temple. Joshua the high priest and Zerubbabel the governor were the leaders of the movement. Many difficulties kept the builders from completing the temple until 515 B.C. At that time they were urged on in the work by the prophets Haggai and Zechariah, and the building was finished. No description of this temple exists. Its dimensions were probably the same as Solomon's, but it was much less ornate and costly.

The Holy Place of the new temple seems to have had a curtain at its front. It had one lampstand, a golden altar of incense, and a table for the bread of the Presence. Another curtain separated the *Hekhal* from the Most Holy Place. According to Josephus, the Most Holy Place was empty. Evidently the ark had been destroyed in 587 B.C. and was never replaced. A single slab of stone marked its place. The Babylonian Talmud asserts that five things were lacking in the new temple: the ark, the sacred fire, the Shekinah, the Holy Spirit, and the Urim and Thummim.

No doubt the temple was repaired and beautified many times in the succeeding centuries, but of this we have no information. Our next knowledge of it comes from the days of Antiochus Epiphanes. In 168 B.C. this Syrian king sought to stamp out the Hebrew religion, robbed the temple of its furniture and desecrated it, forcing the high priest to sacrifice a pig on its altar. This action precipitated the Maccabean revolt. In 165 the Jews, led by the Maccabees, recaptured, cleansed, and rededicated the temple. First Maccabees 4:44–46 tells how they replaced the stone altar of burnt offering with stones that had not been defiled, meanwhile saving the old stones "until there should come a prophet to give an answer concerning them." The story of the rededication of the temple and the miraculous supply of oil for the lamps is perpetuated in the Jewish festival of Hanukkah.

Judas Maccabeus at this time fortified the temple with walls and towers, making it the citadel of Jerusalem. Sometime during the next century a bridge was built across the Tyropoeon Valley connecting the temple with the Hasmonean palace. The Hasmoneans (a later name for the Maccabees) were both high priests and kings, and by this bridge they sought to make the temple easier to defend. All of this points up the fact that the Second Commonwealth period was one of uneasy peace at best, and that the temple henceforth was to be both the religious and military center of the Jews, until, in A.D. 70, Herod's temple fell and the Jews lost both the religious life as they had always known it and their fatherland.

In 63 B.C. the Roman general Pompey captured Jerusalem and took the temple after a hard struggle, breaking down the Hasmonean bridge. Although Pompey did not harm the temple, the Roman consul Crassus plundered it of all its gold nine years later.

IV. Herod's Temple. Our sources of information concerning Herod's temple are Josephus, the Jewish historian and priest who flourished about A.D. 70, and the tract *Middoth* of the Mishnah written at least a century after the final destruction of the temple. Neither can be used uncritically, and many details of the Herodian building and service remain uncertain.

Herod the Great (37–4 B.C.) was an indefatigable builder. Many cities and heathen temples had been rebuilt by him, and it was natural that he should wish to show his own grandeur by replacing the modest restoration temple with a more complex and much more beautiful temple. Other motives probably moved him, especially his desire to ingratiate himself with the more religious Jews, who resented his Idumean origin and his friendliness with the Romans.

Herod began his work in his eighteenth year (20–19 B.C.). The Jews were afraid that the work would interrupt the temple service, but Herod went to great lengths to prevent this, rebuilding the old structure piecemeal, never stopping the ritual observances until an entirely new temple came into being. Since only priests could enter the temple and the inner court, one thousand of them were the masons and the carpenters for that inner area. The "house" itself was finished in a year and a half; eight years were spent on the surrounding buildings and court, which were not finally completed until A.D. 64. The Jews said to Jesus that the temple had been under construction forty-six years (John 2:20); more than thirty more years were to pass before it was really finished, then only to be destroyed. All speak of the grandeur of the building, which was of white marble, its eastern front covered with plates of gold that reflected the rays of the rising sun.

The temple area was probably equivalent to the modern Haram esh-Sherif, except that the north end of the Haram was the location of the fortress Antonia. This area, twice as large as that on which Zerubbabel's temple was situated, was artificially built up by underground arches (the present "Solomon's Stables") and fill held in by retaining walls (the Wailing Wall is a part of Herod's western retaining wall). The area, some twenty-six acres in size, was surrounded by a high wall. Gates on each side led into it, but the principal gates

A reconstruction of the temple mount during the second temple period, based on archeological and historical evidence. Something like this scene is what Jesus and the apostles saw when they came to Jerusalem. Courtesy Carta, Jerusalem.

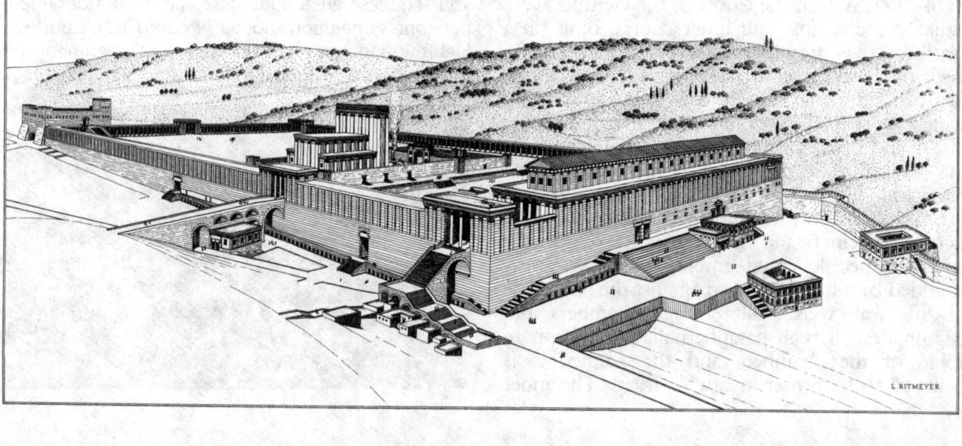

One of the Greek tablets from Herod's temple that forbade strangers from entering the second enclosure. Inscription reads: "No stranger is to enter within the balustrade round the temple and enclosure. Whoever is caught will be responsible to himself for his death, which will ensue." Courtesy Israel Department of Antiquities and Museums.

were in the south and west walls, leading in from the city. The eastern gate may have been the Beautiful Gate (Acts 3:2, 10), perhaps located where the Golden Gate stands today. Around the inside of the walls ran porches. The finest one was on the south side—the Royal Porch—having four rows of dazzling white marble columns in the Corinthian style, 162 columns in all. The eastern porch was called Solomon's Colonnade (John 10:23; Acts 3:11; 5:12). During the feasts the Roman guards used to walk on the roofs of the porches to see that order was kept.

Near the NW corner of the temple area was located the fortress Antonia. It dominated the temple and was the headquarters of the guard so often needed to keep the peace. From the stairs that led from the temple precincts to Antonia, Paul delivered his sermon (Acts 21:31–22:21) after having been rescued by the guard from the mob.

Entering the temple area, one came to four successive walled courts that surrounded the temple, each more exclusive than the one outside it. The first was the Court of the Gentiles. It was not holy ground, and non-Jews were permitted there. Here buying and selling went on; it was here that Jesus cleansed the temple (John 2:14–17). Within the Court of the Gentiles were situated the temple and inner courts, built on a platform twenty-two feet (seven m.) above the floor of the outer court. Stairways led up to this platform. Surrounding it was a stone wall on which were placed stones with inscriptions in Greek and Latin forbidding non-Jews from entering on pain of death. Several of these stones have been found (cf. Acts 21:26–28).

On the platform was the inner court. It was the temple precinct and holy ground. Only the covenant people could enter here. It was surrounded by a high wall, and against the inner side of this wall were built storage chambers and colonnades. Ritual paraphernalia was kept in some of the chambers and the Sanhedrin is believed to have met in one of them. The inner court was divided into two unequal parts by a cross wall running north and south. The eastern and smaller area was the Women's Court. Here women as well as men were permitted and here were located thirteen chests like inverted trumpets, into which offerings for the expenses of the temple services were placed. In this place the poor widow was commended by Jesus when she gave her two copper coins (Mark 12:41–44). For reasons of ceremonial purity only men were allowed in the western area, which contained in its center the temple proper. Around the temple was the Court of the Priests, which contained the altar of burnt offering and the laver. Around the Priests' Court was the Court of Israel, accessible to all Jewish males. Here the men gathered when the service was being carried on, to pray and to observe the offering of the sacrifices (Luke 1:10).

In the center of these many courts within courts stood the temple itself, raised twelve steps above the Court of the Priests. Perhaps the forbidding inaccessibility of the sanctuary was in Paul's mind when he said that Christ "destroyed the barrier, the dividing wall of hostility" to bring the Gentiles into the fellowship of the people of God (Eph 2:14).

The temple porch—one hundred fifty feet (forty-seven m.) in length and breadth and thirty feet (nine m.) deep—faced east. It projected twenty-two and one-half feet (seven m.) beyond the sides of the temple proper, for the temple was only one hundred five feet (thirty-three m.) wide. Above the entrance to the porch (which had no door) Herod had placed a golden eagle, which as a Roman emblem (and an unclean bird) was most distasteful to the Jews. Shortly before his death it was destroyed. In front of the doorway to the *Hekhal* or Holy Place hung a beautifully colored Babylonian curtain or veil. The inner area of the *Hekhal* was sixty feet (nineteen m.) long, thirty feet (nine m.) broad, and ninety feet (twenty-eight m.) high, and it contained the altar of

Hebrew inscription found south of the temple mount: "Le Beth Hatkiyah" believed to mean "To (or belonging to) the Trumpeting Place." At this site trumpets were blown to usher in the Shabbat each week. It was the only coping stone of the second temple to be found among the excavated ruins. "Do you see these great buildings? There will not be left here one stone upon another" (Mark 13:2). Courtesy Hebrew University of Jerusalem, Department of Information and Public Affairs. Photo Glik.

incense in the middle, the table of the bread of the Presence on the north, and the lampstand on the south. Only the officiating priests could enter this room, to bring in the incense morning and evening, to trim the lamps daily, and to replace the bread of the Presence every Sabbath.

Between the *Hekhal* and the *Devir* or the Most Holy Place hung two curtains, with eighteen inches (forty-six cm.) space between them. On the Day of Atonement the high priest entered the *Devir* with his censer by going to the south side, passing between the curtains to the north side, and thus emerging into the Most Holy Place. The Gospels refer to these as one veil, which was torn in two at the time of Jesus' crucifixion (Matt 27:51; Mark 15:38; Luke 23:45). The *Devir* was empty and was entered by the high priest only once a year, on the Day of Atonement.

An upper room, sixty feet (nineteen m.) high, covered the two chambers of the temple. From this room workmen were let down in boxes to effect needed repairs. Probably this was to avoid needless walking through the sacred house. As in Solomon's, so in Herod's temple, there were storerooms along the sides, except for the front or east, where the porch stood. These were used for storage and for the residence of officiating priests. No natural light came into this temple from roof or windows. It depended on the lamps for its light.

In front of the temple, in the Courtyard of the Priests, stood the altar of burnt offering. It is believed that this altar stood on the great rock that is covered today by the building called the Dome of the Rock on the Haram esh-Sherif. It was made of unhewn stones. There was always a fire burning on the altar. At the SW corner was located a drainage channel for the blood to the Kidron Valley. North of the altar were twenty-four rings affixed to the ground. To these were tied the sacrificial victims, and there they were killed by slitting their throats. Still farther to the north were pillars with iron hooks on which the carcasses were hung for dressing. If this reminds us today of a butcher shop rather than a place of worship, we should remember that this antithesis would have been meaningless in the biblical world. Not only did the priests live by eating many of the sacrificial victims, but any killing of an animal for food anywhere was considered a kind of religious act—a sacrifice—and certain rituals were prescribed.

South of the sacrificial altar was the bronze laver or wash basin, where the priests washed their hands and feet. The water was supplied by pipes from the temple spring.

The temple was burned when Jerusalem fell to the Roman armies in August A.D. 70. Pictures on the Triumphal Arch of Titus in Rome show the soldiers carrying off the temple furniture as loot. This destruction made complete and final the break between the temple and the church and thus helped to establish the church as a religion completely separate from Israel. The early Christians saw in this forced cessation of the Jewish ritual a proof of the validity of Christ's claims to

Interior relief of the Arch of Titus in Rome. It shows soldiers carrying the most prized Jewish spoils—first the golden table for the showbread and the pair of long silver trumpets, then the golden candlestick (menorah) with its seven branches. Titus commanded the Roman soldiers at the siege and capture of Jerusalem in 70 A.D. Courtesy Israel Government Press Office.

be the Redeemer foreshadowed by the OT ceremonial law.

In the NT the term *temple* is used figuratively in a number of ways. Jesus spoke of the temple of his body (John 2:19, 21). The individual believer is a temple (1 Cor 6:19). So also is the church; but this temple, unlike the earthly one, is equally accessible to all believers (Heb 6:19; 10:20), now freed by Christ from the ritual limitations of the old covenant (Eph 2:14). The Book of Hebrews (especially chs. 7–10) in great fullness expounds on Christ as the fulfillment of the typology of the temple and its ritual. The culmination of this idea of the "better covenant" is seen in the New Jerusalem where in his vision John "did not see a temple in the city, because the Lord God Almighty and the Lamb are its temple" (Rev 21:22).

Bibliography: F. J. Hollis, *The Archaeology of Herod's Temple,* 1934; A. Cole, *The New Temple,* 1950; J. Simons, *Jerusalem in the Old Testament,* 1952; Y. M. J. Congar, *The Mystery of the Temple,* 1962; R. J. McKelvey, *The New Temple,* 1969.

JBG

TEMPTATION, TESTING (Heb. *massâh,* Gr. *peirasmos*). The idea of putting to the proof–from either a good or bad intention–is found throughout the Bible. Thus the Lord often tests his people with the purpose of strengthening their faith, while Satan tempts them because he wishes to undermine their faith. Jesus, true man, faced both testing from God and temptation from Satan. (Note that it is only in modern English that temptation has come to mean testing for evil purposes: testing and temptation were once synonyms.)

God tests man. The explanation of this testing is provided in Deuteronomy 8:2: "Remember how the LORD your God led you all the way in the desert these forty years, to humble you and to *test* you in order to know what was in your heart,

A typical Bedouin tent made of goat's-hair cloth, in the Negev. Courtesy Zev Radovan.

whether or not you would keep his commandments" (cf. 8:16, "to test you so that in the end it may go well with you"). The Lord tests individuals—Abraham (Gen 22:1), Job (Job 23:10), Hezekiah (2 Chron 32:31)—and nations (Deut 33:8). Sometimes his testing is severe and painful (1 Cor 11:32; Heb 12:4–11; 1 Peter 1:7; 4:8–13), but it originates in holy love.

Satan tempts man. Until Jesus returns, Satan has freedom to tempt people to sin (2 Sam 24:11; 1 Chron 21:1). He is called the tempter (Matt 4:3; 1 Thess 3:5) and the adversary of Christians (1 Tim 5:14; 1 Peter 5:8). God sometimes uses this tempting to test believers. Satan afflicted Job within limits God imposed (Job 1:6–22; 2:1–7). Satan deceived Eve (1 Tim 2:14); Christians are to be constantly watching for temptation (Mark 14:38; Luke 22:40; 2 Cor 2:11; 1 Peter 5:8). They can overcome; they need to remember God's promise: "God is faithful; he will not let you be tempted beyond what you can bear. . . . He will also provide a way out so that you can stand up under it" (1 Cor 10:13).

Satan tempted Jesus (Matt 4:1–11). Although this was genuine testing for evil purposes, the Lord used it for testing Jesus in his vocation as Messiah. Temptation initiated by Satan is not sin: Sin is to submit.

People test God. Satan sought to entice Jesus to put God to the test by tempting him to jump from the pinnacle of the temple, knowing that angels would come to his help (Matt 4:5–6). In response Jesus quoted Deuteronomy 6:16 and said, "Do not test the LORD your God." The name of Massah ("temptation") constituted a reminder of Israel's testing of God in Sinai (Exod 17:7; Deut 6:16). To test God is to assert unbelief and lack of trust in him (see Ps 95:8–11; Acts 5:9; 15:10; 1 Cor 10:9).

Christians are to test themselves. Before partaking of the Lord's Supper believers are to test themselves (1 Cor 11:28) to see whether they are spiritually prepared to participate. Such testing should be a regular feature of the Christian life (2 Cor 13:5; Gal 6:4).

"Lead us not into temptation" (Matt 6:13) is a part of a prayer to be addressed to the Father by his people. Some translations offer, "Do not bring us to the test/trial." This plea seems to ask that we not be forced into tribulation, extreme testing, or great suffering. The next petition is "but deliver us from the evil one," which recognizes that Satan is active in this world, but that God is greater than Satan.

Bibliography: D. Bonhoeffer, *Temptation,* 1953; E. Best, *The Temptation and the Passion,* 1965; P. Doble, "Temptation," ExpT, vol. 72, 1960–61, pp. 91ff. PT

TEN COMMANDMENTS (See COMMANDMENTS, TEN)

TENT (Heb. *'ōhel,* Gr. *skēnē*). A temporary dwelling generally made of strong cloth of goat's hair stretched over poles and held in place by cords reaching out to stakes driven into the ground. It is the typical dwelling of nomadic peoples. Tents are of various shapes—round and tapering, flat and oblong. All of a nomadic family's belongings could normally be carried on one pack animal. A sheik would, of course, have several tents. *Tent* (usually *tabernacle* in KJV) often means any habitation (Gen 9:27; Job 8:22; Ps 84:10) and is often used figuratively (Isa 13:20; 54:2; Jer 10:20).

TENTMAKER (See OCCUPATIONS AND PROFESSIONS)

TENT OF MEETING (See TABERNACLE)

TERAH (tē'rȧ, Heb. *teraḥ*). 1. Son of Nahor and father of Abram (Gen 11:24–32). He lived at Ur of the Chaldees and was an idolater (Josh 24:2). When God called Abram out of Ur with its civilized idolatry, Terah went as far as Haran in Mesopotamia, where he and his family remained until Terah died at 205 years of age; then Abram with his family and his nephew Lot proceeded to Canaan.

2. A stage in Israel's march between Tahath and Mithcah (Num 33:27–28).

TERAPHIM (tĕr′ȧ-phēm, Heb. root and meaning dubious). Used in the KJV for a kind of household god and means of divination. Usually rendered "idol" in NIV. In Genesis 31:19 it is reported that the teraphim of Laban were stolen by Rachel; these were small enough to be concealed in a camel saddle (31:34–35). They were a valuable possession, for their ownership involved the inheritance of the property of Laban, as is illustrated by the Nuzi tablets. In 1 Samuel 19:13–16 Michal, by placing such an object in David's bed, deceived Saul's messengers into thinking that David was there but was too ill to receive visitors. This idol resembled a man in size and appearance sufficiently well to make the ruse temporarily effective. In the time of the judges, Micah had teraphim among the religious articles of his household shrine (Judg 17:5); these furnishings were coveted and seized by the Danites (18:14–20). In the spiritual revival under King Josiah the teraphim and other "abominations" in Judah and Jerusalem were put away (2 Kings 23:24). Zechariah asserted that "the idols speak deceit" (Zech 10:2). Hosea prophesied that "the Israelites will live many days without king or prince, without sacrifice or sacred stones, without ephod or idol" (Hos 3:4). Ezekiel included the consultation of teraphim among the divination practices of the king of Babylon preceding the destruction of Jerusalem (Ezek 21:21). CEDV

TEREBINTH (See PLANTS)

TERESH (tē′rĕsh, Heb. *teresh*). An officer who "guarded the doorway" in the service of Xerxes (KJV Ahasuerus). He plotted to assassinate his master but was discovered by Mordecai and thwarted (Esth 2:21).

TERRACE (Heb. *mesillâh*). Used in the KJV for the steps that Solomon made of algumwood as an approach to the temple (2 Chron 9:11).

TERROR. In ordinary usage this means extreme fear or dread, or sometimes the one who causes such agitation. The word is a translation of about a dozen Hebrew and Greek words that are rendered also by "dread," "fear," "horror," "terribleness," "ruin." Characteristic are Psalm 55:4, "the terrors of death"; Genesis 35:5, "the terror of God"; and 2 Corinthians 5:11 KJV, "the terror of the Lord."

TERTIUS (tûr′shĭ-ŭs, Gr. *Tertios*). The scribe or amanuensis of Paul. At the apostle's dictation, he wrote the Letter to the Romans. He added a personal salutation (Rom 16:22).

TERTULLUS, TERTULIUS (têr-tŭl′ŭs, Gr. *Tertyllos*). A diminutive of Tertius. It was the name of the professional advocate used by the Jews to state their case against Paul before Felix, procurator of Judea (Acts 24:1). Only a few words of Tertullus's elaborate oration are given, but they are enough to reveal the nature of his rhetoric and the character of his accusation. He may have been a Roman, for there is a Latin ring to some of his phrases as they appear in Luke's Greek, and his name is Latin, though this does not necessarily fix his nationality. He was obviously trained in the art of contemporary rhetoric, and what impressed Luke was his elaborate introduction, drawing positive attention toward Felix. (Calvin thought such a subterfuge "a sign of bad faith.") It is rather a traditional courtesy; and the device, without the self-seeking flattery, is to be distinguished also in the opening phrases of Paul's reply (24:10).

TESTAMENT. A word the KJV uses thirteen times to translate the Greek word *diathēkē*, which signifies a testamentary disposition. KJV translates it "covenant" twenty times, as usually the NT uses *diathēkē* in the meaning of its cognate *synthēkē*, which accurately renders the OT *berith*, a binding agreement or contract between one human being and another or between a human being and God. Jesus, at the institution of the Lord's Supper, said, "This cup is the new covenant [testament] in my blood" (Luke 22:20; 1 Cor 11:25), referring to Exodus 24:8. Jesus' death created a new relation between God and believers. The imagery in Hebrews 9:15–20 includes the notion of a testamentary disposition, operative only after the testator's death; only in 9:16–17 does NIV have "will" (testament KJV, MLB, NEB) for *diathēkē* (elsewhere NIV has covenant).

TESTAMENTS OF THE TWELVE PATRIARCHS (See APOCALYPTIC LITERATURE)

TESTIMONY. Generally "a solemn affirmation to establish some fact," and commonly among Christians the statement of one's Christian experience. In Scripture it usually refers to that which was placed in the ark of the covenant (Exod 25:21), or to the Word of God (Ps 119:14, 88, 99 KJV). In Mark 6:11, shaking off the dust of the feet in leaving an unfriendly city was to be considered as a testimony against it.

TESTING (See TEMPTATION, TESTING)

TETRARCH (See OCCUPATIONS AND PROFESSIONS)

TEXTS AND VERSIONS (OLD TESTAMENT). The OT is a book of sacred literature for Jews and Christians and has no rival in quality or scope of influence among other sacred writings of the world today. It is the focal unit of Judaism and the foundation of Christianity's sacred literature. In Jesus' time it was called "the Scriptures," though Jesus himself often referred to it by its divisional terminology. On the day of his resurrection, for example, Jesus declared to the disciples, "Everything must be fulfilled that is written about me in the Law of Moses, the Prophets and the Psalms" (Luke 24:44). It was also the Bible of Peter, Stephen, Philip, Paul, and the other early Christians (Acts 2:7; 8:13).

I. Origin of the Old Testament

A. **General discussion.** The English OT today is identical with the Hebrew Bible but is arranged differently. The customary divisions of the thirty-nine books books in the English version are (1) seventeen historical books, (2) five poetical books, and (3) seventeen (major and minor) prophetical books. The Hebrew Bible was divided into (1) Law (*Torah*, i.e., the Pentateuch), (2) Prophets (*Nebhiim*, including Joshua, Judges, Kings, and Later Prophets, Isaiah, Jeremiah, Ezekiel, and the Twelve Minor Prophets), and (3) Writings (*Kethuvim*, composed of the eleven remaining books). The Hebrew OT—combining certain books that are separate in English—numbered only twenty-four books. Josephus reduced the number to twenty-two by further combinations.

B. **Canonization.** The final confirmation of the books of the Law, the Prophets, and the Writings as exclusively canonical by Jewish scholars cannot be placed later than 400, 200, and 100 B.C. respectively. However, the writing and adoption by consensus doubtless antedated these dates by centuries. Since some contemporary writings were accepted and some rejected during the periods mentioned above, some basis for discrimination was necessary. The critical term for this process is "Canon," derived from the Greek word *Kănon*, "rod," which came from the Hebrew and Old Babylonian words for "reed," meaning "measure." There were no canonical decrees governing selection, but scriptural authority seems to have been derived from usage by devout Jews, and any pronouncements of measuring methods were only confirmations of that authority. Some critics think that the formation of the Canon began in 621 B.C. during Josiah's reign and ended in the Council of Jamnia, A.D. 90. Actually the Council only confirmed the established authority of the books composing our present OT, recognized and accepted before the time of Jesus. The need for some criterion, however, for standardization to protect and preserve Holy Writ was doubtless long in the minds of the rabbis. Probably the first to sense keenly this need were the scribes, the *Sopherim,* who elaborated a theory of inspiration. They said that inspiration belonged to the prophetic office, and the range of prophetic activity began with Moses and ceased with Ezra (though according to rabbinical writings it ended in the time of Alexander the Great). According to these limitations, any writings before Moses or after the prophets would automatically be apocryphal. Consequently the books of the OT were all inspired writings of men chosen by God, spanning a period of approximately a thousand years, embraced within the traditional dates of 1450 to 444 B.C.

C. **Authorship.** Evidences of authorship of the books of the OT are negligible. The traditional view of authorship, as preserved in the Talmud, has basic validity: "Moses wrote his own book and the section concerning Balaam (Num 22:2–25:9) and Job. Joshua wrote his own book and (the last) eight verses of the Torah. Samuel wrote his own book and Judges and Ruth. David wrote the Book of Psalms, incorporating the productions of ten elders: Adam (139), Melchizedek (110), Abraham (89), Moses (90), Heman (88), Jeduthun (39, 62, 77), Asaph (50, 73–83), and the three sons of Korah (42, 44–49, 84, 85, 87). Jeremiah wrote his own book and the Book of Kings and Lamentations. Hezekiah and his company wrote Isaiah, Proverbs, the Song of Songs, and Koheleth. The men of the Great Synagogue wrote Ezekiel, the Twelve, Daniel and Esther. Ezra wrote his own book and the genealogies of the Book of Chronicles, including his own" (MHSM ch. II).

Internal and external evidences combine to give a provisional view of biblical authorship. The cultural development of the Hebrews in correlation with that of their contemporaries may be seen through the eyes of the archaeologists. First, however, the scriptural record should be reviewed.

Belief in special revelation to the authors of the OT as divinely inspired and directed writers has textual bases. In the Pentateuch numerous claims are made to Moses' divine commission and written contributions. "The LORD spoke to Moses" occurs again and again in Leviticus. The earliest reference to writing in the Bible is Exodus 17:14, where "the LORD said to Moses, 'Write this on a scroll as something to be remembered' "; and in 24:4, "Moses then wrote down everything the LORD had said" (cf. 34:28). In Numbers 33:2 (RSV) the record states that "Moses wrote down their starting places, stage by stage." Deuteronomy 31:9 states that "Moses wrote down this law," and 31:24 concludes that "Moses finished writing in a book the words of this law." Other evidences showing that Moses is the substantial author of the Pentateuch are found in several books of the OT and in the Gospels (Josh 1:7–8; Judg 3:4; 2 Chron 25:4; Ezra 6:18; 7:6; Mal 4:4; Matt 8:4; Mark 7:10; 10:5; Luke 20:37; John 5:45–47; 7:19).

In Exodus 24:7 we read concerning Moses, "Then he took the Book of the Covenant and read it to the people." The Book of the Covenant (Exod 20–23) is probably the oldest writing in the OT. It is the nucleus around which the framework of the Pentateuch was built.

II. Texts

A. **Fragmentary scripts.** No autograph texts of any OT writings are known to exist today, but the textual critic tries with all available means to reconstruct texts as nearly like the originals as possible. Until A.D. 1947, when the Dead Sea Scrolls were discovered, the earliest complete extant manuscripts of the Hebrew Bible were dated about 1000. There were, however, fragmentary evidences of considerable value, brought to light from time to time by archaeologists, contributing to the validity of the Bible claims.

B. **The art of writing.** Writing was known as early as 3000 B.C. among the old civilizations of the Near East. Temple inscriptions; the Code of Hammurabi; and the Gilgamesh Epic, with accounts of Creation, original sin, and the Flood, antedate Moses by several centuries. There are numerous examples of early writing that support the claim that Moses, who "was educated in all the wisdom of the Egyptians" (Acts 7:22), could have and did write the passages claimed for him in the Bible.

C. **Antecedents of the Hebrew language.** These may be found in Old Phoenicia, a land on the Mediterranean coast north of Palestine settled by an early wave of Semites. These precocious seafaring people are credited with giving the world its first alphabet. As early as the sixteenth century B.C., evidences of a Hebrew-Phoenician alphabet are found, from which a standarized script emerged about the tenth century. This is the cursive script, used in Old Hebrew and for the original writing of the OT books. This script was replaced by the Hebrew-Aramaic square script probably a century before Christ. However, since the Samaritan Pentateuch is in the old cursive script, the square letters must not have been used until after the schism between Judea and Samaria about 432 (Neh 13:28). Modern scholarship dates the Samaritan Pentateuch at 128 or 122 B.C. Furthermore, the transition seems not to have preceded the Septuagint, though the Aramaic square letters were in use centuries before by the Jews in Egypt. Seemingly, the square Aramaic script was gradually adopted by the Jews after the Exile (536–538 B.C.) and used latest in sacred writing. The letter from Arsham (the Persian satrap of Egypt c. 410 B.C.) is nonbiblical and was written in the square Hebrew letters. Jesus' reference to the "jot" in the law indicates that this type of script was in biblical use in his time (Matt 5:18 KJV).

Other writings discovered in Phoenicia have had valuable bearing on Hebrew philology. Excavations in a mound at Ras Shamra, ancient Ugarit, unearthed a small temple with a library underneath. Among the finds were tablets containing a script of only twenty-seven different characters. This proved to be archaic Hebrew, dated about 1400 B.C., hence one of the earliest alphabetic writings yet known. Another important discovery on the Phoenician coast was made at Byblos, OT Gebal (Ezek 27:9). It was a remarkable alphabetical inscription on the Ahirams sarcophagus (stone coffin), dated about 100. Byblos is the name from which our term *Bible* is derived.

D. **Fragments of the Hebrew language.** From Palestine, the mound of Old Lachish (Josh 10:31–32) yielded a bowl, a jar, and a dagger containing brief inscriptions in alphabetic script similar to that found in Sinai and dating probably between 1750 and 1550 B.C. Similar characters inscribed in ink on a potsherd were found at Beth Shemesh from about the tenth century. Twenty-one letters found at Lachish consisted of broken pieces of pottery on which were inscribed archaic Hebrew by a military commander during the invasion of Nebuchadnezzar in 588. To these may be added fragmentary inscriptions from the Gezer Calendar, c. 900; Moabite Stone, c. 800; Siloam Tunnel, c. 700; and numerous others. Prior to the discovery of the Dead Sea Scrolls, the small sheet known as the Nash Papyrus, dated second to first century B.C., was our earliest biblical Hebrew document. It contains the Ten Commandments and the Shema (Deut 6:4).

Earliest dated Bible manuscript in Maaravic square script, A.D. 946, showing part of 2 Kings 17:15–16. Courtesy Encyclopaedia Judaica Photo Archive, Jerusalem.

E. **The Bible in the Hebrew language.** The OT was originally written in Hebrew, with the exception of a few chapters and verses in the later books. These were written in Aramaic, a kindred language, and are found in Daniel 2:4–7:28; Ezra 4:8–6:18; 7:12–26; and Jeremiah 10:11.

The Scriptures were written on animal skins, called vellum or parchment, or on papyrus. Papyrus comes from a water plant of that name from the marshes of the Nile. The glutinous pith was sliced and the stripes laid at right angles and pressed together, making a very smooth and durable paper.

The Hebrew Bible is the work of many authors over a period of more than a thousand years, roughly between the fifteenth and fifth centuries B.C. As it grew in size it also grew in sacredness and authority for the Jews.

F. **Preservation of the texts.** Two obvious factors have militated against the preservation of original autograph writings and archaic texts. First, when transcriptions were made onto new scrolls, the old deteriorating ones were destroyed lest they fall into the hands of profane and unscrupulous men. Second, attempts were made at different times by the enemies of the Jews to destroy their sacred literature. Antiochus Epiphanes (c. 167 B.C.) burned all the copies he could find, and many rolls were destroyed during the Roman wars (c. A.D. 70).

Another hazard that threatened accurate transmission of the Scriptures was the repeated copying by hand. Scribal errors and explanatory marginal notes doubtless resulted in slight deviations from the original, but the fidelity of the copyist is amazing. Ezra and his school of scribes, the Great Synagogue, and subsequent rabbinical schools and priests and scribes worked diligently to perpetuate the original Scriptures. It was the Masoretic scholars who devised the present vowel system and accentual marks. Before this the consonantal Hebrew Scripture was not vocalized. Chapter divisions came much later, appearing first in the Vulgate, A.D. 1227 or 1248, and transferred to the Hebrew Bible about 1440. Verses were marked in the Vulgate as early as 1558.

G. **The Dead Sea Scrolls.** In A.D. 1947 some Palestinian herdsmen accidentally discovered a cave in the Judean hills that proved to be a veritable treasure house of ancient Scriptures. The discovery of these scrolls was acclaimed by biblical scholars as the greatest manuscript discovery in modern times. From this and other caves by the Wadi Qumran, NW of the Dead Sea, came a hoard of OT parchments dated 200 B.C. to the first century A.D.

The first major find comprised four scrolls. One of the first documents was a copy of the Book of Isaiah in Hebrew, and another a copy of the first two chapters of the Book of Habakkuk in Hebrew, with added commentary. Later discoveries yielded fragments with portions of other biblical books in Hebrew. The Deuteronomy fragments were written in archaic script. Altogether, the manuscript fragments constitute over four hundred books, a few almost intact, and more than forty thousand fragments. Ninety of these books were parts of the Bible, with every OT book except Esther being represented among them.

These scrolls are of great critical value on the basis of such factors as antiquity and authenticity. The scroll of Isaiah A is dated near 200 B.C., while that of Ecclesiastes and the fragments of Exodus and Samuel are estimated by some to be as old as 250 and 225 B.C. respectively.

One valuable contribution of the Dead Sea Scrolls is their provision of a critical basis for the study of the three main lines of transmission by which the text of the OT has come down to us. The first of these, and probably the most trustworthy, is the Masoretic Hebrew text of the eighth and ninth century A.D. The second is the Greek Septuagint, and the third is the Samaritan Pentateuch. The antecedents of these three forms of Hebrew texts seem to have been varying types of texts used by the people of Israel in general in the closing centuries of the Second Jewish Commonwealth, and were in no sense confined to or used by a particular sect. It may be that the Masoretic text was derived from a Babylonian revision, the Septuagint from Egyptian Hebrew, and the Samaritan from a Palestinian text; but it seems obvious that all were used in Judea.

III. Versions of the Old Testament

A. **Greek versions.**

1. **The Septuagint,** whose value can hardly be overestimated, was in popular use in Jesus' time and is often quoted by NT writers. It is a translation of Hebrew into Greek by Jewish scholars in Alexandria, Egypt. The Pentateuch was translated about 250 B.C. and the entire OT completed a hundred years later. The term *Septuagint* is the Latin word for seventy, representing the seventy-two rabbis who did the translating, probably under orders of Ptolemy Philadelphus. The Greek used was not the classical idiom but rather anticipated that of the NT, the *Koinē*. It was designed to preserve the old religion among the dispersed Jews in a language they commonly used. The oldest extant fragments of the Septuagint today are from a papyrus roll of Deuteronomy, dated about A.D. 150, found on an Egyptian mummy, and now in the John Rylands Library, Manchester, England. (See also SEPTUAGINT)

Fragment of a papyrus scroll containing the oldest known copy of the Septuagint today. Shown here is part of Deuteronomy 25:1–3. Dated c. A.D. 150. Found in Egypt. Courtesy John Rylands Library.

2. **Other Greek versions.** Three Greek translations from the Hebrew were made in the second century A.D., but only fragments of them have survived. Aquila, a proselyte Jew, made a very literal translation that became the official Greek version for the Jews. Theodotion, a Christian of Pontus, made a translation between 180 and 192 that seemed to be partially a revision of the Septuagint. It was a free rendering of the idiomatic Greek and became popular in the early Christian churches. In about 200, Symmachus faithfully translated the Hebrew into good, smooth Greek, though it was somewhat a paraphrase. Jerome's commentary on these versions was that "Aquila translates word for word, Symmachus follows the sense, and Theodotion differs slightly from the Septuagint."

3. **The Hexapla** was a translation and six-column arrangement by Origen in Caesarea about A.D. 240. This was a kind of harmony of the translations of Aquila, Theodotion, Symmachus, and the Septuagint. It became the authoritative Greek OT for some churches. Only fragments of this work remain.

4. **Several Greek manuscripts** containing excerpts from the OT have been discovered. The oldest were written on papyrus; and those after the fourth century A.D., on vellum. The script of the latter is in "uncials," capital letters written separately, used generally from the third to the tenth century, and in "cursives," from about the

ninth to the sixteenth century.

A papyrus manuscript of the minor prophets, in uncials, dated the latter part of the third century A.D., was found in Egypt and is now in the Freer collection, Washington, D.C.

Codex Vaticanus, "B," dated about the middle of the fourth century A.D., contains most of the OT and NT. It is in the Vatican Library, where it was known as early as the fifteenth century.

Codex Sinaiticus, א (or *Aleph*), contains a limited fragment of the OT of equal age with "B." It was discovered in 1844 by Tischendorf in the Monastery of St. Catherine at Mount Sinai and placed in the royal library at St. Petersburg (Leningrad). It was later purchased from the Soviet government and placed in the British Museum in 1933.

Codex Alexandrinus, "A," a manuscript in uncials, dated in the fifth century A.D., was a gift to King James I and was brought to England in 1628 and placed in the British Museum.

Codex Ephraemi, "C," contains sixty-four leaves of the OT dated from the fifth century A.D. and is now in the Bibliotheque Nationale in Paris.

B. **Aramaic versions.** The Targums were probably oral translations of the Hebrew Scriptures into Aramaic after the latter replaced the Hebrew as the spoken language of the Jews. The Targums contain religious instructions along with interpretations, which accompanied the reading of Scripture in the synagogues. Compare the procedure followed when Jesus was in the synagogue at Nazareth (Luke 4:16–27). Besides the Targum of Jonathan on the Prophets, there are three on the Pentateuch, all of which were put into written form from about the first to the ninth century A.D. The three are the Onkelos (Babylonian), the Jerusalem Targum, and the Fragmentary Palestinian Targum.

C. **Syriac versions.** The Peshitta is the Syriac Bible of the OT translated in the second or third century A.D. for the benefit of Christians whose language was Syriac. Many manuscripts survive. The earliest data known on any manuscript of the Bible is found on one containing Genesis, Exodus, Numbers, and Deuteronomy, in the British Museum, dating to A.D. 464.

D. **Latin versions.**

1. **The Old Latin versions** probably originated among the Latin-speaking Jews of Carthage and were adopted by the Christians. An entire Bible in "Old Latin" circulated in Carthage by A.D. 250. There were a variety of Latin versions before Jerome's day, representing three types of Old Latin text: African, European, and Italian.

2. **The Vulgate** was produced by the scholarly Jerome in a cave in Bethlehem adjacent to what he believed was the Grotto of the Nativity. Jerome translated directly from the Hebrew with references to the Septuagint and Origen's Hexapla. He was commissioned in A.D. 382 by Pope Damasus to make an official revision of the Old Latin Bible. His work was completed in 405. The Vulgate is a creditable work, though not an infallibly accurate translation of the original text. Rather, it was an interpretation of thought put into idiomatic, graceful Latin. It was virtually without a rival for a thousand years. The Douay Version, translated from the Vulgate, was until recently the only authorized Roman Catholic Bible in English.

E. **Other Eastern versions.** The Coptic versions were made for Christians in Egypt in the second or third century A.D. The Ethiopic version was made in the fourth or fifth century. The Gothic version was prepared by Ulfilas about 350. The Armenian version, beautiful and accurate, was made for Christians of eastern Asia Minor about 400. A twin to the latter was the Georgian version of the fifth or sixth century. The Slavonic version of the ninth century is preserved in the oldest manuscript of the whole Bible in existence today. It is dated 1499 and is known as Codex Gennadius, now in Moscow. The Arabic version, necessitated by the Arabic conquests of the seventh and eighth centuries, was begun by Saadya in the tenth century.

These ancient versions aid the critic in trying to restore the original text and in interpretations. For data on English versions, see BIBLE, ENGLISH VERSIONS.

For bibliography, see next article. GBF

TEXTS AND VERSIONS (NEW TESTAMENT). The Bible, and especially the NT, occupies a unique place in the literature of ancient times, and part of that uniqueness is the history of its transmission through the centuries. No other ancient writing approaches it in the number of copies made of it from the time it was written until the age of printing; its existing MSS approach the date of its origin far more closely than do the MSS of almost any other piece of ancient literature; and the NT (with the OT) stands virtually alone in the literature of antiquity as a work that was translated into other languages. In

Leaf from the Papyrus Bodmer. Courtesy Foundation Martin Bodmer.

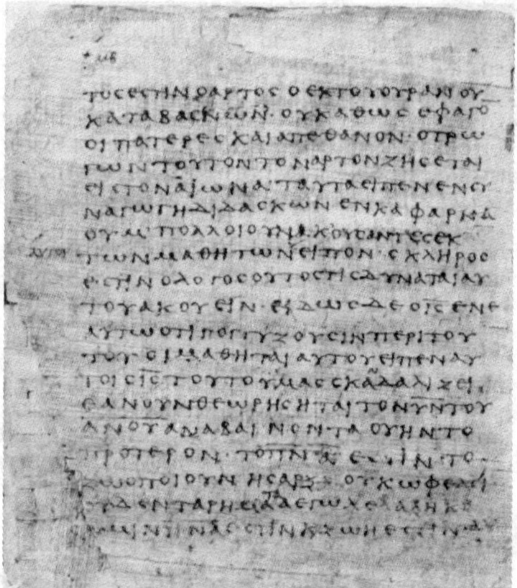

the beginning, of course, there was no "New Testament" as a single volume. The individual books were written over a period of years and afterward were gradually brought together (see CANONICITY).

1. **The Greek manuscripts.** What did a book of the NT look like when it was first written? Its language was Greek. There doubtless were both written and oral records, probably both in Aramaic and in Greek, that lay behind the Gospels. Proof is lacking, however, that any of the NT books as such were originally written in Aramaic.

An original copy of a NT book was probably written on papyrus sheets, either folded into a codex, which is the modern book form, or possibly on a papyrus roll. It was long thought that the earliest copies of the NT books were written in roll form, since this was the regular form for both the OT and for other literary writings of the period. However, even the very oldest NT papyrus MSS or fragments that are now known are in the codex form, not the roll. Although the codex form was used for notes, rough drafts of an author's work, etc., the early Christians were pioneers in using the codex form for literary purposes—i.e., for copies of books of the NT and perhaps for the originals of some of the NT books. The codex was far better suited for ready reference to passages and was generally easier to use than the roll.

The style of the Greek letters in the original of a NT book may have been one of two in common use. Literary works of the period were written in "uncial" or "majuscule" letters, rounded capitals, the letters not connected to each other. A "cursive" or "minuscule" hand, in which the letters were connected, somewhat as in English longhand writing, was used for personal letters, business receipts, and other nonliterary materials. The Greek MSS were written with no separation between words. This was not merely in order to save space, because the size of the letters in many MSS indicates that space was not necessarily an important consideration. It was simply an accepted custom. Latin MSS similarly do not separate words, but Hebrew MSS do. The originals of Paul's letters may therefore have been written in the cursive hand as being simply private correspondence; the Gospels would probably have been originally written in uncial letters. Of course, when Paul's letters began to be copied and recopied, they would be thought of as public writings and would doubtless soon be copied in uncial letters. All of the earliest known MSS of the NT are written in uncial letters.

The first three centuries are the period of the use of papyrus as a writing material. Sheets were made from thin strips of the papyrus reed, which grew along the Nile and in a very few other places in the Mediterranean world. The strips were laid side by side, with a second layer placed on top at right angles to the first layer. Pounded together and dried in the sun, these sheets made very serviceable material for writing with a reed pen. In a roll, the side that normally received the writing was the side on which the strips were horizontal. In the codex form, both sides would be used, but the "verso," where the strips were vertical, would give the writer more difficulty than the "recto."

Page of the Gospel of Matthew from the Codex Sinaiticus, from Sinai, fourth century A.D. The script is in Greek, in uncial letters, on vellum. Courtesy The British Library.

At the beginning of the fourth century A.D., a notable change occurred in the production of NT MSS, when vellum or parchment began to displace papyrus as a writing material. The use of tanned skins for a writing material had long been known and was commonly used for the Hebrew OT. Vellum and parchment, however, are skins that have been treated with lime and made into a thin material having a smooth, firm writing surface. The term "vellum" was applied to the finer skins of calf, kid, or lamb; and "parchment" (from Pergamene, a city prominent in its manufacture) was applied to ordinary skins; but the two terms are now used synonymously. A few papyrus MSS of the NT from the fifth and sixth centuries are known; but apparently papyrus was quickly displaced by the far more durable parchment, and the fourth century may be called the beginning of the parchment period of NT MSS, a period lasting until the introduction of paper as a writing material in the fourteenth century.

In the ninth century A.D. another significant change occurred, with the development of the cursive style of handwriting into a literary hand called "minuscule." By the end of the tenth century the uncial hand had been completely displaced by the minuscule, which remained the regular style of writing until the invention of printing.

In addition to the MSS containing a continuous NT text, many MSS of lectionaries from these centuries have survived. These are MSS that contain NT passages organized for reading on particular days.

We may summarize as follows: From the first to the fourth centuries A.D., NT MSS were written in uncial letters on papyrus; from the fourth to the tenth, in uncial letters on vellum; from the tenth to the fourteenth, in minuscule letters on vellum; from the fourteenth to the invention of printing in the fifteenth century, in minuscule letters on paper.

Almost 70 papyrus MSS and fragments are known, about 250 uncial MSS, 2,500 cursive MSS, and 1,600 lectionaries. Papyri are designated by "P" and a superscript number (e.g., P^{66}). Uncials are designated by capital letters of the English and Greek alphabets plus א (the Hebrew letter *Aleph*) so far as these letters permit; but all uncials are also designated by a number with a zero prefixed (e.g., 047). Cursives are designated by a number only (e.g., 565), and lectionaries by a number with a lower-case letter *l* prefixed and sometimes italicized (e.g., *l*299).

2. **Variant readings.** While these developments in writing were taking place, there were other developments concerning the text of these MSS. Since copies were made individually by hand, mistakes and changes inevitably occurred—omissions, additions, changes of words, word order, and spelling—usually unintentionally made, but sometimes intentionally to clarify, explain, or to avoid a doctrinal misunderstanding. In the MSS now known there are thousands of these "variants." The vast majority, however, make no difference in meaning; and the application of accepted principles of textual criticism makes it possible to determine the original form of the text for all practical purposes, though not to verbal perfection. No fundamental Christian doctrine is left in doubt by any textual variant.

These variants, moreover, tended to group themselves into companies. A MS tended to contain the errors of the MS from which it was copied. As MSS were carried to various cities and lands, and as copies were made from MSS at hand, the MSS of a given region would tend to contain a similar group of variants, and these would be somewhat different from the variants of MSS in another region. Scholars recognize at least three of these "text-types," as they are called, from the fifth century A.D. and earlier: "Alexandrian," "Caesarean," and "Western"—names that are only partially significant geographically. After the official recognition of Christianity in the fourth century A.D., with more opportunity to compare MSS, these "local texts" were gradually displaced by a type of text that tended to smooth out rough constructions, harmonize parallel passages, and make for ease of understanding. This text-type, known as "Byzantine," was dominant by the eighth century. It remained the accepted text, becoming known as the "Textus Receptus" after the invention of printing, and was the principal text behind the King James Version. It was not until the latter part of the nineteenth century that textual scholarship switched to the other text-types.

3. **Patristic quotations.** If every MS of the NT itself were destroyed, the NT could virtually be reconstructed from another significant source: the thousands of quotations of NT passages in the writings of the ancient church fathers, principally in Greek, Latin, and Syriac. These quotations must be consulted with care, as they were often given from memory or simply as a scriptural allusion and hence not verbally exact. Yet many are textually reliable; and these are valuable, because readings quoted by a particular church father can usually be assumed to have been current during that man's lifetime and in the region of his activity.

4. **Ancient versions.** In the case of most ancient writings, when the MSS in the original language of the work have been consulted, the limits of the field have been reached. The Bible, especially the NT, is therefore virtually unique in ancient literature in this respect, for not only was it translated into other languages in the earliest centuries of its history, but these translations are sufficiently accurate to be of help in textual criticism in determining the original text of the NT. Of course, no original MSS of these ancient translations remain, and the copies that are known must first be examined to determine the original text of the translation. However, certain types of Greek variants would not be reflected in certain versions (e.g., the presence or absence of a definite article in Greek would not normally be reflected in Latin, as Latin has no definite article); but in many respects the versions are useful, not least in helping to show the regions in which certain textual readings were current.

The NT must have been translated into Latin, the official language of the Roman Empire, very shortly after the books were written and certainly before the second century A.D. had passed. The forty or so extant MSS of this Old Latin differ extensively among themselves, and it is not clear whether they represent one or several translations. As a result of these variations, in 382 Pope Damasus commissioned Jerome to undertake a revision of the Latin Bible. In the NT Jerome worked cautiously, making changes only where he felt they were absolutely necessary. This revision, the Latin Vulgate, became the official Bible of the Western church and remains the official Roman Catholic Bible. Probably eight thousand MSS are in existence.

Syriac, a dialect related to Aramaic, which was spoken in lands around Palestine, likewise received the NT during the second century A.D. The first such translation seems to have been either the original or a translation of a Greek original of a continuous Gospel account known as the Diatessaron (meaning "through the four"), constructed by combining elements from all four Gospels. It was composed about 160 by Tatian and seems to have been the Syriac Gospel in common use for over a century. There was also made, however, perhaps in the second century, a translation of the four Gospels, known as the Old Syriac, which is now known in two MSS, the Sinaitic and the Curetonian.

The Syriac that is still the standard version is the Peshitta (meaning "simple"), translated in the fifth century A.D., perhaps by Rabbula, bishop of Edessa. Some 250 MSS are known, none of which contains 2 Peter, 2 and 3 John, Jude, or Revelation. The Peshitta was revised in 508 by authority of Philoxenus, bishop of Mabbog. It is thought by some that this Philoxenian version still exists in or is related to the current Syriac text of the four books named above, which were not in the original Peshitta but are now printed in the Syriac NT. The Philoxenian was in turn revised in 616 by Thomas of Harkel. The Harklean Syriac is such an extremely literal translation from the Greek that it even violates Syriac idiom at times to follow the Greek. It is likewise characterized by numerous marginal alternative readings, often in Greek. About fifty MSS of this version are known.

The Palestinian Syriac version was made about the sixth century. It exists in fragmentary MSS, including some lectionary material. The so-called Karkaphensian Syriac, which has sometimes been named as a version, is in fact only a collection of Scripture passages accompanied by notes on spelling and pronunciation.

Likewise significant in textual criticism are the two principal versions of Egypt. The earlier of these is the Sahidic, the dialect of southern Egypt, which probably received its NT in the third century A.D. It exists in numerous but fragmentary MSS. The Bohairic, the dialect of Alexandria and the Nile Delta, was more literary and later displaced the other dialects to become the current Coptic. About one hundred MSS of the Bohairic NT are known. There are fragments of versions in three other Egyptian dialects: Fayumic, Middle Egyptian, and Akhmimic.

The Gothic version, translated very accurately from the Greek by the Gothic Bishop Ulfilas, dates from the fourth century A.D. and is the earliest version representing the Byzantine text-type.

The Armenian version originated about A.D. 400, the work of Mesrop and Sahak, using an alphabet created by Mesrop. The version was probably made from Syriac. A revision was made a century or two later. Many MSS of the Armenian version are known, but only one is earlier than the tenth century.

Christianity became established in Georgia in the fourth century A.D., and the Georgian version of the NT probably was in existence before the middle of the fifth century, apparently translated from Armenian. A thorough revision, based on Greek MSS, was made about the eleventh century.

The Ethiopic version originated about A.D. 600, perhaps translated from Syriac rather than Greek. About one hundred MSS are extant, but the earliest is from the thirteenth century.

The NT was translated into Arabic by about the seventh century. Several translations were made at various periods from the Syriac, Greek, Coptic, and Latin.

The Persian exists in two versions, the earlier made from the Peshitta and the later one from the Greek. They are later than the Arabic, but the exact date is unknown.

The Slavonic version originated in the ninth century A.D., the work of Cyril and Methodius, who translated from Greek into the Macedo-Bulgarian dialect, using an alphabet created by Cyril. This version is only partially extant.

Other translations were made from time to time, but they have virtually no significance for textual study and are more appropriately dealt with under the subject of Bible translations.

See BIBLE, ENGLISH VERSIONS.

Bibliography: W. H. P. Hatch, *The Principal Uncial Manuscripts of the New Testament,* 1939; C. C. Torrey, *Documents of the Primitive Church,* 1941; B. J. Roberts, *The Old Testament Text and Versions,* 1951; E. Wuerthwein, *The Text of the Old Testament,* 1957; H. G. G. Herklots, *How Our Bible Came to Us,* 1954; F. G. Kenyon, *Our Bible and the Ancient Manuscripts,* rev. 1958; F. F. Bruce, *The Books and the Parchments,* rev. 1963; B. M. Metzger, *The Text of the New Testament,* 1964; J. H. Greenlee, *Introduction to New Testament Textual Criticism,* 1964; S. Jellicoe, *The Septuagint and Modern Study,* 1968; P. Walters, *The Text of the Septuagint,* 1973. JHG

THADDAEUS (thă-dē'ŭs, Gr. *Thaddaios*). One of the twelve apostles, mentioned only twice in Scripture—in two of the four lists of the apostles (Matt 10:3; Mark 3:18). In Matthew 10:3, KJV has "Lebbaeus, whose surname was Thaddaeus," NEB has "Lebbaeus," and NASB, NIV, and RSV have "Thaddaeus." The other two lists (Luke 6:16; Acts 1:13) insert Judas, son of (or brother of) James instead of this name. Nothing else is certainly known about him, but he may be mentioned in John 14:22. A spurious "Gospel of Thaddaeus" used to exist.

THAHASH (See TAHASH)

THAMAH (See TEMAH)

THAMAR (See TAMAR)

THANK OFFERING (See SACRIFICE AND OFFERINGS)

THARA (See TERAH)

THARSHISH (See TARSHISH)

THEATER. In spite of a rudimentary dramatic structure discernible in the Book of Job and the Song of Songs, Israel produced no drama and had thus no theaters. The word *theater* is from the Greek and is a noun derived from the verb *theaomai,* "to view," or "to look upon." The Greek theater, and the Roman theater that followed it, were therefore structures designed to seat the viewers at a dramatic representation. The theater was usually an open-air structure, a semicircle of stone seats built into the side of a hill, and seating up to five or six thousand people. The

The famous theater at Ephesus, capable of seating nearly 25,000 spectators and completed in its present form under Trajan. This was the only theater mentioned in the New Testament (Acts 19:29). The Arcadian Way is in the foreground. Courtesy Dan Bahat.

The theater of Dionysus at Athens, first used in the sixth century B.C. Modified in Hellenistic and Roman times, the theater contains 64–78 stone tiers and seats c. 17,500. Courtesy Gerald Nowotny.

seats were cut concentrically, and at the foot of the auditorium a semicircular piece of level pavement provided the "orchestra" or the place where the chorus, an indispensable part of all Greek dramas, and the actors performed. In the more primitive theaters a tent backed the diameter of this semicircle, into which the actors retired to change their masks and, by implication, their roles. (There were only three actors in a Greek tragedy to fill all the roles involved in the play.) On the tent was painted a rough representation of trees or a temple or a house, to indicate that the scene of action was town or country and so on. The Greek for "tent" is *skēnē*, hence "scenery" in the dramatic sense. Surviving Greek theaters are acoustically remarkable. Theaters were commonly

The Roman theater at Hierapolis, overlooking the city where Philip (the apostle) made his home and is buried. Courtesy Dan Bahat.

used for public gatherings, since they were likely to provide the largest places of assembly in the city; hence the use of the only theater mentioned in the NT (Acts 19:29), that of Ephesus. The ruins of this theater, a most imposing structure seating twenty-five thousand people, have been excavated. Roman theaters tended to be more elaborate than those of the Greeks, contained a more finished stage, and, perhaps in conformity with the needs of a severer climate, were at least in part roofed over. EMB

THEBES (See No)

THEBEZ (thē'bĕz, Heb. *tēvēts*). A city in the tribe of Ephraim about halfway from Beth Shan to Shechem. It is mentioned only in connection with the death of Abimelech, son of Gideon, who wanted to be king (Judg 9:50; 2 Sam 11:21). Abimelech had taken the city except for a central tower, from the top of which a woman dropped a millstone on him, causing his death. It is now called Tubas.

THELASAR (See Tel Assar)

THEOCRACY (thē-ŏk'rȧ-sē, Gr. *theokratia*). A government in which God himself is the ruler. The best and perhaps the only illustration among nations is Israel from the time that God redeemed them from the power of the pharaoh by drying the Red Sea (Exod 15:13; 19:5–6) and gave them his law at Mount Sinai, until the time when Samuel acceded to their demand, "Now appoint a king to lead us, such as all the other nations have" (1 Sam 8:5). During this period God ruled through Moses (Exod 19–Deut 34), then through Joshua (Josh 1–24), and finally through "judges" whom he raised up from time to time to deliver his people. From the human standpoint, the power was largely in the hands of the priests, who acted on the basis of laws passed by God, in which were united all the powers of the state—legislative, executive, and judicial. Such a government was, of course, possible only because of God's special revelation of himself to the nation.

THEOPHANY. A visible appearance of God, generally in human form. In the early days of humanity, before people had the written Word, before the Incarnation, and before the Holy Spirit had come to make his abode in human hearts, God sometimes appeared and talked with people. Before man sinned, he walked and talked with God; but after sin entered, Adam and his wife hid when they heard the voice of the Lord God (Gen 3:8). God spoke to Cain (ch. 4), Enoch and Noah "walked with God" (5:24; 6:9), and God gave Noah detailed instructions concerning the ark and the Flood. One of the loveliest and most instructive of the theophanies is found in Genesis 18. From Abraham's time on, theophanies generally occurred when the recipients were asleep, as in Jacob's vision at Bethel (28:10–17), but God addressed Moses "face to face" (Exod 33:11). There is good reason to think that theophanies before the incarnation of Christ were visible manifestations of the preincarnate Son of God. Theophanies ceased with the incarnation of our Lord. ABF

THEOPHILUS (thē-ŏf'ĭ-lŭs, Gr. *Theophilos*). It is reasonable to suppose that Theophilus, to whom Luke dedicated both his gospel (1:3) and the Book of Acts (1:1), was a real person. The title "most excellent" demands this, while the name and title together suggest a person of equestrian rank who became a Christian convert. Theophilus is most probably a baptismal name (see W. M. Ramsay, *St. Paul the Traveller and Roman Citizen,* pp. 388–89). Nothing is known of the man. He was certainly not Seneca, as one rash conjecture would have it. It is impossible to decide whether he was pure Roman, Greek, or Jew, or whether the omission in Acts of the honorable title used in the Gospel indicates a deepening friendship when the second book was dedicated, the abandonment of office, or dismissal from office for professing the Christian faith. EMB

THESSALONIANS, LETTERS TO THE. With the possible exception of Galatians, 1 and 2 Thessalonians are the earliest letters surviving from the correspondence of Paul. They were written to the church in Thessalonica, which was founded by Paul on his second journey en route from Philippi to Achaia. His preaching of Jesus as the Messiah aroused such violent controversy in the synagogue at Thessalonica that the opposing Jewish faction brought him before the city magistrates, charging him with fomenting insurrection against Caesar (Acts 17:5–9). Paul's friends were placed under bond for his good behavior, and to protect their own security, they sent him away from the city. He proceeded to Berea and after a short stay, interrupted by a fanatical group of Jews from Thessalonica, he went on to Athens, leaving Silas and Timothy to continue the preaching (17:10–14). From Athens he sent back instructions that they should join him as quickly as possible (17:15). According to 1 Thessalonians, they did so, and it is possible that he sent Timothy back again to encourage the Thessalonians while he continued at Athens (1 Thess 3:2). In the meantime Paul moved on to Corinth; and there Timothy found him when he returned with the news of the growth of the Thessalonian church (3:6; Acts 18:5). The first letter was prompted by Timothy's report.

I. 1 Thessalonians

A. **Authenticity.** There can be little doubt of the genuineness of this letter. Ignatius (*Ephesians* 10) and the *Shepherd of Hermas* (*Visions* 3.9.10) both contain passages that may have been taken from it, and it is listed in the canon of Marcion (A.D. 140). Irenaeus (c. 180) quoted it by name (*Against Heresies* 5.6.1); Tertullian attributed it to "the apostle" (*On the Resurrection of the Flesh* 24); and his contemporary, Clement of Alexandria, ascribed it directly to Paul (*Instructor* 1.5). As noted above, the autobiographical allusions in

1 Thessalonians correspond well with the data on the life of Paul given in Acts. Furthermore, no forger of the second century would have been likely to stress the imminency of the coming of Christ as Paul did.

B. **Date and Place.** Paul's stay both in Thessalonica and in Athens was brief, and he probably arrived in Corinth about A.D. 50. According to the narrative in Acts, Paul had begun his ministry there while working at the tentmaker's trade with Aquila and Priscilla (Acts 18:1–3). When Silas and Timothy rejoined him after their stay in Macedonia, they brought funds that enabled Paul to stop working and to devote his entire time to evangelism (Acts 18:5; 2 Cor 11:9). Shortly afterward the Jewish opposition to Paul's preaching became so violent that he was forced out of the synagogue. About a year and a half later he was called before the tribunal of Gallio, the Roman proconsul (Acts 18:12). Gallio had taken office only a short time previously, in 51 or 52. The first letter, then, must have been written at Corinth about a year prior to that date, in 50 or 51.

C. **Occasion.** Timothy brought a report concerning the problems of the church, with which Paul dealt in this letter. Some of his Jewish enemies had attacked his character, putting him under obligation to defend himself (1 Thess 2:1–6, 10, 14–16). A few of the converts were still influenced by the lax morality of the paganism from which they had so recently emerged and in which they had to live (4:3–7). Some of the church members had died, causing the rest to worry whether their departed friends would share in the return of Christ (4:13). Still others, anticipating the Second Advent, had given up all regular employment and were idly waiting for the Lord to appear (4:9–12). The letter was intended to encourage the Thessalonians' growth as Christians and to settle the questions that were troubling them.

D. **Outline and Content, 1 Thessalonians**

- I. The Conversion of the Thessalonians (1:1–10)
- II. The Ministry of Paul (2:1–3:13)
  - A. In Founding the Church (2:1–20)
  - B. In Concern for the Church (3:1–13)
- III. The Problems of the Church (4:1–5:22)
  - A. Moral Instruction (4:1–12)
  - B. The Lord's Coming (4:13–5:11)
  - C. Ethical Duties (5:12–22)
- IV. Conclusion (5:23–28)

First Thessalonians is a friendly, personal letter. The persecution in Thessalonica and the uncertainty concerning the coming of Christ that Paul had preached had disturbed the believers. Paul devoted the first half of his letter to reviewing his relationship with them in order to counteract the attacks of his enemies. The body of teaching in the second half of the letter dealt with sexual immorality by insisting on standards of holiness. The chief doctrinal topic was the second coming of Christ. Paul assured his readers that those who had died would not perish, but that they would be resurrected at the return of Christ. In company with the living believers, who would be translated, all would enter into eternal fellowship with Christ (1 Thess 4:13–18). Since the exact time of the return was not known, they were urged to be watchful, that they might not be taken unaware.

II. 2 Thessalonians

A. **Authenticity.** The genuineness of 2 Thessalonians has been challenged because of its difference from 1 Thessalonians: the warning of signs preceding the Day of the Lord (2 Thess 2:1–3) in contrast to a sudden and unannounced appearing (1 Thess 5:1–3); the teaching on the "man of sin" (2 Thess 2:3–9), unique in Paul's letters; and the generally more somber tone of the whole letter have been alleged as reason for rejecting authorship by Paul. None of these is convincing, for the two letters deal with two different aspects of the same general subject, and bear so many resemblances to each other that they are clearly related.

Early evidence for the acceptance of 2 Thessalonians is almost as full as for that of 1 Thessalonians. Shadowy references to it appear in the *Didache* (16), Ignatius (*Romans* 10), and possibly Polycarp (*Philippians* 11). Justin Martyr (A.D. 140) quotes 2 Thessalonians unmistakably in his *Dialogue with Trypho* (110). Irenaeus (A.D. 170) mentions it definitely as one of the letters of Paul in *Against Heresies* (3.7.2), as does Clement of Alexandria (*Stromata* 5.3).

B. **Date and Place.** The second letter was probably sent from Corinth in A.D. 51, not more than a few months after the first letter. Since Silas and Timothy were still with Paul, it is likely that no great interval elapsed between the writing of the two.

C. **Occasion.** Evidently the Thessalonian Christians had been disturbed by the arrival of a letter purporting to come from Paul—a letter he had not authorized (2 Thess 2:2). Some of them were suffering harsh persecution (1:4–5); others were apprehensive that the Last Day was about to arrive (2:2); and there were still a few who were idle and disorderly (3:6–12). The second letter serves to clarify further the problems of the first letter and to confirm the confidence of the readers.

D. **Outline and Content, 2 Thessalonians**

- I. Salutation (1:1–2)
- II. Encouragement in Persecution (1:3–12)
- III. The Signs of the Day of Christ (2:1–17)
  - A. Warning of false rumors (2:1–2)
  - B. The apostasy (2:3)
  - C. The revelation of the man of sin (2:4–12)
  - D. The preservation of God's people (2:13–17)
- IV. Spiritual Counsel (3:1–15)
- V. Conclusion (3:16–18)

Whereas the first letter heralds the resurrection of the righteous dead and the restoration of the living at the return of Christ, the second letter describes the apostasy preceding the coming of Christ to judgment. Paul stated that the "secret power of lawlessness" was already at work and that its climax would be reached with the removal of the "hinderer" (2 Thess 2:6–7), who has been variously identified with the Holy Spirit, the power of the Roman Empire, and the preaching of Paul himself. With the disappearance of any spiritual restraint, the "man of sin" or "lawlessness" will be revealed, who will (2:3–10) deceive all people and will be energized by the power of Satan himself.

In view of this prospect, Paul exhorted the Thessalonians to retain their faith and to improve their conduct. He spoke even more vehemently to those who persisted in idleness (2 Thess 3:6–12), recommending that the Christians withdraw fellowship from them.

Bibliography: L. L. Morris, *The First and Second Epistles to the Thessalonians* (NIC), 1959; E. Best, *The First and Second Epistles to the Thessalonians* (HNTC), 1972; F. F. Bruce, *1 & 2 Thessalonians* (WBC), 1982; I. H. Marshall, *1 and 2 Thessalonians* (NCB), 1983. MCT

THESSALONICA (thĕs'à-lō-nī'kà, Gr. *Thessalonikē*). A Macedonian town founded by Cassander, Alexander's officer who took control of Greece after Alexander's death in 332 B.C. Thessalonica was probably founded toward the end of the century by consolidating small towns at the head of the Thermaic Gulf. It dominated the junction of the northern trade route and the road from the Adriatic to Byzantium, which later became the Via Egnatia. Its comparatively sheltered harbor made it the chief port of Macedonia, after Pella yielded to the silting that was the perennial problem of Greek harbors. It was a fortress that withstood a Roman siege, surrendering only after the battle of Pydna sealed Rome's victory in the Macedonian Wars. In 147 it became the capital of the Roman province and was Pompey's base a century later in the civil war with Julius Caesar. Prolific coinage suggests a high level of prosperity. The population included a large Roman element and a Jewish colony. Paul visited Thessalonica after Philippi and appears to have worked among a composite group, comprising the Jews of the synagogue and Greek proselytes, among whom were some women of high social standing. There was a high degree of emancipation among the women of Macedonia. In Acts 17:6, 8, the "city officials" (so NIV) are called "politarchs." Its use was once dismissed as a mistake of the historian because it was a term unknown elsewhere. There are now sixteen epigraphical examples in modern Salonica, and one is located in the British Museum. It was evidently a Macedonian term, and Luke's use of it was in line with his habit of using accepted terminology. EMB

THEUDAS (thū'dàs, Gr. *Theudas*). Josephus (*Antiq*. 20.5.1) mentions a Theudas who led a considerable revolt in A.D. 44 or 45. This cannot have been the Theudas of Gamaliel's speech, which was made some ten years earlier. To suggest that Luke used Josephus, and confused Theudas and Judas (Acts 5:36–37), reversing their chronological order, is to disregard Luke's customary accuracy. There is little correspondence between Luke's definite "four hundred" and Josephus's account of a more extensive rebellion. It is quite possible that the reference in Josephus was rather an interpolation from Acts. There could have been more than one Theudas, and our knowledge of the history of the province is far too sketchy to dispute this clear possibility. W. M. Ramsay writes, "The period is very obscure; Josephus is practically our only authority. He does not allude or profess to allude, to every little disturbance on the banks of the Jordan. . ." (*Was Christ Born at Bethlehem?* pp. 258–59). Indeed "no testimony could be stronger than that of Josephus himself to the fact that at the time of the Advent Judaea was full of tumults and seditions and pretenders of all kinds" (EGT 2:158). The movements of Theudas and of Judas were probably associated, and both took place in time of Quirinius. EMB

THIEF, THIEVES (Heb. *gannāv, steal,* Gr. *kleptēs, lestēs, thief*). The word is used for anyone who appropriates someone else's property, including petty thieves and highwaymen (Luke 10:30; John 12:6). Under the law of Moses, thieves who were caught were expected to restore twice the amount stolen. The thieves crucified with Jesus must have been robbers or brigands, judging by the severity of the punishment and the fact that one of them acknowledged that the death penalty imposed on them was just (Luke 23:41).

THIGH (Heb. *yarekh, shôq,* Gr. *mēros*). The upper part of a human leg, or the rear leg of a quadruped. To put one's hand under the thigh of another was to enhance the sacredness of an oath (Gen 24:2, 9; 47:29). To "smite hip and thigh" (Judg 15:8 KJV) implied not only slaughter but slaughter with extreme violence. When the Angel of the Lord wrestled with Jacob so that Jacob might know the weakness of his human strength, he touched the hollow of Jacob's thigh and threw it out of joint at the hip, altering Jacob's position from struggling to clinging; when he was thus transformed, God changed his name from Jacob ("supplanter") to Israel ("prince with God"); recalling this event, the Israelites "do not eat the tendon attached to the socket of the hip" (Gen 32:24–32). In Oriental feasts the shoulder or the thigh of the meat is often placed before an honored guest (cf. 1 Sam 9:23–24); he has the privilege of sharing it with those near him. The thigh was the place to strap a sword (Judg 3:16; Ps 45:3; S of Sol 3:8). To smite one's thigh (Jer 31:19; Ezek 21:12 KJV, MLB, NASB, RSV; beat one's breast JB, NEB, NIV) was a sign of amazement or of great shame.

THIMNATHAH (thĭm'nà-thà, Heb. *timnāthâh*). A city in Dan (Josh 19:43 lit., KJV, MOF; Timnah NASB, NIV, RSV). See TIMNAH.

THISTLE (See PLANTS)

THOMAS (tŏm′ăs, Gr. *Thōmas,* from Aram. *te'oma, twin*). One of the twelve apostles (Matt 10:3). He was called "Didymus" or "the Twin" (cf. John 11:16; 20:24; 21:2). The Gospel of John gives the most information about him. When the other apostles tried to dissuade Jesus from going to Bethany to heal Lazarus because of the danger involved from hostile Jews, Thomas said to them, "Let us also go, that we may die with him" (11:16). Shortly before the Passion, Thomas asked, "Lord, we don't know where you are going, so how can we know the way?" (14:1–6). Thomas was not with the other apostles when Jesus presented himself to them on the evening of the Resurrection, and he told them later that he could not believe in Jesus' resurrection (20:24–25). Eight days later he was with the apostles when Jesus appeared to them again, and he exclaimed, "My Lord and my God!" (20:26–29). He was with the six other disciples when Jesus appeared to them at the Sea of Galilee (21:1–8) and was with the rest of the apostles in the Upper Room at Jerusalem after the Ascension (Acts 1:13). According to tradition he afterward labored in Parthia, Persia, and India. A place near Madras is called St. Thomas's Mount. SB

THOMAS, GOSPEL OF. This was the major item in a jar of papyri discovered at Nag Hammadi between Cairo and Luxor in A.D. 1945. It took some fourteen years for the knowledge of the find to reach the West. Some inkling of the Gospel of Thomas had emerged in 1903 from a papyrus discovered by Grenfell and Hunt. The Nag Hammadi document is a collection of 114 sayings of Christ in the form of isolated dicta or brief conversations, some known, some entirely new, the whole work being ascribed to the apostle Thomas. Some of the sayings are inconsiderable and without the edge and distinctiness of the biblical utterances of Christ. Others, on the contrary, are both fresh and pungent and may well represent a genuine tradition. Consider a few illustrations of the latter sort: "Jesus said: Whoever is near me is near the fire, and whoever is far from me is far from the kingdom." The words coincide with more than one warning of the inevitability of persecution, and the consistent claim that discipleship was the path to God. Again: "They said to him: Come and let us pray today and let us fast. But Jesus said: Which then is the sin I have committed, or in what have I been vanquished?" (The fourth Gospel has this question: "Which of you convicts me of sin?") Again: "Jesus said: Become passersby." The words are in tune with a saying of Christ preserved in the arabesques of the Muslim mosque: "Life is a bridge. You pass over it but build no houses on it." The meaning, of course, is that the wise and good avoid entanglements and too great involvement in material things. Such sayings have a ring of authenticity. So do such words as this beatitude from Thomas: "Blessed is the man who suffers. He finds life." And the reproach to the Pharisees, catching up a simile of the Greeks still in common usage: "Woe to them, for they are like a dog sleeping in a manger of oxen, for neither does he eat nor allow the oxen to eat."

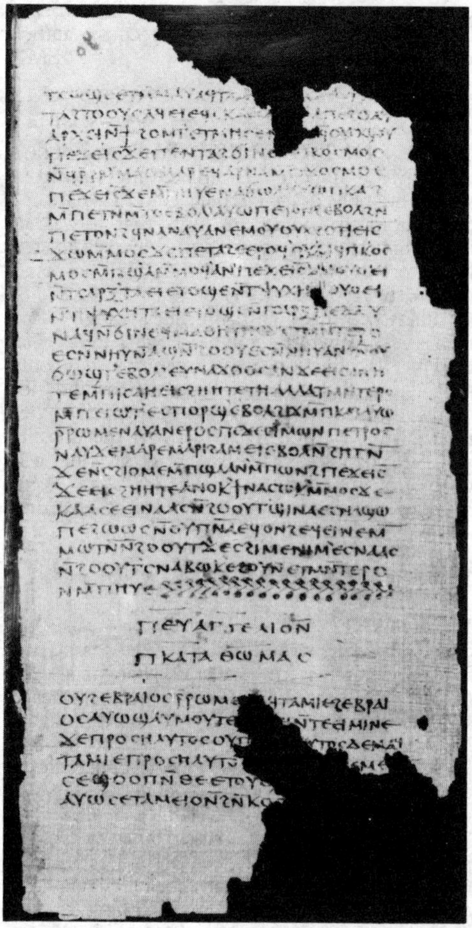

First page of the Gospel of Thomas. Translation: "These are the secret sayings that the living Jesus spoke and Judas Thomas the Twin recorded . . . " (by M. W. Meyer). From the Nag Hamadi library discovered in 1945. Courtesy Institute for Antiquity and Christianity, Claremont, California.

The collection is dated A.D. 140, and it is perhaps not surprising that some well-known sayings have become somewhat worn and altered. Compare, for example, the parable of the sower and the seed in the canonical Gospels with the attenuated version in the Gospel of Thomas: "See the sower went out, he filled his hand, he threw. Some seed fell on the road, the birds came, they gathered them. Others fell on the rock, and did not strike root in the earth, and did not produce ears. Others fell in the thorns. They choked the seed and the worm ate them. Others fell on the good earth, and brought forth good fruit. It bore sixty per measure, and one hundred and twenty per measure." This gospel was held no doubt by a Christian community in Egypt, perhaps a remnant who escaped from Jerusalem before A.D. 70

to live in some measure of isolation in a foreign land. Thomas may, in fact, have been the author of the original document. EMB

THORN (See PLANTS)

THORN IN THE FLESH. Paul's description of a physical ailment that afflicted him and from which he prayed to be relieved (2 Cor 12:7). Some hold that there are hints that it was an inflammation of the eyes. Paul generally dictated his letters, but signed them with his own hand (1 Cor 16:21; 2 Thess 3:17). He wrote the end of Galatians with his own hand, but apologized for the large handwriting ("what large letters," Gal 6:11). His affliction was apparently not only painful but disfiguring. The Galatians did not despise him for it and would have plucked out their own eyes and given them to the apostle, were it possible (4:13–15). He says he was unable to recognize the high priest (Acts 23:5). Ramsay thought it was some form of recurring malarial fever.

THORNS, CROWN OF (See CROWN)

THOUSAND (Heb. *eleph,* Gr. *chilioi*). Frequently used hyperbolically for a very large but indefinite number, or as the division of a tribe (Num 31:5; Josh 22:14). The word was also used as a tribal subdivision known technically as "a father's house" (Num 1:2, 4, 16; Judg 6:15; 1 Sam 10:19, 21).

Photograph of the back panel of the wooden throne of Pharaoh Tut-ankh-amun, overlaid with sheet gold, silver, blue faience, calcite, and glass. The king, wearing a composite crown, broad collar, and pleated skirt, sits on a cushioned throne, as his wife, Queen Ankh-es-en Amen, stands before him holding a bowl in her left hand and touching the king with her right. From tomb No. 91 at Thebes, c. 1370–1353 B.C. Courtesy Egyptian Expedition, The Metropolitan Museum of Art.

THOUSAND YEARS (See KINGDOM OF GOD)

THRACE (thrās, Gr. *Thrakia*). A kingdom and later a Roman province, in SE Europe, east of Macedonia. The name does not appear in the canonical books, but 2 Maccabees 12:35 mentions an unnamed Thracian horseman who rescued Gorgias, the governor of Jamnia, from possible Jewish capture.

THREE HEBREW CHILDREN, SONG OF (See APOCRYPHA)

THREE TAVERNS (Lat. *Tres Tabernae*). This village, which may be translated "Three Shops," was a stopping place on the Via Appia, some thirty-three miles (fifty-five km.) from Rome, at the junction of the road from Antium, near modern Cisterna. It was a place of some importance (Acts 28:15; Cic. *Ad Att.* 2:12).

THRESHING (Heb. *dûsh, to trample out, hāvat, to beat out or off, dārakh, to tread,* Gr. *aloaō, to tread down*). Threshing was done in one of two ways: (1) by beating the sheaves with a rod or flail or (2) by trampling them under the feet of oxen that pulled a wooden sled around the threshing floor (Isa 28:27). Threshing was done out-of-doors on a hard surface of the ground. The word also had a figurative use (Isa 21:10; 41:15; Mic 4:12–13; 1 Cor 9:10). See also AGRICULTURE; FARMING.

THRESHING FLOOR (Heb. *gōren,* Gr. *halōn*). The place where grain was threshed. Usually clay soil was packed to a hard smooth surface. Sheaves of grain were spread on the floor and trampled by oxen often drawing crude wooden sleds with notched rims (Deut 25:4; Isa 28:27; 1 Cor 9:9). A shovel and fan were used in winnowing the grain (Isa 30:24). Since robbers would visit the floor at threshing time (1 Sam 23:1), the laborers slept there (Ruth 3:4–7). Threshing floors were often on hills where the night winds could more easily blow away the chaff.

THRESHOLD (Heb. *saph, threshold, entrance, miphtān, threshold, sill*). The piece of wood or stone that lies below the bottom of a door and has to be crossed on entering a house. The sill of a doorway, hence the entrance to a building.

THRONE (Heb. *kissē',* Gr. *thronos*). A chair of state occupied by one in authority or of high position, such as a high priest, judge, governor, or king (Gen 41:40; 2 Sam 3:10; Neh 3:7; Ps 122:5; Jer 1:15; Matt 19:28). Solomon's throne was an elaborate one (1 Kings 10:18–20; 2 Chron 9:17–19). For ages the throne has been a symbol of authority, exalted position, and majesty (Ps 9:7; 45:6; 94:20; Prov 16:12).

THRUSH (See BIRDS)

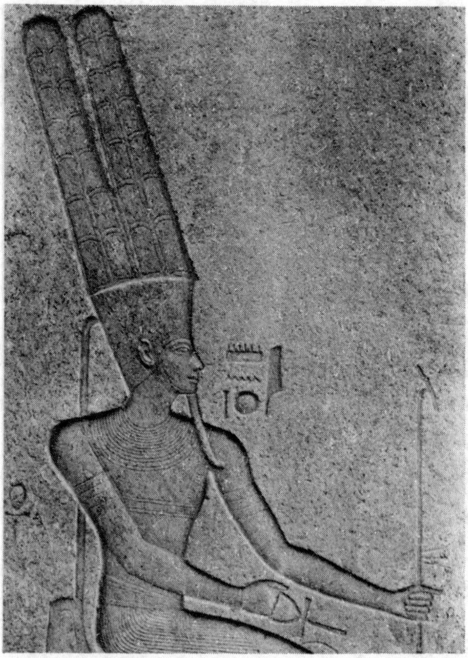

Relief of King Thutmose III, one of the greatest military leaders and administrators of antiquity. Thutmose is a common personal name as well as a great royal name of Egypt. From the temple of Amon at Karnak. Courtesy Bildarchiv Foto, Marburg.

THUMB. Either the great toe of the foot or the thumb of the hand. The Hebrew word *bōhen,* followed by a modifying term, indicates which is meant (Exod 29:20; Lev 8:23; 14:14). To cut off these members was to handicap a victim and brand him. A son of Reuben was named *Bohan,* "thumb" (Josh 15:6).

THUMMIM (See URIM AND THUMMIM)

THUNDER (Heb. *ra'am, qôl,* Gr. *brontē*). The noise that follows a lightning discharge. In Palestine it was a rare phenomenon during summer months, so if it did occur it was considered a sign of divine displeasure (1 Sam 12:17). A spectacular electrical storm accompanied the plague of hail in Egypt (Exod 9:22–26). Such a display was seen at Sinai (19:16–18). Thunder operates according to natural law (Job 28:26; 38:25). Hebrews considered thunder to be a revelation of God's power (Job 37:2–5; 40:9; Ps 18:13; 29:2–9; Isa 30:30), and it represented God's anger and chastening (1 Sam 2:10).

THUNDER, SONS OF (*huioi brontēs*). The title Jesus gave James and John (Mark 3:17) apparently because of their bold and sometimes rash natures (Matt 20:20–23; Luke 9:54).

THUTMOSE (also Tuthmosis, Thotmes). The word does not appear in the Bible but is a common personal name and one of the great royal names of Egypt. It was given to four kings of the Eighteenth Dynasty. The outstanding Thutmose was Thutmose III, one of the greatest military leaders and administrators of antiquity. Thutmose I made a military expedition beyond the Euphrates and also extended the southern boundary to the Third Cataract. He did some building at Karnak; one of his obelisks still stands there. Thutmose II married his half-sister, Hatshepsut, and their daughter became the wife of Thutmose III. Hatshepsut was regent for a period after the death of Thutmose II and even had herself proclaimed "king"; upon her death, Thutmose III burst from obscurity and attempted to eliminate all references to this aunt and mother-in-law. He began his seventeen expeditions to Palestine-Syria with a brilliantly strategic victory over an Asiatic coalition at Megiddo. He reached beyond the Euphrates and set up a stele beside that left by his grandfather (Thutmose I). An ardent sportsman, Thutmose III here engaged in a great elephant hunt. He was also active in the south and pushed the boundary to Gebel Barkal, just below the Fourth Cataract.

The records of his expeditions are preserved in his annals at Karnak. The tribute gained from his successes greatly enriched the priesthood of Amon at Thebes, while the influx of foreign products and peoples effected a cosmopolitanism that eventually contributed to the breakdown of the empire that had been built in large measure by the abilities of Thutmose III. In building activity he is credited with constructions at Karnak: the hall of the annals, a building erected to conceal the obelisks of Hatshepsut; the Sixth Pylon; the Seventh Pylon; and the Festival Hall to the east. On the west bank he built at Thebes, and to the north he erected a mortuary temple that has not survived. He also built temples at other sites in Egypt and Nubia. For various reasons Thutmose III has been considered the Pharaoh of the Oppression, and his successor, Amenhotep II, the Pharaoh of the Exodus. Although this is an attractive hypothesis in many respects, it is burdened with difficulties, and the identity of those pharaohs is still problematic. Thutmose IV, the son of Amenhotep II, is the last of the kings of this name. The Dream Stele, which stills stands between the forelegs of the Sphinx at Giza, relates how he came to the throne. CEDV

THYATIRA (thī'ȧ-tī'rȧ, Gr. *Thyateira*). A city in the province of Asia, on the boundary of Lydia and Mysia. Thyatira has no illustrious history and is scarcely mentioned by ancient writers. Coinage suggests that, lying as it did on a great highway linking two river valleys, Thyatira was a garrison town for many centuries. Its ancient Anatolian deity was a warlike figure armed with a battle-ax and mounted on a charger. An odd coin or two shows a female deity wearing a battlemented crown. The city was a center of commerce, and the records preserve references to more trade guilds than those listed for any other Asian city. Lydia, whom Paul met in Philippi, was a Thyatiran seller of "turkey red," the product of the

General view of modern Tiberias, on the western shore of the Sea of Galilee, first built between A.D. 16 and 22. Courtesy A. Strajmayster.

madder root (Acts 16:14). It is curious to find another woman, nicknamed after the princess who by marriage sealed Ahab's trading partnership with the Phoenicians, leading a party of compromise in the Thyatiran church (Rev 2:20–21). The necessity for membership in a trade guild invited the Christians of Thyatira to compromise and opened the door to manytemptations. Thyatira played a significant part in the later history of the church.

TIBERIAS (tī-bē'rĭ-ăs, Gr. *Tiberias*). A city of Herod Antipas, built between the years A.D. 16 and 22 on the western shore of the Sea of Galilee, or the Sea of Tiberias, as John, writing for non-Jewish readers, calls the lake (John 6:1; 21:1). It was named, of course, after the reigning emperor, Tiberius, reflecting the pro-Roman policy consistently followed by the Herods. The city is said to have occupied the site at Rakkath, an old town of Naphtali, and since Rakkath means "strip" or "coast," this may have been the case. Jewish rumor said Tiberias was built over a graveyard, and the place was therefore dubbed unclean (Josephus, *Antiq.* 18.2.3). Macalister is of the opinion that this proves that no earlier city occupied the site (HDB, p. 934), but Herod could easily have included the burial place Rakkath in his larger foundation. Herod built ambitiously. The ruins indicate a wall three miles (five km.) long. He built a palace, a forum, and a great synagogue, for the foundation illustrates strikingly the dual Herodian policy, which sought to combine pro-Roman loyalty with effective patronage of the Jews. Jewish boycott, however, compelled Herod to populate his new town with the lowest elements of the land. Defended by its strong acropolis, Tiberias survived the passing of the other lakeside towns. Saladin took Tiberias in 1187. The hot springs and baths lay south of the city wall. Their healthful nature is mentioned by the Elder Pliny (H. N. 5:15), and a coin of Tiberias of Trajan's day shows a figure of Hygeia (Health) feeding a serpent (sign of Aesculapius, god of healing) as she sits on a rock over a spring. EMB

TIBERIAS, SEA OF (See GALILEE, SEA OF)

TIBERIUS (tī-bēr'ĭ-ŭs, Gr. *Tiberios*). Tiberius Julius Caesar Augustus succeeded to the principate on the death of Augustus in A.D. 14, becoming thus the second Roman emperor. He was born in 42 B.C., son of Empress Livia, wife of Augustus, by her first husband, Tiberius Claudius Nero. He had a distinguished military career in the East and in Germany, and, in the absence of direct heirs to Augustus, was the logical successor. Augustus, however, did not like Tiberius; and Tiberius for many years, was the passive witness of several attempts to bypass his claims and his abilities. The experience of disapproval and rejection no doubt contributed to the dourness, secretiveness, ambiguity, and suspicious preoccupations that marred the years of Tiberius's power. A morbid fear of disloyalty led to the heavy incidence of treason trials, which were a feature of the Roman principate under its worst incumbents. There is no evidence that Tiberius was unduly tyrannous, but aristocrats and writers of their number blamed the prince for features of later tyranny and for precedents of many subsequent incidents of oppression. This, added to the natural unpopularity of a reticent and lonely man, left Tiberius with a reputation that modern scholarship, discounting Tacitus's brilliant and bitter account, has been at some pains to rehabilitate. Tiberius had great ability and some measure of magnanimity; for, in spite of many unhappy memories, he sought loyally to continue Augustus's policies, foreign and domestic. The rumors of senile debauchery on Capri can be listed with the slanders of earlier years, though there is some evidence of mental disturbance in the later period of the principate. Tiberius died on March 16, A.D. 37. He was the reigning emperor at the time of Christ's death. EMB

TIBHATH (tĭb'hăth, Heb. *tivhath*). In the KJV a city in the kingdom of Zobah, east of the Anti-Lebanon Mountains. David captured it from Hadadezer and sent its treasures to Jerusalem (1 Chron 18:7–9; "Betah" of 2 Sam 8:8). NIV has "Tebah" in both passages.

TIBNI (tĭb'nī, Heb. *tivnî*). A son of Ginath. When Zimri died, he was an unsuccessful competitor for the throne of Israel with Omri (1 Kings 16:15–21). Nothing else is known about him.

TIDAL (tī'dăl, Heb. *tidh'āl*). An unidentified king, mentioned only in Genesis 14:1, 9 where he is called "king of Goiim" ("nations," KJV) and is allied with three other kings, with Kedorlaomer king of Elam as the leader (14:5, 17). Invading westward, they defeated the kings of the cities of the plain and took plunder and captives, including Lot. Abraham routed the coalition in a night raid, rescued the captives, and recovered the goods (14:15–16).

Drawing of a statue of Tiberius Caesar, the Roman emperor who reigned at the time of Christ's death. Courtesy Carta, Jerusalem.

TIGLATH-PILESER (tĭg'lăth-pĭ-lē'zêr, Assyr. *Tukulti-apil-esharra,* Heb. *tiglath-pil'eser, tilleghath-pilne'ser*). A famous name among the Assyrian kings. Tiglath-Pileser I (1114–1074

Tiglath-Pileser III, king of Assyria (745–727 B.C.), standing with driver and third man in chariot led by two footmen. Relief from Nimrud, c. 740 B.C. Reproduced by courtesy of the Trustees of the British Museum.

Engraved bronze band illustrating Shalmaneser III's expedition to the source of the Tigris. From one of the gates of a palace of Shalmaneser III (858–824 B.C.) near Tell Balawat. Reproduced by courtesy of the Trustees of the British Museum.

B.C.) was a conqueror whose campaigns extended northward to the vicinity of Lake Van and westward to the Mediterranean. His annals tell of his efforts to establish a world empire, but his reign was followed by several centuries in which Assyria was weak. In 745 a usurper took the Assyrian throne and assumed the name Tiglath-Pileser. Tiglath-Pileser III (745–727) injected new vigor into the Assyrian Empire, which had suffered another decline after a resurgence of power in the ninth century. He engaged in campaigns to east and west and was recognized as king even in Babylon, where he was known as Pulu. He is referred to as "Pul" in 2 Kings 15:19 and 1 Chronicles 5:26. His annals list Azariah of Judah among the kings from whom he received tribute; the OT does not relate this account. (See D. D. Luckenbill, *Ancient Records of Assyria and Babylonia,* 1926–27, 1:770; hereafter ARAB.) The annals also mention tribute from Menahem of Samaria, who bought him off. Compare the account in 2 Kings 15:19–20: "Then Pul king of Assyria invaded the land, and Menahem gave him a thousand talents of silver to gain his support and strengthen his own hold on the kingdom. . . . So the king of Assyria withdrew and stayed in the land no longer." (Cf. ARAB, 1:772, 815.)

During the reign of the Judean king Ahaz, Pekah of Israel and Rezin of Syria moved against Judah. Ahaz secured the help of Tiglath-Pileser (2 Kings 16:5–8), who captured Damascus, deported its people, and killed Rezin. He took a number of Israelite cities and exiled the inhabitants to Assyria (2 Kings 15:29; cf. ARAB, 1:816: "The land of Bit Humria [= house of Omri = Israel] . . . all its people, together with their goods I carried off to Assyria."). He was also responsible for the deportation of Transjordanian Israelites, whom he brought to "Halah, Habor, Hara and the river of Gozan" (1 Chron 5:6, 26). The transfer of peoples to foreign areas was a practical policy designed to reduce the possibility of revolts in conquered regions (cf. ARAB, 1:770, 772, 777). Ahaz also requested military aid from him because of invasions by Edomites and Philistines; he gave gifts from the temple and the palace to Tiglath-Pileser, "but that did not help him" (2 Chron 28:20–21; cf. ARAB, 1:801). CEDV

TIGRIS (tī'grĭs, Assyr. *Idigalat, arrow,* Heb. *hiddeqel*). One of the two great rivers of the Mesopotamian area. It originates in the Taurus Mountains of Armenia; in its 1,150 miles (1,917 km.) it receives three principal tributaries from the east, the Great Zab, the Little Zab, and the Diyala. It is difficult for navigation, since for some months it is very shallow, yet it is subject to flooding and during the rainy season ranges outside its banks. In antiquity the Tigris and the Euphrates entered the Persian Gulf by separate mouths, but today the Tigris joins the Euphrates at Kurna to form the Shatt el-Arab. The rivers of Iran also have been an important factor in the formation of the delta. Through what was Assyria and Babylonia the Tigris flows past famous cities, living and dead: Mosul, on the west bank, looks across the river to the mounds of Nineveh; farther downstream are Asshur, Samarra, and Baghdad. In the Bible the Tigris is mentioned with the Euphrates and two other streams as rivers that watered the Garden of Eden (Gen 2:14). Daniel 10:4 states that it was while the prophet "was standing on the bank of the great river, the Tigris" that he saw the vision he subsequently recorded. CEDV

TIKVAH (tĭk'vȧ, Heb. *tiqwah*). 1. The father-in-law of the prophetess Huldah, the wife of Shallum (2 Kings 22:8–14).

2. During the reforms under Ezra a son of another Tikvah was a chief leader (Ezra 10:9–15).

TIKVATH (See TIKVAH)

TILE (Heb. *levēnâh, brick,* Gr. *keramos*). Ancient writing was done with a stylus on blocks of soft clay, which varied in size according to need. Ezekiel used such a tile in drawing a prophetic picture of the doom awaiting Jerusalem (Ezek 4:1–8 KJV; NIV "tablet"). When a permanent record was desired, the inscribed tile was baked in a furnace. So skilled were scribes of the day that many of their tiles remain in perfect condition after three thousand years.

Roofing tiles are mentioned in Luke 5:19, where the reference is apparently to clay roofing—tiles with which the roof was covered. Clay tiles were not commonly used as roofing material for houses in Palestine, roofs usually being covered with a mixture of clay and straw. It may be that Luke uses the expression "through the tiles" to mean "through the roof," without reference to the material used for the roof.

TILING (See TILE)

TILLER (See OCCUPATIONS AND PROFESSIONS)

TILON (tī'lŏn, Heb. *tîlôn*). One of the sons of Shimon (1 Chron 4:20), a descendant of Judah.

TIMAEUS (tī-mē'ŭs, Gr. *Timaios*). The father of a blind man whose eyes Jesus opened (Mark 10:46–52), the name Bartimaeus meaning "son of Timaeus."

TIMBREL (see MUSIC AND MUSICAL INSTRUMENTS)

TIME. The history of the development of various measurements for time, and the making of instruments for determining them, is an interesting one. Before the days of Abraham, the Chaldeans had set up a system of days and seasons and had divided the periods of darkness and light into parts. Their seven-day week had been accepted by Egyptians before the time of Moses. Day and night were determined by the sun. The week, no doubt, was determined by the phases of the moon. The month was based on the recurrence of the new moon. In order to provide in the calendar for the extra days of the solar year over the twelve lunar months, the Jews added an intercalary month. They had no way of determining an absolute solar year, so the extra month was added every third year, with adjustments to provide seven extra months each nineteen years. It was added after the spring equinox, hence was called a second Adar (the preceding month being Adar). This method of keeping the lunar and the solar years synchronized was probably learned by the Israelites during the Babylonian captivity.

For ages, years were not numbered consecutively as we number them, but were counted for some outstanding event, such as the founding of Rome. The Hebrews had a civil year that began at the vernal equinox, after the custom of Babylon, and a sacred year that began with the harvest or seventh month (Lev 25:8–9). They divided the year into two seasons, seedtime or winter, and harvest or summer (Gen 8:22; 45:6; Exod 34:21; Prov 10:5).

The Hebrew word for day (*yom*) may mean a period of daylight or a period of twenty-four hours. We have no way of knowing how the period was determined before the solar system was completed (Gen 1:14–19). The Roman day began at midnight and had twelve hours (John 11:9). The Hebrew day was reckoned from sunset. There was the cool of the day (Gen 3:8) or twilight (Job 24:15). Mid-morning was when the sun had become hot (1 Sam 11:9). Noon was the heat of the day (Gen 18:1). Night was divided into watches, so that the length of each varied with changing seasons. The first watch came about 3:30 P.M. Midnight was the middle watch (Judg 7:19). Morning watch began about 9:30 A.M. (Exod 14:24). It was called cockcrow in NT times (Matt 26:34; Mark 13:35). The watch was so named because of the changing of watchmen and was not a very definite period (Ps 90:4; 119:148; Jer 51:12). Roman influence caused a revision of the watches, so in the days of Christ there were four divisions of the night (Matt 14:25; Mark 6:48), these being marked approximately by 7:00 P.M., 9:30 P.M., midnight, 2:30 A.M., and 5:00 A.M.

In the Scriptures the words translated "time" have varied connotations. Temporal existence is "my life" in both Job 7:7 and Psalm 89:47. A period allotted for a special object, task, or cause was its time (Eccl 3:1; 8:6). A special period of life was "a time," as a period of conception (Gen 18:10, 14) or the days of pregnancy (1 Sam 1:20); any special feast or celebration (Ps 81:3); an occasion for the consummation of divine plans (Job 24:1; Jer 2:27; John 7:6, 8; Acts 3:21; Rom 8:22–23; 1 Tim 6:15); a time for showing affection (Eccl 3:8; Ezek 16:8). The dispensation of grace is the time of salvation (Ps 69:13; Isa 49:8; 2 Cor 6:2).

Ancient people had no method of reckoning long periods of time. The Greeks did develop the idea of eras, or connected time elements. The Olympian era dated from 766 B.C.; the Seleucid era from 312 B.C. Their year began on January 1. In Asia Minor the year began with the autumn equinox. It is, therefore, difficult to determine any precise date for events occurring during NT days. Luke's dating of events (1:5; 2:1–2; 3:1) when John the Baptist began his ministry is the only definite fact on which to determine the times of Jesus with any certainty.

The Hebrews used great and well-known events like the Exodus, the Babylonian exile, the building of the temple, and the earthquake (Amos 1:1) as fixed points for indicating the time of other events. In the Maccabean age the beginning of the Seleucid era (312 B.C.) became a starting point. JDF

TIMEUS (See TIMAEUS)

TIMNA (tĭm′nȧ, Heb. *timnaʿ, holding in check*). 1. A concubine of Esau's son Eliphaz (Gen 36:12).

2. A Horite woman, sister of Lotan, who was a son of Seir (Gen 36:20–22; 1 Chron 1:39).

3. A chief or clan descended from Esau (Gen 36:40; Timnah KJV).

4. A son of Eliphaz (1 Chron 1:36).

TIMNAH (tĭm′nȧ, Heb. *timnāh, thimnāthāh*). 1. A town on the border of Judah (Josh 15:10), later given to the tribe of Dan and called Thimnathah (19:43 KJV, MOF; Timnah NASB, NIV, RSV). Located at Tibnah, three miles (five km.) SW of Beth Shemesh, it may be the same as Timnath (Judg 14:1–5 KJV, MOF, NEB).

2. A town in the hill country of Judah (Josh 15:57; Timnath in Gen 38:12–14 KJV, NEB).

3. A duke (chief) in Edom (1 Chron 1:51).

4. A town in south Judah (2 Chron 28:18).

TIMNATH (See TIMNAH)

TIMNATH-HERES (See TIMNATH-SERAH)

TIMNATH-SERAH (tĭm′năth-hē′rēz, Heb. *timnath serah*). The same as Timnath Heres (Judg 2:9). It was a village in Ephraim that Joshua requested as an inheritance (Josh 19:50), that he rebuilt, and where his remains were buried (24:30). It is probably Tibnah, twelve miles (twenty km.) NE of Lydda.

TIMNITE (tĭm′nīt, Heb. *timnî*). A native of Timnah whose daughter was married to Samson (Judg 15:3–6).

TIMON (tī′mŏn, Gr. *Timōn*). One of the seven chosen by the church in Jerusalem to relieve the apostles of having to look after the poor (Acts 6:5).

TIMOTHEUS (See TIMOTHY)

TIMOTHY (tĭm′ō-thē, Gr. *Timotheos, honoring God*). Paul's spiritual child (1 Tim 1:2; 2 Tim 1:2), later the apostle's fellow-traveler and official representative. His character was a blend of amiability and faithfulness in spite of natural timidity. Paul loved Timothy and admired his outstanding personality traits. One must read Philippians 2:19–22 to know how highly the apostle esteemed this young friend. None of Paul's companions is mentioned as often and is with him as constantly as is Timothy. That this relationship was of an enduring nature is clear from 2 Timothy 4:9, 21. Paul knew that he could count on Timothy. He was the kind of person who in spite of his youth—he was Paul's junior by several years (1 Tim 4:12)—his natural reserve and timidity (1 Cor 16:10; 2 Tim 1:7), and his frequent ailments (1 Tim 5:23), was willing to leave his home to accompany the apostle on dangerous journeys, to be sent on difficult errands, and to remain to the very end Christ's faithful servant.

In the popular mind the distinction between Timothy and Titus is not always clear. Both of these men were Paul's worthy fellow workers. The difference, however, is as follows. Titus was more of a leader; Timothy, more of a follower. Titus was resourceful, a man of initiative in a good cause. One finds in him something of the aggressiveness of Paul. (See TITUS.) Timothy, on the other hand, was shy and reserved. Nevertheless, he was ever obedient and cooperative. He manifested his complete willingness even when he was required to do things that ran counter to his natural shyness.

Timothy is first mentioned in Acts 16:1, from which passage it may be inferred that he was an inhabitant of Lystra (cf. 20:4). He was the offspring of a mixed marriage: he had a Greek pagan father and a devout Jewish mother, Eunice (Acts 16:1; 2 Tim 1:5). From the days of his childhood Timothy had been instructed in the sacred writings of the OT (2 Tim 3:15). In the manner of devout Israelites his grandmother Lois and mother Eunice had nurtured him (1:5). Then came Paul, who taught this devout family that Jesus Christ is the fulfillment of the OT. First grandmother Lois and mother Eunice became followers of Christ, then, as a result of their cooperation with Paul, Timothy also did so (1:5). This took place on Paul's first missionary journey. Hence Timothy knew about the persecutions and sufferings that the missionaries (Paul and Barnabas) had experienced on that first journey (3:11), that is, even before Timothy had joined Paul in active missionary labor. When, on the second journey, Paul and Silas came to Derbe and Lystra, Timothy became an active member of the group. Paul took Timothy and circumcised him. Here it must be remembered that Timothy's mother was a Jewess. His case was different, therefore, from that of Titus. Timothy's case was not a test case to determine on what basis Gentiles would be allowed to enter the church. In all probability it was also at this time that Timothy was ordained by the elders of the local church to his new task, Paul himself taking part in this solemn laying on of hands (1 Tim 4:14; 2 Tim 1:6).

Timothy then accompanied the missionaries over into Europe—to Philippi and Thessalonica. He also helped the others in the next place to which they went, Berea. Here he and Silas were left behind to give spiritual support to the infant church, while Paul went on to Athens (Acts 17:10–15). At Paul's request Timothy a little later left Berea and met Paul at Athens. Afterward he was sent back to Thessalonica for the purpose of strengthening the brothers there (1 Thess 3:1–2). After Paul had left Athens and had begun his labors in Corinth, both Silas and Timothy rejoined him (Acts 18:1, 5). At Corinth Timothy worked with Paul. On the third missionary journey Timothy was again with the apostle during the lengthy Ephesus ministry. From there he was sent to Macedonia and to Corinth (Acts 19:21–22; 1 Cor 4:17; 16:10). When Paul arrived in Macedonia, Timothy rejoined him (2 Cor 1:1). Afterward he accompanied the apostle to Corinth (Rom 16:21), was with him on the return to Macedonia (Acts 20:3–4), and was waiting for him at Troas (20:5). He was probably also with Paul in Jerusalem (1 Cor 16:3). During Paul's first imprisonment at Rome the two were again in close contact (Phil 1:1; Col 1:1; Philem 1). When Paul expected to be released in a little while, he told the Philippians that he expected to send Timothy to them soon (Phil 2:19).

Timothy was next found in Ephesus, where the apostle joined him. Paul, on leaving, asked Timothy to remain at this place (1 Tim 1:3). While there, Timothy one day received a letter from Paul, the letter we now call 1 Timothy. Later, in another letter, Paul, writing from Rome as a prisoner facing death, urged his friend to come to him before winter (2 Tim 4:9, 21). Whether the two ever actually saw each other again is not recorded. That Timothy tried to see the apostle is certain. WH

TIMOTHY, LETTERS TO (See PASTORAL EPISTLES)

TIN (See MINERALS)

TINKLING. The sound of small bells that women wore on a chain fastened to anklets. The tinkling (Isa 3:16 JB, KJV, MLB, NASB; jingling NEB, NIV) to) is caused by the affected pose and short, jerky steps. In 1 Corinthians 13:1 the tinkling (KJV; clanging NASB, NEB, NIV, RSV; clashing JB, MLB) is the noise made by a cymbal.

TIPHSAH (tĭf'sȧ, Heb. *tiphsah*). 1. A town on the northern border of Solomon's kingdom (1 Kings 4:24). It was an important city on the Euphrates River where the caravan route from Egypt and Syria passed en route to countries to the east. Greek and Roman records give it as Thapsaeus and indicate that it was strongly fortified. Xenophon tells how Cyrus II crossed the river at this ford (*Anab.* 1.4.2).

2. A town, apparently not far from Tirzah, the inhabitants of which were massacred by Menahem (2 Kings 15:16). It was on the Jordan and is possibly modern Tappuah.

TIRAS (tī'răs, Heb. *tîras*). Youngest son of Japheth (Gen 10:2; 1 Chron 1:5). He is not mentioned elsewhere. Josephus (*Antiq.* 1.6.1) held with other ancients that he was founder of the Thracians. Modern scholars do not agree, but make him founder of a race of pirates called *Tursenich*, who once plied the Aegean Sea. The name Thrusa has been found among Egyptian records, indicating that they invaded the land during the reign of Merneptah about 1250 B.C.

TIRATHITE (tī'răth-īt, Heb. *tîr'āthîm*). A member of a family of scribes from Tirah who lived in Jabeth (1 Chron 2:55).

TIRE (Heb. *pe'ēr, headdress*). An ornamental

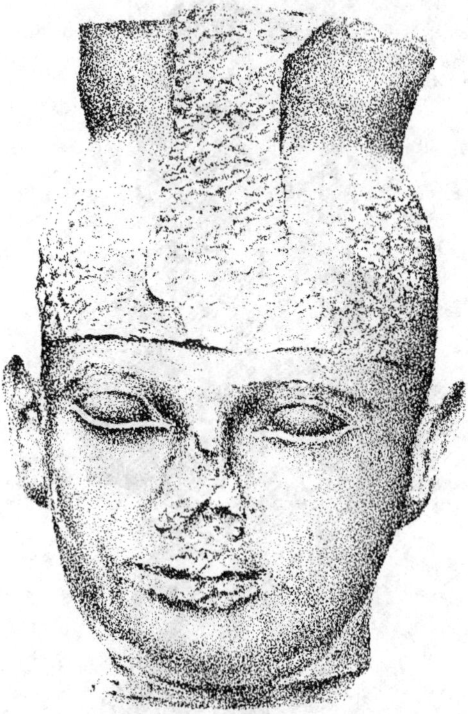

Head from a statue of Tirhakah, Ethiopian king of Egypt, c. 689–664 B.C. Courtesy Carta, Jerusalem.

headdress (Ezek 24:17, 23 KJV; NIV "turban") worn by Aaron (Exod 39:28 ASV; NIV "headbands") and women (Isa 3:20 ASV; NIV "headdresses").

TIRHAKAH (tûr'hȧ-kȧ, Heb. *tirhāqâh*). An Egyptian king, the third and last king of the Twenty-fifth, or Ethiopian, Dynasty. He was the son of Piankhi, whose capital was at Napata, just below the Fourth Cataract. This Nubian kingdom was quite Egyptian in character, and late in the eighth century Piankhi conquered all of Egypt. There was much confusion in the Egyptian political situation (Isa 19), and Isaiah warned about relying on Egypt. Tirhakah was commander of the army of Shabaka, his uncle and first king of the Twenty-fifth Dynasty, and he led the Egyptian armies in their initial conflict with Assyria. Isaiah 37:9 and 2 Kings 19:9 state that Sennacherib, while besieging Judean cities, heard that Tirhakah was coming against him. Sennacherib was successful against Tirhakah, but the loss of his troops forced him back to Assyria (2 Kings 19:35–36; Isa 37:36–37). Tirhakah became king about 689 B.C.and for a number of years was not threatened by the Assyrians, but later he was defeated by Esarhaddon and by Ashurbanipal. Being driven south, he did retain rule of Upper Egypt. CEDV

TIRHANAH (tûr'hȧ-nȧ, Heb. *tirhanâh*). Son of Caleb by his concubine Maacah (1 Chron 2:48).

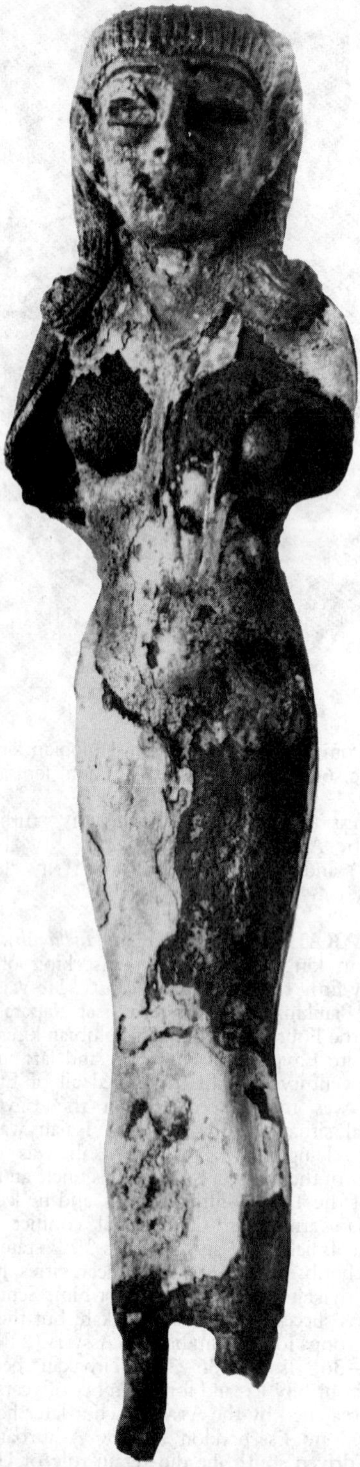

Late Bronze Age silver-plated bronze figurine of a goddess found in a large sanctuary at Tell el-Far'a (Tirzah). Courtesy Israel Department of Antiquities and Museums.

TIRIA (tĭr'ĭ-à, Heb. *tireyā'*). A son of Jehallelel (1 Chron 4:16).

TIRSHATHA (tûr-shā'thà, Heb. *tirshāthā', revered*). In the KJV the title of the governor of Judah under Persia. Zerubbabel (Ezra 2:63; Neh 7:65, 70) and Nehemiah (Neh 8:9; 10:1) bore the title. NIV has "governor."

TIRZAH (tûr'zà, Heb. *tirtsâh*). 1. The youngest daughter of Zelophehad (Num 26:33; Josh 17:3).

2. A town six miles (ten km.) east of Samaria captured by Joshua (Josh 12:24). It must have been noted for its beauty, since Solomon compared his beautiful Shulammite woman to the beauty of Tirzah (Song of Songs 6:4). With the division of the kingdom after the death of Solomon, it became the capital of the northern kingdom (1 Kings 14:17). In it reigned Baasha (15:21–33), his son Elah, and Zimri (16:6–15). Omri defeated Tibni and, since Zimri had destroyed the palace in Tirzah (16:18), moved the capital to Samaria (16:23–24). While Uzziah ruled in Judah, Menahem of Tirzah conspired against Shallum of Israel, killed him, and began a ten-year wicked reign (2 Kings 15:16–18). It is probably to be identified with Tell el-Far'ah about seven miles (eleven and one-half km.) NE of Nablus.

Excavations were done here by R. de Vaux from A.D. 1946 to 1960, revealing remains of an Early-Bronze-Age town with a sanctuary, city wall, and gates. In the Israelite period the city was rebuilt, and in a later phase a palace was constructed but evidently never finished, perhaps because Omri moved the capital from here to Samaria at that time. Large private houses from this period were found. The site was abandoned about 600 B.C.

TISHBITE, TISHBE (tĭsh'bīt, Heb. *tishbī*). Elijah is mentioned as a Tishbite in 1 Kings 17:1. The NIV gives a good reading, "Elijah the Tishbite, from Tishbe in Gilead." The place has been identified, with some probability, with the modern el-Istib, a little west of Mahanaim.

TITHE (tīth, Heb. ma'ăsēr, Gr. *dekatē, the tenth*). Just when and where the idea arose of making the tenth the rate for paying tribute to rulers and of offering gifts as a religious duty cannot be determined. History reveals that it existed in Babylon in ancient times, also in Persia and Egypt, even in China. It is quite certain that Abraham knew of it when he migrated from Ur (Gen 14:17–20). Since Melchizedek was a priest of the Most High, it is certain that by Abraham's day the giving of tithes had been recognized as a holy deed (see Heb 7:4). Dividing the spoils of war with rulers and religious leaders was widespread (1 Macc 10:31). Samuel warned Israel that the king whom they were demanding would exact tithes of their grain and flocks (1 Sam 8:10–18). When Jacob made his covenant with God at

Bethel it included payment of tithes (Gen 28:16–22).

It was a long time before definite legal requirements were set on tithing, hence customs in paying it varied. At first the tither was entitled to share his tithe with the Levites (Deut 14:22–23). After the Levitical code had been completed, tithes belonged exclusively to the Levites (Num 18:21). If a Hebrew lived too far from the temple to make taking his tithes practicable, he could sell his animals and use the money gained to buy substitutes at the temple (Deut 14:24–26). This permit eventually led to gross abuses by priests (Matt 21:12–13; Mark 11:15–17). Tithed animals were shared with the Levites (Deut 15:19–20).

The methods developed for paying the tithes and for their use became somewhat complicated, when to the tithes of the firstfruits (Prov 3:9) were added the firstlings of the flocks (Exod 13:12–13). Then when the Levitical system was established, provision for the upkeep of the sons of Levi was made by tithes (Num 18:21–24). A penalty of twenty percent of the tithe was exacted from one who sold his tithes and refused to use the money to pay for a substitute (Lev 27:31). The Levites in turn gave a tenth to provide for the priests (Num 18:25–32). The temple was the place to which tithes were taken (Deut 12:5–12). One could not partake of his tithes at home, but only when delivered at the temple (12:17–18).

To make sure that no deceit would be practiced regarding tithing, each Hebrew was compelled to make a declaration of honesty before the Lord (Deut 26:13–15). In the tithing of the flocks, every tenth animal that passed under the rod, regardless of its kind, was taken; no substitution was allowed (Lev 27:32–33). Was there only one tithe each year or was the third-year tithe an extra one? Confusion exists about this, even among Hebrew scholars themselves. As the needs for funds increased with the expansion of the temple service, a third-year tithe (all for the use of the Levites and those in need) was exacted. It seems probable that the increase of temple expenses, due to the number of priests and Levites, made it necessary to impose extra tithes. According to Josephus, even a third tithe was collected (*Antiq.* 4.4.3; 8.8.22). Malachi (3:8–10) railed at the Jews for refusing to bring their tithes to the temple storehouse. This did not apply to money but to grains, animals, and fowls, money being deposited in the treasury box (Luke 21:1–4).

By the time of Christ, Roman rule had greatly affected the economic life of Judea, hence it was difficult for people to tithe. But that the laws regarding the tenth were still observed is shown by the fact that the Pharisees tithed even the herbs that were used in seasoning food (Matt 23:23; Luke 11:42). JDF

TITIUS JUSTUS (tĭsh'ŭs jŭs'tŭs). The name of a believer of Corinth with whom Paul lodged for a time (Acts 18:7).

TITTLE (tĭt'l, Gr. *keraia, a horn*). A small, horn-shaped mark used to indicate accent in Hebrew (Matt 5:18; Luke 16:17 KJV). In Matthew 5:18 it is used with "jot" (Gr. *iōta*) to denote a minute requirement of the law.

TITUS (tī'tŭs, Gr. *Titos*). A convert, friend, and helper of Paul (Titus 1:4), in the NT mentioned only in Paul's letters, especially in 2 Corinthians. He was a Greek, a son of Gentile parents (Gal 2:3). After his conversion he accompanied Paul to Jerusalem, where Paul rejected the demand of the Judaists that Titus be circumcised. Hence, Titus became a person of significance for the principle of Gentile admission to the church solely on the basis of faith in Christ. During Paul's third missionary journey Titus was assigned missions to Corinth to solve its vexing problems (1 Cor 1–6; 2 Cor 2:13; 7:5–16) and to encourage material assistance to the needy at Jerusalem (2 Cor 8). Much later Titus was in Crete, left behind there by Paul to organize its churches (Titus 1:4–5). He was requested to meet Paul at Nicopolis (3:12). Titus was consecrated, courageous, resourceful. He knew how to handle the quarrelsome Corinthians, the mendacious Cretans, and the pugnacious Dalmatians (2 Tim 4:10). WH

TITUS, LETTER TO (See PASTORAL LETTERS)

TITUS JUSTUS (See TITIUS JUSTUS)

TIZITE (tī'zīt, Heb. *ha-tîtsî*). The designation of Toha, one of the valiant men of David's army (1 Chron 11:45).

TOAH (tō'ȧ, Heb. *tôah*). An ancestor of Samuel (1 Chron 6:34, Nahath in 6:26). He is called Tohu in 1 Samuel 1:1.

TOB (tŏb, Heb. *tôv*). A fertile district in Syria, extending NE from Gilead. Jephthah, a mighty man of Gilead, took refuge in Tob (Judg 11:1–3). When Israel was beset by Ammonites, the elders in Gilead begged him to return and take charge of their army (11:4–11). When Ammon was preparing to fight David, they hired twelve thousand men of Tob to fight for them (2 Sam 10:6, 8).

TOB-ADONIJAH (tŏb-ăd-ō-nī'jȧ, *tôv 'ădhôn-îyâh, the LORD is good*). A Levite, sent by Jehoshaphat to teach the law to Judah (2 Chron 17:7–9).

TOBIAH (tō-bī'ȧ, Heb. *tôvîyâh, the LORD is good*).

1. A family among the exiles who returned to Jerusalem under Zerubbabel but were not able to prove that they were Israelites (Ezra 2:59–60; Neh 7:61–62).

2. An Ammonite, half Jew, who with Sanballat tried to hinder Nehemiah in repairing Jerusalem (Neh 2:10, 19). Prior to the coming of Nehemiah, Tobiah had connived with a priest named Eliashib, who gave him private quarters in the

Remains of the façade of a temple built by the Tobiad family at Araq el-Emir in Transjordan (c. 190–175 B.C.). It was constructed of huge, stone slabs measuring as large as 20 feet (6 m.) long, 10 feet (3.5 m.) high, with a thickness of 18 inches (45 cm.). At the top are stone reliefs of lions. Courtesy Ecole Biblique et Archéologique Française, Jerusalem.

temple. Nehemiah threw him out and had the rooms purified (13:4ff.).

TOBIJAH (tō-bī'jà, Heb. *tôvîyâh, the LORD is good*). 1. One of the Levites whom Jehoshaphat sent to teach the law in Judah (2 Chron 17:7–9).

2. One of the exiles who returned to Jerusalem from Babylon bringing gold and silver from which Zechariah was instructed to make a crown for the high priest (Zech 6:9–15).

TOBIT, BOOK OF (See APOCRYPHA)

TOCHEN (See TOKEN)

TOGARMAH (tō-gà'mà, Heb. *tôgharmâh*). A man who appears in two genealogies as a son of Gomer (Gen 10:3; 1 Chron 1:6), who is a descendant of Japheth. Ezekiel 27:14 states that Beth Togarmah traded "work horses, war horses and mules" for Tyrian merchandise. Later the prophet lists among the forces of Gog: "Beth Togarmah from the far north with all its troops" (Ezek 38:6). Togarmah is found in the Hittite texts from Boghaz Koi, and some Assyriologists equate Togarmah with Til-Garimmu, a province between the Euphrates River and the Antitaurus Mountains. It appears, however, that the prophet may refer to a people or nation more distant from Palestine. CEDV

TOHU. An ancestor of Samuel (1 Sam 1:1). See NAHATH.

TOI (See TOU)

TOKEN (Heb. *'ôth, sign, token,* Gr. *endeigma, endeixis, syssēmon, sēmeion*). A word that in the KJV of the OT is used practically synonymously with "sign" (so NIV) (Exod 13:9, 16). In Numbers 17:10 and Joshua 2:12 it means a memorial of something past. In the NT (KJV) "token" is self-explanatory: Mark 14:44 (NIV "signal"); Philippians 1:28 (NIV "sign"); 2 Thessalonians 1:5; 3:17 (NIV "evidence," "distinguishing mark").

TOKEN (tō'kĕn, Heb. *tōkhen, a measure*). A town included in the heritage of Simeon (1 Chron 4:32). KJV "Tochen."

TOLA (tō'là, Heb. *tôlā'*). 1. One of Issachar's sons who migrated to Egypt under Jacob and founded a tribal family (Gen 46:1–13).

2. Son of Puah, of the tribe of Issachar, who judged Israel twenty-three years (Judg 10:1–2).

TOLAD (tō'lăd, Heb. *tôladh*). A city occupied by sons of Simeon (1 Chron 4:29).

TOMB (Gr. *taphos*). The word "tomb" is used rather loosely. It may mean a chamber, vault, or crypt, either underground or above. It may refer to a pretentious burying place on a special site. It may be a beehive structure where many bodies can be placed. In general, any burying place is a tomb. The Hebrews were not impressed by the tombs of Egypt, hence their burials remained simple, most burying sites being unmarked. Some kings were interred in a vault in Jerusalem (1 Kings 2:10; 11:43); just where this burial place was located has not been determined. Some mention their "father's tomb" (2 Sam 2:32; Neh 2:3).

Tombs of NT times were either caves or they were holes dug into stone cliffs. Since only grave clothes are mentioned in connection with tombs, it seems certain that the Jews used neither caskets nor sarcophagi. Tombs carried no inscriptions, no paintings. Embalming, learned in Egypt (Gen 50:2), was soon a lost art (John 11:39). A general opening gave access to vaults that opened on ledges to provide support for the stone doors. The door to such a grave weighed from one to three tons (.9 to 2.7 metric tons), hence the miracle of the stone being rolled away from Jesus' tomb (Luke 24:2; John 20:1).

First century A.D. Jewish ossuary, with incised decoration, in which the bones of the dead were placed after the flesh had decayed. Courtesy Zev Radovan.

Roman sarcophagus from Caesarea, with carved relief of a battle between Greeks and Amazons, first-third century A.D. Courtesy Zev Radovan.

TONGS (Heb. *melqāḥayim*). In the Hebrew the word usually means wicktrimmers (KJV "snuffers"), and is used with a tray (KJV "snuffdish") (Exod 25:38; Num 4:9); in Isaiah 6:6 it is "tongs." In 1 Kings 7:49 and 2 Chronicles 4:21 it could be either. In Isaiah 44:12 the KJV "tongs" is translated "axe" in ASV, "tool" in NIV.

TONGUE (Heb. *lāshôn,* Gr. *glōssa*). 1. An organ of the body, used sometimes in drinking (lapping) as Gideon's men did (Judg 7:5; see also Ps 68:23; Zech 14:12; Mark 7:33; Rev 16:10).

2. An organ of speech (Job 27:4; Ps 35:28; Prov 15:2; Mark 7:35).

3. A language or dialect (Gen 10:5, 20; Deut 28:49; Dan 1:4; Acts 1:19; 2:8; 10:46).

4. A people or race having a common language (Isa 66:18; Dan 3:4; Rev 5:9; 10:11).

5. The figurative uses of the word are interesting. The tongue can be sharpened, i.e., made to utter caustic words (Ps 64:3; 140:3). It is a sharp sword (57:4). It is gentle when it uses quieting language (Prov 25:15). Ranting is a rage of tongues (Ps 31:20; Hos 7:16). The tongue is the pen of an eager writer (Ps 45:1), a shrewd antagonist (52:2). The tongue of the just is a treasure (Prov 10:20; 12:18) and a mark of wisdom (Isa 50:4). It is like a bow (Jer 9:3), an arrow (9:8), and a lash (18:18). The miracle at Pentecost included "tongues of fire" (Acts 2:3). The tongue is little but can do great things (James 3:5, 8). In Acts 1:19; 2:8; 21:40; 22:2 the original word is *dialektos,* "dialect," which is translated "language."

TONGUES, CONFUSION OF. The Tower of Babel presents an answer to an otherwise insoluble mystery and reveals God's anger against human vanity and disobedience. That there was originally a common language among people becomes more certain as linguistic research progresses. Many theories have arisen to account for the sudden confusion of tongues at Babel. One is that the whole account is a myth, adapted by Moses to account for the varied speeches that he heard. Another attributes the confusion to a slow change in speech caused by an ancient population explosion resulting in widely scattered peoples who, having no written language, soon developed various forms of speech. But for one to whom miracles exist, it is easy to understand the account in Genesis 11:1–9, for he who designed the media of speech could have, in an instant, made the modifications in speech that caused such confusion.

TONGUES, GIFT OF. A spiritual gift mentioned in Mark 16:17; Acts 2:1–13; 10:44–46; 19:6; 1 Corinthians 12, 14. The gift appeared on the Day of Pentecost with the outpouring of the Holy Spirit on the assembled believers (Acts 2:1–13). The *external* phenomena heralding the Spirit's coming were followed by the *internal* filling of all those gathered together there. The immediate result was that they "began to speak in other tongues." "Began" implies that the phenomenon recorded was now first imparted and that it was afterward repeated (cf. 8:17–18; 10:44–46; 19:6). The context makes it clear that "other tongues" means languages different from their own, and by implication, previously unknown to the speakers, for the amazement of the crowd, coming from many lands, was caused by the fact that *Galileans* could speak these varied languages. Under the Spirit's control they spoke "as the Spirit enabled"; the utterances were praise to God (2:11; 10:46). The gift was not designed merely to facilitate the preaching of the gospel; the message in 2:14–36 was not delivered in more than one language. There is no express NT instance of this gift being used to evangelize others. (At Lystra, Paul and Barnabas preached in Greek, not the native Lycaonian, which they did not understand.) The gift of tongues on Pentecost was a direct witness to God's presence and work in their midst. While the gift came upon all those assembled when the Spirit was poured out (2:4), there is no indication that the three thousand converts at Pentecost received the gift.

It is not stated that the Samaritans received this gift when the Spirit was imparted to them, but the request of Simon to buy the power to bestow the Spirit indicates that some *external* manifestation did result (Acts 8:14–19). The Pentecostal phenomenon clearly appeared again when the Holy Spirit was poured out on the Gentiles in the house of Cornelius (10:44–46). Here again it served as a miraculous token of the divine approval and acceptance of these Gentile believers (11:15–17; 15:7–9). The appearing of the phenomenon in connection with the twelve disciples at Ephesus (19:6), who dispensationally stood before Pentecost, marked the full incorporation of this group into the church and authenticated Paul's teaching.

The gift of tongues is mentioned by Paul as one of the spiritual gifts so richly bestowed on the Corinthian believers. Their reaction to this gift drew forth Paul's discussion of the varied gifts. They are enumerated, compared, and evaluated by their usefulness to the church. He lists the gifts twice and places tongues and their interpretation at the very bottom of the scale (1 Cor 12:8–10, 28–30), thus rebuking the Corinthians' improper evaluation of this spectacular gift. He emphasized the comparative value of tongues and prophecy by insisting that "five intelligible words" spoken in the church were of more value than "ten thousand words in a tongue" not understood (14:19). Paul felt it necessary to regulate the use of tongues in their assembly; the ideal place for their exercise was in private (14:28). He insisted that not more than two or three speak in tongues, and that they do so in turn, and one should interpret; no one was to speak in tongues if no interpreter was present (14:27–28). Speaking in tongues was not prohibited (14:39), but intelligent preaching in understandable words was vastly superior. He further insisted that women were not to speak in their meetings (14:34).

Two views are held as to the exact nature of the Corinthian "tongues." One view holds that they were foreign languages that the speakers were miraculously enabled to speak without having previously learned them. This view is demanded by Acts 2:1–13, unless it is maintained that the two phenomena are quite distinct. That they were intelligible utterances is urged from the fact that they could be interpreted and were the vehicle of prayer, praise, and thanksgiving (1 Cor 14:14–17).

Modern commentators, however, generally hold that the Corinthian tongues were not identical with the tongues at Pentecost but were ecstatic outbursts of prayer and praise in which the utterances often became abnormal and incoherent and the connection with the speaker's own conscious intellectual activity was suspended. It is held that the utterances were incomprehensible to the speaker as well as to the audience (14:14) and that the resultant edification was emotional only (14:4). But 14:4 may only mean that the person's understanding was "unfruitful" to others. Its advocates further hold that this view is indicated in the fact that interpretation was likewise a special gift (12:10).

From 14:27–28 it is clear that this speaking in tongues was not uncontrollable. It was very different from the religious frenzy that marked some pagan rites in which the worshiper lost control both of reason and the power of will. Any manifestation of tongues that is not under the speaker's control is thereby suspect (14:32).

DEH

TONGUES OF FIRE. One of the phenomena that occurred at the outpouring of the Holy Spirit on the Day of Pentecost. Believers assembled in an upper room saw "what seemed to be tongues of fire that separated and came to rest on each of them" (Acts 2:3) as they were all filled with the Holy Spirit. The tongues of fire were symbolic of the Holy Spirit, who came in power on the church.

TOOLS. In the Bible a variety of tools used by the ancients are mentioned. These may be grouped into various categories:

1. Cutting tools: knife (Gen 22:6, 10; Judg 19:29), saw (Isa 10:15), sickle (Joel 3:13), ax (Deut 19:5; 20:19), reaping hook (Isa 44:12), pruning hook (2:4; 18:5).

Assyrian men carrying work tools, on relief from palace of Sennacherib at Nineveh, c. 690 B.C. Reproduced by courtesy of the Trustees of the British Museum.

2. Boring tools: the awl (Exod 21:6; Deut 15:17).

3. Forks and shovels (1 Sam 13:21; 1 Kings 7:40, 45), tongs (Exod 25:38).

4. Carpentry tools: hammer (Judg 5:26), plane (Isa 44:13), plumline (Amos 7:8), level (2 Kings 21:13).

5. Drawing tools: chisel and compass (Isa 44:13).

6. Measuring tools: line (1 Kings 7:23; 2 Kings 21:13), measuring rod (Ezek 40:3–8; Rev 11:1).

7. Tilling tools: plowshare and mattock (1 Sam 13:20–21).

8. Metal-working tools: anvil (Isa 41:7), file (1 Sam 13:21).

9. Stone-working tools: chisel (Exod 20:25), saw (1 Kings 7:9).

TOOTH (See TEETH)

TOPAZ (See MINERALS)

TOPHEL (tō'phĕl, Heb. *tōphel, lime, cement*). A place in the wilderness where Moses addressed the Israelites (Deut 1:1). It is identified by some with modern el-Tafeleh, fifteen miles (twenty-five km.) SE of the Dead Sea.

TOPHETH, TOPHET (tō'phĕth, tō'phĕt, Heb. *tōpheth*). An area in the Valley of Hinnom where human sacrifices were made to Molech (2 Kings 23:10; Jer 7:31). It is mentioned by Isaiah who declared that a topheth, a place of burning, was prepared by the Lord for the king of Assyria (Isa 30:33). Jeremiah predicted that the name of the place would be changed to the Valley of Slaughter because of the many people who would be killed there (Jer 7:32–33; 19:6). Josiah desecrated this place so that it no longer could be used for idolatrous practices (2 Kings 23:10).

TORAH (tō'rȧ, Heb. *tôrâh, direction, instruction, law*). The common Hebrew word for "law." It is so translated over two hundred times in the OT, even though this is far from being the best translation. The word is used for human instruction such as takes place between caring parents and beloved children (e.g., Prov 4:1–2 KJV). In our ears the word "law" carries the overtones of "authoritative imposition"; but while the Torah of the Lord certainly does not lack such authority (Deut 6:1–2), it is rather his loving and caring "instruction" of his people.

The division of the Hebrew Scriptures into the Law (*tôrâh*), the Prophets, and the Writings comes from ancient times. The Samaritans have had only the Pentateuch for their Scripture since ancient times. Perhaps that means that only these five books of Moses were in the sacred canon when the Samaritans began their separate worship. The Torah was divided into 154 sections for use in the synagogue services. It was read through, a section at a time, in three years.

TORCH (See LAMP)

TORMENTOR (Gr. *basanistēs, torturer*). This word occurs only in the NT (Matt 18:34 KJV), where the unforgiving debtor is delivered to tormentors, probably meaning the jailers (so NIV).

TORTOISE (See ANIMALS)

TOU (tō'ū, Heb. *tō'û*). King of Hamath who sent presents to David for conquering their common enemy Hadadezer of Zobah (1 Chron 18:9–10). The variant "Toi" is found in 2 Samuel 8:9–10 KJV.

TOW (Heb. *ne'ōreth*). The coarse and broken part of flax ready for spinning. In the OT it is used as an example of easily inflammable material (Judg 16:9 KJV; NIV "string"; Isa 1:31 KJV; NIV "tinder").

TOWEL (Gr. *lention, linen cloth, towel*). A word occurring only in John 13:4–5. Jesus wrapped himself in a towel and wiped the disciples' feet with it.

TOWER (Heb. *mighdāl, mighdōl, bāhan, misgāv, pinnâh*, Gr. *pyrgos*). A lofty structure used for purposes of protection or attack: to defend a city wall, particularly at a gate or a corner in the wall (2 Chron 14:7; 26:9); to protect flocks and herds and to safeguard roads (2 Kings 17:9; 2 Chron 26:10; 27:4); to observe and to attack a city (Isa 23:13); to protect a vineyard (Matt 21:33).

Round tower unearthed at Samaria, measuring 42.6 feet (13 m.) in diameter and 28 feet (8.5 m.) in height, dating from the Hellenistic period, late fourth century B.C. Courtesy Israel Department of Antiquities and Museums.

TOWN. The translation of several words used in the OT: *bānôth,* literally "daughters," always in the plural, refers to the towns surrounding a city. Cities listed as having towns are: Heshbon, Jazer (Num 21:25, 32; KJV "villages," NIV "settlements"); Ekron, Ashdod (Josh 15:45–47); Beth Shan, Ibleam, Dor, Endor, Taanach, Megiddo (Josh 17:11; Judg 1:27); Areor (Judg 11:26); Jair, Kenath (1 Chron 2:23); Bethel, Gezer, Shechem, Ayyah (7:28); Ono, Lod (8:12); Gath (18:1); Jeshanah, Ephron (2 Chron 13:19); Soco, Timnah, Ginzo (28:18 ASV; KJV and NIV "villages"); Kiriath Arba, Dibon, Jekabzeel, Beersheba, Meconah, Azekah (Neh 11:25–30 ASV, KJV"villages"; NIV "villages" and "settlements"). All the "daughters" of these cities were small towns without walls: *hawwôth,* "village, tent village" (Num 32:41; Josh 13:30; 1 Kings 4:13; 1 Chron 2:23), sometimes in compound names—Havvoth Jair (Deut 3:14; Judg 10:4). These villages may have been the dwelling places of nomads, that is, tent dwellings. *Hātsēr,* "settled abode, village" in Genesis 25:16 was a village of Ishmaelites, probably a movable one made up of tents; but this word usually means villages without walls around them. *'Ir,* the common Hebrew word for "city," can indicate an unwalled town (Deut 3:5); a town with gates and bars (1 Sam 23:7); "country town" (27:5). Other words used are *qîr,* "wall," once translated "town" (Josh 2:15 KJV; ASV and NIV omit); and *perāzôth,* "open region, hamlet" (Zech 2:4, KJV "towns," ASV "villages," NIV "city"). The latter word denotes villages in the open country in contrast to those located in the mountains.

The only NT word that, strictly speaking, means "town" (*kōmopolis*) denotes a community larger than a village but smaller than a city; it occurs only once (Mark 1:38 KJV, RSV; NIV "village"). Another word, *kōmē,* "village," is rendered "town" ten times in KJV (Matt 10:11; Mark 8:23, 26–27; Luke 5:17; 9:6, 12; John 7:42; 11:1, 30). NIV occasionally follows this but usually, like ASV, prefers "village."

TOWN CLERK (See OCCUPATIONS AND PROFESSIONS)

TRACHONITIS, TRACONITIS (trăk-ō-nī'-tĭs, Gr. *Trachōnitis, rough region*). A volcanic region SE of Damascus. It has been identified by inscriptions and is mentioned in Luke 3:1 as the tetrarchy of Philip. The "Rough Region" is still known to the Arabs as "the Refuge" or "the fortress of Allah." It has been likened to "a tempest in stone" or a black, petrified sea. The "region of Argob" (Deut 3:4), part of the realm of Og of Bashan, probably included this wild, infertile area. Josephus, writing in the first century, speaks of the predatory nature of the people of Traconitis (*Antiq.* 16.9.1; 10.1). Trajan in A.D. 106 made it part of the new province of Arabia, based on Bosra.

TRADE AND TRAVEL.

I. Trade in the Old Testament. Abraham came from a trading port, Ur of the Chaldees, which stood in those days at the head of the Persian Gulf, on whose waters man first learned deep-sea navigation. Pottery from Ur has been identified in the ruins of Mohenjo-Daro on the Indus, and Ur was no doubt a trading station between the seaborne commerce of the Gulf and the Arabian Sea, and the caravan routes of the Euphrates Valley. The most negotiable route between East and West ran this way. The fact that Abraham was rich in gold and silver as well as in the nomad wealth of flocks and herds (Gen 13:2; 24:22, 53) is an indication of the wealth of his birthplace and of the commerce that no doubt existed between the desert and the town. The middlemen of this early commerce in the Middle East were the people of the desert.

Egypt, from earliest times, had been a great trading nation. A famous wall painting tells pictorially the story of the exploratory trading expedition sent by Princess Hatshepsut to Punt on the Somali coast fourteen centuries before Christ, and an interesting papyrus speaks of Wen-Amon's quest for fine cedar on the Lebanese shore three centuries later. Hatshepsut's venture had been a quest for myrrh trees, for the embalming practices of the Egyptians needed vast imports of spices and incense. Arabia Felix owed its name to the myrrh and frankincense produced there, and the bulk of this commerce followed the caravan routes NW through the Arabian Peninsula with Egypt as the chief market. Slave trading formed a profitable sideline, and it is significant that Joseph was sold to a company of Ishmaelites carrying myrrh into Egypt (Gen 37:25). The rich imports of the land were balanced by an export trade in corn, and by tribute money from the neighboring spheres of Egyptian dominance. It is recorded that corn was paid for in weighed silver (41:57; 42:3, 25, 35; 43:11). Egypt was a heavy importer of precious stones and metals, some of which must have been of Indian origin brought up the Red Sea and through the canal, which was periodically open between the head of the waterway and the Nile. Egyptian monuments speak of similar commerce with the North and with the Minoan thalassocracy of Crete, the Keftiu of early records.

The first organized commerce of the Hebrew people was under Solomon, whose farsighted trading ventures were inspired by the Phoenician mercantile cities of Tyre and Sidon. It is possible that the building of the temple first made the Phoenicians aware of the market to be found in their own hinterland, and of the profit to be gained from a partnership with the people who dominated the land route to the Gulf of Aqabah. Cedar for the architectural projects of David and Solomon was collected at Tyre from the lumbermen in the ranges and rafted down to Joppa, a distance of seventy-four miles (one hundred twenty-three km.). It was then hauled thirty-two miles (fifty-three km.) up to Jerusalem (1 Kings 5:6, 9; 2 Chron 2:16). The partnership thus begun was extended in a joint venture out of Ezion Geber at the head of the Gulf of Aqabah, down the Red Sea to Ophir and India. Hiram king of Tyre supplied the pilots (1 Kings 9:27–28; 10:11). Ophir was in all probability in southern Arabia, but the cargoes mentioned in 1 Kings 10:22 suggest a trading connection with India. A larger type of vessel was used in this ocean-going commerce, the "ships of Tarshish" (10:22 KJV). Tarshish was probably Tartessos in Spain, and for such distant and exacting voyaging the Phoenicians had developed a sturdy type of vessel called by this name. An "Indiaman" or a "China clipper" in the days of more recent ocean commerce did not necessarily journey to the lands mentioned in the title. They were types of reliable ocean craft. Similarly the Egyptians called the Phoenician galleys engaged on the Cretan run "Keftiu ships." The text quoted seems to imply that Solomon's traders were speedily throwing off the tutelage of Tyre and venturing forth on their own. Judea supplied Phoenicia with wheat, honey, oil, and balm (1 Kings 5:11).

Tyrian traders brought fish into Jerusalem and distressed Nehemiah by their Sabbath trading (Neh 13:16). The timber trade too continued into postcaptivity days, and Ezra made arrangements similar to those of Solomon to secure his supplies of Lebanese timber (1 Kings 5:6, 9; 2 Chron 2:16; Ezra 3:7). Oil was also exported to Egypt (Hos 12:1), and a small domestic export trade in woven goods from Judea seems to be implied in Proverbs 31:24.

When the Hebrew monarchy fell apart after Solomon's death, it is possible that an interesting commercial situation may have arisen. Israel, the northern kingdom, must have inherited the profitable but seductive alliance with the Phoenician trading towns. Jezebel, daughter of the prince of Sidon, married Ahab to seal this partnership. The southern kingdom, however, lay across communication lines to Aqabah and the Red Sea, and there is every evidence that Judah had reverted, after Solomon, to an agricultural economy with nothing more than petty trading. Apart from a half-hearted attempt by Jehoshaphat to revive it (1 Kings 22:48), the eastern trade seems to have vanished with the king who inspired and ordered it. It may have been at this time that Phoenicians, denied the convenient route down the Red Sea, discovered the sea route to India by way of the Cape of Good Hope. A passage in Herodotus (4:42) seems to imply that the intrepid traders succeeded in this amazing achievement. The prosperity of the Phoenician cities certainly continued, and Ezekiel 27 is an eloquent record of the wide and tireless trading activity of Tyre. Ahab's prosperity is also vouched for by the archaeologists' confirmation of the king's "ivory palace" (1 Kings 22:39).

The commercial consequences of the break with Baal worship and the death of Jezebel is an interesting speculation. Tyre, without great difficulty, could strangle the economic life of Israel. Tyre's dependence on the hinterland for primary produce would provide a strong deterrent, but there is no doubt that the choice on Mount Carmel with which Elijah confronted the people involved economic as well as theological considerations. The Hebrew kingdoms from this time onward fell into the background as far as commerce was concerned. The Captivity brought vast depopulation, and the restored Israel was a largely agricultural economy. Internal interchange of goods was vigorous enough from earliest times, and provisions in the law lay stress on fairness of dealing, and honesty in weights and measures (Lev 19:35–36; Deut 25:13–16). The petty trading in the temple, castigated by Christ, was a sample of the seamier side of this internal commerce; but the foreign trade, which invited investment (see Moffatt on Eccl 11:1: "Trust your goods far and wide at sea . . . take shares in several ventures . . . .") and brought great wealth, was no more. Palestine at the close of the OT and in the time of Christ was a poor land.

II. Trade in the New Testament. Trade and commerce have small place in the Gospels. The people of Palestine were aware of the activities of merchant and trader, for such parables as those of the talents, and the merchant who found a "pearl of great price" were obviously meant to be understood by those to whom they were addressed. Trade, in the wider sense of the word, all through NT times, was supremely in the hands of Rome and of Italy. There was a growing interference of the state in matters of commerce. The legal machinery by which a "mark on his right hand or on his forehead" could prevent the nonconformist from buying or selling (Rev 13:16–17) was early apparent.

The foreign trade of the Empire was extensive and varied; it was also one-sided, in important cases, for the hoards of Roman coins commonly found in India are an indication of perilously unbalanced trade and great leakage of bullion. Latin and Greek words in early Irish, German, Iranian, and even in Indian and Mongolian tongues, suggest the influence of trade. Archaeology, especially on the South Indian coast, provides similar evidence. Roman merchants were ubiquitous. There was a Roman market at Delphi outside the sacred precincts for the trade in amulets and souvenirs, and this was probably typical of Italian enterprise abroad wherever crowds were gathered for sacred or profane purposes. From the second century a Roman city stood on Delos, the Aegean center of the slave trade, and when Mithridates in 88 B.C. massacred the Italian residents of Asia Minor and the surrounding coasts, twenty-five thousand fell in Delos alone out of a total of one hundred thousand, mostly traders and the agents of commerce.

Rome itself was a vast market, and a grim satiric chapter in Revelation (18), constructed after the fashion of an OT taunt song, partly in imitation of Ezekiel 27, speaks of the wealth and volume of the capital's trade and the disruption of the world's economy at the fall and passing of a market so rich. Roman trade extended far beyond the boundaries of the Empire. It is certain that merchants from Italy carried their goods into unsubdued Germany, Scandinavia, India, and perhaps China. All this activity sprang from Rome's dominance, the peace that she widely policed, and the absence of political frontiers. There was reason in the merchants' lament predicted in the chapter quoted. Fortunes could be made and lost and made over again. And of Augustus the merchants said that "through him they sailed the seas in safety, through him they could make their wealth, through him they were happy." The fascinating account of the last journey of Paul to Rome (Acts 27), first in a ship from Adramyttium and then in an Alexandrian freighter, probably under charter to the Roman government for the transport of Egyptian corn to the capital, gives a firsthand picture of the hazards of trade, and of the navigation, the ships, and the management of Mediterranean commerce.

There is not much information about the commodities of export trade. Oysters came to Rome from Britain in barrels of sea water. The tin trade of Cornwall, first exploited by the Phoenicians, doubtless continued under Rome. Northern Gaul seems to have had the rudiments of an exporting textile industry, and Gaul certainly exported Samian pottery. Underwater archaeology on wrecked ships has revealed that large cargoes of wine were carried. A monogram of a double "S" seems to indicate that one such freighter, wrecked near Marseilles, was the property of a shipowner who lived at Delos, one Severus Sestius. On the subject of mass production for such trade there is little information, and none concerning the business organization involved. Certain localities, however, became famous for special commodities, and the commerce implied was no doubt in the hands of specialist traders working a market of their own choice and creation. Lydia, for example (Acts 16:14), "a dealer in purple cloth from the city of Thyatira" in Asia Minor, was found at Philippi in Macedonia in pursuit of her trade. Corinthian bronze and the Cilician cloth that was the raw material of Paul's "tentmaking" were probably distributed, locally or abroad, by similar private enterprise (18:3). The imagery of John's apocalyptic letter to Laodicea (Rev 3:14–18) is based partly on trade and industry of the rich Asian town. An important item of trade in Ephesus, now that the harbor was silting and the port losing its trade and prosperity to Smyrna, was the manufacture of silver shrines of Artemis to sell to the pilgrims and tourists who visited the famous temple.

Ramsay's illuminating research revealed a Laodicean trade in valuable wool garments of various kinds. Glossy black fleeces were produced in this district and the neighboring Colosse by some system of crossbreeding, the genetic effects of which were apparent in the Anatolian flocks of the area until comparatively recent times. There is also evidence of a Laodicean eye salve, based probably on the thermal mud of the nearby Hierapolis. Hence the taunt in the letter about "white garments," and the anointing of the eyes of the spirit with a more effective medicine. Another of the seven churches of the Apocalypse was a center of trade and commerce. More trade guilds are named in the records of Thyatira than in those of any other Asian city. Lydia's trade (Acts 16:14) possibly fell under the category of the dyers. They brewed a red dye, perhaps the modern turkey red, from the madder root, which grows abundantly in the district. This "purple" was nearer in color to scarlet than blue, and Lydia's presence in Macedonia, 500 miles (833 km.) away, suggests that the commodity was an important export. It is curious to note in this connection that John uses the figure of Jezebel, the woman given to Ahab of Israel to seal a commercial and political alliance with Phoenicia, to describe a "Nicolaitan" of Thyatira, whose fault may have been some spiritually damaging trade association with the surrounding pagan world.

The trade guilds were a major source of difficulty for Christians who sought in their work and in their social activity to emerge from a pagan world with their conscience intact. The guilds or collegia are mentioned in Acts 19 as a source of organized opposition to the preaching of Christianity. The guilds were not trade unions in the modern sense of the word. Their functions were primarily social, and they covered all trades and professions. There are records of guilds of bankers, doctors, architects, producers of linen and woolen goods, workers in metal or stone or clay, builders, carpenters, farmers, fishers, bakers, pastry cooks, embalmers, and transport workers. Like the modern Rotary Club, the guilds satisfied the need for social intercourse, but in the close-knit society of the ancient world they exercised a function and demonstrated an influence unlike that of any comparable organization today.

In Ephesus the guild of silversmiths and allied trades exerted enough pressure on authority and public opinion to check the free activities of Paul in the city. The famous letter of Pliny (*Ep.* 10.96), in which the repression of vigorous Christian activity in Bithynia in A.D. 112 is vividly described, is fairly clear indication that the guild of the butchers, alarmed at the falling-off in sales of sacrificial meat, was the ally of the pagan priesthoods in rousing the official persecution of the thriving church. Nor was it easy for a Christian to prosper in his trade or business if he attempted to refrain from membership in the appropriate guild or participation in its activities. Since those activities included periodic feasts in the temple of the god or goddess whose patronage was traditionally acknowledged by the trade or calling concerned, what was the faithful Christian to do? Hence the activities of the "Nicolaitans," the "followers of Balaam" and of "Jezebel" of Thyatira, castigated by Jude, Peter, and John. The simple functions and operations of trade and commerce may thus have proved a source of embarrassment, controversy, and division in the early church.

III. Travel. Trade implied travel, and many of the great journeys of the ancient world were made in the pursuit of commerce and remain unrecorded. Those who pioneered the trade routes from the Euphrates and the Persian Gulf to the Indus civilization and Ceylon must have been intrepid

Turn-of-the-century photograph of an Arab merchant from Bethlehem traveling on his donkey. Courtesy University Library, Istanbul.

voyagers. The blazing of the "amber route" from Italy to the Baltic coast, the "incense routes" from Arabia Felix through Petra to Palestine, or the Phoenician seaways to Cornwall and the West African coast, not to mention the circumnavigation of the continent, must have been by experienced and determined travelers. All this voyaging was in the interest of ultimate commercial gain. But there were other motives:

A. **Colonization.** Motivated first by the pressure of increasing population on the limited resources of the Greek homeland, Greek colonies spread around the coasts of the Mediterranean and Black seas, unbroken save for the length of African coastland from the Gulf of Syrtis Major westward. These colonies were places of trade as well as of settlement, and the population often remained distinctive and apart from the natives of the area. Communication was maintained between colony and metropolis, and this was a major occasion of ancient travel. Motives similar to that which sent Abraham's steward to the homeland in search of a bride for Isaac kept people moving over such routes of folk migration.

B. **Exploration.** Curiosity and a desire for knowledge have always been important objects for human wandering. Curiosity accounted for the journey of the queen of Sheba to visit Solomon (1 Kings 10); and if the Magi, as their gifts imply, also came from Arabia Felix, it was the same SE caravan route that, in a nobler curiosity, brought the Nativity visitors to Bethlehem. Curiosity, with historical ends in view, had been the travel motive of the Greek Herodotus in the fifth century before Christ. His journeyings covered a wider area even than those of Paul. Exploration was organized by Hatshepsut around the Somali coast, by Alexander around Arabia, and by Nero up the Nile. Trade and conquest were the motives in mind. Less complex were the aims of the daring party from the Bay of Tripoli who, according to Herodotus (4.174), crossed the Sahara, discovered the Pygmies, and first saw the Niger.

C. **Migration.** Great folk movements fill all ancient history from neolithic times onward, and the Bible mentions directly and indirectly instances of such mass travel. Abraham left Ur by the NW caravan routes that followed the Fertile Crescent in a great curve up the Euphrates Valley and around into Canaan. The same route continued down the Jordan Valley and by the coast road into Egypt, or by way of the Arabah into the Sinai triangle or Egypt. It was along this southern route that Jacob's family journeyed on their various movements into and out of Egypt.

The nomad movements of the Israelites after the Egyptian captivity form a record of mass migration like the "folk-wanderings" of the Indo-European tribes that peopled Europe and determined the character of Iranian and Indian ethnology in the second millennium before Christ. When Abraham's tribe moved into Palestine, a colony from Crete was already established on "the Gaza Strip." After the fall of Crete toward the close of the second millennium before Christ, this movement assumed much more massive shape. A sudden influx of refugees would account for the aggressive imperialism of the Philistines in the time of Saul and David. The movements of conquest and deportation might find a place under this head. It was a policy of Assyria and of Babylon to transfer large masses of subject populations, and such travel, arduous and enforced though it was, occasioned much movement geographically. There was some freedom of communication between the deportees and those who remained behind, as might be illustrated both from the books of Nehemiah and Ezra and from the apocryphal Book of Tobit.

D. **Pilgrimage.** Religious centers like Jerusalem have always been an occasion of travel. The Gospels mention the annual influx from Galilee into Jerusalem, and the account of the Crucifixion speaks of one Simon from Cyrene in Libya who was present in the Holy City as a pilgrim. Paul (Acts 20:16) was anxious to be in Jerusalem in time for Pentecost and was prepared to travel from Greece for the purpose.

E. **Preaching.** The necessities of preaching and teaching caused widespread travel in both Greek and Roman times; and this, of course, is most strikingly illustrated in the well-defined and admirably recorded journeys of Paul. The apostle was only one of many people who traveled for that purpose. It is traditionally believed that Thomas traveled to India, and a large Christian group in that subcontinent is traditionally believed to have descended from his original foundation. Apollos (Acts 18:24–28) had moved about, no doubt on teaching missions, between

Alexandria, Corinth, and Ephesus. The Emperor Claudius, in a stern communication to the Jews of Alexandria, spoke of troublemakers who had journeyed to the delta town by sea from Syria, and it is likely that this is the first reference in secular literature to the widespread missionary travels of early Christian preachers. Acts 11:19 and 28:15 similarly refer to such unrecorded travelers. It is likely that their journeys were very extensive. The tradition, for example, that Joseph of Arimathea traveled to Glastonbury in Britain may not be history, but the story could have arisen only in a world that took for granted the widest and the most distant traveling.

F. **Business.** Search of a livelihood, as distinct from the pursuit of trade, took thousands on long journeys in the ancient world. Juvenal, at the end of the first century, complains that the Orontes had long since flowed into the Tiber, that the city had become so cosmopolitan that native merit could find no place, and that the needy and the bad from the ends of the earth had sought refuge there. The inhabitants of the Roman ghetto were Jews whose business had brought them from Palestine and the many provincial centers of the Dispersion, and such uprooted groups were not necessarily static.

G. **Service.** There were Roman soldiers who had traveled the whole world, and the record of Paul's journey to Rome is an illustration of an official journey of a centurion with an armed escort, engaged on a long and highly responsible courier task. In OT times we find Abraham's steward undertaking a long journey at his master's express command; Tobit acting as agent for the king of Assyria; and Nehemiah adroitly turning a cherished personal project into a royal commission, with all the travel privileges and facilities such a task conferred.

H. **Exile.** Moses' flight into Midian was an early instance of a journey undertaken to escape from justice, and more formal banishment was an accepted penalty in ancient penology. After the troubles in the ghetto, associated, if the Nazareth Decree is rightly interpreted, with the first Christian preaching in Rome, Claudius banished all the Jews of the capital (Acts 18:2); and Aquila and Priscilla are found in Corinth. It is interesting to note that Aquila had come originally from Pontus in Asia Minor.

Travel was not without its hazards, and Paul in an eloquent passage (2 Cor 11:25–27), which finds confirmation in more than one ancient writer, speaks of the perils of road and seaway. Luke's superb account of the voyage and wreck of the Alexandrian grain ship is further illustration (Acts 27). In NT times, however, travel was rather safer by land than it has been at most periods in history.

Roads were the great contribution of the Romans to Mediterranean civilization, and roads promoted the rapid movement of travelers and contributed substantially to their safety by facilitating the rapid movement of troops. The Persians had invented a swift postal system, but it was used mainly for official communications, and no engineering of any major importance was involved. Persia and Babylon relied on the enforced local labor for the opening of highways, and the imagery of Isaiah 40:3–4 is based on the call to such contributions of manpower. The Romans, on the other hand, formed and planned their roads, engineered them boldly, and for the most part paved them. Hence the major contribution to rapid travel. In NT times, in spite of the continuing dangers listed by Paul from his own experience, the roading system was speeding up travel, and the Roman Peace was quelling lawlessness.

Regular passenger services by land or sea were unknown, and there is no evidence that the pattern of procedure changed from OT times to New. "Jonah," the record runs (Jonah 1:3), "ran away from the LORD and headed for Tarshish. He went down to Joppa, where he found a ship bound for that port. After paying the fare, he went aboard and sailed for Tarshish." Nine centuries after the approximate date of Jonah's flight a similar record reads: "When we had sailed across the open sea off the coast of Cilicia and Pamphylia, we land at Myra in Lycia. There the centurion found an Alexandrian ship sailing for Italy and put us on board" (Acts 27:5–6). Travelers evidently made their own arrangements, attached themselves to official parties, accompanied caravans, and coordinated their movements with those of trade and commerce.

The relative convenience of travel by land and sea cannot be estimated. In Claudius's communication to the Alexandrians it is expressly stated that the troublesome envoys who came from Syria came by sea. A perfectly good land route south from Palestine existed, for the Ethiopian eunuch of Queen Candace was using it and riding in a chariot (Acts 8:26ff.). On the other hand, the centurion in charge of Paul disembarked his party at Puteoli and proceeded to Rome probably via the canal through the Pontine Marshes and certainly by the Via Appia (27:11–15), the route described by the poet Horace who negotiated it a century before. Why Paul decided (20:13) to go afoot across the base of Cape Lectum by the Roman road to Assos in Mysia is difficult to explain, unless it was because he sought the privacy for meditation impossible aboard a crowded ship. Discomfort must have been the common lot of travelers by sea. EMB

TRADE GUILDS. Otherwise known as *collegia,* they are first mentioned in Acts 19 as a base of organized opposition to the Christian church. These societies were not trade unions in the modern sense. Their functions were primarily social. Records exist of guilds of bakers, bankers, doctors, architects, producers of linen and woolen goods, dyers, workers in metal or stone or clay, builders, carpenters, farmers, pastry cooks, barbers, embalmers, and transport workers. "No other age," wrote Dill, "felt a greater craving for some form of social life, greater than the family and narrower than the State" (*Roman Society from Nero to Marcus Aurelius,* p. 271; cf. p.267). The *collegia* satisfied the need of the humble for the pleasures of social intercourse and the dignity of self-expression. It was the guild of the silversmiths and associated trades that, adroitly led, forced Paul to withdraw from Ephesus. It was, it appears, the guild of the butchers that precipitated the persecution of A.D. 112 in Bithynia, according to Pliny. The guild banquets, with associated worship of the patron deity and the compromising fellowship involved, were probably the problem of 1 Corinthians. The attempt of certain groups to work out a form of compromise, so essential to the social comfort, and indeed livelihood of many Christians, led to the strong reproaches of 2 Peter, Jude, and Revelation 2–3. EMB

TRADITION (Gr. *paradosis, a giving over*, by word of mouth or in writing). This term does not occur in the Hebrew OT. There are three types of tradition mentioned in the NT. First, the most common use, is the kind of tradition handed down by the Jewish fathers or elders that constituted the oral law, regarded by many of the Jews as of equal authority with the revealed law of Moses. Indeed, the Pharisees tended to make these traditions of even greater authority than the Scriptures (Matt 15:2–3; Mark 7:3–4). The Pharisees were incensed at Christ because he disregarded their traditions and also permitted his disciples to do so. A classic example of their traditions is recorded in the Gospels (Matt 15:2–6; Mark 7:1–13).

Paul refers to his former zeal for the traditions of his fathers (Gal 1:14). Josephus says that "the Pharisees have delivered to the people a great many observances by succession from their fathers which are not written in the law of Moses" (*Antiq.* 12.10.6).

The second type of tradition is mentioned in Colossians 2:8. Some scholars hold that this verse refers to Judaistic heresies, but the emphasis seems to be on the *human*, not necessarily Jewish, origin of these teachings.

The third type of tradition is the gospel truths that the apostle Paul taught. He uses the word three times (1 Cor 11:2 ASV; 2 Thess 2:15; 3:6 KJV). The meaning of this kind of tradition is "instruction" (NIV "teachings"). Paul had taught the believers in Corinth and Thessalonica the doctrines of the gospel, and he urged them to keep those instructions in mind. CEH

TRAIN. 1. Hebrew *hayil*, "army," a much used word that has the meaning of a train or retinue of a monarch, as in the case of the queen of Sheba (1 Kings 10:2 KJV; NIV "caravan").

2. Hebrew *shûl*, "skirt" of a robe; this word, in regard to the Lord whom Isaiah saw in his vision, is best translated "train," as it has been in our versions (Isa 6:1).

3. Hebrew *hānak*, "to train up" is used in connection with rearing a child (Prov 22:6).

4. Greek *sōphronizō*, "to discipline," occurs once in the NT (Titus 2:4).

Drawing of a bust of Trajan, Roman emperor from A.D. 98 to 117. Courtesy Carta, Jerusalem.

TRAJAN (trā'jăn). Trajan, Marcus Ulpius Traianus, was emperor from A.D. 98 to 117. Born in Spain in 53, Trajan was adopted by the emperor Nerva as his heir in 97, after a distinguished military career. The choice of the able and popular soldier was a wise one. Trajan began his rule by dealing firmly with the growing menace of the Roman garrison, the Praetorian Guard; and he succeeded in conciliating the senatorial class, whose loyalty and regard are recorded in Pliny's excessive *Panegyric*. Trajan proved an able financial organizer and a vigorous builder. A large program of public works was financed largely from the loot of the Dacian War. The principate was marked by wide military activity on the Danube, the Parthian, and the African frontiers. During Trajan's reign, in fact, the Empire reached its widest extent and held its frontiers more firmly than ever before or after that time. Provincial administration was economical, strict, humane, and progressive. A volume of correspondence survives between Trajan and Pliny, who was governor of Bithynia just before his death. An interesting reply on the problem of the Christians in the province illustrates strikingly the desire of the emperor to combine firmness with humanity in his legislation (Pliny, *Ep.* 10.79). Conscious of an imperial mission Trajan sought, as few other emperors did so urgently and sincerely, to found a rule of "Felicitas, Securitas, Aequitas, Justitia." He bore, no doubt, too heavy a personal burden, and decided too much from Rome; but the tradition he endeavored to found was a noble one and shows the Empire at its best, not unconscious of a duty to mankind. EMB

TRANCE (Gr. *ekstasis, a throwing of the mind out of its normal state*). A mental state in which the senses are partially or wholly suspended and the person is unconscious of the environment while contemplating some extraordinary object. Peter describes a trance he had in which he saw a vision of unclean animals and heard a voice bidding him kill and eat them because God had cleansed them (Acts 10:9–16). Paul relates how he fell into a trance while praying in the temple and saw the Lord telling him to leave Jerusalem and go to the Gentiles (22:17–21). There are other similar experiences recorded in the Scriptures that are not called trances but must have been such. Balaam, son of Beor, in his third and fourth prophecies said he saw a vision of the Almighty as he fell down with his eyes open (Num 24:4, 16). Isaiah saw a vision of the Lord's glory and heard a call to be his prophet (Isa 6:1–13). Also, Ezekiel's visions (Ezek 8–11, 40–48) must have been given in a trance. In the NT, John, on the Island of Patmos, saw the vision of the revelation of Christ (Rev 4–22). Probably every vision recorded in the Bible that came to a person while awake, came when that person was in a trance. CEH

TRANSFIGURATION. The name given to that singular event recorded in all the Synoptic Gospels (Matt 17:1–8; Mark 9:2–8; Luke 9:28–36), when Jesus was visibly glorified in the presence of three select disciples. The name is derived from the Latin term used to translate the Greek *metamorphoō,* meaning "to change into another form." The accounts portray the transformation as outwardly visible and consisting in an actual physical change in the body of Jesus: "The appearance of his face changed" (Luke 9:29), "his face shone like the sun" (Matt 17:2), while "his clothes became dazzling white" (Mark 9:3). The glory was not caused by the falling of a heavenly light on him from without but by the flashing forth of the radiant splendor within. He had passed into a higher state of existence, his body assuming properties of the resurrection body.

The place is simply identified as "a high mountain" (Mark 9:2). Tradition has identified it with Mount Tabor, but because of its distance from Caesarea Philippi and the fortification on it at that time, a spur of Mount Hermon seems more probable. Jebel Jermuk has also been suggested. Witnessed by Peter, James, and John, the Transfiguration occurred while Jesus "was praying" (Luke 9:29). The natural simplicity of the accounts and their sober insistence on its details powerfully testify to the reality of the event. Its historical reality is also attested by the apostle Peter (2 Peter 1:16–18).

While recorded without interpretation, the uniform dating ("after six days," Matthew and Mark, or inclusively "about eight days after these sayings," Luke) clearly sets the Transfiguration in the context of the crucial events at Caesarea Philippi, Peter's confession, and Christ's announcement of his coming death. The experience gave encouragement to Jesus, who was setting his face to the cross. To the shocked disciples it confirmed the necessity of the cross through the conversation of the heavenly visitors about Christ's coming "departure" (Gr. *exodus,* Luke 9:31) as well as the divine endorsement on Christ's teaching. It inseparably linked the suffering with the glory. It was the crowning with glory of the perfect human life of Jesus, God's stamp of approval on his sinless humanity. The divine approval established his fitness to be our sinbearer on the cross. It was also an entry for Jesus into the glory in which he would reign, thus constituting a typical manifestation of the king coming into his kingdom (Matt 16:28).

Bibliography: G. H. Boobyer, *St. Mark and the Transfiguration Story,* 1942; A. M. Ramsey, *The Glory of God and the Transfiguration of Christ,* 1949; C. Carlston, "Transfiguration and Resurrection," JBL, 80 (1961): 233–40. DEH

TRANSJORDAN (trăns-jôr′dăn). A country included today in the country of Jordan, which is bordered on the west by Israel, on the north by Syria, on the east by Iraq, and on the south by Egypt and Saudi Arabia. In the OT there is no one name given to this area, though the expressions, "this side of the Jordan" and "the other side of the Jordan," appear frequently, their usage depending on the actual or idealized situation of the speaker. Various sections of Transjordan are called by national or ethnic names. The region is essentially a plateau, and ranges from about 2,000 to 3,000 feet (625 to 938 m.) in elevation. Opposite the northern end of the Dead Sea, Mount Nebo, from whose heights Moses viewed the Land of Promise (Deut 34:1–3), rises to 2,664 feet (833 m.).

Nelson Glueck made extensive surveys on the archaeological sites of Transjordan; the results indicate flourishing civilizations during three main periods: (1) c. 2300–1900 B.C.; (2) c. 1200–700; and (3) c. 100 B.C.–A.D. 600 (Nabatean-Byzantine). Rich deposits of iron and copper have been found in the south (Deut 8:9), and ancient mines and smelting furnaces have been discovered. East of the Jordan and in Edom to the south was a road the OT calls "the king's highway," which probably marks the route taken by the eastern kings of Genesis 14. In Numbers 20:17 the Israelites requested permission of Edom to travel through their territory on this route. The king of Edom denied permission, and Israel was forced to skirt the region. Edom was in the southern part of Transjordan, south of the Wadi el-Hesa (the brook Zered; see Num 21:12; Deut 5:13–14), with its capital at Sela ("the Rock," Petra). This region is also called Seir in the OT (see Deut 2:4, 22). It was here that copper mines were found; at Ezion Geber (Tell el-Kheleifeh) Glueck excavated the now-famous smelting center of Solomon. Solomon also used Ezion Geber as a port (1 Kings 9:26–28; 2 Chron 8:17–18). Edom was important also because it controlled the trade routes between Arabia and Syria. The Nabateans developed a powerful kingdom (c. 100 B.C.–A.D. 100) with Petra as their capital; during the NT times their dominion extended to Damascus (2 Cor 11:32).

Adjoining Edom on the north was Moab; at an earlier period Moab extended farther north, but at the time of the Exodus the Arnon River (Wadi el-Mojib) formed the boundary between Moab and the Amorites (Num 21:13, 26). It was to Moab that Elimelech and Naomi went during the famine in Judah (Ruth 1:1). It was also a place of refuge to which David took his parents while he was dodging Saul (1 Sam 22:3–4). The importance of Moab as a grazing land is indicated by

2 Kings 3:4; the Moabite view is given by the Moabite Stone, which was found at Dibon in A.D. 1868.

Further north, between the Arnon and Yarmuk rivers, was Gilead, which was the land of the Amorite king Sihon, whom the Israelites defeated (Num 21:21–26; Deut 2:26–37; Josh 12:12). This territory was given to the tribes of Reuben and Gad (Deut 3; Josh 13). David fled to this region at the time of the rebellion of Absalom (2 Sam 17:22, 24, 26). A number of the cities of the Decapolis, a confederation of independent Hellenized cities, were located in this area. East of Gilead and the Jabbok River was the country of the Ammonites, with their capital at Rabbath Ammon. The northernmost division of Transjordan was Bashan, whose precise northern limits are not certain. Its Amorite king Og was also defeated by the Israelites (Num 21:23–35; Deut 3:1–11; Josh 12:4–5). Bashan was allotted to the half-tribe of Manasseh (Deut 3; Josh 13). CEDV

TRANSLATE (trăns′lāt, Heb. *'āvar, to transfer,* Gr. *metathesis, a transfer, metatithēmi, methistēmi, to remove from one place to another*). The Hebrew word is translated this way once in the OT: "to translate the kingdom from the house of Saul" (2 Sam 3:10 KJV; transfer ASV, NIV). Two Greek words with this same idea occur in Hebrews 11:5—where it is said that Enoch was translated (KJV; taken, taken away NIV) by faith so that he would not die and that before this translation (KJV; he was taken NIV) he pleased God. *Methistēmi* is used to picture regeneration as the believer passing (translated KJV; brought NIV) from the kingdom of darkness into the kingdom of light (Col 1:13).

TRANSPORTATION (See TRADE AND TRAVEL)

TRAVAIL (trăv′āl). "Travail" translates several Hebrew and Greek words in the KJV, all of which are translated with related words and meanings in the NIV. In the OT the word *yalādh,* "to bear a child," is used a few times for literal travail (Gen 35:16; 38:27; 1 Sam 4:19), and many times figuratively. Also figuratively for toil or trouble *hûl,* "anguish" (Isa 23:4; 54:1; 66:7–8); *hālâh,* "to be weak or sick" (Jer 4:31); *'āmāl,* "toil" (Eccl 4:4, 6; Isa 53:11); *'invan,* "occupation, task" only in Ecclesiastes (1:13; 2:23, 26; 3:10; 4:8; 5:14); *hābal,* "writhe, twist" (Ps 7:14; Song of Songs 8:5 ASV); *telā'âh,* "weariness, hardship" (Exod 18:8; Num 20:14; Lam 3:5).

The NT uses various words in this connection (none of which is rendered "travail" by NIV): *ōdinō,* "to be in pain" (Gal 4:19; Rev 12:2); *ōdin,* "pain, labor, sorrow" (1 Thess 5:3); *synōdinō,* "to feel pain together" (Rom 8:22); *tiktō,* "to bring forth" (John 16:21); *mochthos,* "toil, labor, weariness" (1 Thess 2:9; 2 Thess 3:8).

TRAVEL (See TRADE AND TRAVEL)

TREASURE. A word that signifies a collection of objects of value, including stores of provisions (e.g., Jer 41:8; Ezek 28:4; Dan 11:43). The word *ôtzār* has this meaning in two verses—Job 38:22 (treasures KJV; storehouses NIV, RSV) and Psalm 135:7 (treasuries KJV; storehouses NIV, RSV). The treasure cities (store cities NIV) of Exodus 1:11 were arsenals and depots for provisions (cf. Gen 41:48, 56). A similar confusion between the precious store and the place of its storing occurs in the NT. For example, Matthew 2:11 and 19:21 refer to the store of precious things, but Matthew 12:35 clearly refers to the storehouses. In Acts 8:27 both notions are incorporated. The word *gaza'* is a Persian word and is used only in this place in the NT. In Matthew 27:6 the word is derived from Hebrew: the chief priests could not put the polluted silver into the *korbanas,* the sacred treasury, into which the *corban* gifts were paid. This seems to be distinguished from the *gazophylakion,* the treasury of the temple, into which general offerings were cast (Mark 12:41; Luke 21:1). This was simply a collection box. John 8:20 refers to the place where Jesus was teaching in the colonnade, where boxes were placed for the convenient reception of gifts. The metaphorical meaning of treasure is a more common figure of speech in the OT than in the NT (Exod 19:5; Deut 28:12; Ps 17:14; Matt 13:44; Luke 12:21; 2 Cor 4:7). The last reference is to practices such as those illustrated by the Dead Sea Scrolls, the preservation of precious possessions in earthenware jars, sealed for safety. EMB

TREASURER (See OCCUPATIONS AND PROFESSIONS)

TREE (Heb. *'ēts, tree wood,* Gr. *dendron, tree, xylon, timber, wood, tree*). Palestine in ancient times must have been extensively wooded as there are over three hundred references to trees and wood in the Bible. Also over twenty-five different kinds of trees have been identified as having grown in the Holy Land. Most of the wooded areas in Palestine have been cut down.

Trees identified with the holy places were permitted to flourish. Trees were venerated by pagan people who believed gods inhabited them. Sacrifices were often offered under trees (Deut 12:2; 1 Kings 14:23). Planting a tree near a sacred altar was forbidden (Deut 16:21). Trees identified places (Gen 12:6; Deut 11:30; great tree NIV; plain KJV; oak ASV). Tree limbs were used in celebrating the Feast of Tabernacles (Lev 23:40). Jesus used fruit-bearing trees as an illustration of believers' bearing fruit (Matt 7:16–19). See also PLANTS.

TREE OF KNOWLEDGE. A special tree in the Garden of Eden, set apart by the Lord as an instrument to test the obedience of Adam and Eve (Gen 2:9, 17). It must have been a real tree since the test was real, by real people, with real results. Its fruit probably was not much different from that of other trees from which they ate. The sin in eating its fruit did not lie in the tree but in the

Mosaic from Hisham's palace at Jericho that portrays stylized animals eating from the "tree of life." Courtesy Zev Radovan.

disobedience of the persons who ate.

The phrase "to know good and evil" is used in other places: Infants do not know good and evil (Deut 1:39), nor does an old man of failing mind (2 Sam 19:35); but a king does know good and evil (1 Kings 3:9), as do angels (2 Sam 14:17) and God himself (Gen 3:5, 22).

TREE OF LIFE. A special tree in the Garden of Eden (Gen 2:9; 3:22). This tree appears again in Revelation 22:2 as a fruit-bearing tree with leaves. It will have healing in its leaves (22:2). The phrase "tree of life" in Proverbs (3:18; 11:30; 13:12; 15:4) is figurative for an exhilarating experience.

TRENCH. The KJV translation (1 Sam 26:5, 7; 17:20; 2 Sam 20:15) of two Hebrew words—*ma'gāl* and *hēl*—which mean "rampart" and "entrenchment." ASV has "the place of the wagons" for *ma'gāl*. A third Hebrew word, *te'ālâh*, occurs in 1 Kings 18:32, 35, 38, and is given as "trench" in NIV, which uses the same English word to translate *haruts* ("rampart") in Daniel 9:25 (trench NIV; wall KJV). The NT uses *charax* ("palisade, rampart") once (Luke 19:43; trench KJV; embankment NIV).

TRESPASS (Heb. *'ashām*, Gr. *paraptōma*). Used in the KJV of the OT to express the rights of others, whether of God or of another person. In Jewish law acknowledged violation of a person's rights required restoration plus one-fifth of the amount or value of the thing involved and the presentation of a guilt offering (KJV "trespass offering"). Unintentional trespass against God, when the guilty person became aware of it, required a guilt offering to remove guilt. Trespasses against us must be forgiven by us because God has forgiven our sin.

TRESPASS OFFERING (See SACRIFICE AND OFFERINGS)

TRIAL OF JESUS. The tumultuous proceedings before the Jewish and Roman authorities resulting in the crucifixion of Jesus. All four Gospels record at least part of the twofold trial (Matt 26:57–27:31; Mark 14:53–15:20; Luke 22:54–23:25; John 18:12–19:16), but because of the brief and selective nature of their narratives, the precise chronological order of events is not always certain. It is clear that both parts of the trial were marked by great irregularities, but the writers of the Gospels never assert that this or that in the trial was illegal, for they wrote not as lawyers but as witnesses.

Following his arrest in Gethsemane, Jesus was at once taken before the Jewish authorities in Jerusalem. John alone tells us that he was first brought before the former high priest Annas, who conducted a preliminary examination by questioning Jesus about his disciples and teaching. With dignity Jesus reminded him of its illegality, only to be basely struck by an attendant (John 18:12–14, 19–23). Meanwhile the Sanhedrin members had assembled in the palace of Caiaphas, the president of the Sanhedrin, for an illegal night session. Annas sent Jesus to them bound (18:24). The attempt to convict Jesus through false witnesses collected and instructed by the Sanhedrin failed because of their contradictory testimony (Matt 26:59–61; Mark 14:55–59). Before their charges Jesus maintained a dignified silence, even when blustering Caiaphas demanded an answer (Matt 26:62), thus denying the validity of the process. Aware that their case had collapsed, Caiaphas brushed aside the witnesses and put Jesus under oath to tell the court if he was "the Christ, the Son of God" (26:63). The answer, in deliberate self-incrimination, was used to condemn Jesus for blasphemy (26:64–66; Mark 14:61–64). The session broke up in disorder, with indignities being heaped on Jesus (Matt 26:67–68; Mark 14:65; Luke 22:63–65). After dawn the Sanhedrin assembled in its council chamber and reenacted their trial by questioning Jesus on his messianic claims and deity (Luke 22:66–71). This meeting was held to give a semblance of legality to the condemnation.

Since the Romans had deprived the Sanhedrin of the power of capital punishment, it was necessary to secure a confirmatory death sentence from the Roman governor, who found it expedient to be in Jerusalem during the Passover season. Accordingly, "the whole assembly" (Luke 23:1) in formal procession brought Jesus, bound, to Pilate. When Pilate asked their charges, they indicated that they wanted him simply to sanction their condemnation of Jesus without a full trial (John 18:29–32). When Pilate's insisted on knowing what the charges were, the people presented three (Luke 23:2). The charge of treason alone Pilate deemed worthy of investigation. When Jesus explained to him the nature of his kingdom, Pilate concluded that Jesus was harmless and announced a verdict of acquittal (John 18:33–38). This verdict should have ended the trial, but it only evoked a torrent of further charges against Jesus by the Jews, charges that Jesus refused to answer, to Pilate's surprise (Matt 27:12–14). Having learned that he was a Galilean, Pilate decided to be rid of the unpleasant task by sending Jesus to Herod Antipas, also present for the Passover, on the plea that Jesus belonged to Herod's jurisdiction. When Jesus refused to amuse Herod with a miracle, maintaining complete silence before him, Herod mocked him and returned him to Pilate uncondemned (Luke 23:2–12).

With the return of Jesus, Pilate realized that he must handle the trial. Summoning the chief priests "and the people," he reviewed the case to prove the innocence of Jesus, but weakly proposed a compromise by offering to scourge Jesus before releasing him (Luke 23:13–16). When the multitude requested the customary release of one prisoner (Mark 15:8), Pilate offered them the choice between the notorious Barabbas and Jesus (Matt 27:17). He hoped that the crowd would choose Jesus, thus overruling the chief priests. Before the vote was taken, Pilate received an impressive warning from his wife (27:19–21). Meanwhile the Jewish leaders persuaded the people to vote for Barabbas. When asked their choice, the people shouted for Barabbas, demanding that Jesus be crucified (Matt 27:20–21; Luke 23:18–19). Further remonstrance by Pilate proved useless (Luke 23:20–22).

According to John's Gospel, as a last resort to avoid crucifying Jesus, Pilate had him scourged, allowed the soldiers to stage a mock coronation, and then brought out the pathetic figure before the people, hoping that the punishment would satisfy them. It only intensified their shouts for his crucifixion (John 19:1–6). A new charge, that Jesus made himself the Son of God, aroused the superstitious fears of Pilate, causing him to make further futile efforts to release him (19:7–12). Using their last weapon, the Jewish leaders threatened to report Pilate to Caesar if he released Jesus (19:12). This threat, because of Pilate's grievous maladministration, broke all further resistance in the vacillating governor. To his last appeal whether he should crucify their king, the Jews gave the blasphemous answer that they had no king but Caesar (19:15). When Pilate sought to absolve himself of the guilt of Christ's death by publicly washing his hands, the people voluntarily accepted the responsibility (Matt 27:24–26). Keenly conscious of the gross miscarriage of justice, Pilate yielded by releasing Barabbas and sentencing Jesus to the cross. See also CHRIST, JESUS.

Bibliography: J. Stalker, *The Trial and Death of Jesus Christ,* 1894; J. Blinzler, *The Trial of Jesus,* 1959; P. Winter, *On the Trial of Jesus,* 1961; G. S. Sloyan, *Jesus on Trial,* 1973. DEH

TRIBE (Heb. *matteh, rod, staff, tribe, shēvĕt, rod, scepter, tribe,* Gr. *phylē, tribe*). With two exceptions (Isa 19:13; Matt 24:30 KJV) these words always denote a tribe (or the tribes) of Israel. A tribal group comprised all the individuals descended from the same ancestor. As for the Hebrews, each tribe was made up of all the persons descended from one of the sons of the patriarch Jacob. The clan was composed of kinsmen on the father's side. The heads of the tribes are called "rulers" (KJV) or "leaders" (NIV) (Exod 34:31), "heads" (Num 1:16), or "chiefs" (Gen 36:15ff.).

The twelve tribes of Israel (Jacob's new name given in Gen 32:28) were first mentioned by Jacob in prophecy (49:16, 28). While the Hebrews were in Egypt they were grouped according to their fathers' houses (Exod 6:14). After they left Egypt the whole company was conceived of as the twelve tribes of Israel (24:4). The twelve sons of Jacob were Reuben, Simeon, Levi, Judah, Issachar, Dan, Gad, Asher, Naphtali, Joseph, and Benjamin. Although they all had a common father, they had four mothers, Leah and Rachel, who were full wives, and Bilhah and Zilpah, who were concubines. The tribes were called by these names. On the breastplate of the high priest were twelve precious stones arranged in four rows; each stone had the name of a tribe engraved on it (28:21, 29; 39:14).

When the Israelites were counted to find out the number of men of war in each group, the tribe of Levi was left out of this census because the Lord selected them to take care of the keeping and transporting of the tabernacle and its furniture (Num 1). The whole encampment of the Israelites was organized at Sinai and each tribe assigned its place in which to march and to camp (ch. 2).

The leadership of Judah among the tribes was prophesied by Jacob (Gen 49:10), and this tribe was assigned first place in the order of marching (Num 2:3; 10:14). Judah also was the first tribe to bring an offering after the setting up of the tabernacle (7:12).

The withdrawal of the Levites from the group of tribes left only eleven tribes. In the list of leaders from each tribe who were to take the census, the children of Joseph are divided between his two sons to make up the tribe of Ephraim and the tribe of Manasseh (Num 1:10), bringing the total number of tribes back up to twelve.

Before the Israelites entered the Promised Land, the tribes of Reuben and Gad and half of Manasseh chose to settle on the east side of the Jordan (Num 32:33). After the land of Canaan was subdued, the land was divided among the nine and one-half tribes (Josh 15–19). Judah was given the first lot and received the largest area of land (15:1–62). The tribe of Simeon was assigned territory within Judah (19:1). Judah had all the land west of the Dead Sea and south of Kadesh Barnea. North of Judah were Dan and Benjamin. Ephraim was next to them, Manasseh (half-tribe) was next; then Issachar, Zebulun, Naphtali, and Asher were situated north of the Valley of Jezreel, west of the Sea of Galilee, and northward to the Lebanon Mountains. Part of the tribe of Dan went north and seized some territory just south of Mount Hermon, thus settling the farthest north of all the Israelites (Judg 18).

During the period of the judges in Israel the tribes were each a law to themselves. The judges' leadership was sectional. When David became king over the whole land, the twelve tribes were again unified. Jerusalem was conquered and made the capital of the country. There Solomon built the temple. The Lord chose this city as the one place out of all the tribes of Israel where he would put his name (2 Chron 12:13). David appointed a captain over each tribe (1 Chron 27:16–22). He also took a census of the tribes (2 Sam 24:2). Later, when Elijah built an altar in the contest with the prophets of Baal on Mount Carmel, he used twelve stones to represent the twelve tribes of Israel (1 Kings 18:31).

Relief on eastern stairway of the apadana at Persepolis showing part of a large scene of twenty-three groups of nations who sent tribute to Xerxes (485–465 B.C.), king of Persia. Shown here are six bearded Syrians; two bring a team of horses and chariot, and the others carry gifts of metalwork and vases. Courtesy B. Brandl.

The unity of the tribes had a tendency to be disrupted into two factions. After the death of Saul, David reigned over only Judah at first (2 Sam 2:4) and did not become king of all the tribes until later (5:3). After the death of Solomon this same division occurred again: Judah and Benjamin became one nation, the kingdom of Judah, and all the area north of them became another nation, the kingdom of Israel (1 Kings 12:20). This division continued until both kingdoms went into captivity—Israel in 721 B.C. to Assyria, and Judah in 586 to Babylon. These catastrophes wiped out tribal distinctions. The tribes are not mentioned by name again except in the devotional literature of the Psalms and in prophecy.

Jesus says that the apostles of Christ will sit on twelve thrones, judging the twelve tribes of Israel (Matt 19:28; Luke 22:30). The Holy City, the New Jerusalem, will have twelve gates, each bearing the name of one of the tribes of Israel (Rev 21:21). CEH

TRIBULATION, THE GREAT (Heb. *tsar, narrow,* Gr. *thlipsis, pressure*). The Hebrew word for "tribulation" has a large variety of meanings in the OT, but it usually refers to trouble of a general sort (Ps 13:4). Likewise the Greek word refers to tribulation of a general sort (Matt 13:21; John 16:33). Sometimes this suffering is just the natural part of one's life (Rom 12:12; James 1:27), while at other times it is looked on as a definite punishment or chastening from the Lord for misbehavior (Rom 2:9).

The Great Tribulation is a definite period of suffering sent from God on the earth to accomplish several purposes. According to premillennial eschatology, it precedes the millennial reign of Christ. Postmillennial theology places it at the end of the thousand-year reign of Christ. Amillennial theology places it just before the new heavens and the new earth are brought in. This period of suffering will be unlike any other period in the past or future (Dan 12:1; Matt 24:21 KJV; NIV "distress"). See also ESCHATOLOGY.

TRIBUTE (Heb. *mas, forced laborers, middâh, tribute, toll,* Gr. *kēnsos, tax, census, phoros, tax, burden*). The word *mas* occurs twenty-two times in the OT and is usually translated "tribute" in the KJV. Solomon conscripted a force of taskworkers consisting of thirty thousand men (1 Kings 5:13; 9:15, 21). David, too, had forced laborers (4:6; 5:13). Conquered populations were often compelled to render forced labor (Deut 20:11; Josh 16:10). In NT times the *kēnsos*—an annual tax levied on persons, houses, or lands—was paid to a prince or civil governor on behalf of the Roman treasury. The *phoros* was a tax paid by agriculturists.

TRINITY. There is one eternal God, the Lord, who is holy love. Through his self-revelation he has disclosed to his people that he is the Father, the Son, and the Holy Spirit. Yet he is not three deities but one Godhead, since all three Persons share the one Deity/Godhead. The biblical teaching of the Trinity is, in a sense, a mystery; and the more we enter into union with God and deepen our understanding of him, the more we recognize how much there is yet to know. Based on the biblical teaching, the traditional Christian confession is that God is One in Three and Three in One.

I. The Unity of God. God is one. The OT condemns polytheism and declares that God is one and is to be worshiped and loved as such. "Hear, O Israel: The LORD our God, the LORD is one. Love the LORD your God with all your heart and with all your soul and with all your strength" (Deut 6:4–5). He said through Isaiah, "There is no God apart from me, a righteous God and a Savior; there is none but me" (Isa 45:21). And this conviction of the unity of God is continued in

Wall painting from tomb 63 at Thebes, time of Thutmose IV (1421–1413 B.C.) that shows Syrian tribute bearers bringing a quiver, vessels, and a rhyton in the shape of a conventionalized bird (far right). The tribute bearers have bearded faces. On every figure a white shawl edged with red or blue is wound around the body from the waist downward. Reproduced by courtesy of the Trustees of the British Museum.

the NT (see Mark 10:18; 12:29; Gal 3:20; 1 Cor 8:4; 1 Tim 2:5).

II. The Father Is God. God is the Father of Israel (Isa 64:8; Jer 31:9) and of the anointed king of his people (2 Sam 7:14; Ps 2:7; 89:27). Jesus lived in communion with his heavenly Father, always doing his will and recognizing him as truly and eternally God (Matt 11:25–27; Luke 10:21–22; John 10:25–28; Rom 15:6; 2 Cor 1:3; 11:31). Before his ascension, Jesus said he was going to his Father (with whom he had a unique relation) and to the Father of the disciples (John 20:17). He taught his disciples to pray "Our Father . . ." and to live in communion with him.

III. Jesus of Nazareth, the Messiah, Is the Incarnate Son of God. The disciples came to see that Jesus was the long-expected Messiah of Israel (Matt 16:13–20; Mark 8:27–30). Later they came to see also that to be the Messiah, Jesus must also be God made man (see John 1:1–2, 18; 20:28; Rom 9:5; Titus 2:13; Heb 1:8; 2 Peter 1:1). Thus doxologies were offered to him as God (Heb 13:20–21; 2 Peter 3:18; Rev 1:5–6; 5:13; 7:10).

IV. The Spirit Is Also God. He comes in the name of Jesus Christ, Incarnate Son from the Father in heaven. The way in which the apostles, following Jesus, refer to the Holy Spirit shows that they looked on the Spirit as a Person. In the Acts, the Spirit inspires Scripture, is lied to, is tempted, bears witness, is resisted, directs, carries someone away, informs, commands, calls, sends, thinks a certain decision is good, forbids, prevents, warns, appoints, and reveals prophetic truth (see Acts 1:16; 5:3, 9, 32; 7:51; 8:29, 39; 10:19; 11:12; 13:2, 4; 15:28; 16:6, 7; 20:23, 28; 28:25). Paul describes the Spirit as bearing witness, speaking, teaching, and acting as guide (Rom 8:14, 16, 26; Gal 4:6; Eph 4:30). In John's Gospel Jesus calls himself the *paraklētos* (Paraclete), and refers to the Holy Spirit as another *paraklētoṣ* (John 14:16; 15:26–27; 16:13–15).

V. God, the Lord, Is Father, Son, and Holy Spirit. This confession and understanding may be said to be basic to the faith of the writers of the NT, though they rarely express it in precise terms. But in certain passages the doctrine is articulated (Matt 28:19; 1 Cor 12:4–6; 2 Cor 13:14; 2 Thess 2:13–14; 1 Peter 1:2).

VI. Biblical Doctrine and Church Dogma. There is no systematic explanation of the doctrine of God as Trinity in the NT, though the Trinitarian pattern (see no. V and Acts 20:28; Titus 3:4–6; Heb 10:29; Rev 1:4–5) is present. The dogma of the Trinity found in the Nicene Creed may be said to be the systematic presentation of the implications of the Trinitarian suggestions, hints, and patterns of the NT, against the background of the OT. The classic formula is that there is one God and three Persons, and that each Person shares the one Being or Godhead with the two other Persons.

Bibliography: A. W. Wainwright, *The Trinity in the New Testament,* 1975; P. Toon and J. Spiceland (eds.), *One God in Trinity,* 1980. PT

TRIPOLIS (trĭp'ĕ-lĭs) A Greek name meaning tri-city. It was a seaport of Phoenicia, which got its name from the three groups of people who lived there, those from Tyre, Sidon, and Arvad. The city is mentioned in Ezra 4:9 as one whose officials opposed the rebuilding of Jerusalem.

TRIUMPH (Gr. *thriambeuō, to lead in triumph*). In the OT the eight Hebrew words for triumph are all used with reference to God—in praise and prayer and also in discussion concerning him. Paul uses the word twice in his letters (2 Cor 2:14; Col 2:15). In Roman times a triumph was a magnificent procession in honor of a victorious general, the highest military honor he could obtain. He entered the city in a chariot, preceded by the senate and magistrates, musicians, the spoils of his victory, and the captives in chains. Sacrifices were made to Jupiter, and incense was burned by the priests. It was undoubtedly such a triumphal procession that Paul had in mind when he wrote, "Thanks be to God, who always leads us in triumphal procession in Christ" (2 Cor 2:14).

TROAS (trō'ăs, Gr. *Trōas*). A name applied both to a region and a city.

1. The region is the NW corner of Asia Minor, in the district of Mysia and the Roman province of Asia, fronting the Aegean and the entrance to the Dardanelles and backed by the Ida mountain range. In the Troad, or Troas, Alexander first defeated the Persians in the Battle of the Granicus, repeating in recorded history the earlier clash of east and west in the Greek siege of Troy.

2. The city was Alexandria Troas, some ten miles (seventeen km.) from the ruins of ancient Troy at Hissarlik, founded by Lysimachus in 300 B.C. on the site of the earlier Antigoneia. Troas was a Roman colony in Augustus's day and one of the most important cities of NW Asia. It was a port of call on the trade route between Macedonia and Asia (Acts 16:8; 20:5; 2 Cor 2:12). Considerable ruins remain.

TROGYLLIUM (trō-jĭl'ĭ-ŭm, Gr. *Trōgyllion*). The phrase in which Trogyllium is mentioned in Acts 20:15 (JB, KJV, MOF) is the occasion of some textual—but no geographical—difficulty (see W. M. Ramsay, *The Church in the Roman Empire,* p. 155). Trogyllium is a slender promontory thrusting SW from the Asian mainland north of Miletus and overlapping the eastern extension of Samos. The narrow strait forms a protected roadstead in which a small coasting vessel would naturally await suitable wind conditions on the last lap to Miletus. NIV omits the name altogether; RSV also omits it but adds the footnote, "Other ancient authorities add *after remaining at Trogyllium.*"

TROPHIMUS (trŏf'ĭ-mŭs, Gr. *Trophimos, nourishing*). A Gentile Christian of Ephesus (Acts 21:29) and companion of Paul. He was one of

Paul's travel companions apparently chosen by the churches to bear the collection to the poor in Jerusalem (2 Cor 8:19ff.), mentioned in Acts 20:4. In Jerusalem he was the innocent cause of the tumult resulting in Paul's imprisonment when hostile Asian Jews hastily "assumed" that Paul had illegally taken him into the temple itself (Acts 21:29). He is conjectured to be one of the two brothers sent to Corinth with Titus to complete the collection (2 Cor 8:18–22). Shortly before his final Roman imprisonment Paul left Trophimus sick at Miletus (2 Tim 4:20).

TRUMPET (See MUSIC AND MUSICAL INSTRUMENTS)

TRUMPETS, FEAST OF (See FEASTS)

TRUTH. The word "truth," *alētheia* in the NT and a variety of words, chiefly *'emeth* in the OT, always connotes (1) the interrelated consistency of statements and their correspondence with the facts of reality, and (2) the facts themselves. The former may be called propositional truth, and the latter, ontological truth.

The biblical use of the word has rich suggestive meanings that go beyond the literal connotations. When Moses (Exod 18:21 KJV) refers to "able men, such as fear God, men of truth, hating covetousness," there is suggested integrity of character—a kind of reliability that goes beyond the literal meaning to include those aspects of personal behavior that seem to be implied by the love of truth. The concept of truth is assumed to be derived from the character of God and is the exact opposite of the concept of lying. "It is impossible for God to lie" (Heb 6:18; cf. 2 Tim 2:13; Titus 1:2).

Jesus prayed, "Sanctify them by the truth; your word is truth" (John 17:17). And he promised, "If you hold to my teaching, you are really my disciples. Then you will know the truth, and the truth will set you free" (John 8:31–32). In such sayings, "*the* truth" means the most important truth, that is, the gospel of the grace of God.

One of the saddest scenes in the Bible (John 18:37–38) is the one in which Pilate asks Jesus, "What is truth?" and does not even wait for an answer. Jesus had said, "For this reason I was born, and for this I came into the world, to testify to the truth. Everyone on the side of truth listens to me." Jesus' words refer not merely to truth, but to *the* truth. Pilate's question omits the article and expresses skepticism, not merely as to the gospel but as to the very concept of truth.

The gospel invitation to "believe" is always based on the assumption that the evidence is sufficient, and that it is a moral question whether one will accept the grace of God in Christ. Those who disbelieve the gospel are morally reprehensible in the sight of God (John 3:18–19, 36; 2 Thess 2:10–12). Christ is *the truth,* as the sun is *the light*. Those who turn away from Christ, it is assumed, do so willfully and culpably. JOB

TRYPHENA (trī-fē'nȧ, Gr. *Tryphaina, dainty*). A Christian woman who lived in Rome and was known to Paul. He asked the Roman believers to greet her and Tryphosa, her close relative (Rom 16:12). This name has been found on inscriptions of name plates in the burial places of the servants of the royal household of Rome from the time of Paul.

TRYPHOSA (See TRYPHENA)

TUBAL (tū'bȧl, Heb. *tûval*). A tribe descended from Japheth (Gen 10:2). It is mentioned with Javan (Isa 66:19) as trading in the markets of Tyre. The Libareni or Libarenoi of the classical writers are the descendants of Tubal.

TUBAL-CAIN (tū'bȧl-kān). Son of Lamech and Zillah, described as one who "forged all kinds of tools out of bronze and iron" (Gen 4:22).

TUMBLEWEED (See PLANTS)

TUNIC (See DRESS)

TUNNEL (See AQUEDUCT)

TURBAN (See DRESS)

TURQUOISE (See MINERALS)

TURTLEDOVE (See BIRDS)

TWELVE, THE (See APOSTLE)

TYCHICUS (tĭk'ĭ-kŭs, Gr. *Tychikos, fortuitous*). An Asian Christian and close friend and valued helper of Paul. First mentioned in Acts 20:4, he is described as being "of Asia," perhaps a native of Ephesus. As one of the delegates chosen by the churches to bear the collection to the poor in Jerusalem (2 Cor 8:19ff.), he apparently went all the way there with Paul. He was with Paul during the first Roman imprisonment and carried the letters to the Ephesians (Eph 6:21) and the Colossians (Col 4:7–9), being delegated to report to them concerning Paul. Onesimus, returning to his master, accompanied him (Col 4:7–9; Philem). Paul told Titus that he would send either Artemas or Tychicus to replace him in the difficult work on Crete (Titus 3:12). Tychicus was with Paul during his second Roman imprisonment and was sent to Ephesus by him (2 Tim 4:12). Tychicus was a man distinguished for integrity and fidelity; he held the affection and confidence of Paul as an able worker in the service of Christ (Col 4:7).

TYRANNUS (tī-răn'ŭs, Gr. *Tyrannos, tyrant*). According to a well-supported reading of Acts 19:9, Paul taught daily at Ephesus "in the lecture hall of Tyrannus." This could indicate a public building traditionally so named or a school founded by Tyrannus. Another common reading, "in the school of one Tyrannus" (KJV), would refer to the school of a living Ephesian schoolmaster named Tyrannus. W. M. Ramsay discusses the question in *The Church in the Roman Empire*, p. 152, and *St. Paul the Traveller and Roman Citizen*, p. 271.

TYRE (tīr, Heb. *tsôr, a rock,* Gr. *Tyros*). A Phoenician port south of Sidon and north of Carmel. Phoenicia itself is a coastal strip backed by mountains, and Tyre was further defended by rocky promontories (one of them the famous "Ladder of Tyre"), which effectively hampered invasion. Herodotus dates the foundation as early as 2740 B.C., Josephus as late as 1217. Isaiah (23:2, 12) implies that Tyre was a colony of Sidon, and Homer's mention of "Sidonian wares," without reference to Tyre, seems to confirm the greater antiquity of the former city. The Tell El Amarna Letters, apparently refuting Josephus's date, contain an appeal from the ruler of Tyre, dated 1430, imploring help from Amenhotep IV against the invading Habiri. Joshua assigned Tyre to Asher, but in all probability the city was not occupied (Josh 19:29; 2 Sam 24:7).

An obscure period of some four centuries follows, and Tyre emerges into history again with the name of Hiram, friend of David (2 Sam 5:11). This able monarch seems to have rebuilt and fortified Tyre, taking within its boundaries nearby islands and providing the city with two harbors. The trade of Tyre at this time included the exploitation of the cedar forests of the Lebanon range. "Tyrian purple," the product of the murex shellfish, was also a famous export. In addition, the cedar forests provided material for the famous Phoenician galleys. Accepting the challenge of the sea, the one road to wealth for the narrow little land, the Tyrians, like the rest of their kinfolk, ranged far and wide in the search for the precious shellfish and the metals in which they traded. The copper of Cyprus, the silver of Spain, and the tin of Cornwall were carried in Tyrian ships. Under Solomon, who inherited the partnership with Hiram, the Hebrews participated in Tyrian commerce, provided a southern port at Ezion Geber on the Gulf of Aqabah, and shared the trade with Ophir and the East. It was probably the loss of this southern outlet to the Red Sea and the East at the division of Israel after Solomon that stimulated the Tyrian exploration of the coast of Africa and led ultimately to the circumnavigation of the continent. Dynastic troubles followed Hiram's death. A certain Ethbaal emerged victorious after the assassination of his brother. It was Ethbaal's daughter Jezebel who became Ahab's notorious queen (1 Kings 16:31). Renewed troubles after Ethbaal's death led to the emigration of Elissa, the Dido of Vergil's Aeneid IV, and to the founding of Carthage.

The ruins of Tyre, showing remains of the Roman cemetery. The port city's East Gate is in background. Courtesy Zev Radovan.

Remains of the colonnaded main street, or Cardo, at Tyre, from Roman times. Courtesy Zev Radovan.

During the two hundred years of Assyrian aggression, Tyre suffered with the rest of the Middle East but, owing to the strength of her position and her sea power, maintained a measure of independence over much of the troubled era.

She broke free from Nineveh a generation before the last stronghold of the Assyrians fell (606 B.C.). These years were the greatest years of Tyrian glory. Ezekiel's account (Ezek 27–28), set though it is in a context of denunciation and prophecy of ruin, gives a vivid picture of the power and wealth of the great trading port. Ruin eventually came. Babylon succeeded Assyria, and although Tyre seems successfully to have resisted the long siege of Nebuchadnezzar, the strain of her resistance to Babylon and the damage to her commerce brought the city to poverty. She briefly fell under the power of Egypt and then became a dependency of Babylon, a status she held until Babylon fell to Persia. Persia inherited Babylon's rule. Ezra 3:7 contains an order of Cyrus II to Tyre to supply cedar for the restoration of the temple in Jerusalem. Cambyses II conscripted a Tyrian fleet against Egypt, and Tyrian ships fought on the Persian side against the Greeks at Salamis. In 332, in the course of his conquest of the East, Alexander appeared before Tyre. The island stronghold closed her gates, and Alexander was forced to build a causeway. After long months of frustration, he took the city by costly storming. Tyre was broken, and the causeway still remains, now as a place, as Ezekiel foretold, on which fishermen dry their nets (Ezek 26:5, 14; 47:10). Tyre made a measure of political recovery, and for a period functioned as a republic. She struck an early treaty with Rome, and her independence was respected until 20, when Augustus withdrew it. Her remaining history is without significance. EMB

U

UCAL (ū'kăl, Heb. *'ūkhāl*). A word of uncertain meaning found in Proverbs 30:1, regarded as a proper noun by many interpreters. If this is the correct interpretation, it is the name of one of two men to whom Agur addressed his proverbs. Others regard the word as a verb and translate it "I am faint."

UEL (ū'ĕl, Heb. *'ū'ēl, will of God*). One of Bani's sons whom Ezra mentions as having taken a foreign wife (Ezra 10:34).

UGARIT (See Ras Shamra)

ULAI (ū'lī, Heb. *'ûlāy*, meaning uncertain). A river that Daniel mentions twice (8:2, 16). It ran through the province of Elam and flowed through Susa.

ULAM (ū'lăm, Heb. *'ûlām*). 1. A son of Sheresh from the tribe of Manasseh (1 Chron 7:16–17).

2. A descendant of the Benjamite Eshek. His two illustrious sons were known as "brave warriors who could handle the bow" (1 Chron 8:39–40).

ULLA (ŭ'là, Heb. *'ullā'*, meaning unknown). One of Asher's descendants who became the father of three distinguished men of the tribe (1 Chron 7:39).

UMMAH (ŭm'â, Heb. *'ummâh, association*). One of the cities belonging to the tribe of Asher (Josh 19:30). Unless it is to be identified with the modern "Akka," which is at best a mere guess, no other identification is known.

UNCIAL LETTERS (See Texts and Versions; Writing)

UNCIRCUMCISED (ŭn-sûr'kŭm-sīzd, Heb. *'ārēl*, Gr. *akrobystia*). A word used in both OT and NT in several ways. Literally it refers to one who has not submitted to the Jewish rite of circumcision. Figuratively, it signifies a pagan (Judg 14:3; Rom 4:9). In a similar sense it is used of the unresponsive heart (Lev 26:41) and the unhearing ear (Jer 6:10 KJV).

UNCLE (Heb. *dôdh, beloved*). A word used in the OT denoting any kinsman on the father's side (Lev 10:4; Jer 32:7).

The Ulai River, with the ancient mounds of Susa on its bank. The NIV calls it the Ulai Canal, the place Daniel had a vision (Dan 8:2–16). Courtesy The Oriental Institute, University of Chicago.

UNCLEAN, UNCLEANNESS (Heb. *ṭūm'âh, uncleanness, defilement, niddâh, separation, impurity, 'erwâh, 'erwath dāvār, unclean things, tamē', defiled unclean, ṭāmē', to make or declare unclean,* Gr. *akatharsia, miasmos, pollution, akathartos, unclean, koinoō, to defile, mianō, to defile, molynō, to make filthy, spiloō, phtheirō, to corrupt*). Sin arose very early in the history of mankind and brought about changes in both the physical and spiritual life of man. It has greatly affected the entire universe, making the terms "clean" and "unclean" very common in the thinking of the human race from the earliest times. These words have been factors in determining people's diets, friends, and habits, in fact, their entire deportment. These words took on a new meaning when God began to call the nation of Israel into being. They fall largely into two main divisions: spiritual or moral uncleanness and ceremonial uncleanness.

Some have felt that there is a relation between the forbidden foods of other nations and those that the Lord forbade Israel to eat. This could be true, but it does not take away from the fact that the biblical laws on unclean foods came directly from God. All Israel's restricted foods, unlike those of some other nations, involved the flesh of animals. Leviticus 11 is explicit in differentiating the clean from the unclean mammals (11:1–8, 26–28), sea creatures (11:9–12), birds (11:13–25), and creeping things (11:29–38). Nothing that died of itself was fit for their food, nor were they to eat anything strangled. Blood was a forbidden part of their diet. Unclean for Israel were animals that did not chew the cud and part the hoof, fish that did not have both fins and scales, birds that were birds of prey or had unclean habits, and insects that did not have legs above the feet for leaping.

Certain kinds of uncleanness among the Israelites were connected with death. A dead person, regardless of the cause of death, made anyone who touched the body unclean (Num 19:22). Likewise anything the body touched (19:22) or the enclosure in which the person died was made unclean (19:14). Provisions were made for the cleansing of the unclean in this class by sprinkling his body with the ashes of a red heifer on the third and seventh days (19:17–19). Those who touched the carcass of an animal became unclean and could be cleansed only by washing their clothes in water (Lev 11:24–28). Certain types of creeping things that died made anything they touched unclean. Some objects thus touched could be cleansed by washing, whereas others had to be destroyed (11:29–37).

Leprosy, being a type of sin, was looked on as unclean whether it was in people, houses, or clothing. God required the person pronounced leprous by the priest to identify himself in a prescribed manner and to separate himself from the rest of the people. Any time anyone drew near to him, he was to cry "Unclean, unclean." Since this disease was also very contagious, detailed instructions were given for dealing with it (Lev 13–15).

Whatever the seminal fluid that issued from the body touched became unclean. This applied also to certain other kinds of issues (Lev 15:1–18). Issues from women rendered them as well as the things they touched unclean (15:19–33). Regulations for the cleansing of such persons or things were carefully laid down in the two passages above. According to the law, childbirth made a woman unclean, and this uncleanness lasted for different periods of time, depending on whether the child was male or female. In this case too, special instructions were given for cleansing (ch. 13).

In the NT one notes the cumbersome systems of defilement developed by the scribes and Pharisees, which Jesus condemned. Most of the OT regulations passed away with the passing of the Law, and when the matter was discussed at the Jerusalem Council, only four restrictions were placed on the new believers (Acts 15:28–29). In the New Testament era, uncleanness has become moral, not ceremonial.

UNDEFILED (Heb. *tām, perfect,* Gr. *amiantos, unsullied*). A person or thing untainted with moral evil (KJVPs 119:1; S of Sol 5:2; 6:9; Heb 7:26; 13:4; James 1:27; 1 Peter 1:4).

UNDEFILED (Heb. *tām, perfect,* Gr. *amiantos, unsullied*). Used in the KJV for any person or thing not tainted with moral evil (Ps 119:1; Heb 7:26; 13:4; 1 Peter 1:4).

UNICORN (See ANIMALS)

UNITY (Heb. *yāhadh, unitedness,* Gr. *henotēs, oneness*). Used in the OT in the sense of togetherness of persons (Gen 13:6), fellowship (Judg 19:6), and praise (Ps 34:3). Isaiah 11:6–7 tells of a future time when there will be a togetherness among animals. The NT word speaks of the unity of faith that binds together the people of God (Eph 4:13).

UNKNOWN GOD (Gr. *agnōstos theos*). These words occur only in Acts 17:23. When Paul came into Athens on his second missionary journey, he found the city "full of idols." While disputing with the Jews in their synagogues and marketplaces, he was asked by the philosophers concerning his faith. On Mars Hill Paul began his message by saying, "I even found an altar with this inscription: TO AN UNKNOWN GOD" (17:23). This was probably a votive altar erected by some worshiper who did not know what god to thank for some benefit he had received. Using this as a starting point, Paul preached the true God to them. Altars erected to unknown gods were common in Athens.

UNKNOWN TONGUE (Gr. *glōssa, tongue*). The expression "*unknown* tongue" occurs six times in the KJV (1 Cor 14:2, 4, 13–14, 19, 27) where Paul refers to the charismatic gift of speaking in tongues.

UNLEARNED. A word that KJV uses to

translate four different Greek words in the NT: (1) *agrammatos* ("lacking technical rabbinical instruction")—Acts 4:13, (2) *amathēs* ("ignorant, uninstructed")—2 Peter 3:16, (3) *apaideutos* ("an uneducated person")—2 Timothy 2:23; and (4) *idiōtēs* ("private person, nonprofessional")—1 Cor 14:16, 23–24.

UNLEAVENED (Heb. *matstsâh, sweet,* Gr. *azymos*). A word often found in both Testaments, usually in a literal but sometimes in a figurative sense. When used literally, it refers to bread made without any fermented dough (yeast, leaven) or to the Passover Feast, when only unleavened bread could be used. When used figuratively, it means "unmixed" (1 Cor 5:7–8 KJV; NIV reads "without yeast").

UNLEAVENED BREAD, FEAST OF (See FEASTS)

UNNI (ŭn'ī, Heb. *'unnî,* meaning unknown). 1. One of the Levites whom David appointed to play in connection with the tabernacle service (1 Chron 15:18, 20).

2. Another Levite employed in the music service of the temple following the Captivity (Neh 12:9). "Unno" is the corrected spelling.

UNPARDONABLE SIN. Not a phrase used in the Bible, but the usual way of referring to blasphemy against the Holy Spirit (Matt 12:31–32; Mark 3:28–29; Luke 12:10). There is much difference of opinion as to the meaning of this sin, but one of the most popular and likely views is that the sin involves decisively and finally rejecting the testimony of the Holy Spirit regarding the person and work of Jesus Christ.

UNTEMPERED MORTAR (Heb. *tāphēl*). Mortar made of clay instead of slaked lime. It was smeared on the walls of houses made of small stones or mud bricks so as to prolong the life of the building. Ezekiel (13:10ff. KJV; NIV "whitewash") uses the term symbolically to refer to the flimsiness of the work of the false prophets.

UPHARSIN (See MENE, MENE, TEKEL, PARSIN)

UPHAZ (ū'făz, Heb. *'ûphāz,* meaning unknown). A word used of the famous gold-producing region mentioned in Jeremiah 10:9 and Daniel 10:5 (KJV). Its location is still unknown. Perhaps "Ophir" or "and fine gold" should be read instead. NIV omits the place-name in Daniel 10:5.

UPPER CHAMBER, UPPER ROOM (Heb. *'ălîyâh, lofty,* Gr. *anōgeon, a room upstairs, hyperōon, upper*). A room frequently built on the roofs of houses and used in summer because it was cooler than the regular living quarters (Mark 14:15; Luke 22:12; Acts 1:13; 20:8). One of these was the scene of the Lord's Last Supper (Luke 22:12).

UR (ûr, Heb. *'ûr, flame*). The father of Eliphal, one of David's mighty men (1 Chron 11:35).

URBANUS (ûr-băn'ŭs, Gr. *Ourbanos, polite*). A Roman Christian to whom Paul sent greetings (Rom 16:9).

URI (ū'rī, Heb. *'ûrî, fiery*). 1. The father of Bezalel (Exod 31:2; 35:30; 38:22; 1 Chron 2:20; 2 Chron 1:5).

2. The father of Geber, one of the twelve provision officers of Solomon (1 Kings 4:19).

3. A porter of the temple who put away his foreign wife (Ezra 10:24).

URIAH, URIAS, URIJAH (ū-rī'à, ū-rī'ăs, ū-rī'jà, Heb. *'ûrîyâh, Jehovah is light*). 1. A Hittite, the husband of Bathsheba (2 Sam 11:3). The fact that he had married a Hebrew wife, his Hebrew name, and his loyalty and devotion as a soldier (2 Sam 11:11) all indicate that he probably was a worshiper of the Lord. After David had committed adultery with Bathsheba, he recalled Uriah from the battle and sent him to his house, trying in this way to hide his sin. When Uriah refused the comforts of home and wife when his men were on the battlefield, David sent him back to the war with special instructions for Joab to place him in the thick of the fight that he might die. When Uriah was killed, David took Bathsheba for his own wife.

2. A priest during the kingship of Ahaz. He was one of the "reliable witnesses" (Isa 8:2) taken by the king to record the matter concerning Maher-Shalal-Hash-Baz. It also seems highly probable that he was the one who carried out the king's command to build in the temple an Assyrian altar that was to be used for sacrifice (2 Kings 16:10–16; KJV "Urijah").

3. A priest who aided Ezra in carrying on his ministry (Neh 8:4). He may be the Uriah referred to as the father of Meremoth (Ezra 8:33; Neh 3:4, 21, KJV "Urijah").

4. A prophet, the son of Shemaiah of Kiriath Jearim. He predicted the destruction of Judah (Jer 26:20). When the king, angry at his predictions, sought to put him to death, he fled to Egypt, but he was apprehended by the king and killed (Jer 26:21–23, KJV "Urijah").

URIEL (ū'rĭ-ĕl, Heb. *'ûrî'ēl, God is light*). 1. A Levite, the son of Tahash and father of Uzziah from the family of Kohath (1 Chron 6:24).

2. A chief of the Kohathites (1 Chron 15:5, 11). With his 120 brothers he assisted in bring the ark from the house of Obed-Edom.

3. The father of Maacah, wife of Rehoboam. He was from the land of Gibeah (2 Chron 13:2).

URIJAH (See URIAH)

URIM AND THUMMIM (ū'rĭm and thŭm'ĭm, Heb. *hā'ûrîm wehatûmmîm, lights and perfections*). Objects not specifically described, perhaps stones, placed in the breastplate of the high priest, which he wore when he went into the presence of the

Ruins of the great ziggurat temple at Ur, facing southwest. It is a solid tower with a mud-brick core and a fired-brick shell about 70 feet (21 m.) high and served as a religious center of the moon god. Courtesy University Museum, University of Pennsylvania.

Lord and by which he ascertained the will of God in any important matter affecting the nation (Exod 28:30; Lev 8:8). It is uncertain what they were and what they looked like and how they were used. One theory is that they were used as the lot and cast like dice, the manner of their fall somehow revealing the Lord's will (1 Sam 10:19–22; 14:37–42). Another theory is that they served as a symbol of the high priest's authority to seek counsel of the Lord, God's will being revealed to him through inner illumination.

They are first mentioned in Exodus 28:30 with no explanation, showing that Israel was already familiar with them. They seemed to form a necessary part of the equipment of the high priest, for they were passed on from Aaron to Eleazer (Num 20:28). The last reference to them in Scripture is in Nehemiah 7:65.

UR OF THE CHALDEANS. The early home of Abraham, mentioned in Genesis 11:28, 31; 15:7; and in Nehemiah 9:7. Through extensive archaeological excavations it is now known that this city was located in southern Mesopotamia, about 140 miles (233 km.) SE of the site of old Babylon. The most extensive archaeological work was done by Sir Charles Leonard Woolley between A.D. 1922 and 1934.

Education was well developed at Ur, for a school was found there with its array of clay tablets. Students learned to read, write, and do varied forms of arithmetic. Further studies have revealed that commerce was well developed and that ships came into Ur from the Persian Gulf, bringing diorite and alabaster used in statue making, copper ore, ivory, gold, and hard woods.

Much light has been shed on the worship and

Statue (46.5 cm. high, c. 2500 B.C.) of a goat standing upright beside a tree, found in the great death pit at Ur. The great death pit refers to the royal graves at Ur, intricate and beautifully fashioned subterranean palaces sunk deep into the earth and spacious enough to accommodate several persons and artifacts. Reproduced by courtesy of the Trustees of the British Museum.

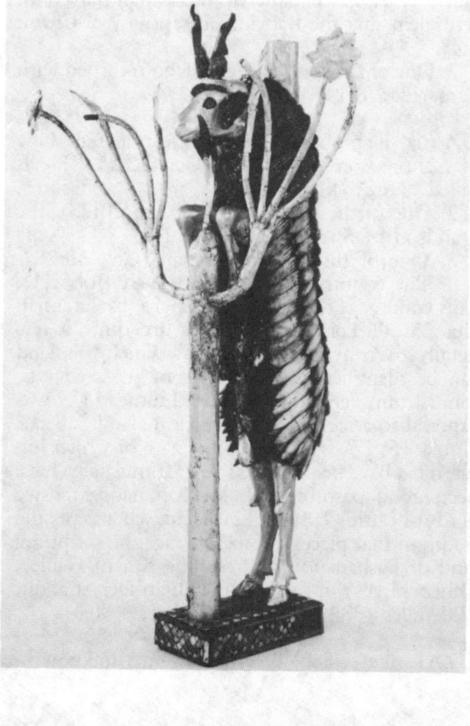

religious life of Abraham's day. Nanna was the moon god worshiped there. The temple, ziggurat, and other buildings used in connection with the worship of this pagan deity have been found. Evidences of worship in the homes of the day are revealed by idols found in private niches in the home walls.

From this city of idolatry God called Abraham and sent him with a promise to the land of Canaan.

USURY (Heb. *neshekh, interest, nāshakh, to bite, to lend on interest, nāshâh, to remove, nash', lead astray,* Gr. *tokos, interest on money*). God gave specific instructions to Israel with regard to interest on money lent. Any money that a Jew lent to his brother was to be without interest (Exod 22:25; Deut 23:19). Money could, however, be lent to a stranger with interest (Deut 23:20). The main purpose for lending money among the Israelites was for the relief of the poor for which, according to law, no interest was to be demanded (Lev 25:35–36). During Israel's time in Babylon many abuses arose regarding the lending of money (Ezek 18:8, 17). Because of this, Nehemiah, after the return from exile, took measures to have the practice stopped (Neh 5:10–12).

In the NT reasonable rates of interest received for money lent are never condemned. It was a common practice in the days of our Lord, and is referred to in the parable of the talents. The meaning of the English word *usury* has changed in recent centuries. While it once meant simply the charging of interest on money lent, it has now come to mean excessive interest..

UTHAI (ū'thī, Heb. *'ûthay,* meaning uncertain). 1. A descendant of Judah who lived in Jerusalem after the Babylonian captivity (1 Chron 9:4).

2. One of the sons of Bigvai who returned with Ezra (Ezra 8:14).

UZ (ŭz, Heb. *'ûts,* meaning uncertain). 1. One of Nahor's sons by Milcah (Gen 22:21). He is called "Huz" (KJV).

2. One of the sons of Aram (Gen 10:23), the grandson of Shem (1 Chron 1:17).

3. One of the sons of Dishan (Gen 36:28).

4. The country in which Job lived (Job 1:1). This country is referred to also twice by Jeremiah (Jer 25:20; Lam 4:21). There are quite a few details given in the Scripture by which this land can be identified. Eliphaz, one of Job's friends, came from Teman located in Idumea. Uz was exposed to attacks by the Chaldeans and Sabeans (Job 1:15, 17). The city, at the gate of which Job sat, must have been located in it. It must also have been good pasture land, for Job had extensive herds of cattle (1:3; 42:12). Delitzsch accepts the tradition that places Uz in Hauran, the scriptural land of Bashan not far from the Sea of Galilee. Others place it in the north Arabian Desert about 200 miles (333 km.) east of Petra.

UZAI (ū'zī, Heb. *'ûzay,* meaning unknown). The father of Palal who aided Nehemiah in rebuilding the walls of Jerusalem (Neh 3:25).

UZAL (ū'zăl, Heb. *'ûzāl,* meaning uncertain). A Shemite, the sixth son of Joktan (Gen 10:27; 1 Chron 1:21). He founded Uzal, the capital of Yemen, probably now the same as Sanaa.

UZZA (ŭz'à, Heb. *'uzzâh, strength*). 1. The eldest son of Ehud (1 Chron 8:7).

2. The caretaker of, owner of, or one in whose memory a garden was named in which Manasseh and his son, Amon, were buried (2 Kings 21:18, 26).

3. One whose children returned under Zerubbabel (Ezra 2:49; Neh 7:51).

UZZA, GARDEN OF. A garden mentioned in 2 Kings 21:18, 26. Manasseh and his son Amon were buried here.

UZZAH (ŭz'à, Heb., *'uzzâh, strength*). 1. One of Abinadab's sons from Kirjath Jearim. He was one of those who accompanied the ark of the Lord when it was being brought from Kirjath Jearim to Jerusalem. The ark was being drawn on a cart pulled by oxen. When something caused the ark to shake, Uzzah took hold of it, thus displeasing the Lord. As a result, he met instant death (2 Sam 6:3–8; 1 Chron 13:6–11, KJV "Uzza").

2. The son of Shimei who became the father of Shimea (1 Chron 6:29; KJV "Uzza").

UZZEN SHEERAH (ŭz'ĕn-shē'ē-rà, Heb. *'uzzēnshe'erâh, plat of Sherah*). A town built by Ephraim's daughter Sheerah (1 Chron 7:24).

UZZI (ŭz'ī, Heb. *'uzzî, strong*). 1. One of Aaron's descendants who became the father of Zerahiah (1 Chron 6:6, 51; Ezra 7:4).

2. Tola's son from the family of Issachar (1 Chron 7:2–3).

3. Bela's son from the tribe of Benjamin (1 Chron 7:7).

4. Another Benjamite, the father of Elah who returned to Jerusalem from the Captivity (1 Chron 9:8).

5. The son of Bani living at Jerusalem and an overseer of the Levites (Neh 11:22).

6. A priest in the family of Jedaiah (Neh 12:19).

UZZIA (ŭ-zī'à, Heb. *'uzzîyā', strength*). One of David's mighty men who was from Ashtaroth (1 Chron 11:44).

UZZIAH (ŭ-zī'à, Heb. *'uzzîyâh, the LORD is strength*). 1. Uzziah, also called Azariah, the son of Amaziah. At the age of sixteen he became Judah's tenth king (2 Kings 14:21) and ruled fifty-two years. He came to the throne at a difficult time. His father, because of a military failure, had been killed (14:19). Uzziah was the people's choice as his successor (14:21). He undertook, very early in his career, an expedition against his father's enemies and won battles against the Edomites, Philistines, Arabians, and

Stone plaque marking resting place of bones of King Uzziah (769–733 B.C.). Aramaic inscription reads "Hither were brought the bones of Uzziah, king of Judah. Do not open." Courtesy Israel Museum, Jerusalem. Photo David Harris.

the Meunites (2 Kings 14:22; 2 Chron 26:1–7). He strengthened his kingdom (26:2), and the report of his strength spread as far as Egypt (26:8). He made many improvements on his home front (26:9–10), and he possessed real ability at organization (26:11–15).

In spite of these successes, he strayed far from the Lord at the end of his life. Apparently as long as the prophet Zechariah lived, his influence was great on the king and "as long as he sought the Lord, God gave him success" (2 Chron 26:5). However, when he became strong, pride filled his heart, and one day he went into the temple, determined to burn incense to the Lord, a duty to be performed only by the priest. The chief priest, Azariah, with eighty priests went into the temple to reason with him, but he would not listen. Because of his self-will, God struck him with leprosy, which stayed with him until his death (26:16–21).

2. A Levite descended from Kohath (1 Chron 6:24).

3. The father of a certain Jonathan in David's time (1 Chron 27:25).

4. One of the sons of Harim who put away his foreign wife when admonished by Ezra the priest (Ezra 10:16–21).

5. The father of Athaiah who came to Jerusalem after the Exile (Neh 11:4).

UZZIEL, UZZIELITE (ŭ-zī′ĕl, ŭ-zī′ĕl-īt, Heb. *'uzzî'ēl, God is strength*). 1. A Levite, son of Kohath (Exod 6:18, 22; Lev 10:4; Num 3:19, 30; 1 Chron 6:2, 18).

2. A captain in the days of Hezekiah from the tribe of Simeon, son of Ishi (1 Chron 4:42).

3. One of Bela's sons and head of a Benjamite family (1 Chron 7:7).

4. One of David's musicians, a son of Heman (1 Chron 25:4).

5. One of the sons of Jeduthun, a Levite, who, heeding King Hezekiah's commandment, assisted in cleansing the temple (2 Chron 29:14–19).

6. The son of Harhaiah, a goldsmith, who aided Nehemiah in repairing the walls of Jerusalem (Neh 3:8).

Anyone who descended from Uzziel the Levite was known as an Uzzielite. This group is referred to in several places (Num 3:27; 1 Chron 26:23). During David's day Amminadab was their chief, and those whom he led numbered 112 (1 Chron 15:10).

V

VAGABOND (Heb. *nûdh, to wander*). A word used in the curse pronounced on Cain (Gen 4:12, 14 KJV; NIV "wanderer"). The plural form is found in the imprecatory prayer in Psalm 109:10 (KJV; NIV "wandering beggars"). The sorcerers mentioned in Acts 19:13 as "vagabond Jews" were professional exorcists (NIV has "Jews who went around driving out evil spirits").

VAIZATHA, VAJEZATHA (vī-ză'thȧ, vȧ-jĕz'ȧ-thȧ, Heb. *wayzāthā', son of the atmosphere*). One of the ten sons of Haman who was hanged by the Jews in Shushan (Esth 9:9).

VALE, VALLEY. 1. *Gaye'*, "a gorge." The word is used to describe the place of Moses' burial (Deut 34:6), the Valley of Hinnom (Josh 15:8; 18:16; 2 Kings 23:10; Jer 7:31), a valley of salt (2 Sam 8:13; 1 Chron 18:12; 2 Chron 25:11), the Valley of Hamon Gog (Ezek 39:11, 15), and the great valley formed when Christ returns to the earth to rule (Zech 14:4–5).

2. *Nahal,* "receiving." Today often translated *wady.* It refers to a valley that is the bed of a brook or river that can be filled quickly by rain. Sudden rains often occur in the climate of Palestine (Gen 26:19; Num 13:23; Josh 12:1).

3. *'Emeq,* "a deep place." This term describes a number of places such as the valleys of Achor (Josh 7:24), Aijalon (10:12), Gibeon (Isa 28:21), Hebron (Gen 37:14), Jehoshaphat (Joel 3:2), Jezreel (Josh 17:16).

4. *Biq'âh,* "a split." A plain between two hills or mountains and in that sense a valley (Deut 34:3; Josh 11:17).

5. *Shephēlâh,* "lowland." It is in reality not a valley but the low-lying hills that stretch from Israel's coast up to the mountains (Josh 10:40; Jer 32:44 KJV).

6. Greek *pharanx,* "a ravine" (Luke 3:5).

VALLEY GATE (Heb. *sha'ar haggay', gate of the Gai*). A gate mentioned in Nehemiah 2:13; 3:13. There is disagreement as to whether it was in the SW or NW corner of the city.

VALLEY OF BEN HINNOM (See GEHENNA)

VANIAH (vȧ-nī'ȧ, Heb. *wanyâh,* meaning unknown). A son of Bani who in response to Ezra's request gave up his Gentile wife (Ezra 10:36).

VANITY (Heb. *hevel, 'āwen, shāw'*, Gr. *kenos, mataiotēs*). A word occurring almost one hundred times in the KJV, but never in the sense of conceit or undue self-esteem. The word *vanity* is not used in the NIV but the Hebrew and Greek words are translated "emptiness," "worthlessness," "futility." These words designate things that are vain and useless, such as the fruitlessness of human endeavors, the worthlessness of idolatry, and the futility of wickedness. This thought appears most often (thirty-seven times) in the Book of Ecclesiastes. Man's natural life is vanity (Job 7:3; Ps 39:5–6). All idolatry is vanity and consequently unprofitable (1 Sam 12:21; 2 Kings 17:15; Isa 41:29; 44:9). The proclamation of false prophets is vanity (Jer 23:16; Ezek 13:1–23; Zech 10:2). In the NT the word *matiotēs* occurs only three times (Rom 8:20; Eph 4:17; 2 Peter 2:18). In the KJV the word "vanity" is sometimes used for one of the Hebrew words that mean iniquity (Job 15:35; Ps 10:7; Prov 22:8). SB

VASHNI (văsh'nī, Heb. *washnî, weak*). The name of the firstborn of Samuel, according to 1 Chronicles 6:28 (KJV). This presents a problem, since another passage says that Samuel's firstborn was Joel and his second Abijah (1 Sam 8:2). The Hebrew text seems to be corrupt, and perhaps *washnî* should be translated "and the second" (so NIV), the name of the first son being accidentally omitted by some copyist.

VASHTI (văsh'tī, Heb. *washtî, beautiful woman, from the Persian*). Xerxes' queen whom he divorced because of her refusal to show herself to the king's guests at a feast. Her place was taken by Esther (Esth 1:11).

VEIL (See DRESS; TEMPLE)

VEIN (Heb. *môtsā', source*). A word found only in Job 28:1 KJV, "a vein for the silver." The NIV "mine" probably conveys the meaning of the Hebrew more accurately. The Hebrew word, however, is found twenty-seven times with a much broader meaning than is indicated in the passage in Job (Num 30:12; Deut 8:3; Ps 19:6).

VENGEANCE (Heb. *nāqam, to grudge*). Any punishment meted out in the sense of retribution. The word occurs in thirty-two OT verses (sixteen of them in Isa and Jer—e.g., Gen 4:15; Deut 32:35, 41, 43; Ps 94:1; 99:8; Jer 50:15, 28; 51:6, 11, 36). In the NT (KJV) the English word translates three Greek words: in two verses *dikē* is translated "vengeance," in both cases in the sense of punishment for wrong done (Acts 28:4; Jude 7), *ekdikēsis* is used in much the same sense (Luke 21:22; Rom 12:19; 2 Thess 1:8; Heb 10:30), and *orgē* is used of God punishing evil in human beings (Rom 3:5).

A hoard of household utensils and containers found in the caves of the Judean Wilderness. Second century A.D. Courtesy Israel Museum, Jerusalem. Photo David Harris.

VENISON (Heb. *tsayidh, tsēdhâh, game of any kind*). Properly the flesh of the deer, but as used in the KJV of Genesis 25:28 and 27:5ff. it could mean any game taken in hunting. NIV "wild game" and "game."

VERMILION (Heb. *shāshār*). A red pigment used for painting walls of palaces (Jer 22:14 KJV, RSV) and for coloring the exotic clothing of the Chaldeans (Ezek 23:14 KJV, RSV). NIV has "red" both times.

A group of limestone vessels, including a two-handled cup and one-handled pitcher, characteristic of the Jerusalem area. Dated c. A.D. 70. Courtesy Reuben and Edith Hecht Museum, University of Haifa. Photo Zev Radovan.

VERSIONS OF THE SCRIPTURES (See BIBLE; BIBLE, ENGLISH VERSIONS; TEXTS AND VERSIONS)

VESSEL (Heb. *kelî*, Gr. *skeuos*). A material object that may have one or more uses, whether it be a tool, an implement, a weapon, or a receptacle. KJV translates *kelî* and *skeuos* 146 times by "vessel," but an almost equal number of times they are translated "armor," "artillery," "bag," "carriage," "furniture," "instrument," "jewel," "pot," "sack," "stuff," "thing," "wares," and "weapon." RSV and NIV translate *kelî* and *skeuos* "utensils" where the context seems to indicate a hollow utensil.

Hosea 13:15 mentions pleasant vessels (KJV; costly treasures NEB; every precious article NASB; precious thing RSV; treasures NIV). In Romans 9:20–24 and 2 Timothy 2:20–21 the term is applied to persons; in 2 Corinthians 4:7 it means the person as an instrument of God's will, and it is used figuratively (1 Thess 4:4) for a man's own body (NIV) or for his wife (NIV footnote), more likely the latter. The weaker vessel (1 Peter 3:7 KJV, MLB, NASB; weaker partner NIV; weaker sex RSV) is a man's wife.

VIA DOLOROSA. "The sorrowful way," the traditional route that our Lord traveled on the day of his crucifixion from the judgment seat of Pilate (Matt 27:26, 31; Mark 15:20; Luke 22:25; John 19:16) to the place of his crucifixion on

Mount Calvary (Matt 27:33; Mark 15:22; Luke 23:33; John 19:18). Nothing is surely known of the exact location of Pilate's judgment hall. Jerusalem was destroyed by the Romans under Titus (A.D. 70), and again at the rebellion of Bar Kokba (A.D. 135), when it was so thoroughly demolished that the very marks of the ancient streets were obliterated. By tradition the "fourteen stations of the cross" are marked in the modern city and also are denoted by pictures or images in many churches and private homes as helps to devotion. The stations are as follows: (1) Christ is condemned to die in Pilate's hall; (2) he receives the cross; (3) he falls under its weight; (4) he meets his mother; (5) Simon of Cyrene is forced to bear the cross (Matt 27:32; Mark 15:21; Luke 23:26); (6) his face is wiped by Veronica; (7) he falls again; (8) he meets the women of Jerusalem (Luke 23:28–31); (9) he falls a third time; (10) he is stripped of his garments (cf. Matt 27:35); (11) he is nailed to the cross (Matt 27:35; Mark 15:24; Luke 23:33; John 19:23); (12) he dies (Matt 27:50; Mark 15:37; Luke 23:46; John 19:30); (13) his body is taken down (Matt 27:59; Mark 15:46; Luke 23:53; John 19:40); (14) and is laid in the tomb (Matt 27:60; Mark 15:46; Luke 23:53; John 19:41–42). ABF

VIAL (Heb. *pakh,* from a root meaning *to pour,* Gr. *phialē*). A hollow vessel used for various purposes. The word occurs thirteen times in the KJV (1 Sam 10:1; Rev 5:8; 15:7; 16:1–4, 8, 10, 12, 17; 17:1; 21:9), where other versions have either "vial" or "bottle, "bowl," or "flask."

VICTORY. The OT associates victory with the God of power and glory and majesty who is in full control of his creation (1 Chron 29:11). That he gives victory in this life to faithful believers is seen throughout Hebrews 11. Faith is the victory that conquers the world (1 John 5:4–5), and through it Christians continually know the victory because of what God has done in Jesus Christ (1 Cor 15:7). They can look unafraid at the vanquishing of sin and death—and they will not suffer the second death (Rev 2:11). All the blessings of the New Jerusalem will be inherited by the overcomers (21:1–7).

VICTUAL (See FOOD)

VIGILANCE. A term most commonly found in verb form: the Christian is urged to be constantly watchful, on his guard. In Gethsemane a particular occasion for watchfulness was stressed by Jesus and was then associated with a rebuke to his sleepy companions (Matt 26:38–41; Mark 14:34, 38). More often, however, watchfulness is directed as a general attitude of preparedness in those who await their Lord's return (Matt 24:42; Mark 13:33–34, 37; Luke 21:36). The KJV uses "watch" in Paul's letters to the Ephesian elders (Acts 20:31), to the Colossians (Col 4:2), and to the Thessalonians (1 Thess 5:6). It is found also three times in John's writing (Rev 3:2–3; 16:15).

Jesus' route ("The Sorrowful Road") from Pilate's judgment hall to Golgotha, the place of crucifixion. Courtesy Zev Radovan.

NIV reads "Be on guard," "alert," "watchful." The word "vigilant" itself is used by KJV in Peter's call for alertness against the diabolical adversary (1 Peter 5:8). NIV has "alert."

VILLAGE. Villages were usually grouped around a fortified town to which the people could flee in time of war. Generally they were unwalled, but in northern Syria even today an agricultural village is often surrounded by a wall, sometimes coinciding with the backs of houses, which face inward; and the farmers walk out daily to their fields, some at quite a distance from the village. In the OT the word is often a translation of the Hebrew *bath*—i.e., "daughter," as in 2 Chronicles 28:18, "with their surrounding villages" (ASV "towns"). The usual OT word (*hātsēr*) signifies an enclosure (Josh 13:23, 28) and is frequently compounded to name a particular village, e.g., Hazar Addar. Its plural may represent a group of hamlets ("Hazeroth," Num 11:35). Another frequent root word is from the verb *kāphār,* signifying shelter or protection, e.g., "Capernaum," i.e., "Village of Nahum." See also TOWN.

VINE, VINEYARD (Heb. *gephen,* usually the cultivated grapevine, *sōrēq, dark grapes, nāzîr, undressed vine,* Gr. *ampelōn, staphylē, botrys*). The common grapevine is mentioned throughout Scripture, often in a figurative sense. It was grown in ancient Egypt and in Canaan prior to the time of Abraham (Gen 14:18; Num 13:20, 24). The mountain regions of Judea and Samaria, largely unsuited for grain, were well adapted for vine growing. A vineyard was usually surrounded with a protecting wall of stones or thorny hedges to keep out destructive animals (Num 22:24; Ps 80:8–13; Prov 24:30–31; Isa 5:5). In every vineyard was a tower for the watchman, a winepress hollowed out of a flat rock, and a vat into which the juice flowed from the winepress (Isa 1:8; 5:1–7; Matt 21:33–41). The vine branches were usually allowed to lie along the ground or to fall over the terraces, but sometimes they were raised above the ground with sticks or supported on poles to form a bower.

Vines required constant care to keep them productive (see PLANTS). They were pruned every spring, and the ground was plowed and kept free of weeds. Pruned branches were gathered and burned (John 15:6). During the harvest season watchmen were stationed in the towers, and sometimes the whole family of the owner took their residence in booths as a protection against thieves. The harvest season was always one of special happiness. The treaders of the winepress shouted and sang as they trod the grapes (Judg 9:27; Isa 16:10; Jer 25:30; 48:33). The gleanings were left to the poor (Lev 19:10; Deut 24:21; Judg 8:2). The wine was stored in new goatskin bags (Matt 9:17) or in large pottery containers. Every seventh year the vines were allowed to lie fallow (Exod 23:11; Lev 25:3).

Grapes were an important part of the diet of the Hebrews. A part of the harvest was preserved in the form of raisin cakes (1 Sam 25:18). Grapes were also their main source of sugar. The juice of the grapes was drunk fresh and fermented.

Figuratively, the vine symbolized prosperity and peace among the ancient Hebrews (1 Kings 4:25; Mic 4:4; Zech 3:10). The vine also symbolized the chosen people, who instead of producing outstanding fruit yielded only wild grapes.

Some of Jesus' parables relate to vines and their culture (Matt 9:17; 20:1–6; 21:28–33; Luke 13:6–9). Jesus referred to himself as the only true vine with whom his disciples are in organic union (John 15).

VINEGAR (Heb. *hōmets,* Gr. *oxos*). With us, generally a sour fluid obtained by fermentation of cider, but in Bible times from wine. The Nazirite was to abstain from drinking it (Num 6:3), and it was used as a condiment on bread (Ruth 2:14). Its action on the teeth (Prov 10:26) and its fizzing with soda (Prov 25:20) are mentioned by Solomon. On the cross Jesus was offered vinegar (NIV "wine") mixed with gall or with myrrh (Matt 27:34; Mark 15:23) in fulfillment of Psalm 69:21, but he refused it. Later he was offered a mixture of water and vinegar on a sponge (Matt 27:48), a drink very popular among the poor and used by Roman soldiers when in camp.

VINEYARDS, PLAIN OF THE. So translated in Judges 11:33 KJV, but transliterated "Abel-cheramim" in ASV, "Abel Keramim" in NIV. A village of the Ammonites east of the Jordan.

VIPER (See ANIMALS)

VIRGIN. The OT has two words that the English versions translate "virgin." The word *bethûlâh* is widely supposed to be the Hebrew technical word for an unmarried and therefore virgin girl, while *'almâh* is said to mean a young woman of marriageable age and, if the context requires, married. The evidence of the way the words are used in the OT is, however, as follows. Nine times *'almâh* is found—four singular (Gen 24:43; Exod 2:8; Prov 30:19; Isa 7:14) and five plural (1 Chron 15:20; Ps 46 title, 68:25; Song of Songs 1:3; 6:8). In the title of Psalm 46 and in 1 Chronicles 15 the word occurs in a way no longer understood and can therefore tell us nothing of its meaning.

Likewise, the context does not help us to understand the meaning in Psalm 68:25 and Song of Songs 1:3. Proverbs 30:19 is best taken as a reference to the mystery of sexual attraction leading to courtship and marriage, in which case the *'almâh* is a virgin. In Genesis 24:43 and Exodus 2:8 the girl is unquestionably a virgin and so also in Song of Songs 6:8, where there is a contrast with queens and concubines, i.e., married women. The evidence so far, then, is that *'almâh* is a virgin, not a woman of some indefinite sexual state; and it may be worth mentioning here that ouside of the Bible, as far as is presently known, the cognates of *'almâh* are never used of a married woman.

Turning now to *bethûlâh,* and leaving aside metaphorical uses (such as references to cities and tribes; e.g., Isa 37:22), there are fourteen occurrences that are noncommittal (e.g., Deut 32:25), grouping girls and young men simply as "young people," without any more implying that the young women are married or unmarried than that the young men are bachelors. There are twenty-one cases where the girls certainly are virgins (e.g., Exod 22:16; Judg 19:24). All that this means is that *bethûlâh* can mean "virgin" where the context requires it; but there are three cases where it is especially important to know that the girl in question is a virgin, and in these the word *bethûlâh* apparently was not by itself sufficient but needed to be amplified by saying that she had never had sexual intercourse (Gen 24:16; Lev 21:3; Judg 21:12). If *bethûlâh* were, as is so confidently claimed by many, a technical term for a virgin, why would the amplifying words ever be needed? By comparison, *'almâh* is never qualified or amplified.

Special importance attaches to Genesis 24, which is the only passage in which the words occur so as to enable comparison. Concerned to find a bride for Isaac, Abraham's servant first prays about the "girl" who would turn out to be the right one. He uses the term *na'arah* (24:14). In verse 16 Rebekah arrives and, knowing only what his eyes tell him, she is described as female (*na'arah*), as of marriageable age (*bethûlâh*), but as unmarried (whom no man had known). If *bethûlâh* necessarily meant "unmarried," no definition would be needed. But in verse 43 the servant, recounting all that has happened, simply describes Rebekah as *'almâh,* i.e., using it as a summary word for all he now knows: female, marriageable, and unmarried.

This conclusion has great bearing on the NT use of *parthenos,* especially as it occurs in Matthew 1:23, and on the virgin birth of the Lord Jesus Christ. See also VIRGIN BIRTH. JAM

VIRGIN BIRTH. The teaching that Mary, the mother of Jesus was a virgin both when she conceived and when she gave birth to Jesus, the child who was Immanuel ("God with us"). The source of this doctrine is threefold: (1) The account in Matthew 1:18–25. Here we learn that before Mary and Joseph came together in marriage "she was found to be with child through the Holy Spirit." Further, an angel of the Lord appeared to Joseph to tell him, "Do not be afraid to take Mary home as your wife, because what is conceived in her is from the Holy Spirit." (2) The account in Luke 1:26–38. Here we learn that the angel told Mary that she had found favor with God and that she would "be with child and give birth to a son." When she asked how this could be since she was a pure virgin, she was told, "The Holy Spirit will come upon you and the power of the Most High will overshadow you. So the holy one to be born will be called the Son of God." (3) The prophecy recorded in Isaiah: "Therefore the Lord himself will give you a sign: The virgin will be with child and will give birth to a son, and will call him Immanuel" (Isa 7:14; Matt 1:23).

Although the conception of Jesus was miraculous and unique, his growth within the womb of Mary and his birth were "normal." The writers of Matthew and Luke probably got their information from Joseph and Mary, and they recorded it with reverence and reticence. Within their accounts several theological motifs may be recognized. First, they record the facts in such a manner as to convey the idea that conception by a virgin was the appropriate way for the eternal Son to become a man, "bone of our bone, flesh of our flesh." Second, as the Holy Spirit had "hovered" over the old creation (Gen 1:2), so now the Holy Spirit is present to superintend the origin of a new creation, of which the Incarnate Son will be the center. Third, the virginal conception points to the unique relation of the Incarnate Son to the human race he came to save: There is a basic continuity with us in that he shares our flesh and was born in the "normal" way. There is a basic discontinuity in that he was conceived in regard to his manhood in a unique way—as a new creation. So he is the same but different, and thus he is one of us, but able to save us, and that is what his name "Jesus" means.

Bibliography: J. Orr, *The Virgin Birth of Christ,* 1907; J. G. Machen, *The Virgin Birth of Jesus Christ,* 1932. PT

VIRTUE (Heb. *hayil, strength, ability,* often involving moral worth, Gr. *aretē,* any excellence of a person or a thing, *dynamis, power, influence*). The phrase "a virtuous woman" found in KJV (Ruth 3:11; Prov 12:4; 31:10) is literally "a woman of worth" (so rendered once by RSV, where NIV has "a woman of noble character"). Sometimes the word is used in its Old English sense of "power" (thus NIV in Mark 5:30; Luke 6:19; 8:46) and "strength" (2 Cor 12:9; Heb 11:11).

VISION (Heb. *hāzôn, hizzāyôn, mar'âh,* Gr. *horama, optasia*). It is impossible to draw a sharp line of demarcation between dreams and visions. The Hebrew and Greek words all have to do with seeing. Visions in the Bible were for the most part given to individuals and were not apprehended by their companions. Through them God revealed to the seers truth in pictorial form. They came under various circumstances, in men's waking hours (Dan 10:7; Acts 9:7), by day (Acts 10:3) or by night (Gen 46:2). In the OT both "writing" and "nonwriting" prophets were recipients of visions (Isa 1:1; Obad 1; Nah 1:1; and 2 Sam 7:17; 1 Kings 22:17–19; 2 Chron 9:29). With perhaps one exception (Num 24:4), they were given only to holy men in the service of God, and those of a revelatory nature were always recognized as coming from God. In the NT Luke especially manifests great interest in visions (Luke 1:22; Acts 9:10; 10:3, 10ff.; 18:9). Biblical visions concerned both immediate situations (Gen 15:1–2; Acts 12:7) and more distant ones connected with the development of the kingdom of God, as may be seen in the writings of Isaiah, Ezekiel, Hosea, Micah, Daniel, and John. In the OT false prophets feigned visions and were denounced by Jeremiah (14:14; 23:16) and Ezekiel (13:7). SB

VISITATION (Heb. *pekuddâh,* Gr. *episkopē*). Used in the KJV for a divine visit for the purpose of rewarding or punishing people for their deeds (Jer 10:15, NIV "judgment"; Luke 19:44, NIV "God's coming"; 1 Peter 2:12, NIV "visits").

VOPHSI (vŏf'sī, Heb. *wopsî*). A man of Naphtali, one of the spies whom Moses sent to Canaan (Num 13:14).

VOW (Heb. *nedher,* Gr. *euchē*). A voluntary promise to God to perform some service or do something pleasing to him, in return for some hoped-for benefits (Gen 28:20–22; Lev 27:2, 8; Num 30; Judg 11:30); or to abstain from certain things (Num 30:3). In the OT vows were never regarded as a religious duty (Deut 23:22); but once they were made, they were considered sacred and binding (Deut 23:21–23; Judg 11:35; Ps 66:13; Eccl 5:4). Fathers could veto vows made by their daughters, and husbands could veto their wives' vows; but if a husband did not veto a wife's vow and then caused her to break it, the blame was his, not hers (Num 30). A vow had to be uttered to be binding (Deut 23:23). Almost anything—people, possessions, oneself—except what was already the Lord's or was an abomination to the Lord (23:18), could be vowed; and all these things could be redeemed with money, their value to be determined by a priest. Houses, lands, and unclean animals that were redeemed had to have a fifth of their value added to make up the redemption money. Jesus referred to vows only once, and that was to condemn the abuse of them (Matt 15:4–6; Mark 7:10–13). Paul's vow in Acts 18:18 was probably a temporary Nazirite vow. SB

VULGATE (See TEXTS AND VERSIONS, OT)

VULTURE (See BIRDS)

W

WADI (wȧ'dē). A valley that forms the bed of a stream during the winter but dries up in the hot season (cf. Gen 26:19). The word is Arabic and does not appear in KJV, but NIV uses it for KJV "river" and RSV "brook" (e.g., Num 34:5; Josh 15:4; 1 Kings 8:65; Isa 27:12; Ezek 47:19). Palestine contains hundreds of these "wadis." Sometimes it is spelled "wady."

WAFERS (Heb. *rāqîq, tsappîhith*). Thin cakes. The word in Exodus 16:31 emphasizes the thinness, but elsewhere what is meant is the process of beating that rendered the cakes thin (Exod 29:2; Lev 2:4; 7:12; 8:26; Num 6:15, 19). The same word is translated "cakes" in 1 Chronicles 23:29 KJV.

WAGES (Heb. *hinnām, maskōreth, pe'ullâh, sākhar*, Gr. *misthos, opsōnion*). Pay given for labor, generally reckoned by the day, and distinguished from fees paid for professional service or salaries that may be paid by the month or the year. In civilizations where slavery was a regular institution, the servant or slave necessarily received his living, but not much more, except when the master was kind and loving and made the servant practically a member of the family. The earliest mention of wages is in the bargaining between Laban and his nephew Jacob (Gen 29). It is implicit in the narrative that he must also have received his living during those fourteen years; then he labored for another six years, receiving as his wages considerable herds and flocks (Gen 29–30). Pharaoh's daughter promised wages to the mother of Moses for acting as his nurse (Exod 2:5–9). In the Mosaic Law a hired servant must be paid at the end of the day (Lev 19:13; Deut 24:14–15), thus implying a hand-to-mouth existence. The same sort of poverty is in the parable of the eleventh-hour laborers (Matt 20:1–16), but too much emphasis should not be put on the supposed value of the denarius (see MONEY), for whether "a penny" as in KJV or "a shilling" as in ASV, the fact remains that the laborer, and presumably his family, could live on it. Mercenary soldiers were advised by John the Baptist to be

Three courses of "Herodian" stones from the Western ("wailing") Wall in Jerusalem. Courtesy Israel Government Press Office.

content with their pay (Luke 3:14). The idea of wages is spiritualized in the statement "The wages of sin is death" (Rom 6:23), where it is contrasted with another: "The gift of God is eternal life in Christ Jesus our Lord." Paul speaks of his gifts from churches at Philippi as "wages" (2 Cor 11:8 KJV; NIV "support"; cf. Phil 4:15–18). He earned his living with his hands, and he teaches the right of the laborer to his wages (1 Tim 5:18). ABF

WAGON (Heb. *'ăghālâh,* from *'aghal, to be round, to roll*). A vehicle with wheels (usually two) used for carrying goods as well as persons. Ancient wagons were crude, with wheels made of wood. They were covered or uncovered, usually drawn by oxen but sometimes horses. Wagons are first mentioned in Genesis 45:19–46:5 (KJV; NIV "carts"), when Pharaoh sent wagons to help move Jacob and his family. Covered wagons, each drawn by two oxen, were used for moving the tabernacle (Num 7:3–9 KJV, NIV "carts") but not the sacred furniture, which was carried on the shoulders of priests.

WAIL (Heb. *mispēdh, nehî,* Gr. *alalazō, pentheō*). In ancient funeral processions wailing relatives, often accompanied by hired female (sometimes male) mourners and musicians, preceded the body to the grave (Jer 9:17–18; Amos 5:16; Matt 9:23).

WALK. More than a dozen Hebrew and Greek verbs are translated "walk." Used hundreds of times, the meaning is generally literal but often figurative (e.g., Ps 1:1). In the NT Letters the word is used uniformly in the figurative sense and refers to the whole manner of life and conduct (Rom 4:12; 2 Cor 6:16; 1 John 1:7) or to the observance of laws or customs (Acts 21:21 KJV).

WALL. In ancient times throughout the East the walls of houses were built of crude or sun-baked brick. Stone was used only in a certain few localities where it was plentiful. In Chaldea stone was entirely absent; in Assyria it was so rare that it was used only as an accessory. In Palestine houses were constructed of crude brick, although sometimes wood, mud-brick, and stone were used in alternate layers. In Egypt houses were built of crude brick mixed with chopped straw. Every ancient city had enormous walls surrounding it, sometimes containing chambers inside. There still exist some of the stones in the wall of the temple enclosure at Jerusalem. They measure thirty feet (nine m.) long, eight feet (two and one-half m.) wide, and three and one-half feet (one m.) high, weighing over eighty tons (seventy-three metric tons). Josephus tells of stones in the temple of Solomon sixty feet (eighteen m.) long.

WAR (Heb. *milhāmâh,* from *laham, to fight,* Gr. *polemos*). Every phase of Israel's life, including their warfare, was bound up with their God. War therefore had religious significance. It was customary for priests to accompany Israel's armies into battle (Deut 20:1–4). Campaigns were begun and engagements entered into with sacrificial rites (1 Sam 7:8–10; 13:9) and after consulting the Lord (Judg 20:18ff.; 1 Sam 14:37; 23:2; 28:6; 30:8). Prophets were sometimes asked for guidance before a campaign (1 Kings 22:5; 2 Kings 3:11).

The blowing of a trumpet throughout the land announced the call to arms (Judg 3:27; 1 Sam 13:3; 2 Sam 15:10), and priests sounded an alarm with trumpets (2 Chron 13:12–16). Weapons included slings, spears, javelins, bows and arrows, swords, and battering rams. Strategical movements included the ambush (Josh 8:3ff.), the feint

Relief from north palace of Ashurbanipal at Kuyunjik (668–633 B.C.) that shows Assyrian forces of Ashurbanipal fighting the Arabs, who seek to escape upon their camels. Assyrians are armed with bows and arrows, shields, spears, and helmets. Reproduced by courtesy of the Trustees of the British Museum.

Military campaign of Tiglath-Pileser III, showing a town being attacked by Assyrian infantry. Weapons include bows and arrows, spears, javelins, and a battering ram. Gypsum relief from Nimrud, 744–727 B.C. Reproduced by courtesy of the Trustees of the British Museum.

(Judg 20:20ff.), the flank movement (2 Sam 5:22ff.), the surprise attack (Josh 11:1–2), the raid (1 Chron 14:9), the foray (2 Sam 3:22), and foraging to secure supplies (23:11). Sometimes when opposing armies were drawn up in battle array, champions from each side fought one another (1 Sam 17). Armies engaged in hand-to-hand combat. Victorious armies pillaged the camp of the enemy, robbed the dead (Judg 8:24–26; 1 Sam 31:9; 2 Chron 20:25), and often killed or mutilated prisoners (Josh 8:23, 29; 10:22–27; Judg 1:6), though prisoners were usually sold into slavery. Booty was divided equally between those who had taken part in the battle and those who had been left behind in camp (Num 31:27; Josh 22:8; 1 Sam 30:24–25), but some of the spoils were reserved for the Levites and for the Lord (Num 31:28, 30).

Clay figure of woman bathing, from Aczib, ninth-early sixth century B.C. Courtesy Israel Department of Antiquities and Museums.

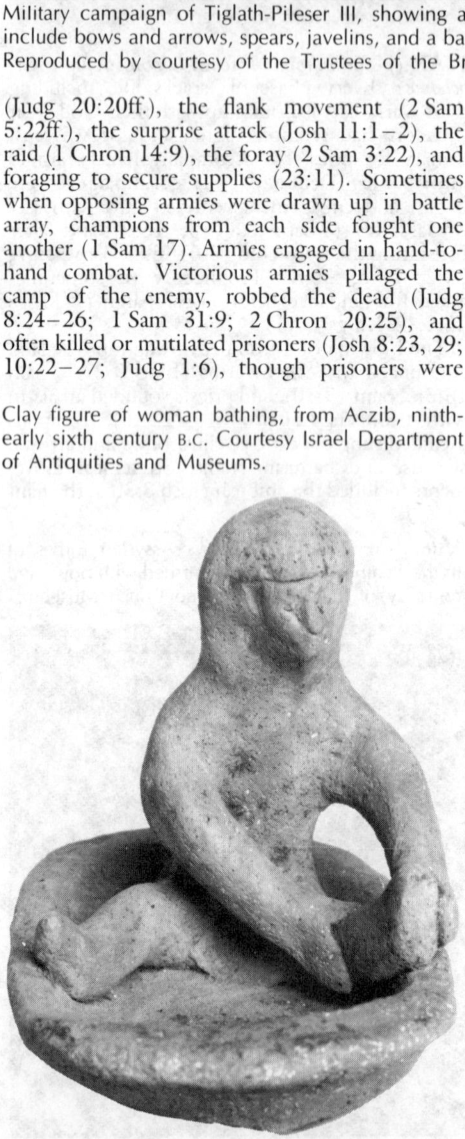

When a city was besieged, the besiegers built up huge mounds of earth against the walls, and from these mounds battering rams were used against the walls (2 Sam 20:15; Ezek 4:2). The besieged tried to drive off the enemy by throwing darts and stones and shooting arrows at them from the walls. Captured cities were often completely destroyed, and victory was celebrated with song and dance (Exod 15:1–21; Judg 5:1; 1 Sam 18:6).

Some point out that Jesus accepted war as an inevitable part of the present sinful world order (Matt 24:6) but warned that those who take the sword must perish by it (26:52). In the NT Letters the Christian is said to be a soldier (2 Tim 2:3; 1 Peter 2:11). The Apocalypse uses the figure of battle and war to describe the final triumph of Christ over Satan (Rev 16:14–16; 17:14; 19:14). SB

WASHERMAN'S FIELD (See FULLER'S FIELD)

WASHING (Heb. *rāhats, kāvas,* Gr. *niptō, louō, loutron*). Frequent bathing was necessary in the warm climate of the East. In Egypt, Syria, and Palestine people washed the dust from their feet when they entered a house (Gen 18:4; John 13:10). Ceremonial defilement was removed by bathing the body and washing the clothing (Lev 14:8; Num 19:7–8). The priests washed their hands and feet before entering the sanctuary or offering a sacrifice (Exod 30:19–21). In the time of Christ the Jews did much ceremonial washing of hands before eating (Mark 7:3–4) and used public baths as the Greeks and Romans did.

WATCH (Heb. *'ashmurâh, 'ashmōreth,* Gr. *phy-*

lakē). A man or group of men set to guard a city. Nehemiah, when building the walls of Jerusalem, set a watch day and night to warn of enemy approaches (Neh 4:9), and after the walls were completed, he set watches near the gates (7:3). Even today in the East, when the crops are ripening in the fields and vineyards, one may see watchmen on guard day and night. The temporary shelters set up by the watchmen in the fields are alluded to in Isaiah 1:8, for they are deserted as soon as the crops have been gathered. Metaphorically, David prays, "Set a guard over my mouth, O LORD; keep watch [restraint] over the door of my lips" (Ps 141:3). The Latin word *custodia,* transliterated in Greek, is used three times (Matt 27:65–66; 28:11 NIV "guard," KJV "watch") for the Roman watch that was set to guard our Lord's tomb.

WATCHES OF THE NIGHT. The divisions into which the twelve hours of the night were divided. The Jews had a threefold division (Judg 7:19), while the Romans had four watches (Mark 6:48).

WATCHMAN (See OCCUPATIONS AND PROFESSIONS)

WATER (Heb. *mayim,* Gr. *hydōr*). Because of its scarcity in Palestine, water is much appreciated there. For its people, absence of water was very serious (1 Kings 17:1ff.; Jer 14:3; Joel 1:20), and rain was a sign of God's favor. The rivers of Palestine are mostly small and have little if any water in summer. Consequently in Bible times the country depended on rain as its source of water. This supplied springs and fountains. Cisterns were a necessity for the storing of water, but if water was stored too long it became brackish and filthy and a menace to health. In the summer there was no rain, so vegetation was dependent on the heavy dews. Irrigation was carried on where there was sufficient water. When water was scarce, as during a time of siege, it had to be rationed. Drinking water, carried in goatskins, was often sold in the streets. Wells and pools, although comparatively scarce, are often mentioned in the Bible (Gen 21:19; 24:11; John 4:6; 9:7). Water was used not only for refreshment, but for ceremonial washings before meals and in the Jewish temple ceremony (Lev 11:32; 16:4; Num 19:7). The Bible uses it as a symbol of the cleansing of the soul from sin (Ezek 16:4, 9; 36:25; John 3:5; Eph 5:26; Heb 10:22; 1 John 5:6, 8). See also MINERALS. SB

Ancient water system at Hazor, comprising an entrance structure, a vertical shaft, and a sloping tunnel extending in depth to about 35 meters. Courtesy Zev Radovan.

WATER HEN (See BIRDS)

WATER OF BITTERNESS; WATER OF JEALOUSY (See JEALOUSY, WATER OF)

WATER OF CLEANSING. Water for the removal of impurity (Num 19:9, 13, 20–21; 31:23). KJV has "water of separation"; ASV, "water of impurity."

WATERPOT (Gr. *hydria*). An earthen jar for carrying or holding water, either for drinking (John 4:28) or for purifying purposes (John 2:6–7). The latter was large, holding eighteen to twenty gallons (sixty-nine to seventy-seven l.). NIV has "water jar."

WATERSPOUT (Heb. *tsinnôr*). Mentioned only in Psalm 42:7 where ASV and NIV have "waterfall." It means a large rush of water sent by God, perhaps great floods of rain.

WAVE OFFERING (See SACRIFICE AND OFFERINGS)

WAY. There are about twenty-five Hebrew and Greek words translated "way" in the Bible. It is often used metaphorically to describe the conduct or manner of life, whether of God or of man (Deut 5:33; Ps 1:6; Prov 16:17). In the NT God's plan of salvation is called "the way of the Lord" (Matt 3:3). The term is also used to mean Christianity or Judaism (Acts 9:2; 19:9; 22:4).

WAYFARING MAN (Heb. *'ōrēah, 'āvar, 'ōrah, hālakh-derekh*). One who walks the roads (Judg 19:17; 2 Sam 12:4; Isa 33:8; 35:8); a traveler (so NIV).

WEALTH (Heb. *hôn, hayil, nekhāsîm,* Gr. *euporia*). Abundance of possessions whether material, social, or spiritual. In the nomadic civilization of the early Hebrews, wealth consisted largely of flocks and herds, silver and gold, brass, iron, and clothing (Josh 22:8). In the days of Job, his sons had houses, but their wealth consisted largely of camels, donkeys, flocks, and herds, and "a large number of servants" (Job 1:3). Wealth can come from sinful endeavors (Acts 19:25). From the beginning of Israel, God taught his people that he was the giver of their wealth (Deut 8:18): "For it is he who gives you the ability to produce wealth." He taught them to be liberal: "One man gives freely, yet gains even more; another withholds unduly, but comes to poverty" (Prov 11:24). NT teaching goes even further: "Nobody should seek his own good, but the good of others" (1 Cor 10:24). Some OT passages give the impression that wealth always went with godliness (Ps 112:3) and that poverty was for the wicked (Prov 13:18), but this outlook can be debated.

WEAN, WEANING (Heb. *gāmal, to complete, wean*). To wean is to accustom a child to depend on other food than his mother's milk. In the East weaning is often deferred for as long as three years (1 Sam 1:22; 2:11). The weaning of a child was celebrated by a feast (Gen 21:8) and with an offering (1 Sam 1:24).

WEAPON (See ARMS AND ARMOR)

WEASEL (See ANIMALS)

WEATHER. There is no Hebrew word corresponding to "weather." The temperature in Palestine varies from the cold at the top of Hermon (9,000 ft. [2,813 m.] above sea level) where there is snow on the ground year around to the oppressive heat of the region near Jericho (1,300 ft. [406 m.] below sea level). The temperature of much of Palestine is comparable to that of California, and so oranges, lemons, and olives are profuse on the coastal plains, figs and grapes a little higher, and most of the hill country is suitable for barley and other crops that mature quickly in a semiarid climate. From about mid-November to mid-January much rain falls, the "former" or "fall" rain of Scripture (Jer 5:24). In late March, if the land is favored, comes the "later" or "spring" rain (Joel 2:23), thus assuring good crops. If the spring rain fails, much of the harvest is lost. The Bible clearly teaches that, at least in OT times, there was a close relationship between the spiritual condition of the people and the weather (1 Kings 8:35–36; Joel 1:17–20). Sin brought physical punishment in famine, plagues of insects, and storms. In the highlands, as at Jerusalem, it became quite cold in winter (Ezra 10:9, 13), especially since the houses were inadequately heated (Jer 36:22). One who has lived on the coast of the Mediterranean soon learns to predict weather conditions by looking out over the sea. When the water looks like bright metallic blue and the horizon is very sharp, he knows that the wind is from the north and he predicts clear, cool weather (Job 37:9, 22; read

Three Arab women weaving a carpet. Courtesy Zev Radovan.

36:24–38:37). When sea and sky seem to blend together, he predicts pleasant warm weather. The occasional hot sirocco is like the breath of an oven.

WEAVING (Heb. *'āragh*). The uniting of threads by crossing each other to produce cloth. The art of weaving is well-nigh universal, even among primitive peoples, and its beginnings are lost in the mists of antiquity. Job complained, "My days are swifter than a weaver's shuttle" (7:6), showing that he not only knew of weaving, but that the art had progressed to the point where the weaver's hands were swift in passing the shuttle back and forth. Jabal, an antediluvian, is called "the father of those who live in tents and raise livestock" (Gen 4:20), implying that the weaving of tents and the taming of cattle had their beginnings nearly at the same time. Weaving, as a fine art, was in the case of Bezelel and Oholiab a gift from God (Exod 35:30–35); and their woven work for the tabernacle, the curtains and veils may have surpassed in beauty anything previously known in cloth. Damascus, one of the oldest cities of the world, was long known for its woven work; and "damask" with its beautifully woven figures takes its name from that city. The lovely acrostic poem on the virtuous woman (Prov 31:10–31) pictures her as acquainted with the work of spinning and weaving, as well as the work of dressmaking; but the heavier work of weaving tentcloth was often done by men. Acts 18:2–3 mentions Paul, with Aquila and his wife Priscilla, as tentmakers. The Oriental tents were generally woven of goats' hair made so well they were nearly waterproof and so strong they lasted for a lifetime. In the "doom of Egypt" (Isa 19) the weavers of both linen and cotton cloth are spoken of as losing hope (19:9), indicating the importance of weaving to the economy of Egypt in her prosperity. In Hezekiah's description of his despair in the days of his sickness (Isa 38:10–18), he spoke of God as cutting off his life as a weaver cuts the thread when his work is complete (38:12). Isaiah speaks of the wicked as weaving the spider's web (59:5), thus indicating the futility of their efforts; and 2 Kings 23:7 speaks with horror of "where women did weaving for Asherah." A giant had a spear like a weaver's rod (1 Chron 11:23).

See also OCCUPATIONS AND PROFESSIONS.

ABF

WEDDING (Gr. *gamos*). An event regarded in Scripture as the ceremony by which a man and a woman were joined together as husband and wife and legally entitled to form a separate family unit. The betrothal was a significant, binding, legal commitment for the forthcoming marriage (Deut 20:7), a commitment that could be broken only by death or divorce. At the time of the betrothal, gifts of jewelry (which were often made of gold set with semiprecious stones) would be presented to the girl and sometimes to her mother, and, depending on the society, the bride price, dowry, or contract would also be exchanged. After the invention of coinage it became increasingly common for gold coins to form part of the betrothal gifts. During the period of the betrothal, which normally lasted for one year, the girl was already deemed to belong to her future husband, and the punishment for any man who violated her sexually was death by stoning.

The wedding of patriarchal times was very similar to that found among nomadic Bedouin tribes today. Often a separate small tent or hut was erected to be used by the bride and groom for the wedding night (2 Sam 16:22; Ps. 19:4–5; Song of Sol 1:16–17). The tent was often round in shape and was pitched in the early evening by the women. To the accompaniment of considerable merriment they also made the bed ready for the bridal pair. For the very poor, who could not afford this privacy, a small section of the groom's parents' tent was partitioned off for the use of the young couple. At sunset, certain female relatives of the groom would go to the tent of the bride's parents and escort the young bride to the nuptial chamber. There the bridegroom would meet her subsequently.

Traditionally, the bride remained veiled and the tent was kept in darkness until after the marriage was consummated. This custom helps to explain the comparative ease with which Laban was able to substitute Leah for her younger and more attractive sister Rachel in the bridal chamber. The public transfer of the bride to the tent of the groom was always a significant part of the wedding ceremony. Genesis 24:67 records that Rebekah accompanied Isaac to his tent and she became his wife. This, in its simplest form, was the wedding, without additional ritual.

With the passage of time, changes in lifestyles and habitation, and the increase in wealth and the desire for ostentation, the wedding ceremony became far more elaborate. The entire village or town would participate in this most memorable event. Bride and groom would be dressed in clothing of fine linen, sometimes decorated by means of gold thread that had been woven into the garment. The bride was also prepared for the nuptials by being bathed and groomed with cosmetic preparations and anointed with sweet-smelling perfumes. By tradition she also wore an elaborate headdress heavily encrusted with jewels and often containing gold in the form of small ornaments. After the invention of coinage the headdress was adorned with gold coins, these sometimes forming part of the bride's dowry. In later biblical times there appear to have been separate processions for bride and groom, where each was accompanied by musicians with drums and tambourines, dancers, torchbearers, well-wishers, and friends, all of whom joined with shouts and songs in celebrating the wedding (Jer 7:34; 16:9; 25:10).

Following the example of king Solomon (Song of Sol 3:11), the bridegroom was crowned king of the festival, and apparently from about the same period (900 B.C.) the bride also submitted to a ceremonial crowning, which in effect made her queen for the period of the celebrations (Ezek 16:8–13). There seem to have been some occasions when, on arrival at the house of the groom, the men participated in the feast (Gen 29:22), while the women, including the bride, had a separate feast at the home of the bride's parents. Traditionally, the feasting lasted for seven days (Judg 14:12, 17), though this period was sometimes doubled in length and was marked by music and entertainment of all kinds, including special poems and songs proclaiming the praises and extolling the charms of the bride and bridegroom. If some Bedouin practices are any guide to the nature of ancient Hebrew marriage proceedings, the songs and poems that were features of the celebrations would be of a decidedly erotic character. The bride would observe all these activities, and might sometimes participate in the dancing with her female attendants. Then, at an approved point in the ceremonies, she was escorted to the specially prepared bridal chamber, to the cheers, laughter, and enthusiasm of the assembled guests.

In the postexilic period, weddings increasingly took place in the middle of the week, so that if, on the wedding night, the bride was found not to be a virgin, her husband could denounce her and bring evidence, or, rather, lack of it, before the magistrates the following day and still have a decision regarding nullity rendered before the Sabbath. The garment stained with hymeneal blood was adopted as the traditional evidence of the bride's virginity and was usually retained as proof by the women of her family.

In Greek times the bridegroom gave a promise neither to maltreat his bride nor to bring any other woman into the house, while the bride promised always to obtain his consent prior to leaving the confines of the house. It was only in Roman times that the groom began to carry the bride over the threshold, a superstitious concession to the belief that it would have been a bad omen for the marriage had she stumbled. This custom was not practiced in Jewish or Christian circles, however.

Although certain aspects of the wedding varied according to the times or local custom, the central theme was the public escorting of the bride to the house of the groom, followed by the celebrating and feasting prior to the wedding night activities in the bridal chamber.

As is the practice today in Jewish circles, the wedding ceremony itself was simple and brief, but the accompanying festivities took on an elaborate ritual that varied somewhat according to the social and economic status of the participants. Where custom demanded that the entire village or town should celebrate the wedding, the occasion became a grand excuse for a magnificently colorful event enhanced by every display of wealth and finery. It also served as a rare opportunity for a feast that included meat and other foods that were not normally a part of the everyday menu. The dancing, laughter, and general merriment that were so characteristic a part of the occasion would have made a welcome break from the rigors of normal daily work.

Bibliography: E. Westermarck, *History of Human Marriage,* 1–3 (1923); R. H. Kennett, *Ancient Hebrew Life and Social Customs* (1933); L. M. Epstein, *Marriage Laws in the Bible and the Talmud* (1942); idem., *Sex Laws and Customs in Judaism* (1948). HWP

WEDGE (Heb. *lāshôn zāhāv, tongue of gold*). The English word occurs only in Joshua 7:21, 24, where the Hebrew word *lashon* ("tongue") indicates the shape. A more accurate translation than "golden wedge" (Isa 13:12 KJV) would be simply "gold" (as in most other versions).

WEEDS (See PLANTS)

WEEK (See CALENDAR)

Bronze lion weight from Khorsabad in Assyria, eighth century B.C. Courtesy Réunion des Musées Nationaux.

WEEKS, FEAST OF (See FEASTS)

WEIGHTS AND MEASURES. The modern reader of the Scriptures lives in a world dominated by the scientific method and the reign of "fact"—measurable fact. Meat is weighed in pounds and ounces on scales checked periodically by a bureau of weights and measures. Exact measurements in miles and fractions of miles state the distance between places. Liquids are measured exactly, from the contents of an oil tanker to that of a hypodermic needle. Such exact measurements cannot be expected in the Bible. The ancient Hebrew lived in a different kind of a world. The lack (for most of biblical times) of a strong, paternalistic central government, the simple life of self-sufficient country folk, and the frequent influence of foreign nations whose standards differed from those of the Hebrews help to account for the lack of consistent and specific measurements. One must be content with round numbers in the study of the weights and measures of the Bible.

Our information is gained from two sources—written and archaeological. Written sources include the Bible and other ancient books such as the works of Josephus, Herodotus, the Talmud, and references in classical literature. Archaeological information is uncovered by the excavator in the lands of the Bible—labeled weight-stones, jars, and other objects that will be mentioned in this article, which attempts a synthesis of the information from all the sources.

I. Measures of Length. Hebrew measures of length arose (as did the English foot) from the simple estimating of distance in terms of the body. Farmers today measure the height of horses by "hands." The ancient Hebrews used the terms *pace* (about a yard), *cubit* (the length of the forearm), *span* (length of a hand; about half a cubit), *palm* (hand-breadth; about one-third of a span), and a *finger* (about one-quarter of a palm). In Egypt a similar system was used.

The ordinary cubit is equivalent to about seventeen and one-half or eighteen inches (forty-five or forty-six cm.) today; it is once referred to as "the cubit of a man"—i.e., the distance that might be measured by a man's forearm (Deut 3:11; RSV "the common cubit"). There was a longer cubit, just as we today have a land mile (5,280 ft. [1,650 m.]) and a nautical mile (6,080 ft. [1,900 m.]). Ezekiel mentions a "long cubit," which he equates with a cubit and a hand-breadth (40:5; 43:13), roughly equivalent to twenty and one-half inches (fifty-three cm.). The Egyptians had two cubits of about the same length (about seventeen and one-half and twenty and one-half in. [forty-five and fifty-three cm.]). The usual cubit in the Bible is the shorter one. The longer cubit is used in Ezekiel's measurements and possibly in Solomon's temple (2 Chron 3:3 may be a reference to it).

The length of Hezekiah's water tunnel underneath Jerusalem is stated by the inscription in the tunnel to be 1,200 cubits. The tunnel is 1,749 feet (547 m.) long according to the most reliable measurement. The cubit length thus arrived at is 17.49 inches (45 cm.). This does not mean, however, that the cubit in Hezekiah's time was exactly 17.49 inches long: the figure of 1,200 cubits is a round number, also it is not certain at what point the ancient measuring of the tunnel began. The Siloam Inscription indicates only that our approximate length for the cubit—a little less than eighteen inches—is not too far off, which is as positive a conclusion as can be hoped for under the circumstances.

Confirmatory evidence for this length of the cubit is also seen in the fact that many ancient buildings have been found on excavation to be measurable in terms of a cubit of about seventeen and one-half inches, or in reeds equivalent to six such cubits.

Some other terms of measurement in the Bible are the *reed,* the *gōmedh,* and the *fathom*. The *reed,* mainly an instrument for measuring rather than a unit of measurement, was six cubits long (Ezek 40:5). The term *gōmedh,* which occurs only in Judges 3:16 and is translated "cubit" (NIV "about a foot and a half" [one-half m.]), is thought by present scholars to refer to a shorter distance—two-thirds of a cubit at most—for a dagger rather than a sword is referred to. The *fathom* (armstretch; Acts 27:28) was about six feet (almost two m.).

II. Measurements of Distance and Area. In OT times distance was usually measured by the length of time necessary to traverse it. Thus we read of the "three-day journey" (Gen 30:36) and "for seven days" (31:23). In the NT these terms are used: stadium ("furlong" KJV, Luke 24:13; John 6:19), about 606 feet (189 m.); mile (Matt 5:41), about 4,860 feet (1,519 m.). About the Sabbath day's journey there is some uncertainty. The term, used to indicate the distance one might walk without breaking the Sabbath law, seems to have been an elastic one. Josephus calls it five stadia in one place and six in another, making it equal 3,000 or 3,600 feet (938 or 1,125 m.). This is about the distance from Jerusalem to the Mount of Olives (Acts 1:12).

Land measurements were indicated in terms of the area that a team of oxen could plow in one day (1 Sam 14:14). This is the meaning of "acre" in Isaiah 5:10, where the Hebrew is *semedh*—"yoke [of oxen]." In Mesopotamia this area equaled two-fifths of an acre. Elsewhere land area was stated as the part of a field that could be seeded with barley in one day (Lev 27:16).

III. Measures of Capacity. Our uncertainty about the units of capacity is understandable when one considers the origin of these terms. They seem to have arisen from common household pots (all handmade locally), or from the farmer's estimate of the carrying ability of a man or beast. The *hin* was a pot and the *ephah* a basket (both words are of Egyptian origin). The *omer* was a sheaf and the *homer* a donkey load. The word *bath* means "daughter"; could this jar be the one that one's daughters carried home from the well? (Gen 24:15).

The student of the English Bible will have difficulty in following this discussion in his Bible because of the untechnical character of his translation. Many of the terms mentioned below are translated "measure" in quite a few places in the standard English versions. The best way to discover which unit the Hebrew or Greek text refers to is to use a comprehensive concordance (such as Strong's or Young's), where the Hebrew and Greek terms are clearly distinguished.

The *bath* was the standard liquid measure in OT times. Its value is a matter of dispute. At present scholars regard it as equal to about six gallons (twenty-three l.), rather than ten gallons (thirty-nine l.) as formerly. The finding of fragments of large jars, inscribed "bath of the king" (perhaps an attempt to standardize the bath for use in tax payments) or simply "bath" have helped to bring about this reduction in size. Unfortunately, these jars cannot be completely restored, hence there is still some uncertainty. Subdivisions of the bath are hin (one-sixth bath) and log (one-twelfth hin).

The liquid measures of NT times are difficult to equate with those of the OT. The English "measure" may equal a *kōr,* as in Luke 16:7, or a *bath,* as in Luke 16:6. The *firkin* of John 2:6 (KJV) held about 10.3 gallons (40 l.).

The *homer* was the standard dry measure of the OT. *Homer* means "donkey," and therefore a donkey-load, or about 6.25 bushels (208 l.) It is to be equated with the *cor.* The *ephah* (about +3/5 bu.—20 l.) is the dry equivalent of the liquid measure *bath* (Ezek 45:10). The *lethekh* is mentioned only in Hosea 3:2 and is probably given its correct value in the KJV, which translates it "half homer."

Three smaller dry measures are: the *se'âh,* about one-fifth bushel (seven l.); the *omer,* four dry pints (two l.); the *'issārôn* (KJV "tenth deal," RSV "tenth measure"), evidently equivalent to the *omer;* and the *cab,* a little more than two dry pints (one l.). However, modern authorities differ greatly as to the value of the dry measures, some inclining toward a substantially higher value for each. The system followed here is substantially that of R. B. Y. Scott in the article referred to at the end of this subject.

NT dry measures are: *bushel* (Matt 5:15), about seven and one-half dry quarts or slightly less than one-half US bushel; *measure* ("quart," RSV), about one dry quart; *pot* (Mark 7:4), about one dry pint.

IV. Weights. Remember that coinage was not used in Palestine until after the Exile. Ezra 2:69 is probably the first mention of coined money in the Bible ("drachmas," NIV; "drams," KJV; "daries," RSV). During most of OT times, barter (Gen 30:27–34; 31:8; 2 Kings 3:4), value determined by precious metal weighed out, was the means of exchange. The *shekel* is a weight in the OT, not a coin (Ezek 4:10), and the verb *shāqal* means "to weigh out," as in Jeremiah 32:10. Simple balance scales were used, and stones of certain weight (often shekels) were used to determine the weight of the silver or gold involved in the transaction. Proverbs 16:11 reads literally, "the stones [Eng-

Assorted Hebrew weights, inscribed with their values. From right to left: 50 shekels, 8 shekels, 4 shekels, 2 shekels, two neseph (5/6 shekel) pieces, and an uncertain weight (perhaps 1/6 shekel). Courtesy Israel Department of Antiquities and Museums.

lish Bible "weights"] in the bag." A good illustration of an ancient business transaction occurs in a Canaanite poem (found at Ras Shamra) that describes the weighing of the marriage price for the wedding of Nikkal and the Moon:

> Her father sets the beam of the balances
> Her mother, the trays of the balances
> Her brothers arrange the ingots(?)
> Her sisters (attend) to the stones of the balances (77:34–39).

In addition to the biblical references to weights, quite a few stone weight-pieces (especially shekels) have been found in the excavations in Palestine, many of them labeled. There is a certain amount of disparity among these. Some have speculated that this is graphic evidence for the necessity of the prophetic indictment of the dishonest merchants who "make the ephah small and the shekel great, and deal deceitfully with false balances" (Amos 8:5 RSV). While this explanation is not to be ruled out completely, it must never be forgotten that life in ancient Palestine was simple, rural, and predominantly agricultural. Most of the time there was no strong central government and certainly no bureau of weights and measures. To some extent, the period of David and Solomon is an exception to this. David seems to have had a "royal standard" (2 Sam 14:26). The standardization that controls every aspect of modern life was completely lacking. Many years ago the writer of this article found farmers in eastern Jordan selling grapes and melons by simple balance scales, with roughly cut stones for weights. No doubt such simple arrangements usually sufficed in Bible times. Esti-

Animal-shaped bronze weights from Palestine: bull's head with nose ring, tortoise, duck, and lion. Fourteenth to sixth century B.C. Courtesy Reuben and Edith Hecht Museum, University of Haifa.

Weight of one mina (60 shekels) with inscription stating that it is an exact replica of a weight made by Nebuchadnezzar II (605–562 B.C.). Reproduced by courtesy of the Trustees of the British Museum.

mates of values of ancient weights must therefore be rather general; taking figures to two decimal places is a futile attempt to reduce ancient people to modern uniformity.

The Hebrews used a modified sexagesimal system of weights modeled on that of the Babylonians. The *shekel* (called by the Babylonians *shiqlu*) was the basic unit. Fifty shekels equaled a *maneh* (or *mina;* Babylonian *manû*) and sixty manehs a *talent* (Heb *kikkār;* Babylonian *biltu*). A *shekel* as made up of twenty *gerahs*. A *bekah* was a half shekel.

The Babylonians had 60 shekels in their maneh, but from Exodus 38:25–26 it appears that the Hebrew maneh consisted of only 50. Half a shekel each was paid by 603,550 men, and totaled 100 talents and 1,775 shekels; this means that the talent here equaled 3,000 shekels. Since the talent was almost 60 manehs, the maneh here equals 50 shekels. Ezekiel uses a different system, with 60 shekels to the maneh (45:12).

When one attempts to define the shekel in terms of presently understood weights, the difficulties are formidable. One of the best recent treatments of the problem is R. B. Y. Scott's (see bibliography at the end of article), which takes into account the many stone weights found in Palestine and computes values in great detail. The weight-pieces discovered vary greatly. In addition to the double standard mentioned above and the generally unregimented style of ancient Israelite life, the standards themselves may have tended to depreciate, as standards do. The influence of foreign systems may also have been a disturbing factor. The larger weights seem to indicate smaller shekel units than do the smaller weights.

The *beqa'* or *half shekel* is the only weight named both in the OT and on discovered weights, and of which the relationship to the shekel is given (Exod 38:26). Several stone weights have been found with Hebrew consonants *BQ* (*beqa*) cut on them, weighing on an average about .21 ounces (6 g.) (actual weights vary from .2 to .23 oz.—5.8 to 6.65 g.). One thing these *beqa* weights indicated is that the shekel weighed about .4 ounces (12 g.). Therefore the numerous stones bearing a symbol resembling a figure-eight with an open loop, weighing about .4 ounces (12 g.), must be shekel weights. This symbol seems to be a representation of a tied bundle of lump silver.

Scott concludes that there were three standards for a shekel: the temple shekel of .35 ounces (about 10 g.), the common or commercial shekel of about .4 ounces (11.5 g.), and a "heavy" shekel of about .45 ounces (13 g.). The last of these was probably used in weighing some special commodity.

Certain recent excavations have yielded weights inscribed *pim,* weighing about two-thirds of a shekel. Thus the name of another unit of Hebrew weight is recovered and light is shed on a difficult statement in 1 Samuel 13:21. This verse contains the word *pim,* which was unknown elsewhere and believed to be a textual corruption. Now that *pim* is known to be the name of a weight, the NIV was able to give an improved translation, which indicates that the Philistines, to keep the Hebrews in subjection, made it difficult for the Hebrews to get iron implements and probably overcharged them for repairing them.

Few weights are mentioned in the NT. *Talent* and *pound* (NIV "mina") in Luke 19:13–25 are sums of money. *Pound* in John 12:3 (NIV "pint") and 19:39 represents another Greek word, *litra,* a weight of some .75 pound avoirdupois (.3 kg.).

Bibliography: R. B. Y. Scott, "Weights and Measures of the Bible," BA, 22 (1951): 22–40, and PEQ, 97, 1965, pp. 128–39; E. W. Heaton, *Everyday Life in Old Testament Times,* 1965, pp. 189–91; D. W. Thomas (ed.), *Documents From Old Testament Times,* 1958, pp. 227–30. JBG

WELL (Heb. *be'ēr,* Gr. *phrear*). A pit or hole dug in the earth down to the water table, i.e., to the level at which the ground is permanently saturated with water. For both safety and permanence, the well was generally surrounded by a wall of stone, and in the case of some famous wells, like that of Jacob at Sychar (John 4), the walls were beautifully constructed with dressed stone. A well is to be distinguished from a cistern (which was merely for storing water, Jer 2:13), a spring (which is found at the surface of the ground), and a fountain (from which water actively flows, Josh 15:9).

WEST (Heb. *yām, sea, māvô', setting of the sun, ma'ărāv, west,* Gr. *dysmē*). *Yām,* "sea," is the Hebrew word usually used for "west," because the Mediterranean Sea lies to the west of Palestine. The word is sometimes used figuratively with "east" to denote great distance (Ps 103:12).

WHALE (See ANIMALS)

WHEAT (See PLANTS)

WHEEL (Heb. *'ôphan, galgal, gilgal, 'ovnayim, pa'am*, Gr. *trochos*). Probably at first just a disk of wood cut from a log, but quite early developed into something resembling the modern device. When the Egyptians with their chariots pursued the Israelites at the Red Sea (Exod 14:24–25), the Lord took off their chariot wheels. In 1 Kings 7:30–33 where the bases of the great "sea" of Solomon's temple are described, reference is made to wheels with their axles, rings, spokes, and hubs, showing that by Solomon's time (c. 1000 B.C.) the wheel was quite developed and was similar to modern wagon wheels. Cart wheels were used for threshing some kinds of grain, but not cummin (Isa 28:27). The word for "potter's wheel" means literally "two stones" (Jer 18:3). In ancient times two circular stone disks were joined by a short shaft, and so spun. Today, the shaft is longer and the wheels are of wood.

WHIP (Heb. *shôt*). An instrument of punishment or inciting to work; generally a lash attached to a handle. This word was used figuratively by Rehoboam in reference to his father (1 Kings 12:14).

WHIRLWIND (Heb. *sûphâh, se'ārâh, sa'ar*). In biblical usage this does not exactly conform to our modern idea of a violent whirling as at the vortex of a tornado, but rather emphasizes the idea of being tossed about. These Hebrew words are often translated "storm" or "tempest," which is a more accurate translation; and they are used figuratively of swift and terrible destruction (Prov 1:27; Isa 5:28; Jer 4:13; Hos 8:7). Elijah was carried to heaven by a whirlwind (2 Kings 2:1, 11).

WHORE (See PROSTITUTE)

WICKED, WICKEDNESS (Heb. *ra, rasha*, Gr. *ponēros, ponēria*). The KJV often uses these words, but later translations prefer "evil," especially in the NT. The idea is that of a person or thing that is bad, worthless, depraved, and corrupt, and especially of a person or thing that opposes God, his will, his Messiah, and his gospel. It can describe a whole people or an individual or the state in which they are (as seen by God). Psalm 37 has many references to wicked or evil people as they are contrasted with the godly or righteous. This Psalm begins, "Do not fret because of evil men . . . for like the grass they will soon wither." Wickedness had been in the world since the entrance of sin, and because of it the Lord sent the great Flood (Gen 6:5), saving only the righteous Noah and his family.

Only wicked people could have killed Jesus the Messiah (Acts 2:23), but also a generation that did not wholeheartedly accept the gospel must be a wicked generation (Matt 16:4). In fact, the whole world is constantly in a state of wickedness (Rom 1:29). The origin and source of wickedness is to be sought, not in the wicked hearts of mankind, but in the work and wiles of the devil,

Detail of mosaic panel from the "Standard" of Ur, c. 2500 B.C., depicting a four-wheeled chariot, each wheel made of two semicircles of wood pegged together by tenons. The earliest wheel was probably made of wooden disks cut from a log. Reproduced by courtesy of the Trustees of the British Museum.

who is the "wicked" or "evil" one (Matt 13:19; Mark 4:15; Luke 8:12; Eph 6:12). Christians are to have nothing to do with the Wicked One or wickedness (1 John 5:18–19; 2:13) and are to use the shield of faith (Eph 6:16).

The certainty of punishment for the wicked is often declared (e.g., Matt 13:49). God permits wickedness in this age but does not condone it, and he will judge those responsible for it.

See also MALICE; EVIL. PT

WIDOW (Heb. *'almānâh*, Gr. *chēra*). Widows in the OT are regarded as being under God's special care (Ps 68:5; 146:9; Prov 15:25). From early times they wore a distinctive garb. The Hebrews were commanded to treat them with special consideration and were punished if they did otherwise (Exod 22:22; Deut 14:29; Isa 1:17; Jer 7:6). The church looked after poor widows in apostolic times (Acts 6:1; James 1:27). Paul gives instructions to Timothy about the care of widows by the church (1 Tim 5:4); but only those were taken care of who were at least sixty years of age, had been married only once, and had a reputation for good works (5:9–10). In the second and third centuries there was an order of widows in the church. Its members looked after the women of the congregation. This order was abolished by the Synod of Laodicea, A.D. 364.

WIFE (See FAMILY; MARRIAGE)

WILDERNESS. In Scripture this word refers either to barren desert or to an uncultivated region suitable for pasturage and occupied by nomads. (1) The most common Hebrew word rendered "wilderness" is *midhbār*, "a place for the driving of cattle" (Num 14:33; Deut 2:8; Judg 1:16 KJV; NIV "desert"). The word may refer to grassy pastures (Ps 65:12; Joel 2:22 KJV; NIV "grasslands") or a wasteland of rock and sand

(Deut 32:10; Job 38:26 KJV; NIV "desert"). (2) *Yeshîmôn,* sometimes rendered as a proper name in KJV (Num 21:20), refers to a dry or riverless region (Isa 43:19–20 KJV; NIV "desert"). (3) *'Arāvâh,* "arid, barren" (Isa 33:9; 51:3), when used with the definite article, denotes the plain of the Jordan and Dead Sea (2 Sam 2:29; Ezek 47:8), and is translated "Arabah" in RV and NIV. (4) *Tsiyyâh,* "land of drought" (Hos 2:3) is translated "desert" in NIV. (5) *Tohû,* "empty waste" (Job 12:24; Ps 107:40 KJV; NIV "trackless waste") refers to barren deserts. (6) Greek *erēmos* is a word that, like *midhbār* above, is used with considerable latitude (Matt 14:13, NIV "solitary place"; Heb 11:38, KJV and NIV "desert").

WILD GOAT (See ANIMALS)

WILD GOURD (See PLANTS)

WILD VINE (See PLANTS)

WILLOW (See PLANTS)

WILLOWS, BROOK OF THE. A brook on the boundary of Moab (Isa 15:7 KJV, RSV), generally identified with the Zered (Wâdi el-Hesā), which flows into the southern end of the Dead Sea and forms the boundary between Edom and Moab. NIV reads "Ravine of the Poplars."

WILLS. Testaments, oral or written, which law courts put into effect, by which property may be disposed of after death. Covenants between living persons might be bilateral, each party making promises, or unilateral, an agreement by one party that the other may accept or reject but may not alter. Wills grew out of the latter. In early times among the Hebrews as among others, property descended according to the laws of inheritance without wills. The only clear Bible reference to a will is in Hebrews 9:16–17, and its meaning is disputed. The context seems to assimilate the testament to a unilateral covenant of God with his people: Greek *diathēkē* always primarily meant a will, but was used in the LXX for Hebrew *berîth,* "covenant." In question here is an instrument that is effective only after the death of the one who made it, and this justifies RSV and NIV in translating it as "will."

WINDOW (See HOUSE)

WINDS. Wind in Hebrew is usually *rûah,* translated also "breath, spirit"; in Greek *anemos,* always "wind." Greek *pneuma,* "breath, wind, spirit" (John 3:8); *pnoē,* "breath" (Acts 2:2); the verb *pneō,* "to blow" (27:40).

Winds are important in the Bible, both literally and figuratively. God causes winds, and he created them (Gen 8:1; Exod 10:13; Num 11:31; Ps 107:25; 135:7; 147:18; Jer 10:13; Jonah 1:4). The four winds are limits of distance or direction (Jer 49:36; Ezek 37:9; Dan 7:2; 8:8; 11:4; Zech 2:6; Matt 24:31; Rev 7:1). Of the cardinal directions, the east wind is most often mentioned (Gen 41:6, 23, 27; Exod 10:13; 14:21; Job 15:2; 27:21; 38:24; Ps 48:7; 78:26; Isa 27:8; Jer 18:17; Ezek 17:10; 19:12; 27:26; Hos 12:1; 13:15; Jonah 4:8; Hab 1:9). Sometimes it is stormy, wrecks ships, withers growing things. The north wind brings rain (Prov 25:23), is refreshing (Song of Songs 4:16), or stormy (Ezek 1:4). The south wind is gentle, helps growth (Job 37:17; Ps 78:26; Song of Songs 4:16). The west wind blew away the plague of locusts (Exod 10:19). Winds brought notable storms (1 Kings 18:45; 19:11; Job 1:9; Matt 8:26–27; 14:24, 32; Acts 27:4, 7, 14–15). In Acts the following winds are named: the south wind (Gr. *notos,* 27:13; 28:13), the northwest wind (*chōros,* 27:12), the southwest wind (*lips,* 27:12), and the "nor'easter" (*eurakylon,* 27:14). The last named is called a "wind of hurricane force" (RSV, NIV). Whirlwinds are mentioned several times. Wind blows chaff (Job 21:18; Ps 1:4; 35:5; 83:13; Isa 17:14; 41:16; Jer 13:24; Dan 2:35); fulfills God's commands (Ps 104:4; 148:8 RSV, NIV); reveals weakness, transitoriness, worthlessness (Job 15:2; Ps 18:42; 78:39; 103:16; Prov 11:29; 25:14; Eccl 5:16; 11:4; Isa 7:2; 26:18; 41:29; Jer 5:13; 22:22; 49:32); clears the sky (Job 37:21); drives ships (James 3:4). Elisha promises water not brought by wind (2 Kings 3:17). God rides on the wings of the wind (2 Sam 22:11; Ps 104:3). The circulation of the wind is recognized (Eccl 1:6). Wind has a drying effect (Isa 11:15; Jer 4:11–12). Princes are to be a hiding place from the wind (Isa 32:2). Wind has an observable effect on animal life (Jer 2:24). Ezekiel scattered hair in the wind to symbolize the scattering of the people (Ezek 5:2, 10, 12; 12:14; 17:21). Winds can be strong and destructive (Jer 51:16; Ezek 13:11, 13; Hos 4:19; 13:15). Wind can represent folly and resulting troubles: "They sow the wind and reap the whirlwind" (Hos 8:7). God controls the force of the wind (Job 28:25). Believers are warned against evil winds of false doctrine (Eph 4:4; Jude 12). Stars will fall like figs shaken from the tree by the wind (Rev 6:13). Wind moved the wings of women carrying a basket (Zech 5:9).

ER

WINE. Several Hebrew words occur, of which two are frequent. These two are (1) *yayin,* wine, as a common drink (Gen 14:18); as a drink offering (Lev 23:13); as intoxicating (Gen 9:21); figuratively of wisdom (Prov 9:2, 5), of wrath (Jer 25:15), of love (Song of Songs 1:2; 4:10) and (2) *tîrôsh,* "must," "fresh or sweet wine"; with approval (Gen 27:28; Judg 9:13; 2 Kings 18:32; Zech 9:17) and once with disapproval (Hos 4:11). Priests were forbidden to drink wine on duty (Lev 10:9; Ezek 44:21). Nazirites were not even to touch grapes while under a vow (Num 6:5, 20; Judg 13:4–14; Luke 1:15). Abuse of wine is condemned in Proverbs (4:17–31:6), also in the Prophets (Isa 5:11), but God offers the wine of his Word (55:1).

In the NT, the primary Greek word is *oinos.* The word *gleukos* ("new, sweet wine") occurs only once (Act 2:13), where the disciples in their

Wall painting from the tomb of Nakht that depicts the gathering of grapes, and the treading and storage of wine in jars with stoppers. Thebes, 18th Dynasty, time of Thutmose IV (?), fourteenth century B.C. Courtesy The Metropolitan Museum of Art (15.5.19e).

exuberant enthusiasm appeared intoxicated. New wine fermenting would burst old wineskins (Matt 9:17). Jesus refused the wine offered him on the cross because it was drugged (Mark 15:25). Jesus contrasts himself with John the Baptist (Luke 7:33–34) as one who ate and drank with others. In OT times wine was not diluted. Before NT times the Hellenistic practice of mixing it with much water was common in Palestine. Wine was a disinfectant (10:34) and medicine (1 Tim 5:23). It is right for a Christian not to drink wine if it causes his brother to stumble (Rom 14:21). Men (1 Tim 3:8) and women (Titus 2:3) church officers were warned against overindulgence. Jesus made water into *oinos* at Cana (John 2:2–11).

At the Last Supper Jesus spoke of "this fruit of the vine" (Matt 26:29; Mark 14:25), as in the Passover liturgy; it may be a studied avoidance of the term "wine," indicating that the drink was unfermented, as the bread was unleavened. Whatever use Jesus or others made of wine is not proof that its use today is wise. The Bible gives more space to the danger than to the benefit of wine.

WINEPRESS. Hebrew *gath* (Judg 6:11; Neh 13:15; Isa 63:2–3), Greek *lēnos* (Matt 21:33). A "trough," usually of stone, cement-lined, from which juice flowed through a hole near the bottom into a vat (Heb. *yeqev;* Num 18:27, 30; Judg 7:25; Isa 5:2; Gr. *hypolēnion,* Mark 12:1). The grapes were pressed by men treading them, the treaders holding onto ropes suspended overhead. The process is compared to the execution of the wrath of God (Lam 1:15; Rev 14:19–20; 19:15).

WINESKIN (See BOTTLE)

WING (Heb. *kānāph,* Gr. *pteryx*). Birds' wings are mentioned in Scripture (Deut 32:11; Job 39:13, 26; Ps 55:6); so also are the wings of the cherubim (1 Kings 6:24) or "living creatures" (Ezek 1:5–25; Rev 4:8). The most significant Bible uses of wings are figurative: God's soaring on the wings of the wind (Ps 18:10), human desire to fly away and be at rest (55:6), our finding refuge in God (17:8; 91:4), an emblem of God's favor and blessing (68:13), the transcience of riches (Prov 23:5), rays of the rising sun (Ps 139:9; Mal 4:2), a promise of renewed strength (Isa 40:31), the compassion of Christ (Matt 23:37).

WINNOW (See FARMING)

WINNOWING FORK (Heb. *mizreh*). A fork with two or more prongs used to throw grain into the air after it had been threshed, so that the chaff might be blown away. The work was done toward evening and at night when a wind came in from the sea and carried away the light chaff. Sometimes a shovel was used for the same purpose. A winnowing fork is referred to in Jeremiah 15:7; Matthew 3:12; Luke 3:17.

WINTER. Hebrew *hōreph,* "harvest time, autumn," and the cold, rainy season following (Gen 8:22; Ps 74:17; Zech 14:8); also the verb "to winter" (Isa 18:6). Hebrew *sethāw,* "winter" (Song of Songs 2:11). Greek *cheimōn,* "winter," the cold, stormy season (Matt 24:20; Mark 13:18; John 10:22; 2 Tim 4:21) and related verbs (Acts 27:12; 28:11; 1 Cor 16:6; Titus 3:12).

WINTER HOUSE (Heb. *bēth ha-hōreph*). Kings and wealthy people had separate residences for hot seasons and residences for cold seasons (Amos 3:15). King Jehoiakim had a fire in the brazier in his winter house (Jer 36:22).

WISDOM. The commonest OT words for wisdom are Hebrew *hākham* and related forms and Greek *sophia.* In God wisdom is the infinite, perfect comprehension of all that is or might be (Rom 11:33–36). God is the source of wisdom as of power, and wisdom is given to people through the fear of the Lord (Job 28:28; Ps 111:10). In man wisdom is an eminently practical attribute, including technical skill (Exod 28:3;

RSV "an able mind"), military prowess (Isa 10:13), and shrewdness for questionable ends (1 Kings 2:6). Wisdom is shown in getting desired ends by effective means. People of the world are often wiser in their generation than the children of light (Luke 16:8). The wisdom of Solomon was far ranging in statesmanship (1 Kings 10:23–24); in understanding of human nature (3:16–25); and in natural history, literature, and popular proverbs (4:29–34). Wisdom is personified (Prov 8) in terms related to the concept of the Word in John 1:1–18, and became one of the names of God the Father and the Son, the Holy Spirit being the Spirit of Wisdom.

Wisdom Literature in the OT consists of Proverbs, Ecclesiastes, and Job, with Psalms 19, 37, 104, 107, 147, 148, and short passages in other books, in the OT Apocrypha, Ecclesiasticus, and Wisdom of Solomon. Hebrew wisdom was not all religious; it dealt, as in Proverbs, with everyday conduct in business, family and social relations, and basic morality. Ecclesiastes ranges farther afield to consider the ultimate value of life. Wise men, unlike prophets, claimed no special inspiration. They exercised no priestly functions and were not, like the scribes, devoted exclusively to the study of the sacred writings. Eventually wise men and scribes coalesced into one class. With worsening political conditions and a deepening sense of moral problems in the period of the prophets and later kings, people came to despise worldly wisdom as irreligious and as characteristic of pagans, who might be superior in secular culture, but were inferior from a moral and religious point of view (Isa 10:12–19). Wisdom is bound up with doing the will of the Lord (Deut 4:6): to forsake his Word is to forfeit one's wisdom (Jer 8:8–9). Although wisdom literature often seems to equate right with advantage (profit, Eccl 1:5), there is clear evidence of the controlling hand and moral interest of God in human affairs. The sayings of Jesus, largely proverbial and parabolical, are the crown of biblical wisdom. Paul calls Jesus "the wisdom of God" (1 Cor 1:24, 30) and says that in him all the treasures of wisdom are hidden (Col 2:3). When Paul compares the wisdom of people with the wisdom of God (1 Cor 2), he is thinking of the former as that of Greek philosophers rather than OT biblical wisdom. James's letter is wisdom literature at its best, a clear mirror of the teaching of Jesus. See also WISE PERSONS.

Bibliography: F. D. Kidner, *Proverbs* (TOTC), 1964; James Wood, *Wisdom Literature,* 1967; K. L. Jensen, *Wisdom the Principal Thing,* 1971. ER

WISDOM OF JESUS, SON OF SIRACH (See APOCRYPHA)

WISDOM OF SOLOMON (See APOCRYPHA)

WISE PERSONS. The name is often applied to people of understanding and skill in ordinary affairs (Job 15:2; Ps 49:10; Prov 1:5; Eccl 2:4; 1 Cor 1:26; 10:15; James 3:13), to Solomon superlatively (1 Kings 2:9; 5:7; 2 Chron 2:12), to the ladies of Sisera's mother (Judg 5:29), and to court women (2 Sam 14:2; 20:16). In a more specialized sense in Israel, the builders of the tabernacle (Exod 28:3; 35:30–35) and the leaders of the tribes (Deut 1:13, 15) were wise men. Wise, understanding, experienced older men came to be recognized as a distinct class, widely esteemed by the discerning. In pagan nations the wise men, grouped with and identified as magicians, sorcerers, enchanters, astrologers, and Chaldeans, appear in Egypt (Gen 41:8; Exod 7:11), Babylon (Dan 2:12–5:15), and Persia (Esth 1:13, NIV "men who understood the laws"). For the wise men of Matthew 2:1–16, see MAGI.

WITCH, WITCHCRAFT. A title commonly linked with those in league with evil spirits and their practices. Hebrew *kāshaph,* "to practice sorcery" is sometimes so translated in NIV, ASV, often in RSV (Exod 22:18; Deut 18:10; 2 Kings 9:22; 2 Chron 33:6; Mic 5:12; Nah 3:4). Hebrew *qesem,* "divination," is once translated "witchcraft" (1 Sam 15:23, KJV, ASV), otherwise "divination." Greek *pharmakeia* (Gal 5:20 ASV; RSV "sorcery") means the use of drugs, charms, or magic words. In Acts 8:9, 11 KJV, "bewitch" is a translation of the Greek *existēmi* (NIV "amazed"). In Galatians 3:1 the Greek *baskainō,* "to use the evil eye on one," is rendered "bewitched." The famous witch of Endor (1 Sam 28:7–25) is not so called in the Bible, but is referred to as a woman who had a "familiar spirit" (KJV, ASV) or who was a "medium" (RSV, NIV). All practices of witchcraft are strictly condemned (Exod 22:18; Deut 18:9–14; 1 Sam 28:3, 9; 2 Kings 23:24; Isa 8:19; Acts 19:18–19).

See MAGIC; OCCUPATIONS AND PROFESSIONS: *Sorcerer.*

WITHE (wĭth, wīth, Heb. *yether, bowstring, cord*). A strong, flexible willow or other twig. The "green withs" that Samson was bound with (Judg 16:7–9 KJV) are translated "fresh thongs" by NIV.

WITHERED HAND (See DISEASES)

WITNESS (Heb. *'ēdh* and related forms, Gr. *martys* and related words and combinations). One who may be called to testify to an event at which he or she was present. Things may be witnesses: a heap of stones (Gen 31:44–52), as a sign that God witnessed Jacob and Laban's covenant; a song (Deut 31:19–21); the law (31:26); an altar (Josh 22:27–34); a stone that has "heard" God speak (24:27); an altar and a pillar on the border of Egypt (Isa 19:20). Bearing false witness is condemned (Exod 20:16; 23:2; Deut 5:20) and punished the same as for the crime of which one accused another (Deut 19:16–18). True and false witnesses are contrasted (Prov 14:5). Two or three witnesses were required in legal proceedings (Deut 19:15; Matt 18:16; 2 Cor 13:1; 1 Tim 5:19; Heb 10:28). Jeremiah (32:6–25, 44) describes the use of witnesses in a transfer of real estate property. The tabernacle of witness, or testimony (Num 17:7–8; 10:2; 2 Chron 24:6), was so named because the witness of God's presence (the shekinah and the tables of the Law) was in it. God is called on as a witness (Gen 31:50; Job 16:19; Jer 29:23; 42:5; Mic 1:2; Mal 3:5; Rom 1:9; 1 Thess 2:5, 10). On solemn occasions men acknowledged themselves witnesses (Josh 24:22; Ruth 4:9–11). God called his people Israel his witnesses (Isa 43:10, 12; 44:8), and the apostles acknowledged themselves to be such (Luke 24:48; Acts 1:8; 2:32; 3:15; 5:32; 10:39–41; 1 Thess 2:10). Peter thought that Judas must be replaced as a witness (Acts 1:22). Paul had a special appointment as a witness (22:15; 26:16). He reminds Timothy of many witnesses (1 Tim 6:12; 2 Tim 2:2). Peter appeals to his readers as a witness of the sufferings of Christ (1 Peter 5:1). John calls Jesus Christ the "faithful witness" (Rev 1:5; 3:14). The cloud of witnesses of Hebrews 12:1 are those who by the lives they lived testify that the life of faith is the only truly worthwhile life. ER

WIZARD (See OCCUPATIONS AND PROFESSIONS)

WOLF (See ANIMALS)

WOMAN (Heb. *'ishshâh,* Gr. *gynē*). The general account of Creation implies the full humanity of Eve (Gen 1:26–27), and the special account of her creation (2:18–24) emphasizes her superiority to all lower animals, Adam's need of her as helper, her intimate relationship to him as a part of his inmost being, and the nature of marriage as a "one flesh" relationship. Though many OT women are not important, three patriarchal wives (Sarah, Rebekah, and Rachel) played significant roles, as did also Moses' sister Miriam (Exod 2:1–9; 15:21; Num 12). In the period of the judges, Deborah exercised unusual leadership (Judg 4–5), and the Moabitess Ruth became a chaste blessing to Israel. Hannah (1 Sam 1:1–2:11) illustrates both the despair of a childless woman and the grace of godly motherhood. The advice of Lemuel's mother to her son (Prov 31) pictures an ideal, industrious wife in a prosperous family. Queens, good and bad, and evil women of other classes of society are frankly portrayed in the Bible. The ancient world was a man's world: such prominence as women attained was achieved by force of character—sometimes, as in the case of Esther, aided by circumstances not of her seeking.

The teaching of Jesus stressed the original nature of marriage and of a man's obligation of purity in his thoughts and actions toward women (Matt 5:27–32). Jesus' example in healing (9:18–26) and in social intercourse (Luke 10:38–42) reinforced his words. The Gospel of Luke is full of evidence of Jesus' understanding and appreciation of women, thus setting a pattern for normal Christian living. Godly women stand out in Jesus' life and ministry: Elizabeth, mother of his forerunner (Luke 1); the Virgin Mary; Anna (2:36–38); the sinner of Luke 7:36–40; Mary Magdalene; Martha and Mary of Bethany; the women who accompanied the disciples on missionary journeys and who provided for them out of their means (8:3). Women remained at the cross until the burial and were first at the empty tomb. Women joined the men in prayer between the Ascension and Pentecost (Acts 1:14). The disciples in Jerusalem met in the house of Mary, mother of John Mark (12:12). Women were the first converts in Europe, including the prosperous business woman Lydia at Philippi (16:13–15). Phoebe, a deaconess, and many other women are greeted in Romans 16. Paul (1 Cor 11:2–16; 14:34–35) urges subordination for Christian women, but he exalts the believing wife as a type of the church, the bride of Christ (Eph 5:21–33). He sets high standards for the wives of church officers and for women in official positions (1 Tim 3:11; Titus 2:3–5). Likewise, 1 Peter 3:1–6 urges a subordinate but noble role for married women. To evaluate Bible teaching with regard to women, it is necessary to consider carefully all the pertinent material and to hold firmly to the normative and authoritative character of the words, deeds, and attitude of Jesus Christ. ER

WOOL (Heb. *tsemer,* Gr. *erion*). The fleece of sheep and some other animals. The first wool was one of the firstfruits that the people of Israel were to give to the priests (Deut 18:4). Israelites were forbidden to wear mixed woolen and linen clothing (Deut 22:11). Wool symbolizes purity (Isa 1:18): "like wool," restored to its original undyed whiteness. It was woven into cloth from which woolen garments were made. It was used principally for the outside garments. Snow is compared to it (Ps 147:16).

WORD (Heb. *dābhār,* Gr. *logos*). The Bible contains much that is literally the word of, and from, the Lord—and so it is called "the Word of the Lord." That expression occurs hundreds of times in the OT and usually denotes the prophetic word (word from God through the mouth of the prophet); however, it also can refer to the law of God (Ps 147:19ff.) and to the creative activity of God, who speaks and causes to be (Gen 1; Ps 33:6–9). In the case of the prophet it is never that the prophet chooses to speak a word, but rather that the word from God takes the prophet into its service so that he becomes a mouthpiece for God (Isa 6; Jer 1:4–10; Ezek 1). And, once uttered, God's word does not return to him empty but accomplishes what he purposes (Isa 55:11). Thus the word of God is the fundamental aspect of God's self-revelation, for by his word he makes known who he is, what he is like, and what his will is for the world.

In the NT the "word of the Lord" or "word of God" (Acts 4:29; 6:2; 1 Thess 1:8) is primarily good news from God (Acts 15:7). It is the word concerning Jesus Christ and God's kingdom in and through him (16:31–32; 17:13); and it is also the word of the cross (1 Cor 1:18), of reconciliation (2 Cor 5:19), of eternal life (Phil 2:16), and of salvation (Acts 13:26). Christians are told to abide in this word (John 8:31), to keep it (8:51; 14:23), and serve it (Acts 6:4).

Jesus himself did not speak like an OT prophet. He said, "I say unto you," not "The Lord says to you" (see Matt 5–7). The words of Jesus are the words of the heavenly Father, and so to receive and accept them is to receive eternal salvation (John 5:24; 8:51; 12:48; 14:24). But not only is the word spoken by Jesus truly the word from heaven—he himself is the true Word who has come to earth from heaven (1:1–14). As the Word (Logos) he is the preexistent Word (Son) who exists eternally and so existed before he became the Incarnate Word, when he was rejected by the world he had made. But as Incarnate Word, truly sharing our human nature and flesh, he achieved the redemption of the world through his life, death, and resurrection.

The reason why John chose to call the eternal Son by the title *Logos* has caused much research. It is generally assumed that there is a Greek background (*logos* was a prominent concept in metaphysical philosophy) and a Hebrew background (for the word of God is virtually personified in parts of the OT—e.g., Prov 8). Thus this title of Jesus appealed to both Jew and Greek. See LOGOS.

Bibliography: H. Ringgren, *Word and Wisdom,* 1947; R. E. Brown, *The Gospel According to John,* vol. 1, 1966, pp. 519ff.; D. Guthrie, *New Testament Theology,* 1981, pp. 321ff. PT

WORK (See LABOR; OCCUPATIONS AND PROFESSIONS)

WORKS (Heb. *ma'aseh, work, deed, pa'al, a work,* Gr. *ergon, work, erga, works*). Used of deeds done by God out of holy love, and by human beings as God's creatures. In the OT the work/works of God (often in the singular, reflecting that the total activity of the Lord is seen as a unity, one work) refer to his creating and preserving the cosmos (Gen 2:2; Ps 8:3), and his deeds of salvation and judgment on behalf of Israel (Ps 28:5; Isa 5:12, 19). God's work is "awesome" (Ps 66:3), is "great" (92:5), is "wonderful" (139:14), and is done in "faithfulness" (33:4). The godly meditate on God's work and works (77:12; 143:5) and praise him for them (72:18; 105:1–2). In the NT God is presented as working in and through the Messiah both in creation (John 1:1–3) and in redemption (9:3–4). By his works Jesus reveals his true identity and from whom he comes (Matt 9:2–5; John 5:36; 10:37–38).

Being made in God's image, human beings perform works as they live in God's world in relationship with other human beings. What deeds they perform cannot be isolated from the state of their hearts and their motivation (Ps 28:3–4). Works done out of evil motivation are "acts of the sinful nature" (Gal 5:19). Works done in order to earn the favorable judgment of God at the end of life—seeking justification by works—are not acceptable for this end (Rom 3:20; Gal 2:16; 2 Tim 1:9). True works, in which God delights, are those that arise from an inward gratitude to God for his goodness and salvation. These spring from faith, the faith that holds to Christ as Savior and Lord (Eph 2:10; Col 1:10). While Paul emphasized the need for faith leading to faithfulness to God in good deeds, James (facing a different situation) emphasized that genuine good works are the evidence of true faith (James 2:14ff.). PT

WORLD. The biblical meanings are best described under the several Hebrew and Greek words. Hebrew *'erets,* "earth, land, country, ground," is translated "world" when it refers to the kingdoms of the world (Isa 23:17; Jer 23:26). There is one occurrence of *hedhel,* thought to mean "land of cessation" (of earthly existence), i.e., Sheol. The word *heledh,* "short duration" (Ps 17:14; 49:1), refers to the ephemeral character of life. Hebrew *'ôlām,* "long duration," past or future (usually translated "ever"), always refers to time; ASV, RSV, NIV "eternity" (Eccl 3:11); RSV, NIV "everlasting" (Isa 45:17); ASV, RSV, "of old," NIV "since ancient times" (64:4). The most common Hebrew word for world is *tēvēl,* "the habitable earth," the earth as made for man, often parallel and synonymous with "earth."

In the NT, Greek *gē,* "earth, land, ground, country," is translated "world" once in KJV (Rev 13:3, ASV, RSV "earth"; NEB, NIV "world"). Greek *aiōn* and derivatives develop in meaning from "life-force, lifetime," to "age, period of time, eternity." Where KJV has "world," ASV sometimes (margin usually) and RSV have "age, forever, of old" or the like. Present and future are contrasted (Matt 13:22; Mark 10:30; Luke 18:30; 20:34–35; Eph 1:21). *Aiōn* and derivatives primarily refer to limited but long periods of time; also, especially in phrases where the word is repeated, to endless time, eternity. Greek *oikomenē* is first geographical (the inhabited earth: Matt 24:14; Luke 4:5; 21:26; Acts 17:31; Rom 10:18; Heb 1:6), then cultural (the Hellenistic world: Acts 19:27), then political (the Roman Empire: Luke 2:1; Acts 11:28; 24:5), though a first-century man felt them practically coextensive (Rev 3:10; 12:9; 16:14). ASV mg has "inhabited earth" in all cases. Hebrews 2:5 uses *oikoumenē* of the world to come. Greek *kosmos* and derivatives range over the meanings "order, beauty, world, universe," never losing their connotation of harmony and beauty. *Kosmos* is one of John's favorite words, used of Jesus as Creator (John 1:10; 17:5), Redeemer (1:29; 3:16–17; 4:42; 6:35, 51; 12:47; 1 John 2:2; 4:9, 14), Light of the world (John 1:9, 3:19; 8:12; 9:5; 12:46), Prophet (6:14), he who was to come (11:27), and Judge (9:39; 12:31; 16:11). The contrast between Jesus and his disciples on the one hand, and the world on the other, is drawn in John 8:23; 14:17–22; 15:18–19; 17:9; 18:36 and often in 1 John. John 17 is rich in references to the relation of believers to the world, considered as a fallen universe hostile to God. In the NT Letters the ethical meaning prevails (e.g., 1 Cor 1:20–28). Other uses are "since the world began" (John 9:32 KJV); the sun as the light of the world

(11:9); the prince of this world (14:30). Hebrew cosmology is not tied in with the concept "world" so much as with "heaven and earth" (Gen 1:1), which embraces the God-oriented universe of sun, moon, planets, stars, and earth, with the abode of God above and Sheol beneath. The Hebrew words for "world" refer either to the earth itself, or as formed for and inhabited by man. Greek cosmology must be reckoned with in the use of such terms as *aiōn* and *kosmos* in the LXX and in the NT. The former term denotes the temporal or durative aspect of that which exists; *kosmos* includes angels, spiritual principalities and powers, men, beasts, earth, heavenly bodies, and Hades. In the NT *kosmos* commonly refers to man and his affairs, especially in an evil sense, over against the new life in Christ, the kingdom God, the body of Christ, the church. As God is in the world but not of it, so are we: God's mode of being penetrates without mixture the world's mode of being, just as iron is penetrated by magnetism or copper by electricity (cf. John 17:14–18). ER

WORM (See ANIMALS)

WORMWOOD (See PLANTS)

WORSHIP (Heb. *shāhâh, bow down, prostrate,* Gr. *proskyneō, to prostrate, do obeisance to*). The honor, reverence, and homage paid to superior beings or powers, whether men, angels, or God. The English word means "worthship" and denotes the worthiness of the individual receiving the special honor due to his worth. While the word is used of men, it is especially used of the divine honors paid to a deity, whether of the heathen religions or the true and living God.

When given to God, worship involves an acknowledgment of divine perfections. It may express itself in the form of direct address, as in adoration or thanksgiving, or in service to God; it may be private, or it may be public, involving a cultus. Worship presupposes that God is, that he can be known by man, and that his perfections set him far above man.

There has always been public worship in the Bible. In patriarchal times there was both the privacy of prayer (e.g., Gen 18) and the public act of setting up an altar (e.g., 12:7). From the patriarchs onward, we can divide the Bible into four periods. First, while Moses established the basis of the public worship of Israel and gave it its focal point in the tabernacle, we know little about the actual performance of worship. As 1 Samuel 1:1, for example, shows, the tabernacle remained the center for the pilgrimage festivals with their round of sacrifices; at the same time it shows the wealth and depth of private devotion that they represented. In the second period worship became highly organized in the temple ritual, which had its origin in the tabernacle set up in the wilderness. It was led by priests assisted by the Levites, and included a complex ritual and system of sacrifices. The third stage was that of the synagogue, which developed among those who remained in exile. This greatly differed from worship in the temple. Whereas the latter was centralized in Jerusalem, the former was found wherever there were Jews. In the synagogues, however, the emphasis was more on instruction than on worship, although the latter was not neglected. The fourth stage was that of the early Christian churches. Jewish Christians continued, as long as they were permitted, to worship in the temple and in the synagogue, though for them the whole ceremonial and sacrificial system ended with the death and resurrection of Jesus. Public Christian worship developed along the lines of the synagogue. It appears that from the first, Christians met in homes for private brotherhood meetings, and the time was the Lord's Day (John 20:19, 26; Acts 20:7; 1 Cor 16:2). Christian public worship consisted of preaching (Acts 20:7; 1 Cor 14:9), reading of Scripture (Col 4:16; James 1:22), prayer (1 Cor 14:14–16), singing (Eph 5:19; Col 3:16), baptism and the Lord's Supper (Acts 2:41; 1 Cor 11:18–34), almsgiving (1 Cor 16:1–2), and sometimes prophesyings and tongues.

Bibliography: R. de Vaux, *Ancient Israel, Its Life and Institutions,* 1961; H. H. Rowley, *Worship in Ancient Israel,* 1967; J. F. White, *Introduction to Christian Worship,* 1980; Ronald Allen, *Worship,* 1982. SB

WRATH. The translation of many Hebrew and Greek words, ranging widely in tone, intensity, and effects (Gen 27:25; 2 Chron 26:19; Esth 1:12; Ps 85:4; Matt 2:16). The first display of human wrath recorded in the Bible (Gen 4:5–6) is followed by numerous accounts of disaster wrought by man's wrath, which never works the righteousness of God (James 1:20) and is never more than tolerated (Eph 4:26; Ps 37:8; Rom 12:19). The wrath of a just, pure, and holy God is dreadful to evildoers (Num 11:1–10; Heb 10:26–31), yet God is slow to anger, eager to forgive (Ps 103:8–9) and so should we be (Eph 4:31–32). Less often mentioned in the NT than in the OT, the wrath of God is no less terrible, is revealed most dramatically in the wrath of the Lamb (John 1:29; Rev 6:16), and abides on "whoever rejects the Son" (John 3:36).

WRESTLE. The Hebrew *pāthal,* with a root meaning "twist" (Gen 30:8), is used of Rachel's wrestling or struggling (emotional and vocal rather than literal) with Leah, leading Rachel to name her handmaid's son Naphtali, "my wrestlings." Hebrew *'āvaq,* "get dusty, wrestle" (Gen 32:24–25), is used of Jacob's wrestling with the angel (physical effect: the dislocation of Jacob's thigh). Greek *palē,* "wrestling," is used later of any kind of fighting; used of the Christian's spiritual conflict with the powers of evil (Eph 6:12 KJV; NIV "struggle").

WRITING. It is generally assumed that the earliest forms of writing were pictographic, not phonetic. That is to say, the ideas were recorded by means of pictures, or sense-symbols, rather than by sound-symbols such as are used in most modern languages. The earliest human beings presumably drew a picture of the idea they wished to represent, rather than using a sign to show how the word in question was to be pronounced. Thus the circle of the sun-disk might indicate either the sun itself (in Egyptian the word *re'*, in Sumerian *ud*) or the span of time during which the sun would shine. The concept of human being was conveyed in Egyptian by the picture of a person sitting with one leg curled under and the other bent with the knee upright. This figure would be accompanied by a single vertical stroke if only one person was involved or by more strokes according to the number of people referred to. In Sumerian the idea of human being (*lu*) was conveyed by a triangular head and a turnip-shaped torso; at first it stood up on end, facing right, but later it lay flat on its back facing upward (for all Sumerian signs underwent a ninety-degree shift in direction from vertical to horizontal sometime between 3000 and 2500 B.C.). This earliest stage in writing was marked by the use of the pure *ideogram*. (This same principle was operative in primitive Chinese, which developed a system of sign language that has endured to the present day; nearly all of its basic characters, or "radicals," represent pictures of the type of object being referred to. This picture may or may not be accompanied by other strokes that indicate the sound value of the word.)

Evidently the next stage in the history of writing was the introduction of the *phonogram*—the type of sign that indicates a sound. At first this was achieved by the *rebus* principle, that is, by using objects that have a name sounding like the sound of the word that the writer wishes to convey, even though the meaning of the object portrayed is entirely different. Thus in an English *rebus* a person becoming "pale" with fear may be indicated by a picture of a "pail." Similarly in Egyptian the sign for "duck" could also represent "son," because in both cases the word was pronounced *sa*. The Sumerian city of Girsu was spelled by a picture of a dagger (*gir*) followed by a piece of hide or skin (*su*).

Both in Sumerian and in Egyptian there was a very early development of this rebus principle, so that the writing system became equipped with a large number of signs that could convey syllabic sounds, independent of meaning, and thus furnish building blocks for words of two or more syllables. Naturally the number of signs necessary to indicate all possible syllables that could occur in the spoken language was very numerous indeed. Both Egyptian and Sumerian writing retained both ideograms and syllabic phonograms right to the end of their history. Moreover, both languages used signs known as *determinatives*, which had no sound value at all but simply indicated the class of object referred to. In Sumerian the name of a city would often be preceded by the sign for "city" (even though it was not to be pronounced aloud as a separate word); similarly a star (standing for *dingir*, or "god") would precede the name of any deity. On the other hand, these determinatives could follow the rest of the word, rather than precede it; thus the Sumerian name of Babylon

Hieroglyphs painted on end board of a coffin found at el-Bersheh (0.248 m. high), 12th Dynasty (1990–1780 B.C.). Courtesy Museum of Fine Arts, Boston.

was written *ka-dingir-ra KI*. *Ka* was an ideogram for "gate," *dingir* was an ideogram for "god," and *ra* was a phonogram indicating that *dingir* ended in an *r* sound and was followed by the genitive particle *-a(k)*; the final *KI* was the sign for "earth," or "land," and served simply as a determinative.

Observe that in this last example the Sumerian name for Babylon (or Babylonia) means "The Gate of God." When the Semitic-speaking Akkadians and Babylonians conquered the Mesopotamian valley, they took over the writing system of the Sumerians and adapted it to their own language. In some cases they took the Sumerian ideograms and gave them the pronunciation of the appropriate words in their own language. Thus the Babylonian for "gate" was *babum* ("gate of" being pronounced *bab*); the word for "god" was *ilu* (in the genitive *ili*). Hence the very same signs that the Sumerians pronounced as *ka-dingir-rak* the Babylonians pronounced as *bab-ili* (which came into Hebrew as *Babel*). Operating on this principle the Babylonians contrived ways of expressing all the necessary sounds in their own language. They would either use the Sumerian phonograms to express the same sound in Akkadian (the language spoken by the Babylonians and Assyrians), or else they would assign new sound values to them. Thus the Sumerian word for "wood" or "tree" was *gish* and was written by four wedges forming a rectangle; the corresponding Akkadian word was *isu*. Hence in Akkadian the sign could furnish the phonetic syllable *gish* (as it did in Sumerian) or else the syllable *is* (derived from the Akkadian word), as for example in the word *is-su-ru* "bird." Thus it was by ingenious adaptation that the Sumerian system of writing was taken over by a nation speaking an entirely different language, and it was used—still in mixed ideographic and phonographic form—to give written expression to their Semitic tongue.

Incidentally, if Abraham's family was residing in Ur back in the twentieth century B.C., this would have coincided with the brilliant Sumerian

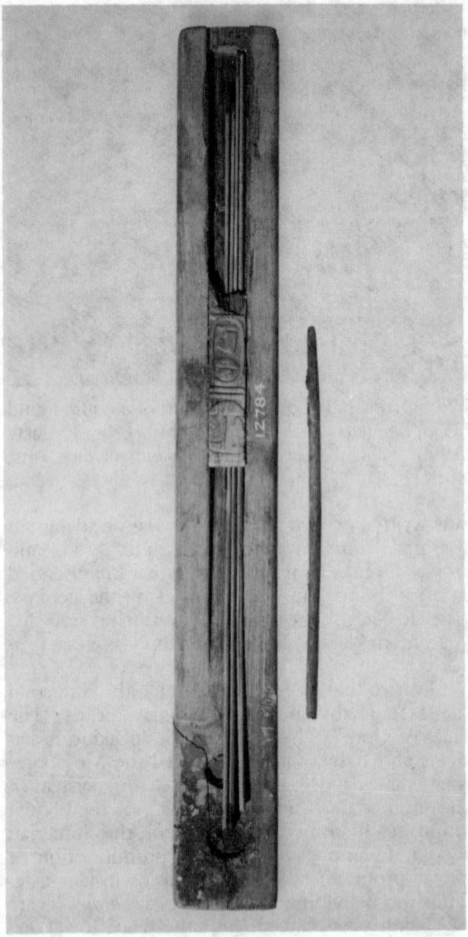

An 18th Dynasty (1550–1350 B.C.) scribe's wooden palette (0.285 m. long) inscribed with the name of Ahmose I (1570–1545 B.C.). Palette is equipped with rushes, which served as pens, and a circular hollow to hold ink or paint. Reproduced by courtesy of the Trustees of the British Museum.

culture that flourished under the Third Dynasty of Ur. It is quite possible not only that he would have learned both to speak and to read Sumerian but also that this was the only type of writing that he knew about, apart from any writing he encountered during the time he lived in Egypt.

The Egyptian system of writing, at least on its monuments, remained in an artistic pictorial form from its earliest rise about 3000 B.C. until its slow demise in the Roman period, 3,200 years later. Its characters never degenerated into combinations of wedges bearing little resemblance to the original pictographs, as was the case in Sumerian and Akkadian. Of course Egyptian was also (at least as early as the Sixth Dynasty) written in a cursive, hieratic (abridged) form, especially in business documents, correspondence, and secular literature. But apart from esthetic considerations, Egyptian writing developed peculiarities of its own that were quite different from the Sumerian-Akkadian system. In the first place, it recorded only the consonants of the spoken language, not its vowels. Some of these consonants were like the so-called vowel letters of Hebrew, Aramaic, and Arabic; that is, the *aleph* or glottal catch, the *y* indicating a neighboring *i* sound, and the *w* indicating a *u* sound before it. On the other hand, the transcriptions of Egyptian names into Akkadian cuneiform and into Greek furnish important evidence as to how Egyptian was vocalized, and these transcriptions do not come out to any consistent pattern of correspondence with these Egyptian "vowel letters." Neither is there any standard relationship between them and their descendants in the Coptic language (which was written in the Greek alphabet and preserved the form of Egyptian as it was spoken in the early Christian centuries). And so it must be recognized that Egyptian hieroglyphic is essentially as consonantal as were the Semitic languages that used the Phoenician alphabet.

A second noteworthy contrast between Egyptian and Sumerian is that it developed genuine alphabetic signs, as well as two-consonant (or three-consonant) syllabic signs. Therefore to the Egyptians goes the credit for being the first to develop an alphabetic system of writing. However, they did not see any need to abandon their ideograms, determinative signs, and syllabic characters just because they had alphabetic letters; and so they simply used all four types of sign in the writing out of their language. Even the more cursive, shorthand type of writing referred to above as *hieratic* introduced virtually no changes in this complicated and cumbersome system; it simply enabled the scribe to write out his four kinds of hieroglyphic signs with a fair degree of rapidity. The same was true of a still more cursive and simplified form of hieratic known as *demotic*, used after 1000 B.C. Not until Egypt was conquered by Alexander the Great (about 332) did the influence of a foreign system of writing make a decisive impact on Egyptian conservatism. By the third century A.D. (the period of the earliest Coptic glosses in the Oxyrychus Papyri) the Egyptians were writing out their vernacular, vowels and all, in the letters of the Greek alphabet, to which they soon added seven more alphabetic signs of their own invention, to represent sounds not found in Greek.

The fact that the Egyptians did develop a full set of alphabetic signs had led some scholars to conclude that the most primitive form of the so-called Phoenician alphabet consisted of modifications of various Egyptian consonantal or syllabic signs. This was a reasonable inference, perhaps, but no convincing list of correspondences could be made up by even the most ingenious advocates of this theory. The true origin of the "Phoenician" alphabet is to be sought rather in the alphabetic hieroglyphs of the Sinaitic Inscriptions of Serabit el-Khadim (written some time between 1900 and 1500 B.C.—for the scholars' estimates vary). These signs are tabulated on Plate A. Since they were inscribed by Semitic miners in the employ of Egypt, and since these documents are found side by side with Egyptian hieroglyphic inscriptions (on statues dedicated to the goddess Hathor), it is fair to conclude that these miners got the idea for their alphabet from the Egyptians themselves. But instead of resorting to ideograms and syllabic signs, they contented themselves with alphabetic symbols chosen on the basis of *acrophony*. That is to say, the first sound of the name of the object represented conveyed the alphabetic unit intended. In Egyptian a sign for "hand" was used as the alphabetic sign for *d,* since the word for "hand" was *dert*. Following this principle, the Semitic miner chose the picture of a hand extended as a sign for *y* (since the word for "hand" was *yadu* in his language). The head of an ox was used for the sound of *aleph* (the glottal catch) because the word for "ox" was *'alpu* (a name that was preserved in the later Hebrew *aleph* and in the still later Greek *alpha*). Interestingly enough, this particular letter has been quite well preserved from 1900 B.C. until the present, for if our capital A is turned upside down, it bears a fairly close similarity to that ancient Sinaitic sign for *aleph,* the ox's head.

During the ensuing centuries this Sinaitic type of script (or modifications of it) was cultivated in Canaan, for household objects like daggers, rings, ewers, pots, and plaques have been found with short inscriptions, mostly of very uncertain interpretation. But a totally different form of alphabetic writing assumed great importance during this period (1800–1400 B.C.), namely the cuneiform alphabet associated with Ras Shamra, or Ugarit. Unlike the cuneiform of Babylonia and Assyria, this kind of cuneiform represented an alphabet of about twenty-nine or thirty characters, all of them consonantal (except that three of them indicated the type of vowel occurring after *aleph,* whether *a, i* [or, *e*], or *u*). This very early dialect of Canaanite (for Ugaritic is much closer to biblical Hebrew than to any other known Semitic language) contained several consonants not appearing in any of the Northwest Semitic scripts; in some cases the sounds are still preserved only in Arabic (such as rough *heth, z* as in Arabic *nazara,* "to see"; *th* as in *thalāthun* "three"), and other sounds are apparently different from any sound found in Arabic (such as *zh* like the English *s* in *pleasure*).

The shapes of characters formed by these wedges bear no consistent similarity to the signs either of Sinaitic letters or the Akkadian syllabary. They are very simple in structure and seem to have no pictographic origin whatever. This type of alphabet flourished not only at Ugarit but also in more southerly localities as well. But after the violent destruction of Ras Shamra in the fifteenth century, the use of the Ugaritic alphabet seems to have declined in favor of the Phoenician.

Several so-called Proto-Phoenician inscriptions have been discovered in Palestinian localities such as Gezer, Lachish, and Shechem, exhibiting forms that could be transitional between the Sinaitic and the authentic Phoenician of the eleventh century B.C. Unfortunately, however, these short lines of

Four clearly incised signs on a bronze dagger from Lachish, showing Proto-Canaanite script, eighteenth to seventeenth centuries B.C. Courtesy Israel Department of Antiquities and Museums.

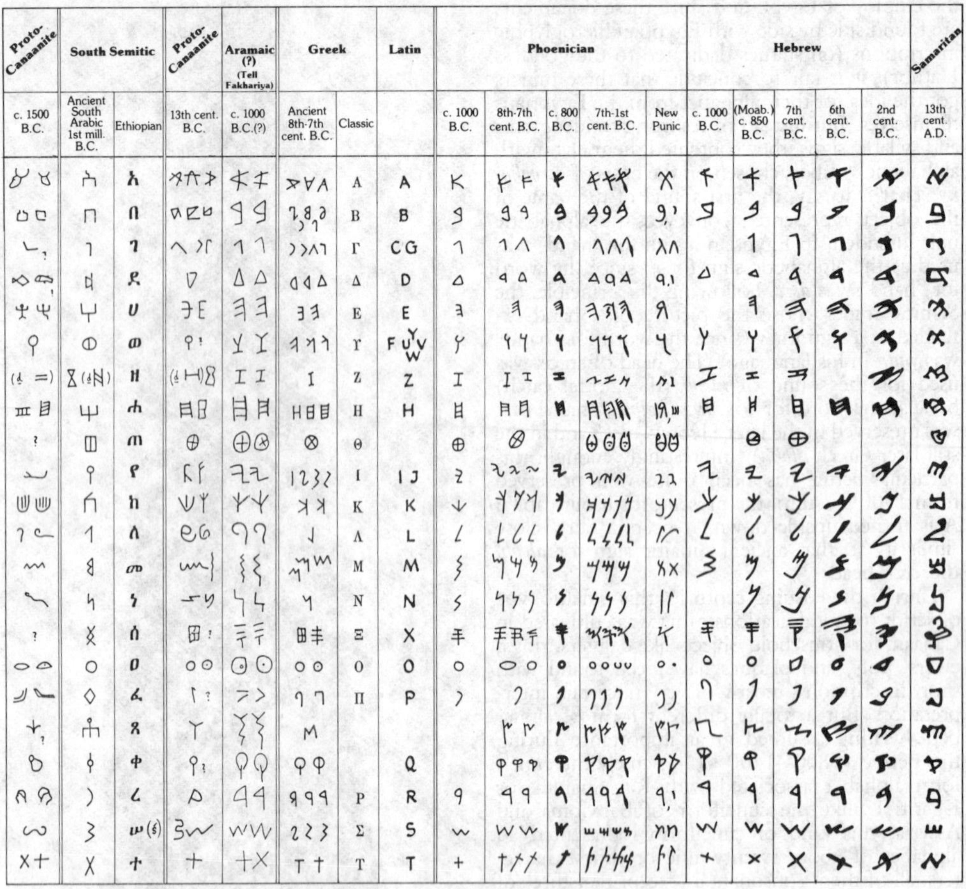

Proto-Canaanite
South Semitic
Proto-Canaanite
Aramaic (?) (Tell Fakhariya)
Greek
Latin
Phoenician
Hebrew
Samaritan
c. 1500 B.C.
Ancient South Arabic 1st mill. B.C.
Ethiopian
13th cent. B.C.
c. 1000 B.C.(?)
Ancient 8th-7th cent. B.C.
Classic
c. 1000 B.C.
8th-7th cent. B.C.
c. 800 B.C.
7th-1st cent. B.C.
New Punic
c. 1000 B.C.
(Moab.) c. 850 B.C.
7th cent. B.C.
6th cent. B.C.
2nd cent. B.C.
13th cent. A.D.

Chronological chart of the alphabet, Plate A. Courtesy Carta, Jerusalem.

Ivory writing boards from Nimrud (715–705 B.C.), linked with hinges and bearing traces of the wax overlay on which a series of astrological omens are written in cuneiform script. Reproduced by courtesy of the Trustees of the British Museum.

writing do not fall into a consistent pattern, and they cannot be deciphered with real certainty. As to the earliest Phoenician inscriptions—those of Shaphatbaal and Ahiram found at Gebal (Byblos) on the coast north of Sidon—there is still much dispute as to the time when they were written.

The inscription on the sarcophagus (stone coffin) of King Ahiram is dated by various authorities from before 1250 to as late as 1000 (the later date being advocated by Dunand, who maintained that the Shaphatbaal inscription was centuries earlier). This writing has the twenty-two-letter alphabet that was to hold the stage from then on in all the northwest Semitic languages (Phoenician, Hebrew, Moabite, Aramaic, and Syriac). The early form of it appears in the left-hand column of Plate A. The earliest Israelite document that has survived in this script is the Gezer Calendar of about 900 B.C. or a few decades earlier. It is a small limestone tablet inscribed with the irregular hand of a schoolboy and containing a list of the successive phases of the agricultural year from season to season. The discovery of this schoolboy's exercise witnesses to the extent of literacy in the reign of Solomon. Unfortunately we have no documents from an earlier period to

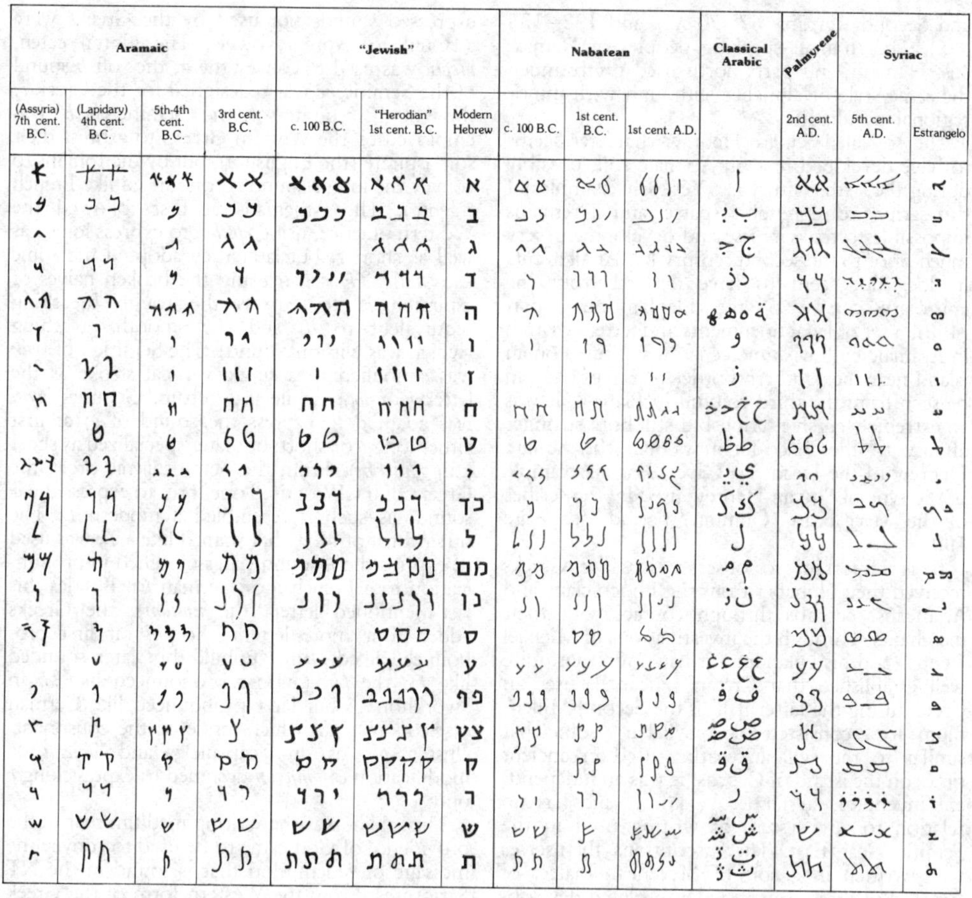

Aramaic
"Jewish"
Nabatean
Classical Arabic
Palmyrene
Syriac
(Assyria) 7th cent. B.C.
(Lapidary) 4th cent. B.C.
5th-4th cent. B.C.
3rd cent. B.C.
c. 100 B.C.
"Herodian" 1st cent. B.C.
Modern Hebrew
c. 100 B.C.
1st cent. B.C.
1st cent. A.D.
2nd cent. A.D.
5th cent. A.D.
Estrangelo

Chronological chart of the alphabet, Plate B. Courtesy Carta, Jerusalem.

serve as a reliable guide, but it is most likely that Moses used a Proto-Phoenician type of script rather than any kind of cuneiform (although the use of Akkadian cuneiform for international correspondence is well attested for the time of Joshua in Palestine). Even in the Tell El Amarna correspondence—which consists of letters in Akkadian addressed by Canaanite princes to the Egyptian court—there were numerous glosses (or explanatory synonyms) in Canaanite or Hebrew, written out in Akkadian cuneiform syllabic signs. Hence this type of writing would also have been known to Moses and available to him. (See HEBREW LANGUAGE.)

The next important Hebrew inscription after the Gezer Calendar was the Siloam Inscription, incised on the wall of the underground tunnel dug through to the Pool of Siloam in preparation (probably) for the siege of Jerusalem by Sennacherib in 701 B.C. Here we see a trend toward the more freely flowing style of manuscript writing, rather than the stern angularity of monumental style. In particular some of the long-tailed letters (like *mem, nun* and *kaph*) curve with a bottom swoop to the left. Examples of the rapid brush-stroked type of script are furnished by the Samaritan Ostraca of about 770 (containing tax receipts paid to the government of Jeroboam II) and the Lachish Ostraca of 588. These last consist of letters written by the captain of a Jewish outpost to Yaosh, commander of Zedekiah's troops in Lachish. Here the letters are formed in a very compressed or flattened form, but they are still of essentially the same pattern as the old Phoenician.

Following the Babylonian exile, this Paleo-Hebrew script (as it is called) was retained for some types of text, such as the books of the Pentateuch, for fragments of Leviticus and Exodus have been discovered in the Qumran Caves, dating from the late fourth century (according to the estimate of some scholars). The Samaritan sect, which originated from the schism of 535 (when Zerubbabel refused to allow the Samaritan heretics to participate in rebuilding the temple at Jerusalem), for some reason developed a special form of this Paleo-Hebrew script all their own; moreover, they retained it for all their religious literature down through the time of the Muslim conquest and even to this day. Paleo-Hebrew was employed on Jewish coinage of the Maccabean period (second century B.C.) and also of the First and Second Revolts (67–70 A.D. and 132–135 A.D.). The Aramaic-speaking peoples of Damascus, Hamath, and parts north used pretty much the same style of alphabet, although with minor regional peculiarities.

The so-called Square Hebrew character seems to have developed first on Aramaic soil, possibly during the sixth century B.C. Yet early examples of this script are regrettably sparse, and it remains impossible to trace its rise and development very much prior to the second century B.C. At all events it does not seem to have derived from the epistolary cursive of the Elephantine Papyri (400), a set of legal documents and letters written in Aramaic by Jewish mercenaries stationed on an island near the southern border of Egypt. As can be seen from the third column in Plate B, it was an extremely cursive script, but still bore stronger affinity to the Paleo-Hebrew than the Square Hebrew of the Dead Sea Caves. For an example of the type of Square Hebrew used by the scribes of the Maccabean (Qumran) period, see page 1001.

It is important to observe that the Greeks received their alphabet from the Phoenicians and Arameans, perhaps through contact with their merchants. Through the investigations of Michael Ventris and his colaborers it has now been quite well established that Cretan Linear B, used in Crete during the latter half of the Second Millennium B.C., consisted of a syllabary somewhat similar to the syllabic writing used in ancient times on the island of Cyprus. It was an independent invention, so far as we know, and has no relation to any system of writing used in the Semitic Near East. The inscriptions themselves were written in a sort of Mycenean dialect of Greek. But these constituted an isolated development without any lasting influence on later times.

Apart from these special developments in Crete and Cyprus, the Hellenic tribal groups found written expression for their language through the Phoenician alphabet, which supplied the first twenty-two letters of the Greek alphabet (i.e., *alpha* through *tau*). Those Semitic letters that expressed sounds not used by the Greeks were adapted to express vowels. The glottal catch, *aleph*, was used to convey the *a*; the soft *h* sound of the Semitic *hē* was redesigned for the Greek *e;* the rough aspirate of the Semitic *heth* was employed by the Western Greeks to express their soft aspirate (the English *h*), but by the Ionians to convey the long *e* sound (pronounced like French *e*-acute). The Athenians at first followed the Western practice, using *epsilon* to express long *e* as well as short *e,* but later they adopted the Ionic use of the *H* as *ēta,* using the broken halves of aspirated *H* to express the rough breathing (equivalent to *h*) and the smooth breathing (which was without sound). The Semitic *y* of *yodh* was simplified to a single vertical stroke as the letter *i* or *iota,* while the guttural Semitic *'ayin* was adapted to express the sound of *o* (at first either long *o* or short, but later specialized as short *o* or *omicron*). From the Semitic *waw*, or *w*, the Greeks of the West used one form to express the *w* sound; as such it resembled a modern *F*. The other form of *waw,* that shaped like a *Υ*, was used to express the *u* sound (later modified in pronunciation to a French *u* or German *ü*). Besides this last-mentioned letter (the *upsilon*), the Greeks added four more letters, the *phi* (at first pronounced liked *ph* in "uphill," but later sounded like *f*); the *khi* (at first pronounced like *kh* in "workhorse," but later pronounced like German or Scots *ch*); *psi,* which rendered the consonant-cluster *p-s* as in "capsule"; and *omega,* a modification of *omicron* designed to express long *o* only.

This, then, was the writing medium that in the providence of God came to be used to convey the message of redemption that is found in the NT Scriptures. From the Western form of the Greek alphabet the Romans derived their Latin alphabet, omitting from it those letters used by the Eastern Greeks that were unnecessary to express the sounds of the Latin tongue. It is this alphabet, therefore, that has descended to us at the present day, ultimately derived from the Semites of the Holy Land. GLA

X

XERXES (zŭrk'sēz, Gr. form of Heb. *'ăhashwērôsh,* Persian *Khshayarsha*). 1. The father of Darius the Mede, mentioned in Daniel 9:1.

Crown Prince Ahasuerus (see Esth 1:1) standing behind the enthroned king of Persia, Darius I. Limestone relief from Persepolis, 521–486 B.C. Courtesy The Oriental Institute, University of Chicago.

2. King of Persia, mentioned in the Book of Esther. There seems to be little doubt that he is the well-known historical Xerxes (KJV, Ahasuerus), who reigned from 486 to 465 B.C. The main support for this identification is to be found in the linguistic equivalence of the names of the KJV "Ahasuerus" and the NIV "Xerxes." In addition, a close similarity has been noted between the character of the historical Xerxes and the character of the king of the Persians portrayed in the Book of Esther. There are also historical correlations. The feast that was held in the third year of the reign of Xerxes at Susa (Esth 1:3) corresponds to an assembly held by Xerxes in his third year in preparation for the invasion of Greece. Herodotus states that Xerxes, following his defeat at Salamis and Plataea, consoled himself in his seventh year with the pleasures of the harem (Herodotus, 9.108). This parallels the biblical account that relates that Ahasuerus replaced Vashti by marrying Esther in his seventh year (Esth 2:16) after gathering all the fair young virgins to Susa. The Xerxes of Ezra 4:6, to whom were written accusations against the Jews of Jerusalem is in all probability this same Xerxes, though sometimes identified with Cambyses, son of Cyrus.

Y

YAHWEH (See YHWH; GOD)

YARN (Heb. *miqweh*). The KJV translation of the Hebrew word that occurs in 1 Kings 10:28 and 2 Chronicles 1:16. In each of these cases "linen yarn" seems to convey the wrong meaning. It is correctly translated in RSV and NIV by the proper name "Kue," the old Assyrian name given to Cilicia, the land located in the SE portion of Asia Minor.

YEAR (See CALENDAR)

YEARLING (See ANIMALS)

YHWH. This is not in reality a word but is known as the "Tetragrammaton," the four consonants standing for the ancient Hebrew name for God commonly referred to as "Jehovah" or "Yahweh." The original Hebrew text was not vocalized. YHWH was considered too sacred to pronounce, so *'adonai* ("my Lord") was substituted in reading. When eventually a vowel system was invented, since the Hebrews had forgotten how to pronounce YHWH, they substituted the vowels for *'adonai*, making "Jehovah," a form first attested at beginning of the twelfth century A.D.

YODH (See JOT)

YOKE (Heb. *môtâh, an oxbow, 'ôl, a yoke, tsemedh, yoke of oxen, an acre,* i.e., as much land as a yoke of oxen could plow in a day, Gr. *zeugos, a team* and *zygos, yoke*). In the literal sense, a bar of wood so constructed as to unite two animals, usually oxen, enabling them to work in the fields. Drawing loads and pulling instruments used in farming, such as the plow, were two chief functions the yoke made possible. Archaeological studies have shown that the yoke was variously constructed in different periods of history. It was commonly used all over the ancient world. Also used figuratively in the sense of servitude (Jer 27–28) and "the law of God."

YOKEFELLOW (Gr. *syzygos, yoked together*). A common word among Greek writers referring to those united by close bonds, as in marriage, labor, etc. It is found only once in the NT (Phil 4:3) and the meaning here is not clear. Some feel that Paul refers here to a fellow worker; others think the word is a proper noun, Syzygos.

YOM KIPPUR (See FEASTS)

Z

ZAANAIM (See ZAANANNIM)

ZAANAN (zā'à-năn, Heb. *tsa'ănān*). A place mentioned by Micah (1:11) in the Shephelah of Judah. The place has never been certainly identified, but it may be Zenan.

ZAANANNIM (zā'à-năn'ĭm, Heb. text uncertain). This place was located on Naphtali's southern border near the spot where Sisera lost his life at the hands of the wife of Heber the Kenite (Josh 19:33; Judg 4:11). KJV has "Zaanaim" in the Judges reference. It is the same as the modern Khan et-Tujjar, located about three miles (five km.) NE of Mount Tabor.

ZAAVAN (zā'à-văn, Heb. *za'ăwān, not quiet*). One of the three sons of Ezer (Gen 36:27; 1 Chron 1:42).

ZABAD (zā'băd, Heb. *zāvādh, the* LORD *has given*). 1. The son of Nathan, who was the son of Attai, who was the son of Ahlai. Hence this man is called the son of Nathan (1 Chron 2:36) and the son of Ahlai (11:41). Note also 1 Chronicles 2:31–37.

2. One from the tribe of Ephraim. He was a son of Tahath (1 Chron 7:21).

3. The son of Shimeath, the Ammonitess. He conspired against King Joash and was later killed by Amaziah (2 Chron 24:26; cf. 25:3–4).

4–6. Three Israelites were given this name, sons of Zattu (Ezra 10:27), Hashum (10:33), and Nebo (10:43). In response to Ezra's plea after the Captivity, they put away their Gentile wives.

ZABBAI (zăb'ā-ī, Heb. *zabbay*, meaning unknown). 1. One of the sons of Bebai who put away his foreign wife at the request of Ezra (Ezra 10:28).

2. The father of Baruch (Neh 3:20).

ZABBUD (See ZACCUR)

ZABDI (zăb'dī, Heb. *zavdî, he [God] has given*). 1. Achan's grandfather, from the tribe of Judah. His father's name was Zerah (Josh 7:1, 17 JB, KJV, MLB, MOF, NASB, NEB, RSV; Zimri NIV).

2. A son of Shimei from the tribe of Benjamin (1 Chron 8:19).

3. One of the officers of David listed as having charge of the wine cellars (1 Chron 27:27). He is called "the Shiphmite."

4. One of the ancestors of Mattaniah, who aided in worship in the days of Nehemiah (Neh 11:17).

ZABDIEL (zăb'dĭ-ĕl, Heb. *zavdî'ēl, God has given*). 1. The father of Jashobeam (1 Chron 27:2).

2. A temple overseer (Neh 11:14).

ZABUD (zā'bŭd, Heb. *zāvûdh, bestowed*). The son of Nathan; a principal officer of Solomon and his best friend (1 Kings 4:5).

ZABULON (See ZEBULUN)

ZACCAI (zăk'ā-ī, Heb. *zakkay*). The ancestral head of a postexilic family whose 760 descendants returned to Jerusalem with Zerubbabel (Ezra 2:9; Neh 7:14).

ZACCHAEUS (ză-kē'ŭs, Gr. *Zakchaios*, from the Hebrew *zakkay, pure*). A publican, referred to only in Luke. He resided at Jericho and is described as a "chief" tax collector. When Jesus was passing through Jericho on one occasion, Zacchaeus wished very much to see him. Being short, he climbed a tree by the side of the path. He must have been quite surprised, therefore, when Jesus paused in his journey beneath this very tree and, looking up, urged Zacchaeus to come down, for he had decided to stay at his house (Luke 19:6). Zacchaeus hurried down gladly and invited Jesus to his home. From that day on his life was changed (19:8).

ZACCUR, ZACCHUR (Heb. *zakkûr, remembered*). 1. The father of the Reubenite spy Shammua (Num 13:4).

2. The son of Hamuel, a Simeonite (1 Chron 4:26), Zacchur in AV.

3. One of the sons of Merari (1 Chron 24:27).

4. One of the sons of Asaph set apart by David for musical service (1 Chron 25:1–2; Neh 12:35).

5. The son of Imri who aided in rebuilding the wall of Jerusalem (Neh 3:2).

6. One of those who, with Nehemiah, sealed the covenant (Neh 10:12).

7. One of the treasurers, father of Hanan (Neh 13:13).

8. A son of Bigvai. He accompanied Ezra to Jerusalem from Babylon (Ezra 8:14 NIV; Zabbud KJV and most versions).

ZACHARIAH, ZACHARIAS (See ZECHARIAH)

ZADOK (zā'dŏk, Heb. *tsādhôq, righteous*). 1. The most familiar Bible character bearing this name is the son of Ahitub. He was a priest in the time of David (2 Sam 8:17) and came to minister to David in Hebron after the death of King Saul (1 Chron 12:23–38). After the death of Uzzah, David called Zadok and asked him to assist, as a Levite, in bringing the ark into its prepared place in Jerusalem (15:11–13). So faithful was he to David that he accompanied him with the ark when he fled from Jerusalem at the rebellion of Absalom and stayed with him until commanded by David to return to Jerusalem to act as a spy for him (2 Sam 15:24–36; 17:15, 17–21).

His continued loyalty was further seen when, at the end of David's life, Adonijah aspired to be king. He followed the instructions of King David and anointed Solomon, David's son, king in Gihon (1 Kings 1:8–45). His loyalty was not forgotten even after David's death, for Solomon favored him by making him the high priest, demoting Abiathar who had been sharing this role with him (2:26–35).

2. The son of Ahitub who is the father of Shallum (1 Chron 6:12), not the same Zadok as no. 1 or the Zadok mentioned earlier in the text (6:8).

3. Jerusha's father (2 Kings 15:33; 2 Chron 27:1).

4. The son of Baana who aided in the construction of the wall of Jerusalem in the time of Nehemiah (Neh 3:4). He is also probably one of those listed as signers of the covenant with Nehemiah (10:21), especially since in both of these instances his name follows the name of Meshezabeel.

5. The son of Immer, another priest who also shared in the labor of rebuilding the Jerusalem walls under Nehemiah (Neh 3:29).

6. One appointed by Nehemiah to be a scribe (Neh 13:13). He may well be one of the two wall-builders mentioned above.

ZAHAM (zā'hăm, Heb. *zāham, odious fool*). Rehoboam's youngest son (2 Chron 11:19).

ZAIR (zā'ĭr, Heb. *tsā'îr, small*). A village somewhere east of the Dead Sea in Idumea where Jehoram conquered the Edomites (2 Kings 8:21). It has not been identified with certainty.

ZALAPH (zā'lăf, Heb. *tsālāph, caper-plant*). The father of Hanun, who aided Nehemiah in repairing the Jerusalem walls (Neh 3:30).

ZALMON (zăl'mōn, Heb. *tsalmôn, dark*). 1. A Benjamite who was one of David's mighty men (2 Sam 23:28). He is also called "Ilai" (1 Chron 11:29), and in both passages "the Ahohite."

2. A forest near Shechem (Judg 9:48) from which wood was taken by Abimelech in the destruction of Shechem. Its exact identity has not been determined.

ZALMONAH (zăl-mō'nȧ, Heb. *tsalmōnâh, gloomy*). One of the places in the wilderness where Israel camped. It lay SE of Edom (Num 33:41–42).

ZALMUNNA (zăl-mŭn'ȧ, Heb. *tsalmunnā', deprived of shade*). One of the two kings of Midian whom Gideon captured and killed during his bold raid on the Midianites (Judg 8:4–21; Ps 83:11).

ZAMZUMMITE, ZAMZUMMIM (zăm-zŭm'īt, zăm-zŭm'ĭm, Heb. *zamzummîn, murmurers*). A name found only in Deuteronomy 2:20. It is used of the race of giants, called Rephaim (2 Sam 5:18, 22), who lived in a spot east of the Jordan. Later on the Ammonites captured them and occupied their land. They are described as "a people strong and numerous, and . . . tall" (Deut 2:21). They may be the same as the Zuzites (Zuzim) in Genesis 14:5.

ZANOAH (zȧ-nō'ȧ, Heb. *zānôah, rejected*). 1. A town located in the lowlying hills of Judah (Josh 15:34). After the Babylonian captivity some Jews returned to lived there (Neh 11:30) and assisted in the rebuilding of the walls of Jerusalem (3:13). It has been identified with Khirbet Zanu and is situated ten miles (seventeen km.) west of Jerusalem.

2. A town located in the mountains of Judah (Josh 15:56), ten or twelve miles (seventeen or twenty km.) SW of Hebron. It was built or rebuilt by Jekuthiel, who is called its "father" (1 Chron 4:18). It is identified with Zenuta.

ZAPHENATH-PANEAH (zăf'ē-năth-pȧ-nē'ȧ, Heb. *tsaphenath-pa'ănēah, the one who furnishes the sustenance of the land*). The name given to Joseph by Pharaoh on the occasion of his promotion for showing the pharaoh the meaning of his dream (Gen 41:45).

ZAPHON (zā'fŏn, Heb. *tsāphôn, north*). A territory east of Jordan allotted by Moses to Gad (Josh 13:27). It is the modern Amateh.

ZARA (zā'rȧ, Gr. *Zara*, meaning unknown). The Greek for the Hebrew Zerah, mentioned in the ancestry of Christ (Matt 1:3).

ZAREAH, ZAREATHITE (See ZORAH)

ZARED (See ZERED)

ZAREDAH (See ZARETHAN)

ZAREPHATH (zăr'ĕ-făth, Heb. *tsārephath, refinement*). An OT town remembered chiefly because Elijah resided there during the latter half of the famine caused by the drought (1 Kings 17:9ff.). Its Greek equivalent "Sarepta" is mentioned in the KJV of Luke 4:26, where it is described as being in the land of Sidon. Here God miraculously sustained the prophet with the help of a widow. Ruins of the ancient town survive south of the modern village of Sarafand, about eight miles (thirteen km.) south of Sidon, fourteen miles (twenty-three km.) north of Tyre.

ZARETHAN (zăr'ĕ-thăn, Heb. *tsārethān*). A place near Beth Shan and Adam that is mentioned in connection with Israel's crossing of the Jordan (Josh 3:16). It is also spelled Zaretan and Zartanah. Bronze castings for the temple were made there (1 Kings 7:46). It is referred to in 1 Kings 4:12 as a means of locating Beth Shan. In 2 Chronicles 4:17 the name is given as Zeredah (ASV, RSV) and Zeredathah (KJV). Its exact site has not been ascertained.

ZARETH-SHAHAR (See ZERETH SHAHAR)

ZARHITES (See ZERAH)

ZARTANAH, ZARTHAN (See ZARETHAN)

ZATTU, ZATTHU (ză'tū, Heb. *zattû'*). Head of a large family of children (Ezra 2:8; Neh 7:13) who returned with Zerubbabel to Jerusalem from the Babylonian captivity and signed the covenant with Nehemiah (Neh 10:14). Several of his children were among those who put away their Gentile wives (Ezra 10:27).

ZAVAN (See ZAAVAN)

ZAZA (zā'zȧ, Heb. *zāzā'*). A Jerahmeelite (1 Chron 2:33).

ZEALOT (zĕl'ŭt, Gr. *zēlōtēs, zealous one*). A member of a Jewish patriotic party started in the time of Quirinius to resist Roman aggression. According to Josephus (*War* 4.3.9; 5.1; 7.8.1), the Zealots resorted to violence and assassination in their hatred of the Romans, their fanatical violence eventually provoking the Roman war. Simon the Zealot was distinguished from Simon Peter by this epithet (Luke 6:15; Acts 1:13).

ZEBADIAH (zĕb'ȧ-dī'ȧ, Heb. *zevadhyāhû, Jehovah has bestowed*). 1. A descendant of Benjamin through Beriah (1 Chron 8:15).

2. Another Benjamite descending from the line of Elpaal (1 Chron 8:17).

3. A Benjamite who joined David at Ziklag to assist him in his defense against Saul. He used bows and arrows as well as stones and was just as adept with his left as with his right hand. He descended through Jeroham of Gedor (1 Chron 12:1–7).

4. One of the Korahite doorkeepers of David's time, son of Meshelemiah (1 Chron 26:2).

5. One of the officers of David's army, son of Joab's brother Asahel (1 Chron 27:7).

6. A Levite sent by King Jehoshaphat to teach the law to the residents of Judah (2 Chron 17:8).

7. Ishamel's son who was head of the house of Judah in all matters that pertained to King Jehoshaphat (2 Chron 19:11).

8. One of those who returned with Ezra from Babylon to Jerusalem with eighty men. He was the son of Michael (Ezra 8:8).

9. A priest who had married a foreign woman after the return from the Babylonian captivity. He was a son of Immer (Ezra 10:20).

ZEBAH (zē'bȧ, Heb. *zevah, sacrifice*). One of the two kings of Midian whom Gideon overthrew, the other being Zalmunna (Judg 8:10, 12; Ps 83:11). The Ephraimites had destroyed 120,000 warriors, the majority of the Midianite forces (Judg 8:10), but these two kings escaped. Gideon captured them and completely routed the rest. Having heard their personal confession that they had killed some of the Israelites (8:18–19), he ordered them executed. The son to whom this command was given, only a boy, refused, and when these kings asked Gideon to kill them, he did so (8:19–21).

ZEBEDEE (zĕb'ĕ-dē, Gr. *Zebedaios,* meaning uncertain). A fisherman on the Sea of Galilee (Mark 1:20), the father of James and John (Matt 4:21; Mark 1:19). He was the husband of Salome and in all probability lived in the vicinity of Bethsaida (Matt 27:56; Mark 15:40). Because of Mark's reference to his hired servants, one would judge that he had been a man of means and influence (Mark 1:20). Our only glimpse of him in the Bible is with his sons in their boat mending their nets (Matt 4:21–22; Mark 1:19–20).

ZEBIDAH (zē-bī'dȧ, Heb. *zevûdhâh,* given). Josiah's wife, the daughter of Pedaiah. She was the mother of Jehoiakim the king (2 Kings 23:36).

ZEBINA (zē-bī'nȧ, Heb. *zevîna', purchased*). A descendant of Nebo. He put away his foreign wife after the Captivity (Ezra 10:43).

ZEBOIIM, ZEBOIM (zē-boi'ĭm, zēbō'ĭm, Heb. *tsevō'îm, gazelles, hyena*). 1. One of the five cities in the Valley of Siddim that God destroyed with Sodom and Gomorrah (Gen 10:19; 14:2, 8; Deut 29:23; Hos 11:8).

2. A ravine in Benjamin not far from Micmash (1 Sam 13:18; Neh 11:34).

ZEBUDAH (See ZEBIDAH)

ZEBUL (zē'bŭl, Heb. *zevul, dwelling*). One who, under Abimelech, ruled the city of Shechem (Judg 9:28, 30, 38). He aided in the overthrow of the enemy led by Gaal and acted as adviser to Abimelech in behalf of the affairs of Shechem.

ZEBULUN (zĕb'ū-lŭn, Heb. *zevûlûn, habitation*). 1. Jacob's tenth son, the sixth and last son of Leah (Gen 30:19–20). Three sons were born to him in the land of his birth (46:14). Aside from this, little is recorded in the Scripture of his personal history.

2. One of the twelve tribes of Israel springing from Zebulun. When God asked Moses to number the able-bodied men at Sinai, the tribe of Zebulun had 57,400 (Num 1:31). The place assigned to this tribe at this period was on the east side of the tabernacle with the standard of Judah (2:7). While the exact boundaries of Zebulun's territory are unknown, its portion lay between the Sea of Galilee and the Mediterranean. This area included many points at which Christ later carried on his ministry, and Matthew records that he thus

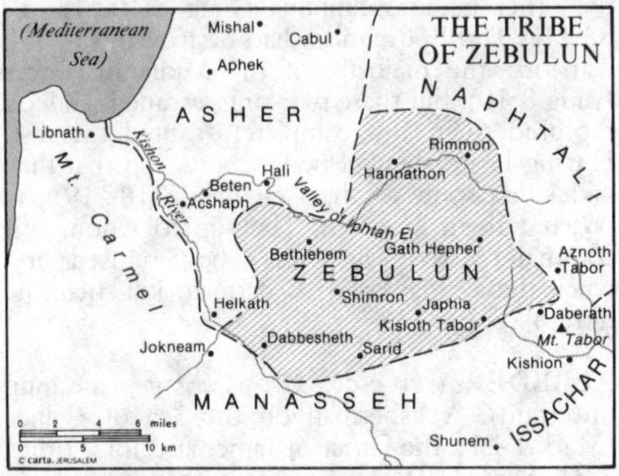

fulfilled the ancient prophecy of Isaiah (Isa 9:1–2; Matt 4:12–16).

3. A city, located in the tribe of Asher between Beth Dagon and the Valley of Iphtah El (Josh 19:27).

ZECHARIAH (zĕk'ā-rī'ā, Heb. *zekharyāhû, Jehovah remembers*). 1. Fourteenth king of Israel, the son of Jeroboam II. In fulfillment of 2 Kings 10:30 he was the last of the house of Jehu. After reigning six months, he was killed by Shallum, his successor (2 Kings 15:8–10).

2. A Reubenite chief (1 Chron 5:7).

3. A Korahite, son of Meshelemiah. He is described as "the gatekeeper at the entrance to the Tent of Meeting" (1 Chron 9:21) and a "a wise counselor" (26:2, 14).

4. A Benjamite, son of Jehiel. He was a brother of Kish (1 Chron 9:37).

5. A Levitical doorkeeper in the time of David (1 Chron 15:17–18) appointed to play the lyre (15:20; 16:5).

6. One of the Davidic priests who was used as a trumpeter to help in bringing the ark from the house of Obed-Edom back to Jerusalem (1 Chron 15:24).

7. A Levite from Uzziel. He was a son of Isshiah (1 Chron 24:25).

8. A Merarite in David's day, son of Hosah (1 Chron 26:11).

9. A Manassite in the time of David. He was the chief of his tribe and the father of Iddo (1 Chron 27:21).

10. One of the princes whom Jehoshaphat sent to teach in the cities of Judah (2 Chron 17:7).

11. The father of the prophet Jahaziel and son of Benaiah (2 Chron 20:14).

12. Jehoshaphat's third son, killed by his brother Jehoram (2 Chron 21:2–4).

13. A son of Jehoiada the high priest who lived in the days of King Joash of Judah. Acting in some official capacity, he sought to check the rising tide of idolatry. A conspiracy was formed against him and, on the king's orders, he was stoned (2 Chron 24:20–22).

14. A prophet whose good influence on King Uzziah was outstanding (2 Chron 26:5).

15. The father of Abijah. Perhaps "Abijah" should be "Abi," thus making him Hezekiah's grandfather through Abi, Hezekiah's mother (2 Chron 29:1).

16. A Levite, the son of Asaph, who in King Hezekiah's day assisted in the purification of the temple (2 Chron 29:13).

17. A Kohathite from among the Levites. He was one of the overseers who faithfully assisted in the repair of the temple in the days of King Josiah (2 Chron 34:12).

18. One of the temple administrators in the time of King Josiah (2 Chron 35:8).

19. One "of the descendants of Parosh" who with 150 men returned to Jerusalem with Ezra (Ezra 8:3).

20. The son of Bebai who returned with Ezra (Ezra 8:11).

21. One of those who stood by Ezra as he read the Law to the people (Neh 8:4); a chief whom he had summoned at the canal that flows toward Ahava and with whom he entered into counsel (Ezra 8:15–16).

22. A son of Elam who at Ezra's suggestion divorced his Gentile wife (Ezra 10:26).

23. A man from the tribe of Judah. He was a son of Amariah and lived in Jerusalem (Neh 11:4).

24. A descendant of Shelah who lived at Jerusalem (Neh 11:5).

25. The son of Pashhur, who with others aided in the work at Jerusalem after the Captivity (Neh 11:12).

26. A son of Iddo. He was one of the priests in the days of Joiakim (Neh 12:16). This man may possibly be identical with the author of the Book of Zechariah mentioned in both Ezra 5:1 and 6:14.

27. A priest, the son of Jonathan. He was one of the trumpeters at the dedication of the wall of Jerusalem under the leadership of Ezra and Nehemiah (Neh 12:35, 41).

28. The son of Jeberekiah, contemporary of Isaiah. He was a "reliable witness" to Isaiah's writing (Isa 8:1–2).

29. The next to the last of the twelve minor prophets. He came from a line of priests, being the son of Berekiah and the grandson of Iddo (Zech 1:1). He was a prophet as well as a priest (1:7). He returned from the Babylonian captivity to Jerusalem under the leadership of Zerubbabel. It was during the eighth month of the second year of the Persian king Darius that he began his prophetic ministry (1:1). He was contemporary with Haggai, beginning his ministry just two months after the latter prophet.

30. The name of the father of John the Baptist (Luke 1:5). He was a priest of the division of Abijah and was childless in his old age. Both he and his wife were righteous. One day while Zechariah was performing his services in the temple, an angel appeared and reported to him that he was to have a son, whom he was to name John. Because of doubt, he was stricken mute until his son was named, at which time his speech was restored (1:67–69).

31. The son of Berakiah, mentioned in Matthew 23:35 and in Luke 11:51 by Christ as

having been murdered between the altar and the temple. His true identity has not been fully determined.

ZECHARIAH, BOOK OF.

I. Historical Background. Zechariah was the grandson of Iddo, the head of one of the priestly families that returned from the Exile (Neh 12:4, 16). Twenty years after the return, the temple still lay a blackened ruin, and the discouraged people did not see how it could be restored. At this critical moment God raised up the prophets Haggai and Zechariah to encourage the Jews to rebuild the temple. The prophecies of the two men were delivered almost at the same time. Haggai appeared first, in August 520 B.C., and within a month after his appeal was made the foundation of the temple was laid. Soon after, Zechariah uttered his first prophecy (Zech 1:1–6). Haggai finished his recorded prophecies the same year. The following year Zechariah gave a message consisting of eight symbolic visions, with an appendix (1:7–6:15). Two years later he gave a third message in answer to an inquiry by the men of Bethel regarding the observance of a fast. The two prophecies found in chapters 9–14 are not dated and were probably given at a much later period.

II. Contents.

A. Zechariah 1–8. Messages delivered on three separate occasions.

1. Zechariah 1:1–6. A general introduction.

2. Zechariah 1:7–6:15. A series of eight symbolic night visions, followed by a coronation scene. These visions were intended to encourage the Israelites to complete the temple.

a. The horsemen among the myrtle trees. They patrol the earth for the Lord and bring him reports from all parts of the earth (1:8–17). The purpose of the vision is to assure the Israelites of God's special care for and interest in them.

b. The four horns and the four craftsmen (1:18–21) teach that Israel's enemies are now destroyed and there is no longer any opposition to the building of God's house.

c. The man with a measuring line (ch. 2) teaches that Jerusalem will expand till it outgrows its walls, and God will be its best defense.

d. Joshua, the high priest, clad in filthy garments, which represent the sins of himself and the people, is cleansed and given charge of the temple. He is a type of the future Messiah-Branch who will take away all iniquity (ch. 3).

e. A seven-branched lampstand fed by two olive trees teaches that the people of God will receive God's grace through their spiritual and temporal leaders, through whose efforts the prosperity of the nation will be accomplished (ch. 4).

f. A flying scroll (5:1–4) teaches that the land will be purified from wickedness when the temple is built and God's law taught.

g. A woman (typifying the besetting sins of Israel) is carried off in a basket to the land of Babylon (5:5–11), teaching that God not only forgives the sins of his people but carries them away from their land.

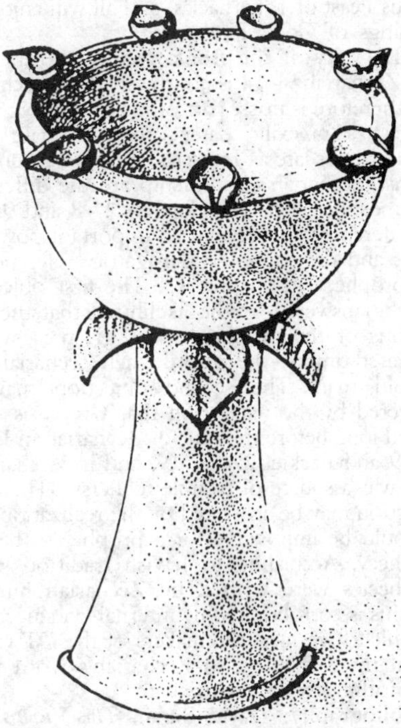

Design of the seven-branched lampstand described in the Book of Zechariah (ch. 4). Courtesy Carta, Jerusalem.

h. Four war chariots go forth to protect God's people (6:1–8), teaching God's protective providence.

These visions are followed by a scene in which a party of Jews has just come from Babylon with silver and gold for the temple. Zechariah is instructed to take part of it and make a crown for the high priest, a type of the Messiah-Branch who is to be both Priest and King to his people.

3. Zechariah 7–8 were spoken two years later than the series of visions described above and represent Zechariah's answer to the questions put to him by certain visitors as to whether the fasts observed in memory of the destruction of Jerusalem should still be kept. The reply is no; for God demands not fasts, but observance of moral laws. God has come to dwell with his people; and even the heathen will desire to worship God in Jerusalem.

B. Zechariah 9–14. This is made up of two distinct prophecies, without dates.

1. Zechariah 9–11. God will visit the nations in judgment and his people in mercy. The Prince of Peace will come and confound the evil shepherds, but he will be rejected by the flock, and they will consequently again experience suffering.

2. Zechariah 12–14. A prophecy describing the victories of the new age and the coming Day of the Lord. Three apocalyptic pictures are presented: (1) Jerusalem will be saved from a siege by her enemies by the intervention of the Lord. (2) A remnant of Israel will be saved. (3) The nations will come to Jerusalem to share in the

joyous Feast of Tabernacles, and all will enjoy the blessings of God's kingdom.

III. Unity of the Book. Many scholars hold that Zechariah 9–14 is not the work of Zechariah and therefore is not a part of his prophecy. Some suggest a preexilic date; others, a date after Zechariah, as late as 160 B.C. The main arguments against Zechariah's authorship are the difference in atmosphere between chapters 1–8 and 9–14, the reference to Greece as an important power in 9:13, and the supposed derogatory reference to the prophecy in chapter 13. The first objection may be answered by the likelihood that the two sections of the prophecy were given at widely separated times—the second when Zechariah was an old man. The second objection may be answered by the realization that Greece is mentioned long before the time of Zechariah in Isaiah 66:19 and Ezekiel 27:13, 19, and in Zechariah's time was a source of trouble to Persia. The third objection may be answered by the realization that it would be impossible for a prophet to belittle prophecy. According to Jewish tradition, these prophecies were written by Zechariah himself, and this is corroborated by internal evidence. It is difficult to see how the makers of the OT canon added these chapters to Zechariah's word if he had nothing to do with them.

Bibliography: David Baran, *The Visions and Prophecies of Zechariah,* 1919; J. G. Baldwin, *Haggai, Zechariah, Malachi* (TOTC), 1972. SB

ZEDAD (zē'dăd, Heb. *tsedhādhâh, a siding*). A city located on the ideal northern boundary of Palestine (Num 34:8; Ezek 47:15).

ZEDEKIAH (zĕd'ĕ-kī'ȧ, Heb. *tsidhqîyahû, the* LORD *is righteous*). 1. The son of Kenaanah, the leader and voice for the four hundred prophets whom Ahab consulted to learn the outcome of his proposed expedition against Ramoth Gilead. In reply to Ahab's question, Zedekiah said that Ahab would be successful in winning a victory over the Syrians. Apparently these were all false prophets, judging from the question raised by Jehoshaphat: "Is there not a prophet of the LORD here whom we can inquire of?" (1 Kings 22:7). When the true prophet was finally called and asked as to the outcome of this planned battle, he revealed the truth and was consequently struck by Zedekiah (1 Kings 22:19–24; 2 Chron 18:10).

2. The last king of Judah, son of Josiah and Hamutal (2 Kings 24:18). Because of the wickedness of Judah, God finally brought on the predicted Babylonian captivity. Nebuchadnezzar came to Jerusalem, took Judah's King Jehoiachin to Babylon, and made Mattaniah, whose name he changed to Zedekiah, king in his place. Having taken away the men of influence from Judah, he felt the remaining Jews would be easily subdued (Ezek 17:11–14). Zedekiah, however, rebelled against the king of Babylon, and as a result he was taken by Nebuchadnezzar and bound. His sons were killed before his eyes, and his own eyes were put out. He was then taken to Babylon where he died (2 Kings 24–25). Because of his evil he was permitted only eleven years of reign, many details of which are given in Jeremiah 34–37.

3. The son of Jehoiachin (1 Chron 3:16).

4. The son of Maaseiah. He was a false prophet who carried on his ruinous work among those who had been deported to Babylon. He was singled out by Jeremiah and publicly denounced for having prophesied lies. His death by being "burned in the fire" was foretold by Jeremiah as a warning to other false prophets (Jer 29:21–23).

5. The son of Hananiah. He was a prince of Israel in the reign of Jehoiakim (Jer 36:12).

6. A high official who sealed the renewed covenant (Neh 10:1). SB

ZEEB (zē'ĕb, Heb. *ze'ev, wolf*). One of the two princes of Midian killed by Gideon's men at a winepress named for him (Judg 7:25ff.).

ZEKER (zē'kêr, Heb. *zākher, memorial*). One of Jehiel's sons (1 Chron 8:31).

ZELAH, ZELA (zē'lȧ, Heb. *tsēla'*). A town in Benjamin probably close to Jerusalem (Josh 18:28). Here David reinterred the bones of Saul and Jonathan in the family tomb, which had belonged to Kish (2 Sam 21:14). "Zela" is closer to the Hebrew.

ZELEK (zē'lĕk, Heb. *tseleq, a fissure*). An Ammonite who served in David's inner circle of mighty men (2 Sam 23:37; 1 Chron 11:39).

ZELOPHEHAD (zē-lō'fē-hăd, Heb. *tselophādh,* meaning unknown). A Manassite who died in the wilderness, leaving five daughters but no sons; in the division of the land, they begged a share in the inheritance (Num 27:1–11). This the Lord granted, and when their tribesmen feared that their property might be alienated from the tribe by marriage (36:1–12), he commanded that they should marry only within their tribe; and this became a general law regarding heiresses.

ZELOTES (See ZEALOT)

ZELZAH (zĕl'zȧ, Heb. *tseltsah*). A town on the southern border of Benjamin near Rachel's tomb (1 Sam 10:2).

ZEMARAIM (zĕm'ȧ-rā'ĭm, Heb. *tsemārayim*). 1. An ancient town allotted to the tribe of Benjamin, about four miles (seven km.) north of Jericho in the Arabah, and long since merely a ruin (Josh 18:22).

2. A mountain in the hill country of Ephraim on which King Abijah stood and rebuked Jeroboam and Israel for their rebellion against Judah and for their idolatry (2 Chron 13:4ff.). Though Jeroboam's army was twice the size of Abijah's, God gave Abijah victory.

ZEMARITES (zĕm'ȧ-rīts, Heb. *ha-tsemārî*). A tribe of Canaanites mentioned in the "Table of the Nations" (Gen 10:18; 1 Chron 1:16) in the Hamite list between the Arvadites and Hamathites. The site was probably modern Sumra, on the coast between Arvad and Tripolis.

ZEMIRAH (zē-mī'rȧ, Heb. *zemîrâh*). A grandson of Benjamin through his son Becher (1 Chron 7:8).

ZENAN (zē'năn, Heb. *tsenān, tsa'ănān*). A place in the lowland of Judah (Josh 15:37), the same as Zaana. See Micah 1:11.

ZENAS (zē'nȧs, Gr. *Zēnas*). A Christian lawyer in Crete whom Paul asked to be sent to him, with Apollos, in Nicopolis (Titus 3:13).

ZEPHANIAH (zĕf'ȧ-nī'ȧ, Heb. *tsephanyâh, hidden of the LORD*). 1. An ancestor of the prophet Samuel (1 Chron 6:36).

2. The author of the Book of Zephaniah. He was very probably related to the kings of Judah as follows (Zeph 1:1): Amariah and King Manasseh were brothers, Gedaliah and King Amon were cousins, Cushi and King Josiah were second cousins, and Zephaniah was third cousin of the three kings Jehoahaz, Jehoiakim, and Zechariah, thus putting the prophet into familiar relationship with the court, to which his message seems to be specially directed (e.g., 1:8). His principal work seems to have been early in Josiah's reign, like that of his contemporaries Nahum and Habakkuk, and before the greater prophecies of his other contemporary, Jeremiah.

3. A priest, son of Masseiah, whom Zedekiah sent to inquire of Jeremiah (2 Kings 25:18–21; Jer 21:1). The Babylonian captain of the guard took him to Riblah where Nebuchadnezzar had him executed.

4. The father of a Josiah in the days of Darius to whom God sent the prophet Zechariah with a message of comfort and encouragement (Zech 6:9–15).

ZEPHANIAH, BOOK OF. Dated in the reign of Josiah (Zeph 1:1), this book was probably written early in his reign, before the religious reformation that began around the period from 640 to 622 B.C. Thus the period from 640 to 622 is the likely time for the giving of the prophecy.

The book is concerned throughout with the Day of the Lord. This prophetic concept refers to any intervention of God in history. The ultimate expression of the Day of the Lord will occur in the end times.

In Zephaniah 1:2–6 the Day of the Lord is seen in its effects on Judah and Jerusalem. It comes as a punishment for the idolatry of the people (1:4–6). In 1:7–13 the prophet pictures the people as though they were coming to a communal sacrifice, but when they arrive, they are suddenly subject to the devastating punishment of God (1:8–9). The punishment is for social crimes as well as for idolatry.

The eschatological Day of the Lord is described in Zephaniah 1:14–18. In chapter 2 the prophet appeals to the humble to return to God, for the Day of the Lord will involve universal destruction. The third chapter continues the same message, but there the prophet includes a message of hope that is centered in a remnant of God's people, who will be kept secure throughout the turmoil predicted by the prophet (3:12–18).

Bibliography: Paul Kleinert, *The Book of Zephaniah,* 1908; G. G. V. Stonehouse, *Zephaniah, Nahum, and Habakkuk* (1929); H. O. Kuhner, *Zephaniah,* 1943. TEM

ZEPHATH (zē'făth, Heb. *tsephath, watchtower*). A Canaanite city about twenty-two miles (thirty-seven km.) SW of the southern end of the Dead Sea, in the territory later occupied by the tribe of Simeon. It was utterly destroyed in the time of the Conquest by the tribes of Judah and Simeon and renamed "Hormah"—i.e., "devoted to God" in the sense of being destroyed (Judg 1:17). Cf. "Hormah" in Numbers 21:3 for the use of the word.

ZEPHATHAH (zĕf'ȧ-thȧ, Heb. *tsephāthâh, watchtower*). A valley near Mareshah in the western part of Judah, where King Asa met the army of Zerah the Cushite, and where, in answer to prayer, God gave a great victory to Judah (2 Chron 14:9–12).

ZEPHO, ZEPHI (zē'fō, zē'fī, Heb. *tsephî, watchtower*). A grandson of Esau through Eliphaz—called Zepho (Gen 36:11, 15) and Zephi (1 Chron 1:36 most versions; Zepho NIV).

ZEPHON, ZIPHION (zē'fŏn, zĭf'ĭ-ŏn, Heb. *tsephôn, watching*). The Gadite ancestor of the Zephonite family—called Zephon (Num 26:15) and Ziphion (Gen 46:16 most versions).

ZEPHONITES (See ZEPHO, ZEPHI)

ZER (zêr, Heb. *tsēr*). A fortified city NW of the Sea of Galilee. It was given in Joshua's time to the tribe of Naphtali (Josh 19:35).

ZERAH (zē'rȧ, Heb. *zerah, rising*). 1. One of twin sons born to Judah (Gen 38:30). Of him came the Zerahite family of Numbers 26:20 (KJV "Zarhites"). He was great-grandfather of Achan, "the troubler of Israel" (Josh 7). He is named with his brother Perez in the genealogy of Jesus (Matt 1:3; KJV "Zara").

2. A cousin of the preceding; son of Simeon (Num 26:13) and head of another Zerahite family.

3. A Gershonite Levite of the sixth generation (1 Chron 6:21).

4. Another Gershonite Levite, but later (1 Chron 6:41).

5. A grandson of Esau through Reuel, son of Basemath (Gen 36:13). He was a chief (36:17; KJV "duke").

6. The father of Jobab, the second of the early kings of Edom (Gen 36:33). He lived at Bozrah several miles south of the Dead Sea.

7. A king of Cush (2 Chron 14:9) in the latter part of the tenth century B.C. who invaded Judah

with an immense army during the reign of Asa, but Asa prayed and the Lord conquered the Cushites and gave Asa victory.

ZERAHIAH (zĕr-à-hī'à, Heb. *zeraḥyâh, the* LORD *is risen*). 1. A Levite in the ancestry of Ezra (1 Chron 6:6, 51).

2. A leader of two hundred men who returned with Ezra (Ezra 8:4).

ZERED (zē'rĕd, Heb. *zeredh*). A valley running northwestward on the border between Moab and Edom and ending at the southern end of the Dead Sea; also the brook that follows the valley. A camping place of Israel at the end of their long wanderings (Num 21:12, KJV "Zared"; Deut 2:13–14). In Isaiah 15:7 it is called "the Ravine of the Poplars"; in Amos 6:14, the "valley of the Arabah."

ZEREDAH, ZEREDA (zĕr-ē'dà, Heb. *tserēdhah*). The birthplace of Jeroboam of Ephraim (1 Kings 11:26). Metalwork for the temple was cast there. It was located somewhere in the Jordan Valley, but the exact site is unknown.

ZEREDATHAH (See ZARETHAN)

ZERERAH (zĕr'ĕ-rà, Heb. *tserērāthâh*). A part of the Valley of Jezreel to which the Midianites went in their flight from Gideon (Judg 7:22). KJV has "Zererath."

ZERESH (zē'rĕsh, Heb. *zeresh, golden*). The wife of Haman the Agagite, the enemy of the Jews. She advised him to build a gallows for Mordecai, but later saw her error (Esth 5:10, 14; 6:13). Her name is Persian.

ZERETH (zē'rĕth, Heb. *tsereth, splendor?*). An early descendant of Judah through Helah, second wife of Ashhur (1 Chron 4:7).

ZERETH SHAHAR (zē'rĕth shā'hàr, Heb. *tsereth hashahar, the glory of dawn*). A city located in the land belonging to Reuben "on the hill in the valley" (Josh 13:19). It has not been identified.

ZERI (zē'rī, Heb. *tserî*). One of the sons of Jeduthun in the days of David. He praised the Lord with harp and voice (1 Chron 25:3). He is perhaps the same as Izri in verse 11.

ZEROR (zē'rôr, Heb. *tserôr*). A Benjamite, great-grandfather of King Saul (1 Sam 9:1).

ZERQA (zêr'kà). A wadi running westward to the Jordan and corresponding to the ancient river Jabbok. Also "Zerka." See JABBOK.

ZERUAH (zê-rū'à, Heb. *tserû'âh, leprous*). The widow of Nebat, father of Jeroboam of Israel (1 Kings 11:26).

ZERUBBABEL (zĕ-rŭb'à-bĕl, Heb. *zerubbāvel, shoot of Babylon*). The son of Shealtiel and the grandson of King Jehoiachin (Ezra 3:2; Hag 1:1; Matt 1:13). In 1 Chronicles 3:19 he is declared to be the son of Pedaiah, Shealtiel's brother. The explanation for this apparent discrepancy is very likely that Shealtiel died without issue; and either his nephew was his legal heir and was therefore called his son (Exod 2:10) or else Pedaiah married his brother's widow and thus Zerubbabel became Shealtiel's son by levirate law (Deut 25:5–10). He was heir to the throne of Judah (1 Chron 3:17–19) and is listed in the genealogy of our Lord (Matt 1:13; Luke 3:27).

When Cyrus allowed the Jews to return to their own land, he appointed Zerubbabel governor of the colony (Ezra 1:8, 11; 5:14). Joshua the high priest was the religious leader. When they reached Jerusalem, they first set up the altar of burnt offering, then they proceeded to lay the foundation of the new temple. Soon, however, opposition arose. The adversaries of the Jews made an apparently friendly offer of assistance (Ezra 4), but Zerubbabel and the other leaders rebuffed them; therefore they wrote to the king and succeeded in stopping the work during the reigns of Cambyses (the Ahasuerus [KJV] or Xerxes [NIV] of Ezra 4:6) and the pseudo-Smerdis (the Artaxerxes of Ezra 4:7ff.). In 520 B.C. the work was resumed and was completed four years later. A great celebration was held at the dedication of the new temple (6:16–22), and as far as the record tells, the work of Zerubbabel was complete. It is not known when he died.

ZERUIAH (zêr'ū-ī'à, Heb. *tserûyâh*). Sister of David and mother of Joab, Abishai, and Asahel. She was probably not a daughter of Jesse, but a daughter of David's mother by an earlier marriage with Nahash (2 Sam 17:25).

ZETHAM (zē'thăm, Heb. *zethām, olive tree*). A Gershonite Levite in David's time. He was son of Ladan (1 Chron 23:8; Laadan KJV, NEB) or the son of Jehieli (26:22); perhaps one was actually his grandfather.

ZETHAN (zē'thăn, Heb. *zethān, olive tree*). A Benjamite, son of Jediael (1 Chron 7:10).

ZETHAR (zē'thàr, Heb. *zēthar*). One of the seven chamberlains of Xerxes (KJV Ahasuerus, Esth 1:10).

ZEUS (zūs, Gr. *Zeus*). The chief of the Olympian gods, corresponding to the Roman Jupiter (see Acts 14:12–13). His ancestry was as follows: Chaos, a heterogeneous mass containing all the seeds of nature, produced Gaea (Earth), who in turn produced Uranus (Heaven) and married him. Among their numerous progeny were Cronos (Saturn), who married his sister Rhea, and they became "Father and mother of the gods." Chief of their children was Zeus, head of the Olympian gods and by various marriages and illicit unions the father of most of the greater gods of the Greek pantheon. One of the crowning

Remains of the altar of Zeus at Pergamum, built in Hellenistic times to commemorate the Attalid victory over the Celtic tribes, late third century B.C. It was decorated with a sculptured representation of the conflict of the gods and giants. The reconstructed altar is now in the Staatliche Museen, Berlin. This may be the same throne-like altar referred to in Revelation 2:13. Courtesy École Biblique et Archéologique Française, Jerusalem.

insults that Antiochus Epiphanes, king of Syria 176–164 B.C., offered to the Jews was his dedication of the temple at Jerusalem to Zeus (2 Macc 6).

ZIA (zī'à, Heb. *zia'*). An early Gadite (1 Chron 5:13).

ZIBA (zī'bà, Heb. *tsîvā', tsivā', a plant*). A servant or slave of King Saul (2 Sam 9:2). He had fifteen sons and twenty servants. David, desiring to show kindness to the house of his departed friend Jonathan, appointed Ziba to work for Mephibosheth, Jonathan's crippled son. When David was in trouble, Ziba brought him supplies (2 Sam 19), but lied and said that Mephibosheth had been disloyal to David. David therefore gave Ziba his master's property; but later (19:24–30) when Mephibosheth declared his innocence, David altered the decree.

ZIBEON (zĭb'ē-ŭn, Heb. *tsiv'ôn, hyena*). A Hivite, grandfather of Oholibamah, a wife of Esau (Gen 36:2, 14). The text should probably be amended to read "Horite."

ZIBIA (zĭb'ĭ-à, Heb. *tsivyā', gazelle*). An early descendant of Benjamin (1 Chron 8:9).

ZIBIAH (zĭb'ĭ-à, Heb. *tsivyāh, gazelle*). A woman of Beersheba who married King Ahaziah and was mother of Joash king of Judah (2 Kings 12:1; 2 Chron 24:1).

ZICRI (zĭk'rī, Heb. *zikhrî*). 1. A Levite, first cousin of Aaron and Moses (Exod 6:21).

2. A Benjamite of the family of Shimei (KJV Shimhi; 1 Chron 8:19–21; cf. 8:13, 21).

3. Another Benjamite, son of Shashak (1 Chron 8:23).

4. Still another Benjamite, son of Jeroham (1 Chron 8:27). All these mentioned were heads of families and so were of some renown in their day.

5. A Levite ancestor of Mattaniah, who returned from captivity (1 Chron 9:15, but called "Zabdi" in Neh 11:17).

6. A descendant of Eliezer, younger son of Moses, in the days of King David (1 Chron 26:25).

7. The father of Eliezer, ruler of the tribe of Reuben in David's time (1 Chron 27:16).

8. The father of Amasiah, the leader of two hundred thousand men of valor of Judah in the time of Jehoshaphat (2 Chron 17:16).

9. The father of Elishaphat, who covenanted with Jehoiada to put Joash on the throne (2 Chron 23:1).

10. A mighty man of Ephraim who, in Pekah's war against Judah, killed the son of Ahaz and other leaders (2 Chron 28:7).

11. The father of Joel, the overseer of the Benjamites under Nehemiah (Neh 11:9).

12. Head of a family of priests in the days of Joiakim (Neh 12:17), a descendant of Abijah.

ZIDDIM (zĭd'ĭm, Heb. *ha-tsiddîm, sides*). A fortified city in Naphtali (Josh 19:35), perhaps less than one-half mile (almost one km.) north of the Horns of Hattin, west of the Sea of Galilee.

ZIDKIJAH (See ZEDEKIAH)

ZIDON, ZIDONIANS (See SIDON)

ZIF (See ZIV)

ZIGGURAT (zĭg'ū-răt, Assyr.-Bab. *ziqquratu*, from the verb *zaqaru*, meaning *to be high* or *raised up;* hence the top of a mountain, or a staged tower). A temple tower of the Babylonians, consisting of a lofty structure in the form of a pyramid, built in successive stages, with staircases on the outside and a shrine at the top. These structures are the most characteristic feature of the temple architecture in Mesopotamia, and the locations of more than two dozen are known

Drawing of the Ziggurat of Anu at Uruk (Erech) in Mesopotamia, crowned by the "white temple" of the Jamdat Nasr period, probably built shortly before 3000 B.C. Courtesy Carta, Jerusalem.

The ziggurat at Choga Zambil, located 37 miles (60 km.) southeast of Susa. One of the best preserved ziggurats found, it measures 492 feet (150 m.) square at the base and was originally 170 feet (52 m.) high. It was built c. 1280 B.C. in honor of the Elamite god In-Shushinak. Courtesy B. Brandl.

today. The oldest one known is at Uruk. It measures 140 by 150 feet (44 by 47 m.) and stands about 30 feet (9 m.) high. At the top was the shrine, 65 feet (20 m.) long, 50 feet (16 m.) wide, and built about a narrow court. It is made of packed clay strengthened with layers of asphalt and unbaked bricks. The ziggurat at Ur was 200 feet (63 m.) long, 150 feet (47 m.) wide, and some 70 feet (22 m.) high. The inside was made of unbaked brick; the outside consisted of about 8 feet (2.5 m.) of baked brick set in bitumen. The Stele of Ur-Nammu is a contemporary record of the building of this ziggurat. The tower of Babel was a ziggurat (Gen 11:1–9). SB

ZIHA (zī'hȧ, Heb. *tsîhā'*). 1. Head of a family of temple servants, (KJV Nethinim), who returned to Jerusalem with Zerubbabel (Ezra 2:43; Neh 7:46).

2. A ruler of the temple servants in Ophel in the days of Nehemiah (Neh 11:21).

ZIKLAG (zĭk'lăg, Heb. *tsiqelagh*). A city in the south of Palestine, given to the tribe of Judah in Joshua's day (Josh 15:31), but subsequently given to or shared by the tribe of Simeon (19:5). Later it was ruled by the Philistines; Achish king of Gath assigned it to David and his men who were fleeing from Saul (1 Sam 27:1–7). During their occupation of the city, David offered to go with Achish against Saul, but the Philistines sent him back. On reaching Ziklag he found that the Amalekites had raided it, burned it, and had carried off the women and children. David recovered his property, returned to Ziklag, and from there began to recruit men of Judah to take his side when they would be needed. Later Ziklag became the property of the kings of Judah until the Captivity.

ZIKRI (See ZICRI)

ZILLAH (zĭl'ȧ, Heb. *tsillâh, shadow*). One of the two wives of Cain's descendant Lamech, the first known polygamist. She was the mother of Tubal-Cain, the patriarch of all workers in brass and iron (Gen 4:19–22).

ZILLETHAI (zĭl'ē-thī, Heb. *tsillethay, shadow of the LORD*). 1. An early Benjamite, a descendant of Shimei (1 Chron 8:20; Zilthai KJV, NEB).

2. A Manassite captain of a thousand. He joined David at Ziklag (1 Chron 12:20).

ZILPAH (zĭl'pȧ, Heb. *zilpâh*, meaning uncertain). Handmaid of Leah, given to her by her father Laban. Later through Jacob she became the mother of Gad and Asher (Gen 29:24; 30:9–13).

ZIMMAH (zĭm'ȧ, Heb. *zimmâh*). A Gershonite Levite (1 Chron 6:20, 42–43; and perhaps 2 Chron 29:12).

ZIMRAN (zĭm'răn, Heb. *zimrān*). A son of Abraham and Keturah (Gen 25:2; 1 Chron 1:32).

ZIMRI (zĭm'rī, Heb. *zimrî*). 1. A prince of the tribe of Simeon who shamelessly brought a

Midianite woman into the camp of Israel to commit adultery with her, even while God was dealing with Israel for this sin (Num 25:14). Phinehas, grandson of Aaron, killed him and the woman.

2. The fifth king of the northern kingdom. He had been captain of half of the chariots of his master Elah (1 Kings 16:9–20). He assassinated the drunken Elah and reigned for seven days, until he himself was besieged by Omri. He committed suicide by burning the king's house over himself. His capital was at Tirzah in the hills of Samaria, and his "reign" was short, wicked, and inglorious.

3. A son of Zerah and grandson of Judah (1 Chron 2:6), possibly the Zimri of Joshua 7:1 (NIV; Zabdi KJV and most versions).

4. A son of Jehoddah or Jarah of the tribe of Benjamin and father of Moza (1 Chron 8:36; 9:42).

5. An unknown tribe in the East (Jer 25:25), but apparently important because its kings were listed with the kings of Elam and of the Medes.

ZIN (zĭn, Heb. *tsin*). A wilderness the Israelites traversed on their way to Canaan. It was close to the borders of Canaan (Num 13:21) and included Kadesh Barnea within its bounds (20:1; 27:14; 33:36). Edom bordered it on the east, Judah on the SE (Josh 15:1–3), and the wilderness of Paran on the south. It was not the same as the wilderness of Sin, Zin and Sin being quite different Hebrew words.

ZINA (See ZIZA)

ZION (zī'ŭn, Heb. *tsîyôn,* Gr. *Siōn,* meaning uncertain, probably *citadel*). One of the hills on which Jerusalem stood. It is first mentioned in the OT as a Jebusite fortress (2 Sam 5:6–9). David captured it and called it the city of David. At this time the citadel probably stood on the long ridge running south of the temple, although not all scholars are agreed on this. This location is near the only known spring; it is suitable for defense; its size is about that of other fortified towns; archaeological remains show that it was inhabited long before David's time; and certain Bible references (1 Kings 8:1; 2 Chron 5:2; 32:30; 33:14) indicate that this was the original Zion. David brought the ark to Zion, and the hill henceforth became sacred (2 Sam 6:10–12). When Solomon later moved the ark to the temple on nearby Mount Moriah, the name Zion was extended to take in the temple (Isa 8:18; 18:7; 24:23; Joel 3:17; Mic 4:7). Zion came to stand for the whole of Jerusalem (2 Kings 19:21; Ps 48; 69:35; 133:3; Isa 1:8). The name is frequently used figuratively for the Jewish church and polity (Ps 126:1; 129:5; Isa 33:14; 34:8; 49:14; 52:8) and for heaven (Heb 12:22; cf. Rev 14:1). SB

ZIOR (zī'ôr, Heb. *tsî'ōr, smallness*). A town in the southern part of the Promised Land given to Judah in the days of Joshua (Josh 15:54). It was probably near Hebron.

ZIPH (zĭf, Heb. *zīph,* meaning unknown). 1. A city in the Negev "toward the border of Edom"

General view of the wilderness area of Zin, which the Israelites crossed on their way to Canaan. Courtesy Zev Radovan.

given to the tribe of Judah in Joshua's division of the land (Josh 15:24). It was probably about four miles (seven km.) south by east from Hebron.

2. The wilderness named from no. 1, which was in the southern part of Jeshimon. David hid here from Saul until the Ziphites betrayed him (1 Sam 23:14–24; 26:1–2).

3. A city in the western part of Judah; Rehoboam fortified it (2 Chron 11:8).

4. Possibly the same as no. 1, though mentioned separately in Joshua 15:55.

5. A Calebite family name (1 Chron 2:42).

6. A son of Jehallelel of the tribe of Judah (1 Chron 4:16). In KJV and NEB his father's name is Jehaleleel.

ZIPHAH (zī′fȧ, Heb. *zīphâh,* fem. of *ziph*). One of the sons of Jehallelel (1 Chron 4:16).

ZIPHIM (See ZIPHITES)

ZIPHION (See ZEPHON, ZIPHION)

ZIPHITES (zĭf′īts, Heb. *zîphî*). The inhabitants of Ziph, whether the name designated the town or the wilderness surrounding it (1 Sam 23:14–23; 26:1–5). Twice, apparently, David hid in their vicinity when being pursued by King Saul. Each time the Ziphites, though of David's tribe, told Saul of his location. They seemed to think it better to support the reigning king than to be kind to David, whom they considered a rebel.

ZIPHRON (zĭf′rŏn, Heb. *ziphrôn*). A place on the ideal northern border of the land of Canaan. It is mentioned as on a line between Zedad and Hazar Enan and is probably not far from the city of Homs (Num 34:9).

ZIPPOR (zĭp′ôr, Heb. *tsippôr, bird*). The father of Balak, king of Moab, and apparently of the Midianites (Num 22:3–4).

ZIPPORAH (zĭ-pō′rȧ, Heb. *tsippōrâh, bird,* fem. of *Zippor*). Daughter of Jethro or Reuel, the priest of Midian, who became the first wife of Moses (Exod 2:21). She was the mother of Gershom and Eliezer (18:1–6). Apparently Moses sent her back to her father during the unsettled and troublous times connected with the Exodus, though she had at least started to Egypt with him (cf. 4:20; 18:2).

ZITHER (See MUSIC AND MUSICAL INSTRUMENTS)

ZITHRI (See SITHRI)

ZIV (Heb. *ziw*). The second month of the old Hebrew calendar, corresponding to Iyyar in the later Jewish calendar (1 Kings 6:1, 37; Zif KJV). See also CALENDAR.

ZIZ (zĭz, Heb. *tsîts, shining*). A cliff near the west side of the Red Sea on the way from En Gedi to Tekoa. A great horde of Moabites, Ammonites, and apparently some Syrians had assembled against Judah at En Gedi. When Jehoshaphat heard of their approach, he feared, but, being a godly man, he also prayed. God, through a prophet, gave him courage and told him he would find the enemy "climbing up the Pass [NIV; ascent NASB, NEB, RSV; cliff KJV; slope JB] of Ziz" and that Judah would not need to fight, "for the LORD will be with you" (2 Chron 20:16–17). Trusting God, Jehoshaphat set his musicians *before* the army; when "they began to sing and praise," the Lord dispersed the enemy, and the Jews gathered the spoil.

ZIZA (zī′zȧ, Heb. *zîzāʾ, abundance*). 1. A son of Shiphi and descendant of Shemaiah. He was a Simeonite in the days of King Hezekiah, and, with others, he drove out the ancient inhabitants of Gedor, SW of Bethlehem, and took their land for pasture (1 Chron 4:37–41).

2. A son of Rehoboam and brother of Abijah, kings of Judah (2 Chron 11:20). His mother was Maacah (KJV Maachah), the favorite wife of his father.

3. The second son of Shimei, a leading Gershonite Levite in the days of David (1 Chron 23:10–11 MOF, NEB, NIV; Zina in v. 10, Zizah in v. 11—JB, KJV, MLB, NASB, RSV).

ZOAN (zō′ăn, Heb. *tsōʿan*). An ancient Egyptian city, built on the east part of the Delta seven years after Hebron was built (Num 13:22). The first kings of the Twelfth Dynasty made it their capital; the Hyksos fortified it and changed the name to Avaris. When the Hyksos were driven out, the city was neglected, but it was reestablished by Sethi I. The Egyptian god Seth had a center of worship there. Moses met Pharaoh at Zoan (Ps 78:12, 43). Isaiah and Ezekiel refer to it as an important city (Isa 19:11, 13; Ezek 30:14). For a time the Assyrians were in control of it. The Greeks called it "Tanis." Eventually it was superseded by the new city of Alexandria. Extensive ruins survive near the modern village of San (i.e., Zoan), about eighteen miles (thirty km.) SE of Damietta.

ZOAR (zō′êr, Heb. *tsōʿar, little*). An ancient Canaanite city now probably under the waters of the bay at the SE part of the Dead Sea. Formerly called "Bela" (Gen 14:2), it was saved from immediate destruction with Sodom and Gomorrah in answer to the prayer of Lot, "It is very small, isn't it?" (19:20–22). When Moses stood on Mount Pisgah to view the Promised Land, Zoar was at the southern limit of his view (Deut 34:3). In the "Doom of Moab" (Isa 15) the fleeing Moabites were to go to Zoar (15:5). We read of its later doom in Jeremiah 48:34. During the Middle Ages it was an important point between Elath and Jerusalem.

ZOBAH, ZOBA (zō′bȧ, Heb. *tsôvâh*). A region in central Syria, sometimes under one king (2 Sam 8:3); but in its first occurrence (1 Sam

14:47) we read that Saul of Israel fought against the kings of Zobah, which may indicate more than one kingdom or possibly successive kings. The kings of Zobah were persistent enemies of Israel, not only fighting against Saul, but also against David (2 Sam 8) and Solomon. Solomon captured Hamath Zobah (2 Chron 8:3), and we hear no more of this kingdom. The servants of Hadadezer in the days of David had shields of gold (2 Sam 8:3–12) and a large army, all of which David captured. Later the Ammonites, in warring against David, hired mercenary troops from Zobah, and these too were badly defeated (2 Sam 10). It lay between Hamath and Damascus. It is called Zoba in Hebrew and KJV.

ZOBEBAH (See HAZZOBEBAH)

ZOHAR (zō'hȧr, Heb. *tsōhar*). 1. A noble Hittite, father of Ephron, from whom Abraham purchased the field of Machpelah where he buried the body of Sarah in a cave (Gen 23:8; 25:9).

2. A son of Simeon, the second son of Jacob (Gen 46:10; Exod 6:15). He is called Zerah in Numbers 26:13 and 1 Chronicles 4:24.

3. A man of Judah (1 Chron 4:7 JB, NIV; Izhar ASV, MLB, RSV; Jezoar KJV, NEB).

ZOHELETH (zō'hē-lĕth, Heb. *zōheleth, serpent*). A stone beside En Rogel where Adonijah, fourth son of David and older than Solomon, gathered his conspirators before David's death. He sacrificed sheep and oxen, attempting to make himself king at or before the death of his father. The plot was revealed to David, who had Solomon anointed, and thus the plot was foiled (1 Kings 1, esp. v. 9). The exact site of Zoheleth is unknown.

ZOHETH (zō'hĕth, Heb. *zohēth*). Son of Ishi, a Judahite (1 Chron 4:20).

ZOPHAH (zō'fȧ, Heb. *tsōphah*). An Asherite, son of Helem (1 Chron 7:35–36).

ZOPHAI (zō'fī, Heb. *tsōphay*). An ancestor of Samuel the prophet (1 Chron 6:26; called Zuph in 6:35).

ZOPHAR (zō'fêr, Heb. *tsōphar*). One of Job's friends who came to comfort him in his affliction (Job 2:11).

ZOPHIM (zō'fĭm, Heb. *tsōphîm, watchers*). A field near the top of Pisgah (Num 23:14). The exact site is unknown.

ZORAH (zō'rȧ, Heb. *tsorâh*). A city about fifteen miles (twenty-five km.) west of Jerusalem on the border of Judah and Dan (Josh 15:33; 19:41), the home of Manoah, father of Samson (Judg 13:2). Samson was buried near there (16:31). From Zorah the Danites sent spies to seek a new home for their tribe (18:2).

ZORATHITES (zō'ră-thīts, Heb. *tsor'āthî*). Inhabitants of Zorah (1 Chron 4:2; in 2:53 NASB, NIV, RSV; Zareathites lit., KJV, NEB).

ZOREAH (See ZORAH)

ZORITES (zō'rīts, Heb. *tsor'î*). In 1 Chronicles 2:54 "Zorathites" should probably be read; otherwise the reference is to a people of some unknown place.

ZUAR (zū'êr, Heb. *tsû'ār, small*). The father of Nethanel of the tribe of Issachar, who was a prince of his tribe (Num 1:8; 2:5).

ZUPH (zŭf, Heb. *tsûph, honeycomb*). 1. An ancestor of the prophet Samuel. He was a Levite descended from Kohath (1 Sam 1:1; 1 Chron 6:35). He is called Zophai in 1 Chronicles 6:26.

2. A district in Benjamin near its northern border (1 Sam 9:5). Location unknown.

ZUR (zûr, Heb. *tsûr, rock*). 1. One of the five kings of the Midianites killed by Israel (Num 25:15; 31:8). Cozbi, his daughter, was killed by Phinehas, grandson of Aaron.

2. An inhabitant of Gibeon in Benjamin; a son of Jeiel (1 Chron 8:30; 9:36).

ZURIEL (zū'rĭ-ĕl, Heb. *tsûrî'ēl, whose rock is God*). A son of Abihail, prince of the Merarite Levites in the wilderness (Num 3:35).

ZURISHADDAI (zū'rĭ-shăd'ī, Heb. *tsûrî-shadday, whose rock is the Almighty*). Father of Shelumiel, head of the tribe of Simeon in the wilderness (Num 1:6; 2:12; 7:36, 41; 10:19).

ZUZIM, ZUZITES (zū'zĭm, zū'zīts, Heb. *zûzîm*). A primitive race of giants conquered by Kedorlaomer and his allies at Ham, an unknown place east of the Jordan, in the days of Abraham (Gen 14:5; Zuzites NIV; Zuzim JB, MLB, NASB, NEB, RSV; Zuzims KJV).

Scripture Index

A page number followed by * indicates that the Scripture reference may be found in the article that begins on that page.

Genesis

Exodus

Leviticus

Numbers

Deuteronomy

Joshua

Judges

Ruth

1 Samuel

2 Samuel

1 Kings

2 Kings

1 Chronicles

2 Chronicles

Ezra

Nehemiah

Esther

Job

Psalms

Proverbs

Ecclesiastes

Song of Songs

Isaiah

Jeremiah

Lamentations

Ezekiel

Daniel

Micah

Nahum

Habakkuk

Zephaniah

Haggai

Zechariah

Malachi

Matthew

Mark

Luke

John

Romans

1 Corinthians

2 Corinthians

Galatians

Ephesians

Philippians

Colossians

1 Thessalonians

2 Thessalonians

1 Timothy

2 Timothy

Titus

Philemon

Hebrews

James

1 Peter

2 Peter

1 John

2 John

3 John

Jude

Revelation

Index to Color Maps

* = Map inset

THE NEAR EAST IN THE TIME OF THE PATRIARCHS

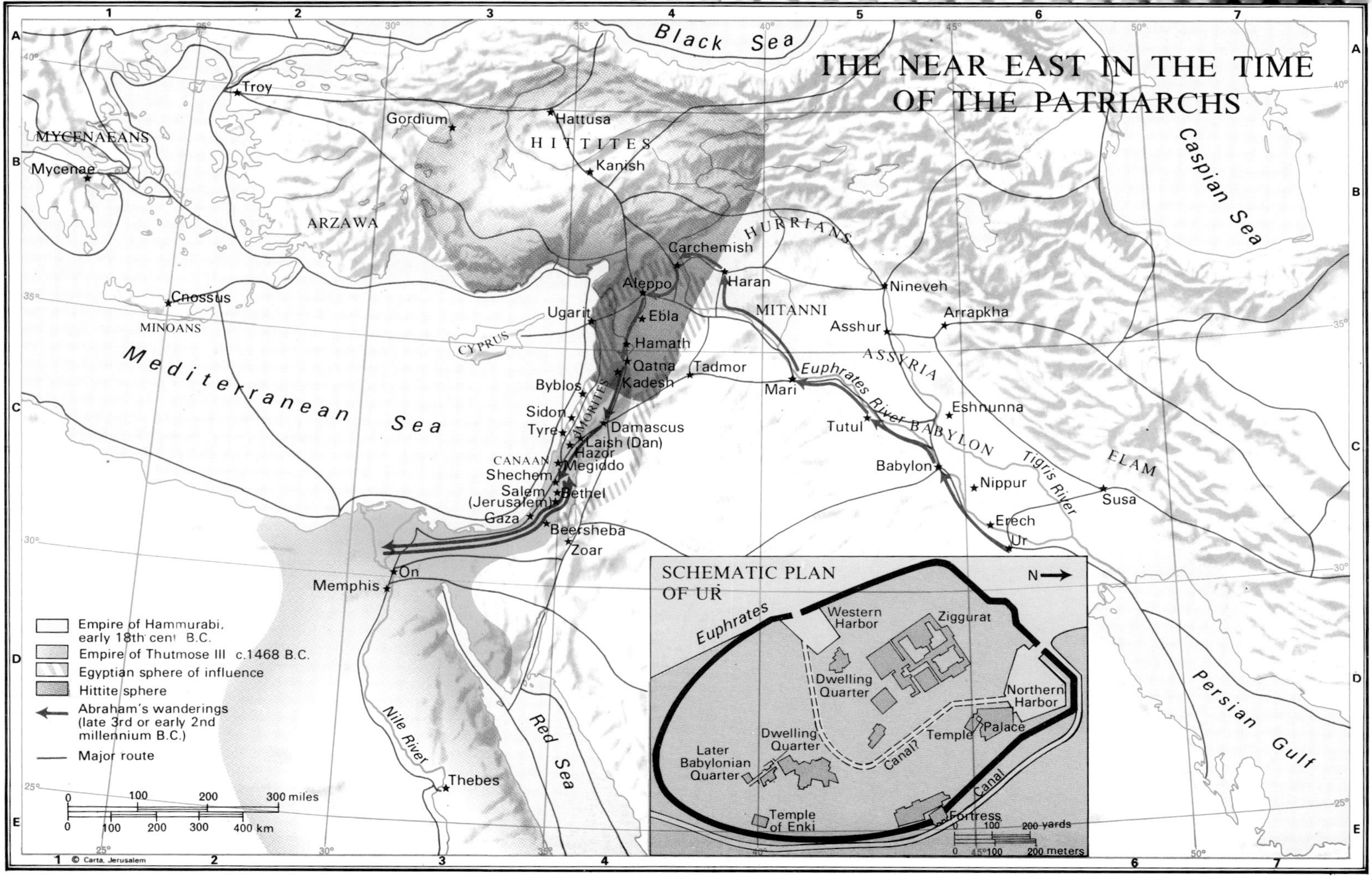

1

THE EXODUS AND CONQUEST OF CANAAN

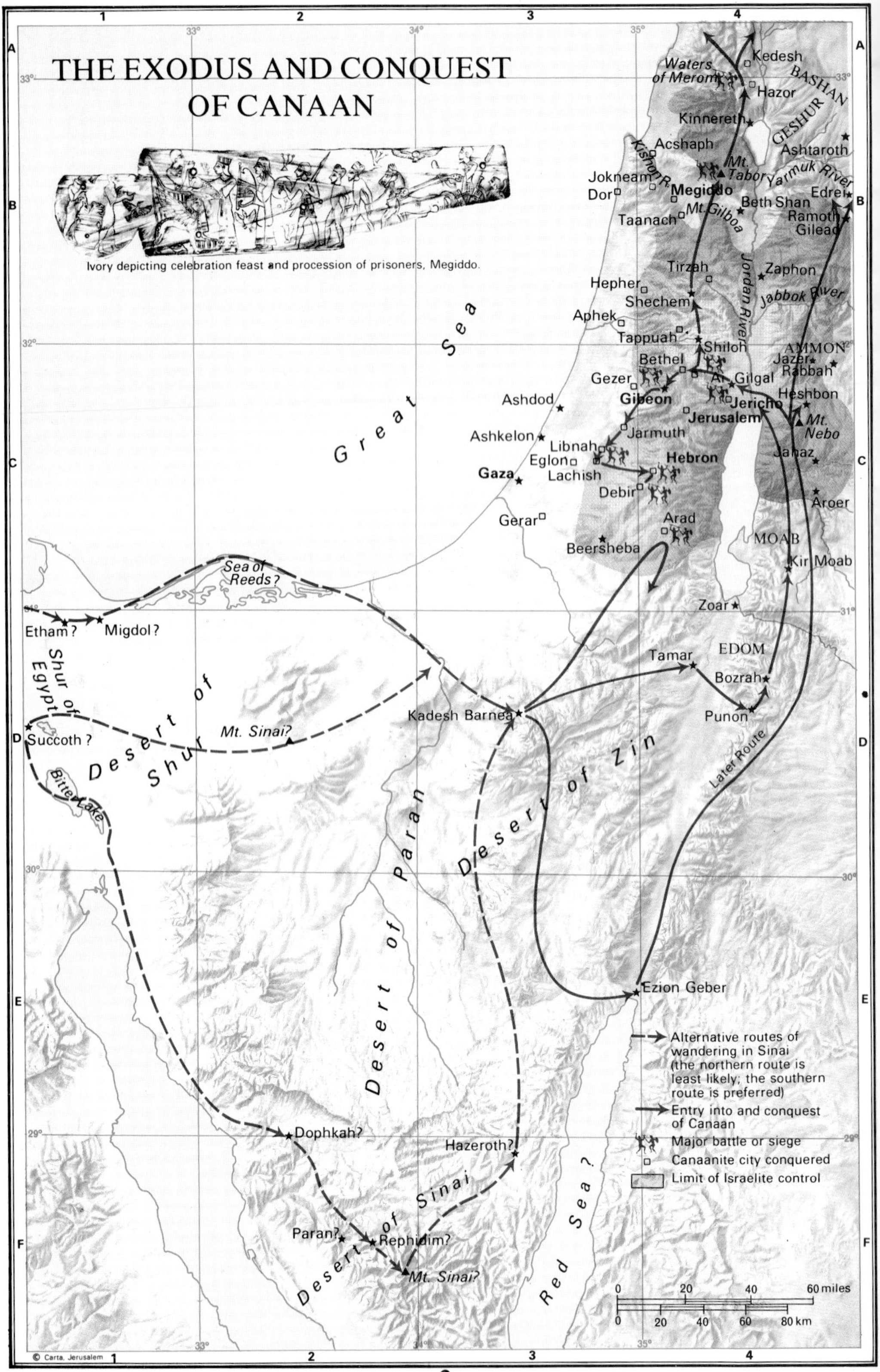
Ivory depicting celebration feast and procession of prisoners, Megiddo.
Great Sea
Kedesh
Waters of Merom
Hazor
BASHAN
GESHUR
Kinnereth
Acshaph
Kishon R.
Mt. Tabor
Ashtaroth
Yarmuk River
Jokneam
Dor
Megiddo
Mt. Gilboa
Beth Shan
Edrei
Taanach
Ramoth Gilead
Tirzah
Jordan River
Zaphon
Hepher
Shechem
Jabbok River
Aphek
Tappuah
Shiloh
AMMON
Bethel
Jazer
Rabbah
Gezer
Ai
Gilgal
Ashdod
Gibeon
Jericho
Heshbon
Jerusalem
Mt. Nebo
Ashkelon
Jarmuth
Libnah
Eglon
Hebron
Jahaz
Gaza
Lachish
Debir
Aroer
Gerar
Arad
MOAB
Beersheba
Kir Moab
Sea of Reeds?
Zoar
Etham?
Migdol?
Shur of Egypt
Tamar
EDOM
Bozrah
Desert of Shur
Kadesh Barnea
Punon
Succoth?
Mt. Sinai?
Desert of Zin
Bitter Lake
Later Route
Desert of Paran
Ezion Geber
Alternative routes of wandering in Sinai (the northern route is least likely; the southern route is preferred)
Entry into and conquest of Canaan
Major battle or siege
Canaanite city conquered
Limit of Israelite control
Dophkah?
Hazeroth?
Desert of Sinai
Red Sea?
Paran?
Rephidim?
Mt. Sinai?
0 20 40 60 miles
0 20 40 60 80 km
© Carta, Jerusalem

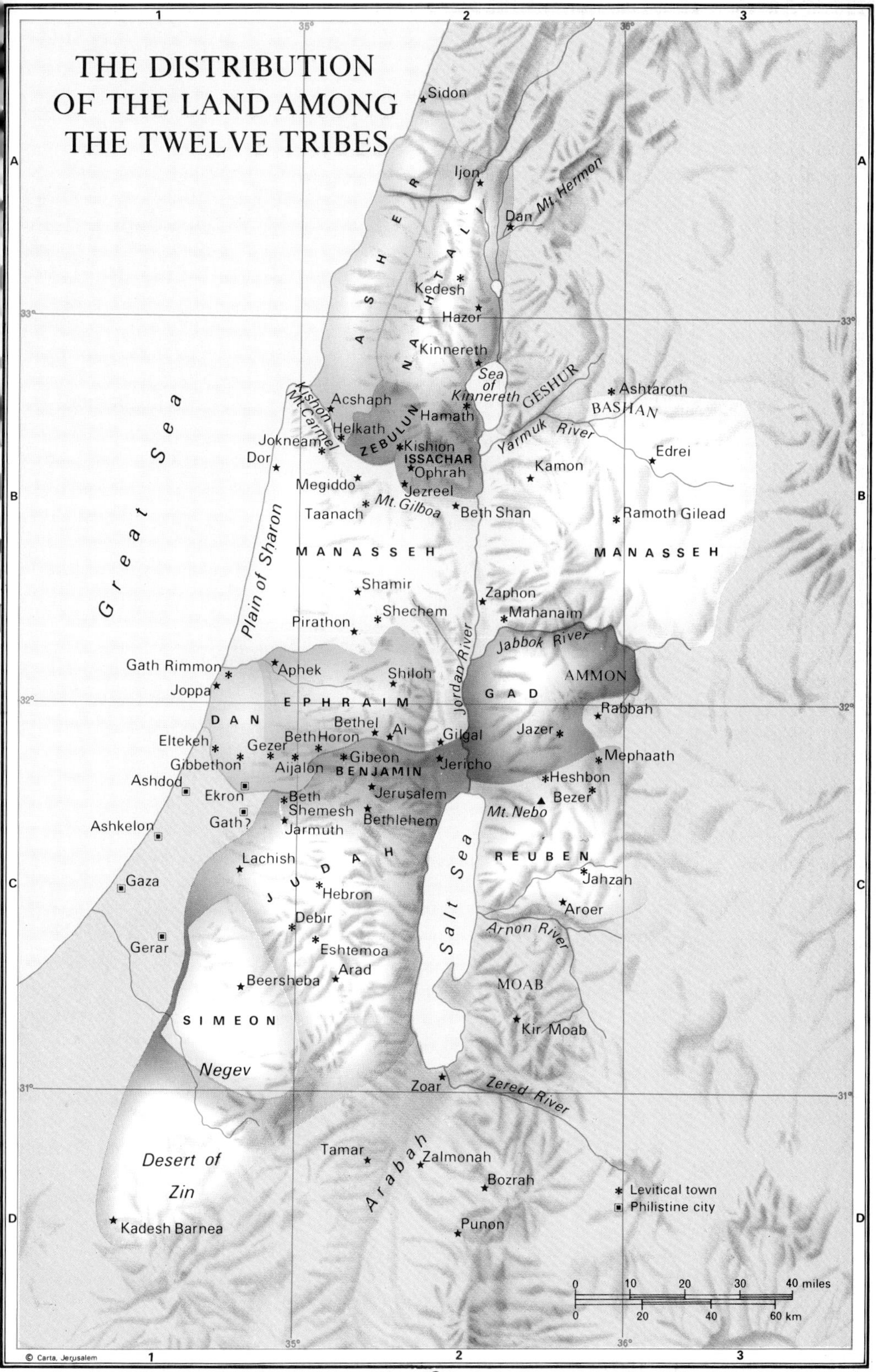
THE DISTRIBUTION OF THE LAND AMONG THE TWELVE TRIBES
Sidon
Ijon
Dan
Mt. Hermon
ASHER
NAPHTALI
Kedesh
Hazor
Kinnereth
Sea of Kinnereth
GESHUR
Ashtaroth
BASHAN
Acshaph
Kishon
Mt. Carmel
Hamath
Helkath
ZEBULUN
Jokneam
Kishion
ISSACHAR
Yarmuk River
Edrei
Dor
Ophrah
Kamon
Megiddo
Jezreel
Great Sea
Taanach
Mt. Gilboa
Beth Shan
Ramoth Gilead
Plain of Sharon
MANASSEH
MANASSEH
Shamir
Zaphon
Shechem
Mahanaim
Pirathon
Jabbok River
Jordan River
Gath Rimmon
Aphek
Shiloh
AMMON
Joppa
EPHRAIM
GAD
Rabbah
DAN
Bethel
Ai
Gilgal
Jazer
Elteked
Gezer
Beth Horon
Gibeon
Mephaath
Gibbethon
Aijalon
BENJAMIN
Jericho
Heshbon
Ashdod
Jerusalem
Bezer
Ekron
Beth Shemesh
Mt. Nebo
Ashkelon
Gath?
Bethlehem
Jarmuth
Salt Sea
Lachish
JUDAH
REUBEN
Gaza
Hebron
Jahzah
Aroer
Debir
Arnon River
Gerar
Eshtemoa
Arad
Beersheba
MOAB
SIMEON
Kir Moab
Negev
Zoar
Zered River
Tamar
Zalmonah
Desert of Zin
Arabah
Bozrah
Levitical town
Philistine city
Kadesh Barnea
Punon
0 10 20 30 40 miles
0 20 40 60 km
© Carta, Jerusalem

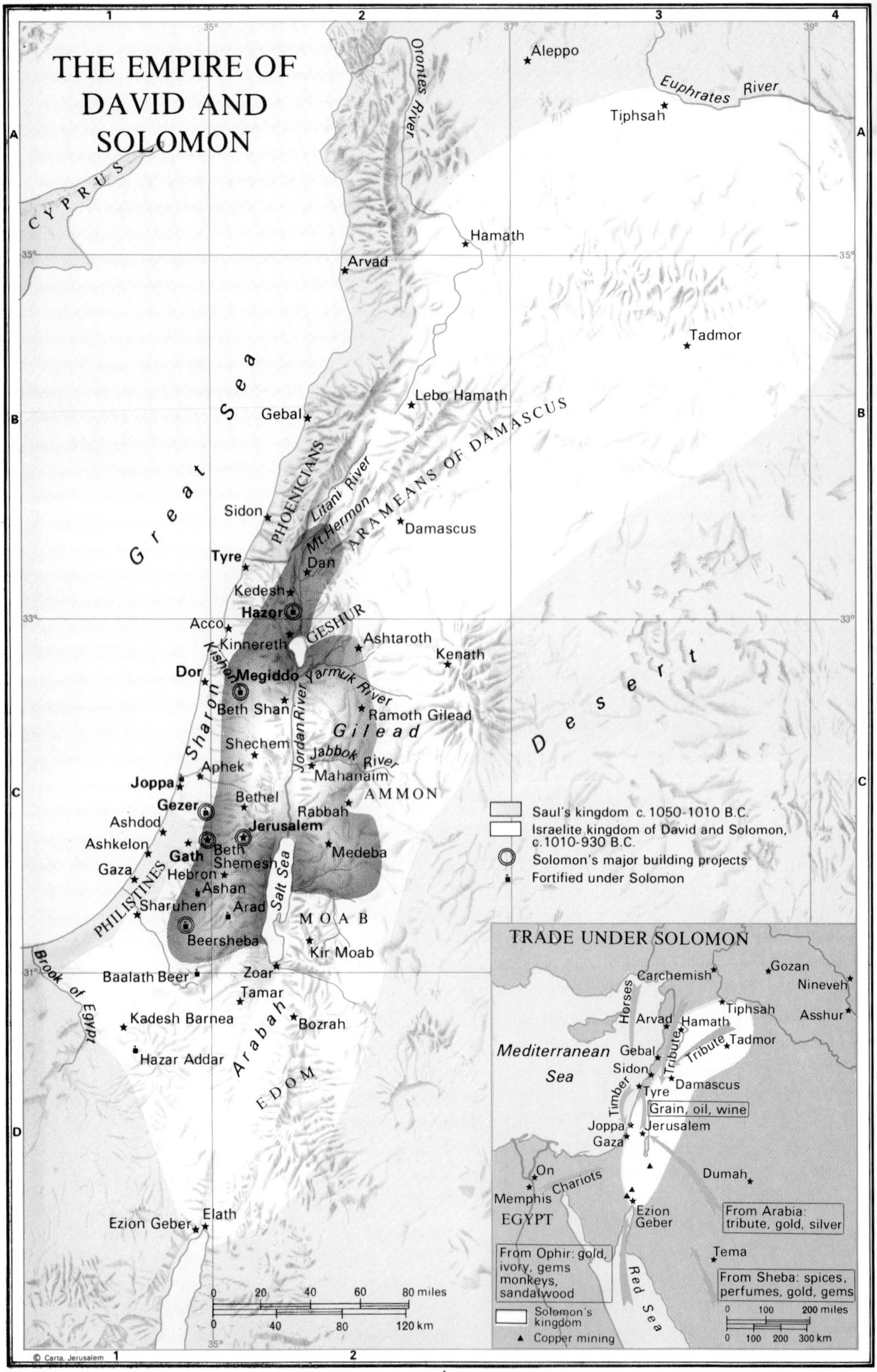
THE EMPIRE OF DAVID AND SOLOMON
CYPRUS
Great Sea
Aleppo
Euphrates River
Tiphsah
Orontes River
Hamath
Arvad
Tadmor
Lebo Hamath
Gebal
PHOENICIANS
Litani River
ARAMEANS OF DAMASCUS
Sidon
Mt.Hermon
Damascus
Tyre
Dan
Kedesh
Hazor
Acco
GESHUR
Kinnereth
Ashtaroth
Kenath
Kishon
Dor
Megiddo
Yarmuk River
Beth Shan
Ramoth Gilead
Jordan River
Gilead
Desert
Sharon
Shechem
Jabbok River
Aphek
Mahanaim
Joppa
Bethel
AMMON
Gezer
Rabbah
Ashdod
Jerusalem
Ashkelon
Beth Shemesh
Medeba
Gath
Gaza
Hebron
Salt Sea
PHILISTINES
Ashan
Sharuhen
Arad
MOAB
Beersheba
Kir Moab
Brook of Egypt
Baalath Beer
Zoar
Tamar
Kadesh Barnea
Arabah
Bozrah
Hazar Addar
EDOM
Elath
Ezion Geber
Saul's kingdom c.1050-1010 B.C.
Israelite kingdom of David and Solomon, c.1010-930 B.C.
Solomon's major building projects
Fortified under Solomon
0 20 40 60 80 miles
0 40 80 120 km
TRADE UNDER SOLOMON
Carchemish
Gozan
Nineveh
Horses
Tiphsah
Asshur
Arvad
Hamath
Tribute
Tadmor
Mediterranean Sea
Gebal
Sidon
Damascus
Tyre
Timber
Grain, oil, wine
Joppa
Jerusalem
Gaza
On
Dumah
Chariots
Memphis
EGYPT
Ezion Geber
From Arabia: tribute, gold, silver
From Ophir: gold, ivory, gems monkeys, sandalwood
Tema
Red Sea
From Sheba: spices, perfumes, gold, gems
Solomon's kingdom
Copper mining
0 100 200 miles
0 100 200 300 km
© Carta, Jerusalem

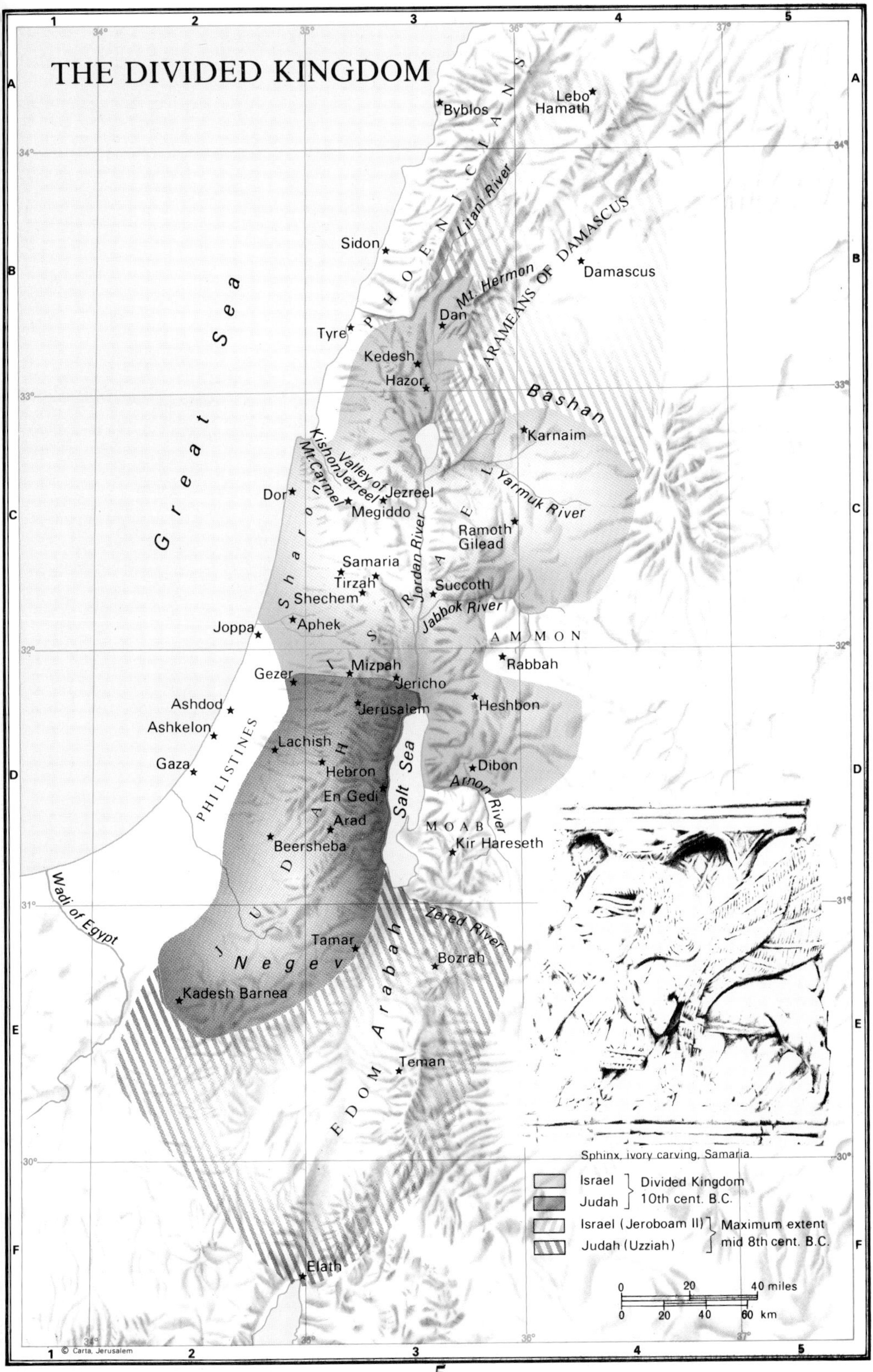
THE DIVIDED KINGDOM
Byblos
Lebo Hamath
PHOENICIANS
Litani River
Sidon
Damascus
ARAMEANS OF DAMASCUS
Mt. Hermon
Dan
Great Sea
Tyre
Kedesh
Hazor
Bashan
Karnaim
Kishon
Mt. Carmel
Valley of Jezreel
Jezreel
Dor
Megiddo
ISRAEL
Yarmuk River
Ramoth Gilead
Sharon
Samaria
Tirzah
Shechem
Jordan River
Succoth
Jabbok River
Aphek
Joppa
AMMON
Rabbah
Gezer
Mizpah
Jericho
Heshbon
Ashdod
Jerusalem
Ashkelon
PHILISTINES
Lachish
JUDAH
Gaza
Hebron
Salt Sea
Dibon
En Gedi
Arnon River
Arad
MOAB
Beersheba
Kir Hareseth
Wadi of Egypt
Zered River
Tamar
Negev
Bozrah
Kadesh Barnea
Arabah
EDOM
Teman
Elath
Sphinx, ivory carving, Samaria.
Israel
Judah
Divided Kingdom 10th cent. B.C.
Israel (Jeroboam II)
Judah (Uzziah)
Maximum extent mid 8th cent. B.C.
0 20 40 miles
0 20 40 60 km
© Carta, Jerusalem

THE NEAR EAST AT THE TIME OF THE ASSYRIAN EMPIRE

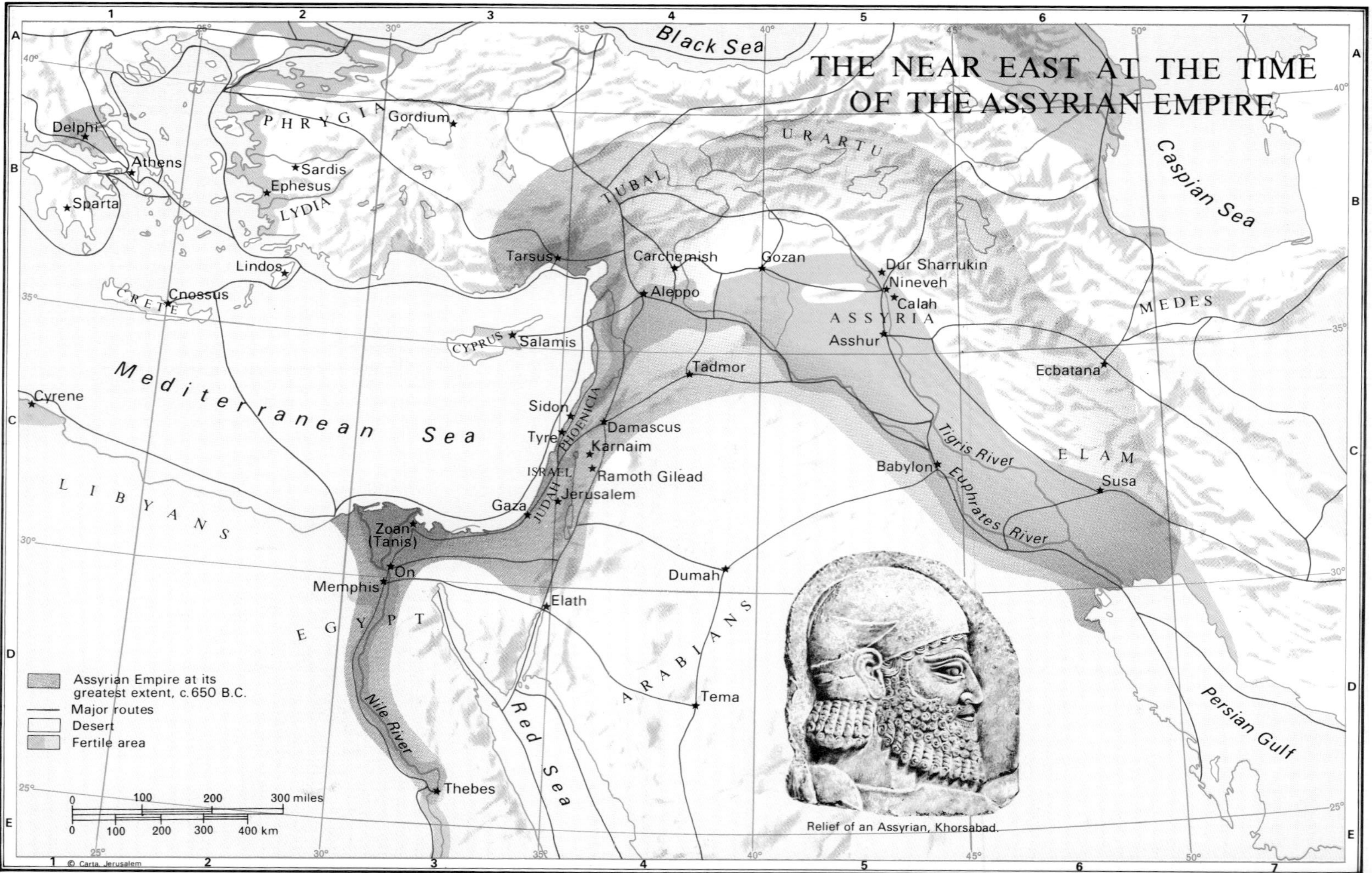

Relief of an Assyrian, Khorsabad.

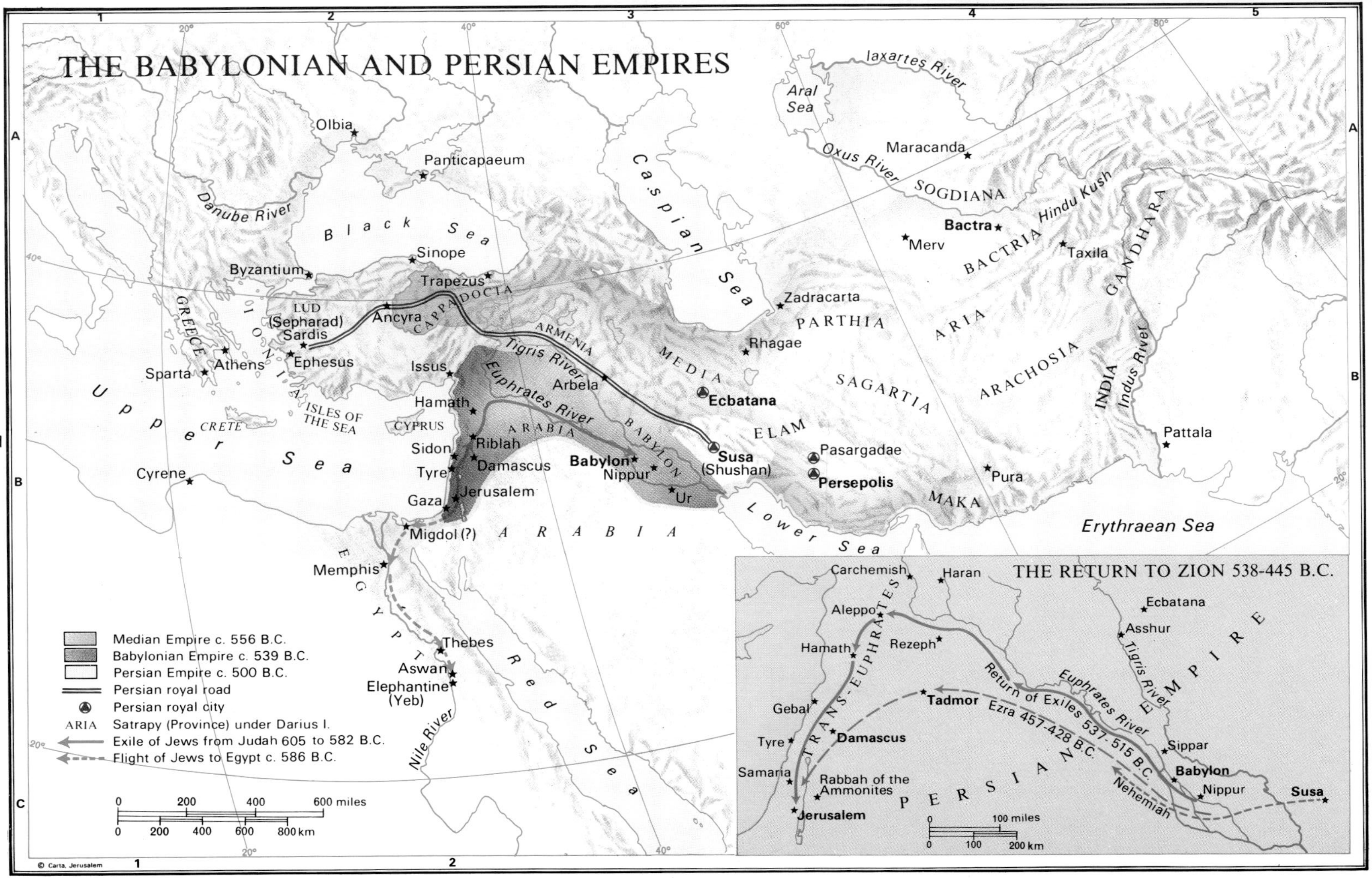
THE BABYLONIAN AND PERSIAN EMPIRES
Median Empire c. 556 B.C.
Babylonian Empire c. 539 B.C.
Persian Empire c. 500 B.C.
Persian royal road
Persian royal city
ARIA Satrapy (Province) under Darius I.
Exile of Jews from Judah 605 to 582 B.C.
Flight of Jews to Egypt c. 586 B.C.
0 200 400 600 miles
0 200 400 600 800 km
Olbia
Panticapaeum
Danube River
Black Sea
Sinope
Byzantium
Trapezus
CAPPADOCIA
LUD (Sepharad)
Ancyra
Sardis
Ephesus
IONIA
GREECE
Athens
Sparta
Upper Sea
CRETE
ISLES OF THE SEA
CYPRUS
Cyrene
Issus
Hamath
Sidon
Riblah
Tyre
Damascus
Gaza
Jerusalem
Migdol (?)
Memphis
EGYPT
Thebes
Aswan
Elephantine (Yeb)
Nile River
Red Sea
ARABIA
ARMENIA
Tigris River
Euphrates River
Arbela
BABYLON
Babylon
Nippur
Ur
Caspian Sea
MEDIA
Ecbatana
Susa (Shushan)
ELAM
Pasargadae
Persepolis
Rhagae
Zadracarta
PARTHIA
SAGARTIA
Lower Sea
Aral Sea
Iaxartes River
Oxus River
Maracanda
SOGDIANA
Merv
Bactra
BACTRIA
Hindu Kush
Taxila
ARIA
ARACHOSIA
GANDHARA
INDIA
Indus River
Pattala
Pura
MAKA
Erythraean Sea
THE RETURN TO ZION 538-445 B.C.
Carchemish
Haran
Ecbatana
Asshur
Tigris River
Aleppo
Rezeph
Hamath
TRANS-EUPHRATES
Return of Exiles 537-515 B.C.
Euphrates River
Ezra 457-428 B.C.
Tadmor
Gebal
Tyre
Damascus
Samaria
Rabbah of the Ammonites
Jerusalem
PERSIAN EMPIRE
Sippar
Babylon
Nippur
Nehemiah
Susa
0 100 miles
0 100 200 km
© Carta, Jerusalem

JERUSALEM AT THE TIME OF DAVID AND SOLOMON

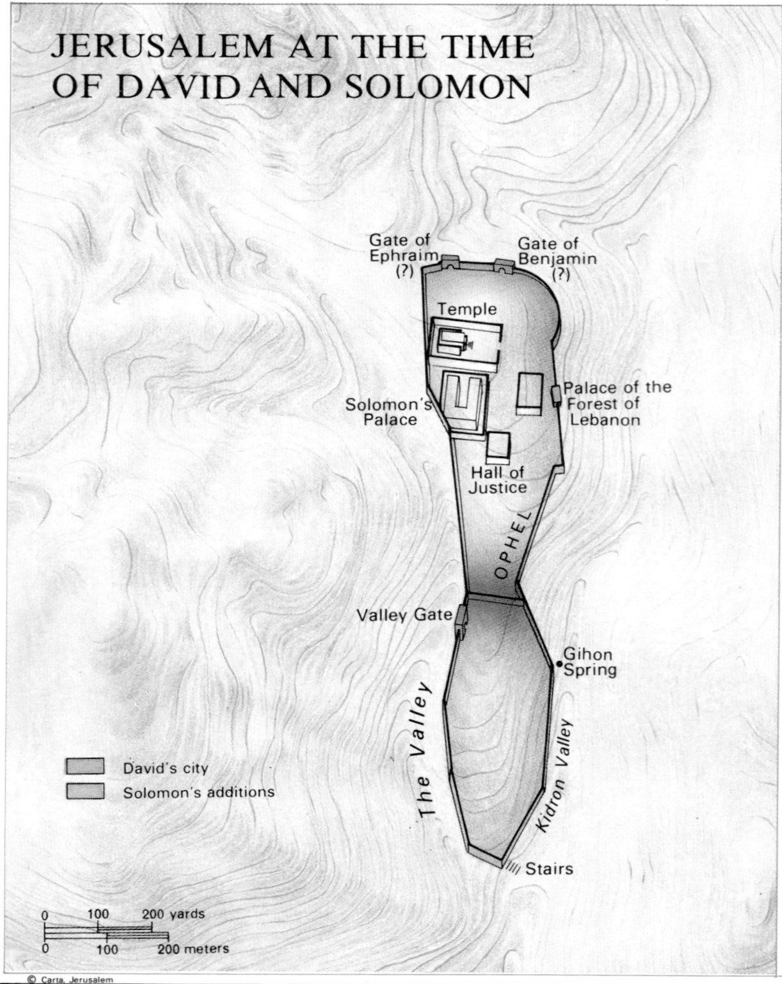

SOLOMON'S TEMPLE

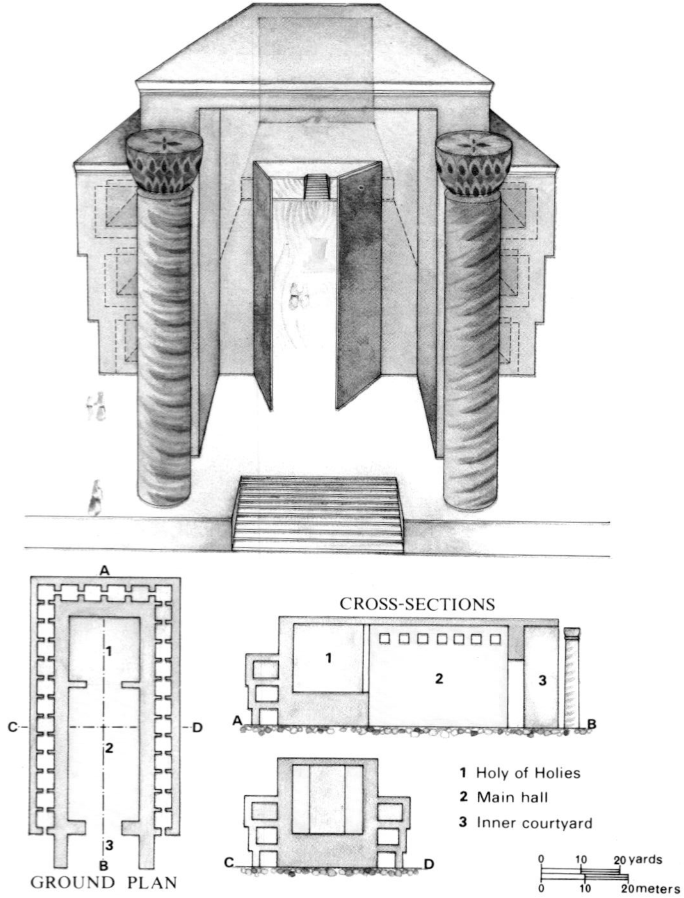

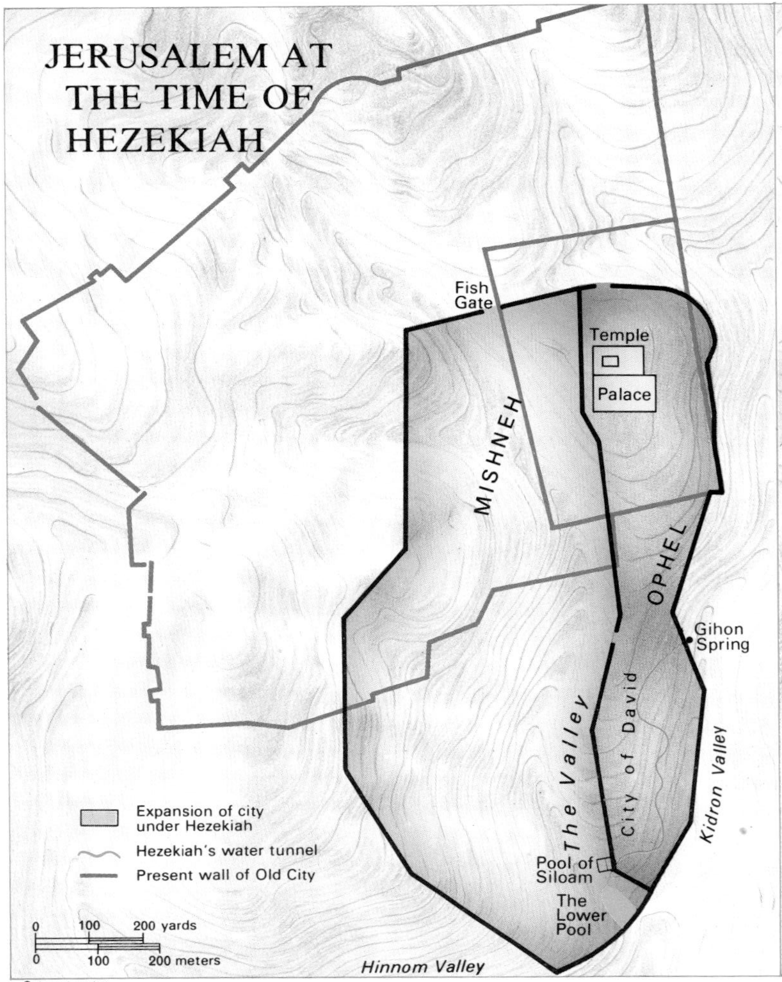
JERUSALEM AT THE TIME OF HEZEKIAH
Fish Gate
Temple
Palace
MISHNEH
OPHEL
Gihon Spring
City of David
The Valley
Kidron Valley
Pool of Siloam
The Lower Pool
Hinnom Valley
Expansion of city under Hezekiah
Hezekiah's water tunnel
Present wall of Old City
0 100 200 yards
0 100 200 meters

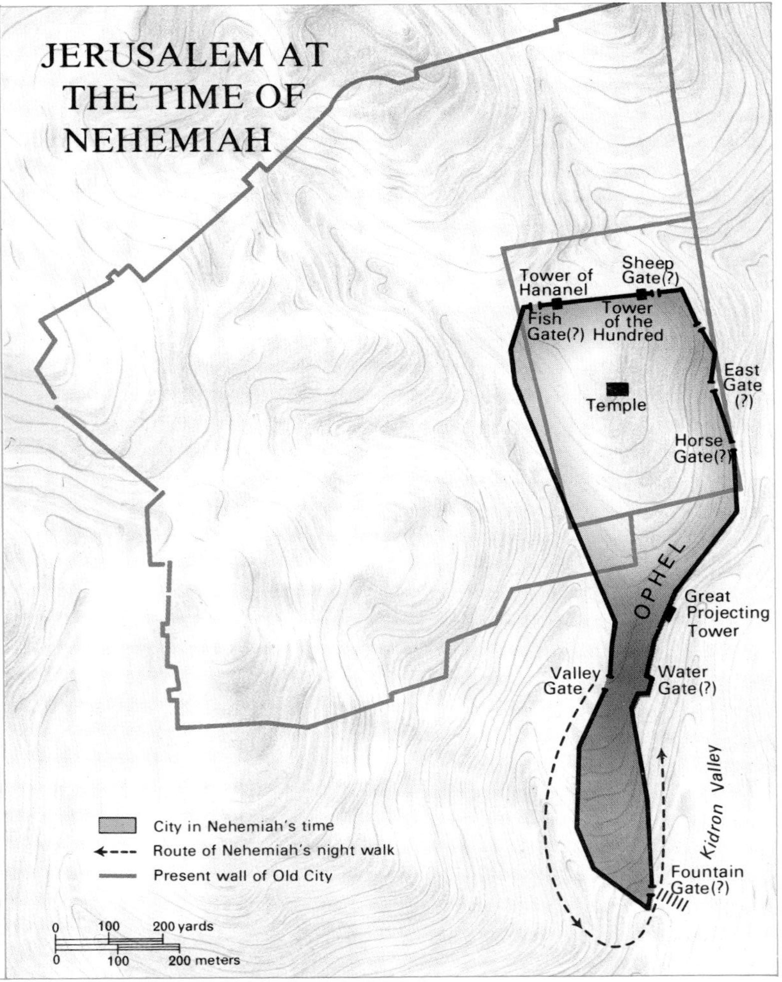
JERUSALEM AT THE TIME OF NEHEMIAH
Tower of Hananel
Sheep Gate(?)
Fish Gate(?)
Tower of the Hundred
East Gate (?)
Temple
Horse Gate(?)
OPHEL
Great Projecting Tower
Valley Gate
Water Gate(?)
Kidron Valley
Fountain Gate(?)
City in Nehemiah's time
Route of Nehemiah's night walk
Present wall of Old City
0 100 200 yards
0 100 200 meters

JESUS' LIFE AND MINISTRY

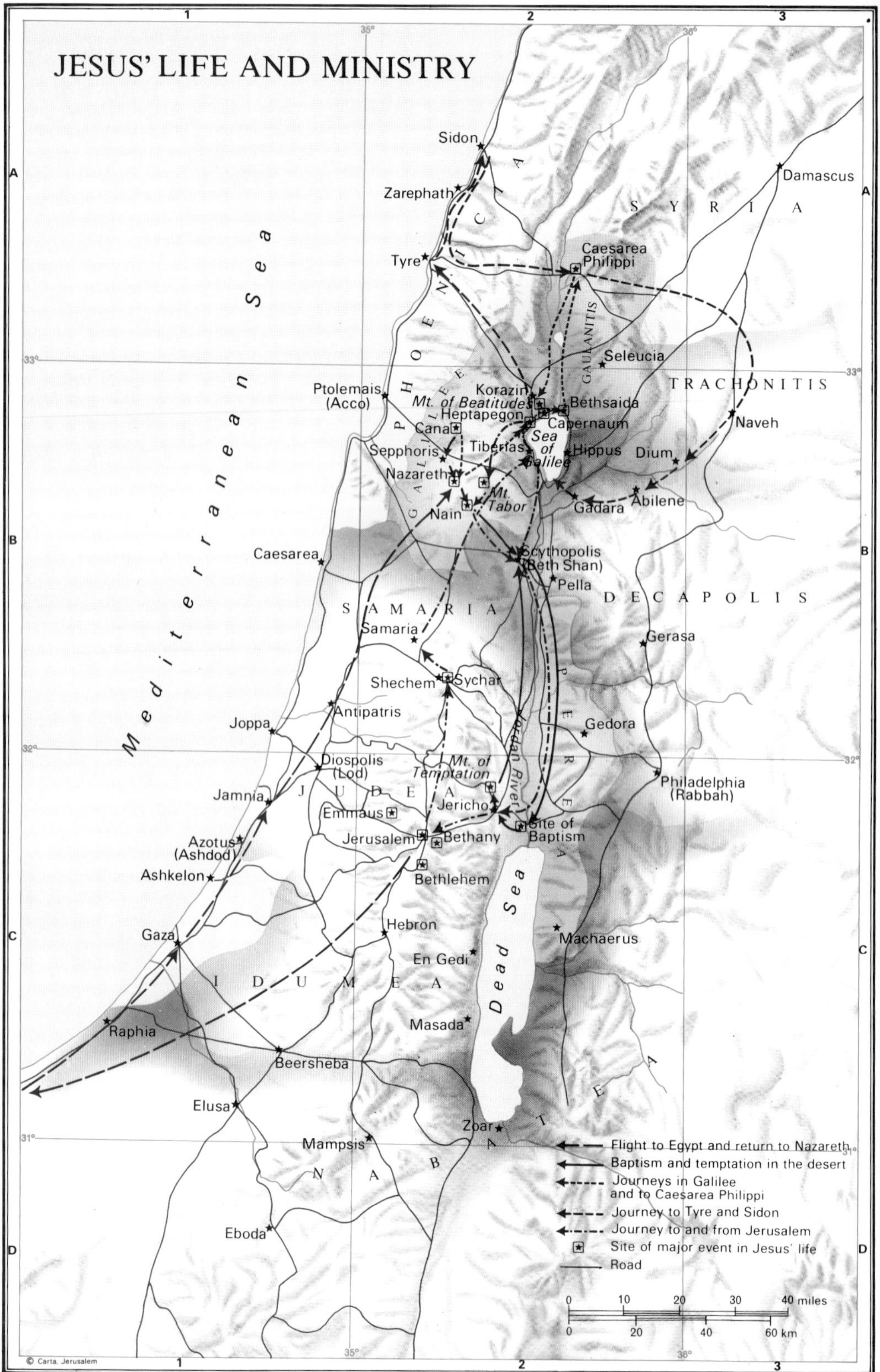

Sidon
Zarephath
Tyre
Damascus
SYRIA
PHOENICIA
Caesarea Philippi
GAULANITIS
Seleucia
TRACHONITIS
Ptolemais (Acco)
Korazin
Mt. of Beatitudes
Bethsaida
Heptapegon
Capernaum
Cana
Sea of Galilee
Naveh
Sepphoris
Tiberias
Hippus
Dium
Nazareth
GALILEE
Mt. Tabor
Gadara
Abilene
Nain
Caesarea
Scythopolis (Beth Shan)
Pella
DECAPOLIS
Mediterranean Sea
SAMARIA
Samaria
Gerasa
Shechem
Sychar
PEREA
Antipatris
Joppa
Gedora
Jordan River
Diospolis (Lod)
Mt. of Temptation
Philadelphia (Rabbah)
JUDEA
Jamnia
Jericho
Emmaus
Site of Baptism
Azotus (Ashdod)
Jerusalem
Bethany
Ashkelon
Bethlehem
Dead Sea
Hebron
Gaza
Machaerus
En Gedi
IDUMEA
Masada
Raphia
Beersheba
NABATEA
Elusa
Zoar
Mampsis
Eboda
Flight to Egypt and return to Nazareth
Baptism and temptation in the desert
Journeys in Galilee and to Caesarea Philippi
Journey to Tyre and Sidon
Journey to and from Jerusalem
Site of major event in Jesus' life
Road
0 10 20 30 40 miles
0 20 40 60 km
35°
36°
33°
32°
31°
1 2 3
A B C D

THE TEMPLE AT THE TIME OF JESUS

After Prof. Avi-Yonah

Viewed from the east

THE TEMPLE MOUNT

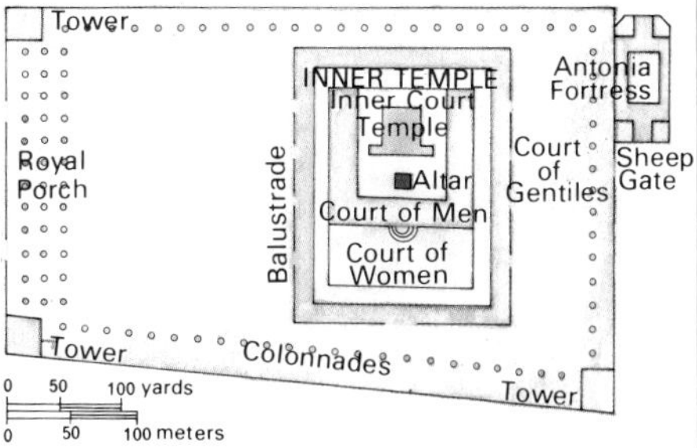

JERUSALEM AT THE TIME OF JESUS

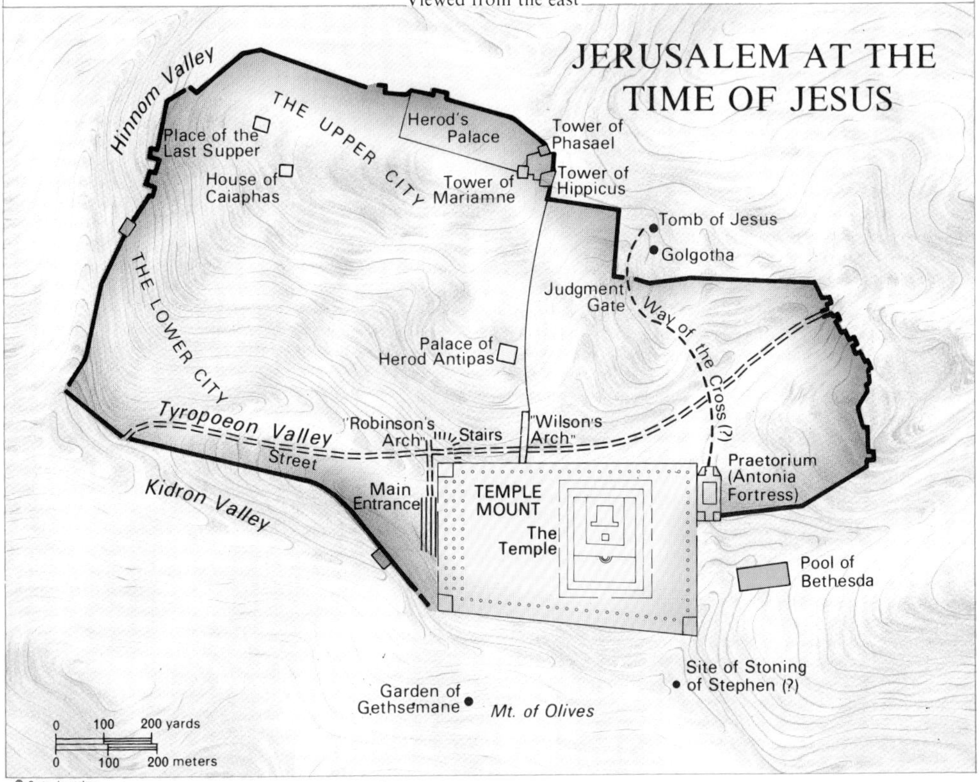

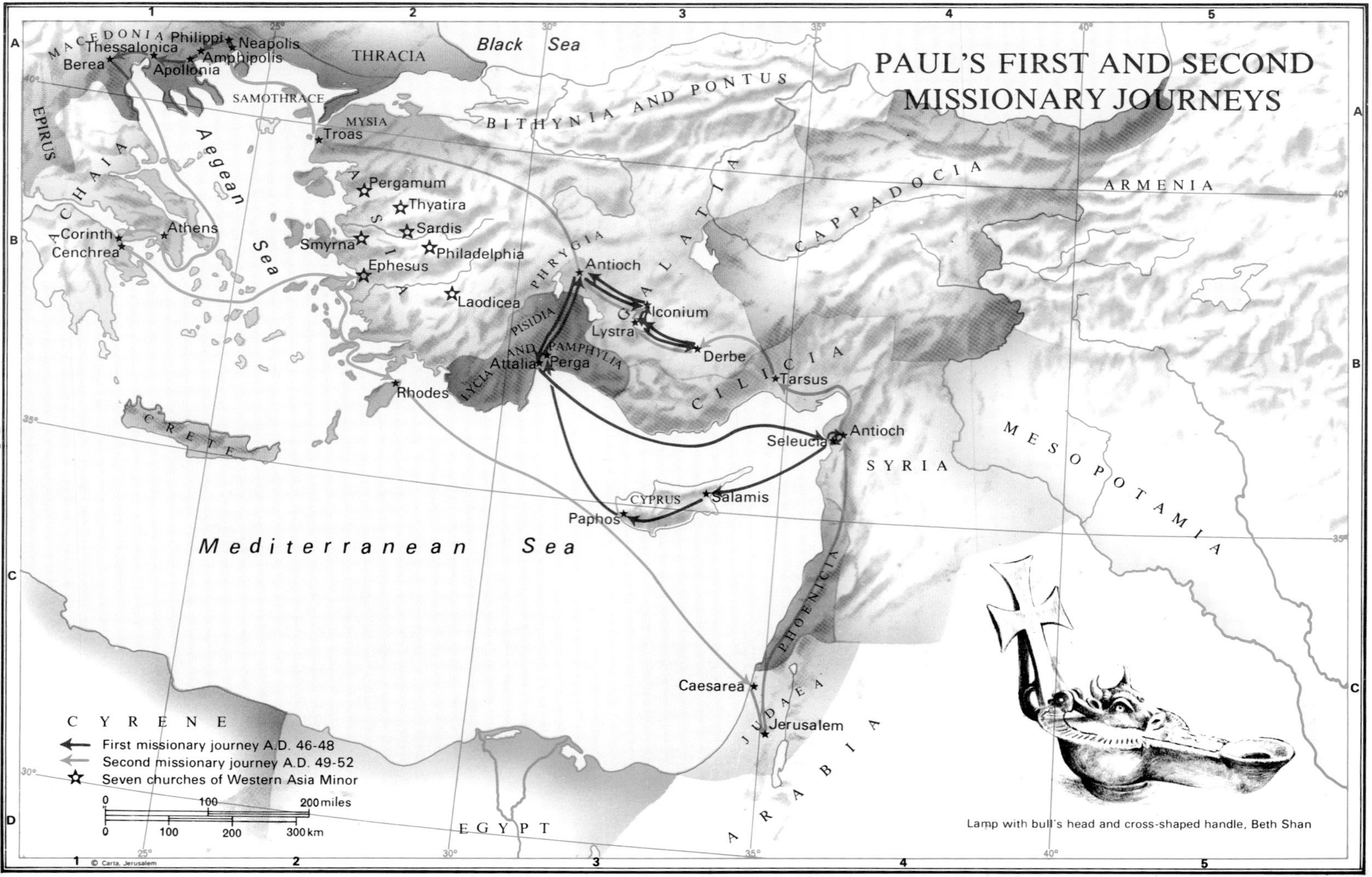
PAUL'S FIRST AND SECOND MISSIONARY JOURNEYS
MACEDONIA
Thessalonica
Philippi
Neapolis
Amphipolis
Apollonia
Berea
THRACIA
Black Sea
SAMOTHRACE
EPIRUS
MYSIA
Troas
BITHYNIA AND PONTUS
ACHAIA
Aegean Sea
Corinth
Cenchrea
Athens
ASIA
Pergamum
Thyatira
Sardis
Smyrna
Philadelphia
Ephesus
Laodicea
PHRYGIA
Antioch
GALATIA
Iconium
Lystra
Derbe
PISIDIA
PAMPHYLIA
Attalia
Perga
LYCIA
Rhodes
CRETE
CAPPADOCIA
ARMENIA
CILICIA
Tarsus
Antioch
Seleucia
SYRIA
MESOPOTAMIA
CYPRUS
Salamis
Paphos
Mediterranean Sea
PHOENICIA
Caesarea
JUDAEA
Jerusalem
ARABIA
CYRENE
EGYPT
First missionary journey A.D. 46-48
Second missionary journey A.D. 49-52
Seven churches of Western Asia Minor
0
100
200 miles
0
100
200
300 km
© Carta, Jerusalem
Lamp with bull's head and cross-shaped handle, Beth Shan

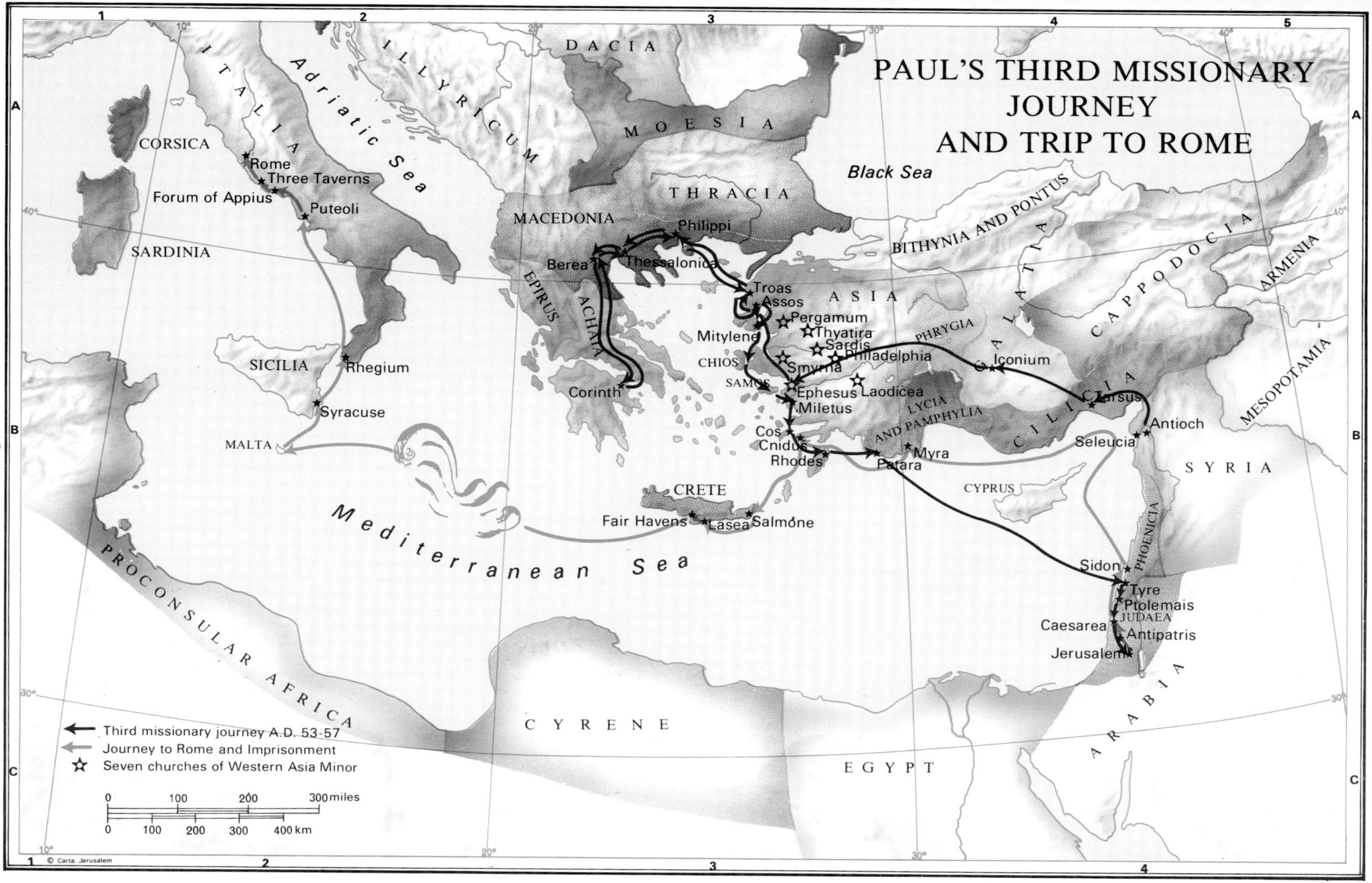
PAUL'S THIRD MISSIONARY JOURNEY AND TRIP TO ROME
Third missionary journey A.D. 53-57
Journey to Rome and Imprisonment
Seven churches of Western Asia Minor
0 100 200 300 miles
0 100 200 300 400 km
© Carta, Jerusalem
DACIA
MOESIA
THRACIA
MACEDONIA
ILLYRICUM
Adriatic Sea
Black Sea
ITALIA
CORSICA
SARDINIA
SICILIA
MALTA
EPIRUS
ACHAIA
ASIA
PHRYGIA
GALATIA
BITHYNIA AND PONTUS
CAPPODOCIA
ARMENIA
MESOPOTAMIA
LYCIA
AND PAMPHYLIA
CILICIA
SYRIA
PHOENICIA
JUDAEA
ARABIA
EGYPT
CYRENE
PROCONSULAR AFRICA
CYPRUS
CRETE
CHIOS
SAMOS
Mediterranean Sea
Rome
Three Taverns
Forum of Appius
Puteoli
Rhegium
Syracuse
Philippi
Thessalonica
Berea
Corinth
Troas
Assos
Pergamum
Thyatira
Sardis
Philadelphia
Smyrna
Ephesus
Laodicea
Mitylene
Miletus
Cos
Cnidus
Rhodes
Patara
Myra
Iconium
Tarsus
Antioch
Seleucia
Fair Havens
Lasea
Salmone
Sidon
Tyre
Ptolemais
Caesarea
Antipatris
Jerusalem

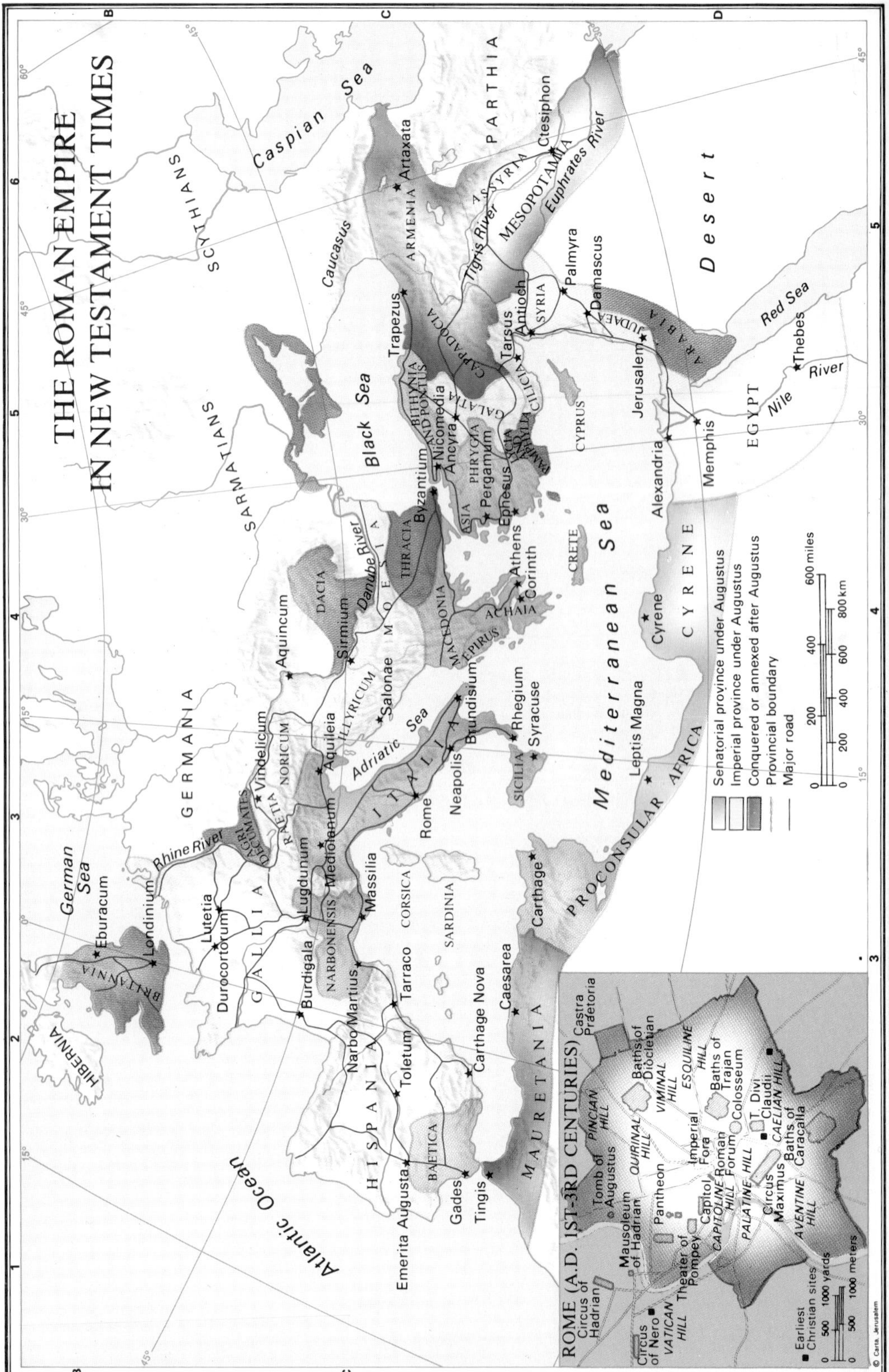
THE ROMAN EMPIRE
IN NEW TESTAMENT TIMES
Senatorial province under Augustus
Imperial province under Augustus
Conquered or annexed after Augustus
Provincial boundary
Major road
0 200 400 600 miles
0 200 400 600 800 km
Atlantic Ocean
German Sea
Mediterranean Sea
Black Sea
Caspian Sea
Adriatic Sea
Red Sea
Desert
Rhine River
Danube River
Tigris River
Euphrates River
Nile River
Caucasus
HIBERNIA
BRITANNIA
Eburacum
Londinium
GALLIA
Lutetia
Durocortorum
Lugdunum
Burdigala
NARBONENSIS
Narbo Martius
Massilia
HISPANIA
BAETICA
Emerita Augusta
Gades
Toletum
Tarraco
Carthage Nova
Tingis
MAURETANIA
Caesarea
Carthage
PROCONSULAR AFRICA
Leptis Magna
CYRENE
Cyrene
GERMANIA
AGRI DECUMATES
RAETIA
Vindelicum
NORICUM
Mediolanum
Aquileia
ILLYRICUM
Salonae
Aquincum
Sirmium
DACIA
MOESIA
THRACIA
MACEDONIA
EPIRUS
ACHAIA
Athens
Corinth
CORSICA
SARDINIA
SICILIA
Syracuse
ITALIA
Rome
Neapolis
Brundisium
Rhegium
CRETE
CYPRUS
SARMATIANS
SCYTHIANS
Byzantium
Nicomedia
BITHYNIA AND PONTUS
Ancyra
GALATIA
ASIA
Pergamum
Ephesus
PHRYGIA
LYCIA
PAMPHYLIA
CILICIA
Tarsus
CAPPADOCIA
Trapezus
ARMENIA
Artaxata
ASSYRIA
MESOPOTAMIA
PARTHIA
Ctesiphon
SYRIA
Antioch
Palmyra
Damascus
JUDAEA
Jerusalem
ARABIA
EGYPT
Alexandria
Memphis
Thebes
ROME (A.D. 1ST-3RD CENTURIES)
Castra Praetoria
Baths of Diocletian
PINCIAN HILL
QUIRINAL HILL
VIMINAL HILL
ESQUILINE HILL
Tomb of Augustus
Mausoleum of Hadrian
Circus of Hadrian
Circus of Nero
VATICAN HILL
Theater of Pompey
Pantheon
Capitol
CAPITOLINE HILL
Imperial Fora
Roman Forum
Baths of Trajan
Colosseum
T. Divi Claudii
CAELIAN HILL
PALATINE HILL
Circus Maximus
Baths of Caracalla
AVENTINE HILL
Earliest Christian sites
0 500 1000 yards
0 500 1000 meters
© Carta, Jerusalem

PHYSICAL MAP OF THE HOLY LAND

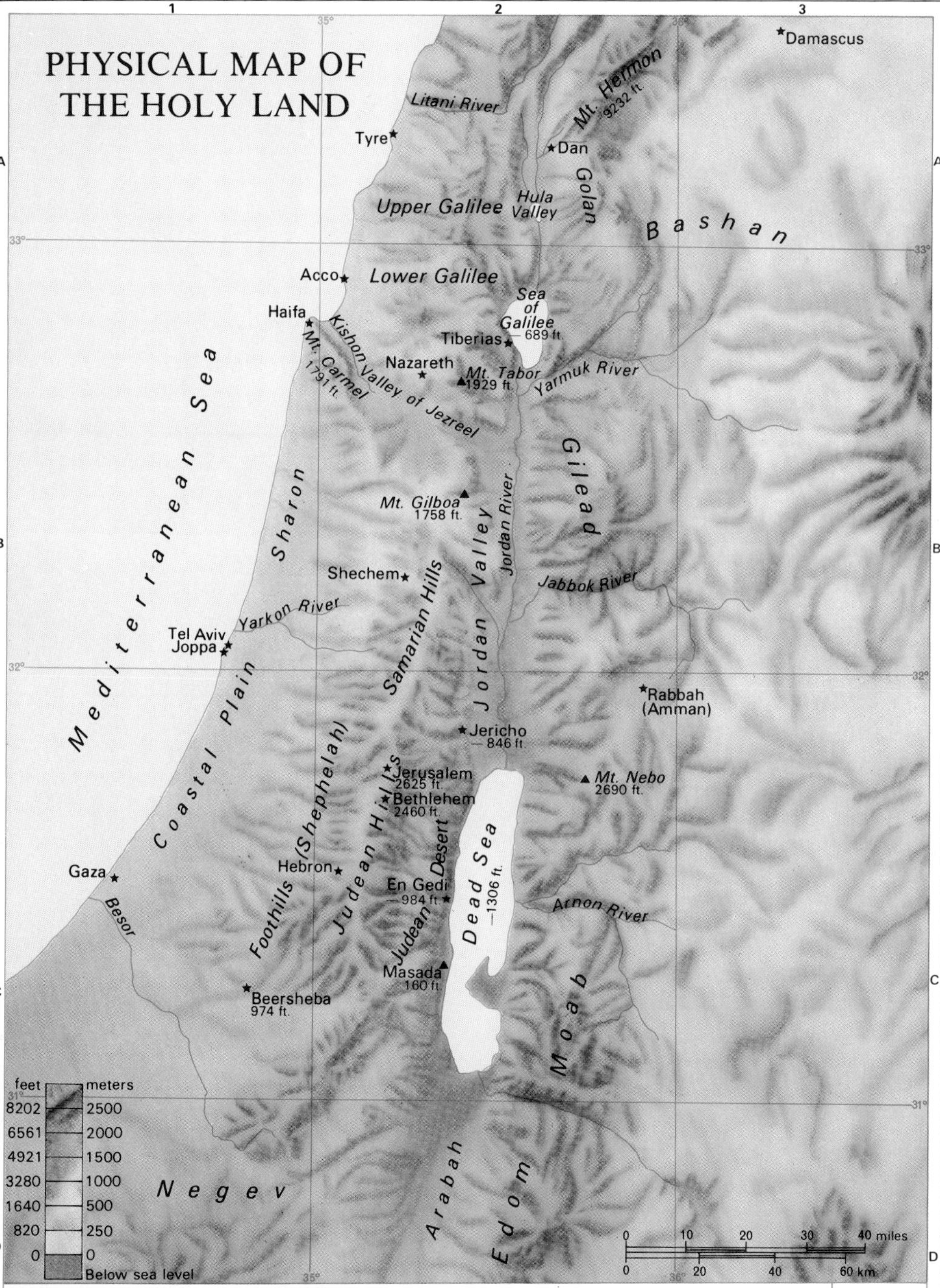

1
2
3
A
B
C
D
35°
36°
33°
32°
31°
Damascus
Mt. Hermon 9232 ft.
Litani River
Tyre
Dan
Golan
Upper Galilee
Hula Valley
Bashan
Acco
Lower Galilee
Sea of Galilee — 689 ft.
Haifa
Kishon
Tiberias
Mt. Carmel 1791 ft.
Nazareth
Mt. Tabor 1929 ft.
Yarmuk River
Valley of Jezreel
Mediterranean Sea
Gilead
Sharon
Mt. Gilboa 1758 ft.
Jordan River
Jordan Valley
Shechem
Samarian Hills
Jabbok River
Yarkon River
Tel Aviv
Joppa
Coastal Plain
Rabbah (Amman)
Jericho — 846 ft.
Foothills (Shephelah)
Jerusalem 2625 ft.
Bethlehem 2460 ft.
Mt. Nebo 2690 ft.
Judean Hills
Judean Desert
Dead Sea —1306 ft.
Gaza
Hebron
En Gedi — 984 ft.
Besor
Arnon River
Masada 160 ft.
Beersheba 974 ft.
Moab
Negev
Arabah
Edom
feet
meters
8202
6561
4921
3280
1640
820
0
2500
2000
1500
1000
500
250
0
Below sea level
0 10 20 30 40 miles
0 20 40 60 km

TOPOGRAPHICAL CROSS-SECTION, JOPPA TO MT. NEBO

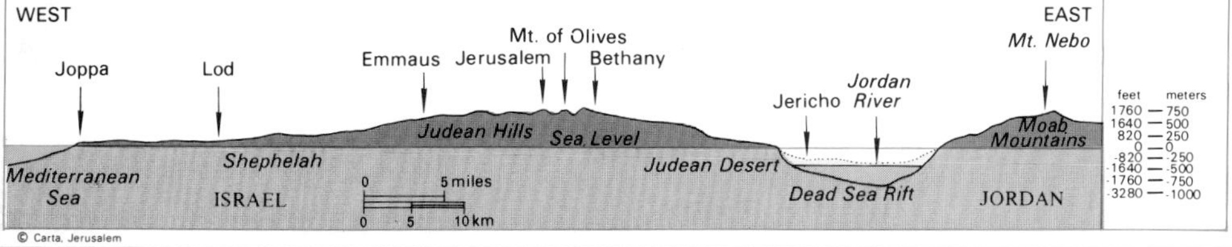

WEST
EAST
Joppa
Lod
Emmaus
Jerusalem
Mt. of Olives
Bethany
Jericho
Jordan River
Mt. Nebo
Judean Hills
Sea Level
Moab Mountains
Mediterranean Sea
Shephelah
ISRAEL
Judean Desert
Dead Sea Rift
JORDAN
0 5 miles
0 5 10 km
feet meters
1760 — 750
1640 — 500
820 — 250
0 — 0
-820 — -250
-1640 — -500
-1760 — -750
-3280 — -1000

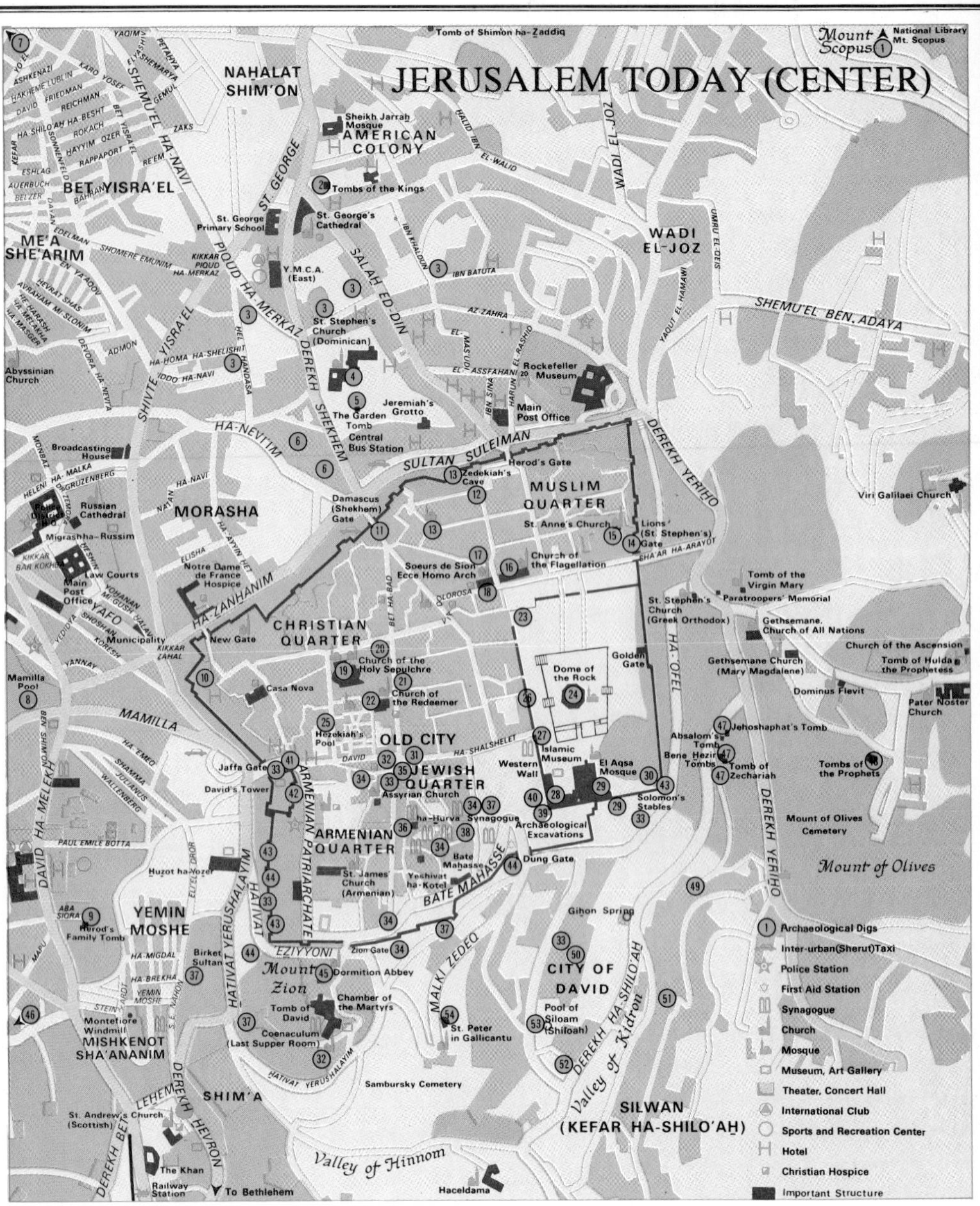

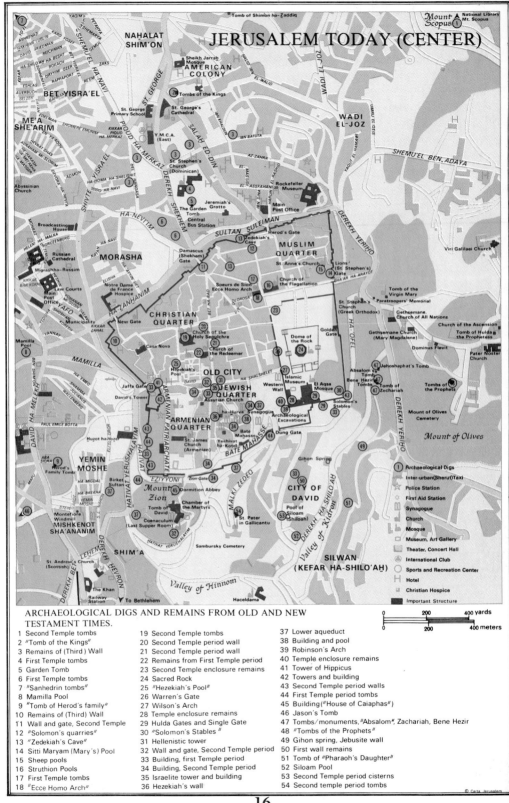

ARCHAEOLOGICAL DIGS AND REMAINS FROM OLD AND NEW TESTAMENT TIMES.

1 Second Temple tombs
2 "Tomb of the Kings"
3 Remains of (Third) Wall
4 First Temple tombs
5 Garden Tomb
6 First Temple tombs
7 "Sanhedrin tombs"
8 Mamilla Pool
9 "Tomb of Herod's family"
10 Remains of (Third) Wall
11 Wall and gate, Second Temple
12 "Solomon's quarries"
13 "Zedekiah's Cave"
14 Sitti Maryam (Mary's) Pool
15 Sheep pools
16 Struthion Pools
17 First Temple tombs
18 "Ecce Homo Arch"
19 Second Temple tombs
20 Second Temple period wall
21 Second Temple period wall
22 Remains from First Temple period
23 Second Temple enclosure remains
24 Sacred Rock
25 "Hezekiah's Pool"
26 Warren's Gate
27 Wilson's Arch
28 Temple enclosure remains
29 Hulda Gates and Single Gate
30 "Solomon's Stables"
31 Hellenistic tower
32 Wall and gate, Second Temple period
33 Building, first Temple period
34 Building, Second Temple period
35 Israelite tower and building
36 Hezekiah's wall
37 Lower aqueduct
38 Building and pool
39 Robinson's Arch
40 Temple enclosure remains
41 Tower of Hippicus
42 Towers and building
43 Second Temple period walls
44 First Temple period tombs
45 Building("House of Caiaphas")
46 Jason's Tomb
47 Tombs/monuments,"Absalom", Zachariah, Bene Hezir
48 "Tombs of the Prophets"
49 Gihon spring, Jebusite wall
50 First wall remains
51 Tomb of "Pharaoh's Daughter"
52 Siloam Pool
53 Second Temple period cisterns
54 Second temple period tombs